CPSIA information can be obtained
at www.ICGtesting.com
Printed in the USA
BVHW012323310721
613343BV00019B/176

9 781286 11628

STATE OF NEVADA

SECOND SUPPLEMENTAL ABSTRACT OF ADDITIONAL AND AMENDED CLAIMS

TO THE

Waters of the Humboldt River and Its Tributaries

Compiled by the Office of State Engineer, Under Authority of Chapter 140, Statutes of 1913, as amended by Chapter 253, Statutes of 1915, as amended by Chapter 106, Statutes of 1921

J. G. SCRUGHAM, State Engineer

CARSON CITY, NEVADA
STATE PRINTING OFFICE—JOE FARNSWORTH, SUPERINTENDENT
1922

1[68]

EXPLANATORY

Subsequent to the preparation and service of the abstract of claims to the waters of the Humboldt River and its Tributaries, dated March 1, 1916, and the preparation of the Supplemental Abstract of Additional and Amended Claims dated December 1, 1918, copies of which have heretofore been mailed to water users, further additional and amended claims have been filed, and this abstract represents such claims so filed.

This Second Supplemental Abstract, together with the original Abstract and the Supplemental Abstract to which reference is above made, gives a complete compilation of all claims filed on the stream system.

J. G. SCRUGHAM,
State Engineer.

STATE OF NEVADA
STATE ENGINEER'S OFFICE

I, J. G. Scrugham, State Engineer of the State of Nevada, duly appointed and qualified, having charge of the records and files of the office of the State Engineer, do hereby certify that the following is a full, complete and true copy of a further abstract of additional and amended claims in and to the waters of the Humboldt River and its Tributaries prepared and filed at said office on or before the 20th day of February, 1922, as appears by the records and files of the office of the State Engineer of Nevada, and nothing more or less.

IN WITNESS WHEREOF, I have hereunto set my hand and affixed my seal of office at the City of Carson, State of Nevada, this 20th day of February, 1922.

J. G. SCRUGHAM,
[SEAL] *State Engineer.*

ABBREVIATIONS

Numbers of proofs not followed by the letter "A" are *new* proofs.

Numbers of proofs followed by the letter "A" are either *supplemental* or *amended* to proofs heretofore filed and abstracted.

LOVELOCK DISTRICT

Claimant—**S. R. Young.** Proof No. **0093**
Source—**Humboldt River.** Ditch—**The Irrigation and Water Power Co.'s Tunnel. and Ditch.**

Date of beneficial use — Nat. mdw.	Date of beneficial use — Cult. area	Construction first initiated — Dams	Construction first initiated — Ditches	Culture—Acres — Harvest crops	Culture—Acres — Meadow pasture	Culture—Acres — Willow and sage pasture	Culture—Acres — Swamp or overflow	Location — Subdivision	Location — Section	Location — Tp.N.	Location — R.E.	Length of season	Duty of water — C.F.S.	Duty of water — Acre-feet
....	.....	.....	1888*											

*Claims 3,000 inches of water for the following uses: 1889 for sluicing and excavating ditch and pumping. In 1901 pits for 1,000 H.P. under 12- and 15-foot heads were excavated and a 100 H.P. water wheel installed; and 1909 a 200 H.P. water wheel was installed.

WINNEMUCCA DISTRICT

Claimant—**Estate of Henry Bain.** Proof No. 00132A
Source—**Rock Creek.** Ditch—**Two small ditches.**

Date of beneficial use: Nat. mdw.	Date of beneficial use: Cult. area	Construction first initiated: Dams	Construction first initiated: Ditches	Culture—Acres: Harvest crops	Culture—Acres: Meadow pasture	Culture—Acres: Willow and sage pasture	Culture—Acres: Swamp or overflow	Location: Subdivision	Location: Section	Location: Tp.N.	Location: R.E.	Length of season	Duty of water: C.F.S.	Duty of water: Acre-feet
	1869		1869	7.47				NW¼SW¼	33	35	40	6 months		
	1869		1869	13.94				NE¼SW¼	33	35	40	6 months		
1869			1869		1.60			NE¼SW¼	33	35	40	6 months		
1869			1869		.30			SE¼SW¼	33	35	40	6 months		
	1869		1869	8.44				SE¼SW¼	33	35	40	6 months		
	1869		1869	15.50				NW¼SE¼	33	35	40	6 months		
	1869		1869	24.07				SW¼NE¼	33	35	40	6 months		
	1869		1869	9.53				SE¼NE¼	33	35	40	6 months		
1869			1869		.17			SE¼NE¼	33	35	40	6 months		
	1869		1869	5.00				NW¼NE¼	33	35	40	6 months		
	1869		1869	20.64				NE¼NE¼	33	35	40	6 months		

Claimant—**A. E. Kent & Co., Inc.** Proof No. 00133
Source—**Rock Creek.** Ditch—**Unnamed.**

Nat. mdw.	Cult. area	Dams	Ditches	Harvest crops	Meadow pasture	Willow and sage pasture	Swamp or overflow	Subdivision	Section	Tp.N.	R.E.	Length of season	C.F.S.	Acre-feet
	1873		1873	*35				NE¼SE¼	32	35	40	6 months		
	1873			*40				NW¼SE¼	32	35	40	6 months		
	1873		1873	*40				NE¼SW¼	32	35	40	6 months		
	1873		1873	*35				NW¼SW¼	32	35	40	6 months		

*Map not yet filed; hence classification of culture may not be entirely correct.

Claimant—**Mary G. Rose.** Proof No. 00117
Source—**Humboldt River.** Ditch—**O'Donnell.**

Nat. mdw.	Cult. area	Dams	Ditches	Harvest crops	Meadow pasture	Willow and sage pasture	Swamp or overflow	Subdivision	Section	Tp.N.	R.E.	Length of season	C.F.S.	Acre-feet
1873		unknown			9.91			NE¼NE¼	35	36	37			
	1873			6.06				SE¼NE¼	35	36	37			
1873					21.29			SE¼NE¼	35	36	37			
	1873			7.65				NE¼SE¼	35	36	37			
	1873			13.23				NW¼SE¼	35	36	37			
	1873			1.36				SW¼SE¼	35	36	37			
	1873			8.94				NE¼SW¼	35	36	37			
	1873			2.65				SE¼SW¼	35	36	37			

BATTLE MOUNTAIN DISTRICT

Claimant—**Lulu K. Burch.** Proof No. 00176
Source—**Humboldt River.** Ditch—**Ward.**

Date of beneficial use: Nat. mdw.	Cult. area	Construction first initiated: Dams	Ditches	Culture—Acres: Harvest crops	Meadow pasture	Willow and sage pasture	Swamp or overflow	Location: Subdivision	Section	Tp.N.	R.E.	Length of season	Duty of water: C.F.S.	Acre-feet
1878			1878		9.80	.47		SW¼NE¼	29	34	44			
1878			1878				4.15	NE¼SE¼	29	34	44			
1878			1878		4.35	2.68	15.05	SE¼SE¼	29	34	44			
1878			1878		8.75	5.60	9.60	NW¼SE¼	29	34	44			
1878	1878		1878	.59	18.31	2.40	5.97	SW¼SE¼	29	34	44			
1878	1878		1878	10.90			10.35	NE¼NW¼	29	34	44			
1878	1878		1878	10.16	10.01		11.32	SE¼NW¼	29	34	44			
1878			1878			10.02	27.42	SW¼NW¼	29	34	44			
1878	1878		1878	3.43	4.10	2.02	20.90	NE¼SW¼	29	34	44			
1878	1878		1878	1.04		13.75	21.60	SE¼SW¼	29	34	44			
1878			1878			25.50	10.00	NW¼SW¼	29	34	44			
1878			1878			11.90	25.08	SW¼SW¼	29	34	44			951.66

Claimant—**Lulu K. Burch.** Proof No. 00176
Source—**Humboldt River.** Ditch—**Wilcox.**

Nat. mdw.	Cult. area	Dams	Ditches	Harvest crops	Meadow pasture	Willow and sage pasture	Swamp or overflow	Subdivision	Section	Tp.N.	R.E.	Length of season	C.F.S.	Acre-feet
	1880		1880	19.60		9.45	6.24	NW¼NW¼	29	34	44			105.87

Claimant—**Ike Erickson.** Proof No. 00173
Source—**Humboldt River.** Ditch—**Argenta Slough and Burge Ditch.**

Nat. mdw.	Cult. area	Dams	Ditches	Harvest crops	Meadow pasture	Willow and sage pasture	Swamp or overflow	Subdivision	Section	Tp.N.	R.E.	Length of season	C.F.S.	Acre-feet
	1874		1874	40				SE¼	17	32	45	3-15—9-15		.

Claimant—**Ellison Ranching Company.** Proof No. 00151A
Source—**Humboldt River.** Ditch—**The Gonzales Slough and other sloughs and ditches.**

Nat. mdw.	Cult. area	Dams	Ditches	Harvest crops	Meadow pasture	Willow and sage pasture	Swamp or overflow	Subdivision	Section	Tp.N.	R.E.	Length of season	C.F.S.	Acre-feet
	1874		1874	1.25				NE¼NW¼	2	35	42	6 months		
	1874		1874	1.52				SE¼NW¼	2	35	42	6 months		
	1874		1874	41.18				NW¼NW¼	2	35	42	6 months		
	1874		1874	39.77				SW¼NW¼	2	35	42	6 months		
	1874		1874	1.20				SE¼SW¼	2	35	42	6 months		
	1874		1874	37.40				SW¼SW¼	2	35	42	6 months		
1874			1874				.44	SW¼SW¼	2	35	42	6 months		
	1874		1874	35.49				NE¼NE¼	3	35	42	6 months		
1874			1874			5.60		NE¼NE¼	3	35	42	6 months		
1874			1874			2.67		SE¼NE¼	3	35	42	6 months		
	1874		1874	36.91				SE¼NE¼	3	35	42	6 months		
	1874		1874	35.05				NW¼NE¼	3	35	42	6 months		
1874			1874			5.88		NW¼NE¼	3	35	42	6 months		
1874			1874		5.68	2.64		SW¼NE¼	3	35	42	6 months		
	1874		1874	29.11				SW¼NE¼	3	35	42	6 months		
	1874		1874	37.61				NE¼SE¼	3	35	42	6 months		

1874			1874			.48		NE¼SE¼	3	35	42	6 months
	1874		1874	37.81				SE¼SE¼	3	35	42	6 months
	1874		1874	35.39				NW¼SE¼	3	35	42	6 months
1874			1874			1.68		NW¼SE¼	3	35	42	6 months
	1874		1874	38.25				SW¼SE¼	3	35	42	6 months
	1874		1874	37.17				NE¼NW¼	3	35	42	6 months
1874			1874			2.16		NE¼NW¼	3	35	42	6 months
1874			1874		4.65	5.69		SE¼NW¼	3	35	42	6 months
	1874		1874	22.91				SE¼NW¼	3	35	42	6 months
	1874		1874	9.18				NW¼NW¼	3	35	42	6 months
1874			1874		19.18			NW¼NW¼	3	35	42	6 months
1874			1874		33.46	1.73		SW¼NW¼	3	35	42	6 months
	1874		1874	39.50				NE¼SW¼	3	35	42	6 months
	1874		1874	39.60				SE¼SW¼	3	35	42	6 months
	1874		1874	30.39				NW¼SW¼	3	35	42	6 months
1874			1874		1.81	3.45		NW¼SW¼	3	35	42	6 months
	1874		1874	37.56				SW¼SW¼	3	35	42	6 months
	1874		1874	.70				SW¼SW¼	34	35	42	6 months
	1874		1874	36.33				NE¼NE¼	10	35	42	6 months
	1874		1874	39.54				SE¼NE¼	10	35	42	6 months
	1874		1874	36.44				NW¼NE¼	10	35	42	6 months
	1874		1874	40.04				SW¼NE¼	10	35	42	6 months
	1874		1874	37.68				NE¼NW¼	10	35	42	6 months
1874			1874			2.12		NE¼NW¼	10	35	42	6 months
	1874		1874	40.65				SE¼NW¼	10	35	42	6 months
	1874		1874	38.28				NW¼NW¼	10	35	42	6 months
	1874		1874	38.94				SW¼NW¼	10	35	42	6 months
1874			1874			2.86		NE¼SE¼	10	35	42	6 months
	1874		1874	40.76				SE¼SE¼	10	35	42	6 months
	1874		1874	40.95				NW¼SE¼	10	35	42	6 months
	1874		1874	38.14				SW¼SE¼	10	35	42	6 months
1874			1874			1.87		SW¼SE¼	10	35	42	6 months
	1874		1874	38.93				NE¼SW¼	10	35	42	6 months
1874			1874			.08		NE¼SW¼	10	35	42	6 months
1874			1874			2.14		SE¼SW¼	10	35	42	6 months
	1874		1874	36				NE¼SE¼	10	35	42	6 months
	1874		1874	36.60				SE¼SW¼	10	35	42	6 months
	1874		1874	31.72				NW¼SW¼	10	35	42	6 months
1874			1874		4	3.83		NW¼SW¼	10	35	42	6 months
1874			1874			.79		SW¼SW¼	10	35	42	6 months
	1874		1874	39.50				SW¼SW¼	10	35	42	6 months
	1874		1874	29.15				SW¼NE¼	14	35	42	6 months
1874			1874			8.95		SW¼NE¼	14	35	42	6 months
	1874		1874	2.14				SE¼NE¼	14	35	42	6 months
1874			1874			.83		NW¼NE¼	14	35	42	6 months
1874			1874			28.88		NE¼SE¼	14	35	42	6 months
	1874		1874	5.22				NE¼SE¼	14	35	42	6 months
1874			1874			37.98		SE¼SE¼	14	35	42	6 months
1874			1874			12.54		NW¼SE¼	14	35	42	6 months
	1874		1874	23.68				NW¼SE¼	14	35	42	6 months
1874			1874		32.58	6.52		SW¼SE¼	14	35	42	6 months
1874			1874		2.07	35.30		NE¼NW¼	14	35	42	6 months
	1874		1874	1.62				NE¼NW¼	14	35	42	6 months

Ellison Ranching Company—Continued. Proof No. 00151A

Date of beneficial use: Nat. mdw.	Date of beneficial use: Cult. area	Construction first initiated: Dams	Construction first initiated: Ditches	Culture—Acres: Harvest crops	Culture—Acres: Meadow pasture	Culture—Acres: Willow and sage pasture	Culture—Acres: Swamp or overflow	Location: Subdivision	Location: Section	Location: Tp.N.	Location: R.E.	Length of season	Duty of water: C.F.S.	Duty of water: Acre-feet
	1874		1874	20.07				SE¼NW¼	14	35	42	6 months		
1874			1874		2.47	17.53		SE¼NW¼	14	35	42	6 months		
1874			1874			34.32		NW¼NW¼	14	35	42	6 months		
	1874		1874	4.85				NW¼NW¼	14	35	42	6 months		
	1874		1874	3.98				SW¼NW¼	14	35	42	6 months		
1874			1874		4.22	30.28		SW¼NW¼	14	35	42	6 months		
1874			1874			.99		NE¼NE¼	15	35	42	6 months		
	1874		1874	.92				NE¼NE¼	15	35	42	6 months		
1874			1874			1.33		SE¼NE¼	15	35	42	6 months		
	1874		1874	5.52				NE¼NE¼	16	35	42	6 months		

Claimant—**Garat and Co.** Proof No. 00175

Source—**Humboldt River.** Ditch—**Antone Joseph and Aztec and Hammond Dam.**

Nat. mdw.	Cult. area	Dams	Ditches	Harvest crops	Meadow pasture	Willow and sage pasture	Swamp or overflow	Subdivision	Section	Tp.N.	R.E.	Length of season	C.F.S.	Acre-feet
1878			1878		1.96			NE¼SW¼	16	36	42			
1878			1878		28.22			NW¼SW¼	16	36	42			
1878			1878			33.87		SE¼SW¼	16	36	42			
1878			1878			40.00		SW¼SW¼	16	36	42			312.15

Claimant—**George Heard.** Proof No. 00174

Source—**Humboldt River. Ditch—Old Clover Valley.**

Nat. mdw.	Cult. area	Dams	Ditches	Harvest crops	Meadow pasture	Willow and sage pasture	Swamp or overflow	Subdivision	Section	Tp.N.	R.E.	Length of season	C.F.S.	Acre-feet
	1879		prior to 1885	2.32				NE¼NE¼	2	35	42	6 months		
1879			1885		34.23	1.73		NE¼NE¼	2	35	42	6 months		
1879			1885		.90			SE¼NE¼	2	35	42	6 months		
	1879		1885	37.00				SE¼NE¼	2	35	42	6 months		
1879			1885		.03	1.36		NW¼NE¼	2	35	42	6 months		
1879			1885		.42	.20		SW¼NE¼	2	35	42	6 months		
	1879		1885	.70				SW¼NE¼	2	35	42	6 months		
	1879		1885	85.87				NE¼SE¼	2	35	42	6 months		
1879			1885			1.21		NE¼SE¼	2	35	42	6 months		
	1879		1885	38.19				SE¼SE¼	2	35	42	6 months		
	1879		1885	1.35				NW¼SE¼	2	35	42	6 months		
	1879		1885	1.37				SW¼SE¼	2	35	42	6 months		

Claimant—**The A. E. Kent & Company, Inc.** Proof No. 00151A

Source—**Humboldt River.** Ditch—**Outside Slough Canal and other sloughs and ditches.**

Nat. mdw.	Cult. area	Dams	Ditches	Harvest crops	Meadow pasture	Willow and sage pasture	Swamp or overflow	Subdivision	Section	Tp.N.	R.E.	Length of season	C.F.S.	Acre-feet
1874			1874			27.79		NE¼NE¼	16	35	42	6 months		
1874			1874			39.50		NW¼NE¼	16	35	42	6 months		
1874			1874			39.46		SE¼NE¼	16	35	42	6 months		
1874			1874		6.93	30.78		SW¼NE¼	16	35	42	6 months		
1874			1874			31.47		NE¼NW¼	16	35	42	6 months		
	1874		1874	5.20				NE¼NW¼	16	35	42	6 months		

……	1874	……	1874	3.77	……	……	……	NW¼NW¼	16	35	42	6 months
1874	……	……	1874	……	……	36.13	……	NW¼NW¼	16	35	42	6 months
1874	……	……	1874	……	……	10.37	……	SW¼NW¼	16	35	42	6 months
……	1874	……	1874	28.82	……	……	……	SW¼NW¼	16	35	42	6 months
……	1874	……	1874	34.46	……	……	……	SE¼NW¼	16	35	42	6 months
1874	……	……	1874	……	……	3.50	……	SE¼NW¼	16	35	42	6 months
1874	……	……	1874	……	……	39.34	……	NE¼SE¼	16	35	42	6 months
1874	……	……	1874	……	……	24.44	……	NW¼SE¼	16	35	42	6 months
……	1874	……	1874	12.28	……	……	……	NW¼SE¼	16	35	42	6 months
……	1874	……	1874	20.43	……	……	……	SW¼SE¼	16	35	42	6 months
1874	……	……	1874	……	……	16.89	……	SW¼SE¼	16	35	42	6 months
1874	……	……	1874	……	……	37.88	1.50	SE¼SE¼	16	35	42	6 months
……	1874	……	1874	39.30	……	……	……	NE¼SW¼	16	35	42	6 months
……	1874	……	1874	26.85	……	……	……	NW¼SW¼	16	35	42	6 months
1874	……	……	1874	……	……	11.97	……	NW¼SW¼	16	35	42	6 months
1874	……	……	1874	……	……	21.68	……	SW¼SW¼	16	35	42	6 months
……	1874	……	1874	17.90	……	……	……	SW¼SW¼	16	35	42	6 months
……	1874	……	1874	39.64	……	……	……	SE¼SW¼	16	35	42	6 months
……	1874	……	1874	1.20	……	……	……	NE¼NE¼	21	35	42	6 months
1874	……	……	1874	……	4.22	31.06	……	NE¼NE¼	21	35	42	6 months
1874	……	……	1874	……	……	3.87	……	NW¼NE¼	21	35	42	6 months
……	1874	……	1874	34.09	……	……	……	NW¼NE¼	21	35	42	6 months
……	1874	……	1874	38.67	……	……	……	SW¼NE¼	21	35	42	6 months
……	1874	……	1874	20.15	……	……	……	SE¼NE¼	21	35	42	6 months
1874	……	……	1874	……	……	16.15	……	SE¼NE¼	21	35	42	6 months
1874	……	……	1874	……	……	1.63	……	NE¼NW¼	21	35	42	6 months
……	1874	……	1874	38.31	……	……	……	NE¼NW¼	21	35	42	6 months
……	1874	……	1874	3.45	……	……	……	NW¼NW¼	21	35	42	6 months
1874	……	……	1874	……	……	36.40	……	NW¼NW¼	21	35	42	6 months
1874	……	……	1874	……	……	38.02	……	SW¼NW¼	21	35	42	6 months
1874	……	……	1874	……	……	25.25	……	SE¼NW¼	21	35	42	6 months
……	1874	……	1874	14.57	……	……	……	SE¼NW¼	21	35	42	6 months
……	1874	……	1874	22.17	……	……	……	NE¼SE¼	21	35	42	6 months
1874	……	……	1874	……	……	14.18	……	NE¼SE¼	21	35	42	6 months
1874	……	……	1874	……	……	11.50	……	NW¼SE¼	21	35	42	6 months
……	1874	……	1874	23.60	……	……	……	NW¼SE¼	21	35	42	6 months
1874	……	……	1874	……	……	35.77	……	SW¼SE¼	21	35	42	6 months
……	1874	……	1874	3.50	……	……	……	SW¼SE¼	21	35	42	6 months
……	1874	……	1874	21.97	……	……	……	SE¼SE¼	21	35	42	6 months
1874	……	……	1874	……	……	16.80	……	SE¼SE¼	21	35	42	6 months
……	1874	……	1874	3.50	……	……	……	SW¼SE¼	21	35	42	6 months
1874	……	……	1874	……	……	35.77	……	SW¼SE¼	21	35	42	6 months
1874	……	……	1874	……	……	40.45	……	NE¼SW¼	21	35	42	6 months
1874	……	……	1874	……	……	38.18	……	NW¼SW¼	21	35	42	6 months
1874	……	……	1874	……	……	39.32	……	SW¼SW¼	21	35	42	6 months
1874	……	……	1874	……	……	38.20	……	SE¼SW¼	21	35	42	6 months
1874	……	……	1874	……	……	36.76	……	NE¼NE¼	28	35	42	6 months
1874	……	……	1874	……	……	37.87	……	NW¼NE¼	28	35	42	6 months
1874	……	……	1874	……	……	39.30	……	SW¼NE¼	28	35	42	6 months
1874	……	……	1874	……	……	39.75	……	SE¼NE¼	28	35	42	6 months

Proof No. 00168A

Claimant—**George B. Williams.**
Source—**Humboldt River.** Ditch—**Argenta Slough.**

Date of beneficial use		Construction first initiated		Culture—Acres				Location				Length of season	Duty of water	
Nat. mdw.	Cult. area	Dams	Ditches	Harvest crops	Meadow pasture	Willow and sage pasture	Swamp or overflow	Subdivision	Section	Tp.N.	R.E.		C.F.S.	Acre-feet
1878	....	....	1878	....	.31	....	....	SW¼SW¼	6	32	47	5 months		
1878	....	....	1878	....	34.40	....	....	NW¼SW¼	6	32	47	5 months		
1878	....	....	1878	....	19.65	....	....	NE¼SW¼	6	32	47	5 months		
1878	....	....	1878	....	4.92	....	....	NW¼SE¼	6	32	47	5 months		

PINE VALLEY DISTRICT

Claimant—**George Goodfellow.** Proof No. 00308

Source—**Pony Creek.** Ditch—**Laterals.**

Date of beneficial use: Nat. mdw.	Date of beneficial use: Cult. area	Construction first initiated: Dams	Construction first initiated: Ditches	Culture—Acres: Harvest crops	Culture—Acres: Meadow pasture	Culture—Acres: Willow and sage pasture	Culture—Acres: Swamp or overflow	Location: Subdivision	Location: Section	Location: Tp.N.	Location: R.E.	Length of season	Duty of water: C.F.S.	Duty of water: Acre-feet
1867	....	....	.. ....	....	*353.32	....	....	NE¼	17	28	52			
1867	.....	....	.....	.	41.34	....	....	SE¼	17	28	52			
....	1887	....	1887	37.48	....	....	....	SW¼	16	28	52			
....	1887	....	1887	111.06	....	....	....	NW¼	21	28	52			
....	1887	....	1887	66.26	....	....	....	NE¼	21	28	52			
....	1887	....	1887	78.72	....	....	....	N½SE¼	21	28	52			
....	1887	....	1887	.20	....	....	....	SW¼NW¼	22	28	52			
....	1887	....	1887	2.47	....	....	....	N½SW¼	22	28	52			
....	1887	....	1887	9.20	....	....	....	NE¼SW¼	21	28	52			

*Probably covers more than the NE¼, Sec. 17, as there is only 160 acres in this tract.

NOTE—Explanation in proof states that water was spread over land by a natural dam in 1867 and used as pasture. Additional dams were constructed in 1887 and possibly earlier. Land under date of 1887 irrigated in lieu of the 1867 pasture land.

EXPLANATORY

Subsequent to the preparation and service of the abstract of claims to the waters of the Humboldt River and its Tributaries, dated March 1, 1916, and the preparation of the Supplemental Abstract of Additional and Amended Claims dated December 1, 1918, copies of which have heretofore been mailed to water users, further additional and amended claims have been filed, and this abstract represents such claims so filed.

This Second Supplemental Abstract, together with the original Abstract and the Supplemental Abstract to which reference is above made, gives a complete compilation of all claims filed on the stream system.

J. G. SCRUGHAM,
State Engineer.

STATE OF NEVADA
STATE ENGINEER'S OFFICE

I, J. G. Scrugham, State Engineer of the State of Nevada, duly appointed and qualified, having charge of the records and files of the office of the State Engineer, do hereby certify that the following is a full, complete and true copy of a further abstract of additional and amended claims in and to the waters of the Humboldt River and its Tributaries prepared and filed at said office on or before the 20th day of February, 1922, as appears by the records and files of the office of the State Engineer of Nevada, and nothing more or less.

IN WITNESS WHEREOF, I have hereunto set my hand and affixed my seal of office at the City of Carson, State of Nevada, this 20th day of February, 1922.

J. G. SCRUGHAM,
[SEAL] *State Engineer.*

ABBREVIATIONS

Numbers of proofs not followed by the letter "A" are *new* proofs.

Numbers of proofs followed by the letter "A" are either *supplemental* or *amended* to proofs heretofore filed and abstracted.

LOVELOCK DISTRICT

Claimant—**S. R. Young.** Proof No. **0093**

Source—**Humboldt River.** Ditch—**The Irrigation and Water Power Co.'s Tunnel. and Ditch.**

Date of beneficial use: Nat. mdw.	Date of beneficial use: Cult. area	Construction first initiated: Dams	Construction first initiated: Ditches	Culture—Acres: Harvest crops	Culture—Acres: Meadow pasture	Culture—Acres: Willow and sage pasture	Culture—Acres: Swamp or overflow	Location: Subdivision	Location: Section	Location: Tp.N.	Location: R.E.	Length of season	Duty of water: C.F.S.	Duty of water: Acre-feet
......	......	......	1888*											

*Claims 3,000 inches of water for the following uses: 1880 for sluicing and excavating ditch and pumping. In 1901 pits for 1,000 H.P. under 12- and 15-foot heads were excavated and a 100 H.P. water wheel installed; and 1909 a 200 H.P. water wheel was installed.

WINNEMUCCA DISTRICT

Claimant—**Estate of Henry Bain.** Proof No. 00132A
Source—**Rock Creek.** Ditch—**Two small ditches.**

Date of beneficial use: Nat. mdw.	Date of beneficial use: Cult. area	Construction first initiated: Dams	Construction first initiated: Ditches	Culture—Acres: Harvest crops	Culture—Acres: Meadow pasture	Culture—Acres: Willow and sage pasture	Culture—Acres: Swamp or overflow	Location: Subdivision	Location: Section	Location: Tp.N.	Location: R.E.	Length of season	Duty of water: C.F.S.	Duty of water: Acre-feet
	1869		1869	7.47				NW¼SW¼	33	35	40	6 months		
	1869		1869	13.94				NE¼SW¼	33	35	40	6 months		
1869			1869	...	1.60			NE¼SW¼	33	35	40	6 months		
1869			1869	...	.30			SE¼SW¼	33	35	40	6 months		
	1869		1869	8.44				SE¼SW¼	33	35	40	6 months		
	1869		1869	15.50				NW¼SE¼	33	35	40	6 months		
	1869		1869	24.07				SW¼NE¼	33	35	40	6 months		
	1869		1869	9.53				SE¼NE¼	33	35	40	6 months		
1869			1869	...	.17			SE¼NE¼	33	35	40	6 months		
	1869		1869	5.00				NW¼NE¼	33	35	40	6 months		
	1869		1869	20.64				NE¼NE¼	33	35	40	6 months		

Claimant—**A. E. Kent & Co., Inc.** Proof No. 00133
Source—**Rock Creek.** Ditch—**Unnamed.**

Date of beneficial use: Nat. mdw.	Date of beneficial use: Cult. area	Construction first initiated: Dams	Construction first initiated: Ditches	Culture—Acres: Harvest crops	Culture—Acres: Meadow pasture	Culture—Acres: Willow and sage pasture	Culture—Acres: Swamp or overflow	Location: Subdivision	Location: Section	Location: Tp.N.	Location: R.E.	Length of season	Duty of water: C.F.S.	Duty of water: Acre-feet
	1873		1873	*35				NE¼SE¼	32	35	40	6 months		
	1873			*40				NW¼SE¼	32	35	40	6 months		
	1873		1873	*40				NE¼SW¼	32	35	40	6 months		
	1873		1873	*35				NW¼SW¼	32	35	40	6 months		

*Map not yet filed; hence classification of culture may not be entirely correct.

Claimant—**Mary G. Rose.** Proof No. 00117
Source—**Humboldt River.** Ditch—**O'Donnell.**

Date of beneficial use: Nat. mdw.	Date of beneficial use: Cult. area	Construction first initiated: Dams	Construction first initiated: Ditches	Culture—Acres: Harvest crops	Culture—Acres: Meadow pasture	Culture—Acres: Willow and sage pasture	Culture—Acres: Swamp or overflow	Location: Subdivision	Location: Section	Location: Tp.N.	Location: R.E.	Length of season	Duty of water: C.F.S.	Duty of water: Acre-feet
1873		unknown		...	9.91			NE¼NE¼	35	36	37			
	1873			6.06				SE¼NE¼	35	36	37			
1873				...	21.29			SE¼NE¼	35	36	37			
	1873			7.65				NE¼SE¼	35	36	37			
	1873			13.23				NW¼SE¼	35	36	37			
	1873			1.36				SW¼SE¼	35	36	37			
	1873			8.94				NE¼SW¼	35	36	37			
	1873			2.65				SE¼SW¼	35	36	37			

BATTLE MOUNTAIN DISTRICT

Claimant—**Lulu K. Burch.** Proof No. 00176
Source—**Humboldt River.** Ditch—**Ward.**

Date of beneficial use: Nat. mdw.	Cult. area	Construction first initiated: Dams	Ditches	Culture—Acres: Harvest crops	Meadow pasture	Willow and sage pasture	Swamp or overflow	Location: Subdivision	Section	Tp.N.	R.E.	Length of season	Duty of water: C.F.S.	Acre-feet
1878			1878		9.80	.47		SW¼NE¼	29	34	44			
1878			1878				4.15	NE¼SE¼	29	34	44			
1878			1878		4.35	2.68	15.05	SE¼SE¼	29	34	44			
1878			1878		8.75	5.60	9.60	NW¼SE¼	29	34	44			
1878	1878		1878	.59	18.31	2.40	5.97	SW¼SE¼	29	34	44			
1878	1878		1878	10.90			10.35	NE¼NW¼	29	34	44			
1878	1878		1878	10.16	10.01		11.32	SE¼NW¼	29	34	44			
1878			1878			10.02	27.42	SW¼NW¼	29	34	44			
1878	1878		1878	3.43	4.10	2.02	20.90	NE¼SW¼	29	34	44			
1878	1878		1878	1.04		13.75	21.60	SE¼SW¼	29	34	44			
1878			1878			25.50	10.00	NW¼SW¼	29	34	44			
1878			1878			11.90	25.08	SW¼SW¼	29	34	44			951.66

Claimant—**Lulu K. Burch.** Proof No. 00176
Source—**Humboldt River.** Ditch—**Wilcox.**

Nat. mdw.	Cult. area	Dams	Ditches	Harvest crops	Meadow pasture	Willow and sage pasture	Swamp or overflow	Subdivision	Section	Tp.N.	R.E.	Length of season	C.F.S.	Acre-feet
	1880		1880	19.60		9.45	6.24	NW¼NW¼	29	34	44			105.87

Claimant—**Ike Erickson.** Proof No. 00173
Source—**Humboldt River.** Ditch—**Argenta Slough and Burge Ditch.**

Nat. mdw.	Cult. area	Dams	Ditches	Harvest crops	Meadow pasture	Willow and sage pasture	Swamp or overflow	Subdivision	Section	Tp.N.	R.E.	Length of season	C.F.S.	Acre-feet
	1874		1874	40				SE¼	17	32	45	3-15—9-15		.

Claimant—**Ellison Ranching Company.** Proof No. 00151A
Source—**Humboldt River.** Ditch—**The Gonzales Slough and other sloughs and ditches.**

Nat. mdw.	Cult. area	Dams	Ditches	Harvest crops	Meadow pasture	Willow and sage pasture	Swamp or overflow	Subdivision	Section	Tp.N.	R.E.	Length of season	C.F.S.	Acre-feet
	1874		1874	1.25				NE¼NW¼	2	35	42	6 months		
	1874		1874	1.52				SE¼NW¼	2	35	42	6 months		
	1874		1874	41.18				NW¼NW¼	2	35	42	6 months		
	1874		1874	39.77				SW¼NW¼	2	35	42	6 months		
	1874		1874	1.20				SE¼SW¼	2	35	42	6 months		
	1874		1874	37.40				SW¼SW¼	2	35	42	6 months		
1874			1874				.44	SW¼SW¼	2	35	42	6 months		
	1874		1874	35.49				NE¼NE¼	3	35	42	6 months		
1874			1874			5.60		NE¼NE¼	3	35	42	6 months		
1874			1874			2.67		SE¼NE¼	3	35	42	6 months		
	1874		1874	36.91				SE¼NE¼	3	35	42	6 months		
	1874		1874	35.05				NW¼NE¼	3	35	42	6 months		
1874			1874			5.88		NW¼NE¼	3	35	42	6 months		
1874			1874		5.68	2.64		SW¼NE¼	3	35	42	6 months		
	1874		4874	29.11				SW¼NE¼	3	35	42	6 months		
	1874		1874	37.61				NE¼SE¼	3	35	42	6 months		

1874			1874			.48		NE¼SE¼	3	35	42	6 months
	1874		1874	37.81				SE¼SE¼	3	35	42	6 months
	1874		1874	35.39				NW¼SE¼	3	35	42	6 months
1874			1874			1.68		NW¼SE¼	3	35	42	6 months
	1874		1874	38.25				SW¼SE¼	3	35	42	6 months
	1874		1874	37.17				NE¼NW¼	3	35	42	6 months
1874			1874			2.16		NE¼NW¼	3	35	42	6 months
1874			1874		4.65	5.69		SE¼NW¼	3	35	42	6 months
	1874		1874	22.91				SE¼NW¼	3	35	42	6 months
	1874		1874	9.18				NW¼NW¼	3	35	42	6 months
1874			1874		19.18			NW¼NW¼	3	35	42	6 months
1874			1874		83.46	1.73		SW¼NW¼	3	35	42	6 months
	1874		1874	39.50				NE¼SW¼	3	35	42	6 months
	1874		1874	39.60				SE¼SW¼	3	35	42	6 months
	1874		1874	30.39				NW¼SW¼	3	35	42	6 months
1874			1874		1.81	3.45		NW¼SW¼	3	35	42	6 months
	1874		1874	37.56				SW¼SW¼	3	35	42	6 months
	1874		1874	.70				SW¼SW¼	34	36	42	6 months
	1874		1874	36.33				NE¼NE¼	10	35	42	6 months
	1874		1874	39.54				SE¼NE¼	10	35	42	6 months
	1874		1874	36.44				NW¼NE¼	10	35	42	6 months
	1874		1874	40.04				SW¼NE¼	10	35	42	6 months
	1874		1874	37.68				NE¼NW¼	10	35	42	6 months
1874			1874			2.12		NE¼NW¼	10	35	42	6 months
	1874		1874	40.65				SE¼NW¼	10	35	42	6 months
	1874		1874	38.28				NW¼NW¼	10	35	42	6 months
	1874		1874	38.94				SW¼NW¼	10	35	42	6 months
1874			1874			2.86		NE¼SE¼	10	35	42	6 months
	1874		1874	40.76				SE¼SE¼	10	35	42	6 months
	1874		1874	40.95				NW¼SE¼	10	35	42	6 months
	1874		1874	38.14				SW¼SE¼	10	35	42	6 months
1874			1874			1.87		SW¼SE¼	10	35	42	6 months
	1874		1874	38.93				NE¼SW¼	10	35	42	6 months
1874			1874			.08		NE¼SW¼	10	35	42	6 months
1874			1874			2.14		SE¼SW¼	10	35	42	6 months
	1874		1874	36				NE¼SE¼	10	35	42	6 months
	1874		1874	36.60				SE¼SW¼	10	35	42	6 months
	1874		1874	31.72				NW¼SW¼	10	35	42	6 months
1874			1874		4	3.83		NW¼SW¼	10	35	42	6 months
1874			1874			.79		SW¼SW¼	10	35	42	6 months
	1874		1874	39.50				SW¼SW¼	10	35	42	6 months
	1874		1874	29.15				SW¼NE¼	14	35	42	6 months
1874			1874			8.95		SW¼NE¼	14	35	42	6 months
	1874		1874	2.14				SE¼NE¼	14	35	42	6 months
1874			1874			.83		NW¼NE¼	14	35	42	6 months
1874			1874			28.88		NE¼SE¼	14	35	42	6 months
	1874		1874	5.22				NE¼SE¼	14	35	42	6 months
1874			1874			37.98		SE¼SE¼	14	35	42	6 months
1874			1874			12.54		NW¼SE¼	14	35	42	6 months
	1874		1874	23.68				NW¼SE¼	14	35	42	6 months
1874			1874		32.58	6.52		SW¼SE¼	14	35	42	6 months
1874			1874		2.07	35.30		NE¼NW¼	14	35	42	6 months
	1874		1874	1.62				NE¼NW¼	14	35	42	6 months

Ellison Ranching Company—Continued. Proof No. 00151A

Date of beneficial use: Nat. mdw.	Cult. area	Construction first initiated: Dams	Ditches	Culture—Acres: Harvest crops	Meadow pasture	Willow and sage pasture	Swamp or overflow	Location: Subdivision	Section	Tp.N.	R.E.	Length of season	Duty of water: C.F.S.	Acre-feet
	1874		1874	20.07				SE¼NW¼	14	35	42	6 months		
1874			1874		2.47	17.53		SE¼NW¼	14	35	42	6 months		
1874			1874			34.32		NW¼NW¼	14	35	42	6 months		
	1874		1874	4.85				NW¼NW¼	14	35	42	6 months		
	1874		1874	3.98				SW¼NW¼	14	35	42	6 months		
1874			1874		4.22	30.28		SW¼NW¼	14	35	42	6 months		
1874			1874			.99		NE¼NE¼	15	35	42	6 months		
	1874		1874	.92				NE¼NE¼	15	35	42	6 months		
1874			1874			1.83		SE¼NE¼	15	35	42	6 months		
	1874		1874	5.52				NE¼NE¼	16	35	42	6 months		

Claimant—**Garat and Co.** Proof No. 00175

Source—**Humboldt River.** Ditch—**Antone Joseph and Artec and Hammond Dam.**

Nat. mdw.	Cult. area	Dams	Ditches	Harvest crops	Meadow pasture	Willow and sage pasture	Swamp or overflow	Subdivision	Section	Tp.N.	R.E.	Length of season	C.F.S.	Acre-feet
1878			1878		1.96			NE¼SW¼	16	36	42			
1878			1878		28.22			NW¼SW¼	16	36	42			
1878			1878			33.87		SE¼SW¼	16	36	42			
1878			1878			40.00		SW¼SW¼	16	36	42			312.15

Claimant—**George Heard.** Proof No. 00174

Source—**Humboldt River. Ditch—Old Clover Valley.**

Nat. mdw.	Cult. area	Dams	Ditches	Harvest crops	Meadow pasture	Willow and sage pasture	Swamp or overflow	Subdivision	Section	Tp.N.	R.E.	Length of season	C.F.S.	Acre-feet
	1879		prior to 1885	2.32				NE¼NE¼	2	35	42	6 months		
1879			1885		34.23	1.73		NE¼NE¼	2	35	42	6 months		
1879			1885		.90			SE¼NE¼	2	35	42	6 months		
	1879		1885	37.00				SE¼NE¼	2	35	42	6 months		
1879			1885		.03	1.36		NW¼NE¼	2	35	42	6 months		
1879			1885		.42	.20		SW¼NE¼	2	35	42	6 months		
	1879		1885	.70				SW¼NE¼	2	35	42	6 months		
	1879		1885	35.87				NE¼SE¼	2	35	42	6 months		
1879			1885			1.21		NE¼SE¼	2	35	42	6 months		
	1879		1885	38.19				SE¼SE¼	2	35	42	6 months		
	1879		1885	1.35				NW¼SE¼	2	35	42	6 months		
	1879		1885	1.37				SW¼SE¼	2	35	42	6 months		

Claimant—**The A. E. Kent & Company, Inc.** Proof No. 00151A

Source—**Humboldt River.** Ditch—**Outside Slough Canal and other sloughs and ditches.**

Nat. mdw.	Cult. area	Dams	Ditches	Harvest crops	Meadow pasture	Willow and sage pasture	Swamp or overflow	Subdivision	Section	Tp.N.	R.E.	Length of season	C.F.S.	Acre-feet
1874			1874			27.79		NE¼NE¼	16	35	42	6 months		
1874			1874			39.50		NW¼NE¼	16	35	42	6 months		
1874			1874			39.46		SE¼NE¼	16	35	42	6 months		
1874			1874		6.93	30.78		SW¼NE¼	16	35	42	6 months		
1874			1874			31.47		NE¼NW¼	16	35	42	6 months		
	1874		1874	5.20				NE¼NW¼	16	35	42	6 months		

...	1874	...	1874	3.77	...	...	...	NW¼NW¼	16	35	42	6 months
1874	...	...	1874	...	...	36.13	...	NW¼NW¼	16	35	42	6 months
1874	...	...	1874	...	...	10.37	...	SW¼NW¼	16	35	42	6 months
...	1874	...	1874	28.82	...	...	...	SW¼NW¼	16	35	42	6 months
...	1874	...	1874	34.46	...	...	...	SE¼NW¼	16	35	42	6 months
1874	...	...	1874	...	...	3.50	...	SE¼NW¼	16	35	42	6 months
1874	...	...	1874	...	...	39.34	...	NE¼SE¼	16	35	42	6 months
1874	...	...	1874	...	...	24.44	...	NW¼SE¼	16	35	42	6 months
...	1874	...	1874	12.28	...	...	...	NW¼SE¼	16	35	42	6 months
...	1874	...	1874	20.43	...	...	...	SW¼SE¼	16	35	42	6 months
1874	...	...	1874	...	...	16.89	...	SW¼SE¼	16	35	42	6 months
1874	...	...	1874	...	...	37.88	1.50	SE¼SE¼	16	35	42	6 months
...	1874	...	1874	39.30	...	...	...	NE¼SW¼	16	35	42	6 months
...	1874	...	1874	26.85	...	...	...	NW¼SW¼	16	35	42	6 months
1874	...	...	1874	...	...	11.97	...	NW¼SW¼	16	35	42	6 months
1874	...	...	1874	...	...	21.68	...	SW¼SW¼	16	35	42	6 months
...	1874	...	1874	17.90	...	...	...	SW¼SW¼	16	35	42	6 months
...	1874	...	1874	39.64	...	...	...	SE¼SW¼	16	35	42	6 months
...	1874	...	1874	1.20	...	...	...	NE¼NE¼	21	35	42	6 months
1874	...	...	1874	...	4.22	31.06	...	NE¼NE¼	21	35	42	6 months
1874	...	...	1874	...	...	3.87	...	NW¼NE¼	21	35	42	6 months
...	1874	...	1874	34.09	...	...	...	NW¼NE¼	21	35	42	6 months
...	1874	...	1874	38.67	...	...	...	SW¼NE¼	21	35	42	6 months
...	1874	...	1874	20.15	...	...	...	SE¼NE¼	21	35	42	6 months
1874	...	...	1874	...	...	16.15	...	SE¼NE¼	21	35	42	6 months
1874	...	...	1874	...	...	1.63	...	NE¼NW¼	21	35	42	6 months
...	1874	...	1874	38.31	...	...	...	NE¼NW¼	21	35	42	6 months
...	1874	...	1874	3.45	...	...	...	NW¼NW¼	21	35	42	6 months
1874	...	...	1874	...	...	36.40	...	NW¼NW¼	21	35	42	6 months
1874	...	...	1874	...	...	38.02	...	SW¼NW¼	21	35	42	6 months
1874	...	...	1874	...	...	25.25	...	SE¼NW¼	21	35	42	6 months
...	1874	...	1874	14.57	...	...	...	SE¼NW¼	21	35	42	6 months
...	1874	...	1874	22.17	...	...	...	NE¼SE¼	21	35	42	6 months
1874	...	...	1874	...	...	14.18	...	NE¼SE¼	21	35	42	6 months
1874	...	...	1874	...	...	11.50	...	NW¼SE¼	21	35	42	6 months
...	1874	...	1874	23.60	...	...	...	NW¼SE¼	21	35	42	6 months
1874	...	...	1874	...	...	35.77	...	SW¼SE¼	21	35	42	6 months
...	1874	...	1874	3.50	...	...	...	SW¼SE¼	21	35	42	6 months
...	1874	...	1874	21.97	...	...	...	SE¼SE¼	21	35	42	6 months
1874	...	...	1874	...	...	16.80	...	SE¼SE¼	21	35	42	6 months
...	1874	...	1874	3.50	...	...	...	SW¼SE¼	21	35	42	6 months
1874	...	...	1874	...	...	35.77	...	SW¼SE¼	21	35	42	6 months
1874	...	...	1874	...	...	40.45	...	NE¼SW¼	21	35	42	6 months
1874	...	...	1874	...	...	38.18	...	NW¼SW¼	21	35	42	6 months
1874	...	...	1874	...	...	39.32	...	SW¼SW¼	21	35	42	6 months
1874	...	...	1874	...	...	38.20	...	SE¼SW¼	21	35	42	6 months
1874	...	...	1874	...	...	36.76	...	NE¼NE¼	28	35	42	6 months
1874	...	...	1874	...	...	37.87	...	NW¼NE¼	28	35	42	6 months
1874	...	...	1874	...	...	39.30	...	SW¼NE¼	28	35	42	6 months
1874	...	...	1874	...	...	39.75	...	SE¼NE¼	28	35	42	6 months

Proof No. 00168A

Claimant—**George B. Williams.**
Source—**Humboldt River.** Ditch—**Argenta Slough.**

Date of beneficial use: Nat. mdw.	Cult. area	Construction first initiated: Dams	Ditches	Culture—Acres: Harvest crops	Meadow pasture	Willow and sage pasture	Swamp or overflow	Location: Subdivision	Section	Tp.N.	R.E.	Length of season	Duty of water: C.F.S.	Acre-feet
1878	......	......	1878	....	.31	......	......	SW¼SW¼	6	32	47	5 months		
1878	......	......	1878	....	34.40	......	......	NW¼SW¼	6	32	47	5 months		
1878	......	......	1878	....	19.65	......	......	NE¼SW¼	6	32	47	5 months		
1878	......	......	1878	....	4.92	......	......	NW¼SE¼	6	32	47	5 months		

PINE VALLEY DISTRICT

Claimant—**George Goodfellow.** Proof No. 00308

Source—**Pony Creek.** Ditch—**Laterals.**

Date of beneficial use		Construction first initiated		Culture—Acres				Location				Length of season	Duty of water	
Nat. mdw.	Cult. area	Dams	Ditches	Harvest crops	Meadow pasture	Willow and sage pasture	Swamp or overflow	Subdivision	Section	Tp.N.	R.E.		C.F.S.	Acre-feet
1867	....	....	....	.	*353.32	....	....	NE¼	17	28	52			
1867	....	....	....	...	41.34	....	....	SE¼	17	28	52			
....	1887	....	1887	37.48	....	....	....	SW¼	16	28	52			
....	1887	....	1887	111.06	....	....	....	NW¼	21	28	52			
....	1887	....	1887	66.26	....	....	....	NE¼	21	28	52			
....	1887	....	1887	78.72	....	....	....	N½SE¼	21	28	52			
....	1887	....	1887	.20	....	....	....	SW¼NW¼	22	28	52			
....	1887	....	1887	2.47	....	....	....	N½SW¼	22	28	52			
....	1887	....	1887	9.20	....	....	....	NE¼SW¼	21	28	52			

*Probably covers more than the NE¼, Sec. 17, as there is only 160 acres in this tract.

NOTE—Explanation in proof states that water was spread over land by a natural dam in 1867 and used as pasture. Additional dams were constructed in 1887 and possibly earlier. Land under date of 1887 irrigated in lieu of the 1867 pasture land.

ELKO DISTRICT

Claimant—**Frank J. Brennen.** Proof No. 00660
Source—**Cottonwood Creek and springs.** Ditch—**Sohlman and Ditch No. 1 and Squires Ditch.**

Date of beneficial use: Nat. mdw.	Cult. area	Construction first initiated: Dams	Ditches	Culture—Acres: Harvest crops	Meadow pasture	Willow and sage pasture	Swamp or overflow	Location: Subdivision	Section	Tp.N.	R.E.	Length of season	Duty of water: C.F.S.	Acre-feet
....	1897	....	prior to 1897	10	....	....	....	SW¼	20	32	57	4-1—7-15		
....	1900	....	1897	9.96	....	....	....	SW¼	20	32	57	4-1—7-15		
....	1903	....	1897	26.50	....	....	....	NW¼	20	32	57	4-1—7-15		

Claimant—**George W. Byers.** Proof No. 00504A
Source—**Spring Canyon Creek and Springs.** Ditch—**Unnamed.**

Date of beneficial use: Nat. mdw.	Cult. area	Construction first initiated: Dams	Ditches	Culture—Acres: Harvest crops	Meadow pasture	Willow and sage pasture	Swamp or overflow	Location: Subdivision	Section	Tp.N.	R.E.	Length of season	Duty of water: C.F.S.	Acre-feet
1889	....	....	....	....	25.10	....	....	E½NE¼	32	37	60	4 months	.251	
1890	....	....	....	....	25.10	....	....	E½NE¼	32	37	60	4 months	.251	

Claimant—**E. Dotta.** Proof No. 00685
Source—**Smith Creek.** Ditch—**West Ditch.**

Date of beneficial use: Nat. mdw.	Cult. area	Construction first initiated: Dams	Ditches	Culture—Acres: Harvest crops	Meadow pasture	Willow and sage pasture	Swamp or overflow	Location: Subdivision	Section	Tp.N.	R.E.	Length of season	Duty of water: C.F.S.	Acre-feet
....	1899	....	1899	248.70	....	....	....		12	31	55			
									13	31	55			
									7	31	56			
									18	31	56	4-1—9-15		

Claimant—**Christene Glaser.** Proof No. 00222A
Source—**Humboldt River.** Ditch—**McCain Ditch.**

Date of beneficial use: Nat. mdw.	Cult. area	Construction first initiated: Dams	Ditches	Culture—Acres: Harvest crops	Meadow pasture	Willow and sage pasture	Swamp or overflow	Location: Subdivision	Section	Tp.N.	R.E.	Length of season	Duty of water: C.F.S.	Acre-feet
....	1875	1875	....	958.12	....	....	....	E½	33	36	58			
....	1887	....	....	31.24	....	....	....	SW¼	33	36	58			
1887	....	....	....	--	....	163.28	....	W½NW¼	33	36	58			
								W½NW¼	34	36	58			
								NW¼SW¼	34	36	58			
								NW¼	4	35	58			
								W½NE¼	4	35	58			
								NE¼NE¼	4	35	58			
								W½SW¼	4	35	58			
								NE¼SW¼	4	35	58			
								E½SE¼	5	35	58			
								SW¼SE¼	5	35	58			
								N½	8	35	58			
								N½NW¼	9	35	58	5 months	11.53	3457.92

Claimant—**Christene Glaser.** Proof No. 00222A

Source—**Humboldt River.** Ditch—**Lamoille Ditch.**

......	1873	......	1872	90.08	......	......	......	NE¼	8	35	58			
								S½NW¼	8	35	58	5 months	1	270.24

Claimant—**Griswold-Henderson Land and Livestock Co.** Proof No. 00369

Source—**Stoffer Creek.** Ditch—**Robert E. Skaggs.**

1884	......	......	1884	66.10	......	......	......	NE¼	30	33	57	4-1—10-1		

Claimant—**Albert Lomori.** Proof No. 00687

Source—**South Fork Humboldt River.** Ditch—**Unnamed.**

......	1902	......	1901	25	......	......	......	SW¼NW¼	30	33	55	4-1—10-1	.25	

Claimant—**Gabriel Rossi.** Proof No. 00461

Source—**Rabbit Creek.** Ditch—**Unnamed.**

......	1887	......	......	53	......	......	......	SE¼	26	34	57
1887	......	......	......	...	29	......	......	SW¼	24	34	57
......	1889	......	......	67	......	......	......	SE¼	24	34	57
......	1889	......	......	4.5	......	......	......	SW¼	24	34	57
......	1889	......	......	58	......	......	......	NW¼	24	34	57
......	1889	......	......	27	......	......	......	NE¼	24	34	57
1889	......	......	......	....	45	......	......	NW¼	24	34	57
1889	......	......	......	....	18.5	......	......	SE¼	24	34	57

STATE OF NEVADA

PRELIMINARY ORDER OF DETERMINATION

OF THE

Waters of the Humboldt River and Its Tributaries

Compiled by the Office of State Engineer, Under Authority of Chapter 140, Statutes of 1913, as amended by Chapter 253, Statutes of 1915, as amended by Chapter 106, Statutes of 1921

J. G. SCRUGHAM, State Engineer

CARSON CITY, NEVADA
STATE PRINTING OFFICE—JOE FARNSWORTH, SUPERINTENDENT
1922

1

PRELIMINARY ORDER OF DETERMINATION OF THE HUMBOLDT RIVER STREAM-SYSTEM AND ITS TRIBUTARIES

The State Engineer of the State of Nevada, having heretofore and under and pursuant to section 18 of chapter 140, Statutes of Nevada, 1913, and Acts amendatory and supplemental thereto, selected in order of its importance for irrigation the Humboldt River stream-system and its tributaries for the determination of the relative rights to the use of the water of said stream-system, and the State Engineer having given and published the notices and filed and made the orders as required by the provisions of sections 18 to 27 of the said chapter 140, Statutes of Nevada, 1913, and Acts amendatory and supplemental thereto, and having made the investigations, prepared the maps, observations and other data, as required by said sections of said Act, and having received and there having been filed with said State Engineer the proofs and statements of claims to the use of water from said stream-system, and all said proofs and evidence taken or given before the State Engineer, or obtained by said State Engineer, having been duly considered, said State Engineer hereby makes this his Preliminary Order of Determination, defining the several rights of claims to the waters of said stream-system and its tributaries.

Except as hereinafter stated, it is recommended the duty of water on the lands irrigated from the Humboldt River stream-system should be as follows:

Class A, Harvest Crops, etc.—3 acre-feet per acre.
Class B, Meadow Pasture—1½ acre-feet per acre.
Class C, Diversified Pasture—¾ acre-foot per acre.

In the following tabulations the calculated rate of flow in Districts 1, 2, and 3 is based upon an irrigating season of 180 days for Class A lands, 90 days for Class B lands, and 45 days for Class C lands. In District 4 the calculated rate of flow is based upon an irrigating season of 120 days for Class A lands, 60 days for Class B lands, and 30 days for Class C lands. Due to the wide variations in conditions of irrigation practice, season, soil, crops, etc., the State Engineer deems it necessary to reserve the right as given under section 36a, chapter 106, Nevada Statutes of 1921, to modify his findings on the duty of water or rate of flow as allocated, where it is afterwards found that such modification is desirable and consistent with the principle that actual and beneficial use is the measure and limit of the right.

In defining this actual and beneficial use the State Engineer will give due consideration to the head required to distribute the water over the land and to the water which returns to the stream-system and becomes available for the use of other appropriators.

Upon lands where conditions render it impossible to measure the amount of water diverted upon the land, the duty of water as allotted will be modified and based upon that time-limit of irrigation which is found to be most consistent with good husbandry. Swamp lands which are allocated a water right in the following tabulations should not carry the right to divert water from the stream-system on to such lands, until the areas become dry or are drained and provision made to return the drainage water to the stream-system.

The parties named in this order of determination, or their successors in

interest, shall not be required to take or use the amount of water allotted to them in a continuous flow, but may cumulate the same or any part thereof in rotation or periodic turn, within the season limits, and with the approval of the Water Commissioner, and subject to the control and direction of the State Engineer.

In addition to water used during the irrigating season, each user should be entitled, in his proper proportion and priority, to the use of water in such reasonable amounts as necessary for fall and spring irrigation and for stock-watering purposes during the nonirrigating season.

In case any water user is dissatisfied with the duty of water as allotted in this preliminary order of determination, he may, either immediately or at any time not later than three years from date of issuance of the court decree, submit to the State Engineer such authenticated measurements as may be necessary to prove the actual and beneficial use of water on his lands. Upon approval of the proof submitted, the Engineer will accordingly modify his findings or, in case the decree has already been entered, he will apply to the Court for a modification of the duty of water allotment in conformity with the proof submitted.

All measurements of amounts diverted are to be made at the point where the main ditch enters or becomes adjacent to the land to be irrigated or as near thereto as practicable, the location if not selected by the State Engineer to be approved by him. Each water user shall install and maintain substantial headgates and weirs in his ditch or ditches. Due allowance for losses in ditches will be made by the State Engineer in case it becomes necessary to divert additional water into said ditches.

LOVELOCK DISTRICT

Claimant—**Antonio J. Alves.** Proof No. 001

Source—**Humboldt River.** Ditch—**Old Channel.**

Date of beneficial use — Nat. mdw.	Date of beneficial use — Cult. area	Construction first initiated — Dams	Construction first initiated — Ditches	Culture—Acres — Harvest crops	Culture—Acres — Meadow pasture	Culture—Acres — Willow and sage pasture	Culture—Acres — Swamp or overflow	Location — Subdivision	Location — Section	Location — Tp.N.	Location — R.E.	Length of season	Duty of water — C.F.S.	Duty of water — Acre-feet
	1904			4				NW¼NW¼	18	27	32	3-15—9-15	.033	12.0
	1904					4.30		NW¼NW¼	18	27	32	3-15—6-13	.035	6.45

Claimant—**Johannes Anderson.** Proof No. 002

Source—**Humboldt River.** Ditch—**Larson Ditch. Union Canal through Reed Ditch.**

Nat. mdw.	Cult. area	Dams	Ditches	Harvest crops	Meadow pasture	Willow and sage pasture	Swamp or overflow	Subdivision	Section	Tp.N.	R.E.	Length of season	C.F.S.	Acre-feet
1874				30				E½NE¼	4	25	31	3-15—9-15	.244	90.0
	1880			10				E½NE¼	4	25	31	3-15—9-15	.081	30.0
	1881			17.25				E½NE¼	4	25	31	3-15—9-15	.140	51.75
	1893			36.25				E½SE¼	4	25	31	3-15—9-15	.295	108.75
	1898			18.25				E½SE¼	4	25	31	3-15—9-15	.118	54.75
	1902			18				E½SE¼	4	25	31	3-15—9-15	.146	54.0

Claimant—**Peter Anker.** Proof No. 003

Source—**Humboldt River.** Ditch—**Union Canal.**

Nat. mdw.	Cult. area	Dams	Ditches	Harvest crops	Meadow pasture	Willow and sage pasture	Swamp or overflow	Subdivision	Section	Tp.N.	R.E.	Length of season	C.F.S.	Acre-feet
	1877					79.40		E½SE¼	22	26	31	3-15—6-13	.646	119.1
	1877			35.45				NE¼	22	26	31	3-15—9-15	.288	106.35
	1878			62.04					22	26	31	3-15—9-15	.504	186.12
	1879			31.02					22	26	31	3-15—9-15	.252	93.06
	1880			35.45					22	26	31	3-15—9-15	.288	106.35
	1881			28.36					22	26	31	3-15—9-15	.231	85.08
	1882			22.16					22	26	31	3-15—9-15	.180	66.48
	1883			35.45					22	26	31	3-15—9-15	.288	106.35
	1886			265.88					22	26	31	3-15—9-15	2.161	797.64
	1890			10.64					22	26	31	3-15—9-15	.225	31.92
	1879			38.60				E½E½	21	26	31	3-15—9-15	.153	116.07
	1880			19.37				E½E½	21	26	31	3-15—9-15	.295	58.11
	1881			19.37				E½E½	21	26	31	3-15—9-15	.295	58.11
	1882			14.50				E½E½	21	26	31	3-15—9-15	.255	43.50
	1883			19.37				E½E½	21	26	31	3-15—9-15	.295	58.11
	1886			30.96				E½E½	21	26	31	3-15—9-15	.380	92.88
	1890			7.74				E½E½	21	26	31	3-15—9-15	.201	23.22

Claimant—**L. R. Bassman.** Proof No. 004
Source—**Humboldt River.** Ditch—**Old Channel.**

1893	86.00			SE¼	14	27	31	3-15—9-15	.837	258.0
1895	22.20			SE¼	14	27	31	3-15—9-15	.319	66.60
1895	2.75			SE¼	14	27	31	3-15—9-15	.160	8.25
1895	24.05			SE¼	14	27	31	3-15—9-15	.834	72.15
1895	60.55			SW¼	14	27	31	3-15—9-15	.630	181.65
1895	78.10			SW¼	14	27	31	3-15—9-15	.773	234.30

Claimant—**Grace S. Jahn.** Proof No. 005
Source—**Humboldt River.** Ditch—**Union Canal through Reed Ditch.**

1880	15			N½	34	26	31	3-15—9-15	.122	45.0
1876	....		96.0	N½	34	26	31	3-15—6-13	.780	144.0
1881	30			N½	34	26	31	3-15—9-15	.244	90.0
1883	55			N½	34	26	31	3-15—9-15	.447	165.0
1887	25			N½	34	26	31	3-15—9-15	.203	75.0
1901	15			N½	34	26	31	3-15—9-15	.122	45.0
1903	20			N½	34	26	31	3-15—9-15	.163	60.0

Claimant—**Pitt and McDonald.** Proof No. 006
Source—**Humboldt River.** Ditch—**Union Canal through Lake Shore Ditch.**

1874	....	44.05		W½NW¼	4	25	31	3-15—6-13	.358	66.75
1874	....		116	NW¼	4	25	31	3-15—6-13	.130	174.0

Claimant—**Ed. Berg.** Proof No. 007
Source—**Humboldt River.** Ditch—**Young Ditch.**

1897	58.14			E½E½	1	27	31	3-15—9-15	.473	174.42

Claimant—**William Loorz.** Proof No. 008
Source—**Humboldt River.** Ditch—**Old Channel.**

1895	30			W½NE¼	13	27	31	3-15—9-15	.244	90.0
1897	20			W½NE¼	13	27	31	3-15—9-15	.165	60.0
1898	15.40			W½NE¼	13	27	31	3-15—9-15	.125	46.20
1895	....	8.75		W½NE¼	13	27	31	3-15—6-13	.071	13.13

Claimant—**W. C. Thorne and Ida M. Thorne.** Proof No. 009
Source—**Humboldt River.** Ditch—**Irish-American.**

1886	4			SW¼SE¼	23	27	31	3-15—9-15	.033	12.0
1888	14.20			SW¼SE¼	23	27	31	3-15—9-15	.115	42.60
1890	....		3.15	SW¼SE¼	23	27	31	3-15—6-13	.026	4.73

Claimant—**Mrs. E. A. Borland.** Proof No. 0010
Source—**Humboldt River.** Ditch—**Irish-American in conjunction with Old Channel.**

Date of beneficial use: Nat. mdw.	Date of beneficial use: Cult. area	Construction first initiated: Dams	Construction first initiated: Ditches	Culture—Acres: Harvest crops	Culture—Acres: Meadow pasture	Culture—Acres: Willow and sage pasture	Culture—Acres: Swamp or over-flow	Location: Subdivision	Location: Section	Location: Tp.N.	Location: R.E.	Length of season	Duty of water: C.F.S.	Duty of water: Acre-feet
	1890			1.69				NW¼NE¼	27	27	31	3-15—9-15	.014	5.07
	1890			37.86				W½NE¼	27	27	31	3-15—9-15	.308	113.58
	1891			29.45				W½NE¼	27	27	31	3-15—9-15	.239	88.35
	1892			110.70				NW¼	27	27	31	3-15—9-15	.900	332.10

Claimant—**F. A. Preston.** Proof No. 0011
Source—**Humboldt River.** Ditch—***Graveyard Slough and Union Canal.**

Nat. mdw.	Cult. area	Dams	Ditches	Harvest crops	Meadow pasture	Willow and sage pasture	Swamp or over-flow	Subdivision	Section	Tp.N.	R.E.	Length of season	C.F.S.	Acre-feet
	1886			9				W½SE¼	29	26	31	3-15—9-15	.073	27.0
	1890			3				W½SE¼	29	26	31	3-15—9-15	.024	9.0
	1900			14.75				W½SE¼	29	26	31	3-15—9-15	.112	44.25
	1886			...		*22.80		W½SE¼	29	26	31	3-15—6-13	.185	34.2

Claimant—**Pitt and McDonald.** Proof No. 0012
Source—**Humboldt River.** Ditch—**Union Canal through Lake Shore Ditch; *Trembly Ditch.**

Nat. mdw.	Cult. area	Dams	Ditches	Harvest crops	Meadow pasture	Willow and sage pasture	Swamp or over-flow	Subdivision	Section	Tp.N.	R.E.	Length of season	C.F.S.	Acre-feet
1874	*1874			227.65				W½SE¼&SW¼	4	25	31	3-15—9-15	1.851	682.95
1874	*1874			...		12.20		W½SE¼&SW¼	4	25	31	3-15—6-13	.099	18.3

Claimant—**L. N. Carpenter.** Proof No. 0013
Source—**Humboldt River.** Ditch—**Rodgers Canal System and †Irish-American.**

Nat. mdw.	Cult. area	Dams	Ditches	Harvest crops	Meadow pasture	Willow and sage pasture	Swamp or over-flow	Subdivision	Section	Tp.N.	R.E.	Length of season	C.F.S.	Acre-feet
	1889			25.55				SW¼NW¼	10	26	31	3-15—9-15	.208	76.65
	1900			17.50				NE¼NW¼	11	26	31	3-15—9-15	.142	52.50
	1897			17.45				E½NW¼	35	27	31	3-15—9-15	.142	52.35
	1877			...		†19.25		E½NW¼	35	27	31	3-15—6-13	.157	28.88
	1877			...		†23.70		S½SW¼	26	27	31	3-15—6-13	.193	35.55
	1877					†6.60		S½SW¼	26	27	31	3-15—6-13	.537	9.9
	1885			25				SE¼NW¼	1	26	31	3-15—9-15	.203	75.0
	1885			75				E½SW¼	1	26	31	3-15—9-15	.610	225.0
	1886			2				W½SW¼	1	26	31	3-15—9-15	.016	6.0
	1886			3				W½NW¼	1	26	31	3-15—9-15	.024	9.0
	1890			40				W½SW¼	1	26	31	3-15—9-15	.325	120.0
	1890			20				NW¼SE¼	1	26	31	3-15—9-15	.163	60.0
	1891			5.75				S½SE¼	1	26	31	3-15—9-15	.047	17.25
	1891			27.65				S½SE¼	1	26	31	3-15—9-15	.225	82.95
	1894			20				NW¼SE¼	1	26	31	3-15—9-15	.163	60.0
	1894			5.40				SW¼SE¼	1	26	31	3-15—9-15	.044	16.20
	1894			3.60				W½NE¼	1	26	31	3-15—9-15	.029	10.8
	1894			5				E½SW¼	1	26	31	3-15—9-15	.041	15.0
	1898			20				NE¼SE¼	1	26	31	3-15—9-15	.163	60.0
	1900			15				S½SE¼	1	26	31	3-15—9-15	.122	45.0
	1900			20				NE¼SE¼	1	26	31	3-15—9-15	.163	60.0
	1900			26.20				S½SE¼	1	26	31	3-15—9-15	.213	08.60
	1900			13.96				E½NE¼	1	26	31	3-15—9-15	.113	40.88

1880				14				E¼NW¼	35	27	31	3-15—9-13	.114	42.0
1880					25.00			SE¼NW¼	1	26	31	3-15—6-13	.203	37.5
1880					1.75			W½SW¼	1	26	31	3-15—6-13	.014	2.63
1880					52.35			S½SE¼	1	26	31	3-15—6-13	.426	78.53
1880					80.00			N½SE¼	1	26	31	3-15—6-13	.650	120.0
1879					47.15			W½SW¼	1	26	31	3-15—6-13	.383	70.73
1879					3.60			S½NE¼	1	26	31	3-15—6-13	.029	5.4
1877				50				W½NE¼ & NW¼SE¼	2	26	31	3-15—9-15	.407	150.0
1877					80.00			E½SW¼	1	26	31	3-15—6-13	.650	120.0
1877					20.00			E½NW¼	2	26	31	3-15—6-13	.163	30.0
1878				31.7				SW¼SW¼	2	26	31	3-15—9-15	.258	95.1
1878				12.7				SE¼SW¼	2	26	31	3-15—9-15	.103	38.1
1878				5.6				NE¼SW¼	2	26	31	3-15—9-15	.046	16.8
1878					16.70			SE¼SW¼	2	26	31	3-15—6-13	.136	25.05
1878					41.95			E½NW¼	2	26	31	3-15—6-13	.341	62.93
1878					11.80			N½SE¼	2	26	31	3-15—6-13	.096	17.7
1878					21.25			W½SW¼	1	26	31	3-15—6-13	.173	31.88
1878					7.85			SE¼NW¼ & NE¼SW¼	2	26	31	3-15—6-13	.064	11.78
1879				3.60				NE¼NW¼	2	26	31	3-15—9-15	.029	10.80
1879				22.70				SE¼SW¼ & SW¼SE¼	2	26	31	3-15—9-15	.185	68.10
1879				7.50				SE¼NW¼ & NE¼SE¼	2	26	31	3-15—9-15	.061	22.50
1879				9.85				NW¼SW¼ & SW¼NW¼	1	26	31	3-15—9-15	.080	29.55
1879				6.35				W½SW¼	2	26	31	3-15—9-15	.052	19.05
1879					49.25			W½SW¼	2	26	31	3-15—6-13	.400	73.88
	1863			10				NE¼SW¼	2	26	31	3-15—9-15	.081	30.0
1863				50				NE¼	2	26	31	3-15—9-15	.407	150.0
1863				50				NW¼	1	26	31	3-15—9-15	.407	150.0
1866				80				N½NE¼	11	26	31	3-15—9-15	.650	240.0
1866				75.90				SE¼	2	26	31	3-15—9-15	.617	227.70
1866				2				SW¼	1	26	31	3-15—9-15	.016	6.0
	1868			20				W½W½	1	26	31	3-15—9-15	.163	60.0
1868				16				S½SW¼	26	27	31	3-15—9-15	.130	48.0
1872					100.00			W½W½	10	26	31	3-15—6-13	.813	150.0
	1872			20				W½SW¼	10	26	31	3-15—9-15	.163	60.0
1871					80.00			N½NW¼	11	26	31	3-15—6-13	.650	120.0
	1875			80				W½NE¼	2	26	31	3-15—9-15	.650	240.0
	1875			25				NE¼NW¼	1	26	31	3-15—9-15	.203	75.0
	1880			25				S½NE¼	1	26	31	3-15—9-15	.203	75.0
	1885			25				SW¼NW¼	1	26	31	3-15—9-15	.203	75.0
	1885			49.25				W½SW¼	2	26	31	3-15—9-15	.400	147.75
	1887			7.85				SE¼NW¼ & NE¼SE¼	2	26	31	3-15—9-15	.064	23.55
	1881			55.45				W½NW¼	27	26	31	3-15—9-15	.451	166.35
	1887			151.80				SW¼	27	26	31	3-15—9-15	1.234	455.40
	1886					154.80		E½	27	26	31	3-15—6-13	1.259	232.2
	1886					47.95		E½	27	26	31	3-15—6-13	.390	71.93
	1884				6.70			NW¼NW¼	27	26	31	3-15—6-13	.054	10.05

Claimant—**C. C. Carpenter.** Proof No. 0014

Source—**Humboldt River.** Ditch—**Union Canal and Lake Shore Ditch.**

	1875			15				E½NE¼	28	26	31	3-15—9-15	.122	45.0
	1881			51.10				E½NE¼	28	26	31	3-15—9-15	.415	153.30

Claimant—**Chris Beck.** Proof No. 0014

Source—**Humboldt River.** Ditch—**Killebrew & Beck Ditch, now Tule Ditch.**

Date of beneficial use: Nat. mdw.	Date of beneficial use: Cult. area	Construction first initiated: Dams	Construction first initiated: Ditches	Culture—Acres: Harvest crops	Culture—Acres: Meadow pasture	Culture—Acres: Willow and sage pasture	Culture—Acres: Swamp or overflow	Location: Subdivision	Location: Section	Location: Tp.N.	Location: R.E.	Length of season	Duty of water: C.F.S.	Duty of water: Acre-feet
....	1901	....	....	80	....	....	....	SW¼	10	25	31	3-15—9-15	.650	240.0

Claimant—**Chris Hanson.** Proof No. 0015

Source—**Humboldt River.** Ditch—***Harrison and Mayes; †Southwest Ditch; ‡Irish-American.**

Nat. mdw.	Cult. area	Dams	Ditches	Harvest crops	Meadow pasture	Willow and sage pasture	Swamp or overflow	Subdivision	Section	Tp.N.	R.E.	Length of season	C.F.S.	Acre-feet
....	‡1885	....	....	10	....	....	....	E½NW¼	28	27	31	3-15—9-15	.061	30.0
....	*†1880	....	....	80	....	....	....	E½NW¼	28	27	31	3-15—9-15	.650	240.0

Claimant—**John G. Taylor.** Proof. No. 0016

Source—**Humboldt River.** Ditch—**Southwest Ditch.**

Nat. mdw.	Cult. area	Dams	Ditches	Harvest crops	Meadow pasture	Willow and sage pasture	Swamp or overflow	Subdivision	Section	Tp.N.	R.E.	Length of season	C.F.S.	Acre-feet
....	1890	....	....	73.14	....	....	....	E½NE¼	28	27	31	3-15—9-15	.595	219.42

Claimant—**John G. Taylor.** Proof No. 0016

Source—**Humboldt River.** Ditch—**Young Ditch in conjunction with Marzen Slough.**

Nat. mdw.	Cult. area	Dams	Ditches	Harvest crops	Meadow pasture	Willow and sage pasture	Swamp or overflow	Subdivision	Section	Tp.N.	R.E.	Length of season	C.F.S.	Acre-feet
....	1890	....	....	67.76	....	....	....	W½NW¼	28	27	31	3-15—9-15	.470	173.28

Claimant—**H. M. Damm.** Proof No. 0017

Source—**Humboldt River.** Ditch—**Old Channel and Humboldt Irrigation and Power Co. Canal.**

Nat. mdw.	Cult. area	Dams	Ditches	Harvest crops	Meadow pasture	Willow and sage pasture	Swamp or overflow	Subdivision	Section	Tp.N.	R.E.	Length of season	C.F.S.	Acre-feet
....	1897	....	....	29.70	....	....	....	NE¼SE¼	11	27	31	3-15—9-15	.241	89.10
....	1897	....	....	33.70	....	....	....	SW¼SW¼	11	27	31	3-15—9-15	.274	101.10
....	1895	....	....	75.81	....	....	....	E½SW¼&NW¼SW¼	11	27	31	3-15—9-15	.616	227.43
....	1897	....	....	30	....	....	....	E½SW¼&NW¼SW¼	11	27	31	3-15—9-15	.244	90.0
....	1895	....	....	82.80	....	....	....	NW¼	11	27	31	3-15—9-15	.673	248.40
....	1895	....	....	11.10	....	....	....	SE¼NW¼	11	27	31	3-15—9-15	.090	33.30
....	1897	....	....	....	1.20	....	....	NE¼SW¼	1	27	31	3-15—6-13	.010	1.8
....	1895	....	....	....	....	8.70	....	NE¼NW¼	11	27	31	3-15—6-13	.071	13.05

Claimant—**J. C. Damm.** Proof No. 0018

Source—**Humboldt River.** Ditch—**Union Canal through Lake Shore Ditch.**

Nat. mdw.	Cult. area	Dams	Ditches	Harvest crops	Meadow pasture	Willow and sage pasture	Swamp or overflow	Subdivision	Section	Tp.N.	R.E.	Length of season	C.F.S.	Acre-feet
....	1877	....	....	5	....	....	....	NW¼	28	26	31	3-15—9-15	.041	15.0
....	1877	....	....	....	....	6.30	....	NW¼	28	26	31	3-15—6-13	.051	9.45
....	1878	....	....	15	....	....	....	NW¼	28	26	31	3-15—9-15	.122	45.0
....	1880	....	....	10	....	....	....	NW¼	28	26	31	3-15—9-15	.081	30.0
....	1883	....	....	46.75	....	....	....	NW¼	28	26	31	3-15—9-15	.380	140.25

Claimant—**E. A. Perez and John Dotta.** Proof No. 0019

Source—**Humboldt River.** Ditch—**Union Canal through Reed Ditch.**

	1884			22				E½NW¼	33	26	31	3-15—9-15	.179	66.0
	1887			33.05				E½NW¼	33	26	31	3-15—9-15	.269	99.15

Claimant—**Lawrence Devita.** Proof No. 0021

Source—**Humboldt River.** Ditch—**Old Channel.**

	1899			29.80				NE¼	13	27	31	3-15—9-15	.242	89.40

Claimant—**Frank Ambrosetti and John Scott.** Proof No. 0022

Source—**Humboldt River.** Ditch—**Old Channel.**

	1896			31.70				W½SW¼	13	27	31	3-15—9-15	.258	95.10
	1896			7.90				W½SW¼	13	27	31	3-15—9-15	.064	23.70
	1896			8.30				W½SW¼	13	27	31	3-15—9-15	.067	24.90
	1896			4.35				W½SW¼	13	27	31	3-15—9-15	.035	13.05
	1896			14.25				W½SW¼	13	27	31	3-15—9-15	.116	42.75
	1896			2.75				NE¼NW¼	24	27	31	3-15—9-15	.022	8.25

Claimant—**Santos and Souza.** Proof No. 0023

Source—**Humboldt River.** Ditch—**Union Canal through Lake Shore Ditch.**

	1899			40				W½SW¼	29	26	31	3-15—9-15	.324	120.0
	1902			20				W½SW¼	29	26	31	3-15—9-15	.163	60.0
	1903			20				W½SW¼	29	26	31	3-15—9-15	.163	60.0

Claimant—**Carl Elges.** Proof No. 0024

Source—**Humboldt River.** Ditch—**Young Ditch.**

	1897			59.75				NE¼	7	27	32	3-15—9-15	.486	179.25
	1897			3.15				NW¼NE¼	7	27	32	3-15—9-15	.026	9.45
	1897			....			6.30	N½NE¼	7	27	32	3-15—6-13	.051	9.45

Claimant—**Frank R. Mancebo.** Proof No. 0025

Source—**Humboldt River.** Ditch—**Old Channel.**

	1894			30				S½SE¼	12	27	31	3-15—9-15	.244	90.0
	1895			46.50				S½SE¼	12	27	31	3-15—9-15	.378	139.50

Claimant—**James Kjeldsen.** Proof No. 0026

Source—**Humboldt River.** Ditch—**Union Canal.**

	1879			18				S½SE¼	28	26	31	3-15—9-15	.146	54.0
	1880			8				S½SE¼	28	26	31	3-15—9-15	.065	24.0
	1882			14				S½SE¼	28	26	31	3-15—9-15	.114	42.0
	1885			12				S½SE¼	28	26	31	3-15—9-15	.098	36.0
	1891			15				S½SE¼	28	26	31	3-15—9-15	.122	45.0
	1891			2.08				S½SE¼	28	26	31	3-15—9-15	.017	6.24

Claimant—**Mary T. Fuss.** Proof No. 0027
Source—**Humboldt River.** Ditch—***Saxenheimer; †Union Canal through Fuss Lateral.**

Date of beneficial use: Nat. mdw.	Date of beneficial use: Cult. area	Construction first initiated: Dams	Construction first initiated: Ditches	Culture—Acres: Harvest crops	Culture—Acres: Meadow pasture	Culture—Acres: Willow and sage pasture	Culture—Acres: Swamp or overflow	Location: Subdivision	Location: Section	Location: Tp.N.	Location: R.E.	Length of season	Duty of water: C.F.S.	Duty of water: Acre-feet
*1866				198.65					12	26	31	3-15—9-15	1.615	595.95
*1866						389.90			12	26	31	3-15—6-13	3.170	584.85
	†1879			‡120					12	26	31	3-15—9-15	.976	360.0
	†1885			‡140					12	26	31	3-15—9-15	1.138	420.0
	†1890			‡100					12	26	31	3-15—9-15	.813	300.0
*1866						‡29.90			12	26	31	3-15—6-13	.243	44.85

‡NOTE—Land originally held water right for pasture as of 1866. Since that time the pasture land has gradually been placed under intensive cultivation in the years mentioned, thus gaining, in addition to the pasture right, right sufficient to give a full water right to the lands listed in tabulation as harvest crops.

The total area for which water is allotted cannot be in excess of 588.55 acres.

Claimant—**C. C. Carpenter.** Proof No. **0028**
Source—**Humboldt River.** Ditch—**Union Canal.**

Nat. mdw.	Cult. area	Dams	Ditches	Harvest crops	Meadow pasture	Willow and sage pasture	Swamp or overflow	Subdivision	Section	Tp.N.	R.E.	Length of season	C.F.S.	Acre-feet
	1877			7				NW¼NE¼	28	26	31	3-15—9-15	.057	21.0
	1878			30				NW¼SE¼	28	26	31	3-15—9-15	.244	90.0
	1878			20				SW¼SE¼	21	26	31	3-15—9-15	.163	60.0
	1883			50				W½SE¼	21	26	31	3-15—9-15	.407	150.0
	1888			50				W½NE¼	21	26	31	3-15—9-15	.407	150.0
	1892			18.50				W½E½	21	26	31	3-15—9-15	.150	55.50
	1892			81.65				W½NE¼&N½SE¼	28	26	31	3-15—9-15	.664	244.95
	1877					4		NW¼SE¼	28	26	31	3-15—6-13	.033	6.0

Claimant—**Hans Westergard.** Proof No. **0031**
Source—**Humboldt River.** Ditch—**Union Canal through Lake Shore Ditch.**

Nat. mdw.	Cult. area	Dams	Ditches	Harvest crops	Meadow pasture	Willow and sage pasture	Swamp or overflow	Subdivision	Section	Tp.N.	R.E.	Length of season	C.F.S.	Acre-feet
	1884			35				W½NW¼	33	26	31	3-15—9-15	.285	105.0
	1890			10				W½NW¼	33	26	31	3-15—9-15	.081	30.0
	1891			10				W½NW¼	33	26	31	3-15—9-15	.081	30.0
	1894			11.40				W½NW¼	33	26	31	3-15—9-15	.093	34.20

Claimant—**Chris Hanson.** Proof No. **0032**
Source—**Humboldt River.** Ditch—**Union Canal through Reed Ditch.**

Nat. mdw.	Cult. area	Dams	Ditches	Harvest crops	Meadow pasture	Willow and sage pasture	Swamp or overflow	Subdivision	Section	Tp.N.	R.E.	Length of season	C.F.S.	Acre-feet
	1882			28.70				E½NE¼	33	26	31	3-15—9-15	.233	86.10
	1885			33.70				E½NE¼	33	26	31	3-15—9-15	.268	101.10
	1905			10				E½NE¼	33	26	31	3-15—9-15	.081	30.0

Claimant—**Nellie Martin.** Proof No. **0033**
Source—**Humboldt River.** Ditch—***Larson Ditch; Union Canal through Reed Ditch.**

Nat. mdw.	Cult. area	Dams	Ditches	Harvest crops	Meadow pasture	Willow and sage pasture	Swamp or overflow	Subdivision	Section	Tp.N.	R.E.	Length of season	C.F.S.	Acre-feet
	*1875			25				S½SE¼	33	26	31	3-15—9-15	.203	75.0
	*1880			44				S½SE¼	33	26	31	3-15—9-15	.358	132.0
	*1875					7.85		S½SE¼	33	26	31	3-15—6-13	.064	11.78

Claimant—**Ingvert Hanson.** Proof No. 0034
Source—**Humboldt River.** Ditch—**Union Canal through Lake Shore Ditch.**

	1878			4				SE¼SW¼	32	26	31	3-15—9-15	.033	12.0
	1879			15.44				SW¼	32	26	31	3-15—9-15	.126	46.32
	1880			4.82				SW¼	32	26	31	3-15—9-15	.039	14.46
	1881			4.82				SW¼	32	26	31	3-15—9-15	.039	14.46
	1882			4.82				SW¼	32	26	31	3-15—9-15	.039	14.46
	1883			4.82				SW¼	32	26	31	3-15—9-15	.039	14.46
	1884			5.79				SW¼	32	26	31	3-15—9-15	.047	17.37
	1890			13.51				SW¼	32	26	31	3-15—9-15	.110	40.53
	1895			27.03				SW¼	32	26	31	3-15—9-15	.220	81.09
	1900			11.60				SW¼	32	26	31	3-15—9-15	.094	34.80
	1880			....		20		SW¼	32	26	31	3-15—6-18	.163	30.0

Claimant—**Andrew Jacobson.** Proof No. 0035
Source—**Humboldt River.** Ditch—**Young Ditch.**

	1897			60				NW¼	7	27	32	3-15—9-15	.488	180.0
	1898			20				NW¼	7	27	32	3-15—9-15	.163	60.0
	1904			40				NW¼	7	27	32	3-15—9-15	.325	120.0
	1904			10				NW¼	7	27	32	3-15—9-15	.081	30.0
	1897			....		2.30		NW¼	7	27	32	3-15—6-13	.019	3.45
	1900			4.30				NW¼NW¼	7	27	32	3-15—9-15	.035	12.90
	1901			1.90				NW¼NW¼	7	27	32	3-15—9-15	.015	5.70

Claimant—**R. Helwinkle.** Proof No. 0036
Source—**Humboldt River.** Ditch—**Southwest Ditch.**

	1887			20				SW¼	23	27	31	3-15—9-15	.163	60.0
	1889			88				SW¼	23	27	31	3-15—9-15	.715	264.0
	1904			29.45				SW¼	23	27	31	3-15—9-15	.239	88.35

Claimant—**J. A. Henrikson.** Proof No. 0037
Source—**Humboldt River.** Ditch—**Union Canal through Reed Ditch.**

	1885			35.60				SE¼	34	26	31	3-15—9-15	.289	106.8
	1886			40.00				SE¼	34	26	31	3-15—9-15	.325	120.0
	1894			47.25				SE¼	34	26	31	3-15—9-15	.384	141.75
	1899			18.90				SE¼	34	26	31	3-15—9-15	.154	56.70

Claimant—**Estate John J. Hill.** Proof No. 0038
Source—**Humboldt River.** Ditch—**Union Canal through Lake Shore Ditch.**

	1880			236				W½	21	26	31	3-15—9-15	.019	708.0
	1880			4.30				SE¼SW¼	21	26	31	3-15—9-15	.035	12.90
	1880			.80				SE¼SW¼	21	26	31	3-15—9-15	.007	2.40
	1880			1.60				NE¼NW¼	21	26	31	3-15—9-15	.013	4.80
	1880			53.50				E½SE¼	20	26	31	3-15—9-15	.435	160.50
	1880			3.55				E½SE¼	20	26	51	3-15—9-15	.029	10.65
	1902			29.10				W½SE¼	20	26	31	3-15—9-15	.237	87.30
	1902			26.00				E¼E½SW¼	20	26	31	3-15—9-15	.211	78.0
	1901			2.30				SW¼NE¼	29	26	31	3-15—9-15	.019	6.90

Claimant—**Joseph Hill.** Proof No. 0039
Source—**Humboldt River.** Ditch—**Union Canal through Reed Ditch.**

Date of beneficial use: Nat. mdw.	Date of beneficial use: Cult. area	Construction first initiated: Dams	Construction first initiated: Ditches	Culture—Acres: Harvest crops	Culture—Acres: Meadow pasture	Culture—Acres: Willow and sage pasture	Culture—Acres: Swamp or overflow	Location: Subdivision	Location: Section	Location: Tp.N.	Location: R.E.	Length of season	Duty of water: C.F.S.	Duty of water: Acre-feet
	1888			35				SW¼	35	26	31	3-15—9-15	.285	105.0
	1893			55				SW¼	35	26	31	3-15—9-15	.447	165.0
	1903			71.60				SW¼	35	26	31	3-15—9-15	.582	214.80

Claimant—**Emil Holmstrom.** Proof No. 0040
Source—**Humboldt River.** Ditch—**Old Channel.**

	1893			50.35				E½NE¼	14	27	31	3-15—9-15	.125	151.05
	1893			23				E½NE¼	14	27	31	3-15—9-15	.187	69.0
	1895			70.95				S½SE¼	11	27	31	3-15—9-15	.577	212.85
	1895			4.70				S½SE¼	11	27	31	3-15—9-15	.038	14.10

Claimant—**Hugh Holmstrom.** Proof No. 0041
Source—**Humboldt River.** Ditch—**Young Ditch.**

	1901			50				N½	2	27	31	3-15—9-15	.407	150.0
	1902			34				N½	2	27	31	3-15—9-15	.276	102.0
	1903			50				N½	2	27	31	3-15—9-15	.407	150.0

Claimant—**John Holmstrom.** Proof No. 0042
Source—**Humboldt River.** Ditch—**Young Ditch.**

	1897			25				E½W½	6	27	32	3-15—9-15	.203	75.0
	1897			35				W½E½	6	27	32	3-15—9-15	.285	105.0
	1898			65				E½	6	27	32	3-15—9-15	.528	195.0
	1899			35				E½	6	27	32	3-15—9-15	.285	105.0
	1897			...		40		E½NE¼	6	27	32	3-15—6-13	.325	60.0
								SE¼SE¼	31	28	32			

Claimant—**Emil Holmstrom.** Proof No. 0043
Source—**Humboldt River.** Ditch—**Young Ditch.**

	1897			47.50				N½NW¼	12	27	31	3-15—9-15	.386	142.50
	1897			9				N½NE¼	11	27	31	3-15—9-15	.073	27.0
	1897			19.35				N½NW¼	12	27	31	3-15—9-15	.157	58.05
	1897			10				N½NE¼	11	27	31	3-15—9-15	.081	30.0

Claimant—**Nels Jensen.** Proof No. 0045
Source—**Humboldt River.** Ditch—**Young Ditch.**

	1903			20				NW¼	11	27	31	3-15—9-15	.163	60.0

Claimant—**James Johnson.** Proof No. 0046

Source—**Humboldt River.** Ditch—**Young Ditch.**

1897	25		E½W½	1	27	31	3-15—9-15	.203	75.0
1901	25		E½W½	1	27	31	3-15—9-15	.203	75.0

Claimant—**M. A. Moreira.** Proof No. 0047

Source—**Humboldt River.** Ditch—**Old Channel.**

1895	65		SW¼	12	27	31	3-15—9-15	.528	195.0
1897	9.30		SW¼	12	27	31	3-15—9-15	.076	27.90

Claimant—**Joe P. Johnson.** Proof No. 0047

Source—**Humboldt River.** Ditch—**Old Channel.**

1895	65		SW¼	12	27	31	3-15—9-15	.528	195.0
1897	9.30		SW¼	12	27	31	3-15—9-15	.076	27.90

Claimant—**Paul Johnson.** Proof No. 0048

Source—**Humboldt River.** Ditch—**Union Canal through Lake Shore Ditch.**

1884	6.76		W½SW¼	33	26	31	3-15—9-15	.055	20.28
1885	10.13		W½SW¼	33	26	31	3-15—9-15	.082	30.39
1886	5.63		W½SW¼	33	26	31	3-15—9-15	.046	16.89
1803	16.89		W½SW¼	33	26	31	3-15—9-15	.137	50.67
1896	5.63		W½SW¼	33	26	31	3-15—9-15	.046	16.89
1897	11.26		W½SW¼	33	26	31	3-15—9-15	.092	33.78
1884	....	1.17	W½SW¼	33	26	31	3-15—6-13	.010	1.76

Claimant—**Mrs. John Chambers.** Proof No. 0048

Source—**Humboldt River.** Ditch—**Union Canal through Lake Shore Ditch.**

1884	4.74		E½SW¼	33	26	31	3-15—9-15	.039	14.22
1885	7.12		E½SW¼	33	26	31	3-15—9-15	.058	21.36
1886	3.95		E½SW¼	33	26	31	3-15—9-15	.032	11.85
1893	11.86		E½SW¼	33	26	31	3-15—9-15	.096	35.68
1896	3.95		E½SW¼	33	26	31	3-15—9-15	.032	11.85
1897	7.90		E½SW¼	33	26	31	3-15—9-15	.064	23.70
1884	....	.83	E½SW¼	33	26	31	3-15—6-13	.007	1.25

Claimant—**Geo. Kennedy.** Proof No. 0049

Source—**Humboldt River.** Ditch—**Old Channel.**

1801	76.50		NW¼	22	27	31	3-15—9-15	.622	229.50
1892	73.70		NW¼	22	27	31	3-15—9-15	.599	221.10
1892	2.80		NW¼	22	27	31	3-15—9-15	.023	8.40

Claimant—**Rachel Killebrew.** Proof No. 0050

Source—**Humboldt River.** Ditch—**Tule Ditch.**

1890	73.15		N½NW¼	10	25	31	3-15—9-15	.595	219.45

Claimant—**H. A. Killebrew.** Proof No. 0050
Source—**Humboldt River.** Ditch—**Tule Ditch.**

Date of beneficial use: Nat. mdw.	Date of beneficial use: Cult. area	Construction first initiated: Dams	Construction first initiated: Ditches	Culture—Acres: Harvest crops	Culture—Acres: Meadow pasture	Culture—Acres: Willow and sage pasture	Culture—Acres: Swamp or overflow	Location: Subdivision	Location: Section	Location: Tp.N.	Location: R.E.	Length of season	Duty of water: C.F.S.	Duty of water: Acre-feet
	1891			78				S½NW¼	10	25	31	3-15—9-15	.634	234.0

Claimant—**H. P. Kruse.** Proof No. 0052
Source—**Humboldt River.** Ditch—**Young Ditch.**

	1895			24.05				NE¼	12	27	31	3-15—9-15	.199	72.15
	1897			100.90				NE¼	12	27	31	3-15—9-15	.820	302.70
	1898			10.56				NE¼	12	27	31	3-15—9-15	.086	31.68

Claimant—**C. C. Larson.** Proof No. 0053
Source—**Humboldt River.** Ditch—**Union Canal through Reed Ditch.**

	1874			45				S½N½	34	26	31	3-15—9-15	.366	135.0
	1876			5				N½SE¼	33	26	31	3-15—9-15	.041	15.0
	1878			29				N½SE¼	33	26	31	3-15—9-15	.163	60.0
	1890			10				N½SE¼	33	26	31	3-15—9-15	.081	30.0
	1894			28.15				N½SE¼	33	26	31	3-15—9-15	.229	84.45

Claimant—**John Greve.** Proof No. 0054
Source—**Humboldt River.** Ditch—***Larson Ditch, Union Canal.**

	*1888			142.03				SE¼	35	26	31	3-15—9-15	1.157	426.09

Claimant—Wm. Loorz. Proof No. 0055
Source—**Humboldt River.** Ditch—**Old Channel.**

	1894			78.10				N½NW¼	13	27	31	3-15—9-15	.635	234.30

Claimant—**John and Domenico Ferritto.** Proof No. 0057
Source—**Humboldt River.** Ditch—**Reed Ditch from Union Canal.**

	1884			8				W½NE¼	33	26	31	3-15—9-15	.065	24.0
	1884					6		W½NE¼	33	26	31	3-15—6-13	.049	9.0
	1887			18				W½NE¼	33	26	31	3-15—9-15	.146	54.0
	1893			25				W½NE¼	33	26	31	3-15—9-15	.203	75.0
	1900			14.60				W½NE¼	33	26	31	3-15—9-15	.119	55.80

Claimant—**Ludwig J. Munk.** Proof No. 0058
Source—**Humboldt River.** Ditch—***Larson Ditch; Union Canal and Reed Ditch.**

	*1874			40				SW¼	34	26	31	3-15—9-15	.325	120.0
	1875			5				SW¼	34	26	31	3-15—9-15	.041	15.0
	1878			65				SW¼	34	26	31	3-15—9-15	.447	165.0
	1881			25				SW¼	34	26	31	3-15—9-15	.203	75.0
	1874			23.70				SW¼	34	26	31	3-15—9-15	.193	71.10

Claimant—**N. C. Munk.** Proof No. 0059
Source—**Humboldt River.** Ditch—***Larson Ditch; Union Canal through Reed Ditch.**

	*1874			35				W½NE¼	4	25	31	3-15—9-15	.285	105.0
	1879			15.35				W½NE¼	4	25	31	3-15—9-15	.125	46.05
	1880			15				W½NE¼	4	25	31	3-15—9-15	.122	45.0
	1874			....	3.60			W½NE¼	4	25	31	3-15—6-13	.029	5.4

Claimant—**Johannes Anderson.** Proof No. 0059
Source—**Humboldt River.** Ditch—***Larson Ditch; Union Canal through Reed Ditch.**

	*1874			20				E½NE¼NE¼	4	25	31	3-15—9-15	.163	60.0

Claimant—**Nevada Land & Livestock Co.** Proof No. 0060
Source—**Humboldt River.** Ditch—**Mayes & Harrison, now Southwest Ditch; Graveyard and Borland Sloughs.**

	1887			20.80				SE¼SW¼	27	27	31	3-15—9-15	.169	62.43
	1887			31.85				W½SW¼	27	27	31	3-15—9-15	.259	95.55
	1887			83.75				SW¼	27	27	31	3-15—9-15	.681	251.25
	1876			65				S½	28	27	31	3-15—9-15	.528	195.0
	1879			25				S½	28	27	31	3-15—9-15	.203	75.0
	1880			70				S½	28	27	31	3-15—9-15	.569	210.0
	1884			57.40				S½	28	27	31	3-15—9-15	.467	172.20
	1894			70.75				W½NE¼	28	27	31	3-15—9-15	.575	212.25
	1891			133.95				SE¼	29	27	31	3-15—9-15	1.089	401.85
	1883			51.20				N½NE¼	32	27	31	3-15—9-15	.416	153.60
	1885			79.90				NE¼	33	27	31	3-15—9-15	.650	239.70
	1895			47.90				NE¼	33	27	31	3-15—9-15	.389	143.70
	1894			....		1.50		SE¼NE¼	28	27	31	3-15—6-13	.012	2.25

Claimant—**John Greve.** Proof No. 0061
Source—**Humboldt River.** Ditch—***Kewley's Slough and Union Canal.**

	*1901			30.65				NW¼SE¼	35	26	31	3-15—9-15	.249	91.95
	1901			....	.60			NW¼SE¼	35	26	31	3-15—6-13	.005	.9

Claimant—**Mrs. Sophia O'Neil.** Proof No. 0062
Source—**Humboldt River.** Ditch—**Southwest Ditch.**

	1885			43.89				*N½NW¼	26	27	31	3-15—9-15	.357	131.67

*West of R. R. track.

Claimant—**Mary Jane Ostrander.** Proof No. 0063
Source—**Humboldt River.** Ditch—**Young Ditch.**

Date of beneficial use: Nat. mdw.	Date of beneficial use: Cult. area	Construction first initiated: Dams	Construction first initiated: Ditches	Culture—Acres: Harvest crops	Culture—Acres: Meadow pasture	Culture—Acres: Willow and sage pasture	Culture—Acres: Swamp or overflow	Location: Subdivision	Location: Section	Location: Tp.N.	Location: R.E.	Length of season	Duty of water: C.F.S.	Duty of water: Acre-feet
	1895			20				N½SE¼	12	27	31	3-15—9-15	.163	60.0
	1897			20				N½SE¼	12	27	31	3-15—9-15	.163	60.0
	1898			38.50				N½SE¼	12	27	31	3-15—9-15	.313	115.50

Claimant—**W. C. Pitt.** Proof No. 0064
Source—**Humboldt River.** Ditch—**Old Channel Ditch.**

Nat. mdw.	Cult. area	Dams	Ditches	Harvest crops	Meadow pasture	Willow and sage pasture	Swamp or overflow	Subdivision	Section	Tp.N.	R.E.	Length of season	C.F.S.	Acre-feet
	1890			38.15				N½	15	27	31	3-15—9-15	.310	114.45
	1890			534.10					15	27	31	3-15—9-15	4.342	1602.30
	1891			39.23				NW¼	23	27	31	3-15—9-15	.319	117.69
	1891			88.27				NW¼	23	27	31	3-15—9-15	.718	264.81
	1895			145.05				NE¼	22	27	31	3-15—9-15	1.179	435.15
	1892			340.95					9	27	31	3-15—9-15	2.772	1022.85
	1900			67				SW¼	10	27	31	3-15—9-15	.545	201.0

Allot sufficient flow of water through Old Channel Ditch, priority of 1900 for generation of 50 H.P.
Allot additional flow of water with priority of 1914 for generation of additional 10 H.P. Location of plant near Old Channel Dam, Lovelock.

Claimant—**W. C. Pitt.** Proof No. 0065
Source—**Humboldt River.** Ditch—**Southwest Ditch.**

Nat. mdw.	Cult. area	Dams	Ditches	Harvest crops	Meadow pasture	Willow and sage pasture	Swamp or overflow	Subdivision	Section	Tp.N.	R.E.	Length of season	C.F.S.	Acre-feet
	1886			50				W½SE¼	27	27	31	3-15—9-15	.407	150.0

Claimant—**U. S. Government Indian School.** Proof. No. 0065
Source—**Humboldt River.** Ditch—**Southwest Ditch.**

Nat. mdw.	Cult. area	Dams	Ditches	Harvest crops	Meadow pasture	Willow and sage pasture	Swamp or overflow	Subdivision	Section	Tp.N.	R.E.	Length of season	C.F.S.	Acre-feet
	1886			17.30				S½SW¼SE¼	27	27	31	3-15—9-15	.141	51.90

Claimant—**A. Reno.** Proof No. 0067
Source—**Humboldt River.** Ditch—**Old Channel.**

Nat. mdw.	Cult. area	Dams	Ditches	Harvest crops	Meadow pasture	Willow and sage pasture	Swamp or overflow	Subdivision	Section	Tp.N.	R.E.	Length of season	C.F.S.	Acre-feet
	1894			66.33				S½NW¼&NE¼SW¼	13	27	31	3-15—9-15	.539	198.99
	1896			33.17				E½SW¼&NE¼SW¼	13	27	31	3-15—9-15	.270	99.51

Claimant—**W. C. Ruddell.** Proof No. 0068
Source—**Humboldt River.** Ditch—**Irish-American.**

Nat. mdw.	Cult. area	Dams	Ditches	Harvest crops	Meadow pasture	Willow and sage pasture	Swamp or overflow	Subdivision	Section	Tp.N.	R.E.	Length of season	C.F.S.	Acre-feet
	1863			20				*E½W¼	26	27	31	3-15—9-15	.163	60.0
1868				43.75				SW¼	26					
								NW¼	35	27	31	3-15—9-15	.356	131.25
1873				45				SE¼	26	27	31	3-15—9-15	.366	135.0
	1873				100.00			*NE¼	26	27	31	3-15—6-13	.813	150.0
	1873				39.61			W½SE¼&E½SW¼	26	27	31	3-15—6-13	.322	59.42
	1885			100				NE¼SW¼						

								SE¼NW¼						
								SW¼NE¼						
								NW¼SE¼	26	27	31	3-15—9-15	.813	300.0
2	1886			35.10				NE¼SE¼	26	27	31	3-15—9-15	.285	105.30
	1887			20.10				NE¼SW¼	26	27	31	3-15—9-15	.163	60.30
								NE¼SW¼						
	1884			5.10				SE¼NW¼						
								SW¼NE¼						
								NW¼SE¼	26	27	31	3-15—9-15	.041	15.30
	1884			7.65				E½SE¼	26	27	31	3-15—9-15	.062	22.95
	1869			....	8.65			NW¼NW¼	35	27	31	3-15—6-13	.070	12.98
	1868			....	42.45			N½NW¼	35	27	31	3-15—6-13	.345	63.68

*Near center.

Claimant—***Millie R. Evans.** Proof No. 0069

Source—**Humboldt River.** Ditch—†**Rodgers Canal System.**

	1890			329.25					24	26	31	3-15—9-15	2.677	987.75
	1890			467.70					25	26	31	3-15—9-15	3.802	1403.10
	1890			158.06				E½	16	26	31	3-15—9-15	1.290	474.18
	1890			11.40				SE¼SE¼	16	26	31	3-15—9-15	.093	34.20
	1891			118					18	26	32	3-15—9-15	.959	354.0
	1891			34.60				W½SW¼	18	26	32	3-15—9-15	.281	103.80
	1891			199.75					18	26	32	3-15—9-15	1.624	599.25
	1891			123.50				NE¼ & W½	19	26	32	3-15—9-15	1.004	370.50
	1891			18.40				NW¼NW¼	19	26	32	3-15—9-15	.150	55.20
	1891			51.10				W½	19	26	32	3-15—9-15	.415	153.30
	1877			277.98					35	26	31	3-15—9-15	2.260	833.94
	1883			173.82				E½W½ & E½	10	26	31	3-15—9-15	1.413	521.46
	1883			....		105.23		N½	10	26	31	3-15—6-13	.856	157.85
	1883					24.84		N½	10	26	31	3-15—6-13	.202	37.26
	1880			143.40					11	26	31	3-15—9-15	1.166	430.20
	1884			244.05					7	26	31	3-15—9-15	1.984	732.15
	1884			8.02					7	26	31	3-15—9-15	.065	24.06
	1876			153.64				SE¼	13	26	31	3-15—9-15	1.249	460.92
	1876			139.92				SW¼	13	26	31	3-15—9-15	1.138	419.76
	1876			19.56				SE¼NW¼	13	26	31	3-15—9-15	.159	58.68
	1876			74.20				S½NE¼	13	26	31	3-15—9-15	.603	222.60
	1876			27.95				NW¼NE¼	13	26	31	3-15—9-15	.227	83.85
	1876			45.28				NE¼NE¼	13	26	31	3-15—9-15	.368	135.84
	1876			....		36.41		NE¼NW¼	13	26	31	3-15—6-13	.296	54.62
	1876			...		92.36		NW¼	13	26	31	3-15—6-13	.751	138.54
	1880			65.67				S½	15	26	31	3-15—9-15	.534	197.01
	1880			218.89				W½ & NE¼	15	26	31	3-15—9-15	1,780	656.67
	1880			6.28				SW¼SW¼	15	26	31	3-15—9-15	.051	18.84
	1880			9.78				NE¼NE¼	15	26	31	3-15—9-15	.080	29.34
	1880			4.52				W½NE¼	15	26	31	3-15—9-15	.037	13.56
	1880			23.99				E½NE¼	15	26	31	3-15—9-15	.195	71.97
	1880			105.80				E½	15	26	31	3-15—9-15	.860	317.40
	1880			3.56				NW¼NW¼	15	26	31	3-15—9-15	.029	10.68
	1880			2.71				W½NE¼	15	26	31	3-15—9-15	.022	8.13
	1880			1.47				NW¼NE¼	15	26	31	3-15—9-15	.012	4.41

Millie R. Evans—Continued.

Date of beneficial use: Nat. mdw.	Cult. area	Construction first initiated: Dams	Ditches	Culture—Acres: Harvest crops	Meadow pasture	Willow and sage pasture	Swamp or overflow	Location: Subdivision	Section	Tp.N.	R.E.	Length of season	Duty of water: C.F.S.	Acre-feet
	1880			44.83				E½E½	15	26	31	3-15—9-15	.364	134.49
	1880			9.77				SW¼SE¼	15	26	31	3-15—9-15	.079	29.31
	1862			70					26	26	31	3-15—9-15	.569	210.0
	1862			40				S½	10	26	31	3-15—9-15	.325	120.0
	1864			20				SW¼	11	26	31	3-15—9-15	.163	60.0
	1867			80				NW¼	23	26	31	3-15—9-15	.650	240.0
	1873			128.90					14	26	31	3-15—9-15	1.048	38.67
	1877			24.84				W½NE¼	23	26	31	3-15—9-15	.202	74.52
	1877			202.90				E½	23	26	31	3-15—9-15	1.650	608.70
	1877			16.43				SW¼SE¼	23	26	31	3-15—9-15	.134	49.29
	1877			43.92				NE¼SW¼	23	26	31	3-15—9-15	.357	131.76
	1877					47.08		NW¼NE¼	23	26	31	3-15—6-13	.383	70.62
	1877					43.53		NW¼SW¼	23	26	31	3-15—6-13	.354	65.30
	1878			289.33					24	26	31	3-15—9-15	2.352	867.99
	1877			42.62				W½NE¼	26	26	31	3-15—9-15	.347	127.86
	1877			16.43				NE¼NE¼	26	26	31	3-15—9-15	.134	49.29
	1877			6.66				SE¼NE¼	26	26	31	3-15—9-15	.054	19.98
	1877					166.54		SW¼	26	26	31	3-15—6-13	1.354	249.81

*Rodgers Canal System was initiated through the following ditches:
(a) Blake Ditch.
(b) Winslow Ditch.
(c) Weikel Ditch.
(d) Kewley Ditch.
(e) McCallum & Andrieux Company Ditch.
(f) McCallum Ditch.
(g) Slaven Ditch.
(h) J. B. Brown Ditch.
(i) Saxenheimer Ditch.
(j) Farmers Ditch.
(k) Marker Ditch.
(l) Fuss Ditch.
(m) J. B. Brown Extension Ditch.
†Rodgers Estate.

Claimant—**Vic Sebbas.** Proof No. 0070
Source—**Humboldt River.** Ditch—**Young Ditch.**

Nat. mdw.	Cult. area	Dams	Ditches	Harvest crops	Meadow pasture	Willow and sage pasture	Swamp or overflow	Subdivision	Section	Tp.N.	R.E.	Length of season	C.F.S.	Acre-feet
	1901			37.25				S½	2	27	31	3-15—9-15	.303	111.75
	1901			38.45				S½	2	27	31	3-15—9-15	.313	115.35
	1901			12.10				S½	2	27	31	3-15—9-15	.098	36.30
	1901			5.55				S½	2	27	31	3-15—9-15	.045	16.65
	1901			9.10				S½	2	27	31	3-15—9-15	.074	27.30
	1901			2.00				S½	2	27	31	3-15—9-15	.016	6.00
	1901			10.00				S½	2	27	31	3-15—9-15	.081	30.00
	1901			1.00				NE¼SE¼	2	27	31	3-15—9-15	.008	3.00

Claimant—**E. W. Sommer.** Proof No. 0071
Source—**Humboldt River.** Ditch—**Highflyer or Arthur Kewley Ditch.**

Nat. mdw.	Cult. area	Dams	Ditches	Harvest crops	Meadow pasture	Willow and sage pasture	Swamp or overflow	Subdivision	Section	Tp.N.	R.E.	Length of season	C.F.S.	Acre-feet
	1877			47.66				NW¼	2	25	31	3-15—9-15	.387	142.98
	1888			100.00				NW¼	2	25	31	3-15—9-15	.813	300.00
	1888					4.84		NW¼	2	25	31	3-15—6-18	.039	7.26

Claimant—**Matt Smith.** Proof No. 0072

Source—**Humboldt River.** Ditch—**Young Ditch.**

	1897			40				W½E½	1	27	31	3-15—9-15	.325	120.00
	1897			8.70				W½E½	1	27	31	3-15—9-15	.071	25.10
	1897			3.15				W½E½	1	27	31	3-15—9-15	.026	9.45
	1904			6.15				W½E½	1	27	31	3-15—9-15	.050	18.45
	1897			....	2.35			W½E½	1	27	31	3-15—6-13	.019	3.53
	1897			....		10.70		W½E½	1	27	31	3-15—6-13	.087	16.05

Claimant—**I. M. Springer, Sr.** Proof No. 0073

Source—**Humboldt River.** Ditch—***Slough ditch 1873 to 1887; †Irish-American 1887 to present.**

	*1873			9.50				W½NE¼&NW¼SE¼	23	27	31	3-15—9-15	.077	28.50
	†1888			19.00				W½NE¼&NW¼SE¼	23	27	31	3-15—9-15	.154	57.00
	1890			19.00				W½NE¼&NW¼SE¼	23	27	31	3-15—9-15	.154	57.00

Claimant—**Wm. A. Stauts.** Proof No. 0074

Source—**Humboldt River.** Ditch—**Irish-American.**

	1891			20.20				SE¼SW¼	22	27	31	3-15—9-15	.164	60.60
	1899			4.00				SW¼SE¼	22	27	31	3-15—9-15	.033	12.00
	1899			26.15				W½SE¼	22	27	31	3-15—9-15	.213	78.45

Claimant—**George C. Stoker.** Proof No. 0076

Source—**Humboldt River.** Ditch—**Old Channel.**

	1896			94.58				SE¼	22	27	31	3-15—9-15	.769	283.74

Claimant—**H. Stoker.** Proof No. 0077

Source—**Humboldt River.** Ditch—**Old Channel.**

	1893			224.70				NW¼&W½NE¼	14	27	31	3-15—9-15	1.827	674.10

Claimant—**Antone Alves and Anna Alves.** Proof No. 0077

Source—**Humboldt River.** Ditch—**Old Channel.**

	1888			45				W½SE¼	10	27	31	3-15—9-15	.366	135.00
	1893			11				W½SE¼	10	27	31	3-15—9-15	.089	33.00
	1896			14.95				W½SE¼	10	27	31	3-15—9-15	.122	44.85

Claimant—**Mary Jane Ostrander.** Proof No. **0063**
Source—**Humboldt River.** Ditch—**Young Ditch.**

Date of beneficial use: Nat. mdw.	Date of beneficial use: Cult. area	Construction first initiated: Dams	Construction first initiated: Ditches	Culture—Acres: Harvest crops	Culture—Acres: Meadow pasture	Culture—Acres: Willow and sage pasture	Culture—Acres: Swamp or overflow	Location: Subdivision	Location: Section	Location: Tp.N.	Location: R.E.	Length of season	Duty of water: C.F.S.	Duty of water: Acre-feet
....	1895	....	....	20	....	....	....	N½SE¼	12	27	31	3-15—9-15	.163	60.0
....	1897	....	....	20	....	....	....	N½SE¼	12	27	31	3-15—9-15	.163	60.0
....	1898	....	....	38.50	....	....	....	N½SE¼	12	27	31	3-15—9-15	.313	115.50

Claimant—**W. C. Pitt.** Proof No. **0064**
Source—**Humboldt River.** Ditch—**Old Channel Ditch.**

Nat. mdw.	Cult. area	Dams	Ditches	Harvest crops	Meadow pasture	Willow and sage pasture	Swamp or overflow	Subdivision	Section	Tp.N.	R.E.	Length of season	C.F.S.	Acre-feet
....	1890	....	....	38.15	....	....	....	N½	15	27	31	3-15—9-15	.310	114.45
....	1890	....	....	534.10	....	....	....		15	27	31	3-15—9-15	4.342	1602.30
....	1891	....	....	39.23	....	....	....	NW¼	23	27	31	3-15—9-15	.319	117.69
....	1891	....	....	88.27	....	....	....	NW¼	23	27	31	3-15—9-15	.718	264.81
....	1895	....	....	145.05	....	....	....	NE¼	22	27	31	3-15—9-15	1.179	435.15
....	1892	....	....	340.95	....	....	....		9	27	31	3-15—9-15	2.772	1022.85
....	1900	....	....	67	....	....	....	SW¼	10	27	31	3-15—9-15	.545	201.0

Allot sufficient flow of water through Old Channel Ditch, priority of 1900 for generation of 50 H.P.
Allot additional flow of water with priority of 1914 for generation of additional 10 H.P. Location of plant near Old Channel Dam, Lovelock.

Claimant—**W. C. Pitt.** Proof No. **0065**
Source—**Humboldt River.** Ditch—**Southwest Ditch.**

Nat. mdw.	Cult. area	Dams	Ditches	Harvest crops	Meadow pasture	Willow and sage pasture	Swamp or overflow	Subdivision	Section	Tp.N.	R.E.	Length of season	C.F.S.	Acre-feet
....	1886	....	....	50	....	....	....	W½SE¼	27	27	31	3-15—9-15	.407	150.0

Claimant—**U. S. Government Indian School.** Proof. No. **0065**
Source—**Humboldt River.** Ditch—**Southwest Ditch.**

Nat. mdw.	Cult. area	Dams	Ditches	Harvest crops	Meadow pasture	Willow and sage pasture	Swamp or overflow	Subdivision	Section	Tp.N.	R.E.	Length of season	C.F.S.	Acre-feet
....	1886	....	....	17.30	....	....	....	S½SW¼SE¼	27	27	31	3-15—9-15	.141	51.90

Claimant—**A. Reno.** Proof No. **0067**
Source—**Humboldt River.** Ditch—**Old Channel.**

Nat. mdw.	Cult. area	Dams	Ditches	Harvest crops	Meadow pasture	Willow and sage pasture	Swamp or overflow	Subdivision	Section	Tp.N.	R.E.	Length of season	C.F.S.	Acre-feet
....	1894	....	....	66.33	....	....	....	S½NW¼&NE¼SW¼	13	27	31	3-15—9-15	.539	198.99
....	1896	....	....	33.17	....	....	....	E½SW¼&NE¼SW¼	13	27	31	3-15—9-15	.270	99.51

Claimant—**W. C. Ruddell.** Proof No. **0068**
Source—**Humboldt River.** Ditch—**Irish-American.**

Nat. mdw.	Cult. area	Dams	Ditches	Harvest crops	Meadow pasture	Willow and sage pasture	Swamp or overflow	Subdivision	Section	Tp.N.	R.E.	Length of season	C.F.S.	Acre-feet
....	1863	....	....	20	....	....	....	*E½W½	26	27	31	3-15—9-15	.163	60.0
1868	....	....	....	43.75	....	....	....	SW¼	26					
								NW¼	35	27	31	3-15—9-15	.356	131.25
1873	....	....	....	45	....	....	....	SE¼	26	27	31	3-15—9-15	.366	135.0
....	1873	....	....	...	100.00	....	....	*NE¼	26	27	31	3-15—6-13	.813	150.0
....	1873	....	....	...	39.61	....	....	W½SE¼&E¼SW¼	26	27	31	3-15—6-13	.322	59.42
....	1885	....	....	100	....	....	....	NE¼SW¼						

269

								SE¼NW¼						
								SW¼NE¼						
								NW¼SE¼	26	27	31	3-15—9-15	.813	300.0
	1886			35.10				NE¼SE¼	26	27	31	3-15—9-15	.285	105.30
	1887			20.10				NE¼SW¼	26	27	31	3-15—9-15	.163	60.30
								NE¼SW¼						
	1884			5.10				SE¼NW¼						
								SW¼NE¼						
								NW¼SE¼	26	27	31	3-15—9-15	.041	15.30
	1884			7.65				E½SE¼	26	27	31	3-15—9-15	.062	22.95
	1869				8.65			NW¼NW¼	35	27	31	3-15—6-13	.070	12.98
	1868				42.45			N½NW¼	35	27	31	3-15—6-13	.345	63.68

*Near center.

Claimant—***Millie R. Evans.** Proof No. 0069

Source—**Humboldt River.** Ditch—†**Rodgers Canal System.**

	1890			329.25					24	26	31	3-15—9-15	2.677	987.75
	1890			467.70					25	26	31	3-15—9-15	3.802	1403.10
	1890			158.06				E½	16	26	31	3-15—9-15	1.290	474.18
	1890			11.40				SE¼SE¼	16	26	31	3-15—9-15	.093	34.20
	1891			118					18	26	32	3-15—9-15	.959	354.0
	1891			34.60				W½SW¼	18	26	32	3-15—9-15	.281	103.80
	1891			199.75					18	26	32	3-15—9-15	1.624	599.25
	1891			123.50				NE¼ & W½	19	26	32	3-15—9-15	1.004	370.50
	1891			18.40				NW¼NW¼	19	26	32	3-15—9-15	.150	55.20
	1891			51.10				W½	19	26	32	3-15—9-15	.415	153.30
	1877			277.98					35	26	31	3-15—9-15	2.260	833.94
	1883			173.82				E½W½&E½	10	26	31	3-15—9-15	1.413	521.46
	1883					105.23		N½	10	26	31	3-15—6-13	.856	157.85
	1883					24.84		N½	10	26	31	3-15—6-13	.202	37.26
	1880			143.40					11	26	31	3-15—9-15	1.166	430.20
	1884			244.05					7	26	31	3-15—9-15	1.984	732.15
	1884			8.02					7	26	31	3-15—9-15	.065	24.06
	1876			153.64				SE¼	13	26	31	3-15—9-15	1.249	460.92
	1876			139.92				SW¼	13	26	31	3-15—9-15	1.138	419.76
	1876			19.56				SE¼NW¼	13	26	31	3-15—9-15	.159	58.68
	1876			74.20				S½NE¼	13	26	31	3-15—9-15	.603	222.60
	1876			27.95				NW¼NE¼	13	26	31	3-15—9-15	.227	83.85
	1876			45.28				NE¼NE¼	13	26	31	3-15—9-15	.368	135.84
	1876					36.41		NE¼NW¼	13	26	31	3-15—6-13	.296	54.62
	1876					92.36		NW¼	13	26	31	3-15—6-13	.751	138.54
	1880			65.67				S½	15	26	31	3-15—9-15	.534	197.01
	1880			218.89				W½&NE¼	15	26	31	3-15—9-15	1.780	656.67
	1880			6.28				SW¼SW¼	15	26	31	3-15—9-15	.051	18.84
	1880			9.78				NE¼NE¼	15	26	31	3-15—9-15	.080	29.34
	1880			4.52				W½NE¼	15	26	31	3-15—9-15	.037	13.56
	1880			23.99				E½NE¼	15	26	31	3-15—9-15	.195	71.97
	1880			105.80				E½	15	26	31	3-15—9-15	.860	317.40
	1880			3.56				NW¼NW¼	15	26	31	3-15—9-15	.029	10.68
	1880			2.71				W½NE¼	15	26	31	3-15—9-15	.022	8.13
	1880			1.47				NW¼NE¼	15	26	31	3-15—9-15	.012	4.41

Millie R. Evans—Continued.

Date of beneficial use: Nat. mdw.	Date of beneficial use: Cult. area	Construction first initiated: Dams	Construction first initiated: Ditches	Culture—Acres: Harvest crops	Culture—Acres: Meadow pasture	Culture—Acres: Willow and sage pasture	Culture—Acres: Swamp or overflow	Location: Subdivision	Location: Section	Location: Tp.N.	Location: R.E.	Length of season	Duty of water: C.F.S.	Duty of water: Acre-feet
	1880			44.83				E½E½	15	26	31	3-15—9-15	.364	134.49
	1880			9.77				SW¼SE¼	15	26	31	3-15—9-15	.079	29.31
	1862			70					26	26	31	3-15—9-15	.569	210.0
	1862			40				S½	10	26	31	3-15—9-15	.325	120.0
	1864			20				SW¼	11	26	31	3-15—9-15	.163	60.0
	1867			80				NW¼	23	26	31	3-15—9-15	.650	240.0
	1873			128.90					14	26	31	3-15—9-15	1.048	38.67
	1877			24.84				W½NE¼	23	26	31	3-15—9-15	.202	74.52
	1877			202.90				E½	23	26	31	3-15—9-15	1.650	608.70
	1877			16.43				SW¼SE¼	23	26	31	3-15—9-15	.134	49.29
	1877			43.92				NE¼SW¼	23	26	31	3-15—9-15	.357	131.76
	1877					47.08		NW¼NE¼	23	26	31	3-15—6-13	.383	70.62
	1877					43.53		NW¼SW¼	23	26	31	3-15—6-13	.354	65.30
	1878			289.33					24	26	31	3-15—9-15	2.352	867.99
	1877			42.62				W½NE¼	26	26	31	3-15—9-15	.347	127.86
	1877			16.43				NE¼NE¼	26	26	31	3-15—9-15	.134	49.29
	1877			6.66				SE¼NE¼	26	26	31	3-15—9-15	.054	19.98
	1877					166.54		SW¼	26	26	31	3-15—6-13	1.354	249.81

*Rodgers Canal System was initiated through the following ditches:
(a) Blake Ditch.
(b) Winslow Ditch.
(c) Weikel Ditch.
(d) Kewley Ditch.
(e) McCallum & Andrieux Company Ditch.
(f) McCallum Ditch.
(g) Slaven Ditch.
(h) J. B. Brown Ditch.
(i) Saxenheimer Ditch.
(j) Farmers Ditch.
(k) Marker Ditch.
(l) Fuss Ditch.
(m) J. B. Brown Extension Ditch.
†Rodgers Estate.

Claimant—Vic Sebbas. Proof No. 0070
Source—Humboldt River. Ditch—Young Ditch.

Nat. mdw.	Cult. area	Dams	Ditches	Harvest crops	Meadow pasture	Willow and sage pasture	Swamp or overflow	Subdivision	Section	Tp.N.	R.E.	Length of season	C.F.S.	Acre-feet
	1901			37.25				S½	2	27	31	3-15—9-15	.303	111.75
	1901			38.45				S½	2	27	31	3-15—9-15	.313	115.35
	1901			12.10				S½	2	27	31	3-15—9-15	.098	36.30
	1901			5.55				S½	2	27	31	3-15—9-15	.045	16.65
	1901			9.10				S½	2	27	31	3-15—9-15	.074	27.30
	1901			2.00				S½	2	27	31	3-15—9-15	.016	6.00
	1901			10.00				S½	2	27	31	3-15—9-15	.081	30.00
	1901			1.00				NE¼SE¼	2	27	31	3-15—9-15	.008	3.00

Claimant—E. W. Sommer. Proof No. 0071
Source—Humboldt River. Ditch—Highflyer or Arthur Kewley Ditch.

Nat. mdw.	Cult. area	Dams	Ditches	Harvest crops	Meadow pasture	Willow and sage pasture	Swamp or overflow	Subdivision	Section	Tp.N.	R.E.	Length of season	C.F.S.	Acre-feet
	1877			47.66				NW¼	2	25	31	3-15—9-15	.387	142.98
	1888			100.00				NW¼	2	25	31	3-15—9-15	.813	300.00
	1888					4.84		NW¼	2	25	31	3-15—6-13	.039	7.26

Claimant—**Matt Smith.** Proof No. 0072

Source—**Humboldt River.** Ditch—**Young Ditch.**

	1897			40				W½E½	1	27	31	3-15—9-15	.325	120.00
	1897			8.70				W½E½	1	27	31	3-15—9-15	.071	25.10
	1897			3.15				W½E½	1	27	31	3-15—9-15	.028	9.45
	1904			6.15				W½E½	1	27	31	3-15—9-15	.050	18.45
	1897				2.35			W½E½	1	27	31	3-15—6-13	.019	3.53
	1897					10.70		W½E½	1	27	31	3-15—6-13	.087	16.05

Claimant—**I. M. Springer, Sr.** Proof No. 0073

Source—**Humboldt River.** Ditch—***Slough ditch 1873 to 1887; †Irish-American 1887 to present.**

	*1873			9.50				W½NE¼ & NW¼SE¼	23	27	31	3-15—9-15	.077	28.50
	†1888			19.00				W½NE¼ & NW¼SE¼	23	27	31	3-15—9-15	.154	57.00
	1890			19.00				W½NE¼ & NW¼SE¼	23	27	31	3-15—9-15	.154	57.00

Claimant—**Wm. A. Stauts.** Proof No. 0074

Source—**Humboldt River.** Ditch—**Irish-American.**

	1891			20.20				SE¼SW¼	22	27	31	3-15—9-15	.164	60.60
	1899			4.00				SW¼SE¼	22	27	31	3-15—9-15	.033	12.00
	1899			26.15				W½SE¼	22	27	31	3-15—9-15	.213	78.45

Claimant—**George C. Stoker.** Proof No. 0076

Source—**Humboldt River.** Ditch—**Old Channel.**

	1898			94.58				SE¼	22	27	31	3-15—9-15	.769	283.74

Claimant—**H. Stoker.** Proof No. 0077

Source—**Humboldt River.** Ditch—**Old Channel.**

	1893			224.70				NW¼ & W½NE¼	14	27	31	3-15—9-15	1.827	674.10

Claimant—**Antone Alves and Anna Alves.** Proof No. 0077

Source—**Humboldt River.** Ditch—**Old Channel.**

	1888			45				W½SE¼	10	27	31	3-15—9-15	.366	135.00
	1893			11				W½SE¼	10	27	31	3-15—9-15	.089	33.00
	1896			14.95				W½SE¼	10	27	31	3-15—9-15	.122	44.85

Claimant—**Pascasio Bilbao.** Proof No. 0078

Source—**Humboldt River.** Ditch—**Union Canal through Lake Shore Ditch.**

Date of beneficial use: Nat. mdw.	Cult. area	Construction first initiated: Dams	Ditches	Culture—Acres: Harvest crops	Meadow pasture	Willow and sage pasture	Swamp or overflow	Location: Subdivision	Section	Tp.N.	R.E.	Length of season	Duty of water: C.F.S.	Acre-feet
....	1883	....	....	5	....	....	....	SE¼NE¼	29	26	31	3-15—9-15	.051	15.0
....	1883	....	....	20	....	....	....	N½NE¼SE¼	29	26	31	3-15—9-15	.163	60.0
....	1884	....	....	5	....	....	....	NE¼SE¼	29	26	31	3-15—9-15	.051	15.0
....	1887	....	....	5	....	....	....	SE¼NE¼	29	26	31	3-15—9-15	.051	15.0
....	1888	....	....	8	....	....	....	E½NE¼	29	26	31	3-15—9-15	.065	24.0
....	1888	....	....	3	....	....	....	E½E½	29	26	31	3-15—9-15	.024	9.0
....	1890	....	....	8	....	....	....	E½E½	29	26	31	3-15—9-15	.065	24.0
....	1891	....	....	10	....	....	....	E½E½	29	26	31	3-15—9-15	.081	30.0
....	1892	....	....	13.20	....	....	....	E½E½	29	26	31	3-15—9-15	.107	39.6
....	1893	....	....	13.20	....	....	....	E½E½	29	26	31	3-15—9-15	.107	39.6
....	1894	....	....	13.20	....	....	....	E½E½	29	26	31	3-15—9-15	.107	39.6
....	1883	....	....	6.50	....	....	....	E½NE¼NE¼	29	26	31	3-15—9-15	.053	19.5
....	1883	....	....	....	....	.80	....	SE¼NE¼	29	26	31	3-15—6-13	.007	1.2

Claimant—**John O'Kane.** Proof No. 0079

Source—**Humboldt River.** Ditch—**Irish-American.**

Date of beneficial use: Nat. mdw.	Cult. area	Construction first initiated: Dams	Ditches	Culture—Acres: Harvest crops	Meadow pasture	Willow and sage pasture	Swamp or overflow	Location: Subdivision	Section	Tp.N.	R.E.	Length of season	Duty of water: C.F.S.	Acre-feet
....	1889	....	....	4.50	....	....	....	W½SE¼NE¼	27	27	31	3-15—9-15	.037	13.5

Claimant—**Lovelock Land and Development Co.** Proof No. 0080

Source—**Humboldt River.** Ditch—***Lovelock Land and Development Co. Ditch System.**

Date of beneficial use: Nat. mdw.	Cult. area	Construction first initiated: Dams	Ditches	Culture—Acres: Harvest crops	Meadow pasture	Willow and sage pasture	Swamp or overflow	Location: Subdivision	Section	Tp.N.	R.E.	Length of season	Duty of water: C.F.S.	Acre-feet
....	1903	....	d-c-i	63.30	....	....	....	N½NE¼	10	25	31	3-15—9-15	.515	189.90
....	1903	....	....	....		d-c-i 52.70	....	S½NE¼	10	25	31	3-15—6-13	1.102	406.65
....	1903	....	....	....		d-c-i 42.05	....	W½SE¼	10	25	31	3-15—6-13	.435	106.65
....	1901	....	....	....	....	a 73.15	....	S½&NE¼	2	25	31	3-15—6-13	.595	108.73
....	1901	....	a-c-d	135.55	....	....	....	SW¼	2	25	31	3-15—9-15	1.102	406.65
....	1903	....	a-c-d	53.55	....	....	....	SE¼	2	25	31	3-15—9-15	.435	160.65
....	1901		a-c-h-e-i	440.25	....	....	....	N½&N½S½	8	25	31	3-15—9-15	3.579	1320.75
....	1903		a-c-h-e-i	155.00	....	....	....	S½S½	8	25	31	3-15—9-15	1.260	465.0
....	1901		a-e-f-g-h	472.50	....	....	....	N½&N½S½	7	25	31	3-15—9-15	3.841	1417.50
....	1903		a-e-f-g-h	155.00	....	....	....	S½S½	7	25	31	3-15—9-15	1.260	465.0
....	1903		a-d-e-i	398.70	....	....	....	A part of	16	25	31	3-15—9-15	3.241	1196.10
....	1903		d-e-i-f-g-h	626.00	....	....	....		11	25	30	3-15—9-15	5.080	1878.0
....	1903		d-e-i-f-g-h	633.40	....	....	....		12	25	30	3-15—9-15	5.150	1900.20
....	1905		a-d-e-i-h-f-g	152.82	....	....	....	NE¼	18	25	31	3-15—9-15	1.242	458.46

*The Lovelock Land and Development Company Ditch System.
- (a) Kewley.
- (b) Highflyer Ditch and Flume.
- (c) Killebrew and Beck.
- (d) Tule Ditch and Flume.
- (e) Levee.
- (f) South Drainage and Waste Ditch.
- (g) Lake Drainage and Waste Ditch.
- (h) Tule Drainage and Waste Ditch.
- (i) Reservoir.

Claimant—**John G. Taylor.** Proof No. 0081
Source—**Humboldt River.** Ditch—**Irish-American in conjunction with Old Channel.**

	1890			97.50				E½	21	27	31	3-15—9-15	.793	292.50
	1890			3.10				SE¼SE¼	21	27	31	3-15—9-15	.025	9.30
	1890			6.30				SE¼SW¼	21	27	31	3-15—9-15	.051	18.90
	1890			4.80				SE¼SW¼	21	27	31	3-15—9-15	.039	14.40
	1895			47.55				W½NE¼	21	27	31	3-15—9-15	.387	142.65
	1895			31.70				E½NW¼	21	27	31	3-15—9-15	.258	95.10

Claimant—**John G. Taylor.** Proof No. 0081
Source—**Humboldt River.** Ditch—**Old Channel in conjunction with Young Ditch.**

	1888			20				N½	3	27	31	3-15—9-15	.163	60.0
	1893			60				N½	3	27	31	3-15—9-15	.488	180.0
	1895			190				S½	3	27	31	3-15—9-15	1.545	570.0
	1898			66.10				N½	3	27	31	3-15—9-15	.537	198.30

Claimant—**John G. Taylor.** Proof No. 0081
Source—**Humboldt River.** Ditch—**Young Ditch.**

	1899			101.05				E½E½	4	27	31	3-15—9-15	.822	303.15
	1888			....		6.75		NW¼NE¼	3	27	31	3-15—6-13	.055	10.13
	1899			9.70				NE¼SW¼	34	28	31	3-15—9-15	.079	29.10
	1899			26				SE¼SE¼	33	28	31	3-15—9-15	.211	78.00

Claimant—**John G. Taylor.** Proof No. 0081
Source—**Humboldt River.** Ditch—**Irish-American in conjunction with Southwest Ditch.**

	1890			136.05				SW¼	22	27	31	3-15—9-15	1.106	408.15

Claimant—**John G.** Taylor. Proof No. 0081
Source—**Humboldt** River. Ditch—**Irish-American in conjunction with Marzen Slough.**

	1893			86				NE¼	29	27	31	3-15—9-15	.699	258.00
	1893			8.70				SE¼NW¼	29	27	31	3-15—9-15	.071	26.10
	1893			16.25				S½NW¼	29	27	31	3-15—9-15	.132	48.75
	1893			128				SW¼	29	27	31	3-15—9-15	1.041	384.00
	1893			39				SE¼SE¼	30	27	31	3-15—9-15	.317	117.00
	1893			15				NE¼	31	27	31	3-15—9-15	.122	45.00
	1898			18.45				NE¼	31	27	31	3-15—9-15	.150	55.35

Claimant—**Bergman and Alfree.** Proof No. 0082
Source—**Humboldt River.** Ditch—**Southwest Ditch; Lovelock and Borland Slough.**

1874				100				N½	34	27	31	3-15—9-15	.813	300.00
	1880			33.70				N½	34	27	31	3-15—9-15	.274	101.10
	1880			79.40				W½SW¼	34	27	31	3-15—9-15	.646	238.20
	1880			47.60				E½SW¼, W½SE¼ & S½NE¼	34	27	31	3-15—9-15	.387	142.80
	1883			....		3.55		NE¼NE¼	34	27	31	3-15—6-13	.029	5.33
	1883			....		108.10		E½NW¼ & W½NE¼	34	27	31	3-15—6-13	.879	162.15
	1883			....		213.10		E½, E½SW¼	34	27	31	3-15—6-13	1.733	319.65

Claimant—**Bergman and Alfree.** Proof No. **0082**

Source—**Humboldt River.** Ditch—**Southwest Ditch.**

Date of beneficial use: Nat. mdw.	Date of beneficial use: Cult. area	Construction first initiated: Dams	Construction first initiated: Ditches	Culture—Acres: Harvest crops	Culture—Acres: Meadow pasture	Culture—Acres: Willow and sage pasture	Culture—Acres: Swamp or overflow	Location: Subdivision	Location: Section	Location: Tp.N.	Location: R.E.	Length of season	Duty of water: C.F.S.	Duty of water: Acre-feet
	1883			52.30				NW¼	3	26	31	3-15—9-15	.425	156.90
	1883					315.75		W½&NE¼	3	26	31	3-15—6-13	2.567	473.63
	1885			49.15				S½SE¼	33	27	31	3-15—9-15	.499	147.45
	1885			48.00				SE¼	33	27	31	3-15—9-15	.390	144.00
	1885			38.90				SE¼&SW¼	33	27	31	3-15—9-15	.316	116.70
	1885			25.95				SE¼SW¼	33	27	31	3-15—9-15	.211	77.85
	1883				22.00			NW¼SW¼	33	27	31	3-15—6-13	.179	33.00
	1885				10.20			SW¼	33	27	31	3-15—6-13	.083	15.30
	1885				14.95			SW¼SW¼	33	27	31	3-15—6-13	.123	22.48
	1885					51.10		S½	33	27	31	3-15—6-13	.415	76.65
	1885					3.95		SW¼SE¼	33	27	31	3-15—6-13	.032	5.93
	1889			60				SE¼	32	27	31	3-15—9-15	.488	180.00
	1883			20				SE¼	32	27	31	3-15—9-15	.163	60.00
	1885			139.80				SE¼,S½NE¼,SW¼	32	27	31	3-15—9-15	1.137	419.40
	1883			59.75				N½	5	26	31	3-15—9-15	.486	179.25
	1883			33.00				NE¼	5	26	31	3-15—9-15	.268	99.00
	1883			47.95				E½E½	5	26	31	3-15—9-15	.390	143.85
	1887			78.65				NE¼	4	26	31	3-15—9-15	.639	235.95
	1877			81.35				S½	4	26	31	3-15—9-15	.661	244.05
	1889			119.95				S½	4	26	31	3-15—9-15	.975	359.85
	1889			128.20				N½	4	26	31	3-15—9-15	1.042	384.60
	1889			77.45				W½NW¼	4	26	31	3-15—9-15	.630	232.35
	1889					38.90		NE¼SE¼	4	26	31	3-15—6-13	.316	58.35
	1889					17.70		SE¼SE¼	4	26	31	3-15—6-13	.144	26.55
	1889					11.00		NE¼NE¼	4	26	31	3-15—6-13	.089	16.50

Claimant—**F. Tessier.** Proof No. **0085**

Source—**Humboldt River.** Ditch—**Old Channel.**

Nat. mdw.	Cult. area	Dams	Ditches	Harvest crops	Meadow pasture	Willow and sage pasture	Swamp or overflow	Subdivision	Section	Tp.N.	R.E.	Length of season	C.F.S.	Acre-feet
	1899			61.48				SE¼	13	27	31	3-15—9-15	.500	184.44
	1900			15.94				SE¼	13	27	31	3-15—9-15	.130	47.82

Claimant—**Morris Nelson.** Proof No. **0086**

Source—**Humboldt River.** Ditch—**Union Canal.**

Nat. mdw.	Cult. area	Dams	Ditches	Harvest crops	Meadow pasture	Willow and sage pasture	Swamp or overflow	Subdivision	Section	Tp.N.	R.E.	Length of season	C.F.S.	Acre-feet
	1887			14.54				W½NW¼	32	26	31	3-15—9-15	.118	43.62
	1888			18.17				W½NW¼	32	26	31	3-15—9-15	.148	54.51
	1892			7.27				W½NW¼	32	26	31	3-15—9-15	.059	21.81
	1900			18.17				W½NW¼	32	26	31	3-15—9-15	.148	54.51
	1888			9.00				SE¼NE¼	31	26	31	3-15—9-15	.073	27.00
	1892			13.85				SE¼NE¼	31	26	31	3-15—9-15	.113	41.55
	1893			9.00				SE¼NE¼	31	26	31	3-15—9-15	.073	27.00
	1890			72.35				N½NE¼	31	26	31	3-15—9-15	.588	217.05

Claimant—**Hans Christensen.** Proof No. 0087
Source—**Humboldt River.** Ditch—**Union Canal through Lake Shore Ditch.**

1878	10		NW¼SW¼	28	26	31	3-15—9-15	.081	30.00
1880	25		SW¼	28	26	31	3-15—9-15	.203	75.00
1885	50		SW¼	28	26	31	3-15—9-15	.407	150.00
1890	13.35		SW¼	28	26	31	3-15—9-15	.109	40.05

Claimant—**Peter Olson.** Proof No. 0088
Source—**Humboldt River.** Ditch—**Old Channel Ditch.**

1895	65.85		S½NW¼	12	27	31	3-15—9-15	.535	107.55
1904	4.70		S½NW¼	12	27	31	3-15—9-15	.038	14.10

Claimant—**W. W. Van Reed.** Proof. No. 0089
Source—**Humboldt River.** Ditch—**Union Canal through Lake Shore Ditch.**

1897	15.00		E½SW¼	29	26	31	3-15—9-15	.122	45.00
1897		5.90	E½SW¼	29	26	31	3-15—6-13	.048	8.85
1898	14.85		E½SW¼	29	26	31	3-15—9-15	.121	44.55
1900	20.50		E½SW¼	29	26	31	3-15—9-15	.167	61.50
1898	5.10		SE¼	29	26	31	3-15—9-15	.041	15.30

Claimant—**Andrew Westfall.** Proof No. 0091
Source—**Humboldt River.** Ditch—**Union Canal through Lake Shore Ditch.**

1878	20.97		SE¼	32	26	31	3-15—9-15	.170	62.91
1878	5.22		NE¼	32	26	31	3-15—9-15	.042	15.66
1885	87.32		SE¼	32	26	31	3-15—9-15	.710	261.96
1885	80.00		E½NE¼	32	26	31	3-15—9-15	.650	240.00
1885	30.00		E½NW¼	32	26	31	3-15—9-15	.244	90.00
1890	11.40		S½SE¼SE¼	29	26	31	3-15—9-15	.093	34.20
1888	35.65		S½	31	26	31	3-15—9-15	.290	106.95
1890	77.79		E½	32	26	31	3-15—9-15	.632	233.37
1890	50.00		E½NW¼	32	26	31	3-15—9-15	.407	150.00
1890		5.10	S½SE¼SE¼	29	26	31	3-15—6-13	.041	7.65
1885		8.25	NW¼NE¼	32	26	31	3-15—6-13	.067	12.38
1888		196.60	S½	31	26	31	3-15—6-13	1.598	291.90

Claimant—**L. P. Johnson.** Proof No. 0092
Source—**Humboldt River.** Ditch—**Old Channel.**

1879	7.00		E½SE¼	10	27	31	3-15—9-15	.057	21.00
1886	15.00		E½SE¼	10	27	31	3-15—9-15	.122	45.00
1887	15.00		E½SE¼	10	27	31	3-15—9-15	.122	45.00
1890	3.80		E½SE¼	10	27	31	3-15—9-15	.031	11.40
1890	31.30		E½SE¼	10	27	31	3-15—9-15	.254	93.90
1889	1.90		E½SE¼	10	27	31	3-15—9-15	.015	5.70

Claimant—**S. R. Young.** Proof No. 0093
Source—**Humboldt River.** Ditch—**Young Ditch.**

Date of beneficial use: Nat. mdw.	Date of beneficial use: Cult. area	Construction first initiated: Dams	Construction first initiated: Ditches	Culture—Acres: Harvest crops	Culture—Acres: Meadow pasture	Culture—Acres: Willow and sage pasture	Culture—Acres: Swamp or overflow	Location: Subdivision	Location: Section	Location: Tp.N.	Location: R.E.	Length of season	Duty of water: C.F.S.	Duty of water: Acre-feet
....	1890	....	....	15.75	....	....	....	SE¼NW¼	28	28	32	3-15—9-15	.120	47.25
....	1902	....	....	11.80	....	....	....	NE¼SW¼	28	28	32	3-15—9-15	.096	35.40
....	1902	....	....	15.00	....	....		NE¼SW¼&SE¼NW¼	28	28	32	3-15—9-15	.122	45.00
....	1902	....	....	31.45	....	....	....	S½NE¼&N½SE¼	28	28	32	3-15—9-15	.256	94.35
....	1902	....	....	66.45				NE¼&NW¼SE¼&NE¼SW¼&SE¼NW¼	28	28	32	3-15—9-15	.540	199.35

Allotted sufficient flow of water through Young Canal, with priority of 1901, for generation of 75 H.P.
Allotted additional flow of water with priority of 1909 for generation of additional 100 H.P. Location of plant on Young Canal in Sec. 28, T. 28 N, R. 32 E.

Claimant—**H. M. Damm.** Proof No. 0094
Source—**Humboldt River.** Ditch—**Old Channel and Humboldt Irrigation and Power Co. Canal.**

Nat. mdw.	Cult. area	Dams	Ditches	Harvest crops	Meadow pasture	Willow and sage pasture	Swamp or overflow	Subdivision	Section	Tp.N.	R.E.	Length of season	C.F.S.	Acre-feet
....	1897	....	....	15	....	....	....	W½W½	1	27	31	3-15—9-15	.122	45.0

Claimant—**E. K. Hanson.** Proof No. 0095
Source—**Humboldt River.** Ditch—**Southwest Ditch.**

Nat. mdw.	Cult. area	Dams	Ditches	Harvest crops	Meadow pasture	Willow and sage pasture	Swamp or overflow	Subdivision	Section	Tp.N.	R.E.	Length of season	C.F.S.	Acre-feet
....	1887	....	....	2.35	....	....	....	SW¼SE¼	23	27	31	3-15—9-15	.019	7.05
....	1883	....	....	3.15	....	....	....	NE¼NW¼	26	27	31	3-15—9-15	.026	9.45
....	1879	....	....	3.55	....	....	....	NE¼NW¼	26	27	31	3-15—9-15	.029	10.65
....	1884	....	....	1.50	....	....	....	NE¼NW¼	26	27	31	3-15—9-15	.012	4.50

Claimant—***Geo. S. Nixon Estate and John Fant.** Proof No. 0099
Source—**Humboldt River.** Ditch—**Rodgers Ditch System—†Riverside Branch.**

Nat. mdw.	Cult. area	Dams	Ditches	Harvest crops	Meadow pasture	Willow and sage pasture	Swamp or overflow	Subdivision	Section	Tp.N.	R.E.	Length of season	C.F.S.	Acre-feet
....	1871	....	....	10.00	....	....	....	NW¼	36	27	31	3-15—9-15	.081	30.00
....	1873	....	....	80.00	....	....	....	NW¼	36	27	31	3-15—9-15	.650	240.00
....	1873	....	....	60.00	....	....	....	SW¼	36	27	31	3-15—9-15	.488	180.00
....	1880	....	....	52.28	....	....	....	NW¼	36	27	31	3-15—9-15	.425	156.84
....	1880	....	....	29.26	....	....	....	SE¼	36	27	31	3-15—9-15	.238	87.78
....	1880	....	....	29.00	....	....	....	NE¼	36	27	21	3-15—9-15	.236	87.00
....	1881	....	....	20.00	....	....	....	SW¼	36	27	31	3-15—9-15	.163	60.00
....	1882	....	....	47.29	....	....	....	SW¼	36	27	31	3-15—9-15	.384	141.87
....	1882	....	....	16.22	....	....	....	NE¼	36	27	31	3-15—9-15	.132	48.66
....	1882	....	....	25.55	....	....	....	SE¼	36	27	31	3-15—9-15	.208	76.65
....	1882	....	....	....	....	30.00	....	N½	36	27	31	3-15—6-13	.244	45.00
....	1883	....	....	28.00	....	....	....	SE¼	35	27	31	3-15—9-15	.228	84.00
....	1883	....	....	52.00	....	....	....	SW¼	35	27	31	3-15—9-15	.423	156.00
....	1885	....	....	153.85	....	....	....	NE¼	35	27	31	3-15—9-15	1.251	461.55
....	1885	....	....	75.00	....	....	....	NE¼	35	27	31	3-15—9-15	.610	225.00
....	1898	....	....	25.72	....	....	....	SW¼	35	27	31	3-15—9-15	.209	77.16
....	1901	....	....	29.77	....	....	....	SE¼	35	27	31	3-15—9-15	.242	89.31

†Riverside Branch.
(a) Silverwood Ditch.
(b) Muttleberry Ditch.
(c) Slough Ditch.
(d) Hazelton-Thies Ditch.
(e) J. H. Thies Ditch.
(f) Thies Reservoir.

*Riverside Ranch.

WINNEMUCCA DISTRICT

Claimant—**Madison Anderson.** Proof No. 00101

Source—**Humboldt River.** Ditch—**North Side Cusick Ditch.**

Date of beneficial use—Nat. mdw.	Date of beneficial use—Cult. area	Construction first initiated—Dams	Construction first initiated—Ditches	Culture—Acres—Harvest crops	Culture—Acres—Meadow pasture	Culture—Acres—Willow and sage pasture	Culture—Acres—Swamp or overflow	Location—Subdivision	Location—Section	Location—Tp.N.	Location—R.E.	Length of season	Duty of water—C.F.S.	Duty of water—Acre-feet
....	1871	....	....	10.00	....	....	....	NE¼SE¼	18	36	40	3-15—9-15	.081	30.00
....	1871	....	....	20.90	....	....	....	SE¼NE¼	18	36	40	3-15—9-15	.170	62.70
....	1870	....	....	38.10	....	....	....	SW¼NE¼	18	36	40	3-15—9-15	.310	114.30
....	1874	....	....	32.00	....	....	....	NW¼NE¼	18	36	40	3-15—9-15	.200	96.00
....	1874	....	....	39.50	....	....	....	NE¼NW¼	18	36	40	3-15—9-15	.331	118.50
....	1872	....	....	20.30	....	....	....	SE¼NW¼	18	36	40	3-15—9-15	.165	60.90
....	1874	....	....	18.75	....	....	....	NW¼NW¼	18	36	40	3-15—9-15	.152	56.25
....	1874	....	....	....	....	8.90	....	NW¼NW¼	18	36	40	3-15—4-28	.072	6.45
....	1873	....	....	2.00	....	....	....	SW¼NW¼	18	36	40	3-15—9-15	.016	6.00
....	1873	....	....	.80	....	....	....	NE¼SW¼	18	36	40	3-15—9-15	.007	2.40

Claimant—**Madison Anderson.** Proof No. 00101

Source—**Humboldt River.** Ditch—**Cusick Ditch.**

Date of beneficial use—Nat. mdw.	Date of beneficial use—Cult. area	Construction first initiated—Dams	Construction first initiated—Ditches	Culture—Acres—Harvest crops	Culture—Acres—Meadow pasture	Culture—Acres—Willow and sage pasture	Culture—Acres—Swamp or overflow	Location—Subdivision	Location—Section	Location—Tp.N.	Location—R.E.	Length of season	Duty of water—C.F.S.	Duty of water—Acre-feet
....	1872	....	....	38.20	....	....	....	SE¼SE¼	18	36	40	3-15—9-15	.311	114.60
....	1871	....	....	5.40	....	....	....	NE¼SE¼	18	36	40	3-15—9-15	.044	16.20
....	1872	....	....	14.80	....	....	....	SW¼SE¼	18	36	40	3-15—9-15	.120	44.40
....	1871	....	....	22.00	....	....	....	NW¼SE¼	18	36	40	3-15—9-15	.179	66.00
....	1870	....	....	.40	....	....	....	SW¼NE¼	18	36	40	3-15—9-15	.003	1.20
....	1873	....	....	6.15	....	....	....	NE¼SW¼	18	36	40	3-15—9-15	.051	18.45
....	1873	....	....	....	....	2.50	....	NE¼SW¼	18	36	40	3-15—4-28	.020	1.88
....	1873	....	....	....	....	.75	....	NW¼SW¼	18	36	40	3-15—4-28	.002	.56
....	1872	....	....	....	....	10.70	....	SE¼NW¼	18	36	40	3-15—4-28	.087	8.03
....	1873	....	....	.20	....	....	....	SW¼NW¼	18	36	40	3-15—9-15	.002	.60
....	1873	....	....	....	....	18.20	....	SW¼NW¼	18	36	40	3-15—4-28	.148	13.65
....	1874	....	....	....	....	6.00	....	NW¼NW¼	18	36	40	3 15—4-28	.049	4.50

Claimant—**Madison Anderson.** Proof No. 00101

Source—**Humboldt River.** Ditch—**Anderson Ditch.**

Date of beneficial use—Nat. mdw.	Date of beneficial use—Cult. area	Construction first initiated—Dams	Construction first initiated—Ditches	Culture—Acres—Harvest crops	Culture—Acres—Meadow pasture	Culture—Acres—Willow and sage pasture	Culture—Acres—Swamp or overflow	Location—Subdivision	Location—Section	Location—Tp.N.	Location—R.E.	Length of season	Duty of water—C.F.S.	Duty of water—Acre-feet
....	1871	....	....	20.00	....	....	....	NE¼SE¼	18	36	40	3-15—9-15	.063	60.00
....	1873	....	....	6.95	....	....	....	NE¼SW¼	18	36	40	3-15—9-15	.057	20.85
....	1873	....	....	....	....	2.50	....	NE¼SW¼	18	36	40	3-15—4-28	.020	1.88
....	1873	....	....	....	....	1.50	....	NW¼SW¼	18	36	40	3-15—4-28	.012	1.13
....	1871	....	....	14.10	....	....	....	NW¼SE¼	18	36	40	3-15—9-15	.115	42.30

Claimant—**Madison Anderson.** Proof No. 00101
Source—**Humboldt River.** Ditch—**Pioneer Slough System.**

Date of beneficial use: Nat. mdw.	Date of beneficial use: Cult. area	Construction first initiated: Dams	Construction first initiated: Ditches	Culture—Acres: Harvest crops	Culture—Acres: Meadow pasture	Culture—Acres: Willow and sage pasture	Culture—Acres: Swamp or overflow	Location: Subdivision	Location: Section	Location: Tp.N.	Location: R.E.	Length of season	Duty of water: C.F.S.	Duty of water: Acre-feet
	1874			7.30				NW¼NE¼	18	36	40	3-15—9-15	.059	21.90
	1874					2.90		NE¼NE¼	20	36	40	3-15—4-28	.025	2.18
	1874					19.70		SE¼SE¼	17	36	40	3-15—4-28	.160	14.78
	1874					33.50		SW¼SE¼	17	36	40	3-15—4-28	.272	25.13
	1874					28.20		NW¼SE¼	17	36	40	3-15—4-28	.229	21.15
	1874			2.60				NE¼SE¼	17	36	40	3-15—9-15	.021	7.80
	1874			3.30				SW¼NE¼	17	36	40	3-15—9-15	.027	9.90
	1874			.80				SE¼SW¼	17	36	40	3-15—9-15	.007	2.40
	1874					21.90		SE¼SW¼	17	36	40	3-15—4-28	.178	16.43
	1874			3.30				SW¼SW¼	17	36	40	3-15—9-15	.027	9.90
	1874					1.00		SW¼SW¼	17	36	40	3-15—4-28	.008	.75
	1874			1.20				NE¼SW¼	17	36	40	3-15—9-15	.010	3.60
	1874					38.80		NE¼SW¼	17	36	40	3-15—4-28	.315	29.10
	1874			29.90				NW¼SW¼	17	36	40	3-15—9-15	.243	89.70
	1874					2.60		NW¼SW¼	17	36	40	3-15—4-28	.021	1.95
	1874			25.70				SE¼NW¼	17	36	40	3-15—9-15	.209	77.10
	1874			4.95				NW¼NW¼	17	36	40	3-15—9-15	.040	14.85
	1874			36.90				SW¼NW¼	17	36	40	3-15—9-15	.300	110.70
	1871			20.00				SE¼NE¼	18	56	40	3-15—9-15	.163	60.00
	1873			29.30				NE¼NE¼	18	36	40	3-15—9-15	.238	87.90

Claimant—**Madison Anderson.** Proof No. 00101
Source—**Humboldt River.** Ditch—**Humboldt River Overflow.**

Date of beneficial use: Nat. mdw.	Date of beneficial use: Cult. area	Construction first initiated: Dams	Construction first initiated: Ditches	Culture—Acres: Harvest crops	Culture—Acres: Meadow pasture	Culture—Acres: Willow and sage pasture	Culture—Acres: Swamp or overflow	Location: Subdivision	Location: Section	Location: Tp.N.	Location: R.E.	Length of season	Duty of water: C.F.S.	Duty of water: Acre-feet
	1874					1.20		SE¼SE¼	17	36	40	3-15—4-28	.010	.90
	1874					2.60		SW¼SE¼	17	36	40	3-15—4-28	.021	1.95
	1874					2.70		NW¼NE¼	20	36	40	3-15—4-28	.023	2.03
	1874			7.20				SE¼SW¼	17	36	40	3-15—9-15	.059	21.60
	1874					5.55		SE¼SW¼	17	36	40	3-15—4-28	.045	4.16
	1874			29.70				SW¼SW¼	17	36	40	3-15—9-15	.241	89.10
	1874			3.60				NW¼SW¼	17	36	40	3-15—9-15	.029	10.80
	1874					.33		SE¼SE¼	27	36	40	3-15—4-28	.003	.25
	1874					10.82		SW¼SE¼	27	36	40	3-15—4-28	.088	8.12

Claimant—**Madison Anderson.** Proof No. 00101
Source—**Humboldt River.** Ditch—**North Side Canal.**

Date of beneficial use: Nat. mdw.	Date of beneficial use: Cult. area	Construction first initiated: Dams	Construction first initiated: Ditches	Culture—Acres: Harvest crops	Culture—Acres: Meadow pasture	Culture—Acres: Willow and sage pasture	Culture—Acres: Swamp or overflow	Location: Subdivision	Location: Section	Location: Tp.N.	Location: R.E.	Length of season	Duty of water: C.F.S.	Duty of water: Acre-feet
	1874					12.49		SE¼NW¼	21	36	40	3-15—4-28	.101	9.30
	1874					4.30		NE¼SW¼	21	36	40	3-15—4-28	.035	3.23
	1874				10.00			NW¼SW¼	21	36	40	3-15—6-13	.091	15.00
	1874					9.20		NW¼SW¼	21	36	40	3-15—4-28	.075	6.90
	1874					31.40		SW¼NW¼	21	36	40	3-15—4-28	.255	23.55
	1874					29.90		NW¼NW¼	21	36	40	3-15—4-28	.243	22.43
	1874					7.70		NE¼NE¼	20	36	40	3-15—4-28	.063	5.78
	1874					11.00		SW¼SW¼	16	36	40	3-15—4-28	.089	8.25

....	1874	....	....	1.12	....	....	....	SE¼SE¼	17	36	40	3-15—0-15	.010	3.36
....	1874	....	....	....	....	12.58	....	SE¼SE¼	17	36	40	3-15—4-28	.102	9.44
....	1874	....	....	25.94	....	....	....	NE¼SE¼	17	36	40	3-15—0-15	.211	77.82
....	1874	....	....	....	....	6.77	....	NE¼SE¼	17	36	40	3-15—4-28	.055	5.08
....	1874	....	....	....	....	10.20	....	NW¼SE¼	17	36	40	3-15—4-28	.083	7.65
....	1874	....	....	17.80	....	....	....	SE¼NE¼	17	36	40	3-15—0-15	.145	53.40
....	1874	....	....	....	....	5.50	....	SE¼NE¼	17	36	40	3-15—4-28	.045	4.13
....	1874	....	....	34.20	....	....	....	SW¼NE¼	17	36	40	3-15—0-15	.278	102.60
....	1874	....	....	11.70	....	....	....	SE¼NW¼	17	36	40	3-15—0-15	.095	35.10
....	1874	....	....	....	....	1.10	....	NE¼NE¼	17	36	40	3-15—4-28	.009	.83
....	1874	....	....	....	....	39.40	....	NE¼NW¼	17	36	40	3-15—4-28	.320	29.55
....	1874	....	....	....	....	.75	....	NE¼SW¼	27	36	40	3-15—4-28	.006	.56
....	1874	....	....	13.45	....	....	....	NW¼SW¼	27	36	40	3-15—0-15	.109	40.35
....	1874	....	....	18.70	....	....	....	SE¼NW¼	27	36	40	3-15—0-15	.152	56.10
....	1874	....	....	34.10	....	....	....	SW¼NW¼	27	36	40	3-15—0-15	.277	102.30
....	1874	....	....	13.22	....	....	....	NW¼NW¼	27	36	40	3-15—0-15	.107	39.66
....	1874	....	....	18.30	....	....	....	NW¼NE¼	17	36	40	3-15—0-15	.149	54.90
....	1874	....	....	....	....	4.40	....	NW¼NE¼	17	36	40	3-15—4-28	.036	3.30
....	1874	....	....	....	....	2.50	....	NW¼SW¼	16	36	40	3-15—4-28	.020	1.88

Claimant—**Madison Anderson.** Proof No. 00101
Source—**Humboldt River.** Ditch—**South Side Swail and Ditch.**

....	1874	....	....	....	....	16.60	....	SE¼SW¼	27	36	40	3-15—4-28	.135	12.45
....	1874	....	....	....	....	27.28	....	SW¼SW¼	27	36	40	3-15—4-28	.222	20.46
....	1874	....	....	....	....	....	3.37	SW¼SW¼	27	36	40	3-15—4-28	.207	2.53
....	1874	....	....	1.00	....	....	....	NW¼SW¼	27	36	40	3-15—0-15	.008	3.00

Claimant—**Madison Anderson.** Proof No. 00101
Source—**Humboldt River.** Ditch—**Big Slough Ditch.**

....	1874	....	....	.36	....	....	....	NE¼SW¼	27	36	40	3-15—0-15	.003	1.08
....	1874	....	....	.10	....	....	....	SE¼SW¼	27	36	40	3-15—0-15	.001	.30
....	1874	....	....	1.82	....	....	....	SW¼SW¼	27	36	40	3-15—0-15	.015	5.46
....	1874	....	....	16.48	....	....	....	NW¼SW¼	27	36	40	3-15—0-15	.134	49.44
....	1874	....	....	....	....	3.86	....	NW¼SW¼	27	36	40	3-15—4-28	.031	2.90
....	1874	....	....	1.90	....	....	....	SW¼SW¼	27	36	40	3-15—0-15	.015	5.70
....	1874	....	....	1.20	....	....	....	SW¼SE¼	8	36	40	3-15—0-15	.010	3.60

Claimant—**Madison Anderson.** Proof No. 00101
Source—**Humboldt River.** Ditch—**North Side Canal.**

....	1874	....	....	27.40	....	....	....	SE¼SW¼	8	36	40	3-15—0-15	.223	82.20
....	1874	....	....	....	....	3.60	....	SE¼SW¼	8	36	40	3-15—4-28	.029	2.70
....	1874	....	....	16.80	....	....	....	NE¼SW¼	8	36	40	3-15—0-15	.137	50.40
....	1874	....	....	....	....	19.60	....	NE¼SW¼	8	36	40	3-15—4-28	.159	14.70
....	1874	....	....	35.00	....	....	....	NW¼SW¼	8	36	40	3-15—0-15	.285	105.00
....	1874	....	....	....	....	1.50	....	NW¼SW¼	8	36	40	3-15—4-28	.012	1.13
....	1874	....	....	2.20	....	....	....	SW¼NW¼	8	36	40	3-15—0-15	.018	6.60
....	1874	....	....	1.20	....	....	....	SE¼NW¼	8	36	40	3-15—0-15	.010	3.60
....	1874	....	....	....	....	.30	....	SE¼NW¼	8	36	40	3-15—4-28	.003	.23
....	1874	....	....	....	....	2.40	....	NW¼SE¼	8	36	40	3-15—4-28	.020	1.80
....	1874	....	....	....	....	10.70	....	SE¼SE¼	27	36	40	3-15—4-28	.087	8.03

Madison Anderson—Continued.

Date of beneficial use: Nat. mdw.	Date of beneficial use: Cult. area	Construction first initiated: Dams	Construction first initiated: Ditches	Culture—Acres: Harvest crops	Culture—Acres: Meadow pasture	Culture—Acres: Willow and sage pasture	Culture—Acres: Swamp or overflow	Location: Subdivision	Location: Section	Location: Tp.N.	Location: R.E.	Length of season	Duty of water: C.F.S.	Duty of water: Acre-feet
	1874			.95				SW¼SE¼	27	36	40	3-15—9-15	.008	2.85
	1874				1.10			SW¼SE¼	27	36	40	3-15—6-13	.009	1.65
	1874					18.65		SW¼SE¼	27	36	40	3-15—4-28	.152	13.99
	1874			.12				NW¼SE¼	27	36	40	3-15—9-15	.001	.36
	1874					16.39		NW¼SE¼	27	36	40	3-15—4-28	.133	12.29
	1874			3.60				SE¼SW¼	27	36	40	3-15—9-15	.029	10.80
	1874					9.30		SE¼SW¼	27	36	40	3-15—4-28	.076	6.98
	1874			35.48				NE¼SW¼	27	36	40	3-15—9-15	.288	106.44

Claimant—**Madison Anderson.** Proof No. 00101

Source—**Humboldt River.** Ditch—**Old South Side House Ditch.**

	1874					.90		NW¼SW¼	21	36	40	3-15—4-28	.007	.68
	1874					1.80		SW¼NW¼	21	36	40	3-15—4-28	.015	1.35
	1874				10.70			NE¼SE¼	20	36	40	3-15—6-13	.087	16.05
	1874					1.60		NE¼SE¼	20	36	40	3-15—4-28	.013	1.20
	1874				27.20			SE¼NE¼	20	36	40	3-15—6-13	.221	40.80
	1874					7.45		SE¼NE¼	20	36	40	3-15—4-28	.061	5.59
	1874				32.15			SW¼NE¼	20	36	40	3-15—6-13	.261	48.23
	1874				28.60			NW¼NE¼	20	36	40	3-15—6-13	.234	43.90
	1874					5.90		NW¼NE¼	20	36	40	3-15—4-28	.048	4.43
	1874				15.40			NE¼NE¼	20	36	40	3-15—6-13	.125	23.10
	1874					7.80		NE¼NE¼	20	36	40	3-15—4-28	.063	5.85

Claimant—**Madison Anderson.** Proof No. 00101

Source—**Humboldt River.** Ditch—**North Side Canal.**

	1874					30.80		NW¼NW¼	17	36	40	3-15—4-28	.250	23.10
	1873					9.25		NE¼NE¼	18	36	40	3-15—4-28	.075	6.94
	1874			37.20				SW¼SW¼	8	36	40	3-15—9-15	.302	111.60

Claimant—**Bliss Brothers.** Proof No. 00101

Source—**Humboldt River.** Ditch—**Anderson Ditch System.**

	1876				32.93			NW¼NE¼	14	36	41	3-15—6-13	.268	49.40
	1877			10.80				NE¼NE¼	14	36	41	3-15—9-15	.088	32.40
	1877				20.89			NE¼NE¼	14	36	41	3-15—6-13	.170	31.34
	1878			4.57				NE¼NW¼	14	36	41	3-15—9-15	.037	13.71
	1878				6.47			NE¼NW¼	14	36	41	3-15—6-13	.053	9.71
	1878					3.92		NE¼NW¼	14	36	41	3-15—4-28	.032	2.94
	1878				.90			SE¼SE¼	11	36	41	3-15—6-13	.007	1.35
	1878				1.70			SW¼SE¼	11	36	41	3-15—6-13	.014	2.55
	1878				1.65			SE¼NW¼	11	36	41	3-15—6-13	.013	2.48
	1878					.20		SE¼NW¼	11	36	41	3-15—4-28	.002	.15
	1878					.95		NW¼NW¼	11	36	41	3-15—4-28	.008	.71
	1878					.80		SW¼SW¼	11	36	41	3-15—4-28	.007	.60

	1878				2.70			SE¼NW¼	12	36	41	3-15—6-13	.022	4.14
	1878						40.04	SE¼NW¼	12	36	41	3-15—4-28	.326	30.03
	1878				4.00			SW¼NW¼	12	36	41	3-15—6-13	.033	6.00
	1878						37.70	SW¼NW¼	12	36	41	3-15—4-28	.307	28.80
	1878				25.53			NW¼SW¼	12	36	41	3-15—6-13	.208	38.30
	1878						10.28	NW¼SW¼	12	36	41	3-15—4-28	.084	7.71
	1879				38.55			SW¼SW¼	12	36	41	3-15—6-13	.313	57.83
	1879				35.26			SE¼SW¼	12	36	41	3-15—6-13	.287	52.89
	1879						.14	SE¼SW¼	12	36	41	3-15—6-13	.001	.12
	1880				35.80			NE¼SW¼	12	36	41	3-15—6-13	.291	58.70
	1880						4.82	NE¼SW¼	12	36	41	3-15—4-28	.039	3.62
	1880				26.10			SW¼SE¼	12	36	41	3-15—6-13	.212	39.15
	1880						12.60	SW¼SE¼	12	36	41	3-15—4-28	.102	9.45
	1874			10.08				SE¼NE¼	14	36	41	3-15—9-15	.082	30.24
	1874				22.96			SE¼NE¼	14	36	41	3-15—6-13	.187	34.44
	1875			4.32				SW¼NE¼	14	36	41	3-15—9-15	.035	12.96
	1875				11.13			SW¼NE¼	14	36	41	3-15—6-13	.090	16.70
	1875					1.50		SW¼NE¼	14	36	41	3-15—6-13	.012	1.13
	1876			2.52				NW¼NE¼	14	36	41	3-15—9-15	.020	7.56

Claimant—**Bliss Brothers.** Proof No. 00102
Source—**Humboldt River.** Ditch—**Pioneer Ditch System.**

	1863			10.00				SW¼NW¼	3	36	39	3-15—9-15	.081	30.00
	1863				10.00			SW¼NW¼	3	36	39	3-15—6-13	.081	15.00
	1863					10.00		SW¼NW¼	3	36	39	3-15—4-28	.081	7.50
	1863						8.43	SW¼NW¼	3	36	39	3-15—4-28	.069	6.32
	1864			10.00				SE¼NW¼	3	36	39	3-15—9-15	.081	30.00
	1864				10.00			SE¼NW¼	3	36	39	3-15—6-13	.081	15.00
	1864					10.00		SE¼NW¼	3	36	39	3-15—4-28	.081	7.50
	1864						8.41	SE¼NW¼	3	36	39	3-15—4-28	.068	6.31
	1868			16.64				SE¼NW¼	2	36	39	3-15—9-15	.135	49.92
	1868					.66		SE¼NW¼	2	36	39	3-15—4-28	.005	.50
	1865			17.78				SE¼NW¼	2	36	39	3-15—9-15	.145	53.34
	1868			31.72				SW¼NE¼	2	36	39	3-15—9-15	.258	95.16
	1868				.86			SW¼NE¼	2	36	39	3-15—6-13	.007	1.29
	1868					.24		SW¼NE¼	2	36	39	3-15—4-28	.002	.18
	1865			3.85				SW¼NE¼	2	36	39	3-15—9-15	.031	11.55
	1865			6.42				NE¼SE¼	2	36	39	3-15—9-15	.052	19.26
	1868				.94			NW¼SE¼	2	36	39	3-15—6-13	.008	1.41
	1865			29.64				NW¼SE¼	2	36	39	3-15—9-15	.241	88.92
	1865				5.06			NW¼SE¼	2	36	39	3-15—6-13	.041	7.59
	1865						1.04	NW¼SE¼	2	36	39	3-15—4-28	.008	.78
	1865			27.32				NE¼SW¼	2	36	39	3-15—9-15	.222	81.96
	1865					11.51		NE¼SW¼	2	36	39	3-15—4-28	.094	8.63
	1865			13.65				NW¼SW¼	2	36	39	3-15—9-15	.111	40.95
	1865					20.05		NW¼SW¼	2	36	39	3-15—4-28	.163	15.04
	1865						.73	NW¼SW¼	2	36	39	3-15—4-28	.006	.55
	1865			2.50				SW¼SE¼	2	36	39	3-15—9-15	.020	7.50
	1865					32.59		SW¼SE¼	2	36	39	3-15—4-28	.265	24.44
	1865			23.35				SE¼SE¼	2	36	39	3-15—9-15	.190	70.05
	1865				1.62			SE¼SE¼	2	36	39	3-15—6-13	.013	2.43
	1865					13.02		SE¼SE¼	2	36	39	3-15—4-28	.106	9.77

Bliss Brothers—Continued.

Date of beneficial use: Nat. mdw.	Cult. area	Construction first initiated: Dams	Ditches	Culture—Acres: Harvest crops	Meadow pasture	Willow and sage pasture	Swamp or overflow	Location: Subdivision	Section	Tp.N.	R.E.	Length of season	Duty of water: C.F.S.	Acre-feet
					7.49			NW¼NW¼	3	36	39	3-15—6-13	.061	11.23
						20.87		NW¼NW¼	3	36	39	3-15—4-28	.170	15.65
					17.86			NE¼NW¼	3	36	39	3-15—6-13	.145	26.79
						18.81		NE¼NW¼	3	36	39	3-15—4-28	.153	14.11
	1868			25.58				NE¼SE¼	2	36	39	3-15—9-15	.208	76.74
	1868					2.08		NE¼SE¼	2	36	39	3-15—4-28	.017	1.56
	1868			4.34				NW¼NW¼	3	36	39	3-15—9-15	.035	13.02
	1868			5.37				SW¼NW¼	1	36	39	3-15—9-15	.044	17.11
	1868				29.08			SW¼NW¼	1	36	39	3-15—6-13	.236	43.62
	1868				30.10			SE¼NW¼	1	36	39	3-15—6-13	.245	45.15
	1868				14.17			NW¼NW¼	1	36	39	3-15—6-13	.115	21.26
	1868				33.86			NE¼SW¼	1	36	39	3-15—6-13	.275	50.79
	1868				28.20			NW¼SW¼	1	36	39	3-15—6-13	.229	42.30
	1868						3.91	SW¼NW¼	33	37	39	3-15—4-28	.032	2.93
	1868						1.77	SE¼NW¼	33	37	39	3-15—4-28	.014	1.33
	1868						4.67	NW¼SW¼	33	37	39	3-15—4-28	.038	3.50
	1868						3.39	NE¼SW¼	33	37	39	3-15—4-28	.028	2.54
	1868						1.23	NW¼SE¼	33	37	39	3-15—4-28	.010	.92

Claimant—**Bliss Brothers.** Proof No. **00102**
Source—**Humboldt River.** Ditch—**Pedroli Ditch System.**

Nat. mdw.	Cult. area	Dams	Ditches	Harvest crops	Meadow pasture	Willow and sage pasture	Swamp or overflow	Subdivision	Section	Tp.N.	R.E.	Length of season	C.F.S.	Acre-feet
	1868			19.02				SW¼SW¼	1	36	39	3-15—9-15	.155	57.06
	1868				11.73			SW¼SW¼	1	36	39	3-15—6-13	.095	17.60

Claimant—**Bliss Brothers.** Proof No. **00102**
Source—**Humboldt River.** Ditch—**Fairbanks Ditch System.**

Nat. mdw.	Cult. area	Dams	Ditches	Harvest crops	Meadow pasture	Willow and sage pasture	Swamp or overflow	Subdivision	Section	Tp.N.	R.E.	Length of season	C.F.S.	Acre-feet
1865				29.33				NE¼NW¼	12	36	39	3-15—9-15	.238	87.99
1865					4.17			NE¼NW¼	12	36	39	3-15—6-13	.034	6.26
1865						1.52		NE¼NW¼	12	36	39	3-15—4-28	.012	4.27
1865							1.67	NE¼NW¼	12	36	39	3-15—4-28	.014	4.38
1865				34.00				NW¼NW¼	12	36	39	3-15—9-15	.276	104.00
1865						4.62		NW¼NW¼	12	36	39	3-15—4-28	.038	6.59
1865							.97	NW¼NW¼	12	36	39	3-15—4-28	.008	.73
1865				3.03				SW¼NW¼	12	36	39	3-15—9-15	.025	9.09
1865						34.27		SW¼NW¼	12	36	39	3-15—4-28	.279	25.70
1865				22.13				SE¼NW¼	12	36	39	3-15—9-15	.180	66.39
1865						15.31		SE¼NW¼	12	36	39	3-15—4-28	.124	11.48
1865				16.40				NE¼SW¼	12	36	39	3-15—9-15	.133	49.20
1865						20.88		NE¼SW¼	12	36	39	3-15—4-28	.170	15.66
1865							2.40	NE¼SW¼	12	36	39	3-15—4-28	.020	1.80

1865				30.67				NW¼SW¼	12	36	39	3-15—9-15	.168	02.01
1865						5.07		NW¼SW¼	12	36	39	3-15—4-28	.041	3.80
1865				8.40				SE¼SW¼	12	36	39	3-15—9-15	.069	25.47
1865						2.40		SE¼SW¼	12	36	39	3-15—4-28	.020	1.80
1865				10.47				NE¼SE¼	12	36	39	3-15—9-15	.085	31.41
1865						24.60		NE¼SE¼	12	36	39	3-15—4-28	.201	18.52
1865				16.10				NW¼SE¼	12	36	39	3-15—9-15	.131	48.30
1865						22.40		NW¼SE¼	12	36	39	3-15—4-28	.182	16.80
1865							.53	NW¼SE¼	12	36	39	3-15—4-28	.004	.38
1865				3.03				SW¼SE¼	12	36	39	3-15—9-15	.025	9.09
1865						21.30		SW¼SE¼	12	36	39	3-15—4-28	.173	15.98
1865							.55	SW¼SE¼	12	36	39	3-15—4-28	.004	.41

Claimant—**Bliss Brothers.** Proof No. 00102

Source—**Humboldt River.** Ditch—**Pedroli Ditch System.**

	1872			.21				SW¼SW¼	32	37	39	3-15—9-15	.002	.63
	1872				6.45			SW¼SW¼	32	37	39	3-15—6-13	.052	9.68
	1872					2.43		SW¼SW¼	32	37	39	3-15—4-28	.020	1.82
	1872			3.13				SW¼SE¼	32	37	39	3-15—9-15	.025	9.39
	1872					11.19		SW¼SE¼	32	37	39	3-15—4-28	.091	8.39
	1873				9.78			SE¼NE¼	4	36	39	3-15—6-13	.080	14.67
	1873					24.40		SE¼NE¼	4	36	39	3-15—4-28	.198	18.30
	1873					22.67		SW¼NE¼	4	36	39	3-15—4-28	.184	17.00
	1873					18.30		SE¼NW¼	4	36	39	3-15—4-28	.149	13.73
	1873					1.78		SW¼NW¼	4	36	39	3-15—4-28	.014	1.34
	1875			28.97				SW¼NE¼	12	36	39	3-15—9-15	.236	86.91
	1875				4.43			SW¼NE¼	12	36	39	3-15—6-13	.036	6.65
	1875						.70	SW¼NE¼	12	36	39	3-15—4-28	.006	1.05
	1875			5.30				SE¼NE¼	12	36	39	3-15—9-15	.043	15.90

Claimant—**Bliss Brothers.** Proof No. 00102

Source—**Humboldt River.** Ditch—**Pioneer Ditch System.**

	1870			28.26				SE¼NE¼	2	36	39	3-15—9-15	.230	84.78
	1870				9.08			SE¼NE¼	2	36	39	3-15—6-13	.074	13.62
	1870					.45		SE¼NE¼	2	36	39	3-15—4-28	.004	.34
	1870					3.05		SW¼SW¼	2	36	39	3-15—4-28	.025	2.29
	1870					20.28		SE¼SW¼	2	36	39	3-15—4-28	.165	15.21
	1870				35.86			SE¼SW¼	1	36	39	3-15—6-13	.292	53.79
	1870				20.17			NW¼SE¼	1	36	39	3-15—6-13	.164	30.26
	1870				19.51			SW¼SE¼	1	36	39	3-15—6-13	.159	29.27
	1870				.33			NE¼NW¼	1	36	39	3-15—6-13	.003	.50
	1870				13.57			SW¼NE¼	1	36	39	3-15—6-13	.110	20.36
	1870			2.49				SE¼NW¼	33	37	39	3-15—9-15	.020	7.47
	1870				23.24			SE¼NW¼	33	37	39	3-15—6-13	.189	34.86
	1870				32.79			SW¼NE¼	33	37	39	3-15—6-13	.267	49.19
	1870						9.38	NW¼NW¼	32	37	39	3-15—4-28	.076	7.04
	1870						10.40	NE¼NW¼	32	37	39	3-15—4-28	.085	7.80
	1871			13.86				SW¼NW¼	33	37	39	3-15—9-15	.113	41.58
	1871				.43			SW¼NW¼	33	37	39	3-15—6-13	.003	.65
	1871				6.90			SE¼NE¼	33	37	39	3-15—6-13	.056	10.35
	1871					4.23		SE¼NE¼	33	37	39	3-15—4-28	.034	8.35

Bliss Brothers—Continued.

Date of beneficial use		Construction first initiated		Culture—Acres				Location					Duty of water	
Nat. mdw.	Cult. area	Dams	Ditches	Harvest crops	Meadow pasture	Willow and sage pasture	Swamp or overflow	Subdivision	Section	Tp. N.	R. E.	Length of season	C.F.S.	Acre-feet
	1871				2.12			NW¼NE¼	33	37	39	3-15—6-13	.017	3.18
	1871			28.69				NW¼SW¼	33	37	39	3-15—9-15	.233	86.07
	1871				3.33			NW¼SW¼	33	37	39	3-15—6-13	.027	5.00
	1871			25.37				NE¼SW¼	33	37	39	3-15—9-15	.206	76.11
	1871				1.23			NE¼SW¼	33	37	39	3-15—6-13	.101	1.85
	1871					6.93		NE¼SW¼	33	37	39	3-15—4-28	.056	7.32
	1871			27.67				NW¼SE¼	33	37	39	3-15—9-15	.225	83.01
	1871				5.77			NW¼SE¼	33	37	39	3-15—6-13	.047	8.66
	1871					1.60		NW¼SE¼	33	37	39	3-15—4-28	.013	1.20
	1871			.63				NE¼SE¼	33	37	39	3-15—9-15	.005	1.89
	1871				6.87			NE¼SE¼	33	37	39	3-15—6-13	.056	10.31
	1871					16.74		NE¼SE¼	33	37	39	3-15—4-28	.136	12.56
	1871			26.60				SW¼SW¼	33	37	39	3-15—9-15	.216	79.80
	1871			36.97				SE¼SW¼	33	37	39	3-15—9-15	.301	110.91
	1871			34.90				SW¼SE¼	33	37	39	3-15—9-15	.284	104.97
	1871						4.54	SW¼SE¼	33	37	39	3-15—4-28	.037	3.41
	1871			26.77				SE¼SE¼	33	37	39	3-15—9-15	.218	80.31
	1871				2.67			SE¼SE¼	33	37	39	3-15—6-13	.022	4.01
	1871					8.10		SE¼SE¼	33	37	39	3-15—4-28	.066	6.08
	1871						.40	SE¼SE¼	33	37	39	3-15—4-28	.004	.30
	1872			20.47				NW¼NW¼	32	37	39	3-15—9-15	.166	61.41
	1872				2.83			NW¼NW¼	32	37	39	3-15—6-13	.023	4.25
	1872			20.56				NE¼NW¼	32	37	39	3-15—9-15	.167	61.68
	1872			22.10				NW¼NE¼	32	37	39	3-15—9-15	.180	66.30
	1872						3.77	NW¼NE¼	32	37	39	3-15—4-28	.031	2.83
	1872			4.00				NE¼NE¼	32	37	39	3-15—9-15	.033	12.00
	1872						1.36	NE¼NE¼	32	37	39	3-15—4-28	.011	1.02
	1872			29.54				SW¼NW¼	32	37	39	3-15—9-15	.240	88.62
	1872						8.03	SW¼NW¼	32	37	39	3-15—4-28	.065	6.02
	1872			27.49				SE¼NW¼	32	37	39	3-15—9-15	.223	82.47
	1872						9.14	SE¼NW¼	32	37	39	3-15—4-28	.074	6.86
	1872			33.88				SW¼NE¼	32	37	39	3-15—9-15	.275	101.64
	1872						3.61	SW¼NE¼	32	37	39	3-15—4-28	.029	2.71
	1872			25.54				SE¼NE¼	32	37	39	3-15—9-15	.208	76.62
	1872						11.66	SE¼NE¼	32	37	39	3-15—4-28	.095	8.75
	1872			20.31				NW¼SW¼	32	37	39	3-15—9-15	.165	60.93
	1872				5.59			NW¼SW¼	32	37	39	3-15—6-13	.045	8.39
	1872					3.54		NW¼SW¼	32	37	39	3-15—4-28	.029	2.66
	1872						7.12	NW¼SW¼	32	37	39	3-15—4-28	.058	5.34
	1872			23.52				NE¼SW¼	32	37	39	3-15—9-15	.191	70.56
	1872						14.18	NE¼SW¼	32	37	39	3-15—4-28	.115	10.64
	1872			29.48				NW¼SE¼	32	37	39	3-15—9-15	.240	88.44
	1872						8.90	NW¼SE¼	32	37	39	3-15—4-28	.072	6.68
	1872			29.18				NE¼SE¼	32	37	39	3-15—9-15	.237	87.54
	1872						9.68	NE¼SE¼	32	37	39	3-15—4-28	.079	7.26
	1872			7.93				SE¼SW¼	32	37	39	3-15—9-15	.064	23.79
	1872				3.11			SE¼SW¼	32	37	39	3-15—6-13	.025	4.67

3[69]

	1872					.81		SE¼SW¼	32	37	39	3-15—4-28	.003	.23
	1872						3.34	SE¼SW¼	32	37	39	3-15—4-28	.027	2.51
	1872			27.39				SE¼SE¼	32	37	39	3-15—9-15	.223	82.17
	1872					5.66		SE¼SE¼	32	37	39	3-15—4-28	.046	4.25
	1873			10.50				NW¼NW¼	4	36	39	3-15—9-15	.085	31.50
	1873					21.15		NW¼NW¼	4	36	39	3-15—4-28	.172	15.86
	1873						.06	NW¼NW¼	4	36	39	3-15—4-28	.001	.05
	1873			23.73				NE¼NW¼	4	36	39	3-15—9-15	.192	71.19
	1873					10.80		NE¼NW¼	4	36	39	3-15—4-28	.088	8.10
	1873						1.10	NE¼NW¼	4	36	39	3-15—4-28	.009	.83
	1873			25.13				NW¼NE¼	4	36	39	3-15—9-15	.204	75.39
	1873					10.45		NW¼NE¼	4	36	39	3-15—4-28	.085	7.84
	1873			31.97				NE¼NE¼	4	36	39	3-15—9-15	.260	95.91
	1873					4.60		NE¼NE¼	4	36	39	3-15—4-28	.037	3.45
	1873					3.53		NE¼SE¼	4	36	39	3-15—4-28	.029	2.65
	1874				.70			SW¼NW¼	7	36	40	3-15—6-13	.006	1.05
	1874					19.97		SW¼NW¼	7	36	40	3-15—4-28	.162	14.98
	1874					6.65		SE¼NW¼	7	36	40	3-15—4-28	.054	5.99
	1874			4.17				NE¼SW¼	7	36	40	3-15—9-15	.034	12.51
	1874				34.06			NE¼SW¼	7	36	40	3-15—6-13	.277	51.09
	1874			10.75				NW¼SW¼	7	36	40	3-15—9-15	.087	32.25
	1874				21.80			NW¼SW¼	7	36	40	3-15—6-13	.177	32.70
	1874					4.83		NW¼SW¼	7	36	40	3-15—4-28	.039	3.62
	1874			10.83				SW¼SW¼	7	36	40	3-15—9-15	.088	32.49
	1874				26.00			SW¼SW¼	7	36	40	3-15—6-13	.211	39.00
	1874					1.12		SW¼SW¼	7	36	40	3-15—4-28	.009	.84
	1874			21.97				SE¼SW¼	7	36	40	3-15—9-15	.179	65.91
	1874				17.14			SE¼SW¼	7	36	40	3-15—6-13	.139	25.71
	1874			35.53				NE¼SE¼	7	36	40	3-15—9-15	.289	106.59
	1874				4.13			NE¼SE¼	7	36	40	3-15—6-13	.034	6.20
	1874			3.20				NW¼SE¼	7	36	40	3-15—9-15	.026	9.60
	1874				36.80			NW¼SE¼	7	36	40	3-15—6-13	.299	55.20
	1874				38.32			SW¼SE¼	7	36	40	3-15—6-13	.312	57.48
	1874				40.10			SE¼SE¼	7	36	40	3-15—6-13	.326	60.15
	1874				5.16			SW¼NE¼	7	36	40	3-15—6-13	.042	7.74
	1874				1.45			SE¼NE¼	7	36	40	3-15—6-13	.012	2.18
	1875			.50				SE¼SW¼	1	36	39	3-15—9-15	.004	1.50
	1875					1.37		SE¼SW¼	1	36	39	3-15—4-28	.011	1.03
	1875					18.47		NW¼SE¼	1	36	39	3-15—4-28	.150	13.85
	1875					14.90		SW¼SE¼	1	36	39	3-15—4-28	.121	11.18
	1875					2.50		SE¼SE¼	1	36	39	3-15—4-28	.120	1.88
	1875					6.60		SW¼NE¼	1	36	39	3-15—4-28	.054	4.95
	1875					2.60		SE¼NE¼	1	36	39	3-15—4-28	.021	1.95
	1875					8.27		NE¼SE¼	1	36	39	3-15—4-28	.007	6.20
	1875			3.90				NW¼NE¼	12	36	39	3-15—9-15	.032	11.70
	1875				2.00			NW¼NE¼	12	36	39	3-15—6-13	.016	3.00
	1875				7.38			NW¼SE¼	3	36	39	3-15—6-13	.060	11.07
	1875					3.12		NW¼SE¼	3	36	39	3-15—4-28	.025	2.34
	1875				22.81			NE¼SE¼	3	36	39	3-15—6-13	.185	34.22
	1876				6.24			NW¼SW¼	34	37	39	3-15—6-13	.051	9.36
	1876				5.81			SW¼SW¼	34	37	39	3-15—6-13	.047	8.72
	1876					22.31		SW¼SW¼	34	37	39	3-15—4-28	.181	16.73
	1876				20.90			SE¼SW¼	34	37	39	3-16—6-13	.170	31.35

Claimant—**Mary Jane Ostrander.** Proof No. 0063

Source—**Humboldt River.** Ditch—**Young Ditch.**

Date of beneficial use: Nat. mdw.	Date of beneficial use: Cult. area	Construction first initiated: Dams	Construction first initiated: Ditches	Culture—Acres: Harvest crops	Culture—Acres: Meadow pasture	Culture—Acres: Willow and sage pasture	Culture—Acres: Swamp or overflow	Location: Subdivision	Location: Section	Location: Tp.N.	Location: R.E.	Length of season	Duty of water: C.F.S.	Duty of water: Acre-feet
....	1895	....	....	20	....	....	....	N¼SE¼	12	27	31	3-15—9-15	.163	60.0
....	1897	....	....	20	....	....	....	N½SE¼	12	27	31	3-15—9-15	.163	60.0
....	1898	....	....	38.50	....	....	....	N½SE¼	12	27	31	3-15—9-15	.313	115.50

Claimant—**W. C. Pitt.** Proof No. 0064

Source—**Humboldt River.** Ditch—**Old Channel Ditch.**

Nat. mdw.	Cult. area	Dams	Ditches	Harvest crops	Meadow pasture	Willow and sage pasture	Swamp or overflow	Subdivision	Section	Tp.N.	R.E.	Length of season	C.F.S.	Acre-feet
....	1890	....	....	38.15	....	....	....	N½	15	27	31	3-15—9-15	.310	114.45
....	1890	....	....	534.10	....	....	....		15	27	31	3-15—9-15	4.342	1602.30
....	1891	....	....	39.23	....	....	....	NW¼	23	27	31	3-15—9-15	.319	117.69
....	1891	....	....	88.27	....	....	....	NW¼	23	27	31	3-15—9-15	.718	264.81
....	1895	....	....	145.05	....	....	....	NE¼	22	27	31	3-15—9-15	1.179	435.15
....	1892	....	....	340.95	....	....	....		9	27	31	3-15—9-15	2.772	1022.85
....	1900	....	....	67	....	....	....	SW¼	10	27	31	3-15—9-15	.545	201.0

Allot sufficient flow of water through Old Channel Ditch, priority of 1900 for generation of 50 H.P.
Allot additional flow of water with priority of 1914 for generation of additional 10 H.P. Location of plant near Old Channel Dam, Lovelock.

Claimant—**W. C. Pitt.** Proof No. 0065

Source—**Humboldt River.** Ditch—**Southwest Ditch.**

Nat. mdw.	Cult. area	Dams	Ditches	Harvest crops	Meadow pasture	Willow and sage pasture	Swamp or overflow	Subdivision	Section	Tp.N.	R.E.	Length of season	C.F.S.	Acre-feet
....	1886	....	....	50	....	....	....	W½SE¼	27	27	31	3-15—9-15	.407	150.0

Claimant—**U. S. Government Indian School.** Proof. No. 0065

Source—**Humboldt River.** Ditch—**Southwest Ditch.**

Nat. mdw.	Cult. area	Dams	Ditches	Harvest crops	Meadow pasture	Willow and sage pasture	Swamp or overflow	Subdivision	Section	Tp.N.	R.E.	Length of season	C.F.S.	Acre-feet
....	1886	....	....	17.30	....	....	....	S½SW¼SE¼	27	27	31	3-15—9-15	.141	51.90

Claimant—**A. Reno.** Proof No. 0067

Source—**Humboldt River.** Ditch—**Old Channel.**

Nat. mdw.	Cult. area	Dams	Ditches	Harvest crops	Meadow pasture	Willow and sage pasture	Swamp or overflow	Subdivision	Section	Tp.N.	R.E.	Length of season	C.F.S.	Acre-feet
....	1894	....	....	66.33	....	....	....	S½NW¼&NE¼SW¼	13	27	31	3-15—9-15	.539	198.99
....	1896	....	....	33.17	....	....	....	E½SW¼&NE¼SW¼	13	27	31	3-15—9-15	.270	99.51

Claimant—**W. C. Buddell.** Proof No. 0068

Source—**Humboldt River.** Ditch—**Irish-American.**

Nat. mdw.	Cult. area	Dams	Ditches	Harvest crops	Meadow pasture	Willow and sage pasture	Swamp or overflow	Subdivision	Section	Tp.N.	R.E.	Length of season	C.F.S.	Acre-feet
....	1863	....	....	20	....	....	....	*E½W½	26	27	31	3-15—9 15	.163	60.0
1868	....	....	....	43.75	....	....	....	SW¼	26					
1873	....	....	....	45	....	....	....	NW¼	35	27	31	3-15—9-15	.356	131.25
....	1873	....	....	....	100.00	....	....	SE¼	28	27	31	3-15—9-15	.366	135.0
....	1873	....	....	....	39.61	....	....	*NE¼	26	27	31	3-15—6-13	.813	150.0
....	1885	....	....	100	....	....	....	W½SE¼ & E½SW¼	26	27	31	3-15—6-13	.822	50.42
								NE¼SW¼						

2[69]

								SE¼NW¼						
								SW¼NE¼						
								NW¼SE¼	26	27	31	3-15—9-15	.813	300.0
	1886			35.10				NE¼SE¼	26	27	31	3-15—9-15	.285	105.30
	1887			20.10				NE¼SW¼	26	27	31	3-15—9-15	.163	60.30
								NE¼SW¼						
	1884			5.10				SE¼NW¼						
								SW¼NE¼						
								NW¼SE¼	26	27	31	3-15—9-15	.041	15.30
	1884			7.65				E½SE¼	26	27	31	3-15—9-15	.062	22.95
	1868				8.65			NW¼NW¼	35	27	31	3-15—6-13	.070	12.98
	1868				42.45			N½NW¼	35	27	31	3-15—6-13	.345	63.68

*Near center.

Claimant—***Millie R. Evans.** Proof No. 0069

Source—**Humboldt River.** Ditch—†**Rodgers Canal System.**

	1890			329.25					24	26	31	3-15—9-15	2.677	987.75
	1890			467.70					25	26	31	3-15—9-15	3.802	1403.10
	1890			158.06				E½	16	26	31	3-15—9-15	1.290	474.18
	1890			11.40				SE¼SE¼	16	26	31	3-15—9-15	.093	34.20
	1891			118					18	26	32	3-15—9-15	.959	354.0
	1891			34.60				W½SW¼	18	26	32	3-15—9-15	.281	103.80
	1891			199.75					18	26	32	3-15—9-15	1.624	599.25
	1891			123.50				NE¼ & W½	19	26	32	3-15—9-15	1.004	370.50
	1891			18.40				NW¼NW¼	19	26	32	3-15—9-15	.150	55.20
	1891			51.10				W½	19	26	32	3-15—9-15	.415	153.30
	1877			277.98					35	26	31	3-15—9-15	2.260	833.94
	1883			173.82				E½W½&E½	10	26	31	3-15—9-15	1.413	521.46
	1883					105.23		N½	10	26	31	3-15—6-13	.856	157.85
	1883					24.84		N½	10	26	31	3-15—6-13	.202	37.26
	1880			143.40					11	26	31	3-15—9-15	1.166	430.20
	1884			244.05					7	26	31	3-15—9-15	1.984	732.15
	1884			8.02					7	26	31	3-15—9-15	.065	24.06
	1876			153.64				SE¼	13	26	31	3-15—9-15	1.249	460.92
	1876			139.92				SW¼	13	26	31	3-15—9-15	1.138	419.76
	1876			19.56				SE¼NW¼	13	26	31	3-15—9-15	.159	58.68
	1876			74.20				S½NE¼	13	26	31	3-15—9-15	.603	222.60
	1876			27.95				NW¼NE¼	13	26	31	3-15—9-15	.227	83.85
	1876			45.28				NE¼NE¼	13	26	31	3-15—9-15	.368	135.84
	1876					36.41		NE¼NW¼	13	26	31	3-15—6-13	.296	54.62
	1876					92.36		NW¼	13	26	31	3-15—6-13	.751	138.54
	1880			65.67				S½	15	26	31	3-15—9-15	.534	197.01
	1880			218.89				W½&NE¼	15	26	31	3-15—9-15	1.780	656.67
	1880			6.28				SW¼SW¼	15	26	31	3-15—9-15	.051	18.84
	1880			9.78				NE¼NE¼	15	26	31	3-15—9-15	.080	29.34
	1880			4.52				W½NE¼	15	26	31	3-15—9-15	.037	13.56
	1880			23.99				E½NE¼	15	26	31	3-15—9-15	.195	71.97
	1880			105.80				E½	15	26	31	3-15—9-15	.860	317.40
	1880			3.56				NW¼NW¼	15	26	31	3-15—9-15	.029	10.68
	1880			2.71				W½NE¼	15	26	31	3-15—9-15	.022	8.13
	1880			1.47				NW¼NE¼	15	26	31	3-15—9-15	.012	4.41

Millie R. Evans—Continued.

Date of beneficial use: Nat. mdw.	Date of beneficial use: Cult. area	Construction first initiated: Dams	Construction first initiated: Ditches	Culture—Acres: Harvest crops	Culture—Acres: Meadow pasture	Culture—Acres: Willow and sage pasture	Culture—Acres: Swamp or overflow	Location: Subdivision	Location: Section	Location: Tp.N.	Location: R.E.	Length of season	Duty of water: C.F.S.	Duty of water: Acre-feet
	1880			44.83				E½E½	15	26	31	3-15—9-15	.364	134.49
	1880			9.77				SW¼SE¼	15	26	31	3-15—9-15	.079	29.31
	1862			70					26	26	31	3-15—9-15	.569	210.0
	1862			40				S½	10	26	31	3-15—9-15	.325	120.0
	1864			20				SW¼	11	26	31	3-15—9-15	.163	60.0
	1867			80				NW¼	23	26	31	3-15—9-15	.650	240.0
	1873			128.90					14	26	31	3-15—9-15	1.048	38.67
	1877			24.84				W½NE¼	23	26	31	3-15—9-15	.202	74.52
	1877			202.90				E½	23	26	31	3-15—9-15	1.650	608.70
	1877			16.43				SW¼SE¼	23	26	31	3-15—9-15	.134	49.29
	1877			43.92				NE¼SW¼	23	26	31	3-15—9-15	.357	131.76
	1877					47.08		NW¼NE¼	23	26	31	3-15—6-13	.383	70.62
	1877					43.53		NW¼SW¼	23	26	31	3-15—6-13	.354	65.30
	1878			280.33					24	26	31	3-15—9-15	2.352	867.99
	1877			42.62				W½NE¼	26	26	31	3-15—9-15	.347	127.86
	1877			16.43				NE¼NE¼	26	26	31	3-15—9-15	.134	49.29
	1877			6.66				SE¼NE¼	26	26	31	3-15—9-15	.054	19.98
	1877					166.54		SW¼	26	26	31	3-15—6-13	1.354	249.81

*Rodgers Canal System was initiated through the following ditches:

(a) Blake Ditch.
(b) Winslow Ditch.
(c) Weikel Ditch.
(d) Kewley Ditch.
(e) McCallum & Andrieux Company Ditch.
(f) McCallum Ditch.
(g) Slaven Ditch.
(h) J. B. Brown Ditch.
(i) Saxenheimer Ditch.
(j) Farmers Ditch.
(k) Marker Ditch.
(l) Fuss Ditch.
(m) J. B. Brown Extension Ditch.

†Rodgers Estate.

Claimant—**Vic Sebbas.** Proof No. 0070

Source—**Humboldt River.** Ditch—**Young Ditch.**

Nat. mdw.	Cult. area	Dams	Ditches	Harvest crops	Meadow pasture	Willow and sage pasture	Swamp or overflow	Subdivision	Section	Tp.N.	R.E.	Length of season	C.F.S.	Acre-feet
	1901			37.25				S½	2	27	31	3-15—9-15	.303	111.75
	1901			38.45				S½	2	27	31	3-15—9-15	.313	115.35
	1901			12.10				S½	2	27	31	3-15—9-15	.098	36.30
	1901			5.55				S½	2	27	31	3-15—9-15	.045	16.65
	1901			9.10				S½	2	27	31	3-15—9-15	.074	27.30
	1901			2.00				S½	2	27	31	3-15—9-15	.016	6.00
	1901			10.00				S½	2	27	31	3-15—9-15	.081	30.00
	1901			1.00				NE¼SE¼	2	27	31	3-15—9-15	.008	3.00

Claimant—**E. W. Sommer.** Proof No. 0071

Source—**Humboldt River.** Ditch—**Highflyer or Arthur Kewley Ditch.**

Nat. mdw.	Cult. area	Dams	Ditches	Harvest crops	Meadow pasture	Willow and sage pasture	Swamp or overflow	Subdivision	Section	Tp.N.	R.E.	Length of season	C.F.S.	Acre-feet
	1877			47.66				NW¼	2	25	31	3-15—9-15	.387	142.98
	1888			100.00				NW¼	2	25	31	3-15—9-15	.813	300.00
	1888					4.84		NW¼	2	25	31	3-15—6-13	.039	7.26

Claimant—**Matt Smith.** Proof No. 0072
Source—**Humboldt River.** Ditch—**Young Ditch.**

...	1897	...	...	40	...	...	...	W½E½	1	27	31	3-15—9-15	.325	120.00
...	1897	...	...	8.70	...	...	...	W½E½	1	27	31	3-15—9-15	.071	25.10
...	1897	...	...	3.15	...	...	...	W½E½	1	27	31	3-15—9-15	.026	9.45
...	1904	...	...	6.15	...	...	...	W½E½	1	27	31	3-15—9-15	.050	18.45
...	1897	...	...	....	2.35	...	...	W½E½	1	27	31	3-15—6-13	.019	3.53
...	1897	...	...	....	...	10.70	...	W½E½	1	27	31	3-15—6-13	.087	16.05

Claimant—**I. M. Springer, Sr.** Proof No. 0073
Source—**Humboldt River.** Ditch—***Slough ditch 1873 to 1887; †Irish-American 1887 to present.**

...	*1873	...	...	9.50	...	...	...	W½NE¼ &NW¼SE¼	23	27	31	3-15—9-15	.077	28.50
...	†1888	...	...	19.00	...	...	...	W½NE¼ &NW¼SE¼	23	27	31	3-15—9-15	.154	57.00
...	1890	...	...	19.00	...	...	...	W½NE¼ &NW¼SE¼	23	27	31	3-15—9-15	.154	57.00

Claimant—**Wm. A. Stauts.** Proof No. 0074
Source—**Humboldt River.** Ditch—**Irish-American.**

...	1891	...	...	20.20	...	...	...	SE¼SW¼	22	27	31	3-15—9-15	.164	60.60
...	1899	...	...	4.00	...	...	...	SW¼SE¼	22	27	31	3-15—9-15	.033	12.00
...	1899	...	...	26.15	...	...	...	W½SE¼	22	27	31	3-15—9-15	.213	78.45

Claimant—**George C. Stoker.** Proof No. 0076
Source—**Humboldt River.** Ditch—**Old Channel.**

...	1896	...	...	94.58	...	...	...	SE¼	22	27	31	3-15—9-15	.769	283.74

Claimant—**H. Stoker.** Proof No. 0077
Source—**Humboldt River.** Ditch—**Old Channel.**

...	1893	...	...	224.70	...	...	...	NW¼&W½NE¼	14	27	31	3-15—9-15	1.827	674.10

Claimant—**Antone Alves and Anna Alves.** Proof No. 0077
Source—**Humboldt River.** Ditch—**Old Channel.**

...	1888	...	...	45	...	...	...	W½SE¼	10	27	31	3-15—9-15	.366	135.00
...	1893	...	...	11	...	...	...	W½SE¼	10	27	31	3-15—9-15	.089	33.00
...	1896	...	...	14.95	...	...	...	W½SE¼	10	27	31	3-15—9-15	.122	44.85

Claimant—**Pascasio Bilbao.** Proof No. 0078
Source—**Humboldt River.** Ditch—**Union Canal through Lake Shore Ditch.**

Date of beneficial use: Nat. mdw.	Date of beneficial use: Cult. area	Construction first initiated: Dams	Construction first initiated: Ditches	Culture—Acres: Harvest crops	Culture—Acres: Meadow pasture	Culture—Acres: Willow and sage pasture	Culture—Acres: Swamp or over-flow	Location: Subdivision	Location: Section	Location: Tp. N.	Location: R. E.	Length of season	Duty of water: C.F.S.	Duty of water: Acre-feet
	1883			5				SE¼NE¼	29	26	31	3-15—9-15	.051	15.0
	1883			20				N½NE¼SE¼	29	26	31	3-15—9-15	.163	60.0
	1884			5				NE¼SE¼	29	26	31	3-15—9-15	.051	15.0
	1887			5				SE¼NE¼	29	26	31	3-15—9-15	.051	15.0
	1888			8				E½NE¼	29	26	31	3-15—9-15	.065	24.0
	1888			3				E½E½	29	26	31	3-15—9-15	.024	9.0
	1890			8				E½E½	29	26	31	3-15—9-15	.065	24.0
	1891			10				E½E½	29	26	31	3-15—9-15	.081	30.0
	1892			13.20				E½E½	29	26	31	3-15—9-15	.107	39.6
	1893			13.20				E½E½	29	26	31	3-15—9-15	.107	39.6
	1894			13.20				E½E½	29	26	31	3-15—9-15	.107	39.6
	1883			6.50				E½NE¼NE¼	29	26	31	3-15—9-15	.053	19.5
	1883					.80		SE¼NE¼	29	26	31	3-15—6-13	.007	1.2

Claimant—**John O'Kane.** Proof No. 0079
Source—**Humboldt River.** Ditch—**Irish-American.**

Date of beneficial use: Nat. mdw.	Date of beneficial use: Cult. area	Construction first initiated: Dams	Construction first initiated: Ditches	Culture—Acres: Harvest crops	Culture—Acres: Meadow pasture	Culture—Acres: Willow and sage pasture	Culture—Acres: Swamp or over-flow	Location: Subdivision	Location: Section	Location: Tp. N.	Location: R. E.	Length of season	Duty of water: C.F.S.	Duty of water: Acre-feet
	1889			4.50				W½SE¼NE¼	27	27	31	3-15—9-15	.037	13.5

Claimant—**Lovelock Land and Development Co.** Proof No. 0080
Source—**Humboldt River.** Ditch—***Lovelock Land and Development Co. Ditch System.**

Date of beneficial use: Nat. mdw.	Date of beneficial use: Cult. area	Construction first initiated: Dams	Construction first initiated: Ditches	Culture—Acres: Harvest crops	Culture—Acres: Meadow pasture	Culture—Acres: Willow and sage pasture	Culture—Acres: Swamp or over-flow	Location: Subdivision	Location: Section	Location: Tp. N.	Location: R. E.	Length of season	Duty of water: C.F.S.	Duty of water: Acre-feet
	1903		d-e-i	63.30				N½NE¼	10	25	31	3-15—9-15	.515	189.90
	1903					d-c-i 52.70		S½NE¼	10	25	31	3-15—6-13	1.102	406.65
	1903					d-c-i 42.05		W½SE¼	10	25	31	3-15—6-13	.435	106.66
	1901					a 73.15		S½&NE¼	2	25	31	3-15—6-13	.595	108.73
	1901		a-c-d	135.55				SW¼	2	25	31	3-15—9-15	1.102	406.65
	1903		a-c-d	53.55				SE¼	2	25	31	3-15—9-15	.435	160.65
	1901		a-c-h-e-i	440.25				N½&N½S½	8	25	31	3-15—9-15	3.579	1320.75
	1903		a-c-h-e-i	155.00				S½S½	8	25	31	3-15—9-15	1.260	465.0
	1901		a-e-f-g-h	472.50				N½&N½S½	7	25	31	3-15—9-15	3.841	1417.50
	1903		a-e-f-g-h	155.00				S½S½	7	25	31	3-15—9-15	1.260	465.0
	1903		a-d-e-i	398.70				A part of	16	25	31	3-15—9-15	3.241	1196.10
	1903		d-e-i-f-g-h	626.00					11	25	30	3-15—9-15	5.089	1878.0
	1903		d-e-i-f-g-h	633.40					12	25	30	3-15—9-15	5.150	1900.20
	1905		a-d-e-i-h-f-g	152.82				NE¼	18	25	31	3-15—9-15	1.242	458.46

*The Lovelock Land and Development Company Ditch System.
(a) Kewley.
(b) Highflyer Ditch and Flume.
(c) Killebrew and Beck.
(d) Tule Ditch and Flume.
(e) Levee.
(f) South Drainage and Waste Ditch.
(g) Lake Drainage and Waste Ditch.
(h) Tule Drainage and Waste Ditch.
(i) Reservoir.

Claimant—**John G. Taylor.** Proof No. 0081

Source—**Humboldt River.** Ditch—**Irish-American in conjunction with Old Channel.**

	1890			97.50				E½	21	27	31	3-15—9-15	.793	292.50
	1890			3.10				SE¼SE¼	21	27	31	3-15—9-15	.025	9.30
	1890			6.30				SE¼SW¼	21	27	31	3-15—9-15	.051	18.90
	1890			4.80				SE¼SW¼	21	27	31	3-15—9-15	.039	14.40
	1895			47.55				W½NE¼	21	27	31	3-15—9-15	.387	142.65
	1895			31.70				E½NW¼	21	27	31	3-15—9-15	.258	95.10

Claimant—**John G. Taylor.** Proof No. 0081

Source—**Humboldt River.** Ditch—**Old Channel in conjunction with Young Ditch.**

	1888			20				N½	3	27	31	3-15—9-15	.163	60.0
	1893			60				N½	3	27	31	3-15—9-15	.488	180.0
	1895			190				S½	3	27	31	3-15—9-15	1.545	570.0
	1898			66.10				N½	3	27	31	3-15—9-15	.537	198.30

Claimant—**John G. Taylor.** Proof No. 0081

Source—**Humboldt River.** Ditch—**Young Ditch.**

	1899			101.05				E½E½	4	27	31	3-15—9-15	.822	303.15
	1898			....		6.75		NW¼NE¼	3	27	31	3-15—6-13	.055	10.13
	1899			9.70				NE¼SW¼	34	28	31	3-15—9-15	.079	29.10
	1899			26				SE¼SE¼	33	28	31	3-15—9-15	.211	78.00

Claimant—**John G. Taylor.** Proof No. 0081

Source—**Humboldt River.** Ditch—**Irish-American in conjunction with Southwest Ditch.**

	1890			136.05				SW¼	22	27	31	3-15—9-15	1.106	408.15

Claimant—**John G. Taylor.** Proof No. 0081

Source—**Humboldt** River. Ditch—**Irish-American in conjunction with Marzen Slough.**

	1893			86				NE¼	29	27	31	3-15—9-15	.699	258.00
	1893			8.70				SE¼NW¼	29	27	31	3-15—9-15	.071	26.10
	1893			16.25				S½NW¼	29	27	31	3-15—9-15	.132	48.75
	1893			128				SW¼	29	27	31	3-15—9-15	1.041	384.00
	1893			39				SE¼SE¼	30	27	31	3-15—9-15	.317	117.00
	1893			15				NE¼	31	27	31	3-15—9-15	.122	45.00
	1898			18.45				NE¼	31	27	31	3-15—9-15	.150	55.35

Claimant—**Bergman and Alfree.** Proof No. 0082

Source—**Humboldt River.** Ditch—**Southwest Ditch; Lovelock and Borland Slough.**

1874				100				N½	34	27	31	3-15—9-15	.813	300.00
	1880			33.70				N½	34	27	31	3-15—9-15	.274	101.10
	1880			79.40				W½SW¼	34	27	31	3-15—9-15	.646	238.20
	1880			47.60				E½SW¼, W½SE¼ & S½NE¼	34	27	31	3-15—9-15	.387	142.80
	1883			....		3.55		NE¼NE¼	34	27	31	3-15—6-13	.029	5.33
	1883			....		108.10		E½NW¼ & W½NE¼	34	27	31	3-15—6-13	.879	162.15
	1883			....		213.10		E½, E½SW¼	34	27	31	3-15—6-13	1.733	319.65

Claimant—**Bergman and Alfree.** Proof No. **0082**

Source—**Humboldt River.** Ditch—**Southwest Ditch.**

Date of beneficial use: Nat. mdw.	Date of beneficial use: Cult. area	Construction first initiated: Dams	Construction first initiated: Ditches	Culture—Acres: Harvest crops	Culture—Acres: Meadow pasture	Culture—Acres: Willow and sage pasture	Culture—Acres: Swamp or overflow	Location: Subdivision	Location: Section	Location: Tp.N.	Location: R.E.	Length of season	Duty of water: C.F.S.	Duty of water: Acre-feet
	1883			52.30				NW¼	3	26	31	3-15—9-15	.425	156.90
	1883					315.75		W½&NE¼	3	26	31	3-15—6-13	2.567	473.63
	1885			49.15				S½SE¼	33	27	31	3-15—9-15	.499	147.45
	1885			48.00				SE¼	33	27	31	3-15—9-15	.390	144.00
	1885			38.90				SE¼&SW¼	33	27	31	3-15—9-15	.316	116.70
	1885			25.95				SE¼SW¼	33	27	31	3-15—9-15	.211	77.85
	1883				22.00			NW¼SW¼	33	27	31	3-15—6-13	.179	33.00
	1885				10.20			SW¼	33	27	31	3-15—6-13	.083	15.30
	1885				14.95			SW¼SW¼	33	27	31	3-15—6-13	.123	22.48
	1885					51.10		S½	33	27	31	3-15—6-13	.415	76.65
	1885					3.95		SW¼SE¼	33	27	31	3-15—6-13	.032	5.93
	1889			60				SE¼	32	27	31	3-15—9-15	.488	180.00
	1883			20				SE¼	32	27	31	3-15—9-15	.163	60.00
	1885			139.80				SE¼,S½NE¼,SW¼	32	27	31	3-15—9-15	1.137	419.40
	1883			59.75				N½	5	26	31	3-15—9-15	.486	179.25
	1883			33.00				NE¼	5	26	31	3-15—9-15	.268	99.00
	1883			47.95				E½E½	5	26	31	3-15—9-15	.390	143.85
	1887			78.65				NE¼	4	26	31	3-15—9-15	.639	235.95
	1877			81.35				S½	4	26	31	3-15—9-15	.661	244.05
	1889			119.95				S½	4	26	31	3-15—9-15	.975	359.85
	1889			128.20				N½	4	26	31	3-15—9-15	1.042	384.60
	1889			77.45				W½NW¼	4	26	31	3-15—9-15	.630	232.35
	1889					38.90		NE¼SE¼	4	26	31	3-15—6-13	.316	58.35
	1889					17.70		SE¼SE¼	4	26	31	3-15—6-13	.144	26.55
	1889					11.00		NE¼NE¼	4	26	31	3-15—6-13	.089	16.50

Claimant—**F. Tessier.** Proof No. **0085**

Source—**Humboldt River.** Ditch—**Old Channel.**

	1899			61.48				SE¼	13	27	31	3-15—9-15	.500	184.44
	1900			15.94				SE¼	13	27	31	3-15—9-15	.130	47.82

Claimant—**Morris Nelson.** Proof No. **0086**

Source—**Humboldt River.** Ditch—**Union Canal.**

	1887			14.54				W½NW¼	32	26	31	3-15—9-15	.118	43.62
	1888			18.17				W½NW¼	32	26	31	3-15—9-15	.148	54.51
	1892			7.27				W½NW¼	32	26	31	3-15—9-15	.059	21.81
	1900			18.17				W½NW¼	32	26	31	3-15—9-15	.148	54.51
	1888			9.00				SE¼NE¼	31	26	31	3-15—9-15	.073	27.00
	1892			18.85				SE¼NE¼	31	26	31	3-15—9-15	.113	41.55
	1893			9.00				SE¼NE¼	31	26	31	3-15—9-15	.073	27.00
	1890			72.35				N½NE¼	31	26	31	3-15—9-15	.588	217.05

Claimant—**Hans Christensen.** Proof No. 0087

Source—**Humboldt River.** Ditch—**Union Canal through Lake Shore Ditch.**

1878	10		NW¼SW¼	28	26	31	3-15—9-15	.081	30.00
1880	25		SW¼	28	26	31	3-15—9-15	.203	75.00
1885	50		SW¼	28	26	31	3-15—9-15	.407	150.00
1890	13.35		SW¼	28	26	31	3-15—9-15	.109	40.05

Claimant—**Peter Olson.** Proof No. 0088

Source—**Humboldt River.** Ditch—**Old Channel Ditch.**

1895	65.85		S½NW¼	12	27	31	3-15—9-15	.535	197.55
1904	4.70		S½NW¼	12	27	31	3-15—9-15	.038	14.10

Claimant—**W. W. Van Reed.** Proof. No. 0089

Source—**Humboldt River. Ditch—Union Canal through Lake Shore Ditch.**

1897	15.00		E½SW¼	29	26	31	3-15—9-15	.122	45.00
1897	...	5.90	E½SW¼	29	26	31	3-15—6-13	.048	8.85
1898	14.85		E½SW¼	29	26	31	3-15—9-15	.121	44.55
1900	20.50		E½SW¼	29	26	31	3-15—9-15	.167	61.50
1898	5.10		SE¼	29	26	31	3-15—9-15	.041	15.30

Claimant—**Andrew Westfall.** Proof No. 0091

Source—**Humboldt River.** Ditch—**Union Canal through Lake Shore Ditch.**

1878	20.97		SE¼	32	26	31	3-15—9-15	.170	62.91
1878	5.22		NE¼	32	26	31	3-15—9-15	.042	15.66
1885	87.32		SE¼	32	26	31	3-15—9-15	.710	261.96
1885	80.00		E½NE¼	32	26	31	3-15—9-15	.650	240.00
1895	30.00		E½NW¼	32	26	31	3-15—9-15	.244	90.00
1893	11.40		S½SE¼SE¼	29	26	31	3-15—9-15	.093	34.20
1888	35.65		S½	31	26	31	3-15—9-15	.290	106.95
1890	77.79		E½	32	26	31	3-15—9-15	.632	233.37
1890	50.00		E½NW¼	32	26	31	3-15—9-15	.407	150.00
1890	...	5.10	S½SE¼SE¼	29	26	31	3-15—6-13	.041	7.65
1885	...	8.25	NW¼NE¼	32	26	31	3-15—6-13	.067	12.38
1888	...	196.60	S½	31	26	31	3-15—6-13	1.598	291.90

Claimant—**L. P. Johnson.** Proof No. 0092

Source—**Humboldt River.** Ditch—**Old Channel.**

1879	7.00		E½SE¼	10	27	31	3-15—9-15	.057	21.00
1886	15.00		E½SE¼	10	27	31	3-15—9-15	.122	45.00
1887	15.00		E½SE¼	10	27	31	3-15—9-15	.122	45.00
1890	3.80		E½SE¼	10	27	31	3-15—9-15	.031	11.40
1890	31.30		E½SE¼	10	27	31	3-15—9-15	.254	93.90
1889	1.90		E½SE¼	10	27	31	3-15—9-15	.015	5.70

Claimant—**S. R. Young.** Proof No. 0093

Source—**Humboldt River.** Ditch—**Young Ditch.**

Date of beneficial use: Nat. mdw.	Date of beneficial use: Cult. area	Construction first initiated: Dams	Construction first initiated: Ditches	Culture—Acres: Harvest crops	Culture—Acres: Meadow pasture	Culture—Acres: Willow and sage pasture	Culture—Acres: Swamp or overflow	Location: Subdivision	Location: Section	Location: Tp.N.	Location: R.E.	Length of season	Duty of water: C.F.S.	Duty of water: Acre-feet
....	1890	....	....	15.75	....	....	....	SE¼NW¼	28	28	32	3-15—9-15	.120	47.25
....	1902	....	....	11.80	....	....	....	NE¼SW¼	28	28	32	3-15—9-15	.096	35.40
....	1902	....	....	15.00	....	....		NE¼SW¼&SE¼NW¼	28	28	32	3-15—9-15	.122	45.00
....	1902	....	....	31.45	....	....	....	S½NE¼&N½SE¼	28	28	32	3-15—9-15	.256	94.35
....	1902	....	....	66.45	....			NE¼&NW¼SE¼&NE¼SW¼&SE¼NW¼	28	28	32	3-15—9-15	.540	199.35

Allotted sufficient flow of water through Young Canal, with priority of 1901, for generation of 75 H.P.
Allotted additional flow of water with priority of 1909 for generation of additional 100 H.P. Location of plant on Young Canal in Sec. 28, T. 28 N, R. 32 E.

Claimant—**H. M. Damm.** Proof No. 0094

Source—**Humboldt River.** Ditch—**Old Channel and Humboldt Irrigation and Power Co. Canal.**

Date of beneficial use: Nat. mdw.	Date of beneficial use: Cult. area	Construction first initiated: Dams	Construction first initiated: Ditches	Culture—Acres: Harvest crops	Culture—Acres: Meadow pasture	Culture—Acres: Willow and sage pasture	Culture—Acres: Swamp or overflow	Location: Subdivision	Location: Section	Location: Tp.N.	Location: R.E.	Length of season	Duty of water: C.F.S.	Duty of water: Acre-feet
....	1897	....	....	15	....	....	....	W½W½	1	27	31	3-15—9-15	.122	45.0

Claimant—**E. K. Hanson.** Proof No. 0095

Source—**Humboldt River.** Ditch—**Southwest Ditch.**

Date of beneficial use: Nat. mdw.	Date of beneficial use: Cult. area	Construction first initiated: Dams	Construction first initiated: Ditches	Culture—Acres: Harvest crops	Culture—Acres: Meadow pasture	Culture—Acres: Willow and sage pasture	Culture—Acres: Swamp or overflow	Location: Subdivision	Location: Section	Location: Tp.N.	Location: R.E.	Length of season	Duty of water: C.F.S.	Duty of water: Acre-feet
....	1887	....	....	2.35	....	....	....	SW¼SE¼	23	27	31	3-15—9-15	.019	7.05
....	1883	....	....	3.15	....	....	....	NE¼NW¼	26	27	31	3-15—9-15	.026	9.45
....	1879	....	....	3.55	....	....	....	NE¼NW¼	26	27	31	3-15—9-15	.029	10.65
....	1884	....	....	1.50	....	....	....	NE¼NW¼	26	27	31	3-15—9-15	.012	4.50

Claimant—***Geo. S. Nixon Estate and John Fant.** Proof No. 0099

Source—**Humboldt River.** Ditch—**Rodgers Ditch System—†Riverside Branch.**

Date of beneficial use: Nat. mdw.	Date of beneficial use: Cult. area	Construction first initiated: Dams	Construction first initiated: Ditches	Culture—Acres: Harvest crops	Culture—Acres: Meadow pasture	Culture—Acres: Willow and sage pasture	Culture—Acres: Swamp or overflow	Location: Subdivision	Location: Section	Location: Tp.N.	Location: R.E.	Length of season	Duty of water: C.F.S.	Duty of water: Acre-feet
....	1871	....	....	10.00	....	....	....	NW¼	36	27	31	3-15—9-15	.081	30.00
....	1873	....	....	80.00	....	....	....	NW¼	36	27	31	3-15—9-15	.650	240.00
....	1873	....	....	60.00	....	....	....	SW¼	36	27	31	3-15—9-15	.488	180.00
....	1880	....	....	52.28	....	....	....	NW¼	36	27	31	3-15—9-15	.425	156.84
....	1880	....	....	29.26	....	....	....	SE¼	36	27	31	3-15—9-15	.238	87.78
....	1880	....	....	29.00	....	....	....	NE¼	36	27	21	3-15—9-15	.236	87.00
....	1881	....	....	20.00	....	....	....	SW¼	36	27	31	3-15—9-15	.163	60.00
....	1882	....	....	47.29	....	....	....	SW¼	36	27	31	3-15—9-15	.384	141.87
....	1882	....	....	16.22	....	....	....	NE¼	36	27	31	3-15—9-15	.132	48.66
....	1882	....	....	25.55	....	....	....	SE¼	36	27	31	3-15—9-15	.208	76.65
....	1882	....	....	...	....	30.00	....	N½	36	27	31	3-15—6-13	.244	45.00
....	1883	....	....	28.00	....	....	....	SE¼	35	27	31	3-15—9-15	.228	84.00
....	1883	....	....	52.00	....	....	....	SW¼	35	27	31	3-15—9-15	.423	156.00
....	1885	....	....	153.85	....	....	....	NE¼	35	27	31	3-15—9-15	1.251	461.55
....	1885	....	....	75.00	....	....	....	NE¼	35	27	31	3-15—9-15	.610	225.00
....	1898	....	....	25.72	....	....	....	SW¼	35	27	31	3-15—9-15	.209	77.16
....	1901	....	....	29.77	....	....	....	SE¼	35	27	31	3-15—9-15	.242	89.31

†Riverside Branch.
(a) Silverwood Ditch.
(b) Muttleberry Ditch.
(c) Slough Ditch.
(d) Hazelton-Thies Ditch.
(e) J. H. Thies Ditch.
(f) Thies Reservoir.

*Riverside Ranch.

WINNEMUCCA DISTRICT

Claimant—**Madison Anderson.** Proof No. 00101
Source—**Humboldt River.** Ditch—**North Side Cusick Ditch.**

Date of beneficial use: Nat. mdw.	Cult. area	Construction first initiated: Dams	Ditches	Culture—Acres: Harvest crops	Meadow pasture	Willow and sage pasture	Swamp or overflow	Location: Subdivision	Section	Tp. N.	R. E.	Length of season	Duty of water: C.F.S.	Acre-feet
	1871			10.00				NE¼SE¼	18	36	40	3-15—9-15	.081	30.00
	1871			20.90				SE¼NE¼	18	36	40	3-15—9-15	.170	62.70
	1870			38.10				SW¼NE¼	18	36	40	3-15—9-15	.310	114.30
	1874			32.00				NW¼NE¼	18	36	40	3-15—9-15	.260	96.00
	1874			39.50				NE¼NW¼	18	36	40	3-15—9-15	.331	118.50
	1872			20.30				SE¼NW¼	18	36	40	3-15—9-15	.165	60.90
	1874			18.75				NW¼NW¼	18	36	40	3-15—9-15	.152	56.25
	1874					8.90		NW¼NW¼	18	36	40	3-15—4-28	.072	6.45
	1873			2.00				SW¼NW¼	18	36	40	3-15—9-15	.016	6.00
	1873			.80				NE¼SW¼	18	36	40	3-15—9-15	.007	2.40

Claimant—**Madison Anderson.** Proof No. 00101
Source—**Humboldt River.** Ditch—**Cusick Ditch.**

Date of beneficial use: Nat. mdw.	Cult. area	Construction first initiated: Dams	Ditches	Culture—Acres: Harvest crops	Meadow pasture	Willow and sage pasture	Swamp or overflow	Location: Subdivision	Section	Tp. N.	R. E.	Length of season	Duty of water: C.F.S.	Acre-feet
	1872			38.20				SE¼SE¼	18	36	40	3-15—9-15	.311	114.60
	1871			5.40				NE¼SE¼	18	36	40	3-15—9-15	.044	16.20
	1872			14.80				SW¼SE¼	18	36	40	3-15—9-15	.120	44.40
	1871			22.00				NW¼SE¼	18	36	40	3-15—9-15	.179	66.00
	1870			.40				SW¼NE¼	18	36	40	3-15—9-15	.003	1.20
	1873			6.15				NE¼SW¼	18	36	40	3-15—9-15	.051	18.45
	1873					2.50		NE¼SW¼	18	36	40	3-15—4-28	.020	1.88
	1873					.75		NW¼SW¼	18	36	40	3-15—4-28	.002	.56
	1872					10.70		SE¼NW¼	18	36	40	3-15—4-28	.087	8.03
	1873			.20				SW¼NW¼	18	36	40	3-15—9-15	.002	.60
	1873					18.20		SW¼NW¼	18	36	40	3-15—4-28	.148	13.65
	1874					6.00		NW¼NW¼	18	36	40	3-15—4-28	.049	4.50

Claimant—**Madison Anderson.** Proof No. 00101
Source—**Humboldt River.** Ditch—**Anderson Ditch.**

Date of beneficial use: Nat. mdw.	Cult. area	Construction first initiated: Dams	Ditches	Culture—Acres: Harvest crops	Meadow pasture	Willow and sage pasture	Swamp or overflow	Location: Subdivision	Section	Tp. N.	R. E.	Length of season	Duty of water: C.F.S.	Acre-feet
	1871			20.00				NE¼SE¼	18	36	40	3-15—9-15	.063	60.00
	1873			6.95				NE¼SW¼	18	36	40	3-15—9-15	.057	20.85
	1873					2.50		NE¼SW¼	18	36	40	3-15—4-28	.020	1.88
	1873					1.50		NW¼SW¼	18	36	40	3-15—4-28	.012	1.13
	1871			14.10				NW¼SE¼	18	36	40	3-15—9-15	.115	42.30

Claimant—**Madison Anderson.** Proof No. 00101

Source—**Humboldt River.** Ditch—**Pioneer Slough System.**

Date of beneficial use: Nat. mdw.	Cult. area	Construction first initiated: Dams	Ditches	Culture—Acres: Harvest crops	Meadow pasture	Willow and sage pasture	Swamp or overflow	Location: Subdivision	Section	Tp.N.	R.E.	Length of season	Duty of water: C.F.S.	Acre-feet
	1874			7.30				NW¼NE¼	18	36	40	3-15—9-15	.059	21.90
	1874					2.90		NE¼NE¼	20	36	40	3-15—4-28	.025	2.18
	1874					19.70		SE¼SE¼	17	36	40	3-15—4-28	.160	14.78
	1874					33.50		SW¼SE¼	17	36	40	3-15—4-28	.272	25.13
	1874					28.20		NW¼SE¼	17	36	40	3-15—4-28	.229	21.15
	1874			2.60				NE¼SE¼	17	36	40	3-15—9-15	.021	7.80
	1874			3.30				SW¼NE¼	17	36	40	3-15—9-15	.027	9.90
	1874			.80				SE¼SW¼	17	36	40	3-15—9-15	.007	2.40
	1874					21.90		SE¼SW¼	17	36	40	3-15—4-28	.178	16.43
	1874			3.30				SW¼SW¼	17	36	40	3-15—9-15	.027	9.90
	1874					1.00		SW¼SW¼	17	36	40	3-15—4-28	.008	.75
	1874			1.20				NE¼SW¼	17	36	40	3-15—9-15	.010	3.60
	1874					38.80		NE¼SW¼	17	36	40	3-15—4-28	.315	29.10
	1874			29.90				NW¼SW¼	17	36	40	3-15—9-15	.243	89.70
	1874					2.60		NW¼SW¼	17	36	40	3-15—4-28	.021	1.95
	1874			25.70				SE¼NW¼	17	36	40	3-15—9-15	.209	77.10
	1874			4.95				NW¼NW¼	17	36	40	3-15—9-15	.040	14.85
	1874			36.90				SW¼NW¼	17	36	40	3-15—9-15	.300	110.70
	1871			20.00				SE¼NE¼	18	36	40	3-15—9-15	.163	60.00
	1873			29.30				NE¼NE¼	18	36	40	3-15—9-15	.238	87.90

Claimant—**Madison Anderson.** Proof No. 00101

Source—**Humboldt River.** Ditch—**Humboldt River Overflow.**

Date of beneficial use: Nat. mdw.	Cult. area	Construction first initiated: Dams	Ditches	Culture—Acres: Harvest crops	Meadow pasture	Willow and sage pasture	Swamp or overflow	Location: Subdivision	Section	Tp.N.	R.E.	Length of season	Duty of water: C.F.S.	Acre-feet
	1874					1.20		SE¼SE¼	17	36	40	3-15—4-28	.010	.90
	1874					2.60		SW¼SE¼	17	36	40	3-15—4-28	.021	1.95
	1874					2.70		NW¼NE¼	20	36	40	3-15—4-28	.023	2.03
	1874			7.20				SE¼SW¼	17	36	40	3-15—9-15	.059	21.60
	1874					5.55		SE¼SW¼	17	36	40	3-15—4-28	.045	4.16
	1874			29.70				SW¼SW¼	17	36	40	3-15—9-15	.241	89.10
	1874			3.60				NW¼SW¼	17	36	40	3-15—9-15	.029	10.80
	1874					.33		SE¼SE¼	27	36	40	3-15—4-28	.003	.25
	1874					10.82		SW¼SE¼	27	36	40	3-15—4-28	.088	8.12

Claimant—**Madison Anderson.** Proof No. 00101

Source—**Humboldt River.** Ditch—**North Side Canal.**

Date of beneficial use: Nat. mdw.	Cult. area	Construction first initiated: Dams	Ditches	Culture—Acres: Harvest crops	Meadow pasture	Willow and sage pasture	Swamp or overflow	Location: Subdivision	Section	Tp.N.	R.E.	Length of season	Duty of water: C.F.S.	Acre-feet
	1874					12.40		SE¼NW¼	21	36	40	3-15—4-28	.101	9.30
	1874					4.30		NE¼SW¼	21	36	40	3-15—4-28	.035	3.23
	1874				10.00			NW¼SW¼	21	36	40	3-15—6-13	.091	15.00
	1874					9.20		NW¼SW¼	21	36	40	3-15—4-28	.075	6.90
	1874					31.40		SW¼NW¼	21	36	40	3-15—4-28	.255	23.55
	1874					29.90		NW¼NW¼	21	36	40	3-15—4-28	.243	22.43
	1874					7.70		NE¼NE¼	20	36	40	3-15—4-28	.063	5.78
	1874					11.00		SW¼SW¼	16	36	40	3-15—4-28	.080	8.25

	1874			1.12				SE¼SE¼	17	36	40	3-15—9-15	.010	3.36
	1874					12.58		SE¼SE¼	17	36	40	3-15—4-28	.102	9.44
	1874			25.94				NE¼SE¼	17	36	40	3-15—9-15	.211	77.82
	1874					6.77		NE¼SE¼	17	36	40	3-15—4-28	.055	5.08
	1874					10.20		NW¼SE¼	17	36	40	3-15—4-28	.083	7.66
	1874			17.80				SE¼NE¼	17	36	40	3-15—9-15	.145	53.40
	1874					5.50		SE¼NE¼	17	36	40	3-15—4-28	.045	4.13
	1874			34.20				SW¼NE¼	17	36	40	3-15—9-15	.278	102.60
	1874			11.70				SE¼NW¼	17	36	40	3-15—9-15	.095	35.10
	1874					1.10		NE¼NE¼	17	36	40	3-15—4-28	.009	.83
	1874					39.40		NE¼NW¼	17	36	40	3-15—4-28	.320	29.55
	1874					.75		NE¼SW¼	27	36	40	3-15—4-28	.006	.56
	1874			13.45				NW¼SW¼	27	36	40	3-15—9-15	.109	40.35
	1874			18.70				SE¼NW¼	27	36	40	3-15—9-15	.152	56.10
	1874			34.10				SW¼NW¼	27	36	40	3-15—9-15	.277	102.30
	1874			13.22				NW¼NW¼	27	36	40	3-15—9-15	.107	39.66
	1874			18.30				NW¼NE¼	17	36	40	3-15—9-15	.149	54.90
	1874					4.40		NW¼NE¼	17	36	40	3-15—4-28	.036	3.30
	1874					2.50		NW¼SW¼	16	36	40	3-15—4-28	.020	1.88

Claimant—**Madison Anderson.** Proof No. 00101
Source—**Humboldt River.** Ditch—**South Side Swail and Ditch.**

	1874					16.60		SE¼SW¼	27	36	40	3-15—4-28	.135	12.45
	1874					27.28		SW¼SW¼	27	36	40	3-15—4-28	.222	20.46
	1874						3.37	SW¼SW¼	27	36	40	3-15—4-28	.207	2.53
	1874			1.00				NW¼SW¼	27	36	40	3-15—9-15	.008	3.00

Claimant—**Madison Anderson.** Proof No. 00101
Source—**Humboldt River.** Ditch—**Big Slough Ditch.**

	1874			.36				NE¼SW¼	27	36	40	3-15—9-15	.003	1.08
	1874			.10				SE¼SW¼	27	36	40	3-15—9-15	.001	.30
	1874			1.82				SW¼SW¼	27	36	40	3-15—9-15	.015	5.46
	1874			16.48				NW¼SW¼	27	36	40	3-15—9-15	.134	49.44
	1874					3.86		NW¼SW¼	27	36	40	3-15—4-28	.031	2.90
	1874			1.90				SW¼SW¼	27	36	40	3-15—9-15	.015	5.70
	1874			1.20				SW¼SE¼	8	36	40	3-15—9-15	.010	3.60

Claimant—**Madison Anderson.** Proof No. 00101
Source—**Humboldt River.** Ditch—**North Side Canal.**

	1874			27.40				SE¼SW¼	8	36	40	3-15—9-15	.223	82.20
	1874					3.60		SE¼SW¼	8	36	40	3-15—4-28	.029	2.70
	1874			16.80				NE¼SW¼	8	36	40	3-15—9-15	.137	50.40
	1874					19.60		NE¼SW¼	8	36	40	3-15—4-28	.159	14.70
	1874			35.00				NW¼SW¼	8	36	40	3-15—9-15	.285	105.00
	1874					1.50		NW¼SW¼	8	36	40	3-15—4-28	.012	1.13
	1874			2.20				SW¼NW¼	8	36	40	3-15—9-15	.018	6.60
	1874			1.20				SE¼NW¼	8	36	40	3-15—9-15	.010	3.60
	1874					.30		SE¼NW¼	8	36	40	3-15—4-28	.003	.23
	1874					2.40		NW¼SE¼	8	36	40	3-15—4-28	.020	1.80
	1874					10.70		SE¼SE¼	27	36	40	3-15—4-28	.087	8.03

Madison Anderson—Continued.

Date of beneficial use: Nat. mdw.	Date of beneficial use: Cult. area	Construction first initiated: Dams	Construction first initiated: Ditches	Culture—Acres: Harvest crops	Culture—Acres: Meadow pasture	Culture—Acres: Willow and sage pasture	Culture—Acres: Swamp or overflow	Location: Subdivision	Location: Section	Location: Tp.N.	Location: R.E.	Length of season	Duty of water: C.F.S.	Duty of water: Acre-feet
	1874			.95				SW¼SE¼	27	36	40	3-15—9-15	.008	2.85
	1874				1.10			SW¼SE¼	27	36	40	3-15—6-13	.009	1.65
	1874					18.65		SW¼SE¼	27	36	40	3-15—4-28	.152	13.99
	1874			.12				NW¼SE¼	27	36	40	3-15—9-15	.001	.36
	1874					16.39		NW¼SE¼	27	36	40	3-15—4-28	.133	12.29
	1874			3.60				SE¼SW¼	27	36	40	3-15—9-15	.029	10.80
	1874					9.30		SE¼SW¼	27	36	40	3-15—4-28	.076	6.98
	1874			35.48				NE¼SW¼	27	36	40	3-15—9-15	.288	106.44

Claimant—**Madison Anderson.** Proof No. 00101

Source—**Humboldt River.** Ditch—**Old South Side House Ditch.**

Nat. mdw.	Cult. area	Dams	Ditches	Harvest crops	Meadow pasture	Willow and sage pasture	Swamp or overflow	Subdivision	Section	Tp.N.	R.E.	Length of season	C.F.S.	Acre-feet
	1874					.90		NW¼SW¼	21	36	40	3-15—4-28	.007	.68
	1874					1.80		SW¼NW¼	21	36	40	3-15—4-28	.015	1.35
	1874				10.70			NE¼SE¼	20	36	40	3-15—6-13	.087	16.05
	1874					1.60		NE¼SE¼	20	36	40	3-15—4-28	.013	1.20
	1874				27.20			SE¼NE¼	20	36	40	3-15—6-13	.221	40.80
	1874					7.45		SE¼NE¼	20	36	40	3-15—4-28	.061	5.59
	1874				32.15			SW¼NE¼	20	36	40	3-15—6-13	.261	48.23
	1874				28.60			NW¼NE¼	20	36	40	3-15—6-13	.234	43.90
	1874					5.90		NW¼NE¼	20	36	40	3-15—4-28	.048	4.43
	1874				15.40			NE¼NE¼	20	36	40	3-15—6-13	.125	23.10
	1874					7.80		NE¼NE¼	20	36	40	3-15—4-28	.063	5.85

Claimant—**Madison Anderson.** Proof No. 00101

Source—**Humboldt River.** Ditch—**North Side Canal.**

Nat. mdw.	Cult. area	Dams	Ditches	Harvest crops	Meadow pasture	Willow and sage pasture	Swamp or overflow	Subdivision	Section	Tp.N.	R.E.	Length of season	C.F.S.	Acre-feet
	1874					30.80		NW¼NW¼	17	36	40	3-15—4-28	.250	23.10
	1873					9.25		NE¼NE¼	18	36	40	3-15—4-28	.075	6.94
	1874			37.20				SW¼SW¼	8	36	40	3-15—9-15	.302	111.60

Claimant—**Bliss Brothers.** Proof No. 00101

Source—**Humboldt River.** Ditch—**Anderson Ditch System.**

Nat. mdw.	Cult. area	Dams	Ditches	Harvest crops	Meadow pasture	Willow and sage pasture	Swamp or overflow	Subdivision	Section	Tp.N.	R.E.	Length of season	C.F.S.	Acre-feet
	1876				32.93			NW¼NE¼	14	36	41	3-15—6-13	.268	49.40
	1877			10.80				NE¼NE¼	14	36	41	3-15—9-15	.088	32.40
	1877				20.89			NE¼NE¼	14	36	41	3-15—6-13	.170	31.34
	1878			4.57				NE¼NW¼	14	36	41	3-15—9-15	.037	13.71
	1878				6.47			NE¼NW¼	14	36	41	3-15—6-13	.053	9.71
	1878					3.92		NE¼NW¼	14	36	41	3-15—4-28	.032	2.94
	1878				.90			SE¼SE¼	11	36	41	3-15—6-13	.007	1.35
	1878				1.70			SW¼SE¼	11	36	41	3-15—6-13	.014	2.55
	1878				1.65			SE¼NW¼	11	36	41	3-15—6-13	.013	2.48
	1878					.20		SE¼NW¼	11	36	41	3-15—4-28	.002	.15
	1878					.95		NW¼NW¼	11	36	41	3-15—4-28	.008	.71
	1878					.80		SW¼SW¼	11	36	41	3-15—4-28	.007	.60

	1878				2.70			SE¼NW¼	12	36	41	3-15—6-13	.022	4.14
	1878						40.04	SE¼NW¼	12	36	41	3-15—4-28	.326	30.03
	1878				4.00			SW¼NW¼	12	36	41	3-15—6-13	.033	6.00
	1878						37.70	SW¼NW¼	12	36	41	3-15—4-28	.307	28.80
	1878				25.53			NW¼SW¼	12	36	41	3-15—6-13	.208	38.30
	1878						10.28	NW¼SW¼	12	36	41	3-15—4-28	.084	7.71
	1879				38.55			SW¼SW¼	12	36	41	3-15—6-13	.313	57.83
	1879				35.26			SE¼SW¼	12	36	41	3-15—6-13	.287	52.89
	1879						.14	SE¼SW¼	12	36	41	3-15—6-13	.001	.12
	1880				35.80			NE¼SW¼	12	36	41	3-15—6-13	.291	53.70
	1880						4.82	NE¼SW¼	12	36	41	3-15—4-28	.039	3.62
	1880				26.10			SW¼SE¼	12	36	41	3-15—6-13	.212	39.15
	1880						12.60	SW¼SE¼	12	36	41	3-15—4-28	.102	9.45
	1874			10.08				SE¼NE¼	14	36	41	3-15—9-15	.082	30.24
	1874				22.96			SE¼NE¼	14	36	41	3-15—6-13	.187	34.44
	1875			4.32				SW¼NE¼	14	36	41	3-15—9-15	.035	12.96
	1875				11.13			SW¼NE¼	14	36	41	3-15—6-13	.090	16.70
	1875					1.50		SW¼NE¼	14	36	41	3-15—6-13	.012	1.13
	1876			2.52				NW¼NE¼	14	36	41	3-15—9-15	.020	7.56

Claimant—**Bliss Brothers.** Proof No. 00102

Source—**Humboldt River.** Ditch—**Pioneer Ditch System.**

	1863			10.00				SW¼NW¼	3	36	39	3-15—9-15	.081	30.00
	1863				10.00			SW¼NW¼	3	36	39	3-15—6-13	.081	15.00
	1863					10.00		SW¼NW¼	3	36	39	3-15—4-28	.081	7.50
	1863						8.43	SW¼NW¼	3	36	39	3-15—4-28	.069	6.32
	1864			10.00				SE¼NW¼	3	36	39	3-15—9-15	.081	30.00
	1864				10.00			SE¼NW¼	3	36	39	3-15—6-13	.081	15.00
	1864					10.00		SE¼NW¼	3	36	39	3-16—4-28	.081	7.50
	1864						8.41	SE¼NW¼	3	36	39	3-15—4-28	.068	6.31
	1868			16.64				SE¼NW¼	2	36	39	3-15—9-15	.135	49.92
	1868					.66		SE¼NW¼	2	36	39	3-15—4-28	.005	.50
	1865			17.78				SE¼NW¼	2	36	39	3-15—9-15	.145	53.34
	1868			31.72				SW¼NE¼	2	36	39	3-15—9-15	.258	95.16
	1868				.86			SW¼NE¼	2	36	39	3-16—6-13	.007	1.29
	1868					.24		SW¼NE¼	2	36	39	3-15—4-28	.002	.18
	1865			3.85				SW¼NE¼	2	36	39	3-15—9-15	.031	11.55
	1865			6.42				NE¼SE¼	2	36	39	3-15—9-15	.052	19.26
	1868				.94			NW¼SE¼	2	36	39	3-15—6-13	.008	1.41
	1865			29.64				NW¼SE¼	2	36	39	3-15—9-15	.241	88.92
	1865				5.06			NW¼SE¼	2	36	39	3-15—6-13	.041	7.59
	1865						1.04	NW¼SE¼	2	36	39	3-15—4-28	.008	.78
	1865			27.32				NE¼SW¼	2	36	39	3-15—9-15	.222	81.96
	1865					11.51		NE¼SW¼	2	36	39	3-15—4-28	.094	8.63
	1865			13.65				NW¼SW¼	2	36	39	3-15—9-15	.111	40.95
	1865					20.05		NW¼SW¼	2	36	39	3-15—4-28	.163	15.04
	1865						.73	NW¼SW¼	2	36	39	3-15—4-28	.006	.55
	1865			2.50				SW¼SE¼	2	36	39	3-15—9-15	.020	7.50
	1865					32.59		SW¼SE¼	2	36	39	3-15—4-28	.265	24.44
	1865			23.35				SE¼SE¼	2	36	39	3-15—9-15	.190	70.05
	1865				1.62			SE¼SE¼	2	36	39	3-15—6-13	.013	2.43
	1865					13.02		SE¼SE¼	2	36	39	3-15—4-28	.106	9.77

Bliss Brothers—Continued.

Date of beneficial use: Nat. mdw.	Date of beneficial use: Cult. area	Construction first initiated: Dams	Construction first initiated: Ditches	Culture—Acres: Harvest crops	Culture—Acres: Meadow pasture	Culture—Acres: Willow and sage pasture	Culture—Acres: Swamp or overflow	Location: Subdivision	Location: Section	Location: Tp.N.	Location: R.E.	Length of season	Duty of water: C.F.S.	Duty of water: Acre-feet
		....	....	....	7.49	....	....	NW¼NW¼	3	36	39	3-15—6-13	.061	11.23
		....	....	....	....	20.87	....	NW¼NW¼	3	36	39	3-15—4-28	.170	15.65
		....	....	....	17.86	....	....	NE¼NW¼	3	36	39	3-15—6-13	.145	26.79
		....	....	....	....	18.81	....	NE¼NW¼	3	36	39	3-15—4-28	.153	14.11
....	1868	....	....	25.58	....	....	....	NE¼SE¼	2	36	39	3-15—9-15	.208	76.74
....	1868	....	....	....	....	2.08	....	NE¼SE¼	2	36	39	3-15—4-28	.017	1.56
....	1868	....	....	4.34	....	....	....	NW¼NW¼	3	36	39	3-15—9-15	.035	13.02
....	1868	....	....	5.37	....	....	....	SW¼NW¼	1	36	39	3-15—9-15	.044	17.11
....	1868	....	....	....	29.08	....	....	SW¼NW¼	1	36	39	3-15—6-13	.236	43.62
....	1868	....	....	....	30.10	....	....	SE¼NW¼	1	36	39	3-15—6-13	.245	45.15
....	1868	....	....	....	14.17	....	....	NW¼NW¼	1	36	39	3-15—6-13	.115	21.26
....	1868	....	....	....	33.86	....	....	NE¼SW¼	1	36	39	3-15—6-13	.275	50.79
....	1868	....	....	....	28.20	....	....	NW¼SW¼	1	36	39	3-15—6-13	.229	42.30
....	1868	....	....	....	....	....	3.91	SW¼NW¼	33	37	39	3-15—4-28	.032	2.93
....	1868	....	....	....	....	....	1.77	SE¼NW¼	33	37	39	3-15—4-28	.014	1.33
....	1868	....	....	....	....	....	4.67	NW¼SW¼	33	37	39	3-15—4-28	.038	3.50
....	1868	....	....	....	....	....	3.89	NE¼SW¼	33	37	39	3-15—4-28	.028	2.54
....	1868	....	....	....	....	....	1.23	NW¼SE¼	33	37	39	3-15—4-28	.010	.92

Claimant—**Bliss Brothers.** Proof No. 00102

Source—**Humboldt River.** Ditch—**Pedroli Ditch System.**

....	1868	....	....	19.02	....	....	....	SW¼SW¼	1	36	39	3-15—9-15	.155	57.06
....	1868	....	....	....	11.73	....	....	SW¼SW¼	1	36	39	3-15—6-13	.095	17.60

Claimant—**Bliss Brothers.** Proof No. 00102

Source—**Humboldt River.** Ditch—**Fairbanks Ditch System.**

1865	....	....	....	29.33	....	....	....	NE¼NW¼	12	36	39	3-15—9-15	.238	87.99
1865	....	....	....	....	4.17	....	....	NE¼NW¼	12	36	39	3-15—6-13	.034	6.26
1865	....	....	....	....	....	1.52	....	NE¼NW¼	12	36	39	3-15—4-28	.012	4.27
1865	....	....	....	....	....	....	1.67	NE¼NW¼	12	36	39	3-15—4-28	.014	4.38
1865	....	....	....	34.00	....	....	....	NW¼NW¼	12	36	39	3-15—9-15	.276	104.00
1865	....	....	....	....	....	4.62	....	NW¼NW¼	12	36	39	3-15—4-28	.038	6.59
1865	....	....	....	....	....	....	.97	NW¼NW¼	12	36	39	3-15—4-28	.008	.73
1865	....	....	....	3.03	....	....	....	SW¼NW¼	12	36	39	3-15—9-15	.025	9.09
1865	....	....	....	....	....	34.27	....	SW¼NW¼	12	36	39	3-15—4-28	.279	25.70
1865	....	....	....	22.13	....	....	....	SE¼NW¼	12	36	39	3-15—9-15	.180	66.39
1865	....	....	....	....	....	15.31	....	SE¼NW¼	12	36	39	3-15—4-28	.124	11.48
1865	....	....	....	16.40	....	....	....	NE¼SW¼	12	36	39	3-15—9-15	.133	49.20
1865	....	....	....	....	....	20.88	....	NE¼SW¼	12	36	39	3-15—4-28	.170	15.66
1865	....	....	....	....	....	....	2.40	NE¼SW¼	12	36	39	3-15—4-28	.020	1.80

1865				20.67				NW¼SW¼	12	36	39	3-15—9-15	.168	62.01
1865						5.07		NW¼SW¼	12	36	39	3-15—4-28	.041	3.80
1865				8.49				SE¼SW¼	12	36	39	3-15—9-15	.069	25.47
1865						2.40		SE¼SW¼	12	36	39	3-15—4-28	.020	1.80
1865				10.47				NE¼SE¼	12	36	39	3-15—9-15	.085	31.41
1865						24.60		NE¼SE¼	12	36	39	3-15—4-28	.201	18.52
1865				16.10				NW¼SE¼	12	36	39	3-15—9-15	.131	48.30
1865						22.40		NW¼SE¼	12	36	39	3-15—4-28	.182	16.80
1865							.53	NW¼SE¼	12	36	39	3-15—4-28	.004	.38
1865				3.03				SW¼SE¼	12	36	39	3-15—9-15	.025	9.09
1865						21.30		SW¼SE¼	12	36	39	3-15—4-28	.173	15.98
1865							.55	SW¼SE¼	12	36	39	3-15—4-28	.004	.41

Claimant—**Bliss Brothers.** Proof No. 00102
Source—**Humboldt River.** Ditch—**Pedroli Ditch System.**

	1872			.21				SW¼SW¼	32	37	39	3-15—9-15	.002	.63
	1872				6.45			SW¼SW¼	32	37	39	3-15—6-13	.052	9.68
	1872					2.43		SW¼SW¼	32	37	39	3-15—4-28	.020	1.82
	1872			3.13				SW¼SE¼	32	37	39	3-15—9-15	.025	9.39
	1872					11.19		SW¼SE¼	32	37	39	3-15—4-28	.091	8.39
	1873				9.78			SE¼NE¼	4	36	39	3-15—6-13	.080	14.67
	1873					24.40		SE¼NE¼	4	36	39	3-15—4-28	.198	18.30
	1873					22.67		SW¼NE¼	4	36	39	3-15—4-28	.184	17.00
	1873					18.30		SE¼NW¼	4	36	39	3-15—4-28	.149	13.73
	1873					1.78		SW¼NW¼	4	36	39	3-15—4-28	.014	1.34
	1875			28.97				SW¼NE¼	12	36	39	3-15—9-15	.236	86.91
	1875				4.43			SW¼NE¼	12	36	39	3-15—6-13	.036	6.65
	1875						.70	SW¼NE¼	12	36	39	3-15—4-28	.006	1.05
	1875			5.30				SE¼NE¼	12	36	39	3-15—9-15	.043	15.90

Claimant—**Bliss Brothers.** Proof No. 00102
Source—**Humboldt River.** Ditch—**Pioneer Ditch System.**

	1870			28.26				SE¼NE¼	2	36	39	3-15—9-15	.230	84.78
	1870				9.08			SE¼NE¼	2	36	39	3-15—6-13	.074	13.62
	1870					.45		SE¼NE¼	2	36	39	3-15—4-28	.004	.34
	1870					3.05		SW¼SW¼	2	36	39	3-15—4-28	.025	2.29
	1870					20.28		SE¼SW¼	2	36	39	3-15—4-28	.165	15.21
	1870				35.86			SE¼SW¼	1	36	39	3-15—6-13	.292	53.79
	1870				20.17			NW¼SE¼	1	36	39	3-15—6-13	.164	30.26
	1870				19.51			SW¼SE¼	1	36	39	3-15—6-13	.159	29.27
	1870				.33			NE¼NW¼	1	36	39	3-15—6-13	.003	.50
	1870				13.57			SW¼NE¼	1	36	39	3-15—6-13	.110	20.36
	1870			2.49				SE¼NW¼	33	37	39	3-15—9-15	.020	7.47
	1870				23.24			SE¼NW¼	33	37	39	3-15—6-13	.189	34.86
	1870				32.79			SW¼NE¼	33	37	39	3-15—6-13	.267	49.19
	1870						9.38	NW¼NW¼	32	37	39	3-15—4-28	.076	7.04
	1870						10.40	NE¼NW¼	32	37	39	3-15—4-28	.085	7.80
	1871			13.86				SW¼NW¼	33	37	39	3-15—9-15	.113	41.58
	1871				.43			SW¼NW¼	33	37	39	3-15—6-13	.003	.65
	1871				6.90			SE¼NE¼	33	37	39	3-15—6-13	.056	10.35
	1871					4.23		SE¼NE¼	33	37	39	3-15—4-28	.034	8.35

Claimant—**Bergman and Alfree.** Proof No. 0082

Source—**Humboldt River.** Ditch—**Southwest Ditch.**

Date of beneficial use: Nat. mdw.	Date of beneficial use: Cult. area	Construction first initiated: Dams	Construction first initiated: Ditches	Culture—Acres: Harvest crops	Culture—Acres: Meadow pasture	Culture—Acres: Willow and sage pasture	Culture—Acres: Swamp or overflow	Location: Subdivision	Location: Section	Location: Tp.N.	Location: R.E.	Length of season	Duty of water: C.F.S.	Duty of water: Acre-feet
	1883			52.30				NW¼	3	26	31	3-15—9-15	.425	156.90
	1883			....		315.75		W½&NE¼	3	26	31	3-15—6-13	2.567	473.63
	1885			49.15				S½SE¼	33	27	31	3-15—9-15	.499	147.45
	1885			48.00				SE¼	33	27	31	3-15—9-15	.390	144.00
	1885			38.90				SE¼&SW¼	33	27	31	3-15—9-15	.316	116.70
	1885			25.95				SE¼SW¼	33	27	31	3-15—9-16	.211	77.85
	1883			....	22.00			NW¼SW¼	33	27	31	3-15—6-13	.179	33.00
	1885			....	10.20			SW¼	33	27	31	3-15—6-13	.083	15.30
	1885			....	14.95			SW¼SW¼	33	27	31	3-15—6-13	.123	22.48
	1885			....		51.10		S½	33	27	31	3-15—6-13	.415	76.65
	1885			....		3.95		SW¼SE¼	33	27	31	3-15—6-13	.032	5.93
	1889			60				SE¼	32	27	31	3-15—9-15	.488	180.00
	1883			20				SE¼	32	27	31	3-15—9-15	.163	60.00
	1885			139.80				SE¼,S½NE¼,SW¼	32	27	31	3-15—9-15	1.137	419.40
	1883			59.75				N½	5	26	31	3-15—9-15	.486	179.25
	1883			33.00				NE¼	5	26	31	3-15—9-15	.268	99.00
	1883			47.95				E¼E½	5	26	31	3-15—9-15	.390	143.85
	1887			78.65				NE¼	4	26	31	3-15—9-15	.639	235.95
	1877			81.35				S½	4	26	31	3-15—9-15	.661	244.05
	1889			119.95				S½	4	26	31	3-15—9-15	.975	359.85
	1889			128.20				N½	4	26	31	3-15—9-15	1.042	384.60
	1889			77.45				W½NW¼	4	26	31	3-15—9-15	.630	232.35
	1889					38.90		NE¼SE¼	4	26	31	3-15—6-13	.316	58.35
	1889					17.70		SE¼SE¼	4	26	31	3-15—6-13	.144	26.55
	1889			....		11.00		NE¼NE¼	4	26	31	3-15—6-13	.089	16.50

Claimant—**F. Tessier.** Proof No. 0085

Source—**Humboldt River.** Ditch—**Old Channel.**

Nat. mdw.	Cult. area	Dams	Ditches	Harvest crops	Meadow pasture	Willow and sage pasture	Swamp or overflow	Subdivision	Section	Tp.N.	R.E.	Length of season	C.F.S.	Acre-feet
	1899			61.48				SE¼	13	27	31	3-15—9-15	.500	184.44
	1900			15.94				SE¼	13	27	31	3-15—9-15	.130	47.82

Claimant—**Morris Nelson.** Proof No. 0086

Source—**Humboldt River.** Ditch—**Union Canal.**

Nat. mdw.	Cult. area	Dams	Ditches	Harvest crops	Meadow pasture	Willow and sage pasture	Swamp or overflow	Subdivision	Section	Tp.N.	R.E.	Length of season	C.F.S.	Acre-feet
	1887			14.54				W½NW¼	32	26	31	3-15—9-15	.118	43.62
	1888			18.17				W½NW¼	32	26	31	3-15—9-15	.148	54.51
	1892			7.27				W½NW¼	32	26	31	3-15—9-15	.060	21.81
	1900			18.17				W½NW¼	32	26	31	3-15—9-15	.148	54.51
	1888			9.00				SE¼NE¼	31	26	31	3-15—9-15	.073	27.00
	1892			13.85				SE¼NE¼	31	26	31	3-15—9-15	.113	41.55
	1893			9.00				SE¼NE¼	31	26	31	3-15—9-15	.073	27.00
	1890			72.35				N½NE¼	31	26	31	3-15—9-15	.588	217.05

Claimant—**Hans Christensen.** Proof No. **0087**

Source—**Humboldt River.** Ditch—**Union Canal through Lake Shore Ditch.**

1878	10		NW¼SW¼	28	26	31	3-15—9-15	.081	30.00
1880	25		SW¼	28	26	31	3-15—9-15	.203	75.00
1885	50		SW¼	28	26	31	3-15—9-15	.407	150.00
1890	13.35		SW¼	28	26	31	3-15—9-15	.109	40.05

Claimant—**Peter Olson.** Proof No. **0088**

Source—**Humboldt River.** Ditch—**Old Channel Ditch.**

1895	65.85		S½NW¼	12	27	31	3-15—9-15	.535	107.55
1904	4.70		S½NW¼	12	27	31	3-15—9-15	.038	14.10

Claimant—**W. W. Van Reed.** Proof. No. **0089**

Source—**Humboldt River. Ditch—Union Canal through Lake Shore Ditch.**

1897	15.00		E½SW¼	29	26	31	3-15—9-15	.122	45.00
1897		5.90	E½SW¼	29	26	31	3-15—6-13	.048	8.85
1898	14.85		E½SW¼	29	26	31	3-15—9-15	.121	44.55
1900	20.50		E½SW¼	29	26	31	3-15—9-15	.167	61.50
1898	5.10		SE¼	29	26	31	3-15—9-15	.041	15.30

Claimant—**Andrew Westfall.** Proof No. **0091**

Source—**Humboldt River.** Ditch—**Union Canal through Lake Shore Ditch.**

1878	20.97		SE¼	32	26	31	3-15—9-15	.170	62.91
1878	5.22		NE¼	32	26	31	3-15—9-15	.042	15.66
1885	87.32		SE¼	32	26	31	3-15—9-15	.710	261.96
1885	80.00		E½NE¼	32	26	31	3-15—9-15	.650	240.00
1885	30.00		E½NW¼	32	26	31	3-15—9-15	.244	90.00
1890	11.40		S½SE¼SE¼	29	26	31	3-15—9-15	.093	34.20
1888	35.65		S½	31	26	31	3-15—9-15	.290	106.95
1890	77.79		E½	32	26	31	3-15—9-15	.632	233.37
1890	50.00		E½NW¼	32	26	31	3-15—9-15	.407	150.00
1890		5.10	S½SE¼SE¼	29	26	31	3-15—6-13	.041	7.65
1885		8.25	NW¼NE¼	32	26	31	3-15—6-13	.067	12.38
1888		196.60	S½	31	26	31	3-15—6-13	1.598	294.90

Claimant—**L. P. Johnson.** Proof No. **0092**

Source—**Humboldt River.** Ditch—**Old Channel.**

1870	7.00		E½SE¼	10	27	31	3-15—9-15	.057	21.00
1886	15.00		E½SE¼	10	27	31	3-15—9-15	.122	45.00
1887	15.00		E½SE¼	10	27	31	3-15—9-15	.122	45.00
1890	3.80		E½SE¼	10	27	31	3-15—9-15	.031	11.40
1890	31.30		E½SE¼	10	27	31	3-15—9-15	.254	93.90
1889	1.90		E½SE¼	10	27	31	3-15—9-15	.015	5.70

Claimant—**S. R. Young.** Proof No. 0093

Source—**Humboldt River.** Ditch—**Young Ditch.**

Date of beneficial use: Nat. mdw.	Date of beneficial use: Cult. area	Construction first initiated: Dams	Construction first initiated: Ditches	Culture—Acres: Harvest crops	Culture—Acres: Meadow pasture	Culture—Acres: Willow and sage pasture	Culture—Acres: Swamp or overflow	Location: Subdivision	Location: Section	Location: Tp. N.	Location: R. E.	Length of season	Duty of water: C.F.S.	Duty of water: Acre-feet
	1890			15.75				SE¼NW¼	28	28	32	3-15—9-15	.120	47.25
	1902			11.80				NE¼SW¼	28	28	32	3-15—9-15	.096	35.40
	1902			15.00				NE¼SW¼&SE¼NW¼	28	28	32	3-15—9-15	.122	45.00
	1902			31.45				S½NE¼&N½SE¼	28	28	32	3-15—9-15	.256	94.35
	1902			66.45				NE¼&NW¼SE¼&NE¼SW¼&SE¼NW¼	28	28	32	3-15—9-15	.540	199.35

Allotted sufficient flow of water through Young Canal, with priority of 1901, for generation of 75 H.P.
Allotted additional flow of water with priority of 1909 for generation of additional 100 H.P. Location of plant on Young Canal in Sec. 28, T. 28 N, R. 32 E.

Claimant—**H. M. Damm.** Proof No. 0094

Source—**Humboldt River.** Ditch—**Old Channel and Humboldt Irrigation and Power Co. Canal.**

Nat. mdw.	Cult. area	Dams	Ditches	Harvest crops	Meadow pasture	Willow and sage pasture	Swamp or overflow	Subdivision	Section	Tp. N.	R. E.	Length of season	C.F.S.	Acre-feet
	1897			15				W½W½	1	27	31	3-15—9-15	.122	45.0

Claimant—**E. K. Hanson.** Proof No. 0095

Source—**Humboldt River.** Ditch—**Southwest Ditch.**

Nat. mdw.	Cult. area	Dams	Ditches	Harvest crops	Meadow pasture	Willow and sage pasture	Swamp or overflow	Subdivision	Section	Tp. N.	R. E.	Length of season	C.F.S.	Acre-feet
	1887			2.85				SW¼SE¼	23	27	31	3-15—9-15	.019	7.05
	1883			3.15				NE¼NW¼	26	27	31	3-15—9-15	.026	9.45
	1879			3.55				NE¼NW¼	26	27	31	3-15—9-15	.029	10.65
	1884			1.50				NE¼NW¼	26	27	31	3-15—9-15	.012	4.50

Claimant—***Geo. S. Nixon Estate and John Fant.** Proof No. 0099

Source—**Humboldt River.** Ditch—**Rodgers Ditch System—†Riverside Branch.**

Nat. mdw.	Cult. area	Dams	Ditches	Harvest crops	Meadow pasture	Willow and sage pasture	Swamp or overflow	Subdivision	Section	Tp. N.	R. E.	Length of season	C.F.S.	Acre-feet
	1871			10.00				NW¼	36	27	31	3-15—9-15	.081	30.00
	1873			80.00				NW¼	36	27	31	3-15—9-15	.650	240.00
	1873			60.00				SW¼	36	27	31	3-15—9-15	.488	180.00
	1880			52.28				NW¼	36	27	31	3-15—9-15	.425	156.84
	1880			29.26				SE¼	36	27	31	3-15—9-15	.238	87.78
	1880			29.00				NE¼	36	27	21	3-15—9-15	.236	87.00
	1881			20.00				SW¼	36	27	31	3-15—9-15	.163	60.00
	1882			47.29				SW¼	36	27	31	3-15—9-15	.384	141.87
	1882			16.22				NE¼	36	27	31	3-15—9-15	.132	48.66
	1882			25.55				SE¼	36	27	31	3-15—9-15	.208	76.65
	1882			....		30.00		N½	36	27	31	3-15—6-13	.244	45.00
	1883			28.00				SE¼	35	27	31	3-15—9-15	.228	84.00
	1883			52.00				SW¼	35	27	31	3-15—9-15	.423	156.00
	1885			153.85				NE¼	35	27	31	3-15—9-15	1.251	461.55
	1885			75.00				NE¼	35	27	31	3-15—9-15	.610	225.00
	1898			25.72				SW¼	35	27	31	3-15—9-15	.209	77.16
	1901			29.77				SE¼	35	27	31	3-15—9-15	.242	89.31

†Riverside Branch.
(a) Silverwood Ditch.
(b) Muttleberry Ditch.
(c) Slough Ditch.
(d) Hazelton-Thies Ditch.
(e) J. H. Thies Ditch.
(f) Thies Reservoir.

*Riverside Ranch.

WINNEMUCCA DISTRICT

Claimant—**Madison Anderson.** Proof No. 00101
Source—**Humboldt River.** Ditch—**North Side Cusick Ditch.**

Date of beneficial use: Nat. mdw.	Cult. area	Construction first initiated: Dams	Ditches	Culture—Acres: Harvest crops	Meadow pasture	Willow and sage pasture	Swamp or overflow	Location: Subdivision	Section	Tp.N.	R.E.	Length of season	Duty of water: C.F.S.	Acre-feet
	1871			10.00				NE¼SE¼	18	36	40	3-15—9-15	.081	30.00
	1871			20.90				SE¼NE¼	18	36	40	3-15—9-15	.170	62.70
	1870			38.10				SW¼NE¼	18	36	40	3-15—9-15	.310	114.30
	1874			32.00				NW¼NE¼	18	36	40	3-15—9-15	.200	96.00
	1874			39.50				NE¼NW¼	18	36	40	3-15—9-15	.331	118.50
	1872			20.30				SE¼NW¼	18	36	40	3-15—9-15	.165	60.90
	1874			18.75				NW¼NW¼	18	36	40	3-15—9-15	.152	56.25
	1874					8.90		NW¼NW¼	18	36	40	3-15—4-28	.072	6.45
	1873			2.00				SW¼NW¼	18	36	40	3-15—9-15	.016	6.00
	1873			.80				NE¼SW¼	18	36	40	3-15—9-15	.007	2.40

Claimant—**Madison Anderson.** Proof No. 00101
Source—**Humboldt River.** Ditch—**Cusick Ditch.**

Nat. mdw.	Cult. area	Dams	Ditches	Harvest crops	Meadow pasture	Willow and sage pasture	Swamp or overflow	Subdivision	Section	Tp.N.	R.E.	Length of season	C.F.S.	Acre-feet
	1872			38.20				SE¼SE¼	18	36	40	3-15—9-15	.311	114.60
	1871			5.40				NE¼SE¼	18	36	40	3-15—9-15	.044	16.20
	1872			14.80				SW¼SE¼	18	36	40	3-15—9-15	.120	44.40
	1871			22.00				NW¼SE¼	18	36	40	3-15—9-15	.179	66.00
	1870			.40				SW¼NE¼	18	36	40	3-15—9-15	.003	1.20
	1873			6.15				NE¼SW¼	18	36	40	3-15—9-15	.051	18.45
	1873					2.50		NE¼SW¼	18	36	40	3-15—4-28	.020	1.88
	1873					.75		NW¼SW¼	18	36	40	3-15—4-28	.002	.56
	1872					10.70		SE¼NW¼	18	36	40	3-15—4-28	.087	8.03
	1873			.20				SW¼NW¼	18	36	40	3-15—9-15	.002	.60
	1873					18.20		SW¼NW¼	18	36	40	3-15—4-28	.148	13.65
	1874					6.00		NW¼NW¼	18	36	40	3-15—4-28	.049	4.50

Claimant—**Madison Anderson.** Proof No. 00101
Source—**Humboldt River.** Ditch—**Anderson Ditch.**

Nat. mdw.	Cult. area	Dams	Ditches	Harvest crops	Meadow pasture	Willow and sage pasture	Swamp or overflow	Subdivision	Section	Tp.N.	R.E.	Length of season	C.F.S.	Acre-feet
	1871			20.00				NE¼SE¼	18	36	40	3-15—9-15	.063	60.00
	1873			6.95				NE¼SW¼	18	36	40	3-15—9-15	.057	20.85
	1873					2.50		NE¼SW¼	18	36	40	3-15—4-28	.020	1.88
	1873					1.50		NW¼SW¼	18	36	40	3-15—4-28	.012	1.13
	1871			14.10				NW¼SE¼	18	36	40	3-15—9-15	.115	42.30

Claimant—**Madison Anderson.** Proof No. 00101

Source—**Humboldt River.** Ditch—**Pioneer Slough System.**

Date of beneficial use: Nat. mdw.	Date of beneficial use: Cult. area	Construction first initiated: Dams	Construction first initiated: Ditches	Culture—Acres: Harvest crops	Culture—Acres: Meadow pasture	Culture—Acres: Willow and sage pasture	Culture—Acres: Swamp or overflow	Location: Subdivision	Location: Section	Location: Tp.N.	Location: R.E.	Length of season	Duty of water: C.F.S.	Duty of water: Acre-feet
	1874			7.30				NW¼NE¼	18	36	40	3-15—9-15	.059	21.90
	1874					2.90		NE¼NE¼	20	36	40	3-15—4-28	.025	2.18
	1874					19.70		SE¼SE¼	17	36	40	3-15—4-28	.160	14.78
	1874					33.50		SW¼SE¼	17	36	40	3-15—4-28	.272	25.13
	1874					28.20		NW¼SE¼	17	36	40	3-15—4-28	.229	21.15
	1874			2.60				NE¼SE¼	17	36	40	3-15—9-15	.021	7.80
	1874			3.30				SW¼NE¼	17	36	40	3-15—9-15	.027	9.90
	1874			.80				SE¼SW¼	17	36	40	3-15—9-15	.007	2.40
	1874					21.90		SE¼SW¼	17	36	40	3-15—4-28	.178	16.43
	1874			3.30				SW¼SW¼	17	36	40	3-15—9-15	.027	9.90
	1874					1.00		SW¼SW¼	17	36	40	3-15—4-28	.008	.75
	1874			1.20				NE¼SW¼	17	36	40	3-15—9-15	.010	3.60
	1874					38.80		NE¼SW¼	17	36	40	3-15—4-28	.315	29.10
	1874			29.90				NW¼SW¼	17	36	40	3-15—9-15	.243	89.70
	1874					2.60		NW¼SW¼	17	36	40	3-15—4-28	.021	1.95
	1874			25.70				SE¼NW¼	17	36	40	3-15—9-15	.209	77.10
	1874			4.95				NW¼NW¼	17	36	40	3-15—9-15	.040	14.85
	1874			36.90				SW¼NW¼	17	36	40	3-15—9-15	.300	110.70
	1871			20.00				SE¼NE¼	18	36	40	3-15—9-15	.163	60.00
	1873			29.30				NE¼NE¼	18	36	40	3-15—9-15	.238	87.90

Claimant—**Madison Anderson.** Proof No. 00101

Source—**Humboldt River.** Ditch—**Humboldt River Overflow.**

Nat. mdw.	Cult. area	Dams	Ditches	Harvest crops	Meadow pasture	Willow and sage pasture	Swamp or overflow	Subdivision	Section	Tp.N.	R.E.	Length of season	C.F.S.	Acre-feet
	1874					1.20		SE¼SE¼	17	36	40	3-15—4-28	.010	.90
	1874					2.60		SW¼SE¼	17	36	40	3-15—4-28	.021	1.95
	1874					2.70		NW¼NE¼	20	36	40	3-15—4-28	.023	2.03
	1874			7.20				SE¼SW¼	17	36	40	3-15—9-15	.059	21.60
	1874					5.55		SE¼SW¼	17	36	40	3-15—4-28	.045	4.16
	1874			29.70				SW¼SW¼	17	36	40	3-15—9-15	.241	89.10
	1874			3.60				NW¼SW¼	17	36	40	3-15—9-15	.029	10.80
	1874					.33		SE¼SE¼	27	36	40	3-15—4-28	.003	.25
	1874					10.82		SW¼SE¼	27	36	40	3-15—4-28	.088	8.12

Claimant—**Madison Anderson.** Proof No. 00101

Source—**Humboldt River.** Ditch—**North Side Canal.**

Nat. mdw.	Cult. area	Dams	Ditches	Harvest crops	Meadow pasture	Willow and sage pasture	Swamp or overflow	Subdivision	Section	Tp.N.	R.E.	Length of season	C.F.S.	Acre-feet
	1874					12.40		SE¼NW¼	21	36	40	3-15—4-28	.101	9.30
	1874					4.30		NE¼SW¼	21	36	40	3-15—4-28	.035	3.23
	1874				10.00			NW¼SW¼	21	36	40	3-15—6-13	.091	15.00
	1874					9.20		NW¼SW¼	21	36	40	3-15—4-28	.075	6.90
	1874					31.40		SW¼NW¼	21	36	40	3-15—4-28	.255	23.55
	1874					20.90		NW¼NW¼	21	36	40	3-15—4-28	.243	22.43
	1874					7.70		NE¼NE¼	20	36	40	3-15—4-28	.063	5.78
	1874					11.00		SW¼SW¼	16	36	40	3-15—4-28	.089	8.25

	1874			1.12				SE¼SE¼	17	36	40	3-15—9-15	.010	3.36
	1874					12.58		SE¼SE¼	17	36	40	3-15—4-28	.102	9.44
	1874			25.94				NE¼SE¼	17	36	40	3-15—9-15	.211	77.82
	1874					6.77		NE¼SE¼	17	36	40	3-15—4-28	.055	5.08
	1874					10.20		NW¼SE¼	17	36	40	3-15—4-28	.083	7.65
	1874			17.80				SE¼NE¼	17	36	40	3-15—9-15	.145	53.40
	1874					5.50		SE¼NE¼	17	36	40	3-15—4-28	.045	4.13
	1874			34.20				SW¼NE¼	17	36	40	3-15—9-15	.278	102.60
	1874			11.70				SE¼NW¼	17	36	40	3-15—9-15	.095	35.10
	1874					1.10		NE¼NE¼	17	36	40	3-15—4-28	.009	.83
	1874					39.40		NE¼NW¼	17	36	40	3-15—4-28	.320	29.55
	1874					.75		NE¼SW¼	27	36	40	3-15—4-28	.006	.56
	1874			13.45				NW¼SW¼	27	36	40	3-15—9-15	.109	40.35
	1874			18.70				SE¼NW¼	27	36	40	3-15—9-15	.152	56.10
	1874			34.10				SW¼NW¼	27	36	40	3-15—9-15	.277	102.30
	1874			13.22				NW¼NW¼	27	36	40	3-15—9-15	.107	39.66
	1874			18.30				NW¼NE¼	17	36	40	3-15—9-15	.149	54.90
	1874					4.40		NW¼NE¼	17	36	40	3-15—4-28	.036	3.30
	1874					2.50		NW¼SW¼	16	36	40	3-15—4-28	.020	1.88

Claimant—**Madison Anderson.** Proof No. **00101**

Source—**Humboldt River.** Ditch—**South Side Swail and Ditch.**

	1874					16.60		SE¼SW¼	27	36	40	3-15—4-28	.135	12.45
	1874					27.28		SW¼SW¼	27	36	40	3-15—4-28	.222	20.46
	1874						3.37	SW¼SW¼	27	36	40	3-15—4-28	.207	2.53
	1874			1.00				NW¼SW¼	27	36	40	3-15—9-15	.008	3.00

Claimant—**Madison Anderson.** Proof No. **00101**

Source—**Humboldt River.** Ditch—**Big Slough Ditch.**

	1874			.36				NE¼SW¼	27	36	40	3-15—9-15	.003	1.08
	1874			.10				SE¼SW¼	27	36	40	3-15—9-15	.001	.30
	1874			1.82				SW¼SW¼	27	36	40	3-15—9-15	.015	5.46
	1874			16.48				NW¼SW¼	27	36	40	3-15—9-15	.134	49.44
	1874					3.86		NW¼SW¼	27	36	40	3-15—4-28	.031	2.90
	1874			1.90				SW¼SW¼	27	36	40	3-15—9-15	.015	5.70
	1874			1.20				SW¼SE¼	8	36	40	3-15—9-15	.010	3.60

Claimant—**Madison Anderson.** Proof No. **00101**

Source—**Humboldt River.** Ditch—**North Side Canal.**

	1874			27.40				SE¼SW¼	8	36	40	3-15—9-15	.223	82.20
	1874					3.60		SE¼SW¼	8	36	40	3-15—4-28	.029	2.70
	1874			16.80				NE¼SW¼	8	36	40	3-15—9-15	.137	50.40
	1874					19.60		NE¼SW¼	8	36	40	3-15—4-28	.159	14.70
	1874			35.00				NW¼SW¼	8	36	40	3-15—9-15	.285	105.00
	1874					1.50		NW¼SW¼	8	36	40	3-15—4-28	.012	1.13
	1874			2.20				SW¼NW¼	8	36	40	3-15—9-15	.018	6.60
	1874			1.20				SE¼NW¼	8	36	40	3-15—9-15	.010	3.60
	1874					.30		SE¼NW¼	8	36	40	3-15—4-28	.003	.23
	1874					2.40		NW¼SE¼	8	36	40	3-15—4-28	.020	1.80
	1874					10.70		SE¼SE¼	27	36	40	3-15—4-28	.087	8.03

Madison Anderson—Continued.

Date of beneficial use: Nat. mdw.	Date of beneficial use: Cult. area	Construction first initiated: Dams	Construction first initiated: Ditches	Culture—Acres: Harvest crops	Culture—Acres: Meadow pasture	Culture—Acres: Willow and sage pasture	Culture—Acres: Swamp or overflow	Location: Subdivision	Location: Section	Location: Tp.N.	Location: R.E.	Length of season	Duty of water: C.F.S.	Duty of water: Acre-feet
	1874			.95				SW¼SE¼	27	36	40	3-15—9-15	.008	2.85
	1874				1.10			SW¼SE¼	27	36	40	3-15—6-13	.009	1.65
	1874					18.65		SW¼SE¼	27	36	40	3-15—4-28	.152	13.99
	1874			.12				NW¼SE¼	27	36	40	3-15—9-15	.001	.36
	1874					16.39		NW¼SE¼	27	36	40	3-15—4-28	.133	12.29
	1874			3.60				SE¼SW¼	27	36	40	3-15—9-15	.029	10.80
	1874					9.30		SE¼SW¼	27	36	40	3-15—4-28	.076	6.98
	1874			35.48				NE¼SW¼	27	36	40	3-15—9-15	.288	106.44

Claimant—**Madison Anderson.** Proof No. 00101

Source—**Humboldt River.** Ditch—**Old South Side House Ditch.**

Nat. mdw.	Cult. area	Dams	Ditches	Harvest crops	Meadow pasture	Willow and sage pasture	Swamp or overflow	Subdivision	Section	Tp.N.	R.E.	Length of season	C.F.S.	Acre-feet
	1874					.90		NW¼SW¼	21	36	40	3-15—4-28	.007	.68
	1874					1.80		SW¼NW¼	21	36	40	3-15—4-28	.015	1.35
	1874				10.70			NE¼SE¼	20	36	40	3-15—6-13	.087	16.05
	1874					1.60		NE¼SE¼	20	36	40	3-15—4-28	.013	1.20
	1874				27.20			SE¼NE¼	20	36	40	3-15—6-13	.221	40.80
	1874					7.45		SE¼NE¼	20	36	40	3-15—4-28	.061	5.59
	1874				32.15			SW¼NE¼	20	36	40	3-15—6-13	.261	48.23
	1874				28.60			NW¼NE¼	20	36	40	3-15—6-13	.234	43.90
	1874					5.90		NW¼NE¼	20	36	40	3-15—4-28	.048	4.43
	1874				15.40			NE¼NE¼	20	36	40	3-15—6-13	.125	23.10
	1874					7.80		NE¼NE¼	20	36	40	3-15—4-28	.063	5.85

Claimant—**Madison Anderson.** Proof No. 00101

Source—**Humboldt River.** Ditch—**North Side Canal.**

Nat. mdw.	Cult. area	Dams	Ditches	Harvest crops	Meadow pasture	Willow and sage pasture	Swamp or overflow	Subdivision	Section	Tp.N.	R.E.	Length of season	C.F.S.	Acre-feet
	1874					30.80		NW¼NW¼	17	36	40	3-15—4-28	.250	23.10
	1873					9.25		NE¼NE¼	18	36	40	3-15—4-28	.075	6.94
	1874			37.20				SW¼SW¼	8	36	40	3-15—9-15	.302	111.60

Claimant—**Bliss Brothers.** Proof No. 00101

Source—**Humboldt River.** Ditch—**Anderson Ditch System.**

Nat. mdw.	Cult. area	Dams	Ditches	Harvest crops	Meadow pasture	Willow and sage pasture	Swamp or overflow	Subdivision	Section	Tp.N.	R.E.	Length of season	C.F.S.	Acre-feet
	1876				32.93			NW¼NE¼	14	36	41	3-15—6-13	.268	49.40
	1877			10.80				NE¼NE¼	14	36	41	3-15—9-15	.088	32.40
	1877				20.89			NE¼NE¼	14	36	41	3-15—6-13	.170	31.34
	1878			4.57				NE¼NW¼	14	36	41	3-15—9-15	.037	13.71
	1878				6.47			NE¼NW¼	14	36	41	3-15—6-13	.053	9.71
	1878					3.92		NE¼NW¼	14	36	41	3-15—4-28	.032	2.94
	1878				.90			SE¼SE¼	11	36	41	3-15—6-13	.007	1.35
	1878				1.70			SW¼SE¼	11	36	41	3-15—6-13	.014	2.55
	1878				1.65			SE¼NW¼	11	36	41	3-15—6-13	.013	2.48
	1878					.20		SE¼NW¼	11	36	41	3-15—4-28	.002	.15
	1878					.95		NW¼NW¼	11	36	41	3-15—4-28	.008	.71
	1878					.80		SW¼SW¼	11	36	41	3-15—4-28	.007	.60

	1878				2.76			SE¼NW¼	12	36	41	3-15—6-13	.022	4.14
	1878						40.04	SE¼NW¼	12	36	41	3-15—4-28	.320	30.03
	1878				4.00			SW¼NW¼	12	36	41	3-15—6-13	.033	6.00
	1878						37.70	SW¼NW¼	12	36	41	3-15—4-28	.307	28.80
	1878				23.53			NW¼SW¼	12	36	41	3-15—6-13	.208	38.30
	1878						10.28	NW¼SW¼	12	36	41	3-15—4-28	.084	7.71
	1879				38.55			SW¼SW¼	12	36	41	3-15—6-13	.313	57.83
	1879				35.26			SE¼SW¼	12	36	41	3-15—6-13	.287	52.89
	1879						.14	SE¼SW¼	12	36	41	3-15—6-13	.001	.12
	1880				35.80			NE¼SW¼	12	36	41	3-15—6-13	.291	53.70
	1880						4.82	NE¼SW¼	12	36	41	3-15—4-28	.039	3.62
	1880				26.10			SW¼SE¼	12	36	41	3-15—6-13	.212	30.15
	1880						12.60	SW¼SE¼	12	36	41	3-15—4-28	.102	9.45
	1874			10.08				SE¼NE¼	14	36	41	3-15—9-15	.082	30.24
	1874				22.96			SE¼NE¼	14	36	41	3-15—6-13	.187	34.44
	1875			4.32				SW¼NE¼	14	36	41	3-15—9-15	.035	12.96
	1875				11.13			SW¼NE¼	14	36	41	3-15—6-13	.090	16.70
	1875					1.50		SW¼NE¼	14	36	41	3-15—6-13	.012	1.13
	1876			2.52				NW¼NE¼	14	36	41	3-15—9-15	.020	7.56

Claimant—**Bliss Brothers.** Proof No. **00102**
Source—**Humboldt River.** Ditch—**Pioneer Ditch System.**

	1863			10.00				SW¼NW¼	3	36	39	3-15—9-15	.081	30.00
	1863				10.00			SW¼NW¼	3	36	39	3-15—6-13	.081	15.00
	1863					10.00		SW¼NW¼	3	36	39	3-15—4-28	.081	7.50
	1863						8.43	SW¼NW¼	3	36	39	3-15—4-28	.069	6.32
	1864			10.00				SE¼NW¼	3	36	39	3-15—9-15	.081	30.00
	1864				10.00			SE¼NW¼	3	36	39	3-15—6-13	.081	15.00
	1864					10.00		SE¼NW¼	3	36	39	3-15—4-28	.081	7.50
	1864						8.41	SE¼NW¼	3	36	39	3-15—4-28	.068	6.31
	1868			16.64				SE¼NW¼	2	36	39	3-15—9-15	.135	49.92
	1868					.66		SE¼NW¼	2	36	39	3-15—4-28	.005	.50
	1865			17.78				SE¼NW¼	2	36	39	3-15—9-15	.145	53.34
	1868			31.72				SW¼NE¼	2	36	39	3-15—9-15	.258	95.16
	1868				.86			SW¼NE¼	2	36	39	3-15—6-13	.007	1.29
	1868					.24		SW¼NE¼	2	36	39	3-15—4-28	.002	.18
	1865			3.85				SW¼NE¼	2	36	39	3-15—9-15	.031	11.55
	1865			6.42				NE¼SE¼	2	36	39	3-15—9-15	.052	19.26
	1868				.04			NW¼SE¼	2	36	39	3-15—6-13	.008	1.41
	1865			29.64				NW¼SE¼	2	36	39	3-15—9-15	.241	88.92
	1865				5.06			NW¼SE¼	2	36	39	3-15—6-13	.041	7.59
	1865						1.04	NW¼SE¼	2	36	39	3-15—4-28	.008	.78
	1865			27.32				NE¼SW¼	2	36	39	3-15—9-15	.222	81.96
	1865					11.51		NE¼SW¼	2	36	39	3-15—4-28	.094	8.63
	1865			13.65				NW¼SW¼	2	36	39	3-15—9-15	.111	40.95
	1865					20.05		NW¼SW¼	2	36	39	3-15—4-28	.163	15.04
	1865						.73	NW¼SW¼	2	36	39	3-15—4-28	.006	.55
	1865			2.50				SW¼SE¼	2	36	39	3-15—9-15	.020	7.50
	1865					32.59		SW¼SE¼	2	36	39	3-15—4-28	.265	24.44
	1865			23.35				SE¼SE¼	2	36	39	3-15—9-15	.190	70.05
	1865				1.62			SE¼SE¼	2	36	39	3-15—6-13	.013	2.43
	1865					13.02		SE¼SE¼	2	36	39	3-15—4-28	.106	9.77

Bliss Brothers—Continued.

Date of beneficial use: Nat. mdw.	Date of beneficial use: Cult. area	Construction first initiated: Dams	Construction first initiated: Ditches	Culture—Acres: Harvest crops	Culture—Acres: Meadow pasture	Culture—Acres: Willow and sage pasture	Culture—Acres: Swamp or overflow	Location: Subdivision	Location: Section	Location: Tp. N.	Location: R. E.	Length of season	Duty of water: C. F. S.	Duty of water: Acre-feet
					7.49			NW¼NW¼	3	36	39	3-15—6-13	.061	11.23
						20.87		NW¼NW¼	3	36	39	3-15—4-28	.170	15.65
					17.86			NE¼NW¼	3	36	39	3-15—6-13	.145	26.79
						18.81		NE¼NW¼	3	36	39	3-15—4-28	.153	14.11
	1868			25.58				NE¼SE¼	2	36	39	3-15—9-15	.208	76.74
	1868					2.08		NE¼SE¼	2	36	39	3-15—4-28	.017	1.56
	1868			4.34				NW¼NW¼	3	36	39	3-15—9-15	.035	13.02
	1868			5.37				SW¼NW¼	1	36	39	3-15—9-15	.044	17.11
	1868				29.08			SW¼NW¼	1	36	39	3-15—6-13	.236	43.62
	1868				30.10			SE¼NW¼	1	36	39	3-15—6-13	.245	45.15
	1868				14.17			NW¼NW¼	1	36	39	3-15—6-13	.115	21.26
	1868				33.86			NE¼SW¼	1	36	39	3-15—6-13	.275	50.79
	1868				28.20			NW¼SW¼	1	36	39	3-15—6-13	.229	42.30
	1868						3.91	SW¼NW¼	33	37	39	3-15—4-28	.032	2.93
	1868						1.77	SE¼NW¼	33	37	39	3-15—4-28	.014	1.33
	1868						4.67	NW¼SW¼	33	37	39	3-15—4-28	.038	3.50
	1868						3.89	NE¼SW¼	33	37	39	3-15—4-28	.028	2.54
	1868						1.23	NW¼SE¼	33	37	39	3-15—4-28	.010	.92

Claimant—**Bliss Brothers.** Proof No. 00102
Source—**Humboldt River.** Ditch—**Pedroli Ditch System.**

Nat. mdw.	Cult. area	Dams	Ditches	Harvest crops	Meadow pasture	Willow and sage pasture	Swamp or overflow	Subdivision	Section	Tp. N.	R. E.	Length of season	C. F. S.	Acre-feet
	1868			19.02				SW¼SW¼	1	36	39	3-15—9-15	.155	57.06
	1868				11.73			SW¼SW¼	1	36	39	3-15—6-13	.095	17.60

Claimant—**Bliss Brothers.** Proof No. 00102
Source—**Humboldt River.** Ditch—**Fairbanks Ditch System.**

Nat. mdw.	Cult. area	Dams	Ditches	Harvest crops	Meadow pasture	Willow and sage pasture	Swamp or overflow	Subdivision	Section	Tp. N.	R. E.	Length of season	C. F. S.	Acre-feet
1865				29.33				NE¼NW¼	12	36	39	3-15—9-15	.238	87.99
1865					4.17			NE¼NW¼	12	36	39	3-15—6-13	.034	6.26
1865						1.52		NE¼NW¼	12	36	39	3-15—4-28	.012	4.27
1865							1.67	NE¼NW¼	12	36	39	3-15—4-28	.014	4.38
1865				34.00				NW¼NW¼	12	36	39	3-15—9-15	.276	104.00
1865						4.62		NW¼NW¼	12	36	39	3-15—4-28	.038	6.59
1865							.97	NW¼NW¼	12	36	39	3-15—4-28	.008	.73
1865				3.03				SW¼NW¼	12	36	39	3-15—9-15	.025	9.09
1865						34.27		SW¼NW¼	12	36	39	3-15—4-28	.279	25.70
1865				22.13				SE¼NW¼	12	36	39	3-15—9-15	.180	66.39
1865						15.31		SE¼NW¼	12	36	39	3-15—4-28	.124	11.48
1865				16.40				NE¼SW¼	12	36	39	3-15—9-15	.133	49.20
1865						20.88		NE¼SW¼	12	36	39	3-15—4-28	.170	15.66
1865							2.40	NE¼SW¼	12	36	39	3-15—4-28	.020	1.80

1865				20.67				NW¼SW¼	12	36	39	3-15—9-15	.108	92.01
1865						5.07		NW¼SW¼	12	36	39	3-15—4-28	.041	3.80
1865				8.49				SE¼SW¼	12	36	39	3-15—9-15	.069	25.47
1865						2.40		SE¼SW¼	12	36	39	3-15—4-28	.020	1.80
1865				10.47				NE¼SE¼	12	36	39	3-15—9-15	.085	31.41
1865						24.60		NE¼SE¼	12	36	39	3-15—4-28	.201	18.52
1865				16.10				NW¼SE¼	12	36	39	3-15—9-15	.131	48.30
1865						22.40		NW¼SE¼	12	36	39	3-15—4-28	.182	16.80
1865							.53	NW¼SE¼	12	36	39	3-15—4-28	.004	.38
1865				3.03				SW¼SE¼	12	36	39	3-15—9-15	.026	9.09
1865						21.30		SW¼SE¼	12	36	39	3-15—4-28	.173	15.98
1865							.55	SW¼SE¼	12	36	39	3-15—4-28	.004	.41

Claimant—**Bliss Brothers.** Proof No. **00102**
Source—**Humboldt River.** Ditch—**Pedroli Ditch System.**

	1872			.21				SW¼SW¼	32	37	39	3-15—9-15	.002	.63
	1872				6.45			SW¼SW¼	32	37	39	3-15—6-13	.052	9.68
	1872					2.43		SW¼SW¼	32	37	39	3-15—4-28	.020	1.82
	1872			3.13				SW¼SE¼	32	37	39	3-15—9-15	.025	9.39
	1872					11.19		SW¼SE¼	32	37	39	3-15—4-28	.091	8.39
	1873				9.78			SE¼NE¼	4	36	39	3-15—6-13	.080	14.67
	1873					24.40		SE¼NE¼	4	36	39	3-15—4-28	.198	18.30
	1873					22.67		SW¼NE¼	4	36	39	3-15—4-28	.184	17.00
	1873					18.30		SE¼NW¼	4	36	39	3-15—4-28	.149	13.73
	1873					1.78		SW¼NW¼	4	36	39	3-15—4-28	.014	1.34
	1875			28.97				SW¼NE¼	12	36	39	3-15—9-15	.236	86.91
	1875				4.43			SW¼NE¼	12	36	39	3-15—6-13	.036	6.65
	1875						.70	SW¼NE¼	12	36	39	3-15—4-28	.006	1.05
	1875			5.30				SE¼NE¼	12	36	39	3-15—9-15	.043	15.90

Claimant—**Bliss Brothers.** Proof No. **00102**
Source—**Humboldt River.** Ditch—**Pioneer Ditch System.**

	1870			28.26				SE¼NE¼	2	36	39	3-15—9-15	.230	84.78
	1870				9.08			SE¼NE¼	2	36	39	3-15—6-13	.074	13.62
	1870					.45		SE¼NE¼	2	36	39	3-15—4-28	.004	.34
	1870					3.05		SW¼SW¼	2	36	39	3-15—4-28	.025	2.29
	1870					20.28		SE¼SW¼	2	36	39	3-15—4-28	.165	15.21
	1870				35.86			SE¼SW¼	1	36	39	3-15—6-13	.292	53.79
	1870				20.17			NW¼SE¼	1	36	39	3-15—6-13	.164	30.26
	1870				19.51			SW¼SE¼	1	36	39	3-15—6-13	.159	29.27
	1870				.33			NE¼NW¼	1	36	39	3-15—6-13	.003	.50
	1870				13.57			SW¼NE¼	1	36	39	3-15—6-13	.110	20.36
	1870			2.49				SE¼NW¼	33	37	39	3-15—9-15	.020	7.47
	1870				23.24			SE¼NW¼	33	37	39	3-15—6-13	.189	34.86
	1870				32.79			SW¼NE¼	33	37	39	3-15—6-13	.267	49.19
	1870						9.38	NW¼NW¼	32	37	39	3-15—4-28	.076	7.04
	1870						10.40	NE¼NW¼	32	37	39	3-15—4-28	.085	7.80
	1871			13.86				SW¼NW¼	33	37	39	3-15—9-15	.113	41.58
	1871				.43			SW¼NW¼	33	37	39	3-15—6-13	.003	.65
	1871				6.90			SE¼NE¼	33	37	39	3-15—6-13	.056	10.35
	1871					4.23		SE¼NE¼	33	37	39	3-15—4-28	.034	8.35

Bliss Brothers—Continued.

Date of beneficial use: Nat. mdw.	Date of beneficial use: Cult. area	Construction first initiated: Dams	Construction first initiated: Ditches	Culture—Acres: Harvest crops	Culture—Acres: Meadow pasture	Culture—Acres: Willow and sage pasture	Culture—Acres: Swamp or overflow	Location: Subdivision	Location: Section	Location: Tp. N.	Location: R. E.	Length of season	Duty of water: C. F. S.	Duty of water: Acre-feet
	1871				2.12			NW¼NE¼	33	37	39	3-15—6-13	.017	3.18
	1871			28.69				NW¼SW¼	33	37	39	3-15—9-15	.233	86.07
	1871				3.33			NW¼SW¼	33	37	39	3-15—6-13	.027	5.00
	1871			25.37				NE¼SW¼	33	37	39	3-15—9-15	.206	76.11
	1871				1.23			NE¼SW¼	33	37	39	3-15—6-13	.101	1.85
	1871					6.93		NE¼SW¼	33	37	39	3-15—4-28	.056	7.32
	1871			27.67				NW¼SE¼	33	37	39	3-15—9-15	.225	83.01
	1871				5.77			NW¼SE¼	33	37	39	3-15—6-13	.047	8.66
	1871					1.60		NW¼SE¼	33	37	39	3-15—4-28	.013	1.20
	1871			.63				NE¼SE¼	33	37	39	3-15—9-15	.005	1.80
	1871				6.87			NE¼SE¼	33	37	39	3-16—6-13	.056	10.31
	1871					16.74		NE¼SE¼	33	37	39	3-15—4-28	.136	12.56
	1871			26.60				SW¼SW¼	33	37	39	3-15—9-15	.216	79.80
	1871			36.97				SE¼SW¼	33	37	39	3-15—9-15	.301	110.91
	1871			34.99				SW¼SE¼	33	37	39	3-15—9-15	.284	104.97
	1871						4.54	SW¼SE¼	33	37	39	3-16—4-28	.037	3.41
	1871			26.77				SE¼SE¼	33	37	39	3-15—9-15	.218	80.31
	1871				2.67			SE¼SE¼	33	37	39	3-15—6-13	.022	4.01
	1871					8.10		SE¼SE¼	33	37	39	3-15—4-28	.066	6.08
	1871						.40	SE¼SE¼	33	37	39	3-15—4-28	.004	.30
	1872			20.47				NW¼NW¼	32	37	39	3-15—9-15	.166	61.41
	1872				2.83			NW¼NW¼	32	37	39	3-15—6-13	.023	4.25
	1872			20.56				NE¼NW¼	32	37	39	3-16—9-15	.167	61.68
	1872			22.10				NW¼NE¼	32	37	39	3-15—9-15	.180	66.30
	1872						3.77	NW¼NE¼	32	37	39	3-15—4-28	.031	2.83
	1872			4.00				NE¼NE¼	32	37	39	3-15—9-15	.033	12.00
	1872						1.36	NE¼NE¼	32	37	39	3-15—4-28	.011	1.02
	1872			29.54				SW¼NW¼	32	37	39	3-15—9-15	.240	88.62
	1872						8.03	SW¼NW¼	32	37	39	3-15—4-28	.065	6.02
	1872			27.49				SE¼NW¼	32	37	39	3-15—9-15	.223	82.47
	1872						9.14	SE¼NW¼	32	37	39	3-15—4-28	.074	6.86
	1872			33.88				SW¼NE¼	32	37	39	3-15—9-15	.275	101.64
	1872						3.61	SW¼NE¼	32	37	39	3-15—4-28	.029	2.71
	1872			25.54				SE¼NE¼	32	37	39	3-15—9-15	.208	76.62
	1872						11.66	SE¼NE¼	32	37	39	3-15—4-28	.095	8.75
	1872			20.31				NW¼SW¼	32	37	39	3-15—9-15	.165	60.93
	1872				5.59			NW¼SW¼	32	37	39	3-15—6-13	.045	8.39
	1872					3.54		NW¼SW¼	32	37	39	3-15—4-28	.029	2.66
	1872						7.12	NW¼SW¼	32	37	39	3-15—4-28	.058	5.34
	1872			23.52				NE¼SW¼	32	37	39	3-15—9-15	.191	70.56
	1872						14.18	NE¼SW¼	32	37	39	3-15—4-28	.115	10.64
	1872			29.48				NW¼SE¼	32	37	39	3-15—9-15	.240	88.44
	1872						8.90	NW¼SE¼	32	37	39	3-15—4-28	.072	6.68
	1872			29.18				NE¼SE¼	32	37	39	3-15—9-15	.237	87.54
	1872						9.68	NE¼SE¼	32	37	39	3-15—4-28	.079	7.26
	1872			7.93				SE¼SW¼	32	37	39	3-16—9-15	.064	23.79
	1872				3.11			SE¼SW¼	32	37	39	3-16—6-13	.025	4.07

	1872					.31		SE¼SW¼	32	37	39	3-15—4-28	.003	.23
	1872						3.34	SE¼SW¼	32	37	39	3-15—4-28	.027	2.51
	1873			27.30				SE¼SE¼	32	37	39	3-15—9-15	.223	82.17
	1872					5.66		SE¼SE¼	32	37	39	3-15—4-28	.046	4.25
	1873			10.50				NW¼NW¼	4	36	39	3-15—9-15	.085	31.50
	1873					21.15		NW¼NW¼	4	36	39	3-15—4-28	.172	15.86
	1873						.06	NW¼NW¼	4	36	39	3-15—4-28	.001	.05
	1873			23.73				NE¼NW¼	4	36	39	3-15—9-15	.192	71.19
	1873					10.80		NE¼NW¼	4	36	39	3-15—4-28	.088	8.10
	1873						1.10	NE¼NW¼	4	36	39	3-15—4-28	.009	.83
	1873			25.13				NW¼NE¼	4	36	39	3-15—9-15	.204	75.39
	1873					10.45		NW¼NE¼	4	36	39	3-15—4-28	.085	7.84
	1873			31.97				NE¼NE¼	4	36	39	3-15—9-15	.260	95.91
	1873					4.60		NE¼NE¼	4	36	39	3-15—4-28	.037	3.45
	1873					3.53		NE¼SE¼	4	36	39	3-15—4-28	.029	2.65
	1874				.70			SW¼NW¼	7	36	40	3-15—6-13	.006	1.05
	1874					19.07		SW¼NW¼	7	36	40	3-15—4-28	.162	14.98
	1874					6.65		SE¼NW¼	7	36	40	3-15—4-28	.054	5.99
	1874			4.17				NE¼SW¼	7	36	40	3-15—9-15	.034	12.51
	1874				34.06			NE¼SW¼	7	36	40	3-15—6-13	.277	51.09
	1874			10.75				NW¼SW¼	7	36	40	3-15—9-15	.087	32.25
	1874				21.80			NW¼SW¼	7	36	40	3-15—6-13	.177	32.70
	1874					4.83		NW¼SW¼	7	36	40	3-15—4-28	.039	3.62
	1874			10.83				SW¼SW¼	7	36	40	3-15—9-15	.088	32.49
	1874				28.00			SW¼SW¼	7	36	40	3-15—6-13	.211	39.00
	1874					1.12		SW¼SW¼	7	36	40	3-15—4-28	.009	.84
	1874			21.97				SE¼SW¼	7	36	40	3-15—9-15	.179	65.91
	1874				17.14			SE¼SW¼	7	36	40	3-15—6-13	.139	25.71
	1874			35.53				NE¼SE¼	7	36	40	3-15—9-15	.289	106.59
	1874				4.13			NE¼SE¼	7	36	40	3-15—6-13	.034	6.20
	1874			3.20				NW¼SE¼	7	36	40	3-15—9-15	.026	9.60
	1874				36.80			NW¼SE¼	7	36	40	3-15—6-13	.299	55.20
	1874				38.32			SW¼SE¼	7	36	40	3-15—6-13	.312	57.48
	1874				40.10			SE¼SE¼	7	36	40	3-15—6-13	.326	60.15
	1874				5.16			SW¼NE¼	7	36	40	3-15—6-13	.042	7.74
	1874				1.45			SE¼NE¼	7	36	40	3-15—6-13	.012	2.18
	1875			.50				SE¼SW¼	1	36	39	3-15—9-15	.004	1.50
	1875					1.37		SE¼SW¼	1	36	39	3-15—4-28	.011	1.03
	1875					18.47		NW¼SE¼	1	36	39	3-15—4-28	.150	13.85
	1875					14.90		SW¼SE¼	1	36	39	3-15—4-28	.121	11.18
	1875					2.50		SE¼SE¼	1	36	39	3-15—4-28	.120	1.88
	1875					6.60		SW¼NE¼	1	36	39	3-15—4-28	.054	4.95
	1875					2.60		SE¼NE¼	1	36	39	3-15—4-28	.021	1.95
	1875					8.27		NE¼SE¼	1	36	39	3-15—4-28	.067	6.20
	1875			3.90				NW¼NE¼	12	36	39	3-15—9-15	.032	11.70
	1875				2.00			NW¼NE¼	12	36	39	3-15—6-13	.016	3.00
	1875				7.38			NW¼SE¼	3	36	39	3-15—6-13	.060	11.07
	1875					3.12		NW¼SE¼	3	36	39	3-15—4-28	.025	2.34
	1875				22.81			NE¼SE¼	3	36	39	3-15—6-13	.185	34.22
	1876				6.24			NW¼SW¼	34	37	39	3-15—6-13	.051	9.36
	1876				5.81			SW¼SW¼	34	37	39	3-15—6-13	.047	8.72
	1876					22.31		SW¼SW¼	34	37	39	3-15—4-28	.181	16.73
	1876				20.90			SE¼SW¼	34	37	39	3-15—6-13	.170	31.35

Bliss Brothers—Continued.

Date of beneficial use: Nat. mdw.	Date of beneficial use: Cult. area	Construction first initiated: Dams	Construction first initiated: Ditches	Culture—Acres: Harvest crops	Culture—Acres: Meadow pasture	Culture—Acres: Willow and sage pasture	Culture—Acres: Swamp or overflow	Location: Subdivision	Location: Section	Location: Tp.N.	Location: R.E.	Length of season	Duty of water: C.F.S.	Duty of water: Acre-feet
	1876					.24		SE¼SW¼	34	37	39	3-15—4-29	.002	.18
	1876				29.87			SW¼SE¼	34	37	39	3-15—6-13	.243	44.81
	1876				2.73			SE¼SE¼	34	37	39	3-15—6-13	.022	4.10
	1876					1.70		SE¼SE¼	34	37	39	3-15—4-28	.014	1.28
	1876			1.17				SW¼SW¼	35	37	39	3-15—9-15	.010	3.51
	1876				12.97			SW¼SW¼	35	37	39	3-15—6-13	.105	19.46
	1876				13.40			SE¼SW¼	35	37	39	3-15—6-13	.109	20.10
	1876				26.10			NW¼NE¼	3	36	39	3-15—6-13	.212	39.15
	1876					11.23		NW¼NE¼	3	36	39	3-15—4-28	.091	8.42
	1876			7.04				NE¼NE¼	3	36	39	3-15—9-15	.057	21.12
	1876				25.72			NE¼NE¼	3	36	39	3-15—6-13	.209	38.58
	1876					.33		NE¼NE¼	3	36	39	3-15—4-28	.003	.25
	1876				28.22			SW¼NE¼	3	36	39	3-15—6-13	.229	42.33
	1876					10.48		SW¼NE¼	3	36	39	3-15—4-28	.085	7.86
	1876				17.40			SE¼NE¼	3	36	39	3-15—6-13	.141	26.10
	1876					19.34		SE¼NE¼	3	36	39	3-15—4-28	.157	14.51
	1876				16.36			NW¼SW¼	3	36	39	3-15—6-13	.133	24.54
	1876				16.32			NE¼SW¼	3	36	39	3-15—6-13	.133	24.48
	1877			0.48				NE¼NE¼	11	36	39	3-15—9-15	.053	19.44
	1877					28.69		NE¼NE¼	11	36	39	3-15—4-28	.233	21.52
	1877					6.42		NW¼NE¼	11	36	39	3-15—4-28	.052	4.82
	1877			4.78				SE¼NE¼	11	36	39	3-15—9-15	.039	14.34
	1877					11.79		SE¼NE¼	11	36	39	3-15—4-28	.096	8.84
	1877			12.97				NE¼SE¼	11	36	39	3-15—9-15	.105	38.91

Claimant—**L. Hirzel.** Proof No. 00103

Source—**Humboldt River.** Ditch—**Sand Hill Slough System.**

Date of beneficial use: Nat. mdw.	Date of beneficial use: Cult. area	Construction first initiated: Dams	Construction first initiated: Ditches	Culture—Acres: Harvest crops	Culture—Acres: Meadow pasture	Culture—Acres: Willow and sage pasture	Culture—Acres: Swamp or overflow	Location: Subdivision	Location: Section	Location: Tp.N.	Location: R.E.	Length of season	Duty of water: C.F.S.	Duty of water: Acre-feet
	1879			25.01				NE¼NE¼	8	35	37	3-15—9-15	.203	75.03
	1879					7.69		NE¼NE¼	8	35	37	3-15—4-28	.063	5.77
	1880			1.00				NW¼NE¼	8	35	37	3-15—9-15	.008	3.00
	1880					33.60		NW¼NE¼	8	35	37	3-15—4-28	.273	25.20
	1880			14.12				SE¼NE¼	8	35	37	3-15—9-15	.115	42.36
	1880					9.98		SE¼NE¼	8	35	37	3-15—4-28	.081	7.49
	1880			6.74				SW¼NE¼	8	35	37	3-15—9-15	.055	20.22
	1880					21.16		SW¼NE¼	8	35	37	3-15—4-28	.172	15.87
	1880			2.56				NW¼SE¼	8	35	37	3-15—9-15	.021	7.68
	1880					30.84		NW¼SE¼	8	35	37	3-15—4-28	.251	23.13
	1880					28.90		NE¼SW¼	8	35	37	3-15—4-28	.235	21.68
	1880			2.01				NW¼SW¼	8	35	37	3-15—9-15	.033	6.03
	1880					31.25		NW¼SW¼	8	35	37	3-15—4-28	.254	23.44
	1880						.14	NW¼SW¼	8	35	37	3-15—4-28	.001	.11
	1880			24.23				SW¼NW¼	8	35	37	3-15—9-15	.197	72.69
	1880					8.39		SW¼NW¼	8	35	37	3-15—4-28	.068	6.29
	1880						1.08	SW¼NW¼	8	35	37	3-15—4-28	.009	.81
	1880			9.86				SE¼NW¼	8	35	37	3-15—9-15	.080	29.58
	1880					20.44		SE¼NW¼	8	35	37	3-15—4-28	.166	15.33

	1881			8.40				NE¼NW¼	8	35	37	3-15—9-15	.069	25.47
	1881					20.15		NE¼NW¼	8	35	37	3-15—4-28	.104	15.11
	1881			8.49				NW¼NW¼	8	35	37	3-15—9-15	.069	25.47
	1881					7,51		NW¼NW¼	8	35	37	3-15—4-28	.061	5.63
	1881			30.16				SE¼NE¼	7	35	37	3-15—9-15	.245	93.48
	1881					4.20		SE¼NE¼	7	35	37	3-15—4-28	.034	3.15
	1881			.68				NE¼SE¼	7	35	37	3-15—9-15	.007	2.04
	1881					32.88		NE¼SE¼	7	35	37	3-15—4-28	.267	21.06
	1881			2.16				NW¼SE¼	7	35	37	3-15—9-15	.018	6.48
	1881					27.59		NW¼SE¼	7	35	37	3-15—4-28	.224	20.69
	1881						.85	NW¼SE¼	7	35	37	3-15—4-28	.007	.64
	1881					2.10		SW¼NW¼	7	35	37	3-15—4-28	.017	1.58
	1881			21.25				NE¼SW¼	7	35	37	3-15—9-15	.173	63.75
	1881					10.21		NE¼SW¼	7	35	37	3-15—4-28	.083	7.66
	1881						.64	NE¼SW¼	7	35	37	3-15—4-28	.005	.48
	1882			34.00				NW¼SW¼	7	35	37	3-15—9-15	.276	102.00
	1882					4.62		NW¼SW¼	7	35	37	3-15—4-28	.038	3.47
	1882			8.33				NE¼SE¼	12	35	36	3-15—9-15	.068	24.99
	1882					21.67		NE¼SE¼	12	35	36	3-15—4-28	.176	16.25
	1882					22.62		SE¼SE¼	12	35	36	3-15—4-28	.184	16.97
	1880			7.56				NW¼SW¼	4	35	37	3-15—9-15	.061	22.68
	1880					20.83		NW¼SW¼	4	35	37	3-15—4-28	.165	15.25
	1880			36.39				SW¼SW¼	4	35	37	3-15—9-15	.296	109.17
	1880					1.51		SW¼SW¼	4	35	37	3-15—4-28	.012	1.13
	1879			25.96				NE¼SW¼	4	35	37	3-15—9-15	.211	77.88
	1879					11.14		NE¼SW¼	4	35	37	3-15—4-28	.091	8.36
	1881					7.91		SE¼NW¼	4	35	37	3-15—4-28	.064	5.93
	1881					19.71		SW¼NE¼	4	35	37	3-15—4-28	.160	14.78
	1881				5.57			SE¼NE¼	4	35	37	3-15—6-13	.045	8.36
	1881					5.39		SE¼NE¼	4	35	37	3-15—4-28	.044	4.04
	1879			15.37				NW¼SE¼	4	35	37	3-15—9-15	.135	46.11
	1879				7.00			NW¼SE¼	4	35	37	3-15—6-13	.057	10.50
	1879					13.63		NW¼SE¼	4	35	37	3-15—4-28	.111	10.22
	1878			14.22				SW¼SE¼	4	35	37	3-15—9-15	.116	42.66
	1878					12.32		SW¼SE¼	4	35	37	3-15—4-28	.100	9.24
	1878						3.28	SW¼SE¼	4	35	37	3-15—4-28	.027	2.46
	1878			32.60				SE¼SW¼	4	35	37	3-15—9-15	.265	97.80
	1878					3.80		SE¼SW¼	4	35	37	3-15—4-28	.031	28.50
	1879			15.99				NE¼SE¼	4	35	37	3-15—9-15	.130	47.97
	1879				11.45			NE¼SE¼	4	35	37	3-15—6-13	.093	17.18
	1879					7.36		NE¼SE¼	4	35	37	3-15—4-28	.060	5.52
	1879			2.51				SE¼SE¼	4	35	37	3-15—9-15	.020	7.53
	1879					21.84		SE¼SE¼	4	35	37	3-15—4-28	.178	16.38
	1879						1.20	SE¼SE¼	4	35	37	3-15—4-28	.010	.90
	1879					14.20		NW¼NE¼	9	35	37	3-15—4-28	.115	10.65
	1878			15.80				NE¼NW¼	9	35	37	3-15—9-15	.128	47.40
	1878					18.30		NE¼NW¼	9	35	37	3-15—4-28	.149	13.73
	1878			33.99				NW¼NW¼	9	35	37	3-15—9-15	.276	101.97
	1878					1.51		NW¼NW¼	9	35	37	3-15—4-28	.012	1.13
	1879			3.63				SW¼NW¼	9	35	37	3-15—9-15	.030	10.89
	1879					18.67		SW¼NW¼	9	35	37	3-15—4-28	.152	14.00

Claimant—**Reinhart Land and Livestock Co.** Proof No. 00103

Source—**Humboldt River.** Ditch—**Unnamed Slough System.**

Date of beneficial use — Nat. mdw.	Date of beneficial use — Cult. area	Construction first initiated — Dams	Construction first initiated — Ditches	Culture—Acres — Harvest crops	Culture—Acres — Meadow pasture	Culture—Acres — Willow and sage pasture	Culture—Acres — Swamp or overflow	Location — Subdivision	Location — Section	Location — Tp.N.	Location — R.E.	Length of season	Duty of water — C.F.S.	Duty of water — Acre-feet
	1870			24.11				NE¼SE¼	25	36	37	3-15—9-15	.196	72.33
	1870					9.67		NE¼SE¼	25	36	37	3-15—4-28	.079	7.25
	1870			2.90				SE¼NE¼	25	36	37	3-15—9-15	.024	8.70
	1870					16.02		SE¼NE¼	25	36	37	3-15—4-28	.130	12.02

Claimant—**Reinhart Land and Livestock Co.** Proof No. 00103

Source—**Humboldt River.** Ditch—**Adrian Dam System.**

Date of beneficial use — Nat. mdw.	Date of beneficial use — Cult. area	Construction first initiated — Dams	Construction first initiated — Ditches	Culture—Acres — Harvest crops	Culture—Acres — Meadow pasture	Culture—Acres — Willow and sage pasture	Culture—Acres — Swamp or overflow	Location — Subdivision	Location — Section	Location — Tp.N.	Location — R.E.	Length of season	Duty of water — C.F.S.	Duty of water — Acre-feet
	1880					20.20		NW¼SE¼	12	35	37	3-15—4-28	.164	15.15
	1880					22.62		SE¼SE¼	12	35	37	3-15—4-28	.184	16.97
	1880			8.33				NE¼SE¼	12	35	37	3-15—9-15	.068	24.99
	1880					21.67		NE¼SE¼	12	35	37	3-15—4-28	.176	16.25
	1882			.14				SE¼SW¼	7	35	37	3-15—9-15	.001	.42
	1882					20.25		SE¼SW¼	7	35	37	3-15—4-28	.165	15.19
	1882			4.15				SW¼SW¼	7	35	37	3-15—9-15	.034	12.45
	1882					20.85		SW¼SW¼	7	35	37	3-15—4-28	.170	15.64
	1882			34.00				NW¼SW¼	7	35	37	3-15—9-15	.276	102.00
	1882					4.62		NW¼SW¼	7	35	37	3-15—4-28	.038	3.47
	1882			21.25				NE¼SW¼	7	35	37	3-15—9-15	.173	63.75
	1882					10.21		NE¼SW¼	7	35	37	3-15—4-28	.083	7.66
	1882						.64	NE¼SW¼	7	35	37	3-15—4-28	.005	.48
	1882					2.10		SW¼NW¼	7	35	37	3-15—4-28	.017	1.58
	1882			8.30				SE¼NW¼	7	35	37	3-15—9-15	.067	24.90
	1882			2.16				NW¼SE¼	7	35	37	3-15—9-15	.018	3.48
	1882					27.50		NW¼SE¼	7	35	37	3-15—4-28	.224	20.60
	1882						.85	NW¼SE¼	7	35	37	3-15—4-28	.007	.64
	1881					13.80		SW¼SE¼	7	35	37	3-15—4-28	.112	10.35
	1881					8.90		SE¼SE¼	7	35	37	3-15—4-28	.072	6.68
	1881			.68				NE¼SE¼	7	35	37	3-15—9-15	.006	2.04
	1881					32.88		NE¼SE¼	7	35	37	3-15—4-28	.267	24.66
	1881			20.58				SW¼NE¼	7	35	37	3-15—9-15	.167	61.74
	1881					10.22		SW¼NE¼	7	35	37	3-15—4-28	.083	7.74
	1881			30.16				SE¼NE¼	7	35	37	3-15—9-15	.245	90.48
	1881					4.20		SE¼NE¼	7	35	37	3-15—4-28	.035	3.15
	1881			.25				NE¼NE¼	7	35	37	3-15—9-15	.002	.75
	1881					1.15		NE¼NE¼	7	35	37	3-15—4-28	.009	.86
	1881			8.49				NW¼NW¼	8	35	37	3-15—9-15	.069	25.47
	1881					7.51		NW¼NW¼	8	35	37	3-15—4-28	.061	5.63
	1881			8.49				NE¼NW¼	8	35	37	3-15—9-15	.069	25.47
	1881					20.15		NE¼NW¼	8	35	37	3-15—4-28	.164	15.11
	1881			9.86				SE¼NW¼	8	35	37	3-15—9-15	.080	29.58
	1881					20.44		SE¼NW¼	8	35	37	3-15—4-28	.166	15.33
	1881			24.23				SW¼NW¼	8	35	37	3-15—9-15	.197	72.69
	1881					8.39		SW¼NW¼	8	35	37	3-15—4-28	.068	6.29
	1881						1.08	SW¼NW¼	8	35	37	3-15—4-28	.009	.81

	1879					10.40		SE¼NW¼	9	35	37	3-15—4-28	.085	7.80
	1880					6.50		NE¼SE¼	5	35	37	3-15—4-28	.063	5.88
	1880			6.40				SE¼SE¼	5	35	37	3-15—9-15	.052	19.20
	1880					27.30		SE¼SE¼	5	35	37	3-15—4-28	.222	20.48
	1880					8.90		SW¼SE¼	5	35	37	3-15—4-28	.072	6.68
	1880			3.80				NE¼SE¼	8	35	37	3-15—9-15	.031	11.40
	1880					4.00		NE¼SE¼	8	35	37	3-15—4-28	.033	3.00
	1880					18.86		NW¼NE¼	20	36	38	3-15—4-28	.153	14.10
	1880					26.72		NE¼NW¼	20	36	38	3-15—4-28	.217	20.04
	1880					13.90		NW¼NW¼	20	36	38	3-15—4-28	.113	10.43
	1880					15.90		SW¼NW¼	20	36	38	3-15—4-28	.129	11.93
	1880					26.90		SE¼NW¼	20	36	38	3-15—4-28	.219	20.18
	1880					.46		SW¼SW¼	17	36	38	3-15—4-28	.004	.35
	1880					8.96		NE¼SW¼	17	36	38	3-15—4-28	.073	6.72
	1878			7.00				NW¼NE¼	17	36	38	3-15—9-15	.057	21.00
	1878					11.60		NW¼NE¼	17	36	38	3-15—4-28	.094	8.70
	1874			24.08				SE¼NE¼	17	36	38	3-15—9-15	.196	72.24
	1874				5.20			SE¼NE¼	17	36	38	3-15—6-13	.042	7.80
	1874					10.00		SE¼NE¼	17	36	38	3-15—4-28	.081	7.50
	1874						2.24	SE¼NE¼	17	36	38	3-15—4-28	.018	1.68
	1875			13.74				SW¼NE¼	17	36	38	3-15—9-15	.112	41.22
	1875				10.94			SW¼NE¼	17	36	38	3-15—6-13	.138	25.41
	1875						4.12	SW¼NE¼	17	36	38	3-15—4-28	.033	3.09
	1880					4.71		SE¼NW¼	17	36	38	3-15—4-28	.038	3.53
	1880					24.14		SE¼SW¼	17	36	38	3-15—4-28	.196	18.11
	1876			11.93				NW¼SE¼	17	36	38	3-15—9-15	.097	35.79
	1876				6.18			NW¼SE¼	17	36	38	3-15—6-13	.050	9.27
	1876					20.26		NW¼SE¼	17	36	38	3-15—4-28	.165	15.20
	1876						.04	NW¼SE¼	17	36	38	3-15—4-28	.000	.03
	1877			3.55				NE¼SE¼	17	36	38	3-15—9-15	.029	10.65
	1877				3.55			NE¼SE¼	17	36	38	3-15—6-13	.029	5.33
	1877					34.00		NE¼SE¼	17	36	38	3-15—4-28	.276	25.50
	1880					26.80		SW¼SE¼	17	36	38	3-15—4-28	.214	20.10
	1873			33.40				NE¼NE¼	17	36	38	3-15—9-15	.272	100.20
	1873						7.74	NE¼NE¼	17	36	38	3-15—4-28	.063	5.81
	1878				3.49			SW¼NW¼	16	36	38	3-15—6-13	.028	5.24
	1878					15.57		SW¼NW¼	16	36	38	3-15—4-28	.127	11.68
	1878			23.93				NW¼NW¼	16	36	38	3-15—9-15	.195	71.79
	1878				6.03			NW¼NW¼	16	36	38	3-15—6-13	.049	9.05
	1878						1.60	NW¼NW¼	16	36	38	3-15—4-28	.013	1.20
	1878			1.23				NE¼NW¼	16	36	38	3-15—9-15	.010	3.69
	1878						4.83	NE¼NW¼	16	36	38	3-15—4-28	.039	3.62
	1878			5.93				SE¼SW¼	9	36	38	3-15—9-15	.048	17.79
	1878					12.73		SE¼SW¼	9	36	38	3-15—4-28	.103	9.55
	1878						3.00	SE¼SW¼	9	36	38	3-15—4-28	.024	2.25
	1872			38.52				SW¼SW¼	9	36	38	3-15—9-15	.313	115.56
	1871			3.20				NW¼SE¼	9	36	38	3-15—9-15	.026	9.60
	1871						4.10	NW¼SE¼	8	36	38	3-15—4-28	.033	3.08
	1869			27.80				NE¼SW¼	9	36	38	3-15—9-15	.226	83.40
	1869					7.80		NE¼SW¼	9	36	38	3-15—4-28	.063	5.85
	1869						2.90	NE¼SW¼	9	36	38	3-15—4-28	.024	2.18
	1871			39.40				NW¼SW¼	9	36	38	3-15—9-15	.320	118.20
	1877			38.90				NE¼NW¼	9	36	38	3-15—9-15	.316	116.70

Reinhart Land and Livestock Co.—Continued.

Date of beneficial use: Nat. mdw.	Date of beneficial use: Cult. area	Construction first initiated: Dams	Construction first initiated: Ditches	Culture—Acres: Harvest crops	Culture—Acres: Meadow pasture	Culture—Acres: Willow and sage pasture	Culture—Acres: Swamp or overflow	Location: Subdivision	Location: Section	Location: Tp.N.	Location: R.E.	Length of season	Duty of water: C.F.S.	Duty of water: Acre-feet
	1878			40.20				SW¼NW¼	9	36	38	3-15—9-15	.327	120.60
	1877			34.41				NW¼NW¼	9	36	38	3-15—9-15	.280	103.23
	1877					3.60		NW¼NW¼	9	36	38	3-15—4-28	.029	2.70
	1874			40.53				SE¼NW¼	9	36	38	3-15—9-15	.330	121.59
	1877			17.78				NW¼SW¼	4	36	38	3-15—9-15	.145	53.34
	1877				1.90			NW¼SW¼	4	36	38	3-15—6-13	.015	2.85
	1877						1.70	NW¼SW¼	4	36	38	3-15—4-28	.014	1.28
	1877			22.10				SW¼SW¼	4	36	38	3-15—9-15	.180	66.30
	1877					9.88		SW¼SW¼	4	36	38	3-15—4-28	.080	7.41
	1877			24.39				NE¼SW¼	4	36	38	3-15—9-15	.198	73.17
	1877					9.15		NE¼SW¼	4	36	38	3-15—4-28	.074	6.86
	1877			24.34				SE¼SW¼	4	36	38	3-15—9-15	.190	73.02
	1877					7.56		SE¼SW¼	4	36	38	3-15—4-28	.061	5.67
	1880			10.28				SE¼SE¼	5	36	38	3-15—9-15	.084	30.84
	1880					3.22		SE¼SE¼	5	36	38	3-15—4-28	.026	2.42
	1878			16.90				NE¼NE¼	8	36	38	3-15—9-15	.137	50.70
	1878					15.60		NE¼NE¼	8	36	38	3-15—4-28	.127	11.70
	1878					1.08		NW¼NE¼	8	36	38	3-15—4-28	.009	.81
	1878					1.53		SW¼NE¼	8	36	38	3-15—4-28	.012	1.15
	1878						.64	SW¼NE¼	8	36	38	3-15—4-28	.005	.48
	1878			28.00				SE¼NE¼	8	36	38	3-15—9-15	.228	84.00
	1878					9.41		SE¼NE¼	8	36	38	3-15—4-28	.077	7.06
	1878					9.00		NW¼SE¼	8	36	38	3-15—4-28	.073	6.75
	1878						3.40	NW¼SE¼	8	36	38	3-15—4-28	.028	2.55
	1878			22.60				NE¼SE¼	8	36	38	3-15—9-15	.184	67.80
	1878					13.28		NE¼SE¼	8	36	38	3-15—4-28	.108	9.96
	1878					17.48		SW¼SE¼	8	36	38	3-15—4-28	.142	13.11
	1878			31.30				SE¼SE¼	8	36	38	3-15—9-15	.254	93.90
	1878					3.80		SE¼SE¼	8	36	38	3-15—4-28	.031	2.85

Claimant—**Reinhart Land & Livestock Co.** Proof No. 00103

Source—**Humboldt River.** Ditch—**Sand Hill Slough.**

Date of beneficial use: Nat. mdw.	Date of beneficial use: Cult. area	Construction first initiated: Dams	Construction first initiated: Ditches	Culture—Acres: Harvest crops	Culture—Acres: Meadow pasture	Culture—Acres: Willow and sage pasture	Culture—Acres: Swamp or overflow	Location: Subdivision	Location: Section	Location: Tp.N.	Location: R.E.	Length of season	Duty of water: C.F.S.	Duty of water: Acre-feet
	1874				5.60			SE¼NE¼	9	36	38	3-15—6-13	.046	8.40
	1877			26.60				SW¼NE¼	9	36	38	3-15—9-15	.216	79.80
	1877				8.80			SW¼NE¼	8	36	38	3-15—6-13	.072	13.20
	1877						3.90	SW¼NE¼	9	36	38	3-15—4-28	.032	2.93
	1874			4.40				NE¼NE¼	9	36	38	3-15—9-15	.036	13.20
	1874				3.40			NE¼NE¼	9	36	38	3-15—6-13	.028	5.10
	1874			39.70				NW¼NE¼	9	36	38	3-15—9-15	.323	119.10
	1877			31.20				NW¼SE¼	4	36	38	3-15—9-15	.254	93.60
	1877					3.10		NW¼SE¼	4	36	38	3-15—4-28	.025	2.83

Claimant—**J. A. Callahan.** Proof No. 00104

Source—**Humboldt River.** Ditch—**St. Mary's Ditch.**

1866							17.56	SW¼SE¼	35	33	33	3-15—4-28	.143	13.17
1866						.34		SE¼SW¼	35	33	33	3-15—4-28	.028	.26
1866							30.34	SE¼SW¼	35	33	33	3-15—4-28	.247	22.75
1866							10.06	SW¼SW¼	35	33	33	3-15—4-28	.082	7.55
1866						10.20		SW¼SW¼	35	33	33	3-15—4-28	.083	7.65
1866							12.22	NE¼SW¼	35	33	33	3-15—4-28	.099	9.17
1866						22.87		NE¼SW¼	35	33	33	3-15—4-28	.186	17.15
1866						40.00		NW¼SW¼	35	33	33	3-15—4-28	.325	30.00
1861					34.00			SE¼NW¼	35	33	33	3-15—6-13	.276	51.00
1861						6.00		SE¼NW¼	35	33	33	3-15—4-28	.049	4.50
1866						35.23		SW¼NW¼	35	33	33	3-15—4-28	.286	26.42
1871						25.66		NE¼NW¼	35	33	33	3-15—4-28	.209	19.25
1871						11.64		NW¼NW¼	35	33	33	3-15—4-28	.095	8.73
1867						1.29		SE¼NE¼	34	33	33	3-15—4-28	.010	.97
1861					23.86			SE¼NE¼	34	33	33	3-15—6-13	.194	35.79
	1867			.31				NE¼NE¼	34	33	33	3-15—9-15	.003	.93
	1867					3.25		NE¼NE¼	34	33	33	3-15—4-28	.026	2.44
1863	1867			31.08				NE¼SE¼	34	33	33	3-15—9-15	.253	93.24
1863	1867				5.82			NE¼SE¼	34	33	33	3-15—6-13	.047	8.73
	1865			2.02				SE¼SE¼	34	33	33	3-15—9-15	.016	6.06
1861							20.12	SE¼SW¼	25	33	33	3-15—4-28	.164	15.09
1861							3.53	NW¼NW¼	36	33	33	3-15—4-28	.029	2.65
1861							32.92	NE¼NW¼	36	33	33	3-15—4-28	.268	24.69
	1861			1.94				SW¼SW¼	25	33	33	3-15—9-15	.016	5.82
1861					2.97			SW¼SW¼	25	33	33	3-15—6-13	.024	4.46
1861						3.00		SW¼SW¼	25	33	33	3-15—4-28	.025	2.32
1861							13.51	SW¼SW¼	25	33	33	3-15—4-28	.110	10.13
	1866			9.92				SE¼SE¼	26	33	33	3-15—9-15	.081	29.76
	1868				10.20			SE¼SE¼	26	33	33	3-15—6-13	.083	15.30
	1878				8.30			SW¼SE¼	26	33	33	3-15—6-13	.068	12.50
1861							12.70	NE¼NE¼	35	33	33	3-15—4-28	.104	9.59
1861						8.51		NE¼NE¼	35	33	33	3-15—4-28	.069	6.38
1861						34.80		NW¼NE¼	35	33	33	3-15—4-28	.283	26.10
1861						29.60		SW¼NE¼	35	33	33	3-15—4-28	.241	22.27
1861							6.23	SW¼NE¼	35	33	33	3-15—4-28	.051	4.67
1861						1.64		SE¼NE¼	35	33	33	3-15—4-28	.013	1.23
	1861			6.67				SE¼NW¼	34	33	33	3-15—9-15	.054	20.01
	1861					2.88		SE¼NW¼	34	33	33	3-15—4-28	.023	2.16
	1867			10.15				SW¼NE¼	34	33	33	3-15—9-15	.083	30.45
	1867				11.36			SW¼NE¼	34	33	33	3-15—6-13	.092	17.04
	1867					8.80		SW¼NE¼	34	33	33	3-15—4-28	.072	6.67
	1861			6.44				NE¼NW¼	34	33	33	3-15—9-15	.052	19.32
1864							22.53	SE¼SE¼	34	33	33	3-15—4-28	.183	16.90
1864							10.25	SW¼SE¼	34	33	33	3-15—4-28	.083	7.69
	1877			2.60				SW¼SE¼	34	33	33	3-15—9-15	.021	7.80
	1867			8.73				SW¼SE¼	34	33	33	3-15—9-15	.071	26.19
	1878					10.80		SW¼SE¼	34	33	33	3-15—4-28	.088	8.10
1866							17.21	SE¼SW¼	34	33	33	3-15—4-28	.140	12.91
	1866			4.98				SE¼SW¼	34	33	33	3-15—9-15	.040	14.94
	1878						18.46	SW¼SW¼	34	33	33	3-15—4-28	.150	13.85

J. A. Callahan—Continued.

Date of beneficial use: Nat. mdw.	Cult. area	Construction first initiated: Dams	Ditches	Culture—Acres: Harvest crops	Meadow pasture	Willow and sage pasture	Swamp or overflow	Location: Subdivision	Section	Tp.N.	R.E.	Length of season	Duty of water: C.F.S.	Acre-feet
	1863			38.09				NW¼SE¼	34	33	33	3-15—9-15	.310	114.27
	1863				.72			NW¼SE¼	34	33	33	3-15—6-13	.006	1.08
	1865			36.70				NE¼SW¼	34	33	33	3-15—9-15	.298	110.10
	1866						.52	NE¼SW¼	34	33	33	3-15—4-28	.004	.39
	1864			29.77				NW¼SW¼	34	33	33	3-15—9-15	.242	89.31
1865							5.57	NW¼SW¼	34	33	33	3-15—4-28	.045	4.18
	1866			21.77				SW¼NW¼	34	33	33	3-15—9-15	.177	65.31
	1862			5.12				SW¼NW¼	34	33	33	3-15—9-15	.042	15.36
	1866			17.45				SE¼NW¼	34	33	33	3-15—9-15	.142	52.35
1861							31.14	SE¼NE¼	35	33	33	3-15—4-28	.253	23.36
1861						2.26		NW¼SE¼	35	33	33	3-15—4-28	.018	1.70
1861							35.05	NW¼SE¼	35	33	33	3-15—4-28	.285	26.29
1866							22.18	NE¼SE¼	35	33	33	3-15—4-28	.180	16.64
1866							.55	SE¼SE¼	35	33	33	3-15—4-28	.004	.41
	1876	Power	Plant—	Quartz	Mill			SW¼SW¼	25	33	33	1-1—12-31	200	

Water discharged without loss into river directly below Mill.

Claimant—**Robt. Robinson.** Proof No. 00105

Source—**Humboldt River.** Ditch—**Reil Dam and Ditches.**

Nat. mdw.	Cult. area	Dams	Ditches	Harvest crops	Meadow pasture	Willow and sage pasture	Swamp or overflow	Subdivision	Section	Tp.N.	R.E.	Length of season	C.F.S.	Acre-feet
	1878			4.15				SW¼NW¼	4	36	38	3-15—9-15	.035	12.45
	1878				4.77			SW¼NW¼	4	36	38	3-15—6-13	.039	7.16
	1878						1.40	SW¼NW¼	4	36	38	3-15—4-28	.011	1.05
	1878			37.74				SE¼NW¼	4	36	38	3-15—9-15	.307	113.22
	1878				.50			SE¼NW¼	4	36	38	3-15—6-13	.004	.75
	1878					.20		SE¼NW¼	4	36	38	3-15—4-28	.002	.15
	1878						2.16	SE¼NW¼	4	36	38	3-15—4-28	.018	1.62
	1878			26.09				SW¼NE¼	4	36	38	3-15—9-15	.212	78.27
	1878					8.53		SW¼NE¼	4	36	38	3-15—4-28	.069	6.40
	1878						2.18	SW¼NE¼	4	36	38	3-15—4-28	.018	1.64
	1878			24.80				SE¼NE¼	4	36	38	3-15—9-15	.202	74.40
	1878					6.40		SE¼NE¼	4	36	38	3-15—4-28	.053	4.80
	1878						5.36	SE¼NE¼	4	36	38	3-15—4-28	.044	4.02
	1878			20.01				NE¼NW¼	4	36	38	3-15—9-15	.163	60.03
	1878				5.60			NE¼NW¼	4	36	38	3-15—6-13	.046	8.40
	1878					10.24		NE¼NW¼	4	36	38	3-15—4-28	.083	7.68
	1878			36.58				NW¼NE¼	4	36	38	3-15—9-15	.297	109.74
	1878				.22			NW¼NE¼	4	36	38	3-15—6-13	.002	.33
	1878			30.64				NE¼NE¼	4	36	38	3-15—9-15	.259	91.92
	1878					1.36		NE¼NE¼	4	36	38	3-15—4-28	.011	1.02
	1878						4.84	NE¼NE¼	4	36	38	3-15—4-28	.039	3.63
	1878			1.92				SW¼NW¼	3	36	38	3-15—9-15	.016	5.76
	1878			5.68				NW¼NW¼	3	36	38	3-15—9-15	.046	17.04
	1877			17.69				SE¼SE¼	33	37	38	3-15—9-15	.144	53.07
	1877				13.20			SE¼SE¼	33	37	38	3-15—6-13	.107	19.80
	1877					.88		SE¼SE¼	33	37	38	3-15—4-28	.007	.66

	1877						2.87	SE¼SE¼	33	37	38	3-15—4-28	.023	2.15
	1877			9.56				SW¼SE¼	33	37	38	3-15—9-15	.078	28.68
	1877				13.32			SW¼SE¼	33	37	38	3-15—6-13	.108	19.98
	1880			27.12				SW¼SW¼	34	37	38	3-15—9-15	.220	81.36
	1880				13.28			SW¼SW¼	34	37	38	3-15—6-13	.108	19.92
	1880						.28	SW¼SW¼	34	37	38	3-15—4-28	.002	.21
	1880			10.68				SE¼SW¼	34	37	38	3-15—9-15	.087	32.04
	1880				27.20			SE¼SW¼	34	37	38	3-15—6-13	.221	40.80
	1880					2.08		SE¼SW¼	34	37	38	3-15—4-28	.017	1.56
	1880				40.24			NE¼SW¼	34	37	38	3-15—6-13	.327	60.36
	1880				30.88			NW¼SW¼	34	37	38	3-15—6-13	.251	46.32
	1880				14.44			SE¼NW¼	34	37	38	3-15—6-13	.117	21.66
	1880				.28			SW¼NW¼	34	37	38	3-15—6-13	.002	.42
	1887				6.08			NE¼SE¼	33	37	38	3-15—6-13	.049	9.12
	1877				3.08			SE¼SW¼	33	37	38	3-15—6-13	.025	4.62
	1878			1.76				NE¼SW¼	4	36	38	3-15—9-15	.014	5.28
	1878			.76				NW¼SW¼	4	36	38	3-15—9-15	.006	2.28

Claimant—**E. J. Thacker.** Proof No. 00106

Source—**Humboldt River.** Ditch—**Flood Water.**

	1875						5.08	SW¼SW¼	34	34	35	3-15—4-28	.041	3.81
	1875						30.09	NW¼NW¼	3	33	35	3-15—4-28	.245	22.57
	1875						6.42	NE¼NW¼	3	33	35	3-15—4-28	.052	4.82
	1875						25.92	SW¼NW¼	3	33	35	3-15—4-28	.211	19.44
	1875						6.12	SE¼NW¼	3	33	35	3-15—4-28	.050	4.59
	1875						24.19	NW¼SW¼	3	33	35	3-15—4-28	.197	18.14
	1875						6.27	NE¼SW¼	3	33	35	3-15—4-28	.051	4.70
	1875						28.49	SW¼SW¼	3	33	35	3-15—4-28	.232	21.37
	1875						6.34	SE¼SE¼	4	33	35	3-15—4-28	.052	4.76
	1882						25.67	NW¼NW¼	10	33	35	3-15—4-28	.208	19.25
	1898						3.89	SW¼NW¼	10	33	35	3-15—4-28	.032	2.92
	1882						29.41	NE¼NE¼	9	33	35	3-15—4-28	.237	22.06
	1898						34.59	SE¼NE¼	9	33	35	3-15—4-28	.281	25.94
	1898						16.30	SW¼NE¼	9	33	35	3-15—4-28	.133	12.23
	1898						21.46	NW¼SE¼	9	33	35	3-15—4-28	.174	16.10
	1898						12.86	NE¼SE¼	9	33	35	3-15—4-28	.105	9.65
	1898						2.78	SW¼SE¼	9	33	35	3-15—4-28	.023	2.09
	1898						13.08	SE¼SE¼	9	33	35	3-15—4-28	.106	9.81
	1898						1.60	NW¼NE¼	16	33	35	3-15—4-28	.013	1.20
	1898						9.39	NE¼NE¼	16	33	35	3-15—4-28	.076	7.04

Claimant—**Russell and Chadwick.** Proof No. 00108

Source—**Humboldt River.** Ditch—**No. 2.**

	1864					15.80		NW¼SW¼	31	33	33	3-15—4-28	.128	11.85
	1864				16.30			SE¼SW¼	31	33	33	3-15—6-13	.133	24.45
	1864					16.43		SE¼SW¼	31	33	33	3-15—4-28	.134	12.32
	1864				2.63			NW¼SE¼	31	33	33	3-15—6-13	.021	3.95
	1864					6.63		NW¼SE¼	31	33	33	3-15—4-28	.054	4.97
	1864					1.80		NE¼NE¼	29	33	33	3-15—4-28	.015	1.35
	1864				11.83			NW¼NE¼	29	33	33	3-15—6-13	.096	17.75
	1864					12.87		NW¼NE¼	29	33	33	3-15—4-28	.105	9.65

Russell and Chadwick—Continued.

Date of beneficial use — Nat. mdw.	Date of beneficial use — Cult. area	Construction first initiated — Dams	Construction first initiated — Ditches	Culture—Acres — Harvest crops	Culture—Acres — Meadow pasture	Culture—Acres — Willow and sage pasture	Culture—Acres — Swamp or overflow	Location — Subdivision	Location — Section	Location — Tp.N.	Location — R.E.	Length of season	Duty of water — C.F.S.	Duty of water — Acre-feet
	1864				15.53			SW¼NE¼	29	33	33	3-15—6-13	.126	23.30
	1864					22.13		SW¼NE¼	29	33	33	3-15—4-28	.180	16.60
	1864				1.17			SE¼NE¼	29	33	33	3-15—6-13	.010	1.76
	1864					33.67		SE¼NE¼	29	33	33	3-15—4-28	.274	25.25
	1864				6.07			NE¼NW¼	29	33	33	3-15—6-13	.049	9.11
	1864					11.91		NE¼NW¼	29	33	33	3-15—4-28	.097	8.93
	1864				29.65			SW¼NW¼	29	33	33	3-15—6-13	.241	44.48
	1864					9.10		SW¼NW¼	29	33	33	3-15—4-28	.074	6.83
	1864				25.22			SE¼NW¼	29	33	33	3-15—6-13	.205	37.83
	1864					11.40		SE¼NW¼	29	33	33	3-15—4-28	.093	8.56
	1864				27.75			NE¼SW¼	29	33	33	3-15—6-13	.226	41.63
	1864					8.56		NE¼SW¼	29	33	33	3-15—4-28	.070	6.42
	1864				35.47			NW¼SW¼	29	33	33	3-15—6-13	.288	53.21
	1864					.70		NW¼SW¼	29	33	33	3-15—4-28	.006	.53
	1864				32.96			NW¼SE¼	29	33	33	3-15—6-13	.268	49.44
	1864					6.60		NW¼SE¼	29	33	33	3-15—4-28	.054	4.95
	1864				34.80			NE¼SE¼	30	33	33	3-15—6-13	.283	52.20
	1864					1.90		NE¼SE¼	30	33	33	3-15—4-28	.015	1.43
	1864				16.63			NW¼SE¼	30	33	33	3-15—6-13	.135	24.95
	1864					1.15		NW¼SE¼	30	33	33	3-15—4-28	.009	.86
	1864				34.87			SW¼SE¼	30	33	33	3-15—6-13	.283	52.31
	1864					.13		SW¼SE¼	30	33	33	3-15—4-28	.001	.10
	1864				37.09			SE¼SE¼	30	33	33	3-15—6-13	.302	55.64
	1864				38.60			NW¼NE¼	31	33	33	3-15—6-13	.314	57.90
	1864			1.50				SW¼NE¼	31	33	33	3-15—9-15	.012	4.50
	1864				7.57			SW¼NE¼	31	33	33	3-15—6-13	.062	11.36
	1864						27.07	SW¼NE¼	31	33	33	3-15—4-28	.220	20.30
	1864			1.20				SE¼NE¼	31	33	33	3-15—9-15	.010	3.60
	1864						5.97	SE¼NE¼	31	33	33	3-15—4-28	.049	4.48
	1864					8.30		NE¼NW¼	31	33	33	3-15—4-28	.067	6.02
	1864				9.82			SW¼NW¼	31	33	33	3-15—6-13	.080	14.73
	1864				29.10			SE¼NW¼	31	33	33	3-15—6-13	.237	43.65
	1864					.77		SE¼NW¼	31	33	33	3-15—4-28	.005	.58
	1864						7.57	SE¼NW¼	31	33	33	3-15—4-28	.062	5.68
	1864				22.93			NW¼NW¼	6	32	33	3-15—6-13	.186	34.40
	1864						5.80	NW¼NW¼	6	32	33	3-15—4-28	.047	4.26
	1864				25.14			SW¼NW¼	6	32	33	3-15—6-13	.204	37.71
	1864					2.90		SW¼NW¼	6	32	33	3-15—4-28	.024	2.18
	1864						4.83	SW¼NW¼	6	32	33	3-15—4-28	.039	3.63

Claimant—**Russell and Chadwick.** Proof No. 00108

Source—**Humboldt River.** Ditch—**Blakeslee.**

Nat. mdw.	Cult. area	Dams	Ditches	Harvest crops	Meadow pasture	Willow and sage pasture	Swamp or overflow	Subdivision	Section	Tp.N.	R.E.	Length of season	C.F.S.	Acre-feet
	1867						32.86	NE¼SE¼	11	32	32	3-15—4-28	.267	24.65
	1867						18.08	NW¼SE¼	11	32	32	3-15—4-28	.147	13.56
	1867						25.43	SW¼SE¼	11	32	32	3-15—4-28	.207	19.07
	1867						27.12	SE¼SE¼	11	32	32	3-15—4-28	.220	20.34

	1867				19.00			SW¼NE¼	1	32	32	3-15—6-13	.154	28.50
	1867					2.00		SW¼NE¼	1	32	32	3-15—4-28	.016	1.50
	1867						5.37	SW¼NE¼	1	32	32	3-15—4-28	.044	40.28
	1867				29.97			NW¼SE¼	1	32	32	3-15—6-13	.244	44.96

Claimant—**Russell and Chadwick.** Proof No. 00108
Source—**Humboldt River.** Ditch—**Overflow.**

	1863					20.90		NE¼NE¼	29	33	33	3-15—4-28	.170	15.68
	1863						14.30	NE¼NE¼	29	33	33	3-15—4-28	.116	10.73
	1863					4.10		NW¼NW¼	29	33	33	3-15—4-28	.033	3.08
	1863						10.63	NW¼NW¼	29	33	33	3-15—4-28	.086	7.97
	1863					1.30		NE¼NE¼	30	33	33	3-15—4-28	.011	.98
	1863						1.53	NE¼NE¼	30	33	33	3-15—4-28	.012	1.15
	1863					20.70		SW¼NE¼	30	33	33	3-15—4-28	.168	15.53
	1863					15.23		SE¼NE¼	30	33	33	3-15—4-28	.124	11.42
	1863						19.11	SE¼NE¼	30	33	33	3-15—4-28	.155	14.33
	1863					4.80		SE¼NW¼	30	33	33	3-15—4-28	.039	3.60
	1863					21.23		NE¼SW¼	30	33	33	3-15—4-28	.173	15.92
	1863						.67	NE¼SW¼	30	33	33	3-15—4-28	.005	.50
	1863					22.23		SE¼SW¼	30	33	33	3-15—4-28	.181	16.67
	1863						9.53	SE¼SW¼	30	33	33	3-15—4-28	.177	7.15
	1863					13.15		NW¼SE¼	30	33	33	3-15—4-28	.107	9.86
	1863						4.01	NW¼SE¼	30	33	33	3-15—4-28	.033	3.01
	1863						2.40	SW¼SE¼	30	33	33	3-15—4-28	.020	1.80
	1863					16.87		NE¼NW¼	31	33	33	3-15—4-28	.137	12.65
	1863						9.20	NE¼NW¼	31	33	33	3-15—4-28	.175	6.90
	1863					3.60		NW¼NW¼	31	33	33	3-15—4-28	.029	2.70
	1863					35.37		NE¼NW¼	12	32	32	3-15—4-28	.288	26.53
	1863					38.20		NW¼NW¼	12	32	32	3-15—4-28	.311	28.65

Claimant—**Russell and Chadwick.** Proof No. 00108
Source—**Humboldt River.** Ditch—**No. 1.**

	1864				6.87			NE¼SW¼	31	33	33	3-15—6-13	.056	10.31
	1864					31.90		NE¼SW¼	31	33	33	3-15—4-28	.259	23.93
	1864				22.42			SW¼SW¼	29	33	33	3-15—6-13	.182	33.63
	1864					1.79		SW¼SW¼	29	33	33	3-15—4-28	.015	1.34
	1864				38.05			SE¼SW¼	29	33	33	3-15—6-13	.309	57.08
	1864				4.60			SW¼SE¼	29	33	33	3-15—6-13	.037	6.90
	1864					.70		SW¼SE¼	29	33	33	3-15—4-28	.006	.53
	1864						31.95	SW¼SE¼	29	33	33	3-15—4-28	.260	23.96
	1864					.80		SE¼SE¼	29	33	33	3-15—4-28	.007	.60
	1864						35.64	SE¼SE¼	29	33	33	3-15—4-28	.290	26.73
	1864				11.76			NE¼NE¼	31	33	33	3-15—6-13	.096	17.64
	1864						2.70	NE¼NE¼	31	33	33	3-15—4-28	.022	2.03
	1864				27.85			NE¼NW¼	6	32	33	3-15—6-13	.226	41.78
	1864			2.90				SW¼SE¼	1	32	32	3-15—0-15	.024	8.70
	1864				33.04			SW¼SE¼	1	32	32	3-15—6-13	.269	49.56
	1864			8.80				SE¼SE¼	1	32	32	3-15—0-15	.072	26.40
	1864				.31			SE¼SE¼	1	32	32	3-15—6-13	.003	.47
	1864				36.14			NW¼NE¼	12	32	32	3-15—6-13	.294	54.21

Russell and Chadwick—Continued.

Date of beneficial use: Nat. mdw.	Cult. area	Construction first initiated: Dams	Ditches	Culture—Acres: Harvest crops	Meadow pasture	Willow and sage pasture	Swamp or overflow	Location: Subdivision	Section	Tp.N.	R.E.	Length of season	Duty of water: C.F.S.	Acre-feet
	1864				33.93			SW¼NE¼	12	32	32	3-15—6-13	.276	50.90
	1864				36.70			SW¼NW¼	12	32	32	3-15—6-13	.298	55.05
	1864				39.40			SE¼NW¼	12	32	32	3-15—6-13	.320	59.10
	1864				19.23			NE¼SW¼	12	32	32	3-15—6-13	.156	28.85
	1864						20.53	NE¼SW¼	12	32	32	3-15—4-28	.167	15.40
	1864				36.63			NW¼SW¼	12	32	32	3-15—6-13	.298	54.95
	1864						2.97	NW¼SW¼	12	32	32	3-15—4-28	.024	2.23
	1864				2.93			SW¼SW¼	12	32	32	3-15—6-13	.024	4.40
	1864						36.95	SW¼SW¼	12	32	32	3-15—4-28	.300	27.71

Claimant—**Rodgers Estate.** Proof No. 00109

Source—**Humboldt River.** Ditch—**St. Mary's.**

Date of beneficial use: Nat. mdw.	Cult. area	Construction first initiated: Dams	Ditches	Culture—Acres: Harvest crops	Meadow pasture	Willow and sage pasture	Swamp or overflow	Location: Subdivision	Section	Tp.N.	R.E.	Length of season	Duty of water: C.F.S.	Acre-feet
	1867				15.66			NW¼NW¼	28	33	33	3-15—6-13	.127	23.34
	1867				.79			NE¼NW¼	28	33	33	3-15—6-13	.006	1.19
	1867				18.11			SW¼NW¼	28	33	33	3-15—6-13	.147	27.17
	1867					16.33		SW¼NW¼	28	33	33	3-15—4-28	.133	12.25
	1867				22.16			SE¼NW¼	28	33	33	3-15—6-13	.180	33.24
	1867					8.05		SE¼NW¼	28	33	33	3-15—4-28	.165	6.04
	1867				31.60			SW¼NE¼	28	33	33	3-15—6-13	.257	47.40
	1867				7.50			SE¼NE¼	28	33	33	3-15—6-13	.061	11.35
	1867					40.00		NW¼SW¼	26	33	33	3-15—4-28	.325	30.00
	1867				15.23			NE¼SW¼	28	33	33	3-15—6-13	.124	22.85
	1867					17.59		NE¼SW¼	28	33	33	3-15—4-28	.143	13.19
	1867					37.71		SW¼SW¼	28	33	33	3-15—4-28	.307	28.28
	1867				15.79			SE¼SW¼	28	33	33	3-15—6-13	.128	23.69
	1867					16.89		SE¼SW¼	28	33	33	3-15—4-28	.137	12.67
	1867				38.66			NW¼SE¼	28	33	33	3-15—6-13	.314	57.99
	1867				29.86			NE¼SE¼	28	33	33	3-15—6-13	.244	44.79
	1867				39.76			SW¼SE¼	28	33	33	3-15—6-13	.323	59.64
	1867				30.14			SE¼SE¼	28	33	33	3-15—6-13	.318	58.71
	1867				1.07			NW¼SW¼	27	33	33	3-15—6-13	.009	1.61
	1867				28.42			SW¼SW¼	27	33	33	3-15—6-13	.231	42.63
	1867					16.25		NW¼NW¼	33	33	33	3-15—4-28	.132	12.19
	1867					31.53		NE¼NW¼	33	33	33	3-15—4-28	.257	23.65
	1867				3.14			NW¼NE¼	33	33	33	3-15—6-13	.026	4.71
	1867					14.95		NW¼NE¼	33	33	33	3-15—4-28	.122	11.21
	1867				10.75			NE¼NE¼	33	33	33	3-15—6-13	.087	16.13
	1867					21.39		NE¼NE¼	33	33	33	3-15—4-28	.174	16.04
	1867					31.90		SE¼NE¼	33	33	33	3-15—4-28	.259	23.93
	1867					22.08		NE¼SE¼	33	33	33	3-15—4-28	.180	16.56
	1867					4.58		SE¼SE¼	33	33	33	3-15—4-28	.037	3.44
	1867				37.91			NW¼NW¼	34	33	33	3-15—6-13	.308	56.87
	1867					1.40		NW¼NW¼	34	33	33	3-15—4-28	.011	1.05

Claimant—**Sarah E. Thacker.** Proof No. **00110**

Source—**Humboldt River.** Ditch—**South Ditch.**

	1868						17.40	SW¼SE¼	33	33	34	3-15—4-28	.141	13.05
	1868						37.52	SE¼SE¼	33	33	34	3-15—4-28	.305	28.14
	1868						20.77	NE¼NE¼	4	32	34	3-15—4-28	.160	15.58
1863	1866					10.82		SE¼SE¼	28	33	34	3-15—4-28	.089	8.12
1863	1866					0.91		SW¼SE¼	28	33	34	3 15—4-28	.081	7.46
1863	1866						7.67	NW¼SE¼	34	33	34	3-15—4-28	.062	5.75
1863	1866						20.35	NE¼SE¼	34	33	34	3-15—4-28	.165	15.41
1863	1866						8.95	SW¼SE¼	34	33	34	3-15—4-28	.073	6.71
1863	1866						13.10	SE¼SE¼	34	33	34	3-15—4-28	.107	9.83
1863	1866						4.45	NW¼SW¼	34	33	34	3-15—4-28	.036	3.34
1863	1866						15.48	NE¼SW¼	34	33	34	3-15—4-28	.126	11.61
1863	1866					2.17		NE¼NE¼	35	33	34	3-15—4-28	.018	1.63
1866	1866				1.32			NW¼NE¼	35	33	34	3-15—6-13	.011	1.98
1863	1866					33.60		NW¼NE¼	35	33	34	3-15—4-28	.273	25.20
1863	1866					6.68		SW¼NE¼	35	33	34	3-15—4-28	.054	5.04
1863	1866					15.53		NE¼NW¼	35	33	34	3-15—4-28	.126	11.65
1863	1864				.73			SE¼NW¼	35	33	34	3-15—6-13	.006	1.10
1863	1864					38.12		SE¼NW¼	35	33	34	3-15—4-28	.310	28.59
1863	1864					14.77		NE¼SW¼	35	33	34	3-15—4-28	.120	11.08
1863	1864					33.00		NW¼SW¼	35	33	34	3-15—4-28	.268	24.75
1863	1864					1.45		SW¼SW¼	35	33	34	3-15—4-28	.012	1.08
	1868						14.15	SE¼NE¼	32	33	34	3-15—4-28	.115	10.61
	1868						12.78	SW¼NE¼	32	33	34	3-15—4-28	.104	9.59
	1868						35.26	NW¼NW¼	32	33	34	3-15—4-28	.287	26.44
	1868						12.46	SW¼NW¼	32	33	34	3-15—4-28	.101	9.35
	1868						15.28	SE¼NW¼	32	33	34	3-15—4-28	.124	11.46
	1868						12.25	NW¼NE¼	31	33	34	3-15—4-28	.100	9.19
	1868						25.93	NE¼NE¼	31	33	34	3-15—4-28	.211	19.45
	1868						3.10	SE¼NE¼	31	33	34	3-15—4-28	.025	2.33
	1868					17.30		NE¼SW¼	30	33	34	3-15—4-28	.141	12.98
	1868					10.34		SE¼SW¼	30	33	34	3-15—4-28	.084	7.76
	1868						34.64	SW¼SE¼	30	33	34	3-15—4-28	.282	25.98
	1868						29.23	SE¼SE¼	30	33	34	3-15—4-28	.238	21.92
	1868						5.01	SE¼SW¼	34	33	34	3-15—4-28	.041	3.76
	1868						19.81	SW¼SW¼	34	33	34	3-15—4-28	.161	14.86
	1868				2.87			SW¼NE¼	33	33	34	3-15—6-13	.023	4.31
	1868						30.18	SW¼NE¼	33	33	34	3-15—4-28	.245	22.64
	1868						11.89	SE¼NE¼	33	33	34	3-15—4-28	.096	8.85
1863	1864						13.39	SW¼NW¼	33	33	34	3-15—4-28	.109	10.04
1863	1864				1.88			SE¼NW¼	33	33	34	3-15—6-13	.015	2.82
1863	1864						22.60	SE¼NW¼	33	33	34	3-15—4-28	.184	17.02
1863	1864						6.78	NW¼SE¼	33	33	34	3-15—4-28	.055	5.09
	1868						21.73	NE¼SE¼	33	33	34	3-15—4-28	.178	16.30
	1868					19.23		NW¼SW¼	25	33	34	3-15—4-28	.156	14.42
	1868					.37		SW¼SW¼	25	33	34	3-15—4-28	.093	.28
	1868					27.09		SE¼SE¼	26	33	34	3-15—4-28	.220	20.32
	1868					20.51		SW¼SE¼	26	33	34	3-15—4-28	.167	15.38

Proof No. 00110

Claimant—**Sarah E. Thacker.**
Source—**Humboldt River.** Ditch—**Center Ditch.**

Date of beneficial use: Nat. mdw.	Date of beneficial use: Cult. area	Construction first initiated: Dams	Construction first initiated: Ditches	Culture—Acres: Harvest crops	Culture—Acres: Meadow pasture	Culture—Acres: Willow and sage pasture	Culture—Acres: Swamp or overflow	Location: Subdivision	Location: Section	Location: Tp.N.	Location: R.E.	Length of season	Duty of water: C.F.S.	Duty of water: Acre-feet
1863	1878				15.30			SE¼SE¼	29	33	34	3-15—6-13	.124	22.95
1863	1878				4.05			SW¼SE¼	29	33	34	3-15—6-13	.033	6.08
1863	1878						11.84	SW¼SE¼	29	33	34	3-15—4-28	.096	8.88
1863	1878						6.49	SE¼SW¼	29	33	34	3-15—4-28	.053	4.87
1863	1878				23.23			NE¼NE¼	32	33	34	3-15—6-13	.189	34.85
1863	1878					14.83		NE¼NE¼	32	33	34	3-15—4-28	.121	11.12
1863	1878				12.24			NW¼NE¼	32	33	34	3-15—6-13	.100	18.36
1863	1878					7.31		NW¼NE¼	32	33	34	3-15—4-28	.059	5.48
1863	1878						15.71	NW¼NE¼	32	33	34	3-15—4-28	.128	11.78
1863	1878				11.16			NE¼NW¼	32	33	34	3-15—6-13	.091	16.74
1863	1878						22.69	NE¼NW¼	32	33	34	3-15—4-28	.185	17.02
1863	1866				35.23			NW¼NE¼	33	33	34	3-15—6-13	.286	52.91
1863	1866						4.23	NW¼NE¼	33	33	34	3-15—4-28	.034	3.17
1863	1866				32.37			NE¼NE¼	33	33	34	3-15—6-13	.263	48.56
1863	1866						6.59	NE¼NE¼	33	33	34	3-15—4-28	.054	4.94
1863	1866				30.47			NW¼NW¼	33	33	34	3-15—6-13	.248	45.71
1863	1866						8.90	NW¼NW¼	33	33	34	3-15—4-28	.072	6.68
1863	1866				35.71			NE¼NW¼	33	33	34	3-15—6-13	.290	53.57
1863	1866						3.81	NE¼NW¼	33	33	34	3-15—4-28	.031	2.86
1863	1866				6.88			SW¼SW¼	27	33	34	3-15—6-13	.056	10.32
1863	1866					2.96		SW¼SW¼	27	33	34	3-15—4-28	.024	2.22
1863	1864				21.57			NE¼NE¼	34	33	34	3-15—6-13	.175	32.36
1863	1864				16.67			NW¼NE¼	34	33	34	3-15—6-13	.136	25.00
1863	1864				16.11			SW¼NE¼	34	33	34	3-15—6-13	.131	24.17
1863	1864						22.57	SW¼NE¼	34	33	34	3-15—4-28	.183	16.93
1863	1864				15.90			SE¼NE¼	34	33	34	3-15—6-13	.129	23.85
1863	1864						22.96	SE¼NE¼	34	33	34	3-15—4-28	.187	17.22
1863	1864				30.30			NW¼NW¼	34	33	34	3-15—6-13	.246	45.45
1863	1864					2.07		NW¼NW¼	34	33	34	3-15—4-28	.017	1.55
1863	1864				25.67			NE¼NW¼	34	33	34	3-15—6-13	.209	38.51
1863	1864					.20		NE¼NW¼	34	33	34	3-15—4-28	.002	.15
1863	1864				18.67			SE¼NW¼	34	33	34	3-15—6-13	.152	28.01
1863	1864					19.24		SE¼NW¼	34	33	34	3-15—4-28	.156	14.43
1863	1864				4.31			SW¼NW¼	34	33	34	3-15—6-13	.035	6.47
1863	1864					8.43		SW¼NW¼	34	33	34	3-15—4-28	.069	6.32
	1864				17.69			NW¼NW¼	35	33	34	3-15—6-13	.144	26.54
	1864					8.17		NW¼NW¼	35	33	34	3-15—4-28	.066	6.13
	1864				20.26			NE¼NW¼	35	33	34	3-15—6-13	.165	30.39
	1864				27.86			SW¼NW¼	35	33	34	3-15—6-13	.227	41.79
	1864					10.52		SW¼NW¼	35	33	34	3-15—4-28	.086	7.90
	1878					13.68		NW¼SE¼	25	33	34	3-15—4-28	.111	10.26
	1878					26.33		NE¼SE¼	25	33	34	3-15—4-28	.214	19.75
	1878					24.26		NE¼SW¼	25	33	34	3-15—4-28	.197	18.09
	1878				4.00			NE¼SE¼	26	33	34	3-15—6-13	.033	6.00
	1878					13.35		NE¼SE¼	26	33	34	3-15—4-28	.109	10.01
	1878				15.60			NW¼SE¼	26	33	34	3-15—6-13	.127	23.40
	1878					18.60		SW¼SE¼	26	33	34	3-15—4-28	.151	13.96

	1878				2.00			NE¼SW¼	26	33	34	3-15—6-13	.016	3.00
	1878					2.00		NE¼SW¼	26	33	34	3-15—4-28	.025	3.18
	1878				18.81			SE¼SW¼	26	33	34	3-15—6-13	.153	28.22
	1878					5.39		SE¼SW¼	26	33	34	3-15—4-28	.044	4.04
	1878					17.31		SE¼SW¼	28	33	34	3-15—4-28	.141	12.98
	1878				7.27			SW¼SW¼	28	33	34	3-15—6-13	.059	10.91
	1878					9.50		SW¼SW¼	28	33	31	3-15—4-28	.077	7.13

Claimant—**Sarah E. Thacker.** Proof No. 00110

Source—**Humboldt River.** Ditch—**Overflow.**

1863	1863						13.46	SE¼SE¼	29	33	34	3-15—4-28	.109	10.10
1863	1863						12.20	SW¼SE¼	29	33	34	3-15—4-28	.090	9.15
1863	1863						13.93	SE¼SW¼	29	33	34	3-15—4-28	.113	10.45
1863	1863						31.17	SW¼SW¼	29	33	34	3-15—4-28	.253	23.38
1863	1863						3.64	SW¼NE¼	30	33	34	3-15—4-28	.030	2.73
1863	1863						13.20	SW¼NW¼	30	33	34	3-15—4-28	.107	9.90
1863	1863						12.23	SE¼NW¼	30	33	34	3-15—4-28	.099	9.17
1863	1863						25.78	NW¼SE¼	30	33	34	3-15—4-28	.210	19.34
1863	1863						.55	SE¼SE¼	30	33	34	3-15—4-28	.005	.41
1863	1863					6.56		NW¼SW¼	30	33	34	3-15—4-28	.053	4.92
1863	1863						9.74	SE¼SE¼	28	33	34	3-15—4-28	.079	7.31
1863	1863						18.90	SW¼SE¼	28	33	34	3-15—4-28	.154	14.18
1863	1863						2.92	NW¼SE¼	28	33	34	3-15—4-28	.024	2.19
1863	1863						2.55	SE¼SE¼	27	33	34	3-15—4-28	.021	1.91
1863	1863				15.04			SW¼SE¼	27	33	34	3-15—6-13	.122	22.56
1863	1863				15.14			SE¼SW¼	27	33	34	3-15—6-13	.123	22.71
1863	1863				1.36			SW¼SW¼	27	33	34	3-15—6-13	.011	2.04
1863	1863						8.06	SW¼SW¼	27	33	34	3-15—4-28	.066	6.05
	1868				7.16			NE¼NE¼	34	33	34	3-15—6-13	.058	10.74
	1868				13.40			NW¼NE¼	34	33	34	3-15—6-13	.109	20.10
	1868				3.17			NW¼NW¼	34	33	34	3-15—6-13	.026	4.76
	1868					8.20		NE¼NW¼	34	33	34	3-15—4-28	.067	6.15
	1868						7.68	NW¼NW¼	35	33	34	3-15—4-28	.062	5.76
	1868						.94	NE¼NW¼	35	33	34	3-15—4-28	.008	.71
	1878						3.13	SE¼NE¼	25	33	34	3-15—4-28	.025	2.35
	1878						7.22	SW¼NE¼	25	33	34	3-15—4-28	.059	5.42
	1878						11.91	NW¼SE¼	25	33	34	3-15—4-28	.097	8.93
	1878						13.11	SE¼NW¼	25	33	34	3-15—4-28	.107	9.83
	1878						18.82	SW¼NW¼	25	33	34	3-15—4-28	.153	14.12
	1868						17.04	SE¼NE¼	26	33	34	3-15—4-28	.139	12.78
	1868						1.05	SW¼NE¼	26	33	34	3-15—4-28	.009	.79
	1868						13.72	NE¼SE¼	26	33	34	3-15—4-28	.111	10.29
	1868						11.60	NW¼SE¼	26	33	34	3-15—4-28	.094	8.70
	1868						6.73	SW¼SW¼	26	33	34	3-15—4-28	.055	5.05
	1868						3.18	SE¼SW¼	26	33	34	3-15—4-28	.026	2.39
1863	1863						2.56	NE¼SW¼	28	33	34	3-15—4-28	.021	1.92
1863	1863						3.06	SE¼SW¼	28	33	34	3-15—4-28	.025	2.30
1863	1863						12.22	SW¼SW¼	28	33	34	3-15—4-28	.107	9.16
1863	1863						.78	NW¼SW¼	28	33	34	3-15—4-28	.006	.59
1863	1863						11.58	NW¼SW¼	29	33	34	3-15—4-28	.094	8.69
1863	1863						20.53	NE¼SE¼	30	33	34	3-15—4-28	.167	15.40

Claimant—**John G. Taylor.** Proof No. 00111
Source—**Humboldt River.** Ditch—**Thacker Dam.**

Date of beneficial use: Nat. mdw.	Cult. area	Construction first initiated: Dams	Ditches	Culture—Acres: Harvest crops	Meadow pasture	Willow and sage pasture	Swamp or overflow	Location: Subdivision	Section	Tp.N.	R.E.	Length of season	Duty of water: C.F.S.	Acre-feet
	1878					15.26		NW¼NW¼	32	33	35	3-15—4-28	.124	11.45
	1878					.92		NE¼NW¼	32	33	35	3-15—4-28	.007	.69
	1878					26.16		SE¼NW¼	32	33	35	3-15—4-28	.213	19.62
	1878					23.64		SW¼NE¼	32	33	35	3-15—4-28	.193	17.73
	1878					16.15		SE¼NE¼	32	33	35	3-15—4-28	.131	12.11

Claimant—**Peter Organ.** Proof No. 00112
Source—**Humboldt River.** Ditch—**Thacker Dam.**

Nat. mdw.	Cult. area	Dams	Ditches	Harvest crops	Meadow pasture	Willow and sage pasture	Swamp or overflow	Subdivision	Section	Tp.N.	R.E.	Length of season	C.F.S.	Acre-feet
	1878						11.51	SW¼NW¼	32	33	35	3-15—4-28	.094	8.63
	1878						3.43	NW¼NE¼	32	33	35	3-15—4-28	.028	2.57

Claimant—**Thos. C. O'Donnell.** Proof. No. 00113
Source—**Humboldt River.** Ditch—**O'Donnell Dam and Ditch. System No. 1.**

Nat. mdw.	Cult. area	Dams	Ditches	Harvest crops	Meadow pasture	Willow and sage pasture	Swamp or overflow	Subdivision	Section	Tp.N.	R.E.	Length of season	C.F.S.	Acre-feet
	1888						24.85	NE¼NW¼	20	33	36	3-15—4-28	.202	18.64
	1888						37.13	SE¼NW¼	20	33	36	3-15—4-28	.302	27.85
	1888						12.38	NE¼SW¼	20	33	36	3-15—4-28	.101	9.29
	1888						36.07	NW¼NE¼	20	33	36	3-15—4-28	.293	27.05
	1888						37.94	NW¼NW¼	21	33	36	3-15—4-28	.318	28.46

Claimant—**Thos. C. O'Donnell.** Proof No. 00113
Source—**Humboldt River.** Ditch—**O'Donnell Dam and Ditch. System No. 2.**

Nat. mdw.	Cult. area	Dams	Ditches	Harvest crops	Meadow pasture	Willow and sage pasture	Swamp or overflow	Subdivision	Section	Tp.N.	R.E.	Length of season	C.F.S.	Acre-feet
	1897						18.33	NE¼SE¼	16	33	36	3-15—4-28	.149	13.75
	1897						38.01	SW¼SE¼	16	33	36	3-15—4-28	.309	28.51
	1897						28.67	SE¼SE¼	16	33	36	3-15—4-28	.233	21.50
	1897						24.32	NE¼NW¼	21	33	36	3-15—4-28	.198	18.24
	1897						17.74	SW¼NW¼	21	33	36	3-15—4-28	.144	13.31
	1897						17.97	NW¼NE¼	21	33	36	3-15—4-28	.146	13.48
	1897						9.06	NE¼NE¼	21	33	36	3-15—4-28	.074	6.80
	1897						1.28	SW¼NW¼	15	33	36	3-15—4-28	.010	.96
	1897						31.72	NW¼SW¼	15	33	36	3-15—4-28	.258	23.79
	1897						27.97	SW¼SW¼	15	33	36	3-15—4-28	.227	22.48
	1897						.35	SE¼SW¼	15	33	36	3-15—4-28	.003	.26
	1897						36.27	NE¼NE¼	20	33	36	3-15—4-28	.295	27.20
	1897						35.93	SW¼NE¼	20	33	36	3-15—4-28	.292	26.95
	1897						30.02	SE¼NE¼	20	33	36	3-15—4-28	.244	22.52
	1897						5.32	NW¼SE¼	20	33	36	3-15—4-28	.043	3.99
	1897						17.93	SW¼SW¼	16	33	36	3-15—4-28	.146	13.45
	1897						22.34	SE¼SW¼	16	33	36	3-15—4-28	.182	16.76

Claimant—**Estate Chas. Pedroli.** Proof No. 00114

Source—**Humboldt River.** Ditch—**Pedroli Dam and Ditch. System No. 1.**

1880	5.73			NE¼SW¼	12	35	36	3-15—0-15	.048	17.10
1880		30.29		NE¼SW¼	12	35	36	3-15—4-28	.246	22.72
1881	28.98			SW¼SW¼	12	35	36	3-15—0-15	.235	86.94
1881		8.17		SW¼SW¼	12	35	36	3-15—4-28	.066	6.13
1881			1.03	SW¼SW¼	12	35	36	3-15—4-28	.008	.77
1881	27.76			SE¼SW¼	12	35	36	3-15—0-15	.226	83.28
1881		10.08		SE¼SW¼	12	35	36	3-15—4-28	.088	7.56
1881	.56			SW¼SE¼	12	35	36	3-15—0-15	.005	1.68
1881		16.05		SW¼SE¼	12	35	36	3-15—4-28	.130	12.04
1881			2.15	SW¼SE¼	12	35	36	3-15—4-28	.017	1.61
1882	9.25			NW¼SE¼	12	35	36	3-15—0-15	.075	27.75
1882		4.73		NW¼SE¼	12	35	36	3-15—4-28	.038	3.55
1880	15.91			SE¼NW¼	12	35	36	3-15—0-15	.129	47.73
1880		1.37		SE¼NW¼	12	35	36	3-15—4-28	.011	1.03
1882		.72		SW¼NE¼	12	35	36	3-15—4-28	.006	.54
1883	10.24			SW¼NE¼	14	35	36	3-15—0-15	.083	30.72
1883		29.68		SW¼NE¼	14	35	36	3-15—4-28	.241	22.26
1883		26.21		SE¼NE¼	14	35	36	3-15—4-28	.213	19.68
1883	30.23			NE¼NE¼	14	35	36	3-15—0-15	.246	90.69
1883		8.81		NE¼NE¼	14	35	36	3-15—4-28	.072	6.61
1883	32.25			NW¼NE¼	14	35	36	3-15—0-15	.264	96.75
1883		6.64		NW¼NE¼	14	35	36	3-15—4-28	.054	4.98
1882	5.75			SE¼SE¼	11	35	36	3-15—0-15	.047	17.25
1882		13.45		SE¼SE¼	11	35	36	3-15—4-28	.100	10.09
1882	.78			SW¼SE¼	11	35	36	3-15—0-15	.006	2.34
1882		4.34		SW¼SE¼	11	35	36	3-15—4-28	.035	3.26
1882	18.78			NW¼NW¼	13	35	36	3-15—0-15	.153	56.34
1882		4.31		NW¼NW¼	13	35	36	3-15—4-28	.035	3.23
1882			4.67	NW¼NW¼	13	35	36	3-15—4-28	.038	3.50
1882		.32		SW¼NW¼	13	35	36	3-15—4-28	.003	.24
1882	20.00			NE¼NW¼	13	35	36	3-15—0-15	.163	60.00
1882			3.45	NE¼NW¼	13	35	36	3-15—4-28	.028	2.59
1880	2.90			NW¼SW¼	12	35	36	3-15—0-15	.024	8.70
1880		13.94		NW¼SW¼	12	35	36	3-15—4-28	.113	10.46
1884	.56			NW¼SE¼	14	35	36	3-15—0-15	.005	1.68
1884		14.40		NW¼SE¼	14	35	36	3-15—4-28	.117	10.80

Claimant—**Estate Chas. Pedroli.** Proof No. 00114

Source—**Humboldt River.** Ditch—**Pedroli Dam and Ditch. System No. 2.**

1884	23.15			NE¼NW¼	14	35	36	3-15—0-15	.188	69.45
1884			2.23	NE¼NW¼	14	35	36	3-15—4-28	.018	1.67
1885	34.50			SW¼NW¼	14	35	36	3-15—0-15	.280	103.50
1885		1.80		SW¼NW¼	14	35	36	3-15—4-28	.015	1.35
1885			.45	SW¼NW¼	14	35	36	3-15—4-28	.004	.34
1885	4.86			NW¼NW¼	14	35	36	3-15—0-15	.040	14.58
1885		17.50		NW¼NW¼	14	35	36	3-15—4-28	.142	13.13
1885			1.72	NW¼NW¼	14	35	36	3-15—4-28	.014	1.29
1886		1.68		NW¼SW¼	15	35	36	3-15—4-28	.014	1.26
1886		31.92		NE¼SW¼	15	35	36	3-15—4-28	.260	23.94

4[69]

Estate Chas. Pedroli—Continued.

Date of beneficial use: Nat. mdw.	Date of beneficial use: Cult. area	Construction first initiated: Dams	Construction first initiated: Ditches	Culture—Acres: Harvest crops	Culture—Acres: Meadow pasture	Culture—Acres: Willow and sage pasture	Culture—Acres: Swamp or overflow	Location: Subdivision	Location: Section	Location: Tp.N.	Location: R.E.	Length of season	Duty of water: C.F.S.	Duty of water: Acre-feet
	1886					15.44		SE¼SW¼	15	35	36	3-15—4-28	.126	11.58
	1886					7.24		SW¼SE¼	15	35	36	3-15—4-28	.059	5.43
	1886					.68		SE¼SE¼	15	35	36	3-15—4-28	.006	.51
	1886			8.44				NE¼SE¼	15	35	36	3-15—9-15	.069	25.32
	1886					31.56		NE¼SE¼	15	35	36	3-15—4-28	.257	23.67
	1887					37.33		NW¼SE¼	15	35	36	3-15—4-28	.303	27.10
	1887			2.86				SE¼NE¼	15	35	36	3-15—9-15	.023	8.58
	1887					24.88		SE¼NE¼	15	35	36	3-15—4-28	.202	18.66
	1887					9.00		SW¼NE¼	15	35	36	3-15—4-28	.073	6.75
	1887					.68		SE¼NE¼	15	35	36	3-15—4-28	.006	.51
	1887					2.12		SE¼NW¼	15	35	36	3-15—4-28	.017	1.59
	1884			5.84				NE¼SW¼	14	35	36	3-15—9-15	.047	17.52
	1884					16.44		NE¼SW¼	14	35	36	3-15—4-28	.134	12.33
	1884			11.36				NW¼SW¼	14	35	36	3-15—9-15	.092	34.08
	1884					19.86		NW¼SW¼	14	35	36	3-15—4-28	.161	14.90
	1884			40.00				SE¼NW¼	14	35	36	3-15—9-15	.325	120.00
	1884					5.89		NE¼NW¼	14	35	36	3-15—4-28	.048	4.42

Claimant—**Chas. Farrel.** Proof No. 00115

Source—**Humboldt River.** Ditch—**Trousdale Dam and Ditches.**

Nat. mdw.	Cult. area	Dams	Ditches	Harvest crops	Meadow pasture	Willow and sage pasture	Swamp or overflow	Subdivision	Section	Tp.N.	R.E.	Length of season	C.F.S.	Acre-feet
	1876					3.58		SE¼SW¼	36	36	37	3-15—4-28	.029	2.69
	1876					.30		NW¼SW¼	36	36	37	3-15—4-28	.002	.23
	1876				10.00			SW¼SW¼	36	36	37	3-15—6-13	.081	15.00
	1876					23.50		SW¼SW¼	36	36	37	3-15—4-28	.191	17.63
	1876					3.50		NW¼NW¼	1	35	37	3-15—4-28	.028	2.63

Claimant—**W. F. and F. H. Pearce.** Proof No. 00116

Source—**Humboldt River.** Ditch—**North Side.**

Nat. mdw.	Cult. area	Dams	Ditches	Harvest crops	Meadow pasture	Willow and sage pasture	Swamp or overflow	Subdivision	Section	Tp.N.	R.E.	Length of season	C.F.S.	Acre-feet
	1880			1.93				SE¼SW¼	35	36	37	3-15—9-15	.016	5.79
	1880					4.70		SE¼SW¼	35	36	37	3-15—4-28	.038	3.53
	1880			14.87				NE¼NE¼	3	35	37	3-15—9-15	.121	44.61
	1880					9.04		NE¼NE¼	3	35	37	3-15—4-28	.074	6.78
	1880						6.47	NE¼NE¼	3	35	37	3-15—4-28	.053	4.85
	1880			19.72				NW¼NE¼	3	35	37	3-15—9-15	.160	59.16
	1880				4.46			NW¼NE¼	3	35	37	3-15—6-13	.036	6.69
	1880						14.20	NW¼NE¼	3	35	37	3-15—6-13	.115	10.65
	1880			10.73				SW¼NE¼	3	35	37	3-15—9-15	.087	32.19
	1880					4.33		SW¼NE¼	3	35	37	3-15—4-28	.035	3.25
	1880					.63		SE¼NE¼	3	35	37	3-15—4-28	.005	.47
	1880			20.40				NE¼NW¼	3	35	37	3-15—9-15	.167	61.20
	1880				7.64			NE¼NW¼	3	35	37	3-15—6-13	.063	11.46
	1880						7.30	NW¼NW¼	3	35	37	3-15—4-28	.059	5.48
	1880			14.63				SW¼NW¼	3	35	37	3-15—9-15	.119	43.89
	1880					25.17		SW¼NW¼	3	35	37	3-15—4-28	.205	18.88

	1880			30.22				SE¼NW¼	3	35	37	3-15—9-15	.246	90.66
	1880					1.43		SE¼NW¼	3	35	37	3-15—4-28	.012	1.07
	1880			20.00				NW¼SW¼	3	35	37	3-15—9-15	.236	87.00
	1880					5.20		NW¼SW¼	3	35	37	3-15—4-28	.042	3.90
	1880			12.36				NE¼SW¼	3	35	37	3-15—9-15	.100	37.08
	1880					1.27		NE¼SW¼	3	35	37	3-15—4-28	.010	.95
	1880					12.63		NE¼SE¼	34	36	37	3-15—4-28	.103	9.47
	1880			2.10				SE¼SE¼	34	36	37	3-15—9-15	.017	6.30
	1880				18.79			SE¼SE¼	34	36	37	3-15—6-13	.153	28.19
	1880					6.34		SE¼SE¼	34	36	37	3-15—4-28	.053	4.76
	1880				13.67			SW¼SE¼	34	36	37	3-15—6-13	.111	20.51
	1880				6.23			SE¼SW¼	34	36	37	3-15—6-13	.051	9.35
	1880						1.53	SE¼SW¼	34	36	37	3-15—4-28	.012	1.15
	1880			7.50				NE¼SW¼	35	36	37	3-15—9-15	.061	22.50
	1880				.30			NE¼SW¼	35	36	37	3-15—6-13	.002	.45
	1880					.63		NE¼SW¼	35	36	37	3-15—4-28	.005	.47
	1880			6.06				NW¼SW¼	35	36	37	3-15—9-15	.049	18.18
	1880					12.40		NW¼SW¼	35	36	37	3-15—4-28	.101	9.30
	1880			27.17				SW¼SW¼	35	36	37	3-15—9-15	.221	81.51
	1880					6.14		SW¼SW¼	35	36	37	3-15—4-28	.050	4.61

Source—**Humboldt River.** Ditch—**South Side.**

1871	1877			.60				SW¼SW¼	2	35	37	3-15—9-15	.005	1.80
1871	1877			2.30				NE¼NE¼	3	35	37	3-15—9-15	.019	6.90
1871	1877					.60		NE¼NE¼	3	35	37	3-15—4-28	.005	.45
1871	1877						6.47	NE¼NE¼	3	35	37	3-15—4-28	.053	4.85
1871	1877			10.00				SW¼NE¼	3	35	37	3-15—9-15	.081	30.00
1871	1877					2.84		SW¼NE¼	3	35	37	3-15—4-28	.023	2.13
1871	1877			33.10				SE¼NE¼	3	35	37	3-15—9-15	.269	99.30
1871	1877					1.72		SE¼NE¼	3	35	37	3-15—4-28	.014	1.29
1871	1877			39.04				NE¼SE¼	3	35	37	3-15—9-15	.317	117.12
1871	1877			36.89				NW¼SE¼	3	35	37	3-15—9-15	.300	110.67
1871	1877			7.90				SW¼SE¼	3	35	37	3-15—9-15	.064	23.70
1871	1877					1.40		SW¼SE¼	3	35	37	3-15—4-28	.011	1.05
1871	1877			14.80				SE¼SE¼	3	35	37	3-15—9-15	.120	44.40
1871	1877					1.00		SE¼SE¼	3	35	37	3-15—4-28	.008	.75
1871	1877			4.33				SE¼NW¼	3	35	37	3-15—9-15	.035	12.49
1871	1877					.60		SE¼NW¼	3	35	37	3-15—4-28	.005	.45
1871	1877			19.86				NE¼SW¼	3	35	37	3-15—9-15	.161	59.58
1871	1877			7.55				SE¼SW¼	3	35	37	3-15—9-15	.061	22.65
1871	1877			14.67				SW¼SW¼	3	35	37	3-15—9-15	.119	44.01
1871	1877				19.70			NE¼SE¼	35	36	37	3-15—6-13	.160	29.55
1871	1877					5.90		NE¼SE¼	35	36	37	3-15—4-28	.048	4.43
1871	1877				23.55			SE¼SE¼	35	36	37	3-15—6-13	.191	35.33
1871	1877					9.10		SE¼SE¼	35	36	37	3-15—4-28	.074	6.83
1871	1877				.63			NW¼NE¼	35	36	37	3-15—6-13	.005	.95
1871	1877					4.60		NW¼NE¼	35	36	37	3-15—4-28	.037	3.45
1871	1877				18.24			SW¼SE¼	35	36	37	3-15—6-13	.148	27.36
1871	1877			12.00				SE¼SW¼	35	36	37	3-15—9-15	.098	36.00
1871	1877				15.90			SE¼SW¼	35	36	37	3-15—6-13	.129	23.85
1871	1877					.63		SE¼SW¼	35	36	37	3-15—4-28	.005	.47
1871	1877					4.56		NW¼NE¼	2	35	37	3-15—4-28	.037	3.42
1871	1877			28.41				NE¼NW¼	2	35	37	3-15—9-15	.231	85.23

W. F. and F. H. Pearce—Continued.

Date of beneficial use: Nat. mdw.	Date of beneficial use: Cult. area	Construction first initiated: Dams	Construction first initiated: Ditches	Culture—Acres: Harvest crops	Culture—Acres: Meadow pasture	Culture—Acres: Willow and sage pasture	Culture—Acres: Swamp or over-flow	Location: Subdivision	Location: Section	Location: Tp.N.	Location: R.E.	Length of season	Duty of water: C.F.S.	Duty of water: Acre-feet
1871	1877					5.91		NE¼NW¼	2	35	37	3-15—4-28	.048	4.43
1871	1877			22.48				NW¼NW¼	2	35	37	3-15—9-15	.183	67.44
1871	1877					7.97		NW¼NW¼	2	35	37	3-15—4-28	.065	5.98
1871	1877			19.33				SE¼NW¼	2	35	37	3-15—9-15	.157	57.99
1871	1877					.97		SE¼NW¼	2	35	37	3-15—4-28	.008	.73
1871	1877			36.72				SW¼NW¼	2	25	37	3-15—9-15	.299	110.16
1871	1877			18.40				NW¼SW¼	2	35	37	3-15—9-15	.150	55.20
1871	1877					5.70		SW¼SW¼	3	35	37	3-15—4-28	.046	4.28
1871	1877				2.10			SE¼SE¼	34	36	37	3-15—6-13	.017	3.15
1871	1877					18.03		SW¼SE¼	34	36	37	3-15—4-28	.147	13.52

Claimant—**Mary G. Rose.** Proof No. 00117

Source—**Humboldt River.** Ditch—**Lower Slough.**

Nat. mdw.	Cult. area	Dams	Ditches	Harvest crops	Meadow pasture	Willow and sage pasture	Swamp or over-flow	Subdivision	Section	Tp.N.	R.E.	Length of season	C.F.S.	Acre-feet
	1877			13.23				NW¼SE¼	35	36	37	3-15—9-15	.108	39.69
	1877			1.36				SW¼SE¼	35	36	37	3-15—9-15	.011	4.08
	1877			8.94				NE¼SW¼	35	36	37	3-15—9-15	.073	26.82
	1877			2.65				SE¼SW¼	35	36	37	3-15—9-15	.022	7.95

Source—**Humboldt River.** Ditch—**Upper Slough.**

Nat. mdw.	Cult. area	Dams	Ditches	Harvest crops	Meadow pasture	Willow and sage pasture	Swamp or over-flow	Subdivision	Section	Tp.N.	R.E.	Length of season	C.F.S.	Acre-feet
	1877				9.90			NE¼NE¼	35	36	37	3-15—6-13	.080	14.85
	1877			6.06				SE¼NE¼	35	36	37	3-15—9-15	.049	18.18
	1877				21.29			SE¼NE¼	35	36	37	3-15—6-13	.173	31.94
	1877			7.65				NE¼SE¼	35	36	37	3-15—9-15	.062	22.95

Source—**Humboldt River.** Ditch—**Miller & Lux Dam.**

Nat. mdw.	Cult. area	Dams	Ditches	Harvest crops	Meadow pasture	Willow and sage pasture	Swamp or over-flow	Subdivision	Section	Tp.N.	R.E.	Length of season	C.F.S.	Acre-feet
	1886				5.36			SE¼SE¼	26	36	37	3-15—6-13	.044	8.04

Claimant—**Pacific Livestock Co.** Proof No. 00118

Source—**Humboldt River.** Ditch—**Miller & Lux Dam and Ditch System.**

Nat. mdw.	Cult. area	Dams	Ditches	Harvest crops	Meadow pasture	Willow and sage pasture	Swamp or over-flow	Subdivision	Section	Tp.N.	R.E.	Length of season	C.F.S.	Acre-feet
	1880						.97	NW¼NE¼	30	36	38	3-15—4-28	.009	.73
	1880					16.30		SW¼NE¼	30	36	38	3-15—4-28	.133	12.23
	1880						.75	SW¼NE¼	30	36	38	3-15—4-28	.006	.56
	1874						3.70	NW¼SE¼	30	26	38	3-15—4-28	.030	2.78
	1880						19.70	NE¼NW¼	30	36	38	3-15—4-28	.160	14.78
	1880					3.53		SE¼NW¼	30	36	38	3-15—4-28	.029	2.65
	1880						28.84	SE¼NW¼	30	36	38	3-15—4-28	.234	21.63
	1880					20.93		SW¼NW¼	30	36	38	3-15—4-28	.170	15.70
	1880						.93	SW¼NW¼	30	36	38	3-15—4-28	.008	.70
	1872			1.40				NE¼SW¼	30	36	38	3-15—9-15	.011	4.20
	1872					34.40		NE¼SW¼	30	36	38	3-15—4-28	.280	25.80
	1872						1.97	NE¼SW¼	30	36	38	3-15—4-28	.016	1.48
	1874			.40				SE¼SW¼	30	36	38	3-15—9-15	.003	1.20
	1874					20.89		SE¼SW¼	30	36	38	3-15—4-28	.169	15.60
	1872			13.97				NW¼SW¼	30	36	38	3-15—9-15	.114	51.91

...	1872	...	...	...	...	17.83	...	NW¼SW¼	30	36	38	3-15—4-28	.145	13.87
...	1872	...	...	...	...	...	1.70	NW¼SW¼	30	36	38	3-15—4-28	.014	1.28
...	1872	...	...	34.93	...	...	...	SW¼SW¼	30	36	38	3-15—9-15	.284	104.79
...	1872	...	...	...	...	1.87	...	SW¼SW¼	30	36	38	3-15—4-28	.015	1.40
...	1872	...	...	...	...	...	1.50	SW¼SW¼	30	36	38	3-15—4-28	.012	1.13
...	1880	...	...	...	...	3.87	...	NE¼NW¼	31	36	38	3-15—4-28	.031	2.90
...	1880	...	...	11.52	...	...	...	NW¼NW¼	31	36	38	3-15—9-15	.094	34.56
...	1880	...	...	...	...	15.29	...	NW¼NW¼	31	36	38	3-15—4-28	.124	11.47
...	1880	...	...	.95	...	...	...	SW¼NW¼	31	36	38	3-15—9-15	.008	2.87
...	1880	...	...	...	...	1.90	...	SW¼NW¼	31	36	38	3-15—4-28	.015	1.43
...	1880	...	...	...	...	...	6.60	SE¼NE¼	25	36	37	3-15—4-28	.054	4.95
...	1880	...	...	5.30	...	...	...	NE¼SE¼	25	36	37	3-15—9-15	.043	15.00
...	1880	...	...	...	...	...	28.20	NE¼SE¼	25	36	37	3-15—4-28	.229	21.15
...	1878	...	...	30.64	...	...	...	SE¼SE¼	25	36	37	3-15—9-15	.249	91.92
...	1878	...	...	...	...	5.52	...	SE¼SE¼	25	36	37	3-15—4-28	.045	4.14
...	1880	...	...	.90	...	...	...	NW¼SE¼	25	36	37	3-15—9-15	.007	2.70
...	1880	...	...	...	...	18.13	...	NW¼SE¼	25	36	37	3-15—4-28	.147	13.60
...	1878	...	...	17.78	...	...	...	SW¼SE¼	25	36	37	3-15—9-15	.145	53.34
...	1878	...	...	...	...	13.23	...	SW¼SE¼	25	36	37	3-15—4-28	.108	9.92
...	1878	...	...	...	...	...	3.20	SW¼SE¼	25	36	37	3-15—4-28	.026	2.40
...	1880	...	...	...	...	2.37	...	NE¼SW¼	25	36	37	3-15—4-28	.019	1.78
...	1880	...	...	3.13	...	...	...	SE¼SW¼	25	36	37	3-15—9-15	.025	9.39
...	1880	...	...	...	...	16.10	...	SE¼SW¼	25	36	37	3-15—4-28	.130	12.08
...	1880	...	...	...	...	...	7.40	SE¼SW¼	25	36	37	3-15—4-28	.060	5.55
...	1873	...	...	33.78	...	...	...	NE¼NE¼	36	36	37	3-15—9-15	.275	101.34
...	1873	...	...	...	...	1.75	...	NE¼NE¼	36	36	37	3-15—4-28	.014	1.31
...	1873	...	...	...	...	...	.97	NE¼NE¼	36	36	37	3-15—4-28	.008	.73
...	1875	...	...	25.63	...	...	...	SE¼NE¼	36	36	37	3-15—9-15	.208	76.89
...	1875	...	...	...	...	3.90	...	SE¼NE¼	36	36	37	3-15—4-28	.032	2.93
...	1873	...	...	35.14	...	...	...	NW¼NE¼	36	36	37	3-15—9-15	.286	105.42
...	1873	...	...	...	...	1.87	...	NW¼NE¼	36	36	37	3-15—4-28	.015	1.40
...	1875	...	...	31.74	...	...	...	SW¼NE¼	36	36	37	3-15—9-15	.258	95.22
...	1875	...	...	...	...	4.36	...	SW¼NE¼	36	36	37	3-15—4-28	.035	3.27
...	1880	...	...	.33	...	...	...	NW¼SE¼	36	36	37	3-15—9-15	.003	.99
...	1886	...	...	18.63	...	...	...	NE¼NW¼	36	36	37	3-15—9-15	.151	55.89
...	1886	...	...	...	...	14.23	...	NE¼NW¼	36	36	37	3-15—4-28	.116	10.67
...	1873	...	...	33.83	...	...	...	SE¼NW¼	36	36	37	3-15—9-15	.276	101.49
...	1873	...	...	...	...	2.50	...	SE¼NW¼	36	36	37	3-15—4-28	.020	1.88
...	1880	...	...	3.07	...	...	...	NW¼NW¼	36	36	37	3-15—9-15	.025	9.21
...	1880	...	...	...	...	11.92	...	NW¼NW¼	36	36	37	3-15—4-28	.097	8.94
...	1880	...	...	28.46	...	...	...	SW¼NW¼	36	36	37	3-15—9-15	.241	85.38
...	1880	...	...	...	...	5.04	...	SW¼NW¼	36	36	37	3-15—4-28	.041	3.78
...	1886	...	...	25.51	...	...	...	NE¼SW¼	36	36	37	3-15—9-15	.207	76.53
...	1886	...	...	...	...	5.90	...	NE¼SW¼	36	36	37	3-15—4-28	.048	4.43
...	1880	...	...	29.51	...	...	...	NW¼SW¼	36	36	37	3-15—9-15	.240	88.53
...	1880	...	...	...	...	6.61	...	NW¼SW¼	36	36	37	3-15—4-28	.054	4.96
...	1880	...	...	...	...	.35	...	NW¼SE¼	36	36	37	3-15—4-28	.004	.26

Claimant—**C. L. Tobin.** Proof No. 00119

Source—**Humboldt River.** Ditch—**Pioneer Slough System.**

Date of beneficial use — Nat. mdw.	Date of beneficial use — Cult. area	Construction first initiated — Dams	Construction first initiated — Ditches	Culture—Acres — Harvest crops	Culture—Acres — Meadow pasture	Culture—Acres — Willow and sage pasture	Culture—Acres — Swamp or overflow	Location — Subdivision	Location — Section	Location — Tp.N.	Location — R.E.	Length of season	Duty of water — C.F.S.	Duty of water — Acre-feet
	1878						26.13	NE¼NE¼	34	37	38	3-15—4-28	.212	19.60
	1878				1.93			NW¼NE¼	34	37	38	3-15—6-13	.016	2.90
	1878						31.54	NW¼NE¼	34	37	38	3-15—4-28	.256	23.66
	1878						36.80	NW¼NE¼	34	37	38	3-15—4-28	.299	27.60
	1878						31.07	SE¼NE¼	34	37	38	3-15—4-28	.253	23.30
	1878				2.07			NE¼NW¼	34	37	38	3-15—6-13	.017	3.11
	1878						.73	NE¼NW¼	34	37	38	3-15—4-28	.006	.55
	1878				1.87			SE¼NW¼	34	37	38	3-15—6-13	.015	2.81
	1878						28.93	SE¼NW¼	34	37	38	3-15—4-28	.235	21.70
	1877			9.07				NE¼SE¼	35	37	38	3-15—9-15	.074	27.21
	1877						6.20	NE¼SE¼	35	37	38	3-15—4-28	.050	4.65
	1877						19.00	NW¼SE¼	35	37	38	3-15—4-28	.154	14.25
	1875			34.59				SW¼SE¼	35	37	38	3-15—9-15	.281	103.77
	1875						4.40	SW¼SE¼	35	37	38	3-15—4-28	.036	3.30
	1875			32.46				SE¼SE¼	35	37	38	3-15—9-15	.264	97.38
	1875						8.67	SE¼SE¼	35	37	38	3-15—4-28	.070	6.50
	1877						23.47	NE¼SW¼	35	37	38	3-15—4-28	.191	17.60
	1877						30.73	NW¼SW¼	35	37	38	3-15—4-28	.250	23.05
	1875						4.94	SW¼SW¼	36	37	38	3-15—4-28	.040	3.71
	1876			29.14				NE¼NE¼	31	37	39	3-15—9-15	.240	87.42
	1876						4.93	NE¼NE¼	31	37	39	3-15—4-28	.040	3.70
	1873			35.62				NW¼NE¼	31	37	39	3-15—9-15	.290	106.86
	1873						4.50	NW¼NE¼	31	37	39	3-15—4-28	.037	3.38
	1876			27.32				SE¼NE¼	31	37	39	3-15—9-15	.222	81.96
	1876						12.26	SE¼NE¼	31	37	39	3-15—4-28	.100	9.20
	1876			37.32				NE¼NW¼	31	37	39	3-15—9-15	.303	111.96
	1876						2.68	NE¼NW¼	31	37	39	3-15—4-29	.022	2.01
	1876			33.54				NW¼NW¼	31	37	39	3-15—9-15	.273	100.62
	1876						5.49	NW¼NW¼	31	37	39	3-15—4-28	.045	4.12
	1879			2.40				SE¼SE¼	25	37	38	3-15—9-15	.020	7.20
	1879				6.00			SE¼SE¼	25	37	38	3-15—6-13	.049	9.00
	1879						1.87	SE¼SE¼	25	37	38	3-15—4-28	.015	1.40
	1879			2.00				SW¼SW¼	30	37	39	3-15—9-15	.016	6.00
	1879				3.00			SW¼SW¼	30	37	39	3-15—6-13	.024	4.50
	1879			1.00				SE¼SW¼	30	37	39	3-15—9-15	.008	3.00
	1879				5.40			SE¼SW¼	30	37	39	3-15—6-13	.044	8.10
	1877			36.60				SW¼SW¼	35	37	38	3-15—9-15	.298	109.80
	1877					.67		SW¼SW¼	35	37	38	3-15—4-28	.005	.50
	1877			38.60				SE¼SW¼	35	37	38	3-15—9-15	.314	115.80
	1877			23.87				NE¼NE¼	36	37	38	3-15—9-15	.194	71.61
	1877				9.14			NE¼NE¼	36	37	38	3-15—6-13	.074	13.71
	1877						1.86	NE¼NE¼	36	37	38	3-15—4-28	.015	1.40
	1877			13.47				NW¼NE¼	36	37	38	3-15—9-15	.110	40.41
	1877				5.67			NW¼NE¼	36	37	38	3-15—6-13	.046	8.51
	1877			36.33				SW¼NE¼	36	37	38	3-15—9-15	.295	108.99

	1877					3.00		SW¼NE¼	36	37	38	3-15—4-28	.024	2.25
	1877			39.46				SE¼NE¼	36	37	38	3-15—9-15	.321	118.38
	1877						.53	SE¼NE¼	36	37	38	3-15—4-28	.004	.40
	1877			2.00				SE¼NW¼	36	37	38	3-15—9-15	.016	6.00
	1877					32.22		SE¼NW¼	36	37	38	3-15—4-28	.262	24.17
	1877			20.53				NE¼SW¼	36	37	38	3-15—9-15	.167	61.59
	1877					15.13		NE¼SW¼	36	37	38	3-15—4-28	.123	11.35
	1877			15.34				NW¼SW¼	36	37	38	3-15—9-15	.125	46.02
	1877						15.81	NW¼SW¼	36	37	38	3-15—4-28	.129	11.86
	1875			35.33				SW¼SW¼	36	37	38	3-15—9-15	.287	105.99

Source—Humboldt River. Ditch—Sloan Dam and Ditch System.

	1872			35.98				SW¼NW¼	31	37	39	3-15—9-15	.293	107.94
	1872						3.88	SW¼NW¼	31	37	39	3-15—4-28	.031	2.91
	1871			34.90				SE¼NW¼	31	37	39	3-15—9-15	.284	104.70
	1871						5.27	SE¼NW¼	31	37	39	3-15—4-28	.043	3.95
	1871			27.20				NE¼SW¼	31	37	39	3-15—9-15	.221	81.60
	1871					3.00		NE¼SW¼	31	37	39	3-15—4-28	.024	2.25
	1871						9.27	NE¼SW¼	31	37	39	3-15—4-28	.075	6.95
	1872			28.97				NW¼SW¼	31	37	39	3-15—9-15	.236	86.91
	1872						11.10	NW¼SW¼	31	37	39	3-15—4-28	.090	8.33
	1876			18.20				SW¼SW¼	31	37	39	3-15—9-15	.148	54.60
	1876					13.47		SW¼SW¼	31	37	39	3-15—4-28	.109	10.10
	1876						4.87	SW¼SW¼	31	37	39	3-15—4-28	.040	3.65
	1876			23.80				SE¼SW¼	31	37	39	3-15—9-15	.193	71.40
	1876					9.93		SE¼SW¼	31	37	39	3-15—4-28	.081	7.45
	1872			23.13				NE¼SE¼	31	37	39	3-15—9-15	.188	69.39
	1872					5.99		NE¼SE¼	31	37	39	3-15—4-28	.049	4.49
	1872						6.26	NE¼SE¼	31	37	39	3-15—4-28	.051	4.70
	1871			29.13				NW¼SE¼	31	37	39	3-15—9-15	.237	87.39
	1871					.73		NW¼SE¼	31	37	39	3-15—4-28	.006	.55
	1871						9.20	NW¼SE¼	31	37	39	3-15—4-28	.075	6.90
	1871			14.60				SW¼SE¼	31	37	39	3-15—9-15	.119	43.80
	1871					9.01		SW¼SE¼	31	37	39	3-15—4-28	.073	6.76
	1871					24.14		SW¼SE¼	31	37	39	3-15—4-28	.196	18.11
	1874			35.92				SE¼SW¼	36	37	38	3-15—9-15	.292	107.76
	1874						4.21	SE¼SW¼	36	37	38	3-15—4-28	.034	3.16
	1873			32.12				NE¼SE¼	36	37	38	3-15—9-15	.261	96.36
	1873						6.02	NE¼SE¼	36	37	38	3-15—4-28	.049	4.52
	1874			37.26				NW¼SE¼	36	37	38	3-15—9-15	.303	111.78
	1874			34.50				SW¼SE¼	36	37	38	3-15—9-15	.281	103.77
	1874				.33			SW¼SE¼	36	57	38	3-15—6-13	.003	.50
	1874						4.21	SW¼SE¼	36	37	38	3-15—4-28	.034	3.16
	1873			31.82				SE¼SE¼	36	37	38	3-15—9-15	.259	95.46
	1873				1.87			SE¼SE¼	36	37	38	3-15—6-13	.015	2.81
	1873						6.31	SE¼SE¼	36	37	38	3-15—4-28	.051	4.73
	1871			25.13				SW¼NE¼	31	37	39	3-15—9-15	.204	75.39
	1871						15.40	SW¼NE¼	31	37	39	3-15—4-28	.125	11.55

Source—Humboldt River. Ditch—Tobin Sloughs.

	1879			6.47				SW¼SE¼	30	37	39	3-15—9-15	.053	19.41
	1879				8.47			SW¼SE¼	30	37	39	3-15—6-13	.069	12.71
	1879			2.93				SE¼SE¼	30	37	39	3-15—9-15	.024	8.79

C. L. Tobin—Continued.

Date of beneficial use: Nat. mdw.	Cult. area	Construction first initiated: Dams	Ditches	Culture—Acres: Harvest crops	Meadow pasture	Willow and sage pasture	Swamp or overflow	Location: Subdivision	Section	Tp.N.	R.E.	Length of season	Duty of water: C.F.S.	Acre-feet
	1879				4.33			SE¼SE¼	30	37	39	3-15—6-13	.035	6.50
	1879			4.93				NE¼NE¼	3	36	38	3-15—9-15	.040	14.79
	1879				7.47			NE¼NE¼	3	36	38	3-15—6-13	.061	11.21
	1879					23.93		NE¼NE¼	3	36	38	3-15—4-28	.195	17.95
	1879			12.61				NE¼NE¼	1	36	38	3-15—9-15	.103	37.83
	1879					5.95		NE¼NE¼	1	36	38	3-15—4-28	.048	4.46
	1879			4.93				NW¼NE¼	1	36	38	3-15—9-15	.040	14.79
	1879				12.93			NW¼NE¼	1	36	38	3-15—6-13	.105	19.40
	1879					10.46		NW¼NE¼	1	36	38	3-15—4-28	.085	7.85
	1879					.40		SW¼NE¼	1	36	38	3-15—4-28	.003	.30
	1879			5.60				NE¼NW¼	1	36	38	3-15—9-15	.046	16.80
	1879				3.80			NE¼NW¼	1	36	38	3-15—6-13	.031	5.70
	1879					14.67		NE¼NW¼	1	36	38	3-15—4-28	.119	11.00
	1879						6.87	NE¼NW¼	1	36	38	3-15—4-28	.056	5.15
	1879			9.00				NW¼NW¼	1	36	38	3-15—9-15	.073	27.00
	1879					28.27		NW¼NW¼	1	36	38	3-15—4-28	.230	21.20
	1879						.33	NW¼NW¼	1	36	38	3-15—4-28	.003	.25
	1879						8.60	SW¼NW¼	1	36	38	3-15—4-28	.070	6.45
	1875			24.20				NE¼NE¼	2	36	38	3-15—9-15	.197	72.60
	1875				4.33			NE¼NE¼	2	36	38	3-15—6-13	.135	6.50
	1875					3.06		NE¼NE¼	2	36	38	3-15—4-28	.030	2.75
	1875						5.20	NE¼NE¼	2	36	38	3-15—4-28	.042	3.90
	1878			3.20				SE¼NE¼	2	36	38	3-15—9-15	.026	9.60
	1878						13.50	SE¼NE¼	2	36	38	3-15—4-28	.110	10.13
	1878			2.00				SW¼NE¼	2	36	38	3-15—9-15	.016	6.00
	1875			28.80				NW¼NE¼	2	36	38	3-15—9-15	.234	86.40
	1875					.33		NW¼NE¼	2	36	38	3-15—4-28	.003	.25
	1875						4.27	NW¼NE¼	2	36	38	3-15—4-28	.035	3.20
	1875			25.20				NE¼NW¼	2	36	38	3-15—9-15	.205	75.60
	1875					3.00		NE¼NW¼	2	36	38	3-15—4-28	.024	2.25
	1875						3.80	NE¼NW¼	2	36	38	3-15—4-28	.031	2.85
	1875			16.20				NW¼NW¼	2	36	38	3-15—9-15	.132	48.60
	1875					3.33		NW¼NW¼	2	36	38	3-15—4-28	.027	2.50
	1875						5.67	NW¼NW¼	2	36	38	3-15—4-28	.046	4.25
	1878						1.53	SE¼NW¼	2	36	38	3-15—4-28	.012	1.15
	1878				28.80			SE¼NE¼	3	36	38	3-15—6-13	.234	43.20
	1878					1.09		SE¼NE¼	3	36	38	3-15—4-28	.009	.82
	1879				27.27			NW¼NE¼	3	36	38	3-15—6-13	.222	40.91
	1879						6.20	NW¼NE¼	3	36	38	3-15—4-28	.050	4-65
	1879						7.20	SW¼NE¼	3	36	38	3-15—4-28	.059	5.40
	1879				30.92			NE¼NW¼	3	36	38	3-15—6-13	.251	46.38
	1879						1.00	NE¼NW¼	3	36	38	3-15—4-28	.008	.75
	1879				7.00			SW¼NW¼	3	36	38	3-15—6-13	.057	1.05
	1879					5.60		SW¼NW¼	5	36	38	3-15—4-28	.045	4.20
	1879						9.13	SW¼NW¼	3	36	38	3-15—4-28	.074	6.85
	1879				3.33			SE¼NW¼	3	36	38	3-15—6-13	.027	5.00
	1879					1.80		SE¼NW¼	3	36	38	3-15—4-28	.015	1.35

	1870						.20	SE¼NW¼	3	36	38	3-15—4-28	.002	.15
	1878				2.87			NE¼SE¼	34	37	38	3-15—6-13	.023	4.31
	1878						36.87	NE¼SE¼	34	37	38	3-15—4-28	.300	27.65
	1878				9.40			NW¼SE¼	34	37	38	3-15—6-13	.076	14.10
	1878						27.90	NW¼SE¼	34	37	38	3-15—4-28	.227	20.93
	1878				33.40			SW¼SE¼	34	37	38	3-15—6-13	.272	50.10
	1878					2.50		SW¼SE¼	34	37	38	3-15—4-28	.020	1.88
	1878				24.77			SE¼SE¼	34	37	38	3-15—6-13	.201	37.16
	1878					6.93		SE¼SE¼	34	37	38	3-15—4-28	.056	5.20
	1878						2.87	SE¼SE¼	34	37	38	3-15—4-28	.023	2.15
	1879					5.87		NE¼NW¼	6	36	39	3-15—4-28	.048	4.40
	1879					15.47		NW¼NW¼	6	36	39	3-15—4-28	.126	11.60
	1879				19.79			NW¼NW¼	3	36	38	3-15—6-13	.161	29.69
	1879						16.87	NW¼NW¼	3	36	38	3-15—4-28	.137	12.65

Claimant—**Taylor and Sheehan.** Proof No. **00120**

Source—**Humboldt River.** Ditch—**Anderson Ditch.**

	1865				33.70			NE¼NW¼	20	36	40	3-15—6-13	.274	50.55
	1865				40.50			NW¼NW¼	20	36	40	3-15—6-13	.329	60.75

Source—**Little Rock Creek.** Ditch—**Rock Creek.**

	1878					.70		SW¼NW¼	32	36	40	3-15—4-28	.006	.53
	1878					22.80		NE¼NW¼	32	36	40	3-15—4-28	.185	17.10
	1878					31.40		NW¼NW¼	32	36	40	3-15—4-28	.255	23.55
	1878			10.65				SE¼SW¼	29	36	40	3-15—9-15	.087	31.95
	1878					15.30		SE¼SW¼	29	36	40	3-15—4-28	.124	11.48
	1878			7.50				SW¼SE¼	29	36	40	3-15—9-15	.061	22.50
	1878					2.75		SW¼SE¼	29	36	40	3-15—4-28	.022	2.06
	1878			21.80				NW¼SE¼	29	36	40	3-15—9-15	.177	65.40
	1878					.40		NW¼SE¼	29	36	40	3-15—4-28	.003	.30
	1878			37.80				NE¼SW¼	29	36	40	3-15—9-15	.307	113.40
	1878			20.45				SE¼NW¼	29	36	40	3-15—9-15	.166	61.35
	1878			25.25				SW¼NW¼	29	36	40	3-15—9-15	.205	75.74
	1878			7.90				NW¼SW¼	29	36	40	3-15—9-15	.064	23.70
	1878					40.05		SW¼SW¼	29	36	40	3-15—4-28	.326	30.04
	1878					.75		SE¼NW¼	32	36	40	3-15—4-28	.006	.56

Source—**Pole Creek.** Ditch—Pole **Creek Ditches.**

	1878					4.30		NE¼NE¼	31	36	40	3-15—4-28	.035	3.23
	1878			4.05				NW¼SW¼	29	36	40	3-15—9-15	.033	12.15
	1878					16.90		NW¼SW¼	29	36	40	3-15—4-28	.137	12.68
	1878					.60		SW¼NW¼	29	36	40	3-15—4-28	.005	.45
	1878					29.75		SE¼SE¼	30	36	40	3-15—4-28	.243	22.31
	1878					37.95		NE¼SE¼	30	36	40	3-15—4-28	.309	28.46
	1878					28.20		SE¼NE¼	30	36	40	3-15—4-28	.229	21.15
	1878					2.45		NE¼NE¼	30	36	40	3-15—4-28	.020	1.84
	1878			8.45				SW¼NE¼	19	36	40	3-15—9-15	.069	25.35
	1878					34.60		SE¼SW¼	19	36	40	3-15—4-28	.281	25.95
	1878					14.30		SW¼SW¼	19	36	40	3-15—4-28	.126	10.73
	1878					16.10		NE¼SW¼	19	36	40	3-15—4-28	.131	12.08
	1878					39.40		NW¼SW¼	19	36	40	3-15—4-28	.320	29.55

Taylor and Sheehan—Continued.
Source—**Humboldt River.** Ditch—**Humboldt Canal.**

Date of beneficial use — Nat. mdw.	Date of beneficial use — Cult. area	Construction first initiated — Dams	Construction first initiated — Ditches	Culture—Acres — Harvest crops	Culture—Acres — Meadow pasture	Culture—Acres — Willow and sage pasture	Culture—Acres — Swamp or overflow	Location — Subdivision	Location — Section	Location — Tp.N.	Location — R.E.	Length of season	Duty of water — C.F.S.	Duty of water — Acre-feet
	1873			13.90				SE¼SW¼	12	36	.39	3-15—9-15	.113	41.70
	1873			5.10				SW¼SW¼	12	36	39	3-15—9-15	.041	15.30
	1873			18.35				NW¼NE¼	13	36	39	3-15—9-15	.149	55.05
	1873			32.80				NE¼NW¼	13	36	39	3-15—9-15	.267	98.40
	1873					.85		NE¼NW¼	13	36	39	3-15—4-28	.007	.64
	1873			1.70				NW¼NW¼	13	36	39	3-15—9-15	.015	5.10
	1873					28.30		NW¼NW¼	13	36	39	3-15—4-28	.230	21.22
	1869			38.25				SW¼NE¼	13	36	39	3-15—9-15	.311	114.75
	1873			21.85				SE¼NE¼	13	36	39	3-15—9-15	.178	65.55
	1873			6.40				SE¼NW¼	13	36	39	3-15—9-15	.052	19.20
	1873					21.80		SE¼NW¼	13	36	39	3-15—4-28	.177	16.35
	1873					23.60		SW¼NW¼	13	36	39	3-15—4-28	.192	17.70
	1868			16.43				NE¼SE¼	13	36	39	3-15—9-15	.134	49.29
	1868			22.87				NE¼SE¼	13	36	39	3-15—9-15	.186	68.61
	1873			13.30				NW¼SE¼	13	36	39	3-15—9-15	.108	39.90
	1873					3.00		NW¼SE¼	13	[illegible]	39	3-15—4-28	.024	2.25
	1868			9.30				SE¼SE¼	13	36	39	3-15—9-15	.076	27.90
	1868			24.48				NW¼SW¼	18	36	40	3-15—9-15	.199	73.44
	1867			5.51				SE¼SW¼	18	36	40	3-15—9-15	.045	16.53
	1873					17.65		NE¼NE¼	13	36	39	3-15—4-28	.143	13.24
	1873					1.20		SE¼NE¼	13	36	39	3-15—4-28	.010	.90
	1867				24.35			NE¼NE¼	19	36	39	3-15—6-13	.198	36.53
	1867				1.85			NW¼NE¼	19	36	40	3-15—6-13	.015	2.78
	1866				33.10			SE¼NW¼	20	36	40	3-15—6-13	.269	49.65
	1866					6.45		SE¼NW¼	20	36	40	3-15—4-28	.052	4.84
	1866				11.10			SW¼NW¼	20	36	40	3-15—6-13	.090	16.65
	1873			4.00				NW¼NE¼	19	36	40	3-15—9-15	.033	12.00
	1867			20.39				SE¼SW¼	18	36	40	3-15—9-15	.166	61.17
	1867					1.35		SW¼SE¼	18	36	40	3-15—4-28	.011	1.01
	1868			21.62				SW¼SW¼	18	36	40	3-15—9-15	.176	64.86
	1868			10.98				SW¼SW¼	18	36	40	3-15—9-15	.089	32.94
	1868			.40				NE¼SW¼	18	36	40	3-15—9-15	.003	1.20
	1867					12.10		NE¼NE¼	19	36	40	3-15—4-28	.098	9.08
	1867					24.20		NW¼NE¼	19	36	40	3-15—4-28	.197	18.15
	1867			12.10				NE¼NW¼	19	36	40	3-15—9-15	.098	36.30
	1867					1.40		NE¼NW¼	19	36	40	3-15—4-28	.011	1.05
	1867					22.85		SE¼NE¼	19	36	40	3-15—4-28	.186	17.14
	1866					25.30		NE¼SE¼	20	36	40	3-15—4-28	.206	18.98
	1866					34.45		NW¼SE¼	20	36	40	3-15—4-28	.280	25.81
	1866				2.85			NE¼SW¼	20	36	40	3-15—6-13	.023	4.28
	1866					16.35		NE¼SW¼	20	36	40	3-15—4-28	.133	12.26
	1866					3.25		NW¼SW¼	20	36	40	3-15—4-28	.026	2.44
	1866					25.15		SW¼NW¼	20	36	40	3-15—4-28	.204	18.86

	1866					13.45		SE¼SE¼	20	36	40	3-15—4-28	.100	10.00
	1866					.70		NW¼SW¼	21	36	40	3-15—4-28	.006	.53
	1866					2.40		SW¼SW¼	21	36	40	3-15—4-28	.020	1.80

Claimant—**Taylor and Sheehan.** Proof No. 00122

Source—**Humboldt River.** Ditch—**Humboldt Canal.**

	1865					2.45		SW¼NE¼	28	36	40	3-15—4-28	.020	1.84
	1865			4.25				SE¼NW¼	28	36	40	3-15—0-15	.035	12.75
	1865					14.30		SE¼NW¼	28	36	40	3-15—4-28	.116	10.73
	1865				12.92			NW¼SE¼	28	36	40	3-15—6-13	.105	19.38
	1865					7.93		NW¼SE¼	28	36	40	3-15—4-28	.064	5.95
	1865						1.20	NW¼SE¼	28	36	40	3-15—4-28	.010	.90
	1865			3.25				NE¼SW¼	28	36	40	3-15—0-15	.026	9.75
	1865				8.30			NE¼SW¼	28	36	40	3-15—6-13	.067	12.45
	1865					.55		NE¼SW¼	28	36	40	3-15—4-28	.004	.41
	1865				18.30			SE¼SE¼	28	36	40	3-15—6-13	.150	27.45
	1865					12.75		SE¼SE¼	28	36	40	3-15—4-28	.104	9.56
	1865				19.25			SW¼SE¼	28	36	40	3-15—6-13	.156	28.88

Source—**Humboldt River.** Ditch—**Pioneer Slough.**

	1870					37.70		NE¼NE¼	28	36	40	3-15—4-28	.307	28.28
	1870					36.75		NW¼NE¼	28	36	40	3-15—4-28	.299	27.56
	1870					35.75		SE¼NE¼	28	36	40	3-15—4-28	.291	26.81
	1870					4.50		SW¼SW¼	22	36	40	3-15—4-28	.037	3.38
	1870			12.50				NE¼NW¼	28	36	40	3-15—0-15	.102	37.50
	1870					17.62		NE¼NW¼	28	36	40	3-15—4-28	.143	13.24
	1870				1.70			NE¼SE¼	28	36	40	3-15—6-13	.014	2.55
	1870					30.66		NE¼SE¼	28	36	40	3-15—4-28	.249	23.00
	1870					3.10		NE¼NE¼	33	36	40	3-15—4-28	.026	2.33
	1870					3.80		SE¼SE¼	28	36	40	3-15—4-28	.031	2.85
	1870					31.10		SW¼NE¼	28	36	40	3-15—4-28	.253	23.33
	1870					6.55		SE¼NW¼	28	36	40	3-15—4-28	.053	4.91
	1870			4.85				NW¼SE¼	28	36	40	3-15—0-15	.039	14.55
	1870					3.45		NW¼SE¼	28	36	40	3-15—4-28	.028	2.59

Claimant—**Paul A. Pinson.** Proof No. 00124

Source—**Humboldt River.** Ditch—**Louis Lay Dam.**

	1885						7.94	SW¼SW¼	25	36	40	3-15—4-28	.065	5.96
	1885						7.50	SE¼SW¼	25	36	40	3-15—4-28	.061	5.63
	1885					11.70		SW¼SE¼	25	36	40	3-15—4-28	.095	8.78
	1885					2.29		NW¼SE¼	25	36	40	3-15—4-28	.018	1.72
	1885					17.92		NE¼SE¼	25	36	40	3-15—4-28	.146	13.44
	1885				4.07			SE¼SE¼	25	36	40	3-15—6-13	.033	6.11
	1885					4.00		SE¼SE¼	25	36	40	3-15—4-28	.033	3.00
	1885					24.97		NW¼SW¼	30	36	41	3-15—4-28	.203	18.73
	1885					2.72		NE¼SW¼	30	36	41	3-15—4-28	.022	2.04
	1885					6.88		SW¼NW¼	30	36	41	3-15—4-28	.056	5.16
	1885					21.18		SE¼NW¼	30	36	41	3-15—4-28	.172	15.89
	1885					5.43		NE¼NW¼	30	36	41	3-15—4-28	.014	4.07

Paul A. Pinson—Continued.
Source—**Humboldt River.** Ditch—**Pinson Dam and Ditch System.**

Date of beneficial use: Nat. mdw.	Date of beneficial use: Cult. area	Construction first initiated: Dams	Construction first initiated: Ditches	Culture—Acres: Harvest crops	Culture—Acres: Meadow pasture	Culture—Acres: Willow and sage pasture	Culture—Acres: Swamp or overflow	Location: Subdivision	Location: Section	Location: Tp. N.	Location: R. E.	Length of season	Duty of water: C. F. S.	Duty of water: Acre-feet
	1900					3.13		SW¼NE¼	30	36	41	3-15—4-28	.025	2.35
	1900				10.00			NW¼NE¼	30	36	41	3-15—6-13	.081	7.50
	1900					10.93		NW¼NE¼	30	36	41	3-15—4-28	.089	8.20
	1900				.37			NE¼NE¼	30	36	41	3-15—6-13	.003	.56
	1900					9.84		SW¼SE¼	19	36	41	3-15—4-28	.080	7.38
	1900				13.77			SE¼SE¼	19	36	41	3-15—6-13	.112	20.66
	1900					1.83		SE¼SE¼	19	36	41	3-15—4-28	.015	1.37
	1900				5.60			NE¼SE¼	19	36	41	3-15—6-13	.046	8.40
	1900				13.08			NW¼SW¼	20	36	41	3-15—6-13	.106	19.62
	1900					12.05		NW¼SW¼	20	36	41	3-15—4-28	.098	9.04
	1900				11.17			SW¼SW¼	20	36	41	3-15—6-13	.091	16.76
	1900					4.29		SW¼SW¼	20	36	41	3-15—4-28	.035	3.22
	1900				4.93			NE¼SW¼	20	36	41	3-15—6-13	.040	7.40
	1900					25.04		NE¼SW¼	20	36	41	3-15—4-28	.204	18.78
	1900				9.39			SE¼SW¼	20	36	41	3-15—6-13	.076	14.09
	1900					3.05		SE¼SW¼	20	36	41	3-15—4-28	.025	2.29
	1892			10.31				NW¼SE¼	20	36	41	3-15—9-15	.084	30.93
	1892					13.90		NW¼SE¼	20	36	41	3-15—4-28	.113	10.43
	1892			23.08				NE¼SE¼	20	36	41	3-15—9-15	.188	69.24
	1892					3.70		NE¼SE¼	20	36	41	3-15—4-28	.030	2.78
	1892			17.72				SW¼SE¼	20	36	41	3-15—9-15	.144	53.16
	1892					4.59		SW¼SE¼	20	36	41	3-15—4-28	.037	3.44
	1892			12.12				SE¼SE¼	20	36	41	3-15—9-15	.099	36.36
	1892					10.89		SE¼SE¼	20	36	41	3-15—4-28	.089	8.17
	1892			7.50				NE¼SW¼	21	36	41	3-15—9-15	.061	22.50
	1892					1.58		NE¼SW¼	21	36	41	3-15—4-28	.013	1.19
	1892			24.62				NW¼SW¼	21	36	41	3-15—9-15	.200	73.86
	1892					4.12		NW¼SW¼	21	36	41	3-15—4-28	.033	3.09
	1892			.20				SW¼SW¼	21	36	41	3-15—9-15	.002	.60
	1892					5.32		SW¼SW¼	21	36	41	3-15—4-28	.043	3.99
	1892			7.80				SE¼NW¼	21	36	41	3-15—9-15	.063	23.40
	1892					1.49		SE¼NW¼	21	36	41	3-15—4-28	.012	1.12
	1892			.98				SW¼NW¼	21	36	41	3-15—9-15	.008	2.94
	1892			20.02				NW¼NE¼	21	36	41	3-15—9-15	.163	60.06
	1892			34.09				SW¼NE¼	21	36	41	3-15—9-15	.277	102.27
	1892					.20		SW¼NE¼	21	36	41	3-15—4-28	.002	.15
	1892			1.44				SE¼NE¼	21	36	41	3-15—9-15	.012	4.32
	1892					5.75		SE¼NE¼	21	36	41	3-15—4-28	.047	4.31
	1892			3.35				NE¼NE¼	21	36	41	3-15—9-15	.027	10.05
	1892					28.58		NE¼NE¼	21	36	41	3-15—4-28	.208	19.19
	1892			3.05				NW¼SE¼	21	36	41	3-15—9-15	.025	9.15

Claimant—**J. J. Trigueiro.** Proof No. 00125
Source—**Humboldt River.** Ditch—**Water Wheel.**

1901	3.50			NW¼NW¼	10	28	32	3-15—9-15	.029	10.77
1901			.36	NW¼NW¼	10	28	32	3-15—4-28	.003	.27
1901	12.09			NE¼NW¼	10	28	32	3-15—9-15	.098	36.27
1901		1.39		NE¼NW¼	10	28	32	3-15—6-13	.011	2.09
1901			3.90	NE¼NW¼	10	28	32	3-15—4-28	.032	2.93
1901	5.09			SW¼NW¼	10	28	32	3-15—9-15	.041	15.27
1901			3.70	SW¼NW¼	10	28	32	3-15—4-28	.030	27.75
1901			2.48	SE¼NW¼	10	28	32	3-15—4-28	.020	1.86
1901			26.41	NW¼NE¼	10	28	32	3-15—4-28	.215	19.81
1901			29.14	NE¼NE¼	10	28	32	3-15—4-28	.237	21.86
1901			20.57	NW¼SW¼	10	28	32	3-15—4-28	.177	15.43
1901			16.36	SW¼SW¼	10	28	32	3-15—4-28	.133	12.27
1901	2.93			SE¼SW¼	3	28	32	3-15—9-15	.024	8.79
1901			12.44	SW¼SE¼	3	28	32	3-15—4-28	.101	9.33
1901			1.01	SE¼SE¼	2	28	32	3-15—4-28	.008	.76
1901			2.26	SW¼SW¼	2	28	32	3-15—4-28	.018	1.70
1901			1.20	NW¼NW¼	11	28	32	3-15—4-28	.010	.90
1901			1.49	SW¼NW¼	11	28	32	3-15—4-28	.012	1.12

Claimant—**Hazel D. Smith.** Proof No. 00127
Source—**Humboldt River.** Ditch—**Miller & Lux Upper Dam.**

1871		5.72		SW¼SE¼	19	36	38	3-15—6-13	.046	8.58
1871			1.59	SW¼SE¼	19	36	38	3-15—4-28	.013	1.19
1871		10.91		NW¼NE¼	30	36	38	3-15—6-13	.089	16.37
1871			6.49	NW¼NE¼	30	36	38	3-15—4-28	.053	4.87

Claimant—**David Giroux.** Proof No. 00130
Source—**Humboldt River.** Ditch—**Gasoline Pump.**

1901	5.66			SE¼SE¼	19	36	38	3-15—9-15	.046	16.98
1901		3.19		SE¼SE¼	19	36	38	3-15—6-13	.026	4.79
1901	.28			NE¼NE¼	30	36	38	3-15—9-15	.002	.84
1901			.94	NE¼NE¼	30	36	38	3-15—4-28	.008	.71

Claimant—**Golconda Cattle Co.** Proof No. 00131
Source—**Little Rock Creek.** Ditch—**Little Rock Creek System.**

1874	12.72			NW¼NW¼	6	34	40	3-15—9-15	.103	38.16
1874			1.05	NW¼NW¼	6	34	40	3-15—4-28	.009	.79
1875	.87			SW¼NW¼	6	34	40	3-15—9-15	.007	2.61
1875	1.45			NW¼SW¼	6	34	40	3-15—9-15	.012	4.35
1875	24.17			NW¼NE¼	6	34	40	3-15—9-15	.197	72.51
1875	14.60			NE¼SW¼	6	34	40	3-15—9-15	.119	43.80

Golconda Cattle Co.—Continued.

Date of beneficial use: Nat. mdw.	Date of beneficial use: Cult. area	Construction first initiated: Dams	Construction first initiated: Ditches	Culture—Acres: Harvest crops	Culture—Acres: Meadow pasture	Culture—Acres: Willow and sage pasture	Culture—Acres: Swamp or overflow	Location: Subdivision	Location: Section	Location: Tp.N.	Location: R.E.	Length of season	Duty of water: C.F.S.	Duty of water: Acre-feet
	1875			4.37				SE¼NE¼	6	34	40	3-15—9-15	.036	13.11
	1874			16.40				NE¼NE¼	6	34	40	3-15—9-15	.133	49.20
	1874					3.50		NE¼NE¼	6	34	40	3-15—4-28	.028	2.63
	1874			29.47				NE¼NW¼	6	34	40	3-15—9-15	.240	88.41
	1868			16.22				SE¼NW¼	6	34	40	3-15—9-15	.132	48.66
	1873			25.85				SW¼NE¼	6	34	40	3-15—9-15	.210	77.55
	1876			19.78				NW¼NW¼	5	34	40	3-15—9-15	.161	59.34
	1876			7.55				SW¼NW¼	5	34	40	3-15—9-15	.061	22.65
	1876			9.20				SE¼NW¼	5	34	40	3-15—9-15	.075	27.60
	1876			35.75				NE¼NW¼	5	34	40	3-15—9-15	.291	107.25
	1878			20.62				NW¼NE¼	5	34	40	3-15—9-15	.168	61.86
	1878					6.50		NW¼NE¼	5	34	40	3-15—4-28	.053	4.88
	1878			8.55				NE¼NE¼	5	34	40	3-15—9-15	.070	25.65
	1878					1.55		NE¼NE¼	5	34	40	3-15—4-28	.013	1.16
	1874			10.82				SE¼SW¼	31	35	40	3-15—9-15	.088	32.46
	1874			31.80				SW¼SE¼	31	35	40	3-15—9-15	.259	95.40
	1874			15.55				NE¼SE¼	31	35	40	3-15—9-15	.126	46.65
	1874			40.00				SE¼SE¼	31	35	40	3-15—9-15	.325	120.00
	1876			40.00				SW¼SW¼	32	35	40	3-15—9-15	.325	120.00
	1876			40.00				SE¼SW¼	32	35	40	3-15—9-15	.325	120.00
	1880			.55				NW¼SW¼	32	35	40	3-15—9-15	.004	1.65
	1880			27.30				SW¼SE¼	32	35	40	3-15—9-15	.222	81.90
	1880					4.57		SW¼SE¼	32	35	40	3-15—4-28	.037	3.43
	1880			27.27				SE¼SE¼	32	35	40	3-15—9-15	.222	81.81
	1880					5.30		SE¼SE¼	32	35	40	3-15—4-28	.043	3.98
	1880			20.97				SW¼SW¼	33	35	40	3-15—9-15	.170	62.91
	1880						15.55	SW¼SW¼	33	35	40	3-15—4-28	.126	11.66
	1875					9.65		NW¼NE¼	1	34	39	3-15—4-28	.078	7.24
	1875					1.00		SW¼NE¼	1	34	39	3-15—4-28	.008	.75
	1875					12.22		NE¼NE¼	1	34	39	3-15—4-28	.099	9.17
	1875					2.95		SE¼NE¼	1	34	39	3-15—4-28	.024	2.21

Claimant—**Estate of Henry Bain.** Proof No. 00132

Source—**Little Rock Creek.** Ditch—**South Side Ditch.**

Nat. mdw.	Cult. area	Dams	Ditches	Harvest crops	Meadow pasture	Willow and sage pasture	Swamp or overflow	Subdivision	Section	Tp.N.	R.E.	Length of season	C.F.S.	Acre-feet
	1877			2.92				NE¼NE¼	33	35	40	3-15—9-15	.024	8.76
	1884			6.13				SE¼NE¼	33	35	40	3-15—9-15	.050	18.30
	1868			6.91				SW¼NE¼	33	35	40	3-15—9-15	.056	20.73
	1882			12.56				NW¼SE¼	33	35	40	3-15—9-15	.102	37.68
	1882			4.49				NE¼SW¼	33	35	40	3-15—9-15	.037	13.47
	1884			1.62				SE¼SW¼	33	35	40	3-15—9-15	.013	4.86
	1884					7.12		SE¼SW¼	33	35	40	3-15—4-28	.059	5.34
	1884			6.67				NW¼SW¼	33	35	40	3-15—9-15	.054	20.01
	1884					.80		NW¼SW¼	33	35	40	3-15—4-28	.007	.60
	1876			6.13				SE¼NE¼	33	35	40	3-15—9-15	.050	18.39

Source—**Little Rock Creek.** Ditch—**North Side Ditch.**

	1877			16.20				NE¼NE¼	33	35	40	3-15—9-15	.132	48.60
	1877				1.52			NE¼NE¼	33	35	40	3-15—6-13	.012	2.28
	1876			5.00				NW¼NE¼	33	35	40	3-15—9-15	.041	15.00
	1876			3.40				SE¼NE¼	33	35	40	3-15—9-15	.028	10.20
	1876					.17		SE¼NE¼	33	35	40	3-15—4-28	.001	.18
	1868			17.11				SW¼NE¼	33	35	40	3-15—9-15	.139	51.33
	1882			2.94				NW¼SE¼	33	35	40	3-15—9-15	.034	8.82
	1882			9.95				NE¼SW¼	33	35	40	3-15—9-15	.081	29.85
	1882					1.10		NE¼SW¼	33	35	40	3-15—4-28	.009	.83

Claimant—**A. E. Kent and Co., Inc.** Proof No. 00133

Source—**Little Rock Creek.** Ditch—**Little Rock Creek System.**

	1880			1.48				NE¼SE¼	32	35	40	3-15—9-15	.012	4.44
	1880			1.60				NW¼SE¼	32	35	40	3-15—9-15	.013	4.80
	1880			23.99				NE¼SW¼	32	35	40	3-15—9-15	.196	71.97
	1880			28.59				NW¼SW¼	32	35	40	3-15—9-15	.232	85.77

Claimant—**Mrs. James Marr.** Proof No. 00134

Source—**Humboldt River.** Ditch—**Water Wheel.**

	1886					30.41		NW¼SW¼	20	36	38	3-15—4-28	.247	22.81
	1886					5.21		NE¼SE¼	19	36	38	3-15—4-28	.042	3.91
	1886					9.02		SE¼SE¼	19	36	38	3-15—4-28	.073	6.77
	1886					1.78		SW¼SE¼	19	36	38	3-15—4-28	.014	1.34

BATTLE MOUNTAIN DISTRICT

Claimant—**Ellison Ranching Co.** Proof No. 00151

Source—**Humboldt River.** Ditch—**Aemes Dam.**

Date of beneficial use: Nat. mdw.	Cult. area	Construction first initiated: Dams	Ditches	Culture—Acres: Harvest crops	Meadow pasture	Willow and sage pasture	Swamp or overflow	Location: Subdivision	Section	Tp.N.	R.E.	Length of season	Duty of water: C.F.S.	Acre-feet
1876	1876					2.14		SE¼SW¼	10	35	42	3-15—4-28	.017	1.61
1876	1876			36.60				SE¼SW¼	10	35	42	3-15—9-15	.298	109.80
1876	1876			31.72				NW¼SW¼	10	35	42	3-15—9-15	.258	95.16
1876	1876					7.83		NW¼SW¼	10	35	42	3-15—4-28	.064	5.87
1876	1876					.79		SW¼SW¼	10	35	42	3-15—4-28	.006	.59
1876	1876			39.50				SW¼SW¼	10	35	42	3-15—9-15	.321	118.50
1876	1876			29.15				SW¼NE¼	14	35	42	3-15—9-15	.237	87.45
1876	1876					8.07		SW¼NE¼	14	35	42	3-15—4-28	.066	6.05
1876	1876						.88	SW¼NE¼	14	35	42	3-15—4-28	.007	.66
1876	1876			2.14				SE¼NE¼	14	35	42	3-15—9-15	.017	6.42
1876	1876						.83	NW¼NE¼	14	35	42	3-15—4-28	.007	.62
1876	1876						9.25	NE¼SE¼	14	35	42	3-15—4-28	.075	6.94
1876	1876			5.22				NE¼SE¼	14	35	42	3-15—9-15	.042	15.66
1876	1876					19.63		NE¼SE¼	14	35	42	3-15—4-28	.160	14.72
1876	1876					37.98		SE¼SE¼	14	35	42	3-15—4-28	.309	28.60
1876	1876					12.54		NW¼SE¼	14	35	42	3-15—4-28	.102	9.41
1876	1876			23.68				NW¼SE¼	14	35	42	3-15—9-15	.193	71.04
1876	1876			35.49				NE¼NE¼	3	35	42	3-15—9-15	.289	106.47
1876	1876						5.60	NE¼NE¼	3	35	42	3-15—4-28	.046	4.20
1876	1876			36.91				SE¼NE¼	3	35	42	3-15—9-15	.300	110.73
1876	1876						2.42	SE¼NE¼	3	35	42	3-15—4-28	.020	1.82
1876	1876						.25	SE¼NE¼	3	35	42	3-15—4-28	.002	.19
1876	1876			35.05				NW¼NE¼	3	35	42	3-15—9-15	.285	105.15
1876	1876					3.05		NW¼NE¼	3	35	42	3-15—4-28	.025	2.29
1876	1876						2.83	NW¼NE¼	3	35	42	3-15—4 28	.023	2.12
1876	1876			29.11				SW¼NE¼	3	35	42	3-15—9-15	.237	87.33
1876	1876				5.68			SW¼NE¼	3	35	42	3-15—6-13	.046	8.52
1876	1876					2.64		SW¼NE¼	3	35	42	3-15—4-28	.021	1.98
1876	1876			37.61				NE¼SE¼	3	35	42	3-15—9-15	.306	112.83
1876	1880				32.58			SW¼SE¼	14	36	42	3-15—6-13	.265	48.87
1876	1880					6.52		SW¼SE¼	14	35	42	3-15—6-13	.053	1.13
1876	1876			39.54				SE¼NE¼	10	35	42	3-15—9-15	.321	118.62
1876	1876			36.44				NW¼NE¼	10	35	42	3-15—9-15	.296	109.32
1876	1876			40.04				SW¼NE¼	10	35	42	3-15—9-15	.326	120.12
1876	1876			37.68				NE¼NW¼	10	35	42	3-15—9-15	.306	113.04
1876	1876						2.12	NE¼NW¼	10	35	42	3-15—4-28	.017	1.59
1876	1876			40.65				SE¼NW¼	10	35	42	3-15—9-15	.330	121.95
1876	1876			38.28				NW¼NW¼	10	35	42	3-15—9-15	.311	114.84
1876	1876			38.94				SW¼NW¼	10	35	42	3-15—9-15	.317	116.82
1876	1876			36.00				NE¼SE¼	10	35	42	3-15—9-15	.293	108.00
1876	1876					2.86		NE¼SE¼	10	35	42	3-15—4-28	.023	2.15

5[69]

1876	1876			40.76				SE¼SE¼	10	35	42	3-15—9-15	.331	122.28
1876	1876			40.95				NW¼SE¼	10	35	42	3-15—9-15	.333	122.85
1876	1876			38.14				SW¼SE¼	10	35	42	3-15—9-15	.310	114.42
1876	1876					1.87		SW¼SE¼	10	35	42	3-15—4-28	.015	1.40
1876	1876			38.93				NE¼SW¼	10	35	42	3-15—9-15	.317	116.79
1876	1876					.08		NE¼SW¼	10	35	42	3-15—4-28	.001	.06
	1876					.48		NE¼SE¼	3	35	42	3-15—4-28	.004	.36
	1876			37.81				SE¼SE¼	3	35	42	3-15—9-15	.307	113.43
	1876			35.39				NW¼SE¼	3	35	42	3-15—9-15	.288	106.17
	1876					1.68		NW¼SE¼	3	35	42	3-15—4-28	.014	1.26
	1876			38.25				SW¼SE¼	3	35	42	3-15—9-15	.311	114.75
	1876					2.00		NE¼NW¼	14	35	42	3-15—4-28	.016	1.50
	1876						33.30	NE¼NW¼	14	35	42	3-15—4-28	.271	24.98
	1876				2.07			NE¼NW¼	14	35	42	3-15—6-13	.017	3.11
	1876			1.62				NE¼NW¼	14	35	42	3-15—9-15	.013	4.86
	1876			20.07				SE¼NW¼	14	35	42	3-15—9-15	.163	60.21
	1876					5.43		SE¼NW¼	14	35	42	3-15—4-28	.044	4.07
	1876						12.10	SE¼NW¼	14	35	42	3-15—4-28	.098	9.08
	1876				2.47			SE¼NW¼	14	35	42	3-15—6-13	.020	3.71
	1876						32.77	NW¼NW¼	14	35	42	3-15—4-28	.266	24.58
	1876			4.85				NW¼NW¼	14	35	42	3-15—9-15	.039	14.55
	1876					1.55		NW¼NW¼	14	35	42	3-15—4-28	.013	1.16
	1876					17.18		SW¼NW¼	14	35	42	3-15—4-28	.140	12.89
	1876						13.10	SW¼NW¼	14	35	42	3-15—4-28	.107	9.83
	1876				4.22			SW¼NW¼	14	35	42	3-15—6-13	.034	6.33
	1876			3.98				SW¼NW¼	14	35	42	3-15—9-15	.032	11.94
	1876			.92				NE¼NE¼	15	35	42	3-15—9-15	.007	2.76
	1876						.99	NE¼NE¼	15	35	42	3-15—4-28	.008	.74
	1876					.83		SE¼NE¼	15	35	42	3-15—4-28	.007	.62
	1876						.50	SE¼NE¼	15	35	42	3-15—4-28	.004	.38
Source—**Humboldt River.** Ditch—**Gonzales Slough.**														
1880	1880			1.25				NE¼NW¼	2	35	42	3-15—9-15	.010	3.75
1880	1880			1.52				SE¼NW¼	2	35	42	3-15—9-15	.012	4.56
1880	1880			41.18				NW¼NW¼	2	35	42	3-15—9-15	.335	123.54
1880	1880			39.77				SW¼NW¼	2	35	42	3-15—9-15	.323	119.31
1880	1880			1.20				SE¼SW¼	2	35	42	3-15—9-15	.010	3.60
1880	1880			37.40				SW¼SW¼	2	35	42	3-15—9-15	.304	112.20
1880	1880				.44			SW¼SW¼	2	35	42	3-15—6-13	.004	.66
1880	1880				35.22			NE¼NW¼	3	35	42	3-15—6-13	.286	52.83
1880	1880			1.59				NE¼NW¼	3	35	42	3-15—9-15	.013	4.77
1880	1880					2.16		NE¼NW¼	3	35	42	3-15—4-28	.018	1.62
1880	1880			13.47				SE¼NW¼	3	35	42	3-15—9-15	.110	40.41
1880	1880				14.09			SE¼NW¼	3	35	42	3-15—6-13	.115	21.14
1880	1880					5.69		SE¼NW¼	3	35	42	3-15—4-28	.046	4.27
1880	1880				29.36			NW¼NW¼	3	35	42	3-15—6-13	.239	44.04
1880	1880				33.46			SW¼NW¼	3	35	42	3-15—6-13	.272	50.19
1880	1880						1.65	SW¼NW¼	3	35	42	3-15—4-28	.013	1.24
1880	1880					.08		SW¼NW¼	3	35	42	3-15—4-28	.001	.06
1880	1880			39.50				NE¼SW¼	3	35	42	3-15—9-15	.321	118.50
1880	1880			39.60				SE¼SW¼	3	35	42	3-15—9-15	.322	118.80
1880	1880			2.33				NW¼SW¼	3	35	42	3-15—9-15	.019	6.99
1880	1880				29.87			NW¼SW¼	3	35	42	3-15—6-13	.243	44.81

Ellison Ranching Co.—Continued.

Date of beneficial use: Nat. mdw.	Date of beneficial use: Cult. area	Construction first initiated: Dams	Construction first initiated: Ditches	Culture—Acres: Harvest crops	Culture—Acres: Meadow pasture	Culture—Acres: Willow and sage pasture	Culture—Acres: Swamp or overflow	Location: Subdivision	Location: Section	Location: Tp.N.	Location: R.E.	Length of season	Duty of water: C.F.S.	Duty of water: Acre-feet
1880	1880	...	...	...	...	...	3.45	NW¼SW¼	3	35	42	3-15—4-28	.028	2.59
1880	1880	...	...	14.86	...	...	...	SW¼SW¼	3	35	42	3-15—9-15	.121	43.98
1880	1880	...	...	...	22.70	...	...	SW¼SW¼	3	35	42	3-15—6-13	.185	34.05
1880	1880	...	...	36.33	...	...	...	NE¼NE¼	10	35	42	3-15—9-15	.295	108.99

Source—**Humboldt River.** Ditch—**Outside Slough.**

...	1887	...	...	...	5.52	...	...	NE¼NE¼	16	35	42	3-15—6-13	.045	8.28

Claimant—**The A. E. Kent Co.** Proof No. 00151

Source—**Humboldt River.** Ditch—**Outside Slough.**

Nat. mdw.	Cult. area	Dams	Ditches	Harvest crops	Meadow pasture	Willow and sage pasture	Swamp or overflow	Subdivision	Section	Tp.N.	R.E.	Length of season	C.F.S.	Acre-feet
*1886	1887	...	...	...	20.15	...	...	SE¼NE¼	21	35	42	3-15—6-13	.164	30.23
*1886	1887	...	...	...	...	16.15	...	SE¼NE¼	21	35	42	3-15—4-28	.131	12.11
*1886	1887	...	...	...	38.31	...	...	NE¼NW¼	21	35	42	3-15—6-13	.311	57.47
*1886	1887	...	...	...	3.45	...	...	NW¼NW¼	21	35	42	3-15—6-13	.028	5.18
*1886	1887	...	...	...	14.57	...	...	SE¼NW¼	21	35	42	3-15—6-13	.118	21.86
*1886	1887	...	...	...	22.17	...	...	NE¼SE¼	21	35	42	3-15—6-13	.180	33.26
*1886	1887	...	...	...	...	14.18	...	NE¼SE¼	21	35	42	3-15—4-28	.115	10.64
*1886	1887	...	...	...	28.60	...	...	NW¼SE¼	21	35	42	3-15—6-13	.233	42.90
*1886	1887	...	...	...	3.50	...	...	SW¼SE¼	21	35	42	3-15—6-13	.028	5.25
*1886	1887	...	...	...	21.97	...	...	SE¼SE¼	21	35	42	3-15—6-13	.179	32.96
*1886	1887	...	...	...	...	1.07	...	SE¼SE¼	21	35	42	3-15—4-28	.009	.80
*1886	1887	...	...	...	3.50	...	...	SW¼SE¼	21	35	42	3-15—6-13	.028	5.25
*1886	1887	...	...	...	...	...	21.30	SE¼SE¼	16	35	42	3-15—4-28	.173	15.98
*1886	1887	...	...	...	39.30	...	...	NE¼SW¼	16	35	42	3-15—6-13	.320	58.95
*1886	1887	...	...	...	26.85	...	...	NW¼SW¼	16	35	42	3-15—6-13	.218	40.28
*1886	1887	...	...	...	17.90	...	...	SW¼SW¼	16	35	42	3-15—6-13	.146	26.85
*1886	1887	...	...	...	39.64	...	...	SE¼SW¼	16	35	42	3-15—6-13	.322	59.46
*1886	1887	...	...	...	1.20	...	...	NE¼NE¼	21	35	42	3-15—6-13	.010	1.86
*1886	1887	...	...	...	...	10.16	...	NE¼NE¼	21	35	42	3-15—4-28	.083	7.62
*1886	1887	...	...	...	...	...	25.12	NE¼NE¼	21	35	42	3-15—4-28	.204	18.84
*1886	1887	...	...	...	34.09	...	...	NW¼NE¼	21	36	42	3-15—6-13	.277	51.14
*1886	1887	...	...	...	...	3.87	...	NW¼NE¼	21	35	42	3-15—4-28	.031	2.90
*1886	1887	...	...	...	38.07	...	...	SW¼NE¼	21	36	42	3-15—6-13	.314	58.01
*1886	1887	...	...	...	...	...	27.79	NE¼NE¼	16	35	42	3-15—4-28	.226	20.84
*1886	1887	...	...	...	...	...	38.80	NW¼NE¼	16	35	42	3-15—4-28	.315	29.10
*1886	1887	...	...	...	...	...	39.46	SE¼NE¼	16	35	42	3-15—4-28	.321	29.60
*1886	1887	...	...	...	...	6.93	...	SW¼NE¼	16	35	42	3-15—4-28	.056	5.20
*1886	1887	...	...	...	...	...	30.78	SW¼NE¼	16	35	42	3-15—4-28	.250	23.09
*1886	1887	...	...	...	5.20	...	...	NE¼NW¼	16	36	42	3-15—6-13	.042	7.80
*1886	1887	...	...	...	...	...	1.02	NE¼NW¼	16	35	42	3-15—4-28	.013	1.22
*1886	1887	...	...	...	3.77	...	...	NW¼NW¼	16	35	42	3-15—6-13	.031	5.66
*1886	1887	...	...	7.32	...	...	...	SW¼NW¼	16	35	42	3-15—9-15	.060	21.96
*1886	1887	...	...	...	21.50	...	...	SW¼NW¼	16	35	42	3-15—6-13	.175	32.25
*1886	1887	...	...	...	34.46	...	...	SE¼NW¼	16	35	42	3-15—6-13	.280	51.69
*1886	1887	...	...	...	...	...	3.50	SE¼NW¼	16	35	42	3-15—4-28	.028	2.63

*1886	1887						30.34	NE¼SE¼	16	35	42	3-15—4-28	.329	20.51
*1886	1887				12.28			NW¼SE¼	16	35	42	3-15—6-13	.100	18.42
*1886	1887						24.44	NW¼SE¼	16	35	42	3-15—4-28	.199	18.33
*1886	1887				20.43			SW¼SE¼	16	35	42	3-15—6-13	.166	30.65
*1886	1887					13.27		SW¼SE¼	16	35	42	3-15—4-28	.108	9.95
*1886	1887						3.62	SW¼SE¼	16	35	42	3-15—4-28	.029	2.72
*1886	1887					8.50		SE¼SE¼	16	35	42	3-15—4-28	.069	6.38

*First irrigation in flood season from Wilcox Dam, NE¼NE¼, sec. 30, T. 34 N, R. 44 E.

Claimant—**C. H. Duborg.** Proof No. 00153
Source—**Humboldt River.** Ditch—**Cluro.**

	1883			4.58				SE¼SE¼	7	31	50	3-15—9-15	.037	13.74
	1883			15.58				SW¼SW¼	8	31	50	3-15—9-15	.127	46.74
	1883			12.79				SE¼SW¼	8	31	50	3-15—9-15	.104	38.37
	1883			10.40				SW¼SE¼	8	31	50	3-15—9-15	.085	31.20
	1883			7.49				NW¼NW¼	16	31	50	3-15—9-15	.061	22.47
	1883			.90				SW¼NW¼	16	31	50	3-15—9-15	.007	2.70
	1883			4.50				NE¼NW¼	17	31	50	3-15—9-15	.037	13.50
	1883					3.22		NE¼NW¼	17	31	50	3-15—4-28	.026	2.42
	1883			1.90				SE¼NW¼	17	31	50	3-15—9-15	.015	5.70
	1883			16.64				NW¼NE¼	17	31	50	3-15—9-15	.135	49.92
	1883					6.36		NW¼NE¼	17	31	50	3-15—4-28	.056	5.15
	1883			22.88				NE¼NE¼	17	31	50	3-15—9-15	.186	68.64
	1883			35.88				SW¼NE¼	17	31	50	3-15—9-15	.292	107.64
	1883			35.60				SE¼NE¼	17	31	50	3-15—9-15	.289	106.80

Claimant—**Humboldt Land & Cattle Co.** Proof No. 00154
Source—**Humboldt River.** Ditch—**Rose Dam.**

	1873						8.20	NW¼NW¼	36	33	48	3-15—4-28	.067	6.15
	1873						1.88	SW¼NW¼	36	33	48	3-15—4-28	.015	1.41
	1873						34.92	NW¼NE¼	36	33	48	3-15—4-28	.284	26.19
	1873						33.40	SW¼NE¼	36	33	48	3-15—4-28	.272	25.05
	1873						29.92	NW¼SE¼	36	33	48	3-15—4-28	.243	22.44
	1873						40.00	NE¼SE¼	36	33	48	3-15—4-28	.325	30.00
	1873						19.14	SW¼SE¼	36	33	48	3-15—4-28	.156	14.36
	1873						39.00	SE¼SE¼	36	33	48	3-15—4-28	.317	29.25
	1873						33.72	NE¼NE¼	1	32	48	3-15—4-28	.274	25.29
	1873					5.20		SW¼NW¼	6	32	49	3-15—4-28	.042	3.90
	1873						9.84	SW¼NW¼	6	32	49	3-15—4-28	.080	7.38
	1873					8.60		NW¼SW¼	6	32	49	3-15—4-28	.070	6.45
	1873						18.49	NW¼SW¼	6	32	49	3-15—4-28	.150	13.87
	1873						25.50	SE¼SW¼	6	32	49	3-15—4-28	.207	19.12
	1873					1.60		SW¼SW¼	6	32	49	3-15—4-28	.013	1.20
	1873						25.36	SW¼SW¼	6	32	49	3-15—4-28	.206	19.02
	1873						30.50	SW¼SE¼	6	32	49	3-15—4-28	.248	22.88
	1873					5.26		SE¼NE¼	1	32	48	3-15—4-28	.043	3.95
	1873						24.50	SE¼NE¼	1	32	48	3-15—4-28	.109	18.38
	1873						1.70	SW¼NE¼	1	32	48	3-15—4-28	.014	1.28
	1873					4.04		NE¼SE¼	1	32	48	3-15—4-28	.033	3.03
	1873						28.16	NE¼SE¼	1	32	48	3-15—4-28	.229	21.12
	1873						31.46	SE¼SE¼	1	32	48	3-15—4-28	.256	23.60

Humboldt Land and Cattle Co.—Continued.

Date of beneficial use — Nat. mdw.	Date of beneficial use — Cult. area	Construction first initiated — Dams	Construction first initiated — Ditches	Culture—Acres — Harvest crops	Culture—Acres — Meadow pasture	Culture—Acres — Willow and sage pasture	Culture—Acres — Swamp or overflow	Location — Subdivision	Location — Section	Location — Tp.N.	Location — R.E.	Length of season	Duty of water — C.F.S.	Duty of water — Acre-feet
	1873						40.00	NW¼NE¼	7	32	49	3-15—4-28	.325	30.00
	1873					22.52		NW¼SE¼	7	32	49	3-15—4-28	.183	16.89
	1873					6.22		SE¼SE¼	7	32	49	3-15—4-28	.051	4.67
	1873						34.79	NW¼NW¼	7	32	49	3-15—4-28	.283	26.09
	1873					35.29		NE¼NW¼	7	32	49	3-15—4-28	.287	26.47
	1873					35.68		SE¼NW¼	7	32	49	3-15—4-28	.290	26.76
	1873					7.98		SW¼NW¼	7	32	49	3-15—4-28	.065	5.99
	1873						20.70	SW¼NW¼	7	32	49	3-15—4-28	.168	15.53
	1873					37.25		NE¼SW¼	7	32	49	3-15—4-28	.303	27.91

Source—**Humboldt River.** Ditch—**High Line Canal.**

Nat. mdw.	Cult. area	Dams	Ditches	Harvest crops	Meadow pasture	Willow and sage pasture	Swamp or overflow	Subdivision	Section	Tp.N.	R.E.	Length of season	C.F.S.	Acre-feet
	1883			2.91				NE¼NW¼	5	31	49	3-15—9-15	.024	8.73
	1883					8.99		NE¼NW¼	5	31	49	3-15—4-28	.073	6.74
	1883						5.72	NE¼NW¼	5	31	49	3-15—4-28	.047	4.29
	1883					3.01		SE¼NW¼	5	31	49	3-15—4-28	.024	2.26
	1883					4.16		NW¼NE¼	5	31	49	3-15—4-28	.034	3.12
	1883						19.76	NW¼NE¼	5	31	49	3-15—4-28	.162	14.82
	1883					8.64		SW¼NE¼	5	31	49	3-15—4-28	.070	6.48
	1883						5.05	SW¼NE¼	5	31	49	3-15—4-28	.041	3.79
	1883						16.64	NE¼NE¼	5	31	49	3-15—4-28	.135	12.48
	1883					2.60		SE¼NE¼	5	31	49	3-15—4-28	.021	1.95
	1883						22.80	SE¼NE¼	5	31	49	3-15—4-28	.186	17.10
	1883			7.28				NE¼NE¼	28	32	49	3-15—9-15	.059	21.84
	1883			29.60				NW¼NE¼	28	32	49	3-15—9-15	.241	88.80
	1883			29.50				NE¼NW¼	28	32	49	3-15—9-15	.240	88.50
	1883			1.00				NW¼NW¼	28	32	49	3-15—9-15	.008	3.00
	1883			30.61				SE¼NW¼	28	32	49	3-15—9-15	.249	91.89
	1883			10.50				SW¼NW¼	28	32	49	3-15—9-15	.085	31.50
	1883			27.00				NE¼SW¼	28	32	49	3-15—9-15	.219	81.00
	1883			24.40				NW¼SW¼	28	32	49	3-15—9-15	.198	73.20
	1883			27.52				SE¼SW¼	28	32	49	3-15—9-15	.224	82.56
	1883			32.72				SW¼SW¼	28	32	49	3-15—9-15	.266	98.16
	1884			40.00				NW¼NW¼	33	32	49	3-15—9-15	.325	120.00
	1884			9.48				NE¼NW¼	33	32	49	3-15—9-15	.077	28.44
	1884			9.48				SW¼NW¼	33	32	49	3-15—9-15	.077	28.44

Source—**Humboldt River.** Ditch—**Overflow.**

Nat. mdw.	Cult. area	Dams	Ditches	Harvest crops	Meadow pasture	Willow and sage pasture	Swamp or overflow	Subdivision	Section	Tp.N.	R.E.	Length of season	C.F.S.	Acre-feet
	1877					19.08		NE¼NE¼	19	32	49	3-15—4-28	.155	14.31
	1877					20.52		SE¼NE¼	19	32	49	3-15—4-28	.167	15.39
	1877					2.60		SW¼SE¼	19	32	49	3-15—4-28	.021	1.95
	1877					21.28		NE¼SE¼	19	32	49	3-15—4-28	.173	15.96
	1877					4.68		NW¼SE¼	19	32	49	3-15—4-28	.038	3.51
	1877					5.20		NW¼NE¼	19	32	49	3-15—4-28	.042	3.90
	1877					5.20		SW¼NE¼	19	32	49	3-15—4-28	.042	3.90

Source—Humboldt River. Ditch—Dwyer Dam.

	1897		31.80		NW¼NE¼	19	32	49	3-15—4-28	.259	23.85
	1897		30.72		SW¼NE¼	19	32	49	3-15—4-28	.231	23.04
	1897		24.50		NE¼NW¼	19	32	49	3-15—4-28	.199	18.38
	1897			2.50	NE¼NW¼	19	32	49	3-15—4-28	.020	1.88
	1897		17.83		SE¼NW¼	19	32	49	3-15—4-28	.155	13.37
	1897			10.16	SE¼NW¼	19	32	49	3-15—4-28	.083	7.62
	1897		1.52		SE¼SW¼	19	32	49	3-15—4-28	.012	1.14
	1897			29.84	SE¼SW¼	19	32	49	3-15—4-28	.243	22.38
	1897		7.72		NE¼SW¼	19	32	49	3-15—4-28	.063	5.79
	1897			20.28	NE¼SW¼	19	32	49	3-15—4-28	.165	15.21
	1897		21.36		SE¼SE¼	19	32	49	3-15—4-28	.174	16.02
	1897		34.40		SW¼SE¼	19	32	49	3-15—4-28	.280	25.80
	1897		26.76		NW¼SE¼	19	32	49	3-15—4-28	.218	20.07
	1897		25.54		SE¼NE¼	18	32	49	3-15—4-28	.208	19.16
	1897		39.00		NE¼SW¼	18	32	49	3-15—4-28	.317	20.25
	1897		6.96		NW¼SW¼	18	32	49	3-15—4-28	.057	5.22
	1897			19.04	NW¼SW¼	18	32	49	3-15—4-28	.155	14.28
	1897		37.00		SE¼SW¼	18	32	49	3-15—4-28	.301	27.75
	1897			39.20	SW¼SW¼	18	32	49	3-15—4-28	.319	29.40
	1897		39.00		SW¼SE¼	18	32	49	3-15—4-28	.317	29.25
	1897		12.00		SE¼SE¼	18	32	49	3-15—4-28	.098	9.00
	1897		38.00		NW¼SE¼	18	32	49	3-15—4-28	.309	28.50
	1897		27.76		NE¼SE¼	18	32	49	3-15—4-28	.226	20.82
	1897			21.20	NW¼NW¼	18	32	49	3-15—4-28	.172	15.90
	1897		39.00		NE¼NW¼	18	32	49	3-15—4-28	.317	29.25
	1897		38.12		SE¼NW¼	18	32	49	3-15—4-28	.310	28.59
	1897			12.00	SW¼NW¼	18	32	49	3-15—4-28	.098	9.00
	1897		12.90		SW¼NW¼	18	32	49	3-15—4-28	.105	9.68
	1897		38.00		NW¼NE¼	18	32	49	3-15—4-28	.309	28.50
	1897		38.65		SW¼NE¼	18	32	49	3-15—4-28	.314	28.99
	1897		12.48		NE¼NE¼	18	32	49	3-15—4-28	.102	9.36
	1897		38.75		SW¼SE¼	7	32	49	3-15—4-28	.315	29.06
	1897		26.40		SE¼SW¼	7	32	49	3-15—4-28	.215	19.80
	1897		38.26		SW¼SW¼	7	32	49	3-15—4-28	.311	28.70
	1897		24.08		NW¼SW¼	7	32	49	3-15—4-28	.196	18.06
	1897		34.54		NE¼NE¼	30	32	49	3-15—4-28	.281	25.91
	1897		32.40		NW¼NE¼	30	32	49	3-15—4-28	.263	24.30
	1897		33.70		SE¼NE¼	30	32	49	3-15—4-28	.274	25.28
	1897		19.12		SW¼NE¼	30	32	49	3-15—4-28	.155	14.34
	1897			6.84	SW¼NE¼	30	32	49	3-15—4-28	.056	5.13
	1897			40.00	SE¼NW¼	30	32	49	3-15—4-28	.325	30.00
	1897		34.72		SE¼SE¼	30	32	49	3-15—4-28	.292	26.04
	1897		30.95		NE¼SE¼	30	32	49	3-15—4-28	.252	23.21
	1897		12.46		NW¼SE¼	30	32	49	3-15—4-28	.101	9.35
	1897		6.00		SW¼SE¼	30	32	49	3-15—4-28	.049	4.50

Source—Humboldt River. Ditch—Beowawe No. 1.

	1879	*40.00			NE¼NE¼	17	32	49	3-15—6-13	.325	60.00
	1879	*40.00			SE¼NE¼	17	32	49	3-15—6-13	.325	60.00
	1879	*40.00			SW¼NE¼	17	32	49	3-15—6-13	.325	60.00

*Third-Class—1874

Humboldt Land and Cattle Co.—Continued.

Date of beneficial use: Nat. mdw.	Date of beneficial use: Cult. area	Construction first initiated: Dams	Construction first initiated: Ditches	Culture—Acres: Harvest crops	Culture—Acres: Meadow pasture	Culture—Acres: Willow and sage pasture	Culture—Acres: Swamp or over-flow	Location: Subdivision	Location: Section	Location: Tp.N.	Location: R.E.	Length of season	Duty of water: C.F.S.	Duty of water: Acre-feet
	1879				*40.00			NW¼NE¼	17	32	49	3-15—6-13	.325	60.00
	1879				*40.00			NW¼NW¼	17	32	49	3-15—6-13	.325	60.00
	1879				*40.00			NE¼NW¼	17	32	49	3-15—6-13	.325	60.00
	1879				*40.00			SE¼NW¼	17	32	49	3-15—6-13	.325	60.00
	1879				*40.00			SW¼NW¼	17	32	49	3-15—6-13	.325	60.00
	1879				40.00			SW¼SW¼	17	32	49	3-15—6-13	.325	60.00
	1879				40.00			SE¼SW¼	17	32	49	3-15—6-13	.325	60.00
	1879				40.00			NW¼SW¼	17	32	49	3-15—6-13	.325	60.00
	1879				40.00			NE¼SW¼	17	32	49	3-15—6-13	.325	60.00
	1879				40.00			SE¼SE¼	17	32	49	3-15—6-13	.325	60.00
	1879				40.00			SW¼SE¼	17	32	49	3-15—6-13	.325	60.00
	1879				40.00			NE¼SE¼	17	32	49	3-15—6-13	.325	60.00
	1879				40.00			NW¼SE¼	17	32	49	3-15—6-13	.325	60.00
	1876					9.38		SE¼NE¼	18	32	49	3-15—4-28	.076	7.04
	1876					23.00		SE¼SE¼	18	32	49	3-15—4-28	.087	17.25
	1876					6.24		NE¼SE¼	18	32	49	3-15—4-28	.051	4.68
	1876					23.56		NE¼NE¼	18	32	49	3-15—4-28	.192	17.67
	1879				*20.92			NE¼NE¼	19	32	49	3-15—6-13	.170	31.38
	1879				*19.48			SE¼NE¼	19	32	49	3-15—6-13	.158	29.22
	1879					*5.72		SE¼SE¼	19	32	49	3-15—4-28	.047	4.29
	1879					*18.72		NE¼SE¼	19	32	49	3-15—4-28	.152	14.04
	1879			*40.00				NE¼NE¼	20	32	49	3-15—9-15	.325	120.00
	1879			*40.00				NW¼NE¼	20	32	49	3-15—9-15	.325	120.00
	1879			*40.00				SE¼NE¼	20	32	49	3-15—9-15	.325	120.00
	1879			*40.00				SW¼NE¼	20	32	49	3-15—9-15	.325	120.00
	1879			*40.00				NE¼NW¼	20	32	49	3-15—9-15	.325	120.00
	1879			*40.00				NW¼NW¼	20	32	49	3-15—9-15	.325	120.00
	1879			*36.30				SE¼NW¼	20	32	49	3-15—9-15	.295	108.90
	1879				*3.70			SE¼NW¼	20	32	49	3-15—6-13	.030	5.55
	1879			*40.00				SW¼NW¼	20	32	49	3-15—9-15	.325	120.00
	1879			*40.00				NE¼SE¼	20	32	49	3-15—9-15	.325	120.00
	1879			*40.00				NW¼SE¼	20	32	49	3-15—9-15	.325	120.00
	1879			*40.00				SE¼SE¼	20	32	49	3-15—9-15	.325	120.00
	1879			*37.00				SW¼SE¼	20	32	49	3-15—9-15	.301	111.00
	1879					*3.00		SW¼SE¼	20	20	49	3-15—4-28	.024	2.25
	1879			*40.00				SW¼SW¼	20	32	49	3-15—9-15	.325	120.00
	1879			*36.00				SE¼SW¼	20	32	49	3-15—9-15	.293	108.00
	1879					*4.00		SE¼SW¼	20	32	49	3-15—4-28	.033	3.00
	1879			*38.30				NW¼SW¼	20	32	49	3-15—9-15	.311	114.90
	1879				*1.70			NW¼SW¼	20	32	49	3-15—6-13	.014	2.55
	1879			*40.00				NE¼SW¼	20	32	49	3-15—9-15	.325	120.00
	1888				40.00			NW¼NW¼	21	32	49	3-15—6-13	.325	60.00
	1888				40.00			NE¼NW¼	21	32	49	3-15—6-13	.325	60.00
	1888				40.00			SE¼NW¼	21	32	49	3-15—6-13	.325	60.00
	1888				40.00			SW¼NW¼	21	32	49	3-15—6-13	.325	60.00
	1888			40.00				SW¼SW¼	21	32	49	3-15—9-15	.325	120.00
	1888			40.00				SE¼SW¼	21	32	49	3-15—9-15	.325	120.00

	1888				40.00			NE¼SW¼	21	32	49	3-15—6-13	.325	60.00
	1888			40.00				NW¼SW¼	21	32	49	3-15—9-15	.325	120.00
	1888			40.00				SW¼SE¼	21	32	49	3-15—9-15	.325	120.00
	1888				40.00			NW¼SE¼	21	32	49	3-15—6-13	.325	60.00
	1888				40.00			SW¼NE¼	21	32	49	3-15—6-13	.325	60.00
	1876			10.50				NE¼NW¼	28	32	49	3-15—9-15	.085	31.50
	1876			12.23				NW¼NW¼	28	32	49	3-15—9-15	.099	36.69
	1876				26.77			NW¼NW¼	28	32	49	3-15—6-13	.218	40.16
	1876			23.78				SW¼NW¼	28	32	49	3-15—9-15	.193	71.34
	1876				5.72			SW¼NW¼	28	32	49	3-15—6-13	.047	8.58
	1876			15.60				NW¼SW¼	28	32	49	3-15—9-15	.127	46.80
	1876			7.28				SW¼SW¼	28	32	49	3-15—9-15	.059	21.84
	1879				*40.00			NE¼NE¼	29	32	49	3-15—6-13	.325	60.00
	1879				*40.00			NW¼NE¼	29	32	49	3-15—6-13	.325	60.00
	1879				*40.00			SE¼NE¼	29	32	49	3-15—6-13	.325	60.00
	1879				*40.00			SW¼NE¼	29	32	49	3-15—6-13	.325	60.00
	1879				*40.00			NE¼NW¼	29	32	49	3-15—6-13	.325	60.00
	1879				*40.00			NW¼NW¼	29	32	49	3-15—6-13	.325	60.00
	1879				*40.00			SE¼NW¼	29	32	49	3-15—6-13	.325	60.00
	1879				*40.00			SW¼NW¼	29	32	49	3-15—6-13	.325	60.00
	1879				*40.00			SE¼SW¼	29	32	49	3-15—6-13	.325	60.00
	1879				*39.75			SW¼SW¼	29	32	49	3-15—6-13	.323	59.63
	1879				*40.00			NE¼SW¼	29	32	49	3-15—6-13	.325	60.00
	1879				*40.00			NW¼SW¼	29	32	49	3-15—6-13	.325	60.00
	1879				*40.00			SE¼SE¼	29	32	49	3-15—6-13	.325	60.00
	1879				*40.00			SW¼SE¼	29	32	49	3-15—6-13	.325	60.00
	1879				*40.00			NE¼SE¼	29	32	49	3-15—6-13	.325	60.00
	1879				*40.00			NW¼SE¼	29	32	49	3-15—6-13	.325	60.00
	1876			15.12				NE¼SW¼	32	32	49	3-15—9-15	.123	45.36
	1876				9.88			NE¼SW¼	32	32	49	3-15—6-13	.080	14.82
	1876					12.75		NE¼SW¼	32	32	49	3-15—4-28	.104	9.56
	1876			8.68				SE¼SW¼	32	32	49	3-15—9-15	.071	26.04
	1876					14.72		SE¼SW¼	32	32	49	3-15—4-28	.120	11.04
	1876						6.24	SE¼SW¼	32	32	49	3-15—4-28	.051	4.68
	1876					2.60		SW¼SW¼	32	32	49	3-15—4-28	.021	1.95
	1876						34.80	SW¼SW¼	32	32	49	3-15—4-28	.283	26.10
	1876						36.47	NW¼SW¼	32	32	49	3-15—4-28	.297	27.35
	1876				27.52			NW¼SE¼	32	32	49	3-15—6-13	.225	41.28
	1876				10.40			NE¼SE¼	32	32	49	3-15—6-13	.085	15.60
	1876				40.00			NW¼NW¼	32	32	49	3-15—6-13	.325	60.00
	1876				40.00			NE¼NW¼	32	32	49	3-15—6-13	.325	60.00
	1876				40.00			SE¼NW¼	32	32	49	3-15—6-13	.325	60.00
	1876				40.00			SW¼NW¼	32	32	49	3-15—6-13	.325	60.00
	1876				40.00			NW¼NE¼	32	32	49	3-15—6-13	.325	60.00
	1876				40.00			NE¼NE¼	32	32	49	3-15—6-13	.325	60.00
	1876				40.00			SE¼NE¼	32	32	49	3-15—6-13	.325	60.00
	1876				40.00			SW¼NE¼	32	32	49	3-15—6-13	.325	60.00

Source—Humboldt River. Ditch—Merchant Canal.

	1898						31.40	NW¼NW¼	8	32	49	3-15—4-28	.255	23.55
	1898						40.00	SW¼NW¼	8	32	49	3-15—4-28	.325	30.00
	1898						40.00	SE¼NW¼	8	32	49	3-15—4-28	.325	30.00

*Third-Class—1874

Humboldt Land and Cattle Co.—Continued.

Date of beneficial use: Nat. mdw.	Date of beneficial use: Cult. area	Construction first initiated: Dams	Construction first initiated: Ditches	Culture—Acres: Harvest crops	Culture—Acres: Meadow pasture	Culture—Acres: Willow and sage pasture	Culture—Acres: Swamp or overflow	Location: Subdivision	Location: Section	Location: Tp.N.	Location: R.E.	Length of season	Duty of water: C.F.S.	Duty of water: Acre-feet
....	1898	....	....	....	....	....	40.00	SW¼NE¼	8	32	49	3-15—4-28	.325	30.00
....	1898	....	....	....	....	....	40.00	SW¼SW¼	8	32	49	3-15—4-28	.325	30.00
....	1898	....	....	....	....	....	40.00	SE¼SW¼	8	32	49	3-15—4-28	.325	30.00
....	1898	....	....	....	....	....	40.00	NE¼SW¼	8	32	49	3-13—4-28	.325	30.00
....	1898	....	....	....	....	....	40.00	NW¼SW¼	8	32	49	3-15—4-28	.325	30.00
....	1898	....	....	....	....	....	40.00	SW¼SE¼	8	32	49	3-15—4-28	.325	30.00
....	1898	....	....	....	*40.00	....	....	SE¼SE¼	8	32	49	3-15—6-13	.325	60.00
....	1898	....	....	....	....	....	40.00	NE¼NE¼	7	32	49	3-15—4-28	.325	30.00
....	1898	....	....	....	....	....	40.00	SE¼NE¼	7	32	49	3-15—4-28	.325	30.00
....	1898	....	....	....	....	....	35.62	SW¼NE¼	7	32	49	3-15—4-28	.290	26.72
....	1898	....	....	....	....	....	40.00	NE¼SE¼	7	32	49	3-15—4-28	.325	30.00
....	1898	....	....	....	....	13.08	....	NW¼SE¼	7	32	49	3-15—4-28	.106	9.81

Source—Humboldt River. Ditch—Beowawe No. 2.

Date of beneficial use: Nat. mdw.	Date of beneficial use: Cult. area	Construction first initiated: Dams	Construction first initiated: Ditches	Culture—Acres: Harvest crops	Culture—Acres: Meadow pasture	Culture—Acres: Willow and sage pasture	Culture—Acres: Swamp or overflow	Location: Subdivision	Location: Section	Location: Tp.N.	Location: R.E.	Length of season	Duty of water: C.F.S.	Duty of water: Acre-feet
....	1897	....	....	*40.00	....	....	....	NE¼NE¼	1	31	48	3-15—9-15	.325	120.00
....	1897	....	....	*40.00	....	....	....	NW¼NE¼	1	31	48	3-15—9-15	.325	120.00
....	1889	....	....	*40.00	....	....	....	SE¼NE¼	1	31	48	3-15—9-15	.325	120.00
....	1897	....	....	*40.00	....	....	....	SW¼NE¼	1	31	48	3-15—9-15	.325	120.00
....	1897	....	....	*40.05	....	....	....	NE¼NW¼	1	31	48	3-15—9-15	.325	120.15
....	1897	....	....	*40.00	....	....	....	SE¼NW¼	1	31	48	3-15—9-15	.325	120.00
....	1897	....	....	*2.70	....	....	....	NW¼NW¼	1	31	48	3-15—9-15	.022	8.10
....	1897	....	....	..	....	....	37.32	NW¼NW¼	1	31	48	3-15—4-28	.303	27.99
....	1897	....	....	*2.08	....	....	....	SW¼NW¼	1	31	48	3-15—9-15	.017	6.24
....	1897	....	....	..	....	....	37.92	SW¼NW¼	1	31	48	3-15—4-28	.308	28.44
....	1897	....	....	*38.96	....	....	....	NE¼SW¼	1	31	48	3-15—9-15	.317	116.88
....	1897	....	....	..	....	....	1.04	NE¼SW¼	1	31	48	3-15—4-28	.008	.78
....	1897	....	....	*2.08	....	....	....	NW¼SW¼	1	31	48	3-15—9-15	.017	6.24
....	1897	....	....	..	....	....	37.92	NW¼SW¼	1	31	48	3-15—4-28	.308	28.44
....	1897	....	....	..	....	....	40.00	SW¼SW¼	1	31	48	3-15—4-28	.325	30.00
....	1897	....	....	*15.67	....	....	....	SE¼SW¼	1	31	48	3-15—9-15	.127	47.01
....	1897	....	....	..	....	....	18.20	SE¼SW¼	1	31	48	3-15—4-28	.148	13.65
....	1883	....	....	*17.57	....	....	....	NE¼SE¼	1	31	48	3-15—9-15	.143	52.71
....	1883	....	....	*39.50	....	....	....	NW¼SE¼	1	31	48	3-15—9-15	.321	118.50
....	1883	....	....	*10.40	....	....	....	SW¼SE¼	1	31	48	3-15—9-15	.085	31.20
....	1886	....	....	..	15.80	....	....	NE¼NE¼	26	32	48	3-15—6-13	.128	23.70
.. .	1886	....	....	..	....	24.20	....	NE¼NE¼	26	32	48	3-15—4-28	.197	18.15
....	1886	....	....	*6.76	....	....	....	SE¼NE¼	26	32	48	3-15—9-15	.055	20.28
....	1886	....	....	....	22.84	....	....	SE¼NE¼	26	32	48	3-15—6-13	.186	34.26
.. .	1886	....	....	..	....	10.40	....	SE¼NE¼	26	32	48	3-15—4-28	.085	7.80
....	1886	....	....	..	17.68	....	....	SW¼NE¼	26	32	48	3-15—6-13	.144	26.52
....	1886	....	....	..	....	....	22.32	SW¼NE¼	26	32	48	3-15—4-28	.181	16.74
....	1886	....	....	*25.48	....	....	....	NE¼SE¼	26	32	48	3-15—9-15	.207	76.44
....	1886	....	....	..	14.52	....	....	NE¼SE¼	26	32	48	3-16—6-13	.118	21.78
....	1886	....	....	..	....	40.00	....	NW¼SE¼	26	32	48	3-15—4-28	.325	30.00
....	1886	....	....	*4.36	....	....	....	SE¼SE¼	26	32	48	3-16—9-15	.035	13.08
....	1886	....	....	...	....	35.34	....	SE¼SE¼	26	32	48	3-15—4-28	.287	26.51

	1877						21.00	SW¼SE¼	20	32	48	3-15—4-28	.203	18.72
	1877						40.00	SE¼SE¼	13	32	48	3-15—4-28	.325	30.00
	1877						39.30	NE¼SE¼	13	32	48	3-15—4-28	.320	29.48
	1877						39.15	NW¼SE¼	13	32	48	3-15—4-28	.318	29.36
	1877						39.00	SW¼SE¼	13	32	48	3-15—4-28	.317	29.25
	1877						11.44	SW¼NE¼	13	32	48	3-15—4-28	.093	8.58
	1877						38.70	SE¼NE¼	13	32	48	3-15—4-28	.314	29.03
	1877						38.10	NE¼NE¼	13	32	48	3-15—4-28	.310	28.58
	1877						11.70	NE¼SW¼	13	32	48	3-15—4-28	.095	8.78
	1877						13.20	SE¼SW¼	13	32	48	3-15—4-28	.107	9.90
	1886						6.24	NE¼NW¼	35	32	48	3-15—4-28	.051	4.68
	1886						40.00	NW¼NE¼	35	32	48	3-15—4-28	.325	30.00
	1886						40.00	NW¼NW¼	35	32	48	3-15—4-28	.325	30.00
	1886						34.49	SW¼NE¼	35	32	48	3-15—4-28	.280	25.87
	1886						40.00	SE¼NE¼	35	32	48	3-15—4-28	.325	30.00
	1886						40.00	NE¼SE¼	35	32	48	3-15—4-28	.325	30.00
	1886						40.00	NW¼SE¼	35	32	48	3-15—4-28	.325	30.00
	1886						40.00	SE¼SE¼	35	32	48	3-15—4-28	.325	30.00
	1886						40.00	SW¼SE¼	35	32	48	3-15—4-28	.325	30.00
	1880						40.00	SW¼SW¼	24	32	48	3-15—4-28	.325	30.00
	1880					12.52		SE¼SW¼	24	32	48	3-15—4-28	.102	9.39
	1880						26.48	SE¼SW¼	24	32	48	3-15—4-28	.215	19.86
	1880						40.00	NW¼SW¼	24	32	48	3-15—4-28	.325	30.00
	1880					7.84		NE¼SW¼	24	32	48	3-15—4-28	.064	5.88
	1880						31.60	NE¼SW¼	24	32	48	3-15—4-28	.256	23.70
	1880					8.32		SE¼NW¼	24	32	48	3-15—4-28	.068	6.24
	1880						31.18	SE¼NW¼	24	32	48	3-15—4-28	.253	23.39
	1880					8.32		NE¼NW¼	24	32	48	3-15—4-28	.068	6.24
	1880						35.24	NE¼NW¼	24	32	48	3-15—4-28	.286	26.43
	1880						38.26	NE¼NE¼	24	32	48	3-15—4-28	.311	28.70
	1880						38.30	SE¼NE¼	24	32	48	3-15—4-28	.311	28.73
	1880					39.25		NW¼NE¼	24	32	48	3-15—4-28	.319	29.44
	1880					39.30		SW¼NE¼	24	32	48	3-15—4-28	.320	29.48
	1880					39.40		NW¼SE¼	24	32	48	3-15—4-28	.320	29.55
	1880					38.20		SW¼SE¼	24	32	48	3-15—4-28	.311	28.65
	1880						40.00	SE¼SE¼	24	32	48	3-15—4-28	.325	30.00
	1880						39.40	NE¼SE¼	24	32	48	3-15—4-28	.320	29.55
	1880						15.30	SE¼SE¼	23	32	48	3-15—4-28	.124	11.48
	1880					38.60		NW¼NE¼	25	32	48	3-15—4-28	.314	28.95
	1880				38.70			SW¼NE¼	25	32	48	3-15—6-13	.315	58.05
	1880				1.04			NW¼NW¼	25	32	48	3-15—6-13	.008	1.56
	1880						38.96	NW¼NW¼	25	32	48	3-15—4-28	.317	29.22
	1880				30.64			NE¼NW¼	25	32	48	3-15—6-13	.249	45.96
	1880						9.36	NE¼NW¼	25	32	48	3-15—4-28	.076	7.02
	1880				22.22			SW¼NW¼	25	32	48	3-15—6-13	.181	33.33
	1880						17.78	SW¼NW¼	25	32	48	3-15—4-28	.145	13.34
	1880				40.00			SE¼NW¼	25	32	48	3-15—6-13	.325	60.00
	1880				38.44			NW¼SW¼	25	32	48	3-15—6-13	.313	57.66
	1880				40.00			NE¼SW¼	25	32	48	3-15—6-13	.325	60.00
	1880				38.48			SW¼SW¼	25	32	48	3-15—6-13	.313	57.72
	1880						1.52	SW¼SW¼	25	32	48	3-15—4-28	.012	1.14
	1880				38.60			SE¼SW¼	25	32	48	3-15—6-13	.314	57.90

*Third-class—1874.

Humboldt Land and Cattle Co.—Continued.

Date of beneficial use: Nat. mdw.	Date of beneficial use: Cult. area	Construction first initiated: Dams	Construction first initiated: Ditches	Culture—Acres: Harvest crops	Culture—Acres: Meadow pasture	Culture—Acres: Willow and sage pasture	Culture—Acres: Swamp or overflow	Location: Subdivision	Location: Section	Location: Tp.N.	Location: R.E.	Length of season	Duty of water: C.F.S.	Duty of water: Acre-feet
	1880				40.00			SW¼SE¼	25	32	48	3-15—6-13	.325	60.00
	1880				38.70			NW¼SE¼	25	32	48	3-15—6-13	.315	58.05
	1880				40.00			SE¼SE¼	25	32	48	3-15—6-13	.325	60.00
	1880				5.72			NE¼SE¼	25	32	48	3-15—6-13	.047	8.58
	1880					34.28		NE¼SE¼	25	32	48	3-15—4-28	.279	25.71
	1880					40.00		SE¼NE¼	25	32	48	3-15—4-28	.325	30.00
	1880					40.00		NE¼NE¼	25	32	48	3-15—4-28	.325	30.00
	1877						38.18	SW¼NW¼	19	32	49	3-15—4-28	.310	28.64
	1877						38.26	NW¼NW¼	19	32	49	3-15—4-28	.311	27.70
	1877						38.03	SW¼SW¼	19	32	49	3-15—4-28	.309	28.52
	1877						38.11	NW¼SW¼	19	32	49	3-15—4-28	.310	28.58
	1877						38.04	NW¼NW¼	30	32	49	3-15—4-28	.309	28.53
	1877						38.40	NE¼NW¼	30	32	49	3-15—4-28	.312	28.80
	1877						38.15	SW¼NW¼	30	32	49	3-15—4-28	.310	28.61
	1877						22.00	SW¼SE¼	30	32	49	3-15—4-28	.179	16.50
	1877						38.31	SW¼SW¼	30	32	49	3-15—4-28	.311	28.73
	1877						40.00	SE¼SW¼	30	32	49	3-15—4-28	.325	30.00
	1877						40.00	NE¼SW¼	30	32	49	3-15—4-28	.325	30.00
	1877						38.72	NW¼SW¼	30	32	49	3-15—4-28	.315	29.04
	1877						15.45	NW¼SE¼	30	32	49	3-15—4-28	.126	11.59
	1880				38.34			NW¼NW¼	31	32	49	3-15—6-13	.312	57.51
	1880				9.36			NE¼NW¼	31	32	49	3-15—6-13	.076	14.04
	1880						30.64	NE¼NW¼	31	32	49	3-15—4-28	.249	22.98
	1882				38.30			SW¼NW¼	31	32	49	3-15—6-13	.311	57.45
	1883				36.30			SE¼NW¼	31	32	49	3-15—6-13	.295	54.45
	1883						2.70	SE¼NW¼	31	32	49	3-15—4-28	.022	2.03
	1878						33.56	NW¼NE¼	31	32	49	3-15—4-28	.273	25.17
	1878						40.00	SW¼NE¼	31	32	49	3-15—4-28	.325	30.00
	1883					*37.60		NE¼NE¼	31	32	49	3-15—4-28	.306	28.20
	1883					*25.50		SE¼NE¼	31	32	49	3-15—4-28	.207	19.13
	1885				*6.13			SE¼SE¼	31	32	49	3-15—6-13	.050	9.20
	1885					*2.60		SE¼SE¼	31	32	49	3-15—4-28	.021	1.96
	1878			*37.53				SW¼SE¼	31	32	49	3-15—9-15	.305	112.59
	1878				*2.47			SW¼SE¼	31	32	49	3-15—6-13	.020	3.71
	1878			*37.60				SE¼SW¼	31	32	49	3-15—9-15	.306	112.80
	1878			*37.60				SW¼SW¼	31	32	49	3-15—9-15	.306	112.80
	1878						31.70	NW¼SE¼	31	32	49	3-15—4-28	.258	23.78
	1886			*17.47				SE¼NW¼	36	32	48	3-15—9-15	.142	52.41
	1886				*0.50			SE¼NW¼	36	32	48	3-15—6-13	.004	.75
	1886						*22.53	SE¼NW¼	36	32	48	3-15—4-28	.183	16.90
	1877				*40.00			NE¼NW¼	36	32	48	3-15—6-13	.325	60.00
	1877					*14.56		NW¼NW¼	36	32	48	3-15—4-28	.128	10.92
	1877						*25.44	NW¼NW¼	36	32	48	3-15—4-28	.207	19.08
	1877			*1.45				NW¼SW¼	36	32	48	3-15—9-15	.012	4.35
	1877						38.55	NW¼SW¼	36	32	48	3-15—4-28	.313	28.91
	1877			*3.64				SW¼SW¼	36	32	48	3-15—9-15	.030	11.07

	1877						36.36	SW¼SW¼	36	32	48	3-15—4-28	.296	27.27
	1879			*40.00				NE¼SW¼	36	32	48	3-15—9-15	.325	120.00
	1880			*40.00				SE¼SW¼	36	32	48	3-15—9-15	.325	120.00
	1878			*40.00				NE¼SE¼	36	32	48	3-15—9-15	.325	120.00
	1878			*40.00				SE¼SE¼	36	32	48	3-15—9-15	.325	120.00
	1878			*40.00				NW¼SE¼	36	32	48	3-15—9-15	.325	120.00
	1878			*40.00				SW¼SE¼	36	32	48	3-15—9-15	.325	120.00
	1882				*22.76			NE¼NE¼	36	32	48	3-15—6-13	.185	34.14
	1882						*17.06	NE¼NE¼	36	32	48	3-15—4-28	.139	12.80
	1878				*40.00			SE¼NE¼	36	32	48	3-15—6-13	.325	60.00
	1883				*40.00			NW¼NE¼	36	32	48	3-15—6-13	.325	60.00
	1884				*34.28			SW¼NE¼	36	32	48	3-15—6-13	.280	51.42
	1884						*5.72	SW¼NE¼	36	32	48	3-15—4-28	.047	4.29
	1886						*39.50	SW¼NW¼	36	32	48	3-15—4-28	.321	29.63
	1878					*18.20		NE¼SE¼	31	32	49	3-15—4-28	.148	13.65
	1878			*40.00				NE¼SW¼	31	32	49	3-15—9-15	.325	120.00
	1878			*38.76				NW¼SW¼	31	32	49	3-15—9-15	.315	116.28

*Third-class—1874.

Claimant—**Sam Broyles.** Proof No. 00155

Source—**Humboldt River.** Ditch—**Altenberg Ditch.**

1880	1875			3.30				SE¼SW¼	16	32	45	3-15—9-15	.027	9.90
1880	1875				3.55			SE¼SW¼	16	32	45	3-15—6-13	.029	5.33
	1875			1.67				NW¼SW¼	16	32	45	3-15—9-15	.014	5.01
	1875				19.03			NW¼SW¼	16	32	45	3-15—6-13	.155	28.95
	1875					.15		NW¼SW¼	16	32	45	3-15—4-28	.001	.11
	1875			15.47				NE¼SW¼	16	32	45	3-15—9-15	.126	46.41
	1875				8.84			NE¼SW¼	16	32	45	3-15—6-13	.072	13.26
	1875					.65		NE¼SW¼	16	32	45	3-15—4-28	.005	.49

Source—**Humboldt River.** Ditch—**McIntyre Starrett.**

1880	1883			30.47				NE¼SE¼	16	32	45	3-15—9-15	.248	91.41
1880	1883					1.60		NE¼SE¼	16	32	45	3-15—4-28	.013	1.20
1880	1883			32.70				NW¼SE¼	16	32	45	3-15—9-15	.266	98.10
1880	1883					3.01		NW¼SE¼	16	32	45	3-15—4-28	.024	2.26
1880	1883			9.25				SE¼SE¼	16	32	45	3-15—9-15	.075	27.75
1880	1883				28.37			SE¼SE¼	16	32	45	3-15—6-13	.231	42.56
1880	1883					.30		SE¼SE¼	16	32	45	3-15—4-28	.002	.23
1880	1883			2.17				SW¼SE¼	16	32	45	3-15—9-15	.018	6.51
1880	1883				18.90			SW¼SE¼	16	32	45	3-15—6-13	.154	28.35
1880	1883				16.45			SW¼SW¼	16	32	45	3-15—6-13	.134	24.68
	1883			7.80				NE¼SW¼	16	32	45	3-15—9-15	.063	23.40

Claimant—**Golconda Cattle Co.** Proof No. 00156

Source—**Humboldt River.** Ditch—**Aemes Dam.**

Date of beneficial use: Nat. mdw.	Date of beneficial use: Cult. area	Construction first initiated: Dams	Construction first initiated: Ditches	Culture—Acres: Harvest crops	Culture—Acres: Meadow pasture	Culture—Acres: Willow and sage pasture	Culture—Acres: Swamp or overflow	Location: Subdivision	Location: Section	Location: Tp.N.	Location: R.E.	Length of season	Duty of water: C.F.S.	Duty of water: Acre-feet
*1875	1878						40.44	NW¼NE¼	30	35	43	3-15—4-28	.329	30.33
*1875	1878					30.61		NE¼NE¼	30	35	43	3-15—4-28	.249	22.96
*1875	1878						9.78	NE¼NE¼	30	35	42	3-15—4-28	.080	7.34
*1876	1886					11.60		SE¼NE¼	30	35	43	3-15—4-28	.094	8.70
*1876	1886						29.48	SE¼NE¼	30	35	43	3-15—4-28	.240	22.11
*1876	1878			5.60				SW¼NE¼	30	35	43	3-15—9-15	.046	16.80
*1876	1878					9.43		SW¼NE¼	30	35	43	3-15—4-28	.077	7.07
*1876	1886					8.64		NE¼SE¼	30	35	43	3-15—4-28	.070	6.48
*1876	1886						31.88	NE¼SE¼	30	35	43	3-15—4-28	.259	23.91
*1876	1886			13.76				NW¼SE¼	30	35	43	3-15—9-15	.112	41.28
*1876	1886				17.56			NW¼SE¼	30	35	43	3-15—6-13	.143	26.34
*1876	1886					4.20		NW¼SE¼	30	35	43	3-15—4-28	.034	3.15
*1876	1886					13.48		SE¼SE¼	30	35	43	3-15—4-28	.110	10.11
*1876	1886						17.40	SE¼SE¼	30	35	43	3-15—4-28	.141	13.05
*1876	1886			11.50				SW¼SE¼	30	35	43	3-15—9-15	.093	34.50
*1876	1886				22.32			SW¼SE¼	30	35	43	3-15—6-13	.181	33.48
*1876	1886					1.92		SW¼SE¼	30	35	43	3-15—4-28	.016	1.24
*1876	1884			29.52				NE¼SW¼	30	35	43	3-15—9-15	.240	88.59
*1876	1884					3.52		NE¼SW¼	30	35	43	3-15—4-28	.029	2.64

Source—**Humboldt River.** Ditch—**Aemes Dam.** (Lands of Duvivier.)

Date of beneficial use: Nat. mdw.	Date of beneficial use: Cult. area	Construction first initiated: Dams	Construction first initiated: Ditches	Culture—Acres: Harvest crops	Culture—Acres: Meadow pasture	Culture—Acres: Willow and sage pasture	Culture—Acres: Swamp or overflow	Location: Subdivision	Location: Section	Location: Tp.N.	Location: R.E.	Length of season	Duty of water: C.F.S.	Duty of water: Acre-feet
*1876	1884						.48	NE¼SW¼	30	35	43	3-15—4-28	.004	.36
*1876	1884			29.68				NW¼SW¼	30	35	43	3-15—9-15	.241	89.04
*1876	1884					2.80		NW¼SW¼	30	35	43	3-15—4-28	.023	2.10
*1876	1884			30.56				SW¼SW¼	30	35	43	3-15—9-15	.248	91.68
*1876	1884				3.88			SW¼SW¼	30	35	43	3-15—6-13	.032	5.82
*1876	1884			28.16				SE¼SW¼	30	35	43	3-15—9-15	.229	81.48
*1876	1884				4.88			SE¼SW¼	30	35	43	3-15—6-13	.040	7.32
*1876	1884					.84		SE¼SW¼	30	35	43	3-15—4-28	.007	.62

*Irrigated first during high water from Aemes Dam.

Source—**Humboldt River.** Ditch—**Henderson.** (Lands of Duvivier.)

Date of beneficial use: Nat. mdw.	Date of beneficial use: Cult. area	Construction first initiated: Dams	Construction first initiated: Ditches	Culture—Acres: Harvest crops	Culture—Acres: Meadow pasture	Culture—Acres: Willow and sage pasture	Culture—Acres: Swamp or overflow	Location: Subdivision	Location: Section	Location: Tp.N.	Location: R.E.	Length of season	Duty of water: C.F.S.	Duty of water: Acre-feet
1886	1887			6.62				NW¼NE¼	36	35	42	3-15—9-15	.054	19.86
1886	1887					32.90		NW¼NE¼	36	35	42	3-15—4-28	.267	24.68
1886	1887			16.23				NE¼NE¼	36	35	42	3-15—9-15	.132	48.69
1886	1887				7.56			NE¼NE¼	36	35	42	3-15—6-13	.061	11.34
1886	1887					16.09		NE¼NE¼	36	35	42	3-15—4-28	.131	12.07
1886	1894			21.33				NE¼SW¼	14	35	42	3-15—9-15	.174	64.08
1886	1894				18.40			NE¼SW¼	14	35	42	3-15—6-13	.150	27.60
1886	1894				41.20			NE¼SW¼	14	35	42	3-15—6-13	.335	61.80
1886	1894				40.16			SE¼SW¼	14	35	42	3-15—6-13	.327	60.24
1886	1894				41.20			NW¼SW¼	14	35	42	3-15—6-13	.335	61.80

Source—**Humboldt River.** Ditch—**Outside Slough.** (Lands of Duvivier.)

1887	1887		8.96				SW¼NE¼	36	35	42	3-15—0-15	.032	11.88
1887	1887				35.72		SW¼NE¼	36	35	42	3-15—4-28	.200	26.79
1887	1887		34.11				SE¼NE¼	36	35	42	3-15—0-15	.277	102.33
1887	1887			2.64			SE¼NE¼	36	35	42	3-15—6-13	.021	3.96
1887	1887				2.37		SE¼NE¼	36	35	12	3-15—4-28	.019	1.78
1888	1894			40.96			SW¼SW¼	14	35	42	3-15—6-13	.333	61.44

Claimant—**Ellison Ranching Co.** Proof No. **00156**

Source—**Humboldt** River. Ditch—**Outside Slough Ditch.** (Humboldt River lands.)

1887				40.60	SW¼SW¼	15	35	42	3-15—4-28	.330	30.45
1887				38.60	NW¼SW¼	15	35	42	3-15—4-28	.314	28.95
1887				35.60	SE¼SW¼	15	35	42	3-15—4-28	.289	26.70
1887				34.72	NE¼SW¼	15	35	42	3-15—4-28	.282	26.05
1887				33.44	SW¼NW¼	15	35	42	3-15—4-28	.272	25.08
1887	14.72				SE¼NW¼	15	35	42	3-15—0-15	.120	44.16
1887			24.64		SE¼NW¼	15	35	42	3-15—4-28	.200	18.48
1887				36.88	SW¼SE¼	15	35	42	3-15—4-28	.300	27.66
1887				39.44	SE¼SE¼	15	35	42	3-15—4-28	.321	29.58
1887				40.08	NE¼SE¼	15	35	42	3-15—4-28	.326	30.06
1887	9.28				NW¼SE¼	15	35	42	3-15—0-15	.075	27.84
1887			29.92		NW¼SE¼	15	35	42	3-15—4-28	.243	22.44
1887				40.24	SE¼SE¼	22	35	42	3-15—4-28	.327	30.18
1887				39.88	SW¼SE¼	22	35	42	3-15—4-28	.324	29.91
1887				39.84	NW¼SE¼	22	35	42	3-15—4-28	.324	29.88
1887				37.28	NE¼SE¼	22	35	42	3-15—4-28	.303	27.96
1887				40.12	NE¼SW¼	22	35	42	3-15—4-28	.326	30.09
1887				39.68	SE¼SW¼	22	35	42	3-15—4-28	.323	29.76
1887				38.60	SW¼NW¼	22	35	42	3-15—4-28	.314	28.95
1887				40.12	SE¼NW¼	22	35	42	3-15—4-28	.326	30.09
1887				40.08	NE¼NW¼	22	35	42	3-15—4-28	.326	30.06
1887				40.00	NW¼NW¼	22	35	42	3-15—4-28	.325	30.00
1887				39.88	SW¼NE¼	22	35	42	3-15—4-28	.324	29.91
1887				31.88	NW¼NE¼	22	35	42	3-15—4-28	.259	23.91
1887				39.00	NE¼NE¼	22	35	42	3-15—4-28	.317	29.25
1887				32.40	SE¼NE¼	22	35	42	3-15—4-28	.263	24.30
1887				41.12	NW¼NW¼	26	35	42	3-15—4-28	.334	30.84
1887	.96				NE¼NW¼	26	35	42	3-15—9-15	.008	2.88
1887			25.24		NE¼NW¼	26	35	42	3-15—4-28	.205	18.93
1887				39.48	SE¼NW¼	26	35	42	3-15—4-28	.321	29.61
1887				41.80	SW¼NW¼	26	35	42	3-15—4-28	.340	31.65
1887				40.80	NW¼NE¼	26	35	42	3-15—4-28	.331	30.60
1887				32.56	SW¼NE¼	26	35	42	3-15—4-28	.265	24.42
1887				41.28	SE¼NE¼	26	35	42	3-15—4-28	.336	30.96
1887				39.84	NW¼SW¼	26	35	42	3-15—4-28	.324	29.88
1887				40.60	NE¼SW¼	26	35	42	3-15—4-28	.330	30.45
1887				38.48	SW¼SW¼	26	35	42	3-15—4-28	.313	28.86
1887				40.64	SE¼SW¼	26	35	42	3-15—4-28	.330	30.48
1887			36.80		NW¼SE¼	26	35	42	3-15—4-28	.299	27.60
1887				35.92	NE¼SE¼	26	35	42	3-15—4-28	.292	26.90
1887			40.16		SW¼SE¼	26	35	42	3-15—4-28	.327	30.12
1887			23.08		SE¼SE¼	26	35	42	3-15—4-28	.188	17.31

Ellison Ranching Co.—Continued.

Date of beneficial use: Nat. mdw.	Date of beneficial use: Cult. area	Construction first initiated: Dams	Construction first initiated: Ditches	Culture—Acres: Harvest crops	Culture—Acres: Meadow pasture	Culture—Acres: Willow and sage pasture	Culture—Acres: Swamp or overflow	Location: Subdivision	Location: Section	Location: Tp.N.	Location: R.E.	Length of season	Duty of water: C.F.S.	Duty of water: Acre-feet
	1887						8.96	SE¼SE¼	26	35	42	3-15—4-28	.073	6.72
	1887						40.36	NE¼NE¼	27	35	42	3-15—4-28	.328	30.27
	1887					39.84		NW¼NW¼	23	35	42	3-15—4-28	.324	29.88
	1887					39.80		SW¼NW¼	23	35	42	3-15—4-28	.324	29.85
	1887			11.12				NW¼SW¼	23	35	42	3-15—9-15	.090	33.36
	1887					20.56		NW¼SW¼	23	35	42	3-15—4-28	.167	15.42
	1887						3.24	NW¼SW¼	23	35	42	3-15—4-28	.026	2.43
	1887			.32				SW¼SW¼	23	35	42	3-15—9-15	.003	.96
	1887					3.76		SW¼SW¼	23	35	42	3-15—4-28	.031	2.82
	1887						25.28	SW¼SW¼	23	35	42	3-15....4-28	.206	18.96
	1887			13.12				NE¼SW¼	23	35	42	3-15—9-15	.107	39.36
	1887					27.20		NE¼SW¼	23	35	42	3-15—4-28	.221	20.40
	1887			18.68				SE¼SW¼	23	35	42	3-15—9-15	.152	56.04
	1887					17.88		SE¼SW¼	23	35	42	3-15—4-28	.145	13.41
	1887						36.88	NE¼NW¼	9	35	42	3-15—4-28	.300	27.66
	1887						10.72	SE¼NW¼	9	35	42	3-15—4-28	.087	8.04
	1887						37.84	NW¼NE¼	9	35	42	3-15—4-28	.308	29.38
	1887					37.80		NE¼NE¼	9	35	42	3-15—4-28	.307	28.35
	1887					37.84		SE¼NE¼	9	35	42	3-15—4-28	.308	28.38
	1887						19.34	NW¼SE¼	9	35	42	3-15—4-28	.157	14.51
	1887					30.48		SE¼SE¼	9	35	42	3-15—4-28	.248	22.86

Source—**Humboldt River.** Ditch—**Aemes Dam.** (Humboldt River lands.)

Date of beneficial use: Nat. mdw.	Date of beneficial use: Cult. area	Construction first initiated: Dams	Construction first initiated: Ditches	Culture—Acres: Harvest crops	Culture—Acres: Meadow pasture	Culture—Acres: Willow and sage pasture	Culture—Acres: Swamp or overflow	Location: Subdivision	Location: Section	Location: Tp.N.	Location: R.E.	Length of season	Duty of water: C.F.S.	Duty of water: Acre-feet
	1876					40.08		NW¼NW¼	25	35	42	3-15—4-28	.326	30.06
	1876			18.20				NE¼NW¼	25	35	42	3-15—9-15	.147	54.60
	1876				.36			NE¼NW¼	25	35	42	3-15—6-13	.003	.54
	1876					20.48		NE¼NW¼	25	35	42	3-15—4-28	.167	15.36
	1876					40.24		SW¼NW¼	25	35	42	3-15—4-28	.327	30.18
	1876			5.80				SE¼NW¼	25	35	42	3-15—9-15	.047	17.40
	1876				2.28			SE¼NW¼	25	35	42	3-15—6-13	.019	3.42
	1876					31.08		SE¼NW¼	25	35	42	3-15—4-28	.253	23.31
	1876			21.32				NW¼NW¼	30	35	43	3-15—9-15	.173	63.96
	1876					6.16		NW¼NW¼	30	35	43	3-15—4-28	.050	4.62
	1876						.86	NW¼NW¼	30	35	43	3-15—4-28	.007	.65
	1876			20.28				SW¼NW¼	30	35	43	3-15—9-15	.165	60.84
	1876					4.24		SW¼NW¼	30	35	43	3-15—4-28	.034	3.18
	1876						7.60	SW¼NW¼	30	35	43	3-15—4-28	.062	5.70
	1876			18.00				SE¼NW¼	30	35	43	3-15—9-15	.146	54.00
	1876					11.52		SE¼NW¼	30	35	43	3-15—4-28	.094	8.64
	1876						2.52	SE¼NW¼	30	35	43	3-15—4-28	.020	1.89
	1876			14.32				NE¼NW¼	30	35	43	3-15—9-15	.116	42.96
	1876					22.92		NE¼NW¼	30	35	43	3-15—4-28	.186	17.19
	1876					6.40		SW¼NE¼	19	35	43	3-15—4-28	.052	4.80
	1876						10.36	SW¼NE¼	19	35	43	3-15—4-28	.084	7.77
	1876			20.72				NW¼SE¼	19	35	43	3-15—9-15	.166	62.16
	1876						9.28	NW¼SE¼	19	35	43	3-15—4-28	.075	6.96

	1876			25.36				SW¼SE¼	19	35	43	3-15—9-15	.206	76.08
	1876						8.20	SW¼SE¼	19	35	43	3-15—4-28	.067	6.22
	1876				27.04			NW¼NW¼	19	35	43	3-15—6-13	.220	40.56
	1876						7.24	NW¼NW¼	19	35	43	3-15—4-28	.050	5.43
	1876				18.24			NE¼NW¼	19	35	43	3-15—6-13	.148	27.36
	1876						21.52	NE¼NW¼	19	35	43	3-15—4-28	.175	16.14
	1876			38.80				NW¼NE¼	24	35	42	3-15—9-15	.315	116.40
	1876			23.84				NE¼NE¼	24	35	42	3-15—9-15	.194	71.52
	1876					10.88		NE¼NE¼	24	35	42	3-15—4-28	.088	8.16
	1876			40.08				SW¼NE¼	24	35	42	3-15—9-15	.326	120.24
	1876			26.44				SE¼NE¼	24	35	42	3-15—9-15	.215	79.32
	1876					3.68		SE¼NE¼	24	35	42	3-15—4-28	.030	2.76
	1876			23.56				NW¼SE¼	24	35	42	3-15—9-15	.192	70.68
	1876					16.56		NW¼SE¼	24	35	42	3-15—4-28	.135	12.42
	1876			40.24				NE¼SE¼	24	35	42	3-15—9-15	.327	120.72
	1876			12.76				SW¼SE¼	24	35	42	3-15—9-15	.104	38.28
	1876					24.76		SW¼SE¼	24	35	42	3-15—4-28	.201	18.57
	1876			39.98				SE¼SE¼	24	35	42	3-15—9-15	.325	119.34
	1876			39.59				NE¼NW¼	24	35	42	3-15—9-15	.322	118.77
	1876			13.12				NW¼NW¼	24	35	42	3-15—9-15	.107	39.36
	1876					25.60		NW¼NW¼	24	35	42	3-15—4-28	.208	19.20
	1876			.48				SW¼NW¼	24	35	42	3-15—9-15	.004	1.44
	1876					35.76		SW¼NW¼	24	35	42	3-15—4-28	.291	26.82
	1876			24.88				SE¼NW¼	24	35	42	3-15—9-15	.202	74.64
	1876					12.52		SE¼NW¼	24	35	42	3-15—4-28	.102	9.40
	1876					30.00		SE¼NW¼	19	35	43	3-15—4-28	.244	22.50
	1876				2.08			SW¼NW¼	19	35	43	3-15—6-13	.017	3.12
	1876					27.92		SW¼NW¼	19	35	43	3-15—4-28	.227	20.94
	1876				18.52			NW¼SW¼	19	35	43	3-15—6-13	.151	27.78
	1876					7.78		NW¼SW¼	19	35	43	3-15—4-28	.063	5.84
	1876				13.08			SW¼SW¼	19	35	43	3-15—6-13	.106	19.62
	1876					6.08		SW¼SW¼	19	35	43	3-15—4-28	.049	4.56
	1876				32.64			SE¼SW¼	19	35	43	3-15—6-13	.265	48.96
	1876					3.64		SE¼SW¼	19	35	43	3-15—4-28	.034	2.73
	1876			31.04				NE¼SW¼	19	35	43	3-15—9-15	.252	93.12
	1876					3.52		NE¼SW¼	19	35	43	3-15—4-28	.029	2.64
	1876			39.72				SE¼SW¼	13	35	42	3-15—9-15	.323	119.16
	1876					1.12		SE¼SE¼	13	35	42	3-15—4-28	.009	.84
	1876			15.12				NE¼SW¼	13	35	42	3-15—9-15	.123	45.36
	1876			33.12				NW¼SW¼	13	35	42	3-15—9-15	.269	99.36
	1876					5.04		NW¼SW¼	13	35	42	3-15—4-28	.041	3.78
	1876			23.80				SW¼SW¼	13	35	42	3-15—9-15	.193	71.40
	1876					14.96		SW¼SW¼	13	35	42	3-15—4-28	.122	11.22
	1876			14.48				SW¼NW¼	13	35	42	3-15—9-15	.117	43.44
	1876				3.96			SW¼NW¼	13	35	42	3-15—6-13	.032	5.94
	1876			.60				SE¼NW¼	13	35	42	3-15—9-15	.005	1.80
	1876					.80		SE¼NW¼	13	35	42	3-15—4-28	.007	.60

Source—**Humboldt River.** Ditch—**Henderson Dam.** (Humboldt River lands.)

1886	1887			15.68				NW¼NW¼	31	35	43	3-15—9-15	.127	47.04
1886	1887				4.48			NW¼NW¼	31	35	43	3-15—6-13	.036	6.72
1886	1887						13.60	NW¼NW¼	31	35	43	3-15—4-28	.111	10.20
1886	1887						34.40	SW¼NW¼	31	35	43	3-15—4-28	.280	25.80

Ellison Ranching Co.—Continued.

Date of beneficial use: Nat. mdw.	Cult. area	Construction first initiated: Dams	Ditches	Culture—Acres: Harvest crops	Meadow pasture	Willow and sage pasture	Swamp or overflow	Location: Subdivision	Section	Tp.N.	R.E.	Length of season	Duty of water: C.F.S.	Acre-feet
1886	1887						33.28	NW¼SW¼	31	35	43	3-15—4-28	.271	24.96
1886	1887						33.84	SW¼SW¼	31	35	43	3-15—4-28	.275	25.38
1886	1887			1.28				SE¼SW¼	31	35	43	3-15—9-15	.010	3.84
1886	1887						38.24	SE¼SW¼	31	35	43	3-15—4-28	.311	28.68
1886	1887			.96				NE¼SW¼	31	35	43	3-15—9-15	.008	2.88
1886	1887				7.48			NE¼SW¼	31	35	43	3-15—6-13	.061	11.22
1886	1887						30.32	NE¼SW¼	31	35	43	3-15—4-28	.247	22.74
1886	1887			10.72				SE¼SE¼	31	35	43	3-15—9-15	.087	32.16
1886	1887						26.28	SE¼SE¼	31	35	43	3-15—4-28	.214	19.71
1886	1887			19.96				SW¼SE¼	31	35	43	3-15—9-15	.162	59.88
1886	1887						13.04	SW¼SE¼	31	35	43	3-15—4-28	.106	9.78
1886	1887						39.48	NE¼SE¼	31	35	43	3-15—4-28	.321	29.61
1886	1887			17.92				NW¼SE¼	31	35	43	3-15—9-15	.146	53.76
1886	1887				2.04			NW¼SE¼	31	35	43	3-15—6-13	.017	3.06
1886	1887						13.76	NW¼SE¼	31	35	43	3-15—4-28	.113	10.32
	1887			17.00				NW¼NW¼	15	35	42	3-15—9-15	.138	51.00
	1887				14.00			NW¼NW¼	15	35	42	3-15—6-13	.114	21.00
	1887					6.24		NW¼NW¼	15	35	42	3-15—4-28	.051	4.68
	1887			39.24				NE¼NW¼	15	35	42	3-15—9-15	.319	117.72
	1887			39.12				NW¼NE¼	15	35	42	3-15—9-15	.318	117.36
	1887			39.76				NE¼NE¼	15	35	42	3-15—9-15	.323	119.28
	1887			25.72				SE¼NE¼	15	35	42	3-15—9-15	.209	77.16
	1887					12.92		SE¼NE¼	15	35	42	3-15—4-28	.105	9.69
	1887			33.12				SW¼NE¼	15	35	42	3-15—9-15	.269	99.36
	1887					5.40		SW¼NE¼	15	35	42	3-15—4-28	.044	4.05
	1887						40.00	NE¼NW¼	23	35	42	3-15—4-28	.325	30.00
	1887						40.40	SE¼NW¼	23	35	42	3-15—4-28	.328	30.30
	1887						40.08	NW¼NE¼	23	35	42	3-15—4-28	.326	30.06
	1887						39.44	NE¼NE¼	23	35	42	3-15—4-28	.321	29.58
	1887						40.48	SW¼NE¼	23	35	42	3-15—4-28	.329	30.36
	1887						40.56	SE¼NE¼	23	35	42	3-15—4-28	.330	30.42
	1887						40.64	NW¼SE¼	23	35	42	3-15—4-28	.330	30.48
	1887						40.96	NE¼SE¼	23	35	42	3-15—4-28	.333	30.72
	1887						41.20	SW¼SE¼	23	35	42	3-15—4-28	.335	30.90
	1887						41.44	SE¼SW¼	23	35	42	3-15—4-28	.337	31.08
	1887			1.20				NE¼SW¼	24	35	42	3-15—9-15	.010	3.60
	1887					36.68		NE¼SW¼	24	35	42	3-15—4-28	.298	27.51
	1887					38.76		NW¼SW¼	24	35	42	3-15—4-28	.315	29.07
	1887			23.80				SW¼SW¼	24	35	42	3-15—9-15	.193	71.40
	1887					14.96		SW¼SW¼	24	35	42	3-15—4-28	.122	11.22
	1887			10.24				SE¼SW¼	24	35	42	3-15—9-15	.083	30.72
	1887					26.84		SE¼SW¼	24	35	42	3-15—4-28	.218	20.13
	1887			21.52				SE¼NW¼	31	35	43	3-15—9-15	.175	64.56
	1887				5.04			SE¼NW¼	31	35	43	3-15—6-13	.041	7.56
	1887					11.80		SE¼NW¼	31	35	43	3-15—4-28	.096	8.85
	1887			33.08				NE¼NW¼	31	35	43	3-15—9-15	.209	99.24
	1887					2.08		NE¼NW¼	31	35	43	3-15—4-28	.017	1.56

	1887			29.64				SW¼NE¼	31	35	43	3-15—9-15	.241	88.92
	1887					2.56		SW¼NE¼	31	35	43	3-15—4-28	.021	1.92
	1887						1.76	SW¼NE¼	31	35	43	3-15—4-28	.014	1.32
	1887			6.60				NW¼NE¼	31	35	43	3-15—9-15	.054	19.80
	1887					24.24		NW¼NE¼	31	35	43	3-15—4-28	.197	18.18
	1887						3.12	NW¼NE¼	31	35	43	3-15—4-28	.025	2.34
	1887			1.52				SE¼NE¼	31	35	43	3-15—9-15	.012	4.56
	1887					2.48		SE¼NE¼	31	35	43	3-15—4-28	.020	1.86
	1887						.24	SE¼NE¼	31	35	43	3-15—4-28	.002	.18
	1887					38.56		NE¼NE¼	31	35	43	3-15—4-28	.313	28.92
	1887						2.00	NE¼NE¼	31	35	43	3-15—4-28	.016	1.50
	1887			8.80				SW¼SE¼	25	35	42	3-15—9-15	.072	26.40
	1887				31.20			SW¼SE¼	25	35	42	3-15—6-13	.254	46.80
	1887			40.80				SE¼SE¼	25	35	42	3-15—9-15	.332	122.40
	1887				40.64			SE¼SW¼	25	35	42	3-15—6-13	.330	60.96
	1887			19.20				NE¼SW¼	25	35	42	3-15—9-15	.156	57.60
	1887					20.64		NE¼SW¼	25	35	42	3-15—4-28	.168	15.48
	1887					40.64		NW¼SW¼	25	35	42	3-15—4-28	.330	30.48
	1887					38.56		SW¼SW¼	25	35	42	3-15—4-28	.313	28.92
	1887			34.48				NE¼SE¼	25	35	42	3-15—9-15	.280	103.44
	1887					3.16		NE¼SE¼	25	35	42	3-15—4-28	.026	2.37
	1887						1.08	NE¼SE¼	25	35	42	3-15—4-28	.009	.81
	1887			14.16				NW¼SE¼	25	35	42	3-15—9-15	.115	42.48
	1887					25.20		NW¼SE¼	25	35	42	3-15—4-28	.205	18.90
	1887			24.00				NE¼NE¼	25	35	42	3-15—9-15	.195	72.00
	1887				10.48			NE¼NE¼	25	35	42	3-15—6-13	.085	15.72
	1887					3.24		NE¼NE¼	25	35	42	3-15—4-28	.026	2.43
	1887			24.80				NW¼NE¼	25	35	42	3-15—9-15	.202	74.40
	1887					14.16		NW¼NE¼	25	35	42	3-15—4-28	.115	10.62
	1887			32.12				SE¼NE¼	25	35	42	3-15—9-15	.261	96.36
	1887				3.52			SE¼NE¼	25	35	42	3-15—6-13	.029	5.28
	1887					1.72		SE¼NE¼	25	35	42	3-15—4-28	.014	1.29
	1887			38.64				SW¼NE¼	25	35	42	3-15—9-15	.314	115.92
	1887			.48				SE¼NE¼	6	34	43	3-15—9-15	.004	1.44
	1887			12.96				NE¼NE¼	6	34	43	3-15—9-15	.105	38.88
	1887					17.54		NE¼NE¼	6	34	43	3-15—4-28	.143	13.16
	1887			8.36				NW¼NE¼	6	34	43	3-15—9-15	.069	25.08
	1887					4.38		NW¼NE¼	6	34	43	3-15—4-28	.036	3.29
	1887						2.56	NW¼NE¼	6	34	43	3-15—4-28	.021	1.92

Source—**Humboldt River.** Ditch—**Bacon Dam.** (Humboldt River lands.)

	1887			11.08				NW¼SE¼	13	35	42	3-15—9-15	.090	33.24
	1887					1.22		NW¼SE¼	13	35	42	3-15—4-28	.010	.92
	1887			32.92				SW¼SE¼	13	35	42	3-15—9-15	.268	98.76
	1887			.32				NE¼SE¼	13	35	42	3-15—9-15	.003	.64
	1887						.24	NE¼SE¼	13	35	42	3-15—4-28	.002	.18

Source—**Humboldt River.** Ditch—**Gonzales Slough.** (Humboldt River lands.)

	1880						40.00	NW¼NW¼	20	36	42	3-15—4-28	.325	30.00
	1880						40.00	NE¼NW¼	20	36	42	3-15—4-28	.325	30.00
	1880						40.00	NW¼NE¼	20	36	42	3-15—4-28	.328	30.30
	1880						39.36	SW¼NW¼	20	36	42	3-15—4-28	.320	29.52

Ellison Ranching Co.—Continued.

Date of beneficial use: Nat. mdw.	Date of beneficial use: Cult. area	Construction first initiated: Dams	Construction first initiated: Ditches	Culture—Acres: Harvest crops	Culture—Acres: Meadow pasture	Culture—Acres: Willow and sage pasture	Culture—Acres: Swamp or overflow	Location: Subdivision	Location: Section	Location: Tp.N.	Location: R.E.	Length of season	Duty of water: C.F.S.	Duty of water: Acre-feet
	1880						40.00	SE¼NW¼	20	36	42	3-15—4-28	.325	30.00
	1880						36.24	NW¼SW¼	20	36	42	3-15—4-28	.295	27.18
	1880						37.44	NE¼SW¼	20	36	42	3-15—4-28	.304	28.08
	1880						39.06	SW¼SW¼	20	36	42	3-15—4-28	.318	29.30
	1880						38.36	SE¼SW¼	20	36	42	3-15—4-28	.312	28.77
	1880						40.00	NE¼SE¼	20	36	42	3-15—4-28	.325	30.00
	1880						38.56	NW¼SE¼	20	36	42	3-15—4-28	.313	28.92
	1880						37.92	SE¼SE¼	20	36	42	3-15—4-28	.308	28.44
	1880						36.00	SW¼SE¼	20	36	42	3-15—4-28	.292	27.00
	1880						40.00	NW¼NW¼	21	36	42	3-15—4-28	.325	30.00
	1880				20.72			NE¼NW¼	21	36	42	3-15—6-13	.169	31.08
	1880						19.44	NE¼NW¼	21	36	42	3-15—4-28	.158	14.58
	1880						39.52	SW¼NW¼	21	36	42	3-15—4-28	.321	29.64
	1880				19.84			SE¼NW¼	21	36	42	3-15—6-13	.161	29.76
	1880						19.32	SE¼NW¼	21	36	42	3-15—4-28	.157	14.49
	1880				23.68			NE¼SW¼	21	36	42	3-15—6-13	.193	35.52
	1880						15.84	NE¼SW¼	21	36	42	3-15—4-28	.129	11.88
	1880						40.00	NW¼SW¼	21	36	42	3-15—4-28	.325	30.00
	1880						39.48	SW¼SW¼	21	36	42	3-15—4-28	.321	29.61
	1880				.48			SE¼SW¼	21	36	42	3-15—6-13	.004	.72
	1880						38.20	SE¼SW¼	21	36	42	3-15—4-28	.310	28.65
	1880			23.36				NW¼NE¼	21	36	42	3-15—9-15	.190	70.08
	1880						11.76	NW¼NE¼	21	36	42	3-15—4-28	.096	8.82
	1880			31.72				SW¼NE¼	21	36	42	3-15—9-15	.258	95.16
	1880						.32	SW¼NE¼	21	36	42	3-15—4-28	.003	.24
	1880			20.40				SE¼NE¼	21	36	42	3-15—9-15	.166	61.20
	1880						.72	SE¼NE¼	21	36	42	3-15—4-28	.006	.54
	1880			15.48				NW¼SE¼	21	36	42	3-15—9-15	.126	46.44
	1880				11.92			NW¼SE¼	21	36	42	3-15—6-13	.097	17.87
	1880						12.48	NW¼SE¼	21	36	42	3-15—4-28	.101	9.36
	1880			34.96				NE¼SE¼	21	36	42	3-15—9-15	.284	104.88
	1880						6.16	NE¼SE¼	21	36	42	3-15—4-28	.050	4.62
	1880				26.40			SW¼SE¼	21	36	42	3-15—6-13	.215	39.60
	1880						12.88	SW¼SE¼	21	36	42	3-15—4-28	.105	9.66
	1880			20.20				SE¼SE¼	21	36	42	3-15—9-15	.164	60.60
	1880						18.20	SE¼SE¼	21	36	42	3-15—4-28	.148	13.65
	1880			5.16				NW¼SW¼	22	36	42	3-15—9-15	.042	15.48
	1880				21.76			NW¼SW¼	22	36	42	3-15—6-13	.177	32.74
	1880						6.08	NW¼SW¼	22	36	42	3-15—4-28	.049	4.56
	1880			1.08				NE¼SW¼	22	36	42	3-15—9-15	.009	3.24
	1880				2.92			NE¼SW¼	22	36	42	3-15—6-13	.024	4.38
	1880						36.52	NE¼SW¼	22	36	42	3-15—4-28	.297	27.39
	1880			19.68				SW¼SW¼	22	36	42	3-15—9-15	.160	59.04
	1880						3.16	SW¼SW¼	22	36	42	3-15—4-28	.026	2.38
	1880						38.44	NW¼SE¼	28	36	42	3-15—4-28	.313	28.83
	1880						38.36	NE¼SE¼	28	36	42	3-15—4-28	.312	28.77
	1880						39.40	SE¼SE¼	28	36	42	3-15—4-28	.320	29.55

...	1880	...	...	...	...	...	39.28	SW¼SE¼	28	36	42	3-15—4-28	.319	20.46
...	1880	...	...	...	...	...	40.00	NW¼SW¼	28	36	42	3-15—4-28	.325	30.00
...	1880	...	...	...	...	...	38.44	NE¼SW¼	28	36	42	3-15—4-28	.313	28.83
...	1880	...	...	...	...	...	39.20	SW¼SW¼	28	36	42	3-15—4-28	.312	29.40
...	1880	...	...	...	...	...	38.52	SE¼SW¼	28	36	42	3-15—4-28	.313	28.89
...	1880	...	...	...	...	...	39.84	NW¼NW¼	28	36	42	3-15—4-28	.324	29.88
...	1880	...	...	...	...	...	39.60	NE¼NW¼	28	36	42	3-15—4-28	.322	29.70
...	1880	...	...	...	...	...	40.00	SW¼NW¼	28	36	42	3-15—4-28	.323	30.00
...	1880	...	...	...	...	...	38.72	SE¼NW¼	28	36	42	3-15—4-28	.315	29.04
...	1880	...	...	...	...	...	40.00	SW¼NE¼	28	36	42	3-15—4-28	.325	30.00
...	1880	...	...	2.00	...	...	...	SE¼NE¼	28	36	42	3-15—9-15	.016	6.00
...	1880	...	...	...	...	...	38.84	SE¼NE¼	28	36	42	3-15—4-28	.316	29.13
...	1880	...	...	10.28	...	...	...	NW¼NE¼	28	36	42	3-15—9-15	.084	30.84
...	1880	...	...	...	...	...	29.68	NW¼NE¼	28	36	42	3-15—4-28	.241	22.26
...	1880	...	...	36.28	...	...	...	NW¼NW¼	34	36	42	3-15—9-15	.295	108.84
...	1880	...	...	...	...	2.24	...	NW¼NW¼	34	36	42	3-15—4-28	.018	1.68
...	1880	...	...	31.92	...	...	...	NE¼NW¼	34	36	42	3-15—9-15	.260	95.76
...	1880	...	...	39.20	...	...	...	SE¼NW¼	34	36	42	3-15—9-15	.319	117.60
...	1880	...	...	35.88	...	...	...	SW¼SW¼	34	36	42	3-15—9-15	.292	107.64
...	1880	...	...	...	...	...	2.40	SW¼SW¼	34	36	42	3-15—4-28	.020	1.80
...	1880	...	...	40.00	...	...	...	SE¼SW¼	34	36	42	3-15—9-15	.325	120.00
...	1880	...	...	38.28	...	...	...	SW¼SW¼	34	36	42	3-15—9-15	.311	114.84
...	1880	...	...	40.00	...	...	...	NE¼SW¼	34	36	42	3-15—9-15	.325	120.00
...	1880	...	...	37.00	...	...	...	NW¼SW¼	34	36	42	3-15—9-15	.301	111.00
...	1880	...	...	...	...	...	3.12	NW¼SW¼	34	36	42	3-15—4-28	.025	2.34

Source—**Humboldt River.** Ditch—**Overflow.** (Humboldt River lands.)

...	1880	...	...	...	...	...	28.80	NE¼NE¼	21	36	42	3-15—4-28	.234	21.60
...	1880	...	...	...	...	...	3.84	SW¼NE¼	21	36	42	3-15—4-28	.028	2.58
...	1880	...	...	...	...	...	12.96	SE¼NE¼	21	36	42	3-15—4-28	.105	9.72
...	1880	...	...	...	...	...	10.08	SW¼SW¼	22	36	42	3-15—4-28	.082	7.56
...	1880	...	...	15.48	...	...	...	SE¼SW¼	22	36	42	3-15—9-15	.126	46.44
...	1880	...	...	...	...	...	23.80	SE¼SW¼	22	36	42	3-15—4-28	.193	17.85

Source—**Humboldt River.** Ditch—**"13" Ditch.** (Humboldt River lands.)

...	1874	...	...	...	17.36	...	...	NE¼SE¼	14	36	41	3-15—6-13	.141	26.04
...	1874	...	...	...	...	...	9.72	NE¼SE¼	14	36	41	3-15—4-28	.079	7.29
...	1874	...	...	...	...	...	27.04	SE¼SE¼	14	36	41	3-15—4-28	.220	20.28

Source—**Humboldt River.** Ditch—**Outside Slough.** (Humboldt River lands.)

...	1887	...	...	...	...	...	2.24	SE¼SE¼	6	34	43	3-15—4-28	.018	1.68
...	1887	...	...	...	...	...	12.40	SW¼SE¼	6	34	43	3-15—4-28	.101	9.30
...	1887	...	...	...	...	...	10.72	NE¼SE¼	6	34	43	3-15—4-28	.087	8.04
...	1887	...	...	...	...	...	15.08	NW¼SE¼	6	34	43	3-15—4-28	.123	11.31
...	1887	...	...	...	...	...	33.70	NE¼SW¼	6	34	43	3-15—4-28	.274	25.28
...	1887	...	...	...	...	...	21.60	NW¼SW¼	6	34	43	3-15—4-28	.176	16.20
...	1887	...	...	...	...	...	7.04	SW¼SW¼	6	34	43	3-15—4-28	.057	5.28
...	1887	...	...	...	...	...	9.32	SE¼SW¼	6	34	43	3-15—4-28	.076	6.99
...	1886	...	...	...	...	...	36.56	NW¼NW¼	32	36	42	3-15—4-28	.297	27.42
...	1886	...	...	...	...	...	37.64	SW¼NW¼	32	36	42	3-15—4-28	.306	28.33
...	1886	...	...	...	...	...	36.86	SE¼NW¼	32	36	42	3-15—4-28	.300	27.65
...	1886	...	...	...	...	...	38.64	NE¼NW¼	32	36	42	3-15—4-28	.314	28.98

Ellison Ranching Co.—Continued.

Date of beneficial use: Nat. mdw.	Date of beneficial use: Cult. area	Construction first initiated: Dams	Construction first initiated: Ditches	Culture—Acres: Harvest crops	Culture—Acres: Meadow pasture	Culture—Acres: Willow and sage pasture	Culture—Acres: Swamp or over-flow	Location: Subdivision	Location: Section	Location: Tp.N.	Location: R.E.	Length of season	Duty of water: C.F.S.	Duty of water: Acre-feet
....	1886	....	....	....	....	....	38.20	NW¼NE¼	32	36	42	3-15—4-28	.311	28.65
....	1886	....	....	....	....	....	37.32	SW¼NE¼	32	36	42	3-15—4-28	.303	27.99
....	1886	....	....	....	....	....	39.00	NE¼NE¼	32	36	42	3-15—4-28	.317	29.25
....	1886	....	....	....	....	....	40.20	SE¼NE¼	32	36	42	3-15—4-28	.327	30.15
....	1886	....	....	....	....	....	38.00	NE¼SW¼	32	36	42	3-15—4-28	.309	28.50
....	1886	....	....	....	....	....	40.32	NW¼SW¼	32	36	42	3-15—4-28	.328	30.24
....	1886	....	....	....	....	....	40.24	SE¼SW¼	32	36	42	3-15—4-28	.327	30.18
....	1886	....	....	....	....	....	27.12	SW¼SW¼	32	36	42	3-15—4-28	.220	20.35
....	1886	....	....	....	....	....	40.32	NE¼SE¼	32	36	42	3-15—4-28	.328	30.24
....	1886	....	....	....	....	....	40.48	SE¼SE¼	32	36	42	3-15—4-28	.329	30.36
....	1886	....	....	....	....	....	35.62	NW¼SE¼	32	36	42	3-15—4-28	.290	26.72
....	1886	....	....	....	....	....	37.64	SW¼SE¼	32	36	42	3-15—4-28	.306	28.23
....	1886	....	....	....	....	....	28.68	NW¼NE¼	5	35	42	3-15—4-28	.233	21.51
....	1886	....	....	....	....	....	38.08	NE¼NE¼	5	35	42	3-15—4-28	.310	28.56
....	1886	....	....	....	....	....	37.10	SE¼SE¼	5	35	42	3-15—4-28	.302	27.83
....	1886	....	....	....	....	....	16.64	NE¼SE¼	5	35	42	3-15—4-28	.135	12.98
....	1886	....	....	....	....	....	4.96	SW¼NE¼	5	35	42	3-15—4-28	.040	3.72
....	1886	....	....	....	....	....	36.80	SE¼NE¼	5	35	42	3-15—4-28	.299	27.60
....	1886	....	....	....	....	....	36.60	NW¼NW¼	4	35	42	3-15—4-28	.298	27.45
....	1886	....	....	....	....	....	36.56	NE¼NW¼	4	35	42	3-15—4-28	.297	27.42
....	1886	....	....	....	....	....	38.96	SW¼NW¼	4	35	42	3-15—4-28	.317	29.22
....	1886	....	....	....	....	....	39.32	SE¼NW¼	4	35	42	3-15—4-28	.320	29.49
....	1886	....	....	....	....	....	38.80	NW¼SE¼	4	35	42	3-15—4-28	.315	29.10
....	1886	....	....	....	....	....	39.28	NE¼SE¼	4	35	42	3-15—4-28	.319	29.46
....	1886	....	....	....	....	....	33.16	SW¼SE¼	4	35	42	3-15—4-28	.270	24.87
....	1886	....	....	....	....	....	39.24	SE¼SE¼	4	35	42	3-15—4-28	.319	29.43
....	1886	....	....	....	....	....	40.08	NW¼NE¼	4	35	42	3-15—4-28	.326	30.06
....	1886	....	....	....	....	....	38.72	NE¼NE¼	4	35	42	3-15—4-28	.315	29.04
....	1886	....	....	....	....	....	39.36	SE¼NE¼	4	35	42	3-15—4-28	.320	29.52
....	1886	....	....	....	....	....	38.88	SW¼NE¼	4	35	42	3-15—4-28	.315	29.16
....	1886	....	....	....	....	....	38.16	SE¼SE¼	4	35	42	3-15—4-28	.310	28.62
....	1886	....	....	....	....	....	37.66	SW¼SE¼	4	35	42	3-15—4-28	.306	28.25
....	1886	....	....	....	....	....	38.88	NE¼SE¼	4	35	42	3-15—4-28	.315	29.16
....	1886	....	....	....	....	....	38.24	NW¼SE¼	4	35	42	3-15—4-28	.311	28.68
....	1887	....	....	....	....	....	12.32	NE¼NW¼	35	35	42	3-15—4-28	.100	9.24
....	1887	....	....	....	....	....	39.60	SE¼NW¼	35	35	42	3-15—4-28	.322	29.70
....	1887	....	....	....	....	....	11.66	NE¼SW¼	35	35	42	3-15—4-28	.095	8.75
....	1887	....	....	....	....	....	40.40	NE¼NE¼	35	35	42	3-15—4-28	.328	30.30
....	1887	....	....	....	....	....	39.12	NW¼SE¼	35	35	42	3-15—4-28	.318	29.34
....	1887	....	....	....	....	....	39.44	NE¼SE¼	35	35	42	3-15—4-28	.321	29.58
1886	1887	....	....	....	....	....	30.64	NE¼SE¼	1	34	42	3-15—4-28	.249	22.98
1886	1887	....	....	....	....	....	10.88	NW¼SE¼	1	34	42	3-15—4-28	.088	8.16
1886	1887	....	....	....	....	....	33.20	SE¼NE¼	1	34	42	3-15—4-28	.270	24.90
1886	1887	....	....	....	....	....	39.36	SW¼NE¼	1	34	42	3-15—4-28	.320	29.52
1886	1887	....	....	....	....	....	26.00	NE¼NE¼	1	34	42	3-15—4-28	.211	19.50
1886	1887	....	....	....	....	....	38.00	NW¼NE¼	1	34	42	3-15—4-28	.309	28.60
1886	1887	....	....	....	....	....	16.48	NE¼NW¼	1	34	42	3-15—4-28	.134	12.36

1886	1887						32.48	SE¼NW¼	1	34	42	3-15—4-28	.264	24.36
	1887					38.80		NW¼NW¼	27	35	42	3-15—4-28	.311	29.10
	1887					35.44		NE¼NW¼	27	35	42	3-15—4-28	.288	26.58
	1887						38.20	SE¼NW¼	27	35	42	3-15—4-28	.311	28.65
	1887						40.40	SW¼NW¼	27	35	42	3-15—4-28	.328	30.30
	1887						40.00	NW¼NE¼	27	35	42	3-15—4-28	.325	30.00
	1887					37.88		NW¼SE¼	27	35	42	3-15—4-28	.308	28.41
	1887						38.96	NE¼SE¼	27	35	42	3-15—4-28	.317	29.22
	1887					37.36		SE¼SE¼	27	35	42	3-15—4-28	.304	28.02
	1887						39.68	SW¼NE¼	27	35	42	3-15—4-28	.323	29.76
	1887						39.88	SE¼NE¼	27	35	42	3-15—4-28	.324	29.91
	1887						37.08	SW¼SW¼	22	35	42	3-15—4-28	.301	27.81
	1887						35.72	NW¼SW¼	22	35	42	3-15—4-28	.290	26.79
	1887						36.71	SE¼SE¼	35	35	42	3-15—4-28	.298	27.53
	1887						1.33	SW¼SE¼	35	35	42	3-15—4-28	.011	1.00
	1887						38.84	NW¼SW¼	36	35	42	3-15—4-28	.316	29.13
	1887						35.40	NE¼SW¼	36	35	42	3-15—4-28	.288	26.55
	1887						37.44	SW¼SW¼	36	35	42	3-15—4-28	.304	28.08
	1887						41.40	SE¼SW¼	36	35	42	3-15—4-28	.337	31.05
	1887						38.80	NW¼SE¼	36	35	42	3-15—4-28	.315	29.10
	1887						40.32	NE¼SE¼	36	35	42	3-15—4-28	.328	30.24
	1887						39.56	SE¼SE¼	36	35	42	3-15—4-28	.322	29.67
	1887						31.04	SW¼SE¼	36	35	42	3-15—4-28	.252	23.28
	1887						31.60	NW¼NW¼	9	35	42	3-15—4-28	.257	23.70
	1887						19.84	SE¼NW¼	9	35	42	3-15—4-28	.161	14.88
	1887						36.80	SW¼NW¼	9	35	42	3-15—4-28	.299	27.60
	1887						.72	SW¼SW¼	9	35	42	3-15—4-28	.006	.54
	1887						37.28	NE¼SW¼	9	35	42	3-15—4-28	.303	27.96
	1887					38.32		SE¼SW¼	9	35	42	3-15—4-28	.312	28.74
	1887						10.68	NW¼SE¼	9	35	42	3-15—4-28	.087	8.01
	1887					38.66		NE¼SE¼	9	35	42	3-15—4-28	.314	29.00
	1887						3.48	SE¼SE¼	9	35	42	3-15—4-28	.028	2.61
	1887						36.36	SW¼SE¼	9	35	42	3-15—4-28	.296	27.27
	1887						37.44	SW¼NE¼	9	35	42	3-15—4-28	.304	28.08

Source—**Rock Creek and Tributaries.** Ditch—**Fraser Creek Canal.** (Squaw Valley lands.)

1876						1.05		NE¼NE¼	26	38	46	3-15—4-28	.009	.79
	1886			23.30				NE¼SE¼	13	38	46	3-15—9-15	.189	69.90
	1886						18.17	NE¼SE¼	13	38	46	3-15—4-28	.148	14.73
	1886			.82				SE¼SE¼	13	38	46	3-15—9-15	.007	2.46
	1886					9.45		SE¼SE¼	13	38	46	3-15—4-28	.077	7.09
	1886						25.97	SE¼SE¼	13	38	46	3-15—4-28	.211	19.49
	1886			34.81				NW¼SE¼	13	38	46	3-15—9-15	.283	104.43
	1886						7.63	NW¼SE¼	13	38	46	3-15—4-28	.062	5.72
	1886			.27				SW¼SE¼	13	38	46	3-15—9-15	.002	.81
	1886						43.55	SW¼SE¼	13	38	46	3-15—4-28	.354	32.66
	1886			1.95				SE¼NW¼	13	38	46	3-15—9-15	.016	5.85
	1886					12.45		SE¼NW¼	13	38	46	3-15—4-28	.101	9.34
	1886			3.44				NE¼SW¼	13	38	46	3-15—9-15	.028	10.32
	1886					7.68		NE¼SW¼	13	38	46	3-15—4-28	.062	7.68
	1886						29.07	NE¼SW¼	13	38	46	3-15—4-28	.236	21.80
	1886						9.26	SE¼SW¼	13	38	46	3-15—4-28	.075	6.95
	1886						30.50	NE¼NE¼	24	38	46	3-15—4-28	.248	22.88

Ellison Ranching Co.—Continued.

Date of beneficial use: Nat. mdw.	Date of beneficial use: Cult. area	Construction first initiated: Dams	Construction first initiated: Ditches	Culture—Acres: Harvest crops	Culture—Acres: Meadow pasture	Culture—Acres: Willow and sage pasture	Culture—Acres: Swamp or overflow	Location: Subdivision	Location: Section	Location: Tp.N.	Location: R.E.	Length of season	Duty of water: C.F.S.	Duty of water: Acre-feet
......	1886	......	......	......	......	......	36.50	SE¼NE¼	24	38	46	3-15—4-28	.297	27.38
......	1886	......	......	......	......	......	41.42	NW¼NE¼	24	38	46	3-15—4-28	.337	31.07
......	1886	......	......	......	......	......	41.10	SW¼NE¼	24	38	46	3-15—4-28	.334	30.83
......	1886	......	......	......	......	......	38.10	NE¼SE¼	24	38	46	3-15—4-28	.310	28.60
......	1886	......	......	......	......	10.98	......	SE¼SE¼	24	28	46	3-15—4-28	.089	8.18
......	1886	......	......	......	......	......	29.74	SE¼SE¼	24	38	46	3-15—4-28	.242	22.31
......	1886	......	......	......	......	......	40.95	NW¼SE¼	24	38	46	3-15—4-28	.333	30.71
......	1886	......	......	......	......	29.31	......	SW¼SE¼	24	38	46	3-15—4-28	.238	21.98
......	1886	......	......	......	......	......	12.06	SW¼SE¼	24	38	46	3-15—4-28	.098	9.05
......	1886	......	......	......	......	......	17.84	NE¼NW¼	24	38	46	3-15—4-28	.145	13.08
......	1886	......	......	......	......	......	7.94	SE¼NW¼	24	38	46	3-15—4-28	.065	5.96
......	1886	......	......	......	......	2.42	......	SE¼NE¼	12	38	46	3-15—4-28	.020	1.82
......	1886	......	......	15.53	......	......	......	NE¼SE¼	12	38	46	3-15—9-15	.126	46.59
......	1886	......	......	......	......	8.64	......	NE¼SE¼	12	38	46	3-15—4-28	.070	6.48
......	1886	......	......	......	......	......	14.00	NE¼SE¼	12	38	46	3-15—4-28	.114	10.50
......	1886	......	......	15.05	......	......	......	SE¼SE¼	12	38	46	3-15—9-15	.122	45.15
......	1886	......	......	......	......	......	9.04	SE¼SE¼	12	38	46	3-15—4-28	.073	6.78
......	1886	......	......	8.00	......	......	......	NE¼NE¼	13	38	46	3-15—9-15	.065	24.00
......	1886	......	......	28.37	......	......	......	NW¼NE¼	13	38	46	3-15—9-15	.231	85.11
......	1886	......	......	......	......	......	6.05	NW¼NE¼	13	38	46	3-15—4-28	.049	4.54
......	1886	......	......	3.10	......	......	......	SE¼NE¼	13	58	46	3-15—9-15	.025	6.30
......	1886	......	......	24.87	......	......	......	SW¼NE¼	13	38	46	3-15—9-15	.202	74.61
......	1886	......	......	.36	......	......	......	NE¼NW¼	13	38	46	3-15—9-15	.003	1.08
......	1886	......	......	......	......	......	1.73	NE¼NW¼	13	38	46	3-15—4-28	.014	1.30
......	1886	......	......	3.90	......	......	......	SE¼NW¼	13	38	46	3-15—9-15	.032	11.70
......	1886	......	......	......	......	6.26	......	SE¼NW¼	13	38	46	3-15—4-28	.051	4.70
......	1886	......	......	......	......	......	2.38	SE¼NW¼	13	38	46	3-15—4-28	.019	1.79
......	1886	......	......	33.52	......	......	......	SW¼SE¼	6	38	47	3-15—9-15	.273	100.56
......	1886	......	......	......	......	3.17	......	SW¼SE¼	6	38	47	3-15—4-28	.026	2.38

Source—**Willow Creek.** Ditch—**Fraser Creek Canal.** (Squaw Valley lands.)

Nat. mdw.	Cult. area	Dams	Ditches	Harvest crops	Meadow pasture	Willow and sage pasture	Swamp or overflow	Subdivision	Section	Tp.N.	R.E.	Length of season	C.F.S.	Acre-feet
......	1886	......	......	......	......	......	1.55	SW¼NW¼	18	38	47	3.15—4-28	.013	1.16
......	1886	......	......	6.95	......	......	......	SE¼NE¼	13	38	46	3-15—9-15	.057	20.85
......	1886	......	......	......	......	......	6.87	SE¼NE¼	13	38	46	3-15—4-28	.055	5.15
......	1886	......	......	14.45	......	......	......	SW¼NE¼	13	38	46	3-15—9-15	.117	43.35

Source—**Rock Creek and Tributaries.** Ditch—**Fraser Creek Canal.** (Squaw Valley lands.)

Nat. mdw.	Cult. area	Dams	Ditches	Harvest crops	Meadow pasture	Willow and sage pasture	Swamp or overflow	Subdivision	Section	Tp.N.	R.E.	Length of season	C.F.S.	Acre-feet
......	1886	......	......	35.50	......	......	......	NE¼NW¼	7	38	47	3 15—9-15	.289	106.50
......	1881	......	......	27.74	......	......	......	SW¼NW¼	7	38	47	3-15—9-15	.226	83.22
......	1881	......	......	......	......	......	8.21	SW¼NW¼	7	38	47	3-15—4-28	.067	6.16
......	1886	......	......	0.46	......	......	......	SW¼SW¼	32	39	47	3-15—9-15	.004	1.38
......	1886	......	......	......	......	......	8.30	SW¼SW¼	32	39	47	3 15—4-28	.007	6.23
......	1886	......	......	......	......	......	12.08	NE¼SW¼	24	38	46	3 15—4-28	.098	9.06
......	1886	......	......	......	......	......	35.35	SE¼SW¼	24	38	46	3-15—4-28	.287	27.61
......	1886	......	......	......	......	16.37	......	SW¼SW¼	24	38	40	3 15—4-28	.133	12.28
......	1886	......	......	......	......	......	9.95	SW¼SW¼	19	38	17	3 15—4-28	.081	7.46

	1886						23.92	NW¼NW¼	30	38	47	3-15—4-28	.194	17.94
	1886						2.42	SW¼NW¼	30	38	47	3-15—4-28	.020	1.82
	1886						1.87	SE¼SE¼	23	38	46	3-15—4-28	.015	1.40

Source—**Rock Creek and Tributaries.** Ditch—**Lakefield Ditch.** (Squaw Valley lands.)

	1880			24.82				SW¼SW¼	7	38	47	3-15—9-15	.202	74.16
	1880						5.62	SW¼SW¼	7	38	47	3-15—4-28	.046	4.22
	1880			16.27				SE¼SW¼	7	38	47	3-15—9-15	.132	48.81
	1880						8.50	SE¼SW¼	7	38	47	3-15—4-28	.070	6.44
	1880			4.03				NE¼NW¼	18	38	47	3-15—9-15	.033	12.09
	1880						6.17	NE¼NW¼	18	38	47	3-15—4-28	.050	4.63
	1880			17.13				NW¼NW¼	18	38	47	3-15—9-15	.139	51.39
	1880						2.30	NW¼NW¼	18	38	47	3-15—4-28	.019	1.73
	1880			4.82				SW¼NW¼	18	38	47	3-15—9-15	.039	14.46
	1880						7.49	SW¼NW¼	18	38	47	3-15—4-28	.061	5.62
	1880						2.70	SE¼NW¼	18	38	47	3-15—4-28	.022	2.03
	1881			29.55				SW¼NE¼	7	38	47	3-15—9-15	.240	88.65
	1881						10.30	SW¼NE¼	7	38	47	3-15—4-28	.084	7.73
	1881			33.87				SE¼NW¼	7	38	47	3-15—9-15	.275	101.61
	1881					3.38		SE¼NW¼	7	38	47	3-15—4-28	.027	2.54
	1881			29.74				NE¼SW¼	7	38	47	3-15—9-15	.242	89.22
	1881						2.16	NE¼SW¼	7	38	47	3-15—4-28	.018	1.62
	1881			34.17				NW¼SW¼	7	38	47	3-15—9-15	.279	102.51
	1881						5.18	NW¼SW¼	7	38	47	3-15—4-28	.042	3.89

Source—**Rock Creek** and Tributaries. Ditch—**Rock Creek Ditch.** (Squaw Valley lands.)

	1880			18.53				NW¼NW¼	8	38	47	3-15—9-15	.151	55.60
	1880					14.36		NW¼NW¼	8	38	47	3-15—4-28	.117	10.77
	1880					2.09		SE¼NW¼	8	38	47	3-15—4-28	.017	1.57
	1880					3.38		SW¼NW¼	8	38	47	3-15—4-28	.027	2.54
	1880						23.12	SW¼NW¼	8	38	47	3-15—4-28	.180	17.34
	1880						1.60	NW¼SW¼	8	38	47	3-15—4-28	.013	1.20
	1880			38.05				NE¼NE¼	7	38	47	3-15—9-15	.309	114.15
	1880			37.00				NW¼NE¼	7	38	47	3-15—9-15	.300	111.00
	1880			24.28				SW¼NE¼	7	38	47	3-15—9-15	.197	72.84
	1880						12.95	SE¼NE¼	7	38	47	3-15—4-28	.105	9.71
	1880						7.05	NE¼SE¼	7	38	47	3-15—4-28	.057	5.29
	1880			4.02				NW¼SE¼	7	38	47	3-15—9-15	.033	12.06
	1880						8.30	NW¼SE¼	7	38	47	3-15—4-28	.067	6.23
	1878			36.80				SE¼NW¼	5	38	47	3-15—9-15	.299	110.40
	1878			17.74				NE¼SW¼	5	38	47	3-15—9-15	.144	53.22
	1878			36.47				NW¼SW¼	5	38	47	3-15—9-15	.297	109.41
	1878					4.75		NW¼SW¼	5	38	47	3-15—4-28	.039	3.56
	1878			37.27				SW¼SW¼	5	38	47	3-15—9-15	.303	111.81

Source—**Rock Creek and Tributaries.** Ditch—**Highline Ditch.** (Squaw Valley lands.)

	1888			18.43				SE¼NW¼	1	38	46	3-15—9-15	.150	55.29
	1888						4.88	SE¼NW¼	1	38	46	3-15—4-28	.040	3.66
	1888			34.92				SW¼NW¼	1	38	46	3-15—9-15	.283	104.76
	1888			15.90				NE¼SW¼	1	38	46	3-15—9-15	.129	47.70

Ellison Ranching Co.—Continued.

Date of beneficial use—Nat. mdw.	Date of beneficial use—Cult. area	Construction first initiated—Dams	Construction first initiated—Ditches	Culture—Acres—Harvest crops	Culture—Acres—Meadow pasture	Culture—Acres—Willow and sage pasture	Culture—Acres—Swamp or overflow	Location—Subdivision	Location—Section	Location—Tp.N.	Location—R.E.	Length of season	Duty of water—C.F.S.	Duty of water—Acre-feet
....	1888	....	....	30.62	....	....	....	NW¼SW¼	1	38	46	3-15—9-15	.249	91.86
....	1888	....	....	8.93	....	....	....	SW¼SW¼	1	38	46	3-15—9-15	.073	26.79
....	1888	....	....	40.87	....	....	....	SE¼NE¼	2	38	46	3-15—9-15	.332	122.61
....	1888	....	....	14.70	....	....	....	SW¼NE¼	2	38	46	3-15—9-15	.120	44.10
....	1888	....	....	....	24.27	....	....	SW¼NE¼	2	38	46	3-15—6-13	.197	36.41
....	1888	....	....	26.03	....	....	....	NE¼SE¼	2	38	46	3-15—9-15	.212	78.09
....	1888	....	....	8.54	....	....	....	NW¼SE¼	2	38	46	3-15—9-15	.069	25.62
....	1888	....	....	....	25.95	....	....	NW¼SE¼	2	38	46	3-15—6-13	.211	38.93
....	1888	....	....	5.04	....	....	....	SE¼SE¼	2	38	46	3-15—9-15	.041	15.12
....	1888	....	....	....	....	....	2.47	SE¼SW¼	32	39	47	3-15—4-28	.020	1.85
....	1888	....	....	....	....	....	9.61	SE¼SW¼	31	39	47	3-15—4-28	.078	7.21
....	1888	....	....	....	....	....	8.54	SW¼SW¼	31	39	47	3-15—4-28	.069	6.41
....	1888	....	....	5.71	....	....	....	NW¼NW¼	5	38	47	3-15—9-15	.046	17.13
....	1888	....	....	....	....	....	17.33	NE¼NW¼	6	38	47	3-15—4-28	.141	13.00
....	1888	....	....	....	....	....	2.31	NW¼NW¼	6	38	47	3-15—4-28	.019	1.73
....	1888	....	....	5.82	....	....	....	NE¼NE¼	2	38	46	3-15—9-15	.047	17.46
....	1888	....	....	12.75	....	....	....	NW¼NE¼	2	38	46	3-15—9-15	.104	38.25
....	1885	....	....	....	....	5.83	....	SE¼NW¼	6	38	47	3-15—4-28	.047	4.38

Source—**Willow Creek.** Ditch—**Overflow.** (Squaw Valley lands.)

Nat. mdw.	Cult. area	Dams	Ditches	Harvest crops	Meadow pasture	Willow and sage pasture	Swamp or overflow	Subdivision	Section	Tp.N.	R.E.	Length of season	C.F.S.	Acre-feet
....	1878	....	....	5.47	....	....	....	NE¼SW¼	18	38	47	3-15—9-15	.044	16.41
....	1878	....	....	....	....	2.28	....	NE¼SW¼	18	38	47	3-15—4-28	.019	1.71
....	1878	....	....	....	....	....	8.47	NE¼SW¼	18	38	47	3-15—4-28	.069	6.35
....	1878	....	....	....	....	....	12.50	NW¼SW¼	18	38	47	3-15—4-28	.101	9.38

Source—**Willow Creek.** Ditch—Deep **Slough.** (Squaw Valley lands.)

Nat. mdw.	Cult. area	Dams	Ditches	Harvest crops	Meadow pasture	Willow and sage pasture	Swamp or overflow	Subdivision	Section	Tp.N.	R.E.	Length of season	C.F.S.	Acre-feet
....	1886	....	....	....	10.90	....	....	SE¼SW¼	8	38	47	3-15—6-13	.089	16.35
....	1886	....	....	....	17.27	....	....	NE¼NW¼	17	38	47	3-15—6-13	.140	25.91
....	1886	....	....	....	20.82	....	....	NW¼NW¼	17	38	47	3-15—6-13	.169	31.23
....	1886	....	....	....	2.42	....	....	SW¼NW¼	17	38	47	3-15—6-13	.020	3.63
....	1886	....	....	....	13.30	....	....	NE¼NE¼	18	38	47	3-15—6-13	.108	19.95
....	1886	....	....	....	0.87	....	....	NW¼NE¼	18	38	47	3-15—6-13	.007	1.31
....	1886	....	....	....	24.77	....	....	SE¼NE¼	18	38	47	3-15—6-13	.201	37.16
....	1886	....	....	....	14.35	....	....	SW¼NE¼	18	38	47	3-15—6-13	.116	21.53
....	1886	....	....	27.27	....	....	....	NE¼SE¼	8	38	47	3-15—9-15	.222	81.81
....	1886	....	....	16.62	....	....	....	SE¼SE¼	8	38	47	3-15—9-15	.135	49.86
....	1886	....	....	7.62	....	....	....	NW¼SE¼	8	38	47	3-15—9-15	.062	22.86
....	1886	....	....	32.87	....	....	....	SW¼SE¼	8	38	47	3-15—9-15	.267	98.61
....	1886	....	....	0.97	....	....	....	NW¼NE¼	17	38	47	3-15—9-15	.008	2.91
....	1886	....	....	1.90	....	....	....	SE¼NE¼	18	38	47	3-15—9-15	.015	5.70
....	1886	....	....	....	....	....	7.49	SE¼NE¼	18	38	17	3-15—4-28	.061	5.62
....	1886	....	....	11.70	....	....	....	SW¼NE¼	18	38	47	3-15—9-15	.095	35.10
....	1886	....	....	....	....	....	0.75	SW¼NE¼	18	38	47	3-15—4-28	.006	.56
....	1886	....	....	....	....	....	1.32	NE¼SE¼	18	38	47	3-15—4-28	.011	.99
....	1886	....	....	3.97	....	....	....	NW¼SE¼	18	38	47	3-15—9-15	.032	12.01*

	1886						11.57	NW¼SE¼	18	38	47	3-15—4-28	.094	8.64
	1886			3.32				SE¼NW¼	18	38	47	3-15—9-15	.027	9.96
	1886					5.85		SE¼NW¼	18	38	47	3.15—4-28	.048	4.39
	1886						0.95	SE¼NW¼	18	38	47	3-15—4-28	.008	.71

Source—Rock Creek and Tributaries. Ditch—**Warm Spring.** (Squaw Valley lands.)

	1876					13.15		NE¼NE¼	25	38	46	3-15—4-28	.107	9.87
	1876						20.17	NE¼NE¼	25	38	46	3-15—4-28	.164	15.13
	1876					13.01		NW¼NE¼	25	38	46	3.15—4-28	.106	9.76
	1876						13.74	NW¼NE¼	25	38	46	3-15—4-28	.112	10.81
	1876					21.62		NE¼NW¼	25	38	46	3-15—4-28	.176	16.22
	1876						3.00	NE¼NW¼	25	38	46	3-15—4-28	.024	2.25
	1876					20.35		NW¼NW¼	25	38	46	3.15—4-28	.165	15.26

Source—Rock Creek. Ditch—**Barleyfield Canal.** (Squaw Valley lands.)

	1888			3.96				NW¼SE¼	21	39	47	3-15—9-15	.032	11.85
	1888			0.47				SW¼SE¼	21	39	47	3-15—9-15	.038	1.41
	1888			32.45				NE¼SW¼	21	39	47	3-15—9-15	.264	97.36
	1888			29.30				SE¼SW¼	21	39	47	3-15—9-15	.238	87.90
	1888			35.95				NW¼SW¼	21	39	47	3-15—9-15	.292	107.85
	1888			36.00				SW¼SW¼	21	39	47	3-15—9-15	.293	108.00
	1888			1.00				SW¼NE¼	20	39	47	3-15—9-15	.008	3.00
	1888			40.55				NE¼SE¼	20	39	47	3-15—9-15	.330	121.65
	1888			36.35				SE¼SE¼	20	39	47	3-15—9-15	.296	109.05
	1888			21.40				NW¼SE¼	20	39	47	3-15—9-15	.174	64.20
	1888			23.30				SW¼SE¼	20	39	47	3-15—9-15	.189	69.90
	1888			2.90				NE¼NW¼	28	39	47	3-15—9-15	.024	8.70
	1888			27.64				NW¼NW¼	28	39	47	3-15—9-15	.225	82.92
	1888			4.73				SW¼NW¼	28	39	47	3-15—9-15	.039	14.19
	1888			39.37				NE¼NE¼	29	39	47	3-15—9-15	.320	118.11
	1888			2.35				SE¼NE¼	29	39	47	3-15—9-15	.019	7.05

Source—Rock Creek and Tributaries. Ditch—**Willow Creek Canal.** (Squaw Valley lands.)

	1880				23.40			SE¼NE¼	1	38	46	3-15—6-13	.190	35.10
	1880						5.26	SE¼NE¼	1	38	46	3-15—4-28	.043	3.95
	1880				23.61			SW¼NE¼	1	38	46	3-15—6-13	.192	35.42
	1880						13.68	SW¼NE¼	1	38	46	3-15—4-28	.111	10.26
	1880			16.56				NE¼SE¼	1	38	46	3-15—9-15	.135	49.68
	1880				17.67			NE¼SE¼	1	38	46	3-15—6-13	.144	26.51
	1880						3.31	NE¼SE¼	1	38	46	3-15—4-28	.027	2.48
	1880			12.12				NW¼SE¼	1	38	46	3-15—9-15	.098	36.36
	1880				7.27			NW¼SE¼	1	38	46	3-15—6-13	.059	10.90
	1880			34.19				SE¼SE¼	1	38	46	3-15—9-15	.278	102.57
	1880						5.76	SE¼SE¼	1	38	46	3-15—4-28	.047	4.32
	1880			40.00				SW¼SE¼	1	38	46	3-15—9-15	.325	120.00
	1888			34.79				SE¼SW¼	1	38	46	3-15—9-15	.283	104.37
	1888				1.51			SE¼SW¼	1	38	46	3-15—6-13	.012	2.27
	1888				3.67			SE¼NW¼	1	38	46	3-15—6-13	.030	5.51
	1888			15.12				NE¼SW¼	1	38	46	3-15—9-15	.123	45.36
	1888				7.06			NE¼SW¼	1	38	46	3-15—6-13	.057	10.59
	1888						1.90	SW¼SW¼	1	38	46	3-15—4-28	.015	1.43
	1885			33.85				SE¼SE¼	6	38	47	3-15—9-15	.275	101.56

Ellison Ranching Co.—Continued.

Date of beneficial use: Nat. mdw.	Date of beneficial use: Cult. area	Construction first initiated: Dams	Construction first initiated: Ditches	Culture—Acres: Harvest crops	Culture—Acres: Meadow pasture	Culture—Acres: Willow and sage pasture	Culture—Acres: Swamp or overflow	Location: Subdivision	Location: Section	Location: Tp. N.	Location: R. E.	Length of season	Duty of water: C. F. S.	Duty of water: Acre-feet
	1885					4.25		SE¼SE¼	6	38	47	3-15—4-28	.035	3.19
	1885			32.48				NE¼SW¼	6	38	47	3-15—9-15	.264	97.44
	1885						8.42	NE¼SW¼	6	32	47	3-15—4-28	.068	6.32
	1885			15.12				NW¼SW¼	6	38	47	3-15—9-15	.122	45.36
	1885						20.47	NW¼SW¼	6	38	47	3-15—4-28	.166	15.35
	1885			40.37				SE¼SW¼	6	38	47	3-15—9-15	.328	121.11
	1885			27.65				SW¼SW¼	6	38	47	3-15—9-15	.225	82.95
	1885						4.54	SW¼SW¼	6	38	47	3-15—4-28	.037	3.41
	1885			0.97				NE¼NE¼	5	38	47	3-15—9-15	.008	2.91
	1885			8.82				NW¼NE¼	5	38	47	3-15—9-15	.072	26.46
	1885						3.70	NW¼NE¼	5	38	47	3-15—4-28	.030	2.78
	1886			18.37				NE¼NW¼	5	38	47	3-15—9-15	.149	55.11
	1885				10.18			NE¼NW¼	5	38	47	3-15—6-13	.083	15.27
	1885						3.22	NE¼NW¼	5	38	47	3-15—4-28	.026	2.42
	1886			29.45				NW¼NW¼	5	38	47	3-15—9-15	.230	88.35
	1885						5.78	NW¼NW¼	5	38	47	3-15—4-28	.047	4.34
	1885			15.10				NE¼NE¼	6	38	47	3-15—9-15	.123	45.30
	1885						11.10	NE¼NE¼	6	38	47	3-15—4-28	.090	8.33
	1885			0.40				SE¼NE¼	5	38	47	3-15—9-15	.003	1.20
	1885			34.09				SW¼NE¼	5	38	47	3-15—9-15	.277	102.27
	1885					0.26		SW¼NE¼	5	38	47	3-15—4-28	.002	0.20
	1885			15.11				NW¼SE¼	5	38	47	3-15—9-15	.123	45.33
	1885					6.51		NW¼SE¼	5	38	47	3-15—4-28	.053	4.88
	1885					2.12		SW¼SE¼	5	38	47	3-15—4-28	.017	1.59
	1886			1.65				SW¼SE¼	3	38	47	3-15—9-15	.013	4.95
	1886			12.45				SE¼SW¼	3	38	47	3-15—9-15	.101	37.35
	1886			33.90				SW¼SW¼	3	38	47	3-15—9-15	.276	101.70
	1886			24.60				SE¼SE¼	4	38	47	3-15—9-15	.200	73.80
	1886			3.00				SW¼SE¼	4	38	47	3-15—9-15	.024	9.00
	1886			0.67				NW¼NW¼	10	38	47	3-15—9-15	.005	2.01
	1886			10.68				NE¼NE¼	9	38	47	3-15—9-15	.087	32.04
	1886						3.93	NE¼NE¼	9	38	47	3-15—4-28	.032	2.97
	1886			30.86				NW¼NE¼	9	38	47	3-15—9-15	.251	92.58
	1886						4.21	NW¼NE¼	9	38	47	3-15—4-28	.034	3.16
	1886			6.77				SW¼NE¼	9	38	47	3-15—9-15	.055	20.31
	1886						7.88	SW¼NE¼	9	38	47	3-15—4-28	.064	5.91
	1886			18.37				NE¼NW¼	8	38	47	3-15—9-15	.149	55.11
	1886			37.40				SE¼NW¼	9	38	47	3-15—9-15	.304	112.20
	1886			20.88				SW¼NW¼	9	38	47	3-15—9-15	.170	62.64
	1886			4.95				NE¼SW¼	9	38	47	3-15—9-15	.040	14.85
	1886			36.72				NW¼SW¼	9	38	47	3-15—9-15	.299	110.16
	1886			1.40				SW¼SW¼	9	38	47	3-15—9-15	.011	4.20
	1886			0.29				SE¼NE¼	8	38	47	3-15—9-15	.002	.87
	1885			6.05				NE¼NW¼	8	38	47	3-15—9-15	.049	18.15
	1885					17.42		NE¼NW¼	8	38	47	3-15—4-28	.142	13.07
	1880			23.82				NW¼NW¼	7	38	47	3-15—9-15	.194	71.46
	1880						3.23	NW¼NW¼	7	38	47	3-15—4-28	.026	2.42

	1885				3.35			NE¼NE¼	1	38	46	3-15—6-13	.026	4.88
	1885				13.56			NW¼NE¼	1	38	46	3-15—6-13	.110	20.34
	1885				2.20			NE¼NW¼	1	38	46	3-15—6-13	.018	3.30
	1885			22.03				NE¼NE¼	12	38	46	3-15—9-15	.179	66.00
	1885						9.65	NE¼NE¼	12	38	46	3-15—4-28	.078	7.24
	1885			28.80				NW¼NE¼	12	38	46	3-15—9-15	.234	86.40
	1885				11.10			NW¼NE¼	12	38	46	3-15—6-13	.090	16.65
	1885			29.23				SE¼NE¼	12	38	46	3-15—9-15	.238	87.60
	1885						4.39	SE¼NE¼	12	38	46	3-15—4-28	.030	3.21
	1885			16.20				SW¼NE¼	12	38	46	3-15—9-15	.132	48.60
	1885						15.12	SW¼NE¼	12	38	46	3-15—4-28	.123	11.34
	1885			4.90				NE¼NW¼	12	38	46	3-15—9-15	.040	14.70
	1885				27.45			NE¼NW¼	12	38	46	3-15—6-13	.223	41.18
	1885						8.42	NE¼NW¼	12	38	46	3-15—4-28	.068	6.32
	1885						13.70	NW¼NW¼	12	38	46	3-15—4-28	.111	10.28
	1885						4.39	SE¼NW¼	12	38	46	3-15—4-28	.036	3.29
	1885						7.06	NW¼SE¼	12	38	46	3-15—4-28	.057	5.30
	1885			1.20				SW¼SE¼	12	38	46	3-15—9-15	.010	3.60
	1885						9.58	SW¼SE¼	12	38	46	3-15—4-28	.078	7.19
	1880			19.14				SW¼NW¼	5	38	47	3-15—9-15	.156	57.42
	1880				22.26			SW¼NW¼	5	38	47	3-15—6-13	.181	33.39
	1880			27.15				SE¼SW¼	5	38	47	3-15—9-15	.221	81.45
	1880					12.99		SE¼SW¼	5	38	47	3-15—4-28	.106	9.74
	1885			29.40				SE¼NE¼	6	38	47	3-15—9-15	.239	88.20
	1885				8.14			SE¼NE¼	6	38	47	3-15—6-13	.066	12.21
	1885					2.81		SE¼NE¼	6	38	47	3-15—4-28	.023	2.11
	1885			23.38				SW¼NE¼	6	38	47	3-15—9-15	.190	70.14
	1885						5.54	SW¼NE¼	6	38	47	3-15—4-28	.045	4.16
	1885			21.66				SE¼NW¼	6	38	47	3-15—9-15	.176	64.98
	1885						8.93	SE¼NW¼	6	38	47	3-15—4-28	.073	6.70
	1885			19.70				NE¼SW¼	5	38	47	3-15—9-15	.160	59.10
	1885				2.38			SW¼NW¼	6	38	47	3-15—6-13	.019	3.57
	1885						13.03	SW¼NW¼	6	38	47	3-15—4-28	.106	9.77
	1885			7.77				NE¼SE¼	6	38	47	3-15—9-15	.063	23.31
	1885				29.62			NE¼SE¼	6	38	47	3-15—6-13	.241	44.39
	1885			28.25				NW¼SE¼	6	38	47	3-15—9-15	.230	84.75
	1885					9.37		NW¼SE¼	6	38	47	3-15—4-28	.076	7.03
	1885						1.37	NW¼SE¼	6	38	47	3-15—4-28	.011	1.03

Claimant—**Clover Valley Land and Stock Co.** Proof No. 00157

Source—**Humboldt River.** Ditch—**Hammond.** (Lands of Hammond Bros.)

1872	1875						38.76	NE¼NE¼	17	36	42	3-15—4-28	.315	29.07
1872	1875			16.90				NW¼NE¼	17	36	42	3-15—9-15	.137	50.70
1872	1875						19.28	NW¼NE¼	17	36	42	3-15—4-28	.157	14.46
1872	1875			17.26				SE¼NE¼	17	36	42	3-15—9-15	.140	51.78
1872	1875				.92			SE¼NE¼	17	36	42	3-15—6-13	.007	1.38
1872	1875						11.60	SE¼NE¼	17	36	42	3-15—4-28	.094	8.70
1872	1875			34.24				SW¼NE¼	17	36	42	3-15—9-15	.278	102.72
1872	1875					1.18		SW¼NE¼	17	36	42	3-15—4-28	.010	.89
1872	1875			37.68				NW¼SE¼	17	36	42	3-15—9-15	.306	113.04
1872	1875					.92		NW¼SE¼	17	36	42	3-15—4-28	.008	.69
1872	1875			39.04				NE¼SE¼	17	36	42	3-15—9-15	.317	117.12

Clover Valley Land and Stock Co.—Continued.

Date of beneficial use: Nat. mdw.	Cult. area	Construction first initiated: Dams	Ditches	Culture—Acres: Harvest crops	Meadow pasture	Willow and sage pasture	Swamp or over-flow	Location: Subdivision	Section	Tp.N.	R.E.	Length of season	Duty of water: C.F.S.	Acre-feet
1872	1875			21.82				SE¼SE¼	17	36	42	3-15—9-15	.177	65.46
1872	1875				1.20			SE¼SE¼	17	36	42	3-15—6-13	.010	1.80
1872	1875						17.36	SE¼SE¼	17	36	42	3-15—4-28	.141	13.02
1872	1875			34.42				SW¼SE¼	17	36	42	3-15—9-15	.280	103.26
1872	1875						6.84	SW¼SE¼	17	36	42	3-15—4-28	.056	5.13
1872	1875			14.00				NW¼NW¼	7	36	42	3-15—9-15	.114	42.00
1872	1875			37.96				NE¼NW¼	7	36	42	3-15—9-15	.309	113.88
1872	1875					2.40		NE¼NW¼	7	36	42	3-15—4-28	.020	1.80
1872	1875			15.12				SW¼NW¼	7	36	42	3-15—9-15	.123	45.36
1872	1875			40.80				SE¼NW¼	7	36	42	3-15—9-15	.332	122.40
1872	1875			8.88				NW¼SW¼	7	36	42	3-15—9-15	.072	26.64
1872	1875			40.00				NE¼SW¼	7	36	42	3-15—9-15	.325	120.00
1872	1875			1.72				SW¼SW¼	7	36	42	3-15—9-15	.014	5.16
1872	1875			34.08				SE¼SW¼	7	36	42	3-15—9-15	.277	102.24
1872	1875						6.24	SE¼SW¼	7	36	42	3-15—4-28	.051	4.68
1872	1875						39.68	NE¼NE¼	7	36	42	3-15—4-28	.323	29.76
1872	1875			7.08				NW¼NE¼	7	36	42	3-15—9-15	.058	21.24
1872	1875						31.97	NW¼NE¼	7	36	42	3-15—4-28	.260	23.98
1872	1875			39.76				SW¼NE¼	7	36	42	3-15—9-15	.323	119.28
1872	1875						0.72	SW¼NE¼	7	36	42	3-15—4-28	.006	.54
1872	1875			13.04				SE¼NE¼	7	36	42	3-15—9-15	.106	39.12
1872	1875						26.53	SE¼NE¼	7	36	42	3-15—4-28	.216	19.90
1872	1875			40.64				NW¼SE¼	7	36	42	3-15—9-15	.330	121.92
1872	1875			38.84				NE¼SE¼	7	36	42	3-15—9-15	.316	116.52
1872	1875						2.16	NE¼SE¼	7	36	42	3-15—4-28	.018	1.62
1872	1875			40.72				SW¼SE¼	7	36	42	3-15—9-15	.331	122.16
1872	1875			41.04				SE¼SE¼	7	36	42	3-15—9-15	.334	123.12
1872	1875			8.80				NW¼SW¼	8	36	42	3-15—9-15	.072	26.40
1872	1875						10.56	NW¼SW¼	8	36	42	3-15—4-28	.086	7.92
1872	1875			38.54				SW¼SW¼	8	36	42	3-15—9-15	.313	115.62
1872	1875						1.60	SW¼SW¼	8	36	42	3-15—4-28	.013	1.20
1872	1875			12.80				SE¼SW¼	8	36	42	3-15—9-15	.104	38.40
1872	1875						27.56	SE¼SW¼	8	36	42	3-15—4-28	.224	20.67
1872	1875			34.92				NW¼NW¼	17	36	42	3-15—9-15	.284	104.76
1872	1875			34.38				NE¼NW¼	17	36	42	3-15—9-15	.280	103.14
1872	1875						1.08	NE¼NW¼	17	36	42	3-15—4-28	.009	.81
1872	1875			26.08				SW¼NW¼	17	36	42	3-15—9-15	.212	78.24
1872	1875					5.80		SW¼NW¼	17	36	42	3-15—4-28	.047	4.35
1872	1875			35.12				SE¼NW¼	17	36	42	3-15—9-15	.289	105.36
1872	1875					.16		SE¼NW¼	17	36	42	3-15—4-28	.001	.12
1872	1875			36.08				NW¼SW¼	17	36	42	3-15—9-15	.293	108.24
1872	1875					1.44		NW¼SW¼	17	36	42	3-15—4-28	.012	1.08
1872	1875			39.76				NE¼SW¼	17	36	42	3-15—9-15	.323	119.28
1872	1875			38.96				SE¼SW¼	17	36	42	3-15—9-15	.317	116.88
1872	1875						1.68	SE¼SW¼	17	36	42	3-15—4-28	.014	1.26
1872	1875			16.24				SW¼SW¼	17	36	42	3-15—9-15	.132	48.72
1872	1875						24.68	SW¼SW¼	17	36	42	3-15—4-28	.200	18.51

Source—**Humboldt River.** Ditch—**Gonzales Slough.** (Russell Land and Cattle Co. lands.)

	1880			10.00				SE¼ NE¼	33	36	42	3-15—9-15	.154	57.00
	1880			1.34				NE¼ NE¼	33	36	42	3-15—9-15	.010	3.72
	1880			26.80				NE¼ SE¼	33	36	42	3-15—9-15	.209	89.40
	1880			25.44				SE¼ SE¼	33	36	42	3-15—9-15	.207	76.82
	1880			27.88				SE¼ SE¼	27	36	42	3-15—9-15	.227	83.54
	1880				4.72			SE¼ SE¼	27	36	42	3-15—6-13	.038	7.08
	1880					1.16		SE¼ SE¼	27	36	42	3-15—4-28	.009	0.87
	1880			37.41				NW¼ SE¼	27	36	42	3-15—9-15	.304	112.23
	1880					0.91		NW¼ SE¼	27	36	42	3-15—4-28	.007	0.68
	1880			17.78				NW¼ SE¼	11	35	42	3-15—9-15	.144	53.34
	1880					15.98		NW¼ SE¼	11	35	42	3-15—4-28	.130	11.99
	1880				14.08			SW¼ SE¼	11	35	42	3-15—6-13	.114	21.12
	1880					21.84		SW¼ SE¼	11	35	42	3-15—4-28	.178	16.38
	1880			28.45				NE¼ SW¼	11	35	42	3-15—9-15	.231	85.35
	1880					10.00		NE¼ SW¼	11	35	42	3-15—4-28	.081	7.50
	1880			0.44				SE¼ SW¼	11	35	42	3-15—9-15	.004	1.32
	1880					39.12		SE¼ SW¼	11	35	42	3-15—4-28	.318	29.34
	1880			14.62				NW¼ SW¼	11	35	42	3-15—9-15	.119	43.92
	1880					24.88		NW¼ SW¼	11	35	42	3-15—4-28	.202	18.06
	1880					40.00		SW¼ SW¼	11	35	42	3-15—4-28	.325	30.00
	1880			35.72				SW¼ SW¼	27	36	42	3-15—9-15	.290	107.16
	1880				3.08			SW¼ SW¼	27	36	42	3-15—6-13	.025	4.62
	1880					13.56		SE¼ NW¼	11	35	42	3-15—4-28	.110	10.17
	1880			38.52				NW¼ NW¼	11	35	42	3-15—9-15	.313	115.56
	1880			39.60				SW¼ NW¼	11	35	42	3-15—9-15	.322	118.80
	1880					0.10		SW¼ NW¼	11	35	42	3-15—4-28	.001	0.08
	1880			35.68				SE¼ NE¼	11	35	42	3-15—9-15	.290	107.04
	1880					3.84		SE¼ NE¼	11	35	42	3-15—4-28	.031	2.88
	1880			38.88				NW¼ NE¼	11	35	42	3-15—9-15	.316	116.64
	1880					1.56		NW¼ NE¼	11	35	42	3-15—4-28	.012	1.18
	1880			39.36				NE¼ NE¼	11	35	42	3-15—9-15	.320	118.08

Source—**Humboldt River.** Ditch—**Aemes Dam.** (Russell Land and Cattle Co. lands.)

	1876			31.12				SE¼ NW¼	2	35	42	3-15—9-15	.253	93.36
	1876					5.04		SE¼ NW¼	2	35	42	3-15—4-28	.041	3.78
	1876			33.69				NE¼ SW¼	2	35	42	3-15—9-15	.274	101.07
	1876					2.90		NE¼ SW¼	2	35	42	3-15—4-28	.024	2.17
	1876			23.42				SE¼ SW¼	2	35	42	3-15—9-15	.190	70.26
	1876					5.80		SE¼ SW¼	2	35	42	3-15—4-28	.047	4.35
	1876			29.92				NW¼ SW¼	2	35	42	3-15—9-15	.243	89.96
	1876			19.68				NE¼ SE¼	11	35	42	3-15—9-15	.160	59.04
	1876					15.02		NE¼ SE¼	11	35	42	3-15—4-28	.122	11.27
	1876						0.50	NE¼ SE¼	11	35	42	3-15—4-28	.004	0.38
	1876					35.41		SE¼ SE¼	11	35	42	3-15—4-28	.288	26.57
	1876						0.31	SE¼ SE¼	11	35	42	3-15—4-28	.003	0.23
	1876					4.18		NE¼ NW¼	11	35	42	3-15—4-28	.034	3.13
	1876			19.50				SE¼ NW¼	11	35	42	3-15—9-15	.159	58.50
	1876			23.88				SW¼ NE¼	11	35	42	3-15—9-15	.194	71.64
	1876					10.68		SW¼ NE¼	11	35	42	3-15—4-28	.087	8.01
	1876			31.68				NE¼ NW¼	11	35	42	3-15—9-15	.258	95.04
	1876			0.09				NE¼ NE¼	10	35	42	3-15—9-15	.001	.27

Clover Valley Land and Stock Co.—Continued.

Date of beneficial use: Nat. mdw.	Date of beneficial use: Cult. area	Construction first initiated: Dams	Construction first initiated: Ditches	Culture—Acres: Harvest crops	Culture—Acres: Meadow pasture	Culture—Acres: Willow and sage pasture	Culture—Acres: Swamp or overflow	Location: Subdivision	Location: Section	Location: Tp.N.	Location: R.E.	Length of season	Duty of water: C.F.S.	Duty of water: Acre-feet
......	1876	......	......	1.51	......	......	......	SE¼NE¼	10	35	42	3-15—9-15	.012	4.53
......	1876	......	......	......	......	0.12	......	SE¼NE¼	10	35	42	3-15—4-28	.001	.09
......	1876	......	......	......	......	1.44	......	NE¼SE¼	10	35	42	3-15—4-28	.012	1.08
......	1876	......	......	......	......	0.48	......	SE¼SE¼	10	35	42	3-15—4-28	.004	.36
......	1876	......	......	15.56	......	......	......	NE¼SW¼	27	36	42	3-15—9-15	.127	46.58
......	1876	......	......	......	......	15.58	......	NE¼SW¼	27	36	42	3-15—4-28	.127	11.69
......	1876	......	......	20.80	......	......	......	NW¼SW¼	27	36	42	3-15—9-15	.218	80.40
......	1876	......	......	3.28	......	......	......	SE¼NE¼	27	36	42	3-15—9-15	.027	9.84
......	1876	......	......	......	2.00	......	......	SE¼NE¼	27	36	42	3-15—6-13	.016	3.00
......	1876	......	......	29.35	......	......	......	SW¼NE¼	27	36	42	3-15—9-15	.239	88.05
......	1876	......	......	......	4.88	......	......	SW¼NE¼	27	36	42	3-15—6-13	.040	7.32
......	1876	......	......	......	......	1.29	......	SW¼NE¼	27	36	42	3-15—4-28	.010	0.97
......	1876	......	......	24.64	......	......	......	SE¼SW¼	27	36	42	3-15—9-15	.200	73.95
......	1876	......	......	......	......	10.20	......	SE¼SW¼	27	36	42	3-15—4-28	.083	7.65
......	1876	......	......	26.64	......	......	......	SE¼NW¼	27	36	42	3-15—9-15	.217	79.92
......	1876	......	......	......	......	6.56	......	SE¼NW¼	27	36	42	3-15—4-28	.053	4.92
......	1876	......	......	30.92	......	......	......	SW¼NW¼	27	36	42	3-15—9-15	.251	92.76
......	1876	......	......	......	......	0.10	......	SE¼NW¼	27	36	42	3-15—4-28	.001	0.08
......	1876	......	......	......	3.84	......	......	NE¼NE¼	27	36	42	3-15—6-13	.031	5.76
......	1876	......	......	......	7.20	......	......	NW¼NE¼	27	36	42	3-15—6-13	.059	10.80
......	1876	......	......	......	......	6.88	......	NW¼NE¼	27	36	42	3-15—4-28	.056	5.16
......	1876	......	......	28.80	......	......	......	NE¼NW¼	27	36	42	3-15—9-15	.227	86.40
......	1876	......	......	......	1.40	......	......	NE¼NW¼	27	36	42	3-15—6-13	.011	2.16
......	1876	......	......	......	......	2.64	......	NE¼NW¼	27	36	42	3-15—4-28	.021	1.98
......	1876	......	......	23.44	......	......	......	NW¼NW¼	27	36	42	3-15—9-15	.191	70.32
......	1876	......	......	......	......	8.40	......	NW¼NW¼	27	36	42	3-15—4-28	.068	6.30
......	1876	......	......	20.70	......	......	......	NE¼NE¼	28	36	42	3-15—9-15	.168	62.10
......	1876	......	......	......	......	......	6.14	NE¼NE¼	28	36	42	3-15—4-28	.050	4.72
......	1876	......	......	39.60	......	......	......	NE¼SE¼	34	36	42	3-15—9-15	.320	118.80
......	1876	......	......	29.64	......	......	......	NE¼NW¼	2	35	42	3-15—9-15	.241	88.92
......	1876	......	......	......	......	6.50	......	NE¼NW¼	2	35	42	3-15—4-28	.053	4.88
......	1876	......	......	27.60	......	......	......	NW¼NE¼	34	36	42	3-15—9-15	.224	82.80
......	1876	......	......	......	3.92	......	......	NW¼NE¼	34	36	42	3-15—6-13	.032	5.88
......	1876	......	......	......	......	1.52	......	NW¼NE¼	34	36	42	3-15—4-28	.012	1.14
......	1876	......	......	40.00	......	......	......	NE¼NW¼	34	36	42	3-15—9-15	.325	120.00
......	1876	......	......	23.44	......	......	......	SW¼SE¼	27	36	42	3-15—9-15	.191	70.32
......	1876	......	......	......	9.84	......	......	SW¼SE¼	27	36	42	3-15—6-13	.080	14.76
......	1876	......	......	......	......	2.96	......	SW¼SE¼	27	36	42	3-15—4-28	.024	2.22
......	1876	......	......	29.57	......	......	......	NE¼SE¼	27	36	42	3-15—9-15	.240	88.71
......	1876	......	......	......	1.40	......	......	NE¼SE¼	27	36	42	3-15—6-13	.011	2.10
......	1876	......	......	......	......	2.67	......	NE¼SE¼	27	36	42	3-15—4-28	.022	2.00
......	1876	......	......	......	......	13.32	......	NE¼NW¼	35	36	42	3-15—4-28	.108	10.00
......	1876	......	......	23.96	......	......	......	SE¼SE¼	34	36	42	3-15—9-15	.196	71.88
......	1876	......	......	......	......	11.12	......	SE¼SE¼	34	36	42	3-15—4-28	.090	8.84
......	1876	......	......	38.64	......	......	......	SW¼SE¼	34	36	42	3-15—9-15	.311	115.92
......	1876	......	......	24.28	......	......	......	NE¼SE¼	34	36	42	3-15—9-15	.197	72.84
......	1876	......	......	......	......	8.68	......	NE¼SE¼	34	36	42	3-15—4-28	.071	6.51

	1876			26.73				SE¼NE¼	34	36	42	3-15—9-15	.217	80.19
	1876					7.86		SE¼NE¼	34	36	42	3-15—4-28	.064	5.90
	1876			26.60				SW¼NE¼	34	36	42	3-15—9-15	.216	79.80
	1876					6.08		SW¼NE¼	34	36	42	3-15—4-28	.049	4.56
	1876			18.68				NE¼NE¼	34	36	42	3-15—9-15	.152	56.04
	1876				11.78			NE¼NE¼	34	36	42	3-15—6-13	.096	17.04
	1876					7.52		NE¼NE¼	34	36	42	3-15—4-28	.061	5.64
	1876				9.21			SW¼SE¼	35	36	42	3-15—6-13	.075	13.81
	1876					2.07		SW¼SE¼	35	36	42	3-15—4-28	.017	1.55
	1876			2.00				NW¼SE¼	35	36	42	3-15—9-15	.016	6.00
	1876			26.27				SE¼SW¼	35	36	42	3-15—9-15	.213	78.81
	1876				7.28			SE¼SW¼	35	36	42	3-15—6-13	.059	10.92
	1876					2.73		SE¼SW¼	35	36	42	3-15—4-28	.022	2.05
	1876			11.68				SW¼SW¼	35	36	42	3-15—9-15	.095	35.04
	1876					20.12		SW¼SW¼	35	36	42	3-15—4-28	.164	15.09
	1876			37.68				NW¼SW¼	35	36	42	3-15—9-15	.306	113.04
	1876					1.36		NW¼SW¼	35	36	42	3-15—4-28	.011	1.03
	1876			36.00				NE¼SW¼	35	36	42	3-15—9-15	.293	108.00
	1876			0.32				SW¼NE¼	35	36	42	3-15—9-15	.003	0.96
	1876			33.92				SE¼NW¼	35	36	42	3-15—9-15	.276	101.76
	1876			38.64				SW¼NW¼	35	36	42	3-15—9-15	.314	115.92
	1876			26.32				NW¼NW¼	35	36	42	3-15—9-15	.214	78.96
	1876					0.74		NW¼NW¼	35	36	42	3-15—4-28	.006	.55
	1876			4.00				NE¼NW¼	35	36	42	3-15—9-15	.033	12.00
	1876				2.72			NE¼NE¼	14	35	42	3-15—6-13	.022	4.08
	1876					31.20		NE¼NE¼	14	35	42	3-15—4-28	.254	23.40
	1876				27.56			SE¼NE¼	14	35	42	3-15—6-13	.224	41.34
	1876					8.84		SE¼NE¼	14	35	42	3-15—4-28	.072	6.63
	1876				16.48			NW¼NE¼	14	35	42	3-15—6-13	.134	24.72
	1876					22.12		NW¼NE¼	14	35	42	3-15—4-28	.180	16.59
	1876				1.12			SW¼NE¼	14	35	42	3-15—6-13	.009	1.68
	1876			0.48				SW¼SW¼	26	36	42	3-15—9-15	.004	1.44
	1876				2.80			SW¼SW¼	26	36	42	3-15—6-13	.023	4.20
	1876				2.24			NW¼SW¼	26	36	42	3-15—6-13	.018	3.36
	1876				2.56			SW¼NW¼	26	36	42	3-15—6-13	.021	3.84

Source—**Humboldt River.** Ditch—**Hot Springs.** (Russel Land and Cattle Co. lands.)

1880					8.16			SE¼NE¼	29	36	42	3-15—6-13	.066	12.24
1880					8.32			SW¼NE¼	29	36	42	3-15—6-13	.068	12.48
1880					28.16			NE¼SE¼	29	36	42	3-15—6-13	.229	42.24
1880					34.76			SE¼SE¼	29	36	42	3-15—6-13	.283	52.14
1880						16.90		NW¼SW¼	29	36	42	3-15—4-28	.137	12.68
1880						19.64		SW¼SW¼	29	36	42	3-15—4-28	.160	14.72

Source—**Humboldt River.** Ditch—**Unnamed Ditch.** (John G. Taylor lands.)

	1875				31.36			NE¼NE¼	13	36	41	3-15—6-13	.255	47.04
	1875				35.36			NW¼NE¼	13	36	41	3-15—6-13	.287	53.14
	1875			12.90				SE¼NE¼	13	36	41	3-15—9-15	.105	38.70
	1875				22.54			SE¼NE¼	13	36	41	3-15—6-13	.183	33.81
	1875					3.56		SE¼NE¼	13	36	41	3-15—4-28	.029	2.67
	1875			3.96				SW¼NE¼	13	36	41	3-15—9-15	.032	11.88
	1875				29.32			SW¼NE¼	13	36	41	3-15—6-13	.238	43.98

Clover Valley Land and Stock Co.—Continued.

Date of beneficial use: Nat. mdw.	Date of beneficial use: Cult. area	Construction first initiated: Dams	Construction first initiated: Ditches	Culture—Acres: Harvest crops	Culture—Acres: Meadow pasture	Culture—Acres: Willow and sage pasture	Culture—Acres: Swamp or overflow	Location: Subdivision	Location: Section	Location: Tp.N.	Location: R.E.	Length of season	Duty of water: C.F.S.	Duty of water: Acre-feet
	1875					1.36		SW¼NE¼	13	36	41	3-15—4-28	.011	1.02
	1875				40.00			NE¼NW¼	13	36	41	3-15—6-13	.325	60.00
	1875				40.88			NW¼NW¼	13	36	41	3-15—6-13	.332	61.32
	1875				39.76			SE¼NW¼	13	36	41	3-15—6-13	.323	59.65
	1875					.48		SE¼NW¼	13	36	41	3-15—4-28	.004	.36
	1875				41.17			SW¼NW¼	13	36	41	3-15—6-13	.335	61.76
	1875			26.40				NE¼SE¼	13	36	41	3-15—9-15	.215	79.20
	1875					6.40		NE¼SE¼	13	36	41	3-15—4-28	.052	4.80
	1875			32.64				SE¼SE¼	13	36	41	3-15—9-15	.265	97.92
	1875				3.20			SE¼SE¼	13	36	41	3-15—6-13	.026	4.80
	1875					1.18		SE¼SE¼	13	36	41	3-15—4-28	.010	.89
	1875				6.26			SW¼SE¼	13	36	41	3-15—6-13	.051	9.39
	1875					.28		SW¼SE¼	13	36	41	3-15—4-28	.002	.21
	1875			33.50				SW¼SE¼	13	36	41	3-15—9-15	.272	100.50
	1875			16.04				NW¼SE¼	13	36	41	3-15—9-15	.130	48.12
	1875				6.64			NW¼SE¼	13	36	41	3-15—6-13	.054	9.96
	1875					12.24		NW¼SE¼	13	36	41	3-15—4-28	.100	9.18
	1875				17.80			SW¼SW¼	13	36	41	3-15—6-13	.145	26.70
	1875					1.76		SW¼SW¼	13	36	41	3-15—4-28	.014	1.32
	1875						12.32	SW¼SW¼	13	36	41	3-15—4-28	.100	9.24
	1875				37.38			SE¼SW¼	13	36	41	3-15—6-13	.304	56.07
	1875			1.44				NE¼SW¼	13	36	41	3-15—9-15	.012	4.32
	1875				16.52			NE¼SW¼	13	36	41	3-15—6-13	.134	24.78
	1875					5.41		NE¼SW¼	13	36	41	3-15—4-28	.044	4.06
	1875				26.17			NW¼SW¼	13	36	41	3-15—6-13	.213	39.26
	1875					8.97		NW¼SW¼	13	36	41	3-15—4-28	.073	6.73
1878	1880				32.08			SE¼SE¼	11	36	41	3-15—6-13	.261	48.12
1878	1880				33.28			SW¼SE¼	11	36	41	3-15—6-13	.271	49.92
1878	1880						39.89	NE¼SE¼	11	36	41	3-15—4-28	.324	29.92
1878	1880						39.73	NW¼SE¼	11	36	41	3-15—4-28	.323	29.80
1878	1880				34.64			SE¼SW¼	11	36	41	3-15—6-13	.282	51.96
1878	1880					.56		SE¼SW¼	11	36	41	3-15—4-28	.005	.42
1878	1880				2.28			SW¼SW¼	11	36	41	3-15—6-13	.019	3.32
1878	1880					13.12		SW¼SW¼	11	36	41	3-15—4-28	.107	9.84
1878	1880				26.40			NW¼SW¼	11	36	41	3-15—6-13	.215	39.60
1878	1880					5.12		NW¼SW¼	11	36	41	3-15—4-28	.042	3.84
1878	1880				36.60			NE¼SW¼	11	36	41	3-15—6-13	.298	55.90
1878	1880					5.12		NE¼SW¼	11	36	41	3-15—4-28	.042	3.84
1878	1880						35.84	SE¼NE¼	11	36	41	3-15—4-28	.291	26.88
1878	1880						25.12	SW¼NE¼	11	36	41	3-15—4-28	.204	18.84
1878	1880						6.16	NE¼NE¼	11	36	41	3-15—4-28	.050	4.62
1878	1880						9.12	SE¼NW¼	11	36	41	3-15—4-28	.074	6.84
1878	1880						15.12	NE¼NW¼	11	36	41	3-15—4-28	.123	11.34
1878	1880						24.24	NW¼NW¼	11	36	41	3-15—4-28	.197	18.18
1878	1880						31.84	SW¼NW¼	11	36	41	3-15—4-28	.259	23.88

Source—**Humboldt** River. Ditch—**Outside Slough.** (John G. Taylor lands.)

1887	14.32		SW¼NW¼	10	36	42	3-15—4-28	.116	11.05
1887		25.56	SW¼NW¼	10	36	42	3-15—4-28	.208	10.17
1887	27.48		SE¼NW¼	10	36	42	3-15—4-28	.223	20.61
1887		9.80	SE¼NW¼	19	36	42	3-15—4-28	.080	7.35
1887	20.06		NW¼SE¼	19	36	42	3-15—4-28	.170	15.72
1887		18.76	NW¼SE¼	19	36	42	3-15—4-28	.153	14.07
1887	5.56		SW¼SE¼	19	36	42	3-15—4-28	.045	4.17
1887		30.18	SW¼SE¼	19	36	42	3-15—4-28	.245	22.64
1887	2.92		SE¼SE¼	19	36	42	3-15—4-28	.024	2.19
1887		35.44	SE¼SE¼	19	36	42	3-15—4-28	.288	26.58
1887		39.60	SW¼SW¼	19	36	42	3-15—4-28	.322	29.70
1887		39.72	SE¼SW¼	19	36	42	3-15—4-28	.323	29.79
1887	5.12		NE¼SW¼	19	36	42	3-15—4-28	.042	3.84
1887		32.68	NE¼SW¼	19	36	42	3-15—4-28	.266	24.51
1887	.28		NW¼SW¼	19	36	42	3-15—4-28	.002	.21
1887		39.52	NW¼SW¼	19	36	42	3-15—4-28	.321	29.64
1887		13.28	NW¼NW¼	19	36	42	3-15—4-28	.108	9.96

Source—**Humboldt River.** Ditch—**Gonzales Slough.** (John G. Taylor lands.)

1880		25.72	NW¼NW¼	19	36	42	3-15—4-28	.209	26.79
1880	36.12		NE¼NW¼	19	26	42	3-15—4-28	.294	27.09
1880		.96	NE¼NW¼	19	36	42	3-15—4-28	.008	.72
1880	38.86		NW¼NE¼	19	36	42	3-15—4-28	.316	29.15
1880	32.44		SW¼NE¼	19	36	42	3-15—4-28	.264	24.33
1880		4.40	SW¼NE¼	19	36	42	3-15—4-28	.036	3.30
1880	10.92		NE¼NE¼	19	36	42	3-15—4-28	.089	8.19
1880		28.16	NE¼NE¼	19	36	42	3-15—4-28	.220	21.12
1880	22.68		SE¼NE¼	19	36	42	3-15—4-28	.184	17.01
1880		16.48	SE¼NE¼	19	36	42	3-15—4-28	.134	12.36
1880	14.36		NE¼SE¼	19	36	42	3-15—4-28	.117	10.77
1880		23.52	NE¼SE¼	19	36	42	3-15—4-28	.191	17.64

Claimant—**W. M. Pettit.** Proof No. 00158

Source—**Humboldt River.** Ditch—**Southside Ditch.**

1875		13.40	SE¼SE¼	10	36	41	3-15—4-28	.109	10.05
1875		4.64	SE¼NW¼	15	36	41	3-15—4-28	.038	3.48
1875		17.35	NW¼NE¼	15	36	41	3-15—4-28	.141	13.01
1875		6.05	NE¼NE¼	15	36	41	3-15—4-28	.049	4.54
1875		37.73	NW¼SW¼	15	36	41	3-15—4-28	.307	28.30

Source—**Humboldt** River. Ditch—**Overflow.**

1883		3.84	SW¼NW¼	10	36	41	3-15—4-28	.031	2.88
1883		4.67	SW¼NE¼	10	36	41	3-15—4-28	.038	3.50
1883		8.11	SE¼NE¼	10	36	41	3-15—4-28	.066	6.08
1883		38.71	NE¼SW¼	10	36	41	3-15—4-28	.315	29.03
1883		40.00	NW¼SE¼	10	36	41	3-15—4-28	.325	30.00
1883		34.72	NE¼SE¼	10	36	41	3-15—4-28	.282	26.04
1883		37.22	SW¼SE¼	10	36	41	3-15—4-28	.303	27.92
1883		39.13	NW¼NW¼	15	36	41	3-15—4-28	.318	29.35
1883		20.64	NE¼NW¼	15	36	41	3-15—4-28	.168	15.48

W. M. Pettit—Continued.

Date of beneficial use: Nat. mdw.	Cult. area	Construction first initiated: Dams	Ditches	Culture—Acres: Harvest crops	Meadow pasture	Willow and sage pasture	Swamp or over-flow	Location: Subdivision	Section	Tp.N.	R.E.	Length of season	Duty of water: C.F.S.	Acre-feet
	1883						36.36	SW¼NW¼	15	36	41	3-15—4-28	.296	27.27
	1883						2.67	NE¼SW¼	15	36	41	3-15—4-28	.022	2.00
	1883						38.30	SW¼SW¼	15	36	41	3-15—4-28	.311	28.73
	1883						5.27	SE¼SW¼	15	36	41	3-15—4-28	.043	3.95

Claimant—**Swan and Foster.** Proof No. 00158

Source—**Humboldt River.** Ditch—**Swan and Foster.**

Nat. mdw.	Cult. area	Dams	Ditches	Harvest crops	Meadow pasture	Willow and sage pasture	Swamp or over-flow	Subdivision	Section	Tp.N.	R.E.	Length of season	C.F.S.	Acre-feet
	1879				9.21			NW¼NW¼	24	36	41	3-15—6-13	.076	13.82
	1879				20.20			NE¼NW¼	24	36	41	3-15—6-13	.164	30.30
	1879				14.76			NW¼NE¼	24	36	41	3-15—6-13	.120	22.14
	1879				34.96			NE¼NE¼	24	36	41	3-15—6-13	.284	52.44
	1879				4.19			SE¼NE¼	24	36	41	3-15—6-13	.034	6.29

Claimant—**John G. Taylor.** Proof No. 00159

Source—**Humboldt River.** Ditch—**Not Named.**

Nat. mdw.	Cult. area	Dams	Ditches	Harvest crops	Meadow pasture	Willow and sage pasture	Swamp or over-flow	Subdivision	Section	Tp.N.	R.E.	Length of season	C.F.S.	Acre-feet
1874	1885			36.70				NE¼NE¼	18	36	42	3-15—9-15	.298	110.10
1874	1885			30.96				SE¼NE¼	18	36	42	3-15—9-15	.252	92.88
1874	1885					1.35		SE¼NE¼	18	36	42	3-15—4-28	.012	1.01
1874	1885						.40	SE¼NE¼	18	36	42	3-15—4-28	.003	.30
1874	1885			13.54				SW¼NE¼	18	36	42	3-15—9-15	.110	40.62
1874	1885					.65		SW¼NE¼	18	36	42	3-15—4-28	.005	.49
1874	1885						21.15	SW¼NE¼	18	36	42	3-15—4-28	.172	15.86
1874	1885			26.13				NW¼NE¼	18	36	42	3-15—9-15	.212	78.39
1874	1885						9.86	NW¼NE¼	18	36	42	3-15—4-28	.080	7.40
1874	1890			18.95				SE¼NW¼	18	36	42	3-15—9-15	.154	56.85
1874	1890						18.95	SE¼NW¼	18	36	42	3-15—4-28	.154	14.21
1874	1890			1.30				NE¼NW¼	18	36	42	3-15—9-15	.011	3.90
1874	1890						31.75	NE¼NW¼	18	36	42	3-15—4-28	.258	23.81
1874	1896			12.74				NW¼NW¼	18	36	42	3-15—9-15	.104	38.22
1874	1896						21.90	NW¼NW¼	18	36	42	3-15—4-28	.178	16.43
1874	1896			38.88				SW¼NW¼	18	36	42	3-15—9-15	.316	116.64
1874	1896						.82	SW¼NW¼	18	36	42	3-15—4-28	.007	.62
1874	1885			38.20				NE¼SE¼	18	36	42	3-15—9-15	.311	114.60
1874	1885					.10		NE¼SE¼	18	36	42	3-15—4-28	.001	.08
1874	1885			8.56				SE¼SE¼	18	36	42	3-15—9-15	.070	25.68
1874	1885			15.14				SW¼SE¼	18	36	42	3-15—9-15	.123	45.42
1874	1885			35.34				NW¼SE¼	18	36	42	3-15—9-15	.287	106.02
1874	1885					.60		NW¼SE¼	18	36	42	3-15—4-28	.005	.45
1874	1885			35.28				NE¼SW¼	18	36	42	3-15—9-15	.287	105.84
1874	1885					.51		NE¼SW¼	18	36	42	3-15—4-28	.004	.38
1874	1885			28.38				NW¼SW¼	18	36	42	3-15—9-15	.231	85.14
1874	1885				3.64			NW¼SW¼	18	36	42	3-15—6-13	.030	5.46
1874	1885					2.55		NW¼SW¼	18	36	42	3-15—4-28	.021	1.91
1874	1885			5.83				SE¼SW¼	18	36	42	3-15—9-15	.047	17.49
1874	1885				3.87			SE¼SW¼	18	36	42	3-15—6-13	.031	5.81
1874	1885			6.60				SW¼SW¼	18	36	42	3-15—9-15	.054	19.80

Claimant—**Land Development Company.** Proof No. 00163

Source—**Humboldt River.** Ditch—**Reese River Slough.**

1871	1886				10.50			NE¼NE¼	7	32	45	3-15—6-13	.085	15.75
1871	1886						14.50	NE¼NE¼	7	32	45	3-15—4-28	.118	10.88
1871	1886						6.20	SE¼NE¼	7	32	45	3-15—4-28	.050	4.65
1871	1886						.50	NW¼NE¼	7	32	45	3-15—4-28	.004	.38
1871	1886				23.30			NE¼NW¼	8	32	45	3-15—6-13	.189	34.95
1871	1886					13.25		NE¼NW¼	8	32	45	3-15—4-28	.108	9.94
1871	1886				31.45			SE¼NW¼	8	32	45	3-15—6-13	.256	47.18
1871	1886						2.80	SE¼NW¼	8	32	45	3-15—4-28	.023	2.10
1871	1886				36.00			NW¼NW¼	8	32	45	3-15—6-13	.293	54.00
1871	1886						1.55	NW¼NW¼	8	32	45	3-15—4-28	.013	1.16
1871	1886				8.37			SW¼NW¼	8	32	45	3-15—6-13	.068	12.56
1871	1886					8.00		SW¼NW¼	8	32	45	3-15—4-28	.065	6.00
1871	1886						18.60	SW¼NW¼	8	32	45	3-15—4-28	.151	13.95
1871	1886				22.30			NE¼SW¼	8	32	45	3-15—6-13	.181	33.45
1871	1886					16.50		NE¼SW¼	8	32	45	3-15—4-28	.134	12.38
1871	1886					26.50		SE¼SW¼	8	32	45	3-15—4-28	.215	19.88
1871	1886					7.20		NW¼SW¼	8	32	45	3-15—4-28	.059	5.40
1871	1886						17.10	NW¼SW¼	8	32	45	3-15—4-28	.139	12.83
1871	1886						3.00	SW¼SW¼	8	32	45	3-15—4-28	.024	2.25
1871	1886					1.05		SE¼SW¼	5	32	45	3-15—4-28	.009	.79
1871	1886				4.33			NW¼SW¼	5	32	45	3-15—6-13	.035	6.50
1871	1886					2.78		NW¼SW¼	5	32	45	3-15—4-28	.023	2.09
1871	1886					11.07		SW¼SW¼	5	32	45	3-15—4-28	.090	8.30
1871	1886			2.05				NE¼SE¼	6	32	45	3-15—9-15	.017	6.15
1871	1886				15.40			NE¼SE¼	6	32	45	3-15—6-13	.125	23.10
1871	1886					13.27		NE¼SE¼	6	32	45	3-15—4-28	.108	9.95
1871	1886				28.70			SE¼SE¼	6	32	45	3-15—6-13	.232	42.75
1871	1886					4.10		SE¼SE¼	6	32	45	3-15—4-28	.033	3.08
1871	1886				5.20			SW¼SE¼	6	32	45	3-15—6-13	.042	7.80
1871	1886					5.40		SW¼SE¼	6	32	45	3-15—4-28	.044	4.05
1871	1886				11.35			NE¼SW¼	6	32	45	3-15—6-13	.092	17.03
1871	1886					25.40		NE¼SW¼	6	32	45	3-15—4-28	.207	19.05
1871	1886					2.35		SE¼SW¼	6	32	45	3-15—4-28	.019	1.76
1871	1886					7.25		NW¼SW¼	6	32	45	3-15—4-28	.059	5.44
1871	1886					1.30		SW¼SW¼	6	32	45	3-15—4-28	.011	.98
1871	1886					38.50		NE¼NE¼	1	32	45	3-15—4-28	.313	28.88
1871	1886					14.90		SE¼NE¼	1	32	45	3-15—4-28	.121	11.18
1871	1886					9.10		NW¼NE¼	1	32	45	3-15—4-28	.074	6.83

Source—**Humboldt River.** Ditch—**South Ditch.**

	1895						17.00	SE¼SW¼	3	32	45	3-15—4-28	.138	12.75
	1895						11.60	NW¼SW¼	3	32	45	3-15—4-28	.094	8.70
	1895						3.80	SW¼SW¼	3	32	45	3-15—4-28	.031	2.85

Source—**Humboldt River.** Ditch—**Layton.**

1871	1886			25.90				SW¼NE¼	5	32	45	3-15—9-15	.211	77.70
1871	1886				5.30			SW¼NE¼	5	32	45	3-15—6-13	.043	7.95
1871	1886				3.09			NE¼SE¼	5	32	45	3-15—6-13	.025	4.64
1871	1886			21.00				SE¼SE¼	5	32	45	3-15—9-15	.171	63.00
1871	1886				10.00			SE¼SE¼	5	32	45	3-15—6-13	.081	15.00

Land Development Co.—Continued.

Date of beneficial use—Nat. mdw.	Date of beneficial use—Cult. area	Construction first initiated—Dams	Construction first initiated—Ditches	Culture—Acres—Harvest crops	Culture—Acres—Meadow pasture	Culture—Acres—Willow and sage pasture	Culture—Acres—Swamp or overflow	Location—Subdivision	Location—Section	Location—Tp.N.	Location—R.E.	Length of season	Duty of water—C.F.S.	Duty of water—Acre-feet
1871	1886			15.00				NW¼SE¼	5	32	45	3-15—9-15	.122	45.00
1871	1886				20.50			NW¼SE¼	5	32	45	3-15—6-13	.167	30.75
1871	1886			29.40				SW¼SE¼	5	32	45	3-15—9-15	.239	88.20
1871	1886				4.85			SW¼SE¼	5	32	45	3-15—6-13	.039	7.28
1871	1888					5.05		SW¼SE¼	5	32	45	3-15—4-28	.041	3.79
1871	1886			40.00				SE¼NW¼	5	32	45	3-15—9-15	.325	120.00
1871	1886			11.50				NW¼NW¼	5	32	45	3-15—9-15	.093	34.50
1871	1886			39.90				SW¼NW¼	5	32	45	3-15—9-15	.324	119.70
1871	1886			39.40				NE¼SW¼	5	32	45	3-15—9-15	.320	118.20
1871	1886					.10		NE¼SW¼	5	32	45	3-15—4-28	.001	.08
1871	1888			16.46				SE¼SW¼	5	32	45	3-15—9-15	.134	49.38
1871	1898					14.85		SE¼SW¼	5	32	45	3-15—4-28	.121	11.14
1871	1886			20.80				NW¼SW¼	5	32	45	3-15—9-15	.169	62.40
1871	1886					4.14		NW¼SW¼	5	32	45	3-15—4-28	.034	3.11
1871	1886				16.38			SW¼SW¼	5	32	45	3-15—6-13	.133	24.57
1871	1886					3.45		SW¼SW¼	5	32	45	3-15—4-28	.028	2.59
1871	1886				2.05			NE¼SE¼	6	32	45	3-15—6-13	.017	3.08
1871	1886					2.60		NE¼SE¼	6	32	45	3-15—4-28	.021	1.95

Source—**Humboldt River.** Ditch—**Big Field.**

Date of beneficial use—Nat. mdw.	Date of beneficial use—Cult. area	Construction first initiated—Dams	Construction first initiated—Ditches	Culture—Acres—Harvest crops	Culture—Acres—Meadow pasture	Culture—Acres—Willow and sage pasture	Culture—Acres—Swamp or overflow	Location—Subdivision	Location—Section	Location—Tp.N.	Location—R.E.	Length of season	Duty of water—C.F.S.	Duty of water—Acre-feet
1873	1895						1.73	NE¼SW¼	7	33	45	3-15—4-28	.014	1.30
1873	1895						12.48	SE¼SW¼	7	33	45	3-15—4-28	.101	9.36
1873	1895						2.02	SW¼SE¼	7	33	45	3-15—4-28	.016	1.52
1873	1895						10.84	NE¼NW¼	18	33	45	3-15—4-28	.088	8.13
1873	1895						32.45	NW¼NE¼	18	33	45	3-15—4-28	.264	24.34
1873	1895						3.94	NE¼NE¼	18	33	45	3-15—4-28	.032	2.96
1873	1895						24.29	SW¼NE¼	18	33	45	3-15—4-28	.197	18.22
1873	1895						25.15	SE¼NE¼	18	33	45	3-15—4-28	.204	18.86
1873	1895						1.87	NE¼SE¼	18	33	45	3-15—4-28	.015	1.40
1873	1895						33.79	NE¼SE¼	18	33	45	3-15—4-28	.275	25.34
1873	1895						21.31	SE¼SE¼	18	33	45	3-15—4-28	.171	15.98
1873	1895						.77	SW¼NW¼	17	33	45	3-15—4-28	.006	.58
1873	1895						.38	NW¼SW¼	17	33	45	3-15—4-28	.003	.29
1873	1895						16.61	SW¼SW¼	17	33	45	3-15—4-28	.135	12.46
1873	1895						4.32	NE¼NE¼	19	33	45	3-15—4-28	.035	3.24
1873	1895						22.76	NW¼NW¼	20	33	45	3-15—4-28	.185	17.07
1873	1895						.19	NE¼NW¼	20	33	45	3-15—4-28	.002	.14
1873	1895						9.16	SW¼NW¼	20	33	45	3-15—4-28	.074	6.87
1873	1895						32.29	SE¼NW¼	20	33	45	3-15—4-28	.263	24.22
1873	1895						29.25	SW¼NE¼	20	33	45	3-15—4-28	.238	21.94
1873	1895						6.52	SE¼NE¼	20	33	45	3-15—4-28	.053	4.89
1873	1895						25.15	NW¼SE¼	20	33	45	3-15—4-28	.204	18.86
1873	1895						31.10	NE¼SE¼	20	33	45	3-15—4-28	.253	23.33
1873	1895						1.24	SW¼SE¼	20	33	45	3-15—4-28	.010	.93
1873	1895						36.48	SE¼SE¼	20	33	45	3-15—4-28	.297	27.36
1873	1895						5.85	NW¼SW¼	21	33	45	3-15—4-28	.048	4.39
1873	1895						31.89	SW¼SW¼	21	33	45	3-15—4-28	.259	23.92
1873	1895						8.16	SE¼SW¼	21	33	45	3-15—4-28	.066	6.12

Source—**Humboldt River.** Ditch—**Blossom Dam.**

1871	1901					4.60		NE¼NE¼	29	33	45	3-15—4-28	.037	3.45
1871	1901			20.75				NW¼SW¼	30	33	45	3-15—9-15	.169	62.25
1871	1901			35.70				SW¼SW¼	30	33	45	3-15—9-15	.290	107.10
1871	1901					1.50		SW¼SW¼	30	33	45	3-15—4-28	.012	1.13
1871	1901			2.75				SE¼SW¼	30	33	45	3-15—9-15	.022	8.25
1871	1901			13.10				SE¼SE¼	31	33	45	3-15—9-15	.107	30.30
1871	1901			9.65				NW¼SE¼	31	33	45	3-15—9-15	.078	28.95
1871	1901			32.45				SW¼SE¼	31	33	45	3-15—9-15	.264	97.35
1871	1901			2.25				NE¼NW¼	31	33	45	3-15—9-15	.018	6.75
1871	1901			7.40				SE¼NW¼	31	33	45	3-15—9-15	.060	22.20
1871	1901					.50		SE¼NW¼	31	33	45	3-15—4-28	.004	.38
1871	1901			29.25				NW¼NW¼	31	33	45	3-15—9-15	.238	87.75
1871	1901					3.90		NW¼NW¼	31	33	45	3-15—4-28	.032	2.93
1871	1901			14.40				SW¼NW¼	31	33	45	3-15—9-15	.117	43.20
1871	1901				2.67			SW¼NW¼	31	33	45	3-15—6-13	.022	4.01
1871	1901					14.40		SW¼NW¼	31	33	45	3-15—4-28	.117	10.80
1871	1901			28.90				NE¼SW¼	31	33	45	3-15—9-15	.235	86.70
1871	1901					8.30		NE¼SW¼	31	33	45	3-15—4-28	.067	6.23
1871	1901			1.75				NW¼SW¼	31	33	45	3-15—9-15	.014	5.25
1871	1901				9.15			NW¼SW¼	31	33	45	3-15—6-13	.074	13.73
1871	1901					20.30		NW¼SW¼	31	33	45	3-15—4-28	.165	15.23
1871	1901			7.15				SE¼SW¼	31	33	45	3-15—9-15	.058	21.45
1871	1901				6.00			SE¼SW¼	31	33	45	3-15—6-13	.049	9.00
1871	1901					19.85		SE¼SW¼	31	33	45	3-15—4-28	.161	14.89
1871	1901				31.48			SW¼SW¼	31	33	45	3-15—6-13	.256	47.22
1871	1901					3.45		SW¼SW¼	31	33	45	3-15—4-28	.028	2.59
1871	1901				35.50			NW¼SE¼	6	32	45	3-15—6-13	.289	53.25
1871	1901					1.50		NW¼SE¼	6	32	45	3-15—4-28	.012	1.13
1871	1901			7.75				NE¼NW¼	6	22	45	3-15—9-15	.063	23.25
1871	1901				14.75			NE¼NW¼	6	32	45	3-15—6-13	.120	22.13
1871	1901					9.90		NE¼NW¼	6	32	45	3-15—4-28	.080	7.43
1871	1901				29.40			SE¼NW¼	6	32	45	3-15—6-13	.239	44.10
1871	1901					8.15		SE¼NW¼	6	32	45	3-15—4-28	.066	6.11
1871	1901				25.53			NW¼NW¼	6	32	45	3-15—6-13	.208	38.30
1871	1901					13.17		NW¼NW¼	6	32	45	3-15—4-28	.107	9.88
1871	1901				4.60			SW¼NW¼	6	32	45	3-15—6-13	.037	6.90
1871	1901					28.70		SW¼NW¼	6	32	45	3-15—4-28	.233	21.53
1871	1901			14.15				NE¼NE¼	6	32	45	3-15—9-15	.115	42.45
1871	1901					1.70		NE¼NE¼	6	32	45	3-15—4-28	.014	1.28
1871	1901			28.25				SE¼NE¼	6	32	45	3-15—9-15	.230	84.75
1871	1901				.10			SE¼NE¼	6	32	45	3-15—6-13	.001	.15
1871	1901					4.90		SE¼NE¼	6	32	45	3-15—4-28	.040	3.68
1871	1901			30.45				NW¼NE¼	6	32	45	3-15—9-15	.248	91.35
1871	1901					8.55		NW¼NE¼	6	32	45	3-15—4-28	.070	6.41
1871	1901			.75				SW¼NE¼	6	32	45	3-15—9-15	.006	2.25
1871	1901				12.70			SW¼NE¼	6	32	45	3-15—6-13	.103	38.10
1871	1901					15.03		SW¼NE¼	6	32	45	3-15—4-28	.122	11.27

Land Development Co.—Continued.

Source—**Humboldt River.** Ditch—**Crum-Blossom Slough.**

Date of beneficial use: Nat. mdw.	Cult. area	Construction first initiated: Dams	Ditches	Culture—Acres: Harvest crops	Meadow pasture	Willow and sage pasture	Swamp or overflow	Location: Subdivision	Section	Tp.N.	R.E.	Length of season	Duty of water: C.F.S.	Acre-feet
1871	1883			1.00				SW¼SE¼	32	33	45	3-15—9-15	.008	3.00
1871	1883			6.95				SE¼SW¼	32	33	45	3-15—9-15	.057	20.85
1871	1883			12.50				SW¼SW¼	32	33	45	3-15—9-15	.102	37.50
1871	1883			20.35				NW¼NE¼	5	32	45	3-15—9-15	.165	61.05
1871	1883			38.10				NE¼NW¼	5	32	45	3-15—9-15	.310	114.30
1871	1883			25.75				NW¼NW¼	5	32	45	3-15—9-15	.209	77.25
1871	1883			23.35				NE¼NE¼	6	32	45	3-15—9-15	.190	70.05

Source—**Humboldt River.** Ditch—**Rocky Point Canal.**

Nat. mdw.	Cult. area	Dams	Ditches	Harvest crops	Meadow pasture	Willow and sage pasture	Swamp or overflow	Subdivision	Section	Tp.N.	R.E.	Length of season	C.F.S.	Acre-feet
1876	1895			9.85				SE¼SW¼	21	33	45	3-15—9-15	.080	29.55
1876	1895					.35		SE¼SW¼	21	33	45	3-15—4-28	.003	.26
1876	1895			5.01				SW¼SW¼	21	33	45	3-15—9-15	.041	15.03
1876	1895					.71		SW¼SW¼	21	33	45	3-15—4-28	.006	.53
1876	1895					.20		SE¼SE¼	22	33	45	3-15—4-28	.002	.15
1876	1895			5.60				NE¼NE¼	28	33	45	3-15—9-15	.046	16.80
1876	1895					1.90		SE¼NE¼	28	33	45	3-15—4-28	.015	1.43
1876	1895						20.10	SE¼NE¼	28	33	45	3-15—4-28	.163	15.08
1876	1895			4.10				NW¼NE¼	28	33	45	3-15—9-15	.033	12.30
1876	1895				3.00			NW¼NE¼	28	33	45	3-15—6-13	.024	4.50
1876	1895			7.80				SW¼NE¼	28	33	45	3-15—9-15	.063	23.40
1876	1895				2.50			SW¼NE¼	28	33	45	3-15—6-13	.020	3.75
1876	1895					25.90		SW¼NE¼	28	33	45	3-15—4-28	.211	19.43
1876	1895			26.70				NE¼SE¼	28	33	45	3-15—9-15	.217	80.10
1876	1895			9.35				SE¼SE¼	28	33	45	3-15—9-15	.076	28.05
1876	1895			24.80				NW¼SE¼	28	33	45	3-15—9-15	.202	74.40
1876	1895					2.20		NW¼SE¼	28	33	45	3-15—4-28	.018	1.65
1876	1895			4.25				SW¼SE¼	28	33	45	3-15—9-15	.035	12.75
1876	1895					8.30		SW¼SE¼	28	33	45	3-15—4-28	.067	6.23
1876	1895			36.40				NE¼NW¼	28	33	45	3-15—9-15	.296	109.20
1876	1895			29.80				SE¼NW¼	28	33	45	3-15—9-15	.242	89.40
1876	1895					6.60		SE¼NW¼	28	33	45	3-15—4-28	.054	4.95
1876	1895			30.05				NW¼NW¼	28	33	45	3-15—9-15	.244	90.15
1876	1895					9.95		NW¼NW¼	28	33	45	3-15—4-28	.081	7.46
1876	1895			19.65				SW¼NW¼	28	33	45	3-15—9-15	.160	58.95
1876	1895					10.05		SW¼NW¼	28	33	45	3-15—4-28	.082	7.54
1876	1895					2.35		NE¼SW¼	28	33	45	3-15—4-28	.019	1.76
1876	1895					1.60		SE¼SW¼	28	33	45	3-15—4-28	.013	1.20
1876	1895					.20		NW¼SW¼	28	33	45	3-15—4-28	.002	.15

Claimant—**Wm. Licking.** Proof No. 00164

Source—**Humboldt River.** Ditch—**Layton.**

Nat. mdw.	Cult. area	Dams	Ditches	Harvest crops	Meadow pasture	Willow and sage pasture	Swamp or overflow	Subdivision	Section	Tp.N.	R.E.	Length of season	C.F.S.	Acre-feet
1870	1871			1.84				NE¼NW¼	16	32	45	3-15—9-15	.015	5.52
1870	1871			7.12				NW¼NW¼	16	32	45	3-15—9-15	.058	21.36
1870	1871					2.18		NW¼NW¼	16	32	45	3-15—4-28	.018	1.64

1870	1871			36.94				NE¼NE¼	17	32	45	3-15—9-15	.300	110.82
1870	1871			10.25				SE¼NE¼	17	32	45	3-15—9-15	.083	30.75
1870	1871				11.30			SE¼NE¼	17	32	45	3-15—6-13	.092	16.95
1870	1871			19.68				NW¼NE¼	17	32	45	3-15—9-15	.160	59.04
1870	1871				17.95			NW¼NE¼	17	32	45	3-15—6-13	.146	26.93
1870	1871				11.80			SW¼NE¼	17	32	45	3-15—6-13	.097	17.84
1870	1871			.31				SW¼SE¼	9	32	45	3-15—9-15	.003	.93
1870	1871						.30	NW¼SE¼	9	32	45	3-15—4-28	.002	.23
1870	1871			30.25				NE¼NE¼	8	32	45	3-15—9-15	.310	117.75
1870	1871					.14		NE¼NE¼	8	32	45	3-15—4-28	.001	.11
1870	1871			30.45				SE¼NE¼	8	32	45	3-15—9-15	.321	118.35
1870	1871			14.45				NW¼NE¼	8	32	45	3-15—9-15	.117	43.35
1870	1871					18.79		NW¼NE¼	8	32	45	3-15—4-28	.153	14.09
1870	1871			18.73				SW¼NE¼	8	32	45	3-15—9-15	.152	56.19
1870	1871					9.29		SW¼NE¼	8	32	45	3-15—4-28	.076	6.97
1870	1871			20.04				NE¼SE¼	8	32	45	3-15—9-15	.236	87.12
1870	1871					4.12		NE¼SE¼	8	32	45	3-15—4-28	.033	3.09
1870	1871			12.06				SE¼SE¼	8	32	45	3-15—9-15	.098	36.18
1870	1871					19.77		SE¼SE¼	8	32	45	3-15—4-28	.161	14.83
1870	1871			30.45				NW¼SE¼	8	32	45	3-15—9-15	.248	91.35
1870	1871					5.33		NW¼SE¼	8	32	45	3-15—4-28	.043	4.00
1870	1871			35.85				SW¼SE¼	8	32	45	3-15—9-15	.291	107.55
	1871			.94				NE¼NW¼	9	32	45	3-15—9-15	.008	2.82
	1871				2.81			NE¼NW¼	9	32	45	3-15—6-13	.023	4.22
	1871						12.58	NE¼NW¼	9	32	45	3-15—4-28	.102	9.44
	1871			22.45				SE¼NW¼	9	32	45	3-15—9-15	.183	67.35
	1871						6.97	SE¼NW¼	9	32	45	3-15—4-28	.057	5.23
	1871			33.07				NW¼NW¼	9	32	45	3-15—9-15	.269	99.21
	1871				5.20			NW¼NW¼	9	32	45	3-15—6-13	.042	7.80
	1871						.94	NW¼NW¼	9	32	45	3-15—4-28	.008	.71
	1871			39.63				SW¼NW¼	9	32	45	3-15—9-15	.322	118.89
	1871			36.41				NE¼SW¼	9	32	45	3-15—9-15	.296	109.23
	1871						.75	NE¼SW¼	9	32	45	3-15—4-28	.006	.56
	1871			38.98				SE¼SW¼	9	32	45	3-15—9-15	.317	116.94
	1871			40.03				NW¼SW¼	9	32	45	3-15—9-15	.325	120.09
	1871			31.90				SW¼SW¼	9	32	45	3-15—9-15	.259	95.70
	1871					4.19		SW¼SW¼	9	32	45	3-15—4-28	.034	3.14
	1871						1.80	SW¼NE¼	9	32	45	3-15—4-28	.015	1.35
	1871			1.98				NW¼SE¼	9	32	45	3-15—9-15	.016	5.94

Claimant—**McIntyre-Starrett Co.** Proof No. 00165

Source—**Humboldt River.** Ditch—**McIntyre-Starrett Dam.**

1878	1883			5.50				NE¼SE¼	9	32	45	3-15—9-15	.045	16.50
1878	1883			38.86				SE¼SE¼	9	32	45	3-15—9-15	.316	116.58
1878	1883			25.90				NW¼SE¼	9	32	45	3-15—9-15	.211	77.70
1878	1883			38.75				SW¼SE¼	9	32	45	3-15—9-15	.315	116.25
1878	1883			39.35				NE¼NE¼	16	32	35	3-15—9-15	.320	119.05
1878	1883			37.30				SE¼NE¼	16	32	35	3-15—9-15	.303	11.90
1878	1883					.50		SE¼NE¼	16	32	35	3-15—4-28	.008	.38
1878	1883			37.06				NW¼NE¼	16	32	35	3-15—9-15	.301	111.18
1878	1883			28.19				SW¼NE¼	16	32	35	3-15—9-15	.237	84.57
1878	1883					.83		SW¼NE¼	16	32	35	3-15—4-28	.007	.62

McIntyre-Starrett Co.—Continued.

Date of beneficial use: Nat. mdw.	Date of beneficial use: Cult. area	Construction first initiated: Dams	Construction first initiated: Ditches	Culture—Acres: Harvest crops	Culture—Acres: Meadow pasture	Culture—Acres: Willow and sage pasture	Culture—Acres: Swamp or overflow	Location: Subdivision	Location: Section	Location: Tp.N.	Location: R.E.	Length of season	Duty of water: C.F.S.	Duty of water: Acre-feet
1878	1883			36.27				NE¼NW¼	16	32	35	3-15—9-15	.295	108.81
1878	1883			16.08				SE¼NW¼	16	32	35	3-15—9-15	.131	48.24
1878	1883					.13		SE¼NW¼	16	32	35	3-15—4-28	.001	.10
1878	1883			13.59				NW¼NW¼	16	32	35	3-15—9-15	.110	40.77
1878	1883					.73		NW¼NW¼	16	32	35	3-15—4-28	.006	.55
1878	1883			6.53				SW¼NW¼	16	32	35	3-15—9-15	.053	19.59
1878	1883					6.55		SW¼NW¼	10	32	35	3-15—4-28	.053	4.91

Source—**Humboldt River.** Ditch—**Altenberg Ditch.**

Nat. mdw.	Cult. area	Dams	Ditches	Harvest crops	Meadow pasture	Willow and sage pasture	Swamp or overflow	Subdivision	Section	Tp.N.	R.E.	Length of season	C.F.S.	Acre-feet
1878	1874			3.26				SW¼NW¼	16	32	35	3-15—9-15	.027	9.78
1878	1874			13.33				SW¼NW¼	16	32	35	3-15—9-15	.108	39.99
1878	1874				4.40			SW¼NW¼	16	32	35	3-15—6-13	.036	6.60
1878	1874					11.35		SE¼NW¼	10	32	35	3-15—4-28	.092	8.51

Claimant—**W. T. Jenkins Co.** **Proof No. 00166**

Source—**Humboldt River.** Ditch—**Rocky Point.**

Nat. mdw.	Cult. area	Dams	Ditches	Harvest crops	Meadow pasture	Willow and sage pasture	Swamp or overflow	Subdivision	Section	Tp.N.	R.E.	Length of season	C.F.S.	Acre-feet
	1873				5.55			NE¼NW¼	6	32	46	3-15—6-13	.045	8.33
	1873				.11			NE¼SE¼	1	32	45	3-15—6-13	.001	.17
	1873					6.61		NE¼SE¼	1	32	45	3-15—4-28	.054	4.96
	1873						6.33	NE¼SE¼	1	32	45	3-15—4-28	.051	4.75
	1873			6.27				NE¼NW¼	1	32	45	3-15—9-15	.051	18.81
	1873			18.57				NW¼NW¼	1	32	45	3-15—9-15	.151	55.71
	1873					5.60		NW¼NW¼	1	32	45	3-15—4-28	.046	4.20

Source—**Humboldt River.** Ditch—**South Ditch.**

Nat. mdw.	Cult. area	Dams	Ditches	Harvest crops	Meadow pasture	Willow and sage pasture	Swamp or overflow	Subdivision	Section	Tp.N.	R.E.	Length of season	C.F.S.	Acre-feet
	1895				7.62			SE¼SE¼	2	32	45	3-15—6-13	.062	11.43
	1895						30.79	SE¼SE¼	2	32	45	3-15—4-28	.250	23.09
	1895			9.45				NW¼SE¼	2	32	45	3-15—9-15	.077	28.35
	1895				19.87			NW¼SE¼	2	32	45	3-15—6-13	.162	29.81
	1895			6.60				SW¼SE¼	2	32	45	3-15—9-15	.054	18.80
	1895				9.93			SW¼SE¼	2	32	45	3-15—6-13	.081	14.90
	1895						5.28	SW¼SE¼	2	32	45	3-15—4-28	.043	3.96
	1895						1.16	NE¼NW¼	2	32	45	3-15—4-28	.009	.87
	1895			11.50				SE¼SW¼	2	32	45	3-15—9-15	.093	34.50
	1895			10.15				SW¼SW¼	2	32	45	3-15—9-15	.083	30.45
	1895			12.04				NW¼SE¼	1	32	45	3-15—9-15	.098	36.12
	1895				3.36			NW¼SE¼	1	32	45	3-15—6-13	.027	5.04
	1895					16.67		NW¼SE¼	1	32	45	3-15—4-28	.136	12.50
	1895						2.21	NW¼SE¼	1	32	45	3-15—4-28	.018	1.66
	1895					1.00		SW¼SE¼	1	32	45	3-15—4-28	.008	.75
	1895			5.70				SW¼NE¼	1	32	45	3-15—9-15	.046	17.10
	1895					4.47		SW¼NE¼	1	32	45	3-15—4-28	.036	3.35
	1895			19.30				SE¼NW¼	1	32	45	3 15—9-15	.157	57.90
	1895			26.50				SW¼NW¼	1	32	45	3-15—9 15	.215	79.50
	1895					13.67		SW¼SW¼	1	32	45	3 15—4-28	.111	10.25

	1895			.55				NE¼SW¼	1	32	45	3-15—9-15	.005	1.65
	1895					39.00		NE¼SW¼	1	32	45	3-15—4-28	.317	29.25
	1895					9.97		SE¼SW¼	1	32	45	3-15—4-28	.081	7.48
	1895						5.82	SE¼SW¼	1	32	45	3-15—4-28	.047	4.37
	1895					40.12		NW¼SW¼	1	32	45	3-15—4-28	.326	30.09
	1895					21.84		SW¼SW¼	1	32	45	3-15—4-28	.178	16.38
	1895			28.30				NE¼NE¼	2	32	45	3-15—9-15	.230	84.90
	1895					13.06		NE¼NE¼	2	32	45	3-15—4-28	.106	9.80
	1895			6.98				SE¼NE¼	2	32	45	3-15—9-15	.057	20.94
	1895				2.16			SE¼NE¼	2	32	45	3-15—6-13	.018	3.24
	1895					30.88		SE¼NE¼	2	32	45	3-15—4-28	.251	23.16
	1895			7.35				NW¼NE¼	2	32	45	3-15—9-15	.060	22.05
	1895					9.14		NW¼NE¼	2	32	45	3-15—4-28	.074	6.87
	1895			6.60				SW¼NE¼	2	32	45	3-15—9-15	.054	19.80
	1895				8.47			NE¼SE¼	2	32	45	3-15—6-13	.069	12.71
	1895					29.60		NE¼SE¼	2	32	45	3-15—4-28	.241	22.20

Areas in sections 6, 1 and 2, T. 32 N, R. 45 E, totaling 871.53 **acres, first flooded artificially during the year 1873 due to Rocky Point Dam when these areas were third-class pasture; therefore has pasture water right of .75 acre-feet per acre from 1873 to 1895.**

Claimant—**Faris Estate.** Proof No. 00167

Source—**Humboldt River.** Ditch—**Faris Ditch System.**

	1873					17.31		SE¼SE¼	5	32	46	3-15—4-28	.141	21.98
1872	1873					6.30		SE¼SE¼	5	32	46	3-15—4-28	.051	4.73
	1873					17.57		SW¼SE¼	5	32	46	3-15—4-28	.143	13.18
1872	1873					4.71		SW¼SE¼	5	32	46	3-15—4-28	.038	3.53
	1873					24.77		SE¼SW¼	5	32	46	3-15—4-28	.201	18.58
1872	1873					.50		SE¼SW¼	5	32	46	3-15—4-28	.004	.38
1875	1876			22.97				NE¼NE¼	20	32	46	3-15—9-15	.187	68.91
	1892					.75		NE¼NE¼	20	32	46	3-15—4-28	.006	.56
	1893					13.15		NE¼NE¼	20	32	46	3-15—4-28	.107	9.86
	1893					33.46		SE¼NE¼	20	32	46	3-15—4-28	.272	25.10
	1892					32.65		NW¼NE¼	20	32	46	3-15—4-28	.265	24.49
	1892					34.69		NE¼NW¼	20	32	46	3-15—4-28	.282	26.02
	1892					35.41		NW¼NW¼	20	32	46	3-15—4-28	.288	26.56
	1892					2.30		SE¼NW¼	20	32	46	3-15—4-28	.019	1.73
	1892					5.85		SW¼NW¼	20	32	46	3-15—4-28	.048	4.39
	1873					36.20		SE¼SE¼	6	32	46	3-15—4-28	.294	27.15
	1873					30.26		SW¼SE¼	6	32	46	3-15—4-28	.246	22.70
	1873					33.37		SE¼SW¼	6	32	46	3-15—4-28	.271	25.03
	1873					10.61		SW¼SW¼	6	32	46	3-15—4-28	.086	7.96
	1892					36.53		NE¼NE¼	19	32	46	3-15—4-28	.297	27.41
	1892					3.75		SE¼NE¼	19	32	46	3-15—4-28	.030	2.81
	1892					11.66		NW¼NE¼	19	32	46	3-15—4-28	.095	8.75
	1890				1.60			NE¼NW¼	19	32	46	3-15—6-13	.013	2.40
	1890					8.25		NE¼NW¼	19	32	46	3-15—4-28	.067	6.19
	1890				.45			SE¼NW¼	19	32	46	3-15—6-13	.004	.68
	1890					18.80		SE¼NW¼	19	32	46	3-15—4-28	.153	14.10
	1890				2.43			NW¼NW¼	19	32	46	3-15—6-13	.020	3.65
	1890					3.30		NW¼NW¼	19	32	46	3-15—4-28	.027	2.48
	1890				26.10			SW¼NW¼	19	32	46	3-15—6-13	.212	39.15
	1890					21.84		SW¼NW¼	19	32	46	3-15—4-28	.178	16.38
	1873					31.30		NE¼NE¼	7	32	46	3-15—4-28	.254	23.48

Faris Estate—Continued.

Date of beneficial use: Nat. mdw.	Date of beneficial use: Cult. area	Construction first initiated: Dams	Construction first initiated: Ditches	Culture—Acres: Harvest crops	Culture—Acres: Meadow pasture	Culture—Acres: Willow and sage pasture	Culture—Acres: Swamp or overflow	Location: Subdivision	Location: Section	Location: Tp.N.	Location: R.E.	Length of season	Duty of water: C.F.S.	Duty of water: Acre-feet
	1873					.50		SE¼NE¼	7	32	46	3-15—4-28	.004	.38
	1873					9.96		NW¼NE¼	7	32	46	3-15—4-28	.081	7.47
	1873					12.83		NE¼NW¼	7	32	46	3-15—4-28	.104	9.62
	1873					41.55		NW¼NW¼	7	32	46	3-15—4-28	.338	31.16
	1873					30.72		SW¼NW¼	7	32	46	3-15—4-28	.250	23.04
	1878						2.90	SE¼SE¼	4	32	46	3-15—4-28	.024	2.18
	1878						18.65	SW¼SE¼	4	32	46	3-15—4-28	.152	13.99
	1878						20.00	SE¼SW¼	4	32	46	3-15—4-28	.163	15.00
	1878						16.37	SW¼SW¼	4	32	46	3-15—4-28	.133	12.28
	1873					3.75		SW¼SW¼	4	32	46	3-15—4-28	.030	2.81
	1893				37.44			NE¼NE¼	21	32	46	3-15—6-13	.304	56.16
	1893				35.22			SE¼NE¼	21	32	46	3-15—6-13	.286	52.83
	1893					3.80		SE¼NE¼	21	32	46	3-15—4-28	.031	2.85
	1893				34.50			NW¼NE¼	21	32	46	3-15—6-13	.280	51.75
	1893					2.92		NW¼NE¼	21	32	46	3-15—4-28	.024	2.19
	1893				2.12			SW¼NE¼	21	32	46	3-15—6-13	.017	3.18
	1893					35.77		SW¼NE¼	21	32	46	3-15—4-28	.291	26.83
	1893				22.51			NE¼NW¼	21	32	46	3-15—6-13	.183	33.77
	1893					14.62		NE¼NW¼	21	32	46	3-15—4-28	.119	10.97
	1893					38.42		SE¼NW¼	21	32	46	3-15—4-28	.312	29.92
	1893			11.40				NW¼NW¼	21	32	46	3-15—9-15	.093	34.20
	1893				5.72			NW¼NW¼	21	32	46	3-15—6-13	.047	8.58
	1893					20.80		NW¼NW¼	21	32	46	3-15—4-28	.169	15.60
	1893					40.00		SW¼NW¼	21	32	46	3-15—4-28	.325	30.00
	1893				39.40			NE¼SE¼	21	32	46	3-15—6-13	.320	59.10
	1893				39.50			NW¼SE¼	21	32	46	3-15—6-13	.321	59.25
	1893				37.20			SE¼SE¼	21	32	46	3-15—6-13	.303	55.94
	1893						1.24	SE¼SE¼	21	32	46	3-15—4-28	.010	.93
	1893				36.40			SW¼SE¼	21	32	46	3-15—6-13	.296	54.60
	1893						3.60	SW¼SE¼	21	32	46	3-15—4-28	.029	2.70
	1893				34.35			NE¼SW¼	21	32	46	3-15—6-13	.279	51.53
	1893					4.90		NE¼SW¼	21	32	46	3-15—4-28	.040	3.68
	1893				20.86			NW¼SW¼	21	32	46	3-15—6-13	.170	21.39
	1893					18.54		NW¼SW¼	21	32	46	3-15—4-28	.150	13.91
	1893				35.40			SE¼SW¼	21	32	46	3-15—6-13	.288	53.10
	1893						4.60	SE¼SW¼	21	32	46	3-15—4-28	.037	3.45
	1893				35.03			SW¼SW¼	21	32	46	3-15—6-13	.285	52.55
	1893						4.97	SW¼SW¼	21	32	46	3-15—4-28	.040	3.73
	1893						1.00	NE¼NE¼	28	32	46	3-15—4-28	.081	.75
	1893						6.96	NW¼NE¼	28	32	46	3-15—4-28	.057	5.22
	1893						8.58	NE¼NW¼	28	32	46	3-15—4-28	.070	6.44
	1893						7.09	NW¼NW¼	28	32	46	3-15—4-28	.058	5.32
	1893					1.86		NE¼NE¼	29	32	46	3-15—4-28	.016	1.40
	1878						3.34	NE¼NE¼	8	32	46	3-15—4-28	.027	2.51
	1878						25.05	SE¼NE¼	8	32	46	3-15—4-28	.204	18.79
	1873					.75		NW¼NE¼	8	32	46	3-15—4-28	.006	.56
	1873						9.47	NW¼NE¼	8	32	40	3-15—4-28	.077	7.10

							8.75	SW¼NE¼	8	32	46	3-15—4-28	.071	6.50
	1878						40.00	NE¼SE¼	8	32	46	3-15—4-28	.325	30.00
	1878			9.42				SE¼SE¼	8	32	46	3-15—9-15	.077	28.26
	1878						30.63	SE¼SE¼	8	32	40	3-15—4-28	.249	22.07
	1878						40.00	NW¼SE¼	8	32	46	3-15—4-28	.325	30.00
	1878			1.30				SW¼SE¼	8	32	46	3-15—9-15	.011	3.90
	1878						38.70	SW¼SE¼	8	32	46	3-15—4-28	.315	29.03
	1878					29.05		NE¼NW¼	8	32	46	3-15—4-28	.236	21.79
	1878					26.95		NW¼NW¼	8	32	46	3-15—4-28	.219	20.21
	1878						33.54	NE¼SW¼	8	32	46	3-15—4-28	.273	25.16
	1878						40.00	SE¼SW¼	8	32	46	3-15—4-28	.325	30.00
	1878						9.70	NW¼SW¼	8	32	46	3-15—4-28	.079	7.28
	1878						40.00	SW¼SW¼	8	32	46	3-15—4-28	.325	30.00
	1878					4.53		SW¼SE¼	9	32	46	3-15—4-28	.037	3.40
	1878					.30		NE¼SW¼	9	32	46	3-15—4-28	.002	3.23
	1878						40.00	NW¼SW¼	9	32	46	3-15—4-28	.325	30.00
	1878			14.40				SE¼SW¼	9	32	46	3-15—9-15	.117	43.20
	1878					18.21		SE¼SW¼	9	32	46	3-15—4-28	.148	13.66
	1878			3.38				SW¼SW¼	9	32	46	3-15—9-15	.027	10.14
	1878					18.16		SW¼SW¼	9	32	46	3-15—4-28	.148	13.95
	1878						18.70	SW¼SW¼	9	32	46	3-15—4-28	.152	14.03
	1878					13.10		NE¼NE¼	9	32	46	3-15—4-28	.107	9.83
	1878			11.40				SE¼NE¼	9	32	16	3-15—9-15	.093	34.20
	1878					23.13		SE¼NE¼	9	32	46	3-15—4-28	.188	17.35
	1878						4.40	NW¼NE¼	9	32	46	3-15—4-28	.036	3.30
	1878					4.00		SW¼NE¼	9	32	46	3-15—4-28	.033	3.00
	1878						33.60	NE¼NW¼	9	32	46	3-15—4-28	.273	25.20
	1878						10.10	SE¼NW¼	9	32	46	3-15—4-28	.082	7.58
	1878						40.00	NW¼NW¼	9	32	46	3-15—4-28	.325	30.00
	1878						40.00	SW¼NW¼	9	32	46	3-15—4-28	.325	30.00
	1878			34.86				NE¼SE¼	9	32	46	3-15—9-15	.283	104.58
	1878					2.43		NE¼SE¼	9	32	46	3-15—4-28	.020	1.82
	1878			37.87				SE¼SE¼	9	32	46	3-15—9-15	.308	113.71
	1878					2.05		SE¼SE¼	9	32	46	3-15—4-28	.017	1.55
	1878			12.27				NW¼SE¼	9	32	46	3-15—9-15	.100	36.81
	1878					21.92		NW¼SE¼	9	32	46	3-15—4-28	.178	16.44
	1878			34.10				SW¼SE¼	8	32	46	3-15—9-15	.277	102.30
1875	1876				7.10			NW¼SW¼	10	32	46	3-15—6-13	.058	10.65
1875	1878			30.34				NW¼SW¼	10	32	46	3-15—9-15	.247	91.02
1875	1878				.90			NW¼SW¼	10	32	46	3-15—6-13	.007	1.35
1875	1876			21.64				SE¼SW¼	10	32	46	3-15—9-15	.176	64.92
1875	1876				18.44			SE¼SW¼	10	32	46	3-15—6-13	.150	27.66
1875	1876				27.58			SW¼SW¼	10	32	46	3-15—6-13	.224	41.37
1875	1878			8.10				SW¼SW¼	10	32	46	3-15—9-15	.066	24.30
1875	1878				3.91			SW¼SW¼	10	32	46	3-15—6-13	.032	5.87
1875	1878			24.62				SE¼NW¼	10	32	46	3-15—9-15	.200	73.86
1875	1878			34.16				SW¼NW¼	10	32	46	3-15—9-15	.278	102.48
1875	1878				4.92			SW¼NW¼	10	32	46	3-15—6-13	.040	7.38
1875	1876			21.50				NE¼SE¼	10	32	46	3-15—9-15	.175	64.50
1875	1876				17.38			NE¼SE¼	10	32	46	3-15—6-13	.141	26.17
1875	1876					.95		NE¼SE¼	10	32	46	3-15—4-28	.008	.71
1875	1876			29.98				NW¼SE¼	10	32	46	3-15—9-15	.244	89.84
1875	1876				10.27			NW¼SE¼	10	32	46	3-15—6-13	.083	15.41

Faris Estate—Continued.

Date of beneficial use: Nat. mdw.	Date of beneficial use: Cult. area	Construction first initiated: Dams	Construction first initiated: Ditches	Culture—Acres: Harvest crops	Culture—Acres: Meadow pasture	Culture—Acres: Willow and sage pasture	Culture—Acres: Swamp or overflow	Location: Subdivision	Location: Section	Location: Tp.N.	Location: R.E.	Length of season	Duty of water: C.F.S.	Duty of water: Acre-feet
1875	1876			4.17				SE¼SE¼	10	32	46	3-15—9-15	.034	12.51
1875	1876				35.83			SE¼SE¼	10	32	46	3-15—6-13	.291	53.75
1875	1876			36.00				SW¼SE¼	10	32	46	3-15—9-15	.293	108.00
1875	1876				3.60			SW¼SE¼	10	32	46	3-15—6-13	.029	5.40
1875	1878			.75				NE¼SW¼	10	32	46	3-15—9-15	.006	2.25
1875	1876			1.04				NE¼SW¼	10	32	46	3-15—9-15	.008	3.12
1875	1876				38.17			NE¼SW¼	10	32	46	3-15—6-13	.310	57.26
1875	1876			20.17				NE¼NE¼	10	32	46	3-15—9-15	.164	60.51
1875	1876				17.04			NE¼NE¼	10	32	46	3-15—6-13	.139	26.56
1875	1878						2.50	NE¼NE¼	10	32	46	3-15—4-28	.020	1.88
1875	1876			16.84				NW¼NE¼	10	32	46	3-15—9-15	.137	50.52
1875	1876				.70			NW¼NE¼	10	32	46	3-15—6-13	.006	1.05
1875	1878			19.77				NW¼NE¼	10	32	46	3-15—9-15	.161	59.31
1875	1878						2.60	NW¼NE¼	10	32	46	3-15—4-28	.021	1.95
1875	1876			32.50				SE¼NE¼	10	32	46	3-15—9-15	.264	97.50
1875	1876				6.07			SE¼NE¼	10	32	46	3-15—6-13	.049	9.11
1875	1876					1.40		SE¼NE¼	10	32	46	3-15—4-28	.011	1.05
1875	1876			8.86				SW¼NE¼	10	32	46	3-15—9-15	.072	26.58
1875	1876				30.38			SW¼NE¼	10	32	46	3-15—6-13	.247	45.57
1875	1878			16.72				NE¼NW¼	10	32	46	3-15—9-15	.136	50.16
1875	1878					21.96		NE¼NW¼	10	32	46	3-15—4-28	.179	16.47
1875	1878			1.63				NW¼NW¼	10	32	46	3-15—9-15	.013	4.89
1875	1878					30.95		NW¼NW¼	10	32	46	3-15—4-28	.252	23.21
1875	1876				14.49			SE¼NW¼	10	32	46	3-15—6-13	.118	21.74
	1893				23.37			NE¼SE¼	15	32	46	3 15—6-13	.190	35.06
	1893				4.00			SE¼SE¼	15	32	46	3-15—6-13	.033	6.00
	1893				35.30			SW¼SE¼	15	32	46	3-15—6-13	.286	52.95
	1893				14.80			NE¼NE¼	22	32	46	3-15—6-13	.120	22.20
	1893				38.50			NE¼NW¼	22	32	46	3-15—6-13	.313	57.75
	1893				28.96			SE¼NW¼	22	32	46	3-15—6-13	.235	43.44
	1893				4.72			NE¼SW¼	22	32	46	3-15—6-13	.038	7.08
	1893				38.28			NW¼SW¼	22	32	46	3-15—6-13	.311	57.42
	1893				15.54			SW¼SW¼	22	32	46	3-15—6-13	.126	23.31
1875	1876				40.00			NE¼NE¼	15	32	46	3-15—6-13	.325	60.00
1875	1876			24.48				NW¼NE¼	15	32	46	3-15—9-15	.199	73.44
1875	1876				15.43			NW¼NE¼	15	32	46	3-15—6-13	.125	23.15
1875	1876				32.96			SE¼NE¼	15	32	46	3-15—6-13	.268	49.44
1875	1893				6.44			SE¼NE¼	15	32	46	3-15—6-13	.052	9.66
1875	1876			3.60				SW¼NE¼	15	32	46	3-15—9-15	.029	10.80
1875	1876				20.08			SW¼NE¼	15	32	46	3-15—6-13	.163	30.12
	1893				16.32			SW¼NE¼	15	32	46	3-15—6-13	.138	24.48
1875	1876			31.75				NE¼NW¼	15	32	46	3-15—9-15	.258	95.45
1875	1876				8.24			NE¼NW¼	15	32	46	3-15—6-13	.067	12.36
	1893				10.00			SE¼NW¼	15	32	46	3-15—6-13	.081	15.00
1875	1876			22.39				SE¼NW¼	15	32	46	3-15—9-15	.182	67.17
1875	1876				5.42			SE¼NW¼	15	32	46	3-15—6-13	.044	8.13
1875	1876			25.38				NW¼NW¼	15	32	46	3-15—9-15	.206	76.14

1875	1876	......	......	......	11.46	2.30	......	NW¼ NW¼	15	32	46	3-15—6-13	.093	17.19
1875	1876	......	......	......	......	......	......	NW¼ NW¼	15	32	46	3-15—4-28	.019	1.79
1875	1876	......	......	37.20	......	......	......	SW¼ NW¼	15	32	46	3-15—9-15	.302	111.60
......	1876	......	......	22.39	......	......	......	SE¼ NW¼	15	32	46	3-15—9-15	.182	67.17
......	1893	......	......	......	15.43	......	......	SE¼ NW¼	15	32	46	3-15—6-13	.125	23.15
......	1893	......	......	......	40.00	......	......	NW¼ SE¼	15	32	46	3-15—6-13	.325	60.00
......	1876	......	......	9.95	......	......	......	NE¼ SW¼	15	32	46	3-15—9-15	.081	29.85
......	1893	......	......	......	30.05	......	......	NE¼ SW¼	15	32	46	3-15—6-13	.244	45.08
......	1876	......	......	31.18	......	......	......	NW¼ SW¼	15	32	46	3-15—9-15	.253	93.54
......	1893	......	......	......	8.82	......	......	NW¼ SW¼	15	32	46	3-15—6-13	.072	13.23
......	1876	......	......	0.20	......	......	......	SE¼ SW¼	15	32	46	3-15—9-15	.002	.60
......	1893	......	......	......	39.80	......	......	SE¼ SW¼	15	32	46	3-15—6-13	.324	59.70
......	1876	......	......	3.75	......	......	......	SW¼ SW¼	15	32	46	3-15—9-15	.030	11.25
......	1893	......	......	......	36.25	......	......	SW¼ SW¼	15	32	46	3-15—6-13	.295	54.38
......	1876	......	......	7.38	......	......	......	NE¼ NE¼	16	32	46	3-15—9-15	.060	22.14
......	1878	......	......	23.60	......	......	......	NE¼ NE¼	16	32	46	3-15—9-15	.192	70.81
......	1878	......	......	......	6.40	......	......	NE¼ NE¼	16	32	46	3-15—6-13	.052	9.20
......	1876	......	......	39.35	......	......	......	SE¼ NE¼	16	32	46	3-15—9-15	.320	118.05
......	1876	......	......	0.67	......	......	......	NW¼ NE¼	16	32	46	3-15—9-15	.005	2.01
......	1878	......	......	34.06	......	......	......	NW¼ NE¼	16	32	46	3-15—9-15	.277	102.18
......	1878	......	......	......	3.53	......	......	NW¼ NE¼	16	32	46	3-15—6-13	.029	5.30
......	1878	......	......	39.67	......	......	......	NE¼ NW¼	16	32	46	3-15—9-15	.323	119.01
......	1876	......	......	3.74	......	......	......	SE¼ NW¼	16	32	46	3-15—9-15	.030	111.22
......	1878	......	......	34.14	......	......	......	SE¼ NW¼	16	32	46	3-15—9-15	.278	102.42
......	1878	......	......	38.88	......	......	......	NW¼ NW¼	16	32	46	3-15—9-15	.316	116.64
......	1878	......	......	......	......	0.55	......	NW¼ NW¼	16	32	46	3-15—4-28	.004	.41
......	1878	......	......	39.50	......	......	......	SW¼ NW¼	16	32	46	3-15—9-15	.321	118.50
......	1876	......	......	31.46	......	......	......	NW¼ SE¼	16	32	46	3-15—9-15	.256	94.38
......	1893	......	......	......	8.54	......	......	NW¼ SE¼	16	32	46	3-15—6-13	.069	12.81
......	1893	......	......	......	23.13	......	......	NE¼ SE¼	16	32	46	3-15—6-13	.188	34.70
......	1876	......	......	16.87	......	......	......	NE¼ SE¼	16	32	46	3-15—9-15	.137	50.81
......	1878	......	......	4.42	......	......	......	NE¼ SW¼	16	32	46	3-15—9-15	.036	13.26
......	1878	......	......	......	1.20	......	......	NE¼ SW¼	16	32	46	3-15—6-13	.010	1.80
......	1876	......	......	31.16	......	......	......	NE¼ SW¼	16	32	46	3-15—9-15	.253	93.48
......	1893	......	......	......	1.67	......	......	NE¼ SW¼	16	32	46	3-15—6-13	.014	2.51
......	1876	......	......	11.20	......	......	......	SE¼ SW¼	16	32	46	3-15—9-15	.091	33.60
......	1893	......	......	......	28.80	......	......	SE¼ SW¼	16	32	46	3-15—6-13	.234	43.20
......	1878	......	......	33.28	......	......	......	NW¼ SW¼	16	32	46	3-15—9-15	.271	99.84
......	1878	......	......	......	2.63	......	......	NW¼ SW¼	16	32	46	3-15—6-13	.021	3.80
......	1876	......	......	2.28	......	......	......	NW¼ SW¼	16	32	46	3-15—9-15	.019	6.84
......	1876	......	......	35.85	......	......	......	SW¼ SW¼	16	32	46	3-15—9-15	.291	107.55
......	1876	......	......	......	......	.60	......	SW¼ SW¼	16	32	46	3-15—4-28	.005	.45
......	1893	......	......	......	2.25	......	......	SW¼ SW¼	16	32	46	3-15—6-13	.018	3.38
......	1893	......	......	......	40.00	......	......	SE¼ SE¼	16	32	46	3-15—6-13	.325	60.00
......	1893	......	......	......	40.00	......	......	SW¼ SE¼	16	32	46	3-15—6-13	.325	60.00
......	1878	......	......	37.37	......	......	......	NE¼ NE¼	17	32	46	3-15—9-15	.304	112.11
......	1878	......	......	39.10	......	......	......	SE¼ NE¼	17	32	46	3-15—9-15	.318	117.30
......	1878	......	......	27.06	......	......	......	NW¼ NE¼	17	32	46	3-15—9-15	.220	81.18
......	1878	......	......	......	......	12.00	......	NW¼ NE¼	17	32	46	3-15—4-28	.098	9.06
......	1878	......	......	38.42	......	......	......	SW¼ NE¼	17	32	46	3-15—9-15	.312	115.26
......	1878	......	......	38.68	......	......	......	NE¼ SE¼	17	32	46	3-15—9-15	.314	116.04
......	1878	......	......	......	0.60	......	......	NE¼ SE¼	17	32	46	3-15—6-13	.005	.90
......	1878	......	......	16.81	......	......	......	SE¼ SE¼	17	32	46	3-15—9-15	.137	50.43

Faris Estate—Continued.

Date of beneficial use—Nat. mdw.	Date of beneficial use—Cult. area	Construction first initiated—Dams	Construction first initiated—Ditches	Culture—Acres—Harvest crops	Culture—Acres—Meadow pasture	Culture—Acres—Willow and sage pasture	Culture—Acres—Swamp or overflow	Location—Subdivision	Location—Section	Location—Tp.N.	Location—R.E.	Length of season	Duty of water—C.F.S.	Duty of water—Acre-feet
	1878					2.00		SE¼SE¼	17	32	46	3-15—4-28	.016	1.50
	1878			39.40				NW¼SE¼	17	32	46	3-15—9-15	.320	118.20
	1878			40.08				SW¼SE¼	17	32	46	3-15—9-15	.326	120.24
	1878			3.97				NE¼NW¼	17	32	46	3-15—9-15	.323	11.91
	1878					36.04		NE¼NW¼	17	32	46	3-15—4-28	.293	27.03
	1878			27.50				SE¼NW¼	17	32	46	3-15—9-15	.224	82.50
	1878					11.56		SE¼NW¼	17	32	46	3-15—4-28	.094	8.67
	1878					40.00		NW¼NW¼	17	32	46	3-15—4-28	.325	30.00
	1878			5.00				SW¼NW¼	17	32	46	3-15—9-15	.041	15.00
	1878					35.00		SW¼NW¼	17	32	46	3-15—4-28	.285	26.25
	1878			38.94				NE¼SW¼	17	32	46	3-15—9-15	.317	116.82
	1878			37.62				SE¼SW¼	17	32	46	3-15—9-15	.306	112.86
	1878					1.50		SE¼SW¼	17	32	46	3-15—4-28	.012	1.13
	1878			9.77				NW¼SW¼	17	32	46	3-15—9-15	.079	29.31
	1878					29.50		NW¼SW¼	17	32	46	3-15—4-28	.240	22.13
	1878			19.43				SW¼SW¼	17	32	46	3-15—9-15	.158	58.29
	1878					18.90		SW¼SW¼	17	32	46	3-15—4-28	.154	14.18
	1876			18.44				SE¼SE¼	17	32	46	3-15—9-15	.150	55.32
	1873					0.75		NW¼SW¼	7	32	46	3-15—4-28	.006	.56
	1878						5.60	SE¼SE¼	7	32	46	3-15—4-28	.046	4.20
	1878						37.44	NE¼NE¼	18	32	46	3-15—4-28	.304	28.08
	1878						7.96	NW¼NE¼	18	32	46	3-15—4-28	.065	5.97
	1878					40.00		SE¼NE¼	18	32	46	3-15—4-28	.325	30.00
	1878					35.45		SW¼NE¼	18	32	46	3-15—4-28	.288	26.59
	1878					9.10		SE¼NW¼	18	32	46	3-15—4-28	.074	6.83
	1878					6.40		SW¼NW¼	18	32	46	3-15—4-28	.052	4.80
	1878					40.00		NE¼SE¼	18	32	46	3-15—4-28	.325	30.00
	1878					39.70		NW¼SE¼	18	32	46	3-15—4-28	.319	29.40
	1878					36.72		SE¼SE¼	18	32	46	3-15—4-28	.299	27.54
	1878					30.83		SW¼SE¼	18	32	46	3-15—4-28	.251	23.12
	1878					36.97		NE¼SW¼	18	32	46	3-15—4-28	.301	27.73
	1878					41.28		NW¼SW¼	18	32	46	3-15—4-28	.336	30.96
	1878					4.32		SE¼SW¼	18	32	46	3-15—4-28	.035	3.24
	1878					2.90		SW¼SW¼	18	32	46	3-15—4-28	.024	2.18
	1893				37.60			NW¼NW¼	22	32	46	3-15—6-13	.306	56.40
	1893				37.90			SW¼NW¼	22	32	46	3-15—6-13	.308	56.85
	1878						41.74	SE¼SE¼	3	32	46	3-15—4-28	.339	31.31
	1876			3.34				SE¼SE¼	3	32	46	3-15—9-15	.027	10.02
	1878			4.43				SW¼SE¼	3	32	46	3-15—9-15	.036	13.29
	1878					25.03		SW¼SE¼	3	32	46	3-15—4-28	.203	18.77
	1878						14.62	SW¼SE¼	3	32	46	3-15—4-28	.119	10.97
	1878					28.05		SE¼SW¼	3	32	46	3-15—4-28	.228	21.04
	1878					0.60		SW¼SW¼	3	32	46	3-15—4-28	.005	.45
	1893					6.84		NE¼SW¼	19	32	46	3-15—4-28	.056	5.13
	1893						6.38	NE¼SW¼	19	32	46	3-15—4-28	.052	4.79
	1893					46.36		NW¼SW¼	19	32	46	3-15—4-28	.377	34.78
	1893						1.23	NW¼SW¼	19	32	46	3-15—4-28	.010	.92

1893			18.04	SE¼SW¼	19	32	46	3-15—4-28	.147	13.53
1893			30.32	SW¼SW¼	19	32	46	3-15—4-28	.295	27.24
1893			.61	NW¼NW¼	30	32	46	3-15—4-28	.005	.46
1893			15.70	SE¼NW¼	30	32	46	3-15—4-28	.128	11.84
1893			31.70	SW¼NW¼	30	32	46	3-15—4-28	.258	23.78
1893			8.20	NW¼SW¼	30	32	46	3-15—4-28	.067	6.15
1893			6.46	NE¼NE¼	30	32	46	3-15—4-28	.053	4.85
1893			2.61	SE¼NE¼	30	32	46	3-15—4-28	.021	1.96
1893			17.40	SW¼NE¼	30	32	46	3-15—4-28	.141	13.05
1893	10.04			NE¼SE¼	20	32	46	3-15—6-13	.082	15.06
1893		20.66		NE¼SE¼	20	32	46	3-15—4-28	.241	22.25
1893		14.48		NW¼SE¼	20	32	46	3-15—4-28	.118	10.86
1893	20.26			SE¼SE¼	20	32	46	3-15—6-13	.165	30.39
1893		16.74		SE¼SE¼	20	32	46	3-15—4-28	.136	12.56
1893		39.20		SW¼SE¼	20	32	46	3-15—4-28	.319	29.40
1893		31.78		SE¼SW¼	20	32	46	3-15—4-28	.258	23.84
1893		14.72		SW¼SW¼	29	32	46	3-15—4-28	.120	11.04
1891	10.18			NE¼SE¼	24	32	45	3-15—6-13	.083	15.27
1891		29.72		NE¼SE¼	24	32	45	3-15—4-28	.242	22.29
1891	12.40			NW¼SE¼	24	32	45	3-15—6-13	.101	18.60
1891		25.86		NW¼SE¼	24	32	45	3-15—4-28	.210	19.40
1893			3.36	NE¼NE¼	29	32	46	3-15—4-28	.027	2.52
1893		4.10		NW¼NE¼	29	32	46	3-15—4-28	.033	3.08
1893		5.22		NE¼NW¼	29	32	46	3-15—4-28	.042	3.92
1893		3.85		NW¼NW¼	29	32	46	3-15—4-28	.031	2.89
1883			14.80	NW¼NE¼	10	32	45	3-15—4-28	.120	11.10
1883			16.60	SE¼NE¼	10	32	45	3-15—4-28	.135	12.45
1883			40.00	SW¼NE¼	10	32	45	3-15—4-28	.325	30.60
1883			20.30	NE¼NW¼	10	32	45	3-15—4-28	.165	15.33
1883			34.93	SE¼NW¼	10	32	45	3-15—4-28	.284	26.20
1883			24.80	NE¼SE¼	10	32	45	3-15—4-28	.202	18.60
1883			29.50	NW¼SE¼	10	32	45	3-15—4-28	.240	22.13
1883		14.64		SE¼SE¼	10	32	45	3-15—4-28	.119	10.98
1883		11.56		SW¼SE¼	10	32	45	3-15—4-28	.094	8.67
1883			17.80	NE¼SW¼	10	32	45	3-15—4-28	.145	13.35
1883		3.20		NW¼SW¼	10	32	45	3-15—4-28	.026	2.40
1883		9.36		SE¼SW¼	10	32	45	3-15—4-28	.076	7.02
1883		23.80		SW¼SW¼	10	32	45	3-15—4-28	.193	17.85
1883		4.95		NE¼SE¼	11	32	45	3-15—4-28	.040	3.71
1883			18.40	NE¼SE¼	11	32	45	3-15—4-28	.150	13.80
1883		2.10		NW¼SE¼	11	32	45	3-15—4-28	.017	1.58
1883			33.40	NW¼SE¼	11	32	45	3-15—4-28	.272	25.05
1883		36.04		SE¼SE¼	11	32	45	3-15—4-28	.293	27.03
1883		23.70		SW¼SE¼	11	32	45	3-15—4-28	.193	17.78
1883			12.03	SW¼SE¼	11	32	45	3-15—4-28	.098	9.02
1883			9.00	SW¼NW¼	11	32	45	3-15—4-28	.073	6.75
1883			40.00	NE¼SW¼	11	32	45	3-15—4-28	.325	30.00
1883			30.50	NW¼SW¼	11	32	45	3-15—4-28	.248	22.88
1883		13.70		SE¼SW¼	11	32	45	3-15—4-28	.111	10.28
1883			21.82	SE¼SW¼	11	32	45	3-15—4-28	.177	16.47
1883		16.00		SW¼SW¼	11	32	45	3-15—4-28	.130	12.00
1873		2.15		NE¼NE¼	12	32	45	3-15—4-28	.017	1.61
1873		25.43		SE¼NE¼	12	32	45	3-15—4-28	.207	19.07

Faris Estate—Continued.

Date of beneficial use: Nat. mdw.	Date of beneficial use: Cult. area	Construction first initiated: Dams	Construction first initiated: Ditches	Culture—Acres: Harvest crops	Culture—Acres: Meadow pasture	Culture—Acres: Willow and sage pasture	Culture—Acres: Swamp or overflow	Location: Subdivision	Location: Section	Location: Tp.N.	Location: R.E.	Length of season	Duty of water: C.F.S.	Duty of water: Acre-feet
	1873					11.96		SW¼ NE¼	12	32	45	3-15—4-28	.097	8.97
	1873					23.17		NE¼ SE¼	12	32	45	3-15—4-28	.188	17.38
	1873					0.45		SE¼ SE¼	12	32	45	3-15—4-28	.004	.35
	1873					37.45		NW¼ SE¼	12	32	45	3-15—4-28	.304	28.09
	1873					30.10		SW¼ SE¼	12	32	45	3-15—4-28	.245	22.58
	1873					3.85		NW¼ NE¼	13	32	45	3-15—4-28	.031	2.89
	1878					12.69		NE¼ SE¼	13	32	45	3-15—4-28	.103	9.52
	1878					14.10		NE¼ SE¼	13	32	45	3-15—4-28	.115	10.58
	1878					0.65		SE¼ SE¼	13	32	45	3-15—4-28	.005	.49
	1878					21.11		NW¼ SE¼	13	32	45	3-15—4-28	.172	15.83
	1878					13.83		SW¼ SE¼	13	32	45	3-15—4-28	.112	10.37
	1891					0.50		NE¼ NE¼	24	32	45	3-15—4-28	.004	.38
	1891				17.76			SE¼ NE¼	24	32	45	3-15—6-13	.144	26.64
	1891					15.56		SE¼ NE¼	24	32	45	3-15—4-28	.127	11.67
	1891				1.16			SW¼ NE¼	24	32	45	3-15—6-13	.009	1.74
	1891					9.30		SW¼ NE¼	24	32	45	3-15—4-28	.076	6.98
	1873					3.10		SE¼ NW¼	12	32	45	3-15—4-28	.025	2.33
	1873					21.20		NE¼ SW¼	12	32	45	3-15—4-28	.172	15.90
	1873						13.45	NE¼ SW¼	12	32	45	3-15—4-28	.109	10.09
	1873					9.63		NW¼ SW¼	12	32	45	3-15—4-28	.078	7.22
	1873						19.00	NW¼ SW¼	12	32	45	3-15—4-28	.154	14.35
	1873					39.99		SE¼ SW¼	12	32	45	3-15—4-28	.325	29.99
	1873					34.50		SW¼ SW¼	12	32	45	3-15—4-28	.280	25.88
	1873					32.80		NE¼ NW¼	13	32	45	3-15—4-28	.267	24.60
	1873					40.00		NW¼ NW¼	13	32	45	3-15—4-28	.325	30.00
	1873					3.29		SE¼ NW¼	13	32	45	3-15—4-28	.026	2.40
	1873					35.00		SW¼ NW¼	13	32	45	3-16—4-28	.285	26.25
	1878					16.37		NE¼ SW¼	13	32	45	3-15—4-28	.133	12.28
	1873					13.18		NW¼ SW¼	13	32	45	3-15—4-28	.107	9.89
	1878					5.20		NW¼ SW¼	13	32	45	3-15—4-28	.042	3.90
	1878					18.61		SE¼ SW¼	13	32	45	3-15—4-28	.151	15.06
	1878					14.44		SW¼ SW¼	13	32	45	3-15—4-28	.117	10.83
	1891					2.00		SW¼ NW¼	24	32	45	3-15—4-28	.016	1.50
	1873					40.00		NE¼ NE¼	14	32	45	3-15—4-28	.325	30.00
	1873					40.00		SE¼ NE¼	14	32	45	3-15—4-28	.325	30.00
	1873			8.70				NW¼ NE¼	14	32	45	3-16—9-15	.071	26.10
	1873					31.26		NW¼ NE¼	14	32	45	3-15—4-28	.254	23.45
	1873			14.50				SW¼ NE¼	14	32	45	3-15—9-15	.118	43.50
	1873					25.50		SW¼ NE¼	14	32	45	3-15—4-28	.207	19.13
	1873			26.05				NE¼ NW¼	14	32	45	3-15—9-15	.212	78.15
	1873					13.18		NE¼ NW¼	14	32	45	3-15—4-28	.107	9.89
	1873			8.35				NW¼ NW¼	11	32	45	3-15—9-15	.008	25.05
	1873				4.75			NW¼ NW¼	14	32	45	3-16—6-13	.039	7.13
	1873					4.50		NW¼ NW¼	14	32	45	3-15—4-28	.037	3.38
	1883			17.90				NW¼ NW¼	14	32	45	3-15—9-15	.146	53.70
	1873			40.00				SE¼ NW¼	14	32	45	3-15—9-15	.325	120.00
	1873			27.60				SW¼ NW¼	11	32	45	3-15—9-15	.224	82.80

1883			3.96	SW¼NW¼	14	32	45	3-15—4-28	.032	2.96
1883	1.70			SW¼NW¼	14	32	45	3-15—9-15	.014	5.10
1873			39.66	NE¼SE¼	14	32	45	3-15—4-28	.322	29.75
1878		12.70		SE¼SE¼	11	32	45	3-15—6-13	.103	19.05
1873			22.12	SE¼SE¼	14	32	45	3-15—4-28	.180	16.59
1873	15.62			NW¼SE¼	14	32	45	3-15—9-15	.127	46.86
1873			23.41	NW¼SE¼	14	32	45	3-15—4-28	.190	17.56
1873	15.00			SW¼SE¼	14	32	45	3-15—9-15	.122	45.00
1873			22.50	SW¼SE¼	14	32	45	3-15—4-28	.183	16.68
1873	38.91			NE¼SW¼	14	32	45	3-15—9-15	.317	116.82
1873	39.00			NW¼SW¼	14	32	45	3-15—9-15	.317	117.00
1873	32.10			SE¼SW¼	14	32	45	3-15—9-15	.261	96.30
1873			4.77	SE¼SW¼	14	32	45	3-15—4-28	.028	3.58
1873	30.91			SW¼SW¼	14	32	45	3-15—9-15	.251	92.73
1873			5.98	SW¼SW¼	14	32	45	3-15—4-28	.049	4.49
1883	36.00			NE¼NE¼	15	32	45	3-15—9-15	.293	108.00
1883			4.15	NE¼NE¼	15	32	45	3-15—4-28	.034	3.11
1883	37.00			NW¼NE¼	15	32	45	3-15—9-15	.301	111.00
1883			3.00	NW¼NE¼	15	32	45	3-15—4-28	.024	2.25
1873	6.15			SE¼NE¼	15	32	45	3-15—9-15	.050	18.45
1883	11.05			SE¼NE¼	15	32	45	3-15—9-15	.090	33.15
1883			16.75	SE¼NE¼	15	32	45	3-15—4-28	.136	12.56
1883	10.50			SW¼NE¼	15	32	45	3-15—9-15	.134	49.50
1883			19.44	SW¼NE¼	15	32	45	3-15—4-28	.158	14.58
1883	37.50			NE¼NW¼	15	32	45	3-15—9-15	.306	112.50
1883			1.85	NE¼NW¼	15	32	45	3-15—4-28	.015	1.39
1883	38.74			NW¼NW¼	15	32	45	3-15—9-15	.315	116.22
1873	0.87			SE¼NW¼	15	32	45	3-15—9-15	.007	2.61
1873			10.50	SE¼NW¼	15	32	45	3-15—4-28	.085	7.80
1883	21.73			SE¼NW¼	15	32	45	3-15—9-15	.170	62.58
1883	33.37			SW¼NW¼	15	32	45	3-15—4-28	.007	.65
1873			1.77	SW¼NW¼	15	32	45	3-15—4-28	.014	1.33
1883			1.70	SW¼NW¼	15	32	45	3-15—4-28	.013	1.27
1873	39.70			NE¼SE¼	15	32	45	3-15—9-15	.323	119.10
1873	40.00			SE¼SE¼	15	32	45	3-15—9-15	.325	120.00
1873	30.00			NW¼SE¼	15	32	45	3-15—9-15	.244	90.00
1883			6.50	NW¼SE¼	15	32	45	3-15—4-28	.053	4.88
1873	38.08			SW¼SE¼	15	32	45	3-15—9-15	.316	116.94
1883			4.20	NE¼NW¼	15	32	45	3-15—4-28	.034	3.15
1873	25.91			NE¼NW¼	15	32	45	3-15—9-15	.211	77.73
1873			5.20	NE¼NW¼	15	32	45	3-15—4-28	.042	3.90
1873	39.07			SE¼SW¼	15	32	45	3-15—9-15	.318	117.21
1873	7.35			NW¼SW¼	15	32	45	3-15—9-15	.060	22.05
1873			18.75	NW¼SW¼	15	32	45	3-15—4-28	.152	14.07
1883			7.70	NW¼SW¼	15	32	45	3-15—4-28	.063	5.75
1873	26.25			SW¼SW¼	15	32	45	3-15—9-15	.213	78.75
1873			11.84	SW¼SW¼	15	32	45	3-15—4-28	.096	8.90
1873	6.95			NE¼NE¼	22	32	45	3-15—9-15	.057	20.85
1873			8.10	NE¼NE¼	22	32	45	3-15—4-28	.066	6.08
1890		23.57		NE¼NE¼	22	32	45	3-15—6-13	.192	35.36
1890			38.82	SE¼NE¼	22	32	45	3-15—4-28	.316	29.12
1873	18.91			NW¼NE¼	22	32	45	3-15—9-15	.154	56.73
1873			6.85	NW¼NE¼	22	32	45	3-15—4-28	.056	5.14

Land Development Co.—Continued.

Source—**Humboldt River.** Ditch—**Crum-Blossom Slough.**

Date of beneficial use: Nat. mdw.	Date of beneficial use: Cult. area	Construction first initiated: Dams	Construction first initiated: Ditches	Culture—Acres: Harvest crops	Culture—Acres: Meadow pasture	Culture—Acres: Willow and sage pasture	Culture—Acres: Swamp or overflow	Location: Subdivision	Location: Section	Location: Tp.N.	Location: R.E.	Length of season	Duty of water: C.F.S.	Duty of water: Acre-feet
1871	1883			1.00				SW¼SE¼	32	33	45	3-15—9-15	.008	3.00
1871	1883			6.95				SE¼SW¼	32	33	45	3-15—9-15	.057	20.85
1871	1883			12.50				SW¼SW¼	32	33	45	3-15—9-15	.102	37.50
1871	1883			20.35				NW¼NE¼	5	32	45	3-15—9-15	.165	61.05
1871	1883			38.10				NE¼NW¼	5	32	45	3-15—9-15	.310	114.30
1871	1883			25.75				NW¼NW¼	5	32	45	3-15—9-15	.209	77.25
1871	1883			23.35				NE¼NE¼	6	32	45	3-15—9-15	.190	70.05

Source—**Humboldt River.** Ditch—**Rocky Point Canal.**

Nat. mdw.	Cult. area	Dams	Ditches	Harvest crops	Meadow pasture	Willow and sage pasture	Swamp or overflow	Subdivision	Section	Tp.N.	R.E.	Length of season	C.F.S.	Acre-feet
1876	1895			9.85				SE¼SW¼	21	33	45	3-15—9-15	.080	29.55
1876	1895					.35		SE¼SW¼	21	33	45	3-15—4-28	.003	.26
1876	1895			5.01				SW¼SW¼	21	33	45	3-15—9-15	.041	15.03
1876	1895					.71		SW¼SW¼	21	33	45	3-15—4-28	.006	.53
1876	1895					.20		SE¼SE¼	22	33	45	3-15—4-28	.002	.15
1876	1895			5.60				NE¼NE¼	28	33	45	3-15—9-15	.046	16.80
1876	1895					1.90		SE¼NE¼	28	33	45	3-15—4-28	.015	1.43
1876	1895						20.10	SE¼NE¼	28	33	45	3-15—4-28	.163	15.08
1876	1895			4.10				NW¼NE¼	28	33	45	3-15—9-15	.033	12.30
1876	1895				3.00			NW¼NE¼	28	33	45	3-15—6-13	.024	4.50
1876	1895			7.80				SW¼NE¼	28	33	45	3-15—9-15	.063	23.40
1876	1895				2.50			SW¼NE¼	28	33	45	3-15—6-13	.020	3.75
1876	1895					25.90		SW¼NE¼	28	33	45	3-15—4-28	.211	19.43
1876	1895			26.70				NE¼SE¼	28	33	45	3-15—9-15	.217	80.10
1876	1895			9.35				SE¼SE¼	28	33	45	3-15—9-15	.076	28.05
1876	1895			24.80				NW¼SE¼	28	33	45	3-15—9-15	.202	74.40
1876	1895					2.20		NW¼SE¼	28	33	45	3-15—4-28	.018	1.65
1876	1895			4.25				SW¼SE¼	28	33	45	3-15—9-15	.035	12.75
1876	1895					8.30		SW¼SE¼	28	33	45	3-15—4-28	.067	6.23
1876	1895			36.40				NE¼NW¼	28	33	45	3-15—9-15	.296	109.20
1876	1895			29.80				SE¼NW¼	28	33	45	3-15—9-15	.242	89.40
1876	1895					6.60		SE¼NW¼	28	33	45	3-15—4-28	.054	4.95
1876	1895			30.05				NW¼NW¼	28	33	45	3-15—9-15	.244	90.15
1876	1895					9.95		NW¼NW¼	28	33	45	3-15—4-28	.081	7.46
1876	1895			19.65				SW¼NW¼	28	33	45	3-15—9-15	.160	58.95
1876	1895					10.05		SW¼NW¼	28	33	45	3-15—4-28	.082	7.54
1876	1895					2.35		NE¼SW¼	28	33	45	3-15—4-28	.019	1.76
1876	1895					1.60		SE¼SW¼	28	33	45	3-15—4-28	.013	1.20
1876	1895					.20		NW¼SW¼	28	33	45	3-15—4-28	.002	.15

Claimant—**Wm. Licking.** Proof No. **00164**

Source—**Humboldt River.** Ditch—**Layton.**

Nat. mdw.	Cult. area	Dams	Ditches	Harvest crops	Meadow pasture	Willow and sage pasture	Swamp or overflow	Subdivision	Section	Tp.N.	R.E.	Length of season	C.F.S.	Acre-feet
1870	1871			1.84				NE¼NW¼	16	32	45	3-15—9-15	.015	5.52
1870	1871			7.12				NW¼NW¼	16	32	45	3-15—9-15	.058	21.36
1870	1871					2.18		NW¼NW¼	10	32	45	3-15—4-28	.018	1.64

1870	1871			36.94				NE¼NE¼	17	32	45	3-15—9-15	.300	110.82
1870	1871			10.25				SE¼NE¼	17	32	45	3-15—9-15	.083	30.75
1870	1871				11.30			SE¼NE¼	17	32	45	3-15—6-13	.092	16.95
1870	1871			19.68				NW¼NE¼	17	32	45	3-15—9-15	.160	59.04
1870	1871				17.95			NW¼NE¼	17	32	45	3-15—6-13	.146	26.93
1870	1871				11.80			SW¼NE¼	17	32	45	3-15—6-13	.097	17.84
1870	1871			.31				SW¼SE¼	9	32	45	3-15—9-15	.003	.93
1870	1871						.30	NW¼SE¼	9	32	45	3-15—4-28	.002	.23
1870	1871			39.25				NE¼NE¼	8	32	45	3-15—9-15	.310	117.75
1870	1871					.14		NE¼NE¼	8	32	45	3-15—4-28	.001	.11
1870	1871			39.45				SE¼NE¼	8	32	45	3-15—9-15	.321	118.35
1870	1871			14.45				NW¼NE¼	8	32	45	3-15—9-15	.117	43.35
1870	1871					18.79		NW¼NE¼	8	32	45	3-15—4-28	.153	14.09
1870	1871			18.73				SW¼NE¼	8	32	45	3-15—9-15	.152	56.19
1870	1871					9.29		SW¼NE¼	8	32	45	3-15—4-28	.076	6.97
1870	1871			29.04				NE¼SE¼	8	32	45	3-15—9-15	.236	87.12
1870	1871					4.12		NE¼SE¼	8	32	45	3-15—4-28	.033	3.09
1870	1871			12.06				SE¼SE¼	8	32	45	3-15—9-15	.098	36.18
1870	1871					19.77		SE¼SE¼	8	32	45	3-15—4-28	.161	14.83
1870	1871			30.45				NW¼SE¼	8	32	45	3-15—9-15	.248	91.35
1870	1871					5.33		NW¼SE¼	8	32	45	3-15—4-28	.043	4.00
1870	1871			35.85				SW¼SE¼	8	32	45	3-15—9-15	.291	107.55
	1871			.94				NE¼NW¼	9	32	45	3-15—9-15	.008	2.82
	1871				2.81			NE¼NW¼	9	32	45	3-15—6-13	.023	4.22
	1871						12.58	NE¼NW¼	9	32	45	3-15—4-28	.102	9.44
	1871			22.45				SE¼NW¼	9	32	45	3-15—9-15	.183	67.35
	1871						6.97	SE¼NW¼	9	32	45	3-15—4-28	.057	5.23
	1871			33.07				NW¼NW¼	9	32	45	3-15—9-15	.269	99.21
	1871				5.20			NW¼NW¼	9	32	45	3-15—6-13	.042	7.80
	1871						.94	NW¼NW¼	9	32	45	3-15—4-28	.008	.71
	1871			39.63				SW¼NW¼	9	32	45	3-15—9-15	.322	118.89
	1871			36.41				NE¼SW¼	9	32	45	3-15—9-15	.296	109.23
	1871						.75	NE¼SW¼	9	32	45	3-15—4-28	.006	.56
	1871			38.98				SE¼SW¼	9	32	45	3-15—9-15	.317	116.94
	1871			40.03				NW¼SW¼	9	32	45	3-15—9-15	.325	120.09
	1871			31.90				SW¼SW¼	9	32	45	3-15—9-15	.259	95.70
	1871					4.19		SW¼SW¼	9	32	45	3-15—4-28	.034	3.14
	1871						1.80	SW¼NE¼	9	32	45	3-15—4-28	.015	1.35
	1871			1.98				NW¼SE¼	9	32	45	3-15—9-15	.016	5.94

Claimant—**McIntyre-Starrett Co.** Proof No. **00165**

Source—**Humboldt River.** Ditch—**McIntyre-Starrett Dam.**

1878	1883			5.50				NE¼SE¼	9	32	45	3-15—9-15	.045	16.50
1878	1883			38.86				SE¼SE¼	9	32	45	3-15—9-15	.316	116.58
1878	1883			25.90				NW¼SE¼	9	32	45	3-15—9-15	.211	77.70
1878	1883			38.75				SW¼SE¼	9	32	45	3-15—9-15	.315	116.25
1878	1883			39.35				NE¼NE¼	16	32	35	3-15—9-15	.320	119.05
1878	1883			37.30				SE¼NE¼	16	32	35	3-15—9-15	.303	11.90
1878	1883					.50		SE¼NE¼	16	32	35	3-15—4-28	.008	.38
1878	1883			37.06				NW¼NE¼	16	32	35	3-15—9-15	.301	111.18
1878	1883			28.19				SW¼NE¼	16	32	35	3-15—9-15	.237	84.57
1878	1883					.83		SW¼NE¼	16	32	35	3-15—4-28	.007	.62

McIntyre-Starrett Co.—Continued.

Date of beneficial use: Nat. mdw.	Date of beneficial use: Cult. area	Construction first initiated: Dams	Construction first initiated: Ditches	Culture—Acres: Harvest crops	Culture—Acres: Meadow pasture	Culture—Acres: Willow and sage pasture	Culture—Acres: Swamp or overflow	Location: Subdivision	Location: Section	Location: Tp.N.	Location: R.E.	Length of season	Duty of water: C.F.S.	Duty of water: Acre-feet
1878	1883			36.27				NE¼NW¼	16	32	35	3-15—9-15	.295	108.81
1878	1883			16.08				SE¼NW¼	16	32	35	3-15—9-15	.131	48.24
1878	1883					.13		SE¼NW¼	16	32	35	3-15—4-28	.001	.10
1878	1883			13.59				NW¼NW¼	16	32	35	3-15—9-15	.110	40.77
1878	1883					.73		NW¼NW¼	16	32	35	3-15—4-28	.006	.55
1878	1883			6.53				SW¼NW¼	16	32	35	3-15—9-15	.053	19.59
1878	1883					6.55		SW¼NW¼	16	32	35	3-15—4-28	.053	4.91
Source—Humboldt River. Ditch—Altenberg Ditch.														
1878	1874			3.26				SW¼NW¼	16	32	35	3-15—9-15	.027	9.78
1878	1874			13.33				SW¼NW¼	16	32	35	3-15—9-15	.108	39.99
1878	1874				4.40			SW¼NW¼	16	32	35	3-15—6-13	.036	6.60
1878	1874					11.35		SE¼NW¼	16	32	35	3-15—4-28	.092	8.51

Claimant—**W. T. Jenkins Co.** **Proof No. 00166**

Date of beneficial use: Nat. mdw.	Date of beneficial use: Cult. area	Construction first initiated: Dams	Construction first initiated: Ditches	Culture—Acres: Harvest crops	Culture—Acres: Meadow pasture	Culture—Acres: Willow and sage pasture	Culture—Acres: Swamp or overflow	Location: Subdivision	Location: Section	Location: Tp.N.	Location: R.E.	Length of season	Duty of water: C.F.S.	Duty of water: Acre-feet
Source—Humboldt River. Ditch—Rocky Point.														
	1873				5.55			NE¼NW¼	6	32	46	3-15—6-13	.045	8.33
	1873				.11			NE¼SE¼	1	32	45	3-15—6-13	.001	.17
	1873					6.61		NE¼SE¼	1	32	45	3-15—4-28	.054	4.96
	1873						6.33	NE¼SE¼	1	32	45	3-15—4-28	.051	4.75
	1873			6.27				NE¼NW¼	1	32	45	3-15—9-15	.051	18.81
	1873			18.57				NW¼NW¼	1	32	45	3-15—9-15	.151	55.71
	1873					5.60		NW¼NW¼	1	32	45	3-15—4-28	.046	4.20
Source—Humboldt River. Ditch—South Ditch.														
	1895				7.62			SE¼SE¼	2	32	45	3-15—6-13	.062	11.43
	1895						30.79	SE¼SE¼	2	32	45	3-15—4-28	.250	23.09
	1895			9.45				NW¼SE¼	2	32	45	3-15—9-15	.077	28.35
	1895				19.87			NW¼SE¼	2	32	45	3-15—6-13	.162	29.81
	1895			6.60				SW¼SE¼	2	32	45	3-15—9-15	.054	18.80
	1895				9.93			SW¼SE¼	2	32	45	3-15—6-13	.081	14.90
	1895						5.28	SW¼SE¼	2	32	45	3-15—4-28	.043	3.96
	1895						1.16	NE¼NW¼	2	32	45	3-15—4-28	.009	.87
	1895			11.50				SE¼SW¼	2	32	45	3-15—9-15	.093	34.50
	1895			10.15				SW¼SW¼	2	32	45	3-15—9-15	.083	30.45
	1895			12.04				NW¼SE¼	1	32	45	3-15—9-15	.098	36.12
	1895				3.36			NW¼SE¼	1	32	45	3-15—6-13	.027	5.04
	1895					16.67		NW¼SE¼	1	32	45	3-15—4-28	.136	12.50
	1895						2.21	NW¼SE¼	1	32	45	3-15—4-28	.018	1.66
	1895					1.00		SW¼SE¼	1	32	45	3-15—4-28	.008	.75
	1895			5.70				SW¼NE¼	1	32	45	3-15—9-15	.046	17.10
	1895					4.47		SW¼NE¼	1	32	45	3-15—4-28	.036	3.35
	1805			19.30				SE¼NW¼	1	32	45	3-15—9-15	.157	57.90
	1895			26.50				SW¼NW¼	1	32	45	3-15—9-15	.215	79.50
	1805					13.67		SW¼SW¼	1	32	45	3-15—4-28	.111	10.25

	1895			.55				NE¼SW¼	1	32	45	3 15—0-15	.005	1.65
	1895					39.00		NE¼SW¼	1	32	45	3 15—4-28	.317	29.25
	1895					9.97		SE¼SW¼	1	32	45	3-15—4-28	.081	7.48
	1895						5.82	SE¼SW¼	1	32	45	3-15—4-28	.047	4.37
	1895					40.12		NW¼SW¼	1	32	45	3 15—4-28	.326	30.09
	1895					21.84		SW¼SW¼	1	32	45	3-15—4-28	.178	16.38
	1895			28.30				NE¼NE¼	2	32	45	3-15—0-15	.230	84.90
	1895					13.06		NE¼NE¼	2	32	45	3-15—4 28	.106	9.80
	1895			6.98				SE¼NE¼	2	32	45	3-15—0-15	.057	20.94
	1895				2.16			SE¼NE¼	2	32	45	3-15—6-13	.018	3.24
	1895					30.88		SE¼NE¼	2	32	45	3-15—4-28	.251	23.16
	1895			7.35				NW¼NE¼	2	32	45	3-15—0-15	.060	22.05
	1895					9.14		NW¼NE¼	2	32	45	3-15—4-28	.074	6.87
	1895			6.60				SW¼NE¼	2	32	45	3-15—0 15	.054	19.80
	1895				8.47			NE¼SE¼	2	32	45	3-15—6-13	.069	12.71
	1895					29.60		NE¼SE¼	2	32	45	3-15—4-28	.241	22.20

Areas in sections 6, 1 and 2, T. 32 N, R. 45 E, totaling 871.53 acres, first flooded artificially during the year 1873 due to Rocky Point Dam when these areas were third-class pasture; therefore has pasture water right of .75 acre-feet per acre from 1873 to 1895.

Claimant—**Faris** Estate. Proof No. **00167**
Source—**Humboldt** River. Ditch—**Faris Ditch System.**

	1873					17.31		SE¼SE¼	5	32	46	3-15—4-28	.141	21.98
1872	1873					6.30		SE¼SE¼	5	32	46	3-15—4-28	.051	4.73
	1873					17.57		SW¼SE¼	5	32	46	3-15—4-28	.143	13.18
1872	1873					4.71		SW¼SE¼	5	32	46	3-15—4-28	.038	3.53
	1873					24.77		SE¼SW¼	5	32	46	3-15—4-28	.201	18.58
1872	1873					.50		SE¼SW¼	5	32	46	3-15—4-28	.004	.38
1875	1876			22.97				NE¼NE¼	20	32	46	3-15—0-15	.187	68.91
	1892					.75		NE¼NE¼	20	32	46	3-15—4-28	.006	.56
	1893					13.15		NE¼NE¼	20	32	46	3-15—4-28	.107	9.86
	1893					33.46		SE¼NE¼	20	32	46	3-15—4-28	.272	25.10
	1892					32.65		NW¼NE¼	20	32	46	3-15—4-28	.265	24.49
	1892					34.69		NE¼NW¼	20	32	46	3-15—4-28	.282	26.02
	1892					35.41		NW¼NW¼	20	32	46	3-15—4-28	.288	26.56
	1892					2.30		SE¼NW¼	20	32	46	3-15—4-28	.019	1.73
	1892					5.85		SW¼NW¼	20	32	46	3-15—4-28	.048	4.39
	1873					36.20		SE¼SE¼	6	32	46	3-15—4-28	.294	27.15
	1873					30.26		SW¼SE¼	6	32	46	3-15—4-28	.246	22.70
	1873					33.37		SE¼SW¼	6	32	46	3-15—4-28	.271	25.03
	1873					10.61		SW¼SW¼	6	32	46	3-15—4-28	.086	7.96
	1892					36.53		NE¼NE¼	19	32	46	3-15—4-28	.297	27.41
	1892					3.75		SE¼NE¼	19	32	46	3-15—4-28	.030	2.81
	1892					11.66		NW¼NE¼	19	32	46	3-15—4-28	.095	8.75
	1890				1.60			NE¼NW¼	19	32	46	3-15—6-13	.013	2.40
	1890					8.25		NE¼NW¼	19	32	46	3-15—4-28	.067	6.19
	1890				.45			SE¼NW¼	19	32	46	3-15—6-13	.004	.68
	1890					18.80		SE¼NW¼	19	32	46	3-15—4-28	.153	14.10
	1890				2.43			NW¼NW¼	19	32	46	3-15—6-13	.020	3.65
	1890					3.30		NW¼NW¼	19	32	46	3-15—4 28	.027	2.48
	1890				26.10			SW¼NW¼	19	32	46	3-15—6-13	.212	39.15
	1890					21.84		SW¼NW¼	19	32	46	3-15—4-28	.178	16.38
	1873					31.30		NE¼NE¼	7	32	46	3-15—4-28	.254	23.48

Faris Estate—Continued.

Date of beneficial use: Nat. mdw.	Date of beneficial use: Cult. area	Construction first initiated: Dams	Construction first initiated: Ditches	Culture—Acres: Harvest crops	Culture—Acres: Meadow pasture	Culture—Acres: Willow and sage pasture	Culture—Acres: Swamp or overflow	Location: Subdivision	Location: Section	Location: Tp.N.	Location: R.E.	Length of season	Duty of water: C.F.S.	Duty of water: Acre-feet
	1873					.50		SE¼NE¼	7	32	46	3-15—4-28	.004	.38
	1873					9.96		NW¼NE¼	7	32	46	3-15—4-28	.081	7.47
	1873					12.83		NE¼NW¼	7	32	46	3-15—4-28	.104	9.62
	1873					41.55		NW¼NW¼	7	32	46	3-15—4-28	.338	31.16
	1873					30.72		SW¼NW¼	7	32	46	3-15—4-28	.250	23.04
	1878						2.10	SE¼SE¼	4	32	46	3-15—4-28	.024	2.18
	1878						18.65	SW¼SE¼	4	32	46	3-15—4-28	.152	13.99
	1878						20.00	SE¼SW¼	4	32	46	3-15—4-28	.163	15.00
	1878						16.37	SW¼SW¼	4	32	46	3-15—4-28	.133	12.28
	1873					3.75		SW¼SW¼	4	32	46	3-15—4-28	.030	2.81
	1893				37.44			NE¼NE¼	21	32	46	3-15—6-13	.304	56.16
	1893				35.22			SE¼NE¼	21	32	46	3-15—6-13	.286	52.83
	1893					3.80		SE¼NE¼	21	32	46	3-15—4-28	.031	2.85
	1893				34.50			NW¼NE¼	21	32	46	3-15—6-13	.280	51.75
	1893					2.92		NW¼NE¼	21	32	46	3-15—4-28	.024	2.19
	1893				2.12			SW¼NE¼	21	32	46	3-15—6-13	.017	3.18
	1893					35.77		SW¼NE¼	21	32	46	3-15—4-28	.291	26.83
	1893				22.51			NE¼NW¼	21	32	46	3-15—6-13	.183	33.77
	1893					14.62		NE¼NW¼	21	32	46	3-15—4-28	.119	10.97
	1893					38.42		SE¼NW¼	21	32	46	3-15—4-28	.312	29.92
	1893			11.40				NW¼NW¼	21	32	46	3-15—9-15	.093	34.20
	1893				5.72			NW¼NW¼	21	32	46	3-15—6-13	.047	8.58
	1893					20.80		NW¼NW¼	21	32	46	3-15—4-28	.169	15.60
	1893					40.00		SW¼NW¼	21	32	46	3-15—4-28	.325	30.00
	1893				39.40			NE¼SE¼	21	32	46	3-15—6-13	.320	59.10
	1893				39.50			NW¼SE¼	21	32	46	3-15—6-13	.321	59.25
	1893				37.29			SE¼SE¼	21	32	46	3-15—6-13	.303	55.94
	1893						1.24	SE¼SE¼	21	32	46	3-15—4-28	.010	.93
	1893				36.40			SW¼SE¼	21	32	46	3-15—6-13	.296	54.60
	1893						3.60	SW¼SE¼	21	32	46	3-15—4-28	.029	2.70
	1893				34.35			NE¼SW¼	21	32	46	3-15—6-13	.279	51.53
	1893					4.00		NE¼SW¼	21	32	46	3-15—4-28	.040	3.68
	1893				20.86			NW¼SW¼	21	32	46	3-15—6-13	.170	21.30
	1893					18.54		NW¼SW¼	21	32	46	3-15—4-28	.150	13.91
	1893				35.40			SE¼SW¼	21	32	46	3-15—6-13	.288	53.10
	1893						4.60	SE¼SW¼	21	32	46	3-15—4-28	.037	3.45
	1893				35.03			SW¼SW¼	21	32	46	3-15—6-13	.285	52.55
	1893						4.97	SW¼SW¼	21	32	46	3-15—4-28	.040	3.73
	1893						1.00	NE¼NE¼	28	32	46	3-15—4-28	.081	.75
	1893						6.96	NW¼NE¼	28	32	46	3-15—4-28	.057	5.22
	1893						8.58	NE¼NW¼	28	32	46	3-15—4-28	.070	6.44
	1893						7.09	NW¼NW¼	28	32	46	3-15—4-28	.058	5.32
	1893					1.86		NE¼NE¼	29	32	46	3-15—4-28	.016	1.40
	1878						3.34	NE¼NE¼	8	32	46	3-15—4-28	.027	2.51
	1878						25.05	SE¼NE¼	8	32	46	3-15—4-28	.204	18.79
	1878					.75		NW¼NE¼	8	32	46	3-15—4-28	.006	.56
	1873						9.47	NW¼NE¼	8	32	46	3-15—4-28	.077	7.10

	1878						8.75	SW¼NE¼	8	32	46	3-15—4-28	.071	6.56
	1878						40.00	NE¼SE¼	8	32	46	3-15—4-28	.325	30.00
	1878			9.42				SE¼SE¼	8	32	46	3-15—9-15	.077	28.26
	1878						30.63	SE¼SE¼	8	32	46	3-15—4-28	.249	22.97
	1878						40.00	NW¼SE¼	8	32	46	3-15—4-28	.325	30.00
	1878			1.30				SW¼SE¼	8	32	46	3-15—9-15	.011	3.90
	1878						38.70	SW¼SE¼	8	32	46	3-15—4-28	.315	29.03
	1873					29.05		NE¼NW¼	8	32	46	3-15—4-28	.236	21.79
	1873					26.95		NW¼NW¼	8	32	46	3-15—4-28	.219	20.21
	1878						33.54	NE¼SW¼	8	32	46	3-15—4-28	.273	25.16
	1878						40.00	SE¼SW¼	8	32	46	3-15—4-28	.325	30.00
	1878						9.70	NW¼SW¼	8	32	46	3-15—4-28	.079	7.28
	1878						40.00	SW¼SW¼	8	32	46	3-15—4-28	.325	30.00
	1878					4.53		SW¼SE¼	9	32	46	3-15—4-28	.037	3.40
	1878					.30		NE¼SW¼	9	32	46	3-15—4-28	.002	3.23
	1878						40.00	NW¼SW¼	9	32	46	3-15—4-28	.325	30.00
	1878			14.40				SE¼SW¼	9	32	46	3-15—9-15	.117	43.20
	1878					18.21		SE¼SW¼	9	32	46	3-15—4-28	.148	13.66
	1878			3.38				SW¼SW¼	9	32	46	3-15—9-15	.027	10.14
	1878					18.16		SW¼SW¼	9	32	46	3-15—4-28	.148	13.95
	1878						18.70	SW¼SW¼	9	32	46	3-13—4-28	.152	14.03
	1878					13.10		NE¼NE¼	9	32	46	3-15—4-28	.107	9.83
	1878			11.40				SE¼NE¼	9	32	16	3-15—9-15	.093	34.20
	1878					23.13		SE¼NE¼	9	32	46	3-15—4-28	.188	17.35
	1878						4.40	NW¼NE¼	9	32	46	3-15—4-28	.036	3.30
	1878					4.00		SW¼NE¼	9	32	46	3-15—4-28	.033	3.00
	1878						33.60	NE¼NW¼	9	32	46	3-15—4-28	.273	25.20
	1878						10.10	SE¼NW¼	9	32	46	3-15—4-28	.082	7.58
	1878						40.00	NW¼NW¼	9	32	46	3-15—4-28	.325	30.00
	1878						40.00	SW¼NW¼	9	32	46	3-15—4-28	.325	30.00
	1878			34.86				NE¼SE¼	9	32	46	3-15—9-15	.283	104.58
	1878					2.43		NE¼SE¼	9	32	46	3-15—4-28	.020	1.82
	1878			37.87				SE¼SE¼	9	32	46	3-15—9-15	.308	113.71
	1878					2.05		SE¼SE¼	9	32	46	3-15—4-28	.017	1.55
	1878			12.27				NW¼SE¼	9	32	46	3-15—9-15	.100	36.81
	1878					21.92		NW¼SE¼	9	32	46	3-15—4-28	.178	16.44
	1878			34.10				SW¼SE¼	8	32	46	3-15—9-15	.277	102.30
1875	1876				7.10			NW¼SW¼	10	32	46	3-15—6-13	.058	10.65
1875	1878			30.34				NW¼SW¼	10	32	46	3-15—9-15	.247	91.02
1875	1878				.90			NW¼SW¼	10	32	46	3-15—6-13	.007	1.35
1875	1876			21.64				SE¼SW¼	10	32	46	3-15—9-15	.176	64.92
1875	1876				18.44			SE¼SW¼	10	32	46	3-15—6-13	.150	27.66
1875	1876				27.58			SW¼SW¼	10	32	46	3-15—6-13	.224	41.37
1875	1878			8.10				SW¼SW¼	10	32	46	3-15—9-15	.066	24.30
1875	1878				3.91			SW¼SW¼	10	32	46	3-15—6-13	.032	5.87
1875	1878			24.62				SE¼NW¼	10	32	46	3-15—9-15	.200	73.86
1875	1878			34.16				SW¼NW¼	10	32	46	3-15—9-15	.278	102.48
1875	1878				4.92			SW¼NW¼	10	32	46	3-15—6-13	.040	7.38
1875	1876			21.50				NE¼SE¼	10	32	46	3-15—9-15	.175	64.50
1875	1876				17.38			NE¼SE¼	10	32	46	3-15—6-13	.141	26.17
1875	1876					.95		NE¼SE¼	10	32	46	3-15—4-28	.008	.71
1875	1876			29.98				NW¼SE¼	10	32	46	3-15—9-15	.244	89.84
1875	1876				10.27			NW¼SE¼	10	32	46	3-15—6-13	.083	15.41

Faris Estate—Continued.

Date of beneficial use: Nat. mdw.	Date of beneficial use: Cult. area	Construction first initiated: Dams	Construction first initiated: Ditches	Culture—Acres: Harvest crops	Culture—Acres: Meadow pasture	Culture—Acres: Willow and sage pasture	Culture—Acres: Swamp or overflow	Location: Subdivision	Location: Section	Location: Tp.N.	Location: R.E.	Length of season	Duty of water: C.F.S.	Duty of water: Acre-feet
1875	1876			4.17				SE¼SE¼	10	32	46	3-15—9-15	.034	12.51
1875	1876				35.83			SE¼SE¼	10	32	46	3-15—6-13	.291	53.75
1875	1876			38.00				SW¼SE¼	10	32	46	3-15—9-15	.293	108.00
1875	1876				3.60			SW¼SE¼	10	32	46	3-15—6-13	.029	5.40
1875	1878			.75				NE¼SW¼	10	32	46	3-15—9-15	.006	2.25
1875	1876			1.04				NE¼SW¼	10	32	46	3-15—9-15	.008	3.12
1875	1876				38.17			NE¼SW¼	10	32	46	3-15—6-13	.310	57.26
1875	1876			20.17				NE¼NE¼	10	32	46	3-15—9-15	.164	60.51
1875	1876				17.04			NE¼NE¼	10	32	46	3-15—6-13	.139	26.56
1875	1878						2.50	NE¼NE¼	10	32	46	3-15—4-28	.020	1.88
1875	1876			16.84				NW¼NE¼	10	32	46	3-15—9-15	.137	50.52
1875	1876				.70			NW¼NE¼	10	32	46	3-15—6-13	.006	1.05
1875	1878			19.77				NW¼NE¼	10	32	46	3-15—9-15	.161	59.31
1875	1878						2.60	NW¼NE¼	10	32	46	3-15—4-28	.021	1.95
1875	1876			32.50				SE¼NE¼	10	32	46	3-15—9-15	.264	97.50
1875	1876				6.07			SE¼NE¼	10	32	46	3-15—6-13	.049	9.11
1875	1876					1.40		SE¼NE¼	10	32	46	3-15—4-28	.011	1.05
1875	1876			8.80				SW¼NE¼	10	32	46	3-15—9-15	.072	26.58
1875	1876				30.38			SW¼NE¼	10	32	46	3-15—6-13	.247	45.57
1875	1878			16.72				NE¼NW¼	10	32	46	3-15—9-15	.136	50.16
1875	1878					21.96		NE¼NW¼	10	32	46	3-15—4-28	.179	16.47
1875	1878			1.63				NW¼NW¼	10	32	46	3-15—9-15	.013	4.89
1875	1878					30.95		NW¼NW¼	10	32	46	3-15—4-28	.252	23.21
1875	1876				14.49			SE¼NW¼	10	32	46	3-15—6-13	.118	21.74
	1893				23.37			NE¼SE¼	15	32	46	3-15—6-13	.190	35.06
	1893				4.00			SE¼SE¼	15	32	46	3-15—6-13	.033	6.00
	1893				35.30			SW¼SE¼	15	32	46	3-15—6-13	.286	52.96
	1893				14.80			NE¼NE¼	22	32	46	3-15—6-13	.120	22.20
	1893				38.50			NE¼NW¼	22	32	46	3-15—6-13	.313	57.75
	1893				28.96			SE¼NW¼	22	32	46	3-15—6-13	.235	43.44
	1893				4.72			NE¼SW¼	22	32	46	3-15—6-13	.038	7.08
	1893				38.28			NW¼SW¼	22	32	46	3-15—6-18	.311	57.42
	1893				15.54			SW¼SW¼	22	32	46	3-15—6-13	.126	23.31
1875	1876				40.00			NE¼NE¼	15	32	46	3-15—6-13	.325	60.00
1875	1876			24.48				NW¼NE¼	15	32	46	3-15—9-15	.199	73.44
1875	1876				15.43			NW¼NE¼	15	32	46	3-15—6-13	.125	23.15
1875	1876				32.96			SE¼NE¼	15	32	46	3-15—6-13	.268	49.44
1875	1893				6.44			SE¼NE¼	15	32	46	3-15—6-13	.052	9.66
1875	1876			3.60				SW¼NE¼	15	32	46	3-15—9-15	.029	10.80
1875	1876				20.08			SW¼NE¼	15	32	46	3-15—6-13	.163	30.12
	1893				16.32			SW¼NE¼	15	32	46	3-15—6-13	.183	24.48
1875	1876			31.75				NE¼NW¼	15	32	46	3-15—9-15	.258	95.45
1875	1876				8.24			NE¼NW¼	15	32	46	3-15—6-13	.067	12.36
	1893				10.00			SE¼NW¼	15	32	46	3-15—6-13	.081	15.00
1875	1876			22.39				SE¼NW¼	15	32	46	3-15—9-15	.182	67.17
1875	1876				5.42			SE¼NW¼	15	32	46	3-15—6-13	.044	8.13
1875	1876			25.38				NW¼NW¼	15	32	46	3-15—9-15	.206	76.14

1875	1876				11.46			NW¼ NW¼	15	32	46	3-15—6-13	.093	17.19
1875	1876					2.30		NW¼ NW¼	15	32	46	3-15—4-28	.019	1.79
1875	1876			37.20				SW¼ NW¼	15	32	46	3-15—9-15	.302	111.60
	1876			22.39				SE¼ NW¼	15	32	46	3-15—9-15	.182	67.17
	1893				15.43			SE¼ NW¼	15	32	46	3-15—6-13	.125	23.16
	1893				40.00			NW¼ SE¼	15	32	46	3-15—6-13	.325	60.00
	1876			9.95				NE¼ SW¼	15	32	46	3-15—9-15	.081	29.85
	1893				30.05			NE¼ SW¼	15	32	46	3-15—6-13	.244	45.08
	1876			31.18				NW¼ SW¼	15	32	46	3-15—9-15	.253	93.54
	1893				8.82			NW¼ SW¼	15	32	46	3-15—6-13	.072	13.23
	1876			0.20				SE¼ SW¼	15	32	46	3-15—9-15	.002	.60
	1893				39.80			SE¼ SW¼	15	32	46	3-15—6-13	.324	59.70
	1876			3.75				SW¼ SW¼	15	32	46	3-15—9-15	.030	11.25
	1893				36.25			SW¼ SW¼	15	32	46	3-15—6-13	.296	54.38
	1876			7.38				NE¼ NE¼	16	32	46	3-15—9-15	.060	22.14
	1878			23.60				NE¼ NE¼	16	32	46	3-15—9-15	.192	70.80
	1878				6.40			NE¼ NE¼	16	32	46	3-15—6-13	.052	9.20
	1876			39.35				SE¼ NE¼	16	32	46	3-15—9-15	.320	118.05
	1876			0.67				NW¼ NE¼	16	32	46	3-15—9-15	.005	2.01
	1878			34.06				NW¼ NE¼	16	32	46	3-15—9-15	.277	102.18
	1878				3.53			NW¼ NE¼	16	32	46	3-15—6-13	.029	5.30
	1878			39.67				NE¼ NW¼	16	32	46	3-15—9-15	.323	119.01
	1876			3.74				SE¼ NW¼	16	32	46	3-15—9-15	.030	111.22
	1878			31.14				SE¼ NW¼	16	32	46	3-15—9-15	.278	102.42
	1878			38.88				NW¼ NW¼	16	32	46	3-15—9-15	.316	116.64
	1878					0.55		NW¼ NW¼	16	32	46	3-15—4-28	.004	.41
	1878			39.50				SW¼ NW¼	16	32	46	3-15—9-15	.321	118.50
	1876			31.46				NW¼ SE¼	16	32	46	3-15—9-15	.256	94.38
	1893				8.54			NW¼ SE¼	16	32	46	3-15—6-13	.060	12.81
	1893				23.13			NE¼ SE¼	16	32	46	3-15—6-13	.188	34.70
	1876			16.87				NE¼ SE¼	16	32	46	3-15—9-15	.137	50.61
	1878			4.42				NE¼ SW¼	16	32	46	3-15—9-15	.036	13.26
	1878				1.20			NE¼ SW¼	16	32	46	3-15—6-13	.010	1.80
	1876			31.16				NE¼ SW¼	16	32	46	3-15—9-15	.253	93.48
	1893				1.67			NE¼ SW¼	16	32	46	3-15—6-13	.014	2.51
	1876			11.20				SE¼ SW¼	16	32	46	3-15—9-15	.091	33.60
	1893				28.80			SE¼ SW¼	16	32	46	3-15—6-13	.234	43.20
	1878			33.28				NW¼ SW¼	16	32	46	3-15—9-15	.271	99.84
	1878				2.63			NW¼ SW¼	16	32	46	3-15—6-13	.021	3.80
	1876			2.28				NW¼ SW¼	16	32	46	3-15—9-15	.019	6.84
	1876			35.85				SW¼ SW¼	16	32	46	3-15—9-15	.291	107.55
	1876					.60		SW¼ SW¼	16	32	46	3-15—4-28	.005	.45
	1893				2.25			SW¼ SW¼	16	32	46	3-15—6-13	.018	3.38
	1893				40.00			SE¼ SE¼	16	32	46	3-15—6-13	.325	60.00
	1893				40.00			SW¼ SE¼	16	32	46	3-15—6-13	.325	60.00
	1878			37.37				NE¼ NE¼	17	32	46	3-15—9-15	.304	112.11
	1878			39.10				SE¼ NE¼	17	32	46	3-15—9-15	.318	117.30
	1878			27.06				NW¼ NE¼	17	32	46	3-15—9-15	.220	81.18
	1878					12.00		NW¼ NE¼	17	32	46	3-15—4-28	.098	9.00
	1878			38.42				SW¼ NE¼	17	32	46	3-15—9-15	.312	115.26
	1878			38.68				NE¼ SE¼	17	32	46	3-15—9-15	.314	116.04
	1878				0.60			NE¼ SE¼	17	32	46	3-15—6-13	.005	.90
	1878			16.81				SE¼ SE¼	17	32	46	3-15—9-15	.137	50.43

Faris Estate—Continued.

Date of beneficial use: Nat. mdw.	Date of beneficial use: Cult. area	Construction first initiated: Dams	Construction first initiated: Ditches	Culture—Acres: Harvest crops	Culture—Acres: Meadow pasture	Culture—Acres: Willow and sage pasture	Culture—Acres: Swamp or overflow	Location: Subdivision	Location: Section	Location: Tp.N.	Location: R.E.	Length of season	Duty of water: C.F.S.	Duty of water: Acre-feet
	1878					2.00		SE¼ SE¼	17	32	46	3-15—4-28	.016	1.50
	1878			39.40				NW¼ SE¼	17	32	46	3-15—9-15	.320	118.20
	1878			40.08				SW¼ SE¼	17	32	46	3-15—9-15	.326	120.24
	1878			3.97				NE¼ NW¼	17	32	46	3-15—9-15	.323	11.91
	1878					36.04		NE¼ NW¼	17	32	46	3-15—4-28	.293	27.03
	1878			27.50				SE¼ NW¼	17	32	46	3-15—9-15	.224	82.50
	1878					11.56		SE¼ NW¼	17	32	46	3-15—4-28	.094	8.67
	1878					40.00		NW¼ NW¼	17	32	46	3-15—4-28	.325	30.00
	1878			5.00				SW¼ NW¼	17	32	46	3-15—9-15	.041	15.00
	1878					35.00		SW¼ NW¼	17	32	46	3-15—4-28	.285	26.25
	1878			38.94				NE¼ SW¼	17	32	46	3-15—9-15	.317	116.82
	1878			37.62				SE¼ SW¼	17	32	46	3-15—9-15	.306	112.86
	1878					1.50		SE¼ SW¼	17	32	46	3-15—4-28	.012	1.13
	1878			9.77				NW¼ SW¼	17	32	46	3-15—9-15	.079	29.31
	1878					29.50		NW¼ SW¼	17	32	46	3-15—4-28	.240	22.13
	1878			19.43				SW¼ SW¼	17	32	46	3-15—9-15	.158	58.29
	1878					18.90		SW¼ SW¼	17	32	46	3-15—4-28	.154	14.18
	1876			18.44				SE¼ SE¼	17	32	46	3-15—9-15	.150	55.32
	1873					0.75		NW¼ SW¼	7	32	46	3-15—4-28	.006	.56
	1878						5.60	SE¼ SE¼	7	32	46	3-15—4-28	.046	4.20
	1878						37.44	NE¼ NE¼	18	32	46	3-15—4-28	.304	28.08
	1878						7.96	NW¼ NE¼	18	32	46	3-15—4-28	.065	5.97
	1878					40.00		SE¼ NE¼	18	32	46	3-15—4-28	.325	30.00
	1878					35.45		SW¼ NE¼	18	32	46	3-15—4-28	.288	26.59
	1878					9.10		SE¼ NW¼	18	32	46	3-15—4-28	.074	6.83
	1878					6.40		SW¼ NW¼	18	32	46	3-15—4-28	.052	4.80
	1878					40.00		NE¼ SE¼	18	32	46	3-15—4-28	.325	30.00
	1878					39.70		NW¼ SE¼	18	32	46	3-15—4-28	.319	29.40
	1878					36.72		SE¼ SE¼	18	32	46	3-15—4-28	.299	27.54
	1878					30.83		SW¼ SE¼	18	32	46	3-15—4-28	.251	23.12
	1878					36.97		NE¼ SW¼	18	32	46	3-15—4-28	.301	27.73
	1878					41.28		NW¼ SW¼	18	32	46	3-15—4-28	.336	30.96
	1878					4.32		SE¼ SW¼	18	32	46	3-15—4-28	.035	3.24
	1878					2.90		SW¼ SW¼	18	32	46	3-15—4-28	.024	2.18
	1893				37.60			NW¼ NW¼	22	32	46	3-15—6-13	.306	56.40
	1893				37.90			SW¼ NW¼	22	32	46	3-15—6-13	.308	56.85
	1878						41.74	SE¼ SE¼	3	32	46	3-15—4-28	.339	31.31
	1876			3.34				SE¼ SE¼	3	32	46	3-15—9-15	.027	10.02
	1878			4.43				SW¼ SE¼	3	32	46	3-15—9-15	.036	13.29
	1878					25.03		SW¼ SE¼	3	32	46	3-16—4-28	.203	18.77
	1878						14.62	SW¼ SE¼	3	32	46	3-15—4-28	.119	10.97
	1878					28.05		SE¼ SW¼	3	32	46	3-15—4-28	.228	21.04
	1878					0.60		SW¼ SW¼	3	32	46	3-15—4-28	.005	.45
	1893					6.84		NE¼ SW¼	19	32	46	3-15—4-28	.056	5.13
	1893						6.38	NE¼ SW¼	19	32	46	3-15—4-28	.052	4.79
	1893					46.36		NW¼ SW¼	19	32	46	3-15—4-28	.377	34.78
	1893						1.23	NW¼ SW¼	19	32	46	3-15—4-28	.010	.02

1893			18.04	SE¼ SW¼	19	32	46	3-15-4-28	.147	13.53
1893			30.32	SW¼ SW¼	19	32	46	3-15-4-28	.295	27.21
1893			.01	NW¼ NW¼	30	32	46	3-15-4-28	.005	.46
1893			15.70	SE¼ NW¼	30	32	46	3-15-4-28	.128	11.84
1893			31.70	SW¼ NW¼	30	32	46	3-15-4-28	.258	23.78
1893			8.20	NW¼ SW¼	30	32	46	3-15-4-28	.067	6.15
1893			6.40	NE¼ NE¼	30	32	46	3-15-4-28	.053	4.85
1893			2.61	SE¼ NE¼	30	32	46	3-15-4-28	.021	1.96
1893			17.40	SW¼ NE¼	30	32	46	3-15-4-28	.141	13.05
1893	10.04			NE¼ SE¼	20	32	46	3-15-6-13	.082	15.06
1893		29.66		NE¼ SE¼	20	32	46	3-15-4-28	.241	22.25
1893		14.48		NW¼ SE¼	20	32	46	3-15-4-28	.118	10.86
1893	20.26			SE¼ SE¼	20	32	46	3-15-6-13	.165	30.39
1893		16.74		SE¼ SE¼	20	32	46	3-15-4-28	.136	12.56
1893		39.20		SW¼ SE¼	20	32	46	3-15-4-28	.319	29.40
1893		31.78		SE¼ SW¼	20	32	46	3-15-4-28	.258	23.84
1893		14.72		SW¼ SW¼	20	32	46	3-15-4-28	.120	11.04
1891	10.18			NE¼ SE¼	24	32	45	3-15-6-13	.083	15.27
1891		29.72		NE¼ SE¼	24	32	45	3-15-4-28	.242	22.29
1891	12.40			NW¼ SE¼	24	32	45	3-15-6-13	.101	18.60
1891		25.86		NW¼ SE¼	24	32	45	3-15-4-28	.210	19.40
1893			3.36	NE¼ NE¼	29	32	46	3-15-4-28	.027	2.52
1893		4.10		NW¼ NE¼	29	32	46	3-15-4-28	.033	3.08
1893		5.22		NE¼ NW¼	29	32	46	3-15-4-28	.042	3.92
1893		8.85		NW¼ NW¼	29	32	46	3-15-4-28	.031	2.89
1883			14.80	NW¼ NE¼	10	32	45	3-15-4-28	.120	11.10
1883			16.60	SE¼ NE¼	10	32	45	3-15-4-28	.135	12.45
1883			40.00	SW¼ NE¼	10	32	45	3-15-4-28	.325	30.00
1883			20.30	NE¼ NW¼	10	32	45	3-15-4-28	.165	15.33
1883			34.93	SE¼ NW¼	10	32	45	3-15-4-28	.284	26.20
1883			24.80	NE¼ SE¼	10	32	45	3-15-4-28	.202	18.60
1883			29.50	NW¼ SE¼	10	32	45	3-15-4-28	.240	22.13
1883		14.64		SE¼ SE¼	10	32	45	3-15-4-28	.119	10.98
1883		11.56		SW¼ SE¼	10	32	45	3-15-4-28	.094	8.67
1883			17.80	NE¼ SW¼	10	32	45	3-15-4-28	.145	13.35
1883		3.20		NW¼ SW¼	10	32	45	3-15-4-28	.026	2.40
1883		9.36		SE¼ SW¼	10	32	45	3-15-4-28	.076	7.02
1883		23.80		SW¼ SW¼	10	32	45	3-15-4-28	.193	17.85
1883		4.95		NE¼ SE¼	11	32	45	3-15-4-28	.040	3.71
1883			18.40	NE¼ SE¼	11	32	45	3-15-4-28	.150	13.80
1883		2.10		NW¼ SE¼	11	32	45	3-15-4-28	.017	1.58
1883			33.40	NW¼ SE¼	11	32	45	3-15-4-28	.272	25.05
1883		36.04		SE¼ SE¼	11	32	45	3-15-4-28	.293	27.03
1883		23.70		SW¼ SE¼	11	32	45	3-15-4-28	.193	17.78
1883			12.03	SW¼ SE¼	11	32	45	3-15-4-28	.098	9.02
1883			9.00	SW¼ NW¼	11	32	45	3-15-4-28	.073	6.75
1883			40.00	NE¼ SW¼	11	32	45	3-15-4-28	.325	30.00
1883			30.50	NW¼ SW¼	11	32	45	3-15-4-28	.248	22.88
1883		13.70		SE¼ SW¼	11	32	45	3-15-4-28	.111	10.28
1883			21.82	SE¼ SW¼	11	32	45	3-15-4-28	.177	16.47
1883		16.00		SW¼ SW¼	11	32	45	3-15-4-28	.130	12.00
1873		2.15		NE¼ NE¼	12	32	45	3-15-4-28	.017	1.61
1873		25.43		SE¼ NE¼	12	32	45	3-15-4-28	.207	19.07

Faris Estate—Continued.

Date of beneficial use — Nat. mdw.	Date of beneficial use — Cult. area	Construction first initiated — Dams	Construction first initiated — Ditches	Culture—Acres — Harvest crops	Culture—Acres — Meadow pasture	Culture—Acres — Willow and sage pasture	Culture—Acres — Swamp or overflow	Location — Subdivision	Location — Section	Location — Tp. N.	Location — R. E.	Length of season	Duty of water — C.F.S.	Duty of water — Acre-feet
	1873					11.96		SW¼NE¼	12	32	45	3-15—4-28	.097	8.97
	1873					23.17		NE¼SE¼	12	32	45	3-15—4-28	.188	17.38
	1873					0.45		SE¼SE¼	12	32	45	3-15—4-28	.004	.35
	1873					37.45		NW¼SE¼	12	32	45	3-15—4-28	.304	28.09
	1873					30.10		SW¼SE¼	12	32	45	3-15—4-28	.245	22.58
	1873					3.85		NW¼NE¼	13	32	45	3-15—4-28	.031	2.89
	1878					12.69		NE¼SE¼	13	32	45	3-15—4-28	.103	9.52
	1878					14.10		NE¼SE¼	13	32	45	3-15—4-28	.115	10.58
	1878					0.65		SE¼SE¼	13	32	45	3-15—4-28	.005	.49
	1878					21.11		NW¼SE¼	13	32	45	3-15—4-28	.172	15.83
	1878					13.83		SW¼SE¼	13	32	45	3-15—4-28	.112	10.37
	1891					0.50		NE¼NE¼	24	32	45	3-15—4-28	.004	.38
	1891				17.76			SE¼NE¼	24	32	45	3-15—6-13	.144	26.64
	1891					15.56		SE¼NE¼	24	32	45	3-15—4-28	.127	11.67
	1891				1.16			SW¼NE¼	24	32	45	3-15—6-13	.009	1.74
	1891					9.30		SW¼NE¼	24	32	45	3-15—4-28	.076	6.98
	1873					3.10		SE¼NW¼	12	32	45	3-15—4-28	.025	2.33
	1873					21.20		NE¼SW¼	12	32	45	3-15—4-28	.172	15.90
	1873						13.45	NE¼SW¼	12	32	45	3-15—4-28	.109	10.09
	1873					9.63		NW¼SW¼	12	32	45	3-15—4-28	.078	7.22
	1873						19.00	NW¼SW¼	12	32	45	3-15—4-28	.154	14.35
	1873					39.99		SE¼SW¼	12	32	45	3-15—4-28	.325	29.99
	1873					34.50		SW¼SW¼	12	32	45	3-15—4-28	.280	25.88
	1873					32.80		NE¼NW¼	13	32	45	3-15—4-28	.267	24.60
	1873					40.00		NW¼NW¼	13	32	45	3-15—4-28	.325	30.00
	1873					3.20		SE¼NW¼	13	32	45	3-15—4-28	.026	2.40
	1873					35.00		SW¼NW¼	13	32	45	3-16—4-28	.285	26.25
	1878					16.37		NE¼SW¼	13	32	45	3-15—4-28	.133	12.28
	1873					13.18		NW¼SW¼	13	32	45	3-15—4-28	.107	9.89
	1878					5.20		NW¼SW¼	13	32	45	3-15—4-28	.042	3.90
	1878					18.61		SE¼SW¼	13	32	45	3-15—4-28	.151	15.06
	1878					14.44		SW¼SW¼	13	32	45	3-15—4-28	.117	10.83
	1891					2.00		SW¼NW¼	24	32	45	3-15—4-28	.016	1.50
	1873					40.00		NE¼NE¼	14	32	45	3-15—4-28	.325	30.00
	1873					40.00		SE¼NE¼	14	32	45	3-15—4-28	.325	30.00
	1873			8.70				NW¼NE¼	14	32	45	3-15—9-15	.071	26.10
	1873					31.26		NW¼NE¼	14	32	45	3-15—4-28	.254	23.45
	1873			14.50				SW¼NE¼	14	32	45	3-15—9-15	.118	43.50
	1873					25.50		SW¼NE¼	14	32	45	3-15—4-28	.207	19.13
	1873			26.05				NE¼NW¼	14	32	45	3-15—9-15	.212	78.15
	1873					13.18		NE¼NW¼	14	32	45	3-15—4-28	.107	9.89
	1873			8.35				NW¼NW¼	14	32	45	3-15—9-15	.068	25.05
	1873				4.75			NW¼NW¼	14	32	45	3-16—6-13	.039	7.13
	1873					4.50		NW¼NW¼	14	32	45	3-15—4-28	.037	3.38
	1883			17.90				NW¼NW¼	14	32	45	3-15—9-15	.146	53.70
	1873			40.00				SE¼NW¼	14	32	45	3-15—9-15	.325	120.00
	1873			27.00				SW¼NW¼	14	32	45	3-15—9-15	.224	82.80

1883			3.96	SW¼NW¼	14	32	45	3-15—4-28	.032	2.96
1883	1.70			SW¼NW¼	14	32	45	3-15—9-15	.014	5.10
1873			39.66	NE¼SE¼	14	32	45	3-15—4-28	.322	20.75
1873		12.70		SE¼SE¼	14	32	45	3-15—6-13	.103	19.05
1873			22.12	SE¼SE¼	14	32	45	3-15—4-28	.180	16.59
1873	15.62			NW¼SE¼	14	32	45	3-15—9-15	.127	46.86
1873			23.41	NW¼SE¼	14	32	45	3-15—4-28	.190	17.56
1878	15.00			SW¼SE¼	14	32	45	3-15—9-15	.122	45.00
1878			22.50	SW¼SE¼	14	32	45	3-15—4-28	.183	16.68
1873	38.94			NE¼SW¼	14	32	45	3-15—9-15	.317	116.82
1873	39.00			NW¼SW¼	14	32	45	3-15—9-15	.317	117.00
1873	32.10			SE¼SW¼	14	32	45	3-15—9-15	.261	96.30
1873			4.77	SE¼SW¼	14	32	45	3-15—4-28	.023	3.58
1873	30.91			SW¼SW¼	14	32	45	3-15—9-15	.251	92.73
1873			5.98	SW¼SW¼	14	32	45	3-15—4-28	.049	4.49
1883	36.00			NE¼NE¼	15	32	45	3-15—9-15	.293	108.00
1883			4.15	NE¼NE¼	15	32	45	3-15—4-28	.034	3.11
1883	37.00			NW¼NE¼	15	32	45	3-15—9-15	.301	111.00
1883			3.00	NW¼NE¼	15	32	45	3-15—4-28	.024	2.25
1873	6.15			SE¼NE¼	15	32	45	3-15—9-15	.050	18.45
1883	11.05			SE¼NE¼	15	32	45	3-15—9-15	.090	33.15
1883			16.75	SE¼NE¼	15	32	45	3-15—4-28	.136	12.56
1883	16.50			SW¼NE¼	15	32	45	3-15—9-15	.134	49.50
1883			19.44	SW¼NE¼	15	32	45	3-15—4-28	.158	14.58
1883	37.50			NE¼NW¼	15	32	45	3-15—9-15	.305	112.50
1883			1.85	NE¼NW¼	15	32	45	3-15—4-28	.015	1.39
1883	38.74			NW¼NW¼	15	32	45	3-15—9-15	.315	116.22
1873	0.87			SE¼NW¼	15	32	45	3-15—9-15	.007	2.61
1873			10.50	SE¼NW¼	15	32	45	3-15—4-28	.085	7.80
1883	21.73			SE¼NW¼	15	32	45	3-15—9-15	.170	62.58
1883	33.37			SW¼NW¼	15	32	45	3-15—4-28	.007	.65
1873			1.77	SW¼NW¼	15	32	45	3-15—4-28	.014	1.33
1883			1.70	SW¼NW¼	15	32	45	3-15—4-28	.013	1.27
1873	39.70			NE¼SE¼	15	32	45	3-15—9-15	.323	119.10
1873	40.00			SE¼SE¼	15	32	45	3-15—9-15	.325	120.00
1873	30.00			NW¼SE¼	15	32	45	3-15—9-15	.244	90.00
1883			6.50	NW¼SE¼	15	32	45	3-15—4-28	.053	4.88
1873	38.98			SW¼SE¼	15	32	45	3-15—9-15	.316	116.94
1883			4.20	NE¼NW¼	15	32	45	3-15—4-28	.034	3.15
1873	25.91			NE¼NW¼	15	32	45	3-15—9-15	.211	77.73
1873			5.20	NE¼NW¼	15	32	45	3-15—4-28	.042	3.90
1873	39.07			SE¼SW¼	15	32	45	3-15—9-15	.318	117.21
1873	7.35			NW¼SW¼	15	32	45	3-15—9-15	.060	22.05
1873			18.75	NW¼SW¼	15	32	45	3-15—4-28	.152	14.07
1883			7.70	NW¼SW¼	15	32	45	3-15—4-28	.063	5.78
1873	26.25			SW¼SW¼	15	32	45	3-15—9-15	.213	78.75
1873			11.84	SW¼SW¼	15	32	45	3-15—4-28	.096	8.90
1873	6.95			NE¼NE¼	22	32	45	3-15—9-15	.057	20.85
1873			8.10	NE¼NE¼	22	32	45	3-15—4-28	.066	6.08
1890		23.57		NE¼NE¼	22	32	45	3-15—6-13	.192	35.36
1890			38.82	SE¼NE¼	22	32	45	3-15—4-28	.316	29.12
1873	18.91			NW¼NE¼	22	32	45	3-15—9-15	.154	56.73
1873			6.85	NW¼NE¼	22	32	45	3-15—4-28	.056	5.14

Faris Estate—Continued.

Date of beneficial use: Nat. mdw.	Date of beneficial use: Cult. area	Construction first initiated: Dams	Construction first initiated: Ditches	Culture—Acres: Harvest crops	Culture—Acres: Meadow pasture	Culture—Acres: Willow and sage pasture	Culture—Acres: Swamp or overflow	Location: Subdivision	Location: Section	Location: Tp.N.	Location: R.E.	Length of season	Duty of water: C.F.S.	Duty of water: Acre-feet
	1890					10.49		NW¼NE¼	22	32	45	3-15—4-28	.085	7.87
	1890					37.89		SW¼NE¼	22	32	45	3-15—4-28	.308	28.42
	1873			22.22				NE¼NW¼	22	32	45	3-15—9-15	.181	66.66
	1873					7.34		NE¼NW¼	22	32	45	3-15—4-28	.060	5.51
	1890					6.52		NE¼NW¼	22	32	45	3-15—4-28	.053	4.89
	1873			8.60				NW¼NW¼	22	32	45	3-15—9-15	.070	25.80
	1873					4.17		NW¼NW¼	22	32	45	3-15—4-28	.034	3.14
	1890					23.24		NW¼NW¼	22	32	45	3-15—4-28	.189	17.43
	1891					38.59		SE¼NW¼	22	32	45	3-15—4-28	.314	28.94
	1890					19.77		SW¼NW¼	22	32	45	3-15—4-28	.161	14.83
	1890					39.97		NE¼SE¼	22	32	45	3-15—4-28	.325	29.98
	1890					19.00		SE¼SE¼	22	32	45	3-15—4-28	.154	14.25
	1890					18.83		NW¼SE¼	22	32	45	3-15—4-28	.153	14.12
	1890					23.47		NE¼SW¼	22	32	45	3-15—4-28	.191	17.60
	1890					1.83		NW¼SW¼	22	32	45	3-15—4-28	.015	1.37
	1890					9.00		NE¼NE¼	23	32	45	3-15—4-28	.073	6.75
	1890					27.82		NW¼NE¼	23	32	45	3-15—4-28	.226	21.87
	1878					7.50		NW¼NE¼	23	32	45	3-15—4-28	.061	5.63
	1890					10.41		SE¼NE¼	23	32	45	3-15—4-28	.085	7.81
	1890					11.50		SW¼NE¼	23	32	45	3-15—4-28	.093	8.03
	1891					21.21		NE¼NW¼	23	32	45	3-15—4-28	.172	15.91
	1878					15.97		NE¼NW¼	23	32	45	3-15—4-28	.130	11.98
	1896			0.37				NW¼NW¼	23	32	45	3-15—9-15	.003	1.11
	1890					23.64		NW¼NW¼	23	32	45	3-15—4-28	.192	17.73
	1878					12.60		NW¼NW¼	23	32	45	3-15—4-28	.102	9.45
	1890					40.00		SE¼NW¼	23	32	45	3-15—4-28	.325	30.00
	1890					38.93		SW¼NW¼	23	32	45	3-15—4-28	.317	29.20
	1890				31.36			NE¼SE¼	23	32	45	3-15—6-13	.255	47.04
	1890					6.84		NE¼SE¼	23	32	45	3-15—4-28	.056	5.15
	1890				11.06			NW¼SE¼	23	32	45	3-15—6-13	.090	16.59
	1890					26.95		NW¼SE¼	23	32	45	3-15—4-28	.219	20.21
	1890				21.25			SE¼SE¼	23	32	45	3-15—6-13	.173	31.88
	1890					17.30		SE¼SE¼	23	32	45	3-15—4-28	.141	12.98
	1890				8.93			SW¼SE¼	23	32	46	3-15—6-13	.073	13.40
	1890					28.94		SW¼SE¼	23	32	45	3-15—4-28	.235	21.71
	1890					38.80		NE¼SW¼	23	32	45	3-15—4-28	.315	29.10
	1890					38.77		NW¼SW¼	23	32	45	3-15—4-28	.315	29.08
	1890					38.38		SE¼SW¼	23	32	45	3-15—4-28	.312	28.79
	1890					36.81		SW¼SW¼	23	32	45	3-15—4-28	.299	27.61
	1891				1.90			NE¼SW¼	24	32	45	3-15—6-13	.015	2.85
	1891					25.17		NE¼SW¼	24	32	45	3-15—4-28	.205	18.88
	1891				5.05			NW¼SW¼	24	32	45	3-15—6-13	.041	7.58
	1891					27.06		NW¼SW¼	24	32	45	3-15—4-28	.220	20.80
	1891				22.50			SE¼SW¼	24	32	45	3-15—6-13	.183	33.76
	1891					16.05		SE¼SW¼	24	32	45	3-15—4-28	.130	12.04
	1891				19.30			SW¼SW¼	24	32	45	3-15—6-13	.157	28.95
	1891					17.82		SW¼SW¼	24	32	45	3-15—4-28	.145	13.37

	1893					17.42		SE¼ SE¼	24	32	45	3-15—4-28	.142	13.06
	1893						22.58	SE¼ SE¼	24	32	45	3-15—4-28	.184	16.94
	1893					37.67		SW¼ SE¼	24	32	45	3-15—4-28	.306	28.25
	1893						2.33	SW¼ SE¼	24	32	45	3-15—4-28	.019	1.75
	1893						5.52	NE¼ NE¼	25	32	45	3-15—4-28	.045	4.14
	1893					7.24		NW¼ NE¼	25	32	45	3-15—4-28	.050	5.43
	1893						2.70	NW¼ NE¼	25	32	45	3-15—4-28	.022	2.03
	1893						20.63	SE¼ NE¼	25	32	45	3-15—4-28	.168	15.47
	1893						10.69	SW¼ NE¼	25	32	45	3-15—4-28	.087	8.02
	1893						2.49	NE¼ SE¼	25	32	45	3-15—4-28	.020	1.87
	1893						2.61	NW¼ SE¼	25	32	45	3-15—4-28	.021	1.96
	1893					22.82		NE¼ NW¼	25	32	45	3-15—4-28	.186	17.12
	1893					32.76		NW¼ NW¼	25	32	45	3-15—4-28	.266	24.57
	1893					7.00		SE¼ NW¼	25	32	45	3-15—4-28	.057	5.25
	1893						3.73	SE¼ NW¼	25	32	45	3-15—4-28	.030	2.80
	1893					1.60		SW¼ NW¼	25	32	45	3-15—4-28	.013	1.20
	1893					33.74		NE¼ NE¼	26	32	45	3-15—4-28	.274	25.31
	1893					4.91		SE¼ NE¼	26	32	45	3-15—4-28	.040	3.68
	1893					25.28		NW¼ NE¼	26	32	45	3-15—4-28	.206	18.96
	1893					28.22		NE¼ NW¼	26	32	45	3-15—4-28	.229	21.17
	1893					10.18		NW¼ NW¼	26	32	45	3-15—4-28	.083	7.64

Claimant—**Geo. B. Williams.** Proof No. **00168**

Source—**Humboldt River.** Ditch—**Upper Slavin Dam.**

	1881					.08		SW¼ SW¼	6	32	47	3-15—4-28	.001	.06
	1881						0.23	SW¼ SW¼	6	32	47	3-15—4-28	.002	.17
	1881						6.20	NW¼ SW¼	6	32	47	3-15—4-28	.050	4.65
	1881					28.20		NW¼ SW¼	6	32	47	3-15—4-28	.229	21.15
	1881					0.81		NE¼ SW¼	6	32	47	3-15—4-28	.007	.61
	1881						18.84	NE¼ SW¼	6	32	47	3-15—4-28	.153	14.13
	1881						4.92	NW¼ SE¼	6	32	47	3-15—4-28	.040	3.60

Source—**Humboldt** River. Ditch—**No. 1.**

1872	1881					23.00		NE¼ SE¼	1	32	46	3-15—4-28	.187	17.25
1872	1881			6.43				SE¼ SE¼	1	32	46	3-15—9-15	.052	19.29
1872	1881					9.25		SE¼ SE¼	1	32	46	3-15—4-28	.076	6.94
1872	1881			13.00				SW¼ SE¼	1	32	46	3-15—9-15	.106	39.00
1872	1881					8.19		SW¼ SE¼	1	32	46	3-15—4-28	.067	6.14
1872	1881			.50				SE¼ SW¼	1	32	46	3-15—9-15	.004	1.50
1872	1881					1.91		SE¼ SW¼	1	32	46	3-15—4-28	.016	1.43
1872	1881			21.50				NW¼ NE¼	12	32	46	3-15—9-15	.175	64.50
1872	1881			.80				SW¼ NE¼	12	32	46	3-15—9-15	.007	2.40
1872	1881			.80				SE¼ NW¼	12	32	46	3-15—9-15	.007	2.40
1872	1881					21.14		SE¼ NW¼	12	32	46	3-15—4-28	.172	14.86
1872	1881			8.02				SW¼ NW¼	12	32	46	3-15—9-15	.065	24.00

Source—**Humboldt River.** Ditch—**No. 2.**

1872	1881			38.48				NE¼ NE¼	1	32	46	3-15—9-15	.313	115.44
1872	1881			39.00				NW¼ NE¼	1	32	46	3-15—9-15	.317	117.00
1872	1881			20.60				SE¼ NE¼	1	32	46	3-15—9-15	.167	61.80
1872	1881				11.45			SE¼ NE¼	1	32	46	3-15—6-13	.093	17.18

Geo. B. Williams—Continued.

Date of beneficial use—Nat. mdw.	Date of beneficial use—Cult. area	Construction first initiated—Dams	Construction first initiated—Ditches	Culture—Acres—Harvest crops	Culture—Acres—Meadow pasture	Culture—Acres—Willow and sage pasture	Culture—Acres—Swamp or overflow	Location—Subdivision	Location—Section	Location—Tp.N.	Location—R.E.	Length of season	Duty of water—C.F.S.	Duty of water—Acre-feet
1872	1881	.....	.....	38.07	.....	.....	.....	SW¼ NE¼	1	32	46	3-15—9-15	.310	114.21
1872	1881	.....	.....	.....	1.70	.....	.....	SW¼ NE¼	1	32	46	3-15—6-13	.014	2.55
1872	1881	.....	.....	39.03	.....	.....	.....	NE¼ NW¼	1	32	46	3-15—9-15	.317	117.09
1872	1881	.....	.....	.....	0.52	.....	.....	NE¼ NW¼	1	32	46	3-15—6-13	.004	.78
1872	1881	.....	.....	18.43	.....	.....	.....	NW¼ NW¼	1	32	46	3-15—9-15	.150	55.29
1872	1881	.....	.....	.....	19.60	.....	.....	NW¼ NW¼	1	32	46	3-15—6-13	.159	29.40
1872	1881	.....	.....	39.57	.....	.....	.....	SE¼ NW¼	1	32	46	3-15—9-15	.322	118.71
1872	1881	.....	.....	37.38	.....	.....	.....	SW¼ NW¼	1	32	46	3-15—9-15	.304	112.14
1872	1881	.....	.....	.....	2.26	.....	.....	SW¼ NW¼	1	32	46	3-15—6-13	.018	3.39
.....	1881	.....	.....	.....	26.00	.....	.....	SE¼ NE¼	2	32	46	3-15—6-13	.211	39.00
.....	1881	.....	.....	3.00	.....	.....	.....	SW¼ NE¼	2	32	46	3-15—9-15	.024	9.00
.....	1881	.....	.....	.....	9.57	.....	.....	SW¼ NE¼	2	32	46	3-15—6-13	.078	14.36
.....	1881	.....	.....	.....	6.34	.....	.....	SE¼ NW¼	2	32	46	3-15—6-13	.052	9.51
.....	1881	.....	.....	.....	9.15	.....	.....	NE¼ SE¼	2	32	46	3-15—6-13	.074	13.73
.....	1881	.....	.....	.....	10.40	.....	.....	NW¼ SE¼	2	32	46	3-15—6-13	.085	15.60
.....	1881	.....	.....	16.48	.....	.....	.....	SW¼ SE¼	2	32	46	3-15—9-15	.119	49.44
.....	1881	.....	.....	.....	5.00	.....	.....	SW¼ SE¼	2	32	46	3-15—6-13	.040	7.50
.....	1881	.....	.....	8.67	.....	.....	.....	SE¼ SW¼	2	32	46	3-15—9-15	.070	26.01
.....	1881	.....	.....	.....	3.43	.....	.....	SE¼ SW¼	2	32	46	3-15—6-13	.028	5.15
.....	1881	.....	.....	2.78	.....	.....	.....	SW¼ SW¼	2	32	46	3-15—9-15	.023	8.34

Source—Humboldt River. Ditch—No. 3.

Date of beneficial use—Nat. mdw.	Date of beneficial use—Cult. area	Construction first initiated—Dams	Construction first initiated—Ditches	Culture—Acres—Harvest crops	Culture—Acres—Meadow pasture	Culture—Acres—Willow and sage pasture	Culture—Acres—Swamp or overflow	Location—Subdivision	Location—Section	Location—Tp.N.	Location—R.E.	Length of season	Duty of water—C.F.S.	Duty of water—Acre-feet
1872	1881	.....	.....	.....	.....	2.15	.....	NW¼ NE¼	11	32	46	3-15—4-28	.017	1.61
1872	1881	.....	.....	20.92	.....	.....	.....	NE¼ NW¼	11	32	46	3-15—9-15	.170	62.76
1872	1881	.....	.....	.....	12.37	.....	.....	NE¼ NW¼	11	32	46	3-15—6-13	.101	18.56
1872	1881	.....	.....	.....	.....	5.96	.....	NE¼ NW¼	11	32	46	3-15—4-28	.048	4.47
1872	1881	.....	.....	14.56	.....	.....	.....	NW¼ NW¼	11	32	46	3-15—9-15	.118	43.68
1872	1881	.....	.....	.....	24.45	.....	.....	NW¼ NW¼	11	32	46	3-15—6-13	.198	36.68
1872	1881	.....	.....	.....	.....	.30	.....	NW¼ NW¼	11	32	46	3-15—4-28	.002	.23
1872	1881	.....	.....	14.15	.....	.....	.....	SW¼ NW¼	11	32	46	3-15—9-15	.115	42.45
1872	1881	.....	.....	.....	25.00	.....	.....	SW¼ NW¼	11	32	46	3-15—6-13	.203	37.50
1872	1881	.....	.....	2.75	.....	.....	.....	NE¼ SE¼	1	32	46	3-15—9-15	.022	8.25
1872	1881	.....	.....	.....	1.77	.....	.....	NE¼ SE¼	1	32	46	3-15—6-13	.014	2.66
1872	1881	.....	.....	.....	.....	8.47	.....	NE¼ SE¼	1	32	46	3-15—4-28	.069	6.35
1872	1881	.....	.....	24.06	.....	.....	.....	NW¼ SE¼	1	32	46	3-15—9-15	.196	72.18
1872	1881	.....	.....	.....	3.81	.....	.....	NW¼ SE¼	1	32	46	3-15—6-13	.032	5.72
1872	1881	.....	.....	.....	.....	11.18	.....	NW¼ SE¼	1	32	46	3-15—4-28	.091	8.39
1872	1881	.....	.....	13.15	.....	.....	.....	SW¼ SE¼	1	32	46	3-15—9-15	.107	39.45
1872	1881	.....	.....	.....	.....	0.65	.....	SW¼ SE¼	1	32	46	3-15—4-28	.005	.49
1872	1881	.....	.....	37.49	.....	.....	.....	NE¼ SW¼	1	32	46	3-15—9-15	.305	112.47
1872	1881	.....	.....	.....	.....	2.41	.....	NE¼ SW¼	1	32	46	3-15—4-28	.020	1.81
1872	1881	.....	.....	37.64	.....	.....	.....	NW¼ SW¼	1	32	46	3-15—9-15	.306	112.92
1872	1881	.....	.....	.....	0.42	.....	.....	NW¼ SW¼	1	32	46	3-15—6-13	.003	.63
1872	1881	.....	.....	21.62	.....	.....	.....	SE¼ SW¼	1	32	46	3-15—9-15	.176	64.86
1872	1881	.....	.....	.....	.....	14.73	.....	SE¼ SW¼	1	32	46	3-15—4-28	.120	11.05
1872	1881	.....	.....	37.29	.....	.....	.....	SW¼ SW¼	1	32	46	3-15—9-15	.303	111.87

1872	1881				1.40			SW¼SW¼	1	32	46	3-15—6-13	.011	2.10
	1881			20.85				SE¼SE¼	2	32	46	3-15—9-15	.170	62.55
	1881				14.25			SE¼SE¼	2	32	46	3-15—6-13	.116	21.38
1872	1881			8.08				NW¼NE¼	11	32	46	3-15—9-15	.066	24.21

Source—**Humboldt River.** Ditch—**No. 4.**

1872	1876			39.67				NE¼NE¼	11	32	46	3-15—9-15	.323	110.01
1872	1876			26.40				SE¼NE¼	11	32	46	3-15—9-15	.215	70.20
1872	1876					12.97		SE¼NE¼	11	32	46	3-15—4-28	.105	9.73
1872	1876			39.64				SW¼NE¼	11	32	46	3-15—9-15	.323	118.92
1872	1876			26.93				NE¼SW¼	11	32	46	3-15—9-15	.219	80.79
1872	1876				12.62			NE¼SW¼	11	32	46	3-15—6-13	.103	18.93
1872	1876			4.42				NW¼SW¼	11	32	46	3-15—9-15	.036	13.26
1872	1876				35.58			NW¼SW¼	11	32	46	3-15—6-13	.289	53.37
1872	1876			16.15				SE¼SW¼	11	32	46	3-15—9-15	.181	48.45
1872	1876					17.35		SE¼SW¼	11	32	46	3-15—4-28	.141	13.01
1872	1876			26.74				SW¼SW¼	11	32	46	3-15—9-15	.217	80.22
1872	1876				13.23			SW¼SW¼	11	32	46	3-15—6-13	.108	19.85
1872	1876			0.79				NE¼NW¼	14	32	46	3-15—9-15	.006	2.37
1872	1876					2.30		NE¼NW¼	14	32	46	3-15—4-28	.019	1.73
1872	1876			23.27				NW¼NW¼	14	32	46	3-15—9-15	.189	69.81
1872	1876				13.56			NW¼NW¼	14	32	46	3-15—6-13	.110	20.34
1872	1876				15.85			SW¼NW¼	14	32	46	3-15—6-13	.129	23.78
1872	1876			28.47				NW¼NE¼	11	32	46	3-15—9-15	.231	85.41
1872	1876			26.07				SE¼NW¼	11	32	46	3-15—9-15	.212	78.21
1872	1876				13.40			SE¼NW¼	11	32	46	3-15—6-13	.109	20.10
1872	1876			12.95				NE¼NW¼	12	32	46	3-15—9-15	.106	38.85
1872	1876					18.48		NE¼NW¼	12	32	46	3-15—4-28	.150	13.86
1872	1876			27.25				NW¼NW¼	12	32	46	3-15—9-15	.222	81.75
1872	1876					12.37		NW¼NW¼	12	32	46	3-15—4-28	.101	9.28
1872	1876					29.14		SW¼NW¼	12	32	46	3-15—4-28	.237	21.86

Source—**Humboldt River.** Ditch—**No. 5.**

1872	1876					31.36		NE¼SE¼	11	32	46	3-15—4-28	.255	23.52
1872	1876			8.05				NW¼SE¼	11	32	46	3-15—9-15	.065	24.15
1872	1876				6.97			NW¼SE¼	11	32	46	3-15—6-13	.057	10.46
1872	1876					23.00		NW¼SE¼	11	32	46	3-15—4-28	.187	17.25
1872	1876					5.17		SW¼SE¼	11	32	46	3-15—4-28	.042	3.88

Claimant—**Dean Estate.** Proof No. **00169**

Source—**Humboldt River.** Ditch—**McConnell & Johnson.**

	1874			27.07				NW¼NW¼	6	31	49	3-15—9-15	.220	81.21
	1874						4.16	NW¼NW¼	6	31	49	3-15—4-28	.034	3.12
	1874			33.15				NE¼NW¼	6	31	49	3-15—9-15	.270	99.45
	1874						5.41	NE¼NW¼	6	31	49	3-15—4-28	.044	4.06
	1874			31.00				SW¼NW¼	6	31	49	3-15—9-15	.252	63.00
	1874			23.38				SE¼NW¼	6	31	49	3-15—9-15	.190	70.14
	1874			26.12				NW¼NE¼	6	31	49	3-15—9-15	.212	78.36
	1874						2.91	NW¼NE¼	6	31	49	3-15—4-28	.024	2.18
	1874			21.55				NE¼NE¼	6	31	49	3-15—9-15	.175	64.05
	1874						4.58	NE¼NE¼	6	31	49	3-15—4-28	.037	3.44

Dean Estate—Continued.

Date of beneficial use: Nat. mdw.	Date of beneficial use: Cult. area	Construction first initiated: Dams	Construction first initiated: Ditches	Culture—Acres: Harvest crops	Culture—Acres: Meadow pasture	Culture—Acres: Willow and sage pasture	Culture—Acres: Swamp or overflow	Location: Subdivision	Location: Section	Location: Tp.N.	Location: R.E.	Length of season	Duty of water: C.F.S.	Duty of water: Acre-feet
	1874			3.85				SW¼ NE¼	6	31	49	3-15—9-15	.031	11.55
	1897			9.58				NE¼ NW¼	8	31	49	3-15—9-15	.078	28.74
	1897			11.65				SE¼ NW¼	8	31	49	3-15—9-15	.095	34.95
	1897						3.02	SE¼ NW¼	8	31	49	3-15—4-28	.025	2.27
	1897			22.98				NW¼ NE¼	8	31	49	3-15—9-15	.187	68.94
	1897						5.72	NW¼ NE¼	8	31	49	3-15—4-28	.047	4.29
	1874			2.96				NE¼ NE¼	8	31	49	3-15—9-15	.024	8.88
	1874						5.10	NE¼ NE¼	8	31	49	3-15—4-28	.041	3.83
	1897			13.41				SE¼ NE¼	8	31	49	3-15—9-15	.109	40.23
	1897						5.83	SE¼ NE¼	8	31	49	3-15—4-28	.047	4.37
	1897			25.06				SW¼ NE¼	8	31	49	3-15—9-15	.204	75.18
	1897						3.43	SW¼ NE¼	8	31	49	3-15—4-28	.028	2.57
	1897			6.90				NE¼ SE¼	8	31	49	3-15—9-15	.056	20.70
	1897						3.74	NE¼ SE¼	8	31	49	3-15—4-28	.030	2.81
	1897			2.95				NW¼ SE¼	8	31	49	3-15—9-15	.024	8.85

Claimant—**Ellison Ranching Co.** Proof No. 00170

Source—**Humboldt River.** Ditch—**Bacon Ditch.**

Nat. mdw.	Cult. area	Dams	Ditches	Harvest crops	Meadow pasture	Willow and sage pasture	Swamp or overflow	Subdivision	Section	Tp.N.	R.E.	Length of season	C.F.S.	Acre-feet
1874	1888			*38.30				NE¼ NW¼	13	35	42	3-15—9-15	.311	114.90
1874	1888					0.95		NE¼ NW¼	13	35	42	3-15—4-28	.008	.71
1874	1888			*27.25				SE¼ NW¼	13	35	42	3-15—9-15	.222	81.75
1874	1888					6.75		SE¼ NW¼	13	35	42	3-15—4-28	.055	5.06
1874	1888			*29.15				NW¼ NW¼	13	35	42	3-15—9-15	.237	87.45
1874	1888					8.00		NW¼ NW¼	13	35	42	3-15—4-28	.065	6.90
1874	1888			*10.00				SW¼ NW¼	13	35	42	3-15—9-15	.081	30.00
1874	1888					3.30		SW¼ NW¼	13	35	42	3-15—4-28	.027	2.48
1874	1888			*0.26				NE¼ SW¼	13	35	42	3-15—9-15	.002	.78
1874	1888					12.52		NE¼ SW¼	13	35	42	3-15—4-28	.102	9.39
1874	1888			*32.99				SE¼ SW¼	12	35	42	3-15—9-15	.268	98.97
1874	1888					2.15		SE¼ SW¼	12	35	42	3-15—4-28	.017	1.61
1874	1888			*39.65				SW¼ SW¼	12	35	42	3-15—9-15	.322	118.95
1874	1888			*1.98				NE¼ NE¼	13	35	42	3-15—9-15	.016	5.94
1874	1888					4.50		NE¼ NE¼	13	35	42	3-15—4-28	.037	3.38
1874	1888			*27.32				SE¼ NE¼	13	35	42	3-15—9-15	.222	81.96
1874	1888					3.00		SE¼ NE¼	13	35	42	3-15—4-28	.024	2.25
1874	1888			*11.45				NW¼ NE¼	13	35	42	3-15—9-15	.093	34.45
1874	1888					22.27		NW¼ NE¼	13	35	42	3-15—4-28	.181	16.70
1874	1888			*21.54				SW¼ NE¼	13	35	42	3-15—9-15	.175	64.62
1874	1888				2.28			SW¼ NE¼	13	35	42	3-15—6-13	.019	3.42
1874	1888					16.05		SW¼ NE¼	13	35	42	3-15—4-28	.130	13.14
1874	1888			*27.60				NE¼ SE¼	13	35	42	3-15—9-15	.224	82.80
1874	1888					0.30		NE¼ SE¼	13	35	42	3-15—4-28	.002	.23
1874	1888						0.35	NE¼ SE¼	13	35	42	3-15—4-28	.003	.26
1874	1888			*33.90				SE¼ SE¼	13	35	42	3-15—9-15	.376	101.70
1874	1888					0.25		SE¼ SE¼	13	35	42	3-15—4-28	.002	.19
1874	1888						1.10	SE¼ SE¼	13	35	42	3-15—4-28	.009	.83

1874	1888			*9.55				NW¼SE¼	13	35	42	3-15—9-15	.070	25.65
1874	1888					9.40		NW¼SE¼	13	35	42	3-15—4-28	.077	7.10
1874	1888			*1.25				SW¼SE¼	13	35	42	3-15—9-15	.010	3.75
1874	1888					0.60		SW¼SE¼	13	35	42	3-15—4-28	.005	.40

*Third-class pasture—1875, due to Aemes Dam overflow in high water.

Source—Humboldt River. Ditch—Big Slough.

	1892			17.02				SE¼SW¼	19	34	44	3-15—9-15	.138	51.06
	1889						8.66	NW¼SW¼	19	34	44	3-15—4-28	.070	6.50
	1892			12.73				SW¼SW¼	19	34	44	3-15—9-15	.103	38.19
	1892			30.36				NE¼NW¼	30	34	44	3-15—9-15	.247	91.68
	1892			12.04				NW¼NW¼	30	34	44	3-15—9-15	.098	36.12
	1892						5.15	NW¼NW¼	30	34	44	3-15—4-28	.042	3.86
	1891				5.95			NE¼NE¼	25	34	43	3-15—6-13	.048	8.93
	1890					15.90		NE¼SE¼	24	34	43	3-15—4-28	.129	11.93
	1890						8.64	NE¼SE¼	24	34	43	3-15—4-28	.070	6.48
	1892			22.93				SE¼SE¼	24	34	43	3-15—9-15	.186	68.79
	1892					7.16		SE¼SE¼	24	34	43	3-15—4-28	.058	5.37
	1892						0.93	SE¼SE¼	24	34	43	3-15—4-28	.008	0.70
	1892			0.54				NW¼SE¼	24	34	43	3-15—9-15	.004	1.62
	1892					37.66		NW¼SE¼	24	'34	43	3-15—4-28	.306	28.25
	1891				22.28			SE¼NW¼	24	34	43	3-15—6-13	.181	33.42
	1891				27.90			SW¼NW¼	24	34	43	3-15—6-13	.227	41.85
	1891					3.45		SW¼NW¼	24	34	43	3-15—4-28	.028	2.50
	1891				17.77			NE¼SW¼	24	34	43	3-15—6-13	.144	26.66
	1891				4.00			NW¼SW¼	24	34	43	3-15—6-13	.032	6.00
	1892			2.20				SW¼SE¼	24	34	44	3-15—9-15	.018	6.60
	1892				0.66			SW¼SE¼	24	34	44	3-15—6-13	.005	0.99
	1892					5.71		SW¼SE¼	24	34	43	3-15—4-28	.046	4.28
	1892						4.32	SW¼SE¼	24	34	43	3-15—4-28	.035	3.24
	1890					12.68		SE¼SE¼	24	34	43	3-15—4-28	.103	9.51
	1890					9.45		SE¼NW¼	14	34	43	3-15—4-28	.077	7.09
	1891				26.50			SW¼NW¼	14	34	43	3-15—6-13	.215	39.75
	1890					27.72		NE¼SW¼	14	34	43	3-15—4-28	.225	21.80
	1891				34.45			SE¼SW¼	14	34	43	3-15—6-13	.280	51.68
	1891					6.78		SE¼SW¼	14	34	43	3-15—4-28	.065	5.09
	1891				23.09			NW¼SW¼	14	34	43	3-15—6-13	.188	34.64
	1891					16.96		NW¼SW¼	14	34	43	3-15—4-28	.139	12.72
	1890					1.95		SW¼SW¼	14	34	43	3-15—4-28	.016	1.46
	1890						21.35	SW¼SW¼	14	34	43	3-15—4-28	.174	16.01
	1890					25.42		SW¼SE¼	10	34	43	3-15—4-28	.207	19.07
	1892			1.19				SE¼NW¼	10	34	43	3-15—9-15	.010	3.57
	1890					23.10		NW¼NW¼	10	34	43	3-15—4-28	.188	17.33
	1892			3.62				SW¼NW¼	10	34	43	3-15—9-15	.029	10.86
	1892				12.28			SW¼NW¼	10	34	43	3-15—6-13	.100	18.42
	1892						24.50	SW¼NW¼	10	34	43	3-15—4-28	.199	18.38
	1892			4.21				NE¼SW¼	10	34	43	3-15—9-15	.034	12.63
	1892						27.38	NE¼SW¼	10	34	43	3-15—4-28	.227	20.53
	1889						38.65	SE¼SW¼	10	34	43	3-15—4-28	.314	28.99
	1891				21.15			NW¼SW¼	10	34	43	3-15—6-13	.172	31.73
	1891						18.85	NW¼SW¼	10	34	43	3-15—4-28	.153	14.14
	1891				39.94			SW¼SW¼	10	34	43	3-15—6-13	.325	59.91

Ellison Ranching Co.—Continued.

Date of beneficial use: Nat. mdw.	Date of beneficial use: Cult. area	Construction first initiated: Dams	Construction first initiated: Ditches	Culture—Acres: Harvest crops	Culture—Acres: Meadow pasture	Culture—Acres: Willow and sage pasture	Culture—Acres: Swamp or overflow	Location: Subdivision	Location: Section	Location: Tp.N.	Location: R.E.	Length of season	Duty of water: C.F.S.	Duty of water: Acre-feet
	1889						40.20	SE¼NE¼	15	34	43	3-15—4-28	.327	30.15
	1889						20.10	NW¼NE¼	15	34	43	3-15—4-28	.163	15.08
	1890					39.57		NE¼NE¼	23	34	43	3-15—4-28	.322	29.68
	1890					12.17		SE¼NE¼	23	34	43	3-15—4-28	.099	9.15
	1890					5.70		NW¼NE¼	23	34	43	3-15—4-28	.046	4.28
	1890						34.50	NW¼NE¼	23	34	43	3-15—4-28	.280	25.88
	1889						40.00	SW¼NE¼	23	34	43	3-15—4-28	.325	30.00
	1890					7.00		NE¼SE¼	23	34	43	3-15—4-28	.057	5.25
	1890					21.70		NW¼SE¼	23	34	43	3-15—4-28	.176	16.28
	1890					18.50		NE¼NW¼	28	34	43	3-15—4-28	.150	13.88
	1890						21.90	NE¼NW¼	23	34	43	3-15—4-28	.178	16.43
	1890					17.00		SE¼NW¼	23	34	43	3-15—4-28	.138	12.75
	1890						19.65	SE¼NW¼	23	34	43	3-15—4-28	.160	14.74
	1890					9.88		NW¼NW¼	23	34	43	3-15—4-28	.080	7.41
	1890					2.65		SW¼NW¼	23	34	43	3-15—4-28	.022	2.00
	1892			1.65				NE¼NE¼	9	34	43	3-15—9-15	.014	4.95
	1892				1.35			NE¼NE¼	9	34	43	3-15—6-13	.011	2.03
	1892					1.44		NE¼NE¼	9	34	43	3-15—4-28	.012	1.08
	1892						35.84	NE¼NE¼	9	34	43	3-15—4-28	.292	26.88
	1892			15.92				SE¼NE¼	9	34	43	3-15—9-15	.129	47.76
	1892				2.23			SE¼NE¼	9	34	43	3-15—6-13	.018	3.35
	1892						19.58	SE¼NE¼	9	34	43	3-15—4-28	.159	14.69
	1892			10.00				NW¼NE¼	9	34	43	3-15—9-15	.081	30.00
	1892				10.68			NW¼NE¼	9	34	43	3-15—6-13	.087	16.02
	1892						19.88	NW¼NE¼	9	34	43	3-15—4-28	.162	14.91
	1892			24.70				SW¼NE¼	9	34	43	3-15—9-15	.201	74.10
	1892						16.00	SW¼NE¼	9	34	43	3-15—4-28	.130	12.00
	1892			23.46				NE¼SE¼	9	34	43	3-15—9-15	.191	70.38
	1892						16.59	NE¼SE¼	9	34	43	3-15—4-28	.135	12.44
	1892			0.25				SE¼SE¼	9	34	43	3-15—9-15	.002	0.75
	1892			5.35				NE¼NW¼	9	34	43	3-15—9-15	.043	16.05
	1892						31.01	NE¼NW¼	9	34	43	3-15—4-28	.277	25.51
	1892			6.60				SE¼NW¼	9	34	43	3-15—9-15	.054	19.80
	1892				33.40			SE¼NW¼	9	34	43	3-15—6-13	.272	50.10
	1891				9.99			NE¼SE¼	4	34	43	3-15—6-13	.081	14.99
	1889						37.40	SE¼SE¼	4	34	43	3-15—4-28	.304	28.05
	1889						15.26	SW¼SE¼	4	34	43	3-15—4-28	.124	11.55
	1891				15.22			NE¼NW¼	4	34	43	3-15—6-18	.124	22.83
	1890					3.55		SE¼SW¼	4	34	43	3-15—4-28	.029	2.66
	1890					11.98		SW¼SW¼	4	34	43	3-15—4-28	.097	8.99

Source—Humboldt River. Ditch—Section 11 Ditch.

Nat. mdw.	Cult. area	Dams	Ditches	Harvest crops	Meadow pasture	Willow and sage pasture	Swamp or overflow	Subdivision	Section	Tp.N.	R.E.	Length of season	C.F.S.	Acre-feet
	1889				8.64			NW¼NE¼	11	34	43	3-15—6-13	.070	12.96
	1890			22.50				SW¼NE¼	11	34	43	3-15—9-15	.183	67.40
	1888					8.74		NE¼SE¼	11	34	43	3-15—4-28	.071	6.56
	1889				22.32			NE¼NW¼	11	34	43	3-15—6-13	.181	33.48

	1890			4.70				NW¼SW¼	2	34	43	3-15—9-15	.038	14.10
	1890					5.65		NW¼SW¼	2	34	43	3-15—4-28	.056	4.24
	1890						7.40	NW¼SW¼	2	34	43	3-15—4-28	.060	5.55
	1890			2.63				SW¼SW¼	2	34	43	3-15—9-15	.021	7.89
	1890						29.80	SW¼SW¼	2	34	43	3-15—4-28	.242	22.35
	1888					21.53		SW¼NE¼	2	34	43	3-15—4-28	.175	16.15
	1890			3.40				NE¼SE¼	2	34	43	3-15—9-15	.028	10.20
	1890					14.93		NE¼SE¼	3	34	43	3-15—4-28	.121	11.20
	1888					1.84		SE¼SE¼	3	34	43	3-15—4-28	.015	1.38
	1888						9.75	SE¼SE¼	3	34	43	3-15—4-28	.079	7.31
	1889				5.78			NW¼SE¼	3	34	43	3-15—6-13	.047	8.67
	1889					26.67		NW¼SE¼	3	34	43	3-15—4-28	.217	20.00
	1887						7.81	SW¼SE¼	3	34	43	3-15—4-28	.063	5.86
	1888					38.14		SE¼NW¼	3	34	43	3-15—4-28	.310	28.61
	1888					14.90		NW¼SW¼	3	34	43	3-15—4-28	.121	11.18
	1888					11.62		NW¼SW¼	3	34	43	3-15—4-28	.094	8.72

Source—Humboldt River. Ditch—Wilcox.

	1880			13.44				NW¼SW¼	19	34	44	3-15—9-15	.109	40.32
	1880			6.29				NE¼SE¼	24	34	43	3-15—9-15	.051	18.87
	1880				9.92			NE¼SE¼	24	34	43	3-15—6-13	.081	14.88
	1878					8.79		SE¼NE¼	24	34	43	3-15—4-28	.071	6.59
	1878					4.50		NW¼NE¼	24	34	43	3-15—4-28	.037	3.38
	1879				18.86			SW¼NE¼	24	34	43	3-15—6-13	.162	28.29
	1878					5.00		NW¼NW¼	13	34	43	3-15—4-28	.041	3.75
	1878					29.48		SW¼NW¼	13	34	43	3-15—4-28	.240	22.11
	1879				16.95			NE¼SW¼	13	34	43	3-15—6-13	.138	25.43
	1879				28.20			SE¼SW¼	13	34	43	3-15—6-13	.229	42.30
	1878					40.00		NW¼SW¼	13	34	43	3-15—4-28	.325	30.00
	1878					38.60		SW¼SW¼	13	34	43	3-15—4-28	.314	28.95
	1877						37.80	NE¼NW¼	24	34	43	3-15—4-28	.307	28.35
	1877						13.35	SE¼NW¼	24	34	43	3-15—4-28	.109	10.01
	1879				40.00			NW¼NW¼	24	34	43	3-15—6-13	.325	60.00
	1877						7.35	SW¼NW¼	24	34	43	3-15—4-28	.060	5.51
	1880			0.40				SE¼SE¼	11	34	43	3-15—9-15	.003	1.20
	1880				1.15			SE¼SE¼	11	34	43	3-15—6-13	.009	1.73
	1880						10.00	SE¼SE¼	11	34	43	3-15—4-28	.081	7.50
	1878					3.40		SW¼SE¼	11	34	43	3-15—4-28	.028	2.55
	1878					9.50		NW¼SW¼	11	34	43	3-15—4-28	.077	7.13
	1878					4.50		SW¼SW¼	11	34	43	3-15—4-28	.037	3.38
	1878					37.21		NE¼NE¼	14	34	43	3-15—4-28	.303	27.91
	1878					40.00		SE¼NE¼	14	34	43	3-15—4-28	.325	30.00
	1878					13.15		NW¼NE¼	14	34	43	3-15—4-28	.107	9.86
	1878					25.90		SW¼NE¼	14	34	43	3-15—4-28	.211	19.42
	1877						40.00	NE¼SE¼	14	34	43	3-15—4-28	.325	30.00
	1878					27.05		SE¼SE¼	14	34	43	3-15—4-28	.220	20.29
	1877						30.50	SE¼NW¼	14	34	43	3-15—4-28	.248	22.88
	1878					8.90		NW¼NW¼	14	34	43	3-15—4-28	.072	6.68
	1878						30.00	NW¼NW¼	14	34	43	3-15—4-28	.244	22.50
	1878					13.90		SW¼NW¼	14	34	43	3-15—4-28	.113	10.43
	1877						12.46	NE¼SW¼	14	34	43	3-15—4-28	.101	9.35
	1879				9.00			NE¼SE¼	4	34	43	3-15—6-13	.073	13.50
	1878					14.85		SW¼SE¼	10	34	43	3-15—4-28	.120	11.14

Ellison Ranching Co.—Continued.

Date of beneficial use: Nat. mdw.	Date of beneficial use: Cult. area	Construction first initiated: Dams	Construction first initiated: Ditches	Culture—Acres: Harvest crops	Culture—Acres: Meadow pasture	Culture—Acres: Willow and sage pasture	Culture—Acres: Swamp or overflow	Location: Subdivision	Location: Section	Location: Tp.N.	Location: R.E.	Length of season	Duty of water: C.F.S.	Duty of water: Acre-feet
	1878					13.95		NE¼NE¼	10	34	43	3-15—4-28	.113	10.46
	1878					17.10		SE¼NE¼	10	34	43	3-15—4-28	.139	12.83
	1877						26.70	NW¼NE¼	10	34	43	3-15—4-28	.217	20.00
	1877						39.25	SW¼NE¼	10	34	43	3-15—4-28	.319	29.44
	1877						40.00	NE¼SE¼	10	34	43	3-15—4-28	.325	30.00
	1877						39.95	SE¼SE¼	10	34	43	3-15—4-28	.325	29.96
	1877						39.60	NW¼SE¼	10	34	43	3-15—4-28	.322	29.70
	1877						40.29	NE¼NW¼	10	34	43	3-15—4-28	.328	30.22
	1877						38.50	SE¼NW¼	10	34	43	3-15—4-28	.313	28.88
	1878					15.59		NW¼NW¼	10	34	43	3-15—4-28	.127	11.69
	1878						8.00	NE¼SW¼	10	34	43	3-15—4-28	.065	6.00
	1878						20.45	SE¼SW¼	3	34	43	3-15—4-28	.166	15.34
	1878						37.82	SW¼SW¼	3	34	43	3-15—4-28	.307	28.37

Source—**Humboldt River.** Ditch—**Overflow.**

Date of beneficial use: Nat. mdw.	Date of beneficial use: Cult. area	Construction first initiated: Dams	Construction first initiated: Ditches	Culture—Acres: Harvest crops	Culture—Acres: Meadow pasture	Culture—Acres: Willow and sage pasture	Culture—Acres: Swamp or overflow	Location: Subdivision	Location: Section	Location: Tp.N.	Location: R.E.	Length of season	Duty of water: C.F.S.	Duty of water: Acre-feet
	1880			6.15				SE¼SE¼	19	34	44	3-15—9-15	.050	18.45
	1880					19.47		SE¼SE¼	19	34	44	3-15—4-28	.158	14.60
	1880			7.23				NW¼SE¼	19	34	44	3-15—9-15	.059	21.69
	1880					5.42		NW¼SE¼	19	34	44	3-15—4-28	.044	4.07
	1880			19.77				SW¼SE¼	19	34	44	3-15—9-15	.161	59.71
	1880					15.40		SW¼SE¼	19	34	44	3-15—4-28	.125	11.55
	1880			11.19				NE¼SW¼	19	34	44	3-15—9-15	.091	33.57
	1880					23.52		NE¼SW¼	19	34	44	3-15—4-28	.191	17.54
	1878					14.34		SE¼SW¼	19	34	44	3-15—4-28	.117	10.76
	1878					12.87		NW¼SW¼	19	34	44	3-15—4-28	.105	9.65
	1879			25.16				NE¼NE¼	30	34	44	3-15—9-15	.205	75.48
	1879					7.60		NE¼NE¼	30	34	44	3-15—4-28	.062	5.70
	1879			16.81				SE¼NE¼	30	34	44	3-15—9-15	.137	50.43
	1879					12.69		SE¼NE¼	30	34	44	3-15—4-28	.103	9.52
	1879			16.66				NW¼NE¼	30	34	44	3-15—9-15	.135	49.98
	1879					16.40		NW¼NE¼	30	34	44	3-15—4-28	.133	12.30
	1879			2.19				SW¼NE¼	30	34	44	3-15—9-15	.018	6.57
	1879					3.36		SW¼NE¼	30	34	44	3-15—4-28	.027	2.52
	1879			7.25				NE¼SE¼	30	34	44	3-15—9-15	.059	21.75
	1879					7.60		NE¼SE¼	30	34	44	3-15—4-28	.062	5.70
	1878					5.20		NE¼NW¼	30	34	44	3-15—4-28	.042	3.90
	1878					9.25		SW¼SW¼	30	34	44	3-15—4-28	.075	6.94
	1878					2.23		NE¼NW¼	19	34	44	3-15—4-28	.018	1.67
	1880			4.67				SE¼NW¼	19	34	44	3-15—9-15	.038	14.01
	1880					4.50		SE¼NW¼	19	34	44	3-15—4-28	.037	3.38
	1880						10.33	SE¼NW¼	19	34	44	3-15—4-28	.084	7.75
	1880			9.34				NW¼NW¼	19	34	44	3-15—9-15	.076	38.02
	1880					2.33		NW¼NW¼	19	34	44	3-15—4-28	.019	1.74
	1880						21.06	NW¼NW¼	19	34	44	3-15—4-28	.176	16.25
	1880			11.65				SW¼NW¼	19	34	44	3-15—9-15	.093	34.95
	1880					18.44		SW¼NW¼	19	34	44	3-15—4-28	.150	13.83

	1880						.66	SW¼NW¼	19	34	44	3-15—4-28	.005	.40
	1878					19.04		NE¼NE¼	24	34	43	3-15—4-28	.155	14.28
	1880			22.00				SE¼NE¼	24	34	43	3-15—9-15	.170	66.00
	1880				6.22			SE¼NE¼	24	34	43	3-15—6-13	.051	9.83
	1880						.42	SE¼NE¼	24	34	43	3-15—4-28	.003	.32
	1879				31.30			NW¼NE¼	24	34	43	3-15—6-13	.254	46.95
	1877						11.15	NW¼SE¼	13	34	43	3-15—4-28	.091	8.30
	1879				5.05			SW¼SE¼	13	34	43	3-15—6-13	.041	7.58
	1879					25.55		SW¼SE¼	13	34	43	3-15—4-28	.208	19.16
	1878					9.11		NE¼NW¼	13	34	43	3-15—4-28	.074	6.83
	1879				24.26			SE¼NW¼	13	34	43	3-15—6-13	.197	36.39
	1879				22.99			NW¼NW¼	13	34	43	3-15—6-13	.187	34.37
	1879				6.47			SW¼NW¼	13	34	43	3-15—6-13	.054	9.71
	1879				23.05			NE¼SW¼	13	34	43	3-15—6-13	.187	34.58
	1879				6.90			SE¼SW¼	13	34	43	3-15—6-13	.056	10.35
	1878					7.20		SW¼SW¼	12	34	43	3-15—4-28	.059	5.40
	1878					5.23		SE¼NE¼	11	34	43	3-15—4-28	.043	3.92
	1878					15.88		NW¼NE¼	11	34	43	3-15—4-28	.129	11.91
	1879				16.29			NE¼SE¼	11	34	43	3-15—6-13	.132	24.44
	1878					22.04		SE¼SE¼	11	34	43	3-15—4-28	.179	16.53
	1880			4.96				NE¼NW¼	11	34	43	3-15—9-15	.040	14.88
	1880					11.63		NE¼NW¼	11	34	43	3-15—4-28	.095	8.83
	1879				2.79			NE¼NE¼	14	34	43	3-15—6-13	.023	4.19
	1879				9.14			NE¼NE¼	4	34	43	3-15—6-13	.074	13.71
	1879					24.11		NE¼NE¼	4	34	43	3-15—4-28	.196	18.08
	1879				4.87			NW¼NE¼	4	24	43	3-15—6-13	.040	7.31
	1879					30.07		NW¼NE¼	4	34	43	3-15—4-28	.244	22.55
	1878					16.07		NE¼NW¼	4	34	43	3-15—4-28	.131	12.05
	1879				21.40			SW¼NW¼	4	34	43	3-15—6-13	.175	32.10
	1879					9.60		SW¼NW¼	4	34	43	3-15—4-28	.078	7.20
	1879				6.80			SW¼SW¼	34	35	43	3-15—6-13	.055	10.20
	1879					13.30		SW¼SW¼	34	35	43	3-15—4-28	.108	9.98
	1878					3.88		SW¼SE¼	2	34	43	3-15—4-28	.032	2.91
	1877						8.83	NE¼SW¼	2	34	43	3-15—4-28	.072	6.62
	1878					3.95		SW¼SW¼	2	34	43	3-15—4-28	.032	2.96
	1880			2.11				SE¼NE¼	3	34	43	3-15—9-15	.017	6.33
	1880						6.12	SE¼NE¼	3	34	43	3-15—4-28	.050	4.59
	1878					9.60		NW¼NE¼	3	34	43	3-15—4-28	.078	7.20
	1878						1.75	NW¼NE¼	3	34	43	3-15—4-28	.014	1.31
	1877						12.80	SW¼NE¼	3	34	43	3-15—4-28	.104	9.60
	1877						14.04	NE¼SE¼	3	34	43	3-15—4-28	.114	10.53
	1877						7.75	NW¼SE¼	3	34	43	3-15—4-28	.063	5.81
	1879				9.63			NE¼NW¼	3	34	43	3-15—6-13	.078	14.45
	1879					23.22		NE¼NW¼	3	34	43	3-15—4-28	.189	17.42
	1878					14.86		NW¼NW¼	3	34	43	3-15—4-28	.121	11.15
	1878						21.21	NW¼NW¼	3	34	43	3-15—4-28	.197	18.16
	1879				1.00			SW¼NW¼	3	34	43	3-15—6-13	.008	1.50
	1879					3.92		SW¼NW¼	3	34	43	3-15—4-28	.032	2.94
	1879					6.92		NE¼SW¼	3	34	43	3-15—4-28	.056	5.19
	1879				4.89			SE¼SW¼	34	35	43	3-15—6-13	.041	7.34
	1879					3.06		SE¼SW¼	34	35	43	3-15—4-28	.025	2.30

Ellison Ranching Co.—Continued.
Source—**Humboldt River.** Ditch—**No. 8.**

Date of beneficial use: Nat. mdw.	Date of beneficial use: Cult. area	Construction first initiated: Dams	Construction first initiated: Ditches	Culture—Acres: Harvest crops	Culture—Acres: Meadow pasture	Culture—Acres: Willow and sage pasture	Culture—Acres: Swamp or overflow	Location: Subdivision	Location: Section	Location: Tp.N.	Location: R.E.	Length of season	Duty of water: C.F.S.	Duty of water: Acre-feet
	1880			13.26				SW¼SW¼	19	34	44	3-15—9-15	.107	39.60
	1880			14.39				NE¼NE¼	24	34	43	3-15—9-15	.117	43.17
	1877						3.45	NW¼NE¼	13	34	43	3-15—4-28	.028	2.59
	1878					14.85		SW¼NE¼	13	34	43	3-15—4-28	.121	11.14
	1878						14.25	SW¼NE¼	13	34	43	3-15—4-28	.117	10.69
	1877						1.01	SE¼NE¼	13	34	43	3-15—4-28	.008	.76
	1879				7.20			NE¼SE¼	13	34	43	3-15—6-13	.059	10.80
	1879						15.45	NE¼SE¼	13	34	43	3-15—4-28	.126	11.59
	1880			13.83				SE¼SE¼	13	34	43	3-15—9-15	.112	41.49
	1880				22.20			SE¼SE¼	13	34	43	3-15—6-13	.180	33.30
	1880					2.26		SE¼SE¼	13	34	43	3-15—4-28	.018	1.70
	1879				24.00			NW¼SE¼	13	34	43	3-15—6-13	.195	36.00
	1879				29.81			NE¼NW¼	13	34	43	3-15—6-13	.242	44.72
	1878					9.19		SE¼NW¼	13	34	43	3-15—4-28	.075	6.89
	1878					6.34		NW¼NW¼	13	34	43	3-15—4-28	.052	4.76
	1879				4.16			SE¼SW¼	12	34	43	3-15—6-13	.034	6.24
	1879					2.91		SE¼SW¼	12	34	43	3-15—4-28	.024	2.18
	1879				21.50			NW¼SW¼	12	34	43	3-15—6-13	.175	32.25
	1879				31.70			SW¼SW¼	12	34	43	3-15—6-13	.258	47.55
	1880			3.96				NE¼NE¼	11	34	43	3-15—9-15	.032	11.88
	1880				25.96			NE¼NE¼	11	34	43	3-15—6-13	.211	38.94
	1880					1.55		NE¼NE¼	11	34	43	3-15—4-28	.013	1.16
	1880			20.70				SE¼NE¼	11	34	43	3-15—9-15	.168	62.10
	1880				12.42			SE¼NE¼	11	34	43	3-15—6-13	.101	18.63
	1880			9.33				NW¼NE¼	11	24	43	3-15—9-15	.076	27.99
	1879					12.25		SW¼NE¼	11	34	43	3-15—4-28	.100	9.19
	1880			11.06				NE¼SE¼	11	34	43	3-15—9-15	.090	33.18
	1880			6.30				SE¼NW¼	11	34	43	3-15—9-15	.051	18.90
	1880				6.70			SE¼NW¼	11	34	43	3-15—6-13	.054	10.05
	1879				14.35			NW¼NW¼	11	34	43	3-15—6-13	.117	21.53
	1878						30.90	SW¼SE¼	2	34	43	3-15—4-28	.251	23.18
	1879			1.37				NE¼SW¼	2	24	43	3-15—9-15	.011	4.11
	1879					3.55		NE¼SW¼	2	34	43	3-15—4-28	.029	2.66
	1878					3.88		SE¼SW¼	2	34	43	3-15—4-28	.032	2.91
	1878						5.60	SE¼SW¼	2	34	43	3-15—4-28	.045	5.20

Claimant—**William Dunphy Estate.** Proof No. 00171
Source—**Humboldt River.** Ditch—**Humboldt Slough No. 2.**

Nat. mdw.	Cult. area	Dams	Ditches	Harvest crops	Meadow pasture	Willow and sage pasture	Swamp or overflow	Subdivision	Section	Tp.N.	R.E.	Length of season	C.F.S.	Acre-feet
1871	1890				2.40			SE¼SE¼	36	33	46	3-15—6-13	.020	3.60
1871	1890				21.70			SE¼SW¼	31	33	47	3-15—6-13	.176	32.55
1871	1890					4.25		SE¼SW¼	31	33	47	3-15—4-28	.035	3.19
1871	1890				20.55			SW¼SW¼	31	33	47	3-15—6-13	.167	30.83
1871	1890					13.80		SW¼SW¼	31	33	47	3-15—4-28	.112	10.35
1871	1890				9.30			SW¼SE¼	31	33	47	3-15—6-13	.176	14.04

1871	1890					8.85		SW¼SE¼	31	33	47	3-15—4-28	.072	6.64
1871	1890				12.00			SE¼SE¼	31	33	47	3-15—6-13	.098	18.00
1871	1890					22.00		SW¼SE¼	31	33	47	3-15—4-28	.184	16.95
1871	1890					24.30		SE¼SW¼	32	33	47	3-15—4-28	.198	18.23
1871	1890					18.80		SW¼SW¼	32	33	47	3-15—4-28	.153	14.10

Source—**Humboldt River.** Ditch—**White House Ditch No. 1.**

1871	1886			4.85				NE¼NW¼	26	33	47	3-15—9-15	.039	14.55
1871	1886			39.25				NW¼NE¼	26	33	47	3-15—9-15	.319	117.75
1871	1886			15.85				SW¼NE¼	26	33	47	3-15—9-15	.129	47.55
1871	1886			15.55				SE¼NE¼	26	33	47	3-15—9-15	.126	46.65
1871	1886			37.20				NE¼NE¼	26	33	47	3-15—9-15	.302	111.60

Source—**Humboldt River.** Ditch—**South Branch White House Slough.**

1871	1887			14.80				SW¼NW¼	27	33	47	3-15—9-15	.120	44.40
1871	1887			16.90				SE¼NW¼	27	33	47	3-15—9-15	.137	50.70
1871	1887			36.15				NE¼NW¼	27	33	47	3-15—9-15	.294	108.45
1871	1887			38.10				NW¼NE¼	27	33	47	3-15—9-15	.310	114.30
1871	1887			16.00				SW¼NE¼	27	33	47	3-15—9-15	.130	48.00
1871	1887			15.45				SE¼NE¼	27	33	47	3-15—9-15	.126	46.35
1871	1887			37.00				NE¼NE¼	27	33	47	3-15—9-15	.301	111.00
1871	1887			37.75				NW¼NW¼	26	33	47	3-15—9-15	.307	113.25
1871	1887			15.50				SW¼NW¼	26	33	47	3-15—9-15	.126	46.50
1871	1887			14.20				SE¼NW¼	26	33	47	3-15—9-15	.115	42.60
1871	1887			32.80				NE¼NW¼	26	33	47	3-15—9-15	.267	98.40
1871	1887			30.30				SE¼SE¼	23	33	47	3-15—9-15	.246	90.90
1871	1887				5.95			SE¼SE¼	23	33	17	3-15—6-13	.048	8.93
1871	1887				35.25			NE¼SE¼	23	33	47	3-15—6-13	.287	52.88
1871	1887			34.70				SW¼SE¼	23	33	47	3-15—9-15	.282	104.10
1871	1887				2.60			SW¼SE¼	23	33	47	3-15—6-13	.021	3.90

Source—**Humboldt River.** Ditch—**Big Slough.**

1871	1902					2.00		NW¼NW¼	26	33	48	3-15—4-28	.016	1.50
1871	1902					8.80		SW¼NW¼	26	33	48	3-15—4-28	.072	6.60
1871	1902				8.20			NE¼NE¼	27	33	48	3-15—6-13	.067	12.30
1871	1902					.70		NE¼NE¼	27	33	48	3-15—4-28	.006	.53
1871	1902				14.85			SE¼NE¼	27	33	48	3-15—6-13	.121	22.38
1871	1902					4.05		SE¼NE¼	27	33	48	3-15—4-28	.033	3.04
1871	1902				.60			NW¼NE¼	27	33	48	3-15—6-13	.005	.90
1871	1902					9.90		NW¼NE¼	27	33	48	3-15—4-28	.080	7.43
1871	1902				5.65			SW¼NE¼	27	33	48	3-15—6-13	.046	8.48
1871	1902					6.85		SW¼NE¼	27	33	48	3-15—4-28	.056	5.14
1871	1902				12.30			NE¼NW¼	27	33	48	3-15—6-13	.100	18.45
1871	1902					7.25		NE¼NW¼	27	33	48	3-15—4-28	.059	5.44
1871	1902				7.95			SE¼NW¼	27	33	48	3-15—6-13	.065	11.93
1871	1902					6.95		SE¼NW¼	27	33	48	3-15—4-28	.057	5.21
1871	1902				7.15			SW¼NW¼	27	33	48	3-15—6-13	.058	10.73
1871	1902					1.50		SW¼NW¼	27	33	48	3-15—4-28	.012	1.13
1871	1902				15.55			SW¼NW¼	26	33	48	3-15—6-13	.126	23.33
1871	1902					3.05		SW¼NW¼	26	33	48	3-15—4-28	.025	2.29
1871	1902				.80			SE¼NW¼	26	33	48	3-15—6-13	.007	1.00

William Dunphy Estate—Continued.
Source—**Humboldt River.** Ditch—**Mosel Slough.**

Date of beneficial use: Nat. mdw.	Cult. area	Construction first initiated: Dams	Ditches	Culture—Acres: Harvest crops	Meadow pasture	Willow and sage pasture	Swamp or overflow	Location: Subdivision	Section	Tp.N.	R.E.	Length of season	Duty of water: C.F.S.	Acre-feet
1873					9.95			NE¼NE¼	3	32	47	3-15—6-13	.081	14.93
1873					18.50			NW¼NE¼	3	32	47	3-15—6-13	.150	27.75
1873					35.45			SE¼NE¼	3	32	47	3-15—6-13	.288	53.18
1873					21.35			SW¼NE¼	3	32	47	3-15—6-13	.174	32.04

Source—**Humboldt River.** Ditch—**South Fork Ditch No. 1.**

Nat. mdw.	Cult. area	Dams	Ditches	Harvest crops	Meadow pasture	Willow and sage pasture	Swamp or overflow	Subdivision	Section	Tp.N.	R.E.	Length of season	C.F.S.	Acre-feet
	1891					5.90		NE¼NW¼	33	33	48	3-15—4-28	.048	4.43
	1891					7.45		NE¼SW¼	28	33	48	3-15—4-28	.061	5.59
	1891					9.00		SE¼SW¼	28	33	48	3-15—4-28	.073	6.75
	1891					26.00		NW¼SE¼	28	33	48	3-15—4-28	.211	19.50
	1891					32.40		SW¼SE¼	28	33	48	3-15—4-28	.263	24.30
	1891					27.95		SE¼SE¼	28	33	48	3-15—4-28	.227	20.96
	1891						2.25	SE¼SE¼	28	33	48	3-15—4-28	.017	1.69
	1891					28.80		NE¼SE¼	28	33	48	3-15—4-28	.234	21.60
	1891					2.85		SW¼NE¼	28	33	48	3-15—4-28	.022	2.14

Source—**Humboldt River.** Ditch—**South Fork Slough.**

Nat. mdw.	Cult. area	Dams	Ditches	Harvest crops	Meadow pasture	Willow and sage pasture	Swamp or overflow	Subdivision	Section	Tp.N.	R.E.	Length of season	C.F.S.	Acre-feet
	1891				10.75			SE¼NW¼	27	33	48	3-15—6-13	.087	16.13
	1891					8.40		SE¼NW¼	27	33	48	3-15—4-28	.068	6.30
	1891				27.60			NW¼SW¼	27	33	48	3-15—6-13	.224	41.40
	1891					5.25		NW¼SW¼	27	33	48	3-15—4-28	.043	3.94
	1891				27.30			SW¼SW¼	27	33	48	3-15—6-13	.222	40.95
	1891				12.95			SE¼SW¼	27	33	48	3-15—6-13	.105	19.43
	1891				36.45			NE¼SW¼	27	33	48	3-15—6-13	.296	54.68
	1891					2.80		NE¼SW¼	27	33	48	3-15—4-28	.023	2.10
	1891				27.85			NW¼SE¼	27	33	48	3-15—6-13	.226	41.78
	1891					2.45		NW¼SE¼	27	23	48	3-15—4-28	.020	1.84
	1891				2.10			SW¼SE¼	27	33	48	3-15—6-13	.017	3.15
	1891					0.40		SW¼SE¼	27	33	48	3-15—4-28	.003	0.30

Source—**Humboldt River.** Ditch—**Farrel Slough.**

Nat. mdw.	Cult. area	Dams	Ditches	Harvest crops	Meadow pasture	Willow and sage pasture	Swamp or overflow	Subdivision	Section	Tp.N.	R.E.	Length of season	C.F.S.	Acre-feet
	1888					32.35		SW¼NW¼	32	33	48	3-15—4-28	.263	24.26
	1888					33.80		SE¼NW¼	32	33	48	3-15—4-28	.275	25.35
	1888					23.10		NW¼SW¼	32	33	48	3-15—4-28	.207	17.33
	1888						5.50	NW¼SW¼	32	33	48	3-15—4-28	.064	4.13
	1888					8.60		NE¼SW¼	32	33	48	3-15—4-28	.089	6.45
	1888						19.10	NE¼SW¼	32	33	48	3-15—4-28	.174	11.33
	1888					35.45		NW¼NE¼	32	33	48	3-15—4-28	.288	26.59
	1888					26.75		SW¼NE¼	32	33	48	3-15—4-28	.217	20.06
	1888					13.55		SE¼NE¼	32	33	48	3-15—4-28	.129	10.16
	1888					37.70		NE¼NE¼	32	33	48	3-15—4-28	.307	28.28
	1888				34.05			SW¼SW¼	28	33	48	3-15—6-13	.277	51.08
	1888					.45		SW¼SW¼	28	33	48	3-15—4-28	.004	0.34

	1888				26.70			SE¼ SW¼	28	33	48	3-15—6-13	.217	40.05
	1888				38.00			NW¼ NW¼	33	33	48	3-15—6-13	.300	57.00
	1888				2.35			SW¼ NW¼	33	33	48	3-15—6-13	.019	3.53
	1888				21.30			NE¼ NW¼	33	33	48	3-15—6-13	.173	31.95
								Source—Humboldt River. Ditch—Old Field Ditch.						
	1904				30.40			NW¼ NW¼	1	32	47	3-15—6-13	.247	45.60
	1904					2.95		NW¼ NW¼	1	32	47	3-15—4-28	.024	2.21
	1904						1.95	NW¼ NW¼	1	32	47	3-15—4-28	.016	1.46
	1904				0.15			SE¼ NW¼	1	32	47	3-15—6-13	.001	0.23
	1904				33.20			NE¼ NW¼	1	32	47	3-15—6-13	.270	49.80
	1904				27.25			NW¼ NE¼	1	32	47	3-15—6-13	.223	40.88
	1904					0.65		NW¼ NW¼	6	32	48	3-15—4-28	.005	0.49
	1904				35.00			SW¼ SE¼	36	32	48	3-15—6-13	.281	52.50
	1904				34.45			SE¼ SE¼	36	32	48	3-15—6-13	.280	51.68
	1904				20.60			NW¼ SW¼	31	32	48	3-15—6-13	.167	30.90
	1904				24.60			SW¼ SW¼	31	32	48	3-15—6-13	.200	36.90
	1904				20.45			SE¼ SW¼	31	32	48	3-15—6-13	.166	30.68
	1904				34.00			NE¼ SW¼	31	32	48	3-15—6-13	.276	51.00
	1904				30.50			NW¼ SE¼	31	32	48	3-15—6-13	.248	45.75
	1904						1.90	NW¼ SE¼	31	32	48	3-15—4-28	.015	1.43
	1904				3.50			SW¼ SE¼	31	32	48	3-15—6-13	.028	4.25
	1904						16.80	SW¼ SE¼	31	32	48	3-15—4-28	.137	12.60
	1904						5.85	SE¼ SE¼	31	32	48	3-15—4-28	.048	4.39
	1904				13.55			NE¼ SE¼	31	32	48	3-15—6-13	.110	20.33
	1904					19.05		NE¼ SE¼	31	32	48	3-15—4-28	.155	14.29
								Source—Humboldt River. Ditch—White House Slough.						
1871	1887				1.70			SE¼ NE¼	22	33	48	3-15—6-13	.014	2.55
1871	1887				2.05			SW¼ NE¼	22	33	48	3-15—6-13	.017	3.08
1871	1887				8.15			NE¼ SE¼	22	33	48	3-15—6-13	.066	12.23
1871	1887				31.10			NW¼ SE¼	22	33	48	3-15—6-13	.253	46.65
1871	1887				2.65			SW¼ SE¼	22	33	48	3-15—6-13	.022	3.98
1871	1887				28.45			NE¼ SW¼	22	33	48	3-15—6-13	.231	42.68
1871	1887				8.95			NW¼ SW¼	22	33	48	3-15—6-13	.073	13.43
1871	1887				0.55			NW¼ SE¼	23	33	48	3-15—6-13	.004	0.83
1871	1887				1.50			SW¼ SE¼	23	33	48	3-15—6-13	.012	2.25
1871	1887				0.60			NE¼ SW¼	23	33	48	3-15—6-13	.005	0.90
1871	1887				17.50			SE¼ SW¼	23	33	48	3-15—6-13	.042	26.25
1871	1887				7.35			NW¼ SW¼	23	33	48	3-15—6-13	.060	11.03
1871	1887				15.55			SW¼ SW¼	23	33	48	3-15—6-13	.126	23.33
1871	1887				5.45			SW¼ NE¼	29	33	47	3-15—6-13	.044	8.18
1871	1887				22.65			SE¼ NE¼	29	33	47	3-15—6-13	.184	33.98
1871	1887				8.05			NW¼ SE¼	29	33	47	3-15—6-13	.065	12.08
1871	1887				35.55			NE¼ SE¼	29	33	47	3-15—6-13	.289	53.33
1871	1887					35.65		NW¼ NW¼	31	33	47	3-15—4-28	.290	26.74
1871	1887					36.45		NE¼ NW¼	31	33	47	3-15—4-28	.296	27.34
1871	1887					28.80		SW¼ SW¼	20	33	47	3-15—4-28	.234	21.60
1871	1887				0.30			SE¼ NE¼	25	33	48	3-15—6-13	.002	.45
1871	1887						4.50	SE¼ NE¼	25	33	48	3-15—4-28	.037	3.37
1871	1887						1.85	SW¼ NE¼	25	33	48	3-15—4-28	.015	1.39

William Dunphy Estate—Continued.

Date of beneficial use: Nat. mdw.	Cult. area	Construction first initiated: Dams	Ditches	Culture—Acres: Harvest crops	Meadow pasture	Willow and sage pasture	Swamp or overflow	Location: Subdivision	Section	Tp.N.	R.E.	Length of season	Duty of water: C.F.S.	Acre-feet
1871	1887				10.25			NW¼SW¼	25	33	48	3-15—6-13	.083	15.38
1871	1887					11.25		NW¼SW¼	25	33	48	3-15—4-28	.091	8.44
1871	1887						9.60	NW¼SW¼	25	33	48	3-15—4-28	.078	7.20
1871	1887				0.95			SW¼SW¼	25	33	48	3-15—6-13	.008	1.43
1871	1887					16.05		SW¼SW¼	25	33	48	3-15—4-28	.130	12.04
1871	1887			1.90				SE¼SW¼	25	33	48	3-15—9-15	.015	5.70
1871	1887				17.45			SE¼SW¼	25	33	48	3-15—6-13	.142	26.18
1871	1887					5.85		SE¼SW¼	25	33	48	3-15—4-28	.048	4.39
1871	1887					1.40		NE¼SW¼	25	33	48	3-15—4-28	.011	1.05
1871	1887						3.20	NE¼SW¼	25	33	48	3-15—4-28	.026	2.40
1871	1887			15.85				SE¼NE¼	28	33	48	3-15—9-15	.129	47.55
1871	1887			35.40				NE¼NE¼	28	33	48	3-15—9-15	.288	106.20
1871	1887			36.45				NW¼NW¼	27	33	48	3-15—9-15	.296	109.35
1871	1887			39.15				NW¼NW¼	25	33	48	3-15—9-15	.318	157.45
1871	1887				0.75			NW¼NW¼	25	33	48	3-15—6-13	.006	1.13
1871	1887			15.20				SW¼NW¼	25	33	48	3-15—9-15	.124	45.60
1871	1887			19.60				NW¼NE¼	25	33	48	3-15—9-15	.159	49.80
1871	1887						11.00	NW¼NE¼	25	33	48	3-15—4-28	.089	8.25
1871	1887			36.25				SE¼SE¼	22	33	47	3-15—9-15	.295	144.75
1871	1887				0.35			SE¼SE¼	22	33	47	3-15—6-13	.003	.53
1871	1887			18.95				SW¼SE¼	22	33	47	3-15—9-15	.154	56.85
1871	1887				18.35			SW¼SE¼	22	33	47	3-15—6-13	.149	27.53
1871	1887			4.00				SE¼SW¼	22	33	47	3-15—9-15	.033	12.00
1871	1887			35.80				SW¼SW¼	22	33	47	3-15—9-15	.291	107.40
1871	1887				2.15			SW¼SW¼	22	33	47	3-15—6-13	.017	3.23
1871	1887				9.45			NE¼NE¼	23	33	47	3-15—6-13	.077	14.18
1871	1887				34.45			SE¼NE¼	23	33	47	3-15—6-13	.280	51.68
1871	1887					1.75		SE¼NE¼	23	33	47	3-15—4-28	.014	1.31
1871	1887				31.75			SW¼NE¼	23	33	47	3-15—6-13	.258	47.63
1871	1887				38.85			NW¼SE¼	23	33	47	3-15—6-13	.316	58.28
1871	1887			14.65				NE¼SW¼	23	33	47	3-15—9-15	.119	43.95
1871	1887				21.20			NE¼SW¼	23	33	47	3-15—6-13	.172	31.80
1871	1887			36.95				SE¼SW¼	23	33	47	3-15—9-15	.300	110.85
1871	1887				1.30			SE¼SW¼	23	33	47	3-15—6-13	.011	1.95
1871	1887			11.55				NW¼SW¼	23	33	47	3-15—9-15	.094	35.65
1871	1887				21.20			NW¼SW¼	23	33	47	3-15—6-13	.172	31.80
1871	1887						4.35	NW¼SW¼	23	33	47	3-15—4-28	.035	3.26
1871	1887			38.90				SW¼SW¼	23	33	47	3-15—9-15	.316	116.70
1871	1887				2.85			NW¼NE¼	24	33	47	3-15—6-13	.023	4.28
1871	1887				15.80			SW¼NE¼	24	33	47	3-15—6-13	.128	23.70
1871	1887						14.70	SW¼NE¼	24	33	47	3-15—4-28	.120	11.03
1871	1887			14.85				SW¼SE¼	24	33	47	3-15—9-15	.121	44.55
1871	1887						14.75	SW¼SE¼	24	33	47	3-15—4-28	.120	11.06
1871	1887				3.30			NE¼NW¼	24	33	47	3-15—6-13	.027	4.95
1871	1887						1.20	NE¼NW¼	24	33	47	3-15—4-28	.010	0.90
1871	1887				20.45			SE¼NW¼	24	33	47	3-15—6-13	.166	30.68

1871	1887						16.00	SE¼NW¼	24	33	47	3-15—4-28	.130	12.00
1871	1887				6.20			NW¼NW¼	24	33	47	3-15—6-18	.050	9.30
1871	1887						2.90	NW¼NW¼	24	33	47	3-15—4-28	.024	2.18
1871	1887				35.25			SW¼NW¼	24	33	47	3-15—6-18	.287	52.88
1871	1887						.70	SW¼NW¼	24	33	47	3-15—4-28	.006	0.53
1871	1887				36.75			NE¼SW¼	24	33	47	3-15—6-13	.299	55.18
1871	1887						.40	NE¼SW¼	24	33	47	3-15—4-28	.003	.30
1871	1887			8.80				SE¼SW¼	24	33	47	3-15—0-15	.072	26.40
1871	1887				14.50			SE¼SW¼	24	33	47	3-15—6-13	.118	21.75
1871	1887						16.05	SE¼SW¼	24	33	47	3-15—4-28	.130	12.04
1871	1887				37.00			NW¼SW¼	24	33	47	3-15—6-18	.301	55.50
1871	1887			1.55				SW¼SW¼	24	33	47	3-15—0-15	.018	4.65
1871	1887				34.65			SW¼SW¼	24	33	47	3-15—6-13	.282	51.98
1871	1887						1.55	SW¼SW¼	24	33	47	3-15—4-28	.013	1.16
1871	1887				1.70			SW¼NE¼	24	33	47	3-15—6-13	.014	2.55
1871	1887						4.05	SW¼NE¼	24	33	47	3-15—4-28	.033	3.04
1871	1887				18.45			SE¼NE¼	24	33	47	3-15—6-13	.150	27.68
1871	1887						4.20	SE¼NE¼	24	33	47	3-15—4-28	.034	3.15
1871	1887				7.60			NW¼SE¼	24	33	47	3-15—6-13	.062	11.40
1871	1887				37.30			NE¼SE¼	24	33	47	3-15—6-18	.303	55.95
1871	1887			3.10				SW¼SE¼	24	33	47	3-15—0-15	.025	9.30
1871	1887						2.15	SW¼SE¼	24	33	47	3-15—4-28	.017	1.61
1871	1887			2.15				SE¼SE¼	24	33	47	3-15—0-15	.017	6.45
1871	1887				11.20			SE¼SE¼	24	33	47	3-15—6-13	.091	16.80
1871	1887						17.65	SE¼SE¼	24	33	47	3-15—4-28	.143	13.24
1871	1887					27.25		SE¼SW¼	29	33	47	3-15—4-28	.222	19.69
1871	1887					26.05		NW¼SE¼	29	33	47	3-15—4-28	.212	19.54
1871	1887			17.30				SW¼NW¼	28	33	47	3-15—0-15	.141	61.90
1871	1887				2.05			SW¼NW¼	28	33	47	3-15—6-13	.017	3.08
1871	1887			18.80				SE¼NW¼	28	33	47	3-15—0-15	.153	56.40
1871	1887			.70				NW¼SW¼	28	33	47	3-15—0-15	.006	2.10
1871	1887				28.00			NW¼SW¼	28	33	47	3-15—6-13	.228	42.00
1871	1887			28.80				NE¼SW¼	28	33	47	3-15—0-15	.234	86.40
1871	1887					1.80		NE¼SW¼	28	33	47	3-15—4-28	.015	1.35
1871	1887			12.40				NW¼SE¼	28	33	47	3-15—0-15	.010	37.20
1871	1887					2.40		NW¼SE¼	28	33	47	3-15—4-28	.020	1.80
1871	1887			19.70				SW¼NE¼	28	33	47	3-15—0-15	.160	59.10
1871	1887			9.25				SE¼NE¼	28	33	47	3-15—0-15	.075	27.75
1871	1887					.40		SE¼NE¼	28	33	47	3-15—4-28	.003	.30
1871	1887			17.30				SW¼NW¼	27	33	47	3-15—0-15	.141	51.90
1871	1887			21.15				SE¼NW¼	27	33	47	3-15—0-15	.172	63.45
1871	1887				7.60			NE¼NW¼	26	33	47	3-15—6-13	.062	11.40
1871	1887						9.35	NE¼NW¼	26	33	47	3-15—4-28	.076	7.01
1871	1887				27.95			NW¼SE¼	26	33	47	3-15—6-13	.227	41.93
1871	1887					2.15		NW¼SE¼	26	33	47	3-15—4-28	.017	1.61
1871	1887				.20			SE¼SE¼	26	33	47	3-15—6-13	.002	.30
1871	1887					3.10		SE¼SE¼	26	33	47	3-15—4-28	.025	2.32
1871	1887				14.70			NE¼SE¼	26	33	47	3-15—6-13	.120	22.05
1871	1887					11.55		NE¼SE¼	26	33	47	3-15—4-28	.094	8.66
1871	1887				11.40			SW¼NE¼	26	33	47	3-15—6-13	.093	17.10
1871	1887						8.80	SW¼NE¼	26	33	47	3-15—4-28	.072	6.60
1871	1887				5.00			SE¼NE¼	26	33	47	3-15—6-13	.048	8.85
1871	1887						10.65	SE¼NE¼	26	33	47	3-15—4-28	.087	7.99

William Dunphy Estate—Continued.

Date of beneficial use: Nat. mdw.	Cult. area	Construction first initiated: Dams	Ditches	Culture—Acres: Harvest crops	Meadow pasture	Willow and sage pasture	Swamp or overflow	Location: Subdivision	Section	Tp. N.	R. E.	Length of season	Duty of water: C.F.S.	Acre-feet
1871	1887					.50		SW¼NW¼	25	33	47	3-15—4-28	.004	.38
1871	1887						.40	SW¼NW¼	25	33	47	3-15—4-28	.003	.30
1871	1887				2.00			SE¼NW¼	25	33	47	3-15—6-13	.016	3.00
1871	1888				13.45			SW¼NW¼	19	33	48	3-15—6-13	.109	27.18
1871	1888				35.95			NE¼SW¼	19	33	48	3-15—6-13	.292	53.93
1871	1888				25.20			SE¼SW¼	19	33	48	3-15—6-13	.205	37.80
1871	1888						.45	SE¼SW¼	19	33	48	3-15—4-28	.004	.34
1871	1888						11.50	SE¼SW¼	19	33	48	3-15—4-28	.093	8.63
1871	1888				35.50			NW¼SW¼	19	33	48	3-15—6-13	.289	53.35
1871	1888				10.35			SW¼SW¼	19	33	48	3-15—6-13	.084	15.53
1871	1888						2.25	SW¼SW¼	19	33	48	3-15—4-28	.018	1.69
1871	1888						24.10	SW¼SW¼	19	33	48	3-15—4-28	.196	18.08
1871	1888				3.15			NE¼NE¼	20	33	48	3-15—6-13	.026	4.73
1871	1888						31.05	NE¼NE¼	20	33	48	3-15—4-28	.252	23.29
1871	1888				9.75			SE¼NE¼	20	33	48	3-15—6-13	.079	14.63
1871	1888						25.65	SE¼NE¼	20	33	48	3-15—4-28	.209	19.24
1871	1888				1.05			NW¼NE¼	20	33	48	3-15—6-13	.009	1.58
1871	1888						38.40	NW¼NE¼	20	33	48	3-15—4-28	.312	25.05
1871	1888				.70			SW¼NE¼	20	33	48	3-15—6-13	.006	1.05
1871	1888						37.95	SW¼NE¼	20	33	48	3-15—4-28	.309	28.46
1871	1888				4.65			NE¼SE¼	20	33	48	3-15—6-13	.038	6.98
1871	1888						33.80	NE¼SE¼	20	33	48	3-15—4-28	.275	25.35
1871	1888				29.70			SE¼SE¼	20	33	48	3-15—6-13	.241	44.55
1871	1888						8.55	SE¼SE¼	20	33	48	3-15—4-28	.070	6.41
1871	1888				20.75			NW¼SE¼	20	33	48	3-15—6-13	.169	31.13
1871	1888						16.20	NW¼SE¼	20	33	48	3-15—4-28	.132	12.15
1871	1888				36.40			SW¼SE¼	20	33	48	3-15—6-13	.296	54.60
1871	1888						1.55	SW¼SE¼	20	33	48	3-15—4-28	.013	1.16
1871	1888				1.30			NE¼NW¼	20	33	48	3-15—6-13	.011	1.95
1871	1888						37.55	NE¼NW¼	20	33	48	3-15—4-28	.305	28.16
1871	1888				.80			SE¼NW¼	29	33	48	3-15—6-13	.007	1.20
1871	1888						38.35	SE¼NW¼	20	33	48	3-15—4-28	.312	28.76
1871	1888				1.30			NW¼NW¼	20	33	48	3-15—6-13	.011	1.95
1871	1888						12.85	NW¼NW¼	20	33	48	3-15—4-28	.104	9.64
1871	1888						24.20	SW¼NW¼	20	33	48	3-15—4-28	.197	18.15
1871	1887				22.05			NE¼SW¼	20	33	48	3-15—6-13	.179	33.08
1871	1887						12.75	NE¼SW¼	20	33	48	3-15—4-28	.104	9.56
1871	1887				28.75			SE¼SW¼	20	33	48	3-15—6-13	.234	43.13
1871	1887						9.25	SE¼SW¼	20	33	48	3-15—4-28	.075	6.94
1871	1887				26.05			NW¼SW¼	20	33	48	3-15—6-13	.212	39.08
1871	1887						9.85	NW¼SW¼	20	33	48	3-15—4-28	.080	7.39
1871	1887				20.05			SW¼SW¼	20	33	48	3-15—6-13	.163	30.08
1871	1887						12.30	SW¼SW¼	20	33	48	3-15—4-28	.100	9.23
1871	1887				2.40			SE¼NE¼	21	33	48	3-15—6-13	.020	3.60
1871	1887						2.90	SE¼NE¼	21	33	48	3-15—4-28	.024	2.18
1871	1887				1.05			SW¼NE¼	21	33	48	3-15—6-13	.009	1.58

1871	1887			11.60	SW¼NE¼	21	33	48	3-15—4-28	.094	8.70
1871	1887	21.10			NE¼SE¼	21	33	48	3-15—6-13	.172	31.65
1871	1887			15.05	NE¼SE¼	21	33	48	3-15—4-28	.122	11.29
1871	1887	38.55			SE¼SE¼	21	33	48	3-15—6-13	.313	57.83
1871	1887	17.50			NW¼SE¼	21	33	48	3-15—6-13	.142	26.35
1871	1887			18.40	NW¼SE¼	21	33	48	3-15—4-28	.150	13.80
1871	1887	38.70			SW¼SE¼	21	33	48	3-15—6-13	.315	58.05
1871	1887	14.85			SE¼NW¼	21	33	48	3-15—6-13	.121	22.28
1871	1887			7.55	SE¼NW¼	21	33	48	3-15—4-28	.061	5.66
1871	1887	19.60			SW¼NW¼	21	33	48	3-15—6-13	.159	29.40
1871	1887			14.25	SW¼NW¼	21	33	48	3-15—4-28	.116	10.60
1871	1887	7.20			NE¼SW¼	21	33	48	3-15—6-13	.059	10.80
1871	1887			30.25	NE¼SW¼	21	33	48	3-15—4-28	.246	22.69
1871	1887	37.85			SE¼SW¼	21	33	48	3-15—6-13	.308	56.78
1871	1887			39.25	NW¼SW¼	21	33	48	3-15—4-28	.319	29.44
1871	1887	24.10			SW¼SW¼	21	33	48	3-15—6-13	.196	36.15
1871	1887			13.50	SW¼SW¼	21	33	48	3-15—4-28	.110	10.13
1871	1887			1.25	NW¼NE¼	19	33	48	3-15—4-28	.010	.94
1871	1887	2.75			SW¼NE¼	19	33	48	3-15—6-13	.022	4.13
1871	1887			1.75	SW¼NE¼	19	33	48	3-15—4-28	.014	1.31
1871	1887	21.95			NE¼SE¼	19	33	48	3-15—6-13	.178	32.93
1871	1887			11.60	NE¼SE¼	10	33	48	3-15—4-28	.094	8.70
1871	1887	15.50			SE¼SE¼	19	33	48	3-15—6-13	.126	23.25
1871	1887		17.35		SE¼SE¼	19	33	48	3-15—4-28	.141	13.01
1871	1887			2.65	SE¼SE¼	19	33	48	3-15—4-28	.022	1.99
1871	1887	23.50			NW¼SE¼	19	33	48	3-15—6-13	.191	35.25
1871	1887			13.60	NW¼SE¼	19	33	48	3-15—4-28	.111	10.20
1871	1887	17.25			SW¼SE¼	19	33	48	3-15—6-13	.140	25.88
1871	1887		20.30		SW¼SE¼	19	33	48	3-15—4-28	.165	15.23
1871	1887	2.00			NE¼NW¼	19	33	48	3-15—6-13	.016	3.00
1871	1887			4.30	NE¼NW¼	19	33	48	3-15—4-28	.035	3.23
1871	1887	3.70			SE¼SW¼	19	33	48	3-15—6-13	.030	5.56
1871	1887	3.10			NW¼NW¼	19	33	48	3-15—6-13	.025	4.65
1871	1887			17.20	NW¼NW¼	19	33	48	3-15—4-28	.140	12.90
1871	1887	7.70			NW¼NW¼	27	33	48	3-15—6-13	.063	11.55
1871	1887	2.40			SW¼NW¼	22	33	48	3-15—6-13	.020	3.60
1871	1887			12.40	SW¼NW¼	22	33	48	3-15—4-28	.101	9.30
1871	1887	6.55			NW¼SW¼	22	33	48	3-15—6-13	.053	9.83
1871	1887			9.95	NW¼SW¼	22	33	48	3-15—4-28	.081	7.46
1871	1887	16.60			SW¼SW¼	22	33	48	3-15—6-13	.135	24.90
1871	1887	20.55			NE¼NE¼	28	33	48	3-15—6-18	.167	30.83
1871	1887	26.85			NW¼NE¼	28	33	48	3-15—6-13	.218	40.28
1871	1887	23.60			NE¼NW¼	28	33	48	3-15—6-13	.192	35.40
1871	1887			9.00	NE¼NW¼	28	33	48	3-15—4-28	.073	6.75
1871	1887	1.80			NW¼NE¼	30	33	48	3-15—6-13	.015	3.70
1871	1887			25.95	NW¼NE¼	30	33	48	3-15—4-29	.211	19.46
1871	1887	3.75			NE¼NW¼	30	33	48	3-15—6-13	.030	5.63
1871	1897			18.75	NE¼NW¼	30	33	48	3-15—4-28	.152	14.06
1871	1887	1.30			NW¼NW¼	30	33	48	3-15—6-13	.011	1.95
1871	1887			13.60	NW¼NW¼	30	33	48	3-15—4-28	.111	10.20
1871	1887			1.25	NE¼NE¼	25	33	48	3-15—4-28	.010	.94

William Dunphy Estate—Continued.
Source—Humboldt River. Ditch—Blue House Slough.

Date of beneficial use: Nat. mdw.	Cult. area	Construction first initiated: Dams	Ditches	Culture—Acres: Harvest crops	Meadow pasture	Willow and sage pasture	Swamp or overflow	Location: Subdivision	Section	Tp.N.	R.E.	Length of season	Duty of water: C.F.S.	Acre-feet
1871	1888				4.95			SW¼SE¼	29	33	47	3-15—6-13	.040	7.43
1871	1888						5.65	SW¼SE¼	29	33	47	3-15—4-28	.046	4.24
1871	1888				24.70			SE¼SE¼	29	33	47	3-15—6-13	.201	37.05
1871	1888			2.70				NW¼NE¼	32	33	47	3-15—9-15	.022	8.10
1871	1888				5.15			NW¼NE¼	32	33	47	3-15—6-13	.042	7.73
1871	1888			3.95				NE¼NE¼	32	33	47	3-15—9-15	.032	11.85
1871	1888				2.70			NE¼NE¼	32	33	47	3-15—6-13	.022	4.05
1871	1888			9.10				SW¼NE¼	32	33	47	3-15—9-15	.074	27.30
1871	1888			27.85				SE¼NE¼	32	33	47	3-15—9-15	.226	83.55
1871	1888					13.50		SW¼NW¼	31	33	47	3-15—4-28	.110	10.13
1871	1888					8.00		SE¼NW¼	31	33	47	3-15—4-28	.065	6.00
1871	1888					37.15		NW¼NE¼	31	33	47	3-15—4-28	.302	27.86
1871	1888					30.55		NE¼NE¼	31	33	47	3-15—4-28	.248	22.91
1871	1888					23.55		SW¼NE¼	31	33	47	3-15—4-28	.191	17.66
1871	1888					12.70		SE¼NE¼	31	33	47	3-15—4-28	.103	9.53
1871	1888				3.30			NW¼SW¼	31	33	47	3-15—6-13	.027	4.95
1871	1888					.85		NW¼SW¼	31	33	47	3-15—4-28	.007	.64
1871	1888						21.35	NW¼SW¼	31	33	47	3-15—4-28	.074	16.01
1871	1888				5.40			NE¼SW¼	31	33	47	3-15—6-13	.044	8.10
1871	1888					4.30		NE¼SW¼	31	33	47	3-15—4-28	.035	3.23
1871	1888					5.65		SW¼SW¼	29	33	47	3-15—4-28	.046	4.24
1871	1888					9.40		SE¼SW¼	29	33	47	3-15—4-28	.076	7.05
1871	1888					23.55		SW¼SE¼	29	33	47	3-15—4-28	.191	17.66
1871	1888					27.10		NW¼NW¼	32	33	47	3-15—4-28	.220	20.33
1871	1888					18.75		NE¼NW¼	32	33	47	3-15—4-28	.152	14.06
1871	1888			3.10				NW¼NE¼	32	33	47	3-15—9-15	.025	.93
1871	1888				3.90			NW¼NE¼	32	33	47	3-15—6-13	.032	5.85
1871	1888					1.20		NE¼SW¼	30	33	48	3-15—4-28	.010	.90
1871	1888						16.60	NE¼SW¼	30	33	48	3-15—4-28	.135	12.45
1871	1888					1.45		NW¼SE¼	30	33	48	3-15—4-28	.012	1.09
1871	1888						28.15	NW¼SE¼	30	33	48	3-15—4-28	.229	21.11
1871	1888					10.40		SW¼SE¼	30	33	48	3-15—4-28	.085	7.80
1871	1888						23.25	SW¼SE¼	30	33	48	3-15—4-28	.189	17.44
1871	1888					2.35		SE¼SE¼	30	33	48	3-15—4-28	.019	1.76
1871	1888						31.35	SE¼SE¼	30	33	48	3-15—4-28	.255	23.51
1871	1888						2.25	NE¼SE¼	30	33	48	3-15—4-28	.018	1.67
1871	1888						34.05	NW¼SW¼	29	33	48	3-15—4-28	.277	25.52
1871	1888				1.05			SW¼SW¼	29	33	48	3-15—6-13	.009	1.58
1871	1888						36.20	SW¼SW¼	29	33	48	3-15—4-28	.294	27.15
1871	1888				4.45			SE¼SW¼	29	33	48	3-15—6-13	.036	6.68
1871	1888						29.30	SE¼SW¼	29	33	48	3-15—4-28	.238	21.98
1871	1888				2.30			NE¼SW¼	29	33	48	3-15—6-13	.019	3.45
1871	1888						30.30	NE¼SW¼	29	33	48	3-15—4-28	.246	22.73
1871	1888				12.50			NW¼SE¼	29	33	48	3-15—6-13	.102	18.75
1871	1888						21.35	NW¼SE¼	29	33	48	3-15—4-28	.174	16.01

1871	1888				11.05			SW¼SE¼	29	33	48	3-15—6-13	.090	16.58
1871	1888					5.45		SW¼SE¼	29	33	48	3-15—4-28	.044	4.09
1871	1888						12.55	SW¼SE¼	29	33	48	3-15—4-28	.102	9.41
1871	1888				28.85			SE¼SE¼	29	33	48	3-15—6-13	.218	40.28
1871	1888						5.95	SE¼SE¼	29	33	48	3-15—4-28	.048	4.46
1871	1888				7.80			NE¼SE¼	29	33	48	3-15—6-13	.063	11.70
1871	1888					10.85		NE¼SE¼	29	33	48	3-15—4-28	.088	8.14
1871	1888						12.45	NE¼SE¼	29	33	48	3-15—4-28	.101	9.34
1871	1888				7.75			NW¼SW¼	29	33	48	3-15—6-13	.063	11.63
1871	1888						25.45	NW¼SW¼	29	33	48	3-15—4-28	.206	19.09
1871	1888			20.35				NW¼SE¼	27	33	47	3-15—9-15	.165	61.05
1871	1888			24.00				NW¼SE¼	27	33	47	3-15—9-15	.195	82.00
1871	1888			11.00				NW¼SE¼	26	33	47	3-15—9-15	.089	33.00
1871	1888						21.50	NW¼SE¼	26	33	47	3-15—4-28	.175	16.13
1871	1888			17.20				NE¼SE¼	26	33	47	3-15—9-15	.140	51.60
1871	1888				16.40			NE¼SE¼	26	33	47	3-15—6-13	.133	24.60
1871	1888			36.45				NW¼SW¼	26	33	47	3-15—9-15	.296	109.35
1871	1888			35.10				SW¼SW¼	26	33	47	3-15—9-15	.285	105.30
1871	1888			26.55				NE¼SW¼	26	33	47	3-15—9-15	.216	79.65
1871	1888				7.70			NE¼SW¼	26	33	47	3-15—6-13	.063	11.55
1871	1888			13.10				NW¼SW¼	25	33	47	3-15—9-15	.107	39.30
1871	1888				11.00			NW¼SW¼	25	33	47	3-15—6-13	.094	17.40
1871	1888						4.95	NW¼SW¼	25	33	47	3-15—4-28	.040	3.71
1871	1888				21.30			SW¼SW¼	25	33	47	3-15—6-13	.173	31.95
1871	1888					8.00		SW¼SW¼	25	33	47	3-15—4-28	.065	6.00
1871	1888						.40	SW¼SW¼	25	33	47	3-15—4-28	.003	.30
1871	1888				20.70			SE¼SW¼	25	33	47	3-15—6-13	.168	31.05
1871	1888						18.20	SE¼SW¼	25	33	47	3-15—4-28	.148	13.65
1871	1888			.60				NE¼SW¼	25	33	47	3-15—9-15	.005	1.80
1871	1888				15.31			NE¼SW¼	25	33	47	3-15—6-13	.124	22.97
1871	1888						21.15	NE¼SW¼	25	33	47	3-15—4-28	.172	15.86
1871	1888				3.15			NW¼SE¼	25	33	47	3-15—6-13	.026	4.73
1871	1888						21.35	NW¼SE¼	25	33	47	3-15—4-28	.174	16.01
1871	1888				6.50			SW¼SE¼	25	33	47	3-15—6-13	.053	9.75
1871	1888						28.85	SW¼SE¼	25	33	47	3-15—4-28	.235	21.64
1871	1888				10.95			SE¼SE¼	25	33	47	3-15—6-13	.089	16.43
1871	1888						22.95	SE¼SE¼	25	33	47	3-15—4-28	.187	17.21
1871	1888				2.40			NE¼SE¼	25	33	47	3-15—6-13	.020	3.60
1871	1888						33.35	NE¼SE¼	25	33	47	3-15—4-28	.271	25.01
1871	1888			12.00				NW¼NW¼	36	33	47	3-15—9-15	.098	36.00
1871	1888					.55		NW¼NW¼	36	33	47	3-15—4-28	.004	.41
1871	1888						.10	NW¼NW¼	36	33	47	3-15—4-28	.001	.08
1871	1888				1.35			NE¼NW¼	36	33	47	3-15—6-13	.011	2.03
1871	1888						7.70	NE¼NW¼	36	33	47	3-15—4-28	.063	5.78
1871	1888				1.30			NW¼SW¼	30	33	47	3-15—6-13	.011	1.95
1871	1888						29.95	NW¼SW¼	30	33	47	3-15—4-28	.243	22.46
1871	1888				10.15			SW¼SW¼	30	33	47	3-15—6-13	.083	15.23
1871	1888						22.90	SW¼SW¼	30	33	47	3-15—4-28	.186	17.18
1871	1888				17.35			SE¼SW¼	30	33	47	3-15—6-13	.141	26.03
1871	1888						17.65	SE¼SW¼	30	33	47	3-15—4-28	.143	13.24
1871	1888			16.75				SW¼NE¼	32	33	47	3-15—9-15	.128	47.25

William Dunphy Estate—Continued.

Date of beneficial use: Nat. mdw.	Cult. area	Construction first initiated: Dams	Ditches	Culture—Acres: Harvest crops	Meadow pasture	Willow and sage pasture	Swamp or overflow	Location: Subdivision	Section	Tp.N.	R.E.	Length of season	Duty of water: C.F.S.	Acre-feet
1871	1888				6.40			SW¼NE¼	32	33	47	3-15—6-13	.052	9.60
1871	1888						1.35	SW¼NE¼	32	33	47	3-15—4-28	.011	1.01
1871	1888				3.10			NW¼SE¼	32	33	47	3-15—6-13	.025	4.65
1871	1888						5.80	NW¼SE¼	32	33	47	3-15—4-28	.047	4.35
1871	1888					15.15		SW¼SE¼	32	33	47	3-15—4-28	.123	11.63
1871	1888				18.35			NW¼SW¼	32	33	47	3-15—6.13	.149	27.53
1871	1888						6.10	NW¼SW¼	32	33	47	3-15—4-28	.050	4.58
1871	1888			6.40				NW¼SW¼	28	33	47	3-15—9-15	.052	19.20
1871	1888				28.00			SW¼SW¼	28	33	47	3-15—6-13	.228	42.00
1871	1888			18.90				SE¼SW¼	28	33	47	3-15—9-15	.154	56.70
1871	1888				13.05			SE¼SW¼	28	33	47	3-15—6-13	.106	19.58
1871	1888			6.65				NE¼SW¼	28	33	47	3-15—9-15	.054	19.95
1871	1888			19.70				NW¼SE¼	28	33	47	3-15—9-15	.160	59.10
1871	1888			25.95				SW¼SE¼	28	33	47	3-15—9-15	.211	77.85
1871	1888			4.00				SE¼SE¼	28	33	47	3-15—9-15	.033	12.00
1871	1888			34.85				NE¼SE¼	28	33	47	3-15—9-15	.283	104.55
1871	1888			7.70				SE¼NE¼	28	33	47	3-15—9-15	.063	23.10
1871	1888			4.60				NE¼NW¼	33	33	47	3-15—9-15	.037	13.80
1871	1888					2.05		SW¼NW¼	27	33	47	3-15—4-28	.017	1.54
1871	1888			26.60				NW¼SW¼	27	33	47	3-15—9-15	.216	79.80
1871	1888					1.50		NW¼SW¼	27	33	47	3-15—4-28	.012	1.13
1871	1888						8.50	NW¼SW¼	27	33	47	3-15—4-28	.069	6.38
1871	1888			6.25				SW¼SW¼	27	33	47	3-15—9-15	.051	18.75
1871	1888						29.20	SW¼SW¼	27	33	47	3-15—4-28	.237	21.90
1871	1888			6.00				SE¼SW¼	27	33	47	3-15—9-15	.049	18.00
1871	1888						27.80	SE¼SW¼	27	33	47	3-15—4-28	.226	20.85
1871	1888			15.05				NE¼SW¼	27	33	47	3-15—9-15	.122	45.15

Source—Humboldt River. Ditch—Blue House Ditch No. 1.

Date of beneficial use: Nat. mdw.	Cult. area	Construction first initiated: Dams	Ditches	Culture—Acres: Harvest crops	Meadow pasture	Willow and sage pasture	Swamp or overflow	Location: Subdivision	Section	Tp.N.	R.E.	Length of season	Duty of water: C.F.S.	Acre-feet
1871	1888			37.75				SE¼SW¼	26	33	47	3-15—9-15	.307	113.25
1871	1888			33.55				SE¼SE¼	27	33	47	3-15—9-15	.273	100.65
1871	1888			14.95				SW¼SE¼	27	33	47	3-15—9-15	.122	44.85
1871	1888				17.6			SW¼SE¼	27	33	47	3-15—6-13	.158	26.40
1871	1888						1.45	SW¼SE¼	27	33	47	3-15—4-28	.011	1.09
1871	1888			7.00				NW¼NW¼	33	33	47	3-15—9-15	.057	21.00
1871	1888				38.90			SW¼SE¼	26	33	47	3-15—6-13	.316	58.35
1871	1888				36.60			SE¼SE¼	26	33	47	3-15—6-13	.298	54.90
1871	1888			25.65				NE¼NW¼	34	33	47	3-15—9-15	.209	76.95
1871	1888				3.50			NE¼NW¼	34	33	47	3-15—6-13	.028	5.25
1871	1888						8.10	NE¼NW¼	34	33	47	3-15—4-28	.066	6.08
1871	1888			6.75				NE¼NE¼	34	33	47	3-15—9-15	.055	20.25
1871	1888				9.50			NE¼NE¼	34	33	47	3-15—6-13	.077	14.25
1871	1888				12.25			NW¼NW¼	35	33	47	3-15—6-13	.100	18.38
1871	1888					3.30		NW¼NW¼	35	33	47	3-15—4-28	.027	2.48
1871	1888				0.70			SE¼NW¼	35	33	47	3-15—6-13	.006	1.05
1871	1888					4.70		SE¼NW¼	35	33	47	3-15—4-28	.038	3.53

1871	1888					3.15		NE¼ NW¼	35	33	47	3-15—4-28	.026	2.36
1871	1888			12.05				NW¼ NE¼	35	33	47	3-15—9-15	.098	36.15
1871	1888				14.60			NW¼ NE¼	35	33	47	3-15—6-13	.119	21.90
1871	1888					1.90		NW¼ NE¼	35	33	47	3-15—4-28	.015	1.43
1871	1888				20.55			SW¼ NE¼	35	33	47	3-15—6-13	.167	30.83
1871	1888					4.30		SW¼ NE¼	35	33	47	3-15—4-28	.035	3.23
1871	1888						.60	SW¼ NE¼	35	33	47	3-15—4-28	.005	0.4"
1871	1888				26.20			SE¼ NE¼	35	33	47	3-15—6-13	.213	39.30
1871	1888					5.10		SE¼ NE¼	35	33	47	3-15—4-28	.041	3.83
1871	1888				10.55			NE¼ NE¼	35	33	47	3-15—6-13	.086	15.83
1871	1888					12.80		NE¼ NE¼	35	33	47	3-15—4-28	.104	9.60
1871	1888				3.60			NW¼ SW¼	25	33	47	3-15—6-13	.029	5.40
1871	1888					1.70		NW¼ SW¼	25	33	47	3-15—4-28	.014	1.28
1871	1888					3.30		SW¼ SW¼	25	33	47	3-15—4-28	.027	2.48
1871	1888					1.50		NW¼ NW¼	36	33	47	3-15—4-28	.012	1.13

Source—**Humboldt River.** Ditch—**Railroad Slough.**

1871	1887			3.25				SW¼ NE¼	25	33	47	3-15—9-15	.026	9.75
1871	1887						8.15	SW¼ NE¼	25	33	47	3-15—4-28	.066	6.11
1871	1887				33.95			NW¼ NW¼	28	33	48	3-15—6-13	.276	59.93
1871	1887						1.05	NW¼ NW¼	28	33	48	3-15—4-28	.008	0.79
1871	1887				36.35			NE¼ NE¼	29	33	48	3-15—6-13	.296	54.53
1871	1887				5.05			SE¼ NE¼	29	33	48	3-15—6-13	.041	7.58
1871	1887				32.45			NW¼ NE¼	29	33	48	3-15—6-13	.264	48.68
1871	1887						4.10	NW¼ NE¼	29	33	48	3-15—4-28	.033	3.08
1871	1887				9.55			SW¼ NE¼	29	33	48	3-15—6-13	.078	14.33
1871	1887				0.10			NE¼ NW¼	29	33	48	3-15—6-13	.001	0.15
1871	1887						37.55	NE¼ NW¼	29	33	48	3-15—4-28	.305	28.16
1871	1887				1.10			SE¼ NW¼	29	33	48	3-15—6-13	.009	1.65
1871	1887						12.90	SE¼ NW¼	29	33	48	3-15—4-28	.105	9.68
1871	1887				0.15			NW¼ NW¼	29	33	48	3-15—6-13	.001	0.23
1871	1887						38.30	NW¼ NW¼	29	33	48	3-15—4-28	.311	28.73
1871	1887				15.60			SW¼ NW¼	29	33	48	3-15—6-13	.127	23.40
1871	1887						13.00	SE¼ NE¼	30	33	48	3-15—4-28	.106	9.75
1871	1887				0.50			SW¼ NE¼	30	33	48	3-15—6-13	.004	0.75
1871	1887				0.90			NE¼ NE¼	30	33	48	3-15—6-13	.007	1.35
1871	1887			0.40				NW¼ SW¼	27	33	47	3-15—9-15	.003	1.20
1871	1887			17.80				NE¼ SW¼	27	33	47	3-15—9-15	.145	53.40
1871	1887			14.95				NW¼ SE¼	27	33	47	3-15—9-15	.122	44.85
1871	1887			10.50				NE¼ SE¼	27	33	47	3-15—9-15	.085	31.50
1871	1887			20.25				SW¼ NE¼	27	33	47	3-15—9-15	.165	60.75
1871	1887			20.00				SE¼ NE¼	27	33	47	3-15—9-15	.162	60.00
1871	1887			21.30				SW¼ NW¼	26	33	47	3-15—9-15	.173	63.90
1871	1887			20.90				SE¼ NW¼	26	33	47	3-15—9-15	.170	62.70
1871	1887			21.20				SW¼ NE¼	26	33	47	3-15—9-15	.172	63.60
1871	1887			20.05				SE¼ NE¼	26	33	47	3-15—9-15	.163	60.15
1871	1887			3.35				SW¼ NW¼	25	33	47	3-15—9-15	.027	10.05
1871	1887			17.65				SW¼ NW¼	25	33	47	3-15—9-15	.143	52.95
1871	1887			11.05				SE¼ NW¼	25	33	47	3-15—9-15	.090	33.15
1871	1887						9.05	SE¼ NW¼	25	33	47	3-15—4-28	.074	6.79
1871	1887						11.95	NW¼ SE¼	25	33	47	3-15—4-28	.097	8.96
1871	1887			0.10				SW¼ NE¼	25	33	47	3-15—9-15	.001	.30

William Dunphy Estate—Continued.

Date of beneficial use: Nat. mdw.	Cult. area	Construction first initiated: Dams	Ditches	Culture—Acres: Harvest crops	Meadow pasture	Willow and sage pasture	Swamp or overflow	Location: Subdivision	Section	Tp.N.	R.E.	Length of season	Duty of water: C.F.S.	Acre-feet
1871	1887						21.25	SW¼ NE¼	26	33	47	3-15—4-28	.172	15.94
1871	1887						20.80	SE¼ NE¼	25	33	47	3-15—4-28	.169	15.60
1871	1887						20.65	SW¼ NW¼	30	33	48	3-15—4-28	.168	15.49
1871	1887						34.90	NE¼ NE¼	30	33	48	3-15—4-28	.283	26.18
1871	1887				0.50			SE¼ NW¼	30	33	48	3-15—6-13	.004	0.75
1871	1887						15.00	SE¼ NW¼	30	33	48	3-15—4-28	.122	11.25
1871	1887				0.45			SW¼ NW¼	30	33	48	3-15—6-13	.004	0.68
1871	1887						15.00	SW¼ NW¼	30	33	48	3-15—4-28	.122	11.25
1871	1887					.20		SE¼ NW¼	30	33	48	3-15—4-28	.002	0.15
1871	1887						17.80	SE¼ NW¼	30	33	48	3-15—4-28	.145	13.35
1871	1887			15.00				SE¼ NW¼	25	33	47	3-15—9-15	.122	45.00

Source—Humboldt River. Ditch—Rose Canal.

Date of beneficial use: Nat. mdw.	Cult. area	Construction first initiated: Dams	Ditches	Culture—Acres: Harvest crops	Meadow pasture	Willow and sage pasture	Swamp or overflow	Location: Subdivision	Section	Tp.N.	R.E.	Length of season	Duty of water: C.F.S.	Acre-feet
	1877				1.05			NE¼ NE¼	23	33	48	3-15—6-13	.009	1.58
	1877				3.35			SE¼ NE¼	23	33	48	3-15—6-13	.027	5.03
	1877				3.20			NW¼ NE¼	23	33	48	3-15—6-13	.026	4.80
	1877				1.30			SE¼ SE¼	23	33	48	3-15—6-13	.011	1.95
	1877				3.50			NE¼ NW¼	23	33	48	3-15—6-13	.028	5.25
	1887				0.95			NW¼ NW¼	23	33	48	3-15—6-13	.008	1.43
	1877			0.20				SW¼ NE¼	24	33	48	3-15—9-15	.002	.60
	1877			3.85				NW¼ SE¼	24	33	48	3-15—9-15	.031	11.55
	1877			25.15				NE¼ NW¼	24	33	48	3-15—9-15	.204	75.45
	1877			28.45				SE¼ NW¼	24	33	48	3-15—9-15	.231	85.35
	1877			27.05				NW¼ NW¼	24	33	48	3-15—9-15	.220	81.15
	1877			33.30				SW¼ NW¼	24	33	48	3-15—9-15	.271	99.90
	1877			37.25				NE¼ SW¼	24	23	48	3-15—9-15	.303	111.75
	1877			9.40				SE¼ SW¼	24	33	48	3-15—9-15	.076	28.20
	1877						1.25	SE¼ SW¼	24	33	48	3-15—4-28	.010	9.38
	1877			18.10				NW¼ SW¼	24	33	48	3-15—9-15	.147	54.30
	1877				0.90			NW¼ SW¼	24	33	48	3-15—6-13	.007	1.35
	1877						19.90	NW¼ SW¼	24	33	48	3-15—4-28	.162	14.93
	1877			1.20				SW¼ SW¼	24	33	48	3-15—9-15	.010	3.60
	1877				2.60			SW¼ SW¼	24	33	48	3-15—6-13	.021	3.90
	1877						26.40	SW¼ SW¼	24	33	48	3-15—4-28	.215	19.80
	1875						1.75	SW¼ NE¼	25	33	48	3-15—4-28	.014	1.42
	1875			0.25				NE¼ SW¼	25	33	48	3-15—9-15	.002	.75
	1875						14.55	NE¼ SW¼	25	33	48	3-15—4-28	.118	10.91
	1875						1.30	SE¼ NW¼	25	33	48	3-15—4-28	.010	.98
	1875				1.10			NW¼ NW¼	25	33	48	3-15—6-13	.009	1.65
	1875						2.05	NW¼ NW¼	25	33	48	3-15—4-28	.017	1.54
	1877				0.35			SW¼ SW¼	11	33	48	3-15—6-13	.003	.53
	1877			10.75				SE¼ SW¼	13	33	48	3-15—9-15	.087	32.25
	1877			18.60				SW¼ SW¼	13	33	48	3-15—9-15	.151	55.80
	1877					0.15		SE¼ NE¼	14	33	48	3-15—4-28	.001	.11
	1877					0.50		SW¼ NE¼	14	33	48	3-15—4-28	.004	.38
	1875					0.35		NE¼ SE¼	14	33	48	3-15—4-28	.003	.26

	1877				0.60			NE¼NW¼	14	33	48	3-15—6-13	.005	.90
	1877				1.00			SE¼NW¼	14	33	48	3-15—6-13	.008	1.50
	1877				1.50			NW¼NW¼	14	33	48	3-15—6-13	.012	2.25
	1877				0.80			SE¼SW¼	14	33	48	3-15—6-13	.007	1.20
	1877				4.05			SW¼SW¼	14	33	48	3-15—6-13	.033	6.08
	1875				0.20			NW¼NE¼	15	33	48	3-15—6-13	.002	.30
	1875				3.10			SW¼NE¼	15	33	48	3-15—6-13	.025	4.65
	1875				1.45			NE¼SE¼	15	33	48	3-15—6-13	.012	2.18
	1875				1.60			SE¼SE¼	15	33	46	3-15—6-13	.013	2.40
	1875				1.40			NW¼SE¼	15	33	48	3-15—6-13	.011	2.10
	1875				5.35			NE¼NW¼	15	33	48	3-15—6-13	.043	8.03
	1875				9.60			NW¼NW¼	15	33	48	3-15—6-13	.078	14.40
	1875				0.20			SW¼NW¼	15	33	48	3-15—6-13	.002	.30
	1875			3.10				SW¼SE¼	25	33	48	3-15—9-15	.025	9.30
	1875				15.60			SW¼SE¼	25	33	48	3-15—6-13	.127	23.40
	1875					10.00		SW¼SE¼	25	33	48	3-15—4-28	.081	7.50
	1875						1.10	SE¼SE¼	25	33	48	3-15—4-28	.009	.83
	1875						2.30	SW¼NE¼	25	33	48	3-15—4-28	.019	1.73
	1875				2.90			NW¼NE¼	36	33	48	3-15—6-13	.024	4.35
	1875						1.00	NW¼NE¼	36	33	48	3-15—4-28	.008	.75
	1875				3.00			NE¼NE¼	36	33	48	3-15—6-13	.024	4.50
	1875						5.30	NE¼NE¼	36	33	48	3-15—4-28	.043	3.98
	1875				5.65			SE¼NE¼	36	33	48	3-15—6-13	.046	8.48
	1875						1.20	SE¼NE¼	36	33	48	3-15—4-28	.010	.90

Source—**Humboldt River.** Ditch—**Flood Area.**

1870	1887					2.35		SW¼NW¼	25	33	48	3-15—4-28	.019	1.76
1870	1887					1.50		NE¼NE¼	26	33	48	3-15—4-28	.012	1.13
1870	1887						3.90	NE¼NE¼	26	33	48	3-15—4-28	.032	2.93
1870	1887					2.15		SE¼NE¼	26	33	48	3-15—4-28	.017	1.61
1870	1887					1.85		NW¼NE¼	26	33	48	3-15—4-28	.015	1.39
1870	1887						15.85	NW¼NE¼	26	33	48	3-15—4-28	.129	11.89
1870	1887				7.95			NE¼SW¼	31	33	47	3-15—6-13	.065	11.93
1870	1887					7.03		NW¼SE¼	31	33	47	3-15—4-28	.057	5.27
1870	1887					3.10		NE¼SE¼	31	33	47	3-15—4-28	.025	2.33
1870	1887				8.30			NW¼NE¼	36	33	47	3-15—6-13	.067	12.45
1870	1887						20.75	NW¼NE¼	36	33	47	3-15—4-28	.169	15.56
1870	1887				2.70			NE¼NE¼	36	33	47	3-15—6-13	.022	4.05
1870	1887					8.35		NE¼NE¼	36	33	47	3-15—4-28	.068	6.26
1870	1887						17.05	NE¼NE¼	36	33	47	3-15—4-28	.139	12.79
1870	1887				5.85			NW¼NW¼	31	33	47	3-15—6-13	.048	8.78
1870	1887						22.95	NW¼NW¼	31	33	47	3-15—4-28	.187	17.21
1870	1887				2.05			NE¼NW¼	31	33	47	3-15—6-13	.017	3.08
1870	1887					13.75		NE¼NW¼	31	33	47	3-15—4-28	.112	10.31
1870	1887						7.95	NE¼NW¼	31	33	47	3-15—4-28	.065	5.96
1870	1887				14.10			NW¼NE¼	31	33	47	3-15—6-13	.115	21.15
1870	1887						7.80	NW¼NE¼	31	33	47	3-15—4-28	.063	5.85
1870	1887				19.35			NE¼NE¼	31	33	47	3-15—6-13	.157	29.03
1870	1887					1.95		NE¼NE¼	31	33	47	3-15—4-28	.016	1.46
1870	1887						4.90	NE¼NE¼	31	33	47	3-15—4-28	.040	3.68
1870	1887				13.85			NW¼NW¼	32	33	47	3-15—6-13	.113	20.78
1870	1887						20.80	NW¼NW¼	32	33	47	3-15—4-28	.169	15.60

William Dunphy Estate—Continued.

Date of beneficial use: Nat. mdw.	Date of beneficial use: Cult. area	Construction first initiated: Dams	Construction first initiated: Ditches	Culture—Acres: Harvest crops	Culture—Acres: Meadow pasture	Culture—Acres: Willow and sage pasture	Culture—Acres: Swamp or overflow	Location: Subdivision	Location: Section	Location: Tp.N.	Location: R.E.	Length of season	Duty of water: C.F.S.	Duty of water: Acre-feet
1870	1887	......	......	....	17.65	......	......	NE¼NW¼	32	33	47	3-15—6-13	.143	26.48
1870	1887	......	......	....	......	7.45	......	NE¼NW¼	32	33	47	3-15—4-28	.061	5.59
1870	1887	......	......	....	......	......	5.80	NE¼NW¼	32	33	47	3-15—4-28	.047	4.35
1870	1887	......	......	....	26.70	......	......	NE¼SW¼	28	33	47	3-15—6-13	.217	40.05
1870	1887	......	......	....	......	4.15	......	NE¼SE¼	28	33	47	3-15—4-28	.034	3.11
1870	1887	......	......	....	......	7.80	......	SW¼NE¼	28	33	47	3-15—4-28	.063	5.85
1870	1887	......	......	....	......	......	5.30	SW¼NE¼	28	33	47	3-15—4-28	.043	3.98
1870	1887	......	......	....	3.35	......	......	SE¼NE¼	28	33	47	3-15—6-13	.027	5.03
1870	1887	......	......	....	......	14.25	......	SE¼NE¼	28	33	47	3-15—4-28	.116	10.69
1870	1887	......	......	....	.25	......	......	SW¼NW¼	27	53	48	3-15—6-13	.002	.38
1870	1887	......	......	....	......	14.45	......	SW¼NW¼	27	33	48	3-15—4-28	.117	8.59
1870	1887	......	......	....	......	.90	......	SE¼NW¼	27	33	48	3-15—4-28	.007	.68
1870	1887	......	......	....	......	.40	......	NW¼SW¼	27	33	48	3-15—4-28	.003	.30
1870	1887	......	......	....	20.70	......	......	NE¼SE¼	27	53	48	3-15—6-13	.168	31.05
1870	1887	......	......	....	......	4.35	......	NE¼SE¼	27	33	48	3-15—4-28	.035	3.26
1870	1887	......	......	....	11.15	......	......	SW¼NE¼	27	33	48	3-15—6-13	.091	16.73
1870	1887	......	......	....	......	5.85	......	SW¼NE¼	27	33	48	3-15—4-28	.048	4.39
1870	1887	......	......	....	......	1.40	......	SW¼NW¼	26	33	48	3-15—4-28	.011	1.05
1870	1887	......	......	....	9.60	......	......	NW¼SW¼	26	33	48	3-15—6-13	.078	14.40
1870	1887	......	......	....	......	9.05	......	NW¼SW¼	26	33	48	3-15—4-28	.074	6.79
1870	1887	......	......	....	10.25	......	......	NE¼SW¼	26	33	48	3-15—6-13	.083	15.38
1870	1887	......	......	....	......	10.10	......	NE¼SW¼	26	33	48	3-15—4-28	.082	7.58

Source—Humboldt River. Ditch—New Dam Ditch.

Date of beneficial use: Nat. mdw.	Date of beneficial use: Cult. area	Construction first initiated: Dams	Construction first initiated: Ditches	Culture—Acres: Harvest crops	Culture—Acres: Meadow pasture	Culture—Acres: Willow and sage pasture	Culture—Acres: Swamp or overflow	Location: Subdivision	Location: Section	Location: Tp.N.	Location: R.E.	Length of season	Duty of water: C.F.S.	Duty of water: Acre-feet
......	1902	......	......	....	21.95	......	......	SE¼SW¼	22	33	48	3-15—6-13	.178	32.93
......	1902	......	......	....	14.15	......	......	SW¼SW¼	22	33	48	3-15—6-13	.115	21.23
......	1902	......	......	....	12.90	......	......	NW¼NE¼	27	33	48	3-15—6-13	.105	19.35
......	1902	......	......	....	15.65	......	......	NW¼NW¼	27	35	48	3-15—6-13	.127	23.48
......	1902	......	......	....	......	......	7.55	NW¼SE¼	30	33	48	3-15—4-28	.061	5.66
......	1902	......	......	....	......	1.70	......	NE¼SE¼	30	33	48	3-15—4-28	.014	1.28
......	1902	......	......	....	......	......	31.75	NE¼SE¼	30	33	48	3-15—4-28	.258	23.81
......	1902	......	......	....	......	3.00	......	SW¼NE¼	30	33	48	3-15—4-28	.024	2.25
......	1902	......	......	....	......	......	13.30	SW¼NE¼	30	33	48	3-15—4-28	.108	9.98
......	1902	......	......	....	......	9.40	......	SE¼NE¼	30	33	48	3-15—4-28	.076	7.05
......	1902	......	......	....	......	......	7.55	SE¼NE¼	30	33	48	3-15—4-28	.061	5.66
......	1902	......	......	....	6.20	......	......	SW¼NW¼	29	33	48	3-15—6-13	.050	9.30
......	1902	......	......	....	......	......	10.90	SW¼NW¼	29	33	48	3-15—4-28	.089	8.18
......	1902	......	......	....	19.05	......	......	SE¼NW¼	29	33	48	3-15—6-13	.155	28.58
......	1902	......	......	....	......	......	.40	SE¼NW¼	29	33	48	3-15—4-28	.003	.30
......	1902	......	......	....	......	......	14.60	NW¼SW¼	29	33	48	3-15—4-28	.119	10.95
......	1902	......	......	....	20.60	......	......	SW¼NE¼	29	33	48	3-15—6-13	.167	30.90
......	1902	......	......	....	18.00	......	......	SE¼NE¼	29	33	48	3-15—6-13	.146	27.00
......	1902	......	......	....	......	......	1.50	SE¼NE¼	29	33	48	3-15—4-28	.012	1.13
......	1902	......	......	....	......	......	18.80	SW¼NW¼	28	33	48	3-15—4-28	.153	14.10
......	1902	......	......	....	4.30	......	......	SE¼NW¼	28	82	48	3-15—6-13	.035	6.45
......	1902	......	......	....	......	......	16.80	SE¼NW¼	28	83	48	3-15—4-28	.187	12.60

	1902				7.75			NW¼SW¼	28	33	48	3-15—6-13	.063	11.62
	1902						25.45	NW¼SW¼	28	33	48	3-15—4-28	.207	19.09
	1902						.95	NE¼SW¼	28	33	48	3-15—4-28	.008	.71
	1902						5.20	NW¼SE¼	28	33	48	3-15—4-28	.042	3.90
	1902				7.20			NW¼NW¼	27	33	48	3-15—6-13	.059	10.80
	1902				6.55			SW¼NW¼	27	33	48	3-15—6-13	.053	9.82
	1902					.20		SW¼NW¼	27	33	48	3-15—4-28	.002	.15
	1902				13.00			NE¼NE¼	28	33	48	3-15—6-13	.106	19.50
	1902				15.20			SE¼NE¼	28	33	48	3-15—6-13	.124	22.80
	1902					1.65		SE¼NE¼	28	33	48	3-15—4-28	.013	1.24
	1902				8.25			NW¼NE¼	28	33	48	3-15—6-13	.067	12.38
	1902				17.10			SW¼NE¼	28	33	48	3-15—6-13	.139	25.65
	1902				3.05			NE¼NW¼	28	33	48	3-15—6-13	.025	4.58
	1902				18.00			SE¼NW¼	28	33	48	3-15—6-13	.146	27.00
	1902						4.85	SW¼NW¼	28	33	48	3-15—4-28	.039	3.64
	1902				9.55			SW¼NW¼	28	33	48	3-15—6-13	.078	14.33
	1902				9.90			SE¼NE¼	29	33	48	3-15—6-13	.080	14.85
	1902				4.25			SW¼NE¼	29	33	48	3-15—6-13	.035	6.38
	1902				.20			SE¼NW¼	29	33	48	3-15—6-13	.002	.30

Source—**Humboldt River.** Ditch—**Argenta Slough.**

1871	1890					11.95		NW¼NE¼	2	32	47	3-15—4-28	.156	8.96
1871	1890					4.95		NE¼NE¼	2	32	47	3-15—4-28	.040	3.71
1871	1890				.70			SE¼SW¼	34	33	47	3-15—6-13	.006	1.05
1871	1890				1.80			SW¼SE¼	34	33	47	3-15—6-13	.015	2.70
1871	1890						18.60	SW¼SE¼	34	33	47	3-15—4-28	.151	13.95
1871	1890				1.50			NW¼SW¼	36	33	47	3-15—6-13	.012	2.25
1871	1890				26.55			SW¼SW¼	36	33	47	3-15—6-13	.216	39.83
1871	1890				37.35			SE¼SW¼	36	33	47	3-15—6-13	.304	56.03
1871	1890				10.20			NE¼SW¼	36	33	47	3-15—6-13	.083	15.30
1871	1890				26.25			NW¼SE¼	36	33	47	3-15—6-13	.213	39.38
1871	1890				21.50			NE¼SE¼	36	33	47	3-15—6-13	.175	32.25
1871	1890						9.75	NE¼SE¼	36	33	47	3-15—4-28	.079	7.31
1871	1890						31.30	SW¼NE¼	36	33	47	3-15—4-28	.254	23.48
1871	1890					2.40		SE¼NE¼	36	33	47	3-15—4-28	.020	1.80
1871	1890						34.30	SE¼NE¼	36	33	47	3-15—4-28	.279	25.73
1871	1890				6.45			SW¼NW¼	31	33	47	3-15—6-13	.052	9.68
1871	1890						29.45	SW¼NW¼	31	33	47	3-15—4-28	.239	22.09
1871	1890				5.90			SE¼NW¼	31	33	47	3-15—6-13	.048	8.85
1871	1890					12.60		SE¼NW¼	31	33	47	3-15—4-28	.102	9.45
1871	1890				4.20			SW¼SW¼	33	33	47	3-15—6-13	.033	6.30
1871	1890					4.65		SW¼SW¼	33	33	47	3-15—4-28	.036	3.49
1871	1890						5.55	SW¼SW¼	33	33	47	3-15—4-28	.043	4.16
1871	1890					16.10		SW¼NW¼	4	32	47	3-15—4-28	.131	12.08
1871	1890					.40		NW¼SW¼	4	32	47	3-15—4-28	.003	.30
1871	1890					4.80		NE¼SW¼	4	32	47	3-15—4-28	.040	3.60
1871	1890					12.35		SE¼NW¼	4	32	47	3-15—4-28	.100	9.26
1871	1890					.20		NW¼SE¼	4	32	47	3-15—4-28	.002	.15
1871	1890					13.10		SW¼NE¼	4	32	47	3-15—4-28	.107	9.83
1871	1890					9.50		SE¼NE¼	4	32	47	3-15—4-28	.077	7.13
1871	1890					14.70		SW¼NW¼	3	32	47	3-15—4-28	.120	11.03
1871	1890					12.50		NW¼SW¼	3	32	47	3-15—4-28	.102	9.38

William Dunphy Estate—Continued.

Date of beneficial use: Nat. mdw.	Cult. area	Construction first initiated: Dams	Ditches	Culture—Acres: Harvest crops	Meadow pasture	Willow and sage pasture	Swamp or overflow	Location: Subdivision	Section	Tp. N.	R. E.	Length of season	Duty of water: C.F.S.	Acre-feet
1871	1890					16.65		SE¼NW¼	3	32	47	3-15—4-28	.135	12.49
1871	1890					13.15		NE¼SW¼	3	32	47	3-15—4-28	.107	10.13
1871	1890				6.50			NW¼SE¼	3	32	47	3-15—6-13	.053	9.75
1871	1890				4.95			NE¼SE¼	3	32	47	3-15—6-13	.040	7.43
1871	1890				15.75			NE¼NE¼	3	32	47	3-15—6-13	.128	23.63
1871	1890				9.00			NW¼NE¼	3	32	47	3-15—6-13	.073	13.50
1871	1890					35.85		NW¼NW¼	2	32	47	3-15—4-28	.291	26.89
1871	1890						4.40	NW¼NE¼	5	33	47	3-15—4-28	.036	3.30
1871	1890						8.15	NE¼NE¼	5	33	47	3-15—4-28	.066	14.88
1871	1890						13.70	SW¼NE¼	5	33	47	3-15—4-28	.111	10.28
1871	1890						30.25	SE¼NE¼	5	33	47	3-15—4-28	.246	22.69
1871	1890						3.50	NW¼SE¼	5	33	47	3-15—4-28	.028	2.68
1871	1890						7.20	NE¼SE¼	5	33	47	3-15—4-28	.059	5.40
1871	1890			34.60				NW¼NW¼	6	32	47	3-15—9-15	.280	103.80
1871	1890						3.00	NW¼NW¼	6	32	47	3-15—4-28	.024	2.25
1871	1890			31.18				NE¼NW¼	6	32	47	3-15—9-15	.252	93.54
1871	1890						2.60	NE¼NW¼	6	32	47	3-15—4-28	.021	1.95
1871	1890			1.18				SW¼NW¼	6	32	47	3-15—9-15	.010	3.54
1871	1890					3.45		SW¼NW¼	6	32	47	3-15—4-28	.020	2.59
1871	1890						34.20	SW¼NW¼	6	32	47	3-15—4-28	.277	25.65
1871	1890			2.15				SE¼NW¼	6	32	47	3-15—9-15	.017	6.45
1871	1890				4.75			SE¼NW¼	6	32	47	3-15—6-13	.039	7.13
1871	1890					8.15		SE¼NW¼	6	32	47	3-15—4-28	.066	6.11
1871	1890						21.60	SE¼NW¼	6	32	47	3-15—4-28	.176	16.20
1871	1890			15.05				NE¼NE¼	6	32	47	3-15—9-15	.122	45.15
1871	1890				7.65			NE¼NE¼	6	32	47	3-15—6-13	.062	11.48
1871	1890					1.15		NE¼NE¼	6	32	47	3-15—4-28	.009	.86
1871	1890			30.45				NW¼NE¼	6	32	47	3-15—9-15	.248	91.35
1871	1890					2.85		NW¼NE¼	6	32	47	3-15—4-28	.023	2.14
1871	1890				12.65			SW¼NE¼	6	32	47	3-15—6-13	.103	18.96
1871	1890			1.55				SE¼NE¼	6	32	47	3-15—9-15	.013	4.65
1871	1890				21.85			SE¼NE¼	6	32	47	3-15—6-13	.178	32.78
1871	1890					14.10		SE¼NE¼	6	32	47	3-15—4-28	.158	10.58
1871	1890						4.90	NE¼NW¼	5	32	47	3-15—4-28	.040	3.68
1871	1890						6.85	NW¼NW¼	5	32	47	3-15—4-28	.056	5.14
1871	1890						14.70	SE¼NW¼	5	32	47	3-15—4-28	.120	11.03
1871	1890						4.15	SW¼NW¼	5	32	47	3-15—4-28	.034	3.11
1871	1890						4.25	NW¼NE¼	5	32	47	3-15—1-28	.035	3.19
1871	1890						19.70	SW¼NE¼	5	32	47	3-15—4-28	.160	14.78
1871	1890					33.60		NE¼NW¼	2	32	47	3-15—4-28	.273	25.20
1871	1890					26.70		SW¼NW¼	2	32	47	3-15—4-28	.217	20.08
1891	1890					9.40		SE¼NW¼	2	32	47	3-15—4-28	.076	7.05
1871	1890						8.15	SE¼NW¼	31	33	47	3-15—4-28	.066	6.11
1871	1890				.35			NW¼SW¼	31	33	47	3-15—6-13	.008	.58
1871	1890						10.95	NW¼SW¼	31	33	47	3-15—4-28	.088	8.21
1871	1890				14.40			SW¼NE¼	31	33	47	3-15—6-13	.117	21.60

1871	1890						13.15	SW¼NE¼	31	33	47	3-15—4-28	.107	9.86
1871	1890				20.55			SE¼NE¼	31	33	47	3-15—6-13	.167	30.83
1871	1890					5.90		SE¼NE¼	31	33	47	3-15—4-28	.048	8.98

Source—Humboldt River. Ditch—Bull Field Slough.

1879	1904				6.20			NE¼NE¼	34	33	47	3-15—6-13	.050	9.30
1879	1904				9.55			NW¼NW¼	35	33	47	3-15—6-13	.078	14.33
1879	1904					1.30		NW¼NW¼	35	33	47	3-15—4-28	.011	.98
1879	1904				15.25			SW¼NW¼	35	33	47	3-15—6-13	.124	22.88
1879	1904						17.65	SW¼NW¼	35	33	47	3-15—4-28	.143	13.24
1879	1904				4.90			SE¼NW¼	35	33	47	3-15—6-13	.048	7.35
1879	1904					4.50		SE¼NW¼	35	33	47	3-15—4-28	.037	3.38
1879	1904						11.70	SE¼NW¼	35	33	47	3-15—4-28	.095	8.79
1879	1904			8.60				NE¼NW¼	35	33	47	3-15—9-15	.070	25.80
1879	1904				19.05			NE¼NW¼	35	33	47	3-15—6-13	.155	28.58
1879	1904				.30			NW¼SW¼	35	33	47	3-15—6-13	.002	.45
1879	1904						31.00	NW¼SW¼	35	33	47	3-15—4-28	.252	23.25
1879	1904				22.15			SW¼SW¼	35	33	47	3-15—6-13	.180	33.23
1879	1904						15.95	SW¼SW¼	35	33	47	3-15—4-28	.130	11.96
1879	1904				1.65			SE¼SW¼	35	33	47	3-15—6-13	.013	2.48
1879	1904						32.35	SE¼SW¼	35	33	47	3-15—4-28	.263	24.38
1879	1904				.80			NE¼SW¼	35	33	47	3-15—6-13	.007	1.20
1879	1904						33.05	NE¼SW¼	35	33	47	3-15—4-28	.269	24.79
1879	1904				11.50			NW¼SE¼	35	33	47	3-15—6-13	.093	17.25
1879	1904				9.45			SE¼SW¼	33	33	47	3-15—6-13	.077	14.18
1879	1904					3.05		SE¼SW¼	33	33	47	3-15—4-28	.025	2.29
1879	1904						20.95	SE¼SW¼	33	33	47	3-15—4-28	.170	15.71
1879	1904				.80			NE¼SW¼	33	33	47	3-15—6-13	.007	1.20
1879	1904					8.30		NE¼SW¼	33	33	47	3-15—4-28	.067	6.23
1879	1904				.10			NE¼NE¼	33	33	47	3-15—6-13	.001	.15
1879	1904				12.30			NW¼SE¼	33	33	47	3-15—6-13	.100	18.45
1879	1904					4.70		NW¼SE¼	33	33	47	3-15—4-28	.038	3.53
1879	1904				7.50			SW¼SE¼	33	33	47	3-15—6-13	.061	11.25
1879	1904						28.45	SW¼SE¼	33	33	47	3-15—4-28	.231	21.34
1879	1904				17.00			SE¼SE¼	33	33	47	3-15—6-13	.138	25.50
1879	1904						18.65	SE¼SE¼	33	33	47	3-15—4-28	.152	13.99
1879	1904				24.45			NE¼SE¼	33	33	47	3-15—6-13	.199	36.68
1879	1904					9.30		NE¼SE¼	33	33	47	3-15—4-28	.076	6.98
1879	1904			21.45				NW¼NE¼	33	33	47	3-15—9-15	.174	64.35
1879	1904						14.15	NW¼NE¼	33	33	47	3-15—4-28	.115	10.61
1879	1904					2.35		SW¼NE¼	33	33	47	3-15—4-28	.019	1.76
1879	1904				.70			SE¼NE¼	33	33	47	3-15—6-13	.006	1.05
1879	1904					5.20		SE¼NE¼	33	33	47	3-15—4-28	.042	3.90
1879	1904				37.65			NW¼SW¼	34	33	47	3-15—6-13	.306	56.48
1879	1904						2.15	NW¼SW¼	34	33	47	3-15—4-28	.017	1.61
1879	1904				4.35			SW¼SW¼	34	33	47	3-15—6-13	.035	6.53
1879	1904						29.85	SW¼SW¼	34	33	47	3-15—4-28	.243	22.40
1879	1904						32.95	SE¼SW¼	34	33	47	3-15—4-28	.268	24.71
1879	1904				15.90			NE¼SW¼	34	33	47	3-15—6-13	.129	23.85
1879	1904					.90		NE¼SW¼	34	33	47	3-15—4-28	.007	.68
1879	1904						19.90	NE¼SW¼	34	33	47	3-15—4-28	.162	14.93
1879	1904				22.10			NW¼SE¼	34	33	47	3-15—6-13	.180	33.15

William Dunphy Estate—Continued.

Date of beneficial use—Nat. mdw.	Cult. area	Construction first initiated—Dams	Ditches	Culture—Acres—Harvest crops	Meadow pasture	Willow and sage pasture	Swamp or overflow	Location—Subdivision	Section	Tp.N.	R.E.	Length of season	Duty of water—C.F.S.	Acre-feet
1879	1904					1.10		NW¼SE¼	34	33	47	3-15—4-28	.009	.83
1879	1904						11.40	NW¼SE¼	34	33	47	3-15—4-28	.093	8.55
1879	1904				13.70			SW¼SE¼	34	33	47	3-15—6-13	.111	20.55
1879	1904				17.30			SE¼SE¼	34	33	47	3-15—6-13	.141	25.97
1879	1904						17.75	SE¼SE¼	34	33	47	3-15—4-28	.144	13.31
1879	1904				17.50			NE¼SE¼	34	33	47	3-15—6-13	.142	26.25
1879	1904						13.00	NE¼SE¼	34	33	47	3-15—4-28	.106	9.75
1879	1904				1.40			SW¼NE¼	34	33	47	3-15—6-13	.011	2.10
1879	1904					1.60		SW¼NE¼	34	33	47	3-15—4-28	.013	1.20
1879	1904						1.20	SW¼NE¼	34	33	47	3-15—4-28	.010	.90
1879	1904						24.40	NW¼SE¼	35	33	47	3-15—4-28	.198	18.30
1879	1904				.30			SW¼SE¼	35	33	47	3-15—6-13	.002	.45
1879	1904						34.60	SW¼SE¼	35	33	47	3-15—4-28	.281	25.95
1879	1904				.30			SE¼SE¼	35	33	47	3-15—6-13	.002	.45
1879	1904						34.15	SE¼SE¼	35	33	47	3-15—4-28	.278	25.61
1879	1904				17.65			NE¼SE¼	35	33	47	3-15—6-13	.143	26.48
1879	1904						14.65	NE¼SE¼	35	33	47	3-15—4-28	.119	10.99
1879	1904					4.50		NW¼NE¼	35	33	47	3-15—4-28	.037	3.38
1879	1904					2.70		SW¼NE¼	35	33	47	3-15—4-28	.022	2.03
1879	1904					4.45		NE¼NE¼	35	33	47	3-15—4-28	.036	3.34
1879	1904				.15			NW¼NW¼	36	33	47	3-15—6-13	.001	.23
1879	1904					2.65		NW¼NW¼	36	33	47	3-15—4-28	.022	1.99
1879	1904				4.45			SW¼NW¼	36	33	47	3-15—6-13	.036	6.68
1879	1904				2.25			NW¼SW¼	36	33	47	3-15—6-13	.018	3.38
1879	1904						2.40	NW¼SW¼	36	33	47	3-15—4-28	.020	1.80
1879	1904						4.55	SW¼SW¼	36	33	47	3-15—4-28	.037	3.41
1879	1904				3.95			NW¼NW¼	36	33	47	3-15—6-13	.032	5.93
1879	1904					8.00		NW¼NW¼	36	33	47	3-15—4-28	.065	6.00
1879	1904						.55	NW¼NW¼	36	33	47	3-15—4-28	.004	.41
1879	1904				25.55			SW¼NW¼	36	33	47	3-15—6-13	.208	38.33
1879	1904						.45	SW¼NW¼	36	33	47	3-15—4-28	.004	.34
1879	1904				22.45			SE¼NW¼	36	33	47	3-15—6-13	.183	33.68
1879	1904						12.55	SE¼NW¼	36	33	47	3-15—4-28	.102	9.41
1879	1904						19.10	NE¼NW¼	36	33	47	3-15—4-28	.155	14.33
1879	1904				14.95			NW¼SW¼	36	33	47	3-15—6-13	.122	22.43
1879	1904						10.60	NW¼SW¼	36	33	47	3-15—4-28	.086	7.95
1879	1904						.20	SW¼SW¼	36	33	47	3-15—4-28	.002	.15
1879	1904				13.05			NE¼SW¼	36	33	47	3-15—6-13	.106	19.58
1879	1904						6.80	NE¼SW¼	36	33	47	3-15—4-28	.055	5.10
1879	1904						5.00	NW¼SE¼	36	33	47	3-15—4-28	.040	3.75
1879	1904				8.90			SE¼NE¼	34	33	47	3-15—6-13	.072	13.35
1879	1904					1.65		SE¼NE¼	34	33	47	3-15—4-28	.013	1.24
1879	1904						17.15	SE¼NE¼	34	33	47	3-15—4-28	.139	12.86

Source Humboldt River. Ditch Kampas Swale.

1871	1886	....	....	.15	....	....	....	NE¼SE¼	32	33	47	3-15-9-15	.001	0.45
1871	1886	....	....	....	2.30	....	....	NE¼SE¼	32	33	47	3-15-6-13	.010	3.45
1871	1886	....	....	....	6.75	....	....	SW¼SE¼	32	33	47	3-15-6-13	.055	10.13
1871	1886	....	....	....	....	4.10	....	SW¼SE¼	32	33	47	3-15-4-28	.033	3.08
1871	1886	....	....	....	14.35	....	....	SE¼SE¼	32	33	47	3-15-6-13	.117	21.53
1871	1886	....	....	....	1.20	....	....	NW¼SE¼	32	33	47	3-15-6-13	.010	1.80
1871	1886	....	....	....	....	7.60	....	SW¼NE¼	31	33	47	3-15-4-28	.062	5.70
1871	1886	....	....	....	....	24.20	....	SE¼NE¼	31	33	47	3-15-4-28	.197	18.15
1871	1886	....	....	....	....	24.17	....	NW¼SE¼	31	33	47	3-15-4-28	.197	18.13
1871	1886	....	....	....	....	28.05	....	NE¼SE¼	31	33	47	3-15-4-28	.228	21.04
1871	1886	....	....	....	....	4.75	....	NW¼NW¼	32	33	47	3-15-4-28	.039	3.56
1871	1886	....	....	....	....	31.80	....	SE¼NW¼	32	33	47	3-15-4-28	.259	23.85
1871	1886	....	....	....	....	38.60	....	SW¼NW¼	32	33	47	3-15-4-28	.314	28.95
1871	1886	....	....	....	14.20	....	....	NE¼SW¼	32	33	47	3-15-6-13	.115	21.30
1871	1886	....	....	....	....	....	4.55	NE¼SW¼	32	33	47	3-15-4-28	.037	3.41
1871	1886	....	....	26.45	....	....	....	SW¼NW¼	33	33	47	3-15-9-15	.215	79.35
1871	1886	....	....	....	....	....	8.50	SW¼NW¼	33	33	47	3-15-4-28	.069	6.38
1871	1886	....	....	24.70	....	....	....	SE¼NW¼	33	33	47	3-15-9-15	.200	74.10
1871	1886	....	....	....	....	....	10.70	SE¼NW¼	33	33	47	3-15-4-28	.087	8.03
1871	1886	....	....	17.75	....	....	....	NE¼NW¼	33	33	47	3-15-9-15	.144	53.25
1871	1886	....	....	....	....	....	10.70	NE¼NW¼	33	33	47	3-15-4-28	.087	8.03
1871	1886	....	....	....	....	1.60	....	NW¼SW¼	33	33	47	3-15-4-28	.013	1.20
1871	1886	....	....	....	....	....	31.90	NW¼SW¼	33	33	47	3-15-4-28	.259	23.93
1871	1886	....	....	....	....	3.90	....	SW¼SW¼	33	33	47	3-15-4-28	.032	2.93
1871	1886	....	....	....	....	....	3.85	SW¼SW¼	33	33	47	3-15-4-28	.031	2.89
1871	1886	....	....	....	....	.60	....	NE¼SW¼	33	33	47	3-15-4-28	.005	0.45
1871	1886	....	....	....	....	....	15.80	NE¼SW¼	33	33	47	3-15-4-28	.128	11.85
1871	1886	....	....	20.85	....	....	....	NE¼NE¼	33	33	47	3-15-9-15	.170	62.55
1871	1886	....	....	....	.30	....	....	NE¼NE¼	33	33	47	3-15-6-13	.002	0.45
1871	1886	....	....	....	....	....	10.70	NE¼NE¼	33	33	47	3-15-4-28	.087	8.03
1871	1886	....	....	....	3.05	....	....	NW¼SE¼	33	33	47	3-15-6-13	.025	4.58
1871	1886	....	....	....	....	....	8.05	NW¼SE¼	33	33	47	3-15-4-28	.065	6.04
1871	1886	....	....	14.90	....	....	....	SW¼NE¼	33	33	47	3-15-9-15	.121	44.70
1871	1886	....	....	....	2.20	....	....	SW¼NE¼	33	33	47	3-15-6-13	.018	3.30
1871	1886	....	....	....	....	....	13.70	SW¼NE¼	33	33	47	3-15-4-28	.111	10.28
1871	1886	....	....	0.70	....	....	....	SE¼NE¼	33	33	47	3-15-9-15	.006	2.10
1871	1886	....	....	....	15.85	....	....	SE¼NE¼	33	33	47	3-15-6-13	.129	23.78
1871	1886	....	....	....	....	2.95	....	SE¼NE¼	33	33	47	3-15-4-28	.024	2.21
1871	1886	....	....	....	....	....	2.10	SE¼NE¼	33	33	47	3-15-4-28	.020	1.80
1871	1886	....	....	....	27.00	....	....	NW¼NW¼	34	33	47	3-15-6-13	.220	40.50
1871	1886	....	....	....	....	2.30	....	NW¼NW¼	34	33	47	3-15-4-28	.017	1.73
1871	1886	....	....	....	....	....	6.10	NW¼NW¼	34	33	47	3-15-4-28	.048	4.58
1871	1886	....	....	....	19.45	....	....	SW¼NW¼	34	33	47	3-15-6-13	.158	29.18
1871	1886	....	....	....	....	9.70	....	SW¼NW¼	34	33	47	3-15-4-28	.077	7.28
1871	1886	....	....	....	27.80	....	....	SE¼NW¼	34	33	47	3-15-6-13	.226	41.70
1871	1886	....	....	....	....	5.70	....	SE¼NW¼	34	33	47	3-15-4-28	.045	4.28
1871	1886	....	....	34.00	....	....	....	NW¼NE¼	34	33	47	3-15-9-15	.276	102.00
1871	1886	....	....	....	2.20	....	....	NW¼NE¼	34	33	47	3-15-6-13	.016	3.30
1871	1886	....	....	....	....	.10	....	NW¼NE¼	34	33	47	3-15-4-28	.001	0.08
1871	1886	....	....	2.95	....	....	....	SW¼NE¼	34	33	47	3-15-9-15	.022	8.85
1871	1886	....	....	....	17.20	....	....	SW¼NE¼	34	33	47	3-15-6-13	.140	25.80
1871	1886	....	....	....	....	4.75	....	SW¼NE¼	34	33	47	3-15-4-28	.037	3.56

Claimant—**Russell Land and Cattle Co.** Proof No. 00172

Source—**Humboldt River.** Ditch—**Southside Ditch, 1879; Northside Ditch, 1887.**

Date of beneficial use: Nat. mdw.	Date of beneficial use: Cult. area	Construction first initiated: Dams	Construction first initiated: Ditches	Culture—Acres: Harvest crops	Culture—Acres: Meadow pasture	Culture—Acres: Willow and sage pasture	Culture—Acres: Swamp or overflow	Location: Subdivision	Location: Section	Location: Tp.N.	Location: R.E.	Length of season	Duty of water: C.F.S.	Duty of water: Acre-feet
	1887			5.10				SE¼SW¼	24	33	44	3-15—9-15	.041	15.30
	1887				29.90			SE¼SW¼	24	33	44	3-15—6-13	.243	44.85
	1887			34.80				SW¼SW¼	24	33	44	3-15—9-15	.283	104.40
	1887				5.20			SW¼SW¼	24	33	44	3-15—6-13	.042	7.80
	1887				5.70			NE¼SW¼	24	33	44	3-15—6-13	.046	8.55
	1887				8.77			NW¼SW¼	24	33	44	3-15—6-13	.071	13.16
	1887					28.27		NW¼SW¼	24	33	44	3-15—4-28	.230	21.20
	1887					9.79		SW¼NW¼	24	33	44	3-15—4-28	.080	7.34
	1879				13.57			SE¼SE¼	23	33	44	3-15—6-13	.110	20.36
	1879					1.33		SE¼SE¼	23	33	44	3-15—4-28	.011	1.00
	1887			13.57				SE¼SE¼	23	33	44	3-15—9-15	.110	40.71
	1887					2.85		SE¼SE¼	23	33	44	3-15—4-28	.023	2.13
	1879			19.58				SW¼SE¼	23	33	44	3-15—9-15	.159	58.74
	1879				15.10			SW¼SE¼	23	33	44	3-15—6-13	.122	22.65
	1879					.41		SW¼SE¼	23	33	44	3-15—4-28	.003	0.31
	1887			2.65				SW¼SE¼	23	33	44	3-15—9-15	.022	7.95
	1887					.82		SW¼SE¼	23	33	44	3-15—4-28	.006	0.62
	1879			7.55				SE¼NE¼	26	33	44	3-15—9-15	.061	22.65
	1879				14.42			SE¼NE¼	26	33	44	3-15—6-13	.117	21.63
	1879					16.44		SE¼NE¼	26	33	44	3-15—4-28	.134	12.33
	1887					1.00		SE¼NE¼	26	33	44	3-15—4-28	.008	0.75
	1879				0.92			SW¼NE¼	26	33	14	3-15—6-13	.007	1.38
	1879					39.08		SW¼NE¼	26	33	44	3-15—4-28	.318	29.31
	1879			18.44				NE¼NE¼	26	33	44	3-15—9-15	.150	55.32
	1879				2.36			NE¼NE¼	26	33	44	3-15—6-13	.019	3.54
	1879					2.55		NE¼NE¼	26	33	44	3-15—4-28	.021	1.91
	1887			8.04				NE¼NE¼	26	33	44	3-15—9-15	.065	24.12
	1887					3.06		NE¼NE¼	26	33	44	3-15—4-28	.025	2.30
	1879				23.50			NW¼NE¼	26	33	44	3-15—6-13	.191	35.25
	1879					16.50		NW¼NE¼	26	33	44	3-15—4-28	.134	12.38
	1879					29.07		SE¼NW¼	26	33	44	3-15—4-28	.236	21.80
	1879					40.00		NE¼NW¼	26	33	44	3-15—4-28	.325	30.00
	1879					21.16		NW¼NW¼	26	33	44	3-15—4-28	.172	15.87
	1887				3.15			SW¼SE¼	24	33	41	3-15—6-13	.026	4.73
	1879					16.93		SE¼SE¼	26	33	44	3-15—4-28	.138	12.69
	1879					40.00		NE¼SE¼	26	33	44	3-15—4-28	.325	30.00
	1879					17.85		NW¼SE¼	26	33	44	3-15—4-28	.145	18.39
	1879					1.02		NE¼SW¼	26	33	44	3-15—4-28	.008	0.77
	1887			1.89				NW¼NE¼	25	33	41	3-15—9-15	.015	5.40
	1887				28.60			NW¼NE¼	25	33	44	3-15—6-13	.233	42.90
	1887			15.50				SE¼NW¼	25	33	44	3-15—9-15	.126	46.50
	1887				12.44			SE¼NW¼	25	38	44	3-15—6-13	.101	18.68
	1887					0.82		SE¼NW¼	25	33	41	3-15—4-28	.007	0.62
	1879			4.90				SE¼NW¼	25	33	44	3-15—9-15	.040	14.70
	1879					2.15		SE¼NW¼	25	33	44	3-15—4-28	.017	1.61

1879	24.08				SW¼ NW¼	26	33	44	3-15—9-15	.201	74.04
1879		1.84			SW¼ NW¼	25	33	44	3-15—6-13	.015	2.76
1879			1.43		SW¼ NW¼	25	33	44	3-15—4-28	.012	1.07
1887	5.92				SW¼ NW¼	25	33	44	3-15—9-15	.048	17.76
1887			1.83		SW¼ NW¼	25	33	44	3-15—4-28	.015	1.37
1887	31.00				NE¼ NW¼	25	33	44	3-15—9-15	.252	93.00
1887		9.00			NE¼ NW¼	25	33	44	3-15—6-13	.073	18.50
1887	34.06				NW¼ NW¼	25	33	44	3-15—9-15	.277	102.18
1879	2.75				NW¼ NW¼	25	33	44	3-15—9-15	.022	8.25
1879			2.35		NW¼ NW¼	25	33	44	3-15—4-28	.019	1.76
1879	12.56				SE¼ SW¼	25	33	44	3-15—9-15	.102	37.68
1879		27.44			SE¼ SW¼	25	33	44	3-15—6-13	.223	41.16
1879		38.84			SW¼ SW¼	25	33	44	3-15—6-13	.316	58.36
1879			.82		SW¼ SW¼	25	33	44	3-15—4-28	.007	0.62
1879	34.51				NE¼ SW¼	25	33	44	3-15—9-15	.281	103.53
1879			0.61		NE¼ SW¼	25	33	44	3-15—4-28	.005	0.46
1887		.70			NE¼ SW¼	25	33	44	3-15—6-13	.006	1.05
1887			1.05		NE¼ SW¼	25	33	44	3-15—4-28	.009	0.79
1879	7.04				NW¼ SW¼	25	33	44	3-15—9-15	.060	21.12
1879		32.96			NW¼ SW¼	25	33	44	3-15—6-13	.268	49.44
1887	12.75				SE¼ NE¼	25	33	44	3-15—9-15	.104	38.25
1887		13.10			SE¼ NE¼	25	33	44	3-15—6-13	.107	19.65
1887	30.00				SW¼ NE¼	25	33	44	3-15—9-15	.244	90.00
1887			0.61		SW¼ NE¼	25	33	44	3-15—4-28	.005	0.46
1879	0.80				SW¼ NE¼	25	33	44	3-15—9-15	.007	2.40
1879			0.61		SW¼ NE¼	25	33	44	3-15—4-28	.005	0.46
1887		1.20			NE¼ NE¼	25	33	44	3-15—6-13	.010	1.80
1879			4.00		NW¼ SW¼	4	33	44	3-15—4-28	.003	3.00
1879				16.63	NW¼ SW¼	4	33	44	3-15—4-28	.135	12.47
1887	6.32				SW¼ SE¼	4	33	44	3-15—9-15	.051	18.96
1887			1.12		SW¼ SE¼	4	33	44	3-15—4-28	.009	0.84
1887	21.29				NE¼ SE¼	4	33	44	3-15—9-15	.173	63.87
1887		18.91			NE¼ SE¼	4	33	44	3-15—6-13	.154	28.37
1887	4.55				NW¼ SE¼	4	33	44	3-15—9-15	.037	13.65
1887		5.02			NW¼ SE¼	4	33	44	3-15—6-13	.041	7.53
1887			3.51		NW¼ SE¼	4	33	44	3-15—4-28	.029	2.63
1879		16.63			NW¼ SE¼	4	33	44	3-15—6-13	.135	24.95
1879			1.25		NW¼ SE¼	4	33	44	3-15—4-28	.010	0.94
1879		28.78			SE¼ SW¼	4	33	44	3-15—6-13	.234	43.17
1879			9.49		SE¼ SW¼	4	33	44	3-15—4-28	.077	7.11
1879		20.71			SW¼ SW¼	4	33	44	3-15—6-13	.168	31.07
1879				18.00	SW¼ SW¼	4	33	44	3-15—4-28	.146	13.50
1879	5.15				NE¼ SW¼	4	33	44	3-15—9-15	.042	15.45
1879		29.01			NE¼ SW¼	4	33	44	3-15—6-13	.236	43.52
1879			5.50		NE¼ SW¼	4	33	44	3-15—4-28	.045	4.13
1879		18.69			NW¼ SW¼	4	33	44	3-15—6-13	.152	28.04
1887		12.83			SW¼ SE¼	3	33	44	3-15—6-13	.104	19.25
1887		20.55			SE¼ SW¼	3	33	44	3-15—6-13	.167	30.83
1887	14.60				SW¼ SW¼	3	33	44	3-15—9-15	.119	43.80
1887		21.80			SW¼ SW¼	3	33	44	3-15—6-13	.177	32.70
1887				3.60	SW¼ SW¼	3	33	44	3-15—4-28	.029	2.70
1887		19.87			NW¼ SW¼	3	33	44	3-15—6-13	.162	29.81

Russell Land and Cattle Co.—Continued.

Date of beneficial use: Nat. mdw.	Date of beneficial use: Cult. area	Construction first initiated: Dams	Construction first initiated: Ditches	Culture—Acres: Harvest crops	Culture—Acres: Meadow pasture	Culture—Acres: Willow and sage pasture	Culture—Acres: Swamp or overflow	Location: Subdivision	Location: Section	Location: Tp.N.	Location: R.E.	Length of season	Duty of water: C.F.S.	Duty of water: Acre-feet
	1887						20.13	NW¼SW¼	3	33	44	3-15—4-28	.164	15.10
	1887				6.56			SW¼NW¼	3	33	44	3-15—6-13	.053	9.84
	1887						33.44	SW¼NW¼	3	33	44	3-15—4-28	.272	25.08
	1887						33.50	NW¼NW¼	3	33	44	3-15—4-28	.272	25.12
	1887			19.07				SE¼SE¼	4	33	44	3-15—9-15	.155	57.21
	1887				12.86			SE¼SE¼	4	33	44	3-15—6-13	.105	19.20
	1887					.45		SE¼SE¼	4	33	44	3-15—4-23	.004	0.34
	1879			2.14				SE¼SE¼	4	33	44	3-15—9-15	.017	6.42
	1879					.41		SE¼SE¼	4	33	44	3-15—4-28	.003	0.31
	1879			20.01				SW¼SE¼	4	33	44	3-15—9-15	.163	60.03
	1879					5.97		SW¼SE¼	4	33	44	3-15—4-28	.047	4.31
	1879						19.40	SE¼NW¼	32	34	44	3-15—4-28	.158	14.55
	1879				3.07			NE¼NW¼	32	34	44	3-15—6-13	.025	5.61
	1879						30.20	NE¼NW¼	32	34	44	3-15—4-28	.246	22.65
	1887					2.20		NE¼NE¼	32	34	44	3-15—4-28	.018	1.65
	1879				13.66			NE¼NE¼	32	34	44	3-15—6-13	.111	20.49
	1879					8.31		NE¼NE¼	32	34	44	3-15—4-28	.068	6.23
	1879				37.32			NW¼NE¼	32	34	44	3-15—6-13	.303	55.98
	1879						1.70	NW¼NE¼	32	34	44	3-15—4-28	.014	1.28
	1879					1.00		SW¼NW¼	33	34	44	3-15—4-28	.008	0.75
	1887				2.50			NE¼NW¼	33	34	44	3-15—6-13	.020	3.75
	1887				18.71			NW¼NW¼	33	34	44	3-15—6-13	.152	28.07
	1879				32.85			SE¼SE¼	32	34	44	3-15—6-13	.267	49.28
	1879						6.19	SE¼SE¼	32	34	44	3-15—4-28	.050	4.64
	1879				0.30			SW¼SE¼	32	34	44	3-15—6-13	.002	0.45
	1879						5.00	SW¼SE¼	32	34	44	3-15—4-28	.046	4.20
	1879				39.10			NE¼SE¼	32	34	44	3-15—6-13	.318	58.65
	1887					.20		NE¼SE¼	32	34	44	3-15—4-28	.002	0.15
	1879				15.44			NW¼SE¼	32	34	44	3-15—6-13	.126	23.16
	1879						6.63	NW¼SE¼	32	34	44	3-15—4-28	.054	4.97
	1879				34.25			SE¼NE¼	32	34	44	3-15—6-13	.278	51.38
	1879					1.00		SE¼NE¼	32	34	44	3-15—4-28	.008	0.75
	1887				3.27			SE¼NE¼	32	34	44	3-15—6-13	.027	4.91
	1879				32.69			SW¼NE¼	32	34	44	3-15—6-13	.266	49.04
	1879						7.20	SW¼NE¼	32	34	44	3-15—4-28	.059	5.40
	1887				10.80			NE¼NE¼	32	34	44	3-15—6-13	.088	16.20
	1879				10.60			SE¼SW¼	33	34	44	3-15—6-13	.086	15.90
	1879					4.64		SE¼SW¼	33	34	44	3-15—4-28	.038	3.18
	1887				18.04			SE¼SW¼	33	34	44	3-15—6-13	.147	27.06
	1887					1.39		SE¼SW¼	33	34	44	3-15—4-28	.011	1.04
	1879				40.00			SW¼SW¼	33	34	44	3-15—6-13	.325	60.00
	1887				35.74			NE¼SW¼	33	34	44	3-15—6-13	.291	53.61
	1887						2.00	NE¼SW¼	33	34	44	3-15—4-28	.016	1.50
	1879					.70		NE¼SW¼	33	34	44	3-15—4-28	.006	0.53
	1879				24.30			NW¼SW¼	33	34	44	3-15—6-13	.198	36.45
	1879					1.39		NW¼SW¼	33	34	44	3-15—4-28	.011	1.04

	1887				9.00			NW¼ SW¼	33	34	44	3-15—6-13	.078	14.40
	1887					1.59		NW¼ SW¼	33	34	44	3-15—4-28	.013	1.19
	1887						16.00	SW¼ NE¼	33	34	44	3-15—4-28	.130	12.00
	1887				18.91			SE¼ NW¼	33	34	44	3-15—6-13	.154	28.87
	1887						21.09	SE¼ NW¼	33	34	44	3-15—4-28	.171	15.81
	1887				34.85			SW¼ NW¼	33	34	44	3-15—6-13	.283	52.28
	1879				1.80			SW¼ NW¼	33	34	44	3-15—6-13	.015	2.79
	1887			9.21				SE¼ NE¼	4	33	44	3-15—9-15	.075	27.63
	1887				30.79			SE¼ NE¼	4	33	44	3-15—6-13	.250	46.19
	1887			19.40				SW¼ NE¼	4	33	44	3-15—9-15	.158	58.20
	1887				8.51			SW¼ NE¼	4	33	44	3-15—6-13	.069	12.77
	1887					2.67		SW¼ NE¼	4	33	44	3-15—4-28	.022	2.00
	1879				3.07			SW¼ NE¼	4	33	44	3-15—6-13	.025	4.61
	1879					1.99		SW¼ NE¼	4	33	44	3-15—4-28	.016	1.40
	1887				29.10			NE¼ NE¼	4	33	44	3-15—6-13	.237	43.65
	1887						10.90	NE¼ NE¼	4	33	44	3-15—4-28	.089	8.18
	1887				40.00			NW¼ NE¼	4	33	44	3-15—6-13	.325	60.00
	1879			25.34				SE¼ NW¼	4	33	44	3-15—9-15	.206	76.02
	1879				5.55			SE¼ NW¼	4	33	44	3-15—6-13	.045	8.25
	1879					.80		SE¼ NW¼	4	33	44	3-15—4-28	.007	0.60
	1887				2.83			SE¼ NW¼	4	33	44	3-15—6-13	.023	4.25
	1887					1.89		SE¼ NW¼	4	33	44	3-15—4-28	.015	1.42
	1879			8.61				SW¼ NW¼	4	33	44	3-15—9-15	.071	25.83
	1879				14.46			SW¼ NW¼	4	33	44	3-15—6-13	.118	21.69
	1879					7.61		SW¼ NW¼	4	33	44	3-15—4-28	.062	5.71
	1879						7.21	SW¼ NW¼	4	33	44	3-15—4-28	.059	5.41
	1879			4.55				NE¼ NW¼	4	33	44	3-15—9-15	.037	13.65
	1879				4.27			NE¼ NW¼	4	33	44	3-15—6-13	.035	6.41
	1879					4.66		NE¼ NW¼	4	33	44	3-15—4-28	.038	3.50
	1887				18.51			NE¼ NW¼	4	33	44	3-15—6-13	.150	27.77
	1887					.40		NE¼ NW¼	4	33	44	3-15—4-28	.003	0.30
	1879			32.17				NW¼ NW¼	4	33	44	3-15—9-15	.262	96.51
	1879				6.93			NW¼ NW¼	4	33	44	3-15—6-13	.056	10.40
	1879						3.00	SE¼ SE¼	5	33	44	3-15—4-28	.024	2.25
	1879						7.48	NE¼ SE¼	5	33	44	3-15—4-28	.059	5.61
	1879				1.30			SE¼ NE¼	5	33	44	3-15—6-13	.011	1.95
	1879					6.25		SE¼ NE¼	5	33	44	3-15—4-28	.051	4.69
	1879						8.30	SE¼ NE¼	5	33	44	3-15—4-28	.067	6.23
	1879				14.66			NE¼ NE¼	5	33	44	3-15—6-13	.111	21.99
	1879						10.30	NE¼ NE¼	5	33	44	3-15—4-28	.084	7.73
	1887						5.00	SW¼ SW¼	34	34	44	3-15—4-28	.041	3.75
	1887				1.35			SE¼ SE¼	33	34	44	3-15—6-13	.011	2.03
	1887						35.09	SE¼ SE¼	33	34	44	3-15—4-28	.285	26.32
	1887				30.52			SW¼ SE¼	33	34	44	3-15—6-13	.248	45.78
	1887						9.48	SW¼ SE¼	33	34	44	3-15—4-28	.077	7.11
	1887						8.25	NE¼ SE¼	33	34	44	3-15—4-28	.067	6.19
	1887				5.70			NW¼ SE¼	33	34	44	3-15—6-13	.046	8.55
	1887						33.30	NW¼ SE¼	33	34	44	3-15—4-28	.271	24.98
	1879					.40		NW¼ SW¼	14	33	44	3-15—4-28	.003	0.30
	1879			38.60				SE¼ SE¼	15	33	44	3-15—9-15	.314	115.80
	1887					.50		SE¼ SE¼	15	33	44	3-15—4-28	.004	0.38
	1879			40.00				SW¼ SE¼	15	33	44	3-15—9-15	.325	120.00
	1879			19.65				NE¼ SE¼	14	33	44	3-15—9-15	.160	58.95

Russell Land and Cattle Co.—Continued.

Date of beneficial use: Nat. mdw.	Date of beneficial use: Cult. area	Construction first initiated: Dams	Construction first initiated: Ditches	Culture—Acres: Harvest crops	Culture—Acres: Meadow pasture	Culture—Acres: Willow and sage pasture	Culture—Acres: Swamp or overflow	Location: Subdivision	Location: Section	Location: Tp. N.	Location: R. E.	Length of season	Duty of water: C. F. S.	Duty of water: Acre-feet
	1887			11.46				NE¼SE¼	14	33	44	3-15—9-15	.093	34.38
	1887					1.80		NE¼SE¼	14	33	44	3-15—4-28	.015	1.35
	1879			39.40				NW¼SE¼	14	33	44	3-15—9-15	.320	118.20
	1879			40.00				SE¼NE¼	22	33	44	3-15—9-15	.325	120.00
	1879			17.62				SW¼NE¼	22	33	44	3-15—9-15	.143	52.86
	1879				22.38			SW¼NE¼	22	33	44	3-15—6-13	.182	33.57
	1879			39.30				NE¼NE¼	22	33	44	3-15—9-15	.320	117.96
	1879			38.00				NW¼NE¼	22	33	44	3-15—9-15	.309	114.00
	1879			13.19				NE¼NW¼	22	33	44	3-15—9-15	.107	39.57
	1887					3.70		SE¼SE¼	14	33	44	3-15—4-28	.030	2.78
	1887					37.30		SW¼SE¼	14	33	44	3-15—4-28	.303	27.98
	1887					18.00		NW¼SE¼	14	33	44	3-15—4-28	.146	13.50
	1887			34.16				SE¼SW¼	14	33	44	3-15—9-15	.278	102.48
	1887					5.84		SE¼SW¼	14	33	44	3-15—4-28	.047	4.38
	1887			27.38				SW¼SW¼	14	33	44	3-15—9-15	.223	82.14
	1879			4.10				SW¼SW¼	14	33	44	3-15—9-15	.033	12.30
	1879					1.00		SW¼SW¼	14	33	44	3-15—4-28	.008	0.75
	1887			17.50				NE¼SW¼	14	33	44	3-15—9-15	.142	52.50
	1887					22.50		NE¼SW¼	14	32	44	3-15—4-28	.181	16.88
	1887			37.40				NW¼SW¼	14	33	44	3-15—9-15	.304	112.20
	1879			10.10				NW¼NE¼	36	33	44	3-15—9-15	.082	30.30
	1879				29.90			NW¼NE¼	36	33	44	3-15—6-13	.243	44.85
	1879				12.07			SE¼NW¼	36	33	44	3-15—6-13	.098	18.11
	1879					22.78		SE¼NW¼	36	33	44	3-15—4-28	.185	17.09
	1879					9.08		SW¼NW¼	36	33	44	3-15—4-28	.074	6.81
	1879				38.00			NE¼NW¼	36	33	44	3-15—6-13	.309	57.00
	1879					1.55		NE¼NW¼	36	33	44	3-15—4-28	.013	1.16
	1879				13.46			NW¼NW¼	36	33	44	3-15—6-13	.109	20.19
	1879					24.15		NW¼NW¼	36	33	44	3-15—4-28	.196	18.11
	1879				1.63			NE¼NE¼	35	33	44	3-15—6-13	.013	2.45
	1879					4.50		NE¼NE¼	35	33	44	3-15—4-28	.037	3.44
	1879			21.23				SE¼SE¼	25	33	44	3-15—9-15	.173	63.69
	1879				13.06			SE¼SE¼	25	33	44	3-15—6-13	.106	19.59
	1879					0.43		SE¼SE¼	25	33	44	3-15—4-28	.003	0.32
	1887			3.65				SE¼SE¼	25	33	44	3-15—9-15	.030	10.95
	1887					1.33		SE¼SE¼	25	33	44	3-15—4-28	.011	1.00
	1879			15.52				SW¼SE¼	25	33	44	3-15—9-15	.126	46.56
	1879				40.00			SE¼SE¼	36	33	44	3-15—6-13	.325	60.00
	1879				2.48			SW¼SE¼	36	33	44	3-15—6-13	.020	3.72
	1879					1.02		SW¼SE¼	36	33	44	3-15—4-28	.008	.77
	1879			10.00				NE¼SE¼	36	33	44	3-15—9-15	.081	30.00
	1879				30.00			NE¼SE¼	36	33	44	3-15—6-13	.244	45.00
	1879			2.10				NW¼SE¼	36	33	44	3-15—9-15	.017	6.30
	1879				24.80			NW¼SE¼	36	33	44	3-15—6-13	.202	37.20
	1879					6.80		NW¼SE¼	36	33	44	3-15—4-28	.055	5.10
	1879			26.75				SE¼NE¼	36	33	44	3-15—9-15	.217	80.25

	1879				9.25			SE¼NE¼	36	33	44	3-15—6-13	.075	13.88
	1879					0.71		SE¼NE¼	36	33	44	3-15—4-28	.006	0.53
	1887					1.33		SE¼NE¼	36	33	44	3-16—4-28	.011	1.00
	1879			14.58				SW¼NE¼	36	33	44	3-15—9-15	.119	44.24
	1879				24.71			SW¼NE¼	36	33	44	3-15—6-13	.201	27.07
	1879			20.48				NE¼NE¼	36	33	44	3-15—9-15	.240	89.44
	1879					1.43		NE¼NE¼	36	33	44	3-15—4-28	.012	1.07
	1887					4.20		NE¼NE¼	36	33	44	3-15—4-28	.034	3.15
	1879				25.00			SE¼NE¼	10	33	44	3-15—6-13	.203	37.50
	1879			20.60				SW¼NE¼	10	33	44	3-15—9-15	.167	61.80
	1879				19.40			SW¼NE¼	10	33	44	3-15—6-13	.158	29.10
	1879				33.17			NE¼NE¼	10	33	44	3-15—6-13	.270	49.76
	1879			2.00				NW¼NE¼	10	33	44	3-15—9-15	.016	6.00
	1879				38.00			NW¼NE¼	10	33	44	3-15—6-13	.309	57.00
	1887			38.50				SE¼NW¼	10	33	44	3-15—9-15	.313	115.50
	1879					.50		SE¼NW¼	10	33	44	3-15—4-28	.004	0.38
	1879			20.10				SW¼NW¼	10	33	44	3-15—9-15	.163	60.30
	1879					11.48		SW¼NW¼	10	33	44	3-15—4-28	.093	8.61
	1887			12.60				SW¼NW¼	10	33	44	3-15—9-15	.102	37.80
	1887					.70		SW¼NW¼	10	33	44	3-13—4-28	.006	0.53
	1879			25.49				NE¼NW¼	10	33	44	3-15—9-15	.207	76.47
	1879				10.81			NE¼NW¼	10	33	44	3-15—6-13	.088	16.22
	1887			38.00				NW¼NW¼	10	33	44	3-15—9-15	.309	114.00
	1879			1.00				NW¼NW¼	10	33	44	3-15—9-15	.008	3.00
	1887			40.00				SE¼SE¼	10	33	44	3-15—9-15	.325	120.00
	1887			38.10				SW¼SE¼	10	33	44	3-15—9-15	.310	114.30
	1879					.40		SW¼SE¼	10	33	44	3-15—4-28	.003	0.30
	1887			40.00				NE¼SE¼	10	33	44	3-15—9-15	.325	120.00
	1887			40.00				NW¼SE¼	10	33	44	3-15—9-15	.325	120.00
	1887			15.18				SE¼SW¼	10	33	44	3-15—9-15	.123	45.54
	1887					1.10		SE¼SW¼	10	33	44	3-15—4-28	.009	0.83
	1879			12.80				SE¼SW¼	10	33	44	3-15—9-15	.100	36.90
	1879					2.80		SE¼SW¼	10	33	44	3-15—4-28	.023	2.10
	1879			38.00				SW¼SW¼	10	33	44	3-16—9-15	.309	114.00
	1887					1.40		SW¼SW¼	10	33	44	3-15—4-28	.011	1.05
	1879			38.70				NE¼SW¼	10	33	44	3-15—9-15	.315	116.10
	1879			25.35				NW¼SW¼	10	33	44	3-15—9-15	.206	76.05
	1879					13.74		NW¼SW¼	10	33	44	3-15—4-28	.112	10.31
	1887			5.35				NW¼SW¼	10	33	44	3-15—9-15	.043	16.05
	1887					2.09		NW¼SW¼	10	33	44	3-15—4-28	.017	1.57
	1879			14.85				SE¼NE¼	10	33	44	3-15—6-15	.121	44.55
	1887			29.80				NE¼SE¼	23	33	44	3-15—9-15	.242	89.40
	1887					10.00		NE¼SE¼	23	33	44	3-15—4-28	.081	7.50
	1887			14.46				NW¼SE¼	23	33	44	3-15—4-28	.118	43.38
	1887					6.49		NW¼SE¼	23	33	44	3-15—4-28	.053	4.87
	1879			6.32				NW¼SE¼	23	33	44	3-15—9-15	.051	18.96
	1879					5.10		NW¼SE¼	23	33	44	3-15—4-28	.041	3.83
	1879				24.48			SW¼SE¼	25	33	44	3-15—6-13	.199	36.72
	1879			10.04				NE¼SE¼	25	33	44	3-15—9-15	.085	30.12
	1879					.71		NE¼SE¼	25	33	44	3-15—4-28	.006	0.53
	1887			24.64				NE¼SE¼	25	33	44	3-15—9-15	.200	73.92
	1887					0.51		NE¼SE¼	25	33	44	3-15—4-28	.004	0.38

Russell Land and Cattle Co.—Continued.

Date of beneficial use: Nat. mdw.	Date of beneficial use: Cult. area	Construction first initiated: Dams	Construction first initiated: Ditches	Culture—Acres: Harvest crops	Culture—Acres: Meadow pasture	Culture—Acres: Willow and sage pasture	Culture—Acres: Swamp or over-flow	Location: Subdivision	Location: Section	Location: Tp.N.	Location: R.E.	Length of season	Duty of water: C.F.S.	Duty of water: Acre-feet
....	1879	....	....	26.72	....	....	....	NW¼SE¼	25	33	44	3-15—9-15	.217	80.16
....	1887	....	....	6.22	....	....	....	NW¼SE¼	25	33	44	3-15—9-15	.051	18.66
....	1887	....	....	....	....	1.36	....	NW¼SE¼	25	33	44	3-15—4-28	.011	1.02
....	1879	....	....	15.54	....	....	....	SE¼SE¼	9	33	44	3-15—9-15	.126	46.62
....	1879	....	....	....	....	23.37	....	SE¼SE¼	9	33	44	3-15—4-28	.190	17.52
....	1879	....	....	....	12.97	....	....	SW¼SE¼	9	33	44	3-15—6-13	.105	19.46
....	1879	....	....	....	....	3.66	....	SW¼SE¼	9	33	44	3-15—4-28	.030	2.75
....	1879	....	....	18.22	....	....	....	NE¼SE¼	9	33	44	3-15—9-15	.148	54.66
....	1879	....	....	....	10.80	....	....	NE¼SE¼	9	33	44	3-15—6-13	.088	16.20
....	1879	....	....	....	....	6.73	....	NE¼SE¼	9	33	44	3-15—4-28	.055	5.05
....	1879	....	....	....	2.60	....	....	NW¼SE¼	9	33	44	3-15—6-13	.021	3.90
....	1879	....	....	....	16.95	....	....	SE¼SW¼	9	33	44	3-15—6-13	.138	25.43
....	1879	....	....	....	28.30	....	....	NE¼SW¼	9	33	44	3-15—6-13	.230	42.45
....	1879	....	....	37.37	....	....	....	SE¼NE¼	9	33	44	3-15—9-15	.304	113.11
....	1879	....	....	....	2.50	....	....	SE¼NE¼	9	33	44	3-15—6-13	.020	3.75
....	1879	....	....	11.32	....	....	....	SW¼NE¼	9	33	44	3-15—9-15	.092	33.96
....	1879	....	....	....	7.28	....	....	SW¼NE¼	9	33	44	3-15—6-13	.059	10.92
....	1879	....	....	....	....	13.60	....	SW¼NE¼	9	33	44	3-15—4-28	.110	10.20
....	1879	....	....	21.83	....	....	....	NE¼NE¼	9	33	44	3-15—9-15	.177	65.46
....	1879	....	....	....	....	2.11	....	NE¼NE¼	9	33	44	3-15—4-28	.017	1.58
....	1879	....	....	39.40	....	....	....	NE¼SE¼	22	33	44	3-15—9-15	.320	118.20
....	1879	....	....	....	0.60	....	....	NE¼SE¼	22	33	44	3-15—6-13	.005	0.90
....	1879	....	....	5.94	....	....	....	NW¼SE¼	22	33	44	3-15—9-15	.048	17.82
....	1879	....	....	....	34.06	....	....	NW¼SE¼	22	33	44	3-15—6-13	.277	51.09
....	1887	....	....	....	....	2.40	....	SE¼NW¼	23	33	44	3-15—4-28	.020	1.80
....	1879	....	....	5.86	....	....	....	SE¼NW¼	23	33	44	3-15—9-15	.048	17.58
....	1879	....	....	....	....	0.80	....	SE¼NW¼	23	33	44	3-15—4-28	.007	.60
....	1879	....	....	25.57	....	....	....	SW¼NW¼	23	33	44	3-15—9-15	.208	76.71
....	1879	....	....	....	....	0.60	....	SW¼NW¼	23	33	44	3-15—4-28	.005	.45
....	1887	....	....	6.45	....	....	....	SW¼NW¼	23	33	44	3-15—9-15	.052	19.35
....	1887	....	....	....	....	1.19	....	SW¼NW¼	23	33	44	3-15—4-28	.010	0.89
....	1879	....	....	35.24	....	....	....	NE¼NW¼	23	33	44	3-15—9-15	.287	105.72
....	1879	....	....	....	4.06	....	....	NE¼NW¼	23	33	44	3-15—6-13	.033	6.09
....	1879	....	....	14.40	....	....	....	NW¼NW¼	23	33	44	3-15—9-15	.117	43.20
....	1879	....	....	....	....	1.99	....	NW¼NW¼	23	33	44	3-15—4-28	.016	1.49
....	1887	....	....	13.50	....	....	....	NW¼NW¼	23	33	44	3-15—9-15	.110	40.50
....	1887	....	....	....	....	.40	....	NW¼NW¼	23	33	44	3-15—4-28	.003	.30
....	1879	....	....	40.00	....	....	....	NW¼SW¼	23	33	44	3-15—9-15	.325	120.00
....	1879	....	....	10.40	....	....	....	SE¼SE¼	22	33	44	3-15—9-15	.085	31.20
....	1879	....	....	....	29.60	....	....	SE¼SE¼	22	33	44	3-15—6-13	.241	44.40
....	1879	....	....	....	18.07	....	....	SW¼SE¼	22	33	44	3-15—6-13	.147	27.11
....	1879	....	....	22.05	....	....	....	SE¼SW¼	23	33	44	3-15—9-15	.179	66.15
....	1879	....	....	....	....	17.95	....	SE¼SW¼	23	33	44	3-15—4-28	.146	18.46
....	1879	....	....	16.94	....	....	....	SW¼SW¼	23	33	44	3-15—9-15	.138	57.72
....	1879	....	....	....	....	23.00	....	SW¼SW¼	23	33	44	3-15—4-28	.187	17.25
....	1879	....	....	20.17	....	....	....	NE¼SW¼	23	33	44	3-15—9-15	.164	60.51

	1870					12.18		NE¼ SW¼	23	33	44	3-15—4-28	.099	9.14
	1887			1.19				NE¼ SW¼	23	33	44	3-15—9-15	.010	3.57
	1887					2.34		NE¼ SW¼	23	33	44	3-15—4-28	.019	1.76
	1887			2.00				SE¼ NE¼	23	33	44	3-15—9-15	.016	6.00
	1887					37.91		SE¼ NE¼	23	33	44	3-15—4-28	.308	28.43
	1887			28.00				SW¼ NE¼	23	33	44	3-15—9-15	.228	84.00
	1887					9.90		SW¼ NE¼	23	33	44	3-15—4-28	.080	7.43
	1879					.50		SW¼ NE¼	23	33	44	3-15—4-28	.004	.38
	1887					27.80		NE¼ NE¼	23	33	44	3-15—4-28	.226	20.85
	1887				3.00			NW¼ NE¼	23	33	44	3-15—6-13	.024	4.50
	1887					37.00		NW¼ NE¼	23	33	44	3-15—4-28	.300	27.75
	1887			24.95				SE¼ NW¼	23	33	44	3-15—9-15	.203	74.85
	1879			25.10				SW¼ NE¼	15	33	44	3-15—9-15	.204	75.30
	1879					1.10		SW¼ NE¼	15	33	44	3-15—4-28	.009	.83
	1887			7.57				SW¼ NE¼	15	33	44	3-15—9-15	.062	22.71
	1887					1.00		SW¼ NE¼	15	33	44	3-15—4-28	.008	.75
	1879			40.00				NE¼ NE¼	15	33	44	3-15—9-15	.325	120.00
	1887			24.50				NW¼ NE¼	15	33	44	3-15—9-15	.199	73.50
	1887					2.08		NW¼ NE¼	15	33	44	3-15—4-28	.017	1.56
	1879			6.75				NW¼ NE¼	15	33	44	3-15—9-15	.055	20.25
	1879					1.70		NW¼ NE¼	15	33	44	3-15—4-28	.014	1.28
	1879			40.00				SE¼ NW¼	15	33	44	3-15—9-15	.325	120.00
	1879			25.70				SW¼ NW¼	15	33	44	3-15—9-15	.200	77.10
	1870					14.30		SW¼ NW¼	15	33	44	3-15—4-28	.116	10.73
	1879			40.00				NE¼ NW¼	15	33	44	3-15—9-15	.325	120.00
	1879			35.64				NW¼ NW¼	15	33	44	3-15—9-15	.290	106.92
	1879					4.36		NW¼ NW¼	15	33	44	3-15—4-28	.035	3.27
	1879					39.00		SE¼ NE¼	16	33	44	3-15—4-28	.317	29.25
	1879				5.95			SW¼ NE¼	16	33	44	3-15—6-13	.048	8.93
	1879			0.40				NE¼ NE¼	16	33	44	3-15—9-15	.003	1.20
	1879					39.00		NE¼ NE¼	16	33	44	3-15—4-28	.317	29.25
	1879				18.90			NW¼ NE¼	16	33	44	3-15—6-13	.154	28.35
	1879					2.47		NW¼ NE¼	16	33	44	3-15—4-28	.020	1.85
	1879				1.60			NE¼ NW¼	16	33	44	3-15—6-13	.013	2.40
	1887			3.15				SE¼ SW¼	11	33	44	3-15—9-15	.026	9.45
	1887			36.70				SW¼ SW¼	11	33	44	3-15—9-15	.298	110.10
	1887			17.15				NW¼ SW¼	11	33	44	3-15—9-15	.139	51.45
	1887				12.55			SW¼ NW¼	11	33	44	3-15—6-13	.102	18.83
	1887				5.30			NW¼ NW¼	11	33	44	3-15—6-13	.043	7.95
	1879			40.00				SE¼ SW¼	15	33	44	3-15—9-15	.325	120.00
	1879			10.95				SW¼ SW¼	15	33	44	3-15—9-15	.089	32.85
	1879			40.00				NE¼ SW¼	15	33	44	3-15—9-15	.325	120.00
	1879			17.00				NW¼ SW¼	15	33	44	3-15—9-15	.138	51.00
	1879					9.21		NW¼ SW¼	15	33	44	3-15—4-28	.075	6.91
	1879					7.00		NE¼ SE¼	16	33	44	3-15—4-28	.057	5.25
	1887				1.25			SW¼ NE¼	14	33	44	3-15—6-13	.010	1.88
	1887			1.19				SE¼ NW¼	14	33	44	3-15—9-15	.010	3.57
	1887				26.33			SE¼ NW¼	14	33	44	3-15—6-13	.214	39.50
	1887					7.82		SE¼ NW¼	14	33	44	3-15—4-28	.064	5.87
	1887			36.00				SW¼ NW¼	14	33	44	3-15—9-15	.293	108.00
	1887				1.98			SW¼ NW¼	14	33	44	3-15—6-13	.016	1.49
	1887					1.98		SW¼ NW¼	14	33	44	3-15—4-28	.016	2.97

Russell Land and Cattle Co.—Continued.

Date of beneficial use: Nat. mdw.	Date of beneficial use: Cult. area	Construction first initiated: Dams	Construction first initiated: Ditches	Culture—Acres: Harvest crops	Culture—Acres: Meadow pasture	Culture—Acres: Willow and sage pasture	Culture—Acres: Swamp or overflow	Location: Subdivision	Location: Section	Location: Tp.N.	Location: R.E.	Length of season	Duty of water: C.F.S.	Duty of water: Acre-feet
	1887			10.00				NE¼NW¼	14	33	44	3-15—9-15	.081	30.00
	1887					11.00		NE¼NW¼	14	33	44	3-15—4-28	.089	8.25
	1887			40.00				NW¼NW¼	14	33	44	3-15—9-15	.325	120.00
	1887			40.00				SE¼NE¼	15	33	44	3-15—9-15	.325	120.00
	1887			9.28				NE¼NE¼	9	33	44	3-15—9-15	.075	27.84
	1887					2.53		NE¼NE¼	9	33	44	3-15—4-28	.021	1.90
	1879			24.68				NW¼NE¼	9	33	44	3-15—9-15	.201	74.04
	1879				7.14			NW¼NE¼	9	33	44	3-15—6-13	.058	10.71
	1879					7.50		NW¼NE¼	9	33	44	3-15—4-28	.061	5.63
	1879				27.64			SE¼NW¼	9	33	44	3-15—6-13	.217	41.46
	1879						12.36	SE¼NW¼	9	33	44	3-15—4-28	.100	9.27
	1879						10.32	SW¼NW¼	9	33	44	3-15—4-28	.084	7.74
	1879				40.00			NE¼NW¼	9	33	44	3-15—6-13	.325	60.00
	1879				4.79			NW¼NW¼	9	33	44	3-15—6-13	.039	7.18
	1879						21.90	NW¼NW¼	9	33	44	3-15—4-28	.170	16.43

Claimant—**Ike Erickson.** Proof No. **00173**
Source—**Humboldt River.** Ditch—**Altenberg.**

Nat. mdw.	Cult. area	Dams	Ditches	Harvest crops	Meadow pasture	Willow and sage pasture	Swamp or overflow	Subdivision	Section	Tp.N.	R.E.	Length of season	C.F.S.	Acre-feet
	1874			20.36				SE¼NE¼	17	32	45	3-15—9-15	.165	61.08
	1874			5.58				NE¼SE¼	17	32	45	3-15—9-15	.045	16.74
	1874					11.44		NE¼SE¼	17	32	45	3-15—4-28	.093	8.58
	1874					.02		SW¼NE¼	17	32	45	3-15—4-28	.000	.02
	1874					.02		NW¼SE¼	17	32	45	3-15—4-28	.000	.02
	1874					.39		SE¼NE¼	17	32	45	3-15—4-28	.003	.29

Claimant—**Geo. Heard.** Proof No. **00174**
Source—**Humboldt River.** Ditch—**Russel Dam.**

Nat. mdw.	Cult. area	Dams	Ditches	Harvest crops	Meadow pasture	Willow and sage pasture	Swamp or overflow	Subdivision	Section	Tp.N.	R.E.	Length of season	C.F.S.	Acre-feet
	1880			2.32				NE¼NE¼	2	35	42	3-15—9-15	.189	6.96
	1880				34.23			NE¼NE¼	2	35	42	3-15—6-13	.278	36.35
	1880					1.73		NE¼NE¼	2	35	42	3-15—4-28	.014	1.30
	1880			37.00				SE¼NE¼	2	35	42	3-15—9-15	.301	111.00
	1880				0.90			SE¼NE¼	2	35	42	3-15—6-13	.007	1.35
	1880				0.03			NW¼NE¼	2	35	42	3-15—6-13	.000	.05
	1880					1.36		NW¼NE¼	2	35	42	3-15—4-28	.011	1.02
	1880			0.70				SW¼NE¼	2	35	42	3-15—9-15	.006	2.10
	1880				0.42			SW¼NE¼	2	35	42	3-15—6-13	.003	.63
	1880					0.20		SW¼NE¼	2	35	42	3-15—4-28	.002	.15
	1880			35.87				NE¼SE¼	2	35	42	3-15—9-15	.292	107.61
	1880					1.21		NE¼SE¼	2	35	42	3-15—4-28	.010	.91
	1890			38.19				SE¼SE¼	2	35	42	3-15—9-15	.310	114.57
	1880			1.35				NW¼SE¼	2	35	42	3-15—9-15	.011	4.05
	1880			1.37				SW¼SE¼	2	35	42	3-15—9-15	.011	4.11

Flooded first in 1874 by Acmes Dam when above area was third class pasture.

								Claimant—Garat and Co.					Proof No. 00175	
								Source—Humboldt River. Ditch—Hammond.						
1872	1875				1.96			NE¼SW¼	16	36	42	3-15—6-13	.016	2.94
1872	1875				28.22			NW¼SW¼	16	36	42	3-15—6-13	.229	42.33
1872	1875					33.87		SE¼SW¼	16	36	42	3-15—4-28	.275	25.40
1872	1875					40.00		SW¼SW¼	16	36	42	3-15—4-28	.325	30.00
								Claimant—Lulu Kattenhorn Burch.					Proof No. 00176	
								Source—Humboldt River. Ditch—Eaton Dam.						
1878					9.80			SW¼NE¼	29	34	44	3-15—6-13	.080	14.70
1878						0.47		SW¼NE¼	29	34	44	3-15—4-28	.004	0.35
1878							4.15	NE¼SE¼	29	34	44	3-15—4-28	.034	3.11
1878					4.35			SE¼SE¼	29	34	44	3-15—6-13	.035	6.53
1878						2.68		SE¼SE¼	29	34	44	3-15—4-28	.022	2.01
1878							15.05	SE¼SE¼	29	34	44	3-15—4-28	.122	11.29
1878					8.75			NW¼SE¼	29	34	44	3-15—6-13	.071	13.13
1878						5.60		NW¼SE¼	29	34	44	3-15—4-28	.046	4.20
1878							9.60	NW¼SE¼	29	34	44	3-15—4-28	.078	7.20
1878				0.59				SW¼SE¼	29	34	44	3-15—9-15	.005	1.77
1878					18.31			SW¼SE¼	29	34	44	3-15—6-13	.149	27.47
1878						2.40		SW¼SE¼	29	34	44	3-15—4-28	.020	1.80
1878							5.97	SW¼SE¼	29	34	44	3-15—4-28	.049	4.48
1878				10.90				NE¼NW¼	29	34	44	3-15—9-15	.089	32.70
1878							10.35	NE¼NW¼	29	34	44	3-15—4-28	.084	7.76
1878				10.16				SE¼NW¼	29	34	44	3-15—9-15	.083	30.48
1878					10.01			SE¼NW¼	29	34	44	3-15—6-13	.081	15.02
1878							11.32	SE¼NW¼	29	34	44	3-15—4-28	.092	8.49
1878						10.02		SW¼NW¼	29	34	44	3-15—4-28	.081	7.52
1878							27.42	SW¼NW¼	29	34	44	3-15—4-28	.223	20.57
1878				3.43				NE¼SW¼	29	34	44	3-15—9-15	.028	10.29
1878					4.10			NE¼SW¼	29	34	44	3-15—6-13	.033	6.15
1878						2.02		NE¼SW¼	29	34	44	3-15—4-28	.016	1.52
1878							20.90	NE¼SW¼	29	34	44	3-15—4-28	.170	15.68
								Source—Humboldt River. Ditch—Ward Ditch.						
1878	1879			1.04				SE¼SW¼	29	34	44	3-15—9-15	.008	3.12
1878	1879					13.75		SE¼SW¼	29	34	44	3-15—4-28	.112	10.31
1878	1879						21.60	SE¼SW¼	29	34	44	3-15—4-28	.176	16.20
1878	1879					25.50		NW¼SW¼	29	34	44	3-15—4-28	.207	19.13
1878	1879						10.00	NW¼SW¼	29	34	44	3-15—4-28	.081	7.50
1878	1879					11.90		SW¼SW¼	29	34	44	3-15—4-28	.097	8.93
1878	1879						25.08	SW¼SW¼	29	34	44	3-15—4-28	.204	18.81
								Source—Humboldt River. Ditch—Wilcox Dam.						
1886	1886			19.60				NW¼NW¼	29	34	44	3-15—9-15	.159	58.80
1886	1886					9.45		NW¼NW¼	29	34	44	3-15—4-28	.077	7.09
1886	1886						6.24	NW¼NW¼	29	34	44	3-15—4-28	.051	4.68

Claimant—**William Dunphy Estate.** Proof No. 00333

Source—**Rock Creek.** Ditch—**Rock Creek Branches.**

Date of beneficial use		Construction first initiated		Culture—Acres				Location				Length of season	Duty of water	
Nat. mdw.	Cult. area	Dams	Ditches	Harvest crops	Meadow pasture	Willow and sage pasture	Swamp or overflow	Subdivision	Section	Tp.N.	R.E.		C.F.S.	Acre-feet
1870	1870					3.50		NE¼NW¼	36	34	47	3-15—4-28	.028	2.63
1870	1870					9.90		SE¼NW¼	36	34	47	3-15—4-28	.080	7.42
1870	1870					9.25		NW¼NW¼	36	34	47	3-15—4-28	.075	6.94
1870	1870					38.55		SW¼NW¼	36	34	47	3-15—4-28	.313	28.91
1870	1870					9.20		NE¼SW¼	36	34	47	3-15—4-28	.075	6.90
1870	1870					9.65		SE¼SW¼	36	34	47	3-15—4-28	.078	7.24
1870	1870					39.80		NW¼SW¼	36	34	47	3-15—4-28	.324	29.85
1870	1870					38.65		SW¼SW¼	36	34	47	3-15—4-28	.314	28.99
1870	1870					36.35		NE¼SE¼	35	34	47	3-15—4-28	.296	27.26
1870	1870				9.65			SE¼SE¼	35	34	47	3-15—6-13	.078	14.48
1870	1870					30.05		SE¼SE¼	35	34	47	3-15—4-28	.278	22.54
1870	1870					6.90		NW¼SE¼	35	34	47	3-15—4-28	.056	5.18
1870	1870				7.45			SW¼SE¼	35	34	47	3-15—6-13	.061	11.18
1870	1870					26.80		SW¼SE¼	35	34	47	3-15—4-28	.218	20.10
1870	1870					8.90		NE¼NW¼	1	33	47	3-15—4-28	.072	6.68
1870	1870					9.65		SE¼NW¼	1	33	47	3-15—4-28	.078	7.24
1870	1870				0.40			NW¼NW¼	1	33	47	3-15—6-13	.003	.60
1870	1870					39.35		NW¼NW¼	1	33	47	3-15—4-28	.320	29.51
1870	1870					37.55		SW¼NW¼	1	33	47	3-15—4-28	.305	28.16
1870	1870					12.95		NE¼NE¼	36	34	47	3-15—4-28	.105	9.71
1870	1870					38.65		SE¼NE¼	36	34	47	3-15—4-28	.314	28.99
1870	1870					14.15		NW¼NE¼	36	34	47	3-15—4-28	.115	10.61
1870	1870					40.45		SW¼NE¼	36	34	47	3-15—4-28	.329	30.34
1870	1870					40.05		NE¼SE¼	36	34	47	3-15—4-28	.326	30.04
1870	1870				3.15			SE¼SE¼	36	34	47	3-15—6-13	.026	4.73
1870	1870					34.20		SE¼SE¼	36	34	47	3-15—4-28	.278	25.65
1870	1870					39.40		NW¼SE¼	36	34	47	3-15—4-28	.320	29.55
1870	1870				10.05			SW¼SE¼	36	34	47	3-15—6-13	.082	15.08
1870	1870					27.90		SW¼SE¼	36	34	47	3-15—4-28	.227	20.93
1870	1870					10.30		NE¼NW¼	36	34	47	3-15—4-28	.084	7.73
1870	1870					29.50		SE¼NW¼	36	34	47	3-15—4-28	.240	22.13
1870	1870					28.40		NE¼SW¼	36	34	47	3-15—4-28	.231	21.30
1870	1870					28.35		SE¼SW¼	36	34	47	3-15—4-28	.230	21.26
1870	1870					41.65		NE¼NE¼	1	33	47	3-15—4-28	.339	31.24
1870	1870					22.00		SE¼NE¼	1	33	47	3-15—4-28	.179	16.50
1870	1870					41.95		NW¼NE¼	1	33	47	3-15—4-28	.341	31.46
1870	1870					14.40		SW¼NE¼	1	33	47	3-15—4-28	.117	10.80
1870	1870					12.00		NW¼NW¼	31	34	48	3-15—4-28	.098	9.00
1870	1870					33.55		SW¼NW¼	31	34	48	3-15—4-28	.273	25.16
1870	1870					12.05		NE¼SW¼	31	34	48	3-15—4-28	.098	9.04
1870	1870					28.75		SE¼SW¼	31	34	48	3-15—4-28	.234	21.56
1870	1870					30.20		NW¼SW¼	31	34	48	3-15—4-28	.294	27.15
1870	1870					36.65		SW¼SW¼	31	34	48	3-15—4-28	.208	27.40
1870	1870					6.40		NW¼NE¼	6	33	48	3-15—4-28	.052	4.80

1870	1870	....	....	....	....	38.50	....	SW¼NE¼	6	33	48	3-15—4-28	.313	28.88
1870	1870	....	....	....	....	19.20	....	NW¼SE¼	6	33	48	3-15—4-28	.156	14.40
1870	1870	....	....	....	....	40.80	....	NE¼NW¼	6	33	48	3-15—4-28	.328	30.23
1870	1870	....	....	....	....	39.40	....	SE¼NW¼	6	33	48	3-15—4-28	.320	29.55
1870	1870	....	....	....	....	40.45	....	NW¼NW¼	6	33	48	3-15—4-28	.329	30.33
1870	1870	....	....	....	....	38.90	....	SW¼NW¼	6	33	48	3-15—4-28	.316	29.18
1870	1870	....	....	....	....	39.20	....	NE¼SW¼	6	33	48	3-15—4-28	.319	29.40
1870	1870	....	....	....	....	27.80	....	SE¼SW¼	6	33	48	3-15—4-28	.226	20.85
1870	1870	....	....	....	....	38.95	....	NW¼SW¼	6	33	48	3-15—4-28	.317	29.21
1870	1870	....	....	....	....	38.65	....	SW¼SW¼	6	33	48	3-15—4-28	.314	28.99
1870	1870	....	....	....	....	10.55	....	NW¼SE¼	25	34	47	3-15—4-28	.086	7.91
1870	1870	....	....	....	....	15.95	....	NE¼SE¼	25	34	47	3-15—4-28	.130	11.96
1870	1870	....	....	....	....	36.50	....	SW¼SE¼	25	34	47	3-15—4-28	.297	27.38
1870	1870	....	....	....	....	39.50	....	SE¼SE¼	25	34	47	3-15—4-28	.321	29.63
1870	1870	....	....	....	....	1.90	....	NW¼NW¼	36	33	47	3-15—4-28	.015	1.43
1870	1870	....	....	....	....	21.60	....	NE¼NW¼	36	33	47	3-15—4-28	.176	16.20
1870	1870	....	....	....	....	26.50	....	NW¼NE¼	36	33	47	3-15—4-28	.215	19.88
1870	1870	....	....	....	....	27.00	....	NE¼NE¼	36	33	47	3-15—4-28	.220	20.25
1870	1870	....	....	....	....	2.00	....	NW¼SW¼	30	34	48	3-15—4-28	.016	1.50
1870	1870	....	....	....	....	12.00	....	NE¼SW¼	30	34	48	3-15—4-28	.098	9.00
1870	1870	....	....	....	....	36.05	....	SW¼SW¼	30	34	48	3-15—4-28	.293	27.04
1870	1870	....	....	....	....	27.45	....	SE¼SW¼	30	34	48	3-15—4-28	.223	20.59
1870	1870	....	....	....	....	1.10	....	NW¼SE¼	30	34	48	3-15—4-28	.009	.83
1870	1870	....	....	....	....	17.50	....	SW¼SE¼	30	34	48	3-15—4-28	.142	13.13
1870	1870	....	....	....	....	26.10	....	NW¼NW¼	31	34	48	3-15—4-28	.212	19.58
1870	1870	....	....	....	....	12.90	....	NE¼NW¼	31	34	48	3-15—4-28	.105	9.68
1870	1870	....	....	....	29.75	....	....	SE¼SE¼	36	33	46	3-15—6-13	.242	44.63
1870	1870	....	....	....	27.25	....	....	SW¼SE¼	36	33	46	3-15—6-13	.226	40.88
1870	1870	....	....	....	9.20	....	....	SE¼SW¼	36	33	46	3-15—6-13	.075	13.80
1870	1870	....	....	....	22.00	....	....	NE¼NE¼	36	33	46	3-15—6-13	.179	33.00
1870	1870	....	....	....	14.35	....	....	SE¼NE¼	36	33	46	3-15—6-13	.117	21.58
1870	1870	....	....	....	....	8.90	....	SE¼NW¼	25	33	46	3-15—4-28	.072	6.68
1870	1870	....	....	....	....	28.30	....	NE¼SW¼	25	33	46	3-15—4-28	.230	21.22
1870	1870	....	....	....	....	4.20	....	SE¼SW¼	25	33	46	3-15—4-28	.034	3.15
1870	1870	....	....	....	....	21.10	....	SW¼NE¼	25	33	46	3-15—4-28	.172	15.83
1870	1870	....	....	....	....	19.20	....	SE¼NE¼	25	33	46	3-15—4-28	.156	14.40
1870	1870	....	....	....	....	35.95	....	NW¼SE¼	25	33	46	3-15—4-28	.292	26.96
1870	1870	....	....	....	....	9.80	....	NE¼SE¼	25	33	46	3-15—4-28	.080	7.35
1870	1870	....	....	....	....	5.45	....	SW¼SE¼	25	33	46	3-15—4-28	.044	4.09
1870	1870	....	....	....	....	8.35	....	SE¼SE¼	25	33	46	3-15—4-28	.068	6.26
1870	1870	....	....	....	....	2.35	....	NW¼SW¼	30	33	47	3-15—4-28	.019	1.76
1870	1870	....	....	....	....	....	20.85	NW¼SW¼	30	33	47	3-15—4-28	.170	15.64
1870	1870	....	....	....	....	25.45	....	NE¼SW¼	30	33	47	3-15—4-28	.207	19.09
1870	1870	....	....	....	....	....	6.55	NE¼SW¼	30	33	47	3-15—4-28	.053	4.91
1870	1870	....	....	....	....	26.75	....	NW¼SE¼	30	33	47	3-15—4-28	.217	20.06
1870	1870	....	....	....	36.10	....	....	NW¼NE¼	19	33	47	3-15—6-13	.293	54.15
1870	1870	....	....	....	36.85	....	....	SW¼NE¼	19	33	47	3-15—6-13	.300	55.28
1870	1870	....	....	....	39.30	....	....	SE¼NE¼	19	33	47	3-15—6-13	.320	58.95
1870	1870	....	....	....	38.25	....	....	NE¼NE¼	19	33	47	3-15—6-13	.311	57.38
1870	1870	....	....	....	4.50	....	....	NE¼SE¼	24	33	46	3-15—6-13	.037	6.75
1870	1870	....	....	....	28.30	....	....	SE¼SE¼	24	33	46	3-15—6-13	.230	42.45
1870	1870	....	....	....	12.70	....	....	NW¼NE¼	25	33	46	3-15—6-13	.103	19.05
1870	1870	....	....	....	36.90	....	....	NE¼NE¼	25	33	46	3-15—6-13	.300	55.35

William Dunphy Estate—Continued.

Date of beneficial use: Nat. mdw.	Date of beneficial use: Cult. area	Construction first initiated: Dams	Construction first initiated: Ditches	Culture—Acres: Harvest crops	Culture—Acres: Meadow pasture	Culture—Acres: Willow and sage pasture	Culture—Acres: Swamp or over-flow	Location: Subdivision	Location: Section	Location: Tp.N.	Location: R.E.	Length of season	Duty of water: C.F.S.	Duty of water: Acre-feet
1870	1870				14.20			SW¼NE¼	25	33	46	3-15—6-13	.115	21.30
1870	1870				14.70			SE¼NE¼	25	33	46	3-15—6-13	.120	22.05
1870	1870				0.40			SE¼NW¼	25	33	46	3-15—6-13	.003	.60
1870	1870				34.90			NW¼NW¼	30	33	47	3-15—6-13	.284	52.35
1870	1870						0.40	NW¼NW¼	30	33	47	3-15—4-28	.003	3.00
1870	1870				12.15			SW¼NW¼	30	33	47	3-15—6-13	.099	18.23
1870	1870						1.40	SW¼NW¼	30	33	47	3-15—4-28	.011	1.05
1870	1870				9.40			SE¼NW¼	30	33	47	3-15—6-13	.076	14.10
1870	1870						5.40	SE¼NW¼	30	33	47	3-15—4-28	.044	4.05
1870	1870				32.15			NE¼NW¼	30	33	47	3-15—6-13	.261	48.23
1870	1870						3.45	NE¼NW¼	30	33	47	3-15—4-28	.028	2.59
1870	1870					5.20		NE¼NW¼	10	33	47	3-15—4-28	.042	3.90
1870	1870				36.65			SE¼NW¼	10	33	47	3-15—6-13	.298	54.98
1870	1870					1.95		SE¼NW¼	10	33	47	3-15—4-28	.016	1.46
1870	1870				21.00			NW¼NW¼	10	33	47	3-15—6-13	.176	32.40
1870	1870					2.00		NW¼NW¼	10	33	47	3-15—4-28	.016	1.50
1870	1870				36.25			SW¼NW¼	10	33	47	3-15—6-13	.295	54.38
1870	1870					3.30		SW¼NW¼	10	33	47	3-15—4-28	.027	2.48
1870	1870				38.95			NE¼SW¼	10	33	47	3-15—6-13	.317	58.43
1870	1870				0.15			SE¼SW¼	10	33	47	3-15—6-13	.001	.23
1870	1870				37.90			NW¼SW¼	10	33	47	3-15—6-13	.308	56.85
1870	1870				2.10			SW¼SW¼	10	33	47	3-15—6-13	.017	3.15
1870	1870				40.65			SW¼SE¼	2	33	47	3-15—6-13	.330	60.98
1870	1870				19.45			NE¼NW¼	2	33	47	3-15—6-13	.158	29.18
1870	1870					15.90		NE¼NW¼	2	33	47	3-15—4-28	.129	11.93
1870	1870				3.30			SE¼NW¼	2	33	47	3-15—6-13	.027	4.95
1870	1870					36.50		SE¼NW¼	2	33	47	3-15—4-28	.297	27.38
1870	1870				11.10			NW¼NW¼	2	33	47	3-15—6-13	.090	16.65
1870	1870					1.80		NW¼NW¼	2	33	47	3-15—4-28	.014	1.35
1870	1870				27.80			SW¼NW¼	2	33	47	3-15—6-13	.226	41.70
1870	1870					12.75		SW¼NW¼	2	33	47	3-15—4-28	.104	9.56
1870	1870				39.75			NW¼NW¼	20	33	47	3-15—6-13	.323	59.63
1870	1870				40.40			NE¼NW¼	20	33	47	3-15—6-13	.328	60.60
1870	1870				40.50			SW¼NW¼	20	33	47	3-15—6-13	.329	60.75
1870	1870				38.85			SE¼NW¼	20	33	47	3-15—6-13	.316	58.28
1870	1870				38.65			NW¼SW¼	20	33	47	3-15—6-13	.314	57.98
1870	1870				25.80			NE¼SW¼	20	33	47	3-15—6-13	.210	38.70
1870	1870				36.30			SW¼SW¼	20	33	47	3-15—6-13	.295	54.45
1870	1870				18.70			SE¼SW¼	20	33	47	3-15—6-13	.152	28.05
1870	1870				16.35			NW¼SE¼	20	33	47	3-15—6-13	.133	24.53
1870	1870				12.70			SW¼SE¼	20	33	47	3-15—6-13	.103	19.05
1870	1870				26.65			SE¼SE¼	20	33	47	3-15—6-13	.217	39.98
1870	1870				5.20			NE¼SE¼	20	33	47	3-15—6-13	.042	7.80
1870	1870				37.00			NW¼NE¼	20	33	47	3-15—6-13	.300	55.50
1870	1870				37.45			SW¼NE¼	20	33	47	3-15—6-13	.304	56.18
1870	1870				17.10			NE¼NE¼	20	33	47	3-15—6-13	.139	25.65

1870	1870	....	....	....	4.80	....	....	NE¼ NE¼	20	33	47	3-15—6-13	.080	7.20
1870	1870	....	....	....	14.55	....	....	SE¼ SW¼	9	33	47	3-15—6-13	.118	21.83
1870	1870	....	....	....	....	1.55	....	SE¼ SW¼	9	33	47	3-15—4-28	.013	1.16
1870	1870	....	....	....	10.55	....	....	SW¼ SE¼	9	33	47	3-15—6-13	.086	15.83
1870	1870	....	....	....	....	26.65	....	SW¼ SE¼	9	33	47	3-15—4-28	.216	19.90
1870	1870	....	....	....	31.40	....	....	SE¼ SE¼	9	33	47	3-15—6-13	.255	47.10
1870	1870	....	....	....	....	4.45	....	SE¼ SE¼	9	33	47	3-15—4-28	.036	3.34
1870	1870	....	....	....	35.90	....	....	SW¼ SW¼	10	33	47	3-15—6-13	.292	53.85
1870	1870	....	....	....	30.15	....	....	SE¼ SW¼	10	33	47	3-15—6-13	.318	58.73
1870	1870	....	....	....	11.15	....	....	SW¼ SE¼	10	33	47	3-15—6-13	.091	16.73
1870	1870	....	....	....	30.45	....	....	SE¼ SE¼	10	33	47	3-15—6-13	.248	45.68
1870	1870	....	....	....	1.90	....	....	NE¼ SE¼	10	33	47	3-15—6-13	.015	2.85
1870	1870	....	....	....	.20	....	....	NW¼ SE¼	10	33	47	3-15—6-13	.002	.30
1870	1870	....	....	....	24.10	....	....	SW¼ SW¼	11	33	47	3-15—6-13	.196	36.15
1870	1870	....	....	....	40.25	....	....	NE¼ NE¼	16	33	47	3-15—6-13	.327	60.38
1870	1870	....	....	....	36.90	....	....	SE¼ NE¼	16	33	47	3-15—6-13	.300	55.35
1870	1870	....	....	....	....	1.90	....	SE¼ NE¼	16	33	47	3-15—4-28	.015	1.43
1870	1870	....	....	....	35.20	....	....	NW¼ NE¼	16	33	47	3-15—6-13	.327	52.80
1870	1870	....	....	....	....	2.95	....	NW¼ NE¼	16	33	47	3-15—4-28	.024	2.21
1870	1870	....	....	....	37.25	....	....	SW¼ NE¼	16	33	47	3-15—6-13	.303	55.88
1870	1870	....	....	....	....	1.50	....	SW¼ NE¼	16	33	47	3-15—4-28	.012	1.13
1870	1870	....	....	....	16.85	....	....	NE¼ NW¼	16	33	47	3-15—6-13	.137	25.28
1870	1870	....	....	....	....	1.80	....	NE¼ NW¼	16	33	47	3-15—4-28	.015	1.85
1870	1870	....	....	....	13.35	....	....	SE¼ NW¼	16	33	47	3-15—6-13	.109	20.03
1870	1870	....	....	....	....	4.85	....	SE¼ NW¼	16	33	47	3-15—4-28	.039	3.64
1870	1870	....	....	....	....	21.35	....	NE¼ SW¼	16	33	47	3-15—4-28	.174	16.01
1870	1870	....	....	....	13.65	....	....	SE¼ SW¼	16	33	47	3-15—6-13	.111	20.48
1870	1870	....	....	....	....	7.80	....	SE¼ SW¼	16	33	47	3-15—4-28	.063	5.85
1870	1870	....	....	....	0.65	....	....	NW¼ SE¼	16	33	47	3-15—6-13	.005	.98
1870	1870	....	....	....	....	37.50	....	NW¼ SE¼	16	33	47	3-15—4-28	.305	28.13
1870	1870	....	....	....	21.90	....	....	SW¼ SE¼	16	33	47	3-15—6-13	.178	32.85
1870	1870	....	....	....	....	16.15	....	SW¼ SE¼	16	33	47	3-15—4-28	.131	12.11
1870	1870	....	....	....	37.25	....	....	SE¼ SE¼	16	33	47	3-15—6-13	.303	55.88
1870	1870	....	....	....	....	1.85	....	SE¼ SE¼	16	33	47	3-15—4-28	.015	1.39
1870	1870	....	....	....	3.30	....	....	NE¼ SE¼	16	33	47	3-15—6-13	.027	4.95
1870	1870	....	....	....	....	34.55	....	NE¼ SE¼	16	33	47	3-15—4-28	.281	25.91
1870	1870	....	....	....	2.35	....	....	NE¼ NE¼	21	33	47	3-15—6-13	.019	3.53
1870	1870	....	....	....	....	35.10	....	NE¼ NE¼	21	33	47	3-15—4-28	.285	26.33
1870	1870	....	....	....	....	37.55	....	SE¼ NE¼	21	33	47	3-15—4-28	.305	28.16
1870	1870	....	....	....	14.15	....	....	NW¼ NE¼	21	33	47	3-15—6-13	.115	21.23
1870	1870	....	....	....	....	22.80	....	NW¼ NE¼	21	33	47	3-15—4-28	.185	17.10
1870	1870	....	....	....	....	39.05	....	SW¼ NE¼	21	33	47	3-15—4-28	.317	29.29
1870	1870	....	....	....	18.65	....	....	NE¼ SE¼	21	33	47	3-15—6-13	.152	27.98
1870	1870	....	....	....	....	18.50	....	NE¼ SE¼	21	33	47	3-15—4-28	.150	13.88
1870	1870	....	....	17.95	....	....	....	SE¼ SE¼	21	33	47	3-15—9-15	.146	53.85
1870	1870	....	....	....	19.50	....	....	SE¼ SE¼	21	33	47	3-15—6-13	.159	29.25
1870	1870	....	....	....	....	0.40	....	SE¼ SE¼	21	33	47	3-15—4-28	.003	.30
1870	1870	....	....	0.60	....	....	....	SW¼ SE¼	21	33	47	3-15—9-15	.005	1.80
1870	1870	....	....	....	28.20	....	....	SW¼ SE¼	21	33	47	3-15—6-13	.229	42.36
1870	1870	....	....	....	....	8.80	....	SW¼ SE¼	21	33	47	3-15—4-28	.072	6.60
1870	1870	....	....	....	....	38.75	....	NW¼ SE¼	21	33	47	3-15—4-28	.315	29.06
1870	1870	....	....	....	9.00	....	....	NE¼ NW¼	21	33	47	3-15—6-13	.073	13.50

William Dunphy Estate—Continued.

Date of beneficial use: Nat. mdw.	Cult. area	Construction first initiated: Dams	Ditches	Culture—Acres: Harvest crops	Meadow pasture	Willow and sage pasture	Swamp or overflow	Location: Subdivision	Section	Tp. N.	R. E.	Length of season	Duty of water: C. F. S.	Acre-feet
1870	1870					12.85		NE¼NW¼	21	33	47	3-15—4-28	.104	9.64
1870	1870					21.35		SE¼NW¼	21	33	47	3-15—4-28	.174	16.01
1870	1870					24.05		NE¼SW¼	21	33	47	3-15—4-28	.196	18.04
1870	1870			1.15				SE¼SW¼	21	33	47	3-15—9-15	.009	3.45
1870	1870				12.50			SE¼SW¼	21	33	47	3-15—6-13	.102	18.75
1870	1870					9.65		SE¼SW¼	21	33	47	3-15—4-28	.078	7.24
1870	1870				14.70			SW¼SW¼	9	33	47	3-15—6-13	.120	22.05
1870	1870				18.55			SE¼SW¼	9	33	47	3-15—6-13	.151	27.82
1870	1870				34.05			NW¼NW¼	16	33	47	3-15—6-13	.277	51.08
1870	1870				19.15			NE¼NW¼	16	33	47	3-15—6-13	.155	28.73
1870	1870				34.00			SW¼NW¼	16	33	47	3-15—6-13	.276	51.00
1870	1870				16.25			SE¼NW¼	16	33	47	3-15—6-13	.132	24.38
1870	1870					1.80		SE¼NW¼	16	33	47	3-15—4-28	.015	1.35
1870	1870				16.60			NW¼SW¼	16	33	47	3-15—6-13	.135	24.90
1870	1870					18.80		NW¼SW¼	16	33	47	3-15—4-28	.153	14.10
1870	1870				2.70			SW¼SW¼	16	33	47	3-15—6-13	.022	4.05
1870	1870					34.20		SW¼SW¼	16	33	47	3-15—4-28	.278	25.65
1870	1870				5.15			SE¼SW¼	16	33	47	3-15—6-13	.042	7.73
1870	1870					10.60		SE¼SW¼	16	33	47	3-15—4-28	.086	7.95
1870	1870					19.10		NE¼SW¼	16	33	47	3-15—4-28	.155	14.33
1870	1870				37.80			NE¼SE¼	17	33	47	3-15—6-13	.307	56.70
1870	1870					0.95		NE¼SE¼	17	33	47	3-15—4-28	.008	.71
1870	1870				20.80			SE¼SE¼	17	33	47	3-15—6-13	.169	31.20
1870	1870					16.05		SE¼SE¼	17	33	47	3-15—4-28	.130	12.04
1870	1870				36.50			NW¼SE¼	17	33	47	3-15—6-13	.297	54.75
1870	1870					1.65		NW¼SE¼	17	33	47	3-15—4-28	.013	1.24
1870	1870				38.00			SW¼SE¼	17	33	47	3-15—6-13	.309	57.00
1870	1870				16.10			NW¼SW¼	17	33	47	3-15—6-13	.131	24.15
1870	1870				37.80			SW¼SW¼	17	33	47	3-15—6-13	.307	56.70
1870	1870				0.35			NW¼NE¼	22	33	47	3-15—6-13	.003	.53
1870	1870						38.00	NW¼NE¼	22	33	47	3-15—4-28	.309	28.50
1870	1870				14.65			SW¼NE¼	22	33	47	3-15—6-13	.119	21.98
1870	1870				8.15			NE¼NW¼	22	33	47	3-15—6-13	.066	12.23
1870	1870						31.10	NE¼NW¼	22	33	47	3-15—4-28	.253	23.33
1870	1870				37.65			SE¼NW¼	22	33	47	3-15—6-13	.306	56.48
1870	1870						1.30	SE¼NW¼	22	33	47	3-15—4-28	.011	.98
1870	1870				0.95			NW¼NW¼	22	33	47	3-15—6-13	.008	1.43
1870	1870						38.70	NW¼NW¼	22	33	47	3-15—4-28	.315	29.03
1870	1870				25.50			SW¼NW¼	22	33	47	3-15—6-13	.183	38.25
1870	1870						12.35	SW¼NW¼	22	33	47	3-15—4-28	.100	9.26
1870	1870			1.40				NE¼SW¼	22	33	47	3-15—9-15	.011	4.20
1870	1870				26.70			NE¼SW¼	22	33	47	3-15—6-13	.217	40.05
1870	1870						8.85	NE¼SW¼	22	33	47	3-15—4-28	.072	6.64
1870	1870			1.50				NW¼SW¼	22	33	47	3-15—9-15	.012	4.50
1870	1870				37.35			NW¼SW¼	22	33	47	3-15—6-13	.304	56.03
1870	1870				8.00			SE¼SW¼	15	33	47	3-15—6-13	.065	12.00

1870	1870						30.55	SE¼SW¼	15	33	47	3-15—4-28	.248	22.01
1870	1870				21.35			NE¼SW¼	15	33	47	3-15—6-13	.108	36.53
1870	1870						15.65	NE¼SW¼	15	33	47	3-15—4-28	.127	11.74
1870	1870						39.55	NW¼SE¼	15	33	47	3-15—4-28	.322	29.66
1870	1870						38.55	SW¼SE¼	15	33	47	3-15—4-28	.313	28.91
1870	1870				0.40			SE¼SE¼	15	33	47	3-15—6-13	.003	.60
1870	1870						38.50	SE¼SE¼	15	33	47	3-15—4-28	.313	28.88
1870	1870						38.05	NE¼SE¼	15	33	47	3-15—4-28	.309	28.54
1870	1870				27.90			NW¼NE¼	15	33	47	3-15—6-13	.227	41.85
1870	1870						11.95	NW¼NE¼	15	33	47	3-15—4-28	.097	8.96
1870	1870				0.60			SW¼NE¼	15	33	47	3-15—6-13	.005	.90
1870	1870						37.70	SW¼NE¼	15	33	47	3-15—4-28	.307	28.28
1870	1870						37.95	SE¼NE¼	15	33	47	3-15—4-28	.308	28.46
1870	1870				4.10			NE¼NE¼	15	33	47	3-15—6-13	.033	6.15
1870	1870						36.55	NE¼NE¼	15	33	47	3-15—4-28	.297	27.41
1870	1870				3.45			NW¼NW¼	14	33	47	3-15—6-13	.028	5.18
1870	1870				4.45			NE¼NW¼	14	33	47	3-15—6-13	.036	6.68
1870	1870				9.60			SW¼NW¼	14	33	47	3-15—6-13	.078	14.40
1870	1870				6.65			SE¼NW¼	14	33	47	3-15—6-13	.054	9.98
1870	1870				1.25			NW¼SW¼	14	33	47	3-15—6-13	.010	1.88
1870	1870				0.30			NE¼SW¼	14	33	47	3-15—6-13	.002	.45
1870	1870				0.50			SW¼SW¼	14	33	47	3-15—6-13	.004	.75
1870	1870					1.30		SE¼NW¼	30	33	47	3-15—4-28	.011	.98
1870	1870						17.50	SE¼NW¼	30	33	47	3-15—4-28	.142	13.13
1870	1870					3.15		SW¼NW¼	30	33	47	3-15—4-28	.026	2.36
1870	1870						11.90	SW¼NW¼	30	33	47	3-15—4-28	.097	8.93
1870	1870					1.00		SW¼NE¼	30	33	47	3-15—4-28	.008	.75
1870	1870						20.20	SW¼NE¼	30	33	47	3-15—4-28	.164	15.15
1870	1870					18.15		SW¼NW¼	20	33	47	3-15—4-28	.148	13.54
1870	1870					15.80		SE¼NW¼	29	33	47	3-15—4-28	.128	11.85
1870	1870					15.00		SW¼NE¼	29	33	47	3-15—4-28	.122	11.25
1870	1870					37.00		NW¼SW¼	29	33	47	3-15—4-28	.300	27.75
1870	1870					37.00		NE¼SW¼	29	33	47	3-15—4-28	.300	27.75
1870	1870			4.80				SE¼NW¼	28	33	47	3-15—9-15	.039	14.40
1870	1870						5.90	SE¼NW¼	28	33	47	3-15—4-28	.048	4.43
1870	1870			20.15				NE¼NW¼	28	33	47	3-15—9-15	.164	60.45
1870	1870				1.45			NE¼NW¼	28	33	47	3-15—6-13	.012	2.18
1870	1870						.70	NE¼NW¼	28	33	47	3-15—4-28	.006	.53
1870	1870			32.45				NW¼NE¼	28	33	47	3-15—9-15	.264	97.35
1870	1870				3.90			NW¼NE¼	28	33	47	3-15—6-13	.032	5.85
1870	1870			13.25				SW¼NE¼	28	33	47	3-15—9-15	.107	39.75
1870	1870						3.55	SW¼NE¼	28	33	47	3-15—4-28	.029	2.66
1870	1870				40.25			NW¼NW¼	15	33	47	3-15—6-13	.327	60.38
1870	1870				38.70			SW¼NW¼	15	33	47	3-15—6-13	.315	58.05
1870	1870				38.20			SE¼NW¼	15	33	47	3-15—6-13	.311	57.30
1870	1870						2.85	SE¼NW¼	15	33	47	3-15—4-28	.023	2.14
1870	1870				40.00			NE¼NW¼	15	33	47	3-15—6-13	.325	60.00
1870	1870				36.50			NW¼SW¼	15	33	47	3-15—6-13	.297	54.75
1870	1870						3.45	NW¼SW¼	15	33	47	3-15—4-28	.028	2.59
1870	1870				36.20			SW¼SW¼	15	33	47	3-15—6-13	.294	54.30
1870	1870						3.90	SW¼SW¼	15	33	47	3-15—4-28	.032	2.93
1870	1870						8.00	NW¼SE¼	30	33	47	3-15—4-28	.065	6.00

William Dunphy Estate—Continued.

Date of beneficial use: Nat. mdw.	Date of beneficial use: Cult. area	Construction first initiated: Dams	Construction first initiated: Ditches	Culture—Acres: Harvest crops	Culture—Acres: Meadow pasture	Culture—Acres: Willow and sage pasture	Culture—Acres: Swamp or overflow	Location: Subdivision	Location: Section	Location: Tp.N.	Location: R.E.	Length of season	Duty of water: C.F.S.	Duty of water: Acre-feet
1870	1870					33.60		NE¼SE¼	30	33	47	3-15—4-28	.273	25.20
1870	1870					20.20		SE¼NE¼	30	33	47	3-15—4-28	.164	15.15
1870	1870						.15	SE¼NE¼	30	33	47	3-15—4-28	.001	.11
1870	1870				32.45			SE¼NE¼	9	33	47	3-15—6-13	.264	48.68
1870	1870					1.42		SE¼NE¼	9	33	47	3-15—4-28	.012	1.07
1870	1870				10.64			SW¼NE¼	9	33	47	3-15—6-13	.087	15.96
1870	1870				26.20			NE¼SE¼	9	33	47	3-15—6-13	.213	39.30
1870	1870					11.35		NE¼SE¼	9	33	47	3-15—4-28	.092	8.51
1870	1870				.85			SE¼SE¼	9	33	47	3-15—6-13	.007	1.28
1870	1870					1.50		SE¼SE¼	9	33	47	3-15—4-28	.012	1.13
1870	1870				32.35			NW¼SE¼	9	33	47	3-15—6-13	.263	48.53
1870	1870					4.50		NW¼SE¼	9	33	47	3-15—4-28	.037	3.38
1870	1870				35.80			NE¼SW¼	2	33	47	3-15—6-13	.291	53.70
1870	1870					3.65		NE¼SW¼	2	33	47	3-15—4-28	.030	2.74
1870	1870				40.90			SE¼SW¼	2	33	47	3-15—6-13	.333	61.35
1870	1870				35.65			NW¼SW¼	2	33	47	3-15—6-13	.290	53.48
1870	1870					4.20		NW¼SW¼	2	33	47	3-15—4-28	.034	3.15
1870	1870				38.55			SW¼SW¼	2	33	47	3-15—6-13	.312	57.83
1870	1870					2.25		SW¼SW¼	2	33	47	3-15—4-28	.018	1.69
1870	1870				15.25			SE¼NE¼	3	33	47	3-15—6-13	.124	22.88
1870	1870					5.16		SE¼NE¼	3	33	47	3-15—4-28	.042	3.87
1870	1870				28.15			NE¼SE¼	3	33	47	3-15—6-13	.229	42.23
1870	1870					11.40		NE¼SE¼	3	33	47	3-15—4-28	.093	8.55
1870	1870				2.65			SE¼SE¼	3	33	47	3-15—6-13	.022	3.98
1870	1870					39.50		SE¼SE¼	3	33	47	3-15—4-28	.321	29.63
1870	1870				5.90			NW¼SE¼	3	33	47	3-15—6-13	.048	8.85
1870	1870					.15		NW¼SE¼	3	33	47	3-15—4-28	.001	.11
1870	1870				18.05			SW¼SE¼	3	33	47	3-15—6-13	.147	27.08
1870	1870					13.90		SW¼SE¼	3	33	47	3-15—4-28	.113	10.43
1870	1870				4.57			SE¼SW¼	3	33	47	3-15—6-13	.037	6.86
1870	1870				3.53			NE¼NE¼	9	33	47	3-15—6-13	.029	5.30
1870	1870					41.25		NE¼SE¼	1	33	47	3-15—4-28	.335	30.94
1870	1870					40.55		SE¼SE¼	1	33	47	3-15—4-28	.330	30.41
1870	1870					39.05		NW¼SE¼	1	33	47	3-15—4-28	.317	29.29
1870	1870					41.00		SW¼SE¼	1	33	47	3-15—4-28	.333	30.75
1870	1870					30.05		NE¼NW¼	1	33	47	3-15—4-28	.244	22.54
1870	1870					30.50		SE¼NW¼	1	33	47	3-15—4-28	.248	22.88
1870	1870					31.70		NE¼SW¼	1	33	47	3-15—4-28	.258	23.78
1870	1870				17.60			SE¼SW¼	1	33	47	3-15—6-13	.143	26.40
1870	1870					14.00		SE¼SW¼	1	33	47	3-15—4-28	.257	10.50
1870	1870					37.55		NE¼NE¼	12	33	47	3-15—4-28	.305	28.16
1870	1870					32.45		SE¼NE¼	12	33	47	3-15—4-28	.264	24.34
1870	1870					40.00		NW¼NE¼	12	33	47	3-15—4-28	.325	30.00
1870	1870					37.55		SW¼NE¼	12	33	47	3-15—4-28	.305	28.16
1870	1870				8.35			NE¼NW¼	12	33	47	3-15—6-13	.068	12.53
1870	1870					20.90		NE¼NW¼	12	33	47	3-15—4-28	.170	15.68

1870	1870				.15			SE¼NW¼	12	33	47	3-15—6-13	.001	.23
1870	1870					15.85		SE¼NW¼	12	33	47	3-15—4-28	.120	11.80
1870	1870					3.00		SW¼SE¼	31	34	48	3-15—4-28	.024	2.25
1870	1870					1.15		NE¼NW¼	31	34	48	3-15—4-28	.009	.86
1870	1870					3.65		SE¼NW¼	31	34	48	3-15—4-28	.030	2.74
1870	1870					5.10		NE¼NW¼	12	33	47	3-15—4-28	.041	3.83
1870	1870				1.25			SE¼NW¼	12	33	47	3-15—6-13	.010	1.88
1870	1870					2.40		SE¼NW¼	12	33	47	3-15—4-28	.020	1.80
1870	1870				21.65			NW¼NW¼	12	33	47	3-15—6-13	.176	32.48
1870	1870					17.80		NW¼NW¼	12	33	47	3-15—4-28	.145	13.35
1870	1870				1.55			SW¼NW¼	12	33	47	3-15—6-13	.013	2.33
1870	1870					19.80		SW¼NW¼	12	33	47	3-15—4-28	.161	14.85
1870	1870				31.80			NE¼NE¼	11	33	47	3-15—6-13	.259	47.70
1870	1870					6.25		NE¼NE¼	11	33	47	3-15—4-28	.051	4.67
1870	1870					38.00		SE¼NE¼	11	33	47	3-15—4-28	.309	28.50
1870	1870				37.65			NW¼NE¼	11	33	47	3-15—6-13	.306	56.48
1870	1870				5.20			SW¼NE¼	11	33	47	3-15—6-13	.042	7.80
1870	1870					31.50		SW¼NE¼	11	33	47	3-15—4-28	.256	23.63
1870	1870					.75		NE¼SE¼	11	33	47	3-15—4-28	.006	.56
1870	1870					21.80		NW¼SE¼	11	33	47	3-15—4-28	.177	16.35
1870	1870				36.95			NE¼NW¼	11	33	47	3-15—6-13	.300	55.43
1870	1870					.15		NE¼NW¼	11	33	47	3-15—4-28	.001	.11
1870	1870				4.15			SE¼NW¼	11	33	47	3-15—6-13	.033	6.23
1870	1870					31.80		SE¼NW¼	11	33	47	3-15—4-28	.259	23.85
1870	1870				32.50			NW¼NW¼	11	33	47	3-15—6-13	.264	48.75
1870	1870					2.75		NW¼NW¼	11	33	47	3-15—4-28	.022	2.06
1870	1870				19.55			SW¼NW¼	11	33	47	3-15—6-13	.159	29.33
1870	1870					16.45		SW¼NW¼	11	33	47	3-15—4-28	.134	12.34
1870	1870					31.75		NE¼SW¼	11	33	47	3-15—4-28	.258	23.81
1870	1870					34.85		NW¼SW¼	11	33	47	3-15—4-28	.202	26.14
1870	1870				3.70			NE¼NW¼	12	33	47	3-15—6-13	.030	5.55
1870	1870					9.80		NE¼SW¼	1	33	47	3-15—4-28	.080	7.35
1870	1870				8.90			SE¼SW¼	1	33	47	3.15—6-13	.072	13.35
1870	1870					.80		SE¼SW¼	1	33	47	3-15—4-28	.007	.60
1870	1870				.25			NW¼SW¼	1	33	47	3-15—6-13	.002	.38
1870	1870					39.90		NW¼SW¼	1	33	47	3-15—4-28	.324	29.93
1870	1870				39.35			SW¼SW¼	1	33	47	3-15—6-13	.320	59.03
1870	1870					1.35		SW¼SW¼	1	33	47	3-15—4-28	.011	1.01
1870	1870					38.50		NE¼NE¼	2	33	47	3-15—4-28	.313	28.88
1870	1870				12.45			SE¼NE¼	2	33	47	3-15—6-13	.101	18.68
1870	1870					25.10		SE¼NE¼	2	33	47	3-15—4-28	.204	26.33
1870	1870				1.60			NW¼NE¼	2	33	47	3-15—6-13	.013	2.40
1870	1870					38.10		NW¼NE¼	2	33	47	3-15—4-28	.310	28.58
1870	1870				4.30			SW¼NE¼	2	33	47	3-15—6-13	.035	6.45
1870	1870					35.30		SW¼NE¼	2	33	47	3-15—4-28	.287	26.48
1870	1870				24.15			NE¼SE¼	2	33	47	3-15—6-13	.196	36.23
1870	1870					14.20		NE¼SE¼	2	33	47	3-15—4-28	.115	10.65
1870	1870				40.60			SE¼SE¼	2	33	47	3-15—6-13	.330	60.90
1870	1870				36.05			NW¼SE¼	2	33	47	3-15—6-13	.293	54.08
1870	1870					3.25		NW¼SE¼	2	33	47	3-15—4-28	.026	2.44
1870	1870				35.55			NW¼NE¼	30	33	47	3-15—6-13	.289	53.33
1870	1870						1.90	NW¼NE¼	30	33	47	3-15—4-28	.015	1.42

William Dunphy Estate—Continued.

Date of beneficial use: Nat. mdw.	Date of beneficial use: Cult. area	Construction first initiated: Dams	Construction first initiated: Ditches	Culture—Acres: Harvest crops	Culture—Acres: Meadow pasture	Culture—Acres: Willow and sage pasture	Culture—Acres: Swamp or overflow	Location: Subdivision	Location: Section	Location: Tp.N.	Location: R.E.	Length of season	Duty of water: C.F.S.	Duty of water: Acre-feet
1870	1870				6.10			SW¼NE¼	30	33	47	3-15—6-13	.050	9.15
1870	1870						6.95	SW¼NE¼	30	33	47	3-15—4-28	.057	5.21
1870	1870				2.25			SW¼SE¼	9	33	47	3-15—6-13	.018	3.38
1870	1870					.45		SW¼SE¼	9	33	47	3-15—4-28	.004	.34
1870	1870				9.70			NE¼SW¼	9	33	47	3-15—6-13	.079	14.55
1870	1870					.40		NE¼SW¼	9	33	47	3-15—4-28	.003	.30
1870	1870				1.05			SE¼SW¼	9	33	47	3-15—6-13	.000	.08
1870	1870					.10		SE¼SW¼	9	33	47	3-15—4-28	.001	.08
1870	1870				1.70			NE¼NE¼	10	33	47	3-15—6-13	.014	2.55
1870	1870					36.05		NE¼NE¼	10	33	47	3-15—4-28	.293	27.04
1870	1870				29.95			SE¼NE¼	10	33	47	3-15—6-13	.243	44.93
1870	1870					8.65		SE¼NE¼	10	33	47	3-15—4-28	.070	6.49
1870	1870				32.10			NW¼NE¼	10	33	47	3-15—6-13	.261	48.15
1870	1870					7.10		NW¼NE¼	10	33	47	3-15—4-28	.058	5.33
1870	1870				36.50			SW¼NE¼	10	33	47	3-15—6-13	.297	54.75
1870	1870					2.25		SW¼NE¼	10	33	47	3-15—4-28	.018	1.69
1870	1870				9.95			NE¼SE¼	10	33	47	3-15—6-13	.081	14.93
1870	1870					26.95		NE¼SE¼	10	33	47	3-15—4-28	.219	20.21
1870	1870				33.00			NW¼SE¼	10	33	47	3-15—6-13	.268	49.50
1870	1870					5.70		NW¼SE¼	10	33	47	3-15—4-28	.046	4.28
1870	1870				32.50			NE¼NW¼	10	33	47	3-15—6-13	.264	48.75
1870	1870						7.35	SE¼NW¼	29	33	47	3-15—4-28	.060	5.51
1870	1870				26.70			NW¼NE¼	29	33	47	3-15—6-13	.217	40.05
1870	1870						10.70	NW¼NE¼	29	33	47	3-15—4-28	.087	8.03
1870	1870			10.75				NE¼NE¼	29	33	47	3-15—9-15	.087	32.25
1870	1870						26.85	NE¼NE¼	29	33	47	3-15—4-28	.218	20.14
1870	1870			0.40				SE¼NE¼	29	33	47	3-15—9-15	.003	1.20
1870	1870				13.15			SE¼NE¼	29	33	47	3-15—6-13	.107	19.73
1870	1870						1.80	SE¼NE¼	29	33	47	3-15—4-28	.015	1.35
1870	1870				15.30			SW¼NE¼	29	33	47	3-15—6-13	.125	23.10
1870	1870				9.85			SE¼NE¼	30	33	47	3-15—6-13	.080	14.78
1870	1870						3.35	SE¼NE¼	30	33	47	3-15—4-28	.027	2.51
1870	1870				29.90			NE¼NE¼	30	33	47	3-15—6-13	.243	44.85
1870	1870						4.25	NE¼NE¼	30	33	47	3-15—4-28	.035	3.19
1870	1870				33.95			NW¼NW¼	21	33	47	3-15—6-13	.276	50.93
1870	1870				14.50			NE¼NW¼	21	33	47	3-15—6-13	.118	21.75
1870	1870				13.90			SW¼NW¼	21	33	47	3-15—6-13	.113	20.85
1870	1870				1.00			SE¼NW¼	21	33	47	3-15—6-13	.008	1.50
1870	1870			9.00				NW¼NW¼	28	33	47	3-15—9-15	.073	27.00
1870	1870			10.85				NE¼NW¼	28	33	47	3-15—9-15	.088	32.55
1870	1870			8.55				SW¼NW¼	28	33	47	3-15—9-15	.070	25.65
1870	1870				1.00			SW¼NW¼	28	33	47	3-15—6-13	.008	1.50
1870	1870			4.40				SE¼NW¼	28	33	47	3-15—9-15	.036	13.20
1870	1870				35.35			NW¼NW¼	29	33	47	3-15—6-13	.287	53.03
1870	1870				28.35			NE¼NW¼	29	33	47	3-15—6-13	.230	42.53
1870	1870						7.70	NE¼NW¼	29	33	47	3-15—4-28	.063	5.76

1870	1870				11.55			SW¼ NW¼	20	33	47	3-15—6-13	.094	17.33
1870	1870						2.80	SW¼ NW¼	20	33	47	3-15—4-28	.023	2.10
1870	1870				6.70			SE¼ NW¼	20	33	47	3-15—6-13	.054	10.05
1870	1870				38.85			SE¼ SW¼	17	33	47	3-15—6-13	.316	58.28
1870	1870				33.55			NE¼ SW¼	17	33	47	3-15—6-13	.273	50.33
1870	1870				11.60			SE¼ NE¼	17	33	47	3-15—6-13	.094	17.40
1870	1870				12.25			SW¼ SE¼	18	33	47	3-15—6-13	.100	18.38
1870	1870				34.35			SE¼ SE¼	18	33	47	3-15—6-13	.279	51.53
1870	1870				1.70			NE¼ SE¼	18	33	47	3-15—6-13	.014	2.55
1870	1870				14.80			SW¼ NW¼	19	33	47	3-15—6-13	.120	22.20
1870	1870				37.10			SE¼ NW¼	19	33	47	3-15—6-13	.302	55.65
1870	1870				15.10			NE¼ NW¼	19	33	47	3-15—6-13	.123	22.65
1870	1870				34.90			NW¼ SW¼	19	33	47	3-15—6-13	.284	52.35
1870	1870				37.20			SW¼ SW¼	19	33	47	3-15—6-13	.302	55.80
1870	1870				39.25			SE¼ SW¼	19	33	47	3-15—6-13	.319	58.88
1870	1870				38.55			NE¼ SW¼	19	33	47	3-15—6-13	.313	57.83
1870	1870				38.50			NW¼ SE¼	19	33	47	3-15—6-13	.313	57.75
1870	1870				40.25			SW¼ SE¼	19	33	47	3-15—6-13	.327	60.38
1870	1870				39.65			SE¼ SE¼	19	33	47	3-15—6-13	.322	59.48
1870	1870				38.75			NE¼ SE¼	19	33	47	3-15—6-13	.315	58.13
1870	1870					15.80		NE¼ SE¼	7	33	48	3-15—4-28	.128	11.85
1870	1870					4.50		NE¼ SW¼	7	33	48	3-15—4-28	.037	3.38
1870	1870					29.60		NW¼ NW¼	7	33	48	3-15—4-28	.241	22.20
1870	1870					0.70		SW¼ NE¼	8	33	48	3-15—4-28	.006	.53
1870	1870					19.70		NE¼ SE¼	8	33	48	3-15—4-28	.160	14.78
1870	1870					32.05		NW¼ SE¼	8	33	48	3-15—4-28	.261	24.04
1870	1870					27.25		NE¼ SW¼	8	33	48	3-15—4-28	.222	20.44
1870	1870					24.50		NW¼ SW¼	8	33	48	3-15—4-28	.199	18.38
1870	1870					24.45		SW¼ NE¼	9	33	48	3-15—4-28	.199	18.34
1870	1870					32.05		NW¼ SE¼	9	33	48	3-15—4-28	.261	24.04
1870	1870					14.75		SE¼ NW¼	9	33	48	3-15—4-28	.120	11.06
1870	1870					36.45		NE¼ SW¼	9	33	48	3-15—4-28	.296	27.34
1870	1870					1.95		SW¼ NW¼	9	33	48	3-15—4-28	.016	1.46
1870	1870					32.70		NW¼ SW¼	9	33	48	3-15—4-28	.266	24.53

Source—Boulder Creek. Ditch—Boulder Creek.

1875	1875						6.10	NE¼ NE¼	34	34	48	3-15—4-28	.050	4.58
1875	1875						33.40	SE¼ NE¼	34	34	48	3-15—4-28	.272	25.05
1875	1875						41.20	NE¼ SE¼	34	34	48	3-15—4-28	.335	30.90
1875	1875						39.05	SE¼ SE¼	34	34	48	3-15—4-28	.317	29.29
1875	1875						3.75	NW¼ SE¼	34	34	48	3-15—4-28	.142	2.81
1875	1875						14.35	SW¼ SE¼	34	34	48	3-15—4-28	.117	10.76
1875	1875						11.30	NE¼ NE¼	35	34	48	3-15—4-28	.092	8.48
1875	1875						38.30	SE¼ NE¼	35	34	48	3-15—4-28	.311	28.73
1875	1875						11.50	NW¼ NE¼	35	34	48	3-15—4-28	.093	8.63
1875	1875						42.45	SW¼ NE¼	35	34	48	3-15—4-28	.345	31.84
1875	1875						6.25	NE¼ SE¼	35	34	48	3-15—4-28	.051	4.69
1875	1875						37.00	NW¼ SE¼	35	34	48	3-15—4-28	.301	27.75
1875	1875						9.00	SW¼ SE¼	35	34	48	3-15—4-28	.073	6.75
1875	1875						11.05	NE¼ NW¼	35	34	48	3-15—4-28	.090	8.29
1875	1875					6.80		SE¼ NW¼	35	34	48	3-15—4-28	.055	5.10
1875	1875						35.35	SE¼ NW¼	35	34	48	3-15—4-28	.287	26.51

William Dunphy Estate—Continued.

Date of beneficial use: Nat. mdw.	Date of beneficial use: Cult. area	Construction first initiated: Dams	Construction first initiated: Ditches	Culture—Acres: Harvest crops	Culture—Acres: Meadow pasture	Culture—Acres: Willow and sage pasture	Culture—Acres: Swamp or overflow	Location: Subdivision	Location: Section	Location: Tp.N.	Location: R.E.	Length of season	Duty of water: C.F.S.	Duty of water: Acre-feet
1875	1875	.....	.....	.....	.....	.....	11.35	NW¼ NW¼	35	34	48	3-15—4-28	.092	8.51
1875	1875	.....	.....	.....	.....	18.15	.....	SW¼ NW¼	35	34	48	3-15—4-28	.148	13.61
1875	1875	.....	.....	.....	.....	.....	24.10	SW¼ NW¼	35	34	48	3-15—4-28	.196	18.08
1875	1875	.....	.....	.....	.....	0.15	.....	NE¼ SW¼	35	34	48	3-15—4-28	.001	.11
1875	1875	.....	.....	.....	.....	.....	41.70	NE¼ SW¼	35	34	48	3-15—4-28	.330	31.28
1875	1875	.....	.....	.....	.....	.....	38.95	SE¼ SW¼	35	34	48	3-15—4-28	.317	29.21
1875	1875	.....	.....	.....	.....	12.00	.....	NW¼ SW¼	35	34	48	3-15—4-28	.098	9.00
1875	1875	.....	.....	.....	.....	.....	29.90	NW¼ SW¼	35	34	48	3-15—4-28	.243	22.43
1875	1875	.....	.....	.....	.....	.....	42.15	SW¼ SW¼	35	34	48	3-15—4-28	.343	31.61
1875	1875	.....	.....	.....	.....	9.55	.....	NE¼ NW¼	2	33	48	3-15—4-28	.081	7.46
1875	1875	.....	.....	.....	.....	.....	1.40	NE¼ NW¼	2	33	48	3-15—4-28	.011	1.05
1875	1875	.....	.....	.....	.....	8.20	.....	SE¼ NW¼	2	33	48	3-15—4-28	.067	6.15
1875	1875	.....	.....	.....	.....	.....	0.20	SE¼ NW¼	2	33	48	3-15—4-28	.002	0.15
1875	1875	.....	.....	.....	.....	24.80	.....	NW¼ NW¼	2	33	48	3-15—4-28	.202	18.60
1875	1875	.....	.....	.....	.....	.....	16.75	NW¼ NW¼	2	33	18	3-15—4-28	.136	12.56
1875	1875	.....	.....	.....	.....	30.00	.....	SW¼ NW¼	2	33	48	3-15—4-28	.244	22.50
1875	1875	.....	.....	.....	.....	.....	11.75	SW¼ NW¼	2	33	18	3-15—4-28	.096	8.81
1875	1875	.....	.....	.....	.....	9.80	.....	NW¼ SW¼	2	33	48	3-15—4-28	.080	7.35
1875	1875	.....	.....	.....	.....	.....	16.50	NW¼ SW¼	2	33	48	3-15—4-28	.134	12.38
1875	1875	.....	.....	.....	.....	6.15	.....	SW¼ SW¼	2	33	48	3-15—4-28	.050	4.61
1875	1875	.....	.....	.....	.....	8.45	.....	NE¼ NE¼	3	33	48	3-15—4-28	.069	6.34
1875	1875	.....	.....	.....	.....	.....	30.60	NE¼ NE¼	3	33	48	3-15—4-28	.249	22.95
1875	1875	.....	.....	.....	.....	31.00	.....	SE¼ NE¼	3	33	48	3-15—4-28	.252	23.25
1875	1875	.....	.....	.....	.....	.....	8.70	SE¼ NE¼	3	33	48	3-15—4-28	.071	6.53
1875	1875	.....	.....	.....	.....	4.90	.....	NW¼ NE¼	3	33	48	3-15—4-28	.045	3.68
1875	1875	.....	.....	.....	.....	.....	22.25	NW¼ NE¼	3	33	48	3-15—4-28	.181	16.69
1875	1875	.....	.....	.....	.....	32.70	.....	SW¼ NE¼	3	33	48	3-15—4-28	.266	24.53
1875	1875	.....	.....	.....	.....	.....	7.35	SW¼ NE¼	3	33	48	3-15—4-28	.060	5.51
1875	1875	.....	.....	.....	.....	18.10	.....	NE¼ SE¼	3	33	48	3-15—4-28	.147	13.58
1875	1875	.....	.....	.....	.....	.....	21.90	NE¼ SE¼	3	33	48	3-15—4-28	.178	16.43
1875	1875	.....	.....	.....	.....	22.70	.....	SE¼ SE¼	3	33	48	3-15—4-28	.185	17.03
1875	1875	.....	.....	.....	.....	.....	15.80	SE¼ SE¼	3	33	48	3-15—4-28	.128	11.85
1875	1875	.....	.....	.....	.....	16.20	.....	NW¼ SE¼	3	33	48	3-15—4-28	.132	12.15
1875	1875	.....	.....	.....	.....	.....	22.85	NW¼ SE¼	3	33	48	3-15—4-28	.186	17.14
1875	1875	.....	.....	.....	.....	.....	38.90	SW¼ SE¼	3	33	48	3-15—4-28	.316	29.18
1875	1875	.....	.....	.....	.....	.....	4.10	NE¼ NW¼	3	33	48	3-15—4-28	.033	3.08
1875	1875	.....	.....	.....	.....	.....	32.50	SE¼ NW¼	3	33	48	3-15—4-28	.264	24.38
1875	1875	.....	.....	.....	.....	.....	22.70	NE¼ SW¼	3	33	48	3-15—4-28	.185	17.03
1875	1875	.....	.....	.....	.....	.....	18.90	SE¼ SW¼	3	33	48	3-15—4-28	.154	14.18
1875	1875	.....	.....	.....	.....	.....	1.75	NE¼ NE¼	9	33	48	3-15—4-28	.014	1.31
1875	1875	.....	.....	.....	.....	.....	38.45	SE¼ NE¼	9	33	48	3-15—4-28	.313	28.84
1875	1875	.....	.....	.....	.....	.....	0.10	NW¼ NE¼	9	33	48	3-15—4-28	.001	.08
1875	1875	.....	.....	.....	.....	.....	4.65	SW¼ NE¼	9	33	48	3-15—4-28	.037	3.48
1875	1875	.....	.....	.....	.....	.....	36.50	NE¼ SE¼	9	33	48	3-15—4-28	.207	27.38
1875	1875	.....	.....	.....	.....	.....	4.10	NW¼ SE¼	9	33	48	3-15—4-28	.033	3.08
1875	1875	.....	.....	.....	.....	2.25	.....	NE¼ NE¼	10	33	48	3-15—4-28	.018	1.69

1875	1875						11.75	NE¼NE¼	10	33	48	3-15—4-28	.096	8.81
1875	1875						38.50	NW¼NE¼	10	33	48	3-15—4-28	.313	28.88
1875	1875						9.05	SW¼NE¼	10	33	48	3-15—4-28	.074	6.79
1875	1875						32.20	NE¼NW¼	10	33	48	3-15—4-28	.262	24.15
1875	1875						32.10	SE¼NW¼	10	33	48	3-15—4-28	.261	24.08
1875	1875					3.00		NW¼NW¼	10	33	48	3-15—4-28	.041	8.75
1875	1875						13.00	NW¼NW¼	10	33	48	3-15—4-28	.106	9.75
1875	1875						39.00	SW¼NW¼	10	33	48	3-15—4-28	.317	20.25
1875	1875						21.90	NE¼SW¼	10	33	48	3-15—4-28	.178	16.43
1875	1875						36.80	NW¼SW¼	10	33	48	3-15—4-28	.299	27.60
1875	1875				1.25			SW¼SW¼	14	33	47	3-15—6-13	.010	1.88
1875	1875				1.30			SE¼SW¼	14	33	47	3-15—6-13	.011	1.95
1875	1875				1.75			SW¼SE¼	14	33	47	3-15—6-13	.014	2.63
1875	1875				16.70			SE¼SE¼	14	33	47	3-15—6-13	.136	25.05
1875	1875				.25			NE¼SE¼	14	33	47	3-15—6-13	.002	.88
1875	1875				1.65			NW¼SW¼	13	33	47	3-15—6-13	.013	2.48
1875	1875				8.95			SW¼SW¼	13	33	47	3-15—6-13	.073	13.43
1875	1875				3.70			NE¼SW¼	13	33	47	3-15—6-13	.030	5.55
1875	1875				16.30			NW¼SE¼	13	33	47	3-15—6-13	.133	24.45
1875	1875				4.90			SW¼SE¼	13	33	47	3-15—6-13	.040	7.85
1875	1875				.40			SE¼SW¼	13	33	47	3-15—6-13	.003	.60
1875	1875						37.70	NE¼NE¼	22	33	47	3-15—4-28	.307	28.28
1875	1875						38.50	SE¼NE¼	22	33	47	3-15—4-28	.313	28.80
1875	1875						22.85	SW¼NE¼	22	33	47	3-15—4-28	.186	17.14
1875	1875			7.95				NE¼SE¼	22	33	47	3-15—9-15	.065	23.85
1875	1875				12.45			NE¼SE¼	22	33	47	3-15—6-13	.101	18.68
1875	1875						16.65	NE¼SE¼	22	33	47	3-15—4-28	.135	12.49
1875	1875				3.70			NW¼SE¼	22	33	47	3-15—6-13	.030	5.55
1875	1875						34.50	NW¼SE¼	22	33	47	3-15—4-28	.280	25.88
1875	1875			21.60				SE¼SW¼	22	33	47	3-15—9-15	.176	64.80
1875	1875				11.85			SE¼SW¼	22	33	47	3-15—6-13	.096	17.78
1875	1875						1.20	SE¼SW¼	22	33	47	3-15—4-28	.010	.90
1875	1875				1.80			NW¼NE¼	23	33	47	3-15—6-13	.015	2.70
1875	1875					1.35		NW¼NE¼	23	33	47	3-15—4-28	.011	1.01
1875	1875						38.35	NE¼NW¼	23	33	47	3-15—4-28	.312	28.76
1875	1875				25.75			SE¼NW¼	23	33	47	3-15—6-13	.209	38.62
1875	1875						13.25	SE¼NW¼	23	33	47	3-15—4-28	.108	9.94
1875	1875						38.50	NW¼NW¼	23	33	47	3-15—4-28	.313	28.88
1875	1875				8.95			SW¼NW¼	23	33	47	3-15—6-13	.073	13.43
1875	1875						28.70	SW¼NW¼	23	33	47	3-15—4-28	.233	21.53
1875	1875				5.30			SE¼NE¼	13	33	47	3-15—6-13	.043	7.95
1875	1875				25.75			NE¼SE¼	13	33	47	3-15—6-13	.209	38.63
1875	1875						11.00	NE¼SE¼	13	33	47	3-15—4-28	.089	8.25
1875	1875				6.50			NW¼SE¼	13	33	47	3-15—6-13	.053	9.75
1875	1875						37.65	NE¼NE¼	18	33	48	3-15—4-28	.306	28.24
1875	1875				19.90			SE¼NE¼	18	33	48	3-15—6-13	.162	29.85
1875	1875						15.60	SE¼NE¼	18	33	48	3-15—4-28	.238	11.70
1875	1875						38.85	NW¼NE¼	18	33	48	3-15—4-28	.316	20.14
1875	1875				27.40			SW¼NE¼	18	33	48	3-15—6-13	.223	41.10
1875	1875						11.00	SW¼NE¼	18	33	48	3-15—4-28	.089	8.25
1875	1875				7.80			NE¼SE¼	18	33	48	3-15—6-13	.063	11.70
1875	1875						30.80	NE¼SE¼	18	33	48	3-15—4-28	.250	23.10

William Dunphy Estate—Continued.

Date of beneficial use: Nat. mdw.	Date of beneficial use: Cult. area	Construction first initiated: Dams	Construction first initiated: Ditches	Culture—Acres: Harvest crops	Culture—Acres: Meadow pasture	Culture—Acres: Willow and sage pasture	Culture—Acres: Swamp or overflow	Location: Subdivision	Location: Section	Location: Tp.N.	Location: R.E.	Length of season	Duty of water: C.F.S.	Duty of water: Acre-feet
1875	1875				1.80			SE¼SE¼	18	33	48	3-15—6-13	.015	2.70
1875	1875						27.40	SE¼SE¼	18	33	48	3-15—4-28	.223	20.55
1875	1875				18.55			NW¼SE¼	18	33	48	3-15—6-13	.151	27.83
1875	1875						19.10	NW¼SE¼	18	33	48	3-15—4-28	.156	14.33
1875	1875				.70			SW¼SE¼	18	33	48	3-15—6-13	.006	1.05
1875	1875						26.05	SW¼SE¼	18	33	48	3-15—4-28	.212	19.54
1875	1875						32.80	NE¼NW¼	18	33	48	3-15—4-28	.267	24.60
1875	1875				28.75			SE¼NW¼	18	33	48	3-15—6-13	.234	43.13
1875	1875						9.40	SE¼NW¼	18	33	48	3-15—4-28	.076	7.05
1875	1875						1.30	NW¼NW¼	18	33	48	3-15—4-28	.011	.98
1875	1875				23.45			SW¼NW¼	18	33	48	3-15—6-13	.191	35.18
1875	1875						3.60	SW¼NW¼	18	33	48	3-15—4-28	.029	2.70
1875	1875				28.20			NE¼SW¼	18	33	48	3-15—6-13	.229	42.30
1875	1875						8.50	NE¼SW¼	18	33	48	3-15—4-28	.069	6.38
1875	1875						36.20	SE¼SW¼	18	33	48	3-15—4-28	.294	27.15
1875	1875				31.10			NW¼SW¼	18	33	48	3-15—6-13	.253	46.65
1875	1875						6.10	NW¼SW¼	18	33	48	3-15—4-28	.050	4.58
1875	1875						33.05	SW¼SW¼	18	33	48	3-15—4-28	.269	24.79
1875	1875						2.65	NE¼SE¼	7	33	48	3-15—4-28	.022	1.99
1875	1875						38.00	SE¼SE¼	7	33	48	3-15—4-28	.309	28.50
1875	1875						27.00	SW¼SE¼	7	33	48	3-15—4-28	.220	20.25
1875	1875						3.90	SE¼SW¼	7	33	48	3-15—4-28	.032	2.93
1875	1875						1.65	NE¼SE¼	8	33	48	3-15—4-28	.013	1.24
1875	1875						39.25	SE¼SE¼	8	33	48	3-15—4-28	.319	29.44
1875	1875						2.10	NW¼SE¼	8	33	48	3-15—4-28	.017	1.58
1875	1875						38.25	SW¼SE¼	8	33	48	3-15—4-28	.311	28.69
1875	1875						2.35	NE¼SW¼	8	33	48	3-15—4-28	.019	1.76
1875	1875						38.50	SE¼SW¼	8	33	48	3-15—4-28	.313	28.88
1875	1875						2.70	NW¼SW¼	8	33	48	3-15—4-28	.022	2.03
1875	1875						39.40	SW¼SW¼	8	33	48	3-15—4-28	.320	29.55
1875	1875						1.30	NE¼SE¼	9	33	48	3-15—4-28	.010	.98
1875	1875					5.15		SE¼SE¼	9	33	48	3-15—4-28	.042	3.86
1875	1875						33.15	SE¼SE¼	9	33	48	3-15—4-28	.270	24.86
1875	1875						1.30	NW¼SE¼	9	33	48	3-15—4-28	.010	.98
1875	1875						38.95	SW¼SE¼	9	33	48	3-15—4-28	.317	29.21
1875	1875						1.45	NE¼SW¼	9	33	48	3-15—4-28	.012	1.09
1875	1875						39.40	SE¼SW¼	9	33	48	3-15—4-28	.320	29.55
1875	1875						1.50	NW¼SW¼	9	33	48	3-15—4-28	.012	1.13
1875	1875						39.30	SW¼SW¼	9	33	48	3-15—4-28	.320	29.48
1875	1875						0.70	NW¼SW¼	10	33	48	3-15—4-28	.006	0.53
1875	1875						18.50	SW¼SW¼	10	33	48	3-15—4-28	.150	13.88
1875	1875					14.45		NW¼NW¼	15	33	48	3-15—4-28	.117	10.84
1875	1875						1.30	NW¼NW¼	15	33	48	3-15—4-28	.011	0.98
1875	1875					0.20		SW¼NW¼	15	33	48	3-15—4-28	.002	0.15
1875	1875					13.95		NE¼NE¼	16	33	48	3-15—4-28	.118	10.46
1875	1875						15.15	NE¼NW¼	16	33	48	3-15—4-28	.123	11.36

1875	1875	....	....	....	....	....	37.35	NW¼ NE¼	16	33	48	3-15—4-28	.304	28.01
1875	1875	....	....	....	....	....	6.30	SW¼ NE¼	16	33	48	3-15—4-28	.061	4.78
1875	1875	....	....	....	....	....	30.50	NE¼ NW¼	16	33	48	3-15—4-28	.321	29.63
1875	1875	....	....	....	....	....	15.30	SE¼ NW¼	16	33	48	3-15—4-28	.125	11.48
1875	1875	....	....	....	....	....	39.35	NW¼ NW¼	16	33	48	3-15—4-28	.321	29.51
1875	1875	....	....	....	....	....	21.25	SW¼ NW¼	16	33	48	3-15—4-28	.174	15.94
1875	1875	....	....	....	....	....	38.90	NE¼ NE¼	17	33	48	3-15—4-28	.317	29.18
1875	1875	....	....	....	....	....	26.30	SE¼ NE¼	17	33	48	3-15—4-28	.215	19.73
1875	1875	....	....		....	....	38.30	NW¼ NE¼	17	33	48	3-15—4-28	.312	28.73
1875	1875	....	....	....	....	....	38.60	SW¼ NE¼	17	33	48	3-15—4-28	.315	28.95
1875	1875	....	....	....	....	....	5.80	NE¼ SE¼	17	33	48	3-15—4-28	.047	4.35
1875	1875	....	....	....	....	....	19.70	SE¼ SE¼	17	31	48	3-15—4-28	.160	14.78
1875	1875	....	....	....	....	....	40.40	NW¼ SE¼	17	33	48	3-15—4-28	.328	30.30
1875	1875	....	....	....	....	....	39.80	SW¼ SE¼	17	33	48	3-15—4-28	.324	29.85
1875	1875	....	....	....	....	....	37.00	NE¼ NW¼	17	33	48	3-15—4-28	.301	27.75
1875	1875	....	....	....	....	....	39.20	SE¼ NW¼	17	33	48	3-15—4-28	.319	29.40
1875	1875	....	....	....	....	....	39.60	NW¼ NW¼	17	33	48	3-15—4-28	.322	29.70
1875	1875	....	....	....	....	....	38.70	SW¼ NW¼	17	33	48	3-15—4-28	.315	29.03
1875	1875	....	....	....	....	....	40.10	NE¼ SW¼	17	33	48	3-15—4-28	.326	30.08
1875	1875	....	....	....	....	0.50	....	SE¼ SW¼	17	33	48	3-15—4-28	.004	0.38
1875	1875	....	....	....	....	....	38.90	SE¼ SW¼	17	33	48	3-15—4-28	.316	29.18
1875	1875	....	....	....	....	....	40.20	NW¼ SW¼	17	33	48	3-15—4-28	.327	30.15
1875	1875	....	....	....	....	0.30	....	SW¼ SW¼	17	33	48	3-15—4-28	.002	0.23
1875	1875	....	....	....	....	....	38.90	SW¼ SW¼	17	33	48	3-15—4-28	.316	29.18
1875	1875	....	....	....	....	....	11.10	NE¼ NE¼	34	34	48	3-15—4-28	.090	8.33
1875	1875	....	....	....	....	....	9.40	SE¼ SE¼	27	34	48	3-15—4-28	.076	7.05
1875	1875	....	....	....	....	....	29.40	NW¼ NW¼	35	34	48	3-15—4-28	.239	22.05
1875	1875	....	....	....	....	....	29.60	NE¼ NW¼	35	34	48	3-15—4-28	.241	22.20
1875	1875	....	....	....	....	....	30.50	NW¼ NE¼	35	34	48	3-15—4-28	.248	22.88
1875	1875	....	....	....	....	....	30.40	NE¼ NE¼	35	34	48	3-15—4-28	.247	22.80

ELKO AND PINE CREEK DISTRICTS

Claimant—**Henderson Banking Company.** **Proof. No. 00201**
Source—**Humboldt River.** Ditch—**Henderson Ditches.**

Date of beneficial use: Nat. mdw.	Date of beneficial use: Cult. area	Construction first initiated: Dams	Construction first initiated: Ditches	Culture—Acres: Harvest crops	Culture—Acres: Meadow pasture	Culture—Acres: Willow and sage pasture	Culture—Acres: Swamp or over-flow	Location: Subdivision	Location: Section	Location: Tp.N.	Location: R.E.	Length of season	Duty of water: C.F.S.	Duty of water: Acre-feet
	1883				63.00			S½	20	35	56	4-15—6-15	.775	94.50
	1888				197.37			N½	29	35	56	4-15—6-15	2.428	296.06

Claimant—**Elko Water Works.** **Proof No. 00202**
Source—**Humboldt River.** Ditch—**Elko Water Works Ditches.**

Nat. mdw.	Cult. area	Dams	Ditches	Harvest crops	Meadow pasture	Willow and sage pasture	Swamp or over-flow	Subdivision	Section	Tp.N.	R.E.	Length of season	C.F.S.	Acre-feet
	1890			15.00				SE¼ NE¼	10	34	55	4-15—8-15	.185	45.00
	1892			15.00				SE¼	10	34	55	4-15—8-15	.185	45.00
	1894			30.00				SW¼	11	34	55	4-15—8-15	.369	90.00
	1896			20.00								4-15—8-15	.246	60.00
	1900			30.00								4-15—8-15	.369	90.00
	1901			15.22								4-15—8-15	.187	45.06
	1903			5.22								4-15—8-15	.064	15.66

NOTE—It is found that Elko Water Works are owners of entire flow of Kitridge Canyon Springs above their point of diversion with priority of 1891, and also all rights from the Humboldt River that were included in that certain Act of Nevada State Legislature entitled "An Act to supply the Town of Elko, Elko County, Nevada, with water for extinguishment of fire and other purposes, and to define said boundaries of said town."

Claimant—**Frank Fernald.** **Proof No.00203**
Source—**Humboldt River.** Ditch—**Frank Fernald Ditches.**

Nat. mdw.	Cult. area	Dams	Ditches	Harvest crops	Meadow pasture	Willow and sage pasture	Swamp or over-flow	Subdivision	Section	Tp.N.	R.E.	Length of season	C.F.S.	Acre-feet
	1879				193.16			S½SW¼	30	35	56			
	1880				193.15			NE¼ SW¼	30	35	56			
								SE¼ SE¼	30	35	56			
								SW¼ NE¼	30	35	56			
								E½ NE¼	30	35	56			
								W½ W½	29	35	56			
								E½SW¼	29	35	56			
								SE¼ NW¼	29	35	56	4-15—6-15	2.376	289.74
								NW¼ SE¼	29	35	56	4-15—6-15	2.376	289.73

Claimant—**M. Aguirre.** **Proof No. 00204**
Source—**Humboldt River.** Ditch—**M. Aguirre Ditches.**

Nat. mdw.	Cult. area	Dams	Ditches	Harvest crops	Meadow pasture	Willow and sage pasture	Swamp or over-flow	Subdivision	Section	Tp.N.	R.E.	Length of season	C.F.S.	Acre-feet
	1882				168.25			SW¼	8	35	57			
								E½ NW¼	8	35	57			
								NE¼	8	35	57			
								NE¼ SE¼	8	35	57			
								SW¼ NW¼	9	35	57			
								W½SW¼	9	35	57	4-15—6-15	2.000	252.39

Claimant—**Mrs. C. Glaser.** Proof No. 00205

Source—**Rabbit & Lamoille Creeks.*** Ditch—**Glaser Ditches.**

1871	34.70		S½	13	35	57	4-15—8-15	.427	114.10

*Priority from Lamoille Creek dated 1894.

Source—**Rabbit Creek.** Ditch—**Glaser Ditches.**

1871	84.30		S½	13	35	57	4-15—8-15	1.037	252.90

Source—**Humboldt River.** Ditch—**Glaser Ditches.**

1872		171.00	N½	14	35	57			
1873		298.50	N¼N½S½	14	35	57			
1874		298.50	N½	13	35	57			
			SE¼	12	35	57	4-15—6-15	2.103	256.50
			SW¼	7	35	58	4-15—6-15	3.672	447.75
			NW¼	18	35	58	4-15—6-15	3.672	447.75

Source—**Lamoille Creek.** Ditch—**Glaser Ditches.**

1873	175.60		S½	14	35	57	4-15—8-15	2.159	526.80
1893	51.50		S½	13	35	57	4-15—8-15	.633	154.50
1894	136.80		NE¼	13	35	57	4-15—8-15	1.682	410.40
1901	46.50		W½	18	35	58	4-15—8-15	.572	139.50
1904	178.20		NE¼	18	35	58	4-15—8-15	2.192	534.60

Claimant—**W. F. Linebarger.** Proof No. 00207

Source—**Humboldt River.** Ditch—**Linebarger Ditch and Overflow.**

1876	14.00		SW¼ NE¼	34	33	52	4-15—8-15	.172	42.00
1876	40.00		NE¼ NE¼	34	33	52	4-15—8-15	.492	120.00
1876	34.00		SE¼ NE¼	34	33	52	4-15—8-15	.418	102.00
1876	18.60		NE¼ SW¼	34	33	52	4-15—8-15	.229	55.80
1876	13.25		SW¼ SW¼	34	33	52	4-15—8-15	.163	39.75
1876	33.80		NW¼ SW¼	34	33	52	4-15—8-15	.416	101.40
1876	15.00		NE¼ SW¼	34	33	52	4-15—8-15	.185	45.00
1876	10.00		NW¼ SE¼	34	33	52	4-15—8-15	.123	30.00
1876	30.00		SW¼ NW¼	35	33	52	4-15—8-15	.370	90.00
1876	22.00		SE¼ NW¼	35	33	52	4-15—8-15	.271	66.00
1876	37.00		NW¼ NW¼	35	33	52	4-15—8-15	.455	111.00
1876	34.00		NE¼ NW¼	35	33	32	4-15—8-15	.492	102.00

Source—**Mary's Creek.** Ditch—**Linebarger Ditches.**

1880	30.00		NW¼ NW¼	34	33	52	4-15—8-15	.369	90.00
1880	3.00		NE¼ NW¼	34	33	52	4-15—8-15	.037	9.00
1880		28.00	NE¼ NW¼	34	32	52	4-15—6-15	.344	42.00
1880	36.00		SW¼ NW¼	34	33	52	4-15—8-15	.443	108.00
1880	8.00		SE¼ NW¼	34	33	52	4-15—8-15	.098	24.00
1880		25.00	SE¼ NW¼	34	33	52	4-15—6-15	.308	37.50
1880		14.00	NW¼ NE¼	34	33	52	4-15—6-15	.172	21.00
1880	15.00		NW¼ NE¼	34	33	52	4-15—8-15	.185	45.00
1880	20.00		SW¼ NE¼	34	33	52	4-15—8-15	.246	60.00

Claimant—**L. L. Redden.** Proof. No. 00208

Source—**Starr Creek.** Ditch—**L. L. Redden Ditches.**

Date of beneficial use—Nat. mdw.	Cult. area	Construction first initiated—Dams	Ditches	Culture—Acres—Harvest crops	Meadow pasture	Willow and sage pasture	Swamp or overflow	Location—Subdivision	Section	Tp.N.	R.E.	Length of season	Duty of water—C.F.S.	Acre-feet
	1879			158.20				S½SE¼	33	37	59			
								W½SW¼	34	37	59			
								NE¼SW¼	34	37	59			
								N½SE¼	34	37	59	4-15—8-15	1.946	474.20

Source—**Starr Creek and Humboldt River.** Ditch—**L. L. Redden Ditches.**

Date of beneficial use—Nat. mdw.	Cult. area	Construction first initiated—Dams	Ditches	Culture—Acres—Harvest crops	Meadow pasture	Willow and sage pasture	Swamp or overflow	Location—Subdivision	Section	Tp.N.	R.E.	Length of season	Duty of water—C.F.S.	Acre-feet
	1879				41.00			S½SE¼	33	37	59			
								NE¼SE¼	33	37	59	4-15—6-15	.504	61.50

Source—**Humboldt River.** Ditch—**L. L. Redden Ditches.**

Date of beneficial use—Nat. mdw.	Cult. area	Construction first initiated—Dams	Ditches	Culture—Acres—Harvest crops	Meadow pasture	Willow and sage pasture	Swamp or overflow	Location—Subdivision	Section	Tp.N.	R.E.	Length of season	Duty of water—C.F.S.	Acre-feet
	1879				63.60			SW¼SE¼	33	37	59			
								NE¼SE¼	33	37	59			
								N½SW¼	34	37	59	4-15—6-15	.782	95.40

Claimant—**M. Aguirre.** Proof No. 00209

Source—**Humboldt River.** Ditch—**M. Aguirre Ditches.**

Date of beneficial use—Nat. mdw.	Cult. area	Construction first initiated—Dams	Ditches	Culture—Acres—Harvest crops	Meadow pasture	Willow and sage pasture	Swamp or overflow	Location—Subdivision	Section	Tp.N.	R.E.	Length of season	Duty of water—C.F.S.	Acre-feet
	1882				146.46			NW¼	7	35	57			
								NE¼SW¼	7	35	57			
								SW¼NE¼	7	35	57			
								SE¼	7	35	57	4-15—6-15	1.801	219.69

Claimant—Union Land and Cattle **Company.** Proof No. 00210

Source—Mary's River, Humboldt **River, Stevens Creek, Reed Creek* and Warm Springs.**

Ditch—Union Land **and Cattle Co. Ditches.**

Date of beneficial use—Nat. mdw.	Cult. area	Construction first initiated—Dams	Ditches	Culture—Acres—Harvest crops	Meadow pasture	Willow and sage pasture	Swamp or overflow	Location—Subdivision	Section	Tp.N.	R.E.	Length of season	Duty of water—C.F.S.	Acre-feet
	1884				649.50				1	36	58			
	1885				649.50				11	36	58			
	1886				649.50				12	36	58			
	1887				649.50				13	36	58			
	1888				649.50				14	36	58			
	1889				649.50				15	36	58			
	1890				649.50				21	36	58			
									22	36	58			
									23	36	58			
									27	36	58			
									28	36	58			
									4	36	59			
									5	36	59	4-15—6-15	7.980	974.25
									6	36	59	4-15—6-15	7.980	974.25
									7	36	59	4-15—6-15	7.980	974.25

									8	36	50	4-15—6-15	7.989	974.25
									31	37	50	4-15—6-15	7.989	974.25
									32	37	59	4-15—6-15	7.989	974.25
									33	37	50	4-15—6-15	7.989	974.25

*Priority from Reed Creek dated 1891.

Claimant—**J. J. Wright.** Proof No. 00211

Source—**Humboldt River.** Ditch—**J. J. Wright Ditches.**

	1872				45.50			SE¼SE¼	9	35	56	4-15—6-15	.560	68.25
	1872				160.90			NE¼	16	35	56	4-15—6-15	1.979	241.35
	1872				60.00			S½NW¼	16	35	56	4-15—6-15	.738	90.00
	1872				87.60			NE¼NW¼	16	35	56	4-15—6-15	1.077	131.40
	1873				45.60			SW¼	16	35	56	4-15—6-15	.561	68.40
	1878				60.00			W½SE¼	16	35	56	4-15—6-15	.738	90.00
	1888				37.60			NE¼SE¼	16	35	56	4-15—6-15	.462	56.40
	1888				247.40			E½	20	35	56	4-15—6-15	3.048	371.10
	1892				54.10			N½NW¼&SW¼NW¼	21	35	56	4-15—6-15	.665	81.15

Claimant—**Griswold-Henderson Livestock Co.** Proof No. 00212

Source—**Humboldt River.** Ditch—**Griswold-Henderson Ditches.**

	1882				770.30			S½	20	34	55			
	1902				86.30			S½NW¼	21	34	55			
								SW¼	21	34	55			
								NW¼	29	34	55			
								NE¼	29	34	55			
								N½SW¼	29	34	55			
								SW¼SW¼	29	34	55			
								NE¼	30	34	55	4-15—6-15	9.475	1155.45
								E½SE¼	30	34	55	4-15—6-15	1.061	129.45

Claimant—**Thomas Hunter.** Proof No. 00213

Source—**Springs and South Fork of Humboldt River.** Ditch—**Thomas Hunter Ditches.**

	1870			20.00				NW¼SW¼	9	33	54	4-15—8-15	.246	60.00
	1871			168.10				SW¼SW¼	9	33	54	4-15—8-15	2.068	504.30
	1872			41.40				E½SW¼	9	33	54	4-15—8-15	.509	124.20
	1876			47.10				SE¼	9	33	54	4-15—8-15	.579	141.30
	1877			47.10				SE¼SE¼	8	33	54	4-15—8-15	.579	141.30
	1879			47.20				NW¼	14	33	54	4-15—8-15	.581	141.60
	1880			47.20				SW¼NE¼	14	33	54	4-15—8-15	.581	141.60
	1882			47.20				N½	15	33	54	4-15—8-15	.581	141.60
	1883			47.20				N½S½	15	33	54	4-15—8-15	.581	141.60
	1885			47.20				N½	16	33	54	4-15—8-15	.581	141.60
	1886			58.80				N½N½	16	33	54	4-15—8-15	.723	176.40
	1887			11.60				NE¼	17	33	54	4-15—8-15	.143	34.80
	1888			58.80				SE¼NW¼	17	33	54	4-15—8-15	.723	176.40
	1889			58.90				NE¼SW¼	17	33	54	4-15—8-15	.724	176.70
	1890			106.10				S½SW¼	17	33	54	4-15—8-15	1.305	318.30
	1900			182.90				SE¼	17	33	54	4-15—8-15	2.250	548.70

Thomas Hunter—Continued.

Date of beneficial use: Nat. mdw.	Date of beneficial use: Cult. area	Construction first initiated: Dams	Construction first initiated: Ditches	Culture—Acres: Harvest crops	Culture—Acres: Meadow pasture	Culture—Acres: Willow and sage pasture	Culture—Acres: Swamp or overflow	Location: Subdivision	Location: Section	Location: Tp.N.	Location: R.E.	Length of season	Duty of water: C.F.S.	Duty of water: Acre-feet
	1901			182.90				N½NW¼	20	33	54	4-15—8-15	2.250	548.70
	1902			182.90				SW¼NW¼	30	33	54	4-15—8-15	2.250	548.70
	1903			183.00				S½NE¼	19	33	54	4-15—8-15	2.251	549.00
	1904			106.30				N½SE¼	19	33	51	4-15—8-15	1.307	318.90
	1905			181.40				SW¼SE¼	19	33	54	4-15—8-15	2.231	544.20

Claimant—**Hunter Banks Company.** Proof No. **00213**

Source—**Humboldt River.** Ditch—**Hunter Banks Co. Ditches.**

Nat. mdw.	Cult. area	Dams	Ditches	Harvest crops	Meadow pasture	Willow and sage pasture	Swamp or overflow	Subdivision	Section	Tp.N.	R.E.	Length of season	C.F.S.	Acre-feet
	1902				17.40			S½S½	3	33	54	4-15—6-15	.214	26.10
	1873				5.00							4-15—6-15	.061	7.50
	1870				55.90			SE¼	4	33	54	4-15—6-15	.688	83.85
	1870				41.20			SW¼	4	33	54	4-15—6-15	.507	61.80
	1902				12.60			NE¼	10	33	54	4-15—6-15	.155	18.90
	1874				200.40			NE¼	8	33	54	4-15—6-15	2.465	300.00
	1875				200.50			S½	8	33	54	4-15—6-15	2.466	300.80
	1881				33.60			SE¼	7	33	54	4-15—6-15	.413	50.40
	1882				33.50			NW¼	17	33	54	4-15—6-15	.412	50.30
	1884				52.80				18	33	54	4-15—6-15	.649	79.20
	1885				52.80							4-15—6-15	.649	79.20
	1887				15.00							4-15—6-15	.185	22.50
	1891				30.30							4-15—6-15	.373	45.45
	1892				25.80							4-15—6-15	.317	38.70
	1893				25.80							4-15—6-15	.317	38.70
	1893				26.10							4-15—6-15	.321	39.15
	1893				42.80							4-15—6-15	.526	64.20
	1890				30.90							4-15—6-15	.380	46.35

Source—**South Fork of Humboldt and Humboldt River.** Ditch—**Hunter Banks Co. Ditches.**

Nat. mdw.	Cult. area	Dams	Ditches	Harvest crops	Meadow pasture	Willow and sage pasture	Swamp or overflow	Subdivision	Section	Tp.N.	R.E.	Length of season	C.F.S.	Acre-feet
	1890				94.10			SE¼	4	33	54	4-15—6-15	1.157	141.15
	1890				154.40			NW¼	9	33	54	4-15—6-15	1.899	231.60
	1890				43.30			SW¼	4	33	54	4-15—6-15	.532	64.95

Claimant—**Batiste Tamara.** Proof No. **00213**

Source—**Humboldt River.** Ditch—**Batiste Tamara Ditches.**

Nat. mdw.	Cult. area	Dams	Ditches	Harvest crops	Meadow pasture	Willow and sage pasture	Swamp or overflow	Subdivision	Section	Tp.N.	R.E.	Length of season	C.F.S.	Acre-feet
	1882				60.00			SE¼SW¼	18	33	54	4-15—6-15	.738	90.00
	1883				60.00			NW¼	19	33	54	4-15—6-15	.738	90.00
	1884				60.00			W½NE¼	19	33	54	4-15—6-15	.738	90.00
	1885				61.50			N½SW¼	19	33	54	4-15—6-15	.756	92.25

Claimant—**Weeks Bros., Inc.** Proof No. **00214**
Source—**Humboldt River, Willow, Bishop, and Burnt Creeks.** Ditch—**Weeks Bros. Ditches.**

1884	116.00		S½SW¼	29	38	61			
1890	172.90		W½SE¼	29	38	61			
			NW¼	32	38	61			
			W½NE¼	32	38	61	4-15—8-15	1.353	330.00
			NE¼NE¼	32	38	61	4-15—8-15	2.127	518.70

Claimant—**A. W. Gobel.** Proof No. **00215**
Source—**Town Creek.** Ditch—**Nos. 1 and 2.**

1897		22.27	W½SW¼	35	38	62			
1900		94.60	SW¼SW¼	34	38	62			
			W½NW¼	3	37	62			
			NE¼NW¼	3	37	62			
			NW¼NE¼	3	37	62	4-15—6-15	.274	33.41
			NW¼SW¼	3	37	62	4-15—6-15	1.165	142.04

Claimant—**H. H. Coryell.** Proof No. **00216**
Source—**Town Creek.** Ditch—**Nos. 1 and 2.**

1890		77.04	S½SE¼	34	38	62			
			SE¼SW¼	34	38	62	4-15—6-15	.948	115.56

Claimant—**Bank of Wells.** Proof No. **00217**
Source—**Humboldt River.** Ditch—**Badt Nos. 1 and 2.**

1873		168.26	NE¼NW¼	4	37	62			
			NE¼	4	37	62	4-15—6-15	2.070	252.30

Claimant—**Mrs. Hattie A. Downey.** Proof No. **00218**
Source—**Humboldt River.** Ditch—**Downey.**

1886		44.52	SE¼SE¼	32	38	62			
			SW¼SW¼	33	38	62			
			NW¼NW¼	4	37	62			
			NE¼NE¼	5	37	62	4-15—6-15	.548	66.78

Claimant—**Batiste Tamara.** Proof No. **00221**
Source—**Humboldt River.** Ditch—**Batiste Tamara Ditches.**

1886		40.39	SE¼	24	33	53	4-15—6-15	.497	60.59
1887		40.39	SE¼SW¼	24	33	53	4-15—6-15	.497	60.59
1888		40.38	N½	25	33	53	4-15—6-15	.497	60.57
1886		2.89	E½	26	33	53	4-15—6-15	.036	4.34
1887		2.80	S½SW¼	26	33	53	4-15—6-15	.036	4.31
1888		2.90	N½NW¼	35	33	53	4-15—6-15	.036	4.35
1889		7.49	E½SE¼	27	33	53	4-15—6-15	.921	11.24
1890		7.49	....	....	....	..	4-15—6-15	.921	11.24
1891		61.15	....	....	....	....	4-15—6-15	.752	91.73

Claimant—**Mrs. C. Glaser.** Proof No. 00222

Source—**Humboldt River.** Ditch—**Glaser Ditches.**

Date of beneficial use: Nat. mdw.	Cult. area	Construction first initiated: Dams	Ditches	Culture—Acres: Harvest crops	Meadow pasture	Willow and sage pasture	Swamp or overflow	Location: Subdivision	Section	Tp.N.	R.E.	Length of season	Duty of water: C.F.S.	Acre-feet
	1875				958.12			E½NW¼	33	36	58			
	1887				31.24			E½	33	36	58			
	1887				103.28			W½W½	33	36	58			
								E½SW¼	33	36	58			
								SW¼SW¼	33	36	58			
								W½NW¼	34	36	58			
								NW¼SW¼	34	36	58			
								NW¼	4	35	58			
								W½NE¼	4	35	58			
								NE¼NE¼	4	35	58			
								W½SW¼	4	35	58			
								NE¼SW¼	4	35	58			
								E½SE¼	5	35	58			
								SW¼SE¼	5	35	58	4-15—6-15	11.785	1437.18
								N½	8	35	58	4-15—6-15	.384	46.86
								N½NW¼	9	35	58	4-15—6-15	2.008	244.92

Source—**Lamoille Creek.** Ditch—**Glaser Ditches.**

Nat. mdw.	Cult. area	Dams	Ditches	Harvest crops	Meadow pasture	Willow and sage pasture	Swamp or overflow	Subdivision	Section	Tp.N.	R.E.	Length of season	C.F.S.	Acre-feet
	1873			90.08				S½NW¼	8	35	58			
								NE¼	8	35	58	4-15—8-15	1.108	270.24

Claimant—**Thomas Griffin.** Proof No. 00223

Source—**Humboldt River.** Ditch—**McIntosh-Griffin Ditches and Sloughs.**

Nat. mdw.	Cult. area	Dams	Ditches	Harvest crops	Meadow pasture	Willow and sage pasture	Swamp or overflow	Subdivision	Section	Tp.N.	R.E.	Length of season	C.F.S.	Acre-feet
	1880			31.59				NW¼NE¼	17	32	52	4-15—8-15	.380	94.77
	1880			19.97				NE¼NW¼	17	32	52	4-15—8-15	.246	59.91
	1880					4.23		NE¼NW¼	17	32	52	4-15—5-15	.052	8.17
	1890			5.72				SW¼NW¼	17	32	52	4-15—8-15	.070	17.16
	1880			40.00				SE¼NW¼	17	32	52	4-15—8-15	.492	120.00
	1890			8.19				SW¼NE¼	17	32	52	4-15—8-15	.101	24.57
	1880					4.34		SW¼NE¼	17	32	52	4-15—5-15	.053	3.26
	1880			2.48				NW¼SE¼	17	32	52	4-15—8-15	.031	7.44
	1880			36.70				NE¼SW¼	17	32	52	4-15—8-15	.451	110.10
	1880			12.18				NW¼SW¼	17	32	52	4-15—8-15	.150	36.54
	1880			9.95				SW¼SW¼	17	32	52	4-15—8-15	.122	29.85
	1880					0.20		SW¼SW¼	17	32	52	4-15—5-15	.002	.15
	1880					0.56		SE¼SW¼	17	32	52	4-15—5-15	.007	.42
	1880			24.80				SE¼SW¼	17	32	52	4-15—8-15	.305	74.40
	1880			11.02				NE¼NW¼	20	32	52	4-15—8-15	.136	33.06
	1880			3.38				NW¼NW¼	20	32	52	4-15—8-15	.042	10.14
	1880			0.10				SE¼NW¼	20	32	52	4-15—8-15	.001	0.30
	1880			1.54				SW¼NW¼	20	32	52	4-15—8-15	.019	4.62
	1880			14.53				NW¼SW¼	20	32	52	4-15—8-15	.179	43.59

	1880			1.43				SW¼SW¼	20	32	52	4-15—8-15	.018	4.20
	1880			2.16				NE¼SE¼	19	32	52	4-15—8-15	.027	6.48
	1880			1.80				SE¼SE¼	19	32	52	4-15—8-15	.022	5.40

Claimant—**Thomas Griffin.** Proof No. 00224

Source—**Humboldt River.** Ditch—**Griffin Ditches and Sloughs and Overflow.**

	1876						3.52	NE¼NE¼	30	33	53	4-15—5-15	.043	2.64
	1876						21.23	NW¼NW¼	29	33	53	4-15—5-15	.261	15.92
	1876						2.24	NE¼NW¼	29	33	53	4-15—5-15	.028	1.68
	1876			19.52				NE¼NW¼	29	33	53	4-15—8-15	.240	58.56
	1876			11.68				SE¼NW¼	29	33	53	4-15—8-15	.144	35.04
	1876						9.53	SE¼NW¼	29	33	53	4-15—5-15	.117	7.15
	1876			9.79				NW¼NE¼	29	33	53	4-15—8-15	.120	29.37
	1876			19.59				SW¼NE¼	29	33	53	4-15—8-15	.241	58.77
	1876			5.10				NW¼SE¼	29	33	53	4-15—8-15	.063	15.30
	1876			9.64				NE¼SW¼	29	33	53	4-15—8-15	.119	28.92
	1876						6.71	NE¼SW¼	29	33	53	4-15—5-15	.083	5.03
	1876					3.75		NE¼SW¼	29	33	53	4-15—5-15	.046	2.81
	1876					1.51		SE¼SW¼	29	33	53	4-15—5-15	.019	1.13
	1876			3.66				SE¼SW¼	29	33	53	4-15—8-15	.045	10.98
	1876						5.36	NE¼SW¼	29	33	53	4-15—5-15	.066	4.02
	1876						1.68	SW¼SW¼	29	33	53	4-15—5-15	.021	1.26
	1876						5.03	NW¼SW¼	29	33	53	4-15—5-15	.062	3.77
	1876					2.15		NW¼SW¼	29	33	53	4-15—5-15	.026	1.61
	1876			3.32				NW¼SW¼	29	33	53	4-15—8-15	.041	9.96
	1876			18.50				NE¼SE¼	30	33	53	4-15—8-15	.228	55.50
	1876					6.85		NE¼SE¼	30	33	53	4-15—5-15	.084	5.14
	1876						1.29	NE¼SE¼	30	33	53	4-15—5-15	.016	.97
	1876					1.33		NW¼SE¼	30	33	53	4-15—5-15	.016	1.00
	1876			15.84				NW¼SE¼	30	33	53	4-15—8-15	.195	47.52
	1876						14.78	SE¼NE¼	30	33	53	4-15—5-15	.182	11.09
	1876					6.07		SE¼NE¼	30	33	53	4-15—5-15	.075	4.55
	1876					2.50		SW¼NE¼	30	33	53	4-15—5-15	.031	1.88
	1876						26.30	SW¼NE¼	30	33	53	4-15—5-15	.323	19.73
	1876			5.30				SW¼NE¼	30	33	53	4-15—8-15	.065	15.90
	1876						9.31	NW¼NE¼	30	33	53	4-15—5-15	.115	6.98
	1876						14.85	NE¼NW¼	30	33	53	4-15—5-15	.183	11.14
	1876					0.84		NE¼NW¼	30	33	53	4-15—5-15	.010	.63
	1876						23.45	NW¼NW¼	30	33	53	4-15—5-15	.288	17.59
	1876						7.18	SW¼NW¼	30	33	53	4-15—5-15	.088	5.39
	1876			4.96				SW¼NW¼	30	33	53	4-15—8-15	.061	14.88
	1876				21.89			SW¼NW¼	30	33	53	4-15—6-15	.269	32.97
	1876			19.19				SE¼NW¼	30	33	53	4-15—8-15	.236	57.57
	1876					8.00		SE¼NW¼	30	33	53	4-15—5-15	.098	6.00
	1876						5.05	SE¼NW¼	30	33	53	4-15—5-15	.062	3.79
	1876			7.71				NE¼SW¼	30	33	53	4-15—8-15	.095	23.13
	1876				.22			NE¼SW¼	30	33	53	4-15—6-15	.003	.33
	1876				9.86			NW¼SW¼	30	33	53	4-15—6-15	.121	14.86
	1876				24.55			NE¼SE¼	25	33	52	4-15—6-15	.302	36.83
	1876				31.64			NW¼SE¼	25	33	52	4-15—6-15	.389	54.96
	1876				3.12			SW¼NE¼	25	33	52	4-15—6-15	.038	2.34

Thomas Griffin—Continued.

Date of beneficial use: Nat. mdw.	Date of beneficial use: Cult. area	Construction first initiated: Dams	Construction first initiated: Ditches	Culture—Acres: Harvest crops	Culture—Acres: Meadow pasture	Culture—Acres: Willow and sage pasture	Culture—Acres: Swamp or overflow	Location: Subdivision	Location: Section	Location: Tp.N.	Location: R.E.	Length of season	Duty of water: C.F.S.	Duty of water: Acre-feet
	1876						28.67	SW¼NE¼	25	33	52	4-15—5-15	.353	21.50
	1876						11.24	SE¼NE¼	25	33	52	4-15—5-15	.138	8.43
	1876				24.44			SE¼NE¼	25	33	52	4-15—6-15	.301	36.66
	1876						16.58	NE¼NE¼	25	33	52	4-15—5-15	.204	12.44
	1876						9.58	NW¼NE¼	25	33	52	4-15—5-15	.118	7.19
	1876						.22	NE¼NW¼	25	33	52	4-15—5-15	.003	0.17
	1876						17.62	SW¼NW¼	25	33	52	4-15—5-15	.217	13.22
	1876						31.80	SE¼NW¼	25	33	52	4-15—5-15	.391	23.85
	1876				.55			SE¼NW¼	25	33	52	4-15—6-15	.007	0.83
	1876				2.61			NE¼SW¼	25	33	52	4-15—6-15	.032	3.92
	1876						2.55	NE¼SW¼	25	33	52	4-15—5-15	.031	1.91
	1876			28.56				NE¼SW¼	25	33	52	4-15—8-15	.351	85.68
	1876			5.21				NW¼SW¼	25	33	52	4-15—8-15	.064	15.63
	1876						17.04	NW¼SW¼	25	33	52	4-15—5-15	.210	12.78

Source—**Humboldt River.** Ditch—**Linebarger Dam and Overflow.**

Date of beneficial use: Nat. mdw.	Date of beneficial use: Cult. area	Construction first initiated: Dams	Construction first initiated: Ditches	Culture—Acres: Harvest crops	Culture—Acres: Meadow pasture	Culture—Acres: Willow and sage pasture	Culture—Acres: Swamp or overflow	Location: Subdivision	Location: Section	Location: Tp.N.	Location: R.E.	Length of season	Duty of water: C.F.S.	Duty of water: Acre-feet
	1876				4.79			NW¼SW¼	25	33	52	4-15—6-15	.059	7.19
	1876				9.55			SW¼SW¼	25	33	52	4-15—6-15	.117	14.33
	1876						2.35	SE¼NE¼	26	23	52	4-15—5-15	.029	1.76
	1876						28.14	NE¼SE¼	26	33	52	4-15—5-15	.346	21.11
	1876				5.36			NE¼SE¼	26	33	52	4-15—6-15	.066	8.04
	1876				22.40			SE¼SE¼	26	33	52	4-15—6-15	.276	33.60
	1876						5.34	SE¼SE¼	26	33	52	4-15—5-15	.066	4.00
	1876						13.89	NW¼SE¼	26	33	52	4-15—5-15	.171	10.42
	1876						0.34	SW¼SE¼	26	33	52	4-15—5-15	.066	0.26
	1876				10.99			SW¼SE¼	26	33	52	4-15—6-15	.135	16.49
	1876				1.20			NW¼NE¼	35	33	52	4-15—6-15	.015	1.80

Claimant—**McIntosh Estate.** Proof No. 00225

Source—**Humboldt River.** Ditch—**McIntosh-Griffin Ditches and Sloughs.**

Date of beneficial use: Nat. mdw.	Date of beneficial use: Cult. area	Construction first initiated: Dams	Construction first initiated: Ditches	Culture—Acres: Harvest crops	Culture—Acres: Meadow pasture	Culture—Acres: Willow and sage pasture	Culture—Acres: Swamp or overflow	Location: Subdivision	Location: Section	Location: Tp.N.	Location: R.E.	Length of season	Duty of water: C.F.S.	Duty of water: Acre-feet
	1880			15.15				NE¼SE¼	5	32	52	4-15—8-15	.186	45.45
	1880			35.08				SE¼SE¼	5	32	52	4-15—8-15	.431	105.24
	1880			3.65				SW¼SE¼	5	32	52	4-15—8-15	.045	10.95
	1880			0.08				NW¼NE¼	8	32	52	4-15—8-15	.001	.24
	1880					0.71		NW¼NE¼	8	32	52	4-15—5-15	.009	.54
	1880					7.86		NE¼NE¼	8	32	52	4-15—5-15	.097	5.90
	1880			21.32				NE¼NE¼	8	32	52	4-15—8-15	.262	63.96
	1880			36.66				SE¼NE¼	8	32	52	4-15—8-15	.451	109.98
	1880			0.61				SW¼NE¼	8	32	52	4-15—8-15	.008	1.83
	1880			1.52				NW¼SE¼	8	32	52	4-15—8-15	.019	4.56
	1880			26.40				NE¼SE¼	8	32	52	4-15—8-15	.325	79.20
	1880			0.32				SE¼SE¼	8	32	52	4-15—8-15	.004	.96
	1880			0.07				SW¼SE¼	8	32	52	4-15—8-15	.001	.21

1880	16.59			SE¼SW¼	8	32	52	4-15—8-15	.204	40.77
1880			10.12	SE¼SW¼	8	32	52	4-15—5-15	.124	7.59
1880			0.85	SW¼SW¼	8	32	52	4-15—5-15	.010	.64
1880			1.10	NW¼NW¼	9	32	52	4-15—5-15	.014	.83
1880	19.85			NW¼NW¼	9	32	52	4-15—8-15	.244	59.55
1880	11.50			SW¼NW¼	9	32	52	4-15—8-15	.141	34.50
1880	.10			NW¼SW¼	9	32	52	4-15—8-15	.001	.30

Claimant—**Mrs. T. D. Griffin.** Proof No. **00226**
Source—**Humboldt River.** Ditch—**Mrs. T. D. Griffin Ditch.**

1880		342.34		SE¼SW¼	33	33	52			
				SW¼SE¼	33	33	52			
				W½	4	32	52			
				W½NE¼	4	32	52			
				NW¼SE¼	4	32	52			
				SE¼NE¼	5	32	52			
				NE¼SE¼	5	32	52			
				SW¼NE¼	8	32	52			
				W½SE¼	8	32	52			
				SE¼SE¼	8	32	52			
				E½SW¼	8	32	52			
				NW¼NW¼	9	32	52	4-15—6-15	4.211	513.51

Source—**Warm Spring Creek.** Ditch—**Mrs. T. D. Griffin Ditches.**

1875		136.98		SE¼SW¼	5	32	52			
				W½SE¼	5	32	52			
				W½NE¼	8	32	52			
				E½W½	8	32	52	4-15—6-15	1.685	205.47

Claimant—**George Arthur.** Proof No. **00227**
Source—**Dwyer Spring.** Ditch—**George Arthur Ditch.**

1876	15.00			S½SE¼	28	33	52			
				N½NE¼	33	33	52	4-15—8-15	.185	45.00

Source—**Humboldt River and Hot Spring.** Ditch—**George Arthur Ditch.**

1876	96.22			SE¼	33	33	52			
				NE¼NE¼	4	32	52	4-15—8-15	1.184	288.66

Claimant—**Paul Giudici.** Proof No. **00229**
Source—**Humboldt River.** Ditches—**Paul Giudici Ditches.**

1873		38.54		NW¼	2	33	54	4-15—6-15	.474	57.81
1874		38.54		SW¼	2	33	54	4-15—6-15	.474	57.81
1875		38.53		S½NE¼	2	33	54	4-15—6-15	.474	57.80
1876		38.53		N½SE¼	2	33	54	4-15—6-15	.474	57.80
1877		38.53						4-15—6-15	.474	57.80
1878		38.53						4-15—6-15	.474	57.80

Paul Guidici—Continued.

Date of beneficial use: Nat. mdw.	Date of beneficial use: Cult. area	Construction first initiated: Dams	Construction first initiated: Ditches	Culture—Acres: Harvest crops	Culture—Acres: Meadow pasture	Culture—Acres: Willow and sage pasture	Culture—Acres: Swamp or overflow	Location: Subdivision	Location: Section	Location: Tp.N.	Location: R.E.	Length of season	Duty of water: C.F.S.	Duty of water: Acre-feet
	1879				38.53							4-15—6-15	.474	57.80
	1880				38.53							4-15—6-15	.474	57.80
	1885				15.05			NW¼NW¼	2	33	54	4-15—6-15	.185	22.58
	1885				17.51			NW¼NW¼	1	33	54	4-15—6-15	.215	26.27
	1885				9.08			SW¼NW¼	1	33	54	4-15—6-15	.112	13.62
	1885				1.27			SW¼NW¼	1	33	54	4-15—6-15	.016	1.91

Claimant—**Chas. Dressi** Proof. No. 00230

Source—**Humboldt River.** Ditch—**Chas. Dressi Ditches.**

Nat. mdw.	Cult. area	Dams	Ditches	Harvest crops	Meadow pasture	Willow and sage pasture	Swamp or overflow	Subdivision	Section	Tp.N.	R.E.	Length of season	C.F.S.	Acre-feet
	1873				72.69			SW¼SW¼	30	34	55			
	1874				72.69			W½W½	31	34	55			
	1875				72.69			S½SE¼	25	34	55			
	1876				72.69			NE¼	36	34	54			
	1877				72.69			W½SW¼	36	34	54			
	1878				72.69			SW¼NW¼	36	34	54	4-15—6-15	.894	109.04
	1879				72.69			E½W½	36	34	54	4-15—6-15	.894	109.04
	1880				72.69			SE¼	36	34	54	4-15—6-15	.894	109.04
								NE¼NW¼	1	33	54	4-15—6-15	.894	109.04
								SE¼	35	34	54	4-15—6-15	.894	109.04
								S½SW¼	35	34	54	4-15—6-15	.894	109.04
								NE¼	2	33	54	4-15—6-15	.894	109.04
								NE¼NW¼	2	33	54	4-15—6-15	.894	109.04
	1882				33.23			NE¼SE¼	36	34	55	4-15—6-15	.409	49.85
	1882				6.51			NW¼SE¼	36	34	55	4-15—6-15	.080	9.77
	1885				7.26			NE¼NW¼	1	33	55	4-15—6-15	.089	10.89
	1887				3.72			NE¼NE¼	36	34	55	4-15—6-15	.046	5.58
	1887				5.12			SE¼NE¼	36	34	55	4-15—6-15	.063	7.68
	1887				11.62			SW¼NE¼	36	34	55	4-15—6-15	.143	17.43
	1887				4.65			NW¼SE¼	36	34	55	4-15—6-15	.057	6.98
	1887				0.47			SE¼NW¼	36	34	55	4-15—6-15	.006	.71
	1887				20.46			NE¼SW¼	36	34	55	4-15—6-15	.252	30.69
	1887				0.93			NW¼SW¼	36	34	55	4-15—6-15	.011	1.40
	1887				5.58			SE¼SW¼	36	34	55	4-15—6-15	.069	8.37
	1887				15.81			SW¼SW¼	36	34	55	4-15—6-15	.194	23.82

Claimant—**Albert Lomori.** Proof No. 00231

Source—**Humboldt River.** Ditch—**Lomori Dam.**

Nat. mdw.	Cult. area	Dams	Ditches	Harvest crops	Meadow pasture	Willow and sage pasture	Swamp or overflow	Subdivision	Section	Tp.N.	R.E.	Length of season	C.F.S.	Acre-feet
	1888				30.27			S½SE¼	36	34	54	4 15—6-15	.372	45.41

Claimant—**Mary Larson.** Proof No. 00232

Source—**Humboldt River.** Ditch—**Dams, Tinker Slough and Mulchay's Ditch.**

Nat. mdw.	Cult. area	Dams	Ditches	Harvest crops	Meadow pasture	Willow and sage pasture	Swamp or overflow	Subdivision	Section	Tp.N.	R.E.	Length of season	C.F.S.	Acre-feet
	1874				94.95			SE¼NW¼	30	34	55			
	1875				94.96			SW¼	30	34	55			

1876	94.95		W½SE¼	30	34	55	4-15—6-15	1.108	142.43
1877	94.95		NW¼NE¼	30	34	55	4-15—6-15	1.108	142.43
			NW¼	31	34	55	4-15—6-15	1.108	142.43
			NW¼NE¼	31	34	55	4-15—6-15	1.108	142.43

Claimant—**H. S. Van Drielen.** Proof No. **00233**

Source—**Humboldt River.** Ditch—**Van Drielen Dam.**

1902	40.32		S½NE¼	21	34	55			
			W½SE¼	21	34	55			
			NE¼SW¼	21	34	55	4-15—6-15	.495	60.48

Claimant—**Estate James Russell.** Proof No. **00234**

Source—**Humboldt River.** Ditch—**Russell Dams.**

1872	17.07		SW¼SE¼	15	34	55	4-15—6-15	.210	25.60
1872	3.89		SE¼SW¼	15	34	55	4-15—6-15	.048	5.84
1872	17.41		NW¼NW¼	22	34	55	4-15—6-15	.214	26.12
1872	12.60		NE¼NW¼	22	34	55	4-15—6-15	.155	18.90
1872	3.97		SW¼NW¼	22	34	55	4-15—6-15	.049	5.96
1872	5.06		NW¼NE¼	22	34	55	4-15—6-15	.062	7.59
1880	21.21		SE¼SE¼	15	34	55	4-15—6-15	.261	31.82
1880	17.38		NE¼NW¼	22	34	55	4-15—6-15	.214	26.07
1880	8.07		SE¼NW¼	22	34	55	4-15—6-15	.099	12.11
1880	7.89		SW¼NW¼	22	34	55	4-15—6-15	.097	11.84
1880	22.15		NW¼NE¼	22	34	55	4-15—6-15	.272	33.23
1880	11.28		NE¼NE¼	22	34	55	4-15—6-15	.139	16.92
1880	2.97		SW¼NE¼	22	34	55	4-15—6-15	.037	4.46

Claimant—**A. G. McBride.** Proof No. **00236**

Source—**Humboldt River.** Ditch—**McBride Dams.**

1882		50.99	SE¼NE¼	11	34	55	4-15—5-15	.627	38.24
1885		50.99	SE¼	11	34	55	4-15—5-15	.627	38.24
1888		50.99	E½NW¼	14	34	55	4-15—5-15	.627	38.24
1889		50.99	NE¼	14	34	55	4-15—5-15	.627	38.24

Claimant—**Mrs. Isabella Dewar.** Proof No. **00238**

Source—**Humboldt River.** Ditch—**Burner Ditch.**

1879	27.30		SW¼	6	34	56	4-15—6-15	.336	40.95
1879	7.50		SW¼	6	34	56	4-15—6-15	.092	11.25
1880	27.30		SW¼	6	34	56	4-15—6-15	.336	40.95
1880	7.50		SW¼	6	34	56	4-15—6-15	.092	11.25
1881	27.30		SW¼	6	34	56	4-15—6-15	.336	40.95

Claimant—**J. N. Phillips.** Proof No. 00239

Source—**Humboldt River.** Ditch—**J. N. Phillips Ditches.**

Date of beneficial use: Nat. mdw.	Date of beneficial use: Cult. area	Construction first initiated: Dams	Construction first initiated: Ditches	Culture—Acres: Harvest crops	Culture—Acres: Meadow pasture	Culture—Acres: Willow and sage pasture	Culture—Acres: Swamp or overflow	Location: Subdivision	Location: Section	Location: Tp. N.	Location: R. E.	Length of season	Duty of water: C.F.S.	Duty of water: Acre-feet
	1881				4.60			NW¼NW¼	6	34	56	4-15—6-15	.057	6.90
	1881				31.80			SW¼NW¼	6	34	56	4-15—6-15	.391	47.70
	1881				5.70			SE¼NE¼	1	34	55	4-15—6-15	.070	8.55
	1881				14.30			NE¼NW¼	6	34	56	4-15—6-15	.176	21.45
	1881				29.60			SE¼NW¼	6	34	56	4-15—6-15	.364	44.40
	1888				34.20			SE¼NW¼	31	35	56	4-15—6-15	.421	51.30
	1888				45.30			NW¼NE¼	31	35	56	4-15—6-15	.557	67.95
	1888				32.80			NE¼NE¼	31	35	56	4-15—6-15	.403	49.20
	1888				42.50			SW¼NE¼	31	35	56	4-15—6-15	.523	63.75
	1888				20.00			SE¼NE¼	31	35	56	4-15—6-15	.246	30.00
	1888				3.50			SW¼NW¼	31	35	56	4-15—6-15	.043	5.25
	1888				6.70			NW¼SW¼	31	35	56	4-15—6-15	.082	10.05
	1888				27.20			NE¼SW¼	31	35	56	4-15—6-15	.335	40.80
	1888				9.30			NW¼SE¼	31	35	56	4-15—6-15	.114	13.95
	1888				7.00			SW¼SW¼	31	35	56	4-15—6-15	.086	10.50
	1888				17.40			SE¼SW¼	31	35	56	4-15—6-15	.214	26.10
	1888				2.80			NW¼NW¼	6	34	56	4-15—6-15	.034	4.20
	1888				8.00			NE¼NW¼	6	34	56	4-15—6-15	.098	12.00
	1873				1.00			NW¼NE¼	31	35	56	4-15—6-15	.012	1.50
	1878				14.70			SW¼SE¼	31	35	56	4-15—6-15	.181	22.05
	1879				14.70			SW¼SE¼	31	35	56	4-15—6-15	.181	22.05
	1879				67.15							4-15—6-15	.826	100.73
	1880				67.15				31	35	56	4-15—6-15	.826	100.73
	1879				2.50				6	34	56	4-15—6-15	.031	3.75
	1880				2.50							4-15—6-15	.031	3.75

Source—**Kittredge Creek.** Ditch—**J. N. Phillips Ditches.**

Date of beneficial use: Nat. mdw.	Date of beneficial use: Cult. area	Construction first initiated: Dams	Construction first initiated: Ditches	Culture—Acres: Harvest crops	Culture—Acres: Meadow pasture	Culture—Acres: Willow and sage pasture	Culture—Acres: Swamp or overflow	Location: Subdivision	Location: Section	Location: Tp. N.	Location: R. E.	Length of season	Duty of water: C.F.S.	Duty of water: Acre-feet
	1869					18.00		NW¼SW¼	31	35	56	4-15—5-15	.221	13.50
	1869					28.90		SW¼NW¼	31	35	56	4-15—5-15	.355	21.68
	1869					19.40		NW¼NW¼	6	34	56	4-15—5-15	.239	14.55
	1869					1.00		SW¼NW¼	6	34	56	4-15—5-15	.012	0.75

Claimant—**Aurelio Papa.** Proof No. 00240

Source—**Humboldt River.** Ditch—**Bett Ditches.**

Date of beneficial use: Nat. mdw.	Date of beneficial use: Cult. area	Construction first initiated: Dams	Construction first initiated: Ditches	Culture—Acres: Harvest crops	Culture—Acres: Meadow pasture	Culture—Acres: Willow and sage pasture	Culture—Acres: Swamp or overflow	Location: Subdivision	Location: Section	Location: Tp. N.	Location: R. E.	Length of season	Duty of water: C.F.S.	Duty of water: Acre-feet
	1901				10.38			NW¼NE¼	20	34	55	4-15—6-15	.128	15.57
	1901				28.37			SW¼NE¼	20	34	55	4-15—6-15	.349	42.56
	1901				13.37			SE¼NE¼	20	34	55	4-17—6-15	.164	20.10
	1901				36.34			NE¼NE¼	20	34	55	4-15—6-15	.447	54.50
	1901				1.16			NW¼NW¼	21	34	55	4-15—6-15	.014	1.74
	1901				0.29			SW¼NW¼	21	34	55	4-15—6-15	.004	0.43

Claimants—**Mildred Elmore, Walter S. Elmore, Mildred C. Clubine, Grace Kendricks.** Proof No. 00241

Source—**Rabbit Creek and Humboldt River.** Ditch—**Elmore Ditches.**

1872			47.70	S¼	15	35	57	4-15—5-15	.587	143.10
1872	74.60			S½	15	35	57	4-15—8-15	.918	223.90
1872		337.10		N½	15	35	57			
				N½NE¼	16	35	57	4-15—6-15	4.146	1011.30

Claimant—**Chas. Clubine.** Proof No. 00242

Source—**Sherman and Jackstone Creeks and Humboldt River.** Ditch—**Chas. Clubine Ditches.**

1872	44.30		N½N½	15	35	56	4-15—6-15	.545	66.45
1872	73.90		SW¼	10	35	56	4-15—6-15	.909	110.85
1872	18.60		W½SE¼	10	35	56	4-15—6-15	.229	27.90
1872	6.20		NE¼SE¼	10	35	56	4-15—6-15	.076	9.30
1872	5.80		NW¼SW¼	11	35	56	4-15—6-15	.071	8.70
1883	18.10		NE¼SW¼	10	35	56	4-15—6-15	.223	27.15
1883		21.80	W½SW¼	10	35	56	4-15—5-15	.268	16.35
1883	42.30		N½SE¼	10	35	56	4-15—6-15	.520	63.45
1883	31.20		S½NE¼	10	35	56	4-15—6-15	.384	46.80
1883	24.80		SW¼NW¼	11	35	56	4-15—6-15	.305	37.20
1883		1.20	SW¼NW¼	11	35	56	4-15—5-15	.015	.90
1883	19.60		NW¼SW¼	11	35	56	4-15—6-15	.241	29.40
1888		12.40	SE¼NE¼	32	35	56	4-15—5-15	.153	9.30
1888		10.80	SW¼NW¼	33	35	56	4-15—5-15	.133	8.10
1887	55.00		S½	3	35	56	4-15—6-15	.677	82.50
1887		12.50	NW¼	10	35	56	4-15—5-15	.154	9.38
1888	55.00		SW¼	10	35	56	4-15—6-15	.677	82.50
1888		12.50	NE¼	10	35	56	4-15—5-15	.154	9.38
1889	55.00		NW¼	11	35	56	4-15—6-15	.677	82.50
1889		12.50					4-15—5-15	.154	9.38
1890	55.00						4-15—6-15	.677	82.50
1890		12.50					4-15—5-15	.154	9.38
1891	55.10						4-15—6-15	.678	82.65
1891		12.40					4-15—5-15	.153	9.30

Claimant—**O'Neill Bros. Land and Stock Co.** Proof. No. 00243

Source—**Town Creek.** Ditch—**O'Neill Bros. Ditches.**

1885	39.75	SE¼SE¼	30	38	62			
		NE¼NE¼	31	38	62			
		NW¼NW¼	32	38	62			
		NE¼NW¼	32	38	62	4-15—6-15	.489	59.62

Claimant—**Chas. W. Clubine.** Proof No. 00244
Source—**Humboldt River and Springs.** Ditch—**Clubine Dams.**

Date of beneficial use: Nat. mdw.	Date of beneficial use: Cult. area	Construction first initiated: Dams	Construction first initiated: Ditches	Culture—Acres: Harvest crops	Culture—Acres: Meadow pasture	Culture—Acres: Willow and sage pasture	Culture—Acres: Swamp or overflow	Location: Subdivision	Location: Section	Location: Tp.N.	Location: R.E.	Length of season	Duty of water: C.F.S.	Duty of water: Acre-feet
	1879				371.70			S½NW¼	1	35	56			
								SW¼	1	35	56			
								SE¼	1	35	56			
								S½NE¼	1	35	56			
								SE¼NE¼	2	35	56			
								E½SE¼	2	35	56			
								W½SW¼	6	35	57			
								SE¼SW¼	6	35	57			
								NE¼NW¼	7	35	57	4-15—6-15	4.572	557.55

Claimant—**J. J. Henderson.** Proof No. 00246
Source—**Humboldt River.** Ditch—**J. J. Henderson Ditches.**

Nat. mdw.	Cult. area	Dams	Ditches	Harvest crops	Meadow pasture	Willow and sage pasture	Swamp or overflow	Subdivision	Section	Tp.N.	R.E.	Length of season	C.F.S.	Acre-feet
	1879				278.40			SE¼NE¼	1	34	55			
	1880				278.30			SE¼	1	34	55			
								E½SW¼	1	34	55			
								SW¼SW¼	1	34	55			
								N½	12	34	55			
								W½SW¼	12	34	55			
								NE¼SW¼	12	34	55			
								NW¼SE¼	12	34	55	4-15—6-15	3.424	417.60
								NW¼SW¼	6	34	56	4-15—6-15	3.423	417.45

Claimant—**Q. D. Boyd.** Proof No. 00247
Source—**Humboldt River.** Ditch—**Q. D. Boyd Ditches.**

Nat. mdw.	Cult. area	Dams	Ditches	Harvest crops	Meadow pasture	Willow and sage pasture	Swamp or overflow	Subdivision	Section	Tp.N.	R.E.	Length of season	C.F.S.	Acre-feet
	1876				60.56			S½NE¼	7	35	58	4-15—6-15	.745	90.84
	1877				17.95			SE¼	7	35	58	4-15—6-15	.221	26.93

Claimant—**J. W. Ebert.** Proof. No. 00301
Source—**Pine Creek.** Ditch—**Ebert Ditch No. 2.**

Nat. mdw.	Cult. area	Dams	Ditches	Harvest crops	Meadow pasture	Willow and sage pasture	Swamp or overflow	Subdivision	Section	Tp.N.	R.E.	Length of season	C.F.S.	Acre-feet
	1879			30.00				S½NE¼	2	31	51	4-15—8-15	.369	90.00
	1885			12.77				S½NE¼	2	31	51	4-15—8-15	.157	38.31
	1885			12.25				SW¼NW¼	1	31	51	4-15—8-15	.151	36.75
	1885			4.65				SE¼NW¼	1	31	51	4-15—8-15	.057	13.95
	1885			2.07				SW¼NW¼	1	31	51	4-15—8-15	.025	6.21

Source—**Pine Creek.** Ditch—**Ebert Ditch No. 1.**

Nat. mdw.	Cult. area	Dams	Ditches	Harvest crops	Meadow pasture	Willow and sage pasture	Swamp or overflow	Subdivision	Section	Tp.N.	R.E.	Length of season	C.F.S.	Acre-feet
	1879			26.14				NE¼	2	31	51	4-15—8-15	.322	78.42
	1885			21.26				E½NE¼	2	31	51	4-15—8-15	.261	63.78
	1885			13.20				W½NW¼	1	31	51	4-15—8-15	.163	39.60
	1890			2.50				NW¼NE¼	2	31	51	4-15—8-15	.031	7.50
	1890			16.53				NE¼	2	31	51	4-15—8-15	.203	49.59

	1899			9.00				E½NW¼	2	31	51	4-15—8-15	.111	27.00
	1899					16.35		W½NW¼	1	31	51	4-15—5-15	.201	12.26
	1899					4.65		SE¼NW¼	1	31	51	4-15—5-15	.057	3.40
	1899					1.00		NE¼SW¼	1	31	51	4-15—5-15	.012	.75

Claimant—**Geo. W. Goodfellow.** Proof No. **00302**

Source—**Hot Creek.** Ditch—**Hale Nos. 1 and 2.**

1868	1868			0.70				SE¼	8	28	52	4-15—8-15	.009	2.10
1868	1868			1.68				SE¼	8	28	52	4-15—8-15	.021	5.04
1868	1868			0.10				SW¼NW¼	16	28	52	4-15—8-15	.001	.30
1868	1868			86.24				NE¼	17	28	52	4-15—8-15	1.061	258.72
1868	1868			80.65				NW¼	17	28	52	4-15—8-15	.992	241.95
1868	1868			25.07				SW¼	8	28	52	4-15—8-15	.308	75.21

Claimant—**T. H. Jewell.** Proof No. **00303**

Source—**Pine Creek.** Ditch—**Pine Creek Ditch No. 1.**

	1877			7.58				NW¼SW¼	17	31	52	4-15—8-15	.093	21.74
	1877			5.32				NE¼SE¼	18	31	52	4-15—8-15	.065	15.96
	1877			1.50				SW¼NW¼	17	31	52	4-15—8-15	.018	4.50
	1877			18.00				E½NE¼	18	31	52	4-15—8-15	.221	54.00
	1898			6.42				E½NE¼	18	31	52	4-15—8-15	.079	19.26
	1898			0.60				NW¼NE¼	18	31	52	4-15—8-15	.007	1.80
	1898			17.63				SE¼	7	31	52	4-15—8-15	.217	52.89

Source—**Pine Creek.** Ditch—**Pine Creek Ditch No. 2.**

	1875			1.95				SW¼NW¼	17	31	52	4-15—8-15	.024	5.85
	1875			2.92				SE¼SE¼	18	31	52	4-15—8-15	.036	6.76
	1877			10.00				NE¼NE¼	18	31	52	4-15—8-15	.123	30.00
	1898			18.00				SE¼	7	31	52	4-15—8-15	.221	54.00
	1898			5.00				SE¼SE¼	7	31	52	4-15—8-15	.062	15.00
	1898			4.00				NE¼NE¼	18	31	52	4-15—8-15	.049	12.00

NOTE—All of the area east of Pine Creek and west of Ditch No. 2 shows no signs of irrigation in recent years, probably not since 1910. The area west of Pine Creek is not in a good state of cultivation.

Source—**Pine Creek.** Ditch—**Cold Creek Ditch.**

	1898			2.00				SE¼	7	31	52	4-15—8-15	.025	6.00

Claimant—**J. P. Raine.** Proof No. **00304**

Source—**Pine Creek.** Ditches—**Nos. 1, 2, 3, and 4.**

	1871			4.41				SE¼SE¼	29	31	52	4-15—8-15	.054	13.23
	1871			17.37				SW¼SE¼	29	31	52	4-15—8-15	.214	52.11
	1871			7.85				SE¼NW¼	29	31	52	4-15—8-15	.097	23.55
	1875			15.24				NE¼NW¼	29	31	52	4-15—8-15	.187	45.72
	1875			37.13				NW¼NE¼	20	31	52	4-15—8-15	.457	81.39
	1875			15.58				SE¼SW¼	20	31	52	4-15—8-15	.192	47.24
	1875			22.64				SW¼SE¼	20	31	52	4-15—8-15	.278	67.92
	1872			28.75				NW¼SE¼	29	31	52	4-15—8-15	.354	86.25
	1875			8.25				NE¼SW¼	29	31	52	4-15—8-15	.101	24.75
	1875			14.43				SE¼NW¼	29	31	52	4-15—8-15	.177	43.29

J. P. Raine—Continued.

Date of beneficial use: Nat. mdw.	Date of beneficial use: Cult. area	Construction first initiated: Dams	Construction first initiated: Ditches	Culture—Acres: Harvest crops	Culture—Acres: Meadow pa-ture	Culture—Acres: Willow and sage pasture	Culture—Acres: Swamp or over-flow	Location: Subdivision	Location: Section	Location: Tp.N.	Location: R.E.	Length of season	Duty of water: C.F.S.	Duty of water: Acre-feet
	1871			37.57				SE¼NW¼	29	31	52	4-15—8-15	.462	113.71
	1874			13.07				NW¼NE¼	29	31	52	4-15—8-15	.161	39.21
	1875			9.96				NW¼SE¼	20	31	52	4-15—8-15	.123	29.88
	1875			7.52				NE¼SW¼	20	31	52	4-15—8-15	.092	22.56
	1875			4.20				SW¼NE¼	20	31	52	4-15—8-15	.052	12.30
	1875			9.60				SE¼NW¼	20	31	52	4-15—8-15	.119	28.98
	1903						10.32	NE¼NW¼	20	31	52	4-15—5-15	.127	7.72
	1889			15.66				NE¼SW¼	29	31	52	4-15—8-15	.192	46.98
	1889			16.78				SE¼NW¼	29	31	52	4-15—8-15	.206	50.34
	1880			1.56				SE¼NW¼	29	31	52	4-15—8-15	.019	4.68

Source—Hot Creek. Ditch—Hot Creek Ditch No. 1.

Nat. mdw.	Cult. area	Dams	Ditches	Harvest crops	Meadow pa-ture	Willow and sage pasture	Swamp or over-flow	Subdivision	Section	Tp.N.	R.E.	Length of season	C.F.S.	Acre-feet
	1871			25.77				SW¼NW¼	16	29	52	4-15—8-15	.317	77.31
	1871			.80				SE¼NW¼	16	29	52	4-15—8-15	.098	2.40
	1871			10.40				NE¼NW¼	16	29	52	4-15—8-15	.128	31.20
	1871			40.00				NW¼NW¼	16	29	52	4-15—8-15	.492	120.00
	1871			1.70				SW¼NW¼	16	29	52	4-15—8-15	.021	5.10
	1871			6.66				SW¼SW¼	16	29	52	4-15—8-15	.082	19.98
	1871					12.53		SW¼NW¼	16	29	52	4-15—5-15	.154	9.40
	1871			40.00				NW¼SW¼	4	29	52	4-15—8-15	.492	120.00
	1871			40.00				SW¼SW¼	4	29	52	4-15—8-15	.492	120.00
	1871			18.93				SE¼SW¼	4	29	52	4-15—8-15	.233	56.79
	1871			8.54				NE¼SW¼	4	29	52	4-15—8-15	.105	25.62
	1871			40.00				SW¼NW¼	9	29	52	4-15—8-15	.492	120.00
	1871			23.80				SE¼NW¼	9	29	52	4-15—8-15	.293	71.40
	1871			23.80				NE¼SW¼	9	29	52	4-15—8-15	.293	71.40
	1871			40.00				NW¼SW¼	9	29	52	4-15—8-15	.492	120.00
	1871			40.00				SW¼SW¼	9	29	52	4-15—8-15	.492	120.00
	1871			24.20				SE¼SW¼	9	29	52	4-15—8-15	.298	72.60
	1871			26.91				NE¼NW¼	9	29	52	4-15—8-15	.331	80.73
	1871			40.00				NW¼NW¼	9	29	52	4-15—8-15	.492	120.00

Source—Hot Creek. Ditch—Hot Creek Ditch No. 2.

Nat. mdw.	Cult. area	Dams	Ditches	Harvest crops	Meadow pa-ture	Willow and sage pasture	Swamp or over-flow	Subdivision	Section	Tp.N.	R.E.	Length of season	C.F.S.	Acre-feet
	1871			32.18				SW¼NE¼	8	29	52	4-15—8-15	.396	96.54
	1871			40.00				SE¼NE¼	8	29	52	4-15—8-15	.492	120.00
	1871			40.00				NE¼SE¼	8	29	52	4-15—8-15	.492	120.00
	1871			9.25				NW¼SE¼	8	29	52	4-15—8-15	.114	27.75
	1871					23.77		NW¼SE¼	8	29	52	4-15—5-15	.292	17.83
	1871					32.78		SW¼SE¼	8	29	52	4-15—5-15	.403	24.59
	1871			32.30				SE¼SE¼	8	29	52	4-15—8-15	.397	96.90
	1871					8.30		SE¼SE¼	8	29	52	4-15—5-15	.102	6.23
	1871			16.80				NE¼NE¼	17	29	52	4-15—8-15	.207	50.40
	1871				16.66			NE¼NE¼	17	29	52	4-15—6-15	.205	24.99
	1871					1.20		NW¼NE¼	17	29	52	4-15—5-15	.015	.90
	1871					17.94		SE¼NE¼	17	29	52	4-15—5-15	.221	13.46
	1871				15.20			NW¼SW¼	16	29	52	4-15—6-15	.187	22.80

1871			7.20	SW¼SW¼	16	29	52	4-15—5-15	.080	5.40
1871			17.40	NW¼SW¼	16	29	52	4-15—5-15	.214	13.05
1871	40.00			SE¼SE¼	5	29	52	4-15—8-15	.492	120.00
1871	40.00			NE¼SE¼	5	29	52	4-15—8-15	.492	120.00
1871	16.80			SW¼NE¼	5	29	52	4-15—8-15	.207	50.40
1871	27.93			NW¼SE¼	5	29	52	4-15—8-15	.344	83.79
1871	31.22			SW¼SE¼	5	29	52	4-15—8-15	.384	93.66
1871	40.00			NE¼NE¼	8	29	52	4-15—8-15	.492	120.00
1871	37.02			NW¼NE¼	8	29	52	4-15—8-15	.418	111.06

Source—**Willow Creek, a tributary of Hot Creek.** Ditch—**Willow Creek.**

1880		6.15		SW¼SW¼	16	29	52	4-15—6-15	.076	0.23
1880		22.37		NW¼NW¼	21	29	52	4-15—6-15	.275	33.56
1880		26.91		SW¼NW¼	21	29	52	4-15—6-15	.331	40.37
1880		24.35		NE¼NW¼	21	29	52	4-15—6-15	.300	36.53
1880		17.08		SE¼NW¼	21	29	52	4-15—6-15	.210	25.62
1880			11.96	NE¼NW¼	21	29	52	4-15—5-15	.147	8.97
1880			13.67	SE¼NW¼	21	29	52	4-15—5-15	.168	10.25

Source—**Dry or Padelford Creek.** Ditch—**Padelford Ditch.**

1871	6.55			SE¼NE¼	29	31	52	4-15—8-15	.081	19.65
1871	5.51			SW¼NE¼	29	31	52	4-15—8-15	.068	16.53
1871	15.00			NW¼SE¼	29	31	52	4-15—8-15	.185	45.00

Source—**Pine Creek.**

1903	8.25			SW¼SE¼	29	31	52	4-15—8-15	.101	24.75
1903	17.89			NE¼NW¼	20	31	52	4-15—8-15	.220	23.67
1875	...	.28		NE¼NW¼	29	31	52	4-15—6-15	.003	.42
1875	5.92			SE¼SW¼	20	31	52	4-15—8-15	.073	17.76
1875	28.33			NE¼SW¼	20	31	52	4-15—8-15	.348	84.99
1875	19.02			SE¼NW¼	20	31	52	4-15—8-15	.234	57.06
1875	2.06			NE¼NW¼	20	31	52	4-15—8-15	.025	6.18
1876	2.15			NE¼SW¼	20	31	52	4-15—8-15	.026	6.45
1876	10.32			SE¼NW¼	20	31	52	4-15—8-15	.127	30.96
1876	4.64			NE¼NW¼	20	31	52	4-15—8-15	.057	13.92

Claimant—**W. S. Yates.** Proof No. 00305

Source—**Smith Creek.** Ditch—**Smith Creek Ditch System.**

1872	2.00			N½NW¼	4	29	52	4-15—8-15	.026	6.00
1878	10.00			W½NW¼	4	29	52	4-15—8-15	.123	30.00
1874	13.07			NW¼NW¼	4	29	52	4-15—8-15	.161	39.21
1874	12.83			E½SE¼	32	30	52	4-15—8-15	.158	38.43
1874	32.96			W½SW¼	33	30	52	4-15—8-15	.405	98.88
1880	.20			NE¼NE¼	5	29	52	4-15—8-15	.002	.60
1880	20.00			SW¼NW¼	4	29	52	4-15—8-15	.246	60.00

W. S. Yates—Continued.
Source—**Pine Creek.** Ditch—**Pine Creek Ditch System.**

Date of beneficial use: Nat. mdw.	Date of beneficial use: Cult. area	Construction first initiated: Dams	Construction first initiated: Ditches	Culture—Acres: Harvest crops	Culture—Acres: Meadow pasture	Culture—Acres: Willow and sage pasture	Culture—Acres: Swamp or overflow	Location: Subdivision	Location: Section	Location: Tp.N.	Location: R.E.	Length of season	Duty of water: C.F.S.	Duty of water: Acre-feet
	1874			75.01				E½NE¼	3	29	52	4-15—8-15	.923	225.03
	1875			29.01				W½NW¼	4	29	52	4-15—8-15	.357	87.03
	1875			13.32				SE¼SE¼	32	30	52	4-15—8-15	.164	39.96
	1875			71.91				SW¼	16	30	52	4-15—8-15	.884	215.73
	1875			....	5.50			SW¼	16	30	52	4-15—6-15	.068	8.25
	1875			35.00				NW¼NW¼	21	30	52	4-15—8-15	.431	105.00
	1875			....	5.00			NW¼NW¼	21	30	52	4-15—6-15	.062	7.50
	1875			....	5.78			NE¼NW¼	21	30	52	4-15—6-15	.071	8.67
	1882			2.00				SW¼	21	30	52	4-15—8-15	.025	6.00

Claimant—**C. H. Rand.** Proof No. 00306
Source—**Pine Creek and Tributaries.** Ditch—**Pine Creek.**

Nat. mdw.	Cult. area	Dams	Ditches	Harvest crops	Meadow pasture	Willow and sage pasture	Swamp or overflow	Subdivision	Section	Tp.N.	R.E.	Length of season	C.F.S.	Acre-feet
	1871			35.89				NW¼	21	30	52	4-15—8-15	.441	107.67
	1871			12.03				SW¼	21	30	52	4-15—8-15	.148	36.09
	1871			55.93				S½NE¼	20	30	52	4-15—8-15	.688	177.79
	1889			....		3.45		SE¼NW¼	20	30	52	4-15—5-15	.042	2.58
	1889			1.95				SE¼NW¼	20	30	52	4-15—8-15	.024	5.85
	1871			74.15				E½SW¼	20	30	52	4-15—8-15	.912	222.45
	1871			137.77				SE¼	20	30	52	4-15—8-15	1.695	413.31
	1889			21.79				SE¼	20	30	52	4-15—8-15	.268	65.37
	1889			6.91				NE¼	29	30	52	4-15—8-15	.085	20.73
	1871			...		8.40		E½SW¼	20	30	52	4-15—5-15	.103	6.30
	1871			36.91				NE¼	29	30	52	4-15—8-15	.454	110.73
	1871			14.96				E½NW¼	29	30	52	4-15—8-15	.184	44.88
	1871			6.60				E½NW¼	29	30	52	4-15—8-15	.071	19.80

Source—**Pine Creek and Tributaries.** Ditch—**Trout Creek.**

Nat. mdw.	Cult. area	Dams	Ditches	Harvest crops	Meadow pasture	Willow and sage pasture	Swamp or overflow	Subdivision	Section	Tp.N.	R.E.	Length of season	C.F.S.	Acre-feet
	1871			....	9.20			NW¼	21	30	52	4-15—6-15	.113	13.80
	1871			....	27.21			SW¼	21	30	52	4-15—6-15	.335	40.81
	1889			14.30				SW¼SW¼	21	30	52	4-15—8-15	.176	32.90
	1871			....			82.29	NE¼	29	30	52	4-15—5-15	1.012	61.72
	1871			....			30.45	N½SE¼	29	30	52	4-15—5-15	.375	22.84

Claimant—**Belle B. Ennor, Herbert B. Ennor, and Sarah P. Ennor.** Proof. No. 00307
Source—**Pine Creek.** Ditch—**Ennor Irrigation System.**

Nat. mdw.	Cult. area	Dams	Ditches	Harvest crops	Meadow pasture	Willow and sage pasture	Swamp or overflow	Subdivision	Section	Tp.N.	R.E.	Length of season	C.F.S.	Acre-feet
	1870			32.07				W½NW¼	16	30	52	4-15—8-15	.394	96.21
	1870			22.60				E½NE¼	17	30	52	4-15—8-15	.278	67.80
	1879			16.60				SW¼NW¼	16	30	52	4-15—8-15	.204	49.80
	1870			29.14				SE¼	8	30	52	4-15—8-15	.358	87.42
	1879			39.90				E½SE¼	17	30	52	4-15—8-15	.491	119.70
	1879			90.57				NE¼	17	30	52	4-15—8-15	1.114	271.71
	1882			49.24				W½SE¼	8	30	52	4-15—8-15	.600	147.72

	1882			6.28				NE¼SW¼	8	30	52	4-15—8-15	.077	18.81
	1882			20.81				E½NW¼	8	30	52	4-15—8-15	.256	62.43
	1882			22.58				W½W½NE¼	8	30	52	4-15—8-15	.278	68.24
	1882			4.12				SE¼SW¼	5	30	52	4-15—8-15	.051	12.36
	1882			15.44				W½SE¼	5	30	52	4-15—8-15	.190	46.32
	1880			13.33				E½SE¼	5	30	52	4-15—8-15	.164	39.99
	1885			10.40				SW¼SE¼	5	30	52	4-15—8-15	.128	31.20
	1885			24.39				E½NE¼	8	30	52	4-15—8-15	.300	73.17
	1885			6.07				NE¼SE¼	8	30	52	4-15—8-15	.075	18.21
	1885			1.40				SW¼NW¼	9	30	52	4-15—8-15	.017	4.20
	1885			.54				NW¼SW¼	9	30	52	4-15—8-15	.007	1.62
	1880			35.50				N½SE¼	8	30	52	4-15—8-15	.437	106.50
	1880			6.00				W½SE¼	8	30	52	4-15—8-15	.074	18.00
	1880			10.10				S½NE¼	8	30	52	4-15—8-15	.124	30.30
	1899			19.20				S½NE¼	8	30	52	4-15—8-15	.236	57.60
	1898			36.40				NE¼	8	30	52	4-15—8-15	.448	109.20
	1882			26.95				W½NE¼	8	30	52	4-15—8-15	.331	88.85
	1898			39.20				SE¼	5	30	52	4-15—8-15	.482	117.60
	1870			19.63				SE¼SE¼	8	30	52	4-15—8-15	.241	58.89

Claimant—**Geo. W. Goodfellow.** **Proof No. 00308**
Source—**Pony Creek.** Ditch—**Goodfellow Ditch System.**

	1888			6.59				NE¼	17	28	52	4-15—8-15	.081	19.77
	1888			41.34				SE¼	17	28	52	4-15—8-15	.508	124.02
	1888			37.48				SW¼	16	28	52	4-15—8-15	.461	112.44
	1888			111.06				NW¼	21	28	52	4-15—8-15	1.360	333.18
	1888			66.26				NE¼	21	28	52	4-15—8-15	.815	198.78
	1888			78.72				N½SE¼	21	28	52	4-15—8-15	.968	236.16
	1888			.20				SW¼NW¼	22	28	52	4-15—8-15	.002	.60
	1888			2.47				N½SW¼	22	28	52	4-15—8-15	.030	7.41
	1888			9.20				NE¼SW¼	21	28	52	4-15—8-15	.113	27.60

Claimant—**George Arthur.** **Proof No. 00321**
Source—**James Creek.** Ditch—**George Arthur Ditches.**

	1882			28.09				SW¼SW¼	2	33	51			
								NE¼NE¼	10	33	51	4-15—8-15	.346	84.27

Claimant—**J. W. Puett.** Proof No. **00322**
Source—**Maggie Creek.** Ditch—**Palmer.**

	1871			20.00				SE¼NW¼	26	33	52	4-15—8-15	.266	60.00

Claimant—**W. T. Jenkins Co.** Proof No. **00323**
Source—**Meadow Creek.** Ditch—**Meadow Creek.**

	1896			7.71				NW¼SW¼	10	37	52	4-15—8-15	.095	23.23
	1896			2.80				NE¼SW¼	10	37	52	4-15—8-15	.034	8.40
	1896			...	3.91			NE¼SW¼	10	37	52	4-15—6-15	.048	5.91
	1896			6.44				NW¼SE¼	10	37	52	4-15—8-15	.079	19.32

W. T. Jenkins Co.—Continued.

Date of beneficial use: Nat. mdw.	Date of beneficial use: Cult. area	Construction first initiated: Dams	Construction first initiated: Ditches	Culture—Acres: Harvest crops	Culture—Acres: Meadow pasture	Culture—Acres: Willow and sage pasture	Culture—Acres: Swamp or overflow	Location: Subdivision	Location: Section	Location: Tp.N.	Location: R.E.	Length of season	Duty of water: C.F.S.	Duty of water: Acre-feet
	1896			4.69				SW¼SE¼	10	37	52	4-15—8-15	.058	14.07
	1896			10.23				SE¼SE¼	10	37	52	4-15—8-15	.126	30.69
	1896			7.76				SW¼SW¼	11	37	52	4-15—8-15	.095	23.28
	1896				6.39			SW¼SW¼	11	37	52	4-15—6-15	.079	9.59
	1896				1.27			SE¼SW¼	11	37	52	4-15—6-15	.016	1.91
Source—Stampede Creek. Ditch—Stampede Creek.														
	1885			1.00				SE¼NW¼	26	38	52	4-15—8-15	.012	3.00
	1885			5.13				SW¼NE¼	26	38	52	4-15—8-15	.063	15.39
	1885			3.62				NE¼SW¼	26	38	52	4-15—8-15	.045	10.86
	1885			.28				NW¼SW¼	26	38	52	4-15—8-15	.003	.84
	1885			.15				SW¼SW¼	26	38	52	4-15—8-15	.002	.45
	1885			7.92				SE¼SW¼	26	38	52	4-15—8-15	.097	23.76
	1885			8.90				NW¼SE¼	26	38	52	4-15—8-15	.109	26.70
	1885			11.23				SW¼SE¼	26	38	52	4-15—8-15	.138	33.69
	1885			2.16				NE¼SE¼	26	38	52	4-15—8-15	.027	6.48
	1885			35.55				SE¼SE¼	26	38	52	4-15—8-15	.437	106.65
	1885			2.98				SW¼SW¼	25	38	52	4-15—8-15	.037	8.94
	1885			20.61				NE¼NE¼	35	38	52	4-15—8-15	.254	61.83
	1885			3.96				NW¼NW¼	36	38	52	4-15—8-15	.048	11.88
	1885			2.92				SE¼NE¼	35	38	52	4-15—8-15	.036	8.76
	1885			13.10				SW¼NW¼	36	38	52	4-15—8-15	.161	39.30
	1885			7.94				NW¼SW¼	36	38	52	4-15—8-15	.098	23.82
Source—Lake Creek. Ditch—Lake Creek.														
	1885			9.22				NE¼SW¼	3	37	52	4-15—8-15	.113	27.66
	1885			2.02				SE¼SW¼	3	37	52	4-15—8-15	.025	6.06
	1885			8.62				NW¼SE¼	3	37	52	4-15—8-15	.106	25.86
	1885			0.72				NE¼SE¼	3	37	52	4-15—8-15	.009	2.16
	1885			15.29				SW¼SE¼	3	37	52	4-15—8-15	.188	45.87
	1885			23.89				SE¼SE¼	3	37	52	4-15—8-15	.294	71.67
	1885			11.60				NE¼SW¼	11	37	52	4-15—8-15	.143	34.80
	1885					2.17		NE¼SW¼	11	37	52	4-15—5-15	.027	3.26
	1885			2.34				NW¼SE¼	11	37	52	4-15—8-15	.029	7.02
	1885				1.38			NW¼SE¼	11	37	52	4-15—6-15	.017	2.07
	1885			13.53				SW¼SW¼	2	37	52	4-15—8-15	.166	40.59
Source—Spring Creek. Ditch—Spring Creek.														
	1885			0.49				NW¼NW¼	35	38	52	4-15—8-15	.006	1.47
	1885				4.34			SW¼NW¼	35	38	52	4-15—6-15	.053	6.51
	1885			18.29				SE¼NW¼	35	38	52	4-15—8-15	.225	54.87
	1885			2.65				NE¼SW¼	35	38	52	4-15—8-15	.033	7.95
	1885			0.22				SW¼NE¼	35	38	52	4-15—8-15	.008	.66
	1885			19.37				NW¼SE¼	35	38	52	4-15—8-15	.238	58.11
	1885			2.38				NE¼SE¼	35	38	52	4-15—8-15	.029	7.14

1885	4.48			SW¼SE¼	35	38	52	4-15—8-15	.055	13.44
1885	9.02			SE¼SE¼	35	38	52	4-15—8-15	.122	29.76
1885		1.45		NE¼SE¼	35	38	52	4-15—6-15	.018	2.18

Areas tabulated under 00323 not correct. Resurvey will add hay lands and pasture, the extent of which is not determinable at this date. Since the land requires early irrigation which added to the short seasonal flow, waters passing through are not of great importance as tributaries to Maggie Creek.

Claimant—**Hunter-Banks Company.** Proof No. 00324

Source—**Camp Creek.** Ditch—**Hunter-Banks Company Ditches.**

1898	13.60			N½NW¼	2	35	53	4-15—8-15	.107	40.80

Source—**Cold Creek and Susie Creek.** Ditch—**Hunter-Banks Company Ditches.**

1897	58.60			SW¼NW¼	8	36	54			
				E½NW¼	8	36	54			
				W½NE¼	8	36	54			
				N½SW¼	8	36	54	4-15—8-15	.721	175.80

Source—**Susie Creek.** Ditch—**Hunter-Banks Company Ditches.**

1876	71.70			S½	9	34	53			
				NW¼	16	34	53	4-15—8-15	.882	215.10

Claimant—**William Dunphy Estate.** Proof No. **00325-00329, Inc.**

Source—**Jack Creek; Indian Creek.**

1883		4.52		NW¼SW¼	33	36	51	4-15—6-15	.056	6.78
1883		2.22		SE¼SE¼	32	36	51	4-15—6-15	.027	3.33
1883		3.50		NW¼SE¼	32	36	51	4-15—6-15	.043	5.25
1883			3.10	NW¼SE¼	32	36	51	4-15—5-15	.038	2.38
1883		8.70		NE¼SE¼	32	36	51	4-15—6-15	.107	13.05
1883			3.80	NE¼SE¼	32	36	51	4-15—5-15	.047	2.85

Source—**Maggie Creek and Tributaries.**

1875			3.48	NW¼SW¼	23	33	52	4-15—5-15	.043	2.61
1875			9.31	SW¼SW¼	23	33	52	4-15—5-15	.115	6.98
1875			7.58	NE¼SW¼	23	33	52	4-15—5-15	.093	5.89
1875			36.77	SE¼SW¼	23	33	52	4-15—5-15	.452	27.58
1875			.20	NW¼SE¼	23	33	52	4-15—5-15	.002	0.15
1875			1.21	SW¼SE¼	23	33	52	4-15—5-15	.015	0.91
1875	2.30			NW¼NW¼	23	33	52	4-15—8-15	.028	6.90
1875			26.46	NW¼NW¼	23	33	52	4-15—5-15	.325	19.85
1875			1.82	NE¼NW¼	23	33	52	4-15—5-15	.022	1.37
1875			34.93	SE¼NW¼	23	33	52	4-15—5-15	.430	26.20
1875	28.21			SW¼NW¼	23	33	52	4-15—8-15	.347	81.63
1875			7.68	SW¼NW¼	23	33	52	4-15—5-15	.094	5.76
1875	18.33			NW¼SW¼	23	33	52	4-15—8-15	.225	54.99
1875			.30	NW¼SW¼	23	33	52	4-15—5-15	.004	.23
1875	4.05			NE¼SW¼	23	33	52	4-15—8-15	.050	12.15
1875			24.12	NE¼SW¼	23	33	52	4-15—5-15	.297	18.09
			1.55	SW¼NE¼	23	33	52	4-15—6-15	.019	1.16
			1.78	NW¼SE¼	23	33	52	4-15—5-15	.022	1.34
1875			19.50	NE¼SE¼	15	33	52	4-15—5-15	.240	14.63

William Dunphy Estate—Continued.

Date of beneficial use: Nat. mdw.	Date of beneficial use: Cult. area	Construction first initiated: Dams	Construction first initiated: Ditches	Culture—Acres: Harvest crops	Culture—Acres: Meadow pasture	Culture—Acres: Willow and sage pasture	Culture—Acres: Swamp or over-flow	Location: Subdivision	Location: Section	Location: Tp.N.	Location: R.E.	Length of season	Duty of water: C.F.S.	Duty of water: Acre-feet
	1875					36.70		SE¼SE¼	15	33	52	4-15—5-15	.451	27.53
	1875			15.45				SW¼SE¼	15	33	52	4-15—8-15	.190	46.35
	1875					23.55		SW¼SE¼	15	33	52	4-15—5-15	.290	17.66
	1875					5.45		SW¼SW¼	14	33	52	4-15—5-15	.067	4.09
	1875			2.85				NE¼NW¼	22	33	52	4-15—8-15	.035	8.55
	1875			24.28				NW¼NE¼	22	33	52	4-15—8-15	.290	72.84
	1875					1.30		NW¼NE¼	22	33	52	4-15—5-15	.016	.98
	1875			22.22				NE¼NE¼	22	33	52	4-15—8-15	.273	66.66
	1875					15.45		NE¼NE¼	22	33	52	4-15—5-15	.190	11.59
	1875			11.75				SE¼NE¼	22	33	52	4-15—8-15	.145	35.25
	1875			.72				NE¼NW¼	15	33	52	4-15—8-15	.009	2.26
	1875					3.70		NE¼NW¼	15	33	52	4-15—5-15	.046	2.78
	1875			27.07				SE¼NW¼	15	33	52	4-15—8-15	.333	81.21
	1875					9.38		SE¼NW¼	15	33	52	4-15—5-15	.115	7.04
	1875			7.75				SW¼NW¼	15	33	52	4-15—8-15	.095	23.25
	1875					4.80		NW¼NE¼	15	33	52	4-15—5-15	.059	3.60
	1875			.40				SW¼NE¼	15	33	52	4-15—8-15	.005	1.20
	1875					30.01		SW¼NE¼	15	33	52	4-15—5-15	.369	22.51
	1875					40.00		SE¼NE¼	15	33	52	4-15—5-15	.492	30.00
	1875			4.90				NW¼SW¼	15	33	52	4-15—8-15	.060	14.70
	1875					5.75		NW¼SW¼	15	33	52	4-15—5-15	.071	4.31
	1875			29.68				NE¼SW¼	15	33	52	4-15—8-15	.365	89.04
	1875					8.82		NE¼SW¼	15	33	52	4-15—5-15	.108	6.62
	1875			17.11				SE¼SW¼	15	33	52	4-15—8-15	.210	51.33
	1875					15.92		SE¼SW¼	15	33	52	4-15—5-15	.196	11.94
	1875			.60				NW¼SE¼	15	33	52	4-15—8-15	.007	1.80
	1875					37.15		NW¼SE¼	15	33	52	4-15—5-15	.457	27.86
	1875			9.73				NW¼NE¼	22	34	51	4-15—8-15	.120	29.19
	1875					3.64		NW¼NE¼	22	34	51	4-15—5-15	.045	2.73
	1875			1.10				NE¼NE¼	22	34	51	4-15—8-15	.014	3.30
	1875					10.40		NE¼NE¼	22	34	51	4-15—5-15	.128	7.80
	1875				8.45			SW¼SW¼	11	34	51	4-15—6-15	.104	12.68
	1875				14.60			NW¼NE¼	11	34	51	4-15—6-15	.180	21.90
	1875					2.30		NW¼NE¼	11	34	51	4-15—5-15	.028	1.73
	1875				3.50			SW¼NE¼	11	34	51	4-15—6-15	.043	5.25
	1875					2.02		SW¼NE¼	11	34	51	4-15—5-15	.025	1.52
	1875				5.85			NW¼NW¼	11	34	51	4-15—6-15	.072	8.78
	1875					8.65		NW¼NW¼	11	34	51	4-15—5-15	.106	6.49
	1875			29.67				SW¼NW¼	11	34	51	4-15—8-15	.365	80.01
	1875					5.55		SW¼NW¼	11	34	51	4-15—5-15	.068	4.16
	1875			22.13				SE¼NW¼	11	34	51	4-15—8-15	.272	66.39
	1875					11.82		SE¼NW¼	11	34	51	4-15—5-15	.144	8.49
	1875				15.84			NE¼NW¼	11	34	51	4-15—6-15	.195	23.70
	1875					9.30		NE¼NW¼	11	34	51	4-15—5-15	.114	6.98
	1875				1.80			NE¼SW¼	11	34	51	4-15—6-15	.022	2.70
	1875					2.15		NE¼SW¼	11	34	51	4-15—5-15	.026	1.61

	1875			31.70				NW¼SW¼	11	34	51	4-15—8-15	.390	95.10
	1875					1.02		NW¼SW¼	11	34	51	4-15—5-15	.013	.77
	1875			6.53				SW¼SW¼	11	34	51	4-15—8-15	.080	10.59
	1875					1.32		SE¼NE¼	10	34	51	4-15—5-15	.016	.09
	1875			29.15				SE¼SE¼	10	34	51	4-15—8-15	.350	87.45
	1875					3.07		SE¼SE¼	10	34	51	4-15—5-15	.038	2.30
	1875			10.67				NE¼SE¼	10	34	51	4-15—8-15	.131	32.01
	1875					7.03		NE¼SE¼	10	34	51	4-15—5-15	.086	5.27
	1875			6.39				NE¼NE¼	15	34	51	4-15—8-15	.079	19.17
	1875				1.18			NE¼NE¼	15	34	51	4-15—6-15	.015	1.77
	1875					22.44		NE¼NE¼	15	34	51	4-15—5-15	.276	16.83
	1875			7.15				NW¼NE¼	15	34	51	4-15—8-15	.088	21.45
	1875					.51		NW¼NE¼	15	34	51	4-15—5-15	.006	.38
	1875			29.15				SW¼NE¼	15	34	51	4-15—8-15	.359	87.45
	1875					3.96		SE¼NW¼	15	34	51	4-15—5-15	.049	2.97
	1875			8.05				NW¼SE¼	15	34	51	4-15—8-15	.099	24.15
	1875					6.69		NW¼SE¼	15	34	51	4-15—5-15	.082	5.02
	1875					9.97		NE¼SE¼	15	34	51	4-15—5-15	.123	7.48
	1875					3.12		SE¼SE¼	15	34	51	4-15—5-15	.038	2.34
	1875			16.51				SW¼SE¼	15	34	51	4-15—8-15	.203	49.53
	1875					2.00		SW¼SE¼	15	34	51	4-15—5-15	.025	1.50
	1875					7.20		NW¼SW¼	15	34	51	4-15—5-15	.089	5.40
	1875			.65				SE¼NE¼	15	34	51	4-15—8-15	.008	1.95
	1875					14.10		SE¼NE¼	15	34	51	4-15—5-15	.173	10.58
	1875				4.30			SE¼NE¼	2	34	51	4-15—6-15	.053	6.45
	1875				2.22			NE¼SE¼	2	34	51	4-15—6-15	.027	3.33
	1875				21.48			SW¼SE¼	2	34	51	4-15—6-15	.264	32.22
	1875				5.00			SE¼SE¼	2	34	51	4-15—6-15	.062	7.50
	1875				2.83			SE¼SW¼	2	34	51	4-15—6-15	.035	4.25
	1875				4.65			NE¼NW¼	11	34	51	4-15—6-15	.057	6.98
	1875				8.74			NW¼NE¼	11	34	51	4-15—6-15	.108	13.11
	1883					.75		NE¼SW¼	15	36	51	4-15—5-15	.009	.56
	1883					7.62		SE¼SW¼	15	36	51	4-15—5-15	.094	5.72
	1883					2.00		SW¼SE¼	15	36	51	4-15—5-15	.025	1.50
	1883				.80			NE¼NW¼	22	36	51	4-15—6-15	.098	1.20
	1883					1.77		NE¼NW¼	22	36	51	4-15—5-15	.022	1.33
	1883				2.60			NW¼NE¼	22	36	51	4-15—6-15	.032	3.90
	1883					6.11		NW¼NE¼	22	36	51	4-15—5-15	.075	4.58
	1883					14.49		SW¼SE¼	36	36	51	4-15—5-15	.178	10.87
	1883				30.18			NW¼SE¼	36	36	51	4-15—6-15	.371	45.27
	1883					2.93		NW¼SE¼	36	36	51	4-15—5-15	.036	2.20
	1883				2.69			NE¼SE¼	36	36	51	4-15—6-15	.033	4.04
	1883					4.78		NE¼SE¼	36	36	51	4-15—5-15	.059	3.59
	1883				3.66			NE¼SW¼	36	36	51	4-15—6-15	.045	5.49
	1883					23.68		NE¼SW¼	36	36	51	4-15—5-15	.291	17.72
	1883				6.42			SE¼NW¼	36	36	51	4-15—6-15	.079	9.63
	1883				11.15			SW¼NE¼	36	36	51	4-15—6-15	.137	16.73
1883					1.38			SW¼SE¼	6	35	52	4-15—6-15	.017	2.07
1883					1.70			NW¼NE¼	7	35	52	4-15—6-15	.021	2.55
1883						6.25		NW¼NE¼	7	35	52	4-15—5-15	.077	4.69
1883					2.95			SW¼NE¼	7	35	52	4-15—6-15	.036	4.43
1883					4.53			NE¼NW¼	7	35	52	4-15—6-15	.056	6.80
1883					10.29			SE¼NW¼	7	35	52	4-15—6-15	.127	15.44

William Dunphy Estate—Continued.

Date of beneficial use: Nat. mdw.	Date of beneficial use: Cult. area	Construction first initiated: Dams	Construction first initiated: Ditches	Culture—Acres: Harvest crops	Culture—Acres: Meadow pasture	Culture—Acres: Willow and sage pasture	Culture—Acres: Swamp or overflow	Location: Subdivision	Location: Section	Location: Tp.N.	Location: R.E.	Length of season	Duty of water: C.F.S.	Duty of water: Acre-feet
1883					.47			SW¼NW¼	7	35	52	4-15—6-15	.006	.71
	1883			6.64				NE¼NE¼	1	35	51	4-15—8-15	.082	19.92
	1883				24.39			NE¼NE¼	13	35	51	4-15—6-15	.300	36.59
	1883					3.85		NE¼NE¼	1	35	51	4-15—5-15	.047	2.80
	1883			.30				NW¼NE¼	1	35	51	4-15—8-15	.004	.90
	1883				16.77			NW¼NE¼	1	35	51	4-15—6-15	.206	25.11
	1883				.20			NE¼NW¼	1	35	51	4-15—6-15	.002	.30
	1883					3.36		NE¼NW¼	1	35	51	4-15—5-15	.041	2.52
	1883				24.65			SE¼SE¼	36	36	51	4-15—6-15	.303	36.98
	1883					5.72		SE¼SE¼	36	36	51	4-15—5-15	.070	4.29
	1883				12.63			SW¼SE¼	36	36	51	4-15—6-15	.155	18.95
1883						4.03		SE¼SE¼	6	35	52	4-15—5-15	.050	3.02
1883					7.00			SE¼SW¼	6	35	52	4-15—6-15	.086	10.50
	1883				14.34			NW¼NW¼	6	35	52	4-15—6-15	.184	21.51
	1883				2.52			SE¼NW¼	6	35	52	4-15—6-15	.031	3.78
	1883				5.65			NE¼NW¼	6	35	52	4-15—6-15	.069	8.48
	1883				.62			NW¼SE¼	6	35	52	4-15—6-15	.008	.93
1883					40.00			SW¼SW¼	29	36	52	4-15—6-15	.492	60.00
1883					3.13			SE¼SE¼	30	36	52	4-15—6-15	.038	4.70
1883					3.39			SW¼SW¼	32	36	52	4-15—6-15	.042	5.09
1883						.75		SW¼SW¼	32	36	52	4-15—5-15	.009	.56
1883						1.03		NE¼NE¼	31	36	52	4-15—5-15	.013	.77
1883						3.17		SE¼NE¼	31	36	52	4-15—5-15	.039	2.38
1883						1.50		NE¼SE¼	31	36	52	4-15—5-15	.018	1.13
1883						4.50		SE¼SE¼	31	36	52	4-15—5-15	.055	3.38
1883						8.55		NW¼SE¼	31	36	52	4-15—5-15	.105	6.41
1883					1.78			SW¼SW¼	31	36	52	4-15—6-15	.022	2.67
1883					7.60			NE¼NE¼	6	35	52	4-15—6-15	.093	11.40
1883						2.80		NE¼NE¼	6	35	52	4-15—5-15	.034	2.10
1883					3.60			SE¼NE¼	6	35	52	4-15—6-15	.044	5.40
1883						5.62		SE¼NE¼	6	35	52	4-15—5-15	.069	4.22
1883					8.92			NE¼SE¼	6	35	52	4-15—6-15	.110	13.38
1883						4.11		NE¼SE¼	6	35	52	4-15—5-15	.051	3.08
1883					4.18			SE¼SE¼	6	35	52	4-15—6-15	.051	6.27
	1883			33.53				NW¼NW¼	29	36	52	4-15—8-15	.412	100.59
	1883					2.07		NW¼NW¼	29	36	52	4-15—5-15	.025	1.55
	1883			24.84				SW¼NW¼	29	36	52	4-15—8-15	.306	74.52
	1883					10.77		SW¼NW¼	29	36	52	4-15—5-15	.132	8.08
	1883			1.40				SE¼NW¼	29	36	52	4-15—8-15	.017	4.20
	1883					28.10		SE¼NW¼	29	36	52	4-15—5-15	.346	21.08
	1883			9.63				NE¼NW¼	29	36	52	4-15—8-15	.118	28.89
	1883					27.20		NE¼NW¼	29	36	52	4-15—5-15	.335	20.40
	1883					13.18		NW¼NE¼	29	36	52	4-15—5-15	.162	9.89
	1883			9.32				NW¼SW¼	29	36	52	4-15—8-15	.115	27.96
	1883					24.25		NW¼SW¼	29	36	52	4-15—5-15	.298	18.19
	1883			4.10				SW¼SW¼	29	36	52	4-15—8-15	.050	12.30

1883		12.25	SW¼SW¼	29	36	52	4-15—5-15	.151	9.19
1883		9.85	SE¼SW¼	29	36	52	4-15—5-15	.121	7.39
1883		25.37	NE¼SW¼	29	36	52	4-15—5-15	.312	19.03
1883	13.68		NW¼SE¼	20	36	52	4-15—8-15	.168	41.04
1883		16.95	NW¼SE¼	20	36	52	4-15—5-15	.208	12.71
1883	4.62		SW¼SE¼	20	36	52	4-15—8-15	.057	13.86
1884		16.85	SW¼SE¼	20	36	52	4-15—5-15	.205	12.49
1883	12.35		NW¼SW¼	20	36	52	4-15—8-15	.152	37.05
1883	26.22		SW¼SW¼	20	36	52	4-15—8-15	.323	78.66
1883	35.12		SE¼SW¼	20	36	52	4-15—8-15	.432	105.36
1883		1.48	SE¼SW¼	20	36	52	4-15—5-15	.018	1.11
1883	36.63		NE¼SW¼	20	36	52	4-15—8-15	.451	109.89
1883		.10	NE¼SW¼	20	36	52	4-15—5-15	.001	.06
1883	28.54		NW¼NE¼	20	36	52	4-15—8-15	.351	85.62
1883		8.31	NW¼NE¼	20	36	52	4-15—5-15	.102	6.23
1883	1.00		NE¼NE¼	20	36	52	4-15—6-15	.012	3.00
1883		3.98	NE¼NE¼	20	36	52	4-15—5-15	.049	2.99
1883	22.96		SW¼NE¼	20	36	52	4-15—8-15	.282	68.88
1883		7.45	SW¼NE¼	20	36	52	4-15—5-15	.092	5.59
1883	22.12		NE¼NW¼	20	36	52	4-15—8-15	.272	66.36
1883		3.30	NE¼NW¼	20	36	52	4-15—5-15	.041	2.48
1883	36.52		SE¼NW¼	20	36	52	4-15—8-15	.449	109.56
1883		3.08	SE¼NW¼	20	36	52	4-15—5-15	.038	2.31
1883	.82		SW¼NW¼	20	36	52	4-15—8-15	.010	2.46
1883		2.75	SW¼NW¼	20	36	52	4-15—5-15	.035	2.06
1883	3.90		NW¼NW¼	20	36	52	4-15—8-15	.048	11.70
1883		14.95	NW¼NW¼	20	36	52	4-15—5-15	.184	11.21
1883	2.92		NE¼NE¼	19	36	52	4-15—8-15	.036	8.76
1883		25.86	NE¼NE¼	19	36	52	4-15—5-15	.318	10.40
1883	.60		SE¼NE¼	19	36	52	4-15—8-15	.007	1.80
1883		4.80	SE¼NE¼	19	36	52	4-15—5-15	.059	3.60
1883		18.65	SE¼SE¼	18	36	52	4-15—5-15	.229	13.99
1883	6.93		SE¼SW¼	17	36	52	4-15—8-15	.085	20.79
1883		11.89	SE¼SW¼	17	36	52	4-15—5-15	.146	8.92
1883		6.40	NE¼SW¼	17	36	52	4-15—5-15	.079	4.80
1883	10.03		SE¼NE¼	17	36	52	4-15—8-15	.123	30.09
1883		5.45	SE¼NE¼	17	36	52	4-15—5-15	.067	4.09
1883	32.23		NE¼SE¼	17	36	52	4-15—8-15	.396	96.69
1883		5.06	NE¼SE¼	17	36	52	4-15—5-15	.062	3.80
1883	11.11		NW¼SE¼	17	36	52	4-15—8-15	.137	33.33
1883		12.40	NW¼SE¼	17	36	52	4-15—5-15	.153	9.30
1883	23.67		SW¼SE¼	17	36	52	4-15—8-15	.291	71.01
1883		13.86	SW¼SE¼	17	36	52	4-15—5-15	.170	10.40
1883	19.25		SE¼SE¼	17	36	52	4-15—8-15	.257	57.75
1883		13.63	SE¼SE¼	17	36	52	4-15—5-15	.168	10.22
1883		1.30	SE¼NE¼	16	36	52	4-15—5-15	.016	.98
1883	1.25		SW¼NE¼	16	36	52	4-15—8-15	.015	3.75
1883	8.41		NW¼NE¼	16	36	52	4-15—8-15	.103	125.23
1883		3.10	NW¼NE¼	16	36	52	4-15—5-15	.038	2.33
1883	15.28		NE¼NW¼	16	36	52	4-15—8-15	.188	45.84
1883		12.37	NE¼NW¼	16	36	52	4-15—5-15	.152	9.28
1883		11.53	NW¼NW¼	16	36	52	4-15—5-15	.142	8.65
1883	24.83		SW¼NW¼	16	36	52	4-15—8-15	.305	74.49

William Dunphy Estate—Continued.

Date of beneficial use: Nat. mdw.	Date of beneficial use: Cult. area	Construction first initiated: Dams	Construction first initiated: Ditches	Culture—Acres: Harvest crops	Culture—Acres: Meadow pasture	Culture—Acres: Willow and sage pasture	Culture—Acres: Swamp or overflow	Location: Subdivision	Location: Section	Location: Tp.N.	Location: R.E.	Length of season	Duty of water: C.F.S.	Duty of water: Acre-feet
	1883					7.78		SW¼NW¼	16	36	52	4-15—5-15	.096	5.84
	1883			22.58				SE¼NW¼	16	36	52	4-15—8-15	.278	67.34
	1883					4.93		SE¼NW¼	16	36	52	4-15—5-15	.061	3.70
	1883					.30		NE¼NW¼	16	36	52	4-15—5-15	.004	.23
	1883			12.14				NW¼SW¼	16	36	52	4-15—8-15	.149	36.42
	1883					15.95		NW¼SW¼	16	36	52	4-15—5-15	.196	11.96
	1883			.28				NE¼SW¼	16	36	52	4-15—8-15	.003	.84
	1883					.25		NW¼SE¼	16	36	52	4-15—5-15	.003	.19
	1883			.35				SW¼SW¼	16	36	52	4-15—8-15	.004	1.05
1883					3.15			NW¼NW¼	10	36	52	4-15—6-15	.039	4.73
1883						1.90		NW¼NW¼	10	36	52	4-15—5-15	.023	1.43
1883					4.70			SW¼NW¼	10	36	52	4-15—6-15	.078	7.05
1883						2.40		SW¼NW¼	10	36	52	4-15—5-15	.025	1.50
1883					6.35			NW¼SW¼	10	36	52	4-15—6-15	.078	9.53
1883						5.91		NW¼SW¼	10	36	52	4-15—5-15	.069	4.43
1883					.30			SW¼SW¼	10	36	52	4-15—6-15	.004	0.45
1883						3.55		SW¼SW¼	10	36	52	4-15—5-15	.044	2.66
1883					23.65			SE¼NE¼	9	36	52	4-15—6-15	.291	35.48
1883						3.05		SE¼NE¼	9	36	52	4-15—5-15	.038	2.29
1883					2.45			NE¼SE¼	9	36	52	4-15—6-15	.030	3.68
1883						17.27		NE¼SE¼	9	36	52	4-15—5-15	.212	12.95
	1883				2.43			NE¼NW¼	16	36	52	4-15—6-15	.030	3.65
	1883				4.60			NW¼NE¼	16	36	52	4-15—6-15	.057	6.90
	1883				2.70			SW¼SE¼	9	36	52	4-15—6-15	.033	4.05
	1883				.82			SE¼SW¼	9	36	52	4-15—6-15	.101	1.23
	1883			8.30				NW¼NE¼	3	36	52	4-15—8-15	.102	24.90
	1883			37.33				NE¼NW¼	3	36	52	4-15—8-15	.459	111.99
	1883			13.02				NW¼NW¼	3	36	52	4-15—8-15	.160	39.06
	1883			7.33				SE¼NW¼	3	36	52	4-15—8-15	.090	28.99
	1883			7.50				SW¼NW¼	3	36	52	4-15—8-15	.092	22.50
	1883					4.15		SE¼SW¼	27	37	52	4-15—5-15	.051	3.11
	1883					16.80		SE¼NE¼	34	37	52	4-15—5-15	.207	12.60
	1883					1.10		NE¼SE¼	34	37	52	4-15—5-15	.014	.83
	1883					7.20		SW¼NE¼	34	37	52	4-15—5-15	.089	5.40
	1883			4.85				NW¼SE¼	34	37	52	4-15—8-15	.060	14.55
	1883					.45		NW¼SE¼	34	37	52	4-15—5-15	.006	.34
	1883			10.37				SW¼SE¼	34	37	52	4-15—8-15	.128	31.11
	1883			22.00				SE¼NW¼	34	37	52	4-15—8-15	.271	66.00
	1883			.80				SW¼NW¼	34	37	52	4-15—8-15	.010	2.40
	1883			5.55				NW¼SW¼	34	37	52	4-15—8-15	.068	16.65
	1883			6.88				SW¼SW¼	34	37	52	4-15—8-15	.085	20.64
	1883			30.26				SE¼SW¼	34	37	52	4-15—8-15	.372	10.78
	1883			33.05				NE¼SW¼	34	37	52	4-15—8-15	.407	99.15
	1883				18.55			NE¼NW¼	34	37	52	4-15—6-15	.228	27.83
	1883					8.80		NE¼NW¼	34	37	52	4-15—5-15	.108	6.60
	1883				1.05			SE¼NW¼	34	37	52	4-15—6-15	.013	1.58

	1883			.80	SE¼NW¼	34	37	52	4-15—5-15	.011	.65
	1883			1.02	SW¼NE¼	34	37	52	4-15—5-15	.020	1.23
	1883			23.37	NW¼NE¼	34	37	52	4-15—5-15	.287	17.53
1883			6.35		NE¼SW¼	23	37	52	4-15—6-15	.078	9.53
1883			.48		NW¼SW¼	23	37	52	4-15—6-15	.006	.72
	1883			36.72	NE¼NE¼	27	37	52	4-15—5-15	.451	27.54
	1883		1.10		SE¼NE¼	27	37	52	4-15—6-15	.014	1.65
	1883			34.90	SE¼NE¼	27	37	52	4-15—5-15	.430	20.22
	1883		.85		SW¼NE¼	27	37	52	4-17—6-15	.010	1.28
	1883			2.55	SW¼NE¼	27	37	52	4-15—5-15	.031	1.91
	1883		5.25		NW¼SE¼	27	37	52	4-15—6-15	.065	7.88
	1883			20.63	NW¼SE¼	27	37	52	4-15—5-15	.253	15.47
	1883		1.50		SW¼SE¼	27	37	52	4-15—6-15	.018	2.25
	1883			35.49	SW¼SE¼	27	37	52	4-15—5-15	.437	26.62
	1883		.65		SE¼SE¼	27	37	52	4-11—6-15	.008	.98
	1883			11.58	SE¼SE¼	27	37	52	4-15—5-15	.142	8.69
	1883		20.75		NE¼SE¼	27	37	52	4-15—6-15	.255	31.13
	1883			7.25	NE¼SE¼	27	37	52	4-15—5-15	.089	5.44
	1883			.10	NE¼SW¼	27	37	52	4-15—5-15	.001	.08
	1883		7.32		SE¼SW¼	27	37	52	4-15—6-15	.090	10.98
1883			4.70		NE¼SE¼	2	37	52	4-15—6-15	.058	3.53
1883			2.34		SE¼SE¼	2	37	52	4-15—6-15	.029	1.76
1883			1.08		SW¼SE¼	2	37	52	4-15—6-15	.013	.80
1883			3.05		NE¼NE¼	11	37	52	4-15—6-15	.038	2.29
1883			11.71		NW¼NE¼	11	37	52	4-15—6-15	.144	8.78
1883			3.60		SE¼SW¼	11	37	52	4-15—6-15	.044	2.70
1883			.50		NW¼NE¼	14	37	52	4-15—6-15	.006	.38
1883			.50		NE¼NE¼	14	37	52	4-15—6-15	.006	.38

Claimant—**Hunter-Banks Company.** Proof No. **00330**

Source—**Cold Creek.** Ditch—**Hunter Banks Company Ditches.**

	1880	26.45			S½SE¼	25	37	53			
					N½NE¼	36	37	53	4-15—8-15	.325	79.35

Claimant—**John** Paleni. Proof No. **00331**

Source—**Springs** Tributary to **Susie Creek.** Ditch—**Paleni Ditches.**

	1870	2.45			SW¼NE¼	15	35	54	4-15—8-15	.030	7.35
	1870	0.31			SW¼NE¼	15	35	54	4-15—8-15	.004	.93
	1870	2.26			NW¼SE¼	15	35	54	4-15—8-15	.028	6.78
	1870	0.11			NE¼NW¼	15	35	54	4-15—8-15	.001	.33
	1870	21.96			SE¼NW¼	15	35	54	4-15—8-15	.270	65.88
	1870	1.97			NE¼SW¼	15	35	54	4-15—8-15	.024	5.97
	1870	16.76			SW¼NW¼	15	35	54	4-15—8-15	.206	50.28
	1870	0.12			NE¼NE¼	16	35	54	4-15—8-15	.001	.36
	1870	13.25			SE¼NE¼	16	35	54	4-15—8-15	.163	39.75
	1870	4.05			SW¼NE¼	16	35	54	4-15—8-15	.049	12.15
	1870	3.62			NW¼NE¼	16	35	54	4-15—8-15	.057	10.86
	1870	9.29			NE¼NW¼	16	35	54	4-15—8-15	.114	27.87
	1870	1.02			SE¼NW¼	16	35	54	4-15—8-15	.010	3.06
	1870	1.42			SW¼NW¼	16	35	54	4-15—8-15	.014	4.26
	1870	0.56			NW¼NW¼	16	35	54	4-15—8-15	.006	1.68

Claimant—**John Paleni.** Proof No. 00332
Source—**Susie Creek.** Ditch—**Paleni Ditches.**

Date of beneficial use: Nat. mdw.	Cult. area	Construction first initiated: Dams	Ditches	Culture—Acres: Harvest crops	Meadow pasture	Willow and sage pasture	Swamp or overflow	Location: Subdivision	Section	Tp.N.	R.E.	Length of season	Duty of water: C.F.S.	Acre-feet
....	1900	....	....	3.92	....	....	....	NE¼NW¼	12	35	53	4-15—8-15	.048	11.76
....	1900	....	....	18.02	....	....	....	SE¼NW¼	12	35	53	4-15—8-15	.222	54.06
....	1900	....	....	1.84	....	....	....	SW¼NE¼	12	35	53	4-15—8-15	.023	5.52
....	1900	....	....	0.41	....	....	....	NW¼SE¼	12	35	53	4-15—8-15	.005	1.23
....	1900	....	....	12.19	....	....	....	NE¼SW¼	12	35	53	4-15—8-15	.150	36.57

Claimant—**Max Arnhold.** Proof. No. 00351
Source—**Pearl Creek.** Ditch—**Max Arnhold Ditches.**

Nat. mdw.	Cult. area	Dams	Ditches	Harvest crops	Meadow pasture	Willow and sage pasture	Swamp or overflow	Subdivision	Section	Tp.N.	R.E.	Length of season	C.F.S.	Acre-feet
....	1869	....	....	33.00	....	....	....	W½	21	28	56	4-15—8-15	.405	99.00
....	1870	....	....	33.00	....	....	....	W½SE½	21	28	56	4-15—8-15	.405	99.00
....	1871	....	....	34.00	....	....	....	SE¼SE¼	21	28	56	4-15—8-15	.418	102.00
....	1879	....	....	50.00	....	....	....	S½S½	22	28	56	4-15—8-15	.615	150.00
....	1885	....	....	50.00	....	....	....	N½NE¼	28	28	56	4-15—8-15	.615	150.00
....	1898	....	....	10.00	....	....	....	....	....	....	....	4-15—8-15	.123	30.00
....	1899	....	....	10.00	....	....	....	....	....	....	....	4-15—8-15	.123	30.00
....	1900	....	....	10.00	....	....	....	....	....	....	....	4-15—8-15	.123	30.00
....	1901	....	....	10.00	....	....	....	....	....	....	....	4-15—8-15	.123	30.00
....	1902	....	....	18.90	....	....	....	....	....	....	....	4-15—8-15	.232	56.70

Claimant—**J. J. Hylton.** Proof No. 00352
Source—**Frost Canyon and Springs.** Ditch—**J. J. Hylton Ditches.**

Nat. mdw.	Cult. area	Dams	Ditches	Harvest crops	Meadow pasture	Willow and sage pasture	Swamp or overflow	Subdivision	Section	Tp.N.	R.E.	Length of season	C.F.S.	Acre-feet
....	1874	....	....	40.00	....	....	....	W½SE¼	8	28	56			
....	1874	....	....	....	44.70	....	....	SE¼SE¼	8	28	56			
....	1895	....	....	7.00	....	....	....	SW¼SW¼	9	28	56	4-15—8-15	.492	120.00
....	1896	....	....	8.00	....	....	....	NE¼SW¼	9	28	56	4-15—6-15	.550	67.05
								NW¼SE¼	9	28	56	4-15—8-15	.086	21.00
								SE¼NE¼	9	28	56	4-15—8-15	.098	24.00

Claimant—**T. F. Brennen.** Proof No. 00353
Source—**Ainley Creek, Ogilvie Creek, Springs, and one-third waters of Young Creek.***
Ditch—**T. F. Brennen Ditches.**

Nat. mdw.	Cult. area	Dams	Ditches	Harvest crops	Meadow pasture	Willow and sage pasture	Swamp or overflow	Subdivision	Section	Tp.N.	R.E.	Length of season	C.F.S.	Acre-feet
....	1869	....	....	40.00	....	....	....	SE¼NW¼	9	32	57	4-15—8-15	.492	120.00
....	1870	....	....	15.00	....	....	....	NE¼SW¼	9	32	57	4-15—8-15	.185	45.00
....	1871	....	....	15.00	....	....	....	S½NE¼	9	32	57	4-15—8-15	.185	45.00
....	1872	....	....	50.00	....	....	....	N½SE¼	9	32	57	4-15—8-15	.615	150.00
....	1873	....	....	50.00	....	....	....	SE¼SE¼	9	32	57	4-15—8-15	.615	150.00
....	1874	....	....	50.00	....	....	....	SW¼NW¼	10	32	57	4-15—8-15	.615	150.00
....	1875	....	....	51.78	....	....	....	NW¼SW¼	10	32	57	4-15—8-15	.637	155.34
....	1872	....	....	20.00	....	....	....	SW¼NW¼	9	32	57	4-15—8-15	.246	60.00
....	1873	....	....	16.00	....	....	....	W½SW¼	9	32	57	4-15—8-15	.197	48.00
....	1873	....	....	40.00	....	....	....	SE¼SW¼	9	32	57	4-15—8-15	.492	120.00

1876	17.00			SW¼SE¼	9	32	57	4-15—8-15	.209	51.00
1879	17.00							4-15—8-15	.209	51.00
1880	35.00							4-15—8-15	.431	105.00
1881	36.63							4-15—8-15	.451	109.80
1898			78.90	SE¼NE¼	8	32	57			
				E½SE¼	8	32	57	4-15—5-15	.970	59.18
1870	100.00			N½	16	32	57	4-15—8-15	1.230	300.00
1871	40.00			N½S½	16	32	57	4-15—8-15	.492	120.00
1872	21.00							4-15—8-15	.258	36.00
1873	21.00							4-15—8-15	.258	36.00
1874	21.00							4-15—8-15	.258	36.00
1875	21.00							4-15—8-15	.258	36.00
1876	21.00							4-15—8-15	.258	36.00
1877	26.53							4-15—8-15	.326	79.59
1877	20.00							4-15—8-15	.246	60.00
1892	13.00							4-15—8-15	.160	39.00
1892		14.00						4-15—6-15	.172	10.50
1900			14.26	W½SW¼	16	32	57	4-15—5-15	.175	10.70

(*)That certain agreement signed by T. F. Brennen and J. Hennen in regard to the division of the waters of Young Creek, as recorded in Elko County, Book 4 of Miscl. Records, pages 180 to 187, is binding as between parties to the agreement. The "miner's inch" referred to shall be defined as being the amount of water that will flow through an opening of one square inch and under a six inch head. The parties to this agreement are to construct and maintain a device in Young Creek in the NW¼NW¼, Sec. 14, T 32 N., R. 57 E., that will automatically divide the stream according to the said agreement, the plans for said device to be approved by the State Engineer.

Claimant—**Mrs. Mary Campbell.** Proof No. 00354

Source—**Bradley or McCutcheon Creek.** Ditch—**Mrs. Mary Campbell Ditches.**

1878	20.00			N½SW¼	31	30	57	4-15—8-15	.246	60.00
1880	25.00			SE¼	31	30	57	4-15—8-15	.308	75.00
1880			56.00	W½SW¼	32	30	57	4-15—5-15	.680	168.00
1881	80.00			SE¼SW¼	32	30	57	4-15—8-15	.984	240.00
1882	64.61			W½NW¼	5	29	57	4-15—8-15	.795	193.83
1890	15.00			E½NE¼	6	29	57	4-15—8-15	.185	45.00
1890			67.50					4-15—5-15	.830	202.50
1890	20.00							4-15—8-15	.246	60.00
1902	28.00							4-15—8-15	.344	84.00
1904	14.05							4-15—8-15	.172	54.00
1905	5.89							4-15—8-15	.072	17.67

Claimant—**J. J. Hylton.** Proof No. 00355

Source—**Peorl Creek and South Fork Humboldt River.** Ditch—**J. J. Hylton Ditches.**

1893	65.60			E½SE¼	19	31	57	4-15—8-15	0.809	196.80
1894	40.00			SW¼	20	31	57	4-15—8-15	0.492	120.00
1895	29.00							4-15—8-15	0.357	87.00
1894	8.00			S½NW¼	20	31	57	4-15—8-15	.980	24.00
1898	13.00			S½SE¼	20	31	57	4-15—8-15	.160	39.00
1905			67.00					4-15—5-15	.824	50.25

J. J. Hylton—Continued.

Date of beneficial use — Nat. mdw.	Date of beneficial use — Cult. area	Construction first initiated — Dams	Construction first initiated — Ditches	Culture—Acres — Harvest crops	Culture—Acres — Meadow pasture	Culture—Acres — Willow and sage pasture	Culture—Acres — Swamp or overflow	Location — Subdivision	Location — Section	Location — Tp.N.	Location — R.E.	Length of season	Duty of water — C.F.S.	Duty of water — Acre-feet
	Source—South Fork Humboldt River. Ditch—J. J. Hylton Ditches.													
....	1871	....	....	30.00	....	....	....	S½	16	31	57	4-15—8-15	.369	90.00
....	1873	....	....	27.06	....	....	....	S½	17	31	57	4-15—8-15	.332	81.10
....	1874	....	....	57.00	....	....	....	N½	20	31	57	4-15—8-15	.701	171.00
....	1875	....	....	4.00	....	....	....	NW¼	21	31	57	4-15—8-15	.049	12.00
....	1876	....	....	1.20	....	....	....	....	....	....	....	4-15—8-15	.015	3.60
....	1878	....	....	196.10	....	....	....	....	....	....	....	4-15—8-15	2.412	588.30
....	1883	....	....	27.70	....	....	....	....	....	....	....	4-15—8-15	.841	83.10
....	1891	....	....	8.80	....	....	....	....	....	....	....	4-15—8-15	.108	26.40
	Source—Rattlesnake Creek. Ditch—J. J. Hylton Ditches.													
....	1869	....	....	64.00	....	....	....	NW¼NW¼	25	31	56	4-15—8-15	.787	192.00
....	1877	....	....	86.00	....	....	....	NW¼	26	31	56	4-15—8-15	1.058	258.00
....	1901	....	....	62.43	....	....	....	NE¼	27	31	56	4-15—8-15	.708	187.29
	Source—South Fork. Ditch—Clayton-Drown.													
....	1897	....	....	51.00	....	....	....	NE¼NE¼	20	31	57	4-15—8-15	.615	153.00
....	1898	....	....	65.96	....	....	....	S½NE¼	20	31	57	4-15—8-15	.811	197.88
....	1901	....	....	32.00	....	....	....	N½SE¼	20	31	57	4-15—8-15	.394	96.00
								NE¼SW¼	20	31	57			
								SE¼NW¼	20	31	57			
	Claimant—J. J. Hylton (Lang Ranch). Proof No. 00355													
	Source—Rattlesnake Creek. Ditch—Company and Ogilvie.													
....	1875	....	....	31.70	....	....	....	SW¼NW¼	19	31	57			
								W½SW¼	19	31	57			
								NE¼SW¼	19	31	57	4-15—8-15	.390	95.10
	Claimant—Pedro Corta. Proof No. 00356													
	Source—Spencer Creek. Ditch—Pedro Corta Ditches.													
....	1871	....	....	2.00	....	....	....	E½W½	12	28	56	4-15—8-15	.025	6.00
....	1883	....	....	91.10	....	....	....	SW¼	1	28	56	4-15—8-15	1.121	273.30
....	1905	....	....	9.00	....	....	....	S½NW¼	1	28	56	4-15—8-15	.111	27.00
	Claimant—Clark Drown. Proof No. 00357													
	Source—Lee Creek and South Fork of Humboldt River.* Ditch—Clark Drown Ditches.													
....	1863	....	....	103.00	....	....	....	SW¼	8	31	57	4-15—8-15	1.267	309.00
....	1883	....	....	22.10	....	....	....	S½SE¼	7	31	57	4-15—8-15	.272	66.30
								N½NE¼	18	31	57			
								N½NW¼	18	31	57			

(*)Priority from South Fork Humboldt River to date, 1908.

Source—**South Fork Humboldt River.** Ditch—**Clark Drown Ditches.**

1868	40.00			SW¼	12	31	56	4-15—8-15	.492	120.00
1870	30.40			SW¼SE¼	12	31	56	4-15—8-15	.374	91.20
1871	30.40			N½	12	31	56	4-15—8-15	.374	91.20
1872	30.40			W½NW¼	18	31	57	4-15—8-15	.374	91.20
1873	30.40							4-15—8-15	.374	91.20
1874	30.30							4-15—8-15	.373	90.90
1875	30.30							4-15—8-15	.373	90.90
1880	46.00							4-15—8-15	.506	138.00
1880	1.50							4-15—8-15	.019	4.50
1880	3.00							4-15—8-15	.037	9.00
1880	4.00							4-15—8-15	.049	12.00
1902	64.27*							4-15—8-15	.791	192.81
1903	45.00*							4-15—8-15	.554	135.00
1905			57.70					4-15—5-15	.710	43.28

*From Company Ditch.

Claimant—**Albert Hankins.** Proof No. 00358

Source—**Smith, South Fork, Smith Creek, McCutcheon, Adams and Dry Creeks.**

Ditch—**Albert Hankins Ditches.**

1872	30.00			NE¼	4	29	56	4-15—8-15	.369	90.00
1875	20.00			N½SE¼	4	29	56	4-15—8-15	.246	60.00
1876	60.60			S½NW¼	3	29	56	4-15—8-15	.745	181.80
1895		104.50		NW¼SW¼	3	29	56	4-15—6-15	1.285	156.75
1904			16.00	NE¼NE¼	10	29	56	4-15—5-15	.197	12.00
1905			33.00	NW¼	11	29	56	4-15—5-15	.406	24.75
1870	80.00			SE¼NW¼	2	29	56	4-15—8-15	.984	240.00
1871	10.00			SW¼	2	29	56	4-15—8-15	.123	30.00
1872	10.00			SE¼	2	29	56	4-15—8-15	.123	30.00
1873	63.00			NW¼SW¼	1	29	56	4-15—8-15	.775	189.00
1874	63.00			N½NW¼	11	29	56	4-15—8-15	.775	189.00
1875	65.00							4-15—8-15	.780	195.00
1867	40.00			NW¼	2	29	56	4-15—8-15	.492	120.00
1868	15.00			NE¼	3	29	56	4-15—8-15	.185	45.00
1869	15.00			SE¼NW¼	3	29	56	4-15—8-15	.185	45.00
1870	15.00			S½	3	29	56	4-15—8-15	.185	45.00
1871	15.00			N½SW¼	2	29	56	4-15—8-15	.185	45.00
1872	30.00			SW¼SW¼	2	29	56	4-15—8-15	.369	90.00
1873	54.00			NW¼NW¼	11	29	56	4-15—8-15	.664	162.00
1877	54.00							4-15—8-15	.664	162.00
1881	54.00							4-15—8-15	.664	162.00
1885	54.00							4-15—8-15	.664	162.00
1889	54.00							4-15—8-15	.664	162.00
1893	57.50							4-15—8-15	.707	172.50

Claimant has vested right in the ditch high up on the Ruby Mountains that was constructed in 1876 and that cuts off some of the drainage water that would naturally flow into McCutcheon Creek.

1875	37.00			W½SW¼	1	29	56	4-15—8-15	.455	111.00
1878	25.50			S½SE¼	2	29	56	4-15—8-15	.314	76.50
1880	40.00			NW¼NE¼	11	29	56	4-15—8-15	.492	120.00
1903	31.50			NW¼	11	29	56	4-15—8-15	.387	94.50

Decree No. 1355, Elko County District Court Records, is binding as between parties to the suit.

Claimant—**J. J. Hylton.** Proof No. 00359

Source—**Smith and Huntington Creeks.** Ditch—**J. J. Hylton Ditches.**

Date of beneficial use: Nat. mdw.	Date of beneficial use: Cult. area	Construction first initiated: Dams	Construction first initiated: Ditches	Culture—Acres: Harvest crops	Culture—Acres: Meadow pasture	Culture—Acres: Willow and sage pasture	Culture—Acres: Swamp or overflow	Location: Subdivision	Location: Section	Location: Tp.N.	Location: R.E.	Length of season	Duty of water: C.F.S.	Duty of water: Acre-feet
	1880			29.00				SE¼	24	30	55	4-15—8-15	.357	87.00
	1870			18.00				NE¼	24	30	55	4-15—8-15	.221	54.00
	1873			18.00				NE¼	24	30	55	4-15—8-15	.221	54.00
	1876			17.00				NE¼	24	30	55	4-15—8-15	.209	51.00
	1880			66.00				NE¼	24	30	55	4-15—8-15	.812	198.00
	1870			21.00				SE¼	13	30	55	4-15—8-15	.258	63.00
	1873			20.00				SE¼	13	30	55	4-15—8-15	.246	60.00
	1876			20.00				SE¼	13	30	55	4-15—8-15	.246	60.00
	188[illegible]			49.00				SE¼	13	30	55	4-15—8-15	.603	147.00
	18[illegible]			38.00				SE¼	13	30	55	4-15—8-15	.467	114.00
	188[illegible]			30.00				NE¼	13	30	55	4-15—8-15	.369	90.00
	188[illegible]			25.00				NE¼	13	30	55	4-15—8-15	.308	75.00
	1878			40.00				NE¼	13	30	55	4-15—8-15	.492	120.00
	1895			9.00				NE¼	13	30	55	4-15—8-15	.111	27.00
	1876			19.50				NE¼	12	30	55	4-15—8-15	.240	58.50
	1876			66.50				SE¼	12	30	55	4-15—8-15	.818	199.50
	1880			35.50				SE¼	12	30	55	4-15—8-15	.437	106.50
	1895			12.00				NW¼	30	30	56	4-15—8-15	.148	36.00
	1896			12.00				NW¼	30	30	56	4-15—8-15	.148	36.00
	1897			12.00				NW¼	30	30	56	4-15—8-15	.148	36.00
	1898			12.00				NW¼	30	30	56	4-15—8-15	.148	36.00
	1899			12.00				NW¼	30	30	56	4-15—8-15	.148	36.00
	1900			9.00				NW¼	30	30	56	4-15—8-15	.111	27.00
	1880			16.00				SW¼	19	30	56	4-15—8-15	.197	48.00
	1895			27.00				SW¼	19	30	56	4-15—8-15	.332	81.00
	1898			25.00				SW¼	19	30	56	4-15—8-15	.308	75.00
	1900			25.00				SW¼	19	30	56	4-15—8-15	.308	75.00
	1870			19.00				SW¼	19	30	56	4-15—8-15	.234	57.00
	1873			17.00				SW¼	19	30	56	4-15—8-15	.209	51.00
	1876			17.00				SW¼	19	30	56	4-15—8-15	.209	51.00
	1879			.50				NW¼	19	30	56	4-15—8-15	.006	1.50
	1870			43.00				NW¼	19	30	56	4-15—8-15	.529	129.00
	1873			43.00				NW¼	19	30	56	4-15—8-15	.529	129.00
	1876			43.00				NW¼	19	30	56	4-15—8-15	.529	129.00
	1890					55.00		NW¼	13	30	55	4-15—5-15	.677	41.25
	1899					74.00		SW¼	12	30	55	4-15—5-15	.910	55.50
	1893					20.50		NW¼	12	30	55	4-15—5-15	.252	15.38

Source—**Huntington Creek.** Ditch—**J. J. Hylton Ditches.**

Nat. mdw.	Cult. area	Dams	Ditches	Harvest crops	Meadow pasture	Willow and sage pasture	Swamp or overflow	Subdivision	Section	Tp.N.	R.E.	Length of season	C.F.S.	Acre-feet
	1802			209.00				SE¼	7	29	56			
								SW¼	7	29	56			
								SE¼	6	29	56			
								SW¼	6	29	56			
								NW¼	6	29	56			
								NE¼	6	29	56	4-15—8-15	2.571	627.00
	1872			781.00				NW¼	6	29	56			

*This land has a priority of 1894 from Smith Creek.

1873		NE¼	6	29	56			
1874		SE¼	6	29	56			
1875			31	30	56			
			30	30	56	4-15—8-15	9.606	2343.00

This land has a divided priority of 1876-77 from Smith Creek, one-half the acreage in each year.

Source—**Smith Creek.** Ditch—**J. J. Hylton Ditches.**

1879	30.70	SW¼	28	30	56	4-15—8-15	.378	92.10
1897	15.30	SW¼	28	30	56	4-15—8-15	.188	45.90
1876	18.50	SW¼	28	30	56	4-15—8-15	.166	40.50
1879	25.00	SW¼	28	30	56	4-15—8-15	.308	75.00
1880	25.00	SW¼	28	30	56	4-15—8-15	.308	75.00
1881	24.00	SW¼	28	30	56	4-15—8-15	.295	72.00
1882	24.50	SW¼	28	30	56	4-15—8-15	.301	73.50
1879	11.00	NW¼	28	30	56	4-15—8-15	.135	33.00
1880	11.00	NW¼	28	30	56	4-15—8-15	.135	33.00
1881	11.00	NW¼	28	30	56	4-15—8-15	.135	33.00
1882	12.00	NW¼	28	30	56	4-15—8-15	.148	36.00
1879	9.00	SE¼	28	30	56	4-15—8-15	.111	27.00
1882	9.00	SE¼	28	30	56	4-15—8-15	.111	27.00
1903	21.00	SE¼	28	30	56	4-15—8-15	.258	63.00
1880	1.00	NW¼	33	30	56	4-15—8-15	.012	3.00
1876	42.00	NW¼	33	30	56	4-15—8-15	.517	126.00
1879	16.60	NW¼	33	30	56	4-15—8-15	.204	49.80
1897	8.40	NW¼	33	30	56	4-15—8-15	.103	25.20
1880	17.00	NW¼	33	30	56	4-15—8-15	.209	51.00
1896	1.00	NW¼	33	30	56	4-15—8-15	.012	3.00
1879	38.00	NW¼	33	30	56	4-15—8-15	.467	114.00
1876	28.00	NE¼	33	30	56	4-15—8-15	.344	84.00
1901	18.00	NE¼	33	30	56	4-15—8-15	.221	54.00
1901	3.00	NE¼	33	30	56	4-15—8-15	.369	9.00
1903	9.00	NE¼	33	30	56	4-15—8-15	.111	27.00
1881	23.00	NE¼	33	30	56	4-15—8-15	.283	69.00
1903	15.00	NE¼	33	30	56	4-15—8-15	.185	45.00
1879	14.00	NE¼	33	30	56	4-15—8-15	.172	52.00
1880	14.00	NE¼	33	30	56	4-15—8-15	.172	52.00
1881	14.00	NE¼	33	30	56	4-15—8-15	.172	52.00
1882	14.00	NE¼	33	30	56	4-15—8-15	.172	52.00
1881	7.00	NW¼	34	30	56	4-15—8-15	.086	21.00
1903	9.00	NW¼	34	30	56	4-15—8-15	.111	27.00
1880	4.00	SW¼	33	30	56	4-15—8-15	.049	12.00
1876	25.50	SW¼	33	30	56	4-15—8-15	.314	76.50
1879	37.33	SW¼	33	30	56	4-15—8-15	.459	111.99
1900	48.00	SW¼	33	30	56	4-15—8-15	.590	144.00
1876	28.50	SE¼	33	30	56	4-15—8-15	.351	75.50
1901	62.50	SE¼	33	30	56	4-15—8-15	.769	187.50
1901	8.00	SE¼	33	30	56	4-15—8-15	.098	24.00
1903	56.50	SE¼	33	30	56	4-15—8-15	.695	169.50
1903	15.00	SW¼	34	30	56	4-15—8-15	.185	45.00
1879	8.67	NW¼	4	29	56	4-15—8-15	.107	26.01
1903	2.00	NE¼	4	29	56	4-15—8-15	.025	6.00
1881	6.00	NE¼	32	30	56	4-15—8-15	.074	18.00
1889	20.00	NE¼	32	30	56	4-15—8-15	.246	60.00

J. J. Hylton—Continued.

Date of beneficial use—Nat. mdw.	Date of beneficial use—Cult. area	Construction first initiated—Dams	Construction first initiated—Ditches	Culture—Acres—Harvest crops	Culture—Acres—Meadow pasture	Culture—Acres—Willow and sage pasture	Culture—Acres—Swamp or overflow	Location—Subdivision	Location—Section	Location—Tp.N.	Location—R.E.	Length of season	Duty of water—C.F.S.	Duty of water—Acre-feet
	1896			56.00				NE¼	32	30	56	4-15—8-15	.689	168.00
	1900			55.00				NE¼	32	30	56	4-15—8-15	.677	165.00
	1894			2.00				SW¼	32	30	56	4-15—8-15	.025	6.00
	1896			13.00				SW¼	32	30	56	4-15—8-15	.160	39.00
	1900			12.00				SW¼	32	30	56	4-15—8-15	.148	36.00
	1896			13.00				SE¼	32	30	56	4-15—8-15	.160	39.00
	1900			13.00				SE¼	32	30	56	4-15—8-15	.160	39.00
	1894			22.50				NW¼	5	29	56	4-15—8-15	.277	67.50
	1894			3.00				SW¼	5	29	56	4-15—8-15	.369	9.00
	1896			34.00				SE¼	30	30	56	4-15—8-15	.418	102.00
	1900			33.00				SE¼	30	30	56	4-15—8-15	.406	99.00
	1889			41.00				SW¼	29	30	56	4-15—8-15	.504	123.00
	1881			4.50				SW¼	29	30	56	4-15—8-15	.055	13.50
	1882			4.50				SW¼	29	30	56	4-15—8-15	.055	13.50
	1896			25.00				SW¼	29	30	56	4-15—8-15	.308	75.00
	1896					30.00		SW¼	29	30	56	4-15—5-15	.369	22.50
	1900			55.00				SW¼	29	30	56	4-15—8-15	.677	40.50
	1881			40.00				SE¼	29	30	56	4-15—8-15	.492	30.00
	1896			20.00				SE¼	29	30	56	4-15—8-15	.246	15.00
	1900			20.00				SE¼	29	30	56	4-15—8-15	.246	15.00
	1870			14.00				SE¼	29	30	56	4-15—8-15	.172	10.50
	1897			7.00				SE¼	29	30	56	4-15—8-15	.086	5.25
	1879			4.30				SE¼	29	30	56	4-15—8-15	.053	3.23
	1882			4.30				SE¼	29	30	56	4-15—8-15	.053	3.23
	1880			20.50				SE¼	29	30	56	4-15—8-15	.252	61.50
	1881			15.00				SE¼	29	30	56	4-15—8-15	.185	45.00
	1882			15.00				SE¼	29	30	56	4-15—8-15	.185	45.00
	1880			1.00				SE¼	29	30	56	4-15—8-15	.012	3.00
	1894			29.00				SE¼	31	30	56	4-15—8-15	.357	87.00
	1896			19.00				SE¼	31	30	56	4-15—8-15	.234	57.00
	1900			18.00				SE¼	31	30	56	4-15—8-15	.221	54.00
	1896			35.00				NW¼	32	30	56	4-15—8-15	.431	105.00
	1900			35.00				NW¼	32	30	56	4-15—8-15	.431	105.00
	1893			2.00				SE¼	6	29	56	4-15—8-15	.025	6.00
	1894			17.00				SE¼	6	29	56	4-15—8-15	.209	51.00
	1894			23.00				SE¼	6	29	56	4-15—8-15	.283	69.00
	1893			9.00				NE¼	6	29	56	4-15—8-15	.111	27.00
	1894			20.00				NE¼	6	29	56	4-15—8-15	.246	60.00
	1894			49.00				NE¼	6	29	56	4-15—8-15	.603	147.00
	1894			43.00				NE¼	7	29	56	4-15—8-15	.529	129.00
	1875			1.00				NE¼	10	30	56	4-15—8-15	.012	3.00
	1873			4.00				SE¼	19	30	56	4-15—8-15	.049	12.00
	1895			10.00				SE¼	19	30	56	4-15—8-15	.123	30.00
	1897			11.00				SE¼	19	30	56	4-15—8-15	.135	33.00
	1900			10.00				SE¼	19	30	56	4-15—8-15	.123	30.00
	1880			8.00				SE¼	10	30	56	4-15—8-15	.098	24.00

	1879	23.00		SW¼	20	30	56	4-15—8-15	.283	60.00
	1880	20.00		SE¼	19	30	56	4-15—8-15	.240	60.00
	1881	18.00		SE¼	19	30	56	4-15—8-15	.221	54.00
	1882	20.00		SE¼	19	30	56	4-15—8-15	.240	60.00
	1880	2.00		NE¼	19	30	56	4-15—8-15	.025	6.00
	1881	2.00		SE¼	19	30	56	4-15—8-15	.025	6.00
	1881	3.25		NE¼	30	30	56	4-15—8-15	.040	9.75
	1880	3.00		NW¼	29	30	56	4-15—8-15	.037	9.00
	1879	15.00		NW¼	29	30	56	4-15—8-15	.185	45.00
	1880	15.00		NW¼	29	30	56	4-15—8-15	.185	45.00
	1881	15.00		NW¼	29	30	56	4-15—8-15	.185	45.00
	1882	15.00		NW¼	29	30	56	4-15—8-15	.185	45.00
	1879	21.00		NE¼	29	30	56	4-15—8-15	.258	63.00
	1880	21.00		NE¼	29	30	56	4-15—8-15	.258	63.00
	1881	21.00		NE¼	29	30	56	4-15—8-15	.258	63.00
	1882	21.00		NE¼	29	30	56	4-15—8-15	.258	63.00
	1896	21.00		NE¼	30	30	56	4-15—8-15	.258	63.00
	1898	21.00		NE¼	30	30	56	4-15—8-15	.258	63.00
	1900	20.50		NE¼	30	30	56	4-15—8-15	.242	61.50
	1871	.75		SE¼	19	30	56	4-15—8-15	.009	2.25
	1871	9.25		NW¼	29	30	56	4-15—8-15	.114	27.75
	1872	18.00		NW¼	29	30	56	4-15—8-15	.221	54.00
	1873	18.00		NW¼	29	30	56	4-15—8-15	.221	54.00
	1874	18.00		NW¼	29	30	56	4-15—8-15	.221	54.00
	1874	6.00		NW¼	29	30	56	4-15—8-15	.074	18.00
	1876	5.00		NW¼	29	30	56	4-15—8-15	.062	15.00
	1878	5.75		NW¼	29	30	56	4-15—8-15	.071	17.25
	1875	13.00		NE¼	29	30	56	4-15—8-15	.160	39.00
	1877	13.00		NE¼	29	30	56	4-15—8-15	.160	39.00
	1879	12.00		NE¼	29	30	56	4-15—8-15	.148	36.00
	1881	12.50		NW¼	29	30	56	4-15—8-15	.154	37.50
	1880	16.50		NE¼	30	30	56	4-15—8-15	.203	49.50
	1896	17.00		NE¼	30	30	56	4-15—8-15	.209	51.00
	1900	17.00		NE¼	30	30	56	4-15—8-15	.209	51.00

Source—**South Fork Humboldt River.** Ditch—**J. J. Hylton Ditches.**

	1870	217.40		SE¼	4	32	55			
	1880	37.30		S½	3	32	55			
	1888	333.40			10	32	55	4-15—8-15	2.674	652.20
	1892	274.50		W½	11	32	55	4-15—8-15	.458	111.90
	1893	79.50		N½	15	32	55	4-15—8-15	4.101	1000.20
	1894	212.40			14	32	55	4-15—8-15	3.376	823.50
	1894		307.00	E½	23	32	55	4-15—8-15	.978	238.50
	1903	56.00		W½	24	32	55	4-15—8-15	2.612	637.20
				SE¼	24	32	55	4-15—6-15	3.776	460.50
					25	32	55	4-15—8-15	.689	168.00
	1895	65.00		S½NE¼	15	31	57	4-15—8-15	.800	195.00
	1896	20.00		SE¼	15	31	57	4-15—8-15	.246	60.00
	1897	20.00		W½SW¼	14	31	57	4-15—8-15	.246	60.00
	1898	15.00		SW¼NW¼	14	31	57	4-15—8-15	.185	45.00
	1898	58.00						4-15—8-15	.713	174.00

Claimant—**Simon A. Merkley.** Proof No. 00360
Source—**McCutcheon Creek and Tributary.** Ditch—**Simon A. Merkley Ditches.**

Date of beneficial use—Nat. mdw.	Cult. area	Construction first initiated—Dams	Ditches	Culture—Acres—Harvest crops	Meadow pasture	Willow and sage pasture	Swamp or overflow	Location—Subdivision	Section	Tp.N.	R.E.	Length of season	Duty of water—C.F.S.	Acre-feet
	1889			5.00				E½SW¼	6	29	57	4-15—8-15	.062	15.00
	1890			5.00				W½SE¼	6	29	57	4-15—8-15	.062	15.00
	1892			7.00								4-15—8-15	.086	21.00
	1900			15.50								4-15—8-15	.191	46.50

Priority on McCutcheon Creek proper starts with 1890.

Claimant—**Merkley & Young.** Proof No. 00361
Source—**Smith Creek.** Ditch—**Merkley & Young Ditches.**

Nat. mdw.	Cult. area	Dams	Ditches	Harvest crops	Meadow pasture	Willow and sage pasture	Swamp or overflow	Subdivision	Section	Tp.N.	R.E.	Length of season	C.F.S.	Acre-feet
	1868			45.00				SE¼NW¼	26	30	56	4-15—8-15	.554	135.00
	1869			5.00				S½NE¼	26	30	56	4-15—8-15	.062	15.00
	1870			5.00				S½	26	30	56	4-15—8-15	.062	15.00
	1871			40.10				S½NW¼	25	30	56	4-15—8-15	.493	120.30
	1872			91.80				S½	25	30	56	4-15—8-15	1.129	275.40
	1872					14.50		E½NW¼	35	30	56	4-15—5-15	.178	43.50
	1873			119.60				NE¼	35	30	56	4-15—8-15	1.471	358.80
	1874			10.00				S½	35	30	56	4-15—8-15	.123	30.00
	1875			60.70				W½	36	30	56	4-15—8-15	.747	182.10
	1876			60.70				NE¼	36	30	56	4-15—8-15	.747	182.10
	1877					19.20		NW¼SE¼	36	30	56	4-15—5-15	.236	57.60
	1878			20.00				NE¼	2	29	56	4-15—8-15	.123	60.00
	1886			59.70				W½NW¼	1	29	56	4-15—8-15	.734	179.10
	1887			57.70								4-15—8-15	.734	179.10
	1888			57.50								4-15—8-15	.707	178.50
	1889			22.70								4-15—8-15	.279	68.10
	1890			265.60								4-15—8-15	3.267	796.80
	1891			41.40								4-15—8-15	.509	124.20
	1892			13.90								4-15—8-15	.171	41.70
	1893			13.90								4-15—8-15	.171	41.70
	1893					66.00						4-15—5-15	.812	198.00
	1893					35.00						4-15—5-15	.431	105.00
	1894					126.00						4-15—5-15	1.550	378.00
	1894					148.30						4-15—5-15	1.824	444.90
	1900					63.30						4-15—5-15	.779	189.90
	1904			7.00								4-15—8-15	.086	21.00
	1894					117.50						4-15—5-15	1.445	352.50
	1894					20.00						4-15—5-15	.246	60.00

Judgment and Decree No. 1355, Elko County District Court Records, is binding as between parties to the suit.

Source—**Huntington Creek.** Ditch—**Merkley & Young Ditches.**

Nat. mdw.	Cult. area	Dams	Ditches	Harvest crops	Meadow pasture	Willow and sage pasture	Swamp or overflow	Subdivision	Section	Tp.N.	R.E.	Length of season	C.F.S.	Acre-feet
	1881			92.52				W½	33	28	55	4-15—8-15	1.138	277.56
	1886			335.79				W½E½	33	28	55	4-15—8-15	4.130	1007.37
	1900			300.00				S½SW¼	28	28	55	4-15—8-15	3.690	900.00
								NW¼	4	27	55			
								SE¼NE¼	5	27	55			

E½SE¼	5	27	55	
SW¼	4	27	55	
E½NE¼	8	27	55	
All	9	27	55	

Reference is made to stipulation between Huntington and Diamond Valley Land and Stock Co. and J. J. Hylton, Merkley & Young and Frank Odiaga, regarding the use of waters of Huntington Creek.

These lands were included in the suit H. H. Porch vs. U. Lani et al., No. 1644 Elko County Records. After listing dates and areas they were pooled and then listed in accordance with the decree.

Claimant—**Chas. Mitchell.** Proof No. 00362

Source—**Springs and Gulch.** Ditch—**Chas. Mitchell Ditches.**

1879	2.80		SE¼NW¼	14	27	56	4-15—8-15	.034	8.40
1879	1.80		SW¼NW¼	14	27	56	4-15—8-15	.022	5.40
1879	11.30		NW¼SW¼	14	27	56	4-15—8-15	.139	33.90
1870	17.50		NE¼SW¼	14	27	56	4-15—8-15	.215	52.50
1879	11.20		NW¼SE¼	14	27	56	4-15—8-15	.138	33.60

Source—**Brown's Creek.** Ditch—**Chas. Mitchell Ditches.**

1876	78.12		NE¼NE¼	30	28	56	4-15—8-15	.961	234.36
1876	50.22		NW¼NW¼	29	28	56	4-15—8-15	.618	150.66
1876		4.65	S½NW¼	29	28	56	4-15—5-15	.057	3.49
1869	34.39		SW¼NE¼	29	28	56	4-15—8-15	.423	103.17
1869		4.34	N½S½	29	28	56	4-15—5-15	.053	3.26
1872	34.39		NE¼SE¼	29	28	56	4-15—8-15	.423	103.17
1872		4.34	N½SW¼	28	28	56	4-15—5-15	.053	3.26
1876	34.38		....	....	....	....	4-15—8-15	.423	103.14
1876		4.34	....	....	....	....	4-15—5-15	.053	3.26
1899	20.92		....	....	....	....	4-15—8-15	.257	62.76
1899		8.37	....	....	....	....	4-15—5-15	.103	6.28
1900	30.23		....	....	....	....	4-15—8-15	.372	90.69
1900	....	8.37	....	....	....	....	4-15—5-15	.103	6.28

Source—**Mitchell Creek.** Ditch—**Chas. Mitchell Ditches.**

1876	5.80	SW¼SW¼	35	27	56	4-15—8-15	.071	17.40
1876	5.00	NW¼SW¼	35	27	56	4-15—8-15	.062	15.00
1876	7.50	NE¼SW¼	35	27	56	4-15—8-15	.092	22.50
1876	31.00	SE¼SW¼	35	27	56	4-15—8-15	.381	93.00
1876	22.80	SW¼SE¼	35	27	56	4-15—8-15	.280	68.40
1876	15.20	SE¼SE¼	35	27	56	4-15—8-15	.187	45.60
1876	7.80	NE¼NE¼	2	26	56	4-15—8-15	.096	23.40
1876	4.00	NW¼NW¼	1	26	56	4-15—8-15	.049	12.00
1876	11.60	SW¼SW¼	36	27	56	4-15—8-15	.143	34.80
1876	10.50	SE¼SW¼	36	27	56	4-15—8-15	.129	31.50
1876	2.80	SW¼SE¼	36	27	56	4-15—8-15	.034	8.40
1876	0.70	NW¼SE¼	36	27	56	4-15—8-15	.009	2.10

Claimant—**F. Odiaga.** Proof No. 00363

Source—**Huntington Creek, Pearl Creek, Brown Creek, and Frost Canyon Creek.**

Ditch—**F. Odiaga Ditches.**

Date of beneficial use: Nat. mdw.	Date of beneficial use: Cult. area	Construction first initiated: Dams	Construction first initiated: Ditches	Culture—Acres: Harvest crops	Culture—Acres: Meadow pasture	Culture—Acres: Willow and sage pasture	Culture—Acres: Swamp or overflow	Location: Subdivision	Location: Section	Location: Tp.N.	Location: R.E.	Length of season	Duty of water: C.F.S.	Duty of water: Acre-feet
	1883			150.00				E½NW¼	1	28	55			
	1884			150.00				SW¼NW¼	1	28	55			
								NW¼SW¼	1	28	55			
								NE¼SE¼	2	28	55			
								E½NE¼	24	29	55			
								SE¼	24	29	55			
								N½SE¼	25	29	55			
								SW¼SE¼	25	29	55			
								SE¼SW¼	25	29	55			
								NW¼	36	29	55	4-15—8-15	1.845	450.00
								E½SW¼	36	29	55	4-15—8-15	1.845	450.00
	1889			101.60				W½SE¼	11	28	55			
	1898			62.31				E½SW¼	11	28	55			
	1900			140.57				SW¼SW¼	11	28	55			
								N½NW¼	14	28	55			
								SW¼NW¼	14	28	55			
								SE¼NE¼	15	28	55			
								N½SE¼	15	28	55			
								SW¼SE¼	15	28	55			
								NE¼SW¼	15	28	55			
								SE¼	24	29	55			
								N½SE¼	25	29	55			
								SW¼SE¼	25	29	55			
								SE¼SW¼	25	29	55	4-15—8-15	1.250	304.80
								NW¼	36	29	55	4-15—8-15	.766	186.93
								W½NE¼	36	29	55	4-15—8-15	1.729	421.71

NOTE—Odiaga acreage and description in accordance with Elko County Court decrees 1548 and 1644, which are binding as between parties to the suits.

Source—**Robinson Creek and Spring.** Ditch—**F. Odiaga Ditches.**

Nat. mdw.	Cult. area	Dams	Ditches	Harvest crops	Meadow pasture	Willow and sage pasture	Swamp or overflow	Subdivision	Section	Tp.N.	R.E.	Length of season	C.F.S.	Acre-feet
	1900			33.10				NW¼	11	28	55	4-15—8-15	.407	99.30

Source—**Huntington Creek and Springs.** Ditch—**F. Odiaga Ditches.**

Nat. mdw.	Cult. area	Dams	Ditches	Harvest crops	Meadow pasture	Willow and sage pasture	Swamp or overflow	Subdivision	Section	Tp.N.	R.E.	Length of season	C.F.S.	Acre-feet
	1869			28.90				NE¼	25	29	55	4-15—8-15	.355	86.70
	1873			28.90				NE¼	25	29	55	4-15—8-15	.355	86.70
	1876			28.95				NE¼	25	29	55	4-15—8-15	.356	86.85
	1900			16.01					13	28	55	4-15—8-15	.197	48.03
	1900			57.51				N½NE¼	15	28	55	4-15—8-15	.707	172.53
	1906			40.00				SW¼NE¼	15	28	55	4-15—8-15	.492	120.00
	1900			2.50				SE¼NW¼	15	28	55	4-15—8-15	.031	7.50

NOTE—Not in court decree, Porch vs. Lani et al. Reference is hereby made to stipulation between Huntington and Diamond Valley Land and Stock Co. and J. J. Hylton, Merkley & Young and Frank Odiaga, regarding the use of waters of Huntington Creek.

			Claimant—**P. J. Ogilvie.**						Proof No. 00364
			Source—**South Fork Humboldt River.** Ditch—**Ogilvie Ditch.**						
1905		11.20	S½	14	31	56	4-15—5-15	.138	8.40
1905		25.00	S½	13	31	56	4-15—5-15	.308	18.75
1868	40.00		N½	24	31	56	4-15—8-15	.492	120.00
1873	3.00		W½NW¼	19	31	57	4-15—8-15	.037	9.00
			Source—**South Fork of Humboldt River and Rattlesnake Creek.*** Ditch—**Ogilvie Ditch.**						
1901	29.00		S½	14	31	56	4-15—8-15	.357	87.00
1901	149.00		S½	13	31	56	4-15—8-15	1.833	447.00
1901	18.20		N½	24	31	56	4-15—8-15	.224	54.00
			W½NW¼	19	31	57			
1875	117.40		S½	14	31	56	4-15—8-15	1.444	352.20
1902	72.00		S½	13	31	56	4-15—8-15	.886	216.00
1903	150.00		N½	24	31	56	4-15—8-15	1.845	450.00
1905	115.00		W½NW¼	19	31	57	4-15—8-15	1.415	345.00
			Source—**South Fork of Humboldt River and Rattlesnake Creek.** Ditch—**Company Ditch.**						
1901	18.60		S½	14	31	56	4-15—8-15	.229	55.80
1901	14.10		S½	13	31	56	4-15—8-15	.173	42.30

Early water only from Rattlesnake Creek.

			Claimant—**D. J. Riordan.**						Proof No. 00365
			Source—**Big Cottonwood and Little Cottonwood Creeks.** Ditch—**D. J. Riordan Ditches.**						
1888		29.50	S½NE¼	24	30	56	4-15—5-15	.363	22.13
1888	63.10		N½SE¼	24	30	56	4-15—8-15	.776	189.30
			Source—**Smith Creek.** Ditch—**D. J. Riordan Ditches.**						
1870	10.00		S½SE¼	24	30	56	4-15—8-15	.123	30.00
1871	10.00		NE¼	25	30	56	4-15—8-15	.123	30.00
1872	11.00		S½SW¼	19	30	57	4-15—8-15	.135	33.00
1873	40.00		NW¼	30	30	57	4-15—8-15	.492	120.00
1879	45.00		N½NE¼	30	30	57	4-15—8-15	.554	135.00
1880	16.80		SE¼NE¼	30	30	57	4-15—8-15	.207	50.40
1882	16.80		W½SW¼	30	30	57	4-15—8-15	.207	50.40
1883	112.80		NE¼SW¼	30	30	57	4-15—8-15	1.387	338.40
1884		27.60	SE¼	30	30	57	4-15—5-15	.339	20.70
1884	16.70		NE¼	31	30	57	4-15—8-15	.205	50.10
1887	112.80		W½NW¼	32	30	57	4-15—8-15	1.387	338.40
1890		64.30					4-15—5-15	.791	48.23
1890	112.70						4-15—8-15	1.386	338.10
1893	12.00						4-15—8-15	.148	36.00
1897	13.00						4-15—8-15	.160	39.00
1900		43.20					4-15—5-15	.531	32.40
1900	8.10						4-15—8-15	.100	24.30

Decree No. 155, Elko County District Court Records, is binding as between parties to the suit.

Source **Young Creek.** Ditch - **Hennen Ditches.**

			4 15 -5 15	.015		
			4 15 -5 15	.158		
			4 15 -5 15			
			4 15 -5 15			

That certain agreement signed by [illegible] Hennen and J. Hennen in regard to the division of the waters of Young Creek, as recorded in Elko County, Book [illegible] of Misc. Records, pages [illegible] and [illegible], is binding as between the parties to agreement. The "miner's inch" referred to shall be defined as being the amount of water that will flow through an opening of one square inch and under a six inch head in Young Creek in the NW¼NW¼, Sec. 11, T. 32 N, R. 57 E, that will automatically divide the stream according to the said agreement, the plans for said device to be approved by the State Engineer.

The parties to this agreement are to construct and maintain a device in Young Creek in the NW¼NW¼, Sec. 11, T. 32 N, R. 57 E, that will automatically divide the stream according to the said agreement, the plans for said device to be approved by the State Engineer.

Source **Butterfield Creek and Young Creek.** Ditch - **Hennen Ditches.**

1865	15.30		NE¼	10	32	57	4 15 5 15	.188	11.
1872		50.00	NE¼NW¼	10	32	57	4 15 5 15	.015	150.

When not sufficient water in Butterfield Creek, balance to be made up from Young Creek.
NOTE: Stock water right from Butterfield Creek dated 1872.

Source—Young Creek. Ditch—Hennen Ditches.

1868	30.00			NW¼	10	32	57	4-15—8-15	.360	90.00
1869	30.00			W½NE¼	10	32	57	4-15—8-15	.369	90.00
1870	30.00			N½SE¼	10	32	57	4-15—8-15	.369	90.00
1871	30.00			NE¼SW¼	10	32	57	4-15—8-15	.369	90.00
1872	32.90			SW¼NE¼	10	32	57	4-15—8-15	.405	98.70
1873	...	110.00		....	....	...	...	4-15—6-15	1.353	165.00

Claimant—**Griswold-Henderson Livestock Co.** Proof No. 00369

Source—**Stoffer Creek.** Ditch—**Griswold-Henderson Ditches.**

1886	66.10			NE¼	30	33	57	4-15—8-15	.813	198.30

Source—**Butterfield Creek and Thompson Creek.** Ditch—**Griswold-Henderson Ditches.**

1868	155.00				2	32	57	4-15—8-15	1.907	465.00
1869	154.00				3	32	57	4-15—8-15	1.894	462.00
1870	154.00				4	32	57	4-15—8-15	1.894	462.00
1871	154.00				11	32	57	4-15—8-15	1.894	462.00
1873	...	152.10			....	....	....	4-15—6-15	1.871	228.15
1874		152.10			....	....	....	4-15—6-15	1.871	228.15
1874	..	97.80			..	....	....	4-15—6-15	1.203	146.70
1875	....	97.80			....	....	....	4-15—6-15	1.203	146.70
1905	...		21.40		.	...	....	4-15—5-15	.263	16.05

Source—**Springs.** Ditch—**Griswold-Henderson Ditches.**

1905	..		81.20	SW¼	11	32	57	4-15—5-15	.999	243.60

Claimant—**Ernest Hodges.** Proof No. 00370

Source—**Stoffer Creek.** Ditch—**Ernest Hodges Ditches.**

1903	99.00			S½NW¼	30	33	57			
				SW¼	30	33	57	4-15—8-15	1.218	207.00

Source—**Dry Creek and Springs.** Ditch—**Ernest Hodges Ditches.**

1901	48.00			SW¼	30	33	57	4-15—8-15	.590	144.00
1902	18.00				....	....	....	4-15—8-15	.221	54.00
1905	21.00				....	...	..	4-15—8-15	.258	63.00

Claimant—**Antone Zunino.** Proof No. 00371

Source—**Cottonwood Creek, Smith Creek, and Natural Draws.**
Ditch—**Antone Zunino Ditches.**

1874	6.00			SW¼	15	30	56	4-15—8-15	.074	18.00
1874	46.00			SW¼SE¼	15	30	56	4-15—8-15	.566	138.00
1875	45.80			E½NW¼	22	30	56	4-15—8-15	.563	137.40
1875	60.70			NE¼	22	30	56	4-15—8-15	.747	182.10
1876	40.00			SE¼	22	30	56	4-15—8-15	.492	120.00
1876	15.00			S½	23	30	56	4-15—8-15	.185	45.00
1877	44.00			SW¼NW¼	24	30	56	4-15—8-15	.541	132.00
1878	42.00			SW¼	24	30	56	4-15—8-15	.517	126.00

Claimant—**Manuel Urrutia.** Proof No. **00366**

Source—**South Fork of Humboldt River and Natural Draw.** Ditch—**Manuel Urrutia.**

Date of beneficial use: Nat. mdw.	Date of beneficial use: Cult. area	Construction—first initiated: Dams	Construction—first initiated: Ditches	Culture—Acres: Harvest crops	Culture—Acres: Meadow pasture	Culture—Acres: Willow and sage pasture	Culture—Acres: Swamp or overflow	Location: Subdivision	Location: Section	Location: Tp.N.	Location: R.E.	Length of season	Duty of water: C.F.S.	Duty of water: Acre-feet
	1888			41.70				SW¼SE¼	25	22	55	4-15—8-15	.550	134.10
	1898			23.63				E½NW¼	36	32	55	4-15—8-15	.291	70.89
	1899			23.62				NE¼	36	32	55	4-15—8-15	.291	70.86
	1905			6.25								4-15—8-15	.077	18.75
	1905			24.60*								4-15—8-15	.303	73.80

*Water from natural draw. Claimant has no right to divert water from South Fork of Humboldt River for this area.

Claimant—**Estate Joseph Hennen.** Proof. No. **00368**

Source—**Mitchell Creek.** Ditch—**Hennen Ditches.**

Nat. mdw.	Cult. area	Dams	Ditches	Harvest crops	Meadow pasture	Willow and sage pasture	Swamp or overflow	Subdivision	Section	Tp.N.	R.E.	Length of season	C.F.S.	Acre-feet
	1883			78.70					7	32	57	4-15—8-15	.968	236.10
	1905					9.10						4-15—5-15	.112	6.83

Source—**Little Valley Spring.** Ditch—**Hennen Ditches.**

Nat. mdw.	Cult. area	Dams	Ditches	Harvest crops	Meadow pasture	Willow and sage pasture	Swamp or overflow	Subdivision	Section	Tp.N.	R.E.	Length of season	C.F.S.	Acre-feet
	1887			39.40				E½SW¼	31	33	57			
								SE¼	31	33	57			
								NW¼SW¼	32	33	57	4-15—8-15	.485	118.20

Source—**Butterfield Creek.** Ditch—**Hennen Ditches.**

Nat. mdw.	Cult. area	Dams	Ditches	Harvest crops	Meadow pasture	Willow and sage pasture	Swamp or overflow	Subdivision	Section	Tp.N.	R.E.	Length of season	C.F.S.	Acre-feet
	1881			59.00				S½NE¼	36	33	56			
	1887			16.90				NE¼SE¼	36	33	56			
								SW¼	31	33	57	4-15—8-15	.726	177.00
								SW¼SE¼	31	33	57	4-15—8-15	.208	50.70

Source—**Young Creek.** Ditch—**Hennen Ditches.**

Nat. mdw.	Cult. area	Dams	Ditches	Harvest crops	Meadow pasture	Willow and sage pasture	Swamp or overflow	Subdivision	Section	Tp.N.	R.E.	Length of season	C.F.S.	Acre-feet
	1873			10.00				S½S½	5	32	57	4-15—8-15	.123	30.00
	1874			20.00				N½NE¼	8	32	57	4-15—8-15	.246	60.00
	1875			25.00				S½S½	4	32	57	4-15—8-15	.308	75.00
	1876			112.40				N½N½	9	32	57	4-15—8-15	1.383	337.20
	1876					17.40						4-15—5-15	.214	13.05
	1877			112.30								4-15—8-15	1.381	336.90
	1877					17.30						4-15—5-15	.214	12.98
	1878					50.00						4-15—5-15	.615	37.50
	1905					12.70						4-15—5-15	.156	9.53

That certain agreement signed by T. F. Brennen and J. Hennen in regard to the division of the waters of Young Creek, as recorded in Elko County, Book 4 of Miscl. Records, pages 186 and 187, is binding as between the parties to agreement. The "miner's inch" referred to shall be defined as being the amount of water that will flow through an opening of one square inch and under a six-inch head.

The parties to this agreement are to construct and maintain a device in Young Creek in the NW¼NW¼, Sec. 14, T. 32 N, R. 57 E, that will automatically divide the stream according to the said agreement, the plans for said device to be approved by the State Engineer.

Source—**Butterfield Creek and Young Creek.** Ditch—**Hennen Ditches.**

Nat. mdw.	Cult. area	Dams	Ditches	Harvest crops	Meadow pasture	Willow and sage pasture	Swamp or overflow	Subdivision	Section	Tp.N.	R.E.	Length of season	C.F.S.	Acre-feet
	1905					15.30		NE¼	10	32	57	4-15—5-15	.188	11.48
	1872			50.00				NE¼NW¼	10	32	57	4-15—5-15	.615	150.00

When not sufficient water in Butterfield Creek, balance to be made up from Young Creek.
NOTE—Stock water-right from Butterfield Creek dated 1872.

Source—**Young Creek.** Ditch—**Hennen Ditches.**

1868	30.00			NW¼	10	32	57	4-15—8-15	.369	90.00
1869	30.00			W¼NE¼	10	32	57	4-15—8-15	.369	90.00
1870	30.00			N½SE¼	10	32	57	4-15—8-15	.369	90.00
1871	30.00			NE¼SW¼	10	32	57	4-15—8-15	.369	90.00
1872	32.00			SW¼NE¼	10	32	57	4-15—8-15	.405	98.70
1873		110.00						4-15—6-15	1.353	165.00

Claimant—**Griswold-Henderson Livestock Co.** Proof No. 00369

Source—**Stoffer Creek.** Ditch—**Griswold-Henderson Ditches.**

1886	66.10			NE¼	30	33	57	4-15—8-15	.813	198.30

Source—**Butterfield Creek and Thompson Creek.** Ditch—**Griswold-Henderson Ditches.**

1868	155.00				2	32	57	4-15—8-15	1.907	465.00
1869	154.00				3	32	57	4-15—8-15	1.894	462.00
1870	154.00				4	32	57	4-15—8-15	1.894	462.00
1871	154.00				11	32	57	4-15—8-15	1.894	462.00
1873		152.10						4-15—6-15	1.871	228.15
1874		152.10						4-15—6-15	1.871	228.15
1874		97.80						4-15—6-15	1.203	146.70
1875		97.80						4-15—6-15	1.203	146.70
1905			21.40					4-15—5-15	.263	16.05

Source—**Springs.** Ditch—**Griswold-Henderson Ditches.**

1905			81.20	SW¼	11	32	57	4-15—5-15	.990	243.60

Claimant—**Ernest Hodges.** Proof No. 00370

Source—**Stoffer Creek.** Ditch—**Ernest Hodges Ditches.**

1903	99.00			S½NW¼	30	33	57			
				SW¼	30	33	57	4-15—8-15	1.218	297.00

Source—**Dry Creek and Springs.** Ditch—**Ernest Hodges Ditches.**

1904	48.00			SW¼	30	33	57	4-15—8-15	.590	144.00
1902	18.00							4-15—8-15	.221	54.00
1905	21.00							4-15—8-15	.258	63.00

Claimant—**Antone Zunino.** Proof No. 00371

Source—**Cottonwood Creek, Smith Creek, and Natural Draws.**

Ditch—**Antone Zunino Ditches.**

1874	6.00			SW¼	15	30	56	4-15—8-15	.074	18.00
1874	46.00			SW¼SE¼	15	30	56	4-15—8-15	.566	138.00
1875	45.80			E½NW¼	22	30	56	4-15—8-15	.563	137.40
1875	60.70			NE¼	22	30	56	4-15—8-15	.747	182.10
1876	40.00			SE¼	22	30	56	4-15—8-15	.492	120.00
1876	15.00			S½	23	30	56	4-15—8-15	.185	45.00
1877	44.00			SW¼NW¼	24	30	56	4-15—8-15	.541	132.00
1878	42.00			SW¼	24	30	56	4-15—8-15	.517	126.00

Antone Zunino—Continued.

Date of beneficial use: Nat. mdw.	Cult. area	Construction first initiated: Dams	Ditches	Culture—Acres: Harvest crops	Meadow pasture	Willow and sage pasture	Swamp or overflow	Location: Subdivision	Section	Tp.N.	R.E.	Length of season	Duty of water: C.F.S.	Acre-feet
	1884			99.00				N½NW¼	25	30	56	4-15—8-15	1.107	270.00
	1897			21.80								4-15—8-15	.268	65.40
	1897			6.80								4-15—8-15	.084	20.40
	1904			57.10								4-15—8-15	.070	171.30
	1905					48.50						4-15—5-15	.597	145.50

Judgment and Decree No. 1355, Elko County District Court Records. is binding as between parties to the suit.

Claimant—**A. M. Griswold.** Proof No. 00372

Source—**South Fork Humboldt River.** Ditch—**Griswold Ditches.**

Date of beneficial use: Nat. mdw.	Cult. area	Construction first initiated: Dams	Ditches	Culture—Acres: Harvest crops	Meadow pasture	Willow and sage pasture	Swamp or overflow	Location: Subdivision	Section	Tp.N.	R.E.	Length of season	Duty of water: C.F.S.	Acre-feet
	1867			45.00				N½NW¼	10	31	56	4-15—8-15	.554	135.00
	1869			27.00				NE¼	10	31	56	4-15—8-15	.332	81.00
	1870			27.00				E½SE¼	10	31	56	4-15—8-15	.332	81.00
	1870			11.00				S½NW¼	11	31	56	4-15—8-15	.123	30.00
	1872			145.50				W½SW¼	11	31	56	4-15—8-15	1.790	436.50
	1904			80.00				N½	14	31	56	4-15—8-15	.984	240.00
	1904					27.00						4-15—5-15	.332	20.25
	1904			7.00								4-15—5-15	.086	5.25
	1904			55.00								4-15—5-15	.677	41.25
	1904			28.00								4-15—5-15	.344	21.00
	1904			25.00								4-15—5-15	.308	18.75
	1904					10.00						4-15—5-15	.123	7.50
	1904			50.00								4-15—5-15	.615	37.50
	1904			55.00								4-15—5-15	.677	41.25
	1904			35.00								4-15—5-15	.431	26.25
	1904			16.00								4-15—5-15	.197	12.00
	1904			15.00								4-15—5-15	.185	11.25
	1871			38.50				S½NE¼	4	31	56	4-15—8-15	.474	114.50
	1872			38.50				N½SE¼	4	31	56	4-15—8-15	.474	114.50
	1873			38.50				SE¼SE¼	4	31	56	4-15—8-15	.474	114.50
	1874			38.50				NW¼SW¼	3	31	56	4-15—8-15	.474	114.50
								S½SW¼	3	31	56			
	1870			9.50				NE¼	4	31	56	4-15—8-15	.117	98.50
	1871			10.00				NE¼SE¼	4	31	56	4-15—8-15	.123	30.00
	1872			8.50				SW¼	3	31	56	4-15—8-15	.105	25.50
	1873			8.50				SW¼NW¼	3	31	56	4-15—8-15	.105	25.50
	1874			9.50				SW¼SE¼	3	31	56	4-15—8-15	.117	28.50
	1875			7.50								4-15—8-15	.092	22.50
	1881			9.00								4-15—8-15	.111	27.00
	1881			8.00								4-15—8-15	.098	24.00
	1900			8.00								4-15—8-15	.098	24.00
	1901			28.50								4-15—8-15	.351	85.50

Claimant—**Arrascada Bros.** Proof No. 00373

Source—**South Fork.** Ditch—**Nos. 2 and 3.**

1903	23.53	E½E½	36	33	54			
1884	39.05	SE¼NE¼	25	33	54	4-15—8-15	.289	70.59
		NE¼SE¼	25	33	54	4-15—8-15	.481	117.15

Claimant—**W. B. Bellinger.** Proof No. 00374

Source—**South Fork Humboldt River.** Ditch—**W. B. Bellinger Ditches.**

1868	40.60	NW¼	4	31	56	4-15—8-15	0.492	120.00
1869	41.00	N½N½	5	31	56	4-15—8-15	0.504	122.00
1870	41.00	SE¼	31	32	56	4-15—8-15	0.504	122.00
1871	41.00	S½S½	32	32	56	4-15—8-15	0.504	122.00
1872	41.00					4-15—8-15	0.504	122.00
1873	41.00					4-15—8-15	0.504	122.00
1874	44.85					4-15—8-15	0.552	134.55
1881	7.00					4-15—8-15	0.086	21.00

NOTE—Fall pasture irrigation right on areas listed from 1868 to 1874.

Source—**South Fork Humboldt River.** Ditch—**Crane-Griswold.**

1870	9.50	N½NW¼	4	31	56	4-15—8-15	0.117	28.50
1871	10.00	S½SE¼	32	32	56	4-15—8-15	0.123	30.00
1872	8.50	SE¼SW¼	32	32	56	4-15—8-15	0.105	25.50
1873	8.50					4-15—8-15	0.105	25.50
1874	9.50					4-15—8-15	0.117	28.50
1875	7.50					4-15—8-15	0.092	22.50
1881	5.00					4-15—8-15	0.062	15.00

Claimants—**Minnie Hankins, Lillie Hankins, Elizabeth Hankins, Estate Jane Bellinger.** Proof No. 00375

Source—**South Fork of Humboldt.** Ditch—**Hankins & Bellinger Ditches.**

1870	22.00	W½	31	32	56	4-15—8-15	.271	66.00
1872	24.01	NE¼NW¼	6	31	56	4-15—8-15	.295	72.03
1873	24.01	N½NE¼	6	31	56	4-15—8-15	.295	72.03
1874	68.34	SE¼NE¼	6	31	56	4-15—8-15	.841	205.02
1903	35.00					4-15—8-15	.431	105.00
1904	31.00					4-15—8-15	.381	93.00
1905	44.36					4-15—8-15	.546	133.08

Claimant—**J. G. Hankins.** Proof No. 00377

Source—**Smith Creek and Willow Creek.** Ditch—**J. G. Hankins Ditches.**

1879	57.86	E½SE¼	25	31	55			
		NE¼	36	31	55			
		SW¼NW¼	30	31	56			
		NW¼SW¼	30	31	56	4-15—8-15	.712	173.58

J. G. Hankins—Continued.

Date of beneficial use—Nat. mdw.	Date of beneficial use—Cult. area	Construction first initiated—Dams	Construction first initiated—Ditches	Culture—Acres—Harvest crops	Culture—Acres—Meadow pasture	Culture—Acres—Willow and sage pasture	Culture—Acres—Swamp or overflow	Location—Subdivision	Location—Section	Location—Tp.N.	Location—R.E.	Length of season	Duty of water—C.F.S.	Duty of water—Acre-feet
Source—Cottonwood Creek and Smith Creek. Ditch—J. G. Hankins Ditches.														
......	1901	......	......	105.90	......	......	......	W½NE¼	1	30	55			
								NE¼NE¼	1	30	55			
								NW¼SE¼	1	30	55			
								SE¼	36	31	55	4-15—8-15	1.303	317.70
......	1879	......	......	110.07	......	......	......	E½SE¼	25	31	55			
								E½NE¼	36	31	55			
								S½NW¼	30	31	56			
								N½SW¼	30	31	56			
								SW¼SW¼	30	31	56			
								SW¼NW¼	31	31	56	4-15—8-15	1.354	330.21

Claimant—**Griswold-Henderson Livestock Co.** Proof No. 00378
Source—**Ten-Mile Creek.** Ditch—**Yowell Ditch.**

Nat. mdw.	Cult. area	Dams	Ditches	Harvest crops	Meadow pasture	Willow and sage pasture	Swamp or overflow	Subdivision	Section	Tp.N.	R.E.	Length of season	C.F.S.	Acre-feet
......	1888	......	......	11.20	......	......	......	NE¼SE¼	26	33	55	4-15—8-15	.138	33.60
......	1888	......	......	3.15	......	......	......	NW¼SE¼	26	33	55	4-15—8-15	.039	9.45
......	1888	......	......	11.10	......	......	......	SW¼SE¼	26	33	55	4-15—8-15	.137	33.30
......	1888	......	......	17.85	......	......	......	SE¼SW¼	26	33	55	4-15—8-15	.220	53.55
......	1888	......	......	12.09	......	......	......	E½E½	26	33	55	4-15—8-15	.149	36.27

Claimant—**J. J. Hylton.** Proof No. 00381
Source—**Cottonwood Creek.** Ditch—**Nos. 1, 2, 3, 5, and 6.**

Nat. mdw.	Cult. area	Dams	Ditches	Harvest crops	Meadow pasture	Willow and sage pasture	Swamp or overflow	Subdivision	Section	Tp.N.	R.E.	Length of season	C.F.S.	Acre-feet
......	1887	......	......	10.00	......	......	......	NE¼NE¼	16	30	56	4-15—8-15	.123	30.00
......	1887	......	......	23.20	......	......	......	NW¼NE¼	16	30	56	4-15—8-15	.285	69.60
......	1887	......	......	10.20	......	......	......	NE¼NW¼	16	30	56	4-15—8-15	.125	30.60
......	1887	......	......	5.40	......	......	......	SE¼SW¼	9	30	56	4-15—8-15	.066	16.20
......	1887	......	......	7.20	......	......	......	NW¼NW¼	16	30	56	4-15—8-15	.080	21.20
......	1888	......	......	4.20	......	......	......	NW¼NE¼	16	30	56	4-15—8-15	.052	12.60
......	1888	......	......	10.10	......	......	......	NE¼NW¼	15	30	56	4-15—8-15	.124	30.30
......	1888	......	......	5.40	......	......	......	SE¼SW¼	9	30	56	4-15—8-15	.066	16.20
......	1888	......	......	7.10	......	......	......	NW¼NW¼	16	30	56	4-15—8-15	.087	21.30
......	1889	......	......	4.20	......	......	......	NW¼NE¼	16	30	56	4-15—8-15	.052	12.60
......	1889	......	......	10.10	......	......	......	NE¼NW¼	16	30	56	4-15—8-15	.124	30.30
......	1889	......	......	5.40	......	......	......	SE¼SW¼	9	30	56	4-15—8-15	.066	16.20
......	1889	......	......	7.10	......	......	......	NW¼NW¼	16	90	56	4-15—8-15	.087	21.30
......	1890	......	......	4.10	......	......	......	NW¼NE¼	16	30	56	4-15—8-15	.050	12.30
......	1890	......	......	10.10	......	......	......	NE¼NW¼	16	30	56	4-15—8-15	.124	30.30
......	1890	......	......	5.40	......	......	......	SE¼SW¼	9	30	56	4-15—8-15	.066	16.20
......	1890	......	......	7.10	......	......	......	NW¼NW¼	16	30	56	4-15—8-15	.087	21.30
......	1890	......	......	2.00	......	......	......	N½SW¼	9	30	56	4-15—8-15	.025	6.00
......	1894	......	......	2.40	......	......	......	NW¼SW¼	15	30	56	4-15—8-15	.030	7.20
......	1894	......	......	7.90	......	......	......	SW¼NW¼	15	30	56	4-15—8-15	.097	28.70
......	1894	......	......	.60	......	......	......	SE¼NE¼	16	30	56	4-15—8-15	.007	1.80
......	1894	......	......	1.40	......	......	......	NE¼NE¼	16	30	56	4-15—8-15	.017	4.20

	1894			1.00				NW¼NW¼	15	30	56	4-15—8-15	.012	3.00
	1899			13.40				NE¼NE¼	16	30	56	4-15—8-15	.166	40.20
	1899			3.50				NE¼SW¼	15	30	56	4-15—8-15	.043	10.50
	1899			7.90				SW¼NW¼	15	30	56	4-15—8-15	.097	23.70
	1899			.50				SE¼NE¼	16	30	56	4-15—8-15	.006	1.50
	1899			1.00				NW¼NW¼	15	30	56	4-15—8-15	.012	3.00
	1900			15.00				NW¼SW¼	15	30	56	4-15—8-15	.185	45.00
	1904			1.30				SE¼NW¼	15	30	56	4-15—8-15	.016	3.90
	1904			7.90				SW¼NW¼	15	30	56	4-15—8-15	.097	23.70
	1904			.50				SE¼NE¼	16	30	56	4-15—8-15	.006	1.50
	1904			1.30				NE¼NE¼	16	30	56	4-15—8-15	.016	3.90
	1904			1.00				NW¼NW¼	15	30	56	4-15—8-15	.012	3.00

Claimant—**Chas. Dressi.** **Proof No. 00382**
Source—**Humboldt River.** Ditch—**Chas. Dressi Ditches.**

	1873				286.10			S½NW¼	3	33	54	4-15—6-15	3.519	429.15
	1881				15.00			NE¼	3	33	54	4-15—6-15	.185	12.50
	1902				41.00			N½SW¼	3	33	54	4-15—6-15	.504	61.50
	1903				42.80			N½SE¼	3	33	54	4-15—6-15	.526	64.20
								SE¼SE¼	3	33	54			
								E½SW¼SE¼	3	33	54			

Claimant—**Hunter Banks Company.** Proof No. 00382
Source—**South Fork of Humboldt.** Ditch—**Hunter Banks Co. Ditches.**

	1869			25.00					10	33	54	4-15—8-15	.308	75.00
	1871			193.70				SE¼	3	33	54	4-15—8-15	2.383	581.10
	1875			179.60				S½SW¼	3	33	54	4-15—8-15	2.209	538.80
	1886			37.20								4-15—8-15	.458	111.60
	1890			81.00								4-15—8-15	.996	243.00
	1890			160.00				NE¼	9	33	54	4-15—8-15	1.968	480.00
	1875			1.60				NW¼	10	33	54	4-15—8-15	.020	4.80

Claimant—**Ed. Carville.** Proof No. 00383
Source—**South Fork Smith Creek and Basin Creek.** Ditch—**Ed. Carville Ditches.**

	1870			56.00				W½	14	29	56	4-15—8-15	.689	168.00
	1871			9.00				SE¼NE¼	15	29	56	4-15—8-15	.111	27.00
	1872			159.68				NE¼SE¼	15	29	56	4-15—8-15	1.964	479.04
	1873			55.00				E½NE¼	22	29	56	4-15—8-15	.677	165.00
	1874			88.11				W½	23	29	56	4-15—8-15	1.084	264.33
	1880			7.00				E½NW¼	26	29	56	4-15—8-15	.086	21.00
	1890			18.45				E½	26	29	56	4-15—8-15	.227	55.35
	1902			87.64								4-15—8-15	1.078	262.92
	1903			34.18								4-15—8-15	.420	112.54

Claimant—**Drown Bros.** Proof No. 00385

Source—**South Fork of Humboldt River.** Ditch—**Drown Bros. Ditches.**

Date of beneficial use: Nat. mdw.	Date of beneficial use: Cult. area	Construction first initiated: Dams	Construction first initiated: Ditches	Culture—Acres: Harvest crops	Culture—Acres: Meadow pasture	Culture—Acres: Willow and sage pasture	Culture—Acres: Swamp or overflow	Location: Subdivision	Location: Section	Location: Tp.N.	Location: R.E.	Length of season	Duty of water: C.F.S.	Duty of water: Acre-feet
	1868			40.00				S½NW¼	10	31	56	4-15—8-15	.492	120.00
	1870			62.70				SW¼	10	31	56	4-15—8-15	.771	188.10
	1880			20.00				W½SE¼	10	31	56	4-15—8-15	.246	60.00
	1889			61.38				SE¼NW¼	11	31	56	4-15—8-15	.755	184.14
	1901			60.00				S½NE¼	11	31	56	4-15—8-15	.738	180.00
	1902			45.00				E½SW¼	11	31	56	4-15—8-15	.554	135.00
	1903			20.00				SE¼	11	31	56	4-15—8-15	.246	60.00
	1904			20.00								4-15—8-15	.246	60.00
	1905			108.00								4-15—8-15	1.328	324.00

NOTE—Fall pasture right with 1874 priority.

Date of beneficial use: Nat. mdw.	Date of beneficial use: Cult. area	Construction first initiated: Dams	Construction first initiated: Ditches	Culture—Acres: Harvest crops	Culture—Acres: Meadow pasture	Culture—Acres: Willow and sage pasture	Culture—Acres: Swamp or overflow	Location: Subdivision	Location: Section	Location: Tp.N.	Location: R.E.	Length of season	Duty of water: C.F.S.	Duty of water: Acre-feet
	1905			30.30				NE¼NW¼	15	31	56	4-15—8-15	.373	90.00

Source—**South Fork of Humboldt,* South Branch of South Fork of Humboldt, Rock Spring Creek, Pearl Creek and Creek east of Pearl Creek.**
Ditch—**Drown Bros. Ditches.**

Date of beneficial use: Nat. mdw.	Date of beneficial use: Cult. area	Construction first initiated: Dams	Construction first initiated: Ditches	Culture—Acres: Harvest crops	Culture—Acres: Meadow pasture	Culture—Acres: Willow and sage pasture	Culture—Acres: Swamp or overflow	Location: Subdivision	Location: Section	Location: Tp.N.	Location: R.E.	Length of season	Duty of water: C.F.S.	Duty of water: Acre-feet
	1873			62.40				NW¼	21	31	57	4-15—8-15	.077	187.20
	1874			6.00				S½	21	31	57	4-15—8-15	.074	18.00
	1875			219.80				NW¼NE¼	21	31	57	4-15—8-15	2.704	659.40
	1876			15.10				S½NE¼	21	31	57	4-15—8-15	.186	45.30
	1879			29.60				N½NW¼	28	31	57	4-15—8-15	.364	88.80
	1880			14.60				NE¼	28	31	57	4-15—8-15	.180	43.80
	1881			14.50				NW¼	27	31	57	4-15—8-15	.178	43.50
	1882			29.50				NE¼SW¼	27	21	57	4-15—8-15	.363	88.50
	1882					77.00						4-15—5-15	.947	57.75
	1884			42.30								4-15—8-15	.520	126.90
	1885			31.00								4-15—8-15	.381	93.00
	1886			32.90								4-15—8-15	.405	98.70
	1887			20.20								4-15—8-15	.248	60.60
	1888			11.20								4-15—8-15	.138	33.60
	1889			23.10								4-15—8-15	.274	69.30
	1892			11.90								4-15—8-15	.146	35.70
	1895			11.90								4-15—8-15	.146	35.70
	1898			11.90								4-15—8-15	.146	35.70
	1898					43.50						4-15—5-15	.535	32.63
	1901			11.90								4-15—8-15	.146	35.70
	1904			11.90								4-15—8-15	.146	35.70
	1904					121.80						4-15—5-15	1.408	91.35

*Right from South Fork and out of Ditch No. 2 to date from 1898.

Source—**Pearl Creek.** Ditch—**Drown Bros. Ditches.**

Date of beneficial use: Nat. mdw.	Date of beneficial use: Cult. area	Construction first initiated: Dams	Construction first initiated: Ditches	Culture—Acres: Harvest crops	Culture—Acres: Meadow pasture	Culture—Acres: Willow and sage pasture	Culture—Acres: Swamp or overflow	Location: Subdivision	Location: Section	Location: Tp.N.	Location: R.E.	Length of season	Duty of water: C.F.S.	Duty of water: Acre-feet
	1877			8.00				S¼NW¼	27	31	57	4-15—8-15	.098	24.00
	1878			3.00				NE¼SW¼	27	31	57	4-15—8-15	.037	18.00
	1890					33.30						4-15—5-15	.410	24.98

Claimant—**X. B. Martin.** Proof No. 00368

Source—**Lee Creek and Welch Creek.** Ditch—**X. B. Martin Ditches.**

1873	150.00		NE¼	8	31	57	4-15—8-15	1.845	450.00
1874	50.00		N½SE¼	8	31	57	4-15—8-15	.615	150.00
1874	20.00			9	51	57	4-15—8-15	.246	60.00
1875	47.46		N½	16	31	57	4-15—8-15	.584	142.38
1876	47.45						4-15—8-15	.584	142.35
1877	47.45						4-15—8-15	.584	142.35
1878	47.45						4-15—8-15	.584	142.85
1879	47.45						4-15—8-15	.584	142.85
1880	47.45						4-15—8-15	.584	142.85
1881	47.45						4-15—8-15	.584	142.35
1882	24.52						4-15—8-15	.302	73.56
1882		30.30					4-15—5-15	.373	22.72
1883		401.88					4-15—5-15	4.943	301.41
1887	15.00						4-15—8-15	.185	45.00
1905	15.00						4-15—8-15	.185	45.00

Claimant—**Albert Hankins.** Proof No. 00387

Source—**Smith, Big Cottonwood and Little Cottonwood Creeks.**

Ditch—**Albert Hankins Ditches.**

1875	35.00		W½NE¼	19	30	57	4-16—8-15	.431	105.06
1876	36.00		S½NW¼	19	30	57	4-15—8-15	.443	108.00
1880	36.00		N½SW¼	19	30	57	4-15—8-15	.443	108.00
1884	36.00		N½SE¼	19	30	57	4-15—8-15	.443	108.09
1888	36.72						4-15—8-15	.452	110.16
1876		24.00					4-15—5-15	.295	18.00
1880		24.00					4-15—5-15	.295	18.00
1884		24.00					4-15—5-15	.295	18.00
1888		25.11					4-15—5-15	.300	18.83

Decree No. 1355, Elko County District Court, is binding as between parties to the suit.

Claimant—**Estate of Mamie Winstead.** Proof No. 00388

Source—**Rattlesnake Creek.** Ditch—**Mamie Winstead Ditches.**

1869	35.00		NE¼	29	31	57	4-15—8-15	.431	105.00
1870	35.00		NW¼NW¼	28	31	57	4-15—8-15	.431	105.00
1871	35.00		S½NW¼	28	31	57	4-15—8-15	.431	105.00
1872	35.00		S½	28	31	57	4-15—8-15	.431	105.00
1873	7.66		W½SW¼	27	31	57	4-15—8-15	.094	22.98
1873		25.51	E½NW¼	33	31	57	4-15—5-15	.314	19.13
1876	90.00		N½NE¼	33	31	57	4-15—8-15	1.107	270.00
1877	29.87						4-15—8-15	.367	89.61
1878	29.87						4-15—8-15	.367	89.61
1879	29.87						4-15—8-15	.367	89.61
1880	29.87						4-15—8-15	.367	89.61
1881	29.87						4-15—8-15	.367	89.61

Estate of Mamie Winstead—Continued.

Date of beneficial use: Nat. mdw.	Date of beneficial use: Cult. area	Construction first initiated: Dams	Construction first initiated: Ditches	Culture—Acres: Harvest crops	Culture—Acres: Meadow pasture	Culture—Acres: Willow and sage pasture	Culture—Acres: Swamp or overflow	Location: Subdivision	Location: Section	Location: Tp.N.	Location: R.E.	Length of season	Duty of water: C.F.S.	Duty of water: Acre-feet
	1882			29.87								4-15—8-15	.367	89.61
	1883			29.88								4-15—8-15	.368	89.64
	1883					145.38						4-15—5-15	1.788	109.04

Source—**Pearl Creek.** Ditch—**Mamie Winstead Ditches.**

Date of beneficial use: Nat. mdw.	Date of beneficial use: Cult. area	Construction first initiated: Dams	Construction first initiated: Ditches	Culture—Acres: Harvest crops	Culture—Acres: Meadow pasture	Culture—Acres: Willow and sage pasture	Culture—Acres: Swamp or overflow	Location: Subdivision	Location: Section	Location: Tp.N.	Location: R.E.	Length of season	Duty of water: C.F.S.	Duty of water: Acre-feet
	1873					15.67		N½NE¼	29	31	57	4-15—5-15	.193	11.75

Claimant—**Leslie Carter.** Proof No. 00388

Source—**Rattlesnake Creek.** Ditch—**Leslie Carter Ditches.**

Date of beneficial use: Nat. mdw.	Date of beneficial use: Cult. area	Construction first initiated: Dams	Construction first initiated: Ditches	Culture—Acres: Harvest crops	Culture—Acres: Meadow pasture	Culture—Acres: Willow and sage pasture	Culture—Acres: Swamp or overflow	Location: Subdivision	Location: Section	Location: Tp.N.	Location: R.E.	Length of season	Duty of water: C.F.S.	Duty of water: Acre-feet
	1868			60.80				S½	19	31	57	4-15—8-15	.748	182.40
	1869			60.70					30	31	57	4-15—8-15	.747	182.10
	1870			60.70				S½SE¼	24	31	56	4-15—8-15	.747	182.10
	1871			60.70				E½	25	31	56	4-15—8-15	.747	182.10
	1872			60.70				E½SW¼	25	31	56	4-15—8-15	.747	182.10
	1873					43.00						4-15—5-15	.529	91.05
	1873			87.00								4-15—8-15	1.070	261.00
	1874			28.60								4-15—8-15	.352	85.80
	1875			53.60								4-15—8-15	.659	160.80
	1876			16.20								4-15—8-15	.199	48.60
	1877			16.20								4-15—8-15	.199	48.60
	1878			16.20								4-15—8-15	.199	48.60
	1880			48.50								4-15—8-15	.597	145.50
	1881				12.20							4-15—6-15	.150	36.60
	1881			118.70								4-15—8-15	1.460	18.30
	1883			10.00								4-15—8-15	.123	30.00
	1890			49.48								4-15—8-15	.609	128.44
	1903					203.10						4-15—5-15	2.498	304.65
	1881				45.00							4-15—6-15	.554	67.50
	1868			15.00				W½	29	31	57	4-15—8-15	.185	45.00
	1870			15.00				NE¼NW¼	32	31	57	4-15—8-15	.185	45.00
	1872			15.00				NW¼NE¼	32	31	57	4-15—8-15	.185	45.00
	1873			2.00								4-15—8-15	.025	6.00
	1874			25.00								4-15—8-15	.308	75.00
	1874			25.00								4-15—8-15	.308	75.00
	1877			25.00								4-15—8-15	.308	75.00
	1890			7.45								4-15—8-15	.092	22.35
	1891			7.45								4-15—8-15	.092	22.35
	1892			7.45								4-15—8-15	.092	22.35
	1893			7.45								4-15—8-15	.092	22.35
	1894			27.45								4-15—8-15	.338	82.35
	1894					5.00						4-15—5-15	.615	3.75
	1895			7.45								4-15—8-15	.092	22.35
	1896			7.45								4-15—8-15	.092	22.35
	1905					54.85						4-15—5-15	.675	41.14

Claimant—**A. J. Dewar.** Proof No. 00388
Source—**South Fork Humboldt River.** Ditch—**A. J. Dewar Ditches.**

	1874			100.00				S½S½	17	31	57	4-15—8-15	1.230	300.00
	1875			12.00				S½	18	31	57	4-15—8-15	.148	36.00
	1876			8.40				SE¼NE¼	19	31	57	4-15—8-15	.108	25.20
	1876			2.00				N½NE¼	19	31	57	4-15—8-15	.025	6.00
	1876			10.00				NE¼NW¼	19	31	57	4-15—8-15	.123	30.00
	1876			.91								4-15—8-15	.011	2.73
	1876			17.50								4-15—8-15	.215	52.50
	1876					25.40						4-15—5-15	.312	19.05
	1876					49.99						4-15—5-15	.615	37.49
	1876					10.20						4-15—5-15	.125	7.65
	1895			20.00								4-15—8-15	.246	60.00
	1895			7.50								4-15—8-15	.092	22.50
	1898					20.00						4-15—5-15	.246	15.00
	1900			53.80								4-15—8-15	.662	161.40
	1902			30.00								4-15—8-15	.369	90.00
	1912					15.40						4-15—5-15	.189	11.55

Claimant—**Pete Genette & Co.** Proof No. 00391
Source—**Big Cottonwood, Little Cottonwood, and Smith Creeks.**
Ditch—**Pete Genette & Co. Ditches.**

	1873			35.00					20	30	57	4-15—8-15	.431	105.00
	1874			35.00				SE¼NE¼	19	30	57	4-15—8-15	.431	105.00
	1875			20.00								4-15—8-15	.246	60.00
	1876			20.00								4-15—8-15	.246	60.00
	1877			19.00								4-15—8-15	.234	57.00
	1888			76.43								4-15—8-15	.940	229.29
	1892			15.62								4-15—8-15	.192	46.86
	1892			1.15								4-15—8-15	.014	3.45
	1875				13.09				20	30	57	4-15—6-15	.161	19.63
	1876				27.90			SE¼NE¼	19	30	57	4-15—6-15	.343	41.85
	1877				49.75							4-15—6-15	.612	74.63
	1888				70.58							4-15—6-15	.868	105.75
	1892				37.12				20	30	57	4-15—6-15	.457	55.68
	1900					36.27		S½SE¼	17	30	57	4-15—5-15	.446	27.20

Decree No. 1355, Elko County District Court Records, is binding as between parties to the suit.

Source—**Big Cottonwood Creek.** Ditch—**Pete Genette & Co. Ditches.**

	1872			30.00					20	30	57			
								SE¼NE¼	19	30	57	4-15—8-15	.369	90.00

Decree No. 1356, Elko County District Court Records, is binding as between parties to the suit.

Source—**Smith Creek.** Ditch—**Pete Genette & Co. Ditches.**

	1871			12.60				SW¼NE¼	29	30	57	4-15—8-15	.155	37.80
	1872			21.45				S½NW¼	29	30	57	4-15—8-15	.264	64.35
	1874			18.00				N½SW¼	29	30	57	4-15—8-15	.221	54.00
	1876			12.00								4-15—8-15	.148	36.00

Pete Genette & Co.—Continued.

Date of beneficial use: Nat. mdw.	Date of beneficial use: Cult. area	Construction first initiated: Dams	Construction first initiated: Ditches	Culture—Acres: Harvest crops	Culture—Acres: Meadow pasture	Culture—Acres: Willow and sage pasture	Culture—Acres: Swamp or overflow	Location: Subdivision	Location: Section	Location: Tp.N.	Location: R.E.	Length of season	Duty of water: C.F.S.	Duty of water: Acre-feet
	1880			2.42								4-15—8-15	.030	7.26
	1881			10.49								4-15—8-15	.129	31.47
	1872				43.06			SW¼NE¼	29	30	57	4-15—6-15	.530	129.18
	1876				5.59			S½NW¼	29	30	57	4-15—6-15	.069	16.77
	1881				12.10			N½SW¼	29	30	57	4-15—6-15	.149	36.30

Claimant—**A. J. Dewar.** Proof No. 00393

Source—**Pearl Creek.** Ditch—**A. J. Dewar Ditches.**

Nat. mdw.	Cult. area	Dams	Ditches	Harvest crops	Meadow pasture	Willow and sage pasture	Swamp or overflow	Subdivision	Section	Tp.N.	R.E.	Length of season	C.F.S.	Acre-feet
	1898			28.70				SE¼NE¼	19	31	57	4-15—8-15	.353	86.10

Claimant—**Chris Baumbach (Peterson Ranch).** Proof No. 00394

Source—**Rattlesnake Creek.** Ditch—**Chris Baumbach Ditches.**

Nat. mdw.	Cult. area	Dams	Ditches	Harvest crops	Meadow pasture	Willow and sage pasture	Swamp or overflow	Subdivision	Section	Tp.N.	R.E.	Length of season	C.F.S.	Acre-feet
								S½NW¼	19	31	57			
	1873			55.60				SW¼NE¼	19	31	57	4-15—8-15	0.684	166.80
	1883			18.84				NE¼SW¼	19	31	57	4-15—8-15	0.232	56.52
	1904			54.86				SE¼	19	31	57	4-15—8-15	0.675	164.58
								SW¼SW¼	20	31	57			

Source—**Pearl Creek.** Ditch—**Chris Baumbach Ditches.**

Nat. mdw.	Cult. area	Dams	Ditches	Harvest crops	Meadow pasture	Willow and sage pasture	Swamp or overflow	Subdivision	Section	Tp.N.	R.E.	Length of season	C.F.S.	Acre-feet
	1880			2.00				SW¼NE¼	19	31	57	4-15—8-15	.025	6.00

Claimant—**Merkley & Young.** Proof No. 00397

Source—**Smith Creek.** Ditch—**Merkley & Young Ditches.**

Nat. mdw.	Cult. area	Dams	Ditches	Harvest crops	Meadow pasture	Willow and sage pasture	Swamp or overflow	Subdivision	Section	Tp.N.	R.E.	Length of season	C.F.S.	Acre-feet
	1895					33.10		E½SE¼	34	30	56	4-15—5-15	.407	24.83
	1895			16.14				SE¼NE¼	34	30	56	4-15—8-15	.199	48.42
	1899			19.61				W½NE¼	35	30	56	4-15—8-15	.241	58.83
	1903			14.00								4-15—8-15	.172	42.00
	1904			6.42								4-15—8-15	.079	19.26
	1905			6.42								4-15—8-15	.079	19.26

Claimant—**Eureka Land and Stock Co.** Proof No. 00398

Source—**Smith Creek No. 2.** Ditch—**Nos. 1-21, Inc.**

Nat. mdw.	Cult. area	Dams	Ditches	Harvest crops	Meadow pasture	Willow and sage pasture	Swamp or overflow	Subdivision	Section	Tp.N.	R.E.	Length of season	C.F.S.	Acre-feet
	1890			2.08				SW¼NW¼	24	29	54	4-15—8-15	.026	6.24
	1890			7.48				SE¼NW¼	24	29	54	4-15—8-15	.092	22.44
	1890			7.15				SW¼NE¼	24	29	54	4-15—8-15	.088	21.45
	1890			2.66				NW¼NE¼	24	29	54	4-15—8-15	.033	7.98
	1890			7.75				NE¼NE¼	24	29	54	4-15—8-15	.095	28.35
	1890			.37				SE¼NE¼	24	29	54	4-15—8-15	.006	1.11
	1890			7.89				NW¼NW¼	10	29	55	4-15—8-15	.097	23.67
	1890			2.82				SW¼NW¼	10	29	55	4-15—8-15	.035	8.46
	1889			10.70				SE¼NW¼	10	29	55	4-15—8-15	.132	32.10
	1889			8.83				NE¼NW¼	10	29	55	4-15—8-15	.109	26.40

1889	13.14		NW¼NE¼	19	29	55	4-15—8-15	.165	40.32
1889	17.30		SW¼NE¼	19	29	55	4-15—8-15	.213	51.90
1890	19.48		NE¼NE¼	19	29	55	4-15—8-15	.240	58.44
1890	3.14		SE¼NE¼	19	29	55	4-15—8-15	.039	9.42
1890	3.62		NW¼NW¼	19	20	55	4-15—8-15	.045	10.86
1890		9.50	NW¼NW¼	19	29	55	4-15—5-15	.117	7.13
1890	.12		SW¼NW¼	19	29	55	4-15—8-15	.001	.36
1890		5.81	NE¼NW¼	19	29	55	4-15—5-15	.071	4.36

Claimant—**C. P. McNew.** Proof No. 00399
Source—**South Fork Humboldt River.** Ditch—**C. P. McNew.**

1881	22.09		NE¼SE¼	13	31	56	4-15—8-15	.272	66.27

Claimant—**A. J. Dewar.** Proof No. 00399
Source—**South Fork Humboldt River.** Ditch—**A. J. Dewar Ditches.**

1881	14.16		NE¼SE¼	13	31	56	4-15—8-15	0.174	42.48
1900	6.60		W½SW¼	18	31	57	4-15—8-15	0.081	19.80

Claimant—**W. S. Griswold.** Proof No. 00400
Source—**Sheep Creek.** Ditch—**Nos. 1-5.**

1904	66.08		N½N½	32	32	57	4-15—8-15	.813	198.24

Claimant—**W. B. Bellinger.** Proof No. 00401
Source—**Lamoille Creek.** Ditch—**W. B. Bellinger Ditches.**

1897	12.00		W½W½	30	33	58	4-15—8-15	.148	36.00
1904	13.00		S½SW¼	30	33	58	4-15—8-15	.160	39.00
1870	.80		E½W½	30	33	58	4-15—8-15	.010	2.40
1871	12.45		....	....	....	....	4-15—8-15	.153	37.35
1872	4.21		....	....	....	....	4-15—8-15	.052	12.63
1873	4.70		....	....	....	....	4-15—8-15	.058	14.10
1874	3.82		....	....	....	....	4-15—8-15	.047	11.46
1875	19.11		....	....	....	....	4-15—8-15	.235	57.33
1876	6.79		....	....	....	....	4-15—8-15	.084	20.37
1877	4.10		....	....	....	....	4-15—8-15	.050	12.30
1878	4.02		....	....	....	....	4-15—8-15	.049	12.06

Claimant—**Mrs. C. Glaser.** Proof No. 00402
Source—**Rabbit Creek.** Ditch—**Glaser Ditches.**

1872	185.10		SW¼	36	35	57			
			NW¼	1	34	57			
			W½SW¼	1	34	57			
			E½SE¼	2	34	57			
			SE¼NE¼	2	34	57	4-15—8-15	2.277	555.30

Claimant—**Manuel Erro.** Proof No. 00404
Source—**Lamoille Creek.** Ditch—**Erro Ditches.**

Date of beneficial use: Nat. mdw.	Date of beneficial use: Cult. area	Construction first initiated: Dams	Construction first initiated: Ditches	Culture—Acres: Harvest crops	Culture—Acres: Meadow pasture	Culture—Acres: Willow and sage pasture	Culture—Acres: Swamp or overflow	Location: Subdivision	Location: Section	Location: Tp. N.	Location: R. E.	Length of season	Duty of water: C. F. S.	Duty of water: Acre-feet
	1900			15.50				SE¼NE¼	13	33	57	4-15—8-15	.194	46.50
	1900			3.70				SE¼NE¼	13	33	57	4-15—8-15	.046	11.10

Claimant—**Hankins-Bellinger Co.** Proof No. 00405
Source—**Lamoille Creek.** Ditch—**Hankins-Bellinger Ditches.**

Date of beneficial use: Nat. mdw.	Date of beneficial use: Cult. area	Construction first initiated: Dams	Construction first initiated: Ditches	Culture—Acres: Harvest crops	Culture—Acres: Meadow pasture	Culture—Acres: Willow and sage pasture	Culture—Acres: Swamp or overflow	Location: Subdivision	Location: Section	Location: Tp. N.	Location: R. E.	Length of season	Duty of water: C. F. S.	Duty of water: Acre-feet
	1865			16.00				SW¼	18	33	58	4-15—8-15	.197	48.00
	1868			4.00				NW¼	19	33	58	4-15—8-15	.049	12.00
	*A1868			19.42				NW¼NW¼	24	33	58	4-15—8-15	.240	58.26
	1869			33.88								4-15—8-15	.417	101.64
	1870			3.54								4-15—8-15	.044	10.62
	1871			54.76								4-15—8-15	.674	164.28
	1872			18.51								4-15—8-15	.228	55.53
	1873			20.68								4-15—8-15	.254	62.04
	1874			16.81								4-15—8-15	.207	61.92
	1875			84.08								4-15—8-15	1.034	252.24
	1876			29.89								4-15—8-15	.368	80.67
	1877			18.03								4-15—8-15	.222	54.09
	1878			17.70								4-15—8-15	.218	53.10

*1868 prior right over A1868.
NOTE—After exchanging dates and areas to conform to Lamoille Court Decree.

Date of beneficial use: Nat. mdw.	Date of beneficial use: Cult. area	Construction first initiated: Dams	Construction first initiated: Ditches	Culture—Acres: Harvest crops	Culture—Acres: Meadow pasture	Culture—Acres: Willow and sage pasture	Culture—Acres: Swamp or overflow	Location: Subdivision	Location: Section	Location: Tp. N.	Location: R. E.	Length of season	Duty of water: C. F. S.	Duty of water: Acre-feet
	1888			1.50				E½NE¼	24	33	57	4-15—8-15	.018	4.50
	1896			8.00				NW¼SW¼	19	33	58	4-15—8-15	.098	24.00
	1900			17.00				SW¼SW¼	18	33	58	4-15—8-15	.209	51.00
	1901			25.10								4-15—8-15	.309	75.30
	1904			8.40								4-15—8-15	.103	25.20

Claimant—**Mrs. Johanna Eisenberg.** Proof No. 00406
Source—**Lamoille Creek.** Ditch—**Mrs. Johanna Eisenberg Ditches.**

Date of beneficial use: Nat. mdw.	Date of beneficial use: Cult. area	Construction first initiated: Dams	Construction first initiated: Ditches	Culture—Acres: Harvest crops	Culture—Acres: Meadow pasture	Culture—Acres: Willow and sage pasture	Culture—Acres: Swamp or overflow	Location: Subdivision	Location: Section	Location: Tp. N.	Location: R. E.	Length of season	Duty of water: C. F. S.	Duty of water: Acre-feet
	1904			33.00				NE¼	31	33	58	4-15—8-15	.406	99.00

Claimant—**Henderson Banking Co.** Proof No. 00407
Source—**Lamoille Creek.** Ditch—**Cahill..Reboule.**

Date of beneficial use: Nat. mdw.	Date of beneficial use: Cult. area	Construction first initiated: Dams	Construction first initiated: Ditches	Culture—Acres: Harvest crops	Culture—Acres: Meadow pasture	Culture—Acres: Willow and sage pasture	Culture—Acres: Swamp or overflow	Location: Subdivision	Location: Section	Location: Tp. N.	Location: R. E.	Length of season	Duty of water: C. F. S.	Duty of water: Acre-feet
	A1868	(a)		32.79				E½W½	20	33	58	4-15—8-15	.403	98.37
	1869			57.21				NE¼	20	33	58	4-15—8-15	.704	171.63
	1870			1.00				SE¼	20	33	58	4-15—8-15	.012	3.00
	1871			15.56				W½NW¼	21	33	58	4-15—8-15	.191	46.68
	1872			5.26								4-15—8-15	.065	15.78
	1873			5.88								4-15—8-15	.072	17.64
	1874			4.78								4-15—8-15	.059	14.34
	1875			23.89								4-15—8-15	.294	71.67
	1876			8.49								4-15—8-15	.104	25.47

1877		5.12					4-15—8-15	.063	15.36
1878		5.02					4-15—8-15	.062	15.06
A1878	(b)	9.78					4-15—8-15	.190	29.34
1879		51.80					4-15—8-15	.637	155.40
1880		79.74					4-15—8-15	.981	239.22
1881		6.12					4-15—8-15	.075	18.36
1882		8.42					4-15—8-15	.104	25.26
1883		12.72					4-15—8-15	.154	38.16
1884		17.69					4-15—8-15	.218	53.07
1885		4.08					4-15—8-15	.050	12.24
1886		5.91					4-15—8-15	.073	17.73
1887		8.16					4-15—8-15	.100	24.48
1888		7.55					4-15—8-15	.093	22.65
1889		7.55					4-15—8-15	.093	22.65
1890		4.08					4-15—8-15	.050	12.24
1894		4.08					4-15—8-15	.050	12.24
1895		32.82					4-15—8-15	.404	98.46

(a) 1868 prior right over A1868.
NOTE—After exchanging dates and areas to conform to Lamoille Court Decree.

(b) 1878 prior right over A1878.
Deed for this property to Mr. Ed. Helth in held in escrow.

Source—**Talbot Creek.** Ditch—**Henderson Ditches.**

1873	20.00	SE¼	20	33	58	4-15—8-15	.246	60.00
1879	10.00	W½W½	21	33	58	4-15—8-15	.123	30.00
1885	12.00					4-15—8-15	.148	36.00
1892	15.00					4-15—8-15	.185	45.00
1898	45.00					4-15—8-15	.555	135.00
1904	45.00					4-15—8-15	.556	135.00
1904	14.30					4-15—8-15	.176	42.90

Claimant—**Lamoille Mercantile Co.** Proof No. **00408**
Source—**Lamoille Creek.** Ditch—**L. M. Co.**

A1868*	3.64	W¼SE¼	19	33	58	4-15—8-15	.045	10.92
1869	6.36	NE¼SW¼	19	33	58	4-15—8-15	.078	19.08
1870	.60					4-15—8-15	.007	1.80
1871	9.34					4-15—8-15	.115	28.02
1872	3.14					4-15—8-15	.039	9.42
1873	3.54					4-15—8-15	.044	10.62
1874	2.87					4-15—8-15	.035	8.61
1875	14.33					4-15—8-15	.176	42.99
1876	5.09					4-15—8-15	.063	15.27
1877	3.07					4-15—8-15	.038	9.21
1878	3.02					4-15—8-15	.037	9.06
1896	46.60					4-15—8-15	.573	139.80
1902	7.60					4-15—8-15	.093	22.80

*1868 prior right over A1868.
NOTE—"After exchanging dates and areas to conform to Lamoille Court Decree."

Claimant—**Samuel McIntyre Investment Company.** Proof No. 00409

Source—**Lamoille Creek.** Ditch—**Samuel McIntyre Investment Company Ditches.**

Date of beneficial use: Nat. mdw.	Date of beneficial use: Cult. area	Construction first initiated: Dams	Construction first initiated: Ditches	Culture—Acres: Harvest crops	Culture—Acres: Meadow pasture	Culture—Acres: Willow and sage pasture	Culture—Acres: Swamp or over-flow	Location: Subdivision	Location: Section	Location: Tp.N.	Location: R.E.	Length of season	Duty of water: C.F.S.	Duty of water: Acre-feet
	1886			208.30				S½	9	35	58	4-15—8-15	3.275	798.90
	1894			165.90				SW¼	10	35	58	4-15—8-15	2.041	497.70
	1890			25.40					15	35	58	4-15—8-15	.312	76.20
	1893					191.10						4-15—5-15	2.351	143.33
	1893					527.70		SW¼	14	35	58	4-15—5-15	6.491	395.78
	1887			707.10					23	35	58	4-15—8-15	8.697	2121.30
	1893			36.00					22	35	58	4-15—8-15	.450	109.80
									26	35	58			
								NE¼	27	35	58			
								N½	35	35	58			
	1872			80.00					21	34	58	4-15—8-15	.984	240.00
	1883			179.00					15	34	58	4-15—8-15	2.202	537.00
	1884			179.00					22	34	58	4-15—8-15	2.202	537.00
	1885			179.00					10	34	58	4-15—8-15	2.202	537.00
	1886			179.00					3	34	58	4-15—8-15	2.202	537.00
	1887			179.00					2	34	58	4-15—8-15	2.202	537.00
	1888			179.00					34	35	58	4-15—8-15	2.202	537.00
	1889			184.60					35	35	58	4-15—8-15	2.271	553.80
	1893					82.20						4-15—5-15	1.011	61.65

Source—**Secret Creek and Lamoille Creek.*** Ditch—**Sam'l. McIntyre Investment Co. Ditches.**

Nat. mdw.	Cult. area	Dams	Ditches	Harvest crops	Meadow pasture	Willow and sage pasture	Swamp or over-flow	Subdivision	Section	Tp.N.	R.E.	Length of season	C.F.S.	Acre-feet
	1887			40.00				N½	9	35	58	4-15—8-15	.492	120.00
	1888			120.00					10	35	58	4-15—8-15	1.476	360.00
	1889			160.00					11	35	58	4-15—8-15	1.968	480.00
	1892			260.60				S½	13	36	58	4-15—8-15	3.205	781.80
	1893			260.60					14	35	58	4-15—8-15	3.205	781.80
	1894			260.60				N½NE¼	15	35	58	4-15—8-15	3.205	781.80
	1895			260.60				N½	24	36	58	4-15—8-15	3.205	781.80
	1896			260.60					19	35	59	4-15—8-15	3.205	781.80
	1897			260.77								4-15—8-15	3.207	782.10
	1897					231.90						4-15—5-15	2.852	173.92

*Priority from Lamoille Creek 1895 on land under "Upper Reservoir Ditch."

Source—**Warm Spring and Cold Creek.** Ditch—**Samuel McIntyre Investment Co. Ditches.**

Nat. mdw.	Cult. area	Dams	Ditches	Harvest crops	Meadow pasture	Willow and sage pasture	Swamp or over-flow	Subdivision	Section	Tp.N.	R.E.	Length of season	C.F.S.	Acre-feet
	1875			2250.00				S½NW¼	36	35	58			
								SW¼NE¼	36	35	58			
								NW¼SW¼	36	35	58			
								SE¼	36	35	58			
								NE¼SE¼	35	35	58			
								W½SW¼	1	35	59			
								W½	6	34	59			
								W½	7	34	59			
								E½	1	34	58			

		E½	12	34	58			
			13	34	58			
			24	34	58			
		W¼W¼	18	34	59			
		SW¼SW¼	30	34	59			
		W½	31	34	59			
		E½	25	34	58			
			36	34	58			
		W½	6	33	59	4-15—8-28	25.00	6750.00

NOTE—Subject to that certain opinion and decision No. 2573, Elko County Records.

Claimant—**O. P. McDermott.** Proof No. 00410

Source—**Lamoille Creek.** Ditch—**O. P. McDermott Ditches.**

A1868*	1.82	SW¼	29	33	58	4-15—8-15	.022	5.46
1869	3.18	NW¼	32	33	58	4-15—8-15	.039	9.54
1870	1.21	....	....	....	....	4-15—8-15	.015	3.63
1871	18.67	....	....	....	....	4-15—8-15	.230	56.01
1872	6.31	....	....	....	....	4-15—8-15	.078	18.91
1873	7.05	....	....	....	....	4-15—8-15	.087	21.15
1874	5.73	....	....	....	....	4-15—8-15	.070	17.19
1875	28.66	....	....	....	....	4-15—8-15	.353	85.98
1876	10.19	....	....	....	....	4-15—8-15	.125	30.57
1877	6.15	....	....	....	....	4-15—8-15	.076	18.45
1878	6.03	....	....	....	....	4-15—8-15	.074	18.09
1896	30.00	....	....	....	....	4-15—8-15	.369	90.00
1898	30.00	....	....	....	....	4-15—8-15	.369	90.00
1901	34.40	....	....	....	....	4-15—8-15	.423	103.20
1904	27.00	....	....	....	....	4-15—8-15	.332	81.00

*1868 prior right over A1868.

NOTE—"After exchanging dates and areas to conform to Lamoille court decree. Also 10 acres dated 1871 from Springs. (Vested right)."

Claimant—**J. E. Myers.** Proof No. 00411

Source—**Lamoille Creek.** Ditch—**J. E. Myers Ditches.**

1885	40.00	SW¼NW¼	13	33	57			
		SE¼NE¼	14	33	57	4-15—8-15	.492	120.00

Source—**Rabbit Creek and Little Rabbit Creek.** Ditch—**J. E. Myers Ditches.**

1873	70.60	W½SE¼	11	33	57	4-15—8-15	.868	211.80
1875	47.70	E½SW¼	11	33	57	4-15—8-15	.587	143.10
1890	10.00	SE¼SE¼	11	33	57	4-15—8-15	.123	30.00
		N½NE¼	14	33	57			

Claimant—**C. E. Noble.** Proof No. 00412
Source—**Lamoille Creek.** Ditch—**C. E. Noble Ditches.**

Date of beneficial use: Nat. mdw.	Date of beneficial use: Cult. area	Construction first initiated: Dams	Construction first initiated: Ditches	Culture—Acres: Harvest crops	Culture—Acres: Meadow pasture	Culture—Acres: Willow and sage pasture	Culture—Acres: Swamp or overflow	Location: Subdivision	Location: Section	Location: Tp.N.	Location: R.E.	Length of season	Duty of water: C.F.S.	Duty of water: Acre-feet
	A1868*			16.93				E½	30	33	58	4-15—8-15	.134	32.79
	1869			19.07				NW¼	29	33	58	4-15—8-15	.235	57.21
	1870			3.81				SE¼SE¼	19	33	58	4-15—8-15	.047	11.43
	1871			59.02				NE¼SE¼	19	33	58	4-15—8-15	.726	177.06
	1872			19.95								4-15—8-15	.245	59.85
	1873			22.29								4-15—8-15	.274	66.87
	1874			18.11								4-15—8-15	.223	54.33
	1875			90.61								4-15—8-15	1.115	271.83
	1876			32.21								4-15—8-15	.396	96.63
	1877			19.43								4-15—8-15	.239	58.29
	1878			19.07								4-15—8-15	.235	57.21
	1890			95.50								4-15—8-15	1.175	286.50
	1898			117.00								4-15—8-15	1.439	351.00
	1900			9.00								4-15—8-15	.111	27.00

*1868 prior right over A1868.

NOTE—After exchanging dates and areas to conform to Lamoille court decree.

NOTE—The amount of water flowing through the swamp ditch is to be deducted from the amount claimant is entitled to divert from Lamoille Creek, but in case swamp ditch becomes dry, claimant is allowed to use water for his entire area as listed from Lamoille Creek.

Swamp Area—No water to be diverted from the creek for any swamp area until the same becomes dry or is drained.

Claimant—**John W. McNew.** Proof No. 00412
Source—**Lamoille Creek.** Ditch—**John W. McNew Ditches.**

Nat. mdw.	Cult. area	Dams	Ditches	Harvest crops	Meadow pasture	Willow and sage pasture	Swamp or overflow	Subdivision	Section	Tp.N.	R.E.	Length of season	C.F.S.	Acre-feet
	1865			4.00				NW¼	18	33	58	4-15—8-15	.049	12.00
	1868			1.00								4-15—8-15	.012	3.00
	A1868*			8.38								4-15—8-15	.103	25.14
	1869			14.62								4-15—8-15	.180	43.86
	1870			1.78								4-15—8-15	.022	5.34
	1871			27.38								4-15—8-15	.337	82.14
	1872			9.25								4-15—8-15	.114	27.75
	1873			10.34								4-15—8-15	.127	31.02
	1874			8.40								4-15—8-15	.103	25.40
	1875			42.04								4-15—8-15	.517	126.12
	1876			14.94								4-15—8-15	.184	44.82
	1877			9.02								4-15—8-15	.111	27.06
	1878			8.85								4-15—8-15	.109	26.55

*1868—Prior right over A1868.

NOTE—After exchanging dates and areas to conform to Lamoille court decree.

Claimant—**John McKinney.** Proof No. 00414
Source—**Talbot Creek.** Ditch—**John McKinney Ditches.**

Nat. mdw.	Cult. area	Dams	Ditches	Harvest crops	Meadow pasture	Willow and sage pasture	Swamp or overflow	Subdivision	Section	Tp.N.	R.E.	Length of season	C.F.S.	Acre-feet
	1868			20.00				SE¼	8	33	58	4-15—8-15	.246	60.00
	1871			103.00				SE¼	8	33	58	4-15—8-15	1.267	309.00
	1887			37.00				SE¼	8	33	58	4-15—8-15	.455	111.00

Claimant—**Ramon Lugea.** Proof No. **00415**
Source—**Talbot Creek.** Ditch—**Ramon Lugea Ditches.**

	1871			10.00				E½SW¼	16	33	58	4-15—8-15	.123	30.00
	1873			5.00				E½SW¼	16	33	58	4-15—8-15	.062	15.00
	1876			5.00				E½SW¼	16	33	58	4-15—8-15	.062	15.00
	1892			17.00				E½SW¼	16	33	58	4-15—8-15	.209	51.00
	1900			17.00				E½SW¼	16	33	58	4-15—8-15	.209	51.00
	1904			8.00				E½SW¼	16	33	58	4-15—8-15	.098	24.00
	1904			1.50				E½SW¼	16	33	58	4-15—8-15	.018	4.50

Claimant—**F. W. Wiggins.** Proof No. **00416**
Source—**Beaver or Thorp Creek.** Ditch—**F. W. Wiggins Ditches.**

	1868			8.20				NW¼NE¼	9	33	58	4-15—8-15	.101	24.60
	1869			8.20				S½NE¼	9	33	58	4-15—8-15	.101	24.60
	1870			8.20				E½SE¼	9	33	58	4-15—8-15	.101	24.60
	1871			8.20				W½SW¼	10	33	58	4-15—8-15	.101	24.60
	1872			8.20				N½NW¼	15	33	58	4-15—8-15	.104	24.60
	1873			18.80								4-15—8-15	.231	56.40
	1874			3.00								4-15—8-15	.037	9.00
	1875			3.00								4-15—8-15	.037	9.00
	1876			15.20								4-15—8-15	.189	45.60
	1877			2.90								4-15—8-15	.036	8.70
	1878			2.90								4-15—8-15	.036	8.70
	1880			15.50								4-15—8-15	.191	46.50
	1881			9.70								4-15—8-15	.119	29.10
	1882			9.70								4-15—8-15	.119	29.10
	1883			9.60								4-15—8-15	.118	28.80
	1884			9.60								4-15—8-15	.118	28.80
	1885			12.60								4-15—8-15	.154	37.80
	1892			7.70								4-15—8-15	.095	23.10
	1893			7.70								4-15—8-15	.095	23.10
	1894			7.70								4-15—8-15	.095	23.10
	1895			7.00								4-15—8-15	.093	22.80
	1895					8.30						4-15—5-15	.102	6.23
	1898			14.10								4-15—8-15	.173	42.30
	1899			12.40								4-15—8-15	.153	37.20
	1900			12.40								4-15—8-15	.153	37.20
	1900					10.00						4-15—5-15	.123	7.50
	1902					9.90						4-15—5-15	.122	7.43
	1902			13.80								4-15—8-15	.170	41.40
	1904			21.20								4-15—8-15	.261	63.60

Claimant—**Antonio Echeverrieta.** Proof No. **00417**
Source—**Talbot Creek.** Ditch—**Antonio Echeverrieta Ditches.**

	1896			5.00				W½E½	21	33	58	4-15—8-15	.062	15.00
	1902			25.00				E½W½	21	33	58	4-15—8-15	.308	75.00
	1904			16.00								4-15—8-15	.197	48.00

Claimant—**J. E. Fraiser.** Proof No. **00418**
Source—**Rabbit Creek.** Ditch—**J. E. Fraiser Ditches.**

Date of beneficial use: Nat. mdw.	Date of beneficial use: Cult. area	Construction first initiated: Dams	Construction first initiated: Ditches	Culture—Acres: Harvest crops	Culture—Acres: Meadow pasture	Culture—Acres: Willow and sage pasture	Culture—Acres: Swamp or overflow	Location: Subdivision	Location: Section	Location: Tp.N.	Location: R.E.	Length of season	Duty of water: C.F.S.	Duty of water: Acre-feet
	1900			47.00				SE¼	14	33	57	4-15—8-15	.478	141.00

Claimant—**Harry Trott.** Proof No. **00420**
Source—**Talbot Creek.** Ditch—**Harry Trott Ditches.**

Nat. mdw.	Cult. area	Dams	Ditches	Harvest crops	Meadow pasture	Willow and sage pasture	Swamp or overflow	Subdivision	Section	Tp.N.	R.E.	Length of season	C.F.S.	Acre-feet
	1873			30.00				NE¼	8	33	58	4-15—8-15	.369	90.00
	1875			30.00				NW¼	8	33	58	4-15—8-15	.369	90.00
	1879			90.00				NE¼SW¼	8	33	58	4-15—8-15	1.107	270.00
	1885			5.00								4-15—8-15	.062	15.00
	1900			25.00								4-15—8-15	.308	75.00
	1902			40.00								4-15—8-15	.492	120.00
	1902			73.90								4-15—8-15	.909	221.70

Source—**Paterson Springs.** Ditch—**Harry Trott Ditches.**

Nat. mdw.	Cult. area	Dams	Ditches	Harvest crops	Meadow pasture	Willow and sage pasture	Swamp or overflow	Subdivision	Section	Tp.N.	R.E.	Length of season	C.F.S.	Acre-feet
	1880				99.50*			W½NW¼	8	33	58			
								N½SW¼	8	33	58	4-15—6-15	1.224	149.25

*No water to be diverted from Lamoille Creek for this 99.50 acres.

Claimant—**Henry Voight.** Proof No. **00421**
Source—**Beaver or Thorpe Creek and Springs.** Ditch—**Henry Voight Ditches.**

Nat. mdw.	Cult. area	Dams	Ditches	Harvest crops	Meadow pasture	Willow and sage pasture	Swamp or overflow	Subdivision	Section	Tp.N.	R.E.	Length of season	C.F.S.	Acre-feet
	1867			100.00				E½	33	34	58	4-15—8-15	1.230	300.00
	1873			98.20				W½W½	3	33	58	4-15—8-15	1.208	294.60
	1874			34.20				E½	4	33	58	4-15—8-15	.421	102.60
	1876			202.40				S½NW¼	4	33	58	4-15—8-15	2.490	307.20
	1877			68.00				SW¼	4	33	58	4-15—8-15	.836	204.00
	1878			105.10				NE¼NE¼	9	33	58	4-15—8-15	1.293	315.30
	1880			72.90				W½NW¼	10	33	58	4-15—8-15	.897	218.70
	1881			41.30								4-15—8-15	.508	123.90
	1884			41.20								4-15—8-15	.508	123.60
	1887			41.20								4-15—8-15	.508	123.60
	1890			41.20								4-15—8-15	.508	123.60
	1901			24.00								4-15—8-15	.295	72.00

Source—**Talbot Creek.** Ditch—**Wines No. 3.**

Nat. mdw.	Cult. area	Dams	Ditches	Harvest crops	Meadow pasture	Willow and sage pasture	Swamp or overflow	Subdivision	Section	Tp.N.	R.E.	Length of season	C.F.S.	Acre-feet
	1870			25.00				W½SW¼	4	33	58	4-15—8-15	.308	75.00

Claimant—**Conrad Smith.** Proof No. **00422**
Source—**Talbot Creek and Branch.** Ditch—**Conrad Smith Ditches.**

Nat. mdw.	Cult. area	Dams	Ditches	Harvest crops	Meadow pasture	Willow and sage pasture	Swamp or overflow	Subdivision	Section	Tp.N.	R.E.	Length of season	C.F.S.	Acre-feet
	1876			15.00				E½E½	21	33	58	4-15—8-15	.185	45.00
	1883			1.00				W½NW¼	22	33	58	4-15—8-15	.012	3.00
	1885			22.00				SE¼NW¼	22	33	58	4-15—8-15	.271	66.00
	1886			6.00				NW¼SW¼	22	33	58	4-15—8-15	.074	18.00

1887	10.00	N½SW¼SW¼	22	33	58	4-15—8-15	.123	30.00
1901	55.00					4-15—8-15	.677	165.00
1904	35.30					4-15—8-15	.434	105.90

Claimant—**Hunter & Lytton.** Proof No. 00423

Source—**Talbot Creek.** Ditch—**Hunter & Lytton Ditches.**

1875	25.00	SE¼NE¼	32	34	58	4-15—8-15	.308	75.00
1875	20.00	S½NW¼	33	34	58	4-15—8-15	.246	60.00
1875	45.00	SW¼	33	34	58	4-15—8-15	.554	135.00
1876	5.00	N½NW¼	4	33	58	4-15—8-15	.062	15.00
1877	40.00	E½	5	33	58	4-15—8-15	.492	120.00
1877	11.00	E½SW¼	5	33	58	4-15—8-15	.135	33.00
1884	10.00					4-15—8-15	.123	30.00
1884	15.00					4-15—8-15	.185	45.00
1885	50.00					4-15—8-15	.615	150.00
1886	60.00					4-15—8-15	.738	180.00
1886	50.00					4-15—8-15	.615	150.00
1887	50.00					4-15—8-15	.615	150.00
1888	26.00					4-15—8-15	.320	78.00
1889	50.00					4-15—8-15	.615	150.00
1890	50.00					4-15—8-15	.615	150.00
1891	50.00					4-15—8-15	.615	150.00
1892	50.00					4-15—8-15	.615	150.00
1892	7.40					4-15—8-15	.091	22.20

Source—**Spring Creek.** Ditch—**Hunter & Lytton Ditches.**

1890	61.40	N½NW¼	4	33	58			
		SE¼SW¼	33	34	58	4-15—8-15	.755	184.20

Source—**Lamoille Creek.** Ditch—**Hunter & Lytton.**

1871	10.00	SW¼NE¼	32	34	58	4-15—8-15	.123	30.00
1872	24.00	W½	32	34	58	4-15—8-15	.295	84.00
1873	36.00	E½	6	33	58	4-15—8-15	.443	108.00
1874	40.00	W½	5	33	58	4-15—8-15	.492	120.00
1875	20.00	W½NE¼	5	33	58	4-15—8-15	.246	60.00
1876	50.00					4-15—8-15	.615	150.00
1877	17.50					4-15—8-15	.215	52.50
1878	34.00					4-15—8-15	.418	102.00
1880	20.00					4-15—8-15	.246	60.00
1881	50.00					4-15—8-15	.615	150.00
1882	115.00					4-15—8-15	1.415	345.00
1883	10.00					4-15—8-15	.123	30.00
1884	75.00					4-15—8-15	.923	225.00
1885	50.00					4-15—8-15	.615	150.00
1886	20.00					4-15—8-15	.246	60.00
1887	75.00					4-15—8-15	.923	225.00
1888	26.70					4-15—8-15	.328	80.10
1889	76.80					4-15—8-15	.945	220.40

Claimant—**Alex. Carden.** Proof No. 00424
Source—**Talbot Creek and Springs.** Ditch—**Carden Ditches.**

Date of beneficial use: Nat. mdw.	Cult. area	Construction first initiated: Dams	Ditches	Culture—Acres: Harvest crops	Meadow pasture	Willow and sage pasture	Swamp or over-flow	Location: Subdivision	Section	Tp.N.	R.E.	Length of season	Duty of water: C.F.S.	Acre-feet
	1872			90.90*				W½E½	17	33	58	4-15—8-15	1.118	272.70
	1873			83.50				NE¼NE¼	17	33	58	4-15—8-15	1.027	250.50
	1873			23.00				NE¼NE¼	17	33	58	4-15—8-15	.283	69.00

*90.90 acres is from swamp ditches and Talbot Creek. All water available from swamp ditches is to be used first and if it is not sufficient to irrigate the extra water is to come from Talbot Creek. 106.5 acres from Talbot Creek.

Claimant—**George Bower.** Proof No. 00426
Source—**Lamoille Creek.** Ditch—**Patterson, Garden, Bowers Nos. 1 and 2.**

Nat. mdw.	Cult. area	Dams	Ditches	Harvest crops	Meadow pasture	Willow and sage pasture	Swamp or over-flow	Subdivision	Section	Tp.N.	R.E.	Length of season	C.F.S.	Acre-feet
	1865			4.00				NE¼	19	33	58	4-15—8-15	.049	12.00
	1868			1.00				NE¼	19	33	58	4-15—8-15	.012	3.00
	A1868*			2.91				NE¼	19	33	58	4-15—8-15	.036	8.73
	1869			5.09				NE¼	19	33	58	4-15—8-15	.063	15.27
	1870			1.00				NE¼	19	33	58	4-15—8-15	.012	3.00
	1871			15.56				NE¼	19	33	58	4-15—8-15	.191	46.68
	1872			5.26				NE¼	19	33	58	4-15—8-15	.065	15.78
	1873			5.88				NE¼	19	33	58	4-15—8-15	.072	17.64
	1874			4.78				NE¼	19	33	58	4-15—8-15	.059	14.34
	1875			23.89				NE¼	19	33	58	4-15—8-15	.294	81.67
	1876			8.48				NE¼	19	33	58	4-15—8-15	.104	25.44
	1877			5.12				NE¼	19	33	58	4-15—8-15	.063	15.36
	1878			5.03				NE¼	19	33	58	4-15—8-15	.062	15.09
	1898			22.76				NE¼	19	33	58	4-15—8-15	.255	62.28
	1899			26.00				NE¼	19	33	58	4-15—8-15	.320	78.00
	1900			21.45				NE¼	19	33	58	4-15—8-15	.264	64.35

*1868 prior right over A1868.
NOTE—"After exchanging dates and areas to conform to Lamoille Court Decree."

Claimant—**John Paleni.** Proof No. 00427
Source—**Lamoille Creek.** Ditch—**Erro-Streeter.**

Nat. mdw.	Cult. area	Dams	Ditches	Harvest crops	Meadow pasture	Willow and sage pasture	Swamp or over-flow	Subdivision	Section	Tp.N.	R.E.	Length of season	C.F.S.	Acre-feet
	1900			13.80				NE¼NE¼	13	33	57	4-15—8-15	.170	41.40

Claimant—**Joe Capriola.** Proof No. 00428
Source—**Lamoille Creek.** Ditch—**Joe Capriola Ditches.**

Nat. mdw.	Cult. area	Dams	Ditches	Harvest crops	Meadow pasture	Willow and sage pasture	Swamp or over-flow	Subdivision	Section	Tp.N.	R.E.	Length of season	C.F.S.	Acre-feet
	1900			46.20				SE¼	13	33	58	4-15—8-15	.568	138.60

Claimant—**Webster Patterson.** Proof No. 00430
Source—**Lamoille Creek.** Ditch—**Patterson, Streeter.**

Nat. mdw.	Cult. area	Dams	Ditches	Harvest crops	Meadow pasture	Willow and sage pasture	Swamp or over-flow	Subdivision	Section	Tp.N.	R.E.	Length of season	C.F.S.	Acre-feet
	1865			16.00				E½	18	33	58	4-15—8-15	.197	48.00
	1868			4.00				W½	17	33	58	4-15—8-15	.049	12.00
	A 1868*			19.42				S½SW¼	8	33	58	4-15—8-15	.239	58.26
	1869			33.88								4-15—8-15	.417	101.64

1870	8.54						4-15—8-15	.044	10.62
1871	54.76						4-15—8-15	.674	104.28
1872	18.51						4-15—8-15	.228	54.58
1873	20.68						4-15—8-15	.254	62.04
1874	16.81						4-15—8-15	.207	50.43
1875	84.08						4-15—8-15	1.034	252.24
1876	29.89						4-15—8-15	.368	89.67
1877	18.03						4-15—8-15	.222	54.09
1878	17.70						4-15—8-15	.218	53.10

*1868 prior right over A1868.

A1878*	14.21						4-15—8-15	.175	42.36
1879	75.20						4-15—8-15	.925	225.60
1880	115.76						4-15—8-15	1.424	347.28
1881	8.88						4-15—8-15	.109	26.64
1882	12.22						4-15—8-15	.150	36.66
1883	18.48						4-15—8-15	.227	55.44
1884	25.68						4-15—8-15	.316	77.04
1885	5.92						4-15—8-15	.073	17.76
1886	8.59						4-15—8-15	.106	25.77
1887	11.84						4-15—8-15	.146	35.52
1888	10.95						4-15—8-15	.135	32.85
1889	10.95						4-15—8-15	.135	32.85
1890	5.92						4-15—8-15	.073	17.76
1894	5.92						4-15—8-15	.073	17.76
1895	47.68						4-15—8-15	.586	143.04

*1878 prior right over A1878.

NOTE—After exchanging dates and areas to conform to Lamoille court decree.
Also stock-watering right from Carden's swamp ditch in SE¼ of SW¼, Sec. 17, T. N. 33, R. E. 58. This right was initiated prior to 1905.

Claimant—**R. B. Stewart.** Proof No. 00431

Source—**Rabbit Creek.** Ditch—**Stewart Ditches.**

1862 to 1869	100.00		E½	36	33	57	4-15—8-15	2.460	600.00
1870	23.00		E½SW¼	36	33	57	4-15—8-15	.566	138.00
1871	23.00		SE¼NW¼	36	33	57	4-15—8-15	.566	138.00
1872	23.00		N½NE¼	1	32	57	4-15—8-15	.566	138.00
1873	23.00		SW¼NE¼	1	32	57	4-15—8-15	.566	138.00
1874	23.00		E½NW¼	1	32	57	4-15—8-15	.566	138.00
1875	24.70						4-15—8-15	.608	148.20
1876	2.00						4-15—8-15	.050	12.00
1877	50.00						4-15—8-15	1.230	300.00
1877		16.00					4-15—8-15	.394	24.00
1898	45.00						4-15—8-15	1.108	270.00
1904	12.80						4-15—8-15	.314	76.80
1904	36.70						4-15—8-15	.902	220.20
1904		115.60					4-15—8-15	2.844	173.40

Claimant—**C. E. Noble.** Proof No. **00437**
Source—**Talbot Creek.** Ditch—**C. E. Noble Ditches.**

Date of beneficial use — Nat. mdw.	Date of beneficial use — Cult. area	Construction first initiated — Dams	Construction first initiated — Ditches	Culture—Acres — Harvest crops	Culture—Acres — Meadow pasture	Culture—Acres — Willow and sage pasture	Culture—Acres — Swamp or overflow	Location — Subdivision	Location — Section	Location — Tp.N.	Location — R.E.	Length of season	Duty of water — C.F.S.	Duty of water — Acre-feet
	1875			25.00				NE¼	28	33	58	4-15—8-15	.308	75.00
	1875			*10.44				N½SE¼	28	33	58	4-15—8-15	.128	31.32
	1876			10.00								4-15—8-15	.123	30.00
	1878			20.00								4-15—8-15	.246	60.00
	1880			41.00								4-15—8-15	.504	123.00
	1887			20.00								4-15—8-15	.246	60.00
	1896			2.00								4-15—8-15	.025	6.00

*Swamp area. No water to be diverted from the creek for any swamp area until the same become dry or is drained.

Claimant—**J. A. Castor.** Proof No. **00438**
Source—**Little Rabbit Creek.** Ditch—**J. A. Castor Ditches.**

Nat. mdw.	Cult. area	Dams	Ditches	Harvest crops	Meadow pasture	Willow and sage pasture	Swamp or overflow	Subdivision	Section	Tp.N.	R.E.	Length of season	C.F.S.	Acre-feet
	1886			20.90				E½SW¼	14	33	57	4-15—8-15	.357	62.70

NOTE—Little Rabbit Creek is branch of Rabbit Creek.

Claimant—**N. R. Castor.** Proof No. **00439**
Source—**Little Rabbit Creek.** Ditch—**N. R. Castor Ditches.**

Nat. mdw.	Cult. area	Dams	Ditches	Harvest crops	Meadow pasture	Willow and sage pasture	Swamp or overflow	Subdivision	Section	Tp.N.	R.E.	Length of season	C.F.S.	Acre-feet
	1873			3.44				E½NW¼	14	33	57	4-15—8-15	.042	10.32
	1886			29.45								4-15—8-15	.362	88.35

NOTE—Little Rabbit Creek is branch of Rabbit Creek.

Claimant—**C. Larrondo & Co.** Proof No. **00441**
Source—**Stoffer Creek and Natural Draws.** Ditch—**C. Larrondo Ditches.**

Nat. mdw.	Cult. area	Dams	Ditches	Harvest crops	Meadow pasture	Willow and sage pasture	Swamp or overflow	Subdivision	Section	Tp.N.	R.E.	Length of season	C.F.S.	Acre-feet
	1806			62.26				NW¼	29	33	57	4-15—8-15	.766	186.78
	1897			62.25				N½NE¼	29	33	57	4-15—8-15	.766	186.75
								S½SE¼	20	33	57			

NOTE—Stoffer Creek is branch of Rabbit Creek.

Claimant—**R. B. Stewart.** Proof No. **00442-00443**
Source—**Rabbit Creek.** Ditch—**Stewart Ditches.**

Nat. mdw.	Cult. area	Dams	Ditches	Harvest crops	Meadow pasture	Willow and sage pasture	Swamp or overflow	Subdivision	Section	Tp.N.	R.E.	Length of season	C.F.S.	Acre-feet
1862 to	1869			50.00				SE¼	35	33	57	4-15—8-15	1.230	300.00
	1869			45.00				S½NE¼	35	33	57	4-15—8-15	1.108	270.00
	1870			45.00				W½W½	36	33	57	4-15—8-15	1.108	270.00
	1871			40.00				NE¼NW¼	36	33	57	4-15—8-15	.984	240.00
	1872			30.00				W½NW¼	1	32	57	4-15—8-15	.738	180.00
	1874			30.00				N½NE¼	2	32	57	4-15—8-15	.738	180.00
	1876			53.50								4-15—8-15	1.316	321.00
	1879			64.60								4-15—8-15	1.590	387.60
	1886			73.30								4-15—8-15	1.804	439.80
	1901			4.00								4-15—8-15	.098	24.00

Claimant—**Andrew Westlund.** Proof No. 00444

Source—**Lamoille Creek.** Ditch—**Andrew Westlund Ditches.**

1870	1.51	W½E½	29	33	58	4-15—8-15	.019	4.53
1871	23.34	W½E½	29	33	58	4-15—8-15	.287	70.02
1872	7.89	W½E½	29	33	58	4-15—8-15	.297	23.67
1873	8.81	W½E½	29	33	58	4-15—8-15	.108	26.43
1874	7.16	W½E½	29	33	58	4-15—8-15	.088	21.48
1875	35.83	W½E½	29	33	58	4-15—8-15	.441	107.49
1876	12.74	W½E½	29	33	58	4-15—8-15	.157	38.22
1877	7.68	W½E½	29	33	58	4-15—8-15	.094	23.04
1878	7.54	W½E½	29	33	58	4-15—8-15	.093	22.62

NOTE—After exchanging dates and areas to conform to Lamoille Court Decree.

Source—**Snell Creek.** Ditch—**Andrew Westlund Ditches.**

1871	47.50	W½E½	29	33	58	4-15—8-15	.584	142.50

Claimant—**Griswold-Henderson Livestock Co.** **Proof No. 00445**

Source—**Cold Creek.** Ditch—**Hamilton and Greenwood.**

1873	10.00		1	33	58	4-15—8-15	.123	30.00
1874	15.00					4-15—8-15	.185	45.00
1875	15.00					4-15—8-15	.185	45.00
1876	15.00					4-15—8-15	.185	45.00
1877	15.00					4-15—8-15	.185	45.00
1879	30.00					4-15—8-15	.369	90.00
1880	10.00					4-15—8-15	.123	30.00
1881	10.00					4-15—8-15	.123	30.00
1882	10.00					4-15—8-15	.123	30.00
1883	10.00					4-15—8-15	.123	30.00
1884	10.00					4-15—8-15	.123	30.00
1885	10.00					4-15—8-15	.123	30.00
1886	10.00					4-15—8-15	.123	30.00
1887	13.00					4-15—8-15	.160	39.00
1869	10.00	S½NE¼SW¼	34	34	58	4-15—8-15	.123	30.00
1870	30.00	SE¼SW¼	34	34	58	4-15—8-15	.369	90.00
1871	30.00	SE¼	34	34	58	4-15—8-15	.369	90.00
1872	30.00	E½NW¼	3	33	58	4-15—8-15	.369	90.00
1873	30.00	E½SW¼	3	33	58	4-15—8-15	.369	90.00
1874	30.00	NE¼	3	33	58	4-15—8-15	.369	90.00
1875	30.00	SE¼	3	33	58	4-15—8-15	.369	90.00
1876	30.00	NW¼SW¼	2	33	58	4-15—8-15	.369	90.00
1877	30.00					4-15—8-15	.369	90.00
1878	34.60					4-15—8-15	.426	103.80
1895	15.00					4-15—8-15	.185	45.00

NOTE—That certain agreement entered into between Henderson Banking Company, Griswold-Henderson Livestock Company, C. W. Griswold, and Samuel McIntyre, as of July 16, 1908, is binding as between parties to agreement.

Claimant—**R. B. Stewart.** Proof No. 00446
Source—**Rabbit Creek.** Ditch—**Stewart Ditches.**

Date of beneficial use: Nat. mdw.	Date of beneficial use: Cult. area	Construction first initiated: Dams	Construction first initiated: Ditches	Culture—Acres: Harvest crops	Culture—Acres: Meadow pasture	Culture—Acres: Willow and sage pasture	Culture—Acres: Swamp or overflow	Location: Subdivision	Location: Section	Location: Tp.N.	Location: R.E.	Length of season	Duty of water: C.F.S.	Duty of water: Acre-feet
....	1869	....	....	40.00	....	....	....	S½	26	33	57	4-15—8-15	.984	240.00
....	1870	....	....	50.00	....	....	....	N½N½	35	33	57	4-15—8-15	1.230	300.00
....	1871	....	....	50.00	....	....	....	S½NW¼	35	33	57	4-15—8-15	1.230	300.00
....	1872	....	....	30.00	....	....	....	....	....	....	....	4-15—8-15	.738	180.00
....	1873	....	....	30.00	....	....	....	....	....	....	....	4-15—8-15	.738	180.00
....	1874	....	....	30.00	....	....	....	....	....	....	....	4-15—8-15	.738	180.00
....	1875	....	....	30.00	....	....	....	....	....	....	....	4-15—8-15	.738	180.00
....	1876	....	....	40.00	....	....	....	....	....	....	....	4-15—8-15	.984	240.00
....	1879	....	....	40.80	....	....	....	....	....	....	....	4-15—8-15	1.004	244.80
....	1880	....	....	20.00	....	....	....	....	....	....	....	4-15—8-15	.492	120.00

Claimant—**C. W. Clubine.** Proof No. 00447
Source—**Talbot Creek.** Ditch—**C. W. Clubine Ditches.**

Nat. mdw.	Cult. area	Dams	Ditches	Harvest crops	Meadow pasture	Willow and sage pasture	Swamp or overflow	Subdivision	Section	Tp.N.	R.E.	Length of season	C.F.S.	Acre-feet
....	1886	....	....	6.00	....	....	....	W½E½	16	33	58	4-15—8-15	.074	18.00
....	1889	....	....	6.00	....	....	....	E½NE¼	16	33	58	4-15—8-15	.074	18.00
....	1895	....	....	20.00	....	....	....	SW¼SE¼	9	33	58	4-15—8-15	.246	60.00
....	1900	....	....	19.50	....	....	....	....	....	....	....	4-15—8-15	.240	58.50
....	1903	....	....	73.00	....	....	....	....	....	....	....	4-15—8-15	.898	219.00
....	1904	....	....	24.00	....	....	....	....	....	....	....	4-15—8-15	.295	72.00

Source—**Beaver or Thorp Creek.** Ditch—**C. W. Clubine Ditches.**

Nat. mdw.	Cult. area	Dams	Ditches	Harvest crops	Meadow pasture	Willow and sage pasture	Swamp or overflow	Subdivision	Section	Tp.N.	R.E.	Length of season	C.F.S.	Acre-feet
....	1867	....	....	100.00	....	....	....	W½	9	33	58	4-15—8-15	1.230	300.00
....	1889	....	....	27.20	....	....	....	W½SE¼	9	33	58	4-15—8-15	.335	81.60
....	1870	....	....	31.40	....	....	....	....	....	....	....	4-15—8-15	.386	94.20
....	1871	....	....	31.30	....	....	....	....	....	....	....	4-15—8-15	.385	93.90
....	1872	....	....	31.30	....	....	....	....	....	....	....	4-15—8-15	.385	93.90
....	1873	....	....	31.30	....	....	....	....	....	....	....	4-15—8-15	.385	93.90
....	1873	....	....	8.90	....	....	....	....	....	....	....	4-15—8-15	.109	26.70
....	1881	....	....	51.20	....	....	....	....	....	....	....	4-15—8-15	.630	153.60
....	1881	....	....	5.00	....	....	....	....	....	....	....	4-15—8-15	.062	15.00
....	1889	....	....	45.80	....	....	....	....	....	....	....	4-15—8-15	.563	137.40

Claimant—**C. H. Reinken.** Proof No. 00448
Source—**Beaver or Thorpe Creek, Holland Slough and Springs.**
Dtich—**C. H. Reinken Ditches.**

Nat. mdw.	Cult. area	Dams	Ditches	Harvest crops	Meadow pasture	Willow and sage pasture	Swamp or overflow	Subdivision	Section	Tp.N.	R.E.	Length of season	C.F.S.	Acre-feet
....	1875	....	....	30.00	....	....	....	N½NE¼	33	34	58	4-15—8-15	.369	90.00
....	1876	....	....	20.00	....	....	....	SE¼	28	34	58	4-15—8-15	.246	60.00
....	1877	....	....	20.00	....	....	....	SE¼NE¼	28	34	58	4-15—8-15	.240	60.00
....	1879	....	....	57.00	....	....	....	SW¼	27	34	58	4-15—8-15	.701	171.00
....	1870	....	....	20.00	....	....	....	E½NW¼	27	34	58	4-15—8-15	.246	60.00
....	1872	....	....	10.00	....	....	....	W½	34	34	58	4-15—8-15	.123	30.00
....	1874	....	....	40.00	....	....	....	SE¼NE¼	33	34	58	4-15—8-15	.492	120.00
....	1875	....	....	22.00	....	....	....	NE¼SE¼	33	34	58	4-15—8-15	.271	66.00

....	1870	....	....	22.00	....	....	....	....	....	....	....	4-15—8-15	.271	66.00
....	1874	....	....	50.00	....	....	....	....	....	....	....	4-15—8-15	.615	150.00
....	1875	....	....	40.00	....	....	....	....	....	....	....	4-15—8-15	.492	120.00
....	1876	....	....	40.00	....	....	....	....	....	....	....	4-15—8-15	.492	120.00
....	1877	....	....	50.00	....	....	....	....	....	....	....	4-15—8-15	.615	150.00
....	1878	....	....	23.50	....	....	....	....	....	....	....	4-15—8-15	.289	70.50
....	1872	....	....	20.00	....	....	....	....	....	....	....	4-15—8-15	.246	60.00
....	1876	....	....	20.00	....	....	....	....	....	....	....	4-15—8-15	.246	60.00
....	1878	....	....	40.00	....	....	....	....	....	....	....	4-15—8-15	.492	120.00
....	1880	....	....	23.00	....	....	....	....	....	....	....	4-15—8-15	.283	69.00
....	1872	....	....	30.00	....	....	....	....	....	....	....	4-15—8-15	.369	90.00
....	1873	....	....	45.00	....	....	....	....	....	....	....	4-15—8-15	.554	135.00
....	1876	....	....	30.00	....	....	....	....	....	....	....	4-15—8-15	.369	90.00
....	1898	....	....	15.00	....	....	....	....	....	....	....	4-15—8-15	.185	45.00
....	1900	....	....	22.00	....	....	....	....	....	....	....	4-15—8-15	.271	66.00

Source—Lamoille Creek.

Ditch No. 4—

....	1900	....	....	30.00	....	....	....	W¼NW¼	28	34	58	4-15—8-15	.369	90.00
....	1901	....	....	27.00	....	....	....	NW¼SW¼	28	34	58	4-15—8-15	.332	81.00
....	1902	....	....	15.00	....	....	....	NE¼SE¼	29	34	58	4-15—8-15	.185	45.00
....	1903	....	....	36.00	....	....	....	....	....	....	....	4-15—8-15	.443	108.00

Ditch No. 3—

....	1873	....	....	2.00	....	....	....	N½NE¼	32	34	58	4-15—8-15	.025	6.00
....	1885	....	....	31.00	....	....	....	S½SE¼	29	34	58	4-15—8-15	.381	93.00
....	1890	....	....	35.00	....	....	....	W½SW¼	28	34	58	4-15—8-15	.431	105.00
....	1895	....	....	36.10	....	....	....	....	....	....	....	4-15—8-15	.444	108.30

Ditches Nos. 7 and 11—

....	1874	....	....	25.00	....	....	....	SW¼	28	34	58	4-15—8-15	.308	75.00
....	1875	....	....	25.00	....	....	....	....	....	....	....	4-15—8-15	.308	75.00
....	1878	....	....	21.00	....	....	....	....	....	....	....	4-15—8-15	.258	63.00

Ditch No. 12—

....	1872	....	....	24.00	....	....	....	E½NW¼	28	34	58	4-15—8-15	.295	72.00
....	1885	....	....	22.00	....	....	....	W½NE¼	28	34	58	4-15—8-15	.271	66.00
....	1890	....	....	22.00	....	....	....	....	....	....	....	4-15—8-15	.271	66.00

Ditch No. 8—

....	1878	....	....	60.00	....	....	....	NE¼	28	34	58	4-15—8-15	.738	180.00
....	1880	....	....	121.00	....	....	....	NW¼	27	34	58	4-15—8-15	1.488	363.00

Ditch not on map—

....	1874	....	....	2.00	....	....	....	NW¼SE¼	28	34	58	4-15—8-15	.025	6.00
....	1876	....	....	6.00	....	....	....	....	....	....	....	4-15—8-15	.074	18.00
....	1878	....	....	15.00	....	....	....	....	....	....	....	4-15—8-15	.185	45.00
....	1880	....	....	13.00	....	....	....	....	....	....	....	4-15—8-15	.160	39.00

C. H. Reinken—Continued.
Source—**Talbot Creek.**

Ditches Nos. 9 and 10—

Date of beneficial use: Nat. mdw.	Cult. area	Construction first initiated: Dams	Ditches	Culture—Acres: Harvest crops	Meadow pasture	Willow and sage pasture	Swamp or overflow	Location: Subdivision	Section	Tp.N.	R.E.	Length of season	Duty of water: C.F.S.	Acre-feet
	1876			20.00				N½NW¼	33	34	58	4-15—8-15	.246	60.00
	1890			40.00				S½SW¼	28	34	58	4-15—8-15	.492	120.00
	1890			42.00								4-15—8-15	.517	126.00

Ditch No. 2—

Date of beneficial use: Nat. mdw.	Cult. area	Construction first initiated: Dams	Ditches	Culture—Acres: Harvest crops	Meadow pasture	Willow and sage pasture	Swamp or overflow	Location: Subdivision	Section	Tp.N.	R.E.	Length of season	Duty of water: C.F.S.	Acre-feet
	1875			20.00				SE¼	28	34	58	4-15—8-15	.246	60.00
	1876			13.00				NW¼NE¼	33	34	58	4-15—8-15	.160	39.00
	1879			9.00				NE¼NW¼	33	34	58	4-15—8-15	.111	27.00
	1880			8.00								4-15—8-15	.098	24.00
	1885			11.00								4-15—8-15	.135	33.00
	1890			11.00								4-15—8-15	.135	33.00
	1905*			2.00				NW¼SE¼	28	34	58	4-15—8-15	.025	6.00

*This ditch not shown, but is flumed across Lamoille Creek.

Claimant—**Dave Morrow.** Proof No. **00449**
Source—**Springs (as below).** Ditch—**Dave Morrow Ditches.**

Date of beneficial use: Nat. mdw.	Cult. area	Construction first initiated: Dams	Ditches	Culture—Acres: Harvest crops	Meadow pasture	Willow and sage pasture	Swamp or overflow	Location: Subdivision	Section	Tp.N.	R.E.	Length of season	Duty of water: C.F.S.	Acre-feet
	1872			12.00*				NE¼	32	33	58	4-15—8-15	.148	36.00
	1878			8.00†				NE¼	32	33	58	4-15—8-15	.098	24.00
	1896			6.68‡				NE¼	32	33	58	4-15—8-15	.082	20.04

This takes practically all of the water from these sources: *From Orchard Spring; †From Big Spring in Trueman Canyon; ‡From Brown Canyon.

Claimant—**Jas. Byers.** Proof No. **00451**
Source—**Talbot Creek.** Ditch—**Jas. Byers Ditches.**

Date of beneficial use: Nat. mdw.	Cult. area	Construction first initiated: Dams	Ditches	Culture—Acres: Harvest crops	Meadow pasture	Willow and sage pasture	Swamp or overflow	Location: Subdivision	Section	Tp.N.	R.E.	Length of season	Duty of water: C.F.S.	Acre-feet
	1876			45.00				SW¼NE¼	22	33	58	4-15—8-15	.554	135.00
	1878			15.00				W½SE¼	22	33	58	4-15—8-15	.185	45.00
	1880			5.00				E½SW¼	22	33	58	4-15—8-15	.062	15.00
	1881			12.00				S½SW¼SW¼	22	33	58	4-15—8-15	.148	36.00
	1887			15.80								4-15—8-15	.194	47.40
	1889			5.00								4-15—8-15	.062	15.00
	1890			12.00								4-15—8-15	.148	36.00
	1895			5.00								4-15—8-15	.062	15.00
	1897			12.00								4-15—8-15	.148	36.00
	1898			12.50								4-15—8-15	.154	37.50
	1899			10.00								4-15—8-15	.123	30.00
	1900			7.00								4-15—8-15	.086	21.00
	1904			8.70								4-15—8-15	.107	26.10

Claimant—**Samuel Cook.** Proof No. 00452

Source—**Little Rabbit Creek and Spring Creek.** Ditch—**Spring Creek and Bellinger Ditch.**

Little Rabbit Creek		SE¼	8	33	57			
1901	25.00	W½SW¼	9	33	57	4-15—8-15	.308	75.00
1902	15.00	W½NW¼	16	33	57	4-15—8-15	.185	45.00
1905	19.56	SE¼NW¼	16	33	57	4-15—8-15	.241	58.68
Spring Creek		NE¼SW¼	16	33	57			
1880	65.00	NW¼SE¼	16	33	57	4-15—8-15	.800	195.00
1903	13.59	N½NE¼	17	33	57	4-15—8-15	.167	40.77
1903	3.50	SE¼NE¼	17	33	57	4-15—8-15	.043	10.50
1903	4.00	NE¼	17	33	57	4-15—8-15	.049	12.00

Before irrigating more land from Spring Creek than the 65 acres dated 1880, claimant is to have ⅝ c.f.s. flowing over a weir in Spring Creek between the water hole on Elko-Lamoille road and the bridge where the Pleasant Valley road cross Spring Creek, up to August 15 of each year. After August 15 there must be ⅝ c.f.s flowing over said weir before irrigation of any more land from Spring Creek other than the 65 acres. These restrictions are in accordance with judgment and decree No. 1621—Yowell v. Bellinger, Elko County Records. Said judgment and decree are binding as between parties to the suit.

Claimant—**R. Lebreski.** Proof No. 00453

Source—**Rabbit Creek and Springs.** Ditch—**Lebreski.**

1873	12.50	SE¼	2	33	57	4-15—8-15	.154	37.50
1890	37.10	SE¼	2	33	57	4-15—8-15	.456	111.30
1890	18.60*	SE¼	2	33	57	4-15—8-15	.229	55.80

*Priority from Rabbit Creek dated 1904.

Source—**Rabbit Creek and *Spring.** Ditch—**Lebreski.**

1896	56.71	E½NW¼	2	33	57	4-15—8-15	.698	170.13
1904	11.56	W½NE¼	2	33	57	4-15—8-15	.142	34.68
1904	2.09*					4-15—8-15	.026	6.27

Claimant—**E. Hankins** (Deed to James Billet in escrow). Proof No. 00454

Source—**Talbot Creek.** Ditch—**E. Hankins Ditches.**

1873	15.00	E½NW¼	16	33	58	4-15—8-15	.185	45.00
1876	5.00					4-15—8-15	.062	15.00
1884	4.40 (a)					4-15—8-15	.054	13.20
1892	10.00					4-15—8-15	.123	30.00
1900	44.00					4-15—8-15	.541	132.00
						4-15—8-15		
1869	10.00	W½NW¼	16	33	58	4-15—8-15	.123	30.00
1870	25.00	SE¼NE¼	17	33	58	4-15—8-15	.308	75.00
1871	5.00	W½SW¼	16	33	58	4-15—8-15	.062	15.00
1872	3.00	E½SE¼	17	33	58	4-15—8-15	.037	9.00
1873	10.00 (a)					4-15—8-15	.123	30.00
1878	30.00					4-15—8-15	.369	90.00
1884	100.00					4-15—8-15	1.230	300.00
1884	22.00 (a)					4-15—8-15	.271	66.00
1893	15.00					4-15—8-15	.185	45.00
1895	30.00					4-15—8-15	.369	90.00

(a) Swamp area. No water to be diverted from the creek for this area until the same becomes dry or is drained.

Claimant—**Q. D. Boyd.** Proof No. 00458

Source—**Lamoille Creek.** Ditch—**Q. D. Boyd Ditches.**

Date of beneficial use: Nat. mdw.	Date of beneficial use: Cult. area	Construction first initiated: Dams	Construction first initiated: Ditches	Culture—Acres: Harvest crops	Culture—Acres: Meadow pasture	Culture—Acres: Willow and sage pasture	Culture—Acres: Swamp or overflow	Location: Subdivision	Location: Section	Location: Tp.N.	Location: R.E.	Length of season	Duty of water: C.F.S.	Duty of water: Acre-feet
	1883			213.55				SE¼	7	35	58	4-15—8-15	2.627	640.65
	1883			12.55				S½	8	35	58	4-15—8-15	.154	37.65
	1884			40.00								4-15—8-15	.492	120.00
	1885			7.16								4-15—8-15	.088	21.48
	1885			53.91								4-15—8-15	.063	161.73
	1888			17.55								4-15—8-15	.216	52.65
	1895					68.52						4-15—5-15	.843	51.39

Claimant—**Albert Trescartes.** Proof No. 00459

Source—**Lamoille Creek.** Ditch—**Albert Trescartes Ditches.**

Nat. mdw.	Cult. area	Dams	Ditches	Harvest crops	Meadow pasture	Willow and sage pasture	Swamp or overflow	Subdivision	Section	Tp.N.	R.E.	Length of season	C.F.S.	Acre-feet
	1900			55.90				N½	26	33	57	4-15—8-15	.688	167.70
	1902			24.00								4-15—8-15	.295	74.00
	1903			27.20								4-15—8-15	.335	81.20

NOTE—Water right initiated prior to 1905 on Section 25 and transferred by permit to Section 26.

Claimant—**Chas. Trescartes.** Proof No. 00459

Source—**Lamoille Creek.** Ditch—**Chas. Trescartes Ditches.**

Nat. mdw.	Cult. area	Dams	Ditches	Harvest crops	Meadow pasture	Willow and sage pasture	Swamp or overflow	Subdivision	Section	Tp.N.	R.E.	Length of season	C.F.S.	Acre-feet
	A1868*			7.29				W½NW¼	20	33	58	4-15—8-15	.090	21.87
	1869			12.71				W½SW¼	20	33	58	4-15—8-15	.156	38.13
	1870			1.21								4-15—8-15	.015	3.63
	1871			18.67								4-15—8-15	.230	56.01
	1872			6.31								4-15—8-15	.078	18.93
	1873			7.05								4-15—8-15	.087	21.15
	1874			5.73								4-15—8-15	.070	17.19
	1875			28.66								4-15—8-15	.353	85.98
	1876			10.19								4-15—8-15	.125	30.57
	1877			6.15								4-15—8-15	.076	18.45
	1878			6.03								4-15—8-15	.074	18.09
	1880			28.00								4-15—8-15	.344	84.00
	1896			17.10								4-15—8-15	.210	51.30

*1868 has priority over A1868.

Claimant—**Albert Trescartes.** Proof No. 00459

Source—**Rabbit Creek, Little Rabbit Creek, and Swamps and Springs.**

Ditch—**Albert Trescartes Ditches.**

Nat. mdw.	Cult. area	Dams	Ditches	Harvest crops	Meadow pasture	Willow and sage pasture	Swamp or overflow	Subdivision	Section	Tp.N.	R.E.	Length of season	C.F.S.	Acre-feet
	1898			5.20*				N½	26	33	57	4-15—8-15	.064	15.60
	1898			22.00*								4-15—8-15	.271	66.00
	1898			17.00†								4-15—8-15	.209	51.00
	1900			20.00‡								4-15—8-15	.240	60.00

NOTE—Little Rabbit Creek is branch of Rabbit Creek. *From Swamps and Springs; †From Rabbit Creek; ‡Little Rabbit Creek.

Claimant—**Chas. Trescartes.** Proof No. 00459

Source—**Lamoille Creek.** Ditch—**Chas. Trescartes Ditches.**

1904	56.30	W½NE¼	24	33	57	4-15—8-15	.692	168.90
1905	40.50	SE¼NE¼	24	33	57	4-15—8-15	.498	121.50

Claimant—**Gabriel Rossi.** Proof No. 00461

Source—**Rabbit Creek.** Ditch—**Gabriel Rossi Ditches.**

1887	82.00	E½NE¼	23	34	57			
1880	220.00	NW¼	24	34	57			
		E½SW¼	24	34	57			
		SW¼NE¼	24	34	57			
		SE¼	24	34	57			
		W½SE¼	26	34	57	4-15—8-15	1.009	246.00
		NE¼SE¼	26	34	57	4-15—8-15	2.706	660.00

Claimant—**James B. Stewart.** Proof No. 00462

Source—**Rabbit Creek and Little Rabbit Creek.** Ditch—**James B. Stewart Ditches.**

1873	35.50	N½	11	33	57	4-15—8-15	.437	106.50
1890	35.60	N½	11	33	57	4-15—8-15	.438	106.80

Claimant—**August Alles.** Proof No. 00476

Source—**Deering or Alles or Lost Creek and Ackler Creek.** Ditch—**August Alles Ditches.**

1888	12.27	NW¼SW¼	23	36	60	4-15—8-15	.151	36.81
1889	9.00	SE¼NE¼	22	36	60	4-15—8-15	.111	27.00
1890	5.85	SE¼NE¼	22	36	60	4-15—8-15	.072	17.55
1890	2.25	NE¼SW¼	23	36	60	4-15—8-15	.028	6.75
1891	5.85	SE¼NE¼	22	36	60	4-15—8-15	.072	17.55
1896	7.50	NE¼SW¼	23	36	60	4-15—8-15	.092	22.50
1897	1.12	NW¼SW¼	23	36	60	4-15—8-15	.014	3.36
1898	14.25	SW¼NE¼	23	36	60	4-15—8-15	.175	42.85
1899	14.25	SW¼NE¼	23	36	60	4-15—8-15	.175	42.85
1900	20.42	SW¼NE¼	22	36	60	4-15—8-15	.251	61.26

NOTE—Water for irrigating above land to be taken first from Alles Creek, and upon its failure to run, enough Ackler Creek is to be drawn upon.

NOTE—That certain Decree No. 1527, Elko County District Court, is binding as between parties to the suit. No water is to be diverted from Deering Creek or its tributaries until decree is satisfied.

Claimant—**W. W. Alles.** Proof No. 00477

Source—**Springs, Swamps, and Natural Draw on Secs. 5 and 6, T. 36 N, R. 60 E.**

Ditch—**W. W. Alles Ditches.**

1901	36.14	S½NE¼	6	36	60	4-15—8-15	.445	108.42

NOTE—Source is as shown above. Claimant not to take water from Ackler or Herder Creek in case of shortage.

Claimant—**J. W. Weathers.** Proof No. 00479

Source—**Right Boulder Creek.** Ditch—**J. W. Weathers Ditches.**

Date of beneficial use: Nat. mdw.	Date of beneficial use: Cult. area	Construction first initiated: Dams	Construction first initiated: Ditches	Culture—Acres: Harvest crops	Culture—Acres: Meadow pasture	Culture—Acres: Willow and sage pasture	Culture—Acres: Swamp or overflow	Location: Subdivision	Location: Section	Location: Tp.N.	Location: R.E.	Length of season	Duty of water: C.F.S.	Duty of water: Acre-feet
	1902			30.94				NW¼ SE¼	32	36	60			
								N½ SW¼	32	36	60	4-15—8-15	.381	92.82

Source—**Left Boulder Creek.** Ditch—**J. W. Weathers Ditches.**

Nat. mdw.	Cult. area	Dams	Ditches	Harvest crops	Meadow pasture	Willow and sage pasture	Swamp or overflow	Subdivision	Section	Tp.N.	R.E.	Length of season	C.F.S.	Acre-feet
	1880			3.90				NE¼	32	36	60	4-15—8-15	.048	11.70
	1903			24.05								4-15—8-15	.296	72.15
	1905			28.73								4-15—8-15	.353	86.19

Claimant—**Mrs. M. E. Goodale and J. H. Goodale.** Proof. No. 00481

Source—**Deering Creek.** Ditch—**Goodale Ditches.**

Nat. mdw.	Cult. area	Dams	Ditches	Harvest crops	Meadow pasture	Willow and sage pasture	Swamp or overflow	Subdivision	Section	Tp.N.	R.E.	Length of season	C.F.S.	Acre-feet
	1873			20.00				SE¼	18	36	60	4-15—8-15	.246	60.00
	1874			5.50				SE¼	18	36	60	4-15—8-15	.068	16.50
	1874			6.00				SE¼	18	36	60	4-15—8-15	.074	18.00
	1882			10.10				SE¼	18	36	60	4-15—8-15	.124	30.30
	1882			5.10				SE¼	18	36	60	4-15—8-15	.063	15.30
	1882			.50				SE¼	18	36	60	4-15—8-15	.006	1.50
	1882			7.00				SE¼	18	36	60	4-15—8-15	.086	21.00
	1882			11.20				SE¼	18	36	60	4-15—8-15	.138	33.60

NOTE—That certain Decree No. 1527, Elko County District Court, is binding as between parties to the suit.

Claimant—**J. W. Johnston.** Proof No. 00482

Source—**Boulder Creek and Branches.** Ditch—**Armstrong 1-6, incl.**

Nat. mdw.	Cult. area	Dams	Ditches	Harvest crops	Meadow pasture	Willow and sage pasture	Swamp or overflow	Subdivision	Section	Tp.N.	R.E.	Length of season	C.F.S.	Acre-feet
	1868			100.00				SW¼	18	36	60	4-15—8-15	1.230	300.00
	1868					103.63		W½SW¼ SE¼	18	36	60	4-15—5-15	1.275	77.72
	1871			20.00				W½NW¼	19	36	60	4-15—8-15	.246	60.00
	1872			10.15				NE¼	19	36	60	4-15—8-15	.125	30.45
	1873			171.00				S½	19	36	60	4-15—8-15	2.103	513.00
	1875			81.25				N¼	30	36	60	4-15—8-15	.999	243.75
								E½NE¼	25	36	59			
								E½SE¼	24	36	59			

Claimant—**H. M. Lane.** Proof No. 00483

Source—**Boulder Creek.** Ditch—**Johnston & Armstrong and Carlson.**

Nat. mdw.	Cult. area	Dams	Ditches	Harvest crops	Meadow pasture	Willow and sage pasture	Swamp or overflow	Subdivision	Section	Tp.N.	R.E.	Length of season	C.F.S.	Acre-feet
	1876			20.00				NW¼	19	36	60	4-15—8-15	.246	60.00
	1878			43.00				NW¼	19	36	60	4-15—8-15	.528	129.00
	1888			17.00				NW¼	19	36	60	4-15—8-15	.209	51.00

Claimant—**Phil Harney.** Proof No. **00484**
Source—**Soldier Creek.** Ditch—**McDermott 1-4, incl.**

1896	22.10			SW¼	20	34	59	4-15—8-15	.272	66.30
1896	15.40			W½SE¼	20	34	59	4-15—8-15	.180	46.20
1896	10.10							4-15—8-15	.124	30.30
1896	21.80							4-15—8-15	.268	65.40
1896			24.20*					4-15—5-15	.298	18.15
1896		22.00						4-15—6-15	.282	34.35
1902	26.20							4-15—8-15	.322	78.60
1902	4.00							4-15—5-15	.049	12.00
1902	8.00							4-15—8-15	.098	24.00
1902		25.30						4-15—6-15	.311	37.95
1902		18.50						4-15—6-15	.228	27.75
1896			20.20					4-15—5-15	.250	15.15
1902			11.30					4-15—5-15	.139	8.48
1902			10.00					4-15—5-15	.123	7.50

*No water is to be diverted onto this land until it becomes dry or is drained.

Claimant—**Earl Green.** Proof No. **00485**
Source—**Soldier Creek.** Ditch—**Earl Green Ditches.**

1902	3.40	E½NE¼	32	34	59	4-15—8-15	.042	10.20
1902	4.40		....	....	....	4-15—8-15	.054	17.60
1902	5.40		....	....	....	4-15—8-15	.066	16.20
1902	5.00		....	....	....	4-15—8-15	.062	15.00
1902	0.80		....	....	....	4-15—8-15	.010	2.40
1894	39.60	SE¼SW¼	28	34	59	4-15—8-15	.487	118.80
1895	20.70	SW¼SE¼	28	34	59	4-15—8-15	.255	62.10
1897	11.50	NW¼	33	34	59	4-15—8-15	.141	34.50
1898	7.50	NW¼NE¼	33	34	59	4-15—8-15	.092	22.50
1899	16.80		....	....	....	4-15—8-15	.207	50.40
1902	17.00		....	....	....	4-15—8-15	.209	51.00
1904	11.50		....	....	....	4-15—8-15	.141	34.50
1904	12.10		....	....	....	4-15—8-15	.149	36.30

Claimant—**W. L. Paul.** Proof No. **00486**
Source—**Deering Creek and Branch of Deering Creek.** Ditch—**W. L. Paul Ditches.**

1876	4.55	SE¼NE¼	28	36	60	4-15—8-15	.055	13.65

Claimant—**L. L. Redden.** Proof No. **00487**
Source—**Herder Creek.** Ditch—**L. L. Redden Ditches.**

1894	13.50	S½N½	5	36	60	4-15—8-15	.166	40.50
1895	27.70		....	....	....	4-15—8-15	.341	80.10
1900	95.30		....	....	....	4-15—8-15	1.172	285.90
1902	23.00		....	....	....	4-15—8-15	.283	69.00

Claimant—**J. M. Riddell.** Proof No. **00488**
Source—**Herder Creek.** Ditch—**J. M. Riddell Ditches.**

Date of beneficial use: Nat. mdw.	Date of beneficial use: Cult. area	Construction first initiated: Dams	Construction first initiated: Ditches	Culture—Acres: Harvest crops	Culture—Acres: Meadow pasture	Culture—Acres: Willow and sage pasture	Culture—Acres: Swamp or overflow	Location: Subdivision	Location: Section	Location: Tp.N.	Location: R.E.	Length of season	Duty of water: C.F.S.	Duty of water: Acre-feet
	1881			25.00				N½SE¼	4	36	60	4-15—8-15	.308	75.00
	1875			9.00								4-15—8-15	.111	27.00
	1892			8.00								4-15—8-15	.098	24.00
	1900			6.00								4-15—8-15	.074	18.00
	1901			1.80								4-15—8-15	.022	5.40
	1883			11.50								4-15—8-15	.141	34.50
	1894			11.50								4-15—8-15	.141	34.50
	1903			4.00								4-15—8-15	.049	12.00
	1901			1.30				SW¼SW¼	3	36	60	4-15—8-15	.016	3.90
	1902			10.00				S½NW¼SW¼	3	36	60	4-15—8-15	.123	30.00
	1903			3.00								4-15—8-15	.037	9.00
	1904			2.30								4-15—8-15	.028	6.90
	1901					28.20						4-15—5-15	.347	21.15

Claimant—**Pete Scott.** Proof No. **00489**
Source—**Soldier Creek.** Ditch—**Scott Ditch.**

Nat. mdw.	Cult. area	Dams	Ditches	Harvest crops	Meadow pasture	Willow and sage pasture	Swamp or overflow	Subdivision	Section	Tp.N.	R.E.	Length of season	C.F.S.	Acre-feet
	1893			16.90				S½NW¼NW¼	28	34	59	4-15—8-15	.207	50.70
	1894			41.00				S½NW¼	28	34	59	4-15—8-15	.504	123.00
	1895			42.10								4-15—8-15	.518	126.30

Claimant—**William Smiley.** Proof No. **00490**
Source—**Smiley Creek, Dry Gulch and Little Hall Canyon Creek.**
Ditch—**Smiley Nos. 1-8, incl.**

Nat. mdw.	Cult. area	Dams	Ditches	Harvest crops	Meadow pasture	Willow and sage pasture	Swamp or overflow	Subdivision	Section	Tp.N.	R.E.	Length of season	C.F.S.	Acre-feet
	1880			197.20				E½SW¼	34	37	60	4-15—8-15	2.426	591.60
	1881			73.10				E½	34	37	60	4-15—8-15	.899	219.10
	1882			93.90				W½W½	35	37	60	4-15—8-15	1.155	291.70
	1883			42.00				E½SW¼	35	37	60	4-15—8-15	.517	126.00
	1885			2.30				NE¼NE¼	3	36	60	4-15—8-15	.028	6.90
	1891			7.90				NW¼NW¼	2	36	60	4-15—8-15	.097	23.70
	1892			27.40								4-15—8-15	.337	82.20
	1894			26.80								4-15—8-15	.330	80.40
	1895			8.60								4-15—8-15	.106	25.80
	1896			18.60								4-15—8-15	.229	55.80
	1897			51.10								4-15—8-15	.029	153.30

As far as possible claimant is to use the waters of Smiley Creek, Dry Gulch, and Little Hall Canyon Creek before taking any water from Herder Creek; the balance of the water required for irrigation to be taken from Herder Creek.

NOTE—In addition to irrigation rights claimant has a vested right from Herder Creek for domestic and stock watering purposes in NE corner of Sec. 33 with a date of 1902. Claimant not to divert water from Herder Creek to the NE corner of Sec. 33 as long as there is sufficient water from other sources for domestic and stockwatering purposes in said section.

Claimant—**W. J. Smiley.** Proof No. **00491**

			Source—Boulder Creek. Ditch—W. J. Smiley Ditches.					
1877	58.49	E½NE¼	13	36	59	4-15—8-15	.718	175.20
			Source—Reed Creek and Sloughs. Ditch—W. J. Smiley Ditches.					
1885	50.00	SW¼	27	36	59	4-15—8-15	.615	150.00
1887	50.00	SE¼	28	36	59	4-15—8-15	.615	150.00
1889	50.00	NE¼	33	36	59	4-15—8-15	.615	150.00
1890	14.15	NW¼	34	36	59	4-15—8-15	.174	42.45
			Source—Starr Creek. Ditch—W. J. Smiley Ditches.					
1871	5.00	SW¼SW¼	7	36	60	4-15—8-15	.062	15.00
1877	79.00	NW¼	18	36	60	4-15—8-15	.972	237.00
			Source—Herder Creek. Ditch—W. J. Smiley Ditches.					
1872	15.00	NW¼	7	36	60	4-15—8-15	.185	45.00
1873	20.00	N½SW¼	7	36	60	4-15—8-15	.246	60.00
1881	25.00	....	...	....	....	4-15—8-15	.308	75.00
			Source—Ackler Creek. Ditch—W. J. Smiley Ditches.					
1872	61.00	SW¼	7	36	60			
...	...	SE¼NW¼	7	36	60	4-15—8-15	.750	183.00
1870	10.60	NW¼NW¼	17	36	60	4-15—8-15	.130	31.80
			Source—Deering Creek. Ditch—W. J. Smiley Ditches.					
1868	10.00	SW¼	7	36	60	4-15—8-15	.123	30.00
1868	20.00	NW¼NW¼	17	36	60	4-15—8-15	.246	60.00
1869	25.00	SW¼NW¼	17	36	60	4-15—8-15	.308	75.00
1870	25.00	N½	18	36	60	4-15—8-15	.308	75.00
1870	8.40	....	...	...	....	4-15—8-15	.103	25.20
1871	20.00	....	...	...	...	4-15—8-15	.246	60.00
1872	25.00	....	...	...	...	4-15—8-15	.308	75.00
1872	25.00	....	...	...	...	4-15—8-15	.308	75.00
1873	25.00	....	...	...	...	4-15—8-15	.308	75.00
1873	13.00	....	...	...	...	4-15—8-15	.160	39.00
1874	25.00	....	...	...	...	4-15—8-15	.308	75.00
1877	80.00	....	...	...	...	4-15—8-15	.984	240.00
1879	31.20	....	...	...	...	4-15—8-15	.384	93.60
1880	10.00*	....	...	...	...	4-15—8-15	.123	30.00
1903	10.00	....	...	...	...	4-15—8-15	.123	30.00

*Was land of defendant Tauffer in suit No.1527, Elko County Records. No water to be diverted for this land until balance of Smiley land and lands of Mrs. M. E. Goodale and J. H. Goodale have been satisfied as per decree.

NOTE—That certain Decree No. 1527, Elko County District Court, is binding as between parties to the suit.

			Source—Boulder Creek. Ditch—Monk's Ditch.					
1887	89.34	....	23	36	59	4-15—8-15	1.099	268.02

Claimant—**W. C. Mills.** Proof No. **00492**
Source—**Deering Creek and Branch of Deering Creek.** Ditch—**W. C. Mills Ditches.**

Date of beneficial use: Nat. mdw.	Date of beneficial use: Cult. area	Construction first initiated: Dams	Construction first initiated: Ditches	Culture—Acres: Harvest crops	Culture—Acres: Meadow pasture	Culture—Acres: Willow and sage pasture	Culture—Acres: Swamp or overflow	Location: Subdivision	Location: Section	Location: Tp.N.	Location: R.E.	Length of season	Duty of water: C.F.S.	Duty of water: Acre-feet
	1873			10.00					28	36	60	4-15—8-15	.123	30.00
	1876			60.00					28	36	60	4-15—8-15	.738	180.00
	1888			10.00					28	36	60	4-15—8-15	.123	30.00
	1889			10.00					28	36	60	4-15—8-15	.123	30.00
	1890			10.00					28	36	60	4-15—8-15	.123	30.00
	1891			10.00					28	36	60	4-15—8-15	.123	30.00
	1892			10.00					28	36	60	4-15—8-15	.123	30.00
	1893			5.20					28	36	60	4-15—8-15	.064	15.60
	1900			3.00					28	36	60	4-15—8-15	.037	9.00

NOTE—That certain Decree No. 1527, Elko County District Court, is binding as between parties to the suit. No water is to be diverted from Deering Creek or its tributaries until decree is satisfied.

Claimant—**John Stiers.** Proof No. **00493**
Source—**Deering Creek.** Ditch—**Left-Hand and Right-Hand Ditches.**

Nat. mdw.	Cult. area	Dams	Ditches	Harvest crops	Meadow pasture	Willow and sage pasture	Swamp or overflow	Subdivision	Section	Tp.N.	R.E.	Length of season	C.F.S.	Acre-feet
	1890			7.40				SW¼NW¼	21	36	60	4-15—8-15	.091	22.20
	1890			4.50				NW¼NW¼	21	36	60	4-15—8-15	.055	13.50
	1891			1.39				SE¼NW¼	21	36	60	4-15—8-15	.017	4.17
	1891			4.00				NW¼NW¼	21	36	60	4-15—8-15	.057	14.80
	1893			1.00				SW¼NW¼	21	36	60	4-15—8-15	.012	3.00

Claimant—**W. B. Tavelle.** Proof No. **00494**
Source—**Left Boulder Creek.** Ditch—**W. B. Tavelle Ditches.**

Nat. mdw.	Cult. area	Dams	Ditches	Harvest crops	Meadow pasture	Willow and sage pasture	Swamp or overflow	Subdivision	Section	Tp.N.	R.E.	Length of season	C.F.S.	Acre-feet
	1881			46.41				SE¼	30	36	60	4-15—8-15	.511	139.23
	1884			6.50				SE¼	30	36	60	4-15—8-15	.080	19.50
	1884			....			18.00	SE¼	30	36	60	4-15—5-15	.221	13.50
	1891			11.40				SE¼	30	36	60	4-15—8-15	.140	34.20
	1891			....			32.93	SE¼	30	36	60	4-15—5-15	.405	24.70

Right Boulder Creek.

Nat. mdw.	Cult. area	Dams	Ditches	Harvest crops	Meadow pasture	Willow and sage pasture	Swamp or overflow	Subdivision	Section	Tp.N.	R.E.	Length of season	C.F.S.	Acre-feet
	1872			2.86				SE¼	30	36	60	4-15—8-15	.035	8.58

Claimant—**W. W. Weathers.** Proof No. **00496**
Source—**Right Boulder Creek.** Ditch—**W. W. Weathers Ditches.**

Nat. mdw.	Cult. area	Dams	Ditches	Harvest crops	Meadow pasture	Willow and sage pasture	Swamp or overflow	Subdivision	Section	Tp.N.	R.E.	Length of season	C.F.S.	Acre-feet
	1868			13.59				SW¼	30	36	60	4-15—8-15	.167	40.77
	1869			14.24				SW¼	30	36	60	4-15—8-15	.175	42.72
	1876			5.32				SW¼	30	36	60	4-15—8-15	.065	15.96
	1876			....			35.23	SW¼	30	36	60	4-15—5-15	.433	26.42

Source—**Left Boulder Creek.** Ditch—**W. W. Weathers Ditches.**

Nat. mdw.	Cult. area	Dams	Ditches	Harvest crops	Meadow pasture	Willow and sage pasture	Swamp or overflow	Subdivision	Section	Tp.N.	R.E.	Length of season	C.F.S.	Acre-feet
	1878			1.17				SW¼	30	36	60	4-15—8-15	.014	3.51

Claimant—**Mrs. Annie M. Wells.** Proof No. 00496

Source—**Right Boulder Creek and Spring.** Ditch—**Wells Ditches.**

Right Boulder Creek—

1879	4.68	NE¼	31	36	60	4-15—8-15	.058	14.04
1879	3.40	NW¼	32	36	60	4-15—8-15	.043	11.47
1879	6.13	NE¼	31	36	60	4-15—8-15	.075	18.39
1879	22.11	NE¼	31	36	60	4-15—8-15	.272	66.33
1905	14.10	NW¼	32	36	60	4-15—8-15	.173	42.80
1905	8.89	NW¼	32	36	60	4-15—8-15	.109	26.67
1905	.42	NE¼	31	36	60	4-15—8-15	.005	1.26

Spring—

1887	27.39	NW¼	32	36	60	4-15—8-15	.337	82.17
1887	11.34	NW¼	32	36	60	4-15—8-15	.139	34.02
1887	1.69	NE¼	31	36	60	4-15—8-15	.021	5.07
1887	5.00	NE¼	32	36	60	4-15—8-15	.062	15.00
1887	2.40	NW¼	32	36	60	4-15—8-15	.030	7.20

Source—**Left Boulder Creek.** Ditch—**Wells Ditches.**

1880	5.33	SW¼	29	36	60	4-15—8-15	.066	15.99
1880	1.30	SE¼	29	36	60	4-15—8-15	.016	3.90
1880	2.34	SW¼	29	36	60	4-15—8-15	.288	7.02
1884	30.94	NE¼	31	36	60	4-15—8-15	.381	92.82
1884	29.22	SW¼	29	36	60	4-15—8-15	.359	87.66
1884	3.90	SW¼	29	36	60	4-15—8-15	.048	11.70
1905	10.28	NW¼	32	36	60	4-15—8-15	.126	30.84
1905	30.94	NW¼	32	36	60	4-15—8-15	.381	92.82
1905	10.00	SW¼	32	36	60	4-15—8-15	.123	30.00
1905	10.13	NE¼	31	36	60	4-15—8-15	.125	30.39

Claimant—**Estate of Mrs. Jane Wright.** Proof No. 00497

Source—**Wright Creek, Dry Creek, Secret Creek and Springs.**

Ditch—**Jane Wright Ditches Nos. 1-8, incl.**

1879	10.00	S½NW¼	10	34	60	4-15—8-15	.123	30.00
1879	59.10	SW¼NE¼	10	34	60	4-15—8-15	.727	177.10
1880	59.20	S½	10	34	60	4-15—8-15	.728	177.60
1881	59.20	N½NW¼	15	34	60	4-15—8-15	.728	177.60
1882	59.20	NW¼NE¼	15	34	60	4-15—8-15	.728	177.60
1883	59.20	SE¼NW¼	15	34	60	4-15—8-15	.728	177.60
1883	15.00	SW¼NE¼	15	34	60	4-15—8-15	.185	45.00
1884	59.20					4-15—8-15	.728	177.60
1900	51.00					4-15—8-15	.627	153.00

Claimant—**John Stiers.** Proof No. **00498**

Source—**Alles Creek.** Ditch—**Stiers Ditch.**

Date of beneficial use: Nat. mdw.	Cult. area	Construction first initiated: Dams	Ditches	Culture—Acres: Harvest crops	Meadow pasture	Willow and sage pasture	Swamp or overflow	Location: Subdivision	Section	Tp.N.	R.E.	Length of season	Duty of water: C.F.S.	Acre-feet
	1890			3.86				NE¼NW¼	21	36	60	4-15—8-15	.047	11.58
	1890			2.00				NW¼NW¼	21	36	60	4-15—8-15	.025	6.00
	1891			3.87				NE¼NW¼	21	36	60	4-15—8-15	.047	11.61

Claimant—**Wm. Goodale.** Proof No. **00499**

Source—**Herder Creek through Brennen Gulch.** Ditch—**Wm. Goodale Ditches.**

Nat. mdw.	Cult. area	Dams	Ditches	Harvest crops	Meadow pasture	Willow and sage pasture	Swamp or overflow	Subdivision	Section	Tp.N.	R.E.	Length of season	C.F.S.	Acre-feet
	1877			19.80				SE¼SE¼	5	36	60	4-15—8-15	.244	59.40
	1877			9.70				SW¼SE¼	5	36	60	4-15—8-15	.119	29.10
	1877			9.80				SE¼SE¼	5	36	60	4-15—8-15	.121	29.40
	1894			10.00				SW¼SE¼	5	36	60	4-15—8-15	.123	30.00
	1894			10.00				SE¼SE¼	5	36	60	4-15—8-15	.123	30.00
	1894			19.70				SW¼SE¼	5	36	60	4-15—8-15	.242	59.10

Claimant—**Ed. Smiley.** Proof No. **00500**

Source—**Hall Canyon Creek, Smiley Springs, and Little Hall Canyon Creek.**

Ditch—**Ed. Smiley Ditches.**

Nat. mdw.	Cult. area	Dams	Ditches	Harvest crops	Meadow pasture	Willow and sage pasture	Swamp or overflow	Subdivision	Section	Tp.N.	R.E.	Length of season	C.F.S.	Acre-feet
	1877			18.70				SW¼SW¼	26	37	60	4-15—8-15	.230	56.10
	1877			8.90				N½NW¼	26	37	60	4-15—8-15	.109	26.70
	1877			4.20				SE¼NW¼	26	37	60	4-15—8-15	.052	12.60
	1877			42.60				E½SW¼	26	37	60	4-15—8-15	.523	127.80
	1897			21.60				SE¼SE¼	26	37	60	4-15—8-15	.266	64.80

NOTE—All lands under Decree No. 2635 to be served with water before diverting any water for this land.

Nat. mdw.	Cult. area	Dams	Ditches	Harvest crops	Meadow pasture	Willow and sage pasture	Swamp or overflow	Subdivision	Section	Tp.N.	R.E.	Length of season	C.F.S.	Acre-feet
	1877			200.00				NW¼	26	37	60			
								SW¼	26	37	60			
								SE¼	26	37	60	4-1—9-1	2.50	
	1897			73.90				S½	26	37	60			
								NW¼	26	37	60	4-1—9-1	.02	
	1904			10.00				S½	26	37	60			
								NW¼	26	37	60	4-1—9-1	.125	

Decree No. 2635 is binding as between parties to the suit.

That certain agreement between H. A. Agee and Ed. Smiley and copy filed with State Engineer July 22, 1921, File No. 00500, is hereby made a part of this finding.

Claimant—**H. A. Agee.** Proof No. **00501**

Source—**Hall Canyon Creek, Gray's Spring and Berger Creek.** Ditch—**Agee Ditches.**

Nat. mdw.	Cult. area	Dams	Ditches	Harvest crops	Meadow pasture	Willow and sage pasture	Swamp or overflow	Subdivision	Section	Tp.N.	R.E.	Length of season	C.F.S.	Acre-feet
	1879			38.00				NE¼NE¼	26	37	60			
	1879			20.00				SE¼NE¼	26	37	60			
	1879			40.00				NW¼NE¼	26	37	60			
	1879			40.00				SW¼NE¼	26	37	60			
	1879			40.00				SE¼SE¼	23	37	60			
	1879			11.50				NW¼NW¼	25	37	60	4-1—9-1	2.370	

1883	40.00		SW¼SW¼	24	37	60	4-1—9-1	.500	
1887	40.00		SW¼SE¼	23	37	60	4-1—9-1	.500	
1902	11.00		NW¼NW¼	24	37	60			
1912	13.50		NE¼NW¼	24	37	60			
1902	19.90		SE¼NW¼	24	37	60			
1902	11.10		SW¼NW¼	24	37	60			
1902	33.50		NW¼SW¼	24	37	60			
1902	35.30		NE¼SW¼	24	37	60			
1902	2.20		SE¼SW¼	24	37	60			
1902	4.80		SE¼NW¼	24	37	60	4-1—9-1	1.640	

Judgment and Decree No. 2635 are binding as between parties to the suit. The above duty of water is set by Decree No. 2635.
That certain agreement between H. A. Agee and Ed. Smiley is binding between said parties.
Claimant has 1879 priority for stock and domestic water.

1879	2.00		NE¼NE¼	26	37	60	4-15—8-15	.025	6.00
1879	4.40		NW¼NW¼	25	37	60	4-15—8-15	.054	13.20
1882	1.70		NE¼SW¼	24	37	60	4-15—8-15	.021	5.10
1882	11.20		NE¼SW¼	24	37	60	4-15—8-15	.138	33.60
1886		7.80	NE¼SW¼	24	37	60	4-15—5-15	.096	5.85
1886		26.50	NE¼SW¼	25	37	60	4-15—5-15	.326	19.88
1886		1.00	SE¼NW¼	25	37	60	4-15—5-15	.012	0.75
1894	2.50		NW¼NW¼	24	37	60	4-15—8-15	.031	7.50
1894		21.20	NW¼NW¼	24	37	60	4-15—5-15	.261	15.90
1894		1.40	NW¼NW¼	24	37	60	4-15—5-15	.017	1.05
1894		5.60	NE¼NW¼	24	37	60	4-15—5-15	.069	4.20
1894		1.50	SW¼NW¼	24	37	60	4-15—5-15	.019	1.13
1894		19.20	SW¼NW¼	24	37	60	4-15—5-15	.236	14.40
1894		14.70	SE¼NW¼	24	37	60	4-15—5-15	.181	11.03
1894		3.40	NW¼SW¼	24	37	60	4-15—5-15	.042	2.55
1902	8.20		SW¼NW¼	24	37	60	4-15—8-15	.101	24.60
1902	3.10		NW¼SW¼	24	37	60	4-15—8-15	.038	9.30
1912	2.00		NE¼SW¼	24	37	60	4-15—8-15	.025	6.00
1902	2.10		SE¼SW¼	24	37	60	4-15—8-15	.026	6.30

NOTE—All lands under Decree No. 2635 to be served with water before diverting any water for this land.

Claimant—**Hylton & Mentz.** Proof No. 00502

Source—**Herder Creek.** Ditch—**Hylton & Mentz Ditches.**

1880	11.80	SE¼	6	36	60	4-15—8-15	.145	35.40
1880	4.00	NE¼SW¼	6	36	60	4-15—8-15	.049	12.00
1882	7.00					4-15—8-15	.086	21.00
1886	1.20					4-15—8-15	.015	3.60
1886	2.90					4-15—8-15	.036	8.70
1897	3.50					4-15—8-15	.043	10.50
1903	21.30					4-15—8-15	.262	63.90
1903	9.70					4-15—8-15	.119	29.10
1905	30.00					4-15—8-15	.369	90.00
1905	14.70					4-15—8-15	.180	44.10

Source—**Deering Creek.** Ditch—**Hylton & Mentz Ditches.**

1878	50.00*	W½SE¼	7	36	60	4-15—8-15	.615	150.00

*No water is to be diverted until swamp becomes dry or is drained.

Hylton & Mentz—Continued.

Source—Ackler Creek. Ditch—Hylton & Mentz Ditches.

Date of beneficial use: Nat. mdw.	Date of beneficial use: Cult. area	Construction first initiated: Dams	Construction first initiated: Ditches	Culture—Acres: Harvest crops	Culture—Acres: Meadow pasture	Culture—Acres: Willow and sage pasture	Culture—Acres: Swamp or overflow	Location: Subdivision	Location: Section	Location: Tp.N.	Location: R.E.	Length of season	Duty of water: C.F.S.	Duty of water: Acre-feet
	1873			16.60				NW¼SE¼	7	36	60	4-15—8-15	.204	49.80
	1873			21.50				S½NE¼	7	36	60	4-15—8-15	.264	64.50
	1878			30.00*				S½NE¼	7	36	60	4-15—8-15	.360	90.00

*No water is to be diverted until swamp becomes dry or is drained.

Source—Ackler Creek and Herder Creek. Ditch—Hylton & Mentz Ditches.

Nat. mdw.	Cult. area	Dams	Ditches	Harvest crops	Meadow pasture	Willow and sage pasture	Swamp or overflow	Subdivision	Section	Tp.N.	R.E.	Length of season	C.F.S.	Acre-feet
	1870			10.60				NE¼	7	36	60	4-15—8-15	.130	31.80
	1871			9.70				N½NW¼	8	36	60	4-15—8-15	.119	29.10
	1872			11.20								4-15—8-15	.138	33.60
	1872			5.00								4-15—8-15	.062	15.00
	1872			8.90								4-15—8-15	.109	26.70
	1873			2.30								4-15—8-15	.028	6.90
	1873			4.00								4-15—8-15	.049	12.00
	1873			21.60								4-15—8-15	.266	64.80
	1873			29.40								4-15—8-15	.362	88.20
	1874			22.20								4-15—8-15	.273	66.60
	1874			1.20								4-15—8-15	.015	3.60
	1874			29.50								4-15—8-15	.363	88.50
	1874			10.40								4-15—8-15	.128	31.20
	1875			5.00								4-15—8-15	.062	15.00
	1875			6.00								4-15—8-15	.074	18.00
	1886			11.60								4-15—8-15	.143	34.80

Source—Herder Creek. Ditch—Hylton & Mentz Ditches.

Nat. mdw.	Cult. area	Dams	Ditches	Harvest crops	Meadow pasture	Willow and sage pasture	Swamp or overflow	Subdivision	Section	Tp.N.	R.E.	Length of season	C.F.S.	Acre-feet
	1873			8.10				SW¼	5	36	60	4-15—8-15	.100	24.30
	1873			6.10								4-15—8-15	.075	18.30
	1873			9.30								4-15—8-15	.114	27.90
	1873			3.20								4-15—8-15	.039	9.60
	1875			10.00								4-15—8-15	.123	30.00
	1876			21.90								4-15—8-15	.269	65.70
	1880			11.70								4-15—8-15	.144	35.10
	1880			19.50								4-15—8-15	.240	58.50
	1881			19.50								4-15—8-15	.240	58.50
	1897			37.00								4-15—8-15	.455	111.00

Claimant—E. C. Riddell. Proof No. 00503

Source—Ackler and Herder Creeks. Ditch—E. C. Riddell Ditches.

Nat. mdw.	Cult. area	Dams	Ditches	Harvest crops	Meadow pasture	Willow and sage pasture	Swamp or overflow	Subdivision	Section	Tp.N.	R.E.	Length of season	C.F.S.	Acre-feet
	1870			28.40				NW¼	9	36	60	4-15—8-15	.340	85.20
	1872			7.00				W½NE¼	9	36	60	4-15—8-15	.086	21.00
	1873			68.60				SE¼NE¼	9	36	60	4-15—8-15	.844	205.80
	1874			20.80				W½NE¼NE¼	9	36	60	4-15—8-15	.256	62.40
	1875			16.20								4-15—8-15	.199	48.60
	1876			40.80								4-15—8-15	.502	122.40

1901	2.70					4-15—8-15	.033	8.10
1904	8.30					4-15—8-15	.102	24.90
1905	1.00					4-15—8-15	.012	3.00

Claimant—**George Byers.** Proof No. 00504

Source—**As Below.** Ditch—**George Byers Ditches.**

Springs, Swamps, and Natural Draw—								
1881	12.18	SE¼SE¼	27	37	60	4-15—8-15	.150	36.54
1881	4.47	SW¼SE¼	27	37	60	4-15—8-15	.055	13.41
Spring and Natural Draw—								
1881	12.00	E½NE¼	27	37	60	4-15—8-15	.148	36.00
Springs and Spring Branch—								
1881	43.40	SW¼NW¼	27	37	60	4-15—8-15	.534	130.20
1905	7.00	N½SW¼	27	37	60	4-15—8-15	.086	21.00
		SE¼SW¼	27	37	60			
		SW¼SE¼	27	37	60			
Blasengame Creek—								
1883	48.30	W½W½	22	37	60	4-15—8-15	.594	144.90
1887	4.00	W½W½	22	37	60	4-15—8-15	.049	12.00
Natural Channel* and Springs Tributary to Blasengame Creek—								
1892	100.00	SW¼	27	37	60	4-15—8-15	1.230	300.00
		W½NW¼	27	37	60			
No rights to divert this natural channel from streams above.								
Spring Canyon and Springs—								
1889	25.10	E½E½	32	37	60	4-15—8-15	.308	75.30
1890	25.10	E½E½	32	37	60	4-15—8-15	.308	75.30
Hall Canyon Creek—								
1883	14.80	N½NW¼	22	37	60	4-15—8-15	.182	44.40
All lands under Decree No. 2635 to be served with water before diverting any water for this land.								
1901	15.10	NE¼SE¼	27	37	60	4-1—9-1		
1901	28.90	NW¼SE¼	27	37	60	4-1—9-1		
1901	12.00	SW¼SE¼	27	37	60	4-1—9-1		
1901	13.30	SE¼SE¼	27	37	60	4-1—9-1	.870	
Decree No. 2635 is binding as between parties to the suit.								

Source—**Hall Canyon Creek and Spring.** Ditch—**Geo. Byers Ditches.**

1876*	22.00†	NE¼SE¼	27	37	60	4-15—8-15	.271	66.00
1876	9.00†	SE¼SE¼	27	37	60	4-15—8-15	.111	27.00
1876	10.10†	NE¼SW¼	27	37	60	4-15—8-15	.124	36.30
1876	1.20†	SE¼NW¼	27	37	60	4-15—8-15	.015	3.60
1876	5.50†	SW¼NW¼	27	37	60	4-15—8-15	.068	16.50

*Priority in Hall Canyon Creek to date 1901.
†All lands under Decree No. 2635 to be served with water before diverting any water from Hall Canyon Creek for this land.

George Byers—Continued.
Source—**Herder Creek.** Ditch—**George Byers Ditches.**

Date of beneficial use: Nat. mdw.	Cult. area	Construction first initiated: Dams	Ditches	Culture—Acres: Harvest crops	Meadow pasture	Willow and sage pasture	Swamp or overflow	Location: Subdivision	Section	Tp.N.	R.E.	Length of season	Duty of water: C.F.S.	Acre-feet
	1892			4.50				NE¼	4	36	60	4-15—8-15	.055	13.50
	1893			16.50				NE¼	4	36	60	4-15—8-15	.208	49.50
	1894			16.70				NE¼	4	36	60	4-15—8-15	.205	50.10
	1894			....		43.50		NE¼	4	36	60	4-15—5-15	.535	32.63

Claimant—**J. L. Bartmess.** Proof No. **00505**
Source—**Ackler Creek and Branch.** Ditches—**Nos. 1-14, incl.**

Nat. mdw.	Cult. area	Dams	Ditches	Harvest crops	Meadow pasture	Willow and sage pasture	Swamp or overflow	Subdivision	Section	Tp.N.	R.E.	Length of season	C.F.S.	Acre-feet
	1872			8.10				SW¼NW¼	8	36	60	4-15—8-15	.100	24.30
	1874			5.90				SE¼NW¼	8	36	60	4-15—8-15	.073	17.70
	1876			5.90								4-15—8-15	.073	17.70
	1878			17.60								4-15—8-15	.216	52.80
	1878			0.70								4-15—8-15	.009	2.10

Claimant—**W. J. Black.** Proof No. **00505**
Source—**Ackler Creek, Brennen Gulch, and Herder Creek.** Ditches—**Nos. 1-14, incl.**

Nat. mdw.	Cult. area	Dams	Ditches	Harvest crops	Meadow pasture	Willow and sage pasture	Swamp or overflow	Subdivision	Section	Tp.N.	R.E.	Length of season	C.F.S.	Acre-feet
	1872			10.00				E½	8	36	60	4-15—8-15	.123	30.00
	1882			10.00				S½NW¼	8	36	60	4-15—8-15	.123	30.00
	1892			10.00				NE¼SW¼	8	36	60	4-15—8-15	.123	30.00
	1902			10.00								4-15—8-15	.123	30.00
Branch Ackler Creek—														
	1872			57.80				E½	8	36	60	4-15—8-15	.711	173.40
	1874			10.00				SE¼NW¼	8	36	60	4-15—8-15	.123	30.00
	1876			10.00				NE¼SW¼	8	36	60	4-15—8-15	.123	30.00
	1878			14.70								4-15—8-15	.181	44.10
Brennen Gulch—														
	1881			5.90								4-15—8-15	.073	17.70
Herder Creek—														
	1875			5.90								4-15—8-15	.073	17.70
	1876			5.90								4-15—8-15	.073	17.70
	1881			2.00								4-15—8-15	.025	6.00

Source—**Ackler Creek.** Ditches—**Nos. 1-14, incl.**

Nat. mdw.	Cult. area	Dams	Ditches	Harvest crops	Meadow pasture	Willow and sage pasture	Swamp or overflow	Subdivision	Section	Tp.N.	R.E.	Length of season	C.F.S.	Acre-feet
	1872			14.20				E½	8	36	60	4-15—8-15	.175	42.60
	1878			10.00				SE¼NW¼	8	36	60	4-15—8-15	.123	30.00
	1886			28.30				NE¼SW¼	8	36	60	4-15—8-15	.348	84.90
	1891			13.00								4-15—8-15	.160	39.00
	1901			10.40								4-15—8-15	.128	31.20
	1902			3.00								4-15—8-15	.037	9.00
	1903			14.80								4-15—8-15	.182	44.40

Claimant—**Jos. Jeanney.** Proof No. 00506
Source—**Branch of Ackler Creek and Alles Creek or Lost Creek.**
Ditch—**St. Clair and Natural Channel.**

Branch of Ackler Creek—								
1872	11.00	NW¼SW¼	8	36	60	4-15—8-15	.135	33.00
1872	17.50	NE¼SE¼	7	36	60	4-15—8-15	.215	52.50
1898	10.60	NW¼NE¼	17	36	60	4-15—8-15	.130	31.80
1904	9.90	NW¼NE¼	17	36	60	4-15—8-15	.122	29.70
1870	25.00	NW¼SW¼	8	36	60	4-15—8-15	.304	75.00
1870	21.00	SW¼SW¼	8	36	60	4-15—8-15	.258	63.00
1872	20.00	NE¼SE¼	7	36	60	4-15—8-15	.246	60.00
1872	2.00	SW¼SW¼	8	36	60	4-15—8-15	.025	6.00
1872	2.50	NE¼SE¼	7	36	60	4-15—8-15	.031	7.50
1872	23.30	SE¼SE¼	7	36	60	4-15—8-15	.287	69.90
1872	16.70	SE¼SE¼	7	36	60	4-15—8-15	.205	50.10
Lost Creek or Alles Creek—								
1899	2.70	NE¼NE¼	17	36	60	4-15—8-15	.022	8.10
1899	1.80	NW¼NE¼	17	36	60	4-15—8-15	.015	5.40

Claimant—**C. H. Black.** Proof. No. 00507
Source—**Herder Creek.** Ditch—**Redden and Black.**

1872	15.00	NW¼	4	36	60	4-15—8-15	.180	45.00
1873	19.00	N½SW¼	4	36	60	4-15—8-15	.234	57.00
1875	42.00	S½SE¼	4	36	60	4-15—8-15	.517	126.00
1879	14.50					4-15—8-15	.178	43.50
1880	49.00					4-15—8-15	.603	147.00
1885	4.00					4-15—8-15	.049	12.00
1890	4.00					4-15—8-15	.049	12.00
1894	29.20					4-15—8-15	.359	87.60
1895	28.90					4-15—8-15	.355	86.70

Source—**Ackler Creek.** Ditch—**C. H. Black Ditches.**

1892	9.00	E½	10	36	60	4-15—8-15	0.111	27.00
1894	3.40	SW¼	10	36	60	4-15—8-15	0.042	10.20
1895	43.00	S½ SE¼NW¼	10	36	60	4-15—8-15	0.529	129.00
1896	17.30					4-15—8-15	0.213	51.90
1898	10.00					4-15—8-15	0.123	30.00
1900	5.00					4-15—8-15	0.062	15.00
1901	4.80					4-15—8-15	0.059	14.40

Claimant—**Isaac Griswold.** Proof No. 00508
Source—**Boulder Creek.** Ditch—**Isaac Griswold Ditch.**

1888	17.30	W½SE¼	2	36	59	4-15—8-15	.213	51.90
1888	9.90	W½SE¼	2	36	59	4-15—8-15	.122	29.70
1888	20.10	W½SE¼	2	36	59	4-15—8-15	.247	60.30

Claimant—**W. W. Weathers.** Proof No. 00508

Source—**Starr Creek.** Ditch—**W. W. Weathers Ditches.**

Date of beneficial use: Nat. mdw.	Date of beneficial use: Cult. area	Construction first initiated: Dams	Construction first initiated: Ditches	Culture—Acres: Harvest crops	Culture—Acres: Meadow pasture	Culture—Acres: Willow and sage pasture	Culture—Acres: Swamp or overflow	Location: Subdivision	Location: Section	Location: Tp.N.	Location: R.E.	Length of season	Duty of water: C.F.S.	Duty of water: Acre-feet
	1879			14.80				NW¼SW¼	1	36	59	4-15—8-15	.182	44.40
	1879			3.00				SE¼SW¼	1	36	59	4-15—8-15	.037	9.00
	1878			25.20				NE¼SE¼	12	36	59	4-15—8-15	.309	75.60
	1875			22.00				NE¼NE¼	2	36	59	4-15—8-15	.271	66.00
	1875			2.80				SE¼NE¼	2	36	59	4-15—8-15	.034	8.40
	1872			32.90				SW¼NW¼	1	36	59	4-15—8-15	.405	98.70
	1872			24.70				NW¼NW¼	1	36	59	4-15—8-15	.304	74.10
	1872			12.50				SE¼SW¼	1	36	59	4-15—8-15	.154	37.50
	1872			2.60				NE¼NE¼	2	36	59	4-15—8-15	.032	8.40
	1875			21.90				NE¼NW¼	12	36	59	4-15—8-15	.269	65.70
	1872			22.90				SW¼SW¼	36	37	59	4-15—8-15	.282	68.70
	1872			7.30				NW¼SW¼	36	37	59	4-15—8-15	.090	21.90
	1872			38.00				NE¼SE¼	35	37	59	4-15—8-15	.467	114.00
	1872			1.00				NW¼SE¼	35	37	59	4-15—8-15	.012	3.00
	1872			32.40				SE¼SE¼	35	37	59	4-15—8-15	.400	97.20
	1879			8.20				SW¼NE¼	35	37	50	4-15—8-15	.101	24.60
	1879			18.40				SW¼NE¼	35	37	59	4-15—8-15	.226	55.20
	1879			40.00				SE¼NE¼	35	37	59	4-15—8-15	.492	120.00
	1879			29.70				SW¼NW¼	35	37	59	4-15—8-15	.365	89.10
	1879			30.40				SE¼NW¼	35	37	59	4-15—8-15	.374	91.20
	1879			12.10				NE¼SW¼	35	37	59	4-15—8-15	.149	36.30
	1879			23.40				NW¼SW¼	35	37	59	4-15—8-15	.288	70.20
	1879			0.70				NW¼SE¼	35	37	59	4-15—8-15	.009	2.10
	1878			3.70				NE¼SE¼	12	36	59	4-15—8-15	.046	11.10

Source—**Natural Draw North of Brennens Gulch.*** Ditch—**W. W. Weathers Ditches.**

Nat. mdw.	Cult. area	Dams	Ditches	Harvest crops	Meadow pasture	Willow and sage pasture	Swamp or overflow	Subdivision	Section	Tp.N.	R.E.	Length of season	C.F.S.	Acre-feet
	1885			5.00				S½SE¼	1	36	59	4-15—8-15	.062	15.00
	1890			7.00								4-15—8-15	.086	21.00
	1894			5.00								4-15—8-15	.062	15.00
	1895			10.00								4-15—8-15	.123	30.00
	1902			13.00								4-15—8-15	.160	30.00

*Water in this source is from springs, swamps and some return water. If supply becomes short, claimant is not to have water from any other natural source.

Source—**Ackler* and Herder Creeks through Brennens Gulch.**
Ditch—**W. W. Weathers Ditches.**

Nat. mdw.	Cult. area	Dams	Ditches	Harvest crops	Meadow pasture	Willow and sage pasture	Swamp or overflow	Subdivision	Section	Tp.N.	R.E.	Length of season	C.F.S.	Acre-feet
	1887			7.00				E½SW¼	1	36	59	4-15—8-15	.093	22.80
	1887			10.00				SW¼SE¼	1	36	50	4-15—8-15	.123	30.00
	1887			6.00								4-15—8-15	.074	18.00
	1887			2.10								4-15—8-15	.026	6.30
	1887			0.20								4-15—8-15	.002	0.60
	1887			4.00								4-15—8-15	.040	12.00
	1887			5.00								4-15—8-15	.062	15.00
	1893			12.00								4-15—8-15	.148	30.00

*Ackler Creek priority 1893.

Source—Ackler Creek. Ditch—**W. W. Weathers Ditches.**

1878	6.00	NE¼SE¼	12	36	59	4-15—8-15	.074	9.00

Source—Boulder and Starr Creek. Ditch—**W. W. Weathers Ditches.**

1878	76.30	SE¼	12	36	59	4-15—8-15	.038	228.00

Source—Boulder Creek. Ditch—**W. W. Weathers Ditches.**

1868	37.20	NE¼NE¼	24	36	59	4-15—8-15	.458	111.60
1868	25.40	SE¼NE¼	24	36	59	4-15—8-15	.312	76.20
1868	37.50	NE¼SE¼	13	36	59	4-15—8-15	.461	112.50
1870	39.00	SE¼SE¼	13	36	59	4-15—8-15	.480	117.00
1870	10.00	SW¼SE¼	13	36	59	4-15—8-15	.123	30.00
1870	2.80	NE¼NE¼	24	36	59	4-15—8-15	.034	8.40
1870	12.80	NW¼SE¼	24	36	59	4-15—8-15	.157	38.40
1872	6.10	NW¼SE¼	24	36	59	4-15—8-15	.075	18.30
1872	12.70	NW¼NE¼	25	36	59	4-15—8-15	.156	38.10
1872	1.00	SE¼SE¼	13	36	59	4-15—8-15	.012	3.00
1872	2.70	SW¼SE¼	13	36	59	4-15—8-15	.033	8.10
1870	14.60	SE¼NE¼	24	36	59	4-15—8-15	.180	43.80
1868	10.00	NW¼SE¼	24	36	59	4-15—8-15	.123	30.00
1869	4.00	NW¼SE¼	24	36	59	4-15—8-15	.049	12.00
1870	5.10	NW¼SE¼	24	36	59	4-15—8-15	.063	15.30
1878	28.50	SW¼NE¼	24	36	59	4-15—8-15	.351	85.50
1878	11.50	SW¼NE¼	24	36	59	4-15—8-15	.141	34.50
1878	22.60	NW¼NE¼	24	36	59	4-15—8-15	.278	67.80
1878	17.40	NW¼NE¼	24	36	59	4-15—8-15	.214	52.20
1878	27.30	SW¼SE¼	13	36	59	4-15—8-15	.336	81.90
1878	38.30	NW¼SE¼	13	36	59	4-15—8-15	.471	114.90
1878	29.00	SW¼NE¼	13	36	59	4-15—8-15	.357	87.00
1878	9.50	NW¼NE¼	13	36	59	4-15—8-15	.117	28.50
1878	1.50	SW¼NE¼	13	36	59	4-15—8-15	.018	4.50
1878	3.90	W½SE¼	12	36	59	4-15—8-15	.048	11.70
1878	1.40	W½SE¼	12	36	59	4-15—8-15	.017	4.20
1878	3.80	W½SE¼	12	36	59	4-15—8-15	.047	11.40
1888	8.60	SE¼SE¼	2	36	59	4-15—8-15	.106	25.80
1888	10.00	NE¼SE¼	2	36	59	4-15—8-15	.123	30.00
1888	19.30	SE¼SE¼	2	36	59	4-15—8-15	.237	57.90
1888	14.90	NE¼SE¼	2	36	59	4-15—8-15	.183	44.70
1888	27.20	SE¼NE¼	2	36	59	4-15—8-15	.335	81.60
1875	15.90	SW¼SW¼	1	36	59	4-15—8-15	.196	47.70
1875	20.70	NW¼SW¼	1	36	59	4-15—8-15	.255	62.10
1875	2.00	NE¼SE¼	2	36	59	4-15—8-15	.025	6.00
1875	24.20	NW¼NW¼	12	36	59	4-15—8-15	.297	72.60
1875	9.70	NE¼NW¼	12	36	59	4-15—8-15	.119	29.10
1875	22.00	SW¼SW¼	1	36	59	4-15—8-15	.271	66.00
1875	8.40	NE¼NW¼	12	36	59	4-15—8-15	.103	25.20
1888	7.60	NW¼NW¼	12	36	59	4-15—8-15	.093	22.80
1876	7.60	SW¼SW¼	30	36	60	4-15—8-15	.093	22.80

Claimant—**G. E. Weathers.** Proof No. **00508**
Source—**Ackler Creek,* Herder Creek, and Brennens Gulch.** Ditch—**G. E. Weathers Ditches.**

Date of beneficial use — Nat. mdw.	Date of beneficial use — Cult. area	Construction first initiated — Dams	Construction first initiated — Ditches	Culture—Acres — Harvest crops	Culture—Acres — Meadow pasture	Culture—Acres — Willow and sage pasture	Culture—Acres — Swamp or overflow	Location — Subdivision	Location — Section	Location — Tp.N.	Location — R.E.	Length of season	Duty of water — C.F.S.	Duty of water — Acre-feet
	1875			8.00				NE¼	12	36	59	4-15—8-15	.098	24.00
	1888			16.00								4-15—8-15	.197	48.00
	1873			14.00								4-15—8-15	.172	42.00
	1902			11.00								4-15—8-15	.135	33.00
	1888			2.40								4-15—8-15	.295	7.20

*Priority from Ackler Creek through Co-Op Ditch to date 1893.

Source—**Ackler Creek and Starr Creek.** Ditch—**G. E. Weathers Ditches.**

	1875			21.00				NE¼	12	36	59	4-15—8-15	.295	72.00
	1873			21.30								4-15—8-15	.262	63.90

Source—**Boulder Creek and Starr Creek.** Ditch—**G. E. Weathers Ditches.**

	1873			5.50				NE¼	12	36	59	4-15—8-15	.068	16.50
	1875			13.10								4-15—8-15	.161	39.30

Source—**Starr Creek.** Ditch—**Starr Ditch.**

	1878			3.50				NE¼	12	36	59	4-15—8-15	.043	10.50

Claimant—**Union Land and Cattle Co.** Proof No. **00510**
Source—**Starvation Creek, Soldier Creek, Murphy Creek, Ross Creek, Dry Creek.**
Ditch—**Union Land and Cattle Co. Ditches.**

	1874			198.00				E½	22	34	59	4-15—8-15	2.435	594.00
	1900					42.00		E½	22	34	59	4-15—5-15	.517	81.50
	1877			100.00				W½	22	34	59	4-15—8-15	1.230	300.00
	1900					220.00		W½	22	34	59	4-15—5-15	2.706	165.00
	1900					237.00		E½	21	34	59	4-15—5-15	2.915	177.75
	1883			185.00					21	34	59	4-15—8-15	2.276	555.00
	1893			53.00					21	34	59	4-15—8-15	.652	159.00
	1898			93.00				NW¼	21	34	59	4-15—8-15	1.144	279.00
	1895			49.00				SW¼	21	34	59	4-15—8-15	.603	147.00
	1891			160.00				NE¼	20	34	59	4-15—8-15	1.968	480.00
	1893			80.00				E½SE¼	20	34	59	4-15—8-15	.984	240.00
	1877			158.00					27	34	59	4-15—8-15	1.943	474.00
	1883					149.00		E½E½	28	34	59	4-15—5-15	1.833	111.75
	1891					179.00		W½NE¼	28	34	59			
								NW¼	28	34	59			
								NW¼SE¼	28	34	59	4-15—5-15	2.202	134.25
	1894					82.00		SW¼	28	34	59	4-15—5-15	1.008	61.50

Source—**Soldier Creek.** Ditch—**Union Land and Cattle Co. Ditches.**

	1915				22.40			S½	5	34	59	4-15—6-15	.275	33.60
	1879			112.00					4	34	59	4-15—8-15	1.378	330.00

	1880			112.00					5	34	59	4-15—8-15	1.378	336.00
	1881			112.00					32	35	59	4-15—8-15	1.378	336.00
	1882			112.00					29	35	59	4-15—8-15	1.378	336.00
	1883			114.40				S½	20	35	59	4-15—8-15	1.407	343.20
	1883					234.70						4-15—5-15	2.887	176.03

Source—**Soldier Creek, Ross Creek, Murphy Creek, Starvation Creek, Springs.**
Ditch—**Union Land and Cattle Co. Ditches.**

	1880			63.00				W¼W½	9	34	59	4-15—8-15	.775	180.00
	1885			63.00				E½E½	8	34	59	4-15—8-15	.775	180.00
	1890			64.00				NE¼	17	34	59	4-15—8-15	.787	192.00
	1899			160.00				E½	17	34	59	4-15—8-15	1.968	480.00
	1900			109.50								4-15—8-15	1.347	328.50
	1897			37.00				NW¼	16	34	59	4-15—8-15	.455	111.00
	1898			37.00								4-15—8-15	.455	111.00
	1899			37.00								4-15—8-15	.455	111.00
	1900			40.00								4-15—8-15	.492	120.00
	1895			38.00				SW¼	16	34	59	4-15—8-15	.467	114.00
	1896			38.00								4-15—8-15	.467	114.00
	1897			38.00								4-15—8-15	.467	114.00
	1898			39.00								4-15—8-15	.480	117.00

Source—**Soldier Creek.** Ditch—**Union Land and Cattle Co. Ditches.**

	1905				136.70			W¼W½	8	34	59	4-15—6-15	1.681	205.05
								W½W½	17	34	59			
	1880					141.00		E½	8	34	59	4-15—5-15	1.734	105.75
	1885					141.00		E¼SW¼	8	34	59	4-15—5-15	1.734	105.75
	1890					143.00		E½W½	17	34	59	4-15—5-15	1.759	107.25
								W½E½	17	34	59			

Source—**Ross Creek, Starvation Creek, Murphy Creek.**
Ditch—**Union Land and Cattle Co. Ditches.**

	1894			45.00				E½	16	34	59	4-15—8-15	.554	135.00
	1896			20.00								4-15—8-15	.246	60.00
	1898			20.00								4-15—8-15	.246	60.00
	1900			23.00								4-15—8-15	.283	69.00
	1880			23.00				SW¼	15	34	59	4-15—8-15	.283	69.00
	1883			23.00								4-15—8-15	.283	69.00
	1886			23.00								4-15—8-15	.283	69.00
	1887			11.00								4-15—8-15	.135	33.00

Source—**Secret Creek.** Ditch—**Union Land and Cattle Co. Ditches.**

	1874			36.74					34	35	59	4-15—8-15	.452	110.22
	1874					140.91			3	34	59	4-15—5-15	1.733	105.68
	1878			86.37								4-15—8-15	1.062	259.11
	1883			25.00								4-15—8-15	.308	75.00
	1891			22.78								4-15—8-15	.280	68.34
	1890				54.00							4-15—6-15	.664	81.00
	1892				54.00							4-15—6-15	.664	81.00
	1894				54.00							4-15—6-15	.664	81.00
	1897				57.55							4-15—6-15	.708	86.33

Union Land and Cattle Co.—Continued.

Date of beneficial use: Nat. mdw.	Date of beneficial use: Cult. area	Construction first initiated: Dams	Construction first initiated: Ditches	Culture—Acres: Harvest crops	Culture—Acres: Meadow pasture	Culture—Acres: Willow and sage pasture	Culture—Acres: Swamp or overflow	Location: Subdivision	Location: Section	Location: Tp.N.	Location: R.E.	Length of season	Duty of water: C.F.S.	Duty of water: Acre-feet
	1897			142.41								4-15—8-15	1.752	427.23
	1897					51.50						4-15—5-15	.663	38.63
	1882				54.00							4-15—6-15	.664	81.00
	1882				54.00							4-15—6-15	.664	81.00
	1882				54.00							4-15—6-15	.664	81.00
	1882				57.55							4-15—6-15	.708	86.33

Claimant—**E. C. Murphy.** Proof No. 00511

Source—**Boulder Creek.** Ditch—**E. C. Murphy Ditches.**

Nat. mdw.	Cult. area	Dams	Ditches	Harvest crops	Meadow pasture	Willow and sage pasture	Swamp or overflow	Subdivision	Section	Tp.N.	R.E.	Length of season	C.F.S.	Acre-feet
	1869			95.00				SW¼	25	36	59	4-15—8-15	1.169	285.00
	1870			26.30				E½SE¼	26	36	59	4-15—8-15	.323	78.90
	1873			1.60				NW¼NW¼	36	36	59	4-15—8-15	.020	4.80
	1880			40.00								4-15—8-15	.492	120.00
	1889			23.70								4-15—8-15	.292	71.10
	1900			16.00								4-15—8-15	.197	48.00

Source—**Stevens Creek.** Ditch—**E. C. Murphy Ditches.**

Nat. mdw.	Cult. area	Dams	Ditches	Harvest crops	Meadow pasture	Willow and sage pasture	Swamp or overflow	Subdivision	Section	Tp.N.	R.E.	Length of season	C.F.S.	Acre-feet
	1868			104.80				SE¼SE¼	26	36	59	4-15—8-15	1.289	314.40
	1876			5.50				E½NE¼	35	36	59	4-15—8-15	.068	16.50
								NW¼	36	36	59			

Source—**Secret, Wright, Lemon, Dry, and Dorsey Creeks and Springs.**
Ditch—**E. C. Murphy Ditches.**

Nat. mdw.	Cult. area	Dams	Ditches	Harvest crops	Meadow pasture	Willow and sage pasture	Swamp or overflow	Subdivision	Section	Tp.N.	R.E.	Length of season	C.F.S.	Acre-feet
	1879			137.43				S½NW¼	4	34	60	4-15—8-15	1.690	412.29
	1880			53.63				SW¼	4	34	60	4-15—8-15	.660	160.89
	1881			53.63				SE¼	4	34	60	4-15—8-15	.660	160.89
	1882			43.63				E½	5	34	60	4-15—8-15	.537	130.89
	1883			126.23				E½	8	34	60	4-15—8-15	1.553	378.69
	1884			59.60					9	34	60	4-15—8-15	.733	178.80
	1886			10.00				NW¼NW¼	16	34	60	4-15—8-15	.123	30.00
	1887			10.35								4-15—8-15	.127	31.05
	1900			50.90								4-15—8-15	.626	152.70
	1900			78.70								4-15—8-15	.968	236.10
	1900			35.10								4-15—8-15	.432	105.30
	1901			61.20								4-15—8-15	.753	183.60
	1903			42.00								4-15—8-15	.517	126.00
	1905			58.70								4-15—8-15	.722	176.10

Claimant—**S. M. Davis.** Proof No. 00512

Source—**Ackler Creek.** Ditch—**S. M. Davis Ditches.**

Nat. mdw.	Cult. area	Dams	Ditches	Harvest crops	Meadow pasture	Willow and sage pasture	Swamp or overflow	Subdivision	Section	Tp.N.	R.E.	Length of season	C.F.S.	Acre-feet
	1873			2.38				NE¼NW¼	9	36	60	4-15—8-15	.029	7.14
	1873			1.00				NE¼NE¼	9	36	60	4-15—8-15	.012	3.00
	1880			3.30				NE¼NW¼	10	36	60	4-15—8-15	.041	9.90

1888	12.00	NW¼NW¼	10	36	60	4-15—8-15	.148	36.00
1888	3.00	NW¼NW¼	10	36	60	4-15—8-15	.037	9.00
1888	.50	SE¼NW¼	10	36	60	4-15—8-15	.008	1.50
1889	11.80	NW¼NW¼	10	36	60	4-15—8-15	.145	35.40
1891	.80	NE¼NW¼	10	36	60	4-15—8-15	.010	2.40
1891	6.00	SE¼NW¼	10	36	60	4-15—8-15	.074	18.00
1896	15.70	SW¼NW¼	10	36	60	4-15—8-15	.193	47.10
1896	11.50	SE¼NW¼	10	36	60	4-15—8-15	.141	34.50
1896	6.30	SW¼NW¼	10	36	60	4-15—8-15	.077	18.90
1896	12.20	NW¼NW¼	10	36	60	4-15—8-15	.150	36.60
1877	3.00	NE¼NE¼	9	36	60	4-15—8-15	.037	9.00
1896	7.80	NE¼NE¼	9	36	60	4-15—8-15	.096	23.40
1896	1.00	NE¼NE¼	9	36	60	4-15—8-15	.012	3.00
1904	2.00	NE¼NW¼	10	36	60	4-15—8-15	.025	6.00

Claimant—**Wm. Goodale.** Proof No. 00513

Source—**Herder Creek.** Ditch—**Wm. Goodale Ditches.**

1872	10.00	....	4 and 5	36	60	4-15—8-15	.123	30.00
1872	4.90	SW¼SW¼	4	36	60	4-15—8-15	.060	14.70
1875	15.00	SE¼SW¼	4	36	60	4-15—8-15	.185	45.00
1892	18.70	SE¼SW¼	4	36	60	4-15—8-15	.230	56.10
1893	10.00	SW¼SW¼	4	36	60	4-15—8-15	.123	30.00
1894	10.00	SW¼SW¼	4	36	60	4-15—8-15	.123	30.00
1894	14.50	NW¼SE¼	5	36	60	4-15—8-15	.178	43.50
1895	20.50	NE¼SE¼	5	36	60	4-15—8-15	.252	61.50
1895	7.00	SW¼SW¼	4	36	60	4-15—8-15	.086	21.00
1895	25.00	NW¼SE¼	5	36	60	4-15—8-15	.308	75.00
1895	5.00	NE¼SE¼	5	36	60	4-15—8-15	.062	15.00
1898	1.30	NE¼SE¼	5	36	60	4-15—8-15	.016	3.90
1905	1.40	NE¼SE¼	5	36	60	4-15—8-15	.017	4.20
1905	0.90	NE¼SE¼	5	36	60	4-15—8-15	.011	2.70
1898	0.90	NE¼SE¼	5	36	60	4-15—8-15	.011	2.70
1896	5.50	NE¼SE¼	5	36	60	4-15—8-15	.068	16.50

Claimant—**Geo. A. Grock.** Proof No. 00514

Source—**Starr Creek.** Ditch—**Geo. A. Grock Ditches.**

1874	48.10	SW¼NW¼	36	37	59	4-15—8-15	.592	144.30
1902	11.20	N½SW¼	36	37	59	4-15—8-15	.138	33.60
1903	23.90	SE¼SW¼	36	37	59	4-15—8-15	.284	71.70
1904	35.10	W½SE¼	36	37	59	4-15—8-15	.432	105.30
1905	8.60	....	....	...	....	4-15—8-15	.106	25.80

Claimant—**Edward Goodale.** Proof No. 00515

Source—**Stevens Creek.** Ditch—**Nos. 1 and 2.**

1904	94.31	S½SE¼	5	36	59			
		NW¼NE¼	8	36	59			
		E½NE¼	8	36	59	4-15—8-15	1.171	282.93

Claimant—**Alex. Gardner.** Proof No. 00516

Source—**Secret, Wolverton, Covert and Wright Creeks and Springs.**

Ditch—**Alex. Gardner Ditches.**

Date of beneficial use: Nat. mdw.	Date of beneficial use: Cult. area	Construction first initiated: Dams	Construction first initiated: Ditches	Culture—Acres: Harvest crops	Culture—Acres: Meadow pasture	Culture—Acres: Willow and sage pasture	Culture—Acres: Swamp or overflow	Location: Subdivision	Location: Section	Location: Tp.N.	Location: R.E.	Length of season	Duty of water: C.F.S.	Duty of water: Acre-feet
....	1883	....	....	32.48	....	....	....	W½SW¼	16	34	60	4-15—8-15	.400	97.44
....	1884	....	....	32.48	....	....	....	E½W½	16	34	60	4-15—8-15	.400	97.44
....	1885	....	....	32.48	....	....	....	E½	16	34	60	4-15—8-15	.400	97.44
....	1886	....	....	97.44	....	....	....	NW¼NW¼	21	34	60	4-15—8-15	1.199	292.32
....	1887	....	....	97.44	....	....	....	....	....	....	....	4-15—8-15	1.199	292.32
....	1888	....	....	97.45	....	....	....	....	....	....	....	4-15—8-15	1.199	292.35

Source—**Secret Creek.** Ditch—**Alex Gardner Ditches.**

Nat. mdw.	Cult. area	Dams	Ditches	Harvest crops	Meadow pasture	Willow and sage pasture	Swamp or overflow	Subdivision	Section	Tp.N.	R.E.	Length of season	C.F.S.	Acre-feet
....	1883	....	....	21.46	....	....	....	SE¼NE¼	10	34	60	4-15—8-15	.264	64.38
....	1884	....	....	21.46	....	....	....	E½SE¼	10	34	60	4-15—8-15	.264	64.38
								SW¼NW¼	11	34	60			
								W½SW¼	11	34	60			

Source—**Wright Creek.** Ditch—**Alex. Gardner Ditches.**

Nat. mdw.	Cult. area	Dams	Ditches	Harvest crops	Meadow pasture	Willow and sage pasture	Swamp or overflow	Subdivision	Section	Tp.N.	R.E.	Length of season	C.F.S.	Acre-feet
....	1888	....	....	16.91	....	....	....	SE¼SW¼	3	34	60	4-15—8-15	.208	50.73
....	1891	....	....	10.00	....	....	....	E½NW¼	10	34	60	4-15—8-15	.123	30.00

Claimant—**Fred and Frank Cleverly.** Proof No. 00517

Source—**Halls Canon Creek, Blasingame Creek.** Ditch—**Cleverly Ditches.**

Nat. mdw.	Cult. area	Dams	Ditches	Harvest crops	Meadow pasture	Willow and sage pasture	Swamp or overflow	Subdivision	Section	Tp.N.	R.E.	Length of season	C.F.S.	Acre-feet
....	1883	....	....	24.00	....	....	....	....	15	37	60	4-15—8-15	.295	72.00
....	1884	....	....	24.00	....	....	....	....	15	37	60	4-15—8-15	.295	72.00
....	1885	....	....	24.00	....	....	....	....	15	37	60	4-15—8-15	.295	72.00
....	1886	....	....	24.00	....	....	....	....	15	37	60	4-15—8-15	.295	72.00
....	1887	....	....	22.82	....	....	....	....	15	37	60	4-15—8-15	.281	68.46

Claimant—**John G. Lewis.** Proof No. 00518

Source—**Springs.** Ditch—**Lewis Ditches.**

Nat. mdw.	Cult. area	Dams	Ditches	Harvest crops	Meadow pasture	Willow and sage pasture	Swamp or overflow	Subdivision	Section	Tp.N.	R.E.	Length of season	C.F.S.	Acre-feet
....	1901	....	....	4.00	....	....	....	SW¼SW¼	19	37	61	4-15—8-15	.049	12.00
....	1901	....	....	6.71	....	....	....	SE¼SW¼	19	37	61	4-15—8-15	.083	20.13
....	1901	....	....	.63	....	....	....	SW¼SE¼	19	37	61	4-15—8-15	.008	1.89

Claimant—**Isaac Griswold.** Proof No. 00519

Source—**Boulder and Monks Creeks.** Ditch—**Isaac Griswold Ditches.**

1875	3.80			S½NW¼	12	36	59			
1877	3.80			SW¼	12	36	59	4-15—8-15	.047	11.40
1879	3.80			W½	13	36	59	4-15—8-15	.047	11.40
1880	3.90			E½	14	36	59	4-15—8-15	.047	11.40
				E½SW¼	14	36	59	4-15—8-15	.048	11.70
1904	...	172.90		N½	11	36	59			
				S½	14	36	59	4-15—5-15	2.127	129.68

Source—**Monks Creek.** Ditch—**Isaac Griswold Ditches.**

1883	83.80			E½SW¼	14	36	59			
				W½E½	14	36	59			
				SE¼SE¼	14	36	59	4-15—8-15	1.081	251.40

Source—**Boulder Creek.** Ditch—**Isaac Griswold Ditches.**

1873	66.00			S½NW¼	12	36	59	4-15—8-15	.812	198.00
1877	77.90			SW¼	12	36	59	4-15—8-15	.958	233.70
1880	103.30			NW¼	13	36	59	4-15—8-15	1.271	309.90
1883	33.40			E½SW¼	13	36	59	4-15—8-15	.411	100.20
1888	178.20			E½	14	36	59	4-15—8-15	2.192	534.60
1894	13.10			...	...	...	...	4-15—8-15	.161	39.30
1904	31.10			...	...	...	...	4-15—8-15	.383	93.30
1904	...		34.40	...	...	...	...	4-15—5-15	.423	103.20

Source—**Branch of Boulder Creek.** Ditch—**Isaac Griswold Ditches.**

1875	59.20			SW¼NW¼	13	36	59	4-15—8-15	.728	177.60
1880	56.60			W½SW¼	13	36	59	4-15—8-15	.696	169.80
1889	62.80			E½E½	14	36	59	4-15—8-15	.772	188.10

Claimant—**Jno. H.** Cazier & **Sons Company.** Proof. No. 00521

Source—**Blasengame** Creek and **Poverty Gulch.** Ditch—**Cazier & Company Ditches.**

1883	210.10			SW¼SW¼	3	37	60			
				E½SW¼	3	37	60			
				W½SE¼	3	37	60			
				N½NW¼	10	37	60			
				SE¼NW¼	10	37	60			
				W½NE¼	10	37	60	4-15—8-15	2.584	630.30

Source—**Humboldt River and Bishop Creek.** Ditch—**Cazier & Company Ditches.**

1878	100.00			NE¼NE¼	2	37	60			
1879	260.79			W½NE¼	2	37	60			
1880	260.78			NW¼	2	37	60			
				N½SW¼	2	37	60			
				NE¼	3	37	60			
				SE¼	3	37	60			
				S½NW¼	3	37	60	4-15—8-15	1.230	300.00
				N½SW¼	3	37	60	4-15—8-15	3.208	782.37
				SW¼SW¼	3	37	60	4-15—8-15	3.208	782.34

Claimant—**Estate of Samuel McMullen.** Proof No. 00522

Source—**Boulder Creek.** Ditch—**McMullen Ditches.**

Date of beneficial use: Nat. mdw.	Date of beneficial use: Cult. area	Construction first initiated: Dams	Construction first initiated: Ditches	Culture—Acres: Harvest crops	Culture—Acres: Meadow pasture	Culture—Acres: Willow and sage pasture	Culture—Acres: Swamp or overflow	Location: Subdivision	Location: Section	Location: Tp.N.	Location: R.E.	Length of season	Duty of water: C.F.S.	Duty of water: Acre-feet
	1868			40.00				E½NE¼	23	36	59	4-15—8-15	.492	120.00
	1868			40.00				NE¼SE¼	23	36	50	4-15—8-15	.492	120.00
	1868			10.20				NW¼	24	36	50	4-15—8-15	.125	30.60
	1868					29.80		SW¼	24	36	50	4-15—6-15	.367	22.35
	1870			15.00				SW¼SE¼	24	36	59	4-15—8-15	.185	45.00
	1870			38.55				NW¼	25	36	59	4-15—8-15	.474	115.65
	1871			40.00				NE¼	26	36	59	4-15—8-15	.492	120.00
	1875			15.00								4-15—8-15	.185	45.00
	1880			15.00								4-15—8-15	.185	45.00
	1882			40.00								4-15—8-15	.492	120.00
	1883			68.95								4-15—8-15	.848	206.85
	1884			137.44								4-15—8-15	1.691	412.32
	1885			40.00								4-15—8-15	.492	120.00
	1885			15.00								4-15—8-15	.185	45.00
	1887			41.25								4-15—8-15	.507	123.75
	1887			11.15								4-15—8-15	.137	33.45
	1888			39.40								4-15—8-15	.485	118.20
	1888			83.93*								4-15—8-15	1.032	251.79

*No water to be diverted for this land until it becomes dry or is drained.

Source—**Boulder Creek and Stevens Creek.** Ditch—**Samuel McMullen Ditches.**

Nat. mdw.	Cult. area	Dams	Ditches	Harvest crops	Meadow pasture	Willow and sage pasture	Swamp or overflow	Subdivision	Section	Tp.N.	R.E.	Length of season	C.F.S.	Acre-feet
	1883			46.86				W½SE¼	26	36	59	4-15—8-15	.576	140.58
	1888			46.86				SW¼	26	36	59	4-15—8-15	.576	140.58
	1893			46.86				NW¼	26	36	59	4-15—8-15	.576	140.58
	1898			46.86				NE¼	27	36	50	4-15—8-15	.576	140.58
	1902			46.86								4-15—8-15	.576	140.58

Source—**Monks Creek, Stevens Creek, Boulder Creek.** Ditch—**Samuel McMullen Ditches.**

Nat. mdw.	Cult. area	Dams	Ditches	Harvest crops	Meadow pasture	Willow and sage pasture	Swamp or overflow	Subdivision	Section	Tp.N.	R.E.	Length of season	C.F.S.	Acre-feet
	1883				35.00			All	22	36	59	4-15—6-15	.431	52.50
	1888				35.00							4-15—6-15	.431	52.50
	1893				35.00							4-15—6-15	.431	52.50
	1898				35.00							4-15—6-15	.431	52.50
	1902				34.57							4-15—6-15	.425	51.86
	1904				571.75				9	36	59			
									10	36	59			
									15	36	59			
									16	36	59	4-15—6-15	7.033	857.03

Claimant—**Quilici Bros.** Proof No. 00524
Source—**Willow Creek, Lake at head of Trout Creek, and Angel Lake.***
Ditch—**Quilici Bros. Ditches.**

1878	108.70	E½NW¼	3	37	61			
1883	76.60	S½NE¼	3	37	61			
1892	91.70	NE¼SE¼	3	37	61			
		W½SW¼	2	37	61			
		SE¼SW¼	2	37	61			
		E½	10	37	61	4-15—8-15	1.337	326.10
		W½	11	37	61	4-15—8-15	.942	229.80
		W½E½	11	37	61	4-15—8-15	1.165	284.10

*Angel Lake is not a natural tributary to Humboldt River, but water was diverted into Humboldt drainage area by artificial means.

Claimant—**W. G. Randolph.** Proof No. 00525
Source—**Secret Creek.** Ditch—**W. G. Randolph Ditches.**

1882	50.00	All	4	35	48	4-15—8-15	.615	150.00
1883	134.25					4-15—8-15	1.651	402.75

Claimant—**Frank Blundell.** Proof No. 00551
Source—**Walker Creek and Springs.** Ditch—**Blundell, Blundell & Connell.**

1893	116.40	SW¼SW¼	28	42	54			
		N½	33	42	54			
		N½SW¼	33	42	54	4-15—8-15	1.373	349.20

Claimant—**Diana Morgan Hill** (Deed to J. J. Hylton in escrow). Proof No. 00552
Source—**North Fork.** Ditch—**McKee & Clayton.**

1889	146.10	E½NE¼	35	40	56			
		NE¼SE¼	35	40	56			
		NW¼	36	40	56			
		N½SW¼	36	40	56			
		SW¼NE¼	36	40	56			
		NW¼SE¼	36	40	56	4-15—8-15	1.797	438.30

Claimant—**R. T. Evans & Brother.** Proof No. 00553
Source—**Foreman Creek.** Ditch—**R. T. Evans Ditches.**

1888	91.75		7	41	54	4-15—8-15	1.129	275.25
1889	33.50	NE¼NE¼	18	41	54	4-15—8-15	.412	100.50
1890	48.73	W½NW¼	17	41	54	4-15—8-15	.599	146.19
1900	22.50	W½	8	41	54	4-15—8-15	.277	67.50
1901	63.55					4-15—8-15	.782	190.65
1902	98.87					4-15—8-15	1.212	296.61

Source—**Walker Creek.** Ditch—**R. T. Evans Ditches.**

1887	2.00		28	42	54	4-15—8-15	.025	6.00
1892	159.30		28	42	54	4-15—8-15	1.959	477.90

R. T. Evans & Brother—Continued.
Source—**Pratt Creek.** Ditch—**R. T. Evans Ditches.**

Date of beneficial use: Nat. mdw.	Date of beneficial use: Cult. area	Construction first initiated: Dams	Construction first initiated: Ditches	Culture—Acres: Harvest crops	Culture—Acres: Meadow pasture	Culture—Acres: Willow and sage pasture	Culture—Acres: Swamp or overflow	Location: Subdivision	Location: Section	Location: Tp.N.	Location: R.E.	Length of season	Duty of water: C.F.S.	Duty of water: Acre-feet
....	1895	....	....	23.47	....	....	....	NW¼NE¼	3	41	54	4-15—8-15	.289	70.41
....	1896	....	....	23.47	....	....	....	N½NW¼	3	41	54	4-15—8-15	.289	70.41
....	1904	....	....	23.46	....	....	....	....	....	....	....	4-15—8-15	.289	70.38

Source—**Foreman Creek, Winters Creek, California Creek, and Springs.**
Ditch—**R. T. Evans Ditches.**

Nat. mdw.	Cult. area	Dams	Ditches	Harvest crops	Meadow pasture	Willow and sage pasture	Swamp or overflow	Subdivision	Section	Tp.N.	R.E.	Length of season	C.F.S.	Acre-feet
....	1889	....	....	20.00	....	....	....	E½W½	17	41	54	4-15—8-15	.246	60.00
....	1890	....	....	...	....	98.50	....	E½	17	41	54	4-15—5-15	1.212	73.88
....	1890	....	....	186.80	....	....	....	W½W½	16	41	54	4-15—8-15	2.298	560.40
....	1891	....	....	73.46	....	....	....	E½NW¼	16	41	54	4-15—8-15	.904	220.38
....	1892	....	....	182.56	....	....	....	NE¼SW¼	16	41	54	4-15—8-15	2.245	547.68
....	1899	....	....	18.20	....	....	....	NE¼	20	41	54	4-15—8-15	.224	54.60
....	1902	....	....		....	200.30	....	E½SE¼	20	41	54	4-15—5-15	2.464	150.22
....	1903	....	....	70.75	....	....	....	W½W½	21	41	54	4-15—8-15	.870	212.25
....	1893	....	....	191.01	....	....	....	NE¼NE¼	29	41	54	4-15—8-15	2.349	573.03
....	1901	....	....	131.62	....	....	....	NW¼	28	41	54	4-15—8-15	1.619	394.86
								E½SW¼	28	41	54			
								NW¼SE¼	28	41	54			

Claimant—**C. B. Evans.** Proof No. 00553
Source—**Forney Creek, Branch of Forney Creek, Pratt Creek, and Springs.**
Ditch—**C. B. Evans Ditches.**

Nat. mdw.	Cult. area	Dams	Ditches	Harvest crops	Meadow pasture	Willow and sage pasture	Swamp or overflow	Subdivision	Section	Tp.N.	R.E.	Length of season	C.F.S.	Acre-feet
....	1903	....	....	945.20	....	....	....	S½	3	41	54			
								S½NW¼	3	41	54			
								SE¼NE¼	3	41	54			
								SE¼NE¼	4	41	54			
								SE¼	4	41	54			
								All	9	41	54			
								N½NE¼	8	41	54			
								All	10	41	54	4-15—8-15	11.626	2835.60

Claimant—**Mrs. C. Glaser.** Proof No. 00555
Source—**Pie Creek.** Ditch—**Nos. 3 and 4.**

Nat. mdw.	Cult. area	Dams	Ditches	Harvest crops	Meadow pasture	Willow and sage pasture	Swamp or overflow	Subdivision	Section	Tp.N.	R.E.	Length of season	C.F.S.	Acre-feet
....	1889	....	....	25.00	....	....	....	NE¼	7	39	56			
....	1890	....	....	32.60	....	....	....	N½SE¼	7	39	56	4-15—8-15	.308	75.00
....	1891	....	....	32.60	....	....	....	SW¼SE¼	7	39	56	4-15—8-15	.401	97.80
....	1892	....	....	32.80	....	....	....	SE¼SW¼	7	39	56	4-15—8-15	.401	97.80
								NE¼NW¼	18	39	56	4-15—8-15	.403	98.40

Claimant—**C. A. & L. M. Laing.** Proof No. 00556

Source—**North Fork Humboldt River.** Ditch—**Laing Ditches.**

....	1870	....	....	79.30	....	....	....	SE¼	25	42	54			
....	1876	....	....	79.30	....	....	....	E½	30	42	54	4-15—8-15	0.975	237.90
....	1880	....	....	79.20	....	....	....	SW¼NW¼	31	42	55	4-15—8-15	0.974	237.60
....	1880	....	....	5.00	....	....	....	SW¼	31	42	55	4-15—8-15	0.974	237.60
....	1884	....	....	144.00	....	....	....	S½SE¼	31	42	55	4-15—8-15	0.062	15.00
....	1886	....	....	39.40	....	....	....	N½NE¼	6	41	55	4-15—8-15	1.771	432.00
....	1898	....	....	39.30	....	....	....	SE¼NE¼	6	41	55	4-15—8-15	0.484	118.20
....	1898	....	....	80.00	....	....	....	SW¼NW¼	5	41	55	4-15—8-15	0.483	117.90
....	1902	....	....	57.00	....	....	....	SW¼	5	41	55	4-15—8-15	0.984	240.00
								E½NW¼	8	41	55	4-15—8-15	0.701	171.00

Source—**Pratt Creek.** Ditch—**Laing Ditches.**

....	1870	....	....	233.50	....	....	....	NW¼SE¼	36	42	54			
....	1876	....	....	233.50	....	....	....	S½SE¼	36	42	54			
....	1880	....	....	233.40	....	....	....	S½SW¼	31	42	55			
								SE¼NW¼	1	41	54			
								NE¼	1	41	54			
								....	6	41	55			
								W½SW¼	5	41	55	4-15—8-15	2.872	700.50
								NE¼NE¼	7	41	55	4-15—8-15	2.872	700.50
								NW¼NW¼	8	41	55	4-15—8-15	2.871	700.20

Claimant—**G. F. McKnight.** Proof No. 00557

Source—**North Fork.** Ditch—**Burns, McKnight, Harrah and Doll.**

....	1896	....	....	41.00	....	....	....	E½NW¼	26	39	57	4-15—8-15	.504	123.00
....	1898	....	....	44.50	....	....	....	SW¼	26	39	57	4-15—8-15	.547	133.50
....	1903	....	....	23.90	....	....	....	SW¼SE¼	26	39	57	4-15—8-15	.294	81.70

Claimant—**Howard Morse.** Proof No. 00558

Source—**Peterson Creek and Springs.** Ditch—**Howard Morse Ditches.**

....	1888	....	....	....	131.00	....	....	E½	8	42	54	4-15—6-15	1.611	196.50
....	1888	....	....	136.80	....	....	....	W½	9	42	54	4-15—8-15	1.683	410.40
....	1889	....	....	....	24.30	....	....	NE¼	9	42	54	4-15—6-15	.299	36.50
....	1889	....	....	26.70	....	....	....	N½SE¼	9	42	54	4-15—8-15	.328	80.10
....	1890	....	....	26.00	....	....	....	W½NW¼	10	42	54	4-15—8-15	.320	78.00
....	1890	....	....	....	11.30	....	....	NW¼SW¼	10	42	54	4-15—6-15	.139	17.00
....	1891	....	....	....	11.30	....	....	S½S½	4	42	54	4-15—6-15	.139	17.00
....	1891	....	....	26.00	....	....	....	....	....	....	....	4-15—8-15	.320	78.00
....	1892	....	....	46.00	....	....	....	....	....	....	....	4-15—8-15	.566	138.00
....	1892	....	....	....	11.30	....	....	....	....	....	....	4-15—6-15	.139	17.00
....	1893	....	....	20.00	....	....	....	....	....	....	....	4-15—8-15	.246	60.00
....	1894	....	....	....	16.70	....	....	....	....	....	....	4-15—6-15	.205	25.05
....	1894	....	....	23.50	....	....	....	....	....	....	....	4-15—8-15	.289	70.50
....	1903	....	....	....	41.40	....	....	....	....	....	....	4-15—6-15	.509	62.20
....	1904	....	....	....	85.00	....	....	....	....	....	....	4-15—6-15	1.046	127.50

Claimant—**Chas. L. Nuckols.** Proof No. 00559
Source—**North Fork Humboldt River and Peterson Creek.** Ditch—**Nuckols.**

Date of beneficial use: Nat. mdw.	Date of beneficial use: Cult. area	Construction first initiated: Dams	Construction first initiated: Ditches	Culture—Acres: Harvest crops	Culture—Acres: Meadow pasture	Culture—Acres: Willow and sage pasture	Culture—Acres: Swamp or overflow	Location: Subdivision	Location: Section	Location: Tp.N.	Location: R.E.	Length of season	Duty of water: C.F.S.	Duty of water: Acre-feet
	1899			7.00				SW¼	3	42	54	4-15—8-15	0.086	21.00
	1899			371.96				E½NW¼	10	42	54	4-15—8-15	4.575	1115.88
	1900			72.43				W½E½	10	42	54	4-15—8-15	0.891	217.29
	1901			28.49				E½SE¼	10	42	54	4-15—8-15	0.350	85.47
	1905			35.95				E½	15	42	54	4-15—8-15	0.442	107.85
								W½SW¼	14	42	54			
								NW¼	23	42	54			

Claimant—**T. S. Park.** Proof No. 00560
Source—**Dorsey Creek.** Ditch—**Park Ditches.**

Date of beneficial use: Nat. mdw.	Date of beneficial use: Cult. area	Construction first initiated: Dams	Construction first initiated: Ditches	Culture—Acres: Harvest crops	Culture—Acres: Meadow pasture	Culture—Acres: Willow and sage pasture	Culture—Acres: Swamp or overflow	Location: Subdivision	Location: Section	Location: Tp.N.	Location: R.E.	Length of season	Duty of water: C.F.S.	Duty of water: Acre-feet
	1865			9.81				NW¼SW¼	13	37	54	4-15—8-15	.121	29.43
	1865			1.09				NE¼SW¼	13	37	54	4-15—8-15	.013	3.27
	1865			16.54				SW¼SW¼	13	37	54	4-15—8-15	.203	49.62
	1865					3.45		SW¼SW¼	13	37	54	4-15—5-15	.042	2.58
	1865			1.27				SE¼SW¼	13	37	54	4-15—8-15	.016	3.81
	1865					18.44		SE¼SW¼	13	37	54	4-15—5-15	.227	13.83
	1865			7.45				SW¼SE¼	13	37	54	4-15—8-15	.092	22.35
	1865					3.99		SW¼SE¼	13	37	54	4-15—5-15	.049	2.99
	1865			12.54				SW¼NE¼	14	37	54	4-15—8-15	.154	67.62
	1865			3.44				SE¼NW¼	14	37	54	4-15—8-15	.042	10.32
	1865			9.63				NW¼SE¼	14	37	54	4-15—8-15	.118	28.89
	1901					19.99		NW¼SE¼	14	37	54	4-15—5-15	.246	14.99
	1865			24.36				NE¼SE¼	14	37	54	4-15—8-15	.300	73.08
	1901					2.36		NE¼SE¼	14	37	54	4-15—5-15	.029	1.77
	1865			3.87				SE¼SE¼	14	37	54	4-15—8-15	.048	11.61
	1901					4.90		SE¼SE¼	14	37	54	4-15—5-15	.060	3.68
	1865			15.63				NE¼NE¼	24	37	54	4-15—8-15	.192	46.89
	1865			11.63				NW¼NE¼	24	37	54	4-15—8-15	.143	34.89
	1865					.90		NW¼NE¼	24	37	54	4-15—5-15	.011	.68
	1865			2.18				SE¼NE¼	24	37	54	4-15—8-15	.027	6.54

Claimant—**Estate** of Thos. Kearns. Proof No. 00561
Source—**North Fork** and Tributaries. Ditch—**Thos. Kearns Ditches.**

Date of beneficial use: Nat. mdw.	Date of beneficial use: Cult. area	Construction first initiated: Dams	Construction first initiated: Ditches	Culture—Acres: Harvest crops	Culture—Acres: Meadow pasture	Culture—Acres: Willow and sage pasture	Culture—Acres: Swamp or overflow	Location: Subdivision	Location: Section	Location: Tp.N.	Location: R.E.	Length of season	Duty of water: C.F.S.	Duty of water: Acre-feet
	1888			10.00				SE¼SW¼	[illegible]	42	54			
								SW¼SE¼	22	42	54			
								NW¼NE¼	[illegible]	42	54	4-15—8-15	.123	30.00
	1888			180.20				SW¼	15	42	54			
	1889			60.10				SE¼SE¼	16	42	54			
								NW¼	[illegible]	42	54	4-15—8-15	2.216	540.60
								W½NE¼	[illegible]	42	54	4-15—8-15	.730	180.30
	1889			15.00				NE¼NE¼	21	42	54	4-15—8-15	.185	45.00
	1889			28.80				N½NW¼	27	42	54			
								NE¼	[illegible]	42	54	4-16—8-15	.354	86.40

1880	90.00		NE¼	27	42	54			
			SE¼NW¼	27	42	54			
			NE¼SW¼	27	42	54			
			NW¼SE¼	27	42	54			
			SW¼NW¼	26	42	54	4-15—8-15	1.107	270.00
1890	21.60		W½NW¼	26	42	54			
			E½NE¼	27	42	54	4-15—8-15	.266	64.80
1894	197.00		E½	21	42	54	4-15—8-15	2.423	591.00
1895	175.70		S½NW¼	26	42	54			
			E½SW¼	26	42	54			
			SE¼	26	42	54	4-15—8-15	2.161	527.10
1895	10.60		S½SW¼	22	42	54			
			NE¼NW¼	27	42	54	4-15—8-15	1.300	31.80
1896	197.10		S½NW¼	22	42	54			
			SW¼	22	42	54			
			W½SE¼	22	42	54			
			N½NE¼	27	42	54	4-15—8-15	2.424	591.30
1896	27.00		W½SE¼	22	42	54	4-15—8-15	.332	81.00
1899	96.80		E½SE¼	22	42	54			
			W½SW¼	23	42	54			
			SW¼SW¼	23	42	54			
			NE¼NE¼	27	42	54			
			NW¼	26	42	54			
			W½NW¼	26	42	54	4-15—8-15	1.190	290.40
1901	20.90		SE¼SW¼	22	42	54			
			SW¼SE¼	22	42	54			
			NE¼NW¼	27	42	54			
			NW¼NE¼	27	42	54	4-15—8-15	.257	62.70
1902	40.50		SE¼	26	42	54	4-15—8-15	.498	121.50
1904	30.10		N½SE¼	26	42	54			
			SE¼SE¼	26	42	54	4-15—8-15	.370	90.30
1905	8.80		N½SE¼	27	42	54	4-15—8-15	.108	26.40
1890	45.10		SW¼	25	42	54	4-15—8-15	.555	135.30
1904	73.00		SW¼	25	42	54			
			N½NW¼	36	42	54	4-15—8-15	.808	219.00
1895	151.80		NW¼	36	42	54	4-15—8-15	1.867	455.40

Tributaries are McAfee Creek, Dell Creek, Spring Creek, Walker Creek Branch of **Walker Creek, and Springs.**

Claimant—**Geo. W. Pratt.** Proof No. 00562

Source—**McAfee Creek.** Ditch—**Geo. W. Pratt Ditches.**

1889	49.00		SE¼NE¼	35	42	54	4-15—8-15	1.033	147.00
1889	....	84.00	N½SW¼	36	42	54	4-15—8-15	.602	63.00

Source—**Pratt Creek and Springs.** Ditch—**Geo. W. Pratt Ditches.**

1887	154.90		SW¼	36	42	54			
1888	96.70		SE¼SE¼	35	42	54			
1889	26.00		NE¼NE¼	2	41	54			
1890	145.70		S½N½	2	41	54	4-15—8-15	1.906	464.70
1898	31.10		N½S½	2	41	54	4-15—8-15	1.189	290.10
			W½NW¼	1	41	54	4-15—8-15	0.319	78.00
			NE¼NW¼	1	41	54	4-15—8-15	1.792	437.10
			SW¼NE¼	3	41	54	4-15—8-15	0.383	93.30

Proof No. 00563

Claimant—**Frank Rutherford.**
Source—**North Fork Humboldt.** Ditch—**Rutherford.**

Date of beneficial use: Nat. mdw.	Date of beneficial use: Cult. area	Construction first initiated: Dams	Construction first initiated: Ditches	Culture—Acres: Harvest crops	Culture—Acres: Meadow pasture	Culture—Acres: Willow and sage pasture	Culture—Acres: Swamp or overflow	Location: Subdivision	Location: Section	Location: Tp.N.	Location: R.E.	Length of season	Duty of water: C.F.S.	Duty of water: Acre-feet
	1890			45.82					4	42	54	4-15—8-15	0.564	137.46
	1892			84.80				NE¼NE¼	5	42	54	4-15—8-15	1.043	254.40
	1893			100.58								4-15—8-15	1.975	481.74
	1899			17.00								4-15—8-15	0.209	51.00

Proof No. 00565

Claimant—**Rose M. Tremewan.**
Source—**Mahala Creek.** Ditch—**Austin Gilruth Ditches.**

Nat. mdw.	Cult. area	Dams	Ditches	Harvest crops	Meadow pasture	Willow and sage pasture	Swamp or overflow	Subdivision	Section	Tp.N.	R.E.	Length of season	C.F.S.	Acre-feet
	1888			144.01				E½W½	1	39	54			
	1897			66.47				SE¼	1	39	54			
	1899			12.38				N½	7	39	55			
								N¼SE¼	7	39	55			
								SW¼SW¼	4	39	55	4-15—8-15	1.771	432.03
								SE¼SE¼	5	39	55	4-15—8-15	.818	199.41
								SE¼NE¼	4	39	56	4-15—8-15	.152	37.14

Proof No. 00566

Source—**East Fork Beaver Creek.** Ditch—**Diana Morgan Hill Ditches.**
Claimant—**Diana Morgan Hill** (Deed to J. J. Hylton in escrow).

Nat. mdw.	Cult. area	Dams	Ditches	Harvest crops	Meadow pasture	Willow and sage pasture	Swamp or overflow	Subdivision	Section	Tp.N.	R.E.	Length of season	C.F.S.	Acre-feet
	1893			20.00				N½NW¼	17	40	57	4-15—8-15	.246	60.00
	1894			21.85				S½SW¼	8	40	57	4-15—8-15	.269	65.55

Proof No. 00567

Claimant—**Williams Estate Company.**
Source—**North Fork Humboldt River and Springs.** Ditch—**Williams Estate Co. Ditches.**

Nat. mdw.	Cult. area	Dams	Ditches	Harvest crops	Meadow pasture	Willow and sage pasture	Swamp or overflow	Subdivision	Section	Tp.N.	R.E.	Length of season	C.F.S.	Acre-feet
	1888			186.14					36	40	55			
									1	39	55			
									6	39	56	4-15—8-15	2.290	558.42

Proof No. 00568

Claimant—**Samuel McIntyre.**
Source—**North Fork of Humboldt.** Ditch—**Samuel McIntyre Ditches.**

Nat. mdw.	Cult. area	Dams	Ditches	Harvest crops	Meadow pasture	Willow and sage pasture	Swamp or overflow	Subdivision	Section	Tp.N.	R.E.	Length of season	C.F.S.	Acre-feet
								W½SE¼ & N½SW¼	36	39	57			
	1888			147.00				E¼NW¼				4-15—8-15	1.808	441.00
	1889			147.00				NW¼SW¼ & SE¼SW¼	1	38	57	4-15—8-15	1.808	441.00
	1890			140.73				E½	12	38	57	4-15—8-15	1.842	449.19

Proof No. 00569

Claimant—**John McKee.**
Source—**North Fork of Humboldt River.** Ditch—**John McKee Ditches.**

Nat. mdw.	Cult. area	Dams	Ditches	Harvest crops	Meadow pasture	Willow and sage pasture	Swamp or overflow	Subdivision	Section	Tp.N.	R.E.	Length of season	C.F.S.	Acre-feet
								SE¼SE¼	27	40	56			
	1889			140.78				E½NE¼	34	40	56	4-15—8-15	1.732	422.84
	1908			71.01				N½	35	40	56	4-15—8-15	.873	213.03

Claimant—**J. Leslie Carter.** Proof No. 00569

Source—**North Fork of Humboldt River.** Ditch—**J. Leslie Carter Ditches.**

1889	72.23	SE¼SW¼	27	40	56			
		SW¼SE¼	27	40	56			
		NW¼	34	40	56			
		NW¼NE¼	34	40	56			
		E½NE¼	33	40	56	4-15—8-15	.888	216.69

Claimant—**G. F. McKnight.** Proof No. 00570

Source—**North Fork Humboldt River.** Ditch—**Doll.**

1903	10.60	SW¼SE¼	15	39	57	4-15—8-15	.112	31.80
1903	0.62	SE¼SE¼	15	39	57	4-15—8-15	.076	1.86
1903	8.66	NW¼NE¼	22	39	57	4-15—8-15	.107	25.98
1903	9.26	NE¼NE¼	22	39	57	4-15—8-15	.114	27.78

Claimant—**Saval Livestock Co.** Proof No. 00571

Source—**Ganz Creek and Springs.** Ditch—**Saval Co.**

1885	10.00		4	39	54	4-15—8-15	0.123	30.00
1886	10.00		5	39	54	4-15—8-15	0.123	30.00
1887	10.00		9	39	54	4-15—8-15	0.123	30.00
1894	100.00		10	39	54	4-15—8-15	1.230	300.00
1895	80.00		15	39	54	4-15—8-15	0.984	240.00
1896	80.00		14	39	54	4-15—8-15	0.984	240.00
1897	90.00		13	39	54	4-15—8-15	1.107	270.00
1905	168.60		24	39	54	4-15—8-15	2.074	505.80

Claimant—**R. B. Stewart.** Proof No. 00572

Source—**Pie, Willow, Clay Hill, and Red Hill Creeks.** Ditch—**R. B. Stewart Ditches.**

1888	254.83	SE¼SW¼	26	39	54
1891	65.61	E½NW¼	35	39	54
		W½NE¼	35	39	54
		SW¼	35	39	54
		W½SE¼	35	39	54
		N½NW¼	2	38	54
		SW¼NW¼	2	38	54
		SE¼NE¼	3	38	54
		NE¼SE¼	3	38	54
		W½NE¼	10	38	54
		NE¼NW¼	10	38	54
		S½NW¼	10	38	54
		N½SW¼	10	38	54
		N½SE¼	9	38	54
		SW¼SE¼	9	38	54
		SE¼SW¼	9	38	54
		NW¼	16	38	54
		N½SW¼	16	38	54
		SW¼SW¼	16	38	54
		E½SE¼	17	38	54

R. B. Stewart—Continued.

Date of beneficial use: Nat. mdw.	Cult. area	Construction first initiated: Dams	Ditches	Culture—Acres: Harvest crops	Meadow pasture	Willow and sage pasture	Swamp or overflow	Location: Subdivision	Section	Tp.N.	R.E.	Length of season	Duty of water: C.F.S.	Acre-feet
								S¼NE¼	19	38	54			
								N¼SE¼	19	38	54			
								SW¼SE¼	19	38	54			
								S¼SW¼	19	38	54			
								NW¼NW¼	30	38	54	4-15—8-15	3.134	764.49
								SE¼NE¼	25	38	53	4-15—8-15	.806	196.83

Claimant—**Warner Griswold.** Proof No. 00573
Source—**Ganz Creek.** Ditch—**Warner Griswold Ditches.**

	1885			67.00					24	39	54			
	1886			67.00					19	39	55	4-15—8-15	0.824	201.00
	1887			67.00					20	39	55	4-15—8-15	0.824	201.00
	1888			67.00					21	39	55	4-15—8-15	0.824	201.00
	1889			69.90					27	39	55	4-15—8-15	0.824	201.00
									28	39	55	4-15—8-15	0.860	209.70

Claimant—**Chas. S. and Aleck Wieland.** Proof No. 00574
Source—**Springs and Pie or McClellan Creek.** Ditch—**Wieland Ditches.**

	1886			106.00					32	39	55	4-15—8-15	1.230	300.00
	1887			185.41					33	39	55	4-15—8-15	2.281	556.23
	1900			39.00					..	....	....	4-15—8-15	0.480	117.00

Claimant—**Williams Estate Company.** Proof No. 00575
Source—**North Fork Humboldt River.** Ditch—**Williams Estate Co. Ditches.**

	1888			239.64				SW¼SE¼	8	41	55	4-15—8-15	2.948	718.02
	1890			116.90				E½	17	41	55	4-15—8-15	1.438	350.70
	1891			40.50				E½	20	41	55	4-15—8-15	0.498	121.50
	1892			214.00				E½	29	41	55	4-15—8-15	2.632	642.00
								E½	32	41	55			

Claimant—**Diana Morgan Hill** (Deed to J. J. Hylton in escrow). Proof No. 00576
Source—**North Fork Humboldt River.** Ditch—**Diana Morgan-Hill Ditches.**

	1872			161.80					16	40	55			
	1873			161.80					21	40	55			
	1890			341.80					28	40	55	4-15—8-15	1.990	485.40
	1902			49.20					27	40	55	4-15—8-15	1.990	485.40
									33	40	55	4-15—8-15	4.204	1025.40
	1873			150.00					34	40	55	4-15—8-15	0.005	117.00
	1888			266.50					2 & 3	36	57			
									10 & 15	36	57			

1892	260.50		21 & 22	36	57			
1896	266.50		34 & 27 & 28	36	57			
1900	266.50		1 & 2 & 10	37	57			
1904	266.40		11 & 12	37	57	4-15—8-15	1.845	450.00
1904	301.60		14 & 15	37	57	4-15—8-15	3.278	799.50
			22 & 23	37	57	4-15—8-15	3.278	799.50
			26 & 27	37	57	4-15—8-15	3.278	799.50
			34 & 35	37	57	4-15—8-15	3.278	799.50
			24 & 25	38	57	4-15—8-15	3.277	799.20
			35 & 36	38	57	4-15—8-15	4.448	1084.80

Source—**Springs.** Ditch—**Diana Morgan-Hill Ditches.**

1898	434.00	W½	15	41	54			
			16	41	54	4-15—8-15	5.338	1302.00
1898	241.00	N¼	21	41	54			
		NW¼	22	41	54	4-15—8-15	2.964	723.00

Source—**Dry Creek and Springs.** Ditch—**Diana Morgan-Hill Ditches.**

1898	125.70	S½	25	41	54			
		SW¼	30	41	55			
		NE¼ NW¼	31	41	55	4-15—8-15	1.546	377.10

Source—**Springs and Foreman Creek.** Ditch—**Diana Morgan-Hill Ditches.**

1876	680.10	SW¼	22	41	54			
		SW¼ NE¼	21	41	54			
		SE¼ NE¼	21	41	54			
		S½	21	41	54			
			27	41	54			
			28	41	54	4-15—8-15	8.365	2040.30
1889	822.80	NE¼ NE¼	33	41	54			
			34	41	54			
		S½	35	41	54			
			2	40	54			
		N½ NE¼	3	40	54			
		W½	1	40	54	4-15—8-15	10.120	2468.40
1886	492.00	E½	1	40	54			
			6	40	55			
			5	40	55			
		SW¼ SW¼	4	40	55	4-15—8-15	6.052	1476.00

Claimant—**J. J. Hylton.** Proof No. 00576

Source—**Stump Creek.** Ditch—**Hylton and Clayton.**

1889	99.65	SE¼ SW¼	3	40	54			
		SE¼	3	40	54			
		N½ SW¼	2	40	54			
		S½ N½	2	40	54	4-15—8-15	1.226	298.95

Claimant—**J. J. Hylton Bros.** Proof No. 00576
Source—**North Fork.** Ditch—**Hylton.**

Date of beneficial use: Nat. mdw.	Cult. area	Construction first initiated: Dams	Ditches	Culture—Acres: Harvest crops	Meadow pasture	Willow and sage pasture	Swamp or overflow	Location: Subdivision	Section	Tp.N.	R.E.	Length of season	Duty of water: C.F.S.	Acre-feet
	1905				6.36			NE¼NE¼	36	38	57	4-15—6-15	.078	9.54
	1905				1.20			SE¼NE¼	36	38	57	4-15—6-15	.015	1.80
	1905				7.60			SE¼SE¼	25	38	57	4-15—6-15	.093	11.41
	1905				2.84			NE¼SE¼	25	38	57	4-15—6-15	.035	4.26
	1905			1.31				SE¼NE¼	25	38	57	4-15—8-15	.016	3.93
	1908				6.88			Lot 2	30	38	58	4-15—6-15	.085	10.32
	1905				8.21			Lot 3	30	38	58	4-15—6-15	.101	12.32
	1905				3.60			Lot 4	30	38	58	4-15—6-15	.044	5.40
	1905			16.70				NW¼NE¼	19	38	57	4-15—8-15	.205	50.10

Claimant—**Union Land and Cattle Co.** Proof No. 00601
Source—**Mary's River.** Ditch—**Cold Spring.**

Nat. mdw.	Cult. area	Dams	Ditches	Harvest crops	Meadow pasture	Willow and sage pasture	Swamp or overflow	Subdivision	Section	Tp.N.	R.E.	Length of season	C.F.S.	Acre-feet
	1896				11.50			SE¼	19	40	60	4-15—6-15	.141	17.25
	1896				12.15			SE¼	19	40	60	4-15—6-15	.149	18.23
	1899				53.21			SE¼	6	39	60	4-15—6-15	.654	79.82
	1899				32.18			E½SW¼	6	39	60	4-15—6-15	.396	48.27
	1896				22.58			NE¼	7	39	60	4-15—6-15	.278	33.87
	1896				9.49			NE¼	7	39	60	4-15—6-15	.117	14.24
	1896				32.22			SE¼	7	39	60	4-15—6-15	.396	48.33
	1896				12.22			SE¼	7	39	60	4-15—6-15	.150	18.33
	1899				32.41			W½NE¼	7	39	60	4-15—6-15	.399	48.62
	1899				7.93			E½SW¼	7	39	60	4-15—6-15	.098	11.90
	1899				4.42			NW¼SE¼	7	39	60	4-15—6-15	.054	6.63
	1899				0.91			NW¼	7	39	60	4-15—6-15	.011	1.37
	1896				10.79			SE¼SW¼	7	39	60	4-15—6-15	.133	16.19
	1896				53.53			E½NE¼	31	40	60	4-15—6-15	.658	81.30
	1896				70.13			SE¼	31	40	60	4-15—6-15	.863	105.20
	1898				78.18			NE¼	31	40	60	4-15—6-15	.962	117.27
	1898					21.76		NE¼	31	40	60	4-15—5-15	.268	16.32
	1898				56.47			NW¼	31	40	60	4-15—6-15	.695	84.71
	1898					19.35		NW¼	31	40	60	4-15—5-15	.238	14.51
	1898				44.63			W½SE¼	31	40	60	4-15—6-15	.549	66.95
	1898					26.80		W½SE¼	31	40	60	4-15—5-15	.330	20.10
	1898				70.41			SW¼	31	40	60	4-15—6-15	.866	105.62
	1898					54.19		SW¼	31	40	60	4-15—5-15	.666	40.64
	1896				9.65			W½NW¼	32	40	60	4-15—6-15	.119	14.48

Source—**Mary's River.** Ditch—**Commatele.**

Nat. mdw.	Cult. area	Dams	Ditches	Harvest crops	Meadow pasture	Willow and sage pasture	Swamp or overflow	Subdivision	Section	Tp.N.	R.E.	Length of season	C.F.S.	Acre-feet
	1899				10.56			SW¼SE¼	18	41	60	4-15—6-15	.180	15.84
	1899				47.90			NE¼	19	41	60	4-15—6-15	.580	71.86
	1899				24.55			E½NW¼	19	41	60	4-15—6-15	.302	30.83
	1899				14.77			SE¼	19	41	60	4-15—6-15	.182	22.10
	1899				92.11			SW¼	19	41	60	4-15—6-15	1.138	188.17

	1899				80.07			SW¼	30	41	60	4-15—6-15	1.006	133.61
	1899					.30		SW¼	30	41	60	4-15—5-15	.004	.23
	1899				88.01			NW¼	30	41	60	4-15—6-15	1.068	132.02
	1899				7.72			SW¼	31	41	60	4-15—6-15	.095	11.58
	1899					23.23		SW¼	31	41	60	4-15—5-15	.286	17.42
	1899				17.91			NW¼	31	41	60	4-15—6-15	.222	26.87
	1899					36.15		NW¼	31	41	60	4-15—5-15	.444	27.22
	1899				.66			SW¼SE¼	31	41	60	4-15—6-15	.008	.99
	1900				2.90			NW¼	8	40	60	4-15—6-15	.036	4.35
	1900				3.73			NW¼	5	40	60	4-15—6-15	.046	5.60
	1899				72.84			NE¼	6	40	60	4-15—6-15	.896	109.26
	1899				32.90			E½SE¼	6	40	60	4-15—6-15	.405	49.35
	1899				51.88			SE¼	6	40	60	4-15—6-15	.638	77.82
	1900				1.05			SE¼NW¼	7	40	60	4-15—6-15	.013	1.58
	1899				3.40			E½NE¼	7	40	60	4-15—6-15	.042	5.10
	1899					21.90		E½NE¼	7	40	60	4-15—5-15	.269	16.43
	1899				84.23			NE¼	7	40	60	4-15—6-15	1.046	126.35
	1900				53.19			SE¼	7	40	60	4-15—6-15	.654	80.79

Source—**Mary's River.** Ditch—**Sloughs formed by Beaver Dams.**

	1885				37.96			W½	18	39	60	4-15—6-15	.467	56.94
	1885				54.47			NE¼	26	39	59	4-15—6-15	.670	81.71
	1885				39.78			SE¼	26	39	59	4-15—6-15	.489	59.67
	1885				9.49			SW¼	26	39	59	4-15—6-15	.117	14.24
	1885				2.08			NW¼	35	39	59	4-15—6-15	.026	3.12
	1885				26.13			NE¼	35	39	59	4-15—6-15	.321	39.20
	1885				52.79			SE¼	55	39	59	4-15—6-15	.649	79.19
	1885				1.56			SE¼	2	38	59	4-15—6-15	.019	2.34
	1885				24.44			NE¼	2	38	59	4-15—6-15	.301	36.66

Source—**Mary's River.** Ditch—**Rosebud.**

	1899				30.60			NW¼	7	39	60	4-15—6-15	.376	45.90
	1899					121.80		NW¼	7	39	60	4-15—5-15	1.498	91.35
	1899				13.39			W½NE¼	7	39	60	4-15—6-15	.165	20.09
	1899				33.05			SW¼	7	39	60	4-15—6-15	.407	49.58
	1899					102.36		SW¼	7	39	60	4-15—5-15	1.259	76.77
	1898				2.12			E½E½	1	39	59	4-15—6-15	.026	3.18
	1898					21.15		E½E½	1	39	59	4-15—5-15	.260	15.86
	1898				36.75			W½W½	31	40	60	4-15—6-15	.452	55.13
	1898				11.01			E½SE¼	36	40	59	4-15—6-15	.135	16.52
	1898					3.24		E½SE¼	36	40	59	4-15—5-15	.040	2.43
	1898				41.41			SW¼	6	39	60	4-15—6-15	.509	62.12
	1898					80.52		SW¼	6	39	60	4-15—5-15	.990	60.50
	1898				26.99			W½NW¼	6	39	60	4-15—6-15	.332	40.49
	1898					20.06		W½NW¼	6	39	60	4-15—5-15	.247	15.05
	1898				2.60			SW¼SE¼	6	39	60	4-15—6-15	.032	3.90
	1901				104.53			NW¼	18	39	60	4-15—6-15	1.287	156.80
	1901					5.97		NW¼	18	39	60	4-15—5-15	.073	4.48
	1901				25.71			SW¼	18	39	60	4-15—6-15	.317	38.61
	1898					76.72		E½E½	12	39	59	4-15—5-15	.944	57.54
	1901					24.14		E½NE¼	13	39	59	4-15—5-15	.300	18.09

Union Land and Cattle Co.—Continued.
Source—**Mary's River.** Ditch—**Pot Hole.**

Date of beneficial use: Nat. mdw.	Cult. area	Construction first initiated: Dams	Ditches	Culture—Acres: Harvest crops	Meadow pasture	Willow and sage pasture	Swamp or overflow	Location: Subdivision	Section	Tp.N.	R.E.	Length of season	Duty of water: C.F.S.	Acre-feet
	1899				55.17			E½NE¼	18	40	60	4-15—6-15	.679	82.76
	1899				38.85			E½SE¼	18	40	60	4-15—6-15	.478	58.28
	1899				10.94			E½SE¼	18	40	60	4-15—6-15	.135	16.41
	1900				32.60			W½SW¼	8	40	60	4-15—6-15	.401	48.90
	1899				8.66			SE¼SE¼	6	40	60	4-15—6-15	.107	12.99
	1899				13.35			NE¼NE¼	7	40	60	4-15—6-15	.164	20.03
	1899				49.63			E½SE¼	7	40	60	4-15—6-15	.610	74.55
	1899				1.85			SE¼	7	40	60	4-15—6-15	.022	2.78
	1899				34.31			W½NW¼	17	40	60	4-15—6-15	.423	51.57
	1899				78.43			W½SW¼	17	40	60	4-15—6-15	.719	87.65
	1899				60.21			E½NE¼	19	40	60	4-15—6-15	.741	90.32
	1899				4.77			NE¼	19	40	60	4-15—6-15	.059	7.16
	1899				50.70			SE¼	19	40	60	4-15—6-15	.624	76.05
	1899				36.92			W½W½	20	40	60	4-15—6-15	.454	55.38
	1899				4.50			NW¼	29	40	60	4-15—6-15	.055	6.75
	1899				8.40			NE¼NE¼	30	40	60	4-15—6-15	.103	12.60

Source—**Mary's River.** Ditch—**Spring Gulch.**

Nat. mdw.	Cult. area	Dams	Ditches	Harvest crops	Meadow pasture	Willow and sage pasture	Swamp or overflow	Subdivision	Section	Tp.N.	R.E.	Length of season	C.F.S.	Acre-feet
	1899				8.66			SW¼SE¼	6	41	60	4-15—6-15	.107	12.99
	1899				2.67			SE¼SW¼	6	41	60	4-15—6-15	.033	4.01
	1899				45.83			NE¼	7	41	60	4-15—6-15	.564	68.75
	1899				21.80			NW¼	7	41	60	4-15—6-15	.268	32.70
	1899				48.55			SW¼	7	41	60	4-15—6-15	.597	72.83
	1899				32.50			SE¼	7	41	60	4-15—6-15	.400	48.75
	1899					43.15		SE¼	7	41	60	4-15—5-15	.531	32.36
	1899				25.34			E½NW¼	18	41	60	4-15—6-15	.312	38.01
	1899				99.65			NE¼	18	41	60	4-15—6-15	1.236	149.48
	1899				62.43			SE¼	18	41	60	4-15—6-15	.768	92.65
	1899				21.12			NE¼SW¼	18	41	60	4-15—6-15	.260	31.68

Source—**Mary's River.** Ditch—**Horse Pasture.**

Nat. mdw.	Cult. area	Dams	Ditches	Harvest crops	Meadow pasture	Willow and sage pasture	Swamp or overflow	Subdivision	Section	Tp.N.	R.E.	Length of season	C.F.S.	Acre-feet
	1884				57.90			NE¼	23	38	59	4-15—6-15	.712	86.85
	1884				19.40			NE¼SE¼	23	38	59	4-15—6-15	.239	29.10
	1885				8.60			SE¼SE¼	23	38	59	4-15—6-15	.106	12.90
	1884				124.90			SW¼	13	38	59	4-15—6-15	1.536	187.35
	1884				50.20			S½NW¼	13	38	59	4-15—6-15	.617	75.30
	1884				62.32			E½NE¼	14	38	59	4-15—6-15	.767	93.48
	1884				0.50			NW¼SE¼	14	38	59	4-15—6-15	.006	.75
	1884				65.30			E½SE¼	14	38	59	4-15—6-15	.803	97.95
	1884				131.60			NW¼	24	38	59	4-15—6-15	1.619	197.40
	1884				54.80			N½SW¼	24	38	59	4-15—6-15	.674	82.20
	1885				43.68			SW¼	24	38	59	4-15—6-15	.537	65.52
	1885				14.40			W½SE¼	24	38	59	4-15—6-15	.177	21.60
	1886				72.17			SE¼	36	38	59	4-15—6-15	.888	108.20

	1886					10.82		SE¼	36	38	59	4-15—5-15	.153	8.12
	1886				58.70			NE¼	36	38	59	4-15—6-15	.723	88.19
	1886					25.98		NE¼	36	38	59	4-15—5-15	.320	19.49
	1886				67.02			NE¼	1	37	59	4-15—6-15	.824	100.53
	1886					8.30		NE¼	1	37	59	4-15—5-15	.102	6.23
	1886				53.04			E½SE¼	1	37	59	4-15—6-15	.652	79.56
	1885				31.70			NW¼	25	38	59	4-15—6-15	.391	47.60
	1886				67.54			W½SE¼	25	38	59	4-15—6-15	.831	101.10
	1886				12.43			SW¼	25	38	59	4-15—6-15	.153	18.65
	1886					26.04		SW¼	25	38	59	4-15—5-15	.320	19.53
	1886				51.56			NW¼	7	37	60	4-15—6-15	.634	77.34
	1886					2.68		NW¼	7	37	60	4-15—5-15	.033	2.01
	1886				0.50			NE¼SW¼	7	37	60	4-15—6-15	.006	.75
	1886				5.83			NE¼NE¼	12	37	59	4-15—6-15	.072	8.75
	1886				9.60			NW¼	6	37	60	4-15—6-15	.118	14.40
	1886					1.82		NW¼	6	37	60	4-15—5-15	.022	1.37
	1886				48.98			SW¼	6	37	60	4-15—6-15	.602	73.47
	1885				16.33			W½NE¼	25	38	59	4-15—6-15	.201	24.50
	1885					26.40		W½NE¼	25	38	59	4-15—5-15	.325	19.80

Source—**Mary's River.** Ditch—**Check Dams and Small Natural Sloughs.**

	1885				102.57			W½	31	42	60	4-15—6-15	1.262	153.86
	1885				70.04			W½E½	31	42	60	4-15—6-15	.861	105.06
	1885				107.42			NW¼	6	41	60	4-15—6-15	1.321	161.13
	1885					17.15		NW¼	6	41	60	4-15—5-15	.211	12.86
	1885				7.65			NE¼	6	41	60	4-15—6-15	.094	11.48
	1885				83.79			SW¼	6	41	60	4-15—6-15	1.031	125.69
	1885				0.79			SE¼	6	41	60	4-15—6-15	.010	1.19
	1885				16.49			SW¼	7	41	60	4-15—6-15	.203	24.74
	1885				0.66			NE¼	7	41	60	4-15—6-15	.008	.99
	1885				42.63			NW¼	7	41	60	4-15—6-15	.524	63.95
	1885				26.26			W½	19	41	60	4-15—6-15	.323	39.39

Source—**Mary's River.** Ditch—**Natural Slough.**

	1885				54.17			NW¼	19	42	60	4-15—6-15	.666	81.26
	1885				28.37			E½SW¼	30	42	60	4-15—6-15	.349	42.56
	1885				13.58			N½SW¼	30	42	60	4-15—6-15	.167	20.37
	1904				4.82			SW¼NE¼	30	42	60	4-15—6-15	.059	7.23
	1904				4.35			SE¼NW¼	30	42	60	4-15—6-15	.054	6.53
	1885				45.91			NE¼	18	40	60	4-15—6-15	.565	68.87
	1885				41.55			S½	18	40	60	4-15—6-15	.511	63.33
	1885				1.84			SE¼NW¼	7	40	60	4-15—6-15	.023	2.76
	1885				26.92			SW¼	7	40	60	4-15—6-15	.311	40.38
	1885				52.77			SE¼	7	40	60	4-15—6-15	.649	79.16

Source—**Mary's River.** Ditch—**Buena Vista.**

	1901				4.22			SW¼SW¼	19	41	60	4-15—6-15	.052	6.33
	1901				51.86			W½NW¼	30	41	60	4-15—6-15	.638	77.79
	1902				55.72			W½SW¼	30	41	60	4-15—6-15	.070	83.58
	1902				93.08			NW¼	31	41	60	4-15—6-15	1.144	139.59
	1902				112.09			SW¼	31	41	60	4-15—6-15	1.379	168.14

Union Land and Cattle Co.—Continued.

Date of beneficial use — Nat. mdw.	Date of beneficial use — Cult. area	Construction first initiated — Dams	Construction first initiated — Ditches	Culture—Acres — Harvest crops	Culture—Acres — Meadow pasture	Culture—Acres — Willow and sage pasture	Culture—Acres — Swamp or overflow	Location — Subdivision	Location — Section	Location — Tp.N.	Location — R.E.	Length of season	Duty of water — C.F.S.	Duty of water — Acre-feet
	1903				10.56			NE¼NW¼	18	40	60	4-15—6-15	.130	15.84
	1902				47.62			W½NE¼	6	40	60	4-15—6-15	.586	71.43
	1902				73.22			E½NW¼	6	40	60	4-15—6-15	.901	109.83
	1902				56.62			W½NW¼	6	40	60	4-15—6-15	.819	84.93
	1902				53.97			E½SW¼	6	40	60	4-15—6-15	.664	80.96
	1902				50.11			E½NW¼	7	40	60	4-15—6-15	.851	88.67
	1902				24.80			W½NE¼	7	40	60	4-15—6-15	.305	37.20
	1903				3.56			W½NE¼	7	40	60	4-15—6-15	.044	5.34
	1902				19.00			W½SW¼	7	40	60	4-15—6-15	.234	28.50
Source—Mary's River. Ditch—Cold Spring.														
	1896				42.58			NE¼	6	39	60	4-15—6-15	.524	63.87
	1896				42.45			SE¼	6	39	60	4-15—6-15	.522	63.68
	1896				2.60			SE¼	6	39	60	4-15—6-15	.034	3.90
	1899				49.50			NE¼	6	39	60	4-15—6-15	.609	74.25
	1899					24.52		NE¼	6	39	60	4-15—5-15	.302	18.39
	1899				99.12			NW¼	6	39	60	4-15—6-15	1.219	148.68
	1899					9.70		NW¼	6	39	60	4-15—5-15	.119	7.28
	1896				4.97			NW¼NE¼	18	39	60	4-15—6-15	.061	7.46
	1896				48.87			W½W½	29	40	60	4-15—6-15	.601	73.31
	1896				61.71			E½NE¼	30	40	60	4-15—6-15	.759	92.57
	1896				29.60			E½SE¼	30	40	60	4-15—6-15	.364	44.40
	1897				45.70			W½SE¼	30	40	60	4-15—6-15	.562	68.55
	1897				3.25			W½NE¼	30	40	60	4-15—6-15	.040	4.88
	1897				3.25			SE¼NW¼	30	40	60	4-15—6-15	.040	4.88
	1897				129.89			SE¼	30	40	60	4-15—6-15	1.598	194.84
	1897				57.80			SW¼	30	40	60	4-15—6-15	.711	86.70
	1897				8.73			SE¼NE¼	30	40	60	4-15—6-15	.107	13.10
Source—Taber and Pole Creeks. Ditch—Nos. 1 and 2.														
	1899				1.27			SE¼NW¼	14	39	60	4-15—6-15	.016	1.91
	1899				102.16			SW¼	14	39	60	4-15—6-15	1.257	153.24
	1899				45.72			W½NW¼	14	39	60	4-15—6-15	.562	68.58
	1899				5.39			E½NE¼	15	39	60	4-15—6-15	.066	8.09
	1899				.30			NE¼SE¼	15	39	60	4-15—6-15	.004	.45
	1899					71.95		N½	23	39	60	4-15—5-15	.885	53.96
	1900					29.10		NW¼	23	39	60	4-15—5-15	.358	21.83
	1900				116.63			SW¼	23	39	60	4-15—6-15	1.435	174.95
Source—Taber and Pole Creeks. Ditch—No. 1.														
	1899				43.73			NW¼	14	39	60	4-15—6-15	.538	65.60
	1899					29.24		NW¼	14	39	60	4-15—5-15	.360	21.93
	1899				37.48			E½SW¼	14	39	60	4-15—6-15	.461	56.22
	1899				31.66			W½SE¼	14	39	60	4-15—6-15	.389	47.40
	1899				37.00			E½NW¼	14	39	60	4-15—6-15	.455	55.50

	1899					51.97		N½	23	39	60	4-15—5-15	.689	38.96
	1899				1.00			NW¼SE¼	23	39	60	4-15—6-15	.012	1.50
	1900				7.00			SW¼NE¼	23	39	60	4-15—6-15	.086	10.50
	1900					113.02		SE¼	23	39	60	4-15—5-15	1.890	84.77
	1900					123.00		NE¼	26	39	60	4-15—5-15	1.513	92.25
	1900					133.00		S½	26	30	60	4-15—6-15	1.635	99.75

Source—**Taber Creek.** Ditch—**No. 1.**

	1893					71.80		E½	12	40	60	4-15—5-15	.883	58.85
	1900					110.00		W½	26	39	60	4-15—5-15	1.353	82.50

Source—**Taber Creek.** Ditch—**Nos. 1, 2 and 3.**

	1899			1.27				SW¼SW¼	31	41	61	4-15—8-15	.016	3.81
	1899			76.00				N½	6	40	61	4-15—8-15	.935	228.00
	1900			38.97				N½	6	40	61	4-15—8-15	.479	86.91
	1899					123.34		W½	6	40	61	4-15—5-15	1.517	92.51

Source—**Taber Creek.** Ditch—**No. 2.**

	1886				8.10			SE¼SW¼	12	40	60	4-15—6-15	.100	12.15
	1886				46.00			E½	12	40	60	4-15—6-15	.566	69.00
	1886				.42			NW¼NE¼	13	40	60	4-15—6-15	.005	.63
	1886				11.50			NE¼NW¼	13	40	60	4-15—6-15	.141	17.25

Source—**Taber Creek.** Ditch—**No. 3.**

	1885				12.63			SW¼NW¼	12	40	60	4-15—6-15	.155	18.95
	1885				24.42			NW¼SE¼	12	40	60	4-15—6-15	.300	36.63
	1885				23.00			NE¼SW¼	12	40	60	4-15—6-15	.283	34.50
	1885				31.38			SE¼SW¼	12	40	60	4-15—6-15	.386	47.07
	1885				4.68			NW¼SW¼	12	40	60	4-15—6-15	.058	7.02
	1885				32.51			SW¼SW¼	12	40	60	4-15—6-15	.400	48.77
	1885				.64			SW¼NW¼	12	40	60	4-15—6-15	.008	.96
	1885				13.77			NE¼NW¼	12	40	60	4-15—6-15	.160	20.66
	1885				33.79			NW¼NW¼	12	40	60	4-15—6-15	.416	50.69
	1885				13.91			SW¼SW¼	12	40	60	4-15—6-15	.171	20.87

Source—**Taber Creek.** Ditch—**No. 4.**

	1901				2.98			NE¼NE¼	14	40	60	4-15—6-15	.037	4.47
	1901				20.30			SE¼NE¼	14	40	60	4-15—6-15	.250	30.45
	1901				18.88			NW¼SE¼	14	40	60	4-15—6-15	.232	28.20
	1901				7.81			NE¼SE¼	14	40	60	4-15—6-15	.096	11.72

Source—**Taber Creek.** Ditch—**Nos. 4 and 5.**

	1901				70.71			E½	11	40	60	4-15—6-15	.870	106.07
	1901				38.78			NW¼NW¼	14	40	60	4-15—6-15	.477	58.17
	1901				35.78			SW¼SE¼	14	40	60	4-15—6-15	.440	53.67

Source—**Taber Creek.** Ditch—**No. 5.**

	1901					50.90		E½	11	40	60	4-15—5-15	.626	38.18
	1901					7.00		NE¼	11	40	60	4-15—5-15	.086	5.25
	1901				2.84			NE¼NW¼	14	40	60	4-15—6-15	.035	4.26

Union Land and Cattle Co.—Continued.

Source—**Curran Creek.** Ditch—**No. (?)**

Date of beneficial use: Nat. mdw.	Date of beneficial use: Cult. area	Construction first initiated: Dams	Construction first initiated: Ditches	Culture—Acres: Harvest crops	Culture—Acres: Meadow pasture	Culture—Acres: Willow and sage pasture	Culture—Acres: Swamp or overflow	Location: Subdivision	Location: Section	Location: Tp.N.	Location: R.E.	Length of season	Duty of water: C.F.S.	Duty of water: Acre-feet
	1902				29.82			W½E½	19	42	60	4-15—6-15	.367	44.73
	1902				15.80			NW¼	19	42	60	4-15—6-15	.194	23.70
	1902					16.50		NW¼	19	42	60	4-15—5-15	.203	12.38
	1902				13.29			E½SW¼	19	42	60	4-15—6-15	.163	19.94
	1902				48.24			W½E½	30	42	60	4-15—6-15	.593	72.36
	1902					48.60		W½E½	30	42	60	4-15—5-15	.598	36.45
	1902				14.12			SW¼	18	42	60	4-15—6-15	.174	21.18
	1902				68.82			SE¼	18	42	60	4-15—6-15	.846	103.23
	1902				17.16			SE¼	18	42	60	4-15—6-15	.211	25.74

Source—**Curran Creek.** Ditch—**No. 1.**

Nat. mdw.	Cult. area	Dams	Ditches	Harvest crops	Meadow pasture	Willow and sage pasture	Swamp or overflow	Subdivision	Section	Tp.N.	R.E.	Length of season	C.F.S.	Acre-feet
	1903				1.87			SW¼NW¼	19	42	60	4-15—6-15	.023	2.81
	1903				5.53			SE¼NW¼	19	42	60	4-15—6-15	.065	8.30
	1903				8.00			NE¼SW¼	19	42	60	4-15—6-15	.098	12.00

Source—**T Creek.** Ditch—**No. 2.**

Nat. mdw.	Cult. area	Dams	Ditches	Harvest crops	Meadow pasture	Willow and sage pasture	Swamp or overflow	Subdivision	Section	Tp.N.	R.E.	Length of season	C.F.S.	Acre-feet
	1901				18.52			SW¼	18	42	60	4-15—6-15	.228	27.78
	1901				6.46			SE¼	18	42	60	4-15—6-15	.079	9.69

Source—**T Creek.** Ditch—**No. 1.**

Nat. mdw.	Cult. area	Dams	Ditches	Harvest crops	Meadow pasture	Willow and sage pasture	Swamp or overflow	Subdivision	Section	Tp.N.	R.E.	Length of season	C.F.S.	Acre-feet
	1901				50.94			SW¼	18	42	60	4-15—6-15	.627	76.41
	1901					6.81		SW¼	18	42	60	4-15—5-15	.084	5.11
	1901				2.83			N½	18	42	60	4-15—6-15	.035	4.25

Source—**T Creek.** Ditch—**Natural Slough.**

Nat. mdw.	Cult. area	Dams	Ditches	Harvest crops	Meadow pasture	Willow and sage pasture	Swamp or overflow	Subdivision	Section	Tp.N.	R.E.	Length of season	C.F.S.	Acre-feet
	1885				28.37			E½SW¼	30	42	60	4-15—6-15	.349	42.56
	1885				13.58			W½SE¼	30	42	60	4-15—6-15	.167	20.37
	1885				4.82			SW¼NE¼	30	42	60	4-15—6-15	.059	7.23
	1885				4.32			SE¼NW¼	30	42	60	4-15—6-15	.054	6.53

Source—**Hank's Creek.** Ditch—**Nos. 1 and 2.**

Nat. mdw.	Cult. area	Dams	Ditches	Harvest crops	Meadow pasture	Willow and sage pasture	Swamp or overflow	Subdivision	Section	Tp.N.	R.E.	Length of season	C.F.S.	Acre-feet
	1899					51.05		S½	36	42	59	4-15—5-15	.628	38.20

Source—**Bishop Creek.** Ditch—**McCausland.**

Nat. mdw.	Cult. area	Dams	Ditches	Harvest crops	Meadow pasture	Willow and sage pasture	Swamp or overflow	Subdivision	Section	Tp.N.	R.E.	Length of season	C.F.S.	Acre-feet
	1883				81.70			NW¼	20	37	60	4-15—6-15	1.004	122.55
	1883				19.60			SW¼	20	37	60	4-15—6-15	.241	29.40
	1883				91.25			SE¼	19	37	60	4-15—6-15	1.122	136.78
	1883				6.24			NE¼	19	37	60	4-15—6-15	.077	9.36
	1883				93.09			NE¼	30	37	60	4-15—6-15	1.145	139.64
	1883				43.09			NW¼	30	37	60	4-15—6-15	.530	64.64
	1883				68.30			SW¼	30	37	60	4-15—6-15	.840	102.45
	1883				5.83			SE¼SE¼	25	37	59	4-15—6-15	.072	8.75

	1883				13.56			NW¼	36	37	59	4-15—6-15	.107	20.34
	1883					13.00		NW¼	36	37	59	4-15—5-15	.100	9.75
	1883				39.55			NE¼	36	37	59	4-15—6-15	.486	59.33
	1883				3.70			NW¼	31	37	59	4-15—6-15	.046	5.55

Source—**Bishop Creek.** Ditch—**Various sloughs and small ditches.**

	1883				27.05			NW¼	20	37	60	4-15—6-15	.333	40.61
	1883				182.19			E½	19	37	60	4-15—6-15	2.241	273.29
	1883				88.00			SW¼	19	37	60	4-15—6-15	1.090	132.90
	1883				163.69			W½	30	37	60	4-15—6-15	2.013	245.42
	1883				181.83			E½	25	37	59	4-15—6-15	2.237	272.75
	1883				40.16			SW¼	25	37	59	4-15—6-15	.497	60.25
	1883				10.85			NE¼	36	37	59	4-15—6-15	.133	16.28
	1883					4.05		NE¼	36	37	59	4-15—5-15	.050	8.04
	1883				26.38			NW¼	36	37	59	4-15—6-15	.324	39.57
	1883					15.91		NW¼	36	37	59	4-15—5-15	.196	11.93

Source—**Mary's River.** Ditch—**No. 1.**

	1904				2.40			SW¼NW¼	19	42	60	4-15—6-15	.030	3.60
	1904				42.10			SW¼	19	42	60	4-15—6-15	.518	63.15
	1904				36.70			SW¼	13	42	59	4-15—6-15	.451	55.05
	1904				21.91			NE¼NW¼	24	42	59	4-15—6-15	.269	32.87
	1904				38.00			NE¼	24	42	59	4-15—6-15	.467	57.00
	1904				27.98			SE¼	24	42	59	4-15—6-15	.344	41.97
	1904				2.64			NW¼NW¼	24	42	59	4-15—6-15	.032	3.96
	1904				15.12			NW¼	30	42	60	4-15—6-15	.186	22.68
	1904					12.32		NW¼	30	42	60	4-15—5-15	.152	9.24
	1904				27.44			SW¼	30	42	60	4-15—6-15	.338	41.16

Source—**Mary's River.** Ditch—**No. 2.**

	1904				41.92			SW¼	19	42	60	4-15—6-15	.505	62.53
	1904					43.96		SW¼	19	42	60	4-15—5-15	.541	32.97
	1904				3.19			SW¼SE¼	19	42	60	4-15—6-15	.039	4.79
	1904				10.52			NW¼	19	42	60	4-15—6-15	.129	15.78
	1904					16.44		NW¼	19	42	60	4-15—5-15	.202	12.33
	1904				19.11			SW¼	13	42	59	4-15—6-15	.235	28.67
	1904				24.27			NE¼	24	42	59	4-15—6-15	.290	36.41
	1904				5.94			NE¼NW¼	24	42	59	4-15—6-15	.073	8.91
	1904				20.76			NW¼	30	42	60	4-15—6-15	.339	31.14
	1904				4.43			NW¼NE¼	30	42	60	4-15—6-15	.054	6.65
	1904				2.37			NE¼SW¼	30	42	60	4-15—6-15	.029	3.56

Source—**Mary's River.** Ditch—**Cross.**

	1900					27.17		NE¼	35	38	59	4-15—5-15	.334	20.38
	1900				14.20			NE¼SE¼	35	38	59	4-15—6-15	.175	21.30
	1900			36.43				W½NE¼	23	38	59	4-15—8-15	.448	109.26
	1900				21.92			W½NE¼	23	38	59	4-15—6-15	.270	32.88
	1900			28.53				E½NW¼	23	38	59	4-15—8-15	.351	85.59
	1900			4.96				NW¼SE¼	23	38	59	4-15—8-15	.061	14.78
	1900				2.44			NW¼SE¼	23	38	59	4-15—6-15	.030	3.66
	1900			19.17				NE¼SW¼	23	38	59	4-15—8-15	.236	57.51

Union Land and Cattle Co.—Continued.

Date of beneficial use: Nat. mdw.	Date of beneficial use: Cult. area	Construction first initiated: Dams	Construction first initiated: Ditches	Culture—Acres: Harvest crops	Culture—Acres: Meadow pasture	Culture—Acres: Willow and sage pasture	Culture—Acres: Swamp or overflow	Location: Subdivision	Location: Section	Location: Tp.N.	Location: R.E.	Length of season	Duty of water: C.F.S.	Duty of water: Acre-feet
	1900			2.30				SE¼SW¼	23	38	59	4-15—8-15	.028	6.90
	1900				0.56			SW¼SE¼	23	38	59	4-15—6-15	.007	.84
	1901			14.20				SW¼SE¼	23	38	59	4-15—8-15	.175	42.60
	1901			17.04				SE¼SW¼	23	38	59	4-15—8-15	.210	51.12
	1901				12.20			W½NW¼	36	38	59	4-15—6-15	.150	18.30
	1901			67.98				NE¼	26	38	59	4-15—8-15	.836	203.94
	1901				10.56			NE¼	26	38	59	4-15—6-15	.130	15.84
	1901			20.10				E½NW¼	26	38	59	4-15—8-15	.247	60.30
	1901			82.89				SE¼	26	38	59	4-15—8-15	1.020	248.67
	1901				4.37			SE¼	26	38	59	4-15—6-15	.054	6.56
	1901					32.37		SE¼	26	38	59	4-15—5-15	.398	24.28
	1900			35.58				NE¼	35	38	59	4-15—8-15	.438	107.24
	1900				20.31			NE¼	35	38	59	4-15—6-15	.250	30.47

Source—**Mary's River.** Ditch—**Cross Ditch and overflow from Beaver Dams.**

Nat. mdw.	Cult. area	Dams	Ditches	Harvest crops	Meadow pasture	Willow and sage pasture	Swamp or overflow	Subdivision	Section	Tp.N.	R.E.	Length of season	C.F.S.	Acre-feet
	1885			1.54				SE¼	14	38	59	4-15—8-15	.056	13.62
	1885				65.60			SE¼	14	38	59	4-15—6-15	.807	98.40
	1885				2.40			SW¼	14	38	59	4-15—6-15	.030	3.60
	1885				68.12			NE¼	11	38	59	4-15—6-15	.838	102.18
	1885				31.50			NW¼	11	38	59	4-15—6-15	.387	47.25
	1885				96.63			SE¼	11	38	59	4-15—6-15	1.189	144.95
	1885				66.83			SW¼	11	38	59	4-15—6-15	.822	100.25
	1885				93.97			NE¼	14	38	59	4-15—6-15	1.156	140.95
	1885				43.50			NW¼	14	38	59	4-15—6-15	.535	65.25

Source—**Mary's River.** Ditch—**Anderson.**

Nat. mdw.	Cult. area	Dams	Ditches	Harvest crops	Meadow pasture	Willow and sage pasture	Swamp or overflow	Subdivision	Section	Tp.N.	R.E.	Length of season	C.F.S.	Acre-feet
	1886				39.20			NE¼	23	38	59	4-15—6-15	.482	58.80
	1886				106.94			SE¼	23	38	59	4-15—6-15	1.315	160.41
	1886				69.94			NW¼	36	38	59	4-15—6-15	.860	104.91
	1886					17.23		NW¼	36	38	59	4-15—5-15	.212	12.92
	1886				121.34			SW¼	36	38	59	4-15—6-15	1.491	182.01
	1886				112.33			NW¼	1	37	59	4-15—6-15	1.382	168.50
	1886					6.98		NW¼	1	37	59	4-15—5-15	.086	5.24
	1886				92.00			SW¼	1	37	59	4-15—6-15	1.132	138.00
	1886				23.19			W½NW¼	25	38	59	4-15—6-15	.285	34.79
	1886					.84		W½NW¼	25	38	59	4-15—5-15	.010	.63
	1886				20.07			W½SW¼	25	38	59	4-15—6-15	.247	30.11
	1886					33.48		W½SW¼	25	38	59	4-15—5-15	.412	25.11
	1886				.20			SE¼SW¼	25	38	59	4-15—6-15	.002	.30
	1886				66.20			NE¼	26	38	59	4-15—6-15	.814	99.30
	1886					8.90		NE¼	26	38	59	4-15—5-15	.109	6.68
	1886					21.47		E½SE¼	26	38	59	4-15—5-15	.264	16.10
	1886				4.70			SE¼SE¼	35	38	59	4-15—6-15	.058	7.05
	1886				66.40			NW¼	12	37	59	4-15—6-15	.817	99.60
	1886				17.00			NE¼SW¼	12	37	59	4-15—6-15	.209	25.50

Source—**Mary's River.** Ditch—**Cabin Field.**

1884	7.17		S½NE¼	20	39	59	4-15—6-15	.088	10.76
1884	35.66		SE¼	26	39	59	4-15—6-15	.438	53.49
1884	55.65		NE¼	35	39	59	4-15—6-15	.684	83.48
1884	37.65		SE¼	35	39	59	4-15—6-15	.463	56.48
1884	.85		SW¼SW¼	30	39	59	4-15—6-15	.010	1.28
1885	44.30		W½W½	1	38	59	4-15—6-15	.545	66.45
1885		8.88	W½W½	1	38	59	4-15—5-15	.209	6.66
1884	1.00		NE¼SE¼	2	38	59	4-15—6-15	.012	1.50
1885	92.17		SE¼	2	38	59	4-15—6-15	1.134	138.26
1885		49.28	SE¼	2	38	59	4-15—5-15	.606	36.96
1885	98.68		NE¼	2	38	59	4-15—6-15	1.214	148.02
1885	16.70		NE¼	11	38	59	4-15—6-15	.200	25.05
1886	49.78		NE¼	11	38	59	4-15—6-15	.612	74.67
1886		17.04	NE¼	11	38	59	4-15—5-15	.210	12.78
1886	52.00		E½SE¼	11	38	59	4-15—6-15	.640	78.00
1885	4.30		W½W½	12	38	59	4-15—6-15	.053	6.45
1886	28.19		W½W½	12	38	50	4-15—6-15	.347	42.29
1886		1.92	W½W½	12	38	59	4-15—5-15	.024	1.44
1880	34.06		NW¼NW¼	13	38	59	4-15—6-15	.419	51.09

Source—**Mary's River.** Ditch—**Greasewood.**

1885	96.06		NW¼	25	38	50	4-15—6-15	1.182	144.09
1885	57.81		SW¼	25	38	59	4-15—6-15	.711	86.72
1885	60.98		SW¼	24	38	59	4-15—6-15	.750	91.47
1885	14.56		NE¼NW¼	36	38	59	4-15—6-15	.179	21.84
1885	1.40		NW¼NE¼	36	38	59	4-15—6-15	.017	2.10

Source—**Mary's River.** Ditch—**Nos. 1 and 2.**

1900	7.25		SE¼SW¼	7	41	60	4-15—6-15	.089	10.88
1900	61.75		NW¼	18	41	60	4-15—6-15	.760	92.63
1900	75.24		SW¼	18	41	60	4-15—6-15	.925	112.36
1900	6.33		SW¼SE¼	18	41	60	4-15—6-15	.078	9.50

Source—**Mary's River.** Ditch—**King Pin.**

1898	9.24		NE¼NW¼	18	40	60	4-15—6-15	.113	13.86
1898	17.55		W½NE¼	18	40	60	4-15—6-15	.216	26.33
1898	38.06		W½NE¼	18	40	60	4-15—6-15	.468	57.09
1898	36.91		E½NW¼	18	40	60	4-15—6-15	.454	55.37
1898	18.48		E½NW¼	18	40	60	4-15—6-15	.227	26.72
1898	81.74		SE¼	18	40	60	4-15—6-15	1.005	122.61
1898	11.07		SE¼	18	40	60	4-15—6-15	.136	16.61
1898	28.11		SW¼	18	40	60	4-15—6-15	.346	42.17
1898	29.30		SW¼	7	40	60	4-15—6-15	.360	43.95
1898	48.69		NE¼	19	40	60	4-15—6-15	.599	73.04
1898		31.38	NE¼	19	40	60	4-15—5-15	.386	23.54
1898	10.41		NE¼	19	40	60	4-15—6-15	.128	15.62
1898	7.93		NE¼NW¼	19	40	60	4-15—6-15	.098	11.90
1898	22.34		SE¼	19	40	60	4-15—6-15	.275	33.51
1898	15.59		SE¼	19	40	60	4-15—6-15	.192	23.39
1899	3.09		E½NW¼	19	40	60	4-15—6-15	.038	4.64

Union Land and Cattle Co.—Continued.

Date of beneficial use: Nat. mdw.	Date of beneficial use: Cult. area	Construction first initiated: Dams	Construction first initiated: Ditches	Culture—Acres: Harvest crops	Culture—Acres: Meadow pasture	Culture—Acres: Willow and sage pasture	Culture—Acres: Swamp or overflow	Location: Subdivision	Location: Section	Location: Tp.N.	Location: R.E.	Length of season	Duty of water: C.F.S.	Duty of water: Acre-feet
	1899					11.84		E½NW¼	19	40	60	4-15—5-15	.146	8.88
	1899				17.02			E½NW¼	19	40	60	4-15—6-15	.209	25.53
	1899				7.57			E½SW¼	19	40	60	4-15—6-15	.093	11.36

Source—Mary's River. Ditch—Island.

Nat. mdw.	Cult. area	Dams	Ditches	Harvest crops	Meadow pasture	Willow and sage pasture	Swamp or overflow	Subdivision	Section	Tp.N.	R.E.	Length of season	C.F.S.	Acre-feet
	1886				92.70			NE¼	13	37	59	4-15—6-15	1.140	139.05
	1886				41.80			W½SE¼	13	37	59	4-15—6-15	.514	62.70
	1886				17.35			NE¼NW¼	36	38	59	4-15—6-15	.213	26.03
	1886				9.00			NE¼	36	38	59	4-15—6-15	.111	13.50
	1886				1.00			NE¼NW¼	36	38	59	4-15—6-15	.012	1.50
	1886				37.20			E½SW¼	36	38	50	4-15—6-15	.458	55.80
	1886				22.86			NW¼	36	38	59	4-15—6-15	.281	34.29
	1886				39.60			W½SE¼	36	38	59	4-15—6-15	.487	59.40
	1886					8.76		W½SE¼	36	38	59	4-15—5-15	.108	6.57
	1886				70.28			NE¼	1	37	59	4-15—6-15	.864	105.42
	1886					8.28		NE¼	1	37	59	4-15—5-15	.102	6.21
	1886				14.01			E½NW¼	1	37	59	4-15—6-15	.172	21.02
	1886					9.88		E½NW¼	1	37	59	4-15—5-15	.122	7.41
	1886				12.45			SE¼	1	37	59	4-15—6-15	.153	18.68
	1886					79.44		SE¼	1	37	59	4-15—5-15	.977	59.58
	1886				2.55			NE¼SW¼	1	37	59	4-15—6-15	.031	3.83
	1887				12.74			W½NW¼	7	37	60	4-15—6-15	.157	19.11
	1887					17.27		W½NW¼	7	37	60	4-15—5-15	.212	12.95
	1887				21.92			NW¼SW¼	7	37	60	4-15—6-15	.270	32.88
	1887				120.14			NE¼	12	37	59	4-15—6-15	1.478	180.21
	1887				82.10			SE¼	12	37	59	4-15—6-15	1.010	123.15

Source—Mary's River. Ditch—King Pin.

Nat. mdw.	Cult. area	Dams	Ditches	Harvest crops	Meadow pasture	Willow and sage pasture	Swamp or overflow	Subdivision	Section	Tp.N.	R.E.	Length of season	C.F.S.	Acre-feet
	1899				56.79			NW¼	30	40	60	4-15—6-15	.699	85.19
	1899				24.36			NW¼	30	40	60	4-15—6-15	.300	36.54
	1899					19.84		NW¼	30	40	60	4-15—5-15	.244	14.88
	1899				5.92			W½NE¼	30	40	60	4-15—6-15	.073	8.88
	1899					9.81		W½NE¼	30	40	60	4-15—5-15	.121	7.36
	1899				0.70			SW¼	30	40	60	4-15—6-15	.009	1.05
	1899				9.94			W½NE¼	30	40	60	4-15—6-15	.122	14.91
	1899				28.14			SW¼	30	40	60	4-15—6-15	.346	42.21
	1899					2.28		SW¼	30	40	60	4-15—5-15	.028	1.71
	1899				32.64			E½SW¼	19	40	60	4-15—6-15	.401	48.96
	1899				20.09			W½SE¼	19	40	60	4-15—6-15	.247	30.14
	1899					12.22		W½SE¼	19	40	60	4-15—5-15	.150	9.17
	1899				13.30			W½SE¼	19	40	60	4-15—6-15	.164	19.95

Source—Mary's River. Ditch—Atchison.

Nat. mdw.	Cult. area	Dams	Ditches	Harvest crops	Meadow pasture	Willow and sage pasture	Swamp or overflow	Subdivision	Section	Tp.N.	R.E.	Length of season	C.F.S.	Acre-feet
	1881				44.38			NW¼	25	37	59	4-15—6-15	.540	66.57
	1881					3.42		NW¼	25	37	59	4-15—5-15	.042	2.57

	1884				4.44			NW¼	24	37	60	4-15—6-15	.055	6.00
	1884					29.63		NW¼	24	37	60	4-15—5-15	.364	22.22
	1884				68.29			SW¼	24	37	59	4-15—6-15	.778	94.94
	1884					18.48		SW¼	24	37	59	4-15—5-15	.227	13.86

Source—**Mary's River.** Ditch—**Slough.**

	1883				0.30			SW¼SW¼	25	37	59	4-15—6-15	.004	.45
	1883				85.31			NE¼	25	37	59	4-15—6-15	1.049	127.97
	1883					0.52		NE¼	25	37	59	4-15—5-15	.006	.39
	1883				7.19			E½NW¼	25	37	59	4-15—6-15	.088	10.79
	1883					39.93		E½NW¼	25	37	59	4-15—5-15	.491	29.95
	1883				7.60			NW¼SE¼	25	37	59	4-15—6-15	.093	11.40
	1883				88.96			SW¼	25	37	59	4-15—6-15	1.094	133.44
	1883				85.04			NE¼	24	37	59	4-15—6-15	1.046	127.56
	1883					42.90		NE¼	24	37	59	4-15—5-15	.528	32.18
	1883				79.16			SE¼	24	37	59	4-15—6-15	.974	118.74
	1883					24.00		SE¼	24	37	59	4-15—5-15	.295	18.00
	1883				11.78			SW¼	24	37	59	4-15—6-15	.145	17.67
	1883					8.44		SW¼	24	37	59	4-15—5-15	.104	6.33
	1883				0.84			SE¼SE¼	24	37	59	4-15—6-15	.010	1.26

Source—**Mary's River.** Ditch—**Various Sloughs and Small Ditches.**

	1883				1.70			SE¼SE¼	13	37	59	4-15—6-15	.021	2.55
	1883				43.70			SW¼	18	37	60	4-15—6-15	.538	65.55
	1883				80.21			W½	19	37	60	4-15—6-15	.987	120.32
	1883					55.84		W½	19	37	60	4-15—5-15	.687	41.88
	1883				51.86			E½	24	37	59	4-15—6-15	.638	77.79
	1883					5.88		E½	24	37	59	4-15—5-15	.072	4.41

Source—**Mary's River.** Ditch—**Mason and Bradley.**

	1901				97.90			NW¼	18	37	60	4-15—6-15	1.204	146.85
	1901				33.80			W½SW¼	18	37	60	4-15—6-15	.416	50.70
	1901				64.48			SW¼	7	37	60	4-15—6-15	.793	96.72
	1901					14.52		SW¼	7	37	60	4-15—5-15	.179	10.89
	1901				32.00			NE¼	13	37	59	4-15—6-15	.394	48.00
	1901				18.16			SE¼	13	37	59	4-15—6-15	.223	27.24
	1901					79.84		SE¼	13	37	59	4-15—5-15	.982	59.88

Source—**Mary's River.** Ditch—**Goodale.**

	1886				.97			E½SW¼	1	37	59	4-15—6-15	.012	1.46
	1886					9.38		E½SW¼	1	37	59	4-15—5-15	.115	7.04
	1886				2.45			W½SE¼	1	37	59	4-15—6-15	.030	3.68
	1886					4.92		W½SE¼	1	37	59	4-15—5-15	.061	3.69
	1886				3.40			E½NW¼	12	37	59	4-15—6-15	.042	5.10
	1886				27.40			W½NE¼	12	37	59	4-15—6-15	.337	41.10
	1886				1.84			NE¼SW¼	12	37	59	4-15—6-15	.023	2.76
	1886				75.12			W½SE¼	12	37	59	4-15—6-15	.924	112.68
	1886				32.30			W½NE¼	13	37	59	4-15—6-15	.397	48.45
	1886				13.20			W½SE¼	13	37	59	4-15—6-15	.162	19.80

Claimant—**Jno. H. Cazier & Sons Company.** Proof. No. 00602
Source—**Bishop Creek and Humboldt River.** Ditch—**Cazier & Company Ditches.**

Date of beneficial use—Nat. mdw.	Date of beneficial use—Cult. area	Construction first initiated—Dams	Construction first initiated—Ditches	Culture—Acres—Harvest crops	Culture—Acres—Meadow pasture	Culture—Acres—Willow and sage pasture	Culture—Acres—Swamp or overflow	Location—Subdivision	Location—Section	Location—Tp.N.	Location—R.E.	Length of season	Duty of water—C.F.S.	Duty of water—Acre-feet
	1879				153.70			NE¼NE¼	35	38	60	4-15—6-15	1.891	230.55
	1880				153.70			S½NE¼	35	38	00	4-15—6-15	1.891	230.55
								SE¼	35	38	60			
								NE¼SW¼	35	38	60			
								S½SW¼	35	38	69			

Claimant—**Mrs. Annie McMullen.** Proof No. 00603
Source—**As below.** Ditch—**Annie McMullen Ditches.**

Nat. mdw.	Cult. area	Dams	Ditches	Harvest crops	Meadow pasture	Willow and sage pasture	Swamp or overflow	Subdivision	Section	Tp.N.	R.E.	Length of season	C.F.S.	Acre-feet
Taber Creek—														
	1905				155.10			W½	4	37	60	4-15—6-15	1.908	232.65
Bishop Creek—														
	1882				78.50			S½SE¼	4	37	60	4-15—6-15	.966	117.75
Bishop and Taber Creeks—														
	1882				181.30				8	37	60	4-15—6-15	2.230	271.95
	1905				47.20				8	37	60	4-15—6-15	.581	70.80

Claimant—**W. B. Gibbs.** Proof No. 00604
Source—**T and Wildcat Creeks.** Ditch—**W. B. Gibbs Ditches.**

Nat. mdw.	Cult. area	Dams	Ditches	Harvest crops	Meadow pasture	Willow and sage pasture	Swamp or overflow	Subdivision	Section	Tp.N.	R.E.	Length of season	C.F.S.	Acre-feet
	1884			90.70				SE¼NW¼	29	43	60	4-15—8-15	1.116	272.10
	1885			74.70				E½SW¼	29	43	60	4-15—8-15	.919	224.10
	1889			79.60				W¼NE¼	32	43	60	4-15—8-15	.979	238.80
	1896			228.20				E¼W½	32	43	60	4-15—8-15	2.807	684.60
	1897			53.40				W½SW¼	32	43	60	4-15—8-15	.657	160.20
								W½	5	42	60			
								SE¼NE¼	6	42	60			
								W½	8	42	60			

Source—**Hot Creek.** Ditch—**W. B. Gibbs Ditches.**

Nat. mdw.	Cult. area	Dams	Ditches	Harvest crops	Meadow pasture	Willow and sage pasture	Swamp or overflow	Subdivision	Section	Tp.N.	R.E.	Length of season	C.F.S.	Acre-feet
	1885			77.71				SE¼SW¼	32	43	60			
								S¼SE¼	32	43	60			
								S¼SW¼	33	43	60			
								NW¼NE¼	5	42	60			
								NE¼NW¼	5	42	60	4-15—8-15	.956	233.13

Claimant—**Hylton & Mentz.** Proof No. 00605
Source—**Bishop Creek, Taber Creek, and Blasengame Creek.** Ditch—**Goodale 1-9, incl.**

Nat. mdw.	Cult. area	Dams	Ditches	Harvest crops	Meadow pasture	Willow and sage pasture	Swamp or overflow	Subdivision	Section	Tp.N.	R.E.	Length of season	C.F.S.	Acre-feet
	1882				711.60			N½	9	37	60			
								N¼SW¼	9	37	60			
								SW¼SW¼	9	37	60			
									17	37	60	4-15—6-15	8.758	1067.40

Claimant—**Robert W. Anderson.** Proof No. **00607**

Source—**Humboldt River.** Ditch—**Robert W. Anderson Ditches.**

1879		40.00		NW¼SE¼	33	37	59	4-15—6-15	.492	60.00

Source—**T Creek and Tributaries.** Ditch—**Robert W. Anderson Ditches.**

1884	76.50			SE¼	9	43	59	4-15—8-15	.912	229.50
1902	....	55.25		SW¼	10	43	59	4-15—6-15	.680	82.88
1904	....	62.20		N½	15	43	59	4-15—6-15	.765	93.30
1904	....	156.17			....	....	....	4-15—6-15	1.921	234.26

Source—**Mary's River, Humboldt River and Tributaries.** Ditch—**Robert W. Anderson.**

1877	....	274.51		S½	26	37	59	4-15—6-15	3.376	411.77
1878	....	68.63		S½S½	27	37	59	4-15—6-15	.844	102.95
1879	....	68.63		N½	34	37	59	4-15—6-15	.844	102.95
1880	....	68.63		N½N½	35	37	59	4-15—6-15	.844	102.95
1881	....	68.63			....	....	....	4-15—6-15	.844	102.95
1881	....		157.12		....	....	....	4-15—5-15	1.933	235.68

Source—**T Creek.** Ditch—**Robert W. Anderson Ditches.**

1895	16.94			SW¼NE¼	36	43	59	4-15—8-15	.208	50.82
1898	238.98			SE¼	36	43	59	4-15—8-15	2.939	716.94
1899	15.00			SW¼	31	43	60	4-15—8-16	.185	45.00
1904	16.03			N½	6	42	60	4-15—8-15	.197	48.09
				NE¼SE¼	6	42	60			
				SW¼NW¼	5	42	60			
				NW¼SW¼	5	42	60			

Claimant—**Metropolis Land Company.** Proof No. **00608**

Source—**Bishop Creek.** Ditch—**Nos. 1, 2, and 3.**

1886	160.00			NW¼SE¼	28	39	62			
1887	61.93			N½SW¼	28	39	62			
1888	61.92			S½SE¼	29	39	62			
1889	61.92			E½NE¼	31	39	62	4-15—8-15	1.968	480.00
1892	42.33			NE¼SE¼	31	39	62	4-15—8-15	.762	185.79
				N½	32	39	62	4-15—8-15	.762	185.75
				N½SW¼	32	39	62	4-15—8-15	.762	185.76
				NW¼SE¼	32	39	62	4-15—8-15	.521	126.99

Source—**Trout Creek and Springs.** Ditch—**Nos. 1, 2, and 3.**

1889	16.94			SW¼SE¼	19	39	62			
1890	16.93			SE¼	30	39	62			
1891	16.93			E½SE¼	30	39	62	4-15—8-15	.208	50.82
1892	16.93			SW¼SE¼	30	39	62	4-15—8-15	.208	50.79
1893	153.47			W½SW¼	29	39	62	4-15—8-15	.208	50.79
				NE¼	31	39	62	4-15—8-15	.208	50.79
				NW¼NW¼	32	39	62	4-15—8-15	1.888	460.41

Metropolis Land Company—Continued.
Source—**Burnt Creek and Spring Creek.** Ditch—**Nos. 1, 2, and 3.**

Date of beneficial use: Nat. mdw.	Date of beneficial use: Cult. area	Construction first initiated: Dams	Construction first initiated: Ditches	Culture—Acres: Harvest crops	Culture—Acres: Meadow pasture	Culture—Acres: Willow and sage pasture	Culture—Acres: Swamp or overflow	Location: Subdivision	Location: Section	Location: Tp. N.	Location: R. E.	Length of season	Duty of water: C. F. S.	Duty of water: Acre-feet
....	1893	....	....	107.67	....	....	....	S½NW¼	25	39	61			
								N½SW¼	25	39	61			
								SW¼SW¼	25	39	61	4-15—8-15	1.324	323.01

NOTE—The above land has a priority from Spring Creek alone of 1889.

Source—**Johnson and Bishop Creeks and Springs.** Ditch—**Nos. 1-6, incl.**

Nat. mdw.	Cult. area	Dams	Ditches	Harvest crops	Meadow pasture	Willow and sage pasture	Swamp or overflow	Subdivision	Section	Tp. N.	R. E.	Length of season	C. F. S.	Acre-feet
....	1883	....	....	15.65	....	....	....	E½SE¼	8	39	63	4-15—8-15	.192	46.95
....	1884	....	....	15.65	....	....	....	W½SW¼	9	39	63	4-15—8-15	.192	46.95
....	1885	....	....	15.65	....	....	....	NW¼NW¼	16	39	63	4-15—8-15	.192	46.95
....	1886	....	....	15.64	....	....	....	NE¼NE¼	17	39	63	4-15—8-15	.192	46.92
....	1887	....	....	15.64	....	....	....	....	...	...	...	4-15—8-15	.192	46.92

Source—**Bishop and Burnt Creeks.** Ditch—**Nos. 5 and 6.**

Nat. mdw.	Cult. area	Dams	Ditches	Harvest crops	Meadow pasture	Willow and sage pasture	Swamp or overflow	Subdivision	Section	Tp. N.	R. E.	Length of season	C. F. S.	Acre-feet
....	1876	....	....	147.44	....	....	....	E½SW¼	2	38	61			
								SE¼	2	38	61			
								SE¼NE¼	2	38	61			
								W½SW¼	1	38	61			
								SW¼NW¼	1	38	61	4-15—8-15	1.814	442.32

Claimant—**H. A. Agee, Steele Bros., S. C. & S. J. Weeks.** Proof No. 00608
Source—**Burnt Creek.** Ditch—**Nos. 1 and 2.**

Nat. mdw.	Cult. area	Dams	Ditches	Harvest crops	Meadow pasture	Willow and sage pasture	Swamp or overflow	Subdivision	Section	Tp. N.	R. E.	Length of season	C. F. S.	Acre-feet
....	1896	....	....	40.79	....	....	....	E½SE¼	26	40	61			
....	1897	....	....	31.30	....	....	....	W½SW¼	25	40	61			
								E½NE¼	35	40	61	4-15—8-15	.502	122.37
								W½NW¼	36	40	61	4-15—8-15	.385	93.90

Claimant—**John H. Cazier & Sons Company.** Proof No. 00609
Source—**Trout Creek and Springs.** Ditch—**John H. Cazier Ditches.**

Nat. mdw.	Cult. area	Dams	Ditches	Harvest crops	Meadow pasture	Willow and sage pasture	Swamp or overflow	Subdivision	Section	Tp. N.	R. E.	Length of season	C. F. S.	Acre-feet
....	1873	....	....	95.00	....	....	....	SW¼	5	37	61	4-15—8-15	1.169	285.00
....	1873	....	....	49.82	....	....	....	E½W½	6	37	61	4-15—8-15	.613	149.46
....	1874	....	....	66.21	....	....	....	W½NE¼	6	37	61	4-15—8-15	.814	198.63
....	1874	....	....	49.82	....	....	....	SE¼	6	37	61	4-15—8-15	.613	149.46
....	1875	....	....	66.20	....	....	....	E½	7	37	61	4-15—8-15	.814	198.60
....	1875	....	....	49.83	....	....	....	W½	8	37	61	4-15—8-15	.613	149.49
....	1876	....	....	66.20	....	....	....	W½NE¼	8	37	61	4-15—8-15	.814	198.60
....	1876	....	....	49.83	....	....	....	SE¼	8	37	61	4-15—8-15	.613	149.49
....	1877	....	....	66.20	....	....	....	W½W½	16	37	61	4-15—8-15	.814	198.60
....	1877	....	....	323.85	....	....	....	E½NW¼	16	37	61	4-15—8-15	3.983	971.55
....	1877	....	....	49.83	....	....	....	W½NE¼	16	37	61	4-15—8-15	.613	149.49
....	1878	....	....	66.20	....	....	....	E½	17	37	61	4-15—8-15	.814	198.60
....	1879	....	....	66.20	....	....	....	....	...	...	...	4-15—8-15	.814	198.60
....	1880	....	....	9.00	....	....	....	....	...	...	...	4-15—8-15	.111	27.00
....	1881	....	....	20.00	....	....	....	....	...	...	...	4-15—8-15	.246	60.00

1881	9.00						4-15—8-15	.111	27.00
1882	9.00						4-15—8-15	.111	27.00
1883	9.00						4-15—8-15	.111	27.00
1884	9.00						4-15—8-15	.111	27.00
1885	9.00						4-15—8-15	.111	27.00
1886	9.00						4-15—8-15	.111	27.00
1887	9.00						4-15—8-15	.111	27.00
1888	9.00						4-15—8-15	.111	27.00
1889	9.00						4-15—8-15	.111	27.00
1890	10.00						4-15—8-15	.123	30.00
	83.70								
	25.92								
	25.93								
	25.80								
	25.80								
	166.20								

Source—**Trout Creek.** Ditch—**John H. Cazier Ditches.**

1889	113.58		S½NW¼	31	38	61			
			N½SW¼	31	38	61			
			SE¼SW¼	31	38	61			
			W½SE¼	31	38	61			
			NE¼SE¼	31	38	61	4-15—8-15	1.397	341.74

Source—**Bishop Creek, Humboldt River, and Trout Creek.** Ditch—**John H. Cazier Ditches.**

1889		287.15	N½	31	38	61	4-15—6-15	3.532	861.45

Source—**Trout Creek, Picnic Grove Creek and Gulch.** Ditch—**Cazier & Company Ditches.**

1881	40.00		E½SE¼	13	37	60			
1882	217.30		NE¼NE¼	24	37	60			
1883	85.65		W½NW¼	18	37	61			
1900	47.20		SE¼NW¼	18	37	61			
	12.00		NE¼	18	37	61			
	129.60		S½	18	37	61	4-15—8-15	.492	120.00
			N½NW¼	19	37	61	4-15—8-15	2.673	651.90
			SW¼NW¼	19	37	61	4-15—8-15	1.053	256.95
			NW¼NE¼	19	37	61	4-15—8-15	.581	141.60

Source—**Humboldt River, Bishop Creek, and West Fork of Trout Creek.**
Ditch—**Cazier & Company Ditches.**

1879		426.50	W½	36	38	60			
			NE¼	36	38	60			
			N½SE¼	36	33	60	4-15—6-15	5.246	639.80

Claimant—**L. L. Redden.** Proof No. 00610
Source—**Mary's River.** Ditch—**L. L. Redden Ditches.**

1898		10.00	SW¼NW¼	10	42	59			
1899		103.60	E½NW¼	10	42	59	4-15—6-15	.123	15.00
1899		62.50	NE¼	10	42	59	4-15—6-15	1.274	155.40
			SW¼NW¼	11	42	59	4-15—6-15	.769	93.75

Claimant—**Huntington and Diamond Valley Stock and Land Company.** Proof No. 00651
Source—**Huntington Creek and Tributaries.**
Ditch—**Huntington and Diamond Valley Ditches.**

Date of beneficial use: Nat. mdw.	Date of beneficial use: Cult. area	Construction first initiated: Dams	Construction first initiated: Ditches	Culture—Acres: Harvest crops	Culture—Acres: Meadow pasture	Culture—Acres: Willow and sage pasture	Culture—Acres: Swamp or overflow	Location: Subdivision	Location: Section	Location: Tp.N.	Location: R.E.	Length of season	Duty of water: C.F.S.	Duty of water: Acre-feet
	1869			345.18					35	27	55	4-15—8-15	4.246	1035.54
	1870			50.00					36	27	55	4-15—8-15	.615	150.00
	1871			50.00					31	27	56	4-15—8-15	.615	150.00
	1873			159.00					26	27	55	4-15—8-15	1.956	477.00
	1874			10.00					23	27	55	4-15—8-15	.123	30.00
	1875			10.00					22	27	55	4-15—8-15	.123	30.00
	1876			175.00					14	27	55	4-15—8-15	2.153	525.00
									15	27	56			
									10	27	55			

See Appendix A.

Claimant—**Bert Stoddart.** Proof No. 00652
Source—**Welch Creek and South Fork of Humboldt River.** Ditch—**Kleckner-Dovel.**

Date of beneficial use: Nat. mdw.	Date of beneficial use: Cult. area	Construction first initiated: Dams	Construction first initiated: Ditches	Culture—Acres: Harvest crops	Culture—Acres: Meadow pasture	Culture—Acres: Willow and sage pasture	Culture—Acres: Swamp or overflow	Location: Subdivision	Location: Section	Location: Tp.N.	Location: R.E.	Length of season	Duty of water: C.F.S.	Duty of water: Acre-feet
	1902			18.50				S½NW¼	10	31	57	4-15—8-15	.229	56.50
	1902			1.00				SW¼	10	31	57	4-15—8-15	.012	3.00
	1902			50.00				NW¼SE¼	10	31	57	4-15—8-15	.615	150.00
	1902			15.50				W½NE¼	10	31	57	4-15—8-15	.191	46.50
	1903			25.90								4-15—8-15	.319	77.70
	1903			35.00								4-15—8-15	.431	105.00
	1904			10.50								4-15—8-15	.129	31.50
	1904			41.00								4-15—8-15	.504	123.00
	1904			1.10								4-15—8-15	.014	3.30

Claimant—**Griswold-Henderson Livestock Co.** Proof No. 00653
Source—**Ten-Mile Creek.** Ditch—**Griswold-Henderson Ditches.**

Date of beneficial use: Nat. mdw.	Date of beneficial use: Cult. area	Construction first initiated: Dams	Construction first initiated: Ditches	Culture—Acres: Harvest crops	Culture—Acres: Meadow pasture	Culture—Acres: Willow and sage pasture	Culture—Acres: Swamp or overflow	Location: Subdivision	Location: Section	Location: Tp.N.	Location: R.E.	Length of season	Duty of water: C.F.S.	Duty of water: Acre-feet
	1885			21.00					4	33	56	4-15—8-15	.258	63.00
	1886			21.00								4-15—8-15	.258	63.00
	1887			21.00								4-15—8-15	.258	63.00
	1888			21.00								4-15—8-15	.258	63.00
	1889			21.41								4-15—8-15	.263	64.23

NOTE—That certain Decree No. 1621, District Court of Elko County, is binding as between parties to the suit.

Source—**Ten-Mile Creek and Mitchell Creek.** Ditch—**Griswold-Henderson Ditches.**

Date of beneficial use: Nat. mdw.	Date of beneficial use: Cult. area	Construction first initiated: Dams	Construction first initiated: Ditches	Culture—Acres: Harvest crops	Culture—Acres: Meadow pasture	Culture—Acres: Willow and sage pasture	Culture—Acres: Swamp or overflow	Location: Subdivision	Location: Section	Location: Tp.N.	Location: R.E.	Length of season	Duty of water: C.F.S.	Duty of water: Acre-feet
	1885			169.80					8	33	56	4-15—8-15	2.089	509.20
	1886			169.80					9	33	56	4-15—8-15	2.089	509.20
	1887			169.93					16	33	56	4-15—8-15	2.090	509.79
									17	33	56			

NOTE—That certain Decree No. 1621, District Court of Elko County, is binding as between parties to the suit.

Claimant—**J. H. Carter.** Proof No. 00654

Source—**Willow Creek.** Ditch—**Toyn Nos. 1-12, incl.**

1904	15.00		NW¼NE¼	3	30	56	4-15—8-15	.186	45.00
1905	5.69		NW¼NE¼	3	30	56	4-15—8-15	.070	17.07
1905	21.11		NE¼NW¼	3	30	56	4-15—8-15	.260	63.83
1905	12.74		NW¼NW¼	3	30	56	4-15—8-15	.157	38.22
1905	9.42		SW¼SW¼	34	31	56	4-15—8-15	.116	28.36

Source—**Willow** Creek, **Swamps, and Springs.** Ditch—**Toyn Nos. 1-12, incl.**

1896	18.42		NW¼SE¼	33	31	56	4-15—8-15	.227	55.26
1896	1.50		NE¼SE¼	33	31	56	4-15—8-15	.018	4.50
1896	35.32		SW¼SE¼	33	31	56	4-15—8-15	.434	105.96
1896	26.98		SE¼SE¼	33	31	56	4-15—8-15	.332	80.94
1896	9.14		NE¼SW¼	33	31	56	4-15—8-15	.112	27.42
1896	33.92		SE¼SW¼	33	31	56	4-15—8-15	.417	101.76
1896	.82		NW¼NW¼	3	30	56	4-15—8-15	.010	2.46
1896	3.55		NE¼NE¼	4	30	56	4-15—8-15	.044	10.65
1896	2.41		NW¼NE¼	4	30	56	4-15—8-15	.030	7.23
1896	21.33		NE¼NW¼	4	30	56	4-15—8-15	.262	63.99
1896	2.38		SE¼NW¼	4	30	56	4-15—8-15	.029	7.14
1896	2.76		NW¼NW¼	4	30	56	4-15—8-15	.034	8.28
1896	18.85		SW¼NW¼	4	30	56	4-15—8-15	.232	56.55
1896	2.82		SE¼NE¼	5	30	56	4-15—8-15	.035	8.46
1896	5.72		NE¼NE¼	5	30	56	4-15—8-15	.070	17.16

Claimant—**J. J. Hylton.** Proof No. 00655

Source—**Pearl Creek, Frost Canyon Creek, and Brown Creek.** Ditch—**J. J. Hylton Ditches.**

1899*	40.00		NW¼	12	28	55	4-15—8-15	.492	120.00
1900*	34.36		SW¼SW¼	1	28	55	4-15—8-15	.423	103.08
1901*	34.36		SE¼SE¼	2	28	55	4-15—8-15	.423	103.08
1902	34.36		NW¼	12	28	55	4-15—8-15	.423	103.08
1900		10.00	NE¼SW¼	12	28	55	4-15—5-15	.123	7.50
1901		10.00	NW¼SE¼	12	28	55	4-15—5-15	.123	7.50
1902		10.00	E½NE¼	11	28	55	4-15—5-15	.123	7.50

*In order to comply with the decree in the case of H. H. Porch and H. F. Porch v. Antone Sestenovich, No. 1548, 80 acres of land now belonging to J. J. Hylton, Claim No. 00655, and being in sections 1, 2, 11 and 12 in T. 28 N. R. 55 E. with dates as follows: 40 acres in 1899, 34.36 acres in 1900, 5.64 acres in 1901, are to be supplied with water from Brown, Pearl, and Frost Canyon Creeks before any water is allowed to flow into Huntington Creek from these streams for the irrigation of land now belonging to Odiaga with a prior date of 1889 from Huntington Creek.

Claimant—**Javier Goyeneche.** Proof No. 00656

Source—**Lindsay Creek and Unnamed Canyon.** Ditch—**Javier Goyeneche Ditches.**

1869	13.98		N½SW¼	11	27	56	4-15—8-15	.172	41.94
1870	13.97		SE¼SW¼	11	27	56	4-15—8-15	.172	41.91
1871	13.97		W½SE¼	11	27	56	4-15—8-15	.172	41.91
1872	13.97		SE¼SE¼	11	27	56	4-15—8-15	.172	41.91
1873	13.97		S½SW¼	12	27	56	4-15—8-15	.172	41.91

Claimant—**V. Juaristi.** Proof No. 00657

Source—**Willow Creek.** Ditch—**Ditches Nos. 1-13, incl.**

Date of beneficial use: Nat. mdw.	Date of beneficial use: Cult. area	Construction first initiated: Dams	Construction first initiated: Ditches	Culture—Acres: Harvest crops	Culture—Acres: Meadow pasture	Culture—Acres: Willow and sage pasture	Culture—Acres: Swamp or overflow	Location: Subdivision	Location: Section	Location: Tp.N.	Location: R.E.	Length of season	Duty of water: C.F.S.	Duty of water: Acre-feet
	1876			18.94				NW¼NW¼	33	26	56	4-15—8-15	.233	56.82
	1876			6.11				SW¼NW¼	33	26	56	4-15—8-16	.075	18.33
	1876			23.53				NE¼NW¼	33	26	56	4-15—8-15	.289	70.59
	1876			13.64				NW¼NE¼	33	26	56	4-15—8-15	.168	40.92
	1876			5.20				NE¼NE¼	33	26	56	4-15—8-15	.064	15.60
	1876			1.02				SW¼SE¼	28	26	56	4-15—8-15	.013	3.06
	1876			.70				SE¼SW¼	28	26	56	4-15—8-15	.009	2.10
	1876			3.13				SE¼SE¼	28	26	56	4-15—8-15	.039	9.39
	1905			.66				SE¼SW¼	29	26	56	4-15—8-15	.008	1.98
	1905			2.90				SW¼SE¼	29	26	56	4-15—8-15	.036	8.70
	1905			1.62				NE¼NW¼	32	26	56	4-15—8-15	.020	4.86
	1905			9.98				NW¼NE¼	32	26	56	4-15—8-15	.123	29.94
	1905			12.44				NE¼NE¼	32	26	56	4-15—8-15	.153	37.32
	1905			7.40				NW¼NW¼	33	26	56	4-15—8-15	.091	22.20

Claimant—**Henry Peters.** Proof No. 00659

Source—**Peters Creek** and Spring. Ditch—**Nos. 1-8, incl.**

Nat. mdw.	Cult. area	Dams	Ditches	Harvest crops	Meadow pasture	Willow and sage pasture	Swamp or overflow	Subdivision	Section	Tp.N.	R.E.	Length of season	C.F.S.	Acre-feet
	1900			2.18				NE¼NW¼	4	26	56	4-15—8-15	.028	6.54
	1900			2.76				NW¼NE¼	4	26	56	4-15—8-15	.034	8.28
	1901			0.43				NW¼NE¼	4	26	56	4-15—8-15	.005	1.29
	1901			0.12				NE¼NE¼	4	26	56	4-15—8-15	.001	.36
	1903			2.54				NE¼NE¼	4	26	56	4-15—8-16	.031	8.62
	1903			1.21				SE¼NE¼	4	26	56	4-15—8-15	.015	3.63
	1903			0.85				NW¼NW¼	3	26	56	4-15—8-15	.010	2.55
	1903			0.74				SW¼NW¼	3	26	56	4-15—8-15	.009	2.21
	1904			0.40				NW¼NW¼	4	26	56	4-15—8-15	.005	1.20
	1904			1.96				SW¼NW¼	4	26	56	4-15—8-15	.024	5.88
	1904			1.49				SE¼NW¼	4	26	56	4-15—8-15	.018	4.47
	1904			0.56				NE¼NW¼	4	26	56	4-15—8-15	.007	1.68
	1904			15.00				N½	4	26	56	4-15—8-15	.185	45.00

Claimant—**Frank Brennen.** Proof No. 00660

Source—**Cottonwood Creek and Springs.** Ditch—**Frank Brennen Ditches.**

Nat. mdw.	Cult. area	Dams	Ditches	Harvest crops	Meadow pasture	Willow and sage pasture	Swamp or overflow	Subdivision	Section	Tp.N.	R.E.	Length of season	C.F.S.	Acre-feet
	1897			10.00*				W½	20	32	57	4-15—8-15	0.123	30.00
	1900			9.96†								4-15—8-15	0.123	29.88
	1903			26.50†								4-15—8-15	0.326	79.50

*From Spring. †Cottonwood Creek and Springs.

Claimant—**Vincente Juaristi.** Proof No. 00662

Source—**Holum Spring in Water Canyon.** Ditch—**Nos. 1-3, incl.**

Nat. mdw.	Cult. area	Dams	Ditches	Harvest crops	Meadow pasture	Willow and sage pasture	Swamp or overflow	Subdivision	Section	Tp.N.	R.E.	Length of season	C.F.S.	Acre-feet
	1890			11.16				SW¼	5	25	56	4-15—8-15	.137	33.48

Claimant—**J. H. Carter.** Proof No. **00663**
Source—**Willow Creek and Rattlesnake Creek.** Ditch—**J. H. Carter Ditches.**

1873	39.00								4-15—8-15	.480	117.00
1874	21.00								4-15—8-15	.258	63.00
1875	13.00								4-15—8-15	.529	129.00
1876	42.00								4-15—8-15	.517	126.00
1877	10.00								4-15—8-15	.123	30.00
1878	10.00					31	31	57	4-15—8-15	.123	30.00
1879	30.00					32	31	57	4-15—8-15	.360	[illegible]
1881	13.60				N½N½	6	30	57	4-15—8-15	.167	40.80
1885	13.60								4-15—8-15	.167	40.80
1885	60.86								4-15—8-15	.749	182.58
1889	13.60								4-15—8-15	.167	40.80
1893	13.60								4-15—8-15	.167	40.80
1897	13.60								4-15—8-15	.167	40.80
1901	13.64								4-15—8-15	.168	40.92
1902	85.00								4-15—8-15	1.046	255.00
1905			2.50						4-15—5-15	.031	1.88
1905			1.86						4-15—5-15	.023	1.40
1876			77.00						4-15—5-15	.947	57.75
1885			51.56						4-15—5-15	.634	38.67

Claimant—**Chas. Toyn.** Proof No. **00664**
Source—**South Fork Smith Creek.** Ditch—**Chas. Toyn Ditches.**

1871	5.00				E½NW¼	35	29	56			
1872	16.53				W½NE¼	35	29	56			
1873	66.11				SE¼NE¼	35	29	56	4-15—8-15	.062	15.00
1874	16.27				E½SE¼	35	29	56	4-15—8-15	.203	49.59
1904	10.67				S½S½	36	29	56	4-15—8-15	.813	198.33
					N½N½	1	28	56	4-15—8-15	.200	48.81
					NE¼NE¼	2	28	56	4-15—8-15	.131	32.01

Claimant—**C. H. Kleckner.** Proof No. **00668**
Source—**South Fork of Humboldt River and Welch Creek.*** Ditch—**C. H. Kleckner Ditches.**

1873	6.26				NW¼	15	31	57	4-15—8-15	.077	18.78
1902	37.70								4-15—8-15	.464	113.10
1902		32.07							4-15—6-15	.394	48.11
1873			8.26						4-15—5-15	.102	6.20

Kleckner Canyon—

1873	1.65				E½NW¼	15	31	57	4-15—8-15	.020	4.95

Springs and Natural Draws and Kleckner Canyon†—

1900	5.00				S½NW¼	15	31	57	4-15—8-15	.062	15.00
1901	40.15				N½SW¼	15	31	57	4-15—8-15	.494	120.45
1905			21.61						4-15—5-15	.266	16.21

*Claimant has ditch diverting water from South Fork into Welch Creek.
†Priority in Kleckner Canyon 1905. Water to be used from natural draws and springs before diverting from Kleckner Canyon.

Claimant—**J. J. Hylton.** Proof No. 00670
Source—**Sherman Canyon.** Ditch—**J. J. Hylton Ditches.**

Date of beneficial use: Nat. mdw.	Date of beneficial use: Cult. area	Construction first initiated: Dams	Construction first initiated: Ditches	Culture—Acres: Harvest crops	Culture—Acres: Meadow pasture	Culture—Acres: Willow and sage pasture	Culture—Acres: Swamp or overflow	Location: Subdivision	Location: Section	Location: Tp.N.	Location: R.E.	Length of season	Duty of water: C.F.S.	Duty of water: Acre-feet
......	1878	......	......	9.46	......	......	......	NE¼NW¼	28	26	56	4-15—8-15	.116	28.38
......	1878	......	......	5.54	......	......	......	NW¼NW¼	28	26	56	4-15—8-15	.068	16.62
......	1878	......	......	1.71	......	......	......	NW¼NW¼	28	26	56	4-15—8-15	.021	5.13
......	1880	......	......	1.71	......	......	......	NW¼NW¼	28	26	56	4-15—8-15	.021	5.13
......	1882	......	......	1.70	......	......	......	NW¼NW¼	28	26	56	4-15—8-15	.021	5.10
......	1878	......	......	2.79	......	......	......	NE¼NE¼	29	26	56	4-15—8-15	.034	8.37
......	1880	......	......	2.79	......	......	......	NE¼NE¼	29	26	56	4-15—8-15	.034	8.27
......	1882	......	......	2.78	......	......	......	NE¼NE¼	29	26	56	4-15—8-15	.034	8.37
......	1878	......	......	0.94	......	......	......	NW¼NE¼	29	26	56	4-15—8-15	.012	2.82
......	1880	......	......	0.94	......	......	......	NW¼NE¼	29	26	56	4-15—8-15	.012	2.82
......	1882	......	......	0.93	......	......	......	NW¼NE¼	29	26	56	4-15—8-15	.012	2.79

Claimant—**Fred Walther.** Proof No. 00671
Source—**Walther Creek.** Ditch—**Nos. 1-3, incl., and Sastanovich Ditch.**

Date of beneficial use: Nat. mdw.	Date of beneficial use: Cult. area	Construction first initiated: Dams	Construction first initiated: Ditches	Culture—Acres: Harvest crops	Culture—Acres: Meadow pasture	Culture—Acres: Willow and sage pasture	Culture—Acres: Swamp or overflow	Location: Subdivision	Location: Section	Location: Tp.N.	Location: R.E.	Length of season	Duty of water: C.F.S.	Duty of water: Acre-feet
......	1875	......	......	0.71	......	......	......	NW¼SW¼	14	26	56	4-15—8-15	.009	2.13
......	1875	......	......	7.27	......	......	......	NE¼SE¼	15	26	56	4-15—8-15	.089	21.81
......	1875	......	......	2.66	......	......	......	SE¼SE¼	15	26	56	4-15—8-15	.033	7.98
......	1875	......	......	1.36	......	......	......	SW¼SE¼	15	26	56	4-15—8-15	.017	4.08
......	1876	......	......	7.99	......	......	......	SW¼SE¼	15	26	56	4-15—8-15	.098	23.97
......	1876	......	......	16.33	......	......	......	SE¼SW¼	15	26	56	4-15—8-15	.201	48.99
......	1876	......	......	24.68	......	......	......	SW¼SW¼	15	26	56	4-15—8-15	.304	74.04
......	1877	......	......	0.64	......	......	......	NW¼SW¼	15	26	56	4-15—8-15	.008	1.92
......	1882	......	......	0.64	......	......	......	NW¼SW¼	15	26	56	4-15—8-15	.008	1.92
......	1887	......	......	0.63	......	......	......	NW¼SW¼	15	26	56	4-15—8-15	.008	1.89
......	1893	......	......	0.63	......	......	......	NW¼SW¼	15	26	56	4-15—8-15	.008	1.89
......	1877	......	......	2.76	......	......	......	SW¼SW¼	15	26	56	4-15—8-15	.034	8.28
......	1882	......	......	2.76	......	......	......	SW¼SW¼	15	26	56	4-15—8-15	.034	8.28
......	1887	......	......	2.75	......	......	......	SW¼SW¼	15	26	56	4-15—8-15	.034	8.25
......	1893	......	......	2.75	......	......	......	SW¼SW¼	15	26	56	4-15—8-15	.034	8.25
......	1877	......	......	0.33	......	......	......	NW¼NW¼	22	26	56	4-15—8-15	.004	0.90
......	1882	......	......	0.33	......	......	......	NW¼NW¼	22	26	56	4-15—8-15	.004	0.99
......	1887	......	......	0.33	......	......	......	NW¼NW¼	22	26	56	4-15—8-15	.004	0.99
......	1893	......	......	0.32	......	......	......	NW¼NW¼	22	26	56	4-15—8-15	.004	0.96
......	1877	......	......	0.81	......	......	......	NE¼SE¼	16	26	56	4-15—8-15	.010	2.43
......	1882	......	......	0.81	......	......	......	NE¼SE¼	16	26	56	4-15—8-15	.010	2.43
......	1887	......	......	0.80	......	......	......	NE¼SE¼	16	26	56	4-15—8-15	.010	2.40
......	1893	......	......	0.80	......	......	......	NE¼SE¼	16	26	56	4-15—8-15	.010	2.40
......	1877	......	......	11.84	......	......	......	S½SE¼	16	26	56	4-15—8-15	.146	35.52
......	1882	......	......	11.84	......	......	......	S½SE¼	16	26	56	4-15—8-15	.146	35.52

1887	11.84	S½SE¼	16	26	56	4-15—8-15	.146	35.52
1893	11.83	S½SE¼	16	26	56	4-15—8-15	.146	35.49
1877	13.45	N½NE¼	21	26	56	4-15—8-15	.165	40.35
1882	13.45	N½NE¼	21	26	56	4-15—8-15	.165	40.35
1887	13.45	N½NE¼	21	26	56	4-15—8-15	.165	40.35
1893	13.46	N½NE¼	21	26	56	4-15—8-15	.165	40.38
1877	20.42	NW¼	21	26	56	4-15—8-15	.251	61.26
1882	20.42	NW¼	21	26	56	4-15—8-15	.251	61.26
1887	20.43	NW¼	21	26	56	4-15—8-15	.251	61.29
1893	20.43	NW¼	21	26	56	4-15—8-15	.251	61.29
1905	3.63	SW¼SW¼	22	26	56	4-15—8-15	.045	10.89
1905	3.77	SE¼SE¼	21	26	56	4-15—8-15	.046	11.31
1905	.69	SE¼SE¼	21	26	56	4-15—8-15	.008	2.07
1905	4.11	SW¼SE¼	21	26	56	4-15—8-15	.051	12.33
1905	2.62	NE¼NE¼	28	26	56	4-15—8-15	.032	7.86
1905	7.42	NW¼NE¼	28	26	56	4-15—8-15	.091	22.42

Claimant—**James Sastanovich.** Proof No. 00673

Source—**Walthers Creek, Sherman Canyon, and Springs.** Ditch—**Nos. 1 to 4, incl.**

1905	1.38	NE¼NE¼	20	26	56	4-15—8-15	.017	4.14
1905	7.23	NE¼NE¼	20	26	56	4-15—8-15	.089	21.69
1905	3.33	NW¼NE¼	20	26	56	4-15—8-15	.041	9.99
1905	1.53	SE¼SE¼	17	26	56	4-15—8-15	.009	4.59
1905	.40	SE¼SE¼	17	26	56	4-15—8-15	.005	1.20
1905	1.62	SW¼SE¼	17	26	56	4-15—8-15	.020	4.86

Claimant—**John C. Hackward.** Proof No. 00674

Source—**Dixie Creek.** Ditch—**John C. Hackward Ditches.**

1883	4.86	NW¼SE¼	17	30	54	4-15—8-15	.060	14.58
1883	8.44	SW¼NE¼	17	30	54	4-15—8-15	.104	25.32
1883	1.85	NE¼NW¼	17	30	54	4-15—8-15	.023	5.55
1883	.51	NE¼NW¼	17	30	54	4-15—8-15	.006	1.53
1884	1.31	NW¼SE¼	17	30	54	4-15—8-15	.016	3.93
1884	16.08	SW¼NE¼	17	30	54	4-15—8-15	.198	48.24
1884	.20	SW¼NE¼	17	30	54	4-15—8-15	.002	.60
1884	2.22	SE¼NE¼	17	30	54	4-15—8-15	.027	6.66
1884	16.35	NW¼NE¼	17	30	54	4-15—8-15	.201	49.05
1884	3.88	NE¼NW¼	17	30	54	4-15—8-15	.048	11.64
1890	2.67	SE¼SW¼	5	30	54	4-15—8-15	.033	8.01
1890	5.32	NE¼NW¼	8	30	54	4-15—8-15	.065	15.96
1890	.88	SE¼NW¼	8	30	54	4-15—8-15	.011	2.64

Claimant—**James Bett.** Proof No. 00675

Source—**Dixie Creek and Tributaries.** Ditch—**James Bett Ditches.**

Date of beneficial use: Nat. mdw.	Date of beneficial use: Cult. area	Construction first initiated: Dams	Construction first initiated: Ditches	Culture—Acres: Harvest crops	Culture—Acres: Meadow pasture	Culture—Acres: Willow and sage pasture	Culture—Acres: Swamp or overflow	Location: Subdivision	Location: Section	Location: Tp.N.	Location: R.E.	Length of season	Duty of water: C.F.S.	Duty of water: Acre-feet
	1882			.14				SE¼SW¼	32	31	54	4-15—8-15	.002	.42
	1882			3.32				SW¼SE¼	32	31	54	4-15—8-15	.041	9.96
	1882			5.90				NW¼SE¼	32	31	54	4-15—8-15	.073	17.70
	1882			6.66				SW¼NE¼	32	31	54	4-15—8-15	.082	19.98
	1882			1.99				SE¼NW¼	32	31	54	4-15—8-15	.024	5.97
	1882			1.99				NE¼NW¼	32	31	54	4-15—8-15	.024	5.97
	1883			42.72					28	31	54	4-15—8-15	.525	128.16
	1884			42.72					29	31	54	4-15—8-15	.525	128.16
	1885			42.71					32	31	54	4-15—8-15	.525	128.13
	1885			3.49*				NW¼SW¼	29	31	54	4-15—8-15	.043	10.47
	1885			2.74*				NE¼SE¼	30	31	54	4-15—8-15	.034	8.22
	1885			14.34								4-15—8-15	.176	43.02
	1887			14.34					21	31	54	4-15—8-15	.176	43.02
	1890			14.33					28	31	54	4-15—8-15	.176	42.99
	1892			14.33								4-15—8-15	.176	42.99

*Water for the irrigation of this land comes from Bullion Creek.

Claimant—**J. J. Hylton.** Proof No. 00676

Source—**Bullion Creek.** Ditch—**Nos. 1-7, incl.**

Nat. mdw.	Cult. area	Dams	Ditches	Harvest crops	Meadow pasture	Willow and sage pasture	Swamp or overflow	Subdivision	Section	Tp.N.	R.E.	Length of season	C.F.S.	Acre-feet
	1874			.25				SE¼SE¼	25	31	53	4-15—8-15	.031	.75
	1874			5.80				SW¼SE¼	25	31	53	4-15—8-15	.071	17.40
	1874			6.20				SE¼SW¼	25	31	53	4-15—8-15	.076	18.60
	1874			5.95				SW¼SW¼	25	31	53	4-15—8-15	.073	17.85
	1874			4.78				SE¼SE¼	26	31	53	4-15—8-15	.059	14.34
	1874			6.39				SW¼SE¼	26	31	53	4-16—8-15	.079	19.17
	1874			1.95				SE¼SW¼	26	31	53	4-16—8-15	.024	5.85

Claimant—**Bett & Papa.** Proof No. 00677

Source—**Creeks** (no name) tributary **to South Fork.** Ditch—**Nos. 1, 2, 3, 4, 5, 6, 7.**

Nat. mdw.	Cult. area	Dams	Ditches	Harvest crops	Meadow pasture	Willow and sage pasture	Swamp or overflow	Subdivision	Section	Tp.N.	R.E.	Length of season	C.F.S.	Acre-feet
	1882			3.25				SW¼SW¼	11	31	53	4-15—8-15	.040	9.75
	1882			6.46				SW¼SE¼	11	31	53	4-15—8-15	.079	19.38
	1882			8.88				SE¼SE¼	11	31	53	4-15—8-15	.109	26.64
	1882			4.70				SW¼SW¼	12	31	53	4-15—8-15	.058	14.10
	1882			.41				NE¼NW¼	13	31	53	4-15—8-15	.005	1.23
	1882			4.91				NW¼NW¼	13	31	53	4-15—8-15	.060	14.73
	1882			3.29				NE¼NE¼	14	31	53	4-15—8-15	.040	9.87
	1882			1.74				SE¼NE¼	14	31	53	4-15—8-15	.021	5.22
	1882			16.63				SW¼NE¼	14	31	53	4-15—8-15	.205	49.89
	1882			1.69				NW¼NE¼	14	31	53	4-15—8-15	.021	5.07
	1882			8.45				NE¼NW¼	14	31	53	4-15—8-15	.106	25.35
	1882			13.22				NW¼NW¼	14	31	53	4-15—8-15	.163	39.66
	1882			10.85				SE¼NW¼	14	31	53	4-15—8-15	.133	32.56
	1882			3.39				NE¼SW¼	14	31	53	4-15—8-15	.042	10.17

1882	5.79	NW¼SW¼	14	31	53	4-15—8-15	.071	17.37
1882	3.43	NW¼SW¼	14	31	53	4-15—8-15	.042	10.29
1882	11.53	SE¼SE¼	15	31	53	4-15—8-15	.142	34.59
1882	4.60	SW¼SE¼	15	31	53	4-15—8-15	.057	13.80
1882	1.06	NE¼NE¼	15	31	53	4-15—8-15	.013	3.18
1882	9.67	NW¼NE¼	22	31	53	4-15—8-15	.119	29.01

Claimant—**Bett & Papa.** Proof No. 00678

Source—**Dixie Creek.** Ditch—**Nos. 1 and 2.**

1882	4.42	NE¼SW¼	3	31	54	4-15—8-15	.054	13.26
1882	15.73	SE¼SW¼	3	31	54	4-15—8-15	.193	47.19
1882	3.40	NW¼NE¼	3	31	54	4-15—8-15	.042	10.20
1882	24.08	SW¼NE¼	3	31	54	4-15—8-15	.206	72.24
1882	39.56	NW¼SE¼	3	31	54	4-15—8-15	.442	118.68
1882	31.62	SW¼SE¼	3	31	54	4-15—8-15	.389	94.86
1882	2.37	NW¼NE¼	10	31	54	4-15—8-15	.029	7.11
1882	6.29	NE¼NW¼	10	31	54	4-15—8-15	.077	18.87
1885	0.69	NE¼NW¼	3	31	54	4-15—8-15	.008	2.07
1885	16.18	SE¼NW¼	3	31	54	4-15—8-15	.199	48.54
1885	16.60	NE¼SW¼	3	31	54	4-15—8-15	.204	49.80
1885	12.33	SE¼SW¼	3	31	54	4-15—8-15	.152	36.99
1885	12.01	NE¼NW¼	3	31	54	4-15—8-15	.148	36.03
1885	2.07	SE¼NW¼	3	31	54	4-15—8-15	.025	6.21

Claimant—**E. E. Elliot.** Proof No. 00679

Source—**North Fork Dixie Creek and Springs.** Ditch—**E. E. Elliot Ditches.**

1878	3.63	NW¼SE¼	13	30	53	4-15—8-15	.044	10.89
1878	3.86	NW¼SW¼	13	30	53	4-15—8-15	.047	11.58
1878	0.48	SW¼SW¼	13	30	53	4-15—8-15	.006	1.44
1878	7.82	SE¼SW¼	13	30	53	4-15—8-15	.096	23.46
1878	21.02	NE¼SW¼	13	30	53	4-15—8-15	.259	63.06

Source—**Cissillini Canyon Creek.** Ditch—**Dixie Creek Ditch.**

1893	1.69	NE¼NW¼	13	30	53	4-15—8-15	.021	5.07
1893	6.23	NW¼NW¼	13	30	53	4-15—8-15	.077	18.69
1893	1.08	NE¼NE¼	14	30	53	4-15—8-15	.013	3.24

Source—**South Fork Dixie Creek.** Ditch—**Dixie Creek Ditch.**

1892	15.13	SE¼SE¼	13	30	53	4-15—8-15	.186	45.39
1892	36.68	NE¼NE¼	24	30	53	4-15—8-15	.451	110.04
1892	26.41	SE¼NE¼	24	30	53	4-15—8-15	.325	79.23
1892	0.30	SW¼NE¼	24	30	53	4-15—8-15	.004	0.90
1892	2.54	NW¼NW¼	19	30	54	4-15—8-15	.031	7.62
1892	0.10	SW¼NW¼	19	30	54	4-15—8-15	.001	0.30

Claimant—**Chas. Hairgrove.** Proof No. 00680

Source—**Rattlesnake Creek.** Ditch—**Chas. Hairgrove Ditches.**

Date of beneficial use: Nat. mdw.	Cult. area	Construction first initiated: Dams	Ditches	Culture—Acres: Harvest crops	Meadow pasture	Willow and sage pasture	Swamp or overflow	Location: Subdivision	Section	Tp.N.	R.E.	Length of season	Duty of water: C.F.S.	Acre-feet
	1902			9.52				SE¼	29	31	57	4-15—8-15	.117	28.56
	1903			5.95				NE¼NE¼	32	31	57	4-15—8-15	.118	17.85
	1905					100.00						4-15—5-15	1.230	75.00

Claimant—**Merkley & Young.** Proof No. 00681

Source—**Lindsay and Twin Creeks.** Ditch—**Merkeley & Young Ditches.**

Date of beneficial use: Nat. mdw.	Cult. area	Construction first initiated: Dams	Ditches	Culture—Acres: Harvest crops	Meadow pasture	Willow and sage pasture	Swamp or overflow	Location: Subdivision	Section	Tp.N.	R.E.	Length of season	Duty of water: C.F.S.	Acre-feet
	1869			11.05				S½S½	6	27	56	4-15—8-15	.136	33.15
	1870			8.70				N½N½	7	27	56	4-15—8-15	.107	26.10
	1871			7.83				SE¼SE¼	1	27	55	4-15—8-15	.096	23.49
	1872			64.70				NE¼NE¼	12	27	55	4-15—8-15	.796	194.10
	1874			22.50								4-15—8-15	.277	67.50
	1889			34.72								4-15—8-15	.427	104.16

NOTE—"It is agreed between Merkley & Young and J. J. Hylton that sufficient water will be allowed to run down Lindsay Creek and Twin Creek at all times for stock-watering purposes in the following described lands: Sec. 35, T 28 N, R 55 E; Sec. 2, T 27 N, R 55 E; Secs. 6 and 7, T 27 N, R 56 E, and Secs. 1 and 12, T 27 N, R 55 E, and such agreement is binding upon parties to agreement."

These lands were included in the suit H. H. Porch v. U. Lani et al., No. 1644, Elko County Records. After listing dates and areas they were pooled and then listed in accordance with the decree.

Claimant—**J. J. Hylton.** Proof No. 00681

Source—**Lindsay and Twin Creeks.** Ditch—**J. J. Hylton Ditches.**

Date of beneficial use: Nat. mdw.	Cult. area	Construction first initiated: Dams	Ditches	Culture—Acres: Harvest crops	Meadow pasture	Willow and sage pasture	Swamp or overflow	Location: Subdivision	Section	Tp.N.	R.E.	Length of season	Duty of water: C.F.S.	Acre-feet
	1869			11.05				SE¼NW¼	35	28	55	4-15—8-15	.136	33.15
	1870			8.70				E½SW¼	35	28	55	4-15—8-15	.107	26.10
	1871			7.82				W½SE¼	35	28	55	4-15—8-15	.096	23.46
	1872			64.70				NE¼	2	27	55	4-15—8-15	.796	194.10
	1874			22.50								4-15—8-15	.277	67.50
	1889			27.59								4-15—8-15	.339	83.77

NOTE—"It is agreed between Merkley & Young and J. J. Hylton that sufficient water will be allowed to run down Lindsay Creek and Twin Creek at all times for stock-watering purposes in the following described lands: Sec. 35, T 28 N, R 55 E; Sec. 2, T 27 N, R 55 E; Secs. 6 and 7, T 27 N, R 56 E, and Secs. 1 and 12, T 27 N, R 56 E."

These lands were included in the suit H. H. Porch v. U. Lani et al., No. 1644, Elko County Records. After listing dates and areas they were pooled and then listed in accordance with the decree.

Claimant—**E. Dotta.** Proof No. 00685

Source—**Smith Creek.** Ditch—**E. Dotta Ditches.**

Date of beneficial use: Nat. mdw.	Cult. area	Construction first initiated: Dams	Ditches	Culture—Acres: Harvest crops	Meadow pasture	Willow and sage pasture	Swamp or overflow	Location: Subdivision	Section	Tp.N.	R.E.	Length of season	Duty of water: C.F.S.	Acre-feet
	1898			248.70				NW¼NE¼	12	31	55			
								E½E½	12	31	55			
								E½E½	13	31	55			
								W½SW¼	7	31	56			
								W½W½	18	31	56			
								NE¼NE¼	24	31	55			
								NW¼NW¼	19	31	56	4-15—8-15	3.059	746.10

Claimant—**J. J. Hylton.** Proof No. **00686**

Source—**Huntington Creek.** Ditch—**Nos. 1, 2, and 3.**

1869	76.15		S½SW¼	15	28	56	4-15—8-15	.937	228.45
1869	86.72		NW¼	22	28	56	4-15—8-15	1.067	260.19
1900	17.30		SE¼SE¼	16	28	55	4-15—8-15	.213	51.90
1900	71.15		NE¼	21	28	55	4-15—8-15	.875	213.45

Claimant—**Albert Lomori.** Proof No. **00687**

Source—**South Fork of Humboldt River.** Ditch—**Albert Lomori Ditches.**

1902	32.60		Lots 1, 2 & 3	30	33	55	4-15—8-15	.401	97.80

Claimant—**Thurber Estate** (Deed in escrow to Nevada Bunker Hill Mining Company).

Source—**Springs.** Ditch—**Thurber Estate Ditches.** Proof No. **00688**

1889			Plant in NW¼NW¼	35	31	53	1-1—12-31	1.00	

For mining and milling purposes.

Claimant—**George Clayton.** Proof No. **00689**

Source—**Ten Mile Creek.** Ditch—**George Clayton Ditches.**

1892	47.37		E½SW¼	34	33	55	4-15—8-15	.583	142.11
1892	....	9.96	W½SE¼	34	33	55	4-15—5-15	.123	7.47
1889	10.00		NE¼SE¼	34	33	55	4-15—8-15	.123	30.00
1888	13.91		S½NE¼	34	33	55	4-15—8-15	.171	41.73
1897	52.55		NW¼	35	33	55	4-15—8-15	.646	157.65
1897	..	4.15	NW¼SW¼	35	33	55	4-15—5-15	.051	3.11
1898	..	38.18	....	....	....	....	4-15—5-15	.470	28.64
1905	7.25		....	....	....	....	4-15—8-15	.089	21.75

APPENDIX A

Stipulation Between Huntington and Diamond Valley Land and Stock Company and J. J. Hylton, Merkley & Young, and Frank Odiaga, Regarding the Use of Waters of Huntington Creek.

"It is stipulated between claimant and J. J. Hylton, S. A. Merkley and S. S. Young and Merkley & Young, a copartnership, and Frank Odiaga, that in order to settle the existing claims to the flood waters of Huntington Creek, they agree as follows: That said Hylton, Merkley, Young, Merkley & Young, and Frank Odiaga claim no right to any of the springs located upon or rising upon the lands of said corporation for irrigating purposes, or for any waters that may be developed by the development of any or all of these springs, and that said waters, if developed, may be used upon any of the lands of said corporation;

"That they do not claim for irrigation purposes any of the waters of Huntington Creek or its tributaries within the lands of the corporation after the flood season, which ends during each year within the period from about March 15 to April 1, and they do not claim any right whatsoever to any of said waters during the irrigating season of each year after said flood season;

"And it is agreed by said corporation that it will during each year allow flood waters to run in their natural courses as they are wont to flow from the place where said flood waters enter the head of the channel to a point in the NW¼NE¼ of 15, 26–55, to the end of said flood season for the use of the other parties to this stipulation below the northern extremity of the lands of said corporation, it being understood that nothing herein contained shall be construed to prevent the said corporation from using said flood waters for the purpose of irrigating lands below the NW¼NE¼ of 15, 26–55, at any time in accordance with their priorities on the stream, and in and to said waters and upon the land shown on map as meadow and pasture to the north of said point;

"And it is understood and agreed that nothing herein contained shall interfere with the turning of sufficient waters by said corporation into the natural watercourses and ditches to provide stock water for the parties immediately adjacent to said lands of said corporation;

"And it is further stipulated, in order to adjust existing claims upon the stream that said corporation will after the hay has been cut and stacked each year, and during and after the dry season, and after supplying its existing and necessary demands for stock-watering pur-

poses, shall prior to distributing any water for irrigation purposes, to wit, on the 1st day of September of each year, turn into the channel water for stock-watering purposes for the use of the other parties to this stipulation, in a quantity sufficient to cause it to flow in its natural channel a distance of one-half mile below the northerly boundary fence on the land of said corporation. This water to be used for stock watering only, and not for irrigation."

APPENDIX B

CO-OP DITCH

The Co-Op Ditch was constructed in 1893 and carries water from Ackler Creek into Herder Creek.

No water is to be turned into said Co-Op Ditch until all rights on Ackler Creek prior to 1893 have been satisfied.

The following claimants have a vested right from Ackler Creek through the Co-Op Ditch into Herder Creek:

Lands of: C. H. Black, S. M. Davis, John Riddell, Wm. Goodale, Hylton & Mentz, W. W. Weathers, James O'Brien, Wilbur Smiley, E. A. Hylton (Lane Estate), John Crossen, W. J. Smiley, E. C. Riddell, Geo. Byers (Priority—1893).

APPENDIX C

The following pages represent the continuation of rights acquired prior to 1905 into the period 1906 to date, or lands upon which the water was not diverted until after 1905:

APPENDIX C—Continued.

Claimant—**Antonio J. Alves.** Proof No. 001
Source—**Humboldt River.** Ditch—**Old Channel.**

Date of beneficial use: Nat. mdw.	Date of beneficial use: Cult. area	Construction first initiated: Dams	Construction first initiated: Ditches	Culture—Acres: Harvest crops	Culture—Acres: Meadow pasture	Culture—Acres: Willow and sage pasture	Culture—Acres: Swamp or overflow	Location: Subdivision	Location: Section	Location: Tp.N.	Location: R.E.	Length of season	Duty of water: C.F.S.	Duty of water: Acre-feet
	1907			15.00				NW¼NW¼	18	27	32	3-15—9-15	.122	45.00
	1908			14.00				NW¼NW¼	18	27	32	3-15—9-15	.114	42.00
	1912			2.00				NW¼NW¼	18	27	32	3-15—9-15	.016	6.00

Claimant—**Grace S. Jahn.** Proof No. 005
Source—**Humboldt River.** Ditch—**Union Canal through Reed Ditch.**

Nat. mdw.	Cult. area	Dams	Ditches	Harvest crops	Meadow pasture	Willow and sage pasture	Swamp or overflow	Subdivision	Section	Tp.N.	R.E.	Length of season	C.F.S.	Acre-feet
	1913			30.00				N½	34	26	31	3-15—9-15	.244	90.00
	1913			28.00				N½	34	26	31	3-15—9-15	.228	84.00
	1913			4.00				N½	34	26	31	3-15—9-15	.033	12.00
	1913			3.00				N½	34	26	31	3-15—9-15	.024	9.00

This area holds water right as of 1876 for willow and sage pasture.

Claimant—**Pitt & McDonald.** Proof No. 006
Source—**Humboldt River.** Ditch—**Union Canal through Lake Shore Ditch.**

Nat. mdw.	Cult. area	Dams	Ditches	Harvest crops	Meadow pasture	Willow and sage pasture	Swamp or overflow	Subdivision	Section	Tp.N.	R.E.	Length of season	C.F.S.	Acre-feet
	1914			70.00				NW¼	4	25	31	3-15—9-15	.569	210.00
	1915			40.00				NW¼	4	25	31	3-15—9-15	.325	120.00
	1920			28.36				NW¼	4	25	31	3-15—9-15	.231	85.08

Claimant—**Ed. Berg.** Proof No. 007
Source—**Humboldt River.** Ditch—**Young Ditch.**

Nat. mdw.	Cult. area	Dams	Ditches	Harvest crops	Meadow pasture	Willow and sage pasture	Swamp or overflow	Subdivision	Section	Tp.N.	R.E.	Length of season	C.F.S.	Acre-feet
	1910			5.00				E½E½	1	27	31	3-15—9-15	.040	15.00
	1913			8.41				E½E½	1	27	31	3-15—9-15	.068	25.23

Claimant—**F. A. Preston.** Proof No. 0011
Source—**Humboldt River.** Ditch—**Graveyard Slough and *Union Canal.**

Nat. mdw.	Cult. area	Dams	Ditches	Harvest crops	Meadow pasture	Willow and sage pasture	Swamp or overflow	Subdivision	Section	Tp.N.	R.E.	Length of season	C.F.S.	Acre-feet
	1906			9.00				W½SE¼	29	26	31	3-15—9-15	.073	27.00
	1915			3.60*				W½SE¼	29	26	31	3-15—9-15	.029	10.80
	1920			22.77*				S½W½ofSE¼	29	26	31	3-15—9-15	.185	68.81
	1920			5.95				N½W½ofSE¼	29	26	31	3-15—9-15	.048	17.85

Claimant—**L. N. Carpenter.** Proof No. 0013
Source—**Humboldt River.** Ditch—**Rodgers Canal System.**

Nat. mdw.	Cult. area	Dams	Ditches	Harvest crops	Meadow pasture	Willow and sage pasture	Swamp or overflow	Subdivision	Section	Tp.N.	R.E.	Length of season	C.F.S.	Acre-feet
	1919			16.70				SE¼SW¼	2	26	31	3-15—9-15	.136	50.10
	1915			11.80				N½SE¼	2	26	31	3-15—9-15	.096	35.40
	1919			35.27				E½NW¼	2	26	31	3-15—9-15	.287	105.81

1912	138.40		NW¼	27	26	31	3-15—9-15	1.125	515.20
1912	6.70		NW¼	27	26	31	3-15—9-15	.054	20.10
1913	6.90		W½SW¼	1	26	31	3-15—9-15	.056	20.70

Claimant—**Chris Beck.** Proof No. 0014

Source—**Humboldt River. Ditch—Tule Ditch.**

1909	45.00		SW¼	10	25	31	8-15—9-15	.366	135.00
1909	....	15.75	SW¼	10	25	31	3-15—6-13	.128	23.63
1909	....	17.30	SW¼	10	25	31	3-15—6-13	.141	25.95

Claimant—**John Christensen.** Proof No. 0015

Source—**Humboldt River.** Ditch—**Irish American.**

1913	5.15		SW¼NW¼	28	27	31	3-15—9-15	.042	15.45
1912	13.45		NE¼NW¼	28	27	31	3-15—9-15	.109	40.35

Claimant—**J. C. Damm.** Proof No. 0018

Source—**Humboldt River.** Ditch—**Union Canal through Lake Shore Ditch.**

1917	32.66		NW¼	28	26	31	3-15—9-15	.266	97.98
1913	15.39		NW¼	28	26	31	3-15—9-15	.125	46.17

Claimant—**Lawrence Devita.** Proof No. 0021

Source—**Humboldt River.** Ditch—**Old Channel.**

1908	13.00		NE¼	13	27	31	3-15—9-15	.106	39.00
1914	12.70		NE¼	13	27	31	3-15—9-15	.103	38.10

Claimant—**Frank Ambrosetti & John Scott.** Proof No. 0022

Source—**Humboldt River.** Ditch—**Old Channel.**

1908	5.95		NW¼NW¼	24	27	31	3-15—9-15	.048	17.85
1910	30.10		NW¼	24	27	31	3-15—9-15	.245	90.30
1910	7.15		NE¼NW¼	24	27	31	3-15—9-15	.058	21.45
1913	14.92		NE¼NW¼	24	27	31	3-16—9-15	.121	44.76
1913	4.59		SE¼NW¼	24	27	31	3-15—9-15	.037	13.77
1913	29.27		SW¼NW¼	24	27	31	3-15—9-15	.238	87.81
1912	1.15		NW¼NW¼	24	27	31	3-15—9-15	.009	3.45

Claimant—**Mrs. Eva Granis.** Proof No. 0030

Source—**Humboldt River.** Ditch—**Southwest Ditch.**

1910	10.20		SE¼SE¼	27	27	31	3-15—9-15	.083	30.60

Claimant—**Nellie Martin.** Proof No. 0033

Source—**Humboldt River.** Ditch—**Larson Ditch; Union Canal through Reed Ditch.**

*1919	3.00		S½SE¼	33	26	31	3-15—9-15	.024	9.00
*1921	4.85		S½SE¼	33	26	31	3-15—9-15	.039	14.55

*This land has a water right as of 1875 for willow and sage pasture.

Date of beneficial use — Nat. mdw.	Date of beneficial use — Cult. area	Construction first initiated — Dams	Construction first initiated — Ditches	Culture—Acres — Harvest crops	Culture—Acres — Meadow pasture	Culture—Acres — Willow and sage pasture	Culture—Acres — Swamp or overflow	Location — Subdivision	Location — Section	Location — Tp.N.	Location — R.E.	Length of season	Duty of water — C.F.S.	Duty of water — Acre-feet
Claimant—**Ingvert Hanson.** Source—**Humboldt River.** Ditch—**Union Canal through Lake Shore Ditch.** Proof No. 0034														
	1906			20.00				SW¼	32	26	31	3-15—9-15	.163	60.00
	1906			18.60				SW¼	32	26	31	3-15—9-15	.151	55.80
Claimant—**Andrew Jacobson.** Source—**Humboldt River.** Ditch—**Young Ditch.** Proof No. 0035														
	1906			3.55				NW¼	7	27	32	3-15—9-15	.029	10.65
	1912			10.20				NE¼NW¼	7	27	32	3-15—9-15	.083	30.60
	1917			1.00				N½NW¼	7	27	32	3-15—9-15	.008	3.00
Claimant—**Estate John J. Hill.** Source—**Humboldt River.** Ditch—**Union Canal through Lake Shore Ditch.** Proof No. 0038														
	1910			77.10				NW¼	29	36	31	3-15—9-15	.627	231.30
Claimant—**Hugh Holmstrom.** Source—**Humboldt River.** Ditch—**Young Ditch.** Proof No. 0041														
	1909			3.85				N½	2	27	31	3-15—9-15	.031	11.55
Claimant—**John Holmstrom.** Source—**Humboldt River.** Ditch—**Young Ditch.** Proof No. 0042														
	1909			80.00				SE¼	31	28	32	3-15—9-15	.650	240.00
	1911			20.00				SE¼	31	28	32	3-15—9-15	.163	60.00
	1914			11.50				E½NW¼	6	28	32	3-15—9-15	.093	34.50
	1914			6.00				W½NE¼	6	27	32	3-15—9-15	.049	18.00
	1914			2.00				E½NE¼	6	27	32	3-15—9-15	.016	6.00
Claimant—**Nels Jensen.** Source—**Humboldt River.** Ditch—**Young Ditch.** Proof No. 0045														
	1909			12.40				NW¼	11	27	31	3-15—9-15	.101	37.20
Claimant—**James Johnson.** Source—**Humboldt River.** Ditch—**Young Ditch.** Proof No. 0046														
	1909			13.75				E½W½	1	27	31	3-15—9-15	.112	41.25
Claimant—**Paul Johnson.** Source—**Humboldt River.** Ditch—**Union Canal through Lake Shore Ditch.** Proof No. 0048														
	1906			9.01				SW¼	33	26	31	3-15—9-15	.073	27.03
	1914			.88				SW¼	33	26	31	3-15—9-15	.007	2.64

Claimant—**Mrs. John Chambers.** Proof No. 0048
Source—**Humboldt River.** Ditch—**Union Canal through Lake Shore Ditch.**

1906	6.32	SW¼	33	26	31	3-15—9-15	.051	18.96
1914	.62	SW¼	33	26	31	3-15—9-15	.005	1.86

Claimant—**H. P. Kruse.** Proof No. 0052
Source—**Humboldt River.** Ditch—**Young Ditch.**

1917	2.00	NE¼	12	27	31	3-15—9-15	.016	6.00
1917	2.00	NE¼	12	27	31	3-15—9-15	.016	6.00
1913	5.00	NE¼	12	27	31	3-15—9-15	.041	15.00
1920	3.00	NE¼	12	27	31	3-15—9-15	.024	9.00

Claimant—**John & Domenico Ferritto.** Proof No. 0057
Source—**Humboldt River.** Ditch—**Reed Ditch from Union Canal.**

1917	4.00*	W½NE¼	33	26	31	3-15—9-15	.033	12.00

***This area has water right as of 1884 for willow and sage pasture.**

Claimant—**N. C. Munk.** Proof No. 0059
Source—**Humboldt River.** Ditch—**Union Canal through Reed Ditch.**

1919	6.00	W½NE¼	4	25	31	3-15—9-15	.049	18.00
1920	5.00	W½NE¼	4	25	31	3-15—9-15	.041	15.00

Claimant—**W. C. Pitt.** Proof No. 0064
Source—**Humboldt River.** Ditch—**Old Channel Ditch.**

1906	213.25	N½&SE¼	16	27	31	3-15—9-15	1.735	639.75
1913	69.44		16	27	31	3-15—9-15	.565	208.32
1913	10.16		16	27	31	3-15—9-15	.083	30.48
1913	10.59		16	27	31	3-15—9-15	.086	31.77

Claimants—**Lawrence Devita.** Proof No. 0066
Source—**Humboldt River.** Ditch—**Old Channel.**

1908	28.30	SW¼NW¼	18	27	32	3-15—9-15	.230	84.90
1912	2.30	SW¼NW¼	18	27	32	3-15—9-15	.019	6.90
1920	5.00	SW¼NW¼	18	27	32	3-15—9-15	.041	15.00

Claimant—**W. C. Ruddell.** Proof No. 0068
Source—**Humboldt River.** Ditch—**Irish American.**

1912	20.85	E¼SE¼	26	27	31	3-15—9-15	.170	62.55
1912	15.75	SE¼SE¼	26	27	31	3-15—9-15	.128	47.25
1912	25.55	S½SE¼	26	27	31	3-15—9-15	.208	76.65
1912	10.20	CenterSE¼	26	27	31	3-15—9-15	.083	30.60

Claimant—**H. M. Damm.** Proof No. 0094
Source—**Humboldt River.** Ditch—**Old Channel and Young.**

Date of beneficial use: Nat. mdw.	Date of beneficial use: Cult. area	Construction first initiated: Dams	Construction first initiated: Ditches	Culture—Acres: Harvest crops	Culture—Acres: Meadow pasture	Culture—Acres: Willow and sage pasture	Culture—Acres: Swamp or overflow	Location: Subdivision	Location: Section	Location: Tp.N.	Location: R.E.	Length of season	Duty of water: C.F.S.	Duty of water: Acre-feet
	1910			5.60				W½W½	1	27	31	3-15—9-15	.046	16.80

Claimant—**Thomas P. Ebert.** Proof No. **00700**
Source—**Humboldt River.** Ditch—**Young Ditch.**

Date of beneficial use: Nat. mdw.	Date of beneficial use: Cult. area	Construction first initiated: Dams	Construction first initiated: Ditches	Culture—Acres: Harvest crops	Culture—Acres: Meadow pasture	Culture—Acres: Willow and sage pasture	Culture—Acres: Swamp or overflow	Location: Subdivision	Location: Section	Location: Tp.N.	Location: R.E.	Length of season	Duty of water: C.F.S.	Duty of water: Acre-feet
	1915			15.70				SW¼SW¼	7	27	32	3-15—9-15	.128	47.10
	1915			20.90				SE¼SW¼&NE¼SW¼	7	27	32	3-15—9-15	.170	62.70
	1915			32.00				SE¼SW¼&NE¼SW¼	7	27	32	3-15—9-15	.260	96.00

Claimant—**Geo. W. Ostrander.** Proof No. **00701**
Source—**Humboldt River.** Ditch—**Young Ditch.**

Date of beneficial use: Nat. mdw.	Date of beneficial use: Cult. area	Construction first initiated: Dams	Construction first initiated: Ditches	Culture—Acres: Harvest crops	Culture—Acres: Meadow pasture	Culture—Acres: Willow and sage pasture	Culture—Acres: Swamp or overflow	Location: Subdivision	Location: Section	Location: Tp.N.	Location: R.E.	Length of season	Duty of water: C.F.S.	Duty of water: Acre-feet
	1914			54.63				SW¼	7	27	32	3-15—9-15	.444	163.89

Claimant—**William M. Biggs.** Proof No. **00702**
Source—**Humboldt River.** Ditch—**Young Ditch.**

Date of beneficial use: Nat. mdw.	Date of beneficial use: Cult. area	Construction first initiated: Dams	Construction first initiated: Ditches	Culture—Acres: Harvest crops	Culture—Acres: Meadow pasture	Culture—Acres: Willow and sage pasture	Culture—Acres: Swamp or overflow	Location: Subdivision	Location: Section	Location: Tp.N.	Location: R.E.	Length of season	Duty of water: C.F.S.	Duty of water: Acre-feet
	1914			65.40				W½SE¼	7	27	32	3-15—9-15	.532	196.20

Claimant—**John G. Taylor.** Proof No. **00111**
Source—**Humboldt River.** Ditch—**Taylor Dam.**

Date of beneficial use: Nat. mdw.	Date of beneficial use: Cult. area	Construction first initiated: Dams	Construction first initiated: Ditches	Culture—Acres: Harvest crops	Culture—Acres: Meadow pasture	Culture—Acres: Willow and sage pasture	Culture—Acres: Swamp or overflow	Location: Subdivision	Location: Section	Location: Tp.N.	Location: R.E.	Length of season	Duty of water: C.F.S.	Duty of water: Acre-feet
	1912					9.53		NW¼SW¼	20	33	35	3-15—4-28	.077	7.15
	1912					19.84		NE¼SW¼	20	33	35	3-15—4-28	.161	14.88
	1912					38.64		SW¼SW¼	20	33	35	3-15—4-28	.314	28.98
	1912					10.45		SE¼SW¼	20	33	35	3-15—4-28	.085	7.84
	1912					37.76		NW¼SE¼	20	33	35	3-15—4-28	.307	28.32
	1912					25.55		NE¼SE¼	20	33	35	3-15—4-28	.208	19.16

Claimant—Taylor & Sheehan. Proof No. **00120**
Source—**Humboldt River.** Ditch—**High Line Canal.**

Date of beneficial use: Nat. mdw.	Date of beneficial use: Cult. area	Construction first initiated: Dams	Construction first initiated: Ditches	Culture—Acres: Harvest crops	Culture—Acres: Meadow pasture	Culture—Acres: Willow and sage pasture	Culture—Acres: Swamp or overflow	Location: Subdivision	Location: Section	Location: Tp.N.	Location: R.E.	Length of season	Duty of water: C.F.S.	Duty of water: Acre-feet
	1912			30.85				NW¼NW¼	19	30	40	3-15—9-15	.251	92.55
	1912					1.80		NW¼NW¼	19	30	40	3-15—4-28	.015	1.35
	1912			20.00				SW¼NE¼	19	30	40	3-15—9-15	.103	60.00

	1912					2.00		SW¼NE¼	19	36	40	3-15—4-28	.024	2.18
	1912			8.25				SW¼NE¼	19	36	40	3-15—9-15	.067	24.75
	1912			36.75				SE¼NW¼	19	36	40	3-15—9-15	.299	110.25
	1912			4.30				SW¼NW¼	19	36	40	3-15—9-15	.085	12.90
	1912					26.25		SW¼NW¼	19	36	40	3-15—4-28	.213	19.69
	1912			35.03				NE¼SE¼	19	36	40	3-15—9-15	.285	105.09
	1912					3.22		NE¼SE¼	19	36	40	3-15—4-28	.026	2.42
	1912			38.30				NW¼SE¼	19	36	40	3-15—9-15	.311	114.90
	1912			10.30				NE¼SW¼	19	36	40	3-15—9-15	.084	30.90
	1912					38.95		NW¼SW¼	13	36	39	3-15—4-28	.317	29.21
	1912					37.85		SW¼SE¼	13	36	39	3-15—4-28	.308	38.20
	1912					40.70		SE¼SW¼	13	36	39	3-15—4-28	.311	30.53
	1912					19.40		SW¼SW¼	13	36	39	3-15—4-28	.158	14.55
	1912					12.85		NE¼NE¼	14	36	39	3-15—4-28	.104	9.64
	1912					40.50		SE¼NE¼	14	36	39	3-15—4-28	.329	80.38
	1912					12.95		SW¼NE¼	14	36	39	3-15—4-28	.105	9.71
	1912					22.45		NE¼SE¼	14	36	39	3-15—4-28	.183	16.84
	1912					.90		NW¼SE¼	14	36	39	3-15—4-28	.007	.68
	1912			.70				NE¼NE¼	24	36	39	3-15—9-15	.006	2.10
	1912					33.90		NE¼NE¼	24	36	39	3-15—4-28	.271	24.98
	1912					39.05		NW¼NE¼	24	36	39	3-15—4-28	.317	29.29
	1912					13.30		NE¼NW¼	24	36	39	3-15—4-28	.108	9.98
	1912					39.80		SE¼NE¼	24	36	39	3-15—4-28	.323	29.85
	1912					16.55		SW¼NE¼	24	36	39	3-15—4-28	.135	12.41
	1912					17.40		NE¼SE¼	24	36	39	3-15—4-28	.141	13.05
	1912			13.00				SE¼SE¼	13	36	39	3-15—9-15	.106	39.00
	1912					6.35		SE¼SE¼	13	36	39	3-15—4-28	.052	4.76
	1912					9.30		NW¼SE¼	13	36	39	3-15—4-28	.086	6.98
	1912					15.20		SW¼NW¼	13	36	39	3-15—4-28	.124	11.40
	1912			8.15				SW¼SW¼	18	36	40	3-15—9-15	.066	24.45
	1912					2.85		NW¼SE¼	20	26	40	3-15—4-28	.023	2.14
	1912			15.00				NE¼SW¼	20	36	40	3-15—9-15	.122	45.00
	1912			32.40				NW¼SW¼	20	36	40	3-15—9-15	.263	97.20
	1912			.15				SW¼NW¼	20	36	40	3-15—9-15	.001	.45
	1912					6.50		SW¼NE¼	20	36	40	3-15—4-28	.053	4.88
	1912					23.85		SE¼SE¼	20	36	40	3-15—4-28	.194	17.89
	1912			25.70				SW¼SE¼	20	36	40	3-15—9-15	.209	77.10
	1912					8.65		SW¼SE¼	20	36	40	3-15—4-28	.071	6.49
	1912					.35		SW¼SE¼	20	36	40	3-15—4-28	.003	.26
	1912			30.35				SE¼SW¼	20	36	40	3-15—9-15	.247	91.05
	1912					4.85		SE¼SW¼	20	36	40	3-15—4-28	.039	3.64
	1912			38.90				SW¼SW¼	20	36	40	3-15—9-15	.316	116.70
	1912					1.50		SW¼SW¼	20	36	40	3-15—4-28	.012	1.13
	1912			3.85				NE¼NE¼	29	36	40	3-15—9-15	.031	11.55
	1912					11.05		NE¼NE¼	29	36	40	3-15—4-28	.090	8.29
	1912			33.55				NW¼NE¼	29	36	40	3-15—9-15	.273	100.65
	1912					1.25		NW¼NE¼	29	36	40	3-15—4-28	.010	.94
	1912			28.85				NE¼NW¼	29	36	40	3-15—9-15	.235	86.55
	1912					9.00		NE¼NW¼	29	36	40	3-15—4-28	.073	6.75
	1912			40.30				SE¼SE¼	19	36	40	3-15—9-15	.328	120.90
	1912			19.80				SW¼SE¼	19	36	40	3-15—9-15	.161	59.40
	1912					8.45		SW¼SE¼	19	36	40	3-15—4-28	.069	6.34
	1912			27.70				NE¼NE¼	30	36	40	3-15—9-15	.225	83.10

Taylor & Sheehan—Continued.

Date of beneficial use: Nat. mdw.	Cult. area	Construction first initiated: Dams	Ditches	Culture—Acres: Harvest crops	Meadow pasture	Willow and sage pasture	Swamp or overflow	Location: Subdivision	Section	Tp.N.	R.E.	Length of season	Duty of water: C.F.S.	Acre-feet
	1912			.40				NW¼NE¼	30	36	40	3-15—9-15	.003	1.20
	1912				6.00			NW¼NE¼	30	36	40	3-15—6-13	.041	9.00
	1912					21.05		NW¼NE¼	30	36	40	3-15—4-28	.171	15.79
	1912			2.95				SE¼NE¼	30	36	40	3-15—9-15	.024	8.85
	1912			38.70				NW¼NW¼	29	36	40	3-15—9-15	.315	116.10
	1912					1.10		NW¼NW¼	29	36	40	3-15—4-28	.009	.83
	1912			1.00				SE¼NE¼	29	36	40	3-15—9-15	.008	3.00
	1912			36.15				SW¼NE¼	29	36	40	3-15—9-15	.294	108.45
	1912			20.50				SE¼NW¼	29	36	40	3-15—9-15	.177	61.50
	1912			10.80				SW¼NW¼	29	36	40	3-15—9-15	.088	32.40
	1912					40.20		NE¼SW¼	13	36	39	3-15—4-28	.327	30.15

Source—**Humboldt River.** Ditch—**Pump from Sink Hole.**

Nat. mdw.	Cult. area	Dams	Ditches	Harvest crops	Meadow pasture	Willow and sage pasture	Swamp or overflow	Subdivision	Section	Tp.N.	R.E.	Length of season	C.F.S.	Acre-feet
	1912					9.85		NW¼NW¼	34	36	40	3-15—4-28	.080	7.39
	1912					7.10		NE¼NW¼	34	36	40	3-15—4-28	.058	5.33
	1912					15.80		NW¼NE¼	34	36	40	3-15—4-28	.128	11.85
	1912					13.90		NE¼NE¼	34	36	40	3-15—4-28	.113	10.43

Source—**Humboldt River.** Ditch—**Pole Creek Ditches.**

Nat. mdw.	Cult. area	Dams	Ditches	Harvest crops	Meadow pasture	Willow and sage pasture	Swamp or overflow	Subdivision	Section	Tp.N.	R.E.	Length of season	C.F.S.	Acre-feet
	1912			12.20				SE¼NE¼	19	36	40	3-15—9-15	.099	36.60
	1912			25.35				NE¼NW¼	19	36	40	3-15—9-15	.206	76.05

Claimant—**Humboldt Land and Cattle Co.** Proof No. 00154

Source—**Humboldt River.** Ditch—**Pump.**

Nat. mdw.	Cult. area	Dams	Ditches	Harvest crops	Meadow pasture	Willow and sage pasture	Swamp or overflow	Subdivision	Section	Tp.N.	R.E.	Length of season	C.F.S.	Acre-feet
	1918			5.20				NE¼NE¼	28	32	49	3-15—9-15	.042	15.60
	1918			1.56				SE¼NE¼	28	32	49	3-15—9-15	.012	4.68
	1918			10.40				NW¼NE¼	28	32	49	3-15—9-15	.085	31.20
	1918			35.84				SW¼NE¼	28	32	49	3-15—9-15	.291	107.52
	1918			9.36				SE¼NW¼	28	32	49	3-15—9-15	.076	28.08
	1918			13.00				NE¼SW¼	28	32	49	3-15—9-15	.106	39.00
	1918			12.48				SE¼SW¼	28	32	49	3-15—9-15	.101	37.44

Claimant—**George Kaeding.** Proof No. 00163

Source—**Humboldt River.** Ditch—**Kaeding.**

Nat. mdw.	Cult. area	Dams	Ditches	Harvest crops	Meadow pasture	Willow and sage pasture	Swamp or overflow	Subdivision	Section	Tp.N.	R.E.	Length of season	C.F.S.	Acre-feet
	1914						40.00	SE¼NE¼	34	33	45	3-15—4-28	.325	30.00
	1914						40.00	SW¼NE¼	34	33	45	3-15—4-28	.325	30.00
	1914						40.00	NE¼NW¼	34	33	45	3-15—4-28	.325	30.00
	1914						40.00	SE¼NW¼	34	33	45	3-15—4-28	.325	30.00
	1914						40.00	NW¼NW¼	34	33	45	3-15—4-28	.325	30.00

	1914						40.00	SW¼NW¼	34	33	45	3-15—4-28	.325	30.00
	1914						39.52	NW¼SW¼	34	33	45	3-15—4-28	.321	29.64
	1914						35.47	SW¼SW¼	34	33	45	3-15—4-28	.288	26.60

Source—**Humboldt River.** Ditch—**South Ditch.**

	1914			0.70				NW¼SE¼	2	32	45	3-15—9-15	.079	29.10
	1914			3.20				SW¼SE¼	2	32	45	3-15—9-15	.026	9.60
	1914			38.28				NE¼NW¼	2	32	45	3-15—9-15	.311	114.84
	1914			39.92				SE¼NW¼	2	32	45	3-15—9-15	.325	119.76
	1914			40.15				NW¼NW¼	2	32	45	3-15—9-15	.326	120.45
	1914			40.07				SW¼NW¼	2	32	45	3-15—9-15	.326	120.21
	1914			40.05				NE¼SW¼	2	32	45	3-15—9-15	.326	120.15
	1914			8.52				SE¼SW¼	2	32	45	3-15—9-15	.069	25.56
	1914			40.00				NW¼SW¼	2	32	45	3-15—9-15	.325	120.00
	1914			9.80				SW¼SW¼	2	32	45	3-15—9-15	.080	29.40
	1914			12.37				SE¼NW¼	1	32	45	3-15—9-15	.101	37.11
	1914					4.47		SE¼NW¼	1	32	45	3-15—4-28	.036	3.35
	1914			5.05				NW¼NW¼	1	32	45	3-15—9-15	.041	15.15
	1914			22.55				NW¼NE¼	2	32	45	3-15—9-15	.183	67.65
	1914			25.59				SW¼NE¼	2	32	45	3-15—9-15	.208	76.77
	1914				3.51			SW¼NE¼	2	32	45	3-15—6-13	.021	5.27
	1914					2.15		SW¼NE¼	2	32	45	3-15—4-28	.017	1.61

Claimant—**J. W. Puett.** Proof No. 00322
Source—**Maggie Creek.** Ditch—**Palmer.**

	1908			10.00				SE¼NW¼	26	33	52	4-15—8-15	.123	30.00
	1909			8.00				SE¼NW¼	26	33	52	4-15—8-15	.098	24.00
	1910			12.00				NW¼SE¼	26	33	52	4-15—8-15	.148	36.00
	1912			14.00				SE¼SW¼	26	33	52	4-15—8-15	.172	42.00

Claimant—**Max Arnhold.** Proof No. 00351
Source—**Pearl Creek.** Ditch—**Max Arnhold Ditches.**

	1911			20.30				W½	21	28	56			
								W½SE¼	21	28	56			
								SE¼SE¼	21	28	56			
								S½S½	22	28	56			
								N½NE¼	28	28	56	4-15—8-15	.250	60.90

Claimant—**T. F. Brennen.** Proof No. 00353
Source—**Ainley, Ogilvie, Young, and Cottonwood Creeks.** Ditch—**Brennen Ditches.**

	1908			14.26*				W½SW¼	10	32	57	4-15—8-15	.175	42.78
	1910			28.52†					....	....	....	4-15—8-15	.351	85.56

*Has flood water right on pasture as of 1900. †From Cottonwood Creek only.

Claimant—**J. J. Hylton.** Proof No. 00355
Source—**South Fork Humboldt River and Rattlesnake Creek.** Ditch—**J. J. Hylton Ditches.**

Date of beneficial use: Nat. mdw.	Cult. area	Construction first initiated: Dams	Ditches	Culture—Acres: Harvest crops	Meadow pasture	Willow and sage pasture	Swamp or overflow	Location: Subdivision	Section	Tp.N.	R.E.	Length of season	Duty of water: C.F.S.	Acre-feet
	1907			28.00				S½	23	31	56	4-15—8-15	0.344	84.00
	1908			2.00				S½	24	31	56	4-15—8-15	0.025	6.00
	1909			30.57				S½NW¼	24	31	56	4-15—8-15	0.374	91.11
	1911			40.91				NW¼NW¼	25	31	56	4-15—8-15	0.503	122.73
	1912			80.91					26	31	56	4-15—8-15	0.995	212.73
	1912			23.70				NE¼	27	31	56	4-15—8-15	0.292	71.10
	1913			100.91								4-15—8-15	1.241	302.73
	1914			95.91								4-15—8-15	1.180	287.73
	1915			140.92								4-15—8-15	1.733	422.76
	1918			53.82								4-15—8-15	0.662	161.46
	1918			36.50								4-15—8-15	0.449	109.50
	1920			17.82								4-15—8-15	0.209	53.46

Early Water only from Rattlesnake Creek.

Source—**Pearl Creek and South Fork Humboldt River.** Ditch—**J. J. Hylton Ditches.**

	1911			15.00				E½SE¼	19	31	57			
								SW¼	20	31	57	4-15—8-15	0.183	45.00

Claimant—**Pedro Corta.** Proof No. 00356
Source—**Spencer Creek.** Ditch—**Pedro Corta Ditches.**

	1907			13.30				E½W½	12	28	56			
								SW¼	1	28	56			
								S½NW¼	1	28	56	4-15—8-15	.164	39.90

Claimant—**Clark Drown.** Proof No. 00357
Source—**South Fork Humboldt River.** Ditch—**Clark Drown Ditches.**

	1909			10.00				S½SW¼	8	31	57	4-15—8-15	.123	30.00
	1910			55.00				N½	17	31	57	4-15—8-15	.677	165.00
	1910			16.00				N½SE¼	17	31	57	4-15—8-15	.197	48.00
	1911			20.00				NE¼SW¼	17	31	57	4-15—8-15	.246	60.00
	1911			51.00				NE¼	18	31	57	4-15—8-15	.627	153.00
	1912			64.50				SE¼NW¼	18	31	57	4-15—8-15	.793	193.50
	1915			22.50								4-15—8-15	.277	67.50
	1916			15.00								4-15—8-15	.185	45.00
	1916			30.00								4-15—8-15	.369	90.00
	1916			35.00								4-15—8-15	.431	105.00
	1916					246.00						4-15—8-15	3.026	184.50

Claimant—**Albert Hankins.** Proof No. 00358
Source—**Smith, South Fork, Smith Creek, McCutcheons, Adams, and Dry Creeks.**
Ditch—**Albert Hankins Ditches.**

1909		70.00	NW¼	2	29	56			
			NE¼	3	29	56	4-15—5-15	.861	52.50

Claimant—**J. J. Hylton.** Proof No. 00359
Source—**South Fork Humboldt River.** Ditch—**J. J. Hylton Ditches.**

1908	40.00	SE¼	4	32	55			
1912	9.50	S½	3	32	55			
1915	40.00		10	32	55			
1920	35.00	W½	11	32	55			
		N½	15	32	55			
			14	32	55			
		E½	23	32	55	4-15—8-15	.492	120.00
		W½	24	32	55	4-15—8-15	.117	28.50
		SE¼	24	32	55	4-15—8-15	.492	120.00
			25	32	55	4-15—9-15	.431	105.00

Source—**Smith Creek.** Ditch—**J. J. Hylton Ditches.**

1909	17.00	NW¼	33	30	56	4-15—8-15	.209	51.00
1912	19.00	NW¼	33	30	56	4-15—8-15	.234	57.00
1909	4.00	SW¼	33	30	56	4-15—8-15	.049	12.00
1915	22.50	SW¼	33	30	56	4-15—8-15	.277	67.50
1912	18.67	SW¼	33	30	56	4-15—8-15	.230	56.01
1915	22.00	NW¼	4	29	56	4-15—8-15	.271	66.00
1912	4.33	NW¼	4	29	56	4-15—8-15	.053	12.99
1909	19.00	NE¼	32	30	56	4-15—8-15	.234	57.00
1915	5.00	NE¼	32	30	56	4-15—8-15	.062	15.00
1915	12.00	SW¼	32	30	56	4-15—8-15	.148	36.00
1916	97.00	SW¼	32	30	56	4-15—8-15	1.193	291.00
1915	73.00	SE¼	32	30	56	4-15—8-15	.898	279.00
1916	6.00	NW¼	5	29	56	4-15—8-15	.074	18.00
1909	1.00	SE¼	29	30	56	4-15—8-15	.012	3.00
1915	10.00	NW¼	32	30	56	4-15—8-15	.123	30.00

Source—**South Fork Humboldt River.** Ditch—**J. J. Hylton Ditches.**

1912	69.00	S½NE¼	15	31	57			
1912	10.50	SE¼	15	31	57			
		W½SW¼	14	31	57	4-15—8-15	.849	207.00
		SW¼NW¼	14	31	57	4-15—8-15	.129	31.50

Claimant—**Chas. Mitchell.** Proof No. 00362

Source—**Brown's Creek.** Ditch—**Chas. Mitchell Ditches.**

Date of beneficial use: Nat. mdw.	Date of beneficial use: Cult. area	Construction first initiated: Dams	Construction first initiated: Ditches	Culture—Acres: Harvest crops	Culture—Acres: Meadow pasture	Culture—Acres: Willow and sage pasture	Culture—Acres: Swamp or overflow	Location: Subdivision	Location: Section	Location: Tp.N.	Location: R.E.	Length of season	Duty of water: C.F.S.	Duty of water: Acre-feet
	1906			36.70				NE¼NE¼	30	28	56			
								NW¼NW¼	29	28	56			
								S½NW¼	20	28	56			
								SW¼NE¼	29	28	56			
								N½S½	29	28	56			
								NE¼SE¼	29	28	56			
								N½SW¼	28	28	56	4-15—8-15	.378	92.10

Claimant—**P. J. Ogilvie.** Proof No. 00364

Source—**South Fork of Humboldt River and Rattlesnake Creek.**

Nat. mdw.	Cult. area	Dams	Ditches	Harvest crops	Meadow pasture	Willow and sage pasture	Swamp or overflow	Subdivision	Section	Tp.N.	R.E.	Length of season	C.F.S.	Acre-feet
	1908			77.00				S½	14	31	56	4-15—8-15	.947	231.00
	1915			53.00				S½	13	31	56	4-15—8-15	.652	159.00
								N½	24	31	56			
								W½NW¼	19	31	57			

Early water only from Rattlesnake Creek.

Claimant—**Ernest Hodges.** Proof No. 00370

Source—**Dry Creek and Springs.** Ditch—**Ernest Hodges Ditches.**

Nat. mdw.	Cult. area	Dams	Ditches	Harvest crops	Meadow pasture	Willow and sage pasture	Swamp or overflow	Subdivision	Section	Tp.N.	R.E.	Length of season	C.F.S.	Acre-feet
	1906			39.00				SW¼	30	33	57	4-15—8-15	.480	117.00

Claimant—**A. M. Griswold.** Proof No. 00372

Source—**South Fork Humboldt River.** Ditch—**Griswold Ditches.**

Nat. mdw.	Cult. area	Dams	Ditches	Harvest crops	Meadow pasture	Willow and sage pasture	Swamp or overflow	Subdivision	Section	Tp.N.	R.E.	Length of season	C.F.S.	Acre-feet
	1906			7.00				N½NW¼	10	31	56	5-15—8-15	.086	21.00
	1908			55.00				NE¼	10	31	56	5-15—8-15	.677	165.00
	1910			28.00				E½SE¼	10	31	56	5-15—8-15	.344	84.00
	1911			25.00				S½NW¼	11	31	56	5-15—8-15	.308	75.00
	1913					10.00		W½SW¼	11	31	56	5-15—6-15	.123	7.50
	1915			50.00				N½	14	31	56	5-15—8-15	.615	150.00
	1915			55.00								5-15—8-15	.677	165.00
	1915			35.00								5-15—8-15	.431	105.00
	1916			16.00								5-15—8-15	.197	48.00
	1917			15.00								5-15—8-15	.185	45.00

Claimant—**Minnie Hankins, Lillie Hankins, Elizabeth Hankins, Estate Jane Bellinger.** Proof No. 00375

Source—**South Fork of Humboldt.** Ditch—**Hankins & Bellinger Ditches.**

Nat. mdw.	Cult. area	Dams	Ditches	Harvest crops	Meadow pasture	Willow and sage pasture	Swamp or overflow	Subdivision	Section	Tp.N.	R.E.	Length of season	C.F.S.	Acre-feet
	1906			44.36				W½	31	32	56			
								NE¼NW¼	6	31	56			

								N½NE¼	6	31	56			
								SE¼NE¼	6	31	56	4-15—8-15	.546	133.08

Claimant—**J. J. Hylton.** Proof No. 00381
Source—**Cottonwood Creek.** Ditch—**Nos. 1, 2, 3, 5, and 6.**

	1909			7.80				SW¼NW¼	15	30	56	4-15—8-15	.096	23.40
	1909			0.50				SE¼NE¼	16	30	56	4-15—8-15	.006	1.50
	1909			1.30				NE¼NE¼	16	30	56	4-15—8-15	.016	3.90
	1909			1.00				NW¼NW¼	15	30	56	4-15—8-15	.012	3.00

Claimant—**Drown Bros.** Proof No. 00385
Source—**South Fork of Humboldt River.** Ditch—**Drown Bros. Ditches.**

								S½NW¼	10	31	56			
	1906			80.00				SW¼	10	31	56			
	1907			26.00				W½SE¼	10	31	56			
	1909			75.00				SE¼NW¼	11	31	56			
								S½NE¼	11	31	56	4-15—8-15	.984	240.00
								E½SW¼	11	31	56	4-15—8-15	.320	78.00
								SE¼	11	31	56	4-15—8-15	.923	225.00
	1906					38.80		N½	22	31	56	4-15—5-15	.477	29.10
	1906			20.00				S½NW¼	23	31	56	4-15—8-15	.246	60.00
	1907			33.50								4-15—8-15	.412	100.50
	1908			30.80								4-15—8-15	.379	92.40
	1909					52.70						4-15—5-15	.648	39.53
	1909			51.80								4-15—8-15	.637	155.40
	1911			15.40								4-15—8-15	.189	46.20
	1912				48.10							4-15—6-15	.592	72.15
	1913				18.40							4-15—6-15	.226	27.60
	1908			10.90				NE¼	15	31	56	4-15—8-15	.134	32.70
	1909			3.00				E½SE¼	15	31	56	4-15—8-15	.037	9.00
	1910			21.80				SW¼SE¼	15	31	56	4-15—8-15	.268	65.40
	1915			110.80				S½SW¼	15	31	56	4-15—8-15	1.363	332.40
	1917			59.50				NW¼SW¼	15	31	56	4-15—8-15	.732	178.50
	1919			21.70				SW¼NW¼	15	31	56	4-15—8-15	.267	65.10
	1918					12.50		NE¼NW¼	9	31	56	4-15—5-15	.154	9.38
	1919					50.00		NE¼	9	31	56	4-15—5-15	.615	37.50
	1920					88.70		NE¼SE¼	9	31	56	4-15—5-15	1.091	66.53

Claimant—**A. J. Dewar.** Proof No. 00388
Source—**South Fork Humboldt River.** Ditch—**A. J. Dewar Ditches.**

	1907			18.00				S½S½	17	31	57			
	1908			17.32				S½	18	31	57			
	1910			6.78				SE¼NE¼	19	31	57	4-15—8-15	.221	54.00
								N½NE¼	19	31	57	4-15—8-15	.213	51.96
								NE¼NW¼	19	31	57	4-15—8-15	.083	20.34

Date of beneficial use — Nat. mdw.	Date of beneficial use — Cult. area	Construction first initiated — Dams	Construction first initiated — Ditches	Culture—Acres — Harvest crops	Culture—Acres — Meadow pasture	Culture—Acres — Willow and sage pasture	Culture—Acres — Swamp or overflow	Location — Subdivision	Location — Section	Location — Tp.N.	Location — R.E.	Length of season	Duty of water — C.F.S.	Duty of water — Acre-feet
Claimant—**Ingvert Hanson.** Source—**Humboldt River.** Ditch—**Union Canal through Lake Shore Ditch.** Proof No. 0034														
	1906			20.00				SW¼	32	26	31	3-15—9-15	.163	60.00
	1906			18.60				SW¼	32	26	31	3-15—9-15	.151	55.80
Claimant—**Andrew Jacobson.** Source—**Humboldt River.** Ditch—**Young Ditch.** Proof No. 0035														
	1906			3.55				NW¼	7	27	32	3-15—9-15	.029	10.65
	1912			10.20				NE¼NW¼	7	27	32	3-15—9-15	.083	30.60
	1917			1.00				N½NW¼	7	27	32	3-15—9-15	.008	3.00
Claimant—**Estate John J. Hill.** Source—**Humboldt River.** Ditch—**Union Canal through Lake Shore Ditch.** Proof No. 0038														
	1910			77.10				NW¼	29	36	31	3-15—9-15	.627	231.30
Claimant—**Hugh Holmstrom.** Source—**Humboldt River.** Ditch—**Young Ditch.** Proof No. 0041														
	1909			3.85				N½	2	27	31	3-15—9-15	.031	11.55
Claimant—**John Holmstrom.** Source—**Humboldt River.** Ditch—**Young Ditch.** Proof No. 0042														
	1909			80.00				SE¼	31	28	32	3-15—9-15	.650	240.00
	1911			20.00				SE¼	31	28	32	3-15—9-15	.163	60.00
	1914			11.50				E½NW¼	6	28	32	3-15—9-15	.093	34.50
	1914			6.00				W½NE¼	6	27	32	3-15—9-15	.049	18.00
	1914			2.00				E½NE¼	6	27	32	3-15—9-15	.016	6.00
Claimant—**Nels Jensen.** Source—**Humboldt River.** Ditch—**Young Ditch.** Proof No. 0045														
	1909			12.40				NW¼	11	27	31	3-15—9-15	.101	37.20
Claimant—**James Johnson.** Source—**Humboldt River.** Ditch—**Young Ditch.** Proof No. 0046														
	1909			13.75				E½W½	1	27	31	3-15—9-15	.112	41.25
Claimant—**Paul Johnson.** Source—**Humboldt River.** Ditch—**Union Canal through Lake Shore Ditch.** Proof No. 0048														
	1906			9.01				SW¼	33	26	31	3-15—9-15	.073	27.03
	1914			.88				SW¼	33	26	31	3-15—9-15	.007	2.64

Claimant—**Mrs. John Chambers.** Proof No. 0048

Source—**Humboldt River.** Ditch—**Union Canal through Lake Shore Ditch.**

1906	6.32	SW¼	33	26	31	3-15—9-15	.051	18.96
1914	.62	SW¼	33	26	31	3-15—9-15	.005	1.86

Claimant—**H. P. Kruse.** Proof No. 0052

Source—**Humboldt River.** Ditch—**Young Ditch.**

1917	2.00	NE¼	12	27	31	3-15—9-15	.016	6.00
1917	2.00	NE¼	12	27	31	3-15—9-15	.016	6.00
1913	5.00	NE¼	12	27	31	3-15—9-15	.041	15.00
1920	3.00	NE¼	12	27	31	3-15—9-15	.024	9.00

Claimant—**John & Domenico Ferritto.** Proof No. 0057

Source—**Humboldt River.** Ditch—**Reed Ditch from Union Canal.**

1917	4.00*	W½NE¼	33	26	31	3-15—9-15	.033	12.00

*This area has water right as of 1884 for willow and sage pasture.

Claimant—**N. C. Munk.** Proof No. 0059

Source—**Humboldt River.** Ditch—**Union Canal through Reed Ditch.**

1919	6.00	W½NE¼	4	25	31	3-15—9-15	.049	18.00
1920	5.00	W½NE¼	4	25	31	3-15—9-15	.041	15.00

Claimant—**W. C. Pitt.** Proof No. 0064

Source—**Humboldt River.** Ditch—**Old Channel Ditch.**

1906	213.25	N½&SE¼	16	27	31	3-15—9-15	1.735	639.75
1913	69.44		16	27	31	3-15—9-15	.565	208.32
1913	10.16		16	27	31	3-15—9-15	.083	30.48
1913	10.59		16	27	31	3-15—9-15	.086	31.77

Claimants—**Lawrence Devita.** Proof No. 0066

Source—**Humboldt River.** Ditch—**Old Channel.**

1908	28.30	SW¼NW¼	18	27	32	3-15—9-15	.230	84.90
1912	2.30	SW¼NW¼	18	27	32	3-15—9-15	.019	6.90
1920	5.00	SW¼NW¼	18	27	32	3-15—9-15	.041	15.00

Claimant—**W. C. Ruddell.** Proof No. 0068

Source—**Humboldt River.** Ditch—**Irish American.**

1912	20.85	E¼SE¼	26	27	31	3-15—9-15	.170	62.55
1912	15.75	SE¼SE¼	26	27	31	3-15—9-15	.128	47.25
1912	25.55	S½SE¼	26	27	31	3-15—9-15	.208	76.65
1912	10.20	CenterSE¼	26	27	31	3-15—9-15	.083	30.60

Claimant—**Millie R. Evans (Rodger Estate).** Proof No. 0069
Source—**Humboldt River.** Ditch—**Rodgers Canal System.**

Date of beneficial use: Nat. mdw.	Date of beneficial use: Cult. area	Construction first initiated: Dams	Construction first initiated: Ditches	Culture—Acres: Harvest crops	Culture—Acres: Meadow pasture	Culture—Acres: Willow and sage pasture	Culture—Acres: Swamp or overflow	Location: Subdivision	Location: Section	Location: Tp.N.	Location: R.E.	Length of season	Duty of water: C.F.S.	Duty of water: Acre-feet
	1909			56.45					25	26	31	3-15—9-15	.459	169.35
	1918			65.16					7	26	32	3-15—9-15	.530	195.48
	1919			61.42				N½	10	26	31	3-15—9-15	.499	184.26
	1918			70.33					19	26	32	3-15—9-15	.572	210.99
	1918			105.09				N½	30	26	32	3-15—9-15	.854	315.27

Claimant—**Matt Smith.** Proof No. 0072
Source—**Humboldt River.** Ditch—**Young Ditch.**

Nat. mdw.	Cult. area	Dams	Ditches	Harvest crops	Meadow pasture	Willow and sage pasture	Swamp or overflow	Subdivision	Section	Tp.N.	R.E.	Length of season	C.F.S.	Acre-feet
	1909			6.15				W½E½	1	27	31	3-15—9-15	.050	18.45
	1912			3.00				W½E½	1	27	31	3-15—9-15	.024	9.00

Claimant—**I. M. Springer, Sr.** Proof No. 0073
Source—**Humboldt River.** Ditch—**Irish American.**

Nat. mdw.	Cult. area	Dams	Ditches	Harvest crops	Meadow pasture	Willow and sage pasture	Swamp or overflow	Subdivision	Section	Tp.N.	R.E.	Length of season	C.F.S.	Acre-feet
	1906			9.50				W½NE¼&NW¼SE¼	23	27	31	3-15—9-15	.077	28.50
	1906			38.00				E½NE¼	23	27	31	3-15—9-15	.309	104.00
	1909			14.35				W½NE¼&NW¼SE¼	23	27	31	3-15—9-15	.117	43.05
	1914			3.00				W½SE¼	23	27	31	3-15—9-15	.024	9.00
	1915			3.00				NW¼SE¼	23	27	31	3-15—9-15	.024	9.00

Claimant—**B. E. Stoker.** Proof No. 0075
Source—**Humboldt River.** Ditch—**Union Canal.**

Nat. mdw.	Cult. area	Dams	Ditches	Harvest crops	Meadow pasture	Willow and sage pasture	Swamp or overflow	Subdivision	Section	Tp.N.	R.E.	Length of season	C.F.S.	Acre-feet
	1911			6.00				SW¼SW¼	24	27	31	3-15—9-15	.049	18.00
	1912			41.50				E½SE¼	23	27	31	3-15—9-15	.362	133.50
	1913			9.55				E½SE¼	23	27	31	3-15—9-15	.078	28.65

Claimant—**Pascasio Bilbao.** Proof No. 0078
Source—**Humboldt River.** Ditch—**Union Canal through Lake Shore Ditch.**

Nat. mdw.	Cult. area	Dams	Ditches	Harvest crops	Meadow pasture	Willow and sage pasture	Swamp or overflow	Subdivision	Section	Tp.N.	R.E.	Length of season	C.F.S.	Acre-feet
	1911					5.50		W½NE¼NE¼	29	26	31	3-15—6-13	.045	8.25

Claimant—**Lovelock Land and Development Co.** Proof. No. 0080
Source—**Humboldt River.** Ditch—**Lovelock Land and Development Company Ditch System.**

Nat. mdw.	Cult. area	Dams	Ditches	Harvest crops	Meadow pasture	Willow and sage pasture	Swamp or overflow	Subdivision	Section	Tp.N.	R.E.	Length of season	C.F.S.	Acre-feet
	1908			85.30				NE¼	2	25	31	3-15—9-15	.698	255.90
	1906			458.48				W½&SE¼	18	25	31	3-15—9-15	3.727	1375.44

Claimant—**John G. Taylor.** Proof No. 0081
Source—**Humboldt River.** Ditch—**Marsen Slough.**

Nat. mdw.	Cult. area	Dams	Ditches	Harvest crops	Meadow pasture	Willow and sage pasture	Swamp or overflow	Subdivision	Section	Tp.N.	R.E.	Length of season	C.F.S.	Acre-feet
	1917			60.78				N½NW¼	32	27	31	3-15—9-15	.494	182.34
	1917			20.14				S½NW¼	32	27	31	3-15—9-15	.164	60.42

Source—**Humboldt River.** Ditch—**Young Ditch.**

1913	167.80		S½S½	34	28	31	3-15—9-15	1.364	503.40
1913	36.51		E½S½	34	28	31	3-15—9-15	.297	109.53
1917	145.81		NE¼	34	28	31	3-15—9-15	1.186	437.43

Claimant—**Bergman & Alfree.** Proof No. 0082

Source—**Humboldt River.** Ditch—**Southwest Ditch, Lovelock and Borland Slough.**

1914	42.55		SE¼	34	27	31	3-15—9-15	.346	127.65
1916	44.48		SE¼	34	27	31	3-15—9-15	.362	133.44

Source—**Humboldt River.** Ditch—**Southwest Ditch.**

1913		3.95	SW¼SE¼	33	27	31	3-15—6-13	.032	5.93
1913	40.50		S½NE¼	32	27	31	3-15—9-15	.329	121.50
1914	22.78		NE¼NE¼	3	26	31	3-15—9-15	.185	68.34
1916	59.00		N½	3	26	31	3-15—9-15	.480	177.00

Claimant—**F. Tessier.** Proof No. 0085

Source—**Humboldt River.** Ditch—**Old Channel Ditch.**

1910	22.70		SW¼&SE¼	13	27	31	3-15—9-15	.185	68.10
1912	15.93		SE¼&SW¼	13	27	31	3-15—9-15	.130	47.79
1912	18.00		SW¼SE¼	13	27	31	3-15—9-15	.146	54.00
1912	9.98		SE¼SE¼	13	27	31	3-15—9-15	.081	29.94
1913	8.95		SE¼SW¼	13	27	31	3-15—9-15	.073	26.85

Claimant—**Peter Olson.** Proof No. 0088

Source—**Humboldt River.** Ditch—**Old Channel Ditch.**

1920	8.00		S½NW¼	12	27	31	3-15—9-15	.065	24.00

Claimant—**W. W. Van Reed.** Proof No. 0089

Source—**Humboldt River.** Ditch—**Union Canal through Lake Shore Ditch.**

1918	5.90*		E½SW¼	29	26	31	3-15—9-15	.048	17.70
1918	15.00		NW¼SE¼SW¼	29	26	31	3-15—9-15	.122	45.00

*This area holds water right as of 1897 for willow and sage pasture.

Claimant—**Emil Hostman.** Proof No. 0090

Source—**Humboldt River.** Ditch—**Old Channel.**

1910	7.80*		E½NW¼	18	27	32	3-15—9-15	.063	23.40
1911	43.65		E½NW¼	18	27	32	3-15—9-15	.355	130.95
1912	24.11		E½NW¼&W½NW¼	18	27	32	3-15—9-15	.196	72.33
1912	5.57		E½NW¼	18	27	32	3-15—9-15	.045	16.71

*South and west of ditch.

Claimant—**Andrew Westfall.** Proof No. 0091

Source—**Humboldt River.** Ditch—**Union Canal through Lake Shore Ditch.**

1914	10.00		E½E½	31	26	31	3-15—9-15	.081	30.00

This area holds water right as of 1888 for willow and sage pasture.

Date of beneficial use: Nat. mdw.	Date of beneficial use: Cult. area	Construction first initiated: Dams	Construction first initiated: Ditches	Culture—Acres: Harvest crops	Culture—Acres: Meadow pasture	Culture—Acres: Willow and sage pasture	Culture—Acres: Swamp or overflow	Location: Subdivision	Location: Section	Location: Tp.N.	Location: R.E.	Length of season	Duty of water: C.F.S.	Duty of water: Acre-feet
Claimant—H. M. Damm. Source—**Humboldt River.** Ditch—**Old Channel and Young.** Proof No. 0094														
	1910			5.60				W½W½	1	27	31	3-15—9-15	.046	16.80
Claimant—Thomas P. Ebert. Source—**Humboldt River.** Ditch—**Young Ditch.** Proof No. 00700														
	1915			15.70				SW¼SW¼	7	27	32	3-15—9-15	.128	47.19
	1915			20.90				SE¼SW¼&NE¼SW¼	7	27	32	3-15—9-15	.170	62.70
	1915			32.00				SE¼SW¼&NE¼SW¼	7	27	32	3-15—9-15	.260	96.00
Claimant—Geo. W. Ostrander. Source—**Humboldt River.** Ditch—**Young Ditch.** Proof No. 00701														
	1914			54.63				SW¼	7	27	32	3-15—9-15	.444	163.89
Claimant—William M. Biggs. Source—**Humboldt River.** Ditch—**Young Ditch.** Proof No. 00702														
	1914			65.40				W½SE¼	7	27	32	3-15—9-15	.532	196.20
Claimant—John G. Taylor. Source—**Humboldt River.** Ditch—**Taylor Dam.** Proof No. 00111														
	1912					9.53		NW¼SW¼	20	33	35	3-15—4-28	.077	7.15
	1912					19.84		NE¼SW¼	20	33	35	3-15—4-28	.161	14.88
	1912					38.64		SW¼SW¼	20	33	35	3-15—4-28	.314	28.98
	1912					10.45		SE¼SW¼	20	33	35	3-15—4-28	.085	7.84
	1912					37.76		NW¼SE¼	20	33	35	3-15—4-28	.307	28.32
	1912					25.55		NE¼SE¼	20	33	35	3-15—4-28	.208	19.16
Claimant—Taylor & Sheehan. Source—**Humboldt River.** Ditch—**High Line Canal.** Proof No. 00120														
	1912			30.85				NW¼NW¼	19	36	40	3-15—9-15	.251	92.55
	1912					1.80		NW¼NW¼	19	36	40	3-15—4-28	.015	1.35
	1912			20.00				SW¼NE¼	19	36	40	3-15—9-15	.163	60.00

	1912					2.90		SW¼NE¼	19	36	40	3-15—4-28	.024	2.18
	1912			8.25				SW¼NE¼	19	36	40	3-15—9-15	.067	24.75
	1912			36.75				SE¼NW¼	19	36	40	3-15—9-15	.290	110.25
	1912			4.30				SW¼NW¼	19	36	40	3-15—9-15	.035	12.90
	1912					26.25		SW¼NW¼	19	36	40	3-15—4-28	.213	19.69
	1912			35.03				NE¼SE¼	19	36	40	3-15—9-15	.285	105.69
	1912					3.22		NE¼SE¼	19	36	40	3-15—4-28	.026	2.42
	1912			38.30				NW¼SE¼	19	36	40	3-15—9-15	.311	114.90
	1912			10.30				NE¼SW¼	19	36	40	3-15—9-15	.084	30.90
	1912					38.95		NW¼SW¼	13	36	39	3-15—4-28	.317	29.21
	1912					37.85		SW¼SE¼	13	36	39	3-15—4-28	.308	38.20
	1912					40.70		SE¼SW¼	13	36	39	3-15—4-28	.311	30.53
	1912					19.40		SW¼SW¼	13	36	39	3-15—4-28	.158	14.55
	1912					12.85		NE¼NE¼	14	36	39	3-15—4-28	.104	9.64
	1912					40.50		SE¼NE¼	14	36	39	3-15—4-28	.329	30.38
	1912					12.95		SW¼NE¼	14	36	39	3-15—4-28	.105	9.71
	1912					22.45		NE¼SE¼	14	36	39	3-15—4-28	.183	16.84
	1912					.90		NW¼SE¼	14	36	39	3-15—4-28	.007	.68
	1912			.70				NE¼NE¼	24	36	39	3-15—9-15	.006	2.10
	1912					33.30		NE¼NE¼	24	36	39	3-15—4-28	.271	24.98
	1912					39.05		NW¼NE¼	24	36	39	3-15—4-28	.317	29.29
	1912					13.30		NE¼NW¼	24	36	39	3-15—4-28	.108	9.98
	1912					39.80		SE¼NE¼	24	36	39	3-15—4-28	.323	29.85
	1912					16.55		SW¼NE¼	24	36	39	3-15—4-28	.135	12.41
	1912					17.40		NE¼SE¼	24	36	39	3-15—4-28	.141	13.05
	1912			13.00				SE¼SE¼	13	36	39	3-15—9-15	.106	39.00
	1912					6.35		SE¼SE¼	13	36	39	3-15—4-28	.052	4.76
	1912					9.30		NW¼SE¼	13	36	39	3-15—4-28	.086	6.98
	1912					15.20		SW¼NW¼	13	36	39	3-15—4-28	.124	11.40
	1912			8.15				SW¼SW¼	18	36	40	3-15—9-15	.066	24.45
	1912					2.85		NW¼SE¼	20	36	40	3-15—4-28	.023	2.14
	1912			15.00				NE¼SW¼	20	36	40	3-15—9-15	.122	45.00
	1912			32.40				NW¼SW¼	20	36	40	3-15—9-15	.263	97.20
	1912			.15				SW¼NW¼	20	36	40	3-15—9-15	.001	.45
	1912					6.50		SW¼NE¼	20	36	40	3-15—4-28	.053	4.88
	1912					23.85		SE¼SE¼	20	36	40	3-15—4-28	.194	17.89
	1912			25.70				SW¼SE¼	20	36	40	3-15—9-15	.209	77.10
	1912					8.65		SW¼SE¼	20	36	40	3-15—4-28	.071	6.49
	1912					.35		SW¼SE¼	20	36	40	3-15—4-28	.003	.26
	1912			30.35				SE¼SW¼	20	36	40	3-15—9-15	.247	91.05
	1912					4.85		SE¼SW¼	20	36	40	3-15—4-28	.039	3.64
	1912			38.90				SW¼SW¼	20	36	40	3-15—9-15	.316	116.70
	1912					1.50		SW¼SW¼	20	36	40	3-15—4-28	.012	1.13
	1912			3.85				NE¼NE¼	29	36	40	3-15—9-15	.031	11.55
	1912					11.05		NE¼NE¼	29	36	40	3-15—4-28	.090	8.29
	1912			33.55				NW¼NE¼	29	36	40	3-15—9-15	.273	100.65
	1912					1.25		NW¼NE¼	29	36	40	3-15—4-28	.010	.94
	1912			28.85				NE¼NW¼	29	36	40	3-15—9-15	.235	86.55
	1912					9.00		NE¼NW¼	29	36	40	3-15—4-28	.073	6.75
	1912			40.30				SE¼SE¼	19	36	40	3-15—9-15	.328	120.90
	1912			19.80				SW¼SE¼	19	36	40	3-15—9-15	.161	59.40
	1912					8.45		SW¼SE¼	19	36	40	3-15—4-28	.069	6.34
	1912			27.70				NE¼NE¼	30	36	40	3-15—9-15	.225	83.10

Taylor & Sheehan—Continued.

Date of beneficial use: Nat. mdw.	Date of beneficial use: Cult. area	Construction first initiated: Dams	Construction first initiated: Ditches	Culture—Acres: Harvest crops	Culture—Acres: Meadow pasture	Culture—Acres: Willow and sage pasture	Culture—Acres: Swamp or overflow	Location: Subdivision	Location: Section	Location: Tp.N.	Location: R.E.	Length of season	Duty of water: C.F.S.	Duty of water: Acre-feet
	1912			.40				NW¼NE¼	30	36	40	3-15—9-15	.003	1.20
	1912				6.00			NW¼NE¼	30	36	40	3-15—6-13	.041	9.00
	1912					21.05		NW¼NE¼	30	36	40	3-15—4-28	.171	15.79
	1912			2.95				SE¼NE¼	30	36	40	3-15—9-15	.024	8.85
	1912			38.70				NW¼NW¼	29	36	40	3-15—9-15	.315	116.10
	1912					1.10		NW¼NW¼	29	36	40	3-15—4-28	.009	.83
	1912			1.00				SE¼NE¼	29	36	40	3-15—9-15	.008	3.00
	1912			36.15				SW¼NE¼	29	36	40	3-15—9-15	.294	108.45
	1912			20.50				SE¼NW¼	29	36	40	3-15—9-15	.177	61.50
	1912			10.80				SW¼NW¼	29	36	40	3-15—9-15	.088	32.40
	1912					40.20		NE¼SW¼	13	36	39	3-15—4-28	.327	30.15

Source—**Humboldt River.** Ditch—**Pump from Sink Hole.**

Nat. mdw.	Cult. area	Dams	Ditches	Harvest crops	Meadow pasture	Willow and sage pasture	Swamp or overflow	Subdivision	Section	Tp.N.	R.E.	Length of season	C.F.S.	Acre-feet
	1912					9.85		NW¼NW¼	34	36	40	3-15—4-28	.080	7.39
	1912					7.10		NE¼NW¼	34	36	40	3-15—4-28	.058	5.33
	1912					15.80		NW¼NE¼	34	36	40	3-15—4-28	.128	11.85
	1912					13.90		NE¼NE¼	34	36	40	3-15—4-28	.113	10.43

Source—**Humboldt River.** Ditch—**Pole Creek Ditches.**

Nat. mdw.	Cult. area	Dams	Ditches	Harvest crops	Meadow pasture	Willow and sage pasture	Swamp or overflow	Subdivision	Section	Tp.N.	R.E.	Length of season	C.F.S.	Acre-feet
	1912			12.20				SE¼NE¼	19	36	40	3-15—9-15	.099	36.60
	1912			25.35				NE¼NW¼	19	36	40	3-15—9-15	.206	76.05

Claimant—**Humboldt Land and Cattle Co.** Proof No. 00154

Source—**Humboldt River.** Ditch—**Pump.**

Nat. mdw.	Cult. area	Dams	Ditches	Harvest crops	Meadow pasture	Willow and sage pasture	Swamp or overflow	Subdivision	Section	Tp.N.	R.E.	Length of season	C.F.S.	Acre-feet
	1918			5.20				NE¼NE¼	28	32	49	3-15—9-15	.042	15.60
	1918			1.56				SE¼NE¼	28	32	49	3-15—9-15	.012	4.68
	1918			10.40				NW¼NE¼	28	32	49	3-15—9-15	.085	31.20
	1918			35.84				SW¼NE¼	28	32	49	3-15—9-15	.291	107.52
	1918			9.36				SE¼NW¼	28	32	49	3-15—9-15	.076	28.08
	1918			13.00				NE¼SW¼	28	32	49	3-15—9-15	.106	39.00
	1918			12.48				SE¼SW¼	28	32	49	3-15—9-15	.101	37.44

Claimant—**George Kaeding.** Proof No. 00163

Source—**Humboldt River.** Ditch—**Kaeding.**

Nat. mdw.	Cult. area	Dams	Ditches	Harvest crops	Meadow pasture	Willow and sage pasture	Swamp or overflow	Subdivision	Section	Tp.N.	R.E.	Length of season	C.F.S.	Acre-feet
	1914						40.00	SE¼NE¼	34	33	45	3-15—4-28	.325	30.00
	1914						40.00	SW¼NE¼	34	33	45	3-15—4-28	.325	30.00
	1914						40.00	NE¼NW¼	34	33	45	3-15—4-28	.325	30.00
	1914						40.00	SE¼NW¼	34	33	45	3-15—4-28	.325	30.00
	1914						40.00	NW¼NW¼	34	33	45	3-15—4-28	.325	30.00

...	1914	...	...	...	...	...	40.00	SW¼NW¼	34	33	45	3-15—4-28	.325	30.00
...	1914	...	...	...	...	...	39.52	NW¼SW¼	34	33	45	3-15—4-28	.321	29.64
...	1914	...	...	...	...	...	35.47	SW¼SW¼	34	33	45	3-15—4-28	.288	26.60

Source—**Humboldt River.** Ditch—**South Ditch.**

...	1914	...	...	9.70	...	...	...	NW¼SE¼	2	32	45	3-15—9-15	.079	29.10
...	1914	...	...	3.20	...	...	...	SW¼SE¼	2	32	45	3-15—9-15	.026	9.60
...	1914	...	...	38.28	...	...	...	NE¼NW¼	2	32	45	3-15—9-15	.311	114.84
...	1914	...	...	39.92	...	...	...	SE¼NW¼	2	32	45	3-15—9-15	.325	119.76
...	1914	...	...	40.15	...	...	...	NW¼NW¼	2	32	45	3-15—9-15	.326	120.45
...	1914	...	...	40.07	...	...	...	SW¼NW¼	2	32	45	3-15—9-15	.326	120.21
...	1914	...	...	40.05	...	...	...	NE¼SW¼	2	32	45	3-15—9-15	.326	120.15
...	1914	...	...	8.52	...	...	...	SE¼SW¼	2	32	45	3-15—9-15	.069	25.56
...	1914	...	...	40.00	...	...	...	NW¼SW¼	2	32	45	3-15—9-15	.325	120.00
...	1914	...	...	9.80	...	...	...	SW¼SW¼	2	32	45	3-15—9-15	.080	29.40
...	1914	...	...	12.37	...	...	...	SE¼NW¼	1	32	45	3-15—9-15	.101	37.11
...	1914	...	...	....	...	4.47	...	SE¼NW¼	1	32	45	3-15—4-28	.036	3.35
...	1914	...	...	5.05	...	...	...	NW¼NW¼	1	32	45	3-15—9-15	.041	15.15
...	1914	...	...	22.55	...	...	...	NW¼NE¼	2	32	45	3-15—9-15	.183	67.65
...	1914	...	...	25.59	...	...	...	SW¼NE¼	2	32	45	3-15—9-15	.208	76.77
...	1914	...	...	....	3.51	...	...	SW¼NE¼	2	32	45	3-15—6-13	.021	5.27
...	1914	...	...	....	...	2.15	...	SW¼NE¼	2	32	45	3-15—4-28	.017	1.61

Claimant—**J. W. Puett.** Proof No. **00322**
Source—**Maggie Creek.** Ditch—**Palmer.**

...	1908	...	...	10.00	...	...	...	SE¼NW¼	26	33	52	4-15—8-15	.123	30.00
...	1909	...	...	8.00	...	...	...	SE¼NW¼	26	33	52	4-15—8-15	.098	24.00
...	1910	...	...	12.00	...	...	...	NW¼SE¼	26	33	52	4-15—8-15	.148	36.00
...	1912	...	...	14.00	...	...	...	SE¼SW¼	26	33	52	4-15—8-15	.172	42.00

Claimant—**Max Arnhold.** Proof No. **00351**
Source—**Pearl Creek.** Ditch—**Max Arnhold Ditches.**

...	1911	...	...	20.39	...	...	...	W½	21	28	56			
								W½SE¼	21	28	56			
								SE¼SE¼	21	28	56			
								S½S½	22	28	56			
								N½NE¼	28	28	56	4-15—8-15	.250	60.90

Claimant—**T. F. Brennen.** Proof No. **00353**
Source—**Ainley, Ogilvie, Young, and Cottonwood Creeks.** Ditch—**Brennen Ditches.**

...	1908	...	...	14.26*	...	...	...	W½SW¼	16	32	57	4-15—8-15	.175	42.78
...	1910	...	...	28.52†	...	...	...	...	....	....	...	4-15—8-15	.351	85.56

*Has flood water right on pasture as of 1900. †From Cottonwood Creek only.

Claimant—**J. J. Hylton.** Proof No. 00355

Source—**South Fork Humboldt River and Rattlesnake Creek.** Ditch—**J. J. Hylton Ditches.**

Date of beneficial use: Nat. mdw.	Date of beneficial use: Cult. area	Construction first initiated: Dams	Construction first initiated: Ditches	Culture—Acres: Harvest crops	Culture—Acres: Meadow pasture	Culture—Acres: Willow and sage pasture	Culture—Acres: Swamp or over-flow	Location: Subdivision	Location: Section	Location: Tp.N.	Location: R.E.	Length of season	Duty of water: C.F.S.	Duty of water: Acre-feet
	1907			28.00				S½	23	31	56	4-15—8-15	0.344	84.00
	1908			2.00				N½	24	31	56	4-15—8-15	0.025	6.00
	1909			30.37				S½NW¼	24	31	56	4-15—8-15	0.374	91.11
	1911			40.91				NW¼NW¼	25	31	56	4-15—8-15	0.503	122.73
	1912			80.91					26	31	56	4-15—8-15	0.995	212.73
	1912			23.70				NE¼	27	31	56	4-15—8-15	0.292	71.10
	1913			100.91								4-15—8-15	1.241	302.73
	1914			95.91								4-15—8-15	1.180	287.73
	1915			140.92								4-15—8-15	1.733	422.76
	1918			53.82								4-15—8-15	0.662	161.46
	1918			36.50								4-15—8-15	0.449	109.50
	1920			17.82								4-15—8-15	0.209	53.46

Early Water only from Rattlesnake Creek.

Source—**Pearl Creek and South Fork Humboldt River.** Ditch—**J. J. Hylton Ditches.**

Nat. mdw.	Cult. area	Dams	Ditches	Harvest crops	Meadow pasture	Willow and sage pasture	Swamp or over-flow	Subdivision	Section	Tp.N.	R.E.	Length of season	C.F.S.	Acre-feet
	1911			15.00				E½SE¼	19	31	57			
								SW¼	20	31	57	4-15—8-15	0.183	45.00

Claimant—**Pedro Corta.** Proof No. 00356

Source—**Spencer Creek.** Ditch—**Pedro Corta Ditches.**

Nat. mdw.	Cult. area	Dams	Ditches	Harvest crops	Meadow pasture	Willow and sage pasture	Swamp or over-flow	Subdivision	Section	Tp.N.	R.E.	Length of season	C.F.S.	Acre-feet
	1907			13.30				E½W½	12	28	56			
								SW¼	1	28	56			
								S½NW¼	1	28	56	4-15—8-15	.164	39.90

Claimant—**Clark Drown.** Proof No. 00357

Source—**South Fork Humboldt River.** Ditch—**Clark Drown Ditches.**

Nat. mdw.	Cult. area	Dams	Ditches	Harvest crops	Meadow pasture	Willow and sage pasture	Swamp or over-flow	Subdivision	Section	Tp.N.	R.E.	Length of season	C.F.S.	Acre-feet
	1909			10.00				S½SW¼	8	31	57	4-15—8-15	.123	30.00
	1910			55.00				N½	17	31	57	4-15—8-15	.677	165.00
	1910			16.00				N½SE¼	17	31	57	4-15—8-15	.197	48.00
	1911			20.00				NE¼SW¼	17	31	57	4-15—8-15	.246	60.00
	1911			51.00				NE¼	18	31	57	4-15—8-15	.627	153.00
	1912			64.50				SE¼NW¼	18	31	57	4-15—8-15	.793	193.50
	1915			22.50								4-15—8-15	.277	67.50
	1916			15.00								4-15—8-15	.185	45.00
	1916			30.00								4-15—8-15	.369	90.00
	1916			35.00								4-15—8-15	.431	105.00
	1916					246.00						4-15—5-15	3.020	184.50

Claimant—**Albert Hankins.** Proof No. 00358
Source—**Smith, South Fork, Smith Creek, McCutcheons, Adams, and Dry Creeks.**
Ditch—**Albert Hankins Ditches.**

1909	70.00	NW¼	2	29	56			
		NE¼	3	29	56	4-15—5-15	.861	52.50

Claimant—**J. J. Hylton.** Proof No. 00359
Source—**South Fork Humboldt River.** Ditch—**J. J. Hylton Ditches.**

1908	40.00	SE¼	4	32	55			
1912	9.50	S½	3	32	55			
1915	40.00		10	32	55			
1920	35.00	W½	11	32	55			
		N½	15	32	55			
			14	32	55			
		E½	23	32	55	4-15—8-15	.492	120.00
		W½	24	32	55	4-15—8-15	.117	28.50
		SE¼	24	32	55	4-15—8-15	.492	120.00
			25	32	55	4-15—9-15	.431	105.00

Source—**Smith Creek.** Ditch—**J. J. Hylton Ditches.**

1909	17.00	NW¼	33	30	56	4-15—8-15	.209	51.00
1912	19.00	NW¼	33	30	56	4-15—8-15	.234	57.00
1909	4.00	SW¼	33	30	56	4-15—8-15	.049	12.00
1915	22.50	SW¼	33	30	56	4-15—8-15	.277	67.50
1912	18.67	SW¼	33	30	56	4-15—8-15	.230	56.01
1915	22.00	NW¼	4	29	56	4-15—8-15	.271	66.00
1912	4.33	NW¼	4	29	56	4-15—8-15	.053	12.99
1909	19.00	NE¼	32	30	56	4-15—8-15	.234	57.00
1915	5.00	NE¼	32	30	56	4-15—8-15	.062	15.00
1915	12.00	SW¼	32	30	56	4-15—8-15	.148	36.00
1916	97.00	SW¼	32	30	56	4-15—8-15	1.193	291.00
1915	73.00	SE¼	32	30	56	4-15—8-15	.898	279.00
1916	6.00	NW¼	5	29	56	4-15—8-15	.074	18.00
1909	1.00	SE¼	29	30	56	4-15—8-15	.012	3.00
1915	10.00	NW¼	32	30	56	4-15—8-15	.123	30.00

Source—**South Fork Humboldt River.** Ditch—**J. J. Hylton Ditches.**

1912	69.00	S½NE¼	15	31	57			
1912	10.50	SE¼	15	31	57			
		W½SW¼	14	31	57	4-15—8-15	.849	207.00
		SW¼NW¼	14	31	57	4-15—8-15	.129	31.50

Claimant—**Chas. Mitchell.** Proof No. 00362
Source—**Brown's Creek.** Ditch—**Chas. Mitchell Ditches.**

Date of beneficial use: Nat. mdw.	Date of beneficial use: Cult. area	Construction first initiated: Dams	Construction first initiated: Ditches	Culture—Acres: Harvest crops	Culture—Acres: Meadow pasture	Culture—Acres: Willow and sage pasture	Culture—Acres: Swamp or overflow	Location: Subdivision	Location: Section	Location: Tp.N.	Location: R.E.	Length of season	Duty of water: C.F.S.	Duty of water: Acre-feet
......	1906	......	......	30.70	......	......	......	NE¼NE¼	30	28	56			
								NW¼NW¼	29	28	56			
								S½NW¼	29	28	56			
								SW¼NE¼	29	28	56			
								N½S½	29	28	56			
								NE¼SE¼	29	28	56			
								N½SW¼	28	28	56	4-15—8-15	.378	92.10

Claimant—**P. J. Ogilvie.** Proof No. 00364
Source—**South Fork of Humboldt River and Rattlesnake Creek.**

Nat. mdw.	Cult. area	Dams	Ditches	Harvest crops	Meadow pasture	Willow and sage pasture	Swamp or overflow	Subdivision	Section	Tp.N.	R.E.	Length of season	C.F.S.	Acre-feet
......	1908	......	......	77.00	......	......	......	S½	14	31	56	4-15—8-15	.947	231.00
......	1915	......	......	53.00	......	......	......	S½	13	31	56	4-15—8-15	.652	159.00
								N½	24	31	56			
								W½NW¼	19	31	57			

Early water only from Rattlesnake Creek.

Claimant—**Ernest Hodges.** Proof No. 00370
Source—**Dry Creek and Springs.** Ditch—**Ernest Hodges Ditches.**

Nat. mdw.	Cult. area	Dams	Ditches	Harvest crops	Meadow pasture	Willow and sage pasture	Swamp or overflow	Subdivision	Section	Tp.N.	R.E.	Length of season	C.F.S.	Acre-feet
......	1906	......	......	39.00	......	......	......	SW¼	30	33	57	4-15—8-15	.480	117.00

Claimant—**A. M. Griswold.** Proof No. 00372
Source—**South Fork Humboldt River.** Ditch—**Griswold Ditches.**

Nat. mdw.	Cult. area	Dams	Ditches	Harvest crops	Meadow pasture	Willow and sage pasture	Swamp or overflow	Subdivision	Section	Tp.N.	R.E.	Length of season	C.F.S.	Acre-feet
......	1906	......	......	7.00	......	......	......	N½NW¼	10	31	56	5-15—8-15	.086	21.00
......	1908	......	......	55.00	......	......	......	NE¼	10	31	56	5-15—8-15	.677	165.00
......	1910	......	......	28.00	......	......	......	E½SE¼	10	31	56	5-15—8-15	.344	84.00
......	1911	......	......	25.00	......	......	......	S½NW¼	11	31	56	5-15—8-15	.308	75.00
......	1913	......	......	...	......	10.00	......	W½SW¼	11	31	56	5-15—6-15	.123	7.50
......	1915	......	......	50.00	......	......	......	N½	14	31	56	5-15—8-15	.615	150.00
......	1915	......	......	55.00	......	......	......	......	....	....	....	5-15—8-15	.677	165.00
......	1915	......	......	35.00	......	......	......	......	....	....	....	5-15—8-15	.431	105.00
......	1916	......	......	16.00	......	......	......	......	....	....	....	5-15—8-15	.197	48.00
......	1917	......	......	15.00	......	......	......	......	....	....	....	5-15—8-15	.185	45.00

Claimant—**Minnie Hankins, Lillie Hankins, Elizabeth Hankins, Estate Jane Bellinger.** Proof No. 00375
Source—**South Fork of Humboldt.** Ditch—**Hankins & Bellinger Ditches.**

Nat. mdw.	Cult. area	Dams	Ditches	Harvest crops	Meadow pasture	Willow and sage pasture	Swamp or overflow	Subdivision	Section	Tp.N.	R.E.	Length of season	C.F.S.	Acre-feet
......	1906	......	......	44.36	......	......	......	W½	31	32	56			
								NE¼NW¼	6	31	56			

									N½NE¼	6	31	56			
									SE¼NE¼	6	31	56	4-15—8-15	.546	183.08
									Claimant—J. J. Hylton.					Proof No. 00381	
									Source—Cottonwood Creek. Ditch—**Nos. 1, 2, 3, 5, and 6.**						
	1909			7.80					SW¼NW¼	15	30	56	4-15—8-15	.096	23.40
	1909			0.50					SE¼NE¼	16	30	56	4-15—8-15	.006	1.50
	1909			1.30					NE¼NE¼	16	30	56	4-15—8-15	.016	3.90
	1909			1.00					NW¼NW¼	15	30	56	4-15—8-15	.012	3.00
									Claimant—Drown Bros.					Proof No. 00385	
									Source—South Fork of Humboldt River. Ditch—**Drown Bros. Ditches.**						
									S½NW¼	10	31	56			
	1906			80.00					SW¼	10	31	56			
	1907			26.00					W½SE¼	10	31	56			
	1909			75.00					SE¼NW¼	11	31	56			
									S½NE¼	11	31	56	4-15—8-15	.984	240.00
									E½SW¼	11	31	56	4-15—8-15	.320	78.00
									SE¼	11	31	56	4-15—8-15	.923	225.00
	1906						38.80		N½	22	31	56	4-15—5-15	.477	29.10
	1906			20.00					S½NW¼	23	31	56	4-15—8-15	.246	60.00
	1907			33.50									4-15—8-15	.412	100.50
	1908			30.80									4-15—8-15	.379	92.40
	1909						52.70						4-15—5-15	.648	39.53
	1909			51.80									4-15—8-15	.637	155.40
	1911			15.40									4-15—8-15	.189	46.20
	1912					48.10							4-15—6-15	.592	72.15
	1913					18.40							4-15—6-15	.226	27.60
	1908			10.90					NE¼	15	31	56	4-15—8-15	.134	32.70
	1909			3.00					E½SE¼	15	31	56	4-15—8-15	.037	9.00
	1910			21.80					SW¼SE¼	15	31	56	4-15—8-15	.268	65.40
	1915			110.80					S½SW¼	15	31	56	4-15—8-15	1.363	332.40
	1917			59.50					NW¼SW¼	15	31	56	4-15—8-15	.732	178.50
	1919			21.70					SW¼NW¼	15	31	56	4-15—8-15	.267	65.10
	1918						12.50		NE¼NW¼	9	31	56	4-15—5-15	.154	9.38
	1919						50.00		NE¼	9	31	56	4-15—5-15	.615	37.50
	1920						88.70		NE¼SE¼	9	31	56	4-15—5-15	1.091	66.53
									Claimant—A. J. Dewar.					Proof No. 00388	
									Source—South Fork Humboldt River. Ditch—**A. J. Dewar Ditches.**						
	1907			18.00					S½S½	17	31	57			
	1908			17.32					S½	18	31	57			
	1910			6.78					SE¼NE¼	19	31	57	4-15—8-15	.221	54.00
									N½NE¼	19	31	57	4-15—8-15	.213	51.96
									NE¼NW¼	19	31	57	4-15—8-15	.083	20.34

Claimant—**Chris Baumbach.** Proof No. 00394
Source—**Rattlesnake Creek.** Ditch—**Chris Baumbach Ditches.**

Date of beneficial use: Nat. mdw.	Date of beneficial use: Cult. area	Construction first initiated: Dams	Construction first initiated: Ditches	Culture—Acres: Harvest crops	Culture—Acres: Meadow pasture	Culture—Acres: Willow and sage pasture	Culture—Acres: Swamp or overflow	Location: Subdivision	Location: Section	Location: Tp.N.	Location: R.E.	Length of season	Duty of water: C.F.S.	Duty of water: Acre-feet
	1910			37.15				S½NW¼	19	31	57			
								SW¼NE¼	19	31	57			
								NE¼SW¼	19	31	57			
								SE¼	19	31	57			
								SW¼SW¼	20	31	57	4-15—8-15	.457	111.45

Claimant—**W. R. Bellinger.** Proof No. 00401
Source—**Lamoille Creek.** Ditch—**W. R. Bellinger Ditches.**

Nat. mdw.	Cult. area	Dams	Ditches	Harvest crops	Meadow pasture	Willow and sage pasture	Swamp or overflow	Subdivision	Section	Tp.N.	R.E.	Length of season	C.F.S.	Acre-feet
	1907			30.00				W½W½	30	33	58	4-15—8-15	.309	90.00
	1908			11.00				S½SW¼	19	33	58	4-15—8-15	.135	33.00
	1909			10.00								4-15—8-15	.123	30.00
	1910			9.20								4-15—8-15	.113	27.60
	1911			26.50								4-15—8-15	.826	79.50
	1914			105.00								4-15—8-15	1.292	315.00
	1915			8.00								4-15—8-15	.098	24.00
	1918			42.00								4-15—8-15	.517	126.00

Claimant—**Hankins-Bellinger Co.** Proof No. 00405
Source—**Lamoille Creek.** Ditch—**Hankins-Bellinger Ditches.**

Nat. mdw.	Cult. area	Dams	Ditches	Harvest crops	Meadow pasture	Willow and sage pasture	Swamp or overflow	Subdivision	Section	Tp.N.	R.E.	Length of season	C.F.S.	Acre-feet
	1911			10.00				E½NE¼	24	33	57	4-15—8-15	.123	30.00
	1912			20.00				NW¼SW¼	19	33	58	4-15—8-15	.246	60.00
	1914			15.00				SW¼SW¼	19	33	58	4-15—8-15	.185	45.00

Claimant—**Samuel McIntyre Investment Company.** Proof No. 00409
Source—**Lamoille Creek.** Ditch—**Samuel McIntyre Investment Company Ditches.**

Nat. mdw.	Cult. area	Dams	Ditches	Harvest crops	Meadow pasture	Willow and sage pasture	Swamp or overflow	Subdivision	Section	Tp.N.	R.E.	Length of season	C.F.S.	Acre-feet
	1910			60.00				S½	9	35	58	4-15—8-15	.738	180.00
	1909			....		131.50		SW¼	10	35	58	4-15—5-15	1.617	98.63
									15	35	58			

Claimant—**R. B. Stewart.** Proof No. 00446
Source—**Rabbit Creek.** Ditch—**Stewart Ditches.**

Nat. mdw.	Cult. area	Dams	Ditches	Harvest crops	Meadow pasture	Willow and sage pasture	Swamp or overflow	Subdivision	Section	Tp.N.	R.E.	Length of season	C.F.S.	Acre-feet
	1907			30.00				S½	26	33	57	4-15—8-15	.738	180.00
	1909			30.00				N½N½	35	33	57	4-15—8-15	.738	180.00
								S½NW¼	35	33	57			

Claimant—**Albert Trescartes.** Proof No. 00459

Source—**Lamoille Creek.** Ditch—**Albert Trescartes Ditches.**

1911	87.00		N½	26	33	57	4-15—8-15	1.070	261.00
1912	61.70						4-15—8-15	.750	185.10

Water right initiated prior to 1905 on Sec. 25 and transferred by permit to Sec. 26.

Claimant—**Chas. Trescartes.** Proof No. 00459

Source—**Lamoille Creek.** Ditch—**Chas Trescartes Ditches.**

1907	59.20		W½NE¼	24	33	57	4-15—8-15	.728	177.60
1913	18.00		SE¼NE¼	24	33	57	4-15—8-15	.221	54.00
1916	11.00						4-15—8-15	.135	33.00

Claimant—**W. W. Alles.** Proof No. 00477

Source—**Springs, Swamps and Natural Draw on Secs. 5 and 6, T. 36 N, R. 60 E.**

Ditch—**W. W. Alles Ditches.**

1911	18.06		S½NE¼	6	36	60	4-15—8-15	.222	54.18

NOTE—Source is as shown above. Claimant not to take water from Ackler or Herder Creek in case of shortage.

Claimant—**Phil Harney.** Proof No. 00484

Source—**Soldier Creek.** Ditch—**McDermott 1-4, incl.**

1906	20.20*		SW¼	20	34	59	4-15—8-15	.250	60.60
1915		11.30†	W½SE¼	20	34	59	4-15—5-15	.139	33.90
1915		10.00†					4-15—5-15	.123	30.00

***Was pasture in 1896. †Was pasture in 1902.**

Claimant—**W. J. Smiley.** Proof No. 00491

Source—**Herder Creek.** Ditch—**W. J. Smiley Ditches.**

1910	73.00		NW¼	7	36	60	4-15—8-15	.898	213.00
1910	9.80		N½SW¼	7	36	60	4-15—8-15	.121	29.40

"This land was subirrigated from irrigation of older land, but water not directly applied on surface until 1910. No water to be applied directly to this land until all vested rights are served, nor until all permits with date prior to 1910 have been served. Agreed to by all users in settlement of disputes."

Claimant—**Hylton & Mentz.** Proof No. 00502

Source—**Herder Creek.** Ditch—**Hylton & Mentz Ditches.**

1909	5.60		SE¼	6	36	60	4-15—8-15	.060	16.80
1909	15.00		NE¼SW¼	6	36	60	4-15—8-15	.185	45.00
1909	1.00						4-15—8-15	.012	3.00

Date of beneficial use: Nat. mdw.	Date of beneficial use: Cult. area	Construction first initiated: Dams	Construction first initiated: Ditches	Culture—Acres: Harvest crops	Culture—Acres: Meadow pasture	Culture—Acres: Willow and sage pasture	Culture—Acres: Swamp or overflow	Location: Subdivision	Location: Section	Location: Tp.N.	Location: R.E.	Length of season	Duty of water: C.F.S.	Duty of water: Acre-feet
Claimant—W. J.' Black. Proof No. 00505														
Source—**Ackler Creek, Brennen Gulch, and Herder Creek.** Ditches—**Nos. 1-14, incl.**														
...	1909	...	...	10.00	...	...	...	E½	8	36	60			
								S½NW¼	8	36	60			
								NE¼SW¼	8	36	60	4-15—8-15	.123	30.00
Source—**Ackler Creek.** Ditches—**Nos. 1-14, incl.**														
...	1909	...	...	5.10	...	...	...	E½	8	36	60			
								SE¼NW¼	8	36	60			
								NE¼SW¼	8	36	60	4-15—8-15	.063	15.30
Claimant—Isaac Griswold. Proof No. 00519														
Source—**Branch of Boulder Creek.** Ditch—**Isaac Griswold Ditches.**														
...	1909	...	...	7.00	...	...	...	SW¼NW¼	13	36	59	4-15—8-15	.086	21.00
...	1910	...	...	7.00	...	...	...	W½SW¼	13	36	59	4-15—8-15	.086	21.00
								E½E½	14	36	59			
Claimant—Diana Morgan-Hill (Deed to J. J. Hylton in escrow). Proof No. 00552														
Source—**North Fork.** Ditch—**McKee & Clayton.**														
...	1913	...	...	83.50	...	...	...	E½NE¼	35	40	56			
								NE¼SE¼	35	40	56			
								NW¼	36	40	56			
								N½SW¼	36	40	56			
								SW¼NE¼	36	40	56			
								NW¼SE¼	36	40	56	4-15—8-15	1.027	250.50
Claimant—C. A. & L. M. Laing. Proof No. 00556														
Source—**Pratt Creek.** Ditch—**Laing Ditches.**														
...	1914	...	...	53.00	...	...	...	NW¼SE¼	36	42	54			
								S½SE¼	36	42	54			
								S½SW¼	31	42	55			
								SE¼NW¼	1	41	54			
								NE¼	1	41	54			
									6	41	55			
								W½SW¼	5	41	55			
								NE¼NE¼	7	41	55			
								NW¼NW¼	8	41	55	4-15—8-15	.652	159.00
Claimant—Union Land and Cattle Co. **Proof No. 00601**														
Source—**Taber Creek.** Ditch—**Nos. 1, 2, and 3.**														
...	1911	...	...	34.07	...	...	...	N½	6	40	61	4-15—8-15	.426	104.01

Claimant—**Metropolis Land Company.** Proof No. 00608
Source—**Bishop Creek.** Ditch—**Nos. 1, 2, and 3.**

1911	9.09	NW¼SE¼	28	39	62			
		N½SW¼	28	39	62			
		S½SE¼	29	39	62			
		E½NE¼	31	39	62			
		NE¼SE¼	31	39	62			
		N½	32	39	62			
		N½SW¼	32	39	62			
		NW¼SE¼	32	39	62	4-15—8-15	.112	27.27

Claimant—**Ambrose Truett.** Proof No. 00611
Source—**Tom Cain Creek.** Ditch—**Ambrose Truett Ditches.**

1908	31.43	E½SW¼	31	42	61			
		S½SE¼	31	42	61	5-1—8-31	.400	

Decree in Case 2580, records of District Court of Elko County, is binding as between parties to such suit.

Claimant—**Chas. Toyn.** Proof No. 00664
Source—**South Fork Smith Creek.** Ditch—**Chas. Toyn Ditches.**

1907	9.75	E½NW¼	35	29	56			
		W½NE¼	35	29	56			
		SE¼NE¼	35	29	56			
		E½SE¼	35	29	56			
		S½S½	36	29	56			
		N½N½	1	28	56			
		NE¼NE¼	2	28	56	4-15—8-15	.120	29.25

Claimant—**Thomas Griffin.** Proof No. 00224
Source—**Maggie Creek.** Ditch—**Griffin Ditch.**

1908	4.41	NE¼SW¼	26	33	52	4-15—8-15	.054	13.23
1908	3.55	NW¼SE¼	26	33	52	4-15—8-15	.044	10.65
1908	6.20	SW¼SE¼	26	33	52	4-15—8-15	.076	18.60
1908	4.43	SE¼SW¼	26	33	52	4-15—8-15	.054	13.29

Any person claiming any interest in said Humboldt River stream-system and its tributaries involved in the determination of the relative rights above set forth and to the use of the water thereof, claiming under vested right or under permit from the State Engineer, may object to any finding, part or portion of foregoing Preliminary Order of Determination of said Humboldt River stream-system and its tributaries by filing objections with the State Engineer within thirty days after said evidence and proofs heretofore taken, received, and filed by the State Engineer shall have been open to public inspection. You are further notified that all evidence and proofs of claims received or considered by the State Engineer will be open to the inspection of any and all interested persons for a continuous period of twenty (20) days in the office of the State Engineer at Carson City, Nevada, between the hours of 9 a. m. and 4:30 p. m. of each business day during said period. Any and all persons interested may inspect such evidence and proofs of claims as have been filed with or taken by or considered by the State Engineer in accordance with the provisions of said Chapter 140, Statutes of Nevada, 1913, and Acts amendatory or supplemental thereto.

Dated this 23d day of March, 1922, at Carson City, Nevada.

By order of J. G. SCRUGHAM,
State Engineer.

APPENDIX D

Procedure for the Finding of Title to Water Rights

CHAPTER 140, STATUTES OF 1913

All water public property.

SECTION 1. The water of all sources of water supply within the boundaries of the state, whether above or beneath the surface of the ground, belongs to the public.

Beneficial use.

SEC. 2. Subject to existing rights, all such water may be appropriated for beneficial use as provided in this act and not otherwise.

Basis.

SEC. 3. Beneficial use shall be the basis, the measure and the limit of the right to the use of water.

Provisions for use of water.

SEC. 4. All water used in this state for beneficial purposes shall remain appurtenant to the place of use; *provided*, that if for any reason it should at any time become impracticable to beneficially or economically use water at the place to which it is appurtenant, said right may be severed from such place of use and simultaneously transferred and become appurtenant to other place or places of use, in the manner provided in this act, and not otherwise, without losing priority of right heretofore established; *and provided*, that the provisions of this section shall not apply in cases of ditch or canal companies which have appropriated water for diversion and transmission to the lands of private persons at an annual charge.

Right to divert ceases, when.

SEC. 5. When the necessity for the use of water does not exist, the right to divert it ceases and no person shall be permitted to divert or use the waters of this state except at such times as the water is required for a beneficial purpose.

Right of eminent domain.

SEC. 6. The beneficial use of water is hereby declared a public use, and any person may exercise the right of eminent domain to condemn all lands and other property or rights required for the construction, use and maintenance of any works for the lawful diversion, conveyance and storage of waters.

Relative to storage of water.

SEC. 7. Water may be stored for a beneficial purpose. Water turned into any natural channel or watercourse by any person entitled to the use thereof, whether stored in Nevada or in an adjoining state, may be claimed for beneficial use below, and diverted from said channel or watercourse by such person, subject to existing rights, due allowance for losses to be made, as determined by the state engineer.

Standards of measurement.

SEC. 9. A cubic foot of water per second of time shall be the legal standard for the measurement of water in this state. The unit of volume shall be an acre-foot defined as 43,560 cubic feet. Where necessary to transpose miner's inches to cubic feet per second, one cubic foot per second shall be considered equal to forty miner's inches; but the term "miner's inch" shall not be used henceforth in any permit or adjudicated right issuing from the office of the state engineer without first naming the amount in cubic feet per second or in acre-feet.

[NOTE—Statutes 1913, 197, Section 10, repealed, Statutes 1919, 197. Section 1, Chap. 108, Statutes 1919, 197, is a substitute for Section 10.]

Determination of rights to water, how effected.

SEC. 18. Upon a petition to the state engineer, signed by one or more water users of any stream or stream system, requesting the determination of the relative rights of the various claimants to the waters thereof, it shall be the duty of the state engineer, if upon investigation he finds the facts and conditions justify it, to enter an order granting said petition and to make proper arrangements to proceed with such determination; *provided, however*, that it shall be the duty of the state engineer, in the absence of such a petition requesting a determination of relative rights, to enter an order for the determination of the relative rights to the use of water of any stream selected by him; commencing on the streams in the order of their importance for irrigation. As soon as practicable after said order is made and entered, it shall be the duty of the state engineer to proceed with such determination as hereinafter provided. A water user upon or from any stream or body of water shall be held and deemed to be a water user upon the stream system of which said stream or body of water is a part or tributary.

Publication of orders.

SEC. 19. As soon as practicable after the state engineer shall make and enter the order granting the said petition or selecting the streams upon which the determination of rights is to begin, he shall prepare a notice setting forth the fact of the entry of the said order and of the pendency of the said proceedings, which notice shall name a date when the state engineer or his assistants shall begin said examination, and shall set forth that all claimants to rights in the waters of said stream system are required, as in this act provided, to make proof of their claims, which notice shall be published for a period of four consecutive weeks in one or more newspapers of general circulation within the boundaries of said stream system.

Investigation of flow of streams and ditches.

SEC. 20. At the time set in said notice, the state engineer shall begin an investigation of the flow of the stream and of the ditches diverting water, and of the lands irrigated therefrom, and shall gather such other data and information as may be essential to the proper determination of the water rights in the stream. He shall reduce his observations and measurements to writing, and execute, or cause to be executed, surveys, and shall prepare, or cause to be prepared, maps from the observations of such surveys in accordance with such uniform

rules and regulations as he may adopt, which surveys and maps shall show with substantial accuracy the course of the said stream, the location of each ditch or canal diverting water therefrom, together with the point of diversion thereof, the area and outline of each parcel of land upon which the water of the stream has been employed for the irrigation of crops or pasture, and indicating the kind of culture upon each of the said parcels of land, which map shall be prepared as the surveys and observations progress, and which when completed shall be filed and made of record in the office of the state engineer; *provided, however,* that such map for original filing in his office shall be on tracing linen on a scale of not less than one thousand feet to the inch.

Data of U S. geological survey may be used—Provisions regarding maps.

SEC. 21. In the event that satisfactory data are available from the measurements and areas compiled by the United States geological survey, or other persons, the state engineer may dispense with the execution of such surveys and the preparation of such maps and stream measurements, except in so far as is necessary to prepare them to conform with the rules and regulations, as above provided. In the further event that said surveys are executed and maps are prepared and filed with the state engineer at the instance of the person claiming a right to the use of water, the proportionate cost thereof, as determined by the state engineer, to be assessed and collected for the adjudication of the relative rights, as hereinafter provided, shall be remitted to said claimant after the completion of the determination; *provided,* however, that the map must conform with the rules and regulations of the state engineer and shall be accepted only after the state engineer is satisfied that the data shown thereon are substantially correct. Such measurements, maps, and determinations shall be exhibited for inspection at the time of taking proofs and during the period during which such proofs and evidence are kept open for inspection in accordance with the provisions of this act.

Proofs, procedure regarding—Publication of notice.

SEC. 22. Upon the filing of such measurements, maps, and determinations, the state engineer shall prepare a notice setting forth the date when the said state engineer is to commence the taking of said proofs, as to the rights in and to the waters of said stream system, and the date prior to which the same must be filed; *provided, however,* that the date set prior to which said proofs must be filed shall not be less than sixty days from the date set for the commencement of the taking of said proofs, which notice shall be deemed to be an order of the state engineer as to its contents, and which notice the state engineer shall cause to be published for a period of four consecutive weeks in one or more newspapers of general circulation within the boundaries of the said stream system, the date of the last publication of said notice to be not less than fifteen (15) days prior to the date fixed for the commencement of the taking of proofs by the said state engineer. At or near the time of the first publication of said notice it shall be the duty of the said state engineer to send by registered mail to each person, or deliver to each person, in person, hereinafter designated as claimant, claiming rights in or to the waters of said stream system in so far as such claimants can be reasonably ascertained, a notice equiva-

lent in terms to the said published notice setting forth the date when the said state engineer will commence the said taking of proofs, and the date prior to which said proofs must be filed with the state engineer. Said notice must be mailed at least thirty (30) days prior to the date fixed for the commencement of the taking of said proofs.

Statement regarding rights to water—What statement shall contain.

SEC. 23. The state engineer shall, in addition, enclose with the notice to be mailed as aforesaid, blank forms upon which said claimant shall present in writing all particulars necessary for the determination of his right in or to the waters of said stream system, the said statement to include the following:

(a) The name and postoffice address of the claimant.

(b) The nature of the right or use on which the claim for appropriation is based.

(c) The time of the initiation of such right and a description of works of diversion and distribution.

(d) The date of beginning of construction.

(e) The date when completed.

(f) The dates of beginning and completion of enlargements.

(g) The dimensions of the ditch as originally constructed and as enlarged.

(h) The date when water was first used for irrigation or other beneficial purposes, and if used for irrigation, the amount of land reclaimed the first year, the amount in subsequent years, with the dates of reclamation, and the area and location of the lands which are intended to be irrigated.

(i) The character of the soil and the kind of crops cultivated, the number of acre-feet of water per annum required to irrigate the land, and such other facts as will show the extent and nature of the right and a compliance with the law in acquiring the same, as may be required by the state engineer.

Statements to be under oath.

SEC. 24. Each claimant shall be required to certify to his statements under oath, and the state engineer and his assistants authorized to take proofs are hereby authorized to administer such oaths, which shall be done without charge to the claimant, as shall also the furnishing of blank forms for said statement.

CHAPTER 253, STATUTES OF 1915

Various duties of state engineer enumerated.

SEC. 25. It shall be the duty of the state engineer to commence the taking of proofs on the date fixed and named in the notice provided for herein for the commencement of the taking of proofs, and he shall proceed therewith during the period fixed by him and named in the said notice, after which no proofs shall be received by or filed with the said state engineer; *provided, however,* that the state engineer may in his discretion, for cause shown, extend the time in which proofs may be filed. Upon neglect or refusal of any person to make proof of his claim or rights in or to the waters of such stream system, as required by this act, prior to the expiration of the period fixed by said state

engineer during which proofs may be filed, the state engineer shall determine the right of such person from such evidence as he may obtain or may have on file in his office in the way of maps, plats, surveys and transcripts, and exceptions to such determination may be filed in court, as hereinafter provided.

CHAPTER 140, STATUTES OF 1913

Petition of intervention, when.

SEC. 26. Any person interested in the water of any stream upon whom no service of notice shall have been had of the pendency of proceedings for the determination of the relative rights to the use of water of said stream system, and who shall have no actual knowledge or notice of the pendency of said proceedings, may at any time prior to the expiration of six months after the entry of the determinations of the state engineer, file a petition to intervene in said proceedings. Such petition shall be under oath and shall contain, among other things, all matters required by this act of claimants who have been duly served with notice of said proceedings, and also a statement that the intervener had no actual knowledge or notice of the pendency of said proceedings. Upon the filing of said petition in intervention granted by the state engineer, the petitioner shall be allowed to intervene upon such terms as may be equitable, and thereafter shall have all rights vouchsafed by this act to claimants who have been duly served.

CHAPTER 106, STATUTES OF 1921

Fees to be collected by state engineer.

SEC. 27. At the time of submission of proofs of appropriation, where the necessary maps are prepared by the state engineer, the fee collected from such claimants shall be seventy-five cents for each acre of irrigated land up to and including one hundred acres; fifty cents for each acre from one hundred acres to and including five hundred acres; thirty-five cents for each acre from five hundred acres to and including one thousand acres; and twenty-five cents per acre for each acre in excess of one thousand acres; seventy-five cents for each theoretical horsepower up to and including one hundred horsepower; fifty cents for each horsepower from one hundred horsepower to and including five hundred horsepower; thirty-five cents for each horsepower from five hundred horsepower to and including one thousand horsepower; and twenty-five cents for each horsepower in excess of one thousand horsepower; as set forth in such proof, the minimum fee, however, for any claimant to be ten dollars ($10). The state engineer shall collect a fee of ten dollars ($10) for a proof of water used for domestic purposes or any other character of claim to water. Such fee shall include the cost of recording the water-right certificate in the office of the county recorder, should such certificate of water right issue. All fees collected as above set forth shall be accounted for in detail and deposited with the state treasurer once in each month; *provided, however,* that the state engineer shall deduct and hold such an amount from said fees as may be estimated to recover the cost of recording the certificates of water right.

State engineer shall assemble proofs and have same printed.

SEC. 28. As soon as practicable after the expiration of the period fixed in which proofs may be filed, the state engineer shall assemble all proofs which have been filed with him, and prepare and certify an abstract of all of said proofs, which shall be printed in the state printing office. The state engineer shall also prepare from the proofs and evidence taken or given before him, or obtained by him, a preliminary order of determination establishing the several rights of claimants to the waters of the stream. When said abstract of proofs and said preliminary order of determination shall be completed, the state engineer shall then prepare a notice fixing and setting a time and place when and where the evidence taken by or filed with him and the proofs of claims shall be open to the inspection of all interested persons, said period of inspection to be not less than twenty days, which notice shall be deemed an order of the state engineer as to the matters contained therein. A copy of said notice, together with a printed copy of the preliminary order of determination and a printed copy of the said abstract of proofs, shall be delivered by the state engineer, or sent by registered mail, at least thirty days prior to the first day of such period of inspection, to each person who has appeared and filed proof, as herein provided. The state engineer shall be present at the time and place designated in said notice and allow, during said period, any person interested to inspect such evidence and proof as have been filed with or taken by him in accordance with this act.

Contest, how instituted.

SEC. 29. Any person claiming any interest in the stream system involved in the determination of relative rights and to the use of water, whether claiming under vested right or under permit from the state engineer, may object to any finding, part, or portion of the preliminary order of determination made by the state engineer, by filing objections with the state engineer within thirty days after said evidence and proofs, as provided in section 28 of this act, shall have been opened to public inspection, or within such further time as for good cause shown may be allowed by the state engineer upon application. Said objections shall be verified by the affidavit of the objector, his agent or attorney, and shall state with reasonable certainty the grounds of objection.

Hearings for determination of water rights.

SEC. 30. The state engineer shall fix a time and place for the hearing of objections, which date shall not be less than thirty (30) days, nor more than sixty (60) days from the date the notice is served on the persons who are, or may be, affected thereby. Said notice may be sent by registered mail to the persons to be affected by said objections, and the receipt therefor shall constitute legal and valid proof of service. Said notice may also be served by the state engineer, or by any person qualified and competent to serve a summons in civil actions, appointed by him, and return thereof made in the same manner as in civil actions in the district courts of the state. The state engineer shall have power to adjourn hearings from time to time upon reasonable notice to all parties interested, and to issue subpenas and compel the attendance of witnesses to testify at such hearings,

which shall be served in the same manner as subpenas issued out of the district courts of the state. Depositions may be taken by any officer authorized to administer oaths and designated by the state engineer or the parties of interest, and oral testimony may be introduced in all hearings. The state engineer or his deputy shall have the power to administer oaths to witnesses. In case of neglect or refusal on the part of any person to comply with any order of the state engineer or any subpena, or on the refusal of any witness to testify to any matter regarding which he may be lawfully interrogated, it shall be the duty of the district court of any county, or any judge thereof, on application of the state engineer, to issue attachment proceedings for contempt, as in the case of disobedience of a subpena issued from such court or a refusal to testify therein. Witnesses shall receive fees as in civil cases, to be paid by the party calling such witnesses. The evidence in such proceedings shall be confined to the subjects enumerated in the objections and preliminary order of determination. All testimony taken at such hearings shall be reported and transcribed in its entirety.

CHAPTER 140, STATUTES OF 1913

State engineer to make rules governing contests.

SEC. 31. The state engineer shall have power to make rules, not in conflict herewith, governing the practice and procedure in all contests before his office to insure the proper and orderly exercise of the powers herein granted, and the speedy accomplishment of the purposes of this act. Such rules of practice and procedure shall be furnished to any person upon application therefor.

CHAPTER 106, STATUTES OF 1921

Contestants to pay expenses of contests.

SEC. 32. The state engineer shall require a deposit of five dollars ($5) per day from each party while engaged in taking evidence on said objections. The amount received from such fee, or so much as may be necessary, shall be used in paying the cost of reporting and transcribing testimony; the balance, if any, shall be turned into the general fund of the state treasury upon the next monthly transmittal of fees by the state engineer to said state treasurer.

State engineer to make and record order determining water rights.

SEC. 33. As soon as practicable after the hearing of objections to the preliminary order of determination, the state engineer shall make and cause to be entered of record in his office an order of determination, defining the several rights to the waters of the stream or stream system. Said order of determination, when filed with the clerk of the district court as provided in section 34 of this act, shall have the legal effect of a complaint in a civil action. The order of determination shall be certified by the state engineer and as many copies as required printed in the state printing office. A copy of said order of determination shall be sent by registered mail or delivered in person to each person who has filed proof of claim and to each person who has become interested, through intervention or through filing objections under the provisions of section 26 or section 29 of this act.

CHAPTER 253, STATUTES OF 1915

Order to be filed with county clerks of counties where stream system is situated—Proviso—Further regulations concerning order—Order published, when—What deemed full notice.

SEC. 34. As soon as practicable thereafter a certified copy of the order of determination, together with the original evidence and transcript of testimony filed with, or taken before the state engineer, as aforesaid, duly certified by him, shall be filed with the clerk of the county, as ex officio clerk of the district court, in which said stream system is situated, or if in more than one county but all within one judicial district, then with the said clerk of the county wherein reside the largest number of parties in interest. But if such stream system shall be in two or more judicial districts, then the state engineer shall notify the district judge of each of such judicial districts of his intent to file such order of determination, whereupon, within ten days after receipt of such notice, such judges shall confer and agree where the court proceedings under this act shall be held and upon the judge who shall preside, and on notification thereof the state engineer shall file said order of determination, evidence, and transcripts with the clerk of the court so designated; *provided,* that if such district judges fail to notify the state engineer of their agreement, as aforesaid, within five days after the expiration of such ten days, then, and in that event, the state engineer may file such order of determination, evidence, and transcript with the clerk of any county he may elect, and the district judge of such county shall have jurisdiction over the proceedings in relation thereto. In all instances a certified copy of the order of determination shall be filed with the county clerk of each county in which such stream system, or any part thereof, is situated. Upon the filing of the certified copy of said order, evidence, and transcript with the clerk of the court in which the proceedings are to be had, the state engineer shall procure an order from said court setting the time for hearing. The clerk of such court shall immediately furnish the state engineer with a certified copy thereof. It shall be the duty of the state engineer immediately thereupon to mail a copy of such certified order of the court, by registered mail, addressed to each such party in interest at his last known place of residence, and to cause the same to be published at least once a week for four consecutive weeks in some newspaper of general circulation published in each county in which such stream system or any part thereof is located, and the state engineer shall file with the clerk of the court proof of such service by registered mail and by publication. And such service by registered mail and by publication shall be deemed full and sufficient notice to all parties in interest of the date and purpose of such hearing.

CHAPTER 106, STATUTES OF 1921

Exceptions to order, how made—Decree of court, when.

SEC. 25. At least five days prior to the date set for hearing, all parties in interest who are aggrieved or dissatisfied with the order of determination of the state engineer shall file with the clerk of said court notice of exceptions to the order of determination of the state engineer, which notice shall state briefly the exceptions taken, and the prayer for relief, and a copy thereof shall be served upon or trans-

mitted to the state engineer by registered mail. The order of determination by the state engineer and the statements or claims of claimants and exceptions made to the order of determination shall constitute the pleadings, and there shall be no other pleadings in the cause. If no exceptions shall have been filed with the clerk of the court as aforesaid, then on the day set for hearing the court may take further testimony if deemed proper, and shall then enter its findings of facts and judgment and decree. On the day set for hearing, all parties in interest who have filed notices of exceptions as aforesaid shall appear in person or by counsel, and it shall be the duty of the court to hear the same or set the time for hearing, until such exceptions are disposed of, and all proceedings thereunder including the taking of testimony shall be as nearly as may be in accordance with the rules governing civil actions.

CHAPTER 253, STATUTES OF 1915

Expert witnesses may be called by court—Costs, how assessed.

SEC. 36. For further information on any subject in controversy the court may employ one or more qualified persons to investigate and report thereon under oath, subject to examination by any party in interest as to his competency to give expert testimony thereon. The court, may, if necessary, refer the case or any part thereof for such further evidence to be taken by the state engineer as it may direct, and may require a further determination by him, subject to the court's instructions. After the hearing, the court shall enter a decree affirming or modifying the order of the state engineer. Upon the hearing the court may assess and adjudge against any party such costs as it may deem just and equitable, or may assess the costs in proportion to the amount of water right allotted. Appeals from such decree may be taken to the supreme court by the state engineer or any party in interest, in the same manner and with the same effect as in civil cases.

CHAPTER 106, STATUTES OF 1921

Court decree final—Proviso—Time limit.

SEC. 36A. The decree entered by the court, as provided by section 36 of this act, shall be final and shall be conclusive upon all persons and rights lawfully embraced within the adjudication; *provided, however,* that the state engineer, or any party or adjudicated claimant upon any stream or stream system affected by such decree, may, at any time within three years from the entry thereof, apply to the court for a modification of said decree, in so far only as said decree fixed the duty of water, and upon the hearing of such motion the court may modify such decree increasing or decreasing the duty of water, consistent with good husbandry, and consistent with the principle that actual and beneficial use shall be the measure and limit of the right. Notice of application shall be given as in civil cases.

State engineer may make order without notice, when.

SEC. 36B. Whenever there are ten or less appropriators or claimants upon a stream system, and all of such claimants or appropriators in writing waive the provisions of this act with reference to notices and the service and publication thereof, as provided in preceding sections,

Such certificate shall be transmitted by the state engineer in person or by registered mail to the county recorder of the county in which said right is located, and it shall be the duty of the county recorder upon the receipt of a recording fee of one dollar, collected as hereinbefore provided, to record the same in a book especially prepared and kept for that purpose, and thereupon immediately transmit the certificate to the respective owners.

CHAPTER 106, STATUTES OF 1921

Governor to appoint water commissioners—Duties of water commissioners—Charges, how based—Minimum charge—Defaulted payments lien on property—Water commissioners paid by county.

SEC. 52. There shall be appointed by the governor, on the recommendation of the state engineer, one or more water commissioners for each district, who shall receive a salary to be fixed by the state engineer, but not to exceed $5 per day and necessary travel expense while actually employed in the performance of their duties; *provided, however,* that a sum not to exceed $10 per day may be paid to water commissioners whose duties require special training and experience, and when such higher compensation is approved by the board of county commissioners of the county or counties in which the district is situated. Such water commissioners shall execute the laws prescribed in sections 52 to 58, inclusive, of this act, under the direction of the state engineer. The salary of such water commissioners shall be paid by the county in which the water district is situated, out of a fund as hereinafter provided. If the water district lies in more than one county, such salary and expenses shall be apportioned ratably to the counties, in the proportion the water rights in the county bear to the aggregate rights in the district and served by the water district. The state engineer shall, between the first Monday of January and the first Monday of April of each year, prepare a budget of the amount of money estimated to be necessary to pay the expenses of each water district for the then current year. Said budget shall be prepared and show the following detail: The aggregate amount estimated to be necessary to pay the expenses of said district; the aggregate water rights in the district as determined by the state engineer or the court, and the proportion that each claimant's right bears to the aggregate rights in the district, and the charge against each water user, which shall be based upon the proportion which his water right bears to the aggregate water rights in the district; *provided, however,* that the minimum charge shall be one dollar. Upon receipt of such budget by the board of county commissioners, it shall be their duty to certify the respective charges contained therein to the assessor of the county or counties in which the land or property is situate, and it shall be the duty of such assessor to enter the amount of such charge or charges on the assessment roll against said claimants and the property or acreage served. It shall be the duty of the proper officers of the county to collect such tax as other taxes are levied and collected, and such charge shall be a lien upon the property so served, and shall be collected in the same manner as other taxes are collected. The taxes and charges hereinabove provided for, when collected, shall be deposited in a fund in the county treasury which shall be known as "........................ Water District

Fund." All bills against said fund shall be certified by the state engineer, and, when so certified, the board of county commissioners shall approve such bills and authorize the auditor of the county to draw his warrant therefor against such water district fund. Any moneys remaining in the water district fund at the end of the current year shall remain in such fund and be available for use in the following year. Whenever any appropriator by reason of shortage of water shall not receive the amount of water to which he is entitled or that the water commissioner rendered a materially lessened service than that assessed to such user, he may apply to, and the board of county commissioners shall have authority to make such equalization of the charge made against him as shall be equitable.

CHAPTER 140, STATUTES OF 1913

State divided into districts by state engineer, when.

SEC. 53. The state engineer shall divide the state into water districts to be so constituted as to insure the best protection for the water user, and the most economical water supervision on the part of the state. Said water districts shall not be created until a necessity therefor shall arise and shall be created from time to time as the priorities and claims to the streams of the state shall be determined.

State engineer to insure proper distribution of water—Mode of procedure.

SEC. 54. It shall be the duty of the state engineer to divide or cause to be divided the waters of the natural streams or other sources of supply in the state among the several ditches and reservoirs taking water therefrom, according to the rights of each respectively, in whole or in part, and to shut or fasten, or cause to be shut or fastened, the head-gates or ditches, and to regulate or cause to be regulated, the controlling works of reservoirs, as may be necessary to insure a proper distribution of the waters thereof. Such state engineer shall have authority to regulate the distribution of water among the various users under any partnership ditch or reservoir where rights have been adjudicated in accordance with existing decrees. Whenever, in pursuance of his duties the water commissioner regulates a head-gate to a ditch or the controlling works of reservoirs, it shall be his duty to attach to such head-gate or controlling works a written notice properly dated or signed, setting forth the fact that such head-gate or controlling works has been properly regulated and is wholly under his control, and such notice shall be a legal notice to all parties interested in the diversion and distribution of the water of such ditch or reservoir. It shall be the duty of the district attorney to appear for or in behalf of the state engineer or his duly authorized assistants in any case which may arise in the pursuance of the official duties of any such officer within the jurisdiction of said district attorney.

Misdemeanor to interfere with water officers—Prima-facie evidence.

SEC. 55. Any person who shall wilfully open, close, change or interfere with any lawfully established head-gate or water-box without authority, or who shall wilfully use water or conduct water into or through his ditch which has been lawfully denied him by the state engineer, his assistants or water commissioners, shall be deemed guilty of a misdemeanor.

The possession or use of water when the same shall have been lawfully denied by the state engineer or other competent authority shall be prima-facie evidence of the guilt of the person using it.

Head-gates to be maintained by owners—Measuring device must be maintained.

SEC. 56. The owner or owners of any ditch or canal shall maintain to the satisfaction of the state engineer of the division in which the irrigation works are located, a substantial head-gate at or near the point where the water is diverted, which shall be of such construction that it can be locked and kept closed by the water commissioner; and such owners shall construct and maintain, when required by the state engineer, suitable measuring devices at such points along such ditch as may be necessary for the purpose of. assisting the water commissioner in determining the amount of water that is to be diverted into said ditch from the stream, or taken from it by the various users. Any and every owner or manager of a reservoir located across or upon the bed of a natural stream or of a reservoir which requires the use of a natural stream channel, shall be required to construct and maintain, when required by the state engineer, a measuring device of a plan to be approved by the state engineer, below such reservoir, and a measuring device above such reservoir, on each or every stream or source of supply discharging into such reservoir, for the purpose of assisting the state engineer or water commissioners in determining the amount of water to which appropriators are entitled and thereafter diverting it for such appropriators' use. When it may be necessary for the protection of other water users, the state engineer may require flumes to be installed along the line of any ditch. If any such owner or owners of irrigation works shall refuse or neglect to construct and put in such head-gates, flumes, or measuring devices after ten (10) days' notice. the state engineer may close such ditch, and the same shall not be opened or any water diverted from the source of supply, under the penalties prescribed by law for the opening of head-gates, lawfully closed until the requirements of the state engineer as to such headgate, flume, or measuring device have been complied with, and if any owner or manager of a reservoir, which requires the use of a natural stream channel, shall neglect or refuse to put in such measuring device after ten (10) days' notice by the state engineer, such state engineer may open the sluice-gate or outlet of such reservoir and the same shall not be closed under the penalties of the law for changing or interfering with head-gates, until the requirements of the state engineer as to such measuring device are complied with.

State engineer or assistants may arrest violators of water law.

SEC. 57. The state engineer or his assistants shall have power to arrest any person violating any of the provisions of this act, and to turn them over to the sheriff, or other competent police officer within the county, and immediately on delivering any such person so arrested into the custody of the sheriff, it shall be the duty of said state engineer or his assistant making such arrest to immediately, in writing, and upon oath, make complaint before the justice of the peace against the person so arrested.

Penalties for violation.

SEC. 58. Any person violating any of the provisions of this act shall be deemed guilty of a misdemeanor, and upon conviction thereof shall be fined in a sum not less than twenty-five dollars ($25), nor more than two hundred and fifty dollars ($250), together with the costs, or imprisoned in the county jail not exceeding six months, and not less than ten (10) days, or by both such fine and imprisonment.

CHAPTER 106, STATUTES OF 1921

Permits subject to existing rights.

SEC. 72A. Every permit to appropriate water, and every certificate of appropriation granted under any permit by the state engineer upon any stream or stream system which shall have been adjudicated under the provisions of sections 18 to 39 of this act, shall be, and the same is hereby declared to be subject to existing rights and to the decree and modifications thereof entered in such adjudication proceedings, and the same shall be subject to regulation and control by the state engineer and the water commissioners in the same manner and to the same extent as rights which have been adjudicated and decreed under the provisions of this act, and every such holder of certificate or permit shall in like manner be subject to all of the provisions of sections 52 to 58, inclusive.

CHAPTER 140, STATUTES OF 1913

Use of bed of stream, how regulated—Expenses, how met.

SEC. 77. Whenever the owner, manager or lessee of a reservoir constructed under the provisions of this act shall desire to use the bed of a stream or other watercourse for the purpose of carrying stored or impounded water from the reservoir to the consumer thereof, he shall, in writing, notify the state engineer, and the water commissioner of the district in which said water is to be used, giving the date when it is proposed to discharge water from said reservoir, its volume, and the names of all the persons and ditches entitled to its use, and it shall then be the duty of the said state engineer, or his assistant, to regulate the said works and head-gates, of all ditches from the stream or watercourse not entitled to the use of such stored water as will enable those having the right to secure the volume to which they are entitled. The state engineer shall keep a true and distinct account of the time spent by him in the discharge of his duties, as defined in this section, and to present a certified statement thereof to the county commissioners of the county wherein the expense is incurred. Said county commissioners shall present a bill for the expense so incurred to the reservoir owner, manager, or lessee, and if such owner, manager, or lessee shall neglect for thirty (30) days after the presentation of such bill of costs, to pay the same, the said costs shall be made a charge upon the said reservoir and shall be collected as delinquent taxes until payment of such bill of costs has been made.

Negligent coowners may be compelled to pay share of expenses.

SEC. 79. In all cases where ditches are owned by two or more persons, and one or more of such persons shall fail or neglect to do a

proportionate share of the work necessary for the proper maintenance and operation of such ditch or ditches, or to construct suitable head-gates, or other devices at the point where water is diverted from the main ditch, such owner or owners desiring the performance of such work, may, after giving ten days' written notice to such other owner or owners who have failed to perform such proportionate share of the work necessary for the operation and maintenance of said ditch or ditches, perform such share of the work, and recover therefor from such person or persons in default, the reasonable expense of such work.

Statement of expenses to constitute valid lien against property of delinquent.

SEC. 80. Upon the failure of any coowner to pay his proportionate share of such expense, as mentioned in the preceding section, within thirty days after receiving the statement of the same as performed by his coowners or owners, such person or persons so performing such labor may secure payment of said claim by filing an itemized and sworn statement thereof, setting forth the date of the performance and the nature of the labor so performed, with the county clerk of the county wherein said ditch is situated, and when so filed it shall constitute a valid lien against the interest of such person or persons in default, which said lien may be established and enforced in the same manner as provided by law for the enforcement of mechanics' liens.

Unauthorized use or wilful waste of water prima-facie evidence of guilt.

SEC. 81. The unauthorized use of water to which another person is entitled, or the wilful waste of water to the detriment of another, shall be a misdemeanor, and the possession or use of such water without legal right, shall be prima-facie evidence of the guilt of the person using or diverting it.

Obstruction unlawful.

SEC. 82. Whenever any appropriator of water has the lawful right of way for the storage, diversion, or carriage of water, it shall be unlawful to place or maintain any obstruction that shall interfere with the use of his works, or prevent convenient access thereto. Any violation of the provisions of this section shall be a misdemeanor.

Misdemeanor to violate these provisions.

SEC. 83. All violations of the provisions of this act declared herein to be a misdemeanor, shall be punished by a fine not exceeding two hundred and fifty dollars ($250), and not less than ten dollars ($10), or by imprisonment in the county jail not exceeding six months, or by both such fine and imprisonment.

Vested rights to water not impaired.

SEC. 84. Nothing in this act contained shall impair the vested right of any person to the use of water, nor shall the right of any person to take and use water be impaired or affected by any of the provisions of this act where appropriations have been initiated in accordance with law prior to the approval of this act. Any and all appropriations based upon applications and permits now on file in the state engineer's office, shall be perfected in accordance with the laws in force at the time of their filing.

Rotation in use of water.

Sec. 85. To bring about a more economical use of the available water supply, it shall be lawful for water users, owning lands to which water is appurtenant, to rotate in the use of the supply to which they may be collectively entitled; or a single water user, having lands to which water rights of a different priority attach, may in like manner rotate in use, when such rotation can be made without injury to lands enjoying an earlier priority, to the end that each user may have an irrigation head of at least two (2) cubic feet per second.

State engineer to make rules.

Sec. 86. The state engineer is hereby empowered to make such reasonable rules and regulations as may be necessary for the proper and orderly execution of the powers conferred by this act.

Each section of this law declared independent.

Sec. 87. Each section of this act and every part of each section is hereby declared to be independent sections, and parts of sections, and the holding of any section or part thereof to be void or ineffective for any cause shall not be deemed to affect any other section or any part thereof.

CHAPTER 253, STATUTES OF 1915

All documentary evidence, maps, etc., admissible in court—Proviso—All evidence to be considered.

Sec. 88a. Any and all maps, plats, surveys, and evidence on file in the office of the state engineer relating to any proof of appropriation involved in the proceedings for the determination of the relative rights in and to the waters of any stream system, obtained or filed under the provisions of this or any preceding act relating to the office of state engineer, shall be admissible in court, and shall have the same force and effect as though obtained and submitted under the provisions of this act as amended; *provided,* that at least ninety days prior to the rendering of his order of determination of the relative rights in and to the waters of any stream system, the state engineer shall notify all parties in interest of his intention to consider such maps, plats, and evidence, and of his intention to submit his findings to the court under the provisions of this act as amended; such notice to be given in the manner prescribed in section 22 of this act. Within sixty days after such notice, any such party in interest may file with the state engineer any additional or supplementary maps, plats, surveys, or evidence, or objections to the admissibility of any evidence hitherto presented and on file in the office of the state engineer, in relation to his claim of water right or adverse to the claim or claims of the water right of any other party or parties in interest, in order so to perfect his claim in accordance with the provisions of this amended act, and the state engineer shall consider the whole thereof in rendering such order of determination, and the same shall become a part of the record which shall be submitted to the court as provided by sections 34 to 39, inclusive, of this act.

USEFUL EQUIVALENTS

The following equivalents of the terms, second-foot and acre-foot and miner's inch, will serve as a guide where necessary to transpose them:

1 acre-foot of water is the quantity that will cover an area of 1 acre 1 foot deep.

1 second-foot of water is the quantity that will fill a space of 1 cubic foot in 1 second of time.

1 second-foot equals 40 miners' inches.

1 second-foot equals 7.4805 gallons per second, or 448.83 gallons per minute.

1 acre-foot equals 43,560 cubic feet.

1 miner's inch equals 0.186+ gallons per second.

1 miner's inch equals 11.21 gallons per minute.

1 miner's inch equals 672.60 gallons per hour.

1 miner's inch equals 16,142.40 gallons per day of 24 hours.

1 miner's inch flowing 20.16 days will cover an acre of land 1 foot deep, or it will be the equivalent of 1 acre-foot.

1 miner's inch flowing 150 days (5 months of 30 days each) will cover an acre of land 7.4 feet deep.

1 second-foot of water flowing 150 days equals 297.06 acre-feet, or enough water to cover 100 acres of land 2.9706 feet deep.

1 second-foot of water flowing 24 hours equals 86,400 cubic feet, or 1.98 acre-feet, or approximately 1 acre 2 feet deep.

1 acre-foot equals 325,850 gallons.

MEASUREMENTS OF WATER

In everyday practice water measurements are accomplished by means of weirs, and the current meter. Other methods are used, such as the float, or measurement through an orifice; however, they are never used when it is possible to use a current meter or a weir.

Weirs should invariably be used where the flow of the ditch or stream is not so large that they are impracticable. This method affords the most accurate measurement, besides being what might be termed an automatic measuring device, which enables every water user to know at all times the quantity of water flowing in his ditch, by simply referring to tables which give the discharge according to the length of the weir and the depth of water flowing over it.

On large streams it is not feasible to construct weirs, and measurements are taken by means of the current meter, an instrument for obtaining the velocity of the water. The cross-section of the stream, multiplied by the velocity obtained by the current meter, gives the dis-

charge. The cross-section is usually taken in square feet, the velocity in feet per second, and the discharge given in cubic feet per second.

WEIRS

There are several forms of weirs which may be used for the measurement of water. The most common forms in use, however, are the rectangular weir and the trapezoidal or "Cippoletti weir."

The rectangular weir requires corrections for the different heights of water flowing over the crest, and for this reason the Cippoletti weir is recommended wherever it is necessary to accurately measure the discharge of any ditch or stream.

The Cippoletti weir receives its name from its inventor. The design of the weir is such that the sloping ends of the notch correct automatically the changes for the different heights of water flowing over it, as compared with the rectangular weir.

The Cippoletti weir has been adopted as the standard form by the office of the State Engineer, and a set of plans for a four-foot weir have been prepared for free distribution upon application.

The size of the weir required for any given discharge may be found by referring to the table of discharges. The proportions of the weir shown on the standard form should be maintained for the different sizes to insure correct measurements. In the construction of any weir the rules herewith given should be followed as closely as conditions will permit.

The location of weirs in a channel should be selected with care. The channel should be straight and of uniform cross-section for a distance of 50 to 100 feet leading to the weir. The center of the stream should meet the center of the weir and be perpendicular to it.

The water above the weir should be without current, or as nearly so as possible. This may be accomplished by widening the channel immediately above the weir, forming a pond or reservoir. By so enlarging the channel the velocity of approach is reduced to minimum.

The area of the channel should be from eight to ten times the area of the notch of the weir.

The upstream side of the weir plane should be sharp and rigid. Usually this is accomplished by beveling the crest and ends of the weir. A galvanized-iron sheet, cut to form and attached to the upper side of the notch by means of screws or bolts, makes an excellent crest.

The width of the weir crest should be three times the maximum depth of water that will pass over it. Thin sheets of water passing over weirs may cause inaccurate measurements. The distance from the end of the weir notch to the edge of the channel should be two times the depth of water passing over the crest. Dirt should not be allowed to accumulate against the upstream side of the structure. The canal bottom should

be three times the depth of water passing over the crest below the top of the crest.

The overflow should have full contractions. By constructing the faces of the weir at right angles to the stream on both sides and bottom equal to two times the depth of water expected to pass over it, air will pass under the overflow sheet of water and produce the contractions. The water should have a clear fall to insure this perfect air-space.

The depth of water passing over the weir should be measured some distance up stream from the crest. A peg should be driven in the bed of the stream at such a distance above the weir that the curve formed by the water flowing over it will not affect the surface of the peg.

The zero mark of the peg should be exactly level with the top of the crest. Numerous devices may be used for gages to read the depth of water. Simple graduations in feet and decimals thereof may be placed on the peg and the depth read directly. Brass-headed tacks may be used as the markers for the different graduations.

Care should be exercised in reading the gage, as a slight error in reading produces a considerable error in the quantity of discharge. For accuracy the gage should be read to at least $^{1}/_{100}$ of a foot. In every-day practice the errors will usually be compensated, as on one occasion the reading may be too high and again it may be too low.

FORMULA FOR COMPUTING THE DISCHARGE OVER CIPPOLETTI'S TRAPEZOIDAL WEIRS

Q equals $3.3^{2}/_{3}LH^{3}/_{2}$.

Q equals the discharge in cubic feet per second.

L equals the length of the weir in feet.

H equals the depth of water passing over the crest measured to the quiet surface.

INDEX

STATE OF NEVADA

OBJECTIONS

TO

PRELIMINARY ORDER OF DETERMINATION

OF THE

Waters of the Humboldt River and Its Tributaries

J. G. SCRUGHAM, State Engineer

CARSON CITY, NEVADA
STATE PRINTING OFFICE : : JOE FARNSWORTH, SUPERINTENDENT
1922

170

IN THE OFFICE OF THE STATE ENGINEER OF THE STATE OF NEVADA

IN THE MATTER OF THE DETERMINATION OF THE RELATIVE RIGHTS IN AND TO THE WATERS OF THE HUMBOLDT RIVER AND ITS TRIBUTARIES.

To the Water Users of the Humboldt River and its Tributaries:

You will please take notice that each of the parties named in the schedule, which is hereto annexed and hereby made a part hereof, has, within the time allowed by law and by the order of the State Engineer, made and filed with the State Engineer objections to the Preliminary Order of Determination made by the State Engineer on the 10th day of April, 1922, in the above-entitled matter.

You will further take notice that, commencing on the 14th day of August, 1922, at 10 a. m., in the office of the State Engineer of the State of Nevada, at Carson City, Nevada, the State Engineer will hold a hearing on the objections so made and filed against said preliminary order of determination, in the numerical order specified in said schedule.

Dated this 30th day of June, 1922.

By Order of J. G. SCRUGHAM,
State Engineer.

No. 1

IN THE OFFICE OF THE STATE ENGINEER OF NEVADA

OBJECTIONS OF W. C. RUDDELL, JOHN G. TAYLOR, JOHN HOLMSTROM, H. P. KRUSE, AND H. M. DAMM

In the Matter of the Determination of the Relative Rights in and to the Waters of the Humboldt River Stream-System

Come now W. C. Ruddell, John G. Taylor, John Holmstrom, H. P. Kruse and H. M. Damm, whose postoffice address is Lovelock, Nevada, and object to the whole, and to each and every part or portion of and to the several findings set out in the "Preliminary Order of Determination Establishing the Several Rights of Claimants to the Waters of the" Humboldt River and its tributaries, as made by the State Engineer of the State of Nevada under date of April ...., 1922, in the above-entitled matter, and as grounds of said objections, specify the following:

1. That the undersigned objectors are, and each of them is, an appropriator and user of water from the above-mentioned stream-system; that the water claimed by each of us has been beneficially used by each of us, or each of our predecessors, in interest continuously for many years last past and is now being so used through and by means of the following-named ditches or ditch systems, to wit: the Last Chance or Irish American Ditch, or other ditch system; the Union Canal Ditch, or other ditch system; the Southwest Ditch, or other ditch system; the Old Channel Ditch, or other ditch system; the Young Ditch or other ditch system.

2. That said preliminary order of determination is invalid, in that it appears from the face of said preliminary order of determination that it was made in violation of and does not comply with or conform to the requirements of the statutes of the State of Nevada, under which it purports to have been made.

3. That said preliminary order of determination is invalid, in that it appears from the face thereof that the several rights of the claimants to the waters of the Humboldt River and its tributaries cannot be ascertained therefrom, because no dates or data is stated therein as to when the several rights of the objectors or of any of the claimants to the waters of said Humboldt River and its tributaries was initiated by the commencement of the construction, completion or enlargement of any of the works by means of which the waters claimed by the objectors or any other claimants to the waters of said stream-system where diverted from the source for the beneficial uses claimed by the objectors or any of the claimants to the waters of said Humboldt River and its tributaries.

4. That said preliminary order of determination is invalid, in that no date or number of priority of the objectors or any of the claimants to the waters of the Humboldt River and its tributaries is stated therein; neither is there any fact or facts stated in said preliminary order of determination from which the priority of the objectors or any of the claimants to the waters of the Humboldt River and its tributaries can be ascertained or determined.

5. That said preliminary order of determination is invalid, in that it appears from the face of said preliminary order of determination

that one of the fundamental and essential elements in determining and establishing the several rights of the claimants to the waters of said Humboldt River and its tributaries, viz, the "doctrine of relation" is not considered, but has been rejected by the State Engineer in making said preliminary order of determination establishing the several rights of claimants to the waters of said Humboldt River and its tributaries.

6. That said preliminary order of determination is invalid, in that it does not appear therefrom, nor can it be ascertaind or determined from said preliminary order of determination where the point of diversion is located, by means of which said objectors or any of the claimants to the waters of said Humboldt River and its tributaries divert the water claimed from said source for beneficial uses.

7. That said preliminary order of determination is invalid, in that said State Engineer has failed, neglected and refused to apply in said preliminary order of determination establishing the several rights of claimants to the waters of said Humboldt River and its tributaries court decrees rendered and entered by the United States Federal Court of the District of Nevada, and by the District Courts of the State of Nevada, wherein and whereby the rights of claimants to the waters of the said Humboldt River and its tributaries have been adjudicated and determined; and also because in the making of said preliminary order of determination said State Engineer has neglected and refused to give due and proper consideration, weight and effect to various agreements made and entered into by and between the several claimants to the waters of said Humboldt River and its tributaries.

8. That said preliminary order of determination is invalid, in that it appears therefrom that said State Engineer has neglected and refused to consider as tributaries of said Humboldt River certain known and well-defined tributaries thereof, viz, the Little Humboldt River and its tributaries, as well as other tributaries of said Humboldt River.

9. That said preliminary order of determination is defective, indefinite, uncertain and insufficient, and does not state facts sufficient to constitute an order of determination establishing the several rights of the objectors or any of the claimants to the waters of said Humboldt River and its tributaries for and because of all and each of the reasons hereinabove stated as to why said preliminary order of determination is invalid.

10. That said preliminary order of determination is invalid, erroneous and defective:

a. In that by said preliminary order of determination a water right is attempted to be awarded to overflow lands; and

b. In that by said preliminary order of determination a water right is attempted to be awarded to swamp lands, both of which attempted awards is contrary to and in violation of the law in re water rights.

11. That said preliminary order of determination is invalid, erroneous and defective in that it appears therefrom that in many instances a water right is attempted to be awarded for acres of lands. but the lands for which such water right is attempted to be awarded are not described or mentioned; such condition appears especially in District No. 4, Elko and Pine Creek; as illustrating this objection, reference is made to findings beginning on pages 168, 170, 171, 172,

177, 196, 197, 204, 206, 210, 213, 214, 215, 216, 217, 220, 221, 222, 223, 224, 225, 227, 228, 229, 231, 232, 236, 245, 252, 258, 281, 282, 284, 287, of said preliminary order of determination.

12. That said preliminary order of determination is invalid, erroneous and defective, in that it appears therefrom that in many instances the number of acres mentioned and for which a water right is attempted to be awarded exceeds the total number of acres of land described by local subdivisions in said preliminary order of determination; as illustrating this objection, reference is made to pages 38, 84, 85, 86, 88, 90, 170, 213, 215, 216, 222 of said preliminary order of determination.

13. That said preliminary order of determination is erroneous, defective and incorrect in that it does not award to said objectors and each of them the water rights to which they are entitled, and for which claim was made by them and each of them, as is set out in the statement of claim filed in the office of the State Engineer of the State of Nevada.

14. That said preliminary order of determination is erroneous, defective and incorrect in that excessive water rights are thereby attempted to be awarded to a great number of persons as appears from the findings, set out in said preliminary order of determination, and beginning on pages 25, 28, 36, 41, 44, 46, 50, 52, 64, 67, 99, 105 to 115, 117, 124, 144, 154, 183, 189, 197, 204, 246, 250, 258, 262, 268, 282, 284, 292, and at other pages, which will be designated before or at the time of hearing this objection. For reasons, among others, that the amount of water attempted to be awarded is excessive; that during the several years for which a water right is attempted to be awarded a large portion of the lands for which a water right is attempted to be awarded was either the United States Government or Central Pacific Railway Company's lands and was not irrigated or reclaimed; that no valid appropriation of water for said lands was initiated during or prior to the said years designated in said preliminary order of determination; that to award to said lands the water right as stated in said preliminary order of determination would be to impair and invade vested rights of other appropriators of water from said stream-system.

Wherefore, objectors pray that the objections hereinabove made may, upon hearing, be sustained, and that said preliminary order of determination be modified, changed, and corrected in conformity with said objections, and that said preliminary order of determination as it now exists be declared and held to be invalid, erroneous and defective and of no force, virtue and effect; and further that it be declared to be a cloud and encumbrance upon and as impairing and invading the vested rights of the objectors herein named.

W. C. RUDDELL,
JOHN G. TAYLOR,
JOHN HOLMSTROM,
H. P. KRUSE,
H. M. DAMM.
By CHENEY, PRICE, HAWKINS & LUNSFORD,
Attorneys for Objectors.

State of Nevada, County of Washoe, ss.

W. C. Noteware, being first duly sworn, deposes and says: That he is the agent for the above-named objectors, and as such makes this

affidavit; that he has read the foregoing objections and knows the contents thereof, and that the same are true and well founded to the best of his knowledge, information and belief.

W. C. NOTEWARE,

Subscribed and sworn to before me, this 14th day of June, 1922.

[SEAL] PRINCE A. HAWKINS, *Notary Public.*

No. 2

IN THE OFFICE OF THE STATE ENGINEER OF NEVADA

OBJECTIONS OF JOHN G. TAYLOR

In the Matter of the Determination of the Relative Rights in and to the Waters of the Humboldt River Stream-System

Comes now John G. Taylor, whose postoffice address, for the purposes of this objection, is Reno, Nevada, care of Prince A. Hawkins, and objects to that part or portion of the preliminary order of determination establishing the several rights of claimants to the waters of the Humboldt River and its tributaries, as made by the State Engineer of the State of Nevada, under date April ...., 1922, in the above-entitled matter, and as grounds for said objection specifies the following:

1. That the West ½ of the Northwest ¼ of Section 28, Township 27 North, Range 31 East, referred to on page 8 of said preliminary order of determination, should be through the Southwest and Irish American Ditches in conjunction with Marzen Slough, and not through Young Ditch as there stated.

2. That in the preliminary order of determination 320 acres in the North ½ and 85 acres in the South ½ of Section 10, Township 27 North, Range 31 East, M. D. M. are omitted from said preliminary order of determination and said preliminary order of determination should be corrected by the addition of said lands described fixing the priority of 40 acres in the South ½ of said Section as of date 1890, and that said 320 acres in the North ½ of said Section should have a priority of 1894; that 155 acres in the West ½ of Section 6, Township 27 North, Range 32 East, should be included in said preliminary order of determination with a priority of 1896; that 117 acres in the West ½ of the Northwest ¼ and Northwest ¼ of Southwest ¼ of Section 30, Township 28 North, Range 32 East, should be included in said preliminary order of determination with a priority of ....; that said 155 acres in the West ½ of Section 6, Township 27 North, Range 32 East, is now owned by H. P. Kruse; that all the above-mentioned lands which were omitted from said preliminary order of determination were mentioned and described in statement of claims heretofore filed in the office of said State Engineer and are designated and specified in proof No. 0081 and in the abstract of claims March 1, 1916, and supplemental abstract of additional and amended claims, November 1, 1918.

Wherefore, objectors pray that the objections hereinabove made may, upon hearing, be sustained, and that said preliminary order of determination be modified, changed and corrected in conformity with said objections, and that said preliminary order of determination as it now exists be declared and held to be invalid, erroneous and defective and of no force, virtue and effect; and further that it be declared

to be a cloud and encumbrance upon and as impairing and invading the vested rights of the objector herein named.

JOHN G. TAYLOR,
By CHENEY, PRICE, HAWKINS & LUNSFORD,
Attorneys for Objector.

State of Nevada, County of Washoe, ss.

W. C. Noteware, being first duly sworn, deposes and says: That he is the agent for the above-named objector, and as such makes this affidavit; that he has read the foregoing objections and knows the contents thereof, and that the same are true and well founded to the best of his knowledge, information and belief.

W. C. NOTEWARE,

Subscribed and sworn to before me, this 14th day of June, 1922.

[SEAL] PRINCE A. HAWKINS, *Notary Public.*

No. 3

IN THE OFFICE OF THE STATE ENGINEER OF NEVADA

OBJECTIONS OF LOVELOCK LAND AND DEVELOPMENT COMPANY (a Corporation)

In the Matter of the Determination of the Relative Rights in and to the Waters of the Humboldt River Stream-System

Comes now Lovelock Land and Development Company, a corporation organized and existing under the laws of the State of Nevada, principal office, Reno, Nevada, and objects to the preliminary order of determination establishing the several rights of claimants to the waters of the Humboldt River and its tributaries, as made by the State Engineer of the State of Nevada, under date April ...., 1922, in the above-entitled matter, and as grounds for said objection specifies the following:

1. That by said preliminary order of determination said objector is denied and deprived of water rights initiated and perfected by diversion of water from said Humboldt River and the application of waters so diverted to beneficial use, to wit, the irrigation of portions of Sections 1 and 2, Township 25 North, Range 30 East, M. D. M.; and portions of Sections 2, 9, 11, and 17, in Township 25 North, Range 31 East, M. D. M.; as appears from the statement of claim and proof No. 0080 heretofore filed in the office of the State Engineer of the State of Nevada and listed and allowed by the State Engineer of the State of Nevada in the abstract of claims to the waters of the Humboldt River and its tributaries published in 1916, as appears on pages 13 and 14 of said abstract of claims.

2. That said objector objects to said preliminary order of determination for the further reason that it fails to include and recognize the water right of said objector initiated and perfected by virtue of a diversion and application during the year 1917, of water from said Humboldt River and the application of waters so diverted in the irrigation of portions of Sections 20 and 21, Township 25 North, Range 31 East, M. D. M.; and portions of Sections 13 and 14, Township 25 North, Range 30 East, M. D. M.; also said objector objects

to said preliminary order of determintaion for the reason that the reservoir right of said objector initiated and constructed and completed and water stored therein in the year 1902 and thereafter drawn from said reservoir and applied to beneficial use in the irrigation of land of said objector during the year 1903 and each and every year thereafter.

Wherefore, objector prays that the objections hereinabove made may, upon hearing be sustained, and that said preliminary order of determination be modified, changed and corrected in conformity with said objections, and that said preliminary order of determination as it now exists be declared and held to be invalid, erroneous and defective and of no force, virtue and effect; and further that it be declared to be a cloud and encumbrance upon and as impairing and invading the vested rights of the objector herein named.

LOVELOCK LAND AND DEVELOPMENT COMPANY
(a Corporation).

By CHENEY, PRICE, HAWKINS & LUNSFORD,
Attorneys for Objector.

State of Nevada, County of Washoe, ss.

W. C. Noteware, being first duly sworn, deposes and says: That he is the Secretary of and agent for the above-named objector and as such makes this affidavit; that said objector is a corporation organized and existing under and by virtue of the laws of the State of Nevada; that he has read the foregoing objections, knows the contents thereof and that the same are true and well founded to the best of his knowledge, information and belief.

W. C. NOTEWARE.

Subscribed and sworn to before me, this 14th day of June, 1922.

[SEAL] PRINCE A. HAWKINS, *Notary Public.*

No. 4

IN THE OFFICE OF THE STATE ENGINEER OF NEVADA

OBJECTIONS OF JOHN G. TAYLOR AND J. SHEEHAN

In the Matter of the Determination of the Relative Rights in and to the Waters of the Humboldt River Stream-System

Come now John G. Taylor and J. Sheehan, whose postoffice address, for the purposes of this objection, is Reno, Nevada, care of Prince A. Hawkins, and object to that part or portion of the preliminary order of determination establishing the several rights of claimants to the waters of the Humboldt River and the tributaries as made by the State Engineer of the State of Nevada, under date April ...., 1922, in the above-entitled matter, and as grounds for said objections specify the following:

1. That said objectors are the appropriators and users of the entire flow of Pole and Little Rock Creeks, with a priority of 1878, for the irrigation of lands owned and possessed by them; that all the water of said Little Rock and Pole Creeks were, during the year 1878, and have been each and every year thereafter, diverted from the source and

applied to beneficial uses, to wit, the irrigation of lands, watering stock, and domestic purposes; that the culture of the lands so irrigated is erroneously classified in said preliminary order of determination, as appears on page 57 thereof.

Wherefore, objectors pray that the objections hereinabove made may, upon hearing, be sustained, and that said preliminary order of determination be modified, changed and corrected in conformity with said objections, and that said preliminary order of determination as it now exists be declared and held to be invalid, erroneous and defective and of no force, virtue and effect; and further that it be declared to be a cloud and encumbrance upon and as impairing and invading the vested rights of the objectors herein named.

JOHN G. TAYLOR,
J. SHEEHAN,
By CHENEY, PRICE, HAWKINS & LUNSFORD,
Attorneys for Objectors.

State of Nevada, County of Washoe, ss.

W. C. Noteware, being first duly sworn, deposes and says: That he is the agent for the above-named objectors, and as such makes this affidavit; that he has read the foregoing objections and knows the contents thereof, and that the same are true and well founded to the best of his knowledge, information and belief.

W. C. NOTEWARE,

Subscribed and sworn to before me, this 14th day of June, 1922.

[SEAL] PRINCE A. HAWKINS, *Notary Public.*

No. 5

BEFORE THE STATE ENGINEER OF THE STATE OF NEVADA

In the Matter of the Determination of the Water Rights of the Humboldt River and its Tributaries

File No. 00167

OBJECTIONS OF THE ESTATE OF JAMES FARIS, DECEASED, TO THE STATE ENGINEER'S PRELIMINARY ORDER OF DETERMINATION

The Estate of James Faris, deceased, and William H. Devlin and Ethel Faris Adams, administrators of said Estate, persons claiming an interest in the waters of Humboldt River, herewith pursuant to section 29 of chapter 140 of the Statutes of 1913 of the State of Nevada, as amended by section 3 of chapter 106 of the Statutes of the State of Nevada of the year 1921, file their objections to the said preliminary order of determination made by the State Engineer and to each and every finding, part and portion of said order.

Said objections are:

I. That said preliminary order should be withdrawn because (1) it has been made in departure, to the prejudice of this estate, from assurances given to this estate by the State Engineer; and (2) it has been made in departure from sections 28 to 33, inclusive, of said statutes and is therefore insufficient as a preliminary order upon which to base a final order; and (3) it is in excess of the jurisdiction

of the State Engineer under articles III to VI, inclusive, of the Constitution of the State of Nevada.

II. That said preliminary order is erroneous for failure to find a prescriptive right in said Faris Estate for the irrigation of all of its lands in pages 105–115, inclusive, of said findings described as against all persons whose lands or points of diversion lie below the said lands of said estate upon said river.

III. That said preliminary order is erroneous for failure to find rights existing by agreements and judicial decrees.

IV. That said preliminary order is erroneous in its findings of the dates of commencement of beneficial use of water.

V. That said preliminary order is erroneous in its findings of irrigated area.

VI. That said preliminary order is erroneous in its findings of duty of water and length of irrigation season.

VII. That said preliminary order is erroneous for failure to find rights for stock-watering and domestic use.

VIII. That said preliminary order takes property from the Faris Estate without due process of law, and takes property of said Estate for public use without just compensation, in violation of section 84 of said statute of 1913 enacting that vested rights shall not be impaired, and in violation of section 8 of article I of the Constitution of the State of Nevada and amendment XIV of the Constitution of the United States.

The grounds of said objection are:

I

GROUNDS OF THE OBJECTION THAT SAID PRELIMINARY ORDER SHOULD BE WITHDRAWN BECAUSE (1) IT HAS BEEN MADE IN DEPARTURE, TO THE PREJUDICE OF THIS ESTATE, FROM ASSURANCES GIVEN TO THIS ESTATE BY THE STATE ENGINEER; AND (2) IT HAS BEEN MADE IN DEPARTURE FROM SECTIONS 28 TO 33, INCLUSIVE, OF SAID STATUTES AND IS THEREFORE INSUFFICIENT AS A PRELIMINARY ORDER UPON WHICH TO BASE A FINAL ORDER: AND (3) IT IS IN EXCESS OF THE JURISDICTION OF THE STATE ENGINEER UNDER ARTICLES III TO VI, INCLUSIVE, OF THE CONSTITUTION OF THE STATE OF NEVADA.

1. *It is respectfully urged that said preliminary order has been made in departure, to the prejudice of this Estate, from assurances given to this Estate by the State Engineer.*

At the request of the State Engineer, Col. J. G. Scrugham, made personally to the undersigned attorney for this Estate at his office in San Francisco, California, this Estate contributed to the payment of the State Engineer's expenses of collecting evidence and examining witnesses in the matter of said adjudication. At the time, the circumstances were noted in a letter to the State Engineer as follows:

> I would, in fact, like to put it somewhat more strongly, and say that the making of this contribution toward the expenses is being done upon your assurance that I shall be informed by your office of all matters that may affect the Faris Estate so far as they come to your knowledge. (Letter of August 11, 1920, from Samuel C. Wiel to the State Engineer.)

In reply thereto, under date of August 13, 1920, the State Engineer wrote: "We will also inform you in detail as to the progress of the work, particularly in so far as it has reference to the Faris Estate."

A year later under date of October 3, 1921, the Estate's said attorney wrote to the State Engineer, Mr. Scrugham: "Enclosed please find copy of a letter which I am today sending to Mr. MacFarland, Deputy State Engineer. The point is that I would like to be kept posted in sufficient time, and to have sufficient information, to enable me to proceed in such matter as may require attention." The therein-mentioned letter to Mr. Ira MacFarland further contained the following: "I presume that your session at Battle Mountain is for the purpose of arriving at issues, and that information what the issues are and an opportunity to present argument or discussion thereon will be given by the State Engineer a reasonable time before he takes the issues up for decision." In reply, under date of October 5, 1921, the State Engineer, Mr. Scrugham, wrote: "You will be kept posted in sufficient time to enable you to proceed in such matters as may require your attention."

On the 20th of the same month (October) the Estate's said attorney wrote to Mr. Ira MacFarland, Deputy State Engineer, a letter containing the following passage:

> I would naturally be reluctant to make the trip from here to Battle Mountain so long as there is no issue raised. Your letters seem to concur that there are no conflicts between the Faris Ranch and its neighbors. If the same should unexpectedly arise, would it not be possible, as I have heretofore suggested, to inform me of them and give me an opportunity to deal with them first by correspondence?

—to which, on the 26th of the same month, Mr. Ira MacFarland, Deputy State Engineer, replied that "from my knowledge of this claim I doubt if it will be necessary for you to appear at Battle Mountain because of the fact that there are no conflicts between the Faris Ranch and its neighbors; but if you do not come please see that some one is authorized to appear and represent the Estate at the hearing."

As a consequence of said assurances and in reliance thereon, the only representatives of this Estate at said hearing were Mr. George D. Adams, a farmer by occupation, and Mr. L. H. Taylor, a civil engineer, and no attorney of said Estate was present at said hearing, or at any of the various hearings, in the matter of said adjudication, at which witnesses were heard by the State Engineer and evidence was received.

The State Engineer thereafter made said preliminary order, differing very much adversely from the claim of said Estate, without further communication with this Estate. The Estate's said attorney wrote to the State Engineer in regard thereto under date of January 9, 1922, but received no reply other than a registry receipt dated January 12 for the letter, and a subsequent possible reference to its receipt in a letter of February 16.

It was no doubt the magnitude of the work and the large number of persons with whom the State Engineer has had to deal that caused the situation. But it was this that caused the assurance to be asked and given. The contribution of this estate to payment of the expenses of bringing witnesses to the hearings in said correspondence mentioned was substantial, and probably would not otherwise have been made.

It is respectfully submitted that a final order or other action affecting the rights of said Estate should not be made by said State Engineer without recalling free of expense to this Estate the witnesses upon

whom the State Engineer may have relied in conflict with the said Estate's claim, and affording to the Estate's attorney the promised opportunity of cross-examination and of argument.

2. *Said preliminary order was made in departure from sections 28 to 33 inclusive of said statute of 1913 and the amendments thereof in said statute of 1921, and is therefore insufficient as a preliminary order upon which to base a final order.*

The statutes last above mentioned require the final order of the State Engineer to be preceded by a preliminary order. Matters upon which the State Engineer has not made a preliminary order cannot, it is suggested, be taken up in a final order. This seems to be the letter and the spirit of the statute—the letter of it because the statute requires the preliminary order to be one of determination establishing the several rights (section 28), and it is therefore comprehensive in its wording; and the spirit of it because its purpose is to afford inspection of the intended provisions of the final order in advance of their becoming such.

It is respectfully submitted that the State Engineer has failed to make his preliminary order contain a number of matters that are thus essential. We will hereafter note—and we here refer to the following pages relative thereto—the failure to find prescriptive rights, the failure to find rights based upon existing agreements or decrees between various claimants; the failure to find rights for stock-watering and domestic use. Reference is here also made to the omission to find a proper amount for head of water mentioned on page 2 of said preliminary order; the failure to find a specific time limit of irrigation consistent with good husbandry also on said page 2 mentioned; the failure to find a specific allowance for losses in ditches mentioned in the last paragraph upon page 3 of said findings.

The omission of the State Engineer to make a preliminary order upon rights by prescription, agreements or judicial decrees heretofore rendered, we assume, represents an intention of the State Engineer not to regard them as rights, for his said order states upon page 2 thereof that it defines all the rights upon the river. Upon nonessentials we assume that discretion to omit rests in a public officer. But the matters in this objection mentioned, we respectfully submit, are essential matters in the sense that there can be no "determination establishing the several rights" without them. The draft upon the common supply by these omitted factors must necessarily be great, and in the absence of a determination of them there can be no knowledge of the residue for entitlement to any person either in quantity of water or time of use or other respect, and the statute is seriously departed from.

In the same connection we respectfully submit that the preliminary order lacks a compilation of rights by years and amounts of water and upper or lower location of place of diversion or use, such as to enable a comparison of the award to the Faris Estate with the award to other claimants upon said river. In the absence of such compilation the preliminary order cannot but remain unintelligible to a substantial degree, and the statute is not effectuated.

3. *Said preliminary order is in excess of the jurisdiction of the*

State Engineer under articles III to VI, inclusive, of the Constitution of the State of Nevada.

(a) Sections 29, 30, 31 and 32 of said Statutes of 1913 and 1915 were held in Pitt v. Scrugham (Nevada), 195 Pac. 1101, to be unconstitutional relative to contests before the State Engineer because they attempt to confer judicial powers upon him to hear and determine questions properly and only determinable by a regularly organized court. The amendments thereof in said statute of 1921 appear to be rather a change of form than of substance in that regard.

(b) Under said decision the State Engineer has no jurisdiction involving "not relative but vested rights," and the said preliminary order shows that the right of this Estate has remained vested since at least 1893.

(c) Sections 29 to 39, inclusive, deny to the District Courts, when the matter reaches them, power to make an independent decree. Adverse action of the courts upon the State Engineer's determination of rights is by section 36 limited to modifying it; a stipulation of degree which stops at changing the identity of the order or abolishing it. In the reluctance with which the doors of the courts were approached by the statute's numerous successive amendments, made only under pressure of the Constitution, the statute remains unwilling, notwithstanding the distribution of governmental powers by the Nevada Constitution, to commit the State Engineer's determination of water rights fully to the supremacy in such matters of another department of the government. The compliance with the Constitution is not complete and has a string to it. The courts are commanded to leave the State Engineer's order untouched to some extent that must be substantial.

Therein the statute, it seems to us, still attempts, in capital matters, to oust the jurisdiction of the courts and transfer it to the State Engineer. Although in this instance the ouster is of a part and not the whole of their jurisdiction, it is an essential and not merely incidental part, and goes to the root of the proceedings and of the establishment and declaration of the right and title to private property.

In so doing, the statute, it seems to us, has violated said articles III and VI of the Constitution of the State of Nevada. The effect of said articles is to vest in the courts therein mentioned all of the judicial power of the State in that matter.

(d) For the same reasons said sections 29 to 39, inclusive, of the statute are in conflict with section 6 of article VI of the Constitution of Nevada providing that the District Courts shall have original jurisdiction in all cases in equity; also in all cases at law which involve the title or the right to possession of real property, and shall have power to issue all writs proper and necessary to the complete exercise of their jurisdiction.

(e) For the same reasons said sections of the statute are in conflict with section 20 of section IV of the Constitution of the State of Nevada prohibiting the Legislature from passing special laws regulating the practice of courts of justice.

The several foregoing objections go to the State Engineer's authority to proceed, and, if they are sound, their operation would appear to be a discontinuance of the proceedings, and we respectfully make said request accordingly.

II

GROUNDS OF THE OBJECTION THAT SAID PRELIMINARY ORDER IS ERRONEOUS FOR FAILURE TO FIND A PRESCRIPTIVE RIGHT IN SAID FARIS ESTATE FOR THE IRRIGATION OF ALL OF ITS SAID LANDS AS AGAINST ALL PERSONS WHOSE LANDS OR POINTS OF DIVERSION LIE BELOW THE LANDS OF SAID ESTATE UPON SAID RIVER.

The said preliminary order of determination finds in, and proposes to award to, various persons whose lands lie below the lands of said Faris Estate upon said river, rights in the waters of said river prior and superior to those of this Estate.

The said findings show at the same time that the Faris Estate has used water continuously upon all of its said lands in said order described, since at least the year 1893. The proofs and evidence filed and made of record in the office of the State Engineer show that said use has ever since said date, at least, been open, notorious, under claim of right and under color of title, exclusive of all claimants lower down the stream and uninterrupted by any of them; and hostile to and an invasion of right of all such claimants lower down the stream who may have previously had a priority of right.

The right of the Faris Estate to continue irrigating all of its land from Humboldt River has thereby ripened into a prescriptive title against such lower owners, as full, legal and complete as title by other source.

Prescription has its foundation in that the lower owners must press their claims at the time they are first invaded, for otherwise there would be no end to the possibility of litigation. Even when the acquisition of water by the upper ranches was originally wrongful, the dispossession of them, after a generation has elapsed, by the pressing of claims below which has long been allowed by their owners to remain dormant, would be a greater private and public mischief than leaving the antiquated wrong without atonement. It may seem hard that the claim of lower owners, if originally just, should be defeated by their mere inaction, but there is a time after which the balance of injustice turns the other way. In no human transactions, not even the simplest and clearest, does it follow that a claim is fit to be recognized now because it was fit for that a dim vista of years ago, and "time out of mind" in the contemplation of the law of this State is five years. It is respectfully submitted that in confining itself to determining a former instead of the present status the preliminary order is not a determination of existing rights but a redistribution upon a different system than now lawfully obtains.

The said preliminary order of determination is therefore objected to for failure to find that the Faris Estate has a right by prescription to irrigate all the lands of said estate as against claimants whose lands or points of diversion are situated lower down upon Humboldt River, and for awarding, as it does, to such persons or some of them a right superior to the right of this Estate.

III

GROUNDS OF THE OBJECTION THAT SAID PRELIMINARY ORDER IS ERRONEOUS FOR FAILURE TO FIND RIGHTS EXISTING BY AGREEMENTS AND JUDICIAL DECREES.

The said preliminary order of the State Engineer makes no mention and takes no account of the decree rendered between the Estate of

James Faris and the Estate of William Dunphy by the United States Circuit Court at Carson City, Nevada. A certified copy of said decree has heretofore been filed with the State Engineer and is now contained in his file number 00167 in the matter of the determination of water rights upon said Humboldt River, and said decree and said certified copy thereof are hereby referred to and make a part hereof. The State Engineer's preliminary order of determination is objected to for the failure to incorporate the said decree therein.

Said preliminary order of the State Engineer further makes no mention and takes no account of the order and judgment rendered by the District Court of Nevada in and for the Second Judicial District (as it then was) sitting at Winnemucca on September 2, 1890, in favor of George W. Crum, predecessor in interest of this Estate, and against George D. Bliss, dismissing the actions entitled Bliss v. Grayson and others, number .... in said District Court and Bliss v. Dunphy and others, number 1066 in said District Court, as set forth in the opinion of the Supreme Court of the State of Nevada entitled Bliss v. Grayson, number 1533 in said Supreme Court and appearing upon page 236 of the report of said opinion in volume 56 Pacific Reporter, pages 231 to 243. Said dismissal, being an absolute dismissal without reservation, constituted a final determination of title to water rights in said river in favor of said Crum as against said Bliss. The State Engineer's Preliminary Order of Determination is objected to for failure to incorporate therein the said judgment as between said Bliss and his successors and this Estate.

Nor does said preliminary order find or determine or establish rights of other claimants by agreements or existing decrees between such other claimants, except in one or two instances. Any such omitted agreements or decrees render the findings of the State Engineer, in disregard of them, contrary to the rights of such parties and no establishment of their rights, and any such occurrence respecting other claimants is a miscarriage also as to the Faris Estate because a river is a common supply in which the rights of all claimants are mutually dependent. The said preliminary order is therefore objected to for failure to find, determine and establish the rights of all claimants upon said river under existing agreements and judicial decrees.

IV

GROUNDS OF THE OBJECTION THAT SAID PRELIMINARY ORDER IS ERRONEOUS IN ITS FINDINGS OF THE DATES OF COMMENCEMENT OF BENEFICIAL USE OF WATER.

1. *The beneficial use of water upon said Faris lands and all thereof began in 1869 and said preliminary order is erroneous in finding a later date of commencement thereof, or of any part thereof.*

(a) The evidence on file shows that the irrigation of said Faris lands and all thereof began in 1869.

The location of this ranch is, and from the beginning has been, particularly favorable for and susceptible to irrigation by fills in the river and sloughs. All of it has therefore been easily irrigable from the outset. Small fills in the river and sloughs answered the purpose and constituted a legitimate means of actual appropriation. When dams came to be put in, the occasion for them was the natural deepening and widening of the channel of Humboldt River and the decrease of its

flow by diversion of increasing quantities above. The dams were thus but a continuance of the original diversion by fills. The testimony of Mr. Fulkerton in file 00167 we understand to be that an area equal to that now irrigated was already under irrigation on the Faris Ranch when he came there in 1875, and to this there is added in said file the affidavits of the former owners (now deceased) James Faris and George W. Crum. They are not contradicted by anything appearing in said file, so far as we know. They state that the irrigation thereon of an area equal to that irrigated today was completed in 1871, and the affidavit of James Faris further states that said irrigation was begun in the year 1869. Reference is particularly made to the following passages in the affidavit of said James Faris:

> 4. The construction of the ditches and other works was begun in 1869 and completed in 1871.
>
> 13–14. The water was first used for irrigation by claimant or his grantors in the year 1869, the intention being at that time to gradually increase the use until all the said water was used; and by 1871 substantially all of said water was put to use by claimant and his predecessors in interest upon the lands herein described, either by surface irrigation or by subirrigation, both natural and artificial. The quantity of land irrigated remained substantially the same from 1871 to the present time, the water being used from time to time upon the different parts of the land herein described according to the varying needs for haying and grazing land.
>
> 16. The water claimed has been used for irrigation each and every year since the right was initiated.
>
> 17. There were no years during which no water was used for irrigation or during which the full water-right was not used.
>
> (On page 8:) As the positions of some of said ditches and sloughs changed from time to time since 1871 the claimant and his predecessors in interest continued without interruption to maintain them as artificial conduits and to make therefrom the beneficial uses herein set forth.

(b) The preliminary order departs from the evidence on file, and draws upon other undisclosed sources, in departure from the statute.

The said statute of 1913, in section 28 thereof as amended by section 2 of said statute of 1921, requires that the said preliminary order of determination shall be made by the State Engineer from "proofs and evidence taken or given before him or obtained by him." Section 20 of said statute of 1913 requires that said proofs and evidence "shall be filed and made of record in the office of the said State Engineer," and similar provisions for said filing are enacted in section 21 to and including 27 of said statute of 1913 and in the amendments of sections 25 and 27 thereof as said amendments appear respectively in chapter 253 of the Statutes of 1915 and chapter 106 of the Statutes of 1921 of said State; and similar provisions for said filing are enacted in section 88a of said statute of 1913 as added by section 14 of chapter 253 of the Statutes of 1915 of said State.

The said preliminary order of determination divides the Faris Ranch into nine segregated areas with a different priority of water right for

all but two of such areas. The Estate is informed that a map was used by the State Engineer at the hearing of said Faris Ranch at Battle Mountain in December, 1921, upon which map there appeared markings of boundaries of segregations of said ranch. Those markings vary from the segregations made in said preliminary order, nor has the Faris Estate or its administrators knowledge how said segregations came to be made in said order or how said markings came to be made or located upon said map. A request has heretofore been made by this Estate to the State Engineer for information how said markings upon said map were arrived at, namely (referring to the report of the Battle Mountain hearing):

> There is nothing in the report showing what the areas marked on the map are intended to designate. Could you inform me what designation is intended, how the boundaries of the areas as they appear on the map were ascertained, how accurately they appear there, and how they compare with the list of cultural areas accompanying the map? (Letter of January 9, 1922, from Samuel C. Wiel to the State Engineer.)

—but the State Engineer has not replied to said request.

If the State Engineer has based his segregation of priorities upon dates of permanent dams, whether on the Faris Ranch or on neighboring ranches, we believe that such basis is contrary to the evidence in these objections mentioned, and the law applicable thereto, that such dams were not the first diversion works.

We furthermore respectfully submit that the Estate should have had its attention called by the State Engineer, in conformity with the assurances heretofore mentioned, to his intention to base segregations upon such dams and to the time and place where the evidence upon such dams and the area to be segregated under them respectively would be taken and that an opportunity of examining the witnesses and presenting argument should have been given to the Estate. At the time of the hearing in December 1921, at Battle Mountain, Mr. Mueller, Deputy State Engineer in charge of the hearing, held the record open for further attention, and preparatory thereto this Estate's attorney sent the following letter to the State Engineer (Mr. Griswold, therein referred to, being an associate of the State Engineer):

> Mr. Griswold requested the incorporation of the records of the Williams Estate, Jenkins Ranch, Blossom Ranch and McIntyre-Starrett Ranch, as showing dates of dams on those ranches. Are copies of those records available to be sent to me for examination? Whether we would desire to introduce further testimony or to make further comment after examining those records, I cannot say in advance of having seem them. (Letter of January 9, 1922 from Samuel C. Wiel to the State Engineer.)

—which received no reply.

In reference to the area assigned by said preliminary order a date of 1873, this is apparently the area of bottom land along the banks of Humboldt River, and the fixing of the date of commencement of water use thereon as 1873 may have been based upon a belief by the State Engineer, obtained in a way of which this Estate is not informed nor

disclosed so far as we know by said State Engineer's file 00167, that this was the date of first settlement upon this ranch. The records of the State Treasurer of the State of Nevada show that payments by predecessors of the Faris Estate were made, for lands within this area, in 1871 on account of applications to purchase said lands from the State of Nevada under section 9 of a statute of said State of March 4, 1871; and the legitimate inference is that first settlement preceded the application. Reference is particularly made to receipts that are in the Faris Estate's possession for payments upon the following lands in Township 32 North, Range 45 East, namely the South half of section 12 and all of section 14, and the following lands in Township 32 North, Range 46 East, namely all of section 8. There may be other lands within that area upon which the same or earlier payments were made.

In reference to the area assigned by said preliminary order a date of 1876, this is apparently the area on the eastern end of the ranch adjacent to the south branch of the river, or Argenta Slough. If the fixing of the date as 1876 has been based upon a belief by the State Engineer of the date of the building of the lower Slavin Dam on the Williams Estate east of the Faris Estate, the comment heretofore directed to the matter of dams is directed hereby to said lower Slavin Dam. So far as shown by the record in said file 00167 of the hearing held by the State Engineer on the rights of the Faris Estate in December, 1921, at Battle Mountain, as we understand said record, said lower Slavin Dam may have been built earlier than 1876, and so much of the area in question as is comprised within the area labeled "A" on the map used by the State Engineer at said last-named hearing was irrigated before 1876 by fills employed prior to the building of lower Slavin Dam. Mr. Fulkerson, as we understand said record, testified that he first saw said area A in 1875, and—

> Q. That hay land at that time had the appearance of being old or new land when you saw it? A. It was old irrigated land. Q. Was it or was it not well irrigated at the time you first saw it? A. Well irrigated.

Furthermore, receipts of the State Treasurer of the State of Nevada above mentioned disclose that land in the area for which the said preliminary order has found a priority as of 1876 was taken up by predecessors of the Faris Estate on or prior to the year 1871, namely, north half of section 10, township 32 north, range 46 east. A receipt for this payment is in the possession of the Faris Estate; and the legitimate inference is that first settlement preceded the application. There may be other lands within this area upon which the same or earlier payments were made.

In reference to the area assigned by said preliminary order a date of 1878, this is apparently the area lying between the two areas next above mentioned. If the fixing of the date as 1878 has been based upon a like belief by the State Engineer of the building of the upper Slavin Dam on the said Williams Estate, the foregoing comment upon the lower Slavin Dam is hereby directed also to the upper Slavin Dam. So far as shown by the record in said file 00167 of the hearing held by the State Engineer on the rights of the Faris Estate in December, 1921, at Battle Mountain, as we understand said record, said upper Slavin Dam may have been built earlier than 1878, and so much of the area

in question which is comprised within the area labeled "B" on the map used by the State Engineer at said last-named hearing, was irrigated before 1878 by fills employed prior to the building of said upper Slavin Dam. Mr. Fulkerson, as we understand said record, testified that he first saw said area B in 1875, and—

> *Before the upper Slavin Dam was built* this land was cut for hay land, and was irrigated for hay land *by other dams and ditches.*

Furthermore, receipts of the State Treasurer of the State of Nevada above mentioned disclose that land in the area for which said preliminary order has found a priority of 1878 was taken up by predecessors of the Faris Estate on or prior to the year 1871, namely, all of section 8, north half of section 10, and all of section 16, township 32 north, range 46 east. A receipt for this payment is in the possession of the Faris Estate; and the legitimate inference is that first settlement preceded the application. There may be other lands within this area upon which the same or earlier payments were made.

In reference to the area assigned by said preliminary order a date of 1883, this is apparently the area on the northwest corner of the ranch. If the source from which the year 1883 as taken by the State Engineer is based upon a dam upon some other ranch, the comment heretofore directed to the matter of dams is hereby directed to such dam. So far as shown by the record in said file 00167 of the hearing held by the State Engineer of the rights of the Faris Estate in December, 1921, at Battle Mountain, as we understand said record, the land within said area to which the State Engineer has assigned a priority as of 1883 was being irrigated in 1875 by a dam in section 6 of township 32 north, range 46 east. Mr. Fulkerson, the witness produced at said hearing upon that question, speaking of said dam irrigating areas J and K on the map used by the State Engineer at said hearing (which areas include land to which the State Engineer's said preliminary order assigns priority of 1883), testified as of the year 1875, as we understand his testimony:

> It may have been constructed *prior to* that time, but this was the first time I saw it.

Furthermore, there may be receipts issued by the State Treasurer for payments prior to 1883 by the predecessors of the Faris Estate on lands within this area.

In reference to the area assigned by said preliminary order a date of 1890, receipts of the State Treasurer of the State of Nevada, above mentioned, disclose that land in this area was taken up by predecessors of the Faris Estate on or prior to the year 1871, namely, the east half (½) of section 22, in township 32 north, range 45 east. A receipt for this payment is in the possession of the Faris Estate; and the legitimate inference is that first settlement preceded the application. There may be other lands within that area upon which the same or earlier payments were made.

In reference to the area assigned by said preliminary order a date of 1891, receipts of the State Treasurer of the State of Nevada, above mentioned, disclose that land in this area was taken up by predecessors of the Faris Estate on or prior to the year 1871, namely, the south half (½) of section 24, and the east half (½) of the northeast quar-

ter (¼) of the same section (24) in township 32 north, range 45 east. A receipt for this payment is in the possession of the Faris Estate, and the legitimate inference is that first settlement preceded the application. There may be other lands within that area upon which the same or earlier payments were made.

In reference to the area assigned by said preliminary order a date of 1892, receipts of the State Treasurer of the State of Nevada, above mentioned, disclose that land in this area was taken up by predecessors of the Faris Estate on or prior to the year 1871, namely, the north half (½) of the northeast quarter (¼) and the north half (½) of the northwest quarter (¼) of section 20 in township 32 north, range 46 east. A receipt for this payment is in the possession of the Faris Estate; and the legitimate inference is that first settlement preceded the application. There may be other lands within that area upon which the same or earlier payments were made.

In reference to the area assigned by said preliminary order a date of 1893, receipts of the State Treasurer of the State of Nevada, above mentioned, disclose that land in this area was taken up by predecessors of the Faris Estate on or prior to the year 1871, namely, all of section 16 and the north half (½) of the northeast quarter (¼), and the north half (½) of the northwest quarter (¼) of section 20, in said township 32 north, range 46 east. A receipt for this payment is in the possession of the Faris Estate, and the legitimate inference is that first settlement preceded the application. There may be other lands within that area upon which the same or earlier payments were made.

2. *Priority of commencement of beneficial use of water erroneously found and erroneously awarded to other claimants adversely to the Faris Estate.*

A large number of ranches, aggregating 300,000 to 400,000 acres of irrigated land, and about 700 claimants, are involved in these proceedings. The natural limit upon the total supply, especially in seasons of shortage, causes each claimant to be reduced, in his enjoyment of water in such seasons, by the rights that are awarded to others as prior in right to him. The Faris Estate is as adversely affected by excessive allowances of that nature as it is by deficient allowance to itself.

We have elsewhere herein presented cause to believe that such errors exist, beside which the magnitude and complexity of the data in the State Engineer's files make some error in handling them inherently unavoidable. At the same time the same magnitude and complexity place the handling of an examination of those files, for checking and designation of the particulars of error in this matter, beyond the power of an individual claimant. The designation of error in this connection we therefore make in general form under the principle that the statute provides that objections may be filed, and where the law provides for a thing it never requires impossibilities. For the protection of its rights against errors there may be, Ethel Faris Adams and William H. Devlin, administrators of the Estate of James Faris, deceased, by the undersigned, their attorney, hereby object to all and singular, in whole and in every part, the said preliminary order of determination by the State Engineer of the rights of all or any other person or persons who are in said preliminary order given a date of commencement of beneficial use of water earlier than or the same as the Faris Estate.

V

GROUNDS OF THE OBJECTION THAT SAID PRELIMINARY ORDER IS ERRONEOUS IN ITS FINDINGS OF IRRIGATED AREAS

1. *It is respectfully presented that the cultural areas in the State Engineer's said preliminary order of determination differ adversely to the Faris Estate in the following respects from the data as checked in December, 1921, by J. V. Mueller, Deputy State Engineer, with L. H. Taylor representing the Estate, and that the said preliminary order is in said respects erroneous.*

State Engineer's Finding	Omitted Area
T. 32 N, R. 45 E.	
Section 12—	
NE¼SW¼—13.45 acres in third column should be in first column.	
NW¼SW¼—19 acres in third column should be in first column.	
Section 15—	
NE¼NW¼—25.91 acres in first column and 5.20 acres in second column and 9.40 in third column should read NE¼SW¼.	
SE¼NW¼—22.60 acres in column 1 and 10.50 acres in column 3 should be SE¼SW¼.	
Section 22—	
NW¼NW¼—8.60 acres in column 1 should read 9.60 acres........	1.00 acre
T. 32 N. R. 46 E.	
Section 5—	
SW¼SW¼—Omission of 25.09 acres in third column..................	25.09 acres
Section 8—	
NW¼NE¼—Columns 2 and 3 are reversed.	
T. 32 N, R. 46 E.	
Section 9—	
NE¼SE¼—2.43 acres in column 2 should be 3.42 acres.............	.99 acres
Section 16—	
SW¼NE¼—Omission of 29.49 acres in column 1 and 7.85 acres in column 2..	37.34 acres
Section 17—	
NW¼NW¼—9.77 acres in column 1 should be 9.97 acres...........	.20 acre
Section 22—	
NE¼NE¼—14.80 acres in column 2 should be NW¼ of NE¼.	
Section 29—	
NE¼NE¼—Omission of 1.86 acres in column 2........................	1.86 acres
Total omitted area..	66.48 acres

2. *The findings of cultural areas on the said Faris Ranch are not possible of observance in practice.* Said cultural areas are often designated in said preliminary order as numerous small portions of varied cultures within the same quarter-section with different allotted duties and amounts of water. The ranch can only be irrigated by broad flooding, which makes it impossible to confine the irrigation of such mingled areas to the separated water use designated in said order. Furthermore, said preliminary order, in designating said acres within quarter-sections, fails to designate what acres they are.

3. *Cultural areas erroneously found and awarded upon the lands of other claimants.* The grounds set forth in subdivision 2 of objection IV, above stated, are referred to and made a part hereof, and upon said grounds objection is hereby made likewise to the preliminary order and its findings in reference to the cultural areas therein found or awarded to persons other than the Faris Estate, all and singular.

VI

GROUNDS OF THE OBJECTION THAT SAID PRELIMINARY ORDER IS ERRONEOUS IN ITS FINDINGS OF DUTY OF WATER AND LENGTH OF IRRIGATION SEASON.

1. *Error in equivalent employed in computing the water allowances from the duty of water prescribed.* The duty of water adopted by the State Engineer is stated on the first page of said Preliminary Order of Determination as follows:

Class A—Harvested Crops, etc.	3.00 acre-feet per acre in	180 days
Class B—Meadow Pasture	1.50 acre-feet per acre in	90 days
Class C—Diversified Pasture	0.75 acre-feet per acre in	45 days
Class C—Swamp or Overflow	...... acre-feet per acre in	.... days

This in each case equals a uniform flow of 0.8403 second-feet per 100 acres of land, equal to 1.00 second-foot per 119.01 acres.

The computation used in the State Engineer's said Preliminary Order of Determination employs a different equivalent, namely, 0.8125 second-feet for each 100 acres, equal to 1.00 second-foot for 123,077 acres.

The discrepancy is 0.0278 second-feet per 100 acres, equal to 4.067 acres per second-foot, which appears to be inadvertent and contrary to the said first page of the order. The water allowance for the Faris lands is affected adversely to the Faris Estate to said extent by this inadvertence in the State Engineer's computation.

2. *The duties of water and the irrigation season on said Faris Ranch were fixed in said order without taking evidence thereof.* There is no proof or evidence in said file 00167, so far as we know, of the duty of water upon said Faris Ranch or of the irrigation season thereon, nor was any evidence upon either thereof taken or obtained by said State Engineer so far as known to the Faris Estate. The duties specified by the State Engineer's said preliminary order are apparently based on the State Engineer's belief of the requirements of the *average* lands along the main Humboldt River, and on the *assumption* that certain classes of lands usually receive water only during certain periods, such as *moderately* high water for the better class of pasture and the tule lands, and when the river is at *flood stage* for the willow and sage pasture lands. In so doing the preliminary order is based upon matters of degree that are undetermined, and fails to be an order, and it is further in conflict with the statutory requirement that the said preliminary order should be based upon evidence and proof.

3. *The findings of the said State Engineer in said preliminary order allowing only three-quarters (¾) of an acre-foot per acre for diversified pasture and one and one-half (1½) feet per acre for meadow pasture are not in accordance with the rights of the said Faris Estate.* The said quantity of water is not sufficient for the irrigation of the said Faris lands, and the said Faris Estate has beneficially used on its said land, and all thereof, at least three acre-feet per acre and the last said quantity is reasonably necessary for the irrigation thereof.

4. *The findings of the said State Engineer in said preliminary order as to the length of the irrigating season, if said findings are intended to limit the right of the said Faris Estate to the said periods therein designated, are not in accordance with the rights of the said Faris Estate.* The said Faris Estate is entitled to take and divert water from

the said river for its land at any time in the year when water is in said river, and the limitation of time in said preliminary order contained is without support, and is not in accordance with the actual use or necessities or beneficial use of or by said Faris Estate.

5. *Differences in calculation of water allowance upon lands of others.* There seem to be differences in computation upon the lands of other claimants, varying from but similar to the difference pointed out in the first subdivision of this objection; and the preliminary order is therefore objected to in reference to the water allowance in cubic feet per second and in acre-feet found or awarded to persons other than the Faris Estate, all and singular.

VII

GROUNDS OF THE OBJECTION THAT SAID PRELIMINARY ORDER IS ERRONEOUS FOR FAILURE TO FIND RIGHTS FOR STOCK-WATERING AND DOMESTIC USE

No reference in the State Engineer's findings is made to determination of the amount of water which may be consumed by any of the claimants to water on the Humboldt River for stock-watering purposes or for domestic purposes, excepting the statement of the State Engineer on page 3 of said preliminary determination reading:

> In addition to water used during the irrigating season, each user should be entitled, in his proper proportion and priority, to the use of water in such reasonable amounts as necessary for fall and spring irrigation and for stock-watering purposes during the nonirrigating season.

The foregoing is objected to on the following grounds:

1. *No allowance is made therein or in any part of the said order of determination, to this estate, for domestic uses of water.*

2. *No allowance is made therein for stock-watering purposes during the irrigation season, but only during the nonirrigating season.*

3. *Said allowance for fall and spring irrigation and for stock-watering purposes during the nonirrigating season does not comply with the statute.* Said allowance is that "each user should be entitled, in his proper proportion and priority, to the use of water in such reasonable amounts as necessary." It is respectfully submitted, as heretofore more particularly noted under subdivision 2 of objection I to which reference is hereby made, that this is too uncertain to constitute an allowance either in amount or priority, but is a failure to make any such determination as the statute requires.

VIII

GROUNDS OF THE OBJECTION THAT SAID PRELIMINARY ORDER TAKES PROPERTY FROM THE FARIS ESTATE WITHOUT DUE PROCESS OF LAW, AND TAKES PROPERTY OF SAID ESTATE FOR PUBLIC USE WITHOUT COMPENSATION, IN VIOLATION OF SECTION 84 OF SAID STATUTE OF 1913 ENACTING THAT VESTED RIGHTS SHALL NOT BE IMPAIRED, AND IN VIOLATION OF SECTION 8 OF ARTICLE I OF THE CONSTITUTION OF THE STATE OF NEVADA AND AMENDMENT XIV OF THE CONSTITUTION OF THE UNITED STATES.

1. *The preliminary order requires the Faris Estate to drain flood waters in the spring of the year and early irrigation season.*

The proofs and evidence filed and made of record in the office of the said State Engineer show that owing to the natural configuration of the locality in which the lands of this Estate are situated, flood waters

coming down Humboldt River easterly of this ranch when said river is in flood in the spring of the year and the early irrigation season spread out over this ranch and a very large additional area. It is impossible to prevent said floods from so spreading over the Battle Mountain area, including this Faris Ranch. If any engineering knowledge exists of means of accomplishing this extreme undertaking, the cost of putting the same into operation would be so great as to many times exceed the value of all of the lands in the Battle Mountain district, including the lands of this Estate.

Furthermore, the drainage of such flood waters from these lands in the said flood stages of the river would be of no great benefit to this ranch, and, if of benefit to any one, said benefit would accrue mostly to other ranches lower down upon the river; and such enterprise would be for the benefit of the public so situated and constitute a taking of property of the Faris Estate for public use. Said taking would consist partly in the loss to said Estate of the benefit of said flood waters, and partly in the loss to said Estate of the ruinous cost of the drainage of said flood waters if said cost were placed upon said Estate.

The enforcement upon said Faris Estate of the cost of such drainage would therefore be a taking of the property of said Faris Estate without compensation, contrary to said section 8 of Article I of the Constitution of the State of Nevada enacting that private property shall not be taken for public use without just compensation, and contrary to the other statutory and constitutional provisions hereinbefore set forth.

It is not believed by this Estate that it is the intention of the State Engineer to make findings, or a preliminary or final order, requiring this Estate to undertake such drainage. The existence of said findings and preliminary order in their present form making no qualification so expressing, is probably an inadvertence on the part of the State Engineer.

The said preliminary order of determination is therefore objected to in its present form for limiting the quantity of water upon the lands of said Faris Estate, during the said flood stages of the river, to the quantity stated in said preliminary order of determination, during which flood stage it is impossible to restrict the water upon said lands to the quantities which the State Engineer's said order prescribes.

2. *The preliminary order proposes to deprive the said Faris Estate of its property without due process of law in all the respects heretofore in any of these objections set forth*, and said order is therefore objected to in all said respects upon the further ground that it is in conflict with section 84 of said statute of 1913, and Section 8 of Article I of the Constitution of Nevada, and subdivision I of Amendment XIV of the Constitution of the United States.

IX

CONCLUSION

The administrators of this Estate, and its said attorney, reside at a distance from the State Engineer's office in Carson City, Nevada, being residents of California. They have been unable to examine State Engineer's file 00167 or other files because of the distance, the amount of time necessarily consumed in studying the preliminary order in the

first instance, and the time necessarily consumed in formulating objections, the State Engineer, in reply to a request by the Estate for an extension of time, having expressed the wish that the objections be filed without such extension.

These objections are filed, as likewise stated in the proof of claim of this Estate filed June 14, 1915, in compliance with the request of the State Engineer in view of the penalties which the statutes of Nevada undertake to impose or to authorize the State Engineer to impose for failure to file objections, and this Estate does not waive any rights it may have to urge now or hereafter, in any tribunal, the objections herein stated or any other objections, or to act in any manner that may exist for the protection of its property.

SAMUEL C. WIEL,
Attorney for the Estate of James Faris, deceased, and William H. Devlin and Ethel Faris Adams, administrators of said Estate.

State of California, City and County of San Francisco, ss.

Samuel C. Wiel, being first duly sworn deposes and says: That he is the attorney for the Estate of James Faris, deceased, and William H. Devlin and Ethel Faris Adams, administrators of said Estate; that he has read the foregoing document and knows the contents thereof, and that the same is true to the best of his knowledge, information and belief; that as such attorney he has personally conducted proceedings on behalf of said Estate in the matters in said document set forth, and that he is therefore more conversant with said proceedings and matters than are said administrators, and he makes this verification in the place of said administrators, for said reason.

SAMUEL C. WIEL.

In witness whereof, I have hereunto affixed my hand and official seal in my office in the City and County of San Francisco, State of California this 9th day of June, 1922.

[SEAL] GRACE SONNTAG,
Notary Public in and for the City and County of San Francisco, State of California.

My commission expires December 12, 1925.

State of California, City and County of San Francisco, ss.

I, H. I. Mulcrevy, County Clerk of the City and County of San Francisco, State of California, and ex officio Clerk of the Superior Court thereof, the same being a court of record having by law a seal, do hereby certify that Grace Sonntag, whose name is subscribed to the certificate of the proof or acknowledgement of the annexed instrument and thereon written, was, at the time of taking such proof and acknowledgment, a Notary Public, in and for said City and County, residing therein, duly commissioned and sworn, and duly authorized by the laws of said State to take the acknowledgments and proofs of deeds or conveyances, for land, tenements or hereditaments in said State, to be recorded therein. And further that I am well acquainted with the handwriting of such Notary Public, and verily believe that the signature to said certificate of proof or acknowledgment is genuine, and that said instrument is executed and acknowledged according to the laws of said State.

In testimony whereof, I have hereunto set my hand and affixed the seal of the said Superior Court, dated June 9, 1922.

I further certify that an impression of the seals of Notaries Public are not required by law to be filed in my office.

[SEAL] H. I. MULCREVY, *Clerk.*

No. 6

BEFORE THE STATE ENGINEER OF THE STATE OF NEVADA

In the Matter of the Determination of the Water Rights of the Humboldt River and its Tributaries

File No. 00167

OBJECTIONS OF WILLIAM DUNPHY ESTATE TO THE STATE ENGINEER'S PRELIMINARY ORDER OF DETERMINATION

Jennie C. D. Meyer, Mary D. Flood, James C. Dunphy, Viola P. Burnett, and Jennie C. D. Meyer as trustee under the will of William Dunphy, deceased, owners of the property described in the above-mentioned Preliminary Order as belonging to "William Dunphy Estate," and therein and hereinafter designated as "William Dunphy Estate" or as "said Estate," and persons claiming an interest in the waters of Humboldt River, pursuant to section 29 of chapter 140 of the Statutes of 1913 of the State of Nevada, as amended by section 3 of chapter 106 of the Statutes of the State of Nevada of the year 1921, hereby file these, their objections to the said preliminary order of determination made by the State Engineer and to each and every finding, part and portion of said order.

Said objections are:

I. That said preliminary order should be withdrawn because (1) it has been made in departure from sections 28 to 33, inclusive, of said statutes and is therefore insufficient as a preliminary order upon which to base a final order; and (2) it is in excess of the jurisdiction of the State Engineer under articles III to VI, inclusive, of the Constitution of the State of Nevada.

II. That said preliminary order is erroneous for failure to find a prescriptive right in said Estate for the irrigation of all of its lands in said findings described as against all persons whose lands or points of diversion lie below the said lands of said Estate upon said river.

III. That said preliminary order is erroneous for failure to find rights existing by agreements and judicial decrees.

IV. That said preliminary order is erroneous in its findings of the dates of commencement of beneficial use of water by the persons whose rights are therein designated as commencing prior to those of said Estate.

V. That said preliminary order is erroneous in its findings of irrigated area of the lands of said persons in that excessive areas are designated.

VI. That said preliminary order is erroneous in its findings of duty of water and length of irrigation season as to the lands of said Estate.

VII. That said preliminary order is erroneous for failure to find

rights for stock-watering and domestic use for said Estate or for any other person.

VIII. That said preliminary order takes property from said Estate without due process of law, and takes property of said Estate for public use without just compensation, in violation of section 84 of said statute of 1913 enacting that vested rights shall not be impaired, and in violation of section 8 of Article I of the Constitution of the State of Nevada and amendment XIV of the Constitution of the United States.

The following are some of the especial points upon which said objections are based:

1. The said preliminary order is made in a manner incapable of supporting a final order, for lack of compilation of relative rights by years and amounts of water and upper or lower location of place of diversion or use, such as to enable a comparison of the award to the said Estate with the award to other claimants upon said river. In the absence of such compilation the preliminary order cannot but remain unintelligible to a substantial degree, and is not the preliminary order that the said statute directs.

2. Sections 29, 30, 31 and 32 of said Statutes of 1913 and 1915 are unconstitutional relative to contests before the State Engineer because they attempt to confer judicial powers upon him to hear and determine questions properly and only determinable by a regularly organized court. The amendments thereof in said statute of 1921 appear to be rather a change of form than of substance in that regard,

3. Sections 29 to 39, inclusive, of said statutes deny to the district courts, when the matter reaches them, power to make an independent decree. Adverse action of the courts upon the State Engineer's determination of rights is by section 36 limited to modifying it; a stipulation of degree which stops at changing the identity of the order or abolishing it.

4. The said preliminary order finds that said Estate has used water continuously upon all of its said lands in said order described for over twenty years last past. The proofs and evidence filed and made of record in the office of the State Engineer show that said use has during all of said time been open, notorious, under claim of right and under color of title, exclusive of all claimants lower down the stream and uninterrupted by any of them; and hostile to and an invasion of right of all such claimants lower down the stream who may have previously had a priority of right.

The right of said Estate to continue irrigating all of its land from Humboldt River has thereby ripened into a prescriptive title against such lower owners, as full, legal and complete as title by other source.

The said preliminary order of determination is therefore objected to for failure to find that said Estate has a right by prescription to irrigate all the lands of said Estate as against claimants whose lands or points of diversion are situated lower down upon Humboldt River, and for awarding, as it does, to such persons or some of them rights superior to the right of this Estate.

5. Said preliminary order of the State Engineer makes no mention and takes no account of the order and judgment rendered by the District Court of Nevada in and for the Second Judicial District (as it then was) sitting at Winnemucca on September 2, 1890, in favor of

William Dunphy, predecessor in interest of this Estate, and against George D. Bliss, dismissing the actions entitled Bliss v. Grayson and others, number............in said District Court and Bliss v. Dunphy and others, number 1066 in said District Court, as set forth in the opinion of the Supreme Court of the State of Nevada entitled Bliss v. Grayson, number 1533 in said Supreme Court and appearing upon page 236 of the report of said opinion in volume 56, Pacific Reporter, pages 231 to 243. Said dismissal, being an absolute dismissal without reservation, constituted a final determination of title to water rights in said river in favor of said Dunphy as against said Bliss. The State Engineer's Preliminary Order of Determination is objected to for failure to incorporate therein the said judgment as between said Bliss and his successors and this Estate.

6. The said preliminary order is objected to for failure to find, determine and establish the rights of all claimants upon said river under existing agreements and judicial decrees.

7. The preliminary order departs from the evidence on file, and draws upon other undisclosed sources, in departure from the statute.

8. Because of the large number of ranches along said river, aggregating 300,000 to 400,000 acres of irrigated land, and the large and complex and elaborate amount of data involved in the determination of their rights, it is physically impossible for said Estate to examine the files of all the other claimants along the river. It is impossible for any one ranch to become acquainted with the data regarding all of the other ranches without consuming the same time as the State Engineer has consumed, now approaching twenty years, and the same labor involving the employment of many assistants in the way of office organization, surveyors, and attorneys, and expense amounting to many thousands of dollars which have been so expended on the part of the State Engineer. For the protection of its property against any errors there may be said Estate feels that it should not be bound to concurrence or acquiescence in any errors which may hereafter come to light. In a stream of water the right of any one claimant is inextricably dependent upon what rights are allowed to other claimants, and the rights of said Estate are adversely affected by every excessive allowance to any other person which there may be in the said preliminary order of the State Engineer. For this reason said Estate hereby objects to all and singular, in whole and in every part, the said preliminary order of determination by the State Engineer of the rights of all or any other person or persons who are in said preliminary order given a date of commencement of beneficial use of water earlier than or the same as said Estate.

9. The findings of cultural areas on the lands of said Estate are not possible of observance in practice. Said cultural areas are often designated in said preliminary order as numerous small portions of varied cultures within the same quarter-section with different allotted duties and amounts of water. The ranch can only be irrigated by broad flooding, which makes it impossible to confine the irrigation of such mingled areas to the separated water use designated in said order. Furthermore, said preliminary order, in designating said acres within quarter-sections, fails to designate what acres they are.

10. The duty of water adopted by the State Engineer, as stated on the first page of said Preliminary Order of Determination, equals a

uniform flow of 0.8403 second-feet per 100 acres of land, equal to 1 second-foot per 119.01 acres.

The computation used in the State Engineer's said Preliminary Order of Determination employs a different equivalent, namely, 0.8125 second-feet for each 100 acres, equal to 1 second-foot for 123.077 acres.

The discrepancy is 0.0278 second-feet per 100 acres, equal to 4.067 acres per second-foot, which appears to be inadvertent and contrary to the said first page of the order. The water allowance for said Estate is affected adversely to said Estate to said extent by this inadvertence in the State Engineer's computation.

11. The duties of water and the irrigation season on the lands of said Estate were fixed in said order without taking evidence thereof. There is no proof or evidence in said file 00167, so far as we know, of the duty of water upon the lands of said Estate or of the irrigation season thereon, nor was any evidence upon either thereof taken or obtained by said State Engineer so far as known to said Estate.

12. The findings of the said State Engineer in said preliminary order allowing only three-quarters (¾) of an acre-foot per acre for diversified pasture and one and one-half (1½) feet per acre for meadow pasture are not in accordance with the rights of the said Estate. The said Estate is entitled to take and divert water from the said river for its land at any time in the year when water is in said river, and the limitation of time in said preliminary order contained is without support, and is not in accordance with the actual use or necessities or beneficial use of or by said Estate.

13. The findings of the said State Engineer in said preliminary order as to the length of the irrigating season, if said findings are intended to limit the right of the said Estate to the said periods therein designated, are not in accordance with the rights of the said Estate. The said Estate is entitled to take and divert water from the said river for its land at any time in the year when water is in said river, and the limitation of time in said preliminary order contained is without support, and is not in accordance with the actual use or necessities or beneficial use of or by said Estate.

14. No allowance is made therein or in any part of the said order of determination, to this Estate, for domestic uses of water.

No allowance is made therein for stock-watering purposes during the irrigation season, but only during the nonirrigating season.

Said allowance for fall and spring irrigation and for stock-watering purposes during the nonirrigating season does not comply with the statute. Said allowance is that "each user should be entitled, in his proper proportion and priority, to the use of water in such reasonable amounts as necessary." It is respectfully submitted, that this is too uncertain to constitute an allowance either in amount or priority, but is a failure to make any such determination as the statute requires.

15. The preliminary order appears to require said Estate to drain flood waters in the spring of the year and early irrigation season.

The proofs and evidence filed and made of record in the office of the said State Engineer show that owing to the natural configuration of the locality in which the lands of this Estate are situated, flood waters coming down Humboldt River easterly of this ranch when said river is in flood in the spring of the year and the early irrigation season spread

out over this ranch and a very large additional area. It is impossible to prevent said floods from so spreading over the Battle Mountain area, including this ranch. If any engineering knowledge exists of means of accomplishing this extreme undertaking, the cost of putting the same into operation would be so great as to many times exceed the value of all of the lands in the Battle Mountain district, including the lands of this Estate.

Furthermore, the drainage of such flood waters from these lands in the said flood stages of the river would be of no great benefit to this ranch, and if of benefit to any one said benefit would accrue mostly to other ranches lower down upon the river; and such enterprise would be for the benefit of the public so situated and constitute a taking of property of said Estate for public use. Said taking would consist partly in the loss to said Estate of the benefit of said flood waters, and partly in the loss to said Estate of the ruinous cost of the drainage of said flood waters if said cost were placed upon said Estate.

The enforcement upon said Estate of the cost of such drainage would therefore be a taking of the property of said Estate without compensation, contrary to said section 8 of Article I of the Constitution of the State of Nevada enacting that private property shall not be taken for public use without just compensation, and contrary to the other statutory and constitutional provisions hereinbefore set forth.

The said preliminary order of determination is therefore objected to in its present form for limiting the quantity of water upon the lands of said Estate, during the said flood stages of the river, to the quantity stated in said preliminary order of determination, during which flood stage it is impossible to restrict the water upon said lands to the quantities which the State Engineer's said order prescribes.

CONCLUSION

16. The owners of said Estate, and their attorney, reside at a distance from the State Engineer's office in Carson City, being all residents of California, and the extent of the contents of the files of the State Engineer in the matter of said adjudication is great. Because of this the said Estate requested of the State Engineer an extension of time for the examination of said files as preparatory to the preparation of these objections. This request being unfavorably acted upon by the State Engineer, this Estate has had to prepare these objections hurriedly and without such examination. The Estate therefore asks an extension of time of thirty days from the time it receives notice from the State Engineer of such extension, in which to file supplementary objections hereafter if it should so desire.

These objections are filed in compliance with the request of the State Engineer in view of the penalties which the statutes of Nevada undertake to impose or to authorize the State Engineer to impose for failure to file objections, and this Estate does not waive any rights it may have to urge now or hereafter, in any tribunal, the objections herein stated or any other objections, or to act in any manner that may exist for the protection of its property.

Dated June 10, 1922.

JENNIE C. D. MEYER,
MARY D. FLOOD,
JAMES C. DUNPHY,
VIOLA P. BURNETT;

JENNIE C. D. MEYER,
As Trustee under the will of William Dunphy, deceased.

By PERRY EVANS, *Their Attorney.*

State of California, City and County of San Francisco, ss.

X. R. Meyer, being first duly sworn, deposes and says: That he is the agent for the owners of the William Dunphy Estate, named in the foregoing document; that he has read the foregoing document and knows the contents thereof, and that the same is true to the best of his knowledge, information and belief; that as such agent he has personally conducted proceedings on behalf of said Estate in the matters in said document set forth, and that he is therefore more conversant with said proceedings and matters than are said owners, and he makes this verification in the place of said owners for said reason.

X. R. MEYER.

Subscribed and sworn to before me this 12th day of June, 1922,

MARIE FORMAN,

Notary Public in and for the City and County of San Francisco, State of California.

My commission expires January 10, 1925.

State of California, City and County of San Francisco, ss.

I, H. I. Mulcrevy, County Clerk of the City and County of San Francisco, State of California, and ex officio Clerk of the Superior Court thereof, the same being a court of record, having by law a seal, the officer authorized by the laws of the State of California to make the following certificate, do hereby certify, that Marie Forman of the City and County of San Francisco, whose name is subscribed to the annexed instrument and thereon written and before whom the annexed oath or affidavit was taken, was at the time of taking such oath or affidavit, a Notary Public in and for the said City and County of San Francisco, residing in said City and County, duly authorized to take the same, and an officer duly authorized by the laws of said State to take and certify the acknowledgment and proof of deeds to be recorded in said State. And further that I am well acquainted with the handwriting of said officer, and verily believe that the signature to such jurat or certificate is genuine.

In testimony whereof, I have hereunto set my hand and affixed the seal of the said Superior Court, dated June 12, 1922.

I further certify that an impression of the seals of Notaries Public are not required by law to be filed in my office.

[SEAL] H. I. MULCREVY, *Clerk.*

No. 7

IN THE OFFICE OF THE STATE ENGINEER OF THE STATE OF NEVADA

In the Matter of the Adjudication of the Water Rights of the Humboldt River

OBJECTIONS PROPOSED BY HUMBOLDT LAND AND CATTLE COMPANY

The Humboldt Land and Cattle Company, a corporation, hereby respectfully proposes and makes the following objections to the Preliminary Determination made by the State Engineer in the foregoing matter, in so far as the said determination affects the rights, titles, and interests of said corporation.

Said objections are as follows:

1. Inasmuch as the Preliminary Order fails to make any finding upon the prescriptive rights of this corporation, as to which a mass of evidence was introduced and is now in the record, the said Order fails to determine the *present* status of the said rights, with relation to the rights of others lying below us on said river. The said Preliminary Order is therefore erroneous for failure to find upon the prescriptive rights of this corporation.

The evidence and record show that this corporation or its predecessor in interest, immediately after the completion of its respective ditches, dams, levees, etc., irrigated, by flooding all the land covered by each ditch, dam, levee respectively, and ever since has continued to annually irrigate such land to the extent that the water in the river would fill such dam or ditch, or reach such levee. That such use of the river water has been open, notorious, under claim of right, adverse to all claimants below us on the river as well as to those above us; that it has been exclusive and uninterrupted by any; that it has been hostile to them and an invasion of their right, if any they had or claimed. Our right to so continue to use such river water has therefore ripened into a title to such use against all owners or claimants below us, and such right or title is supreme over all other water rights or priorities. If any lower owners had or claimed water rights superior or prior to ours, the legal duty rested upon them to have pressed them. Having failed to press their rights, and by acquiescing in our use of these waters for forty and more years, they have lost the right to question our title to such waters. It is respectfully suggested that the method followed by the Engineer in adjusting rights on the basis of priorities as of original use, establishes a former instead of the present status, and seeks to effect a redistribution of the water rights on a basis other than now lawfully obtains. This method works a particular hardship upon the lands located on the upper reaches of the river, whose rights have ripened by many years of a customary use. This does not necessarily mean that users on the lower river have had no water, but it means that such use has been secondary to those located above. It does not mean that our use of the water deprives those next below us of water, even if we divert all the river carries in the late season, for such water largely drains back into the river and is used again below us. Thus our right to the primary use may be absolute, yet those below are entitled to the water that may reach them after the said use by us. The method of establishing water rights upon a basis of *priorities* of use *only* would oblige us to permit water to run past our intakes without use by us, in order to supply those prior to us, although they might have forfeited such priority by acquiescing for forty years in our first use as above described.

We claim, therefore, that all the lands covered by the High Line ditch, which was finished in 1883, have acquired a water right by annual use since that time to the extent of the capacity of the ditch, and a like right is claimed by us of the following ditches and dams by reason of an annual use since the dates hereafter respectively given:

Beowawe No. 1 by an annual use to capacity since 1876.
Beowawe No. 2 by an annual use to capacity since 1877.
Merchant Canal by an annual use to capacity since 1898.

Dwyer Dam by an annual use since 1897.

Rose Dam by an annual use since 1873.

Overflow waters from the river have been used whenever the water stage permitted over a large section of land, and it has been the custom to use such waters whenever available.

The physical condition of the Horseshoe Ranch is such that very large proportions of the water taken into ditches and used for irrigation return to the river either by drainage or through springs that are caused by irrigation, and it is submitted that we have the right to continue such use and such methods of drainage in the future as in the past, assuming such to be economical and in accord with the demands of the land and crops.

Reference is hereby made to the testimony of Louis Freamonth, who testified that for about the last 18 years he had each year irrigated the lands of this ranch, and that each and every year he had diverted and used all the water in the river up to the capacity of the various ditches and the supply in the river.

2. We desire to object to the amount of water set aside by the Engineer for use on the various parcels of land, inasmuch as it is impossible to secure such distribution on the said parcels by reason of the physical lay of the land. Heretofore the ranch has been divided into two general divisions for irrigation purposes, one lying on each side of the river, and each piece has been flooded quite equally, because it was impossible to do otherwise. To measure the quantity of water allotted to various 40-acre pieces adjoining each other and divert it as desired would present work impossible of accomplishment.

3. The Preliminary Order does not appear to have any table establishing relative rights of the various water users, showing rights by years or of the relative amounts which each shall have during the low period of water, when there is not enough for all.

4. It appears to us that when the State Engineer attempts to decide disputed titles or rights in matters essential to these entire proceedings he is asserting judicial functions, which are forbidden to any but the courts by the State Constitution in Articles III and VI. The Legislature had no power to give such functions to the Engineer, and any action herein taken that seeks to decide a dispute relating to such essential matters as title by prescription, and to effect a new distribution of titles and rights to the waters of the river, is beyond the power of the Legislature to give and of the Engineer to exercise, and the preliminary order would be of no value as a basis for a final order under such circumstances, even if the final order be from a court.

5. We respectfully object to the general form of the Order because it fails to incorporate in it rights existing by agreement and by judicial decree. There have been numerous court decrees settling water rights and the relative privileges of users on the river, and as the rights of all users are intermingled and relative, each is affected by said judicial decisions. There is no mention made of the rulings by the court in the action of Bliss v. Grayson, reported in 56 Pac. Rep., page 231, *et seq.*

6. We contend that it is erroneous for the Preliminary Order to find the commencement of beneficial use of water by others to be prior to ours, and thereby deprive us of the future use of waters which we have

been making beneficial use for more than forty years, and to which use these so-called prior users have acquiesced in. Inasmuch as we are interested in the amount of water allotted to every user on the river as affecting our allotment during low stage of the river, it becomes necessary to protect our interests properly that an examination be made of the priorities allowed to every user, if the water distribution is to be on such a basis. To perform such a prodigious task would consume years of time and many thousands of dollars. We therefore desire to reserve an objection to the priorities and quantities allotted to every other user, and to take advantage of the same in event such becomes necessary to our defense.

7. The findings in the preliminary order allotting three-quarters of an acre-foot per acre for diversified pasture and one and one-half acre-feet per acre for meadow pasture, to be taken from the river during a certain limited time of year, are not in accord with our rights, nor do they take note of the natural conditions. We claim the right to take water at any season of the year, so long as there is water in the river to be taken, and so long as the use is necessary or beneficial.

8. We object to the said order inasmuch as it makes no rulings on our evidence for stock water and water for domestic use, nor any general ruling that is applicable to our every purpose, nor for stock water during the irrigating season.

9. The Dean Estate owns land lying just above the lands of the Humboldt Land and Cattle Company, which is watered through two separate ditches, known as the McConnell Ditch and the Johnson Ditch. The evidence showed the McConnell Ditch was first used in or about 1874 and the Johnson Ditch in 1897. Disputes have arisen between the Dean Estate and ourselves relating to the distribution of water to the Johnson Ditch, which dispute will be affected by the fixing of the priority of the Johnson Ditch. The preliminary order refers to these two ditches as one ditch, the "McConnell and Johnson Ditch" (see page 117). Inasmuch as the priorities of use of the two ditches are so different by many years, we desire to object to such combining of the two ditches under one name and likewise under one date of priority, as seriously affecting the priority of our right in the High Line Ditch, which diverts water in the immediate neighborhood of said two Dean Ditches, with an allotted priority of 1883.

10. Numerous disputes have been had between ourselves and the Dean Estate relating to the obstruction of flow of water to the headgate of our High Line Canal, and several hearings have been held before the State Engineer in an effort to get these disputes settled. Pursuant to our request that the Engineer notify us of the date of hearing of the testimony of the Dean Estate relating to the Johnson Ditch, a notice was received by us from the Engineer that the Dean hearing would be held in Battle Mountain on a certain day, viz,............ That on said day the attorney for said Humboldt Land and Cattle Company went from San Francisco to Battle Mountain to attend said hearing to protect the interests of his client in the matter of said dispute and of the water rights incident thereto. On arriving at said Battle Mountain, said attorney was informed by the Engineer that the hearing had been held the day previous, having been advanced without notice at the request of said Dean Estate, for the reason that all

the witnesses were then present, and that such advance in the time of hearing would be to the great convenience of such parties.

We, therefore, being absent from said hearing, and being now for the first time advised of the combining of the two ditches under one designation, desire to object to the order in the respect named.

11. The preliminary order proposes to deprive the Humboldt Land and Cattle Company of its property without due process of law, and the said order is therefore objected to in those respects, and particularly in that respect as to which said order seeks to effect a redistribution of water rights along the said Humboldt River in accord with certain pre-existing priorities, and to deprive said corporation of the very valuable rights which it has acquired through very many years of beneficial use of the waters of said river. If such a redistribution of rights is sought to be effected by said order, the right of said engineer to so order is hereby challenged and objected to as beyond his powers and beyond the power of the Legislature to vest in him, as the Constitution of the State limits the use of such power to the courts.

ALBERT C. AIKEN,
Attorney for Humboldt Land and Cattle Co.

State of California, County of Inyo, ss.

Albert C. Aiken, being first duly sworn, deposes and says that he is the attorney for the Humboldt Land and Cattle Company, the owner of the ranch property described and referred to in the foregoing set of objections; that he has read the said objections and knows the contents of the foregoing document embodying the said objections; that the same is true to the best of his knowledge, information and belief; that he has conducted personally the proceedings in the matter of the adjudication referred to therein on behalf of the said Humboldt Land and Cattle Company, and is therefore more conversant with the matters set forth in said document than are his said clients, and he makes this affidavit in place of said corporation for that reason.

ALBERT C. AIKEN.

In witness whereof, I have hereunto set hand and affixed my official seal in my office in the County of Inyo, State of California, this 13th day of June, 1922.

[SEAL] CHAS. BROWN,
Notary Public in and for Inyo County, California.

My commission expires July 19, 1925.

No. 8

IN THE OFFICE OF THE STATE ENGINEER OF NEVADA

In the Matter of the Determination of the Relative Rights to the Waters of Humboldt River and its Tributaries

OBJECTIONS TO PRELIMINARY ORDER OF DETERMINATION

Comes now Old Channel Ditch Company, a corporation, Union Canal Ditch Company, a corporation, Southwest Ditch Company, Irish-American Ditch Company and John Fant, whose postoffice addresses are Lovelock, Pershing County, Nevada, and object on behalf of them-

selves and each and every other water-user or appropriator in Lovelock Valley, to the Preliminary Order of Determination of the waters of the Humboldt River and its tributaries, as published by the State Engineer of the State of Nevada, and as grounds of objection allege as follows:

First—That said Preliminary Order of Determination does not definitely define and determine what streams, creeks and rivers are tributaries to the Humboldt River, part of the Humboldt River System, and as such included in and affected by said order of determination.

Second—That said Preliminary Order of Determination does not state determine or fix the date of initiation of each of the several water rights therein described as established by the doctrine of relation, and does not determine the dates of initiation of the rights of the various ditches.

Third—That said Preliminary Order of Determination in districts one, two and three does not observe court decrees and existing contracts in force between water-users, and no mention or reference is made to the same and such decrees and contracts have not been taken into consideration in determining the relative rights of water-users.

Fourth—That said Preliminary Order of Determination fails to allow or determine the storage and power rights of various appropriators both in the natural flow and in the flood waters of the Humboldt River.

Fifth—That the absence of the dates of construction of ditches and dams and the initiation of the rights of the various users renders it impossible to intelligently check the said order for the purpose of making an admission or objection to the correctness thereof. That said order is also indefinite and uncertain in describing the location of the various parcels of land allowed water rights.

Wherefore, your objectors, being aggrieved by said order, pray that the same be modified and changed to conform to said objections and that to that end the said order be added to and corrected in the particulars mentioned.

OLD CHANNEL DITCH COMPANY (a Corporation).
By W. C. PITT, *President*.

UNION CANAL DITCH COMPANY (a Corporation).
By A. WESTFALL, *President*.

SOUTHWEST DITCH COMPANY,
By BERGMAN BROS.; by JOSEPH HILL.

IRISH-AMERICAN DITCH COMPANY (a Partnership),
By W. C. RUDDELL, SR.

JOHN FANT.

State of Nevada, County of Pershing, ss.

W. C. Noteware, being duly sworn, deposes and says that he has read the foregoing objections and knows the contents thereof: that the same is true of his own knowledge excepting as to matters therein stated upon information and belief and as to such matters he believes it to be true; that he makes this verification as agent of the Old Channel Ditch Company.

W. C. NOTEWARE.

Subscribed and sworn to before me this 12th day of June, 1922.

[SEAL] BOOTH B. GOODMAN, *Notary Public*.

No. 9

IN THE OFFICE OF THE STATE ENGINEER OF NEVADA

In the Matter of the Determination of the Relative Rights to the Waters of Humboldt River and its Tributaries

OBJECTIONS TO PRELIMINARY ORDER OF DETERMINATION

Comes now Old Channel Ditch Company, a corporation organized and existing under and by virtue of the laws of the State of Nevada, whose postoffice address is Lovelock, Nevada, by Booth B. Goodman, its attorney, and objects to the Preliminary Order of Determination of the Waters of the Humboldt River and its Tributaries, as published by the State Engineer, and as grounds of objection alleges:

First—That said Preliminary Order of Adjudication fails to mention, enforce or take into consideration the decrees of court enforced between water-users, as well as contracts and agreements enforced between water-users in Lovelock Valley, and particularly that certain judgment and decree of the United States District Court, in and for the District of Nevada, made and entered in the suit of Arthur Rogers v. W. C. Pitt, et al., and the decrees and judgments entered in the District Court of the State of Nevada in certain suits wherein the Southwest Ditch Company and the Union Canal Ditch Company were plaintiffs and the Old Channel Ditch Company was defendant, and that certain agreement for the diversion and division of water made in the year 1910 by and between Union Canal Ditch Company and the water-users thereunder, and the Southwest Ditch Company and the water-users thereunder, on the one part, and your objector, Old Channel Ditch Company, on the other part, which decrees and agreement are now in full force and effect. Said order also fails to determine and establish the date of construction and initiation of this objector's dam, ditch and water right.

Wherefore, your objector prays that the said Order of Adjudication be modified and amended to comply with the objections herein set forth.

BOOTH B. GOODMAN,
Attorney for Old Channel Ditch Co.

State of Nevada, County of Pershing, ss.

R. J. Pierson, being first duly sworn, deposes and says: That he is Assistant Secretary of the Old Channel Ditch Company, the corporation named in the foregoing objection; that he has read the foregoing statement of objection and knows the contents thereof, and that the same is true of his own knowledge, excepting as to matters stated upon information and belief, and as to such matters he believes it to be true.

R. J. PIERSON.

Subscribed and sworn to before me this 13th day of June, A. D. 1922.

[SEAL] J. A. McIntosh, *Notary Public.*

No. 10

BEFORE THE STATE ENGINEER OF THE STATE OF NEVADA

In the Matter of the Termination of the Rights to the Waters of the Humboldt River and its Tributaries

OBJECTIONS OF PACIFIC LIVE STOCK COMPANY TO PRELIMINARY ORDER OF DETERMINATION

To the State Engineer of the State of Nevada, and to Whom It May Concern:

Now comes the Pacific Live Stock Company, a corporation, a person claiming an interest in the waters of the Humboldt River, and objects to the preliminary order of determintaion therein and to the portions thereof set forth in these objections, to wit:

To all of the findings regarding the rights of the Pacific Live Stock Company, contained in pages 52 and 53 of said preliminary order on the following grounds:

1. That the evidence shows that the said right was initiated in the year 1871 and that the said Pacific Live Stock Company was entitled to a priority of 1871 with respect to all of its said land.

2. That the findings of the said State Engineer allowing only three-quarters of an acre-foot per acre for diversified pasture and one and one-half acre feet per acre for meadow pasture are not in accordance with the rights of the said Pacific Live Stock Company and the said quantity of water is not sufficient for the irrigation of the said land and the said Pacific Live Stock Company has beneficially used on the said land, and all thereof, at least three acre-feet per acre and the said quantity is reasonably necessary for the irrigation thereof.

3. That the findings of the said State Engineer as to the length of the irrigating season, if said findings are intended to limit the right of the said Pacific Live Stock Company to the said periods therein designated, are not in accordance with the rights of the said Pacific Live Stock Company and the said Pacific Live Stock Company is entitled to take and divert water from the said river for its said land at any time in the year when the said water is available and the limitation of time therein contained is entirely without support and is not in accordance with the actual use or necessities or beneficial use of the said Pacific Live Stock Company.

Wherefore, said Pacific Live Stock Company prays that said preliminary order of determination be modified and corrected in accordance herewith.

PACIFIC LIVE STOCK COMPANY,

[SEAL] By J. LEROY NICKOL, *President.*

EDWARD F. TREADWELL,
Attorney for Pacific Live Stock Company.

State of California, City and County of San Francisco, ss.

W. H. Trump, being first duly sworn, says: That he is the Secretary of the Pacific Live Stock Company and makes this verification on its behalf; that he has read the foregoing objections and knows the con-

etnts thereof and that the same are true to the best of his knowledge, information and belief.

W. H. TRUMP.

Subscribed and sworn to before me this 8th day of May, 1922.

[SEAL] JAMES MASON,
Notary Public in and for the City and County of San Francisco, State of California.

No. 11

In the Matter of the Adjudication of the Water Rights of the Humboldt River and its Tributaries. And referring more particularly to pages 85 to 91, inclusive, of the finding of the office of the State Engineer of Nevada and of the Preliminary Order of Determination of the Waters of the Humboldt River and its Tributaries, as prepared and printed for the year 1922, and issued out of said office of said State Engineer, in so far as said findings and preliminary orders affect the water rights of the protestant hereinafter named appurtenant to the lands hereinafter described.

PROTEST OF THE ELLISON RANCHING COMPANY AGAINST SAID FINDINGS AND AGAINST SAID PRELIMINARY ORDERS

Now comes the Ellison Ranching Company, a corporation, by its duly authorized agent, R. E. Tilden, and protests against the findings and preliminary orders of determination of the waters of the Humboldt River and its tributaries, as the same are found on pages 85 to 91, inclusive, of the printed preliminary orders of the determination of the State Engineer's office of the State of Nevada for the year 1922, particularly and in so far as said findings and preliminary orders affect protestant's rights to said waters as heretofore used by protestant upon, in and about what is commonly known as and called "Squaw Valley Ranch," the lands more particularly situated in Sections 1, 7, 15, 17, 18, 20, 21, 28, 29, 30, 31, 32 and 33 of Township 39 North of Range 47 East, Mount Diablo Base and Meridian; also situated in Sections 2, 3, 4, 5, 6, 7, 8, 9, 10, 17, 18, 19 and 30 of Township 38 North of Range 47 East, same base and meridian; also situated in Sections 1, 2, 11, 12, 13, 23, 24, 25, 26 of Township 38 North of Range 46 East, same base and meridian; also situated in Sections 35 and 36 of Township 39 North of Range 47 East, said base and meridian; also situated in Sections 28, 29, 30 and 27 of Township 39 North of Range 48 East, said base and meridian, and containing in all eight thousand acres, more or less, of irrigated lands, artificially irrigated by the waters of Rock Creek, Willow Creek, and Frasier Creek and other small tributaries of the Humboldt River.

That said protestant protests as aforesaid for the following causes and upon the following grounds, to wit:

1. That the amount of water allowed and found on the pages aforesaid of said printed preliminary order of determination, and concerning the lands hereinbefore described, are not sufficient to irrigate the said lands of the said Squaw Valley Ranch as said amounts of water are set forth in said preliminary order as aforesaid.

2. That said preliminary orders, and order and findings therein contained, in so far as the same affect the said Squaw Valley Ranch and lands, are erroneous for the reasons hereinbefore stated and are based upon erroneous data, for the reason that said State Engineer has inadvertently overlooked and ignored the data concerning said ranch and irrigated lands shown on culture maps filed with the State Engineer showing the lands so irrigated and accepted by former State Engineer William Kearney.

3. That said preliminary orders and findings as printed are erroneous for all of the reasons aforesaid and are based upon erroneous data, for the following reasons: That affidavits now on file in the State Engineer's office, verified by former owners of said Squaw Valley Ranch, and said lands and the waters used in connection therewith for irrigating the same, contain true and accurate data as to the said irrigated areas; which said affidavits have been inadvertently overlooked and ignored by the State Engineer in arriving at said findings and preliminary orders.

4. That said findings and preliminary orders as printed are erroneous for all of the reasons aforesaid and for the further reason that the discharge of Rock and Willow Creek has been completely used up in the irrigation of said lands during the irrigating season of each year, and that during the latter part of July of each year Rock Creek is dry and the lands on the upper part of said Squaw Valley Ranch are higher lands, have to be irrigated by Frasier Creek or ditch and the waters of the reservoir formed by what is commonly known as and called the Squaw Valley Dam, and protestant maintains and claims that said ranch and the lands belonging thereto as the same are hereinbefore described require the entire supply of water flowing in said creeks for the irrigation thereof, and further shows that much of the water so used in the irrigation of said lands flows back into said creeks and may be used by other appropriators lower down on the stream.

5. That said findings and preliminary orders are erroneous for all of the reasons aforesaid and for the further following reason: That it requires all of the waters in Squaw Valley and flowing in the creeks thereof or contained in the reservoirs situated therein to keep and maintain said lands in a properly irrigated condition, for the reason that said lands have considerable slope carrying off the irrigating waters rapidly from the surface, and for the further reason that the said lands are very porous and full of gravel, and that the water sinks away to lower depths rapidly.

Wherefore, having fully and completely protested against the findings and preliminary orders heretofore made by said office and said State Engineer and as printed and published in a book or pamphlet hereinbefore described, said protestant prays that a hearing be had on this protest and the matters and things herein alleged either before said State Engineer, or before a court of competent jurisdiction, and that upon said hearing said preliminary findings and orders be modified to conform to the facts hereinbefore stated and alleged, and that upon said hearing a water right be given to this protestant to the waters flowing in the creeks aforesaid sufficient for the irrigation for all of the lands heretofore irrigated and composing and being what is known as the Squaw Valley Ranch and lands around about owned by this protestant

and irrigated as aforesaid; and that protestant have such other and further relief as may be meet and proper in the premises.

R. E. TILDEN,
Agent for the said Ellison Ranching Company.

State of Nevada, Humboldt County, ss.

R. E. Tilden, being first duly sworn, on oath deposes and says: That he is the duly authorized agent of the Ellison Ranching Company, a corporation, protestant above named, and makes this verification of said protest as such agent; that he has read said protest and knows the contents thereof; that the same is true of his own knowledge except as to the matters therein stated upon information and belief and as to them that he believes it to be true.

R. E. TILDEN.

Subscribed and sworn to before me this 6th day of June, A. D. 1922.

[SEAL] T. A. BRANDON, *Notary Public.*

No. 12

IN THE OFFICE OF THE STATE ENGINEER OF NEVADA

In the Matter of the Determination of the Relative Rights to the Waters of the Humboldt River and its Tributaries

Comes now the Land Development Company, a corporation, whose postoffice address is Battle Mountain Nevada, business of which is, among other things, ranching and stock-raising, and hereby objects to the preliminary order of determination of the State Engineer as set forth in the pamphlet entitled: "Preliminary Order of Determination of the Waters of the Humboldt River and its Tributaries," upon the following grounds and for the following reasons, to wit:

I

That the objector is an appropriator and user of water from the above-mentioned stream-system; that the water claimed by objector has been beneficially used as set forth in its proofs filed in this matter and said water has been used continuously to the present time.

II

That the said preliminary order of determination tends to establish a priority for the water rights of this claimant for its lands referred to in its proof of appropriation on file with the State Engineer later than the date on which said lands were irrigated and water rights appropriated; that the actual date of appropriation, as this claimant is informed and believes and therefore alleges, is as set forth in the proof already on file and that there is no legal evidence to the contrary, and that a prima facie proof established the date as in said original affidavit "Proof of Appropriation" on file.

III

That the areas of land named in said preliminary order of determination is far below the actual area irrigated and that said order

erroneously establishes a reduced figure of irrigated lands; that the area irrigated by claimant is in conformity with the area referred to in the proof of appropriation of claimant on file herein.

IV

That the said preliminary order of determination tends to establish a duty of water for the lands of objector far below the requirements of said lands; that, if said allotment of water as set forth in said preliminary order of determination be confirmed, objector will be deprived of the use of sufficient water to irrigate and mature its crops and that it will be deprived of a large part of the water lawfully appropriated, diverted and beneficially used under the methods common to the district, which said methods are reasonable and economical under all present and past conditions within the period named in said proof.

V

That the lands of this claimant lie in the Battle Mountain territory which consists of a broad expanse of valley land traversed by the winding and changing course of the Humboldt River; that owing to the many changes of said river during the past fifty years the land is cut up by numerous winding sloughs, all of which are now used by claimant as part of its irrigation system; that, owing to the topography of the land in the Battle Mountain basin, the Humboldt River overflows its banks and spreads over the lands during times of flood, and by reason of such conditions has built up the banks of the river with silt, thus making it impossible, under reasonable costs, to control with any degree of certainty or definiteness the waters that are applied to the lands during portions of the year; that, owing to the character of the flow, large quantities of water have in the past been diverted and used beneficially during the flood season so that all of said lands claimed could be irrigated while the water was available.

For the reasons aforesaid, and the character of soil and crops, the quantity of water allotted in the said preliminary order of determination is insufficient and below the appropriated amount.

VI

That the irrigation season fixed in said order of determination is shorter than the period during which claimant has established a vested right to the use of water.

VII

That the priorities as fixed in the said preliminary order of determination are indefinite and uncertain in that it cannot be ascertained whether the priorities date from the year under beneficial use, under meadow or on cultivated areas or from the date construction was initiated.

Wherefore, objector prays that the priority and extent of the appropriation be fixed in accordance with the proof already on file herein and that said preliminary order of determination be modified so as to award and grant to this claimant additional amounts of water as set forth in the proof on file.

W. M. KEARNEY,
Attorney for Objector.

State of Nevada, County of Washoe, ss.

W. M. Kearney, being first duly sworn, deposes and says: That he is attorney for the objector herein and makes this certification for and on behalf of the objector for the reason that the officers of the objector reside out of the State of Nevada and in the City of Salt Lake, State of Utah; that the only other representative of the company resides out of the County of Washoe wherein affiant resides, and for those reasons the officers and manager of objector are unable to verify this pleading; that affiant has read the foregoing objection and knows the contents thereof and that the same is true except as to those matters stated on information and belief, and as to those matters he believes it to be true.

W. M. KEARNEY.

Subscribed and sworn to before me, this 9th day of June, A. D. 1922.

[SEAL] GEORGIA NEWMAN, *Notary Public.*

No. 13

BEFORE THE STATE ENGINEER, AT CARSON CITY, NEVADA

In the Matter of the Preliminary Order of Determination of the Waters of the Humboldt River and its Tributaries

PROTEST OF GEO. L. KAEDING (Under Proof No. 00163)

Now comes Geo. L. Kaeding of Glendale, California, and here protests to the order of determination of the waters of the Humboldt River and its tributaries of the State Engineer of Nevada, in so far as the same affects his lands, waters and water rights as they are referred to on pages 304 and 305 thereof, and respectfully shows:

1. That said order of determination is contrary to the evidence and is against law;

2. That said order of determination adjudicates to protestant lands, waters and water rights, which he does not own, and in which he has no interest whatever;

3. That said order of determination fails to adjudicate to protestant lands, waters and water rights which he does own, and which subsists as a valid and legal title of record; and

In this connection, protestant alleges that, during all the times herein mentioned, by himself and his predecessors in interest, he was and is now the owner of, in the possession of and entitled to the immediate possession of all and singular, the NW¼ and the S½ of the NE¼ of Section 34, T. 33 N, R 45 E, M. D. B. & M., and also a certain undivided one-fifth interest in the S½ of the NW¼ of Section 6, T. 32 N, R. 46 E, M. D. B. & M., and that the protestant's water right to the lands hereinabove described issues out of the Rocky Point Canal, which commences at the Rock Dam situate on the S½ of the NW¼ of said Section 6, and in which said dam, said Rocky Point Canal and a certain eighty acres of land, included in the lands hereinabove described, protestant has a certain one-fifth undivided interest subsisting of record; and that the water and water rights for the irrigation and cultivation of said lands were duly appropriated, and appear by record title, in the year 1873; and

That protestant's waters and water rights do not issue or depend upon the socalled Kaeding Ditch, but said ditch is merely an instrument of conveying said waters to said lands under appropriation in the year 1873, and continuous application to a beneficial use thereafter to the present date.

Accordingly, protestant claims his waters, water rights and the date of appropriation and application thereof to a beneficial use as hereinabove alleged in the premises, and from the year 1873, and that their determination as specified in said order of the State Engineer is incorrect, in so far as said order conflicts with this protest; and in this behalf protestant hereby specially refers to and annexes hereto his certain letter now on file and of record in the office of the State Engineer tendered to him as a preliminary protest in the premises, and hereby makes the same a part hereof.

Wherefore, protestant prays that a hearing be had on this protest, of which due notice be given to protestant and all other parties interest, and that evidence be adduced, and that protestant have his lands, waters and water rights adjudicated in accordance with evidence and the facts as the same appear on such hearing, and that such further order be made as may be just.

GEO. L. KAEDING, *Protestant.*

By Platt & Sanford, *Attorneys for Protestant.*

State of Nevada, County of Ormsby, ss.

Geo. L. Sanford, being first duly sworn, deposes and says: That he is the acting attorney and agent of Geo. L. Kaeding, said protestant, hereunto duly authorized, who is not present in said county of Ormsby, but who resides at Glendale, California, and is therefore unable to make this verification, for which reason said acting attorney and agent makes this verification.

That he has read the above and foregoing protest and knows the contents thereof; that the same is true of his own knowledge, except those matters of information and belief or stated on information and belief, and as to such matters he believes such protest to be true.

GEORGE L. SANFORD.

Subscribed and sworn to before me this 20th day of June, A. D. 1922.

[SEAL] Mabel H. Stewart, *Notary Public.*

Glendale, Calif., June the tenth, 1922.

Subject—Water Right of G. L. Kaeding.

State Engineer of Nevada, Carson City, Nevada.

Dear Sir: Under the conditions of your adjudication of the Waters of the Humboldt River and its Tributaries, this letter will have to be considered in the light of a protest regarding the adjudication of my water rights. I intend it rather as a request for a correction of what appears to me to be error.

I appreciate the difficulties under which you labored in these matters and congratulate you on having arrived at some definite conclusions and at least made a start toward an adjudication.

Not being able to be present when data was presented at Battle Mountain, I left my case in the hands of the Battle Mountain Water-Users Association and they seem to have gotten greatly mixed up in my case, although I endeavored to present it to them clearly.

First, by comparing the data herewith submitted with your printed

adjudication, you will see that they have adjudicated to me water rights on lands that I do not own. I am the owner, by deed, of the NW¼ and the S½ of the NE¼ of Section 34, Tp. 33 N, R. 45 E; also own a one-fifth interest in the S½ of the NW¼ of Section 6, in Tp. 32 N, R. 46 E, all Mount Diablo Base and Meridian.

You will notice in the adjudication I am given water right for land other than the above.

In October or the first part of November, 1920, I sent to the State Engineer's office certified copies of my deeds to the above lands.

My water right to the above lands is out of the Rocky Point Canal, which commences at the Rock Dam which is situated on the S½ of the NW¼ of Section 6, Tp. 32 N, R. 46 E. As above noted, I own, by deed, a one-fifth interest in this dam, Rocky Point Canal, and 80 acres of land. The original location notice of this water right, written out by Daniel McIntyre, in 1873, and recorded by him in Austin, Nevada, is now in my possession and has descended to me through the various owners by deed.

The land that I own was the first land ever put under cultivation from the Rocky Point Canal, and the old diversion points from the canal to the land are plainly visible to this day, though not now in use.

In the adjudication my water right reads as coming out of the "Kaeding Ditch" dating from 1914, while the water right of the W. T. Jenkins Company on sections 1 and 2 in Tp. 32 N, R. 45 E, and the Land Development Company on sections 28 and 21 in Tp. 33 N, R. 45 E, reads as coming out of the Rocky Point Canal, and dating from 1873 to 1895.

Now the ditch referred to in the Jenkins water right as the Rocky Point Canal, and in my case as the Kaeding Ditch, and in the case of the Land Development Company as the Rocky Point Canal, are all one and the same ditch. The Jenkins Company gets the water first, I get it next, and then the Land Development Company gets it.

All my deeds refer to the Rocky Point Canal so the interjection of the name "Kaeding Ditch" is simply confusing.

Inasmuch as my land was the first land ever put under actual plowed cultivation on any of the above-mentioned sections, growing crops of barley and sweet corn (alfalfa was not known in the district at the time), and as I had the entire area under cultivation and irrigation when I entered the army in 1917, I feel that my water right should read as set forth below.

I organized the Land Development Company, bought for them the land they now own, sold to the W. T. Jenkins Company for the account of James A. Blossom the land they now own and irrigate from the Rocky Point Canal, and made a careful study of the water rights of the district during my residence there from 1912 to 1917, and I feel that I am better posted on the history of the local water rights there than any one else.

In a few days I will be able to get at my maps and other data and I will then make up for you a detailed statement, with accompanying map, of my water rights. In the meantime I ask that you correct the statement of my water rights to conform to the statement submitted herewith.

Yours very truly,

GEO. L. KAEDING.

227 North Central Ave., Glendale, Calif.

No. 14

IN THE OFFICE OF THE STATE ENGINEER OF THE STATE OF NEVADA

In the Matter of the Determination of the Relative Rights of the Various Water Users to the Waters of the Humboldt River of said State and its Tributaries.

Now comes George B. Williams, whose postoffice address is Fallon, Churchill County, Nevada, and whose business, among other things, is ranching and livestock raising, and hereby objects to the preliminary order of determination of the State Engineer of the State of Nevada as set forth in the pamphlet entitled: "Preliminary Order of Determination of the Waters of the Humboldt River and its Tributaries," upon the following grounds and for the following reasons, to wit:

I

That the objector herein is an appropriator and user of water from the above-mentioned stream and water-system; that the water claimed by said objector has been beneficially used as set forth in its proofs filed in the above-entitled matter and proceeding, and said water has been continuously so used to the present time.

II

That the said preliminary order of determination tends to establish a priority for the water rights of said claimant for the lands referred to in his proof of appropriation on file in the office of the State Engineer later than the dates on which said lands were irrigated and the use of said waters so appropriated; that the actual dates or date of appropriation, as this claimant is informed and believes, and therefore alleges, is as set forth in the proof now on file in the office of said State Engineer, and that there is no sufficient evidence to the contrary, and that a prima-facie proof has established the date or dates as in said original affidavit proof of appropriation on file in this matter.

III

That the areas of land named and described in said preliminary order of determination are far less than the actual irrigated areas by said objector and his predecessors and that said order of determination erroneously establishes a reduced aggregate of irrigated lands of said claimant; and that the areas of lands irrigated by claimant is in conformity with the areas referred to in the proof of appropriation of said claimant on file herein.

IV

That the said preliminary order of determination tends to establish a duty of water or water use for the said lands of objector far less than the necessary requirements of proper use of water on said lands of claimant, or to which he is entitled under the law; that, if said allotment of water under and by said preliminary order of determination as set forth therein be confirmed, said claimant will be deprived of the use of sufficient water to irrigate and mature his harvest crops and pasturage, and that he will be deprived of a large part of the

water lawfully and necessarily appropriated, diverted, and beneficially used heretofore under methods of irrigation appropriate and common to the necessary use of water in said water district and locality, which said methods of irrigation are reasonable and economical under all present and past, and as claimant believes and alleges, actual conditions within the time or times designated in said proofs now on file in said matter.

V

That the said lands of this claimant lie in the Battle Mountain territory, or water district, which consists of a broad expanse of river-bottom lands of said Humboldt River traversed by the winding and frequently changing course of said river, and that, owing to the many changes of the main channel of said river during the past half-century and more, the said lands of claimant are cut up by numerous winding sloughs, all of which are now used by claimant as parts of his irrigation system for said lands. That owing to the natural surface of the land in the said Battle Mountain water district and river basin, the Humboldt River overflows its banks and spreads widely over the adjacent lands during all times of flood, and by reason of such conditions has often changed the banks of said river in places, as to make it impossible, under reasonable costs, to control with any degree of certainty or definite manner the waters that are used for irrigating said lands during certain portions of the year; that, owing to the character of the flow of said waters, large quantities of the same have in all the past time referred to in the evidence on file herein been diverted as far as possible under the circumstances and used beneficially during the flood season, so that more than four-fifths of said lands claimed received irrigation to a certain extent while the said waters were available. And for the reasons aforesaid, and the kind of soil and crops to be produced thereon, the quantity of water so allotted in the said preliminary order of determination is insufficient and far less than the amount heretofore annually appropriated by claimant and his predecessors, as claimant is informed and believes, and therefore alleges to be the facts.

VI

That the irrigation season fixed in said order of determination is much shorter in some particulars and different than in the period during which said claimant has established a vested right to the use of said waters.

VII

That the priorities of the use of the said waters, as fixed in the said preliminary order of determination, are indefinite and uncertain in that it cannot be ascertained whether the said priorities date from the year designated as the time of beneficial use under the heading of natural meadow, or beneficial use on cultivated areas, or from use of water under construction first initiated.

Wherefore, claimant and objector prays that the priority and extent of his appropriation of the said waters for irrigation be fixed in accordance with the proofs now on file herein, and that said preliminary order of determination be modified so as to award and give to this claimant additional quantities of water for the lands of claimant

designated in said order of determination, and for the designation of further and additional lands to be included in the final order of the determination herein, as set forth in the proof of claimant on file in this matter, and any other and further change in said order which shall be meet and proper in the premises.

E. L. WILLIAMS,
Attorney for Objector.

State of Nevada, County of Washoe, ss.

George B. Williams, being duly sworn, deposes and says: That he is the objector herein and makes this verification for and on behalf of himself; that affiant has read the foregoing objections and protest and knows the contents thereof, and that the same is true except as to those matters stated on information and belief, and as to those matters he believes it to be true.

GEORGE B. WILLIAMS.

Subscribed and sworn to before me this 15th day of June, A. D. 1922.

[SEAL] WALTER M. KENNEDY,
Notary Public in and for Washoe County, State of Nevada.

No. 15

IN THE OFFICE OF THE STATE ENGINEER OF THE STATE OF NEVADA, CARSON CITY, NEVADA

In the Matter of the Adjudication of the Humboldt River and its Tributaries, under the Preliminary Order of Determination, in re Proofs Nos. 00213, 00330 and 00382.

OBJECTION AS TO LISTING OF ACREAGES AND DATES OF PRIORITY

Comes now Hunter-Banks Company, a corporation, whose lands and water rights are listed under Proofs Nos. 00213, 00330 and 00382, in the Preliminary Order of Determination, in the matter of the Adjudication of the Humboldt River and its Tributaries, recently issued by the honorable State Engineer of the State of Nevada, by Edwin E. Caine, its attorney, and respectfully calls the attention of the honorable State Engineer to the fact that there is a possibility of question as to the priorities and acreages claimed by it, and as the same appear in said Preliminary Order of Determination, in that it may not be possible to determine therefrom to just what subdivision certain acreages and priorities should be applied, and respectfully represents that its understanding of the lists as they appear in said Preliminary Order of Determination is that, where the water is not definitely listed as appurtenant to a particular subdivision, such water may be applied to the irrigated lands belonging to the undersigned, as the same appear in said Preliminary Order of Determination, and respectfully represents that, if such understanding is not correct, it hereby

notifies the State Engineer that it does not waive any rights in connection with said matter, and respectfully objects to the manner in which said claims appear in said Preliminary Order of Determination, and asks that the same be corrected, in accordance with the above understanding, or that said water be definitely listed to the land upon which the right attaches, as shown by said priorities and acreages.

Dated this 13th day of June, 1922.

HUNTER-BANKS CO.
By EDWIN E. CAINE, *Its Attorney.*

No. 16

IN THE OFFICE OF THE STATE ENGINEER OF THE STATE OF NEVADA, CARSON CITY, NEVADA

In the Matter of the Adjudication of the Humboldt River and its Tributaries, Under the Preliminary Order of Determination, in re Proof No. 00241

OBJECTION AS TO LISTING OF ACREAGES AND DATES OF PRIORITY

Come now Mildred Elmore, Walter S. Elmore, Mildred C. Clubine, and Grace Kendricks, whose lands and water rights are listed under Proof No. 00241, in the Preliminary Order of Determination, in the matter of the Adjudication of the Humboldt River and its Tributaries, recently issued by the honorable State Engineer of the State of Nevada, by Edwin E. Caine, their attorney, and respectfully call the attention of the honorable State Engineer to the fact that there is a possibility of question as to the priorities and acreages claimed by them, and as the same appear in said Preliminary Order of Determination, in that it may not be possible to determine therefrom to just what subdivision certain acreages and priorities should be applied, and respectfully represent that their understanding of the lists as they appear in said Preliminary Order of Determination is that, where the water is not definitely listed as appurtenant to a particular subdivision, such water may be applied to the irrigated lands belonging to the undersigned, as the same appear in said Preliminary Order of Determination, and respectfully represents that, if such understanding is not correct, they hereby notify the State Engineer that they do not waive any rights in connection with said matter, and respectfully object to the manner in which said claims appear in said Preliminary Order of Determination, and asks that the same be corrected in accordance with the above understanding, or that said water be definitely listed to the land upon which the right attaches, as shown by said priorities and acreages.

Dated June 13, 1922.

MILDRED ELMORE,
WALTER S. ELMORE,
MILDRED C. CLUBINE,
GRACE KENDRICKS.
By EDWIN E. CAINE, *Their Attorney.*

No. 17

IN THE OFFICE OF THE STATE ENGINEER OF THE STATE OF NEVADA, CARSON CITY, NEVADA

In the Matter of the Adjudication of the Humboldt River and its Tributaries, Under the Preliminary Order of Determination, in re Proofs Nos. 00242, 00244, 00447, and 00421.

OBJECTION AS TO LISTING OF ACREAGES AND DATES OF PRIORITY

Comes now Charles W. Clubine, whose lands and water rights are listed under Proofs Nos. 00242, 00244, 00447 and 00421, in the Preliminary Order of Determination, in the matter of the Adjudication of the Humboldt River and its Tributaries, recently issued by the honorable State Engineer of the State of Nevada, by Edwin E. Caine, his attorney, and respectfully calls the attention of the honorable State Engineer to the fact that there is a possibility of question as to the priorities and acreages claimed by him, and as the same appear in said Preliminary Order of Determination, in that it may not be possible to determine therefrom to just what subdivision certain acreages and priorities should be applied, and respectfully represents that his understanding of the lists as they appear in said Preliminary Order of Determination is that, where the water is not definitely listed as appurtenant to a particular subdivision, such water may be applied to the irrigated lands belonging to the undersigned, as the same appear in said Preliminary Order of Determination, and respectfully represents that, if such understanding is not correct, he hereby notifies the State Engineer that he does not waive any rights in connection with said matter, and respectfully objects to the manner in which said claims appear in said Preliminary Order of Determination, and asks that the same be corrected in accordance with the above understanding, or that said water be definitely listed to the land upon which the right attaches, as shown by said priorities and acreages.

Dated this 13th day of June, 1922.

CHARLES W. CLUBINE,
By Edwin E. Caine, *His Attorney.*

No. 18

IN THE OFFICE OF THE STATE ENGINEER OF NEVADA

OBJECTIONS OF R. F. RAINE, AS ADMINISTRATOR OF THE ESTATE OF J. P. RAINE, DECEASED, AND ALSO IN HIS INDIVIDUAL CAPACITY.

In the Matter of the Preliminary Order of Determination of the Relative Rights in and to the Waters of the Humboldt River and its Tributaries

Comes now R. F. Raine, as administrator of the estate of J. P. Raine, deceased, and R. F. Raine in his individual capacity, whose postoffice address is Palisade, Eureka County, Nevada, and objects to the whole and to each and every part or portion of and to the several findings set out in the Preliminary Order of Determination establishing the

several rights of claimants to the waters of Humboldt River and its tributaries, as made by the State Engineer of the State of Nevada, under date April ...., 1922, in the above-entitled matter, and as grounds of said objections specify the following:

1. That the undersigned objector and the estate of J. P. Raine, deceased, of which he is administrator, are the owners of an usufruct in the waters of Pine Creek, a tributary of the Humboldt River, by appropriation, which said appropriation was made in the month of May, 1868; that said appropriation was made by the building of a dam in Pine Creek, and the construction of a ditch leading therefrom into the lands now owned by said objector situated in Sections 20, 29 and 32, Township 31 North, Range 52 East, M. D. B. & M., and by means of said dam and ditch conducting the water to and distributing it over the lands of said objector situated in said Sections 20, 29 and 32 above mentioned; that said dam and ditch was constructed by the predecessors in interest of said objectors during the month of May, A. D. 1868; that said ditch at the time of its construction was six (6) feet wide on top, four (4) feet wide on the bottom, two (2) feet deep, and was capable of conveying approximately seventeen and one-half (17½) cubic feet of water per second; that said ditch was constructed for the purpose of reclaiming and irrigating approximately one thousand (1,000) acres of land now owned by said objectors, and the waters of Pine Creek, by the using of said ditch, have been conveyed upon the lands of plaintiff every year since its construction, and said waters have been applied to a beneficial use and to the reclamation and irrigation of approximately five hundred (500) acres of the lands belonging to said objectors situated in Sections 20, 29 and 32, and said objectors are entitled by virtue of said appropriation to the prior use of seventeen and one-half (17½) cubic feet per second of the waters of Pine Creek, to irrigate their lands situated in Sections 20, 29, and 32, Township 31 North, Range 52 East.

2. That said Preliminary Order of Determination is invalid in that it appears from the face of said Preliminary Order of Determination that it was made in violation of and does not comply with or conform to the requirements of the statutes of the State of Nevada, under which it purports to have been made.

3. That said Preliminary Order of Determination is invalid in that it appears from the face thereof that the several rights of the claimants to the waters of Pine Creek cannot be ascertained therefrom because no dates or data is stated therein as to when the several rights of the objectors or any of the claimants to the waters of said Pine Creek, a tributary of said Humboldt River, was initiated by the commencement of the construction, completion or enlargement of any of the works by means of which the waters claimed by the objector or any other claimants to the waters of said stream were diverted from the source for the beneficial use claimed by the objector or any of the claimants to the waters of said Pine Creek and its tributaries.

4. That said Preliminary Order of Determination is invalid in that no date or number of priority of the objector or any of the claimants to the waters of Pine Creek is stated therein; neither is there any fact or facts stated in said Preliminary Order of Determination from which the priority of the objector or any of the claimants to the waters of Pine Creek can be ascertained or determined.

5. That said Preliminary Order of Determination is invalid in that it appears from the face of said Preliminary Order of Determination that one of the fundamental and essential elements in determining and establishing the several rights of the claimants to the waters of said Pine Creek, namely, the "doctrine of relation," is not considered, but has been rejected by the State Engineer in making said Preliminary Order of Determination, establishing the several rights of claimants to the waters of Pine Creek and its tributaries.

6. That said Preliminary Order of Determination is invalid in that it does not appear therefrom nor can it be ascertained or determined from said Preliminary Order of Determination where the point of diversion is located, by means of which said objector or any of the claimants to the waters of said Pine Creek and its tributaries divert the water claimed from said source for beneficial uses.

7. That said Preliminary Order of Determination is invalid in that said State Engineer has failed, neglected and refused to apply in said Preliminary Order of Determination establishing the several rights of claimants to the waters of said Pine Creek and its tributaries, court decrees and judgments rendered and entered by the District Court of the State of Nevada, wherein and whereby the rights of said objector and the several claimants to the waters of Pine Creek and its tributaries have been adjudicated and determined.

8. That said Preliminary Order of Determination is defective, indefinite, uncertain and insufficient, and does not state facts sufficient to constitute an order of determination establishing the several rights of the objector or any of the claimants to the waters of Pine Creek and its tributaries for and because of all and each of the reasons hereinbefore stated as to why said Preliminary Order of Determination is invalid.

10. That said Preliminary Order of Determination is invalid, erroneous and defective:

a. In that by said Preliminary Order of Determination a water right is attempted to be awarded to Bell B. Ennor, Hurburt B. Ennor and Sarah P. Ennor, dating back to the year 1870, for lands that were swampy and overflowed lands up to the year 1910, and for which no attempted appropriation of water was made to irrigate said lands prior to the year 1910.

b. In that by said Preliminary Order of Determination a water right is attempted to be awarded to swamp lands belonging to other claimants upon Pine Creek and its tributaries, all of which attempted awards is contrary to and in violation of the law governing water rights in the State of Nevada.

11. That said Preliminary Order of Determination is erroneous, defective and incorrect in that it does not award to said objector the water rights to which he is entitled and for which claim was made by him as a set-out in a statement of claim filed in the office of the State Engineer of the State of Nevada.

12. That said Preliminary Order of Determination is invalid in that it attempts to determine the priorities of the right to the use of the waters of Pine Creek as between the objector and Bell B. Ennor, Hurburt B. Ennor and Sarah P. Ennor, at a time when a suit is pending in the Fourth Judicial District Court of the State of Nevada, in and for the County of Elko, wherein the said objector is plaintiff and the said Bell B. Ennor, Hurburt B. Ennor and Sarah P. Ennor are defen-

dants, which suit was brought and is being prosecuted to determine, among other things, the priority of rights of the several parties above mentioned to the waters of Pine Creek and its tributaries, and at a time when an injunction is in full force and effect, preventing the said Bell B. Ennor, Hurburt B. Ennor and Sarah P. Ennor from interfering with the use by the said objector to the waters of Pine Creek and its tributaries for irrigating purposes.

13. That said Preliminary Order of Determination is invalid in this, that it attempts to determine the relative rights to the use of the waters of Pine Creek and their priorities in disregard of the fact that there is a prior suit pending between the parties over the same subject-matter and within the same jurisdiction.

Wherefore, objector prays that the objections hereinabove made upon hearing be sustained and that said Preliminary Order of Determination be modified, changed and corrected in conformity with said objections, and that said Preliminary Order of Determination as it now exists be declared and held to be invalid, erroneous and defective and of no force, virtue, and effect, and further, that it be declared to be a cloud and encumbrance upon and as impairing and invading the vested rights of the objector named herein.

R. F. RAINE.

By B. F. CURLER, *Attorney for Objector.*

State of Nevada, County of Washoe, ss.

R. F. Raine, being duly sworn, deposes and says: That in his individual capacity and as administrator of the estate of J. P. Raine, deceased, he claims an interest in the stream-system comprising the waters of the Humboldt River and its tributaries, involved in the determination of relative rights, the Preliminary Order of Determination of which has been made by the State Engineer; that such claim to the waters of the said stream-system is under vested rights; that he has read the foregoing objections to the findings and the portion of the Preliminary Order of Determination made with respect to the claims of Bell B. Ennor, Herbert B. Ennor and Sarah P. Ennor, found on pages 186 and 187 of the Preliminary Order of Determination of the Waters of the Humboldt River and its Tributaries, the source being Pine Creek, and to the Preliminary Order of Determination of J. P. Raine, claimant, found on pages 183, 184 and 185 of the Preliminary Order of Determination of the Waters of Humboldt River and its Tributaries, and that the said objections are true, except as to the matters therein stated on his information and belief, and as to those matters he believes it to be true.

R. F. RAINE.

Subscribed and sworn to before me this 15th day of June, 1922.

[SEAL] B. F. CURLER, *Notary Public.*

No. 19

OBJECTION

To the Hon. J. G. Scrugham, State Engineer, Carson City, Nevada.

State of Nevada, County of Eureka, ss.

W. S. Yates, being first duly sworn, on oath deposes and says:

That he is a resident of Palisade, County of Eureka, State of

Nevada, and hereby files objections against the Preliminary Order of Determination of the waters of Humboldt River and its tributaries as compiled by the State Engineer in 1922, as shown on pages 185 and 186, under the name of W. S. Yates, for the waters of Smith and Pine Creeks, together with tributaries;

That there should be listed 260.81 acres in Sections 4 and 5, Township 29 North, Range 52 East, M. D. B. & M., and Sections 16, 21, 32, and 33, Township 30 North, Range 52 East, M. D. B. & M., with the date of 1871;

That said area of 260.81 acres is meadow and pasture land that was first cultivated in 1871, as shown by the testimony on file in the office of the State Engineer at Carson City, Nevada, and that the testimony, documentary evidence and proofs produced at the hearing of the State Engineer by your affiant and other water-users on Pine Creek show and substantiate the claim of your affiant and establish the date of 1871 as the first known irrigation of said lands; that the State Engineer made typographical error in the preliminary findings above referred to and that none of the above lands referred to bear date of 1871, but bear dates subsequent thereto; that the oral testimony and documentary evidence make it possible for definite corrections and that more proof is now available than was available at the time of the testimony taken by the deputy from the office of the State Engineer;

That by reason of this objection your affiant also claims the right to correct any and all other dates and areas that are listed, if witnesses are available to prove the same.

Wherefore, your affiant respectfully requests that the State Engineer review the testimony, documentary evidence and proofs on file in his office, and make such other and further corrections as may be meet and just.

W. S. YATES.

Subscribed and sworn to before me this 14th day of June, 1922.

ROBERT A. ALLEN, *Assistant State Engineer.*

No. 20

IN THE OFFICE OF THE STATE ENGINEER OF NEVADA

In the Matter of the Preliminary Order of Determination of the Relative Rights in and to the Waters of the Humboldt River and its Tributaries

OBJECTIONS OF R. F. RAINE, AS ADMINISTRATOR OF THE ESTATE OF J. P. RAINE, DECEASED, AND ALSO IN HIS INDIVIDUAL CAPACITY.

Comes now R. F. Raine, as administrator of the estate of J. P. Raine, deceased, and in his individual capacity, whose postoffice address is Palisade, Eureka County, Nevada, and objects to the Preliminary Order of Determination, establishing the rights of Bell B. Ennor, Hurburt B. Ennor and Sarah P. Ennor, to the waters of Pine Creek, a

tributary of the Humboldt River, made by the State Engineer of the State of Nevada, under date April ...., 1922, and as grounds for said objections alleges as follows, to wit:

1. That said objector, both as administrator and in his individual capacity, is an owner of an usufruct in the waters of Pine Creek, a tributary of the Humboldt River, and the said J. P. Raine, during his lifetime, and the said R. F. Raine, as administrator of the estate of J. P. Raine, deceased, and in his individual capacity, and the predecessors in interest of the said J. P. Raine, were and are appropriators and users of water from Pine Creek, a tributary of the Humboldt River; that the water claimed by the said R. F. Raine, aforesaid, was appropriated by the said J. P. Raine, and his predecessors in interest, at various times during the year from and including the year 1868 and has been by said objector, the said J. P. Raine, and the predecessors in interest of the said J. P. Raine, beneficially used continuously since the years in which said water was appropriated to the present time for a beneficial use.

2. That as to the rights between said objector and C. H. Rand to the waters of Trout and Pine Creek, the same were settled and adjusted in that certain action entitled J. P. Raine, plaintiff v. Frank Perry, defendant, tried and determined in the District Court of the Fourth Judicial District of the State of Nevada, in and for the County of of Elko, on the 17th day of September, 1896, and that the rights of said objector, so far as the claims of said C. H. Rand are concerned, were and are settled and determined as between said parties by virtue of the fact that the said objector has succeeded to the rights of J. P. Raine growing out of said suit, and that C. H. Rand, has derived his title to the water and land described in the Preliminary Order of Determination by mesne conveyance from the said Frank A. Perry; that said decree has never been modified and is in full force and effect and, as between the said objector and the said C. H. Rand, is res adjudicata.

Wherefore, said objector prays that said Preliminary Order of Determination be modified after the hearing had thereon, and that said claim of C. H. Rand adjusted in accordance with the proof to be adduced upon said hearing.

R. F. RAINE.

By B. F. Curler, *Attorney for Objector.*

State of Nevada, County of Washoe, ss.

B. F. Curler, being duly sworn, deposes and says: That he is the attorney of the objector in the foregoing objection; that he has read the same and knows the contents thereof, and that the same is true of his own knowledge except as to the matter therein stated on his information and belief, and that as to those matters he believes it to be true.

B. F. CURLER,

Subscribed and sworn to before me this 20th day of June, A. D. 1922.

Robert A. Allen, *Assistant State Engineer.*

No. 21

IN THE OFFICE OF THE STATE ENGINEER OF NEVADA

In the Matter of the Preliminary Order of Determination of the Relative Rights in and to the Waters of the Humboldt River and its Tributaries

OBJECTIONS OF R. F. RAINE, AS ADMINISTRATOR OF THE ESTATE OF J. P. RAINE, DECEASED, AND ALSO IN HIS INDIVIDUAL CAPACITY.

Comes now R. F. Raine, as administrator of the estate of J. P. Raine, deceased, and in his individual capacity, whose postoffice address is Palisade, Eureka County, Nevada, and objects to the Preliminary Order of Determination, establishing the rights of Bell B. Ennor, Hurburt B. Ennor and Sarah P. Ennor, to the waters of Pine Creek, a tributary of the Humboldt River, made by the State Engineer of the State of Nevada, under date April ...., 1922, and as grounds for said objections alleges as follows, to wit:

1. That said objector, both as administrator and in his individual capacity, is an owner of an usufruct in the waters of Pine Creek, a tributary of the Humboldt River, and the said J. P. Raine, during his lifetime, and the said R. F. Raine, as administrator of the estate of J. P. Raine, deceased, and in his individual capacity, and the predecessors in interest of the said J. P. Raine, were and are appropriators and users of water from Pine Creek, a tributary of the Humboldt River; that the water claimed by the said R. F. Raine, aforesaid, was appropriated by the said J. P. Raine, and his predecessors in interest, at various times during the year from and including the year 1868, and has been by said objector, the said J. P. Raine, and the predecessors in interest of the said J. P. Raine, beneficially used continuously since the years in which said water was appropriated to the present time for a beneficial use.

2. That during the year 1896 in a suit then pending and determined by the Third Judicial District Court of the State of Nevada, in and for the County of Eureka, in which the prior right to the waters of Pine Creek and its tributaries, as between the predecessors in interest of your objector and the predecessor in interest of the said Bell B. Ennor, Hurburt B. Ennor and Sarah P. Ennor, were involved, and judgment was rendered by which it was determined that the said predecessor in interest of your objector had a prior right over the predecessor in interest of the said Bell B. Ennor, Hurburt B. Ennor and Sarah P. Ennor, to the use of the waters of Pine Creek, and its tributaries, to the extent of seven hundred (700) miners' inches of water; that said judgment upon appeal was affirmed by the Supreme Court of the State of Nevada; that said judgment has never been set aside or in any particular modified, and as between the said objector and the said Bell B. Ennor, Hurburt B. Ennor and Sarah P. Ennor, is res adjudicata; that, despite said judgment and in disregard thereof, said Preliminary Order of Determination attempts to give to said Bell B. Ennor, Huburt B. Ennor and Sarah P. Ennor, a priority to the use of the waters of Pine Creek and its tributaries, over your objector.

3. That said Preliminary Order of Determination pretends to grant to the said Bell B. Ennor, Hurburt B. Ennor and Sarah P. Ennor a priority for the irrigation of 32.07 acres in the W$\frac{1}{2}$ of the NW$\frac{1}{4}$ of

Section 16; and for 32.60 acres in the E½ of the NE¼ of Section 17; and for 29.14 acres in the SE¼ of Section 8; and for 19.63 acres in the SE¼ of the SE¼ of Section 8, all in Township 30 North, Range 52 East, M. D. B. & M., under date of 1870, whereas, in truth and in fact, said land was not settled upon or any ditch taken out of Pine Creek on the said or any portion of said land prior to the year 1872, and that any ditch taken out of Pine Creek in the year 1872 was not of sufficient capacity to irrigate to exceed fifteen (15) acres of land, and that no more than fifteen (15) acres of said or any land upon the Ennor Ranch was irrigated by said ditch or otherwise prior to the year 1888.

3. That prior to the year 1888 all of said land excepting about fifteen (15) acres was swamp and tule land, and until drained did not need water for irrigation, and no water was used on said land for irrigation prior to the year 1888 except for about fifteen (15) acres.

4. That said undersigned objector objects to the Preliminary Order of Determination wherein the said Bell B. Ennor, Hurburt B. Ennor and Sarah P. Ennor are granted a right to irrigate 478.42 acres in Sections 5, 8, 9, 17 and 17 of Township 30 North, Range 52 East, M. D. B. & M. under priorities dating from the year 1879 to 1898, on the ground that prior to the year 1910 all of said land was swamp and tule and did not need irrigation, and no water was conducted through any ditches or by any artificial works over or upon said land for irrigation, but that any and all ditches upon said land were constructed and used for drainage purposes exclusively, and that no ditches were constructed upon said land prior to the year 1883, and said ditches were used after their construction and up to the year 1919 for drainage purposes only; and upon the further ground that the land in Section 5 was purchased by the predecessors in interest of said Bell B. Ennor, Hurburt B. Ennor and Sarah P. Ennor from J. P. Raine, now deceased, in the year 1882, and in the deed of conveyance conveying to the predecessors in interest of the said Bell B. Ennor, Hurburt B. Ennor and Sarah P. Ennor all water and water rights theretofore used by the said J. P. Raine was expressly reserved from said deed.

5. And in connection with this objection said objector alleges that all of said matters set forth in his grounds of objections are true of his own knowledge since the year 1889, and that as to all other matters contained in this objection said objector is informed and believes and upon such information and belief alleges the fact to be that said grounds of objection are based upon the actual facts as they then existed, and are true.

Wherefore, said objector prays that said Preliminary Order of Determination be modified after the hearing had thereon and that said claims be rejected in accordance with the proof to be adduced upon said hearing.

R. F. RAINE.
By B. F. CURLER, *Attorney for Objector.*

State of Nevada, County of Washoe, ss.

B. F. Curler, being duly sworn, deposes and says: That he is the attorney for the objector in the above-entitled objection; that he has read the same and knows the contents thereof; that your affiant has been familiar with the matters involved in the determination of the

waters of Pine Creek, a tributary of the Humboldt River, for a great many years; that since the year 1896 he has been very familiar with the conditions existing with respect to said land and the water rights involved; that he has examined the testimony taken in previous controversies respecting the water rights and the judgments entered therein; that he has also examined many witnesses respecting the conditions existing in Pine Valley, said witnesses claiming to know the condition existing therein since 1868; that to the best of your affiant's knowledge, information and belief, said objections are true; that this affidavit is made by said attorney because the objector is not now present in Washoe County Nevada.

B. F. CURLER,

Subscribed and sworn to before me this..........day of June, A. D. 1922.

[SEAL] JOHN S. SINAI, *Notary Public.*

No. 22

IN THE OFFICE OF THE STATE ENGINEER OF THE STATE OF NEVADA, CARSON CITY, NEVADA

In the Matter of the Adjudication of the Humboldt River and its Tributaries, under the Preliminary Order of Determination, in re Proof No. 00375

OBJECTION AS TO LISTING OF ACREAGE AND DATES OF PRIORITY

Come now Minnie Hankins, Lillie Hankins, Elizabeth Hankins and Estate of Jane Bellinger, whose lands and water rights are listed under Proof No. 00375, in the Preliminary Order of Determination, in the Matter of the Adjudication of the Humboldt River and its Tributaries, recently issued by the honorable State Engineer of the State of Nevada, by Edwin E. Caine, their attorney, and respectfully call the attention of the honorable State Engineer to the fact that there is a possibility of question as to the priorities and acreages claimed by them, and as the same appear in said Preliminary Order of Determination, in that it may not be possible to determine therefrom to just what subdivision certain acreages and priorities should be applied, and respectfully represent that their understanding of the lists, as they appear in said Preliminary Order of Determination, is that, where the water is not definitely listed as appurtenant to a particular subdivision, such water may be applied to the irrigated lands belonging to the undersigned, as the same appear in said Preliminary Order of Determination, and respectfully represent that, if such understanding is not correct, they hereby notify the State Engineer that they do not waive any right in connection with said matter, and respectfully object to the manner in which said claims appear in said Preliminary Order of Determination, and ask that the same be corrected in accordance with the above understanding, or that said

water be definitely listed to the land upon which the right attaches, as shown by said priorities and acreages.

Dated this 13th day of June, 1922.

MINNIE HANKINS,
LILLIE HANKINS,
ELIZABETH HANKINS,
ESTATE OF JANE BELLINGER.
By Edwin E. Caine, *Their Attorney.*

No. 23

IN THE OFFICE OF THE STATE ENGINEER OF THE STATE OF NEVADA, CARSON CITY, NEVADA

In the Matter of the Adjudication of the Humboldt River and its Tributaries, under the Preliminary Order of Determination, in re Proof No. 00405

OBJECTION AS TO LISTING OF ACREAGES AND DATES OF PRIORITY

Comes now Hankins-Bellinger Company, a corporation, whose lands and water rights are listed under Proof No. 00405, in the Preliminary Order of Determination, in the Matter of the Adjudication of the Humboldt River and its Tributaries, recently issued by the honorable State Engineer of the State of Nevada, by Edwin E. Caine, its attorney, and respectfully calls the attention of the honorable State Engineer to the fact that there is a possibility of question as to the priorities and acreages claimed by it, and as the same appear in said Preliminary Order of Determination, in that it may not be possible to determine therefrom to just what subdivision certain acreages and priorities should be applied, and respectfully represents that its understanding of the lists, as they appear in said Preliminary Order of Determination, is that, where the water is not definitely listed as appurtenant to a particular subdivision, such water may be applied to the irrigated lands belonging to the undersigned, as the same appear in said Preliminary Order of Determination, and respectfully represents that, if such understanding is not correct, it hereby notifies the State Engineer that it does not waive any rights in connection with said matter, and respectfully objects to the manner in which said claims appear in said Preliminary Order of Determination, and asks that the same be corrected, in accordance with the above understanding, or that said water be definitely listed to the land upon which the right attaches, as shown by said priorities and acreages.

Dated this 13th day of June, 1922.

HANKINS-BELLINGER COMPANY.
By Edwin E. Caine, *Its Attorney.*

No. 24

IN THE OFFICE OF THE STATE ENGINEER OF THE STATE OF NEVADA

In the Matter of the Preliminary Order of Determination of the Waters of Humboldt River and its Tributaries

OBJECTION OF SAMUEL McINTYRE INVESTMENT COMPANY

Samuel McIntyre Investment Company, a corporation, hereinafter called the objector, and being the successor in interest of all rights of Samuel McIntyre, objects to the findings of the State Engineer of the State of Nevada as made in his Preliminary Order of Determination of the Waters of the Humboldt River and its Tributaries, and particularly to those parts or portions of said Preliminary Order as hereinafter more specifically set forth; and said objector respectfully shows:

I

That it claims an interest in the said stream-system and claims a right to the use of waters thereof under vested rights vesting in said objector and its predecessors in interest prior to 1905.

II

That said objector has heretofore filed proofs of claim with the State Engineer of the State of Nevada and hereby refers to and makes a part hereof all of the said objector's proofs, amended proofs, maps and amended maps on file with the State Engineer in said matter and particularly the copy of the judgment and decision of the Fourth Judicial District Court of the State of Nevada, in and for the County of Elko, in that certain action entitled Samuel McIntyre Investment Company, plaintiff, v. Benard Pearson, defendant.

III

That said objector particularly objects to that part or portion of the said Preliminary Order as (A) contained on page 222 thereof under the priorities listed as 1872, 1883, 1884, 1885, 1886, 1887, 1888, 1889, aggregating 1,338.5 acres. Said objection is made upon the ground that only eighty acres are here given a priority of 1872 and that the following lands should be given a priority of said year of 1872, or earlier, to wit:

18.90 acres in SE¼SW¼ of Sec. 15, T. 34 N, R. 58 E.
39.10 acres in NE¼NW¼ of Sec. 22, T. 34 N, R. 58 E.
37.90 acres in NW¼NW¼ of Sec. 22, T. 34 N, R. 58 E.
39.60 acres in SE¼NW¼ of Sec. 22, T. 34 N, R. 58 E.
40.00 acres in SW¼NW¼ of Sec. 22, T. 34 N, R. 58 E.
80.00 acres in N½SW¼ of Sec. 22, T. 34 N, R. 58 E.
36.00 acres in SE¼SW¼ of Sec. 22, T. 34 N, R. 58 E.
37.00 acres in SW¼SW¼ of Sec. 22, T. 34 N, R. 58 E.
25.80 acres in SE¼NE¼ of Sec. 21, T. 34 N, R. 58 E.
25.00 acres in NE¼NE¼ of Sec. 21, T. 34 N, R. 58 E.
37.90 acres in NE¼SE¼ of Sec. 21, T. 34 N, R. 58 E.
3.60 acres in NE¼SE¼ of Sec. 21, T. 34 N, R. 58 E.
11.95 acres in SW¼SE¼ of Sec. 21, T. 34 N, R. 58 E.
37.00 acres in SE¼SE¼ of Sec. 21, T. 34 N, R. 58 E.

Objector alleges that the waters of Lamoille Creek were appropriated, diverted and beneficially used upon said acreages commencing with the year 1872.

(B) That said objector objects to the classification and listing of said lands under Secret Creek and Lamoille Creek as shown on page 222 of said Preliminary Order and alleges that the following lands should be listed under the source "Secret Creek and Soldier Creek," to wit: All of the listed lands shown in Section 19, T. 35 N, R. 59 E, and thirty acres in NE¼NE¼ of Section 24 and 32.9 acres in SE¼NE¼ of Section 24, T. 35 N, R. 58 E, being the lands irrigated by Secret and Soldier Creeks before any Lamoille water is merged with said creeks from that certain ditch referred to in the Gorlinski maps as Upper Ditch from Reservoir and likewise indicated upon the Taylor & Jepson map; that the lands below the junction of said Lamoille ditch with Secret Creek in Section 13 and 24, 10, 11, 14 and 15, T. 35 N, R. 58 E, should be listed under Lamoille, Secret and Soldier.

(C) That the said lands as listed on page 264 of said Preliminary Order to claimant Samuel McIntyre, source North Fork of Humboldt, to wit, an aggregate of 443.73 acres, should be given a priority dating from 1870. Said objection is made upon the ground that said land was irrigated from said source and the water from said source appropriated and beneficially used upon said lands by objector and its predecessors commencing with said year of 1870, to the best of said objector's knowledge, information and belief.

(D) That the lands listed to claimant Griswold-Henderson Livestock Company on page 231 under source Cold Creek should be listed under "Hamilton Creek, a fork of Cold Creek"; that such change is in accordance with the agreement referred to in the foot-note on said page and in accordance with views expressed by counsel for said claimant.

IV

That it has been impossible for said objector to make a complete examination and checking of all lands listed to objector or of allowances made to other claimants upon the same sources; that objector reserves the right to make further checking and to insist that its acreages be further increased and its priorities allowed as of earlier dates, and that the filing of these objections shall not be construed as a waiver of such right or a waiver of the right of said objector to show that the acreages allowed to other claimants are excessive or the priorities too early.

V

Said objector further alleges that the length of the irrigating season as fixed for all of its said lands under classification of Harvest Crops, to wit, from April 15 to August 15, does not embrace the limits of the full irrigating season during which water is diverted from the said sources upon the said lands of objector; and in this respect objector alleges that the irrigating season varies from year to year and often commences early in the month of March and ends after the 15th of October.

VI

Said objector further alleges that these objections are made for the reasons herein stated and are not to be construed as a waiver on the

part of said objector of its right to object to the legality or validity of the said Preliminary Order on the ground that the same is not made in the manner provided by statute or upon the ground that the said statute whereunder the same is purported to be made is unconstitutional and void.

Wherefore, said objector prays that these objections be set for hearing in the manner provided by law and that notice of such hearing be duly given and that after a full hearing of said objections the same be sustained and allowed and the said Preliminary Order modified accordingly.

MILTON B. BADT & JAMES DYSART,
Attorneys for Objector.

State of Nevada, County of Elko, ss.

Frank McIntyre, being first duly sworn, deposes and says that he is an officer, to wit, the Vice-President and Secretary of Samuel McIntyre Investment Company, the objector named in the foregoing objections: that he has read said objections and knows the contents thereof and that the same are true of his own knowledge, except as to those matters therein stated on his information and belief, and that as to such matters he believes them to be true.

FRANK McINTYRE.

Subscribed and sworn to before me, this 9th day of June, A. D. 1922.
[SEAL] MILTON B. BADT, *Notary Public.*

No. 25

IN THE OFFICE OF THE STATE ENGINEER OF THE STATE OF NEVADA, CARSON CITY, NEVADA

In the Matter of the Adjudication of the Humboldt River and its Tributaries, under the Preliminary Order of Determination, in re Proof No. 00421

OBJECTION AS TO LISTING OF ACREAGES AND DATES OF PRIORITY

Comes now Henry Voight, whose lands and water rights are listed under Proof No. 00421, in the Preliminary Order of Determination, in the matter of the adjudication of the Humboldt River and its tributaries, recently issued by the honorable State Engineer of the State of Nevada, by Edwin E. Caine, his attorney, and respectfully calls the attention of the honorable State Engineer to the fact that there is a possibility of question as to the priorities and acreages claimed by him, and as the same appear in said Preliminary Order of Determination, in that it may not be possible to determine therefrom to just what subdivison certain acreages and priorities should be applied, and respectfully represents that his understanding of the lists, as they appear in said Preliminary Order of Determination, is that, where the water is not definitely listed as appurtenant to a particular subdivision, such water may be applied to the irrigated lands belonging to the undersigned as the same appear in said Preliminary Order of Determination,

and respectfully represents that, if such understanding is not correct, he hereby notifies the State Engineer that he does not waive any rights in connection with said matter, and respectfully objects to the manner in which said claims appear in said Preliminary Order of Determination, and asks that the same be corrected in accordance with the above understanding, or that said water be definitely listed to the land upon which the right attaches, as shown by said priorities and acreages.

Dated this 13th day of June, 1922.

HENRY VOIGHT.
By Edwin E. Caine, *His Attorney.*

No. 26

IN THE OFFICE OF THE STATE ENGINEER OF THE STATE OF NEVADA, CARSON CITY, NEVADA

In the Matter of the Adjudication of the Humboldt River and its Tributaries, under the Preliminary Order of Determination, in re Proof No. 00423

OBJECTION AS TO LISTING OF ACREAGES AND DATES OF PRIORITY

Comes now Hunter & Lytton, a copartnership, whose lands and water rights are listed under Proof No. 00423, in the Preliminary Order of Determination, in the matter of the adjudication of the Humboldt River and its tributaries, recently issued by the honorable State Engineer of the State of Nevada, by Edwin E. Caine, its attorney, and respectfully calls the attention of the honorable State Engineer to the fact that there is a possibility of question as to the priorities and acreages claimed by it, and as the same appear in said Preliminary Order of Determination, in that it may not be possible to determine therefrom to just what subdivision certain acreages and priorities should be applied, and respectfully represents that its understanding of the lists, as they appear in said Preliminary Order of Determination, is that, where the water is not definitely listed as appurtenant to a particular subdivison, such water may be applied to the irrigated lands belonging to the undersigned, as the same appear in said Preliminary Order of Determination, and respectfully represents that, if such understanding is not correct, it hereby notifies the State Engineer that it does not waive any rights in connection with said matter, and respectfully objects to the manner in which said claim appears in said Preliminary Order of Determination, and asks that the same be corrected in accordance with the above understanding, or that said water be definitely listed to the land upon which the right attaches, as shown by said priorities and acreages.

Dated this 13th day of June, 1922.

HUNTER & LYTTON.
By Edwin E. Caine, *Its Attorney.*

No. 27

IN THE OFFICE OF THE STATE ENGINEER OF THE STATE OF NEVADA, CARSON CITY, NEVADA

In the Matter of the Adjudication of the Humboldt River and its Tributaries, under the Preliminary Order of Determination, in re Proof No. 00430

OBJECTION AS TO LISTING OF ACREAGES AND DATES OF PRIORITY

Comes now Webster Patterson, whose lands and water rights are listed under Proof No. 00430, in the Preliminary Order of Determination, in the matter of the adjudication of the Humboldt River and its tributaries, recently issued by the honorable State Engineer of the State of Nevada, by Edwin E. Caine, his attorney, and respectfully calls the attention of the honorable State Engineer to the fact that there is a possibility of question as to the priorities and acreages claimed by him, and as the same appear in said Preliminary Order of Determination, in that it may not be possible to determine therefrom to just what subdivision certain acreages and priorities should be applied, and respectfully represents that his understanding of the lists, as they appear in said Preliminary Order of Determination, is that, where the water is not definitely listed as appurtenant to a particular subdivision, such water may be applied to the irrigated lands belonging to the undersigned, as the same appear in said Preliminary Order of Determination, and respectfully represents that, if such understanding is not correct, he hereby notifies the State Engineer that he does not waive any rights in connection with said matter, and respectfully objects to the manner in which said claims appear in said Preliminary Order of Determination, and asks that the same be corrected in accordance with the above understanding, or that said water be definitely listed to the land upon which the right attaches, as shown by said priorities and acreages.

Dated this 13th day of June, 1922.

WEBSTER PATTERSON,
By Edwin E. Caine, *His Attorney.*

No. 28

IN THE OFFICE OF THE STATE ENGINEER OF THE STATE OF NEVADA, CARSON CITY, NEVADA

In the Matter of the Adjudication of the Humboldt River and its Tributaries, under the Preliminary Order of Determination, in re Proofs Nos. 00431, 00442, 00443, 00446 and 00572.

OBJECTION AS TO LISTING OF ACREAGES AND DATES OF PRIORITY

Comes now Robert B. Stewart, whose lands and water rights are listed under Proofs Nos. 00431, 00442, 00443, 00446, and 00572, in the Preliminary Order of Determination, in the matter of the Adjudication

of the Humboldt River and its Tributaries, recently issued by the honorable State Engineer of the State of Nevada, by Edwin E. Caine, his attorney, and respectfully calls the attention of the honorable Engineer to the fact that there is a possibility of question as to the priorities and acreages claimed by him, and as the same appear in said Preliminary Order of Determination, in that it may not be possible to determine therefrom to just what subdivision certain acreages and priorities should be applied, and respectfully represents that his understanding of the lists, as they appear in said Preliminary Order of Determination, is that, where the water is not definitely listed as appurtenant to a particular subdivision, such water may be applied to the irrigated lands belonging to the undersigned, as the same appear in said Preliminary Order of Determination, and respectfully represents that, if such understanding is not correct, he hereby notifies the State Engineer that he does not waive any rights in connection with said matter, and respectfully objects to the manner in which said claims appear in said Preliminary Order of Determination, and asks that the same be corrected in accordance with the above understanding, or that said water be definitely listed to the land upon which the right attaches, as shown by said priorities and acreages.

Dated this 13th day of June, 1922.

ROBERT B. STEWART.
By EDWIN E. CAINE, *His Attorney.*

No. 29

IN THE OFFICE OF THE STATE ENGINEER OF THE STATE OF NEVADA

In the Matter of Proof No. 00444 of Andrew Westlund, as compiled by the Office of the State Engineer and issued in the year 1922

PROTEST OF RALPH McCOY AND JAMES DYSART

Ralph McCoy and James Dysart hereby protest against the proof of appropriation of Andrew Westlund, being Proof No. 00444 filed in the office of the State Engineer of the State of Nevada, and for grounds of protest allege:

1. That the protestants' names are Ralph McCoy and James Dysart.
2. That the proof against which this protest is filed is Proof No. 00444 filed by Andrew Westlund in the office of the State Engineer of the State of Nevada, in connection with the adjudication of the waters of the Humboldt River system.
3. That the source of the water supply mentioned in said proof is Lamoille Creek and Snell Creek, located in Elko County, Nevada.
4. That the grounds for protest are as follows: That the said Andrew Westlund claims a water right from said Lamoille Creek for one hundred twelve and fifty hundredths (112.50) acres for the irrigation of a portion of the West half (W½) of the East half (E½) of Section 29, Township 33 North, Range 58 East, M. D. B. & M., and claims a water

right from Snell Creek for forty-seven and fifty hundredths (47.50) acres to irrigate a portion of the West half (W½) of the East half (E½) of Section 29, Township 33 North, Range 58 East, M. D. B. & M.

That heretofore the said Andrew Weslund has made an application to change the place of use of certain waters from Snell Creek from the East half (E½) of the Northeast quarter (NE¼) of Section 29, Township 33 North, Range 58 East, to the West half (W½) of the East half (E½) of said section, township and range. That if said Andrew Westlund has owned a vested right to these waters for the East half (E½) of the Northeast quarter (NE¼) of said section, township and range, he abandoned the same by his failure to use said waters upon said lands for a period of more than five (5) years prior to the date of his said application.

That protestants are informed and believe, and therefore allege, that it is impossible for the said Andrew Westlund to irrigate a portion of the West half (W½) of the East half (E½) of said section, township and range, from either Snell Creek or Lamoille Creek, on account of the contour of the lands in this particular vicinity.

That protestants are informed and believe, and therefore allege, that the whole irrigated area of the lands belonging to Andrew Westlund shown under said proof do not exceed one hundred twelve and fifty hundredths (112.50) acres, and that there is at least forty-seven and fifty hundredths (47.50) acres within his lands for which he claims ownership upon which no water has ever been diverted and used and for which no water right exists.

That if said Andrew Westlund has a water right of one hundred twelve and fifty hundredths (112.50) acres from Lamoille Creek, it covers all of the land that he has under cultivation and irrigation on his property, and the said Andrew Westlund does not own a vested water right in and to the waters of Snell Creek in an amount sufficient to irrigate forty-seven and fifty hundredths (47.50) acres, or any other amount of water, or the right to the use of any waters of Snell Creek, as protestants are informed and believe and therefore allege.

Wherefore, protestants pray that said proof be disallowed and that protestants be given an opportunity to prove the conditions herein mentioned.

E. P. CARVILLE,
JAMES DYSART,
Attorneys for Protestants.

State of Nevada, County of Elko, ss.

Ralph McCoy and James Dysart, being first duly sworn, each for himself deposes and says: That he has read the foregoing instrument and knows the contents thereof, and the same is true to his own knowledge, except as to matters therein stated on information and belief and as to those matters he believes it to be true.

JAMES DYSART.
RALPH McCOY.

Subscribed and sworn to before me this 13th day of June, A. D. 1922.

[SEAL] E. P. CARVILLE, *Notary Public.*

No. 30

IN THE OFFICE OF THE STATE ENGINEER OF THE STATE OF NEVADA, CARSON CITY, NEVADA

In the Matter of the Adjudication of the Humboldt River and its Tributaries, under the Preliminary Order of Determination, in re Proof No. 00454

OBJECTION AS TO LISTING OF ACREAGES AND DATES OF PRIORITY

Comes now James Billet, whose lands and water rights are listed under Proof No. 00454, under the name of E. Hankins, in the Preliminary Order of Determination, in the Matter of the Adjudication of the Humboldt River and its Tributaries, recently issued by the honorable State Engineer of the State of Nevada, by Edwin E. Caine, his attorney, and respectfully calls the attention of the honorable State Engineer to the fact that there is a possibility of question as to the priorities and acreages claimed by him, and as the same appear in said Preliminary Order of Determination, in that it may not be possible to determine therefrom to just what subdivision certain acreages and priorities should be applied, and respectfully represents that his understanding of the lists, as they appear in said Preliminary Order of Determination, is that, where the water is not definitely listed as appurtenant to a particular subdivision, such water may be applied to the irrigated lands belonging to the undersigned, as the same appear in said Preliminary Order of Determination, and respectfully represents that, if such understanding is not correct, he hereby notifies the State Engineer that he does not waive any rights in connection with said matter, and respectfully objects to the manner in which said claims appear in said Preliminary Order of Determination, and asks that the same be corrected in accordance with the above understanding. or that said water be definitely listed to the land upon which the right attaches, as shown by said priorities and acreages.

Dated this 13th day of June, 1922.

JAMES BILLET.
By Edwin E. Caine, *His Attorney.*

No. 31
No. 32

IN THE OFFICE OF THE STATE ENGINEER OF THE STATE OF NEVADA

In the Matter of the Preliminary Order of Determination of the Waters of Humboldt River and its Tributaries

OBJECTION OF H. A. AGEE

Office Note: 00500—Agee. 00501—Smiley.

H. A. Agee, hereinafter called the objector, objects to the findings of the State Engineer of the State of Nevada as made in his Preliminary Order of Determination of the Waters of the Humboldt River

and its Tributaries, and particularly to that part or portion of said Preliminary Order as hereinafter more specifically set forth; and said objector respectfully shows:

I

That he claims an interest in the said stream-system and claims a right to the use of waters thereof under vested rights vesting in him and his predecessors in interest prior to 1905.

II

That said objector has heretofore filed proofs of claim with the State Engineer of the State of Nevada and hereby refers to and makes a part hereof all of the said objector's proofs, amended proofs, maps and amended maps on file with the State Engineer in said matter, and particularly the certified copy of judgment, findings and decree in that certain action entitled Ed Smiley and H. A. Agee, plaintiffs, v. Geo. Byers, et al., defendants, in the Fourth Judicial District Court of the State of Nevada, in and for the County of Elko, and to the copy of that certain agreement dated October 30, 1920, between said objector and one Ed. Smiley, all of which are on file in the office of said State Engineer.

III

That objector particularly objects to that part or portion of the said Preliminary Order as contained on pages 244 and 245 thereof under the caption "Claimant—H. A. Agee; Source—Hall Canyon Creek, Gray's Spring and Berger Creek; Proof No. 00501"; and particularly as follows:

A. On page 245 in column "Swamp or Overflow" the following are apparently typographical errors:

7.80 acres in NE¼SW¼—24, should be in SE¼SW¼—24
26.50 acres in NE¼SW¼—25, should be in NE¼NW¼—25

B. On said page the following acreages are listed and classed under the caption "Swamp or Overflow," to wit: 7.80, 26.50, 1.00, 21.20, 1.40, 5.60, 1.50, 19.20, 14.70, and 3.40, all being in Sections 24 and 25, T. 37 N, R. 60 E. All of said lands so listed should be listed and classified under the first column under caption of "Culture," to wit, as "Harvest Crops." Said objection is made upon the ground that the nature and character of said land and the nature and character of the culture thereon and irrigation thereof would thus be properly shown in place of being shown in the manner recited in said Preliminary Order: that all of said land so listed has been irrigated, cultivated and used by objector and his predecessors in interest from the dates, and long prior to the dates, as set forth opposite said respective acreages on page 245 of said Preliminary Order.

Said objection is further based upon the ground that the nature of the use of water on these acreages cannot be distinguished from the nature of its use on the lands of earlier priority. After the satisfaction of the first priority to Agee and Smiley for 543.40 acres, and the second priority to Byers for 69.30 acres, then the lands listed under paragraph III (B) hereof are entitled, as Class A lands, to such water as may be available, without increase of duty of water or shortening of length of irrigation season.

C. That all of the said acreages listed under subdivision B of paragraph III hereof should have an irrigation season from April 15 to

August 15 as provided for lands of similar class, in place of being given an irrigation season of from April 15 to May 15 as set forth on page 245 of said Preliminary Order; that this paragraph is not to be construed as a waiver on the part of said objector to claim that a longer irrigation season should be provided for all of his said lands listed on pages 244 and 245 of said order.

D. That to the note following the lands listed for Ed Smiley on page 244 of said Preliminary Order and listed for H. A. Agee on page 245 of said order and for lands listed under Hall Canyon Creek for Geo. Byers under said order should be added an additional note as follows, to wit:

> As between Ed Smiley, H. A. Agee and Geo. Byers in their claims to the waters of Hall Canyon Creek the said decree and contract provide as follows: That the said claimants Agee and Smiley are entitled to a first priority for an aggregate of 6.79 cubic feet per second for the irrigation of 543.40 acres of land; that the said claimant Byers is entitled to a second priority of .87 cubic feet per second for 69.30 acres of land; that the claimants Smiley and Agee are entitled to a third priority of 1.765 cubic feet per second for 141.30 acres of land; that said priorities are subject to certain deductions through the rights of said respective parties to divert the waters of certain other sources upon said respective acreages.

That the objections in this paragraph contained are upon the ground that the changes thus suggested in the said Preliminary Order will more closely conform with the said decree and will be more intelligible if so recited.

E. That the date of 1876 as recited in the last five lines on page 247 of said Preliminary Order should read 1886. This objection is made upon the ground that the said date 1876 is probably a typographical error, and that 1886 is the correct date for the first appropriation of water from said springs.

F. That the said acreages in the said last five lines of said page 247 should be listed under the caption "Source—Spring" instead of under the caption "Source—Hall Canyon Creek and Spring." Said objection is made upon the ground that such change or correction will correct the fact that said last five lines as shown are contrary to said decree.

G. That, in any event, the said last four lines of said page should likewise be indicated by an asterisk to refer to the foot-note immediately following, as well as the fifth line from the last.

IV

That said objector further objects to the said finding and particularly that portion thereof appearing under the title of "Fred and Frank Cleverly," on page 256 of said Preliminary Order, and in this respect alleges that the caption "Source—Hall's Canyon Creek, Blasingame Creek" should read "Source—Blasingame Creek." The ground of this objection is that the said claimants divert their said water, if any they do divert, and if any right so to divert such water the said claimants or either of them may have, from what is known as Blasingame Creek and not from Hall's Canyon Creek; that the said Blasingame Creek may be to some extent fed at certain seasons of the year from the flood waters of Hall's Canyon Creek, but that the said Blasingame

Creek is likewise fed to a greater extent by the waters from certain springs, draws, canyons and other sources than the said Hall's Canyon Creek; that in no event can the said claimants have any right to divert the waters of Hall's Canyon Creek or any right to be awarded such priority as might ripen into a right on their part to insist at any time or for any reason that this objector, or the said Ed. Smiley, cease or curtail his diversion of the waters of Hall's Canyon Creek for any reason whatsoever.

And as a further ground for this objection, said objector alleges that any rights that might have been initiated by the predecessors of said claimants for the waters of said Blasingame Creek were abandoned and forfeited by continuous nonuser for many years and that the only rights of said claimants to the waters of said Blasingame Creek are, if any, by way of appropriation or application to the State Engineer by the said present claimants themselves.

And as a further ground for this objection, said objector alleges that certain protests and contests were pending against the claims of the said Fred and Frank Cleverly at the time of the making of the said Preliminary Order of Adjudication and that said State Engineer made the said Preliminary Order without any hearing upon the said protests and contests and without any determination thereof.

These objections are made for the specific reasons herein set forth, and are not to be construed as a waiver on the part of said objector to the legality or validity of the said Preliminary Order on the grounds that the same is not made in the manner provided by statute or upon the grounds that the said statute whereunder the same is purported to be made is unconstitutional and void.

Wherefore, said objector prays that these objections be set for hearing in the manner provided by law and that notice of such hearing be duly given and that after a full hearing of said objections, the same be sustained and allowed and the said Preliminary Order modified accordingly.

H. A. AGEE.

MILTON B. BADT & JAMES DYSART, *Attorneys for Objector.*

State of Nevada, County of Elko, ss.

H. A. Agee, being first duly sworn, deposes and says that he is the objector named in the foregoing objections; that he has read said objections and knows the contents thereof and that the same are true of his own knowledge, except as to those matters therein stated on his information and belief, and that as to such matters he believes them to be true.

H. A. AGEE.

Subscribed and sworn to before me this 7th day of June, 1922.

[SEAL] D. A. HUGHES, *Notary Public.*

State of Nevada, County of Elko, ss.

Ed Smiley, being first duly sworn, deposes and says that he claims an interest in the said stream-system and a right to the use of the waters thereof under vested rights vesting in him and his predecessors in interest long prior to 1905; that he has heretofore filed proofs of claim herein, and hereby refers to his original and amended maps and proofs and to the said decree and agreement; that he has read the foregoing objections of the said H. A. Agee; that affiant joins in the

said objections and likewise prays that the said Preliminary Order be modified as therein prayed; that affiant has read said objections and knows the contents thereof and that the same are true of his own knowledge, except as those matters therein stated on his information and belief and that as to such matters he believes them to be true.

ED SMILEY.

Subscribed and sworn to before me this 7th day of June, 1922.

[SEAL] D. A. HUGHES, *Notary Public.*

No. 33

OBJECTION

To the Honorable J. G. Scrugham, State Engineer, Carson City, Nevada.

State of Nevada, County of Elko, ss.

S. M. Davis, being first duly sworn, on oath deposes and says:

That he is a resident of Deeth, Elko County, Nevada, and hereby files objection against the preliminary order of determination of the waters of the Humboldt River and its tributaries as compiled by the State Engineer in 1922, as shown on page 254, under the name of S. M. Davis, Ackler Creek;

That there should be listed 15 acres in the Northeast Quarter of Section 9, Township 36 North, Range 60 East, M. D. B. & M., with the date of 1873; also some area of pasture land that was omitted by the engineer making the survey, and should take the date the same as the adjoining land that is shown as meadow; that if the maps and notes that were used in the adjudication were available at this time it would be possible to make the definite corrections, but until such time as the copies are available it will be impossible to designate the exact areas and dates; that more proof is now available than was available at the time of the investigation by the deputy from your office;

That by reason of this objection protestant also claims the right to correct any other dates or areas that are listed, if witnesses are available to prove the same.

S. M. DAVIS.

Subscribed and sworn to before me this 10th day of June, 1922.

[SEAL] BERNICE H. WALTERS, *Notary Public.*

No. 34

IN THE OFFICE OF THE STATE ENGINEER OF THE STATE OF NEVADA, CARSON CITY, NEVADA

In the Matter of the Claim of Fred and Frank Cleverly, and being Proof No. 00517

PROTEST

To the Honorable the State Engineer of the State of Nevada:

Comes now Jno. H. Cazier & Sons Company, a corporation, duly organized under and existing by virtue of the laws of the State of

Nevada, a claimant and the owner of certain waters of the Humboldt River and its tributaries, and protests against the granting of the claim of Fred and Frank Cleverly, for the waters of Hall's Canyon Creek and Blasingame Creek, as the same appear on page 256 of the Preliminary Order of Determination of the waters of the Humboldt River and its tributaries, recently made by Hon. J. G. Scrugham, State Engineer, and being Proof No. 00517, and for ground of protest alleges:

That said Fred and Frank Cleverly have no water right whatever, or at all, under the ditches and for any of the land, as the same appears in said Proof No. 00517.

Wherefore, Protestant prays that said claim of Fred and Frank Cleverly, being Proof No. 00517, appearing as aforesaid, be stricken from said order by the honorable State Engineer.

Dated this 7th day of June, 1922.

[SEAL] JNO. H. CAZIER & SONS CO.,

By JNO. H. CAZIER, *President.*

Attest: H. H. CAZIER, *Secretary.*

No. 35

IN THE OFFICE OF THE STATE ENGINEER OF THE STATE OF NEVADA, CARSON CITY, NEVADA

In the Matter of the Adjudication of the Humboldt River and its Tributaries, under the Preliminary Order of Determination, in re Proofs Nos. 00521, 00602, and 00609.

OBJECTION AS TO LISTING OF ACREAGES AND DATES OF PRIORITY

Comes now Jno. H. Cazier & Sons Company, a corporation, whose lands and water rights are listed under Proofs Nos. 00521, 00602 and 00609, in the Preliminary Order of Determination, in the matter of the Adjudication of the Humboldt River and its Tributaries, recently issued by the honorable State Engineer of the State of Nevada, by Edwin E. Caine, its attorney, and respectfully calls the attention of the honorable State Engineer to the fact that there is a possibility of question as to the priorities and acreages claimed by it, and as the same appear in said Preliminary Order of Determination, in that it may not be possible to determine therefrom to just what subdivision certain acreages and priorities should be applied, and respectfully represents that its understanding of the lists, as they appear in said Preliminary Order of Determination, is that, where the water is not definitely listed as appurtenant to a particular subdivision, such water may be applied to the irrigated lands belonging to the undersigned, as the same appear in said Preliminary Order of Determination, and respectfully represents that, if such understanding is not correct, it hereby notifies the State Engineer that it does not waive any rights

in connection with said matter, and respectfully objects to the manner in which said claims appear in said Preliminary Order of Determination. and asks that the same be corrected, in accordance with the above understanding, or that said water be definitely listed to the land upon which the right attaches, as shown by said priorities and acreages.

Dated this 13th day of June, 1922.

JNO. H. CAZIER & SONS CO.
By EDWIN E. CAINE, *Its Attorney.*

No. 36

IN THE OFFICE OF THE STATE ENGINEER OF THE STATE OF NEVADA, CARSON CITY, NEVADA

In the Matter of the Adjudication of the Humboldt River and its Tributaries, under the Preliminary Order of Determination, in re Proof No. 00561

OBJECTION AS TO LISTING OF ACREAGES AND DATES OF PRIORITY

Comes now the Estate of Thomas Kearns, deceased, whose lands and water rights are listed under Proof No. 00561, in the Preliminary Order of Determination, in the Matter of the Adjudication of the Humboldt River and its Tributaries, recently issued by the honorable State Engineer of the State of Nevada, by Edwin E. Caine, its attorney, and respectfully calls the attention of the honorable State Engineer to the fact that there is a possibility of question as to the priorities and acreages claimed by it, and as the same appear in said Preliminary Order of Determination, in that it may not be possible to determine therefrom to just what subdivision certain acreages and priorities should be applied, and respectfully represents that its understanding of the lists, as they appear in said Preliminary Order of Determination, is that, where the water is not definitely listed as appurtenant to a particular subdivision, such water may be applied to the irrigated lands belonging to the undersigned, as the same appear in said Preliminary Order of Determination, and respectfully represents that, if such understanding is not correct, it hereby notifies the State Engineer that it does not waive any rights in connection with said matter, and respectfully objects to the manner in which said claims appear in said Preliminary Order of Determination, and asks that the same be corrected in accordance with the above understanding. or that said water be definitely listed to the land upon which the right attaches, as shown by said priorities and acreages.

Dated this 13th day of June, 1922.

ESTATE OF THOMAS KEARNS.
By EDWIN E. CAINE, *Its Attorney.*

No. 37

IN THE OFFICE OF THE STATE ENGINEER OF THE STATE OF NEVADA, CARSON CITY, NEVADA

In the Matter of the Determination of the Relative Rights in and to the Waters of the Humboldt River Stream-System

OBJECTION AND PROTEST

To the Honorable State Engineer of the State of Nevada, Carson City, Nevada:

Comes now the Elko County Water-Users Association, an organization composed of all of the water-users of the Humboldt River and its tributaries, who reside in the County of Elko, State of Nevada, by its President, Webster Patterson, whose residence and postoffice address is Lamoille, Elko County, State of Nevada, and pursuant to Section 29, Chapter 140, Statutes of 1913, State of Nevada, as amended by Section 33, Chapter 106, Statutes of the State of Nevada of the year 1921, and all other statutes or part of statutes or laws of the State of Nevada, in such cases made and provided, and files its objections and protests for and on behalf of each and every member of said Association and organization, to the Preliminary Order of Determination made by the State Engineer, in the above-entitled matter, and on the following grounds:

1. That the members of said Elko County Water-Users Association and each and every one of them, and all and singular, is an appropriator and user of the waters from the above mentioned stream-system:

That the waters claimed by them, and by each of them, have been beneficially used by them, and each of them, and their predecessors in interest, and the predecessors in interest of each of them all and singular, continuously and for many years last past, and is being now so diverted and used by them, and each of them, by means of dams, ditches, laterals and other lawful means of appropriation and diverson and use.

2. That said Preliminary Order of Determination is erroneous, defective and incorrect, in that excessive water rights are thereby attempted to be awarded to divers and different people as appear from the findings set out in the Preliminary Order of Determination, and particularly in so far as the same refers to the pretended and purported claim or claims of one H. M. Damm, and as the same appears on pages 8 and 24 of said Preliminary Order of Determination:

The pretended and purported claim or claims of one W. C. Ruddell, as the same appears on pages 16 and 17 of said Preliminary Order of Determination;

The pretended and purported claim or claims of Bergman and Alfree, as the same appear on pages 21 and 22 of said Preliminary Order of Determination:

The pretended and purported claim or claims of Emil Holmstrom, as the same appear on page 12 of said Preliminary Order of Determination;

The pretended and purported claim or claims of Hugh Holstrom,

as the same appears upon page 12 of said Preliminary Order of Determination;

The pretended and purported claim or claims of John Holmstrom, as the same appears on page 12 of said Preliminary Order of Determination, and the pretended and purported claims of H. P. Kruse, as the same appears on page 14 of said Preliminary Order of Determination, and in the purported and alleged and pretended claims of other claimants, as appearing and set forth on other pages of said Preliminary Order of Determination, as will be more particularly designated before or at the time of the hearing of this objection.

As grounds for these protests and objections, among others, are:

That the amount of water attempted to be awarded to said above-named claimants and others to be specified, as hereinbefore set forth, is excessive.

That during the several years for which a water right is attempted, or purported to be awarded, portions of the lands set forth in said claims, as protestants and objectors are advised and believe, and therefore allege, belonged either to the United States Government, or to the Central Pacific Railway Company, and were not irrigated, reclaimed or water appropriated therefor.

That your protestants are informed and believe, and therefore allege, that during or prior to the years designated in said Preliminary Order of Determination no valid appropriation of the waters of said Humboldt River, or its tributaries, adverse to the rights of the protestants herein, was initiated by any of the said claimants hereinbefore mentioned, and whose claims or pretended claims are hereby and herein objected to.

That to award water rights to the lands of said claimants, as stated in said Preliminary Order of Determination, will impair and invade the vested rights of the members of the Elko County Water-Users Association, and each and every one of them, and will likewise impair and invade the vested rights of other appropriators upon said streams.

3. That the Elko County Water-Users Association, and each and every member thereof, all and singular, reserves the right to make further checking and to insist that the acreages of its members be further increased, and that they be allowed priorities as of earlier dates than appear therein, and dates which are not subordinate in any manner whatever, or at all, to the alleged and purported claims of the claimants hereinbefore named, and against whom this protest is filed, and that the filing of this objection and protest shall not be construed as a waiver of the rights of the members of the Elko County Water-Users Association, or each and every one of them, to show that the acreages allowed to other claimants are excessive or the priorities too early.

4. The Elko County Water-Users Association further states, for and on behalf of each and every member thereof, that the objections herein made for the reasons hereinbefore set forth are not to be construed as a waiver upon the part of such protestants to his or their right to object to the validity or the legality of said Preliminary Order of Determination, on the ground that the same is not made in the manner provided by statute, or upon the ground that the said statute whereunder the same is purported to be made is unconstitutional and void.

Wherefore, the Elko County Water-Users Association, by its President, Webster Patterson, for and on behalf of each and every member thereof, prays that objections and protests hereinabove made, upon hearing be sustained, and that the said Preliminary Order of Determination be modified, changed and corrected in conformity with said protests and objections, and said Preliminary Order of Determination, as it now exists, be declared and held to be of no further force, virtue and effect, and, further, that it be hereby declared to be a cloud and encumbrance upon and as impairing and invading the vested rights of each and every member of said Elko County Water-Users Association.

Dated this 19th day of June, A. D. 1922.

ELKO COUNTY WATER-USERS ASSOCIATION,
By WEBSTER PATTERSON, *President.*

State of Nevada, County of Elko, ss.

Webster Patterson, being first duly sworn according to law, deposes and says: That he is the duly elected, qualified and acting President of the Elko County Water-Users Association, and that he has read the foregoing objection and protest, and knows the contents thereof; and that the same is true of his own knowledge, except as to those matters therein stated on information and belief, and that as to those matters, he believes it to be true.

WEBSTER PATTERSON.

Subscribed and sworn to before me this 19th day of June, A. D. 1922.

[SEAL] DELPHA M. JEWELL,
Notary Public in and for the County of Elko, State of Nevada.
My commission expires June 18, 1923.

No. 38

IN THE OFFICE OF THE STATE ENGINEER OF NEVADA

OBJECTIONS OF J. H. CARTER

In the Matter of the Determination of the Relative Rights in and to the Waters of the Humboldt River Stream-System

Now comes J. H. Carter, whose postoffice address is Elko, Elko County, Nevada, care of Morley Griswold, attorney at law, and pursuant to Section 29, Chapter 140, Statutes of 1913, State of Nevada, as amended by Section 34, Chapter 106, Statutes of the State of Nevada in the year 1921, and files his objections to the said Preliminary Order of Determination made by the State Engineer in the following manner and on the following ground:

1. That the undersigned objector is an appropriator and user of water from the above-mentioned stream-system; that the water claimed by him has been beneficially used by him and his predecessors in interest continuously and for many years last past and is now being so used through and by means of dams, ditches and laterals;

2. That the said Preliminary Order of Determination is erroneous, defective and incorrect in that excessive water rights are thereby attempted to be awarded to a great number of persons as appears from the findings, set out in said Preliminary Order of Determination and beginning on pages 8, 16, 17, 21, 12, 14, and 24, and at other pages which will be designated before or at the time of hearing this objection. For reasons, among others, that the amount of water attempted to be awarded is excessive; that during the several years for which a water right is attempted to be awarded was either the United States Government or Central Pacific Railway Company's lands and was not irrigated or reclaimed; that no valid appropriation of water for said lands was initiated during or prior to the said years designated in said Preliminary Order of Determination; that to award to said lands as stated in said Preliminary Order of Determination would be to impair and invade vested rights of other appropriators of water from said stream-system;

3. That objector reserves the right to make further checking and to insist that its acreages be further increased and its priorities allowed as of earlier dates and that the filing of these objections shall not be construed as a waiver of the right of said objector to show that the acreages allowed to other claimants are excessive or the priorities too early;

4. And on the further ground that objector further alleges that these objections are made for the reasons herein stated and are not to be construed as a waiver on the part of said objector of his right to object to the legality or validity of the said Preliminary Order of Determination on the ground that the same is not made in the manner provided by statute or upon the ground that the said statute whereunder the same is purported to be made is unconstitutional and void.

Wherefore, objector prays that the objections herein above made may, upon hearing, be sustained, and that said Preliminary Order of Determination be modified, changed and corrected in conformity with said objections, and that said Preliminary Order of Determination as it now exists be declared and held to be of no force, virtue and effect; and further that it be held to be a cloud and encumbrance upon and as impairing and invading the vested rights of the objector herein named.

J. H. CARTER.
By Morley Griswold.

State of Nevada, County of Ormsby, ss.

Morley Griswold, being first duly sworn, deposes and says that he is the agent for the above-named objector and as such makes this affidavit; that he has read the forgeoing objection and knows the contents thereof, and that the same are true and well founded to the best of his knowledge, information and belief.

MORLEY GRISWOLD.

Subscribed and sworn to before me, this 15th day of June, 1922.

Robert A. Allen, *Assistant State Engineer.*

No. 39

IN THE OFFICE OF THE STATE ENGINEER OF NEVADA

OBJECTIONS OF FLORA DEAN HOBART AND ETHEL D. HUSSEY, COPARTNERS DOING BUSINESS UNDER THE NAME AND TITLE OF THE DEAN ESTATE.

In the Matter of the Determination of the Relative Rights in and to the Waters of the Humboldt River Stream-System

Now come Flora Dean Hobart and Ethel D. Hussey, copartners, doing business under the name and title of the "Dean Estate," whose postoffice address is Elko, Elko County, Nevada, care of Morley Griswold, attorney at law, and pursuant to Section 29, Chapter 140, Statutes of 1913, State of Nevada, as amended by Section 34, Chapter 106, Statutes of the State of Nevada in the year 1921, and file their objections to the said Preliminary Order of Determination made by the State Engineer in the following manner and on the following ground:

1. That the undersigned objectors are appropriators and users of water from the above-mentioned stream-system; that the water claimed by them has been beneficially used by them and their predecessors in interest continuously and for many years last past and is now being so used through and by means of dams, ditches and laterals;

2. That the said Preliminary Order of Determination is erroneous, defective and incorrect in that excessive water rights are thereby attempted to be awarded to a great number of persons as appears from the findings, set out in said Preliminary Order of Determination and beginning on pages 8, 16, 17, 21, 12, 14 and 24, and at other pages which will be designated before or at the time of hearing this objection. For reasons, among others, that the amount of water attempted to be awarded is excessive; that during the several years for which a water right is attempted to be awarded was either the United States Government or Central Pacific Railway Company's lands and was not irrigated or reclaimed; that no valid appropriation of water for said lands was initiated during or prior to the said years designated in said Preliminary Order of Determination; that to award to said lands as stated in said Preliminary Order of Determination would be to impair and invade vested rights of other appropriators of water from said stream-system;

3. That objectors reserve the right to make further checking and to insist that their acreages be further increased and their priorities allowed as of earlier dates and that the filing of these objections shall not be construed as a waiver of the right of said objectors to show that the acreages allowed to other claimants are excessive or the priorities too early;

4. And on the further ground that objectors further allege that these objections are made for the reasons herein stated and are not to be construed as a waiver on the part of said objectors of their right to object to the legality or validity of the said Preliminary Order of Determination on the ground that the same is not made in the manner provided by statute or upon the ground that the said statute whereunder the same is purported to be made is unconstitutional and void.

Wherefore, objectors pray that the objections hereinabove made may,

upon hearing, be sustained, and that said Preliminary Order of Determination be modified, changed, and corrected in conformity with said objections, and that said Preliminary Order of Determination as it now exists be declared and held to be of no force, virtue and effect; and further that it be held to be a cloud and encumbrance upon and as impairing and invading the vested rights of the objectors herein named.

FLORA DEAN HOBART,
ETHEL DEAN HUSSEY,
By MORLEY GRISWOLD.

State of Nevada, County of Ormsby, ss.

Morley Griswold, being first duly sworn, deposes and says that he is the agent for the above-named objectors and as such makes this affidavit; that he has read the foregoing objection and knows the contents thereof, and that the same are true and well founded to the best of his knowledge, information and belief.

MORLEY GRISWOLD.

Subscribed and sworn to before me, this 15th day of June, 1922.

ROBERT A. ALLEN, *Assistant State Engineer.*

STATE OF NEVADA

STATE ENGINEER'S OFFICE

I, J. G. SCRUGHAM, State Engineer of the State of Nevada, duly appointed and qualified, having charge of the records and files of the office of State Engineer, do hereby certify that the foregoing objections are all the objections against the Preliminary Order of Determination in and to the Waters of the Humboldt River and its Tributaries, filed in the office of the State Engineer of the State of Nevada during the statutory period as provided by law, as appears by the records and files of the office of the State Engineer of Nevada, and nothing more or less.

IN WITNESS WHEREOF, I have hereunto set my hand and affixed my seal of office at the City of Carson, State of Nevada, this 30th day of June, 1922.

J. G. SCRUGHAM,
State Engineer.

STATE OF NEVADA

ORDER OF DETERMINATION

OF THE

Waters of the Humboldt River and Its Tributaries

Compiled by the Office of State Engineer, Under Authority of Chapter 140, Statutes of 1913, as amended by Chapter 253, Statutes of 1915, as amended by Chapter 106, Statutes of 1921

J. G. SCRUGHAM, State Engineer

CARSON CITY, NEVADA
STATE PRINTING OFFICE—JOE FARNSWORTH, SUPERINTENDENT
1922

171

IN THE OFFICE OF THE STATE ENGINEER OF THE STATE OF NEVADA

In the Matter of the Determination of the Relative Rights of Claimants and Appropriators of Waters of the Humboldt River Stream-System and its Tributaries.

ORDER OF DETERMINATION

The State Engineer of the State of Nevada having heretofore and under and pursuant to Section 18 of Chapter 140 of the Statutes of Nevada, 1913, and Acts amendatory and supplemental thereto, selected in order of its importance for irrigation the Humboldt River Stream-System and its tributaries, for determination of the relative rights of the various claimants to the waters thereof, and the State Engineer, having duly given, published, and served the notices, and having duly filed and made his orders as required by the provisions of each and all of Sections 18 to 27 of said Chapter 140 of the Statutes of Nevada, 1913, and Acts amendatory and supplemental thereto, and having made the investigations, prepared the maps, observations, and other data as required by said sections of said Act, and having received and there having been filed with said State Engineer the proofs and statements of claims to the use of water from said stream-system, and all said proofs and evidence taken or given before the State Engineer or obtained by the State Engineer, having been duly considered, and the State Engineer having heretofore assembled all of the proofs which have been filed with him, and having prepared and certified an abstract of said proofs and the same having been duly and regularly printed in the State Printing Office, and the State Engineer, from the proofs and evidence taken or given before him or obtained by him, having made a Preliminary Order of Determination establishing the several rights of claimants to the waters of said Humboldt River Stream-System, and said State Engineer, after said abstract of proofs and said Preliminary Order of Determination were completed, having given due and proper notice fixing and setting a time and place when and where evidence taken by or filed with him and the proofs of claims shall be open to the inspection of all interested parties, and said State Engineer, pursuant to said notice, having duly opened to inspection of all interested parties the evidence taken by or filed with him, and the proofs of claims of the various claimants to said stream-system, and a copy of

the notice fixing and setting the time and place for the inspection of the evidence aforesaid, together with a printed copy of the Preliminary Order of Determination and a printed copy of said abstract of proofs having been duly delivered by the State Engineer or sent by registered mail at least thirty days prior to the first day of such period of inspection, to each person who had appeared and filed proofs of claims to the right to the use of the waters of the Humboldt River Stream-System, and the State Engineer having been present at the time and place designated in said notice, and having allowed during said period any and all persons interested to inspect such evidence and proof as filed or taken by him in accordance with the provisions of Chapter 140, Statutes of 1913, and Acts amendatory and supplemental thereto;

And certain persons claiming interests in the Humboldt River Stream-System having duly filed objections to certain findings, parts, or portions of the Preliminary Order of Determination, and said objections having been duly and regularly considered after hearing, upon due notice served upon each and every claimant upon said stream-system, as required by the provisions of said Chapter 140 of the Statutes of 1913, and Acts amendatory and supplemental thereto;

Now, therefore, and pursuant thereto, the State Engineer of the State of Nevada hereby makes and files in the office of the State Engineer, and causes to be entered of record in his office, this Order of Determination defining the several rights of the appropriators and claimants to the waters of the Humboldt River Stream-System and its tributaries, as follows:

LOVELOCK DISTRICT

Claimant—**Antonio J. Alves.** Proof No. 001
Source—**Humboldt River.** Ditch—**Old Channel.**

Year of priority	Culture—Acres: Harvest crops	Culture—Acres: Meadow pasture	Culture—Acres: Diversified pasture	Location: Subdivision	Location: Section	Location: Tp.N.	Location: R.E.	Length of season	Duty of water: C.F.S.	Duty of water: Acre-feet
1904	4	....	....	NW¼NW¼	18	27	32	3-15—9-15	.033	12.0
1904		....	4.30	NW¼NW¼	18	27	32	3-15—6-13	.035	6.45

Claimant—**Johannes Anderson.** Proof No. 002
Source—**Humboldt River.** Ditch—***Larson Ditch. Union Canal through Reed Ditch.**

Year of priority	Culture—Acres: Harvest crops	Culture—Acres: Meadow pasture	Culture—Acres: Diversified pasture	Location: Subdivision	Location: Section	Location: Tp.N.	Location: R.E.	Length of season	Duty of water: C.F.S.	Duty of water: Acre-feet
*1874	30	....	....	E½NE¼	4	25	31	3-15—9-15	.244	90.0
1876	10	....	....	E½NE¼	4	25	31	3-15—9-15	.081	30.0
1876	17.25	....	....	E½NE¼	4	25	31	3-15—9-15	.140	51.75
1893	36.25	....	....	E½SE¼	4	25	31	3-15—9-15	.295	108.75
1898	18.25	....	....	E½SE¼	4	25	31	3-15—9-15	.148	54.75
1902	18	....	....	E½SE¼	4	25	31	3-15—9-15	.146	54.0

Claimant—**Peter Anker Estate.** Proof No. 003
Source—**Humboldt River.** Ditch—**Union Canal.**

Year of priority	Culture—Acres: Harvest crops	Culture—Acres: Meadow pasture	Culture—Acres: Diversified pasture	Location: Subdivision	Location: Section	Location: Tp.N.	Location: R.E.	Length of season	Duty of water: C.F.S.	Duty of water: Acre-feet
1876	....	....	79.40	E½SE¼	22	26	31	3-15—6-13	.646	119.1
1876	35.45	....	....	NE¼	22	26	31	3-15—9-15	.288	106.35
1876	62.04	....	....		22	26	31	3-15—9-15	.504	186.12
1876	31.02	....	....		22	26	31	3-15—9-15	.252	93.06
1876	35.45	....	....		22	26	31	3-15—9-15	.288	106.35
1876	28.36	....	....		22	26	31	3-15—9-15	.231	85.08
1876	22.16	....	....		22	26	31	3-15—9-15	.180	66.48
1883	35.45	....	....		22	26	31	3-15—9-15	.288	106.35
1886	265.88	....	....		22	26	31	3-15—9-15	2.161	797.64
1890	10.64	....	....		22	26	31	3-15—9-15	.225	31.92
1876	38.69	....	....	E½E½	21	26	31	3-15—9-15	.453	116.07
1876	19.37	....	....	E½E½	21	20	31	3-15—9-15	.295	58.11
1876	19.37	....	....	E½E½	21	26	31	3-15—9-15	.295	58.11
1876	14.50	....	....	E½E½	21	26	31	3-15—9-15	.255	43.50
1883	19.37	....	....	E½E½	21	26	31	3-15—9-15	.295	58.11
1886	30.00	....	....	E½E½	21	26	31	3-15—9-15	.380	92.88
1890	7.74	....	....	E½E½	21	20	31	3-15—9-15	.201	23.[illegible]

Claimant—**L. B. Bassman.** Proof No. 004
Source—**Humboldt River.** Ditch—**Old Channel.**

	1888			86.00				SE¼	14	27	31	3-15—9-15	.837	258.0
	1888			22.20				SE¼	14	27	31	3-15—9-15	.319	66.60
	1888			2.75				SE¼	14	27	31	3-15—9-15	.160	8.25
	1888			24.05				SE¼	14	27	31	3-15—9-15	.334	72.15
	1888			60.55				SW¼	14	27	31	3-15—9-15	.630	181.65
	1888			78.10				SW¼	14	27	31	3-15—9-15	.773	234.30

Claimant—**Grace S. Jahn.** Proof No. 005
Source—**Humboldt River.** Ditch—**Union Canal through Reed Ditch.**

	1876			15				N½	34	26	31	3-15—9-15	.122	45.0
	1876			....		96.0		N½	34	26	31	3-15—6-13	.780	144.0
	1876			30				N½	34	26	31	3-15—9-15	.244	90.0
	1883			55				N½	34	26	31	3-15—9-15	.447	165.0
	1887			25				N½	34	26	31	3-15—9-15	.203	75.0
	1901			15				N½	34	26	31	3-15—9-15	.122	45.0
	1903			20				N½	34	26	31	3-15—9-15	.163	60.0

Claimant—**Pitt and McDonald.** Proof No. 006
Source—**Humboldt River.** Ditch—**Union Canal through Lake Shore Ditch.**

	1876			....	44.05			W½NW¼	4	25	31	3-15—6-13	.358	66.75
	1876			....		116		NW¼	4	25	31	3-15—6-13	.130	174.0

Claimant—**Ed. Berg.** Proof No. 007
Source—**Humboldt River.** Ditch—**Young Ditch.**

	1888			58.14				E½E½	1	27	31	3-15—9-15	.473	174.42

Claimant—**William Loorz.** Proof No. 008
Source—**Humboldt River.** Ditch—**Old Channel.**

	1888			30				W½NE¼	13	27	31	3-15—9-15	.244	90.0
	1897			20				W½NE¼	13	27	31	3-15—9-15	.165	60.0
	1898			15.40				W½NE¼	13	27	31	3-15—9-15	.125	46.20
	1888			....	8.75			W½NE¼	13	27	31	3-15—6-13	.071	13.13

Claimant—**W. C. Thorne and Ida M. Thorne.** Proof No. 009
Source—**Humboldt River.** Ditch—**Irish American or Last Chance and *Southwest.**

	*1883			*4				SW¼SE¼	23	27	31	3-15—9-15	.033	12.0
	1887			14.20				SW¼SE¼	23	27	31	3-15—9-15	.115	42.60
	1887			....		8.15		SW¼SE¼	23	27	31	3-15—6-13	.026	4.73

Claimant—**Mrs. E. A. Borland.** Proof No. 0010
Source—**Humboldt River.** Ditch—**Irish-American (in conjunction with Old Channel from 1898 to date).**

Year of priority	Culture—Acres: Harvest crops	Meadow pasture	Diversified pasture	Location: Subdivision	Section	Tp.N.	R.E.	Length of season	Duty of water: C.F.S.	Acre-feet
1887	1.69			NW¼NE¼	27	27	31	3-15—9-15	.014	5.07
1887	37.86			W½NE¼	27	27	31	3-15—9-15	.308	113.58
1887	29.45			W½NE¼	27	27	31	3-15—9-15	.239	88.35
1887	110.70			NW¼	27	27	31	3-15—9-15	.900	332.10

Claimant—**F. A. Preston.** Proof No. 0011
Source—**Humboldt River.** Ditch—***Graveyard Slough and Union Canal.**

Year of priority	Harvest crops	Meadow pasture	Diversified pasture	Subdivision	Section	Tp.N.	R.E.	Length of season	C.F.S.	Acre-feet
1886	9			W½SE¼	29	26	31	3-15—9-15	.073	27.0
1890	3			W½SE¼	29	26	31	3-15—9-15	.024	9.0
1900	14.75			W½SE¼	29	26	31	3-15—9-15	.112	44.25
1886	—		*22.80	W½SE¼	29	26	31	3-15—6-13	.185	34.2

Claimant—**Pitt and McDonald.** Proof No. 0012
Source—**Humboldt River.** Ditch—**Union Canal through Lake Shore Ditch; *Trembly Ditch.**

Year of priority	Harvest crops	Meadow pasture	Diversified pasture	Subdivision	Section	Tp.N.	R.E.	Length of season	C.F.S.	Acre-feet
*1874	227.65			W½SE¼ & SW¼	4	25	31	3-15—9-15	1.851	682.95
*1874	—		12.20	W½SE¼ & SW¼	4	25	31	3-15—6-13	.099	18.3

Claimant—**L. N. Carpenter.** Proof No. 0013
Source—**Humboldt River.** Ditch—**Rodgers Canal System and †Irish-American.**

Year of priority	Harvest crops	Meadow pasture	Diversified pasture	Subdivision	Section	Tp.N.	R.E.	Length of season	C.F.S.	Acre-feet
1889	25.55			SW¼NW¼	10	26	31	3-15—9-15	.208	76.65
1900	17.50			NE¼NW¼	11	26	31	3-15—9-15	.142	52.50
†1897	†17.45			E½NW¼	35	27	31	3-15—9-15	.142	52.35
1877	—		†19.25	E½NW¼	35	27	31	3-15—6-13	.157	28.88
1877	—		†23.70	S½SW¼	26	27	31	3-15—6-13	.193	35.55
1877			†6.60	S½SW¼	26	27	31	3-15—6-13	.537	9.9
1885	25			SE¼NW¼	1	26	31	3-15—9-15	.203	75.0
1885	75			E½SW¼	1	26	31	3-15—9-15	.610	225.0
1886	2			W½SW¼	1	26	31	3-15—9-15	.016	6.0
1886	3			W½NW¼	1	26	31	3-15—9-15	.024	9.0
1890	40			W½SW¼	1	26	31	3-15—9-15	.325	120.0
1890	20			NW¼SE¼	1	26	31	3-15—9-15	.163	60.0
1891	5.75			S½SE¼	1	26	31	3-15—9-15	.047	17.25
1891	27.65			S½SE¼	1	26	31	3-15—9-15	.225	82.95
1894	20			NW¼SE¼	1	26	31	3-15—9-15	.163	60.0
1894	5.40			SW¼SE¼	1	26	31	3-15—9-15	.044	16.20
1894	3.60			W½NE¼	1	26	31	3-15—9-15	.029	10.8
1894	5			E½SW¼	1	26	31	3-15—9-15	.011	15.0
1898	20			NE¼SE¼	1	26	31	3-15—9-15	.163	60.0
1900	15			S½SE¼	1	26	31	3-15—9-15	.122	45.0
1900	20			NE¼SE¼	1	26	31	3-15—9-15	.163	60.0
1900	26.20			S½SE¼	1	26	31	3-15—9-15	.213	98.00
1900	13.00			E½NE¼	1	26	31	3-15—9-15	.113	40.88

1880	14			E½NW¼	35	27	31	3-15—9-15	.114	42.0
1880		25.00		SE¼NW¼	1	26	31	3-15—6-13	.203	37.5
1880		1.75		W½SW¼	1	26	31	3-15—6-13	.014	2.63
1880		52.35		S½SE¼	1	26	31	3-15—6-13	.426	78.53
1880		80.00		N½SE¼	1	26	31	3-15—6-13	.650	120.0
1879		47.15		W½SW¼	1	26	31	3-15—6-13	.383	70.73
1879		3.60		S½NE¼	1	26	31	3-15—6-13	.029	5.4
1877	50			W½NE¼ & NW¼SE¼	2	26	31	3-15—9-15	.407	150.0
1877		80.00		E½SW¼	1	26	31	3-15—6-13	.650	120.0
1877		20.00		E½NW¼	2	26	31	3-15—6-13	.163	30.0
1878	31.7			SW¼SW¼	2	26	31	3-15—9-15	.258	95.1
1878	12.7			SE¼SW¼	2	26	31	3-15—9-15	.103	38.1
1878	5.6			NE¼SW¼	2	26	31	3-15—9-15	.046	16.8
1878		16.70		SE¼SW¼	2	26	31	3-15—6-13	.136	25.05
1878		41.95		E½NW¼	2	26	31	3-15—6-13	.341	62.93
1878		11.80		N½SE¼	2	26	31	3-15—6-13	.096	17.7
1878		21.25		W½SW¼	1	26	31	3-15—6-13	.173	31.88
1878		7.85		SE¼NW¼ & NE¼SW¼	2	26	31	3-15—6-13	.064	11.78
1879	3.60			NE¼NW¼	2	26	31	3-15—9-15	.029	10.80
1879	22.70			SE¼SW¼ & SW¼SE¼	2	26	31	3-15—9-15	.185	68.10
1879	7.50			SE¼NW¼ & NE¼SE¼	2	26	31	3-15—9-15	.061	22.50
1879	9.85			NW¼SW¼ & SW¼NW¼	1	26	31	3-15—9-15	.080	29.55
1879	6.35			W½SW¼	2	26	31	3-15—9-15	.052	19.05
1879		49.25		W½SW¼	2	26	31	3-15—6-13	.400	73.88
1863	10			NE¼SW¼	2	26	31	3-15—9-15	.081	30.0
1863	50			NE¼	2	26	31	3-15—9-15	.407	150.0
1863	50			NW¼	1	26	31	3-15—9-15	.407	150.0
1890	80			N½NE¼	11	26	31	3-15—9-15	.650	240.0
1890	75.90			SE¼	2	26	31	3-15—9-15	.617	227.70
1890	2			SW¼	1	26	31	3-15—9-15	.016	6.0
1868	20			W½W½	1	26	31	3-15—9-15	.163	60.0
†1868	†16			S½SW¼	26	27	31	3-15—9-15	.130	48.0
1872		100.00		W½W½	10	26	31	3-15—6-13	.813	150.0
1872	20			W½SW¼	10	26	31	3-15—9-15	.163	60.0
1871		80.00		N½NW¼	11	26	31	3-15—6-13	.650	120.0
1875	80			W½NE¼	2	26	31	3-15—9-15	.650	240.0
1875	25			NE¼NW¼	1	26	31	3-15—9-15	.203	75.0
1880	25			S½NE¼	1	26	31	3-15—9-15	.203	75.0
1885	25			SW¼NW¼	1	26	31	3-15—9-15	.203	75.0
1885	49.25			W½SW¼	2	26	31	3-15—9-15	.400	147.75
1887	7.85			SE¼NW¼ & NE¼SE¼	2	26	31	3-15—9-15	.064	23.55
1884	55.45			W½NW¼	27	26	31	3-15—9-15	.451	166.35
1887	151.80			SW¼	27	26	31	3-15—9-15	1.234	455.40
1886			154.80	E½	27	26	31	3-15—6-13	1.259	232.2
1886			47.95	E½	27	26	31	3-15—6-13	.390	71.93
1884		6.70		NW¼NW¼	27	26	31	3-15—6-13	.054	10.05

Claimant—**C. C. Carpenter.** Proof No. **0014**

Source—**Humboldt River.** Ditch—**Union Canal and Lake Shore Ditch.**

1876	15			E½NE¼	28	26	31	3-15—9-15	.122	45.0
1876	51.10			E½NE¼	28	26	31	3-15—9-15	.415	153.30

Year of priority	Harvest crops	Meadow pasture	Diversified pasture	Subdivision	Section	Tp.N.	R.E.	Length of season	C.F.S.	Acre-feet
Claimant—Chris Beck. Proof No. 0014										
Source—Humboldt River. Ditch—Killebrew & Beck Ditch, now Tule Ditch.										
1901	80			SW¼	10	25	31	3-15—9-15	.650	240.0
Claimant—Chris Hanson. Proof No. 0015										
Source—Humboldt River. Ditch—*Harrison and Mayes; now †Southwest Ditch; ‡Irish-American.										
‡1883	10			E½NW¼	28	27	31	3-15—9-15	.081	30.0
†1877	80			E½NW¼	28	27	31	3-15—9-15	.650	240.0
Claimant—John G. Taylor. Proof. No. 0016										
Source—Humboldt River. Ditch—Southwest Ditch.										
1890	73.14			E½NE¼	28	27	31	3-15—9-15	.595	219.42
Claimant—John G. Taylor. Proof No. 0016										
Source—Humboldt River. Ditch—Southwest in conjunction with Marzen Slough.										
1890	57.76			W½NW¼	28	27	31	3-15—9-15	.470	173.28
Claimant—H. M. Damm. Proof No. 0017										
Source—Humboldt River. Ditch—Old Channel and Humboldt Irrigation and Power Co. Canal.										
1888	29.70			NE¼SE¼	11	27	31	3-15—9-15	.241	89.10
1888	33.70			SW¼SW¼	11	27	31	3-15—9-15	.274	101.10
1888	75.81			E½SW¼ & NW¼SW¼	11	27	31	3-15—9-15	.616	227.43
1888	30			E½SW¼ & NW¼SW¼	11	27	31	3-15—9-15	.244	90.0
1888	82.80			NW¼	11	27	31	3-15—9-15	.673	248.40
1888	11.10			SE¼NW¼	11	27	31	3-15—9-15	.090	33.30
1888	....	1.20		NE¼SW¼	1	27	31	3-15—6-13	.010	1.8
1888	....		8.70	NE¼NW¼	11	27	31	3-15—6-13	.071	13.05
Claimant—J. C. Damm. Proof No. 0018										
Source—Humboldt River. Ditch—Union Canal through Lake Shore Ditch.										
1876	5			NW¼	28	26	31	3-15—9-15	.041	15.0
1876	....		6.30	NW¼	28	26	31	3-15—6-13	.051	9.45
1876	15			NW¼	28	26	31	3-15—9-15	.122	45.0
1876	10			NW¼	28	26	31	3-15—9-15	.081	30.0
1883	46.75			NW¼	28	26	31	3-15—9-15	.380	140.25

Claimant—**E. A. Perez and John Dotta.** Proof No. **0019**
Source—**Humboldt River.** Ditch—**Union Canal through Reed Ditch.**

	1884			22				E½NW¼	33	26	31	3-15—9-15	.179	66.0
	1887			33.05				E½NW¼	33	26	31	3-15—9-15	.269	99.15

Claimant—**Lawrence Devita.** Proof No. **0021**
Source—**Humboldt River.** Ditch—**Old Channel.**

	1899			29.80				NE¼	13	27	31	3-15—9-15	.242	89.40

Claimant—**Frank Ambrosetti and John Scott.** Proof No. **0022**
Source—**Humboldt River.** Ditch—**Old Channel.**

	1888			31.70				W½SW¼	13	27	31	3-15—9-15	.258	95.10
	1888			7.90				W½SW¼	13	27	31	3-15—9-15	.064	23.70
	1888			8.30				W½SW¼	13	27	31	3-15—9-15	.067	24.90
	1888			4.35				W½SW¼	13	27	31	3-15—9-15	.035	13.05
	1888			14.25				W½SW¼	13	27	31	3-15—9-15	.116	42.75
	1888			2.75				NE¼NW¼	24	27	31	3-15—9-15	.022	8.25

Claimant—**Santos and Souza.** Proof No. **0023**
Source—**Humboldt River.** Ditch—**Union Canal through Lake Shore Ditch.**

	1899			40				W½SW¼	29	26	31	3-15—9-15	.324	120.0
	1902			20				W½SW¼	29	26	31	3-15—9-15	.163	60.0
	1903			20				W½SW¼	29	26	31	3-15—9-15	.163	60.0

Claimant—**Carl Elges.** Proof No. **0024**
Source—**Humboldt River.** Ditch—**Young Ditch.**

	1888			59.75				NE¼	7	27	32	3-15—9-15	.486	179.25
	1888			3.15				NW¼NE¼	7	27	32	3-15—9-15	.026	9.45
	1888			....			6.30	N½NE¼	7	27	32	3-15—6-13	.051	9.45

Claimant—**Frank R. Mancebo.** Proof No. **0025**
Source—**Humboldt River.** Ditch—**Old Channel.**

	1888			30				S½SE¼	12	27	31	3-15—9-15	.244	90.0
	1888			46.50				S½SE¼	12	27	31	3-15—9-15	.378	139.50

Claimant—**James Kjeldsen.** Proof No. **0026**
Source—**Humboldt River.** Ditch—**Union Canal.**

	1876			18				S½SE¼	28	26	31	3-15—9-15	.146	54.0
	1876			8				S½SE¼	28	26	31	3-15—9-15	.065	24.0
	1876			14				S½SE¼	28	26	31	3-15—9-15	.114	42.0
	1885			12				S½SE¼	28	26	31	3-15—9-15	.098	36.0
	1891			15				S½SE¼	28	26	31	3-15—9-15	.122	45.0
	1891			2.08				S½SE¼	28	26	31	3-15—9-15	.017	6.24

Claimant—**Mary T. Fuss.** Proof No. **0027**
Source—**Humboldt River.** Ditch—***Saxenheimer; †Union Canal through Fuss Lateral.**

Year of priority	Culture—Acres: Harvest crops	Meadow pasture	Diversified pasture	Location: Subdivision	Section	Tp.N.	R.E.	Length of season	Duty of water: C.F.S.	Acre-feet
*1866	198.65				12	26	31	3-15—9-15	1.615	595.95
*1866	....		389.90		12	26	31	3-15—6-13	3.170	584.85
†1876	‡120				12	26	31	3-15—9-15	.976	360.0
†1885	‡140				12	26	31	3-15—9-15	1.138	420.0
†1890	‡100				12	26	31	3-15—9-15	.813	300.0
*1866	....		‡29.90		12	26	31	3-15—6-13	.243	44.85

‡NOTE—Land originally held water right for pasture as of 1866. Since that time the pasture land has gradually been placed under intensive cultivation in the years mentioned, thus gaining, in addition to the pasture right, right sufficient to give a full water right to the lands listed in tabulation as harvest crops.

The total area for which water is allotted cannot be in excess of 588.55 acres.

Claimant—**C. C. Carpenter.** Proof No. **0028**
Source—**Humboldt River.** Ditch—**Union Canal.**

Year of priority	Harvest crops	Meadow pasture	Diversified pasture	Subdivision	Section	Tp.N.	R.E.	Length of season	C.F.S.	Acre-feet
1876	7			NW¼NE¼	28	26	31	3-15—9-15	.057	21.0
1876	30			NW¼SE¼	28	26	31	3-15—9-15	.244	90.0
1876	20			SW¼SE¼	21	26	31	3-15—9-15	.163	60.0
1883	50			W½SE¼	21	26	31	3-15—9-15	.407	150.0
1888	50			W½NE¼	21	26	31	3-15—9-15	.407	150.0
1892	18.50			W½E½	21	26	31	3-15—9-15	.150	55.50
1892	81.65			W½NE¼&N½SE¼	28	26	31	3-15—9-15	.664	244.95
1876			4	NW¼SE¼	28	26	31	3-15—6-13	.033	6.0

Claimant—**Hans Westergard.** Proof No. **0031**
Source—**Humboldt River.** Ditch—**Union Canal through Lake Shore Ditch.**

Year of priority	Harvest crops	Meadow pasture	Diversified pasture	Subdivision	Section	Tp.N.	R.E.	Length of season	C.F.S.	Acre-feet
1884	35			W½NW¼	33	26	31	3-15—9-15	.285	105.0
1891	10			W½NW¼	33	26	31	3-15—9-15	.081	30.0
1891	10			W½NW¼	33	26	31	3-15—9-15	.081	30.0
1894	11.40			W½NW¼	33	26	31	3-15—9-15	.093	34.20

Claimant—**Chris Hanson.** Proof No. **0032**
Source—**Humboldt River.** Ditch—**Union Canal through Reed Ditch.**

Year of priority	Harvest crops	Meadow pasture	Diversified pasture	Subdivision	Section	Tp.N.	R.E.	Length of season	C.F.S.	Acre-feet
1876	28.70			E½NE¼	33	26	31	3-15—9-15	.233	86.10
1885	33.70			E½NE¼	33	26	31	3-15—9-15	.268	101.10
1905	10			E½NE¼	33	26	31	3-15—9-15	.081	30.0

Claimant—**Nellie Martin.** Proof No. **0033**
Source—**Humboldt River.** Ditch—***Larson Ditch; Union Canal through Reed Ditch.**

Year of priority	Harvest crops	Meadow pasture	Diversified pasture	Subdivision	Section	Tp.N.	R.E.	Length of season	C.F.S.	Acre-feet
*1875	25			S½SE¼	33	26	31	3-15—9-15	.203	75.0
*1875	44			S½SE¼	33	26	31	3-15—9-15	.358	132.0
*1875			7.86	S½SE¼	33	26	31	3-15—6-13	.064	11.78

Claimant—**Ingvert Hanson.** Proof No. 0034

Source—**Humboldt River.** Ditch—**Union Canal through Lake Shore Ditch.**

1876	4		SE¼SW¼	32	26	31	3-15—9-15	.033	12.0
1876	15.44		SW¼	32	26	31	3-15—9-15	.126	46.32
1876	4.82		SW¼	32	26	31	3-15—9-15	.039	14.46
1876	4.82		SW¼	32	26	31	3-15—9-15	.039	14.46
1876	4.82		SW¼	32	26	31	3-15—9-15	.039	14.46
1883	4.82		SW¼	32	26	31	3-15—9-15	.039	14.46
1884	5.79		SW¼	32	26	31	3-15—9-15	.047	17.37
1890	13.51		SW¼	32	26	31	3-15—9-15	.110	40.53
1895	27.03		SW¼	32	26	31	3-15—9-15	.220	81.09
1900	11.60		SW¼	32	26	31	3-15—9-15	.094	34.80
1876	....	20	SW¼	32	26	31	3-15—6-13	.163	30.0

Claimant—**Andrew Jacobson.** Proof No. 0035

Source—**Humboldt River.** Ditch—**Young Ditch.**

1888	60		NW¼	7	27	32	3-15—9-15	.488	180.0
1888	20		NW¼	7	27	32	3-15—9-15	.163	60.0
1904	40		NW¼	7	27	32	3-15—9-15	.325	120.0
1904	10		NW¼	7	27	32	3-15—9-15	.081	30.0
1888	..	2.30	NW¼	7	27	32	3-15—6-13	.019	3.45
1888	4.30		NW¼NW¼	7	27	32	3-15—9-15	.035	12.90
1888	1.90		NW¼NW¼	7	27	32	3-15—9-15	.015	5.70

Claimant—**B. Helwinkle.** Proof No. 0036

Source—**Humboldt River.** Ditch—**Southwest Ditch.**

1883	20	SW¼	23	27	31	3-15—9-15	.163	60.0
1880	88	SW¼	23	27	31	3-15—9-15	.715	264.0
1904	29.45	SW¼	23	27	31	3-15—9-15	.239	88.35

Claimant—**J. A. Henrikson.** Proof No. 0037

Source—**Humboldt River.** Ditch—**Union Canal through Reed Ditch.**

1885	35.60	SE¼	34	26	31	3-15—9-15	.289	106.8
1886	40.00	SE¼	34	26	31	3-15—9-15	.325	120.0
1894	47.25	SE¼	34	26	31	3-15—9-15	.384	141.75
1899	18.90	SE¼	34	26	31	3-15—9-15	.154	56.70

Claimant—**Estate John J. Hill.** Proof No. 0038

Source—**Humboldt River.** Ditch—**Union Canal through Lake Shore Ditch.**

1876	236	W½	21	26	31	3-15—9-15	.019	708.0
1876	4.30	SE¼SW¼	21	26	31	3-15—9-15	.035	12.90
1876	.80	SE¼SW¼	21	26	31	3-15—9-15	.007	2.40
1876	1.60	NE¼NW¼	21	26	31	3-15—9-15	.013	4.80
1876	53.50	E½SE¼	20	26	31	3-15—9-15	.435	160.50
1876	3.55	E½SE¼	20	26	31	3-15—9-15	.029	10.65
1902	29.10	W½SE¼	20	26	31	3-15—9-15	.237	87.30
1902	26.00	E½E½SW¼	20	26	31	3-15—9-15	.211	78.0
1901	2.30	SW¼NE¼	29	26	31	3-15—9-15	.019	6.90

Claimant—**Joseph Hill.** Proof No. 0039
Source—**Humboldt River.** Ditch—**Union Canal through Reed Ditch.**

Year of priority	Culture—Acres: Harvest crops	Meadow pasture	Diversified pasture	Location: Subdivision	Section	Tp.N.	R.E.	Length of season	Duty of water: C.F.S.	Acre-feet
1888	35			SW¼	35	26	31	3-15—9-15	.285	105.0
1893	55			SW¼	35	26	31	3-15—9-15	.447	165.0
1903	71.60			SW¼	35	26	31	3-15—9-15	.582	214.80

Claimant—**Emil Holmstrom.** Proof No. 0040
Source—**Humboldt River.** Ditch—**Old Channel.**

Year of priority	Harvest crops	Meadow pasture	Diversified pasture	Subdivision	Section	Tp.N.	R.E.	Length of season	C.F.S.	Acre-feet
1888	50.35			E½NE¼	14	27	31	3-15—9-15	.125	151.05
1888	23			E½NE¼	14	27	31	3-15—9-15	.187	69.0
1888	70.95			S½SE¼	11	27	31	3-15—9-15	.577	212.85
1888	4.70			S½SE¼	11	27	31	3-15—9-15	.038	14.10

Claimant—**Hugh Holmstrom.** Proof No. 0041
Source—**Humboldt River.** Ditch—**Young Ditch.**

Year of priority	Harvest crops	Meadow pasture	Diversified pasture	Subdivision	Section	Tp.N.	R.E.	Length of season	C.F.S.	Acre-feet
1888	50			N½	2	27	31	3-15—9-15	.407	150.0
1888	34			N½	2	27	31	3-15—9-15	.276	102.0
1888	50			N½	2	27	31	3-15—9-15	.407	150.0

Claimant—**John Holmstrom.** Proof No. 0042
Source—**Humboldt River.** Ditch—**Young Ditch.**

Year of priority	Harvest crops	Meadow pasture	Diversified pasture	Subdivision	Section	Tp.N.	R.E.	Length of season	C.F.S.	Acre-feet
1888	25			E½W½	6	27	32	3-15—9-15	.203	75.0
1888	35			W½E½	6	27	32	3-15—9-15	.285	105.0
1888	65			E½	6	27	32	3-15—9-15	.528	195.0
1888	35			E½	6	27	32	3-15—9-15	.285	105.0
1888	....		40	E½NE¼ / SE¼SE¼	6 / 31	27 / 28	32 / 32	3-15—6-13	.325	60.0

Claimant—**Hans P. Kruse.** Proof No. 0042

Year of priority	Harvest crops	Meadow pasture	Diversified pasture	Subdivision	Section	Tp.N.	R.E.	Length of season	C.F.S.	Acre-feet
1888	....		154.47	W½	6	27	32	3-15—6-13	1.255	115.85

Claimant—**Emil Holmstrom.** Proof No. 0043
Source—**Humboldt River.** Ditch—**Young Ditch.**

Year of priority	Harvest crops	Meadow pasture	Diversified pasture	Subdivision	Section	Tp.N.	R.E.	Length of season	C.F.S.	Acre-feet
1888	47.50			N½NW¼	12	27	31	3-15—9-15	.386	142.50
1888	9			N½NE¼	11	27	31	3-15—9-15	.073	27.0
1888	19.35			N½NW¼	12	27	31	3-15—9-15	.157	58.05
1888	10			N½NE¼	11	27	31	3-15—9-15	.081	30.0

Claimant—**Nels Jensen.** Proof No. 0045
Source—**Humboldt River.** Ditch—**Young Ditch.**

Year of priority	Harvest crops	Meadow pasture	Diversified pasture	Subdivision	Section	Tp.N.	R.E.	Length of season	C.F.S.	Acre-feet
1903	20			NW¼	11	27	31	3-15—9-15	.163	60.0

Claimant—**James Johnson.** Proof No. 0046
Source—**Humboldt River.** Ditch—**Young Ditch.**

	1888			25				E½W½	1	27	31	3-15—9-15	.203	75.0
	1888			25				E½W½	1	27	31	3-15—9-15	.203	75.0

Claimant—**M. A. Moreira.** Proof No. 0047
Source—**Humboldt River.** Ditch—**Old Channel.**

	1888			65				SW¼	12	27	31	3-15—9-15	.528	195.0
	1897			9.30				SW¼	12	27	31	3-15—9-15	.076	27.90

Claimant—**Joe P. Johnson.** Proof No. 0047
Source—**Humboldt River.** Ditch—**Old Channel.**

	1888			65				SW¼	12	27	31	3-15—9-15	.528	195.0
	1897			9.30				SW¼	12	27	31	3-15—9-15	.076	27.90

Claimant—**Paul Johnson.** Proof No. 0048
Source—**Humboldt River.** Ditch—**Union Canal through Lake Shore Ditch.**

	1884			6.76				W½SW¼	33	26	31	3-15—9-15	.055	20.28
	1885			10.13				W½SW¼	33	26	31	3-15—9-15	.082	30.39
	1886			5.63				W½SW¼	33	26	31	3-15—9-15	.046	16.89
	1893			16.89				W½SW¼	33	26	31	3-15—9-15	.137	50.67
	1896			5.63				W½SW¼	33	26	31	3-15—9-15	.046	16.89
	1897			11.26				W½SW¼	33	26	31	3-15—9-15	.092	33.78
	1884			—		1.17		W½SW¼	33	26	31	3-15—6-13	.010	1.76

Claimant—**Mrs. John Chambers.** Proof No. 0048
Source—**Humboldt River.** Ditch—**Union Canal through Lake Shore Ditch.**

	1884			4.74				E½SW¼	33	26	31	3-15—9-15	.039	14.22
	1885			7.12				E½SW¼	33	26	31	3-15—9-15	.058	21.36
	1886			3.95				E½SW¼	33	26	31	3-15—9-15	.032	11.85
	1893			11.86				E½SW¼	33	26	31	3-15—9-15	.096	35.68
	1896			3.95				E½SW¼	33	26	31	3-15—9-15	.032	11.85
	1897			7.90				E½SW¼	33	26	31	3-15—9-15	.064	23.70
	1884			—		.83		E½SW¼	33	26	31	3-15—6-13	.007	1.25

Claimant—**Geo. Kennedy.** Proof No. 0049
Source—**Humboldt River.** Ditch—**Old Channel.**

	1888			70.50				NW¼	22	27	31	3-15—9-15	.622	229.50
	1888			73.70				NW¼	22	27	31	3-15—9-15	.599	221.10
	1888			2.80				NW¼	22	27	31	3-15—9-15	.023	8.40

Claimant—**Rachel Killebrew.** Proof No. 0050
Source—**Humboldt River.** Ditch—**Tule Ditch.**

	1890			73.15				N½NW¼	10	25	31	3-15—9-15	.595	219.45

Claimant—**H. A. Killebrew.** Proof No. 0050
Source—**Humboldt River.** Ditch—**Tule Ditch.**

Year of priority	Culture—Acres: Harvest crops	Meadow pasture	Diversified pasture	Location: Subdivision	Section	Tp.N.	R.E.	Length of season	Duty of water: C.F.S.	Acre-feet
1891	78			S½NW¼	10	25	31	3-15—9-15	.634	234.0

Claimant—**H. P. Kruse.** Proof No. 0052
Source—**Humboldt River.** Ditch—**Young Ditch.**

Year of priority	Harvest crops	Meadow pasture	Diversified pasture	Subdivision	Section	Tp.N.	R.E.	Length of season	C.F.S.	Acre-feet
1888	24.05			NE¼	12	27	31	3-15—9-15	.199	72.15
1888	100.90			NE¼	12	27	31	3-15—9-15	.820	302.70
1888	10.56			NE¼	12	27	31	3-15—9-15	.086	31.68

Claimant—**C. C. Larson.** Proof No. 0053
Source—**Humboldt River.** Ditch—**Union Canal through *Reed Ditch.**

Year of priority	Harvest crops	Meadow pasture	Diversified pasture	Subdivision	Section	Tp.N.	R.E.	Length of season	C.F.S.	Acre-feet
*1874	45			S½N½	34	26	31	3-15—9-15	.366	135.0
1876	5			N½SE¼	33	26	31	3-15—9-15	.041	15.0
1876	20			N½SE¼	33	26	31	3-15—9-15	.163	60.0
1890	10			N½SE¼	33	26	31	3-15—9-15	.081	30.0
1894	28.15			N½SE¼	33	26	31	3-15—9-15	.229	84.45

Claimant—**John Greve.** Proof No. 0054
Source—**Humboldt River.** Ditch—***Larson Ditch, Union Canal.**

Year of priority	Harvest crops	Meadow pasture	Diversified pasture	Subdivision	Section	Tp.N.	R.E.	Length of season	C.F.S.	Acre-feet
*1888	142.03			SE¼	35	26	31	3-15—9-15	1.157	426.09

Claimant—Wm. Loorz. Proof No. 0055
Source—**Humboldt River.** Ditch—**Old Channel.**

Year of priority	Harvest crops	Meadow pasture	Diversified pasture	Subdivision	Section	Tp.N.	R.E.	Length of season	C.F.S.	Acre-feet
1888	78.10			N½NW¼	13	27	31	3-15—9-15	.635	234.30

Claimant—**John and Domenico Ferretto.** Proof No. 0057
Source—**Humboldt River.** Ditch—**Reed Ditch from Union Canal.**

Year of priority	Harvest crops	Meadow pasture	Diversified pasture	Subdivision	Section	Tp.N.	R.E.	Length of season	C.F.S.	Acre-feet
1884	8			W½NE¼	33	26	31	3-15—9-15	.065	24.0
1884		6		W½NE¼	33	26	31	3-15—6-13	.049	9.0
1887	18			W½NE¼	33	26	31	3-15—9-15	.146	54.0
1893	25			W½NE¼	33	26	31	3-15—9-15	.203	75.0
1900	14.60			W½NE¼	33	26	31	3-15—9-15	.119	55.80

Claimant—**Ludwig J. Munk.** Proof No. 0058
Source—**Humboldt River.** Ditch—***Larson Ditch; Union Canal and Reed Ditch.**

	*1874			40				SW¼	34	26	31	3-15—0-15	.325	120.0
	1876			5				SW¼	34	26	31	3-15—9-15	.041	15.0
	1876			55				SW¼	34	26	31	3-15—0-15	.447	165.0
	1881			25				SW¼	34	26	31	3-15—9-15	.203	75.0
	1874			23.70				SW¼	34	26	31	3-15—0-15	.193	71.10

Claimant—**N. C. Munk.** Proof No. 0059
Source—**Humboldt River.** Ditch—***Larson Ditch; Union Canal through Reed Ditch.**

	*1874			35				W½NE¼	4	25	31	3-15—9-15	.285	105.0
	1876			15.35				W½NE¼	4	25	31	3-15—9-15	.125	46.05
	1876			15				W½NE¼	4	25	31	3-15—0-15	.122	45.0
	1874			—	3.60			W½NE¼	4	25	31	3-15—6-13	.029	5.4

Claimant—**Johannes Anderson.** Proof No. 0059
Source—**Humboldt River.** Ditch—***Larson Ditch; Union Canal through Reed Ditch.**

	*1874			20				E½NE¼NE¼	4	25	31	3-15—0-15	.163	60.0

Claimant—**Nevada Land & Livestock Co.** Proof No. 0060
Source—**Humboldt River.** Ditch—**†Mayes and Harrison, now Southwest Ditch; Graveyard and Borland Sloughs, *Irish-American.**

	1883			20.80				SE¼SW¼	27	27	31	3-15—0-15	.169	62.43
	1883			31.85				W½SW¼	27	27	31	3-15—9-15	.259	95.55
	1883			83.75				SW¼	27	27	31	3-15—9-15	.681	251.25
	1876			†65				S½	28	27	31	3-15—9-15	.528	195.0
	1878			†25				S½	28	27	31	3-15—0-15	.203	75.0
	1880			†70				S½	28	27	31	3-15—9-15	.569	210.0
	1883			57.40				S½	28	27	31	3-15—0-15	.467	172.20
	1887			*70.75				W½NE¼	28	27	31	3-15—9-15	.575	212.25
	1891			133.95				SE¼	29	27	31	3-15—9-15	1.089	401.85
	1883			51.20				N½NE¼	32	27	31	3-15—9-15	.416	153.60
	1883			79.90				NE¼	33	27	31	3-15—9-15	.650	239.70
	1895			47.90				NE¼	33	27	31	3-15—9-15	.389	143.70
	1894			—		1.50		SE¼NE¼	28	27	31	3-15—6-13	.012	2.25

Claimant—**John Greve.** Proof No. 0061
Source—**Humboldt River.** Ditch—***Kewley's Slough and Union Canal.**

	*1901			30.65				NW¼SE¼	35	26	31	3-15—9-15	.249	91.95
	1901			—	.60			NW¼SE¼	35	26	31	3-15—6-13	.005	.9

Claimant—**Mrs. Sophia O'Neil.** Proof No. 0062
Source—**Humboldt River.** Ditch—**Southwest Ditch.**

	1883			43.80				*N½NW¼	26	27	31	3-15—9-15	.357	131.67

*West of R. R. track.

Claimant—**Mary Jane Ostrander.** Proof No. 0063
Source—**Humboldt River.** Ditch—**Young Ditch.**

Year of priority	Culture—Acres: Harvest crops	Meadow pasture	Diversified pasture	Location: Subdivision	Section	Tp.N.	R.E.	Length of season	Duty of water: C.F.S.	Acre-feet
1888	20			N½SE¼	12	27	31	3-15—9-15	.163	60.0
1888	20			N½SE¼	12	27	31	3-15—9-15	.163	60.0
1888	38.50			N½SE¼	12	27	31	3-15—9-15	.313	115.50

Claimant—**W. C. Pitt.** Proof No. 0064
Source—**Humboldt River.** Ditch—**Old Channel Ditch.**

Year of priority	Harvest crops	Meadow pasture	Diversified pasture	Subdivision	Section	Tp.N.	R.E.	Length of season	C.F.S.	Acre-feet
1888	38.15			N½	15	27	31	3-15—9-15	.310	114.45
1888	534.10				15	27	31	3-15—9-15	4.342	1602.30
1888	39.23			NW¼	23	27	31	3-15—9-15	.319	117.69
1888	88.27			NW¼	23	27	31	3-15—9-15	.718	264.81
1888	145.05			NE¼	22	27	31	3-15—9-15	1.179	435.15
1888	340.95				9	27	31	3-15—9-15	2.772	1022.85
1900	67			SW¼	10	27	31	3-15—9-15	.545	201.0
1888	Sufficient water to develop 50 H.P.							1-1—12-31		
1914	Sufficient water to develop 10 H.P.							1-1—12-31		

Water so diverted to be returned to stream undiminished in quantity immediately below power plant near Old Channel Dam.

Claimant—**W. C. Pitt.** Proof No. 0065
Source—**Humboldt River.** Ditch—**Southwest Ditch.**

Year of priority	Harvest crops	Meadow pasture	Diversified pasture	Subdivision	Section	Tp.N.	R.E.	Length of season	C.F.S.	Acre-feet
1883	50			W½SE¼	27	27	31	3-15—9-15	.407	150.0

Claimant—**U. S. Government Indian School.** Proof. No. 0065
Source—**Humboldt River.** Ditch—**Southwest Ditch.**

Year of priority	Harvest crops	Meadow pasture	Diversified pasture	Subdivision	Section	Tp.N.	R.E.	Length of season	C.F.S.	Acre-feet
1883	17.30			S½SW¼SE¼	27	27	31	3-15—9-15	.141	51.90

Claimant—**A. Reno.** Proof No. 0067
Source—**Humboldt River.** Ditch—**Old Channel.**

Year of priority	Harvest crops	Meadow pasture	Diversified pasture	Subdivision	Section	Tp.N.	R.E.	Length of season	C.F.S.	Acre-feet
1888	66.33			S½NW¼&NE¼SW¼	13	27	31	3-15—9-15	.539	198.99
1888	33.17			E½SW¼&NE¼SW¼	13	27	31	3-15—9-15	.270	99.51

Claimant—**W. C. Ruddell.** Proof No. 0068
Source—**Humboldt River.** Ditch—**Irish-American or Last Chance.**

Year of priority	Harvest crops	Meadow pasture	Diversified pasture	Subdivision	Section	Tp.N.	R.E.	Length of season	C.F.S.	Acre-feet
1863	20			*E½W½	26	27	31	3-15—9-15	.163	60.0
1869	43.75			SW¼	26					
				NW¼	35	27	31	3-15—9-15	.356	131.25
1873	45			SE¼	26	27	31	3-15—9-15	.300	135.0
1873		100.00		*NE¼	26	27	31	3-15—9-13	.813	150.0
1873		39.61		W¼SE¼ & E¼SW¼	26	27	31	3-15—9-13	.292	59.42
1885	100			NE¼SW¼						

								SE¼NW¼						
								SW¼NE¼						
								NW¼SE¼	26	27	31	3-15—9-15	.813	300.0
	1886			35.10				NE¼SE¼	26	27	31	3-15—9-15	.285	105.80
	1887			20.10				NE¼SW¼	26	27	31	3-15—9-15	.163	60.80
								NE¼SW¼						
	1884			5.10				SE¼NW¼						
								SW¼NE¼						
								NW¼SE¼	26	27	31	3-15—9-15	.041	15.30
	1884			7.65				E½SE¼	26	27	31	3-15—9-15	.062	22.95
	1869			...	8.65			NW¼NW¼	35	27	31	3-15—6-13	.070	12.98
	1868			...	42.45			N½NW¼	35	27	31	3-15—6-13	.345	63.68

*Near center.

Claimant—***Millie R. Evans.** Proof No. 0069

Source—**Humboldt River.** Ditch—†**Rodgers Canal System.**

	1890			320.25					24	26	31	3-15—9-15	2.677	987.75
	1890			467.70					25	26	31	3-15—9-15	3.802	1403.10
	1890			158.06				E½	16	26	31	3-15—9-15	1.290	474.18
	1890			11.40				SE¼SE¼	16	26	31	3-15—9-15	.093	34.20
	1891			118					18	26	32	3-15—9-15	.959	354.0
	1891			34.60				W½SW¼	18	26	32	3-15—9-15	.281	103.80
	1891			199.75					18	26	32	3-15—9-15	1.624	599.25
	1891			123.50				NE¼ & W½	19	26	32	3-15—9-15	1.004	370.50
	1891			18.40				NW¼NW¼	19	26	32	3-15—9-15	.150	55.20
	1891			51.10				W½	19	26	32	3-15—9-15	.415	153.30
	1877			277.98					35	26	31	3-15—9-15	2.260	833.94
	1883			173.82				E½W½ & E½	10	26	31	3-15—9-15	1.413	521.46
	1883			...		105.23		N½	10	26	31	3-15—6-13	.856	157.85
	1883			...		24.84		N½	10	26	31	3-15—6-13	.202	37.26
	1880			143.40					11	26	31	3-15—9-15	1.166	430.20
	1884			214.05					7	26	31	3-15—9-15	1.984	732.15
	1884			8.02					7	26	31	3-15—9-15	.065	24.06
	1876			153.64				SE¼	13	26	31	3-15—9-15	1.249	460.92
	1876			139.92				SW¼	13	26	31	3-15—9-15	1.138	419.76
	1876			19.56				SE¼NW¼	13	26	31	3-15—9-15	.159	58.68
	1876			74.20				S½NE¼	13	26	31	3-15—9-15	.603	222.60
	1876			27.95				NW¼NE¼	13	26	31	3-15—9-15	.227	83.85
	1876			45.28				NE¼NE¼	13	26	31	3-15—9-15	.368	135.84
	1876			...		36.41		NE¼NW¼	13	26	31	3-15—6-13	.296	54.62
	1876			...		92.36		NW¼	13	26	31	3-15—6-13	.751	138.54
	1880			65.67				S½	15	26	31	3-15—9-15	.534	197.01
	1880			218.89				W½ & NE¼	15	26	31	3-15—9-15	1,780	656.67
	1880			6.28				SW¼SW¼	15	26	31	3-15—9-15	.051	18.84
	1880			9.78				NE¼NE¼	15	26	31	3-15—9-15	.080	29.34
	1880			4.52				W½NE¼	15	26	31	3-15—9-15	.037	13.56
	1880			23.99				E½NE¼	15	26	31	3-15—9-15	.195	71.97
	1880			105.80				E½	15	26	31	3-15—9-15	.860	317.40
	1880			3.56				NW¼NW¼	15	26	31	3-15—9-15	.029	10.68
	1880			2.71				W½NE¼	15	26	31	3-15—9-15	.022	8.13
	1880			1.47				NW¼NE¼	15	26	31	3-15—9-15	.012	4.41

271

Millie R. Evans—Continued.

Year of priority	Culture—Acres: Harvest crops	Meadow pasture	Diversified pasture	Location: Subdivision	Section	Tp.N.	R.E.	Length of season	Duty of water: C.F.S.	Acre-feet
1880	44.83			E½E½	15	26	31	3-15—9-15	.364	134.49
1880	9.77			SW¼SE¼	15	26	31	3-15—9-15	.079	29.31
1862	70				26	26	31	3-15—9-15	.569	210.0
1862	40			S½	10	26	31	3-15—9-15	.325	120.0
1864	20			SW¼	11	26	31	3-15—9-15	.163	60.0
1867	80			NW¼	23	26	31	3-15—9-15	.650	240.0
1873	128.90				14	26	31	3-15—9-15	1.048	38.67
1877	24.84			W½NE¼	23	26	31	3-15—9-15	.202	74.52
1877	202.90			E½	23	26	31	3-15—9-15	1.650	608.70
1877	16.43			SW¼SE¼	23	26	31	3-15—9-15	.134	49.29
1877	43.92			NE¼SW¼	23	26	31	3-15—9-15	.357	131.76
1877			47.08	NW¼NE¼	23	26	31	3-15—6-13	.383	70.62
1877			43.53	NW¼SW¼	23	26	31	3-15—6-13	.354	65.30
1878	289.33				24	26	31	3-15—9-15	2.352	867.99
1877	42.62			W½NE¼	26	26	31	3-15—9-15	.347	127.86
1877	16.43			NE¼NE¼	26	26	31	3-15—9-15	.134	49.29
1877	6.66			SE¼NE¼	26	26	31	3-15—9-15	.054	19.98
1877			166.54	SW¼	26	26	31	3-15—6-13	1.354	249.81

*Rodgers Canal System was initiated through the following ditches:
- (a) Blake Ditch.
- (b) Winslow Ditch.
- (c) Weikel Ditch.
- (d) Kewley Ditch.
- (e) McCallum & Andrieux Company Ditch.
- (f) McCallum Ditch.
- (g) Slaven Ditch.
- (h) J. B. Brown Ditch.
- (i) Saxenheimer Ditch.
- (j) Farmers Ditch.
- (k) Marker Ditch.
- (l) Fuss Ditch.
- (m) J. B. Brown Extension Ditch.

†Rodgers Estate.

Claimant—**Vic Sebbas.** Proof No. 0070
Source—**Humboldt River.** Ditch—**Young Ditch.**

Year of priority	Harvest crops	Meadow pasture	Diversified pasture	Subdivision	Section	Tp.N.	R.E.	Length of season	C.F.S.	Acre-feet
1888	37.25			S½	2	27	31	3-15—9-15	.303	111.75
1888	38.45			S½	2	27	31	3-15—9-15	.313	115.35
1888	12.10			S½	2	27	81	3-15—9-15	.098	36.30
1888	5.55			S½	2	27	31	3-15—9-15	.045	16.65
1888	9.10			S½	2	27	31	3-15—9-15	.074	27.30
1888	2.00			S½	2	27	31	3-15—9-15	.016	6.00
1888	10.00			S½	2	27	31	3-15—9-15	.081	30.00
1888	1.00			NE¼SE¼	2	27	31	3-15—9-15	.008	3.00

Claimant—**E. W. Sommer.** Proof No. 0071
Source—**Humboldt River.** Ditch—**Highflyer or Arthur Kewley Ditch.**

Year of priority	Harvest crops	Meadow pasture	Diversified pasture	Subdivision	Section	Tp.N.	R.E.	Length of season	C.F.S.	Acre-feet
1887	47.00			NW¼	2	25	31	3-15—9-15	.387	142.08
1888	100.00			NW¼	2	25	31	3-15—9-15	.818	300.00
1888			4.84	NW¼	2	25	31	3-15—6-13	.030	7.26

Claimant—**Matt Smith.** Proof No. 0072
Source—**Humboldt River.** Ditch—**Young Ditch.**

	1888			40				W½E½	1	27	31	3-15—9-15	.325	120.00
	1888			8.70				W½E½	1	27	31	3-15—9-15	.071	25.10
	1888			3.15				W½E½	1	27	31	3-15—9-15	.026	9.45
	1904			6.15				W½E½	1	27	31	3-15—9-15	.050	18.45
	1888			....	2.36			W½E½	1	27	31	3-15—6-13	.019	3.53
	1888			....		10.70		W½E½	1	27	31	3-15—6-13	.087	16.05

Claimant—**I. M. Springer, Sr.** Proof No. 0073
Source—**Humboldt River.** Ditch—***Slough ditch 1873 to 1887; †Irish-American 1887 to present.**

	*1873			9.50				W½NE¼&NW¼SE¼	23	27	31	3-15—9-15	.077	28.50
	†1887			19.00				W½NE¼&NW¼SE¼	23	27	31	3-15—9-15	.154	57.00
	†1887			19.00				W½NE¼&NW¼SE¼	23	27	31	3-15—9-15	.154	57.00

Claimant—**Wm. A. Stauts.** Proof No. 0074
Source—**Humboldt River.** Ditch—**Irish-American.**

	1887			20.20				SE¼SW¼	22	27	31	3-15—9-15	.164	60.60
	1899			4.00				SW¼SE¼	22	27	31	3-15—9-15	.033	12.00

Claimant—**George C. Stoker.** Proof No. 0076
Source—**Humboldt River.** Ditch—**Old Channel.**

	1896			94.58				SE¼	22	27	31	3-15—9-15	.769	283.74

Claimant—**Wm. A. Stauts.** Proof No. 0076
Source—**Humboldt River.** Ditch—**Old Channel.**

	1899			26.15				W½SE¼	22	27	31	3-15—9-15	.213	78.45

Claimant—**H. Stoker.** Proof No. 0077
Source—**Humboldt River.** Ditch—**Old Channel.**

	1888			224.70				NW¼&W½NE¼	14	27	31	3-15—9-15	1.827	674.10

Claimant—**Antone Alves and Anna Alves.** Proof No. 0077
Source—**Humboldt River.** Ditch—**Old Channel.**

	1888			45				W½SE¼	10	27	31	3-15—9-15	.366	135.00
	1888			11				W½SE¼	10	27	31	3-15—9-15	.089	33.00
	1896			14.95				W½SE¼	10	27	31	3-15—9-15	.122	44.85

Claimant—**Pascasio Bilbao.** Proof No. **0078**

Source—**Humboldt River.** Ditch—**Union Canal through Lake Shore Ditch.**

Year of priority	Culture—Acres: Harvest crops	Meadow pasture	Diversified pasture	Location: Subdivision	Section	Tp.N.	R.E.	Length of season	Duty of water: C.F.S.	Acre-feet
1883	5			SE¼NE¼	29	26	31	3-15—9-15	.051	15.0
1883	20			N½NE¼SE¼	29	26	31	3-15—9-15	.163	60.0
1884	5			NE¼SE¼	29	26	31	3-15—9-15	.051	15.0
1887	5			SE¼NE¼	29	26	31	3-15—9-15	.051	15.0
1888	8			E½NE¼	29	26	31	3-15—9-15	.065	24.0
1888	3			E½E½	29	26	31	3-15—9-15	.024	9.0
1899	8			E½E½	29	26	31	3-15—9-15	.065	24.0
1891	10			E½E½	29	26	31	3-15—9-15	.081	30.0
1892	13.20			E½E½	29	26	31	3-15—9-15	.107	39.6
1893	13.20			E½E½	29	26	31	3-15—9-15	.107	39.6
1894	13.20			E½E½	29	26	31	3-15—9-15	.107	39.6
1883	6.50			E½NE¼NE¼	29	26	31	3-15—9-15	.053	19.5
1883	....		.80	SE¼NE¼	29	26	31	3-15—6-13	.007	1.2

Claimant—**John O'Kane.** Proof No. **0079**

Source—**Humboldt River.** Ditch—**Irish-American.**

Year of priority	Harvest crops	Meadow pasture	Diversified pasture	Subdivision	Section	Tp.N.	R.E.	Length of season	C.F.S.	Acre-feet
1887	4.50			W½SE¼NE¼	27	27	31	3-15—9-15	.037	13.5

Claimant—**Lovelock Land and Development Co.** Proof No. **0080**

Source—**Humboldt River.** Ditch—***Lovelock Land and Development Co. Ditch System.**

Year of priority	Harvest crops	Meadow pasture	Diversified pasture	Subdivision	Section	Tp.N.	R.E.	Length of season	C.F.S.	Acre-feet
1900	63.30			N½NE¼	10	25	31	3-15—9-15	.515	189.90
1900	....		52.70	S½NE¼	10	25	31	3-15—6-13	1.102	406.65
1900	....		42.05	W½SE¼	10	25	31	3-15—6-13	.435	106.65
1900	....		73.15	S½&NE¼	2	25	31	3-15—6-13	.595	108.73
1900	135.55			SW¼	2	25	31	3-15—9-15	1.102	406.65
1900	53.55			SE¼	2	25	31	3-15—9-15	.435	160.65
1900	440.25			N½&N½S½	8	25	31	3-15—9-15	3.579	1320.75
1900	155.00			S½S½	8	25	31	3-15—9-15	1.260	465.0
1900	472.50			N½&N½S½	7	25	31	3-15—9-15	3.841	1417.50
1900	155.00			S½S½	7	25	31	3-15—9-15	1.260	465.0
1900	420.00			A part of	16	25	31	3-15—9-15	3.413	1260.00
1900	626.00				11	25	30	3-15—9-15	5.080	1878.0
1900	633.40				12	25	30	3-15—9-15	5.150	1900.20
1900	611.30				18	25	31	3-15—9-15	4.937	1833.90
1900	Reservoir Storage									4800.00

*The Lovelock Land and Development Company Ditch System.
(a) Kewley.
(b) Highflyer Ditch and Flume.
(c) Killebrew and Beck.
(d) Tule Ditch and Flume.
(e) Levee.
(f) South Drainage and Waste Ditch.
(g) Lake Drainage and Waste Ditch.
(h) Tule Drainage and Waste Ditch.
(i) Reservoir.

Claimant—John G. Taylor.
Source—Humboldt River. Ditch—*Irish-American in conjunction with Old Channel.

	1887			*97.50				E½	21	27	31	3-15—9-15	.793	292.50
	1887			*3.10				SE¼SE¼	21	27	31	3-15—9-15	.025	9.30
	1887			*6.30				SE¼SW¼	21	27	31	3-15—9-15	.051	18.90
	1887			*4.80				SE¼SW¼	21	27	31	3-15—9-15	.039	14.40
	1888			47.55				W½NE¼	21	27	31	3-15—9-15	.387	142.65
	1888			31.70				E½NW¼	21	27	31	3-15—9-15	.258	95.10

Claimant—John G. Taylor. Proof No. 0081
Source—Humboldt River. Ditch—Old Channel in conjunction with Young Ditch.

	1888			20				N½	3	27	31	3-15—9-15	.163	60.0
	1888			60				N½	3	27	31	3-15—9-15	.488	180.0
	1888			190				S½	3	27	31	3-15—9-15	1.545	570.0
	1888			66.10				N½	3	27	31	3-15—9-15	.537	198.30
	1888			388.75					10	27	31	3-15—9-15	3.159	1166.25

Claimant—John G. Taylor. Proof No. 0081
Source—Humboldt River. Ditch—Young Ditch.

	1888			101.05				E½E½	4	27	31	3-15—9-15	.822	303.15
	1888			—		6.75		NW¼NE¼	3	27	31	3-15—6-13	.055	10.13
	1888			176.80				S½S½	34	28	31	3-15—9-15	1.437	530.40
	1888			26				SE¼SE¼	33	28	31	3-15—9-15	.211	78.00

Claimant—John G. Taylor. Proof No. 0081
Source—Humboldt River. Ditch—Irish-American in conjunction with Union Canal.

	1887			136.05				SW¼	22	27	31	3-15—9-15	1.106	408.15

Claimant—John G. Taylor. Proof No. 0081
Source—Humboldt River. Ditch—Irish-American in conjunction with Marzen Slough.

	1887			86				NE¼	29	27	31	3-15—9-15	.699	258.00
	1887			8.70				SE¼NW¼	29	27	31	3-15—9-15	.071	26.10
	1887			16.25				S½NW¼	29	27	31	3-15—9-15	.132	48.75
	1887			128				SW¼	29	27	31	3-15—9-15	1.041	384.00
	1887			39				SE¼SE¼	30	27	31	3-15—9-15	.317	117.00
	1887			15				NE¼	31	27	31	3-15—9-15	.122	45.00
	1898			18.45				NE¼	31	27	31	3-15—9-15	.150	55.35

Claimant—Bergman and Alfree. Proof No. 0082
Source—Humboldt River. Ditch—Southwest Ditch; Lovelock and Borland Slough.

1874				100				N½	34	27	31	3-15—9-15	.813	300.00
	1880			33.70				N½	34	27	31	3-15—9-15	.274	101.10
	1880			79.40				W½SW¼	34	27	31	3-15—9-15	.646	238.20
	1890			47.60				E½SW¼, W½SE¼ &S½NE¼	34	27	31	3-15—9-15	.387	142.80
	1883					3.55		NE¼NE¼	34	27	31	3-15—6-13	.029	5.33
	1883					108.10		E½NW¼ &W½NE¼	34	27	31	3-15—6-13	.879	162.15
	1883					213.10		E½, E½SW¼	34	27	31	3-15—6-13	1.733	319.65

Claimant—**Bergman and Alfree.** Proof No. 0082

Source—**Humboldt River.** Ditch—**Southwest Ditch.**

Year of priority	Culture—Acres: Harvest crops	Meadow pasture	Diversified pasture	Location: Subdivision	Section	Tp.N.	R.E.	Length of season	Duty of water: C.F.S.	Acre-feet
1883	52.30			NW¼	3	26	31	3-15—9-15	.425	156.90
1883			315.75	W½&NE¼	3	26	31	3-15—6-13	2.567	473.63
1883	49.15			S½SE¼	33	27	31	3-15—9-15	.499	147.45
1883	48.00			SE¼	33	27	31	3-15—9-15	.390	144.00
1883	38.90			SE¼&SW¼	33	27	31	3-15—9-15	.316	116.70
1883	25.95			SE¼SW¼	33	27	31	3-15—9-15	.211	77.85
1883		22.00		NW¼SW¼	33	27	31	3-15—6-13	.179	33.00
1883		10.20		SW¼	33	27	31	3-15—6-13	.083	15.30
1883		14.95		SW¼SW¼	33	27	31	3-15—6-13	.123	22.48
1883			51.10	S½	33	27	31	3-15—6-13	.415	76.65
1883			3.95	SW¼SE¼	33	27	31	3-15—6-13	.032	5.93
1880	60			SE¼	32	27	31	3-15—9-15	.488	180.00
1883	20			SE¼	32	27	31	3-15—9-15	.163	60.00
1883	139.80			SE¼,S½NE¼,SW¼	32	27	31	3-15—9-15	1.137	419.40
1883	59.75			N½	5	26	31	3-15—9-15	.486	179.25
1883	33.00			NE¼	5	26	31	3-15—9-15	.268	99.00
1883	47.95			E½E½	5	26	31	3-15—9-15	.390	143.85
1883	78.65			NE¼	4	26	31	3-15—9-15	.639	235.95
1877	81.35			S½	4	26	31	3-15—9-15	.661	244.05
1880	119.95			S½	4	26	31	3-15—9-15	.975	359.85
1880	128.20			N½	4	26	31	3-15—9-15	1.042	384.60
1880	77.45			W½NW¼	4	26	31	3-15—9-15	.630	232.35
1880			38.90	NE¼SE¼	4	26	31	3-15—6-13	.316	58.35
1880			17.70	SE¼SE¼	4	26	31	3-15—6-13	.144	26.55
1880			11.00	NE¼NE¼	4	26	31	3-15—6-13	.089	16.50

Claimant—**F. Tessier.** Proof No. 0085

Source—**Humboldt River.** Ditch—**Old Channel.**

Year of priority	Harvest crops	Meadow pasture	Diversified pasture	Subdivision	Section	Tp.N.	R.E.	Length of season	C.F.S.	Acre-feet
1899	61.48			SE¼	13	27	31	3-15—9-15	.500	184.44
1900	15.94			SE¼	13	27	31	3-15—9-15	.130	47.82

Claimant—**Morris Nelson.** Proof No. 0086

Source—**Humboldt River.** Ditch—**Union Canal.**

Year of priority	Harvest crops	Meadow pasture	Diversified pasture	Subdivision	Section	Tp.N.	R.E.	Length of season	C.F.S.	Acre-feet
1887	14.54			W½NW¼	32	26	31	3-15—9-15	.118	43.62
1888	18.17			W½NW¼	32	26	31	3-15—9-15	.148	54.51
1892	7.27			W½NW¼	32	26	31	3-15—9-15	.059	21.81
1900	18.17			W½NW¼	32	26	31	3-15—9-15	.148	54.51
1888	9.00			SE¼NE¼	31	26	31	3-15—9-15	.073	27.00
1892	13.85			SE¼NE¼	31	26	31	3-15—9-15	.113	41.55
1893	9.00			SE¼NE¼	31	26	31	3-15—9-15	.073	27.00
1890	72.35			N½NE¼	31	26	31	3-15—9-15	.588	217.05

Claimant—**Hans Christensen.** Proof No. **0087**

Source—**Humboldt River.** Ditch—**Union Canal through Lake Shore Ditch.**

	1876			10				NW¼SW¼	28	26	31	3-15—9-15	.081	30.00
	1876			25				SW¼	28	26	31	3-15—9-15	.203	75.00
	1885			50				SW¼	28	26	31	3-15—9-15	.407	150.00
	1890			13.35				SW¼	28	26	31	3-15—9-15	.109	40.05

Claimant—**Peter Olson.** Proof No. **0088**

Source—**Humboldt River.** Ditch—**Old Channel Ditch.**

	1888			65.85				S½NW¼	12	27	31	3-15—9-15	.535	197.55
	1904			4.70				S½NW¼	12	27	31	3-15—9-15	.038	14.10

Claimant—**W. W. Van Reed.** Proof. No. **0089**

Source—**Humboldt River. Ditch—Union Canal through Lake Shore Ditch.**

	1897			15.00				E½SW¼	29	26	31	3-15—9-15	.122	45.00
	1897					5.90		E½SW¼	29	26	31	3-15—6-13	.048	8.85
	1898			14.85				E½SW¼	29	26	31	3-15—9-15	.121	44.55
	1900			20.50				E½SW¼	29	26	31	3-15—9-15	.167	61.50
	1898			5.10				SE¼	29	26	31	3-15—9-15	.041	15.30

Claimant—**Andrew Westfall.** Proof No. **0091**

Source—**Humboldt River.** Ditch—**Union Canal through Lake Shore Ditch.**

	1876			20.97				SE¼	32	26	31	3-15—9-15	.170	62.91
	1876			5.22				NE¼	32	26	31	3-15—9-15	.042	15.66
	1885			87.32				SE¼	32	26	31	3-15—9-15	.710	261.96
	1885			80.00				E½NE¼	32	26	31	3-15—9-15	.650	240.00
	1885			30.00				E½NW¼	32	26	31	3-15—9-15	.244	90.00
	1890			11.40				S½SE¼SE¼	29	26	31	3-15—9-15	.093	34.20
	1888			35.65				S½	31	26	31	3-15—9-15	.290	106.95
	1890			77.79				E½	32	26	31	3-15—9-15	.632	233.37
	1890			50.00				E½NW¼	32	26	31	3-15—9-15	.407	150.00
	1890					5.10		S½SE¼SE¼	29	26	31	3-15—6-13	.041	7.65
	1885					8.25		NW¼NE¼	32	26	31	3-15—6-13	.067	12.38
	1888					196.60		S½	31	26	31	3-15—6-13	1.598	294.90

Claimant—**L. P. Johnson.** Proof No. **0092**

Source—**Humboldt River.** Ditch—**Old Channel.**

	1888			7.00				E½SE¼	10	27	31	3-15—9-15	.057	21.00
	1888			15.00				E½SE¼	10	27	31	3-15—9-15	.122	45.00
	1888			15.00				E½SE¼	10	27	31	3-15—9-15	.122	45.00
	1888			3.80				E½SE¼	10	27	31	3-15—9-15	.031	11.40
	1888			31.30				E½SE¼	10	27	31	3-15—9-15	.254	93.90
	1888			1.90				E½SE¼	10	27	31	3-15—9-15	.015	5.70

Claimant—**S. R. Young.** Proof No. 0093

Source—**Humboldt River.** Ditch—**Young Ditch.**

Year of priority	Culture—Acres: Harvest crops	Meadow pasture	Diversified pasture	Location: Subdivision	Section	Tp.N.	R.E.	Length of season	Duty of water: C.F.S.	Acre-feet
1888	15.75			SE¼NW¼	28	28	32	3-15—9-15	.120	47.25
1888	11.80			NE¼SW¼	28	28	32	3-15—9-15	.096	35.40
1888	15.00			NE¼SW¼&SE¼NW¼	28	28	32	3-15—9-15	.122	45.00
1888	31.45			S½NE¼&N½SE¼	28	28	32	3-15—9-15	.256	94.35
1888	66.45			NE¼&NW¼SE¼&NE¼SW¼&SE¼NW¼	28	28	32	3-15—9-15	.540	199.35
1888	Sufficient water to develop 75 H.P.							1-1—12-31		
1909	Sufficient water to develop 100 H.P.							1-1—12-31		

Water so diverted to be returned to stream undiminished in quantity immediately below power plant.

Claimant—**H. M. Damm.** Proof No. 0094

Source—**Humboldt River.** Ditch—**Humboldt Irrigation and Power Co. Canal.**

Year of priority	Harvest crops	Meadow pasture	Diversified pasture	Subdivision	Section	Tp.N.	R.E.	Length of season	C.F.S.	Acre-feet
1888	15			W½W½	1	27	31	3-15—9-15	.122	45.0

Claimant—**E. K. Hanson.** Proof No. 0095

Source—**Humboldt River.** Ditch—**Southwest Ditch.**

Year of priority	Harvest crops	Meadow pasture	Diversified pasture	Subdivision	Section	Tp.N.	R.E.	Length of season	C.F.S.	Acre-feet
1883	2.35			SW¼SE¼	23	27	31	3-15—9-15	.019	7.05
1883	3.15			NE¼NW¼	26	27	31	3-15—9-15	.026	9.45
1879	3.55			NE¼NW¼	26	27	31	3-15—9-15	.029	10.65
1883	1.50			NE¼NW¼	26	27	31	3-15—9-15	.012	4.50

Claimant—***Geo. S. Nixon Estate and John Fant.** Proof No. 0099

Source—**Humboldt River.** Ditch—**Rodgers Ditch System—†Riverside Branch.**

Year of priority	Harvest crops	Meadow pasture	Diversified pasture	Subdivision	Section	Tp.N.	R.E.	Length of season	C.F.S.	Acre-feet
1871	10.00			NW¼	36	27	31	3-15—9-15	.081	30.00
1873	80.00			NW¼	36	27	31	3-15—9-15	.650	240.00
1873	60.00			SW¼	36	27	31	3-15—9-15	.488	180.00
1880	52.28			NW¼	36	27	31	3-15—9-15	.425	156.84
1880	29.26			SE¼	36	27	31	3-15—9-15	.238	87.78
1880	29.00			NE¼	36	27	21	3-15—9-15	.236	87.00
1881	20.00			SW¼	36	27	31	3-15—9-15	.163	60.00
1882	47.29			SW¼	36	27	31	3-15—9-15	.384	141.87
1882	16.22			NE¼	36	27	31	3-15—9-15	.132	48.66
1882	25.55			SE¼	36	27	31	3-15—9-15	.208	76.65
1882	....		30.00	N½	36	27	31	3-15—6-13	.244	45.00
1883	28.00			SE¼	35	27	31	3-15—9-15	.228	84.00
1883	52.00			SW¼	35	27	31	3-15—9-15	.423	156.00
1885	153.85			NE¼	35	27	31	3-15—9-15	1.251	461.55
1885	75.00			NE¼	35	27	31	3-15—9-15	.610	225.00
1898	25.72			SW¼	35	27	31	3-15—9-15	.209	77.16
1901	29.77			SE¼	35	27	31	3-15—9-15	.242	89.31

†Riverside Branch.
(a) Silverwood Ditch.
(b) Muttleberry Ditch.
(c) Slough Ditch.
(d) Hazelton-Thies Ditch.
(e) J. H. Thies Ditch.
(f) Thies Reservoir.

*Riverside Ranch.

WINNEMUCCA DISTRICT

Claimant—**Edna Anderson.** Proof No. 00101

Source—**Humboldt River.** Ditch—**North Side Cusick Ditch.**

1870	10.00		NE¼SE¼	18	36	40	3-15—9-15	.081	30.00
1870	20.90		SE¼NE¼	18	36	40	3-15—9-15	.170	62.70
1870	38.10		SW¼NE¼	18	36	40	3-15—9-15	.310	114.30
1870	32.00		NW¼NE¼	18	36	40	3-15—9-15	.260	96.00
1870	39.50		NE¼NW¼	18	36	40	3-15—9-15	.331	118.50
1870	20.30		SE¼NW¼	18	36	40	3-15—9-15	.165	60.90
1870	18.75		NW¼NW¼	18	36	40	3-15—9-15	.152	56.25
1870	....	8.90	NW¼NW¼	18	36	40	3-15—4-28	.072	6.45
1870	2.00		SW¼NW¼	18	36	40	3-15—9-15	.016	6.00
1870	.80		NE¼SW¼	18	36	40	3-15—9-15	.007	2.40

Claimant—**Edna Anderson.** Proof No. 00101

Source—**Humboldt River.** Ditch—**Cusick Ditch.**

1870	38.20		SE¼SE¼	18	36	40	3-15—9-15	.311	114.60
1870	5.40		NE¼SE¼	18	36	40	3-15—9-15	.044	16.20
1870	14.80		SW¼SE¼	18	36	40	3-15—9-15	.120	44.40
1870	22.00		NW¼SE¼	18	36	40	3-15—9-15	.179	66.00
1870	.40		SW¼NE¼	18	36	40	3-15—9-15	.003	1.20
1870	6.15		NE¼SW¼	18	36	40	3-15—9-15	.051	18.45
1870	....	2.50	NE¼SW¼	18	36	40	3-15—4-28	.020	1.88
1870	....	.75	NW¼SW¼	18	36	40	3-15—4-28	.002	.56
1870	....	10.70	SE¼NW¼	18	36	40	3-15—4-28	.087	8.03
1870	.20		SW¼NW¼	18	36	40	3-15—9-15	.002	.60
1870	....	18.20	SW¼NW¼	18	36	40	3-15—4-28	.148	13.65
1870	....	6.00	NW¼NW¼	18	36	40	3-15—4-28	.049	4.50

Claimant—**Edna Anderson.** Proof No. 00101

Source—**Humboldt River.** Ditch—**Anderson Ditch.**

1871	20.00		NE¼SE¼	18	36	40	3-15—9-15	.063	60.00
1871	6.95		NE¼SW¼	18	36	40	3-15—9-15	.057	20.85
1871	....	2.50	NE¼SW¼	18	36	40	3-15—4-28	.020	1.88
1871	....	1.50	NW¼SW¼	18	36	40	3-15—4-28	.012	1.13
1871	14.10		NW¼SE¼	18	36	40	3-15—9-15	.115	42.30

Claimant—**Edna** Anderson. Proof No. 00101

Source—**Humboldt River.** Ditch—**Pioneer Slough System.**

1871	7.30		NW¼NE¼	18	36	40	3-15—9-15	.059	21.90
1871	....	2.90	NE¼NE¼	20	36	40	3-15—4-28	.025	2.18
1871	....	19.70	SE¼SE¼	17	36	40	3-15—4-28	.160	14.78
1871	....	33.50	SW¼SE¼	17	36	40	3-15—4-28	.272	25.13
1871	....	28.20	NW¼SE¼	17	36	40	3-15—4-28	.229	21.15
1871	2.60		NE¼SE¼	17	36	40	3-15—9-15	.021	7.80
1871	3.30		SW¼NE¼	17	36	40	3-15—9-15	.027	9.90
1871	.80		SE¼SW¼	17	36	40	3-15—9-15	.007	2.40

Edna Anderson—Continued.

Year of priority	Harvest crops (Culture—Acres)	Meadow pasture (Culture—Acres)	Diversified pasture (Culture—Acres)	Subdivision (Location)	Section (Location)	Tp.N. (Location)	R.E. (Location)	Length of season	C.F.S. (Duty of water)	Acre-feet (Duty of water)
1871			21.90	SE¼SW¼	17	36	40	3-15—4-28	.178	16.43
1871	3.30			SW¼SW¼	17	36	40	3-15—9-15	.027	9.90
1871			1.00	SW¼SW¼	17	36	40	3-15—4-28	.008	.75
1871	1.20			NE¼SW¼	17	36	40	3-15—9-15	.010	3.60
1871			38.80	NE¼SW¼	17	36	40	3-15—4-28	.315	29.10
1871	29.90			NW¼SW¼	17	36	40	3-15—9-15	.243	89.70
1871			2.60	NW¼SW¼	17	36	40	3-15—4-28	.021	1.95
1871	25.70			SE¼NW¼	17	36	40	3-15—9-15	.209	77.10
1871	4.95			NW¼NW¼	17	36	40	3-15—9-15	.040	14.85
1871	36.90			SW¼NW¼	17	36	40	3-15—9-15	.300	110.70
1871	20.00			SE¼NE¼	18	36	40	3-15—9-15	.163	60.00
1871	29.30			NE¼NE¼	18	36	40	3-15—9-15	.238	87.90
1871	4.17			NE¼SW¼	7	36	40	3-15—9-15	.034	12.51
1871		34.06		NE¼SW¼	7	36	40	3-15—6-13	.277	51.09
1871	10.75			NW¼SW¼	7	36	40	3-15—9-15	.087	32.25
1871		21.80		NW¼SW¼	7	36	40	3-15—6-13	.177	32.70
1871			4.83	NW¼SW¼	7	36	40	3-15—4-28	.039	3.62
1871	10.83			SW¼SW¼	7	36	40	3-15—9-15	.088	32.49
1871		26.00		SW¼SW¼	7	36	40	3-15—6-13	.211	39.00
1871			1.12	SW¼SW¼	7	36	40	3-15—4-28	.009	.84
1871	21.97			SE¼SW¼	7	36	40	3-15—9-15	.179	65.91
1871		17.14		SE¼SW¼	7	36	40	3-15—6-13	.139	25.71
1871	35.53			NE¼SE¼	7	36	40	3-15—9-15	.289	106.59
1871		4.13		NE¼SE¼	7	36	40	3-15—6-13	.034	6.20
1871	3.20			NW¼SE¼	7	36	40	3-15—9-15	.026	9.60
1871		36.80		NW¼SE¼	7	36	40	3-15—6-13	.299	55.20
1871		38.32		SW¼SE¼	7	36	40	3-15—6-13	.312	57.48
1871		40.10		SE¼SE¼	7	36	40	3-15—6-13	.326	60.15

Claimant—**Edna Anderson.** Proof No. 00101
Source—**Humboldt River.** Ditch—**Humboldt River Overflow.**

Year of priority	Harvest crops	Meadow pasture	Diversified pasture	Subdivision	Section	Tp.N.	R.E.	Length of season	C.F.S.	Acre-feet
1874			1.20	SE¼SE¼	17	36	40	3-15—4-28	.010	.90
1874			2.60	SW¼SE¼	17	36	40	3-15—4-28	.021	1.95
1874			2.70	NW¼NE¼	20	36	40	3-15—4-28	.023	2.03
1874	7.20			SE¼SW¼	17	36	40	3-15—9-15	.059	21.60
1874			5.55	SE¼SW¼	17	36	40	3-15—4-28	.045	4.16
1874	20.70			SW¼SW¼	17	36	40	3-15—9-15	.241	89.10
1874	3.60			NW¼SW¼	17	36	40	3-15—9-15	.029	10.80
1874			.33	SE¼SE¼	27	36	40	3-15—4-28	.003	.25
1874			10.82	SW¼SE¼	27	36	40	3-15—4-28	.088	8.12

Claimant—**Edna Anderson.** Proof No. 00101
Source—**Humboldt River.** Ditch—**North Side Canal.**

Year of priority	Harvest crops	Meadow pasture	Diversified pasture	Subdivision	Section	Tp.N.	R.E.	Length of season	C.F.S.	Acre-feet
1874			12.40	SE¼NW¼	21	36	40	3-15—4-28	.101	9.30
1874			4.30	NE¼SW¼	21	36	40	3-15—4-28	.035	3.23
1874		10.00		NW¼SW¼	21	36	40	3-15—6-13	.081	15.00

	1874					9.20		NW¼SW¼	21	36	40	3-15—4-28	.075	6.90
	1874					31.40		SW¼NW¼	21	36	40	3-15—4-28	.255	23.55
	1874					20.90		NW¼NW¼	21	36	40	3-15—4-28	.243	22.43
	1874					7.70		NE¼NE¼	20	36	40	3-15—4-28	.063	5.78
	1874					11.00		SW¼SW¼	16	36	40	3-15—4-28	.089	8.25
	1874			1.12				SE¼SE¼	17	36	40	3-15—9-15	.010	3.36
	1874					12.58		SE¼SE¼	17	36	40	3-15—4-28	.102	9.44
	1874			25.94				NE¼SE¼	17	36	40	3-15—9-15	.211	77.82
	1874					6.77		NE¼SE¼	17	36	40	3-15—4-28	.055	5.08
	1874					10.20		NW¼SE¼	17	36	40	3-15—4-28	.083	7.65
	1874			17.80				SE¼NE¼	17	36	40	3-15—9-15	.145	53.40
	1874					5.50		SE¼NE¼	17	36	40	3-15—4-28	.045	4.13
	1874			34.20				SW¼NE¼	17	36	40	3-15—9-15	.278	102.60
	1874			11.70				SE¼NW¼	17	36	40	3-15—9-15	.095	35.10
	1874					1.10		NE¼NE¼	17	36	40	3-15—4-28	.009	.83
	1874					39.40		NE¼NW¼	17	36	40	3-15—4-28	.320	29.55
	1874					.75		NE¼SW¼	27	36	40	3-15—4-28	.006	.56
	1874			13.45				NW¼SW¼	27	36	40	3-15—0-15	.109	40.35
	1874			18.70				SE¼NW¼	27	36	40	3-15—9-15	.152	56.10
	1874			34.10				SW¼NW¼	27	36	40	3-15—9-15	.277	102.30
	1874			13.22				NW¼NW¼	27	36	40	3-15—9-15	.107	39.66
	1874			18.30				NW¼NE¼	17	36	40	3-15—0-15	.149	54.90
	1874					4.40		NW¼NE¼	17	36	40	3-15—4-28	.036	3.30
	1874					2.50		NW¼SW¼	16	36	40	3-15—4-28	.020	1.88

Claimant—**Edna Anderson.** Proof No. 00101
Source—**Humboldt River.** Ditch—**South Side Swail and Ditch.**

	1874					16.60		SE¼SW¼	27	36	40	3-15—4-28	.135	12.45
	1874					27.28		SW¼SW¼	27	36	40	3-15—4-28	.222	20.46
	1874						3.37	SW¼SW¼	27	36	40	3-15—4-28	.207	2.53
	1874			1.00				NW¼SW¼	27	36	40	3-15—9-15	.008	3.00

Claimant—**Edna Anderson.** Proof No. 00101
Source—**Humboldt River.** Ditch—**Big Slough Ditch.**

	1874			.36				NE¼SW¼	27	36	40	3-15—9-15	.003	1.08
	1874			.10				SE¼SW¼	27	36	40	3-15—9-15	.001	.30
	1874			1.82				SW¼SW¼	27	36	40	3-15—9-15	.015	5.46
	1874			16.48				NW¼SW¼	27	36	40	3-15—9-15	.134	49.44
	1874					3.86		NW¼SW¼	27	36	40	3-15—4-28	.031	2.90
	1874			1.90				SW¼SW¼	27	36	40	3-15—9-15	.015	5.70
	1874			1.20				SW¼SE¼	8	36	40	3-15—9-15	.010	3.60

Claimant—**Edna Anderson.** Proof No. 00101
Source—**Humboldt River.** Ditch—**North Side Canal.**

	1874			27.40				SE¼SW¼	8	36	40	3-15—9-15	.223	82.20
	1874					3.60		SE¼SW¼	8	36	40	3-15—4-28	.029	2.70
	1874			16.80				NE¼SW¼	8	36	40	3-15—9-15	.137	50.40
	1874					19.60		NE¼SW¼	8	36	40	3-15—4-28	.150	14.70
	1874			35.00				NW¼SW¼	8	36	40	3-15—9-15	.285	105.00

Edna Anderson—Continued.

Year of priority	Culture—Acres: Harvest crops	Culture—Acres: Meadow pasture	Culture—Acres: Diversified pasture	Location: Subdivision	Location: Section	Location: Tp.N.	Location: R.E.	Length of season	Duty of water: C.F.S.	Duty of water: Acre-feet
1874			1.50	NW¼SW¼	8	36	40	3-15—4-28	.012	1.13
1874	2.20			SW¼NW¼	8	36	40	3-15—9-15	.018	6.60
1874	1.20			SE¼NW¼	8	36	40	3-15—9-15	.010	3.60
1874			.30	SE¼NW¼	8	36	40	3-15—4-28	.003	.23
1874			2.40	NW¼SE¼	8	36	40	3-15—4-28	.020	1.80
1874			10.70	SE¼SE¼	27	36	40	3-15—4-28	.087	8.03
1874	.95			SW¼SE¼	27	36	40	3-15—9-15	.008	2.85
1874		1.10		SW¼SE¼	27	36	40	3-15—6-13	.009	1.65
1874			18.65	SW¼SE¼	27	36	40	3-15—4-28	.152	13.99
1874	.12			NW¼SE¼	27	36	40	3-15—9-15	.001	.36
1874			16.39	NW¼SE¼	27	36	40	3-15—4-28	.133	12.29
1874	3.60			SE¼SW¼	27	36	40	3-15—9-15	.029	10.80
1874			9.30	SE¼SW¼	27	36	40	3-15—4-28	.076	6.98
1874	35.48			NE¼SW¼	27	36	40	3-15—9-15	.288	106.44

Claimant—**Edna Anderson.** Proof No. 00101

Source—**Humboldt River.** Ditch—**Old South Side House Ditch.**

Year of priority	Harvest crops	Meadow pasture	Diversified pasture	Subdivision	Section	Tp.N.	R.E.	Length of season	C.F.S.	Acre-feet
1874			.90	NW¼SW¼	21	36	40	3-15—4-28	.007	.68
1874			1.80	SW¼NW¼	21	36	40	3-15—4-28	.015	1.35
1874		10.70		NE¼SE¼	20	36	40	3-15—6-13	.087	16.05
1874			1.60	NE¼SE¼	20	36	40	3-15—4-28	.013	1.20
1874		27.20		SE¼NE¼	20	36	40	3-15—6-13	.221	40.80
1874			7.45	SE¼NE¼	20	36	40	3-15—4-28	.061	5.59
1874		32.15		SW¼NE¼	20	36	40	3-15—6-13	.261	48.23
1874		28.60		NW¼NE¼	20	36	40	3-15—6-13	.234	43.90
1874			5.90	NW¼NE¼	20	36	40	3-15—4-28	.048	4.43
1874		15.40		NE¼NE¼	20	36	40	3-15—6-13	.125	23.10
1874			7.80	NE¼NE¼	20	36	40	3-15—4-28	.063	5.85

Claimant—**Edna Anderson.** Proof No. 00101

Source—**Humboldt River.** Ditch—**North Side Canal.**

Year of priority	Harvest crops	Meadow pasture	Diversified pasture	Subdivision	Section	Tp.N.	R.E.	Length of season	C.F.S.	Acre-feet
1874			30.80	NW¼NW¼	17	36	40	3-15—4-28	.250	23.10
1873			9.25	NE¼NE¼	18	36	40	3-15—4-28	.075	6.94
1874	37.20			SW¼SW¼	8	36	40	3-15—0-15	.302	111.60

Claimant—**Edna Anderson.** Proof No. 00101

Source—**Humboldt River.** Ditch—**Fairbanks Ditch System.**

Year of priority	Harvest crops	Meadow pasture	Diversified pasture	Subdivision	Section	Tp.N.	R.E.	Length of season	C.F.S.	Acre-feet
1874	10.47			NE¼SE¼	12	36	39	3-15—9-15	.086	31.41
1874			24.09	NE¼SE¼	12	36	39	3-15—4-28	.201	18.52

Claimant—**Bliss Brothers.** Proof No. 00101
Source—**Humboldt River.** Ditch—**Anderson Ditch System.**

1874		32.93			NW¼NE¼	14	36	41	3-15—6-13	.268	49.40
1874	10.80				NE¼NE¼	14	36	41	3-15—9-15	.088	32.40
1874		20.89			NE¼NE¼	14	36	41	3-15—6-13	.170	31.34
1874	4.57				NE¼NW¼	14	36	41	3-15—9-15	.037	13.71
1874		6.47			NE¼NW¼	14	36	41	3-15—6-13	.053	9.71
1874			3.92		NE¼NW¼	14	36	41	3-15—4-28	.032	2.94
1874		.90			SE¼SE¼	11	36	41	3-15—6-13	.007	1.35
1874		1.70			SW¼SE¼	11	36	41	3-15—6-13	.014	2.55
1874		1.65			SE¼NW¼	11	36	41	3-15—6-13	.013	2.48
1874			.20		SE¼NW¼	11	36	41	3-15—4-28	.002	.15
1874			.95		NW¼NW¼	11	36	41	3-15—4-28	.008	.71
1874			.80		SW¼SW¼	11	36	41	3-15—4-28	.007	.60
1874		2.76			SE¼NW¼	12	36	41	3-15—6-13	.022	4.14
1874				40.04	SE¼NW¼	12	36	41	3-15—4-28	.326	30.03
1874		4.00			SW¼NW¼	12	36	41	3-15—6-13	.033	6.00
1874				37.70	SW¼NW¼	12	36	41	3-15—4-28	.307	28.80
1874		25.53			NW¼SW¼	12	36	41	3-15—6-13	.208	38.30
1874				10.28	NW¼SW¼	12	36	41	3-15—4-28	.084	7.71
1874		38.55			SW¼SW¼	12	36	41	3-15—6-13	.313	57.83
1874		35.26			SE¼SW¼	12	36	41	3-15—6-13	.287	52.89
1874				.14	SE¼SW¼	12	36	41	3-15—6-13	.001	.12
1880		35.80			NE¼SW¼	12	36	41	3-15—6-13	.291	53.70
1880				4.82	NE¼SW¼	12	36	41	3-15—4-28	.039	3.62
1880		26.10			SW¼SE¼	12	36	41	3-15—6-13	.212	39.15
1880				12.60	SW¼SE¼	12	36	41	3-15—4-28	.102	9.45
1874	10.08				SE¼NE¼	14	36	41	3-15—9-15	.082	30.24
1874		22.96			SE¼NE¼	14	36	41	3-15—6-13	.187	34.44
1874	4.32				SW¼NE¼	14	36	41	3-15—9-15	.035	12.96
1874		11.13			SW¼NE¼	14	36	41	3-15—6-13	.090	16.70
1874			1.50		SW¼NE¼	14	36	41	3-15—6-13	.012	1.13
1874	2.52				NW¼NE¼	14	36	41	3-15—9-15	.020	7.56

Claimant—**Bliss Brothers.** Proof No. 00102
Source—**Humboldt River.** Ditch—**Pioneer Ditch System.**

1863	10.00				SW¼NW¼	3	36	39	3-15—9-15	.081	30.00
1863		10.00			SW¼NW¼	3	36	39	3-15—6-13	.081	15.00
1863			10.00		SW¼NW¼	3	36	39	3-15—4-28	.081	7.50
1863				8.43	SW¼NW¼	3	36	39	3-15—4-28	.069	6.32
1863	10.00				SE¼NW¼	3	36	39	3-15—9-15	.081	30.00
1863		10.00			SE¼NW¼	3	36	39	3-15—6-13	.081	15.00
1863			10.00		SE¼NW¼	3	36	39	3-15—4-28	.081	7.50
1863				8.41	SE¼NW¼	3	36	39	3-15—4-28	.068	6.31
1863	16.64				SE¼NW¼	2	36	39	3-15—9-15	.135	49.92
1863			.66		SE¼NW¼	2	36	39	3-15—4-28	.005	.50
1863	17.78				SE¼NW¼	2	36	39	3-15—9-15	.145	53.34
1863	31.72				SW¼NE¼	2	36	39	3-15—9-15	.258	95.16
1863		.86			SW¼NE¼	2	36	39	3-15—6-13	.007	1.29
1863			.24		SW¼NE¼	2	36	39	3-15—4-28	.002	.18

Millie R. Evans—Continued.

Year of priority	Culture—Acres: Harvest crops	Culture—Acres: Meadow pasture	Culture—Acres: Diversified pasture	Location: Subdivision	Location: Section	Location: Tp.N.	Location: R.E.	Length of season	Duty of water: C.F.S.	Duty of water: Acre-feet
1880	44.83			E½E½	15	26	31	3-15—9-15	.364	134.49
1880	9.77			SW¼SE¼	15	26	31	3-15—9-15	.079	29.31
1862	70				26	26	31	3-15—9-15	.569	210.0
1862	40			S½	10	26	31	3-15—9-15	.325	120.0
1864	20			SW¼	11	26	31	3-15—9-15	.163	60.0
1867	80			NW¼	23	26	31	3-15—9-15	.650	240.0
1873	128.90				14	26	31	3-15—9-15	1.048	38.67
1877	24.84			W½NE¼	23	26	31	3-15—9-15	.202	74.52
1877	202.90			E½	23	26	31	3-15—9-15	1.650	608.70
1877	16.43			SW¼SE¼	23	26	31	3-15—9-15	.134	49.29
1877	43.92			NE¼SW¼	23	26	31	3-15—9-15	.357	131.76
1877	....		47.08	NW¼NE¼	23	26	31	3-15—6-13	.383	70.02
1877	...		43.53	NW¼SW¼	23	26	31	3-15—6-13	.354	65.30
1878	289.33				24	26	31	3-15—9-15	2.352	867.99
1877	42.62			W½NE¼	26	26	31	3-15—9-15	.347	127.86
1877	16.43			NE¼NE¼	26	26	31	3-15—9-15	.134	49.29
1877	6.66			SE¼NE¼	26	26	31	3-15—9-15	.054	19.98
1877	....		166.54	SW¼	26	26	31	3-15—6-13	1.354	249.81

*Rodgers Canal System was initiated through the following ditches:
(a) Blake Ditch.
(b) Winslow Ditch.
(c) Weikel Ditch.
(d) Kewley Ditch.
(e) McCallum & Andrieux Company Ditch.
(f) McCallum Ditch.
(g) Slaven Ditch.
(h) J. B. Brown Ditch.
(i) Saxenheimer Ditch.
(j) Farmers Ditch.
(k) Marker Ditch.
(l) Fuss Ditch.
(m) J. B. Brown Extension Ditch.
†Rodgers Estate.

Claimant—**Vic Sebbas.** Proof No. 0070
Source—**Humboldt River.** Ditch—**Young Ditch.**

1888	37.25			S½	2	27	31	3-15—9-15	.303	111.75
1888	38.45			S½	2	27	31	3-15—9-15	.313	115.35
1888	12.10			S½	2	27	31	3-15—9-15	.098	36.30
1888	5.55			S½	2	27	31	3-15—9-15	.045	16.65
1888	9.10			S½	2	27	31	3-15—9-15	.074	27.30
1888	2.00			S½	2	27	31	3-15—9-15	.016	6.00
1888	10.00			S½	2	27	31	3-15—9-15	.081	30.00
1888	1.00			NE¼SE¼	2	27	31	3-15—9-15	.008	3.00

Claimant—**E. W. Sommer.** Proof No. 0071
Source—**Humboldt River.** Ditch—**Highflyer or Arthur Kewley Ditch.**

1887	47.66			NW¼	2	25	31	3-15—9-15	.387	142.98
1888	100.00			NW¼	2	25	31	3-15—9-15	.813	300.00
1888	....		4.84	NW¼	2	25	31	3-15—6-13	.039	7.20

Claimant—**Matt Smith.** Proof No. 0072
Source—**Humboldt River.** Ditch—**Young Ditch.**

	1888			40				W½E½	1	27	31	3-15—9-15	.325	120.00
	1888			8.70				W½E½	1	27	31	3-15—9-15	.071	25.10
	1888			3.15				W½E½	1	27	31	3-15—9-15	.026	9.45
	1904			6.15				W½E½	1	27	31	3-15—9-15	.050	18.45
	1888				2.35			W½E½	1	27	31	3-15—6-13	.019	3.53
	1888					10.70		W½E½	1	27	31	3-15—6-13	.087	16.05

Claimant—**I. M. Springer, Sr.** Proof No. 0073
Source—**Humboldt River.** Ditch—***Slough ditch 1873 to 1887; †Irish-American 1887 to present.**

	*1873			9.50				W¼NE¼&NW¼SE¼	23	27	31	3-15—9-15	.077	28.50
	†1887			19.00				W¼NE¼&NW¼SE¼	23	27	31	3-15—9-15	.154	57.00
	†1887			19.00				W½NE¼&NW¼SE¼	23	27	31	3-15—9-15	.154	57.00

Claimant—**Wm. A. Stauts.** Proof No. 0074
Source—**Humboldt River.** Ditch—**Irish-American.**

	1887			20.20				SE¼SW¼	22	27	31	3-15—9-15	.164	60.60
	1899			4.00				SW¼SE¼	22	27	31	3-15—9-15	.033	12.00

Claimant—**George C. Stoker.** Proof No. 0076
Source—**Humboldt River.** Ditch—**Old Channel.**

	1806			94.58				SE¼	22	27	31	3-15—9-15	.769	283.74

Claimant—**Wm. A. Stauts.** Proof No. 0076
Source—**Humboldt River.** Ditch—**Old Channel.**

	1899			26.15				W½SE¼	22	27	31	3-15—9-15	.213	78.45

Claimant—**H. Stoker.** Proof No. 0077
Source—**Humboldt River.** Ditch—**Old Channel.**

	1888			224.70				NW¼&W½NE¼	14	27	31	3-15—9-15	1.827	674.10

Claimant—**Antone Alves and Anna Alves.** Proof No. 0077
Source—**Humboldt River.** Ditch—**Old Channel.**

	1888			45				W½SE¼	10	27	31	3-15—9-15	.366	135.00
	1888			11				W½SE¼	10	27	31	3-15—9-15	.089	33.00
	1896			14.95				W½SE¼	10	27	31	3-15—9-15	.122	44.85

Claimant—**Pascasio Bilbao.** Proof No. 0078
Source—**Humboldt River.** Ditch—**Union Canal through Lake Shore Ditch.**

Year of priority	Culture—Acres: Harvest crops	Meadow pasture	Diversified pasture	Location: Subdivision	Section	Tp.N.	R.E.	Length of season	Duty of water: C.F.S.	Acre-feet
1883	5			SE¼NE¼	29	26	31	3-15—9-15	.051	15.0
1883	20			N½NE¼SE¼	29	26	31	3-15—9-15	.163	60.0
1884	5			NE¼SE¼	29	26	31	3-15—9-15	.051	15.0
1887	5			SE¼NE¼	29	26	31	3-15—9-15	.051	15.0
1888	8			E½NE¼	29	26	31	3-15—9-15	.065	24.0
1888	3			E½E½	29	26	31	3-15—9-15	.024	9.0
1890	8			E½E½	29	26	31	3-15—9-15	.065	24.0
1891	10			E½E½	29	26	31	3-15—9-15	.081	30.0
1892	13.20			E½E½	29	26	31	3-15—9-15	.107	39.6
1893	13.20			E½E½	29	26	31	3-15—9-15	.107	39.6
1894	13.20			E½E½	29	26	31	3-15—9-15	.107	39.6
1883	6.50			E½NE¼NE¼	29	26	31	3-15—9-15	.053	19.5
1883	....		.80	SE¼NE¼	29	26	31	3-15—6-13	.007	1.2

Claimant—**John O'Kane.** Proof No. 0079
Source—**Humboldt River.** Ditch—**Irish-American.**

Year of priority	Harvest crops	Meadow pasture	Diversified pasture	Subdivision	Section	Tp.N.	R.E.	Length of season	C.F.S.	Acre-feet
1887	4.50			W½SE¼NE¼	27	27	31	3-15—9-15	.037	13.5

Claimant—**Lovelock Land and Development Co.** Proof No. 0080
Source—**Humboldt River.** Ditch—***Lovelock Land and Development Co. Ditch System.**

Year of priority	Harvest crops	Meadow pasture	Diversified pasture	Subdivision	Section	Tp.N.	R.E.	Length of season	C.F.S.	Acre-feet
1900	63.30			N½NE¼	10	25	31	3-15—9-15	.515	189.90
1900	....		52.70	S½NE¼	10	25	31	3-15—6-13	1.102	406.65
1900	....		42.05	W½SE¼	10	25	31	3-15—6-13	.435	106.65
1900	....		73.15	S½&NE¼	2	25	31	3-15—6-13	.595	108.73
1900	135.55			SW¼	2	25	31	3-15—9-15	1.102	406.65
1900	53.55			SE¼	2	25	31	3-15—9-15	.435	160.65
1900	440.25			N½&N½S½	8	25	31	3-15—9-15	3.579	1320.75
1900	155.00			S½S½	8	25	31	3-15—9-15	1.260	465.0
1900	472.50			N½&N½S½	7	25	31	3-15—9-15	3.841	1417.50
1900	155.00			S½S½	7	25	31	3-15—9-15	1.260	465.0
1900	420.00			A part of	16	25	31	3-15—9-15	3.413	1260.00
1900	626.00				11	25	30	3-15—9-15	5.089	1878.0
1900	633.40				12	25	30	3-15—9-15	5.150	1900.20
1900	611.30				18	25	31	3-15—9-15	4.957	1833.90
1900	Reservoir Storage									4800.00

*The Lovelock Land and Development Company Ditch System.
(a) Kewley.
(b) Highflyer Ditch and Flume.
(c) Killebrew and Beck.
(d) Tule Ditch and Flume.
(e) Levee.
(f) South Drainage and Waste Ditch.
(g) Lake Drainage and Waste Ditch.
(h) Tule Drainage and Waste Ditch.
(i) Reservoir.

Claimant—John G. Taylor.
Source—Humboldt River. Ditch—*Irish-American in conjunction with Old Channel.

	1887			*97.50				E¼	21	27	31	3-15—9-15	.793	292.50
	1887			*3.10				SE¼SE¼	21	27	31	3-15—9-15	.025	9.30
	1887			*6.30				SE¼SW¼	21	27	31	3-15—9-15	.051	18.90
	1887			*4.80				SE¼SW¼	21	27	31	3-15—9-15	.039	14.40
	1888			47.55				W½NE¼	21	27	31	3-15—9-15	.387	142.65
	1888			31.70				E½NW¼	21	27	31	3-15—9-15	.258	95.10

Claimant—John G. Taylor. Proof No. 0081
Source—Humboldt River. Ditch—Old Channel in conjunction with Young Ditch.

	1888			20				N½	3	27	31	3-15—9-15	.163	60.0
	1888			60				N½	3	27	31	3-15—9-15	.488	180.0
	1888			190				S½	3	27	31	3-15—9-15	1.545	570.0
	1888			66.10				N½	3	27	31	3-15—9-15	.537	198.30
	1888			388.75					10	27	31	3-15—9-15	3.159	1166.25

Claimant—John G. Taylor. Proof No. 0081
Source—Humboldt River. Ditch—Young Ditch.

	1888			101.05				E½E½	4	27	31	3-15—9-15	.822	303.15
	1888			....		6.75		NW¼NE¼	3	27	31	3-15—6-13	.055	10.13
	1888			176.80				S½S½	34	28	31	3-15—9-15	1.437	530.40
	1888			26				SE¼SE¼	33	28	31	3-15—9-15	.211	78.00

Claimant—John G. Taylor. Proof No. 0081
Source—Humboldt River. Ditch—Irish-American in conjunction with Union Canal.

	1887			136.05				SW¼	22	27	31	3-15—9-15	1.106	408.15

Claimant—John G. Taylor. Proof No. 0081
Source—Humboldt River. Ditch—Irish-American in conjunction with Marzen Slough.

	1887			86				NE¼	29	27	31	3-15—9-15	.699	258.00
	1887			8.70				SE¼NW¼	29	27	31	3-15—9-15	.071	26.10
	1887			16.25				S½NW¼	29	27	31	3-15—9-15	.132	48.75
	1887			128				SW¼	29	27	31	3-15—9-15	1.041	384.00
	1887			39				SE¼SE¼	30	27	31	3-15—9-15	.317	117.00
	1887			15				NE¼	31	27	31	3-15—9-15	.122	45.00
	1898			18.45				NE¼	31	27	31	3-15—9-15	.150	55.35

Claimant—Bergman and Alfree. Proof No. 0082
Source—Humboldt River. Ditch—Southwest Ditch; Lovelock and Borland Slough.

1874				100				N½	34	27	31	3-15—9-15	.813	300.00
	1880			33.70				N½	34	27	31	3-15—9-15	.274	101.10
	1880			79.40				W½SW¼	34	27	31	3-15—9-15	.646	238.20
	1880			47.60				E½SW¼, W½SE¼ & S½NE¼	34	27	31	3-15—9-15	.387	142.80
	1883			....		3.55		NE¼NE¼	34	27	31	3-15—6-13	.029	5.33
	1883			....		108.10		E½NW¼ & W½NE¼	34	27	31	3-15—6-13	.879	162.15
	1883			....		213.10		E½, E½SW¼	34	27	31	3-15—6-13	1.733	319.65

Claimant—**Bergman and Alfree.** Proof No. 0082

Source—**Humboldt River.** Ditch—**Southwest Ditch.**

Year of priority	Culture—Acres: Harvest crops	Culture—Acres: Meadow pasture	Culture—Acres: Diversified pasture	Location: Subdivision	Location: Section	Location: Tp.N.	Location: R.E.	Length of season	Duty of water: C.F.S.	Duty of water: Acre-feet
1883	52.30			NW¼	3	26	31	3-15—9-15	.425	156.90
1883	....		315.75	W½&NE¼	3	26	31	3-15—6-13	2.567	473.63
1883	49.15			S½SE¼	33	27	31	3-15—9-15	.499	147.45
1883	48.00			SE¼	33	27	31	3-15—9-15	.390	144.00
1883	38.90			SE¼&SW¼	33	27	31	3-15—9-15	.316	116.70
1883	25.95			SE¼SW¼	33	27	31	3-15—9-15	.211	77.85
1883	....	22.00		NW¼SW¼	33	27	31	3-15—6-13	.179	33.00
1883	....	10.20		SW¼	33	27	31	3-15—6-13	.083	15.30
1883	....	14.95		SW¼SW¼	33	27	31	3-15—6-13	.123	22.48
1883	....		51.10	S½	33	27	31	3-15—6-13	.415	76.65
1883	...		3.95	SW¼SE¼	33	27	31	3-15—6-13	.032	5.93
1889	60			SE¼	32	27	31	3-15—9-15	.488	180.00
1883	20			SE¼	32	27	31	3-15—9-15	.163	60.00
1883	139.80			SE¼.S½NE¼.SW¼	32	27	31	3-15—9-15	1.137	419.40
1883	59.75			N½	5	26	31	3-15—9-15	.486	179.25
1883	33.00			NE¼	5	26	31	3-15—9-15	.268	99.00
1883	47.95			E½E½	5	26	31	3-15—9-15	.390	143.85
1883	78.65			NE¼	4	26	31	3-15—9-15	.639	235.95
1877	81.35			S½	4	26	31	3-15—9-15	.661	244.05
1880	119.95			S½	4	26	31	3-15—9-15	.975	359.85
1889	128.20			N½	4	26	31	3-15—9-15	1.042	384.60
1889	77.45			W½NW¼	4	26	31	3-15—9-15	.630	232.35
1880	....		38.90	NE¼SE¼	4	26	31	3-15—6-13	.316	58.35
1880	....		17.70	SE¼SE¼	4	26	31	3-15—6-13	.144	26.55
1889	....		11.00	NE¼NE¼	4	26	31	3-15—6-13	.089	16.50

Claimant—**F. Tessier.** Proof No. 0085

Source—**Humboldt River.** Ditch—**Old Channel.**

Year of priority	Harvest crops	Meadow pasture	Diversified pasture	Subdivision	Section	Tp.N.	R.E.	Length of season	C.F.S.	Acre-feet
1899	61.48			SE¼	13	27	31	3-15—9-15	.500	184.44
1900	15.94			SE¼	13	27	31	3-15—9-15	.130	47.82

Claimant—**Morris Nelson.** Proof No. 0086

Source—**Humboldt River.** Ditch—**Union Canal.**

Year of priority	Harvest crops	Meadow pasture	Diversified pasture	Subdivision	Section	Tp.N.	R.E.	Length of season	C.F.S.	Acre-feet
1887	14.54			W½NW¼	32	26	31	3-15—9-15	.118	43.62
1888	18.17			W½NW¼	32	26	31	3-15—9-15	.148	54.51
1802	7.27			W½NW¼	32	26	31	3-15—9-15	.059	21.81
1900	18.17			W½NW¼	32	26	31	3-15—9-16	.148	54.51
1888	9.00			SE¼NE¼	31	26	31	3-15—9-15	.073	27.00
1892	13.85			SE¼NE¼	31	26	31	3-16—9-15	.11[illegible]	41.55
1803	9.00			SE¼NE¼	31	26	31	3-15—9-15	.073	27.00
1890	72.35			N½NE¼	31	26	31	3-15—9-15	.588	217.05

Claimant—**Hans Christensen.** Proof No. 0087

Source—**Humboldt River.** Ditch—**Union Canal through Lake Shore Ditch.**

1876	10		NW¼SW¼	28	26	31	3-15—9-15	.081	30.00
1876	25		SW¼	28	26	31	3-15—9-15	.203	75.00
1885	50		SW¼	28	26	31	3-15—9-15	.407	150.00
1890	13.35		SW¼	28	26	31	3-15—9-15	.109	40.05

Claimant—**Peter Olson.** Proof No. 0088

Source—**Humboldt River.** Ditch—**Old Channel Ditch.**

1888	65.85		S½NW¼	12	27	31	3-15—9-15	.535	107.55
1904	4.70		S½NW¼	12	27	31	3-15—9-15	.038	14.10

Claimant—**W. W. Van Reed.** Proof. No. 0089

Source—**Humboldt River. Ditch—Union Canal through Lake Shore Ditch.**

1897	15.00		E½SW¼	29	26	31	3-15—9-15	.122	45.00
1897	....	5.90	E½SW¼	29	26	31	3-15—6-13	.048	8.85
1898	14.85		E½SW¼	29	26	31	3-15—9-15	.121	44.55
1900	20.50		E½SW¼	29	26	31	3-15—9-15	.167	61.50
1898	5.10		SE¼	29	26	31	3-15—9-15	.041	15.30

Claimant—**Andrew Westfall.** Proof No. 0091

Source—**Humboldt River.** Ditch—**Union Canal through Lake Shore Ditch.**

1876	20.97		SE¼	32	26	31	3-15—9-15	.170	62.91
1876	5.22		NE¼	32	26	31	3-15—9-15	.042	15.66
1885	87.32		SE¼	32	26	31	3-15—9-15	.710	261.96
1885	80.00		E½NE¼	32	26	31	3-15—9-15	.650	240.00
1885	30.00		E½NW¼	32	26	31	3-15—9-15	.244	90.00
1890	11.40		S½SE¼SE¼	29	26	31	3-15—9-15	.093	34.20
1888	35.65		S½	31	26	31	3-15—9-15	.290	106.95
1890	77.79		E½	32	26	31	3-15—9-15	.632	233.37
1890	50.00		E½NW¼	32	26	31	3-15—9-15	.407	150.00
1890	....	5.10	S½SE¼SE¼	29	26	31	3-15—6-13	.041	7.65
1885	....	8.25	NW¼NE¼	32	26	31	3-15—6-13	.067	12.38
1888	....	196.60	S½	31	26	31	3-15—6-13	1.598	294.90

Claimant—**L. P. Johnson.** Proof No. 0092

Source—**Humboldt River.** Ditch—**Old Channel.**

1888	7.00		E½SE¼	10	27	31	3-15—9-15	.057	21.00
1888	15.00		E½SE¼	10	27	31	3-15—9-15	.122	45.00
1888	15.00		E½SE¼	10	27	31	3-15—9-15	.122	45.00
1888	3.80		E½SE¼	10	27	31	3-15—9-15	.031	11.40
1888	31.30		E½SE¼	10	27	31	3-15—9-15	.254	93.90
1888	1.90		E½SE¼	10	27	31	3-15—9-15	.015	5.70

Claimant—**S. R. Young.** Proof No. 0093
Source—**Humboldt River.** Ditch—**Young Ditch.**

Year of priority	Culture—Acres: Harvest crops	Meadow pasture	Diversified pasture	Location: Subdivision	Section	Tp.N.	R.E.	Length of season	Duty of water: C.F.S.	Acre-feet
1888	15.75			SE¼NW¼	28	28	32	3-15—9-15	.120	47.25
1888	11.80			NE¼SW¼	28	28	32	3-15—9-15	.096	35.40
1888	15.00			NE¼SW¼&SE¼NW¼	28	28	32	3-15—9-15	.122	45.00
1888	31.45			S½NE¼&N½SE¼	28	28	32	3-15—9-15	.256	94.35
1888	66.45			NE¼&NW¼SE¼&NE¼SW¼&SE¼NW¼	28	28	32	3-15—9-15	.540	199.35
1888	Sufficient water to develop 75 H.P.							1-1—12-31		
1909	Sufficient water to develop 100 H.P.							1-1—12-31		

Water so diverted to be returned to stream undiminished in quantity immediately below power plant.

Claimant—**H. M. Damm.** Proof No. 0094
Source—**Humboldt River.** Ditch—**Humboldt Irrigation and Power Co. Canal.**

Year of priority	Harvest crops	Meadow pasture	Diversified pasture	Subdivision	Section	Tp.N.	R.E.	Length of season	C.F.S.	Acre-feet
1888	15			W½W½	1	27	31	3-15—9-15	.122	45.0

Claimant—**E. K. Hanson.** Proof No. 0095
Source—**Humboldt River.** Ditch—**Southwest Ditch.**

Year of priority	Harvest crops	Meadow pasture	Diversified pasture	Subdivision	Section	Tp.N.	R.E.	Length of season	C.F.S.	Acre-feet
1883	2.35			SW¼SE¼	23	27	31	3-15—9-15	.019	7.05
1883	3.15			NE¼NW¼	26	27	31	3-15—9-15	.026	9.45
1879	3.55			NE¼NW¼	26	27	31	3-15—9-15	.029	10.65
1883	1.50			NE¼NW¼	26	27	31	3-15—9-15	.012	4.50

Claimant—***Geo. S. Nixon Estate and John Fant.** Proof No. 0099
Source—**Humboldt River.** Ditch—**Rodgers Ditch System—†Riverside Branch.**

Year of priority	Harvest crops	Meadow pasture	Diversified pasture	Subdivision	Section	Tp.N.	R.E.	Length of season	C.F.S.	Acre-feet
1871	10.00			NW¼	36	27	31	3-15—9-15	.081	30.00
1873	80.00			NW¼	36	27	31	3-15—9-15	.650	240.00
1873	60.00			SW¼	36	27	31	3-15—9-15	.488	180.00
1880	52.28			NW¼	36	27	31	3-15—9-15	.425	156.84
1880	29.26			SE¼	36	27	31	3-15—9-15	.238	87.78
1880	29.00			NE¼	36	27	31	3-15—9-15	.236	87.00
1881	20.00			SW¼	36	27	31	3-15—9-15	.163	60.00
1882	47.29			SW¼	36	27	31	3-15—9-15	.384	141.87
1882	16.22			NE¼	36	27	31	3-15—9-15	.132	48.66
1882	25.55			SE¼	36	27	31	3-15—9-15	.208	76.65
1882	....		30.00	N½	36	27	31	3-15—6-13	.244	45.00
1883	28.00			SE¼	35	27	31	3-15—9-15	.228	84.00
1883	52.00			SW¼	35	27	31	3-15—9-15	.423	156.00
1885	153.85			NE¼	35	27	31	3-15—9-15	1.251	461.55
1885	75.00			NE¼	35	27	31	3-15—9-15	.610	225.00
1898	25.72			SW¼	35	27	31	3-15—9-15	.209	77.16
1901	29.77			SE¼	35	27	31	3-15—9-15	.242	89.31

†Riverside Branch.
(a) Silverwood Ditch.
(b) Muttleberry Ditch.
(c) Slough Ditch.
(d) Hazelton-Thies Ditch.
(e) J. H. Thies Ditch.
(f) Thies Reservoir.
*Riverside Ranch.

WINNEMUCCA DISTRICT

Claimant—**Edna Anderson.** Proof No. 00101
Source—Humboldt River. Ditch—**North Side Cusick Ditch.**

1870	10.00		NE¼SE¼	18	36	40	3-15—9-15	.081	30.00
1870	20.90		SE¼NE¼	18	36	40	3-15—9-15	.170	62.70
1870	38.10		SW¼NE¼	18	36	40	3-15—9-15	.310	114.30
1870	32.00		NW¼NE¼	18	36	40	3-15—9-15	.200	96.00
1870	39.50		NE¼NW¼	18	36	40	3-15—9-15	.331	118.50
1870	20.30		SE¼NW¼	18	36	40	3-15—9-15	.165	60.90
1870	18.75		NW¼NW¼	18	36	40	3-15—9-15	.152	56.25
1870		8.90	NW¼NW¼	18	36	40	3-15—4-28	.072	6.45
1870	2.00		SW¼NW¼	18	36	40	3-15—9-15	.016	6.00
1870	.80		NE¼SW¼	18	36	40	3-15—9-15	.007	2.40

Claimant—**Edna Anderson.** Proof No. 00101
Source—Humboldt River. Ditch—**Cusick Ditch.**

1870	38.20		SE¼SE¼	18	36	40	3-15—9-15	.311	114.60
1870	5.40		NE¼SE¼	18	36	40	3-15—9-15	.044	16.20
1870	14.80		SW¼SE¼	18	36	40	3-15—9-15	.120	44.40
1870	22.00		NW¼SE¼	18	36	40	3-15—9-15	.179	66.00
1870	.40		SW¼NE¼	18	36	40	3-15—9-15	.003	1.20
1870	6.15		NE¼SW¼	18	36	40	3-15—9-15	.051	18.45
1870		2.50	NE¼SW¼	18	36	40	3-15—4-28	.020	1.88
1870		.75	NW¼SW¼	18	36	40	3-15—4-28	.002	.56
1870		10.70	SE¼NW¼	18	36	40	3-15—4-28	.087	8.03
1870	.20		SW¼NW¼	18	36	40	3-15—9-15	.002	.60
1870		18.20	SW¼NW¼	18	36	40	3-15—4-28	.148	13.65
1870		6.00	NW¼NW¼	18	36	40	3-15—4-28	.049	4.50

Claimant—**Edna** Anderson. Proof No. 00101
Source—Humboldt River. Ditch—**Anderson Ditch.**

1871	20.00		NE¼SE¼	18	36	40	3-15—9-15	.063	60.00
1871	6.95		NE¼SW¼	18	36	40	3-15—9-15	.057	20.85
1871		2.50	NE¼SW¼	18	36	40	3-15—4-28	.020	1.88
1871		1.50	NW¼SW¼	18	36	40	3-15—4-28	.012	1.13
1871	14.10		NW¼SE¼	18	36	40	3-15—9-15	.115	42.30

Claimant—**Edna Anderson.** Proof No. 00101
Source—Humboldt River. Ditch—**Pioneer Slough System.**

1871	7.30		NW¼NE¼	18	36	40	3-15—9-15	.059	21.90
1871		2.90	NE¼NE¼	20	36	40	3-15—4-28	.025	2.18
1871		19.70	SE¼SE¼	17	36	40	3-15—4-28	.160	14.78
1871		33.50	SW¼SE¼	17	36	40	3-15—4-28	.272	25.13
1871		28.20	NW¼SE¼	17	36	40	3-15—4-28	.229	21.15
1871	2.60		NE¼SE¼	17	36	40	3-15—9-15	.021	7.80
1871	3.30		SW¼NE¼	17	36	40	3-15—9-15	.027	9.90
1871	.80		SE¼SW¼	17	36	40	3-15—9-15	.007	2.40

Edna Anderson—Continued.

Year of priority	Culture—Acres: Harvest crops	Meadow pasture	Diversified pasture	Location: Subdivision	Section	Tp.N.	R.E.	Length of season	Duty of water: C.F.S.	Acre-feet
1871			21.90	SE¼SW¼	17	36	40	3-15—4-28	.178	16.43
1871	3.30			SW¼SW¼	17	36	40	3-15—9-15	.027	9.90
1871			1.00	SW¼SW¼	17	36	40	3-15—4-28	.008	.75
1871	1.20			NE¼SW¼	17	36	40	3-15—9-15	.010	3.60
1871			38.80	NE¼SW¼	17	36	40	3-15—4-28	.315	29.10
1871	29.90			NW¼SW¼	17	36	40	3-15—9-15	.243	89.70
1871			2.60	NW¼SW¼	17	36	40	3-15—4-28	.021	1.95
1871	25.70			SE¼NW¼	17	36	40	3-15—9-15	.209	77.10
1871	4.95			NW¼NW¼	17	36	40	3-15—9-15	.040	14.85
1871	36.90			SW¼NW¼	17	36	40	3-15—9-15	.300	110.70
1871	20.00			SE¼NE¼	18	56	40	3-15—9-15	.163	60.00
1871	29.30			NE¼NE¼	18	36	40	3-15—9-15	.238	87.90
1871	4.17			NE¼SW¼	7	36	40	3-15—9-15	.034	12.51
1871		34.06		NE¼SW¼	7	36	40	3-15—6-13	.277	51.09
1871	10.75			NW¼SW¼	7	36	40	3-15—9-15	.087	32.25
1871		21.80		NW¼SW¼	7	36	40	3-15—6-13	.177	32.70
1871			4.83	NW¼SW¼	7	36	40	3-15—4-28	.039	3.62
1871	10.83			SW¼SW¼	7	36	40	3-15—9-15	.088	32.49
1871		26.00		SW¼SW¼	7	36	40	3-15—6-13	.211	39.00
1871			1.12	SW¼SW¼	7	36	40	3-15—4-28	.009	.84
1871	21.97			SE¼SW¼	7	36	40	3-15—9-15	.179	65.91
1871		17.14		SE¼SW¼	7	36	40	3-15—6-13	.139	25.71
1871	35.53			NE¼SE¼	7	36	40	3-15—9-15	.289	106.59
1871		4.13		NE¼SE¼	7	36	40	3-15—6-13	.034	6.20
1871	3.20			NW¼SE¼	7	36	40	3-15—9-15	.026	9.60
1871		36.80		NW¼SE¼	7	36	40	3-15—6-13	.299	55.20
1871		38.32		SW¼SE¼	7	36	40	3-15—6-13	.312	57.48
1871		40.10		SE¼SE¼	7	36	40	3-15—6-13	.326	60.15

Claimant—**Edna Anderson.** Proof No. 00101

Source—**Humboldt River.** Ditch—**Humboldt River Overflow.**

1874			1.20	SE¼SE¼	17	36	40	3-15—4-28	.010	.90
1874			2.60	SW¼SE¼	17	36	40	3-15—4-28	.021	1.95
1874			2.70	NW¼NE¼	20	36	40	3-15—4-28	.023	2.03
1874	7.20			SE¼SW¼	17	36	40	3-15—9-15	.059	21.60
1874			5.55	SE¼SW¼	17	36	40	3-15—4-28	.045	4.16
1874	29.70			SW¼SW¼	17	36	40	3-15—9-15	.241	89.10
1874	3.60			NW¼SW¼	17	36	40	3-15—9-15	.029	10.80
1874			.33	SE¼SE¼	27	36	40	3-15—4-28	.003	.25
1874			10.82	SW¼SE¼	27	36	40	3-15—4-28	.088	8.12

Claimant—**Edna Anderson.** Proof No. 00101

Source—**Humboldt River.** Ditch—**North Side Canal.**

1874			12.40	SE¼NW¼	21	36	40	3-15—4-28	.101	9.30
1874			4.30	NE¼SW¼	21	36	40	3-15—4-28	.035	3.23
1874		10.00		NW¼SW¼	21	36	40	3-15—6-13	.081	15.00

	1874				9.20		NW¼SW¼	21	36	40	3-15—4-28	.075	6.00
	1874				31.40		SW¼NW¼	21	36	40	3-15—4-28	.255	23.55
	1874				20.90		NW¼NW¼	21	36	40	3-15—4-28	.243	22.43
	1874				7.70		NE¼NE¼	20	36	40	3-15—4-28	.063	5.78
	1874				11.00		SW¼SW¼	16	36	40	3-15—4-28	.089	8.25
	1874			1.12			SE¼SE¼	17	36	40	3-15—9-15	.010	3.36
	1874				12.58		SE¼SE¼	17	36	40	3-15—4-28	.102	9.44
	1874			25.94			NE¼SE¼	17	36	40	3-15—9-15	.211	77.82
	1874				6.77		NE¼SE¼	17	36	40	3-15—4-28	.055	5.08
	1874				10.20		NW¼SE¼	17	36	40	3-15—4-28	.083	7.65
	1874			17.80			SE¼NE¼	17	36	40	3-15—9-15	.145	53.40
	1874				5.50		SE¼NE¼	17	36	40	3-15—4-28	.045	4.13
	1874			34.20			SW¼NE¼	17	36	40	3-15—9-15	.278	102.60
	1874			11.70			SE¼NW¼	17	36	40	3-15—9-15	.095	35.10
	1874				1.10		NE¼NE¼	17	36	40	3-15—4-28	.009	.83
	1874				39.40		NE¼NW¼	17	36	40	3-15—4-28	.320	29.55
	1874				.75		NE¼SW¼	27	36	40	3-15—4-28	.006	.56
	1874			13.45			NW¼SW¼	27	36	40	3-15—9-15	.109	40.35
	1874			18.70			SE¼NW¼	27	36	40	3-15—9-15	.152	56.10
	1874			34.10			SW¼NW¼	27	36	40	3-15—9-15	.277	102.30
	1874			13.22			NW¼NW¼	27	36	40	3-15—9-15	.107	39.66
	1874			18.30			NW¼NE¼	17	36	40	3-15—9-15	.149	54.90
	1874				4.40		NW¼NE¼	17	36	40	3-15—4-28	.036	3.30
	1874				2.50		NW¼SW¼	16	36	40	3-15—4-28	.020	1.88

Claimant—**Edna Anderson.** Proof No. **00101**
Source—**Humboldt River.** Ditch—**South Side Swail and Ditch.**

	1874				16.60		SE¼SW¼	27	36	40	3-15—4-28	.135	12.45
	1874				27.28		SW¼SW¼	27	36	40	3-15—4-28	.222	20.46
	1874					3.37	SW¼SW¼	27	36	40	3-15—4-28	.207	2.53
	1874			1.00			NW¼SW¼	27	36	40	3-15—9-15	.008	3.00

Claimant—**Edna Anderson.** Proof No. **00101**
Source—**Humboldt River.** Ditch—**Big Slough Ditch.**

	1874			.36			NE¼SW¼	27	36	40	3-15—9-15	.003	1.08
	1874			.10			SE¼SW¼	27	36	40	3-15—9-15	.001	.30
	1874			1.82			SW¼SW¼	27	36	40	3-15—9-15	.015	5.46
	1874			16.48			NW¼SW¼	27	36	40	3-15—9-15	.134	49.44
	1874				3.86		NW¼SW¼	27	36	40	3-15—4-28	.031	2.90
	1874			1.90			SW¼SW¼	27	36	40	3-15—9-15	.015	5.70
	1874			1.20			SW¼SE¼	8	36	40	3-15—9-15	.010	3.60

Claimant—**Edna Anderson.** Proof No. **00101**
Source—**Humboldt River.** Ditch—**North Side Canal.**

	1874			27.40			SE¼SW¼	8	36	40	3-15—9-15	.223	82.20
	1874				3.60		SE¼SW¼	8	36	40	3-15—4-28	.029	2.70
	1874			16.80			NE¼SW¼	8	36	40	3-15—9-15	.137	50.40
	1874				19.60		NE¼SW¼	8	36	40	3-15—4-28	.159	14.70
	1874			35.00			NW¼SW¼	8	36	40	3-15—9-15	.285	105.00

Edna Anderson—Continued.

Year of priority	Culture—Acres: Harvest crops	Meadow pasture	Diversified pasture	Location: Subdivision	Section	Tp.N.	R.E.	Length of season	Duty of water: C.F.S.	Acre-feet
1874	....	....	1.50	NW¼SW¼	8	36	40	3-15—4-26	.012	1.13
1874	2.20	....	....	SW¼NW¼	8	36	40	3-15—9-15	.018	6.60
1874	1.20	....	....	SE¼NW¼	8	36	40	3-15—9-15	.010	3.60
1874	....	....	.30	SE¼NW¼	8	36	40	3-15—4-28	.003	.23
1874	....	....	2.40	NW¼SE¼	8	36	40	3-15—4-28	.020	1.80
1874	....	....	10.70	SE¼SE¼	27	36	40	3-15—4-28	.087	8.03
1874	.95	....	....	SW¼SE¼	27	36	40	3-15—9-15	.008	2.85
1874	....	1.10	....	SW¼SE¼	27	36	40	3-15—6-13	.009	1.65
1874	....	....	18.65	SW¼SE¼	27	36	40	3-15—4-28	.152	13.99
1874	.12	....	....	NW¼SE¼	27	36	40	3-15—9-15	.001	.36
1874	....	....	16.39	NW¼SE¼	27	36	40	3-15—4-28	.133	12.29
1874	3.60	....	....	SE¼SW¼	27	36	40	3-15—9-15	.029	10.80
1874	....	....	9.30	SE¼SW¼	27	36	40	3-15—4-28	.076	6.98
1874	35.48	....	....	NE¼SW¼	27	36	40	3-15—9-15	.288	106.44

Claimant—**Edna Anderson.** Proof No. 00101
Source—**Humboldt River.** Ditch—**Old South Side House Ditch.**

Year of priority	Harvest crops	Meadow pasture	Diversified pasture	Subdivision	Section	Tp.N.	R.E.	Length of season	C.F.S.	Acre-feet
1871	....	....	.90	NW¼SW¼	21	36	40	3-15—4-28	.007	.68
1874	....	....	1.80	SW¼NW¼	21	36	40	3-15—4-28	.015	1.35
1874	....	10.70	....	NE¼SE¼	20	36	40	3-15—6-13	.087	16.05
1874	....	....	1.60	NE¼SE¼	20	36	40	3-15—4-28	.013	1.20
1874	....	27.20	....	SE¼NE¼	20	36	40	3-15—6-13	.221	40.80
1874	....	....	7.45	SE¼NE¼	20	36	40	3-15—4-28	.061	5.59
1874	....	32.15	....	SW¼NE¼	20	36	40	3-15—6-13	.261	48.23
1874	....	28.60	....	NW¼NE¼	20	36	40	3-15—6-13	.234	43.90
1874	....	....	5.90	NW¼NE¼	20	36	40	3-15—4-28	.048	4.43
1874	....	15.40	....	NE¼NE¼	20	36	40	3-15—6-13	.125	23.10
1874	....	....	7.80	NE¼NE¼	20	36	40	3-15—4-28	.063	5.85

Claimant—**Edna Anderson.** Proof No. 00101
Source—**Humboldt River.** Ditch—**North Side Canal.**

Year of priority	Harvest crops	Meadow pasture	Diversified pasture	Subdivision	Section	Tp.N.	R.E.	Length of season	C.F.S.	Acre-feet
1874	....	....	30.80	NW¼NW¼	17	36	40	3-15—4-28	.250	23.10
1873	....	....	9.25	NE¼NE¼	18	36	40	3-15—4-28	.075	6.94
1874	37.20	....	....	SW¼SW¼	8	36	40	3-15—9-15	.302	111.00

Claimant—**Edna Anderson.** Proof No. 00101
Source—**Humboldt River.** Ditch—**Fairbanks Ditch System.**

Year of priority	Harvest crops	Meadow pasture	Diversified pasture	Subdivision	Section	Tp.N.	R.E.	Length of season	C.F.S.	Acre-feet
1874	10.47	....	....	NE¼SE¼	12	36	39	3-15—9-15	.085	31.41
1871	...	....	24.09	NE¼SE¼	12	36	39	3-15—4-28	.201	18.62

Claimant—**Bliss Brothers.** Proof No. 00101
Source—**Humboldt River.** Ditch—**Anderson Ditch System.**

1874		32.93			NW¼NE¼	14	36	41	3-15—6-13	.268	49.40
1874	10.80				NE¼NE¼	14	36	41	3-15—9-15	.088	32.40
1874		20.89			NE¼NE¼	14	36	41	3-15—6-13	.170	31.34
1874	4.57				NE¼NW¼	14	30	41	3-15—9-15	.037	13.71
1874		6.47			NE¼NW¼	14	36	41	3-15—6-13	.053	9.71
1874			3.92		NE¼NW¼	14	36	41	3-15—4-28	.032	2.94
1874		.90			SE¼SE¼	11	36	41	3-15—6-13	.007	1.35
1874		1.70			SW¼SE¼	11	36	41	3-15—6-13	.014	2.55
1874		1.65			SE¼NW¼	11	36	41	3-15—6-13	.013	2.48
1874			.20		SE¼NW¼	11	36	41	3-15—4-28	.002	.15
1874			.95		NW¼NW¼	11	36	41	3-15—4-28	.008	.71
1874			.80		SW¼SW¼	11	36	41	3-15—4-28	.007	.60
1874		2.76			SE¼NW¼	12	36	41	3-15—6-13	.022	4.14
1874				40.04	SE¼NW¼	12	36	41	3-15—4-28	.326	30.03
1874		4.00			SW¼NW¼	12	36	41	3-15—6-13	.033	6.00
1874				37.70	SW¼NW¼	12	36	41	3-15—4-28	.307	28.80
1874		25.53			NW¼SW¼	12	36	41	3-15—6-13	.208	38.30
1874				10.28	NW¼SW¼	12	36	41	3-15—4-28	.084	7.71
1874		38.55			SW¼SW¼	12	36	41	3-15—6-13	.313	57.83
1874		35.26			SE¼SW¼	12	36	41	3-15—6-13	.287	52.89
1874				.14	SE¼SW¼	12	30	41	3-15—6-13	.001	.12
1880		35.80			NE¼SW¼	12	36	41	3-15—6-13	.291	53.70
1880				4.82	NE¼SW¼	12	36	41	3-15—4-28	.039	3.62
1880		26.10			SW¼SE¼	12	30	41	3-15—6-13	.212	39.15
1880				12.60	SW¼SE¼	12	36	41	3-15—4-28	.102	9.45
1874	10.08				SE¼NE¼	14	36	41	3-15—9-15	.082	30.24
1874		22.96			SE¼NE¼	14	36	41	3-15—6-13	.187	34.44
1874	4.32				SW¼NE¼	14	36	41	3-15—9-15	.035	12.96
1874		11.13			SW¼NE¼	14	36	41	3-15—6-13	.090	16.70
1874			1.50		SW¼NE¼	14	36	41	3-15—6-13	.012	1.13
1874	2.52				NW¼NE¼	14	36	41	3-15—9-15	.020	7.56

Claimant—**Bliss Brothers.** Proof No. 00102
Source—**Humboldt River.** Ditch—**Pioneer Ditch System.**

1863	10.00				SW¼NW¼	3	36	39	3-15—9-15	.081	30.00
1863		10.00			SW¼NW¼	3	36	39	3-15—6-13	.081	15.00
1863			10.00		SW¼NW¼	3	36	30	3-15—4-28	.081	7.50
1863				8.43	SW¼NW¼	3	36	39	3-15—4-28	.069	6.32
1863	10.00				SE¼NW¼	3	36	39	3-15—9-15	.081	30.00
1863		10.00			SE¼NW¼	3	36	39	3-15—6-13	.081	15.00
1863			10.00		SE¼NW¼	3	36	39	3-15—4-28	.081	7.50
1863				8.41	SE¼NW¼	3	36	39	3-15—4-28	.068	6.31
1863	16.64				SE¼NW¼	2	36	39	3-15—9-15	.135	49.92
1863			.66		SE¼NW¼	2	36	39	3-15—4-28	.005	.50
1863	17.78				SE¼NW¼	2	36	39	3-15—9-15	.145	53.34
1863	31.72				SW¼NE¼	2	36	39	3-15—9-15	.258	95.16
1863		.86			SW¼NE¼	2	36	39	3-15—6-13	.007	1.29
1863			.24		SW¼NE¼	2	36	39	3-15—4-28	.002	.18

Bliss Brothers—Continued.

Year of priority	Culture—Acres: Harvest crops	Meadow pasture	Diversified pasture		Location: Subdivision	Section	Tp.N.	R.E.	Length of season	Duty of water: C.F.S.	Acre-feet
1863	3.85				SW¼NE¼	2	36	39	3-15—9-15	.031	11.55
1863	6.42				NE¼SE¼	2	36	39	3-15—9-15	.052	19.26
1863		.94			NW¼SE¼	2	36	39	3-15—6-13	.008	1.41
1863	29.64				NW¼SE¼	2	36	39	3-15—9-15	.241	88.92
1863		5.06			NW¼SE¼	2	36	39	3-15—6-13	.041	7.59
1863				1.04	NW¼SE¼	2	36	39	3-15—4-28	.008	.78
1863	27.32				NE¼SW¼	2	36	39	3-15—9-15	.222	81.96
1863			11.51		NE¼SW¼	2	36	39	3-15—4-28	.094	8.63
1863	13.65				NW¼SW¼	2	36	39	3-15—9-15	.111	40.95
1863			20.05		NW¼SW¼	2	36	39	3-15—4-28	.163	15.04
1863				.73	NW¼SW¼	2	36	39	3-15—4-28	.006	.55
1863	2.50				SW¼SE¼	2	36	39	3-15—9-15	.020	7.50
1863			32.59		SW¼SE¼	2	36	39	3-15—4-28	.265	24.44
1863	23.35				SE¼SE¼	2	36	39	3-15—9-15	.190	70.05
1863		1.62			SE¼SE¼	2	36	39	3-15—6-13	.013	2.43
1863			13.02		SE¼SE¼	2	36	39	3-15—4-28	.106	9.77
1863		7.49			NW¼NW¼	3	36	39	3-15—6-13	.061	11.23
1863			20.87		NW¼NW¼	3	36	39	3-15—4-28	.170	15.65
1863		17.86			NE¼NW¼	3	36	39	3-15—6-13	.145	26.79
1863			18.81		NE¼NW¼	3	36	39	3-15—4-28	.153	14.11
1863	25.58				NE¼SE¼	2	36	39	3-15—9-15	.208	76.74
1863			2.08		NE¼SE¼	2	36	39	3-15—4-28	.017	1.56
1863	4.34				NW¼NW¼	3	36	39	3-15—9-15	.035	13.02
1863	5.37				SW¼NW¼	1	36	39	3-15—9-15	.044	17.11
1863		29.08			SW¼NW¼	1	36	39	3-15—6-13	.236	43.62
1863		30.10			SE¼NW¼	1	36	39	3-15—6-13	.245	45.15
1863		14.17			NW¼NW¼	1	36	39	3-15—6-13	.115	21.26
1863		33.86			NE¼SW¼	1	36	39	3-15—6-13	.275	50.79
1863		28.20			NW¼SW¼	1	36	39	3-15—6-13	.229	42.30
1863				3.91	SW¼NW¼	33	37	39	3-15—4-28	.032	2.93
1863				1.77	SE¼NW¼	33	37	39	3-15—4-28	.014	1.33
1863				4.67	NW¼SW¼	33	37	39	3-15—4-28	.038	3.50
1863				3.39	NE¼SW¼	33	37	39	3-15—4-28	.028	2.54
1863				1.23	NW¼SE¼	33	37	39	3-15—4-28	.010	.92

Claimant—**Bliss Brothers.** Proof No. 00102
Source—**Humboldt River.** Ditch—**Pedroli Ditch System.**

1868	19.02				SW¼SW¼	1	36	39	3-15—9-15	.155	57.06
1868		11.73			SW¼SW¼	1	36	39	3-15—6-13	.095	17.60

Claimant—**Bliss Brothers.** Proof No. 00102
Source—**Humboldt River.** Ditch—**Fairbanks Ditch System.**

1865	20.33				NE¼NW¼	12	36	39	3-15—9-15	.238	87.90
1865		4.17			NE¼NW¼	12	36	39	3-15—6-13	.034	6.21
1865			1.52		NE¼NW¼	12	36	39	3-15—4-28	.012	4.27

	1865						1.67	NE¼NW¼	12	36	39	3-15—4-28	.014	4.38
	1865			34.00				NW¼NW¼	12	36	39	3-15—9-15	.276	104.00
	1865					4.62		NW¼NW¼	12	36	39	3-15—4-28	.038	6.59
	1865						.97	NW¼NW¼	12	36	39	3-15—4-28	.008	.73
	1865			3.03				SW¼NW¼	12	36	39	3-15—9-15	.025	9.09
	1865					34.27		SW¼NW¼	12	36	39	3-15—4-28	.279	25.70
	1865			22.13				SE¼NW¼	12	36	39	3-15—9-15	.180	66.39
	1865					15.31		SE¼NW¼	12	36	39	3-15—4-28	.124	11.48
	1865			16.40				NE¼SW¼	12	36	39	3-15—9-15	.133	49.20
	1865					20.88		NE¼SW¼	12	36	39	3-15—4-28	.170	15.66
	1865						2.40	NE¼SW¼	12	36	39	3-15—4-28	.020	1.80
	1865			20.67				NW¼SW¼	12	36	39	3-15—9-15	.168	62.01
	1865					8.72		NW¼SW¼	12	36	39	3-15—4-28	.071	6.54
	1865			18.96				SE¼SW¼	12	36	39	3-15—9-15	.154	56.88
	1865					21.08		SE¼SW¼	12	36	39	3-15—4-28	.171	15.81
	1865			16.10				NW¼SE¼	12	36	39	3-15—9-15	.131	48.30
	1865					22.40		NW¼SE¼	12	36	39	3-15—4-28	.182	16.80
	1865						.53	NW¼SE¼	12	36	39	3-15—4-28	.004	.38
	1865			3.03				SW¼SE¼	12	36	39	3-15—9-15	.025	9.09
	1865					21.30		SW¼SE¼	12	36	39	3-15—4-28	.173	15.98
	1865						.55	SW¼SE¼	12	36	39	3-15—4-28	.004	.41

Claimant—**Bliss Brothers.** Proof No. 00102
Source—**Humboldt River.** Ditch—**Pedroli Ditch System.**

	1868			.21				SW¼SW¼	32	37	39	3-15—9-15	.002	.63
	1868				6.45			SW¼SW¼	32	37	39	3-15—6-13	.052	9.68
	1868					2.43		SW¼SW¼	32	37	39	3-15—4-28	.020	1.82
	1868			3.13				SW¼SE¼	32	37	39	3-15—9-15	.025	9.39
	1868					11.19		SW¼SE¼	32	37	39	3-15—4-28	.091	8.39
	1868				9.78			SE¼NE¼	4	36	39	3-15—6-13	.080	14.67
	1868					24.40		SE¼NE¼	4	36	39	3-15—4-28	.198	18.30
	1868					22.67		SW¼NE¼	4	36	39	3-15—4-28	.184	17.00
	1868					18.30		SE¼NW¼	4	36	39	3-15—4-28	.149	13.73
	1868					1.78		SW¼NW¼	4	36	39	3-15—4-28	.014	1.34
	1875			28.97				SW¼NE¼	12	36	39	3-15—9-15	.236	86.91
	1875				4.43			SW¼NE¼	12	36	39	3-15—6-13	.036	6.65
	1875						.70	SW¼NE¼	12	36	39	3-15—4-28	.006	1.05
	1875			5.30				SE¼NE¼	12	36	39	3-15—9-15	.043	15.90

Claimant—**Bliss Brothers.** Proof No. 00102
Source—**Humboldt River.** Ditch—**Pioneer Ditch System.**

	1870			28.26				SE¼NE¼	2	36	39	3-15—9-15	.230	84.78
	1870				9.08			SE¼NE¼	2	36	39	3-15—6-13	.074	13.62
	1870					.45		SE¼NE¼	2	36	39	3-15—4-28	.004	.34
	1870					3.05		SW¼SW¼	2	36	39	3-15—4-28	.025	2.29
	1870					20.28		SE¼SW¼	2	36	39	3-15—4-28	.165	15.21

Bliss Brothers—Continued.

Year of priority	Culture—Acres: Harvest crops	Meadow pasture	Diversified pasture		Location: Subdivision	Section	Tp. N.	R. E.	Length of season	Duty of water: C. F. S.	Acre-feet
1870	....	35.86			SE¼SW¼	1	36	39	3-15—6-13	.292	53.79
1870	....	20.17			NW¼SE¼	1	36	39	3-15—6-13	.164	30.26
1870	....	19.51			SW¼SE¼	1	36	39	3-15—6-13	.159	29.27
1870	....	.33			NE¼NW¼	1	36	39	3-15—6-13	.003	.50
1870	....	13.57			SW¼NE¼	1	36	39	3-15—6-13	.110	20.36
1870	2.49				SE¼NW¼	33	37	39	3-15—9-15	.020	7.47
1870	....	23.24			SE¼NW¼	33	37	39	3-15—6-13	.180	34.86
1870	....	32.79			SW¼NE¼	33	37	39	3-15—6-13	.367	49.19
1870	....			9.38	NW¼NW¼	32	37	39	3-15—4-28	.076	7.04
1870	....			10.40	NE¼NW¼	32	37	39	3-15—4-28	.085	7.80
1871	13.86				SW¼NW¼	33	37	39	3-15—9-15	.113	41.58
1871	....	.43			SW¼NW¼	33	37	39	3-15—6-13	.003	.66
1871	....	6.90			SE¼NE¼	33	37	39	3-15—6-13	.056	10.35
1871	....		4.23		SE¼NE¼	33	37	39	3-15—4-28	.034	8.35
1871	....	2.12			NW¼NE¼	33	37	39	3-16—6-13	.017	3.18
1871	28.60				NW¼SW¼	33	37	39	3-15—9-15	.233	86.07
1871	....	3.33			NW¼SW¼	33	37	39	3-15—6-13	.027	5.00
1871	25.37				NE¼SW¼	33	37	39	3-15—9-15	.206	76.11
1871	....	1.23			NE¼SW¼	33	37	39	3-15—6-13	.101	1.85
1871	....		6.93		NE¼SW¼	33	37	39	3-15—4-28	.056	7.32
1871	27.67				NW¼SE¼	33	37	39	3-15—9-15	.225	83.01
1871	....	5.77			NW¼SE¼	33	37	39	3-15—6-13	.047	8.66
1871	....		1.60		NW¼SE¼	33	37	39	3-15—4-28	.013	1.20
1871	.63				NE¼SE¼	33	37	39	3-15—9-15	.005	1.89
1871	....	6.87			NE¼SE¼	33	37	39	3-16—6-13	.056	10.81
1871	....		16.74		NE¼SE¼	33	37	39	3-15—4-28	.138	12.56
1871	26.60				SW¼SW¼	33	37	39	3-15—9-15	.216	79.80
1871	36.97				SE¼SW¼	33	37	39	3-15—9-15	.301	110.91
1871	34.99				SW¼SE¼	33	37	39	3-15—9-15	.284	104.97
1871	....			4.54	SW¼SE¼	33	37	39	3-16—4-28	.037	3.41
1871	26.77				SE¼SE¼	33	37	39	3-15—9-15	.218	80.31
1871	....	2.67			SE¼SE¼	33	37	39	3-15—6-13	.022	4.01
1871	....		8.10		SE¼SE¼	33	37	39	3-15—4-28	.066	6.08
1871	....			.40	SE¼SE¼	33	37	39	3-15—4-28	.004	.30
1871	20.47				NW¼NW¼	32	37	39	3-15—9-15	.166	61.41
1871	....	2.83			NW¼NW¼	32	37	39	3-15—6-13	.023	4.25
1871	20.56				NE¼NW¼	32	37	39	3-15—9-15	.167	61.68
1871	22.10				NW¼NE¼	32	37	39	3-15—9-15	.180	66.30
1871	....			3.77	NW¼NE¼	32	37	39	3-15—4-28	.031	2.83
1871	4.00				NE¼NE¼	32	37	39	3-15—9-15	.033	12.00
1871				1.36	NE¼NE¼	32	37	39	3-15—4-28	.011	1.02
1871	29.54				SW¼NW¼	32	37	39	3-15—9-15	.240	88.02
1871				8.03	SW¼NW¼	32	37	39	3-15—4-28	.065	6.02
1871	27.49				SE¼NW¼	32	37	39	3-15—9-15	.223	82.47
1871				9.14	SE¼SW¼	32	37	39	3-15—4-28	.074	6.86
1871	33.88				SW¼NE¼	32	37	39	3-15—9-15	.275	101.61
1871				3.61	SW¼NE¼	32	37	39	3-15—4-28	.020	2.71

1871	25.54				SE¼NE¼	32	37	39	3-15—9-15	.908	76.62
1871				11.66	SE¼NE¼	32	37	39	3-15—4-28	.005	8.75
1871	20.31				NW¼SW¼	32	37	39	3-15—9-15	.165	60.93
1871		5.59			NW¼SW¼	32	37	39	3-15—6-13	.045	8.39
1871			3.54		NW¼SW¼	32	37	39	3-15—4-28	.029	2.66
1871				7.12	NW¼SW¼	32	37	39	3-15—4-28	.058	5.34
1871	23.52				NE¼SW¼	32	37	39	3-15—9-15	.191	70.56
1871				14.18	NE¼SW¼	32	37	39	3-15—4-28	.115	10.64
1871	29.48				NW¼SE¼	32	37	39	3-15—9-15	.240	88.44
1871				8.90	NW¼SE¼	32	37	39	3-15—4-28	.072	6.68
1871	29.18				NE¼SE¼	32	37	39	3-15—9-15	.237	87.54
1871				9.68	NE¼SE¼	32	37	39	3-15—4-28	.079	7.26
1871	7.93				SE¼SW¼	32	37	39	3-15—9-15	.064	23.79
1871		3.11			SE¼SW¼	32	37	39	3-15—6-13	.025	4.67
1871			.31		SE¼SW¼	32	37	39	3-15—4-28	.003	.23
1871				3.34	SE¼SW¼	32	37	39	3-15—4-28	.027	2.51
1871	27.39				SE¼SE¼	32	37	39	3-15—9-15	.223	82.17
1871			5.66		SE¼SE¼	32	37	39	3-15—4-28	.046	4.25
1871	10.50				NW¼NW¼	4	36	39	3-15—9-15	.085	31.50
1871			21.15		NW¼NW¼	4	36	39	3-15—4-28	.172	15.86
1871				.06	NW¼NW¼	4	36	39	3-15—4-28	.001	.05
1871	23.73				NE¼NW¼	4	36	39	3-15—9-15	.192	71.19
1871			10.80		NE¼NW¼	4	36	39	3-15—4-28	.088	8.10
1871				1.10	NE¼NW¼	4	36	39	3-15—4-28	.009	.83
1871	25.13				NW¼NE¼	4	36	39	3-15—9-15	.204	75.39
1871			10.45		NW¼NE¼	4	36	39	3-15—4-28	.085	7.84
1871	31.97				NE¼NE¼	4	36	39	3-15—9-15	.260	95.91
1871			4.60		NE¼NE¼	4	36	39	3-15—4-28	.037	3.45
1871			3.53		NE¼SE¼	4	36	39	3-15—4-28	.029	2.65
1871		.70			SW¼NW¼	7	36	40	3-15—6-13	.006	1.05
1871			19.97		SW¼NW¼	7	36	40	3-15—4-28	.162	14.98
1871			6.65		SE¼NW¼	7	36	40	3-15—4-28	.054	5.99
1871		5.16			SW¼NE¼	7	36	40	3-15—6-13	.042	7.74
1871		1.45			SE¼NE¼	7	36	40	3-15—6-13	.012	2.18
1871	.50				SE¼SW¼	1	36	39	3-15—9-15	.004	1.50
1871			1.37		SE¼SW¼	1	36	39	3-15—4-28	.011	1.03
1871			18.47		NW¼SE¼	1	36	39	3-15—4-28	.150	13.85
1871			14.90		SW¼SE¼	1	36	39	3-15—4-28	.121	11.18
1871			2.50		SE¼SE¼	1	36	39	3-15—4-28	.120	1.88
1871			6.60		SW¼NE¼	1	36	39	3-15—4-28	.054	4.95
1871			2.60		SE¼NE¼	1	36	39	3-15—4-28	.021	1.95
1871			8.27		NE¼SE¼	1	36	39	3-15—4-28	.067	6.20
1871	3.90				NW¼NE¼	12	36	39	3-15—9-15	.032	11.70
1871		2.00			NW¼NE¼	12	36	39	3-15—6-13	.016	3.00
1871		7.38			NW¼SE¼	3	36	39	3-15—6-13	.060	11.07
1871			3.12		NW¼SE¼	3	36	39	3-15—4-28	.025	2.34
1871		22.81			NE¼SE¼	3	36	39	3-15—6-13	.185	34.22
1871		6.24			NW¼SW¼	34	37	39	3-15—6-13	.051	9.36
1871		5.81			SW¼SW¼	34	37	39	3-15—6-13	.047	8.72
1871			22.31		SW¼SW¼	34	37	39	3-15—4-28	.181	16.73
1871		20.90			SE¼SW¼	34	37	39	3-15—6-13	.170	31.85

Bliss Brothers—Continued.

Year of priority	Culture—Acres: Harvest crops	Culture—Acres: Meadow pasture	Culture—Acres: Diversified pasture		Location: Subdivision	Location: Section	Location: Tp.N.	Location: R.E.	Length of season	Duty of water: C.F.S.	Duty of water: Acre-feet
1876			.24		SE¼SW¼	34	37	39	3-15—4-29	.002	.18
1876		29.87			SW¼SE¼	34	37	39	3-15—6-13	.243	44.81
1876		2.73			SE¼SE¼	34	37	39	3-15—6-13	.022	4.10
1876			1.70		SE¼SE¼	34	37	39	3-15—4-28	.014	1.28
1876	1.17				SW¼SW¼	35	37	39	3-15—9-15	.010	3.51
1876		12.97			SW¼SW¼	35	37	39	3-15—6-13	.105	19.46
1876		13.40			SE¼SW¼	35	37	39	3-15—6-13	.109	20.10
1876		26.10			NW¼NE¼	3	36	39	3-15—6-13	.212	39.15
1876			11.23		NW¼NE¼	3	36	39	3-15—4-28	.091	8.42
1876	7.04				NE¼NE¼	3	36	39	3-15—9-15	.057	21.12
1876		25.72			NE¼NE¼	3	36	39	3-15—6-13	.209	38.58
1876			.33		NE¼NE¼	3	36	39	3-15—4-28	.003	.25
1876		28.22			SW¼NE¼	3	36	39	3-15—6-13	.229	42.33
1876			10.48		SW¼NE¼	3	36	39	3-15—4-28	.085	7.86
1876		17.40			SE¼NE¼	3	36	39	3-15—6-13	.141	26.10
1876			19.34		SE¼NE¼	3	36	39	3-15—4-28	.157	14.51
1876		16.36			NW¼SW¼	3	36	39	3-15—6-13	.133	24.54
1876		16.32			NE¼SW¼	3	36	39	3-15—6-13	.133	24.48
1877	6.48				NE¼NE¼	11	36	39	3-15—9-15	.053	19.44
1877			28.69		NE¼NE¼	11	36	39	3-15—4-28	.233	21.52
1877			6.42		NW¼NE¼	11	36	39	3-15—4-28	.052	4.82
1877	4.78				SE¼NE¼	11	36	39	3-15—9-15	.039	14.34
1877			11.79		SE¼NE¼	11	36	39	3-15—4-28	.096	8.84
1877	12.97				NE¼SE¼	11	36	39	3-15—9-15	.105	38.91

Claimant—**L. Hirzel.** Proof No. 00103

Source—**Humboldt River.** Ditch—**Sand Hill Slough System.**

Year of priority	Harvest crops	Meadow pasture	Diversified pasture		Subdivision	Section	Tp.N.	R.E.	Length of season	C.F.S.	Acre-feet
1874	25.01				NE¼NE¼	8	35	37	3-15—9-15	.203	75.03
1874			7.69		NE¼NE¼	8	35	37	3-15—4-28	.063	5.77
1880	1.00				NW¼NE¼	8	35	37	3-15—9-15	.008	3.00
1880			33.60		NW¼NE¼	8	35	37	3-15—4-28	.273	25.20
1880	14.12				SE¼NE¼	8	35	37	3-15—9-15	.115	42.36
1880			9.98		SE¼NE¼	8	35	37	3-15—4-28	.081	7.49
1880	6.74				SW¼NE¼	8	35	37	3-15—9-15	.055	20.22
1880			21.16		SW¼NE¼	8	35	37	3-15—4-28	.172	15.87
1880	2.56				NW¼SE¼	8	35	37	3-15—9-15	.021	7.68
1880			30.84		NW¼SE¼	8	35	37	3-15—4-28	.251	23.13
1880			28.90		NE¼SW¼	8	35	37	3-15—4-28	.235	21.68
1880	2.01				NW¼SW¼	8	35	37	3-15—9-15	.033	6.03
1880			31.25		NW¼SW¼	8	35	37	3-15—4-28	.254	23.44
1880				.14	NW¼SW¼	8	35	37	3-15—4-28	.001	.11
1880	24.23				SW¼NW¼	8	35	37	3-15—9-15	.197	72.69
1880			8.39		SW¼NW¼	8	35	37	3-15—4-28	.068	6.29
1880				1.08	SW¼NW¼	8	35	37	3-15—4-28	.009	.81
1880	9.86				SE¼NW¼	8	35	37	3-15—9-15	.080	29.58
1880			20.44		SE¼NW¼	8	35	37	3-15—4-28	.100	15.83

	1881			8.49				NE¼NW¼	8	35	37	3-15—9-15	.009	25.47
	1881					20.15		NE¼NW¼	8	35	37	3-15—4-28	.164	15.11
	1881			8.49				NW¼NW¼	8	35	37	3-15—9-15	.009	25.47
	1881					7.51		NW¼NW¼	8	35	37	3-15—4-28	.061	5.63
	1881			30.16				SE¼NE¼	7	35	37	3-15—9-15	.245	90.48
	1881					4.20		SE¼NE¼	7	35	37	3-15—4-28	.034	3.15
	1881			.68				NE¼SE¼	7	35	37	3-15—9-15	.007	2.04
	1881					32.88		NE¼SE¼	7	35	37	3-15—4-28	.267	24.66
	1881			2.16				NW¼SE¼	7	35	37	3-15—9-15	.018	6.48
	1881					27.59		NW¼SE¼	7	35	37	3-15—4-28	.224	20.69
	1881						.85	NW¼SE¼	7	35	37	3-15—4-28	.007	.64
	1881					2.10		SW¼NW¼	7	35	37	3-15—4-28	.017	1.58
	1881			21.25				NE¼SW¼	7	35	37	3-15—9-15	.173	63.75
	1881					10.21		NE¼SW¼	7	35	37	3-15—4-28	.083	7.66
	1881						.64	NE¼SW¼	7	35	37	3-15—4-28	.005	.48
	1882			34.00				NW¼SW¼	7	35	37	3-15—9-15	.276	102.00
	1882					4.62		NW¼SW¼	7	35	37	3-15—4-28	.038	3.47
	1882			8.33				NE¼SE¼	12	35	36	3-15—9-15	.068	24.99
	1882					21.67		NE¼SE¼	12	35	36	3-15—4-28	.176	16.25
	1882					22.62		SE¼SE¼	12	35	36	3-15—4-28	.184	16.97
	1880			7.56				NW¼SW¼	4	35	37	3-15—9-15	.061	22.68
	1880					20.33		NW¼SW¼	4	35	37	3-15—4-28	.165	15.25
	1880			36.39				SW¼SW¼	4	35	37	3-15—9-15	.296	109.17
	1880					1.51		SW¼SW¼	4	35	37	3-15—4-28	.012	1.13
	1874			25.96				NE¼SW¼	4	35	37	3-15—9-15	.211	77.88
	1874					11.14		NE¼SW¼	4	35	37	3-15—4-28	.091	8.36
	1881					7.91		SE¼NW¼	4	35	37	3-15—4-28	.064	5.93
	1881					19.71		SW¼NE¼	4	35	37	3-15—4-28	.160	14.78
	1881				5.57			SE¼NE¼	4	35	37	3-15—6-13	.045	8.36
	1881					5.39		SE¼NE¼	4	35	37	3-15—4-28	.044	4.04
	1874			15.37				NW¼SE¼	4	35	37	3-15—9-15	.135	46.11
	1874				7.00			NW¼SE¼	4	35	37	3-15—6-13	.057	10.50
	1874					13.63		NW¼SE¼	4	35	37	3-15—4-28	.111	10.22
	1874			14.22				SW¼SE¼	4	35	37	3-15—9-15	.116	42.66
	1874					12.32		SW¼SE¼	4	35	37	3-15—4-28	.100	9.24
	1874						3.28	SW¼SE¼	4	35	37	3-15—4-28	.027	2.46
	1874			32.60				SE¼SW¼	4	35	37	3-15—9-15	.265	97.80
	1874					3.80		SE¼SW¼	4	35	37	3-15—4-28	.031	28.50
	1874			15.99				NE¼SE¼	4	35	37	3-15—9-15	.130	47.97
	1874				11.45			NE¼SE¼	4	35	37	3-15—6-13	.093	17.18
	1874					7.36		NE¼SE¼	4	35	37	3-15—4-28	.060	5.52
	1874			2.51				SE¼SE¼	4	35	37	3-15—9-15	.020	7.53
	1874					21.84		SE¼SE¼	4	35	37	3-15—4-28	.178	16.38
	1874						1.20	SE¼SE¼	4	35	37	3-15—4-28	.010	.90
	1874					14.20		NW¼NE¼	9	35	37	3-15—4-28	.115	10.65
	1874			15.80				NE¼NW¼	9	35	37	3-15—9-15	.128	47.40
	1874					18.30		NE¼NW¼	9	35	37	3-15—4-28	.149	13.73
	1874			33.99				NW¼NW¼	9	35	37	3-15—9-15	.276	101.97
	1874					1.51		NW¼NW¼	9	35	37	3-15—4-28	.012	1.13
	1874			3.63				SW¼NW¼	9	35	37	3-15—9-15	.030	10.89
	1874					18.67		SW¼NW¼	9	35	37	3-15—4-28	.152	14.00

Claimant—**Reinhart Land and Livestock Co.** Proof No. 00103

Source—**Humboldt River.** Ditch—**Unnamed Slough System.**

Year of priority	Culture—Acres: Harvest crops	Culture—Acres: Meadow pasture	Culture—Acres: Diversified pasture		Location: Subdivision	Location: Section	Location: Tp.N.	Location: R.E.	Length of season	Duty of water: C.F.S.	Duty of water: Acre-feet
1870	24.11				NE¼SE¼	25	36	37	3-15—9-15	.196	72.33
1870			9.67		NE¼SE¼	25	36	37	3-15—4-28	.079	7.25
1870	2.90				SE¼NE¼	25	36	37	3-15—9-15	.024	8.70
1870			16.02		SE¼NE¼	25	36	37	3-15—4-28	.130	12.02

Claimant—**Reinhart Land and Livestock Co.** Proof No. 00103

Source—**Humboldt River.** Ditch—**Adrian Dam System.**

Year of priority	Harvest crops	Meadow pasture	Diversified pasture		Subdivision	Section	Tp.N.	R.E.	Length of season	C.F.S.	Acre-feet
1880			20.20		NW¼SE¼	12	35	37	3-15—4-28	.164	15.15
1880			22.62		SE¼SE¼	12	35	37	3-15—4-28	.184	16.97
1880	8.33				NE¼SE¼	12	35	37	3-15—9-15	.068	24.99
1880			21.67		NE¼SE¼	12	35	37	3-15—4-28	.176	16.25
1882	.14				SE¼SW¼	7	35	37	3-15—9-15	.001	.42
1882			20.25		SE¼SW¼	7	35	37	3-15—4-28	.165	15.19
1882	4.15				SW¼SW¼	7	35	37	3-15—9-15	.034	12.45
1882			20.85		SW¼SW¼	7	35	37	3-15—4-28	.170	15.64
1882	34.00				NW¼SW¼	7	35	37	3-15—9-15	.276	102.00
1882			4.62		NW¼SW¼	7	35	37	3-15—4-28	.038	3.47
1882	21.25				NE¼SW¼	7	35	37	3-15—9-15	.173	63.75
1882			10.21		NE¼SW¼	7	35	37	3-15—4-28	.083	7.66
1882				.64	NE¼SW¼	7	35	37	3-15—4-28	.005	.48
1882			2.10		SW¼NW¼	7	35	37	3-15—4-28	.017	1.58
1882	8.30				SE¼NW¼	7	35	37	3-15—9-15	.067	24.90
1882	2.16				NW¼SE¼	7	35	37	3-15—9-15	.018	3.48
1882			27.59		NW¼SE¼	7	35	37	3-15—4-28	.224	20.60
1882				.85	NW¼SE¼	7	35	37	3-15—4-28	.007	.64
1881			13.80		SW¼SE¼	7	35	37	3-15—4-28	.112	10.35
1881			8.90		SE¼SE¼	7	35	37	3-15—4-28	.072	6.68
1881	.68				NE¼SE¼	7	35	37	3-15—9-15	.006	2.04
1881			32.88		NE¼SE¼	7	35	37	3-15—4-28	.267	24.66
1881	20.58				SW¼NE¼	7	35	37	3-15—9-15	.167	61.74
1881			10.22		SW¼NE¼	7	35	37	3-15—4-28	.083	7.74
1881	30.16				SE¼NE¼	7	35	37	3-15—9-15	.245	90.48
1881			4.20		SE¼NE¼	7	35	37	3-15—4-28	.035	3.15
1881	.25				NE¼NE¼	7	35	37	3-15—9-15	.002	.75
1881			1.15		NE¼NE¼	7	35	37	3-15—4-28	.009	.86
1881	8.49				NW¼NW¼	8	35	37	3-15—9-15	.069	25.47
1881			7.51		NW¼NW¼	8	35	37	3-15—4-28	.061	5.63
1881	8.40				NE¼NW¼	8	35	37	3-15—9-15	.069	25.47
1881			20.15		NE¼NW¼	8	35	37	3-15—4-28	.164	15.11
1881	9.86				SE¼NW¼	8	35	37	3-15—9-15	.080	29.58
1881			20.44		SE¼NW¼	8	35	37	3-15—4-28	.166	15.33
1881	21.23				SW¼NW¼	8	35	37	3-15—9-15	.197	72.00
1881			8.39		SW¼NW¼	8	35	37	3-15—4-28	.068	6.29
1881				1.08	SW¼NW¼	8	35	37	3-15—4-28	.009	.81
1879			10.40		SE¼NW¼	9	35	37	3-15—4-28	.085	7.80

	1880					6.50		NE¼SE¼	5	35	37	3-15—4-28	.053	5.88
	1880			6.40				SE¼SE¼	5	35	37	3-15—9-15	.052	19.20
	1880					27.30		SE¼SE¼	5	35	37	3-15—4-28	.222	20.48
	1880					8.90		SW¼SE¼	5	35	37	3-15—4-28	.072	6.68
	1880			3.80				NE¼SE¼	8	35	37	3-15—9-15	.031	11.40
	1880					4.00		NE¼SE¼	8	35	37	3-15—4-28	.033	3.00
	1880					18.86		NW¼NE¼	20	36	38	3-15—4-28	.153	14.10
	1880					26.72		NE¼NW¼	20	36	38	3-15—4-28	.217	20.04
	1880					13.90		NW¼NW¼	20	36	38	3-15—4-28	.113	10.43
	1880					15.90		SW¼NW¼	20	36	38	3-15—4-28	.129	11.93
	1880					26.90		SE¼NW¼	20	36	38	3-15—4-28	.219	20.18
	1880					.46		SW¼SW¼	17	36	38	3-15—4-28	.004	.35
	1880					8.96		NE¼SW¼	17	36	38	3-15—4-28	.073	6.72
	1878			7.00				NW¼NE¼	17	36	38	3-15—9-15	.057	21.00
	1878					11.60		NW¼NE¼	17	36	38	3-15—4-28	.094	8.70
	1869			21.08				SE¼NE¼	17	36	38	3-15—9-15	.196	72.24
	1869				5.20			SE¼NE¼	17	36	38	3-15—6-13	.042	7.80
	1869					10.00		SE¼NE¼	17	36	38	3-15—4-28	.081	7.50
	1869						2.24	SE¼NE¼	17	36	38	3-15—4-28	.018	1.68
	1875			13.74				SW¼NE¼	17	36	38	3-15—9-15	.112	41.22
	1875				16.94			SW¼NE¼	17	36	38	3-15—6-13	.138	25.41
	1875						4.12	SW¼NE¼	17	36	38	3-15—4-28	.033	3.09
	1880					4.71		SE¼NW¼	17	36	38	3-15—4-28	.038	3.53
	1880					24.14		SE¼SW¼	17	36	38	3-15—4-28	.196	18.11
	1876			11.93				NW¼SE¼	17	36	38	3-15—9-15	.097	35.79
	1876				6.18			NW¼SE¼	17	36	38	3-15—6-13	.050	9.27
	1876					20.26		NW¼SE¼	17	36	38	3-15—4-28	.165	15.20
	1876						.04	NW¼SE¼	17	36	38	3-15—4-28	.000	.03
	1877			3.55				NE¼SE¼	17	36	38	3-15—9-15	.029	10.65
	1877				3.55			NE¼SE¼	17	36	38	3-15—6-13	.029	5.33
	1877					34.00		NE¼SE¼	17	36	38	3-15—4-28	.276	25.50
	1880					26.80		SW¼SE¼	17	36	38	3-15—4-28	.214	20.10
	1869			33.40				NE¼NE¼	17	36	38	3-15—9-15	.272	100.20
	1869						7.74	NE¼NE¼	17	36	38	3-15—4-28	.063	5.81
	1878				3.49			SW¼NW¼	16	36	38	3-15—6-13	.028	5.24
	1878					15.57		SW¼NW¼	16	36	38	3-15—4-28	.127	11.68
	1878			23.93				NW¼NW¼	16	36	38	3-15—9-15	.195	71.79
	1878				6.03			NW¼NW¼	16	36	38	3-15—6-13	.049	9.05
	1878						1.60	NW¼NW¼	16	36	38	3-15—4-28	.013	1.20
	1878			1.23				NE¼NW¼	16	36	38	3-15—9-15	.010	3.69
	1878						4.83	NE¼NW¼	16	36	38	3-15—4-28	.039	3.62
	1878			5.93				SE¼SW¼	9	36	38	3-15—9-15	.048	17.79
	1878					12.73		SE¼SW¼	9	36	38	3-15—4-28	.103	9.55
	1878						3.00	SE¼SW¼	9	36	38	3-15—4-28	.024	2.25
	1869			38.52				SW¼SW¼	9	36	38	3-15—9-15	.313	115.56
	1869			3.20				NW¼SE¼	9	36	38	3-15—9-15	.026	9.60
	1869						4.10	NW¼SE¼	8	36	38	3-15—4-28	.033	3.08
	1869			27.80				NE¼SW¼	9	36	38	3-15—9-15	.226	83.40
	1869					7.80		NE¼SW¼	9	36	38	3-15—4-28	.063	5.85
	1869						2.90	NE¼SW¼	9	36	38	3-15—4-28	.024	2.18
	1869			39.40				NW¼SW¼	9	36	38	3-15—9-15	.320	118.20
	1877			38.90				NE¼NW¼	9	36	38	3-15—9-15	.316	116.70

Reinhart Land and Livestock Co.—Continued.

Year of priority	Culture—Acres: Harvest crops	Culture—Acres: Meadow pasture	Culture—Acres: Diversified pasture	Location: Subdivision	Location: Section	Location: Tp.N.	Location: R.E.	Length of season	Duty of water: C.F.S.	Duty of water: Acre-feet
1878	40.20			SW¼NW¼	9	36	38	3-15—9-15	.327	120.60
1877	34.41			NW¼NW¼	9	36	38	3-15—9-15	.280	103.23
1877			3.60	NW¼NW¼	9	36	38	3-15—4-28	.029	2.70
1869	40.53			SE¼NW¼	9	36	38	3-15—9-15	.330	121.59
1877	17.78			NW¼SW¼	4	36	38	3-15—9-15	.145	53.34
1877		1.90		NW¼SW¼	4	36	38	3-15—6-13	.015	2.85
1877			1.70	NW¼SW¼	4	36	38	3-15—4-28	.014	1.28
1877	22.10			SW¼SW¼	4	36	38	3-15—9-15	.180	66.30
1877			9.88	SW¼SW¼	4	36	38	3-15—4-28	.080	7.41
1877	24.39			NE¼SW¼	4	36	38	3-15—9-15	.198	73.17
1877			9.15	NE¼SW¼	4	36	38	3-15—4-28	.074	6.86
1877	24.34			SE¼SW¼	4	36	38	3-15—9-15	.190	73.02
1877			7.56	SE¼SW¼	4	36	38	3-15—4-28	.061	5.67
1880	10.28			SE¼SE¼	5	36	38	3-15—9-15	.084	30.84
1880			3.22	SE¼SE¼	5	36	38	3-15—4-28	.026	2.42
1878	16.90			NE¼NE¼	8	36	38	3-15—9-15	.137	50.70
1878			15.60	NE¼NE¼	8	36	38	3-15—4-28	.127	11.70
1878			1.08	NW¼NE¼	8	36	38	3-15—4-28	.009	.81
1878			1.53	SW¼NE¼	8	36	38	3-15—4-28	.012	1.15
1878			.64	SW¼NE¼	8	36	38	3-15—4-28	.005	.48
1878	28.00			SE¼NE¼	8	36	38	3-15—9-15	.228	84.00
1878			9.41	SE¼NE¼	8	36	38	3-15—4-28	.077	7.06
1878			9.00	NW¼SE¼	8	36	38	3-15—4-28	.073	6.75
1878			3.40	NW¼SE¼	8	36	38	3-15—4-28	.028	2.55
1878	22.60			NE¼SE¼	8	36	38	3-15—9-15	.184	67.80
1878			13.28	NE¼SE¼	8	36	38	3-15—4-28	.108	9.96
1878			17.48	SW¼SE¼	8	36	38	3-15—4-28	.142	13.11
1878	31.30			SE¼SE¼	8	36	38	3-15—9-15	.254	93.90
1878			3.80	SE¼SE¼	8	36	38	3-15—4-28	.031	2.85

Claimant—**Reinhart Land & Livestock Co.** Proof No. 00103

Source—**Humboldt River.** Ditch—**Sand Hill Slough.**

Year of priority	Harvest crops	Meadow pasture	Diversified pasture	Subdivision	Section	Tp.N.	R.E.	Length of season	C.F.S.	Acre-feet
1874		5.60		SE¼NE¼	9	36	38	3-15—6-13	.046	8.40
1874	26.60			SW¼NE¼	9	36	38	3-15—9-15	.216	79.80
1874		8.80		SW¼NE¼	8	36	38	3-15—6-13	.072	13.20
1874			3.90	SW¼NE¼	9	36	38	3-15—4-28	.032	2.93
1874	4.40			NE¼NE¼	9	36	38	3-15—9-15	.036	13.20
1874		3.40		NE¼NE¼	9	36	38	3-15—6-13	.028	5.10
1874	39.70			NW¼NE¼	9	36	38	3-15—9-15	.323	119.10
1874	31.20			NW¼SE¼	4	36	38	3-15—9-15	.254	93.60
1874			3.10	NW¼SE¼	4	36	38	3-15—4-28	.025	2.33

Claimant—**J. A. Callahan.** Proof No. 00104

Source—**Humboldt River.** Ditch—**St. Mary's Ditch.**

1861				17.56	SW¼SE¼	35	33	33	3-15—4-28	.143	13.17
1861			.34		SE¼SW¼	35	33	33	3-15—4-28	.028	.26
1861				30.34	SE¼SW¼	35	33	33	3-15—4-28	.247	22.75
1861				10.06	SW¼SW¼	35	33	33	3-15—4-28	.082	7.55
1861			10.20		SW¼SW¼	35	33	33	3-15—4-28	.083	7.65
1861				12.22	NE¼SW¼	35	33	33	3-15—4-28	.099	9.17
1861			22.87		NE¼SW¼	35	33	33	3-15—4-28	.186	17.15
1861			40.00		NW¼SW¼	35	33	33	3-15—4-28	.325	30.00
1861		34.00			SE¼NW¼	35	33	33	3-15—6-13	.276	51.00
1861			6.00		SE¼NW¼	35	33	33	3-15—4-28	.049	4.50
1861			35.23		SW¼NW¼	35	33	33	3-15—4-28	.286	26.42
1871			25.66		NE¼NW¼	35	33	33	3-15—4-28	.209	19.25
1871			11.64		NW¼NW¼	35	33	33	3-15—4-28	.095	8.73
1867			1.29		SE¼NE¼	34	33	33	3-15—4-28	.010	.97
1861		23.86			SE¼NE¼	34	33	33	3-15—6-13	.194	35.79
1867	.31				NE¼NE¼	34	33	33	3-15—9-15	.003	.93
1867			3.25		NE¼NE¼	34	33	33	3-15—4-28	.026	2.41
1861	31.08				NE¼SE¼	34	33	33	3-15—9-15	.253	93.24
1861		5.82			NE¼SE¼	34	33	33	3-15—6-13	.047	8.73
1861	2.02				SE¼SE¼	34	33	33	3-15—9-15	.016	6.06
1861				20.12	SE¼SW¼	25	33	33	3-15—4-28	.164	15.09
1861				3.53	NW¼NW¼	36	33	33	3-15—4-28	.029	2.65
1861				32.92	NE¼NW¼	36	33	33	3-15—4-28	.268	24.69
1861	1.94				SW¼SW¼	25	33	33	3-15—9-15	.016	5.82
1861		2.97			SW¼SW¼	25	33	33	3-15—6-13	.024	4.46
1861			3.09		SW¼SW¼	25	33	33	3-15—4-28	.025	2.32
1861				13.51	SW¼SW¼	25	33	33	3-15—4-28	.110	10.13
1861	9.92				SE¼SE¼	26	33	33	3-15—9-15	.081	29.76
1868		10.20			SE¼SE¼	26	33	33	3-15—6-13	.083	15.30
1878		8.39			SW¼SE¼	26	33	33	3-15—6-13	.068	12.59
1861				12.79	NE¼NE¼	35	33	33	3-15—4-28	.104	9.59
1861			8.51		NE¼NE¼	35	33	33	3-15—4-28	.069	6.38
1861			34.80		NW¼NE¼	35	33	33	3-15—4-28	.283	26.10
1861			29.60		SW¼NE¼	35	33	33	3-15—4-28	.241	22.27
1861				6.23	SW¼NE¼	35	33	33	3-15—4-28	.051	4.67
1861			1.64		SE¼NE¼	35	33	33	3-15—4-28	.013	1.23
1861	6.67				SE¼NW¼	34	33	33	3-15—9-15	.054	20.01
1861			2.88		SE¼NW¼	34	33	33	3-15—4-28	.023	2.16
1867	10.15				SW¼NE¼	34	33	33	3-15—9-15	.083	30.45
1867		11.36			SW¼NE¼	34	33	33	3-15—6-13	.092	17.04
1867			8.89		SW¼NE¼	34	33	33	3-15—4-28	.072	6.67
1861	6.44				NE¼NW¼	34	33	33	3-15—9-15	.052	19.32
1861				22.53	SE¼SE¼	34	33	33	3-15—4-28	.183	16.90
1861				10.25	SW¼SE¼	34	33	33	3-15—4-28	.083	7.69
1877	2.60				SW¼SE¼	34	33	33	3-15—9-15	.021	7.80
1867	8.73				SW¼SE¼	34	33	33	3-15—9-15	.071	26.19
1878			10.80		SW¼SE¼	34	33	33	3-15—4-28	.088	8.10
1861				17.21	SE¼SW¼	34	33	33	3-15—4-28	.140	12.91
1861	4.98				SE¼SW¼	34	33	33	3-15—9-15	.040	14.94
1878				18.46	SW¼SW¼	34	33	33	3-15—4-28	.150	13.85

J. A. Callahan—Continued.

Year of priority	Culture—Acres: Harvest crops	Culture—Acres: Meadow pasture	Culture—Acres: Diversified pasture		Location: Subdivision	Location: Section	Location: Tp.N.	Location: R.E.	Length of season	Duty of water: C.F.S.	Duty of water: Acre-feet
1861	38.09				NW¼SE¼	34	33	33	3-15—9-15	.310	114.27
1861		.72			NW¼SE¼	34	33	33	3-15—6-13	.006	1.08
1861	36.70				NE¼SW¼	34	33	33	3-15—9-15	.298	110.10
1861				.52	NE¼SW¼	34	33	33	3-15—4-28	.004	.39
1861	29.77				NW¼SW¼	34	33	33	3-15—9-15	.242	89.31
1861				5.57	NW¼SW¼	34	33	33	3-15—4-28	.045	4.18
1861	21.77				SW¼NW¼	34	33	33	3-15—9-15	.177	65.31
1861	5.12				SW¼NW¼	34	33	33	3-15—9-15	.042	15.36
1861	17.45				SE¼NW¼	34	33	33	3-15—9-15	.142	52.35
1861				31.14	SE¼NE¼	35	33	33	3-15—4-28	.253	23.36
1861			2.26		NW¼SE¼	35	33	33	3-15—4-28	.018	1.70
1861				35.05	NW¼SE¼	35	33	33	3-15—4-28	.285	26.29
1861				22.18	NE¼SE¼	35	33	33	3-15—4-28	.180	16.64
1861				.55	SE¼SE¼	35	33	33	3-15—4-28	.004	.41
1876	Power Plant—Quartz Mill				SW¼SW¼	25	33	33	1-1—12-31	200	

Water discharged without loss into river directly below Mill.

Claimant—**Robt. Robinson.** Proof No. 00105

Source—**Humboldt River.** Ditch—**Reil Dam and Ditches.**

Year of priority	Harvest crops	Meadow pasture	Diversified pasture		Subdivision	Section	Tp.N.	R.E.	Length of season	C.F.S.	Acre-feet
1877	4.15				SW¼NW¼	4	36	38	3-15—9-15	.035	12.45
1877		4.77			SW¼NW¼	4	36	38	3-15—6-13	.039	7.16
1877				1.40	SW¼NW¼	4	36	38	3-15—4-28	.011	1.05
1877	37.74				SE¼NW¼	4	36	38	3-15—9-15	.307	113.22
1877		.50			SE¼NW¼	4	36	38	3-15—6-13	.004	.75
1877			.20		SE¼NW¼	4	36	38	3-15—4-28	.002	.15
1877				2.16	SE¼NW¼	4	36	38	3-15—4-28	.018	1.62
1877	26.09				SW¼NE¼	4	36	38	3-15—9-15	.212	78.27
1877			8.53		SW¼NE¼	4	36	38	3-15—4-28	.069	6.40
1877				2.18	SW¼NE¼	4	36	38	3-15—4-28	.018	1.64
1877	24.80				SE¼NE¼	4	36	38	3-15—9-15	.202	74.40
1877			6.40		SE¼NE¼	4	36	38	3-15—4-28	.053	4.80
1877				5.36	SE¼NE¼	4	36	38	3-15—4-28	.044	4.02
1877	20.01				NE¼NW¼	4	36	38	3-15—9-15	.163	60.03
1877		5.60			NE¼NW¼	4	36	38	3-15—6-13	.046	8.40
1877			10.24		NE¼NW¼	4	36	38	3-15—4-28	.083	7.68
1877	36.58				NW¼NE¼	4	36	38	3-15—9-15	.297	109.74
1877		.22			NW¼NE¼	4	36	38	3-15—6-13	.002	.33
1877	30.64				NE¼NE¼	4	36	38	3-15—9-15	.259	91.92
1877			1.36		NE¼NE¼	4	36	38	3-15—4-28	.011	1.02
1877				4.84	NE¼NE¼	4	36	38	3-15—4-28	.039	3.63
1877	1.92				SW¼NW¼	3	36	38	3-15—9-15	.016	5.76
1877	5.68				NW¼NW¼	3	56	38	3-15—9-15	.046	17.04
1877	17.09				SE¼SE¼	33	37	38	3-15—9-15	.144	53.07
1877		13.20			SE¼SE¼	33	37	38	3-15—6-13	.107	19.80
1877			.88		SE¼SE¼	33	37	38	3-15—4-28	.007	.66

	1877						2.87	SE¼SE¼	33	37	38	3-15—4-28	.023	2.15
	1877			9.56				SW¼SE¼	33	37	38	3-15—9-15	.078	28.68
	1877				13.32			SW¼SE¼	33	37	38	3-15—6-13	.108	19.08
	1877			27.12				SW¼SW¼	34	37	38	3-15—9-15	.220	81.36
	1877				13.28			SW¼SW¼	34	37	38	3-15—6-13	.108	19.92
	1877						.28	SW¼SW¼	34	37	38	3-15—4-28	.002	.21
	1877			10.68				SE¼SW¼	34	37	38	3-15—9-15	.087	32.01
	1877				27.20			SE¼SW¼	34	37	38	3-15—6-13	.221	40.80
	1877					2.08		SE¼SW¼	34	37	38	3-15—4-28	.017	1.56
	1877				40.24			NE¼SW¼	34	37	38	3-15—6-13	.327	60.36
	1877				30.88			NW¼SW¼	34	37	38	3-15—6-13	.251	46.32
	1877				14.44			SE¼NW¼	34	37	38	3-15—6-13	.117	21.66
	1877				.28			SW¼NW¼	34	37	38	3-15—6-13	.002	.42
	1887				6.08			NE¼SE¼	33	37	38	3-15—6-13	.049	9.12
	1877				3.08			SE¼SW¼	33	37	38	3-15—6-13	.025	4.62
	1877			1.76				NE¼SW¼	4	36	38	3-15—9-15	.014	5.28
	1877			.76				NW¼SW¼	4	36	38	3-15—9-15	.006	2.28

Claimant—**E. J. Thacker.** Proof No. **00106**

Source—**Humboldt River.** Ditch—**Flood Water.**

	1875						5.08	SW¼SW¼	34	34	35	3-15—4-28	.041	3.81
	1875						30.09	NW¼NW¼	3	33	35	3-15—4-28	.245	22.57
	1875						6.42	NE¼NW¼	3	33	35	3-15—4-28	.052	4.82
	1875						25.92	SW¼NW¼	3	33	35	3-15—4-28	.211	19.44
	1875						6.12	SE¼NW¼	3	33	35	3-15—4-28	.050	4.59
	1875						24.19	NW¼SW¼	3	33	35	3-15—4-28	.197	18.14
	1875						6.27	NE¼SW¼	3	33	35	3-15—4-28	.051	4.70
	1875						28.49	SW¼SW¼	3	33	35	3-15—4-28	.232	21.37
	1875						6.34	SE¼SE¼	4	33	35	3-15—4-28	.052	4.76
	1882						25.67	NW¼NW¼	10	33	35	3-15—4-28	.208	19.25
	1898						3.89	SW¼NW¼	10	33	35	3-15—4-28	.032	2.92
	1882						29.41	NE¼NE¼	9	33	35	3-15—4-28	.237	22.06
	1898						34.59	SE¼NE¼	9	33	35	3-15—4-28	.281	25.94
	1898						16.30	SW¼NE¼	9	33	35	3-15—4-28	.133	12.23
	1898						21.46	NW¼SE¼	9	33	35	3-15—4-28	.174	16.10
	1898						12.86	NE¼SE¼	9	33	35	3-15—4-28	.105	9.65
	1898						2.78	SW¼SE¼	9	33	35	3-15—4-28	.023	2.09
	1898						13.08	SE¼SE¼	9	33	35	3-15—4-28	.106	9.81
	1898						1.60	NW¼NE¼	16	33	35	3-15—4-28	.013	1.20
	1898						9.39	NE¼NE¼	16	33	35	3-15—4-28	.076	7.04

Claimant—**Russell and Chadwick.** Proof No. **00108**

Source—**Humboldt River.** Ditch—**No. 2.**

	1864					15.80		NW¼SW¼	31	33	33	3-15—4-28	.128	11.85
	1864				16.30			SE¼SW¼	31	33	33	3-15—6-13	.133	24.45
	1864					16.43		SE¼SW¼	31	33	33	3-15—4-28	.134	12.32
	1864				2.63			NW¼SE¼	31	33	33	3-15—6-13	.021	3.95
	1864					6.63		NW¼SE¼	31	33	33	3-15—4-28	.054	4.97
	1864					1.80		NE¼NE¼	29	33	33	3-15—4-28	.015	1.35
	1864				11.83			NW¼NE¼	29	33	33	3-15—6-13	.096	17.75
	1864					12.87		NW¼NE¼	29	33	33	3-15—4-28	.105	9.65

Russell and Chadwick—Continued.

Year of priority	Culture—Acres: Harvest crops	Meadow pasture	Diversified pasture		Location: Subdivision	Section	Tp.N.	R.E.	Length of season	Duty of water: C.F.S.	Acre-feet
1864		15.53			SW¼NE¼	29	33	33	3-15—6-13	.126	23.30
1864			22.13		SW¼NE¼	29	33	33	3-15—4-28	.180	16.60
1864		1.17			SE¼NE¼	29	33	33	3-15—6-13	.010	1.76
1864			33.67		SE¼NE¼	29	33	33	3-15—4-28	.274	25.25
1864		6.07			NE¼NW¼	29	33	33	3-15—6-13	.049	9.11
1864			11.91		NE¼NW¼	29	33	33	3-15—4-28	.097	8.93
1864		29.65			SW¼NW¼	29	33	33	3-15—6-13	.241	44.48
1864			9.10		SW¼NW¼	29	33	33	3-15—4-28	.074	6.83
1864		25.22			SE¼NW¼	29	33	33	3-15—6-13	.205	37.83
1864			11.40		SE¼NW¼	29	33	33	3-15—4-28	.093	8.55
1864		27.75			NE¼SW¼	29	33	33	3-15—6-13	.226	41.63
1864			8.56		NE¼SW¼	29	33	33	3-15—4-28	.070	6.42
1864		35.47			NW¼SW¼	29	33	33	3-15—6-13	.288	53.21
1864			.70		NW¼SW¼	29	33	33	3-15—4-28	.006	.53
1864		32.96			NW¼SE¼	29	33	33	3-15—6-13	.268	49.44
1864			6.60		NW¼SE¼	29	33	33	3-15—4-28	.054	4.95
1864		34.80			NE¼SE¼	30	33	33	3-15—6-13	.283	52.20
1864			1.90		NE¼SE¼	30	33	33	3-15—4-28	.015	1.43
1864		16.63			NW¼SE¼	30	33	33	3-15—6-13	.135	24.95
1864			1.15		NW¼SE¼	30	33	33	3-15—4-28	.009	.86
1864		34.87			SW¼SE¼	30	33	33	3-15—6-13	.283	52.31
1864			.13		SW¼SE¼	30	33	33	3-15—4-28	.001	.10
1864		37.09			SE¼SE¼	30	33	33	3-15—6-13	.302	55.64
1864		38.60			NW¼NE¼	31	33	33	3-15—6-13	.314	57.90
1864	1.50				SW¼NE¼	31	33	33	3-15—9-15	.012	4.50
1864		7.57			SW¼NE¼	31	33	33	3-15—6-13	.062	11.36
1864				27.07	SW¼NE¼	31	33	33	3-15—4-28	.220	20.30
1864	1.20				SE¼NE¼	31	33	33	3-15—9-15	.010	3.60
1864				5.97	SE¼NE¼	31	33	33	3-15—4-28	.049	4.48
1864			8.30		NE¼NW¼	31	33	33	3-15—4-28	.067	6.02
1864		9.82			SW¼NW¼	31	33	33	3-15—6-13	.080	14.73
1864		29.10			SE¼NW¼	31	33	33	3-15—6-13	.237	43.65
1864			.77		SE¼NW¼	31	33	33	3-15—4-28	.005	.58
1864				7.57	SE¼NW¼	31	33	33	3-15—4-28	.062	5.68
1864		22.93			NW¼NW¼	6	32	33	3-15—6-13	.186	34.40
1864				5.80	NW¼NW¼	6	32	33	3-15—4-28	.047	4.26
1864		25.14			SW¼NW¼	6	32	33	3-15—6-13	.204	37.71
1864			2.90		SW¼NW¼	6	32	33	3-15—4-28	.024	2.18
1864				4.83	SW¼NW¼	6	32	33	3-15—4-28	.039	3.63

Claimant—**Russell and Chadwick.** Proof No. 00108

Source—**Humboldt River.** Ditch—**Blakeslee.**

1867				32.86	NE¼SE¼	11	32	32	3-15—4-28	.267	24.65
1867				18.08	NW¼SE¼	11	32	32	3-15—4-28	.147	13.58
1867				25.43	SW¼SE¼	11	32	32	3-15—4-28	.207	19.07
1867				27.12	SE¼SE¼	11	32	32	3-15—4-28	.220	20.34

	1867				19.00			SW¼NE¼	1	32	32	3-15—6-13	.154	28.50
	1867					2.00		SW¼NE¼	1	32	32	3-15—4-28	.016	1.50
	1867						5.37	SW¼NE¼	1	32	32	3-15—4-28	.044	40.28
	1867				29.97			NW¼SE¼	1	32	32	3-15—6-13	.244	44.96

Claimant—**Russell and Chadwick.** Proof No. 00108

Source—**Humboldt River.** Ditch—**Overflow.**

	1863					20.90		NE¼NE¼	29	33	33	3-15—4-28	.170	15.68
	1863						14.30	NE¼NE¼	29	33	33	3-15—4-28	.116	10.73
	1863					4.10		NW¼NW¼	29	33	33	3-15—4-28	.033	3.08
	1863						10.63	NW¼NW¼	29	33	33	3-15—4-28	.086	7.97
	1863					1.30		NE¼NE¼	30	33	33	3-15—4-28	.011	.98
	1863						1.53	NE¼NE¼	30	33	33	3-15—4-28	.012	1.15
	1863					20.70		SW¼NE¼	30	33	33	3-15—4-28	.168	15.53
	1863					15.23		SE¼NE¼	30	33	33	3-15—4-28	.124	11.42
	1863						19.11	SE¼NE¼	30	33	33	3-15—4-28	.155	14.33
	1863					4.80		SE¼NW¼	30	33	33	3-15—4-28	.039	3.60
	1863					21.23		NE¼SW¼	30	33	33	3-15—4-28	.173	15.92
	1863						.67	NE¼SW¼	30	33	33	3-15—4-28	.005	.50
	1863					22.23		SE¼SW¼	30	33	33	3-15—4-28	.181	16.67
	1863						9.53	SE¼SW¼	30	33	33	3-15—4-28	.177	7.15
	1863					13.15		NW¼SE¼	30	33	33	3-15—4-28	.107	9.86
	1863						4.01	NW¼SE¼	30	33	33	3-15—4-28	.033	3.01
	1863						2.40	SW¼SE¼	30	33	33	3-15—4-28	.020	1.80
	1863					16.87		NE¼NW¼	31	33	33	3-15—4-28	.137	12.65
	1863						9.20	NE¼NW¼	31	33	33	3-15—4-28	.175	6.90
	1863					3.60		NW¼NW¼	31	33	33	3-15—4-28	.029	2.70
	1863					35.37		NE¼NW¼	12	32	32	3-15—4-28	.288	26.53
	1863					38.20		NW¼NW¼	12	32	32	3-15—4-28	.311	28.65

Claimant—**Russell and Chadwick.** Proof No. 00108

Source—**Humboldt River.** Ditch—**No. 1.**

	1864				6.87			NE¼SW¼	31	33	33	3-15—6-13	.056	10.31
	1864					31.90		NE¼SW¼	31	33	33	3-15—4-28	.259	23.93
	1864				22.42			SW¼SW¼	29	33	33	3-15—6-13	.182	33.63
	1864					1.79		SW¼SW¼	29	33	33	3-15—4-28	.015	1.34
	1864				38.05			SE¼SW¼	29	33	33	3-15—6-13	.309	57.08
	1864				4.60			SW¼SE¼	29	33	33	3-15—6-13	.037	6.90
	1864					.70		SW¼SE¼	29	33	33	3-15—4-28	.006	.53
	1864						31.95	SW¼SE¼	29	33	33	3-15—4-28	.260	23.96
	1864					.80		SE¼SE¼	29	33	33	3-15—4-28	.007	.60
	1864						35.64	SE¼SE¼	29	33	33	3-15—4-28	.290	26.73
	1864				11.76			NE¼NE¼	31	33	33	3-15—6-13	.096	17.64
	1864						2.70	NE¼NE¼	31	33	33	3-15—4-28	.022	2.03
	1864				27.85			NE¼NW¼	6	32	33	3-15—6-13	.226	41.78
	1864			2.90				SW¼SE¼	1	32	32	3-15—9-15	.024	8.70
	1864				33.04			SW¼SE¼	1	32	32	3-15—6-13	.269	49.56
	1864			8.80				SE¼SE¼	1	32	32	3-15—9-15	.072	26.40
	1864				.31			SE¼SE¼	1	32	32	3-15—6-13	.003	.47
	1864				36.14			NW¼NE¼	12	32	32	3-15—6-13	.294	54.21

Russell and Chadwick—Continued.

Year of priority	Harvest crops	Culture—Acres Meadow pasture	Diversified pasture	Location Subdivision	Section	Tp.N.	R.E.	Length of season	Duty of water C.F.S.	Acre-feet
1864	....	33.93		SW¼NE¼	12	32	32	3-15—6-13	.276	50.90
1864	....	36.70		SW¼NW¼	12	32	32	3-15—6-13	.298	55.05
1864	....	39.40		SE¼NW¼	12	32	32	3-15—6-13	.320	59.10
1864	....	19.23		NE¼SW¼	12	32	32	3-15—6-13	.156	28.85
1864	....		20.53	NE¼SW¼	12	32	32	3-15—4-28	.167	15.40
1864	....	36.63		NW¼SW¼	12	32	32	3-15—6-13	.298	54.95
1864	....		2.97	NW¼SW¼	12	32	32	3-15—4-28	.024	2.23
1864	....	2.93		SW¼SW¼	12	32	32	3-15—6-13	.024	4.40
1864	....		36.95	SW¼SW¼	12	32	32	3-15—4-28	.300	27.71

Claimant—**Rodgers Estate.** Proof No. 00109

Source—**Humboldt** River. Ditch—St. **Mary's.**

Year of priority	Harvest crops	Culture—Acres Meadow pasture	Diversified pasture	Location Subdivision	Section	Tp.N.	R.E.	Length of season	Duty of water C.F.S.	Acre-feet
1867	....	15.66		NW¼NW¼	28	33	33	3-15—6-13	.127	23.34
1867	....	.79		NE¼NW¼	28	33	33	3-15—6-13	.006	1.19
1867	....	18.11		SW¼NW¼	28	33	33	3-15—6-13	.147	27.17
1867	....		16.33	SW¼NW¼	28	33	33	3-15—4-28	.133	12.25
1867	....	22.16		SE¼NW¼	28	33	33	3-15—6-13	.180	33.24
1867	....		8.05	SE¼NW¼	28	33	33	3-15—4-28	.165	6.04
1867	....	31.60		SW¼NE¼	28	33	33	3-15—6-13	.257	47.40
1867	....	7.50		SE¼NE¼	28	33	33	3-15—6-13	.061	11.35
1867	....		40.00	NW¼SW¼	28	33	33	3-15—4-28	.325	30.00
1867	....	15.23		NE¼SW¼	28	33	33	3-15—6-13	.124	22.85
1867	....		17.59	NE¼SW¼	28	33	33	3-15—4-28	.143	13.19
1867	....		37.71	SW¼SW¼	28	33	33	3-15—4-28	.307	28.28
1867	....	15.79		SE¼SW¼	28	33	33	3-15—6-13	.128	23.69
1867	....		16.89	SE¼SW¼	28	33	33	3-15—4-28	.137	12.67
1867	....	38.66		NW¼SE¼	28	33	33	3-15—6-13	.314	57.99
1867	....	29.86		NE¼SE¼	28	33	33	3-15—6-13	.244	44.79
1867	....	39.76		SW¼SE¼	28	33	33	3-15—6-13	.323	59.64
1867	....	39.14		SE¼SE¼	28	33	33	3-15—6-13	.318	58.71
1867	....	1.07		NW¼SW¼	27	33	33	3-15—6-13	.009	1.61
1867	....	28.42		SW¼SW¼	27	33	33	3-15—6-13	.231	42.63
1867	....		16.25	NW¼NW¼	33	33	33	3-15—4-28	.132	12.19
1867	....		31.53	NE¼NW¼	33	33	33	3-15—4-28	.257	23.65
1867	....	3.14		NW¼NE¼	33	33	33	3-15—6-13	.026	4.71
1867	....		14.95	NW¼NE¼	33	33	33	3-15—4-28	.122	11.21
1867	....	10.75		NE¼NE¼	33	33	33	3-15—6-13	.087	16.13
1867	....		21.89	NE¼NE¼	33	33	33	3-15—4-28	.174	16.04
1867	..		31.90	SE¼NE¼	33	33	33	3-15—4-28	.259	23.93
1867	....		22.08	NE¼SE¼	33	33	33	3-15—4-28	.180	16.56
1867	....		4.58	SE¼SE¼	33	33	33	3-15—4-28	.037	3.44
1867	..	87.91		NW¼NW¼	34	33	33	3-15—6-13	.308	56.87
1867	...		1.40	NW¼NW¼	34	33	33	3-15—4-28	.011	1.05

Proof No. 00110

Claimant—**Sarah E. Thacker.**
Source—**Humboldt River.** Ditch—**South Ditch.**

1864			17.40	SW¼ SE¼	33	33	34	3-15—4-28	.141	13.05
1864			37.52	SE¼ SE¼	33	33	34	3-15—4-28	.305	28.14
1864			20.77	NE¼ NE¼	4	32	34	3-15—4-28	.169	15.58
1864		10.82		SE¼ SE¼	28	33	34	3-15—4-28	.089	8.12
1864		9.91		SW¼ SE¼	28	33	34	3-15—4-28	.081	7.46
1864			7.67	NW¼ SE¼	34	33	34	3-15—4-28	.062	5.75
1864			20.35	NE¼ SE¼	34	33	34	3-15—4-28	.165	15.41
1864			8.95	SW¼ SE¼	34	33	34	3-15—4-28	.073	6.71
1864			13.10	SE¼ SE¼	34	33	34	3-15—4-28	.107	9.83
1864			4.45	NW¼ SW¼	34	33	34	3-15—4-28	.036	3.34
1864			15.48	NE¼ SW¼	34	33	34	3-15—4-28	.126	11.61
1864		2.17		NE¼ NE¼	35	33	34	3-15—4-28	.018	1.63
1864	1.32			NW¼ NE¼	35	33	34	3-15—6-13	.011	1.98
1864		33.60		NW¼ NE¼	35	33	34	3-15—4-28	.273	25.20
1864		6.68		SW¼ NE¼	35	33	34	3-15—4-28	.054	5.04
1864		15.53		NE¼ NW¼	35	33	34	3-15—4-28	.126	11.65
1864	.73			SE¼ NW¼	35	33	34	3-15—6-13	.006	1.10
1864		38.12		SE¼ NW¼	35	33	34	3-15—4-28	.310	28.59
1864		14.77		NE¼ SW¼	35	33	34	3-15—4-28	.120	11.08
1864		33.00		NW¼ SW¼	35	33	34	3-15—4-28	.268	24.75
1864		1.45		SW¼ SW¼	35	33	34	3-15—4-28	.012	1.08
1864			14.15	SE¼ NE¼	32	33	34	3-15—4-28	.115	10.61
1864			12.78	SW¼ NE¼	32	33	34	3-15—4-28	.104	9.59
1864			35.26	NW¼ NW¼	32	33	34	3-15—4-28	.287	26.44
1864			12.46	SW¼ NW¼	32	33	34	3-15—4-28	.101	9.35
1864			15.28	SE¼ NW¼	32	33	34	3-15—4-28	.124	11.46
1864			12.25	NW¼ NE¼	31	33	34	3-15—4-28	.100	9.19
1864			25.93	NE¼ NE¼	31	33	34	3-15—4-28	.211	19.45
1864			3.10	SE¼ NE¼	31	33	34	3-15—4-28	.025	2.33
1864		17.30		NE¼ SW¼	30	33	34	3-15—4-28	.141	12.98
1864		10.34		SE¼ SW¼	30	33	34	3-15—4-28	.084	7.76
1864			34.64	SW¼ SE¼	30	33	34	3-15—4-28	.282	25.98
1864			29.23	SE¼ SE¼	30	33	34	3-15—4-28	.238	21.92
1864			5.01	SE¼ SW¼	34	33	34	3-15—4-28	.041	3.76
1864			19.81	SW¼ SW¼	34	33	34	3-15—4-28	.161	14.86
1864	2.87			SW¼ NE¼	33	33	34	3-15—6-13	.023	4.31
1864			30.18	SW¼ NE¼	33	33	34	3-15—4-28	.245	22.64
1864			11.80	SE¼ NE¼	33	33	34	3-15—4-28	.096	8.85
1864			13.30	SW¼ NW¼	33	33	34	3-15—4-28	.109	10.04
1864	1.88			SE¼ NW¼	33	33	34	3-15—6-13	.015	2.82
1864			22.69	SE¼ NW¼	33	33	34	3-15—4-28	.184	17.02
1864			6.78	NW¼ SE¼	33	33	34	3-15—4-28	.055	5.09
1864			21.73	NE¼ SE¼	33	33	34	3-15—4-28	.178	16.30
1864		19.23		NW¼ SW¼	25	33	34	3-15—4-28	.156	14.42
1864		.37		SW¼ SW¼	25	33	34	3-15—4-28	.003	.28
1864		27.09		SE¼ SE¼	26	33	34	3-15—4-28	.220	20.32
1864		20.51		SW¼ SE¼	26	33	34	3-15—4-28	.167	15.38

Claimant—**Sarah E. Thacker.** Proof No. 00110

Source—**Humboldt River.** Ditch—**Center Ditch.**

Year of priority	Culture—Acres: Harvest crops	Meadow pasture	Diversified pasture		Location: Subdivision	Section	Tp.N.	R.E.	Length of season	Duty of water: C.F.S.	Acre-feet
1878		15.30			SE¼SE¼	29	33	34	3-15—6-13	.124	22.95
1878		4.05			SW¼SE¼	29	33	34	3-15—6-13	.033	6.08
1878				11.84	SW¼SE¼	29	33	34	3-15—4-28	.096	8.88
1878				6.49	SE¼SW¼	29	33	34	3-15—4-28	.053	4.87
1878		23.23			NE¼NE¼	32	33	34	3-15—6-13	.189	34.85
1878			14.83		NE¼NE¼	32	33	34	3-15—4-28	.121	11.12
1878		12.24			NW¼NE¼	32	33	34	3-15—6-13	.100	18.36
1878			7.31		NW¼NE¼	32	33	34	3-15—4-28	.059	5.48
1878				15.71	NW¼NE¼	32	33	34	3-15—4-28	.128	11.78
1878		11.16			NE¼NW¼	32	33	34	3-15—6-13	.094	16.74
1878				22.69	NE¼NW¼	32	33	34	3-15—4-28	.185	17.02
1864		35.23			NW¼NE¼	33	33	34	3-15—6-13	.286	52.91
1864				4.23	NW¼NE¼	33	33	34	3-15—4-28	.034	3.17
1864		32.37			NE¼NE¼	33	33	34	3-15—6-13	.263	48.56
1864				6.59	NE¼NE¼	33	33	34	3-15—4-28	.054	4.94
1864		30.47			NW¼NW¼	33	33	34	3-15—6-13	.248	45.71
1864				8.90	NW¼NW¼	33	33	34	3-15—4-28	.072	6.68
1864		35.71			NE¼NW¼	33	33	34	3-15—6-13	.290	53.57
1864				3.81	NE¼NW¼	33	33	34	3-15—4-28	.031	2.86
1864		6.88			SW¼SW¼	27	33	34	3-15—6-13	.056	10.32
1864			2.96		SW¼SW¼	27	33	34	3-15—4-28	.024	2.22
1864		21.57			NE¼NE¼	34	33	34	3-15—6-13	.175	32.36
1864		16.67			NW¼NE¼	34	33	34	3-15—6-13	.136	25.00
1864		16.11			SW¼NE¼	34	33	34	3-15—6-13	.131	24.17
1864				22.57	SW¼NE¼	34	33	34	3-15—4-28	.183	16.93
1864		15.90			SE¼NE¼	34	33	34	3-15—6-13	.129	23.85
1864				22.96	SE¼NE¼	34	33	34	3-15—4-28	.187	17.22
1864		30.30			NW¼NW¼	34	33	34	3-15—6-13	.246	45.45
1864			2.07		NW¼NW¼	34	33	34	3-15—4-28	.017	1.55
1864		25.67			NE¼NW¼	34	33	34	3-15—6-13	.209	38.51
1864			.20		NE¼NW¼	34	33	34	3-15—4-28	.002	.15
1864		18.67			SE¼NW¼	34	33	34	3-15—6-13	.152	28.01
1864			19.24		SE¼NW¼	34	33	34	3-15—4-28	.156	14.43
1864		4.31			SW¼NW¼	34	33	34	3-15—6-13	.085	6.47
1864			8.43		SW¼NW¼	34	33	34	3-15—4-28	.069	6.32
1864		17.69			NW¼NW¼	35	33	34	3-15—6-13	.144	26.54
1864			8.17		NW¼NW¼	35	53	34	3-15—4-28	.066	6.13
1864		20.26			NE¼NW¼	35	33	34	3-15—6-13	.165	30.39
1864		27.86			SW¼NW¼	35	33	34	3-15—6-13	.227	41.79
1864			10.52		SW¼NW¼	35	33	34	3-15—4-28	.086	7.90
1878			13.68		NW¼SE¼	25	33	34	3-15—4-28	.111	10.26
1878			26.33		NE¼SE¼	25	33	34	3-15—4-28	.214	19.75
1878			24.26		NE¼SW¼	25	33	34	3-15—4-28	.197	18.09
1878		4.00			NE¼SE¼	26	33	34	3-15—6-13	.033	6.00
1878			13.35		NE¼SE¼	26	33	34	3-15—4-28	.109	10.01
1878		15.60			NW¼SE¼	20	33	34	3-15—6-13	.127	23.40
1878			18.60		SW¼SE¼	20	33	34	3-15—4-28	.151	13.95

1878	2.00			NE¼SW¼	26	33	34	3-15—6-13	.016	3.00
1878		2.90		NE¼SW¼	26	33	34	3-15—4-28	.025	3.18
1878	18.81			SE¼SW¼	26	33	34	3-15—6-13	.153	28.22
1878		5.39		SE¼SW¼	26	33	34	3-15—4-28	.044	4.04
1878		17.31		SE¼SW¼	28	33	34	3-15—4-28	.111	12.98
1878	7.27			SW¼SW¼	28	33	34	3-15—6-13	.059	10.91
1878		9.50		SW¼SW¼	28	33	34	3-15—4-28	.077	7.13

Claimant—**Sarah E. Thacker.** Proof No. 00110
Source—**Humboldt River.** Ditch—**Overflow.**

1863			13.46	SE¼SE¼	29	33	34	3-15—4-28	.109	10.10
1863			12.20	SW¼SE¼	29	33	34	3-15—4-28	.090	9.15
1863			13.93	SE¼SW¼	29	33	34	3-15—4-28	.113	10.45
1863			31.17	SW¼SW¼	29	33	34	3-15—4-28	.253	23.38
1863			3.64	SW¼NE¼	30	33	34	3-15—4-28	.030	2.73
1863			13.20	SW¼NW¼	30	33	34	3-15—4-28	.107	9.90
1863			12.23	SE¼NW¼	30	33	34	3-15—4-28	.099	9.17
1863			25.78	NW¼SE¼	30	33	34	3-15—4-28	.210	19.34
1863			.55	SE¼SE¼	30	33	34	3-15—4-28	.005	.41
1863		6.56		NW¼SW¼	30	33	34	3-15—4-28	.053	4.92
1863			9.74	SE¼SE¼	28	33	34	3-15—4-28	.079	7.31
1863			18.90	SW¼SE¼	28	33	34	3-15—4-28	.154	14.18
1863			2.92	NW¼SE¼	28	33	34	3-15—4-28	.024	2.19
1863			2.55	SE¼SE¼	27	33	34	3-15—4-28	.021	1.91
1863	15.04			SW¼SE¼	27	33	34	3-15—6-13	.122	22.56
1863	15.14			SE¼SW¼	27	33	34	3-15—6-13	.123	22.71
1863	1.36			SW¼SW¼	27	33	34	3-15—6-13	.011	2.04
1863			8.06	SW¼SW¼	27	33	34	3-15—4-28	.066	6.05
1863	7.16			NE¼NE¼	34	33	34	3-15—6-13	.058	10.74
1863	13.40			NW¼NE¼	34	33	34	3-15—6-13	.109	20.10
1863	3.17			NW¼NW¼	34	33	34	3-15—6-13	.026	4.76
1863		8.20		NE¼NW¼	34	33	34	3-15—4-28	.067	6.15
1863			7.68	NW¼NW¼	35	33	34	3-15—4-28	.062	5.76
1863			.94	NE¼NW¼	35	33	34	3-15—4-28	.008	.71
1878			3.13	SE¼NE¼	25	33	34	3-15—4-28	.025	2.35
1878			7.22	SW¼NE¼	25	33	34	3-15—4-28	.050	5.42
1878			11.91	NW¼SE¼	25	33	34	3-15—4-28	.097	8.93
1878			13.11	SE¼NW¼	25	33	34	3-15—4-28	.107	9.83
1878			18.82	SW¼NW¼	25	33	34	3-15—4-28	.153	14.12
1863			17.04	SE¼NE¼	26	33	34	3-15—4-28	.139	12.78
1863			1.05	SW¼NE¼	26	33	34	3-15—4-28	.009	.79
1863			13.72	NE¼SE¼	26	33	34	3-15—4-28	.111	10.29
1863			11.60	NW¼SE¼	26	33	34	3-15—4-28	.094	8.70
1863			6.73	SW¼SW¼	26	33	34	3-15—4-28	.055	5.05
1863			3.18	SE¼SW¼	26	33	34	3-15—4-28	.026	2.39
1863			2.56	NE¼SW¼	28	33	34	3-15—4-28	.021	1.92
1863			3.06	SE¼SW¼	28	33	34	3-15—4-28	.025	2.30
1863			12.22	SW¼SW¼	28	33	34	3-15—4-28	.107	9.16
1863			.78	NW¼SW¼	28	33	34	3-15—4-28	.006	.59
1863			11.58	NW¼SW¼	29	33	34	3-15—4-28	.094	8.69
1863			20.53	NE¼SE¼	30	33	34	3-15—4-28	.167	15.40

Claimant—**John G. Taylor.** Proof No. 00111
Source—**Humboldt River.** Ditch—**Thacker Dam.**

Year of priority	Culture—Acres: Harvest crops	Meadow pasture	Diversified pasture	Location: Subdivision	Section	Tp.N.	R.E.	Length of season	Duty of water: C.F.S.	Acre-feet
1878			15.26	NW¼NW¼	32	33	35	3-15—4-28	.124	11.45
1878			.92	NE¼NW¼	32	33	35	3-15—4-28	.007	.69
1878			26.16	SE¼NW¼	32	33	35	3-15—4-28	.213	19.62
1878			23.64	SW¼NE¼	32	33	35	3-15—4-28	.193	17.73
1878			16.15	SE¼NE¼	32	33	35	3-15—4-28	.131	12.11

Claimant—**Peter Organ.** Proof No. 00112
Source—**Humboldt River.** Ditch—**Thacker Dam.**

Year of priority	Harvest crops	Meadow pasture	Diversified pasture	Subdivision	Section	Tp.N.	R.E.	Length of season	C.F.S.	Acre-feet
1878			11.51	SW¼NW¼	32	33	35	3-15—4-28	.094	8.63
1878			3.43	NW¼NE¼	32	33	35	3-15—4-28	.028	2.57

Claimant—**Thos. C. O'Donnell.** Proof. No. 00113
Source—**Humboldt River.** Ditch—**O'Donnell Dam and Ditch. System No. 1.**

Year of priority	Harvest crops	Meadow pasture	Diversified pasture	Subdivision	Section	Tp.N.	R.E.	Length of season	C.F.S.	Acre-feet
1888			24.85	NE¼NW¼	20	33	36	3-15—4-28	.202	18.64
1888			37.13	SE¼NW¼	20	33	36	3-15—4-28	.302	27.85
1888			12.38	NE¼SW¼	20	33	36	3-15—4-28	.101	9.29
1888			36.07	NW¼NE¼	20	33	36	3-15—4-28	.293	27.05
1888			37.94	NW¼NW¼	21	33	36	3-15—4-28	.318	28.46

Claimant—**Thos. C. O'Donnell.** Proof No. 00113
Source—**Humboldt River.** Ditch—**O'Donnell Dam and Ditch. System No. 2.**

Year of priority	Harvest crops	Meadow pasture	Diversified pasture	Subdivision	Section	Tp.N.	R.E.	Length of season	C.F.S.	Acre-feet
1897			18.33	NE¼SE¼	16	33	36	3-15—4-28	.149	13.75
1897			38.01	SW¼SE¼	16	33	36	3-15—4-28	.309	28.51
1897			28.67	SE¼SE¼	16	33	36	3-15—4-28	.233	21.50
1897			24.32	NE¼NW¼	21	33	36	3-15—4-28	.198	18.24
1897			17.74	SW¼NW¼	21	33	36	3-15—4-28	.144	13.31
1897			17.97	NW¼NE¼	21	33	36	3-15—4-28	.146	13.48
1897			9.06	NE¼NE¼	21	33	36	3-15—4-28	.074	6.80
1897			1.28	SW¼NW¼	15	33	36	3-15—4-28	.010	.96
1897			31.72	NW¼SW¼	15	33	36	3-15—4-28	.258	23.70
1897			27.97	SW¼SW¼	15	33	36	3-15—4-28	.227	22.48
1807			.35	SE¼SW¼	15	33	36	3-16—4-28	.003	.26
1897			36.27	NE¼NE¼	20	33	36	3-16—4-28	.295	27.20
1807			35.93	SW¼NE¼	20	33	36	3-15—4-28	.292	26.95
1897			30.02	SE¼NE¼	20	33	36	3-15—4-28	.244	22.52
1897			5.32	NW¼SE¼	20	33	36	3-16—4-28	.043	3.90
1897			17.93	SW¼SW¼	16	33	36	3-15—4-28	.146	13.45
1897			22.34	SE¼SW¼	16	33	36	3-15—4-28	.182	16.76

471

Claimant—**Estate Chas. Pedroli.** Proof No. 00114

Source—**Humboldt River.** Ditch—**Pedroli Dam and Ditch. System No. 1.**

1880	5.73			NE¼SW¼	12	35	36	3-15—0-15	.048	17.19
1890		30.29		NE¼SW¼	12	35	36	3-15—4-28	.246	22.72
1881	28.98			SW¼SW¼	12	35	36	3-15—0-15	.235	86.94
1881		8.17		SW¼SW¼	12	35	36	3-15—4-28	.066	6.13
1881			1.03	SW¼SW¼	12	35	36	3-15—4-28	.008	.77
1881	27.76			SE¼SW¼	12	35	36	3-15—0-15	.226	83.28
1881		10.08		SE¼SW¼	12	35	36	3-15—4-28	.088	7.56
1881	.56			SW¼SE¼	12	35	36	3-15—0-15	.005	1.68
1881		16.05		SW¼SE¼	12	35	36	3-15—4-28	.130	12.04
1881			2.15	SW¼SE¼	12	35	36	3-15—4-28	.017	1.61
1882	9.25			NW¼SE¼	12	35	36	3-15—0-15	.075	27.75
1882		4.73		NW¼SE¼	12	35	36	3-15—4-28	.038	3.55
1880	15.91			SE¼NW¼	12	35	36	3-15—0-15	.129	47.73
1880		1.37		SE¼NW¼	12	35	36	3-15—4-28	.011	1.03
1882		.72		SW¼NE¼	12	35	36	3-15—4-28	.006	.54
1883	10.24			SW¼NE¼	14	35	36	3-15—0-15	.083	30.72
1883		29.68		SW¼NE¼	14	35	36	3-15—4-28	.241	22.26
1883		26.24		SE¼NE¼	14	35	36	3-15—4-28	.213	19.68
1883	30.23			NE¼NE¼	14	35	36	3-15—0-15	.246	90.69
1883		8.81		NE¼NE¼	14	35	36	3-15—4-28	.072	6.61
1883	32.25			NW¼NE¼	14	35	36	3-15—0-15	.264	96.75
1883		6.64		NW¼NE¼	14	35	36	3-15—4-28	.054	4.98
1882	5.75			SE¼SE¼	11	35	36	3-15—0-15	.047	17.25
1882		13.45		SE¼SE¼	11	35	36	3-15—4-28	.109	10.09
1882	.78			SW¼SE¼	11	35	36	3-15—0-15	.006	2.34
1882		4.34		SW¼SE¼	11	35	36	3-15—4-28	.035	3.26
1882	18.78			NW¼NW¼	13	35	36	3-15—0-15	.153	56.34
1882		4.31		NW¼NW¼	13	35	36	3-15—4-28	.035	3.23
1882			4.67	NW¼NW¼	13	35	36	3-15—4-28	.038	3.50
1882		.32		SW¼NW¼	13	35	36	3-15—4-28	.003	.24
1882	20.00			NE¼NW¼	13	35	36	3-15—0-15	.163	60.00
1882			3.45	NE¼NW¼	13	35	36	3-15—4-28	.028	2.59
1880	2.90			NW¼SW¼	12	35	36	3-15—0-15	.024	8.70
1880		13.94		NW¼SW¼	12	35	36	3-15—4-28	.113	10.46
1884	.56			NW¼SE¼	14	35	36	3-15—0-15	.005	1.68
1884		14.40		NW¼SE¼	14	35	36	3-15—4-28	.117	10.80

Claimant—**Estate Chas. Pedroli.** Proof No. 00114

Source—**Humboldt River.** Ditch—**Pedroli Dam and Ditch. System No. 2.**

1884	23.15			NE¼NW¼	14	35	36	3-15—0-15	.188	69.45
1884			2.23	NE¼NW¼	14	35	36	3-15—4-28	.018	1.67
1885	34.50			SW¼NW¼	14	35	36	3-15—0-15	.280	103.50
1885		1.80		SW¼NW¼	14	35	36	3-15—4-28	.015	1.35
1885			.45	SW¼NW¼	14	35	36	3-15—4-28	.004	.34
1885	4.86			NW¼NW¼	14	35	36	3-15—0-15	.040	14.58
1885		17.50		NW¼NW¼	14	35	36	3-15—4-28	.142	13.13
1885			1.72	NW¼NW¼	14	35	36	3-15—4-28	.014	1.29
1886		1.68		NW¼SW¼	15	35	36	3-15—4-28	.014	1.26
1886		31.92		NE¼SW¼	15	35	36	3-15—4-28	.260	23.94

Estate Chas. Pedroli—Continued.

Year of priority	Culture—Acres: Harvest crops	Meadow pasture	Diversified pasture		Location: Subdivision	Section	Tp.N.	R.E.	Length of season	Duty of water: C.F.S.	Acre-feet
1886			15.44		SE¼SW¼	15	35	36	3-15—4-28	.126	11.58
1886			7.24		SW¼SE¼	15	35	36	3-15—4-28	.059	5.43
1886			.68		SE¼SE¼	15	35	36	3-15—4-28	.006	.51
1886	8.41				NE¼SE¼	15	35	36	3-15—9-15	.069	25.32
1886			31.56		NE¼SE¼	15	35	36	3-15—4-28	.257	23.67
1887			37.33		NW¼SE¼	15	35	36	3-15—4-28	.303	27.10
1887	2.86				SE¼NE¼	15	35	36	3-15—9-15	.023	8.58
1887			24.88		SE¼NE¼	15	35	36	3-15—4-28	.202	18.66
1887			9.00		SW¼NE¼	15	35	36	3-15—4-28	.073	6.75
1887			.68		SE¼NE¼	15	35	36	3-15—4-28	.006	.51
1887			2.12		SE¼NW¼	15	35	36	3-15—4-28	.017	1.59
1884	5.84				NE¼SW¼	14	35	36	3-15—9-15	.047	17.52
1884			16.44		NE¼SW¼	14	35	36	3-15—4-28	.134	12.33
1884	11.36				NW¼SW¼	14	35	36	3-15—9-15	.092	34.08
1884			19.86		NW¼SW¼	14	35	36	3-15—4-28	.161	14.90
1884	40.00				SE¼NW¼	14	35	36	3-15—9-15	.325	120.00
1884			5.89		NE¼NW¼	14	35	36	3-15—4-28	.048	4.42

Claimant—**Chas. Farrel.** Proof No. 00115

Source—**Humboldt River.** Ditch—**Trousdale Dam and Ditches.**

Year of priority	Harvest crops	Meadow pasture	Diversified pasture		Subdivision	Section	Tp.N.	R.E.	Length of season	C.F.S.	Acre-feet
1876			3.58		SE¼SW¼	36	36	37	3-15—4-28	.029	2.69
1876			.30		NW¼SW¼	36	36	37	3-15—4-28	.002	.23
1876		10.00			SW¼SW¼	36	36	37	3-15—6-13	.081	15.00
1876			23.50		SW¼SW¼	36	36	37	3-15—4-28	.191	17.63
1876			3.50		NW¼NW¼	1	35	37	3-15—4-28	.028	2.63

Claimant—**W. F. and F. H. Pearce.** Proof No. 00116

Source—**Humboldt River.** Ditch—**North Side.**

Year of priority	Harvest crops	Meadow pasture	Diversified pasture		Subdivision	Section	Tp.N.	R.E.	Length of season	C.F.S.	Acre-feet
1880	1.93				SE¼SW¼	35	36	37	3-15—9-15	.016	5.79
1880			4.70		SE¼SW¼	35	36	37	3-15—4-28	.038	3.53
1880	14.87				NE¼NE¼	3	35	37	3-15—9-15	.121	44.61
1880			9.04		NE¼NE¼	3	35	37	3-15—4-28	.074	6.78
1880				6.47	NE¼NE¼	3	35	37	3-15—4-28	.053	4.85
1880	19.72				NW¼NE¼	3	35	37	3-15—9-15	.160	59.16
1880		4.46			NW¼NE¼	3	35	37	3-15—6-13	.036	6.69
1880				14.20	NW¼NE¼	3	35	37	3-15—6-13	.115	10.65
1880	10.73				SW¼NE¼	3	35	37	3-15—9-15	.087	32.19
1880			4.33		SW¼NE¼	3	35	37	3-15—4-28	.035	3.25
1880			.63		SE¼NE¼	3	35	37	3-15—4-28	.005	.47
1880	20.40				NE¼NW¼	3	35	37	3-15—9-15	.167	61.20
1880		7.64			NE¼NW¼	3	35	37	3-15—6-13	.063	11.46
1880				7.30	NW¼NW¼	3	35	37	3-15—4-28	.059	5.48
1880	14.63				SW¼NW¼	3	35	37	3-15—9-15	.119	43.89
1880			25.17		SW¼NW¼	3	35	37	3-15—4-28	.205	18.88

1880			30.22				SE¼NW¼	3	35	37	3-15—9-15	.246	90.66
1880					1.43		SE¼NW¼	3	35	37	3-15—4-28	.012	1.07
1880			20.00				NW¼SW¼	3	35	37	3-15—9-15	.236	87.00
1880					5.20		NW¼SW¼	3	35	37	3-15—4-28	.012	3.90
1880			12.36				NE¼SW¼	3	35	37	3-15—9-15	.100	37.08
1880					1.27		NE¼SW¼	3	35	37	3-15—4-28	.010	.95
1880					12.63		NE¼SE¼	34	36	37	3-15—4-28	.103	9.47
1880			2.10				SE¼SE¼	34	36	37	3-15—9-15	.017	6.30
1880				18.79			SE¼SE¼	34	36	37	3-15—6-13	.153	28.19
1880					6.34		SE¼SE¼	34	36	37	3-15—4-28	.053	4.76
1880				13.67			SW¼SE¼	34	36	37	3-15—6-13	.111	20.51
1880				6.23			SE¼SW¼	34	36	37	3-15—6-13	.051	9.35
1880						1.53	SE¼SW¼	34	36	37	3-15—4-28	.012	1.15
1880			7.50				NE¼SW¼	35	36	37	3-15—9-15	.061	22.50
1880				.30			NE¼SW¼	35	36	37	3-15—6-13	.002	.45
1880					.63		NE¼SW¼	35	36	37	3-15—4-28	.005	.47
1880			6.06				NW¼SW¼	35	36	37	3-15—9-15	.049	18.18
1880					12.40		NW¼SW¼	35	36	37	3-15—4-28	.101	9.30
1880			27.17				SW¼SW¼	35	36	37	3-15—9-15	.221	81.51
1880					6.14		SW¼SW¼	35	36	37	3-15—4-28	.050	4.61

Source—**Humboldt River.** Ditch—**South Side.**

1877			.60				SW¼SW¼	2	35	37	3-15—9-15	.005	1.80
1877			2.30				NE¼NE¼	3	35	37	3-15—9-15	.019	6.90
1877					.60		NE¼NE¼	3	35	37	3-15—4-28	.005	.45
1877						6.47	NE¼NE¼	3	35	37	3-15—4-28	.053	4.85
1877			10.00				SW¼NE¼	3	35	37	3-15—9-15	.081	30.00
1877					2.84		SW¼NE¼	3	35	37	3-15—4-28	.023	2.13
1877			33.10				SE¼NE¼	3	35	37	3-15—9-15	.269	99.30
1877					1.72		SE¼NE¼	3	35	37	3-15—4-28	.014	1.29
1877			39.04				NE¼SE¼	3	35	37	3-15—9-15	.317	117.12
1877			36.89				NW¼SE¼	3	35	37	3-15—9-15	.300	110.67
1877			7.90				SW¼SE¼	3	35	37	3-15—9-15	.064	23.70
1877					1.40		SW¼SE¼	3	35	37	3-15—4-28	.011	1.05
1877			14.80				SE¼SE¼	3	35	37	3-15—9-15	.120	44.40
1877					1.00		SE¼SE¼	3	35	37	3-15—4-28	.008	.75
1877			4.33				SE¼NW¼	3	35	37	3-15—9-15	.035	12.49
1877					.60		SE¼NW¼	3	35	37	3-15—4-28	.005	.45
1877			19.86				NE¼SW¼	3	35	37	3-15—9-15	.161	59.58
1877			7.55				SE¼SW¼	3	35	37	3-15—9-15	.061	22.65
1877			14.67				SW¼SW¼	3	35	37	3-15—9-15	.119	44.01
1877				19.70			NE¼SE¼	35	36	37	3-15—6-13	.160	29.55
1877					5.90		NE¼SE¼	35	36	37	3-15—4-28	.048	4.43
1877				23.55			SE¼SE¼	35	36	37	3-15—6-13	.191	35.33
1877					9.10		SE¼SE¼	35	36	37	3-15—4-28	.074	6.83
1877				.63			NW¼NE¼	35	36	37	3-15—6-13	.005	.95
1877					4.60		NW¼NE¼	35	36	37	3-15—4-28	.037	3.45
1877				18.24			SW¼SE¼	35	36	37	3-15—6-13	.148	27.36
1877			12.00				SE¼SW¼	35	36	37	3-15—9-15	.098	36.00
1877				15.90			SE¼SW¼	35	36	37	3-15—6-13	.129	23.85
1877					.63		SE¼SW¼	35	36	37	3-15—4-28	.005	.47
1877					4.56		NW¼NE¼	2	35	37	3-15—4-28	.037	3.42
1877			28.41				NE¼NW¼	2	35	37	3-15—9-15	.231	85.23

W. F. and F. H. Pearce—Continued.

Year of priority	Culture—Acres: Harvest crops	Meadow pasture	Diversified pasture		Location: Subdivision	Section	Tp. N.	R. E.	Length of season	Duty of water: C.F.S.	Acre-feet
1877			5.91		NE¼NW¼	2	35	37	3-15—4-28	.048	4.43
1877	22.48				NW¼NW¼	2	35	37	3-15—9-15	.183	67.44
1877			7.97		NW¼NW¼	2	35	37	3-15—4-28	.065	5.98
1877	19.33				SE¼NW¼	2	35	37	3-15—9-15	.157	57.99
1877			.97		SE¼NW¼	2	35	37	3-15—4-28	.008	.73
1877	36.72				SW¼NW¼	2	25	37	3-15—9-15	.299	110.16
1877	18.40				NW¼SW¼	2	35	37	3-15—9-15	.150	55.20
1877			5.70		SW¼SW¼	3	35	37	3-15—4-28	.046	4.28
1877		2.10			SE¼SE¼	34	36	37	3-15—6-13	.017	3.15
1877			18.03		SW¼SE¼	34	36	37	3-15—4-28	.147	13.52

Claimant—**Mary G. Rose.** Proof No. 00117

Source—**Humboldt River.** Ditch—**Lower Slough.**

Year of priority	Harvest crops	Meadow pasture	Diversified pasture		Subdivision	Section	Tp. N.	R. E.	Length of season	C.F.S.	Acre-feet
1877	13.23				NW¼SE¼	35	36	37	3-15—9-15	.108	39.69
1877	1.36				SW¼SE¼	35	36	37	3-15—9-15	.011	4.08
1877	8.94				NE¼SW¼	35	36	37	3-15—9-15	.073	26.82
1877	2.65				SE¼SW¼	35	36	37	3-16—9-15	.022	7.95

Source—**Humboldt River.** Ditch—**Upper Slough.**

Year of priority	Harvest crops	Meadow pasture	Diversified pasture		Subdivision	Section	Tp. N.	R. E.	Length of season	C.F.S.	Acre-feet
1877		9.90			NE¼NE¼	35	36	37	3-15—6-13	.080	14.85
1877	6.06				SE¼NE¼	35	36	37	3-15—9-15	.049	18.18
1877		21.29			SE¼NE¼	35	36	37	3-15—6-13	.173	31.94
1877	7.65				NE¼SE¼	35	36	37	3-15—9-15	.062	22.95

Source—**Humboldt River.** Ditch—**Miller & Lux Dam.**

Year of priority	Harvest crops	Meadow pasture	Diversified pasture		Subdivision	Section	Tp. N.	R. E.	Length of season	C.F.S.	Acre-feet
1886		5.36			SE¼SE¼	26	36	37	3-15—6-13	.044	8.04

Claimant—**Pacific Livestock Co.** Proof No. 00118

Source—**Humboldt River.** Ditch—**Miller & Lux Dam and Ditch System.**

Year of priority	Harvest crops	Meadow pasture	Diversified pasture		Subdivision	Section	Tp. N.	R. E.	Length of season	C.F.S.	Acre-feet
1872				.97	NW¼NE¼	30	36	38	3-15—4-28	.009	.73
1872			16.30		SW¼NE¼	30	36	38	3-15—4-28	.133	12.23
1872				.75	SW¼NE¼	30	36	38	3-15—4-28	.006	.56
1872				3.70	NW¼SE¼	30	26	38	3-15—4-28	.030	2.78
1872				19.70	NE¼NW¼	30	36	38	3-15—4-28	.160	14.78
1872			3.53		SE¼NW¼	30	36	38	3-15—4-28	.029	2.65
1872				28.84	SE¼NW¼	30	36	38	3-15—4-28	.234	21.63
1872			20.93		SW¼NW¼	30	36	38	3-15—4-28	.170	15.70
1872				.93	SW¼NW¼	30	36	38	3-15—4-28	.008	.70
1872	1.40				NE¼SW¼	30	36	38	3-15—9-15	.011	4.20
1872			34.40		NE¼SW¼	30	36	38	3-15—4-28	.280	25.80
1872				1.07	NE¼SW¼	30	36	38	3-15—4-28	.010	1.48
1872	.40				SE¼SW¼	30	36	38	3-15—9-15	.003	1.20
1872			20.80		SE¼SW¼	30	36	38	3-15—4-28	.160	15.60
1872	18.97				NW¼SW¼	30	36	38	3-15—9-15	.114	51.91

	1872					17.83		NW¼SW¼	30	36	38	3-15—4-28	.145	13.37
	1872						1.70	NW¼SW¼	30	36	38	3-15—4-28	.014	1.28
	1872			34.03				SW¼SW¼	30	36	38	3-15—9-15	.284	104.70
	1872					1.87		SW¼SW¼	30	36	38	3-15—4-28	.015	1.40
	1872						1.50	SW¼SW¼	30	36	38	3-15—4-28	.012	1.13
	1872					3.87		NE¼NW¼	31	36	38	3-15—4-28	.031	2.90
	1872			11.52				NW¼NW¼	31	36	38	3-15—9-15	.094	34.56
	1872					15.29		NW¼NW¼	31	36	38	3-15—4-28	.124	11.47
	1872			.95				SW¼NW¼	31	36	38	3-15—9-15	.008	2.87
	1872					1.90		SW¼NW¼	31	36	38	3-15—4-28	.015	1.43
	1872						6.60	SE¼NE¼	25	36	37	3-15—4-28	.054	4.95
	1872			5.30				NE¼SE¼	25	36	37	3-15—9-15	.043	15.90
	1872						28.20	NE¼SE¼	25	36	37	3-15—4-28	.229	21.15
	1872			30.64				SE¼SE¼	25	36	37	3-15—9-15	.249	91.92
	1872					5.52		SE¼SE¼	25	36	37	3-15—4-28	.045	4.14
	1872			.90				NW¼SE¼	25	36	37	3-15—9-15	.007	2.70
	1872					18.13		NW¼SE¼	25	36	37	3-15—4-28	.147	13.60
	1872			17.78				SW¼SE¼	25	36	37	3-15—9-15	.145	53.34
	1872					13.23		SW¼SE¼	25	36	37	3-15—4-28	.108	9.92
	1872						3.20	SW¼SE¼	25	36	37	3-15—4-28	.026	2.40
	1872					2.37		NE¼SW¼	25	36	37	3-15—4-28	.019	1.78
	1872			3.13				SE¼SW¼	25	36	37	3-15—9-15	.025	9.39
	1872					16.10		SE¼SW¼	25	36	37	3-15—4-28	.130	12.08
	1872						7.40	SE¼SW¼	25	36	37	3-15—4-28	.060	5.55
	1872			33.78				NE¼NE¼	36	36	37	3-15—9-15	.275	101.34
	1872					1.75		NE¼NE¼	36	36	37	3-15—4-28	.014	1.31
	1872						.97	NE¼NE¼	36	36	37	3-15—4-28	.008	.73
	1872			25.63				SE¼NE¼	36	36	37	3-15—9-15	.208	76.89
	1872					3.90		SE¼NE¼	36	36	37	3-15—4-28	.032	2.93
	1872			35.14				NW¼NE¼	36	36	37	3-15—9-15	.286	105.42
	1872					1.87		NW¼NE¼	36	36	37	3-15—4-28	.015	1.40
	1872			31.74				SW¼NE¼	36	36	37	3-15—9-15	.258	95.22
	1872					4.36		SW¼NE¼	36	36	37	3-15—4-28	.035	3.27
	1872			.33				NW¼SE¼	36	36	37	3-15—9-15	.003	.99
	1872			18.63				NE¼NW¼	36	36	37	3-15—9-15	.151	55.80
	1872					14.23		NE¼NW¼	36	36	37	3-15—4-28	.116	10.67
	1872			33.83				SE¼NW¼	36	36	37	3-15—9-15	.276	101.49
	1872					2.50		SE¼NW¼	36	36	37	3-15—4-28	.020	1.88
	1872			3.07				NW¼NW¼	36	36	37	3-15—9-15	.025	9.21
	1872					11.92		NW¼NW¼	36	36	37	3-15—4-28	.097	8.94
	1872			28.46				SW¼NW¼	36	36	37	3-15—9-15	.241	85.38
	1872					5.04		SW¼NW¼	36	36	37	3-15—4-28	.041	3.78
	1872			25.51				NE¼SW¼	36	36	37	3-15—9-15	.207	76.53
	1872					5.90		NE¼SW¼	36	36	37	3-15—4-28	.048	4.43
	1872			29.51				NW¼SW¼	36	36	37	3-15—9-15	.240	88.53
	1872					6.61		NW¼SW¼	36	36	37	3-15—4-28	.054	4.96
	1872					.35		NW¼SE¼	36	36	37	3-15—4-28	.004	.26

Claimant—**C. L. Tobin.** Proof No. 00119

Source—**Humboldt River.** Ditch—**Pioneer Slough System.**

Year of priority	Culture—Acres: Harvest crops	Culture—Acres: Meadow pasture	Culture—Acres: Diversified pasture	Location: Subdivision	Location: Section	Location: Tp.N.	Location: R.E.	Length of season	Duty of water: C.F.S.	Duty of water: Acre-feet
1878			26.13	NE¼NE¼	34	37	38	3-15—4-28	.212	19.60
1878		1.93		NW¼NE¼	34	37	38	3-15—6-13	.016	2.90
1878			31.54	NW¼NE¼	34	37	38	3-15—4-28	.256	23.66
1878			36.80	NW¼NE¼	34	37	38	3-15—4-28	.299	27.60
1878			31.07	SE¼NE¼	34	37	38	3-15—4-28	.253	23.30
1878		2.07		NE¼NW¼	34	37	38	3-15—6-13	.017	3.11
1878			.73	NE¼NW¼	34	37	36	3-15—4-28	.006	.55
1878		1.87		SE¼NW¼	34	37	38	3-15—6-13	.015	2.81
1878			28.93	SE¼NW¼	34	37	38	3-15—4-28	.235	21.70
1877	9.07			NE¼SE¼	35	37	38	3-15—9-15	.074	27.21
1877			6.20	NE¼SE¼	35	37	38	3-15—4-28	.050	4.65
1877			19.00	NW¼SE¼	35	37	38	3-15—4-28	.154	14.25
1871	34.59			SW¼SE¼	35	37	38	3-15—9-15	.281	103.77
1871			4.40	SW¼SE¼	35	37	38	3-15—4-28	.036	3.30
1871	32.46			SE¼SE¼	35	37	38	3-15—9-15	.264	97.38
1871			8.67	SE¼SE¼	35	37	38	3-15—4-28	.070	6.50
1877			23.47	NE¼SW¼	35	37	38	3-15—4-28	.191	17.60
1877			30.73	NW¼SW¼	35	37	38	3-15—4-28	.250	23.05
1871			4.94	SW¼SW¼	36	37	38	3-15—4-28	.040	3.71
1871	29.14			NE¼NE¼	31	37	39	3-15—9-15	.240	87.42
1871			4.93	NE¼NE¼	31	37	39	3-15—4-28	.040	3.70
1871	35.62			NW¼NE¼	31	37	39	3-15—9-15	.290	106.86
1871			4.50	NW¼NE¼	31	37	39	3-15—4-28	.037	3.38
1871	27.32			SE¼NE¼	31	37	39	3-15—9-15	.222	81.96
1871			12.26	SE¼NE¼	31	37	39	3-15—4-28	.100	9.20
1871	37.32			NE¼NW¼	31	37	39	3-15—9-15	.303	111.96
1871			2.68	NE¼NW¼	31	37	39	3-15—4-28	.022	2.01
1871	33.54			NW¼NW¼	31	37	39	3-15—9-15	.273	100.62
1871			5.49	NW¼NW¼	31	37	39	3-15—4-28	.045	4.12
1879	2.40			SE¼SE¼	25	37	38	3-15—9-15	.020	7.20
1879		6.00		SE¼SE¼	25	37	38	3-15—6-13	.049	9.00
1879			1.87	SE¼SE¼	25	37	38	3-15—4-28	.015	1.40
1879	2.00			SW¼SW¼	30	37	39	3-15—9-15	.016	6.00
1879		3.00		SW¼SW¼	30	37	39	3-15—6-13	.024	4.50
1879	1.00			SE¼SW¼	30	37	39	3-15—9-15	.008	3.00
1879		5.40		SE¼SW¼	30	37	39	3-15—6-13	.044	8.10
1877	36.60			SW¼SW¼	35	37	38	3-15—9-15	.298	109.80
1877		.67		SW¼SW¼	35	37	38	3-15—4-28	.005	.50
1877	38.00			SE¼SW¼	35	37	38	3-15—9-15	.314	115.80
1877	23.87			NE¼NE¼	36	37	38	3-15—9-15	.194	71.61
1877		9.14		NE¼NE¼	36	37	38	3-15—6-13	.074	13.71
1877			1.80	NE¼NE¼	36	37	38	3-15—4-28	.015	1.40
1877	13.47			NW¼NE¼	36	37	38	3-15—9-15	.110	40.41
1877		5.67		NW¼NE¼	36	37	38	3-15—6-13	.046	8.51
1877	36.33			SW¼NE¼	36	37	38	3-15—9-15	.295	108.99

	1877					3.00		SW¼NE¼	36	37	38	3-15—4-28	.021	2.25
	1877			30.46				SE¼NE¼	36	37	38	3-15—9-15	.321	118.38
	1877						.53	SE¼NE¼	36	37	38	3-15—4-28	.004	.40
	1877			2.00				SE¼NW¼	36	37	38	3-15—9-15	.016	6.00
	1877					32.22		SE¼NW¼	36	37	38	3-15—4-28	.262	24.17
	1877			20.53				NE¼SW¼	36	37	38	3-15—9-15	.167	61.59
	1877					15.13		NE¼SW¼	36	37	38	3-15—4-28	.123	11.35
	1877			15.34				NW¼SW¼	36	37	38	3-15—9-15	.125	46.02
	1877						15.81	NW¼SW¼	36	37	38	3-15—4-28	.129	11.86
	1871			35.33				SW¼SW¼	36	37	38	3-15—9-15	.287	105.99

Source—**Humboldt River.** Ditch—**Sloan Dam and Ditch System.**

	1871			35.08				SW¼NW¼	31	37	39	3-15—9-15	.293	107.94
	1871						3.88	SW¼NW¼	31	37	39	3-15—4-28	.031	2.01
	1871			34.00				SE¼NW¼	31	37	39	3-15—9-15	.284	104.70
	1871						5.27	SE¼NW¼	31	37	39	3-15—4-28	.043	3.95
	1871			27.20				NE¼SW¼	31	37	39	3-15—9-15	.221	81.60
	1871					3.00		NE¼SW¼	31	37	39	3-15—4-28	.024	2.25
	1871						9.27	NE¼SW¼	31	37	39	3-15—4-28	.075	6.95
	1871			28.97				NW¼SW¼	31	37	39	3-15—9-15	.236	86.91
	1871						11.10	NW¼SW¼	31	37	39	3-15—4-28	.090	8.33
	1871			18.20				SW¼SW¼	31	37	39	3-15—9-15	.148	54.60
	1871					13.47		SW¼SW¼	31	37	39	3-15—4-28	.109	10.10
	1871						4.87	SW¼SW¼	31	37	39	3-15—4-28	.040	3.65
	1871			23.80				SE¼SW¼	31	37	39	3-15—9-15	.193	71.40
	1871					9.93		SE¼SW¼	31	37	39	3-15—4-28	.081	7.45
	1871			23.13				NE¼SE¼	31	37	39	3-15—9-15	.188	69.39
	1871					5.99		NE¼SE¼	31	37	39	3-15—4-28	.049	4.49
	1871						6.26	NE¼SE¼	31	37	39	3-15—4-28	.051	4.70
	1871			29.13				NW¼SE¼	31	37	39	3-15—9-15	.237	87.39
	1871					.73		NW¼SE¼	31	37	39	3-15—4-28	.006	.55
	1871						9.20	NW¼SE¼	31	37	39	3-15—4-28	.075	6.90
	1871			14.60				SW¼SE¼	31	37	39	3-15—9-15	.119	43.89
	1871					9.01		SW¼SE¼	31	37	39	3-15—4-28	.073	6.76
	1871					24.14		SW¼SE¼	31	37	39	3-15—4-28	.196	18.11
	1871			35.92				SE¼SW¼	36	37	38	3-15—9-15	.292	107.76
	1871						4.21	SE¼SW¼	36	37	38	3-15—4-28	.034	3.16
	1871			32.12				NE¼SE¼	36	37	38	3-15—9-15	.261	96.36
	1871						6.02	NE¼SE¼	36	37	38	3-15—4-28	.049	4.52
	1871			37.26				NW¼SE¼	36	37	38	3-15—9-15	.303	111.78
	1871			34.50				SW¼SE¼	36	37	38	3-15—9-15	.281	103.77
	1871				.33			SW¼SE¼	36	37	38	3-15—6-13	.003	.50
	1871						4.21	SW¼SE¼	36	37	38	3-15—4-28	.034	3.16
	1871			31.82				SE¼SE¼	36	37	38	3-15—9-15	.259	95.46
	1871				1.87			SE¼SE¼	36	37	38	3-15—6-13	.015	2.81
	1871						6.31	SE¼SE¼	36	37	38	3-15—4-28	.051	4.73
	1871			25.13				SW¼NE¼	31	37	39	3-15—9-15	.204	75.39
	1871						15.40	SW¼NE¼	31	37	39	3-15—4-28	.125	11.55

Source—**Humboldt River.** Ditch—**Tobin Sloughs.**

	1875			6.47				SW¼SE¼	30	37	39	3-15—9-15	.053	19.41
	1875				8.47			SW¼SE¼	30	37	39	3-15—6-13	.069	12.71
	1875			2.93				SE¼SE¼	30	37	39	3-15—9-15	.024	8.79

C. L. Tobin—Continued.

Year of priority	Culture—Acres: Harvest crops	Culture—Acres: Meadow pasture	Culture—Acres: Diversified pasture		Location: Subdivision	Location: Section	Location: Tp.N.	Location: R.E.	Length of season	Duty of water: C.F.S.	Duty of water: Acre-feet
1875		4.33			SE¼SE¼	30	37	39	3-15—6-13	.035	6.50
1875	4.93				NE¼NE¼	3	36	38	3-15—9-15	.040	14.79
1875		7.47			NE¼NE¼	3	36	38	3-15—6-13	.061	11.21
1875			23.93		NE¼NE¼	3	36	38	3-15—4-28	.195	17.95
1875	12.61				NE¼NE¼	1	36	38	3-15—9-15	.103	37.83
1875			5.95		NE¼NE¼	1	36	38	3-15—4-28	.048	4.46
1875	4.93				NW¼NE¼	1	36	38	3-15—9-15	.040	14.79
1875		12.93			NW¼NE¼	1	36	38	3-15—6-13	.105	19.40
1875			10.46		NW¼NE¼	1	36	38	3-15—4-28	.085	7.85
1875			.40		SW¼NE¼	1	36	38	3-15—4-28	.003	.30
1875	5.60				NE¼NW¼	1	36	38	3-15—9-15	.046	16.80
1875		3.80			NE¼NW¼	1	36	38	3-15—6-13	.031	5.70
1875			14.67		NE¼NW¼	1	36	38	3-15—4-28	.119	11.00
1875				6.87	NE¼NW¼	1	36	38	3-15—4-28	.056	5.15
1875	9.00				NW¼NW¼	1	36	38	3-15—9-15	.073	27.00
1875			28.27		NW¼NW¼	1	36	38	3-15—4-28	.230	21.20
1875				.33	NW¼NW¼	1	36	38	3-15—4-28	.003	.25
1875				8.60	SW¼NW¼	1	36	38	3-15—4-28	.070	6.45
1875	24.20				NE¼NE¼	2	36	38	3-15—9-15	.197	72.60
1875		4.33			NE¼NE¼	2	36	38	3-15—6-13	.135	6.50
1875			3.66		NE¼NE¼	2	36	38	3-15—4-28	.030	2.75
1875				5.20	NE¼NE¼	2	36	38	3-15—4-28	.042	3.90
1875	3.20				SE¼NE¼	2	36	38	3-15—9-15	.026	9.60
1875				13.50	SE¼NE¼	2	36	38	3-15—4-28	.110	10.13
1875	2.00				SW¼NE¼	2	36	38	3-15—9-15	.016	6.00
1875	28.80				NW¼NE¼	2	36	38	3-15—9-15	.234	86.40
1875			.33		NW¼NE¼	2	36	38	3-15—4-28	.003	.25
1875				4.27	NW¼NE¼	2	36	38	3-15—4-28	.035	3.20
1875	25.20				NE¼NW¼	2	36	38	3-15—9-15	.205	75.60
1875			3.00		NE¼NW¼	2	36	38	3-15—4-28	.024	2.25
1875				3.80	NE¼NW¼	2	36	38	3-15—4-28	.031	2.85
1875	16.20				NW¼NW¼	2	36	38	3-15—9-15	.132	48.60
1875			3.33		NW¼NW¼	2	36	38	3-15—4-28	.027	2.50
1875				5.67	NW¼NW¼	2	36	38	3-15—4-28	.046	4.25
1875				1.53	SE¼NW¼	2	36	38	3-15—4-28	.012	1.15
1875		28.80			SE¼NE¼	3	36	38	3-15—6-13	.234	43.20
1875			1.09		SE¼NE¼	3	36	38	3-15—4-28	.009	.82
1875		27.27			NW¼NE¼	3	36	38	3-15—6-13	.222	40.91
1875				6.20	NW¼NE¼	3	36	38	3-15—4-28	.050	4.65
1875				7.20	SW¼NE¼	3	36	38	3-15—4-28	.059	5.40
1875		30.92			NE¼NW¼	3	36	38	3-15—6-13	.251	46.38
1875				1.00	NE¼NW¼	3	36	38	3-15—4-28	.008	.75
1875		7.00			SW¼NW¼	3	36	38	3-15—6-13	.057	1.05
1875			5.60		SW¼NW¼	3	36	38	3-15—4-28	.045	4.20
1875				9.13	SW¼NW¼	3	36	38	3-15—4-28	.074	6.85
1875		3.33			SE¼NW¼	3	36	38	3-15—6-13	.027	5.00
1875			1.80		SE¼NW¼	3	36	38	3-15—4-28	.015	1.36

	1875						.20	SE¼NW¼	3	36	38	3-15—4-28	.002	.15
	1875				2.87			NE¼SE¼	34	37	38	3-15—6-13	.023	4.31
	1875						30.87	NE¼SE¼	34	37	38	3-15—4-28	.300	27.65
	1875				0.40			NW¼SE¼	34	37	38	3-15—6-13	.076	14.10
	1875						27.90	NW¼SE¼	34	37	38	3-15—4-28	.227	20.93
	1875				33.40			SW¼SE¼	34	37	38	3-15—6-13	.272	50.10
	1875					2.50		SW¼SE¼	34	37	38	3-15—4-28	.020	1.88
	1875				24.77			SE¼SE¼	34	37	38	3-15—6-13	.201	37.16
	1875					6.93		SE¼SE¼	34	37	38	3-15—4-28	.056	5.20
	1875						2.87	SE¼SE¼	34	37	38	3-15—4-28	.023	2.15
	1875					5.87		NE¼NW¼	6	36	39	3-15—4-28	.048	4.40
	1875					15.47		NW¼NW¼	6	36	39	3-15—4-28	.126	11.60
	1875				19.79			NW¼NW¼	3	36	38	3-15—6-13	.161	29.69
	1875						16.87	NW¼NW¼	3	36	38	3-15—4-28	.137	12.65

Claimant—**Taylor and Sheehan.** Proof No. **00120**

Source—**Humboldt River.** Ditch—**Anderson Ditch.**

	1865				33.70			NE¼NW¼	20	36	40	3-15—6-13	.274	50.55
	1865				40.50			NW¼NW¼	20	36	40	3-15—6-13	.329	60.75

Source—**Little Rock** Creek. Ditch—**Rock Creek.**

	1878			.70				SW¼NW¼	32	36	40	3-15—9-15	.006	2.10
	1878			30.15				NE¼NW¼	32	36	40	3-15—9-15	.250	90.45
	1878			31.40				NW¼NW¼	32	36	40	3-15—9-15	.255	94.20
	1878			25.95				SE¼SW¼	29	36	40	3-15—9-15	.211	77.85
	1878			10.25				SW¼SE¼	29	36	40	3-15—9-15	.083	30.75
	1878			22.20				NW¼SE¼	29	36	40	3-15—9-15	.180	66.60
	1878			37.80				NE¼SW¼	29	36	40	3-15—9-15	.307	113.40
	1878			20.45				SE¼NW¼	29	36	40	3-15—9-15	.166	61.35
	1878			25.25				SW¼NW¼	29	36	40	3-15—9-15	.205	75.74
	1878			7.90				NW¼SW¼	29	36	40	3-15—9-15	.064	23.70
	1878			40.05				SW¼SW¼	29	36	40	3-15—9-15	.326	120.15
	1878			.75				SE¼NW¼	32	36	40	3-15—9-15	.006	2.25

Source—**Pole Creek.** Ditch—**Pole Creek Ditches.**

	1878			4.30				NE¼NE¼	31	36	40	3-15—9-15	.035	12.90
	1878			20.95				NW¼SW¼	29	36	40	3-15—9-15	.170	62.85
	1878			.60				SW¼NW¼	29	36	40	3-15—9-15	.005	1.80
	1878			29.75				SE¼SE¼	30	36	40	3-15—9-15	.243	89.25
	1878			37.95				NE¼SE¼	30	36	40	3-15—9-15	.309	113.85
	1878			28.20				SE¼NE¼	30	36	40	3-15—9-15	.229	84.60
	1878			2.45				NE¼NE¼	30	36	40	3-15—9-15	.020	7.35
	1878			8.45				SW¼NE¼	19	36	40	3-15—9-15	.069	25.35
	1878			34.60				SE¼SW¼	19	36	40	3-15—9-15	.281	103.80
	1878			14.30				SW¼SW¼	19	36	40	3-15—9-15	.126	42.90
	1878			16.10				NE¼SW¼	19	36	40	3-15—9-15	.131	48.30
	1878			39.40				NW¼SW¼	19	36	40	3-15—9-15	.320	118.20

NOTE—Pole and Rock Creeks are small streams of variable flow and the culture area and character of the culture varies. Claimants Taylor and Sheehan and their predecessors have at all times used the entire flow of said streams, reaching their points of diversion, increasing and decreasing the amount of culture area and changing the character thereof to adapt themselves to the amount of the flow. The claimants are entitled to the entire flow of said streams reaching their points of diversion for irrigation of the land specified.

Taylor and Sheehan—Continued.
Source—**Humboldt River.** Ditch—**Humboldt Canal.**

Year of priority	Culture—Acres: Harvest crops	Meadow pasture	Diversified pasture	Location: Subdivision	Section	Tp.N.	R.E.	Length of season	Duty of water: C.F.S.	Acre-feet
1873	13.90			SE¼SW¼	12	36	39	3-15—9-15	.113	41.70
1873	5.10			SW¼SW¼	12	36	39	3-15—9-15	.041	15.30
1873	18.35			NW¼NE¼	13	36	39	3-15—9-15	.149	55.05
1873	32.80			NE¼NW¼	13	36	39	3-15—9-15	.267	98.40
1873			.85	NE¼NW¼	13	36	39	3-15—4-28	.007	.64
1873	1.70			NW¼NW¼	13	36	39	3-15—9-15	.015	5.10
1873			28.30	NW¼NW¼	13	36	39	3-15—4-28	.230	21.22
1864	38.25			SW¼NE¼	13	36	39	3-15—9-15	.311	114.75
1873	21.85			SE¼NE¼	13	36	39	3-15—9-15	.178	65.55
1873	6.40			SE¼NW¼	13	36	39	3-15—9-15	.052	19.20
1873			21.80	SE¼NW¼	13	36	39	3-15—4-28	.177	16.35
1873			23.60	SW¼NW¼	13	36	39	3-15—4-28	.192	17.70
1864	16.43			NE¼SE¼	13	36	39	3-15—9-15	.134	49.29
1864	22.87			NE¼SE¼	13	36	39	3-15—9-15	.186	68.61
1873	13.30			NW¼SE¼	13	36	39	3-15—9-15	.108	39.90
1873			3.00	NW¼SE¼	13	36	39	3-15—4-28	.024	2.25
1864	9.30			SE¼SE¼	13	36	39	3-15—9-15	.076	27.90
1864	24.48			NW¼SW¼	18	36	40	3-15—9-15	.199	73.44
1864	5.51			SE¼SW¼	18	36	40	3-15—9-15	.045	16.53
1873			17.65	NE¼NE¼	13	36	39	3-15—4-28	.143	13.24
1873			1.20	SE¼NE¼	13	36	39	3-15—4-28	.010	.90
1864		24.35		NE¼NE¼	19	36	39	3-15—6-13	.198	36.53
1864		1.85		NW¼NE¼	19	36	40	3-15—6-13	.015	2.78
1864		33.10		SE¼NW¼	20	36	40	3-15—6-13	.269	49.65
1864			6.45	SE¼NW¼	20	36	40	3-15—4-28	.052	4.84
1864		11.10		SW¼NW¼	20	36	40	3-15—6-13	.090	16.65
1873	4.00			NW¼NE¼	19	36	40	3-15—9-15	.033	12.00
1864	20.39			SE¼SW¼	18	36	40	3-15—9-15	.166	61.17
1864			1.35	SW¼SE¼	18	36	40	3-15—4-28	.011	1.01
1864	21.62			SW¼SW¼	18	36	40	3-15—9-15	.176	64.86
1864	10.98			SW¼SW¼	18	36	40	3-15—9-15	.089	32.94
1864	.40			NE¼SW¼	18	36	40	3-15—9-15	.003	1.20
1864			12.10	NE¼NE¼	19	36	40	3-15—4-28	.098	9.08
1864			24.20	NW¼NE¼	19	36	40	3-15—4-28	.197	18.15
1864	12.10			NE¼NW¼	19	36	40	3-15—9-15	.098	36.30
1864			1.40	NE¼NW¼	19	36	40	3-15—4-28	.011	1.05
1864			22.85	SE¼NE¼	19	36	40	3-15—4-28	.186	17.14
1864			25.30	NE¼SE¼	20	36	40	3-15—4-28	.206	18.98
1864			31.45	NW¼SE¼	20	36	40	3-15—4-28	.280	25.81
1864		2.85		NE¼SW¼	20	36	40	3-15—6-13	.023	4.28
1864			16.35	NE¼SW¼	20	36	40	3-15—4-28	.133	12.26
1864			3.25	NW¼SW¼	20	36	40	3-15—4-28	.026	2.44
1864			25.15	SW¼NW¼	20	36	40	3-15—4-28	.204	18.86

......	1864	......	......	....	......	13.45	......	SE¼SE¼	20	36	40	3-15—4-28	.109	10.09
......	1864	......	......	....	......	.70	......	NW¼SW¼	21	36	40	3-15—4-28	.006	.53
......	1864	......	......	....	......	2.40	......	SW¼SW¼	21	36	40	3-15—4-28	.020	1.80

Claimant—**Taylor and Sheehan.** Proof No. **00122**

Source—**Humboldt River.** Ditch—**Humboldt Canal.**

......	1864	......	......	2.45	......	......	......	SW¼NE¼	28	36	40	3-15—9-15	.020	7.35
......	1864	......	......	18.55	......	......	......	SE¼NW¼	28	36	40	3-15—9-15	.151	55.65
......	1864	......	......	22.05	......	......	......	NW¼SE¼	28	36	40	3-15—9-15	.179	66.15
......	1864	......	......	3.25	......	......	......	NE¼SW¼	28	36	40	3-15—9-15	.026	9.75
......	1864	......	......	8.85	......	......	......	NE¼SW¼	28	36	40	3-15—9-15	.071	26.45
......	1864	......	......	18.30	......	......	......	SE¼SE¼	28	36	40	3-15—9-15	.150	54.90
......	1864	......	......	....	......	12.75	......	SE¼SE¼	28	36	40	3-15—4-28	.104	9.56
......	1864	......	......	19.25	......	......	......	SW¼SE¼	28	36	40	3-15—9-15	.156	57.75

Source—**Humboldt River.** Ditch—**Pioneer Slough.**

......	1870	......	......	37.70	......	......	......	NE¼NE¼	28	36	40	3-15—9-15	.307	113.10
......	1870	......	......	35.20	......	......	......	NW¼NE¼	28	36	40	3-15—9-15	.286	105.60
......	1870	......	......	35.75	......	......	......	SE¼NE¼	28	36	40	3-15—9-15	.291	107.25
......	1870	......	......	....	......	4.50	......	SW¼SW¼	22	36	40	3-15—4-28	.037	3.38
......	1870	......	......	30.12	......	......	......	NE¼NW¼	28	36	40	3-15—9-15	.245	90.36
......	1870	......	......	22.46	......	......	......	NE¼SE¼	28	36	40	3-15—9-15	.183	67.38
......	1870	......	......	....	......	3.10	......	NE¼NE¼	33	36	40	3-15—4-28	.026	2.33
......	1870	......	......	....	......	3.80	......	SE¼SE¼	28	36	40	3-15—4-28	.031	2.85
......	1870	......	......	23.85	......	......	......	SW¼NE¼	28	36	40	3-15—9-15	.194	71.55
......	1870	......	......	6.55	......	......	......	SE¼NW¼	28	36	40	3-15—9-15	.053	19.65
......	1870	......	......	8.30	......	......	......	NW¼SE¼	28	36	40	3-15—9-15	.068	24.90

Claimant—**Paul A. Pinson.** Proof No. **00124**

Source—**Humboldt River.** Ditch—**Louis Lay Dam.**

......	1885	......	......	....	......	......	7.94	SW¼SW¼	25	36	40	3-15—4-28	.065	5.96
......	1885	......	......	....	......	......	7.50	SE¼SW¼	25	36	40	3-15—4-28	.061	5.63
......	1885	......	......	....	......	11.70	......	SW¼SE¼	25	36	40	3-15—4-28	.095	8.78
......	1885	......	......	....	......	2.29	......	NW¼SE¼	25	36	40	3-15—4-28	.018	1.72
......	1885	......	......	....	......	17.92	......	NE¼SE¼	25	36	40	3-15—4-28	.146	13.44
......	1885	......	......	....	4.07	......	......	SE¼SE¼	25	36	40	3-15—6-13	.033	6.11
......	1885	......	......	....	......	4.00	......	SE¼SE¼	25	36	40	3-15—4-28	.033	3.00
......	1885	......	......	....	......	24.97	......	NW¼SW¼	30	36	41	3-15—4-28	.203	18.73
......	1885	......	......	....	......	2.72	......	NE¼SW¼	30	36	41	3-15—4-28	.022	2.04
......	1885	......	......	....	......	6.88	......	SW¼NW¼	30	36	41	3-15—4-28	.056	5.16
......	1885	......	......	....	......	21.18	......	SE¼NW¼	30	36	41	3-15—4-28	.172	15.89
......	1885	......	......	....	......	5.43	......	NE¼NW¼	30	36	41	3-15—4-28	.044	4.07

Paul A. Pinson—Continued.

Source—**Humboldt River.** Ditch—**Pinson Dam and Ditch System.**

Year of priority	Culture—Acres: Harvest crops	Meadow pasture	Diversified pasture	Location: Subdivision	Section	Tp. N.	R. E.	Length of season	Duty of water: C. F. S.	Acre-feet
1900			3.13	SW¼NE¼	30	36	41	3-15—4-28	.025	2.35
1900		10.00		NW¼NE¼	30	36	41	3-15—6-13	.081	7.50
1900			10.93	NW¼NE¼	30	36	41	3-15—4-28	.089	8.20
1900		.37		NE¼NE¼	30	36	41	3-15—6-13	.003	.56
1900			9.84	SW¼SE¼	19	36	41	3-15—4-28	.080	7.38
1900		13.77		SE¼SE¼	19	36	41	3-15—6-13	.112	20.66
1900			1.83	SE¼SE¼	19	36	41	3-15—4-28	.015	1.37
1900		5.60		NE¼SE¼	19	36	41	3-15—6-13	.046	8.40
1900		13.08		NW¼SW¼	20	36	41	3-15—6-13	.106	19.62
1900			12.05	NW¼SW¼	20	36	41	3-15—4-28	.098	9.04
1900		11.17		SW¼SW¼	20	36	41	3-15—6-13	.091	16.76
1900			4.29	SW¼SW¼	20	36	41	3-15—4-28	.035	3.22
1900		4.93		NE¼SW¼	20	36	41	3-15—6-13	.040	7.40
1900			25.04	NE¼SW¼	20	36	41	3-15—4-28	.204	18.78
1900		9.39		SE¼SW¼	20	36	41	3-15—6-13	.076	14.09
1900			3.05	SE¼SW¼	20	36	41	3-15—4-28	.025	2.29
1892	10.31			NW¼SE¼	20	36	41	3-15—9-15	.084	30.93
1892			13.90	NW¼SE¼	20	36	41	3-15—4-28	.113	10.43
1892	23.08			NE¼SE¼	20	36	41	3-15—9-15	.188	69.24
1892			3.70	NE¼SE¼	20	36	41	3-15—4-28	.030	2.78
1892	17.72			SW¼SE¼	20	36	41	3-15—9-15	.144	53.16
1892			4.59	SW¼SE¼	20	36	41	3-15—4-28	.037	3.44
1892	12.12			SE¼SE¼	20	36	41	3-15—9-15	.099	36.36
1892			10.89	SE¼SE¼	20	36	41	3-15—4-28	.089	8.17
1892	7.50			NE¼SW¼	21	36	41	3-15—9-15	.061	22.50
1892			1.58	NE¼SW¼	21	36	41	3-15—4-28	.013	1.19
1892	24.62			NW¼SW¼	21	36	41	3-15—9-15	.200	73.86
1892			4.12	NW¼SW¼	21	36	41	3-15—4-28	.033	3.09
1892	.20			SW¼SW¼	21	36	41	3-15—9-15	.002	.60
1892			5.32	SW¼SW¼	21	36	41	3-15—4-28	.043	3.99
1892	7.80			SE¼NW¼	21	36	41	3-15—9-15	.063	23.40
1892			1.49	SE¼NW¼	21	36	41	3-15—4-28	.012	1.12
1892	.98			SW¼NW¼	21	36	41	3-15—9-15	.008	2.94
1892	20.02			NW¼NE¼	21	36	41	3-15—9-15	.163	60.06
1892	34.09			SW¼NE¼	21	36	41	3-15—9-15	.277	102.27
1892			.20	SW¼NE¼	21	36	41	3-15—4-28	.002	.15
1892	1.44			SE¼NE¼	21	36	41	3-15—9-15	.012	4.32
1892			5.75	SE¼NE¼	21	36	41	3-15—4-28	.047	4.31
1892	3.35			NE¼NE¼	21	36	41	3-15—9-15	.027	10.05
1892			28.58	NE¼NE¼	21	36	41	3-15—4-28	.208	19.19
1892	3.05			NW¼SE¼	21	36	41	3-15—9-15	.025	9.15

Claimant—**J. J. Trigueiro.** Proof No. 00125
Source—**Humboldt River.** Ditch—**Water Wheel.**

	1901			3.59				NW¼NW¼	10	28	32	3-15—9-15	.020	10.77
	1901					.36		NW¼NW¼	10	28	32	3-15—4-28	.003	.27
	1901			12.00				NE¼NW¼	10	28	32	3-15—9-15	.098	36.27
	1901				1.39			NE¼NW¼	10	28	32	3-15—6-13	.011	2.09
	1901					3.90		NE¼NW¼	10	28	32	3-15—4-28	.032	2.93
	1901			5.00				SW¼NW¼	10	28	32	3-15—9-15	.041	15.27
	1901					3.70		SW¼NW¼	10	28	32	3-15—4-28	.030	27.75
	1901					2.48		SE¼NW¼	10	28	32	3-15—1-28	.020	1.86
	1901					26.41		NW¼NE¼	10	28	32	3-15—4-28	.215	19.81
	1901					29.14		NE¼NE¼	10	28	32	3-15—4-28	.237	21.86
	1901					20.57		NW¼SW¼	10	28	32	3-15—4-28	.177	15.43
	1901					16.36		SW¼SW¼	10	28	32	3-15—4-28	.133	12.27
	1901			2.03				SE¼SW¼	3	28	32	3-15—9-15	.024	8.79
	1901					12.44		SW¼SE¼	3	28	32	3-15—4-28	.101	9.33
	1901					1.01		SE¼SE¼	2	28	32	3-15—4-28	.008	.76
	1901					2.26		SW¼SW¼	2	28	32	3-15—4-28	.018	1.70
	1901					1.20		NW¼NW¼	11	28	32	3-15—4-28	.010	.90
	1901					1.49		SW¼NW¼	11	28	32	3-15—4-28	.012	1.12

Claimant—**Hazel D. Smith.** Proof No. 00127
Source—**Humboldt River.** Ditch—**Miller & Lux Upper Dam.**

	1871				5.72			SW¼SE¼	19	36	38	3-15—6-13	.046	8.58
	1871					1.59		SW¼SE¼	19	36	38	3-15—4-28	.013	1.19
	1871				10.01			NW¼NE¼	30	36	38	3-15—6-13	.080	16.37
	1871					6.49		NW¼NE¼	30	36	38	3-15—4-28	.053	4.87

Claimant—**David Giroux.** Proof No. 00130
Source—**Humboldt River.** Ditch—**Gasoline Pump.**

	1901			5.66				SE¼SE¼	19	36	38	3-15—9-15	.046	16.98
	1901				3.19			SE¼SE¼	19	36	38	3-15—6-13	.026	4.79
	1901			.28				NE¼NE¼	30	36	38	3-15—9-15	.002	.84
	1901					.94		NE¼NE¼	30	36	38	3-15—4-28	.008	.71

Claimant—**Golconda Cattle Co.** Proof No. 00131
Source—**Little Rock Creek.** Ditch—**Little Rock Creek System.**

	1873			12.72				NW¼NW¼	6	34	40	3-15—9-15	.103	38.16
	1873					1.05		NW¼NW¼	6	34	40	3-15—4-28	.009	.79
	1873			.87				SW¼NW¼	6	34	40	3-15—9-15	.007	2.61
	1873			1.45				NW¼SW¼	6	34	40	3-15—9-15	.012	4.35
	1873			24.17				NW¼NE¼	6	34	40	3-15—9-15	.197	72.51
	1873			14.60				NE¼SW¼	6	34	40	3-15—9-15	.119	43.80

Golconda Cattle Co.—Continued.

Year of priority	Culture—Acres: Harvest crops	Meadow pasture	Diversified pasture		Location: Subdivision	Section	Tp.N.	R.E.	Length of season	Duty of water: C.F.S.	Acre-feet
1875	4.37				SE¼NE¼	6	34	40	3-15—9-15	.036	13.11
1874	16.40				NE¼NE¼	6	34	40	3-15—9-15	.133	49.20
1874			3.50		NE¼NE¼	6	34	40	3-15—4-28	.028	2.63
1874	29.47				NE¼NW¼	6	34	40	3-15—9-15	.240	88.41
1868	16.22				SE¼NW¼	6	34	40	3-15—9-15	.132	48.66
1868	25.85				SW¼NE¼	6	34	40	3-15—9-15	.210	77.55
1876	19.78				NW¼NW¼	5	34	40	3-15—9-15	.161	59.34
1876	7.55				SW¼NW¼	5	34	40	3-15—9-15	.061	22.65
1876	9.20				SE¼NW¼	5	34	40	3-15—9-15	.075	27.60
1876	35.75				NE¼NW¼	5	34	40	3-15—9-15	.291	107.25
1878	20.62				NW¼NE¼	5	34	40	3-15—9-15	.168	61.86
1878			6.50		NW¼NE¼	5	34	40	3-15—4-28	.053	4.88
1878	8.55				NE¼NE¼	5	34	40	3-15—9-15	.070	25.65
1878			1.55		NE¼NE¼	5	34	40	3-15—4-28	.013	1.16
1874	10.82				SE¼SW¼	31	35	40	3-15—9-15	.088	32.46
1874	31.80				SW¼SE¼	31	35	40	3-15—9-15	.259	95.40
1874	15.55				NE¼SE¼	31	35	40	3-15—9-15	.126	46.65
1874	40.00				SE¼SE¼	31	35	40	3-15—9-15	.325	120.00
1876	40.00				SW¼SW¼	32	35	46	3-15—9-15	.325	120.00
1876	40.00				SE¼SW¼	32	35	40	3-15—9-15	.325	120.00
1880	.55				NW¼SW¼	32	35	40	3-15—9-15	.004	1.65
1880	27.30				SW¼SE¼	32	35	40	3-15—9-15	.222	81.90
1880			4.57		SW¼SE¼	32	35	40	3-15—4-28	.037	3.43
1880	27.27				SE¼SE¼	32	35	40	3-15—9-15	.222	81.81
1880			5.30		SE¼SE¼	32	35	40	3-15—4-28	.043	3.98
1880	20.97				SW¼SW¼	33	35	40	3-15—9-15	.170	62.91
1880				15.55	SW¼SW¼	33	35	40	3-15—4-28	.126	11.66
1875			9.65		NW¼NE¼	1	34	39	3-15—4-28	.078	7.24
1875			1.00		SW¼NE¼	1	34	39	3-15—4-28	.008	.75
1875			12.22		NE¼NE¼	1	34	39	3-15—4-28	.099	9.17
1875			2.95		SE¼NE¼	1	34	39	3-15—4-28	.024	2.21

Claimant—**Estate of Henry Bain.** Proof No. 00132

Source—**Little Rock Creek.** Ditch—**South Side Ditch.**

Year of priority	Harvest crops	Meadow pasture	Diversified pasture		Subdivision	Section	Tp.N.	R.E.	Length of season	C.F.S.	Acre-feet
1877	2.92				NE¼NE¼	33	35	40	3-15—9-15	.024	8.76
1884	6.13				SE¼NE¼	33	35	40	3-15—9-15	.050	18.39
1808	6.91				SW¼NE¼	33	35	40	3-15—9-15	.056	20.73
1882	12.56				NW¼SE¼	33	35	40	3-15—9-15	.102	37.68
1882	4.49				NE¼SW¼	33	35	40	3-15—9-15	.037	13.47
1884	1.62				SE¼SW¼	33	35	40	3-15—9-15	.013	4.86
1881			7.12		SE¼SW¼	33	35	40	3-15—4-28	.059	5.34
1884	6.67				NW¼SW¼	33	35	40	3-15—9-15	.054	20.01
1884			.80		NW¼SW¼	33	35	40	3-15—4-28	.007	[illegible]
1876	6.13				SE¼NE¼	33	35	40	3-15—9-15	.050	[illegible]

....	1877	....	....	16.20	....	....	....	NE¼NE¼	33	35	40	3-15—9-15	.1-2	48.60
....	1877	....	....	....	1.52	....	....	NE¼NE¼	33	35	40	3-15—6-15	.012	2.28
....	1876	....	....	5.00	....	....	....	NW¼NE¼	33	35	40	3-15—9-15	.041	15.00
....	1876	....	....	3.40	....	....	....	SE¼NE¼	33	35	40	3-15—9-15	.028	10.20
....	1876	....	....	...	....	.17	....	SE¼NE¼	33	35	40	3-15—4-28	.001	.13
....	1868	....	....	17.11	....	....	....	SW¼NE¼	33	35	40	3-15—9-15	.139	51.33
....	1882	....	....	2.94	....	....	....	NW¼SE¼	33	35	40	3-15—9-15	.034	8.82
....	1882	....	....	9.95	....	....	....	NE¼SW¼	33	35	40	3-15—9-15	.081	29.85
....	1882	....	....	..	....	1.10	....	NE¼SW¼	33	35	40	3-15—4-28	.009	.83

Claimant—**A. E. Kent and Co., Inc.** Proof No. **00133**

Source—**Little Rock Creek.** Ditch—**Little Rock Creek System.**

....	1880	....	....	1.48	....	....	....	NE¼SE¼	32	35	40	3-15—9-15	.012	4.44
....	1880	....	....	1.60	....	....	....	NW¼SE¼	32	35	40	3-15—9-15	.013	4.80
....	1880	....	....	23.99	....	....	....	NE¼SW¼	32	35	40	3-15—9-15	.195	71.97
....	1880	....	....	28.59	....	....	....	NW¼SW¼	32	35	40	3-15—9-15	.232	85.77

Claimant—**Mrs. James Marr.** Proof No. **00134**

Source—**Humboldt River.** Ditch—**Water Wheel.**

....	1886	....	....	...	....	30.41	....	NW¼SW¼	20	36	38	3-15—4-28	.247	22.81
....	1886	....	....	...	....	5.21	....	NE¼SE¼	19	36	38	3-15—4-28	.042	3.91
....	1886	....	....	...	....	9.02	....	SE¼SE¼	19	36	38	3-15—4-28	.073	6.77
....	1886	....	....	...	....	1.78	....	SW¼SE¼	19	36	38	3-15—4-28	.014	1.34

BATTLE MOUNTAIN DISTRICT

Claimant—**Ellison Ranching Co.** Proof No. 00151

Source—**Humboldt River.** Ditch—**Aemes Dam.**

Year of priority	Culture—Acres: Harvest crops	Culture—Acres: Meadow pasture	Culture—Acres: Diversified pasture		Location: Subdivision	Location: Section	Location: Tp.N.	Location: R.E.	Length of season	Duty of water: C.F.S.	Duty of water: Acre-feet
1876			2.14		SE¼SW¼	10	35	42	3-15—4-28	.017	1.61
1876	36.60				SE¼SW¼	10	35	42	3-15—9-15	.298	109.80
1876	31.72				NW¼SW¼	10	35	42	3-15—9-15	.258	95.16
1876			7.83		NW¼SW¼	10	35	42	3-15—4-28	.064	5.87
1876			.79		SW¼SW¼	10	35	42	3-15—4-28	.006	.59
1876	39.50				SW¼SW¼	10	35	42	3-15—9-15	.321	118.50
1876	29.15				SW¼NE¼	14	35	42	3-15—9-15	.237	87.45
1876			8.07		SW¼NE¼	14	35	42	3-15—4-28	.066	6.05
1876				.88	SW¼NE¼	14	35	42	3-15—4-28	.007	.66
1876	2.14				SE¼NE¼	14	35	42	3-15—9-15	.017	6.42
1876				.83	NW¼NE¼	14	35	42	3-15—4-28	.007	.62
1876				9.25	NE¼SE¼	14	35	42	3-15—4-28	.075	6.94
1876	5.22				NE¼SE¼	14	35	42	3-15—9-15	.042	15.66
1876			19.63		NE¼SE¼	14	35	42	3-15—4-28	.160	14.72
1876			37.98		SE¼SE¼	14	35	42	3-15—4-28	.309	28.60
1876			12.54		NW¼SE¼	14	35	42	3-15—4-28	.102	9.41
1876	23.68				NW¼SE¼	14	35	42	3-15—9-15	.193	71.04
1876	35.49				NE¼NE¼	3	35	42	3-15—9-15	.289	106.47
1876				5.60	NE¼NE¼	3	35	42	3-15—4-28	.046	4.20
1876	36.91				SE¼NE¼	3	35	42	3-15—9-15	.300	110.73
1876				2.42	SE¼NE¼	3	35	42	3-15—4-28	.020	1.82
1876				.25	SE¼NE¼	3	35	42	3-15—4-28	.002	.19
1876	35.05				NW¼NE¼	3	35	42	3-15—9-15	.285	105.15
1876			3.05		NW¼NE¼	3	35	42	3-15—4-28	.025	2.29
1876				2.83	NW¼NE¼	3	35	42	3-15—4-28	.023	2.12
1876	29.11				SW¼NE¼	3	35	42	3-15—9-15	.237	87.33
1876		5.68			SW¼NE¼	3	35	42	3-15—6-13	.046	8.52
1876			2.64		SW¼NE¼	3	35	42	3-15—4-28	.021	1.98
1876	37.61				NE¼SE¼	3	35	42	3-15—9-15	.306	112.83
1876		32.58			SW¼SE¼	14	35	42	3-15—6-13	.265	48.87
1876			6.52		SW¼SE¼	14	35	42	3-15—6-13	.053	1.13
1876	39.54				SE¼NE¼	10	35	42	3-15—9-15	.321	118.62
1876	36.44				NW¼NE¼	10	35	42	3-15—9-15	.296	109.32
1876	40.04				SW¼NE¼	10	35	42	3-15—9-15	.326	120.12
1876	37.68				NE¼NW¼	10	35	42	3-15—9-15	.306	113.04
1876				2.12	NE¼NW¼	10	35	42	3-15—4-28	.017	1.59
1876	40.65				SE¼NW¼	10	35	42	3-15—9-15	.330	121.95
1876	38.28				NW¼NW¼	10	35	42	3-15—9-15	.311	114.84
1876	38.94				SW¼NW¼	10	35	42	3-15—9-15	.317	116.82
1876	36.00				NE¼SE¼	10	35	42	3-15—9-15	.293	108.00
1876			2.80		NE¼SE¼	10	35	42	3-15—4-28	.023	2.15

1876			40.76				SE¼SE¼	10	35	42	3-15—0-15	.331	122.28
1876			40.05				NW¼SE¼	10	35	42	3-15—0-15	.333	122.85
1876			38.14				SW¼SE¼	10	35	42	3-15—0-15	.310	114.42
1876					1.87		SW¼SE¼	10	35	42	3-15—4-28	.015	1.40
1876			38.93				NE¼SW¼	10	35	42	3-15—0-15	.317	116.79
1876					.08		NE¼SW¼	10	35	42	3-15—4-28	.001	.06
1876					.48		NE¼SE¼	3	35	42	3-15—4-28	.004	.36
1876			37.81				SE¼SE¼	3	35	42	3-15—0-15	.307	113.43
1876			35.39				NW¼SE¼	3	35	42	3-15—0-15	.288	106.17
1876					1.68		NW¼SE¼	3	35	42	3-15—4-28	.014	1.26
1876			38.25				SW¼SE¼	3	35	42	3-15—0-15	.311	114.75
1876					2.00		NE¼NW¼	14	35	42	3-15—4-28	.016	1.50
1876						33.30	NE¼NW¼	14	35	42	3-15—4-28	.271	24.98
1876				2.07			NE¼NW¼	14	35	42	3-15—6-13	.017	3.11
1876			1.62				NE¼NW¼	14	35	42	3-15—0-15	.013	4.86
1876			20.07				SE¼NW¼	14	35	42	3-15—0-15	.163	60.21
1876					5.43		SE¼NW¼	14	35	42	3-15—4-28	.044	4.07
1876						12.10	SE¼NW¼	14	35	42	3-15—4-28	.098	9.08
1876				2.47			SE¼NW¼	14	35	42	3-15—6-13	.020	3.71
1876						32.77	NW¼NW¼	14	35	42	3-15—4-28	.266	24.58
1876			4.85				NW¼NW¼	14	35	42	3-15—0-15	.039	14.55
1876					1.55		NW¼NW¼	14	35	42	3-15—4-28	.013	1.16
1876					17.18		SW¼NW¼	14	35	42	3-15—4-28	.140	12.80
1876						13.10	SW¼NW¼	14	35	42	3-15—4-28	.107	9.83
1876				4.22			SW¼NW¼	14	35	42	3-15—6-13	.034	6.33
1876			3.98				SW¼NW¼	14	35	42	3-15—0-15	.032	11.94
1876			.92				NE¼NE¼	15	35	42	3-15—0-15	.007	2.76
1876						.99	NE¼NE¼	15	35	42	3-15—4-28	.008	.74
1876					.83		SE¼NE¼	15	35	42	3-15—4-28	.007	.62
1876						.50	SE¼NE¼	15	35	42	3-15—4-28	.004	.38

Source—**Humboldt River.** Ditch—**Gonzales Slough.**

1880			1.25				NE¼NW¼	2	35	42	3-15—9-16	.010	3.75
1880			1.52				SE¼NW¼	2	35	42	3-15—0-15	.012	4.56
1880			41.18				NW¼NW¼	2	35	42	3-15—0-15	.335	123.54
1880			39.77				SW¼NW¼	2	35	42	3-15—0-15	.323	119.31
1880			1.20				SE¼SW¼	2	35	42	3-15—9-15	.010	3.60
1880			37.40				SW¼SW¼	2	35	42	3-15—0-16	.304	112.20
1880				.44			SW¼SW¼	2	35	42	3-15—6-13	.004	.66
1880				35.22			NE¼NW¼	3	35	42	3-15—6-13	.286	52.83
1880			1.50				NE¼NW¼	3	35	42	3-15—9-15	.013	4.77
1880					2.16		NE¼NW¼	3	35	42	3-15—4-28	.018	1.62
1880			13.47				SE¼NW¼	3	35	42	3-15—0-15	.110	40.41
1880				14.09			SE¼NW¼	3	35	42	3-15—6-13	.115	21.14
1880					5.60		SE¼NW¼	3	35	42	3-15—4-28	.046	4.27
1880				29.36			NW¼NW¼	3	35	42	3-15—6-13	.239	44.04
1880				33.46			SW¼NW¼	3	35	42	3-15—6-13	.272	50.19
1880						1.65	SW¼NW¼	3	35	42	3-15—4-28	.013	1.24
1880					.08		SW¼NW¼	3	35	42	3-15—4-28	.001	.06
1880			39.50				NE¼SW¼	3	35	42	3-15—9-15	.321	118.50
1880			39.60				SE¼SW¼	3	35	42	3-15—9-15	.322	118.80
1880			2.33				NW¼SW¼	3	35	42	3-15—0-15	.019	6.99
1880				29.87			NW¼SW¼	3	35	42	3-15—6-13	.243	44.81

Ellison Ranching Co.—Continued.

Year of priority	Culture—Acres: Harvest crops	Meadow pasture	Diversified pasture		Location: Subdivision	Section	Tp.N.	R.E.	Length of season	Duty of water: C.F.S.	Acre-feet
1880				3.45	NW¼SW¼	3	35	42	3-15—4-28	.028	2.59
1880	14.86				SW¼SW¼	3	35	42	3-15—9-15	.121	43.98
1880		22.70			SW¼SW¼	3	35	42	3-15—6-13	.185	34.05
1880	36.33				NE¼NE¼	10	35	42	3-15—9-15	.295	108.99

Source—**Humboldt River.** Ditch—**Outside Slough.**

Year of priority	Harvest crops	Meadow pasture	Diversified pasture		Subdivision	Section	Tp.N.	R.E.	Length of season	C.F.S.	Acre-feet
1887		5.52			NE¼NE¼	16	35	42	3-15—6-13	.045	8.28

Claimant—**The A. E. Kent Co.** Proof No. 00151

Source—**Humboldt River.** Ditch—**Outside Slough.**

Year of priority	Harvest crops	Meadow pasture	Diversified pasture		Subdivision	Section	Tp.N.	R.E.	Length of season	C.F.S.	Acre-feet
1886		20.15			SE¼NE¼	21	35	42	3-15—6-13	.164	30.23
1886			16.15		SE¼NE¼	21	35	42	3-15—4-28	.131	12.11
1886		38.31			NE¼NW¼	21	35	42	3-15—6-13	.311	57.47
1886		3.45			NW¼NW¼	21	35	42	3-15—6-13	.028	5.18
1886		14.57			SE¼NW¼	21	35	42	3-15—6-13	.118	21.86
1886		22.17			NE¼SE¼	21	35	42	3-15—6-13	.180	33.26
1886			14.18		NE¼SE¼	21	35	42	3-15—4-28	.115	10.64
1886		28.60			NW¼SE¼	21	35	42	3-15—6-13	.233	42.90
1886		3.50			SW¼SE¼	21	35	42	3-15—6-13	.028	5.25
1886		21.97			SE¼SE¼	21	35	42	3-15—6-13	.179	32.96
1886			1.07		SE¼SE¼	21	35	42	3-15—4-28	.009	.80
1886		3.50			SW¼SE¼	21	35	42	3-15—6-13	.028	5.25
1886				21.30	SE¼SE¼	16	35	42	3-15—4-28	.173	15.98
1886		39.30			NE¼SW¼	16	35	42	3-15—6-13	.320	58.95
1886		26.85			NW¼SW¼	16	35	42	3-15—6-13	.218	40.28
1886		17.90			SW¼SW¼	16	35	42	3-15—6-13	.146	26.85
1886		39.64			SE¼SW¼	16	35	42	3-15—6-13	.322	59.46
1886		1.20			NE¼NE¼	21	25	42	3-15—6-13	.010	1.86
1886			10.16		NE¼NE¼	21	35	42	3-15—4-28	.083	7.62
1886				25.12	NE¼NE¼	21	35	42	3-15—4-28	.204	18.84
1886		34.09			NW¼NE¼	21	35	42	3-15—6-13	.277	51.14
1886			3.87		NW¼NE¼	21	35	42	3-15—4-28	.031	2.90
1886		38.67			SW¼NE¼	21	36	42	3-15—6-13	.314	58.01
1886				27.79	NE¼NE¼	16	35	42	3-15—4-28	.226	20.84
1886				38.80	NW¼NE¼	16	35	42	3-15—4-28	.315	29.10
1886				39.46	SE¼NE¼	16	35	42	3-15—4-28	.321	29.60
1886			6.93		SW¼NE¼	16	35	42	3-15—4-28	.056	5.20
1886				30.78	SW¼NE¼	16	35	42	3-15—4-28	.250	23.09
1886		5.20			NE¼NW¼	16	36	42	3-15—6-13	.042	7.80
1886				1.62	NE¼NW¼	16	35	42	3-15—4-28	.013	1.22
1886		3.77			NW¼NW¼	16	35	42	3-15—6-13	.031	5.66
1886	7.32				SW¼NW¼	16	35	42	3-15—9-15	.060	21.06
1886		21.50			SW¼NW¼	16	35	42	3-15—6-13	.175	32.25
1886		34.40			SE¼NW¼	16	35	42	3-15—6-13	.280	51.60
1886				3.50	SE¼NW¼	16	35	42	3-15—4-28	.028	2.63

....	1886	....	....	....	....	....	89.34	NE¼SE¼	16	35	42	3-15—4-28	.320	29.51
....	1886	....	....	....	12.28	....	....	NW¼SE¼	16	35	42	3-15—6-13	.100	18.42
....	1886	....	....	....	....	....	24.44	NW¼SE¼	16	35	42	3-15—4-28	.199	18.33
....	1886	....	....	....	20.43	....	....	SW¼SE¼	16	35	42	3-15—6-13	.166	30.65
....	1886	....	....	....	....	13.27	....	SW¼SE¼	16	35	42	3-15—4-28	.108	9.95
....	1886	....	....	....	....	....	3.62	SW¼SE¼	16	35	42	3-15—4-28	.029	2.72
....	1886	....	....	....	....	8.50	....	SE¼SE¼	16	35	42	3-15—4-28	.069	6.38

Claimant—C. H. Duborg. Proof No. 00153
Source—Humboldt River. Ditch—Cluro.

....	1883	....	....	4.58	....	....	....	SE¼SE¼	7	31	50	3-15—9-15	.037	13.74
....	1883	....	....	15.58	....	....	....	SW¼SW¼	8	31	50	3-15—9-15	.127	46.74
....	1883	....	....	12.79	....	....	....	SE¼SW¼	8	31	50	3-15—9-15	.104	38.37
....	1883	....	....	10.40	....	....	....	SW¼SE¼	8	31	50	3-15—9-15	.085	31.20
....	1883	....	....	7.49	....	....	....	NW¼NW¼	16	31	50	3-15—9-15	.061	22.47
....	1883	....	....	.90	....	....	....	SW¼NW¼	16	31	50	3-15—9-15	.007	2.70
....	1883	....	....	4.50	....	....	....	NE¼NW¼	17	31	50	3-15—9-15	.037	13.50
....	1883	....	....	....	....	3.22	....	NE¼NW¼	17	31	50	3-15—4-28	.026	2.42
....	1883	....	....	1.90	....	....	....	SE¼NW¼	17	31	50	3-15—9-15	.015	5.70
....	1883	....	....	16.64	....	....	....	NW¼NE¼	17	31	50	3-15—9-15	.135	49.92
....	1883	....	....	....	....	6.86	....	NW¼NE¼	17	31	50	3-15—4-28	.056	5.15
....	1883	....	....	22.88	....	....	....	NE¼NE¼	17	31	50	3-15—9-15	.186	68.64
....	1883	....	....	35.88	....	....	....	SW¼NE¼	17	31	50	3-15—9-15	.292	107.64
....	1883	....	....	35.60	....	....	....	SE¼NE¼	17	31	50	3-15—9-15	.289	106.80

Claimant—Humboldt Land & Cattle Co. Proof No. 00154
Source—Humboldt River. Ditch—Rose Dam.

....	1873	....	....	....	....	....	8.20	NW¼NW¼	36	33	48	3-15—4-28	.067	6.15
....	1873	....	....	....	....	....	1.88	SW¼NW¼	36	33	48	3-15—4-28	.015	1.41
....	1873	....	....	....	....	....	34.92	NW¼NE¼	36	33	48	3-15—4-28	.284	26.19
....	1873	....	....	....	....	....	33.40	SW¼NE¼	36	33	48	3-15—4-28	.272	25.05
....	1873	....	....	....	....	....	29.92	NW¼SE¼	36	33	48	3-15—4-28	.243	22.44
....	1873	....	....	....	....	....	40.00	NE¼SE¼	36	33	48	3-15—4-28	.325	30.00
....	1873	....	....	....	....	....	19.14	SW¼SE¼	36	33	48	3-15—4-28	.156	14.36
....	1873	....	....	....	....	....	39.00	SE¼SE¼	36	33	48	3-15—4-28	.317	29.25
....	1873	....	....	....	....	....	33.72	NE¼NE¼	1	32	48	3-15—4-28	.274	25.29
....	1873	....	....	....	....	5.20	....	SW¼NW¼	6	32	49	3-15—4-28	.042	3.90
....	1873	....	....	....	....	....	9.84	SW¼NW¼	6	32	49	3-15—4-28	.080	7.38
....	1873	....	....	....	....	8.60	....	NW¼SW¼	6	32	49	3-15—4-28	.070	6.45
....	1873	....	....	....	....	....	18.49	NW¼SW¼	6	32	49	3-15—4-28	.150	13.87
....	1873	....	....	....	....	....	25.50	SE¼SW¼	6	32	49	3-15—4-28	.207	19.12
....	1873	....	....	....	....	1.60	....	SW¼SW¼	6	32	49	3-15—4-28	.013	1.20
....	1873	....	....	....	....	....	25.36	SW¼SW¼	6	32	49	3-15—4-28	.206	19.02
....	1873	....	....	....	....	....	30.50	SW¼SE¼	6	32	49	3-15—4-28	.248	22.88
....	1873	....	....	....	....	5.26	....	SE¼NE¼	1	32	48	3-15—4-28	.043	3.95
....	1873	....	....	....	....	....	24.50	SE¼NE¼	1	32	48	3-15—4-28	.199	18.38
....	1873	....	....	....	....	....	1.70	SW¼NE¼	1	32	48	3-15—4-28	.014	1.28
....	1873	....	....	....	....	4.04	....	NE¼SE¼	1	32	48	3-15—4-28	.033	3.03
....	1873	....	....	....	....	....	28.16	NE¼SE¼	1	32	48	3-15—4-28	.229	21.12
....	1873	....	....	....	....	....	31.46	SE¼SE¼	1	32	48	3-15—4-28	.256	23.60

Humboldt Land and Cattle Co.—Continued.

Year of priority	Culture—Acres: Harvest crops	Culture—Acres: Meadow pasture	Culture—Acres: Diversified pasture		Location: Subdivision	Location: Section	Location: Tp.N.	Location: R.E.	Length of season	Duty of water: C.F.S.	Duty of water: Acre-feet
1873				40.00	NW¼NE¼	7	32	49	3-15—4-28	.325	30.00
1873			22.52		NW¼SE¼	7	32	49	3-15—4-28	.183	16.80
1873			6.22		SE¼SE¼	7	32	49	3-15—4-28	.051	4.67
1873				34.79	NW¼NW¼	7	32	49	3-15—4-28	.283	26.09
1873			35.29		NE¼NW¼	7	32	49	3-15—4-28	.287	26.47
1873			35.68		SE¼NW¼	7	32	49	3-15—4-28	.290	26.76
1873			7.98		SW¼NW¼	7	32	49	3-15—4-28	.065	5.99
1873				20.70	SW¼NW¼	7	32	49	3-15—4-28	.168	15.53
1873			37.25		NE¼SW¼	7	32	49	3-15—4-28	.303	27.94

Source—**Humboldt River.** Ditch—**High Line Canal.**

Year of priority	Harvest crops	Meadow pasture	Diversified pasture		Subdivision	Section	Tp.N.	R.E.	Length of season	C.F.S.	Acre-feet
1883	2.91				NE¼NW¼	5	31	49	3-15—9-15	.024	8.73
1883			8.99		NE¼NW¼	5	31	49	3-15—4-28	.073	6.74
1883				5.72	NE¼NW¼	5	31	49	3-15—4-28	.047	4.29
1883			3.01		SE¼NW¼	5	31	49	3-15—4-28	.024	2.26
1883			4.16		NW¼NE¼	5	31	49	3-15—4-28	.034	3.12
1883				19.76	NW¼NE¼	5	31	49	3-15—4-28	.162	14.82
1883			8.64		SW¼NE¼	5	31	49	3-15—4-28	.070	6.48
1883				5.05	SW¼NE¼	5	31	49	3-15—4-28	.041	3.70
1883				16.64	NE¼NE¼	5	31	49	3-15—4-28	.135	12.48
1883			2.60		SE¼NE¼	5	31	49	3-15—4-28	.021	1.95
1883				22.80	SE¼NE¼	5	31	49	3-15—4-28	.186	17.10
1883	7.28				NE¼NE¼	28	32	49	3-15—9-15	.079	21.84
1883	29.60				NW¼NE¼	28	32	49	3-15—9-15	.241	88.80
1883	29.50				NE¼NW¼	28	32	49	3-15—9-15	.240	88.50
1883	1.00				NW¼NW¼	28	32	49	3-15—9-15	.008	3.00
1883	30.64				SE¼NW¼	28	32	49	3-15—9-15	.249	91.80
1883	10.50				SW¼NW¼	28	32	49	3-15—9-15	.085	31.50
1883	27.00				NE¼SW¼	28	32	49	3-15—9-15	.219	81.00
1883	24.40				NW¼SW¼	28	32	49	3-15—9-15	.198	73.20
1883	27.52				SE¼SW¼	28	32	49	3-15—9-15	.224	82.56
1883	32.72				SW¼SW¼	28	32	49	3-15—9-15	.266	98.16
1883	40.00				NW¼NW¼	33	32	49	3-15—9-15	.325	120.00
1883	9.48				NE¼NW¼	33	32	49	3-15—9-15	.077	28.44
1883	9.48				SW¼NW¼	33	32	49	3-15—9-15	.077	28.44

Source—**Humboldt** River. Ditch—**Overflow.**

Year of priority	Harvest crops	Meadow pasture	Diversified pasture		Subdivision	Section	Tp.N.	R.E.	Length of season	C.F.S.	Acre-feet
1877			19.08		NE¼NE¼	10	32	49	3-15—4-28	.155	14.31
1877			20.52		SE¼NE¼	10	32	49	3-15—4-28	.167	15.39
1877			2.00		SW¼SE¼	10	32	49	3-15—4-28	.021	1.95
1877			21.28		NE¼SE¼	10	32	49	3-15—4-28	.173	15.96
1877			4.68		NW¼SE¼	10	32	49	3-15—4-28	.038	3.51
1877			5.20		NW¼NE¼	10	32	49	3-15—4-28	.042	3.90
1877			5.20		SW¼NE¼	10	32	49	3-15—4-28	[illegible]	3.90

Source—Humboldt River. Ditch—Dwyer Dam.

	1897					31.80		NW¼NE¼	19	32	49	3-15-4-28	.259	23.85
	1897					30.72		SW¼NE¼	19	32	49	3-15-4-28	.251	23.01
	1897					24.50		NE¼NW¼	19	32	49	3-15-4-28	.199	18.38
	1897						2.50	NE¼NW¼	19	32	49	3-15-4-28	.020	1.88
	1897					17.83		SE¼NW¼	19	32	49	3-15-4-28	.155	13.37
	1897						10.16	SE¼NW¼	19	32	49	3-15-4-28	.083	7.62
	1897					1.52		SE¼SW¼	19	32	49	3-15-4-28	.012	1.14
	1897						29.84	SE¼SW¼	19	32	49	3-15-4-28	.243	22.38
	1897					7.72		NE¼SW¼	19	32	49	3-15-4-28	.063	5.79
	1897						20.28	NE¼SW¼	19	32	49	3-15-4-28	.165	15.21
	1897					21.36		SE¼SE¼	19	32	49	3-15-4-28	.174	16.02
	1897					34.40		SW¼SE¼	19	32	49	3-15-4-28	.280	25.80
	1897					26.76		NW¼SE¼	19	32	49	3-15-4-28	.218	20.07
	1897					25.54		SE¼NE¼	18	32	49	3-15-4-28	.208	19.16
	1897					39.00		NE¼SW¼	18	32	49	3-15-4-28	.317	29.25
	1897					6.96		NW¼SW¼	18	32	49	3-15-4-28	.057	5.22
	1897						19.04	NW¼SW¼	18	32	49	3-15-4-28	.155	14.28
	1897					37.00		SE¼SW¼	18	32	49	3-15-4-28	.301	27.75
	1897						39.20	SW¼SW¼	18	32	49	3-15-4-28	.319	29.40
	1897					39.00		SW¼SE¼	18	32	49	3-15-4-28	.317	29.25
	1897					12.00		SE¼SE¼	18	32	49	3-15-4-28	.098	9.00
	1897					38.00		NW¼SE¼	18	32	49	3-15-4-28	.309	28.50
	1897					27.76		NE¼SE¼	18	32	49	3-15-4-28	.226	20.82
	1897						21.20	NW¼NW¼	18	32	49	3-15-4-28	.172	15.90
	1897					39.00		NE¼NW¼	18	32	49	3-15-4-28	.317	29.25
	1897					38.12		SE¼NW¼	18	32	49	3-15-4-28	.310	28.59
	1897						12.00	SW¼NW¼	18	32	49	3-15-4-28	.098	9.00
	1897					12.90		SW¼NW¼	18	32	49	3-15-4-28	.105	9.68
	1897					38.00		NW¼NE¼	18	32	49	3-15-4-28	.309	28.50
	1897					38.65		SW¼NE¼	18	32	49	3-15-4-28	.314	28.99
	1897					12.48		NE¼NE¼	18	32	49	3-15-4-28	.102	9.36
	1897					38.75		SW¼SE¼	7	32	49	3-15-4-28	.315	29.06
	1897					26.40		SE¼SW¼	7	32	49	3-15-4-28	.215	19.80
	1897					38.26		SW¼SW¼	7	32	49	3-15-4-28	.311	28.70
	1897					24.08		NW¼SW¼	7	32	49	3-15-4-28	.196	18.06
	1897					34.54		NE¼NE¼	30	32	49	3-15-4-28	.281	25.91
	1897					32.40		NW¼NE¼	30	32	49	3-15-4-28	.263	24.30
	1897					33.70		SE¼NE¼	30	32	49	3-15-4-28	.274	25.28
	1897					19.12		SW¼NE¼	30	32	49	3-15-4-28	.155	14.34
	1897						6.84	SW¼NE¼	30	32	49	3-15-4-28	.056	5.13
	1897						40.00	SE¼NW¼	30	32	49	3-15-4-28	.325	30.00
	1897					34.72		SE¼SE¼	30	32	49	3-15-4-28	.292	26.04
	1897					30.95		NE¼SE¼	30	32	49	3-15-4-28	.252	23.21
	1897					12.46		NW¼SE¼	30	32	49	3-15-4-28	.101	9.35
	1897					6.00		SW¼SE¼	30	32	49	3-15-4-28	.049	4.50

Source—Humboldt River. Ditch—Beowawe No. 1.

	1874				40.00			NE¼NE¼	17	32	49	3-15-6-13	.325	60.00
	1874				40.00			SE¼NE¼	17	32	49	3-15-6-13	.325	60.00
	1874				40.00			SW¼NE¼	17	32	49	3-15-6-13	.325	60.00

Humboldt Land and Cattle Co.—Continued.

Year of priority	Culture—Acres: Harvest crops	Meadow pasture	Diversified pasture	Location: Subdivision	Section	Tp.N.	R.E.	Length of season	Duty of water: C.F.S.	Acre-feet
1874		40.00		NW¼NE¼	17	32	49	3-15—6-13	.325	60.00
1874		40.00		NW¼NW¼	17	32	49	3-15—6-13	.325	60.00
1874		40.00		NE¼NW¼	17	32	49	3-15—6-13	.325	60.00
1874		40.00		SE¼NW¼	17	32	49	3-15—6-13	.325	60.00
1874		40.00		SW¼NW¼	17	32	49	3-15—6-13	.325	60.00
1874		40.00		SW¼SW¼	17	32	49	3-15—6-13	.325	60.00
1874		40.00		SE¼SW¼	17	32	49	3-15—6-13	.325	60.00
1874		40.00		NW¼SW¼	17	32	49	3-15—6-13	.325	60.00
1874		40.00		NE¼SW¼	17	32	49	3-15—6-13	.325	60.00
1874		40.00		SE¼SE¼	17	32	49	3-15—6-13	.325	60.00
1874		40.00		SW¼SE¼	17	32	49	3-15—6-13	.325	60.00
1874		40.00		NE¼SE¼	17	32	49	3-15—6-13	.325	60.00
1874		40.00		NW¼SE¼	17	32	49	3-15—6-13	.325	60.00
1874			9.38	SE¼NE¼	18	32	49	3-15—4-28	.076	7.04
1874			23.00	SE¼SE¼	18	32	49	3-15—4-28	.087	17.25
1874			6.24	NE¼SE¼	18	32	49	3-15—4-28	.051	4.68
1874			23.56	NE¼NE¼	18	32	49	3-15—4-28	.192	17.67
1874		20.92		NE¼NE¼	19	32	49	3-15—6-13	.170	31.38
1874		19.48		SE¼NE¼	19	32	49	3-15—6-13	.158	29.22
1874			5.72	SE¼SE¼	19	32	49	3-15—4-28	.047	4.29
1874			18.72	NE¼SE¼	19	32	49	3-15—4-28	.152	14.04
1874	40.00			NE¼NE¼	20	32	49	3-15—9-15	.325	120.00
1874	40.00			NW¼NE¼	20	32	49	3-15—9-15	.325	120.00
1874	40.00			SE¼NE¼	20	32	49	3-15—9-15	.325	120.00
1874	40.00			SW¼NE¼	20	32	49	3-15—9-15	.325	120.00
1874	40.00			NE¼NW¼	20	32	49	3-15—9-15	.325	120.00
1874	40.00			NW¼NW¼	20	32	49	3-15—9-15	.325	120.00
1874	36.30			SE¼NW¼	20	32	19	3-15—9-15	.295	108.90
1874		3.70		SE¼NW¼	20	32	49	3-15—6-13	.030	5.55
1874	40.00			SW¼NW¼	20	32	49	3-15—9-15	.325	120.00
1874	40.00			NE¼SE¼	20	32	49	3-15—9-15	.325	120.00
1874	40.00			NW¼SE¼	20	32	49	3-15—9-15	.325	120.00
1874	40.00			SE¼SE¼	20	32	49	3-15—9-15	.325	120.00
1874	37.00			SW¼SE¼	20	32	49	3-15—9-15	.301	111.00
1874			3.00	SW¼SE¼	20	20	49	3-15—4-28	.024	2.25
1874	40.00			SW¼SW¼	20	32	49	3-15—9-15	.325	120.00
1874	36.00			SE¼SW¼	20	32	49	3-15—9-15	.293	108.00
1874			4.00	SE¼SW¼	20	32	49	3-15—4-28	.033	3.00
1874	38.30			NW¼SW¼	20	32	49	3-15—9-15	.311	114.90
1874		1.70		NW¼SW¼	20	32	49	3-15—6-13	.014	2.55
1874	40.00			NE¼SW¼	20	32	49	3-15—9-15	.325	120.00
1888		40.00		NW¼NW¼	21	32	49	3-15—6-13	.325	60.00
1888		40.00		NE¼NW¼	21	32	49	3-15—6-13	.325	60.00
1888		40.00		SE¼NW¼	21	32	49	3-15—6-13	.325	60.00
1888		40.00		SW¼NW¼	21	32	49	3-15—6-13	.325	60.00
1888	40.00			SW¼SW¼	21	32	49	3-15—9-15	.325	120.00
1888	40.00			SE¼SW¼	[illegible]	[illegible]	49	3-15—9-15	.325	120.00

	1888				40.00			NE¼SW¼	21	32	49	3-15—6-13	.325	60.00
	1888			40.00				NW¼SW¼	21	32	49	3-15—0-15	.325	120.00
	1838			40.00				SW¼SE¼	21	32	49	3-15—9-15	.325	120.00
	1888				40.00			NW¼SE¼	21	32	49	3-15—6-13	.325	60.00
	1888				40.00			SW¼NE¼	21	32	49	3-15—6-13	.325	60.00
	1874			10.50				NE¼NW¼	28	32	49	3-15—9-15	.085	31.50
	1874			12.23				NW¼NW¼	28	32	49	3-15—9-15	.099	36.69
	1874				26.77			NW¼NW¼	28	32	49	3-15—6-13	.218	40.16
	1874			23.78				SW¼NW¼	28	32	49	3-15—9-15	.193	71.34
	1874				5.72			SW¼NW¼	28	32	49	3-15—6-13	.047	8.58
	1874			15.60				NW¼SW¼	28	32	49	3-15—9-15	.127	46.80
	1874			7.28				SW¼SW¼	28	32	49	3-15—9-15	.059	21.84
	1874				40.00			NE¼NE¼	29	32	49	3-15—6-13	.325	60.00
	1874				40.00			NW¼NE¼	29	32	49	3-15—6-13	.325	60.00
	1874				40.00			SE¼NE¼	29	32	49	3-15—6-13	.325	60.00
	1874				40.00			SW¼NE¼	29	32	49	3-15—6-13	.325	60.00
	1874				40.00			NE¼NW¼	29	32	49	3-15—6-13	.325	60.00
	1874				40.00			NW¼NW¼	29	32	49	3-15—6-13	.325	60.00
	1874				40.00			SE¼NW¼	29	32	49	3-15—6-13	.325	60.00
	1874				40.00			SW¼NW¼	29	32	49	3-15—6-13	.325	60.00
	1874				40.00			SE¼SW¼	29	32	49	3-15—6-13	.325	60.00
	1874				39.75			SW¼SW¼	29	32	49	3-15—6-13	.323	59.63
	1874				40.00			NE¼SW¼	29	32	49	3-15—6-13	.325	60.00
	1874				40.00			NW¼SW¼	29	32	49	3-15—6-13	.325	60.00
	1874				40.00			SE¼SE¼	29	32	49	3-15—6-13	.325	60.00
	1874				40.00			SW¼SE¼	29	32	49	3-15—6-13	.325	60.00
	1874				40.00			NE¼SE¼	29	32	49	3-15—6-13	.325	60.00
	1874				40.00			NW¼SE¼	29	32	49	3-15—6-13	.325	60.00
	1874			15.12				NE¼SW¼	32	32	49	3-15—9-15	.123	45.36
	1874				9.88			NE¼SW¼	32	32	49	3-15—6-13	.080	14.82
	1874					12.75		NE¼SW¼	32	32	49	3-15—4-28	.104	9.56
	1874			8.68				SE¼SW¼	32	32	49	3-15—9-15	.071	26.04
	1874					14.72		SE¼SW¼	32	32	49	3-15—4-28	.120	11.04
	1874						6.24	SE¼SW¼	32	32	49	3-15—4-28	.051	4.68
	1874					2.60		SW¼SW¼	32	32	49	3-15—4-28	.021	1.95
	1874						34.80	SW¼SW¼	32	32	49	3-15—4-28	.283	26.10
	1874						36.47	NW¼SW¼	32	32	49	3-15—4-28	.297	27.35
	1874				27.52			NW¼SE¼	32	32	49	3-15—6-13	.225	41.28
	1874				10.40			NE¼SE¼	32	32	49	3-15—6-13	.085	15.60
	1874				40.00			NW¼NW¼	32	32	49	3-15—6-13	.325	60.00
	1874				40.00			NE¼NW¼	32	32	49	3-15—6-13	.325	60.00
	1874				40.00			SE¼NW¼	32	32	49	3-15—6-13	.325	60.00
	1874				40.00			SW¼NW¼	32	32	49	3-15—6-13	.325	60.00
	1874				40.00			NW¼NE¼	32	32	49	3-15—6-13	.325	60.00
	1874				40.00			NE¼NE¼	32	32	49	3-15—6-13	.325	60.00
	1874				40.00			SE¼NE¼	32	32	49	3-15—6-13	.325	60.00
	1874				40.00			SW¼NE¼	32	32	49	3-15—6-13	.325	60.00

Source—**Humboldt River.** Ditch—**Merchant Canal.**

	1898						31.40	NW¼NW¼	8	32	49	3-15—4-28	.255	23.55
	1898						40.00	SW¼NW¼	8	32	49	3-15—4-28	.325	30.00
	1898						40.00	SE¼NW¼	8	32	49	3-15—4-28	.325	30.00

Humboldt Land and Cattle Co.—Continued.

Year of priority	Culture—Acres: Harvest crops	Meadow pasture	Diversified pasture		Location: Subdivision	Section	Tp.N.	R.E.	Length of season	Duty of water: C.F.S.	Acre-feet
1898	....			40.00	SW¼NE¼	8	32	49	3-15—4-28	.325	30.00
1898	....			40.00	SW¼SW¼	8	32	49	3-15—4-28	.325	30.00
1898	....			40.00	SE¼SW¼	8	32	49	3-15—4-28	.325	30.00
1898	....			40.00	NE¼SW¼	8	32	49	3-15—4-28	.325	30.00
1898	....			40.00	NW¼SW¼	8	32	49	3-15—4-28	.325	30.00
1898	....			40.00	SW¼SE¼	8	32	49	3-15—4-28	.325	30.00
1898	....	*40.00			SE¼SE¼	8	32	49	3-15—6-13	.325	60.00
1898	....			40.00	NE¼NE¼	7	32	49	3-15—4-28	.325	30.00
1898	....			40.00	SE¼NE¼	7	32	49	3-15—4-28	.325	30.00
1898	....			35.62	SW¼NE¼	7	32	49	3-15—4-28	.200	26.72
1898	....			40.00	NE¼SE¼	7	32	49	3-15—4-28	.325	30.00
1898	....		13.08		NW¼SE¼	7	32	49	3-15—4-28	.106	9.81
Source—Humboldt River. Ditch—Beowawe No. 2.											
1897	*40.00				NE¼NE¼	1	31	48	3-15—9-15	.325	120.00
1897	*40.00				NW¼NE¼	1	31	48	3-15—9-15	.325	120.00
1889	*40.00				SE¼NE¼	1	31	48	3-15—9-15	.325	120.00
1897	*40.00				SW¼NE¼	1	31	48	3-15—9-15	.325	120.00
1897	*40.05				NE¼NW¼	1	31	48	3-15—9-15	.325	120.15
1897	*40.00				SE¼NW¼	1	31	48	3-15—9-15	.325	120.00
1897	*2.70				NW¼NW¼	1	31	48	3-15—9-15	.022	8.10
1897	....			37.32	NW¼NW¼	1	31	48	3-15—4-28	.303	27.99
1897	*2.08				SW¼NW¼	1	31	48	3-15—9-15	.017	6.24
1897	....			37.92	SW¼NW¼	1	31	48	3-15—4-28	.308	28.44
1897	*38.96				NE¼SW¼	1	31	48	3-15—9-15	.317	116.88
1897	....			1.04	NE¼SW¼	1	31	48	3-15—4-28	.008	.78
1897	*2.08				NW¼SW¼	1	31	48	3-15—9-15	.017	6.24
1897	....			37.92	NW¼SW¼	1	31	48	3-15—4-28	.308	28.44
1897	....			40.00	SW¼SW¼	1	31	48	3-15—4-28	.325	30.00
1897	*15.67				SE¼SW¼	1	31	48	3-15—9-15	.127	47.01
1897	....			18.20	SE¼SW¼	1	31	48	3-15—4-28	.148	13.65
1883	*17.57				NE¼SE¼	1	31	48	3-15—9-15	.143	52.71
1883	*39.50				NW¼SE¼	1	31	48	3-15—9-15	.321	118.50
1883	*10.40				SW¼SE¼	1	31	48	3-15—9-15	.085	31.20
1886	....	15.80			NE¼NE¼	26	32	48	3-15—6-13	.128	23.70
1886	....		24.20		NE¼NE¼	26	32	48	3-15—4-28	.197	18.15
1886	*6.76				SE¼NE¼	26	32	48	3-15—9-15	.055	20.28
1886	....	22.84			SE¼NE¼	26	32	48	3-15—6-13	.186	34.26
1886	....		10.40		SE¼NE¼	26	32	48	3-15—4-28	.085	7.80
1886	....	17.68			SW¼NE¼	26	32	48	3-15—6-13	.144	26.52
1886	....			22.32	SW¼NE¼	26	32	48	3-15—4-28	.181	16.74
1866	*25.48				NE¼SE¼	26	32	48	3-15—9-15	.207	76.44
1886	....	14.52			NE¼SE¼	26	32	48	3-15—6-13	.118	21.78
1886	....		40.00		NW¼SE¼	26	32	48	3-15—4-28	.325	30.00
1886	*4.36				SE¼SE¼	26	32	48	3-15—9-15	.035	13.08
1886	....		35.34		SE¼SE¼	26	32	48	3-15—4-28	.287	26.51

	1874						24.96	SW¼SE¼	26	32	48	3-15—4-28	.203	18.72
	1874						40.00	SE¼SE¼	13	32	48	3-15—4-28	.325	30.00
	1874						39.30	NE¼SE¼	13	32	48	3-15—4-28	.320	29.48
	1874						39.15	NW¼SE¼	13	32	48	3-15—4-28	.318	29.36
	1874						39.00	SW¼SE¼	13	32	48	3-15—4-28	.317	29.25
	1874						11.41	SW¼NE¼	13	32	48	3-15—4-28	.093	8.58
	1874						38.70	SE¼NE¼	13	32	48	3-15—4-28	.314	29.03
	1874						38.10	NE¼NE¼	13	32	48	3-15—4-28	.310	28.58
	1874						*11.70	NE¼SW¼	13	32	48	3-15—4-28	.095	8.78
	1874						13.20	SE¼SW¼	13	32	48	3-15—4-28	.107	9.90
	1886						6.24	NE¼NW¼	35	32	48	3-15—4-28	.051	4.68
	1886						40.00	NW¼NE¼	35	32	48	3-15—4-28	.325	30.00
	1886						40.00	NW¼NW¼	35	32	48	3-15—4-28	.325	30.00
	1886						34.49	SW¼NE¼	35	32	48	3-15—4-28	.280	25.87
	1886						40.00	SE¼NE¼	35	32	48	3-15—4-28	.325	30.00
	1886						40.00	NE¼SE¼	35	32	48	3-15—4-28	.325	30.00
	1886						40.00	NW¼SE¼	35	32	48	3-15—4-28	.325	30.00
	1886						40.00	SE¼SE¼	35	32	48	3-15—4-28	.325	30.00
	1886						40.00	SW¼SE¼	35	32	48	3-15—4-28	.325	30.00
	1880						40.00	SW¼SW¼	24	32	48	3-15—4-28	.325	30.00
	1880					12.52		SE¼SW¼	24	32	48	3-15—4-28	.102	9.39
	1880						26.48	SE¼SW¼	24	32	48	3-15—4-28	.215	19.86
	1880						40.00	NW¼SW¼	24	32	48	3-15—4-28	.325	30.00
	1880					7.84		NE¼SW¼	24	32	48	3-15—4-28	.064	5.88
	1880						31.60	NE¼SW¼	24	32	48	3-15—4-28	.256	23.70
	1880					8.32		SE¼NW¼	24	32	48	3-15—4-28	.068	6.24
	1880						31.18	SE¼NW¼	24	32	48	3-15—4-28	.253	23.39
	1880					8.32		NE¼NW¼	24	32	48	3-15—4-28	.068	6.24
	1880						35.24	NE¼NW¼	24	32	48	3-15—4-28	.286	26.43
	1880						38.26	NE¼NE¼	24	32	48	3-15—4-28	.311	28.70
	1880						38.30	SE¼NE¼	24	32	48	3-15—4-28	.311	28.73
	1880					39.25		NW¼NE¼	24	32	48	3-15—4-28	.319	29.44
	1880					39.30		SW¼NE¼	24	32	48	3-15—4-28	.320	29.48
	1880					39.40		NW¼SE¼	24	32	48	3-15—4-28	.320	29.55
	1880					38.20		SW¼SE¼	24	32	48	3-15—4-28	.311	28.65
	1880						40.00	SE¼SE¼	24	32	48	3-15—4-28	.325	30.00
	1880						39.40	NE¼SE¼	24	32	48	3-15—4-28	.320	29.55
	1880						15.30	SE¼SE¼	23	32	48	3-15—4-28	.124	11.48
	1880					38.60		NW¼NE¼	25	32	48	3-15—4-28	.314	28.95
	1880				38.70			SW¼NE¼	25	32	48	3-15—6-13	.315	58.05
	1880				1.04			NW¼NW¼	25	32	48	3-15—6-13	.008	1.56
	1880						38.96	NW¼NW¼	25	32	48	3-15—4-28	.317	29.22
	1880				30.64			NE¼NW¼	25	32	48	3-15—6-13	.249	45.96
	1880						9.36	NE¼NW¼	25	32	48	3-15—4-28	.076	7.02
	1880				22.22			SW¼NW¼	25	32	48	3-15—6-13	.181	33.33
	1880						17.78	SW¼NW¼	25	32	48	3-15—4-28	.145	13.34
	1880				40.00			SE¼NW¼	25	32	48	3-15—6-13	.325	60.00
	1880				38.44			NW¼SW¼	25	32	48	3-15—6-13	.313	57.66
	1880				40.00			NE¼SW¼	25	32	48	3-15—6-13	.325	60.00
	1880				38.48			SW¼SW¼	25	32	48	3-15—6-13	.313	57.72
	1880						1.52	SW¼SW¼	25	32	48	3-15—4-28	.012	1.14
	1880				38.60			SE¼SW¼	25	32	48	3-15—6-13	.314	57.90

*Was Class C—1874.

Humboldt Land and Cattle Co.—Continued.

Year of priority	Culture—Acres: Harvest crops	Culture—Acres: Meadow pasture	Culture—Acres: Diversified	Culture—Acres: pasture	Location: Subdivision	Location: Section	Location: Tp.N.	Location: R.E.	Length of season	Duty of water: C.F.S.	Duty of water: Acre-feet
1880	....	40.00	....	....	SW¼SE¼	25	32	48	3-15—6-13	.325	60.00
1880	....	38.70	....	....	NW¼SE¼	25	32	48	3-15—6-13	.315	58.05
1880	....	40.00	....	....	SE¼SE¼	25	32	48	3-15—6-13	.325	60.00
1880	....	5.72	....	....	NE¼SE¼	25	32	48	3-15—6-13	.047	8.58
1889	....	....	34.28	....	NE¼SE¼	25	32	48	3-15—4-28	.279	25.71
1880	....	....	40.00	....	SE¼NE¼	25	32	48	3-15—4-28	.325	30.00
1880	....	....	40.00	....	NE¼NE¼	25	32	48	3-15—4-28	.325	30.00
1874	....	....	....	38.18	SW¼NW¼	19	32	49	3-15—4-28	.310	28.64
1874	....	....	....	38.26	NW¼NW¼	19	32	49	3-15—4-28	.311	27.70
1874	....	....	....	38.03	SW¼SW¼	19	32	49	3-15—4-28	.309	28.52
1874	....	....	....	38.11	NW¼SW¼	19	32	49	3-15—4-28	.310	28.58
1874	....	....	....	38.04	NW¼NW¼	30	32	49	3-15—4-28	.309	28.53
1874	....	....	....	38.40	NE¼NW¼	30	32	49	3-15—4-28	.312	28.80
1874	....	....	....	38.15	SW¼NW¼	30	32	49	3-15—4-28	.310	28.61
1874	....	....	....	22.00	SW¼SE¼	30	32	49	3-15—4-28	.179	16.50
1874	....	....	....	38.31	SW¼SW¼	30	32	49	3-15—4-28	.311	28.73
1874	....	....	....	40.00	SE¼SW¼	30	32	49	3-15—4-28	.325	30.00
1874	....	....	....	40.00	NE¼SW¼	30	32	49	3-15—4-28	.325	30.00
1874	....	....	....	38.72	NW¼SW¼	30	32	49	3-15—4-28	.315	29.04
1874	....	....	....	15.45	NW¼SE¼	30	32	49	3-15—4-28	.126	11.59
1880	....	38.34	....	....	NW¼NW¼	31	32	49	3-15—6-13	.312	57.51
1880	....	9.36	....	....	NE¼NW¼	31	32	49	3-15—6-13	.076	14.04
1880	....	....	....	30.64	NE¼NW¼	31	32	49	3-15—4-28	.249	22.98
1882	....	38.30	....	....	SW¼NW¼	31	32	49	3-15—6-13	.311	57.45
1883	....	36.30	....	....	SE¼NW¼	31	32	49	3 15—6-13	.295	54.45
1883	....	....	....	2.70	SE¼NW¼	31	32	49	3-15—4-28	.022	2.03
1874	....	....	....	33.56	NW¼NE¼	31	32	49	3-15—4-28	.273	25.17
1874	....	....	....	40.00	SW¼NE¼	31	32	49	3-15—4-28	.325	30.00
1883	....	....	*37.60	....	NE¼NE¼	31	32	49	3-15—4-28	.306	28.20
1883	....	....	*25.50	....	SE¼NE¼	31	32	49	3-15—4-28	.207	19.13
1885	....	*6.13	....	....	SE¼SE¼	31	32	49	3-15—6-13	.050	9.20
1885	....	....	*2.60	....	SE¼SE¼	31	32	49	3 15—4-28	.021	1.95
1874	37.53	....	....	....	SW¼SE¼	31	32	49	3-15—9-15	.305	112.59
1874	....	*2.47	....	....	SW¼SE¼	31	32	40	3-15—6-13	.020	3.71
1874	37.60	....	....	....	SE¼SW¼	31	32	49	3 15—9-15	.306	112.80
1874	37.60	....	....	....	SW¼SW¼	31	32	49	3-15—9-15	.306	112.80
1874	....	....	....	31.70	NW¼SE¼	31	32	49	3-15—4-28	.258	23.78
1886	*17.47	....	....	....	SE¼NW¼	36	32	48	3-15—9-15	.142	52.41
1886	....	*0.50	....	....	SE¼NW¼	36	32	48	3 15—6-13	.004	.75
1886	..	....	....	*22.53	SE¼NW¼	36	32	48	3 15—4 28	.183	16.90
1871	..	*40.00	....	....	NE¼NW¼	36	32	48	3 15—6 13	.325	60.00
1871	..	....	*14.56	....	NW¼NW¼	36	32	48	3 15—4 28	.128	10.92
1871		....	....	*25.44	SW¼NW¼	36	32	48	3 15—4 28	.207	19.08
1874	1.45	....	....		NW¼SW¼	36	32	48	3 15—9 15	.012	4.35
1871				38.55	NW¼SW¼	36	32	48	3 15—4 28	[illegible]	28.91
1871	[illegible]				SW¼SW¼	36	32	48	3 15—9 15	[illegible]	11.07

1874				36.36	SW¼SW¼	36	32	48	3-15—1-28	.206	27.27
1874	40.00				NE¼SW¼	36	32	48	3-15—9-15	.325	120.00
1880	*40.00				SE¼SW¼	36	32	48	3-15—9-15	.325	120.00
1874	40.00				NE¼SE¼	36	32	48	3-15—9-15	.325	120.00
1874	40.00				SE¼SE¼	36	32	48	3-15—9-15	.325	120.00
1874	40.00				NW¼SE¼	36	32	48	3-15—9-15	.325	120.00
1874	40.00				SW¼SE¼	36	32	48	3-15—9-15	.325	120.00
1882		*22.76			NE¼NE¼	36	32	48	3-15—6-13	.185	34.14
1882				*17.06	NE¼NE¼	36	32	48	3-15—4-28	.139	12.80
1874		40.00			SE¼NE¼	36	32	48	3-15—6-13	.325	60.00
1883		*40.00			NW¼NE¼	36	32	48	3-15—6-13	.325	60.00
1884		*34.28			SW¼NE¼	36	32	48	3-15—6-13	.289	51.42
1884				*5.72	SW¼NE¼	36	32	48	3-15—4-28	.047	4.29
1886				*39.50	SW¼NW¼	36	32	48	3-15—4-28	.321	29.63
1874			18.20		NE¼SE¼	31	32	49	3-15—4-28	.148	13.65
1874	40.00				NE¼SW¼	31	32	49	3-15—9-15	.325	120.00
1874	38.76				NW¼SW¼	31	32	49	3-15—9-15	.315	116.28

*Was Class C—1874.

Claimant—**Sam Broyles.** Proof No. 00155

Source—**Humboldt River.** Ditch—**Altenberg Ditch.**

1875	3.30				SE¼SW¼	16	32	45	3-15—9-15	.027	9.90
1875		3.55			SE¼SW¼	16	32	45	3-15—6-13	.020	5.33
1875	1.67				NW¼SW¼	16	32	45	3-15—9-15	.014	5.01
1875		19.03			NW¼SW¼	16	32	45	3-15—6-13	.155	28.95
1875			.15		NW¼SW¼	16	32	45	3-15—4-28	.001	.11
1875	15.47				NE¼SW¼	16	32	45	3-15—9-15	.126	46.41
1875		8.84			NE¼SW¼	16	32	45	3-15—6-13	.072	13.26
1875			.65		NE¼SW¼	16	32	45	3-15—4-28	.005	.49

Source—**Humboldt River.** Ditch—**McIntyre Starrett.**

1883	30.47				NE¼SE¼	16	32	45	3-15—9-15	.248	91.41
1883			1.60		NE¼SE¼	16	32	45	3-15—4-28	.013	1.20
1883	32.70				NW¼SE¼	16	32	45	3-15—9-15	.266	98.10
1883			3.01		NW¼SE¼	16	32	45	3-15—4-28	.024	2.26
1883	9.25				SE¼SE¼	16	32	45	3-15—9-15	.075	27.75
1883		28.37			SE¼SE¼	16	32	45	3-15—6-13	.231	42.56
1883			.30		SE¼SE¼	16	32	45	3-15—4-28	.002	.23
1883	2.17				SW¼SE¼	16	32	45	3-15—9-15	.018	6.51
1883		18.90			SW¼SE¼	16	32	45	3-15—6-13	.154	28.35
1883		16.45			SW¼SW¼	16	32	45	3-15—6-13	.134	24.68
1883	7.80				NE¼SW¼	16	32	45	3-15—9-15	.063	23.40

Claimant—**Golconda Cattle Co.** Proof No. 00156

Source—**Humboldt River.** Ditch—***Aemes Dam.**

Year of priority	Culture—Acres: Harvest crops	Meadow pasture	Diversified pasture		Location: Subdivision	Section	Tp.N.	R.E.	Length of season	Duty of water: C.F.S.	Acre-feet
1876				40.44	NW¼NE¼	30	35	43	3-15—4-28	.329	30.33
1876			30.61		NE¼NE¼	30	35	43	3-15—4-28	.249	22.96
1876				9.78	NE¼NE¼	30	35	42	3-15—4-28	.080	7.34
1886			11.60		SE¼NE¼	30	35	43	3-15—4-28	.094	8.70
1886				29.48	SE¼NE¼	30	35	43	3-15—4-28	.240	22.11
1876	5.00				SW¼NE¼	30	35	43	3-15—9-15	.046	16.80
1876			9.43		SW¼NE¼	30	35	43	3-15—4-28	.077	7.07
1886			8.64		NE¼SE¼	30	35	43	3-15—4-28	.070	6.48
1886				31.88	NE¼SE¼	30	35	43	3-15—4-28	.259	23.91
1886	13.76				NW¼SE¼	30	35	43	3-15—9-15	.112	41.28
1886		17.56			NW¼SE¼	30	35	43	3-15—6-13	.143	26.34
1886			4.20		NW¼SE¼	30	35	43	3-15—4-28	.034	3.15
1886			13.48		SE¼SE¼	30	35	43	3-15—4-28	.110	10.11
1886				17.40	SE¼SE¼	30	35	43	3-15—4-28	.141	13.05
1886	11.50				SW¼SE¼	30	35	43	3-15—9-15	.093	34.50
1886		22.32			SW¼SE¼	30	35	43	3-15—6-13	.181	33.48
1886			1.92		SW¼SE¼	30	35	43	3-15—4-28	.016	1.24
1884	29.52				NE¼SW¼	30	35	43	3-15—9-15	.240	88.59
1884			3.52		NE¼SW¼	30	35	43	3-15—4-28	.029	2.64

Source—**Humboldt River.** Ditch—***Aemes Dam.** (Lands of Duviver.)

Year of priority	Harvest crops	Meadow pasture	Diversified pasture		Subdivision	Section	Tp.N.	R.E.	Length of season	C.F.S.	Acre-feet
1884				.48	NE¼SW¼	30	35	43	3-15—4-28	.004	.36
1884	29.68				NW¼SW¼	30	35	43	3-15—9-15	.241	89.04
1884			2.80		NW¼SW¼	30	35	43	3-15—4-28	.023	2.10
1884	30.56				SW¼SW¼	30	35	43	3-15—9-15	.248	91.68
1884		3.88			SW¼SW¼	30	35	43	3-15—6-13	.032	5.82
1884	28.16				SE¼SW¼	30	35	43	3-15—9-15	.229	84.48
1884		4.88			SE¼SW¼	30	35	43	3-15—6-13	.040	7.32
1884			.84		SE¼SW¼	30	35	43	3-15—4-28	.007	.62

*Was Class C—1876.

Source—**Humboldt River.** Ditch—**Henderson.** (Lands of Duvivier.)

Year of priority	Harvest crops	Meadow pasture	Diversified pasture		Subdivision	Section	Tp.N.	R.E.	Length of season	C.F.S.	Acre-feet
1887	6.62				NW¼NE¼	36	35	42	3-15—9-15	.054	19.86
1887			32.90		NW¼NE¼	36	35	42	3-15—4-28	.267	24.68
1887	16.23				NE¼NE¼	36	35	42	3-15—9-15	.132	48.69
1887		7.56			NE¼NE¼	36	35	42	3-15—6-13	.061	11.34
1887			16.09		NE¼NE¼	36	35	42	3-15—4-28	.131	12.07
1894	21.33				NE¼SW¼	14	35	42	3-15—9-15	.174	61.08
1894		18.40			NE¼SW¼	14	35	42	3-15—6-13	.150	27.60
1894		41.20			NE¼SW¼	14	35	42	3-15—6-13	.335	61.80
1894		40.16			SE¼SW¼	14	35	42	3-15—6-13	.327	60.24
1894		41.20			NW¼SW¼	14	35	42	3-15—6-13	.335	61.80

Source—**Humboldt River.** Ditch—**Outside Slough.** (Lands of Duvivier.)

1887			3.96				SW¼NE¼	36	35	42	3-15—9-15	.032	11.88
1887					35.72		SW¼NE¼	36	35	42	3-15—4-28	.200	26.79
1887			34.11				SE¼NE¼	36	35	42	3-15—9-15	.277	102.33
1887				2.64			SE¼NE¼	36	35	42	3-15—6-13	.021	3.96
1887					2.37		SE¼NE¼	36	35	42	3-15—4-28	.019	1.78
1894				40.96			SW¼SW¼	14	35	42	3-15—6-13	.333	61.44

Claimant—**Ellison Ranching Co.** Proof No. 00156

Source—**Humboldt River.** Ditch—**Outside Slough Ditch.** (Humboldt River lands.)

1887						40.60	SW¼SW¼	15	35	42	3-15—4-28	.330	30.45
1887						38.60	NW¼SW¼	15	35	42	3-15—4-28	.314	28.95
1887						35.60	SE¼SW¼	15	35	42	3-15—4-28	.289	26.70
1887						34.72	NE¼SW¼	15	35	42	3-15—4-28	.282	26.05
1887						33.44	SW¼NW¼	15	35	42	3-15—4-28	.272	25.08
1887			14.72				SE¼NW¼	15	35	42	3-15—9-15	.120	44.16
1887					24.64		SE¼NW¼	15	35	42	3-15—4-28	.200	18.48
1887						36.88	SW¼SE¼	15	35	42	3-15—4-28	.300	27.66
1887						39.44	SE¼SE¼	15	35	42	3-15—4-28	.321	29.58
1887						40.08	NE¼SE¼	15	35	42	3-15—4-28	.326	30.06
1887			9.28				NW¼SE¼	15	35	42	3-15—9-15	.075	27.84
1887					29.92		NW¼SE¼	15	35	42	3-15—4-28	.243	22.44
1887						40.24	SE¼SE¼	22	35	42	3-15—4-28	.327	30.18
1887						39.88	SW¼SE¼	22	35	42	3-15—4-28	.324	29.91
1887						39.84	NW¼SE¼	22	75	42	3-15—4-28	.324	29.88
1887						37.28	NE¼SE¼	22	35	42	3-15—4-28	.303	27.96
1887						40.12	NE¼SW¼	22	35	42	3-15—4-28	.326	30.09
1887						39.68	SE¼SW¼	22	35	42	3-15—4-28	.323	29.76
1887						38.60	SW¼NW¼	22	35	42	3-15—4-28	.314	28.95
1887						40.12	SE¼NW¼	22	35	42	3-15—4-28	.326	30.09
1887						40.08	NE¼NW¼	22	35	42	3-15—4-28	.326	30.06
1887						40.00	NW¼NW¼	22	35	42	3-15—4-28	.325	30.00
1887						39.88	SW¼NE¼	22	35	42	3-15—4-28	.324	29.91
1887						31.88	NW¼NE¼	22	35	42	3-15—4-28	.259	23.91
1887						39.00	NE¼NE¼	22	35	42	3-15—4-28	.317	29.25
1887						32.40	SE¼NE¼	22	35	42	3-15—4-28	.263	24.30
1887						41.12	NW¼NW¼	26	35	42	3-15—4-28	.334	30.84
1887			.96				NE¼NW¼	26	35	42	3-15—9-15	.008	2.88
1887					25.24		NE¼NW¼	26	35	42	3-15—4-28	.205	18.93
1887						39.48	SE¼NW¼	26	35	42	3-15—4-28	.321	29.61
1887						41.80	SW¼NW¼	26	35	42	3-15—4-28	.340	31.65
1887						40.80	NW¼NE¼	26	35	42	3-15—4-28	.331	30.60
1887						32.56	SW¼NE¼	26	35	42	3-15—4-28	.265	24.42
1887						41.28	SE¼NE¼	26	35	42	3-15—4-28	.336	30.96
1887						39.84	NW¼SW¼	26	35	42	3-15—4-28	.324	29.88
1887						40.60	NE¼SW¼	26	35	42	3-15—4-28	.330	30.45
1887						38.48	SW¼SW¼	26	35	42	3-15—4-28	.313	28.86
1887						40.64	SE¼SW¼	26	35	42	3-15—4-28	.330	30.48
1887					36.80		NW¼SE¼	26	35	42	3-15—4-28	.299	27.60
1887						35.92	NE¼SE¼	26	35	42	3-15—4-28	.292	26.90
1887					40.16		SW¼SE¼	26	35	42	3-15—4-28	.327	30.12
1887					23.08		SE¼SE¼	26	35	42	3-15—4-28	.188	17.31

Ellison Ranching Co.—Continued.

Year of priority	Culture—Acres: Harvest crops	Meadow pasture	Diversified	pasture	Location: Subdivision	Section	Tp. N.	R. E.	Length of season	Duty of water: C. F. S.	Acre-feet
1887				8.96	SE¼SE¼	26	35	42	3-15—4-28	.073	6.72
1887				40.36	NE¼NE¼	27	35	42	3-15—4-28	.328	30.27
1887			39.84		NW¼NW¼	23	35	42	3-15—4-28	.324	29.88
1887			39.80		SW¼NW¼	23	35	42	3-15—4-28	.324	29.85
1887	11.12				NW¼SW¼	23	35	42	3-15—9-15	.090	33.36
1887			20.56		NW¼SW¼	23	35	42	3-15—4-28	.167	15.42
1887				3.24	NW¼SW¼	23	35	42	3-15—4-28	.026	2.43
1887	.32				SW¼SW¼	23	35	42	3-15—9-15	.003	.96
1887			3.76		SW¼SW¼	23	35	42	3-15—4-28	.031	2.82
1887				25.28	SW¼SW¼	23	35	42	3-15—4-28	.206	18.96
1887	13.12				NE¼SW¼	23	35	42	3-15—9-15	.107	39.36
1887			27.20		NE¼SW¼	23	35	42	3-15—4-28	.221	20.40
1887	18.68				SE¼SW¼	23	35	42	3-15—9-15	.152	56.04
1887			17.88		SE¼SW¼	23	35	42	3-15—4-28	.145	13.41
1887				36.88	NE¼NW¼	9	35	42	3-15—4-28	.300	27.66
1887				10.72	SE¼NW¼	9	35	42	3-15—4-28	.087	8.04
1887				37.84	NW¼NE¼	9	35	42	3-15—4-28	.308	29.38
1887			37.80		NE¼NE¼	9	35	42	3-15—4-28	.307	28.35
1887			37.84		SE¼NE¼	9	35	42	3-15—4-28	.308	28.38
1887				19.34	NW¼SE¼	9	35	42	3-15—4-28	.157	14.51
1887			30.48		SE¼SE¼	9	35	42	3-15—4-28	.248	22.86

Source—**Humboldt River.** Ditch—**Aemes Dam.** (Humboldt River lands.)

Year of priority	Harvest crops	Meadow pasture	Diversified	pasture	Subdivision	Section	Tp. N.	R. E.	Length of season	C. F. S.	Acre-feet
1876			40.08		NW¼NW¼	25	35	42	3-15—4-28	.326	30.06
1876	18.20				NE¼NW¼	25	35	42	3-15—9-15	.147	54.60
1876		.36			NE¼NW¼	25	35	42	3-15—6-13	.003	.54
1876			20.48		NE¼NW¼	25	35	42	3-15—4-28	.167	15.36
1876			40.24		SW¼NW¼	25	35	42	3-15—4-28	.327	30.18
1876	5.80				SE¼NW¼	25	35	42	3-15—9-15	.047	17.40
1876		2.28			SE¼NW¼	25	35	42	3-15—6-13	.019	3.42
1876			31.08		SE¼NW¼	25	35	42	3-15—4-28	.253	23.31
1876	21.32				NW¼NW¼	30	35	43	3-15—9-15	.173	63.96
1876			6.16		NW¼NW¼	30	35	43	3-15—4-28	.050	4.62
1876				.86	NW¼NW¼	30	35	43	3-15—4-28	.007	.65
1876	20.28				SW¼NW¼	30	35	43	3-15—9-15	.165	60.84
1876			4.24		SW¼NW¼	30	35	43	3-15—4-28	.034	3.18
1876				7.60	SW¼NW¼	30	35	43	3-15—4-28	.062	5.70
1876	18.00				SE¼NW¼	30	35	43	3-15—9-15	.146	54.00
1876			11.52		SE¼NW¼	30	35	43	3-15—4-28	.094	8.64
1876				2.52	SE¼NW¼	30	35	43	3-15—4-28	.020	1.89
1876	14.32				NE¼NW¼	30	35	43	3-15—9-15	.116	42.96
1876			22.92		NE¼NW¼	30	35	43	3-15—4-28	.186	17.19
1876			6.40		SW¼NE¼	19	35	43	3-15—4-28	.052	4.80
1876				10.36	SW¼NE¼	19	35	43	3-15—4-28	.084	7.77
1876	20.72				NW¼SE¼	19	35	43	3-15—9-15	.100	62.10
1876				9.28	NW¼SE¼	19	35	43	3-15—4-28	.075	6.90

	1876			25.36				SW¼SE¼	19	35	43	3-15-9-15	.206	76.08
	1876						8.29	SW¼SE¼	19	35	43	3-15-4-28	.007	6.22
	1876				27.04			NW¼NW¼	19	35	43	3-15-6-13	.220	40.56
	1876						7.21	NW¼NW¼	19	35	43	3-15-4-28	.050	5.43
	1876				18.21			NE¼NW¼	19	35	43	3-15-6-13	.148	27.36
	1876						21.52	NE¼NW¼	19	35	43	3-15-4-28	.175	16.11
	1876			38.80				NW¼NE¼	24	35	42	3-15-9-15	.315	116.40
	1876			23.84				NE¼NE¼	24	35	42	3-15-9-15	.194	71.52
	1876					10.88		NE¼NE¼	24	35	42	3-15-4-28	.088	8.16
	1876			40.08				SW¼NE¼	24	35	42	3-15-9-15	.326	120.24
	1876			26.44				SE¼NE¼	24	35	42	3-15-9-15	.215	79.32
	1876					3.68		SE¼NE¼	24	35	42	3-15-4-28	.030	2.76
	1876			23.56				NW¼SE¼	24	35	42	3-15-9-15	.192	70.68
	1876					16.56		NW¼SE¼	24	35	42	3-15-4-28	.135	12.42
	1876			40.24				NE¼SE¼	24	35	42	3-15-9-15	.327	120.72
	1876			12.76				SW¼SE¼	24	35	42	3-15-9-15	.104	38.28
	1876					24.76		SW¼SE¼	24	35	42	3-15-4-28	.201	18.57
	1876			39.98				SE¼SE¼	24	35	42	3-15-9-15	.325	119.34
	1876			39.59				NE¼NW¼	24	35	42	3-15-9-15	.322	118.77
	1876			13.12				NW¼NW¼	24	35	42	3-15-9-15	.107	39.36
	1876					25.60		NW¼NW¼	24	35	42	3-15-4-28	.208	19.20
	1876			.48				SW¼NW¼	24	35	42	3-15-9-15	.004	1.44
	1876					35.76		SW¼NW¼	24	35	42	3-15-4-28	.291	26.82
	1876			24.88				SE¼NW¼	24	35	42	3-15-9-15	.202	74.64
	1876					12.52		SE¼NW¼	24	35	42	3-15-4-28	.102	9.40
	1876					30.00		SE¼NW¼	19	35	43	3-15-4-28	.244	22.50
	1876				2.08			SW¼NW¼	19	35	43	3-15-6-13	.017	3.12
	1876					27.92		SW¼NW¼	19	35	43	3-15-4-28	.227	20.94
	1876				18.52			NW¼SW¼	19	35	43	3-15-6-13	.151	27.78
	1876					7.78		NW¼SW¼	19	35	43	3-15-4-28	.063	5.84
	1876				13.08			SW¼SW¼	19	35	43	3-15-6-13	.106	19.62
	1876					6.08		SW¼SW¼	19	35	43	3-15-4-28	.049	4.56
	1876				32.64			SE¼SW¼	19	35	43	3-15-6-13	.265	48.96
	1876					3.64		SE¼SW¼	19	35	43	3-15-4-28	.034	2.73
	1876			31.04				NE¼SW¼	19	35	43	3-15-9-15	.252	93.12
	1876					3.52		NE¼SW¼	19	35	43	3-15-4-28	.029	2.64
	1876			39.72				SE¼SW¼	13	35	42	3-15-9-15	.323	119.16
	1876					1.12		SE¼SE¼	13	35	42	3-15-4-28	.009	.84
	1876			15.12				NE¼SW¼	13	35	42	3-15-9-15	.123	45.36
	1876			33.12				NW¼SW¼	13	35	42	3-15-9-15	.269	99.36
	1876					5.04		NW¼SW¼	13	35	42	3-15-4-28	.041	3.78
	1876			23.80				SW¼SW¼	13	35	42	3-15-9-15	.193	71.40
	1876					14.96		SW¼SW¼	13	35	42	3-15-4-28	.122	11.22
	1876			14.48				SW¼NW¼	13	35	42	3-15-9-15	.117	43.44
	1876				3.96			SW¼NW¼	13	35	42	3-15-6-13	.032	5.94
	1876			.60				SE¼NW¼	13	35	42	3-15-9-15	.005	1.80
	1876					.80		SE¼NW¼	13	35	42	3-15-4-28	.007	.60

Source—**Humboldt River.** Ditch—**Henderson Dam.** (Humboldt River lands.)

	1887			15.68				NW¼NW¼	31	35	43	3-15-9-15	.127	47.04
	1887				4.48			NW¼NW¼	31	35	43	3-15-6-13	.036	6.72
	1887						13.60	NW¼NW¼	31	35	43	3-15-4-28	.111	10.20
	1887						34.40	SW¼NW¼	31	35	43	3-15-4-28	.280	25.80

Ellison Ranching Co.—Continued.

Year of priority	Culture—Acres: Harvest crops	Culture—Acres: Meadow pasture	Culture—Acres: Diversified	Culture—Acres: Diversified pasture	Location: Subdivision	Location: Section	Location: Tp. N.	Location: R. E.	Length of season	Duty of water: C. F. S.	Duty of water: Acre-feet
1887				33.28	NW¼SW¼	31	35	43	3-15—4-28	.271	21.96
1887				33.84	SW¼SW¼	31	35	43	3-15—4-28	.275	25.38
1887	1.28				SE¼SW¼	31	35	43	3-15—9-15	.010	3.84
1887				38.24	SE¼SW¼	31	35	43	3-15—4-28	.311	28.68
1887	.96				NE¼SW¼	31	35	43	3-15—9-15	.008	2.88
1887		7.48			NE¼SW¼	31	35	43	3-15—6-13	.061	11.22
1887				30.32	NE¼SW¼	31	35	43	3-15—4-28	.247	22.74
1887	10.72				SE¼SE¼	31	35	43	3-15—9-15	.087	32.16
1887				26.28	SE¼SE¼	31	35	43	3-15—4-28	.214	19.71
1887	19.96				SW¼SE¼	31	35	43	3-15—9-15	.162	59.88
1887				13.04	SW¼SE¼	31	35	43	3-15—4-28	.106	9.78
1887				39.48	NE¼SE¼	31	35	43	3-15—4-28	.321	29.61
1887	17.92				NW¼SE¼	31	35	43	3-15—9-15	.146	53.76
1887		2.04			NW¼SE¼	31	35	43	3-15—6-13	.017	3.06
1887				13.76	NW¼SE¼	31	35	43	3-15—4-28	.113	10.32
1887	17.00				NW¼NW¼	15	35	42	3-15—9-15	.138	51.00
1887		14.00			NW¼NW¼	15	35	42	3-15—6-13	.114	21.00
1887			6.24		NW¼NW¼	15	35	42	3-15—4-28	.051	4.68
1887	39.24				NE¼NW¼	15	35	42	3-15—9-15	.319	117.72
1887	39.12				NW¼NE¼	15	35	42	3-15—9-15	.318	117.36
1887	39.76				NE¼NE¼	15	35	42	3-15—9-15	.323	119.28
1887	25.72				SE¼NE¼	15	35	42	3-15—9-15	.209	77.16
1887			12.92		SE¼NE¼	15	35	42	3-15—4-28	.105	9.69
1887	33.12				SW¼NE¼	15	35	42	3-15—9-15	.269	99.36
1887			5.40		SW¼NE¼	15	35	42	3-15—4-28	.044	4.05
1887				40.00	NE¼NW¼	23	35	42	3-15—4-28	.325	30.00
1887				40.40	SE¼NW¼	23	35	42	3-15—4-28	.328	30.30
1887				40.08	NW¼NE¼	23	35	42	3-15—4-28	.326	30.06
1887				39.44	NE¼NE¼	23	35	42	3-15—4-28	.321	29.58
1887				40.48	SW¼NE¼	23	35	42	3-15—4-28	.329	30.36
1887				40.56	SE¼NE¼	23	35	42	3-15—4-28	.330	30.42
1887				40.64	NW¼SE¼	23	35	42	3-15—4-28	.330	30.48
1887				40.96	NE¼SE¼	23	35	42	3-15—4-28	.333	30.72
1887				41.20	SW¼SE¼	23	35	42	3-15—4-28	.335	30.90
1887				41.44	SE¼SW¼	23	35	42	3-15—4-28	.337	31.08
1887	1.20				NE¼SW¼	24	35	42	3-15—9-15	.010	3.60
1887			36.68		NE¼SW¼	24	35	42	3-15—4-28	.208	27.51
1887			38.76		NW¼SW¼	24	35	42	3-15—4-28	.315	29.07
1887	23.80				SW¼SW¼	24	35	42	3-15—9-15	.193	71.40
1887			14.96		SW¼SW¼	24	35	42	3-15—4-28	.122	11.22
1887	10.24				SE¼SW¼	24	35	42	3-15—9-15	.083	30.72
1887			26.84		SE¼SW¼	24	35	42	3-15—4-28	.218	20.13
1887	21.52				SE¼NW¼	31	35	43	3-15—9-15	.175	64.56
1887		5.04			SE¼NW¼	31	35	43	3-15—6-13	.041	7.56
1887			11.90		SE¼NW¼	31	35	43	3-15—4-28	.088	8.85
1887	33.68				NE¼NW¼	31	35	43	3-15—9-15	.200	[illegible]
1887			2.08		NE¼NW¼	31	35	43	3-15—4-28	.017	1.56

6[71]

	1887			29.64				SW¼NE¼	31	35	43	3-15—9-15	.241	88.92
	1887					2.56		SW¼NE¼	31	35	43	3-15—4-28	.021	1.02
	1887						1.76	SW¼NE¼	31	35	43	3-15—4-28	.014	1.32
	1887			6.60				NW¼NE¼	31	35	43	3-15—9-15	.054	19.80
	1887					24.24		NW¼NE¼	31	35	43	3-15—4-28	.197	18.18
	1887						3.12	NW¼NE¼	31	35	43	3-15—4-28	.025	2.34
	1887			1.52				SE¼NE¼	31	35	43	3-15—9-15	.012	4.56
	1887					2.48		SE¼NE¼	31	35	43	3-15—4-28	.020	1.86
	1887						.24	SE¼NE¼	31	35	43	3-15—4-28	.002	.18
	1887					38.56		NE¼NE¼	31	35	43	3-15—4-28	.313	28.92
	1887						2.00	NE¼NE¼	31	35	43	3-15—4-28	.016	1.50
	1887			8.80				SW¼SE¼	25	35	42	3-15—9-15	.072	26.40
	1887				31.20			SW¼SE¼	25	35	42	3-15—6-13	.254	46.80
	1887			40.80				SE¼SE¼	25	35	42	3-15—9-15	.332	122.40
	1887				40.64			SE¼SW¼	25	35	42	3-15—6-13	.330	60.96
	1887			19.20				NE¼SW¼	25	35	42	3-15—9-15	.156	57.60
	1887					20.64		NE¼SW¼	25	35	42	3-15—4-28	.168	15.48
	1887					40.64		NW¼SW¼	25	35	42	3-15—4-28	.330	30.48
	1887					38.56		SW¼SW¼	25	35	42	3-15—4-28	.313	28.92
	1887			34.48				NE¼SE¼	25	35	42	3-15—9-15	.280	103.44
	1887					3.16		NE¼SE¼	25	35	42	3-15—4-28	.026	2.37
	1887						1.08	NE¼SE¼	25	35	42	3-15—4-28	.009	.81
	1887			14.16				NW¼SE¼	25	35	42	3-15—9-15	.115	42.48
	1887					25.20		NW¼SE¼	25	35	42	3-15—4-28	.205	18.90
	1887			24.00				NE¼NE¼	25	35	42	3-15—9-15	.195	72.00
	1887				10.48			NE¼NE¼	25	35	42	3-15—6-13	.085	15.72
	1887					3.24		NE¼NE¼	25	35	42	3-15—4-28	.026	2.43
	1887			24.80				NW¼NE¼	25	35	42	3-15—9-15	.202	74.40
	1887					14.16		NW¼NE¼	25	35	42	3-15—4-28	.115	10.62
	1887			32.12				SE¼NE¼	25	35	42	3-15—9-15	.261	96.36
	1887				3.52			SE¼NE¼	25	35	42	3-15—6-13	.029	5.28
	1887					1.72		SE¼NE¼	25	35	42	3-15—4-28	.014	1.29
	1887			38.64				SW¼NE¼	25	35	42	3-15—9-15	.314	115.92
	1887			.48				SE¼NE¼	6	34	43	3-15—9-15	.004	1.44
	1887			12.96				NE¼NE¼	6	34	43	3-15—9-15	.105	38.88
	1887					17.54		NE¼NE¼	6	34	43	3-15—4-28	.143	13.16
	1887			8.36				NW¼NE¼	6	34	43	3-15—9-15	.069	25.08
	1887					4.38		NW¼NE¼	6	34	43	3-15—4-28	.036	3.29
	1887						2.56	NW¼NE¼	6	34	43	3-15—4-28	.021	1.92

Source—**Humboldt River.** Ditch—**Bacon Dam.** (Humboldt River lands.)

	1887			11.08				NW¼SE¼	13	35	42	3-15—9-15	.090	33.24
	1887					1.22		NW¼SE¼	13	35	42	3-15—4-28	.010	.92
	1887			32.92				SW¼SE¼	13	35	42	3-15—9-15	.268	98.76
	1887			.32				NE¼SE¼	13	35	42	3-15—9-15	.003	.64
	1887						.24	NE¼SE¼	13	35	42	3-15—4-28	.002	.18

Source—**Humboldt River.** Ditch—**Gonzales Slough.** (Humboldt River lands.)

	1880						40.00	NW¼NW¼	20	36	42	3-15—4-28	.325	30.00
	1880						40.00	NE¼NW¼	20	36	42	3-15—4-28	.325	30.00
	1880						40.00	NW¼NE¼	20	36	42	3-15—4-28	.328	30.30
	1880						39.36	SW¼NW¼	20	36	42	3-15—4-28	.320	29.52
	1880						40.00	SE¼NW¼	20	36	42	3-15—4-28	.325	30.00

Ellison Ranching Co.—Continued.

Year of priority	Culture—Acres: Harvest crops	Meadow pasture	Diversified pasture	Location: Subdivision	Section	Tp.N.	R.E.	Length of season	Duty of water: C.F.S.	Acre-feet
1880			36.24	NW¼SW¼	20	36	42	3-15—4-28	.295	27.18
1880			37.44	NE¼SW¼	20	36	42	3-15—4-28	.304	28.08
1880			39.06	SW¼SW¼	20	36	42	3-15—4-28	.318	29.30
1880			38.36	SE¼SW¼	20	36	42	3-15—4-28	.312	28.77
1880			40.00	NE¼SE¼	20	36	42	3-15—4-28	.325	30.00
1880			38.56	NW¼SE¼	20	36	42	3-15—4-28	.313	28.92
1880			37.92	SE¼SE¼	20	36	42	3-15—4-28	.308	28.44
1880			36.00	SW¼SE¼	20	36	42	3-15—4-28	.292	27.00
1880			40.00	NW¼NW¼	21	36	42	3-15—4-28	.325	30.00
1880		20.72		NE¼NW¼	21	36	42	3-15—6-13	.169	31.08
1880			19.44	NE¼NW¼	21	36	42	3-15—4-28	.158	14.58
1880			39.52	SW¼NW¼	21	36	42	3-15—4-28	.321	29.64
1880		19.84		SE¼NW¼	21	36	42	3-15—6-13	.161	29.76
1880			19.32	SE¼NW¼	21	36	42	3-15—4-28	.157	14.49
1880		23.68		NE¼SW¼	21	36	42	3-15—6-13	.193	35.52
1880			15.84	NE¼SW¼	21	56	42	3-15—4-28	.129	11.88
1880			40.00	NW¼SW¼	21	36	42	3-15—4-28	.325	30.00
1880			39.48	SW¼SW¼	21	36	42	3-15—4-28	.321	29.61
1880		.48		SE¼SW¼	21	36	42	3-15—6-13	.004	.72
1880			38.20	SE¼SW¼	21	36	42	3-15—4-28	.310	28.65
1880	23.36			NW¼NE¼	21	:6	42	3-15—9-15	.190	70.08
1880			11.76	NW¼NE¼	21	36	42	3-15—4-28	.096	8.82
1880	31.72			SW¼NE¼	21	36	42	3-15—9-15	.258	95.16
1880			.32	SW¼NE¼	21	36	42	3-15—4-28	.003	.24
1880	20.40			SE¼NE¼	21	36	42	3-15—9-15	.166	61.20
1880			.72	SE¼NE¼	21	36	42	3-15—4-28	.006	.54
1880	15.48			NW¼SE¼	21	36	42	3-15—9-15	.126	46.44
1880		11.92		NW¼SE¼	21	36	42	3-15—6-13	.097	17.87
1880			12.48	NW¼SE¼	21	36	42	3-15—4-28	.101	9.36
1880	34.96			NE¼SE¼	21	36	42	3-15—9-15	.284	104.88
1880			6.16	NE¼SE¼	21	36	42	3-15—4-28	.050	4.62
1880		26.40		SW¼SE¼	21	36	42	3-15—6-13	.215	39.60
1880			12.88	SW¼SE¼	21	36	42	3-15—4-28	.105	9.66
1880	20.20			SE¼SE¼	21	36	42	3-15—9-15	.164	60.60
1880			18.20	SE¼SE¼	21	36	42	3-15—4-28	.148	13.65
1880	5.16			NW¼SW¼	22	36	42	3-15—9-15	.042	15.48
1880		21.76		NW¼SW¼	22	56	42	3-15—6-13	.177	32.74
1880			6.08	NW¼SW¼	22	36	42	3-15—4-28	.049	4.56
1880	1.08			NE¼SW¼	22	36	42	3-15—9-15	.009	3.24
1880		2.92		NE¼SW¼	22	36	42	3-15—6-13	.024	4.38
1880			36.52	NE¼SW¼	22	?0	42	3-15—4-28	.297	27.39
1880	19.68			SW¼SW¼	22	36	42	3-15—9-15	.160	59.04
1880			3.16	SW¼SW¼	22	36	42	3-15—4-28	.026	2.38
1880			38.44	NW¼SE¼	28	36	42	3-15—4-28	.313	28.83
1880			38.36	NE¼SE¼	28	36	42	3-15—4-28	.312	28.77
1880			39.40	SE¼SE¼	28	36	42	3-15—4-28	.320	29.55
1880			39.28	SW¼SE¼	28	36	42	3-15—4-28	.319	29.46
1880			40.00	NW¼SW¼	28	36	42	3-15—4-28	.325	30.00
1880			38.44	NE¼SW¼	28	36	42	3-15—4-28	.313	28.83

	1880						30.20	SW¼SW¼	28	36	42	3-15—4-28	.312	29.40
	1880						39.52	SE¼SW¼	28	36	42	3-15—4-28	.313	28.80
	1880						39.84	NW¼NW¼	28	36	42	3-15—4-28	.324	29.88
	1880						39.00	NE¼NW¼	28	36	42	3-15—4-28	.322	29.70
	1880						40.00	SW¼NW¼	28	36	42	3-15—4-28	.325	30.00
	1880						38.72	SE¼NW¼	28	36	42	3-15—4-28	.315	29.04
	1880						40.00	SW¼NE¼	28	36	42	3-15—4-28	.325	30.00
	1880			2.00				SE¼NE¼	28	36	42	3-15—0-15	.016	6.00
	1880						38.84	SE¼NE¼	28	36	42	3-15—4-28	.316	29.13
	1880			10.28				NW¼NE¼	28	36	42	3-15—0-15	.084	30.84
	1880						29.68	NW¼NE¼	28	36	42	3-15—4-28	.241	22.26
	1880			36.28				NW¼NW¼	34	36	42	3-15—0-15	.295	108.84
	1880					2.24		NW¼NW¼	34	36	42	3-15—4-28	.018	1.68
	1880			31.92				NE¼NW¼	34	36	42	3-15—0-15	.260	95.76
	1880			39.20				SE¼NW¼	34	36	42	3-15—0-15	.319	117.60
	1880			35.88				SW¼SW¼	34	36	42	3-15—0-15	.292	107.64
	1880						2.40	SW¼SW¼	34	36	42	3-15—4-28	.020	1.80
	1880			40.00				SE¼SW¼	34	56	42	3-15—0-15	.325	120.00
	1880			38.28				SW¼SW¼	34	36	42	3-15—0-15	.311	114.84
	1880			40.00				NE¼SW¼	34	36	42	3-15—0-15	.325	120.00
	1880			37.00				NW¼SW¼	34	36	42	3-15—0-15	.301	111.00
	1880						3.12	NW¼SW¼	34	36	42	3-15—4-28	.025	2.34

Source—Humboldt River. Ditch—**Overflow.** (Humboldt River lands.)

	1880						28.80	NE¼NE¼	21	36	42	3-15—4-28	.234	21.60
	1880						3.84	SW¼NE¼	21	36	42	3-15—4-28	.028	2.58
	1880						12.96	SE¼NE¼	21	36	42	3-15—4-28	.105	9.72
	1880						10.08	SW¼SW¼	22	36	42	3-15—4-28	.082	7.56
	1880			15.48				SE¼SW¼	22	36	42	3-15—0-15	.126	46.44
	1880						23.80	SE¼SW¼	22	36	42	3-15—4-28	.193	17.85

Source—Humboldt River. Ditch—**"13" Ditch.** (Humboldt River lands.)

	1874				17.36			NE¼SE¼	14	36	41	3-15—6-13	.141	26.04
	1874						9.72	NE¼SE¼	14	36	41	3-15—4-28	.079	7.29
	1874						27.04	SE¼SE¼	14	36	41	3-15—4-28	.220	20.28

Source—Humboldt River. Ditch—**Outside Slough.** (Humboldt River lands.)

	1887						2.24	SE¼SE¼	6	34	43	3-15—4-28	.018	1.68
	1887						12.40	SW¼SE¼	6	54	43	3-15—4-28	.101	9.30
	1887						10.72	NE¼SE¼	6	34	43	3-15—4-28	.087	8.04
	1887						15.08	NW¼SE¼	6	34	43	3-15—4-28	.123	11.31
	1887						33.70	NE¼SW¼	6	34	43	3-15—4-28	.274	25.28
	1887						21.60	NW¼SW¼	6	34	43	3-15—4-28	.176	16.20
	1887						7.04	SW¼SW¼	6	34	43	3-15—4-28	.057	5.28
	1887						9.32	SE¼SW¼	6	34	43	3-15—4-28	.076	6.99
	1886						36.56	NW¼NW¼	32	36	42	3-15—4-28	.297	27.42
	1886						37.64	SW¼NW¼	32	36	42	3-15—4-28	.306	28.33
	1886						36.86	SE¼NW¼	32	36	42	3-15—4-28	.300	27.65
	1886						38.64	NE¼NW¼	32	36	42	3-15—4-28	.314	28.98
	1886						38.20	NW¼NE¼	32	36	42	3-15—4-28	.311	28.65
	1886						37.32	SW¼NE¼	32	36	42	3-15—4-28	.303	27.99
	1886						39.00	NE¼NE¼	32	36	42	3-15—4-28	.317	29.25
	1886						40.20	SE¼NE¼	32	36	42	3-15—4-28	.327	30.15

Ellison Ranching Co.—Continued.

Year of priority	Culture—Acres: Harvest crops	Culture—Acres: Meadow pasture	Culture—Acres: Diversified pasture		Location: Subdivision	Location: Section	Location: Tp.N.	Location: R.E.	Length of season	Duty of water: C.F.S.	Duty of water: Acre-feet
1886				38.00	NE¼SW¼	32	35	42	3-15—4-28	.309	28.50
1886				40.32	NW¼SW¼	32	35	42	3-15—4-28	.328	30.24
1886				40.24	SE¼SW¼	32	35	42	3-15—4-28	.327	30.18
1886				27.12	SW¼SW¼	32	35	42	3-15—4-28	.220	20.35
1886				40.32	NE¼SE¼	32	35	42	3-15—4-28	.328	30.24
1886				40.48	SE¼SE¼	32	35	42	3-15—4-28	.329*	30.36
1886				35.62	NW¼SE¼	32	35	42	3-15—4-28	.290	26.72
1886				37.64	SW¼SE¼	32	35	42	3-15—4-28	.306	28.23
1886				28.68	NW¼NE¼	5	35	42	3-15—4-28	.233	21.51
1886				38.08	NE¼NE¼	5	35	42	3-15—4-28	.310	28.56
1886				37.10	SE¼SE¼	5	35	42	3-15—4-28	.302	27.83
1886				16.64	NE¼SE¼	5	35	42	3-15—4-28	.135	12.98
1886				4.96	SW¼NE¼	5	35	42	3-15—4-28	.040	3.72
1886				36.80	SE¼NE¼	5	35	42	3-15—4-28	.299	27.60
1886				36.60	NW¼NW¼	4	35	42	3-15—4-28	.298	27.45
1886				36.56	NE¼NW¼	4	35	42	3-15—4-28	.297	27.42
1886				38.96	SW¼NW¼	4	35	42	3-15—4-28	.317	29.22
1886				39.32	SE¼NW¼	4	35	42	3-15—4-28	.320	29.49
1886				38.80	NW¼SE¼	4	35	42	3-15—4-28	.315	29.10
1886				39.28	NE¼SE¼	4	35	42	3-15—4-28	.319	29.46
1886				33.16	SW¼SE¼	4	35	42	3-15—4-28	.270	24.87
1886				39.24	SE¼SE¼	4	35	42	3-15—4-28	.319	29.43
1886				40.08	NW¼NE¼	4	35	42	3-15—4-28	.326	30.06
1886				38.72	NE¼NE¼	4	35	42	3-15—4-28	.315	29.04
1886				39.36	SE¼NE¼	4	35	42	3-15—4-28	.320	29.52
1886				38.88	SW¼NE¼	4	35	42	3-15—4-28	.315	29.16
1886				38.16	SE¼SE¼	4	35	42	3-15—4-28	.310	28.62
1886				37.66	SW¼SE¼	4	35	42	3-15—4-28	.306	28.25
1886				38.88	NE¼SE¼	4	35	42	3-15—4-28	.315	29.16
1886				38.24	NW¼SE¼	4	35	42	3-15—4-28	.311	28.68
1887				12.32	NE¼NW¼	35	35	42	3-15—4-28	.100	9.24
1887				39.60	SE¼NW¼	35	35	42	3-15—4-28	.322	29.70
1887				11.66	NE¼SW¼	35	35	42	3-15—4-28	.095	8.75
1887				40.40	NE¼NE¼	35	35	42	3-15—4-28	.328	30.30
1887				39.12	NW¼SE¼	35	35	42	3-15—4-28	.318	29.34
1887				39.44	NE¼SE¼	35	35	42	3-15—4-28	.321	29.58
1887				30.64	NE¼SE¼	1	34	42	3-15—4-28	.249	22.98
1887				10.88	NW¼SE¼	1	34	42	3-15—4-28	.088	8.16
1887				33.20	SE¼NE¼	1	34	42	3-15—4-28	.270	24.90
1887				39.36	SW¼NE¼	1	34	42	3-15—4-28	.320	29.52
1887				26.00	NE¼NE¼	1	34	42	3-15—4-28	.211	19.50
1887				38.00	NW¼NE¼	1	34	42	3-15—4-28	.309	28.60
1887				16.48	NE¼NW¼	1	34	42	3-15—4-28	.134	12.36
1887				32.48	SE¼NW¼	1	34	42	3-15—4-28	.264	24.30
1887			38.80		NW¼NW¼	27	[illegible]	42	3-15—4-28	.311	29.10
1887			35.44		NE¼NW¼	27	[illegible]	42	3-15—4-28	.288	26.58
1887				38.20	SE¼NW¼	27	[illegible]	42	3-15—4-28	.311	28.65
1887				40.40	SW¼NW¼	27	[illegible]	42	3-15—4-28	[illegible]	30.30
1887				40.00	NW¼NE¼	27	[illegible]	42	3-15—4-28	[illegible]	[illegible]

	1887					37.88		NW¼SE¼	27	35	42	3-15—4-28	.308	28.41
	1887						38.06	NE¼SE¼	27	35	42	3-15—4-28	.317	29.22
	1887					37.30		SE¼SE¼	27	35	42	3-15—4-28	.304	28.02
	1887						39.08	SW¼NE¼	27	35	42	3-15—4-28	.323	29.76
	1887						39.88	SE¼NE¼	27	35	42	3-15—4-28	.324	29.91
	1887						37.08	SW¼SW¼	22	35	42	3-15—4-28	.301	27.81
	1887						35.72	NW¼SW¼	22	35	42	3-15—4-28	.290	26.79
	1887						36.71	SE¼SE¼	35	35	42	3-15—4-28	.298	27.53
	1887						1.33	SW¼SE¼	35	35	42	3-15—4-28	.011	1.00
	1887						38.84	NW¼SW¼	36	35	42	3-15—4-28	.316	29.13
	1887						35.40	NE¼SW¼	36	35	42	3-15—4-28	.288	26.55
	1887						37.44	SW¼SW¼	36	35	42	3-15—4-28	.304	28.08
	1887						41.40	SE¼SW¼	36	35	42	3-15—4-28	.337	31.05
	1887						38.80	NW¼SE¼	36	35	42	3-15—4-28	.315	29.10
	1887						40.32	NE¼SE¼	36	35	42	3-15—4-28	.328	30.24
	1887						39.56	SE¼SE¼	36	35	42	3-15—4-28	.322	29.67
	1887						31.04	SW¼SE¼	36	35	42	3-15—4-28	.252	23.28
	1887						31.60	NW¼NW¼	9	35	42	3-15—4-28	.257	23.70
	1887						19.84	SE¼NW¼	9	35	42	3-15—4-28	.161	14.88
	1887						36.80	SW¼NW¼	9	35	42	3-15—4-28	.299	27.60
	1887						.72	SW¼SW¼	9	35	42	3-15—4-28	.006	.54
	1887						37.28	NE¼SW¼	9	35	42	3-15—4-28	.303	27.96
	1887					38.32		SE¼SW¼	9	35	42	3-15—4-28	.312	28.74
	1887						10.68	NW¼SE¼	9	35	42	3-15—4-28	.087	8.01
	1887					38.66		NE¼SE¼	9	35	42	3-15—4-28	.314	29.00
	1887						3.48	SE¼SE¼	9	35	42	3-15—4-28	.028	2.61
	1887						36.36	SW¼SE¼	9	35	42	3-15—4-28	.296	27.27
	1887						37.44	SW¼NE¼	9	35	42	3-15—4-28	.304	28.08

Source—**Rock Creek** and Tributaries. Ditch—**Fraser Creek Canal.** (Squaw Valley lands.)

	1886					1.05		NE¼NE¼	26	38	46	3-15—4-28	.009	.79
	1886			23.30				NE¼SE¼	13	38	46	3-15—9-15	.189	69.90
	1886						18.17	NE¼SE¼	13	38	46	3-15—4-28	.148	14.73
	1886			.82				SE¼SE¼	13	38	46	3-15—9-15	.007	2.46
	1886					9.45		SE¼SE¼	13	38	46	3-15—4-28	.077	7.09
	1886						25.97	SE¼SE¼	13	38	46	3-15—4-28	.211	19.49
	1886			34.81				NW¼SE¼	13	38	46	3-15—9-15	.283	104.43
	1886						7.63	NW¼SE¼	13	38	46	3-15—4-28	.062	5.72
	1886			.27				SW¼SE¼	13	38	46	3-15—9-15	.002	.81
	1886						43.56	SW¼SE¼	13	38	46	3-15—4-28	.354	32.66
	1886			1.95				SE¼NW¼	13	38	46	3-15—9-15	.016	5.85
	1886					12.45		SE¼NW¼	13	38	46	3-15—4-28	.101	9.34
	1886			3.44				NE¼SW¼	13	38	46	3-15—9-15	.028	10.32
	1886					7.68		NE¼SW¼	13	38	46	3-15—4-28	.062	7.68
	1886						29.07	NE¼SW¼	13	38	46	3-15—4-28	.236	21.80
	1886						9.26	SE¼SW¼	13	38	46	3-15—4-28	.075	6.95
	1886						30.50	NE¼NE¼	24	38	46	3-15—4-28	.248	22.88
	1886						36.50	SE¼NE¼	24	38	46	3-15—4-28	.297	27.38
	1886						41.42	NW¼NE¼	24	38	46	3-15—4-28	.337	31.07
	1886						41.10	SW¼NE¼	24	38	46	3-15—4-28	.334	30.83
	1886						38.10	NE¼SE¼	24	38	46	3-15—4-28	.310	28.60
	1886					10.98		SE¼SE¼	24	38	46	3-15—4-28	.089	8.18
	1886						29.74	SE¼SE¼	24	38	46	3-15—4-28	.242	22.31

Ellison Ranching Co.—Continued.

Year of priority	Culture—Acres: Harvest crops	Meadow pasture	Diversified pasture		Location: Subdivision	Section	Tp. N.	R. E.	Length of season	Duty of water: C. F. S.	Acre-feet
1886				40.95	NW¼SE¼	24	38	46	3-15—4-28	.333	30.71
1886			29.31		SW¼SE¼	24	38	46	3-15—4-28	.238	21.98
1886				12.06	SW¼SE¼	24	38	46	3-15—4-28	.098	9.05
1886				17.84	NE¼NW¼	24	38	46	3-15—4-28	.145	13.08
1886				7.94	SE¼NW¼	24	38	46	3-15—4-28	.065	5.96
1886			2.42		SE¼NE¼	12	38	46	3-15—4-28	.020	1.82
1886	15.53				NE¼SE¼	12	38	46	3-15—9-15	.126	46.59
1886			8.64		NE¼SE¼	12	38	46	3-15—4-28	.070	6.48
1886				14.00	NE¼SE¼	12	38	46	3-15—4-28	.114	10.50
1886	15.05				SE¼SE¼	12	38	46	3-15—9-15	.122	45.15
1886				9.09	SE¼SE¼	12	38	46	3-15—4-28	.074	6.82
1886	8.00				NE¼NE¼	13	38	46	3-15—9-15	.065	24.00
1886	28.37				NW¼NE¼	13	38	46	3-15—9-15	.231	85.11
1886				6.05	NW¼NE¼	13	38	46	3-15—4-28	.049	4.54
1886	3.10				SE¼NE¼	13	38	46	3-15—9-15	.025	6.30
1886	24.87				SW¼NE¼	13	38	46	3-15—9-15	.202	74.61
1886	.36				NE¼NW¼	13	38	46	3-15—9-15	.003	1.08
1886				1.73	NE¼NW¼	13	38	46	3-15—4-28	.014	1.30
1886	3.90				SE¼NW¼	13	38	46	3-15—9-15	.032	11.70
1886			6.26		SE¼NW¼	13	38	46	3-15—4-28	.051	4.70
1886				2.38	SE¼NW¼	13	38	46	3-15—4-28	.019	1.79
1886	33.52				SW¼SE¼	6	38	47	3-15—9-15	.273	100.56
1886			3.17		SW¼SE¼	6	38	47	3-15—4-28	.026	2.38

Source—**Willow Creek.** Ditch—**Fraser Creek Canal.** (Squaw Valley lands.)

Year of priority	Harvest crops	Meadow pasture	Diversified pasture		Subdivision	Section	Tp. N.	R. E.	Length of season	C. F. S.	Acre-feet
1886				1.55	SW¼NW¼	18	38	47	3-15—4-28	.013	1.16
1886	6.95				SE¼NE¼	13	38	46	3-15—9-15	.057	20.85
1886				6.87	SE¼NE¼	13	38	46	3-15—4-28	.056	5.15
1886	14.45				SW¼NE¼	13	38	46	3-15—9-15	.117	43.35

Source—**Rock Creek and Tributaries.** Ditch—**Fraser Creek Canal.** (Squaw Valley lands.)

Year of priority	Harvest crops	Meadow pasture	Diversified pasture		Subdivision	Section	Tp. N.	R. E.	Length of season	C. F. S.	Acre-feet
1881	35.50				NE¼NW¼	7	38	47	3-15—9-15	.289	106.50
1881	27.74				SW¼NW¼	7	38	47	3-15—9-15	.226	83.22
1881				8.21	SW¼NW¼	7	38	47	3-15—4-28	.067	6.16
1881	0.46				SW¼SW¼	32	39	47	3-15—9-15	.004	1.38
1881				9.60	SW¼SW¼	32	39	47	3-15—4-28	.078	7.20
1881				12.08	NE¼SW¼	24	38	46	3-15—4-28	.098	9.06
1881				40.35	SE¼SW¼	24	38	46	3-15—4-28	.328	30.26
1881			16.37		SW¼SW¼	24	38	46	3-15—4-28	.133	12.28
1881				9.95	SW¼SW¼	19	38	47	3-15—4-28	.081	7.46
1881				23.92	NW¼NW¼	20	38	47	3-15—4-28	.194	17.94
1881				2.42	SW¼NW¼	30	38	47	3-15—4-28	.020	1.82
1881				1.87	SE¼SE¼	23	38	46	3-15—4-28	.015	1.40

Source—**Rock Creek and Tributaries.** Ditch **Lakefield Ditch.** (Squaw Valley lands.)

Year of priority	Harvest crops	Meadow pasture	Diversified pasture		Subdivision	Section	Tp. N.	R. E.	Length of season	C. F. S.	Acre-feet
1880	24.82				SW¼SW¼	7	38	47	3-15—9-15	.202	74.46
1880				5.02	SW¼SW¼	7	38	47	3-15—4-28	.040	4.22
1880	16.27				SE¼SW¼	7	38	47	3-15—9-15	.132	48.81
1880				8.59	SE¼SW¼	7	38	47	3-15—4-28	.070	6.44

	1880			4.03				NE¼NW¼	18	38	47	3-15—9-15	.033	12.99
	1880						6.17	NE¼NW¼	18	38	47	3-15—4-28	.050	4.63
	1880			17.13				NW¼NW¼	18	38	47	3-15—9-15	.130	51.39
	1880						2.30	NW¼NW¼	18	38	47	3-15—4-28	.019	1.73
	1880			4.82				SW¼NW¼	18	38	47	3-15—9-15	.039	14.46
	1880						7.40	SW¼NW¼	18	38	47	3-15—4-28	.061	5.62
	1880						2.70	SE¼NW¼	18	38	47	3-15—4-28	.022	2.03
	1880			29.55				SW¼NE¼	7	38	47	3-15—9-15	.240	88.65
	1880						10.30	SW¼NE¼	7	38	47	3-15—4-28	.084	7.73
	1880			33.02				SE¼NW¼	7	38	47	3-15—9-15	.276	101.76
	1880					3.38		SE¼NW¼	7	38	47	3-15—4-28	.027	2.54
	1880			29.74				NE¼SW¼	7	38	47	3-15—9-15	.242	89.22
	1880						2.16	NE¼SW¼	7	38	47	3-15—4-28	.018	1.62
	1880			34.17				NW¼SW¼	7	38	47	3-15—9-15	.279	102.51
	1880						5.18	NW¼SW¼	7	38	47	3-15—4-28	.042	3.80

Source—**Rock Creek** and Tributaries. Ditch—**Rock Creek Ditch.** (Squaw Valley lands.)

	1878			18.53				NW¼NW¼	8	38	47	3-15—9-15	.151	55.69
	1878					14.36		NW¼NW¼	8	38	47	3-15—4-28	.117	10.77
	1878					2.09		SE¼NW¼	8	38	47	3-15—4-28	.017	1.57
	1878					3.38		SW¼NW¼	8	38	47	3-15—4-28	.027	2.54
	1878						23.12	SW¼NW¼	8	38	47	3-15—4-28	.189	17.34
	1878						1.60	NW¼SW¼	8	38	47	3-15—4-28	.013	1.20
	1878			38.05				NE¼NE¼	7	38	47	3-15—9-15	.309	114.15
	1878			37.00				NW¼NE¼	7	38	47	3-15—9-15	.300	111.00
	1878			24.28				SE¼NE¼	7	38	47	3-15—9-15	.197	72.84
	1878						12.95	SE¼NE¼	7	38	47	3-15—4-28	.105	9.71
	1878						7.05	NE¼SE¼	7	38	47	3-15—4-28	.057	5.29
	1878			1.72				NW¼SE¼	7	38	47	3-15—9-15	.014	5.16
	1878						8.30	NW¼SE¼	7	38	47	3-15—4-28	.067	6.23
	1878			36.80				SE¼NW¼	5	38	47	3-15—9-15	.290	110.40
	1878			17.74				NE¼SW¼	5	38	47	3-15—9-15	.144	53.22
	1878			36.47				NW¼SW¼	5	38	47	3-15—9-15	.297	109.41
	1878					4.75		NW¼SW¼	5	38	47	3-15—4-28	.039	3.56
	1878			37.27				SW¼SW¼	5	38	47	3-15—9-15	.303	111.81

Source—**Rock Creek and Tributaries.** Ditch—**Highline Ditch.** (Squaw Valley lands.)

	1887			.50				NW¼NW¼	1	38	46	3-15—9-15	.004	1.50
	1887			18.43				SE¼NW¼	1	38	46	3-15—9-15	.150	55.29
	1887						4.88	SE¼NW¼	1	38	46	3-15—4-28	.040	3.66
	1887			34.92				SW¼NW¼	1	38	46	3-15—9-15	.283	104.76
	1887			15.90				NE¼SW¼	1	38	46	3-15—9-15	.129	47.70
	1887			30.62				NW¼SW¼	1	38	46	3-15—9-15	.249	91.86
	1887			8.93				SW¼SW¼	1	38	46	3-15—9-15	.073	26.79
	1887			40.87				SE¼NE¼	2	38	46	3-15—9-15	.332	122.61
	1887			14.70				SW¼NE¼	2	38	46	3-15—9-15	.120	44.10
	1887			24.27				SW¼NE¼	2	38	46	3-15—9-15	.197	72.81
	1887			26.03				NE¼SE¼	2	38	46	3-15—9-15	.212	78.09
	1887			21.06				NW¼SE¼	2	38	46	3-15—9-15	.171	63.18
	1887						19.41	NW¼SE¼	2	38	46	3-15—4-28	.158	14.56
	1887			5.04				SE¼SE¼	2	38	46	3-15—9-15	.041	15.12
	1887						13.88	SE¼SW¼	32	39	47	3-15—4-28	.113	10.41
	1887				9.61			SE¼SW¼	31	39	47	3-15—6-13	.078	14.42

Claimant—**Golconda Cattle Co.** Proof No. 00156

Source—**Humboldt River.** Ditch—***Aemes Dam.**

Year of priority	Culture—Acres: Harvest crops	Culture—Acres: Meadow pasture	Culture—Acres: Diversified	Culture—Acres: pasture	Location: Subdivision	Location: Section	Location: Tp.N.	Location: R.E.	Length of season	Duty of water: C.F.S.	Duty of water: Acre-feet
1876	....	....	....	40.44	NW¼NE¼	30	35	43	3-15—4-28	.329	30.33
1876	....	....	30.61	....	NE¼NE¼	30	35	43	3-15—4-28	.249	22.96
1876	....	....	....	9.78	NE¼NE¼	30	35	42	3-15—4-28	.080	7.34
1886	....	....	11.60	....	SE¼NE¼	30	35	43	3-15—4-28	.094	8.70
1886	....	....	....	29.48	SE¼NE¼	30	35	43	3-15—4-28	.240	22.11
1876	5.60	....	....	....	SW¼NE¼	30	35	43	3-15—9-15	.046	16.80
1876	....	....	9.43	....	SW¼NE¼	30	35	43	3-15—4-28	.077	7.07
1886	....	....	8.64	....	NE¼SE¼	30	35	43	3-15—4-28	.070	6.48
1886	....	....	....	31.88	NE¼SE¼	30	35	43	3-15—4-28	.259	23.91
1886	13.76	....	....	....	NW¼SE¼	30	35	43	3-15—9-15	.112	41.28
1886	....	17.56	....	....	NW¼SE¼	30	35	43	3-15—6-13	.143	26.34
1886	....	....	4.20	....	NW¼SE¼	30	35	43	3-15—4-28	.034	3.15
1886	....	....	13.48	....	SE¼SE¼	30	35	43	3-15—4-28	.110	10.11
1886	....	....	....	17.40	SE¼SE¼	30	35	43	3-15—4-28	.141	13.05
1886	11.50	....	....	....	SW¼SE¼	30	35	43	3-15—9-15	.093	34.50
1886	....	22.32	....	....	SW¼SE¼	30	35	43	3-15—6-13	.181	33.48
1886	....	....	1.92	....	SW¼SE¼	30	35	43	3-15—4-28	.016	1.24
1884	29.52	....	....	....	NE¼SW¼	30	35	43	3-15—9-15	.240	88.59
1884	....	....	3.52	....	NE¼SW¼	30	35	43	3-15—4-28	.029	2.64

Source—**Humboldt River.** Ditch—***Aemes Dam.** (Lands of Duviver.)

Year of priority	Harvest crops	Meadow pasture	Diversified	pasture	Subdivision	Section	Tp.N.	R.E.	Length of season	C.F.S.	Acre-feet
1884	....	....	....	.48	NE¼SW¼	30	35	43	3-15—4-28	.004	.36
1884	29.68	....	....	....	NW¼SW¼	30	35	43	3-15—9-15	.241	89.04
1884	....	....	2.80	....	NW¼SW¼	30	35	43	3-15—4-28	.023	2.10
1884	30.56	....	....	....	SW¼SW¼	30	35	43	3-15—9-15	.248	91.68
1884	....	3.88	....	....	SW¼SW¼	30	35	43	3-15—6-13	.032	5.82
1884	28.16	....	....	....	SE¼SW¼	30	35	43	3-15—9-15	.229	81.48
1884	....	4.88	....	....	SE¼SW¼	30	35	43	3-15—6-13	.040	7.32
1884	....	....	.84	....	SE¼SW¼	30	35	43	3-15—4-28	.007	.62

*Was Class C—1876.

Source—**Humboldt River.** Ditch—**Henderson.** (Lands of Duvivior.)

Year of priority	Harvest crops	Meadow pasture	Diversified	pasture	Subdivision	Section	Tp.N.	R.E.	Length of season	C.F.S.	Acre-feet
1887	6.62	....	....	....	NW¼NE¼	36	35	42	3-15—9-15	.054	19.86
1887	....	....	32.90	....	NW¼NE¼	36	35	42	3-15—4-28	.267	24.68
1887	16.23	....	....	....	NE¼NE¼	36	35	42	3-15—9-15	.132	48.69
1887	....	7.56	....	....	NE¼NE¼	36	35	42	3-15—6-13	.061	11.34
1887	....	....	16.09	....	NE¼NE¼	36	35	42	3-15—4-28	.131	12.07
1894	21.33	....	....	....	NE¼SW¼	14	35	42	3-15—9-15	.174	64.08
1894	....	18.40	....	....	NE¼SW¼	14	35	42	3-15—6-13	.150	27.60
1894	....	41.20	....	....	NE¼SW¼	14	35	42	3-15—6-13	.335	61.80
1894	....	40.16	....	....	SE¼SW¼	14	35	42	3-15—6-13	.327	60.24
1894	....	41.20	....	....	NW¼SW¼	14	35	42	3-15—6-13	.335	61.80

Source—**Humboldt River.** Ditch—**Outside Slough.** (Lands of Duvivier.)

1887			3.90				SW¼NE¼	36	35	42	3-15—9-15	.032	11.88
1887					35.72		SW¼NE¼	36	35	42	3-15—4-28	.290	26.79
1887			34.11				SE¼NE¼	36	35	42	3-15—9-15	.277	102.33
1887				2.64			SE¼NE¼	36	35	42	3-15—6-13	.021	3.96
1887					2.37		SE¼NE¼	36	35	12	3-15—4-28	.019	1.78
1894				40.96			SW¼SW¼	14	35	42	3-15—6-13	.333	61.44

Claimant—**Ellison Ranching Co.** Proof No. **00156**

Source—**Humboldt River.** Ditch—**Outside Slough Ditch.** (Humboldt River lands.)

1887						40.60	SW¼SW¼	15	35	42	3-15—4-28	.330	30.45
1887						38.60	NW¼SW¼	15	35	42	3-15—4-28	.314	28.95
1887						35.60	SE¼SW¼	15	35	42	3-15—4-28	.289	26.70
1887						34.72	NE¼SW¼	15	35	42	3-15—4-28	.282	26.05
1887						33.44	SW¼NW¼	15	35	42	3-15—4-28	.272	25.08
1887			14.72				SE¼NW¼	15	35	42	3-15—9-15	.120	44.16
1887					24.64		SE¼NW¼	15	35	42	3-15—4-28	.200	18.48
1887						36.88	SW¼SE¼	15	35	42	3-15—4-28	.300	27.66
1887						39.44	SE¼SE¼	15	35	42	3-15—4-28	.321	29.58
1887						40.08	NE¼SE¼	15	35	42	3-15—4-28	.326	30.06
1887			9.28				NW¼SE¼	15	35	42	3-15—9-15	.075	27.84
1887					29.92		NW¼SE¼	15	35	42	3-15—4-28	.243	22.44
1887						40.24	SE¼SE¼	22	35	42	3-15—4-28	.327	30.18
1887						39.88	SW¼SE¼	22	35	42	3-15—4-28	.324	29.91
1887						39.84	NW¼SE¼	22	35	42	3-15—4-28	.324	29.88
1887						37.28	NE¼SE¼	22	35	42	3-15—4-28	.303	27.96
1887						40.12	NE¼SW¼	22	35	42	3-15—4-28	.326	30.09
1887						39.68	SE¼SW¼	22	35	42	3-15—4-28	.323	29.76
1887						38.60	SW¼NW¼	22	35	42	3-15—4-28	.314	28.95
1887						40.12	SE¼NW¼	22	35	42	3-15—4-28	.326	30.09
1887						40.08	NE¼NW¼	22	35	42	3-15—4-28	.326	30.06
1887						40.00	NW¼NW¼	22	35	42	3-15—4-28	.325	30.00
1887						39.88	SW¼NE¼	22	35	42	3-15—4-28	.324	29.91
1887						31.88	NW¼NE¼	22	35	42	3-15—4-28	.259	23.91
1887						39.00	NE¼NE¼	22	35	42	3-15—4-28	.317	29.25
1887						32.40	SE¼NE¼	22	35	42	3-15—4-28	.263	24.30
1887						41.12	NW¼NW¼	26	35	42	3-15—4-28	.334	30.84
1887			.96				NE¼NW¼	26	35	42	3-15—9-15	.008	2.88
1887					25.24		NE¼NW¼	26	35	42	3-15—4-28	.205	18.93
1887						39.48	SE¼NW¼	26	35	42	3-15—4-28	.321	29.61
1887						41.80	SW¼NW¼	26	35	42	3-15—4-28	.340	31.65
1887						40.80	NW¼NE¼	26	35	42	3-15—4-28	.331	30.60
1887						32.56	SW¼NE¼	26	35	42	3-15—4-28	.265	24.42
1887						41.28	SE¼NE¼	26	35	42	3-15—4-28	.336	30.96
1887						39.84	NW¼SW¼	26	35	42	3-15—4-28	.324	29.88
1887						40.60	NE¼SW¼	26	35	42	3-15—4-28	.330	30.45
1887						38.48	SW¼SW¼	26	35	42	3-15—4-28	.313	28.86
1887						40.64	SE¼SW¼	26	35	42	3-15—4-28	.330	30.48
1887					36.80		NW¼SE¼	26	35	42	3-15—4-28	.299	27.60
1887						35.92	NE¼SE¼	26	35	42	3-15—4-28	.292	26.90
1887					40.16		SW¼SE¼	26	35	42	3-15—4-28	.327	30.12
1887					23.08		SE¼SE¼	26	35	42	3-15—4-28	.188	17.31

Ellison Ranching Co.—Continued.

Year of priority	Culture—Acres: Harvest crops	Meadow pasture	Diversified pasture		Location: Subdivision	Section	Tp.N.	R.E.	Length of season	Duty of water: C.F.S.	Acre-feet
1887				8.96	SE¼SE¼	26	35	42	3-15—4-28	.073	6.72
1887				40.36	NE¼NE¼	27	35	42	3-15—4-28	.328	30.27
1887			39.84		NW¼NW¼	23	35	42	3-15—4-28	.324	29.88
1887			39.80		SW¼NW¼	23	35	42	3-15—4-28	.324	29.85
1887	11.12				NW¼SW¼	23	35	42	3-15—9-15	.090	33.36
1887			20.56		NW¼SW¼	23	35	42	3-15—4-28	.167	15.42
1887				3.24	NW¼SW¼	23	35	42	3-15—4-28	.026	2.43
1887	.32				SW¼SW¼	23	35	42	3-15—9-15	.003	.96
1887			3.76		SW¼SW¼	23	35	42	3-15—4-28	.031	2.82
1887				25.28	SW¼SW¼	23	35	42	3-15—4-28	.206	18.96
1887	13.12				NE¼SW¼	23	35	42	3-15—9-15	.107	39.36
1887			27.20		NE¼SW¼	23	35	42	3-15—4-28	.221	20.40
1887	18.68				SE¼SW¼	23	35	42	3-15—9-15	.152	56.04
1887			17.88		SE¼SW¼	23	35	42	3-15—4-28	.145	13.41
1887				36.88	NE¼NW¼	9	35	42	3-15—4-28	.300	27.66
1887				10.72	SE¼NW¼	9	35	42	3-15—4-28	.087	8.04
1887				37.84	NW¼NE¼	9	35	42	3-15—4-28	.308	29.38
1887			37.80		NE¼NE¼	9	35	42	3-15—4-28	.307	28.35
1887			37.84		SE¼NE¼	9	35	42	3-15—4-28	.308	28.38
1887				19.34	NW¼SE¼	9	35	42	3-15—4-28	.157	14.51
1887			30.48		SE¼SE¼	9	35	42	3-15—4-28	.248	22.86

Source—**Humboldt River.** Ditch—**Aemes Dam.** (Humboldt River lands.)

Year of priority	Harvest crops	Meadow pasture	Diversified pasture		Subdivision	Section	Tp.N.	R.E.	Length of season	C.F.S.	Acre-feet
1876			40.08		NW¼NW¼	25	35	42	3-15—4-28	.326	30.06
1876	18.20				NE¼NW¼	25	35	42	3-15—9-15	.147	54.60
1876		.36			NE¼NW¼	25	35	42	3-15—6-13	.003	.54
1876			20.48		NE¼NW¼	25	35	42	3-15—4-28	.167	15.36
1876			40.24		SW¼NW¼	25	35	42	3-15—4-28	.327	30.18
1876	5.80				SE¼NW¼	25	35	42	3-15—9-15	.047	17.40
1876		2.28			SE¼NW¼	25	35	42	3-15—6-13	.019	3.42
1876			31.08		SE¼NW¼	25	35	42	3-15—4-28	.253	23.31
1876	21.32				NW¼NW¼	30	35	43	3-15—9-15	.173	63.96
1876			6.16		NW¼NW¼	30	35	43	3-15—4-28	.050	4.62
1876				.86	NW¼NW¼	30	35	43	3-15—4-28	.007	.65
1876	20.28				SW¼NW¼	30	35	43	3-15—9-15	.165	60.84
1876			4.24		SW¼NW¼	30	35	43	3-15—4-28	.034	3.18
1876				7.60	SW¼NW¼	30	35	43	3-15—4-28	.062	5.70
1876	18.00				SE¼NW¼	30	35	43	3-15—9-15	.146	54.00
1876			11.52		SE¼NW¼	30	35	43	3-15—4-28	.094	8.64
1876				2.52	SE¼NW¼	30	35	43	3-15—4-28	.020	1.89
1876	14.32				NE¼NW¼	30	35	43	3-15—9-15	.116	42.96
1876			22.92		NE¼NW¼	30	35	43	3-15—4-28	.186	17.19
1876			6.40		SW¼NE¼	19	35	43	3-15—4-28	.052	4.80
1876				10.36	SW¼NE¼	19	35	43	3-15—4-28	.084	7.77
1876	20.72				NW¼SE¼	19	35	43	3-15—9-15	.166	62.16
1876				9.28	NW¼SE¼	19	35	43	3-15—4-28	.075	6.00

	1876			25.36				SW¼SE¼	19	35	43	3-15—9-15	.206	70.08
	1876						8.29	SW¼SE¼	19	35	43	3-15—4-28	.067	6.22
	1876				27.04			NW¼NW¼	19	35	43	3-15—6-13	.220	40.56
	1876						7.21	NW¼NW¼	19	35	43	3-15—4-28	.059	5.43
	1876				18.24			NE¼NW¼	19	35	43	3-15—6-13	.148	27.36
	1876						21.52	NE¼NW¼	19	35	43	3-15—4-28	.175	16.11
	1876			38.80				NW¼NE¼	24	35	42	3-15—9-15	.315	116.40
	1876			23.84				NE¼NE¼	24	35	42	3-15—9-15	.194	71.52
	1876					10.88		NE¼NE¼	24	35	42	3-15—4-28	.088	8.16
	1876			40.08				SW¼NE¼	24	35	42	3-15—9-15	.326	120.24
	1876			26.44				SE¼NE¼	24	35	42	3-15—9-15	.215	79.32
	1876					3.68		SE¼NE¼	24	35	42	3-15—4-28	.030	2.76
	1876			23.56				NW¼SE¼	24	35	42	3-15—9-15	.192	70.68
	1876					16.56		NW¼SE¼	24	35	42	3-15—4-28	.135	12.42
	1876			40.24				NE¼SE¼	24	35	42	3-15—9-15	.327	120.72
	1876			12.76				SW¼SE¼	24	35	42	3-15—9-15	.104	38.28
	1876					24.76		SW¼SE¼	24	35	42	3-15—4-28	.201	18.57
	1876			39.96				SE¼SE¼	24	35	42	3-15—9-15	.325	119.34
	1876			39.59				NE¼NW¼	24	35	42	3-15—9-15	.322	118.77
	1876			13.12				NW¼NW¼	24	35	42	3-15—9-15	.107	39.36
	1876					25.60		NW¼NW¼	24	35	42	3-15—4-28	.208	19.20
	1876			.48				SW¼NW¼	24	35	42	3-15—9-15	.004	1.44
	1876					35.76		SW¼NW¼	24	35	42	3-15—4-28	.291	26.82
	1876			24.88				SE¼NW¼	24	35	42	3-15—9-15	.202	74.64
	1876					12.52		SE¼NW¼	24	35	42	3-15—4-28	.102	9.40
	1876					30.00		SE¼NW¼	19	35	43	3-15—4-28	.244	22.50
	1876				2.08			SW¼NW¼	19	35	43	3-15—6-13	.017	3.12
	1876					27.92		SW¼NW¼	19	35	43	3-15—4-28	.227	20.94
	1876				18.52			NW¼SW¼	19	35	43	3-15—6-13	.151	27.78
	1876					7.78		NW¼SW¼	19	35	43	3-15—4-28	.063	5.84
	1876				13.08			SW¼SW¼	19	35	43	3-15—6-13	.106	19.62
	1876					6.08		SW¼SW¼	19	35	43	3-15—4-28	.049	4.56
	1876				32.64			SE¼SW¼	19	35	43	3-15—6-13	.265	48.96
	1876					3.64		SE¼SW¼	19	35	43	3-15—4-28	.034	2.73
	1876			31.04				NE¼SW¼	19	35	43	3-15—9-15	.252	93.12
	1876					3.52		NE¼SW¼	19	35	43	3-15—4-28	.029	2.64
	1876			39.72				SE¼SW¼	13	35	42	3-15—9-15	.323	119.16
	1876					1.12		SE¼SE¼	13	35	42	3-15—4-28	.009	.84
	1876			15.12				NE¼SW¼	13	35	42	3-15—9-15	.123	45.36
	1876			33.12				NW¼SW¼	13	35	42	3-15—9-15	.269	99.36
	1876					5.04		NW¼SW¼	13	35	42	3-15—4-28	.041	3.78
	1876			23.80				SW¼SW¼	13	35	42	3-15—9-15	.193	71.40
	1876					14.96		SW¼SW¼	13	35	42	3-15—4-28	.122	11.22
	1876			14.48				SW¼NW¼	13	35	42	3-15—9-15	.117	43.44
	1876				3.96			SW¼NW¼	13	35	42	3-15—6-13	.032	5.94
	1876			.60				SE¼NW¼	13	35	42	3-15—9-15	.005	1.80
	1876					.80		SE¼NW¼	13	35	42	3-15—4-28	.007	.60

Source—**Humboldt River.** Ditch—**Henderson Dam.** (Humboldt River lands.)

	1887			15.68				NW¼NW¼	31	35	43	3-15—9-15	.127	47.04
	1887				4.48			NW¼NW¼	31	35	43	3-15—6-13	.036	6.72
	1887						13.60	NW¼NW¼	31	35	43	3-15—4-28	.111	10.20
	1887						34.40	SW¼NW¼	31	35	43	3-15—4-28	.280	25.80

Ellison Ranching Co.—Continued.

Year of priority	Culture—Acres: Harvest crops	Culture—Acres: Meadow pasture	Culture—Acres: Diversified	Culture—Acres: pasture	Location: Subdivision	Location: Section	Location: Tp.N.	Location: R.E.	Length of season	Duty of water: C.F.S.	Duty of water: Acre-feet
1887	....			33.28	NW¼SW¼	31	35	43	3-15—4-28	.271	24.96
1887	....			33.84	SW¼SW¼	31	35	43	3-15—4-28	.275	25.38
1887	1.28				SE¼SW¼	31	35	43	3-15—9-15	.010	3.84
1887	....			38.24	SE¼SW¼	31	35	43	3-15—4-28	.311	28.68
1887	.96				NE¼SW¼	31	35	43	3-15—9-15	.008	2.88
1887	...	7.48			NE¼SW¼	31	35	43	3-15—6-13	.061	11.22
1887				30.32	NE¼SW¼	31	35	43	3-15—4-28	.247	22.74
1887	10.72				SE¼SE¼	31	35	43	3-15—9-15	.087	32.16
1887	....			26.28	SE¼SE¼	31	35	43	3-15—4-28	.214	19.71
1887	19.96				SW¼SE¼	31	35	43	3-15—9-15	.162	59.88
1887	....			13.04	SW¼SE¼	31	35	43	3-15—4-28	.106	9.78
1887	...			39.48	NE¼SE¼	31	35	43	3-15—4-28	.321	29.61
1887	17.92				NW¼SE¼	31	35	43	3-15—9-15	.146	53.76
1887	....	2.04			NW¼SE¼	31	35	43	3-15—6-13	.017	3.06
1887	...			13.76	NW¼SE¼	31	35	43	3-15—4-28	.113	10.32
1887	17.00				NW¼NW¼	15	35	42	3-15—9-15	.138	51.00
1887	....	14.00			NW¼NW¼	15	35	42	3-15—6-13	.114	21.00
1887	....		6.24		NW¼NW¼	15	35	42	3-15—4-28	.051	4.68
1887	39.24				NE¼NW¼	15	35	42	3-15—9-15	.319	117.72
1887	39.12				NW¼NE¼	15	35	42	3-15—9-15	.318	117.36
1887	39.76				NE¼NE¼	15	35	42	3-15—9-15	.323	119.28
1887	25.72				SE¼NE¼	15	35	42	3-15—9-15	.209	77.16
1887	....		12.92		SE¼NE¼	15	35	42	3-15—4-28	.105	9.69
1887	33.12				SW¼NE¼	15	35	42	3-15—9-15	.269	99.36
1887	....		5.40		SW¼NE¼	15	35	42	3-15—4-28	.044	4.05
1887	....			40.00	NE¼NW¼	23	35	42	3-15—4-28	.325	30.00
1887	....			40.40	SE¼NW¼	23	35	42	3-15—4-28	.328	30.30
1887	....			40.08	NW¼NE¼	23	35	42	3-15—4-28	.326	30.06
1887	....			39.44	NE¼NE¼	23	35	42	3-15—4-28	.321	29.58
1887	....			40.48	SW¼NE¼	23	35	42	3-15—4-28	.329	30.36
1887	...			40.56	SE¼NE¼	23	35	42	3-15—4-28	.330	30.42
1887	..			40.64	NW¼SE¼	23	35	42	3-15—4-28	.330	30.48
1887	..			40.96	NE¼SE¼	23	35	42	3-15—4-28	.333	30.72
1887	....			41.20	SW¼SE¼	23	35	42	3-15—4-28	.335	30.90
1887	....			41.44	SE¼SE¼	23	35	42	3-15—4-28	.337	31.08
1887	1.20				NE¼SW¼	24	35	42	3-15—9-15	.010	3.60
1887	....		36.68		NE¼SW¼	24	35	42	3-15—4-28	.298	27.51
1887	....		38.76		NW¼SW¼	24	35	42	3-15—4-28	.315	29.07
1887	23.80				SW¼SW¼	24	35	42	3-15—9-15	.193	71.40
1887	...		14.96		SW¼SW¼	24	35	42	3-15—4-28	.122	11.22
1887	10.24				SE¼SW¼	24	35	42	3-15—9-15	.083	30.72
1887			26.84		SE¼SW¼	24	35	42	3-15—4-28	.218	20.13
1887	21.52				SE¼NW¼	31	35	43	3-15—9-15	.175	61.56
1887		5.04			SE¼NW¼	31	35	43	3-15—6-13	.041	7.56
1887			11.90		SE¼NW¼	31	35	43	3-15—4-28	.006	8.85
1887	33.68				NE¼NW¼	31	35	43	3-15—9-15	.200	90.24
1887			2.08		NE¼NW¼	31	35	43	3-15—4-28	.017	1.56

	1887			20.64				SW¼NE¼	31	35	43	3-15—9-15	.241	88.92
	1887					2.56		SW¼NE¼	31	35	43	3-15—4-28	.021	1.92
	1887						1.76	SW¼NE¼	31	35	43	3-15—4-28	.014	1.32
	1887			6.60				NW¼NE¼	31	35	43	3-15—9-15	.054	19.80
	1887					24.24		NW¼NE¼	31	35	43	3-15—4-28	.197	18.18
	1887						3.12	NW¼NE¼	31	35	43	3-15—4-28	.025	2.34
	1887			1.52				SE¼NE¼	31	35	43	3-15—9-15	.012	4.56
	1887					2.48		SE¼NE¼	31	35	43	3-15—4-28	.020	1.86
	1887						.24	SE¼NE¼	31	35	43	3-15—4-28	.002	.18
	1887					38.56		NE¼NE¼	31	35	43	3-15—4-28	.313	28.92
	1887						2.00	NE¼NE¼	31	35	43	3-15—4-28	.016	1.50
	1887			8.80				SW¼SE¼	25	35	42	3-15—9-15	.072	26.40
	1887				31.20			SW¼SE¼	25	35	42	3-15—6-13	.254	46.80
	1887			40.80				SE¼SE¼	25	35	42	3-15—9-15	.332	122.40
	1887				40.64			SE¼SW¼	25	35	42	3-15—6-13	.330	60.96
	1887			19.20				NE¼SW¼	25	35	42	3-15—9-15	.156	57.60
	1887					20.64		NE¼SW¼	25	35	42	3-15—4-28	.168	15.48
	1887					40.64		NW¼SW¼	25	35	42	3-15—4-28	.330	30.48
	1887					38.56		SW¼SW¼	25	35	42	3-15—4-28	.313	28.92
	1887			34.48				NE¼SE¼	25	35	42	3-15—9-15	.280	103.44
	1887					3.16		NE¼SE¼	25	35	42	3-15—4-28	.026	2.37
	1887						1.08	NE¼SE¼	25	35	42	3-15—4-28	.009	.81
	1887			14.16				NW¼SE¼	25	35	42	3-15—9-15	.115	42.48
	1887					25.20		NW¼SE¼	25	35	42	3-15—4-28	.205	18.90
	1887			24.00				NE¼NE¼	25	35	42	3-15—9-15	.195	72.00
	1887				10.48			NE¼NE¼	25	35	42	3-15—6-13	.085	15.72
	1887					3.24		NE¼NE¼	25	35	42	3-15—4-28	.026	2.43
	1887			24.80				NW¼NE¼	25	35	42	3-15—9-15	.202	74.40
	1887					14.16		NW¼NE¼	25	35	42	3-15—4-28	.115	10.62
	1887			32.12				SE¼NE¼	25	35	42	3-15—9-15	.261	96.36
	1887				3.52			SE¼NE¼	25	35	42	3-15—6-13	.029	5.28
	1887					1.72		SE¼NE¼	25	35	42	3-15—4-28	.014	1.29
	1887			38.64				SW¼NE¼	25	35	42	3-15—9-15	.314	115.92
	1887			.48				SE¼NE¼	6	34	43	3-15—9-15	.004	1.44
	1887			12.96				NE¼NE¼	6	34	43	3-15—9-15	.105	38.88
	1887					17.54		NE¼NE¼	6	34	43	3-15—4-28	.143	13.16
	1887			8.36				NW¼NE¼	6	34	43	3-15—9-15	.069	25.08
	1887					4.38		NW¼NE¼	6	34	43	3-15—4-28	.036	3.29
	1887						2.56	NW¼NE¼	6	34	43	3-15—4-28	.021	1.92

Source—**Humboldt River.** Ditch—**Bacon Dam.** (Humboldt River lands.)

	1887			11.08				NW¼SE¼	13	35	42	3-15—9-15	.090	33.24
	1887					1.22		NW¼SE¼	13	35	42	3-15—4-28	.010	.92
	1887			32.92				SW¼SE¼	13	35	42	3-15—9-15	.268	98.76
	1887			.32				NE¼SE¼	13	35	42	3-15—9-15	.003	.64
	1887						.24	NE¼SE¼	13	35	42	3-15—4-28	.002	.18

Source—**Humboldt River.** Ditch—**Gonzales Slough.** (Humboldt River lands.)

	1880						40.00	NW¼NW¼	20	36	42	3-15—4-28	.325	30.00
	1880						40.00	NE¼NW¼	20	36	42	3-15—4-28	.325	30.00
	1880						40.00	NW¼NE¼	20	36	42	3-15—4-28	.328	30.30
	1880						39.36	SW¼NW¼	20	36	42	3-15—4-28	.320	29.52
	1880						40.00	SE¼NW¼	20	36	42	3-15—4-28	.325	30.00

Ellison Ranching Co.—Continued.

Year of priority	Culture—Acres: Harvest crops	Culture—Acres: Meadow pasture	Culture—Acres: Diversified pasture	Location: Subdivision	Location: Section	Location: Tp.N.	Location: R.E.	Length of season	Duty of water: C.F.S.	Duty of water: Acre-feet
1880			36.24	NW¼SW¼	20	36	42	3-15—4-28	.295	27.18
1880			37.44	NE¼SW¼	20	36	42	3-15—4-28	.304	28.08
1880			39.06	SW¼SW¼	20	36	42	3-15—4-28	.318	29.30
1880			38.36	SE¼SW¼	20	36	42	3-15—4-28	.312	28.77
1880			40.00	NE¼SE¼	20	36	42	3-15—4-28	.325	30.00
1880			38.56	NW¼SE¼	20	36	42	3-15—4-28	.313	28.92
1880			37.92	SE¼SE¼	20	36	42	3-15—4-28	.308	28.44
1880			36.00	SW¼SE¼	20	36	42	3-15—4-28	.292	27.00
1880			40.00	NW¼NW¼	21	36	42	3-15—4-28	.325	30.00
1880		20.72		NE¼NW¼	21	36	42	3-15—6-13	.169	31.08
1880			19.44	NE¼NW¼	21	36	42	3-15—4-28	.158	14.58
1880			39.52	SW¼NW¼	21	36	42	3-15—4-28	.321	29.04
1880		19.84		SE¼NW¼	21	36	42	3-15—6-13	.161	29.76
1880			19.32	SE¼NW¼	21	36	42	3-15—4-28	.157	[illegible].49
1880		23.68		NE¼SW¼	21	36	42	3-15—6-13	.193	35.52
1880			15.84	NE¼SW¼	21	36	42	3-15—4-28	.129	11.88
1880			40.00	NW¼SW¼	21	36	42	3-15—4-28	.325	30.00
1880			39.48	SW¼SW¼	21	36	42	3-15—4-28	.321	29.61
1880		.48		SE¼SW¼	21	36	42	3-15—6-13	.004	.72
1880			38.20	SE¼SW¼	21	36	42	3-15—4-28	.310	28.65
1880	23.36			NW¼NE¼	21	36	42	3-15—9-15	.190	70.08
1880			11.76	NW¼NE¼	21	36	42	3-15—4-28	.096	8.82
1880	31.72			SW¼NE¼	21	36	42	3-15—9-15	.258	95.16
1880			.32	SW¼NE¼	21	36	42	3-15—4-28	.003	.24
1880	20.40			SE¼NE¼	21	36	42	3-15—9-15	.166	61.20
1880			.72	SE¼NE¼	21	36	42	3-15—4-28	.006	.54
1880	15.48			NW¼SE¼	21	36	42	3-15—9-15	.126	46.44
1880		11.92		NW¼SE¼	21	36	42	3-15—6-13	.097	17.87
1880			12.48	NW¼SE¼	21	36	42	3-15—4-28	.101	9.36
1880	34.96			NE¼SE¼	21	36	42	3-15—9-15	.284	104.88
1880			6.16	NE¼SE¼	21	36	42	3-15—4-28	.050	4.62
1880		26.40		SW¼SE¼	21	36	42	3-15—6-13	.215	39.60
1880			12.88	SW¼SE¼	21	36	42	3-15—4-28	.105	9.66
1880	20.20			SE¼SE¼	21	36	42	3-15—9-15	.164	60.60
1880			18.20	SE¼SE¼	21	36	42	3-15—4-28	.148	13.65
1880	5.16			NW¼SW¼	22	36	42	3-15—9-15	.042	15.48
1880		21.76		NW¼SW¼	22	36	42	3-15—6-13	.177	32.74
1880			6.08	NW¼SW¼	22	36	42	3-15—4-28	.049	4.56
1880	1.08			NE¼SW¼	22	36	42	3-15—9-15	.009	3.24
1880		2.92		NE¼SW¼	22	36	42	3-15—6-13	.024	4.38
1880			36.52	NE¼SW¼	22	36	42	3-15—4-28	.297	27.39
1880	19.68			SW¼SW¼	22	36	42	3-15—9-15	.160	59.04
1880			3.16	SW¼SW¼	22	36	42	3-15—4-28	.026	2.38
1880			38.44	NW¼SE¼	28	36	42	3-15—4-28	.313	28.83
1880			38.36	NE¼SE¼	28	36	42	3-15—4-28	.312	28.77
1880			39.40	SE¼SE¼	28	36	42	3-15—4-28	.320	29.55
1880			39.28	SW¼SE¼	28	36	42	3-15—4-28	.310	29.46
1880			40.00	NW¼SW¼	28	36	42	3-15—4-28	.325	30.00
1880			38.44	NE¼SW¼	28	36	42	3-15—4-28	.313	28.83

	1880						30.20	SW¼SW¼	28	36	42	3-15—4-28	.312	29.40
	1880						38.52	SE¼SW¼	28	36	42	3-15—4-28	.313	28.80
	1880						39.84	NW¼NW¼	28	36	42	3-15—4-28	.324	29.88
	1880						39.60	NE¼NW¼	28	36	42	3-15—4-28	.322	29.70
	1880						40.00	SW¼NW¼	28	36	42	3-15—4-28	.325	30.00
	1880						38.72	SE¼NW¼	28	36	42	3-15—4-28	.315	29.04
	1880						40.00	SW¼NE¼	28	36	42	3-15—4-28	.325	30.00
	1880			2.00				SE¼NE¼	28	36	42	3-15—9-15	.016	6.00
	1880						38.84	SE¼NE¼	28	36	42	3-15—4-28	.316	29.13
	1880			10.28				NW¼NE¼	28	36	42	3-15—9-15	.084	30.84
	1880						29.68	NW¼NE¼	28	36	42	3-15—4-28	.241	22.26
	1880			36.28				NW¼NW¼	34	36	42	3-15—9-15	.295	108.84
	1880					2.24		NW¼NW¼	34	36	42	3-15—4-28	.018	1.68
	1880			31.92				NE¼NW¼	34	36	42	3-15—9-15	.260	95.76
	1880			39.20				SE¼NW¼	34	36	42	3-15—9-15	.319	117.60
	1880			35.88				SW¼SW¼	34	36	42	3-15—9-15	.292	107.64
	1880						2.40	SW¼SW¼	34	36	42	3-15—4-28	.020	1.80
	1880			40.00				SE¼SW¼	34	36	42	3-15—9-15	.325	120.00
	1880			38.28				SW¼SW¼	34	36	42	3-15—9-15	.311	114.84
	1880			40.00				NE¼SW¼	34	36	42	3-15—9-15	.325	120.00
	1880			37.00				NW¼SW¼	34	36	42	3-15—9-15	.301	111.00
	1880						3.12	NW¼SW¼	34	36	42	3-15—4-28	.025	2.34

Source—Humboldt River. Ditch—**Overflow.** (Humboldt River lands.)

	1880						28.80	NE¼NE¼	21	36	42	3-15—4-28	.234	21.60
	1880						3.84	SW¼NE¼	21	36	42	3-15—4-28	.028	2.58
	1880						12.96	SE¼NE¼	21	36	42	3-15—4-28	.105	9.72
	1880						10.08	SW¼SW¼	22	36	42	3-15—4-28	.082	7.56
	1880			15.48				SE¼SW¼	22	36	42	3-15—9-15	.126	46.44
	1880						23.80	SE¼SW¼	22	36	42	3-15—4-28	.193	17.85

Source—Humboldt River. Ditch—**"13" Ditch.** (Humboldt River lands.)

	1874				17.38			NE¼SE¼	14	36	41	3-15—6-13	.141	26.04
	1874						9.72	NE¼SE¼	14	36	41	3-15—4-28	.079	7.29
	1874						27.04	SE¼SE¼	14	36	41	3-15—4-28	.220	20.28

Source—Humboldt River. Ditch—**Outside Slough.** (Humboldt River lands.)

	1887						2.24	SE¼SE¼	6	34	43	3-15—4-28	.018	1.68
	1887						12.40	SW¼SE¼	6	34	43	3-15—4-28	.101	9.30
	1887						10.72	NE¼SE¼	6	34	43	3-15—4-28	.087	8.04
	1887						15.08	NW¼SE¼	6	34	43	3-15—4-28	.123	11.31
	1887						33.70	NE¼SW¼	6	34	43	3-15—4-28	.274	25.28
	1887						21.60	NW¼SW¼	6	34	43	3-15—4-28	.176	16.20
	1887						7.04	SW¼SW¼	6	34	43	3-15—4-28	.057	5.28
	1887						9.32	SE¼SW¼	6	34	43	3-15—4-28	.076	6.99
	1886						36.56	NW¼NW¼	32	36	42	3-15—4-28	.297	27.42
	1886						37.64	SW¼NW¼	32	36	42	3-15—4-28	.306	28.33
	1886						36.86	SE¼NW¼	32	36	42	3-15—4-28	.300	27.65
	1886						38.64	NE¼NW¼	32	36	42	3-15—4-28	.314	28.98
	1886						38.20	NW¼NE¼	32	36	42	3-15—4-28	.311	28.65
	1886						37.32	SW¼NE¼	32	36	42	3-15—4-28	.303	27.99
	1886						39.00	NE¼NE¼	32	36	42	3-15—4-28	.317	29.25
	1886						40.20	SE¼NE¼	32	36	42	3-15—4-28	.327	30.15

Ellison Ranching Co.—Continued.

Year of priority	Culture—Acres: Harvest crops	Meadow pasture	Diversified pasture	Location: Subdivision	Section	Tp. N.	R. E.	Length of season	Duty of water: C. F. S.	Acre-feet
1886			38.00	NE¼SW¼	32	36	42	3-15—4-28	.309	28.50
1886			40.32	NW¼SW¼	32	36	42	3-15—4-28	.328	30.24
1886			40.24	SE¼SW¼	32	36	42	3-15—4-28	.327	30.18
1886			27.12	SW¼SW¼	32	36	42	3-15—4-28	.220	20.35
1886			40.32	NE¼SE¼	32	36	42	3-15—4-28	.328	30.24
1886			40.48	SE¼SE¼	32	36	42	3-15—4-28	.329	30.36
1886			35.62	NW¼SE¼	32	36	42	3-15—4-28	.290	26.72
1886			37.64	SW¼SE¼	32	36	42	3-15—4-28	.306	28.23
1886			28.68	NW¼NE¼	5	35	42	3-15—4-28	.233	21.51
1886			38.08	NE¼NE¼	5	35	42	3-15—4-28	.310	28.56
1886			37.10	SE¼SE¼	5	35	42	3-15—4-28	.302	27.83
1886			16.64	NE¼SE¼	5	35	42	3-15—4-28	.135	12.98
1886			4.96	SW¼NE¼	5	35	42	3-15—4-28	.040	3.72
1886			36.80	SE¼NE¼	5	35	42	3-15—4-28	.299	27.60
1886			36.60	NW¼NW¼	4	35	42	3-15—4-28	.298	27.45
1886			36.56	NE¼NW¼	4	35	42	3-15—4-28	.297	27.42
1886			38.96	SW¼NW¼	4	35	42	3-15—4-28	.317	29.22
1886			39.32	SE¼NW¼	4	35	42	3-15—4-28	.320	29.49
1886			38.80	NW¼SE¼	4	35	42	3-15—4-28	.315	29.10
1886			39.28	NE¼SE¼	4	35	42	3-15—4-28	.319	29.46
1886			33.16	SW¼SE¼	4	35	42	3-15—4-28	.270	24.87
1886			39.24	SE¼SE¼	4	35	42	3-15—4-28	.319	29.43
1886			40.08	NW¼NE¼	4	35	42	3-15—4-28	.326	30.06
1886			38.72	NE¼NE¼	4	35	42	3-15—4-28	.315	29.04
1886			39.36	SE¼NE¼	4	35	42	3-15—4-28	.320	29.52
1886			38.88	SW¼NE¼	4	35	42	3-15—4-28	.315	29.16
1886			38.16	SE¼SE¼	4	35	42	3-15—4-28	.310	28.62
1886			37.66	SW¼SE¼	4	35	42	3-15—4-28	.306	28.25
1886			38.88	NE¼SE¼	4	35	42	3-15—4-28	.315	29.16
1886			38.24	NW¼SE¼	4	35	42	3-15—4-28	.311	28.68
1887			12.32	NE¼NW¼	35	35	42	3-15—4-28	.100	9.24
1887			39.60	SE¼NW¼	35	35	42	3-15—4-28	.322	29.70
1887			11.66	NE¼SW¼	35	35	42	3-15—4-28	.095	8.75
1887			40.40	NE¼NE¼	35	35	42	3-15—4-28	.328	30.30
1887			39.12	NW¼SE¼	35	35	42	3-15—4-28	.318	29.34
1887			39.44	NE¼SE¼	35	35	42	3-15—4-28	.321	29.58
1887			30.64	NE¼SE¼	1	34	42	3-15—4-28	.249	22.98
1887			10.88	NW¼SE¼	1	34	42	3-15—4-28	.088	8.16
1887			33.20	SE¼NE¼	1	34	42	3-15—4-28	.270	24.90
1887			39.36	SW¼NE¼	1	34	42	3-15—4-28	.320	29.52
1887			26.00	NE¼NE¼	1	34	42	3-15—4-28	.211	19.50
1887			38.00	NW¼NE¼	1	34	42	3-15—4-28	.309	28.60
1887			16.48	NE¼NW¼	1	34	42	3-15—4-28	.134	12.36
1887			32.48	SE¼NW¼	1	34	42	3-15—4-28	.264	24.36
1887		38.80		NW¼NW¼	27	35	42	3-15—4-28	.311	29.10
1887		35.41		NE¼NW¼	27	35	42	3-15—4-28	.288	26.58
1887			38.20	SE¼NW¼	27	35	42	3-15—4-28	.311	28.65
1887			40.40	SW¼NW¼	27	35	42	3-15—4-28	.328	30.30
1887			40.00	NW¼NE¼	27	35	42	3-15—4-28	.325	30.00

	1887					37.88		NW¼SE¼	27	35	42	3-15—4-28	.308	28.41
	1887						38.96	NE¼SE¼	27	35	42	3-15—4-28	.317	29.22
	1887					37.36		SE¼SE¼	27	35	42	3-15—4-28	.304	28.02
	1887						39.68	SW¼NE¼	27	35	42	3-15—4-28	.323	29.76
	1887						39.88	SE¼NE¼	27	35	42	3-15—4-28	.324	29.91
	1887						37.08	SW¼SW¼	22	35	42	3-15—4-28	.301	27.81
	1887						35.72	NW¼SW¼	22	35	42	3-15—4-28	.290	26.79
	1887						36.71	SE¼SE¼	35	35	42	3-15—4-28	.298	27.53
	1887						1.33	SW¼SE¼	35	35	42	3-15—4-28	.011	1.00
	1887						38.84	NW¼SW¼	36	35	42	3-15—4-28	.316	29.13
	1887						35.40	NE¼SW¼	36	35	42	3-15—4-28	.288	26.55
	1887						37.44	SW¼SW¼	36	35	42	3-15—4-28	.304	28.08
	1887						41.40	SE¼SW¼	36	35	42	3-15—4-28	.337	31.05
	1887						38.80	NW¼SE¼	36	35	42	3-15—4-28	.315	29.10
	1887						40.32	NE¼SE¼	36	35	42	3-15—4-28	.328	30.24
	1887						39.56	SE¼SE¼	36	35	42	3-15—4-28	.322	29.67
	1887						31.04	SW¼SE¼	36	35	42	3-15—4-28	.252	23.28
	1887						31.60	NW¼NW¼	9	35	42	3-15—4-28	.257	23.70
	1887						19.84	SE¼NW¼	9	35	42	3-15—4-28	.161	14.88
	1887						36.80	SW¼NW¼	9	35	42	3-15—4-28	.299	27.60
	1887						.72	SW¼SW¼	9	35	42	3-15—4-28	.006	.54
	1887						37.28	NE¼SW¼	9	35	42	3-15—4-28	.303	27.96
	1887					38.32		SE¼SW¼	9	35	42	3-15—4-28	.312	28.74
	1887						10.68	NW¼SE¼	9	35	42	3-15—4-28	.087	8.01
	1887					38.66		NE¼SE¼	9	35	42	3-15—4-28	.314	29.00
	1887						3.48	SE¼SE¼	9	35	42	3-15—4-28	.028	2.61
	1887						36.36	SW¼SE¼	9	35	42	3-15—4-28	.296	27.27
	1887						37.44	SW¼NE¼	9	35	42	3-15—4-28	.304	28.08

Source—**Rock Creek and Tributaries.** Ditch—**Fraser Creek Canal.** (Squaw Valley lands.)

	1883					1.05		NE¼NE¼	26	38	46	3-15—4-28	.009	.79
	1886			23.30				NE¼SE¼	13	38	46	3-15—9-15	.189	69.90
	1886						18.17	NE¼SE¼	13	38	46	3-15—4-28	.148	14.73
	1886			.82				SE¼SE¼	13	38	46	3-15—9-15	.007	2.46
	1886					9.45		SE¼SE¼	13	38	46	3-15—4-28	.077	7.09
	1886						25.97	SE¼SE¼	13	38	46	3-15—4-28	.211	19.49
	1886			34.81				NW¼SE¼	13	38	46	3-15—9-15	.283	104.43
	1886						7.63	NW¼SE¼	13	38	46	3-15—4-28	.062	5.72
	1886			.27				SW¼SE¼	13	38	46	3-15—9-15	.002	.81
	1886						43.55	SW¼SE¼	13	38	46	3-15—4-28	.354	32.66
	1886			1.95				SE¼NW¼	13	38	46	3-15—9-15	.016	5.85
	1886					12.45		SE¼NW¼	13	38	46	3-15—4-28	.101	9.34
	1886			3.44				NE¼SW¼	13	38	46	3-15—9-15	.028	10.32
	1886					7.68		NE¼SW¼	13	38	46	3-15—4-28	.062	7.68
	1886						29.07	NE¼SW¼	13	38	46	3-15—4-28	.236	21.80
	1886						9.26	SE¼SW¼	13	38	46	3-15—4-28	.075	6.95
	1886						30.50	NE¼NE¼	24	38	46	3-15—4-28	.248	22.88
	1886						36.50	SE¼NE¼	24	38	46	3-15—4-28	.297	27.38
	1886						41.42	NW¼NE¼	24	38	46	3-15—4-28	.337	31.07
	1886						41.10	SW¼NE¼	24	38	46	3-15—4-28	.334	30.83
	1886						38.10	NE¼SE¼	24	38	46	3-15—4-28	.310	28.60
	1886					10.98		SE¼SE¼	24	38	46	3-15—4-28	.089	8.18
	1886						29.74	SE¼SE¼	24	38	46	3-15—4-28	.242	22.31

Ellison Ranching Co.—Continued.

Year of priority	Culture—Acres: Harvest crops	Meadow pasture	Diversified	pasture	Location: Subdivision	Section	Tp.N.	R.E.	Length of season	Duty of water: C.F.S.	Acre-feet
1886				40.95	NW¼SE¼	24	38	46	3-15—4-28	.333	30.71
1886			29.31		SW¼SE¼	24	38	46	3-15—4-28	.238	21.98
1886				12.06	SW¼SE¼	24	38	46	3-15—4-28	.098	9.05
1886				17.84	NE¼NW¼	24	38	46	3-15—4-28	.145	13.08
1886				7.94	SE¼NW¼	24	38	46	3-15—4-28	.065	5.96
1886			2.42		SE¼NE¼	12	38	46	3-15—4-28	.020	1.82
1886	15.53				NE¼SE¼	12	38	46	3-15—9-15	.126	46.59
1886			8.64		NE¼SE¼	12	38	46	3-15—4-28	.070	6.48
1886				14.00	NE¼SE¼	12	38	46	3-15—4-28	.114	10.50
1886	15.05				SE¼SE¼	12	38	46	3-15—9-15	.122	45.15
1886				9.09	SE¼SE¼	12	38	46	3-15—4-28	.074	6.82
1886	8.00				NE¼NE¼	13	38	46	3-15—9-15	.065	24.00
1886	28.37				NW¼NE¼	13	38	46	3-15—9-15	.231	85.11
1886				6.05	NW¼NE¼	13	38	46	3-15—4-28	.049	4.54
1886	3.10				SE¼NE¼	13	38	46	3-15—9-15	.025	6.30
1886	24.87				SW¼NE¼	13	38	46	3-15—9-15	.202	74.61
1886	.36				NE¼NW¼	13	38	46	3-15—9-15	.003	1.08
1886				1.73	NE¼NW¼	13	38	46	3-15—4-28	.014	1.30
1886	3.90				SE¼NW¼	13	38	46	3-15—9-15	.032	11.70
1886			6.26		SE¼NW¼	13	38	46	3-15—4-28	.051	4.70
1886				2.38	SE¼NW¼	13	38	46	3-15—4-28	.019	1.79
1886	33.52				SW¼SE¼	6	38	47	3-15—9-15	.273	100.56
1886			3.17		SW¼SE¼	6	38	47	3-15—4-28	.026	2.38

Source—**Willow Creek.** Ditch—**Fraser Creek Canal.** (Squaw Valley lands.)

1886				1.55	SW¼NW¼	18	38	47	3-15—4-28	.013	1.16
1886	6.95				SE¼NE¼	13	38	46	3-15—9-15	.057	20.85
1886				6.87	SE¼NE¼	13	38	46	3-15—4-28	.056	5.15
1846	14.45				SW¼NE¼	13	38	46	3-15—9-15	.117	43.35

Source—**Rock Creek and Tributaries.** Ditch—**Fraser Creek Canal.** (Squaw Valley lands.)

1881	35.50				NE¼NW¼	7	38	47	3-15—9-15	.289	106.50
1881	27.74				SW¼NW¼	7	38	47	3-15—9-15	.226	83.22
1881				8.21	SW¼NW¼	7	38	47	3-15—4-28	.067	6.16
1881	0.46				SW¼SW¼	32	39	47	3-15—9-15	.004	1.38
1881				9.60	SW¼SW¼	32	39	47	3-15—4-28	.078	7.20
1881				12.08	NE¼SW¼	24	38	46	3-15—4-28	.098	9.06
1881				40.35	SE¼SW¼	24	38	46	3-15—4-28	.328	30.26
1881			16.37		SW¼SW¼	24	38	46	3-15—4-28	.133	12.28
1881				9.95	SW¼SW¼	19	38	47	3-15—4-28	.081	7.46
1881				23.92	NW¼NW¼	20	38	47	3-15—4-28	.194	17.94
1881				2.42	SW¼NW¼	30	38	47	3-15—4-28	.020	1.82
1881				1.87	SE¼SE¼	23	38	46	3-15—4-28	.015	1.40

Source—**Rock Creek and Tributaries.** Ditch—**Lakefield Ditch.** (Squaw Valley lands.)

1880	24.82				SW¼SW¼	7	38	47	3-15—9-15	.202	74.46
1880				6.62	SW¼SW¼	7	38	47	3-15—4-28	.010	4.22
1880	16.27				SE¼SW¼	7	38	47	3-15—9-15	.132	48.81
1880				8.50	SE¼SW¼	7	38	47	3-15—4-28	.070	6.14

	1880			4.03				NE¼NW¼	18	38	47	3-15—9-15	.033	12.09
	1880						6.17	NE¼NW¼	18	38	47	3-15—4-28	.050	4.63
	1880			17.13				NW¼NW¼	18	38	47	3-15—9-15	.139	51.39
	1880						2.39	NW¼NW¼	18	38	47	3-15—4-28	.019	1.73
	1880			4.82				SW¼NW¼	18	38	47	3-15—9-15	.039	14.46
	1880						7.49	SW¼NW¼	18	38	47	3-15—4-28	.061	5.62
	1880						2.70	SE¼NW¼	18	38	47	3-15—4-28	.022	2.03
	1880			29.55				SW¼NE¼	7	38	47	3-15—9-15	.240	88.65
	1880						10.30	SW¼NE¼	7	38	47	3-15—4-28	.084	7.73
	1880			33.92				SE¼NW¼	7	38	47	3-15—9-15	.276	101.76
	1880					3.38		SE¼NW¼	7	38	47	3-15—4-28	.027	2.54
	1880			20.74				NE¼SW¼	7	38	47	3-15—9-15	.242	80.22
	1880						2.16	NE¼SW¼	7	38	47	3-15—4-28	.018	1.62
	1880			34.17				NW¼SW¼	7	38	47	3-15—9-15	.279	102.51
	1880						5.18	NW¼SW¼	7	38	47	3-15—4-28	.042	3.89

Source—**Rock Creek and Tributaries.** Ditch—**Rock Creek Ditch.** (Squaw Valley lands.)

	1878			18.53				NW¼NW¼	8	38	47	3-15—9-15	.151	55.60
	1878					14.36		NW¼NW¼	8	38	47	3-15—4-28	.117	10.77
	1878					2.09		SE¼NW¼	8	38	47	3-15—4-28	.017	1.57
	1878					3.38		SW¼NW¼	8	38	47	3-15—4-28	.027	2.54
	1878						23.12	SW¼NW¼	8	38	47	3-15—4-28	.189	17.34
	1878						1.60	NW¼SW¼	8	38	47	3-15—4-28	.013	1.20
	1878			38.05				NE¼NE¼	7	38	47	3-15—9-15	.309	114.15
	1878			37.00				NW¼NE¼	7	38	47	3-15—9-15	.300	111.00
	1878			24.28				SE¼NE¼	7	38	47	3-15—9-15	.197	72.81
	1878						12.95	SE¼NE¼	7	38	47	3-15—4-28	.105	9.71
	1878						7.05	NE¼SE¼	7	38	47	3-15—4-28	.057	5.29
	1878			1.72				NW¼SE¼	7	38	47	3-15—9-15	.014	5.16
	1878						8.30	NW¼SE¼	7	38	47	3-15—4-28	.067	6.23
	1878			36.80				SE¼NW¼	5	38	47	3-15—9-15	.290	110.40
	1878			17.74				NE¼SW¼	5	38	47	3-15—9-15	.144	53.22
	1878			36.47				NW¼SW¼	5	38	47	3-15—9-15	.297	109.41
	1878					4.75		NW¼SW¼	5	38	47	3-15—4-28	.039	3.56
	1878			37.27				SW¼SW¼	5	38	47	3-15—9-15	.303	111.81

Source—**Rock Creek and Tributaries.** Ditch—**Highline Ditch.** (Squaw Valley lands.)

	1887			.50				NW¼NW¼	1	38	46	3-15—9-15	.004	1.50
	1887			18.43				SE¼NW¼	1	38	46	3-15—9-15	.150	55.29
	1887						4.88	SE¼NW¼	1	38	46	3-15—4-28	.040	3.66
	1887			34.92				SW¼NW¼	1	38	46	3-15—9-15	.283	104.76
	1887			15.90				NE¼SW¼	1	38	46	3-15—9-15	.129	47.70
	1887			30.62				NW¼SW¼	1	38	46	3-15—9-15	.249	91.86
	1887			8.93				SW¼SW¼	1	38	46	3-16—9-15	.073	26.79
	1887			40.87				SE¼NE¼	2	38	46	3-15—9-15	.332	122.61
	1887			14.70				SW¼NE¼	2	38	46	3-15—9-15	.120	44.10
	1887			24.27				SW¼NE¼	2	38	46	3-15—9-15	.197	72.81
	1887			26.03				NE¼SE¼	2	38	46	3-15—9-15	.212	78.09
	1887			21.06				NW¼SE¼	2	38	46	3-15—9-15	.171	63.18
	1887						19.41	NW¼SE¼	2	38	46	3-15—4-28	.158	14.56
	1887			5.04				SE¼SE¼	2	38	46	3-15—9-15	.041	15.12
	1887						13.88	SE¼SW¼	32	39	47	3-15—4-28	.113	10.41
	1887				9.61			SE¼SW¼	31	39	47	3-15—6-13	.078	14.42

Ellison Ranching Co.—Continued.

Year of priority	Culture—Acres: Harvest crops	Culture—Acres: Meadow pasture	Culture—Acres: Diversified pasture		Location: Subdivision	Location: Section	Location: Tp. N.	Location: R. E.	Length of season	Duty of water: C. F. S.	Duty of water: Acre-feet
1887		8.54			SW¼SW¼	31	39	47	3-15—6-13	.069	12.81
1887		17.33			NE¼NW¼	6	38	47	3-15—6-13	.141	26.00
1887		2.31			NW¼NW¼	6	38	47	3-15—6-13	.019	3.47
1887	5.82				NE¼NE¼	2	38	46	3-15—9.15	.047	17.46
1887	12.75				NW¼NE¼	2	38	46	3-15—9-15	.104	38.25
1887			11.29		SE¼SE¼	2	38	46	3-15—4-28	.092	8.46
1887			14.04		NE¼SE¼	2	38	46	3-15—4-28	.114	10.53
1887	2.35				SE¼NW¼	2	38	46	3-15—6-13	.019	3.53
1887	5.34				NE¼SW¼	2	38	46	3-15—6-13	.043	8.01
1887			4.86		NE¼SW¼	2	38	46	3-15—4-28	.039	3.65
1887			8.45		SW¼SE¼	2	38	46	3-15—4-28	.069	6.34
1887			7.00		NW¼SW¼	2	38	46	3-15—4-28	.057	5.25
1887			2.80		SW¼SW¼	2	38	46	3-15—4-28	.023	2.10
1887			6.75		SW¼SE¼	31	39	47	3 15—4-28	.055	5.06
1887			5.95		SE¼SE¼	31	39	47	3-15—4-28	.048	4.46
1887			3.20		NE¼NE¼	6	38	47	3-15—4-28	.026	2.40

Source—**Willow Creek.** Ditch—**Overflow.** (Squaw Valley lands.)

Year of priority	Harvest crops	Meadow pasture	Diversified pasture		Subdivision	Section	Tp. N.	R. E.	Length of season	C. F. S.	Acre-feet
1878	5.47				NE¼SW¼	18	38	47	3-15—9 15	.044	16.41
1878			2.28		NE¼SW¼	18	38	47	3-15—4-28	.019	1.71
1878				8.47	NE¼SW¼	18	38	47	3-15—4-28	.069	6.35
1878				12.50	NW¼SW¼	18	38	47	3-15—4 28	.101	9.38

Source—**Willow Creek.** Ditch—**Deep Slough.** (Squaw Valley lands.)

Year of priority	Harvest crops	Meadow pasture	Diversified pasture		Subdivision	Section	Tp. N.	R. E.	Length of season	C. F. S.	Acre-feet
1883	5.55				SE¼SW¼	8	38	47	3-15—9-15	.045	16.05
1886		10.90			SE¼SW¼	8	38	47	3-15—6-13	.089	16.35
1886		17.27			NE¼NW¼	17	38	47	3-15—6-13	.140	25.91
1886		20.82			NW¼NW¼	17	38	47	3.15—6-13	.160	31.23
1886		2.42			SW¼NW¼	17	38	47	3-15—6-13	.020	3.63
1886		13.30			NE¼NE¼	18	38	47	3-15—6-13	.108	19.95
1886		0.87			NW¼NE¼	18	38	47	3-15—6-13	.007	1.31
1886		24.77			SE¼NE¼	18	38	47	3.15—6-13	.201	37.16
1886		14.85			SW¼NE¼	18	38	47	3-15—6-13	.116	21.53
1886	27.27				NE¼SE¼	8	38	47	3-15—9-15	.222	81.81
1886	16.62				SE¼SE¼	8	38	47	3-15—9-15	.135	49.86
1886	7.62				NW¼SE¼	8	38	47	3.15—9-15	.062	22.86
1886	32.87				SW¼SE¼	8	38	47	3-15—9-15	.267	98.61
1886	0.97				NW¼NE¼	17	38	47	3-15—9 15	.008	2.91
1886	1.90				SE¼NE¼	18	38	47	3-15—9-15	.015	5.70
1886				7.49	SE¼NE¼	18	38	47	3.15—4-28	.061	5.62
1886	11.70				SW¼NE¼	18	38	47	3-15—9-15	.095	35.10
1886				0.75	SW¼NE¼	18	38	47	3-15—4-28	.006	.56
1886				1.32	NE¼SE¼	18	88	47	3 15—4-28	.011	.99
1886	3.97				NW¼SE¼	18	38	47	3-15—9-15	.032	12.01
1886				11.57	NW¼SE¼	18	38	47	3-15—4 28	.094	8.64
1883	3.02				SE¼NW¼	18	38	47	3 15—9-15	.029	10.86
1886			5.85		SE¼NW¼	18	38	47	3 15—4 28	.048	4.30
1884				1.25	SE¼NW¼	18	38	47	3 15—4 28	.010	[illegible]

Source—**Rock Creek and Tributaries.** Ditch—**Warm Spring.** (Squaw Valley lands.)

	1876					13.15		NE¼NE¼	25	38	46	3-15—4-28	.107	9.87
	1876						20.17	NE¼NE¼	25	38	46	3-15—4-28	.164	15.13
	1876					13.01		NW¼NE¼	25	38	46	3-15—4-28	.106	9.76
	1876						13.74	NW¼NE¼	25	38	46	3-15—4-28	.112	10.31
	1876					21.02		NE¼NW¼	25	38	46	3-15—4-28	.176	16.22
	1876						3.00	NE¼NW¼	25	38	46	3-15—4-28	.024	2.25
	1876					20.35		NW¼NW¼	25	38	46	3-15—4-28	.165	15.26

Source—**Rock Creek.** Ditch—**Barleyfield Canal.** (Squaw Valley lands.)

	1888					3.96		NW¼SE¼	21	39	47	3-15—4-28	.032	2.96
	1888					0.47		SW¼SE¼	21	39	47	3-15—4-28	.038	0.35
	1888					32.45		NE¼SW¼	21	39	47	3-15—4-28	.264	24.34
	1888					29.30		SE¼SW¼	21	39	47	3-15—4-28	.238	21.98
	1888					35.95		NW¼SW¼	21	39	47	3-15—4-28	.292	26.96
	1888					36.00		SW¼SW¼	21	39	47	3-15—4-28	.293	27.00
	1888					1.00		SW¼NE¼	20	39	47	3-15—4-28	.008	0.75
	1888					40.55		NE¼SE¼	20	39	47	3-15—4-28	.330	30.41
	1888					36.35		SE¼SE¼	20	39	47	3-15—4-28	.296	27.26
	1888					21.40		NW¼SE¼	20	39	47	3-15—4-28	.174	16.30
	1888					23.30		SW¼SE¼	20	39	47	3-15—4-28	.189	17.48
	1888					2.90		NE¼NW¼	28	39	47	3-15—4-28	.024	2.18
	1888					27.64		NW¼NW¼	28	39	47	3-15—4-28	.225	20.73
	1888					4.73		SW¼NW¼	28	39	47	3-15—4-28	.039	3.55
	1888					39.37		NE¼NE¼	29	39	47	3-15—4-28	.320	29.53
	1888					2.35		SE¼NE¼	29	39	47	3-15—4-28	.019	1.76

Source—**Rock Creek and Tributaries.** Ditch—**Willow Creek Canal.** (Squaw Valley lands.)

	1880				23.40			SE¼NE¼	1	38	46	3-15—6-13	.190	35.10
	1880						5.26	SE¼NE¼	1	38	46	3-15—4-28	.043	3.95
	1880				23.61			SW¼NE¼	1	38	46	3-15—6-13	.192	35.42
	1880						13.68	SW¼NE¼	1	38	46	3-15—4-28	.111	10.26
	1880			16.56				NE¼SE¼	1	38	46	3-15—9-15	.135	49.68
	1880				17.67			NE¼SE¼	1	38	46	3-15—6-12	.144	26.51
	1880						3.31	NE¼SE¼	1	38	46	3-15—4-28	.027	2.48
	1880			12.12				NW¼SE¼	1	38	46	3-15—9-15	.098	36.36
	1880				7.27			NW¼SE¼	1	38	46	3-15—6-13	.059	10.90
	1880			34.19				SE¼SE¼	1	38	46	3-15—9-15	.278	102.57
	1880						5.76	SE¼SE¼	1	38	46	3-15—4-28	.047	4.32
	1880			40.00				SW¼SE¼	1	38	46	3-15—9-15	.325	120.00
	1888			34.79				SE¼SW¼	1	38	46	3-15—9-15	.283	[illegible]
	1888				1.51			SE¼SW¼	1	38	46	3-15—6-13	.012	2.27
	1888				3.67			SE¼NW¼	1	38	46	3-15—6-13	.030	5.51
	1888			15.12				NE¼SW¼	1	38	46	3-15—9-15	.123	45.36
	1888				7.06			NE¼SW¼	1	38	46	3-15—6-13	.057	10.59
	1888						1.90	SW¼SW¼	1	38	46	3-15—4-28	.015	1.43
	1880			33.85				SE¼SE¼	6	38	47	3-15—9-15	.275	101.55
	1880					4.25		SE¼SE¼	6	38	47	3-15—4-28	.035	3.19
	1880			32.48				NE¼SW¼	6	38	47	3-15—9-15	.264	97.44
	1880						8.42	NE¼SW¼	6	38	47	3-15—4-28	.068	6.32
	1880			15.12				NW¼SW¼	6	38	47	3-15—9-15	.122	45.36
	1880						20.47	NW¼SW¼	6	38	47	3-15—4-28	.166	15.35
	1880			40.37				SE¼SW¼	6	38	47	3-15—9-15	.328	121.11

Ellison Ranching Co.—Continued.

Year of priority	Culture—Acres: Harvest crops	Culture—Acres: Meadow pasture	Culture—Acres: Diversified pasture		Location: Subdivision	Location: Section	Location: Tp. N.	Location: R. E.	Length of season	Duty of water: C. F. S.	Duty of water: Acre-feet
1889	27.65				SW¼SW¼	6	38	47	3-15—9-15	.225	82.95
1889				4.54	SW¼SW¼	6	38	47	3-15—4-28	.037	3.41
1889	0.07				NE¼NE¼	5	38	47	3-15—9-15	.008	2.91
1889	8.82				NW¼NE¼	5	38	47	3-15—9-15	.072	26.46
1889				4.48	NW¼NE¼	5	38	47	3-15—4-28	.036	3.36
1889	18.37				NE¼NW¼	5	38	47	3-15—9-15	.149	55.11
1889		10.18			NE¼NW¼	5	38	47	3-15—6-13	.083	15.27
1889				6.29	NE¼NW¼	5	38	47	3-15—4-28	.051	4.70
1880	11.29				NW¼NW¼	5	38	47	3-15—9-15	.092	33.87
1889				5.78	NW¼NW¼	5	38	47	3-15—4-28	.047	4.34
1889	15.10				NE¼NE¼	6	38	47	3-15—9-15	.123	45.30
1889				11.10	NE¼NE¼	6	38	47	3-15—4-28	.090	8.33
1889	0.40				SE¼NE¼	5	38	47	3-15—9-15	.003	1.20
1889	34.09				SW¼NE¼	5	38	47	3-15—9-15	.277	102.27
1889			0.26		SW¼NE¼	5	38	47	3-15—4-28	.002	0.20
1889	15.11				NW¼SE¼	5	38	47	3-15—9-15	.123	45.33
1889			6.51		NW¼SE¼	5	38	47	3-15—4-28	.053	4.88
1889			3.46		SW¼SE¼	5	38	47	3-15—4-28	.028	2.60
1886	1.65				SW¼SE¼	3	38	47	3-15—9-15	.013	4.95
1886	12.45				SE¼SW¼	3	38	47	3-15—9-15	.101	37.35
1886	33.90				SW¼SW¼	3	38	47	3-15—9-15	.276	101.70
1886	24.60				SE¼SE¼	4	38	47	3-15—9-15	.200	73.80
1886	3.00				SW¼SE¼	4	38	47	3-15—9-15	.024	9.00
1886	0.67				NW¼NW¼	10	38	47	3-15—9-15	.005	2.01
1886	10.68				NE¼NE¼	9	38	47	3-15—9-15	.067	32.04
1886				3.93	NE¼NE¼	9	38	47	3-15—4-28	.032	2.95
1886	30.86				NW¼NE¼	9	38	47	3-15—9-15	.251	92.58
1886				4.21	NW¼NE¼	9	38	47	3-15—4-28	.034	3.16
1886	6.77				SW¼NE¼	9	38	47	3-15—9-15	.055	20.31
1886				7.88	SW¼NE¼	9	38	47	3-15—4-28	.064	5.91
1886	18.37				NE¼NW¼	8	38	47	3-15—9-15	.149	55.11
1886	37.40				SE¼NW¼	9	38	47	3-15—9-15	.304	112.20
1886	20.88				SW¼NW¼	9	38	47	3-15—9-15	.170	62.64
1886	4.95				NE¼SW¼	9	38	47	3-15—9-15	.040	14.85
1886	36.72				NW¼SW¼	9	38	47	3-15—9-15	.299	110.16
1886	1.46				SW¼SW¼	9	38	47	3-15—9-15	.011	4.20
1886	0.29				SE¼NE¼	8	38	47	3-15—9-15	.002	.87
1889	6.05				NE¼NW¼	8	38	47	3-15—9-15	.049	18.15
1880			21.08		NE¼NW¼	8	38	47	3-15—4-28	.171	15.81
1880	23.82				NW¼NW¼	7	38	47	3-15—9-15	.194	71.46
1880				3.23	NW¼NW¼	7	38	47	3-15—4-28	.026	2.42
1880		21.27			NW¼NW¼	5	38	47	3-15—6-13	.173	31.91
1880			1.12		SW¼SE¼	3	38	47	3-15—4-28	.009	0.84
1880			0.33		SW¼SW¼	3	38	47	3-15—4-28	.003	0.25
1880			0.15		NW¼SW¼	3	38	47	3-15—4-28	.001	0.11
1880			8.91		NE¼SW¼	3	38	47	3-15—4-28	.072	6.68
1880			14.51		NW¼SE¼	3	38	47	3-15—4-28	.118	10.88
1880			1.40		NE¼SE¼	3	38	47	3-15—4-28	.011	1.05
1880			4.25		SE¼SW¼	3	38	47	3-15—4-28	.035	[illegible]

.....	1880	.....	.....	....	3.25	.....	.....	NE¼NE¼	1	38	46	3-15—6-13	.026	1.88
.....	1881	.....	.....	....	15.06	.....	.....	NW¼NE¼	1	38	46	3-15—6-13	.122	2.26
.....	1880	.....	.....	....	2.74	.....	.....	NE¼NW¼	1	38	46	3-15—6-13	.022	0.41
.....	1880	.....	.....	22.03	.....	.....	.....	NE¼NE¼	12	38	46	3-15—9-15	.179	66.09
.....	1880	.....	.....	....	.....	.....	9.65	NE¼NE¼	12	38	46	3-15—4-28	.078	7.24
.....	1880	.....	.....	28.80	.....	.....	.....	NW¼NE¼	12	38	46	3-15—9-15	.234	86.40
.....	1880	.....	.....	....	11.10	.....	.....	NW¼NE¼	12	38	46	3-15—6-13	.090	16.65
.....	1880	.....	.....	29.23	.....	.....	.....	SE¼NE¼	12	38	46	3-15—9-15	.238	87.69
.....	1880	.....	.....	....	.....	.....	4.39	SE¼NE¼	12	38	46	3-15—4-28	.036	3.21
.....	1880	.....	.....	16.20	.....	.....	.....	SW¼NE¼	12	38	46	3-15—9-15	.132	48.60
.....	1880	.....	.....	....	.....	.....	15.12	SW¼NE¼	12	38	46	3-15—4-28	.123	11.34
.....	1880	.....	.....	4.90	.....	.....	.....	NE¼NW¼	12	38	46	3-15—9-15	.040	14.70
.....	1880	.....	.....	....	27.45	.....	.....	NE¼NW¼	12	38	46	3-15—6-13	.223	41.18
.....	1880	.....	.....	....	.....	.....	8.42	NE¼NW¼	12	38	46	3-15—4-28	.068	6.32
.....	1880	.....	.....	....	.....	.....	13.70	NW¼NW¼	12	38	46	3-15—4-28	.111	10.28
.....	1880	.....	.....	....	.....	.....	4.39	SE¼NW¼	12	38	46	3-15—4-28	.036	3.29
.....	1880	.....	.....	....	.....	.....	7.06	NW¼SE¼	12	38	46	3-15—4-28	.057	5.30
.....	1880	.....	.....	1.20	.....	.....	.....	SW¼SE¼	12	38	46	3-15—9-15	.010	3.60
.....	1880	.....	.....	....	.....	.....	9.58	SW¼SE¼	12	38	46	3-15—4-28	.078	7.19
.....	1880	.....	.....	19.14	.....	.....	.....	SW¼NW¼	5	38	47	3-15—9-15	.156	57.42
.....	1880	.....	.....	....	22.26	.....	.....	SW¼NW¼	5	38	47	3-15—6-13	.181	33.39
.....	1880	.....	.....	27.15	.....	.....	.....	SE¼SW¼	5	38	47	3-15—9-15	.221	81.45
.....	1880	.....	.....	....	.....	13.70	.....	SE¼SW¼	5	38	47	3-15—4-28	.111	10.28
.....	1880	.....	.....	29.40	.....	.....	.....	SE¼NE¼	6	38	47	3-15—9-15	.239	88.20
.....	1880	.....	.....	....	8.14	.....	.....	SE¼NE¼	6	38	47	3-15—6-13	.066	12.21
.....	1880	.....	.....	....	.....	2.81	.....	SE¼NE¼	6	38	47	3-15—4-28	.023	2.11
.....	1881	.....	.....	23.38	.....	.....	.....	SW¼NE¼	6	38	47	3-15—9-15	.190	70.14
.....	1881	.....	.....	....	.....	.....	5.54	SW¼NE¼	6	38	47	3-15—4-28	.045	4.16
.....	1881	.....	.....	21.66	.....	.....	.....	SE¼NW¼	6	38	47	3-15—9-15	.176	64.98
.....	1881	.....	.....	....	.....	.....	8.93	SE¼NW¼	6	38	47	3-15—4-28	.073	6.70
.....	1881	.....	.....	19.70	.....	.....	.....	NE¼SW¼	5	38	47	3-15—9-15	.160	59.10
.....	1881	.....	.....	....	2.38	.....	.....	SW¼NW¼	6	38	47	3-15—6-13	.019	3.57
.....	1880	.....	.....	....	.....	.....	13.03	SW¼NW¼	6	38	47	3-15—4-28	.106	9.77
.....	1880	.....	.....	7.77	.....	.....	.....	NE¼SE¼	6	38	47	3-15—9-15	.063	23.31
.....	1880	.....	.....	....	29.62	.....	.....	NE¼SE¼	6	38	47	3-15—6-13	.241	44.39
.....	1880	.....	.....	28.25	.....	.....	.....	NW¼SE¼	6	38	47	3-15—9-15	.230	84.75
.....	1880	.....	.....	....	.....	9.37	.....	NW¼SE¼	6	38	47	3-15—4-28	.076	7.03
.....	1880	.....	.....	....	.....	.....	1.37	NW¼SE¼	6	38	47	3-15—4-28	.011	1.03

Claimant—**Clover Valley Land and Stock Co.** Proof No. 00157
Source—**Humboldt River.** Ditch—**Hammond.** (Lands of Hammond Bros.)

.....	1875	.....	.....	....	.....	.....	38.76	NE¼NE¼	17	36	42	3-15—4-28	.315	29.07
.....	1875	.....	.....	16.90	.....	.....	.....	NW¼NE¼	17	36	42	3-15—9-15	.137	50.70
.....	1875	.....	.....	....	.....	.....	19.28	NW¼NE¼	17	36	42	3-15—4-28	.157	14.46
.....	1875	.....	.....	17.26	.....	.....	.....	SE¼NE¼	17	36	42	3-15—9-15	.140	51.78
.....	1875	.....	.....	....	.92	.....	.....	SE¼NE¼	17	36	42	3-15—6-13	.007	1.38
.....	1875	.....	.....	....	.....	.....	11.60	SE¼NE¼	17	36	42	3-15—4-28	.094	8.70
.....	1875	.....	.....	34.24	.....	.....	.....	SW¼NE¼	17	36	42	3-15—9-15	.278	102.72
.....	1875	.....	.....	....	.....	1.18	.....	SW¼NE¼	17	36	42	3-15—4-28	.010	.89
.....	1875	.....	.....	37.68	.....	.....	.....	NW¼SE¼	17	36	42	3-15—9-15	.306	113.04
.....	1875	.....	.....	....	.....	.92	.....	NW¼SE¼	17	36	42	3-15—4-28	.008	.69
.....	1875	.....	.....	39.04	.....	.....	.....	NE¼SE¼	17	36	42	3-15—9-15	.317	117.12

Humboldt Land and Cattle Co.—Continued.

Year of priority	Culture—Acres: Harvest crops	Culture—Acres: Meadow pasture	Culture—Acres: Diversified pasture		Location: Subdivision	Location: Section	Location: Tp.N.	Location: R.E.	Length of season	Duty of water: C.F.S.	Duty of water: Acre-feet
1880	....	40.00			SW¼SE¼	25	32	48	3-15—6-13	.325	60.00
1880	....	38.70			NW¼SE¼	25	32	48	3-15—6-13	.315	58.05
1880	....	40.00			SE¼SE¼	25	32	48	3-15—6-13	.325	60.00
1880	....	5.72			NE¼SE¼	25	32	48	3-15—6-13	.047	8.58
1880	....		34.28		NE¼SE¼	25	32	48	3-15—4-28	.279	25.71
1880	....		40.00		SE¼NE¼	25	32	48	3-15—4-28	.325	30.00
1880	....		40.00		NE¼NE¼	25	32	48	3-15—4-28	.325	30.00
1874	....			38.18	SW¼NW¼	19	32	49	3-15—4-28	.310	28.64
1874	....			38.26	NW¼NW¼	19	32	49	3-15—4-28	.311	27.70
1874	....			38.03	SW¼SW¼	19	32	49	3-15—4-28	.309	28.52
1874	....			38.11	NW¼SW¼	19	32	49	3-15—4-28	.310	28.58
1874	....			38.04	NW¼NW¼	30	32	49	3-15—4-28	.309	28.53
1874	....			38.40	NE¼NW¼	30	32	40	3-15—4-28	.312	28.80
1874	....			38.15	SW¼NW¼	30	32	49	3-15—4-28	.310	28.61
1874	....			22.00	SW¼SE¼	30	32	49	3-15—4-28	.179	16.50
1874	....			38.31	SW¼SW¼	30	32	49	3-15—4-28	.311	28.73
1874	....			40.00	SE¼SW¼	30	32	49	3-15—4-28	.325	30.00
1874	....			40.00	NE¼SW¼	30	32	49	3-15—4-28	.325	30.00
1874	....			38.72	NW¼SW¼	30	32	49	3-15—4-28	.315	29.04
1874	....			15.45	NW¼SE¼	39	52	49	3-15—4-28	.126	11.59
1880	....	38.34			NW¼NW¼	31	32	49	3-15—6-13	.312	57.51
1880	....	9.36			NE¼NW¼	31	32	49	3-15—6-13	.076	14.04
1880	....			30.64	NE¼NW¼	31	32	49	3-15—4-28	.249	22.98
1882	....	38.30			SW¼NW¼	31	32	49	3-15—6-13	.311	57.45
1883	....	36.30			SE¼NW¼	31	32	49	3-15—6-13	.295	54.45
1883	....			2.70	SE¼NW¼	31	32	49	3-15—4-28	.022	2.03
1874	....			33.56	NW¼NE¼	31	32	49	3-15—4-28	.273	25.17
1874	....			40.00	SW¼NE¼	31	32	49	3-15—4-28	.325	30.00
1883	....		*37.60		NE¼NE¼	31	32	49	3-15—4-28	.306	28.20
1883	....		*25.50		SE¼NE¼	31	32	49	3-15—4-28	.207	19.13
1885	....	*6.13			SE¼SE¼	31	32	49	3-15—6-13	.050	9.20
1885	....		*2.60		SE¼SE¼	31	32	49	3-15—4-28	.021	1.95
1874	37.53				SW¼SE¼	31	32	40	3-15—9-15	.305	112.59
1874	....	*2.47			SW¼SE¼	31	32	40	3-15—6-13	.020	3.71
1874	37.60				SE¼SW¼	31	32	49	3-15—9-15	.306	112.80
1874	37.60				SW¼SW¼	31	32	40	3-15—9-15	.306	112.80
1874	...			31.70	NW¼SE¼	31	32	40	3-15—4-28	.258	23.78
1886	*17.47				SE¼NW¼	36	32	48	3-15—9-15	.142	52.41
1886	....	*0.50			SE¼NW¼	36	32	48	3-15—6-13	.004	.75
1886	....			*22.53	SE¼NW¼	36	32	48	3-15—4-28	.183	16.90
1874	...	*40.00			NE¼NW¼	36	32	48	3-15—6-13	.325	60.00
1874	...		*11.56		NW¼NW¼	36	32	48	3-15—4-28	.128	10.92
1874				*25.44	NW¼NW¼	36	32	48	3-15—4-28	.207	19.08
1874	1.45				NW¼SW¼	36	32	48	3-15—9-15	.012	4.35
1874				38.55	NW¼SW¼	36	32	48	3-15—4-28	.313	28.91
1874	3.64				SW¼SW¼	36	32	48	3-15—9-15	.030	11.07

1874				36.36	SW¼SW¼	36	32	48	3-15—4-28	.296	27.27
1874	40.00				NE¼SW¼	36	32	48	3-15—9-15	.325	120.00
1880	*40.00				SE¼SW¼	36	32	48	3-15—9-15	.325	120.00
1874	40.00				NE¼SE¼	36	32	48	3-15—9-15	.325	120.00
1874	40.00				SE¼SE¼	36	32	48	3-15—9-15	.325	120.00
1874	40.00				NW¼SE¼	36	32	48	3-15—9-15	.325	120.00
1874	40.00				SW¼SE¼	36	32	48	3-15—9-15	.325	120.00
1882		*22.76			NE¼NE¼	36	32	48	3-15—6-13	.185	34.14
1882				*17.06	NE¼NE¼	36	32	48	3-15—4-28	.139	12.80
1874		40.00			SE¼NE¼	36	32	48	3-15—6-13	.325	60.00
1883		*40.00			NW¼NE¼	36	22	48	3-15—6-13	.325	60.00
1884		*34.28			SW¼NE¼	36	32	48	3-15—6-13	.280	51.42
1884				*5.72	SW¼NE¼	36	32	48	3-15—4-28	.047	4.29
1886				*39.50	SW¼NW¼	36	32	48	3-15—4-28	.321	29.63
1874			18.20		NE¼SE¼	31	32	49	3-15—4-28	.148	13.65
1874	40.00				NE¼SW¼	31	32	49	3-15—9-15	.325	120.00
1874	38.70				NW¼SW¼	31	32	49	3-15—9-15	.315	116.28

*Was Class C—1874.

Claimant—**Sam Broyles.** Proof No. 00155

Source—**Humboldt River.** Ditch—**Altenberg Ditch.**

1875	3.30				SE¼SW¼	16	32	45	3-15—9-15	.027	9.90
1875		3.55			SE¼SW¼	16	32	45	3-15—6-13	.029	5.33
1875	1.67				NW¼SW¼	16	32	45	3-15—9-15	.014	5.01
1875		19.03			NW¼SW¼	16	32	45	3-15—6-13	.155	28.95
1875			.15		NW¼SW¼	16	32	45	3-15—4-28	.001	.11
1875	15.47				NE¼SW¼	16	32	45	3-15—9-15	.126	46.41
1875		8.84			NE¼SW¼	16	32	45	3-15—6-13	.072	13.26
1875			.65		NE¼SW¼	16	32	45	3-15—4-28	.005	.49

Source—**Humboldt River.** Ditch—**McIntyre Starrett.**

1883	30.47				NE¼SE¼	16	32	45	3-15—9-15	.248	91.41
1883			1.60		NE¼SE¼	16	32	45	3-15—4-28	.013	1.20
1883	32.70				NW¼SE¼	16	32	45	3-15—9-15	.266	98.10
1883			3.01		NW¼SE¼	16	32	45	3-15—4-28	.024	2.26
1883	9.25				SE¼SE¼	16	32	45	3-15—9-15	.075	27.75
1883		28.37			SE¼SE¼	16	32	45	3-15—6-13	.231	42.56
1883			.30		SE¼SE¼	16	32	45	3-15—4-28	.002	.23
1883	2.17				SW¼SE¼	16	32	45	3-15—9-15	.018	6.51
1883		18.90			SW¼SE¼	16	32	45	3-15—6-13	.154	28.35
1883		16.45			SW¼SW¼	16	32	45	3-15—6-13	.134	24.68
1883	7.80				NE¼SW¼	16	32	45	3-15—9-15	.063	23.40

Claimant—**Golconda Cattle Co.** Proof No. 00156

Source—**Humboldt River.** Ditch—***Aemes Dam.**

Year of priority	Culture—Acres: Harvest crops	Culture—Acres: Meadow pasture	Culture—Acres: Diversified pasture	Culture—Acres: Diversified pasture	Location: Subdivision	Location: Section	Location: Tp.N.	Location: R.E.	Length of season	Duty of water: C.F.S.	Duty of water: Acre-feet
1876				40.44	NW¼NE¼	30	35	43	3-15—4-28	.329	30.33
1876			30.61		NE¼NE¼	30	35	43	3-15—4-28	.249	22.96
1876				9.78	NE¼NE¼	30	35	42	3-15—4-28	.080	7.34
1886			11.60		SE¼NE¼	30	35	43	3-15—4-28	.094	8.70
1886				29.48	SE¼NE¼	30	35	43	3-15—4-28	.240	22.11
1876	5.60				SW¼NE¼	30	35	43	3-15—9-15	.046	16.80
1876			9.43		SW¼NE¼	30	35	43	3-15—4-28	.077	7.07
1886			8.64		NE¼SE¼	30	35	43	3-15—4-28	.070	6.48
1886				31.88	NE¼SE¼	30	35	43	3-15—4-28	.259	23.91
1886	13.76				NW¼SE¼	30	35	43	3-15—9-15	.112	41.28
1886		17.56			NW¼SE¼	30	35	43	3-15—6-13	.143	26.34
1886			4.20		NW¼SE¼	30	35	43	3-15—4-28	.034	3.15
1886			13.48		SE¼SE¼	30	35	43	3-15—4-28	.110	10.11
1886				17.40	SE¼SE¼	30	35	43	3-15—4-28	.141	13.05
1886	11.50				SW¼SE¼	30	35	43	3-15—9-15	.093	34.50
1886		22.32			SW¼SE¼	30	35	43	3-15—6-13	.181	33.48
1886			1.92		SW¼SE¼	30	35	43	3-15—4-28	.016	1.24
1884	29.52				NE¼SW¼	30	35	43	3-15—9-15	.240	88.59
1884			3.52		NE¼SW¼	30	35	43	3-15—4-28	.029	2.64

Source—**Humboldt River.** Ditch—***Aemes Dam.** (Lands of Duviver.)

Year of priority	Harvest crops	Meadow pasture	Diversified pasture	Diversified pasture	Subdivision	Section	Tp.N.	R.E.	Length of season	C.F.S.	Acre-feet
1884				.48	NE¼SW¼	30	35	43	3-15—4-28	.004	.36
1884	29.68				NW¼SW¼	30	35	43	3-15—9-15	.241	89.04
1884			2.80		NW¼SW¼	30	35	43	3-15—4-28	.023	2.10
1884	30.56				SW¼SW¼	30	35	43	3-15—9-15	.248	91.68
1884		3.88			SW¼SW¼	30	35	43	3-15—6-13	.032	5.82
1884	28.16				SE¼SW¼	30	35	43	3-15—9-15	.229	84.48
1884		4.88			SE¼SW¼	30	35	43	3-15—6-13	.040	7.32
1884			.84		SE¼SW¼	30	35	43	3-15—4-28	.007	.62

*Was Class C—1876.

Source—**Humboldt River.** Ditch—**Henderson.** (Lands of Duvivier.)

Year of priority	Harvest crops	Meadow pasture	Diversified pasture	Diversified pasture	Subdivision	Section	Tp.N.	R.E.	Length of season	C.F.S.	Acre-feet
1887	6.62				NW¼NE¼	36	35	42	3-15—9-15	.054	19.86
1887			32.90		NW¼NE¼	36	35	42	3-15—4-28	.267	24.68
1887	16.23				NE¼NE¼	36	35	42	3-15—9-15	.132	48.69
1887		7.56			NE¼NE¼	36	35	42	3-15—6-13	.061	11.34
1887			16.09		NE¼NE¼	36	35	42	3-15—4-28	.131	12.07
1894	21.33				NE¼SW¼	14	35	42	3-15—9-15	.174	64.08
1894		18.40			NE¼SW¼	14	35	42	3-15—6-13	.150	27.60
1894		41.20			NE¼SW¼	14	35	42	3-15—6-13	.335	61.80
1894		40.16			SE¼SW¼	14	45	42	3-15—6-13	.327	60.24
1894		41.90			NW¼SW¼	14	35	42	3-15—6-13	.335	61.80

Source—**Humboldt River.** Ditch—**Outside Slough.** (Lands of Duvivier.)

1887			3.96				SW¼NE¼	36	35	42	3-15—9-15	.032	11.88
1887					35.72		SW¼NE¼	36	35	42	3-15—4-28	.290	26.79
1887			34.11				SE¼NE¼	36	35	42	3-15—9-15	.277	102.33
1887				2.64			SE¼NE¼	36	35	42	3-15—6-13	.021	3.96
1887					2.37		SE¼NE¼	36	35	42	3-15—4-28	.019	1.78
1894				40.96			SW¼SW¼	14	35	42	3-15—6-13	.333	61.44

Claimant—**Ellison Ranching Co.** Proof No. **00156**

Source—**Humboldt River.** Ditch—**Outside Slough Ditch.** (Humboldt River lands.)

1887						40.60	SW¼SW¼	15	35	42	3-15—4-28	.330	30.45
1887						38.60	NW¼SW¼	15	35	42	3-15—4-28	.314	28.95
1887						35.60	SE¼SW¼	15	35	42	3-15—4-28	.289	26.70
1887						34.72	NE¼SW¼	15	35	42	3-15—4-28	.282	26.05
1887						33.44	SW¼NW¼	15	35	42	3-15—4-28	.272	25.08
1887			14.72				SE¼NW¼	15	35	42	3-15—9-15	.120	44.16
1887					24.64		SE¼NW¼	15	35	42	3-15—4-28	.200	18.48
1887						36.88	SW¼SE¼	15	35	42	3-15—4-28	.300	27.66
1887						39.44	SE¼SE¼	15	35	42	3-15—4-28	.321	29.58
1887						40.08	NE¼SE¼	15	35	42	3-15—4-28	.326	30.06
1887			9.28				NW¼SE¼	15	35	42	3-15—9-15	.075	27.84
1887					29.92		NW¼SE¼	15	35	42	3-15—4-28	.243	22.44
1887						40.24	SE¼SE¼	22	35	42	3-15—4-28	.327	30.18
1887						39.88	SW¼SE¼	22	35	42	3-15—4-28	.324	29.91
1887						39.84	NW¼SE¼	22	25	42	3-15—4-28	.324	29.88
1887						37.28	NE¼SE¼	22	35	42	3-15—4-28	.303	27.96
1887						40.12	NE¼SW¼	22	35	42	3-15—4-28	.326	30.09
1887						39.68	SE¼SW¼	22	35	42	3-15—4-28	.323	29.76
1887						38.60	SW¼NW¼	22	35	42	3-15—4-28	.314	28.95
1887						40.12	SE¼NW¼	22	35	42	3-15—4-28	.326	30.09
1887						40.08	NE¼NW¼	22	35	42	3-15—4-28	.326	30.06
1887						40.00	NW¼NW¼	22	35	42	3-15—4-28	.325	30.00
1887						39.88	SW¼NE¼	22	35	42	3-15—4-28	.324	29.91
1887						31.88	NW¼NE¼	22	35	42	3-15—4-28	.259	23.91
1887						39.00	NE¼NE¼	22	35	42	3-15—4-28	.317	29.25
1887						32.40	SE¼NE¼	22	35	42	3-15—4-28	.263	24.30
1887						41.12	NW¼NW¼	26	35	42	3-15—4-28	.334	30.84
1887			.96				NE¼NW¼	26	35	42	3-15—9-15	.008	2.88
1887					25.24		NE¼NW¼	26	35	42	3-15—4-28	.205	18.93
1887						39.48	SE¼NW¼	26	35	42	3-15—4-28	.321	29.61
1887						41.80	SW¼NW¼	26	35	42	3-15—4-28	.340	31.65
1887						40.80	NW¼NE¼	26	35	42	3-15—4-28	.331	30.60
1887						32.56	SW¼NE¼	26	35	42	3-15—4-28	.265	24.42
1887						41.28	SE¼NE¼	26	35	42	3-15—4-28	.336	30.96
1887						39.84	NW¼SW¼	26	35	42	3-15—4-28	.324	29.88
1887						40.60	NE¼SW¼	26	35	42	3-15—4-28	.330	30.45
1887						38.48	SW¼SW¼	26	35	42	3-15—4-28	.313	28.86
1887						40.64	SE¼SW¼	26	35	42	3-15—4-28	.330	30.48
1887					36.80		NW¼SE¼	26	35	42	3-15—4-28	.299	27.60
1887						35.92	NE¼SE¼	26	35	42	3-15—4-28	.292	26.90
1887					40.16		SW¼SE¼	26	35	42	3-15—4-28	.327	30.12
1887					23.08		SE¼SE¼	26	35	42	3-15—4-28	.188	17.31

Ellison Ranching Co.—Continued.

Year of priority	Culture—Acres: Harvest crops	Meadow pasture	Diversified pasture		Location: Subdivision	Section	Tp.N.	R.E.	Length of season	Duty of water: C.F.S.	Acre-feet
1887				8.96	SE¼SE¼	26	35	42	3-15—4-28	.073	6.72
1887				40.36	NE¼NE¼	27	35	42	3-15—4-28	.328	30.27
1887			39.84		NW¼NW¼	23	35	42	3-15—4-28	.324	29.88
1887			39.80		SW¼NW¼	23	35	42	3-15—4-28	.324	29.85
1887	11.12				NW¼SW¼	23	35	42	3-15—9-15	.090	33.36
1887			20.56		NW¼SW¼	23	35	42	3-15—4-28	.167	15.42
1887				3.24	NW¼SW¼	23	35	42	3-15—4-28	.026	2.43
1887	.32				SW¼SW¼	23	35	42	3-15—9-15	.003	.96
1887			3.76		SW¼SW¼	23	35	42	3-15—4-28	.031	2.82
1887				25.28	SW¼SW¼	23	35	42	3-15...4-28	.206	18.96
1887	13.12				NE¼SW¼	23	35	42	3-15—9-15	.107	39.36
1887			27.20		NE¼SW¼	23	35	42	3-15—4-28	.221	20.40
1887	18.68				SE¼SW¼	23	35	42	3-15—9-15	.152	56.04
1887			17.88		SE¼SW¼	23	35	42	3-15—4-28	.145	13.41
1887				36.88	NE¼NW¼	9	35	42	3-15—4-28	.300	27.66
1887				10.72	SE¼NW¼	9	35	42	3-15—4-28	.087	8.04
1887				37.84	NW¼NE¼	9	35	42	3-15—4-28	.308	29.38
1887			37.80		NE¼NE¼	9	35	42	3-15—4-28	.307	28.35
1887			37.84		SE¼NE¼	9	35	42	3-15—4-28	.308	28.38
1887				19.34	NW¼SE¼	9	35	42	3-15—4-28	.157	14.51
1887			30.48		SE¼SE¼	9	35	42	3-15—4-28	.248	22.86

Source—**Humboldt River.** Ditch—**Aemes Dam.** (Humboldt River lands.)

Year of priority	Harvest crops	Meadow pasture	Diversified pasture		Subdivision	Section	Tp.N.	R.E.	Length of season	C.F.S.	Acre-feet
1876			40.08		NW¼NW¼	25	35	42	3-15—4-28	.326	30.06
1876	18.20				NE¼NW¼	25	35	42	3-15—9-15	.147	54.60
1876		.36			NE¼NW¼	25	35	42	3-15—6-13	.003	.54
1876			20.48		NE¼NW¼	25	35	42	3-15—4-28	.167	15.36
1876			40.24		SW¼NW¼	25	35	42	3-15—4-28	.327	30.18
1876	5.80				SE¼NW¼	25	35	42	3-15—9-15	.047	17.40
1876		2.28			SE¼NW¼	25	35	42	3-15—6-13	.019	3.42
1876			31.08		SE¼NW¼	25	35	42	3-15—4-28	.253	23.31
1876	21.32				NW¼NW¼	30	35	43	3-15—9-15	.173	63.96
1876			6.16		NW¼NW¼	30	35	43	3-15—4-28	.050	4.62
1876				.86	NW¼NW¼	30	35	43	3-15—4-28	.007	.65
1876	20.28				SW¼NW¼	30	35	43	3-15—9-15	.165	60.84
1876			4.24		SW¼NW¼	30	35	43	3-15—4-28	.034	3.18
1876				7.60	SW¼NW¼	30	35	43	3-15—4-28	.062	5.70
1876	18.00				SE¼NW¼	30	35	43	3-15—9-15	.146	54.00
1876			11.52		SE¼NW¼	30	35	43	3-15—4-28	.091	8.64
1876				2.52	SE¼NW¼	30	35	43	3-15—4-28	.020	1.89
1876	14.32				NE¼NW¼	30	35	43	3-15—9-15	.116	42.96
1876			22.92		NE¼NW¼	30	35	43	3-15—4-28	.186	17.19
1876			6.40		SW¼NE¼	19	35	43	3-15—4-28	.052	4.80
1876				10.36	SW¼NE¼	19	35	43	3-15—4-28	.084	7.77
1876	20.72				NW¼SE¼	19	35	43	3-15—9-15	.100	[illegible]
1876				9.28	NW¼SE¼	19	35	43	3-15—4-28	.075	6.90

	1876			25.36				SW¼SE¼	19	35	43	3-15—9-15	.206	76.08
	1876						8.29	SW¼SE¼	19	35	43	3-15—4-28	.067	6.22
	1876				27.04			NW¼NW¼	19	35	43	3-15—6-13	.220	40.56
	1876						7.24	NW¼NW¼	19	35	43	3-15—4-28	.059	5.43
	1876				18.24			NE¼NW¼	19	35	43	3-15—6-13	.148	27.36
	1876						21.52	NE¼NW¼	19	35	43	3-15—4-28	.175	16.14
	1876			38.80				NW¼NE¼	24	35	42	3-15—9-15	.315	116.40
	1876			23.84				NE¼NE¼	24	35	42	3-15—9-15	.194	71.52
	1876					10.88		NE¼NE¼	24	35	42	3-15—4-28	.088	8.16
	1876			40.08				SW¼NE¼	24	35	42	3-15—9-15	.326	120.24
	1876			26.44				SE¼NE¼	24	35	42	3-15—9-15	.215	79.32
	1876					3.68		SE¼NE¼	24	35	42	3-15—4-28	.030	2.76
	1876			23.56				NW¼SE¼	24	35	42	3-15—9-15	.192	70.68
	1876					16.56		NW¼SE¼	24	35	42	3-15—4-28	.135	12.42
	1876			40.24				NE¼SE¼	24	35	42	3-15—9-15	.327	120.72
	1876			12.76				SW¼SE¼	24	35	42	3-15—9-15	.104	38.28
	1876					24.76		SW¼SE¼	24	35	42	3-15—4-28	.201	18.57
	1876			39.98				SE¼SE¼	24	35	42	3-15—9-15	.325	119.34
	1876			39.59				NE¼NW¼	24	35	42	3-15—9-15	.322	118.77
	1876			13.12				NW¼NW¼	24	35	42	3-15—9-15	.107	39.36
	1876					25.60		NW¼NW¼	24	35	42	3-15—4-28	.208	19.20
	1876			.48				SW¼NW¼	24	35	42	3-15—9-15	.004	1.44
	1876					35.76		SW¼NW¼	24	35	42	3-15—4-28	.291	26.82
	1876			24.88				SE¼NW¼	24	35	42	3-15—9-15	.202	74.64
	1876					12.52		SE¼NW¼	24	35	42	3-15—4-28	.102	9.40
	1876					30.00		SE¼NW¼	19	35	43	3-15—4-28	.244	22.50
	1876				2.08			SW¼NW¼	19	35	43	3-15—6-13	.017	3.12
	1876					27.92		SW¼NW¼	19	35	43	3-15—4-28	.227	20.94
	1876				18.52			NW¼SW¼	19	35	43	3-15—6-13	.151	27.78
	1876					7.78		NW¼SW¼	19	35	43	3-15—4-28	.063	5.84
	1876				13.08			SW¼SW¼	19	35	43	3-15—6-13	.106	19.62
	1876					6.08		SW¼SW¼	19	35	43	3-15—4-28	.049	4.56
	1876				32.64			SE¼SW¼	19	45	43	3-15—6-13	.265	48.96
	1876					3.64		SE¼SW¼	19	35	43	3-15—4-28	.034	2.73
	1876			31.04				NE¼SW¼	19	35	43	3-15—9-15	.252	93.12
	1876					3.52		NE¼SW¼	19	35	43	3-15—4-28	.029	2 64
	1876			39.72				SE¼SW¼	13	35	42	3-15—9-15	.323	119.16
	1876					1.12		SE¼SE¼	13	35	42	3-15—4-28	.009	.84
	1876			15.12				NE¼SW¼	13	35	42	3-15—9-15	.123	45.36
	1876			33.12				NW¼SW¼	13	35	42	3-15—9-15	.209	99.36
	1876					5.04		NW¼SW¼	13	35	42	3-15—4-28	.041	3.78
	1876			23.80				SW¼SW¼	13	35	42	3-15—9-15	.193	71.40
	1876					14.96		SW¼SW¼	13	35	42	3-15—4-28	.122	11.22
	1876			14.48				SW¼NW¼	13	35	42	3-15—9-15	.117	43.44
	1876				3.96			SW¼NW¼	13	35	42	3-15—6-13	.032	5.94
	1876			.60				SE¼NW¼	13	35	42	3-15—9-15	.005	1.80
	1876					.80		SE¼NW¼	13	35	42	3-15—4-28	.007	.60
								Source—Humboldt River. Ditch—Henderson Dam. (Humboldt River lands.)						
	1887			15.68				NW¼NW¼	31	35	43	3-15—9-15	.127	47.04
	1887				4.48			NW¼NW¼	31	35	43	3-15—6-13	.036	6.72
	1887						13.60	NW¼NW¼	31	35	43	3-15—4-28	.111	10.20
	1887						34.40	SW¼NW¼	31	35	43	3-15—4-28	.280	25.80

Ellison Ranching Co.—Continued.

Year of priority	Culture—Acres: Harvest crops	Meadow pasture	Diversified pasture		Location: Subdivision	Section	Tp. N.	R. E.	Length of season	Duty of water: C.F.S.	Acre-feet
1887				33.28	NW¼SW¼	31	35	43	3-15—4-28	.271	24.06
1887				33.81	SW¼SW¼	31	35	43	3-15—4-28	.275	25.38
1887	1.28				SE¼SW¼	31	35	43	3-15—9-15	.010	3.84
1887				38.24	SE¼SW¼	31	35	43	3-15—4-28	.311	28.68
1887	.96				NE¼SW¼	31	35	43	3-15—9-15	.008	2.88
1887		7.48			NE¼SW¼	31	35	43	3-15—6-13	.061	11.22
1887				30.32	NE¼SW¼	31	35	43	3-15—4-28	.247	22.74
1887	10.72				SE¼SE¼	31	35	43	3-15—9-15	.087	32.16
1887				26.28	SE¼SE¼	31	35	43	3-15—4-28	.214	10.71
1887	19.96				SW¼SE¼	31	35	43	3-15—9-15	.162	59.88
1887				13.04	SW¼SE¼	31	35	43	3-15—4-28	.106	9.78
1887				39.48	NE¼SE¼	31	35	43	3-15—4-28	.321	29.61
1887	17.92				NW¼SE¼	31	35	43	3-15—9-15	.146	53.76
1887		2.04			NW¼SE¼	31	35	43	3-15—6-13	.017	3.06
1887				13.76	NW¼SE¼	31	35	43	3-15—4-28	.113	10.32
1887	17.00				NW¼NW¼	15	35	42	3-15—9-15	.138	51.00
1887		14.00			NW¼NW¼	15	35	42	3-15—6-13	.114	21.00
1887			6.24		NW¼NW¼	15	35	42	3-15—4-28	.051	4.68
1887	39.24				NE¼NW¼	15	35	42	3-15—9-15	.319	117.72
1887	39.12				NW¼NE¼	15	35	42	3-15—9-15	.318	117.36
1887	39.76				NE¼NE¼	15	35	42	3-15—9-15	.323	119.28
1887	25.72				SE¼NE¼	15	35	42	3-15—9-15	.209	77.16
1887			12.92		SE¼NE¼	15	35	42	3-15—4-28	.105	9.69
1887	33.12				SW¼NE¼	15	35	42	3-15—9-15	.269	99.36
1887			5.40		SW¼NE¼	15	35	42	3-15—4-28	.044	4.05
1887				40.00	NE¼NW¼	23	35	42	3-15—4-28	.325	30.00
1887				40.40	SE¼NW¼	23	35	42	3-15—4-28	.328	30.30
1887				40.08	NW¼NE¼	23	35	42	3-15—4-28	.326	30.06
1887				39.44	NE¼NE¼	23	35	42	3-15—4-28	.321	29.58
1887				40.48	SW¼NE¼	23	35	42	3-15—4-28	.320	30.36
1887				40.56	SE¼NE¼	23	35	42	3-15—4-28	.330	30.42
1887				40.64	NW¼SE¼	23	35	42	3-15—4-28	.330	30.48
1887				40.96	NE¼SE¼	23	35	42	3-15—4-28	.333	30.72
1887				41.20	SW¼SE¼	23	35	42	3-15—4-28	.335	30.90
1887				41.44	SE¼SW¼	23	35	42	3-15—4-28	.337	31.08
1887	1.20				NE¼SW¼	24	35	42	3-15—9-15	.010	3.60
1887			36.68		NE¼SW¼	21	35	42	3-15—4-28	.298	27.51
1887			38.76		NW¼SW¼	24	35	42	3-15—4-28	.315	29.07
1887	23.80				SW¼SW¼	24	35	42	3-15—9-15	.193	71.40
1887			14.06		SW¼SW¼	24	35	42	3-15—4-28	.122	11.22
1887	10.24				SE¼SW¼	24	35	42	3-15—9-15	.083	30.72
1887			26.84		SE¼SW¼	24	35	42	3-15—4-28	.218	20.13
1887	21.52				SE¼NW¼	[illegible]	[illegible]	[illegible]	3-15—9-15	.175	61.56
1887		5.04			SE¼NW¼	[illegible]	[illegible]	[illegible]	3-15—6-13	.041	7.56
1887			11.80		SE¼NW¼	[illegible]	[illegible]	[illegible]	3-15—4-28	.096	8.85
1887	34.08				NE¼NW¼	1	[illegible]	[illegible]	3-15—9-15	.269	90.24
1887			2.08		NE¼NW¼	1	[illegible]	[illegible]	3-15—4-28	.017	1.56

1887	29.64				SW¼NE¼	31	35	43	3-15—0-15	.241	88.92
1887			2.56		SW¼NE¼	31	35	43	3-15—4-28	.021	1.92
1887				1.76	SW¼NE¼	31	35	43	3-15—4-28	.014	1.32
1887	6.60				NW¼NE¼	31	35	43	3-15—0-15	.054	19.80
1887			24.24		NW¼NE¼	31	35	43	3-15—4-28	.107	18.18
1887				3.12	NW¼NE¼	31	35	43	3-15—4-28	.025	2.34
1887	1.52				SE¼NE¼	31	35	43	3-15—0-15	.012	4.56
1887			2.48		SE¼NE¼	31	35	43	3-15—4-28	.020	1.86
1887				.24	SE¼NE¼	31	35	43	3-15—4-28	.002	.18
1887			38.56		NE¼NE¼	31	35	43	3-15—4-28	.313	28.92
1887				2.00	NE¼NE¼	31	35	43	3-15—4-28	.016	1.50
1887	8.80				SW¼SE¼	25	35	42	3-15—0-15	.072	26.40
1887		31.20			SW¼SE¼	25	35	42	3-15—6-13	.254	46.80
1887	40.80				SE¼SE¼	25	35	42	3-15—0-15	.332	122.40
1887		40.64			SE¼SW¼	25	35	42	3-15—6-13	.330	60.96
1887	19.20				NE¼SW¼	25	35	42	3-15—0-15	.156	57.60
1887			20.64		NE¼SW¼	25	35	42	3-15—4-28	.168	15.48
1887			40.64		NW¼SW¼	25	35	42	3-15—4-28	.330	30.48
1887			38.56		SW¼SW¼	25	35	42	3-15—4-28	.313	28.92
1887	34.48				NE¼SE¼	25	35	42	3-15—0-15	.280	103.44
1887			3.16		NE¼SE¼	25	35	42	3-15—4-28	.026	2.37
1887				1.08	NE¼SE¼	25	35	42	3-15—4-28	.009	.81
1887	14.16				NW¼SE¼	25	35	42	3-15—0-15	.115	42.48
1887			25.20		NW¼SE¼	25	35	42	3-15—4-28	.205	18.90
1887	24.00				NE¼NE¼	25	35	42	3-15—0-15	.195	72.00
1887		10.48			NE¼NE¼	25	35	42	3-15—6-13	.085	15.72
1887			3.24		NE¼NE¼	25	35	42	3-15—4-28	.026	2.43
1887	24.80				NW¼NE¼	25	35	42	3-15—0-15	.202	74.40
1887			14.16		NW¼NE¼	25	35	42	3-15—4-28	.115	10.62
1887	32.12				SE¼NE¼	25	35	42	3-15—0-15	.261	96.36
1887		3.52			SE¼NE¼	25	35	42	3-15—6-13	.029	5.28
1887			1.72		SE¼NE¼	25	35	42	3-15—4-28	.014	1.29
1887	38.64				SW¼NE¼	25	35	42	3-15—0-15	.314	115.92
1887	.48				SE¼NE¼	6	34	43	3-15—0-15	.004	1.44
1887	12.96				NE¼NE¼	6	34	43	3-15—0-15	.105	38.88
1887			17.54		NE¼NE¼	6	34	43	3-15—4-28	.143	18.16
1887	8.36				NW¼NE¼	6	34	43	3-15—0-15	.069	25.08
1887			4.38		NW¼NE¼	6	34	43	3-15—4-28	.036	3.29
1887				2.56	NW¼NE¼	6	34	43	3-15—4-28	.021	1.92

Source—**Humboldt River.** Ditch—**Bacon Dam.** (Humboldt River lands.)

1887	11.08				NW¼SE¼	13	35	42	3-15—0-15	.090	33.24
1887			1.22		NW¼SE¼	13	35	42	3-15—4-28	.010	.92
1887	32.92				SW¼SE¼	13	35	42	3-15—0-15	.268	98.76
1887	.32				NE¼SE¼	13	35	42	3-15—0-15	.003	.64
1887				.24	NE¼SE¼	13	35	42	3-15—4-28	.002	.18

Source—**Humboldt River.** Ditch—**Gonzales Slough.** (Humboldt River lands.)

1880				40.00	NW¼NW¼	20	36	42	3-15—4-28	.325	30.00
1880				40.00	NE¼NW¼	20	36	42	3-15—4-28	.325	30.00
1880				40.00	NW¼NE¼	20	36	42	3-15—4-28	.328	30.30
1880				39.36	SW¼NW¼	20	36	42	3-15—4-28	.320	29.52
1880				40.00	SE¼NW¼	20	36	42	3-15—4-28	.325	30.00

Ellison Ranching Co.—Continued.

Year of priority	Culture—Acres: Harvest crops	Meadow pasture	Diversified pasture	Location: Subdivision	Section	Tp. N.	R. E.	Length of season	Duty of water: C. F. S.	Acre-feet
1880			36.21	NW¼SW¼	20	36	42	3-15—4-28	.295	27.18
1880			37.44	NE¼SW¼	20	36	42	3-15—4-28	.304	28.08
1880			39.06	SW¼SW¼	20	36	42	3-15—4-28	.318	29.30
1880			38.36	SE¼SW¼	20	36	42	3-15—4-28	.312	28.77
1880			40.00	NE¼SE¼	20	36	42	3-15—4-28	.325	30.00
1880			38.56	NW¼SE¼	20	36	42	3-15—4-28	.313	28.92
1880			37.92	SE¼SE¼	20	36	42	3-15—4-28	.308	28.44
1880			36.00	SW¼SE¼	20	36	42	3-15—4-28	.292	27.00
1880			40.00	NW¼NW¼	21	36	42	3-15—4-28	.325	30.00
1880		20.72		NE¼NW¼	21	36	42	3-15—6-13	.169	31.08
1880			19.44	NE¼NW¼	21	36	42	3-15—4-28	.158	14.58
1880			39.52	SW¼NW¼	21	36	42	3-15—4-28	.321	29.64
1880		19.84		SE¼NW¼	21	36	42	3-15—6-13	.161	29.76
1880			19.32	SE¼NW¼	21	36	42	3-15—4-28	.157	14.49
1880		23.68		NE¼SW¼	21	36	42	3-15—6-13	.193	35.52
1880			15.84	NE¼SW¼	21	36	42	3-15—4-28	.129	11.88
1880			40.00	NW¼SW¼	21	36	42	3-15—4-28	.325	30.00
1880			39.48	SW¼SW¼	21	36	42	3-15—4-28	.321	29.61
1880		.48		SE¼SW¼	21	36	42	3-15—6-13	.004	.72
1880			38.20	SE¼SW¼	21	36	42	3-15—4-28	.310	28.65
1880	23.36			NW¼NE¼	21	36	42	3-15—9-15	.190	70.08
1880			11.76	NW¼NE¼	21	36	42	3-15—4-28	.096	8.82
1880	31.72			SW¼NE¼	21	36	42	3-15—9-15	.258	95.16
1880			.32	SW¼NE¼	21	36	42	3-15—4-28	.003	.24
1880	20.40			SE¼NE¼	21	36	42	3-15—9-15	.166	61.20
1880			.72	SE¼NE¼	21	36	42	3-15—4-28	.006	.54
1880	15.48			NW¼SE¼	21	36	42	3-15—9-15	.126	46.44
1880		11.92		NW¼SE¼	21	36	42	3-15—6-13	.097	17.87
1880			12.48	NW¼SE¼	21	36	42	3-15—4-28	.101	9.36
1880	34.96			NE¼SE¼	21	36	42	3-15—9-15	.284	104.88
1880			6.16	NE¼SE¼	21	36	42	3-15—4-28	.050	4.62
1880		26.40		SW¼SE¼	21	36	42	3-15—6-13	.215	39.60
1880			12.88	SW¼SE¼	21	36	42	3-15—4-28	.105	9.66
1880	20.20			SE¼SE¼	21	36	42	3-15—9-15	.164	60.60
1880			18.20	SE¼SE¼	21	36	42	3-15—4-28	.148	13.65
1880	5.16			NW¼SW¼	22	36	42	3-15—9-15	.042	15.48
1880		21.76		NW¼SW¼	22	36	42	3-15—6-13	.177	32.74
1880			6.08	NW¼SW¼	22	36	42	3-15—4-28	.049	4.56
1880	1.08			NE¼SW¼	22	36	42	3-15—9-15	.009	3.24
1880		2.92		NE¼SW¼	22	36	42	3-15—6-13	.024	4.38
1880			36.52	NE¼SW¼	22	36	42	3-15—4-28	.297	27.39
1880	19.68			SW¼SW¼	22	36	42	3-15—9-15	.160	59.04
1880			3.16	SW¼SW¼	22	36	42	3-15—4-28	.026	2.38
1880			38.44	NW¼SE¼	28	36	42	3-15—4-28	.313	28.83
1880			38.36	NE¼SE¼	28	36	42	3-15—4-28	.312	28.77
1880			39.40	SE¼SE¼	28	36	42	3-15—4-28	.320	29.55
1880			39.28	SW¼SE¼	28	36	42	3-15—4-28	.319	29.46
1880			40.00	NW¼SW¼	28	36	42	3-15—4-28	.325	30.00
1880			38.44	NE¼SW¼	28	36	42	3-15—4-28	.313	28.83

....	1880	....	....	....	....	....	30.20	SW¼SW¼	28	36	42	3-15—4-28	.312	29.40
....	1880	....	....	....	....	....	38.52	SE¼SW¼	28	36	42	3-15—4-28	.313	28.89
....	1880	....	....	....	....	....	39.84	NW¼NW¼	28	36	42	3-15—4-28	.324	29.88
....	1880	....	....	....	....	....	39.60	NE¼NW¼	28	36	42	3-15—4-28	.322	29.70
....	1880	....	....	....	....	....	40.00	SW¼NW¼	28	36	42	3-15—4-28	.325	30.00
....	1880	....	....	....	....	....	38.72	SE¼NW¼	28	36	42	3-15—4-28	.315	29.04
....	1880	....	....	....	....	....	40.00	SW¼NE¼	28	36	42	3-15—4-28	.325	30.00
....	1880	....	....	2.00	....	....	....	SE¼NE¼	28	36	42	3-15—0-15	.016	6.00
....	1880	....	....	....	....	....	38.84	SE¼NE¼	28	36	42	3-15—4-28	.316	29.13
....	1880	....	....	10.28	....	....	....	NW¼NE¼	28	36	42	3-15—0-15	.084	30.84
....	1880	....	....	....	....	....	29.68	NW¼NE¼	28	36	42	3-15—4-28	.241	22.26
....	1880	....	....	36.28	....	....	....	NW¼NW¼	34	36	42	3-15—0-15	.295	108.84
....	1880	....	....	....	....	2.24	....	NW¼NW¼	34	36	42	3-15—4-28	.018	1.68
....	1880	....	....	31.92	....	....	....	NE¼NW¼	34	36	42	3-15—0-15	.260	95.76
....	1880	....	....	39.20	....	....	....	SE¼NW¼	34	36	42	3-15—0-15	.319	117.60
....	1880	....	....	35.88	....	....	....	SW¼SW¼	34	36	42	3-15—0-15	.292	107.64
....	1880	....	....	....	....	....	2.40	SW¼SW¼	34	36	42	3-15—4-28	.020	1.80
....	1880	....	....	40.00	....	....	....	SE¼SW¼	34	36	42	3-15—0-15	.325	120.00
....	1880	....	....	38.28	....	....	....	SW¼SW¼	34	36	42	3-15—0-15	.311	114.84
....	1880	....	....	40.00	....	....	....	NE¼SW¼	34	36	42	3-15—0-15	.325	120.00
....	1880	....	....	37.00	....	....	....	NW¼SW¼	34	36	42	3-15—0-15	.301	111.00
....	1880	....	....	....	....	....	3.12	NW¼SW¼	34	36	42	8-15—4-28	.025	2.34
Source—**Humboldt River.** Ditch—**Overflow.** (Humboldt River lands.)														
....	1880	....	....	....	....	....	28.80	NE¼NE¼	21	36	42	3-15—4-28	.234	21.60
....	1880	....	....	....	....	....	3.84	SW¼NE¼	21	36	42	3-15—4-28	.028	2.58
....	1890	....	....	....	....	....	12.96	SE¼NE¼	21	36	42	3-15—4-28	.105	9.72
....	1880	....	....	....	....	....	10.08	SW¼SW¼	22	36	42	3-15—4-28	.082	7.56
....	1880	....	....	15.48	....	....	....	SE¼SW¼	22	36	42	3-15—0-15	.126	46.44
....	1880	....	....	....	....	....	23.80	SE¼SW¼	22	36	42	3-15—4-28	.193	17.85
Source—**Humboldt River.** Ditch—**"13" Ditch.** (Humboldt River lands.)														
....	1874	....	....	....	17.36	....	....	NE¼SE¼	14	36	41	3-15—6-13	.141	26.04
....	1874	....	....	....	....	....	9.72	NE¼SE¼	14	36	41	3-15—4-28	.079	7.29
....	1874	....	....	....	....	....	27.04	SE¼SE¼	14	36	41	3-15—4-28	.220	20.28
Source—**Humboldt River.** Ditch—**Outside Slough.** (Humboldt River lands.)														
....	1887	....	....	....	....	....	2.24	SE¼SE¼	6	34	43	3-15—4-28	.018	1.68
....	1887	....	....	....	....	....	12.40	SW¼SE¼	6	34	43	3-15—4-28	.101	9.30
....	1887	....	....	....	....	....	10.72	NE¼SE¼	6	34	43	3-15—4-28	.087	8.04
....	1887	....	....	....	....	....	15.08	NW¼SE¼	6	34	43	3-15—4-28	.123	11.31
....	1887	....	....	....	....	....	33.70	NE¼SW¼	6	34	43	3-15—4-28	.274	25.28
....	1887	....	....	....	....	....	21.60	NW¼SW¼	6	34	43	3-15—4-28	.176	16.20
....	1887	....	....	....	....	....	7.04	SW¼SW¼	6	34	43	3-15—4-28	.057	5.28
....	1887	....	....	....	....	....	9.32	SE¼SW¼	6	34	43	3-15—4-28	.076	6.99
....	1886	....	....	....	....	....	36.56	NW¼NW¼	32	36	42	3-15—4-28	.297	27.42
....	1886	....	....	....	....	....	37.64	SW¼NW¼	32	36	42	3-15—4-28	.306	28.33
....	1886	....	....	....	....	....	36.86	SE¼NW¼	32	36	42	3-15—4-28	.300	27.65
....	1886	....	....	....	....	....	38.64	NE¼NW¼	32	36	42	3-15—4-28	.314	28.98
....	1886	....	....	....	....	....	38.20	NW¼NE¼	32	36	42	3-15—4-28	.311	28.65
....	1886	....	....	....	....	....	37.32	SW¼NE¼	32	36	42	3-15—4-28	.303	27.99
....	1886	....	....	....	....	....	39.00	NE¼NE¼	32	36	42	3-15—4-28	.317	29.25
....	1886	....	....	....	....	....	40.20	SE¼NE¼	32	36	42	3-15—4-28	.327	30.15

Ellison Ranching Co.—Continued.

Year of priority	Culture—Acres: Harvest crops	Culture—Acres: Meadow pasture	Culture—Acres: Diversified pasture	Location: Subdivision	Location: Section	Location: Tp. N.	Location: R. E.	Length of season	Duty of water: C. F. S.	Duty of water: Acre-feet
1886			38.00	NE¼SW¼	32	36	42	3-15—4-28	.309	28.50
1886			40.32	NW¼SW¼	32	36	42	3-15—4-28	.328	30.24
1886			40.24	SE¼SW¼	32	36	42	3-15—4-28	.327	30.18
1886			27.12	SW¼SW¼	32	36	42	3-15—4-28	.220	20.35
1886			40.32	NE¼SE¼	32	36	42	3-15—4-28	.328	30.24
1886			40.48	SE¼SE¼	32	36	42	3-15—4-28	.329*	30.36
1886			35.62	NW¼SE¼	32	36	42	3-15—4-28	.290	26.72
1886			37.64	SW¼SE¼	32	36	42	3-15—4-28	.306	28.23
1886			28.68	NW¼NE¼	5	35	42	3-15—4-28	.233	21.51
1886			38.08	NE¼NE¼	5	35	42	3-15—4-28	.310	28.56
1886			37.10	SE¼SE¼	5	35	42	3-15—4-28	.302	27.83
1886			16.64	NE¼SE¼	5	35	42	3-15—4-28	.135	12.98
1886			4.96	SW¼NE¼	5	35	42	3-15—4-28	.040	3.72
1886			36.80	SE¼NE¼	5	35	42	3-15—4-28	.290	27.60
1886			36.60	NW¼NW¼	4	35	42	3-15—4-28	.298	27.45
1886			36.56	NE¼NW¼	4	35	42	3-15—4-28	.297	27.42
1886			38.96	SW¼NW¼	4	35	42	3-15—4-28	.317	29.22
1886			39.32	SE¼NW¼	4	35	42	3-15—4-28	.320	29.49
1886			38.80	NW¼SE¼	4	35	42	3-15—4-28	.315	29.10
1886			39.28	NE¼SE¼	4	35	42	3-15—4-28	.319	29.46
1886			33.16	SW¼SE¼	4	35	42	3-15—4-28	.270	24.87
1886			39.24	SE¼SE¼	4	35	42	3-15—4-28	.319	29.43
1886			40.08	NW¼NE¼	4	35	42	3-15—4-28	.326	30.06
1886			38.72	NE¼NE¼	4	35	42	3-15—4-28	.315	29.04
1886			39.36	SE¼NE¼	4	35	42	3-15—4-28	.320	29.52
1886			38.88	SW¼NE¼	4	35	42	3-15—4-28	.315	29.16
1886			38.16	SE¼SE¼	4	35	42	3-15—4-28	.310	28.62
1886			37.66	SW¼SE¼	4	35	42	3-15—4-28	.306	28.25
1886			38.88	NE¼SE¼	4	35	42	3-15—4-28	.315	29.16
1886			38.24	NW¼SE¼	4	35	42	3-15—4-28	.311	28.68
1887			12.32	NE¼NW¼	35	35	42	3-15—4-28	.100	9.24
1887			39.60	SE¼NW¼	35	35	42	3-15—4-28	.322	29.70
1887			11.66	NE¼SW¼	35	35	42	3-15—4-28	.095	8.75
1887			40.40	NE¼NE¼	35	35	42	3-15—4-28	.328	30.30
1887			39.12	NW¼SE¼	35	35	42	3-15—4-28	.318	29.34
1887			39.44	NE¼SE¼	35	35	42	3-15—4-28	.321	29.58
1887			30.64	NE¼SE¼	1	34	42	3-15—4-28	.249	22.98
1887			10.88	NW¼SE¼	1	34	42	3-15—4-28	.088	8.16
1887			33.20	SE¼NE¼	1	34	42	3-15—4-28	.270	24.90
1887			39.36	SW¼NE¼	1	34	42	3-15—4-28	.320	29.52
1887			26.00	NE¼NE¼	1	34	42	3-15—4-28	.211	19.50
1887			38.00	NW¼NE¼	1	34	42	3-15—4-28	.309	28.60
1887			16.48	NE¼NW¼	1	34	42	3-15—4-28	.134	12.36
1887			32.48	SE¼NW¼	1	34	42	3-15—4-28	.264	24.36
1887			38.80	NW¼NW¼	27	[illegible]	42	3-15—4-28	.311	29.10
1887			35.41	NE¼NW¼	27	[illegible]	42	3-15—4-28	.288	26.58
1887			38.20	SE¼NW¼	27	[illegible]	42	3-15—4-28	.311	28.65
1887			40.40	SW¼NW¼	27	[illegible]	42	3-15—4-28	.328	30.30
1887			40.00	NW¼NE¼	27	[illegible]	42	3-15—4-28	.325	30.00

	1887					37.88		NW¼SE¼	27	35	42	3-15—4-28	.308	28.41
	1887						38.96	NE¼SE¼	27	35	42	3-15—4-28	.317	29.22
	1887					37.36		SE¼SE¼	27	35	42	3-15—4-28	.304	28.02
	1887						39.68	SW¼NE¼	27	35	42	3-15—4-28	.324	29.76
	1887						39.88	SE¼NE¼	27	35	42	3-15—4-28	.321	29.91
	1887						37.08	SW¼SW¼	22	35	42	3-15—4-28	.301	27.81
	1887						35.72	NW¼SW¼	22	35	42	3-15—4-28	.290	26.79
	1887						36.71	SE¼SE¼	35	35	42	3-15—4-28	.298	27.53
	1887						1.33	SW¼SE¼	35	35	42	3-15—4-28	.011	1.00
	1887						38.84	NW¼SW¼	36	35	42	3-15—4-28	.316	29.13
	1887						35.40	NE¼SW¼	36	35	42	3-15—4-28	.288	26.55
	1887						37.44	SW¼SW¼	36	35	42	3-15—4-28	.304	28.08
	1887						41.40	SE¼SW¼	36	35	42	3-15—4-28	.337	31.05
	1887						38.80	NW¼SE¼	36	35	42	3-15—4-28	.315	29.10
	1887						40.32	NE¼SE¼	36	35	42	3-15—4-28	.328	30.24
	1887						39.56	SE¼SE¼	36	35	42	3-15—4-28	.322	29.67
	1887						31.04	SW¼SE¼	36	35	42	3-15—4-28	.252	23.28
	1887						31.60	NW¼NW¼	9	35	42	3-15—4-28	.257	23.70
	1887						19.84	SE¼NW¼	9	35	42	3-15—4-28	.161	14.88
	1887						36.80	SW¼NW¼	9	35	42	3-15—4-28	.299	27.60
	1887						.72	SW¼SW¼	9	35	42	3-16—4-28	.006	.54
	1887						37.28	NE¼SW¼	9	35	42	3-15—4-28	.303	27.96
	1887					38.32		SE¼SW¼	9	35	42	3-15—4-28	.312	28.74
	1887						10.68	NW¼SE¼	9	35	42	3-15—4-28	.087	8.01
	1887					38.66		NE¼SE¼	9	35	42	3-15—4-28	.314	29.00
	1887						3.48	SE¼SE¼	9	35	42	3-15—4-28	.028	2.61
	1887						36.36	SW¼SE¼	9	35	42	3-15—4-28	.296	27.27
	1887						37.44	SW¼NE¼	9	35	42	3-15—4-28	.304	28.08

Source—**Rock Creek and Tributaries.** Ditch—**Fraser Creek Canal.** (Squaw Valley lands.)

	1883					1.05		NE¼NE¼	26	38	46	3-15—4-28	.009	.79
	1886			23.30				NE¼SE¼	13	38	46	3-15—9-15	.189	69.90
	1886						18.17	NE¼SE¼	13	38	46	3-15—4-28	.148	14.73
	1886			.82				SE¼SE¼	13	38	46	3-15—9-15	.007	2.46
	1886					9.45		SE¼SE¼	13	38	46	3-15—4-28	.077	7.09
	1886						25.97	SE¼SE¼	13	38	46	3-15—4-28	.211	19.49
	1886			34.81				NW¼SE¼	13	38	46	3-15—9-15	.283	104.43
	1886						7.63	NW¼SE¼	13	38	46	3-15—4-28	.062	5.72
	1886			.27				SW¼SE¼	13	38	46	3-15—9-15	.002	.81
	1886						43.55	SW¼SE¼	13	38	46	3-15—4-28	.354	32.66
	1886			1.95				SE¼NW¼	13	38	46	3-15—9-15	.016	5.85
	1886					12.45		SE¼NW¼	13	38	46	3-15—4-28	.101	9.34
	1886			3.44				NE¼SW¼	13	38	46	3-15—9-15	.028	10.32
	1886					7.68		NE¼SW¼	13	38	46	3-15—4-28	.062	7.68
	1886						29.07	NE¼SW¼	13	38	46	3-15—4-28	.236	21.80
	1886						9.26	SE¼SW¼	13	38	46	3-15—4-28	.075	6.95
	1886						30.50	NE¼NE¼	24	28	46	3-15—4-28	.248	22.88
	1886						36.50	SE¼NE¼	24	38	46	3-15—4-28	.297	27.38
	1886						41.42	NW¼NE¼	24	38	46	3-15—4-28	.337	31.07
	1886						41.10	SW¼NE¼	24	38	46	3-15—4-28	.334	30.83
	1886						38.10	NE¼SE¼	24	38	46	3-15—4-28	.310	28.60
	1886					10.98		SE¼SE¼	24	38	46	3-15—4-28	.089	8.18
	1886						29.74	SE¼SE¼	24	38	46	3-15—4-28	.242	22.31

Ellison Ranching Co.—Continued.

Year of priority	Culture—Acres: Harvest crops	Meadow pasture	Diversified pasture		Location: Subdivision	Section	Tp.N.	R.E.	Length of season	Duty of water: C.F.S.	Acre-feet
1886				40.95	NW¼SE¼	24	38	46	3-15—4-28	.333	30.71
1886			29.31		SW¼SE¼	24	38	46	3-15—4-28	.238	21.98
1886				12.06	SW¼SE¼	24	38	46	3-15—4-28	.098	9.05
1886				17.84	NE¼NW¼	24	38	46	3-15—4-28	.145	13.08
1886				7.94	SE¼NW¼	24	38	46	3-15—4-28	.065	5.96
1886			2.42		SE¼NE¼	12	38	46	3-15—4-28	.020	1.82
1886	15.53				NE¼SE¼	12	38	46	3-15—9-15	.126	46.59
1886			8.64		NE¼SE¼	12	38	46	3-15—4-28	.070	6.48
1886				14.00	NE¼SE¼	12	38	46	3-15—4-28	.114	10.50
1886	15.05				SE¼SE¼	12	38	46	3-15—9-15	.122	45.15
1886				9.09	SE¼SE¼	12	38	46	3-15—4-28	.074	6.82
1886	8.00				NE¼NE¼	13	38	46	3-15—9-15	.065	24.00
1886	28.37				NW¼NE¼	13	38	46	3-15—9-15	.231	85.11
1886				6.05	NW¼NE¼	13	38	46	3-15—4-28	.049	4.54
1886	3.10				SE¼NE¼	13	38	46	3-15—9-15	.025	6.30
1886	24.87				SW¼NE¼	13	38	46	3-15—9-15	.202	74.61
1886	.36				NE¼NW¼	13	38	46	3-15—9-15	.003	1.08
1886				1.73	NE¼NW¼	13	38	46	3-15—4-28	.014	1.30
1886	3.90				SE¼NW¼	13	38	46	3-15—9-15	.032	11.70
1886			6.26		SE¼NW¼	13	38	46	3-15—4-28	.051	4.70
1886				2.38	SE¼NW¼	13	38	46	3-15—4-28	.019	1.79
1886	33.52				SW¼SE¼	6	38	47	3-15—9-15	.273	100.56
1886			3.17		SW¼SE¼	6	38	47	3-15—4-28	.026	2.38

Source—**Willow Creek.** Ditch—**Fraser Creek Canal.** (Squaw Valley lands.)

Year of priority	Harvest crops	Meadow pasture	Diversified pasture		Subdivision	Section	Tp.N.	R.E.	Length of season	C.F.S.	Acre-feet
1886				1.55	SW¼NW¼	18	38	47	3-15—4-28	.013	1.16
1886	6.95				SE¼NE¼	13	38	46	3-15—9-15	.057	20.85
1886				6.87	SE¼NE¼	13	38	46	3-15—4-28	.055	5.15
1846	14.45				SW¼NE¼	13	38	46	3-15—9-15	.117	43.35

Source—**Rock Creek** and **Tributaries.** Ditch—**Fraser Creek Canal.** (Squaw Valley lands.)

Year of priority	Harvest crops	Meadow pasture	Diversified pasture		Subdivision	Section	Tp.N.	R.E.	Length of season	C.F.S.	Acre-feet
1881	35.50				NE¼NW¼	7	38	47	3-15—9-15	.289	106.50
1881	27.74				SW¼NW¼	7	38	47	3-15—9-15	.226	83.22
1881				8.21	SW¼NW¼	7	38	47	3-15—4-28	.067	6.16
1881	0.46				SW¼SW¼	32	39	47	3-15—9-15	.004	1.38
1881				9.60	SW¼SW¼	32	39	47	3-15—4-28	.078	7.20
1881				12.08	NE¼SW¼	24	38	46	3-15—4-28	.098	9.06
1881				40.35	SE¼SW¼	24	38	46	3-15—4-28	.328	30.26
1881			16.37		SW¼SW¼	24	38	46	3-15—4-28	.133	12.28
1881				9.95	SW¼SW¼	19	38	47	3-15—4-28	.081	7.46
1881				23.92	NW¼NW¼	30	38	47	3-15—4-28	.194	17.94
1881				2.42	SW¼NW¼	30	38	47	3-15—4-28	.020	1.82
1881				1.87	SE¼SE¼	23	38	46	3-15—4-28	.015	1.40

Source—**Rock Creek and Tributaries.** Ditch—**Lakefield Ditch.** (Squaw Valley lands.)

Year of priority	Harvest crops	Meadow pasture	Diversified pasture		Subdivision	Section	Tp.N.	R.E.	Length of season	C.F.S.	Acre-feet
1880	24.82				SW¼SW¼	7	38	47	3-15—9-15	.202	74.46
1880				5.62	SW¼SW¼	7	38	47	3-15—4-28	.046	4.22
1880	16.27				SE¼SW¼	7	38	47	3-15—9-15	.132	48.81
1880				8.60	SE¼SW¼	7	38	47	3-15—4-28	.070	6.44

	1880			4.03				NE¼NW¼	18	38	47	3-15—0-15	.033	12.09
	1880						6.17	NE¼NW¼	18	38	47	3-15—4-28	.050	4.63
	1880			17.13				NW¼NW¼	18	38	47	3-15—0-15	.139	51.39
	1880						2.30	NW¼NW¼	18	38	47	3-15—4-28	.019	1.73
	1880			4.82				SW¼NW¼	18	38	47	3-15—0-15	.039	14.46
	1880						7.40	SW¼NW¼	18	38	47	3-15—4-28	.061	5.62
	1880						2.70	SE¼NW¼	18	38	47	3-15—4-28	.022	2.03
	1880			29.55				SW¼NE¼	7	38	47	3-15—0-15	.240	88.65
	1880						10.30	SW¼NE¼	7	38	47	3-15—4-28	.084	7.73
	1880			33.92				SE¼NW¼	7	38	47	3-15—0-15	.276	101.76
	1880					3.38		SE¼NW¼	7	38	47	3-15—4-28	.027	2.54
	1880			29.74				NE¼SW¼	7	38	47	3-15—0-15	.242	89.22
	1880						2.16	NE¼SW¼	7	38	47	3-15—4-28	.018	1.62
	1880			34.17				NW¼SW¼	7	38	47	3-15—0-15	.279	102.51
	1880						5.18	NW¼SW¼	7	38	47	3-15—4-28	.042	3.80

Source—**Rock Creek and Tributaries.** Ditch—**Rock Creek Ditch.** (Squaw Valley lands.)

	1878			18.53				NW¼NW¼	8	38	47	3-15—0-15	.151	55.60
	1878					14.36		NW¼NW¼	8	38	47	3-15—4-28	.117	10.77
	1878					2.09		SE¼NW¼	8	38	47	3-15—4-28	.017	1.57
	1878					3.38		SW¼NW¼	8	38	47	3-15—4-28	.027	2.54
	1878						23.12	SW¼NW¼	8	38	47	3-15—4-28	.189	17.31
	1878						1.60	NW¼SW¼	8	38	47	3-15—4-28	.013	1.20
	1878			38.05				NE¼NE¼	7	38	47	3-15—0-15	.309	114.15
	1878			37.00				NW¼NE¼	7	38	47	3-15—0-15	.300	111.00
	1878			24.28				SE¼NE¼	7	38	47	3-15—0-15	.197	72.84
	1878						12.95	SE¼NE¼	7	38	47	3-15—4-28	.105	9.71
	1878						7.05	NE¼SE¼	7	38	47	3-15—4-28	.057	5.29
	1878			1.72				NW¼SE¼	7	38	47	3-15—0-15	.014	5.16
	1878						8.30	NW¼SE¼	7	38	47	3-15—4-28	.067	6.23
	1878			36.80				SE¼NW¼	5	38	47	3-15—0-15	.290	110.40
	1878			17.74				NE¼SW¼	5	38	47	3-15—0-15	.144	53.22
	1878			36.47				NW¼SW¼	5	38	47	3-15—0-15	.297	109.41
	1878					4.75		NW¼SW¼	5	38	47	3-15—4-28	.039	3.56
	1878			37.27				SW¼SW¼	5	38	47	3-15—0-15	.303	111.81

Source—**Rock Creek and Tributaries.** Ditch—**Highline Ditch.** (Squaw Valley lands.)

	1887			.50				NW¼NW¼	1	38	46	3-15—0-15	.004	1.50
	1887			18.43				SE¼NW¼	1	38	46	3-15—0-15	.150	55.29
	1887						4.88	SE¼NW¼	1	38	46	3-15—4-28	.040	3.66
	1887			34.92				SW¼NW¼	1	38	46	3-15—0-15	.283	104.76
	1887			15.90				NE¼SW¼	1	38	46	3-15—0-15	.129	47.70
	1887			30.62				NW¼SW¼	1	38	46	3-15—0-15	.249	91.86
	1887			8.93				SW¼SW¼	1	38	46	3-15—0-15	.073	26.79
	1887			40.87				SE¼NE¼	2	38	46	3-15—0-15	.332	122.61
	1887			14.70				SW¼NE¼	2	38	46	3-15—0-15	.120	44.10
	1887			24.27				SW¼NE¼	2	38	46	3-15—0-15	.197	72.81
	1887			26.03				NE¼SE¼	2	38	46	3-15—0-15	.212	78.09
	1887			21.06				NW¼SE¼	2	38	46	3-15—0-15	.171	63.18
	1887						19.41	NW¼SE¼	2	38	46	3-15—4-28	.158	14.56
	1887			5.04				SE¼SE¼	2	38	46	3-15—0-15	.041	15.12
	1887						13.88	SE¼SW¼	32	39	47	3-15—4-28	.113	10.41
	1887				9.61			SE¼SW¼	31	39	47	3-15—6-13	.078	14.42

Ellison Ranching Co.—Continued.

Year of priority	Culture—Acres: Harvest crops	Meadow pasture	Diversified pasture		Location: Subdivision	Section	Tp.N.	R.E.	Length of season	Duty of water: C.F.S.	Acre-feet
1887		8.54			SW¼SW¼	31	39	47	3-15—6-13	.069	12.81
1887		17.33			NE¼NW¼	6	38	47	3-15—6-13	.141	26.00
1887		2.31			NW¼NW¼	6	38	47	3-15—6-13	.019	3.47
1887	5.82				NE¼NE¼	2	38	46	3-15—9.15	.047	17.46
1887	12.75				NW¼NE¼	2	38	46	3-15—9-15	.104	38.25
1887			11.20		SE¼SE¼	2	38	46	3-15—4-28	.092	8.46
1887			14.04		NE¼SE¼	2	38	46	3-15—4-28	.114	10.53
1887	2.35				SE¼NW¼	2	38	46	3-15—6-13	.019	3.53
1887	5.34				NE¼SW¼	2	38	46	3-15—6-13	.043	8.01
1887			4.86		NE¼SW¼	2	38	46	3-15—4-28	.039	3.65
1887			8.45		SW¼SE¼	2	38	46	3-15—4-28	.069	6.34
1887			7.00		NW¼SW¼	2	38	46	3-15—4-28	.057	5.25
1887			2.80		SW¼SW¼	2	38	46	3-15—4-28	.023	2.10
1887			6.75		SW¼SE¼	31	39	47	3 15—4-28	.055	5.06
1887			5.95		SE¼SE¼	31	39	47	3-15—4-28	.048	4.46
1887			3.20		NE¼NE¼	6	38	47	3-15—4-28	.026	2.40

Source—**Willow Creek.** Ditch—**Overflow.** (Squaw Valley lands.)

Year of priority	Harvest crops	Meadow pasture	Diversified pasture		Subdivision	Section	Tp.N.	R.E.	Length of season	C.F.S.	Acre-feet
1878	5.47				NE¼SW¼	18	38	47	3-15—9 15	.044	16.41
1878			2.28		NE¼SW¼	18	38	47	3-15—4-28	.019	1.71
1878				8.47	NE¼SW¼	18	38	47	3-15—4-28	.069	6.35
1878				12.50	NW¼SW¼	18	38	47	3-15—4.28	.101	9.38

Source—**Willow Creek.** Ditch—**Deep Slough.** (Squaw Valley lands.)

Year of priority	Harvest crops	Meadow pasture	Diversified pasture		Subdivision	Section	Tp.N.	R.E.	Length of season	C.F.S.	Acre-feet
1886	5.55				SE¼SW¼	8	38	47	3-15—9-15	.045	16.65
1886		10.90			SE¼SW¼	8	38	47	3-15—6-13	.089	16.35
1886		17.27			NE¼NW¼	17	38	47	3-15—6-13	.140	25.91
1886		20.82			NW¼NW¼	17	38	47	3. 15—6-13	.169	31.23
1886		2.42			SW¼NW¼	17	38	47	3-15—6-13	.020	3.63
1886		13.30			NE¼NE¼	18	38	47	3-15—6-13	.108	19.96
1886		0.87			NW¼NE¼	18	38	47	3-15—6-13	.007	1.31
1886		24.77			SE¼NE¼	18	38	47	3 15—6-13	.201	37.16
1886		14.35			SW¼NE¼	18	38	47	3-15—6-13	.116	21.53
1886	27.27				NE¼SE¼	8	38	47	3-15—9-15	.222	81.81
1886	16.62				SE¼SE¼	8	38	47	3-15—9-15	.135	49.96
1886	7.62				NW¼SE¼	8	38	47	3.15—9-15	.062	22.86
1886	32.87				SW¼SE¼	8	38	47	3-15—9-15	.267	98.61
1886	0.97				NW¼NE¼	17	38	47	3-15—9-15	.008	2.91
1886	1.90				SE¼NE¼	18	38	47	3-15—9-15	.015	5.70
1886				7.49	SE¼NE¼	18	38	47	3 15—4 28	.061	5.02
1886	11.70				SW¼NE¼	18	38	47	3-15—9-15	.095	35.10
1886				0.75	SW¼NE¼	18	38	47	3 15—4 28	.006	.56
1886				1.32	NE¼SE¼	18	88	47	3 15—4 28	.011	.99
1886	3.97				NW¼SE¼	18	38	47	3-15—9-15	.032	12.01
1886				11.57	NW¼SE¼	18	38	47	3-15—4 28	.094	8.64
1886	3.02				SE¼NW¼	18	38	47	3 15—9 15	.029	10.86
1886			5.85		SE¼NW¼	18	38	47	3.15—4 28	.048	4.39
1886				1.25	SE¼NW¼	18	38	47	3 15—4 28	.010	[illegible]

Year						Sec.					
			Source—**Rock Creek and Tributaries.** Ditch—**Warm Spring.** (Squaw Valley lands.)								
1876			13.15		NE¼ NE¼	25	38	46	3-15—4 28	.107	9.87
1876				20.17	NE¼ NE¼	25	38	46	3 15—4 28	.161	15.13
1876			13.01		NW¼ NE¼	25	38	46	3 15—4 28	.106	9.76
1876				13.74	NW¼ NE¼	25	38	46	3 15—4 28	.112	10.31
1876			21.02		NE¼ NW¼	25	38	46	3 15—4 28	.176	16.22
1876				3.00	NE¼ NW¼	25	38	46	3-15—4 28	.024	2.25
1876			20.35		NW¼ NW¼	25	38	46	3 15—4 28	.165	15.26
			Source—**Rock Creek.** Ditch—**Barleyfield Canal.** (Squaw Valley lands.)								
1888			3.96		NW¼ SE¼	21	39	47	3-15—4-28	.032	2.96
1888			0.47		SW¼ SE¼	21	39	47	3-15—4-28	.038	0.35
1888			32.45		NE¼ SW¼	21	39	47	3-15—4-28	.264	24.34
1888			29.30		SE¼ SW¼	21	39	47	3-15—4-28	.238	21.98
1888			35.95		NW¼ SW¼	21	39	47	3-15—4-28	.292	26.96
1888			36.00		SW¼ SW¼	21	39	47	3-15—4-28	.293	27.00
1888			1.00		SW¼ NE¼	20	39	47	3-15—4-28	.008	0.75
1888			40.55		NE¼ SE¼	20	39	47	3-15—4 28	.330	30.41
1888			36.35		SE¼ SE¼	20	39	47	3-15—4-28	.296	27.26
1888			21.40		NW¼ SE¼	20	39	47	3-15—4-28	.174	16.30
1888			23.30		SW¼ SE¼	20	39	47	3-15—4-28	.180	17.48
1888			2.90		NE¼ NW¼	28	39	47	3-15—4-28	.024	2.18
1888			27.64		NW¼ NW¼	28	39	47	3-15—4-28	.225	20.73
1888			4.73		SW¼ NW¼	28	39	47	3-15—4-28	.039	3.55
1888			39.37		NE¼ NE¼	29	39	47	3-15—4-28	.320	29.53
1888			2.35		SE¼ NE¼	29	39	47	3-15—4-28	.019	1.76
			Source—**Rock Creek and Tributaries.** Ditch—**Willow Creek Canal.** (Squaw Valley lands.)								
1880		23.40			SE¼ NE¼	1	38	46	3-15—6-13	.190	35.10
1880				5.26	SE¼ NE¼	1	38	46	3-15—4-28	.043	3.95
1880		23.61			SW¼ NE¼	1	38	46	3-15—6-13	.192	35.42
1880				13.68	SW¼ NE¼	1	38	46	3 15—4-28	.111	10.26
1880	16.56				NE¼ SE¼	1	38	46	3-15—9-15	.135	49.68
1880		17.67			NE¼ SE¼	1	38	46	3-15—6-13	.144	26.51
1880				3.31	NE¼ SE¼	1	38	46	3-15—4-28	.027	2.48
1880	12.12				NW¼ SE¼	1	38	46	3-15—9 15	.098	36.36
1880		7.27			NW¼ SE¼	1	38	46	3-15—6-13	.059	10.90
1880	34.19				SE¼ SE¼	1	38	46	3-15—9-15	.278	102.57
1880				5.76	SE¼ SE¼	1	38	46	3 15—4 28	.047	4.32
1880	40.00				SW¼ SE¼	1	38	46	3-15—9-15	.325	120.00
1888	34.79				SE¼ SW¼	1	38	46	3-15—9-15	.283	104.37
1888		1.51			SE¼ SW¼	1	38	46	3 15—6-13	.012	2.27
1888		3.67			SE¼ NW¼	1	38	46	3-15—6-13	.030	5.51
1888	15.12				NE¼ SW¼	1	38	46	3 15—9-15	.123	45.36
1888		7.06			NE¼ SW¼	1	38	46	3-15—6-13	.057	10.59
1888				1.90	SW¼ SW¼	1	38	46	3-15—4-28	.015	1.43
1880	33.85				SE¼ SE¼	6	38	47	3-15—9 15	.275	101.55
1880			4.25		SE¼ SE¼	6	38	47	3 15—4 28	.035	3.19
1880	32.48				NE¼ SW¼	6	38	47	3-15—9-15	.264	97.44
1880				8.42	NE¼ SW¼	6	38	47	3-15—4-28	.068	6.32
1880	15.12				NW¼ SW¼	6	38	47	3 15—9 15	.122	45.36
1880				20.47	NW¼ SW¼	6	38	47	3 15—4 28	.166	15.35
1880	40.37				SE¼ SW¼	6	38	47	3-15—9-15	.328	121.11

Ellison Ranching Co.—Continued.

Year of priority	Culture—Acres: Harvest crops	Meadow pasture	Diversified pasture		Location: Subdivision	Section	Tp. N.	R. E.	Length of season	Duty of water: C. F. S.	Acre-feet
[illegible]	27.65				SW¼ SW¼	6	38	47	3-15—9-15	.225	82.95
[illegible]				4.54	SW¼ SW¼	6	38	47	3-15—4-28	.037	3.41
[illegible]	6.97				NE¼ NE¼	5	38	47	3-15—9-15	.008	2.91
[illegible]	8.82				NW¼ NE¼	5	38	47	3-15—9-15	.072	26.46
[illegible]				4.48	NW¼ NE¼	5	38	47	3-15—4-28	.036	3.36
[illegible]	18.37				NE¼ NW¼	5	38	47	3-15—9-15	.149	55.11
[illegible]		10.18			NE¼ NW¼	5	38	47	3-15—6-13	.083	15.27
[illegible]				6.29	NE¼ NW¼	5	38	47	3-15—4-28	.051	4.70
1880	11.29				NW¼ NW¼	5	38	47	3-15—9-15	.092	33.87
1880				5.78	NW¼ NW¼	5	38	47	3-15—4-28	.047	4.34
1880	15.10				NE¼ NE¼	6	38	47	3-15—9-15	.123	45.30
1880				11.10	NE¼ NE¼	6	38	47	3-15—4-28	.090	8.33
1880	0.40				SE¼ NE¼	5	38	47	3-15—9-15	.003	1.20
1880	34.09				SW¼ NE¼	5	38	47	3-15—9-15	.277	102.27
1880			0.26		SW¼ NE¼	5	38	47	3-15—4-28	.002	0.20
1880	15.11				NW¼ SE¼	5	38	47	3-15—9-15	.123	45.33
1880			6.51		NW¼ SE¼	5	38	47	3-15—4-28	.053	4.88
1880			3.46		SW¼ SE¼	5	38	47	3-15—4-28	.028	2.60
1886	1.65				SW¼ SE¼	3	38	47	3-15—9-15	.013	4.95
1886	12.45				SE¼ SW¼	3	38	47	3-15—9-15	.101	37.35
1886	33.90				SW¼ SW¼	3	38	47	3-15—9-15	.276	101.70
1886	24.60				SE¼ SE¼	4	38	47	3-15—9-15	.200	73.80
1886	3.00				SW¼ SE¼	4	38	47	3-15—9-15	.024	9.00
1886	0.67				NW¼ NW¼	10	38	47	3-15—9-15	.005	2.01
1886	10.68				NE¼ NE¼	9	38	47	3-15—9-15	.087	32.04
1886				3.93	NE¼ NE¼	9	38	47	3-15—4-28	.032	2.95
1886	30.86				NW¼ NE¼	9	38	47	3-15—9-15	.251	92.58
1886				4.21	NW¼ NE¼	9	38	47	3-15—4-28	.034	3.16
1886	6.77				SW¼ NE¼	9	38	47	3-15—9-15	.055	20.31
1886				7.88	SW¼ NE¼	9	38	47	3-15—4-28	.064	5.91
1886	18.37				NE¼ NW¼	8	38	47	3-15—9-15	.149	55.11
1886	37.40				SE¼ NW¼	9	38	47	3-15—9-15	.304	112.20
1886	20.88				SW¼ NW¼	9	38	47	3-15—9-15	.170	62.64
1886	4.95				NE¼ SW¼	9	38	47	3-15—9-15	.040	14.85
1886	36.72				NW¼ SW¼	9	38	47	3-15—9-15	.299	110.16
1886	1.46				SW¼ SW¼	9	38	47	3-15—9-15	.011	4.20
1886	0.29				SE¼ NE¼	8	38	47	3-15—9-15	.002	.87
1880	6.05				NE¼ NW¼	8	38	47	3-15—9-15	.049	18.15
1880			21.08		NE¼ NW¼	8	38	47	3-15—4-28	.171	15.81
1880	23.82				NW¼ NW¼	7	38	47	3-15—9-15	.191	71.46
1880				3.23	NW¼ NW¼	7	38	47	3-15—4-28	.026	2.42
1880		21.27			NW¼ NW¼	5	38	47	3-15—6-13	.173	31.91
1880			1.12		SW¼ SE¼	3	38	47	3-15—4-28	.009	0.84
1880			0.33		SW¼ SW¼	3	38	47	3-15—4-28	.003	0.25
1880			0.15		NW¼ SW¼	3	38	47	3-15—4-28	.001	0.11
1880			8.01		NE¼ SW¼	3	38	47	3-15—4-28	[illegible]	6.08
1880			14.51		NW¼ SE¼	3	38	47	3-15—4-28	.118	10.88
1880			1.40		NE¼ SE¼	3	38	47	3-15—4-28	.011	1.05
1880			1.25		SE¼ SW¼	[illegible]	38	47	3-15—4-28	.015	[illegible]

	1880				3.25			NE¼ NE¼	1	38	46	3-15—6-13	.026	4.88
	1880				15.06			NW¼ NE¼	1	38	46	3-15—6-13	.122	2.26
	1880				2.74			NE¼ NW¼	1	38	46	3-15—6-13	.022	0.41
	1880			22.03				NE¼ NE¼	12	38	46	3-15—9-15	.179	66.09
	1880						9.65	NE¼ NE¼	12	38	46	3-15—4-28	.078	7.24
	1880			28.89				NW¼ NE¼	12	38	46	3-15—9-15	.234	86.40
	1880				11.10			NW¼ NE¼	12	38	46	3-15—6-13	.090	16.65
	1880			29.23				SE¼ NE¼	12	38	46	3-15—9-15	.238	87.60
	1880						4.39	SE¼ NE¼	12	38	46	3-15—4-28	.036	3.21
	1880			16.20				SW¼ NE¼	12	38	46	3-15—9-15	.132	48.60
	1880						15.12	SW¼ NE¼	12	38	46	3-15—4-28	.123	11.34
	1880			4.90				NE¼ NW¼	12	38	46	3-15—9-15	.040	14.70
	1880				27.45			NE¼ NW¼	12	38	46	3-15—6-13	.223	41.18
	1880						8.42	NE¼ NW¼	12	38	46	3-15—4-28	.068	6.32
	1880						13.70	NW¼ NW¼	12	38	46	3-15—4-28	.111	10.28
	1880						4.39	SE¼ NW¼	12	38	46	3-15—4-28	.036	3.29
	1880						7.06	NW¼ SE¼	12	38	46	3-15—4-28	.057	5.30
	1880			1.20				SW¼ SE¼	12	38	46	3-15—9-15	.010	3.60
	1880						9.58	SW¼ SE¼	12	38	46	3-15—4-28	.078	7.19
	1880			19.14				SW¼ NW¼	5	38	47	3-15—9-15	.156	57.42
	1880				22.26			SW¼ NW¼	5	38	47	3-15—6-13	.181	33.39
	1880			27.15				SE¼ SW¼	5	38	47	3-15—9-15	.221	81.45
	1880					13.70		SE¼ SW¼	5	38	47	3-15—4-28	.111	10.28
	1880			29.40				SE¼ NE¼	6	38	47	3-15—9-15	.239	88.20
	1880				8.14			SE¼ NE¼	6	38	47	3-15—6-13	.066	12.21
	1880					2.81		SE¼ NE¼	6	38	47	3-15—4-28	.023	2.11
	1880			23.38				SW¼ NE¼	6	38	47	3-15—9-15	.190	70.14
	1880						5.54	SW¼ NE¼	6	38	47	3-15—4-28	.045	4.16
	1880			21.66				SE¼ NW¼	6	38	47	3-15—9-15	.176	64.98
	1880						8.93	SE¼ NW¼	6	38	47	3-15—4-28	.073	6.70
	1880			19.70				NE¼ SW¼	5	38	47	3-15—9-15	.160	59.10
	1880				2.38			SW¼ NW¼	6	38	47	3-15—6-13	.019	3.57
	1880						13.03	SW¼ NW¼	6	38	47	3-15—4-28	.106	9.77
	1880			7.77				NE¼ SE¼	6	38	47	3-15—9-15	.063	23.31
	1880				29.62			NE¼ SE¼	6	38	47	3-15—6-13	.241	44.43
	1880			28.25				NW¼ SE¼	6	38	47	3-15—9-15	.230	84.75
	1880					9.37		NW¼ SE¼	6	38	47	3-15—4-28	.076	7.03
	1880						1.37	NW¼ SE¼	6	38	47	3-15—4-28	.011	1.03

Claimant—**Clover Valley Land and Stock Co.** Proof No. **00157**

Source—**Humboldt River.** Ditch—**Hammond.** (Lands of Hammond Bros.)

	1875						38.76	NE¼ NE¼	17	36	42	3-15—4-28	.315	29.07
	1875			16.90				NW¼ NE¼	17	36	42	3-15—9-15	.137	50.70
	1875						19.28	NW¼ NE¼	17	36	42	3-15—4-28	.157	14.46
	1875			17.26				SE¼ NE¼	17	36	42	3-15—9-15	.140	51.78
	1875				.92			SE¼ NE¼	17	36	42	3-15—6-13	.007	1.38
	1875						11.60	SE¼ NE¼	17	36	42	3-15—4-28	.094	8.70
	1875			34.24				SW¼ NE¼	17	36	42	3-15—9-15	.278	102.72
	1875					1.18		SW¼ NE¼	17	36	42	3-15—4-28	.010	.89
	1875			37.68				NW¼ SE¼	17	36	42	3-15—9-15	.306	113.04
	1875					.92		NW¼ SE¼	17	36	42	3-15—4-28	.008	.69
	1875			30.04				NE¼ SE¼	17	30	42	3-15—9-15	.317	117.12

Ellison Ranching Co.—Continued.

Year of priority	Culture—Acres: Harvest crops	Culture—Acres: Meadow pasture	Culture—Acres: Diversified pasture		Location: Subdivision	Location: Section	Location: Tp. N.	Location: R.E.	Length of season	Duty of water: C.F.S.	Duty of water: Acre-feet
1880	27.65				SW¼ SW¼	6	38	47	3-15—9-15	.225	82.95
1880				4.54	SW¼ SW¼	6	38	47	3-15—4-28	.037	3.41
1880	0.97				NE¼ NE¼	7	38	47	3-15—9-15	.008	2.91
1880	8.82				NW¼ NE¼	7	38	47	3-15—9-15	.072	26.46
1880				4.48	NW¼ NE¼	5	38	47	3-15—4-28	.036	3.36
1880	18.37				NE¼ NW¼	[illegible]	38	47	3-15—9-15	.149	55.11
1880		10.18			NE¼ NW¼	5	38	47	3-15—6-13	.083	15.27
1880				6.29	NE¼ NW¼	[illegible]	38	47	3-15—4-28	.051	4.70
1880	11.29				NW¼ NW¼	5	38	47	3-15—9-15	.092	33.87
1880				5.78	NW¼ NW¼	7	38	47	3-15—4-28	.047	4.34
1880	15.10				NE¼ NE¼	6	38	47	3-16—9-15	.123	45.30
1880				11.10	NE¼ NE¼	6	38	47	3-15—4-28	.090	8.33
1880	0.40				SE¼ NE¼	7	38	47	3-15—9-15	.003	1.20
1880	34.09				SW¼ NE¼	5	38	47	3-15—9-15	.277	102.27
1880			0.26		SW¼ NE¼	5	38	47	3-15—4-28	.002	0.20
1880	15.11				NW¼ SE¼	5	38	47	3-15—9-15	.123	45.33
1880			6.51		NW¼ SE¼	[illegible]	38	47	3-15—4-28	.063	4.88
1880			3.46		SW¼ SE¼	5	38	47	3 15—4-28	.028	2.60
1880	1.65				SW¼ SE¼	[illegible]	38	47	3-15—9-15	.013	4.95
1886	12.45				SE¼ SW¼	[illegible]	38	47	3-15—9-15	.101	37.35
1886	33.90				SW¼ SW¼	[illegible]	38	47	3-15—9-15	.276	101.70
1886	24.60				SE¼ SE¼	4	38	47	3-15—9-15	.200	73.80
1886	3.00				SW¼ SE¼	4	38	47	3-15—9-16	.024	9.00
1886	0.67				NW¼ NW¼	1	38	47	3-15—9-15	.005	2.01
1886	10.68				NE¼ NE¼	9	38	47	3-15—9-15	.087	32.04
1886				3.93	NE¼ NE¼	9	38	47	3-15—4-28	.032	2.97
1886	30.86				NW¼ NE¼	9	38	47	3-15—9-15	.251	92.58
1886				4.21	NW¼ NE¼	9	38	47	3 15—4-28	.034	3.16
1886	6.77				SW¼ NE¼	9	38	47	3-15—9-15	.055	20.31
1886				7.88	SW¼ NE¼	9	38	47	3-15—4-28	.064	5.91
1886	18.37				NE¼ NW¼	8	38	47	3-15—9 15	.149	55.11
1886	37.40				SE¼ NW¼	9	38	47	3-15—9-15	.304	112.20
1886	20.88				SW¼ NW¼	9	38	47	3-15—9-15	.170	62.64
1886	4.95				NE¼ SW¼	9	38	47	3 15—9-15	.040	14.85
1886	36.72				NW¼ SW¼	9	38	47	3-15—9-15	.299	110.16
1886	1.46				SW¼ SW¼	9	38	47	3-15—9-15	.011	4.20
1886	0.20				SE¼ NE¼	8	38	47	3-15—9 15	.002	.87
1880	6.05				NE¼ NW¼	8	38	47	3-15—9-15	.049	18.15
1880			21.08		NE¼ NW¼	8	38	47	3-15—4-28	.171	15.81
1880	23.82				NW¼ NW¼	7	38	47	3-15—9-15	.191	71.46
1880				3.23	NW¼ NW¼	7	38	47	3-15—4-28	.026	2.42
1880		21.27			NW¼ NW¼	7	38	47	3-15—6 13	.173	31.01
1880			1.12		SW¼ SE¼	[illegible]	38	47	3-15—4-28	.009	0.84
1880			0.33		SW¼ SW¼	[illegible]	38	47	3-15—4-28	.003	0.25
1880			0.15		NW¼ SW¼	[illegible]	38	47	3-15—4-28	.001	0.11
1880			8.91		NE¼ SW¼	[illegible]	38	47	3-15—4-28	.072	6.68
1880			14.51		NW¼ SE¼	[illegible]	38	47	3-15—4-28	.118	10.88
1880			1.40		NE¼ SE¼	[illegible]	38	47	3-15—4-28	.011	1.05
1880			1.95		SE¼ SW¼	[illegible]	[illegible]	47	3-15—4-28	.015	3.10

	1880				3.25			NE¼ NE¼	1	38	46	3-15—6-13	.026	4.88
	1880				15.06			NW¼ NE¼	1	38	46	3-15—6-13	.122	2.26
	1880				2.74			NE¼ NW¼	1	38	46	3-15—6-13	.022	0.41
	1880			22.03				NE¼ NE¼	12	38	46	3-15—9-15	.179	66.09
	1880						9.65	NE¼ NE¼	12	38	46	3-15—4-28	.078	7.24
	1880			28.80				NW¼ NE¼	12	38	46	3-15—9-15	.234	86.40
	1880				11.10			NW¼ NE¼	12	38	46	3-15—6-13	.090	16.65
	1880			29.23				SE¼ NE¼	12	38	46	3-15—9-15	.238	87.69
	1880						4.39	SE¼ NE¼	12	38	46	3-15—4-28	.036	3.21
	1880			16.20				SW¼ NE¼	12	38	46	3-15—9-15	.132	48.60
	1880						15.12	SW¼ NE¼	12	38	46	3-15—4-28	.123	11.34
	1880			4.90				NE¼ NW¼	12	38	46	3-15—9-15	.040	14.70
	1880				27.45			NE¼ NW¼	12	38	46	3-15—6-13	.223	41.18
	1880						8.42	NE¼ NW¼	12	38	46	3-15—4-28	.068	6.32
	1880						13.70	NW¼ NW¼	12	38	46	3-15—4-28	.111	10.28
	1880						4.39	SE¼ NW¼	12	38	46	3-15—4-28	.036	3.29
	1880						7.06	NW¼ SE¼	12	38	46	3-15—4-28	.057	5.30
	1880			1.20				SW¼ SE¼	12	38	46	3-15—9-15	.010	3.60
	1880						9.58	SW¼ SE¼	12	38	46	3-15—4-28	.078	7.19
	1880			19.14				SW¼ NW¼	5	38	47	3-15—9-15	.156	57.42
	1880				22.26			SW¼ NW¼	5	38	47	3-15—6-13	.181	33.39
	1880			27.15				SE¼ SW¼	5	38	47	3-15—9-15	.221	81.45
	1880					13.70		SE¼ SW¼	5	38	47	3-15—4-28	.111	10.28
	1880			29.40				SE¼ NE¼	6	38	47	3-15—9-15	.239	88.20
	1880				8.14			SE¼ NE¼	6	38	47	3-15—6-13	.066	12.21
	1880					2.81		SE¼ NE¼	6	38	47	3-15—4-28	.023	2.11
	1880			23.38				SW¼ NE¼	6	38	47	3-15—9-15	.190	70.14
	1880						5.54	SW¼ NE¼	6	38	47	3-15—4-28	.045	4.16
	1880			21.66				SE¼ NW¼	6	38	47	3-15—9-15	.176	64.98
	1880						8.93	SE¼ NW¼	6	38	47	3-15—4-28	.073	6.70
	1880			19.70				NE¼ SW¼	5	38	47	3-15—9-15	.160	59.10
	1880				2.38			SW¼ NW¼	6	38	47	3-15—6-13	.019	3.57
	1880						13.03	SW¼ NW¼	6	38	47	3-15—4-28	.106	9.77
	1880			7.77				NE¼ SE¼	6	38	47	3-15—9-15	.063	23.31
	1880				29.62			NE¼ SE¼	6	38	47	3-15—6-13	.241	44.39
	1880			28.25				NW¼ SE¼	6	38	47	3-15—9-15	.230	84.75
	1880					9.37		NW¼ SE¼	6	38	47	3-15—4-28	.076	7.03
	1880						1.37	NW¼ SE¼	6	38	47	3-15—4-28	.011	1.03

Claimant—**Clover Valley Land and Stock Co.** Proof No. 00157
Source—**Humboldt River.** Ditch—**Hammond.** (Lands of Hammond Bros.)

	1875						38.76	NE¼ NE¼	17	36	42	3-15—4-28	.315	29.07
	1875			16.90				NW¼ NE¼	17	36	42	3-15—9-15	.137	50.70
	1875						19.28	NW¼ NE¼	17	36	42	3-15—4-28	.157	14.46
	1875			17.26				SE¼ NE¼	17	36	42	3-15—9-15	.140	51.78
	1875				.92			SE¼ NE¼	17	36	42	3-15—6-13	.007	1.38
	1875						11.60	SE¼ NE¼	17	36	42	3-15—4-28	.094	8.70
	1875			34.24				SW¼ NE¼	17	36	42	3-15—9-15	.278	102.72
	1875					1.18		SW¼ NE¼	17	36	42	3-15—4-28	.010	.89
	1875			37.68				NW¼ SE¼	17	36	42	3-15—9-15	.306	113.04
	1875					.92		NW¼ SE¼	17	36	42	3-15—4-28	.008	.69
	1875			39.04				NE¼ SE¼	17	36	42	3-15—9-15	.317	117.12

Ellison Ranching Co.—Continued.

Year of priority	Culture—Acres: Harvest crops	Meadow pasture	Diversified pasture		Location: Subdivision	Section	Tp.N.	R.E.	Length of season	Duty of water: C.F.S.	Acre-feet
1886				40.95	NW¼SE¼	24	38	46	3-15—4-28	.333	30.71
1886			29.31		SW¼SE¼	24	38	46	3-15—4-28	.238	21.98
1886				12.06	SW¼SE¼	24	38	46	3-15—4-28	.098	9.05
1886				17.84	NE¼NW¼	24	38	46	3-15—4-28	.145	13.08
1886				7.94	SE¼NW¼	24	38	46	3-15—4-28	.065	5.96
1886			2.42		SE¼NE¼	12	38	46	3-15—4-28	.020	1.82
1886	15.53				NE¼SE¼	12	38	46	3-15—9-15	.126	46.59
1886			8.64		NE¼SE¼	12	38	46	3-15—4-28	.070	6.48
1886				14.00	NE¼SE¼	12	38	46	3-15—4-28	.114	10.50
1886	15.05				SE¼SE¼	12	38	46	3-15—9-15	.122	45.15
1886				9.09	SE¼SE¼	12	38	46	3-15—4-28	.074	6.82
1886	8.00				NE¼NE¼	13	38	46	3-15—9-15	.065	24.00
1886	28.37				NW¼NE¼	13	38	46	3-15—9-15	.231	85.11
1886				6.05	NW¼NE¼	13	38	46	3-15—4-28	.049	4.54
1886	3.10				SE¼NE¼	13	38	46	3-15—9-15	.025	6.30
1886	24.87				SW¼NE¼	13	38	46	3-15—9-15	.202	74.61
1886	.36				NE¼NW¼	13	38	46	3-15—9-15	.003	1.08
1886				1.73	NE¼NW¼	13	38	46	3-15—4-28	.014	1.30
1886	3.90				SE¼NW¼	13	38	46	3-15—9-15	.032	11.70
1886			6.26		SE¼NW¼	13	38	46	3-15—4-28	.051	4.70
1886				2.38	SE¼NW¼	13	38	46	3-15—4-28	.019	1.79
1886	33.52				SW¼SE¼	6	38	47	3-15—9-15	.273	100.56
1886			3.17		SW¼SE¼	6	38	47	3-15—4-28	.026	2.38

Source—**Willow Creek.** Ditch—**Fraser Creek Canal.** (Squaw Valley lands.)

Year of priority	Harvest crops	Meadow pasture	Diversified pasture		Subdivision	Section	Tp.N.	R.E.	Length of season	C.F.S.	Acre-feet
1886				1.55	SW¼NW¼	18	38	47	3-15—4-28	.013	1.16
1886	6.95				SE¼NE¼	13	38	46	3-15—9-15	.057	20.85
1886				6.87	SE¼NE¼	13	38	46	3-15—4-28	.055	5.15
1886	14.45				SW¼NE¼	13	38	46	3-15—9-15	.117	43.35

Source—**Rock Creek and Tributaries.** Ditch—**Fraser Creek Canal.** (Squaw Valley lands.)

Year of priority	Harvest crops	Meadow pasture	Diversified pasture		Subdivision	Section	Tp.N.	R.E.	Length of season	C.F.S.	Acre-feet
1881	35.50				NE¼NW¼	7	38	47	3-15—9-15	.289	106.50
1881	27.74				SW¼NW¼	7	38	47	3-15—9-15	.226	83.22
1881				8.21	SW¼NW¼	7	38	47	3-15—4-28	.067	6.16
1881	0.46				SW¼SW¼	32	39	47	3-15—9-15	.004	1.38
1881				9.60	SW¼SW¼	32	39	47	3-15—4-28	.078	7.20
1881				12.08	NE¼SW¼	24	38	46	3-15—4-28	.098	9.06
1881				40.35	SE¼SW¼	24	38	46	3-15—4-28	.328	30.26
1881			16.37		SW¼SW¼	24	38	46	3-15—4-28	.133	12.28
1881				9.95	SW¼SW¼	19	38	47	3-15—4-28	.081	7.46
1881				23.92	NW¼NW¼	30	38	47	3-15—4-28	.194	17.94
1881				2.42	SW¼NW¼	30	38	47	3-15—4-28	.020	1.82
1881				1.87	SE¼SE¼	23	38	46	3-15—4-28	.015	1.40

Source—**Rock Creek and Tributaries.** Ditch—**Lakefield Ditch.** (Squaw Valley lands.)

Year of priority	Harvest crops	Meadow pasture	Diversified pasture		Subdivision	Section	Tp.N.	R.E.	Length of season	C.F.S.	Acre-feet
1880	24.82				SW¼SW¼	7	38	47	3-15—9-15	.202	74.46
1880				5.02	SW¼SW¼	7	38	47	3-15—4-28	.040	4.22
1880	16.27				SE¼SW¼	7	38	47	3-15—9-15	.132	48.81
1880				8.50	SE¼SW¼	7	38	47	3-15—4-28	.070	6.44

	1880			4.03				NE¼NW¼	18	38	47	3-15—9-15	.023	12.99
	1880						6.17	NE¼NW¼	18	38	47	3-15—4-28	.050	4.63
	1880			17.13				NW¼NW¼	18	38	47	3-15—9-15	.139	51.39
	1880						2.30	NW¼NW¼	18	38	47	3-15—4-28	.019	1.73
	1880			4.82				SW¼NW¼	18	38	47	3-15—9-15	.039	14.46
	1880						7.49	SW¼NW¼	18	38	47	3-15—4-28	.061	5.62
	1880						2.70	SE¼NW¼	18	38	47	3-15—4-28	.022	2.03
	1880			29.55				SW¼NE¼	7	38	47	3-15—9-15	.240	88.65
	1880						10.30	SW¼NE¼	7	38	47	3-15—4-28	.084	7.73
	1880			33.92				SE¼NW¼	7	38	47	3-15—9-15	.276	101.76
	1880					3.38		SE¼NW¼	7	38	47	3-15—4-28	.027	2.54
	1880			29.74				NE¼SW¼	7	38	47	3-15—9-15	.242	89.22
	1880						2.16	NE¼SW¼	7	38	47	3-15—4-28	.018	1.62
	1880			34.17				NW¼SW¼	7	38	47	3-15—9-15	.279	102.51
	1880						5.18	NW¼SW¼	7	38	47	3-15—4-28	.042	3.80
Source—**Rock Creek** and **Tributaries.** Ditch—**Rock Creek Ditch.** (Squaw Valley lands.)														
	1878			18.53				NW¼NW¼	8	38	47	3-15—9-15	.151	55.69
	1878					14.36		NW¼NW¼	8	38	47	3-15—4-28	.117	10.77
	1878					2.09		SE¼NW¼	8	38	47	3-15—4-28	.017	1.57
	1878					3.38		SW¼NW¼	8	38	47	3-15—4-28	.027	2.54
	1878						23.12	SW¼NW¼	8	38	47	3-15—4-28	.189	17.34
	1878						1.60	NW¼SW¼	8	38	47	3-15—4-28	.013	1.20
	1878			38.05				NE¼NE¼	7	38	47	3-15—9-15	.309	114.15
	1878			37.00				NW¼NE¼	7	38	47	3-15—9-15	.300	111.00
	1878			24.28				SE¼NE¼	7	38	47	3-15—9-15	.197	72.84
	1878						12.95	SE¼NE¼	7	38	47	3-15—4-28	.105	9.71
	1878						7.05	NE¼SE¼	7	38	47	3-15—4-28	.057	5.29
	1878			1.72				NW¼SE¼	7	38	47	3-15—9-15	.014	5.16
	1878						8.30	NW¼SE¼	7	38	47	3-15—4-28	.067	6.23
	1878			36.80				SE¼NW¼	5	38	47	3-15—9-15	.290	110.40
	1878			17.74				NE¼SW¼	5	38	47	3-15—9-15	.144	53.22
	1878			36.47				NW¼SW¼	5	38	47	3-15—9-15	.297	109.41
	1878					4.75		NW¼SW¼	5	38	47	3-15—4-28	.039	3.56
	1878			37.27				SW¼SW¼	5	38	47	3-15—9-15	.303	111.81
Source—**Rock Creek** and **Tributaries.** Ditch—**Highline Ditch.** (Squaw Valley lands.)														
	1887			.50				NW¼NW¼	1	38	46	3-15—9-15	.004	1.50
	1887			18.43				SE¼NW¼	1	38	46	3-15—9-15	.150	55.29
	1887						4.88	SE¼NW¼	1	38	46	3-15—4-28	.040	3.66
	1887			34.92				SW¼NW¼	1	38	46	3-15—9-15	.283	104.76
	1887			15.90				NE¼SW¼	1	38	46	3-15—9-15	.129	47.70
	1887			30.62				NW¼SW¼	1	38	46	3-15—9-15	.249	91.86
	1887			8.93				SW¼SW¼	1	38	46	3-16—9-15	.073	26.79
	1887			40.87				SE¼NE¼	2	38	46	3-15—9-15	.332	122.61
	1887			14.70				SW¼NE¼	2	38	46	3-15—9-15	.120	44.10
	1887			24.27				SW¼NE¼	2	38	46	3-15—9-15	.197	72.81
	1887			26.03				NE¼SE¼	2	38	46	3-15—9-15	.212	78.09
	1887			21.06				NW¼SE¼	2	38	46	3-15—9-15	.171	63.18
	1887						19.41	NW¼SE¼	2	38	46	3-15—4-28	.158	14.56
	1887			5.04				SE¼SE¼	2	38	46	3-15—9-15	.041	15.12
	1887						13.88	SE¼SW¼	32	39	47	3-15—4-28	.113	10.41
	1887				9.61			SE¼SW¼	31	39	47	3-15—6-13	.078	14.42

Ellison Ranching Co.—Continued.

Year of priority	Culture—Acres: Harvest crops	Meadow pasture	Diversified pasture		Location: Subdivision	Section	Tp.N.	R.E.	Length of season	Duty of water: C.F.S.	Acre-feet
1887		8.54			SW¼SW¼	31	39	47	3-15—6-13	.069	12.81
1887		17.33			NE¼NW¼	6	38	47	3-15—6-13	.141	26.00
1887		2.31			NW¼NW¼	6	38	47	3-15—6-13	.019	3.47
1887	5.82				NE¼NE¼	2	38	46	3-15—9-15	.047	17.46
1887	12.75				NW¼NE¼	2	38	46	3-15—9-15	.104	38.25
1887			11.29		SE¼SE¼	2	38	46	3-15—4-28	.092	8.46
1887			14.04		NE¼SE¼	2	38	46	3-15—4-28	.114	10.53
1887	2.35				SE¼NW¼	2	38	46	3-15—6-13	.019	3.53
1887	5.34				NE¼SW¼	2	38	46	3-15—6-13	.043	8.01
1887			4.86		NE¼SW¼	2	38	46	3-15—4-28	.039	3.65
1887			8.45		SW¼SE¼	2	38	46	3-15—4-28	.069	6.34
1887			7.00		NW¼SW¼	2	38	46	3-15—4-28	.057	5.25
1887			2.80		SW¼SW¼	2	38	46	3-15—4-28	.023	2.10
1887			6.75		SW¼SE¼	31	39	47	3-15—4-28	.055	5.06
1887			5.95		SE¼SE¼	31	39	47	3-15—4-28	.048	4.46
1887			3.20		NE¼NE¼	6	38	47	3-15—4-28	.026	2.40

Source—**Willow Creek.** Ditch—**Overflow.** (Squaw Valley lands.)

Year of priority	Harvest crops	Meadow pasture	Diversified pasture		Subdivision	Section	Tp.N.	R.E.	Length of season	C.F.S.	Acre-feet
1878	5.47				NE¼SW¼	18	38	47	3-15—9-15	.044	16.41
1878			2.28		NE¼SW¼	18	38	47	3-15—4-28	.019	1.71
1878				8.47	NE¼SW¼	18	38	47	3-15—4-28	.069	6.35
1878				12.50	NW¼SW¼	18	38	47	3-15—4-28	.101	9.38

Source—**Willow Creek.** Ditch—Deep **Slough.** (Squaw Valley lands.)

Year of priority	Harvest crops	Meadow pasture	Diversified pasture		Subdivision	Section	Tp.N.	R.E.	Length of season	C.F.S.	Acre-feet
1883	5.55				SE¼SW¼	8	38	47	3-15—9-15	.045	16.65
1886		10.90			SE¼SW¼	8	38	47	3-15—6-13	.089	16.35
1886		17.27			NE¼NW¼	17	38	47	3-15—6-13	.140	25.91
1886		20.82			NW¼NW¼	17	38	47	3.15—6-13	.169	31.23
1886		2.42			SW¼NW¼	17	38	47	3-15—6-13	.020	3.63
1886		13.30			NE¼NE¼	18	38	47	3-15—6-13	.108	19.95
1886		0.87			NW¼NE¼	18	38	47	3-15—6-13	.007	1.31
1886		24.77			SE¼NE¼	18	38	47	3 15—6-13	.201	37.16
1886		14.35			SW¼NE¼	18	38	47	3-15—6-13	.116	21.53
1886	27.27				NE¼SE¼	8	38	47	3-15—9-15	.222	81.81
1886	16.62				SE¼SE¼	8	38	47	3-15—9-15	.135	49.86
1886	7.62				NW¼SE¼	8	38	47	3.15—9-15	.062	22.86
1886	32.87				SW¼SE¼	8	38	47	3-15—9-15	.267	98.61
1886	0.97				NW¼NE¼	17	38	47	3-15—9-15	.008	2.91
1886	1.90				SE¼NE¼	18	38	47	3-15—9-15	.015	5.70
1886				7.49	SE¼NE¼	18	88	47	3.15—4 28	.061	5.62
1886	11.70				SW¼NE¼	18	38	47	3-15—9-15	.095	35.10
1886				0.75	SW¼NE¼	18	38	47	3-15—4-28	.006	.56
1886				1.32	NE¼SE¼	18	68	47	3.15—4-28	.011	.99
1886	3.97				NW¼SE¼	18	38	47	3 15—9-15	.032	12.01
1886				11.57	NW¼SE¼	18	38	47	3-15—4 28	.094	8.64
1883	3.62				SE¼NW¼	18	38	47	3 15—9-15	.029	10.86
1886			5.85		SE¼NW¼	18	38	47	3.15—4 28	.048	4.39
1883				1.25	SE¼NW¼	18	38	47	3 15—4 28	.010	.038

Source—**Rock Creek and Tributaries.** Ditch—**Warm Spring.** (Squaw Valley lands.)

....	1876	....	....	....	....	13.15	....	NE¼NE¼	25	38	46	3-15—4-28	.107	9.87
....	1876	....	....	....	....	....	20.17	NE¼NE¼	25	38	46	3-15—4-28	.164	15.13
....	1876	....	....	....	....	13.01	....	NW¼NE¼	25	38	46	3-15—4-28	.106	9.76
....	1876	....	....	....	....	....	13.74	NW¼NE¼	25	38	46	3-15—4-28	.112	10.31
....	1876	....	....	....	....	21.02	....	NE¼NW¼	25	38	46	3-15—4-28	.176	16.22
....	1876	....	....	....	....	....	3.00	NE¼NW¼	25	38	46	3-15—4-28	.024	2.25
....	1876	....	....	....	....	20.35	....	NW¼NW¼	25	38	46	3-15—4-28	.165	15.26

Source—**Rock Creek.** Ditch—**Barleyfield Canal.** (Squaw Valley lands.)

....	1888	....	....	....	....	3.96	....	NW¼SE¼	21	39	47	3-15—4-28	.032	2.96
....	1888	....	....	....	....	0.47	....	SW¼SE¼	21	39	47	3-15—4-28	.038	0.35
....	1888	....	....	....	....	32.45	....	NE¼SW¼	21	39	47	3-15—4-28	.264	24.34
....	1888	....	....	....	....	29.30	....	SE¼SW¼	21	39	47	3-15—4-28	.238	21.98
....	1888	....	....	....	....	35.95	....	NW¼SW¼	21	39	47	3-15—4-28	.292	26.96
....	1888	....	....	....	....	36.00	....	SW¼SW¼	21	39	47	3-15—4-28	.293	27.00
....	1888	....	....	....	....	1.00	....	SW¼NE¼	20	39	47	3-15—4-28	.008	0.75
....	1888	....	....	....	....	40.55	....	NE¼SE¼	20	39	47	3-15—4-28	.330	30.41
....	1888	....	....	....	....	36.35	....	SE¼SE¼	20	39	47	3-15—4-28	.296	27.26
....	1888	....	....	....	....	21.40	....	NW¼SE¼	20	39	47	3-15—4-28	.174	16.30
....	1888	....	....	....	....	23.30	....	SW¼SE¼	20	39	47	3-15—4-28	.180	17.48
....	1888	....	....	....	....	2.90	....	NE¼NW¼	28	39	47	3-15—4-28	.024	2.18
....	1888	....	....	....	....	27.64	....	NW¼NW¼	28	39	47	3-15—4-28	.225	20.73
....	1888	....	....	....	....	4.73	....	SW¼NW¼	28	39	47	3-15—4-28	.039	3.55
....	1888	....	....	....	....	39.37	....	NE¼NE¼	29	39	47	3-15—4-28	.320	29.53
....	1888	....	....	....	....	2.35	....	SE¼NE¼	29	39	47	3-15—4-28	.019	1.76

Source—**Rock Creek and Tributaries.** Ditch—**Willow Creek Canal.** (Squaw Valley lands.)

....	1880	....	....	....	23.40	....	....	SE¼NE¼	1	38	46	3-15—6-13	.190	35.10
....	1880	....	....	....	....	....	5.26	SE¼NE¼	1	38	46	3-15—4-28	.043	3.95
....	1880	....	....	....	23.61	....	....	SW¼NE¼	1	38	46	3-15—6-13	.192	35.42
....	1880	....	....	....	....	....	13.68	SW¼NE¼	1	38	46	3-15—4-28	.111	10.26
....	1880	....	....	16.56	....	....	....	NE¼SE¼	1	38	46	3-15—9-15	.135	49.68
....	1880	....	....	....	17.67	....	....	NE¼SE¼	1	38	46	3-15—6-13	.144	26.51
....	1880	....	....	....	....	....	3.31	NE¼SE¼	1	38	46	3-15—4-28	.027	2.48
....	1880	....	....	12.12	....	....	....	NW¼SE¼	1	38	46	3-15—9-15	.098	36.36
....	1880	....	....	....	7.27	....	....	NW¼SE¼	1	38	46	3-15—6-13	.059	10.90
....	1880	....	....	34.19	....	....	....	SE¼SE¼	1	38	46	3-15—9-15	.278	102.57
....	1880	....	....	....	....	....	5.76	SE¼SE¼	1	38	46	3-15—4-28	.047	4.32
....	1880	....	....	40.00	....	....	....	SW¼SE¼	1	38	46	3-15—9-15	.325	120.00
....	1888	....	....	34.79	....	....	....	SE¼SW¼	1	38	46	3-15—9-15	.283	104.37
....	1888	....	....	....	1.51	....	....	SE¼SW¼	1	38	46	3-15—6-13	.012	2.27
....	1888	....	....	....	3.67	....	....	SE¼NW¼	1	38	46	3-15—6-13	.030	5.51
....	1888	....	....	15.12	....	....	....	NE¼SW¼	1	38	46	3-15—9-15	.123	45.36
....	1888	....	....	....	7.06	....	....	NE¼SW¼	1	38	46	3-15—6-13	.057	10.59
....	1888	....	....	....	....	....	1.90	SW¼SW¼	1	38	46	3-15—4-28	.015	1.43
....	1880	....	....	33.85	....	....	....	SE¼SE¼	6	38	47	3-15—9-15	.275	101.55
....	1880	....	....	....	....	4.25	....	SE¼SE¼	6	38	47	3-15—4-28	.035	3.19
....	1880	....	....	32.48	....	....	....	NE¼SW¼	6	38	47	3-15—9-15	.264	97.44
....	1880	....	....	....	....	....	8.42	NE¼SW¼	6	38	47	3-15—4-28	.068	6.32
....	1880	....	....	15.12	....	....	....	NW¼SW¼	6	38	47	3-15—9-15	.122	45.36
....	1880	....	....	....	....	....	20.47	NW¼SW¼	6	38	47	3-15—4-28	.166	15.35
....	1880	....	....	40.37	....	....	....	SE¼SW¼	6	38	47	3-15—9-15	.328	121.11

Ellison Ranching Co.—Continued.

Year of priority	Culture—Acres: Harvest crops	Meadow pasture	Diversified pasture		Location: Subdivision	Section	Tp.N.	R.E.	Length of season	Duty of water: C.F.S.	Acre-feet
1880	27.65				SW¼SW¼	6	38	47	3-15—9-15	.225	82.95
1880				4.54	SW¼SW¼	6	38	47	3-15—4-28	.037	3.41
1880	0.97				NE¼NE¼	5	38	47	3-15—9-15	.008	2.91
1880	8.82				NW¼NE¼	5	38	47	3-15—9-15	.072	26.40
1880				4.48	NW¼NE¼	5	38	47	3-15—4-28	.036	3.36
1880	18.37				NE¼NW¼	5	38	47	3-15—9-15	.149	55.11
1880		10.18			NE¼NW¼	5	38	47	3-15—6-13	.083	15.27
1880				6.29	NE¼NW¼	5	38	47	3-15—4-28	.051	4.70
1880	11.29				NW¼NW¼	5	38	47	3-15—9-15	.092	33.87
1880				5.78	NW¼NW¼	5	38	47	3-15—4-28	.047	4.34
1880	15.10				NE¼NE¼	6	38	47	3-15—9-15	.123	45.30
1880				11.10	NE¼NE¼	6	38	47	3-15—4-28	.090	8.33
1880	0.40				SE¼NE¼	5	38	47	3-15—9-15	.003	1.20
1880	34.09				SW¼NE¼	5	38	47	3-15—9-15	.277	102.27
1880			0.26		SW¼NE¼	5	38	47	3-15—4-28	.002	0.20
1880	15.11				NW¼SE¼	5	38	47	3-15—9-15	.123	45.33
1880			6.51		NW¼SE¼	5	38	47	3-15—4-28	.053	4.88
1880			3.46		SW¼SE¼	5	38	47	3-15—4-28	.028	2.60
1886	1.65				SW¼SE¼	3	38	47	3-15—9-15	.013	4.95
1886	12.45				SE¼SW¼	3	38	47	3-15—9-15	.101	37.35
1886	33.90				SW¼SW¼	3	38	47	3-15—9-15	.276	101.70
1886	24.60				SE¼SE¼	4	38	47	3-15—9-15	.200	73.80
1886	3.00				SW¼SE¼	4	38	47	3-15—9-15	.024	9.00
1886	0.67				NW¼NW¼	10	38	47	3-15—9-15	.005	2.01
1886	10.68				NE¼NE¼	9	38	47	3-15—9-15	.087	32.04
1886				3.93	NE¼NE¼	9	38	47	3-15—4-28	.032	2.95
1886	30.86				NW¼NE¼	9	38	47	3-15—9-15	.251	92.58
1886				4.21	NW¼NE¼	9	38	47	3-15—4-28	.034	3.16
1886	6.77				SW¼NE¼	9	38	47	3-15—9-15	.055	20.31
1886				7.88	SW¼NE¼	9	38	47	3-15—4-28	.064	5.91
1886	18.37				NE¼NW¼	8	38	47	3-15—9-15	.149	55.11
1886	37.40				SE¼NW¼	9	38	47	3-15—9-15	.304	112.20
1886	20.88				SW¼NW¼	9	38	47	3-15—9-15	.170	62.64
1886	4.95				NE¼SW¼	9	38	47	3-15—9-15	.040	14.85
1886	36.72				NW¼SW¼	9	38	47	3-15—9-15	.299	110.16
1886	1.40				SW¼SW¼	9	38	47	3-15—9-15	.011	4.20
1886	0.29				SE¼NE¼	8	38	47	3-15—9-15	.002	.87
1880	6.05				NE¼NW¼	8	38	47	3-15—9-15	.049	18.15
1880			21.08		NE¼NW¼	8	38	47	3-15—4-28	.171	15.81
1880	23.82				NW¼NW¼	7	38	47	3-15—9-15	.194	71.46
1880				3.23	NW¼NW¼	7	38	47	3-15—4-28	.026	2.42
1890		21.27			NW¼NW¼	5	38	47	3-15—6-13	.173	31.91
1880			1.12		SW¼SE¼	3	38	47	3-15—4-28	.009	0.84
1880			0.33		SW¼SW¼	3	38	47	3-15—4-28	.003	0.25
1880			0.15		NW¼SW¼	3	38	47	3-15—4-28	.001	0.11
1880			8.91		NE¼SW¼	3	38	47	3-15—4-28	.072	6.68
1880			14.51		NW¼SE¼	3	38	47	3-15—4-28	.118	10.88
1880			1.40		NE¼SE¼	3	38	47	3-15—4-28	.011	1.05
1880			4.25		SE¼SW¼	3	38	47	3-15—4-28	.035	3.19

	1880				3.25			NE¼NE¼	1	38	46	3-15—6-13	.026	4.88
	1881				15.06			NW¼NE¼	1	38	46	3-15—6-13	.122	2.26
	1880				2.74			NE¼NW¼	1	38	46	3-15—6-13	.022	0.41
	1880			22.03				NE¼NE¼	12	38	46	3-15—9-15	.179	66.09
	1880						9.65	NE¼NE¼	12	38	46	3-15—4-28	.078	7.24
	1880			28.80				NW¼NE¼	12	38	46	3-15—9-15	.234	86.40
	1880				11.10			NW¼NE¼	12	38	46	3-15—6-13	.090	16.65
	1880			29.23				SE¼NE¼	12	38	46	3-15—9-15	.238	87.69
	1880						4.39	SE¼NE¼	12	38	46	3-15—4-28	.036	3.21
	1880			16.20				SW¼NE¼	12	38	46	3-15—9-15	.132	48.60
	1880						15.12	SW¼NE¼	12	38	46	3-15—4-28	.123	11.34
	1880			4.90				NE¼NW¼	12	38	46	3-15—9-15	.040	14.70
	1889				27.45			NE¼NW¼	12	38	46	3-15—6-13	.223	41.18
	1880						8.42	NE¼NW¼	12	38	46	3-15—4-28	.068	6.32
	1889						13.70	NW¼NW¼	12	38	46	3-15—4-28	.111	10.28
	1880						4.39	SE¼NW¼	12	38	46	3-15—4-28	.036	3.29
	1889						7.06	NW¼SE¼	12	38	46	3-15—4-28	.057	5.30
	1889			1.20				SW¼SE¼	12	38	46	3-15—9-15	.010	3.60
	1880						9.58	SW¼SE¼	12	38	46	3-15—4-28	.078	7.19
	1889			19.14				SW¼NW¼	5	38	47	3-15—9-15	.156	57.42
	1880				22.26			SW¼NW¼	5	38	47	3-15—6-13	.181	33.39
	1880			27.15				SE¼SW¼	5	38	47	3-15—9-15	.221	81.45
	1880					13.70		SE¼SW¼	5	38	47	3-15—4-28	.111	10.28
	1880			20.40				SE¼NE¼	6	38	47	3-15—9-15	.239	88.20
	1889				8.14			SE¼NE¼	6	38	47	3-15—6-13	.066	12.21
	1889					2.81		SE¼NE¼	6	38	47	3-15—4-28	.023	2.11
	1889			23.38				SW¼NE¼	6	38	47	3-15—9-15	.190	70.14
	1881						5.54	SW¼NE¼	6	38	47	3-15—4-28	.045	4.16
	1889			21.66				SE¼NW¼	6	38	47	3-15—9-15	.176	64.08
	1889						8.93	SE¼NW¼	6	38	47	3-15—4-28	.073	6.70
	1889			19.70				NE¼SW¼	5	38	47	3-15—9-15	.160	59.10
	1881				2.38			SW¼NW¼	6	38	47	3-15—6-13	.019	3.57
	1889						13.03	SW¼NW¼	6	38	47	3-15—4-28	.106	9.77
	1889			7.77				NE¼SE¼	6	38	47	3-15—9-15	.063	23.31
	1889				20.62			NE¼SE¼	6	38	47	3-15—6-13	.241	44.30
	1889			28.25				NW¼SE¼	6	38	47	3-15—9-15	.230	81.75
	1889					9.37		NW¼SE¼	6	38	47	3-15—4-28	.076	7.03
	1889						1.37	NW¼SE¼	6	38	47	3-15—4-28	.011	1.03

Claimant—**Clover Valley Land and Stock Co.** Proof No. 00157

Source—**Humboldt River.** Ditch—**Hammond.** (Lands of Hammond Bros.)

	1875						38.76	NE¼NE¼	17	36	42	3-15—4-28	.315	29.07
	1875			16.90				NW¼NE¼	17	36	42	3-15—9-15	.137	50.70
	1875						19.28	NW¼NE¼	17	36	42	3-15—4-28	.157	14.46
	1875			17.26				SE¼NE¼	17	36	42	3-15—9-15	.140	51.78
	1875				.02			SE¼NE¼	17	36	42	3-15—6-13	.007	1.38
	1875						11.60	SE¼NE¼	17	36	42	3-15—4-28	.094	8.70
	1875			31.24				SW¼NE¼	17	36	42	3-15—9-15	.278	102.72
	1875					1.18		SW¼NE¼	17	36	42	3-15—4-28	.010	.80
	1875			37.68				NW¼SE¼	17	36	42	3-15—9-15	.366	113.04
	1875					.92		NW¼SE¼	17	36	42	3-15—4-28	.008	.69
	1875			39.04				NE¼SE¼	17	36	42	3-15—9-15	.317	117.12

Clover Valley Land and Stock Co.—Continued.

Year of priority	Culture—Acres: Harvest crops	Meadow pasture	Diversified pasture		Location: Subdivision	Section	Tp.N.	R.E.	Length of season	Duty of water: C.F.S.	Acre-feet
1875	21.82				SE¼SE¼	17	36	42	3-15—9-15	.177	65.46
1875		1.20			SE¼SE¼	17	36	42	3-15—6-13	.070	1.80
1875				17.36	SE¼SE¼	17	36	42	3-15—4-28	.141	13.02
1875	34.42				SW¼SE¼	17	36	42	3-15—9-15	.280	103.26
1875				6.84	SW¼SE¼	17	36	42	3-15—4-28	.056	5.13
1875	14.00				NW¼NW¼	7	36	42	3-15—9-15	.114	42.00
1875	37.96				NE¼NW¼	7	36	42	3-15—9-15	.309	113.88
1875			2.40		NE¼NW¼	7	36	42	3-15—4-28	.020	1.80
1875	15.12				SW¼NW¼	7	36	42	3-15—9-15	.123	45.36
1875	40.80				SE¼NW¼	7	36	42	3-15—9-15	.332	122.40
1875	8.88				NW¼SW¼	7	36	42	3-15—9-15	.072	26.64
1875	40.00				NE¼SW¼	7	36	42	3-15—9-15	.325	120.00
1875	1.72				SW¼SW¼	7	36	42	3-15—9-15	.014	5.16
1875	34.08				SE¼SW¼	7	36	42	3-15—9-15	.277	102.24
1875				6.24	SE¼SW¼	7	36	42	3-15—4-28	.051	4.68
1875				39.68	NE¼NE¼	7	36	42	3-15—4-28	.323	29.76
1875	7.08				NW¼NE¼	7	36	42	3-15—9-15	.058	21.24
1875				31.97	NW¼NE¼	7	36	42	3-15—4-28	.260	23.98
1875	39.76				SW¼NE¼	7	36	42	3-15—9-15	.323	119.28
1875				0.72	SW¼NE¼	7	36	42	3-15—4-28	.006	.54
1875	13.04				SE¼NE¼	7	36	42	3-15—9-15	.106	39.12
1875				26.53	SE¼NE¼	7	36	42	3-15—4-28	.216	19.90
1875	40.64				NW¼SE¼	7	36	42	3-15—9-15	.330	121.92
1875	38.84				NE¼SE¼	7	36	42	3-15—9-15	.316	116.52
1875				2.16	NE¼SE¼	7	36	42	3-15—4-28	.018	1.62
1875	40.72				SW¼SE¼	7	36	42	3-15—9-15	.331	122.16
1875	41.04				SE¼SE¼	7	36	42	3-15—9-15	.334	123.12
1875	8.80				NW¼SW¼	8	36	42	3-15—9-15	.072	26.40
1875				10.56	NW¼SW¼	8	36	42	3-15—4-28	.086	7.92
1875	38.54				SW¼SW¼	8	36	42	3-15—9-15	.313	115.62
1875				1.60	SW¼SW¼	8	36	42	3-15—4-28	.013	1.20
1875	12.80				SE¼SW¼	8	36	42	3-15—9-15	.104	38.40
1875				27.56	SE¼SW¼	8	36	42	3-15—4-28	.224	20.67
1875	34.92				NW¼NW¼	17	36	42	3-15—9-15	.284	104.76
1875	34.38				NE¼NW¼	17	36	42	3-15—9-15	.280	103.14
1875				1.08	NE¼NW¼	17	36	42	3-15—4-28	.009	.81
1875	26.08				SW¼NW¼	17	36	42	3-15—9-15	.212	78.24
1875			5.80		SW¼NW¼	17	36	42	3-15—4-28	.047	4.35
1875	35.12				SE¼NW¼	17	36	42	3-15—0-15	.289	105.36
1875			.16		SE¼NW¼	17	36	42	3-15—4-28	.001	.12
1875	36.08				NW¼SW¼	17	36	42	3-15—9-15	.293	108.24
1875			1.44		NW¼SW¼	17	36	42	3-15—4-28	.012	1.08
1875	39.76				NE¼SW¼	17	36	42	3-15—0-15	.323	119.28
1875	38.96				SE¼SW¼	17	36	42	3-15—9-15	.317	116.88
1875				1.68	SE¼SW¼	17	36	42	3-15—4-28	.014	1.26
1875	16.24				SW¼SW¼	17	36	42	3-15—9-15	[illegible]	18.72
1875				24.68	SW¼SW¼	17	36	42	3-15—4-28	[illegible]	18.51

Source—**Humboldt River.** Ditch—**Gonzales Slough.** (Russell Land and Cattle Co. lands.)

1880			19.00				SE¼NE¼	33	36	42	3-15—9-15	.154	57.00
1880			1.24				NE¼NE¼	33	36	42	3-15—9-15	.010	3.72
1880			26.80				NE¼SE¼	33	36	42	3-15—9-15	.209	80.40
1880			25.44				SE¼SE¼	33	36	42	3-15—9-15	.207	76.32
1880			27.88				SE¼SE¼	27	36	42	3-15—9-15	.227	83.54
1880				4.72			SE¼SE¼	27	36	42	3-15—6-13	.038	7.08
1880					1.16		SE¼SE¼	27	36	42	3-15—4-28	.009	0.87
1880			37.41				NW¼SE¼	27	36	42	3-15—9-15	.304	112.23
1880					0.91		NW¼SE¼	27	36	42	3-15—4-28	.007	0.68
1880			17.78				NW¼SE¼	11	35	42	3-15—9-15	.144	53.34
1880					15.98		NW¼SE¼	11	35	42	3-15—4-28	.130	11.99
1880				14.08			SW¼SE¼	11	35	42	3-15—6-13	.114	21.12
1880					21.84		SW¼SE¼	11	35	42	3-15—4-28	.178	16.38
1880			28.45				NE¼SW¼	11	35	42	3-15—9-15	.231	85.35
1880					10.00		NE¼SW¼	11	35	42	3-15—4-28	.081	7.50
1880			0.44				SE¼SW¼	11	35	42	3-15—9-15	.004	1.32
1880					39.12		SE¼SW¼	11	35	42	3-15—4-28	.318	29.34
1880			14.62				NW¼SW¼	11	35	42	3-15—9-15	.119	43.92
1880					24.88		NW¼SW¼	11	35	42	3-15—4-28	.202	18.66
1880					40.00		SW¼SW¼	11	35	42	3-15—4-28	.325	30.00
1880			35.72				SW¼SW¼	27	36	42	3-15—9-15	.290	107.16
1880				3.08			SW¼SW¼	27	36	42	3-15—6-13	.025	4.62
1880					13.56		SE¼NW¼	11	35	42	3-15—4-28	.110	10.17
1880			38.52				NW¼NW¼	11	35	42	3-15—9-15	.313	115.56
1880			39.60				SW¼NW¼	11	35	42	3-15—9-15	.322	118.80
1880					0.10		SW¼NW¼	11	35	42	3-15—4-28	.001	0.08
1880			35.68				SE¼NE¼	11	35	42	3-15—9-15	.290	107.04
1880					3.84		SE¼NE¼	11	35	42	3-15—4-28	.031	2.88
1880			38.88				NW¼NE¼	11	35	42	3-15—9-15	.316	116.64
1880					1.56		NW¼NE¼	11	35	42	3-15—4-28	.012	1.18
1880			39.36				NE¼NE¼	11	35	42	3-15—9-15	.320	118.08

Source—**Humboldt** River. Ditch—**Aemes Dam.** (Russell Land and Cattle Co. lands.)

1876			31.12				SE¼NW¼	2	35	42	3-15—9-15	.253	93.36
1876					5.04		SE¼NW¼	2	35	42	3-15—4-28	.041	3.78
1876			33.69				NE¼SW¼	2	35	42	3-15—9-15	.274	101.07
1876					2.90		NE¼SW¼	2	35	42	3-15—4-28	.024	2.17
1876			23.42				SE¼SW¼	2	35	42	3-15—9-15	.190	70.26
1876					5.80		SE¼SW¼	2	35	42	3-15—4-28	.047	4.35
1876			29.92				NW¼SW¼	2	35	42	3-15—9-15	.243	89.06
1876			19.68				NE¼SE¼	11	35	42	3-15—9-15	.160	59.04
1876					15.02		NE¼SE¼	11	35	42	3-15—4-28	.122	11.27
1876						0.50	NE¼SE¼	11	36	42	3-15—4-28	.004	0.38
1876					35.41		SE¼SE¼	11	35	42	3-15—4-28	.288	26.57
1876						0.31	SE¼SE¼	11	35	42	3-15—4-28	.003	0.23
1876					4.18		NE¼NW¼	11	35	42	3-15—4-28	.034	3.13
1876			19.50				SE¼NW¼	11	35	42	3-15—9-15	.159	58.50
1876			23.88				SW¼NE¼	11	35	42	3-15—9-15	.194	71.64
1876					10.68		SW¼NE¼	11	35	42	3-15—4-28	.087	8.01
1876			31.68				NE¼NW¼	11	35	42	3-15—9-15	.258	95.04
1876			0.09				NE¼NE¼	10	35	42	3-15—9-15	.001	.27

Clover Valley Land and Stock Co.—Continued.

Year of priority	Culture—Acres: Harvest crops	Culture—Acres: Meadow pasture	Culture—Acres: Diversified pasture		Location: Subdivision	Location: Section	Location: Tp. N.	Location: R. E.	Length of season	Duty of water: C. F. S.	Duty of water: Acre-feet
1876	1.51				SE¼NE¼	10	35	42	3-15—9-15	.012	4.53
1876			0.12		SE¼NE¼	10	35	42	3-15—4-28	.001	.09
1876			1.44		NE¼SE¼	10	35	42	3-15—4-28	.012	1.08
1876			0.48		SE¼SE¼	10	35	42	3-15—4-28	.004	.36
1876	15.56				NE¼SW¼	27	36	42	3-15—9-15	.127	46.58
1876			15.58		NE¼SW¼	27	36	42	3-15—4-28	.127	11.69
1876	20.80				NW¼SW¼	27	36	42	3-15—9-15	.218	80.40
1876	3.28				SE¼NE¼	27	36	42	3-15—9-15	.027	9.84
1876		2.00			SE¼NE¼	27	36	42	3-15—6-13	.016	3.00
1876	29.35				SW¼NE¼	27	36	42	3-15—9-15	.239	88.05
1876		4.88			SW¼NE¼	27	36	42	3-15—6-13	.040	7.32
1876			1.29		SW¼NE¼	27	36	42	3-15—4-28	.010	0.97
1876	24.64				SE¼SW¼	27	36	42	3-15—9-15	.200	73.95
1876			10.20		SE¼SW¼	27	36	42	3-15—4-28	.083	7.65
1876	26.64				SE¼NW¼	27	36	42	3-15—9-15	.217	79.92
1876			6.56		SE¼NW¼	27	36	42	3-15—4-28	.053	4.92
1876	30.92				SW¼NW¼	27	36	42	3-15—9-15	.251	92.76
1876			0.10		SE¼NW¼	27	36	42	3-15—4-28	.001	0.08
1876		3.84			NE¼NE¼	27	36	42	3-15—6-13	.031	5.76
1876		7.20			NW¼NE¼	27	36	42	3-15—6-13	.059	10.80
1876			6.88		NW¼NE¼	27	36	42	3-15—4-28	.056	5.16
1876	28.80				NE¼NW¼	27	36	42	3-15—9-15	.227	86.40
1876		1.40			NE¼NW¼	27	36	42	3-15—6-13	.011	2.10
1876			2.64		NE¼NW¼	27	36	42	3-15—4-28	.021	1.98
1876	23.44				NW¼NW¼	27	36	42	3-15—9-15	.191	70.32
1876			8.40		NW¼NW¼	27	36	42	3-15—4-28	.068	6.30
1876	20.70				NE¼NE¼	28	36	42	3-15—9-15	.168	62.10
1876				6.14	NE¼NE¼	28	36	42	3-15—4-28	.050	4.72
1876	39.60				NE¼SE¼	34	35	42	3-15—9-15	.320	118.80
1876	29.64				NE¼NW¼	2	35	42	3-15—9-15	.241	88.92
1876			6.50		NE¼NW¼	2	35	42	3-15—4-28	.053	4.88
1876	27.60				NW¼NE¼	34	36	42	3-15—9-15	.224	82.80
1876		3.92			NW¼NE¼	34	36	42	3-15—6-13	.032	5.88
1876			1.52		NW¼NE¼	34	36	42	3-15—4-28	.012	1.14
1876	40.00				NE¼NW¼	34	36	42	3-15—9-15	.325	120.00
1876	23.44				SW¼SE¼	27	36	42	3-15—9-15	.191	70.32
1876		9.84			SW¼SE¼	27	36	42	3-15—6-13	.080	14.76
1876			2.96		SW¼SE¼	27	36	42	3-15—4-28	.024	2.22
1876	29.57				NE¼SE¼	27	36	42	3-15—9-15	.240	88.71
1876		1.40			NE¼SE¼	27	36	42	3-15—6-13	.011	2.10
1876			2.67		NE¼SE¼	27	36	42	3-15—4-28	.022	2.00
1876			13.32		NE¼NW¼	36	36	42	3-15—4-28	.108	10.00
1876	23.96				SE¼SE¼	34	36	42	3-15—9-15	.195	71.88
1876			11.12		SE¼SE¼	34	36	42	3-15—4-28	.090	8.34
1876	38.64				SW¼SE¼	34	36	42	3-15—9-15	.314	115.92
1876	24.28				NE¼SE¼	34	36	42	3-15—9-15	.197	72.84
1876			8.68		NE¼SE¼	34	36	42	3-15—4-28	.071	6.51

	1876			26.73				SE¼ NE¼	34	36	42	3-15—9-15	.217	80.19
	1876					7.86		SE¼ NE¼	34	36	42	3-15—4-28	.064	5.00
	1876			26.60				SW¼ NE¼	34	36	42	3-15—9-15	.216	79.8
	1876					6.08		SW¼ NE¼	34	36	42	3-15—4-28	.049	4.56
	1876			18.68				NE¼ NE¼	34	36	42	3-15—9-15	.152	56.04
	1876				11.76			NE¼ NE¼	34	36	42	3-15—6-13	.096	17.64
	1876					7.52		NE¼ NE¼	34	36	42	3-15—4-28	.061	5.64
	1876				9.21			SW¼ SE¼	35	36	42	3-15—6-13	.075	13.81
	1876					2.07		SW¼ SE¼	35	36	42	3-15—4-28	.017	1.55
	1876			2.00				NW¼ SE¼	35	36	42	3-15—9-15	.016	6.00
	1876			26.27				SE¼ SW¼	35	36	42	3-15—9-15	.213	78.81
	1876				7.28			SE¼ SW¼	35	36	42	3-15—6-13	.059	10.92
	1876					2.73		SE¼ SW¼	35	36	42	3-15—4-28	.022	2.05
	1876			11.68				SW¼ SW¼	35	36	42	3-15—9-15	.095	35.04
	1876					20.12		SW¼ SW¼	35	36	42	3-15—4-28	.164	15.09
	1876			37.60				NW¼ SW¼	35	36	42	3-15—9-15	.306	113.04
	1876					1.36		NW¼ SW¼	35	36	42	3-15—4-28	.011	1.03
	1876			36.05				NE¼ SW¼	35	36	42	3-15—9-15	.293	108.00
	1876			0.32				SW¼ NE¼	35	36	42	3-15—9-15	.003	0.96
	1876			33.92				SE¼ NW¼	35	36	42	3-15—9-15	.276	101.76
	1876			38.64				SW¼ NW¼	35	36	42	3-15—9-15	.314	115.92
	1876			26.32				NW¼ NW¼	35	36	42	3-15—9-15	.214	78.96
	1876					0.74		NW¼ NW¼	35	36	42	3-15—4-28	.006	.55
	1876			4.00				NE¼ NW¼	35	36	42	3-15—9-15	.033	12.00
	1876				2.72			NE¼ NE¼	14	35	42	3-15—6-13	.022	4.08
	1876					31.20		NE¼ NE¼	14	35	42	3-15—4-28	.254	23.40
	1876				27.56			SE¼ NE¼	14	35	42	3-15—6-13	.224	41.34
	1876					8.84		SE¼ NE¼	14	35	42	3-15—4-28	.072	6.63
	1876				16.48			NW¼ NE¼	14	35	42	3-15—6-13	.134	24.72
	1876					22.12		NW¼ NE¼	14	35	42	3-15—4-28	.180	16.59
	1876				1.12			SW¼ NE¼	14	35	42	3-15—6-13	.009	1.68
	1876			0.48				SW¼ SW¼	26	36	42	3-15—9-15	.004	1.44
	1876				2.80			SW¼ SW¼	26	36	42	3-15—6-13	.023	4.20
	1876				2.24			NW¼ SW¼	26	36	42	3-15—6-13	.018	3.36
	1876				2.56			SW¼ NW¼	26	36	42	3-15—6-13	.021	3.84

Source—**Humboldt River.** Ditch—**Hot Springs.** (Russel Land and Cattle Co. lands.)

	1880				8.16			SE¼ NE¼	29	36	42	3-15—6-13	.066	12.24
	1880				8.32			SW¼ NE¼	29	36	42	3-15—6-13	.068	12.48
	1880				28.16			NE¼ SE¼	29	36	42	3-15—6-13	.229	42.24
	1880				34.76			SE¼ SE¼	29	36	42	3-15—6-13	.283	52.14
	1880					16.90		NW¼ SW¼	29	36	42	3-15—4-28	.137	12.68
	1880					19.64		SW¼ SW¼	29	36	42	3-15—4-28	.160	14.72

Source—**Humboldt** River. Ditch—**Unnamed Ditch.** (John G. Taylor lands.)

	1875				31.36			NE¼ NE¼	13	36	41	3-15—6-13	.255	47.04
	1875				35.96			NW¼ NE¼	13	36	41	3-15—6-13	.287	53.14
	1875			12.90				SE¼ NE¼	13	36	41	3-15—9-15	.105	38.70
	1875				22.54			SE¼ NE¼	13	36	41	3-15—6-13	.183	33.81
	1875					3.56		SE¼ NE¼	13	36	41	3-15—4-28	.029	2.67
	1875			3.96				SW¼ NE¼	13	36	41	3-15—9-15	.032	11.88
	1875				29.32			SW¼ NE¼	13	36	41	3-15—6-13	.238	43.98

Clover Valley Land and Stock Co.—Continued.

Year of priority	Culture—Acres: Harvest crops	Meadow pasture	Diversified pasture		Location: Subdivision	Section	Tp.N.	R.E.	Length of season	Duty of water: C.F.S.	Acre-feet
1875			1.36		SW¼NE¼	13	36	41	3-15—4-28	.011	1.02
1875		40.00			NE¼NW¼	13	36	41	3-15—6-13	.325	60.00
1875		40.88			NW¼NW¼	13	36	41	3-15—6-13	.332	61.32
1875		39.76			SE¼NW¼	13	36	41	3-15—6-13	.323	59.65
1875			.48		SE¼NW¼	13	36	41	3-15—4-28	.004	.36
1875		41.17			SW¼NW¼	13	36	41	3-15—6-13	.335	61.76
1875	26.40				NE¼SE¼	13	36	41	3-15—9-15	.215	79.20
1875			6.40		NE¼SE¼	13	36	41	3-15—4-28	.052	4.80
1875	32.64				SE¼SE¼	13	36	41	3-15—9-15	.265	97.92
1875		3.20			SE¼SE¼	13	36	41	3-15—6-13	.026	4.80
1875			1.18		SE¼SE¼	13	36	41	3-15—4-28	.010	.89
1875		6.26			SW¼SE¼	13	36	41	3-15—6-13	.051	9.39
1875			.28		SW¼SE¼	13	36	41	3-15—4-28	.002	.21
1875	33.50				SW¼SE¼	13	36	41	3-15—9-15	.272	100.50
1875	16.04				NW¼SE¼	13	36	41	3-15—9-15	.130	48.12
1875		6.64			NW¼SE¼	13	36	41	3-15—6-13	.054	9.96
1875			12.24		NW¼SE¼	13	36	41	3-15—4-28	.100	9.18
1875		17.80			SW¼SW¼	13	36	41	3-15—6-13	.145	26.70
1875			1.76		SW¼SW¼	13	36	41	3-15—4-28	.014	1.32
1875				12.32	SW¼SW¼	13	36	41	3-15—4-28	.100	9.24
1875		37.38			SE¼SW¼	13	36	41	3-15—6-13	.304	56.07
1875	1.44				NE¼SW¼	13	36	41	3-15—9-15	.012	4.32
1875		16.52			NE¼SW¼	13	36	41	3-15—6-13	.134	24.78
1875			5.41		NE¼SW¼	13	36	41	3-15—4-28	.044	4.06
1875		26.17			NW¼SW¼	13	36	41	3-15—6-13	.213	39.26
1875			8.97		NW¼SW¼	13	36	41	3-15—4-28	.073	6.73
1875		32.08			SE¼SE¼	11	36	41	3-15—6-13	.261	48.12
1875		33.28			SW¼SE¼	11	36	41	3-15—6-13	.271	49.92
1875				39.89	NE¼SE¼	11	36	41	3-15—4-28	.324	29.92
1875				39.73	NW¼SE¼	11	36	41	3-15—4-28	.323	29.80
1875		34.64			SE¼SW¼	11	36	41	3-15—6-13	.282	51.96
1875			.56		SE¼SW¼	11	36	41	3-15—4-28	.005	.42
1875		2.28			SW¼SW¼	11	36	41	3-15—6-13	.019	3.32
1875			13.12		SW¼SW¼	11	36	41	3-15—4-28	.107	9.84
1875		26.40			NW¼SW¼	11	36	41	3-15—6-13	.215	30.00
1875			5.12		NW¼SW¼	11	36	41	3-15—4-28	.042	3.84
1875		36.60			NE¼SW¼	11	36	41	3-15—6-13	.298	55.90
1875			5.12		NE¼SW¼	11	36	41	3-15—4-28	.042	3.84
1875				37.84	SE¼NE¼	11	36	41	3-15—4-28	.291	26.88
1875				25.12	SW¼NE¼	11	36	41	3-15—4-28	.204	18.84
1875				6.16	NE¼NE¼	11	36	41	3-15—4-28	.050	4.62
1875				9.12	SE¼NW¼	11	36	41	3-15—4-28	.071	6.84
1875				15.12	NE¼NW¼	11	36	41	3-15—4-28	.123	11.34
1875				24.24	NW¼NW¼	11	36	41	3-15—4-28	.107	18.18
1875				31.84	SW¼NW¼	11	36	41	3-15—4-28	.250	23.04

Source—**Humboldt River.** Ditch—**Outside Slough.** (John G. Taylor lands.)

1887		14.32		SW¼NW	19	36	42	3-15-4-28	.116	11.05
1887			25.56	SW¼NW¼	19	36	42	3-15-4-28	.208	19.17
1887		27.48		SE¼NW¼	19	36	42	3-15-4-28	.223	20.61
1887			9.80	SE¼NW¼	19	36	42	3-15-4-28	.080	7.35
1887		20.96		NW¼SE¼	19	36	42	3-15-4-28	.170	15.72
1887			18.76	NW¼SE¼	19	36	42	3-15-4-28	.153	14.07
1887		5.56		SW¼SE¼	19	36	42	3-15-4-28	.045	4.17
1887			30.18	SW¼SE¼	19	36	42	3-15-4-28	.245	22.64
1887		2.92		SE¼SE¼	19	36	42	3-15-4-28	.024	2.19
1887			35.44	SE¼SE¼	19	36	42	3-15-4-28	.288	26.58
1887			39.60	SW¼SW¼	19	36	42	3-15-4-28	.322	29.70
1887			39.72	SE¼SW¼	19	36	42	3-15-4-28	.323	29.79
1887		5.12		NE¼SW¼	19	36	42	3-15-4-28	.042	3.84
1887			32.68	NE¼SW¼	19	36	42	3-15-4-28	.266	24.51
1887		.28		NW¼SW¼	19	36	42	3-15-4-28	.002	.21
1887			39.52	NW¼SW¼	19	36	42	3-15-4-28	.321	29.64
1887			13.28	NW¼NW¼	19	36	42	3-15-4-28	.108	9.96

Source—**Humboldt River.** Ditch—**Gonzales Slough.** (John G. Taylor lands.)

1880			25.72	NW¼NW¼	19	36	42	3-15-4-28	.209	26.79
1880		36.12		NE¼NW¼	19	36	42	3-15-4-28	.294	27.09
1880			.96	NE¼NW¼	19	36	42	3-15-4-28	.008	.72
1880		38.86		NW¼NE¼	19	36	42	3-15-4-28	.316	29.15
1880		32.44		SW¼NE¼	19	36	42	3-15-4-28	.264	24.33
1880			4.40	SW¼NE¼	19	36	42	3-15-4-28	.036	3.30
1880		10.92		NE¼NE¼	19	36	42	3-15-4-28	.089	8.19
1880			28.16	NE¼NE¼	19	36	42	3-15-4-28	.229	21.12
1880		22.68		SE¼NE¼	19	36	42	3-15-4-28	.184	17.01
1880			16.48	SE¼NE¼	19	36	42	3-15-4-28	.134	12.36
1880		14.36		NE¼SE¼	19	36	42	3-15-4-28	.117	10.77
1880			23.52	NE¼SE¼	19	36	42	3-15-4-28	.191	17.64

Claimant—**W. M. Pettit.** Proof No. 00158

Source—**Humboldt River.** Ditch—**Southside Ditch.**

1875			13.40	SE¼SE¼	10	36	41	3-15-4-28	.109	10.05
1875			4.64	SE¼NW¼	15	36	41	3-15-4-28	.038	3.48
1875			17.35	NW¼NE¼	15	36	41	3-15-4-28	.141	13.01
1875			6.05	NE¼NE¼	15	36	41	3-15-4-28	.049	4.54
1875			37.73	NW¼SW¼	15	36	41	3-15-4-28	.307	28.30

Source—**Humboldt River.** Ditch—**Overflow.**

1883			3.84	SW¼NW¼	10	36	41	3-15-4-28	.031	2.88
1883			4.67	SW¼NE¼	10	36	41	3-15-4-28	.038	3.50
1883			8.11	SE¼NE¼	10	36	41	3-15-4-28	.066	6.08
1883			38.71	NE¼SW¼	10	36	41	3-15-4-28	.315	29.03
1883			40.00	NW¼SE¼	10	36	41	3-15-4-28	.325	30.00
1883			34.72	NE¼SE¼	10	36	41	3-15-4-28	.282	26.04
1883			37.22	SW¼SE¼	10	36	41	3-15-4-28	.303	27.92
1883			39.13	NW¼NW¼	15	36	41	3-15-4-28	.318	29.35
1883			20.64	NE¼NW¼	15	36	41	3-15-4-28	.168	15.48

W. M. Pettit—Continued.

Year of priority	Culture—Acres: Harvest crops	Meadow pasture	Diversified pasture		Location: Subdivision	Section	Tp. N.	R. E.	Length of season	Duty of water: C.F.S.	Acre-feet
1883				36.36	SW¼NW¼	15	36	41	3-15—4-28	.296	27.27
1883				2.67	NE¼SW¼	15	36	41	3-15—4-28	.022	2.00
1883				38.30	SW¼SW¼	15	36	41	3-15—4-28	.311	28.73
1883				5.27	SE¼SW¼	15	36	41	3-15—4-28	.043	3.95

Claimant—**Swan and Foster.** Proof No. 00158

Source—**Humboldt River.** Ditch—**Swan and Foster.**

Year of priority	Harvest crops	Meadow pasture	Diversified pasture		Subdivision	Section	Tp. N.	R. E.	Length of season	C.F.S.	Acre-feet
1879		9.21			NW¼NW¼	24	36	41	3-15—6-13	.076	13.82
1879		20.20			NE¼NW¼	24	36	41	3-15—6-13	.164	30.30
1879		14.76			NW¼NE¼	24	36	41	3-15—6-13	.120	22.14
1879		34.96			NE¼NE¼	24	36	41	3-15—6-13	.284	52.44
1879		4.19			SE¼NE¼	24	36	41	3-15—6-13	.034	6.29

Claimant—**John G. Taylor.** Proof No. 00159

Source—**Humboldt** River. Ditch—Not **Named.**

Year of priority	Harvest crops	Meadow pasture	Diversified pasture		Subdivision	Section	Tp. N.	R. E.	Length of season	C.F.S.	Acre-feet
1885	36.70				NE¼NE¼	18	36	42	3-15—9-15	.298	110.10
1885	30.96				SE¼NE¼	18	36	42	3-15—9-15	.252	92.88
1885			1.35		SE¼NE¼	18	36	42	3-15—4-28	.012	1.01
1885				.40	SE¼NE¼	18	36	42	3-15—4-28	.003	.30
1885	13.54				SW¼NE¼	18	36	42	3-15—9-15	.110	40.62
1885			.65		SW¼NE¼	18	36	42	3-15—4-28	.005	.49
1885				21.15	SW¼NE¼	18	36	42	3-15—4-28	.172	15.86
1885	26.13				NW¼NE¼	18	36	42	3-15—9-15	.212	78.39
1885				9.86	NW¼NE¼	18	36	42	3-15—4-28	.080	7.40
1885	18.95				SE¼NW¼	18	36	42	3-15—9-15	.154	56.85
1885				18.96	SE¼NW¼	18	36	42	3-15—4-28	.154	14.21
1885	1.30				NE¼NW¼	18	36	42	3-15—9-15	.011	3.90
1887				31.75	NE¼NW¼	18	36	42	3-15—4-28	.258	23.81
1896	12.74				NW¼NW¼	18	26	42	3-15—9-15	.104	38.22
1896				21.90	NW¼NW¼	18	36	42	3-15—4-28	.178	16.43
1896	38.88				SW¼NW¼	18	36	42	3-15—9-15	.316	116.64
1896				.82	SW¼NW¼	18	36	42	3-15—4-28	.007	.62
1885	38.20				NE¼SE¼	18	36	42	3-15—9-15	.311	114.60
1885			.10		NE¼SE¼	18	36	42	3-15—4-28	.001	.08
1885	8.56				SE¼SE¼	18	36	42	3-15—9-15	.070	25.68
1885	15.14				SW¼SE¼	18	36	42	3-15—9-15	.123	45.42
1885	35.34				NW¼SE¼	18	36	42	3-15—9-15	.287	106.02
1885			.60		NW¼SE¼	18	36	42	3-15—4-28	.005	.45
1885	35.28				NE¼SW¼	18	36	42	3-15—9-15	.287	105.84
1885			.51		NE¼SW¼	18	36	42	3-15—4-28	.004	.38
1885	28.38				NW¼SW¼	18	36	42	3-15—9-15	.231	85.14
1885		3.64			NW¼SW¼	18	36	43	3-15—6-13	.030	5.46
1885			2.55		NW¼SW¼	18	36	47	3-15—4-28	.021	1.01
1885	5.83				SE¼SW¼	18	36	42	3-15—9-15	.047	17.40
1887		3.87			SE¼SW¼	18	36	42	3-15—6-13	.031	5.81
1885	0.60				SW¼SW¼	18	36	42	3-15—9-15	[illegible]	10.80

Proof No. 00163

Claimant—**Land Development Company.**

Source—**Humboldt River.** Ditch—**Reese River Slough.**

1886				10.50			NE¼NE¼	7	32	45	3-15-6-13	.085	15.75
1886						14.50	NE¼NE¼	7	32	45	3-15-4-28	.118	10.88
1886						6.20	SE¼NE¼	7	32	45	3-15-4-28	.050	4.65
1886						.50	NW¼NE¼	7	32	45	3-15-4-28	.004	.38
1886				23.30			NE¼NW¼	8	32	45	3-15-6-13	.180	34.95
1886					13.25		NE¼NW¼	8	32	45	3-15-4-28	.108	9.94
1886				31.45			SE¼NW¼	8	32	45	3-15-6-13	.256	47.18
1886						2.80	SE¼NW¼	8	32	45	3-15-4-28	.023	2.10
1886				36.00			NW¼NW¼	8	32	45	3-15-6-13	.293	54.00
1886						1.56	NW¼NW¼	8	32	45	3-15-4-28	.013	1.16
1886				8.37			SW¼NW¼	8	32	45	3-15-6-13	.068	12.56
1886					8.00		SW¼NW¼	8	32	45	3-15-4-28	.065	6.00
1886						18.60	SW¼NW¼	8	32	45	3-15-4-28	.151	13.95
1886				22.30			NE¼SW¼	8	32	45	3-15-6-13	.181	33.45
1886					16.50		NE¼SW¼	8	32	45	3-15-4-28	.134	12.38
1886					26.50		SE¼SW¼	8	32	45	3-15-4-28	.215	19.88
1886					7.20		NW¼SW¼	8	32	45	3-15-4-28	.060	5.40
1886						17.10	NW¼SW¼	8	32	45	3-15-4-28	.139	12.83
1886						3.00	SW¼SW¼	8	32	45	3-15-4-28	.024	2.25
1886					1.05		SE¼SW¼	5	32	45	3-15-4-28	.009	.79
1886				4.33			NW¼SW¼	5	32	45	3-15-6-13	.035	6.50
1886					2.78		NW¼SW¼	5	32	45	3-15-4-28	.023	2.09
1886					11.07		SW¼SW¼	5	32	45	3-15-4-28	.090	8.30
1886			2.05				NE¼SE¼	6	32	45	3-15-9-15	.017	6.15
1886				15.40			NE¼SE¼	6	32	45	3-15-6-13	.125	23.10
1886					13.27		NE¼SE¼	6	32	45	3-15-4-28	.108	9.95
1886				28.50			SE¼SE¼	6	32	45	3-15-6-13	.232	42.75
1886					4.10		SE¼SE¼	6	22	45	3-15-4-28	.033	3.08
1886				5.20			SW¼SE¼	6	32	45	3-15-6-13	.042	7.80
1886					5.40		SW¼SE¼	6	32	45	3-15-4-28	.044	4.05
1886				11.35			NE¼SW¼	6	32	45	3-15-6-13	.092	17.03
1886					25.40		NE¼SW¼	6	32	45	3-15-4-28	.207	19.05
1886					2.35		SE¼SW¼	6	32	45	3-15-4-28	.019	1.76
1886					7.25		NW¼SW¼	6	32	45	3-15-4-28	.059	5.44
1886					1.30		SW¼SW¼	6	32	45	3-15-4-28	.011	.98
1886					38.50		NE¼NE¼	1	32	45	3-15-4-28	.313	28.88
1886					14.90		SE¼NE¼	1	32	45	3-15-4-28	.121	11.18
1886					9.10		NW¼NE¼	1	32	45	3-15-4-28	.074	6.83

Source—**Humboldt River.** Ditch—**South Ditch.**

1895						17.00	SE¼SW¼	3	32	45	3-15-4-28	.138	12.75
1895						11.60	NW¼SW¼	3	32	45	3-15-4-28	.094	8.70
1895						3.80	SW¼SW¼	3	32	45	3-15-4-28	.031	2.85

Source—**Humboldt River.** Ditch—**Layton.**

1886			25.90				SW¼NE¼	5	32	45	3-15-9-15	.211	77.70
1886				5.30			SW¼NE¼	5	32	45	3-15-6-13	.043	7.95
1886				3.09			NE¼SE¼	5	32	45	3-15-6-13	.025	4.64
1886			21.00				SE¼SE¼	5	32	45	3-15-9-15	.171	63.00
1886				10.00			SE¼SE¼	5	32	45	3-15-6-13	.081	15.00

Land Development Co.—Continued.

Year of priority	Culture—Acres: Harvest crops	Meadow pasture	Diversified pasture		Location: Subdivision	Section	Tp.N.	R.E.	Length of season	Duty of water: C.F.S.	Acre-feet
1886	15.00				NW¼SE¼	5	32	45	3-15—9-15	.122	45.00
1886		20.50			NW¼SE¼	5	32	45	3-15—6-13	.167	30.75
1886	29.40				SW¼SE¼	5	32	45	3-15—9-15	.239	88.20
1886		4.85			SW¼SE¼	5	32	45	3-15—6-13	.039	7.28
1886			5.05		SW¼SE¼	5	32	45	3-15—4-28	.041	3.79
1886	40.00				SE¼NW¼	5	32	45	3-15—9-15	.325	120.00
1886	11.50				NW¼NW¼	5	32	45	3-15—9-15	.093	34.50
1886	39.90				SW¼NW¼	5	32	45	3-15—9-15	.324	119.70
1886	39.40				NE¼SW¼	5	32	45	3-15—9-15	.320	118.20
1886			.10		NE¼SW¼	5	32	45	3-15—4-28	.001	.08
1886	16.46				SE¼SW¼	5	32	45	3-15—9-15	.134	49.38
1886			14.85		SE¼SW¼	5	32	45	3-15—4-28	.121	11.14
1886	20.80				NW¼SW¼	5	32	45	3-15—9-15	.169	62.40
1886			4.14		NW¼SW¼	5	32	45	3-15—4-28	.034	3.11
1886		16.38			SW¼SW¼	5	32	45	3-15—6-13	.133	24.57
1886			3.45		SW¼SW¼	5	32	45	3-15—4-28	.028	2.59
1886		2.05			NE¼SE¼	6	32	45	3-15—6-13	.017	3.08
1886			2.60		NE¼SE¼	6	32	45	3-15—4-28	.021	1.95

Source—**Humboldt River.** Ditch—**Big Field.**

Year of priority	Harvest crops	Meadow pasture	Diversified pasture		Subdivision	Section	Tp.N.	R.E.	Length of season	C.F.S.	Acre-feet
1895				1.73	NE¼SW¼	7	33	45	3-15—4-28	.014	1.30
1895				12.48	SE¼SW¼	7	33	45	3-15—4-28	.101	9.36
1895				2.02	SW¼SE¼	7	33	45	3-15—4-28	.016	1.52
1895				10.84	NE¼NW¼	18	33	45	3-15—4-28	.088	8.13
1895				32.45	NW¼NE¼	18	33	45	3-15—4-28	.264	24.34
1895				3.94	NE¼NE¼	18	33	45	3-15—4-28	.032	2.96
1895				24.29	SW¼NE¼	18	33	45	3-15—4-28	.197	18.22
1895				25.15	SE¼NE¼	18	33	45	3-15—4-28	.204	18.86
1895				1.87	NE¼SE¼	18	33	45	3-15—4-28	.015	1.40
1895				33.79	NE¼SE¼	18	33	45	3-15—4-28	.275	25.34
1895				21.31	SE¼SE¼	18	33	45	3-15—4-28	.171	15.98
1895				.77	SW¼NW¼	17	33	45	3-15—4-28	.006	.58
1895				.38	NW¼SW¼	17	33	45	3-15—4-28	.003	.29
1895				16.61	SW¼SW¼	17	33	45	3-15—4-28	.135	12.46
1895				4.32	NE¼NE¼	19	33	45	3-15—4-28	.035	3.24
1895				22.76	NW¼NW¼	20	33	45	3-15—4-28	.185	17.07
1895				.19	NE¼NW¼	20	33	45	3-15—4-28	.002	.14
1895				9.16	SW¼NW¼	20	33	45	3-15—4-28	.074	6.87
1895				32.29	SE¼NW¼	20	33	45	3-15—4-28	.263	24.22
1895				29.25	SW¼NE¼	20	33	45	3-15—4-28	.238	21.94
1895				6.52	SE¼NE¼	20	33	45	3-15—4-28	.053	4.89
1895				25.15	NW¼SE¼	20	33	45	3-15—4-28	.204	18.86
1895				31.10	NE¼SE¼	20	33	45	3-15—4-28	.253	23.33
1895				1.24	SW¼SE¼	20	33	45	3-15—4-28	.010	.93
1895				36.48	SE¼SE¼	20	33	45	3-15—4-28	.297	27.36
1895				5.86	NW¼SW¼	21	33	45	3-15—4-28	.048	4.39
1895				31.89	SW¼SW¼	21	33	45	3-15—4-28	.259	23.92
1895				8.16	SE¼SW¼	21	33	45	3-15—4-28	.066	6.12

Source—Humboldt River. Ditch—Blossom Dam.

1901					4.60		NE¼NE¼	29	33	45	3-15—4-28	.037	3.45
1901			20.75				NW¼SW¼	30	33	45	3-15—9-15	.169	62.25
1901			35.70				SW¼SW¼	30	33	45	3-15—9-15	.290	107.10
1901					1.50		SW¼SW¼	30	33	45	3-15—4-28	.012	1.13
1901			2.75				SE¼SW¼	30	33	45	3-15—9-15	.022	8.25
1901			13.10				SE¼SE¼	31	33	45	3-15—9-15	.107	39.30
1901			9.65				NW¼SE¼	31	33	45	3-15—9-15	.078	28.95
1901			32.45				SW¼SE¼	31	33	45	3-15—9-15	.264	97.35
1901			2.25				NE¼NW¼	31	33	45	3-15—9-15	.018	6.75
1901			7.40				SE¼NW¼	31	33	45	3-15—9-15	.060	22.20
1901					.50		SE¼NW¼	31	33	45	3-15—4-28	.004	.38
1901			29.25				NW¼NW¼	31	33	45	3-15—9-15	.238	87.75
1901					3.90		NW¼NW¼	31	33	45	3-15—4-28	.032	2.93
1901			14.40				SW¼NW¼	31	33	45	3-15—9-15	.117	43.20
1901				2.67			SW¼NW¼	31	33	45	3-15—6-13	.022	4.01
1901					14.40		SW¼NW¼	31	33	45	3-15—4-28	.117	10.80
1901			28.90				NE¼SW¼	31	33	45	3-15—9-15	.235	86.70
1901					8.30		NE¼SW¼	31	33	45	3-15—4-28	.067	6.23
1901			1.75				NW¼SW¼	31	33	45	3-15—9-15	.014	5.25
1901				9.15			NW¼SW¼	31	33	45	3-15—6-13	.074	13.73
1901					20.30		NW¼SW¼	31	33	45	3-15—4-28	.165	15.23
1901			7.15				SE¼SW¼	31	33	45	3-15—9-15	.058	21.45
1901				6.00			SE¼SW¼	31	33	45	3-15—6-13	.049	9.00
1901					19.85		SE¼SW¼	31	33	45	3-15—4-28	.161	14.89
1901				31.48			SW¼SW¼	31	33	45	3-15—6-13	.256	47.22
1901					3.45		SW¼SW¼	31	33	45	3-15—4-28	.028	2.59
1901				35.50			NW¼SE¼	6	32	45	3-15—6-13	.289	53.25
1901					1.50		NW¼SE¼	6	32	45	3-15—4-28	.012	1.13
1901			7.75				NE¼NW¼	6	22	45	3-15—9-15	.063	23.25
1901				14.75			NE¼NW¼	6	32	45	3-15—6-13	.120	22.13
1901					9.90		NE¼NW¼	6	32	45	3-15—4-28	.080	7.43
1901				29.40			SE¼NW¼	6	32	45	3-15—6-13	.239	44.10
1901					8.15		SE¼NW¼	6	32	45	3-15—4-28	.066	6.11
1901				25.53			NW¼NW¼	6	32	45	3-15—6-13	.208	38.30
1901					13.17		NW¼NW¼	6	32	45	3-15—4-28	.107	9.88
1901				4.60			SW¼NW¼	6	32	45	3-15—6-13	.037	6.90
1901					28.70		SW¼NW¼	6	32	45	3-15—4-28	.233	21.53
1901			14.15				NE¼NE¼	6	32	45	3-15—9-15	.115	42.45
1901					1.70		NE¼NE¼	6	32	45	3-15—4-28	.014	1.28
1901			28.25				SE¼NE¼	6	32	45	3-15—9-15	.230	84.75
1901				.10			SE¼NE¼	6	32	45	3-15—6-13	.001	.15
1901					4.90		SE¼NE¼	6	32	45	3-15—4-28	.040	3.68
1901			30.45				NW¼NE¼	6	32	45	3-15—9-15	.248	91.35
1901					8.55		NW¼NE¼	6	32	45	3-15—4-28	.070	6.41
1901			.75				SW¼NE¼	6	32	45	3-15—9-15	.006	2.25
1901				12.70			SW¼NE¼	6	32	45	3-15—6-13	.103	38.10
1901					15.03		SW¼NE¼	6	32	45	3-15—4-28	.122	11.27

Land Development Co.—Continued.

Source—**Humboldt River.** Ditch—**Crum-Blossom Slough.**

Year of priority	Harvest crops (Culture—Acres)	Meadow pasture	Diversified pasture		Subdivision (Location)	Section	Tp.N.	R.E.	Length of season	C.F.S. (Duty of water)	Acre-feet
1883	1.00				SW¼SE¼	32	33	45	3-15—9-15	.008	3.00
1883	6.95				SE¼SW¼	32	33	45	3-15—9-15	.057	20.85
1883	12.50				SW¼SW¼	32	33	45	3-15—9-15	.102	37.50
1883	20.35				NW¼NE¼	5	32	45	3-15—9-15	.165	61.05
1883	38.10				NE¼NW¼	5	32	45	3-15—9-15	.310	114.30
1883	25.75				NW¼NW¼	5	32	45	3-15—9-15	.209	77.25
1883	23.35				NE¼NE¼	6	32	45	3-15—9-15	.190	70.05

Source—**Humboldt River.** Ditch—**Rocky Point Canal.**

Year of priority	Harvest crops	Meadow pasture	Diversified pasture		Subdivision	Section	Tp.N.	R.E.	Length of season	C.F.S.	Acre-feet
1895	9.85				SE¼SW¼	21	33	45	3-15—9-15	.080	29.55
1895			.35		SE¼SW¼	21	33	45	3-15—4-28	.003	.26
1895	5.01				SW¼SW¼	21	33	45	3-15—9-15	.041	15.03
1895			.71		SW¼SW¼	21	33	45	3-15—4-28	.006	.53
1895			.20		SE¼SE¼	22	33	45	3-15—4-28	.002	.15
1895	5.60				NE¼NE¼	28	33	45	3-15—9-15	.046	16.80
1895			1.90		SE¼NE¼	28	33	45	3-15—4-28	.015	1.43
1895				20.10	SE¼NE¼	28	33	45	3-15—4-28	.163	15.08
1895	4.10				NW¼NE¼	28	33	45	3-15—9-15	.033	12.30
1895		3.00			NW¼NE¼	28	33	45	3-15—6-13	.024	4.50
1895	7.80				SW¼NE¼	28	33	45	3-15—9-15	.063	23.40
1895		2.50			SW¼NE¼	28	33	45	3-15—6-13	.020	3.75
1895			25.90		SW¼NE¼	28	33	45	3-15—4-28	.211	19.43
1895	26.70				NE¼SE¼	28	33	45	3-15—9-15	.217	80.10
1895	9.35				SE¼SE¼	28	33	45	3-15—9-15	.076	28.05
1895	24.80				NW¼SE¼	28	33	45	3-15—9-15	.202	74.40
1895			2.20		NW¼SE¼	28	33	45	3-15—4-28	.018	1.65
1895	4.25				SW¼SE¼	28	33	45	3-15—9-15	.035	12.75
1895			8.30		SW¼SE¼	28	33	45	3-15—4-28	.067	6.23
1895	36.40				NE¼NW¼	28	33	45	3-15—9-15	.296	109.20
1895	29.80				SE¼NW¼	28	33	45	3-15—9-15	.242	89.40
1895			6.60		SE¼NW¼	28	33	45	3-15—4-28	.054	4.95
1895	30.05				NW¼NW¼	28	33	45	3-15—9-15	.244	90.15
1895			9.95		NW¼NW¼	28	33	45	3-15—4-28	.081	7.46
1895	19.65				SW¼NW¼	28	33	45	3-15—9-15	.160	58.95
1895			10.05		SW¼NW¼	28	33	45	3-15—4-28	.082	7.54
1895			2.35		NE¼SW¼	28	33	45	3-15—4-28	.019	1.76
1895			1.60		SE¼SW¼	28	33	45	3-15—4-28	.013	1.20
1895			.20		NW¼SW¼	28	33	45	3-15—4-28	.002	.15

Claimant—**Wm. Licking.** Proof No. 00164

Source—**Humboldt River.** Ditch—**Layton.**

Year of priority	Harvest crops	Meadow pasture	Diversified pasture		Subdivision	Section	Tp.N.	R.E.	Length of season	C.F.S.	Acre-feet
1871	1.84				NE¼NW¼	16	32	45	3-15—9-15	.015	5.52
1871	7.12				NW¼NW¼	16	32	45	3-15—9-15	.058	21.36
1871			2.18		NW¼NW¼	16	32	45	3-15—4-28	.018	1.64

1871			30.94				NE¼NE¼	17	32	45	3-15—9-15	.300	110.82
1871			10.25				SE¼NE¼	17	32	45	3-15—9-15	.083	30.75
1871				11.30			SE¼NE¼	17	32	45	3-15—6-13	.092	16.95
1871			19.68				NW¼NE¼	17	32	45	3-15—9-15	.160	59.04
1871				17.95			NW¼NE¼	17	32	45	3-15—6-13	.146	26.93
1871				11.80			SW¼NE¼	17	32	45	3-15—6-13	.097	17.81
1871			.31				SW¼SE¼	9	32	45	3-15—9-15	.003	.93
1871						.30	NW¼SE¼	9	32	45	3-15—4-28	.002	.23
1871			39.25				NE¼NE¼	8	32	45	3-15—9-15	.319	117.75
1871					.14		NE¼NE¼	8	32	45	3-15—4-28	.001	.11
1871			39.45				SE¼NE¼	8	32	45	3-15—9-15	.321	118.35
1871			14.45				NW¼NE¼	8	32	45	3-15—9-15	.117	43.35
1871					18.79		NW¼NE¼	8	32	45	3-15—4-28	.153	14.09
1871			18.73				SW¼NE¼	8	32	45	3-15—9-15	.152	56.19
1871					9.29		SW¼NE¼	8	32	45	3-15—4-28	.076	6.97
1871			29.04				NE¼SE¼	8	32	45	3-15—9-15	.236	87.12
1871					4.12		NE¼SE¼	8	32	45	3-15—4-28	.033	3.09
1871			12.06				SE¼SE¼	8	32	45	3-15—9-15	.098	36.18
1871					19.77		SE¼SE¼	8	32	45	3-15—4-28	.161	14.83
1871			30.45				NW¼SE¼	8	32	45	3-15—9-15	.248	91.35
1871					5.33		NW¼SE¼	8	32	45	3-15—4-28	.043	4.00
1871			35.85				SW¼SE¼	8	32	45	3-15—9-15	.291	107.55
1871			.94				NE¼NW¼	9	32	45	3-15—9-15	.008	2.82
1871				2.81			NE¼NW¼	9	32	45	3-15—6-13	.023	4.22
1871						12.58	NE¼NW¼	9	32	45	3-15—4-28	.102	9.44
1871			22.45				SE¼NW¼	9	32	45	3-15—9-15	.183	67.35
1871						6.97	SE¼NW¼	9	32	45	3-15—4-28	.057	5.23
1871			33.07				NW¼NW¼	9	32	45	3-15—9-15	.269	99.21
1871				5.20			NW¼NW¼	9	32	45	3-15—6-13	.042	7.80
1871						.94	NW¼NW¼	9	32	45	3-15—4-28	.008	.71
1871			39.63				SW¼NW¼	9	32	45	3-15—9-15	.322	118.89
1871			36.41				NE¼SW¼	9	32	45	3-15—9-15	.296	109.23
1871						.75	NE¼SW¼	9	32	45	3-15—4-28	.006	.56
1871			38.98				SE¼SW¼	9	32	45	3-15—9-15	.317	116.94
1871			40.03				NW¼SW¼	9	32	45	3-15—9-15	.325	120.09
1871			31.90				SW¼SW¼	9	32	45	3-15—9-15	.259	95.70
1871					4.19		SW¼SW¼	9	32	45	3-15—4-28	.034	3.14
1871						1.80	SW¼NE¼	9	32	45	3-15—4-28	.015	1.35
1871			1.98				NW¼SE¼	9	32	45	3-15—9-15	.016	5.94

Claimant—**McIntyre-Starrett Co.** Proof No. 00165
Source—**Humboldt River.** Ditch—**McIntyre-Starrett Dam.**

1883			5.50				NE¼SE¼	9	32	45	3-15—9-15	.045	16.50
1883			38.86				SE¼SE¼	9	32	45	3-15—9-15	.316	116.58
1883			25.90				NW¼SE¼	9	32	45	3-15—9-15	.211	77.70
1883			38.75				SW¼SE¼	9	32	45	3-15—9-15	.315	116.25
1883			39.35				NE¼NE¼	16	32	35	3-15—9-15	.320	119.05
1883			37.30				SE¼NE¼	16	32	35	3-15—9-15	.303	11.90
1883					.50		SE¼NE¼	16	32	35	3-15—4-28	.008	.38
1883			37.06				NW¼NE¼	16	32	35	3-15—9-15	.301	111.18
1883			28.19				SW¼NE¼	16	32	35	3-15—9-15	.237	84.57
1883					.83		SW¼NE¼	16	32	35	3-15—4-28	.007	.62

McIntyre-Starrett Co.—Continued.

Year of priority	Harvest crops (Culture—Acres)	Meadow pasture (Culture—Acres)	Diversified pasture (Culture—Acres)		Subdivision (Location)	Section (Location)	Tp.N. (Location)	R.E. (Location)	Length of season	C.F.S. (Duty of water)	Acre-feet (Duty of water)
1883	36.27				NE¼NW¼	16	32	35	3-15—9-15	.295	108.81
1883	16.08				SE¼NW¼	16	32	35	3-15—9-15	.131	48.24
1883			.13		SE¼NW¼	16	32	35	3-15—4-28	.001	.10
1883	13.59				NW¼NW¼	16	32	35	3-15—9-15	.110	40.77
1883			.73		NW¼NW¼	16	32	35	3-15—4-28	.006	.55
1883	6.53				SW¼NW¼	16	32	35	3-15—9-15	.053	19.59
1883			6.55		SW¼NW¼	16	32	35	3-15—4-28	.053	4.91

Source—**Humboldt River.** Ditch—**Altenberg Ditch.**

Year of priority	Harvest crops	Meadow pasture	Diversified pasture		Subdivision	Section	Tp.N.	R.E.	Length of season	C.F.S.	Acre-feet
1874	3.26				SW¼NW¼	16	32	35	3-15—9-15	.027	9.78
1874	13.33				SW¼NW¼	16	32	35	3-15—9-15	.108	39.99
1874		4.40			SW¼NW¼	16	32	35	3-15—6-13	.036	6.60
1874			11.35		SE¼NW¼	16	32	35	3-15—4-28	.092	8.51

Claimant—**W. T. Jenkins Co.** **Proof No. 00166**

Source—**Humboldt River.** Ditch—**Rocky Point.**

Year of priority	Harvest crops	Meadow pasture	Diversified pasture		Subdivision	Section	Tp.N.	R.E.	Length of season	C.F.S.	Acre-feet
1873		5.55			NE¼SW¼	6	32	46	3-15—6-13	.045	8.33
1873		.11			NE¼SE¼	1	32	45	3-15—6-13	.001	.17
1873			6.61		NE¼SE¼	1	32	45	3-15—4-28	.054	4.96
1873				6.33	NE¼SE¼	1	32	45	3-15—4-28	.051	4.75
1873	6.27				NE¼NW¼	1	32	45	3-15—9-15	.051	18.81
1873	18.57				NW¼NW¼	1	32	45	3-15—9-15	.151	55.71
1873			5.60		NW¼NW¼	1	32	45	3-15—4-28	.046	4.20

Source—**Humboldt River.** Ditch—**South Ditch.**

Year of priority	Harvest crops	Meadow pasture	Diversified pasture		Subdivision	Section	Tp.N.	R.E.	Length of season	C.F.S.	Acre-feet
1895		7.62			SE¼SE¼	2	32	45	3-15—6-13	.062	11.43
1895				30.79	SE¼SE¼	2	32	45	3-15—4-28	.250	23.09
1895	9.45				NW¼SE¼	2	32	45	3-15—9-15	.077	28.35
1895		19.87			NW¼SE¼	2	32	45	3-15—6-13	.162	29.81
1895	6.60				SW¼SE¼	2	32	45	3-15—9-15	.054	18.80
1895		9.93			SW¼SE¼	2	32	45	3-15—6-13	.081	14.90
1895				5.28	SW¼SE¼	2	32	45	3-15—4-28	.043	3.96
1895				1.16	NE¼NW¼	2	32	45	3-15—4-28	.000	.87
1895	11.50				SE¼SW¼	2	32	45	3-15—9-15	.093	34.50
1895	10.15				SW¼SW¼	2	32	45	3-15—9-15	.083	30.45
1895	12.04				NW¼SE¼	1	32	45	3-15—9-15	.098	36.12
1895		3.36			NW¼SE¼	1	32	45	3-15—6-13	.027	5.04
1895			16.67		NW¼SE¼	1	32	45	3-15—4-28	.136	12.50
1895				2.21	NW¼SE¼	1	32	45	3-15—4-28	.018	1.66
1895			1.00		SW¼SE¼	1	32	45	3-15—4-28	.008	.75
1895	5.70				SW¼NE¼	1	32	45	3-15—9-15	.046	17.10
1895			4.47		SW¼NE¼	1	32	45	3-15—4-28	.036	3.35
1895	19.30				SE¼NW¼	1	32	45	3-15—9-15	.157	57.90
1895	26.50				SW¼NW¼	1	32	45	3-15—9-15	.216	79.50
1895			13.67		SW¼SW¼	1	32	45	3-15—4-28	.111	10.35

1895	....	....	.55	....	....	....	NE¼SW¼	1	32	45	3-15—9-15	.005	1.65
1895	....	....	....	....	39.00	....	NE¼SW¼	1	32	45	3-15—4-28	.317	29.25
1895	....	....	....	....	9.97	....	SE¼SW¼	1	32	45	3-15—4-28	.081	7.48
1895	....	....	....	....	....	5.82	SE¼SW¼	1	32	45	3-15—4-28	.047	4.37
1895	....	....	....	....	40.12	....	NW¼SW¼	1	32	45	3-15—4-28	.326	30.09
1895	....	....	....	....	21.84	....	SW¼SW¼	1	32	45	3-15—4-28	.178	16.38
1895	....	....	28.30	....	....	....	NE¼NE¼	2	32	45	3-15—9-15	.230	84.90
1895	....	....	....	....	13.06	....	NE¼NE¼	2	32	45	3-15—4-28	.106	9.80
1895	....	....	6.98	....	....	....	SE¼NE¼	2	32	45	3-15—9-15	.057	20.94
1895	....	....	....	2.16	....	....	SE¼NE¼	2	32	45	3-15—6-13	.018	3.24
1895	....	....	....	....	30.88	....	SE¼NE¼	2	32	45	3-15—4-28	.251	23.16
1895	....	....	7.35	....	....	....	NW¼NE¼	2	32	45	3-15—9-15	.060	22.05
1895	....	....	....	....	9.14	....	NW¼NE¼	2	32	45	3-15—4-28	.074	6.87
1895	....	....	6.60	....	....	....	SW¼NE¼	2	32	45	3-15—9-15	.054	19.80
1895	....	....	....	8.47	....	....	NE¼SE¼	2	32	45	3-15—6-13	.069	12.71
1895	....	....	....	....	29.60	....	NE¼SE¼	2	32	45	3-15—4-28	.241	22.20

Areas in sections 6, 1 and 2, T. 32 N, R. 45 E, totaling 871.53 acres, first flooded artificially during the year 1873 due to Rocky Point Dam when these areas were Class C pasture; therefore has pasture water right of .75 acre-feet per acre from 1873 to 1895.

Claimant—**Faris Estate.** Proof No. 00167

Source—**Humboldt River.** Ditch—**Faris Ditch System.**

1873	....	....	....	....	17.31	....	SE¼SE¼	5	32	46	3-15—4-28	.141	21.98
1873	....	....	....	....	6.30	....	SE¼SE¼	5	32	46	3-15—4-28	.051	4.73
1873	....	....	....	....	22.28	....	SW¼SE¼	5	32	46	3-15—4-28	.181	16.71
1873	....	....	....	....	25.09	....	SW¼SW¼	5	32	46	3-15—4-28	.204	18.82
1873	....	....	....	....	24.77	....	SE¼SW¼	5	32	46	3-15—4-28	.201	18.58
1873	....	....	....	....	.50	....	SE¼SW¼	5	32	46	3-15—4-28	.004	.38
1876	....	....	22.97	....	....	....	NE¼NE¼	20	32	46	3-15—9-15	.187	68.91
1892	....	....	....	....	.75	....	NE¼NE¼	20	32	46	3-15—4-28	.006	.56
1893	....	....	....	....	13.15	....	NE¼NE¼	20	32	46	3-15—4-28	.107	9.86
1893	....	....	....	....	33.46	....	SE¼NE¼	20	32	46	3-15—4-28	.272	25.10
1892	....	....	....	....	32.65	....	NW¼NE¼	20	32	46	3-15—4-28	.265	24.49
1892	....	....	....	....	34.69	....	NE¼NW¼	20	32	46	3-15—4-28	.282	26.02
1892	....	....	....	....	35.41	....	NW¼NW¼	20	32	46	3-15—4-28	.288	26.56
1892	....	....	....	....	2.30	....	SE¼NW¼	20	32	46	3-15—4-28	.019	1.73
1892	....	....	....	....	5.85	....	SW¼NW¼	20	32	46	3-15—4-28	.048	4.39
1873	....	....	....	....	36.20	....	SE¼SE¼	6	32	46	3-15—4-28	.294	27.15
1873	....	....	....	....	30.26	....	SW¼SE¼	6	32	46	3-15—4-28	.246	22.70
1873	....	....	....	....	33.37	....	SE¼SW¼	6	32	46	3-15—4-28	.271	25.03
1873	....	....	....	....	10.61	....	SW¼SW¼	6	32	46	3-15—4-28	.086	7.96
1892	....	....	....	....	36.53	....	NE¼NE¼	19	32	46	3-15—4-28	.297	27.41
1892	....	....	....	....	3.75	....	SE¼NE¼	19	32	46	3-15—4-28	.030	2.81
1892	....	....	....	....	11.66	....	NW¼NE¼	19	32	46	3-15—4-28	.095	8.75
1890	....	....	....	1.60	....	....	NE¼NW¼	19	32	46	3-15—6-13	.013	2.40
1890	....	....	....	....	8.25	....	NE¼NW¼	19	32	46	3-15—4-28	.067	6.19
1890	....	....	....	.45	....	....	SE¼NW¼	19	32	46	3-15—6-13	.004	.68
1890	....	....	....	....	18.80	....	SE¼NW¼	19	32	46	3-15—4-28	.153	14.10
1890	....	....	....	2.43	....	....	NW¼NW¼	19	32	46	3-15—6-13	.020	3.65
1890	....	....	....	....	3.30	....	NW¼NW¼	19	32	46	3-15—4-28	.027	2.48
1890	....	....	....	26.10	....	....	SW¼NW¼	19	32	46	3-15—6-13	.212	39.15
1890	....	....	....	....	21.84	....	SW¼NW¼	19	32	46	3-15—4-28	.178	16.38
1873	....	....	....	....	31.30	....	NE¼NE¼	7	32	46	3-15—4-28	.254	23.48

Faris Estate—Continued.

Year of priority	Culture—Acres: Harvest crops	Meadow pasture	Diversified pasture		Location: Subdivision	Section	Tp. N.	R. E.	Length of season	Duty of water: C. F. S.	Acre-feet
1873			.50		SE¼NE¼	7	32	46	3-15—4-28	.004	.38
1873			9.96		NW¼NE¼	7	32	46	3-15—4-28	.081	7.47
1873			12.83		NE¼NW¼	7	32	46	3-15—4-28	.104	9.62
1873			41.55		NW¼NW¼	7	32	46	3-15—4-28	.338	31.16
1873			30.72		SW¼NW¼	7	32	46	3-15—4-28	.250	23.04
1878				2.90	SE¼SE¼	4	32	46	3-15—4-28	.024	2.18
1878				18.65	SW¼SE¼	4	32	46	3-15—4-28	.152	13.99
1878				20.00	SE¼SW¼	4	32	46	3-15—4-28	.163	15.00
1878				16.37	SW¼SW¼	4	32	46	3-15—4-28	.133	12.28
1873			3.75		SW¼SW¼	4	32	46	3-15—4-28	.030	2.81
1893		37.44			NE¼NE¼	21	32	46	3-15—6-13	.304	56.16
1893		35.22			SE¼NE¼	21	32	46	3-15—6-13	.286	52.83
1893			3.80		SE¼NE¼	21	32	46	3-15—4-28	.031	2.85
1893		34.50			NW¼NE¼	21	32	46	3-15—6-13	.280	51.75
1893			2.92		NW¼NE¼	21	32	46	3-15—4-28	.024	2.19
1893		2.12			SW¼NE¼	21	32	46	3-15—6-13	.017	3.18
1893			35.77		SW¼NE¼	21	32	46	3-15—4-28	.291	26.83
1893		22.51			NE¼NW¼	21	32	46	3-15—6-13	.183	33.77
1893			14.62		NE¼NW¼	21	32	46	3-15—4-28	.119	10.97
1893			38.42		SE¼NW¼	21	32	46	3-15—4-28	.312	29.92
1893	11.40				NW¼NW¼	21	32	46	3-15—9-15	.093	34.20
1893		5.72			NW¼NW¼	21	32	46	3-15—6-13	.047	8.58
1893			20.80		NW¼NW¼	21	32	46	3-15—4-28	.169	15.60
1893			40.00		SW¼NW¼	21	32	46	3-15—4-28	.325	30.00
1893		39.40			NE¼SE¼	21	32	46	3-15—6-13	.320	59.10
1893		39.50			NW¼SE¼	21	32	46	3-15—6-13	.321	59.25
1893		37.29			SE¼SE¼	21	32	46	3-15—6-13	.303	55.94
1893				1.24	SE¼SE¼	21	32	46	3-15—4-28	.010	.93
1893		36.40			SW¼SE¼	21	32	46	3-15—6-13	.296	54.60
1893				3.60	SW¼SE¼	21	32	46	3-15—4-28	.029	2.70
1893		34.35			NE¼SW¼	21	32	46	3-15—6-13	.279	51.53
1893			4.90		NE¼SW¼	21	32	46	3-15—4-28	.040	3.68
1893		20.86			NW¼SW¼	21	32	46	3-15—6-13	.170	21.39
1893			18.54		NW¼SW¼	21	32	46	3-15—4-28	.150	13.91
1893		35.40			SE¼SW¼	21	32	46	3-15—6-13	.288	53.10
1893				4.60	SE¼SW¼	21	32	46	3-15—4-28	.037	3.45
1893		35.03			SW¼SW¼	21	32	46	3-15—6-13	.285	52.55
1893				4.97	SW¼SW¼	21	32	46	3-15—4-28	.040	3.73
1893				1.00	NE¼NE¼	28	32	46	3-15—4-28	.081	.75
1893				6.96	NW¼NE¼	28	32	46	3-15—4-28	.057	5.22
1893				8.58	NE¼NW¼	28	32	46	3-15—4-28	.070	6.44
1893				7.09	NW¼NW¼	28	32	46	3-15—4-28	.058	5.32
1893			1.86		NE¼NE¼	29	32	46	3-15—4-28	.016	1.40
1893				3.30	NE¼NE¼	29	32	46	3-15—4-28	.027	2.52
1878				3.31	NE¼NE¼	8	32	46	3-15—4-28	.027	2.51
1878				25.05	SE¼NE¼	8	32	46	3-15—4-28	.204	18.79
1873		0.75			NW¼NE¼	8	32	46	3-15—9-13	.006	1.13
1873				0.47	NW¼NE¼	8	32	46	3-15—4-28	.077	7.10

1878				8.75	SW¼NE¼	8	32	46	3-15—4-28	.071	6.56
1878				40.00	NE¼SE¼	8	32	46	3-15—4-28	.325	30.00
1878	9.42				SE¼SE¼	8	32	46	3-15—9-15	.077	28.26
1878				30.63	SE¼SE¼	8	22	46	3-15—4-28	.240	22.07
1878				40.00	NW¼SE¼	8	32	46	3-15—4-28	.325	30.00
1878	1.30				SW¼SE¼	8	32	46	3-15—9-15	.011	3.90
1878				38.70	SW¼SE¼	8	32	46	3-15—4-28	.315	29.03
1873			29.05		NE¼NW¼	8	32	46	3-15—4-28	.236	21.70
1873			26.95		NW¼NW¼	8	32	46	3-15—4-28	.219	20.21
1878				33.54	NE¼SW¼	8	32	46	3-15—4-28	.273	25.16
1878				40.00	SE¼SW¼	8	32	46	3-15—4-28	.325	30.00
1878				9.70	NW¼SW¼	8	32	46	3-15—4-28	.079	7.28
1878				40.00	SW¼SW¼	8	32	46	3-15—4-28	.325	30.00
1878			4.53		SW¼SE¼	9	32	46	3-15—4-28	.037	3.40
1878			.30		NE¼SW¼	9	32	46	3-15—4-28	.002	3.23
1878				40.00	NW¼SW¼	9	32	46	3-15—4-28	.325	30.00
1878	14.40				SE¼SW¼	9	32	46	3-15—9-15	.117	43.20
1878			18.21		SE¼SW¼	9	32	46	3-15—4-28	.148	13.66
1878	3.38				SW¼SW¼	9	32	46	3-15—9-15	.027	10.14
1878			18.16		SW¼SW¼	9	32	46	3-15—4-28	.148	13.95
1878				18.70	SW¼SW¼	9	32	46	3-15—4-28	.152	14.03
1878			13.10		NE¼NE¼	9	32	46	3-15—4-28	.107	9.83
1878	11.40				SE¼NE¼	9	32	16	3-15—9-15	.093	34.20
1878			23.13		SE¼NE¼	9	32	46	3-15—4-28	.188	17.35
1878				4.40	NW¼NE¼	9	32	46	3-15—1-28	.036	3.30
1878			4.00		SW¼NE¼	9	32	46	3-15—1-28	.033	3.00
1878				33.60	NE¼NW¼	9	32	46	3-15—4 28	.273	25.20
1878				10.10	SE¼NW¼	9	32	46	3-15—4-28	.082	7.58
1878				40.00	NW¼NW¼	9	32	46	3-15—4-28	.325	30.00
1878				40.00	SW¼NW¼	9	32	46	3-15—4-28	.325	30.00
1878	34.86				NE¼SE¼	9	32	46	3-15—9-15	.283	104.58
1878			3.42		NE¼SE¼	9	32	46	3-15—1-28	.028	2.57
1878	37.87				SE¼SE¼	9	32	46	3-15—9-15	.308	113.71
1878			2.05		SE¼SE¼	9	32	46	3-15—4-28	.017	1.55
1878	12.27				NW¼SE¼	9	32	46	3-15—9-15	.100	36.81
1878			21.92		NW¼SE¼	9	32	46	3-15—4-28	.178	16.44
1878	34.10				SW¼SE¼	8	32	46	3-15—9-15	.277	102.30
1876		7.10			NW¼SW¼	10	32	46	3-15—6-13	.058	10.65
1878	30.34				NW¼SW¼	10	32	46	3-15—9-15	.247	91.02
1878		.90			NW¼SW¼	10	32	46	3-15—6-13	.007	1.35
1876	21.64				SE¼SW¼	10	32	46	3-15—9-15	.176	64.92
1876		18.44			SE¼SW¼	10	32	46	3-15—6-13	.150	27.66
1876		27.58			SW¼SW¼	10	32	46	3-15—6-13	.224	41.37
1878	8.10				SW¼SW¼	10	32	46	3-15—9-15	.066	24.30
1878		3.91			SW¼SW¼	10	32	46	3-15—6-13	.032	5.87
1878	24.62				SE¼NW¼	10	32	46	3-15—9-15	.200	73.86
1878	34.16				SW¼NW¼	10	32	46	3-15—9-15	.278	102.48
1878		4.92			SW¼NW¼	10	32	46	3-15—6 13	.040	7.38
1876	21.50				NE¼SE¼	10	32	46	3-15—9-15	.175	64.50
1876		17.38			NE¼SE¼	10	52	46	3-15—6-13	.141	26.17
1876			.95		NE¼SE¼	10	32	46	3-15—4 28	.008	.71
1876	20.98				NW¼SE¼	10	32	46	3-15—9-15	.244	89.84
1876		10.27			NW¼SE¼	10	32	46	3-15—6-13	.083	15.41

Faris Estate—Continued.

Year of priority	Culture—Acres: Harvest crops	Culture—Acres: Meadow pasture	Culture—Acres: Diversified pasture		Location: Subdivision	Location: Section	Location: Tp. N.	Location: R. E.	Length of season	Duty of water: C. F. S.	Duty of water: Acre-feet
1876	4.17				SE¼SE¼	10	32	46	3-15—9-15	.034	12.51
1876		35.83			SE¼SE¼	10	32	46	3-15—6-13	.291	53.75
1876	36.00				SW¼SE¼	10	32	46	3-15—9-15	.293	108.00
1876		3.60			SW¼SE¼	10	32	46	3-15—6-13	.029	5.40
1878	.75				NE¼SW¼	10	32	46	3-15—9-15	.006	2.25
1876	1.04				NE¼SW¼	10	32	46	3-15—9-15	.008	3.12
1876		38.17			NE¼SW¼	10	32	46	3-15—6-13	.310	57.26
1876	20.17				NE¼NE¼	10	32	46	3-15—9-15	.164	60.51
1876		17.04			NE¼NE¼	10	32	46	3-15—6-13	.139	26.56
1878				2.50	NE¼NE¼	10	32	46	3-15—4-28	.020	1.88
1876	16.84				NW¼NE¼	10	32	46	3-15—9-15	.137	50.52
1876		.70			NW¼NE¼	10	32	46	3-15—6-13	.006	1.05
1878	19.77				NW¼NE¼	10	32	46	3-15—9-15	.161	59.31
1878				2.60	NW¼NE¼	10	32	46	3-15—4-28	.021	1.95
1876	32.50				SE¼NE¼	10	32	46	3-15—9-15	.264	97.50
1876		6.07			SE¼NE¼	10	32	46	3-15—6-13	.049	9.11
1876			1.40		SE¼NE¼	10	32	46	3-15—4-28	.011	1.05
1876	8.86				SW¼NE¼	10	32	46	3-15—9-15	.072	26.58
1876		30.38			SW¼NE¼	10	32	46	3-15—6-13	.247	45.57
1878	16.72				NE¼NW¼	10	32	46	3-15—9-15	.136	50.16
1878			21.96		NE¼NW¼	10	32	46	3-15—4-28	.179	16.47
1878	1.63				NW¼NW¼	10	32	46	3-15—9-15	.013	4.89
1878			30.95		NW¼NW¼	10	32	46	3-15—4-28	.252	23.21
1876		14.49			SE¼NW¼	10	32	46	3-15—6-13	.118	21.74
1893		23.37			NE¼SE¼	15	32	46	3-15—6-13	.190	35.06
1893		4.00			SE¼SE¼	15	32	46	3-15—6-13	.033	6.00
1893		35.30			SW¼SE¼	15	32	46	3-15—6-13	.286	52.95
1893		14.80			NW¼NE¼	22	32	46	3-15—6-13	.120	22.20
1893		38.50			NE¼NW¼	22	32	46	3-15—6-13	.313	57.75
1893		28.96			SE¼NW¼	22	32	46	3-15—6-13	.235	43.44
1893		4.72			NE¼SW¼	22	32	46	3-15—6-13	.038	7.08
1893		38.28			NW¼SW¼	22	32	46	3-15—6-13	.311	57.42
1893		15.54			SW¼SW¼	22	32	46	3-15—6-13	.126	23.31
1876		40.00			NE¼NE¼	15	32	46	3-15—6-13	.325	60.00
1876	24.48				NW¼NE¼	15	32	46	3-15—9-15	.199	73.44
1876		15.43			NW¼NE¼	15	32	46	3-15—6-13	.125	23.15
1876		32.96			SE¼NE¼	15	32	46	3-15—6-13	.268	49.44
1893		6.44			SE¼NE¼	15	32	46	3-15—6-13	.052	9.06
1876	3.60				SW¼NE¼	15	32	46	3-15—9-15	.029	10.80
1876		20.08			SW¼NE¼	15	32	46	3-15—6-13	.163	30.12
1893		16.32			SW¼NE¼	15	32	46	3-15—6-13	.133	24.48
1876	31.75				NE¼NW¼	15	32	46	3-15—9-15	.258	95.45
1876		8.24			NE¼NW¼	15	32	46	3-15—6-13	.067	12.36
1893		10.00			SE¼NW¼	15	32	46	3-15—6-13	.081	15.00
1876	22.39				SE¼NW¼	15	32	46	3-15—9-15	.182	67.17
1876		5.42			SE¼NW¼	15	32	46	3-15—6-13	.044	8.13
1876	25.38				NW¼NW¼	15	32	46	3-15—9-15	.206	76.14

1876				11.46			NW¼NW¼	15	32	46	3 15—6-13	.093	17.19
1876					2.39		NW¼NW¼	15	32	46	3 15—4-28	.019	1.79
1876			37.20				SW¼NW¼	15	32	46	3-15—9-15	.302	111.60
1876			22.39				SE¼NW¼	15	32	46	3-15—9-15	.182	67.17
1893				15.43			SE¼NW¼	15	32	46	3-15—6-13	.125	23.15
1893				40.00			NW¼SE¼	15	32	46	3-15—6-13	.325	60.00
1876			9.95				NE¼SW¼	15	32	46	3-15—9-15	.081	29.85
1893				30.05			NE¼SW¼	15	32	46	3-15—6-13	.244	45.08
1876			31.18				NW¼SW¼	15	32	46	3-15—9-15	.253	93.54
1893				8.82			NW¼SW¼	15	32	46	3-15—6-13	.072	13.23
1876			0.20				SE¼SW¼	15	32	46	3 15—9-15	.002	.60
1893				39.80			SE¼SW¼	15	32	46	3-15—6-13	.324	59.76
1876			3.75				SW¼SW¼	15	32	46	3-15—9-15	.030	11.25
1893				36.25			SW¼SW¼	15	32	46	3-15—6-13	.295	54.38
1876			7.38				NE¼NE¼	16	32	46	3-15—9-15	.060	22.14
1878			23.60				NE¼NE¼	16	32	46	3-15—9-15	.192	70.80
1878				6.40			NE¼NE¼	16	32	46	3-15—6-13	.052	9.20
1876			39.35				SE¼NE¼	16	32	46	3-15—9-15	.320	118.05
1876			0.67				NW¼NE¼	16	32	46	3-15—9-15	.005	2.01
1878			34.06				NW¼NE¼	16	32	46	3-15—9-15	.277	102.18
1878				3.53			NW¼NE¼	16	32	46	3-15—6-13	.029	5.30
1878			29.49				SW¼NE¼	16	32	46	3-15—9-15	.240	88.47
1878				7.85			SW¼NE¼	16	32	46	3-15—6-13	.064	11.78
1878			39.67				NE¼NW¼	16	32	46	3-15—9-15	.323	119.01
1876			3.74				SE¼NW¼	16	32	46	3-15—9-15	.030	11.22
1878			34.14				SE¼NW¼	16	32	46	3-15—9-15	.278	102.42
1878			38.88				NW¼NW¼	16	32	46	3-15—9-15	.316	116.64
1878					0.55		NW¼NW¼	16	32	46	3-15—4-28	.004	.41
1878			39.50				SW¼NW¼	16	32	46	3-15—9-15	.321	118.50
1876			31.46				NW¼SE¼	16	32	46	3-15—9-15	.256	94.38
1893				8.54			NW¼SE¼	16	32	46	3-15—6-13	.069	12.81
1893				23.13			NE¼SE¼	16	32	46	3-15—6-13	.188	34.76
1876			16.87				NE¼SE¼	16	32	46	3-15—9-15	.137	50.61
1878			4.42				NE¼SW¼	16	32	46	3-15—9-15	.036	13.26
1878				1.20			NE¼SW¼	16	32	46	3-15—6-13	.010	1.80
1876			31.16				NE¼SW¼	16	32	46	3-15—9-15	.253	93.48
1893				1.67			NE¼SW¼	16	32	46	3-15—6-13	.014	2.51
1876			11.20				SE¼SW¼	16	32	46	3-15—9-15	.091	33.60
1893				28.80			SE¼SW¼	16	32	46	3 15—6-13	.234	43.20
1878			33.28				NW¼SW¼	16	32	46	3 15—9-15	.271	99.84
1878				2.63			NW¼SW¼	16	32	46	3-15—6-13	.021	3.80
1876			2.28				NW¼SW¼	16	32	46	3-15—9-15	.019	6.84
1876			35.85				SW¼SW¼	16	32	46	3-15—9-15	.291	107.55
1876					.60		SW¼SW¼	16	32	46	3-15—4-28	.005	.45
1893				2.25			SW¼SW¼	16	32	46	3-15—6-13	.018	3.38
1893				40.00			SE¼SE¼	16	32	46	3-15—6-13	.325	60.00
1893				40.00			SW¼SE¼	16	32	46	3-15—6-13	.325	60.00
1878			37.37				NE¼NE¼	17	32	46	3-15—9-15	.304	112.11
1878			39.10				SE¼NE¼	17	32	46	3-15—9-15	.318	117.30
1878			27.06				NW¼NE¼	17	32	46	3-15—9-15	.220	81.18
1878					12.00		NW¼NE¼	17	32	46	3-15—4-28	.098	9.06
1878			38.42				SW¼NE¼	17	32	46	3-15—9-15	.312	115.26
1878			38.68				NE¼SE¼	17	32	46	3-15—9-15	.314	116.04

Faris Estate—Continued.

Year of priority	Culture—Acres: Harvest crops	Meadow pasture	Diversified pasture		Location: Subdivision	Section	Tp.N.	R.E.	Length of season	Duty of water: C.F.S.	Acre-feet
1878		0.60			NE¼SE¼	17	32	46	3-15—6-13	.005	.90
1878	16.81				SE¼SE¼	17	32	46	3-15—9-15	.137	50.43
1878			2.00		SE¼SE¼	17	32	46	3-15—4-28	.016	1.50
1878	39.40				NW¼SE¼	17	32	46	3-15—9-15	.320	118.20
1878	40.08				SW¼SE¼	17	32	46	3-15—9-15	.326	120.24
1878	3.97				NE¼NW¼	17	32	46	3-15—9-15	.323	11.91
1878			36.04		NE¼NW¼	17	32	46	3-15—4-28	.293	27.03
1878	27.50				SE¼NW¼	17	32	46	3-15—9-15	.224	82.50
1878			11.56		SE¼NW¼	17	32	46	3-15—4-28	.094	8.67
1878			40.00		NW¼NW¼	17	32	46	3-15—4-28	.325	30.00
1878	5.00				SW¼NW¼	17	32	46	3-15—9-15	.041	15.00
1878			35.00		SW¼NW¼	17	32	46	3-15—4-28	.285	26.25
1878	38.94				NE¼SW¼	17	32	46	3-15—9-15	.317	116.82
1878	37.62				SE¼SW¼	17	32	46	3-15—9-15	.306	112.86
1878			1.50		SE¼SW¼	17	32	46	3-15—4-28	.012	1.13
1878	9.97				NW¼SW¼	17	32	46	3-15—9-15	.081	29.91
1878			29.50		NW¼SW¼	17	32	46	3-15—4-28	.240	22.13
1878	19.43				SW¼SW¼	17	32	46	3-15—9-15	.158	58.29
1878			18.90		SW¼SW¼	17	32	46	3-15—4-28	.154	14.18
1876	18.44				SE¼SE¼	17	32	46	3-15—9-15	.150	55.32
1873			0.75		NW¼SW¼	7	32	46	3-15—4-28	.006	.56
1878				5.60	SE¼SE¼	7	32	46	3-15—4-28	.046	4.20
1878				37.44	NE¼NE¼	18	32	46	3-15—4-28	.304	28.08
1878				7.96	NW¼NE¼	18	32	46	3-15—4-28	.065	5.97
1878			40.00		SE¼NE¼	18	32	46	3-15—4-28	.325	30.00
1878			35.45		SW¼NE¼	18	32	46	3-15—4-28	.288	26.59
1878			9.10		SE¼NW¼	18	32	46	3-15—4-28	.074	6.83
1878			6.40		SW¼NW¼	18	32	46	3-15—4-28	.052	4.80
1878			40.00		NE¼SE¼	18	32	46	3-15—4-28	.325	30.00
1878			39.70		NW¼SE¼	18	32	46	3-15—4-28	.319	29.40
1878			36.72		SE¼SE¼	18	32	46	3-15—4-28	.299	27.54
1878			30.83		SW¼SE¼	18	32	46	3-15—4-28	.251	23.12
1878			36.97		NE¼SW¼	18	32	46	3-15—4-28	.301	27.73
1878			41.28		NW¼SW¼	18	32	46	3-15—4-28	.336	30.96
1878			4.32		SE¼SW¼	18	32	46	3-15—4-28	.035	3.24
1878			2.90		SW¼SW¼	18	32	46	3-15—4-28	.024	2.18
1893		37.60			NW¼NW¼	22	32	46	3-15—6-13	.306	56.40
1893		37.90			SW¼NW¼	22	32	46	3-15—6-13	.308	56.85
1878				41.74	SE¼SE¼	3	32	46	3-15—4-28	.339	31.31
1876	3.34				SE¼SE¼	3	32	46	3-15—9-15	.027	10.02
1878	4.43				SW¼SE¼	3	32	46	3-15—9-15	.036	13.20
1878			25.03		SW¼SE¼	3	32	46	3-15—4-28	.203	18.77
1878				14.62	SW¼SE¼	3	32	46	3-15—4-28	.119	10.97
1878			28.05		SE¼SW¼	3	32	46	3-15—4-28	.228	21.04
1878			0.60		SW¼SW¼	3	32	46	3-15—4-28	.005	.45
1893			6.84		NE¼SW¼	19	32	46	3-15—4-28	.056	5.13
1893				6.38	NE¼SW¼	19	32	46	3-15—4-28	.052	4.79
1893			46.36		NW¼SW¼	19	32	46	3-15—4-28	.377	34.78
1893				1.23	NW¼SW¼	19	32	46	3-15—4-28	.010	[illegible]

	1893						18.04	SE¼ SW¼	19	32	46	3-15—4-28	.147	13.53
	1893						36.32	SW¼ SW¼	19	32	46	3-15—4-28	.295	27.24
	1893						.61	NW¼ NW¼	30	32	46	3-15—4-28	.005	.46
	1893						15.79	SE¼ NW¼	30	32	46	3-15—4-28	.128	11.84
	1893						31.70	SW¼ NW¼	30	32	46	3-15—4-28	.258	23.78
	1893						8.20	NW¼ SW¼	30	32	46	3-15—4-28	.007	6.15
	1893						6.46	NE¼ NE¼	30	32	46	3-15—4-28	.053	4.85
	1893						2.61	SE¼ NE¼	30	32	46	3-15—4-28	.021	1.96
	1893						17.40	SW¼ NE¼	30	32	46	3-15—4-28	.141	13.05
	1893				10.04			NE¼ SE¼	20	32	46	3-15—6-13	.082	15.06
	1893					29.66		NE¼ SE¼	20	32	46	3-15—4-28	.241	22.25
	1893					14.48		NW¼ SE¼	20	32	46	3-15—4-28	.118	10.86
	1893				20.26			SE¼ SE¼	20	32	46	3-15—6-13	.165	30.39
	1893					16.74		SE¼ SE¼	20	32	46	3-15—4-28	.130	12.56
	1893					39.20		SW¼ SE¼	20	32	46	3-15—4-28	.319	29.40
	1893					31.78		SE¼ SW¼	20	32	46	3-15—4-28	.258	23.84
	1893					14.72		SW¼ SW¼	20	32	46	3-15—4-28	.120	11.04
	1891				10.18			NE¼ SE¼	24	32	45	3-15—6-13	.083	15.27
	1891					29.72		NE¼ SE¼	24	32	45	3-15—4-28	.242	22.29
	1891				12.40			NW¼ SE¼	24	32	45	3-15—6-13	.101	18.60
	1891					25.86		NW¼ SE¼	24	32	45	3-15—4-28	.210	19.40
	1893						3.36	NE¼ NE¼	29	32	46	3-15—4-28	.027	2.52
	1893					4.10		NW¼ NE¼	29	32	46	3-15—4-28	.033	3.08
	1893					5.22		NE¼ NW¼	29	32	46	3-15—4-28	.042	3.92
	1893					3.85		NW¼ NW¼	29	32	46	3-15—4-28	.031	2.89
	1883						14.80	NW¼ NE¼	10	32	45	3-15—4-28	.120	11.10
	1883						16.60	SE¼ NE¼	10	32	45	3-15—4-28	.135	12.45
	1883						40.00	SW¼ NE¼	10	32	45	3-15—4-28	.325	30.00
	1883						20.30	NE¼ NW¼	10	32	45	3-15—4-28	.165	15.33
	1883						34.93	SE¼ NW¼	10	32	45	3-15—4-28	.284	26.20
	1883						24.80	NE¼ SE¼	10	32	45	3-15—4-28	.202	18.60
	1883						29.50	NW¼ SE¼	10	32	45	3-15—4-28	.240	22.13
	1883					14.64		SE¼ SE¼	10	32	45	3-15—4-28	.119	10.98
	1883					11.56		SW¼ SE¼	10	32	45	3-15—4-28	.094	8.67
	1883						17.80	NE¼ SW¼	10	32	45	3-15—4-28	.145	13.35
	1883					3.20		NW¼ SW¼	10	32	45	3-15—4-28	.026	2.40
	1883					9.36		SE¼ SW¼	10	32	45	3-15—4-28	.076	7.02
	1883					23.80		SW¼ SW¼	10	32	45	3-15—4-28	.193	17.85
	1883					4.95		NE¼ SE¼	11	32	45	3-15—4-28	.040	3.71
	1883						18.40	NE¼ SE¼	11	32	45	3-15—4-28	.150	13.80
	1883					2.10		NW¼ SE¼	11	32	45	3-15—4-28	.017	1.58
	1883						33.40	NW¼ SE¼	11	32	45	3-15—4-28	.272	25.05
	1883					36.04		SE¼ SE¼	11	32	45	3-15—4-28	.293	27.03
	1883					23.70		SW¼ SE¼	11	32	45	3-15—4-28	.193	17.78
	1883						12.03	SW¼ SE¼	11	32	45	3-15—4-28	.098	9.02
	1883						9.00	SW¼ NW¼	11	32	45	3-15—4-28	.073	6.75
	1883						40.00	NE¼ SW¼	11	32	45	3-15—4-28	.325	30.00
	1883						30.50	NW¼ SW¼	11	32	45	3-15—4-28	.248	22.88
	1883					13.70		SE¼ SW¼	11	32	45	3-15—4-28	.111	10.28
	1883						21.82	SE¼ SW¼	11	32	45	3-15—4-28	.177	16.47
	1883					16.00		SW¼ SW¼	11	32	45	3-15—4-28	.130	12.00
	1873					2.15		NE¼ NE¼	12	32	45	3-15—4-28	.017	1.61
	1873					25.43		SE¼ NE¼	12	32	45	3-15—4-28	.207	19.07

Faris Estate—Continued.

Year of priority	Culture—Acres: Harvest crops	Culture—Acres: Meadow pasture	Culture—Acres: Diversified pasture	Location: Subdivision	Location: Section	Location: Tp. N.	Location: R. E.	Length of season	Duty of water: C.F.S.	Duty of water: Acre-feet
1873			11.96	SW¼ NE¼	12	32	45	3-15—4-28	.097	8.97
1873			23.17	NE¼ SE¼	12	32	45	3-15—4-28	.188	17.38
1873			0.45	SE¼ SE¼	12	32	45	3-15—4-28	.004	.35
1873			37.45	NW¼ SE¼	12	32	45	3-15—4-28	.304	28.09
1873			30.10	SW¼ SE¼	12	32	45	3-15—4-28	.245	22.58
1873			3.85	NW¼ NE¼	13	32	45	3-15—4-28	.031	2.89
1878			12.69	NE¼ SE¼	13	32	45	3-15—4-28	.103	9.52
1878			14.10	NE¼ SE¼	13	32	45	3-15—4-28	.115	10.58
1878			0.65	SE¼ SE¼	13	32	45	3-15—4-28	.005	.49
1878			21.11	NW¼ SE¼	13	32	45	3-15—4-28	.172	15.83
1878			13.83	SW¼ SE¼	13	32	45	3-15—4-28	.112	10.37
1891			0.50	NE¼ NE¼	24	32	45	3-15—4-28	.004	.38
1891		17.76		SE¼ NE¼	24	32	45	3-15—6-13	.144	26.64
1891			15.56	SE¼ NE¼	24	32	45	3-15—4-28	.127	11.67
1891		1.16		SW¼ NE¼	24	32	45	3-15—6-13	.009	1.74
1891			9.30	SW¼ NE¼	24	32	45	3-15—4-28	.076	6.98
1873			3.10	SE¼ NW¼	12	32	45	3-15—4-28	.025	2.33
1873			21.20	NE¼ SW¼	12	32	45	3-15—4-28	.172	15.99
1873	13.45			NE¼ SW¼	12	32	45	3-15—9-15	.109	40.35
1873			9.63	NW¼ SW¼	12	32	45	3-15—4-28	.078	7.22
1873	19.00			NW¼ SW¼	12	32	45	3-15—9-15	.154	57.00
1873			39.99	SE¼ SW¼	12	32	45	3-15—4-28	.325	29.99
1873			34.50	SW¼ SW¼	12	32	45	3-15—4-28	.280	25.88
1873			32.80	NE¼ NW¼	13	32	45	3-15—4-28	.267	24.60
1873			40.00	NW¼ NW¼	13	32	45	3-15—4-28	.325	30.00
1873			3.20	SE¼ NW¼	13	32	45	3-15—4-28	.026	2.40
1873			35.00	SW¼ NW¼	13	32	45	3-15—4-28	.285	26.25
1878			16.37	NE¼ SW¼	13	32	45	3-15—4-28	.133	12.28
1873			13.18	NW¼ SW¼	13	32	45	3-15—4-28	.107	9.89
1878			5.20	NW¼ SW¼	13	32	45	3-15—4-28	.042	3.90
1878			18.61	SE¼ SW¼	13	32	45	3-15—4-28	.151	15.06
1878			14.44	SW¼ SW¼	13	32	45	3-15—4-28	.117	10.83
1891			2.00	SW¼ NW¼	24	32	45	3-15—4-28	.016	1.50
1873			40.00	NE¼ NE¼	14	32	45	3-15—4-28	.325	30.00
1873			40.00	SE¼ NE¼	14	32	45	3-15—4-28	.325	30.00
1873	8.70			NW¼ NE¼	14	32	45	3-15—9-15	.071	26.10
1873			31.26	NW¼ NE¼	14	32	45	3-15—4-28	.254	23.45
1873	14.50			SW¼ NE¼	14	32	45	3-15—9-15	.118	43.50
1873			25.50	SW¼ NE¼	14	32	45	3-15—4-28	.207	19.13
1873	26.05			NE¼ NW¼	14	32	45	3-15—9-15	.212	78.15
1873			13.18	NE¼ NW¼	14	32	45	3-15—4-28	.107	9.89
1873	8.35			NW¼ NW¼	14	32	45	3-15—9-15	.068	25.05
1873		4.75		NW¼ NW¼	14	32	45	3-15—6-13	.030	7.13
1873			4.50	NW¼ NW¼	14	32	45	3-15—4-28	.037	3.38
1891	17.00			NW¼ NW¼	14	32	45	3-15—9-15	.140	63.70
1873	40.00			SE¼ NW¼	14	32	45	3-15—9-15	.325	120.00
1873	27.00			SW¼ NW¼	14	32	45	3-15—9-15	.224	82.80

8[71]

1883			3.95	SW¼ NW¼	14	32	45	3-15—4-28	.032	2.06
1883	1.70			SW¼ NW¼	14	32	45	3-15—0-15	.014	5.10
1873			39.66	NE¼ SE¼	14	32	45	3-15—4-28	.322	29.75
1873		12.70		SE¼ SE¼	11	32	45	3-15—6-13	.103	19.05
1873			22.12	SE¼ SE¼	14	32	45	3-15—4-28	.180	16.59
1873	15.62			NW¼ SE¼	14	32	45	3-15—0-15	.127	46.86
1873			23.41	NW¼ SE¼	14	32	45	3-15—4-28	.190	17.56
1873	15.00			SW¼ SE¼	14	32	45	3-15—0-15	.122	45.00
1873			22.50	SW¼ SE¼	14	32	45	3-15—4-28	.183	16.68
1873	38.91			NE¼ SW¼	14	32	45	3-15—0-15	.317	116.82
1873	39.00			NW¼ SW¼	14	32	45	3-15—0-15	.317	117.00
1873	32.10			SE¼ SW¼	14	32	45	3-15—0-15	.261	96.30
1873			4.77	SE¼ SW¼	14	32	45	3-15—4-28	.023	3.58
1873	30.91			SW¼ SW¼	14	32	45	3-15—0-15	.251	92.73
1873			5.98	SW¼ SW¼	14	32	45	3-15—4-28	.049	4.49
1883	36.00			NE¼ NE¼	15	32	45	3-15—0-15	.293	108.00
1883			4.15	NE¼ NE¼	15	32	45	3-15—4-28	.034	3.11
1883	37.00			NW¼ NE¼	15	32	45	3-15—0-15	.301	111.00
1883			3.00	NW¼ NE¼	15	32	45	3-15—4-28	.024	2.25
1873	6.15			SE¼ NE¼	15	32	45	3-15—0-15	.050	18.45
1883	11.05			SE¼ NE¼	15	32	45	3-15—0-15	.090	33.15
1883			16.75	SE¼ NE¼	15	32	45	3-15—4-28	.136	12.56
1883	16.50			SW¼ NE¼	15	32	45	3-15—0-15	.134	49.50
1883			19.44	SW¼ NE¼	15	32	45	3-15—4-28	.158	14.58
1883	37.50			NE¼ NW¼	15	32	45	3-15—0-15	.305	112.50
1883			1.85	NE¼ NW¼	15	32	45	3-15—4-28	.015	1.39
1883	38.74			NW¼ NW¼	15	32	45	3-15—0-15	.315	116.22
1873	0.87			SE¼ SW¼	15	32	45	3-15—0-15	.007	2.61
1873			10.50	SE¼ SW¼	15	32	45	3-15—4-28	.085	7.80
1883	21.73			SE¼ SW¼	15	32	45	3-15—0-15	.170	62.58
1883	33.37			SW¼ NW¼	15	32	45	3-15—4-28	.007	.65
1873			1.77	SW¼ NW¼	15	32	45	3-15—4-28	.014	1.33
1883			1.70	SW¼ NW¼	15	32	45	3-15—4-28	.013	1.27
1873	39.70			NE¼ SE¼	15	32	45	3-15—0-15	.323	119.10
1873	40.00			SE¼ SE¼	15	32	45	3-15—0-15	.325	120.00
1873	30.00			NW¼ SE¼	15	32	45	3-15—0-15	.244	90.00
1883			6.50	NW¼ SE¼	15	32	45	3-15—4-28	.053	4.88
1873	38.98			SW¼ SE¼	15	32	45	3-15—0-15	.316	116.94
1883			4.20	NE¼ SW¼	15	32	45	3-15—4-28	.034	3.15
1873	25.91			NE¼ SW¼	15	32	45	3-15—0-15	.211	77.73
1873			5.20	NE¼ SW¼	15	32	45	3-15—4-28	.042	3.90
1873	39.07			SE¼ SW¼	15	32	45	3-15—0-15	.318	117.21
1873	7.35			NW¼ SW¼	15	32	45	3-15—0-15	.060	22.05
1873			18.75	NW¼ SW¼	15	32	45	3-15—4-28	.152	14.07
1883			7.70	NW¼ SW¼	15	32	45	3-15—4-28	.063	5.78
1873	26.25			SW¼ SW¼	15	32	45	3-15—0-15	.213	78.75
1873			11.84	SW¼ SW¼	15	32	45	3-15—4-28	.096	8.90
1873	6.95			NE¼ NE¼	22	32	45	3-15—0-15	.057	20.85
1873			8.10	NE¼ NE¼	22	32	45	3-15—4-28	.066	6.08
1890		23.57		NE¼ NE¼	22	32	45	3-15—6-13	.192	35.36
1890			38.82	SE¼ NE¼	22	32	45	3-15—4-28	.316	29.12
1873	18.91			NW¼ NE¼	22	32	45	3-15—0-15	.154	56.73
1873			6.85	NW¼ NE¼	22	32	45	3-15—4-28	.056	5.14

Faris Estate—Continued.

Year of priority	Culture—Acres: Harvest crops	Culture—Acres: Meadow pasture	Culture—Acres: Diversified pasture	Location: Subdivision	Location: Section	Location: Tp. N.	Location: R. E.	Length of season	Duty of water: C.F.S.	Duty of water: Acre-feet
1890	....	....	10.49	NW¼ NE¼	22	32	45	3-15—4-28	.085	7.87
1890	....	....	37.89	SW¼ NE¼	22	32	45	3-15—4-28	.308	28.42
1873	22.22	....	....	NE¼ NW¼	22	32	45	3-15—9-15	.181	66.66
1873	....	....	7.34	NE¼ NW¼	22	32	45	3-15—4-28	.060	5.51
1890	....	....	6.52	NE¼ NW¼	22	32	45	3-15—4-28	.053	4.80
1873	9.60	....	....	NW¼ NW¼	22	32	45	3-15—9-15	.078	28.80
1873	....	....	4.17	NW¼ NW¼	22	32	45	3-15—4-28	.034	3.14
1890	....	....	23.24	NW¼ NW¼	22	32	45	3-15—4-28	.189	17.43
1890	....	....	38.59	SE¼ NW¼	22	32	45	3-15—4-28	.314	28.94
1890	....	....	19.77	SW¼ NW¼	22	32	45	3-15—4-28	.161	14.83
1890	....	....	39.97	NE¼ SE¼	22	32	45	3-15—4-28	.325	29.98
1890	....	....	19.00	SE¼ SE¼	22	32	45	3-15—4-28	.154	14.25
1890	....	....	18.83	NW¼ SE¼	22	32	45	3-15—4-28	.153	14.12
1890	....	....	23.47	NE¼ SW¼	22	32	45	3-15—4-28	.191	17.60
1890	....	....	1.83	NW¼ SW¼	22	32	45	3-15—4-28	.015	1.37
1890	....	....	9.00	NE¼ NE¼	23	32	45	3-15—4-28	.073	6.75
1890	....	....	27.82	NW¼ NE¼	23	32	45	3-15—4-28	.226	21.87
1878	....	....	7.50	NW¼ NE¼	23	32	45	3-15—4-28	.061	5.63
1890	....	....	10.41	SE¼ NE¼	23	32	45	3-15—4-28	.085	7.81
1890	....	....	11.50	SW¼ NE¼	23	32	45	3-15—4-28	.093	8.63
1890	....	....	21.21	NE¼ NW¼	23	32	45	3-15—4-28	.172	15.91
1878	....	....	15.97	NE¼ NW¼	23	32	45	3-15—4-28	[illegible]	11.98
1890	0.37	....	....	NW¼ NW¼	23	32	45	3-15—9-15	[illegible]	1.11
1890	....	....	23.64	NW¼ NW¼	23	32	45	3-15—4-28	[illegible]	17.73
1878	....	....	12.60	NW¼ NW¼	23	32	45	3-15—4-28	[illegible]	9.45
1890	....	....	40.00	SE¼ NW¼	23	32	45	3-15—4-28	.325	30.00
1890	....	....	38.93	SW¼ NW¼	23	32	45	3-15—4-28	.317	29.20
1890	....	31.38	....	NE¼ SE¼	23	32	45	3-15—6-13	.255	47.04
1890	....	....	6.84	NE¼ SE¼	23	32	45	3-15—4-28	.056	5.15
1890	....	11.06	....	NW¼ SE¼	23	32	45	3-15—6-13	.090	16.59
1890	....	....	26.95	NW¼ SE¼	23	32	45	3-15—4-28	.219	20.21
1890	....	21.25	....	SE¼ SE¼	23	32	45	3-15—6-13	.173	31.88
1890	....	....	17.30	SE¼ SE¼	23	32	45	3-15—4-28	.141	12.98
1890	....	8.93	....	SW¼ SE¼	23	32	45	3-15—6-13	.073	13.40
1890	....	....	28.94	SW¼ SE¼	23	32	45	3-15—4-28	.235	21.71
1890	....	....	38.80	NE¼ SW¼	23	32	45	3-15—4-28	.315	29.10
1890	....	....	38.77	NW¼ SW¼	23	32	45	3-15—4-28	.316	29.08
1890	....	....	38.38	SE¼ SW¼	23	32	45	3-15—4-28	.312	28.79
1890	....	....	36.81	SW¼ SW¼	23	32	45	3-15—4-28	.299	27.61
1891	....	1.90	....	NE¼ SW¼	24	32	45	3-15—6-13	.015	2.85
1891	....	....	25.17	NE¼ SW¼	24	32	45	3-15—4-28	.205	18.88
1891	....	5.05	....	NW¼ SW¼	24	32	45	3-15—6-13	.041	7.58
1891	....	....	27.06	NW¼ SW¼	24	32	45	3-15—4-28	.220	20.30
1891	....	22.50	....	SE¼ SW¼	24	32	45	3-15—6-13	.183	33.75
1891	....	....	16.05	SE¼ SW¼	24	32	45	3-15—4-28	.130	12.04
1891	....	19.30	....	SW¼ SW¼	24	32	45	3-15—6-13	.157	28.05
1891	....	....	17.82	SW¼ SW¼	24	32	45	3-15—4-28	.140	13.87

	1893					17.42		SE¼ SE¼	24	32	45	3-15—4-28	.142	13.06
	1893						22.58	SE¼ SE¼	24	32	45	3-15—4-28	.184	16.94
	1893					37.67		SW¼ SE¼	24	32	45	3-15—4-28	.306	28.25
	1893						2.33	SW¼ SE¼	24	32	45	3-15—4-28	.019	1.75
	1893						5.52	NE¼ NE¼	25	32	45	3-15—4-28	.045	4.14
	1893					7.24		NW¼ NE¼	25	32	45	3-15—4-28	.059	5.43
	1893						2.70	NW¼ NE¼	25	32	45	3-15—4-28	.022	2.03
	1893						20.63	SE¼ NE¼	25	32	45	3-15—4-28	.168	15.47
	1893						10.69	SW¼ NE¼	25	32	45	3-15—4-28	.087	8.02
	1893						2.49	NE¼ SE¼	25	32	45	3-15—4-28	.020	1.87
	1893						2.61	NW¼ SE¼	25	32	45	3-15—4-28	.021	1.96
	1893					22.82		NE¼ NW¼	25	32	45	3-15—4-28	.186	17.12
	1893					32.76		NW¼ NW¼	25	32	45	3-15—4-28	.266	24.57
	1893					7.00		SE¼ NW¼	25	32	45	3-15—4-28	.057	5.25
	1893						3.73	SE¼ NW¼	25	32	45	3-15—4-28	.030	2.80
	1893					1.60		SW¼ NW¼	25	32	45	3-15—4-28	.013	1.20
	1893					33.74		NE¼ NE¼	26	32	45	3-15—4-28	.274	25.31
	1893					4.91		SE¼ NE¼	26	32	45	3-15—4-28	.040	3.68
	1893					25.28		NW¼ NE¼	26	32	45	3-15—4-28	.206	18.96
	1893					28.22		NE¼ NW¼	26	32	45	3-15—4-28	.229	21.17
	1893					10.18		NW¼ NW¼	26	32	45	3-15—4-28	.083	7.64

Claimant—**Geo. B. Williams.** Proof No. 00168

Source—**Humboldt River.** Ditch—**Upper Slavin Dam.**

	1881					.08		SW¼ SW¼	6	32	47	3-15—4-28	.001	.06
	1881						0.23	SW¼ SW¼	6	32	47	3-15—4-28	.002	.17
	1881						6.20	NW¼ SW¼	6	32	47	3-15—4-28	.050	4.65
	1881					28.20		NW¼ SW¼	6	32	47	3-15—4-28	.229	21.15
	1881					0.81		NE¼ SW¼	6	32	47	3-15—4-28	.007	.61
	1881						18.84	NE¼ SW¼	6	32	47	3-15—4-28	.153	14.13
	1881						4.92	NW¼ SE¼	6	32	47	3-15—4-28	.040	3.69

Source—**Humboldt River.** Ditch—**No. 1.**

	1881					23.00		NE¼ SE¼	1	32	46	3-15—4-28	.187	17.25
	1881			6.43				SE¼ SE¼	1	32	46	3-15—9-15	.052	19.29
	1881					9.25		SE¼ SE¼	1	32	46	3-15—4-28	.076	6.94
	1881			13.00				SW¼ SE¼	1	32	46	3-15—9-15	.106	39.00
	1881					8.19		SW¼ SE¼	1	32	46	3-15—4-28	.067	6.14
	1881			.50				SE¼ SW¼	1	32	46	3-15—9-15	.004	1.50
	1881					1.91		SE¼ SW¼	1	32	46	3-15—4-28	.016	1.43
	1881			21.50				NW¼ NE¼	12	32	46	3-15—9-15	.175	64.50
	1881			.80				SW¼ NE¼	12	32	46	3-15—9-15	.007	2.40
	1881			.80				SE¼ NW¼	12	32	46	3-15—9-15	.007	2.40
	1881					21.14		SE¼ NW¼	12	32	46	3-15—4-28	.172	14.86
	1881			8.02				SW¼ NW¼	12	32	46	3-15—9-15	.065	24.06

Source—**Humboldt River.** Ditch—**No. 2.**

	1881			38.48				NE¼ NE¼	1	32	46	3-15—9-15	.313	115.44
	1881			39.00				NW¼ NE¼	1	32	46	3-15—9-15	.317	117.00
	1881			20.60				SE¼ NE¼	1	32	46	3-15—9-15	.167	61.80
	1881				11.45			SE¼ NE¼	1	32	46	3-15—6-13	.093	17.18

Geo. B. Williams—Continued.

Year of priority	Culture—Acres: Harvest crops	Meadow pasture	Diversified pasture	Location: Subdivision	Section	Tp. N.	R. E.	Length of season	Duty of water: C. F. S.	Acre-feet
1881	38.07			SW¼ NE¼	1	32	46	3-15—9-15	.310	114.21
1881		1.70		SW¼ NE¼	1	32	46	3-15—6-13	.014	2.55
1881	39.03			NE¼ NW¼	1	32	46	3-15—9-15	.317	117.09
1881		0.52		NE¼ NW¼	1	32	46	3-15—6-13	.004	.78
1881	18.43			NW¼ NW¼	1	32	46	3-15—9-15	.150	55.29
1881		19.60		NW¼ NW¼	1	32	46	3-15—6-13	.159	29.40
1881	39.57			SE¼ NW¼	1	32	46	3-15—9-15	.322	118.71
1881	37.38			SW¼ NW¼	1	32	46	3-15—9-15	.304	112.14
1881		2.26		SW¼ NW¼	1	32	46	3-15—6-13	.018	3.39
1881		26.00		SE¼ NE¼	2	32	46	3-15—6-13	.211	39.00
1881	3.00			SW¼ NE¼	2	32	46	3-15—9-15	.024	9.00
1881		9.57		SW¼ NE¼	2	32	46	3-15—6-13	.078	14.36
1881		6.34		SE¼ NW¼	2	32	46	3-15—6-13	.052	9.51
1881		9.15		NE¼ SE¼	2	32	46	3-15—6-13	.074	13.73
1881		10.40		NW¼ SE¼	2	32	46	3-15—6-13	.085	15.60
1881	16.48			SW¼ SE¼	2	32	46	3-15—9-15	.119	49.44
1881		5.00		SW¼ SE¼	2	32	46	3-15—6-13	.040	7.50
1881	8.67			SE¼ SW¼	2	32	46	3-15—9-15	.070	26.01
1881		3.43		SE¼ SW¼	2	32	46	3-15—6-13	.028	5.15
1881	2.78			SW¼ SW¼	2	32	46	3-15—9-15	.023	8.34
Source—Humboldt River. Ditch—**No. 3.**										
1881			2.15	NW¼ NE¼	11	32	46	3-15—4-28	.017	1.61
1881	20.92			NE¼ NW¼	11	32	46	3-15—9-15	.170	62.76
1881		12.37		NE¼ NW¼	11	32	46	3-15—6-13	.101	18.56
1881			5.96	NE¼ NW¼	11	32	46	3-15—4-28	.048	4.47
1881	14.56			NW¼ NW¼	11	32	46	3-15—9-15	.118	43.68
1881		24.45		NW¼ NW¼	11	32	46	3-15—6-13	.198	36.68
1881			.30	NW¼ NW¼	11	32	46	3-15—4-28	.002	.23
1881	14.15			SW¼ NW¼	11	32	46	3-15—9-15	.115	42.45
1881		25.00		SW¼ NW¼	11	32	46	3-15—6-13	.203	37.50
1881	2.75			NE¼ SE¼	1	32	46	3-15—9-15	.022	8.25
1881		1.77		NE¼ SE¼	1	32	46	3-15—6-13	.014	2.66
1881			8.47	NE¼ SE¼	1	32	46	3-15—4-28	.060	6.35
1881	24.06			NW¼ SE¼	1	32	46	3-15—9-15	.196	72.18
1881		3.81		NW¼ SE¼	1	32	46	3-15—6-13	.032	5.72
1881			11.18	NW¼ SE¼	1	32	46	3-15—4-28	.091	8.39
1881	13.15			SW¼ SE¼	1	32	46	3-15—9-15	.107	39.45
1881			0.65	SW¼ SE¼	1	32	46	3-15—4-28	.005	.49
1881	37.49			NE¼ SW¼	1	32	46	3-15—9-15	.305	112.47
1881			2.41	NE¼ SW¼	1	32	46	3-15—4-28	.020	1.81
1881	37.64			NW¼ SW¼	1	32	46	3-15—9-15	.306	112.92
1881		0.42		NW¼ SW¼	1	32	46	3-15—6-13	.003	.63
1881	21.62			SE¼ SW¼	1	32	46	3-15—9-15	.176	64.86
1881			14.73	SE¼ SW¼	1	32	46	3-15—4-28	.120	11.05
1881	37.29			SW¼ SW¼	1	32	46	3-15—9-15	.303	111.87

1881	....	....		1.40	....	....	SW¼SW¼	1	32	46	3-15—6-13	.011	2.10
1881	....	....	20.85	....	....	....	SE¼SE¼	2	32	46	3-15—9-15	.170	62.55
1881	....	....		14.25	....	....	SE¼SE¼	2	32	46	3-15—6-13	.116	21.38
1881	....	....	8.08	....	....	....	NW¼NE¼	11	32	46	3-15—9-15	.066	24.24

Source—**Humboldt River.** Ditch—**No. 4.**

1876	....	....	39.67	....	....	....	NE¼NE¼	11	32	46	3-15—9-15	.323	119.01
1876	....	....	26.40	....	....	....	SE¼NE¼	11	32	46	3-15—9-15	.215	79.20
1876	....	....	....	....	12.97	....	SE¼NE¼	11	32	46	3-15—4-28	.105	9.73
1876	....	....	39.64	....	....	....	SW¼NE¼	11	32	46	3-15—9-15	.323	118.92
1876	....	....	26.93	....	....	....	NE¼SW¼	11	32	46	3-15—9-15	.219	80.79
1876	....	....	....	12.62	....	....	NE¼SW¼	11	32	46	3-15—6-13	.103	18.93
1876	....	....	4.42	....	....	....	NW¼SW¼	11	32	46	3-15—9-15	.036	13.26
1876	....	....	....	35.58	....	....	NW¼SW¼	11	32	46	3-15—6-13	.289	53.37
1876	....	....	16.15	....	....	....	SE¼SW¼	11	32	46	3-15—9-15	.131	48.45
1876	....	....	....	....	17.35	....	SE¼SW¼	11	32	46	3-15—4-28	.141	13.01
1876	....	....	26.74	....	....	....	SW¼SW¼	11	32	46	3-15—9-15	.217	80.22
1876	....	....	....	13.23	....	....	SW¼SW¼	11	32	46	3-15—6-13	.108	19.85
1876	....	....	0.79	....	....	....	NE¼NW¼	14	32	46	3-15—9-15	.006	2.37
1876	....	....	....	....	2.30	....	NE¼NW¼	14	32	46	3-15—4-28	.019	1.73
1876	....	....	23.27	....	....	....	NW¼NW¼	14	32	46	3-15—9-15	.189	69.81
1876	....	....	....	13.56	....	....	NW¼NW¼	14	32	46	3-15—6-13	.110	20.34
1876	....	....	....	15.85	....	....	SW¼NW¼	14	32	46	3-15—6-13	.129	23.78
1876	....	....	28.47	....	....	....	NW¼NE¼	11	32	46	3-15—9-15	.231	85.41
1876	....	....	26.07	....	....	....	SE¼NW¼	11	32	46	3-15—9-15	.212	78.21
1876	....	....	....	13.40	....	....	SE¼NW¼	11	32	46	3-15—6-13	.109	20.10
1876	....	....	12.95	....	....	....	NE¼NW¼	12	32	46	3-15—9-15	.106	38.85
1876	....	....	....	....	18.48	....	NE¼NW¼	12	32	46	3-15—4-28	.150	13.86
1876	....	....	27.25	....	....	....	NW¼NW¼	12	32	46	3-15—9-15	.222	81.75
1876	....	....	....	....	12.37	....	NW¼NW¼	12	32	46	3-15—4-28	.101	9.28
1876	....	....	....	....	29.14	....	SW¼NW¼	12	32	46	3-15—4-28	.237	21.86

Source—**Humboldt River.** Ditch—**No. 5.**

1876	....	....	....	....	31.36	....	NE¼SE¼	11	32	46	3-15—4-28	.255	23.52
1876	....	....	8.05	....	....	....	NW¼SE¼	11	32	46	3-15—9-15	.065	24.15
1876	....	....	....	6.97	....	....	NW¼SE¼	11	32	46	3-15—6-13	.057	10.46
1876	....	....	....	....	23.00	....	NW¼SE¼	11	32	46	3-15—4-28	.187	17.25
1876	....	....	....	....	5.17	....	SW¼SE¼	11	32	46	3-15—4-28	.042	3.88

Claimant—**Dean Estate.** Proof No. 00169

Source—**Humboldt River.** Ditch—**McConnell, Johnson.**

1874	....	....	27.07	....	....	....	NW¼NW¼	6	31	49	3-15—9-15	.220	81.21
1874	....	....	....	....	....	4.16	NW¼NW¼	6	31	49	3-15—4-28	.034	3.12
1874	....	....	33.15	....	....	....	NE¼NW¼	6	31	49	3-15—9-15	.270	99.45
1874	....	....	....	....	....	5.41	NE¼NW¼	6	31	49	3-15—4-28	.044	4.06
1874	....	....	31.00	....	....	....	SW¼NW¼	6	31	49	3-15—9-15	.252	63.00
1874	....	....	23.38	....	....	....	SE¼NW¼	6	31	49	3-15—9-15	.190	70.14
1874	....	....	26.12	....	....	....	NW¼NE¼	6	31	49	3-15—9-15	.212	78.36
1874	....	....	....	....	....	2.91	NW¼NE¼	6	31	49	3-15—4-28	.024	2.18
1874	....	....	21.55	....	....	....	NE¼NE¼	6	31	49	3-15—9-15	.175	64.65
1874	....	....	....	....	....	4.58	NE¼NE¼	6	31	49	3-15—4-28	.037	3.44

Dean Estate—Continued.

Year of priority	Culture—Acres: Harvest crops	Meadow pasture	Diversified pasture		Location: Subdivision	Section	Tp.N.	R.E.	Length of season	Duty of water: C.F.S.	Acre-feet
1874	3.85				SW¼NE¼	6	31	49	3-15—9-15	.031	11.55
1897	9.58				NE¼NW¼	8	31	49	3-15—9-15	.078	28.74
1897	11.65				SE¼NW¼	8	31	49	3-15—9-15	.095	31.95
1897	....			3.02	SE¼NW¼	8	31	49	3-15—4-28	.025	2.27
1897	22.98				NW¼NE¼	8	31	49	3-15—9-15	.187	68.94
1897	....			5.72	NW¼NE¼	8	31	49	3-15—4-28	.047	4.29
1874	2.96				NE¼NE¼	8	31	49	3-15—9-15	.024	8.88
1874	....			5.10	NE¼NE¼	8	31	49	3-15—4-28	.041	3.83
1897	13.41				SE¼NE¼	8	31	49	3-15—9-15	.109	40.23
1897	....			5.83	SE¼NE¼	8	31	49	3-15—4-28	.047	4.37
1897	25.06				SW¼NE¼	8	31	49	3-15—9-15	.204	75.18
1897	....			3.43	SW¼NE¼	8	31	49	3-15—4-28	.028	2.57
1897	6.90				NE¼SE¼	8	31	49	3-15—9-15	.056	20.70
1897	....			3.74	NE¼SE¼	8	31	49	3-15—4-28	.030	2.81
1897	2.95				NW¼SE¼	8	31	49	3-15—9-15	.024	8.85

McConnell, 1874. Johnson, 1897.

Claimant—**Ellison Ranching Co.** Proof No. 00170

Source—**Humboldt River.** Ditch—**Bacon Ditch.**

Year of priority	Harvest crops	Meadow pasture	Diversified pasture		Subdivision	Section	Tp.N.	R.E.	Length of season	C.F.S.	Acre-feet
1888	*38.30				NE¼NW¼	13	35	42	3-15—9-15	.311	114.90
1888	....		0.95		NE¼NW¼	13	35	42	3-15—4-28	.008	.71
1888	*27.25				SE¼NW¼	13	35	42	3-15—9-15	.222	81.75
1888	....		6.75		SE¼NW¼	13	35	42	3-15—4-28	.055	5.06
1888	*29.15				NW¼NW¼	13	35	42	3-15—9-15	.237	87.45
1888	....		8.00		NW¼NW¼	13	35	42	3-15—4-28	.065	6.00
1888	*10.00				SW¼NW¼	13	35	42	3-15—9-15	.081	30.00
1888	....		3.30		SW¼NW¼	13	35	42	3-15—4-28	.027	2.48
1888	*0.26				NE¼SW¼	13	35	42	3-15—9-15	.002	.78
1888	....		12.52		NE¼SW¼	13	35	42	3-15—4-28	.102	9.39
1888	*32.99				SE¼SW¼	12	35	42	3-15—9-15	.268	98.97
1888	....		2.15		SE¼SW¼	12	35	42	3-15—4-28	.017	1.61
1888	*39.65				SW¼SW¼	12	35	42	3-15—9-15	.322	118.95
1888	*1.98				NE¼NE¼	13	35	42	3-15—9-15	.016	5.94
1888	....		4.50		NE¼NE¼	13	35	42	3-15—4-28	.037	3.38
1888	*27.32				SE¼NE¼	13	35	42	3-15—9-15	.222	81.96
1888	....		3.00		SE¼NE¼	13	35	42	3-15—4-28	.024	2.25
1888	*11.45				NW¼NE¼	13	35	42	3-15—9-15	.093	34.45
1888	....		22.27		NW¼NE¼	13	35	42	3-15—4-28	.181	16.70
1888	*21.54				SW¼NE¼	13	35	42	3-15—9-15	.175	61.62
1888	....	2.28			SW¼NE¼	13	35	42	3-15—6-13	.019	3.42
1888	....		16.05		SW¼NE¼	13	35	42	3-15—4-28	.130	13.14
1888	*27.00				NE¼SE¼	13	35	42	3-15—9-15	.224	82.80
1888			0.30		NE¼SE¼	13	35	42	3-15—4-28	.002	.23
1888				0.35	NE¼SE¼	13	35	42	3-15—4-28	.003	.26
1888	*33.90				SE¼SE¼	13	35	42	3-15—9-15	.276	101.70
1888			0.25		SE¼SE¼	13	35	42	3-15—4-28	.002	.19
1888				1.10	SE¼SE¼	13	35	42	3-15—4-28	.009	.83

1888			*8.55				NW¼SE¼	13	35	42	3-15—9-15	.070	25.65
1888					9.46		NW¼SE¼	13	35	42	3-15—4-28	.077	7.10
1888			*1.25				SW¼SE¼	13	35	42	3-15—9-15	.010	3.75
1888					0.60		SW¼SE¼	13	35	42	3-15—4-28	.005	.40

*Was Class C pasture—1876.

Source—**Humboldt River.** Ditch—**Big Slough.**

1880			17.02				SE¼SW¼	19	34	44	3-15—9-15	.138	51.06
1880						8.66	NW¼SW¼	19	34	44	3-15—4-28	.070	6.50
1880			12.73				SW¼SW¼	19	34	44	3-15—9-15	.103	38.19
1880			30.36				NE¼NW¼	30	34	44	3-15—9-15	.247	91.08
1880			12.04				NW¼NW¼	30	34	44	3-15—9-15	.098	36.12
1880						5.15	NW¼NW¼	30	34	44	3-15—4-28	.042	3.86
1880				5.95			NE¼NE¼	25	34	43	3-15—6-13	.048	8.93
1880					15.90		NE¼SE¼	24	34	43	3-15—4-28	.129	11.93
1880						8.64	NE¼SE¼	24	34	43	3-15—4-28	.070	6.48
1880			22.93				SE¼SE¼	24	34	43	3-15—9-15	.186	68.79
1880					7.16		SE¼SE¼	24	34	43	3-15—4-28	.058	5.37
1880						0.93	SE¼SE¼	24	34	43	3-15—4-28	.008	0.70
1880			0.54				NW¼SE¼	24	34	43	3-15—9-15	.004	1.62
1880					37.66		NW¼SE¼	24	34	43	3-15—4-28	.306	28.25
1880				22.28			SE¼NW¼	24	34	43	3-15—6-13	.181	33.12
1880				27.90			SW¼NW¼	24	34	43	3-15—6-13	.227	41.85
1880					3.45		SW¼NW¼	24	34	43	3-15—4-28	.028	2.50
1880				17.77			NE¼SW¼	24	34	43	3-15—6-13	.144	26.66
1880				4.00			NW¼SW¼	24	34	43	3-15—6-13	.032	6.00
1880			2.20				SW¼SE¼	24	34	44	3-15—9-15	.018	6.60
1880				0.66			SW¼SE¼	24	34	44	3-15—6-13	.005	0.90
1880					5.71		SW¼SE¼	24	34	43	3-15—4-28	.046	4.28
1880						4.32	SW¼SE¼	24	34	43	3-15—4-28	.035	3.24
1880					12.68		SE¼SE¼	24	34	43	3-15—4-28	.103	9.51
1880					9.45		SE¼NW¼	14	34	43	3-15—4-28	.077	7.09
1880				26.50			SW¼NW¼	14	34	43	3-15—6-13	.215	39.75
1880					27.72		NE¼SW¼	14	34	43	3-15—4-28	.225	21.89
1880				34.45			SE¼SW¼	14	34	43	3-15—6-13	.280	51.68
1880					6.78		SE¼SW¼	14	34	43	3-15—4-28	.065	5.09
1880				23.09			NW¼SW¼	14	34	43	3-15—6-13	.188	34.64
1880					16.96		NW¼SW¼	14	34	43	3-15—4-28	.139	12.72
1880					1.95		SW¼SW¼	14	34	43	3-15—4-28	.016	1.46
1880						21.35	SW¼SW¼	14	34	43	3-15—4-28	.174	16.01
1880					25.42		SW¼SE¼	10	34	43	3-15—4-28	.207	19.07
1880			1.19				SE¼NW¼	10	34	43	3-15—9-15	.010	3.57
1880					23.10		NW¼NW¼	10	34	43	3-15—4-28	.188	17.33
1880			3.62				SW¼NW¼	10	34	43	3-15—9-15	.029	10.86
1880				12.28			SW¼NW¼	10	34	43	3-15—6-13	.100	18.42
1880						24.50	SW¼NW¼	10	34	43	3-15—4-28	.199	18.38
1880			4.21				NE¼SW¼	10	34	43	3-15—9-15	.034	12.63
1880						27.38	NE¼SW¼	10	34	43	3-15—4-28	.227	20.53
1880						38.65	SE¼SW¼	10	34	43	3-15—4-28	.314	28.99
1880				21.15			NW¼SW¼	10	34	43	3-15—6-13	.172	31.73
1880						18.85	NW¼SW¼	10	34	43	3-15—4-28	.153	14.14
1880				39.94			SW¼SW¼	10	34	43	3-15—6-13	.325	59.91

Ellison Ranching Co.—Continued.

Year of priority	Culture—Acres: Harvest crops	Meadow pasture	Diversified pasture		Location: Subdivision	Section	Tp. N.	R. E.	Length of season	Duty of water: C. F. S.	Acre-feet
1889				40.20	SE¼ NE¼	15	34	43	3-15—4-28	.327	30.15
1889				20.10	NW¼ NE¼	15	34	43	3-15—4-28	.163	15.08
1889			30.57		NE¼ NE¼	23	34	43	3-15—4-28	.322	29.68
1889			12.17		SE¼ NE¼	23	34	43	3-15—4-28	.099	9.15
1889			5.70		NW¼ NE¼	23	34	43	3-15—4-28	.046	4.28
1889				34.50	NW¼ NE¼	23	34	43	3-15—4-28	.280	25.88
1889				40.00	SW¼ NE¼	23	34	43	3-15—4-28	.325	30.00
1889			7.00		NE¼ SE¼	23	34	43	3-15—4-28	.057	5.25
1889			21.70		NW¼ SE¼	23	34	43	3-15—4-28	.176	16.28
1889			18.50		NE¼ NW¼	23	34	43	3-15—4-28	.150	13.88
1889				21.90	NE¼ NW¼	23	34	43	3-15—4-28	.178	16.43
1889			17.00		SE¼ NW¼	23	34	43	3-15—4-28	.138	12.75
1889				19.65	SE¼ NW¼	23	34	43	3-15—4-28	.160	14.74
1889			9.88		NW¼ NW¼	23	34	43	3-15—4-28	.080	7.41
1889			2.65		SW¼ NW¼	23	34	43	3-15—4-28	.022	2.00
1889	1.65				NE¼ NE¼	9	34	43	3-15—9-15	.014	4.95
1889		1.35			NE¼ NE¼	9	34	43	3-15—6-13	.011	2.03
1889			1.44		NE¼ NE¼	9	34	43	3-15—4-28	.012	1.08
1889				35.84	NE¼ NE¼	9	34	43	3-15—4-28	.292	26.88
1889	15.92				SE¼ NE¼	9	34	43	3-15—9-15	.129	47.76
1889		2.23			SE¼ NE¼	9	34	43	3-15—6-13	.018	3.35
1889				19.58	SE¼ NE¼	9	34	43	3-15—4-28	.159	14.69
1889	10.00				NW¼ NE¼	9	34	43	3-15—9-15	.081	30.00
1889		10.68			NW¼ NE¼	9	34	43	3-15—6-13	.087	16.02
1889				19.88	NW¼ NE¼	9	34	43	3-15—4-28	.162	14.91
1889	24.70				SW¼ NE¼	9	34	43	3-15—9-15	.201	74.10
1889				16.00	SW¼ NE¼	9	34	43	3-15—4-28	.130	12.00
1889	23.46				NE¼ SE¼	9	34	43	3-15—9-15	.191	70.38
1889				16.59	NE¼ SE¼	9	34	43	3-15—4-28	.135	12.44
1889	0.25				SE¼ SE¼	9	34	43	3-15—9-15	.002	0.75
1889	5.35				NE¼ NW¼	9	34	43	3-15—9-15	.043	16.05
1889				34.01	NE¼ NW¼	9	34	43	3-15—4-28	.277	25.51
1889	6.60				SE¼ NW¼	9	34	43	3-15—9-15	.054	19.80
1889		33.40			SE¼ NW¼	9	34	43	3-15—6-13	.272	50.10
1889		9.99			NE¼ SE¼	4	34	43	3-15—6-13	.081	14.99
1889				37.40	SE¼ SE¼	4	34	43	3-15—4-28	.304	28.05
1889				15.26	SW¼ SE¼	4	34	43	3-15—4-28	.124	11.55
1889		15.22			NE¼ NW¼	4	34	43	3-15—6-13	.124	22.83
1889			3.55		SE¼ SW¼	4	34	43	3-15—4-28	.029	2.66
1889			11.98		SW¼ SW¼	4	34	43	3-15—4-28	.097	8.99

Source—Humboldt River. Ditch—Section 11 Ditch.

Year of priority	Harvest crops	Meadow pasture	Diversified pasture		Subdivision	Section	Tp. N.	R. E.	Length of season	C. F. S.	Acre-feet
1887		8.64			NW¼ NE¼	11	34	43	3-15—6-13	.070	12.96
1887	22.50				SW¼ NE¼	11	34	43	3-15—9-15	.183	67.40
1887			8.74		NE¼ SE¼	11	34	43	3-15—4-28	.071	6.56
1887		22.32			NE¼ NW¼	11	34	43	3-15—6-13	.181	33.48

	1887			4.70				NW¼SW¼	2	34	43	3-15—9-15	.038	14.10
	1887					5.65		NW¼SW¼	2	34	43	3-15—4-28	.056	4.21
	1887						7.40	NW¼SW¼	2	34	43	3-15—4-28	.000	5.55
	1887			2.63				SW¼SW¼	2	34	43	3-15—9-15	.021	7.80
	1887						29.80	SW¼SW¼	2	34	43	3-15—4-28	.212	22.35
	1887					21.53		SW¼NE¼	3	34	43	3-15—4-28	.175	16.15
	1887			3.40				NE¼SE¼	3	34	43	3-15—9-15	.028	10.20
	1887					14.93		NE¼SE¼	3	34	43	3-15—4-28	.121	11.20
	1887					1.84		SE¼SE¼	3	34	43	3-15—4-28	.015	1.38
	1887						9.75	SE¼SE¼	3	34	43	3-15—4-28	.079	7.31
	1887				5.78			NW¼SE¼	3	34	43	3-15—6-13	.047	8.67
	1887					26.67		NW¼SE¼	3	34	43	3-15—4-28	.217	20.00
	1887						7.81	SW¼SE¼	3	34	43	3-15—4-28	.063	5.86
	1887					38.14		SE¼NW¼	3	34	43	3-15—4-28	.310	28.61
	1887					14.90		NW¼SW¼	3	34	43	3-15—4-28	.121	11.18
	1887					11.62		NW¼SW¼	3	34	43	3-15—4-28	.094	8.72

Source—Humboldt River. Ditch—Wilcox.

	1877			13.44				NW¼SW¼	19	34	44	3-15—9-15	.109	40.32
	1877			6.29				NE¼SE¼	24	34	43	3-15—9-15	.051	18.87
	1877				9.92			NE¼SE¼	24	34	43	3-15—6-13	.081	14.88
	1877					8.79		SE¼NE¼	24	34	43	3-15—4-28	.071	6.59
	1877					4.50		NW¼NE¼	24	34	43	3-15—4-28	.037	3.38
	1877				18.86			SW¼NE¼	24	34	43	3-15—6-13	.163	28.29
	1877					5.00		NW¼NW¼	13	34	43	3-15—4-28	.041	3.75
	1877					29.48		SW¼NW¼	13	34	43	3-15—4-28	.240	22.11
	1877				16.95			NE¼SW¼	13	34	43	3-15—6-13	.138	25.43
	1877				28.20			SE¼SW¼	13	34	43	3-15—6-18	.229	42.30
	1877					40.00		NW¼SW¼	13	34	43	3-15—4-28	.325	30.00
	1877					38.60		SW¼SW¼	13	34	43	3-15—4-28	.314	28.96
	1877						37.80	NE¼NW¼	24	34	43	3-15—4-28	.307	28.35
	1877						13.35	SE¼NW¼	24	34	43	3-15—4-28	.109	10.01
	1877				40.00			NW¼NW¼	24	34	43	3-15—6-13	.325	60.00
	1877						7.35	SW¼NW¼	24	34	43	3-15—4-28	.000	5.51
	1877			0.40				SE¼SE¼	11	34	43	3-15—9-15	.003	1.20
	1877				1.15			SE¼SE¼	11	34	43	3-15—6-13	.009	1.73
	1877						10.00	SE¼SE¼	11	34	43	3-15—4-28	.081	7.50
	1877					3.40		SW¼SE¼	11	34	43	3-15—4-28	.028	2.55
	1877					9.50		NW¼SW¼	11	34	43	3-15—4-28	.077	7.13
	1877					4.50		SW¼SW¼	11	34	43	3-15—4-28	.037	3.38
	1877					37.21		NE¼NE¼	14	34	43	3-15—4-28	.303	27.91
	1877					40.00		SE¼NE¼	14	34	43	3-15—4-28	.325	30.00
	1877					18.15		NW¼NE¼	14	34	43	3-15—4-28	.107	9.86
	1877					25.90		SW¼NE¼	14	34	43	3-15—4-28	.211	19.42
	1877						40.00	NE¼SE¼	14	34	43	3-15—4-28	.325	30.00
	1877					27.05		SE¼SE¼	14	34	43	3-15—4-28	.220	20.29
	1877						30.50	SE¼NW¼	14	34	43	3-15—4-28	.248	22.88
	1877					8.90		NW¼NW¼	14	34	43	3-15—4-28	.072	6.68
	1877						30.00	NW¼NW¼	14	34	43	3-15—4-28	.244	22.50
	1877					13.90		SW¼NW¼	14	34	43	3-15—4-28	.113	10.43
	1877						12.46	NE¼SW¼	14	34	43	3-15—4-28	.101	9.35
	1877				9.00			NE¼SE¼	4	34	43	3-15—6-13	.073	13.50
	1877					14.85		SW¼SE¼	10	34	43	3-15—4-28	.120	11.14

Ellison Ranching Co.—Continued.

Year of priority	Culture—Acres: Harvest crops	Meadow pasture	Diversified pasture		Location: Subdivision	Section	Tp.N.	R.E.	Length of season	Duty of water: C.F.S.	Acre-feet
1877			13.95		NE¼NE¼	10	34	43	3-15—4-28	.113	10.46
1877			17.10		SE¼NE¼	10	34	43	3-15—4-28	.139	12.83
1877				26.70	NW¼NE¼	10	34	43	3-15—4-28	.217	20.00
1877				39.25	SW¼NE¼	10	34	43	3-15—4-28	.319	29.44
1877				40.00	NE¼SE¼	10	34	43	3-15—4-28	.325	30.00
1877				39.95	SE¼SE¼	10	34	43	3-15—4-28	.325	29.96
1877				39.60	NW¼SE¼	10	34	43	3-15—4-28	.322	29.70
1877				40.29	NE¼NW¼	10	34	43	3-15—4-28	.328	30.22
1877				38.50	SE¼NW¼	10	34	43	3-15—4-28	.313	28.88
1877			15.59		NW¼NW¼	10	34	43	3-15—4-28	.127	11.69
1877				8.00	NE¼SW¼	10	34	43	3-15—4-28	.065	6.00
1877				20.45	SE¼SW¼	3	34	43	3-15—4-28	.166	15.34
1877				37.82	SW¼SW¼	3	34	43	3-15—4-28	.307	28.37

Source—**Humboldt River.** Ditch—**Overflow.**

Year of priority	Harvest crops	Meadow pasture	Diversified pasture		Subdivision	Section	Tp.N.	R.E.	Length of season	C.F.S.	Acre-feet
1880	6.15				SE¼SE¼	19	34	44	3-15—9-15	.050	18.45
1880			19.47		SE¼SE¼	19	34	44	3-15—4-28	.158	14.60
1880	7.23				NW¼SE¼	19	34	44	3-15—9-15	.059	21.69
1880			5.42		NW¼SE¼	19	34	44	3-15—4-28	.044	4.07
1880	19.77				SW¼SE¼	19	34	44	3-15—9-15	.161	59.71
1880			15.40		SW¼SE¼	19	34	44	3-15—4-28	.125	11.55
1880	11.19				NE¼SW¼	19	34	44	3-15—9-15	.091	33.57
1880			23.52		NE¼SW¼	19	34	44	3-15—4-28	.191	17.54
1878			14.34		SE¼SW¼	19	34	44	3-15—4-28	.117	10.76
1878			12.87		NW¼SW¼	19	34	44	3-15—4-28	.105	9.65
1879	25.16				NE¼NE¼	30	34	44	3-15—9-15	.205	75.48
1879			7.60		NE¼NE¼	30	34	44	3-15—4-28	.062	5.70
1879	16.81				SE¼NE¼	30	34	44	3-15—9-15	.137	50.43
1879			12.69		SE¼NE¼	30	34	44	3-15—4-28	.103	9.52
1879	16.66				NW¼NE¼	30	34	44	3-15—9-15	.135	49.98
1879			16.40		NW¼NE¼	30	34	44	3-15—4-28	.133	12.30
1879	2.19				SW¼NE¼	30	34	44	3-15—9-15	.018	6.57
1879			3.36		SW¼NE¼	30	34	44	3-15—4-28	.027	2.52
1879	7.25				NE¼SE¼	30	34	44	3-15—9-15	.059	21.75
1879			7.60		NE¼SE¼	30	34	44	3-15—4-28	.062	5.70
1878			5.20		NE¼NW¼	30	34	44	3-15—4-28	.042	3.90
1878			9.25		SW¼SW¼	30	34	44	3-15—4-28	.075	6.94
1878			2.23		NE¼NW¼	19	34	44	3-15—4-28	.018	1.67
1880	4.67				SE¼NW¼	19	34	44	3-15—9-15	.038	14.01
1880			4.50		SE¼NW¼	19	34	44	3-15—4-28	.037	3.38
1880				10.33	SE¼NW¼	19	34	44	3-15—4-28	.084	7.75
1880	9.34				NW¼NW¼	19	34	44	3-15—9-15	.070	[illegible]
1880			2.33		NW¼NW¼	19	34	44	3-15—4-28	.019	1.71
1880				21.00	NW¼NW¼	19	34	44	3-15—4-28	.170	10.25
1880	11.65				SW¼NW¼	19	34	44	3-15—9-15	[illegible]	[illegible]
1880			18.14		SW¼NW¼	19	34	44	3-15—4-28	[illegible]	[illegible]

	1880						.66	SW¼NW¼	19	34	41	3 15—4-28	.005	.40
	1878					19.04		NE¼NE¼	24	34	43	3-15—4-28	.135	14.28
	1880			22.00				SE¼NE¼	24	34	43	3-15—9-15	.179	66.00
	1880				6.22			SE¼NE¼	24	34	43	3-15—6-13	.051	9.33
	1880						.42	SE¼NE¼	24	34	43	3-15—4-28	.003	.32
	1879				31.30			NW¼NE¼	24	34	43	3-15—6-13	.254	46.95
	1877						11.15	NW¼SE¼	13	34	43	3-15—4-28	.091	8.36
	1879				5.05			SW¼SE¼	13	34	43	3-15—6-13	.041	7.58
	1879					25.55		SW¼SE¼	13	34	43	3-15—4-28	.208	10.16
	1878					9.11		NE¼NW¼	13	34	43	3-15—4-28	.074	6.83
	1879				24.26			SE¼NW¼	13	34	43	3-15—6-13	.197	36.30
	1879				22.99			NW¼NW¼	13	34	43	3-15—6-13	.187	34.37
	1879				6.47			SW¼NW¼	13	34	43	3-15—6-13	.054	9.71
	1879				23.05			NE¼SW¼	13	34	43	3-15—6-13	.187	34.58
	1879				6.90			SE¼SW¼	13	34	43	3-15—6-13	.056	10.35
	1878					7.20		SW¼SW¼	12	34	43	3-15—4-28	.059	5.40
	1878					5.23		SE¼NE¼	11	34	43	3-15—4-28	.043	3.92
	1878					15.88		NW¼NE¼	11	34	43	3-15—4-28	.129	11.91
	1879				16.29			NE¼SE¼	11	34	43	3-15—6-13	.132	24.44
	1878					22.04		SE¼SE¼	11	34	43	3-15—4-28	.179	16.53
	1880			4.96				NE¼NW¼	11	34	43	3-15—9-15	.040	14.88
	1880					11.63		NE¼NW¼	11	34	43	3-15—4-28	.095	8.83
	1879				2.79			NE¼NE¼	14	34	43	3-15—6-13	.023	4.19
	1879				9.14			NE¼NE¼	4	34	43	3-15—6-13	.074	13.71
	1879					24.11		NE¼NE¼	4	34	43	3-15—4-28	.196	18.08
	1879				4.87			NW¼NE¼	4	24	43	3-15—6-13	.040	7.31
	1879					30.07		NW¼NE¼	4	34	43	3-15—4-28	.244	22.55
	1878					16.07		NE¼NW¼	4	34	43	3-15—4-28	.131	12.05
	1879				21.40			SW¼NW¼	4	34	43	3-15—6-13	.175	32.10
	1879					9.60		SW¼NW¼	4	34	43	3-15—4-28	.078	7.20
	1879				6.80			SW¼SW¼	34	35	43	3-15—6-13	.055	10.20
	1879					13.30		SW¼SW¼	34	35	43	3-15—4-28	.108	9.98
	1878					3.88		SW¼SE¼	2	34	43	3-15—4-28	.032	2.91
	1877						8.83	NE¼SW¼	2	34	43	3-15—4-28	.072	6.62
	1878					3.95		SW¼SW¼	2	34	43	3-15—4-28	.032	2.96
	1880			2.11				SE¼NE¼	3	34	43	3-15—9-15	.017	6.33
	1880						6.12	SE¼NE¼	3	34	43	3-15—4-28	.050	4.59
	1878					9.60		NW¼NE¼	3	34	43	3-15—4-28	.078	7.20
	1878						1.75	NW¼NE¼	3	34	43	3-15—4-28	.014	1.31
	1877						12.80	SW¼NE¼	3	34	43	3-15—4-28	.104	9.60
	1877						14.04	NE¼SE¼	3	34	43	3-15—4-28	.114	10.53
	1877						7.75	NW¼SE¼	3	34	43	3-15—4-28	.063	5.81
	1879				9.63			NE¼NW¼	3	34	43	3-15—6-13	.078	14.45
	1879					23.22		NE¼NW¼	3	34	43	3-15—4-28	.189	17.42
	1878					14.86		NW¼NW¼	3	34	43	3-15—4-28	.121	11.15
	1878						21.21	NW¼NW¼	3	34	43	3-15—4-28	.197	18.16
	1879				1.00			SW¼NW¼	3	34	43	3-15—6-13	.008	1.50
	1879					3.92		SW¼NW¼	3	34	43	3-15—4-28	.032	2.94
	1879					6.92		NE¼SW¼	3	34	43	3-15—4-28	.056	5.19
	1879				4.80			SE¼SW¼	34	35	43	3-15—6-13	.041	7.34
	1879					3.06		SE¼SW¼	34	35	43	3-15—4-28	.025	2.30

Ellison Ranching Co.—Continued.
Source—**Humboldt River.** Ditch—**No. 8.**

Year of priority	Culture—Acres: Harvest crops	Meadow pasture	Diversified pasture		Location: Subdivision	Section	Tp. N.	R. E.	Length of season	Duty of water: C. F. S.	Acre-feet
1877	13.20				SW¼SW¼	19	34	44	3-15—9-15	.107	39.60
1877	14.39				NE¼NE¼	24	34	43	3-15—9-15	.117	43.17
1877				3.45	NW¼NE¼	13	34	43	3-15—4-28	.028	2.59
1877			14.85		SW¼NE¼	13	34	43	3-15—4-28	.121	11.14
1877				14.25	SW¼NE¼	13	34	43	3-15—4-28	.117	10.69
1877				1.01	SE¼NE¼	13	34	43	3-15—4-28	.008	.76
1877		7.20			NE¼SE¼	13	34	43	3-15—6-13	.059	10.80
1877				15.45	NE¼SE¼	13	34	43	3-15—4-28	.126	11.59
1877	13.83				SE¼SE¼	13	34	43	3-15—9-15	.112	41.49
1877		22.20			SE¼SE¼	13	34	43	3-15—6-13	.180	33.30
1877			2.26		SE¼SE¼	13	34	43	3-15—4-28	.018	1.70
1877		24.00			NW¼SE¼	13	34	43	3-15—6-13	.195	36.00
1877		29.81			NE¼NW¼	13	34	43	3-15—6-13	.242	44.72
1877			9.19		SE¼NW¼	13	34	43	3-15—4-28	.075	6.89
1877			6.34		NW¼NW¼	13	34	43	3-15—4-28	.052	4.76
1877		4.16			SE¼SW¼	12	34	43	3-15—6-13	.034	6.24
1877			2.91		SE¼SW¼	12	34	43	3-15—4-28	.024	2.18
1877		21.50			NW¼SW¼	12	34	43	3-15—6-13	.175	32.25
1877		31.70			SW¼SW¼	12	34	43	3-15—6-13	.258	47.55
1877	3.96				NE¼NE¼	11	34	43	3-15—9-15	.032	11.88
1877		25.96			NE¼NE¼	11	34	43	3-15—6-13	.211	38.94
1877			1.55		NE¼NE¼	11	34	43	3-15—4-28	.013	1.16
1877	20.70				SE¼NE¼	11	34	43	3-15—9-15	.168	62.10
1877		12.42			SE¼NE¼	11	34	43	3-15—6-13	.101	18.63
1877	9.33				NW¼NE¼	11	34	43	3-15—9-15	.076	27.99
1877			12.25		SW¼NE¼	11	34	43	3-15—4-28	.100	9.19
1877	11.06				NE¼SE¼	11	34	43	3-15—9-15	.090	33.18
1877	6.30				SE¼NW¼	11	34	43	3-15—9-15	.051	18.90
1877		6.70			SE¼NW¼	11	34	43	3-15—6-13	.054	10.05
1877		14.35			NW¼NW¼	11	34	43	3-15—6-13	.117	21.53
1877				30.90	SW¼SE¼	2	34	43	3-15—4-28	.251	23.18
1877	1.37				NE¼SW¼	2	24	43	3-15—9-15	.011	4.11
1877			3.55		NE¼SW¼	2	34	43	3-15—4-28	.029	2.66
1877			3.88		SE¼SW¼	2	34	43	3-15—4-28	.032	2.91
1877				5.60	SE¼SW¼	2	34	43	3-15—4-28	.045	5.20

Claimant—**William Dunphy Estate.** Proof No. 00171
Source—**Humboldt River.** Ditch—**Humboldt Slough No. 2.**

1890		2.40			SE¼SE¼	36	33	46	3-15—6-13	.020	3.00
1890		21.70			SE¼SW¼	31	33	47	3-15—6-13	.176	32.55
1890			4.25		SE¼SW¼	31	33	47	3-15—4-28	.035	3.19
1890		20.55			SW¼SW¼	31	33	47	3-15—6-13	.167	30.83
1890			13.80		SW¼SW¼	31	33	47	3-15—4-28	.112	10.35
1890		9.30			SW¼SE¼	31	33	47	3-15—6-13	.170	14.04

1890					8.85		SW¼SE¼	31	33	47	3-15—4-28	.072	6.64
1890				12.00			SE¼SE¼	31	33	47	3-15—6-13	.098	18.00
1890					22.60		SE¼SE¼	31	33	47	3-15—4-28	.184	16.95
1890					24.30		SE¼SW¼	32	33	47	3-15—4-28	.198	18.23
1890					18.80		SW¼SW¼	32	33	47	3-15—4-28	.153	14.10

Source—**Humboldt River.** Ditch—**White House Ditch No. 1.**

1886			4.85				NE¼NW¼	26	33	47	3-15—9-15	.039	14.55
1886			39.25				NW¼NE¼	26	33	47	3-15—9-15	.319	117.75
1886			15.85				SW¼NE¼	26	33	47	3-15—9-15	.129	47.55
1886			15.55				SE¼NE¼	26	33	47	3-15—9-15	.126	46.65
1886			37 20				NE¼NE¼	26	33	47	3-15—9-15	.302	111.60

Source—**Humboldt River.** Ditch—**South Branch White House Slough.**

1887			14.80				SW¼NW¼	27	33	47	3-15—9-15	.120	44.40
1887			16.90				SE¼NW¼	27	?3	47	3-15—9-15	.137	50.70
1887			36.15				NE¼NW¼	27	33	47	3-15—9-15	.294	108.45
1887			38.10				NW¼NE¼	27	33	47	3-15—9-15	.310	114.30
1887			16.00				SW¼NE¼	27	33	47	3-15—9-15	.130	48.00
1887			15.45				SE¼NE¼	27	33	47	3-15—9-15	.126	46.35
1887			37.00				NE¼NE¼	27	33	47	3-15—9-15	.301	111.00
1887			37.75				NW¼NW¼	26	33	47	3-15—9-15	.307	113.25
1887			15.50				SW¼NW¼	26	33	47	3-15—9-15	.126	46.50
1887			14.20				SE¼NW¼	26	33	47	3-15—9-15	.115	42.60
1887			32.80				NE¼NW¼	26	33	47	3-15—9-15	.267	98.40
1887			30.30				SE¼SE¼	23	33	47	3-15—9-15	.246	90.90
1887				5.95			SE¼SE¼	23	33	47	3-15—6-13	.048	8.93
1887				35.25			NE¼SE¼	23	33	47	3-15—6-13	.287	52.88
1887			34.70				SW¼SE¼	23	33	47	3-15—9-15	.282	104.10
1887				2.60			SW¼SE¼	23	33	47	3-15—6-13	.021	3.90

Source—**Humboldt River.** Ditch—**Big Slough.**

1902					2.00		NW¼NW¼	26	33	48	3-15—4-28	.016	1.50
1902					8.80		SW¼NW¼	26	33	48	3-15—4-28	.072	6.60
1902				8.20			NE¼NE¼	27	33	48	3-15—6-13	.067	12.30
1902					.70		NE¼NE¼	27	33	48	3-15—4-28	.006	.53
1902				14.85			SE¼NE¼	27	33	48	3-15—6-13	.121	22.38
1902					4.05		SE¼NE¼	27	33	48	3-15—4-28	.033	3.04
1902				.60			NW¼NE¼	27	33	48	3-15—6-13	.005	.90
1902					9.90		NW¼NE¼	27	33	48	3-15—4-28	.080	7.43
1902				5.65			SW¼NE¼	27	33	48	3-15—6-13	.046	8.48
1902					6.85		SW¼NE¼	27	33	48	3-15—4-28	.056	5.14
1902				12.30			NE¼NW¼	27	33	48	3-15—6-13	.100	18.45
1902					7.25		NE¼NW¼	27	33	48	3-15—4-28	.059	5.44
1902				7.95			SE¼NW¼	27	33	48	3-15—6-13	.065	11.93
1902					6.95		SE¼NW¼	27	33	48	3-15—4-28	.057	5.21
1902				7.15			SW¼NW¼	27	33	48	3-15—6-13	.058	10.73
1902					1.50		SW¼NW¼	27	33	48	3-15—4-28	.012	1.13
1902				15.55			SW¼NW¼	26	33	48	3-15—6-13	.126	23.33
1902					3.05		SW¼NW¼	26	33	48	3-15—4-28	.025	2.29
1902				.80			SE¼NW¼	26	33	48	3-15—6-13	.007	1.00

William Dunphy Estate—Continued.

Source—**Humboldt River.** Ditch—**Mosel Slough.**

Year of priority	Culture—Acres: Harvest crops	Culture—Acres: Meadow pasture	Culture—Acres: Diversified pasture		Location: Subdivision	Location: Section	Location: Tp.N.	Location: R.E.	Length of season	Duty of water: C.F.S.	Duty of water: Acre-feet
1873		9.95			NE¼NE¼	3	32	47	3-15—6-13	.081	14.93
1873		18.50			NW¼NE¼	3	32	47	3-15—6-13	.150	27.75
1873		35.45			SE¼NE¼	3	32	47	3-15—6-13	.288	53.18
1873		21.35			SW¼NE¼	3	32	47	3-15—6-13	.174	32.04

Source—**Humboldt** River. Ditch—**South Fork Ditch No. 1.**

Year of priority	Harvest crops	Meadow pasture	Diversified pasture		Subdivision	Section	Tp.N.	R.E.	Length of season	C.F.S.	Acre-feet
1891			5.90		NE¼NW¼	33	33	48	3-15—4-28	.048	4.43
1891			7.45		NE¼SW¼	28	33	48	3-15—4-28	.061	5.59
1891			9.00		SE¼SW¼	28	33	48	3-15—4-28	.073	6.75
1891			26.00		NW¼SE¼	28	33	48	3-15—4-28	.211	19.50
1891			32.40		SW¼SE¼	28	33	48	3-15—4-28	.263	24.30
1891			27.95		SE¼SE¼	28	33	48	3-15—4-28	.227	20.96
1891				2.25	SE¼SE¼	28	33	48	3-15—4-28	.017	1.69
1891			28.80		NE¼SE¼	28	33	48	3-15—4-28	.234	21.60
1891			2.85		SW¼NE¼	28	33	48	3-15—4-28	.022	2.14

Source—**Humboldt River.** Ditch—**South Fork Slough.**

Year of priority	Harvest crops	Meadow pasture	Diversified pasture		Subdivision	Section	Tp.N.	R.E.	Length of season	C.F.S.	Acre-feet
1891		10.75			SE¼NW¼	27	33	48	3-15—6-13	.087	16.13
1891			8.40		SE¼NW¼	27	33	48	3-15—4-28	.068	6.30
1891		27.60			NW¼SW¼	27	33	48	3-15—6-13	.224	41.40
1891			5.25		NW¼SW¼	27	33	48	3-15—4-28	.043	3.94
1891		27.30			SW¼SW¼	27	33	48	3-15—6-13	.222	40.95
1891		12.95			SE¼SW¼	27	33	48	3-15—6-13	.105	19.43
1891		36.45			NE¼SW¼	27	33	48	3-15—6-13	.296	54.68
1801			2.80		NE¼SW¼	27	33	48	3-15—4-28	.023	2.10
1891		27.85			NW¼SE¼	27	33	48	3-15—6-13	.226	41.78
1891			2.45		NW¼SE¼	27	23	48	3-15—4-28	.020	1.84
1891		2.10			SW¼SE¼	27	33	48	3-15—6-13	.017	3.15
1891			0.40		SW¼SE¼	27	33	48	3-15—4-28	.003	0.30

Source—**Humboldt River.** Ditch—**Farrel Slough.**

Year of priority	Harvest crops	Meadow pasture	Diversified pasture		Subdivision	Section	Tp.N.	R.E.	Length of season	C.F.S.	Acre-feet
1888			32.35		SW¼NW¼	32	33	48	3-15—4-28	.263	24.26
1888			33.80		SE¼NW¼	32	33	48	3-15—4-28	.275	25.35
1888			23.10		NW¼SW¼	32	33	48	3-15—4-28	.207	17.33
1888				5.50	NW¼SW¼	32	33	48	3-15—4-28	.064	4.13
1888			8.60		NE¼SW¼	32	33	48	3-15—4-28	.080	6.45
1888				19.10	NE¼SW¼	32	33	48	3-15—4-28	.174	14.33
1888			35.45		NW¼NE¼	32	33	48	3-15—4-28	.288	26.59
1898			26.75		SW¼NE¼	32	33	48	3-15—4-28	.217	20.06
1888			13.55		SE¼NE¼	32	33	48	3-15—4-28	.129	10.16
1888			37.70		NE¼NE¼	32	33	48	3-15—4-28	.307	28.28
1888		34.05			SW¼SW¼	28	33	48	3-15—6-13	.277	51.08
1888			.45		SW¼SW¼	28	33	48	3-15—4-28	.004	0.34

1888	26.70			SE¼SW¼	28	33	48	3-15—6-13	.217	40.05
1888	38.00			NW¼NW¼	33	33	48	3-15—6-13	.309	57.00
1888	2.35			SW¼NW¼	33	33	48	3-15—6-13	.019	3.53
1888	21.30			NE¼NW¼	33	33	48	3-15—6-13	.173	31.95

Source—Humboldt River. Ditch—Old Field Ditch.

1904	30.40			NW¼NW¼	1	32	47	3-15—6-13	.217	45.60
1904		2.95		NW¼NW¼	1	32	47	3-15—4-28	.024	2.21
1904			1.95	NW¼NW¼	1	32	47	3-15—4-28	.016	1.46
1904	0.15			SE¼NW¼	1	32	47	3-15—6-13	.001	0.23
1904	33.20			NE¼NW¼	1	32	47	3-15—6-13	.270	49.80
1904	27.25			NW¼NE¼	1	32	47	3-15—6-13	.223	40.88
1904		0.65		NW¼NW¼	6	32	48	3-15—4-28	.005	0.49
1904	35.00			SW¼SE¼	36	32	48	3-15—6-13	.284	52.50
1904	34.45			SE¼SE¼	36	32	48	3-15—6-13	.280	51.68
1904	20.60			NW¼SW¼	31	32	48	3-15—6-13	.167	30.90
1904	24.60			SW¼SW¼	31	32	48	3-15—6-13	.200	36.90
1904	20.45			SE¼SW¼	31	32	48	3-15—6-13	.166	30.68
1904	34.00			NE¼SW¼	31	32	48	3-15—6-13	.276	51.00
1904	30.50			NW¼SE¼	31	32	48	3-15—6-13	.248	45.75
1904			1.90	NW¼SE¼	31	32	48	3-15—4-28	.015	1.43
1904	3.50			SW¼SE¼	31	32	48	3-15—6-13	.028	4.25
1904			16.80	SW¼SE¼	31	32	48	3-15—4-28	.137	12.60
1904			5.85	SE¼SE¼	31	32	48	3-15—4-28	.048	4.39
1904	13.55			NE¼SE¼	31	32	48	3-15—6-13	.110	20.33
1904		19.05		NE¼SE¼	31	32	48	3-15—4-28	.155	14.29

Source—Humboldt River. Ditch—White House Slough.

1887	1.70			SE¼NE¼	22	33	48	3-15—6-13	.014	2.55
1887	2.05			SW¼NE¼	22	33	48	3-15—6-13	.017	3.08
1887	8.15			NE¼SE¼	22	33	48	3-15—6-13	.066	12.23
1887	31.10			NW¼SE¼	22	33	48	3-15—6-13	.253	46.65
1887	2.65			SW¼SE¼	22	33	48	3-15—6-13	.022	3.98
1887	28.45			NE¼SW¼	22	33	48	3-15—6-13	.231	42.68
1887	8.95			NW¼SW¼	22	33	48	3-15—6-13	.073	13.43
1887	0.55			NW¼SE¼	23	33	48	3-15—6-13	.004	0.83
1887	1.50			SW¼SE¼	23	33	48	3-15—6-13	.012	2.25
1887	0.60			NE¼SW¼	23	33	48	3-15—6-13	.005	0.90
1887	17.50			SE¼SW¼	23	33	48	3-15—6-13	.042	26.25
1887	7.35			NW¼SW¼	23	33	48	3-15—6-13	.060	11.03
1887	15.55			SW¼SW¼	23	33	48	3-15—6-13	.126	23.33
1887	5.45			SW¼NE¼	29	33	47	3-15—6-13	.044	8.18
1887	22.65			SE¼NE¼	29	33	47	3-15—6-13	.184	33.98
1887	8.05			NW¼SE¼	29	33	47	3-15—6-13	.065	12.08
1887	35.55			NE¼SE¼	29	33	47	3-15—6-13	.280	53.33
1887		35.65		NW¼NW¼	31	33	47	3-15—4-28	.290	26.74
1887		36.45		NE¼NW¼	31	33	47	3-15—4-28	.296	27.34
1887		28.80		SW¼SW¼	29	33	47	3-15—4-28	.234	21.60
1887	0.30			SE¼NE¼	25	33	48	3-15—6-13	.002	.45
1887			4.50	SE¼NE¼	25	33	48	3-15—4-28	.037	3.37
1887			1.85	SW¼NE¼	25	33	48	3-15—4-28	.015	1.39

William Dunphy Estate—Continued.

Year of priority	Culture—Acres: Harvest crops	Meadow pasture	Diversified pasture		Location: Subdivision	Section	Tp. N.	R. E.	Length of season	Duty of water: C. F. S.	Acre-feet
1887		10.25			NW¼SW¼	25	33	48	3-15—6-13	.083	15.38
1887			11.25		NW¼SW¼	25	33	48	3-15—4-28	.091	8.44
1887				9.60	NW¼SW¼	25	33	48	3-15—4-28	.078	7.20
1887		0.95			SW¼SW¼	25	33	48	3-15—6-13	.008	1.43
1887			16.05		SW¼SW¼	25	33	48	3-15—4-28	.130	12.04
1887	1.90				SE¼SW¼	25	33	48	3-15—9-15	.015	5.70
1887		17.45			SE¼SW¼	25	33	48	3-15—6-13	.142	26.18
1887			5.85		SE¼SW¼	25	33	48	3-15—4-28	.048	4.39
1887			1.40		NE¼SW¼	25	33	48	3-15—4-28	.011	1.05
1887				3.20	NE¼SW¼	25	33	48	3-15—4-28	.026	2.40
1887	15.85				SE¼NE¼	28	33	48	3-15—9-15	.129	47.55
1887	35.40				NE¼NE¼	28	33	48	3-15—9-15	.288	106.20
1887	36.45				NW¼NW¼	27	33	48	3-15—9-15	.296	109.35
1887	30.15				NW¼NW¼	25	33	48	3-15—9-15	.318	157.45
1887		0.75			NW¼NW¼	25	33	48	3-15—6-13	.006	1.13
1887	15.20				SW¼NW¼	25	33	48	3-15—9-15	.124	45.60
1887	19.60				NW¼NE¼	25	33	48	3-15—9-15	.159	49.80
1887				11.00	NW¼NE¼	25	33	48	3-15—4-28	.089	8.25
1887	36.25				SE¼SE¼	22	33	47	3-15—9-15	.295	144.75
1887		0.35			SE¼SE¼	22	33	47	3-15—6-13	.003	.53
1887	18.95				SW¼SE¼	22	33	47	3-15—9-15	.154	56.85
1887		18.35			SW¼SE¼	22	33	47	3-15—6-13	.149	27.53
1887	4.00				SE¼SW¼	22	33	47	3-15—9-15	.033	12.00
1887	35.80				SW¼SW¼	22	33	47	3-15—9-15	.291	107.40
1887		2.15			SW¼SW¼	22	33	47	3-15—6-13	.017	3.23
1887		9.45			NE¼NE¼	23	33	47	3-15—6-13	.077	14.18
1887		34.45			SE¼NE¼	23	33	47	3-15—6-13	.280	51.68
1887			1.75		SE¼NE¼	23	33	47	3-15—4-28	.014	1.31
1887		31.75			SW¼NE¼	23	33	47	3-15—6-13	.258	47.63
1887		38.85			NW¼SE¼	23	33	47	3-15—6-13	.316	58.28
1887	14.65				NE¼SW¼	23	33	47	3-15—9-15	.119	43.95
1887		21.20			NE¼SW¼	23	33	47	3-15—6-13	.172	31.80
1887	36.95				SE¼SW¼	23	33	47	3-15—9-15	.300	110.85
1887		1.30			SE¼SW¼	23	33	47	3-15—6-13	.011	1.95
1887	11.55				NW¼SW¼	23	33	47	3-15—9-15	.094	35.65
1887		21.20			NW¼SW¼	23	33	47	3-15—6-13	.172	31.80
1887				4.35	NW¼SW¼	23	33	47	3-15—4-28	.035	3.26
1887	38.90				SW¼SW¼	23	33	47	3-15—9-15	.316	116.70
1887		2.85			NW¼NE¼	24	33	47	3-15—6-13	.023	4.28
1887		15.80			SW¼NE¼	24	33	47	3-15—6-13	.128	23.70
1887				14.70	SW¼NE¼	24	33	47	3-15—4-28	.120	11.03
1887	14.85				SW¼SE¼	24	33	47	3-15—9-15	.121	44.55
1887				14.75	SW¼SE¼	24	33	47	3-15—4-28	.120	11.06
1887		3.30			NE¼NW¼	24	33	47	3-15—6-13	.027	4.95
1887				1.20	NE¼NW¼	24	33	47	3-15—4-28	.010	0.90
1887		20.45			SE¼NW¼	24	33	47	3-15—6-13	.166	30.68

1887						16.00	SE¼NW¼	24	33	47	3-15—4-28	.130	12.00
1887				6.90			NW¼NW¼	24	33	47	3-15—6-13	.050	9.30
1887						2.90	NW¼NW¼	24	33	47	3-15—4-28	.024	2.18
1887				35.25			SW¼NW¼	24	33	47	3-15—6-13	.287	52.88
1887						.70	SW¼NW¼	24	33	47	3-15—4-28	.006	0.53
1887				36.75			NE¼SW¼	24	33	47	3-15—6-13	.299	55.13
1887						.40	NE¼SW¼	24	33	47	3-15—4-28	.003	.30
1887			8.80				SE¼SW¼	24	33	47	3-15—9-15	.072	26.40
1887				14.50			SE¼SW¼	24	33	47	3-15—6-13	.118	21.75
1887						16.05	SE¼SW¼	24	33	47	3-15—4-28	.130	12.04
1887				37.00			NW¼SW¼	24	33	47	3-15—6-13	.301	55.50
1887			1.55				SW¼SW¼	24	33	47	3-15—9-15	.013	4.65
1887				34.65			SW¼SW¼	24	33	47	3-15—6-13	.282	51.98
1887						1.56	SW¼SW¼	24	33	47	3-15—4-28	.013	1.16
1887				1.70			SW¼NE¼	24	33	47	3-15—6-13	.014	2.55
1887						4.05	SW¼NE¼	24	33	47	3-15—4-28	.033	3.04
1887				18.45			SE¼NE¼	24	33	47	3-15—6-13	.150	27.68
1887						4.20	SE¼NE¼	24	33	47	3-15—4-28	.034	3.15
1887				7.60			NW¼SE¼	24	33	47	3-15—6-13	.002	11.40
1887				37.30			NE¼SE¼	24	33	47	3-15—6-13	.303	55.95
1887			3.10				SW¼SE¼	24	33	47	3-15—9-15	.025	9.30
1887						2.15	SW¼SE¼	24	33	47	3-15—4-28	.017	1.61
1887			2.15				SE¼SE¼	24	33	47	3-15—9-15	.017	6.45
1887				11.20			SE¼SE¼	24	33	47	3-15—6-13	.091	16.80
1887						17.65	SE¼SE¼	24	33	47	3-15—4-28	.143	13.24
1887					27.25		SE¼SW¼	29	33	47	3-15—4-28	.222	19.69
1887					26.05		NW¼SE¼	29	33	47	3-15—4-28	.212	19.54
1887			17.30				SW¼NW¼	28	33	47	3-15—9-15	.141	61.90
1887				2.05			SW¼NW¼	28	33	47	3-15—6-13	.017	3.08
1887			18.80				SE¼NW¼	28	33	47	3-15—9-15	.153	56.40
1887			.70				NW¼SW¼	28	33	47	3-15—9-15	.006	2.10
1887				28.00			NW¼SW¼	28	33	47	3-15—6-13	.228	42.00
1887			28.80				NE¼SW¼	28	33	47	3-15—9-15	.234	86.40
1887					1.80		NE¼SW¼	28	33	47	3-15—4-28	.015	1.35
1887			12.40				NW¼SE¼	28	33	47	3-15—9-15	.010	37.20
1887					2.40		NW¼SE¼	28	33	47	3-15—4-28	.020	1.80
1887			19.70				SW¼NE¼	28	33	47	3-15—9-15	.160	59.10
1887			9.25				SE¼NE¼	28	33	47	3-15—9-15	.075	27.75
1887					.40		SE¼NE¼	28	33	47	3-15—4-28	.003	.30
1887			17.30				SW¼NW¼	27	33	47	3-15—9-15	.141	51.90
1887			21.15				SE¼NW¼	27	33	47	3-15—9-15	.172	63.45
1887				7.60			NE¼NW¼	26	33	47	3-15—6-13	.062	11.40
1887						9.35	NE¼NW¼	26	33	47	3-15—4-28	.076	7.01
1887				27.95			NW¼SE¼	26	33	47	3-15—6-13	.227	41.93
1887					2.15		NW¼SE¼	26	33	47	3-15—4-28	.017	1.61
1887				.20			SE¼SE¼	26	33	47	3-15—6-13	.002	.30
1887					3.10		SE¼SE¼	26	33	47	3-15—4-28	.025	2.32
1887				14.70			NE¼SE¼	26	33	47	3-15—6-13	.120	22.05
1887					11.55		NE¼SE¼	26	33	47	3-15—4-28	.094	8.66
1887				11.40			SW¼NE¼	26	33	47	3-15—6-13	.093	17.10
1887						8.80	SW¼NE¼	26	33	47	3-15—4-28	.072	6.60
1887				5.90			SE¼NE¼	26	33	47	3-15—6-13	.048	8.85
1887						10.65	SE¼NE¼	26	33	47	3-15—4-28	.087	7.99

William Dunphy Estate—Continued.

Year of priority	Culture—Acres: Harvest crops	Meadow pasture	Diversified pasture		Location: Subdivision	Section	Tp. N.	R. E.	Length of season	Duty of water: C. F. S.	Acre-feet
1887			.50		SW¼NW¼	25	33	47	3-15—4-28	.004	.38
1887				.40	SW¼NW¼	25	33	47	3-15—4-28	.003	.30
1887		2.00			SE¼NW¼	25	33	47	3-15—6-13	.016	3.00
1887		13.45			SW¼NW¼	19	33	48	3-15—6-13	.109	27.18
1887		35.95			NE¼SW¼	19	33	48	3-15—6-13	.292	53.93
1887		25.20			SE¼SW¼	19	33	48	3-15—6-13	.205	37.80
1887				.45	SE¼SW¼	19	33	48	3-15—4-28	.004	.34
1887				11.50	SE¼SW¼	19	33	48	3-15—4-28	.093	8.63
1887		35.50			NW¼SW¼	19	33	48	3-15—6-13	.289	53.35
1887		10.35			SW¼SW¼	19	33	48	3-15—6-13	.084	15.53
1887				2.25	SW¼SW¼	19	33	48	3-15—4-28	.018	1.69
1887				24.10	SW¼SW¼	19	33	48	3-15—4-28	.196	18.08
1887		3.15			NE¼NE¼	20	33	48	3-15—6-13	.026	4.73
1887				31.05	NE¼NE¼	20	33	48	3-15—4-28	.252	23.29
1887		9.75			SE¼NE¼	20	33	48	3-15—6-13	.079	14.63
1887				25.65	SE¼NE¼	20	33	48	3-15—4-28	.209	19.24
1887		1.05			NW¼NE¼	20	33	48	3-15—6-13	.009	1.58
1887				38.40	NW¼NE¼	20	33	48	3-15—4-28	.312	25.05
1887		.70			SW¼NE¼	20	33	48	3-15—6-13	.006	1.05
1887				37.95	SW¼NE¼	20	33	48	3-15—4-28	.309	28.46
1887		4.65			NE¼SE¼	20	33	48	3-15—6-13	.038	6.98
1887				33.80	NE¼SE¼	20	33	48	3-15—4-28	.275	25.35
1887		29.70			SE¼SE¼	20	33	48	3-15—6-13	.241	44.55
1887				8.55	SE¼SE¼	20	33	48	3-15—4-28	.070	6.41
1887		20.75			NW¼SE¼	20	33	48	3-15—6-13	.169	31.13
1887				16.20	NW¼SE¼	20	33	48	3-15—4-28	.132	12.15
1887		36.40			SW¼SE¼	20	33	48	3-15—6-13	.296	54.60
1887				1.55	SW¼SE¼	20	33	48	3-15—4-28	.013	1.16
1887		1.30			NE¼NW¼	20	33	48	3-15—6-13	.011	1.95
1887				37.55	NE¼NW¼	20	33	48	3-15—4-28	.305	28.16
1887		.80			SE¼NW¼	20	33	48	3-15—6-13	.007	1.20
1887				38.35	SE¼NW¼	20	33	48	3-15—4-28	.312	28.76
1887		1.30			NW¼NW¼	20	33	48	3-15—6-13	.011	1.95
1887				12.85	NW¼NW¼	20	33	48	3-15—4-28	.104	9.64
1887				24.20	SW¼NW¼	20	33	48	3-15—4-28	.197	18.15
1887		22.05			NE¼SW¼	20	33	48	3-15—6-13	.179	33.08
1887				12.75	NE¼SW¼	20	33	48	3-15—4-28	.104	9.56
1887		28.75			SE¼SW¼	20	33	48	3-15—6-13	.234	43.13
1887				9.25	SE¼SW¼	20	33	48	3-15—4-28	.075	6.91
1887		26.05			NW¼SW¼	20	33	48	3-15—6-13	.212	39.08
1887				9.85	NW¼SW¼	20	33	48	3-15—4-28	.080	7.39
1887		20.05			SW¼SW¼	20	33	48	3-15—6-13	.163	30.08
1887				12.30	SW¼SW¼	20	33	48	3-15—4-28	.100	9.23
1887		2.40			SE¼NE¼	21	33	48	3-15—6-13	.020	3.60
1887				2.90	SE¼NE¼	21	33	48	3-15—4-28	.024	2.18
1887		1.05			SW¼NE¼	21	33	48	3-15—6-13	.009	1.58

1887						11.60	SW¼NE¼	21	33	48	3-15—4-28	.094	8.70
1887				21.10			NE¼SE¼	21	33	48	3-15—6-13	.172	31.65
1887						15.05	NE¼SE¼	21	33	48	3-15—4-28	.122	11.20
1887				38.55			SE¼SE¼	21	33	48	3-15—6-13	.313	57.83
1887				17.50			NW¼SE¼	21	33	48	3-15—6-13	.142	26.35
1887						18.40	NW¼SE¼	21	33	48	3-15—4-28	.150	13.80
1887				38.70			SW¼SE¼	21	33	48	3-15—6-13	.315	58.05
1887				14.85			SE¼NW¼	21	33	48	3-15—6-13	.121	22.28
1887						7.55	SE¼NW¼	21	33	48	3-15—4-28	.061	5.66
1887				10.60			SW¼NW¼	21	33	48	3-15—6-13	.159	29.40
1887						14.25	SW¼NW¼	21	33	48	3-15—4-28	.116	10.60
1887				7.20			NE¼SW¼	21	33	48	3-15—6-13	.059	10.90
1887						30.25	NE¼SW¼	21	33	48	3-15—4-28	.246	22.69
1887				37.85			SE¼SW¼	21	33	48	3-15—6-13	.308	56.78
1887						39.25	NW¼SW¼	21	33	48	3-15—4-28	.319	29.44
1887				24.10			SW¼SW¼	21	33	48	3-15—6-13	.196	36.15
1887						13.50	SW¼SW¼	21	33	48	3-15—4-28	.110	10.13
1887						1.25	NW¼NE¼	19	33	48	3-15—4-28	.010	.94
1887				2.75			SW¼NE¼	19	33	48	3-15—6-13	.022	4.13
1887						1.75	SW¼NE¼	19	33	48	3-15—4-28	.014	1.31
1887				21.95			NE¼SE¼	19	33	48	3-15—6-13	.178	32.93
1887						11.60	NE¼SE¼	19	33	48	3-15—4-28	.094	8.70
1887				15.50			SE¼SE¼	19	33	48	3-15—6-13	.126	23.25
1887					17.35		SE¼SE¼	19	33	48	3-15—4-28	.141	13.01
1887						2.65	SE¼SE¼	19	33	48	3-15—4-28	.022	1.99
1887				23.50			NW¼SE¼	19	33	48	3-15—6-13	.191	35.25
1887						13.60	NW¼SE¼	19	33	48	3-15—4-28	.111	10.20
1887				17.25			SW¼SE¼	19	33	48	3-15—6-13	.140	25.88
1887					20.30		SW¼SE¼	19	33	48	3-15—4-28	.165	15.23
1887				2.00			NE¼NW¼	19	33	48	3-15—6-13	.016	3.00
1887						4.30	NE¼NW¼	19	33	48	3-15—4-28	.035	3.23
1887				3.70			SE¼SW¼	19	33	48	3-15—6-13	.030	5.55
1887				3.10			NW¼NW¼	19	33	48	3-15—6-13	.025	4.65
1887						17.20	NW¼NW¼	19	33	48	3-15—4-28	.140	12.90
1887				7.70			NW¼NW¼	27	33	48	3-15—6-13	.063	11.55
1887				2.40			SW¼NW¼	22	33	48	3-15—6-13	.020	3.60
1887						12.40	SW¼NW¼	22	33	48	3-15—4-28	.101	9.30
1887				6.55			NW¼SW¼	22	33	48	3-15—6-13	.053	9.83
1887						9.95	NW¼SW¼	22	33	48	3-15—4-28	.081	7.46
1887				16.60			SW¼SW¼	22	33	48	3-15—6-13	.135	24.90
1887				20.55			NE¼NE¼	28	33	48	3-15—6-13	.167	30.83
1887				26.85			NW¼NE¼	28	33	48	3-15—6-13	.218	40.28
1887				23.60			NE¼NW¼	28	33	48	3-15—6-13	.192	35.40
1887						9.00	NE¼NW¼	28	33	48	3-15—4-28	.073	6.75
1887				1.80			NW¼NE¼	30	33	48	3-15—6-13	.015	3.70
1887						25.95	NW¼NE¼	30	33	48	3-15—4-28	.211	19.46
1887				3.75			NE¼NW¼	30	33	48	3-15—6-13	.030	5.63
1887						18.75	NE¼NW¼	30	33	48	3-15—4-28	.152	14.06
1887				1.30			NW¼NW¼	30	33	48	3-15—6-13	.011	1.95
1887						13.60	NW¼NW¼	30	33	48	3-15—4-28	.111	10.20
1887						1.25	NE¼NE¼	25	33	48	3-15—4-28	.010	.94

William Dunphy Estate—Continued.
Source—**Humboldt River.** Ditch—**Blue House Slough.**

Year of priority	Culture—Acres: Harvest crops	Meadow pasture	Diversified pasture		Location: Subdivision	Section	Tp. N.	R. E.	Length of season	Duty of water: C.F.S.	Acre-feet
1888		4.95			SW¼SE¼	29	33	47	3-15—6-13	.040	7.43
1888				5.65	SW¼SE¼	29	33	47	3-15—4-28	.046	4.24
1888		24.70			SE¼SE¼	29	33	47	3-15—6-13	.201	37.05
1888	2.70				NW¼NE¼	32	33	47	3-15—9-15	.022	8.10
1888		5.15			NW¼NE¼	32	33	47	3-15—6-13	.042	7.73
1888	3.95				NE¼NE¼	32	33	47	3-15—9-15	.032	11.85
1888		2.70			NE¼NE¼	32	33	47	3-15—6-13	.022	4.05
1888	9.10				SW¼NE¼	32	33	47	3-15—9-15	.074	27.30
1888	27.85				SE¼NE¼	32	33	47	3-15—9-15	.226	83.55
1888			13.50		SW¼NW¼	31	33	47	3-15—4-28	.110	10.13
1888			8.00		SE¼NW¼	31	33	47	3-15—4-28	.065	6.00
1888			37.15		NW¼NE¼	31	33	47	3-15—4-28	.302	27.86
1888			30.55		NE¼NE¼	31	33	47	3-15—4-28	.248	22.91
1888			23.55		SW¼NE¼	31	33	47	3-15—4-28	.191	17.66
1888			12.70		SE¼NE¼	31	33	47	3-15—4-28	.103	9.53
1888		3.30			NW¼SW¼	31	33	47	3-15—6-13	.027	4.95
1888			.85		NW¼SW¼	31	33	47	3-15—4-26	.007	.64
1888				21.35	NW¼SW¼	31	33	47	3-15—4-28	.074	16.01
1888		5.40			NE¼SW¼	31	33	47	3-15—6-13	.044	8.10
1888			4.30		NE¼SW¼	31	33	47	3-15—4-28	.035	3.23
1888			5.65		SW¼SW¼	29	33	47	3-15—4-28	.046	4.24
1888			9.40		SE¼SW¼	29	33	47	3-15—4-28	.076	7.05
1888			23.55		SW¼SE¼	29	33	47	3-15—4-28	.191	17.66
1888			27.10		NW¼NW¼	32	33	47	3-15—4-28	.220	20.33
1888			18.75		NE¼NW¼	32	33	47	3-15—4-28	.152	14.06
1888	3.10				NW¼NE¼	32	33	47	3-15—9-15	.025	.93
1888		3.90			NW¼NE¼	32	33	47	3-15—6-13	.032	5.85
1888			1.20		NE¼SW¼	30	33	48	3-15—4-28	.010	.90
1888				16.60	NE¼SW¼	30	33	48	3-15—4-28	.135	12.45
1888			1.45		NW¼SE¼	30	33	48	3-15—4-28	.012	1.09
1888				28.15	NW¼SE¼	30	33	48	3-15—4-28	.229	21.11
1888			10.40		SW¼SE¼	30	33	48	3-15—4-28	.085	7.80
1888				23.25	SW¼SE¼	30	33	48	3-15—4-28	.180	17.44
1888			2.35		SE¼SE¼	30	33	48	3-15—4-28	.019	1.76
1888				31.35	SE¼SE¼	30	33	48	3-15—1-28	.255	23.51
1888				2.25	NE¼SE¼	30	33	48	3-15—4-28	.018	1.67
1888				34.05	NW¼SW¼	29	33	48	3-15—4-28	.277	25.52
1888		1.05			SW¼SW¼	29	33	48	3-15—6-13	.009	1.58
1888				36.20	SW¼SW¼	29	33	48	3-15—4-28	.294	27.15
1888		4.45			SE¼SW¼	29	33	48	3-15—6-13	.036	6.68
1888				29.30	SE¼SW¼	29	33	48	3-15—4-28	.238	21.98
1888		2.30			NE¼SW¼	29	33	48	3-15—6-13	.019	3.45
1888				30.30	NE¼SW¼	29	33	48	3-15—4-28	.246	22.73
1888		12.50			NW¼SE¼	29	33	48	3-15—6-13	.102	18.75
1888				21.35	NW¼SE¼	29	33	48	3-15—4-28	.171	16.01

1888				11.05			SW¼SE¼	29	33	48	3-15—6-13	.090	16.58
1888					5.45		SW¼SE¼	29	33	48	3-15—4-28	.044	4.09
1888						12.55	SW¼SE¼	29	33	48	3-15—4-28	.102	9.41
1888				26.85			SE¼SE¼	29	33	48	3-15—6-13	.218	40.28
1888						5.95	SE¼SE¼	29	33	48	3-15—4-28	.048	4.46
1888				7.80			NE¼SE¼	29	33	48	3-15—6-13	.063	11.70
1888					10.85		NE¼SE¼	29	33	48	3-15—4-28	.088	8.14
1888						12.45	NE¼SE¼	29	33	48	3-15—4-28	.101	9.34
1888				7.75			NW¼SW¼	29	33	48	3-15—6-13	.063	11.63
1888						25.45	NW¼SW¼	29	33	48	3-15—4-28	.206	19.09
1888			20.35				NW¼SE¼	27	33	47	3-15—9-15	.165	61.05
1888			24.00				NW¼SE¼	27	33	47	3-15—9-15	.195	82.00
1888			11.00				NW¼SE¼	26	33	47	3-15—9-15	.089	33.00
1888						21.50	NW¼SE¼	26	33	47	3-15—4-28	.175	16.13
1888			17.20				NE¼SE¼	26	33	47	3-15—9-15	.140	51.60
1888				16.40			NE¼SE¼	26	33	47	3-15—6-13	.133	24.60
1888			36.45				NW¼SW¼	26	33	47	3-15—9-15	.296	109.35
1888			35.10				SW¼SW¼	26	33	47	3-15—9-15	.285	105.30
1888			26.55				NE¼SW¼	26	33	47	3-15—9-15	.216	79.65
1888				7.70			NE¼SW¼	26	33	47	3-15—6-13	.063	11.55
1888			13.10				NW¼SW¼	25	33	47	3-15—9-15	.107	39.30
1888				11.60			NW¼SW¼	25	33	47	3-15—6-13	.094	17.40
1888						4.95	NW¼SW¼	25	33	47	3-15—4-28	.040	3.71
1888				21.30			SW¼SW¼	25	33	47	3-15—6-13	.173	31.95
1888					8.00		SW¼SW¼	25	33	47	3-15—4-28	.065	6.00
1888						.40	SW¼SW¼	25	33	47	3-15—4-28	.003	.30
1888				20.70			SE¼SW¼	25	33	47	3-15—6-13	.168	31.05
1888						18.20	SE¼SW¼	25	33	47	3-15—4-28	.148	13.65
1888			.60				NE¼SW¼	25	33	47	3-15—9-15	.005	1.80
1888				15.31			NE¼SW¼	25	33	47	3-15—6-13	.124	22.97
1888						21.15	NE¼SW¼	25	33	47	3-15—4-28	.172	15.86
1888				3.15			NW¼SE¼	25	33	47	3-15—6-13	.026	4.73
1888						21.35	NW¼SE¼	25	33	47	3-15—4-28	.174	16.01
1888				6.50			SW¼SE¼	25	33	47	3-15—6-13	.053	9.75
1888						28.85	SW¼SE¼	25	33	47	3-15—4-28	.235	21.64
1888				10.95			SE¼SE¼	25	33	47	3-15—6-13	.089	16.43
1888						22.95	SE¼SE¼	25	33	47	3-15—4-28	.187	17.21
1888				2.40			NE¼SE¼	25	33	47	3-15—6-13	.020	3.60
1888						33.35	NE¼SE¼	25	33	47	3-15—4-28	.271	25.01
1888			12.00				NW¼NW¼	36	33	47	3-15—9-15	.098	36.00
1888					.55		NW¼NW¼	36	33	47	3-15—4-28	.004	.41
1888						.10	NW¼NW¼	36	33	47	3-15—4-28	.001	.08
1888				1.35			NE¼NW¼	36	33	47	3-15—6-13	.011	2.03
1888						7.70	NE¼NW¼	36	33	47	3-15—4-28	.063	5.78
1888				1.30			NW¼SW¼	30	33	47	3-15—6-13	.011	1.95
1888						29.95	NW¼SW¼	30	33	47	3-15—4-28	.243	22.46
1888				10.15			SW¼SW¼	30	33	47	3-15—6-13	.083	15.23
1888						22.90	SW¼SW¼	30	33	47	3-15—4-28	.186	17.18
1888				17.35			SE¼SW¼	30	33	47	3-15—6-13	.141	26.03
1888						17.65	SE¼SW¼	30	33	47	3-15—4-28	.143	13.24
1888			15.75				SW¼NE¼	32	33	47	3-15—9-15	.128	47.25

William Dunphy Estate—Continued.

Year of priority	Culture—Acres: Harvest crops	Meadow pasture	Diversified pasture		Location: Subdivision	Section	Tp. N.	R. E.	Length of season	Duty of water: C. F. S.	Acre-feet
1888		6.40			SW¼ NE¼	32	33	47	3-15—6-13	.052	9.60
1888				1.35	SW¼ NE¼	32	33	47	3-15—4-28	.011	1.01
1888		3.10			NW¼ SE¼	32	33	47	3-15—6-13	.025	4.65
1888				5.80	NW¼ SE¼	32	33	47	3-15—4-28	.047	4.35
1888			15.15		SW¼ SE¼	32	33	47	3-15—4-28	.123	11.63
1888		18.35			NW¼ SW¼	32	33	47	3-15—6.13	.149	27.53
1888				6.10	NW¼ SW¼	32	33	47	3-15—4-28	.050	4.58
1888	6.40				NW¼ SW¼	28	33	47	3-15—9-15	.052	19.20
1888		28.00			SW¼ SW¼	28	33	47	3-15—6-13	.228	42.00
1888	18.90				SE¼ SW¼	28	33	47	3-15—9-15	.154	56.70
1888		13.05			SE¼ SW¼	28	33	47	3-15—6-13	.106	19.58
1888	6.65				NE¼ SW¼	28	33	47	3-15—9-15	.054	19.95
1888	19.70				NW¼ SE¼	28	33	47	3-15—9-15	.160	59.10
1888	25.95				SW¼ SE¼	28	33	47	3-15—9-15	.211	77.85
1888	4.00				SE¼ SE¼	28	33	47	3-15—9-15	.033	12.00
1888	34.85				NE¼ SE¼	28	33	47	3-15—9-15	.283	104.55
1888	7.70				SE¼ NE¼	28	33	47	3-15—9-15	.063	23.10
1888	4.60				NE¼ NW¼	33	33	47	3-15—9-15	.037	13.80
1888			2.05		SW¼ NW¼	27	33	47	3-15—4-28	.017	1.54
1888	26.60				NW¼ SW¼	27	33	47	3-15—9-15	.216	79.80
1888			1.50		NW¼ SW¼	27	33	47	3-15—4-28	.012	1.13
1888				8.50	NW¼ SW¼	27	33	47	3-15—4-28	.069	6.38
1888	6.25				SW¼ SW¼	27	33	47	3-15—9-15	.051	18.75
1888				29.20	SW¼ SW¼	27	33	47	3-15—4-28	.237	21.90
1888	6.00				SE¼ SW¼	27	33	47	3-15—9-15	.049	18.00
1888				27.80	SE¼ SW¼	27	33	47	3-15—4-28	.226	20.85
1888	15.05				NE¼ SW¼	27	33	47	3-15—9-15	.122	45.15

Source—**Humboldt River.** Ditch—**Blue House Ditch No. 1.**

Year of priority	Harvest crops	Meadow pasture	Diversified pasture		Subdivision	Section	Tp. N.	R. E.	Length of season	C. F. S.	Acre-feet
1888	37.75				SE¼ SW¼	26	33	47	3-15—9-15	.307	113.25
1888	33.55				SE¼ SE¼	27	33	47	3-15—9-15	.273	100.65
1888	14.95				SW¼ SE¼	27	33	47	3-15—9-15	.122	44.85
1888		17.6			SW¼ SE¼	27	33	47	3-15—6-13	.158	26.40
1888				1.45	SW¼ SE¼	27	33	47	3-15—4-28	.011	1.09
1888	7.00				NW¼ NW¼	33	33	47	3-15—9-15	.057	21.00
1888		38.90			SW¼ SE¼	26	33	47	3-15—6-13	.316	58.35
1888		36.60			SE¼ SE¼	26	33	47	3-15—6-13	.298	54.90
1888	25.65				NE¼ NW¼	34	33	47	3-15—9-15	.209	76.95
1888		3.50			NE¼ NW¼	34	33	47	3-15—6-13	.028	5.25
1888				8.10	NE¼ NW¼	34	33	47	3-15—4-28	.066	6.08
1888	6.75				NE¼ NE¼	34	33	47	3-15—9-15	.055	20.25
1888		9.50			NE¼ NE¼	34	33	47	3-15—6-13	.077	11.25
1888		12.25			NW¼ NW¼	35	33	47	3-15—6-13	.100	18.38
1888			3.30		NW¼ NW¼	35	33	47	3-15—4-28	.027	2.48
1888		0.70			SE¼ NW¼	35	33	47	3-15—6-13	[illegible]	1.05
1888			4.70		SE¼ NW¼	35	33	47	3-15—4-28	[illegible]	[illegible]

1888					3.15		NE¼NW¼	35	33	47	3-15—4-28	.026	2.36
1888			12.05				NW¼NE¼	35	33	47	3-15—9-15	.008	36.15
1888				14.60			NW¼NE¼	35	33	47	3-15—6-13	.119	21.90
1888					1.90		NW¼NE¼	35	33	47	3-15—4-28	.015	1.43
1888				20.55			SW¼NE¼	35	33	47	3-15—6-13	.167	30.83
1888					4.30		SW¼NE¼	35	33	47	3-15—4-28	.035	3.23
1888						.60	SW¼NE¼	35	33	47	3-15—4-28	.005	0.47
1888				26.20			SE¼NE¼	35	33	47	3-15—6-13	.213	39.30
1888					5.10		SE¼NE¼	35	33	47	3-15—4-28	.041	3.83
1888				10.55			NE¼NE¼	35	33	47	3-15—6-13	.086	15.83
1888					12.80		NE¼NE¼	35	33	47	3-15—4-28	.104	9.60
1888				3.60			NW¼SW¼	25	33	47	3-15—6-13	.029	5.40
1888					1.70		NW¼SW¼	25	33	47	3-15—4-28	.014	1.28
1888					3.30		SW¼SW¼	25	33	47	3-15—4-28	.027	2.48
1888					1.50		NW¼NW¼	36	33	47	3-15—4-28	.012	1.13

Source—Humboldt River. Ditch—Railroad Slough.

1887			3.25				SW¼NE¼	25	33	47	3-15—9-15	.026	0.75
1887						8.15	SW¼NE¼	25	33	47	3-15—4-28	.066	6.11
1887				33.95			NW¼NW¼	28	33	48	3-15—6-13	.276	59.93
1887						1.05	NW¼NW¼	28	33	48	3-15—4-28	.008	0.79
1887				38.35			NE¼NE¼	29	33	48	3-15—6-13	.296	54.53
1887				5.05			SE¼NE¼	29	33	48	3-15—6-13	.041	7.58
1887				32.45			NW¼NE¼	29	33	48	3-15—6-13	.264	48.68
1887						4.10	NW¼NE¼	29	33	48	3-15—4-28	.033	3.08
1887				9.55			SW¼NE¼	29	33	48	3-15—6-13	.078	14.33
1887				0.10			NE¼NW¼	29	33	48	3-15—6-13	.001	0.15
1887						37.55	NE¼NW¼	29	33	48	3-15—4-28	.305	28.16
1887				1.10			SE¼NW¼	29	33	48	3-15—6-13	.009	1.65
1887						12.90	SE¼NW¼	29	33	48	3-15—4-28	.105	9.68
1887				0.15			NW¼NW¼	29	33	48	3-15—6-13	.001	0.23
1887						38.30	NW¼NW¼	29	33	48	3-15—4-28	.311	28.73
1887				15.60			SW¼NW¼	29	33	48	3-15—6-13	.127	23.40
1887						13.00	SE¼NE¼	30	33	48	3-15—4-28	.106	9.75
1887				0.50			SW¼NE¼	30	33	48	3-15—6-13	.004	0.75
1887				0.90			NE¼NE¼	30	33	48	3-15—6-13	.007	1.35
1887			0.40				NW¼SW¼	27	33	47	3-15—9-15	.003	1.20
1887			17.80				NE¼SW¼	27	33	47	3-15—9-15	.145	53.40
1887			14.95				NW¼SE¼	27	33	47	3-15—9-15	.122	44.85
1887			10.50				NE¼SE¼	27	33	47	3-15—9-15	.085	31.50
1887			20.25				SW¼NE¼	27	33	47	3-15—9-15	.165	60.75
1887			20.00				SE¼NE¼	27	33	47	3-15—9-15	.162	60.00
1887			21.30				SW¼NW¼	26	33	47	3-15—9-15	.173	63.90
1887			20.90				SE¼NW¼	26	33	47	3-15—9-15	.170	62.70
1887			21.20				SW¼NE¼	26	33	47	3-15—9-15	.172	63.60
1887			20.05				SE¼NE¼	26	33	47	3-15—9-15	.163	60.15
1887			3.35				SW¼NW¼	25	33	47	3-15—9-15	.027	10.05
1887			17.65				SW¼NW¼	25	33	47	3-15—9-15	.143	52.95
1887			11.05				SE¼NW¼	25	33	47	3-15—9-15	.090	33.15
1887						9.05	SE¼NW¼	25	33	47	3-15—4-28	.074	6.79
1887						11.95	NW¼SE¼	25	33	47	3-15—4-28	.097	8.96
1887			0.10				SW¼NE¼	25	33	47	3-15—9-15	.001	.30

William Dunphy Estate—Continued.

Year of priority	Culture—Acres: Harvest crops	Meadow pasture	Diversified pasture	Location: Subdivision	Section	Tp.N.	R.E.	Length of season	Duty of water: C.F.S.	Acre-feet
1887			21.25	SW¼ NE¼	26	33	47	3-15—4-28	.172	15.94
1887			20.80	SE¼ NE¼	25	33	47	3-15—4-28	.169	15.60
1887			20.65	SW¼ NW¼	30	33	48	3-15—4-28	.168	15.49
1887			34.90	NE¼ NE¼	30	33	48	3-15—4-28	.283	26.18
1887		0.50		SE¼ NW¼	30	33	48	3-15—6-13	.004	0.75
1887			15.00	SE¼ NW¼	30	33	48	3-15—4-28	.122	11.25
1887		0.45		SW¼ NW¼	30	33	48	3-15—6-13	.004	0.68
1887			15.00	SW¼ NW¼	30	33	48	3-15—4-28	.122	11.25
1887			.20	SE¼ NW¼	30	33	48	3-15—4-28	.002	0.15
1887			17.80	SE¼ NW¼	30	33	48	3-15—4-28	.145	13.35
1887	15.00			SE¼ NW¼	25	33	47	3-15—9-15	.122	45.00

Source—Humboldt River. Ditch—Rose Canal.

Year of priority	Harvest crops	Meadow pasture	Diversified pasture	Subdivision	Section	Tp.N.	R.E.	Length of season	C.F.S.	Acre-feet
1873		1.05		NE¼ NE¼	23	33	48	3-15—6-13	.009	1.58
1873		3.35		SE¼ NE¼	23	33	48	3-15—6-13	.027	5.03
1873		3.20		NW¼ NE¼	23	33	48	3-15—6-13	.026	4.80
1873		1.30		SE¼ SE¼	23	33	48	3-15—6-13	.011	1.95
1873		3.50		NE¼ NW¼	23	33	48	3-15—6-13	.028	5.25
1873		0.95		NW¼ NW¼	23	33	48	3-15—6-13	.008	1.43
1873	0.20			SW¼ NE¼	24	33	48	3-15—9-15	.002	.60
1873	3.85			NW¼ SE¼	24	33	48	3-15—9-15	.031	11.55
1873	25.15			NE¼ NW¼	24	33	48	3-15—9-15	.204	75.45
1873	28.45			SE¼ NW¼	24	33	48	3-15—9-15	.231	85.35
1873	27.05			NW¼ NW¼	24	33	48	3-15—9-15	.220	81.15
1873	33.30			SW¼ NW¼	24	33	48	3-15—9-15	.271	99.90
1873	37.25			NE¼ SW¼	24	33	48	3-15—9-15	.303	111.75
1873	9.40			SE¼ SW¼	24	33	48	3-15—9-15	.076	28.20
1873			1.25	SE¼ SW¼	24	33	48	3-15—4-28	.010	9.38
1873	18.10			NW¼ SW¼	24	33	48	3-15—9-15	.147	54.30
1873		0.90		NW¼ SW¼	24	33	48	3-15—6-13	.007	1.35
1873			19.90	NW¼ SW¼	24	33	48	3-15—4-28	.162	14.93
1873	1.20			SW¼ SW¼	24	33	48	3-15—9-15	.010	3.60
1873		2.60		SW¼ SW¼	24	33	48	3-15—6-13	.021	3.90
1873			26.40	SW¼ SW¼	24	33	48	3-15—4-28	.215	19.80
1873			1.75	SW¼ NE¼	25	33	48	3-15—4-28	.014	1.42
1873	0.25			NE¼ NW¼	25	33	48	3-15—9-15	.002	.75
1873			14.55	NE¼ NW¼	25	33	48	3-15—4-28	.118	10.91
1873			1.30	SE¼ NW¼	25	33	48	3-15—4-28	.010	.98
1873		1.10		NW¼ NW¼	25	33	48	3-15—6-13	.009	1.65
1873			2.05	NW¼ NW¼	25	33	48	3-15—4-28	.017	1.54
1873		0.35		SW¼ SW¼	11	33	48	3-15—6-13	.003	.53
1873	10.75			SE¼ SW¼	13	33	48	3-15—9-15	.087	32.25
1873	18.60			SW¼ SW¼	13	33	48	3-15—9-15	.151	55.80
1873			0.15	SE¼ NE¼	14	33	48	3-15—4-28	.001	.11
1873			0.50	SW¼ NE¼	14	33	48	3-15—4-28	.004	.38
1873			0.35	NE¼ SE¼	14	33	48	3-15—4-28	.003	.26

1873				0.60			NE¼NW¼	14	33	48	3-15—6-13	.005	.90
1873				1.00			SE¼NW¼	14	33	48	3-15—6-13	.008	1.50
1873				1.50			NW¼NW¼	14	33	48	3-15—6-13	.012	2.25
1873				0.80			SE¼SW¼	14	33	48	3-15—6-13	.007	1.20
1873				4.05			SW¼SW¼	14	33	48	3-15—6-13	.033	6.08
1873				0.20			NW¼NE¼	15	33	48	3-15—6-13	.002	.30
1873				3.10			SW¼NE¼	15	33	48	3-15—6-13	.025	4.65
1873				1.45			NE¼SE¼	15	33	48	3-15—6-13	.012	2.18
1873				1.60			SE¼SE¼	15	33	48	3-15—6-13	.013	2.40
1873				1.40			NW¼SE¼	15	33	48	3-15—6-13	.011	2.10
1873				5.35			NE¼NW¼	15	33	48	3-15—6-13	.043	8.03
1873				9.60			NW¼NW¼	15	33	48	3-15—6-13	.078	11.40
1873				0.20			SW¼NW¼	15	33	48	3-15—6-13	.002	.30
1873			3.10				SW¼SE¼	25	33	48	3-15—9-15	.025	9.30
1873				15.60			SW¼SE¼	25	33	48	3-15—6-13	.127	23.40
1873					10.00		SW¼SE¼	25	33	48	3-15—4-28	.081	7.50
1873						1.10	SE¼SE¼	25	33	48	3-15—4-28	.009	.83
1873						2.30	SW¼NE¼	25	33	48	3-15—4-28	.019	1.73
1873				2.90			NW¼NE¼	36	33	48	3-15—6-13	.024	4.35
1873						1.00	NW¼NE¼	36	33	48	3-15—4-28	.008	.75
1873				3.00			NE¼NE¼	36	33	48	3-15—6-13	.024	4.50
1873						5.30	NE¼NE¼	36	33	48	3-15—4-28	.043	3.98
1873				5.65			SE¼NE¼	36	33	48	3-15—6-13	.046	8.48
1873						1.20	SE¼NE¼	36	33	48	3-15—4-28	.010	.90

Source—**Humboldt** River. Ditch—**Flood Area.**

1887					2.35		SW¼NW¼	25	33	48	3-15—4-28	.019	1.76
1887					1.50		NE¼NE¼	26	33	48	3-15—4-28	.012	1.13
1887						3.90	NE¼NE¼	26	33	48	3-15—4-28	.032	2.93
1887					2.15		SE¼NE¼	26	33	48	3-15—4-28	.017	1.61
1887					1.85		NW¼NE¼	26	33	48	3-15—4-28	.015	1.39
1887						15.85	NW¼NE¼	26	33	48	3-15—4-28	.129	11.89
1887				7.95			NE¼SW¼	31	33	47	3-15—6-13	.065	11.93
1887					7.03		NW¼SE¼	31	33	47	3-15—4-28	.057	5.27
1887					3.10		NE¼SE¼	31	33	47	3-15—4-28	.025	2.33
1887				8.30			NW¼NE¼	36	33	47	3-15—6-13	.067	12.45
1887						20.75	NW¼NE¼	36	33	47	3-15—4-28	.169	15.56
1887				2.70			NE¼NE¼	36	33	47	3-15—6-13	.022	4.05
1887					8.35		NE¼NE¼	36	33	47	3-15—4-28	.068	6.26
1887						17.05	NE¼NE¼	36	33	47	3-15—4-28	.139	12.79
1887				5.85			NW¼NW¼	31	33	47	3-15—6-13	.048	8.78
1887						22.95	NW¼NW¼	31	33	47	3-15—4-28	.187	17.21
1887				2.05			NE¼NW¼	31	33	47	3-15—6-13	.017	3.08
1887					13.75		NE¼NW¼	31	33	47	3-15—4-28	.112	10.31
1887						7.95	NE¼NW¼	31	33	47	3-15—4-28	.065	5.96
1887				14.10			NW¼NE¼	31	33	47	3-15—6-13	.115	21.15
1887						7.80	NW¼NE¼	31	33	47	3-15—4-28	.063	5.85
1887				19.35			NE¼NE¼	31	33	47	3-15—6-13	.157	29.03
1887					1.95		NE¼NE¼	31	33	47	3-15—4-28	.016	1.46
1887						4.90	NE¼NE¼	31	33	47	3-15—4-28	.040	3.68
1887				13.85			NW¼NW¼	32	33	47	3-15—6-13	.113	20.78
1887						20.80	NW¼NW¼	32	33	47	3-15—4-28	.169	15.60

William Dunphy Estate—Continued.

Year of priority	Harvest crops	Meadow pasture	Diversified pasture (1)	Diversified pasture (2)	Subdivision	Section	Tp.N.	R.E.	Length of season	C.F.S.	Acre-feet
1887		17.65			NE¼NW¼	32	33	47	3-15—6-13	.143	26.48
1887			7.45		NE¼NW¼	32	33	47	3-15—4-28	.061	5.59
1887				5.80	NE¼NW¼	32	33	47	3-15—4-28	.047	4.35
1887		26.70			NE¼SW¼	28	33	47	3-15—6-13	.217	40.05
1887			4.15		NE¼SE¼	28	33	47	3-15—4-28	.034	3.11
1887			7.80		SW¼NE¼	28	33	47	3-15—4-28	.063	5.85
1887				5.30	SW¼NE¼	28	33	47	3-15—4-28	.043	3.98
1887		3.35			SE¼NE¼	28	33	47	3-15—6-13	.027	5.03
1887			14.25		SE¼NE¼	28	33	47	3-15—4-28	.116	10.60
1887		.25			SW¼NW¼	27	53	48	3-15—6-13	.002	.38
1887			14.45		SW¼NW¼	27	33	48	3-15—4-28	.117	8.59
1887			.90		SE¼NW¼	27	33	48	3-15—4-28	.007	.68
1887			.40		NW¼SW¼	27	33	48	3-15—4-28	.003	.30
1887		20.70			NE¼SE¼	27	53	48	3-15—6-13	.168	31.05
1887			4.35		NE¼SE¼	27	33	48	3-15—4-28	.035	3.26
1887		11.15			SW¼NE¼	27	33	48	3-15—6-13	.091	16.73
1887			5.85		SW¼NE¼	27	33	48	3-15—4-28	.048	4.39
1887			1.40		SW¼NW¼	26	33	48	3-15—4-28	.011	1.05
1887		9.60			NW¼SW¼	26	33	48	3-15—6-13	.078	14.40
1887			9.05		NW¼SW¼	26	33	48	3-15—4-28	.074	6.79
1887		10.25			NE¼SW¼	26	33	48	3-15—6-13	.083	15.38
1887			10.10		NE¼SW¼	26	33	48	3-15—4-28	.082	7.58

Source—Humboldt River. Ditch—New Dam Ditch.

Year of priority	Harvest crops	Meadow pasture	Diversified pasture (1)	Diversified pasture (2)	Subdivision	Section	Tp.N.	R.E.	Length of season	C.F.S.	Acre-feet
1902		21.95			SE¼SW¼	22	33	48	3-15—6-13	.178	32.93
1902		14.15			SW¼SW¼	22	33	48	3-15—6-13	.115	21.23
1902		12.90			NW¼NE¼	27	33	48	3-15—6-13	.105	19.35
1902		15.65			NW¼NW¼	27	35	48	3-15—6-13	.127	23.48
1902				7.55	NW¼SE¼	30	33	48	3-15—4-28	.061	5.66
1902			1.70		NE¼SE¼	30	33	48	3-15—4-28	.014	1.28
1902				31.75	NE¼SE¼	30	33	48	3-15—4-28	.258	23.81
1902			3.00		SW¼NE¼	30	33	48	3-15—4-28	.024	2.25
1902				13.30	SW¼NE¼	30	33	48	3-15—4-28	.108	9.98
1902			9.40		SE¼NE¼	30	33	48	3-15—4-28	.076	7.05
1902				7.55	SE¼NE¼	30	33	48	3-15—4-28	.061	5.66
1902		6.20			SW¼NW¼	29	33	48	3-15—6-13	.050	9.30
1902				10.90	SW¼NW¼	29	33	48	3-15—4-28	.089	8.18
1902		19.05			SE¼NW¼	29	33	48	3-15—6-13	.155	28.58
1902				.40	SE¼NW¼	29	33	48	3-15—4-28	.003	.30
1902				14.60	NW¼SW¼	29	33	48	3-15—4-28	.119	10.95
1902		20.60			SW¼NE¼	29	33	48	3-15—6-13	.167	30.90
1902		18.00			SE¼NE¼	29	33	48	3-15—6-13	.146	27.00
1902				1.50	SE¼NE¼	29	33	48	3-15—4-28	.012	1.13
1902				18.80	SW¼NW¼	28	33	48	3-15—4-28	.153	14.10
1902		4.30			SE¼NW¼	28	33	48	3-15—6-13	.035	6.45
1902				10.80	SE¼NW¼	28	33	48	3-15—4-28	.137	12.00

1902				7.75			NW¼SW¼	28	33	48	3-15—6-13	.063	11.62
1902						25.45	NW¼SW¼	28	33	48	3-15—4-28	.207	19.00
1902						.95	NE¼SW¼	28	33	48	3-15—4-28	.008	.71
1902						5.20	NW¼SE¼	28	33	48	3-15—4-28	.042	3.90
1902				7.20			NW¼NW¼	27	33	48	3-15—6-13	.059	10.80
1902				6.55			SW¼NW¼	27	33	48	3-15—6-13	.053	9.82
1902					.20		SW¼NW¼	27	33	48	3-15—4-28	.002	.15
1902				13.00			NE¼NE¼	28	33	48	3-15—6-13	.106	19.50
1902				15.20			SE¼NE¼	28	33	48	3-15—6-13	.124	22.80
1902					1.65		SE¼NE¼	28	33	48	3-15—4-28	.013	1.24
1902				8.25			NW¼NE¼	28	33	48	3-15—6-13	.067	12.38
1902				17.10			SW¼NE¼	28	33	48	3-15—6-13	.139	25.65
1902				3.05			NE¼NW¼	28	33	48	3-15—6-13	.025	4.58
1902				18.00			SE¼NW¼	28	33	48	3-15—6-13	.146	27.00
1902						4.85	SW¼NW¼	28	33	48	3-15—4-28	.039	3.64
1902				9.55			SW¼NW¼	28	33	48	3-15—6-13	.078	14.33
1902				9.90			SE¼NE¼	29	33	48	3-15—6-13	.080	14.85
1902				4.25			SW¼NE¼	29	33	48	3-15—6-13	.035	6.38
1902				.20			SE¼NW¼	29	33	48	3-15—6-13	.002	.30

Source—**Humboldt River.** Ditch—**Argenta Slough.**

1890					11.95		NW¼NE¼	2	32	47	3-15—4-28	.156	8.96
1890					4.95		NE¼NE¼	2	32	47	3-15—4-28	.040	3.71
1890				.70			SE¼SW¼	34	33	47	3-15—6-13	.006	1.05
1890				1.80			SW¼SE¼	34	33	47	3-15—6-13	.015	2.70
1890						18.60	SW¼SE¼	34	33	47	3-15—4-28	.151	13.95
1890				1.50			NW¼SW¼	36	33	47	3-15—6-13	.012	2.25
1890				26.55			SW¼SW¼	36	33	47	3-15—6-13	.216	39.83
1890				37.35			SE¼SW¼	36	33	47	3-15—6-13	.304	56.03
1890				10.20			NE¼SW¼	36	33	47	3-15—6-13	.083	15.30
1890				26.25			NW¼SE¼	36	33	47	3-15—6-13	.213	39.38
1890				21.50			NE¼SE¼	36	33	47	3-15—6-13	.175	32.25
1890						9.75	NE¼SE¼	36	33	47	3-15—4-28	.079	7.31
1890						31.30	SW¼NE¼	36	33	47	3-15—4-28	.254	23.48
1890					2.40		SE¼NE¼	36	33	47	3-15—4-28	.020	1.80
1890						34.30	SE¼NE¼	36	33	47	3-15—4-28	.279	25.73
1890				6.45			SW¼NW¼	31	33	47	3-15—6-13	.052	9.68
1890						29.45	SW¼NW¼	31	33	47	3-15—4-28	.239	22.09
1890				5.90			SE¼NW¼	31	33	47	3-15—6-13	.048	8.85
1890					12.60		SE¼NW¼	31	33	47	3-15—4-28	.102	9.45
1890				4.20			SW¼SW¼	33	33	47	3-15—6-13	.033	6.30
1890					4.65		SW¼SW¼	33	33	47	3-15—4-28	.036	3.49
1890						5.55	SW¼SW¼	33	33	47	3-15—4-28	.043	4.16
1890					16.10		SW¼NW¼	4	32	47	3-15—4-28	.131	12.08
1890					.40		NW¼SW¼	4	32	47	3-15—4-28	.003	.30
1890					4.80		NE¼SW¼	4	32	47	3-15—4-28	.040	3.60
1890					12.35		SE¼NW¼	4	32	47	3-15—4-28	.100	9.26
1890					.20		NW¼SE¼	4	32	47	3-15—4-28	.002	.15
1890					13.10		SW¼NE¼	4	32	47	3-15—4-28	.107	9.83
1890					9.50		SE¼NE¼	4	32	47	3-15—4-28	.077	7.13
1890					14.70		SW¼NW¼	3	32	47	3-15—4-28	.120	11.03
1890					12.50		NW¼SW¼	3	32	47	3-15—4-28	.102	9.38

William Dunphy Estate—Continued.

Year of priority	Culture—Acres: Harvest crops	Culture—Acres: Meadow pasture	Culture—Acres: Diversified pasture		Location: Subdivision	Location: Section	Location: Tp. N.	Location: R. E.	Length of season	Duty of water: C. F. S.	Duty of water: Acre-feet
1890			16.65		SE¼NW¼	3	32	47	3-15—4-28	.135	12.49
1890			13.15		NE¼SW¼	3	32	47	3-15—4-28	.107	10.13
1890		6.50			NW¼SE¼	[illegible]	32	47	3-15—6-13	.053	9.75
1890		4.95			NE¼SE¼	3	32	47	3-15—6-13	.040	7.43
1890		15.75			NE¼NE¼	3	32	47	3-15—6-13	.128	23.63
1890		9.00			NW¼NE¼	3	32	47	3-15—6-13	.073	13.50
1890			35.85		NW¼NW¼	2	32	47	3-15—4-28	.291	26.89
1890				4.40	NW¼NE¼	5	32	47	3-15—4-28	.030	3.30
1890				8.15	NE¼NE¼	5	32	47	3-15—4-28	.066	14.88
1890				13.70	SW¼NE¼	5	32	47	3-15—4-28	.111	10.28
1890				30.25	SE¼NE¼	5	32	47	3-15—4-28	.246	22.69
1890				3.50	NW¼SE¼	5	32	47	3-15—4-28	.028	2.68
1890				7.20	NE¼SE¼	5	32	47	3-15—4-28	.059	5.40
1890	34.60				NW¼NW¼	6	32	47	3-15—9-15	.280	103.80
1890				3.00	NW¼NW¼	6	32	47	3-15—4-28	.024	2.25
1890	31.18				NE¼NW¼	6	32	47	3-15—9-15	.252	93.54
1890				2.60	NE¼NW¼	6	32	47	3-15—4-28	.021	1.95
1890	1.18				SW¼NW¼	6	32	47	3-15—9-15	.010	3.54
1890			3.45		SW¼NW¼	6	32	47	3-15—4-28	.020	2.59
1890				34.20	SW¼NW¼	6	32	47	3-15—4-28	.277	25.65
1893	2.15				SE¼NW¼	6	32	47	3-15—9-15	.017	6.45
1890		4.75			SE¼NW¼	6	32	47	3-15—6-13	.039	7.13
1890			8.15		SE¼NW¼	6	32	47	3-15—4-28	.066	6.11
1890				21.60	SE¼NW¼	6	32	47	3-15—4-28	.176	16.20
1890	15.05				NE¼NE¼	6	32	47	3-15—9-15	.122	45.15
1890		7.65			NE¼NE¼	6	32	47	3-15—6-13	.062	11.48
1890			1.15		NE¼NE¼	6	32	47	3-15—4-28	.009	.86
1890	30.45				NW¼NE¼	6	32	47	3-15—9-15	.248	91.35
1890			2.85		NW¼NE¼	6	32	47	3-15—4-28	.023	2.14
1890		12.65			SW¼NE¼	6	32	47	3-15—6-13	.103	18.98
1890	1.55				SE¼NE¼	6	32	47	3-15—9-15	.013	4.65
1890		21.85			SE¼NE¼	6	32	47	3-15—6-13	.178	32.78
1890			14.10		SE¼NE¼	6	32	47	3-15—4-28	.158	10.58
1890				4.90	NE¼NW¼	5	32	47	3-15—4-28	.040	3.68
1890				6.85	NW¼NW¼	5	32	47	3-15—4-28	.056	5.14
1890				14.70	SE¼NW¼	5	32	47	3-15—4-28	.120	11.03
1890				4.15	SW¼NW¼	5	32	47	3-15—4-28	.034	3.11
1890				4.25	NW¼NE¼	5	32	47	3-15—4-28	.035	3.19
1890				19.70	SW¼NE¼	5	32	47	3-15—4-28	.160	14.78
1890			33.60		NE¼NW¼	2	32	47	3-15—4-28	.273	25.20
1890			26.70		SW¼NW¼	2	32	47	3-15—4-28	.217	20.03
1890			9.40		SE¼NW¼	2	32	47	3-15—4-28	.076	7.05
1890				8.15	SE¼NW¼	21	33	47	3-15—4-28	.066	6.11
1890		.35			NW¼SW¼	31	33	47	3-15—6-13	.003	.53
1890				10.95	NW¼SW¼	31	[illegible]	47	3-15—4-28	.088	8.21
1890		14.40			SW¼NE¼	31	[illegible]	47	3-15—6-13	.117	21.00

1890						13.15	SW¼NE¼	31	33	47	3-15—4-28	.107	9.86
1890				20.55			SE¼NE¼	31	33	47	3-15—6-13	.167	30.83
1890					5.30		SE¼NE¼	31	33	47	3-15—4-28	.043	3.98

Source—**Humboldt River.** Ditch—**Bull Field Slough.**

1904				6.20			NE¼NE¼	34	33	47	3-15—6-13	.050	9.30
1904				9.55			NW¼NW¼	35	33	47	3-15—6-13	.078	14.33
1904					1.30		NW¼NW¼	35	33	47	3-15—4-28	.011	.98
1904				15.25			SW¼NW¼	35	33	47	3-15—6-13	.124	22.88
1904						17.65	SW¼NW¼	35	33	47	3-15—4-28	.143	13.24
1904				4.90			SE¼NW¼	35	33	47	3-15—6-13	.048	7.35
1904					4.50		SE¼NW¼	35	33	47	3-15—4-28	.037	3.38
1904						11.70	SE¼NW¼	35	33	47	3-15—4-28	.095	8.79
1904			8.60				NE¼NW¼	35	33	47	3-15—9-15	.070	25.80
1904				19.05			NE¼NW¼	35	33	47	3-15—6-13	.155	28.58
1904				.30			NW¼SW¼	35	33	47	3-15—6-13	.002	.45
1904						31.00	NW¼SW¼	35	33	47	3-15—4-28	.252	23.25
1904				22.15			SW¼SW¼	35	33	47	3-15—6-13	.180	33.23
1904						15.95	SW¼SW¼	35	33	47	3-15—4-28	.130	11.96
1904				1.65			SE¼SW¼	35	33	47	3-15—6-13	.013	2.48
1904						32.35	SE¼SW¼	35	33	47	3-15—4-28	.263	24.36
1904				.80			NE¼SW¼	35	33	47	3-15—6-13	.007	1.20
1904						33.05	NE¼SW¼	35	33	47	3-15—4-28	.269	24.79
1904				11.50			NW¼SE¼	35	33	47	3-15—6-13	.093	17.25
1904				9.45			SE¼SW¼	33	33	47	3-15—6-13	.077	14.18
1904					3.05		SE¼SW¼	33	33	47	3-15—4-28	.025	2.29
1904						20.95	SE¼SW¼	33	33	47	3-15—4-28	.170	15.71
1904				.80			NE¼SW¼	33	33	47	3-15—6-13	.007	1.20
1904					8.30		NE¼SW¼	33	33	47	3-15—4-28	.067	6.23
1904				.10			NE¼NE¼	33	33	47	3-15—6-13	.001	.15
1904				12.30			NW¼SE¼	33	33	47	3-15—6-13	.100	18.45
1904					4.70		NW¼SE¼	33	33	47	3-15—4-28	.038	3.53
1904				7.50			SW¼SE¼	33	33	47	3-15—6-13	.061	11.25
1904						28.45	SW¼SE¼	33	33	47	3-15—4-28	.231	21.34
1904				17.00			SE¼SE¼	33	33	47	3-15—6-13	.138	25.50
1904						18.65	SE¼SE¼	33	33	47	3-15—4-28	.152	13.99
1904				24.45			NE¼SE¼	33	33	47	3-15—6-13	.190	36.68
1904					9.30		NE¼SE¼	33	33	47	3-15—4-28	.076	6.98
1904			21.45				NW¼NE¼	33	33	47	3-15—9-15	.174	64.35
1904						14.15	NW¼NE¼	33	33	47	3-15—4-28	.115	10.61
1904					2.35		SW¼NE¼	33	33	47	3-15—4-28	.019	1.76
1904				.70			SE¼NE¼	33	33	47	3-15—6-13	.006	1.05
1904					5.20		SE¼NE¼	33	33	47	3-15—4-28	.042	3.90
1904				37.65			NW¼SW¼	34	33	47	3-15—6-13	.306	56.48
1904						2.15	NW¼SW¼	34	33	47	3-15—4-28	.017	1.61
1904				4.35			SW¼SW¼	34	33	47	3-15—6-13	.035	6.53
1904						29.85	SW¼SW¼	34	33	47	3-15—4-28	.243	22.40
1904						32.95	SE¼SW¼	34	33	47	3-15—4-28	.268	24.71
1904				15.90			NE¼SW¼	34	33	47	3-15—6-13	.129	23.85
1904					.90		NE¼SW¼	34	33	47	3-15—4-28	.007	.68
1904						19.90	NE¼SW¼	34	33	47	3-15—4-28	.162	14.93
1904				22.10			NW¼SE¼	34	33	47	3-15—6-13	.180	33.15

William Dunphy Estate—Continued.

Year of priority	Culture—Acres: Harvest crops	Meadow pasture	Diversified pasture		Location: Subdivision	Section	Tp.N.	R.E.	Length of season	Duty of water: C.F.S.	Acre-feet
1904	....	....	1.10	....	NW¼SE¼	34	33	47	3-15—4-28	.009	.83
1904	....	....	....	11.40	NW¼SE¼	34	33	47	3-15—4-28	.093	8.55
1904	....	13.70	....	....	SW¼SE¼	34	33	47	3-15—6-13	.111	20.55
1904	....	17.30	....	....	SE¼SE¼	34	33	47	3-15—6-13	.141	25.95
1904	....	....	....	17.75	SE¼SE¼	34	33	47	3-15—4-28	.144	13.31
1904	....	17.50	....	....	NE¼SE¼	34	33	47	3-15—6-13	.142	26.25
1904	....	....	....	13.00	NE¼SE¼	34	33	47	3-15—4-28	.106	9.75
1904	....	1.40	....	....	SW¼NE¼	34	33	47	3-15—6-13	.011	2.10
1904	....	....	1.60	....	SW¼NE¼	34	33	47	3-15—4-28	.013	1.20
1904	....	....	....	1.20	SW¼NE¼	34	33	47	3-15—4-28	.010	.90
1904	....	....	....	24.40	NW¼SE¼	35	33	47	3-15—4-28	.198	18.30
1904	....	.30	....	....	SW¼SE¼	35	33	47	3-15—6-13	.002	.45
1904	....	....	....	34.60	SW¼SE¼	35	33	47	3-15—4-28	.281	25.95
1904	....	.30	....	....	SE¼SE¼	35	33	47	3-15—6-13	.002	.45
1904	....	....	....	34.15	SE¼SE¼	35	33	47	3-15—4-28	.278	25.61
1904	....	17.65	....	....	NE¼SE¼	35	33	47	3-15—6-13	.143	26.48
1904	....	....	....	14.65	NE¼SE¼	35	33	47	3-15—4-28	.119	10.99
1904	....	....	4.50	....	NW¼NE¼	35	33	47	3-15—4-28	.037	3.38
1904	....	....	2.70	....	SW¼NE¼	35	33	47	3-15—4-28	.022	2.03
1904	....	....	4.45	....	NE¼NE¼	35	33	47	3-15—4-28	.036	3.34
1904	....	.15	....	....	NW¼NW¼	36	33	47	3-15—6-13	.001	.28
1904	....	....	2.65	....	NW¼NW¼	36	33	47	3-15—4-28	.022	1.99
1904	....	4.45	....	....	SW¼NW¼	36	33	47	3-15—6-13	.036	6.68
1904	....	2.25	....	....	NW¼SW¼	86	33	47	3-15—6-13	.018	3.38
1904	....	....	....	2.40	NW¼SW¼	36	33	47	3-15—4-28	.020	1.80
1904	....	....	....	4.55	SW¼SW¼	36	33	47	3-15—4-28	.037	3.41
1904	....	3.95	....	....	NW¼NW¼	36	33	47	3-15—6-13	.032	5.93
1904	....	....	8.00	....	NW¼NW¼	36	33	47	3-15—4-28	.065	6.00
1904	....	....	....	.55	NW¼NW¼	36	33	47	3-15—4-28	.004	.41
1904	....	25.55	....	....	SW¼NW¼	36	33	47	3-15—6-13	.208	38.33
1904	....	....	....	.45	SW¼NW¼	36	33	47	3-15—4-28	.001	.34
1904	....	22.45	....	....	SE¼NW¼	36	33	47	3-15—6-13	.183	33.68
1904	....	....	....	12.55	SE¼NW¼	36	33	47	3-15—4-28	.102	9.41
1904	....	....	....	19.10	NE¼NW¼	36	33	47	3-15—4-28	.155	14.33
1904	....	14.95	....	....	NW¼SW¼	36	83	47	3-15—6-13	.122	22.43
1904	....	....	....	10.60	NW¼SW¼	86	33	47	3-15—4-28	.086	7.95
1904	....	....	....	.20	SW¼SW¼	36	33	47	3-15—4-28	.002	.15
1904	....	13.05	....	....	NE¼SW¼	36	33	47	3-15—6-13	.106	19.58
1904	....	....	....	6.80	NE¼SW¼	36	33	47	3-15—4-28	.055	5.10
1904	....	....	....	5.00	NW¼SE¼	36	33	47	3-15—4-28	.040	3.75
1904	....	8.90	....	....	SE¼NE¼	34	33	47	3-15—6-13	.072	13.35
1904	....	....	1.65	....	SE¼NE¼	34	33	47	3-15—4-28	.018	1.24
1904	....	....	....	17.15	SE¼NE¼	34	33	47	3-15—4-28	.150	12.[illegible]

Source—Humboldt River.

1886			.15				NE¼ SE¼	32	33	47	3-15—9-15	.001	0.15
1886				2.30			NE¼ SE¼	32	33	47	3-15—6-13	.019	3.45
1886				6.75			SW¼ SE¼	32	33	47	3-15—6-13	.055	10.13
1886					4.10		SW¼ SE¼	32	33	47	3-15—4-28	.031	3.08
1886				14.35			SE¼ SE¼	32	33	47	3-15—6-13	.117	21.53
1886				1.20			NW¼ SE¼	32	33	47	3-15—6-13	.010	1.80
1886					7.60		SW¼ NE¼	31	33	47	3-15—4-28	.062	5.70
1886					24.20		SE¼ NE¼	31	33	47	3-15—4-28	.197	18.15
1886					24.17		NW¼ SE¼	31	33	47	3-15—4-28	.197	18.13
1886					28.05		NE¼ SE¼	31	33	47	3-15—4-28	.228	21.04
1886					4.75		NW¼ NW¼	32	33	47	3-15—4-28	.039	3.56
1886					31.80		SE¼ NW¼	32	33	47	3-15—4-28	.259	23.85
1886					38.60		SW¼ NW¼	32	33	47	3-15—4-28	.314	28.95
1886				14.20			NE¼ SW¼	32	33	47	3-15—6-13	.115	21.30
1886						4.56	NE¼ SW¼	32	33	47	3-15—4-28	.037	3.41
1886			26.45				SW¼ NW¼	33	33	47	3-15—9-15	.215	79.35
1886						8.50	SW¼ NW¼	33	33	47	3-15—4-28	.069	6.38
1886			24.70				SE¼ NW¼	33	33	47	3-15—9-15	.200	74.10
1886						10.70	SE¼ NW¼	33	33	47	3-15—4-28	.087	8.03
1886			17.75				NE¼ NW¼	33	33	47	3-15—9-15	.144	53.25
1886						10.70	NE¼ NW¼	33	33	47	3-15—4-28	.087	8.03
1886					1.60		NW¼ SW¼	33	33	47	3-15—4-28	.013	1.20
1886						31.90	NW¼ SW¼	33	33	47	3-15—4-28	.259	23.93
1886					3.90		SW¼ SW¼	33	33	47	3-15—4-28	.032	2.93
1886						3.85	SW¼ SW¼	33	33	47	3-15—4-28	.031	2.89
1886					.60		NE¼ SW¼	33	33	47	3-15—4-28	.005	0.45
1886						15.80	NE¼ SW¼	33	33	47	3-15—4-28	.128	11.85
1886			20.85				NE¼ NE¼	33	33	47	3-15—9-15	.170	62.55
1886				.30			NE¼ NE¼	33	33	47	3-15—6-13	.002	0.45
1886						10.70	NE¼ NE¼	33	33	47	3-15—4-28	.087	8.03
1886				3.05			NW¼ SE¼	33	33	47	3-15—6-13	.025	4.58
1886						8.05	NW¼ SE¼	33	33	47	3-15—4-28	.065	6.04
1886			14.90				SW¼ NE¼	33	33	47	3-15—9-15	.121	44.70
1886				2.20			SW¼ NE¼	33	33	47	3-15—6-13	.018	3.30
1886						13.70	SW¼ NE¼	33	33	47	3-15—4-28	.111	10.28
1886			0.70				SE¼ NE¼	33	33	47	3-15—9-15	.006	2.10
1886				15.85			SE¼ NE¼	33	33	47	3-15—6-13	.129	23.78
1886					2.95		SE¼ NE¼	33	33	47	3-15—4-28	.024	2.21
1886						2.40	SE¼ NE¼	33	33	47	3-15—4-28	.020	1.80
1886				27.00			NW¼ NW¼	34	33	47	3-15—6-13	.220	40.50
1886					2.30		NW¼ NW¼	34	33	47	3-15—4-28	.017	1.73
1886						6.10	NW¼ NW¼	34	33	47	3-15—4-28	.048	4.58
1886				19.45			SW¼ NW¼	34	33	47	3-15—6-13	.158	29.18
1886					9.70		SW¼ NW¼	34	33	47	3-15—4-28	.077	7.28
1886				27.80			SE¼ NW¼	34	33	47	3-15—6-13	.226	41.70
1886					5.70		SE¼ NW¼	34	33	47	3-15—4-28	.045	4.28
1886			34.00				NW¼ NE¼	34	33	47	3-15—9-15	.276	102.00
1886				2.20			NW¼ NE¼	34	33	47	3-15—6-13	.016	3.30
1886					.10		NW¼ NE¼	34	33	47	3-15—4-28	.001	0.08
1886			2.95				SW¼ NE¼	34	33	47	3-15—9-15	.022	8.85
1886				17.20			SW¼ NE¼	34	33	47	3-15—6-13	.140	25.80
1886					4.75		SW¼ NE¼	34	33	47	3-15—4-28	.037	3.56

William Dunphy Estate—Continued.

Year of priority	Culture—Acres: Harvest crops	Meadow pasture	Diversified pasture		Location: Subdivision	Section	Tp.N.	R.E.	Length of season	Duty of water: C.F.S.	Acre-feet
1904			1.10		NW¼ SE¼	34	33	47	3-15—4-28	.009	.83
1904				11.40	NW¼ SE¼	34	33	47	3-15—4-28	.093	8.55
1904		13.70			SW¼ SE¼	34	33	47	3-15—6-13	.111	20.55
1904		17.30			SE¼ SE¼	34	33	47	3-15—6-13	.141	25.95
1904				17.75	SE¼ SE¼	34	33	47	3-15—4-28	.144	13.31
1904		17.50			NE¼ SE¼	34	33	47	3-15—6-13	.142	26.25
1904				13.00	NE¼ SE¼	34	33	47	3-15—4-28	.106	9.75
1904		1.40			SW¼ NE¼	34	33	47	3-15—6-13	.011	2.10
1904			1.60		SW¼ NE¼	34	33	47	3-15—4-28	.013	1.20
1904				1.20	SW¼ NE¼	34	33	47	3-15—4-28	.010	.90
1904				24.40	NW¼SE¼	35	33	47	3-15—4-28	.196	18.30
1904		.30			SW¼SE¼	35	33	47	3-15—6-13	.002	.45
1904				34.60	SW¼SE¼	35	33	47	3-15—4-28	.281	25.95
1904		.30			SE¼SE¼	35	33	47	3-15—6-13	.002	.45
1904				34.15	SE¼SE¼	35	33	47	3-15—4-28	.278	25.61
1904		17.65			NE¼SE¼	35	33	47	3-15—6-13	.143	26.48
1904				14.65	NE¼SE¼	35	33	47	3-15—4-28	.119	10.99
1904			4.50		NW¼NE¼	35	33	47	3-15—4-28	.037	3.38
1904			2.70		SW¼NE¼	35	33	47	3-15—4-28	.022	2.03
1904			4.45		NE¼NE¼	35	33	47	3-15—4-28	.036	3.34
1904		.15			NW¼NW¼	36	33	47	3-15—6-13	.001	.23
1904			2.65		NW¼NW¼	36	33	47	3-15—4-28	.022	1.99
1904		4.45			SW¼NW¼	36	33	47	3-15—6-13	.036	6.68
1904		2.25			NW¼SW¼	36	33	47	3-15—6-13	.018	3.38
1904				2.40	NW¼SW¼	36	33	47	3-15—4-28	.020	1.80
1904				4.55	SW¼SW¼	36	33	47	3-15—4-28	.037	3.41
1904		3.95			NW¼NW¼	36	33	47	3-15—6-13	.032	5.93
1904			8.00		NW¼NW¼	36	33	47	3-15—4-28	.065	6.00
1904				.55	NW¼NW¼	36	33	47	3-15—4-28	.004	.41
1904		25.55			SW¼NW¼	36	33	47	3-15—6-13	.208	38.33
1904				.45	SW¼NW¼	36	33	47	3-15—4-28	.004	.34
1904		22.45			SE¼NW¼	36	33	47	3-15—6-13	.183	33.68
1904				12.55	SE¼NW¼	36	33	47	3-15—4-28	.102	9.41
1904				19.10	NE¼NW¼	36	33	47	3-15—4-28	.155	14.33
1904		14.95			NW¼SW¼	36	33	47	3-15—6-13	.122	22.43
1904				10.60	NW¼SW¼	36	33	47	3-15—4-28	.086	7.95
1904				.20	SW¼SW¼	36	33	47	3-15—4-28	.002	.15
1904		13.05			NE¼SW¼	36	33	47	3-15—6-13	.106	19.58
1904				6.80	NE¼SW¼	36	33	47	3-15—4-28	.055	5.10
1904				5.00	NW¼SE¼	36	33	47	3-15—4-28	.040	3.75
1904		8.90			SE¼ NE¼	34	33	47	3-15—6-13	.072	13.35
1904			1.65		SE¼ NE¼	34	33	47	3-15—4-28	.013	1.24
1904				17.15	SE¼ NE¼	34	33	47	3-15—4-28	.139	12.86

Source—

1886			.15				NE¼ SE¼	32	33	47	3-15—9-15	.001	0.45
1886				2.30			NE¼ SE¼	32	33	47	3-15—6-13	.019	3.45
1886				6.75			SW¼ SE¼	32	33	47	3-15—6-13	.055	10.13
1886					4.10		SW¼ SE¼	32	33	47	3-15—4-28	.033	2.08
1886				11.35			SE¼ SE¼	32	33	47	3-15—6-13	.117	21.53
1886				1.20			NW¼ SE¼	32	33	47	3-15—6-13	.010	1.80
1886					7.00		SW¼ NE¼	31	33	47	3-15—4-28	.062	5.70
1886					24.20		SE¼ NE¼	31	33	47	3-15—4-28	.197	18.15
1886					24.17		NW¼ SE¼	31	33	47	3-15—4-28	.197	18.13
1886					28.05		NE¼ SE¼	31	33	47	3-15—4-28	.228	21.04
1886					4.75		NW¼ NW¼	32	33	47	3-15—4-28	.039	3.56
1886					31.80		SE¼ NW¼	32	33	47	3-15—4-28	.259	23.85
1886					38.60		SW¼ NW¼	32	33	47	3-15—4-28	.314	28.95
1886				14.20			NE¼ SW¼	32	33	47	3-15—6-13	.115	21.30
1886						4.56	NE¼ SW¼	32	33	47	3-15—4-28	.037	3.41
1886			26.45				SW¼ NW¼	33	33	47	3-15—9-15	.215	79.35
1886						8.50	SW¼ NW¼	33	33	47	3-15—4-28	.069	6.38
1886			24.70				SE¼ NW¼	33	33	47	3-15—9-15	.200	74.10
1886						10.70	SE¼ NW¼	33	33	47	3-15—4-28	.087	8.03
1886			17.75				NE¼ NW¼	33	33	47	3-15—9-15	.144	53.25
1886						10.70	NE¼ NW¼	33	33	47	3-15—4-28	.087	8.03
1886					1.60		NW¼ SW¼	33	33	47	3-15—4-28	.013	1.20
1886						31.90	NW¼ SW¼	33	33	47	3-15—4-28	.259	23.93
1886					3.90		SW¼ SW¼	33	33	47	3-15—4-28	.032	2.93
1886						3.85	SW¼ SW¼	33	33	47	3-15—4-28	.031	2.89
1886					.60		NE¼ SW¼	33	33	47	3-15—4-28	.005	0.45
1886						15.80	NE¼ SW¼	33	33	47	3-15—4-28	.128	11.85
1886			20.85				NE¼ NE¼	33	33	47	3-15—9-15	.170	62.55
1886				.30			NE¼ NE¼	33	33	47	3-15—6-13	.002	0.45
1886						10.70	NE¼ NE¼	33	33	47	3-15—4-28	.087	8.03
1886				3.05			NW¼ SE¼	33	33	47	3-15—6-13	.025	4.58
1886						8.05	NW¼ SE¼	33	33	47	3-15—4-28	.065	6.04
1886			14.90				SW¼ NE¼	33	33	47	3-15—9-15	.121	44.70
1886				2.20			SW¼ NE¼	33	33	47	3-15—6-13	.018	3.30
1886						13.70	SW¼ NE¼	33	33	47	3-15—4-28	.111	10.28
1886			0.70				SE¼ NE¼	33	33	47	3-15—9-15	.006	2.10
1886				15.85			SE¼ NE¼	33	33	47	3-15—6-13	.129	23.78
1886					2.95		SE¼ NE¼	33	33	47	3-15—4-28	.024	2.21
1886						2.40	SE¼ NE¼	33	33	47	3-15—4-28	.020	1.80
1886				27.00			NW¼ NW¼	34	33	47	3-15—6-13	.220	40.50
1886					2.30		NW¼ NW¼	34	33	47	3-15—4-28	.017	1.73
1886						6.10	NW¼ NW¼	34	33	47	3-15—4-28	.048	4.58
1886				19.45			SW¼ NW¼	34	33	47	3-15—6-13	.158	29.18
1886					9.70		SW¼ NW¼	34	33	47	3-15—4-28	.077	7.28
1886				27.80			SE¼ NW¼	34	33	47	3-15—6-13	.226	41.70
1886					5.70		SE¼ NW¼	34	33	47	3-15—4-28	.045	4.28
1886			34.00				NW¼ NE¼	34	33	47	3-15—9-15	.276	102.00
1886				2.20			NW¼ NE¼	34	33	47	3-15—6-13	.016	3.30
1886					.10		NW¼ NE¼	34	33	47	3-15—4-28	.001	0.08
1886			2.95				SW¼ NE¼	34	33	47	3-15—9-15	.022	8.85
1886				17.20			SW¼ NE¼	34	33	47	3-15—6-13	.140	25.80
1886					4.75		SW¼ NE¼	34	33	47	3-15—4-28	.037	3.56

Claimant—**Russell Land and Cattle Co.** Proof No. 00172

Source—Humboldt River. Ditch—**Southside Ditch, 1879; Northside Ditch, 1887.**

Year of priority	Culture—Acres: Harvest crops	Meadow pasture	Diversified pasture	Location: Subdivision	Section	Tp.N.	R.E.	Length of season	Duty of water: C.F.S.	Acre-feet
1887	5.10			SE¼ SW¼	24	33	44	3-15—9-15	.041	15.30
1887		29.90		SE¼ SW¼	24	33	44	3-15—6-13	.243	44.85
1887	34.80			SW¼ SW¼	24	33	44	3-15—9-15	.283	104.40
1887		5.20		SW¼ SW¼	24	33	44	3-15—6-13	.042	7.80
1887		5.70		NE¼ SW¼	24	33	44	3-15—6-13	.046	8.55
1887		8.77		NW¼ SW¼	24	33	44	3-15—6-13	.071	13.16
1887			28.27	NW¼ SW¼	24	33	44	3-15—4-28	.230	21.20
1887			9.79	SW¼ NW¼	24	33	44	3-15—4-28	.080	7.34
1879		13.57		SE¼ SE¼	23	33	44	3-15—6-13	.110	20.36
1879			1.33	SE¼ SE¼	23	33	44	3-15—4-28	.011	1.00
1887	13.57			SE¼ SE¼	23	33	44	3-15—9-15	.110	40.71
1887			2.85	SE¼ SE¼	23	33	44	3-15—4-28	.023	2.13
1879	19.58			SW¼ SE¼	23	33	44	3-15—9-15	.150	58.74
1879		15.10		SW¼ SE¼	23	33	44	3-15—6-13	.122	22.65
1879			.41	SW¼ SE¼	23	33	44	3-15—4-28	.003	0.31
1887	2.65			SW¼ SE¼	23	33	44	3-15—9-15	.022	7.95
1887			.82	SW¼ SE¼	23	33	44	3-15—4-28	.006	0.62
1879	7.55			SE¼ NE¼	26	33	44	3-15—9-15	.061	22.65
1879		14.42		SE¼ NE¼	26	33	44	3-15—6-13	.117	21.63
1879			16.44	SE¼ NE¼	26	33	44	3-15—4-28	.134	12.33
1887			1.00	SE¼ NE¼	26	33	44	3-15—4-28	.008	0.75
1879		0.92		SW¼ NE¼	26	33	44	3-15—6-13	.007	1.38
1879			39.08	SW¼ NE¼	26	33	44	3-15—4-28	.318	29.31
1879	18.44			NE¼ NE¼	26	33	44	3-15—9-15	.150	55.32
1879		2.36		NE¼ NE¼	26	33	44	3-15—6-13	.019	3.54
1879			2.55	NE¼ NE¼	26	33	44	3-15—4-28	.021	1.91
1887	8.04			NE¼ NE¼	26	33	44	3-15—9-15	.065	24.12
1887			3.06	NE¼ NE¼	26	33	44	3-15—4-28	.025	2.30
1879		23.50		NW¼ NE¼	26	33	44	3-15—6-13	.191	35.25
1879			16.50	NW¼ NE¼	26	33	44	3-15—4-28	.134	12.38
1879			29.07	SE¼ NW¼	26	33	44	3-15—4-28	.236	21.80
1879			40.00	NE¼ NW¼	26	33	44	3-15—4-28	.325	30.00
1879			21.16	NW¼ NW¼	26	33	44	3-15—4-28	.172	15.87
1887		3.15		SW¼ SE¼	24	33	44	3-15—6-13	.026	4.73
1879			16.93	SE¼ SE¼	26	33	44	3-15—4-28	.138	12.60
1879			40.00	NE¼ SE¼	26	33	44	3-15—4-28	.325	30.00
1879			17.85	NW¼ SE¼	26	33	44	3-15—4-28	.145	13.39
1879			1.02	NE¼ SW¼	26	33	44	3-15—4-28	.008	0.77
1887	1.80			NW¼ NE¼	25	33	44	3-15—9-15	.015	5.40
1887		28.60		NW¼ NE¼	25	33	44	3-15—6-13	.233	42.90
1887	15.50			SE¼ NW¼	25	33	44	3-15—9-15	.126	46.50
1887		12.41		SE¼ NW¼	25	33	44	3-15—6-13	.101	18.62
1887			0.82	SE¼ NW¼	25	33	44	3-15—4-28	.007	0.62
1879	4.90			SE¼ NW¼	25	33	44	3-15—9-15	.040	14.70
1879			2.15	SE¼ NW¼	25	33	44	3-15—4-28	.017	1.61

	1879			24.68				SW¼NW¼	25	33	44	3-15—9-15	.201	74.04
	1879				1.84			SW¼NW¼	25	33	44	3-15—6-13	.015	2.76
	1879					1.43		SW¼NW¼	25	33	44	3-15—4-28	.012	1.07
	1887			5.92				SW¼NW¼	25	33	44	3-15—9-15	.048	17.76
	1887					1.83		SW¼NW¼	25	33	44	3-15—4-28	.015	1.37
	1887			31.00				NE¼NW¼	25	33	44	3-15—9-15	.252	93.00
	1887				9.00			NE¼NW¼	25	33	44	3-15—6-13	.073	13.50
	1887			34.06				NW¼NW¼	25	33	44	3-15—9-15	.277	102.18
	1879			2.75				NW¼NW¼	25	33	44	3-15—9-15	.022	8.25
	1879					2.35		NW¼NW¼	25	33	44	3-15—4-28	.019	1.76
	1879			12.56				SE¼SW¼	25	33	44	3-15—9-15	.102	87.68
	1879				27.44			SE¼SW¼	25	33	44	3-15—6-13	.223	41.16
	1879				38.84			SW¼SW¼	25	33	44	3-15—6-13	.316	58.36
	1879					.82		SW¼SW¼	25	33	44	3-15—4-28	.007	0.62
	1879			34.51				NE¼SW¼	25	33	44	3-15—9-15	.281	103.53
	1879					0.61		NE¼SW¼	25	33	44	3-15—4-28	.005	0.46
	1887				.70			NE¼SW¼	25	33	44	3-15—6-13	.006	1.05
	1887					1.05		NE¼SW¼	25	33	44	3-15—4-28	.009	0.79
	1879			7.04				NW¼SW¼	25	33	44	3-15—9-15	.060	21.12
	1879				32.96			NW¼SW¼	25	33	44	3-15—6-13	.268	49.44
	1887			12.75				SE¼NE¼	25	33	44	3-15—9-15	.104	38.25
	1887				13.10			SE¼NE¼	25	33	44	3-15—6-13	.107	19.65
	1887			30.00				SW¼NE¼	25	33	44	3-15—9-15	.244	90.00
	1887					0.61		SW¼NE¼	25	33	44	3-15—4-28	.005	0.46
	1879			0.80				SW¼NE¼	25	33	44	3-15—9-15	.007	2.40
	1879					0.61		SW¼NE¼	25	33	44	3-15—4-28	.005	0.46
	1887				1.20			NE¼NE¼	25	33	44	3-15—6-13	.010	1.80
	1879					4.00		NW¼SW¼	4	33	44	3-15—4-28	.003	3.00
	1879						16.63	NW¼SW¼	4	33	44	3-15—4-28	.135	12.47
	1887			6.32				SW¼SE¼	4	33	44	3-15—9-15	.051	18.96
	1887					1.12		SW¼SE¼	4	33	44	3-15—4-28	.000	0.84
	1887			21.29				NE¼SE¼	4	33	44	3-15—9-15	.173	63.87
	1887				18.91			NE¼SE¼	4	33	44	3-15—6-13	.154	28.37
	1887			4.55				NW¼SE¼	4	33	44	3-15—9-15	.037	13.65
	1887				5.02			NW¼SE¼	4	33	44	3-15—6-13	.041	7.53
	1887					3.51		NW¼SE¼	4	33	44	3-15—4-28	.029	2.63
	1879				16.63			NW¼SE¼	4	33	44	3-15—6-13	.135	24.95
	1879					1.25		NW¼SE¼	4	33	44	3-15—4-28	.010	0.94
	1879				28.78			SE¼SW¼	4	33	44	3-15—6-13	.234	43.17
	1879					9.49		SE¼SW¼	4	33	44	3-15—4-28	.077	7.11
	1879				20.71			SW¼SW¼	4	33	44	3-15—6-13	.168	31.07
	1879						18.00	SW¼SW¼	4	33	44	3-15—4-28	.146	13.50
	1879			5.15				NE¼SW¼	4	33	44	3-15—9-15	.042	15.45
	1879				29.01			NE¼SW¼	4	33	44	3-15—6-13	.236	43.52
	1879					5.50		NE¼SW¼	4	33	44	3-15—4-28	.045	4.13
	1879				18.69			NW¼SW¼	4	33	44	3-15—6-13	.152	28.04
	1887				12.83			SW¼SE¼	3	33	44	3-15—6-13	.104	19.25
	1887				20.55			SE¼SW¼	3	33	44	3-15—6-13	.167	30.83
	1887			11.60				SW¼SW¼	3	33	44	3-15—9-15	.119	43.80
	1887				21.80			SW¼SW¼	3	33	44	3-15—6-13	.177	32.70
	1887						3.00	SW¼SW¼	3	33	44	3-15—4-28	.029	2.70
	1887				19.87			NW¼SW¼	3	33	44	3-15—6-13	.162	29.81

Russell Land and Cattle Co.—Continued.

Year of priority	Culture—Acres: Harvest crops	Meadow pasture	Diversified pasture		Location: Subdivision	Section	Tp. N.	R. E.	Length of season	Duty of water: C. F. S.	Acre-feet
1887				20.13	NW¼SW¼	5	33	44	3-15—4-28	.164	15.10
1887		6.56			SW¼NW¼	5	33	44	3-15—6-13.	.053	9.84
1887				33.44	SW¼NW¼	5	33	44	3-15—4-28	.272	25.08
1887				33.50	NW¼NW¼	5	33	44	3-15—4-28	.272	25.12
1887	19.07				SE¼SE¼	4	33	44	3-15—9-15	.155	57.21
1887		12.86			SE¼SE¼	4	33	44	3-15—6-13	.105	19.29
1887			.45		SE¼SE¼	4	33	44	3-15—4-28	.004	0.34
1879	2.14				SE¼SE¼	4	33	44	3-15—9-15	.017	6.42
1879			.41		SE¼SE¼	4	33	44	3-15—4-28	.003	0.31
1879	20.01				SW¼SE¼	4	33	44	3-15—9-15	.163	60.03
1879			5.97		SW¼SE¼	4	33	44	3-15—4-28	.047	4.31
1879				19.40	SE¼NW¼	32	34	44	3-15—4-28	.158	14.55
1879		3.07			SE¼NW¼	32	34	44	3-15—6-13	.025	5.61
1879				30.20	NE¼NW¼	32	34	44	3-15—4-28	.246	22.65
1887			2.20		NE¼NE¼	32	34	44	3-15—4-28	.018	1.65
1879		13.66			NE¼NE¼	32	34	44	3-15—6-13	.111	20.49
1879			8.31		NE¼NE¼	32	34	44	3-15—4-28	.068	6.23
1879		37.32			NW¼NE¼	32	34	44	3-15—6-13	.303	55.98
1879				1.70	NW¼NE¼	32	34	44	3-15—4-28	.014	1.28
1879			1.00		SW¼NW¼	33	34	44	3-15—4-28	.008	0.75
1887		2.50			NE¼NW¼	33	34	44	3-15—6-13	.020	3.75
1887		18.71			NW¼NW¼	33	34	44	3-15—6-13	.152	28.07
1879		32.85			SE¼SE¼	32	34	44	3-15—6-13	.267	49.28
1879				6.19	SE¼SE¼	32	34	44	3-15—4-28	.050	4.64
1879		0.30			SW¼SE¼	32	34	44	3-15—6-13	.002	0.45
1879				5.60	SW¼SE¼	32	34	44	3-15—4-28	.046	4.20
1879		39.10			NE¼SE¼	32	34	44	3-15—6-13	.318	58.65
1887			.20		NE¼SE¼	32	34	44	3-15—4-28	.002	0.15
1879		15.44			NW¼SE¼	32	34	44	3-15—6-13	.126	23.16
1879				6.63	NW¼SE¼	32	34	44	3-15—4-28	.054	4.97
1879		34.25			SE¼NE¼	32	34	44	3-15—6-13	.278	51.38
1879			1.00		SE¼NE¼	32	34	44	3-15—4-28	.008	0.75
1887		3.27			SE¼NE¼	32	34	44	3-15—6-13	.027	4.91
1879		32.69			SW¼NE¼	32	34	44	3-15—6-13	.266	49.04
1879				7.20	SW¼NE¼	32	34	44	3-15—4-28	.059	5.40
1887		10.80			NE¼NE¼	32	34	44	3-15—6-13	.088	16.20
1879		10.60			SE¼SW¼	33	34	44	3 15—6-13	.086	15.90
1879			4.64		SE¼SW¼	33	34	44	3-15—4-28	.038	3.18
1887		18.04			SE¼SW¼	33	34	44	3-15—6-13	.147	27.06
1887			1.39		SE¼SW¼	33	34	44	3-15—4-28	.011	1.01
1879		40.00			SW¼SW¼	33	34	44	3-15—6-13	.325	60.00
1887		35.74			NE¼SW¼	33	34	44	3-15—6-13	.291	53.61
1887				2.00	NE¼SW¼	33	34	44	3-15—4-28	.016	1.50
1879			.70		NE¼SW¼	33	34	44	3 15—4-28	.006	0.53
1879		24.30			NW¼SW¼	33	34	44	3 15—6-13	.198	36.45
1879			1.39		NW¼SW¼	33	34	44	3 15—4 28	.011	1.04

1887		9.00			NW¼SW¼	33	34	44	3-15—6-13	.078	14.40
1887			1.59		NW¼SW¼	33	34	44	3-15—4-28	.013	1.10
1887				16.00	SW¼NE¼	33	34	44	3-15—4-28	.130	12.00
1887		18.91			SE¼NW¼	33	34	44	3-15—6-13	.154	28.37
1887				21.09	SE¼NW¼	33	34	44	3-15—4-28	.171	15.81
1887		34.85			SW¼NW¼	33	34	44	3-15—6-13	.283	52.28
1879		1.80			SW¼NW¼	33	34	44	3-15—6-13	.015	2.79
1887	9.21				SE¼NE¼	4	33	44	3-15—9-15	.075	27.63
1887		30.79			SE¼NE¼	4	33	44	3-15—6-13	.250	46.19
1887	19.40				SW¼NE¼	4	33	44	3-15—9-15	.158	58.20
1887		8.51			SW¼NE¼	4	33	44	3-15—6-13	.069	12.77
1887			2.67		SW¼NE¼	4	33	44	3-15—4-28	.022	2.00
1879		3.07			SW¼NE¼	4	33	44	3-15—6-13	.025	4.61
1879			1.99		SW¼NE¼	4	33	44	3-15—4-28	.016	1.49
1887		29.10			NE¼NE¼	4	33	44	3-15—6-13	.237	43.65
1887				10.90	NE¼NE¼	4	33	44	3-15—4-28	.089	8.18
1887		40.00			NW¼NE¼	4	33	44	3-15—6-13	.325	60.00
1879	25.34				SE¼NW¼	4	33	44	3-15—9-15	.206	76.02
1879		5.55			SE¼NW¼	4	33	44	3-15—6-13	.045	8.25
1879			.80		SE¼NW¼	4	33	44	3-15—4-28	.007	0.60
1887		2.83			SE¼NW¼	4	33	44	3-15—6-13	.023	4.25
1887			1.89		SE¼NW¼	4	33	44	3-15—4-28	.015	1.42
1879	8.61				SW¼NW¼	4	33	44	3-15—9-15	.071	25.83
1879		14.46			SW¼NW¼	4	33	44	3-15—6-13	.118	21.69
1879			7.61		SW¼NW¼	4	33	44	3-15—4-28	.062	5.71
1879				7.21	SW¼NW¼	4	33	44	3-15—4-28	.059	5.41
1879	4.55				NE¼NW¼	4	33	44	3-15—9-15	.037	13.65
1879		4.27			NE¼NW¼	4	33	44	3-15—6-13	.035	6.41
1879			4.66		NE¼NW¼	4	33	44	3-15—4-28	.038	3.50
1887		18.51			NE¼NW¼	4	33	44	3-15—6-13	.150	27.77
1887			.40		NE¼NW¼	4	33	44	3-15—4-28	.003	0.30
1879	32.17				NW¼NW¼	4	33	44	3-15—9-15	.262	96.51
1879		6.93			NW¼NW¼	4	33	44	3-15—6-13	.056	10.40
1879				3.00	SE¼SE¼	5	33	44	3-15—4-28	.024	2.25
1879				7.48	NE¼SE¼	5	33	44	3-15—4-28	.059	5.61
1879		1.30			SE¼NE¼	5	33	44	3-15—6-13	.011	1.95
1879			6.25		SE¼NE¼	5	33	44	3-15—4-28	.051	4.69
1879				8.30	SE¼NE¼	5	33	44	3-15—4-28	.067	6.23
1879		14.66			NE¼NE¼	5	33	44	3-15—6-13	.111	21.99
1879				10.30	NE¼NE¼	5	33	44	3-15—4-28	.084	7.73
1887				5.00	SW¼SW¼	34	34	44	3-15—4-28	.041	3.75
1887		1.35			SE¼SE¼	33	34	44	3-15—6-13	.011	2.03
1887				35.09	SE¼SE¼	33	34	44	3-15—4-28	.285	26.32
1887		30.52			SW¼SE¼	33	34	44	3-15—6-13	.248	45.78
1887				9.48	SW¼SE¼	33	34	44	3-15—4-28	.077	7.11
1887				8.25	NE¼SE¼	33	34	44	3-15—4-28	.067	6.19
1887		5.70			NW¼SE¼	33	34	44	3-15—6-13	.046	8.55
1887				33.30	NW¼SE¼	33	34	44	3-15—4-28	.271	24.98
1879			.40		NW¼SW¼	14	33	44	3-15—4-28	.003	0.30
1879	38.60				SE¼SE¼	15	33	44	3-15—9-15	.314	115.80
1887			.50		SE¼SE¼	15	33	44	3-15—4-28	.004	0.38
1879	40.00				SW¼SE¼	15	33	44	3-15—9-15	.325	120.00
1879	19.65				NE¼SE¼	14	33	44	3-15—9-15	.160	58.95

Russell Land and Cattle Co.—Continued.

Year of priority	Culture—Acres: Harvest crops	Culture—Acres: Meadow pasture	Culture—Acres: Diversified pasture	Location: Subdivision	Location: Section	Location: Tp.N.	Location: R.E.	Length of season	Duty of water: C.F.S.	Duty of water: Acre-feet
1887	11.46			NE¼ SE¼	14	33	44	3-15—9-15	.093	34.38
1887			1.80	NE¼ SE¼	14	33	44	3-15—4-28	.015	1.35
1879	39.40			NW¼ SE¼	14	33	44	3-15—9-15	.320	118.20
1879	40.00			SE¼ NE¼	22	33	44	3-15—9-15	.325	120.00
1879	17.62			SW¼ NE¼	22	33	44	3-15—9-15	.143	52.86
1879		22.38		SW¼ NE¼	22	33	44	3-15—6-13	.182	33.57
1879	39.30			NE¼ NE¼	22	33	44	3-15—9-15	.320	117.90
1879	38.00			NW¼ NE¼	22	33	44	3-15—9-15	.309	114.00
1879	13.19			NE¼ NW¼	22	33	44	3-15—9-15	.107	39.57
1887			3.70	SE¼ SE¼	14	33	44	3-15—4-28	.030	2.78
1887			37.30	SW¼ SE¼	14	33	44	3-15—4-28	.303	27.98
1887			18.00	NW¼ SE¼	14	33	44	3-15—4-28	.146	13.50
1887	34.16			SE¼ SW¼	14	33	44	3-15—9-15	.278	102.48
1887			5.84	SE¼ SW¼	14	33	44	3-15—4-28	.047	4.38
1887	27.38			SW¼ SW¼	14	33	44	3-15—9-15	.223	82.14
1879	4.10			SW¼ SW¼	14	33	44	3-15—9-15	.033	12.30
1879			1.00	SW¼ SW¼	14	33	44	3-15—4-28	.008	0.75
1887	17.50			NE¼ SW¼	14	33	44	3-15—9-15	.142	52.50
1887			22.50	NE¼ SW¼	14	33	44	3-15—4-28	.183	16.88
1887	37.40			NW¼ SW¼	14	33	44	3-15—9-15	.304	112.20
1879	10.10			NW¼ NE¼	36	33	44	3-15—9-15	.082	30.30
1879		29.90		NW¼ NE¼	36	33	44	3-15—6-13	.243	44.85
1879		12.07		SE¼ NW¼	36	33	44	3-15—6-13	.098	18.11
1879			22.78	SE¼ NW¼	36	33	44	3-15—4-28	.185	17.09
1879			9.08	SW¼ NW¼	36	33	44	3-15—4-28	.074	6.81
1879		38.00		NE¼ NW¼	36	33	44	3-15—6-13	.309	57.00
1879			1.55	NE¼ NW¼	36	33	44	3-15—4-28	.013	1.16
1879		13.46		NW¼ NW¼	36	33	44	3-15—6-13	.109	20.19
1879			24.15	NW¼ NW¼	36	33	44	3-15—4-28	.196	18.11
1879		1.63		NE¼ NE¼	35	33	44	3-15—6-13	.013	2.45
1879			4.59	NE¼ NE¼	35	33	44	3-15—4-28	.037	3.44
1879	21.23			SE¼ SE¼	25	33	44	3-15—9-15	.173	63.69
1879		13.06		SE¼ SE¼	25	33	44	3-15—6-13	.106	19.59
1879			0.43	SE¼ SE¼	25	33	44	3-15—4-28	.003	0.32
1887	3.65			SE¼ SE¼	25	33	44	3-15—9-15	.030	10.95
1887			1.33	SE¼ SE¼	25	33	44	3-15—4-28	.011	1.00
1879	15.52			SW¼ SE¼	25	33	44	3-15—9-15	.126	46.56
1879		40.00		SE¼ SE¼	36	33	44	3-15—6-13	.325	60.00
1879		2.48		SW¼ SE¼	36	33	44	3-15—6-13	.020	3.72
1879			1.02	SW¼ SE¼	36	33	44	3-15—4-28	.008	.77
1879	10.00			NE¼ SE¼	36	33	44	3-15—9-15	.081	30.00
1879		30.00		NE¼ SE¼	36	33	44	3-15—6-13	.244	45.00
1879	2.10			NW¼ SE¼	36	33	44	3-15—9-15	.017	6.30
1879		24.80		NW¼ SE¼	36	33	44	3-15—6-13	.202	37.20
1879			6.80	NW¼ SE¼	36	33	44	3-15—4-28	.055	5.10
1879	26.75			SE¼ NE¼	36	33	44	3-15—9-15	.217	80.25

	1879				9.25			SE¼NE¼	36	33	41	3-15—6-13	.075	13.88
	1879					0.71		SE¼NE¼	36	33	44	3-15—4-28	.006	0.53
	1887					1.33		SE¼NE¼	36	33	44	3-15—4-28	.011	1.00
	1879			14.58				SW¼NE¼	36	33	41	3-15—9-15	.119	44.24
	1879				24.71			SW¼NE¼	36	33	44	3-15—6-13	.201	27.07
	1879			29.48				NE¼NE¼	36	33	44	3-15—9-15	.240	89.44
	1879					1.43		NE¼NE¼	36	33	44	3-15—4-28	.012	1.07
	1887					4.20		NE¼NE¼	36	33	44	3-15—4-28	.034	3.15
	1879				25.00			SE¼NE¼	10	33	41	3-15—6-13	.203	37.50
	1879			20.60				SW¼NE¼	10	33	44	3-15—9-15	.167	61.80
	1879				19.40			SW¼NE¼	10	33	44	3-15—6-13	.158	29.10
	1879				38.17			NE¼NE¼	10	33	44	3-15—6-13	.270	49.76
	1879			2.00				NW¼NE¼	10	33	44	3-15—9-15	.016	6.00
	1879				38.00			NW¼NE¼	10	33	44	3-15—6-13	.309	57.00
	1887			28.50				SE¼NW¼	10	33	44	3-15—9-15	.313	115.50
	1879					.50		SE¼NW¼	10	33	44	3-15—4-28	.004	0.38
	1879			20.10				SW¼NW¼	10	33	44	3-15—9-15	.163	60.30
	1879					11.48		SW¼NW¼	10	33	44	3-15—4-28	.093	8.61
	1887			12.60				SW¼NW¼	10	33	44	3-15—9-15	.102	37.80
	1887					.70		SW¼NW¼	10	33	44	3-15—4-28	.006	0.53
	1879			25.49				NE¼NW¼	10	33	44	3-15—9-15	.207	76.47
	1879				10.81			NE¼NW¼	10	33	44	3-15—6-13	.088	16.22
	1887			38.00				NW¼NW¼	10	33	44	3-15—9-15	.309	114.00
	1879			1.00				NW¼NW¼	10	33	44	3-15—9-15	.008	3.00
	1887			40.00				SE¼SE¼	10	33	44	3-15—9-15	.325	120.00
	1887			38.10				SW¼SE¼	10	33	44	3-15—9-15	.310	114.30
	1879					.40		SW¼SE¼	10	33	44	3-15—4-28	.003	0.30
	1887			40.00				NE¼SE¼	10	33	44	3-15—9-15	.325	120.00
	1887			40.00				NW¼SE¼	10	33	44	3-15—9-15	.325	120.00
	1887			15.18				SE¼SW¼	10	33	44	3-15—9-15	.123	45.54
	1887					1.10		SE¼SW¼	10	33	44	3-15—4-28	.009	0.83
	1879			12.30				SE¼SW¼	10	33	44	3-15—9-15	.100	36.90
	1879					2.80		SE¼SW¼	10	33	44	3-15—4-28	.023	2.10
	1879			38.00				SW¼SW¼	10	33	44	3-15—9-15	.309	114.00
	1887					1.40		SW¼SW¼	10	33	44	3-15—4-28	.011	1.05
	1879			38.70				NE¼SW¼	10	33	44	3-15—9-15	.315	116.10
	1879			25.35				NW¼SW¼	10	33	44	3-15—9-15	.206	76.05
	1879					13.74		NW¼SW¼	10	33	44	3-15—4-28	.112	10.31
	1887			5.35				NW¼SW¼	10	33	44	3-15—9-15	.043	16.05
	1887					2.09		NW¼SW¼	10	33	44	3-15—4-28	.017	1.57
	1879			14.85				SE¼NE¼	10	33	44	3-15—9-15	.121	44.55
	1887			29.80				NE¼SE¼	23	33	44	3-15—9-15	.242	89.40
	1887					10.00		NE¼SE¼	23	33	44	3-15—4-28	.081	7.50
	1887			14.46				NW¼SE¼	23	33	44	3-15—4-28	.118	43.38
	1887					6.49		NW¼SE¼	23	33	44	3-15—4-28	.053	4.87
	1879			6.32				NW¼SE¼	23	33	44	3-15—9-15	.051	18.96
	1879					5.10		NW¼SE¼	23	33	44	3-15—4-28	.041	3.83
	1879				24.48			SW¼SE¼	25	33	44	3-15—6-13	.199	36.72
	1879			10.04				NE¼SE¼	25	33	44	3-15—9-15	.085	30.12
	1879					.71		NE¼SE¼	25	33	44	3-15—4-28	.006	0.53
	1887			24.64				NE¼SE¼	25	33	44	3-15—9-15	.200	73.92
	1887					0.51		NE¼SE¼	25	33	44	3-15—4-28	.004	0.38

Russell Land and Cattle Co.—Continued.

Year of priority	Culture—Acres: Harvest crops	Culture—Acres: Meadow pasture	Culture—Acres: Diversified pasture	Location: Subdivision	Location: Section	Location: Tp. N.	Location: R. E.	Length of season	Duty of water: C. F. S.	Duty of water: Acre-feet
1879	26.72			NW¼SE¼	25	33	44	3-15—9-15	.217	80.16
1887	6.22			NW¼SE¼	25	33	44	3-15—9-15	.051	18.66
1887			1.36	NW¼SE¼	25	33	44	3-15—4-28	.011	1.02
1879	15.54			SE¼SE¼	9	33	44	3-15—9-15	.126	46.62
1879			23.37	SE¼SE¼	9	33	44	3-15—4-28	.190	17.52
1879		12.97		SW¼SE¼	9	33	44	3-15—6-13	.105	19.46
1879			3.66	SW¼SE¼	9	33	44	3-15—4-28	.030	2.75
1879	18.22			NE¼SE¼	9	33	44	3-15—9-15	.148	54.66
1879		10.80		NE¼SE¼	9	33	44	3-15—6-13	.088	16.20
1879			6.73	NE¼SE¼	9	33	44	3-15—4-28	.055	5.05
1879		2.60		NW¼SE¼	9	33	44	3-15—6-13	.021	3.90
1879		16.95		SE¼SW¼	9	33	44	3-15—6-13	.138	25.43
1879		28.30		NE¼SW¼	9	33	44	3-15—6-13	.230	42.45
1879	37.37			SE¼NE¼	9	33	44	3-15—9-15	.304	113.11
1879		2.50		SE¼NE¼	9	33	44	3-15—6-13	.020	3.75
1879	11.32			SW¼NE¼	9	33	44	3-15—9-15	.092	33.96
1879		7.28		SW¼NE¼	9	33	44	3-15—6-13	.059	10.92
1879			13.60	SW¼NE¼	9	33	44	3-15—4-28	.110	10.20
1879	21.83			NE¼NE¼	9	33	44	3-15—9-15	.177	65.46
1879			2.11	NE¼NE¼	9	33	44	3-15—4-28	.017	1.58
1879	39.40			NE¼SE¼	22	33	44	3-15—9-15	.320	118.20
1879		0.60		NE¼SE¼	22	33	44	3-15—6-13	.005	0.90
1879	5.94			NW¼SE¼	22	33	44	3-15—9-15	.048	17.82
1879		34.06		NW¼SE¼	22	33	44	3-15—6-13	.277	51.09
1887			2.40	SE¼NW¼	23	33	44	3-15—4-28	.020	1.80
1879	5.86			SE¼NW¼	23	33	44	3-15—9-15	.048	17.58
1879			0.80	SE¼NW¼	23	33	44	3-15—4-28	.007	.60
1879	25.57			SW¼NW¼	23	33	44	3-15—9-15	.208	76.71
1879			0.60	SW¼NW¼	23	33	44	3-15—4-28	.005	.45
1887	6.45			SW¼NW¼	23	33	44	3-15—9-15	.052	19.35
1887			1.19	SW¼NW¼	23	33	44	3-15—4-28	.010	0.89
1879	35.24			NE¼NW¼	23	33	44	3-15—9-15	.287	105.72
1879		4.06		NE¼NW¼	23	33	44	3-15—6-13	.033	6.09
1879	14.40			NW¼NW¼	23	33	44	3-15—9-15	.117	43.20
1879			1.99	NW¼NW¼	23	33	44	3-15—4-28	.016	1.49
1887	13.50			NW¼NW¼	23	33	44	3-15—9-15	.110	40.50
1887			.40	NW¼NW¼	23	33	44	3-15—4-28	.003	.30
1879	40.00			NW¼SW¼	23	33	44	3-15—9-15	.325	120.00
1879	10.40			SE¼SE¼	22	33	44	3-15—9-15	.085	31.20
1879		29.60		SE¼SE¼	22	33	44	3-15—6-13	.241	44.40
1879		18.07		SW¼SE¼	22	33	44	3-15—6-13	.147	27.11
1879	22.05			SE¼SW¼	23	33	44	3-15—9-15	.179	66.15
1879			17.95	SE¼SW¼	23	33	44	3-15—4-28	.146	13.46
1879	19.04			SW¼SW¼	23	33	44	3-15—9-15	.138	57.72
1879			23.00	SW¼SW¼	23	33	44	3-15—4-28	.187	17.25
1879	20.17			NE¼SW¼	23	33	44	3-15—9-15	.164	60.51

....	1879	....	....			12.18	....	NE¼SW¼	23	33	44	3-15-4-28	.090	9.14
....	1887	....	....	1.19			....	NE¼SW¼	23	33	44	3-15-9-15	.010	3.57
....	1887	....	....			2.84	....	NE¼SW¼	23	33	44	3-15-4-28	.019	1.70
....	1887	....	....	2.00			....	SE¼NE¼	23	33	44	3-15-9-15	.016	6.00
....	1887	....	....			37.91	....	SE¼NE¼	23	33	44	3-15-4-28	.308	28.43
....	1887	....	....	28.00			....	SW¼NE¼	23	33	44	3-15-9-15	.228	84.00
....	1887	....	....			9.90	....	SW¼NE¼	23	33	44	3-15-4-28	.089	7.43
....	1879	....	....			.50	....	SW¼NE¼	23	33	44	3-15-4-28	.004	.38
....	1887	....	....			27.80	....	NE¼NE¼	23	33	44	3-15-4-28	.226	20.85
....	1887	....	....		3.00		....	NW¼NE¼	23	33	44	3-15-6-13	.024	4.50
....	1887	....	....			37.00	....	NW¼NE¼	23	33	44	3-15-4-28	.300	27.75
....	1887	....	....	24.95			....	SE¼NW¼	23	33	44	3-15-9-15	.203	74.85
....	1879	....	....	25.10			....	SW¼NE¼	15	33	44	3-15-9-15	.204	75.30
....	1879	....	....			1.10	....	SW¼NE¼	15	33	44	3-15-4-28	.009	.83
....	1887	....	....	7.57			....	SW¼NE¼	15	33	44	3-15-9-15	.062	22.71
....	1887	....	....			1.00	....	SW¼NE¼	15	33	44	3-15-4-28	.008	.75
....	1879	....	....	40.00			....	NE¼NE¼	15	33	44	3-15-9-15	.325	120.00
....	1887	....	....	24.50			....	NW¼NE¼	15	33	44	3-15-9-15	.199	73.50
....	1887	....	....			2.08	....	NW¼NE¼	15	33	44	3-15-4-28	.017	1.56
....	1879	....	....	6.75			....	NW¼NE¼	15	33	44	3-15-9-15	.055	20.25
....	1879	....	....			1.70	....	NW¼NE¼	15	33	44	3-15-4-28	.014	1.28
....	1879	....	....	40.00			....	SE¼NW¼	15	33	44	3-15-9-15	.325	120.00
....	1879	....	....	25.70			....	SW¼NW¼	15	33	44	3-15-9-15	.209	77.10
....	1879	....	....			14.30	....	SW¼NW¼	15	33	44	3-15-4-28	.116	10.73
....	1879	....	....	40.00			....	NE¼NW¼	15	33	44	3-15-9-15	.325	120.00
....	1879	....	....	35.64			....	NW¼NW¼	15	33	44	3-15-9-15	.290	106.92
....	1879	....	....			4.36	....	NW¼NW¼	15	33	44	3-15-4-28	.035	3.27
....	1879	....	....			39.00	....	SE¼NE¼	16	33	44	3-15-4-28	.317	29.25
....	1879	....	....		5.95		....	SW¼NE¼	16	33	44	3-15-6-13	.048	8.93
....	1879	....	....	0.40			....	NE¼NE¼	16	33	44	3-15-9-15	.003	1.20
....	1879	....	....			39.00	....	NE¼NE¼	16	33	44	3-15-4-28	.317	20.25
....	1879	....	....		18.90		....	NW¼NE¼	16	33	44	3-15-6-13	.154	28.35
....	1879	....	....			2.47	....	NW¼NE¼	16	33	44	3-15-4-28	.020	1.85
....	1879	....	....		1.60		....	NE¼NW¼	16	33	44	3-15-6-13	.013	2.40
....	1887	....	....	3.15			....	SE¼SW¼	11	33	44	3-15-9-15	.026	9.45
....	1887	....	....	36.70			....	SW¼SW¼	11	33	44	3-15-9-15	.298	110.10
....	1887	....	....	17.15			....	NW¼SW¼	11	33	44	3-15-9-15	.139	51.45
....	1887	....	....		12.55		....	SW¼NW¼	11	33	44	3-15-6-13	.102	18.83
....	1887	....	....		5.30		....	NW¼NW¼	11	33	44	3-15-6-13	.043	7.95
....	1879	....	....	40.00			....	SE¼SW¼	15	33	44	3-15-9-15	.325	120.00
....	1879	....	....	10.95			....	SW¼SW¼	15	33	44	3-15-9-15	.080	32.85
....	1879	....	....	40.00			....	NE¼SW¼	15	33	44	3-15-9-15	.325	120.00
....	1879	....	....	17.00			....	NW¼SW¼	15	33	44	3-15-9-15	.138	51.00
....	1879	....	....			9.21	....	NW¼SW¼	15	33	44	3-15-4-28	.075	6.91
....	1879	....	....			7.00	....	NE¼SE¼	16	33	44	3-15-4-28	.057	5.25
....	1887	....	....		1.25		....	SW¼NE¼	14	33	44	3-15-6-13	.010	1.88
....	1887	....	....	1.19			....	SE¼NW¼	14	33	44	3-15-9-15	.010	3.57
....	1887	....	....		26.33		....	SE¼NW¼	14	33	44	3-15-6-13	.214	39.50
....	1887	....	....			7.82	....	SE¼NW¼	14	33	44	3-15-4-28	.064	5.87
....	1887	....	....	36.00			....	SW¼NW¼	14	33	44	3-15-9-15	.293	108.00
....	1887	....	....		1.98		....	SW¼NW¼	14	33	44	3-15-6-13	.016	1.49
....	1887	....	....			1.98	....	SW¼NW¼	14	33	44	3-15-4-28	.016	2.97

Russell Land and Cattle Co.—Continued.

Year of priority	Culture—Acres: Harvest crops	Meadow pasture	Diversified pasture		Location: Subdivision	Section	Tp.N.	R.E.	Length of season	Duty of water: C.F.S.	Acre-feet
1887	10.00				NE¼NW¼	14	33	44	3-15—9-15	.081	30.00
1887			11.00		NE¼NW¼	14	33	44	3-15—4-28	.089	8.25
1887	40.00				NW¼NW¼	14	33	44	3-15—9-15	.325	120.00
1887	40.00				SE¼NE¼	15	33	44	3-15—9-15	.325	120.00
1887	9.28				NE¼NE¼	9	33	44	3-15—9-15	.075	27.84
1887			2.53		NE¼NE¼	9	33	44	3-15—4-28	.021	1.90
1879	24.68				NW¼NE¼	9	33	44	3-15—9-15	.201	74.04
1879		7.14			NW¼NE¼	9	33	44	3-15—6-13	.058	10.71
1879			7.50		NW¼NE¼	9	33	44	3-15—4-28	.061	5.63
1879		27.64			SE¼NW¼	9	33	44	3-15—6-13	.217	41.46
1879				12.36	SE¼NW¼	9	33	44	3-15—4-28	.100	9.27
1879				10.32	SW¼NW¼	9	33	44	3-15—4-28	.084	7.74
1879		40.00			NE¼NW¼	9	33	44	3-15—6-13	.325	60.00
1879		4.79			NW¼NW¼	9	33	44	3-15—6-13	.039	7.18
1879				21.90	NW¼NW¼	9	33	44	3-15—4-28	.170	16.43

Claimant—**Ike Erickson.** Proof No. 00173

Source—**Humboldt River.** Ditch—**Altenberg.**

Year of priority	Harvest crops	Meadow pasture	Diversified pasture		Subdivision	Section	Tp.N.	R.E.	Length of season	C.F.S.	Acre-feet
1874	20.36				SE¼NE¼	17	32	45	3-15—9-15	.165	61.08
1874	5.58				NE¼SE¼	17	32	45	3-15—9-15	.045	16.74
1874			11.44		NE¼SE¼	17	32	45	3-15—4-28	.093	8.58
1874			.02		SW¼NE¼	17	32	45	3-15—4-28	.000	.02
1874			.02		NW¼SE¼	17	32	45	3-15—4-28	.000	.02
1874			.39		SE¼NE¼	17	32	45	3-15—4-28	.003	.29

Claimant—**Geo. Heard.** **Proof No.** 00174

Source—**Humboldt** River. Ditch—**Russel Dam.**

Year of priority	Harvest crops	Meadow pasture	Diversified pasture		Subdivision	Section	Tp.N.	R.E.	Length of season	C.F.S.	Acre-feet
1876	2.32				NE¼NE¼	2	35	42	3-15—9-15	.189	6.96
1876		34.23			NE¼NE¼	2	35	42	3-15—6-13	.278	36.35
1876			1.73		NE¼NE¼	2	35	42	3-15—4-28	.014	1.30
1876	37.00				SE¼NE¼	2	35	42	3-15—9-15	.301	111.00
1876		0.90			SE¼NE¼	2	35	42	3-15—6-13	.007	1.35
1876		0.03			NW¼NE¼	2	35	42	3-15—6-13	.000	.05
1876			1.36		NW¼NE¼	2	35	42	3-15—4-28	.011	1.02
1876	0.70				SW¼NE¼	2	35	42	3-15—9-15	.006	2.10
1876		0.42			SW¼NE¼	2	35	42	3-15—6-13	.003	.63
1876			0.20		SW¼NE¼	2	35	42	3-15—4-28	.002	.15
1876	35.87				NE¼SE¼	2	35	42	3-15—9-15	.292	107.61
1876			1.21		NE¼SE¼	2	35	42	3-15—4-28	.010	.91
1876	38.19				SE¼SE¼	2	35	42	3-15—9-15	.310	114.57
1876	1.35				NW¼SE¼	2	35	42	3-15—9-15	.011	4.05
1876	1.37				SW¼SE¼	2	35	42	3-15—9-15	.011	4.11

Claimant—**Garat and Co.** Proof No. 00175

Source—**Humboldt River.** Ditch—**Hammond.**

1875		1.96			NE¼SW¼	16	36	42	3-15-6-13	.016	2.94
1875		28.22			NW¼SW¼	16	36	42	3-15-6-13	.229	42.33
1875			33.87		SE¼SW¼	16	36	42	3-15-4-28	.275	25.40
1875			40.00		SW¼SW¼	16	36	42	3-15-4-28	.325	30.00

Claimant—**Lulu Kattenhorn Burch.** Proof No. 00176

Source—**Humboldt River.** Ditch—**Eaton Dam.**

1878		9.80			SW¼NE¼	29	34	44	3-15-6-13	.080	14.70
1878			0.47		SW¼NE¼	29	34	44	3-15-4-28	.004	0.35
1878				4.15	NE¼SE¼	29	34	44	3-15-4-28	.034	3.11
1878		4.35			SE¼SE¼	29	34	44	3-15-6-13	.035	6.53
1878			2.68		SE¼SE¼	29	34	44	3-15-4-28	.022	2.01
1878				15.05	SE¼SE¼	29	34	44	3-15-4-28	.122	11.29
1878		8.75			NW¼SE¼	29	34	44	3-15-6-13	.071	13.13
1878			5.60		NW¼SE¼	29	34	44	3-15-4-28	.046	4.20
1878				9.60	NW¼SE¼	29	34	44	3-15-4-28	.078	7.20
1878	0.59				SW¼SE¼	29	34	44	3-15-0-15	.005	1.77
1878		18.31			SW¼SE¼	29	34	44	3-15-6-13	.149	27.47
1878			2.40		SW¼SE¼	29	34	44	3-15-4-28	.020	1.80
1878				5.97	SW¼SE¼	29	34	44	3-15-4-28	.049	4.48
1878	10.90				NE¼NW¼	29	34	44	3-15-0-15	.089	32.70
1878				10.35	NE¼NW¼	29	34	44	3-15-4-28	.084	7.76
1878	10.16				SE¼NW¼	29	34	44	3-15-0-15	.083	30.48
1878		10.01			SE¼NW¼	29	34	44	3-15-6-13	.081	15.02
1878				11.32	SE¼NW¼	29	34	44	3-15-4-28	.092	8.49
1878			10.02		SW¼NW¼	29	34	44	3-15-4-28	.081	7.52
1878				27.42	SW¼NW¼	29	34	44	3-15-4-28	.223	20.57
1878	3.43				NE¼SW¼	29	34	44	3-15-0-15	.028	10.29
1878		4.10			NE¼SW¼	29	34	44	3-15-6-13	.033	6.15
1878			2.02		NE¼SW¼	29	34	44	3-15-4-28	.016	1.52
1878				20.90	NE¼SW¼	29	34	44	3-15-4-28	.170	15.68

Source—**Humboldt River.** Ditch—**Ward Ditch.**

1879	1.04				SE¼SW¼	29	34	44	3-15-0-15	.008	3.12
1879			13.75		SE¼SW¼	29	34	44	3-15-4-28	.112	10.31
1879				21.60	SE¼SW¼	29	34	44	3-15-4-28	.176	16.20
1879			25.50		NW¼SW¼	29	34	44	3-15-4-28	.207	19.13
1879				10.00	NW¼SW¼	29	34	44	3-15-4-28	.081	7.50
1879			11.90		SW¼SW¼	29	34	44	3-15-4-28	.097	8.93
1879				25.08	SW¼SW¼	29	34	44	3-15-4-28	.204	18.81

Source—**Humboldt River.** Ditch—**Wilcox Dam.**

1883	19.60				NW¼NW¼	29	34	44	3-15-0-15	.159	58.80
1883			9.45		NW¼NW¼	29	34	44	3-15-4-28	.077	7.09
1883				6.24	NW¼NW¼	29	34	44	3-15-4-28	.051	4.68

Claimant—**William Dunphy Estate.** Proof No. 00333

Source—**Rock Creek.** Ditch—**Rock Creek Branches.**

Year of priority	Culture—Acres: Harvest crops	Meadow pasture	Diversified pasture	Location: Subdivision	Section	Tp.N.	R.E.	Length of season	Duty of water: C.F.S.	Acre-feet
1870			3.50	NE¼NW¼	26	34	47	3-15—4-28	.028	2.63
1870			9.90	SE¼NW¼	26	34	47	3-15—4-28	.080	7.42
1870			9.25	NW¼NW¼	26	34	47	3-15—4-28	.075	6.94
1870			38.55	SW¼NW¼	26	34	47	3-15—4-28	.313	28.91
1870			9.20	NE¼SW¼	26	34	47	3-15—4-28	.075	6.00
1870			9.65	SE¼SW¼	26	34	47	3-15—4-28	.078	7.24
1870			39.80	NW¼SW¼	26	34	47	3-15—4-28	.324	29.85
1870			38.65	SW¼SW¼	26	34	47	3-15—4-28	.314	28.99
1870			36.35	NE¼SE¼	35	34	47	3-15—4-28	.296	27.26
1870		9.65		SE¼SE¼	35	34	47	3-15—6-13	.078	14.48
1870			30.05	SE¼SE¼	35	34	47	3-15—4-28	.278	22.54
1870			6.90	NW¼SE¼	35	34	47	3-15—4-28	.056	5.18
1870		7.45		SW¼SE¼	35	34	47	3-15—6-13	.061	11.18
1870			26.80	SW¼SE¼	35	34	47	3-15—4-28	.218	20.10
1870			8.90	NE¼NW¼	1	33	47	3-15—4-28	.072	6.68
1870			9.65	SE¼NW¼	1	33	47	3-15—4-28	.078	7.24
1870		0.40		NW¼NW¼	1	33	47	3-15—6-13	.003	.60
1870			39.35	NW¼NW¼	1	33	47	3-15—4-28	.320	29.51
1870			37.55	SW¼NW¼	1	33	47	3-15—4-28	.305	28.16
1870			12.95	NE¼NE¼	36	34	47	3-15—4-28	.105	9.71
1870			33.65	SE¼NE¼	36	34	47	3-15—4-28	.314	28.99
1870			14.15	NW¼NE¼	36	34	47	3-15—4-28	.115	10.61
1870			40.45	SW¼NE¼	36	34	47	3-15—4-28	.329	30.34
1870			40.05	NE¼SE¼	36	34	47	3-15—4-28	.326	30.04
1870		3.15		SE¼SE¼	36	34	47	3-15—6-13	.026	4.73
1870			34.20	SE¼SE¼	36	34	47	3-15—4-28	.278	25.65
1870			39.40	NW¼SE¼	36	34	47	3-15—4-28	.320	29.55
1870		10.05		SW¼SE¼	36	34	47	3-15—6-13	.082	15.08
1870			27.90	SW¼SE¼	36	34	47	3-15—4-28	.227	20.93
1870			10.30	NE¼NW¼	36	34	47	3-15—4-28	.084	7.73
1870			29.50	SE¼NW¼	36	34	47	3-15—4-28	.240	22.13
1870			28.40	NE¼SW¼	36	34	47	3-15—4-28	.231	21.30
1870			28.35	SE¼SW¼	36	34	47	3-15—4-28	.230	21.26
1870			41.65	NE¼NE¼	1	33	47	3-15—4-28	.339	31.24
1870			22.00	SE¼NE¼	1	33	47	3-15—4-28	.179	16.50
1870			41.95	NW¼NE¼	1	33	47	3-15—4-28	.341	31.46
1870			14.40	SW¼NE¼	1	33	47	3-15—4-28	.117	10.80
1870			12.00	NW¼NW¼	31	34	48	3-15—4-28	.098	9.00
1870			33.55	SW¼NW¼	31	34	48	3-15—4-28	.273	25.16
1870			12.05	NE¼SW¼	31	34	48	3-15—4-28	.098	9.04
1870			28.75	SE¼SW¼	31	34	48	3-15—4-28	.234	21.56
1870			30.20	NW¼SW¼	31	34	48	3-15—4-28	.204	27.15
1870			30.65	SW¼SW¼	31	34	48	3-15—4-28	.208	27.40
1870			6.40	NW¼NE¼	6	[illegible]	48	3-15—4-28	.052	4.80

1870	....	....	....	....	38.50	....	SW¼NE¼	6	33	48	3-15—4-28	.313	28.88
1870	....	....	....	....	19.20	....	NW¼SE¼	6	33	48	3-15—4-28	.156	14.40
1870	....	....	....	....	40.30	....	NE¼NW¼	6	33	48	3-15—4-28	.328	30.23
1870	....	....	....	....	39.40	....	SE¼NW¼	6	33	48	3-15—4-28	.320	29.55
1870	....	....	....	....	40.45	....	NW¼NW¼	6	33	48	3-15—4-28	.329	30.33
1870	....	....	....	....	38.90	....	SW¼NW¼	6	33	48	3-15—4-28	.316	29.18
1870	....	....	....	....	39.20	....	NE¼SW¼	6	33	48	3-15—4-28	.319	29.40
1870	....	....	....	....	27.80	....	SE¼SW¼	6	33	48	3-15—4-28	.226	20.85
1870	....	....	....	....	38.95	....	NW¼SW¼	6	33	48	3-15—4-28	.317	29.21
1870	....	....	....	....	38.65	....	SW¼SW¼	6	33	48	3-15—4-28	.314	28.99
1870	....	....	....	....	10.55	....	NW¼SE¼	25	34	47	3-15—4-28	.086	7.91
1870	....	....	....	....	15.95	....	NE¼SE¼	25	34	47	3-15—4-28	.130	11.96
1870	....	....	....	....	36.50	....	SW¼SE¼	25	34	47	3-15—4-28	.297	27.38
1870	....	....	....	....	39.50	....	SE¼SE¼	25	34	47	3-15—4-28	.321	29.63
1870	....	....	....	....	1.90	....	NW¼NW¼	36	33	47	3-15—4-28	.015	1.43
1870	....	....	....	....	21.60	....	NE¼NW¼	36	33	47	3-15—4-28	.176	16.20
1870	....	....	....	....	26.50	....	NW¼NE¼	36	33	47	3-15—4-28	.215	19.88
1870	....	....	....	....	27.00	....	NE¼NE¼	36	33	47	3-15—4-28	.220	20.25
1870	....	....	....	....	2.00	....	NW¼SW¼	30	34	48	3-15—4-28	.016	1.50
1870	....	....	....	....	12.00	....	NE¼SW¼	30	34	48	3-15—4-28	.098	9.00
1870	....	....	....	....	36.05	....	SW¼SW¼	30	34	48	3-15—4-28	.293	27.04
1870	....	....	....	....	27.45	....	SE¼SW¼	30	34	48	3-15—4-28	.223	20.59
1870	....	....	....	....	1.10	....	NW¼SE¼	30	34	48	3-15—4-28	.009	.83
1870	....	....	....	....	17.50	....	SW¼SE¼	30	34	48	3-15—4-28	.142	13.13
1870	....	....	....	....	26.10	....	NW¼NW¼	31	34	48	3-15—4-28	.212	19.58
1870	....	....	....	....	12.90	....	NE¼NW¼	31	34	48	3-15—4-28	.105	9.68
1870	....	....	....	29.75	....	....	SE¼SE¼	36	33	46	3-15—6-13	.242	44.63
1870	....	....	....	27.25	....	....	SW¼SE¼	36	33	46	3-15—6-13	.226	40.88
1870	....	....	....	9.20	....	....	SE¼SW¼	36	33	46	3-15—6-13	.075	13.80
1870	....	....	....	22.00	....	....	NE¼NE¼	36	33	46	3-15—6-13	.179	33.00
1870	....	....	....	14.35	....	....	SE¼NE¼	36	33	46	3-15—6-13	.117	21.58
1870	....	....	....	....	8.90	....	SE¼NW¼	25	33	46	3-15—4-28	.072	6.68
1870	....	....	....	....	28.30	....	NE¼SW¼	25	33	46	3-15—4-28	.230	21.22
1870	....	....	....	....	4.20	....	SE¼SW¼	25	33	46	3-15—4-28	.034	3.15
1870	....	....	....	....	21.10	....	SW¼NE¼	25	33	46	3-15—4-28	.172	15.83
1870	....	....	....	....	19.20	....	SE¼NE¼	25	33	46	3-15—4-28	.156	14.40
1870	....	....	....	....	35.95	....	NW¼SE¼	25	33	46	3-15—4-28	.292	26.96
1870	....	....	....	....	9.80	....	NE¼SE¼	25	33	46	3-15—4-28	.080	7.35
1870	....	....	....	....	5.45	....	SW¼SE¼	25	33	46	3-15—4-28	.044	4.09
1870	....	....	....	....	8.35	....	SE¼SE¼	25	33	46	3-15—4-28	.068	6.26
1870	....	....	....	....	2.35	....	NW¼SW¼	30	33	47	3-15—4-28	.019	1.76
1870	....	....	....	....	....	20.85	NW¼SW¼	30	33	47	3-15—4-28	.170	15.64
1870	....	....	....	....	25.45	....	NE¼SW¼	30	33	47	3-15—4-28	.207	19.09
1870	....	....	....	....	....	6.55	NE¼SW¼	30	33	47	3-15—4-28	.053	4.91
1870	....	....	....	....	26.75	....	NW¼SE¼	30	33	47	3-15—4-28	.217	20.06
1870	....	....	....	36.10	....	....	NW¼NE¼	19	33	47	3-15—6-13	.293	54.15
1870	....	....	....	36.85	....	....	SW¼NE¼	19	33	47	3-15—6-13	.300	55.28
1870	....	....	....	39.30	....	....	SE¼NE¼	19	33	47	3-15—6-13	.320	58.95
1870	....	....	....	38.25	....	....	NE¼NE¼	19	33	47	3-15—6-13	.311	57.38
1870	....	....	....	4.50	....	....	NE¼SE¼	24	33	46	3-15—6-13	.037	6.75
1870	....	....	....	28.30	....	....	SE¼SE¼	24	33	46	3-15—6-13	.230	42.45
1870	....	....	....	12.70	....	....	NW¼NE¼	25	33	46	3-15—6-13	.103	19.05
1870	....	....	....	36.90	....	....	NE¼NE¼	25	33	46	3-15—6-13	.300	55.35

William Dunphy Estate—Continued.

Year of priority	Culture—Acres: Harvest crops	Culture—Acres: Meadow pasture	Culture—Acres: Diversified pasture		Location: Subdivision	Location: Section	Location: Tp. N.	Location: R. E.	Length of season	Duty of water: C.F.S.	Duty of water: Acre-feet
1870	....	14.20			SW¼ NE¼	25	33	46	3-15—6-13	.115	21.30
1870	....	14.70			SE¼ NE¼	25	33	46	3-15—6-13	.120	22.05
1870	....	0.40			SE¼ NW¼	25	33	46	3-15—6-13	.003	.60
1870	....	34.90			NW¼ NW¼	30	33	47	3-15—6-13	.284	52.35
1870	....			0.40	NW¼ NW¼	30	33	47	3-15—4-28	.003	3.00
1870	....	12.15			SW¼ NW¼	30	33	47	3-15—6-13	.099	18.23
1870	....			1.40	SW¼ NW¼	30	33	47	3-15—4-28	.011	1.05
1870	....	9.40			SE¼ NW¼	30	33	47	3-15—6-13	.076	14.10
1870	....			5.40	SE¼ NW¼	30	33	47	3-15—4-28	.044	4.05
1870	....	32.15			NE¼ NW¼	30	33	47	3-15—6-13	.261	48.23
1870	....			3.45	NE¼ NW¼	30	33	47	3-15—4-28	.028	2.59
1870	....		5.20		NE¼ NW¼	16	33	47	3-15—4-28	.042	3.90
1870	....	36.65			SE¼ NW¼	16	33	47	3-15—6-13	.298	54.98
1870	....		1.95		SE¼ NW¼	16	33	47	3-15—4-28	.016	1.46
1870	....	21.60			NW¼ NW¼	16	33	47	3-15—6-13	.176	32.40
1870	....		2.00		NW¼ NW¼	16	33	47	3-15—4-28	.016	1.50
1870	....	36.25			SW¼ NW¼	16	33	47	3-15—6-13	.295	54.38
1870	....		3.30		SW¼ NW¼	16	33	47	3-15—4-28	.027	2.48
1870	....	38.95			NE¼ SW¼	16	33	47	3-15—6-13	.317	58.43
1870	....	0.15			SE¼ SW¼	16	33	47	3-15—6-13	.001	.23
1870	....	37.90			NW¼ SW¼	16	33	47	3-15—6-13	.308	56.85
1870	....	2.10			SW¼ SW¼	16	33	47	3-15—6-13	.017	3.15
1870	....	40.65			SW¼ SE¼	2	33	47	3-15—6-13	.330	60.98
1870	....	19.45			NE¼ NW¼	2	33	47	3-15—6-13	.158	29.18
1870	....		15.90		NE¼ NW¼	2	33	47	3-15—4-28	.129	11.93
1870	....	3.30			SE¼ NW¼	2	33	47	3-15—6-13	.027	4.95
1870	....		36.50		SE¼ NW¼	2	33	47	3-15—4-28	.297	27.38
1870	....	11.10			NW¼ NW¼	2	33	47	3-15—6-13	.090	16.65
1870	....		1.80		NW¼ NW¼	2	33	47	3-15—4-28	.014	1.35
1870	....	27.80			SW¼ NW¼	2	33	47	3-15—6-13	.226	41.70
1870	....		12.75		SW¼ NW¼	2	33	47	3-15—4-28	.104	9.56
1870	....	39.75			NW¼ NW¼	20	33	47	3-15—6-13	.323	59.63
1870	....	40.40			NE¼ NW¼	20	33	47	3-15—6-13	.328	60.60
1870	....	40.50			SW¼ NW¼	20	33	47	3-15—6-13	.329	60.75
1870	....	38.85			SE¼ NW¼	20	33	47	3-15—6-13	.316	58.28
1870	....	38.65			NW¼ SW¼	20	33	47	3-15—6-13	.314	57.98
1870	....	25.80			NE¼ SW¼	20	33	47	3-15—6-13	.210	38.70
1870	....	36.30			SW¼ SW¼	20	33	47	3-15—6-13	.295	54.45
1870	....	18.70			SE¼ SW¼	20	33	47	3-15—6-13	.152	28.05
1870	....	16.35			NW¼ SE¼	20	33	47	3-15—6-13	.133	24.53
1870	....	12.70			SW¼ SE¼	20	33	47	3-15—6-13	.103	19.05
1870	....	26.65			SE¼ SE¼	20	33	47	3-15—6-13	.217	39.98
1870	....	5.20			NE¼ SE¼	20	33	47	3-15—6-13	.042	7.80
1870	....	37.00			NW¼ NE¼	20	33	47	3-15—6-13	.300	55.50
1870	....	37.45			SW¼ NE¼	20	33	47	3-15—6-13	.304	56.18
1870	....	17.10			SE¼ NE¼	20	33	47	3-15—6-13	.139	25.65

1870				4.80			NE¼NE¼	20	33	47	3-15—6-13	.039	7.20
1870				14.55			SE¼SW¼	9	33	47	3-15—6-13	.118	21.83
1870					1.55		SE¼SW¼	9	33	47	3-15—4-28	.013	1.16
1870				10.55			SW¼SE¼	9	33	47	3-15—6-13	.086	15.83
1870					26.65		SW¼SE¼	9	33	47	3-15—4-28	.216	19.99
1870				31.40			SE¼SE¼	9	33	47	3-15—6-13	.255	47.10
1870					4.45		SE¼SE¼	9	33	47	3-15—4-28	.036	3.34
1870				35.90			SW¼SW¼	10	33	47	3-15—6-13	.292	53.85
1870				39.15			SE¼SW¼	10	33	47	3-15—6-13	.318	58.73
1870				11.15			SW¼SE¼	10	33	47	3-15—6-13	.091	16.73
1870				30.45			SE¼SE¼	10	33	47	3-15—6-13	.248	15.68
1870				1.90			NE¼SE¼	10	33	47	3-15—6-13	.015	2.85
1870				.20			NW¼SE¼	10	33	47	3-15—6-13	.002	.30
1870				24.10			SW¼SW¼	11	33	47	3-15—6-13	.196	36.15
1870				40.25			NE¼NE¼	16	33	47	3-15—6-13	.327	60.38
1870				36.90			SE¼NE¼	16	33	47	3-15—6-13	.300	55.35
1870					1.90		SE¼NE¼	16	33	47	3-15—4-28	.015	1.43
1870				35.20			NW¼NE¼	16	33	47	3-15—6-13	.327	52.80
1870					2.95		NW¼NE¼	16	33	47	3-15—4-28	.024	2.21
1870				37.25			SW¼NE¼	16	33	47	3-15—6-13	.303	55.88
1870					1.50		SW¼NE¼	16	33	47	3-15—4-28	.012	1.13
1870				16.85			NE¼NW¼	16	33	47	3-15—6-13	.137	25.28
1870					1.80		NE¼NW¼	16	33	47	3-15—4-28	.015	1.35
1870				13.35			SE¼NW¼	16	33	47	3-15—6-13	.109	20.03
1870					4.85		SE¼NW¼	16	33	47	3-15—4-28	.039	3.64
1870					21.35		NE¼SW¼	16	33	47	3-15—4-28	.174	16.01
1870				13.65			SE¼SW¼	16	33	47	3-15—6-13	.111	20.48
1870					7.80		SE¼SW¼	16	33	47	3-15—4-28	.068	5.85
1870				0.65			NW¼SE¼	16	33	47	3-15—6-13	.005	.98
1870					37.50		NW¼SE¼	16	33	47	3-15—4-28	.305	28.13
1870				21.90			SW¼SE¼	16	33	47	3-15—6-13	.178	32.85
1870					16.15		SW¼SE¼	16	33	47	3-15—4-28	.131	12.11
1870				37.25			SE¼SE¼	16	33	47	3-15—6-13	.303	55.88
1870					1.85		SE¼SE¼	16	33	47	3-15—4-28	.015	1.39
1870				3.30			NE¼SE¼	16	33	47	3-15—6-13	.027	4.95
1870					34.55		NE¼SE¼	16	33	47	3-15—4-28	.281	25.91
1870				2.35			NE¼NE¼	21	33	47	3-15—6-13	.019	3.53
1870					35.10		NE¼NE¼	21	33	47	3-15—4-28	.285	26.33
1870					37.55		SE¼NE¼	21	33	47	3-15—4-28	.305	28.16
1870				14.15			NW¼NE¼	21	33	47	3-15—6-13	.115	21.23
1870					22.80		NW¼NE¼	21	33	47	3-15—4-28	.185	17.10
1870					39.05		SW¼NE¼	21	33	47	3-15—4-28	.317	29.29
1870				18.65			NE¼SE¼	21	33	47	3-15—6-13	.152	27.98
1870					18.50		NE¼SE¼	21	33	47	3-15—4-28	.150	13.88
1870			17.95				SE¼SE¼	21	33	47	3-15—9-15	.146	53.85
1870				19.50			SE¼SE¼	21	33	47	3-15—6-13	.159	29.25
1870					0.40		SE¼SE¼	21	33	47	3-15—4-28	.003	.30
1870			0.60				SW¼SE¼	21	33	47	3-15—9-15	.005	1.80
1870				28.20			SW¼SE¼	21	33	47	3-15—6-13	.229	42.30
1870					8.80		SW¼SE¼	21	33	47	3-15—4-28	.072	6.60
1870					38.75		NW¼SE¼	21	33	47	3-15—4-28	.315	29.06
1870				9.00			NE¼NW¼	21	33	47	3-15—6-13	.073	13.50

William Dunphy Estate—Continued.

Year of priority	Culture—Acres: Harvest crops	Meadow pasture	Diversified pasture		Location: Subdivision	Section	Tp. N.	R. E.	Length of season	Duty of water: C. F. S.	Acre-feet
1870			12.85		NE¼ NW¼	21	33	47	3-15—4-28	.104	9.64
1870			21.35		SE¼ NW¼	21	33	47	3-15—4-28	.174	16.01
1870			24.05		NE¼ SW¼	21	33	47	3-15—4-28	.196	18.04
1870	1.15				SE¼ SW¼	21	33	47	3-15—9-15	.009	3.45
1870		12.50			SE¼ SW¼	21	33	47	3-15—6-13	.102	18.75
1870			9.65		SE¼ SW¼	21	33	47	3-15—4-28	.078	7.24
1870		14.70			SW¼ SW¼	9	33	47	3-15—6-13	.120	22.05
1870		18.55			SE¼ SW¼	9	33	47	3-15—6-13	.151	27.82
1870		34.05			NW¼ NW¼	16	33	47	3-15—6-13	.277	51.08
1870		19.15			NE¼ NW¼	16	33	47	3-15—6-13	.155	28.73
1870		34.00			SW¼ NW¼	16	33	47	3-15—6-13	.276	51.00
1870		16.25			SE¼ NW¼	16	33	47	3-15—6-13	.132	24.38
1870			1.80		SE¼ NW¼	16	33	47	3-15—4-28	.015	1.35
1870		16.60			NW¼ SW¼	16	33	47	3-15—6-13	.135	24.90
1870			18.80		NW¼ SW¼	16	33	47	3-15—4-28	.153	14.10
1870		2.70			SW¼ SW¼	16	33	47	3-15—6-13	.022	4.05
1870			34.20		SW¼ SW¼	16	33	47	3-15—4-28	.278	25.65
1870		5.15			SE¼ SW¼	16	33	47	3-15—6-13	.042	7.73
1870			10.60		SE¼ SW¼	16	33	47	3-15—4-28	.086	7.95
1870			19.10		NE¼ SW¼	16	33	47	3-15—4-28	.155	14.33
1870		37.80			NE¼ SE¼	17	33	47	3-15—6-13	.307	56.70
1870			0.95		NE¼ SE¼	17	33	47	3-15—4-28	.008	.71
1870		20.80			SE¼ SE¼	17	33	47	3-15—6-13	.169	31.20
1870			16.05		SE¼ SE¼	17	33	47	3-15—4-28	.130	12.04
1870		36.50			NW¼ SE¼	17	33	47	3-15—6-13	.297	54.75
1870			1.65		NW¼ SE¼	17	33	47	3-15—4-28	.013	1.24
1870		38.00			SW¼ SE¼	17	33	47	3-15—6-13	.309	57.00
1870		16.10			NW¼ SW¼	17	33	47	3-15—6-13	.131	24.15
1870		37.80			SW¼ SW¼	17	33	47	3-15—6-13	.307	56.70
1870		0.35			NW¼ NE¼	22	33	47	3-15—6-13	.003	.53
1870				38.00	NW¼ NE¼	22	33	47	3-15—4-28	.309	28.50
1870		14.65			SW¼ NE¼	22	33	47	3-15—6-13	.119	21.98
1870		8.15			NE¼ NW¼	22	33	47	3-15—6-13	.066	12.23
1870				31.10	NE¼ NW¼	22	33	47	3-15—4-28	.253	23.33
1870		37.65			SE¼ NW¼	22	33	47	3-15—6-13	.306	56.48
1870				1.30	SE¼ NW¼	22	33	47	3-15—4-28	.011	.98
1870		0.95			NW¼ NW¼	22	33	47	3-15—6-13	.008	1.43
1870				38.70	NW¼ NW¼	22	33	47	3-15—4-28	.315	29.03
1870		25.50			SW¼ NW¼	22	33	47	3-15—6-13	.183	38.25
1870				12.35	SW¼ NW¼	22	33	47	3-15—4-28	.100	9.26
1870	1.40				NE¼ SW¼	22	33	47	3-15—9-15	.011	4.20
1870		26.70			NE¼ SW¼	22	33	47	3-15—6-13	.217	40.05
1870				8.85	NE¼ SW¼	22	33	47	3-15—4-28	.072	6.64
1870	1.50				NW¼ SW¼	22	33	47	3-15—9-15	.012	4.50
1870		37.35			NW¼ SW¼	22	33	47	3-15—6-13	.304	56.03
1870		8.00			SE¼ SW¼	[illegible]	[illegible]	47	3-15—6-13	.005	12.00

1870						30.55	SE¼SW¼	15	33	47	3-15-4-28	.248	22.91
1870				24.35			NE¼SW¼	15	33	47	3-15-6-13	.198	36.53
1870						15.05	NE¼SW¼	15	33	47	3-15-4-28	.127	11.71
1870						39.55	NW¼SE¼	15	33	47	3-15-4-28	.322	29.66
1870						38.55	SW¼SE¼	15	33	47	3-15-4-28	.313	28.91
1870				0.40			SE¼SE¼	15	33	47	3-15-6-13	.003	.69
1870						38.50	SE¼SE¼	15	33	47	3-15-4-28	.313	28.88
1870						38.05	NE¼SE¼	15	33	47	3-15-4-28	.309	28.54
1870				27.90			NW¼NE¼	15	33	47	3-15-6-13	.227	41.85
1870						11.95	NW¼NE¼	15	33	47	3-15-4-28	.097	8.96
1870				0.60			SW¼NE¼	15	33	47	3-15-6-13	.005	.90
1870						37.70	SW¼NE¼	15	33	47	3-15-4-28	.307	28.28
1870						37.95	SE¼NE¼	15	33	47	3-15-4-28	.308	28.46
1870				4.10			NE¼NE¼	15	33	47	3-15-6-13	.033	6.15
1870						36.55	NE¼NE¼	15	33	47	3-15-4-28	.297	27.41
1870				3.45			NW¼NW¼	14	33	47	3-15-6-13	.028	5.18
1870				4.45			NE¼NW¼	14	33	47	3-15-6-13	.036	6.68
1870				9.60			SW¼NW¼	14	33	47	3-15-6-13	.078	14.40
1870				6.65			SE¼NW¼	14	33	47	3-15-6-13	.054	9.98
1870				1.25			NW¼SW¼	14	33	47	3-15-6-13	.010	1.88
1870				0.30			NE¼SW¼	14	33	47	3-15-6-13	.002	.45
1870				0.50			SW¼SW¼	14	33	47	3-15-6-13	.004	.75
1870					1.30		SE¼NW¼	30	33	47	3-15-4-28	.011	.98
1870						17.50	SE¼NW¼	30	33	47	3-15-4-28	.142	13.13
1870					3.15		SW¼NW¼	30	33	47	3-15-4-28	.026	2.36
1870						11.90	SW¼NW¼	30	33	47	3-15-4-28	.097	8.93
1870					1.00		SW¼NE¼	30	33	47	3-15-4-28	.008	.75
1870						20.20	SW¼NE¼	30	33	47	3-15-4-28	.164	15.15
1870					18.15		SW¼NW¼	20	33	47	3-15-4-28	.148	13.54
1870					15.80		SE¼NW¼	29	33	47	3-15-4-28	.128	11.85
1870					15.00		SW¼NE¼	29	33	47	3-15-4-28	.122	11.25
1870					37.00		NW¼SW¼	29	33	47	3-15-4-28	.300	27.75
1870					37.00		NE¼SW¼	29	33	47	3-15-4-28	.300	27.75
1870			4.80				SE¼NW¼	28	33	47	3-15-0-15	.039	14.40
1870						5.90	SE¼NW¼	28	33	47	3-15-4-28	.048	4.43
1870			20.15				NE¼NW¼	28	33	47	3-15-9-15	.164	60.45
1870				1.45			NE¼NW¼	28	33	47	3-15-6-13	.012	2.18
1870						.70	NE¼NW¼	28	33	47	3-15-4-28	.006	.53
1870			32.45				NW¼NE¼	28	33	47	3-15-9-15	.264	97.35
1870				3.90			NW¼NE¼	28	33	47	3-15-6-13	.032	5.85
1870			13.25				SW¼NE¼	28	33	47	3-15-9-15	.107	39.75
1870						3.55	SW¼NE¼	28	33	47	3-15-4-28	.029	2.66
1870				40.25			NW¼NW¼	15	33	47	3-15-6-13	.327	60.38
1870				38.70			SW¼NW¼	15	33	47	3-15-6-13	.315	58.05
1870				38.20			SE¼NW¼	15	33	47	3-15-6-13	.311	57.30
1870						2.85	SE¼NW¼	15	33	47	3-15-4-28	.023	2.14
1870				40.00			NE¼NW¼	15	33	47	3-15-6-13	.325	60.00
1870				36.50			NW¼SW¼	15	33	47	3-15-6-13	.297	54.75
1870						3.45	NW¼SW¼	15	33	47	3-15-4-28	.028	2.59
1870				36.20			SW¼SW¼	15	33	47	3-15-6-13	.294	54.30
1870						3.90	SW¼SW¼	15	33	47	3-15-4-28	.032	2.93
1870						8.00	NW¼SE¼	30	33	47	3-15-4-28	.065	6.00

William Dunphy Estate—Continued.

Year of priority	Harvest crops	Culture—Acres: Meadow pasture	Culture—Acres: Diversified pasture		Location: Subdivision	Section	Tp.N.	R.E.	Length of season	Duty of water: C.F.S.	Duty of water: Acre-feet
1870			33.60		NE¼SE¼	30	33	47	3-15—4-28	.273	25.20
1870			20.20		SE¼NE¼	30	33	47	3-15—4-28	.164	15.15
1870				.15	SE¼NE¼	30	33	47	3-15—4-28	.001	.11
1870		32.45			SE¼NE¼	9	33	47	3-15—6-13	.264	48.68
1870			1.42		SE¼NE¼	9	33	47	3-15—4-28	.012	1.07
1870		10.64			SW¼NE¼	9	33	47	3-15—6-13	.087	15.96
1870		26.20			NE¼SE¼	9	33	47	3-15—6-13	.213	39.30
1870			11.35		NE¼SE¼	9	33	47	3-15—4-28	.092	8.51
1870		.85			SE¼SE¼	9	33	47	3-15—6-13	.007	1.28
1870			1.50		SE¼SE¼	9	33	47	3-15—4-28	.012	1.13
1870		32.35			NW¼SE¼	9	33	47	3-15—6-13	.263	48.53
1870			4.50		NW¼SE¼	9	33	47	3-15—4-28	.037	3.38
1870		35.80			NE¼SW¼	2	33	47	3-15—6-13	.291	53.70
1870			3.65		NE¼SW¼	2	33	47	3-15—4-28	.030	2.74
1870		40.90			SE¼SW¼	2	33	47	3-15—6-13	.333	61.35
1870		35.65			NW¼SW¼	2	33	47	3-15—6-13	.290	53.48
1870			4.20		NW¼SW¼	2	33	47	3-15—4-28	.034	3.15
1870		38.55			SW¼SW¼	2	33	47	3-15—6-13	.312	57.83
1870			2.25		SW¼SW¼	2	33	47	3-15—4-28	.018	1.69
1870		15.25			SE¼NE¼	3	33	47	3-15—6-13	.124	22.88
1870			5.16		SE¼NE¼	3	33	47	3-15—4-28	.042	3.87
1870		28.15			NE¼SE¼	3	33	47	3-15—6-13	.229	42.23
1870			11.40		NE¼SE¼	3	33	47	3-15—4-28	.093	8.55
1870		2.65			SE¼SE¼	3	33	47	3-15—6-13	.022	3.98
1870			39.50		SE¼SE¼	3	33	47	3-15—4-28	.321	29.63
1870		5.90			NW¼SE¼	3	33	47	3-15—6-13	.048	8.85
1870			.15		NW¼SE¼	3	33	47	3-15—4-28	.001	.11
1870		18.05			SW¼SE¼	3	33	47	3-15—6-13	.147	27.08
1870			13.90		SW¼SE¼	3	33	47	3-15—4-28	.113	10.43
1870		4.57			SE¼SW¼	3	33	47	3-15—6-13	.037	6.86
1870		3.53			NE¼NE¼	9	33	47	3-15—6-13	.029	5.30
1870			41.25		NE¼SE¼	1	33	47	3-15—4-28	.335	30.94
1870			40.55		SE¼SE¼	1	33	47	3-15—4-28	.330	30.41
1870			39.05		NW¼SE¼	1	33	47	3-15—4-28	.317	29.29
1870			41.00		SW¼SE¼	1	33	47	3-15—4-28	.333	30.75
1870			30.05		NE¼NW¼	1	33	47	3-15—4-28	.244	22.54
1870			30.50		SE¼NW¼	1	33	47	3-15—4-28	.248	22.88
1870			31.70		NE¼SW¼	1	33	47	3-15—4-28	.258	23.78
1870		17.60			SE¼SW¼	1	33	47	3-15—6-13	.143	26.40
1870			14.00		SE¼SW¼	1	33	47	3-15—4-28	.257	10.50
1870			37.55		NE¼NE¼	12	33	47	3-15—4-28	.305	28.16
1870			32.45		SE¼NE¼	12	33	47	3-15—4-28	.264	24.34
1870			40.00		NW¼NE¼	12	33	47	3-15—4-28	.325	30.00
1870			37.55		SW¼NE¼	12	33	47	3-15—4-28	.305	28.16
1870		8.35			NE¼NW¼	12	33	47	3-15—6-13	.068	12.53
1870			20.00		NE¼NW¼	12	33	47	3-15—4-28	.170	15.08

1870				.15			SE¼NW¼	12	33	47	3-15—6-13	.001	.23
1870					15.85		SE¼NW¼	12	33	47	3-15—4-28	.129	11.80
1870					3.00		SW¼SE¼	31	34	48	3-15—4-28	.024	2.25
1870					1.15		NE¼NW¼	31	34	48	3-15—4-28	.009	.86
1870					3.65		SE¼NW¼	31	34	48	3-15—4-28	.030	2.74
1870					5.10		NE¼NW¼	12	33	47	3-15—4-28	.041	3.83
1870				1.25			SE¼NW¼	12	33	47	3-15—6-13	.010	1.88
1870					2.40		SE¼NW¼	12	33	47	3-15—4-28	.020	1.80
1870				21.65			NW¼NW¼	12	33	47	3-15—6-13	.176	32.48
1870					17.80		NW¼NW¼	12	33	47	3-15—4-28	.145	13.35
1870				1.55			SW¼NW¼	12	33	47	3-15—6-13	.013	2.33
1870					19.80		SW¼NW¼	12	33	47	3-15—4-28	.161	14.85
1870				31.80			NE¼NE¼	11	33	47	3-15—6-13	.259	47.70
1870					6.25		NE¼NE¼	11	33	47	3-15—4-28	.051	4.67
1870					38.00		SE¼NE¼	11	33	47	3-15—4-28	.309	28.50
1870				37.65			NW¼NE¼	11	33	47	3-15—6-13	.306	56.48
1870				5.20			SW¼NE¼	11	33	47	3-15—6-13	.042	7.80
1870					31.50		SW¼NE¼	11	33	47	3-15—4-28	.256	23.63
1870					.75		NE¼SE¼	11	33	47	3-15—4-28	.006	.56
1870					21.80		NW¼SE¼	11	33	47	3-15—4-28	.177	16.35
1870				36.95			NE¼NW¼	11	33	47	3-15—6-13	.300	55.43
1870					.15		NE¼NW¼	11	33	47	3-15—4-28	.001	.11
1870				4.15			SE¼NW¼	11	33	47	3-15—6-13	.033	6.23
1870					31.80		SE¼NW¼	11	33	47	3-15—4-28	.259	23.85
1870				32.50			NW¼SW¼	11	33	47	3-15—6-13	.264	48.75
1870					2.75		NW¼NW¼	11	33	47	3-15—4-28	.022	2.06
1870				19.55			SW¼NW¼	11	33	47	3-15—6-13	.159	29.33
1870					16.45		SW¼NW¼	11	33	47	3-15—4-28	.134	12.34
1870					31.75		NE¼SW¼	11	33	47	3-15—4-28	.258	23.81
1870					34.85		NW¼SW¼	11	33	47	3-15—4-28	.202	26.14
1870				3.70			NE¼NW¼	12	33	47	3-15—6-13	.030	5.55
1870					9.80		NE¼SW¼	1	33	47	3-15—4-28	.080	7.35
1870				8.90			SE¼SW¼	1	33	47	3.15—6-13	.072	13.35
1870					.80		SE¼SW¼	1	33	47	3-15—4-28	.007	.60
1870				.25			NW¼SW¼	1	33	47	3-15—6-13	.002	.38
1870					39.90		NW¼SW¼	1	33	47	3-15—4-28	.324	29.93
1870				39.35			SW¼SW¼	1	33	47	3-15—6-13	.320	59.03
1870					1.35		SW¼SW¼	1	33	47	3-15—4-28	.011	1.01
1870					38.50		NE¼NE¼	2	33	47	3-15—4-28	.313	28.88
1870				12.45			SE¼NE¼	2	33	47	3-15—6-13	.101	18.68
1870					25.10		SE¼NE¼	2	33	47	3-15—4-28	.204	26.33
1870				1.60			NW¼NE¼	2	33	47	3-15—6-13	.013	2.40
1870					38.10		NW¼NE¼	2	33	47	3-15—4-28	.310	28.58
1870				4.30			SW¼NE¼	2	33	47	3-15—6-13	.035	6.45
1870					35.30		SW¼NE¼	2	33	47	3-15—4-28	.287	26.48
1870				24.15			NE¼SE¼	2	33	47	3-15—6-13	.196	36.23
1870					14.20		NE¼SE¼	2	33	47	3-15—4-28	.115	10.65
1870				40.60			SE¼SE¼	2	33	47	3-15—6-13	.330	60.90
1870				36.05			NW¼SE¼	2	33	47	3-15—6-13	.293	54.08
1870					3.25		NW¼SE¼	2	33	47	3-15—4-28	.026	2.44
1870				35.55			NW¼NE¼	30	33	47	3-15—6-13	.289	53.33
1870						1.90	NW¼NE¼	30	33	47	3-15—4-28	.015	1.42

William Dunphy Estate—Continued.

	Culture—Acres				Location					Duty of water	
Year of priority	Harvest crops	Meadow pasture	Diversified	pasture	Subdivision	Section	Tp.N.	R.E.	Length of season	C.F.S.	Acre-feet
1870		6.10			SW¼NE¼	30	33	47	3-15—6-13	.050	9.15
1870				6.95	SW¼NE¼	30	33	47	3-15—4-28	.057	5.21
1870		2.25			SW¼SE¼	9	33	47	3-15—6-13	.018	3.38
1870			.45		SW¼SE¼	9	33	47	3-15—4-28	.004	.34
1870		9.70			NE¼SW¼	9	33	47	3-15—6-13	.079	14.55
1870			.40		NE¼SW¼	9	33	47	3-15—4-28	.003	.30
1870		1.05			SE¼SW¼	9	33	47	3-15—6-13	.000	.08
1870			.10		SE¼SW¼	9	33	47	3-15—4-28	.001	.08
1870		1.70			NE¼NE¼	10	33	47	3-15—6-13	.014	2.55
1870			36.05		NE¼NE¼	10	33	47	3-15—4-28	.293	27.04
1870		29.95			SE¼NE¼	10	33	47	3-15—6-13	.243	44.93
1870			8.65		SE¼NE¼	10	33	47	3-15—4-28	.070	6.49
1870		32.10			NW¼NE¼	10	33	47	3-15—6-13	.261	48.15
1870			7.10		NW¼NE¼	10	33	47	3-15—4-28	.058	5.33
1870		36.50			SW¼NE¼	10	33	47	3-15—6-13	.297	54.75
1870			2.25		SW¼NE¼	10	33	47	3-15—4-28	.018	1.69
1870		9.95			NE¼SE¼	10	33	47	3-15—6-13	.081	14.93
1870			26.95		NE¼SE¼	10	33	47	3-15—4-28	.219	20.21
1870		33.00			NW¼SE¼	10	33	47	3-15—6-13	.268	49.50
1870			5.70		NW¼SE¼	10	33	47	3-15—4-28	.046	4.28
1870		32.50			NE¼NW¼	10	33	47	3-15—6-13	.264	48.75
1870				7.35	SE¼NW¼	29	33	47	3-15—4-28	.060	5.51
1870		26.70			NW¼NE¼	29	33	47	3-15—6-13	.217	40.05
1870				10.70	NW¼NE¼	29	33	47	3-15—4-28	.087	8.03
1870	10.75				NE¼NE¼	29	33	47	3-15—9-15	.087	32.25
1870				26.85	NE¼NE¼	29	33	47	3-15—4-28	.218	20.14
1870	0.40				SE¼NE¼	29	33	47	3-15—9-15	.003	1.20
1870		13.15			SE¼NE¼	29	33	47	3-15—6-13	.107	19.73
1870				1.80	SE¼NE¼	29	33	47	3-15—4-28	.015	1.35
1870		15.80			SW¼NE¼	29	33	47	3-15—6-13	.125	23.10
1870		9.85			SE¼NE¼	30	33	47	3-15—6-13	.080	14.78
1870				3.35	SE¼NE¼	30	33	47	3-15—4-28	.027	2.51
1870		29.90			NE¼NE¼	30	33	47	3-15—6-13	.243	44.85
1870				4.25	NE¼NE¼	30	33	47	3-15—4-28	.035	3.19
1870		33.95			NW¼NW¼	21	33	47	3-15—6-13	.276	50.93
1870		14.50			NE¼NW¼	21	33	47	3-15—6-13	.118	21.75
1870		13.90			SW¼NW¼	21	33	47	3-15—6-13	.113	20.85
1870		1.00			SE¼NW¼	21	33	47	3-15—6-13	.008	1.50
1870	9.00				NW¼NW¼	28	33	47	3-15—9-15	.073	27.00
1870	10.85				NE¼NW¼	28	33	47	3-15—9-15	.088	32.55
1870	8.55				SW¼NW¼	28	33	47	3-15—9-15	.070	25.05
1870		1.00			SW¼NW¼	28	33	47	3-15—6-13	.008	1.50
1870	4.40				SE¼NW¼	28	33	47	3-15—9-15	.036	13.20
1870		35.35			NW¼NW¼	29	33	47	3-15—6-13	.287	53.03
1870		28.85			NE¼NW¼	29	33	47	3-15—6-13	.230	[illegible]
1870				7.70	NE¼NW¼	29	33	47	3-15—4-28	[illegible]	[illegible]

1870	....	....	....	11.55	....	....	SW¼ NW¼	29	33	47	3-15—6-13	[illegible]	[illegible]
1870	....	....	....	....	....	2.80	SW¼ NW¼	29	33	47	3-15—4-28	.023	2.10
1870	....	....	....	6.70	....	....	SE¼ NW¼	29	33	47	3-15—6-13	.054	10.05
1870	....	....	....	38.85	....	....	SE¼ SW¼	17	33	47	3-15—6-13	.316	58.28
1870	....	....	....	33.55	....	....	NE¼ SW¼	17	33	47	3-15—6-13	.273	50.33
1870	....	....	....	11.60	....	....	SE¼ NE¼	17	33	47	3-15—6-13	.094	17.40
1870	....	....	....	12.25	....	....	SW¼ SE¼	18	33	47	3-15—6-13	.100	18.38
1870	....	....	....	34.35	....	....	SE¼ SE¼	18	33	47	3-15—6-13	.279	51.53
1870	....	....	....	1.70	....	....	NE¼ SE¼	18	33	47	3-15—6-13	.014	2.55
1870	....	....	....	14.80	....	....	SW¼ NW¼	19	33	47	3-15—6-13	.120	22.20
1870	....	....	....	37.10	....	....	SE¼ NW¼	19	33	47	3-15—6-13	.302	55.65
1870	....	....	....	15.10	....	....	NE¼ NW¼	19	33	47	3-15—6-13	.123	22.65
1870	....	....	....	34.90	....	....	NW¼ SW¼	19	33	47	3-15—6-13	.284	52.35
1870	....	....	....	37.20	....	....	SW¼ SW¼	19	33	47	3-15—6-13	.302	55.80
1870	....	....	....	39.25	....	....	SE¼ SW¼	19	33	47	3-15—6-13	.319	58.88
1870	....	....	....	38.55	....	....	NE¼ SW¼	19	33	47	3-15—6-13	.313	57.83
1870	....	....	....	38.50	....	....	NW¼ SE¼	19	33	47	3-15—6-13	.313	57.75
1870	....	....	....	40.25	....	....	SW¼ SE¼	19	33	47	3-15—6-13	.327	60.38
1870	....	....	....	39.65	....	....	SE¼ SE¼	19	33	47	3-15—6-13	.322	59.48
1870	....	....	....	38.75	....	....	NE¼ SE¼	19	33	47	3-15—6-13	.315	58.13
1870	....	....	....	....	15.80	....	NE¼ SE¼	7	33	48	3-15—4-28	.128	11.85
1870	....	....	....	....	4.50	....	NE¼ SW¼	7	33	48	3-15—4-28	.037	3.38
1870	....	....	....	....	29.60	....	NW¼ NW¼	7	33	48	3-15—4-28	.241	22.20
1870	....	....	....	....	0.70	....	SW¼ NE¼	8	33	48	3-15—4-28	.006	.53
1870	....	....	....	....	19.70	....	NE¼ SE¼	8	33	48	3-15—4-28	.160	14.78
1870	....	....	....	....	32.05	....	NW¼ SE¼	8	33	48	3-15—4-28	.261	24.04
1870	....	....	....	....	27.25	....	NE¼ SW¼	8	33	48	3-15—4-28	.222	20.44
1870	....	....	....	....	24.50	....	NW¼ SW¼	8	33	48	3-15—4-28	.199	18.38
1870	....	....	....	....	24.45	....	SW¼ NE¼	9	33	48	3-15—4-28	.199	18.34
1870	....	....	....	....	32.05	....	NW¼ SE¼	9	33	48	3-15—4-28	.261	24.04
1870	....	....	....	....	14.75	....	SE¼ NW¼	9	33	48	3-15—4-28	.120	11.06
1870	....	....	....	....	36.45	....	NE¼ SW¼	9	33	48	3-15—4-28	.296	27.34
1870	....	....	....	....	1.95	....	SW¼ NW¼	9	33	48	3-15—4-28	.016	1.46
1870	....	....	....	....	32.70	....	NW¼ SW¼	9	33	48	3-15—4-28	.266	24.53

Source—Boulder Creek. Ditch—Boulder Creek.

1875	....	....	....	....	....	6.10	NE¼ NE¼	34	34	48	3-15—4-28	.050	4.58
1875	....	....	....	....	....	33.40	SE¼ NE¼	34	34	48	3-15—4-28	.272	25.05
1875	....	....	....	....	....	41.20	NE¼ SE¼	34	34	48	3-15—4-28	.335	30.90
1875	....	....	....	....	....	39.05	SE¼ SE¼	34	34	48	3-15—4-28	.317	29.29
1875	....	....	....	....	....	3.75	NW¼ SE¼	34	34	48	3-15—4-28	.142	2.81
1875	....	....	....	....	....	14.35	SW¼ SE¼	34	34	48	3-15—4-28	.117	10.76
1875	....	....	....	....	....	11.30	NE¼ NE¼	35	34	48	3-15—4-28	.092	8.48
1875	....	....	....	....	....	38.30	SE¼ NE¼	35	34	48	3-15—4-28	.311	28.73
1875	....	....	....	....	....	11.50	NW¼ NE¼	35	34	48	3-15—4-28	.093	8.63
1875	....	....	....	....	....	42.45	SW¼ NE¼	35	34	48	3-15—4-28	.345	31.84
1875	....	....	....	....	....	6.25	NE¼ SE¼	35	34	48	3-15—4-28	.051	4.69
1875	....	....	....	....	....	37.00	NW¼ SE¼	35	34	48	3-15—4-28	.301	27.75
1875	....	....	....	....	....	9.00	SW¼ SE¼	35	34	48	3-15—4-28	.073	6.75
1875	....	....	....	....	....	11.05	NE¼ NW¼	35	34	48	3-15—4-28	.090	8.29
1875	....	....	....	....	6.80	....	SE¼ NW¼	35	34	48	3-15—4-28	.055	5.10
1875	....	....	....	....	....	35.35	SE¼ NW¼	35	34	48	3-15—4-28	.287	26.51

William Dunphy Estate—Continued.

Year of priority	Culture—Acres: Harvest crops	Meadow pasture	Diversified pasture		Location: Subdivision	Section	Tp. N.	R. E.	Length of season	Duty of water: C. F. S.	Acre-feet
1875				11.35	NW¼NW¼	35	34	48	3-15—4-28	.092	8.51
1875			18.15		SW¼NW¼	35	34	48	3-15—4-28	.148	13.61
1875				24.10	SW¼NW¼	35	34	48	3-15—4-28	.196	18.08
1875			0.15		NE¼SW¼	35	34	48	3-15—4-28	.001	.11
1875				41.70	NE¼SW¼	35	34	48	3-15—4-28	.339	31.28
1875				38.95	SE¼SW¼	35	34	48	3-15—4-28	.317	29.21
1875			12.00		NW¼SW¼	35	34	48	3-15—4-28	.098	9.00
1875				29.90	NW¼SW¼	35	34	48	3-15—4-28	.243	22.43
1875				42.15	SW¼SW¼	35	34	48	3-15—4-28	.343	31.61
1875			9.55		NE¼NW¼	2	33	48	3-15—4-28	.081	7.46
1875				1.40	NE¼NW¼	2	33	48	3-15—4-28	.011	1.05
1875			8.20		SE¼NW¼	2	33	48	3-15—4-28	.067	6.15
1875				0.20	SE¼NW¼	2	33	48	3-15—4-28	.002	0.15
1875			24.80		NW¼NW¼	2	33	48	3-15—4-28	.202	18.60
1875				16.75	NW¼NW¼	2	33	48	3-15—4-28	.136	12.56
1875			30.00		SW¼NW¼	2	33	48	3-15—4-28	.244	22.50
1875				11.75	SW¼NW¼	2	33	48	3-15—4-28	.096	8.81
1875			9.80		NW¼SW¼	2	33	48	3-15—4-28	.080	7.35
1875				16.50	NW¼SW¼	2	33	48	3-15—4-28	.134	12.38
1875			6.15		SW¼SW¼	2	33	48	3-15—4-28	.050	4.61
1875			8.45		NE¼NE¼	3	33	48	3-15—4-28	.069	6.34
1875				30.60	NE¼NE¼	3	33	48	3-15—4-28	.249	22.95
1875			31.00		SE¼NE¼	3	33	48	3-15—4-28	.252	23.25
1875				8.70	SE¼NE¼	3	33	48	3-15—4-28	.071	6.53
1875			4.90		NW¼NE¼	3	33	48	3-15—4-28	.049	3.68
1875				22.25	NW¼NE¼	3	33	48	3-15—4-28	.181	16.69
1875			32.70		SW¼NE¼	3	33	48	3-15—4-28	.266	24.53
1875				7.35	SW¼NE¼	3	33	48	3-15—4-28	.060	5.51
1875			18.10		NE¼SE¼	3	33	48	3-15—4-28	.147	13.58
1875				21.90	NE¼SE¼	3	33	48	3-15—4-28	.178	16.43
1875			22.70		SE¼SE¼	3	33	48	3-15—4-28	.185	17.03
1875				15.80	SE¼SE¼	3	33	48	3-15—4-28	.128	11.85
1875			16.20		NW¼SE¼	3	33	48	3-15—4-28	.132	12.15
1875				22.85	NW¼SE¼	3	33	48	3-15—4-28	.186	17.14
1875				38.90	SW¼SE¼	3	33	48	3-15—4-28	.316	29.18
1875				4.10	NE¼NW¼	3	33	48	3-15—4-28	.033	3.08
1875				32.50	SE¼NW¼	3	33	48	3-15—4-28	.264	24.38
1875				22.70	NE¼SW¼	3	33	48	3-15—4-28	.185	17.03
1875				18.90	SE¼SW¼	3	33	48	3-15—4-28	.154	14.18
1875				1.75	NE¼NE¼	9	33	48	3-15—4-28	.014	1.31
1875				38.45	SE¼NE¼	9	33	48	3-15—4-28	.313	28.84
1875				0.10	NW¼NE¼	9	33	48	3-15—4-28	.001	.08
1875				4.65	SW¼NE¼	9	33	48	3-15—4-28	.037	3.48
1875				30.50	NE¼SE¼	9	33	48	3-15—4-28	.207	27.38
1875				4.10	NW¼SE¼	9	33	48	3-15—4-28	.033	3.08
1875			2.25		NE¼NE¼	10	33	48	3-15—4-28	.018	[illegible]

1875						11.75	NE¼NE¼	10	33	48	3-15—4-28	.096	8.81
1875						38.50	NW¼NE¼	10	33	48	3-15—4-28	.313	28.88
1875						9.05	SW¼NE¼	10	33	48	3-15—4-28	.074	6.79
1875						32.20	NE¼NW¼	10	33	48	3-15—4-28	.262	24.15
1875						32.10	SE¼NW¼	10	33	48	3-15—4-28	.261	24.08
1875					5.00		NW¼NW¼	10	33	48	3-15—4-28	.041	3.75
1875						13.00	NW¼NW¼	10	33	48	3-15—4-28	.106	9.75
1875						39.00	SW¼NW¼	10	33	48	3-15—4-28	.317	29.25
1875						21.90	NE¼SW¼	10	33	48	3-15—4-28	.178	16.43
1875						36.80	NW¼SW¼	10	33	48	3-15—4-28	.299	27.60
1875				1.25			SW¼SW¼	14	33	47	3-15—6-13	.010	1.88
1875				1.30			SE¼SW¼	14	33	47	3-15—6-13	.011	1.95
1875				1.75			SW¼SE¼	14	33	47	3-15—6-13	.014	2.63
1875				16.70			SE¼SE¼	14	33	47	3-15—6-13	.136	25.05
1875				.25			NE¼SE¼	14	33	47	3-15—6-13	.002	.38
1875				1.65			NW¼SW¼	13	33	47	3-15—6-13	.013	2.48
1875				8.95			SW¼SW¼	13	33	47	3-15—6-13	.073	13.43
1875				3.70			NE¼SW¼	13	33	47	3-15—6-13	.030	5.55
1875				16.30			NW¼SE¼	13	33	47	3-15—6-13	.133	24.45
1875				4.90			SW¼SE¼	13	33	47	3-15—6-13	.040	7.35
1875				.40			SE¼SW¼	13	33	47	3-15—6-13	.003	.60
1875						37.70	NE¼NE¼	22	33	47	3-15—4-28	.307	28.28
1875						38.50	SE¼NE¼	22	33	47	3-15—4-28	.313	28.80
1875						22.85	SW¼NE¼	22	33	47	3-15—4-28	.186	17.14
1875			7.95				NE¼SE¼	22	33	47	3-15—9-15	.065	23.85
1875				12.45			NE¼SE¼	22	33	47	3-15—6-13	.101	18.68
1875						16.65	NE¼SE¼	22	33	47	3-15—4-28	.135	12.49
1875				3.70			NW¼SE¼	22	33	47	3-15—6-13	.030	5.55
1875						34.50	NW¼SE¼	22	33	47	3-15—4-28	.280	25.88
1875			21.60				SE¼SW¼	22	33	47	3-15—9-15	.176	64.80
1875				11.85			SE¼SW¼	22	33	47	3-15—6-13	.096	17.78
1875						1.20	SE¼SW¼	22	33	47	3-15—4-28	.010	.90
1875				1.80			NW¼NE¼	23	33	47	3-15—6-13	.015	2.70
1875					1.35		NW¼NE¼	23	33	47	3-15—4-28	.011	1.01
1875						38.35	NE¼NW¼	23	33	47	3-15—4-28	.312	28.76
1875				25.75			SE¼NW¼	23	33	47	3-15—6-13	.209	38.62
1875						13.25	SE¼NW¼	23	33	47	3-15—4-28	.108	9.94
1875						38.50	NW¼NW¼	23	33	47	3-15—4-28	.313	28.88
1875				8.95			SW¼NW¼	23	33	47	3-15—6-13	.073	13.43
1875						28.70	SW¼NW¼	23	33	47	3-15—4-28	.233	21.53
1875				5.30			SE¼NE¼	13	33	47	3-15—6-13	.043	7.95
1875				25.75			NE¼SE¼	13	33	47	3-15—6-13	.209	38.63
1875						11.00	NE¼SE¼	13	33	47	3-15—4-28	.089	8.25
1875				6.50			NW¼SE¼	13	33	47	3-15—6-13	.053	9.75
1875						37.65	NE¼NE¼	18	33	48	3-15—4-28	.306	28.24
1875				19.90			SE¼NE¼	18	33	48	3-15—6-13	.162	29.85
1875						15.60	SE¼NE¼	18	33	48	3-15—4-28	.238	11.70
1875						38.85	NW¼NE¼	18	33	48	3-15—4-28	.316	29.14
1875				27.40			SW¼NE¼	18	33	48	3-15—6-13	.223	41.10
1875						11.00	SW¼NE¼	18	33	48	3-15—4-28	.089	8.25
1875				7.80			NE¼SE¼	18	33	48	3-15—6-13	.063	11.70
1875						30.80	NE¼SE¼	18	33	48	3-15—4-28	.250	23.10

William Dunphy Estate—Continued.

Year of priority	Culture—Acres: Harvest crops	Meadow pasture	Diversified pasture		Location: Subdivision	Section	Tp.N.	R.E.	Length of season	Duty of water: C.F.S.	Acre-feet
1875		1.80			SE¼SE¼	18	33	48	3-15—6-13	.015	2.70
1875				27.40	SE¼SE¼	18	33	48	3-15—4-28	.223	20.55
1875		18.55			NW¼SE¼	18	33	48	3-15—6-13	.151	27.83
1875				19.10	NW¼SE¼	18	33	48	3-15—4-28	.155	14.33
1875		.70			SW¼SE¼	18	33	48	3-15—6-13	.006	1.05
1875				26.05	SW¼SE¼	18	33	48	3-15—4-28	.212	19.54
1875				32.80	NE¼NW¼	18	33	48	3-15—4-28	.267	24.60
1875		28.75			SE¼NW¼	18	33	48	3-15—6-13	.234	43.13
1875				9.40	SE¼NW¼	18	33	48	3-15—4-28	.076	7.05
1875				1.30	NW¼NW¼	18	33	48	3-15—4-28	.011	.98
1875		23.45			SW¼NW¼	18	33	48	3-15—6-13	.191	35.18
1875				3.60	SW¼NW¼	18	33	48	3-15—4-28	.029	2.70
1875		28.20			NE¼SW¼	18	33	48	3-15—6-13	.229	42.30
1875				8.50	NE¼SW¼	18	33	48	3-15—4-28	.069	6.38
1875				36.20	SE¼SW¼	18	33	48	3-15—4-28	.294	27.15
1875		31.10			NW¼SW¼	18	33	48	3-15—6-13	.253	46.65
1875				6.10	NW¼SW¼	18	33	48	3-15—4-28	.050	4.58
1875				33.05	SW¼SW¼	18	33	48	3-15—4-28	.269	24.79
1875				2.65	NE¼SE¼	7	33	48	3-15—4-28	.022	1.90
1875				38.00	SE¼SE¼	7	33	48	3-15—4-28	.309	28.50
1875				27.00	SW¼SE¼	7	33	48	3-15—4-28	.220	20.25
1875				3.90	SE¼SW¼	7	33	48	3-15—4-28	.032	2.93
1875				1.65	NE¼SE¼	8	33	48	3-15—4-28	.013	1.24
1875				39.25	SE¼SE¼	8	33	48	3-15—4-28	.319	20.44
1875				2.10	NW¼SE¼	8	33	48	3-15—4-28	.017	1.58
1875				38.25	SW¼SE¼	8	33	48	3-15—4-28	.311	28.69
1875				2.35	NE¼SW¼	8	33	48	3-15—4-28	.019	1.76
1875				38.50	SE¼SW¼	8	33	48	3-15—4-28	.313	28.88
1875				2.70	NW¼SW¼	8	33	48	3-15—4-28	.022	2.03
1875				39.40	SW¼SW¼	8	33	48	3-15—4-28	.320	29.55
1875				1.30	NE¼SE¼	9	33	48	3-15—4-28	.010	.98
1875			5.15		SE¼SE¼	9	33	48	3-15—4-28	.042	3.86
1875				33.15	SE¼SE¼	9	33	48	3-15—4-28	.270	24.86
1875				1.30	NW¼SE¼	9	33	48	3-15—4-28	.010	.98
1875				38.95	SW¼SE¼	9	33	48	3-15—4-28	.317	29.21
1875				1.45	NE¼SW¼	9	33	48	3-15—4-28	.012	1.09
1875				39.40	SE¼SW¼	9	33	48	3-15—4-28	.320	20.55
1875				1.50	NW¼SW¼	9	33	48	3-15—4-28	.012	1.13
1875				39.30	SW¼SW¼	9	33	48	3-15—4-28	.320	20.48
1875				0.70	NW¼SW¼	10	33	48	3-15—4-28	.006	0.53
1875				18.50	SW¼SW¼	10	33	48	3-15—4-28	.150	13.88
1875			14.45		NW¼NW¼	15	33	48	3-15—4-28	.117	10.84
1875				1.30	NW¼NW¼	15	33	48	3-15—4-28	.011	0.98
1875			0.20		SW¼NW¼	15	33	48	3-15—4-28	.002	0.15
1876			13.95		NE¼NE¼	16	33	48	3-15—4-28	.113	[illegible]
1875				15.15	NE¼NE¼	[illegible]	[illegible]	[illegible]	3-15—4-28	[illegible]	[illegible]

1875						37.35	NW¼NE¼	16	33	48	3-15—4-28	.304	28.01
1875						6.30	SW¼NE¼	16	33	48	3-15—4-28	.051	4.73
1875						39.50	NE¼NW¼	16	33	48	3-15—4-28	.321	29.63
1875						15.30	SE¼NW¼	16	33	48	3-15—4-28	.125	11.48
1875						39.35	NW¼NW¼	16	33	48	3-15—4-28	.321	29.51
1875						21.25	SW¼NW¼	16	33	48	3-15—4-28	.174	15.94
1875						38.90	NE¼NE¼	17	33	48	3-15—4-28	.317	29.18
1875						26.30	SE¼NE¼	17	33	48	3-15—4-28	.215	19.73
1875						38.30	NW¼NE¼	17	33	48	3-15—4-28	.312	28.73
1875						38.60	SW¼NE¼	17	33	48	3-15—4-28	.315	28.95
1875						5.80	NE¼SE¼	17	33	48	3-15—4-28	.047	4.35
1875						19.70	SE¼SE¼	17	34	48	3-15—4-28	.160	14.78
1875						40.40	NW¼SE¼	17	33	48	3-15—4-28	.328	30.30
1875						39.80	SW¼SE¼	17	33	48	3-15—4-28	.324	29.85
1875						37.00	NE¼NW¼	17	33	48	3-15—4-28	.301	27.75
1875						39.20	SE¼NW¼	17	33	48	3-15—4-28	.319	29.40
1875						39.60	NW¼NW¼	17	33	48	3-15—4-28	.322	29.70
1875						38.70	SW¼NW¼	17	33	48	3-15—4-28	.315	29.03
1875						40.10	NE¼SW¼	17	33	48	3-15—4-28	.326	30.08
1875					0.50		SE¼SW¼	17	33	48	3-15—4-28	.004	0.38
1875						38.90	SE¼SW¼	17	33	48	3-15—4-28	.316	29.18
1875						40.20	NW¼SW¼	17	33	48	3-15—4-28	.327	30.15
1875					0.30		SW¼SW¼	17	33	48	3-15—4-28	.002	0.23
1875						38.90	SW¼SW¼	17	33	48	3-15—4-28	.316	29.18
1875						11.10	NE¼NE¼	34	34	48	3-15—4-28	.090	8.33
1875						9.40	SE¼SE¼	27	34	48	3-15—4-28	.076	7.05
1875						29.40	NW¼NW¼	35	34	48	3-15—4-28	.239	22.05
1875						29.60	NE¼NW¼	35	34	48	3-15—4-28	.241	22.20
1875						30.50	NW¼NE¼	35	34	48	3-15—4-28	.248	22.88
1875						30.40	NE¼NE¼	35	34	48	3-15—4-28	.247	22.80

ELKO AND PINE CREEK DISTRICTS

Claimant—**Henderson Banking Company.** Proof. No. 00201

Source—**Humboldt River.** Ditch—**Henderson Ditches.**

Year of priority	Culture—Acres: Harvest crops	Culture—Acres: Meadow pasture	Culture—Acres: Diversified pasture	Location: Subdivision	Location: Section	Location: Tp.N.	Location: R.E.	Length of season	Duty of water: C.F.S.	Duty of water: Acre-feet
1883	....	63.00		S½	20	35	56	4-15—6-15	.775	94.50
1888	....	197.37		N½	29	35	56	4-15—6-15	2.428	206.06

Claimant—**Elko Water Works.** Proof No. 00202

Source—**Humboldt River.** Ditch—**Elko Water Works Ditches.**

Year of priority	Harvest crops	Meadow pasture	Diversified pasture	Subdivision	Section	Tp.N.	R.E.	Length of season	C.F.S.	Acre-feet
1890	15.00			SE¼ NE¼	10	34	55	4-15—8-15	.185	45.00
1892	15.00			SE¼	10	34	55	4-15—8-15	.185	45.00
1894	30.00			SW¼	11	34	55	4-15—8-15	.369	90.00
1896	20.00							4-15—8-15	.246	60.00
1900	30.00							4-15—8-15	.369	90.00
1901	15.22							4-15—8-15	.187	45.66
1903	5.22							4-15—8-15	.064	15.66

NOTE—It is found that Elko Water Works are owners of entire flow of Kitridge Canyon Springs above their point of diversion with priority of 1891, and also all rights from the Humboldt River that were included in that certain Act of Nevada State Legislature entitled "An Act to supply the Town of Elko, Elko County, Nevada, with water for extinguishment of fire and other purposes, and to define said boundaries of said town."

Claimant—**Frank Fernald.** Proof No.00203

Source—**Humboldt River.** Ditch—**Frank Fernald Ditches.**

Year of priority	Harvest crops	Meadow pasture	Diversified pasture	Subdivision	Section	Tp.N.	R.E.	Length of season	C.F.S.	Acre-feet
1879	....	193.16		S½ SW¼	30	35	56			
1880	....	193.15		NE¼ SW¼	30	35	56			
				SE¼ SE¼	30	35	56			
				SW¼ NE¼	30	35	56			
				E½ NE¼	30	35	56			
				W½ W½	29	35	56			
				E½ SW¼	29	35	56			
				SE¼ NW¼	29	35	56	4-15—6-15	2.376	289.74
				NW¼ SE¼	29	35	56	4-15—6-15	2.376	299.73

Claimant—**M. Aguirre.** Proof No. 00204

Source—**Humboldt River.** Ditch—**M. Aguirre Ditches.**

Year of priority	Harvest crops	Meadow pasture	Diversified pasture	Subdivision	Section	Tp.N.	R.E.	Length of season	C.F.S.	Acre-feet
1882	...	108.25		SW¼	8	35	57			
				E½ NW¼	8	35	57			
				NE¼	8	35	57			
				NE¼ SW¼	8	35	57			
				SW¼ NW¼	9	35	57			
				W½ SW¼	9	35	57	4-15—6-15	2.000	252.89

Claimant—**Mrs. C. Glaser.** Proof No. **00205**

Source—**Rabbit & Lamoille Creeks.*** Ditch—**Glaser Ditches.**

1871	34.70		S½	13	35	57	4-15—8-15	.427	114.10

*Priority from Lamoille Creek dated 1891.

Source—**Rabbit Creek.** Ditch—**Glaser Ditches.**

1871	84.30		S½	13	35	57	4-15—8-15	1.037	252.90

Source—**Humboldt River.** Ditch—**Glaser Ditches.**

1872		171.00	N½	14	35	57			
1873		298.50	N¼N½S½	14	35	57			
1874		298.50	N½	13	35	57			
			SE¼	12	35	57	4-15—6-15	2.103	250.50
			SW¼	7	35	58	4-15—6-15	3.672	447.75
			NW¼	18	35	58	4-15—6-15	3.672	447.75

Source—**Lamoille Creek.** Ditch—**Glaser Ditches.**

1873	175.60		S½	14	35	57	4-15—8-15	2.159	526.90
1893	51.50		S½	13	35	57	4-15—8-15	.633	154.50
1894	136.80		NE¼	13	35	57	4-15—8-15	1.682	410.40
1901	46.50		W½	18	35	58	4-15—8-15	.572	139.50
1904	178.20		NE¼	18	35	58	4-15—8-15	2.192	534.60

Claimant—W. F. Linebarger. Proof No. **00207**

Source—**Humboldt River.** Ditch—**Linebarger Ditch and Overflow.**

1876	14.00		SW¼NE¼	34	33	52	4-15—8-15	.172	42.00
1876	40.00		NE¼NE¼	34	33	52	4-15—8-15	.492	120.00
1876	34.00		SE¼NE¼	34	33	52	4-15—8-15	.418	102.00
1876	18.60		NE¼SW¼	34	33	52	4-15—8-15	.229	55.80
1876	13.25		SW¼SW¼	34	33	52	4-15—8-15	.163	39.75
1876	33.80		NW¼SW¼	34	33	52	4-15—8-15	.416	101.40
1876	15.00		NE¼SW¼	34	33	52	4-15—8-15	.185	45.00
1876	10.00		NW¼SE¼	34	33	52	4-15—8-15	.123	30.00
1876	30.00		SW¼NW¼	35	33	52	4-15—8-15	.370	90.00
1876	22.00		SE¼NW¼	35	33	52	4-15—8-15	.271	66.00
1876	37.00		NW¼NW¼	35	33	52	4-15—8-15	.455	111.00
1876	34.00		NE¼NW¼	35	33	52	4-15—8-15	.492	102.00

Source—**Mary's Creek.** Ditch—**Linebarger Ditches.**

1880	30.00		NW¼NW¼	34	33	52	4-15—8-15	.369	90.00
1880	3.00		NE¼NW¼	34	33	52	4-15—8-15	.037	9.00
1880		28.00	NE¼NW¼	34	33	52	4-15—6-15	.344	42.00
1880	36.00		SW¼NW¼	34	33	52	4-15—8-15	.443	108.00
1880	8.00		SE¼NW¼	34	33	52	4-15—8-15	.098	24.00
1880		25.00	SE¼NW¼	34	33	52	4-15—6-15	.308	37.50
1880		14.00	NW¼NE¼	34	33	52	4-15—6-15	.172	21.00
1880	15.00		NW¼NE¼	34	33	52	4-15—8-15	.185	45.00
1880	20.00		SW¼NE¼	34	33	52	4-15—8-15	.246	60.00

William Dunphy Estate—Continued.

Year of priority			Culture—Acres: Harvest crops	Meadow pasture	Diversified pasture		Location: Subdivision	Section	Tp.N.	R.E.	Length of season	Duty of water: C.F.S.	Acre-feet
1870	......	......	....	6.10	......	......	SW¼NE¼	30	33	47	3-15—6-13	.050	9.15
1870	......	......	....	......	......	6.95	SW¼NE¼	30	33	47	3-15—4-28	.057	5.21
1870	......	......	....	2.25	......	......	SW¼SE¼	9	33	47	3-15—6-13	.018	3.38
1870	......	......	....	......	.45	......	SW¼SE¼	9	33	47	3-15—4-28	.004	.34
1870	......	......	....	9.70	......	......	NE¼SW¼	9	33	47	3-15—6-13	.079	14.55
1870	......	......	....	......	.40	......	NE¼SW¼	9	33	47	3-15—4-28	.003	.30
1870	......	......	....	1.05	......	......	SE¼SW¼	9	33	47	3-15—6-13	.000	.08
1870	......	......	....	......	.10	......	SE¼SW¼	9	33	47	3-15—4-28	.001	.08
1870	......	......	....	1.70	......	......	NE¼NE¼	10	33	47	3-15—6-13	.014	2.55
1870	......	......	....	......	36.05	......	NE¼NE¼	10	33	47	3-15—4-28	.293	27.04
1870	......	......	....	29.95	......	......	SE¼NE¼	10	33	47	3-15—6-13	.243	44.93
1870	......	......	....	......	8.65	......	SE¼NE¼	10	33	47	3-15—4-28	.070	6.49
1870	......	......	....	32.10	......	......	NW¼NE¼	10	33	47	3-15—6-13	.261	48.15
1870	......	......	....	......	7.10	......	NW¼NE¼	10	33	47	3-15—4-28	.058	5.33
1870	......	......	....	36.50	......	......	SW¼NE¼	10	33	47	3-15—6-13	.297	54.75
1870	......	......	....	......	2.25	......	SW¼NE¼	10	33	47	3-15—4-28	.018	1.69
1870	......	......	....	9.95	......	......	NE¼SE¼	10	33	47	3-15—6-13	.081	14.93
1870	......	......	....	......	26.95	......	NE¼SE¼	10	33	47	3-15—4-28	.219	20.21
1870	......	......	....	33.00	......	......	NW¼SE¼	10	33	47	3-15—6-13	.268	49.50
1870	......	......	....	......	5.70	......	NW¼SE¼	10	33	47	3-15—4-28	.046	4.28
1870	......	......	....	32.50	......	......	NE¼NW¼	10	33	47	3-15—6-13	.264	48.75
1870	......	......	....	......	......	7.35	SE¼NW¼	29	33	47	3-15—4-28	.060	5.51
1870	......	......	....	26.70	......	......	NW¼NE¼	29	33	47	3-15—6-13	.217	40.05
1870	......	......	....	......	......	10.70	NW¼NE¼	29	33	47	3-15—4-28	.087	8.03
1870	......	......	10.75	......	......	......	NE¼NE¼	29	33	47	3-15—9-15	.087	32.25
1870	......	......	....	......	......	26.85	NE¼NE¼	29	33	47	3-15—4-28	.218	20.14
1870	......	......	0.40	......	......	......	SE¼NE¼	29	33	47	3-15—9-15	.003	1.20
1870	......	......	....	13.15	......	......	SE¼NE¼	29	33	47	3-15—6-13	.107	19.73
1870	......	......	....	......	......	1.80	SE¼NE¼	29	33	47	3-15—4-28	.015	1.35
1870	......	......	....	15.30	......	......	SW¼NE¼	29	33	47	3-15—6-13	.125	23.10
1870	......	......	....	9.85	......	......	SE¼NE¼	30	33	47	3-16—6-13	.080	14.78
1870	......	......	....	......	......	3.35	SE¼NE¼	30	33	47	3-16—4-28	.027	2.51
1870	......	......	....	29.90	......	......	NE¼NE¼	30	33	47	3-15—6-13	.243	44.85
1870	......	......	....	......	......	4.25	NE¼NE¼	30	33	47	3-15—4-28	.035	3.19
1870	......	......	....	33.95	......	......	NW¼NW¼	21	33	47	3-15—6-13	.276	50.93
1870	......	......	....	14.50	......	......	NE¼NW¼	21	33	47	3-15—6-13	.118	21.75
1870	......	......	....	13.90	......	......	SW¼NW¼	21	33	47	3-15—6-13	.113	20.85
1870	......	......	....	1.00	......	......	SE¼NW¼	21	33	47	3-15—6-13	.008	1.50
1870	......	......	9.00	......	......	......	NW¼NW¼	28	33	47	3-15—9-15	.073	27.00
1870	......	......	10.85	......	......	......	NE¼NW¼	28	33	47	3-15—9-15	.088	32.55
1870	......	......	8.55	......	......	......	SW¼NW¼	28	33	47	3-15—9-15	.070	25.65
1870	......	......	....	1.00	......	......	SW¼NW¼	28	33	47	3-15—6-13	.008	1.50
1870	......	......	4.40	......	......	......	SE¼NW¼	28	33	47	3-15—9-15	.036	13.20
1870	......	......	....	35.35	......	......	NW¼NW¼	29	33	47	3-15—6-13	.287	53.03
1870	......	......	....	28.35	......	......	NE¼NW¼	29	33	47	3-16—6-13	.230	42.53
1870	......	......	....	......	......	7.70	NE¼NW¼	29	33	47	3-15—4-28	.063	5.78

1870				11.55			SW¼NW¼	29	33	47	3-15—6-13	.094	17.33
1870						2.80	SW¼NW¼	29	33	47	3-15—4-28	.023	2.10
1870				6.70			SE¼NW¼	29	33	47	3-15—6-13	.054	10.05
1870				38.85			SE¼SW¼	17	33	47	3-15—6-13	.316	58.28
1870				33.55			NE¼SW¼	17	33	47	3-15—6-13	.273	50.33
1870				11.60			SE¼NE¼	17	33	47	3-15—6-13	.094	17.40
1870				12.25			SW¼SE¼	18	33	47	3-15—6-13	.100	18.38
1870				34.35			SE¼SE¼	18	33	47	3-15—6-13	.279	51.53
1870				1.70			NE¼SE¼	18	33	47	3-15—6-13	.014	2.55
1870				14.80			SW¼NW¼	19	33	47	3-15—6-13	.120	22.20
1870				37.10			SE¼NW¼	19	33	47	3-15—6-13	.302	55.65
1870				15.10			NE¼NW¼	19	33	47	3-15—6-13	.123	22.65
1870				34.90			NW¼SW¼	19	33	47	3-15—6-13	.284	52.35
1870				37.20			SW¼SW¼	19	33	47	3-15—6-13	.302	55.80
1870				39.25			SE¼SW¼	19	33	47	3-15—6-13	.319	58.88
1870				38.55			NE¼SW¼	19	33	47	3-15—6-13	.313	57.83
1870				38.50			NW¼SE¼	19	33	47	3-15—6-13	.313	57.75
1870				40.25			SW¼SE¼	19	33	47	3-15—6-13	.327	60.38
1870				39.65			SE¼SE¼	19	33	47	3-15—6-13	.322	59.48
1870				38.75			NE¼SE¼	19	33	47	3-15—6-13	.315	58.13
1870					15.80		NE¼SE¼	7	33	48	3-15—4-28	.128	11.85
1870					4.50		NE¼SW¼	7	33	48	3-15—4-28	.037	3.38
1870					29.60		NW¼NW¼	7	33	48	3-15—4-28	.241	22.20
1870					0.70		SW¼NE¼	8	33	48	3-15—4-28	.006	.53
1870					19.70		NE¼SE¼	8	33	48	3-15—4-28	.160	14.78
1870					32.05		NW¼SE¼	8	33	48	3-15—4-28	.261	24.04
1870					27.25		NE¼SW¼	8	33	48	3-15—4-28	.222	20.44
1870					24.50		NW¼SW¼	8	33	48	3-15—4-28	.199	18.38
1870					24.45		SW¼NE¼	9	33	48	3-15—4-28	.199	18.34
1870					32.05		NW¼SE¼	9	33	48	3-15—4-28	.261	24.04
1870					14.75		SE¼NW¼	9	33	48	3-15—4-28	.120	11.06
1870					36.45		NE¼SW¼	9	33	48	3-15—4-28	.296	27.34
1870					1.95		SW¼NW¼	9	33	48	3-15—4-28	.016	1.46
1870					32.70		NW¼SW¼	9	33	48	3-15—4-28	.266	24.53

Source—Boulder Creek. Ditch—Boulder Creek.

1875						6.10	NE¼NE¼	34	34	48	3-15—4-28	.050	4.58
1875						33.40	SE¼NE¼	34	34	48	3-15—4-28	.272	25.05
1875						41.20	NE¼SE¼	34	34	48	3-15—4-28	.335	30.90
1875						39.05	SE¼SE¼	34	34	48	3-15—4-28	.317	29.29
1875						3.75	NW¼SE¼	34	34	48	3-15—4-28	.142	2.81
1875						14.35	SW¼SE¼	34	34	48	3-15—4-28	.117	10.76
1875						11.30	NE¼NE¼	35	34	48	3-15—4-28	.092	8.48
1875						38.30	SE¼NE¼	35	34	48	3-15—4-28	.311	28.73
1875						11.50	NW¼NE¼	35	34	48	3-15—4-28	.093	8.63
1875						42.45	SW¼NE¼	35	34	48	3-15—4-28	.345	31.84
1875						6.25	NE¼SE¼	35	34	48	3-15—4-28	.051	4.69
1875						37.00	NW¼SE¼	35	34	48	3-15—4-28	.301	27.75
1875						9.00	SW¼SE¼	35	34	48	3-15—4-28	.073	6.75
1875						11.05	NE¼NW¼	35	34	48	3-15—4-28	.090	8.29
1875					6.80		SE¼NW¼	35	34	48	3-15—4-28	.055	5.10
1875						35.35	SE¼NW¼	35	34	48	3-15—4-28	.287	26.51

William Dunphy Estate—Continued.

Year of priority	Culture—Acres: Harvest crops	Culture—Acres: Meadow pasture	Culture—Acres: Diversified pasture		Location: Subdivision	Location: Section	Location: Tp. N.	Location: R. E.	Length of season	Duty of water: C.F.S.	Duty of water: Acre-feet
1875				11.35	NW¼NW¼	35	34	48	3-15—4-28	.092	8.51
1875			18.15		SW¼NW¼	35	34	48	3-15—4-28	.148	13.61
1875				24.10	SW¼NW¼	35	34	48	3-15—4-28	.196	18.08
1875			0.15		NE¼SW¼	35	34	48	3-15—4-28	.001	.11
1875				41.70	NE¼SW¼	35	34	48	3-15—4-28	.339	31.28
1875				38.95	SE¼SW¼	35	34	48	3-15—4-28	.317	29.21
1875			12.00		NW¼SW¼	35	34	48	3-15—4-28	.098	9.09
1875				29.90	NW¼SW¼	35	34	48	3-15—4-28	.243	22.43
1875				42.15	SW¼SW¼	35	34	48	3-15—4-28	.343	31.61
1875			9.55		NE¼NW¼	2	33	48	3-15—4-28	.081	7.46
1875				1.40	NE¼NW¼	2	33	48	3-15—4-28	.011	1.05
1875			8.20		SE¼NW¼	2	33	48	3-15—4-28	.067	6.15
1875				0.20	SE¼NW¼	2	33	48	3-15—4-28	.002	0.15
1875			24.80		NW¼NW¼	2	33	48	3-15—4-28	.202	18.60
1875				16.75	NW¼NW¼	2	33	48	3-15—4-28	.136	12.50
1875			30.00		SW¼NW¼	2	33	48	3-15—4-28	.244	22.50
1875				11.75	SW¼NW¼	2	33	48	3-15—4-28	.096	8.81
1875			9.80		NW¼SW¼	2	33	48	3-15—4-28	.080	7.35
1875				16.50	NW¼SW¼	2	33	48	3-15—4-28	.134	12.38
1875			6.15		SW¼SW¼	2	33	48	3-15—4-28	.050	4.61
1875			8.45		NE¼NE¼	3	33	48	3-15—4-28	.069	6.34
1875				30.60	NE¼NE¼	3	33	48	3-15—4-28	.249	22.95
1875			31.00		SE¼NE¼	3	33	48	3-15—4-28	.252	23.25
1875				8.70	SE¼NE¼	3	33	48	3-15—4-28	.071	6.53
1875			4.90		NW¼NE¼	3	33	48	3-15—4-28	.040	3.68
1875				22.25	NW¼NE¼	3	33	48	3-15—4-28	.181	16.69
1875			32.70		SW¼NE¼	3	33	48	3-15—4-28	.266	24.51
1875				7.35	SW¼NE¼	3	33	48	3-15—4-28	.060	5.51
1875			18.10		NE¼SE¼	3	33	48	3-15—4-28	.147	13.58
1875				21.90	NE¼SE¼	3	33	48	3-15—4-28	.178	16.43
1875			22.70		SE¼SE¼	3	33	48	3-15—4-28	.185	17.03
1875				15.80	SE¼SE¼	3	33	48	3-15—4-28	.128	11.85
1875			16.20		NW¼SE¼	3	33	48	3-15—4-28	.132	12.15
1875				22.85	NW¼SE¼	3	33	48	3-15—4-28	.186	17.14
1875				38.90	SW¼SE¼	3	33	48	3-15—4-28	.316	29.18
1875				4.10	NE¼NW¼	3	33	48	3-15—4-28	.033	3.08
1875				32.50	SE¼NW¼	3	33	48	3-15—4-28	.264	24.38
1875				22.70	NE¼SW¼	3	33	48	3-15—4-28	.185	17.03
1875				18.90	SE¼SW¼	3	33	48	3-15—4-28	.154	14.18
1875				1.75	NE¼NE¼	10	33	48	3-15—4-28	.014	1.31
1875				38.45	SE¼NE¼	10	33	48	3-15—4-28	.313	28.84
1875				0.10	NW¼NE¼	10	33	48	3-15—4-28	.001	.08
1875				4.65	SW¼NE¼	10	33	48	3-15—4-28	.037	3.48
1875				30.50	NE¼SE¼	10	33	48	3-15—4-28	.297	27.38
1875				4.10	NW¼SE¼	10	33	48	3-15—4-28	.033	3.08
1875			2.25		NE¼NE¼	[illegible]	[illegible]	[illegible]	3-15—4-28	.018	[illegible]

1875						11.75	NE¼NE¼	10	33	48	3-15—4-28	.096	8.81
1875						38.50	NW¼NE¼	10	33	48	3-15—4-28	.313	28.88
1875						9.05	SW¼NE¼	10	33	48	3-15—4-28	.074	6.79
1875						32.20	NE¼NW¼	10	33	48	3-15—4-28	.262	21.15
1875						32.10	SE¼NW¼	10	33	48	3-15—4-28	.261	24.08
1875					5.00		NW¼NW¼	10	33	48	3-15—4-28	.041	3.75
1875						13.00	NW¼NW¼	10	33	48	3-15—4-28	.106	9.75
1875						39.00	SW¼NW¼	10	33	48	3-15—4-28	.317	29.25
1875						21.90	NE¼SW¼	10	33	48	3-15—4-28	.178	16.43
1875						36.80	NW¼SW¼	10	33	48	3-15—4-28	.299	27.60
1875				1.25			SW¼SW¼	14	33	47	3-15—6-13	.010	1.88
1875				1.30			SE¼SW¼	14	33	47	3-15—6-13	.011	1.95
1875				1.75			SW¼SE¼	14	33	47	3-15—6-13	.014	2.63
1875				16.70			SE¼SE¼	14	33	47	3-15—6-13	.136	25.05
1875				.25			NE¼SE¼	14	33	47	3-15—6-13	.002	.38
1875				1.65			NW¼SW¼	13	33	47	3-15—6-13	.013	2.48
1875				8.95			SW¼SW¼	13	33	47	3-15—6-13	.073	13.43
1875				3.70			NE¼SW¼	13	33	47	3-15—6-13	.030	5.55
1875				16.30			NW¼SE¼	13	33	47	3-15—6-13	.133	24.45
1875				4.90			SW¼SE¼	13	33	47	3-15—6-13	.040	7.36
1875				.40			SE¼SW¼	13	33	47	3-15—6-13	.003	.60
1875						37.70	NE¼NE¼	22	33	47	3-15—4-28	.307	28.28
1875						38.50	SE¼NE¼	22	33	47	3-15—4-28	.313	28.80
1875						22.85	SW¼NE¼	22	33	47	3-15—4-28	.186	17.14
1875			7.95				NE¼SE¼	22	33	47	3-15—9-15	.065	23.85
1875				12.45			NE¼SE¼	22	33	47	3-15—6-13	.101	18.68
1875						16.65	NE¼SE¼	22	33	47	3-15—4-28	.135	12.49
1875				3.70			NW¼SE¼	22	33	47	3-15—6-13	.030	5.55
1875						34.50	NW¼SE¼	22	33	47	3-15—4-28	.280	25.88
1875			21.60				SE¼SW¼	22	33	47	3-15—9-15	.176	64.80
1875				11.85			SE¼SW¼	22	33	47	3-15—6-13	.096	17.78
1875						1.20	SE¼SW¼	22	33	47	3-15—4-28	.010	.90
1875				1.80			NW¼NE¼	23	33	47	3-15—6-13	.015	2.70
1875					1.35		NW¼NE¼	23	33	47	3-15—4-28	.011	1.01
1875						38.35	NE¼NW¼	23	33	47	3-15—4-28	.312	28.76
1875				25.75			SE¼NW¼	23	33	47	3-15—6-13	.209	38.62
1875						13.25	SE¼NW¼	23	33	47	3-15—4-28	.108	9.94
1875						38.50	NW¼NW¼	23	33	47	3-15—4-28	.313	28.88
1875				8.95			SW¼NW¼	23	33	47	3-15—6-13	.073	13.43
1875						28.70	SW¼NW¼	23	33	47	3-15—4-28	.233	21.53
1875				5.30			SE¼NE¼	13	33	47	3-15—6-13	.043	7.95
1875				25.75			NE¼SE¼	13	33	47	3-15—6-13	.209	38.63
1875						11.00	NE¼SE¼	13	33	47	3-15—4-28	.089	8.25
1875				6.50			NW¼SE¼	13	33	47	3-15—6-13	.053	9.75
1875						37.65	NE¼NE¼	18	33	48	3-15—4-28	.306	28.24
1875				19.90			SE¼NE¼	18	33	48	3-15—6-13	.162	29.85
1875						15.60	SE¼NE¼	18	33	48	3-15—4-28	.238	11.70
1875						38.85	NW¼NE¼	18	33	48	3-15—4-28	.316	29.14
1875				27.40			SW¼NE¼	18	33	48	3-15—6-13	.223	41.10
1875						11.00	SW¼NE¼	18	33	48	3-15—4-28	.089	8.25
1875				7.80			NE¼SE¼	18	33	48	3-15—6-13	.063	11.70
1875						30.80	NE¼SE¼	18	33	48	3-15—4-28	.250	23.10

William Dunphy Estate—Continued.

Year of priority	Culture—Acres: Harvest crops	Culture—Acres: Meadow pasture	Culture—Acres: Diversified pasture		Location: Subdivision	Location: Section	Location: Tp. N.	Location: R. E.	Length of season	Duty of water: C. F. S.	Duty of water: Acre-feet
1875		1.80			SE¼SE¼	18	33	48	3-15—6-13	.015	2.70
1875				27.40	SE¼SE¼	18	33	48	3-15—4-28	.223	20.55
1875		18.55			NW¼SE¼	18	33	48	3-15—6-13	.151	27.83
1875				19.10	NW¼SE¼	18	33	48	3-15—4-28	.155	14.33
1875		.70			SW¼SE¼	18	33	48	3-15—6-13	.006	1.05
1875				26.05	SW¼SE¼	18	33	48	3-15—4-28	.212	19.54
1875				32.80	NE¼NW¼	18	33	48	3-15—4-28	.267	24.60
1875		28.75			SE¼NW¼	18	33	48	3-15—6-13	.234	43.13
1875				9.40	SE¼NW¼	18	33	48	3-15—4-28	.076	7.05
1875				1.30	NW¼NW¼	18	33	48	3-15—4-28	.011	.98
1875		23.45			SW¼NW¼	18	33	48	3-15—6-13	.191	35.18
1875				3.60	SW¼NW¼	18	33	48	3-15—4-28	.029	2.70
1875		28.20			NE¼SW¼	18	33	48	3-15—6-13	.229	42.30
1875				8.50	NE¼SW¼	18	33	48	3-15—4-28	.069	6.38
1875				36.20	SE¼SW¼	18	33	48	3-15—4-28	.294	27.15
1875		31.10			NW¼SW¼	18	33	48	3-15—6-13	.253	46.65
1875				6.10	NW¼SW¼	18	33	48	3-15—4-28	.050	4.58
1875				33.05	SW¼SW¼	18	33	48	3-15—4-28	.269	24.79
1875				2.65	NE¼SE¼	7	33	48	3-15—4-28	.022	1.90
1875				38.00	SE¼SE¼	7	33	48	3-15—4-28	.309	28.50
1875				27.00	SW¼SE¼	7	33	48	3-15—4-28	.220	20.25
1875				3.90	SE¼SW¼	7	33	48	3-15—4-28	.032	2.93
1875				1.65	NE¼SE¼	8	33	48	3-15—4-28	.013	1.24
1875				39.25	SE¼SE¼	8	33	48	3-15—4-28	.319	29.44
1875				2.10	NW¼SE¼	8	33	48	3-15—4-28	.017	1.58
1875				38.25	SW¼SE¼	8	33	48	3-15—4-28	.311	28.69
1875				2.35	NE¼SW¼	8	33	48	3-15—4-28	.019	1.76
1875				38.50	SE¼SW¼	8	33	48	3-15—4-28	.313	28.88
1875				2.70	NW¼SW¼	8	33	48	3-15—4-28	.022	2.03
1875				39.40	SW¼SW¼	8	33	48	3-15—4-28	.320	29.55
1875				1.30	NE¼SE¼	9	33	48	3-15—4-28	.010	.98
1875			5.15		SE¼SE¼	9	33	48	3-15—4-28	.042	3.86
1875				33.15	SE¼SE¼	9	33	48	3-15—4-28	.270	24.86
1875				1.30	NW¼SE¼	9	33	48	3-15—4-28	.010	.98
1875				38.95	SW¼SE¼	9	33	48	3-15—4-28	.317	29.21
1875				1.45	NE¼SW¼	9	33	48	3-15—4-28	.012	1.00
1875				39.40	SE¼SW¼	9	33	48	3-15—4-28	.320	29.55
1875				1.50	NW¼SW¼	9	33	48	3-15—4-28	.012	1.13
1875				39.30	SW¼SW¼	9	33	48	3-15—4-28	.320	29.48
1875				0.70	NW¼SW¼	10	33	48	3-15—4-28	.006	0.53
1875				18.50	SW¼SW¼	10	33	48	3-15—4-28	.150	13.88
1875			14.45		NW¼NW¼	15	33	48	3-15—4-28	.117	10.84
1875				1.30	NW¼NW¼	15	33	48	3-15—4-28	.011	0.98
1875			0.20		SW¼NW¼	15	33	48	3-15—4-28	.002	0.15
1876			13.05		NE¼NE¼	16	33	48	3-15—4-28	.113	10.46
1875				10.15	NE¼NE¼	16	33	48	3-15—4-28	.123	11.90

1875						37.35	NW¼NE¼	16	33	48	3-15—4-28	.304	28.01
1875						6.30	SW¼NE¼	16	33	48	3-15—4-28	.051	4.73
1875						39.50	NE¼NW¼	16	33	48	3-15—4-28	.321	29.63
1875						15.30	SE¼NW¼	16	33	48	3-15—4-28	.125	11.48
1875						39.35	NW¼NW¼	16	33	48	3-15—4-28	.321	29.51
1875						21.25	SW¼NW¼	16	33	48	3-15—4-28	.174	15.94
1875						38.90	NE¼NE¼	17	33	48	3-15—4-28	.317	29.18
1875						26.30	SE¼NE¼	17	33	48	3-15—4-28	.215	19.73
1875						38.30	NW¼NE¼	17	33	48	3-15—4-28	.312	28.73
1875						38.60	SW¼NE¼	17	33	48	3-15—4-28	.315	28.95
1875						5.80	NE¼SE¼	17	33	48	3-15—4-28	.047	4.35
1875						19.70	SE¼SE¼	17	33	48	3-15—4-28	.160	14.78
1875						40.40	NW¼SE¼	17	33	48	3-15—4-28	.328	30.30
1875						39.80	SW¼SE¼	17	33	48	3-15—4-28	.324	29.85
1875						37.00	NE¼NW¼	17	33	48	3-15—4-28	.301	27.75
1875						30.20	SE¼NW¼	17	33	48	3-15—4-28	.319	29.40
1875						39.60	NW¼NW¼	17	33	48	3-15—4-28	.322	29.70
1875						38.70	SW¼NW¼	17	33	48	3-15—4-28	.315	29.03
1875						40.10	NE¼SW¼	17	33	48	3-15—4-28	.326	30.08
1875					0.50		SE¼SW¼	17	33	48	3-15—4-28	.004	0.38
1875						38.90	SE¼SW¼	17	33	48	3-15—4-28	.316	29.18
1875						40.20	NW¼SW¼	17	33	48	3-15—4-28	.327	30.15
1875					0.30		SW¼SW¼	17	33	48	3-15—4-28	.002	0.23
1875						38.90	SW¼SW¼	17	33	48	3-15—4-28	.316	29.18
1875						11.10	NE¼NE¼	34	31	48	3-15—4-28	.090	8.33
1875						9.40	SE¼SE¼	27	34	48	3-15—4-28	.076	7.05
1875						29.40	NW¼NW¼	35	34	48	3-15—4-28	.239	22.05
1875						29.60	NE¼NW¼	35	34	48	3-15—4-28	.241	22.20
1875						30.50	NW¼NE¼	35	34	48	3-15—4-28	.248	22.88
1875						30.40	NE¼NE¼	35	34	48	3-15—4-28	.247	22.80

ELKO AND PINE CREEK DISTRICTS

Claimant—**Henderson Banking Company.** Proof. No. 00201
Source—**Humboldt River.** Ditch—**Henderson Ditches.**

Year of priority	Culture—Acres: Harvest crops	Meadow pasture	Diversified pasture	Location: Subdivision	Section	Tp.N.	R.E.	Length of season	Duty of water: C.F.S.	Acre-feet
1883	....	63.00		S½	20	35	56	4-15—6-15	.775	94.50
1888	....	197.37		N½	29	35	56	4-15—6-15	2.428	296.06

Claimant—**Elko Water Works.** Proof No. 00202
Source—**Humboldt River.** Ditch—**Elko Water Works Ditches.**

Year of priority	Harvest crops	Meadow pasture	Diversified pasture	Subdivision	Section	Tp.N.	R.E.	Length of season	C.F.S.	Acre-feet
1886	15.00			SE¼ NE¼	10	34	55	4-15—8-15	.185	45.00
1892	15.00			SE¼	10	34	55	4-15—8-15	.185	45.00
1894	30.00			SW¼	11	34	55	4-15—8-15	.369	90.00
1896	20.00				....	....	....	4-15—8-15	.246	60.00
1900	30.00				....	....	....	4-15—8-15	.369	90.00
1901	15.22				....	....	....	4-15—8-15	.187	45.66
1903	5.22						....	4-15—8-15	.064	15.66

NOTE—It is found that Elko Water Works are owners of entire flow of Kitridge Canyon Springs above their point of diversion with priority of 1891, and also all rights from the Humboldt River that were included in that certain Act of Nevada State Legislature entitled "An Act to supply the Town of Elko, Elko County, Nevada, with water for extinguishment of fire and other purposes, and to define said boundaries of said town."

Claimant—**Frank Fernald.** Proof No.00203
Source—**Humboldt River.** Ditch—**Frank Fernald Ditches.**

Year of priority	Harvest crops	Meadow pasture	Diversified pasture	Subdivision	Section	Tp.N.	R.E.	Length of season	C.F.S.	Acre-feet
1870	....	193.16		S½ SW¼	30	35	56			
1880	....	193.15		NE¼ SW¼	30	35	56			
				SE¼ SE¼	30	35	56			
				SW¼ NE¼	30	35	56			
				E½ NE¼	30	35	56			
				W½ W½	29	35	56			
				E½ SW¼	29	35	56			
				SE¼ NW¼	29	35	56	4-15—6-15	2.376	289.74
				NW¼ SE¼	29	35	56	4-15—6-15	2.376	299.73

Claimant—**M. Aguirre.** Proof No. 00204
Source—**Humboldt River.** Ditch—**M. Aguirre Ditches.**

Year of priority	Harvest crops	Meadow pasture	Diversified pasture	Subdivision	Section	Tp.N.	R.E.	Length of season	C.F.S.	Acre-feet
1882	...	108.25		SW¼	8	35	57			
				E½ NW¼	8	35	57			
				NE¼	8	35	57			
				NE¼ SE¼	8	35	57			
				SW¼ NW¼	9	35	57			
				W½ SW¼	9	35	57	4-15—6-15	2.060	252.39

Claimant—**Mrs. C. Glaser.** Proof No. 00205

Source—**Rabbit & Lamoille Creeks.*** Ditch—**Glaser Ditches.**

1871	34.70		S½	13	35	57	4-15—8-15	.427	114.10

*Priority from Lamoille Creek dated 1864.

Source——**Rabbit Creek.** Ditch—**Glaser Ditches.**

1871	84.30		S½	13	35	57	4-15—8-15	1.037	252.90

Source—**Humboldt River.** Ditch—**Glaser Ditches.**

1872		171.00	N½	14	35	57			
1873		298.50	N½N½S½	14	35	57			
1874		298.50	N½	13	35	57			
			SE¼	12	35	57	4-15—6-15	2.103	256.50
			SW¼	7	35	58	4-15—6-15	3.672	447.75
			NW¼	18	35	58	4-15—6-15	3.672	447.75

Source—**Lamoille Creek.** Ditch—**Glaser Ditches.**

1873	175.60		S½	14	35	57	4-15—8-15	2.159	526.90
1893	51.50		S½	13	35	57	4-15—8-15	.633	154.50
1894	136.80		NE¼	13	35	57	4-15—8-15	1.682	410.40
1901	46.50		W½	18	35	58	4-15—8-15	.572	139.50
1904	178.20		NE¼	18	35	58	4-15—8-15	2.192	534.60

Claimant—**W. F. Linebarger.** Proof No. 00207

Source—**Humboldt River.** Ditch—**Linebarger Ditch and Overflow.**

1876	14.00		SW¼NE¼	34	33	52	4-15—8-15	.172	42.00
1876	40.00		NE¼NE¼	34	33	52	4-15—8-15	.492	120.00
1876	34.00		SE¼NE¼	34	33	52	4-15—8-15	.418	102.00
1876	18.60		NE¼SW¼	34	33	52	4-15—8-15	.229	55.80
1876	13.25		SW¼SW¼	34	33	52	4-15—8-15	.163	39.75
1876	33.80		NW¼SW¼	34	33	52	4-15—8-15	.416	101.40
1876	15.00		NE¼SW¼	34	33	52	4-15—8-15	.185	45.00
1876	10.00		NW¼SE¼	34	33	52	4-15—8-15	.123	30.00
1876	30.00		SW¼NW¼	35	33	52	4-15—8-15	.370	90.00
1876	22.00		SE¼NW¼	35	33	52	4-15—8-15	.271	66.00
1876	37.00		NW¼NW¼	35	33	52	4-15—8-15	.455	111.00
1876	34.00		NE¼NW¼	35	33	52	4-15—8-15	.492	102.00

Source—**Mary's Creek.** Ditch—**Linebarger Ditches.**

1880	30.00		NW¼NW¼	34	33	52	4-15—8-15	.369	90.00
1880	3.00		NE¼NW¼	34	33	52	4-15—8-15	.037	9.00
1880	....	28.00	NE¼NW¼	34	33	52	4-15—6-15	.344	42.00
1880	36.00		SW¼NW¼	34	33	52	4-15—8-15	.443	108.00
1880	8.00		SE¼NW¼	34	33	52	4-15—8-15	.098	24.00
1880	....	25.00	SE¼NW¼	34	33	52	4-15—6-15	.308	37.50
1880		14.00	NW¼NE¼	34	33	52	4-15—6-15	.172	21.00
1880	15.00		NW¼NE¼	34	33	52	4-15—8-15	.185	45.00
1880	20.00		SW¼NE¼	34	33	52	4-15—8-15	.246	60.00

Claimant—**L. L. Redden.** Proof. No. 00208

Source—**Starr Creek.** Ditch—**L. L. Redden Ditches.**

Year of priority	Culture—Acres: Harvest crops	Culture—Acres: Meadow pasture	Culture—Acres: Diversified pasture	Location: Subdivision	Location: Section	Location: Tp.N.	Location: R.E.	Length of season	Duty of water: C.F.S.	Duty of water: Acre-feet
1879	158.20			S½SE¼	33	37	59			
				W½SW¼	34	37	59			
				NE¼SW¼	34	37	59			
				N½SE¼	34	37	59	4-15—8-15	1.946	474.20

Source—**Starr Creek and Humboldt River.** Ditch—**L. L. Redden Ditches.**

Year of priority	Harvest crops	Meadow pasture	Diversified pasture	Subdivision	Section	Tp.N.	R.E.	Length of season	C.F.S.	Acre-feet
1879		41.00		S½SE¼	33	37	59			
				NE¼SE¼	33	37	59	4-15—6-15	.504	61.50

Source—**Humboldt River.** Ditch—**L. L. Redden Ditches.**

Year of priority	Harvest crops	Meadow pasture	Diversified pasture	Subdivision	Section	Tp.N.	R.E.	Length of season	C.F.S.	Acre-feet
1879		63.60		SW¼SE¼	33	37	59			
				NE¼SE¼	33	37	59			
				N½SW¼	34	37	59	4-15—6-15	.782	95.40

Claimant—**M. Aguirre.** Proof No. 00209

Source—**Humboldt River.** Ditch—**M. Aguirre Ditches.**

Year of priority	Harvest crops	Meadow pasture	Diversified pasture	Subdivision	Section	Tp.N.	R.E.	Length of season	C.F.S.	Acre-feet
1882		146.46		NW¼	7	35	57			
				NE¼SW¼	7	35	57			
				SW¼NE¼	7	35	57			
				SE¼	7	35	57	4-15—6-15	1.801	219.69

Claimant—**Union Land and Cattle Company.** Proof No. 00210

Source—**Mary's River, Humboldt River, Stevens Creek, Reed Creek* and Warm Springs.**

Ditch—**Union Land and Cattle Co. Ditches.**

Year of priority	Harvest crops	Meadow pasture	Diversified pasture	Subdivision	Section	Tp.N.	R.E.	Length of season	C.F.S.	Acre-feet
1881		649.50			1	36	58			
1885		649.50			11	36	58			
1886		649.50			12	36	58			
1887		649.50			13	36	58			
1888		649.50			14	36	58			
1889		649.50			15	36	58			
1890		649.50			21	36	58			
					22	36	58			
					23	36	58			
					27	36	58			
					28	36	58			
					4	36	59			
					5	36	59	4-15—6-15	7.980	974.25
					6	36	59	4-15—6-15	7.980	974.25
					7	36	59	4-15—6-15	7.980	974.25

				8	36	59	4-15—6-15	7.989	974.25
				31	37	59	4-15—6-15	7.989	974.25
				32	37	59	4-15—6-15	7.989	974.25
				33	37	59	4-15—6-15	7.989	974.25

*Priority from Reed Creek dated 1891.

Claimant—**J. J. Wright.** Proof No. 00211

Source—**Humboldt River.** Ditch—**J. J. Wright Ditches.**

1872		45.50	SE¼SE¼	9	35	56	4-15—6-15	.560	68.25
1872		160.90	NE¼	16	35	56	4-15—6-15	1.979	241.35
1872		60.00	S½NW¼	16	35	56	4-15—6-15	.738	90.00
1872		87.60	NE¼NW¼	16	35	56	4-15—6-15	1.077	131.40
1873		45.60	SW¼	16	35	56	4-15—6-15	.561	68.40
1873		60.00	W½SE¼	16	35	56	4-15—6-15	.738	90.00
1888		37.60	NE¼SE¼	16	35	56	4-15—6-15	.462	56.40
1888		247.40	E½	20	35	56	4-15—6-15	3.043	371.10
1892		54.10	N½NW¼&SW¼NW¼	21	35	56	4-15—6-15	.665	81.15

Claimant—**Griswold-Henderson Livestock Co.** Proof No. 00212

Source—**Humboldt River.** Ditch—**Griswold-Henderson Ditches.**

1882		770.30	S½	20	34	55			
1902		86.30	S½NW¼	21	34	55			
			SW¼	21	34	55			
			NW¼	29	34	55			
			NE¼	29	34	55			
			N½SW¼	29	34	55			
			SW¼SW¼	29	34	55			
			NE¼	30	34	55	4-15—6-15	9.475	1155.45
			E½SE¼	30	34	55	4-15—6-15	1.061	129.45

Claimant—**Thomas Hunter.** Proof No. 00213

Source—**Springs and South Fork of Humboldt River.** Ditch—**Thomas Hunter Ditches.**

1870	20.00		NW¼SW¼	9	33	54	4-15—8-15	.246	60.00
1871	168.10		SW¼SW¼	9	33	54	4-15—8-15	2.068	504.30
1872	41.40		E½SW¼	9	33	54	4-15—8-15	.509	124.20
1876	47.10		SE¼	9	33	54	4-15—8-15	.579	141.30
1877	47.10		SE¼SE¼	8	33	54	4-15—8-15	.579	141.30
1879	47.20		NW¼	14	33	54	4-15—8-15	.581	141.60
1880	47.20		SW¼NE¼	14	33	54	4-15—8-15	.581	141.60
1882	47.20		N½	15	33	54	4-15—8-15	.581	141.60
1883	47.20		N½S½	15	33	54	4-15—8-15	.581	141.60
1885	47.20		N½	16	33	54	4-15—8-15	.581	141.60
1886	78.80		N½N½	16	33	54	4-15—8-15	.723	176.40
1887	11.60		NE¼	17	33	54	4-15—8-15	.143	34.80
1888	58.80		SE¼NW¼	17	33	54	4-15—8-15	.723	176.40
1890	58.90		NE¼SW¼	17	33	54	4-15—8-15	.724	176.70
1890	106.10		S½SW¼	17	33	54	4-15—8-15	1.305	318.30
1900	182.90		SE¼	17	33	54	4-15—8-15	2.250	548.70

Thomas Hunter—Continued.

Year of priority	Culture—Acres: Harvest crops	Meadow pasture	Diversified pasture	Location: Subdivision	Section	Tp. N.	R. E.	Length of season	Duty of water: C.F.S.	Acre-feet
1901	182.90			N½NW¼	20	33	54	4-15—8-15	2.250	548.70
1902	182.90			SW¼NW¼	20	33	54	4-15—8-15	2.250	548.70
1903	183.00			S½NE¼	19	33	54	4-15—8-15	2.251	549.00
1904	106.30			N½SE¼	19	33	54	4-15—8-15	1.307	318.90
1905	181.40			SW¼SE¼	19	33	54	4-15—8-15	2.231	544.20

Claimant—**Hunter Banks Company.** Proof No. 00213

Source—**Humboldt River.** Ditch—**Hunter Banks Co. Ditches.**

Year of priority	Harvest crops	Meadow pasture	Diversified pasture	Subdivision	Section	Tp. N.	R. E.	Length of season	C.F.S.	Acre-feet
1902		17.40		S½S½	3	33	54	4-15—6-15	.214	26.10
1873		5.00						4-15—6-15	.061	7.50
1870		55.90		SE¼	4	33	54	4-15—6-15	.688	83.85
1870		41.20		SW¼	4	33	54	4-15—6-15	.507	61.80
1902		12.60		NE¼	10	33	54	4-15—6-15	.155	18.90
1874		200.40		NE¼	8	33	54	4-15—6-15	2.465	300.00
1875		200.50		S½	8	33	54	4-15—6-15	2.466	300.80
1881		33.60		SE¼	7	33	54	4-15—6-15	.413	50.40
1882		33.50		NW¼	17	33	54	4-15—6-15	.412	50.30
1884		52.80			18	33	54	4-15—6-15	.649	79.20
1885		52.80						4-15—6-15	.649	79.20
1887		15.00						4-15—6-15	.185	22.50
1891		30.30						4-15—6-15	.373	45.45
1892		25.80						4-15—6-15	.317	38.70
1893		25.80						4-15—6-15	.317	38.70
1893		26.10						4-15—6-15	.321	39.15
1893		42.80						4-15—6-15	.526	64.20
1890		30.90						4-15—6-15	.380	46.35

Source—**South Fork of Humboldt and Humboldt River.** Ditch—**Hunter Banks Co. Ditches.**

Year of priority	Harvest crops	Meadow pasture	Diversified pasture	Subdivision	Section	Tp. N.	R. E.	Length of season	C.F.S.	Acre-feet
1890		94.10		SE¼	4	33	54	4-15—6-15	1.157	141.15
1890		154.40		NW¼	9	33	54	4-15—6-15	1.899	231.60
1890		43.30		SW¼	4	33	54	4-15—6-15	.532	64.95

Claimant—**Batiste Tamara.** Proof No. 00213

Source—**Humboldt River.** Ditch—**Batiste Tamara Ditches.**

Year of priority	Harvest crops	Meadow pasture	Diversified pasture	Subdivision	Section	Tp. N.	R. E.	Length of season	C.F.S.	Acre-feet
1882		60.00		SE¼SW¼	18	33	54	4-15—6-15	.738	90.00
1883		60.00		NW¼	19	33	54	4-15—6-15	.738	90.00
1884		60.00		W½NE¼	19	33	54	4-15—6-15	.738	90.00
1885		61.50		N½SW¼	19	33	54	4-15—6-15	.756	92.25

Claimant—**Weeks Bros., Inc.** Proof No. 00214
Source—**Humboldt River, Willow, Bishop, and Burnt Creeks.** Ditch—**Weeks Bros. Ditches.**

1884	110.00	S½SW¼	20	38	61			
1890	172.90	W½SE¼	29	38	61			
		NW¼	32	38	61			
		W½NE¼	32	38	61	4-15—6-15	1.353	165.00
		NE¼NE¼	32	38	61	4-15—6-15	2.127	259.35

Claimant—**A. W. Gobel.** Proof No. 00215
Source—**Town Creek.** Ditch—**Nos. 1 and 2.**

1897	22.27	W½SW¼	35	38	62			
1900	94.69	SW¼SW¼	34	38	62			
		W½NW¼	3	37	62			
		NE¼NW¼	3	37	62			
		NW¼NE¼	3	37	62	4-15—6-15	.274	33.41
		NW¼SW¼	3	37	62	4-15—6-15	1.165	142.04

Claimant—**H. H. Coryell.** Proof No. 00216
Source—**Town Creek.** Ditch—**Nos. 1 and 2.**

1890	77.04	S½SE¼	34	38	62			
		SE¼SW¼	34	38	62	4-15—6-15	.948	115.56

Claimant—**Bank of Wells.** Proof No. 00217
Source—**Humboldt River.** Ditch—**Badt Nos. 1 and 2.**

1873	168.26	NE¼NW¼	4	37	62			
		NE¼	4	37	62	4-15—6-15	2.070	252.39

Claimant—**Mrs. Hattie A. Downey.** Proof No. 00218
Source—**Humboldt River.** Ditch—**Downey.**

1886	44.52	SE¼SE¼	32	38	62			
		SW¼SW¼	33	38	62			
		NW¼NW¼	4	37	62			
		NE¼NE¼	5	37	62	4-15—6-15	.548	66.78

Claimant—**Batiste Tamara.** Proof No. 00221
Source—**Humboldt River.** Ditch—**Batiste Tamara Ditches.**

1886	40.39	SE¼	24	33	53	4-15—6-15	.497	60.50
1887	40.39	SE¼SW¼	24	33	53	4-15—6-15	.497	60.50
1888	40.38	N½	25	33	53	4-15—6-15	.497	60.57
1886	2.89	E½	26	33	53	4-15—6-15	.036	4.34
1887	2.89	S½SW¼	26	33	53	4-15—6-15	.036	4.34
1888	2.90	N½NW¼	35	33	53	4-15—6-15	.036	4.35
1890	7.49	E½SE¼	27	33	53	4-15—6-15	.921	11.24
1890	7.49	......	....	....	....	4-15—6-15	.921	11.24
1894	61.15	......	....	....	....	4-15—6-15	.752	91.73

Claimant—**Mrs. C. Glaser.** Proof No. 00222

Source—**Humboldt River.** Ditch—**Glaser Ditches.**

Year of priority	Culture—Acres: Harvest crops	Culture—Acres: Meadow pasture	Culture—Acres: Diversified pasture	Location: Subdivision	Location: Section	Location: Tp.N.	Location: R.E.	Length of season	Duty of water: C.F.S.	Duty of water: Acre-feet
1875		958.12		E½NW¼	33	36	58			
1887		31.24		E½	33	36	58			
1887		163.28		W½W½	33	36	58			
				E½SW¼	33	36	58			
				SW¼SW¼	33	36	58			
				W½NW¼	34	36	58			
				NW¼SW¼	34	36	58			
				NW¼	4	35	58			
				W½NE¼	4	35	58			
				NE¼NE¼	4	35	58			
				W½SW¼	4	35	58			
				NE¼SW¼	4	35	58			
				E½SE¼	5	35	58			
				SW¼SE¼	5	35	58	4-15—6-15	11.785	1437.18
				N½	8	35	58	4-15—6-15	.384	46.86
				N½NW¼	9	35	58	4-15—6-15	2.008	214.92

Source—**Lamoille Creek.** Ditch—**Glaser Ditches.**

Year of priority	Harvest crops	Meadow pasture	Diversified pasture	Subdivision	Section	Tp.N.	R.E.	Length of season	C.F.S.	Acre-feet
1873	90.08			S½NW¼	8	35	58			
				NE¼	8	35	58	4-15—8-15	1.108	270.24

Claimant—**Thomas Griffin.** Proof No. 00223

Source—**Humboldt River.** Ditch—**McIntosh-Griffin Ditches and Sloughs.**

Year of priority	Harvest crops	Meadow pasture	Diversified pasture	Subdivision	Section	Tp.N.	R.E.	Length of season	C.F.S.	Acre-feet
1880	31.59			NW¼NE¼	17	32	52	4-15—8-15	.389	94.77
1880	19.97			NE¼NW¼	17	32	52	4-15—8-15	.246	59.91
1880			4.23	NE¼NW¼	17	32	52	4-15—5-15	.052	3.17
1880	5.72			SW¼NW¼	17	32	52	4-15—8-15	.070	17.16
1880	40.00			SE¼NW¼	17	32	52	4-15—8-15	.492	120.00
1880	8.19			SW¼NE¼	17	32	52	4-15—8-15	.101	24.57
1880			4.34	SW¼NE¼	17	32	52	4-15—5-15	.053	3.26
1880	2.48			NW¼SE¼	17	32	52	4-15—8-15	.031	7.44
1880	30.70			NE¼SW¼	17	32	52	4-15—8-15	.451	110.10
1880	12.18			NW¼SW¼	17	32	52	4-15—8-15	.150	36.54
1880	9.06			SW¼SW¼	17	32	52	4-15—8-15	.122	29.85
1880			0.20	SW¼SW¼	17	32	52	4-15—5-15	.002	.15
1880			0.56	SE¼SW¼	17	32	52	4-15—5-15	.007	.42
1880	24.80			SE¼SW¼	17	32	52	4-15—8-15	.305	74.40
1880	11.02			NE¼NW¼	20	32	52	4-15—8-15	.136	33.06
1880	3.38			NW¼NW¼	20	32	52	4-15—8-15	.042	10.14
1880	0.10			SE¼NW¼	20	32	52	4-15—8-15	.001	0.36
1880	1.54			SW¼NW¼	20	32	52	4-15—8-15	.019	4.02
1880	14.09			NW¼SW¼	20	32	52	4-15—8-15	.179	43.59

	1880			1.43				SW¼SW¼	20	32	52	4-15—8-15	.018	4.29
	1880			2.16				NE¼SE¼	19	32	52	4-15—8-15	.027	6.48
	1880			1.80				SE¼SE¼	19	32	52	4-15—8-15	.022	5.40

Claimant—**Thomas Griffin.** Proof No. 00224

Source—**Humboldt River.** Ditch—**Griffin Ditches and Sloughs and Overflow.**

	1876						3.52	NE¼NE¼	30	33	53	4-15—5-15	.043	2.64
	1876						21.23	NW¼NW¼	29	33	53	4-15—5-15	.261	15.92
	1876						2.24	NE¼NW¼	29	33	53	4-15—5-15	.028	1.68
	1876			19.52				NE¼NW¼	29	33	53	4-15—8-15	.240	58.56
	1876			11.68				SE¼NW¼	29	33	53	4-15—8-15	.144	35.04
	1876						9.53	SE¼NW¼	29	33	53	4-15—5-15	.117	7.15
	1876			9.79				NW¼NE¼	29	33	53	4-15—8-15	.120	29.37
	1876			19.59				SW¼NE¼	29	33	53	4-15—8-15	.241	58.77
	1876			5.10				NW¼SE¼	29	33	53	4-15—8-15	.063	15.30
	1876			9.64				NE¼SW¼	29	33	53	4-15—8-15	.119	28.92
	1876						6.71	NE¼SW¼	29	33	53	4-15—5-15	.083	5.03
	1876					3.75		NE¼SW¼	29	33	53	4-15—5-15	.046	2.81
	1876					1.51		SE¼SW¼	29	33	53	4-15—5-15	.019	1.13
	1876			3.66				SE¼SW¼	29	33	53	4-15—8-15	.045	10.98
	1876						5.36	NE¼SW¼	29	33	53	4-15—5-15	.066	4.02
	1876						1.68	SW¼SW¼	20	33	53	4-15—5-15	.021	1.26
	1876						5.03	NW¼SW¼	29	33	53	4-15—5-15	.062	3.77
	1876					2.15		NW¼SW¼	20	33	53	4-15—5-15	.026	1.61
	1876			3.32				NW¼SW¼	29	33	53	4-15—8-15	.041	9.96
	1876			18.50				NE¼SE¼	30	33	53	4-15—8-15	.228	55.50
	1876					6.85		NE¼SE¼	30	33	53	4-15—5-15	.084	5.14
	1876						1.29	NE¼SE¼	30	33	53	4-15—5-15	.016	.97
	1876					1.33		NW¼SE¼	30	33	53	4-15—5-15	.016	1.00
	1876			15.84				NW¼SE¼	30	33	53	4-15—8-15	.195	47.52
	1876						14.78	SE¼NE¼	30	33	53	4-15—5-15	.182	11.09
	1876					6.07		SE¼NE¼	30	33	53	4-15—5-15	.075	4.55
	1876					2.50		SW¼NE¼	30	33	53	4-15—5-15	.031	1.88
	1876						26.30	SW¼NE¼	30	33	53	4-15—5-15	.323	19.73
	1876			5.30				SW¼NE¼	30	33	53	4-15—8-15	.065	15.90
	1876						9.31	NW¼NE¼	30	33	53	4-15—5-15	.115	6.98
	1876						14.85	NE¼NW¼	30	33	53	4-15—5-15	.183	11.14
	1876					0.84		NE¼NW¼	30	33	53	4-15—5-15	.010	.63
	1876						23.45	NW¼NW¼	30	33	53	4-15—5-15	.288	17.59
	1876						7.18	SW¼NW¼	30	33	53	4-15—5-15	.088	5.39
	1876			4.96				SW¼NW¼	30	33	53	4-15—8-15	.061	14.88
	1876				21.89			SW¼NW¼	30	33	53	4-15—6-15	.209	32.97
	1876			19.19				SE¼NW¼	30	33	53	4-15—8-15	.236	57.57
	1876					8.00		SE¼NW¼	30	33	53	4-15—5-15	.098	6.00
	1876						5.05	SE¼NW¼	30	33	53	4-15—5-15	.062	3.79
	1876			7.71				NE¼SW¼	30	33	53	4-15—8-15	.095	23.13
	1876				.22			NE¼SW¼	30	33	53	4-15—6-15	.003	.33
	1876				9.86			NW¼SW¼	30	33	53	4-15—6-15	.121	14.86
	1876				24.55			NE¼SE¼	25	33	52	4-15—6-15	.302	36.83
	1876				31.64			NW¼SE¼	25	33	52	4-15—6-15	.389	54.96
	1876				3.12			SW¼NE¼	25	83	52	4-15—6-15	.038	2.34

Thomas Griffin—Continued.

Year of priority	Culture—Acres: Harvest crops	Meadow pasture	Diversified pasture	Location: Subdivision	Section	Tp.N.	R.E.	Length of season	Duty of water: C.F.S.	Acre-feet
1876			28.67	SW¼NE¼	25	33	52	4-15—5-15	.353	21.50
1876			11.24	SE¼NE¼	25	33	52	4-15—5-15	.138	8.43
1876		24.44		SE¼NE¼	25	33	52	4-15—6-15	.301	36.66
1876			16.58	NE¼NE¼	25	33	52	4-15—5-15	.204	12.44
1876			9.58	NW¼NE¼	25	33	52	4-15—5-15	.118	7.19
1876			.22	NE¼NW¼	25	33	52	4-15—5-15	.003	0.17
1876			17.62	SW¼NW¼	25	33	52	4-15—5-15	.217	13.22
1876			31.80	SE¼NW¼	25	33	52	4-15—5-15	.391	23.85
1876		.55		SE¼NW¼	25	33	52	4-15—6-15	.007	0.83
1876		2.61		NE¼SW¼	25	33	52	4-15—6-15	.032	3.92
1876			2.55	NE¼SW¼	25	33	52	4-15—5-15	.031	1.91
1876	28.56			NE¼SW¼	25	33	52	4-15—8-15	.351	85.68
1876	5.21			NW¼SW¼	25	33	52	4-15—8-15	.064	15.63
1876			17.04	NW¼SW¼	25	33	52	4-15—5-15	.210	12.78

Source—**Humboldt River.** Ditch—**Linebarger Dam and Overflow.**

Year of priority	Harvest crops	Meadow pasture	Diversified pasture	Subdivision	Section	Tp.N.	R.E.	Length of season	C.F.S.	Acre-feet
1876		4.79		NW¼SW¼	25	33	52	4-15—6-15	.059	7.19
1876		9.55		SW¼SW¼	25	33	52	4-15—6-15	.117	14.33
1876			2.35	SE¼NE¼	26	23	52	4-15—5-15	.029	1.76
1876			28.14	NE¼SE¼	26	33	52	4-15—5-15	.346	21.11
1876		5.36		NE¼SE¼	26	33	52	4-15—6-15	.066	8.04
1876		22.40		SE¼SE¼	26	33	52	4-15—6-15	.276	33.60
1876			5.34	SE¼SE¼	26	33	53	4-15—5-15	.066	4.00
1876			13.89	NW¼SE¼	26	33	52	4-15—5-15	.171	10.42
1876			0.34	SW¼SE¼	26	33	52	4-15—5-15	.066	0.26
1876		10.99		SW¼SE¼	26	33	52	4-15—6-15	.135	16.49
1876		1.20		NW¼NE¼	35	33	52	4-15—6-15	.015	1.80

Claimant—**McIntosh Estate.** Proof No. 00225

Source—**Humboldt River.** Ditch—**McIntosh-Griffin Ditches and Sloughs.**

Year of priority	Harvest crops	Meadow pasture	Diversified pasture	Subdivision	Section	Tp.N.	R.E.	Length of season	C.F.S.	Acre-feet
1880	15.15			NE¼SE¼	5	32	52	4-15—8-15	.186	45.45
1880	35.08			SE¼SE¼	5	32	52	4-15—8-15	.431	105.24
1880	3.65			SW¼SE¼	5	32	52	4-15—8-15	.045	10.95
1880	0.08			NW¼NE¼	8	32	52	4-15—8-15	.001	.24
1880			0.71	NW¼NE¼	8	32	52	4-15—5-15	.000	.54
1880			7.86	NE¼NE¼	8	32	52	4-15—5-15	.097	5.90
1880	21.32			NE¼NE¼	8	32	52	4-15—8-15	.262	63.96
1880	30.66			SE¼NE¼	8	32	52	4-15—8-15	.451	109.98
1880	0.61			SW¼NE¼	8	32	52	4-15—8-15	.008	1.83
1880	1.52			NW¼SE¼	8	32	52	4-15—8-15	.019	4.56
1880	26.40			NE¼SE¼	8	32	52	4-15—8-15	.325	79.20
1880	0.32			SE¼SE¼	8	32	52	4-15—8-15	.004	.96
1880	0.07			SW¼SE¼	8	32	52	4-15—8-15	.001	.21

	1880			16.59				SE¼SW¼	8	32	52	4-15—8-15	.204	49.77
	1880					10.12		SE¼SW¼	8	32	52	4-15—5-15	.124	7.59
	1880					0.85		SW¼SW¼	8	32	52	4-15—5-15	.010	.61
	1880					1.10		NW¼NW¼	9	32	52	4-15—5-15	.014	.83
	1880			19.85				NW¼NW¼	9	32	52	4-15—8-15	.244	59.55
	1880			11.50				SW¼NW¼	9	32	52	4-15—8-15	.141	34.50
	1880			.10				NW¼SW¼	9	32	52	4-15—8-15	.001	.30

Claimant—**Mrs. T. D. Griffin.** Proof No. **00226**

Source—**Humboldt River.** Ditch—**Mrs. T. D. Griffin Ditch.**

	1880				342.34			SE¼SW¼	33	33	52			
								SW¼SE¼	33	33	52			
								W½	4	32	52			
								W½NE¼	4	32	52			
								NW¼SE¼	4	32	52			
								SE¼NE¼	5	32	52			
								NE¼SE¼	5	32	52			
								SW¼NE¼	8	32	52			
								W½SE¼	8	32	52			
								SE¼SE¼	8	32	52			
								E½SW¼	8	32	52			
								NW¼NW¼	9	32	52	4-15—6-15	4.211	513.51

Source—**Warm Spring Creek.** Ditch—**Mrs. T. D. Griffin Ditches.**

	1875				136.08			SE¼SW¼	5	32	52			
								W½SE¼	5	32	52			
								W½NE¼	8	32	52			
								E½W½	8	32	52	4-15—6-15	1.685	205.47

Claimant—**George Arthur.** Proof No. **00227**

Source—**Dwyer Spring.** Ditch—**George Arthur Ditch.**

	1870			15.00				S½SE¼	28	33	52			
								N½NE¼	33	33	52	4-15—8-15	.185	45.00

Source—**Humboldt River and Hot Spring.** Ditch—**George Arthur Ditch.**

	1876			96.22				SE¼	33	33	52			
								NE¼NE¼	4	32	52	4-15—8-15	1.184	288.66

Claimant—**Paul Giudici.** Proof No. **00229**

Source—**Humboldt River.** Ditches—**Paul Giudici Ditches.**

	1873				38.54			NW¼	2	33	54	4-15—6-15	.474	57.81
	1874				38.54			SW¼	2	33	54	4-15—6-15	.474	57.81
	1875				38.53			S½NE¼	2	33	54	4-15—6-15	.474	57.80
	1876				38.53			N½SE¼	2	33	54	4-15—6-15	.474	57.80
	1877				38.53							4-15—6-15	.474	57.80
	1878				38.53							4-15—6-15	.474	57.80

Paul Guidici—Continued.

Year of priority	Culture—Acres: Harvest crops	Meadow pasture	Diversified pasture	Location: Subdivision	Section	Tp.N.	R.E.	Length of season	Duty of water: C.F.S.	Acre-feet
1879	....	38.53	....	....	....	....	....	4-15—6-15	.474	57.80
1880	..	38.53	....	....	....	....	....	4-15—6-15	.474	57.80
1885	....	15.05	....	NW¼NW¼	2	33	54	4-15—6-15	.185	22.58
1885	....	17.51	....	NW¼NW¼	1	33	54	4-15—6-15	.215	26.27
1885	....	9.08	....	SW¼NW¼	1	33	54	4-15—6-15	.112	13.62
1885	....	1.27	....	SW¼NW¼	1	33	54	4-15—6-15	.016	1.91

Claimant—**Chas. Dressi** Proof. No. 00230

Source—**Humboldt River.** Ditch—**Chas. Dressi Ditches.**

Year of priority	Harvest crops	Meadow pasture	Diversified pasture	Subdivision	Section	Tp.N.	R.E.	Length of season	C.F.S.	Acre-feet
1873	....	72.69	....	SW¼SW¼	30	34	55			
1874	....	72.69	....	W½W½	31	34	55			
1875	....	72.69	....	S½SE¼	25	34	55			
1876	...	72.69	....	NE¼	36	34	54			
1877	....	72.69	....	W½SW¼	36	34	54			
1878	....	72.69	....	SW¼NW¼	36	34	54	4-15—6-15	.894	109.04
1879	....	72.69	....	E½W½	36	34	54	4-15—6-15	.894	109.04
1880	....	72.69	....	SE¼	36	34	54	4-15—6-15	.894	109.04
				NE¼NW¼	1	33	54	4-15—6-15	.894	109.04
				SE¼	35	34	54	4-15—6-15	.894	109.04
				S½SW¼	35	34	54	4-15—6-15	.894	109.04
				NE¼	2	33	54	4-15—6-15	.894	109.04
				NE¼NW¼	2	33	54	4-15—6-15	.894	109.04
1882	....	33.23	....	NE¼SE¼	36	34	55	4-15—6-15	.409	49.85
1882	....	6.51	....	NW¼SE¼	36	34	55	4-15—6-15	.080	9.77
1885	....	7.26	....	NE¼NW¼	1	33	55	4-15—6-15	.080	10.89
1887	....	3.72	....	NE¼NE¼	36	34	55	4-15—6-15	.046	5.58
1887	....	5.12	....	SE¼NE¼	36	34	55	4-15—6-15	.063	7.68
1887	....	11.62	....	SW¼NE¼	36	34	55	4-15—6-15	.143	17.43
1887	....	4.65	....	NW¼SE¼	36	34	55	4-15—6-15	.057	6.98
1887	....	0.47	....	SE¼NW¼	36	34	55	4-15—6-15	.006	.71
1887	....	20.46	....	NE¼SW¼	36	34	55	4-15—6-15	.252	30.69
1887	....	0.93	....	NW¼SW¼	36	34	55	4-15—6-15	.011	1.40
1887	...	5.58	....	SE¼SW¼	36	34	55	4-15—6-15	.069	8.37
1887	....	15.81	....	SW¼SW¼	36	34	55	4-15—6-15	.194	23.82

Claimant—**Albert Lomori.** Proof No. 00231

Source—**Humboldt River.** Ditch—**Lomori Dam.**

Year of priority	Harvest crops	Meadow pasture	Diversified pasture	Subdivision	Section	Tp.N.	R.E.	Length of season	C.F.S.	Acre-feet
1888	....	30.27	....	S½SE¼	36	34	54	4-15—6-15	.372	45.41

Claimant—**Mary Larson.** Proof No. 00232

Source—**Humboldt River.** Ditch—**Dams, Tinker Slough and Mulchay's Ditch.**

Year of priority	Harvest crops	Meadow pasture	Diversified pasture	Subdivision	Section	Tp.N.	R.E.	Length of season	C.F.S.	Acre-feet
1874	...	94.95	....	SE¼NW¼	30	34	55			
1875	....	94.95	....	SW¼	30	34	55			

	1876				94.95			W½SE¼	30	34	55	4-15—6-15	1.168	142.43
	1877				94.95			NW¼NE¼	30	34	55	4-15—6-15	1.168	142.43
								NW¼	31	34	55	4-15—6-15	1.168	142.43
								NW¼NE¼	31	34	55	4-15—6-15	1.168	142.43

Claimant—**H. S. Van Drielen.** Proof No. 00233

Source—**Humboldt River.** Ditch—**Van Drielen Dam.**

	1902				40.32			S½NE¼	21	34	55			
								W½SE¼	21	34	55			
								NE¼SW¼	21	34	55	4-15—6-15	.495	60.48

Claimant—**Estate James Russell.** Proof No. 00234

Source—**Humboldt River.** Ditch—**Russell Dams.**

	1872				17.07			SW¼SE¼	15	34	55	4-15—6-15	.210	25.60
	1872				3.89			SE¼SW¼	15	34	55	4-15—6-15	.048	5.81
	1872				17.41			NW¼NW¼	22	34	56	4-15—6-15	.214	26.12
	1872				12.60			NE¼NW¼	22	34	55	4-15—6-15	.155	18.90
	1872				3.97			SW¼NW¼	22	34	55	4-15—6-15	.049	5.96
	1872				5.06			NW¼NE¼	22	34	55	4-15—6-15	.062	7.59
	1880				21.21			SE¼SE¼	15	34	56	4-15—6-15	.261	31.82
	1880				17.38			NE¼NW¼	22	34	55	4-15—6-15	.214	26.07
	1880				8.07			SE¼NW¼	22	34	55	4-15—6-15	.099	12.11
	1880				7.89			SW¼NW¼	22	34	55	4-15—6-15	.097	11.84
	1880				22.15			NW¼NE¼	22	34	56	4-15—6-15	.272	33.23
	1880				11.28			NE¼NE¼	22	34	55	4-15—6-15	.139	16.92
	1880				2.97			SW¼NE¼	22	34	55	4-15—6-15	.037	4.46

Claimant—**A. G. McBride.** Proof No. 00236

Source—**Humboldt River.** Ditch—**McBride Dams.**

	1882					50.99		SE¼NE¼	11	34	55	4-15—5-15	.627	38.24
	1885					50.99		SE¼	11	34	55	4-15—5-15	.627	38.24
	1888					50.99		E½NW¼	14	34	55	4-15—5-15	.627	38.24
	1889					50.99		NE¼	14	34	55	4-15—5-15	.627	38.24

Claimant—**Mrs. Isabella Dewar.** Proof No. 00238

Source—**Humboldt River.** Ditch—**Burner Ditch.**

	1879				27.30			SW¼	6	34	56	4-15—6-15	.336	40.95
	1879				7.50			SW¼	6	34	56	4-15—6-15	.092	11.25
	1880				27.30			SW¼	6	34	56	4-15—6-15	.336	40.95
	1880				7.50			SW¼	6	34	56	4-15—6-15	.092	11.25
	1881				27.30			SW¼	6	34	56	4-15—6-15	.336	40.95

Claimant—**J. N. Phillips.** Proof No. 00239

Source—**Humboldt River.** Ditch—**J. N. Phillips Ditches.**

Year of priority	Harvest crops	Culture—Acres: Meadow pasture	Diversified pasture	Location: Subdivision	Section	Tp.N.	R.E.	Length of season	Duty of water: C.F.S.	Acre-feet
1881	....	4.60	....	NW¼NW¼	6	34	56	4-15—6-15	.057	6.90
1881	....	31.80	....	SW¼NW¼	6	34	56	4-15—6-15	.391	47.70
1881	....	5.70	....	SE¼NE¼	1	34	55	4-15—6-15	.070	8.55
1881	....	14.30	....	NE¼NW¼	6	34	56	4-15—6-15	.176	21.45
1881	....	29.60	....	SE¼NW¼	6	34	56	4-15—6-15	.364	44.40
1888	....	34.20	....	SE¼NW¼	31	35	56	4-15—6-15	.421	51.30
1888	....	45.30	....	NW¼NE¼	31	35	56	4-15—6-15	.557	67.95
1888	....	32.80	....	NE¼NE¼	31	35	56	4-15—6-15	.403	49.20
1888	....	42.50	....	SW¼NE¼	31	35	56	4-15—6-15	.523	63.75
1888	....	20.00	....	SE¼NE¼	31	35	56	4-15—6-15	.246	30.00
1888	....	3.50	....	SW¼NW¼	31	35	56	4-15—6-15	.043	5.25
1888	....	6.70	....	NW¼SW¼	31	35	56	4-15—6-15	.082	10.05
1888	....	27.20	....	NE¼SW¼	31	35	56	4-15—6-15	.335	40.80
1888	....	9.30	....	NW¼SE¼	31	35	56	4-15—6-15	.114	13.95
1888	....	7.00	....	SW¼SW¼	31	35	56	4-15—6-15	.086	10.50
1888	....	17.40	....	SE¼SW¼	31	35	56	4-15—6-15	.214	26.10
1888	....	2.80	....	NW¼NW¼	6	34	56	4-15—6-15	.034	4.20
1888	....	8.00	....	NE¼NW¼	6	34	56	4-15—6-15	.098	12.00
1873	....	1.00	....	NW¼NE¼	31	35	56	4-15—6-15	.012	1.50
1878	....	14.70	....	SW¼SE¼	31	35	56	4-15—6-15	.181	22.05
1879	....	14.70	....	SW¼SE¼	31	35	56	4-15—6-15	.181	22.05
1870	....	67.15	....	....	....	....	..	4-15—6-15	.826	100.73
1880	....	67.15	....	....	31	35	56	4-15—6-15	.826	100.73
1879	....	2.50	....	....	6	34	56	4-15—6-15	.031	3.75
1880	....	2.50	....	....	....	....	....	4-15—6-15	.031	3.75

Source—**Kittredge Creek.** Ditch—**J. N. Phillips Ditches.**

Year of priority	Harvest crops	Meadow pasture	Diversified pasture	Subdivision	Section	Tp.N.	R.E.	Length of season	C.F.S.	Acre-feet
1869	....	....	18.00	NW¼SW¼	31	35	56	4-15—5-15	.221	13.50
1869	....	....	28.90	SW¼NW¼	31	35	56	4-15—5-15	.355	21.68
1869	....	....	19.40	NW¼NW¼	6	34	56	4-15—5-15	.230	14.55
1869	....	....	1.00	SW¼NW¼	6	34	56	4-15—5-15	.012	0.75

Claimant—**Aurelio Papa.** Proof No. 00240

Source—**Humboldt River.** Ditch—**Bett Ditches.**

Year of priority	Harvest crops	Meadow pasture	Diversified pasture	Subdivision	Section	Tp.N.	R.E.	Length of season	C.F.S.	Acre-feet
1901	....	10.38	....	NW¼NE¼	20	34	55	4-15—6-15	.128	15.57
1901	....	28.37	....	SW¼NE¼	20	34	55	4-15—6-15	.349	42.56
1901	....	13.37	....	SE¼NE¼	20	34	55	4-15—6-15	.164	20.10
1901	....	36.34	....	NE¼NE¼	20	34	55	4-15—6-15	.447	54.50
1901	....	1.16	....	NW¼NW¼	21	34	55	4-15—6-15	.014	1.74
1901	....	0.29	....	SW¼NW¼	21	34	55	4-15—6-15	.004	0.43

Claimants—**Mildred Elmore, Walter S. Elmore, Mildred C. Clubine, Grace Kendricks.** Proof No. 00241

Source—**Rabbit Creek and Humboldt River.** Ditch—**Elmore Ditches.**

	1872					47.70		S¼	15	35	57	4-15—5-15	.587	143.10
	1872			74.00				S½	15	35	57	4-15—8-15	.918	223.90
	1872				337.10			N½	15	35	57			
								N½NE¼	16	35	57	4-15—6-15	4.146	1011.30

Claimant—**Chas. Clubine.** Proof No. 00242

Source—**Sherman and Jackstone Creeks and Humboldt River.** Ditch—**Chas. Clubine Ditches.**

	1872				44.30			N½N½	15	35	56	4-15—6-15	.545	66.45
	1872				73.90			SW¼	10	35	56	4-15—6-15	.909	110.85
	1872				18.60			W½SE¼	10	35	56	4-15—6-15	.229	27.90
	1872				6.20			NE¼SE¼	10	35	56	4-15—6-15	.076	9.30
	1872				5.80			NW¼SW¼	11	35	56	4-15—6-15	.071	8.70
	1883				18.10			NE¼SW¼	10	35	56	4-15—6-15	.223	27.15
	1883					21.80		W½SW¼	10	35	56	4-15—5-15	.268	16.35
	1883				42.30			N½SE¼	10	35	56	4-15—6-15	.520	63.45
	1883				31.20			S½NE¼	10	35	56	4-15—6-15	.384	46.80
	1883				24.80			SW¼NW¼	11	35	56	4-15—6-15	.305	37.20
	1883					1.20		SW¼NW¼	11	35	56	4-15—5-15	.015	.90
	1883				19.60			NW¼SW¼	11	35	56	4-15—6-15	.241	29.40
	1888					12.40		SE¼NE¼	32	35	56	4-15—5-15	.153	9.30
	1888					10.80		SW¼NW¼	33	35	56	4-15—5-15	.133	8.10
	1887				55.00			S½	3	35	56	4-15—6-15	.677	82.50
	1887					12.50		NW¼	10	35	56	4-15—5-15	.154	9.38
	1888				55.00			SW¼	10	35	56	4-15—6-15	.677	82.50
	1888					12.50		NE¼	10	35	56	4-15—5-15	.154	9.38
	1889				55.00			NW¼	11	35	56	4-15—6-15	.677	82.50
	1889					12.50						4-15—5-15	.154	9.38
	1890				55.00							4-15—6-15	.677	82.50
	1890					12.50						4-15—5-15	.154	9.38
	1891				55.10							4-15—6-15	.678	82.65
	1891					12.40						4-15—5-15	.153	9.30

Claimant—**O'Neill Bros. Land and Stock Co.** Proof. No. 00243

Source—**Town Creek.** Ditch—**O'Neill Bros. Ditches.**

	1885				39.75			SE¼SE¼	30	38	62			
								NE¼NE¼	31	38	62			
								NW¼NW¼	32	38	62			
								NE¼NW¼	32	38	62	4-15—6-15	.489	59.62

Claimant—**Chas. W. Clubine.** Proof No. 00244

Source—**Humboldt River and Springs.** Ditch—**Clubine Dams.**

Year of priority	Culture—Acres: Harvest crops	Culture—Acres: Meadow pasture	Culture—Acres: Diversified pasture	Location: Subdivision	Location: Section	Location: Tp.N.	Location: R.E.	Length of season	Duty of water: C.F.S.	Duty of water: Acre-feet
1879	...	371.70	...	S½NW¼	1	35	56			
				SW¼	1	35	56			
				SE¼	1	35	56			
				S½NE¼	1	35	56			
				SE¼NE¼	2	35	56			
				E½SE¼	2	35	56			
				W½SW¼	6	35	57			
				SE¼SW¼	6	35	57			
				NE¼NW¼	7	35	57	4-15—6-15	4.572	557.55

Claimant—**J. J. Henderson.** Proof No. 00246

Source—**Humboldt River.** Ditch—**J. J. Henderson Ditches.**

Year of priority	Harvest crops	Meadow pasture	Diversified pasture	Subdivision	Section	Tp.N.	R.E.	Length of season	C.F.S.	Acre-feet
1879	...	278.40	...	SE¼NE¼	1	34	55			
1880	...	278.30	...	SE¼	1	34	55			
				E½SW¼	1	34	55			
				SW¼SW¼	1	34	55			
				N½	12	34	55			
				W½SW¼	12	34	55			
				NE¼SW¼	12	34	55			
				NW¼SE¼	12	34	55	4-15—6-15	3.424	417.60
				NW¼SW¼	6	34	56	4-15—6-15	3.423	417.45

Claimant—**Q. D. Boyd.** Proof No. 00247

Source—**Humboldt River.** Ditch—**Q. D. Boyd Ditches.**

Year of priority	Harvest crops	Meadow pasture	Diversified pasture	Subdivision	Section	Tp.N.	R.E.	Length of season	C.F.S.	Acre-feet
1876	...	60.56	...	S½NE¼	7	35	58	4-15—6-15	.745	90.84
1877	...	17.06	...	SE¼	7	35	58	4-15—6-15	.221	26.93

Claimant—**J. W. Ebert.** Proof. No. 00301

Source—**Pine Creek.** Ditch—**Ebert Ditch No. 2.**

Year of priority	Harvest crops	Meadow pasture	Diversified pasture	Subdivision	Section	Tp.N.	R.E.	Length of season	C.F.S.	Acre-feet
1879	30.00	...	...	S½NE¼	2	31	51	4-15—8-15	.369	90.00
1885	12.77	...	...	S½NE¼	2	31	51	4-15—8-15	.157	38.31
1885	12.25	...	...	SW¼NW¼	1	31	51	4-15—8-15	.151	36.75
1885	4.65	...	...	SE¼NW¼	1	31	51	4-15—8-15	.057	13.95
1885	2.07	...	...	SW¼NW¼	1	31	51	4-15—8-15	.025	6.21

Source—**Pine Creek.** Ditch—**Ebert Ditch No. 1.**

Year of priority	Harvest crops	Meadow pasture	Diversified pasture	Subdivision	Section	Tp.N.	R.E.	Length of season	C.F.S.	Acre-feet
1879	26.14	...	...	NE¼	2	31	51	4-15—8-15	.322	78.42
1885	21.26	...	...	E½NE¼	2	31	51	4-15—8-15	.261	63.78
1885	13.20	...	...	W½NW¼	1	31	51	4-15—8-15	.103	39.60
1890	2.50	...	...	NW¼NE¼	2	31	51	4-15—8-15	.031	7.50
1890	10.53	...	...	NE¼	2	31	51	4-15—8-15	.204	40.50

1890	9.00		E½NW¼	2	31	51	4-15—8-15	.111	27.00
1890		16.35	W½NW¼	1	31	51	4-15—5-15	.201	12.26
1809		4.65	SE¼NW¼	1	31	51	4-15—5-15	.057	3.49
1809		1.00	NE¼SW¼	1	31	51	4-15—5-15	.012	.75

Claimant—**Geo. W. Goodfellow.** Proof No. 00302

Source—**Hot Creek.** Ditch—**Hale Nos. 1 and 2.**

1868	0.70		SE¼	8	28	52	4-15—8-15	.009	2.10
1868	1.68		SE¼	8	28	52	4-15—8-15	.021	5.04
1868	0.10		SW¼NW¼	16	28	52	4-15—8-15	.001	.30
1868	86.24		NE¼	17	28	52	4-15—8-15	1.061	258.72
1868	80.65		NW¼	17	28	52	4-15—8-15	.902	241.95
1868	25.07		SW¼	8	28	52	4-15—8-15	.308	75.21

Claimant—**T. H. Jewell.** Proof No. 00303

Source—**Pine Creek.** Ditch—**Pine Creek Ditch No. 1.**

1877	7.58		NW¼SW¼	17	31	52	4-15—8-15	.093	21.74
1877	5.32		NE¼SE¼	18	31	52	4-15—8-15	.065	15.96
1877	1.50		SW¼NW¼	17	31	52	4-15—8-15	.018	4.50
1877	18.00		E½NE¼	18	31	52	4-15—8-15	.221	54.00
1898	6.42		E½NE¼	18	31	52	4-15—8-15	.079	19.26
1898	0.60		NW¼NE¼	18	31	52	4-15—8-15	.007	1.80
1898	17.63		SE¼	7	31	52	4-15—8-15	.217	52.89

Source—**Pine Creek.** Ditch—**Pine Creek Ditch No. 2.**

1875	1.95		SW¼NW¼	17	31	52	4-15—8-15	.024	5.85
1875	2.92		SE¼SE¼	18	31	52	4-15—8-15	.036	6.76
1875	10.00		NE¼NE¼	18	31	52	4-15—8-15	.123	30.00
1898	18.00		SE¼	7	31	52	4-15—8-15	.221	54.00
1898	5.00		SE¼SE¼	7	31	52	4-15—8-15	.062	15.00
1898	4.00		NE¼NE¼	18	31	52	4-15—8-15	.049	12.00

NOTE—All of the area east of Pine Creek and west of Ditch No. 2 shows no signs of irrigation in recent years, probably not since 1910. The area west of Pine Creek is not in a good state of cultivation.

Source—**Pine Creek.** Ditch—**Cold Creek Ditch.**

1898	2.00		SE¼	7	31	52	4-15—8-15	.025	6.00

Claimant—**J. P. Raine.** Proof No. 00304

Source—**Pine Creek.** Ditches—**Nos. 1, 2, 3, and 4.**

1868	4.41		SE¼SE¼	29	31	52	4-15—8-15	.054	13.23
1868	17.37		SW¼SE¼	29	31	52	4-15—8-15	.214	52.11
1868	7.85		SE¼NW¼	29	31	52	4-15—8-15	.097	23.55
1875	15.24		NE¼NW¼	29	31	52	4-15—8-15	.187	45.72
1875	37.13		NW¼NE¼	29	31	52	4-15—8-15	.457	81.39
1875	15.58		SE¼SW¼	20	31	52	4-15—8-15	.192	47.24
1875	22.64		SW¼SE¼	20	31	52	4-15—8-15	.278	67.92
1868	28.75		NW¼SE¼	20	31	52	4-15—8-15	.354	86.25
1875	8.25		NE¼SW¼	29	31	52	4-15—8-15	.101	24.75
1875	14.43		SE¼NW¼	29	31	52	4-15—8-15	.177	43.29

J. P. Raine—Continued.

Year of priority	Culture—Acres—Harvest crops	Meadow pasture	Diversified pasture		Location—Subdivision	Section	Tp.N.	R.E.	Length of season	Duty of water—C.F.S.	Acre-feet
1868	37.57				SE¼NW¼	29	31	52	4-15—8-15	.462	113.71
1874	13.07				NW¼NE¼	29	51	52	4-15—8-15	.161	39.21
1875	9.96				NW¼SE¼	20	31	52	4-15—8-15	.123	29.88
1875	7.52				NE¼SW¼	20	31	52	4-15—8-15	.092	22.56
1875	4.20				SW¼NE¼	20	31	52	4-15—8-15	.052	12.30
1875	9.60				SE¼NW¼	20	31	52	4-15—8-15	.119	28.98
1903	...			10.32	NE¼NW¼	20	31	52	4-15—5-15	.127	7.72
1880	15.66				NE¼SW¼	29	31	52	4-15—8-15	.192	46.98
1886	16.78				SE¼NW¼	29	31	52	4-15—8-15	.206	50.34
1880	1.56				SE¼NW¼	29	31	52	4-15—8-15	.019	4.68

Source—Hot Creek. Ditch— Hot **Creek Ditch No. 1.**

Year of priority	Harvest crops	Meadow pasture	Diversified pasture		Subdivision	Section	Tp.N.	R.E.	Length of season	C.F.S.	Acre-feet
1871	25.77				SW¼NW¼	16	29	52	4-15—8-15	.317	77.31
1871	.80				SE¼NW¼	16	29	52	4-15—8-15	.098	2.40
1871	10.40				NE¼NW¼	16	29	52	4-15—8-15	.128	31.20
1871	40.00				NW¼NW¼	16	29	52	4-15—8-15	.492	120.00
1871	1.70				SW¼NW¼	16	29	52	4-15—8-15	.021	5.10
1871	6.66				SW¼SW¼	16	29	52	4-15—8-15	.082	19.98
1871	...		12.53		SW¼NW¼	16	29	52	4-15—5-15	.154	9.40
1871	40.00				NW¼SW¼	4	29	52	4-15—8-15	.492	120.00
1871	40.00				SW¼SW¼	4	29	52	4-15—8-15	.492	120.00
1871	18.93				SE¼SW¼	4	29	52	4-15—8-15	.233	56.79
1871	8.54				NE¼SW¼	4	29	52	4-15—8-15	.105	25.62
1871	40.00				SW¼NW¼	9	29	52	4-15—8-15	.492	120.00
1871	23.80				SE¼NW¼	9	29	52	4-15—8-15	.293	71.40
1871	23.80				NE¼SW¼	9	29	52	4-15—8-15	.293	71.40
1871	40.00				NW¼SW¼	9	29	52	4-15—8-15	.492	120.00
1871	40.00				SW¼SW¼	9	29	52	4-15—8-15	.492	120.00
1871	24.20				SE¼SW¼	9	29	52	4-15—8-15	.298	72.60
1871	26.91				NE¼NW¼	9	29	52	4-15—8-15	.331	80.73
1871	40.00				NW¼NW¼	9	29	52	4-15—8-15	.492	120.00

Source—Hot Creek. Ditch— Hot **Creek Ditch No. 2.**

Year of priority	Harvest crops	Meadow pasture	Diversified pasture		Subdivision	Section	Tp.N.	R.E.	Length of season	C.F.S.	Acre-feet
1871	32.18				SW¼NE¼	8	29	52	4-15—8-15	.396	96.54
1871	40.00				SE¼NE¼	8	29	52	4-15—8-15	.492	120.00
1871	40.00				NE¼SE¼	8	29	52	4-15—8-15	.492	120.00
1871	9.25				NW¼SE¼	8	29	52	4-15—8-15	.114	27.75
1871	...		23.77		NW¼SE¼	8	29	52	4-15—5-15	.292	17.83
1871	...		32.78		SW¼SE¼	8	29	52	4-15—5-15	.403	24.59
1871	32.30				SE¼SE¼	8	29	52	4-15—8-15	.397	96.90
1871	...		8.30		SE¼SE¼	8	29	52	4-15—5-15	.102	6.23
1871	16.80				NE¼NE¼	17	29	52	4-15—8-15	.207	50.40
1871	...	16.66			NE¼NE¼	17	29	52	4-15—6-15	.205	24.99
1871	...		1.20		NW¼NE¼	17	29	52	4-15—5-15	.015	.90
1871			17.94		SE¼NE¼	17	29	52	4-15—5-15	.221	18.46
1871		15.20			NW¼SW¼	10	29	52	4-15—6-15	.187	22.80

1871					7.20		SW¼SW¼	16	29	52	4-15—5-15	.080	5.40
1871					17.40		NW¼SW¼	16	29	52	4-15—5-15	.214	13.05
1871			40.00				SE¼SE¼	5	29	52	4-15—8-15	.492	120.00
1871			40.00				NE¼SE¼	5	29	52	4-15—8-15	.492	120.00
1871			16.80				SW¼NE¼	5	29	52	4-15—8-15	.207	50.40
1871			27.93				NW¼SE¼	5	29	52	4-15—8-15	.344	83.79
1871			31.22				SW¼SE¼	5	29	52	4-15—8-15	.384	93.66
1871			40.00				NE¼NE¼	8	29	52	4-15—8-15	.492	120.00
1871			37.02				NW¼NE¼	8	29	52	4-15—8-15	.418	111.06

Source—**Willow Creek, a tributary of Hot Creek.** Ditch—**Willow Creek.**

1880				6.15			SW¼SW¼	16	29	52	4-15—6-15	.076	9.23
1880				22.37			NW¼NW¼	21	29	52	4-15—6-15	.275	33.56
1880				26.91			SW¼NW¼	21	29	52	4-15—6-15	.331	40.37
1880				24.35			NE¼NW¼	21	29	52	4-15—6-15	.300	36.53
1880				17.08			SE¼NW¼	21	29	52	4-15—6-15	.210	25.62
1880					11.96		NE¼NW¼	21	29	52	4-15—5-15	.147	8.97
1880					13.67		SE¼NW¼	21	29	52	4-15—5-15	.168	10.25

Source—**Dry or Padelford Creek.** Ditch—**Padelford Ditch.**

1871			6.55				SE¼NE¼	29	31	52	4-15—8-15	.081	19.65
1871			5.51				SW¼NE¼	29	31	52	4-15—8-15	.068	16.53
1871			15.00				NW¼SE¼	29	31	52	4-15—8-15	.185	45.00

Source—**Pine Creek.**

1903			8.25				SW¼SE¼	29	31	52	4-15—8-15	.101	24.75
1903			17.89				NE¼NW¼	20	31	52	4-15—8-15	.220	23.67
1875				.28			NE¼NW¼	29	31	52	4-15—6-15	.003	.42
1875			5.92				SE¼SW¼	20	31	52	4-15—8-15	.073	17.76
1875			28.33				NE¼SW¼	20	31	52	4-15—8-15	.348	84.99
1875			19.02				SE¼NW¼	20	31	52	4-15—8-15	.234	57.06
1875			2.06				NE¼NW¼	20	31	52	4-15—8-15	.025	6.18
1876			2.15				NE¼SW¼	20	31	52	4-15—8-15	.026	6.45
1876			10.32				SE¼NW¼	20	31	52	4-15—8-15	.127	30.96
1876			4.64				NE¼NW¼	20	31	52	4-15—8-15	.057	13.92

Claimant—**W. S. Yates.** Proof No. 00305

Source—**Smith Creek.** Ditch—**Smith Creek Ditch System.**

1872			2.00				N½NW¼	4	29	52	4-15—8-15	.026	6.00
1878			10.00				W½NW¼	4	29	52	4-15—8-15	.123	30.00
1872			13.07				NW¼NW¼	4	29	52	4-15—8-15	.161	39.21
1872			12.83				E½SE¼	32	30	52	4-15—8-15	.158	38.43
1872			32.96				W½SW¼	33	30	52	4-15—8-15	.405	98.88
1880			.20				NE¼NE¼	5	29	52	4-15—8-15	.002	.60
1880			20.00				SW¼NW¼	4	29	52	4-15—8-15	.246	60.00

W. S. Yates—Continued.
Source—**Pine Creek.** Ditch—**Pine Creek Ditch System.**

Year of priority	Culture—Acres: Harvest crops	Culture—Acres: Meadow pasture	Culture—Acres: Diversified pasture	Location: Subdivision	Location: Section	Location: Tp.N.	Location: R.E.	Length of season	Duty of water: C.F.S.	Duty of water: Acre-feet
1872	75.01			E½NE¼	5	29	52	4-15—8-15	.923	225.03
1872	29.01			W½NW¼	4	29	52	4-15—8-15	.357	87.03
1872	13.32			SE¼SE¼	32	30	52	4-15—8-15	.164	39.96
1872	71.91			SW¼	16	30	52	4-15—8-15	.884	215.73
1872	....	5.50		SW¼	16	30	52	4-15—6-15	.068	8.25
1872	35.00			NW¼NW¼	21	30	52	4-15—8-15	.431	105.00
1872	....	5.00		NW¼NW¼	21	30	52	4-15—6-15	.062	7.50
1872	....	5.78		NE¼NW¼	21	30	52	4-15—6-15	.071	8.67
1882	2.00			SW¼	21	30	52	4-15—8-15	.025	6.00

Claimant—**C. H. Rand.** Proof No. **00306**
Source—**Pine Creek and Tributaries.** Ditch—**Pine Creek.**

Year of priority	Harvest crops	Meadow pasture	Diversified pasture	Subdivision	Section	Tp.N.	R.E.	Length of season	C.F.S.	Acre-feet
1869	35.89			NW¼	21	30	52	4-15—8-15	.441	107.67
1869	12.03			SW¼	21	30	52	4-15—8-15	.148	36.09
1869	55.93			S½NE¼	20	30	52	4-15—8-15	.688	177.79
1880	....		3.45	SE¼NW¼	20	30	52	4-15—5-15	.042	2.58
1880	1.95			SE¼NW¼	20	30	52	4-15—8-15	.024	5.85
1869	74.15			E½SW¼	20	30	52	4-15—8-15	.912	222.45
1869	137.77			SE¼	20	30	52	4-15—8-15	1.695	413.31
1889	21.79			SE¼	20	30	52	4-15—8-15	.268	65.37
1889	6.91			NE¼	29	30	52	4-15—8-15	.085	20.73
1869	....		8.40	E½SW¼	20	30	52	4-15—5-15	.103	6.30
1839	36.91			NE¼	29	30	52	4-15—8-15	.454	110.73
1869	14.96			E½NW¼	29	30	52	4-15—8-15	.184	44.88
1869	6.60			E½NW¼	29	30	52	4-15—8-15	.071	19.80

Source—**Pine Creek and Tributaries.** Ditch—**Trout Creek.**

Year of priority	Harvest crops	Meadow pasture	Diversified pasture	Subdivision	Section	Tp.N.	R.E.	Length of season	C.F.S.	Acre-feet
1869	....	9.20		NW¼	21	30	52	4-15—6-15	.113	13.80
1869	....	27.21		SW¼	21	30	52	4-15—6-15	.335	40.81
1889	14.30			SW¼SW¼	21	30	52	4-15—8-15	.176	32.90
1869	....		82.29	NE¼	29	30	32	4-15—5-15	1.012	61.72
1869	....		30.45	N½SE¼	29	30	52	4-15—5-15	.375	22.84

Claimant—**Belle B. Ennor, Herbert B. Ennor, and Sarah P. Ennor.** Proof. No. **00307**
Source—**Pine Creek.** Ditch—**Ennor Irrigation System.**

Year of priority	Harvest crops	Meadow pasture	Diversified pasture	Subdivision	Section	Tp.N.	R.E.	Length of season	C.F.S.	Acre-feet
1870	32.07			W½NW¼	16	30	52	4-15—8-15	.394	96.21
1870	22.60			E½NE¼	17	30	52	4-15—8-15	.278	67.80
1870	16.60			SW¼NW¼	16	30	52	4-15—8-15	.204	40.80
1870	29.14			SE¼	8	30	52	4-15—8-15	.358	87.42
1870	39.90			E½SE¼	17	30	52	4-15—8-15	.491	119.70
1870	90.57			NE¼	17	30	52	4-15—8-15	1.114	271.71
1882	49.24			W½SE¼	8	30	52	4-15—8-15	.600	147.74

	1882			6.28				NE¼SW¼	8	30	52	4-15—8-15	.077	18.81
	1882			20.81				E½NW¼	8	30	52	4-15—8-15	.256	62.43
	1882			22.58				W½W½NE¼	8	30	52	4-15—8-15	.278	68.24
	1882			4.12				SE½SW¼	5	30	52	4-15—8-15	.051	12.36
	1882			15.44				W½SE¼	5	30	52	4-15—8-15	.190	46.32
	1880			13.33				E½SE¼	5	30	52	4-15—8-15	.164	39.09
	1885			10.40				SW¼SE¼	5	30	52	4-15—8-15	.128	31.20
	1885			24.39				E½NE¼	8	30	52	4-15—8-15	.300	73.17
	1885			6.07				NE¼SE¼	8	30	52	4-15—8-15	.075	18.21
	1885			1.40				SW¼NW¼	9	30	52	4-15—8-15	.017	4.20
	1885			.54				NW¼SW¼	9	30	52	4-15—8-15	.007	1.62
	1880			35.50				N½SE¼	8	30	52	4-15—8-15	.437	106.50
	1880			6.00				W½SE¼	8	30	52	4-15—8-15	.074	18.00
	1880			10.10				S½NE¼	8	30	52	4-15—8-15	.124	30.30
	1890			19.20				S½NE¼	8	30	52	4-15—8-15	.236	57.60
	1898			36.40				NE¼	8	30	52	4-15—8-15	.448	109.20
	1882			26.95				W½NE¼	8	30	52	4-15—8-15	.331	88.85
	1898			39.20				SE¼	5	30	52	4-15—8-15	.482	117.60
	1870			19.63				SE½SE¼	8	30	52	4-15—8-15	.241	58.89

Claimant—**Geo. W. Goodfellow.** **Proof No. 00308**
Source—**Pony Creek.** Ditch—**Goodfellow Ditch System.**

	1888			6.59				NE¼	17	28	52	4-15—8-15	.081	19.77
	1888			41.34				SE¼	17	28	52	4-15—8-15	.508	124.02
	1888			37.48				SW¼	16	28	52	4-15—8-15	.461	112.44
	1888			111.06				NW¼	21	28	52	4-15—8-15	1.360	333.18
	1888			66.26				NE¼	21	28	52	4-15—8-15	.815	198.78
	1888			78.72				N½SE¼	21	28	52	4-15—8-15	.968	236.16
	1888			.20				SW¼NW¼	22	28	52	4-15—8-15	.002	.60
	1888			2.47				N½SW¼	22	28	52	4-15—8-15	.030	7.41
	1888			9.29				NE¼SW¼	21	28	52	4-15—8-15	.113	27.60

Claimant—**George Arthur.** **Proof No. 00321**
Source—**James Creek.** Ditch—**George Arthur Ditches.**

	1882			28.09				SW¼SW¼	2	33	51			
								NE¼NE¼	10	33	51	4-15—8-15	.346	84.27

Claimant—**J. W. Puett.** Proof No. 00322
Source—**Maggie Creek.** Ditch—**Palmer.**

	1871			20.00				SE¼NW¼	26	33	52	4-15—8-15	.266	60.00

Claimant—**W. T. Jenkins Co.** Proof No. 00323
Source—**Meadow Creek.** Ditch—**Meadow Creek.**

	1896			7.71				NW¼SW¼	10	37	52	4-15—8-15	.095	23.23
	1896			2.80				NE¼SW¼	10	37	52	4-15—8-15	.034	8.40
	1896				3.94			NE¼SW¼	10	37	52	4-15—6-15	.048	5.91
	1896			6.44				NW¼SE¼	10	37	52	4-15—8-15	.079	19.32

W. T. Jenkins Co.—Continued.

Year of priority	Culture—Acres: Harvest crops	Meadow pasture	Diversified pasture	Location: Subdivision	Section	Tp.N.	R.E.	Length of season	Duty of water: C.F.S.	Acre-feet
1896	4.69			SW¼SE¼	10	37	52	4-15—8-15	.058	14.07
1896	10.23			SE¼SE¼	10	37	52	4-15—8-15	.126	30.69
1896	7.76			SW¼SW¼	11	37	52	4-15—8-15	.095	23.28
1896	....	6.39		SW¼SW¼	11	37	52	4-15—6-15	.079	9.59
1896	....	1.27		SE¼SW¼	11	37	52	4-15—6-15	.016	1.91

Source—**Stampede Creek.** Ditch—**Stampede Creek.**

Year of priority	Harvest crops	Meadow pasture	Diversified pasture	Subdivision	Section	Tp.N.	R.E.	Length of season	C.F.S.	Acre-feet
1885	1.00			SE¼NW¼	26	38	52	4-15—8-15	.012	3.00
1885	5.13			SW¼NE¼	26	38	52	4-15—8-15	.063	15.39
1885	3.62			NE¼SW¼	26	38	52	4-15—8-15	.045	10.86
1885	.28			NW¼SW¼	26	38	52	4-15—8-15	.003	.84
1885	.15			SW¼SW¼	26	38	52	4-15—8-15	.002	.45
1885	7.92			SE¼SW¼	26	38	52	4-15—8-15	.097	23.76
1885	8.90			NW¼SE¼	26	38	52	4-15—8-15	.109	26.70
1885	11.23			SW¼SE¼	26	38	52	4-15—8-15	.138	33.69
1885	2.16			NE¼SE¼	26	38	52	4-15—8-15	.027	6.48
1885	35.55			SE¼SE¼	26	38	52	4-15—8-15	.437	106.65
1885	2.98			SW¼SW¼	25	38	52	4-15—8-15	.037	8.94
1885	20.61			NE¼NE¼	35	38	52	4-15—8-15	.254	61.83
1885	3.96			NW¼NW¼	36	38	52	4-15—8-15	.048	11.88
1885	2.92			SE¼NE¼	35	38	52	4-15—8-15	.036	8.76
1885	13.10			SW¼NW¼	36	38	52	4-15—8-15	.161	39.30
1885	7.94			NW¼SW¼	36	38	52	4-15—8-15	.098	23.82

Source—**Lake Creek.** Ditch—**Lake Creek.**

Year of priority	Harvest crops	Meadow pasture	Diversified pasture	Subdivision	Section	Tp.N.	R.E.	Length of season	C.F.S.	Acre-feet
1885	9.22			NE¼SW¼	3	37	52	4-15—8-15	.113	27.66
1885	2.02			SE¼SW¼	3	37	52	4-15—8-15	.025	6.06
1885	8.62			NW¼SE¼	3	37	52	4-15—8-15	.106	25.86
1885	0.72			NE¼SE¼	3	37	52	4-15—8-15	.009	2.16
1885	15.29			SW¼SE¼	3	37	52	4-15—8-15	.188	45.87
1885	23.89			SE¼SE¼	3	37	52	4-15—8-15	.294	71.67
1885	11.60			NE¼SW¼	11	37	52	4-15—8-15	.143	34.80
1885	....		2.17	NE¼SW¼	11	37	52	4-15—5-16	.027	3.26
1885	2.34			NW¼SE¼	11	37	52	4-15—8-15	.029	7.02
1885	....	1.38		NW¼SE¼	11	37	52	4-15—6-15	.017	2.07
1885	13.53			SW¼SW¼	2	37	52	4-15—8-15	.106	40.59

Source—**Spring Creek.** Ditch—**Spring Creek.**

Year of priority	Harvest crops	Meadow pasture	Diversified pasture	Subdivision	Section	Tp.N.	R.E.	Length of season	C.F.S.	Acre-feet
1885	0.49			NW¼NW¼	35	38	52	4-15—8-15	.006	1.47
1885	...	4.34		SW¼NW¼	35	38	52	4-15—6-15	.053	6.51
1885	18.29			SE¼NW¼	35	38	52	4-15—8-15	.225	54.87
1885	2.65			NE¼SW¼	35	38	52	4-15—8-15	.033	7.95
1885	0.22			SW¼NE¼	35	38	52	4-15—8-15	.003	.66
1885	19.37			NW¼SE¼	35	38	52	4-15—8-15	.238	58.11
1885	2.38			NE¼SE¼	35	38	52	4-15—8-15	.029	7.14

	1885			4.48				SW¼SE¼	35	38	52	4-15—8-15	.055	13.44
	1885			9.02				SE¼SE¼	35	38	52	4-15—8-15	.122	29.76
	1885				1.45			SE¼SE¼	35	38	52	4-15—6-15	.018	2.18

Claimant—**Hunter-Banks Company.** Proof No. 00324

Source—**Camp Creek.** Ditch—**Hunter-Banks Company Ditches.**

	1898			13.60				N½NW¼	2	35	53	4-15—8-15	.167	40.80

Source—**Cold Creek and Susie Creek.** Ditch—**Hunter-Banks Company Ditches.**

	1897			58.60				SW¼NW¼	8	36	54			
								E½NW¼	8	36	54			
								W½NE¼	8	36	54			
								N½SW¼	8	36	54	4-15—8-15	.721	175.80

Source—**Susie Creek.** Ditch—**Hunter-Banks Company Ditches.**

	1876			71.70				S½	9	34	53			
								NW¼	16	34	53	4-15—8-15	.882	215.10

Claimant—**William Dunphy Estate.** Proof No. **00325-00329, Inc.**

Source—**Jack Creek; Indian Creek.**

	1883				4.52			NW¼SW¼	33	36	51	4-15—6-15	.056	6.78
	1883				2.22			SE¼SE¼	32	36	51	4-15—6-15	.027	3.33
	1883				3.50			NW¼SE¼	32	36	51	4-15—6-15	.043	5.25
	1883					3.10		NW¼SE¼	32	36	51	4-15—5-15	.038	2.38
	1883				8.70			NE¼SE¼	32	36	51	4-15—6-15	.107	13.05
	1883					3.80		NE¼SE¼	32	36	51	4-15—5-15	.047	2.85

Source—**Maggie** Creek and **Tributaries.**

	1875					3.48		NW¼SW¼	23	33	52	4-15—5-15	.043	2.61
	1875					9.31		SW¼SW¼	23	33	52	4-15—6-15	.115	6.98
	1875					7.58		NE¼SW¼	23	33	52	4-15—5-15	.093	5.80
	1875					36.77		SE¼SW¼	23	33	52	4-15—5-15	.452	27.58
	1875					.20		NW¼SE¼	23	33	52	4-15—5-15	.002	0.15
	1875					1.21		SW¼SE¼	23	33	52	4-15—5-15	.015	0.91
	1875			2.30				NW¼NW¼	23	33	52	4-15—8-15	.028	6.90
	1875					26.46		NW¼NW¼	23	33	52	4-15—5-15	.325	19.85
	1875					1.82		NE¼NW¼	23	33	52	4-15—5-15	.022	1.37
	1875					34.93		SE¼NW¼	23	33	52	4-15—5-15	.430	26.20
	1875			28.21				SW¼NW¼	23	33	52	4-15—8-15	.347	81.63
	1875					7.68		SW¼NW¼	23	33	52	4-15—5-15	.094	5.76
	1875			18.33				NW¼SW¼	23	33	52	4-15—8-15	.225	54.90
	1875					.30		NW¼SW¼	23	33	52	4-15—5-15	.004	.23
	1875			4.05				NE¼SW¼	23	33	52	4-15—8-15	.050	12.15
	1875					24.12		NE¼SW¼	23	33	52	4-15—5-15	.297	18.09
	1875					1.55		SW¼NE¼	23	33	52	4-15—5-15	.019	1.16
	1875					1.78		NW¼SE¼	23	33	52	4-15—5-15	.022	1.34
	1875					19.50		NE¼SE¼	15	33	52	4-15—5-15	.240	14.63

William Dunphy Estate—Continued.

Year of priority	Culture—Acres: Harvest crops	Meadow pasture	Diversified pasture	Location: Subdivision	Section	Tp.N.	R.E.	Length of season	Duty of water: C.F.S.	Acre-feet
1875			36.70	SE¼SE¼	15	33	52	4-15—5-15	.451	27.53
1875	15.45			SW¼SE¼	15	33	52	4-15—8-15	.190	46.35
1875			23.55	SW¼SE¼	15	33	52	4-15—5-15	.290	17.66
1875			5.45	SW¼SW¼	14	33	52	4-15—5-15	.067	4.09
1875	2.85			NE¼NW¼	22	33	52	4-15—8-15	.035	8.55
1875	24.28			NW¼NE¼	22	33	52	4-15—8-15	.299	72.84
1875			1.30	NW¼NE¼	22	33	52	4-15—5-15	.016	.98
1875	22.22			NE¼NE¼	22	33	52	4-15—8-15	.273	66.66
1875			15.45	NE¼NE¼	22	33	52	4-15—5-15	.190	11.59
1875	11.75			SE¼NE¼	22	33	52	4-15—8-15	.145	35.25
1875	.72			NE¼NW¼	15	33	52	4-15—8-15	.009	2.20
1875			3.70	NE¼NW¼	15	33	52	4-15—5-15	.046	2.78
1875	27.07			SE¼NW¼	15	33	52	4-15—8-15	.333	81.21
1875			9.38	SE¼NW¼	15	33	52	4-15—5-15	.115	7.04
1875	7.75			SW¼NW¼	16	33	52	4-15—8-15	.095	23.25
1875			4.80	NW¼NE¼	15	33	52	4-15—5-15	.059	3.60
1875	.40			SW¼NE¼	15	33	52	4-15—8-15	.005	1.20
1875			30.01	SW¼NE¼	15	33	52	4-15—5-15	.309	22.51
1876			40.00	SE¼NE¼	15	33	52	4-15—5-15	.492	30.00
1875	4.90			NW¼SW¼	15	33	52	4-15—8-15	.060	14.70
1875			5.75	NW¼SW¼	15	33	52	4-15—5-15	.071	4.31
1875	29.68			NE¼SW¼	15	33	52	4-15—8-15	.365	89.04
1875			8.82	NE¼SW¼	15	33	52	4-15—5-15	.108	6.62
1875	17.11			SE¼SW¼	15	33	52	4-15—8-15	.210	51.33
1875			15.92	SE¼SW¼	15	33	52	4-15—5-15	.196	11.94
1875	.60			NW¼SE¼	15	33	52	4-15—8-15	.007	1.80
1875			37.15	NW¼SE¼	15	33	52	4-15—5-15	.457	27.86
1875	9.73			NW¼NE¼	22	34	51	4-15—8-15	.120	29.19
1875			3.64	NW¼NE¼	22	34	51	4-15—5-15	.045	2.73
1875	1.10			NE¼NE¼	22	34	51	4-15—8-15	.014	3.30
1875			10.40	NE¼NE¼	22	34	51	4-15—5-15	.128	7.80
1875		8.45		SW¼SW¼	11	34	51	4-15—6-15	.104	12.68
1875		14.60		NW¼NE¼	11	34	51	4-15—6-15	.180	21.90
1875			2.30	NW¼NE¼	11	34	51	4-15—5-15	.028	1.73
1875		3.50		SW¼NE¼	11	34	51	4-15—6-15	.043	5.25
1875			2.02	SW¼NE¼	11	34	51	4-15—5-15	.025	1.52
1875		5.85		NW¼NW¼	11	34	51	4-15—6-15	.072	8.78
1875			8.65	NW¼NW¼	11	34	51	4-15—5-15	.106	6.49
1875	29.67			SW¼NW¼	11	34	51	4-15—8-15	.365	89.01
1875			5.55	SW¼NW¼	11	34	51	4-15—5-15	.068	4.16
1875	22.13			SE¼NW¼	11	34	51	4-15—8-15	.272	66.39
1875			11.82	SE¼NW¼	11	34	51	4-15—5-15	.144	8.49
1875		15.84		NE¼NW¼	11	34	51	4-15—6-15	.195	23.70
1875			9.30	NE¼NW¼	11	34	51	4-15—5-15	.114	6.98
1875		1.80		NE¼SW¼	11	34	51	4-15—6-15	.022	2.70
1875			2.15	NE¼SW¼	11	34	51	4-15—5-15	.026	1.61

	1875			31.70				NW¼SW¼	11	34	51	4-15—8-15	.390	95.10
	1875					1.02		NW¼SW¼	11	34	51	4-15—5-15	.013	.77
	1875			6.53				SW¼SW¼	11	34	51	4-15—8-15	.080	19.50
	1875					1.32		SE¼NE¼	10	34	51	4-15—5-15	.016	.99
	1875			29.15				SE¼SE¼	10	34	51	4-15—8-15	.359	87.45
	1875					3.07		SE¼SE¼	10	34	51	4-15—5-15	.038	2.30
	1875			19.67				NE¼SE¼	10	34	51	4-15—8-15	.131	32.61
	1875					7.03		NE¼SE¼	10	34	51	4-15—5-15	.086	5.27
	1875			6.39				NE¼NE¼	15	34	51	4-15—8-15	.079	19.17
	1875				1.18			NE¼NE¼	15	34	51	4-15—6-15	.015	1.77
	1876					22.44		NE¼NE¼	15	34	51	4-15—5-15	.276	16.83
	1875			7.15				NW¼NE¼	15	34	51	4-15—8-15	.088	21.45
	1875					.51		NW¼NE¼	15	34	51	4-15—5-15	.006	.38
	1876			29.15				SW¼NE¼	15	34	51	4-15—8-15	.359	87.45
	1875					3.96		SE¼NW¼	15	34	51	4-15—5-15	.049	2.97
	1875			8.05				NW¼SE¼	16	34	51	4-15—8-15	.099	24.15
	1875					6.69		NW¼SE¼	15	34	51	4-15—5-15	.082	5.02
	1875					9.97		NE¼SE¼	15	34	51	4-15—5-15	.123	7.48
	1875					3.12		SE¼SE¼	15	34	51	4-15—5-15	.038	2.34
	1875			16.51				SW¼SE¼	15	34	51	4-15—8-15	.203	49.53
	1875					2.00		SW¼SE¼	15	34	51	4-15—5-15	.025	1.50
	1875					7.20		NW¼SW¼	15	34	51	4-15—5-15	.080	5.40
	1875			.65				SE¼NE¼	15	34	51	4-15—8-15	.008	1.95
	1875					14.10		SE¼NE¼	15	34	51	4-15—5-15	.173	10.58
	1875				4.30			SE¼NE¼	2	34	51	4-15—6-15	.053	6.45
	1875				2.22			NE¼SE¼	2	34	51	4-15—6-15	.027	3.33
	1875				21.48			SW¼SE¼	2	34	51	4-15—6-15	.264	32.22
	1875				5.00			SE¼SE¼	2	34	51	4-15—6-15	.062	7.50
	1875				2.83			SE¼SW¼	2	34	51	4-15—6-15	.035	4.25
	1875				4.65			NE¼NW¼	11	34	51	4-15—6-15	.057	6.98
	1875				8.74			NW¼NE¼	11	34	51	4-15—6-15	.108	13.11
	1883					.75		NE¼SW¼	15	36	51	4-15—5-15	.009	.56
	1883					7.62		SE¼SW¼	15	36	51	4-15—5-15	.094	5.72
	1883					2.00		SW¼SE¼	15	36	51	4-15—5-15	.025	1.50
	1883				.80			NE¼NW¼	22	36	51	4-15—6-15	.098	1.20
	1883					1.77		NE¼NW¼	22	36	51	4-15—5-15	.022	1.33
	1883				2.60			NW¼NE¼	22	36	51	4-15—6-15	.032	3.90
	1883					6.11		NW¼NE¼	22	36	51	4-15—5-15	.075	4.58
	1883					14.49		SW¼SE¼	36	36	51	4-15—5-15	.178	10.87
	1883				30.18			NW¼SE¼	36	36	51	4-15—6-15	.371	45.27
	1883					2.93		NW¼SE¼	36	36	51	4-15—5-15	.036	2.20
	1883				2.69			NE¼SE¼	36	36	51	4-15—6-15	.033	4.04
	1883					4.78		NE¼SE¼	36	36	51	4-15—5-15	.059	3.59
	1883				3.66			NE¼SW¼	36	36	51	4-15—6-15	.045	5.49
	1883					23.63		NE¼SW¼	36	36	51	4-15—5-15	.291	17.72
	1883				6.42			SE¼NW¼	36	36	51	4-15—6-15	.079	9.63
	1883				11.15			SW¼NE¼	36	36	51	4-15—6-15	.137	16.73
	1883				1.38			SW¼SE¼	6	35	52	4-15—6-15	.017	2.07
	1883				1.70			NW¼NE¼	7	35	52	4-15—6-15	.021	2.55
	1883					6.25		NW¼NE¼	7	35	52	4-15—5-15	.077	4.09
	1883				2.95			SW¼NE¼	7	35	52	4-15—6-15	.036	4.43
	1883				4.53			NE¼NW¼	7	35	52	4-15—6-15	.056	6.80
	1883				10.29			SE¼NW¼	7	35	52	4-15—6-15	.127	15.44

William Dunphy Estate—Continued.

Year of priority	Culture—Acres: Harvest crops	Culture—Acres: Meadow pasture	Culture—Acres: Diversified pasture	Location: Subdivision	Location: Section	Location: Tp.N.	Location: R.E.	Length of season	Duty of water: O.F.S.	Duty of water: Acre-feet
1883		.47		SW¼NW¼	7	35	52	4-15—6-15	.006	.71
1883	6.64			NE¼NE¼	1	35	51	4-15—8-15	.082	19.92
1883		24.39		NE¼NE¼	13	35	51	4-15—6-15	.300	36.59
1883			3.85	NE¼NE¼	1	35	51	4-15—5-15	.017	2.89
1883	.30			NW¼NE¼	1	35	51	4-15—8-15	.004	.90
1883		16.77		NW¼NE¼	1	35	51	4-15—6-15	.206	25.11
1883		.20		NE¼NW¼	1	35	51	4-15—6-15	.002	.30
1883			3.36	NE¼NW¼	1	35	51	4-15—5-15	.041	2.52
1883		24.65		SE¼SE¼	36	36	51	4-15—6-15	.303	36.98
1883			5.72	SE¼SE¼	36	36	51	4-15—5-15	.070	4.29
1883		12.63		SW¼SE¼	36	36	51	4-15—6-15	.155	18.95
1883			4.03	SE¼SE¼	6	35	52	4-15—5-15	.050	3.02
1883		7.00		SE¼SW¼	6	35	52	4-15—6-15	.086	10.50
1883		14.34		NW¼NW¼	6	35	52	4-15—6-15	.184	21.51
1883		2.52		SE¼NW¼	6	35	52	4-15—6-15	.031	3.78
1883		5.65		NE¼NW¼	6	35	52	4-15—6-15	.069	8.48
1883		.62		NW¼SE¼	6	35	52	4-15—6-15	.008	.93
1883		40.00		SW¼SW¼	29	36	52	4-15—6-15	.492	60.00
1883		3.13		SE¼SE¼	30	36	52	4-15—6-15	.038	4.70
1883		3.39		SW¼SW¼	32	36	52	4-15—6-15	.042	5.09
1883			.75	SW¼SW¼	32	36	52	4-15—5-15	.009	.56
1883			1.03	NE¼NE¼	31	36	52	4-15—5-15	.013	.77
1883			3.17	SE¼NE¼	31	36	52	4-15—5-15	.039	2.38
1883			1.50	NE¼SE¼	31	36	52	4-15—5-15	.018	1.13
1883			4.50	SE¼SE¼	31	36	52	4-15—5-15	.055	3.38
1883			8.55	NW¼SE¼	31	36	52	4-15—5-15	.105	6.41
1883		1.78		SW¼SW¼	31	36	52	4-15—6-15	.022	2.67
1883		7.60		NE¼NE¼	6	35	52	4-15—6-15	.093	11.40
1883			2.80	NE¼NE¼	6	35	52	4-15—5-15	.034	2.10
1883		3.60		SE¼NE¼	6	35	52	4-15—6-15	.044	5.40
1883			5.62	SE¼NE¼	6	35	52	4-15—5-15	.069	4.22
1883		8.92		NE¼SE¼	6	35	52	4-15—6-15	.110	13.38
1883			4.11	NE¼SE¼	6	35	52	4-15—5-15	.051	3.08
1883		4.18		SE¼SE¼	6	35	52	4-15—6-15	.051	6.27
1883	33.53			NW¼NW¼	29	36	52	4-15—8-15	.412	100.50
1883			2.07	NW¼NW¼	29	36	52	4-15—5-15	.025	1.55
1883	24.84			SW¼NW¼	29	36	52	4-15—8-15	.306	74.52
1883			10.77	SW¼NW¼	29	36	52	4-15—5-15	.132	8.08
1883	1.40			SE¼NW¼	20	36	52	4-15—8-15	.017	4.20
1883			28.10	SE¼NW¼	29	36	52	4-15—5-15	.346	21.08
1883	9.63			NE¼NW¼	29	36	52	4-15—8-15	.118	28.89
1883			27.20	NE¼NW¼	29	36	52	4-15—5-15	.335	20.40
1883			13.18	NW¼NE¼	29	36	52	4-15—6-15	.162	9.89
1883	9.32			NW¼SW¼	[illegible]	36	52	4-15—8-15	.115	27.96
1883			24.27	NW¼SW¼	29	36	52	4-15—5-15	.298	18.20
1883	4.10			SW¼SW¼	29	36	52	4-15—8-15	.050	12.30

	Year					Sec.	Twp.	Rge.	Date		
	1883		12.25		SW¼SW¼	20	36	52	4-15—5-15	.151	9.19
	1883		9.85		SE¼SW¼	29	36	52	4-15—5-15	.121	7.39
	1883		25.37		NE¼SW¼	29	36	52	4-15—5-15	.312	19.03
	1883	13.68			NW¼SE¼	20	36	52	4-15—8-15	.168	41.04
	1883		16.95		NW¼SE¼	20	36	52	4-15—5-15	.208	12.71
	1883	4.62			SW¼SE¼	20	36	52	4-15—8-15	.057	13.86
	1883		16.65		SW¼SE¼	20	36	52	4-15—5-15	.205	12.49
	1883	12.35			NW¼SW¼	20	36	52	4-15—8-15	.152	37.05
	1883	26.22			SW¼SW¼	20	36	52	4-15—8-15	.323	78.66
	1883	35.12			SE¼SW¼	20	36	52	4-15—8-15	.432	105.36
	1883		1.48		SE¼SW¼	20	36	52	4-15—5-15	.018	1.11
	1883	36.63			NE¼SW¼	20	36	52	4-15—8-15	.451	109.89
	1883		.10		NE¼SW¼	20	56	52	4-15—5-15	.001	.06
	1883	28.54			NW¼NE¼	20	36	52	4-15—8-15	.351	85.62
	1883		8.31		NW¼NE¼	20	36	52	4-15—5-15	.102	6.23
	1883	1.00			NE¼NE¼	20	36	52	4-15—8-15	.012	3.00
	1883		3.98		NE¼NE¼	20	36	52	4-15—5-15	.049	2.99
	1883	22.96			SW¼NE¼	20	36	52	4-15—8-15	.282	68.88
	1883		7.45		SW¼NE¼	20	36	52	4-15—5-15	.092	5.59
	1883	22.12			NE¼NW¼	20	36	52	4-15—8-15	.272	66.36
	1883		3.30		NE¼NW¼	20	36	52	4-15—5-15	.041	2.48
	1883	36.52			SE¼NW¼	20	36	52	4-15—8-15	.449	109.56
	1883		3.08		SE¼NW¼	20	36	52	4-15—5-15	.038	2.31
	1883	.82			SW¼NW¼	20	36	52	4-15—8-15	.010	2.46
	1883		2.75		SW¼NW¼	20	36	52	4-15—5-15	.035	2.06
	1883	3.90			NW¼NW¼	20	36	52	4-15—8-15	.048	11.70
	1883		14.95		NW¼NW¼	20	36	52	4-15—5-15	.184	11.21
	1883	2.92			NE¼NE¼	19	36	52	4-15—8-15	.036	8.76
	1883		25.86		NE¼NE¼	19	36	52	4-15—5-15	.318	19.40
	1883	.60			SE¼NE¼	19	36	52	4-15—8-15	.007	1.80
	1883		4.80		SE¼NE¼	19	36	52	4-15—5-15	.059	3.60
	1883		18.65		SE¼SE¼	18	36	52	4-15—5-15	.229	13.00
	1883	6.93			SE¼SW¼	17	36	52	4-15—8-15	.085	20.79
	1883		11.89		SE¼SW¼	17	36	52	4-15—5-15	.146	8.92
	1883		6.40		NE¼SW¼	17	36	52	4-15—5-15	.079	4.80
	1883	10.03			SE¼NE¼	17	36	52	4-15—8-15	.123	30.09
	1883		5.45		SE¼NE¼	17	36	52	4-15—5-15	.067	4.09
	1883	32.23			NE¼SE¼	17	36	52	4-15—8-15	.396	96.69
	1883		5.06		NE¼SE¼	17	36	52	4-15—5-15	.062	3.80
	1883	11.11			NW¼SE¼	17	36	52	4-15—8-15	.137	33.33
	1883		12.40		NW¼SE¼	17	36	52	4-15—5-15	.153	9.30
	1883	23.67			SW¼SE¼	17	36	52	4-15—8-15	.291	71.01
	1883		13.86		SW¼SE¼	17	36	52	4-15—5-15	.170	10.40
	1883	19.25			SE¼SE¼	17	36	52	4-15—8-15	.257	57.75
	1883		13.63		SE¼SE¼	17	36	52	4-15—5-15	.168	10.22
	1883		1.30		SE¼NE¼	16	36	52	4-15—5-15	.016	.98
	1883	1.25			SW¼NE¼	16	36	52	4-15—8-15	.015	3.75
	1883	8.41			NW¼NE¼	16	36	52	4-15—8-15	.103	125.23
	1883		3.10		NW¼NE¼	16	36	52	4-15—5-15	.038	2.33
	1883	15.28			NE¼NW¼	16	36	52	4-15—8-15	.188	45.84
	1883		12.37		NE¼NW¼	16	36	52	4-15—5-15	.152	9.28
	1883		11.53		NW¼NW¼	16	36	52	4-15—5-15	.142	8.65
	1883	24.83			SW¼NW¼	16	36	52	4-15—8-15	.305	74.49

William Dunphy Estate—Continued.

Year of priority	Culture—Acres: Harvest crops	Culture—Acres: Meadow pasture	Culture—Acres: Diversified pasture	Location: Subdivision	Location: Section	Location: Tp.N.	Location: R.E.	Length of season	Duty of water: C.F.S.	Duty of water: Acre-feet
1883			7.78	SW¼NW¼	16	36	52	4-15—5-15	.096	5.84
1883	22.58			SE¼NW¼	16	36	52	4-15—8-15	.278	67.34
1883			4.93	SE¼NW¼	16	36	52	4-15—5-15	.061	3.70
1883			.30	NE¼NW¼	16	36	52	4-15—5-15	.004	.23
1883	12.14			NW¼SW¼	16	36	52	4-15—8-15	.149	36.42
1883			15.95	NW¼SW¼	16	36	52	4-15—5-15	.196	11.96
1883	.28			NE¼SW¼	16	36	52	4-15—8-15	.003	.84
1883			.25	NW¼SE¼	16	36	52	4-15—5-15	.003	.19
1883	.35			SW¼SW¼	16	36	52	4-15—8-15	.004	1.05
1883		3.15		NW¼NW¼	10	36	52	4-15—6-15	.039	4.73
1883			1.90	NW¼NW¼	10	36	52	4-15—5-15	.023	1.43
1883		4.70		SW¼NW¼	10	36	52	4-15—6-15	.058	7.05
1883			2.00	SW¼NW¼	10	36	52	4-15—5-15	.025	1.50
1883		6.35		NW¼SW¼	10	36	52	4-15—6-15	.078	9.53
1883			5.91	NW¼SW¼	10	36	52	4-15—5-15	.069	4.43
1883		.30		SW¼SW¼	10	36	52	4-15—6-15	.004	0.45
1883			3.55	SW¼SW¼	10	36	52	4-15—5-15	.044	2.66
1883		23.65		SE¼NE¼	9	36	52	4-15—6-15	.291	35.48
1883			3.05	SE¼NE¼	9	36	52	4-15—5-15	.038	2.29
1883		2.45		NE¼SE¼	9	36	52	4-15—6-15	.030	3.68
1883			17.27	NE¼SE¼	9	36	52	4-15—5-15	.212	12.95
1883		2.43		NE¼NW¼	16	36	52	4-15—6-15	.030	3.65
1883		4.60		NW¼NE¼	16	36	52	4-15—6-15	.057	6.90
1883		2.70		SW¼SE¼	9	36	52	4-15—6-15	.033	4.05
1883		.82		SE¼SW¼	9	36	52	4-15—6-15	.101	1.23
1883	8.30			NW¼NE¼	3	36	52	4-15—8-15	.102	24.90
1883	37.33			NE¼NW¼	3	36	52	4-15—8-15	.459	111.99
1883	13.02			NW¼NW¼	3	36	52	4-15—8-15	.160	39.06
1883	7.33			SE¼NW¼	3	36	52	4-15—8-15	.090	26.99
1883	7.50			SW¼NW¼	3	36	52	4-15—8-15	.092	22.50
1883			4.15	SE¼SW¼	27	37	52	4-15—5-15	.051	3.11
1883			16.80	SE¼NE¼	34	37	52	4-15—5-15	.207	12.60
1883			1.10	NE¼SE¼	34	37	52	4-15—5-15	.014	.83
1883			7.20	SW¼NE¼	34	37	52	4-15—5-15	.089	5.40
1883	4.85			NW¼SE¼	34	37	52	4-15—8-15	.060	14.55
1883			.45	NW¼SE¼	34	37	52	4-15—5-15	.006	.34
1883	10.37			SW¼SE¼	34	37	52	4-15—8-15	.128	31.11
1883	22.00			SE¼NW¼	34	37	52	4-15—8-15	.271	66.00
1883	.80			SW¼NW¼	34	37	52	4-15—8-15	.010	2.40
1883	5.55			NW¼SW¼	34	37	52	4-15—8-15	.068	16.65
1883	6.88			SW¼SW¼	34	37	52	4-15—8-15	.085	20.64
1883	30.26			SE¼SW¼	34	37	52	4-15—8-15	.372	10.78
1883	33.05			NE¼SW¼	34	37	52	4-15—8-15	.407	99.15
1883		18.55		NE¼NW¼	34	37	52	4-15—6-15	.228	27.83
1883			8.80	NE¼NW¼	34	37	52	4-15—5-15	.108	6.00
1883		1.05		SE¼NW¼	34	37	52	4-15—6-15	.013	1.58

	1883					.86		SE¼NW¼	34	37	52	4-15—5-15	.011	.65
	1883					1.62		SW¼NE¼	34	37	52	4-15—5-15	.020	1.23
	1883					23.37		NW¼NE¼	34	37	52	4-15—5-15	.287	17.53
	1883				6.35			NE¼SW¼	23	37	52	4-15—6-15	.078	9.53
	1883				.48			NW¼SW¼	23	37	52	4-15—6-15	.006	.72
	1883					36.72		NE¼NE¼	27	37	52	4-15—5-15	.451	27.54
	1883				1.10			SE¼NE¼	27	37	52	4-15—6-15	.014	1.65
	1883					34.96		SE¼NE¼	27	37	52	4-15—5-15	.430	26.22
	1883				.85			SW¼NE¼	27	37	52	4-15—6-15	.010	1.28
	1883					2.56		SW¼NE¼	27	37	52	4-15—5-15	.031	1.91
	1883				5.25			NW¼SE¼	27	37	52	4-15—6-15	.065	7.88
	1883					20.63		NW¼SE¼	27	37	52	4-15—5-15	.253	15.47
	1883				1.50			SW¼SE¼	27	37	52	4-15—6-15	.018	2.25
	1883					36.49		SW¼SE¼	27	37	52	4-15—5-15	.437	26.62
	1883				.65			SE¼SE¼	27	37	52	4-11—6-15	.008	.98
	1883					11.58		SE¼SE¼	27	37	52	4-15—5-15	.142	8.69
	1883				20.75			NE¼SE¼	27	37	52	4-15—6-15	.255	31.13
	1883					7.25		NE¼SE¼	27	37	52	4-15—5-15	.089	5.44
	1883					.10		NE¼SW¼	27	37	52	4-15—5-15	.001	.08
	1883				7.32			SE¼SW¼	77	37	52	4-15—6-15	.090	10.98
	1883				4.70			NE¼SE¼	2	37	53	4-15—6-15	.058	3.53
	1883				2.34			SE¼SE¼	2	37	52	4-15—6-15	.029	1.76
	1883				1.08			SW¼SE¼	2	37	52	4-15—6-15	.013	.89
	1883				3.05			NE¼NE¼	11	37	52	4-15—6-15	.038	2.29
	1883				11.71			NW¼NE¼	11	37	52	4-15—6-15	.144	8.78
	1883				3.60			SE¼SW¼	11	37	52	4-15—6-15	.044	2.70
	1883				.50			NW¼NE¼	14	37	52	4-15—6-15	.006	.38
	1883				.50			NE¼NE¼	14	37	52	4-15—6-15	.006	.38

Claimant—**Hunter-Banks Company.** Proof No. **00330**

Source—**Cold Creek.** Ditch—**Hunter Banks Company Ditches.**

	1880			26.45				S½SE¼	25	37	53			
								N½NE¼	36	37	53	4-15—8-15	.325	79.35

Claimant—**John** Paleni. Proof No. **00331**

Source—**Springs** Tributary to **Susie Creek.** Ditch—**Paleni Ditches.**

	1870			2.45				SW¼NE¼	15	35	54	4-15—8-15	.030	7.35
	1870			0.31				SW¼NE¼	15	35	54	4-15—8-15	.004	.93
	1870			2.26				NW¼SE¼	15	35	54	4-15—8-15	.028	6.78
	1870			0.11				NE¼NW¼	15	35	54	4-15—8-15	.001	.33
	1870			21.96				SE¼NW¼	15	35	54	4-15—8-15	.270	65.88
	1870			1.97				NE¼SW¼	15	35	54	4-15—8-15	.024	5.97
	1870			16.76				SW¼NW¼	15	35	54	4-15—8-15	.206	50.28
	1870			0.12				NE¼NE¼	16	35	54	4-15—8-15	.001	.36
	1870			13.25				SE¼NE¼	16	35	54	4-15—8-15	.163	39.75
	1870			4.05				SW¼NE¼	16	35	54	4-15—8-15	.049	12.15
	1870			3.62				NW¼NE¼	16	35	54	4-15—8-15	.057	10.86
	1870			9.29				NE¼NW¼	16	35	54	4-15—8-15	.114	27.87
	1870			1.02				SE¼NW¼	16	35	54	4-15—8-15	.010	3.06
	1870			1.42				SW¼NW¼	16	35	54	4-15—8-15	.014	4.26
	1870			0.56				NW¼NW¼	16	35	54	4-15—8-15	.006	1.68

Claimant—**John Paleni.** Proof No. 00332

Source—**Susie Creek.** Ditch—**Paleni Ditches.**

Year of priority	Culture—Acres: Harvest crops	Meadow pasture	Diversified pasture	Location: Subdivision	Section	Tp.N.	R.E.	Length of season	Duty of water: C.F.S.	Acre-feet
1900	3.92			NE¼NW¼	12	35	53	4-15—8-15	.048	11.76
1900	18.02			SE¼NW¼	12	35	53	4-15—8-15	.222	54.06
1900	1.84			SW¼NE¼	12	35	53	4-15—8-15	.023	5.52
1900	0.41			NW¼SE¼	12	35	53	4-15—8-15	.005	1.23
1900	12.19			NE¼SW¼	12	35	53	4-15—8-15	.150	36.57

Claimant—**Max Arnhold.** Proof. No. 00351

Source—**Pearl Creek.** Ditch—**Max Arnhold Ditches.**

Year of priority	Harvest crops	Meadow pasture	Diversified pasture	Subdivision	Section	Tp.N.	R.E.	Length of season	C.F.S.	Acre-feet
1869	33.00			W½	21	28	56	4-15—8-15	.405	99.00
1870	33.00			W½SE¼	21	28	56	4-15—8-15	.405	99.00
1871	34.00			SE¼SE¼	21	28	56	4-15—8-15	.418	102.00
1879	50.00			S½S½	22	28	56	4-15—8-15	.615	150.00
1880	50.00			N½NE¼	28	28	56	4-15—8-15	.615	150.00
1898	10.00							4-15—8-15	.123	30.00
1899	10.00							4-15—8-16	.123	30.00
1900	10.00							4-15—8-16	.123	30.00
1901	10.00							4-15—8-16	.123	30.00
1902	18.90							4-15—8-15	.232	56.70

Claimant—**J. J. Hylton.** Proof No. 00352

Source—**Frost Canyon and Springs.** Ditch—**J. J. Hylton Ditches.**

Year of priority	Harvest crops	Meadow pasture	Diversified pasture	Subdivision	Section	Tp.N.	R.E.	Length of season	C.F.S.	Acre-feet
1874	40.00			W½SE¼	8	28	56			
1874		44.70		SE¼SE¼	8	28	56			
1895	7.00			SW¼SW¼	9	28	56	4-15—8-15	.492	120.00
1896	8.00			NE¼SW¼	9	28	56	4-15—6-15	.550	67.05
				NW¼SE¼	9	28	56	4-15—8-15	.086	21.00
				SE¼NE¼	9	28	56	4-15—8-15	.098	24.00

Claimant—**T. F. Brennen.** Proof No. 00353

Source—**Ainley Creek, Ogilvie Creek, Springs, and one-third waters of Young Creek.***

Ditch—**T. F. Brennen Ditches.**

Year of priority	Harvest crops	Meadow pasture	Diversified pasture	Subdivision	Section	Tp.N.	R.E.	Length of season	C.F.S.	Acre-feet
1869	40.00			SE¼NW¼	9	32	57	4-15—8-15	.492	120.00
1870	15.00			NE¼SW¼	9	32	57	4-15—8-15	.185	45.00
1871	15.00			S½NE¼	9	32	57	4-15—8-15	.185	45.00
1872	50.00			N½SE¼	9	32	57	4-15—8-15	.615	150.00
1873	50.00			SE¼SE¼	9	32	57	4-15—8-15	.615	150.00
1874	50.00			SW¼NW¼	10	32	57	4-15—8-15	.615	150.00
1875	51.78			NW¼SW¼	10	32	57	4-15—8-15	.637	155.34
1872	20.00			SW¼NW¼	9	32	57	4-15—8-15	.240	60.00
1873	16.00			W½SW¼	9	32	57	4-15—8-15	.197	48.00
1873	40.00			SE¼SW¼	9	32	57	4-15—8-15	.492	120.00

	1876			17.00				SW¼SE¼	9	32	57	4-15—8-15	.209	51.00
	1879			17.00								4-15—8-15	.209	51.00
	1880			35.00								4-15—8-15	.431	105.00
	1881			36.63								4-15—8-15	.451	109.89
	1898			....		78.90		SE¼NE¼	8	32	57			
								E½SE¼	8	32	57	4-15—5-15	.970	59.18
	1870			100.00				N½	16	32	57	4-15—8-15	1.230	309.00
	1871			40.00				N½S½	16	32	57	4-15—8-15	.492	120.00
	1872			21.00								4-15—8-15	.258	36.00
	1873			21.00								4-15—8-15	.258	36.00
	1874			21.00								4-15—8-15	.258	36.00
	1875			21.00								4-15—8-15	.258	36.00
	1876			21.00								4-15—8-15	.258	36.00
	1877			26.53								4-15—8-15	.326	79.59
	1877			20.00								4-15—8-15	.246	60.00
	1892			13.00								4-15—8-15	.160	39.00
	1892			....	14.00							4-15—6-15	.172	10.50
	1900					14.26		W½SW¼	16	32	57	4-16—5-16	.175	10.70

(*)That certain agreement signed by T. F. Brennen and J. Hennen in regard to the division of the waters of Young Creek, as recorded in Elko County, Book 4 of Miscl. Records, pages 186 to 187, is binding as between parties to the agreement. The "miner's inch" referred to shall be defined as being the amount of water that will flow through an opening of one square inch and under a six-inch head. The parties to this agreement are to construct and maintain a device in Young Creek in the NW¼NW¼, Sec. 14, T 32 N, R. 57 E, that will automatically divide the stream according to the said agreement, the plans for said device to be approved by the State Engineer.

Claimant—**Mrs. Mary Campbell.** Proof No. 00354

Source—**Bradley or McCutcheon Creek.** Ditch—**Mrs. Mary Campbell Ditches.**

	1878			20.00				N½SW¼	31	30	57	4-15—8-15	.246	60.00
	1880			25.00				SE¼	31	30	57	4-15—8-15	.308	75.00
	1880			....		56.00		W½SW¼	32	30	57	4-15—5-15	.689	168.00
	1881			80.00				SE¼SW¼	32	30	57	4-15—8-15	.984	240.00
	1882			64.61				W½NW¼	5	29	57	4-15—8-15	.795	193.83
	1890			15.00				E½NE¼	6	29	57	4-15—8-15	.185	45.00
	1890			....		67.50						4-15—5-15	.830	202.50
	1899			20.00								4-15—8-15	.246	60.00
	1902			28.00								4-15—8-15	.344	84.00
	1904			14.00								4-15—8-15	.172	54.00
	1905			5.89								4-15—8-15	.072	17.67

Claimant—**J. J. Hylton.** Proof No. 00355

Source—**Peorl Creek and South Fork Humboldt River.** Ditch—**J. J. Hylton Ditches.**

	1893			65.60				E½SE¼	19	31	57	4-15—8-15	0.809	196.80
	1894			40.00				SW¼	20	31	57	4-15—8-15	0.492	120.00
	1895			29.00								4-15—8-15	0.357	87.00
	1894			8.00				S½NW¼	20	31	57	4-15—8-15	.980	24.00
	1898			13.00				S½SE¼	20	31	57	4-15—8-15	.160	39.00
	1905			....		67.00						4-15—5-15	.824	50.25

J. J. Hylton—Continued.

Source—**South Fork Humboldt River.** Ditch—**J. J. Hylton Ditches.**

Year of priority	Culture—Acres: Harvest crops	Meadow pasture	Diversified pasture	Location: Subdivision	Section	Tp.N.	R.E.	Length of season	Duty of water: C.F.S.	Acre-feet
1871	30.00			S½	16	31	57	4-15—8-15	.369	90.00
1873	27.00			S½	17	31	57	4-15—8-15	.332	81.10
1874	57.00			N½	20	31	57	4-15—8-15	.701	171.00
1875	4.00			NW¼	21	31	57	4-15—8-15	.049	12.00
1876	1.20							4-15—8-15	.015	3.60
1878	196.10							4-15—8-15	2.412	588.30
1883	27.70							4-15—8-15	.841	83.10
1891	8.80							4-15—8-15	.108	26.40

Source—**Rattlesnake Creek.** Ditch—**J. J. Hylton Ditches.**

Year of priority	Harvest crops	Meadow pasture	Diversified pasture	Subdivision	Section	Tp.N.	R.E.	Length of season	C.F.S.	Acre-feet
1869	64.00			NW¼NW¼	25	31	56	4-15—8-15	.787	192.00
1877	86.00			NW¼	26	31	56	4-15—8-15	1.058	258.00
1901	62.43			NE¼	27	31	56	4-15—8-15	.768	187.29

Source—**South Fork.** Ditch—**Clayton-Drown.**

Year of priority	Harvest crops	Meadow pasture	Diversified pasture	Subdivision	Section	Tp.N.	R.E.	Length of season	C.F.S.	Acre-feet
1897	50.00			NE¼NE¼	20	31	57	4-15—8-15	.615	150.00
1898	65.96			S½NE¼	20	31	57	4-15—8-15	.811	197.88
1901	32.00			N½SE¼	20	31	57	4-15—8-15	.394	96.00
				NE¼SW¼	20	31	57			
				SE¼NW¼	20	31	57			

Claimant—**J. J. Hylton (Lang Ranch).** **Proof No. 00355**

Source—**Rattlesnake Creek.** Ditch—**Company and Ogilvie.**

Year of priority	Harvest crops	Meadow pasture	Diversified pasture	Subdivision	Section	Tp.N.	R.E.	Length of season	C.F.S.	Acre-feet
1875	31.70			SW¼NW¼	19	31	57			
				W½SW¼	19	31	57			
				NE¼SW¼	19	31	57	4-15—8-15	.390	95.10

Claimant—**Pedro Corta.** Proof No. **00356**

Source—**Spencer Creek.** Ditch—**Pedro Corta Ditches.**

Year of priority	Harvest crops	Meadow pasture	Diversified pasture	Subdivision	Section	Tp.N.	R.E.	Length of season	C.F.S.	Acre-feet
1871	2.00			E½W½	12	28	56	4-15—8-15	.025	6.00
1884	91.10			SW¼	1	28	56	4-15—8-15	1.121	273.30
1905	9.00			S½NW¼	1	28	56	4-15—8-15	.111	27.00

Claimant—**Clark Drown.** Proof No. **00357**

Source—**Lee Creek and South Fork of Humboldt River.*** Ditch—**Clark Drown Ditches.**

Year of priority	Harvest crops	Meadow pasture	Diversified pasture	Subdivision	Section	Tp.N.	R.E.	Length of season	C.F.S.	Acre-feet
1883	103.00			SW¼	8	31	57	4-15—8-15	1.267	300.00
1883	22.10			S½SE¼	7	31	57	4-15—8-15	.272	66.30
				N½NE¼	18	31	57			
				N½NW¼	18	31	57			

(*)Priority from South Fork Humboldt River to date, 1908.

Source—**South Fork Humboldt River.** Ditch—**Clark Drown Ditches.**

Year											
1868	40.00				SW¼	12	31	56	4-15—8-15	.492	120.00
1870	30.40				SW¼SE¼	12	31	56	4-15—8-15	.374	91.20
1871	30.40				N½	12	31	56	4-15—8-15	.374	91.20
1872	30.40				W½NW¼	18	31	57	4-15—8-15	.374	91.20
1873	30.40								4-15—8-15	.374	91.20
1874	30.30								4-15—8-15	.373	90.90
1875	30.30								4-15—8-15	.373	90.90
1880	46.00								4-15—8-15	.566	138.00
1880	1.50								4-15—8-15	.019	4.50
1880	3.00								4-15—8-15	.037	9.00
1880	4.00								4-15—8-15	.049	12.00
1902	64.27*								4-15—8-15	.791	192.81
1903	45.00*								4-15—8-15	.554	135.00
1905			57.70						4-15—5-15	.710	43.28

*From Company Ditch.

Claimant—**Albert Hankins.** Proof No. 00358

Source—**Smith, South Fork, Smith Creek, McCutcheon, Adams and Dry Creeks.**

Ditch—**Albert Hankins Ditches.**

Year											
1872	30.00				NE¼	4	29	56	4-15—8-15	.369	90.00
1875	20.00				N½SE¼	4	29	56	4-15—8-15	.246	60.00
1876	60.60				S½NW¼	3	29	56	4-15—8-15	.745	181.80
1895		104.50			NW¼SW¼	3	29	56	4-15—6-15	1.285	156.75
1904			16.00		NE¼NE¼	10	29	56	4-15—5-15	.197	12.00
1903			33.00		NW¼	11	29	56	4-15—5-15	.406	24.75
1870	80.00				SE¼NW¼	2	29	56	4-15—8-15	.984	240.00
1871	10.00				SW¼	2	29	56	4-15—8-15	.123	30.00
1872	10.00				SE¼	2	29	56	4-15—8-15	.123	30.00
1873	63.00				NW¼SW¼	1	29	56	4-15—8-15	.775	189.00
1874	63.00				N½NW¼	11	29	56	4-15—8-15	.775	189.00
1875	65.00								4-15—8-15	.780	195.00
1867	40.00				NW¼	2	29	56	4-15—8-15	.492	120.00
1868	15.00				NE¼	3	29	56	4-15—8-15	.185	45.00
1869	15.00				SE¼NW¼	3	29	56	4-15—8-15	.185	45.00
1870	15.00				S½	3	29	56	4-15—8-15	.185	45.00
1871	15.00				N½SW¼	2	29	56	4-15—8-15	.185	45.00
1872	30.00				SW¼SW¼	2	29	56	4-15—8-15	.369	90.00
1873	54.00				NW¼NW¼	11	29	56	4-15—8-15	.664	162.00
1877	54.00								4-15—8-15	.664	162.00
1881	54.00								4-15—8-15	.664	162.00
1885	54.00								4-15—8-15	.664	162.00
1889	54.00								4-15—8-15	.664	162.00
1893	57.50								4-15—8-15	.707	172.50

Claimant has vested right in the ditch high up on the Ruby Mountains that was constructed in 1876 and that cuts off some of the drainage water that would naturally flow into McCutcheon Creek.

Year											
1875	37.00				W½SW¼	1	29	56	4-15—8-15	.455	111.00
1878	25.50				S½SE¼	2	29	56	4-15—8-15	.314	76.50
1880	40.00				NW¼NE¼	11	29	56	4-15—8-15	.492	120.00
1903	31.50				NW¼	11	29	56	4-15—8-15	.387	94.50

Decree No. 1355, Elko County District Court Records, is binding as between parties to the suit.

Proof No. 00359

Claimant—**J. J. Hylton.**
Source—**Smith and Huntington Creeks.** Ditch—**J. J. Hylton Ditches.**

Year of priority	Culture—Acres: Harvest crops	Meadow pasture	Diversified pasture	Location: Subdivision	Section	Tp.N.	R.E.	Length of season	Duty of water: C.F.S.	Acre-feet
1880	29.00			SE¼	24	30	55	4-15—8-15	.357	87.00
1870	18.00			NE¼	24	30	55	4-15—8-15	.221	54.00
1873	18.00			NE¼	24	30	55	4-15—8-15	.221	54.00
1876	17.00			NE¼	24	30	55	4-15—8-15	.209	51.00
1880	66.00			NE¼	24	30	55	4-15—8-15	.812	198.00
1870	21.00			SE¼	13	30	55	4-15—8-15	.258	63.00
1873	20.00			SE¼	13	30	55	4-15—8-15	.246	60.00
1876	20.00			SE¼	13	30	55	4-15—8-15	.246	60.00
1880	49.00			SE¼	13	30	55	4-15—8-15	.603	147.00
1895	38.00			SE¼	13	30	55	4-15—8-15	.467	114.00
1880	30.00			NE¼	13	30	55	4-15—8-15	.369	90.00
1880	25.00			NE¼	13	30	55	4-15—8-15	.308	75.00
1878	40.00			NE¼	13	30	55	4-15—8-15	.492	120.00
1895	9.00			NE¼	13	30	55	4-15—8-15	.111	27.00
1876	19.50			NE¼	12	30	55	4-15—8-15	.240	58.50
1876	66.50			SE¼	12	30	55	4-15—8-15	.818	199.50
1880	35.50			SE¼	12	30	55	4-15—8-15	.437	106.50
1895	12.00			NW¼	30	30	56	4-15—8-15	.148	36.00
1896	12.00			NW¼	30	30	56	4-15—8-15	.148	36.00
1897	12.00			NW¼	30	30	56	4-15—8-15	.148	36.00
1898	12.00			NW¼	30	30	56	4-15—8-15	.148	36.00
1899	12.00			NW¼	30	30	56	4-15—8-15	.148	36.00
1900	9.00			NW¼	30	30	56	4-15—8-15	.111	27.00
1880	16.00			SW¼	19	30	56	4-15—8-15	.197	48.00
1895	27.00			SW¼	19	30	56	4-15—8-15	.332	81.00
1898	25.00			SW¼	19	30	56	4-15—8-15	.308	75.00
1900	25.00			SW¼	19	30	56	4-15—8-15	.308	75.00
1870	19.00			SW¼	19	30	56	4-15—8-15	.234	57.00
1873	17.00			SW¼	19	30	56	4-15—8-15	.209	51.00
1876	17.00			SW¼	19	30	56	4-15—8-15	.209	51.00
1879	.50			NW¼	19	30	56	4-15—8-15	.006	1.50
1870	43.00			NW¼	19	30	56	4-15—8-15	.529	129.00
1873	43.00			NW¼	10	30	56	4-15—8-15	.529	129.00
1876	43.00			NW¼	19	30	56	4-15—8-15	.529	129.00
1890	....		55.00	NW¼	13	30	55	4-15—5-15	.677	41.25
1890	....		74.00	SW¼	12	30	55	4-15—5-15	.910	55.50
1890	....		20.50	NW¼	12	30	55	4-15—5-15	.252	15.38

Source—**Huntington Creek.** Ditch—**J. J. Hylton Ditches.**

Year of priority	Harvest crops	Meadow pasture	Diversified pasture	Subdivision	Section	Tp.N.	R.E.	Length of season	C.F.S.	Acre-feet
1892	209.00			SE¼	7	29	56			
				SW¼	7	29	56			
				SE¼	6	29	56			
				SW¼	6	29	56			
				NW¼	6	29	56			
This land has a priority of 1894 from Smith Creek.				NE¼	6	29	56	4-15—8-15	2.571	627.00
1872	781.00			NW¼	6	29	56			

1873		NE¼	6	29	56			
1874		SE¼	6	29	56			
1875			31	30	56			
			30	30	56	4 15—8 15	9.606	2343.00

This land has a divided priority of 1876-77 from Smith Creek, one-half the acreage in each year.

Source—Smith Creek. Ditch—J. J. Hylton Ditches.

1879	30.70	SW¼	28	30	56	4-15—8-15	.378	92.10
1897	15.30	SW¼	28	30	56	4-15—8-15	.188	45.90
1876	13.50	SW¼	28	30	56	4-15—8-15	.166	40.50
1879	25.00	SW¼	28	30	56	4-15—8-15	.308	75.00
1880	25.00	SW¼	28	30	56	4-15—8-15	.308	75.00
1881	24.00	SW¼	28	30	56	4-15—8-15	.295	72.00
1882	24.50	SW¼	28	30	56	4-15—8-15	.301	73.50
1879	11.00	NW¼	28	30	56	4-15—8-15	.135	33.00
1880	11.00	NW¼	28	30	56	4-15—8-15	.135	33.00
1881	11.00	NW¼	28	30	56	4-15—8-15	.135	33.00
1882	12.00	NW¼	28	30	56	4-15—8-15	.148	36.00
1879	9.00	SE¼	28	30	56	4-15—8-15	.111	27.00
1882	9.00	SE¼	28	30	56	4-15—8-15	.111	27.00
1903	21.00	SE¼	28	30	56	4-15—8-15	.258	63.00
1880	1.00	NW¼	33	30	56	4-15—8-15	.012	3.00
1876	42.00	NW¼	33	30	56	4-15—8-15	.517	126.00
1879	16.60	NW¼	33	30	56	4-15—8-15	.204	49.80
1897	8.40	NW¼	33	30	56	4-15—8-15	.103	25.20
1880	17.00	NW¼	33	30	56	4-15—8-15	.209	51.00
1896	1.00	NW¼	33	30	56	4-15—8-15	.012	3.00
1879	38.00	NW¼	33	30	56	4-15—8-15	.467	114.00
1876	28.00	NE¼	33	30	56	4-15—8-15	.344	84.00
1901	18.00	NE¼	33	30	56	4-15—8-15	.221	54.00
1901	3.00	NE¼	33	30	56	4-15—8-15	.369	9.00
1903	9.00	NE¼	33	30	56	4-15—8-15	.111	27.00
1881	23.00	NE¼	33	30	56	4-15—8-15	.283	69.00
1903	15.00	NE¼	33	30	56	4-15—8-15	.185	45.00
1879	14.00	NE¼	33	30	56	4-15—8-15	.172	52.00
1880	14.00	NE¼	33	30	56	4-15—8-15	.172	52.00
1881	14.00	NE¼	33	30	56	4-15—8-15	.172	52.00
1882	14.00	NE¼	33	30	56	4-15—8-15	.172	52.00
1881	7.00	NW¼	34	30	56	4-15—8-15	.086	21.00
1903	9.00	NW¼	34	30	56	4-15—8-15	.111	27.00
1880	4.00	SW¼	33	30	56	4-15—8-15	.049	12.00
1876	25.50	SW¼	33	30	56	4-15—8-15	.314	76.50
1879	37.33	SW¼	33	30	56	4-15—8-15	.459	111.99
1900	48.00	SW¼	33	30	56	4-15—8-15	.590	144.00
1876	28.50	SE¼	33	30	56	4-15—8-15	.351	75.50
1901	62.50	SE¼	33	30	56	4-15—8-15	.769	187.50
1901	8.00	SE¼	33	30	56	4-15—8-15	.098	24.00
1903	56.50	SE¼	33	30	56	4-15—8-15	.695	169.50
1903	15.00	SW¼	34	30	56	4-15—8-15	.185	45.00
1879	8.67	NW¼	4	29	56	4-15—8-15	.107	26.01
1903	2.00	NE¼	4	29	56	4-15—8-15	.025	6.00
1881	6.00	NE¼	32	30	56	4-15—8-15	.074	18.00
1880	20.00	NE¼	32	30	56	4-15—8-15	.246	60.00

J. J. Hylton—Continued.

Year of priority	Culture—Acres: Harvest crops	Meadow pasture	Diversified pasture	Location: Subdivision	Section	Tp.N.	R.E.	Length of season	Duty of water: C.F.S.	Acre-feet
1896	56.00			NE¼	32	30	56	4-15—8-15	.689	168.00
1900	55.00			NE¼	32	30	56	4-15—8-15	.677	165.00
1894	2.00			SW¼	32	30	56	4-15—8-15	.025	6.00
1896	13.00			SW¼	32	30	56	4-15—8-15	.160	39.00
1900	12.00			SW¼	32	30	56	4-15—8-15	.148	36.00
1896	13.00			SE¼	32	30	56	4-15—8-15	.160	39.00
1900	13.00			SE¼	32	30	56	4-15—8-15	.160	39.00
1894	22.50			NW¼	5	29	56	4-15—8-15	.277	67.50
1894	3.00			SW¼	5	29	56	4-15—8-15	.369	9.00
1896	34.00			SE¼	30	30	56	4-15—8-15	.418	102.00
1900	33.00			SE¼	30	30	56	4-15—8-15	.406	99.00
1880	41.00			SW¼	29	30	56	4-15—8-15	.504	123.00
1881	4.50			SW¼	29	30	56	4-15—8-15	.055	13.50
1882	4.50			SW¼	29	30	56	4-15—8-15	.055	13.50
1896	25.00			SW¼	29	30	56	4-15—8-15	.308	75.00
1896	...		30.00	SW¼	29	30	56	4-15—5-15	.369	22.50
1900	55.00			SW¼	29	30	56	4-15—8-15	.677	40.50
1881	40.00			SE¼	29	30	56	4-15—8-15	.492	30.00
1896	20.00			SE¼	29	30	56	4-15—8-15	.246	15.00
1900	20.00			SE¼	29	30	56	4-15—8-15	.246	15.00
1879	14.00			SE¼	29	30	56	4-15—8-15	.172	10.50
1897	7.00			SE¼	29	30	56	4-15—8-15	.086	5.25
1879	4.30			SE¼	29	30	56	4-15—8-15	.053	3.23
1882	4.30			SE¼	29	30	56	4-15—8-15	.053	3.23
1880	20.50			SE¼	29	30	56	4-15—8-15	.252	61.50
1881	15.00			SE¼	29	30	56	4-15—8-15	.185	45.00
1882	15.00			SE¼	29	30	56	4-15—8-15	.185	45.00
1880	1.00			SE¼	29	30	56	4-15—8-15	.012	3.00
1894	29.00			SE¼	31	30	56	4-15—8-15	.357	87.00
1896	19.00			SE¼	31	30	56	4-15—8-15	.234	57.00
1900	18.00			SE¼	31	30	56	4-15—8-15	.221	54.00
1896	35.00			NW¼	32	30	56	4-15—8-15	.431	105.00
1900	35.00			NW¼	32	30	56	4-15—8-15	.431	105.00
1893	2.00			SE¼	6	29	56	4-15—8-15	.025	6.00
1891	17.00			SE¼	6	29	56	4-15—8-15	.209	51.00
1894	23.00			SE¼	6	29	56	4-15—8-15	.283	69.00
1893	9.00			NE¼	6	29	56	4-15—8-15	.111	27.00
1894	20.00			NE¼	6	29	56	4-15—8-15	.246	60.00
1894	49.00			NE¼	6	29	56	4-15—8-15	.603	147.00
1894	43.00			NE¼	7	29	56	4-15—8-15	.529	120.00
1875	1.00			NE¼	19	30	56	4-15—8-15	.012	3.00
1873	4.00			SE¼	19	30	56	4-15—8-15	.049	12.00
1895	10.00			SE¼	19	30	56	4-15—8-15	.123	30.00
1897	11.00			SE¼	19	30	56	4-15—8-15	.135	33.00
1900	10.00			SE¼	19	30	56	4-15—8-15	.123	30.00
1890	8.00			SE¼	19	30	56	4-15—8-15	.098	24.00

......	1879	......	......	23.00	......	......	......	SW¼	20	30	56	4-15—8-15	.283	69.00
......	1880	......	......	20.00	......	......	......	SE¼	19	30	56	4-15—8-15	.246	60.00
......	1881	......	......	18.00	......	......	......	SE¼	19	30	56	4-15—8-15	.221	54.00
......	1882	......	......	20.00	......	......	......	SE¼	19	30	56	4-15—8-15	.246	60.00
......	1880	......	......	2.00	......	......	......	NE¼	19	30	56	4-15—8-15	.025	6.00
......	1881	......	......	2.00	......	......	......	SE¼	19	30	56	4-15—8-15	.025	6.00
......	1881	......	......	3.25	......	......	......	NE¼	30	30	56	4-15—8-15	.040	9.75
......	1880	......	......	3.00	......	......	......	NW¼	29	30	56	4-15—8-15	.037	9.00
......	1879	......	......	15.00	......	......	......	NW¼	29	30	56	4-15—8-15	.185	45.00
......	1880	......	......	15.00	......	......	......	NW¼	29	30	56	4-15—8-15	.185	45.00
......	1881	......	......	15.00	......	......	......	NW¼	29	30	56	4-15—8-15	.185	45.00
......	1882	......	......	15.00	......	......	......	NW¼	29	30	56	4-15—8-15	.185	45.00
......	1879	......	......	21.00	......	......	......	NE¼	29	30	56	4-15—8-15	.258	63.00
......	1880	......	......	21.00	......	......	......	NE¼	29	30	56	4-15—8-15	.258	63.00
......	1881	......	......	21.00	......	......	......	NE¼	29	30	56	4-15—8-15	.258	63.00
......	1882	......	......	21.00	......	......	......	NE¼	29	30	56	4-15—8-15	.258	63.00
......	1896	......	......	21.00	......	......	......	NE¼	30	30	56	4-15—8-15	.258	63.00
......	1898	......	......	21.00	......	......	......	NE¼	30	30	56	4-15—8-15	.258	63.00
......	1900	......	......	20.50	......	......	......	NE¼	30	30	56	4-15—8-15	.242	61.50
......	1871	......	......	.75	......	......	......	SE¼	19	30	56	4-15—8-15	.009	2.25
......	1871	......	......	9.25	......	......	......	NW¼	29	30	56	4-15—8-15	.114	27.75
......	1872	......	......	18.00	......	......	......	NW¼	29	30	56	4-15—8-15	.221	54.00
......	1873	......	......	18.00	......	......	......	NW¼	29	30	56	4-15—8-15	.221	54.00
......	1874	......	......	18.00	......	......	......	NW¼	29	30	56	4-15—8-15	.221	54.00
......	1874	......	......	6.00	......	......	......	NW¼	29	30	56	4-15—8-15	.074	18.00
......	1876	......	......	5.00	......	......	......	NW¼	29	30	56	4-15—8-15	.062	15.00
......	1878	......	......	5.75	......	......	......	NW¼	29	30	56	4-15—8-15	.071	17.25
......	1875	......	......	13.00	......	......	......	NE¼	29	30	56	4-15—8-15	.160	39.00
......	1877	......	......	13.00	......	......	......	NE¼	29	30	56	4-15—8-15	.160	39.00
......	1879	......	......	12.00	......	......	......	NE¼	29	30	56	4-15—8-15	.148	36.00
......	1880	......	......	12.50	......	......	......	NW¼	29	30	56	4-15—8-15	.154	37.50
......	1880	......	......	16.50	......	......	......	NE¼	30	30	56	4-15—8-15	.203	49.50
......	1896	......	......	17.00	......	......	......	NE¼	30	30	56	4-15—8-15	.209	51.00
......	1900	......	......	17.00	......	......	......	NE¼	30	30	56	4-15—8-15	.209	51.00

Source—**South Fork Humboldt River.** Ditch—**J. J. Hylton Ditches.**

......	1870	......	......	217.40	......	......	......	SE¼	4	32	55			
......	1880	......	......	37.30	......	......	......	S½	3	32	55			
......	1888	......	......	333.40	......	......	......	......	10	32	55	4-15—8-15	2.674	652.20
......	1892	......	......	274.50	......	......	......	W½	11	32	55	4-15—8-15	.458	111.00
......	1893	......	......	79.50	......	......	......	N½	15	32	55	4-15—8-15	4.101	1000.20
......	1894	......	......	212.40	......	......	......	......	14	32	55	4-15—8-15	3.376	823.50
......	1894	......	......	..	307.00	......	......	E½	23	32	55	4-15—8-15	.978	238.50
......	1903	......	......	56.00	......	......	......	W½	24	32	55	4-15—8-15	2.612	637.20
								SE¼	24	32	55	4-15—8-15	3.776	460.50
								......	25	32	55	4-15—8-15	.689	168.00
......	1895	......	......	65.00	......	......	......	S½NE¼	15	31	57	4-15—8-15	.800	195.00
......	1896	......	......	20.00	......	......	......	SE¼	15	31	57	4-15—8-15	.246	60.00
......	1897	......	......	20.00	......	......	......	W½SW¼	14	31	57	4-15—8-15	.246	60.00
......	1898	......	......	15.00	......	......	......	SW¼NW¼	14	31	57	4-15—8-15	.185	45.00
......	1898	......	......	58.00	......	......	......	......	....	....	....	4-15—8-15	.713	174.00

Claimant—**Simon A. Merkley.** Proof No. 00360

Source—**McCutcheon Creek and Tributary.** Ditch—**Simon A. Merkley Ditches.**

Year of priority	Culture—Acres: Harvest crops	Culture—Acres: Meadow pasture	Culture—Acres: Diversified pasture	Location: Subdivision	Location: Section	Location: Tp.N.	Location: R.E.	Length of season	Duty of water: C.F.S.	Duty of water: Acre-feet
1889	5.00			E½SW¼	6	29	57	4-15—8-15	.062	15.00
1890	5.00			W½SE¼	6	29	57	4-15—8-15	.062	15.00
1892	7.00				....	....	....	4-15—8-15	.086	21.00
1900	15.50				....	....	....	4-15—8-15	.191	46.50

Priority on McCutcheon Creek proper starts with 1890.

Claimant—**Merkley & Young.** Proof No. 00361

Source—**Smith Creek.** Ditch—**Merkley & Young Ditches.**

Year of priority	Harvest crops	Meadow pasture	Diversified pasture	Subdivision	Section	Tp.N.	R.E.	Length of season	C.F.S.	Acre-feet
1868	45.00			SE¼NW¼	26	30	56	4-15—8-15	.554	135.00
1869	5.00			S½NE¼	26	30	56	4-15—8-15	.062	15.00
1870	5.00			S½	26	30	56	4-15—8-15	.062	15.00
1871	40.10			S½NW¼	25	30	56	4-15—8-15	.493	120.30
1872	91.80			S½	25	30	56	4-15—8-15	1.129	275.40
1872	....		14.50	E½NW¼	35	30	56	4-15—5-15	.178	43.50
1873	119.60			NE¼	35	30	56	4-15—8-15	1.471	358.80
1874	10.00			S½	35	30	56	4-15—8-15	.123	30.00
1875	60.70			W½	36	30	56	4-15—8-15	.747	182.10
1876	60.70			NE¼	36	30	56	4-15—8-15	.747	182.10
1877	....		19.20	NW¼SE¼	36	30	56	4-15—5-15	.236	57.60
1878	20.00			NE¼	2	29	56	4-15—8-15	.123	60.00
1886	59.70			W½NW¼	1	29	56	4-15—8-15	.734	179.10
1887	57.70				....	....	....	4-15—8-15	.734	179.10
1888	57.50				....	....	....	4-15—8-15	.707	178.50
1889	22.70				....	....	....	4-15—8-15	.279	68.10
1890	265.60				....	....	....	4-15—8-15	3.267	796.80
1891	41.40				....	....	....	4-15—8-15	.509	124.20
1892	13.90				....	....	....	4-15—8-15	.171	41.70
1893	13.90				....	....	....	4-15—8-15	.171	41.70
1893	....		66.00		....	....	....	4-15—5-15	.812	198.00
1893	....		35.00		....	....	....	4-15—5-15	.431	105.00
1894	....		126.00		....	....	....	4-15—5-15	1.550	378.00
1894	....		148.30		....	....	....	4-15—5-15	1.824	444.90
1900	....		63.30		....	....	....	4-15—5-15	.779	189.90
1904	7.00				....	....	....	4-15—8-15	.086	21.00
1894	....		117.50		....	....	....	4-15—5-15	1.445	352.50
1894			20.00		....	....	....	4-15—5-15	.246	60.00

Judgment and Decree No. 1355, Elko County District Court Records, is binding as between parties to the suit.

Source—**Huntington Creek.** Ditch—**Merkley & Young Ditches.**

Year of priority	Harvest crops	Meadow pasture	Diversified pasture	Subdivision	Section	Tp.N.	R.E.	Length of season	C.F.S.	Acre-feet
1884	92.52			W½	33	28	55	4-15—8-15	1.138	277.56
1886	335.79			W½E½	33	28	55	4-15—8-15	4.130	1007.37
1900	300.00			S½SW¼	28	28	55	4-15—8-15	3.000	900.00
				NW¼	4	27	55			
				SE¼NE¼	6	27	55			

E½SE¼	5	27	55
SW¼	4	27	55
E½NE¼	8	27	55
All	9	27	55

Reference is made to stipulation between Huntington and Diamond Valley Land and Stock Co. and J. J. Hylton, Merkley & Young and Frank Odiaga, regarding the use of waters of Huntington Creek. See Appendix A.

These lands were included in the suit H. H. Porch vs. U. Lani et al., No. 1614 Elko County Records. After listing dates and areas they were pooled and then listed in accordance with the decree.

Claimant—**Chas. Mitchell.** Proof No. **00362**

Source—**Springs and Gulch.** Ditch—**Chas. Mitchell Ditches.**

....	1879	....	....	2.80	....	....	....	SE¼NW¼	14	27	56	4-15—8-15	.034	8.40
....	1879	....	....	1.80	....	....	....	SW¼NW¼	14	27	56	4-15—8-15	.022	5.40
....	1879	....	....	11.30	....	....	....	NW¼SW¼	14	27	56	4-15—8-15	.139	33.90
....	1879	....	....	17.50	....	....	....	NE¼SW¼	14	27	56	4-15—8-15	.215	52.50
....	1879	....	....	11.20	....	....	....	NW¼SE¼	14	27	56	4-15—8-15	.138	33.60

Source—**Brown's Creek.** Ditch—**Chas. Mitchell Ditches.**

....	1876	....	....	78.12	....	....	....	NE¼NE¼	30	28	56	4-15—8-15	.961	234.36
....	1876	....	....	50.22	....	....	....	NW¼NW¼	29	28	56	4-15—8-15	.618	150.66
....	1876	....	....	...	....	4.65	....	S½NW¼	29	28	56	4-15—5-15	.057	3.49
....	1869	....	....	34.39	....	....	....	SW¼NE¼	29	28	56	4-15—8-15	.423	103.17
....	1869	....	....	....	....	4.34	....	N½S½	29	28	56	4-15—5-15	.053	3.26
....	1872	....	....	34.39	....	....	....	NE¼SE¼	29	28	56	4-15—8-15	.423	103.17
....	1872	....	....	...	....	4.34	....	N½SW¼	28	28	56	4-15—5-15	.053	3.26
....	1876	....	....	34.38	....	....	....	....	....	....	....	4-15—8-15	.423	103.14
....	1876	....	....	...	....	4.34	....	....	....	....	....	4-15—5-15	.053	3.26
....	1899	....	....	20.92	....	....	....	....	....	....	....	4-15—8-15	.257	62.76
....	1899	....	....	...	....	8.37	....	....	....	....	....	4-15—5-15	.103	6.28
....	1900	....	....	30.23	....	....	....	....	....	....	....	4-15—8-15	.372	90.69
....	1900	....	....	....	....	8.37	....	....	....	....	....	4-15—5-15	.103	6.28

Source—**Mitchell Creek.** Ditch—**Chas. Mitchell Ditches.**

....	1876	....	....	5.80	....	....	....	SW¼SW¼	35	27	56	4-15—8-15	.071	17.40
....	1876	....	....	5.00	....	....	....	NW¼SW¼	35	27	56	4-15—8-15	.062	15.00
....	1876	....	....	7.50	....	....	....	NE¼SW¼	35	27	56	4-15—8-15	.092	22.50
....	1876	....	....	31.00	....	....	....	SE¼SW¼	35	27	56	4-15—8-15	.381	93.00
....	1876	....	....	22.80	....	....	....	SW¼SE¼	35	27	56	4-15—8-15	.280	68.40
....	1876	....	....	15.20	....	....	....	SE¼SE¼	35	27	56	4-15—8-15	.187	45.60
....	1876	....	....	7.80	....	....	....	NE¼NE¼	2	26	56	4-15—8-15	.096	23.40
....	1876	....	....	4.00	....	....	....	NW¼NW¼	1	26	56	4-15—8-15	.049	12.00
....	1876	....	....	11.60	....	....	....	SW¼SW¼	36	27	56	4-15—8-15	.143	34.80
....	1876	....	....	10.50	....	....	....	SE¼SW¼	36	27	56	4-15—8-15	.129	31.50
....	1876	....	....	2.80	....	....	....	SW¼SE¼	36	27	56	4-15—8-15	.034	8.40
....	1876	....	....	0.70	....	....	....	NW¼SE¼	36	27	56	4-15—8-15	.009	2.10

Claimant—**F. Odiaga.** Proof No. 00363

Source—**Huntington Creek, Pearl Creek, Brown Creek, and Frost Canyon Creek.**

Ditch—**F. Odiaga Ditches.**

Year of priority	Culture—Acres: Harvest crops	Culture—Acres: Meadow pasture	Culture—Acres: Diversified pasture	Location: Subdivision	Location: Section	Location: Tp.N.	Location: R.E.	Length of season	Duty of water: C.F.S.	Duty of water: Acre-feet
1883	150.00			E½NW¼	1	28	55			
1884	150.00			SW¼NW¼	1	28	55			
				NW¼SW¼	1	28	55			
				NE¼SE¼	2	28	55			
				E½NE¼	24	29	55			
				SE¼	24	29	55			
				N½SE¼	25	29	55			
				SW¼SE¼	25	29	55			
				SE¼SW¼	25	29	55			
				NW¼	36	29	55	4-15—8-15	1.845	450.00
				E½SW¼	36	29	55	4-15—8-15	1.845	450.00
1889	101.60			W½SE¼	11	28	55			
1898	62.31			E½SW¼	11	28	55			
1900	140.57			SW¼SW¼	11	28	55			
				N½NW¼	14	28	55			
				SW¼NW¼	14	28	55			
				SE¼NE¼	15	28	55			
				N½SE¼	15	28	55			
				SW¼SE¼	15	28	55			
				NE¼SW¼	15	28	55			
				SE¼	24	29	55			
				N½SE¼	25	29	55			
				SW¼SE¼	25	29	55			
				SE¼SW¼	25	29	55	4-15—8-15	1.250	304.80
				NW¼	36	29	55	4-15—8-15	.766	186.93
				W½NE¼	36	29	55	4-15—8-15	1.729	421.71

NOTE—Odiaga acreage and description in accordance with Elko County Court decrees 1548 and 1644, which are binding as between parties to the suits.

Source—**Robinson Creek and Spring.** Ditch—**F. Odiaga Ditches.**

Year of priority	Harvest crops	Meadow pasture	Diversified pasture	Subdivision	Section	Tp.N.	R.E.	Length of season	C.F.S.	Acre-feet
1900	33.10			NW¼	11	28	55	4-15—8-15	.407	99.30

Source—**Huntington Creek and Springs.** Ditch—**F. Odiaga Ditches.**

Year of priority	Harvest crops	Meadow pasture	Diversified pasture	Subdivision	Section	Tp.N.	R.E.	Length of season	C.F.S.	Acre-feet
1869	28.90			NE¼	25	29	55	4-15—8-15	.355	86.70
1873	28.90			NE¼	25	29	55	4-15—8-15	.355	86.70
1876	28.95			NE¼	25	29	55	4-15—8-15	.356	86.85
1900	16.01				10	28	55	4-15—8-15	.197	48.03
1900	57.51			N½NE¼	15	28	55	4-15—8-15	.707	172.53
1900	40.00			SW¼NE¼	15	28	55	4-15—8-15	.492	120.00
1900	2.50			SE¼NW¼	15	28	55	4-15—8-15	.031	7.50

NOTE—Not in court decree, Porch vs. Lani et al. Reference is hereby made to stipulation between Huntington and Diamond Valley Land and Stock Co. and J. J. Hylton, Merkley & Young and Frank Odiaga, regarding the use of waters of Huntington Creek. See Appendix A.

Claimant—**P. J. Ogilvie.** Proof No. 00364

Source—**South Fork Humboldt River.** Ditch—**Ogilvie Ditch.**

	1905					11.20		S½	14	31	56	4-15—5-15	.138	8.40
	1905					25.00		S½	13	31	56	4-15—5-15	.308	18.75
	1868			40.06				N½	24	31	56	4-15—8-15	.492	120.00
	1873			3.00				W½NW¼	19	31	57	4-15—8-15	.037	9.00

Source—**South Fork of Humboldt River and Rattlesnake Creek.*** Ditch—**Ogilvie Ditch.**

	1901			29.00				S½	14	31	56	4-15—8-15	.357	87.00
	1901			149.00				S½	13	31	56	4-15—8-15	1.833	447.00
	1901			18.20				N½	24	31	56	4-15—8-15	.224	54.60
								W½NW¼	19	31	57			
	1875			117.40				S½	14	31	56	4-15—8-15	1.444	352.20
	1902			72.00				S½	13	31	56	4-15—8-15	.886	216.00
	1903			150.00				N½	24	31	56	4-15—8-15	1.845	450.00
	1905			115.00				W½NW¼	19	31	57	4-15—8-15	1.415	345.00

Source—**South Fork of Humboldt River and Rattlesnake Creek.** Ditch—**Company Ditch.**

	1901			18.60				S½	14	31	56	4-15—8-15	.229	55.80
	1901			14.10				S½	13	31	56	4-15—8-15	.173	42.30

Early water only from Rattlesnake Creek.

Claimant—**D. J. Riordan.** Proof No. 00365

Source—**Big Cottonwood and Little Cottonwood Creeks.** Ditch—**D. J. Riordan Ditches.**

	1888			....		29.50		S½NE¼	24	30	56	4-15—5-15	.363	22.13
	1888			63.10				N½SE¼	24	30	56	4-15—8-15	.776	189.30

Source—**Smith Creek.** Ditch—**D. J. Riordan Ditches.**

	1870			10.00				S½SE¼	24	30	56	4-15—8-15	.123	30.00
	1871			10.00				NE¼	25	30	56	4-15—8-15	.123	30.00
	1872			11.00				S½SW¼	19	30	57	4-15—8-15	.135	33.00
	1873			40.00				NW¼	30	30	57	4-15—8-15	.492	120.00
	1879			45.00				N½NE¼	30	30	57	4-15—8-15	.554	135.00
	1880			16.80				SE¼NE¼	30	30	57	4-15—8-15	.207	50.40
	1882			16.80				W½SW¼	30	30	57	4-15—8-15	.207	50.40
	1883			112.80				NE¼SW¼	30	30	57	4-15—8-15	1.387	338.40
	1884			....		27.60		SE¼	30	30	57	4-15—5-15	.339	20.70
	1884			16.70				NE¼	31	30	57	4-15—8-15	.205	50.10
	1887			112.80				W½NW¼	32	30	57	4-15—8-15	1.387	338.40
	1890			....		64.30			....	....	....	4-15—5-15	.791	48.23
	1890			112.70					....	....	....	4-15—8-15	1.386	338.10
	1893			12.00					....	....	....	4-15—8-15	.148	36.00
	1897			13.00					....	....	....	4-15—8-15	.160	39.00
	1900			....		43.20			....	....	....	4-15—5-15	.531	32.40
	1900			8.10					....	....	....	4-15—8-15	.100	24.30

Decree No. 1355, Elko County District Court Records, is binding as between parties to the suit.

Claimant—**Manuel Urrutia.** Proof No. 00366

Source—**South Fork of Humboldt River and Natural Draw.** Ditch—**Manuel Urrutia.**

Year of priority	Culture—Acres: Harvest crops	Meadow pasture	Diversified pasture	Location: Subdivision	Section	Tp.N.	R.E.	Length of season	Duty of water: C.F.S.	Acre-feet
1888	41.70			SW¼SE¼	25	22	55	4-15—8-15	.550	134.10
1898	23.63			E½NW¼	36	32	55	4-15—8-15	.291	70.89
1899	23.62			NE¼	36	32	55	4-15—8-15	.291	70.86
1905	6.25				...	...	...	4-15—8-15	.077	18.75
1905	24.60*				...	...	...	4-15—8-15	.303	73.80

*Water from natural draw. Claimant has no right to divert water from South Fork of Humboldt River for this area.

Claimant—**Estate Joseph Hennen.** Proof. No. 00368

Source—**Mitchell Creek.** Ditch—**Hennen Ditches.**

Year of priority	Harvest crops	Meadow pasture	Diversified pasture	Subdivision	Section	Tp.N.	R.E.	Length of season	C.F.S.	Acre-feet
1883	78.70				7	32	57	4-15—8-15	.968	236.10
1905	...		9.10		...	...	...	4-15—5-15	.112	6.83

Source—**Little Valley Spring.** Ditch—**Hennen Ditches.**

Year of priority	Harvest crops	Meadow pasture	Diversified pasture	Subdivision	Section	Tp.N.	R.E.	Length of season	C.F.S.	Acre-feet
1887	39.40			E½SW¼	31	33	57			
				SE¼	31	33	57			
				NW¼SW¼	32	33	57	4-15—8-15	.485	118.20

Source—**Butterfield Creek.** Ditch—**Hennen Ditches.**

Year of priority	Harvest crops	Meadow pasture	Diversified pasture	Subdivision	Section	Tp.N.	R.E.	Length of season	C.F.S.	Acre-feet
1881	59.00			S½NE¼	36	33	56			
1887	16.90			NE¼SE¼	36	33	56			
				SW¼	31	33	57	4-15—8-15	.726	177.00
				SW¼SE¼	31	33	57	4-15—8-15	.208	50.70

Source—**Young Creek.** Ditch—**Hennen Ditches.**

Year of priority	Harvest crops	Meadow pasture	Diversified pasture	Subdivision	Section	Tp.N.	R.E.	Length of season	C.F.S.	Acre-feet
1873	10.00			S½S½	5	32	57	4-15—8-15	.123	30.00
1874	20.00			N½NE¼	8	32	57	4-15—8-15	.246	60.00
1875	25.00			S½S½	4	32	57	4-15—8-15	.308	75.00
1876	112.40			N½N½	9	32	57	4-15—8-15	1.383	337.20
1876	...		17.40		...	...	...	4-15—5-15	.214	13.05
1877	112.30				...	...	...	4-15—8-15	1.381	336.90
1877	...		17.30		...	...	...	4-15—5-15	.214	12.98
1878	...		50.00		...	...	...	4-15—5-15	.615	37.50
1905	...		12.70		...	...	...	4-15—5-15	.156	9.53

That certain agreement signed by T. F. Brennen and J. Hennen in regard to the division of the waters of Young Creek, as recorded in Elko County, Book 4 of Misc. Records, pages 186 and 187, is binding as between the parties to agreement. The "miner's inch" referred to shall be defined as being the amount of water that will flow through an opening of one square inch and under a six-inch head.

The parties to this agreement are to construct and maintain a device in Young Creek in the NW¼NW¼, Sec. 14, T. 32 N, R. 57 E, that will automatically divide the stream according to the said agreement, the plans for said device to be approved by the State Engineer.

Source—**Butterfield Creek and Young Creek.** Ditch—**Hennen Ditches.**

Year of priority	Harvest crops	Meadow pasture	Diversified pasture	Subdivision	Section	Tp.N.	R.E.	Length of season	C.F.S.	Acre-feet
1905	...		15.30	NE¼	10	32	57	4-15—5-15	.188	11.48
1872	50.00			NE¼NW¼	10	32	57	4-15—5-15	.615	150.00

When not sufficient water in Butterfield Creek, balance to be made up from Young Creek.
NOTE. Stock water right from Butterfield Creek dated 1873.

Source—**Young Creek.** Ditch—**Hennen Ditches.**

1868	30.00			NW¼	10	32	57	4-15—8-15	.360	90.00
1869	30.00			W½NE¼	10	32	57	4-15—8-15	.360	90.00
1870	30.00			N½SE¼	10	32	57	4-15—8-15	.360	90.00
1871	30.00			NE¼SW¼	10	32	57	4-15—8-15	.369	90.00
1872	32.90			SW¼NE¼	10	32	57	4-15—8-15	.405	98.70
1873	....	110.00			....	....	...	4-15—8-15	1.353	165.00

Claimant—**Griswold-Henderson Livestock Co.** Proof No. 00369

Source—**Stoffer Creek.** Ditch—**Griswold-Henderson Ditches.**

1886	66.10			NE¼	30	33	57	4-15—8-15	.813	198.30

Source—**Butterfield Creek and Thompson Creek.** Ditch—**Griswold-Henderson Ditches.**

1868	155.00				2	32	57	4-15—8-15	1.907	465.00
1869	154.00				3	32	57	4-15—8-15	1.894	462.00
1870	154.00				4	32	57	4-15—8-15	1.894	462.00
1871	154.00				11	32	57	4-15—8-15	1.894	462.00
1873	...	152.10			...	....	....	4-15—6-15	1.871	228.15
1874	...	152.10			...	....	....	4-15—6-15	1.871	228.15
1874	..	97.80			...	....	....	4-15—6-15	1.203	146.70
1875	....	97.80			....	....	....	4-15—6-15	1.203	146.70
1905	...		21.40		....	...	....	4-15—5-15	.263	16.05

Source—**Springs.** Ditch—**Griswold-Henderson Ditches.**

1905	..		81.20	SW¼	11	32	57	4-15—5-15	.900	243.60

Claimant—**Ernest Hodges.** Proof No. 00370

Source—**Stoffer Creek.** Ditch—**Ernest Hodges Ditches.**

1903	99.00			S½NW¼	30	33	57			
				SW¼	30	33	57	4-15—8-15	1.218	297.00

Source—**Dry Creek and Springs.** Ditch—**Ernest Hodges Ditches.**

1901	48.00			SW¼	30	33	57	4-15—8-15	.500	144.00
1902	18.00				....	....	....	4-15—8-15	.221	54.00
1905	21.00				....	...	....	4-15—8-15	.258	63.00

Claimant—**Antone Zunino.** Proof No. 00371

Source—**Cottonwood Creek, Smith Creek, and Natural Draws.**
Ditch—**Antone Zunino Ditches.**

1874	6.00			SW¼	15	30	56	4-15—8-15	.074	18.00
1874	46.00			SW¼SE¼	15	30	56	4-15—8-15	.566	138.00
1875	45.80			E½NW¼	22	30	56	4-15—8-15	.563	137.40
1875	60.70			NE¼	22	30	56	4-15—8-15	.747	182.10
1876	40.00			SE¼	22	30	56	4-15—8-15	.492	120.00
1876	15.00			S½	23	30	56	4-15—8-15	.185	45.00
1877	44.00			SW¼NW¼	24	30	56	4-15—8-15	.541	132.00
1878	42.00			SW¼	24	30	56	4-15—8-15	.517	126.00

Antone Zunino—Continued.

Year of priority	Culture—Acres: Harvest crops	Meadow pasture	Diversified pasture	Location: Subdivision	Section	Tp.N.	R.E.	Length of season	Duty of water: C.F.S.	Acre-feet
1884	90.00			N½NW¼	25	30	56	4-15—8-15	1.107	270.00
1897	21.80							4-15—8-15	.268	65.40
1897	6.80							4-15—8-15	.084	20.40
1904	57.10							4-15—8-15	.070	171.30
1905			48.50					4-15—5-15	.597	145.50

Judgment and Decree No. 1355, Elko County District Court Records, is binding as between parties to the suit.

Claimant—**A. M. Griswold.** Proof No. 00372

Source—**South Fork Humboldt River.** Ditch—**Griswold Ditches.**

Year of priority	Harvest crops	Meadow pasture	Diversified pasture	Subdivision	Section	Tp.N.	R.E.	Length of season	C.F.S.	Acre-feet
1867	45.00			N½NW¼	10	31	56	4-15—8-15	.554	135.00
1869	27.00			NE¼	10	31	56	4-15—8-15	.332	81.00
1870	27.00			E½SE¼	10	31	56	4-15—8-15	.332	81.00
1870	10.00			S½NW¼	11	31	56	4-15—8-15	.123	30.00
1872	145.50			W½SW¼	11	31	56	4-15—8-15	1.790	436.50
1904	80.00			N½	14	31	56	4-15—8-15	.984	240.00
1904			27.00					4-15—5-15	.332	20.25
1904	7.00							4-15—8-15	.086	5.25
1904	55.00							4-15—8-15	.677	41.25
1904	28.00							4-15—8-15	.344	21.00
1904	25.00							4-15—8-15	.308	18.75
1904			10.00					4-15—5-15	.123	7.50
1904	50.00							4-15—8-15	.615	37.50
1904	55.00							4-15—8-15	.677	41.25
1904	35.00							4-15—8-15	.431	26.25
1904	16.00							4-15—8-15	.197	12.00
1904	15.00							4-15—8-15	.185	11.25
1871	38.50			S½NE¼	4	31	56	4-15—8-15	.474	114.50
1872	38.50			N½SE¼	4	31	56	4-15—8-15	.474	114.50
1873	38.50			SE¼SE¼	4	31	56	4-15—8-15	.474	114.50
1874	38.50			NW¼SW¼	3	31	56	4-15—8-15	.474	114.50
				S½SW¼	3	31	56			
1870	9.50			NE¼	4	31	56	4-15—8-15	.117	28.50
1871	10.00			NE¼SE¼	4	31	56	4-15—8-15	.123	30.00
1872	8.50			SW¼	3	31	56	4-15—8-15	.105	25.50
1873	8.50			SW¼NW¼	3	31	56	4-15—8-15	.105	25.50
1874	9.50			SW¼SE¼	3	31	56	4-15—8-15	.117	28.50
1875	7.50							4-15—8-15	.092	22.50
1881	9.00							4-15—8-15	.111	27.00
1881	8.00							4-15—8-15	.098	24.00
1900	8.00							4-15—8-15	.098	24.00
1901	28.50							4-15—8-15	.351	85.50

Claimant—**Arrascada Bros.** Proof No. 00373

Source—**South Fork.** Ditch—**Nos. 2 and 3.**

1883			23.53				E½E½	36	33	54			
1884			30.05				SE¼NE¼	25	33	54	4-15—8-15	.280	70.59
							NE¼SE¼	25	33	54	4-15—8-15	.480	117.15

Claimant—**W. R. Bellinger.** Proof No. 00374

Source—**South Fork Humboldt River.** Ditch—**W. R. Bellinger Ditches.**

1868			40.00				NW¼	4	31	56	4-15—8-15	0.492	120.00
1869			41.00				N½N½	5	31	56	4-15—8-15	0.504	122.00
1870			41.00				SE¼	31	32	56	4-15—8-15	0.504	122.00
1871			41.00				S½S½	32	32	56	4-15—8-15	0.504	122.00
1872			41.00								4-15—8-15	0.504	122.00
1873			41.00								4-15—8-15	0.504	122.00
1874			44.85								4-15—8-15	0.552	134.55
1881			7.00								4-15—8-15	0.086	21.00

NOTE—Fall pasture irrigation right on areas listed from 1868 to 1874.

Source—**South Fork Humboldt River.** Ditch—**Crane-Griswold.**

1870			9.50				N½NW¼	4	31	56	4-15—8-15	0.117	28.50
1871			10.00				S½SE¼	32	32	56	4-15—8-15	0.123	30.00
1872			8.50				SE¼SW¼	32	32	56	4-15—8-15	0.105	25.50
1873			8.50								4-15—8-15	0.105	25.50
1874			9.50								4-15—8-15	0.117	28.50
1875			7.50								4-15—8-15	0.092	22.50
1881			5.00								4-15—8-15	0.062	15.00

Claimants—**Minnie Hankins, Lillie Hankins, Elizabeth Hankins, Estate Jane Bellinger.** Proof No. 00375

Source—**South Fork of Humboldt.** Ditch—**Hankins & Bellinger Ditches.**

1870			22.00				W½	31	32	56	4-15—8-15	.271	66.00
1872			24.01				NE¼NW¼	6	31	56	4-15—8-15	.295	72.03
1873			24.01				N½NE¼	6	31	56	4-15—8-15	.295	72.03
1874			68.34				SE¼NE¼	6	31	56	4-15—8-15	.841	205.02
1903			35.00								4-15—8-15	.431	105.00
1904			31.00								4-15—8-15	.381	93.00
1905			44.36								4-15—8-15	.546	133.08

Claimant—**J. G. Hankins.** Proof No. 00377

Source—**Smith Creek and Willow Creek.** Ditch—**J. G. Hankins Ditches.**

1879			57.86				E½SE¼	25	31	55			
							NE¼	36	31	55			
							SW¼NW¼	30	31	56			
							NW¼SW¼	30	31	56	4-15—8-15	.712	173.58

J. G. Hankins—Continued.
Source—**Cottonwood Creek and Smith Creek.** Ditch—**J. G. Hankins Ditches.**

Year of priority	Culture—Acres: Harvest crops	Culture—Acres: Meadow pasture	Culture—Acres: Diversified pasture	Location: Subdivision	Location: Section	Location: Tp.N.	Location: R.E.	Length of season	Duty of water: C.F.S.	Duty of water: Acre-feet
1901	105.90			W½NE¼	1	30	55			
				NE¼NE¼	1	30	55			
				NW¼SE¼	1	30	55			
				SE¼	36	31	55	4-15—8-15	1.303	317.70
1879	110.07			E½SE¼	25	31	55			
				E½NE¼	36	31	55			
				S½NW¼	30	31	56			
				N½SW¼	30	31	56			
				SW¼SW¼	30	31	56			
				SW¼NW¼	31	31	56	4-15—8-15	1.354	330.21

Claimant—**Griswold-Henderson Livestock Co.** Proof No. **00378**
Source—**Ten-Mile Creek.** Ditch—**Yowell Ditch.**

Year of priority	Harvest crops	Meadow pasture	Diversified pasture	Subdivision	Section	Tp.N.	R.E.	Length of season	C.F.S.	Acre-feet
1888	11.20			NE¼SE¼	26	33	55	4-15—8-15	.138	33.60
1888	3.15			NW¼SE¼	26	33	55	4-15—8-15	.039	9.45
1888	11.10			SW¼SE¼	26	33	55	4-15—8-15	.137	33.30
1888	17.85			SE¼SW¼	26	33	55	4-15—8-15	.220	53.55
1888	12.09			E½E½	26	33	55	4-15—8-15	.149	36.27

Claimant—**J. J. Hylton.** Proof No. **00381**
Source—**Cottonwood Creek.** Ditch—**Nos. 1, 2, 3, 5, and 6.**

Year of priority	Harvest crops	Meadow pasture	Diversified pasture	Subdivision	Section	Tp.N.	R.E.	Length of season	C.F.S.	Acre-feet
1887	10.00			NE¼NE¼	16	30	56	4-15—8-15	.123	30.00
1887	23.20			NW¼NE¼	16	30	56	4-15—8-15	.285	69.60
1887	10.20			NE¼NW¼	16	30	56	4-15—8-15	.125	30.60
1887	5.40			SE¼SW¼	9	30	56	4-15—8-15	.066	16.20
1887	7.20			NW¼NW¼	16	30	56	4-15—8-15	.080	21.20
1888	4.20			NW¼NE¼	16	30	56	4-15—8-15	.052	12.60
1888	10.10			NE¼NW¼	15	30	56	4-15—8-15	.124	30.30
1888	5.40			SE¼SW¼	9	30	56	4-15—8-15	.066	16.20
1888	7.10			NW¼NW¼	16	30	56	4-15—8-15	.087	21.30
1889	4.20			NW¼NE¼	16	30	56	4-15—8-15	.052	12.60
1889	10.10			NE¼NW¼	16	30	56	4-15—8-15	.124	30.30
1889	5.40			SE¼SW¼	9	30	56	4-15—8-15	.066	16.20
1889	7.10			NW¼NW¼	16	30	56	4-15—8-15	.087	21.30
1890	4.10			NW¼NE¼	16	30	56	4-15—8-15	.050	12.30
1890	10.10			NE¼NW¼	16	30	56	4-15—8-15	.124	30.30
1890	5.40			SE¼SW¼	9	30	56	4-15—8-15	.066	16.20
1890	7.10			NW¼NW¼	16	30	56	4-15—8-15	.087	21.30
1890	2.00			N½SW¼	9	30	56	4-15—8-15	.025	6.00
1894	2.40			NW¼SW¼	15	30	56	4-15—8-15	.030	7.20
1894	7.90			SW¼NW¼	15	30	56	4-15—8-15	.097	23.70
1894	.60			SE¼NE¼	16	30	56	4-15—8-15	.007	1.80
1894	1.40			NE¼NE¼	16	30	56	4-15—8-15	.017	4.20

1894	1.00		NW¼NW¼	15	30	56	4-15—8-15	.012	3.00
1899	13.40		NE¼NE¼	16	30	56	4-15—8-15	.165	40.20
1899	3.50		NE¼SW¼	15	30	56	4-15—8-15	.043	10.50
1899	7.90		SW¼NW¼	15	30	56	4-15—8-15	.097	23.70
1899	.50		SE¼NE¼	16	30	56	4-15—8-15	.006	1.50
1899	1.00		NW¼NW¼	15	30	56	4-15—8-15	.012	3.00
1900	15.00		NW¼SW¼	15	30	56	4-15—8-15	.185	45.00
1904	1.30		SE¼NW¼	15	30	56	4-15—8-15	.016	3.90
1904	7.90		SW¼NW¼	15	30	56	4-15—8-15	.097	23.70
1904	.50		SE¼NE¼	16	30	56	4-15—8-15	.006	1.50
1904	1.30		NE¼NE¼	16	30	56	4-15—8-15	.016	3.90
1904	1.00		NW¼NW¼	15	30	56	4-15—8-15	.012	3.00

Claimant—**Chas. Dressi.** Proof No. 00382
Source—**Humboldt River.** Ditch—**Chas. Dressi Ditches.**

1873	....	286.10	S½NW¼	3	33	54	4-15—6-15	3.519	429.15
1881	....	15.00	NE¼	3	33	54	4-15—6-15	.185	12.50
1902	....	41.00	N½SW¼	3	33	54	4-15—6-15	.504	61.50
1903	....	42.80	N½SE¼	3	33	54	4-15—6-15	.526	64.20
			SE¼SE¼	3	33	54			
			E½SW¼SE¼	3	33	54			

Claimant—**Hunter Banks Company.** Proof No. 00382
Source—**South Fork of Humboldt.** Ditch—**Hunter Banks Co. Ditches.**

1869	25.00		....	10	33	54	4-15—8-15	.308	75.00
1871	193.70		SE¼	3	33	54	4-15—8-15	2.383	581.10
1875	179.60		S½SW¼	3	33	54	4-15—8-15	2.209	538.80
1886	37.20		....	—	—	—	4-15—8-15	.458	111.60
1890	81.00		....	....	....	....	4-15—8-15	.996	243.00
1890	160.00		NE¼	9	33	54	4-15—8-15	1.968	480.00
1875	1.60		NW¼	10	33	54	4-15—8-15	.020	4.80

Claimant—**Ed. Carville.** Proof No. 00383
Source—**South Fork Smith Creek and Basin Creek.** Ditch—**Ed. Carville Ditches.**

1870	56.00		W½	14	29	56	4-15—8-15	.689	168.00
1871	9.00		SE¼NE¼	15	29	56	4-15—8-15	.111	27.00
1872	159.68		NE¼SE¼	15	29	56	4-15—8-15	1.964	479.04
1873	55.00		E½NE¼	22	29	56	4-15—8-15	.677	165.00
1874	88.11		W½	23	29	56	4-15—8-15	1.084	264.33
1880	7.00		E½NW¼	26	29	56	4-15—8-15	.086	21.00
1890	18.45		E½	26	29	56	4-15—8-15	.227	55.35
1902	87.64		....	....	....	....	4-15—8-15	1.078	202.92
1903	34.18		....	....	....	....	4-15—8-15	.420	112.54

Claimant—**Drown Bros.** Proof No. 00385

Source—**South Fork of Humboldt River.** Ditch—**Drown Bros. Ditches.**

Year of priority	Culture—Acres: Harvest crops	Meadow pasture	Diversified pasture	Location: Subdivision	Section	Tp.N.	R.E.	Length of season	Duty of water: C.F.S.	Acre-feet
1868	40.00			S½NW¼	10	31	56	4-15—8-15	.492	120.00
1870	62.70			SW¼	10	31	56	4-15—8-15	.771	188.10
1880	20.00			W½SE¼	10	31	56	4-15—8-15	.246	60.00
1889	61.38			SE¼NW¼	11	31	56	4-15—8-15	.755	184.14
1901	60.00			S½NE¼	11	31	56	4-15—8-15	.738	180.00
1902	45.00			E½SW¼	11	31	56	4-15—8-15	.554	135.00
1903	20.00			SE¼	11	31	56	4-15—8-15	.246	60.00
1904	20.00							4-15—8-15	.246	60.00
1905	108.00							4-15—8-15	1.328	324.00
NOTE—Fall pasture right with 1874 priority.										
1905	30.30			NE¼NW¼	15	31	56	4-15—8-15	.373	90.00

Source—**South Fork of Humboldt,* South Branch of South Fork of Humboldt, Rock Spring Creek, Pearl Creek and Creek east of Pearl Creek.**
Ditch—**Drown Bros. Ditches.**

Year of priority	Harvest crops	Meadow pasture	Diversified pasture	Subdivision	Section	Tp.N.	R.E.	Length of season	C.F.S.	Acre-feet
1873	62.40			NW¼	21	31	57	4-15—8-15	.077	187.20
1874	6.00			S½	21	31	57	4-15—8-15	.074	18.00
1875	219.80			NW¼NE¼	21	31	57	4-15—8-15	2.704	659.40
1876	15.10			S½NE¼	21	31	57	4-15—8-15	.186	45.30
1879	29.60			N½NW¼	28	31	57	4-15—8-15	.364	88.80
1880	14.60			NE¼	28	31	57	4-15—8-15	.180	43.80
1881	14.50			NW¼	27	31	57	4-15—8-15	.178	43.50
1882	29.50			NE¼SW¼	27	31	57	4-15—8-15	.363	88.50
1882	...		77.00					4-15—5-15	.947	57.75
1884	42.30							4-15—8-15	.520	126.90
1885	31.00							4-15—8-15	.381	93.00
1886	32.90							4-15—8-15	.405	98.70
1887	20.20							4-15—8-15	.248	60.60
1888	11.20							4-15—8-15	.138	33.60
1889	23.10							4-15—8-15	.274	69.30
1892	11.90							4-15—8-15	.146	35.70
1895	11.90							4-15—8-15	.146	35.70
1898	11.90							4-15—8-15	.146	35.70
1898	...		43.50					4-15—5-15	.535	32.63
1901	11.90							4-15—8-15	.146	35.70
1904	11.90							4-15—8-15	.146	35.70
1904	...		121.80					4-15—5-15	1.498	91.35

*Right from South Fork and out of Ditch No. 2 to date from 1898.

Source—**Pearl Creek.** Ditch—**Drown Bros. Ditches.**

Year of priority	Harvest crops	Meadow pasture	Diversified pasture	Subdivision	Section	Tp.N.	R.E.	Length of season	C.F.S.	Acre-feet
1877	8.00			S½NW¼	27	31	57	4-15—8-15	.098	24.00
1878	3.00			NE¼SW¼	27	31	57	4-15—8-15	.037	18.00
1890	...		33.30					4-15—5-15	.410	24.98

Claimant—**X. B. Martin.** Proof No. 00368
Source—**Lee Creek and Welch Creek.** Ditch—**X. B. Martin Ditches.**

	1873	150.00		NE¼	8	31	57	4-15—8-15	1.845	450.00
	1874	50.00		N½SE¼	8	31	57	4-15—8-15	.615	150.00
	1874	20.00			9	51	57	4-15—8-15	.246	60.00
	1875	47.46		N½	10	31	57	4-15—8-15	.584	142.38
	1876	47.45						4-15—8-15	.584	142.35
	1877	47.45						4-15—8-15	.584	142.35
	1878	47.45						4-15—8-15	.584	142.35
	1879	47.45						4-15—8-15	.584	142.35
	1880	47.45						4-15—8-15	.584	142.35
	1881	47.45						4-15—8-15	.584	142.35
	1882	24.52						4-15—8-15	.302	73.56
	1882		30.30					4-15—5-15	.373	22.72
	1883		401.88					4-15—5-15	4.943	301.41
	1887	15.00						4-15—8-15	.185	45.00
	1905	15.00						4-15—8-15	.185	45.00

Claimant—**Albert Hankins.** Proof No. 00387
Source—**Smith, Big Cottonwood and Little Cottonwood Creeks.**
Ditch—**Albert Hankins Ditches.**

1875	35.00		W½NE¼	19	30	57	4-15—8-15	.431	105.00
1876	36.00		S½NW¼	19	30	57	4-15—8-15	.443	108.00
1880	36.00		N½SW¼	19	30	57	4-15—8-15	.443	108.00
1884	36.00		N½SE¼	19	30	57	4-15—8-15	.443	108.00
1888	36.72						4-15—8-15	.452	110.16
1876		24.00					4-15—5-15	.295	18.00
1880		24.00					4-15—5-15	.295	18.00
1884		24.00					4-15—5-15	.295	18.00
1888		25.11					4-15—5-15	.309	18.83

Decree No. 1355, Elko County District Court, is binding as between parties to the suit.

Claimant—**Estate of** Mamie **Winstead.** Proof No. 00388
Source—**Rattlesnake** Creek. Ditch—**Mamie Winstead Ditches.**

1869	35.00		NE¼	29	31	57	4-15—8-15	.431	105.00
1870	35.00		NW¼NW¼	28	31	57	4-15—8-15	.431	105.00
1871	35.00		S½NW¼	28	31	57	4-15—8-15	.431	105.00
1872	35.00		S½	28	31	57	4-15—8-15	.431	105.00
1873	7.66		W½SW¼	27	31	57	4-15—8-15	.094	22.98
1873		25.51	E½NW¼	33	31	57	4-15—5-15	.314	19.13
1876	90.00		N½NE¼	33	31	57	4-15—8-15	1.107	270.00
1877	29.87						4-15—8-15	.367	89.61
1878	29.87						4-15—8-15	.367	89.61
1879	29.87						4-15—8-15	.367	89.61
1880	29.87						4-15—8-15	.367	89.61
1881	29.87						4-15—8-15	.367	89.61

Estate of Mamie Winstead—Continued.

Year of priority	Harvest crops	Meadow pasture	Diversified pasture	Subdivision	Section	Tp. N.	R. E.	Length of season	C. F. S.	Acre-feet
1882	29.87							4-15—8-15	.367	89.61
1883	29.88							4-15—8-15	.368	89.64
1883			145.38					4-15—5-15	1.788	109.04

Source—**Pearl Creek.** Ditch—**Mamie Winstead Ditches.**

Year of priority	Harvest crops	Meadow pasture	Diversified pasture	Subdivision	Section	Tp. N.	R. E.	Length of season	C. F. S.	Acre-feet
1873			15.67	N½NE¼	29	31	57	4-15—5-15	.193	11.75

Claimant—**Leslie Carter.** Proof No. 00388

Source—**Rattlesnake Creek.** Ditch—**Leslie Carter Ditches.**

Year of priority	Harvest crops	Meadow pasture	Diversified pasture	Subdivision	Section	Tp. N.	R. E.	Length of season	C. F. S.	Acre-feet
1868	60.80			S½	19	31	57	4-15—8-15	.748	182.40
1869	60.70				30	31	57	4-15—8-15	.747	182.10
1870	60.70			S½SE¼	24	31	56	4-15—8-15	.747	182.10
1871	60.70			E½	25	31	56	4-15—8-15	.747	182.10
1872	60.70			E½SW¼	25	31	56	4-15—8-15	.747	182.10
1873			43.00					4-15—5-15	.529	91.05
1873	87.00							4-15—8-15	1.070	261.00
1874	28.60							4-15—8-15	.352	85.80
1875	53.60							4-15—8-15	.659	160.80
1876	16.20							4-15—8-15	.199	48.60
1877	16.20							4-15—8-15	.199	48.60
1878	16.20							4-15—8-15	.199	48.60
1880	48.50							4-15—8-15	.597	145.50
1881		12.20						4-15—6-15	.150	36.60
1881	118.70							4-15—8-15	1.460	18.30
1883	10.00							4-15—8-15	.123	30.00
1890	49.48							4-15—8-15	.600	128.44
1903			203.10					4-15—5-15	2.498	304.65
1881		45.00						4-15—6-15	.554	67.50
1868	15.00			W½	29	31	57	4-15—8-15	.185	45.00
1870	15.00			NE¼NW¼	32	31	57	4-15—8-15	.185	45.00
1872	15.00			NW¼NE¼	32	31	57	4-15—8-15	.185	45.00
1873	2.00							4-15—8-15	.025	6.00
1874	25.00							4-15—8-15	.308	75.00
1874	25.00							4-15—8-15	.308	75.00
1877	25.00							4-15—8-15	.308	75.00
1890	7.45							4-15—8-15	.092	22.35
1891	7.45							4-15—8-15	.092	22.35
1892	7.45							4-15—8-15	.092	22.35
1893	7.45							4-15—8-15	.092	22.35
1891	27.45							4-15—8-15	.338	82.35
1894			5.00					4-15—5-15	.615	3.75
1895	7.45							4-15—8-15	.092	22.35
1896	7.45							4-15—8-15	.092	22.35
1905			54.85					4-15—5-15	.075	41.14

Claimant—**A. J. Dewar.** Proof No. **00388**

Source—**South Fork Humboldt River.** Ditch—**A. J. Dewar Ditches.**

1874	100.00			S½S½	17	31	57	4-15—8-15	1.230	300.00
1875	12.00			S½	18	31	57	4-15—8-15	.148	36.00
1876	8.40			SE¼NE¼	19	31	57	4-15—8-15	.103	25.20
1876	2.00			N½NE¼	19	31	57	4-15—8-15	.025	6.00
1876	10.00			NE¼NW¼	19	31	57	4-15—8-15	.123	30.00
1876	.91							4-15—8-15	.011	2.73
1876	17.50							4-15—8-15	.215	52.50
1876			25.40					4-15—5-15	.312	19.05
1876			49.99					4-15—5-15	.615	37.49
1876			10.20					4-15—5-15	.125	7.65
1895	20.00							4-15—8-15	.246	60.00
1895	7.50							4-15—8-15	.092	22.50
1898			20.00					4-15—5-15	.246	15.00
1900	53.80							4-15—8-15	.662	161.40
1902	30.00							4-15—8-15	.369	90.00
1902			15.40					4-15—5-15	.189	11.55

Claimant—**Pete Genette & Co.** Proof No. **00391**

Source—**Big Cottonwood, Little Cottonwood, and Smith Creeks.**

Ditch—**Pete Genette & Co. Ditches.**

1873	35.00				20	30	57	4-15—8-15	.431	105.00
1874	35.00			SE¼NE¼	19	30	57	4-15—8-15	.431	105.00
1875	20.00							4-15—8-15	.246	60.00
1876	20.00							4-15—8-15	.246	60.00
1877	19.00							4-15—8-15	.234	57.00
1888	76.43							4-15—8-15	.940	229.29
1892	15.62							4-15—8-15	.192	46.86
1892	1.15							4-15—8-15	.014	3.45
1875		13.09			20	30	57	4-15—6-15	.161	19.63
1876		27.90		SE¼NE¼	19	30	57	4-15—6-15	.343	41.85
1877		49.75						4-15—6-15	.612	74.03
1888		70.58						4-15—6-15	.868	105.75
1892		37.12			20	30	57	4-15—6-15	.457	55.68
1900			36.27	S½SE¼	17	30	57	4-15—5-15	.446	27.20

Decree No. 1355, Elko County District Court Records, is binding as between parties to the suit.

Source—**Big Cottonwood Creek.** Ditch—**Pete Genette & Co. Ditches.**

1872	30.00				20	30	57			
				SE¼NE¼	19	30	57	4-15—8-15	.369	90.00

Decree No. 1355, Elko County District Court Records, is binding as between parties to the suit.

Source—**Smith Creek.** Ditch—**Pete Genette & Co. Ditches.**

1871	12.60			SW¼NE¼	29	30	57	4-15—8-15	.155	37.80
1872	21.45			S½NW¼	29	30	57	4-15—8-15	.264	64.35
1874	18.00			N½SW¼	29	30	57	4-15—8-15	.221	54.00
1876	12.00							4-15—8-15	.148	36.00

Pete Genette & Co.—Continued.

Year of priority	Culture—Acres: Harvest crops	Meadow pasture	Diversified pasture	Location: Subdivision	Section	Tp.N.	R.E.	Length of season	Duty of water: C.F.S.	Acre feet
1880	2.42							4 15 8 15	.030	7.26
1881	10.40							4 15 8 15	.120	31.47
1873		43.06		SW¼NE¼	29	30	57	4 15 6 15	.500	129.18
1870		6.50		S½NW¼	29	30	57	4 15 6 15	.060	16.77
1881		12.10		N½SW¼	29	30	57	4 15 6 15	.140	30.30

Claimant **A. J. Dewar.** Proof No. 00303

Source **Pearl Creek.** Ditch **A. J. Dewar Ditches.**

Year of priority	Harvest crops	Meadow pasture	Diversified pasture	Subdivision	Section	Tp.N.	R.E.	Length of season	C.F.S.	Acre feet
1898	28.70			SE¼NE¼	19	31	57	4 15 8 15	.363	86.10

Claimant **Chris Baumbach (Peterson Ranch).** Proof No. 00304

Source **Rattlesnake Creek.** Ditch **Chris Baumbach Ditches.**

Year of priority	Harvest crops	Meadow pasture	Diversified pasture	Subdivision	Section	Tp.N.	R.E.	Length of season	C.F.S.	Acre feet
				S½NW¼	19	31	57			
1873	55.00			SW¼NE¼	19	31	57	4 15 8 15	0.064	100.00
1881	18.84			NE¼SW¼	19	31	57	4 15 8 15	0.222	50.59
1904	54.80			SE¼	19	31	57	4 15 8 15	0.075	104.58
				SW¼SW¼	20	31	57			

Source **Pearl Creek.** Ditch **Chris Baumbach Ditches.**

Year of priority	Harvest crops	Meadow pasture	Diversified pasture	Subdivision	Section	Tp.N.	R.E.	Length of season	C.F.S.	Acre feet
1880	2.00			NW¼NE¼	19	31	57	4 15 8 15	.020	6.00

Claimant **Merkley & Young.** Proof No. 00307

Source **Smith Creek.** Ditch **Merkley & Young Ditches.**

Year of priority	Harvest crops	Meadow pasture	Diversified pasture	Subdivision	Section	Tp.N.	R.E.	Length of season	C.F.S.	Acre feet
1905			33.10	E½NE¼	34	30	56	4 15 5 15	.407	91.80
1905	16.14			SE¼NE¼	34	30	56	4 15 8 15	.100	48.42
1900	10.61			W½NE¼	35	30	56	4 15 8 15	.241	68.00
1908	14.00							4 15 8 15	.179	42.00
1904	6.42							4 15 8 15	.079	10.90
1905	6.42							4 15 8 15	.079	10.90

Claimant **Eureka Land and Stock Co.** Proof No. 00308

Source **Smith Creek No. 2.** Ditch **Nos. 1-21, Inc.**

Year of priority	Harvest crops	Meadow pasture	Diversified pasture	Subdivision	Section	Tp.N.	R.E.	Length of season	C.F.S.	Acre feet
1900	2.06			NW¼NW¼	24	20	54	4 15 8 15	.020	6.24
1900	7.40			NE¼NW¼	24	20	54	4 15 8 15	.062	22.44
1900	7.15			SW¼NE¼	24	20	54	4 15 8 15	.068	21.45
1900	2.00			NW¼NE¼	24	20	54	4 15 8 15	.030	7.00
1900	7.75			NE¼NE¼	24	20	54	4 15 8 15	.065	23.25
1900	.37			SE¼NE¼	24	20	54	4 15 8 15	.005	1.11
1900	7.80			NW¼NW¼	19	20	55	4 15 8 15	.067	23.07
1900	2.82			SW¼NW¼	19	20	55	4 15 8 15	.025	8.46
1900	10.70			SE¼NW¼	19	20	55	4 15 8 15	.100	32.10
1900	[illegible]			NE¼NW¼	19	20	55	4 15 8 15	[illegible]	[illegible]

	1889			13.44				NW¼NE¼	19	20	55	4-15—8-15	.165	40.32
	1880			17.30				SW¼NE¼	19	29	55	4-15—8-15	.213	51.90
	1890			19.48				NE¼NE¼	19	29	55	4-15—8-15	.240	58.44
	1890			3.14				SE¼NE¼	19	20	55	4-15—8-15	.039	9.42
	1890			3.62				NW¼NW¼	19	20	55	4-15—8-15	.045	10.86
	1890			....		9.50		NW¼NW¼	19	29	55	4-15—8-15	.117	7.13
	1890			.12				SW¼NW¼	19	29	55	4-15—8-15	.001	.36
	1890			....		5.81		NE¼NW¼	19	20	55	4-15—8-15	.071	4.36

Claimant—**C. P. McNew.** Proof No. 00399
Source—**South Fork Humboldt River.** Ditch—**C. P. McNew.**

	1881			22.09				NE¼SE¼	13	31	56	4-15—8-15	.272	66.27

Claimant—**A. J. Dewar.** Proof No. 00399
Source—**South Fork Humboldt River.** Ditch—**A. J. Dewar Ditches.**

	1881			14.16				NE¼SE¼	13	31	56	4-15—8-15	0.174	42.48
	1900			6.60				W½SW¼	18	31	57	4-15—8-15	0.081	19.80

Claimant—**W. S. Griswold.** Proof No. 00400
Source—**Sheep Creek.** Ditch—**Nos. 1-5.**

	1904			66.08				N½N½	32	32	57	4-15—8-15	.813	198.24

Claimant—**W. R. Bellinger.** Proof No. 00401
Source—**Lamoille Creek.** Ditch—**W. R. Bellinger Ditches.**

	1897			12.00				W½W½	30	33	58	4-15—8-15	.148	36.00
	1904			13.00				S½SW¼	30	33	58	4-15—8-15	.160	39.00
	1870			.80				E½W½	30	33	58	4-15—8-15	.010	2.40
	1871			12.45					....	....	....	4-15—8-15	.153	37.35
	1872			4.21					....	....	....	4-15—8-15	.052	12.63
	1873			4.70					....	....	....	4-15—8-15	.058	14.10
	1874			3.82					....	....	....	4-15—8-15	.047	11.46
	1875			19.11					....	....	....	4-15—8-15	.235	57.33
	1876			6.79					....	....	....	4-15—8-15	.084	20.37
	1877			4.10					....	....	....	4-15—8-15	.050	12.30
	1878			4.02					....	....	....	4-15—8-15	.049	12.06

Claimant—**Mrs. C. Glaser.** Proof No. 00402
Source—**Rabbit Creek.** Ditch—**Glaser Ditches.**

	1872			185.10				SW¼	36	35	57			
								NW¼	1	34	57			
								W½SW¼	1	34	57			
								E½SE¼	2	34	57			
								SE¼NE¼	2	34	57	4-15—8-15	2.277	555.30

Estate of Mamie Winstead—Continued.

Year of priority	Culture—Acres: Harvest crops	Meadow pasture	Diversified pasture	Location: Subdivision	Section	Tp.N.	R.E.	Length of season	Duty of water: C.F.S.	Acre-feet
1882	29.87							4-15—8-15	.367	89.61
1883	29.88							4-15—8-15	.368	89.64
1883			145.38					4-15—5-15	1.788	109.04

Source—**Pearl Creek.** Ditch—**Mamie Winstead Ditches.**

Year of priority	Harvest crops	Meadow pasture	Diversified pasture	Subdivision	Section	Tp.N.	R.E.	Length of season	C.F.S.	Acre-feet
1873			15.67	N½NE¼	29	31	57	4-15—5-15	.193	11.75

Claimant—**Leslie Carter.** Proof No. 00388

Source—**Rattlesnake Creek.** Ditch—**Leslie Carter Ditches.**

Year of priority	Harvest crops	Meadow pasture	Diversified pasture	Subdivision	Section	Tp.N.	R.E.	Length of season	C.F.S.	Acre-feet
1868	60.80			S½	19	31	57	4-15—8-15	.748	182.40
1869	60.70				30	31	57	4-15—8-15	.747	182.10
1870	60.70			S½SE¼	24	31	56	4-15—8-15	.747	182.10
1871	60.70			E½	25	31	56	4-15—8-15	.747	182.10
1872	60.70			E½SW¼	25	31	56	4-15—8-15	.747	182.10
1873			43.00					4-15—5-15	.529	91.05
1873	87.00							4-15—8-15	1.070	261.00
1874	28.60							4-15—8-15	.352	85.80
1875	53.60							4-15—8-15	.659	160.80
1876	16.20							4-15—8-15	.199	48.60
1877	16.20							4-15—8-15	.199	48.60
1878	16.20							4-15—8-15	.199	48.60
1880	48.50							4-15—8-15	.597	145.50
1881		12.20						4-15—6-15	.150	36.60
1881	118.70							4-15—8-15	1.460	18.30
1883	10.00							4-15—8-15	.123	30.00
1890	49.48							4-15—8-15	.609	128.44
1903			203.10					4-15—5-15	2.498	304.65
1881		45.00						4-15—6-15	.554	67.50
1868	15.00			W½	29	31	57	4-15—8-15	.185	45.00
1870	15.00			NE¼NW¼	32	31	57	4-15—8-15	.185	45.00
1872	15.00			NW¼NE¼	32	31	57	4-15—8-15	.185	45.00
1873	2.00							4-15—8-15	.025	6.00
1874	25.00							4-15—8-15	.308	75.00
1874	25.00							4-15—8-15	.308	75.00
1877	25.00							4-15—8-15	.308	75.00
1890	7.45							4-15—8-15	.092	22.35
1891	7.45							4-15—8-15	.092	22.35
1892	7.45							4-15—8-15	.092	22.35
1893	7.45							4-15—8-15	.092	22.35
1894	27.45							4-15—8-15	.338	82.35
1894			5.00					4-15—5-15	.615	3.75
1895	7.45							4-15—8-15	.092	22.35
1896	7.45							4-15—8-15	.092	22.35
1905			54.85					4-15—5-15	.070	41.14

Claimant—**A. J. Dewar.** Proof No. **00388**

Source—**South Fork Humboldt River.** Ditch—**A. J. Dewar Ditches.**

	1874			100.00				S½S½	17	31	57	4-15—8-15	1.230	300.00
	1875			12.00				S½	18	31	57	4-15—8-15	.148	36.00
	1876			8.40				SE¼NE¼	19	31	57	4-15—8-15	.103	25.20
	1876			2.00				N½NE¼	19	31	57	4-15—8-15	.025	6.00
	1876			10.00				NE¼NW¼	19	31	57	4-15—8-15	.123	30.00
	1876			.91								4-15—8-15	.011	2.73
	1876			17.50								4-15—8-15	.215	52.50
	1876					25.40						4-15—5-15	.312	19.05
	1876					49.99						4-15—5-15	.615	37.49
	1876					10.20						4-15—5-15	.125	7.65
	1895			20.00								4-15—8-15	.246	60.00
	1895			7.50								4-15—8-15	.092	22.50
	1898					20.00						4-15—5-15	.246	15.00
	1900			53.80								4-15—8-15	.662	161.40
	1902			30.00								4-15—8-15	.369	90.00
	1902					15.40						4-15—5-15	.189	11.55

Claimant—**Pete Genette & Co.** Proof No. **00391**

Source—**Big Cottonwood, Little Cottonwood, and Smith Creeks.**

Ditch—**Pete Genette & Co. Ditches.**

	1873			35.00					20	30	57	4-15—8-15	.431	105.00
	1874			35.00				SE¼NE¼	19	30	57	4-15—8-15	.431	105.00
	1875			20.00								4-15—8-15	.246	60.00
	1876			20.00								4-15—8-15	.246	60.00
	1877			19.00								4-15—8-15	.234	57.00
	1888			76.43								4-15—8-15	.940	229.29
	1892			15.62								4-15—8-15	.192	46.86
	1892			1.15								4-15—8-15	.014	3.45
	1875				13.09				20	30	57	4-15—6-15	.161	19.63
	1876				27.90			SE¼NE¼	19	30	57	4-15—6-15	.343	41.85
	1877				49.75							4-15—6-15	.612	74.63
	1888				70.58							4-15—6-15	.868	105.75
	1892				37.12				20	30	57	4-15—6-15	.457	55.68
	1900					36.27		S½SE¼	17	30	57	4-15—5-15	.446	27.20

Decree No. 1355, Elko County District Court Records, is binding as between parties to the suit.

Source—**Big Cottonwood Creek.** Ditch—**Pete Genette & Co. Ditches.**

	1872			30.00					20	30	57			
								SE¼NE¼	19	30	57	4-15—8-15	.369	90.00

Decree No. 1356, Elko County District Court Records, is binding as between parties to the suit.

Source—**Smith Creek.** Ditch—**Pete Genette & Co. Ditches.**

	1871			12.60				SW¼NE¼	29	30	57	4-15—8-15	.155	37.80
	1872			21.45				S½NW¼	29	30	57	4-15—8-15	.264	64.35
	1874			18.00				N½SW¼	29	30	57	4-15—8-15	.221	54.00
	1876			12.00								4-15—8-15	.148	36.00

Pete Genette & Co.—Continued.

Year of priority	Culture—Acres: Harvest crops	Meadow pasture	Diversified pasture	Location: Subdivision	Section	Tp.N.	R.E.	Length of season	Duty of water: C.F.S.	Acre-feet
1880	2.42							4-15—8-15	.030	7.26
1881	10.49							4-15—8-15	.129	31.47
1872		43.06		SW¼NE¼	29	30	57	4-15—6-15	.530	129.18
1876		5.59		S½NW¼	29	30	57	4-15—6-15	.069	16.77
1881		12.10		N½SW¼	29	30	57	4-15—6-15	.149	36.30

Claimant—**A. J. Dewar.** Proof No. 00393
Source—**Pearl Creek.** Ditch—**A. J. Dewar Ditches.**

Year of priority	Harvest crops	Meadow pasture	Diversified pasture	Subdivision	Section	Tp.N.	R.E.	Length of season	C.F.S.	Acre-feet
1898	28.70			SE¼NE¼	19	31	57	4-15—8-15	.353	86.10

Claimant—**Chris Baumbach (Peterson Ranch).** Proof No. 00394
Source—**Rattlesnake Creek.** Ditch—**Chris Baumbach Ditches.**

Year of priority	Harvest crops	Meadow pasture	Diversified pasture	Subdivision	Section	Tp.N.	R.E.	Length of season	C.F.S.	Acre-feet
				S½NW¼	19	31	57			
1873	55.60			SW¼NE¼	19	31	57	4-15—8-15	0.684	166.80
1883	18.84			NE¼SW¼	19	31	57	4-15—8-15	0.232	56.52
1904	54.86			SE¼	19	31	57	4-15—8-15	0.675	164.58
				SW¼SW¼	20	31	57			

Source—**Pearl Creek.** Ditch—**Chris Baumbach Ditches.**

Year of priority	Harvest crops	Meadow pasture	Diversified pasture	Subdivision	Section	Tp.N.	R.E.	Length of season	C.F.S.	Acre-feet
1880	2.00			SW¼NE¼	19	31	57	4-15—8-15	.025	6.00

Claimant—**Merkley & Young.** Proof No. 00397
Source—**Smith Creek.** Ditch—**Merkley & Young Ditches.**

Year of priority	Harvest crops	Meadow pasture	Diversified pasture	Subdivision	Section	Tp.N.	R.E.	Length of season	C.F.S.	Acre-feet
1895			33.10	E½SE¼	34	30	56	4-15—5-15	.407	24.83
1895	16.14			SE¼NE¼	34	30	56	4-15—8-15	.199	48.42
1899	19.61			W½NE¼	35	30	56	4-15—8-15	.241	58.83
1903	14.00							4-15—8-15	.172	42.00
1904	6.42							4-15—8-15	.079	19.26
1905	6.42							4-15—8-15	.079	19.26

Claimant—**Eureka Land and Stock Co.** Proof No. 00398
Source—**Smith Creek No. 2.** Ditch—**Nos. 1-21, Inc.**

Year of priority	Harvest crops	Meadow pasture	Diversified pasture	Subdivision	Section	Tp.N.	R.E.	Length of season	C.F.S.	Acre-feet
1890	2.08			SW¼NW¼	24	29	54	4-15—8-15	.026	6.24
1890	7.48			SE¼NW¼	24	29	54	4-15—8-15	.092	22.44
1890	7.15			SW¼NE¼	24	29	54	4-15—8-15	.088	21.45
1890	2.66			NW¼NE¼	24	29	54	4-15—8-15	.033	7.98
1890	7.75			NE¼NE¼	24	29	54	4-15—8-15	.095	23.25
1890	.37			SE¼NE¼	24	29	54	4-15—8-15	.005	1.11
1890	7.89			NW¼NW¼	19	29	55	4-15—8-15	.097	23.67
1890	2.82			SW¼NW¼	19	29	55	4-15—8-15	.035	8.46
1890	10.70			SE¼NW¼	19	29	55	4-15—8-15	.132	[illegible]
1890	8.80			NE¼NW¼	19	29	55	4-15—8-15	.109	26.40

	1889			13.44				NW¼NE¼	19	29	55	4-15—8-15	.165	40.32
	1889			17.30				SW¼NE¼	19	29	55	4-15—8-15	.213	51.90
	1890			19.48				NE¼NE¼	19	29	55	4-15—8-15	.240	58.44
	1890			3.14				SE¼NE¼	19	29	55	4 15—8-15	.039	9.42
	1890			3.62				NW¼NW¼	19	29	55	4-15—8-15	.045	10.86
	1890			....		9.50		NW¼NW¼	19	29	55	4-15—6-15	.117	7.13
	1890			.12				SW¼NW¼	19	29	55	4-15—8-15	.001	.36
	1890			....		5.81		NE¼NW¼	19	29	55	4-15—6-15	.071	4.36

Claimant—**C. P. McNew.** Proof No. 00399
Source—**South Fork Humboldt River.** Ditch—**C. P. McNew.**

	1881			22.09				NE¼SE¼	13	31	56	4-15—8-15	.272	66.27

Claimant—**A. J. Dewar.** Proof No. 00399
Source—**South Fork Humboldt River.** Ditch—**A. J. Dewar Ditches.**

	1881			14.16				NE¼SE¼	13	31	56	4-15—8-15	0.174	42.48
	1900			6.60				W½SW¼	18	31	57	4-15—8-15	0.081	19.80

Claimant—**W. S. Griswold.** Proof No. 00400
Source—**Sheep Creek.** Ditch—**Nos. 1-5.**

	1904			66.08				N½N½	32	32	57	4-15—8-15	.813	198.24

Claimant—**W. R. Bellinger.** Proof No. 00401
Source—**Lamoille Creek.** Ditch—**W. R. Bellinger Ditches.**

	1867			12.00				W½W½	30	33	58	4-15—8-15	.148	36.00
	1904			13.00				S½SW¼	30	33	58	4-15—8-15	.100	39.00
	1870			.80				E½W½	30	33	58	4-15—8-15	.010	2.40
	1871			12.45					....	....	....	4-15—8-15	.153	37.35
	1872			4.21					....	....	....	4-15—8-15	.052	12.63
	1873			4.70					....	....	....	4-15—8-15	.058	14.10
	1874			3.82					....	....	....	4-15—8-15	.047	11.46
	1875			19.11					....	....	....	4-15—8-15	.235	57.33
	1876			6.79					....	....	....	4-15—8-15	.084	20.37
	1877			4.10					....	....	....	4-15—8-15	.050	12.30
	1878			4.02					....	....	....	4-15—8-15	.049	12.06

Claimant—**Mrs. C. Glaser.** Proof No. 00402
Source—**Rabbit Creek.** Ditch—**Glaser Ditches.**

	1872			185.10				SW¼	36	35	57			
								NW¼	1	34	57			
								W½SW¼	1	34	57			
								E½SE¼	2	34	57			
								SE¼NE¼	2	34	57	4-15—8-15	2.277	555.30

Claimant—**Manuel Erro.** Proof No. 00404
Source—**Lamoille Creek.** Ditch—**Erro Ditches.**

Year of priority	Harvest crops (Culture—Acres)	Meadow pasture (Culture—Acres)	Diversified pasture (Culture—Acres)	Subdivision (Location)	Section (Location)	Tp.N. (Location)	R.E. (Location)	Length of season	C.F.S. (Duty of water)	Acre-feet (Duty of water)
1900	15.50			SE¼ NE¼	13	33	57	4-15—8-15	.194	46.50
1900	3.70			SE¼ NE¼	13	33	57	4-15—8-15	.046	11.10

Claimant—**Hankins-Bellinger Co.** Proof No. 00405
Source—**Lamoille Creek.** Ditch—**Hankins-Bellinger Ditches.**

Year of priority	Harvest crops	Meadow pasture	Diversified pasture	Subdivision	Section	Tp.N.	R.E.	Length of season	C.F.S.	Acre-feet
1865	16.00			SW¼	18	33	58	4-15—8-15	.197	48.00
1868	4.00			NW¼	19	33	58	4-15—8-15	.049	12.00
*A1868	19.42			NW¼ NW¼	24	33	58	4-15—8-15	.240	58.26
1869	33.88							4-15—8-15	.417	101.64
1870	3.54							4-15—8-15	.044	10.62
1871	54.76							4-15—8-15	.674	164.28
1872	18.51							4-15—8-15	.228	55.53
1873	20.68							4-15—8-15	.254	62.04
1874	16.81							4-15—8-15	.207	61.92
1875	84.08							4-15—8-15	1.034	252.24
1876	29.89							4-15—8-15	.368	80.67
1877	18.03							4-15—8-15	.222	54.09
1878	17.70							4-15—8-15	.218	53.10

*1868 prior right over A1868.
NOTE—After exchanging dates and areas to conform to Lamoille Court Decree No. 1311 Elko County District Court.

Year of priority	Harvest crops	Meadow pasture	Diversified pasture	Subdivision	Section	Tp.N.	R.E.	Length of season	C.F.S.	Acre-feet
1888	1.50			E½ NE¼	24	33	57	4-15—8-15	.018	4.50
1896	8.00			NW¼ SW¼	19	33	58	4-15—8-15	.098	24.00
1900	17.00			SW¼ SW¼	18	33	58	4-15—8-15	.209	51.00
1901	25.10							4-15—8-15	.309	75.30
1904	8.40							4-15—8-15	.103	25.20

Claimant—**Mrs. Johanna Eisenberg.** Proof No. 00406
Source—**Lamoille Creek.** Ditch—**Mrs. Johanna Eisenberg Ditches.**

Year of priority	Harvest crops	Meadow pasture	Diversified pasture	Subdivision	Section	Tp.N.	R.E.	Length of season	C.F.S.	Acre-feet
1904	33.00			NE¼	31	33	58	4-15—8-15	.406	99.00

Claimant—**Henderson Banking Co.** Proof No. 00407
Source—**Lamoille Creek.** Ditch—**Cahill Reboule.**

Year of priority	Harvest crops	Meadow pasture	Diversified pasture	Subdivision	Section	Tp.N.	R.E.	Length of season	C.F.S.	Acre-feet
A1868 (a)	32.79			E½ W½	20	33	58	4-15—8-15	.403	98.37
1869	57.21			NE¼	20	33	58	4-15—8-15	.704	171.63
1870	1.00			SE¼	20	33	58	4-15—8-15	.012	3.00
1871	15.56			W½ NW¼	21	33	58	4-15—8-15	.191	46.68
1872	5.26							4-15—8-15	.065	15.78
1873	5.88							4-15—8-15	.072	17.64
1874	4.78							4-15—8-15	.059	14.34
1875	23.69							4-15—8-15	.294	71.07
1876	8.49							4-15—8-15	.104	25.47

1877		5.12					4-15—8-15	.063	15.36
1878		5.02					4-15—8-15	.062	15.06
A1878	(b)	9.78					4-15—8-15	.120	29.34
1879		51.80					4-15—8-15	.637	155.40
1880		79.74					4-15—8-15	.981	239.22
1881		6.12					4-15—8-15	.075	18.36
1882		8.42					4-15—8-15	.104	25.26
1883		12.72					4-15—8-15	.154	38.16
1884		17.69					4-15—8-15	.218	53.07
1885		4.08					4-15—8-15	.050	12.24
1896		5.91					4-15—8-15	.073	17.73
1887		8.16					4-15—8-15	.100	24.48
1888		7.55					4-15—8-15	.093	22.65
1889		7.55					4-15—8-15	.093	22.65
1890		4.08					4-15—8-15	.050	12.24
1894		4.08					4-15—8-15	.050	12.24
1895		32.82					4-15—8-15	.404	98.46

(a) 1868 prior right over A1868. (b) 1878 prior right over A1878.
NOTE—After exchanging dates and areas to conform to Lamoille Court Decree No. 1311 Elko District Court.

Source—**Talbot Creek.** Ditch—**Henderson Ditches.**

1873	20.00	SE¼	20	33	58	4-15—8-15	.246	60.00
1879	10.00	W½W½	21	33	58	4-15—8-15	.123	30.00
1885	12.00					4-15—8-15	.148	36.00
1892	15.00					4-15—8-15	.185	45.00
1898	45.00					4-15—8-15	.556	135.00
1904	45.00					4-15—8-15	.556	135.00
1904	14.30					4-15—8-15	.176	42.90

Claimant—**Lamoille Mercantile Co.** Proof No. 00408
Source—**Lamoille Creek.** Ditch—**L. M. Co.**

A1868*	3.64	W¼SE¼	19	33	58	4-15—8-15	.045	10.92
1869	6.36	NE¼SW¼	19	33	58	4-15—8-15	.078	19.08
1870	.60					4-15—8-15	.007	1.80
1871	9.34					4-15—8-15	.115	28.02
1872	3.14					4-15—8-15	.039	9.42
1873	3.54					4-15—8-15	.044	10.62
1874	2.87					4-15—8-15	.035	8.61
1875	14.33					4-15—8-15	.176	42.99
1876	5.09					4-15—8-15	.063	15.27
1877	3.07					4-15—8-15	.038	9.21
1878	3.02					4-15—8-15	.037	9.06
1896	46.60					4-15—8-15	.573	139.80
1902	7.60					4-15—8-15	.093	22.80

*1868 prior right over A1868.
NOTE—"After exchanging dates and areas to conform to Lamoille Court Decree No. 1311 Elko District Court.

Claimant—**Samuel McIntyre Investment Company.** Proof No. 00409

Source—**Lamoille Creek.** Ditch—**Samuel McIntyre Investment Company Ditches.**

Year of priority	Culture—Acres: Harvest crops	Meadow pasture	Diversified pasture	Location: Subdivision	Section	Tp.N.	R.E.	Length of season	Duty of water: C.F.S.	Acre-feet
1886	266.30			S½	9	35	58	4-15—8-15	3.275	796.90
1894	165.90			SW¼	10	35	58	4-15—8-15	2.041	497.70
1890	25.40				15	35	58	4-15—8-15	.312	76.20
1893	....		191.10		....	....	....	4-15—5-15	2.351	143.33
1893	....		527.70	SW¼	14	36	56	4-15—5-15	6.491	395.78
1887	707.10				23	35	58	4-15—8-15	8.697	2121.30
1893	36.60				22	35	58	4-15—8-15	.450	109.80
					26	35	58			
				NE¼	27	35	58			
				N½	35	35	58			
1872	375.00				21	34	58	4-15—8-15	4.613	1025.00
1883	137.00				15	34	58	4-15—8-15	1.685	411.00
1884	137.00				22	34	56	4-15—8-15	1.685	411.00
1885	137.00				10	34	58	4-15—8-15	1.685	411.00
1886	137.00				3	34	58	4-15—8-15	1.685	411.00
1887	137.00				2	34	58	4-15—8-15	1.685	411.00
1888	137.00				34	35	58	4-15—8-15	1.685	411.00
1889	141.60				35	35	58	4-15—8-15	1.742	424.80
1893	....		82.20		....	....	....	4-15—5-15	1.011	61.65

Source—***Secret Creek and Soldier Creek.** Ditch—**Sam'l. McIntyre Investment Co. Ditches.**

Year of priority	Harvest crops	Meadow pasture	Diversified pasture	Subdivision	Section	Tp.N.	R.E.	Length of season	C.F.S.	Acre-feet
1887	40.00			N½	9	35	58	4-15—8-15	.492	120.00
1888	120.00				10	35	58	4-15—8-15	1.476	360.00
1889	160.00				11	35	58	4-15—8-15	1.968	480.00
1892	260.60			*S½	*13	35	58	4-15—8-15	3.205	781.80
1893	260.60				14	35	58	4-15—8-15	3.205	781.80
1894	260.60			N½NE¼	15	35	58	4-15—8-15	3.205	781.80
1895	260.60			*N½	*24	35	58	4-15—8-15	3.205	781.80
1896	260.60				*19	35	59	4-15—8-15	3.205	781.80
1897	260.70				....	....	....	4-15—8-15	3.207	782.10
1807	....		231.90		....	....	....	4-15—5-15	2.852	173.92

Priority from Lamoille Creek 1895 on land under "Upper Reservoir Ditch." *Lands irrigated from Secret Creek only.

Source—**Warm Spring and Cold Creek.** Ditch—**Samuel McIntyre Investment Co. Ditches.**

Year of priority	Harvest crops	Meadow pasture	Diversified pasture	Subdivision	Section	Tp.N.	R.E.	Length of season	C.F.S.	Acre-feet
1873	2250.00			S½NW¼	36	35	58			
				SW¼NE¼	36	35	58			
				NW¼SW¼	36	35	58			
				SE¼	36	35	58			
				NE¼SE¼	35	35	58			
				W½SW¼	1	35	59			
				W½	6	34	59			
				W½	7	34	59			
				E½	1	34	58			

Priority	Acres	Subdivision	Sec.	T.	R.	Period	Duty	Acre-feet
		E½	12	34	58			
			13	34	58			
			24	34	58			
		W¼W½	18	34	59			
		SW¼SW¼	30	34	59			
		W½	31	34	59			
		E½	25	34	58			
			36	34	58			
		W½	6	33	59	*4-15—8-28	*25.00	*6750.00

*NOTE—Subject to that certain opinion and decision No. 2573, Elko County Records.

Claimant—**O. P. McDermott.** Proof No. 00410

Source—**Lamoille Creek.** Ditch—**O. P. McDermott Ditches.**

Priority	Acres	Subdivision	Sec.	T.	R.	Period	Duty	Acre-feet
A1868*	1.82	SW¼	29	33	58	4-15—8-15	.022	5.46
1869	3.18	NW¼	32	33	58	4-15—8-15	.039	9.54
1870	1.21	....	....	....	....	4-15—8-15	.015	3.63
1871	18.67	....	....	....	....	4-15—8-15	.230	56.01
1872	6.31	....	....	....	....	4-15—8-15	.078	18.91
1873	7.05	....	....	....	....	4-15—8-15	.087	21.15
1874	5.73	....	....	....	....	4-15—8-15	.070	17.19
1875	28.66	....	....	....	....	4-15—8-15	.353	85.98
1876	10.19	....	....	....	....	4-15—8-15	.125	30.57
1877	6.15	....	....	....	....	4-15—8-15	.076	18.45
1878	6.03	....	....	....	....	4-15—8-15	.074	18.09
1896	30.00	....	....	....	....	4-15—8-15	.369	90.00
1898	30.00	....	....	....	....	4-15—8-15	.369	90.00
1901	34.40	....	....	....	....	4-15—8-15	.423	103.20
1904	27.00	....	....	....	....	4-15—8-15	.332	81.00

*1868 prior right over A1868.

NOTE—"After exchanging dates and areas to conform to Lamoille court decree. Also 10 acres dated 1871 from Springs. (Vested right)." Elko District Court decree No. 1311.

Claimant—**J. E. Myers.** Proof No. 00411

Source—**Lamoille Creek.** Ditch—**J. E. Myers Ditches.**

Priority	Acres	Subdivision	Sec.	T.	R.	Period	Duty	Acre-feet
1885	40.00	SW¼NW¼	13	33	57			
		SE¼NE¼	14	33	57	4-15—8-15	.492	120.00

Source—**Rabbit Creek and Little Rabbit Creek.** Ditch—**J. E. Myers Ditches.**

Priority	Acres	Subdivision	Sec.	T.	R.	Period	Duty	Acre-feet
1873	70.60	W½SE¼	11	33	57	4-15—8-15	.868	211.80
1875	47.70	E½SW¼	11	33	57	4-15—8-15	.587	143.10
1890	10.00	SE¼SE¼	11	33	57	4-15—8-15	.123	30.00
		N½NE¼	14	33	57			

Claimant—**C. E. Noble.** Proof No. 00412
Source—**Lamoille Creek.** Ditch—**C. E. Noble Ditches.**

Year of priority	Culture—Acres: Harvest crops	Meadow pasture	Diversified pasture	Location: Subdivision	Section	Tp.N.	R.E.	Length of season	Duty of water: C.F.S.	Acre-feet
A1868*	16.93			E½	30	33	58	4-15—8-15	.134	32.79
1869	19.07			NW¼	29	33	58	4-15—8-15	.235	57.21
1870	3.81			SE¼ SE¼	19	33	58	4-15—8-15	.047	11.43
1871	59.02			NE¼ SE¼	19	33	58	4-15—8-15	.726	177.06
1872	19.95							4-15—8-15	.245	59.85
1873	22.29							4-15—8-15	.274	66.87
1874	18.11							4-15—8-15	.223	54.33
1875	90.61							4-15—8-15	1.115	271.83
1876	32.21							4-15—8-15	.396	96.63
1877	19.43							4-15—8-15	.239	58.29
1878	19.07							4-15—8-15	.235	57.21
1886	95.50							4-15—8-15	1.175	286.50
1888	117.00							4-15—8-15	1.439	351.00
1900	9.00							4-15—8-15	.111	27.00

*1868 prior right over A1868.
NOTE—After exchanging dates and areas to conform to Lamoille court decree, Elko District Court No. 1311.
NOTE—The amount of water flowing through the swamp ditch is to be deducted from the amount claimant is entitled to divert from Lamoille Creek, but in case swamp ditch becomes dry, claimant is allowed to use water for his entire area as listed from Lamoille Creek.
Swamp Area—No water to be diverted from the creek for any swamp area until the same becomes dry or is drained.

Claimant—**John W. McNew.** Proof No. 00412
Source—**Lamoille Creek.** Ditch—**John W. McNew Ditches.**

Year of priority	Harvest crops	Meadow pasture	Diversified pasture	Subdivision	Section	Tp.N.	R.E.	Length of season	C.F.S.	Acre-feet
1865	4.00			NW¼	18	33	58	4-15—8-15	.049	12.00
1869	1.00							4-15—8-15	.012	3.00
A1868*	8.38							4-15—8-15	.103	25.14
1869	14.62							4-15—8-15	.180	43.86
1870	1.78							4-15—8-15	.022	5.34
1871	27.38							4-15—8-15	.337	82.14
1872	9.25							4-15—8-15	.114	27.75
1873	10.34							4-15—8-15	.127	31.02
1874	8.40							4-15—8-15	.103	25.40
1875	42.04							4-15—8-15	.517	126.12
1876	14.94							4-15—8-15	.184	44.82
1877	9.02							4-15—8-15	.111	27.06
1878	8.85							4-15—8-15	.109	26.55

*1868—Prior right over A1868.
NOTE—After exchanging dates and areas to conform to Lamoille court decree.

Claimant—**John McKinney.** Proof No. 00414
Source—**Talbot Creek.** Ditch—**John McKinney Ditches.**

Year of priority	Harvest crops	Meadow pasture	Diversified pasture	Subdivision	Section	Tp.N.	R.E.	Length of season	C.F.S.	Acre-feet
1868	20.00			SE¼	8	33	58	4-15—8-15	.246	60.00
1871	103.00			SE¼	8	33	58	4-15—8-15	1.267	309.00
1887	37.00			SE¼	8	33	58	4-15—8-15	.455	111.00

15[71]

Claimant—**Ramon Lugea.** Proof No. 00415

Source—**Talbot Creek.** Ditch—**Ramon Lugea Ditches.**

	1871			10.00				E½SW¼	16	33	58	4-15—8-15	.123	30.00
	1873			5.00				E½SW¼	16	33	58	4-15—8-15	.062	15.00
	1876			5.00				E½SW¼	16	33	58	4-15—8-16	.062	15.00
	1892			17.00				E½SW¼	16	33	58	4-15—8-15	.209	51.00
	1900			17.00				E½SW¼	16	33	58	4-15—8-15	.209	51.00
	1904			8.00				E½SW¼	16	33	58	4-15—8-15	.098	24.00
	1904			1.50				E½SW¼	16	33	58	4-15—8-15	.018	4.50

Claimant—**F. W. Wiggins.** Proof No. 00416

Source—**Beaver or Thorp Creek.** Ditch—**F. W. Wiggins Ditches.**

	1868			8.20				NW¼NE¼	9	33	58	4-15—8-15	.101	24.60
	1869			8.20				S½NE¼	9	33	58	4-15—8-15	.101	24.60
	1870			8.20				E½SE¼	9	33	58	4-15—8-15	.101	24.60
	1871			8.20				W½SW¼	10	33	58	4-15—8-15	.101	24.60
	1872			8.20				N½NW¼	15	33	58	4-15—8-15	.101	24.60
	1873			18.80								4-15—8-16	.231	56.40
	1874			3.00								4-15—8-15	.037	9.00
	1875			3.00								4-15—8-15	.037	9.00
	1876			15.20								4-15—8-15	.189	45.60
	1877			2.90								4-15—8-15	.036	8.70
	1878			2.90								4-15—8-15	.036	8.70
	1880			15.50								4-15—8-15	.191	46.50
	1881			9.70								4-15—8-15	.119	29.10
	1882			9.70								4-15—8-15	.119	29.10
	1883			9.60								4-15—8-15	.118	28.80
	1884			9.60								4-15—8-15	.118	28.80
	1885			12.60								4-15—8-15	.154	37.80
	1892			7.70								4-15—8-15	.095	23.10
	1893			7.70								4-15—8-15	.095	23.10
	1894			7.70								4-15—8-15	.095	23.10
	1895			7.60								4-15—8-15	.093	22.80
	1895					8.30						4-15—5-16	.102	6.23
	1898			14.10								4-15—8-15	.173	42.30
	1899			12.40								4-15—8-15	.153	37.20
	1900			12.40								4-15—8-15	.153	37.20
	1900					10.00						4-15—5-15	.123	7.50
	1902					9.90						4-15—5-15	.122	7.43
	1902			13.80								4-15—8-15	.170	41.40
	1904			21.20								4-15—8-15	.261	63.60

Claimant—**Antonio Echeverrieta.** Proof No. 00417

Source—**Talbot Creek.** Ditch—**Antonio Echeverrieta Ditches.**

	1896			5.00				W½E½	21	33	58	4-15—8-15	.062	15.00
	1902			25.00				E½W½	21	33	58	4-15—8-15	.308	75.00
	1904			16.00								4-15—8-15	.197	48.00

Claimant—**J. E. Fraiser.** Proof No. 00418

Source—**Rabbit Creek.** Ditch—**J. E. Fraiser Ditches.**

Year of priority	Culture—Acres: Harvest crops	Culture—Acres: Meadow pasture	Culture—Acres: Diversified pasture	Location: Subdivision	Location: Section	Location: Tp.N.	Location: R.E.	Length of season	Duty of water: C.F.S.	Duty of water: Acre-feet
1900	47.00			SE¼	14	33	57	4-15—8-15	.478	141.00

Claimant—**Harry Trott.** Proof No. 00420

Source—**Talbot Creek.** Ditch—**Harry Trott Ditches.**

Year of priority	Harvest crops	Meadow pasture	Diversified pasture	Subdivision	Section	Tp.N.	R.E.	Length of season	C.F.S.	Acre-feet
1873	30.00			NE¼	8	33	58	4-15—8-15	.369	90.00
1875	30.00			NW¼	8	33	58	4-15—8-15	.369	90.00
1879	90.00			NE¼SW¼	8	33	58	4-15—8-15	1.107	270.00
1895	5.00							4-15—8-15	.062	15.00
1900	25.00							4-15—8-15	.308	75.00
1902	40.00							4-15—8-15	.492	120.00
1902	73.90							4-15—8-15	.909	221.70

Source—**Paterson Springs.** Ditch—**Harry Trott Ditches.**

Year of priority	Harvest crops	Meadow pasture	Diversified pasture	Subdivision	Section	Tp.N.	R.E.	Length of season	C.F.S.	Acre-feet
1889	—	99.50*		W½NW¼	8	33	56			
				N½SW¼	8	33	58	4-15—6-15	1.224	149.25

*No water to be diverted from Lamoille Creek for this 99.50 acres.

Claimant—**Henry Voight.** Proof No. 00421

Source—**Beaver or Thorpe Creek and Springs.** Ditch—**Henry Voight Ditches.**

Year of priority	Harvest crops	Meadow pasture	Diversified pasture	Subdivision	Section	Tp.N.	R.E.	Length of season	C.F.S.	Acre-feet
1867	100.00			E½	33	34	58	4-15—8-15	1.230	300.00
1873	98.20			W½W½	3	33	58	4-15—8-15	1.208	294.60
1874	34.20			E½	4	33	58	4-15—8-15	.421	102.60
1876	202.40			S½NW¼	4	33	58	4-15—8-15	2.490	607.20
1877	68.00			SW¼	4	33	58	4-15—8-15	.836	204.00
1878	105.10			NE¼NE¼	9	33	58	4-15—8-15	1.293	315.30
1880	72.90			W½NW¼	10	33	58	4-15—8-15	.897	218.70
1881	41.30							4-15—8-15	.508	123.90
1884	41.20							4-15—8-15	.508	123.60
1887	41.20							4-15—8-15	.508	123.00
1890	41.30							4-15—8-15	.508	123.00
1901	24.00							4-15—8-15	.295	72.00

Source—**Talbot Creek.** Ditch—**Wines No. 3.**

Year of priority	Harvest crops	Meadow pasture	Diversified pasture	Subdivision	Section	Tp.N.	R.E.	Length of season	C.F.S.	Acre-feet
1870	25.00			W½SW¼	4	33	58	4-15—8-15	.308	75.00

Claimant—**Conrad Smith.** Proof No. 00422

Source—**Talbot Creek and Branch.** Ditch—**Conrad Smith Ditches.**

Year of priority	Harvest crops	Meadow pasture	Diversified pasture	Subdivision	Section	Tp.N.	R.E.	Length of season	C.F.S.	Acre-feet
1876	15.00			E½E½	21	33	58	4-15—8-15	.185	45.00
1883	1.00			W½NW¼	22	33	58	4-15—8-15	.012	3.00
1885	22.00			SE¼NW¼	22	33	58	4-15—8-15	.271	66.00
1886	6.00			NW¼SW¼	22	33	58	4-15—8-15	.074	18.00
1887	10.00			N½SW¼SW¼	22	33	58	4-15—8-15	.123	30.00
1901	55.00							4-15—8-15	.677	[illegible]
1904	36.30							4-15—8-15	[illegible]	[illegible]

1875	25.00	SE¼NE¼	32	34	58	4-15—8-15	.308	75.00
1875	20.00	S¼NW¼	33	34	58	4-15—8-15	.246	60.00
1875	45.00	SW¼	33	34	58	4-15—8-15	.554	135.00
1876	5.00	N½NW¼	4	33	58	4-15—8-15	.062	15.00
1877	40.00	E½	5	33	58	4-15—8-15	.492	120.00
1877	11.00	E½SW¼	5	33	58	4-15—8-15	.135	33.00
1884	10.00					4-15—8-15	.123	30.00
1884	15.00					4-15—8-15	.185	45.00
1885	50.00					4-15—8-15	.615	150.00
1886	60.00					4-15—8-15	.738	180.00
1886	50.00					4-15—8-15	.615	150.00
1887	50.00					4-15—8-15	.615	150.00
1888	26.00					4-15—8-15	.320	78.00
1889	50.00					4-15—8-15	.615	150.00
1890	50.00					4-15—8-15	.615	150.00
1891	50.00					4-15—8-15	.615	150.00
1892	50.00					4-15—8-15	.615	150.00
1892	7.40					4-15—8-15	.091	22.20

Source—**Spring Creek.** Ditch—**Hunter & Lytton Ditches.**

1890	61.40	N½NW¼	4	33	58			
		SE¼SW¼	33	34	58	4-15—8-15	.755	184.20

Source—**Lamoille Creek.** Ditch—**Hunter & Lytton.**

1871	10.00	SW¼NE¼	32	34	58	4-15—8-15	.123	30.00
1872	24.00	W½	32	34	58	4-15—8-15	.295	84.00
1873	36.00	E½	6	33	58	4-15—8-15	.443	108.00
1874	40.00	W¼	5	33	58	4-15—8-15	.492	120.00
1875	20.00	W¼NE¼	5	33	58	4-15—8-15	.246	60.00
1876	50.00					4-15—8-15	.615	150.00
1877	17.50					4-15—8-15	.215	52.50
1878	34.00					4-15—8-15	.418	102.00
1880	20.00					4-15—8-15	.246	60.00
1881	50.00					4-15—8-15	.615	150.00
1882	115.00					4-15—8-15	1.415	345.00
1883	10.00					4-15—8-15	.123	30.00
1884	75.00					4-15—8-15	.923	225.00
1885	50.00					4-15—8-15	.615	150.00
1886	20.00					4-15—8-15	.246	60.00
1887	75.00					4-15—8-15	.923	225.00
1888	26.70					4-15—8-15	.328	80.10
1889	76.80					4-15—8-15	.945	220.40

Claimant—**Alex. Carden.** Proof No. 00424

Source—**Talbot Creek and Springs.** Ditch—**Carden Ditches.**

1872	90.90*	W½E½	17	33	58	4-15—8-15	1.118	272.70
1873	83.50	NE¼NE¼	17	33	58	4-15—8-15	1.027	250.50
1873	23.00	NE¼NE¼	17	33	58	4-15—8-15	.283	69.00

*90.90 acres is from swamp ditches and Talbot Creek. All water available from swamp ditches is to be used first and if it is not sufficient to irrigate the extra water is to come from Talbot Creek. 106.5 acres from Talbot Creek.

Claimant—**C. E. Noble.** Proof No. 00412

Source—**Lamoille Creek.** Ditch—**C. E. Noble Ditches.**

Year of priority	Culture—Acres: Harvest crops	Meadow pasture	Diversified pasture	Location: Subdivision	Section	Tp.N.	R.E.	Length of season	Duty of water: C.F.S.	Acre-feet
A1868*	16.93			E½	30	33	58	4-15—8-15	.134	32.79
1869	19.07			NW¼	29	33	58	4-15—8-15	.235	57.21
1870	3.81			SE¼ SE¼	19	33	58	4-15—8-15	.047	11.43
1871	59.02			NE¼ SE¼	19	33	58	4-15—8-15	.726	177.06
1872	19.95							4-15—8-15	.245	59.85
1873	22.29							4-15—8-15	.274	66.87
1874	18.11							4-15—8-15	.223	54.33
1875	90.61							4-15—8-15	1.115	271.83
1876	32.21							4-15—8-15	.396	96.63
1877	19.43							4-15—8-15	.239	58.29
1878	19.07							4-15—8-15	.235	57.21
1896	95.50							4-15—8-15	1.175	286.50
1898	117.00							4-15—8-15	1.439	351.00
1900	9.00							4-15—8-15	.111	27.00

*1868 prior right over A1868.

NOTE—After exchanging dates and areas to conform to Lamoille court decree, Elko District Court No. 1311.

NOTE—The amount of water flowing through the swamp ditch is to be deducted from the amount claimant is entitled to divert from Lamoille Creek, but in case swamp ditch becomes dry, claimant is allowed to use water for his entire area as listed from Lamoille Creek.

Swamp Area—No water to be diverted from the creek for any swamp area until the same becomes dry or is drained.

Claimant—**John W. McNew.** Proof No. 00412

Source—**Lamoille Creek.** Ditch—**John W. McNew Ditches.**

Year of priority	Harvest crops	Meadow pasture	Diversified pasture	Subdivision	Section	Tp.N.	R.E.	Length of season	C.F.S.	Acre-feet
1865	4.00			NW¼	18	33	58	4-15—8-15	.049	12.00
1868	1.00							4-15—8-15	.012	3.00
A1868*	8.38							4-15—8-15	.103	25.14
1869	14.62							4-15—8-15	.180	43.86
1870	1.78							4-15—8-15	.022	5.34
1871	27.38							4-15—8-15	.337	82.14
1872	9.25							4-15—8-15	.114	27.75
1873	10.34							4-15—8-15	.127	31.02
1874	8.40							4-15—8-15	.103	25.40
1875	42.04							4-15—8-15	.517	126.12
1876	14.94							4-15—8-15	.184	44.82
1877	9.02							4-15—8-15	.111	27.06
1878	8.85							4-15—8-15	.109	26.55

*1868—Prior right over A1868.

NOTE—After exchanging dates and areas to conform to Lamoille court decree.

Claimant—**John McKinney.** Proof No. 00414

Source—**Talbot Creek.** Ditch—**John McKinney Ditches.**

Year of priority	Harvest crops	Meadow pasture	Diversified pasture	Subdivision	Section	Tp.N.	R.E.	Length of season	C.F.S.	Acre-feet
1868	20.00			SE¼	8	33	58	4-15—8-15	.240	60.00
1871	103.00			SE¼	8	33	58	4-15—8-15	1.207	309.00
1887	37.00			SE¼	8	33	58	4-15—8-15	.455	111.00

Claimant—**Ramon Lugea.**
Source—**Talbot Creek.** Ditch—**Ramon Lugea Ditches.**

Proof No. 00415

	1871			10.00				E½SW¼	16	33	58	4-15—8-15	.123	30.00
	1873			5.00				E½SW¼	16	33	58	4-15—8-15	.062	15.00
	1876			5.00				E½SW¼	16	33	58	4-15—8-15	.062	15.00
	1892			17.00				E½SW¼	16	33	58	4-15—8-15	.209	51.00
	1900			17.00				E½SW¼	16	33	58	4-15—8-15	.209	51.00
	1904			8.00				E½SW¼	16	33	58	4-15—8-15	.098	24.00
	1904			1.50				E½SW¼	16	33	58	4-15—8-15	.018	4.50

Claimant—**F. W. Wiggins.**
Source—**Beaver or Thorp Creek.** Ditch—**F. W. Wiggins Ditches.**

Proof No. 00416

	1868			8.20				NW¼NE¼	9	33	58	4-15—8-15	.101	24.60
	1869			8.20				S½NE¼	9	33	58	4-15—8-15	.101	24.60
	1870			8.20				E½SE¼	9	33	58	4-15—8-15	.101	24.60
	1871			8.20				W½SW¼	10	33	58	4-15—8-15	.101	24.60
	1872			8.20				N½NW¼	15	33	58	4-15—8-15	.101	24.60
	1873			18.80				....	....	....	....	4-15—8-15	.231	56.40
	1874			3.00				....	....	....	....	4-15—8-15	.037	9.00
	1875			3.00				....	....	....	....	4-15—8-15	.037	9.00
	1876			15.20				....	....	....	....	4-15—8-15	.189	45.60
	1877			2.90				....	....	....	....	4-15—8-15	.036	8.70
	1878			2.90				....	....	....	....	4-15—8-15	.036	8.70
	1880			15.50				....	....	....	....	4-15—8-15	.191	46.50
	1881			9.70				....	....	....	....	4-15—8-15	.119	29.10
	1882			9.70				....	....	....	....	4-15—8-15	.119	29.10
	1883			9.60				....	....	....	....	4-15—8-15	.118	28.80
	1884			9.60				....	....	....	....	4-15—8-15	.118	28.80
	1885			12.60				....	....	....	....	4-15—8-15	.154	37.80
	1892			7.70				....	....	....	....	4-15—8-15	.095	23.10
	1893			7.70				....	....	....	....	4-15—8-15	.095	23.10
	1894			7.70				....	....	....	....	4-15—8-15	.095	23.10
	1895			7.60				....	....	....	....	4-15—8-15	.093	22.80
	1895			....		8.30		....	....	....	....	4-15—5-15	.102	6.23
	1898			14.10				....	....	....	....	4-15—8-15	.173	42.30
	1899			12.40				....	....	....	....	4-15—8-15	.153	37.20
	1900			12.40				....	....	....	....	4-15—8-15	.153	37.20
	1900			....		10.00		....	....	....	....	4-15—5-15	.123	7.50
	1902			....		9.90		....	....	....	....	4-15—5-15	.122	7.43
	1902			13.80				....	....	....	....	4-15—8-15	.170	41.40
	1904			21.20				....	....	....	....	4-15—8-15	.261	63.60

Claimant—**Antonio Echeverrieta.**
Source—**Talbot Creek.** Ditch—**Antonio Echeverrieta Ditches.**

Proof No. 00417

	1896			5.00				W½E½	21	33	58	4-15—8-15	.062	15.00
	1902			25.00				E½W½	21	33	58	4-15—8-15	.308	75.00
	1904			16.00				....	....	....	....	4-15—8-15	.197	48.00

1571

Claimant—**C. E. Noble.** Proof No. 00412
Source—**Lamoille Creek.** Ditch—**C. E. Noble Ditches.**

Year of priority	Culture—Acres: Harvest crops	Meadow pasture	Diversified pasture	Location: Subdivision	Section	Tp.N.	R.E.	Length of season	Duty of water: C.F.S.	Acre-feet
A1868*	10.93			E½	30	33	58	4-15—8-15	.134	32.79
1869	19.07			NW¼	29	33	58	4-15—8-15	.235	57.21
1870	3.81			SE¼SE¼	19	33	58	4-15—8-15	.047	11.43
1871	59.02			NE¼SE¼	19	33	58	4-15—8-15	.726	177.06
1872	19.95							4-15—8-15	.245	59.85
1873	22.29							4-15—8-15	.274	66.87
1874	18.11							4-15—8-15	.223	54.33
1875	90.61							4-15—8-15	1.115	271.83
1876	32.21							4-15—8-15	.396	96.63
1877	19.43							4-15—8-15	.239	58.29
1878	19.07							4-15—8-15	.235	57.21
1896	95.50							4-15—8-15	1.175	286.50
1898	117.00							4-15—8-15	1.439	351.00
1900	9.00							4-15—8-15	.111	27.00

*1868 prior right over A1868.

NOTE—After exchanging dates and areas to conform to Lamoille court decree, Elko District Court No. 1311.

NOTE—The amount of water flowing through the swamp ditch is to be deducted from the amount claimant is entitled to divert from Lamoille Creek, but in case swamp ditch becomes dry, claimant is allowed to use water for his entire area as listed from Lamoille Creek.

Swamp Area—No water to be diverted from the creek for any swamp area until the same becomes dry or is drained.

Claimant—**John W. McNew.** Proof No. 00412
Source—**Lamoille Creek.** Ditch—**John W. McNew Ditches.**

Year of priority	Harvest crops	Meadow pasture	Diversified pasture	Subdivision	Section	Tp.N.	R.E.	Length of season	C.F.S.	Acre-feet
1865	4.00			NW¼	18	33	58	4-15—8-15	.049	12.00
1868	1.00							4-15—8-15	.012	3.00
A1868*	8.38							4-15—8-15	.103	25.14
1869	14.62							4-15—8-15	.180	43.86
1870	1.78							4-15—8-15	.022	5.34
1871	27.38							4-15—8-15	.337	82.14
1872	9.25							4-15—8-15	.114	27.75
1873	10.34							4-15—8-15	.127	31.02
1874	8.40							4-15—8-15	.103	25.40
1875	42.04							4-15—8-15	.517	126.12
1876	14.94							4-15—8-15	.184	44.82
1877	9.02							4-15—8-15	.111	27.06
1878	8.85							4-15—8-15	.109	26.55

*1868—Prior right over A1868.

NOTE—After exchanging dates and areas to conform to Lamoille court decree.

Claimant—**John McKinney.** Proof No. 00414
Source—**Talbot Creek.** Ditch—**John McKinney Ditches.**

Year of priority	Harvest crops	Meadow pasture	Diversified pasture	Subdivision	Section	Tp.N.	R.E.	Length of season	C.F.S.	Acre-feet
1868	20.00			SE¼	8	33	58	4-15—8-15	.246	60.00
1871	103.00			SE¼	8	33	58	4-15—8-15	1.267	309.00
1887	37.00			SE¼	8	33	58	4-15—8-15	.455	111.00

Claimant—**Ramon Lugea.** Proof No. 00415

Source—**Talbot Creek.** Ditch—**Ramon Lugea Ditches.**

1871	10.00		E½SW¼	16	33	58	4-15—8-15	.123	30.00
1873	5.00		E½SW¼	16	33	58	4-15—8-15	.062	15.00
1876	5.00		E½SW¼	16	33	58	4-15—8-15	.062	15.00
1892	17.00		E½SW¼	16	33	58	4-15—8-15	.209	51.00
1900	17.00		E½SW¼	16	33	58	4-15—8-15	.209	51.00
1904	8.00		E½SW¼	16	33	58	4-15—8-15	.098	24.00
1904	1.50		E½SW¼	16	33	58	4-15—8-15	.018	4.50

Claimant—**F. W. Wiggins.** Proof No. 00416

Source—**Beaver or Thorp Creek.** Ditch—**F. W. Wiggins Ditches.**

1868	8.20		NW¼NE¼	9	33	58	4-15—8-15	.101	24.60
1869	8.20		S½NE¼	9	33	58	4-15—8-15	.101	24.60
1870	8.20		E½SE¼	9	33	58	4-15—8-15	.101	24.60
1871	8.20		W½SW¼	10	33	58	4-15—8-15	.101	24.60
1872	8.20		N½NW¼	15	33	58	4-15—8-15	.101	24.60
1873	18.80						4-15—8-15	.231	56.40
1874	3.00						4-15—8-15	.037	9.00
1875	3.00						4-15—8-15	.037	9.00
1876	15.20						4-15—8-15	.189	45.60
1877	2.90						4-15—8-15	.036	8.70
1878	2.90						4-15—8-15	.036	8.70
1880	15.50						4-15—8-15	.191	46.50
1881	9.70						4-15—8-15	.119	29.10
1882	9.70						4-15—8-15	.119	29.10
1883	9.60						4-15—8-15	.118	28.80
1884	9.60						4-15—8-15	.118	28.80
1885	12.60						4-15—8-15	.154	37.80
1892	7.70						4-15—8-15	.095	23.10
1893	7.70						4-15—8-15	.095	23.10
1894	7.70						4-15—8-15	.095	23.10
1895	7.60						4-15—8-15	.093	22.80
1895	....	8.30					4-15—5-15	.102	6.23
1898	14.10						4-15—8-15	.173	42.30
1899	12.40						4-15—8-15	.153	37.20
1900	12.40						4-15—8-15	.153	37.20
1900	....	10.00					4-15—5-15	.123	7.50
1902	....	9.90					4-15—5-15	.122	7.43
1902	13.80						4-15—8-15	.170	41.40
1904	21.20						4-15—8-15	.261	63.60

Claimant—**Antonio Echeverrieta.** Proof No. 00417

Source—**Talbot Creek.** Ditch—**Antonio Echeverrieta Ditches.**

1896	5.00		W½E½	21	33	58	4-15—8-15	.062	15.00
1902	25.00		E½W½	21	33	58	4-15—8-15	.308	75.00
1904	16.00						4-15—8-15	.197	48.00

Claimant—**J. E. Fraiser.** Proof No. 00418

Source—**Rabbit Creek.** Ditch—**J. E. Fraiser Ditches.**

Year of priority	Culture—Acres: Harvest crops	Meadow pasture	Diversified pasture	Location: Subdivision	Section	Tp.N.	R.E.	Length of season	Duty of water: C.F.S.	Acre-feet
1900	47.00	......	......	SE¼	14	33	57	4-15—8-15	.478	141.00

Claimant—**Harry Trott.** Proof No. 00420

Source—**Talbot Creek.** Ditch—**Harry Trott Ditches.**

Year of priority	Harvest crops	Meadow pasture	Diversified pasture	Subdivision	Section	Tp.N.	R.E.	Length of season	C.F.S.	Acre-feet
1873	30.00	......	......	NE¼	8	33	58	4-15—8-15	.369	90.00
1875	30.00	......	......	NW¼	8	33	58	4-15—8-15	.369	90.00
1879	90.00	......	......	NE¼SW¼	8	33	58	4-15—8-15	1.107	270.00
1886	5.00	......	......	......	....	....	....	4-15—8-15	.062	15.00
1900	25.00	......	......	......	....	....	....	4-15—8-15	.308	75.00
1902	40.00	......	......	......	....	....	....	4-15—8-15	.492	120.00
1902	73.90	......	......	......	....	....	....	4-15—8-15	.909	221.70

Source—**Paterson Springs.** Ditch—**Harry Trott Ditches.**

Year of priority	Harvest crops	Meadow pasture	Diversified pasture	Subdivision	Section	Tp.N.	R.E.	Length of season	C.F.S.	Acre-feet
1889	....	99.50*	......	W¼NW¼	8	33	56			
				N½SW¼	8	33	58	4-15—6-15	1.224	149.25

*No water to be diverted from Lamoille Creek for this 99.50 acres.

Claimant—**Henry Voight.** Proof No. 00421

Source—**Beaver or Thorpe Creek and Springs.** Ditch—**Henry Voight Ditches.**

Year of priority	Harvest crops	Meadow pasture	Diversified pasture	Subdivision	Section	Tp.N.	R.E.	Length of season	C.F.S.	Acre-feet
1867	100.00	......	......	E½	33	34	58	4-15—8-15	1.230	300.00
1873	98.20	......	......	W½W½	3	33	58	4-15—8-15	1.208	291.00
1874	34.20	......	......	E½	4	33	58	4-15—8-15	.421	102.60
1876	202.40	......	......	S½NW¼	4	33	58	4-15—8-15	2.490	307.20
1877	68.00	......	......	SW¼	4	33	58	4-15—8-15	.836	204.00
1878	105.10	......	......	NE¼NE¼	9	33	58	4-15—8-15	1.293	315.30
1880	72.90	......	......	W½NW¼	10	33	58	4-15—8-15	.897	218.70
1881	41.30	......	......	......	....	....	....	4-15—8-15	.508	123.90
1884	41.20	......	......	......	....	....	....	4-15—8-15	.508	123.60
1887	41.20	......	......	......	....	....	....	4-15—8-15	.508	123.60
1890	41.20	......	......	......	....	....	....	4-15—8-15	.508	123.60
1901	24.00	......	......	......	....	....	....	4-15—8-15	.295	72.00

Source—**Talbot Creek.** Ditch—**Wines No. 3.**

Year of priority	Harvest crops	Meadow pasture	Diversified pasture	Subdivision	Section	Tp.N.	R.E.	Length of season	C.F.S.	Acre-feet
1870	25.00	......	......	W½SW¼	4	33	58	4-15—8-15	.308	75.00

Claimant—**Conrad Smith.** Proof No. 00422

Source—**Talbot Creek and Branch.** Ditch—**Conrad Smith Ditches.**

Year of priority	Harvest crops	Meadow pasture	Diversified pasture	Subdivision	Section	Tp.N.	R.E.	Length of season	C.F.S.	Acre-feet
1870	15.00	......	......	E½E½	21	33	58	4-15—8-15	.185	45.00
1883	1.00	......	......	W½NW¼	22	33	58	4-15—8-15	.012	3.00
1885	22.00	......	......	SE¼NW¼	22	33	58	4-15—8-15	.271	66.00
1890	6.00	......	......	NW¼SW¼	22	33	58	4-15—8-15	.074	18.00
1887	10.00	......	......	N½SW¼SW¼	22	33	58	4-15—8-15	.123	30.00
1901	65.00	......	......	......	....	....	....	4-15—8-15	.077	105.00
1904	35.30	......	......	......	....	....	....	4-15—8-15	.434	105.00

Source—Talbot Creek. Ditch—Hunter & Lytton Ditches.

1875	25.00	SE¼NE¼	32	34	58	4-15—8-15	.308	75.00
1875	20.00	S½NW¼	33	34	58	4-15—8-15	.246	60.00
1875	45.00	SW¼	33	34	58	4-15—8-15	.554	135.00
1876	5.00	N½NW¼	4	33	58	4-15—8-15	.062	15.00
1877	40.00	E½	5	33	58	4-15—8-15	.492	120.00
1877	11.00	E½SW¼	5	33	58	4-15—8-15	.135	33.00
1884	10.00					4-15—8-15	.123	30.00
1884	15.00					4-15—8-15	.185	45.00
1885	50.00					4-15—8-15	.615	150.00
1886	60.00					4-15—8-15	.738	180.00
1886	50.00					4-15—8-15	.615	150.00
1887	50.00					4-15—8-15	.615	150.00
1888	26.00					4-15—8-15	.320	78.00
1889	50.00					4-15—8-15	.615	150.00
1890	50.00					4-15—8-15	.615	150.00
1891	50.00					4-15—8-15	.615	150.00
1892	50.00					4-15—8-15	.615	150.00
1892	7.40					4-15—8-15	.091	22.20

Source—**Spring Creek.** Ditch—**Hunter & Lytton Ditches.**

1890	61.40	N½NW¼	4	33	58			
		SE¼SW¼	33	34	58	4-15—8-15	.755	184.20

Source—**Lamoille Creek.** Ditch—**Hunter & Lytton.**

1871	10.00	SW¼NE¼	32	34	58	4-15—8-15	.123	30.00
1872	24.00	W½	32	34	58	4-15—8-15	.295	84.00
1873	36.00	E½	6	33	58	4-15—8-15	.443	108.00
1874	40.00	W½	5	33	58	4-15—8-15	.492	120.00
1875	20.00	W½NE¼	5	33	58	4-15—8-15	.246	60.00
1876	50.00					4-15—8-15	.615	150.00
1877	17.50					4-15—8-15	.215	52.50
1878	34.00					4-15—8-15	.418	102.00
1880	20.00					4-15—8-15	.246	60.00
1881	50.00					4-15—8-15	.615	150.00
1882	115.00					4-15—8-15	1.415	345.00
1883	10.00					4-15—8-15	.123	30.00
1884	75.00					4-15—8-15	.923	225.00
1885	50.00					4-15—8-15	.615	150.00
1886	20.00					4-15—8-15	.246	60.00
1887	75.00					4-15—8-15	.923	225.00
1888	26.70					4-15—8-15	.328	80.10
1889	76.80					4-15—8-15	.945	220.40

Claimant—**Alex. Carden.** Proof No. 00424

Source—**Talbot Creek and Springs.** Ditch—**Carden Ditches.**

1872	90.90*	W½E½	17	33	58	4-15—8-15	1.118	272.70
1873	83.50	NE¼NE¼	17	33	58	4-15—8-15	1.027	250.50
1873	23.00	NE¼NE¼	17	33	58	4-15—8-15	.283	69.00

*90.90 acres is from swamp ditches and Talbot Creek. All water available from swamp ditches is to be used first and if it is not sufficient to irrigate the extra water is to come from Talbot Creek. 106.5 acres from Talbot Creek.

Claimant—**George Bower.** Proof No. 00426

Source—**Lamoille Creek.** Ditch—**Patterson, Garden, Bowers Nos. 1 and 2.**

Year of priority	Culture—Acres: Harvest crops	Meadow pasture	Diversified pasture	Location: Subdivision	Section	Tp.N.	R.E.	Length of season	Duty of water: C.F.S.	Acre-feet
1865	4.00			NE¼	19	33	58	4-15—8-15	.049	12.00
1868	1.00			NE¼	19	33	58	4-15—8-15	.012	3.00
A1868*	2.91			NE¼	19	33	58	4-15—8-15	.036	8.73
1869	5.09			NE¼	19	33	58	4-15—8-15	.063	15.27
1870	1.00			NE¼	19	33	58	4-15—8-15	.012	3.00
1871	15.56			NE¼	19	33	58	4-15—8-15	.101	46.68
1872	5.26			NE¼	19	33	58	4-15—8-15	.065	15.78
1873	5.88			NE¼	19	33	58	4-15—8-15	.072	17.64
1874	4.78			NE¼	19	33	58	4-15—8-15	.059	14.34
1875	23.89			NE¼	19	33	58	4-15—8-15	.294	81.67
1876	8.48			NE¼	19	33	58	4-15—8-15	.104	25.44
1877	5.12			NE¼	19	33	58	4-15—8-15	.063	15.36
1878	5.03			NE¼	19	33	58	4-15—8-15	.062	15.09
1896	20.76			NE¼	19	33	58	4-15—8-15	.255	62.28
1899	26.00			NE¼	19	33	58	4-15—8-15	.320	78.00
1900	21.45			NE¼	19	33	58	4-15—8-15	.264	64.35

*1868 prior right over A1868.

NOTE—"After exchanging dates and areas to conform to Lamoille Court Decree." Elko District Court No. 1311.

Claimant—**John Paleni.** Proof No. 00427

Source—**Lamoille Creek.** Ditch—**Erro-Streeter.**

Year of priority	Harvest crops	Meadow pasture	Diversified pasture	Subdivision	Section	Tp.N.	R.E.	Length of season	C.F.S.	Acre-feet
1900	13.80			NE¼NE¼	13	33	57	4-15—8-15	.170	41.40

Claimant—**Joe Capriola.** Proof No. 00428

Source—**Lamoille Creek.** Ditch—**Joe Capriola Ditches.**

Year of priority	Harvest crops	Meadow pasture	Diversified pasture	Subdivision	Section	Tp.N.	R.E.	Length of season	C.F.S.	Acre-feet
1900	46.20			SE¼	13	33	58	4-15—8-15	.568	138.60

Claimant—**Webster Patterson.** Proof No. 00430

Source—**Lamoille Creek.** Ditch—**Patterson, Streeter.**

Year of priority	Harvest crops	Meadow pasture	Diversified pasture	Subdivision	Section	Tp.N.	R.E.	Length of season	C.F.S.	Acre-feet
1865	16.00			E½	18	33	58	4-15—8-15	.197	48.00
1868	4.00			W½	17	33	58	4-15—8-15	.049	12.00
A 1868*	19.42			S½SW¼	8	33	58	4-15—8-15	.239	58.26
1869	33.88							4-15—8-15	.417	101.64

Source—**Lamoille Creek.** Ditch—**Webster Patterson.**

Year of priority	Harvest crops	Meadow pasture	Diversified pasture	Subdivision	Section	Tp.N.	R.E.	Length of season	C.F.S.	Acre-feet
1874	5.00				7	33	58	4-15—8-15	.062	15.00
1876	50.00				7	33	58	4-15—8-15	.615	150.00
1877	5.00				7	33	58	4-15—8-15	.062	15.00
1880	20.00				7	33	58	4-15—8-15	.246	60.00
1882	25.00				7	33	58	4-15—8-15	.308	75.00
1886	40.00				7	33	58	4-15—8-15	.492	120.00
1888	40.00				7	33	58	4-15—8-15	.492	120.00
1890	40.00				7	33	58	4-15—8-15	.492	120.00
1891	90.00				7	33	58	4-15—8-15	1.107	270.00

	1863			40.00					7	33	58	4-15—8-15	.492	120.00
	1867			40.00					7	33	58	4-15—8-15	.492	120.00
	1904			83.20					7	33	58	4-15—8-15	1.023	249.60
	1870			3.54								4-15—8-15	.044	10.62
	1871			54.76								4-15—8-15	.674	164.28
	1872			18.51								4-15—8-15	.228	51.53
	1873			20.68								4-15—8-15	.254	62.04
	1874			16.81								4-15—8-15	.207	50.43
	1875			84.08								4-15—8-15	1.034	252.24
	1876			29.89								4-15—8-15	.368	89.67
	1877			18.03								4-15—8-15	.222	54.09
	1878			17.70								4-15—8-15	.218	53.10

*1868 prior right over A1868.

	A1878*			14.21								4-15—8-15	.175	42.36
	1879			75.20								4-15—8-15	.925	225.60
	1880			115.76								4-15—8-15	1.424	347.28
	1881			8.88								4-15—8-15	.109	26.64
	1882			12.22								4-15—8-15	.150	36.66
	1883			18.48								4-15—8-15	.227	55.44
	1884			25.68								4-15—8-15	.316	77.04
	1885			5.92								4-15—8-15	.073	17.76
	1886			8.59								4-15—8-15	.106	25.77
	1887			11.84								4-15—8-15	.146	35.52
	1888			10.95								4-15—8-15	.135	32.85
	1889			10.95								4-15—8-15	.135	32.85
	1890			5.92								4-15—8-15	.073	17.76
	1894			5.92								4-15—8-15	.073	17.76
	1895			47.68								4-15—8-15	.586	143.04

*1878 prior right over A1878.

NOTE—After exchanging dates and areas to conform to Lamoille court decree, Elko District Court No. 1311. Also stock-watering right from Carden's swamp ditch in SE¼ of SW¼, Sec. 17, T. N. 33, R. E. 58. This right was initiated prior to 1905.

Claimant—**R. B. Stewart.** Proof No. 00431

Source—**Rabbit Creek.** Ditch—**Stewart Ditches.**

	1862			100.00				E½	36	33	57	4-15—8-15	2.460	600.00
	1870			23.00				E½SW¼	36	33	57	4-15—8-15	.566	138.00
	1871			23.00				SE¼NW¼	36	33	57	4-15—8-15	.566	138.00
	1872			23.00				N½NE¼	1	32	57	4-15—8-15	.566	138.00
	1873			23.00				SW¼NE¼	1	32	57	4-15—8-15	.566	138.00
	1874			23.00				E½NW¼	1	32	57	4-15—8-15	.566	138.00
	1875			24.70								4-15—8-15	.608	148.20
	1876			2.00								4-15—8-15	.050	12.00
	1877			50.00								4-15—8-15	1.230	300.00
	1877			...		16.00						4-15—8-15	.394	24.00
	1898			45.00								4-15—8-15	1.108	270.00
	1904			12.80								4-15—8-15	.314	76.80
	1904			36.70								4-15—8-15	.902	220.20
	1904			...		115.60						4-15—8-15	2.844	173.40

Claimant—**C. E. Noble.** Proof No. **00437**

Source—**Talbot Creek.** Ditch—**C. E. Noble Ditches.**

Year of priority	Culture—Acres: Harvest crops	Meadow pasture	Diversified pasture	Location: Subdivision	Section	Tp.N.	R.E.	Length of season	Duty of water: C.F.S.	Acre-feet
1875	25.00			NE¼	28	33	58	4-15—8-15	.308	75.00
1875	*10.44			N½SE¼	28	33	58	4-15—8-15	.128	31.32
1876	10.00							4-15—8-15	.123	30.00
1878	20.00							4-15—8-15	.246	60.00
1880	41.00							4-15—8-15	.504	123.00
1887	20.00							4-15—8-15	.246	60.00
1896	2.00							4-15—8-15	.025	6.00

*Swamp area. No water to be diverted from the creek for any swamp area until the same become dry or is drained.

Claimant—**J. A. Castor.** Proof No. **00438**

Source—**Little Rabbit Creek.** Ditch—**J. A. Castor Ditches.**

Year of priority	Harvest crops	Meadow pasture	Diversified pasture	Subdivision	Section	Tp.N.	R.E.	Length of season	C.F.S.	Acre-feet
1886	20.90			E½SW¼	14	33	57	4-15—8-15	.357	62.70

NOTE—Little Rabbit Creek is branch of Rabbit Creek.

Claimant—**N. R. Castor.** Proof No. **00439**

Source—**Little Rabbit Creek.** Ditch—**N. R. Castor Ditches.**

Year of priority	Harvest crops	Meadow pasture	Diversified pasture	Subdivision	Section	Tp.N.	R.E.	Length of season	C.F.S.	Acre-feet
1873	3.44			E½NW¼	14	33	57	4-15—8-15	.042	10.32
1886	29.45							4-15—8-15	.362	88.35

NOTE—Little Rabbit Creek is branch of Rabbit Creek.

Claimant—**C. Larrondo & Co.** Proof No. **00441**

Source—**Stoffer Creek and Natural Draws.** Ditch—**C. Larrondo Ditches.**

Year of priority	Harvest crops	Meadow pasture	Diversified pasture	Subdivision	Section	Tp.N.	R.E.	Length of season	C.F.S.	Acre-feet
1806	62.26			NW¼	29	33	57	4-15—8-15	.766	186.78
1807	62.25			N½NE¼	20	33	57	4-15—8-15	.766	186.75
				S½SE¼	20	33	57			

NOTE—Stoffer Creek is branch of Rabbit Creek.

Claimant—**R. B. Stewart.** Proof No. **00442-00443**

Source—**Rabbit Creek.** Ditch—**Stewart Ditches.**

Year of priority	Harvest crops	Meadow pasture	Diversified pasture	Subdivision	Section	Tp.N.	R.E.	Length of season	C.F.S.	Acre-feet
1862	50.00			SE¼	35	33	57	4-15—8-15	1.230	300.00
1869	45.00			S½NE¼	35	33	57	4-15—8-15	1.108	270.00
1870	45.00			W½W½	36	33	57	4-15—8-15	1.108	270.00
1871	40.00			NE¼NW¼	36	33	57	4-15—8-15	.984	240.00
1872	30.00			W½NW¼	1	32	57	4-15—8-15	.738	180.00
1874	30.00			N½NE¼	2	32	57	4-15—8-15	.738	180.00
1876	53.50							4-15—8-15	1.316	321.00
1879	64.60							4-15—8-15	1.590	387.60
1886	73.30							4-15—8-15	1.804	439.80
1901	4.00							4-15—8-15	.098	24.00

Claimant—**Andrew Westlund.** Proof No. 00444

Source—**Lamoille Creek.** Ditch—**Andrew Westlund Ditches.**

1870	1.51	W½E½	29	33	58	4-15—8-15	.019	4.53
1871	23.34	W½E½	29	33	58	4-15—8-15	.287	70.02
1872	7.89	W½E½	29	33	58	4-15—8-15	.297	23.67
1873	8.81	W½E½	29	33	58	4-15—8-15	.108	26.43
1874	7.16	W½E½	29	33	58	4-15—8-15	.088	21.48
1875	35.83	W½E½	29	33	58	4-15—8-15	.441	107.49
1876	12.74	W½E½	29	33	58	4-15—8-15	.157	38.22
1877	7.68	W½E½	29	33	58	4-15—8-15	.094	23.04
1878	7.54	W½E½	29	33	58	4-15—8-15	.093	22.62

NOTE—After exchanging dates and areas to conform to Lamoille Court Decree, Elko District Court No. 1311.

Source—**Snell Creek.** Ditch—**Andrew Westlund Ditches.**

1871	14.00	W½E½	29	33	58	4-15—8-15	.172	42.00

Claimant—**Griswold-Henderson Livestock Co.** **Proof No. 00445**

Source—**Hamilton Creek, a branch of Cold Creek.** Ditch—**Hamilton and Greenwood.**

1873	10.00		1	33	58	4-15—8-15	.123	30.00
1874	15.00					4-15—8-15	.185	45.00
1875	15.00					4-15—8-15	.185	45.00
1876	15.00					4-15—8-15	.185	45.00
1877	15.00					4-15—8-15	.185	45.00
1879	30.00					4-15—8-15	.369	90.00
1880	10.00					4-15—8-15	.123	30.00
1881	10.00					4-15—8-15	.123	30.00
1882	10.00					4-15—8-15	.123	30.00
1883	10.00					4-15—8-15	.123	30.00
1884	10.00					4-15—8-15	.123	30.00
1885	10.00					4-15—8-15	.123	30.00
1886	10.00					4-15—8-15	.123	30.00
1887	13.00					4-15—8-15	.160	39.00
1869	10.00	S½NE¼SW¼	34	34	58	4-15—8-15	.123	30.00
1870	30.00	SE¼SW¼	34	34	58	4-15—8-15	.369	90.00
1871	30.00	SE¼	34	34	58	4-15—8-15	.369	90.00
1872	30.00	E½NW¼	3	33	58	4-15—8-15	.369	90.00
1873	30.00	E½SW¼	3	33	58	4-15—8-15	.369	90.00
1874	30.00	NE¼	3	33	58	4-15—8-15	.369	90.00
1875	30.00	SE¼	3	33	58	4-15—8-15	.369	90.00
1876	30.00	NW¼SW¼	2	33	58	4-15—8-15	.369	90.00
1877	30.00					4-15—8-15	.369	90.00
1878	34.60					4-15—8-15	.426	103.80
1895	15.00					4-15—8-15	.185	45.00

NOTE—That certain agreement entered into between Henderson Banking Company, Griswold-Henderson Livestock Company, C. W. Griswold, and Samuel McIntyre, as of July 16, 1908, is binding as between parties to agreement.

Claimant—**R. B. Stewart.** Proof No. 00446

Source—**Rabbit Creek.** Ditch—**Stewart Ditches.**

Year of priority	Culture—Acres: Harvest crops	Meadow pasture	Diversified pasture	Location: Subdivision	Section	Tp.N.	R.E.	Length of season	Duty of water: C.F.S.	Acre-feet
1869	40.00			S½	26	33	57	4-15—8-15	.984	240.00
1870	50.00			N½N½	35	33	57	4-15—8-15	1.230	300.00
1871	50.00			S½NW¼	35	33	57	4-15—8-15	1.230	300.00
1872	30.00							4-15—8-15	.738	180.00
1873	30.00							4-15—8-15	.738	180.00
1874	30.00							4-15—8-15	.738	180.00
1875	30.00							4-15—8-15	.738	180.00
1876	40.00							4-15—8-15	.984	240.00
1879	40.80							4-15—8-15	1.004	244.80
1880	20.00							4-15—8-15	.492	120.00

Claimant—**C. W. Clubine.** Proof No. 00447

Source—**Talbot Creek.** Ditch—**C. W. Clubine Ditches.**

Year of priority	Harvest crops	Meadow pasture	Diversified pasture	Subdivision	Section	Tp.N.	R.E.	Length of season	C.F.S.	Acre-feet
1886	6.00			W½E½	16	33	58	4-15—8-15	.074	18.00
1889	6.00			E½NE¼	16	33	58	4-15—8-15	.074	18.00
1895	20.00			SW¼SE¼	9	33	58	4-15—8-15	.246	60.00
1900	19.50							4-15—8-15	.240	58.50
1903	73.00							4-15—8-15	.898	219.00
1904	24.00							4-15—8-15	.295	72.00

Source—**Beaver or Thorp Creek.** Ditch—**C. W. Clubine Ditches.**

Year of priority	Harvest crops	Meadow pasture	Diversified pasture	Subdivision	Section	Tp.N.	R.E.	Length of season	C.F.S.	Acre-feet
1867	100.00			W½	9	33	58	4-15—8-15	1.230	300.00
1889	27.20			W½SE¼	9	33	58	4-15—8-15	.335	81.60
1870	31.40							4-15—8-15	.386	94.20
1871	31.30							4-15—8-15	.385	93.90
1872	31.30							4-15—8-15	.385	93.90
1873	31.30							4-15—8-15	.385	93.90
1873	8.90							4-15—8-15	.109	26.70
1881	51.20							4-15—8-15	.630	153.00
1881	5.00							4-15—8-15	.062	15.00
1889	45.80							4-15—8-15	.563	137.40

Claimant—**C. H. Reinken.** Proof No. 00448

Source—**Beaver or Thorpe Creek, Holland Slough and Springs.**

Dtich—**C. H. Reinken Ditches.**

Year of priority	Harvest crops	Meadow pasture	Diversified pasture	Subdivision	Section	Tp.N.	R.E.	Length of season	C.F.S.	Acre-feet
1875	30.00			N½NE¼	33	34	58	4-15—8-15	.369	90.00
1876	20.00			SE¼	28	34	58	4-15—8-15	.246	60.00
1877	20.00			SE¼NE¼	28	34	58	4-15—8-15	.246	60.00
1879	57.00			SW¼	27	34	58	4-15—8-15	.701	171.00
1870	20.00			E½NW¼	27	34	58	4-15—8-15	.246	60.00
1872	10.00			W½	34	34	58	4-15—8-15	.123	30.00
1874	40.00			SE¼NE¼	33	34	58	4-15—8-15	.492	120.00
1875	22.00			NE¼SE¼	33	34	58	4-15—8-15	.271	66.00

	1876			22.00								4-15—8-15	.271	60.00
	1874			50.00								4-15—8-15	.615	150.00
	1875			40.00								4-15—8-15	.492	120.00
	1876			40.00								4-15—8-15	.492	120.00
	1877			50.00								4-15—8-15	.615	150.00
	1878			23.50								4-15—8-15	.289	70.50
	1872			20.00								4-15—8-15	.246	60.00
	1876			20.00								4-15—8-15	.246	60.00
	1878			40.00								4-15—8-15	.492	120.00
	1880			23.00								4-15—8-15	.283	69.00
	1872			30.00								4-15—8-15	.369	90.00
	1873			45.00								4-15—8-15	.554	135.00
	1876			30.00								4-15—8-15	.369	90.00
	1898			15.00								4-15—8-15	.185	45.00
	1900			22.00								4-15—8-15	.271	60.00

Source—**Lamoille Creek.**

Ditch No. 4—

	1900			30.00				W¼NW¼	28	34	58	4-15—8-15	.369	90.00
	1901			27.00				NW¼SW¼	28	34	58	4-15—8-15	.332	81.00
	1902			15.00				NE¼SE¼	29	34	58	4-15—8-15	.185	45.00
	1903			36.00								4-15—8-15	.443	108.00

Ditch No. 3—

	1873			2.00				N½NE¼	32	34	58	4-15—8-15	.025	6.00
	1885			31.00				S½SE¼	29	34	58	4-15. 8-15	.381	93.00
	1890			35.00				W½SW¼	28	34	58	4-15—8-15	.431	105.00
	1895			36.10								4-15—8-15	.444	108.30

Ditches Nos. 7 and 11—

	1874			25.00				SW¼	28	34	58	4-15—8-15	.308	75.00
	1875			25.00								4-15—8-15	.308	75.00
	1878			21.00								4-15—8-15	.258	63.00

Ditch No. 12—

	1872			24.00				E½NW¼	28	34	58	4-15—8-15	.295	72.00
	1885			22.00				W½NE¼	28	34	58	4-15—8-15	.271	66.00
	1890			22.00								4-15—8-15	.271	66.00

Ditch No. 8—

	1878			60.00				NE¼	28	34	58	4-15—8-15	.738	180.00
	1880			121.00				NW¼	27	34	58	4-15—8-15	1.488	363.00

Ditch not on map—

	1874			2.00				NW¼SE¼	28	34	58	4-15—8-15	.025	6.00
	1876			6.00								4-15—8-15	.074	18.00
	1878			15.00								4-15—8-15	.185	45.00
	1880			13.00								4-15—8-15	.160	39.00

C. H. Reinken—Continued.
Source—**Talbot Creek.**

Ditches Nos. 9 and 10—

Year of priority	Culture—Acres: Harvest crops	Meadow pasture	Diversified pasture	Location: Subdivision	Section	Tp.N.	R.E.	Length of season	Duty of water: C.F.S.	Acre-feet
1876	20.00			N½NW¼	33	34	58	4-15—8-15	.246	60.00
1880	40.00			S½SW¼	28	34	58	4-15—8-15	.492	120.00
1890	42.00							4-15—8-15	.517	126.00

Ditch No. 2—

Year of priority	Harvest crops	Meadow pasture	Diversified pasture	Subdivision	Section	Tp.N.	R.E.	Length of season	C.F.S.	Acre-feet
1875	20.00			SE¼	28	34	58	4-15—8-15	.246	60.00
1876	13.00			NW¼NE¼	33	34	58	4-15—8-15	.160	39.00
1879	9.00			NE¼NW¼	33	34	58	4-15—8-15	.111	27.00
1880	8.00							4-15—8-15	.098	24.00
1885	11.00							4-15—8-15	.135	33.00
1890	11.00							4-15—8-15	.135	33.00
1905*	2.00			NW¼SE¼	28	34	58	4-15—8-15	.025	6.00

*This ditch not shown, but is flumed across Lamoille Creek.

Claimant—**Dave Morrow.** Proof No. 00449
Source—**Springs (as below).** Ditch—**Dave Morrow Ditches.**

Year of priority	Harvest crops	Meadow pasture	Diversified pasture	Subdivision	Section	Tp.N.	R.E.	Length of season	C.F.S.	Acre-feet
1872	12.00*			NE¼	32	33	58	4-15—8-15	.148	36.00
1878	8.00†			NE¼	32	33	58	4-15—8-15	.098	24.00
1896	6.68‡			NE¼	32	33	58	4-15—8-15	.082	20.04

This takes practically all of the water from these sources: *From Orchard Spring; †From Big Spring in Trueman Canyon; ‡From Brown Canyon.

Claimant—**Jas. Byers.** Proof No. 00451
Source—**Talbot Creek.** Ditch—**Jas. Byers Ditches.**

Year of priority	Harvest crops	Meadow pasture	Diversified pasture	Subdivision	Section	Tp.N.	R.E.	Length of season	C.F.S.	Acre-feet
1876	45.00			SW¼NE¼	22	33	58	4-15—8-15	.554	135.00
1878	15.00			W½SE¼	22	33	58	4-15—8-15	.185	45.00
1880	5.00			E½SW¼	22	33	58	4-15—8-15	.062	15.00
1881	12.00			S½SW¼SW¼	22	33	58	4-15—8-15	.148	36.00
1887	15.80							4-15—8-15	.194	47.40
1889	5.00							4-15—8-15	.062	15.00
1890	12.00							4-15—8-15	.148	36.00
1895	5.00							4-15—8-15	.002	15.00
1897	12.00							4-15—8-15	.148	36.00
1898	12.50							4-15—8-15	.154	37.50
1899	10.00							4-15—8-15	.123	30.00
1900	7.00							4-15—8-15	.086	21.00
1904	8.70							4-15—8-15	.107	26.10

Claimant—**Samuel Cook.** Proof No. 00452

Source—**Little Rabbit Creek and Spring Creek.** Ditch—**Spring Creek and Bellinger Ditch.**

Little Rabbit Creek		SE¼	8	33	57			
1901	25.00	W½SW¼	9	33	57	4-15—8-15	.308	75.00
1902	15.00	W½NW¼	16	33	57	4-15—8-15	.185	45.00
1905	19.56	SE¼NW¼	16	33	57	4-15—8-15	.241	58.68
Spring Creek		NE¼SW¼	16	33	57			
1880	65.00	NW¼SE¼	16	33	57	4-15—8-15	.800	195.00
1903	13.59	N½NE¼	17	33	57	4-15—8-15	.167	40.77
1903	3.50	SE¼NE¼	17	33	57	4-15—8-15	.043	10.50
1903	4.00	NE¼	17	33	57	4-15—8-15	.049	12.00

Before irrigating more land from Spring Creek than the 65 acres dated 1880, claimant is to have ⅝ c.f.s. flowing over a weir in Spring Creek between the water hole on Elko-Lamoille road and the bridge where the Pleasant Valley road cross Spring Creek, up to August 15 of each year. After August 15 there must be ⅝ c.f.s flowing over said weir before irrigation of any more land from Spring Creek other than the 65 acres. These restrictions are in accordance with judgment and decree No. 1621—Yowell v. Bellinger, Elko County Records. Said judgment and decree are binding as between parties to the suit.

Claimant—**R. Lebreski.** Proof No. 00453

Source—**Rabbit Creek and Springs.** Ditch—**Lebreski.**

1873	12.50	SE¼	2	33	57	4-15—8-15	.154	37.50
1890	37.10	SE¼	2	33	57	4-15—8-15	.456	111.30
1890	18.60*	SE¼	2	33	57	4-15—8-15	.229	55.80

*Priority from Rabbit Creek dated 1904.

Source—**Rabbit Creek and *Spring.** Ditch—**Lebreski.**

1896	56.71	E½NW¼	2	33	57	4-15—8-15	.698	170.13
1904	11.56	W½NE¼	2	33	57	4-15—8-15	.142	34.68
1904	2.09*					4-15—8-15	.026	6.27

Claimant—**E. Hankins** (Deed to James Billet in escrow). Proof No. 00454

Source—**Talbot Creek.** Ditch—**E. Hankins Ditches.**

1873	15.00	E½NW¼	16	33	58	4-15—8-15	.185	45.00
1876	5.00					4-15—8-15	.062	15.00
1884	4.40 (a)					4-15—8-15	.054	13.20
1892	10.00					4-15—8-15	.123	30.00
1900	44.00					4-15—8-16	.541	132.00
						4-15—8-15		
1869	10.00	W½NW¼	16	33	58	4-15—8-15	.123	30.00
1870	25.00	SE¼NE¼	17	33	58	4-15—8-15	.308	75.00
1871	5.00	W½SW¼	16	33	58	4-15—8-15	.062	15.00
1872	3.00	E½SE¼	17	33	58	4-15—8-15	.037	9.00
1873	10.00 (a)					4-15—8-15	.123	30.00
1878	30.00					4-15—8-15	.369	90.00
1884	100.00					4-15—8-15	1.230	300.00
1884	22.00 (a)					4-15—8-15	.271	66.00
1893	15.00					4-15—8-15	.185	45.00
1895	30.00					4-15—8-15	.369	90.00

(a) Swamp area. No water to be diverted from the creek for this area until the same becomes dry or is drained.

Claimant—**Q. D. Boyd.** Proof No. 00458

Source—**Lamoille Creek.** Ditch—**Q. D. Boyd Ditches.**

Year of priority	Culture—Acres: Harvest crops	Meadow pasture	Diversified pasture	Location: Subdivision	Section	Tp.N.	R.E.	Length of season	Duty of water: C.F.S.	Acre-feet
1883	213.55			SE¼	7	35	58	4-15—8-15	2.627	640.65
1883	12.55			S½	8	35	58	4-15—8-15	.154	37.65
1884	40.00							4-15—8-15	.492	120.00
1885	7.16							4-15—8-15	.088	21.48
1885	53.91							4-15—8-15	.663	161.73
1888	17.55							4-15—8-15	.216	52.65
1895			68.52					4-15—5-15	.843	51.39

Claimant—**Albert Trescartes.** Proof No. 00459

Source—**Lamoille Creek.** Ditch—**Albert Trescartes Ditches.**

Year of priority	Harvest crops	Meadow pasture	Diversified pasture	Subdivision	Section	Tp.N.	R.E.	Length of season	C.F.S.	Acre-feet
1900	55.90			N½	26	33	57	4-15—8-15	.688	167.70
1902	24.00							4-15—8-15	.295	74.00
1903	27.20							4-15—8-15	.335	81.20

NOTE—Water right initiated prior to 1905 on Section 25 and transferred by permit to Section 26.

Claimant—**Chas. Trescartes.** Proof No. 00459

Source—**Lamoille Creek.** Ditch—**Chas. Trescartes Ditches.**

Year of priority	Harvest crops	Meadow pasture	Diversified pasture	Subdivision	Section	Tp.N.	R.E.	Length of season	C.F.S.	Acre-feet
A1868*	7.29			W½NW¼	20	33	58	4-15—8-15	.090	21.87
1869	12.71			W½SW¼	20	33	58	4-15—8-15	.156	38.13
1870	1.21							4-15—8-15	.015	3.63
1871	18.67							4-15—8-15	.230	56.01
1872	6.31							4-15—8-15	.078	18.93
1873	7.05							4-15—8-15	.087	21.15
1874	5.73							4-15—8-15	.070	17.19
1875	28.66							4-15—8-15	.353	85.98
1876	10.19							4-15—8-15	.125	30.57
1877	6.15							4-15—8-15	.076	18.45
1878	6.03							4-15—8-15	.074	18.09
1880	28.00							4-15—8-15	.344	84.00
1896	17.10							4-15—8-15	.210	51.30

*1868 has priority over A1868.

Claimant—**Albert Trescartes.** Proof No. 00459

Source—**Rabbit Creek, Little Rabbit Creek, and Swamps and Springs.**

Ditch—**Albert Trescartes Ditches.**

Year of priority	Harvest crops	Meadow pasture	Diversified pasture	Subdivision	Section	Tp.N.	R.E.	Length of season	C.F.S.	Acre-feet
1898	5.20*			N½	26	33	57	4-15—8-15	.064	15.60
1898	22.00*							4-15—8-15	.271	66.00
1898	17.00†							4-15—8-15	.209	51.00
1900	20.00‡							4-15—8-15	.246	60.00

NOTE—Little Rabbit Creek is branch of Rabbit Creek. *From Swamps and Springs; †From Rabbit Creek; ‡Little Rabbit Creek.

Claimant—**Chas. Trescartes.** Proof No. 00450

Source—**Lamoille Creek.** Ditch—**Chas. Trescartes Ditches.**

1904	56.30	W½NE¼	24	33	57	4-15—8-15	.692	168.90
1905	40.50	SE¼NE¼	24	33	57	4-15—8-15	.498	121.50

Claimant—**Gabriel Rossi.** Proof No. 00461

Source—**Rabbit Creek.** Ditch—**Gabriel Rossi Ditches.**

1887	82.00	E½NE¼	23	34	57			
1880	220.00	NW¼	24	34	57			
		E½SW¼	24	34	57			
		SW¼NE¼	24	34	57			
		SE¼	24	34	57			
		W½SE¼	26	34	57	4-15—8-15	1.009	246.00
		NE¼SE¼	26	34	57	4-15—8-15	2.706	660.00

Claimant—**James B. Stewart.** Proof No. 00462

Source—**Rabbit Creek and Little Rabbit Creek.** Ditch—**James B. Stewart Ditches.**

1873	35.50	N½	11	33	57	4-15—8-15	.437	106.50
1890	35.60	N½	11	33	57	4-15—8-15	.438	106.80

Claimant—**August Alles.** Proof No. 00476

Source—**Deering or Alles or Lost Creek and Ackler Creek.** Ditch—**August Alles Ditches.**

1888	12.27	NW¼SW¼	23	36	60	4-15—8-15	.151	36.81
1889	9.00	SE¼NE¼	22	36	60	4-15—8-15	.111	27.00
1890	5.85	SE¼NE¼	22	36	60	4-15—8-15	.072	17.55
1890	2.25	NE¼SW¼	23	36	60	4-15—8-15	.028	6.75
1891	5.85	SE¼NE¼	22	36	60	4-15—8-15	.072	17.55
1896	7.50	NE¼SW¼	23	36	60	4-15—8-15	.092	22.50
1897	1.12	NW¼SW¼	23	36	60	4-15—8-15	.014	3.36
1898	14.25	SW¼NE¼	23	36	60	4-15—8-15	.175	42.85
1899	14.25	SW¼NE¼	23	36	60	4-15—8-15	.175	42.85
1900	20.42	SW¼NE¼	22	36	60	4-15—8-15	.251	61.26

NOTE—Water for irrigating above land to be taken first from Alles Creek, and upon its failure to run, enough Ackler Creek is to be drawn upon.

NOTE—That certain Decree No. 1527, Elko County District Court, is binding as between parties to the suit. No water is to be diverted from Deering Creek or its tributaries until decree is satisfied.

Claimant—**W. W. Alles.** Proof No. 00477

Source—**Springs, Swamps, and Natural Draw on Secs. 5 and 6, T. 36 N, R. 60 E.**

Ditch—**W. W. Alles Ditches.**

1901	36.14	S½NE¼	6	36	60	4-15—8-15	.445	108.42

NOTE—Source is as shown above. Claimant not to take water from Ackler or Herder Creek in case of shortage.

Claimant—**J. W. Weathers.** Proof No. 00479

Source—**Right Boulder Creek.** Ditch—**J. W. Weathers Ditches.**

Year of priority	Culture—Acres: Harvest crops	Meadow pasture	Diversified pasture	Location: Subdivision	Section	Tp.N.	R.E.	Length of season	Duty of water: C.F.S.	Acre-feet
1902	30.94			NW¼SE¼	32	36	60			
				N½SW¼	32	36	60	4-15—8-15	.381	92.82

Source—**Left Boulder Creek.** Ditch—**J. W. Weathers Ditches.**

Year of priority	Harvest crops	Meadow pasture	Diversified pasture	Subdivision	Section	Tp.N.	R.E.	Length of season	C.F.S.	Acre-feet
1880	3.90			NE¼	32	36	60	4-15—8-15	.048	11.70
1903	24.05							4-15—8-15	.296	72.15
1905	28.73							4-15—8-15	.353	86.19

Claimant—**Mrs. M. E. Goodale and J. H. Goodale.** Proof. No. 00481

Source—**Deering Creek.** Ditch—**Goodale Ditches.**

Year of priority	Harvest crops	Meadow pasture	Diversified pasture	Subdivision	Section	Tp.N.	R.E.	Length of season	C.F.S.	Acre-feet
1873	20.00			SE¼	18	36	60	4-15—8-15	.246	60.00
1874	5.50			SE¼	18	36	60	4-15—8-15	.068	16.50
1874	6.00			SE¼	18	36	60	4-15—8-15	.074	18.00
1882	10.10			SE¼	18	36	60	4-15—8-15	.124	30.30
1882	5.10			SE¼	18	36	60	4-15—8-15	.063	15.30
1882	.50			SE¼	18	36	60	4-15—8-15	.006	1.50
1882	7.00			SE¼	18	36	60	4-15—8-15	.086	21.00
1882	11.20			SE¼	18	36	60	4-15—8-15	.138	33.60

NOTE—That certain Decree No. 1527, Elko County District Court, is binding as between parties to the suit.

Claimant—**J. W. Johnston.** Proof No. 00482

Source—**Boulder Creek and Branches.** Ditch—**Armstrong 1-6, incl.**

Year of priority	Harvest crops	Meadow pasture	Diversified pasture	Subdivision	Section	Tp.N.	R.E.	Length of season	C.F.S.	Acre-feet
1868	100.00			SW¼	18	36	60	4-15—8-15	1.230	300.00
1868	...		103.63	W½SW¼SE¼	18	36	60	4-15—5-15	1.275	77.72
1871	20.00			W½NW¼	19	36	60	4-15—8-15	.246	60.00
1872	10.15			NE¼	19	36	60	4-15—8-15	.125	30.45
1873	171.00			S½	19	36	60	4-15—8-15	2.103	513.00
1875	81.25			N½	30	36	60	4-15—8-15	.909	243.75
				E½NE¼	25	36	59			
				E½SE¼	24	36	59			

Claimant—**H. M. Lane.** Proof No. 00483

Source—**Boulder Creek.** Ditch—**Johnston & Armstrong and Carlson.**

Year of priority	Harvest crops	Meadow pasture	Diversified pasture	Subdivision	Section	Tp.N.	R.E.	Length of season	C.F.S.	Acre-feet
1876	20.00			NW¼	19	36	60	4-15—8-15	.246	60.00
1878	43.00			NW¼	19	36	60	4-15—8-15	.528	129.00
1888	17.00			NW¼	19	36	60	4-15—8-15	.209	51.00

Claimant—**Phil Harney.** Proof No. 00484
Source—**Soldier Creek.** Ditch—**McDermott 1-4, incl.**

	1896			22.10				SW¼	20	34	59	4-15—8-15	.272	66.30
	1896			15.40				W½SE¼	20	34	59	4-15—8-15	.180	46.20
	1896			10.10								4-15—8-15	.124	30.30
	1896			21.80								4-15—8-15	.268	65.40
	1896					21.20*						4-15—5-15	.298	18.15
	1896				22.90							4-15—6-15	.282	34.35
	1902			26.20								4-15—8-15	.322	78.60
	1902			4.00								4-15—5-15	.049	12.00
	1902			8.00								4-15—8-15	.098	24.00
	1902				25.30							4-15—6-15	.311	37.65
	1902				18.50							4-15—6-15	.228	27.75
	1896					20.20						4-15—5-15	.250	15.15
	1902					11.30						4-15—5-15	.139	8.48
	1902					10.00						4-15—5-15	.123	7.50

*No water is to be diverted onto this land until it becomes dry or is drained.

Claimant—**Earl Green.** Proof No. 00485
Source—**Soldier Creek.** Ditch—**Earl Green Ditches.**

	1902			3.40				E½NE¼	32	34	59	4-15—8-15	.042	10.20
	1902			4.40								4-15—8-15	.054	17.60
	1902			5.40								4-15—8-15	.066	16.20
	1902			5.00								4-15—8-15	.062	15.00
	1902			0.80								4-15—8-15	.010	2.40
	1894			39.60				SE¼SW¼	28	34	59	4-15—8-15	.487	118.80
	1895			20.70				SW¼SE¼	28	34	59	4-15—8-15	.255	62.10
	1897			11.50				NW¼	33	34	59	4-15—8-15	.141	34.50
	1898			7.50				NW¼NE¼	33	34	59	4-15—8-15	.092	22.50
	1899			16.80								4-15—8-15	.207	50.40
	1902			17.00								4-15—8-15	.209	51.00
	1904			11.50								4-15—8-15	.141	34.50
	1904			12.10								4-15—8-15	.149	36.30

Claimant—**W. L. Paul.** Proof No. 00486
Source—**Deering Creek and Branch of Deering Creek.** Ditch—**W. L. Paul Ditches.**

	1876			4.55				SE¼NE¼	28	36	60	4-15—8-15	.055	13.65

Claimant—**L. L. Redden.** Proof No. 00487
Source—**Herder Creek.** Ditch—**L. L. Redden Ditches.**

	1894			13.50				S½N½	5	36	60	4-15—8-15	.166	40.50
	1895			27.70								4-15—8-15	.341	80.10
	1900			95.30								4-15—8-15	1.172	285.90
	1902			23.00								4-15—8-15	.283	69.00

Claimant—**J. M. Riddell.** Proof No. 00488
Source—**Herder Creek.** Ditch—**J. M. Riddell Ditches.**

Year of priority	Culture—Acres: Harvest crops	Meadow pasture	Diversified pasture	Location: Subdivision	Section	Tp.N.	R.E.	Length of season	Duty of water: C.F.S.	Acre-feet
1881	25.00			N½SE¼	4	36	60	4-15—8-15	.308	75.00
1875	9.00							4-15—8-15	.111	27.00
1892	8.00							4-15—8-15	.098	24.00
1900	6.00							4-15—8-15	.074	18.00
1901	1.80							4-15—8-15	.022	5.40
1893	11.50							4-15—8-15	.141	34.50
1894	11.50							4-15—8-15	.141	34.50
1903	4.00							4-15—8-15	.049	12.00
1901	1.30			SW¼SW¼	3	36	60	4-15—8-15	.016	3.90
1902	10.00			S½NW¼SW¼	3	36	60	4-15—8-15	.123	30.00
1903	3.00							4-15—8-15	.037	9.00
1904	2.30							4-15—8-15	.028	6.90
1901			28.20					4-15—5-15	.347	21.15

Claimant—**Pete Scott.** Proof No. 00489
Source—**Soldier Creek.** Ditch—**Scott Ditch.**

Year of priority	Harvest crops	Meadow pasture	Diversified pasture	Subdivision	Section	Tp.N.	R.E.	Length of season	C.F.S.	Acre-feet
1893	16.00			S½NW¼NW¼	28	34	59	4-15—8-15	.207	50.70
1894	41.00			S½NW¼	28	34	59	4-15—8-15	.504	123.00
1895	42.10							4-15—8-15	.518	126.30

Claimant—**William Smiley.** Proof No. 00490
Source—**Smiley Creek, Dry Gulch and Little Hall Canyon Creek.**
Ditch—**Smiley Nos. 1-8, incl.**

Year of priority	Harvest crops	Meadow pasture	Diversified pasture	Subdivision	Section	Tp.N.	R.E.	Length of season	C.F.S.	Acre-feet
1880	197.20			E½SW¼	34	37	60	4-15—8-15	2.426	591.60
1881	73.10			E½	34	37	60	4-15—8-15	.899	219.10
1882	93.90			W½W½	35	37	60	4-15—8-15	1.155	291.70
1883	42.00			E½SW¼	35	37	60	4-15—8-15	.517	126.00
1885	2.30			NE¼NE¼	3	36	60	4-15—8-15	.028	6.90
1891	7.90			NW¼NW¼	2	36	60	4-15—8-15	.097	23.70
1892	27.40							4-15—8-15	.337	82.20
1894	26.80							4-15—8-15	.330	80.40
1895	8.60							4-15—8-15	.106	25.80
1896	18.60							4-15—8-15	.229	55.80
1897	51.10							4-15—8-15	.629	153.30

As far as possible claimant is to use the waters of Smiley Creek, Dry Gulch, and Little Hall Canyon Creek before taking any water from Herder Creek; the balance of the water required for irrigation to be taken from Herder Creek.

NOTE—In addition to irrigation rights claimant has a vested right from Herder Creek for domestic and stock watering purposes in NE corner of Sec. 33 with a date of 1902. Claimant not to divert water from Herder Creek to the NE corner of Sec. 33 as long as there is sufficient water from other sources for domestic and stockwatering purposes in said section.

16[71]

Claimant—**W. J. Smiley.** Proof No. 00491

Source—**Boulder Creek.** Ditch—**W. J. Smiley Ditches.**

1877	58.40	E½NE¼	13	36	50	4-15—8-15	.718	175.20

Source—**Reed Creek and Sloughs.** Ditch—**W. J. Smiley Ditches.**

1885	50.00	SW¼	27	36	59	4-15—8-15	.615	150.00
1887	50.00	SE¼	28	36	59	4-15—8-15	.615	150.00
1889	50.00	NE¼	33	36	59	4-15—8-15	.615	150.00
1890	14.15	NW¼	34	36	59	4-15—8-15	.174	42.45

Source—**Starr Creek.** Ditch—**W. J. Smiley Ditches.**

1871	5.00	SW¼SW¼	7	36	60	4-15—8-15	.062	15.00
1877	79.00	NW¼	18	36	60	4-15—8-15	.972	237.00

Source—**Herder Creek.** Ditch—**W. J. Smiley Ditches.**

1872	15.00	NW¼	7	36	60	4-15—8-15	.185	45.00
1873	20.00	N½SW¼	7	36	60	4-15—8-15	.246	60.00
1884	25.00					4-15—8-15	.308	75.00

Source—**Ackler Creek.** Ditch—**W. J. Smiley Ditches.**

1872	61.00	SW¼	7	36	60			
		SE¼NW¼	7	36	60	4-15—8-15	.750	183.00
1870	10.60	NW¼NW¼	17	36	60	4-15—8-15	.130	31.80

Source—**Deering Creek.** Ditch—**W. J. Smiley Ditches.**

1868	10.00	SW¼	7	36	60	4-15—8-15	.123	30.00
1868	20.00	NW¼NW¼	17	36	60	4-15—8-15	.246	60.00
1869	25.00	SW¼NW¼	17	36	60	4-15—8-15	.308	75.00
1870	25.00	N½	18	36	60	4-15—8-15	.308	75.00
1870	8.40					4-15—8-15	.103	25.20
1871	20.00					4-15—8-15	.246	60.00
1872	25.00					4-15—8-15	.308	75.00
1872	25.00					4-15—8-15	.308	75.00
1873	25.00					4-15—8-15	.308	75.00
1873	13.00					4-15—8-15	.160	30.00
1874	25.00					4-15—8-15	.308	75.00
1877	80.00					4-15—8-15	.984	240.00
1879	31.20					4-15—8-15	.384	93.60
1889	10.00*					4-15—8-15	.123	30.00
1903	10.00					4-15—8-15	.123	30.00

*Was land of defendant Tauffer in suit No. 1527, Elko County Records. No water to be diverted for this land until balance of Smiley land and lands of Mrs. M. E. Goodale and J. H. Goodale have been satisfied as per decree.

NOTE—That certain Decree No. 1527, Elko County District Court, is binding as between parties to the suit.

Source—**Boulder Creek.** Ditch—**Monk's Ditch.**

1887	89.34		23	36	59	4-15—8-15	1.099	268.02

Claimant—**W. C. Mills.** Proof No. 00492

Source—**Deering Creek and Branch of Deering Creek.** Ditch—**W. C. Mills Ditches.**

Year of priority	Culture—Acres: Harvest crops	Meadow pasture	Diversified pasture	Location: Subdivision	Section	Tp.N.	R.E.	Length of season	Duty of water: C.F.S.	Acre-feet
1873	10.00				28	36	60	4-15—8-15	.123	30.00
1876	60.00				28	36	60	4-15—8-15	.738	180.00
1888	10.00				28	36	60	4-15—8-15	.123	30.00
1889	10.00				28	36	60	4-15—8-15	.123	30.00
1890	10.00				28	36	60	4-15—8-15	.123	30.00
1891	10.00				28	36	60	4-15—8-15	.123	30.00
1892	10.00				28	36	60	4-15—8-15	.123	30.00
1893	5.20				28	36	60	4-15—8-15	.064	15.60
1900	3.00				28	36	60	4-15—8-15	.037	9.00

NOTE—That certain Decree No. 1527, Elko County District Court, is binding as between parties to the suit. No water is to be diverted from Deering Creek or its tributaries until decree is satisfied.

Claimant—**John Stiers.** Proof No. 00493

Source—**Deering Creek.** Ditch—**Left-Hand and Right-Hand Ditches.**

Year of priority	Harvest crops	Meadow pasture	Diversified pasture	Subdivision	Section	Tp.N.	R.E.	Length of season	C.F.S.	Acre-feet
1890	7.40			SW¼NW¼	21	36	60	4-15—8-15	.091	22.20
1890	4.50			NW¼NW¼	21	36	60	4-15—8-15	.055	13.50
1891	1.39			SE¼NW¼	21	36	60	4-15—8-15	.017	4.17
1891	4.60			NW¼NW¼	21	36	60	4-15—8-15	.057	14.80
1893	1.00			SW¼NW¼	21	36	60	4-15—8-15	.012	3.00

Claimant—**W. B. Tavelle.** Proof No. 00494

Source—**Left Boulder Creek.** Ditch—**W. B. Tavelle Ditches.**

Year of priority	Harvest crops	Meadow pasture	Diversified pasture	Subdivision	Section	Tp.N.	R.E.	Length of season	C.F.S.	Acre-feet
1881	46.41			SE¼	30	36	60	4-15—8-15	.511	139.23
1884	6.50			SE¼	30	36	60	4-15—8-15	.080	19.50
1884	....		18.00	SE¼	30	36	60	4-15—6-15	.221	13.50
1891	11.40			SE¼	30	36	60	4-15—8-15	.140	34.20
1891	....		32.93	SE¼	30	36	60	4-15—6-15	.405	24.70

Right Boulder Creek.

Year of priority	Harvest crops	Meadow pasture	Diversified pasture	Subdivision	Section	Tp.N.	R.E.	Length of season	C.F.S.	Acre-feet
1872	2.86			SE¼	30	36	60	4-15—8-15	.035	8.58

Claimant—**W. W. Weathers.** Proof No. 00496

Source—**Right Boulder Creek.** Ditch—**W. W. Weathers Ditches.**

Year of priority	Harvest crops	Meadow pasture	Diversified pasture	Subdivision	Section	Tp.N.	R.E.	Length of season	C.F.S.	Acre-feet
1868	13.59			SW¼	30	36	60	4-15—8-15	.107	40.77
1869	14.24			SW¼	30	36	60	4-15—8-15	.175	42.72
1870	5.32			SW¼	30	36	60	4-15—8-15	.065	15.96
1870	....		35.23	SW¼	30	36	60	4-15—6-15	.433	20.42

Source—**Left Boulder Creek.** Ditch—**W. W. Weathers Ditches.**

Year of priority	Harvest crops	Meadow pasture	Diversified pasture	Subdivision	Section	Tp.N.	R.E.	Length of season	C.F.S.	Acre-feet
1878	1.17			SW¼	30	36	60	4-15—8-15	.014	3.51

Claimant—**Mrs. Annie M. Wells.** Proof No. 00496

Source—**Right Boulder Creek and Spring.** Ditch—**Wells Ditches.**

Right Boulder Creek—

	1879			4.68				NE¼	31	36	60	4-15—8-15	.058	14.04
	1879			3.49				NW¼	32	36	60	4-15—8-15	.043	11.47
	1879			6.13				NE¼	31	36	60	4-15—8-15	.075	18.39
	1879			22.11				NE¼	31	36	60	4-15—8-15	.272	66.33
	1905			14.10				NW¼	32	36	60	4-15—8-15	.173	42.30
	1905			8.89				NW¼	32	36	60	4-15—8-15	.109	26.67
	1905			.42				NE¼	31	36	60	4-15—8-15	.005	1.26

Spring—

	1887			27.39				NW¼	32	36	60	4-15—8-15	.337	82.17
	1887			11.34				NW¼	32	36	60	4-15—8-15	.139	34.02
	1887			1.69				NE¼	31	36	60	4-15—8-15	.021	5.07
	1887			5.00				NE¼	32	36	60	4-15—8-15	.062	15.00
	1887			2.40				NW¼	32	36	60	4-15—8-15	.030	7.20

Source—**Left Boulder Creek.** Ditch—**Wells Ditches.**

	1880			5.33				SW¼	29	36	60	4-15—8-15	.066	15.99
	1880			1.30				SE¼	29	36	60	4-15—8-15	.016	3.90
	1880			2.34				SW¼	29	36	60	4-15—8-15	.288	7.02
	1884			30.94				NE¼	31	36	60	4-15—8-15	.381	92.82
	1884			29.22				SW¼	29	36	60	4-15—8-15	.359	87.66
	1884			3.90				SW¼	29	36	60	4-15—8-15	.048	11.70
	1905			10.28				NW¼	32	36	60	4-15—8-15	.126	30.84
	1905			30.94				NW¼	32	36	60	4-15—8-15	.381	92.82
	1905			10.00				SW¼	32	36	60	4-15—8-15	.123	30.00
	1905			10.13				NE¼	31	36	60	4-15—8-15	.125	30.39

Claimant—**Estate of Mrs. Jane Wright.** Proof No. 00497

Source—**Wright Creek, Dry Creek, Secret Creek and Springs.**

Ditch—**Jane Wright Ditches Nos. 1-8, incl.**

	1879			10.00				S½NW¼	10	34	60	4-15—8-15	.123	30.00
	1879			59.10				SW¼NE¼	10	34	60	4-15—8-15	.727	177.10
	1880			59.20				S½	10	34	60	4-15—8-15	.728	177.60
	1881			59.20				N½NW¼	15	34	60	4-15—8-15	.728	177.60
	1882			59.20				NW¼NE¼	15	34	60	4-15—8-15	.728	177.60
	1883			59.20				SE¼NW¼	15	34	60	4-15—8-15	.728	177.60
	1883			15.00				SW¼NE¼	15	34	60	4-15—8-15	.185	45.00
	1884			59.20								4-15—8-15	.728	177.60
	1900			51.00								4-15—8-15	.627	153.00

Claimant—**John Stiers.** Proof No. 00498

Source—**Alles Creek.** Ditch—**Stiers Ditch.**

Year of priority	Culture—Acres: Harvest crops	Meadow pasture	Diversified pasture	Location: Subdivision	Section	Tp. N.	R. E.	Length of season	Duty of water: C. F. S.	Acre-feet
1890	3.86			NE¼NW¼	21	36	60	4-15—8-15	.047	11.58
1890	2.00			NW¼NW¼	21	36	60	4-15—8-15	.025	6.00
1891	3.87			NE¼NW¼	21	36	60	4-15—8-15	.047	11.61

Claimant—**Wm. Goodale.** Proof No. 00499

Source—**Herder Creek through Brennen Gulch.** Ditch—**Wm. Goodale Ditches.**

Year of priority	Harvest crops	Meadow pasture	Diversified pasture	Subdivision	Section	Tp. N.	R. E.	Length of season	C. F. S.	Acre-feet
1877	19.80			SE¼SE¼	5	36	60	4-15—8-15	.244	59.40
1877	9.70			SW¼SE¼	5	36	60	4-15—8-15	.119	29.10
1877	9.80			SE¼SE¼	5	36	60	4-15—8-15	.121	20.40
1894	10.00			SW¼SE¼	5	36	60	4-15—8-15	.123	30.00
1894	10.00			SE¼SE¼	5	36	60	4-15—8-15	.123	30.00
1894	19.70			SW¼SE¼	5	36	60	4-15—8-15	.242	59.10

Claimant—**Ed. Smiley.** Proof No. 00500

Source—**Hall Canyon Creek, Smiley Springs, and Little Hall Canyon Creek.**

Ditch—**Ed. Smiley Ditches.**

Year of priority	Harvest crops	Meadow pasture	Diversified pasture	Subdivision	Section	Tp. N.	R. E.	Length of season	C. F. S.	Acre-feet
1877	18.70			SW¼SW¼	26	37	60	4-15—8-15	.230	56.10
1877	8.90			N½NW¼	26	37	60	4-15—8-15	.109	26.70
1877	4.20			SE¼NW¼	26	37	60	4-15—8-15	.052	12.60
1877	42.60			E½SW¼	26	37	60	4-15—8-15	.523	127.80
1897	21.60			SE¼SE¼	26	37	60	4-15—8-15	.266	64.80

NOTE—All lands under Elko District Court Decree No. 2635 to be served with water before diverting any water for this land.

Year of priority	Harvest crops	Meadow pasture	Diversified pasture	Subdivision	Section	Tp. N.	R. E.	Length of season	C. F. S.	Acre-feet
1877	200.00			NW¼	26	37	60			
				SW¼	26	37	60			
				SE¼	26	37	60	4-1—9-1	2.50	
1897	73.90			S½	26	37	60			
				NW¼	26	37	60	4-1—9-1	.92	
1904	10.00			S½	26	37	60			
				NW¼	26	37	60	4-1—9-1	.125	

Elko District Court Decree No. 2635 is binding as between parties to the suit.

That certain agreement between H. A. Agee and Ed. Smiley and copy filed with State Engineer July 22, 1921, File No. 00500, is binding as between parties.

Claimant—**H. A. Agee.** Proof No. 00501

Source—**Hall Canyon Creek, Gray's Spring and Berger Creek.** Ditch—**Agee Ditches.**

Year of priority	Harvest crops	Meadow pasture	Diversified pasture	Subdivision	Section	Tp. N.	R. E.	Length of season	C. F. S.	Acre-feet
1879	38.00			NE¼NE¼	26	37	60			
1879	20.00			SE¼NE¼	26	37	60			
1879	40.00			NW¼NE¼	26	37	60			
1879	40.00			SW¼NE¼	26	37	60			
1879	40.00			SE¼SE¼	23	37	60			
1879	11.50			NW¼NW¼	25	37	60	4-1—9-1	2.370	

1883	40.00	SW¼SW¼	24	37	60	4-1—9-1	.500	
1887	40.00	SW¼SE¼	23	37	60	4-1—9-1	.500	
1902	11.00	NW¼NW¼	24	37	60			
1902	13.50	NE¼NW¼	24	37	60			
1902	19.90	SE¼NW¼	24	37	60			
1902	11.10	SW¼NW¼	24	37	60			
1902	33.50	NW¼SW¼	24	37	60			
1902	35.30	NE¼SW¼	24	37	60			
1902	2.20	SE¼SW¼	24	37	60			
1902	4.80	SE¼NW¼	24	37	60	4-1—9-1	1.640	

Judgment and Decree No. 2635 are binding as between parties to the suit. The above duty of water is set by Decree No. 2635, Elko District Court.
That certain agreement between H. A. Agee and Ed. Smiley is binding between said parties.
Claimant has 1879 priority for stock and domestic water.

1879	2.00	NE¼NE¼	26	37	60	4-15—8-15	.025	6.00
1879	4.40	NW¼NW¼	25	37	60	4-15—8-15	.054	13.20
1882	1.70	NE¼SW¼	24	37	60	4-15—8-15	.021	5.10
1882	11.20	NE¼SW¼	24	37	60	4-15—8-15	.138	33.60
1886	7.80	NE¼SW¼	24	37	60	4-15—8-15	.096	23.40
1886	26.50	NE¼SW¼	25	37	60	4-15—8-15	.326	79.50
1886	1.00	SE¼NW¼	25	37	60	4-15—8-15	.012	3.00
1894	2.50	NW¼NW¼	24	37	60	4-15—8-15	.031	7.50
1894	21.20	NW¼NW¼	24	37	60	4-15—8-15	.261	63.60
1894	1.40	NW¼NW¼	24	37	60	4-15—8-15	.017	4.20
1894	5.60	NE¼NW¼	24	37	60	4-15—8-15	.069	16.80
1894	1.50	SW¼NW¼	24	37	60	4-15—8-15	.019	4.50
1894	19.20	SW¼NW¼	24	37	60	4-15—8-15	.236	57.00
1894	14.70	SE¼NW¼	24	37	60	4-15—8-15	.181	44.10
1894	3.40	NW¼SW¼	24	37	60	4-16—8-15	.042	10.20
1902	8.20	SW¼NW¼	24	37	60	4-15—8-15	.101	24.60
1902	3.10	NW¼SW¼	24	37	60	4-15—8-15	.038	9.30
1902	2.00	NE¼SW¼	24	37	60	4-15—8-15	.025	6.00
1902	2.10	SE¼SW¼	24	37	60	4-15—8-15	.026	6.30

NOTE—All lands under Elko District Court Decree No. 2635 to be served with water before diverting any water for this land.

Claimant—**Hylton & Mentz.** Proof No. 00502

Source—**Herder Creek.** Ditch—**Hylton & Mentz Ditches.**

1880	11.80	SE¼	6	36	60	4-15—8-15	.145	35.40
1880	4.00	NE¼SW¼	6	36	60	4-15—8-15	.049	12.00
1882	7.00					4-16—8-15	.086	21.00
1886	1.20					4-15—8-15	.015	3.60
1886	2.90					4-15—8-15	.036	8.70
1897	3.50					4-15—8-15	.043	10.50
1903	21.30					4-15—8-15	.262	63.90
1903	9.70					4-15—8-15	.119	29.10
1903	30.00					4-15—8-15	.369	90.00
1905	14.70					4-15—8-15	.180	44.10

Source—**Deering Creek.** Ditch—**Hylton & Mentz Ditches.**

1878	50.00*	W½SE¼	7	36	60	4-15—8-15	.615	150.00

*No water is to be diverted until swamp becomes dry or is drained.

Hylton & Mentz—Continued.

Source—**Ackler Creek.** Ditch—**Hylton & Mentz Ditches.**

Year of priority	Culture—Acres: Harvest crops	Meadow pasture	Diversified pasture	Location: Subdivision	Section	Tp.N.	R.E.	Length of season	Duty of water: C.F.S.	Acre-feet
1873	16.60			NW¼SE¼	7	36	60	4-15—8-15	.204	49.80
1873	21.50			S½NE¼	7	36	60	4-15—8-15	.264	64.50
1878	30.00*			S½NE¼	7	36	60	4-15—8-15	.369	90.00

*No water is to be diverted until swamp becomes dry or is drained.

Source—**Ackler Creek and Herder Creek.** Ditch—**Hylton & Mentz Ditches.**

Year of priority	Harvest crops	Meadow pasture	Diversified pasture	Subdivision	Section	Tp.N.	R.E.	Length of season	C.F.S.	Acre-feet
1870	10.60			NE¼	7	36	60	4-15—8-15	.130	31.80
1871	9.70			N½NW¼	8	36	60	4-15—8-15	.119	29.10
1872	11.20							4-15—8-15	.138	33.60
1872	5.00							4-15—8-15	.062	15.00
1872	8.90							4-15—8-15	.109	26.70
1873	2.30							4-15—8-15	.028	6.90
1873	4.00							4-15—8-15	.049	12.00
1873	21.60							4-15—8-15	.266	64.80
1873	29.40							4-15—8-16	.362	88.20
1874	22.20							4-15—8-15	.273	66.60
1874	1.20							4-15—8-15	.015	3.60
1874	29.50							4-15—8-15	.363	88.50
1874	10.40							4-15—8-15	.128	31.20
1875	5.00							4-15—8-15	.062	15.00
1875	6.00							4-15—8-15	.074	18.00
1886	11.60							4-15—8-15	.143	34.80

Source—**Herder Creek.** Ditch—**Hylton & Mentz Ditches.**

Year of priority	Harvest crops	Meadow pasture	Diversified pasture	Subdivision	Section	Tp.N.	R.E.	Length of season	C.F.S.	Acre-feet
1873	8.10			SW¼	5	36	60	4-15—8-15	.100	24.30
1873	6.10							4-15—8-15	.075	18.30
1873	9.30							4-15—8-15	.114	27.90
1873	3.20							4-15—8-15	.039	9.60
1875	10.00							4-15—8-15	.123	30.00
1876	21.90							4-15—8-15	.269	65.70
1880	11.70							4-15—8-15	.144	35.10
1880	19.50							4-15—8-15	.240	58.50
1881	19.50							4-15—8-15	.240	58.50
1897	37.00							4-15—8-15	.455	111.00

Claimant—**E. C. Riddell.** Proof No. 00503

Source—**Ackler and Herder Creeks.** Ditch—**E. C. Riddell Ditches.**

Year of priority	Harvest crops	Meadow pasture	Diversified pasture	Subdivision	Section	Tp.N.	R.E.	Length of season	C.F.S.	Acre-feet
1870	28.40			NW¼	9	36	60	4-15—8-15	.349	85.20
1872	7.00			W½NE¼	9	36	60	4-15—8-15	.086	21.00
1873	68.60			SE¼NE¼	9	36	60	4-15—8-15	.844	205.80
1874	20.80			W½NE¼NE¼	9	36	60	4-15—8-15	.256	62.40
1875	10.20							4-15—8-15	.100	18.00
1876	40.80							4-15—8-15	[illegible]	[illegible]

1901	2.70					4-15—8-15	.033	8.10
1904	8.30					4-15—8-15	.102	24.90
1905	1.00					4-15—8-15	.012	3.00

Claimant—**George Byers.** Proof No. 00504

Source—**As Below.** Ditch—**George Byers Ditches.**

Springs, Swamps, and Natural Draw—

1881	12.18	SE¼SE¼	27	37	60	4-15—8-15	.150	36.54
1881	4.47	SW¼SE¼	27	37	60	4-15—8-15	.055	13.41

Spring and Natural Draw—

1881	12.00	E½NE¼	27	37	60	4-15—8-15	.148	36.00

Springs and Spring Branch—

1881	43.40	SW¼NW¼	27	37	60	4-15—8-15	.534	130.20
1905	7.00	N½SW¼	27	37	60	4-15—8-15	.086	21.00
		SE¼SW¼	27	37	60			
		SW¼SE¼	27	37	60			

Blasengame Creek—

1883	48.30	W½W½	22	37	60	4-15—8-15	.594	144.90
1887	4.00	W½W½	22	37	60	4-15—8-15	.049	12.00

Natural Channel and Springs Tributary to Blasengame Creek—

1892	100.00	SW¼	27	37	60	4-15—8-15	1.230	300.00
		W½NW¼	27	37	60			

No rights to divert this natural channel from streams above.

Spring Canyon and Springs—

1889	25.10	E½E½	32	37	60	4-15—8-15	.308	75.30
1890	25.10	E½E½	32	37	60	4-15—8-15	.308	75.30

Hall Canyon Creek—

1883	14.80	N½NW¼	22	37	60	4-15—8-15	.182	44.40

All lands under Elko District Court Decree No. 2635 to be served with water before diverting any water for this land.

1901	15.10	NE¼SE¼	27	37	60	4-1—9-1		
1901	28.90	NW¼SE¼	27	37	60	4-1—9-1		
1901	12.00	SW¼SE¼	27	37	60	4-1—9-1		
1901	13.30	SE¼SE¼	27	37	60	4-1—9-1	.870	

Elko District Court Decree No. 2635 is binding as between parties to the suit.

Source—**Spring.** Ditch—**Geo. Byers Ditches.**

1886	22.00†	NE¼SE¼	27	37	60	4-15—8-15	.271	66.00
1886	9.00†	SE¼SE¼	27	37	60	4-15—8-15	.111	27.00
1886	10.10†	NE¼SW¼	27	37	60	4-15—8-15	.124	30.30
1886	1.20†	SE¼NW¼	27	37	60	4-15—8-15	.015	3.60
1886	5.50†	SW¼NW¼	27	37	60	4-15—8-15	.068	16.50

†All lands under Elko District Court decree No. 2635 to be served with water before diverting any water from Hall Canyon Creek for this land.

George Byers—Continued.
Source—**Herder Creek.** Ditch—**George Byers Ditches.**

Year of priority	Culture—Acres: Harvest crops	Culture—Acres: Meadow pasture	Culture—Acres: Diversified pasture	Location: Subdivision	Location: Section	Location: Tp.N.	Location: R.E.	Length of season	Duty of water: C.F.S.	Duty of water: Acre-feet
1892	4.50			NE¼	4	36	60	4-15—8-15	.055	13.50
1893	16.50			NE¼	4	36	60	4-15—8-15	.203	49.50
1894	16.70			NE¼	4	36	60	4-15—8-15	.205	50.10
1894	...		43.50	NE¼	4	36	60	4-15—5-15	.535	32.63

Claimant—**J. L. Bartmess.** Proof No. **00505**
Source—**Ackler Creek and Branch.** Ditches—**Nos. 1-14, incl.**

Year of priority	Harvest crops	Meadow pasture	Diversified pasture	Subdivision	Section	Tp.N.	R.E.	Length of season	C.F.S.	Acre-feet
1872	8.10			SW¼NW¼	8	36	60	4-15—8-15	.100	24.30
1874	5.90			SE¼NW¼	8	36	60	4-15—8-15	.073	17.70
1876	5.90				...	...	...	4-15—8-15	.073	17.70
1878	17.60				...	...	...	4-15—8-15	.216	52.80
1878	0.70				...	...	...	4-15—8-15	.009	2.10

Claimant—**W. J. Black.** Proof No. **00505**
Source—**Ackler Creek, Brennen Gulch, and Herder Creek.** Ditches—**Nos. 1-14, incl.**

Year of priority	Harvest crops	Meadow pasture	Diversified pasture	Subdivision	Section	Tp.N.	R.E.	Length of season	C.F.S.	Acre-feet
1872	10.00			E½	8	36	60	4-15—8-15	.123	30.00
1882	10.00			S½NW¼	8	36	60	4-15—8-15	.123	30.00
1892	10.00			NE¼SW¼	8	36	60	4-15—8-15	.123	30.00
1902	10.00				...	...	...	4-15—8-15	.123	30.00
Branch Ackler Creek—										
1872	57.80			E½	8	36	60	4-15—8-15	.711	173.40
1874	10.00			SE¼NW¼	8	36	60	4-15—8-15	.123	30.00
1876	10.00			NE¼SW¼	8	36	60	4-15—8-15	.123	30.00
1878	14.70				...	...	...	4-15—8-15	.181	44.10
Brennen Gulch—										
1881	5.90				...	...	...	4-15—8-15	.073	17.70
Herder Creek—										
1875	5.90				...	...	...	4-15—8-15	.073	17.70
1876	5.90				...	...	...	4-15—8-15	.073	17.70
1881	2.00				...	...	...	4-15—8-15	.025	6.00

Source—**Ackler Creek.** Ditches—**Nos. 1-14, incl.**

Year of priority	Harvest crops	Meadow pasture	Diversified pasture	Subdivision	Section	Tp.N.	R.E.	Length of season	C.F.S.	Acre-feet
1872	14.20			E½	8	36	60	4-15—8-15	.175	42.60
1878	10.00			SE¼NW¼	8	36	60	4-15—8-15	.123	30.00
1880	28.30			NE¼SW¼	8	36	60	4-15—8-15	.348	84.90
1891	13.00				...	...	...	4-15—8-15	.100	30.00
1901	10.40					...	...	4-15—8-15	.128	31.20
1902	8.00					...	...	4-15—8-15	.037	9.00
1903	14.80					...	...	4-15—8-15	.182	44.40

Claimant—**Jos. Jeanney.** Proof No. 00506

Source—**Branch of Ackler Creek and Alles Creek or Lost Creek.**

Ditch—**St. Clair and Natural Channel.**

Branch of Ackler Creek—							
1872	11.00	NW¼SW¼	8	36	60	4-15—8-15	.135	33.00
1872	17.50	NE¼SE¼	7	36	60	4-15—8-15	.215	52.50
1898	10.60	NW¼NE¼	17	36	60	4-15—8-15	.130	31.80
1904	9.90	NW¼NE¼	17	36	60	4-15—8-15	.122	29.70
1870	25.00	NW¼SW¼	8	36	60	4-15—8-15	.304	75.00
1870	21.00	SW¼SW¼	8	36	60	4-15—8-15	.258	63.00
1872	20.00	NE¼SE¼	7	36	60	4-15—8-15	.246	60.00
1872	2.00	SW¼SW¼	8	36	60	4-15—8-15	.025	6.00
1872	2.50	NE¼SE¼	7	36	60	4-15—8-15	.031	7.50
1872	23.30	SE¼SE¼	7	36	60	4-15—8-15	.287	69.90
1872	16.70	SE¼SE¼	7	36	60	4-15—8-15	.205	50.10
Lost Creek or Alles Creek—							
1899	2.70	NE¼NE¼	17	36	60	4-15—8-15	.022	8.10
1899	1.80	NW¼NE¼	17	36	60	4-15—8-15	.015	5.40

Claimant—**C. H. Black.** Proof. No. 00507

Source—**Herder Creek.** Ditch—**Redden and Black.**

1872	15.00	NW¼	4	36	60	4-15—8-15	.180	45.00
1873	19.00	N½SW¼	4	36	60	4-15—8-15	.234	57.00
1875	42.00	S½SE¼	4	36	60	4-15—8-15	.517	126.00
1879	14.50					4-15—8-15	.178	43.50
1880	49.00					4-15—8-15	.603	147.00
1885	4.00					4-15—8-15	.049	12.00
1890	4.00					4-15—8-15	.049	12.00
1894	29.20					4-15—8-15	.359	87.60
1895	28.90					4-15—8-15	.355	86.70

Source—**Ackler Creek.** Ditch—**C. H. Black Ditches.**

1892	9.00	E½	10	36	60	4-15—8-15	0.111	27.00
1894	3.40	SW¼	10	36	60	4-15—8-15	0.042	10.20
1895	43.00	S½ SE¼NW¼	10	36	60	4-15—8-15	0.529	129.00
1896	17.30					4-15—8-15	0.213	51.90
1898	10.00					4-15—8-15	0.123	30.00
1900	5.00					4-15—8-15	0.062	15.00
1901	4.80					4-15—8-15	0.059	14.40

Claimant—**Isaac Griswold.** Proof No. 00508

Source—**Boulder Creek.** Ditch—**Isaac Griswold Ditch.**

1888	17.30	W½SE¼	2	36	59	4-15—8-15	.213	51.90
1888	9.90	W½SE¼	2	36	59	4-15—8-15	.122	29.70
1888	20.10	W½SE¼	2	36	59	4-15—8-15	.247	60.30

Claimant—**W. W. Weathers.** Proof No. 00508

Source—**Starr Creek.** Ditch—**W. W. Weathers Ditches.**

Year of priority	Culture—Acres: Harvest crops	Culture—Acres: Meadow pasture	Culture—Acres: Diversified pasture	Location: Subdivision	Location: Section	Location: Tp.N.	Location: R.E.	Length of season	Duty of water: C.F.S.	Duty of water: Acre-feet
1879	14.80			NW¼SW¼	1	36	59	4-15—8-15	.182	44.40
1879	3.00			SE¼SW¼	1	36	59	4-15—8-15	.037	9.00
1878	25.20			NE¼SE¼	12	36	59	4-15—8-15	.309	75.60
1875	22.00			NE¼NE¼	2	36	59	4-15—8-15	.271	66.00
1875	2.80			SE¼NE¼	2	36	59	4-15—8-15	.034	8.40
1872	32.90			SW¼NW¼	1	36	59	4-15—8-15	.405	98.70
1872	24.70			NW¼NW¼	1	36	59	4-15—8-15	.304	74.10
1872	12.50			SE¼SW¼	1	36	59	4-15—8-15	.154	37.50
1872	2.60			NE¼NE¼	2	36	59	4-15—8-15	.032	8.40
1875	21.90			NE¼NW¼	12	36	59	4-15—8-15	.269	65.70
1872	22.90			SW¼SW¼	36	37	59	4-15—8-15	.282	68.70
1872	7.30			NW¼SW¼	36	37	59	4-15—8-15	.090	21.90
1872	38.00			NE¼SE¼	35	37	59	4-15—8-15	.467	114.00
1872	1.00			NW¼SE¼	35	37	59	4-15—8-15	.012	3.00
1872	32.40			SE¼SE¼	35	37	59	4-15—8-15	.400	97.20
1879	8.20			SW¼NE¼	35	37	59	4-15—8-15	.101	24.60
1879	18.40			SW¼NE¼	35	37	59	4-15—8-15	.226	55.20
1879	40.00			SE¼NE¼	35	37	59	4-15—8-15	.492	120.00
1879	29.70			SW¼NW¼	35	37	59	4-15—8-15	.365	89.10
1879	30.40			SE¼NW¼	35	37	59	4-15—8-15	.374	91.20
1879	12.10			NE¼SW¼	35	37	59	4-15—8-15	.149	36.30
1879	23.40			NW¼SW¼	35	37	59	4-15—8-15	.288	70.20
1879	0.70			NW¼SE¼	35	37	59	4-15—8-15	.009	2.10
1878	3.70			NE¼SE¼	12	36	59	4-15—8-15	.046	11.10

Source—**Natural Draw North of Brennens Gulch.*** Ditch—**W. W. Weathers Ditches.**

Year of priority	Harvest crops	Meadow pasture	Diversified pasture	Subdivision	Section	Tp.N.	R.E.	Length of season	C.F.S.	Acre-feet
1885	5.00			S½SE¼	1	36	59	4-15—8-15	.062	15.00
1890	7.00							4-15—8-15	.086	21.00
1894	5.00							4-15—8-15	.062	15.00
1895	10.00							4-15—8-15	.123	30.00
1902	13.00							4-15—8-15	.160	39.00

*Water in this source is from springs, swamps and some return water. If supply becomes short, claimant is not to have water from any other natural source.

Source—**Ackler* and Herder Creeks through Brennens Gulch.**
Ditch—**W. W. Weathers Ditches.**

Year of priority	Harvest crops	Meadow pasture	Diversified pasture	Subdivision	Section	Tp.N.	R.E.	Length of season	C.F.S.	Acre-feet
1887	7.00			E½SW¼	1	36	59	4-15—8-15	.093	22.80
1887	10.00			SW¼SE¼	1	36	59	4-15—8-15	.123	30.00
1887	6.00							4-15—8-15	.071	18.00
1887	2.10							4-15—8-15	.026	6.30
1887	0.20							4-15—8-15	.002	0.60
1887	4.00							4-15—8-15	.049	12.00
1887	5.00							4-15—8-15	.062	15.00
1903	12.00							4-15—8-15	.148	30.00

*Ackler Creek priority 1903.

Source—Ackler Creek. Ditch—W. W. Weathers Ditches.														
	1878			6.00				NE¼SE¼	12	36	59	4-15—8-15	.074	9.00
Source—Boulder and Starr Creek. Ditch—W. W. Weathers Ditches.														
	1878			76.30				SE¼	12	36	59	4-15—8-15	.938	228.90
Source—Boulder Creek. Ditch—W. W. Weathers Ditches.														
	1868			37.20				NE¼NE¼	24	36	59	4-15—8-15	.458	111.60
	1868			25.40				SE¼NE¼	24	36	59	4-15—8-15	.312	76.20
	1868			37.50				NE¼SE¼	13	36	59	4-15—8-15	.461	112.50
	1870			39.00				SE¼SE¼	13	36	59	4-15—8-15	.480	117.00
	1870			10.00				SW¼SE¼	13	36	59	4-15—8-15	.123	30.00
	1870			2.80				NE¼NE¼	24	36	59	4-15—8-15	.034	8.40
	1870			12.80				NW¼SE¼	24	36	59	4-15—8-15	.157	38.40
	1872			6.10				NW¼SE¼	24	36	59	4-15—8-15	.075	18.30
	1872			12.70				NW¼NE¼	25	36	59	4-15—8-15	.156	38.10
	1872			1.00				SE¼SE¼	13	36	59	4-15—8-15	.012	3.00
	1872			2.70				SW¼SE¼	13	36	59	4-15—8-15	.033	8.10
	1870			14.60				SE¼NE¼	24	36	59	4-15—8-15	.180	43.80
	1868			10.00				NW¼SE¼	24	36	59	4-15—8-15	.123	30.00
	1869			4.00				NW¼SE¼	24	36	59	4-15—8-15	.049	12.00
	1870			5.10				NW¼SE¼	24	36	59	4-15—8-15	.063	15.30
	1878			28.50				SW¼NE¼	24	36	59	4-15—8-15	.351	85.50
	1878			11.50				SW¼NE¼	24	36	59	4-15—8-15	.141	34.50
	1878			22.60				NW¼NE¼	24	36	59	4-15—8-15	.278	67.80
	1878			17.40				NW¼NE¼	24	36	59	4-15—8-15	.214	52.20
	1878			27.30				SW¼SE¼	13	36	59	4-15—8-15	.336	81.90
	1878			38.30				NW¼SE¼	13	36	59	4-15—8-15	.471	114.90
	1878			29.00				SW¼NE¼	13	36	59	4-15—8-15	.357	87.00
	1878			9.50				NW¼NE¼	13	36	59	4-15—8-15	.117	28.50
	1878			1.50				SW¼NE¼	13	36	59	4-15—8-15	.018	4.50
	1878			3.90				W½SE¼	12	36	59	4-15—8-15	.048	11.70
	1878			1.40				W½SE¼	12	36	59	4-15—8-15	.017	4.20
	1878			3.80				W½SE¼	12	36	59	4-15—8-15	.047	11.40
	1888			8.60				SE¼SE¼	2	36	59	4-15—8-15	.106	25.80
	1888			10.00				NE¼SE¼	2	36	59	4-15—8-15	.123	30.00
	1888			19.30				SE¼SE¼	2	36	59	4-15—8-15	.237	57.90
	1888			14.90				NE¼SE¼	2	36	59	4-15—8-15	.183	44.70
	1888			27.20				SE¼NE¼	2	36	59	4-15—8-15	.335	81.60
	1875			15.90				SW¼SW¼	1	36	59	4-15—8-15	.196	47.70
	1875			20.70				NW¼SW¼	1	36	59	4-15—8-15	.255	62.10
	1875			2.00				NE¼SE¼	2	36	59	4-15—8-15	.025	6.00
	1875			24.20				NW¼NW¼	12	36	59	4-15—8-15	.297	72.60
	1875			9.70				NE¼NW¼	12	36	59	4-15—8-15	.119	29.10
	1875			22.00				SW¼SW¼	1	36	59	4-15—8-15	.271	66.00
	1875			8.40				NE¼NW¼	12	36	59	4-15—8-15	.103	25.20
	1888			7.60				NW¼NW¼	12	36	59	4-15—8-15	.093	22.80
	1876			7.60				SW¼SW¼	30	36	60	4-15—8-15	.093	22.80

Claimant—**G. E. Weathers.** Proof No. 00508

Source—**Ackler Creek,* Herder Creek, and Brennens Gulch.** Ditch—**G. E. Weathers Ditches.**

Year of priority	Culture—Acres: Harvest crops	Meadow pasture	Diversified pasture	Location: Subdivision	Section	Tp.N.	R.E.	Length of season	Duty of water: C.F.S.	Acre-feet
1875	8.00			NE¼	12	36	59	4-15—8-15	.098	24.00
1888	16.00							4-15—8-15	.197	48.00
1873	14.00							4-15—8-15	.172	42.00
1902	11.00							4-15—8-15	.135	33.00
1888	2.40							4-15—8-15	.295	7.20

*Priority from Ackler Creek through Co-Op Ditch to date 1893.

Source—**Ackler Creek and Starr Creek.** Ditch—**G. E. Weathers Ditches.**

Year of priority	Harvest crops	Meadow pasture	Diversified pasture	Subdivision	Section	Tp.N.	R.E.	Length of season	C.F.S.	Acre-feet
1875	21.00			NE¼	12	36	59	4-15—8-15	.295	72.00
1873	21.30							4-15—8-15	.262	63.90

Source—**Boulder Creek and Starr Creek.** Ditch—**G. E. Weathers Ditches.**

Year of priority	Harvest crops	Meadow pasture	Diversified pasture	Subdivision	Section	Tp.N.	R.E.	Length of season	C.F.S.	Acre-feet
1873	5.50			NE¼	12	36	59	4-15—8-15	.068	16.50
1875	13.10							4-15—8-15	.161	39.30

Source—**Starr Creek.** Ditch—**Starr Ditch.**

Year of priority	Harvest crops	Meadow pasture	Diversified pasture	Subdivision	Section	Tp.N.	R.E.	Length of season	C.F.S.	Acre-feet
1878	3.50			NE¼	12	36	59	4-15—8-15	.043	10.50

Claimant—**Union Land and Cattle Co.** Proof No. 00510

Source—**Starvation Creek, Soldier Creek, Murphy Creek, Ross Creek, Dry Creek.**

Ditch—**Union Land and Cattle Co. Ditches.**

Year of priority	Harvest crops	Meadow pasture	Diversified pasture	Subdivision	Section	Tp.N.	R.E.	Length of season	C.F.S.	Acre-feet
1874	198.00			E½	22	34	59	4-15—8-15	2.435	594.00
1900			42.00	E½	22	34	59	4-15—5-15	.517	31.50
1877	100.00			W½	22	34	59	4-15—8-15	1.230	300.00
1900			220.00	W½	22	34	59	4-15—5-15	2.706	165.00
1900			237.00	E½	21	34	59	4-15—5-15	2.915	177.75
1883	185.00				21	34	59	4-15—8-15	2.276	555.00
1893	53.00				21	34	59	4-15—8-15	.652	159.00
1898	93.00			NW¼	21	34	59	4-15—8-15	1.144	279.00
1895	49.00			SW¼	21	34	59	4-15—8-15	.603	147.00
1891	160.00			NE¼	20	34	59	4-15—8-15	1.968	480.00
1893	80.00			E½SE¼	20	34	59	4-15—8-15	.984	240.00
1877	158.00				27	34	59	4-15—8-15	1.943	474.00
1883			149.00	E¼E½	28	34	59	4-15—5-15	1.833	111.75
1891			179.00	W½NE¼	28	34	59			
				NW¼	28	34	59			
				NW¼SE¼	28	34	59	4-15—5-15	2.202	134.25
1894			82.00	SW¼	28	34	59	4-15—5-15	1.008	61.50

Source—**Soldier Creek.** Ditch—**Union Land and Cattle Co. Ditches.**

Year of priority	Harvest crops	Meadow pasture	Diversified pasture	Subdivision	Section	Tp.N.	R.E.	Length of season	C.F.S.	Acre-feet
1905		22.40		S½	5	34	60	4-15—6-15	.273	33.60
1879	112.00				4	34	59	4-15—8-15	1.378	[illegible]

	1880			112.00					5	34	59	4-15—8-15	1.378	336.00
	1881			112.00					32	35	59	4-15—8-15	1.378	336.00
	1882			112.00					29	35	59	4-15—8-15	1.378	336.00
	1883			114.40				8½	20	35	59	4-15—8-15	1.407	343.20
	1883			....		234.70			....	....	....	4-15—6-15	2.887	176.03

Source—**Soldier Creek, Ross Creek, Murphy Creek, Starvation Creek, Springs.**
Ditch—**Union Land and Cattle Co. Ditches.**

	1880			63.00				W½W½	9	34	59	4-15—8-15	.775	189.00
	1885			63.00				E½E½	8	34	59	4-15—8-15	.775	189.00
	1890			61.00				NE¼	17	34	59	4-15—8-15	.787	192.00
	1899			160.00				E½	17	34	59	4-15—8-15	1.968	480.00
	1900			109.50					...	...	...	4-15—8-15	1.347	328.50
	1897			37.00				NW¼	16	34	59	4-15—8-15	.455	111.00
	1898			37.00					....	....	....	4-15—8-15	.455	111.00
	1899			37.00					....	....	....	4-15—8-15	.455	111.00
	1900			40.00					....	....	....	4-15—8-15	.492	120.00
	1895			38.00				SW¼	16	34	59	4-15—8-15	.467	114.00
	1896			38.00					....	....	....	4-15—8-15	.467	114.00
	1897			38.00					....	....	....	4-15—8-15	.467	114.00
	1898			39.00					....	....	....	4-15—8-15	.480	117.00

Source—**Soldier Creek.** Ditch—**Union Land and Cattle Co. Ditches.**

	1905			....	136.70			W½W½	8	34	59	4-15—6-15	1.681	205.05
								W½W½	17	34	59			
	1880			....		141.00		E½	8	34	59	4-15—5-15	1.734	105.75
	1885			....		141.00		E½SW¼	8	34	59	4-15—5-15	1.734	105.75
	1890			....		143.00		E½W½	17	34	59	4-15—5-15	1.750	107.25
								W½E½	17	34	59			

Source—**Ross Creek, Starvation Creek, Murphy Creek.**
Ditch—**Union Land and Cattle Co. Ditches.**

	1894			45.00				E½	16	34	59	4-15—8-15	.554	135.00
	1896			20.00					....	....	....	4-15—8-15	.246	60.00
	1898			20.00					....	....	....	4-15—8-15	.246	60.00
	1900			23.00					....	....	....	4-15—8-15	.283	69.00
	1889			23.00				SW¼	15	34	59	4-15—8-15	.283	69.00
	1883			23.00					....	....	....	4-15—8-15	.283	69.00
	1886			23.00					....	....	....	4-15—8-15	.283	69.00
	1887			11.00					....	....	....	4-15—8-15	.135	33.00

Source—**Secret Creek.** Ditch—**Union Land and Cattle Co. Ditches.**

	1874			36.74					34	35	59	4-15—8-15	.452	110.22
	1874			..		140.91			3	34	59	4-15—5-15	1.733	105.68
	1878			86.37					..	....	...	4-15—8-15	1.062	259.11
	1883			25.00					....	....	....	4-15—8-15	.308	75.00
	1891			22.78					....	....	....	4-15—8-15	.280	68.34
	1890			....	54.00				....	....	....	4-15—6-15	.664	81.00
	1892			....	54.00				....	....	....	4-15—6-15	.664	81.00
	1894			....	54.00				....	....	....	4-15—6-15	.664	81.00
	1897			....	57.55				....	....	....	4-15—6-15	.708	86.33

Union Land and Cattle Co.—Continued.

Year of priority	Culture—Acres: Harvest crops	Meadow pasture	Diversified pasture	Location: Subdivision	Section	Tp.N.	R.E.	Length of season	Duty of water: C.F.S.	Acre-feet
1897	142.41							4-15—8-15	1.752	427.23
1897			51.50					4-15—5-15	.633	38.63
1882		54.00						4-15—6-15	.664	81.00
1882		54.00						4-15—6-15	.664	81.00
1882		54.00						4-15—6-15	.664	81.00
1882		57.55						4-15—6-15	.708	86.33

Claimant—**E. C. Murphy.** Proof No. 00511

Source—**Boulder Creek.** Ditch—**E. C. Murphy Ditches.**

Year of priority	Harvest crops	Meadow pasture	Diversified pasture	Subdivision	Section	Tp.N.	R.E.	Length of season	C.F.S.	Acre-feet
1869	95.00			SW¼	25	36	59	4-15—8-15	1.169	285.00
1870	26.30			E½SE¼	26	36	59	4-15—8-15	.323	78.90
1873	1.60			NW¼NW¼	36	36	59	4-15—8-15	.020	4.80
1880	40.00							4-15—8-15	.492	120.00
1889	23.70							4-15—8-15	.292	71.10
1900	16.00							4-15—8-15	.197	48.00

Source—**Stevens Creek.** Ditch—**E. C. Murphy Ditches.**

Year of priority	Harvest crops	Meadow pasture	Diversified pasture	Subdivision	Section	Tp.N.	R.E.	Length of season	C.F.S.	Acre-feet
1868	104.80			SE¼SE¼	26	36	59	4-15—8-15	1.289	314.40
1876	5.50			E½NE¼	35	36	59	4-15—8-15	.068	16.50
				NW¼	36	36	59			

Source—**Secret, Wright, Lemon, Dry, and Dorsey Creeks and Springs.** Ditch—**E. C. Murphy Ditches.**

Year of priority	Harvest crops	Meadow pasture	Diversified pasture	Subdivision	Section	Tp.N.	R.E.	Length of season	C.F.S.	Acre-feet
1879	137.43			S½NW¼	4	34	60	4-15—8-15	1.690	412.29
1880	53.63			SW¼	4	34	60	4-15—8-15	.660	160.89
1881	53.63			SE¼	4	34	60	4-15—8-15	.660	160.89
1882	43.63			E½	5	34	60	4-15—8-15	.537	130.89
1883	126.23			E½	8	34	60	4-15—8-15	1.553	378.69
1884	59.60				9	34	60	4-15—8-15	.733	178.80
1886	10.00			NW¼NW¼	16	34	60	4-15—8-15	.123	30.00
1887	10.35							4-15—8-15	.127	31.05
1900	50.90							4-15—8-15	.626	152.70
1900	78.70							4-15—8-15	.968	236.10
1900	35.10							4-15—8-15	.432	105.30
1901	61.20							4-15—8-15	.753	183.60
1903	42.00							4-15—8-15	.517	126.00
1905	58.70							4-15—8-15	.722	176.10

Claimant—**S. M. Davis.** Proof No. 00512

Source—**Ackler Creek.** Ditch—**S. M. Davis Ditches.**

Year of priority	Harvest crops	Meadow pasture	Diversified pasture	Subdivision	Section	Tp.N.	R.E.	Length of season	C.F.S.	Acre-feet
1873	2.38			NE¼NW¼	9	36	60	4-15—8-15	.029	7.14
1873	1.00			NE¼NE¼	9	36	60	4-15—8-15	.012	3.00
1880	3.30			NE¼NW¼	10	36	60	4-15—8-15	.041	9.90

1888	12.00	NW¼NW¼	10	36	60	4-15—8-15	.148	36.00
1888	3.00	NW¼NW¼	10	36	60	4-15—8-15	.037	9.00
1888	.50	SE¼NW¼	10	36	60	4-15—8-15	.006	1.50
1880	11.80	NW¼NW¼	10	36	60	4-15—8-15	.145	35.40
1891	.80	NE¼NW¼	10	36	60	4-15—8-15	.010	2.40
1891	6.00	SE¼NW¼	10	36	60	4-15—8-15	.074	18.00
1896	15.70	SW¼NW¼	10	36	60	4-15—8-15	.193	47.10
1896	11.50	SE¼NW¼	10	36	60	4-15—8-15	.141	34.50
1896	6.30	SW¼NW¼	10	36	60	4-15—8-15	.077	18.90
1896	12.20	NW¼NW¼	10	36	60	4-15—8-15	.150	36.60
1877	18.00	NE¼NE¼	9	36	60	4-15—8-15	.221	54.00
1896	7.80	NE¼NE¼	9	36	60	4-15—8-15	.096	23.40
1896	1.00	NE¼NE¼	9	36	60	4-15—8-15	.012	3.00
1904	2.00	NE¼NW¼	10	36	60	4-15—8-15	.025	6.00

Claimant—**Wm. Goodale.** Proof No. 00513

Source—**Herder Creek.** Ditch—**Wm. Goodale Ditches.**

1872	10.00		4 and 5	36	60	4-15—8-15	.123	30.00
1872	4.90	SW¼SW¼	4	36	60	4-15—8-15	.000	14.70
1875	15.00	SE¼SW¼	4	36	60	4-15—8-15	.185	45.00
1892	18.70	SE¼SW¼	4	36	60	4-15—8-15	.230	56.10
1893	10.00	SW¼SW¼	4	36	60	4-15—8-15	.123	30.00
1894	10.00	SW¼SW¼	4	36	60	4-15—8-15	.123	30.00
1894	14.50	NW¼SE¼	5	36	60	4-15—8-15	.178	43.50
1895	20.50	NE¼SE¼	5	36	60	4-15—8-15	.252	61.50
1895	7.00	SW¼SW¼	4	36	60	4-15—8-15	.086	21.00
1895	25.00	NW¼SE¼	5	36	60	4-15—8-15	.308	75.00
1895	5.00	NE¼SE¼	5	36	60	4-15—8-15	.062	15.00
1898	1.30	NE¼SE¼	5	36	60	4-15—8-15	.016	3.90
1905	1.40	NE¼SE¼	5	36	60	4-15—8-15	.017	4.20
1905	0.90	NE¼SE¼	5	36	60	4-15—8-15	.011	2.70
1898	0.90	NE¼SE¼	5	36	60	4-15—8-15	.011	2.70
1896	5.50	NE¼SE¼	5	36	60	4-15—8-15	.068	16.50

Claimant—**Geo. A. Grock.** Proof No. **00514**

Source—**Starr Creek.** Ditch—**Geo. A. Grock Ditches.**

1874	48.10	SW¼NW¼	36	37	59	4-15—8-15	.592	144.30
1902	11.20	N½SW¼	36	37	59	4-15—8-15	.138	33.60
1903	23.90	SE¼SW¼	36	37	59	4-15—8-15	.284	71.70
1904	35.10	W½SE¼	36	37	59	4-15—8-15	.432	105.30
1905	8.60	...	...	...	...	4-15—8-15	.106	25.80

Claimant—**Edward Goodale.** Proof No. 00515

Source—**Stevens Creek.** Ditch—**Nos. 1 and 2.**

1904	94.31	S½SE¼	5	36	50			
		NW¼NE¼	8	36	50			
		E½NE¼	8	36	50	4-15—8-15	1.171	282.93

Claimant—**Alex. Gardner.** Proof No. 00516

Source—**Secret, Wolverton, Covert and Wright Creeks and Springs.**
Ditch—**Alex. Gardner Ditches.**

Year of priority	Culture—Acres: Harvest crops	Culture—Acres: Meadow pasture	Culture—Acres: Diversified pasture	Location: Subdivision	Location: Section	Location: Tp. N.	Location: R. E.	Length of season	Duty of water: C. F. S.	Duty of water: Acre-feet
1883	32.48	....	....	W½SW¼	16	34	60	4-15—8-15	.400	97.44
1884	32.48	....	....	E½W½	16	34	60	4-15—8-15	.400	97.44
1885	32.48	....	....	E½	16	34	60	4-15—8-15	.400	97.44
1886	97.44	....	....	NW¼NW¼	21	34	60	4-15—8-15	1.199	292.32
1887	97.44	....	....	....	....	....	....	4-15—8-15	1.199	292.32
1888	97.45	....	....	....	....	....	....	4-15—8-15	1.199	292.35

Source—**Secret Creek.** Ditch—**Alex Gardner Ditches.**

Year of priority	Harvest crops	Meadow pasture	Diversified pasture	Subdivision	Section	Tp. N.	R. E.	Length of season	C. F. S.	Acre-feet
1883	21.46	....	....	SE¼NE¼	10	34	60	4-15—8-15	.264	61.38
1884	21.46	....	....	E½SE¼	10	34	60	4-15—8-15	.264	64.38
				SW¼NW¼	11	34	60			
				W½SW¼	11	34	60			

Source—**Wright Creek.** Ditch—**Alex. Gardner Ditches.**

Year of priority	Harvest crops	Meadow pasture	Diversified pasture	Subdivision	Section	Tp. N.	R. E.	Length of season	C. F. S.	Acre-feet
1888	16.91	....	....	SE¼SW¼	3	34	60	4-15—8-15	.208	50.73
1891	10.00	....	....	E½NW¼	10	34	60	4-15—8-15	.123	30.00

Claimant—**John G. Lewis.** Proof No. 00518

Source—**Springs.** Ditch—**Lewis Ditches.**

Year of priority	Harvest crops	Meadow pasture	Diversified pasture	Subdivision	Section	Tp. N.	R. E.	Length of season	C. F. S.	Acre-feet
1901	4.00	....	....	SW¼SW¼	19	37	61	4-15—8-15	.049	12.00
1901	6.71	....	....	SE¼SW¼	19	37	61	4-15—8-15	.083	20.13
1901	.63	....	....	SW¼SE¼	19	37	61	4-15—8-15	.008	1.89

Claimant—**Isaac Griswold.** Proof No. 00519

Source—**Boulder and Monks Creeks.** Ditch—**Isaac Griswold Ditches.**

Year of priority	Harvest crops	Meadow pasture	Diversified pasture	Subdivision	Section	Tp. N.	R. E.	Length of season	C. F. S.	Acre-feet
1875	3.80	....	....	S½NW¼	12	36	59			
1877	3.80	....	....	SW¼	12	36	50	4-15—8-15	.047	11.40
1879	3.80	....	....	W½	13	36	59	4-15—8-15	.047	11.40
1880	3.90	....	....	E½	14	36	50	4-15—8-15	.047	11.40
				E½SW¼	14	36	50	4-15—8-15	.048	11.70
1904	....	....	172.90	N½	11	36	59			
				S½	14	36	59	4-15—5-15	2.127	120.68

Source—**Monks Creek.** Ditch—**Isaac Griswold Ditches.**

Year of priority	Harvest crops	Meadow pasture	Diversified pasture	Subdivision	Section	Tp. N.	R. E.	Length of season	C. F. S.	Acre-feet
1883	83.80	....	....	E½SW¼	14	36	59			
				W½E½	14	36	59			
				SE¼SE¼	14	36	59	4-15—8-15	1.031	251.40

Source—**Boulder Creek.** Ditch—**Isaac Griswold Ditches.**

Year of priority	Harvest crops	Meadow pasture	Diversified pasture	Subdivision	Section	Tp. N.	R. E.	Length of season	C. F. S.	Acre-feet
1873	66.00	....	....	S½NW¼	12	36	59	4-15—8-15	.812	198.00
1877	77.90	....	....	SW¼	12	36	59	4-15—8-15	.958	233.70
1880	103.30	....	....	NW¼	13	36	59	4-15—8-15	1.271	310.00
1883	33.40	....	....	E½SW¼	13	36	59	4-15—8-15	.411	100.20
[illegible]	178.20	....	....	E½	14	36	59	4-15—8-15	2.192	[illegible]

Source—**Branch of Boulder Creek.** Ditch—**Isaac Griswold Ditches.**

	1875			59.20				SW¼NW¼	13	36	59	4-15—8-15	.728	177.60
	1880			56.60				W½SW¼	13	36	59	4-15—8-15	.696	169.80
	1880			62.80				E½E½	14	36	59	4-15—8-15	.772	188.40

Claimant—**Jno. H. Cazier & Sons Company.** Proof. No. 00521

Source—**Blasengame Creek and Poverty Gulch.** Ditch—**Cazier & Company Ditches.**

	1880			299.10				SW¼SW¼	3	37	60			
								E½SW¼	3	37	60			
								W½SE¼	3	37	60			
								N½NW¼	10	37	60			
								SE¼NW¼	10	37	60			
								W½NE¼	10	37	60			
								SW¼SE¼	10	37	60			
								NW¼SE¼	10	37	60			
								SW¼NW¼	10	37	60	4-15—8-15	3.679	897.30

Source—**Humboldt River and Bishop Creek.** Ditch—**Cazier & Company Ditches.**

	1878			100.00				NE¼NE¼	2	37	60			
	1879			260.79				W½NE¼	2	37	60			
	1880			260.78				NW¼	2	37	60			
	1878						100.00	N½SW¼	2	37	60			
								NE¼	3	37	60			
								SE¼	3	37	60			
								S½NW¼	3	37	60	4-15—8-15	1.230	300.00
								N½SW¼	3	37	60	4-15—8-15	3.208	782.37
								SW¼SW¼	3	37	60	4-15—8-15	3.208	782.34
									10	37	60	4-15—5-15	1.230	75.00

Claimant—**Estate of Samuel McMullen.** Proof No. 00522

Source—**Boulder Creek.** Ditch—**McMullen Ditches.**

	1868			40.00				E½NE¼	23	36	59	4-15—8-15	.492	120.00
	1868			40.00				NE¼SE¼	23	36	59	4-15—8-15	.492	120.00
	1868			10.20				NW¼	24	36	59	4-15—8-15	.125	30.60
	1868			....		29.80		SW¼	24	36	59	4-15—6-15	.367	22.35
	1870			15.00				SW¼SE¼	24	36	59	4-15—8-15	.185	45.00
	1870			38.55				NW¼	25	36	59	4-15—8-15	.474	115.65
	1871			40.00				NE¼	26	36	59	4-15—8-15	.492	120.00
	1875			15.00					....	....	....	4-15—8-15	.185	45.00
	1880			15.00					....	....	....	4-15—8-15	.185	45.00
	1882			40.00					....	....	....	4-15—8-15	.492	120.00
	1883			68.95					....	....	....	4-15—8-15	.848	206.85
	1883			137.44					....	....	....	4-15—8-15	1.691	412.32
	1885			40.00					....	....	....	4-15—8-15	.492	120.00
	1885			15.00					....	....	....	4-15—8-15	.185	45.00
	1887			41.25					....	....	....	4-15—8-15	.507	123.75
	1887			11.15					....	....	....	4-15—8-15	.137	33.45
	1888			39.40					....	....	....	4-15—8-15	.485	118.20
	1888			83.93*					....	....	....	4-15—8-15	1.032	251.79

*No water to be diverted for this land until it becomes dry or is drained.

Estate of Samuel McMullen—Continued.
Source—**Boulder Creek and Stevens Creek.** Ditch—**Samuel McMullen Ditches.**

Year of priority	Culture—Acres: Harvest crops	Meadow pasture	Diversified pasture	Location: Subdivision	Section	Tp.N.	R.E.	Length of season	Duty of water: C.F.S.	Acre-feet
1883	46.86	....	....	W½SE¼	26	36	59	4-15—8-15	.576	140.58
1888	46.86	....	....	SW¼	26	36	59	4-15—8-15	.576	140.58
1893	46.86	....	....	NW¼	26	36	59	4-15—8-15	.576	140.58
1898	46.86	....	....	NE¼	27	36	59	4-15—8-15	.576	140.58
1902	46.86	....	....	....	----	----	----	4-15—8-15	.576	140.58

Source—**Monks Creek, Stevens Creek, Boulder Creek.** Ditch—**Samuel McMullen Ditches.**

Year of priority	Harvest crops	Meadow pasture	Diversified pasture	Subdivision	Section	Tp.N.	R.E.	Length of season	C.F.S.	Acre-feet
1883	....	35.00	....	All	22	36	59	4-15—6-15	.431	52.50
1888	....	35.00	....	....	....	....	....	4-15—6-15	.431	52.50
1893	....	35.00	....	....	....	....	....	4-15—6-15	.431	52.50
1898	....	35.00	....	....	....	....	....	4-15—6-15	.431	52.50
1902	....	34.57	....	....	....	....	....	4-15—6-15	.425	51.86
1904	....	571.75	....	....	9	36	59			
				....	10	36	59			
				....	15	36	59			
				....	16	36	59	4-15—6-15	7.033	857.63

Claimant—**Quilici Bros.** Proof No. 00524
Source—**Willow Creek, Lake at head of Trout Creek, and Angel Lake.***
Ditch—**Quilici Bros. Ditches.**

Year of priority	Harvest crops	Meadow pasture	Diversified pasture	Subdivision	Section	Tp.N.	R.E.	Length of season	C.F.S.	Acre-feet
1878	108.70	....	....	E½NW¼	8	37	61			
1883	76.60	....	....	S½NE¼	8	37	61			
1892	91.70	....	....	NE¼SE¼	3	37	61			
				W½SW¼	2	37	61			
				SE¼SW¼	2	37	61			
				E½	10	37	61	4-15—8-15	1.337	326.10
				W½	11	37	61	4-15—8-15	.942	229.80
				W½E½	11	37	61	4-15—8-15	1.165	284.10

*Angel Lake is not a natural tributary to Humboldt River, but water was diverted into Humboldt drainage area by artificial means.

Claimant—**W. G. Randolph.** Proof No. 00525
Source—**Secret Creek.** Ditch—**W. G. Randolph Ditches.**

Year of priority	Harvest crops	Meadow pasture	Diversified pasture	Subdivision	Section	Tp.N.	R.E.	Length of season	C.F.S.	Acre-feet
1882	50.00	....	....	All	4	35	48	4-15—8-15	.615	150.00
1883	134.25	....	....	....	....	....	....	4-15—8-15	1.651	402.75

Claimant—**Frank Blundell.** Proof No. 00551
Source—**Walker Creek and Springs.** Ditch—**Blundell, Blundell & Connell.**

Year of priority	Harvest crops	Meadow pasture	Diversified pasture	Subdivision	Section	Tp.N.	R.E.	Length of season	C.F.S.	Acre-feet
1893	116.40	....	....	SW¼SW¼	28	42	54			
				N½	33	42	54			
				N½SW¼	30	42	54	4-15—8-15	1.873	340.20

Claimant—**Diana Morgan Hill** (Deed to J. J. Hylton in escrow). Proof No. 00552
Source—**North Fork.** Ditch—**McKee & Clayton.**

	1889			146.10				E¼NE¼	35	40	56			
								NE¼SE¼	35	40	56			
								NW¼	36	40	56			
								N½SW¼	36	40	56			
								SW¼NE¼	36	40	56			
								NW¼SE¼	36	40	56	4-15—8-15	1.797	438.30

Claimant—**R. T. Evans & Brother.** Proof No. 00553
Source—**Foreman Creek.** Ditch—**R. T. Evans Ditches.**

	1888			91.75					7	41	54	4-15—8-15	1.129	275.25
	1889			33.50				NE¼NE¼	18	41	54	4-15—8-15	.412	100.50
	1890			48.73				W½NW¼	17	41	54	4-15—8-15	.599	146.19
	1900			22.50				W½	8	41	54	4-15—8-15	.277	67.50
	1901			63.55					....	....	....	4-15—8-15	.782	190.65
	1902			98.87					....	....	....	4-15—8-15	1.212	296.61

Source—**Walker Creek.** Ditch—**R. T. Evans Ditches.**

	1887			2.00					28	42	54	4-15—8-15	.025	6.00
	1892			159.30					28	42	54	4-15—8-15	1.959	477.90

Source—**Pratt Creek.** Ditch—**R. T. Evans Ditches.**

	1895			23.47				NW¼NE¼	3	41	54	4-15—8-15	.289	70.41
	1896			23.47				N½NW¼	3	41	54	4-15—8-15	.289	70.41
	1904			23.46					....	....	....	4-15—8-15	.289	70.38

Source—**Foreman Creek, Winters Creek, California Creek, and Springs.**
Ditch—**R. T. Evans Ditches.**

	1889			20.00				E½W½	17	41	54	4-15—8-15	.246	60.00
	1890			....		98.50		E½	17	41	54	4-15—5-15	1.212	73.88
	1890			186.80				W½W½	16	41	54	4-15—8-15	2.298	560.40
	1891			73.46				E½NW¼	16	41	54	4-15—8-15	.904	220.38
	1892			182.56				NE¼SW¼	16	41	54	4-15—8-15	2.245	547.68
	1899			18.20				NE¼	20	41	54	4-15—8-15	.224	54.60
	1902			...		200.30		E½SE¼	20	41	54	4-15—5-15	2.464	150.22
	1903			70.75				W½W½	21	41	54	4-15—8-15	.870	212.25
	1893			191.01				NE¼NE¼	29	41	54	4-15—8-15	2.349	573.03
	1901			131.62				NW¼	28	41	54	4-15—8-15	1.619	394.86
								E½SW¼	28	41	54			
								NW¼SE¼	28	41	54			

Claimant—**C. B. Evans.** Proof No. 00553

Source—**Forney Creek, Branch of Forney Creek, Pratt Creek, and Springs.**

Ditch—**C. B. Evans Ditches.**

Year of priority	Culture—Acres: Harvest crops	Culture—Acres: Meadow pasture	Culture—Acres: Diversified pasture	Location: Subdivision	Location: Section	Location: Tp.N.	Location: R.E.	Length of season	Duty of water: C.F.S.	Duty of water: Acre-feet
1903	945.20			S½	3	41	54			
				S½NW¼	3	41	54			
				SE¼NE¼	3	41	54			
				SE¼NE¼	4	41	54			
				SE¼	4	41	54			
				All	9	41	54			
				N½NE¼	8	41	54			
				All	10	41	54	4-15—8-15	11.626	2835.60

Claimant—**G. E. Truett.** Proof No. 00554

Source—***North Fork Humboldt River and Pratt Creek.**

Ditch—**Williams, Laing and Doherty.**

Year of priority	Culture—Acres: Harvest crops	Culture—Acres: Meadow pasture	Culture—Acres: Diversified pasture	Location: Subdivision	Location: Section	Location: Tp.N.	Location: R.E.	Length of season	Duty of water: C.F.S.	Duty of water: Acre-feet
1892	*9.00			NW¼SE¼	8	41	55	4-15—8-15	.111	27.00
1900	*12.50			SE¼NE¼	8	41	55	4-15—8-15	.159	37.50
1894	*13.00			SE¼NE¼	8	41	55	4-15—8-15	.160	39.00
1894	*18.00			NW¼SE¼	8	41	55	4-15—8-15	.221	54.00
1894	*9.50			Lot 3	8	41	55	4-15—8-15	.117	28.50
1894	*3.00			Lot 4	8	41	55	4-15—8-15	.037	9.00
1902	24.60			N½SE¼	7	41	55	4-15—8-15	.303	73.80
1902	23.10			S½NW¼	11	41	54	4-15—8-15	.284	69.30
1902	31.50			N½S½	11	41	54	4-15—8-15	.387	94.50
1902	87.70			N½S½	12	41	54	4-15—8-15	1.079	263.10
1902			14.00	N½S½	7	41	55	4-15—5-15	.172	10.50
1902			33.50	N½S½	12	41	54	4-15—5-15	.412	25.13
1902			22.10	N½S½	11	41	54	4-15—5-15	.272	16.58
1902			5.30	S½N½	11	41	54	4-15—5-15	.065	3.98

Claimant—**Mrs. C. Glaser.** Proof No. 00555

Source—**Pie Creek.** Ditch—**Nos. 3 and 4.**

Year of priority	Culture—Acres: Harvest crops	Culture—Acres: Meadow pasture	Culture—Acres: Diversified pasture	Location: Subdivision	Location: Section	Location: Tp.N.	Location: R.E.	Length of season	Duty of water: C.F.S.	Duty of water: Acre-feet
1889	25.00			NE¼	7	39	56			
1890	32.60			N½SE¼	7	39	56	4-15—8-15	.308	75.00
1891	32.60			SW¼SE¼	7	39	56	4-15—8-15	.401	97.80
1892	32.80			SE¼SW¼	7	39	56	4-15—8-15	.401	97.80
				NE¼NW¼	18	39	56	4-15—8-15	.403	98.40

Claimant—**C. A. & L. M. Laing.** Proof No. 00556

Source—**North Fork Humboldt River.** Ditch—**Laing Ditches.**

1870	79.30	SE¼	25	42	54			
1876	79.20	E½	36	42	54	4-15—8-15	0.975	237.90
1880	79.20	SW¼NW¼	31	42	55	4-15—8-15	0.974	237.60
1880	5.00	SW¼	31	42	55	4-15—8-15	0.974	237.60
1884	144.00	S½SE¼	31	42	55	4-15—8-15	0.062	15.00
1886	39.40	N½NE¼	6	41	55	4-15—8-15	1.771	432.00
1898	39.30	SE¼NE¼	6	41	55	4-15—8-15	0.484	118.20
1898	80.00	SW¼NW¼	5	41	55	4-15—8-15	0.483	117.96
1902	57.00	SW¼	5	41	55	4-15—8-15	0.984	240.00
		E½NW¼	8	41	55	4-15—8-15	0.701	171.00

Source—**Pratt Creek.** Ditch—**Laing Ditches.**

1870	233.50	NW¼SE¼	36	42	54			
1876	233.50	S½SE¼	36	42	54			
1880	233.40	S½SW¼	31	42	55			
		SE¼NW¼	1	41	54			
		NE¼	1	41	54			
		......	6	41	55			
		W½SW¼	5	41	55	4-15—8-15	2.872	700.50
		NE¼NE¼	7	41	55	4-15—8-15	2.872	700.50
		NW¼NW¼	8	41	55	4-15—8-15	2.871	700.20

Claimant—**G. F. McKnight.** Proof No. 00557

Source—**North Fork.** Ditch—**Burns, McKnight, Harrah and Doll.**

1896	41.00	E½NW¼	26	39	57	4-15—8-15	.504	123.00
1898	44.50	SW¼	26	39	57	4-15—8-15	.547	133.50
1903	23.90	SW¼SE¼	26	39	57	4-15—8-15	.294	81.70

Claimant—**Howard Morse.** Proof No. 00558

Source—**Peterson Creek and Springs.** Ditch—**Howard Morse Ditches.**

1886	....	131.00	E½	8	42	54	4-15—6-15	1.611	196.50
1888	136.80		W½	9	42	54	4-15—8-15	1.683	410.40
1889	....	24.30	NE¼	9	42	54	4-15—6-15	.299	38.50
1889	26.70		N½SE¼	9	42	54	4-15—8-15	.328	80.10
1890	26.00		W½NW¼	10	42	54	4-15—8-15	.320	78.00
1890	....	11.30	NW¼SW¼	10	42	54	4-15—6-15	.139	17.00
1891	....	11.30	S½S½	4	42	54	4-15—6-15	.139	17.00
1891	26.00			....	....	....	4-15—8-15	.320	78.00
1892	46.00			....	....	....	4-15—8-15	.566	138.00
1892	....	11.30		....	....	....	4-15—6-15	.139	17.00
1893	20.00			....	....	....	4-15—8-15	.246	60.00
1894	....	16.70		....	....	....	4-15—6-15	.205	25.05
1894	23.50			....	....	....	4-15—8-15	.289	70.50
1903	....	41.40		....	....	....	4-15—6-15	.509	62.20
1904	....	85.00		....	....	....	4-15—6-15	1.046	127.50

Claimant—**Chas. L. Nuckols.** Proof No. **00559**
Source—**North Fork Humboldt River and Peterson Creek.** Ditch—**Nuckols.**

Year of priority	Culture—Acres: Harvest crops	Meadow pasture	Diversified pasture	Location: Subdivision	Section	Tp.N.	R.E.	Length of season	Duty of water: C.F.S.	Acre-feet
1899	7.00			SW¼	3	42	54	4-15—8-15	0.086	21.00
1899	371.96			E½NW¼	10	42	54	4-15—8-15	4.575	1115.88
1900	72.43			W½E½	10	42	54	4-15—8-15	0.891	217.29
1901	28.49			E½SE¼	10	42	54	4-15—8-15	0.350	85.47
1905	35.95			E½	15	42	54	4-15—8-15	0.442	107.85
				W½SW¼	14	42	54			
				NW¼	23	42	54			

Claimant—**T. S. Park.** Proof No. **00560**
Source—**Dorsey Creek.** Ditch—**Park Ditches.**

Year of priority	Harvest crops	Meadow pasture	Diversified pasture	Subdivision	Section	Tp.N.	R.E.	Length of season	C.F.S.	Acre-feet
1865	9.81			NW¼SW¼	13	37	54	4-15—8-15	.121	29.43
1865	1.09			NE¼SW¼	13	37	54	4-15—8-15	.013	3.27
1865	16.54			SW¼SW¼	13	37	54	4-15—8-15	.203	49.62
1865	....		3.45	SW¼SW¼	13	37	54	4-15—5-15	.042	2.58
1865	1.27			SE¼SW¼	13	37	54	4-15—8-15	.016	3.81
1865	....		18.44	SE¼SW¼	13	37	54	4-15—5-15	.227	13.83
1865	7.45			SW¼SE¼	13	37	54	4-15—8-15	.092	22.35
1865	....		3.99	SW¼SE¼	13	37	54	4-15—5-15	.049	2.99
1865	12.54			SW¼NE¼	14	37	54	4-15—8-15	.154	67.62
1865	3.44			SE¼NW¼	14	37	54	4-15—8-15	.042	10.32
1865	9.63			NW¼SE¼	14	37	54	4-15—8-15	.118	28.89
1901	....		19.99	NW¼SE¼	14	37	54	4-15—5-15	.246	14.99
1865	24.36			NE¼SE¼	14	37	54	4-15—8-15	.300	73.08
1901	....		2.36	NE¼SE¼	14	37	54	4-15—5-15	.029	1.77
1865	3.87			SE¼SE¼	14	37	54	4-15—8-15	.048	11.61
1901	....		4.90	SE¼SE¼	14	37	54	4-15—5-15	.060	3.68
1865	15.63			NE¼NE¼	24	37	54	4-15—8-15	.192	46.89
1865	11.63			NW¼NE¼	24	37	54	4-15—8-15	.143	34.89
1865	....		.90	NW¼NE¼	24	37	54	4-15—5-15	.011	.68
1865	2.18			SE¼NE¼	24	37	54	4-15—8-15	.027	6.54

Claimant—**Estate of Thos. Kearns.** Proof No. **00561**
Source—**North Fork and Tributaries.** Ditch—**Thos. Kearns Ditches.**

Year of priority	Harvest crops	Meadow pasture	Diversified pasture	Subdivision	Section	Tp.N.	R.E.	Length of season	C.F.S.	Acre-feet
1888	10.00			SE¼SW¼	22	42	54			
				SW¼SE¼	22	42	54			
				NW¼NE¼	27	42	54	4-15—8-15	.123	30.00
1888	180.20			SW¼	15	42	54			
1890	00.10			SE¼SE¼	16	42	54			
				NW¼	22	42	54	4-15—8-15	2.210	540.00
1890	15.00			W½NE¼	22	42	54	4-15—8-15	.730	180.30
1890	28.80			NE¼NE¼	21	42	54	4-15—8-15	.185	45.00
				N½NW¼	27	42	54			
				NE¼	28	42	54	4-15—8-15	.354	90.40

1880			90.00				NE¼	27	42	54			
							SE¼NW¼	27	42	54			
							NE¼SW¼	27	42	54			
							NW¼SE¼	27	42	54			
							SW¼NW¼	26	42	54	4-15—8-15	1.107	270.00
1890			21.60				W½NW¼	26	42	54			
							E½NE¼	27	42	54	4-15—8-15	.266	64.80
1894			197.00				E½	21	42	54	4-15—8-15	2.423	591.00
1895			175.70				S½NW¼	26	42	54			
							E½SW¼	26	42	54			
							SE¼	26	42	54	4-15—8-15	2.161	527.10
1895			10.60				S½SW¼	22	42	54			
							NE¼NW¼	27	42	54	4-15—8-15	1.300	31.80
1896			197.10				S½NW¼	22	42	54			
							SW¼	22	42	54			
							W½SE¼	22	42	54			
							N½NE¼	27	42	54	4-15—8-15	2.424	591.36
1896			27.00				W½SE¼	22	42	54	4-15—8-15	.332	81.00
1899			96.80				E½SE¼	22	42	54			
							W½SW¼	23	42	54			
							SW¼SW¼	23	42	54			
							NE¼NE¼	27	42	54			
							NW¼	26	42	54			
							W½NW¼	26	42	54	4-15—8-15	1.190	290.40
1901			20.90				SE¼SW¼	22	42	54			
							SW¼SE¼	22	42	54			
							NE¼NW¼	27	42	54			
							NW¼NE¼	27	42	54	4-15—8-15	.257	62.70
1902			40.50				SE¼	26	42	54	4-15—8-15	.498	121.50
1904			30.10				N½SE¼	26	42	54			
							SE¼SE¼	26	42	54	4-15—8-15	.370	90.30
1905			8.80				N½SE¼	27	42	54	4-15—8-15	.108	26.40
1890			45.10				SW¼	25	42	54	4-15—8-15	.555	135.30
1904			73.00				SW¼	25	42	54			
							N½NW¼	36	42	54	4-15—8-15	.808	219.00
1895			151.80				NW¼	36	42	54	4-15—8-15	1.867	455.40

Tributaries are McAfee Creek, Dell Creek, Spring Creek, Walker Creek, Branch of Walker Creek, and Springs.

Claimant—**Geo. W. Pratt.** Proof No. 00562

Source—**McAfee Creek.** Ditch—**Geo. W. Pratt Ditches.**

1880			49.00				SE¼NE¼	35	42	54	4-15—8-15	1.033	147.00
1880						84.00	N½SW¼	36	42	54	4-15—8-15	.602	63.00

Source—**Pratt Creek and Springs.** Ditch—**Geo. W. Pratt Ditches.**

1887			154.90				SW¼	36	42	54			
1888			96.70				SE¼SE¼	35	42	54			
1889			26.00				NE¼NE¼	2	41	54			
1890			145.70				S½N½	2	41	54	4-15—8-15	1.906	464.70
1898			31.10				N½S½	2	41	54	4-15—8-15	1.189	290.10
							W½NW¼	1	41	54	4-15—8-15	0.319	78.00
							NE¼NW¼	1	41	54	4-15—8-15	1.792	437.10
							SW¼NE¼	3	41	54	4-15—8-15	0.383	93.30

Claimant—**Frank Rutherford.** Proof No. **00563**
Source—**North Fork Humboldt.** Ditch—**Rutherford.**

Year of priority	Culture—Acres: Harvest crops	Meadow pasture	Diversified pasture	Location: Subdivision	Section	Tp.N.	R.E.	Length of season	Duty of water: C.F.S.	Acre-feet
1890	45.82				4	42	54	4-15—8-15	0.564	137.46
1892	84.80			NE¼NE¼	5	42	54	4-15—8-15	1.043	254.40
1893	160.58							4-15—8-15	1.975	481.74
1899	17.00							4-15—8-15	0.209	51.00

Claimant—**Rose M. Tremewan.** Proof No. **00565**
Source—**Mahala Creek.** Ditch—**Austin Gilruth Ditches.**

Year of priority	Harvest crops	Meadow pasture	Diversified pasture	Subdivision	Section	Tp.N.	R.E.	Length of season	C.F.S.	Acre-feet
1888	144.01			E½W½	1	39	54			
1897	66.47			SE¼	1	39	54			
1899	12.38			N½	7	39	55			
				N½SE¼	7	39	55			
				SW¼SW¼	4	39	55	4-15—8-15	1.771	432.03
				SE¼SE¼	5	39	55	4-15—8-15	.818	199.41
				SE¼NE¼	4	39	55	4-15—8-15	.152	37.14

Source—**East Fork Beaver Creek.** Ditch—**Diana Morgan Hill Ditches.**
Claimant—**Diana Morgan Hill** (Deed to J. J. Hylton in escrow). Proof No. **00566**

Year of priority	Harvest crops	Meadow pasture	Diversified pasture	Subdivision	Section	Tp.N.	R.E.	Length of season	C.F.S.	Acre-feet
1893	20.00			N½NW¼	17	40	57	4-15—8-15	.246	60.00
1894	21.85			S½SW¼	8	40	57	4-15—8-15	.269	65.55

Claimant—**Williams Estate Company.** Proof No. **00567**
Source—**North Fork Humboldt River and Springs.** Ditch—**Williams Estate Co. Ditches.**

Year of priority	Harvest crops	Meadow pasture	Diversified pasture	Subdivision	Section	Tp.N.	R.E.	Length of season	C.F.S.	Acre-feet
1888	186.14				36	40	55			
					1	39	55			
					6	39	56	4-15—8-15	2.290	558.42

Claimant—**Samuel McIntyre.** Proof No. **00568**
Source—**North Fork of Humboldt.** Ditch—**Samuel McIntyre Ditches.**

Year of priority	Harvest crops	Meadow pasture	Diversified pasture	Subdivision	Section	Tp.N.	R.E.	Length of season	C.F.S.	Acre-feet
1887	10.29			SE¼NE¼&NE¼SE¼	35	39	57	4-15—8-15	.127	30.87
1887	102.17			S½NW¼,N½SW¼,SE¼SW¼,W½SE¼	36	39	57	4-15—8-15	1.257	306.51
1887	94.93			NW¼NE¼,NW¼,SW¼,&SW¼SE¼	1	38	57	4-15—8-15	1.168	284.79
1887	163.31			E½NW¼,NE¼,&N½SE¼	12	38	57	4-15—8-15	2.009	480.93
1872	39.02			S½SE¼&SE¼SW¼	12	38	57	4-15—8-15	.480	117.06
1872	33.71			NE¼NW¼,W½NE¼	13	38	57	4-15—8-15	.415	101.13

Claimant—**John McKee.** Proof No. **00569**
Source—**North Fork of Humboldt River.** Ditch—**John McKee Ditches.**

Year of priority	Harvest crops	Meadow pasture	Diversified pasture	Subdivision	Section	Tp.N.	R.E.	Length of season	C.F.S.	Acre-feet
1889	140.78			SE¼SE¼	27	40	56			
1903	71.01			E½NE¼	34	40	56	4-15—8-15	1.732	422.34
				N½	35	40	56	4-15—8-15	.873	213.03

Claimant—**J. Leslie Carter.** Proof No. **00569**

Source—**North Fork of Humboldt River.** Ditch—**J. Leslie Carter Ditches.**

1889	72.23	SE¼SW¼	27	40	56			
		SW¼SE¼	27	40	56			
		NW¼	34	40	56			
		NW¼NE¼	34	40	56			
		E½NE¼	33	40	56	4-15—8-15	.888	216.09

Claimant—**G. F. McKnight.** Proof No. **00570**

Source—**North Fork Humboldt River.** Ditch—**Doll.**

1903	10.60	SW¼SE¼	15	39	57	4-15—8-15	.112	31.80
1903	0.62	SE¼SE¼	15	39	57	4-15—8-15	.076	1.86
1903	8.66	NW¼NE¼	22	39	57	4-15—8-15	.107	25.98
1903	9.26	NE¼NE¼	22	39	57	4-15—8-15	.114	27.78

Claimant—**Saval Livestock Co.** Proof No. **00571**

Source—**Ganz Creek and Springs.** Ditch—**Saval Co.**

1885	10.00		4	39	54	4-15—8-15	0.123	30.00
1886	10.00		5	39	54	4-15—8-15	0.123	30.00
1887	10.00		9	39	54	4-15—8-15	0.123	30.00
1894	100.00		10	39	54	4-15—8-15	1.230	300.00
1895	80.00		15	39	54	4-15—8-15	0.984	240.00
1896	80.00		14	39	54	4-15—8-15	0.984	240.00
1897	90.00		13	39	54	4-15—8-15	1.107	270.00
1905	168.60		24	39	54	4-15—8-15	2.074	505.80

Claimant—**R. B. Stewart.** Proof No. **00572**

Source—**Pie, Willow, Clay Hill, and Red Hill Creeks.** Ditch—**R. B. Stewart Ditches.**

1888	254.83	SE¼SW¼	26	39	54
1891	65.61	E½NW¼	35	39	54
		W½NE¼	35	39	54
		SW¼	35	39	54
		W½SE¼	35	39	54
		N½NW¼	2	38	54
		SW¼NW¼	2	38	54
		SE¼NE¼	3	38	54
		NE¼SE¼	3	38	54
		W½NE¼	10	38	54
		NE¼NW¼	10	38	54
		S½NW¼	10	38	54
		N½SW¼	10	38	54
		N½SE¼	9	38	54
		SW¼SE¼	9	38	54
		SE¼SW¼	9	38	54
		NW¼	16	38	54
		N½SW¼	16	38	54
		SW¼SW¼	16	38	54
		E½SE¼	17	38	54

R. B. Stewart—Continued.

Year of priority	Culture—Acres: Harvest crops	Meadow pasture	Diversified pasture	Location: Subdivision	Section	Tp.N.	R.E.	Length of season	Duty of water: C.F.S.	Acre-feet
				S¼NE¼	19	38	54			
				N¼SE¼	19	38	54			
				SW¼SE¼	19	38	54			
				S½SW¼	19	38	54			
				NW¼NW¼	30	38	54	4-15—8-15	3.134	764.49
				SE¼NE¼	25	38	53	4-15—8-15	.806	196.83

Claimant—**Warner Griswold.** Proof No. **00573**
Source—**Ganz Creek.** Ditch—**Warner Griswold Ditches.**

Year of priority	Harvest crops	Meadow pasture	Diversified pasture	Subdivision	Section	Tp.N.	R.E.	Length of season	C.F.S.	Acre-feet
1885	67.00				24	39	54			
1886	67.00				19	39	55	4-15—8-15	0.824	201.00
1887	67.00				20	39	55	4-15—8-15	0.824	201.00
1888	67.00				21	39	55	4-15—8-15	0.824	201.00
1889	69.90				27	39	55	4-15—8-15	0.824	201.00
					28	39	55	4-15—8-15	0.860	209.70

Claimant—**Chas. S. and Aleck Wieland.** Proof No. **00574**
Source—**Springs and Pie or McClellan Creek.** Ditch—**Wieland Ditches.**

Year of priority	Harvest crops	Meadow pasture	Diversified pasture	Subdivision	Section	Tp.N.	R.E.	Length of season	C.F.S.	Acre-feet
1886	100.00				32	39	55	4-15—8-15	1.230	300.00
1887	185.41				33	39	55	4-15—8-16	2.281	556.23
1900	39.00				....	...	...	4-15—8-15	0.480	117.00

Claimant—**Williams Estate Company.** Proof No. **00575**
Source—**North Fork Humboldt River.** Ditch—**Williams Estate Co. Ditches.**

Year of priority	Harvest crops	Meadow pasture	Diversified pasture	Subdivision	Section	Tp.N.	R.E.	Length of season	C.F.S.	Acre-feet
1888	230.64			SW¼SE¼	8	41	55	4-15—8-15	2.948	718.92
1890	116.90			E½	17	41	55	4-15—8-15	1.438	350.70
1891	40.50			E½	20	41	55	4-15—8-15	0.498	121.50
1892	214.00			E½	29	41	55	4-15—8-15	2.632	642.00
				E½	32	41	55			

Claimant—**Diana Morgan Hill** (Deed to J. J. Hylton in escrow). Proof No. **00576**
Source—**North Fork Humboldt River.** Ditch—**Diana Morgan-Hill Ditches.**

Year of priority	Harvest crops	Meadow pasture	Diversified pasture	Subdivision	Section	Tp.N.	R.E.	Length of season	C.F.S.	Acre-feet
1872	161.80				16	40	55			
1873	101.80				21	40	55			
1890	341.80				28	40	55	4-15—8-15	1.990	485.40
1902	49.20				27	40	55	4-15—8-15	1.990	485.40
					33	40	55	4-15—8-15	4.201	1025.40
					34	40	55	4-15—8-15	0.605	147.60
1873	150.00				2 & 3	39	57			
1888	206.50				10 & 15	39	57			

1892	266.50		21&22	36	57			
1896	266.50		34&27&28	36	57			
1900	266.50		1&2&10	37	57			
1904	266.40		11&12	37	57	4-15—8-15	1.845	450.00
1904	361.60		14&15	37	57	4-15—8-15	3.278	799.50
			22&23	37	57	4-15—8-15	3.278	799.50
			26&27	37	57	4-15—8-15	3.278	799.50
			34&35	37	57	4-15—8-15	3.278	799.50
			24&25	38	57	4-15—8-15	3.277	799.20
			35&36	38	57	4-15—8-15	4.448	1084.80

Source—**Springs.** Ditch—**Diana Morgan-Hill Ditches.**

1898	434.00	W½	15	41	54			
			16	41	54	4-15—8-15	5.338	1302.00
1898	241.00	N½	21	41	54			
		NW¼	22	41	54	4-15—8-15	2.964	723.00

Source—**Dry Creek and Springs.** Ditch—**Diana Morgan-Hill Ditches.**

1898	125.70	S½	25	41	54			
		SW¼	30	41	55			
		NE¼NW¼	31	41	55	4-15—8-15	1.546	377.10

Source—**Springs and Foreman Creek.** Ditch—**Diana Morgan-Hill Ditches.**

1876	680.10	SW¼	22	41	54			
		SW¼NE¼	21	41	54			
		SE¼NE¼	21	41	54			
		S½	21	41	54			
			27	41	54			
			28	41	54	4-15—8-15	8.365	2040.30
1880	822.50	NE¼NE¼	33	41	54			
			34	41	54			
		S½	35	41	54			
			2	40	54			
		N½NE¼	3	40	54			
		W½	1	40	54	4-15—8-15	10.120	2468.40
1886	402.00	E½	1	40	54			
			6	40	55			
			5	40	55			
		SW¼SW¼	4	40	55	4-15—8-15	6.052	1476.00

Claimant—**J. J. Hylton.** Proof No. 00576

Source—**Stump Creek.** Ditch—**Hylton and Clayton.**

1889	99.65	SE¼SW¼	3	40	54			
		SE¼	3	40	54			
		N½SW¼	2	40	54			
		S½N½	2	40	54	4-15—8-15	1.226	298.95

Claimant—**J. J. Hylton Bros.** Proof No. 00576

Source—**North Fork.** Ditch—**Hylton.**

Year of priority	Culture—Acres: Harvest crops	Culture—Acres: Meadow pasture	Culture—Acres: Diversified pasture	Location: Subdivision	Location: Section	Location: Tp.N.	Location: R.E.	Length of season	Duty of water: C.F.S.	Duty of water: Acre-feet
1905		6.36		NE¼NE¼	36	38	57	4-15—6-15	.078	9.54
1905		1.20		SE¼NE¼	36	38	57	4-15—6-15	.015	1.80
1905		7.60		SE¼SE¼	25	38	57	4-15—6-15	.093	11.41
1905		2.84		NE¼SE¼	25	38	57	4-15—6-15	.035	4.26
1905	1.31			SE¼NE¼	25	38	57	4-15—8-15	.016	3.93
1908		6.88		Lot 2	30	38	58	4-15—6-15	.085	10.32
1905		8.21		Lot 3	30	38	58	4-15—6-15	.101	12.32
1905		3.60		Lot 4	30	38	58	4-15—6-15	.044	5.40
1905	16.70			NW¼NE¼	19	38	57	4-15—8-15	.205	50.10

Claimant—**Union Land and Cattle Co.** Proof No. 00601

Source—**Mary's River.** Ditch—**Cold Spring.**

Year of priority	Harvest crops	Meadow pasture	Diversified pasture	Subdivision	Section	Tp.N.	R.E.	Length of season	C.F.S.	Acre-feet
1896		11.50		SE¼	19	40	60	4-15—6-15	.141	17.25
1896		12.15		SE¼	19	40	60	4-15—6-15	.149	18.23
1899		53.21		SE¼	6	39	60	4-15—6-15	.654	79.82
1899		32.18		E½SW¼	6	39	60	4-15—6-15	.396	48.27
1896		22.58		NE¼	7	39	60	4-15—6-15	.278	33.87
1896		9.49		NE¼	7	39	60	4-15—6-15	.117	14.24
1896		32.22		SE¼	7	39	60	4-15—6-15	.396	48.33
1896		12.22		SE¼	7	39	60	4-15—6-15	.150	18.33
1899		32.41		W½NE¼	7	39	60	4-15—6-15	.399	48.62
1899		7.93		E½SW¼	7	39	60	4-15—6-15	.098	11.90
1899		4.42		NW¼SE¼	7	39	60	4-15—6-15	.054	6.63
1899		0.91		NW¼	7	39	60	4-15—6-15	.011	1.37
1896		10.79		SE¼SW¼	7	39	60	4-15—6-15	.133	16.19
1896		53.53		E½NE¼	31	40	60	4-15—6-15	.658	81.30
1896		70.13		SE¼	31	40	60	4-15—6-15	.863	105.20
1898		78.18		NE¼	31	40	60	4-15—6-15	.962	117.27
1898			21.76	NE¼	31	40	60	4-15—5-15	.268	16.32
1898		56.47		NW¼	31	40	60	4-15—6-15	.695	84.71
1898			19.35	NW¼	31	40	60	4-15—5-15	.238	14.51
1898		44.63		W½SE¼	31	40	60	4-15—6-15	.549	66.95
1898			26.80	W½SE¼	31	40	60	4-15—5-15	.330	20.10
1898		70.41		SW¼	31	40	60	4-15—6-15	.866	105.62
1898			54.19	SW¼	31	40	60	4-15—5-15	.666	40.64
1896		9.65		W½NW¼	32	40	60	4-15—6-15	.119	14.48

Source—**Mary's River.** Ditch—**Commatele.**

Year of priority	Harvest crops	Meadow pasture	Diversified pasture	Subdivision	Section	Tp.N.	R.E.	Length of season	C.F.S.	Acre-feet
1899		10.56		SW¼SE¼	18	41	60	4-15—6-15	.130	15.84
1899		47.90		NE¼	19	41	60	4-15—6-15	.580	71.85
1899		24.55		E½NW¼	19	41	60	4-15—6-15	.302	36.83
1899		14.77		SE¼	19	41	60	4-15—6-15	.182	22.16
1899		92.11		SW¼	19	41	60	4-15—6-15	1.180	138.17

	1899				80.07			SW¼	30	41	60	4-15—6-15	1.096	133.61
	1899					.30		SW¼	30	41	60	4-15—5-15	.004	.23
	1899				88.01			NW¼	30	41	60	4-15—6-15	1.083	132.02
	1899				7.72			SW¼	31	41	60	4-15—6-15	.095	11.58
	1899					23.23		SW¼	31	41	60	4-15—5-15	.286	17.42
	1899				17.91			NW¼	31	41	60	4-15—6-15	.222	26.87
	1899					36.15		NW¼	31	41	60	4-15—5-15	.444	27.22
	1899				.66			SW¼SE¼	31	41	60	4-15—6-15	.008	.99
	1900				2.90			NW¼	8	40	60	4-15—6-15	.036	4.35
	1900				3.73			NW¼	5	40	60	4-15—6-15	.046	5.60
	1899				72.84			NE¼	6	40	60	4-15—6-15	.896	109.26
	1899				32.90			E½SE¼	6	40	60	4-15—6-15	.405	49.35
	1899				51.88			SE¼	6	40	60	4-15—6-15	.638	77.82
	1900				1.05			SE¼NW¼	7	40	60	4-15—6-15	.013	1.56
	1899				3.40			E½NE¼	7	40	60	4-15—6-15	.042	5.10
	1899					21.90		E½NE¼	7	40	60	4-15—5-15	.269	16.43
	1899				84.23			NE¼	7	40	60	4-15—6-15	1.046	126.35
	1900				53.19			SE¼	7	40	60	4-15—6-15	.654	80.79

Source—**Mary's River.** Ditch—**Sloughs formed by Beaver Dams.**

	1885				37.96			W½	18	39	60	4-15—6-15	.467	56.94
	1885				54.47			NE¼	26	39	59	4-15—6-15	.670	81.71
	1885				39.78			SE¼	26	39	59	4-15—6-15	.489	59.67
	1885				9.49			SW¼	26	39	59	4-15—6-15	.117	14.24
	1885				2.08			NW¼	35	39	59	4-15—6-15	.026	3.12
	1885				26.13			NE¼	35	39	59	4-15—6-15	.321	39.20
	1885				52.79			SE¼	35	39	59	4-15—6-15	.649	79.19
	1885				1.56			SE¼	2	38	59	4-15—6-15	.019	2.34
	1885				24.44			NE¼	2	38	59	4-15—6-15	.301	36.66

Source—**Mary's River.** Ditch—**Rosebud.**

	1899				30.60			NW¼	7	39	60	4-15—6-15	.376	45.90
	1899					121.80		NW¼	7	39	60	4-15—5-15	1.498	91.35
	1899				13.39			W½NE¼	7	39	60	4-15—6-15	.165	20.09
	1899				33.05			SW¼	7	39	60	4-15—6-15	.407	49.58
	1899					102.36		SW¼	7	39	60	4-15—5-15	1.259	76.77
	1898				2.12			E½E½	1	39	59	4-15—6-15	.026	3.18
	1898					21.15		E½E½	1	39	59	4-15—5-15	.260	15.86
	1898				36.75			W½W½	31	40	60	4-15—6-15	.452	55.13
	1898				11.01			E½SE¼	36	40	59	4-15—6-15	.135	16.52
	1898					3.24		E½SE¼	36	40	59	4-15—5-15	.040	2.43
	1898				41.41			SW¼	6	39	60	4-15—6-15	.509	62.12
	1898					80.52		SW¼	6	39	60	4-15—5-15	.990	60.50
	1898				26.99			W½NW¼	6	39	60	4-15—6-15	.332	40.49
	1898					20.06		W½NW¼	6	39	60	4-15—5-15	.247	15.05
	1898				2.60			SW¼SE¼	6	39	60	4-15—6-15	.032	3.90
	1901				104.53			NW¼	18	39	60	4-15—6-15	1.287	156.80
	1901					5.97		NW¼	18	39	60	4-15—5-15	.073	4.48
	1901				25.74			SW¼	18	39	60	4-15—6-15	.317	38.61
	1898					76.72		E½E½	12	39	59	4-15—5-15	.944	57.54
	1901					24.14		E½NE¼	13	39	59	4-15—5-15	.300	18.09

Union Land and Cattle Co.—Continued.
Source—**Mary's River.** Ditch—**Pot Hole.**

Year of priority	Culture—Acres: Harvest crops	Culture—Acres: Meadow pasture	Culture—Acres: Diversified pasture	Location: Subdivision	Location: Section	Location: Tp.N.	Location: R.E.	Length of season	Duty of water: C.F.S.	Duty of water: Acre-feet
1899		55.17		E½NE¼	18	40	60	4-15—6-15	.679	82.76
1899		38.85		E½SE¼	18	40	60	4-15—6-15	.478	58.28
1899		10.94		E½SE¼	18	40	60	4-15—6-15	.135	16.41
1900		32.60		W½SW¼	8	40	60	4-15—6-15	.401	48.90
1899		8.66		SE¼SE¼	6	40	60	4-15—6-15	.107	12.99
1899		13.35		NE¼NE¼	7	40	60	4-15—6-15	.164	20.03
1899		49.63		E½SE¼	7	40	60	4-15—6-15	.610	74.55
1899		1.85		SE¼	7	40	60	4-15—6-15	.022	2.78
1899		34.31		W½NW¼	17	40	60	4-15—6-15	.423	51.57
1899		58.43		W½SW¼	17	40	60	4-15—6-15	.719	87.65
1899		60.21		E½NE¼	19	40	60	4-15—6-15	.741	90.32
1899		4.77		NE¼	19	40	60	4-15—6-15	.059	7.16
1899		50.70		SE¼	19	40	60	4-15—6-15	.624	76.05
1899		36.92		W½W½	20	40	60	4-15—6-15	.454	55.38
1899		4.50		NW¼	29	40	60	4-15—6-15	.055	6.75
1899		8.40		NE¼NE¼	30	40	60	4-15—6-15	.103	12.60

Source—**Mary's River.** Ditch—**Spring Gulch.**

Year of priority	Harvest crops	Meadow pasture	Diversified pasture	Subdivision	Section	Tp.N.	R.E.	Length of season	C.F.S.	Acre-feet
1899		8.66		SW¼SE¼	6	41	60	4-15—6-15	.107	12.99
1899		2.67		SE¼SW¼	6	41	60	4-15—6-15	.033	4.01
1899		45.83		NE¼	7	41	60	4-15—6-15	.564	68.75
1899		21.80		NW¼	7	41	60	4-15—6-15	.268	32.70
1899		48.55		SW¼	7	41	60	4-15—6-15	.597	72.83
1899		32.50		SE¼	7	41	60	4-15—6-15	.400	48.75
1899			43.15	SE¼	7	41	60	4-15—6-15	.531	32.36
1899		25.34		E½NW¼	18	41	60	4-15—6-15	.312	38.01
1899		99.65		NE¼	18	41	60	4-15—6-15	1.236	149.48
1899		62.43		SE¼	18	41	60	4-15—6-15	.768	92.65
1899		21.12		NE¼SW¼	18	41	60	4-15—6-15	.260	31.68

Source—**Mary's River.** Ditch—**Horse Pasture.**

Year of priority	Harvest crops	Meadow pasture	Diversified pasture	Subdivision	Section	Tp.N.	R.E.	Length of season	C.F.S.	Acre-feet
1884		57.90		NE¼	23	38	59	4-15—6-15	.712	86.85
1884		19.40		NE¼SE¼	23	38	59	4-15—6-15	.239	29.10
1885		8.60		SE¼SE¼	23	88	59	4-15—6-15	.106	12.90
1884		124.90		SW¼	13	38	59	4-15—6-15	1.536	187.35
1884		50.20		S½NW¼	13	38	59	4-15—6-15	.617	75.30
1884		62.32		E½NE¼	14	38	59	4-15—6-15	.767	93.48
1884		0.50		NW¼SE¼	14	38	59	4-15—6-15	.006	.75
1884		65.30		E½SE¼	14	38	59	4-15—6-15	.803	97.95
1884		131.60		NW¼	24	38	59	4-15—6-15	1.619	197.40
1884		54.80		N½SW¼	24	38	59	4-15—6-15	.674	82.20
1885		43.68		SW¼	24	38	59	4-15—6-15	.537	65.52
1886		14.40		W½SE¼	24	38	59	4-15—6-15	.177	21.60
1886		72.17		SE¼	[illegible]	38	59	4-15—6-15	[illegible]	[illegible]

...	1886	...	...	...	...	10.82	...	SE¼	36	38	59	4-15—5-15	.133	8.12
...	1886	...	...	...	58.79	...	...	NE¼	36	38	59	4-15—6-15	.723	88.19
...	1886	...	...	...	...	25.98	...	NE¼	36	38	59	4-15—5-15	.320	19.49
...	1886	...	...	...	67.02	...	...	NE¼	1	37	59	4-15—6-15	.824	100.53
...	1886	...	...	...	...	8.30	...	NE¼	1	37	59	4-15—5-15	.102	6.23
...	1886	...	...	...	53.04	...	...	E½SE¼	1	37	59	4-15—6-15	.652	79.56
...	1885	...	...	...	31.79	...	...	NW¼	25	38	59	4-15—6-15	.391	47.69
...	1886	...	...	...	67.54	...	...	W½SE¼	25	38	59	4-15—6-15	.811	101.10
...	1886	...	...	...	12.43	...	...	SW¼	25	38	59	4-15—6-15	.153	18.65
...	1886	...	...	...	...	26.04	...	SW¼	25	38	59	4-15—5-15	.320	19.53
...	1886	...	...	...	51.56	...	...	NW¼	7	37	60	4-15—6-15	.634	77.34
...	1886	...	...	...	...	2.68	...	NW¼	7	37	60	4-15—5-15	.033	2.01
...	1886	...	...	...	0.50	...	...	NE¼SW¼	7	37	60	4-15—6-15	.006	.75
...	1886	...	...	...	5.83	...	...	NE¼NE¼	12	37	59	4-15—6-15	.072	8.75
...	1886	...	...	...	9.60	...	...	NW¼	6	37	60	4-15—6-15	.118	14.40
...	1886	...	...	...	...	1.82	...	NW¼	6	37	60	4-15—5-15	.022	1.37
...	1886	...	...	...	48.98	...	...	SW¼	6	37	60	4-15—6-15	.602	73.47
...	1885	...	...	...	16.33	...	...	W½NE¼	25	38	59	4-15—6-15	.201	24.50
...	1885	...	...	...	...	26.40	...	W½NE¼	25	38	59	4-15—5-15	.325	19.80

Source—**Mary's River.** Ditch—**Check Dams and Small Natural Sloughs.**

...	1885	...	...	...	102.57	...	...	W½	31	42	60	4-15—6-15	1.262	153.86
...	1885	...	...	...	70.04	...	...	W½E½	31	42	60	4-15—6-15	.861	105.06
...	1885	...	...	...	107.42	...	...	NW¼	6	41	60	4-15—6-15	1.321	161.13
...	1885	...	...	...	...	17.15	...	NW¼	6	41	60	4-15—5-15	.211	12.86
...	1885	...	...	...	7.65	...	...	NE¼	6	41	60	4-15—6-15	.094	11.48
...	1885	...	...	...	83.79	...	...	SW¼	6	41	60	4-15—6-15	1.031	125.69
...	1885	...	...	...	0.79	...	...	SE¼	6	41	60	4-15—6-15	.010	1.19
...	1885	...	...	...	16.49	...	...	SW¼	7	41	60	4-15—6-15	.203	24.74
...	1885	...	...	...	0.66	...	...	NE¼	7	41	60	4-15—6-15	.008	.99
...	1885	...	...	...	42.63	...	...	NW¼	7	41	60	4-15—6-15	.524	63.95
...	1885	...	...	...	26.26	...	...	W½	19	41	60	4-15—6-15	.323	39.39

Source—**Mary's River.** Ditch—**Natural Slough.**

...	1885	...	...	...	54.17	...	...	NW¼	19	42	60	4-15—6-15	.666	81.26
...	1885	...	...	...	28.37	...	...	E½SW¼	30	42	60	4-15—6-15	.349	42.56
...	1885	...	...	...	13.58	...	...	N½SW¼	30	42	60	4-15—6-15	.167	20.37
...	1904	...	...	...	4.82	...	...	SW¼NE¼	30	42	60	4-15—6-15	.059	7.23
...	1904	...	...	...	4.35	...	...	SE¼NW¼	30	42	60	4-15—6-15	.054	6.53
...	1885	...	...	...	45.91	...	...	NE¼	18	40	60	4-15—6-15	.565	68.87
...	1885	...	...	...	41.55	...	...	S½	18	40	60	4-15—6-15	.511	63.33
...	1885	...	...	...	1.84	...	...	SE¼NW¼	7	40	60	4-15—6-15	.023	2.76
...	1885	...	...	...	26.92	...	...	SW¼	7	40	60	4-15—6-15	.311	40.38
...	1885	...	...	...	52.77	...	...	SE¼	7	40	60	4-15—6-15	.649	79.16

Source—**Mary's River.** Ditch—**Buena Vista.**

...	1901	...	...	...	4.22	...	...	SW¼SW¼	19	41	60	4-15—6-15	.052	6.33
...	1901	...	...	...	51.86	...	...	W½NW¼	30	41	60	4-15—6-15	.638	77.79
...	1902	...	...	...	55.72	...	...	W½SW¼	30	41	60	4-15—6-15	.070	83.58
...	1902	...	...	...	93.03	...	...	NW¼	31	41	60	4-15—6-15	1.144	139.59
...	1902	...	...	...	112.09	...	...	SW¼	31	41	60	4-15—6-15	1.379	168.14

Union Land and Cattle Co.—Continued.

Year of priority	Culture—Acres: Harvest crops	Culture—Acres: Meadow pasture	Culture—Acres: Diversified pasture	Location: Subdivision	Location: Section	Location: Tp.N.	Location: R.E.	Length of season	Duty of water: C.F.S.	Duty of water: Acre-feet
1903		10.56		NE¼NW¼	18	40	60	4-15—6-15	.130	15.84
1902		47.62		W½NE¼	6	40	60	4-15—6-15	.586	71.43
1902		73.22		E½NW¼	6	40	60	4-15—6-15	.901	109.83
1902		56.62		W½NW¼	6	40	60	4-15—6-15	.819	84.93
1902		53.97		E½SW¼	6	40	60	4-15—6-15	.664	80.96
1902		59.11		E½NW¼	7	40	60	4-15—6-15	.851	88.67
1902		24.80		W½NE¼	7	40	60	4-15—6-15	.305	37.20
1903		3.56		W½NE¼	7	40	60	4-15—6-15	.044	5.34
1902		19.00		W½SW¼	7	40	60	4-15—6-15	.234	28.50

Source—**Mary's River.** Ditch—**Cold Spring.**

Year of priority	Harvest crops	Meadow pasture	Diversified pasture	Subdivision	Section	Tp.N.	R.E.	Length of season	C.F.S.	Acre-feet
1896		42.58		NE¼	6	39	60	4-15—6-15	.524	63.87
1896		42.45		SE¼	6	39	60	4-15—6-15	.522	63.68
1896		2.60		SE¼	6	39	60	4-15—6-15	.034	3.90
1899		49.50		NE¼	6	39	60	4-15—6-15	.609	74.25
1899			24.52	NE¼	6	39	60	4-15—5-15	.302	18.39
1899		99.12		NW¼	6	39	60	4-15—6-15	1.219	148.68
1899			9.70	NW¼	6	39	60	4-15—5-15	.119	7.28
1896		4.97		NW¼NE¼	18	39	60	4-15—6-15	.061	7.46
1896		48.87		W½W½	29	40	60	4-15—6-15	.601	73.31
1896		61.71		E½NE¼	30	40	60	4-15—6-15	.759	92.57
1896		29.60		E½SE¼	30	40	60	4-15—6-15	.364	44.40
1897		45.70		W½SE¼	30	40	60	4-15—6-15	.562	68.55
1897		3.25		W½NE¼	30	40	60	4-15—6-15	.040	4.88
1897		3.25		SE¼NW¼	30	40	60	4-15—6-15	.040	4.88
1897		129.89		SE¼	30	40	60	4-15—6-15	1.598	194.84
1897		57.80		SW¼	30	40	60	4-15—6-15	.711	86.70
1897		8.73		SE¼NE¼	30	40	60	4-15—6-15	.107	13.10

Source—**Taber and Pole Creeks.** Ditch—**Nos. 1 and 2.**

Year of priority	Harvest crops	Meadow pasture	Diversified pasture	Subdivision	Section	Tp.N.	R.E.	Length of season	C.F.S.	Acre-feet
1899		1.27		SE¼NW¼	14	39	60	4-15—6-15	.016	1.91
1899		102.16		SW¼	14	39	60	4-15—6-15	1.257	153.24
1899		45.72		W½NW¼	14	39	60	4-15—6-15	.562	68.58
1899		5.39		E½NE¼	15	39	60	4-15—6-15	.066	8.09
1899		.30		NE¼SE¼	15	39	60	4-15—6-15	.004	.45
1899			71.95	N½	23	39	60	4-15—5-15	.885	53.96
1900			29.10	NW¼	23	39	60	4-15—5-15	.358	21.83
1900		116.63		SW¼	23	39	60	4-15—6-15	1.435	174.95

Source—**Taber and Pole Creeks.** Ditch—**No. 1.**

Year of priority	Harvest crops	Meadow pasture	Diversified pasture	Subdivision	Section	Tp.N.	R.E.	Length of season	C.F.S.	Acre-feet
1899		43.73		NW¼	14	39	60	4-15—6-15	.538	65.60
1899			29.24	NW¼	14	39	60	4-15—5-15	.360	21.93
1899		37.48		E½SW¼	14	39	60	4-15—6-15	.461	56.22
1899		31.60		W½SE¼	14	39	60	4-15—6-15	.389	47.40
1899		37.00		E½NW¼	14	39	60	4-15—6-15	.455	55.50

18[71]

	1899					51.97		N½	23	39	60	4-15—5-15	.639	38.98
	1899				1.00			NW¼SE¼	23	39	60	4-15—6-15	.012	1.50
	1900				7.00			SW¼NE¼	23	39	60	4-15—6-15	.086	10.50
	1900					113.02		SE¼	23	39	60	4-15—5-15	1.390	84.77
	1900					123.00		NE¼	26	39	60	4-15—5-15	1.513	92.25
	1900					133.00		S½	26	39	60	4-15—5-15	1.635	99.75
						Source—**Taber Creek.**		Ditch—**No. 1.**						
	1893					71.80		E½	12	40	60	4-15—5-15	.883	53.85
	1900					110.00		W½	26	39	60	4-15—5-15	1.353	82.50
						Source—**Taber Creek.**		Ditch—**Nos. 1, 2 and 3.**						
	1899			1.27				SW¼SW¼	31	41	61	4-15—8-15	.016	3.81
	1899			76.00				N½	6	40	61	4-15—8-15	.935	228.00
	1900			38.97				N½	6	40	61	4-15—8-15	.479	86.91
	1899					123.34		W½	6	40	61	4-15—5-15	1.517	92.51
						Source—**Taber Creek.**		Ditch—**No. 2.**						
	1886				8.10			SE¼SW¼	12	40	60	4-15—6-15	.100	12.15
	1886				46.00			E½	12	40	60	4-15—6-15	.566	60.00
	1886				.42			NW¼NE¼	13	40	60	4-15—6-15	.005	.63
	1886				11.50			NE¼NW¼	13	40	60	4-15—6-15	.141	17.25
						Source—**Taber Creek.**		Ditch—**No. 3.**						
	1885				12.63			SW¼NW¼	12	40	60	4-15—6-15	.155	18.95
	1885				24.42			NW¼SE¼	12	40	60	4-15—6-15	.300	36.63
	1885				23.00			NE¼SW¼	12	40	60	4-15—6-15	.283	34.50
	1885				31.38			SE¼SW¼	12	40	60	4-15—6-15	.386	47.07
	1885				4.68			NW¼SW¼	12	40	60	4-15—6-15	.058	7.02
	1885				32.51			SW¼SW¼	12	40	60	4-15—6-15	.400	48.77
	1885				.64			SW¼NW¼	12	40	60	4-15—6-15	.008	.96
	1885				13.77			NE¼NW¼	12	40	60	4-15—6-15	.169	20.66
	1885				33.79			NW¼NW¼	12	40	60	4-15—6-15	.416	50.69
	1885				13.91			SW¼SW¼	12	40	60	4-15—6-15	.171	20.87
						Source—**Taber Creek.**		Ditch—**No. 4.**						
	1901				2.98			NE¼NE¼	14	40	60	4-15—6-15	.037	4.47
	1901				20.30			SE¼NE¼	14	40	60	4-15—6-15	.250	30.45
	1901				18.88			NW¼SE¼	14	40	60	4-15—6-15	.232	28.20
	1901				7.81			NE¼SE¼	14	40	60	4-15—6-15	.096	11.72
						Source—**Taber Creek.**		Ditch—**Nos. 4 and 5.**						
	1901				70.71			E½	11	40	60	4-15—6-15	.870	106.07
	1901				38.78			NW¼NW¼	14	40	60	4-15—6-15	.477	58.17
	1901				35.78			SW¼SE¼	14	40	60	4-15—6-15	.440	53.67
						Source—**Taber Creek.**		Ditch—**No. 5.**						
	1901					50.90		E½	11	40	60	4-15—5-15	.626	38.18
	1901					7.00		NE¼	11	40	60	4-15—5-15	.086	5.25
	1901				2.84			NE¼NW¼	14	40	60	4-15—6-15	.035	4.26

Union Land and Cattle Co.—Continued.

Year of priority	Harvest crops	Culture—Acres Meadow pasture	Diversified pasture	Location Subdivision	Section	Tp.N.	R.E.	Length of season	Duty of water C.F.S.	Acre-feet
1903	....	10.56	....	NE¼NW¼	18	40	60	4-15—6-15	.130	15.84
1902	....	47.62	....	W½NE¼	6	40	60	4-15—6-15	.586	71.43
1902	....	73.22	....	E½NW¼	6	40	60	4-15—6-15	.901	109.83
1902	....	56.62	....	W½NW¼	6	40	60	4-15—6-15	.819	81.93
1902	....	53.97	....	E½SW¼	6	40	60	4-15—6-15	.664	80.96
1902	....	59.11	....	E½NW¼	7	40	60	4-15—6-15	.851	88.67
1902	....	24.80	....	W½NE¼	7	40	60	4-15—6-15	.305	37.20
1903	....	3.56	....	W½NE¼	7	40	60	4-15—6-15	.044	5.34
1902	....	19.00	....	W½SW¼	7	40	60	4-15—6-15	.234	28.50
Source—Mary's River. Ditch—Cold Spring.										
1896	....	42.58	....	NE¼	6	39	60	4-15—6-15	.524	63.87
1896	....	42.45	....	SE¼	6	39	60	4-15—6-15	.522	63.68
1896	....	2.60	....	SE¼	6	39	60	4-15—6-15	.034	3.90
1899	....	49.50	....	NE¼	6	39	60	4-15—6-15	.609	74.25
1899	....	....	24.52	NE¼	6	39	60	4-15—5-15	.302	18.30
1899	....	99.12	....	NW¼	6	39	60	4-15—6-15	1.219	148.68
1899	....	....	9.70	NW¼	6	39	60	4-15—5-15	.119	7.28
1896	....	4.97	....	NW¼NE¼	18	39	60	4-15—6-15	.061	7.46
1896	....	48.87	....	W½W½	29	40	60	4-15—6-15	.601	73.31
1896	....	61.71	....	E½NE¼	30	40	60	4-15—6-15	.759	92.57
1896	....	29.60	....	E½SE¼	30	40	60	4-15—6-15	.364	44.40
1897	....	45.70	....	W½SE¼	30	40	60	4-15—6-15	.562	68.55
1897	....	3.25	....	W½NE¼	30	40	60	4-15—6-15	.040	4.88
1897	....	3.25	....	SE¼NW¼	30	40	60	4-15—6-15	.040	4.88
1897	....	129.89	....	SE¼	30	40	60	4-15—6-15	1.598	194.84
1897	....	57.80	....	SW¼	30	40	60	4-15—6-15	.711	86.70
1897	....	8.73	....	SE¼NE¼	30	40	60	4-15—6-15	.107	13.10
Source—Taber and Pole Creeks. Ditch—Nos. 1 and 2.										
1899	....	1.27	....	SE¼NW¼	14	39	60	4-15—6-15	.016	1.91
1899	....	102.16	....	SW¼	14	39	60	4-15—6-15	1.257	153.24
1899	....	45.72	....	W½NW¼	14	39	60	4-15—6-15	.562	68.58
1899	....	5.39	....	E½NE¼	15	39	60	4-15—6-15	.066	8.09
1899	....	.30	....	NE¼SE¼	15	39	60	4-15—6-15	.004	.45
1899	....	....	71.95	N½	23	39	60	4-15—5-15	.885	53.06
1900	....	....	29.10	NW¼	23	39	60	4-15—5-15	.358	21.83
1900	....	116.63	....	SW¼	23	39	60	4-15—6-15	1.435	174.95
Source—Taber and Pole Creeks. Ditch—No. 1.										
1899	....	43.73	....	NW¼	14	39	60	4-15—6-15	.538	65.60
1899	....	....	29.24	NW¼	14	39	60	4-15—5-15	.360	21.93
1899	....	37.48	....	E½SW¼	14	39	60	4-15—6-15	.461	56.22
1899	....	31.66	....	W½SE¼	14	39	60	4-15—6-15	.389	47.49
1899	....	37.00	....	E½NW¼	14	39	60	4-15—6-15	.455	55.50

18[71]

....	1899	....	....	....	....	51.97	....	N½	23	39	60	4-15—5-15	.689	38.08
....	1899	....	....	....	1.00	....	....	NW¼SE¼	23	39	60	4-15—6-15	.012	1.50
....	1900	....	....	....	7.00	....	....	SW¼NE¼	23	39	60	4-15—6-15	.086	10.50
....	1900	....	....	....	....	113.02	....	SE¼	23	39	60	4-15—5-15	1.390	84.77
....	1900	....	....	....	....	123.00	....	NE¼	26	39	60	4-15—5-15	1.513	92.25
....	1900	....	....	....	....	133.00	....	S½	26	39	60	4-15—5-15	1.035	99.75

Source—**Taber Creek.** Ditch—**No. 1.**

....	1893	....	....	....	....	71.80	....	E½	12	40	60	4-15—5-15	.883	53.85
....	1900	....	....	....	....	110.00	....	W½	26	39	60	4-15—5-15	1.353	82.50

Source—**Taber Creek.** Ditch—**Nos. 1, 2 and 3.**

....	1899	....	....	1.27	....	....	....	SW¼SW¼	31	41	61	4-15—8-15	.016	3.81
....	1899	....	....	76.00	....	....	....	N½	6	40	61	4-15—8-15	.935	228.00
....	1900	....	....	38.97	....	....	....	N½	6	40	61	4-15—8-15	.479	86.91
....	1899	....	....	....	....	123.34	....	W½	6	40	61	4-15—5-15	1.517	92.51

Source—**Taber Creek.** Ditch—**No. 2.**

....	1886	....	....	....	8.10	....	....	SE¼SW¼	12	40	60	4-15—6-15	.100	12.15
....	1886	....	....	....	46.00	....	....	E½	12	40	60	4-15—6-15	.566	69.00
....	1886	....	....	....	.42	....	....	NW¼NE¼	13	40	60	4-15—6-15	.005	.63
....	1886	....	....	....	11.50	....	....	NE¼NW¼	13	40	60	4-15—6-15	.141	17.25

Source—**Taber Creek.** Ditch—**No. 3.**

....	1885	....	....	....	12.63	....	....	SW¼NW¼	12	40	60	4-15—6-15	.156	18.95
....	1885	....	....	....	24.42	....	....	NW¼SE¼	12	40	60	4-15—6-15	.300	36.63
....	1885	....	....	....	23.00	....	....	NE¼SW¼	12	40	60	4-15—6-15	.283	34.50
....	1885	....	....	....	31.38	....	....	SE¼SW¼	12	40	60	4-15—6-15	.386	47.07
....	1885	....	....	....	4.68	....	....	NW¼SW¼	12	40	60	4-15—6-15	.058	7.02
....	1885	....	....	....	32.51	....	....	SW¼SW¼	12	40	60	4-15—6-15	.400	48.77
....	1885	....	....	....	.64	....	....	SW¼NW¼	12	40	60	4-15—6-15	.008	.96
....	1885	....	....	....	13.77	....	....	NE¼NW¼	12	40	60	4-15—6-15	.169	20.66
....	1885	....	....	....	33.79	....	....	NW¼NW¼	12	40	60	4-15—6-15	.416	50.69
....	1885	....	....	....	13.91	....	....	SW¼SW¼	12	40	60	4-15—6-15	.171	20.87

Source—**Taber Creek.** Ditch—**No. 4.**

....	1901	....	....	....	2.98	....	....	NE¼NE¼	14	40	60	4-15—6-15	.037	4.47
....	1901	....	....	....	20.30	....	....	SE¼NE¼	14	40	60	4-15—6-15	.250	30.45
....	1901	....	....	....	18.88	....	....	NW¼SE¼	14	40	60	4-15—6-15	.232	28.20
....	1901	....	....	....	7.81	....	....	NE¼SE¼	14	40	60	4-15—6-15	.096	11.72

Source—**Taber Creek.** Ditch—**Nos. 4 and 5.**

....	1901	....	....	....	70.71	....	....	E½	11	40	60	4-15—6-15	.870	106.07
....	1901	....	....	....	38.78	....	....	NW¼NW¼	14	40	60	4-15—6-15	.477	58.17
....	1901	....	....	....	35.78	....	....	SW¼SE¼	14	40	60	4-15—6-15	.440	53.67

Source—**Taber Creek.** Ditch—**No. 5.**

....	1901	....	....	....	....	50.90	....	E½	11	40	60	4-15—5-15	.626	38.18
....	1901	....	....	....	....	7.00	....	NE¼	11	40	60	4-15—5-15	.086	5.25
....	1901	....	....	....	2.84	....	....	NE¼NW¼	14	40	60	4-15—6-15	.035	4.26

Union Land and Cattle Co.—Continued.
Source—**Mary's River.** Ditch—**Pot Hole.**

Year of priority	Culture—Acres: Harvest crops	Culture—Acres: Meadow pasture	Culture—Acres: Diversified pasture	Location: Subdivision	Location: Section	Location: Tp.N.	Location: R.E.	Length of season	Duty of water: C.F.S.	Duty of water: Acre-feet
1899	....	55.17	....	E½NE¼	18	40	60	4-15—6-15	.679	82.76
1899	....	38.85	....	E½SE¼	18	40	60	4-15—6-15	.478	58.28
1899	....	10.94	....	E½SE¼	18	40	60	4-15—6-15	.135	16.41
1900	....	32.60	....	W½SW¼	8	40	60	4-15—6-15	.401	48.90
1899	....	8.66	....	SE¼SE¼	6	40	60	4-15—6-15	.107	12.99
1899	....	13.36	....	NE¼NE¼	7	40	60	4-15—6-15	.164	20.03
1899	....	49.63	....	E½SE¼	7	40	60	4-15—6-15	.610	74.55
1899	....	1.85	....	SE¼	7	40	60	4-15—6-15	.022	2.78
1899	....	34.31	....	W½NW¼	17	40	60	4-15—6-15	.423	51.57
1899	....	58.43	....	W½SW¼	17	40	60	4-15—6-15	.719	87.65
1899	....	60.21	....	E½NE¼	19	40	60	4-15—6-15	.741	90.32
1899	....	4.77	....	NE¼	19	40	60	4-15—6-15	.059	7.16
1899	....	50.70	....	SE¼	19	40	60	4-15—6-15	.624	76.05
1899	....	36.92	....	W½W½	20	40	60	4-15—6-15	.454	55.38
1899	....	4.50	....	NW¼	29	40	60	4-15—6-15	.055	6.75
1899	....	8.40	....	NE¼NE¼	30	40	60	4-15—6-15	.103	12.60

Source—**Mary's River.** Ditch—**Spring Gulch.**

Year of priority	Harvest crops	Meadow pasture	Diversified pasture	Subdivision	Section	Tp.N.	R.E.	Length of season	C.F.S.	Acre-feet
1899	....	8.66	....	SW¼SE¼	6	41	60	4-15—6-15	.107	12.99
1899	....	2.67	....	SE¼SW¼	6	41	60	4-15—6-15	.033	4.01
1899	....	45.83	....	NE¼	7	41	60	4-15—6-15	.564	68.75
1899	....	21.80	....	NW¼	7	41	60	4-15—6-15	.268	32.70
1899	....	48.55	....	SW¼	7	41	60	4-15—6-15	.597	72.83
1899	....	32.50	....	SE¼	7	41	60	4-15—6-15	.400	48.75
1899	....	....	43.15	SE¼	7	41	60	4-15—6-15	.531	32.36
1899	....	25.34	....	E½NW¼	18	41	60	4-15—6-15	.312	38.01
1899	....	99.65	....	NE¼	18	41	60	4-15—6-15	1.236	149.48
1899	....	62.43	....	SE¼	18	41	60	4-15—6-15	.768	92.65
1899	....	21.12	....	NE¼SW¼	18	41	60	4-15—6-15	.260	31.68

Source—**Mary's River.** Ditch—**Horse Pasture.**

Year of priority	Harvest crops	Meadow pasture	Diversified pasture	Subdivision	Section	Tp.N.	R.E.	Length of season	C.F.S.	Acre-feet
1884	....	57.90	....	NE¼	23	39	59	4-15—6-15	.712	86.85
1884	....	19.40	....	NE¼SE¼	23	38	59	4-15—6-15	.239	29.10
1885	....	8.60	....	SE¼SE¼	23	68	59	4-15—6-15	.106	12.90
1884	....	124.90	....	SW¼	13	38	59	4-15—6-15	1.536	187.35
1884	....	50.20	....	S½NW¼	13	38	59	4-15—6-15	.617	75.30
1884	....	62.32	....	E½NE¼	14	38	59	4-15—6-15	.767	93.48
1884	....	0.50	....	NW¼SE¼	14	38	59	4-15—6-15	.006	.75
1884	....	65.30	....	E½SE¼	14	39	59	4-15—6-15	.803	97.95
1884	....	131.60	....	NW¼	24	38	59	4-15—6-15	1.619	197.40
1884	....	54.80	....	N½SW¼	24	38	59	4-15—6-15	.074	82.20
1885	....	43.68	....	SW¼	24	38	59	4-15—6-15	.537	65.52
1885	....	14.40	....	W½SE¼	24	38	59	4-15—6-15	.177	21.60
1886	....	72.17	....	SE¼	26	38	59	4-15—6-15	.888	108.26

	1886					10.82	SE¼	36	38	50	4-15—5-15	.133	8.12
	1886				58.79		NE¼	36	38	50	4-15—6-15	.723	88.19
	1886					25.98	NE¼	36	38	50	4-15—5-15	.320	19.49
	1886				67.02		NE¼	1	37	50	4-15—6-15	.824	100.53
	1886					8.30	NE¼	1	37	50	4-15—5-15	.102	6.23
	1886				53.04		E½SE¼	1	37	59	4-15—6-15	.652	79.56
	1885				31.79		NW¼	25	38	59	4-15—6-15	.391	47.69
	1886				67.54		W½SE¼	25	38	59	4-15—6-15	.831	101.10
	1886				12.43		SW¼	25	38	59	4-15—6-15	.153	18.65
	1886					26.04	SW¼	25	38	59	4-15—5-15	.320	19.53
	1886				51.56		NW¼	7	37	60	4-15—6-15	.634	77.34
	1886					2.68	NW¼	7	37	60	4-15—5-15	.033	2.01
	1886				0.50		NE¼SW¼	7	37	60	4-15—6-15	.006	.75
	1886				5.83		NE¼NE¼	12	37	59	4-15—6-15	.072	8.75
	1886				9.60		NW¼	6	37	60	4-15—6-15	.118	14.40
	1886					1.82	NW¼	6	37	60	4-15—5-15	.022	1.37
	1886				48.98		SW¼	6	37	60	4-15—6-15	.602	73.47
	1885				16.33		W½NE¼	25	38	59	4-15—6-15	.201	24.50
	1885					26.40	W½NE¼	25	38	59	4-15—5-15	.325	19.80

Source—**Mary's River.** Ditch—**Check Dams and Small Natural Sloughs.**

	1885				102.57		W½	31	42	60	4-15—6-15	1.262	153.86
	1885				70.04		W½E½	31	42	60	4-15—6-15	.861	105.06
	1885				107.42		NW¼	6	41	60	4-15—6-15	1.321	161.13
	1885					17.15	NW¼	6	41	60	4-15—5-15	.211	12.86
	1885				7.65		NE¼	6	41	60	4-15—6-15	.094	11.48
	1885				83.79		SW¼	6	41	60	4-15—6-15	1.031	125.69
	1885				0.79		SE¼	6	41	60	4-15—6-15	.010	1.19
	1885				16.49		SW¼	7	41	60	4-15—6-15	.203	24.74
	1885				0.66		NE¼	7	41	60	4-15—6-15	.008	.99
	1885				42.63		NW¼	7	41	60	4-15—6-15	.524	63.95
	1885				26.26		W½	19	41	60	4-15—6-15	.323	39.39

Source—**Mary's River.** Ditch—**Natural Slough.**

	1885				54.17		NW¼	19	42	60	4-15—6-15	.666	81.26
	1885				28.37		E½SW¼	30	42	60	4-15—6-15	.349	42.56
	1885				13.58		N½SW¼	30	42	60	4-15—6-15	.167	20.37
	1904				4.82		SW¼NE¼	30	42	60	4-15—6-15	.059	7.23
	1904				4.35		SE¼NW¼	30	42	60	4-15—6-15	.054	6.53
	1885				45.91		NE¼	18	40	60	4-15—6-15	.565	68.87
	1885				41.55		S½	18	40	60	4-15—6-15	.511	63.33
	1885				1.84		SE¼NW¼	7	40	60	4-15—6-15	.023	2.76
	1885				26.92		SW¼	7	40	60	4-15—6-15	.311	40.38
	1885				52.77		SE¼	7	40	60	4-15—6-15	.649	79.16

Source—**Mary's River.** Ditch—**Buena Vista.**

	1901				4.22		SW¼SW¼	19	41	60	4-15—6-15	.052	6.33
	1901				51.86		W½NW¼	30	41	60	4-15—6-15	.638	77.79
	1902				55.72		W½SW¼	30	41	60	4-15—6-15	.070	83.58
	1902				93.08		NW¼	31	41	60	4-15—6-15	1.144	139.59
	1902				112.09		SW¼	31	41	60	4-15—6-15	1.379	168.14

Union Land and Cattle Co.—Continued.

Year of priority	Culture—Acres: Harvest crops	Culture—Acres: Meadow pasture	Culture—Acres: Diversified pasture	Location: Subdivision	Location: Section	Location: Tp.N.	Location: R.E.	Length of season	Duty of water: C.F.S.	Duty of water: Acre-feet
1903		10.56		NE¼NW¼	18	40	60	4-15—6-15	.130	15.84
1902		47.62		W½NE¼	6	40	60	4-15—6-15	.586	71.43
1902		73.22		E½NW¼	6	40	60	4-15—6-15	.901	109.83
1902		56.62		W½NW¼	6	40	60	4-15—6-15	.819	84.93
1902		53.97		E½SW¼	6	40	60	4-15—6-15	.664	80.96
1902		59.11		E½NW¼	7	40	60	4-15—6-15	.851	88.67
1902		24.80		W½NE¼	7	40	60	4-15—6-15	.305	37.20
1903		3.56		W½NE¼	7	40	60	4-15—6-15	.044	5.34
1902		19.00		W½SW¼	7	40	60	4-15—6-15	.234	28.50

Source—**Mary's River.** Ditch—**Cold Spring.**

Year of priority	Harvest crops	Meadow pasture	Diversified pasture	Subdivision	Section	Tp.N.	R.E.	Length of season	C.F.S.	Acre-feet
1896		42.58		NE¼	6	39	60	4-15—6-15	.524	63.87
1896		42.45		SE¼	6	39	60	4-15—6-15	.522	63.68
1896		2.60		SE¼	6	39	60	4-15—6-15	.034	3.90
1899		49.50		NE¼	6	39	60	4-15—6-15	.609	74.25
1899			24.52	NE¼	6	39	60	4-15—5-15	.302	18.39
1899		99.12		NW¼	6	39	60	4-15—6-15	1.219	148.68
1899			9.70	NW¼	6	39	60	4-15—5-15	.119	7.28
1896		4.97		NW¼NE¼	18	39	60	4-15—6-15	.061	7.46
1896		48.87		W½W½	29	40	60	4-15—6-15	.601	73.31
1896		61.71		E½NE¼	30	40	60	4-15—6-15	.759	92.57
1896		29.60		E½SE¼	30	40	60	4-15—6-15	.364	44.40
1897		45.70		W½SE¼	30	40	60	4-15—6-15	.562	68.55
1897		3.25		W½NE¼	30	40	60	4-15—6-15	.040	4.88
1897		3.25		SE¼NW¼	30	40	60	4-15—6-15	.040	4.88
1897		129.89		SE¼	30	40	60	4-15—6-15	1.598	194.84
1897		57.80		SW¼	30	40	60	4-15—6-15	.711	86.70
1897		8.73		SE¼NE¼	30	40	60	4-15—6-15	.107	13.10

Source—**Taber and Pole Creeks.** Ditch—**Nos. 1 and 2.**

Year of priority	Harvest crops	Meadow pasture	Diversified pasture	Subdivision	Section	Tp.N.	R.E.	Length of season	C.F.S.	Acre-feet
1899		1.27		SE¼NW¼	14	39	60	4-15—6-15	.016	1.91
1899		102.16		SW¼	14	39	60	4-15—6-15	1.257	153.24
1899		45.72		W½NW¼	14	39	60	4-15—6-15	.562	68.58
1899		5.39		E½NE¼	15	39	60	4-15—6-15	.066	8.09
1899		.30		NE¼SE¼	15	39	60	4-15—6-15	.004	.45
1899			71.95	N½	23	39	60	4-15—5-15	.885	53.06
1900			29.10	NW¼	23	39	60	4-15—5-15	.358	21.83
1900		116.63		SW¼	23	39	60	4-15—6-15	1.435	174.95

Source—**Taber and Pole Creeks.** Ditch—**No. 1.**

Year of priority	Harvest crops	Meadow pasture	Diversified pasture	Subdivision	Section	Tp.N.	R.E.	Length of season	C.F.S.	Acre-feet
1899		43.73		NW¼	14	39	60	4-15—6-15	.538	65.60
1899			29.24	NW¼	14	39	60	4-15—5-15	.360	21.93
1899		37.48		E½SW¼	14	39	60	4-15—6-15	.461	56.22
1899		31.66		W½SE¼	14	39	60	4-15—4-15	.389	47.49
1899		37.00		E½NW¼	14	39	60	4-15—6-15	.455	55.50

	1899					51.97		N½	23	39	60	4-15—5-15	.639	38.08
	1899				1.00			NW¼SE¼	23	39	60	4-15—6-15	.012	1.50
	1900				7.00			SW¼NE¼	23	39	60	4-15—6-15	.086	10.50
	1900					113.02		SE¼	23	39	60	4-15—5-15	1.390	84.77
	1900					123.00		NE¼	26	39	60	4-15—5-15	1.513	92.25
	1900					133.00		S½	26	39	60	4-15—5-15	1.035	90.75

Source—**Taber Creek.** Ditch—**No. 1.**

	1893					71.80		E½	12	40	60	4-15—5-15	.883	53.85
	1900					110.00		W½	26	39	60	4-15—5-15	1.353	82.50

Source—**Taber Creek.** Ditch—**Nos. 1, 2 and 3.**

	1899			1.27				SW¼SW¼	31	41	61	4-15—8-15	.016	3.81
	1899			76.00				N½	6	40	61	4-15—8-15	.935	228.00
	1900			38.97				N½	6	40	61	4-15—8-15	.479	86.91
	1899					123.34		W½	6	40	61	4-15—5-15	1.517	92.51

Source—**Taber Creek.** Ditch—**No. 2.**

	1886				8.10			SE¼SW¼	12	40	60	4-15—6-15	.100	12.15
	1886				46.00			E½	12	40	60	4-15—6-15	.566	60.00
	1886				.42			NW¼NE¼	13	40	60	4-15—6-15	.005	.63
	1886				11.50			NE¼NW¼	13	40	60	4-15—6-15	.141	17.25

Source—**Taber Creek.** Ditch—**No. 3.**

	1885				12.63			SW¼NW¼	12	40	60	4-15—6-15	.155	18.95
	1885				24.42			NW¼SE¼	12	40	60	4-15—6-15	.300	36.63
	1885				23.00			NE¼SW¼	12	40	60	4-15—6-15	.283	34.50
	1885				31.38			SE¼SW¼	12	40	60	4-15—6-15	.386	47.07
	1885				4.68			NW¼SW¼	12	40	60	4-15—6-15	.058	7.02
	1885				32.51			SW¼SW¼	12	40	60	4-15—6-15	.400	48.77
	1885				.64			SW¼NW¼	12	40	60	4-15—6-15	.008	.96
	1885				13.77			NE¼NW¼	12	40	60	4-15—6-15	.169	20.66
	1885				33.79			NW¼NW¼	12	40	60	4-15—6-15	.416	50.69
	1885				13.91			SW¼SW¼	12	40	60	4-15—6-15	.171	20.87

Source—**Taber Creek.** Ditch—**No. 4.**

	1901				2.98			NE¼NE¼	14	40	60	4-15—6-15	.037	4.47
	1901				20.30			SE¼NE¼	14	40	60	4-15—6-15	.250	30.45
	1901				18.88			NW¼SE¼	14	40	60	4-15—6-15	.232	28.20
	1901				7.81			NE¼SE¼	14	40	60	4-15—6-15	.096	11.72

Source—**Taber Creek.** Ditch—**Nos. 4 and 5.**

	1901				70.71			E½	11	40	60	4-15—6-15	.870	106.07
	1901				38.78			NW¼NW¼	14	40	60	4-15—6-15	.477	58.17
	1901				35.78			SW¼SE¼	14	40	60	4-15—6-15	.440	53.67

Source—**Taber Creek.** Ditch—**No. 5.**

	1901					50.90		E½	11	40	60	4-15—5-15	.626	38.18
	1901					7.00		NE¼	11	40	60	4-15—5-15	.086	5.25
	1901				2.84			NE¼NW¼	14	40	60	4-15—6-15	.035	4.26

Union Land and Cattle Co.—Continued.

Year of priority	Harvest crops	Culture—Acres: Meadow pasture	Culture—Acres: Diversified pasture	Location: Subdivision	Location: Section	Location: Tp. N.	Location: R. E.	Length of season	Duty of water: C. F. S.	Duty of water: Acre-feet
Source—Curran Creek. Ditch—No. (?)										
1902	....	29.82	....	W½E½	19	42	60	4-15—6-15	.367	44.73
1902	....	15.80	....	NW¼	19	42	60	4-15—6-15	.194	23.70
1902	....	....	16.50	NW¼	19	42	60	4-15—5-15	.203	12.38
1902	....	13.29	....	E½SW¼	19	42	60	4-15—6-15	.163	19.94
1902	....	48.24	....	W½E½	30	42	60	4-15—6-15	.593	72.36
1902	....	....	48.60	W½E½	30	42	60	4-15—5-15	.598	36.45
1902	....	14.12	....	SW¼	18	42	60	4-15—6-15	.174	21.18
1902	....	68.82	....	SE¼	18	42	60	4-15—6-15	.846	103.23
1902	....	17.16	....	SE¼	18	42	60	4-15—6-15	.211	25.74
Source—Curran Creek. Ditch—No. 1.										
1903	....	1.87	....	SW¼NW¼	19	42	60	4-15—6-15	.023	2.81
1903	....	5.53	....	SE¼NW¼	19	42	60	4-15—6-15	.065	8.30
1903	....	8.00	....	NE¼SW¼	19	42	60	4-15—6-15	.098	12.00
Source—T Creek. Ditch—No. 2.										
1901	....	18.52	....	SW¼	18	42	60	4-15—6-15	.228	27.78
1901	....	6.46	....	SE¼	18	42	60	4-15—6-15	.079	9.69
Source—T Creek. Ditch—No. 1.										
1901	....	50.94	....	SW¼	18	42	60	4-15—6-15	.627	76.41
1901	....	....	6.81	SW¼	18	42	60	4-15—5-15	.084	5.11
1901	....	2.83	....	N½	18	42	60	4-15—6-15	.035	4.25
Source—T Creek. Ditch—Natural Slough.										
1885	....	28.37	....	E½SW¼	30	42	60	4-15—6-15	.349	42.56
1885	....	13.58	....	W½SE¼	30	42	60	4-15—6-15	.167	20.37
1885	....	4.82	....	SW¼NE¼	30	42	60	4-15—6-15	.059	7.23
1885	....	4.32	....	SE¼NW¼	30	42	60	4-15—6-15	.054	6.53
Source—Hank's Creek. Ditch—Nos. 1 and 2.										
1899	....	....	51.05	S½	36	42	59	4-15—5-15	.628	38.20
Source—Bishop Creek. Ditch—McCausland.										
1883	....	81.70	....	NW¼	20	37	60	4-15—6-15	1.004	122.55
1883	....	19.60	....	SW¼	20	37	60	4-15—6-15	.241	29.40
1883	....	91.25	....	SE¼	19	37	60	4-15—6-15	1.122	136.78
1883	....	6.24	....	NE¼	19	37	60	4-15—6-15	.077	9.36
1883	....	93.00	....	NE¼	30	37	60	4-15—6-15	1.145	139.64
1883	....	43.00	....	NW¼	30	37	60	4-15—6-15	.530	64.64
1883	....	68.30	....	SW¼	30	37	60	4-15—6-15	.840	102.45
1881	....	5.83	....	SE¼SE¼	25	37	59	4-15—6-15	.072	8.75

	1883				13.56			NW¼	36	37	59	4-15—6-15	.107	20.34
	1883					13.00		NW¼	36	37	59	4-15—5-15	.100	9.75
	1883				39.55			NE¼	36	37	59	4-15—6-15	.486	59.33
	1883				3.70			NW¼	31	37	59	4-15—6-15	.046	5.55

Source—**Bishop Creek.** Ditch—**Various sloughs and small ditches.**

	1883				27.05			NW¼	20	37	60	4-15—6-15	.333	40.61
	1883				182.19			E½	19	37	60	4-15—6-15	2.241	273.29
	1883				88.60			SW¼	19	37	60	4-15—6-15	1.090	132.90
	1883				163.69			W½	30	37	60	4-15—6-15	2.013	245.42
	1883				181.83			E½	25	37	59	4-15—6-15	2.237	272.75
	1883				40.16			SW¼	25	37	59	4-15—6-15	.497	00.25
	1883				10.85			NE¼	36	37	59	4-15—6-15	.133	16.28
	1883					4.05		NE¼	36	37	59	4-15—5-15	.050	3.04
	1883				26.38			NW¼	36	37	59	4-15—6-15	.324	39.57
	1883					15.91		NW¼	36	37	59	4-15—5-15	.196	11.93

Source—**Mary's River.** Ditch—**No. 1.**

	1904				2.40			SW¼NW¼	19	42	60	4-15—6-15	.030	3.60
	1904				42.10			SW¼	19	42	60	4-15—6-15	.518	63.15
	1904				36.70			SW¼	13	42	59	4-15—6-15	.451	55.05
	1904				21.91			NE¼NW¼	24	42	59	4-15—6-15	.269	32.87
	1904				38.00			NE¼	24	42	59	4-15—6-15	.467	57.00
	1904				27.98			SE¼	24	42	59	4-15—6-15	.344	41.97
	1904				2.64			NW¼NW¼	24	42	59	4-15—6-15	.032	3.96
	1904				15.12			NW¼	30	42	60	4-15—6-15	.186	22.68
	1904					12.32		NW¼	30	42	60	4-15—5-15	.152	9.24
	1904				27.44			SW¼	30	42	60	4-15—6-15	.338	41.16

Source—**Mary's River.** Ditch—**No. 2.**

	1904				41.92			SW¼	19	42	60	4-15—6-15	.505	62.53
	1904					43.96		SW¼	19	42	60	4-15—5-15	.541	32.97
	1904				3.19			SW¼SE¼	19	42	60	4-15—6-15	.039	4.79
	1904				10.52			NW¼	19	42	60	4-15—6-15	.129	15.78
	1904					16.44		NW¼	19	42	60	4-15—5-15	.202	12.33
	1904				19.11			SW¼	13	42	59	4-15—6-15	.235	28.67
	1904				24.27			NE¼	24	42	59	4-15—6-15	.299	36.41
	1904				5.94			NE¼NW¼	24	42	59	4-15—6-15	.073	8.91
	1904				20.76			NW¼	30	42	60	4-15—6-15	.339	31.14
	1904				4.43			NW¼NE¼	30	42	60	4-15—6-15	.054	6.65
	1904				2.37			NE¼SW¼	30	42	60	4-15—6-15	.029	3.56

Source—**Mary's River.** Ditch—**Cross.**

	1900					27.17		NE¼	35	38	59	4-15—5-15	.334	20.38
	1900				14.20			NE¼SE¼	35	38	59	4-15—6-15	.175	21.30
	1900			36.43				W½NE¼	23	38	59	4-15—8-15	.448	109.26
	1900				21.92			W½NE¼	23	38	59	4-15—6-15	.270	32.88
	1900			28.53				E½NW¼	23	38	59	4-15—8-15	.351	85.59
	1900			4.96				NW¼SE¼	23	38	59	4-15—8-15	.061	14.78
	1900				2.44			NW¼SE¼	23	38	59	4-15—6-15	.030	3.66
	1900			19.17				NE¼SW¼	23	38	59	4-15—8-15	.236	57.51

Union Land and Cattle Co.—Continued.

Year of priority	Culture—Acres: Harvest crops	Culture—Acres: Meadow pasture	Culture—Acres: Diversified pasture		Location: Subdivision	Location: Section	Location: Tp.N.	Location: R.E.	Length of season	Duty of water: C.F.S.	Duty of water: Acre-feet
1900	2.30				SE¼SW¼	23	38	59	4-15—8-15	.028	6.90
1900		0.56			SW¼SE¼	23	38	59	4-15—6-15	.007	.84
1901	14.20				SW¼SE¼	23	38	59	4-15—8-15	.175	42.60
1901	17.04				SE¼SW¼	23	38	59	4-15—8-15	.210	51.12
1901		12.20			W½NW¼	36	38	59	4-15—6-15	.150	18.30
1901	67.08				NE¼	26	38	59	4-15—8-15	.836	203.94
1901		10.56			NE¼	26	38	59	4-15—6-15	.130	15.84
1901	20.10				E½NW¼	26	38	59	4-15—8-15	.247	60.30
1901	82.89				SE¼	26	38	59	4-15—8-15	1.020	248.67
1901		4.37			SE¼	26	38	59	4-15—6-15	.054	6.56
1901			32.37		SE¼	26	38	59	4-15—5-15	.398	24.28
1900	35.58				NE¼	35	38	59	4-15—8-15	.438	107.24
1900		20.31			NE¼	35	38	59	4-15—6-15	.250	30.47

Source—**Mary's River.** Ditch—**Cross Ditch and overflow from Beaver Dams.**

Year of priority	Harvest crops	Meadow pasture	Diversified pasture		Subdivision	Section	Tp.N.	R.E.	Length of season	C.F.S.	Acre-feet
1885	1.54				SE¼	14	38	59	4-15—8-15	.056	13.62
1885		65.60			SE¼	14	38	59	4-15—6-15	.807	98.40
1885		2.40			SW¼	14	38	59	4-15—6-15	.030	3.60
1885		68.12			NE¼	11	38	59	4-15—6-15	.838	102.18
1885		31.50			NW¼	11	38	59	4-15—6-15	.387	47.25
1885		96.63			SE¼	11	38	59	4-15—6-15	1.189	144.95
1885		66.83			SW¼	11	38	59	4-15—6-15	.822	100.25
1885		93.97			NE¼	14	38	59	4-15—6-15	1.156	140.95
1885		43.50			NW¼	14	38	59	4-15—6-15	.535	65.25

Source—**Mary's River.** Ditch—**Anderson.**

Year of priority	Harvest crops	Meadow pasture	Diversified pasture		Subdivision	Section	Tp.N.	R.E.	Length of season	C.F.S.	Acre-feet
1886		39.20			NE¼	23	38	59	4-15—6-15	.482	58.80
1886		106.94			SE¼	23	38	59	4-15—6-15	1.315	160.41
1886		69.94			NW¼	36	38	59	4-15—6-15	.860	104.91
1886			17.23		NW¼	36	38	59	4-15—5-15	.212	12.92
1886		121.34			SW¼	36	38	59	4-15—6-15	1.491	182.01
1886		112.33			NW¼	1	37	59	4-15—6-15	1.382	168.50
1886			6.98		NW¼	1	37	59	4-15—5-15	.086	5.24
1886		92.00			SW¼	1	37	59	4-15—6-15	1.132	138.00
1886		23.19			W½NW¼	25	38	59	4-15—6-15	.285	34.70
1886			.84		W½NW¼	25	38	59	4-15—5-15	.010	.63
1886		20.07			W½SW¼	25	38	59	4-15—6-15	.247	30.11
1886			33.48		W½SW¼	25	38	59	4-15—5-15	.412	25.11
1886		.20			SE¼SW¼	25	38	59	4-15—6-15	.002	.30
1886		66.20			NE¼	26	38	59	4-15—6-15	.814	99.30
1886			8.90		NE¼	26	38	59	4-15—5-15	.109	6.68
1886			21.47		E½SE¼	26	38	59	4-15—5-15	.264	16.10
1886		4.70			SE¼SE¼	35	38	59	4-15—6-15	.058	7.05
1886		60.40			NW¼	12	37	59	4-15—6-15	.817	[illegible]
1886		17.00			NE¼SW¼	12	37	59	4-15—6-15	.200	[illegible]

Source—**Mary's River.** Ditch—**Cabin Field.**														
	1884				7.17			S½NE¼	26	39	59	4-15—6-15	.088	10.76
	1884				35.66			SE¼	26	39	59	4-15—6-15	.438	53.49
	1884				55.65			NE¼	35	39	59	4-15—6-15	.684	83.48
	1884				37.65			SE¼	35	39	59	4-15—6-15	.463	56.48
	1884				.85			SW¼SW¼	36	39	59	4-15—6-15	.010	1.28
	1885				44.30			W½W½	1	28	59	4-15—6-15	.545	66.45
	1885					8.88		W½W½	1	38	59	4-15—5-15	.209	6.66
	1884				1.00			NE¼SE¼	2	38	59	4-15—6-15	.012	1.50
	1885				92.17			SE¼	2	38	59	4-15—6-15	1.134	138.26
	1885					49.28		SE¼	2	38	59	4-15—5-15	.006	36.96
	1885				98.68			NE¼	2	38	59	4-15—6-15	1.214	148.02
	1885				16.70			NE¼	11	38	59	4-15—6-15	.200	25.05
	1886				49.78			NE¼	11	38	59	4-15—6-15	.612	74.67
	1886					17.04		NE¼	11	38	59	4-15—5-15	.210	12.78
	1886				52.00			E½SE¼	11	38	59	4-15—6-15	.640	78.00
	1885				4.30			W½W½	12	38	59	4-15—6-15	.053	6.45
	1886				28.19			W½W½	12	38	59	4-15—6-15	.347	42.29
	1886					1.92		W½W½	12	38	59	4-15—5-15	.024	1.44
	1886				34.06			NW¼NW¼	13	38	59	4-15—6-15	.419	51.09
Source—**Mary's River.** Ditch—**Greasewood.**														
	1885				96.06			NW¼	25	38	59	4-15—6-15	1.182	144.09
	1885				57.81			SW¼	25	38	59	4-15—6-15	.711	86.72
	1885				60.98			SW¼	24	38	59	4-15—6-15	.750	91.47
	1885				14.56			NE¼NW¼	36	38	59	4-15—6-15	.179	21.84
	1885				1.40			NW¼NE¼	36	38	59	4-15—6-15	.017	2.10
Source—**Mary's River.** Ditch—**Nos. 1 and 2.**														
	1900				7.25			SE¼SW¼	7	41	60	4-15—6-15	.089	10.88
	1900				61.75			NW¼	18	41	60	4-15—6-15	.760	92.63
	1900				75.24			SW¼	18	41	60	4-15—6-15	.925	112.36
	1900				6.33			SW¼SE¼	18	41	60	4-15—6-15	.078	9.50
Source—**Mary's River.** Ditch—**King Pin.**														
	1898				9.24			NE¼NW¼	18	40	60	4-15—6-15	.113	13.86
	1898				17.55			W½NE¼	18	40	60	4-15—6-15	.216	26.33
	1898				38.06			W½NE¼	18	40	60	4-15—6-15	.468	57.09
	1898				36.91			E½NW¼	18	40	60	4-15—6-15	.454	55.37
	1898				18.48			E½NW¼	18	40	60	4-15—6-15	.227	26.72
	1898				81.74			SE¼	18	40	60	4-15—6-15	1.005	122.61
	1898				11.07			SE¼	18	40	00	4-15—6-15	.136	16.61
	1898				28.11			SW¼	18	40	60	4-15—6-15	.346	42.17
	1898				29.30			SW¼	7	40	60	4-15—6-15	.360	43.95
	1898				48.69			NE¼	19	40	60	4-15—6-15	.599	73.04
	1898					31.38		NE¼	19	40	60	4-15—5-15	.386	23.54
	1898				10.41			NE¼	19	40	60	4-15—6-15	.128	15.62
	1898				7.93			NE¼NW¼	19	40	60	4-15—6-15	.098	11.90
	1898				22.34			SE¼	19	40	60	4-15—6-15	.275	33.51
	1898				15.59			SE¼	19	40	60	4-15—6-15	.192	23.39
	1899				3.09			E½NW¼	19	40	60	4-15—6-15	.038	4.64

Union Land and Cattle Co.—Continued.

Year of priority	Culture—Acres: Harvest crops	Culture—Acres: Meadow pasture	Culture—Acres: Diversified pasture	Location: Subdivision	Location: Section	Location: Tp.N.	Location: R.E.	Length of season	Duty of water: C.F.S.	Duty of water: Acre-feet
1899	....	....	11.84	E½NW¼	19	40	60	4-15—5-15	.146	8.88
1899	....	17.02	....	E½NW¼	19	40	60	4-15—6-15	.209	25.53
1899	....	7.57	....	E½SW¼	19	40	60	4-15—6-15	.093	11.36
Source—Mary's River. Ditch—Island.										
1886	....	92.70	....	NE¼	13	37	59	4-15—6-15	1.140	139.05
1886	....	41.80	....	W½SE¼	13	37	50	4-15—6-15	.514	62.70
1886	....	17.35	....	NE¼NW¼	36	38	59	4-15—6-15	.213	26.03
1886	....	9.00	....	NE¼	36	38	59	4-15—6-15	.111	13.50
1886	....	1.00	....	NE¼NW¼	36	38	59	4-15—6-15	.012	1.50
1886	....	37.20	....	E½SW¼	36	38	59	4-15—6-15	.458	55.80
1886	....	22.86	....	NW¼	36	38	59	4-15—6-15	.281	34.29
1886	....	39.60	....	W½SE¼	36	38	50	4-15—6-15	.487	59.40
1886	....	....	8.76	W½SE¼	36	38	50	4-15—5-15	.108	6.57
1886	....	70.28	....	NE¼	1	37	59	4-15—6-15	.864	105.42
1886	....	....	8.28	NE¼	1	37	59	4-15—5-15	.102	6.21
1886	....	14.01	....	E½NW¼	1	37	59	4-15—6-15	.172	21.02
1886	....	....	9.88	E½NW¼	1	37	59	4-15—5-15	.122	7.41
1886	....	12.45	....	SE¼	1	37	56	4-15—6-15	.153	18.68
1886	....	....	79.44	SE¼	1	37	59	4-15—5-15	.977	59.58
1886	....	2.55	....	NE¼SW¼	1	37	59	4-15—6-15	.031	3.83
1887	....	12.74	....	W½NW¼	7	37	60	4-15—6-15	.157	19.11
1887	....	....	17.27	W½NW¼	7	37	60	4-15—5-15	.212	12.95
1887	....	21.92	....	NW¼SW¼	7	37	60	4-15—6-15	.270	32.88
1887	....	120.14	....	NE¼	12	37	50	4-15—6-15	1.478	180.21
1887	....	82.10	....	SE¼	12	37	50	4-15—6-15	1.010	123.15
Source—Mary's River. Ditch—King Pin.										
1899	....	56.79	....	NW¼	30	40	60	4-15—6-15	.699	85.10
1899	....	24.36	....	NW¼	30	40	60	4-15—6-15	.300	36.54
1899	....	....	19.84	NW¼	30	40	60	4-15—5-15	.244	14.88
1899	....	5.92	....	W½NE¼	30	40	60	4-15—6-15	.073	8.88
1899	....	....	9.81	W½NE¼	30	40	60	4-15—5-15	.121	7.36
1899	....	0.70	....	SW¼	30	40	60	4-15—6-15	.009	1.05
1899	....	9.94	....	W½NE¼	30	40	60	4-15—6-15	.122	14.91
1899	....	28.14	....	SW¼	30	40	60	4-15—6-15	.346	42.21
1899	....	....	2.28	SW¼	30	40	60	4-15—5-15	.028	1.71
1899	....	32.64	....	E½SW¼	19	40	60	4-15—6-15	.401	48.96
1899	....	20.09	....	W½SE¼	19	40	60	4-15—6-15	.247	30.14
1899	....	....	12.22	W½SE¼	19	40	60	4-15—5-15	.150	9.17
1899	....	13.30	....	W½SE¼	19	40	60	4-15—6-15	.164	19.95
Source—Mary's River. Ditch—Atchison.										
1884		44.38	....	NW¼	25	37	50	4-15—6-15	.540	66.57
1884		...	3.42	NW¼	25	37	50	4-15—5-15	.042	2.57

	1884				4.44			NW¼	24	37	59	4-15—6-15	.055	6.60
	1884					29.63		NW¼	24	37	59	4-15—5-15	.364	22.22
	1884				63.20			SW¼	24	37	59	4-15—6-15	.778	94.04
	1884					18.48		SW¼	24	37	59	4-15—5-15	.227	13.86

Source—**Mary's River.** Ditch—**Slough.**

	1883				0.30			SW¼SW¼	25	37	59	4-15—6-15	.004	.45
	1883				85.31			NE¼	25	37	59	4-15—6-15	1.049	127.97
	1883					0.52		NE¼	25	37	50	4-15—5-15	.006	.39
	1883				7.19			E½NW¼	25	37	59	4-15—6-15	.088	10.79
	1883					39.93		E½NW¼	25	37	59	4-15—5-15	.491	29.95
	1883				7.60			NW¼SE¼	25	37	59	4-15—6-15	.093	11.40
	1883				88.96			SW¼	25	37	59	4-15—6-15	1.094	133.44
	1883				85.04			NE¼	24	37	59	4-15—6-15	1.046	127.56
	1883					42.90		NE¼	24	37	59	4-15—5-15	.528	32.18
	1883				79.16			SE¼	24	37	59	4-15—6-15	.974	118.74
	1883					24.00		SE¼	24	37	59	4-15—5-15	.295	18.00
	1883				11.78			SW¼	24	37	59	4-15—6-15	.145	17.67
	1883					8.44		SW¼	24	37	59	4-15—5-15	.104	6.33
	1883				0.84			SE¼SE¼	24	37	59	4-15—6-15	.010	1.26

Source—**Mary's River.** Ditch—**Various Sloughs and Small Ditches.**

	1883				1.70			SE¼SE¼	13	37	59	4-15—6-15	.021	2.55
	1883				43.70			SW¼	18	37	60	4-15—6-15	.538	65.55
	1883				80.21			W½	19	37	60	4-15—6-15	.987	120.32
	1883					55.84		W½	19	37	60	4-15—5-15	.687	41.88
	1883				51.86			E½	24	37	59	4-15—6-15	.638	77.79
	1883					5.88		E½	24	37	59	4-15—5-15	.072	4.41

Source—**Mary's River.** Ditch—**Mason and Bradley.**

	1901				97.90			NW¼	18	37	60	4-15—6-15	1.204	146.85
	1901				33.80			W½SW¼	18	37	60	4-15—6-15	.416	50.70
	1901				64.48			SW¼	7	37	60	4-15—6-15	.793	96.72
	1901					14.52		SW¼	7	37	60	4-15—5-15	.179	10.89
	1901				32.00			NE¼	13	37	59	4-15—6-15	.394	48.00
	1901				18.16			SE¼	13	37	59	4-15—6-15	.223	27.24
	1901					79.84		SE¼	13	37	59	4-15—5-15	.982	59.88

Source—**Mary's River.** Ditch—**Goodale.**

	1886				.97			E½SW¼	1	37	59	4-15—6-15	.012	1.46
	1886					9.38		E½SW¼	1	37	59	4-15—5-15	.115	7.04
	1886				2.45			W½SE¼	1	37	59	4-15—6-15	.030	3.68
	1886					4.92		W½SE¼	1	37	59	4-15—5-15	.061	3.69
	1886				3.40			E½NW¼	12	37	59	4-15—6-15	.042	5.10
	1886				27.40			W½NE¼	12	37	59	4-15—6-15	.337	41.10
	1886				1.84			NE¼SW¼	12	37	59	4-15—6-15	.023	2.76
	1886				75.12			W½SE¼	12	37	59	4-15—6-15	.924	112.68
	1886				32.30			W½NE¼	13	37	59	4-15—6-15	.397	48.45
	1886				13.20			W½SE¼	13	37	59	4-15—6-15	.162	19.80

Claimant—**Jno. H. Cazier & Sons Company.** Proof. No. 00602
Source—**Bishop Creek and Humboldt River.** Ditch—**Cazier & Company Ditches.**

Year of priority	Culture—Acres: Harvest crops	Meadow pasture	Diversified pasture	Location: Subdivision	Section	Tp.N.	R.E.	Length of season	Duty of water: C.F.S.	Acre-feet
1879	....	153.70		NE¼NE¼	35	38	60	4-15—6-15	1.891	230.55
1880	....	153.70		S½NE¼	35	38	00	4-15—6-15	1.891	230.55
				SE¼	35	38	60			
				NE¼SW¼	35	38	60			
				S½SW¼	35	38	60			

Claimant—**Mrs. Annie McMullen.** Proof No. 00603
Source—**As below.** Ditch—**Annie McMullen Ditches.**

Year of priority	Harvest crops	Meadow pasture	Diversified pasture	Subdivision	Section	Tp.N.	R.E.	Length of season	C.F.S.	Acre-feet
Taber Creek—										
1905	....	155.10		W½	4	37	60	4-15—6-15	1.908	232.65
Bishop Creek—										
1882	....	78.50		S½SE¼	4	37	60	4-15—6-15	.960	117.75
Bishop and Taber Creeks—										
1882	....	181.30		....	8	37	60	4-15—6-15	2.230	271.95
1905	....	47.20		....	8	27	60	4-15—6-15	.581	70.80

Claimant—**W. B. Gibbs.** Proof No. 00604
Source—**T and Wildcat Creeks.** Ditch—**W. B. Gibbs Ditches.**

Year of priority	Harvest crops	Meadow pasture	Diversified pasture	Subdivision	Section	Tp.N.	R.E.	Length of season	C.F.S.	Acre-feet
1884	90.70			SE¼NW¼	29	43	60	4-15—8-15	1.116	272.10
1885	74.70			E½SW¼	29	43	60	4-15—8-15	.919	224.10
1889	79.60			W½NE¼	32	43	60	4-15—8-15	.979	238.80
1896	228.20			E½W½	32	43	60	4-15—8-15	2.807	684.60
1897	53.40			W½SW¼	32	43	60	4-15—8-15	.657	160.20
				W½	5	42	60			
				SE¼NE¼	6	42	60			
				W½	8	42	60			

Source—**Hot Creek.** Ditch—**W. B. Gibbs Ditches.**

Year of priority	Harvest crops	Meadow pasture	Diversified pasture	Subdivision	Section	Tp.N.	R.E.	Length of season	C.F.S.	Acre-feet
1885	77.71			SE¼SW¼	32	43	60			
				S½SE¼	32	43	60			
				S½SW¼	33	43	60			
				NW¼NE¼	5	42	60			
				NE¼NW¼	5	42	60	4-15—8-15	.956	233.13

Claimant—**Hylton & Mentz.** Proof No. 00605
Source—**Bishop Creek, Taber Creek, and Blasengame Creek.** Ditch—**Goodale 1-9, incl.**

Year of priority	Harvest crops	Meadow pasture	Diversified pasture	Subdivision	Section	Tp.N.	R.E.	Length of season	C.F.S.	Acre-feet
1882		711.60		N½	9	37	60			
				N½SW¼	9	37	00			
				SW¼SW¼	9	37	60			
					17	37	60	4-15—6-15	8.753	1007.40

Claimant—**Robert W. Anderson.** Proof No. 00607

Source—**Humboldt River.** Ditch—**Robert W. Anderson Ditches.**

....	1879	....	....	....	40.00	....	....	NW¼SE¼	33	37	59	4-15—6-15	.492	60.00

Source—**T Creek and Tributaries.** Ditch—**Robert W. Anderson Ditches.**

....	1884	....	....	76.50	....	....	....	SE¼	9	43	59	4-15—8-15	.912	229.50
....	1902	....	....	....	55.25	....	....	SW¼	10	43	59	4-15—6-15	.680	82.88
....	1904	....	....	....	62.20	....	....	N½	15	43	59	4-15—6-15	.765	93.30
....	1904	....	....	....	156.17	....	....	....	....	....	....	4-15—6-15	1.921	234.26

Source—**Mary's River, Humboldt River and Tributaries.** Ditch—**Robert W. Anderson.**

....	1877	....	....	....	274.51	....	....	S½	26	37	59	4-15—6-15	3.376	411.77
....	1878	....	....	....	68.63	....	....	S½S½	27	37	59	4-15—6-15	.844	102.95
....	1879	....	....	....	68.63	....	....	N½	34	37	59	4-15—6-15	.844	102.95
....	1880	....	....	....	68.63	....	....	N½N½	35	37	59	4-15—6-15	.844	102.95
....	1881	....	....	....	68.63	....	....	....	....	....	....	4-15—6-15	.844	102.95
....	1881	....	....	....	....	157.12	....	....	....	....	....	4-15—5-15	1.933	235.68

Source—**T Creek.** Ditch—**Robert W. Anderson Ditches.**

....	1895	....	....	16.94	....	....	....	SW¼NE¼	36	43	59	4-15—8-15	.208	50.82
....	1898	....	....	238.98	....	....	....	SE¼	36	43	59	4-15—8-15	2.939	716.94
....	1899	....	....	15.00	....	....	....	SW¼	31	43	60	4-15—8-15	.185	45.00
....	1904	....	....	16.03	....	....	....	N½	6	42	60	4-15—8-15	.197	48.09
								NE¼SE¼	6	42	60			
								SW¼NW¼	5	42	60			
								NW¼SW¼	5	42	60			

Claimant—**Metropolis Land Company.** Proof No. 00608

Source—**Bishop Creek.** Ditch—**Nos. 1, 2, and 3.**

....	1886	....	....	160.00	....	....	....	NW¼SE¼	28	39	62			
....	1887	....	....	61.93	....	....	....	N½SW¼	28	39	62			
....	1888	....	....	61.92	....	....	....	S½SE¼	29	39	62			
....	1889	....	....	61.92	....	....	....	E½NE¼	31	39	62	4-15—8-15	1.968	480.00
....	1892	....	....	42.33	....	....	....	NE¼SE¼	31	39	62	4-15—8-15	.762	185.79
								N½	32	39	62	4-15—8-15	.762	185.75
								N½SW¼	32	39	62	4-15—8-15	.762	185.76
								NW¼SE¼	32	39	62	4-15—8-15	.521	126.99

Source—**Trout Creek and Springs.** Ditch—**Nos. 1, 2, and 3.**

....	1889	....	....	16.94	....	....	....	SW¼SE¼	19	39	62			
....	1890	....	....	16.93	....	....	....	SE¼	30	39	62			
....	1891	....	....	16.93	....	....	....	E½SE¼	30	39	62	4-15—8-15	.208	50.82
....	1892	....	....	16.93	....	....	....	SW¼SE¼	30	39	62	4-15—8-15	.208	50.79
....	1893	....	....	153.47	....	....	....	W½SW¼	29	39	62	4-15—8-15	.208	50.79
								NE¼	31	39	62	4-15—8-15	.208	50.79
								NW¼NW¼	32	39	62	4-15—8-15	1.888	460.11

Metropolis Land Company—Continued.

Source—**Burnt Creek and Spring Creek.** Ditch—**Nos. 1, 2, and 3.**

Year of priority	Culture—Acres: Harvest crops	Meadow pasture	Diversified pasture	Location: Subdivision	Section	Tp.N.	R.E.	Length of season	Duty of water: C.F.S.	Acre-feet
1893	107.67			S½NW¼	25	39	61			
				N½SW¼	25	39	61			
				SW¼SW¼	25	39	61	4-15—8-15	1.324	323.01

NOTE—The above land has a priority from Spring Creek alone of 1889.

Source—**Johnson and Bishop Creeks and Springs.** Ditch—**Nos. 1-6, incl.**

Year of priority	Harvest crops	Meadow pasture	Diversified pasture	Subdivision	Section	Tp.N.	R.E.	Length of season	C.F.S.	Acre-feet
1883	15.65			E½SE¼	8	39	63	4-15—8-15	.192	46.95
1884	15.65			W½SW¼	9	39	63	4-15—8-15	.192	46.95
1885	15.65			NW¼NW¼	16	39	63	4-15—8-15	.192	46.95
1886	15.64			NE¼NE¼	17	39	63	4-15—8-15	.192	46.92
1887	15.64			......	...	...	...	4-15—8-15	.192	46.92

Source—**Bishop and Burnt Creeks.** Ditch—**Nos. 5 and 6.**

Year of priority	Harvest crops	Meadow pasture	Diversified pasture	Subdivision	Section	Tp.N.	R.E.	Length of season	C.F.S.	Acre-feet
1876	147.44			E½SW¼	2	38	61			
				SE¼	2	38	61			
				SE¼NE¼	2	38	61			
				W½SW¼	1	38	61			
				SW¼NW¼	1	38	61	4-15—8-15	1.814	442.32

Claimant—**H. A. Agee, Steele Bros., S. C. & S. J. Weeks.** Proof No. 00608

Source—**Burnt Creek.** Ditch—**Nos. 1 and 2.**

Year of priority	Harvest crops	Meadow pasture	Diversified pasture	Subdivision	Section	Tp.N.	R.E.	Length of season	C.F.S.	Acre-feet
1896	40.79			E½SE¼	26	40	61			
1897	31.30			W½SW¼	25	40	61			
				E½NE¼	35	40	61	4-15—8-15	.502	122.37
				W½NW¼	36	40	61	4-15—8-15	.385	93.90

Claimant—**John H. Cazier & Sons Company.** Proof No. 00609

Source—**Trout Creek and Springs.** Ditch—**John H. Cazier Ditches.**

Year of priority	Harvest crops	Meadow pasture	Diversified pasture	Subdivision	Section	Tp.N.	R.E.	Length of season	C.F.S.	Acre-feet
1873	95.60			SW¼	5	37	61	4-15—8-15	1.169	285.00
1873	49.82			E½W½	6	37	61	4-15—8-15	.613	149.46
1874	66.21			W½NE¼	6	37	61	4-15—8-15	.814	198.63
1874	49.82			SE¼	6	37	61	4-15—8-15	.613	149.46
1875	66.20			E½	7	37	61	4-15—8-15	.814	198.60
1875	49.83			W½	8	37	61	4-15—8-15	.613	149.49
1876	66.20			W½NE¼	8	37	61	4-15—8-15	.814	198.60
1876	49.83			SE¼	8	37	61	4-15—8-15	.613	149.49
1877	66.20			W½W½	16	37	61	4-15—8-15	.814	198.60
1877	323.85			E½NW¼	16	37	61	4-15—8-15	3.983	971.55
1877	49.83			W½NE¼	16	37	61	4-15—8-15	.613	149.49
1878	66.20			E½	17	37	61	4-15—8-15	.814	198.60
1879	66.20			......	...	...	...	4-15—8-15	.814	198.60
1880	9.00			......	...	...	...	4-15—8-15	.111	27.00
1881	20.00			......	...	...	...	4-15—8-15	.246	60.00

	1881			9.00								4-15—8-15	.111	27.00
	1882			9.00								4-15—8-15	.111	27.00
	1883			9.00								4-15—8-15	.111	27.00
	1884			9.00								4-15—8-15	.111	27.00
	1885			9.00								4-15—8-15	.111	27.00
	1886			9.00								4-15—8-15	.111	27.00
	1887			9.00								4-15—8-15	.111	27.00
	1888			9.00								4-15—8-15	.111	27.00
	1889			9.00								4-15—8-15	.111	27.00
	1890			10.00								4-15—8-15	.123	30.00
				83.70										
				25.92										
				25.93										
				25.80										
				25.80										
				166.20										

Source—**Trout Creek.** Ditch—**John H. Cazier Ditches.**

	1880			113.58				S½NW¼	31	38	61			
								N½SW¼	31	38	61			
								SE¼SW¼	31	38	61			
								W½SE¼	31	38	61			
								NE¼SE¼	31	38	61	4-15—8-15	1.307	341.74

Source—**Bishop Creek, Humboldt River, and Trout Creek.** Ditch—**John H. Cazier Ditches.**

	1880			287.15				N½	31	38	61	4-15—8-15	3.532	861.45

Source—**Trout Creek, Picnic Grove Creek and Gulch.** Ditch—**Cazier & Company Ditches.**

	1881			40.00				E½SE¼	13	37	60			
	1882			217.30				NE¼NE¼	24	37	60			
	1884			85.65				W½NW¼	18	37	61			
	1900			130.56				SE¼NW¼	18	37	61			
				12.00				NE¼	18	37	61			
				120.60				N½	18	37	61			
								S½	18	37	61	4-15—8-15	.492	120.00
								N½NW¼	19	37	61	4-15—8-15	2.673	651.90
								SW¼NW¼	19	37	61	4-15—8-15	1.053	256.95
								NW¼NE¼	19	37	61	4-15—8-15	1.606	391.68

Source—**Humboldt River, Bishop Creek, and West Fork of Trout Creek.**
Ditch—**Cazier & Company Ditches.**

	1879				426.50			W½	36	38	60			
								NE¼	36	38	60			
								N½SE¼	36	38	60	4-15—6-15	5.246	639.80

Claimant—**L. L. Redden.** Proof No. **00610**
Source—**Mary's River.** Ditch—**L. L. Redden Ditches.**

	1898				10.00			SW¼NW¼	10	42	59			
	1899				103.60			E½NW¼	10	42	59	4-15—6-15	.123	15.00
	1899				62.50			NE¼	10	42	59	4-15—6-15	1.274	155.40
								SW¼NW¼	11	42	59	4-15—6-15	.760	93.75

Claimant—**Huntington and Diamond Valley Stock and Land Company.** Proof No. 00651
Source—**Huntington Creek and Tributaries.**
Ditch—**Huntington and Diamond Valley Ditches.**

Year of priority	Culture—Acres: Harvest crops	Meadow pasture	Diversified pasture	Location: Subdivision	Section	Tp.N.	R.E.	Length of season	Duty of water: C.F.S.	Acre-feet
1869	345.18				35	27	55	4-15—8-15	4.246	1035.54
1870	50.00				36	27	55	4-15—8-15	.615	150.00
1871	50.00				31	27	56	4-15—8-15	.615	150.00
1873	159.00				26	27	55	4-15—8-15	1.956	477.00
1874	10.00				23	27	55	4-15—8-15	.123	30.00
1875	10.00				22	27	55	4-15—8-15	.123	30.00
1876	175.00				14	27	55	4-15—8-15	2.153	525.00
					15	27	55			
					10	27	55			

See Appendix A.

Claimant—**Bert Stoddart.** Proof No. 00652
Source—**Welch Creek and South Fork of Humboldt River.** Ditch—**Kleckner-Dovel.**

Year of priority	Harvest crops	Meadow pasture	Diversified pasture	Subdivision	Section	Tp.N.	R.E.	Length of season	C.F.S.	Acre-feet
1902	18.50			S½NW¼	10	31	57	4-15—8-15	.229	56.50
1902	1.00			SW¼	10	31	57	4-15—8-15	.012	3.00
1902	50.00			NW¼SE¼	10	31	57	4-15—8-15	.615	150.00
1902	15.50			W½NE¼	10	31	57	4-15—8-15	.191	46.50
1903	25.90							4-15—8-15	.319	77.70
1903	27.00							4-15—8-15	.332	81.00
1903			8.00					4-15—5-15	.098	6.00
1904	10.50							4-15—8-15	.129	31.50
1904			41.00					4-15—5-15	.504	30.75
1904	1.10							4-15—8-15	.014	3.30

Claimant—**Griswold-Henderson Livestock Co.** Proof No. 00653
Source—**Ten-Mile Creek.** Ditch—**Griswold-Henderson Ditches.**

Year of priority	Harvest crops	Meadow pasture	Diversified pasture	Subdivision	Section	Tp.N.	R.E.	Length of season	C.F.S.	Acre-feet
1885	21.00				4	33	56	4-15—8-15	.258	63.00
1886	21.00							4-15—8-15	.258	63.00
1887	21.00							4-15—8-15	.258	63.00
1888	21.00							4-15—8-15	.258	63.00
1889	21.41							4-15—8-15	.263	64.23

NOTE—That certain Decree No. 1621, District Court of Elko County, is binding as between parties to the suit.

Source—**Ten-Mile Creek and Mitchell Creek.** Ditch—**Griswold-Henderson Ditches.**

Year of priority	Harvest crops	Meadow pasture	Diversified pasture	Subdivision	Section	Tp.N.	R.E.	Length of season	C.F.S.	Acre-feet
1885	169.80				8	33	56	4-15—8-15	2.080	509.20
1886	169.80				9	33	56	4-15—8-15	2.080	509.20
1887	169.93				16	33	56	4-15—8-15	2.090	509.79
					17	33	56			

NOTE—That certain Decree No. 1621, District Court of Elko County, is binding as between parties to the suit.

Claimant—**J. H. Carter.** Proof No. 00654

Source—**Willow Creek.** Ditch—**Toyn Nos. 1-12, incl.**

1904	15.00		NW¼NE¼	3	30	56	4-15—8-15	.185	45.00
1905	5.69		NW¼NE¼	3	30	56	4-15—8-15	.070	17.07
1905	21.11		NE¼NW¼	3	30	56	4-15—8-15	.260	63.33
1905	12.74		NW¼NW¼	3	30	56	4-15—8-15	.157	38.22
1905	9.42		SW¼SW¼	34	31	56	4-15—8-15	.116	28.36

Source—**Willow** Creek, Swamps, **and Springs.** Ditch—**Toyn Nos. 1-12, incl.**

1896	18.42		NW¼SE¼	33	31	56	4-15—8-15	.227	55.26
1896	1.50		NE¼SE¼	33	31	56	4-15—8-15	.018	4.50
1896	35.32		SW¼SE¼	33	31	56	4-15—8-15	.434	105.96
1896	26.98		SE¼SE¼	33	31	56	4-15—8-15	.332	80.94
1896	9.14		NE¼SW¼	33	31	56	4-15—8-15	.112	27.42
1896	33.92		SE¼SW¼	33	31	56	4-15—8-15	.417	101.76
1896	.82		NW¼NW¼	3	30	56	4-15—8-15	.010	2.46
1896	3.55		NE¼NE¼	4	30	56	4-15—8-15	.044	10.65
1896	2.41		NW¼NE¼	4	30	56	4-15—8-15	.030	7.23
1896	21.33		NE¼NW¼	4	30	56	4-15—8-15	.262	63.99
1896	2.38		SE¼NW¼	4	30	56	4-15—8-15	.029	7.14
1896	2.76		NW¼NW¼	4	30	56	4-15—8-15	.034	8.28
1896	18.85		SW¼NW¼	4	30	56	4-15—8-15	.232	56.55
1896	2.82		SE¼NE¼	5	30	56	4-15—8-15	.035	8.46
1896	5.72		NE¼NE¼	5	30	56	4-15—8-15	.070	17.16

Claimant—**J. J. Hylton.** Proof No. 00655

Source—**Pearl Creek, Frost Canyon Creek, and Brown Creek.** Ditch—**J. J. Hylton Ditches.**

1890*	40.00		NW¼	12	28	55	4-15—8-15	.492	120.00
1900*	34.36		SW¼SW¼	1	28	55	4-15—8-15	.423	103.08
1901*	34.36		SE¼SE¼	2	28	55	4-15—8-15	.423	103.08
1902	34.36		NW¼	12	28	55	4-15—8-15	.423	103.08
1900		10.00	NE¼SW¼	12	28	55	4-15—5-15	.123	7.50
1901		10.00	NW¼SE¼	12	28	55	4-15—5-15	.123	7.50
1902		10.00	E½NE¼	11	28	55	4-15—5-15	.123	7.50

*In order to comply with the decree in the case of H. H. Porch and H. F. Porch v. Antone Sestenovich, No. 1548, 80 acres of land now belonging to J. J. Hylton, Claim No. 00655, and being in sections 1, 2, 11 and 12 in T. 28 N, R. 55 E, with dates as follows: 40 acres in 1899, 34.36 acres in 1900, 5.64 acres in 1901, are to be supplied with water from Brown, Pearl, and Frost Canyon Creeks before any water is allowed to flow into Huntington Creek from these streams for the irrigation of land now belonging to Odiaga with a prior date of 1889 from Huntington Creek. Decrees mentioned are of Elko District Court.

Claimant—**Javier Goyeneche.** Proof No. 00656

Source—**Lindsay Creek and Unnamed Canyon.** Ditch—**Javier Goyeneche Ditches.**

1869	13.98		N½SW¼	11	27	56	4-15—8-15	.172	41.94
1870	13.97		SE¼SW¼	11	27	56	4-15—8-15	.172	41.91
1871	13.97		W½SE¼	11	27	56	4-15—8-15	.172	41.91
1872	13.97		SE¼SE¼	11	27	56	4-15—8-15	.172	41.91
1873	13.97		S½SW¼	12	27	56	4-15—8-15	.172	41.91

Claimant—**V. Juaristi.** Proof No. **00657**

Source—**Willow Creek.** Ditch—**Ditches Nos. 1-13, incl.**

Year of priority	Culture—Acres: Harvest crops	Meadow pasture	Diversified pasture	Location: Subdivision	Section	Tp.N.	R.E.	Length of season	Duty of water: C.F.S.	Acre-feet
1876	18.94			NW¼NW¼	33	26	56	4-15—8-15	.233	56.82
1876	6.11			SW¼NW¼	33	26	56	4-15—8-15	.075	18.33
1876	23.53			NE¼NW¼	33	26	56	4-15—8-15	.289	70.59
1876	13.64			NW¼NE¼	33	26	56	4-15—8-15	.168	40.92
1876	5.20			NE¼NE¼	33	26	56	4-15—8-15	.064	15.60
1876	1.02			SW¼SE¼	28	26	56	4-15—8-15	.013	3.06
1876	.70			SE¼SW¼	28	26	56	4-15—8-15	.009	2.10
1876	3.13			SE¼SE¼	28	26	56	4-15—8-15	.039	9.39
1905	.66			SE¼SW¼	29	26	56	4-15—8-15	.008	1.98
1905	2.90			SW¼SE¼	29	26	56	4-15—8-15	.036	8.70
1905	1.62			NE¼NW¼	32	26	56	4-15—8-15	.020	4.86
1905	9.98			NW¼NE¼	32	26	56	4-15—8-15	.123	29.94
1905	12.44			NE¼NE¼	32	26	56	4-15—8-15	.153	37.32
1905	7.40			NW¼NW¼	33	26	56	4-15—8-15	.091	22.20

Claimant—**Henry Peters.** Proof No. **00659**

Source—**Peters Creek and Spring.** Ditch—**Nos. 1-8, incl.**

Year of priority	Harvest crops	Meadow pasture	Diversified pasture	Subdivision	Section	Tp.N.	R.E.	Length of season	C.F.S.	Acre-feet
1900	2.18			NE¼NW¼	4	26	56	4-15—8-15	.028	6.54
1900	2.76			NW¼NE¼	4	26	56	4-15—8-15	.034	8.28
1901	0.43			NW¼NE¼	4	26	56	4-15—8-15	.005	1.29
1901	0.12			NE¼NE¼	4	26	56	4-15—8-15	.001	.36
1903	2.54			NE¼NE¼	4	26	56	4-15—8-15	.031	8.62
1903	1.21			SE¼NE¼	4	26	56	4-15—8-15	.015	3.63
1903	0.85			NW¼NW¼	3	26	56	4-15—8-15	.010	2.55
1903	0.74			SW¼NW¼	3	26	56	4-15—8-15	.009	2.21
1904	0.40			NW¼NW¼	4	26	56	4-15—8-15	.005	1.20
1904	1.96			SW¼NW¼	4	26	56	4-15—8-15	.024	5.88
1904	1.49			SE¼NW¼	4	26	56	4-15—8-15	.018	4.47
1904	0.56			NE¼NW¼	4	26	56	4-15—8-15	.007	1.68
1904	15.00			N½	4	26	56	4-15—8-15	.185	45.00

Claimant—**Frank Brennen.** Proof No. **00660**

Source—**Cottonwood Creek and Springs.** Ditch—**Frank Brennen Ditches.**

Year of priority	Harvest crops	Meadow pasture	Diversified pasture	Subdivision	Section	Tp.N.	R.E.	Length of season	C.F.S.	Acre-feet
1897	10.00*			W½	20	32	57	4-15—8-15	0.123	30.00
1900	9.96†			....	....	....	....	4-15—8-15	0.123	29.88
1903	26.50†			....	....	....	....	4-15—8-15	0.320	79.50

*From Spring. †Cottonwood Creek and Springs.

Claimant—**Vincente Juaristi.** Proof No. **00662**

Source—**Holum Spring in Water Canyon.** Ditch—**Nos. 1-3, incl.**

Year of priority	Harvest crops	Meadow pasture	Diversified pasture	Subdivision	Section	Tp.N.	R.E.	Length of season	C.F.S.	Acre-feet
1900	11.16			SW¼	5	25	56	4-15—8-15	.137	33.48

Claimant—**J. H. Carter.** Proof No. 00663

Source—**Willow Creek and Rattlesnake Creek.** Ditch—**J. H. Carter Ditches.**

	1873			39.00								4-15—8-15	.480	117.00
	1874			21.00								4-15—8-15	.258	63.00
	1875			43.00								4-15—8-15	.529	129.00
	1876			42.00								4-15—8-15	.517	126.00
	1877			10.00								4-15—8-15	.123	30.00
	1878			10.00					31	31	57	4-15—8-15	.123	30.00
	1879			30.00					32	31	57	4-15—8-15	.369	97.00
	1881			13.60				N½N½	6	30	57	4-15—8-15	.167	40.80
	1885			13.60								4-15—8-15	.167	40.80
	1885			60.86								4-15—8-15	.749	182.58
	1889			13.60								4-15—8-15	.167	40.80
	1893			13.60								4-15—8-15	.167	40.80
	1897			13.60								4-15—8-15	.167	40.80
	1901			13.64								4-15—8-15	.168	40.92
	1902			85.00								4-15—8-15	1.046	255.00
	1905					2.50						4-15—5-15	.031	1.88
	1905					1.86						4-15—5-15	.023	1.40
	1876					77.00						4-15—5-15	.947	57.75
	1885					51.56						4-15—5-15	.634	38.67

Claimant—**Chas. Toyn.** Proof No. 00664

Source—**South Fork Smith Creek.** Ditch—**Chas. Toyn Ditches.**

	1871			5.00				E½NW¼	35	29	56			
	1872			16.53				W½NE¼	35	29	56			
	1873			66.11				SE¼NE¼	35	29	56	4-15—8-15	.062	15.00
	1874			16.27				E½SE¼	35	29	56	4-15—8-15	.203	49.59
	1904			10.67				S½S½	36	29	56	4-15—8-15	.813	198.33
								N½N½	1	28	56	4-15—8-15	.200	48.81
								NE¼NE¼	2	28	56	4-15—8-15	.131	32.01

Claimant—**C. H. Kleckner.** Proof No. 00668

Source—**South Fork of Humboldt River and Welch Creek.*** Ditch—**C. H. Kleckner Ditches.**

	1873			6.26				NW¼	15	31	57	4-15—8-15	.077	18.78
	1902			37.70								4-15—8-15	.464	113.10
	1902				32.07							4-15—6-15	.394	48.11
	1873					8.26						4-15—5-15	.102	6.20
Kleckner Canyon—														
	1873			1.65				E½NW¼	15	31	57	4-15—8-15	.020	4.95
Springs and Natural Draws and Kleckner Canyon†—														
	1900			5.00				S½NW¼	15	31	57	4-15—8-15	.062	15.00
	1901			40.15				N½SW¼	15	31	57	4-15—8-15	.494	120.45
	1905					21.61						4-15—5-15	.266	16.21

*Claimant has ditch diverting water from South Fork into Welch Creek.

†Priority in Kleckner Canyon 1905. Water to be used from natural draws and springs before diverting from Kleckner Canyon.

Claimant—**J. J. Hylton.** Proof No. 00670

Source—**Sherman Canyon.** Ditch—**J. J. Hylton Ditches.**

Year of priority	Culture—Acres: Harvest crops	Culture—Acres: Meadow pasture	Culture—Acres: Diversified pasture	Location: Subdivision	Location: Section	Location: Tp.N.	Location: R.E.	Length of season	Duty of water: C.F.S.	Duty of water: Acre-feet
1878	9.46			NE¼NW¼	28	26	56	4-15—8-15	.116	28.38
1878	5.54			NW¼NW¼	28	26	56	4-15—8-15	.068	16.62
1878	1.71			NW¼NW¼	28	26	56	4-15—8-16	.021	5.13
1880	1.71			NW¼NW¼	28	26	56	4-15—8-16	.021	5.13
1882	1.70			NW¼NW¼	28	26	56	4-15—8-15	.021	5.10
1878	2.79			NE¼NE¼	29	26	56	4-15—8-15	.034	8.37
1880	2.79			NE¼NE¼	29	26	56	4-15—8-15	.034	8.27
1882	2.78			NE¼NE¼	29	26	56	4-15—8-15	.034	8.37
1878	0.94			NW¼NE¼	29	26	56	4-15—8-15	.012	2.82
1880	0.94			NW¼NE¼	29	26	56	4-15—8-15	.012	2.82
1882	0.93			NW¼NE¼	29	26	56	4-15—8-15	.012	2.79

Claimant—**Fred Walther.** Proof No. 00671

Source—**Walther Creek.** Ditch—**Nos. 1-3, incl., and Sastanovich Ditch.**

Year of priority	Culture—Acres: Harvest crops	Culture—Acres: Meadow pasture	Culture—Acres: Diversified pasture	Location: Subdivision	Location: Section	Location: Tp.N.	Location: R.E.	Length of season	Duty of water: C.F.S.	Duty of water: Acre-feet
1875	0.71			NW¼SW¼	14	26	56	4-15—8-15	.009	2.13
1875	7.27			NE¼SE¼	15	26	56	4-15—8-16	.089	21.81
1875	2.66			SE¼SE¼	15	26	56	4-15—8-15	.033	7.98
1875	1.36			SW¼SE¼	15	26	56	4-15—8-15	.017	4.08
1876	7.99			SW¼SE¼	15	26	56	4-15—8-15	.098	23.97
1876	16.33			SE¼SW¼	15	26	56	4-15—8-15	.201	48.99
1876	24.68			SW¼SW¼	15	26	56	4-15—8-15	.304	74.04
1877	0.64			NW¼SW¼	15	26	56	4-15—8-15	.008	1.92
1882	0.64			NW¼SW¼	15	26	56	4-15—8-15	.008	1.92
1887	0.63			NW¼SW¼	15	26	56	4-15—8-16	.008	1.89
1893	0.63			NW¼SW¼	15	26	56	4-15—8-15	.008	1.89
1877	2.76			SW¼SW¼	15	26	56	4-15—8-15	.034	8.28
1882	2.76			SW¼SW¼	15	26	56	4-15—8-15	.034	8.28
1887	2.75			SW¼SW¼	15	26	56	4-15—8-15	.034	8.25
1893	2.75			SW¼SW¼	15	26	56	4-15—8-15	.034	8.25
1877	0.33			NW¼NW¼	22	26	56	4-15—8-15	.004	0.90
1882	0.33			NW¼NW¼	22	26	56	4-15—8-15	.004	0.99
1887	0.33			NW¼NW¼	22	26	56	4-15—8-15	.004	0.99
1893	0.32			NW¼NW¼	22	26	56	4-15—8-15	.004	0.96
1877	0.81			NE¼SE¼	16	26	56	4-15—8-15	.010	2.43
1882	0.81			NE¼SE¼	16	26	56	4-15—8-15	.010	2.43
1887	0.80			NE¼SE¼	16	26	56	4-15—8-15	.010	2.40
1893	0.80			NE¼SE¼	16	26	56	4-15—8-15	.010	2.40
1877	11.84			S½SE¼	16	26	56	4-15—8-15	.140	35.52
1882	11.84			S½SE¼	16	26	56	4-15—8-15	.140	35.52

1887	11.84	S½SE¼	16	26	56	4-15—8-15	.146	35.52
1893	11.83	S½SE¼	16	26	56	4-15—8-15	.146	35.49
1877	13.45	N½NE¼	21	26	56	4-15—8-15	.165	40.35
1882	13.45	N½NE¼	21	26	56	4-15—8-15	.165	40.35
1887	13.45	N½NE¼	21	26	56	4-15—8-15	.165	40.35
1893	13.46	N½NE¼	21	26	56	4-15—8-15	.165	40.38
1877	20.42	NW¼	21	26	56	4-15—8-15	.251	61.26
1882	20.42	NW¼	21	26	56	4-15—8-15	.251	61.26
1887	20.43	NW¼	21	26	56	4-15—8-15	.251	61.29
1893	20.43	NW¼	21	26	56	4-15—8-15	.251	61.29
1905	3.63	SW¼SW¼	22	26	56	4-15—8-15	.045	10.89
1905	3.77	SE¼SE¼	21	26	56	4-15—8-15	.046	11.31
1905	.69	SE¼SE¼	21	26	56	4-15—8-15	.008	2.07
1905	4.11	SW¼SE¼	21	26	56	4-15—8-15	.051	12.33
1905	2.62	NE¼NE¼	28	26	56	4-15—8-15	.032	7.86
1905	7.42	NW¼NE¼	28	26	56	4-15—8-15	.091	22.42

Claimant—**James Sastanovich.** Proof No. 00673

Source—**Walthers Creek, Sherman Canyon, and Springs.** Ditch—**Nos. 1 to 4, incl.**

1905	1.38	NE¼NE¼	20	26	56	4-15—8-15	.017	4.14
1905	7.23	NE¼NE¼	20	26	56	4-15—8-15	.089	21.69
1905	3.33	NW¼NE¼	20	26	56	4-15—8-15	.041	9.99
1905	1.53	SE¼SE¼	17	26	56	4-15—8-15	.009	4.50
1905	.40	SE¼SE¼	17	26	56	4-15—8-15	.005	1.20
1905	1.62	SW¼SE¼	17	26	56	4-15—8-15	.020	4.86

Claimant—**John C. Hackward.** Proof No. 00674

Source—**Dixie Creek.** Ditch—**John C. Hackward Ditches.**

1883	4.86	NW¼SE¼	17	30	54	4-15—8-15	.060	14.58
1883	8.44	SW¼NE¼	17	30	54	4-15—8-15	.104	25.32
1883	1.85	NE¼NW¼	17	30	54	4-15—8-15	.023	5.55
1883	.51	NE¼NW¼	17	30	54	4-15—8-15	.006	1.53
1884	1.31	NW¼SE¼	17	30	54	4-15—8-15	.016	3.93
1884	16.08	SW¼NE¼	17	30	54	4-15—8-15	.198	48.24
1884	.20	SW¼NE¼	17	30	54	4-15—8-15	.002	.60
1884	2.22	SE¼NE¼	17	30	54	4-15—8-15	.027	6.66
1884	16.35	NW¼NE¼	17	30	54	4-15—8-15	.201	49.05
1884	3.88	NE¼NW¼	17	30	54	4-15—8-15	.048	11.64
1890	2.67	SE¼SW¼	5	30	54	4-15—8-15	.033	8.01
1890	5.32	NE¼NW¼	8	30	54	4-15—8-15	.065	15.96
1890	.88	SE¼NW¼	8	30	54	4-15—8-15	.011	2.64

Claimant—**James Bett.** Proof No. 00675
Source—**Dixie Creek and Tributaries.** Ditch—**James Bett Ditches.**

Year of priority	Culture—Acres: Harvest crops	Meadow pasture	Diversified pasture	Location: Subdivision	Section	Tp.N.	R.E.	Length of season	Duty of water: C.F.S.	Acre-feet
1882	.14			SE¼SW¼	32	31	54	4-15—8-15	.002	.42
1882	3.32			SW¼SE¼	32	31	54	4-15—8-15	.041	9.96
1882	5.90			NW¼SE¼	32	31	54	4-15—8-15	.073	17.70
1882	6.66			SW¼NE¼	32	31	54	4-15—8-15	.082	19.98
1882	1.99			SE¼NW¼	32	31	54	4-15—8-15	.024	5.97
1882	1.99			NE¼NW¼	32	31	54	4-15—8-15	.024	5.97
1883	42.72				28	31	54	4-15—8-15	.525	128.16
1884	42.72				29	31	54	4-15—8-15	.525	128.16
1885	42.71				32	31	54	4-15—8-15	.525	128.13
1885	3.49*			NW¼SW¼	29	31	54	4-15—8-15	.043	10.47
1885	2.74*			NE¼SE¼	30	31	54	4-15—8-15	.034	8.22
1885	14.34				....	....	....	4-15—8-15	.176	43.02
1887	14.34				21	31	54	4-15—8-16	.176	43.02
1890	14.33				28	31	54	4-15—8-15	.176	42.99
1892	14.33				....	....	....	4-15—8-15	.176	42.99

*Water for the irrigation of this land comes from Bullion Creek.

Claimant—**J. J. Hylton.** Proof No. 00676
Source—**Bullion Creek.** Ditch—**Nos. 1-7, incl.**

Year of priority	Harvest crops	Meadow pasture	Diversified pasture	Subdivision	Section	Tp.N.	R.E.	Length of season	C.F.S.	Acre-feet
1874	.25			SE¼SE¼	25	31	53	4-15—8-15	.031	.75
1874	5.80			SW¼SE¼	25	31	53	4-15—8-15	.071	17.40
1874	6.20			SE¼SW¼	25	31	53	4-15—8-15	.076	18.60
1874	5.95			SW¼SW¼	25	31	53	4-15—8-15	.073	17.85
1874	4.78			SE¼SE¼	26	31	53	4-15—8-15	.059	14.34
1874	6.39			SW¼SE¼	26	31	53	4-15—8-15	.079	19.17
1874	1.95			SE¼SW¼	26	31	53	4-15—8-15	.024	5.85

Claimant—**Bett & Papa.** Proof No. 00677
Source—**Creeks** (no name) tributary **to South Fork.** Ditch—**Nos. 1, 2, 3, 4, 5, 6, 7.**

Year of priority	Harvest crops	Meadow pasture	Diversified pasture	Subdivision	Section	Tp.N.	R.E.	Length of season	C.F.S.	Acre-feet
1882	3.25			SW¼SW¼	11	31	53	4-15—8-15	.040	9.75
1882	6.46			SW¼SE¼	11	31	53	4-15—8-15	.079	19.38
1882	8.88			SE¼SE¼	11	31	53	4-15—8-15	.109	26.64
1882	4.70			SW¼SW¼	12	31	53	4-15—8-15	.058	14.10
1882	.41			NE¼NW¼	13	31	53	4-15—8-15	.005	1.23
1882	4.91			NW¼NW¼	13	31	53	4-15—8-15	.060	14.73
1882	3.29			NE¼NE¼	14	31	53	4-15—8-15	.040	9.87
1882	1.74			SE¼NE¼	14	31	53	4-15—8-15	.021	5.22
1882	16.63			SW¼NE¼	14	31	53	4-15—8-15	.205	49.89
1882	1.69			NW¼NE¼	14	31	53	4-15—8-15	.021	5.07
1882	8.45			NE¼NW¼	14	31	53	4-15—8-15	.104	25.35
1882	13.22			NW¼NW¼	14	31	53	4-15—8-15	.163	39.66
1882	10.85			SE¼NW¼	14	31	53	4-15—8-15	[illegible]	[illegible]
1882	3.39			[illegible]	14	31	53	4-15—8-15	[illegible]	10.17

	1882			5.79				NW¼SW¼	14	31	53	4 15—8-15	.071	17.37
	1882			3.43				SW¼SW¼	14	31	53	4-15—8-15	.042	10.29
	1882			11.53				SE¼SE¼	15	31	53	4-15—8-15	.142	34.59
	1882			4.00				SW¼SE¼	15	31	53	4-15—8-15	.057	13.80
	1882			1.06				NE¼NE¼	15	31	53	4-15—8-15	.013	3.18
	1882			9.67				NW¼NE¼	22	31	53	4-15—8-15	.119	29.01

Claimant—**Bett & Papa.** Proof No. **00678**

Source—**Dixie Creek.** Ditch—**Nos. 1 and 2.**

	1882			4.42				NE¼SW¼	3	31	54	4-15—8-15	.054	13.28
	1882			15.73				SE¼SW¼	3	31	54	4-15—8-15	.193	47.19
	1882			3.40				NW¼NE¼	3	31	54	4-15—8-15	.042	10.20
	1882			24.08				SW¼NE¼	3	31	54	4-15—8-15	.296	72.24
	1882			39.56				NW¼SE¼	3	31	54	4-15—8-15	.442	118.68
	1882			31.62				SW¼SE¼	3	31	54	4-15—8-15	.389	94.86
	1882			2.37				NW¼NE¼	10	31	54	4-15—8-15	.029	7.11
	1882			6.29				NE¼NW¼	10	31	54	4-15—8-15	.077	18.87
	1885			0.69				NE¼NW¼	3	31	54	4-15—8-15	.008	2.07
	1885			16.18				SE¼NW¼	3	31	54	4-15—8-15	.199	48.54
	1885			16.60				NE¼SW¼	3	31	54	4-15—8-15	.204	49.80
	1885			12.33				SE¼SW¼	3	31	54	4-15—8-15	.152	36.99
	1885			12.01				NE¼NW¼	3	31	54	4-15—8-15	.148	36.03
	1885			2.07				SE¼NW¼	3	31	54	4-15—8-15	.025	6.21

Claimant—**E. E. Elliot.** Proof No. **00679**

Source—**North Fork Dixie Creek and Springs.** Ditch—**E. E. Elliot Ditches.**

	1878			3.63				NW¼SE¼	13	30	53	4-15—8-15	.044	10.89
	1878			3.86				NW¼SW¼	13	30	53	4-15—8-15	.047	11.58
	1878			0.48				SW¼SW¼	13	30	53	4-15—8-15	.006	1.44
	1878			7.82				SE¼SW¼	13	30	53	4-15—8-15	.096	23.46
	1878			21.02				NE¼SW¼	13	30	53	4-15—8-15	.259	63.06

Source—**Cissillini Canyon Creek.** Ditch—**Dixie Creek Ditch.**

	1893			1.69				NE¼NW¼	13	30	53	4-15—8-15	.021	5.07
	1893			6.23				NW¼NW¼	13	30	53	4-15—8-15	.077	18.69
	1893			1.08				NE¼NE¼	14	30	53	4-15—8-15	.013	3.24

Source—**South Fork Dixie Creek.** Ditch—**Dixie Creek Ditch.**

	1892			15.13				SE¼SE¼	13	30	53	4-15—8-15	.186	45.39
	1892			36.68				NE¼NE¼	24	30	53	4-15—8-15	.451	110.04
	1892			26.41				SE¼NE¼	24	30	53	4-15—8-15	.325	79.23
	1892			0.30				SW¼NE¼	24	30	53	4-15—8-15	.004	0.90
	1892			2.54				NW¼NW¼	19	30	54	4-15—8-15	.031	7.62
	1892			0.10				SW¼NW¼	19	30	54	4-15—8-15	.001	0.30

Claimant—**Chas. Hairgrove.** Proof No. 00680

Source—**Rattlesnake Creek.** Ditch—**Chas. Hairgrove Ditches.**

Year of priority	Culture—Acres: Harvest crops	Culture—Acres: Meadow pasture	Culture—Acres: Diversified pasture	Location: Subdivision	Location: Section	Location: Tp.N.	Location: R.E.	Length of season	Duty of water: C.F.S.	Duty of water: Acre-feet
1902	9.52			SE¼	29	31	57	4-15—8-15	.117	28.56
1903	5.95			NE¼NE¼	32	31	57	4-15—8-15	.118	17.85
1905	....		100.00		....	....	....	4-15—5-15	1.230	75.00

Claimant—**Merkley & Young.** Proof No. 00681

Source—**Lindsay and Twin Creeks.** Ditch—**Merkeley & Young Ditches.**

Year of priority	Harvest crops	Meadow pasture	Diversified pasture	Subdivision	Section	Tp.N.	R.E.	Length of season	C.F.S.	Acre-feet
1869	11.05			S½S½	6	27	56	4-15—8-15	.136	33.15
1870	8.70			N½N½	7	27	56	4-15—8-15	.107	26.10
1871	7.83			SE¼SE¼	1	27	55	4-15—8-15	.096	23.49
1872	64.70			NE¼NE¼	12	27	55	4-15—8-15	.796	194.10
1874	22.50				....	....	....	4-15—8-15	.277	67.50
1880	34.72				....	....	....	4-15—8-15	.427	104.16

NOTE—"It is agreed between Merkley & Young and J. J. Hylton that sufficient water will be allowed to run down Lindsay Creek and Twin Creek at all times for stock-watering purposes in the following described lands: Sec. 35, T 28 N, R 55 E; Sec. 2, T 27 N, R 55 E; Secs. 6 and 7, T 27 N, R 56 E, and Secs. 1 and 12, T 27 N, R 55 E, and such agreement is binding upon parties to agreement."

These lands were included in the suit H. H. Porch v. U. Lani et al., No. 1644, Elko County Records. After listing dates and areas they were pooled and then listed in accordance with the decree.

Claimant—**J. J. Hylton.** Proof No. 00681

Source—**Lindsay and Twin Creeks.** Ditch—**J. J. Hylton Ditches.**

Year of priority	Harvest crops	Meadow pasture	Diversified pasture	Subdivision	Section	Tp.N.	R.E.	Length of season	C.F.S.	Acre-feet
1869	11.05			SE¼NW¼	35	28	55	4-15—8-15	.136	33.15
1870	8.70			E½SW¼	35	28	55	4-15—8-15	.107	26.10
1871	7.82			W½SE¼	35	28	55	4-15—8-15	.096	23.46
1872	64.70			NE¼	2	27	55	4-15—8-15	.796	194.10
1874	22.50				....	....	....	4-15—8-15	.277	67.50
1880	27.50				....	....	....	4-15—8-15	.339	83.77

NOTE—"It is agreed between Merkley & Young and J. J. Hylton that sufficient water will be allowed to run down Lindsay Creek and Twin Creek at all times for stock-watering purposes in the following described lands: Sec. 35, T 28 N, R 55 E; Sec. 2, T 27 N, R 55 E; Secs. 6 and 7, T 27 N, R 56 E, and Secs. 1 and 12, T 27 N, R 56 E."

These lands were included in the suit H. H. Porch v. U. Lani et al., No. 1644, Elko County Records. After listing dates and areas they were pooled and then listed in accordance with the decree.

Claimant—**E. Dotta.** Proof No. 00685

Source—**Smith Creek.** Ditch—**E. Dotta Ditches.**

Year of priority	Harvest crops	Meadow pasture	Diversified pasture	Subdivision	Section	Tp.N.	R.E.	Length of season	C.F.S.	Acre-feet
1898	248.70			NW¼NE¼	12	31	55			
				E½E½	12	31	55			
				E½E½	13	31	55			
				W½SW¼	7	31	56			
				[illegible]	18	31	56			
				[illegible]	24	31	55			
				NW¼NW¼	19	31	56	4-15—8-[illegible]	3.050	740.10

Claimant—**J. J. Hylton.** Proof No. 00686

Source—**Huntington Creek.** Ditch—**Nos. 1, 2, and 3.**

	1869			76.15				S½SW¼	15	28	55	4-15—8-15	.937	228.45
	1869			86.72				NW¼	22	28	55	4-15—8-15	1.067	260.19
	1900			17.30				SE¼SE¼	16	28	55	4-15—8-15	.213	51.90
	1900			71.15				NE¼	21	28	55	4-15—8-15	.875	213.45

Claimant—**Albert Lomori.** Proof No. 00687

Source—**South Fork of Humboldt River.** Ditch—**Albert Lomori Ditches.**

	1902			32.60				Lots 1, 2 & 3	30	33	55	4-15—8-15	.401	97.80

Claimant—**Thurber Estate** (Deed in escrow to Nevada Bunker Hill Mining Company).

Source—**Springs.** Ditch—**Thurber Estate Ditches.** Proof No. 00688

	1889							Plant in NW¼NW¼	35	31	53	1-1—12-31	1.00	

For mining and milling purposes.

Claimant—**George Clayton.** Proof No. 00689

Source—**Ten Mile Creek.** Ditch—**George Clayton Ditches.**

	1892			47.37				E½SW¼	34	33	55	4-15—8-15	.583	142.11
	1892					9.96		W½SE¼	34	33	55	4-15—6-15	.123	7.47
	1889			10.00				NE¼SE¼	34	33	55	4-15—8-15	.123	30.00
	1888			13.91				S½NE¼	34	33	55	4-15—8-15	.171	41.73
	1897			52.55				NW¼	35	33	55	4-15—8-15	.646	157.65
	1897					4.15		NW¼SW¼	36	33	55	4-15—6-15	.051	3.11
	1898					38.18						4-15—6-15	.470	28.64
	1905			7.25								4-15—8-15	.089	21.75

APPENDIX A

Stipulation Between Huntington and Diamond Valley Land and Stock Company and J. J. Hylton, Merkley & Young, and Frank Odiaga, Regarding the Use of Waters of Huntington Creek.

"It is stipulated between claimant and J. J. Hylton, S. A. Merkley and S. S. Young and Merkley & Young, a copartnership, and Frank Odiaga, that in order to settle the existing claims to the flood waters of Huntington Creek, they agree as follows: That said Hylton, Merkley. Young, Merkley & Young, and Frank Odiaga claim no right to any of the springs located upon or rising upon the lands of said corporation for irrigating purposes, or for any waters that may be developed by the development of any or all of these springs, and that said waters, if developed, may be used upon any of the lands of said corporation:

"That they do not claim for irrigation purposes any of the waters of Huntington Creek or its tributaries within the lands of the corporation after the flood season, which ends during each year within the period from about March 15 to April 1, and they do not claim any right whatsoever to any of said waters during the irrigating season of each year after said flood season;

"And it is agreed by said corporation that it will during each year allow flood waters to run in their natural courses as they are wont to flow from the place where said flood waters enter the head of the channel to a point in the NW¼NE¼ of 15, 26–55, to the end of said flood season for the use of the other parties to this stipulation below the northern extremity of the lands of said corporation, it being understood that nothing herein contained shall be construed to prevent the said corporation from using said flood waters for the purpose of irrigating lands below the NW¼NE¼ of 15, 26–55, at any time in accordance with their priorities on the stream, and in and to said waters and upon the land shown on map as meadow and pasture to the north of said point;

"And it is understood and agreed that nothing herein contained shall interfere with the turning of sufficient waters by said corporation into the natural watercourses and ditches to provide stock water for the parties immediately adjacent to said lands of said corporation;

"And it is further stipulated, in order to adjust existing claims upon the stream that said corporation will after the hay has been cut and stacked each year, and during and after the dry season, and after supplying its existing and necessary demands for stock-watering pur-

poses, shall prior to distributing any water for irrigation purposes, to wit, on the 1st day of September of each year, turn into the channel water for stock-watering purposes for the use of the other parties to this stipulation, in a quantity sufficient to cause it to flow in its natural channel a distance of one-half mile below the northerly boundary fence on the land of said corporation. This water to be used for stock watering only, and not for irrigation."

APPENDIX B

CO-OP DITCH

The Co-Op Ditch was constructed in 1893 and carries water from Ackler Creek into Herder Creek.

No water is to be turned into said Co-Op Ditch until all rights on Ackler Creek prior to 1893 have been satisfied.

The following claimants have a vested right from Ackler Creek through the Co-Op Ditch into Herder Creek:

Lands of: C. H. Black, S. M. Davis, John Riddell, Wm. Goodale, Hylton & Mentz, W. W. Weathers, James O'Brien, Wilbur Smiley, E. A. Hylton (Lane Estate), John Crossen, W. J. Smiley, E. C. Riddell, Geo. Byers (Priority—1893).

APPENDIX C

The following pages represent the continuation of rights acquired prior to 1905 into the period 1906 to date, or lands upon which the water was not diverted until after 1905; also rights by permit under which certificates have issued, or proofs of beneficial use and cultural maps have been filed between 1905 and date of this order:

APPENDIX C—Continued.

Claimant—**Antonio J. Alves.** Proof No. 001
Source—**Humboldt River.** Ditch—**Old Channel.**

Year of priority	Culture—Acres: Harvest crops	Culture—Acres: Meadow pasture	Culture—Acres: Diversified pasture	Location: Subdivision	Location: Section	Location: Tp.N.	Location: R.E.	Length of season	Duty of water: C.F.S.	Duty of water: Acre-feet
1907	15.00			NW¼NW¼	18	27	32	3-15—9-15	.122	45.00
1908	14.00			NW¼NW¼	18	27	32	3-15—9-15	.114	42.00
1912	2.00			NW¼NW¼	18	27	32	3-15—9-15	.016	6.00

Claimant—**Grace S. Jahn.** Proof No. 005
Source—**Humboldt River.** Ditch—**Union Canal through Reed Ditch.**

Year of priority	Harvest crops	Meadow pasture	Diversified pasture	Subdivision	Section	Tp.N.	R.E.	Length of season	C.F.S.	Acre-feet
1913	30.00			N½	34	26	31	3-15—9-15	.244	90.00
1913	28.00			N½	34	26	31	3-15—9-15	.228	84.00
1913	4.00			N½	34	26	31	3-15—9-15	.033	12.00
1913	3.00			N½	34	26	31	3-15—9-15	.024	9.00

This area holds water right as of 1876 for willow and sage pasture.

Claimant—**Pitt & McDonald.** Proof No. 006
Source—**Humboldt River.** Ditch—**Union Canal through Lake Shore Ditch.**

Year of priority	Harvest crops	Meadow pasture	Diversified pasture	Subdivision	Section	Tp.N.	R.E.	Length of season	C.F.S.	Acre-feet
1914	70.00			NW¼	4	25	31	3-15—9-15	.569	210.00
1915	40.60			NW¼	4	25	31	3-15—9-15	.325	120.00
1920	28.36			NW¼	4	25	31	3-15—9-15	.231	85.08

Claimant—**Ed. Berg.** Proof No. 007
Source—**Humboldt River.** Ditch—**Young Ditch.**

Year of priority	Harvest crops	Meadow pasture	Diversified pasture	Subdivision	Section	Tp.N.	R.E.	Length of season	C.F.S.	Acre-feet
1910	5.00			E½E½	1	27	31	3-15—9-15	.040	15.00
1913	8.41			E½E½	1	27	31	3-15—9-15	.068	25.23

Claimant—**F. A. Preston.** Proof No. 0011
Source—**Humboldt River.** Ditch—**Graveyard Slough and *Union Canal.**

Year of priority	Harvest crops	Meadow pasture	Diversified pasture	Subdivision	Section	Tp.N.	R.E.	Length of season	C.F.S.	Acre-feet
1906	9.00			W½SE¼	29	26	31	3-15—9-15	.073	27.00
1915	3.60*			W½SE¼	29	26	31	3-15—9-15	.029	10.80
1920	22.77*			S½W½ofSE¼	29	26	31	3-15—9-15	.185	68.31
1920	5.95			N½W½ofSE¼	29	26	31	3-15—9-15	.048	17.85

Claimant—**L. N. Carpenter.** Proof No. 0013
Source—**Humboldt River.** Ditch—**Rodgers Canal System.**

Year of priority	Harvest crops	Meadow pasture	Diversified pasture	Subdivision	Section	Tp.N.	R.E.	Length of season	C.F.S.	Acre-feet
1919	16.70			SE¼SW¼	2	26	31	3-15—9-15	.136	50.10
1915	11.80			N½SE¼	2	26	31	3-15—9-15	.096	35.40
1919	36.27			E½NW¼	2	26	31	3-15—9-15	.287	105.81

	1912			138.40				NW¼	27	26	31	3-15—9-15	1.125	515.20
	1912			6.70				NW¼	27	26	31	3-15—9-15	.054	20.10
	1913			6.90				W½SW¼	1	26	31	3-15—9-15	.056	20.70

Claimant—**Chris Beck.** Proof No. 0014
Source—**Humboldt River.** Ditch—**Tule Ditch.**

	1909			45.00				SW¼	10	25	31	3-15—9-15	.366	135.00
	1909			—		15.75		SW¼	10	25	31	3-15—6-13	.128	23.63
	1909			—		17.30		SW¼	10	25	31	3 15—6-13	.141	25.95

Claimant—**John Christensen.** Proof No. 0015
Source—**Humboldt River.** Ditch—**Irish American.**

	1913			5.15				SW¼NW¼	28	27	31	3 15—9-15	.042	15.45
	1912			13.45				NE¼NW¼	28	27	31	3-15—9-15	.109	40.35

Claimant—**J. C. Damm.** Proof No. 0018
Source—**Humboldt River.** Ditch—**Union Canal through Lake Shore Ditch.**

	1917			32.66				NW¼	28	26	31	3-15—9-15	.266	97.98
	1913			15.39				NW¼	28	26	31	3-15—9-15	.125	46.17

Claimant—**Lawrence Devita.** Proof No. 0021
Source—**Humboldt River.** Ditch—**Old Channel.**

	1908			13.00				NE¼	13	27	31	3-15—9-15	.106	39.00
	1914			12.70				NE¼	13	27	31	3-16—9-15	.103	38.10

Claimant—**Frank Ambrosetti & John Scott.** Proof No. 0022
Source—**Humboldt River.** Ditch—**Old Channel.**

	1908			5.95				NW¼NW¼	24	27	31	3-15—9-15	.048	17.85
	1910			30.10				NW¼	24	27	31	3-15—9-15	.245	90.30
	1910			7.15				NE¼NW¼	24	27	31	3-15—9-15	.058	21.45
	1913			14.92				NE¼NW¼	24	27	31	3-15—9-15	.121	44.76
	1913			4.59				SE¼NW¼	24	27	31	3-15—9-15	.037	13.77
	1913			29.27				SW¼NW¼	24	27	31	3-15—9-15	.238	87.81
	1912			1.15				NW¼NW¼	24	27	31	3-15—9-15	.009	3.45

Claimant—**Mrs. Eva Granis.** Proof No. 0030
Source—**Humboldt River.** Ditch—**Southwest Ditch.**

	1910			10.20				SE¼SE¼	27	27	31	3-15—9-15	.083	30.60

Claimant—**Nellie Martin.** Proof No. 0033
Source—**Humboldt River.** Ditch—**Larson Ditch; Union Canal through Reed Ditch.**

	*1919			3.00				S½SE¼	33	26	31	3-15—9-15	.024	9.00
	*1921			4.85				S½SE¼	33	26	31	3-15—9-15	.039	14.55

*This land has a water right as of 1875 for willow and sage pasture.

Claimant—**Ingvert Hanson.** Proof No. 0034
Source—**Humboldt River.** Ditch—**Union Canal through Lake Shore Ditch.**

Year of priority	Culture—Acres: Harvest crops	Culture—Acres: Meadow pasture	Culture—Acres: Diversified pasture	Location: Subdivision	Location: Section	Location: Tp.N.	Location: R.E.	Length of season	Duty of water: C.F.S.	Duty of water: Acre-feet
1906	20.00			SW¼	32	26	31	3-15—9-15	.163	60.00
1906	18.60			SW¼	32	26	31	3-15—9-15	.151	55.80

Claimant—**Andrew Jacobson.** Proof No. 0035
Source—**Humboldt River.** Ditch—**Young Ditch.**

Year of priority	Harvest crops	Meadow pasture	Diversified pasture	Subdivision	Section	Tp.N.	R.E.	Length of season	C.F.S.	Acre-feet
1906	3.55			NW¼	7	27	32	3-15—9-15	.029	10.65
1912	10.20			NE¼NW¼	7	27	32	3-15—9-15	.083	30.60
1917	1.00			N½NW¼	7	27	32	3-15—9-15	.008	3.00

Claimant—**Estate John J. Hill.** Proof No. 0038
Source—**Humboldt River.** Ditch—**Union Canal through Lake Shore Ditch.**

Year of priority	Harvest crops	Meadow pasture	Diversified pasture	Subdivision	Section	Tp.N.	R.E.	Length of season	C.F.S.	Acre-feet
1910	77.10			NW¼	29	36	31	3-15—9-15	.627	231.30

Claimant—**Hugh Holmstrom.** Proof No. 0041
Source—**Humboldt River.** Ditch—**Young Ditch.**

Year of priority	Harvest crops	Meadow pasture	Diversified pasture	Subdivision	Section	Tp.N.	R.E.	Length of season	C.F.S.	Acre-feet
1909	3.85			N½	2	27	31	3-15—9-15	.031	11.55

Claimant—**John Holmstrom.** Proof No. 0042
Source—**Humboldt River.** Ditch—**Young Ditch.**

Year of priority	Harvest crops	Meadow pasture	Diversified pasture	Subdivision	Section	Tp.N.	R.E.	Length of season	C.F.S.	Acre-feet
1909	80.00			SE¼	31	28	32	3-15—9-15	.650	240.00
1911	20.00			SE¼	31	28	32	3-15—9-15	.163	60.00
1914	11.50			E½NW¼	6	28	32	3-15—9-15	.093	34.50
1914	6.00			W½NE¼	6	27	32	3-15—9-15	.049	18.00
1914	2.00			E½NE¼	6	27	32	3-15—9-15	.016	6.00

Claimant—**Nels Jensen.** Proof No. 0045
Source—**Humboldt River.** Ditch—**Young Ditch.**

Year of priority	Harvest crops	Meadow pasture	Diversified pasture	Subdivision	Section	Tp.N.	R.E.	Length of season	C.F.S.	Acre-feet
1909	12.40			NW¼	11	27	31	3-15—9-15	.101	37.20

Claimant—**James Johnson.** Proof No. 0046
Source—**Humboldt River.** Ditch—**Young Ditch.**

Year of priority	Harvest crops	Meadow pasture	Diversified pasture	Subdivision	Section	Tp.N.	R.E.	Length of season	C.F.S.	Acre-feet
1909	13.75			E½W½	1	27	31	3-15—9-15	.112	41.25

Claimant—**Paul Johnson.** Proof No. 0048
Source—**Humboldt River.** Ditch—**Union Canal through Lake Shore Ditch.**

Year of priority	Harvest crops	Meadow pasture	Diversified pasture	Subdivision	Section	Tp.N.	R.E.	Length of season	C.F.S.	Acre-feet
1908	9.01			SW¼	33	26	31	3-15—9-15	.073	27.03
1914	.88			SW¼	33	26	31	3-15—9-15	.007	2.64

Claimant—**Mrs. John Chambers.** Proof No. 0048

Source—**Humboldt River.** Ditch—**Union Canal through Lake Shore Ditch.**

1906	6.32	SW¼	33	26	31	3-15—9-15	.051	18.96
1914	.62	SW¼	33	26	31	3-15—9-15	.005	1.86

Claimant—**H. P. Kruse.** Proof No. 0052

Source—**Humboldt River.** Ditch—**Young Ditch.**

1917	2.00	NE¼	12	27	31	3-15—9-15	.016	6.00
1917	2.00	NE¼	12	27	31	3-15—9-15	.016	6.00
1913	5.00	NE¼	12	27	31	3-15—9-15	.041	15.00
1920	3.00	NE¼	12	27	31	3-15—9-15	.024	9.00

Claimant—**John & Domenico Ferritto.** Proof No. 0057

Source—**Humboldt River.** Ditch—**Reed Ditch from Union Canal.**

1917	4.00*	W½NE¼	33	26	31	3-15—9-15	.033	12.00

*This area has water right as of 1884 for willow and sage pasture.

Claimant—**N. C. Munk.** Proof No. 0059

Source—**Humboldt River.** Ditch—**Union Canal through Reed Ditch.**

1919	6.00	W½NE¼	4	25	31	3-15—9-15	.049	18.00
1920	5.00	W½NE¼	4	25	31	3-15—9-15	.041	15.00

Claimant—**W. C. Pitt.** Proof No. 0064

Source—**Humboldt River.** Ditch—**Old Channel Ditch.**

1906	213.25	N½&SE¼	16	27	31	3-15—9-15	1.735	639.75
1913	69.44		16	27	31	3-15—9-15	.565	208.32
1913	10.16		16	27	31	3-15—9-15	.083	30.48
1913	10.59		16	27	31	3-15—9-15	.086	31.77

Claimants—**Lawrence Devita.** Proof No. 0066

Source—**Humboldt River.** Ditch—**Old Channel.**

1908	28.30	SW¼NW¼	18	27	32	3-15—9-15	.230	84.90
1912	2.30	SW¼NW¼	18	27	32	3-15—9-15	.019	6.90
1920	5.00	SW¼NW¼	18	27	32	3-15—9-15	.041	15.00

Claimant—**W. C. Buddell.** Proof No. 0068

Source—**Humboldt River.** Ditch—**Irish American.**

1912	20.85	E½SE¼	26	27	31	3-15—9-15	.170	62.55
1912	15.75	SE¼SE¼	26	27	31	3-15—9-15	.128	47.25
1912	25.55	S½SE¼	26	27	31	3-15—9-15	.208	76.65
1912	10.20	CenterSE¼	26	27	31	3-15—9-15	.083	30.60

Claimant—**Millie R. Evans (Rodger Estate).** Proof No. 0069
Source—**Humboldt River.** Ditch—**Rodgers Canal System.**

Year of priority	Culture—Acres: Harvest crops	Meadow pasture	Diversified pasture	Location: Subdivision	Section	Tp.N.	R.E.	Length of season	Duty of water: C.F.S.	Acre-feet
1909	56.45				25	26	31	3-15—9-15	.459	169.35
1918	65.16				7	26	32	3-15—9-15	.530	195.48
1919	61.42			N½	10	26	31	3-15—9-15	.499	184.26
1918	70.33				19	26	32	3-15—9-15	.572	210.99
1918	105.09			N½	30	26	32	3-15—9-15	.854	315.27

Claimant—**Matt Smith.** Proof No. 0072
Source—**Humboldt River.** Ditch—**Young Ditch.**

Year of priority	Culture—Acres: Harvest crops	Meadow pasture	Diversified pasture	Location: Subdivision	Section	Tp.N.	R.E.	Length of season	Duty of water: C.F.S.	Acre-feet
1909	6.15			W½E½	1	27	31	3-15—9-15	.050	18.45
1912	3.00			W½E½	1	27	31	3-15—9-15	.024	9.00

Claimant—**I. M. Springer, Sr.** Proof No. 0073
Source—**Humboldt River.** Ditch—**Irish American.**

Year of priority	Culture—Acres: Harvest crops	Meadow pasture	Diversified pasture	Location: Subdivision	Section	Tp.N.	R.E.	Length of season	Duty of water: C.F.S.	Acre-feet
1906	9.50			W¼NE¼&NW¼SE¼	23	27	31	3-15—9-15	.077	28.50
1906	38.00			E½NE¼	23	27	31	3-15—9-15	.309	104.00
1909	14.35			W¼NE¼&NW¼SE¼	23	27	31	3-15—9-15	.117	43.05
1914	3.00			W½SE¼	23	27	31	3-15—9-15	.024	9.00
1915	3.00			NW¼SE¼	23	27	31	3-15—9-15	.024	9.00

Claimant—**B. E. Stoker.** Proof No. 0075
Source—**Humboldt River.** Ditch—**Union Canal.**

Year of priority	Culture—Acres: Harvest crops	Meadow pasture	Diversified pasture	Location: Subdivision	Section	Tp.N.	R.E.	Length of season	Duty of water: C.F.S.	Acre-feet
1911	6.00			SW¼SW¼	24	27	31	3-15—9-15	.049	18.00
1912	44.50			E½SE¼	23	27	31	3-15—9-15	.362	133.50
1913	9.55			E½SE¼	23	27	31	3-15—9-15	.078	28.65

Claimant—**Pascasio Bilbao.** Proof No. 0078
Source—**Humboldt River.** Ditch—**Union Canal through Lake Shore Ditch.**

Year of priority	Culture—Acres: Harvest crops	Meadow pasture	Diversified pasture	Location: Subdivision	Section	Tp.N.	R.E.	Length of season	Duty of water: C.F.S.	Acre-feet
1911	—		5.50	W¼NE¼NE¼	29	26	31	3-15—6-13	.045	8.25

Claimant—**Lovelock Land and Development Co.** Proof. No. 0080
Source—**Humboldt River.** Ditch—**Lovelock Land and Development Company Ditch System.**

Year of priority	Culture—Acres: Harvest crops	Meadow pasture	Diversified pasture	Location: Subdivision	Section	Tp.N.	R.E.	Length of season	Duty of water: C.F.S.	Acre-feet
1908	85.30			NE¼	2	25	31	3-15—9-15	.693	255.90

Claimant—**John G. Taylor.** Proof No. 0081
Source—**Humboldt River.** Ditch—**Marzen Slough.**

Year of priority	Culture—Acres: Harvest crops	Meadow pasture	Diversified pasture	Location: Subdivision	Section	Tp.N.	R.E.	Length of season	Duty of water: C.F.S.	Acre-feet
1917	60.78			N½NW¼	32	27	31	3-15—9-15	.491	182.34
1917	20.14			S½NW¼	32	27	31	3-15—9-15	.164	60.42

Source—**Humboldt River.** Ditch—**Young Ditch.**

1913	60.00		S½	34	28	31	3-15—9-15	.495	182.70
1913	27.51		E½S½	34	28	31	3-15—9-15	.224	82.53
1917	145.81		NE¼	34	28	31	3-15—9-15	1.185	437.43

Claimant—**Bergman & Alfree.** Proof No. 0082

Source—**Humboldt River.** Ditch—**Southwest Ditch, Lovelock and Borland Slough.**

1914	42.56		SE¼	34	27	31	3-15—9-15	.346	127.65
1916	44.48		SE¼	34	27	31	3-15—9-15	.362	133.44

Source—**Humboldt River.** Ditch—**Southwest Ditch.**

1913		3.95	SW¼SE¼	33	27	31	3-15—6-13	.032	5.93
1913	40.50		S½NE¼	32	27	31	3-15—9-15	.329	121.50
1914	22.78		NE¼NE¼	3	26	31	3-15—9-15	.185	68.34
1916	59.00		N½	3	26	31	3-15—9-15	.480	177.00

Claimant—**F. Tessier.** Proof No. 0085

Source—**Humboldt River.** Ditch—**Old Channel Ditch.**

1910	22.70		SW¼&SE¼	13	27	31	3-15—9-15	.185	68.10
1912	15.93		SE¼&SW¼	13	77	31	3-15—9-15	.130	47.79
1912	18.00		SW¼SE¼	13	:7	31	3-15—9-15	.146	54.00
1918	9.98		SE¼SE¼	13	27	31	3-15—9-15	.081	29.94
1913	8.95		SE¼SW¼	13	27	31	3-15—9-15	.073	26.85

Claimant—**Peter Olson.** Proof No. 0088

Source—**Humboldt River.** Ditch—**Old Channel Ditch.**

1920	8.00		S½NW¼	12	27	31	3-15—9-15	.065	24.00

Claimant—**W. W. Van Reed.** Proof No. 0089

Source—**Humboldt River.** Ditch—**Union Canal through Lake Shore Ditch.**

1918	5.90*		E½SW¼	29	26	31	3-15—9-15	.048	17.70
1918	15.00		NW¼SE¼SW¼	29	26	31	3-15—9-15	.122	45.00

*This area holds water right as of 1897 for willow and sage pasture.

Claimant—**Emil Hostman.** Proof No. 0090

Source—**Humboldt River.** Ditch—**Old Channel.**

1910	7.80*		E½NW¼	18	27	32	3-15—9-15	.063	23.40
1911	43.65		E½NW¼	18	27	32	3-15—9-15	.355	130.95
1912	24.11		E½NW¼&W½NW¼	18	27	32	3-15—9-15	.196	72.33
1912	5.57		E½NW¼	18	27	32	3-15—9-15	.045	16.71

*South and west of ditch.

Claimant—**Andrew Westfall.** Proof No. 0091

Source—**Humboldt River.** Ditch—**Union Canal through Lake Shore Ditch.**

1914	10.00		E½E½	31	26	31	3-15—9-15	.081	30.00

This area holds water right as of 1886 for willow and sage pasture.

Claimant—**H. M. Damm.** Proof No. 0094
Source—**Humboldt River.** Ditch—**Young.**

Year of priority	Culture—Acres: Harvest crops	Meadow pasture	Diversified pasture	Location: Subdivision	Section	Tp.N.	R.E.	Length of season	Duty of water: C.F.S.	Acre-feet
1910	5.60	....	....	W½W½	1	27	31	3-15—9-15	.046	16.80

Claimant—**Thomas P. Ebert.** Proof No. 00700
Source—**Humboldt River.** Ditch—**Young Ditch.**

Year of priority	Harvest crops	Meadow pasture	Diversified pasture	Subdivision	Section	Tp.N.	R.E.	Length of season	C.F.S.	Acre-feet
1915	15.70	....	....	SW¼SW¼	7	27	32	3-15—9-15	.128	47.10
1915	20.90	....	....	SE¼SW¼&NE¼SW¼	7	27	32	3-15—9-15	.170	62.70
1915	32.00	....	....	SE¼SW¼&NE¼SW¼	7	27	32	3-15—9-15	.260	96.00

Claimant—**Geo. W. Ostrander.** Proof No. 00701
Source—**Humboldt River.** Ditch—**Young Ditch.**

Year of priority	Harvest crops	Meadow pasture	Diversified pasture	Subdivision	Section	Tp.N.	R.E.	Length of season	C.F.S.	Acre-feet
1914	54.63	....	....	SW¼	7	27	32	3-15—9-15	.444	163.89

Claimant—**William M. Biggs.** Proof No. 00702
Source—**Humboldt River.** Ditch—**Young Ditch.**

Year of priority	Harvest crops	Meadow pasture	Diversified pasture	Subdivision	Section	Tp.N.	R.E.	Length of season	C.F.S.	Acre-feet
1914	65.40	....	....	W½SE¼	7	27	32	3-15—9-15	.532	196.20

Claimant—**John G. Taylor.** Proof No. 00111
Source—**Humboldt River.** Ditch—**Taylor Dam.**

Year of priority	Harvest crops	Meadow pasture	Diversified pasture	Subdivision	Section	Tp.N.	R.E.	Length of season	C.F.S.	Acre-feet
1912	....	....	9.53	NW¼SW¼	20	33	35	3-15—4-28	.077	7.15
1912	....	....	19.84	NE¼SW¼	20	33	35	3-15—4-28	.161	14.88
1912	....	....	38.64	SW¼SW¼	20	33	35	3-15—4-28	.314	28.98
1912	....	....	10.45	SE¼SW¼	20	33	35	3-15—4-28	.085	7.84
1912	....	....	37.76	NW¼SE¼	20	33	35	3-15—4-28	.307	28.32
1912	....	....	25.55	NE¼SE¼	20	33	35	3-15—4-28	.208	19.16

Claimant—Taylor & Sheehan. Proof No. 00120
Source—**Humboldt River.** Ditch—**High Line Canal.**

Year of priority	Harvest crops	Meadow pasture	Diversified pasture	Subdivision	Section	Tp.N.	R.E.	Length of season	C.F.S.	Acre-feet
1912	30.85	....	....	NW¼NW¼	19	36	40	3-15—9-15	.251	92.55
1912	...	....	1.80	NW¼NW¼	19	36	40	3-15—4-28	.015	1.35
1912	20.00	....	....	SW¼NE¼	19	30	40	3-15—9-15	.103	60.00

	1912					2.90		SW¼NE¼	19	36	40	3-15—4-28	.024	2.18
	1912			8.25				SW¼NE¼	19	36	40	3-15—9-15	.067	24.75
	1912			36.75				SE¼NW¼	19	36	40	3-15—9-15	.200	110.25
	1912			4.30				SW¼NW¼	19	36	40	3-15—9-15	.035	12.90
	1912					26.25		SW¼NW¼	19	36	40	3-15—4-28	.213	19.69
	1912			35.03				NE¼SE¼	19	36	40	3-15—9-15	.285	105.09
	1912					3.22		NE¼SE¼	19	36	40	3-15—4-28	.026	2.42
	1912			38.30				NW¼SE¼	19	36	40	3-15—9-15	.311	114.90
	1912			10.30				NE¼SW¼	19	36	40	3-15—9-15	.084	30.90
	1912					38.95		NW¼SW¼	13	36	39	3-15—4-28	.317	29.21
	1912					37.85		SW¼SE¼	13	36	39	3-15—4-28	.308	38.29
	1912					40.70		SE¼SW¼	13	36	39	3-15—4-28	.311	30.53
	1912					19.40		SW¼SW¼	13	36	39	3-15—4-28	.158	14.55
	1912					12.85		NE¼NE¼	14	36	39	3-15—4-28	.104	9.64
	1912					40.50		SE¼NE¼	14	36	39	3-15—4-28	.329	30.38
	1912					12.95		SW¼NE¼	14	36	39	3-15—4-28	.105	9.71
	1912					22.45		NE¼SE¼	14	36	39	3-15—4-28	.183	16.84
	1912					.90		NW¼SE¼	14	36	39	3-15—4-28	.007	.68
	1912			.70				NE¼NE¼	24	36	39	3-15—9-15	.006	2.10
	1912					33.30		NE¼NE¼	24	36	39	3-15—4-28	.271	24.98
	1912					39.05		NW¼NE¼	24	36	39	3-15—4-28	.317	29.29
	1912					13.30		NE¼NW¼	24	36	39	3-15—4-28	.108	9.98
	1912					39.80		SE¼NE¼	24	36	39	3-15—4-28	.323	29.85
	1912					16.55		SW¼NE¼	24	36	39	3-15—4-28	.135	12.41
	1912					17.40		NE¼SE¼	24	36	39	3-15—4-28	.141	13.05
	1912			13.00				SE¼SE¼	13	36	39	3-15—9-15	.106	39.00
	1912					6.35		SE¼SE¼	13	36	39	3-15—4-28	.052	4.76
	1912					9.30		NW¼SE¼	13	36	39	3-15—4-28	.086	6.98
	1912					15.20		SW¼NW¼	13	36	39	3-15—4-28	.124	11.40
	1912			8.15				SW¼SW¼	18	36	40	3-15—9-15	.066	24.45
	1912					2.85		NW¼SE¼	20	36	40	3-15—4-28	.023	2.14
	1912			15.00				NE¼SW¼	20	36	40	3-15—9-15	.122	45.00
	1912			32.40				NW¼SW¼	20	36	40	3-15—9-15	.263	97.20
	1912			.15				SW¼NW¼	20	36	40	3-15—9-15	.001	.45
	1912					6.50		SW¼NE¼	20	36	40	3-15—4-28	.053	4.88
	1912					23.85		SE¼SE¼	20	36	40	3-15—4-28	.194	17.89
	1912			25.70				SW¼SE¼	20	36	40	3-15—9-15	.209	77.10
	1912					8.65		SW¼SE¼	20	36	40	3-15—4-28	.071	6.49
	1912					.35		SW¼SE¼	20	36	40	3-15—4-28	.003	.26
	1912			30.35				SE¼SW¼	20	36	40	3-15—9-15	.247	91.05
	1912					4.85		SE¼SW¼	20	36	40	3-15—4-28	.039	3.64
	1912			38.90				SW¼SW¼	20	36	40	3-15—9-15	.316	116.70
	1912					1.50		SW¼SW¼	20	36	40	3-15—4-28	.012	1.13
	1912			3.85				NE¼NE¼	29	36	40	3-15—9-15	.031	11.55
	1912					11.05		NE¼NE¼	29	36	40	3-15—4-28	.090	8.29
	1912			33.55				NW¼NE¼	29	36	40	3-15—9-15	.273	100.65
	1912					1.25		NW¼NE¼	29	36	40	3-15—4-28	.010	.94
	1912			28.85				NE¼NW¼	29	36	40	3-15—9-15	.235	86.55
	1912					9.00		NE¼NW¼	29	36	40	3-15—4-28	.073	6.75
	1912			40.30				SE¼SE¼	19	36	40	3-15—9-15	.328	120.90
	1912			19.80				SW¼SE¼	19	36	40	3-15—9-15	.161	59.40
	1912					8.45		SW¼SE¼	19	36	40	3-15—4-28	.069	6.34
	1912			27.70				NE¼NE¼	30	36	40	3-15—9-15	.225	83.10

Taylor & Sheehan—Continued.

Year of priority	Culture—Acres: Harvest crops	Meadow pasture	Diversified pasture	Location: Subdivision	Section	Tp.N.	R.E.	Length of season	Duty of water: C.F.S.	Acre-feet
1912	.40			NW¼NE¼	30	36	40	3-15—9-15	.003	1.20
1912		6.00		NW¼NE¼	30	36	40	3-15—6-13	.041	9.00
1912			21.05	NW¼NE¼	30	36	40	3-15—4-28	.171	15.79
1912	2.95			SE¼NE¼	30	36	40	3-15—9-15	.024	8.85
1912	38.70			NW¼NW¼	29	36	40	3-15—9-15	.315	116.10
1912			1.10	NW¼NW¼	29	36	40	3-15—4-28	.009	.83
1912	1.00			SE¼NE¼	29	36	40	3-15—9-15	.008	3.00
1912	36.15			SW¼NE¼	29	36	40	3-15—9-15	.294	168.45
1912	20.50			SE¼NW¼	29	36	40	3-15—9-15	.177	61.50
1912	10.80			SW¼NW¼	29	36	40	3-15—9-15	.088	32.40
1912			40.20	NE¼SW¼	13	36	39	3-15—4-28	.327	30.15
Source—Humboldt River. Ditch—Pump from Sink Hole.										
1912			9.85	NW¼NW¼	34	36	40	3-15—4-28	.080	7.30
1912			7.10	NE¼NW¼	34	36	40	3-15—4-28	.058	5.33
1912			15.80	NW¼NE¼	34	36	40	3-15—4-28	.128	11.85
1912			13.90	NE¼NE¼	34	36	40	3-15—4-28	.113	10.43
Source—Humboldt River. Ditch—Pole Creek Ditches.										
1912	12.20			SE¼NE¼	19	36	40	3-15—9-15	.099	36.60
1912	25.35			NE¼NW¼	19	36	40	3-15—9-15	.206	76.05

Claimant—**Humboldt Land and Cattle Co.** Proof No. 00154

Source—**Humboldt River.** Ditch—**Pump.**

Year of priority	Harvest crops	Meadow pasture	Diversified pasture	Subdivision	Section	Tp.N.	R.E.	Length of season	C.F.S.	Acre-feet
1918	5.20			NE¼NE¼	28	32	40	3-15—9-15	.042	15.60
1918	1.56			SE¼NE¼	28	32	49	3-15—9-15	.012	4.68
1918	10.40			NW¼NE¼	28	32	49	3-15—9-15	.085	31.20
1918	35.84			SW¼NE¼	28	32	40	3-15—9-15	.291	107.52
1918	9.36			SE¼NW¼	28	32	49	3-15—9-15	.076	28.08
1918	13.00			NE¼SW¼	28	32	49	3-15—9-15	.106	39.00
1918	12.48			SE¼SW¼	28	22	49	3-15—9-15	.101	37.44

Claimant—**George Kaeding.** Proof No. 00163

Source—**Humboldt River.** Ditch—**Kaeding Branch, Rocky Point Canal.**

Year of priority	Harvest crops	Meadow pasture	Diversified pasture	Subdivision	Section	Tp.N.	R.E.	Length of season	C.F.S.	Acre-feet
1914			40.00	SE¼NE¼	34	33	45	3-15—4-28	.325	30.00
1914			40.00	SW¼NE¼	34	33	45	3-15—4-28	.325	30.00
1914			40.00	NE¼NW¼	34	33	45	3-15—4-28	.325	30.00
1914			40.00	SE¼NW¼	34	33	45	3-15—4-28	.325	30.00
1914			40.00	NW¼NW¼	34	34	45	3-15—4-28	.325	30.00
1914			40.00	SW¼NW¼	34	33	45	3-15—4-28	.325	30.00

Claimant—**Land Development Co.** Proof No. 00163

Source—**Humboldt River.** Ditch—**Rocky Point.**

	1914						39.52	NW¼SW¼	34	33	45	3-15—4-28	.321	29.64
	1914						35.47	SW¼SW¼	34	33	45	3-15—4-28	.288	26.60

Claimant—**W. T. Jenkins Co.** Proof No. 00166

Source—**Humboldt River.** Ditch—**South Ditch.**

	1914			9.70				NW¼SE¼	2	32	45	3-15—9-15	.079	29.10
	1914			3.20				SW¼SE¼	2	32	45	3-15—9-15	.026	9.60
	1914			38.28				NE¼NW¼	2	32	45	3-15—9-15	.311	114.84
	1914			39.92				SE¼NW¼	2	32	45	3-15—9-15	.325	119.76
	1914			40.15				NW¼NW¼	2	32	45	3-15—9-15	.326	120.45
	1914			40.07				SW¼NW¼	2	32	45	3-15—9-15	.326	120.21
	1914			40.05				NE¼SW¼	2	32	45	3-15—9-15	.326	120.15
	1914			8.52				SE¼SW¼	2	32	45	3-15—9-15	.069	25.56
	1914			40.00				NW¼SW¼	2	32	45	3-15—9-15	.325	120.00
	1914			9.80				SW¼SW¼	2	32	45	3-15—9-15	.080	29.40
	1914			12.37				SE¼NW¼	1	32	45	3-15—9-15	.101	37.11
	1914					4.47		SE¼NW¼	1	32	45	3-15—4-28	.036	3.35
	1914			5.05				NW¼NW¼	1	32	45	3-15—9-15	.041	15.15
	1914			22.55				NW¼NE¼	2	32	45	3-15—9-15	.183	67.65
	1914			25.59				SW¼NE¼	2	32	45	3-15—9-15	.208	76.77
	1914				3.51			SW¼NE¼	2	32	45	3-15—6-13	.021	5.27
	1914					2.15		SW¼NE¼	2	32	45	3-15—4-28	.017	1.61

Claimant—**J. W. Puett.** Proof No. 00322

Source—**Maggie Creek.** Ditch—**Palmer.**

	1908			10.00				SE¼NW¼	26	33	52	4-15—8-15	.123	30.00
	1909			8.00				SE¼NW¼	26	33	52	4-15—8-15	.098	24.00
	1910			12.00				NW¼SE¼	26	33	52	4-15—8-15	.148	36.00
	1912			14.00				SE¼SW¼	26	33	52	4-15—8-15	.172	42.00

Claimant—**Max Arnhold.** Proof No. 00351

Source—**Pearl Creek.** Ditch—**Max Arnhold Ditches.**

	1911			20.30				W½	21	28	56			
								W½SE¼	21	28	56			
								SE¼SE¼	21	28	56			
								S½S½	22	28	56			
								N½NE¼	28	28	56	4-15—8-15	.250	60.90

Claimant—**T. F. Brennen.** Proof No. 00353

Source—**Ainley, Ogilvie, Young, and Cottonwood Creeks.** Ditch—**Brennen Ditches.**

	1908			14.26*				W½SW¼	16	32	57	4-15—8-15	.175	42.78
	1910			28.52†								4-15—8-15	.351	85.56

*Has flood water right on pasture as of 1900. †From Cottonwood Creek only.

Claimant—**J. J. Hylton.** Proof No. 00355
Source—**South Fork Humboldt River and Rattlesnake Creek.** Ditch—**J. J. Hylton Ditches.**

Year of priority	Culture—Acres: Harvest crops	Meadow pasture	Diversified pasture	Location: Subdivision	Section	Tp.N.	R.E.	Length of season	Duty of water: C.F.S.	Acre-feet
1907	28.00			S½	23	31	56	4-15—8-15	0.344	84.00
1908	2.00			S½	24	31	56	4-15—8-15	0.025	6.00
1909	30.37			S½NW¼	24	31	56	4-15—8-15	0.374	91.11
1911	40.91			NW¼NW¼	25	31	56	4-15—8-15	0.503	122.73
1912	80.91				26	31	56	4-15—8-15	0.995	242.73
1912	23.70			NE¼	27	31	56	4-15—8-15	0.292	71.10
1913	100.91							4-15—8-15	1.241	302.73
1914	95.91							4-15—8-15	1.180	287.73
1915	140.92							4-15—8-15	1.733	422.76
1918	53.82							4-15—8-15	0.662	161.46
1918	36.50							4-15—8-15	0.449	109.50
1920	17.82							4-15—8-15	0.200	53.46

Early Water only from Rattlesnake Creek.

Source—**Pearl Creek and South Fork Humboldt River.** Ditch—**J. J. Hylton Ditches.**

Year of priority	Harvest crops	Meadow pasture	Diversified pasture	Subdivision	Section	Tp.N.	R.E.	Length of season	C.F.S.	Acre-feet
1911	15.00			E½SE¼	19	31	57			
				SW¼	20	31	57	4-15—8-15	0.183	45.00

Claimant—**Pedro Corta.** Proof No. 00356
Source—**Spencer Creek.** Ditch—**Pedro Corta Ditches.**

Year of priority	Harvest crops	Meadow pasture	Diversified pasture	Subdivision	Section	Tp.N.	R.E.	Length of season	C.F.S.	Acre-feet
1907	13.30			E½W½	12	28	56			
				SW¼	1	28	56			
				S½NW¼	1	28	56	4-15—8-15	.164	39.90

Claimant—**Clark Drown.** Proof No. 00357
Source—**South Fork Humboldt River.** Ditch—**Clark Drown Ditches.**

Year of priority	Harvest crops	Meadow pasture	Diversified pasture	Subdivision	Section	Tp.N.	R.E.	Length of season	C.F.S.	Acre-feet
1909	10.00			S½SW¼	8	31	57	4-15—8-15	.123	36.00
1910	55.00			N½	17	31	57	4-15—8-15	.677	165.00
1910	16.00			N½SE¼	17	31	57	4-15—8-15	.197	48.00
1911	20.00			NE¼SW¼	17	31	57	4-15—8-15	.246	60.00
1911	51.00			NE¼	18	31	57	4-15—8-15	.627	153.00
1912	64.50			SE¼NW¼	18	31	57	4-15—8-15	.793	193.50
1915	22.50							4-15—8-15	.277	67.50
1916	15.00							4-15—8-15	.185	45.00
1916	30.00							4-15—8-15	.369	90.00
1916	35.00							4-15—8-15	.431	105.00
1916			246.00					4-15—8-15	3.026	181.50

Claimant—**Albert Hankins.** Proof No. 00358

Source—**Smith, South Fork, Smith Creek, McCutcheons, Adams, and Dry Creeks.**

Ditch—**Albert Hankins Ditches.**

....	1909	....	....	....	....	70.00	....	NW¼	2	29	56			
								NE¼	3	29	56	4-15—5-15	.861	52.50

Claimant—**J. J. Hylton.** Proof No. 00359

Source—**South Fork Humboldt River.** Ditch—**J. J. Hylton Ditches.**

....	1908	....	....	40.00	....	....	....	SE¼	4	32	55			
....	1912	....	....	9.50	....	....	....	S½	3	32	55			
....	1915	....	....	40.00	....	....	....		10	32	55			
....	1920	....	....	35.00	....	....	....	W½	11	32	55			
								N½	15	32	55			
									14	32	55			
								E½	23	32	55	4-15—8-15	.492	120.00
								W½	24	32	55	4-15—8-15	.117	28.50
								SE¼	24	32	55	4-15—8-15	.492	120.00
									25	32	55	4-15—9-15	.431	105.00

Source—**Smith Creek.** Ditch—**J. J. Hylton Ditches.**

....	1909	....	....	17.00	....	....	....	NW¼	33	30	56	4-15—8-15	.209	51.00
....	1912	....	....	19.00	....	....	....	NW¼	33	30	56	4-15—8-15	.234	57.00
....	1909	....	....	4.00	....	....	....	SW¼	33	30	56	4-15—8-15	.049	12.00
....	1915	....	....	22.50	....	....	....	SW¼	33	30	56	4-15—8-15	.277	67.50
....	1912	....	....	18.67	....	....	....	SW¼	33	30	56	4-15—8-15	.230	56.01
....	1915	....	....	22.00	....	....	....	NW¼	4	29	56	4-15—8-15	.271	66.00
....	1912	....	....	4.33	....	....	....	NW¼	4	29	56	4-15—8-15	.053	12.99
....	1909	....	....	19.00	....	....	....	NE¼	32	30	56	4-15—8-15	.234	57.00
....	1915	....	....	5.00	....	....	....	NE¼	32	30	56	4-15—8-15	.062	15.00
....	1915	....	....	12.00	....	....	....	SW¼	32	30	56	4-15—8-15	.148	36.00
....	1916	....	....	97.00	....	....	....	SW¼	32	30	56	4-15—8-15	1.193	291.00
....	1915	....	....	73.00	....	....	....	SE¼	32	30	56	4-15—8-15	.898	279.00
....	1916	....	....	6.00	....	....	....	NW¼	5	29	56	4-15—8-15	.074	18.00
....	1909	....	....	1.00	....	....	....	SE¼	29	30	56	4-15—8-15	.012	3.00
....	1915	....	....	10.00	....	....	....	NW¼	32	30	56	4-15—8-15	.123	30.00

Source—**South Fork Humboldt River.** Ditch—**J. J. Hylton Ditches.**

....	1912	....	....	69.00	....	....	....	S½NE¼	15	31	57			
....	1912	....	....	10.50	....	....	....	SE¼	15	31	57			
								W½SW¼	14	31	57	4-15—8-15	.849	207.00
								SW¼NW¼	14	31	57	4-15—8-15	.129	31.50

Claimant—**Chas. Mitchell.** Proof No. 00362

Source—**Brown's Creek.** Ditch—**Chas. Mitchell Ditches.**

Year of priority	Culture—Acres: Harvest crops	Meadow pasture	Diversified pasture	Location: Subdivision	Section	Tp.N.	R.E.	Length of season	Duty of water: C.F.S.	Acre-feet
1906	36.70			NE¼NE¼	30	28	56			
				NW¼NW¼	29	28	56			
				S½NW¼	29	28	56			
				SW¼NE¼	29	28	56			
				N½S½	29	28	56			
				NE¼SE¼	29	28	56			
				N½SW¼	28	28	56	4-15—8-15	.378	92.10

Claimant—**P. J. Ogilvie.** Proof No. 00364

Source—**South Fork of Humboldt River and Rattlesnake Creek.**

Year of priority	Harvest crops	Meadow pasture	Diversified pasture	Subdivision	Section	Tp.N.	R.E.	Length of season	C.F.S.	Acre-feet
1908	77.00			S½	14	31	56	4-15—8-15	.947	231.00
1915	53.00			S½	13	31	56	4-15—8-15	.652	159.00
				N½	24	31	56			
				W½NW¼	19	31	57			

Early water only from Rattlesnake Creek.

Claimant—**Ernest Hodges.** Proof No. 00370

Source—**Dry Creek and Springs.** Ditch—**Ernest Hodges Ditches.**

Year of priority	Harvest crops	Meadow pasture	Diversified pasture	Subdivision	Section	Tp.N.	R.E.	Length of season	C.F.S.	Acre-feet
1906	39.00			SW¼	30	33	57	4-15—8-15	.480	117.00

Claimant—**A. M. Griswold.** Proof No. 00372

Source—**South Fork Humboldt River.** Ditch—**Griswold Ditches.**

Year of priority	Harvest crops	Meadow pasture	Diversified pasture	Subdivision	Section	Tp.N.	R.E.	Length of season	C.F.S.	Acre-feet
1906	7.00			N½NW¼	10	31	56	5-15—8-15	.086	21.00
1908	55.00			NE¼	10	31	56	5-15—8-15	.677	165.00
1910	28.00			E½SE¼	10	31	56	5-15—8-15	.344	84.00
1911	25.00			S½NW¼	11	31	56	5-15—8-15	.308	75.00
1913	....		10.00	W½SW¼	11	31	56	5-15—6-15	.123	7.50
1915	50.00			N½	14	31	56	5-15—8-15	.615	150.00
1915	55.00				....	....	....	5-15—8-15	.677	165.00
1915	35.00				....	....	....	5-15—8-15	.431	105.00
1916	16.00				....	....	....	5-15—8-15	.197	48.00
1917	15.00				....	....	....	5-15—8-15	.185	45.00

Claimant—**Minnie Hankins, Lillie Hankins, Elizabeth Hankins, Estate Jane Bellinger.** Proof No. 00375

Source—**South Fork of Humboldt.** Ditch—**Hankins & Bellinger Ditches.**

Year of priority	Harvest crops	Meadow pasture	Diversified pasture	Subdivision	Section	Tp.N.	R.E.	Length of season	C.F.S.	Acre-feet
1906	44.36			W½	31	32	56			
				NE¼NW¼	6	31	56			

								N½NE¼	6	31	56			
								SE¼NE¼	6	31	56	4-15—8-15	.546	133.08

Claimant—**J. J. Hylton.** Proof No. 00381
Source—**Cottonwood Creek.** Ditch—**Nos. 1, 2, 3, 5, and 6.**

	1909			7.80				SW¼NW¼	15	30	56	4-15—8-15	.096	23.40
	1909			0.50				SE¼NE¼	16	30	56	4-15—8-15	.006	1.50
	1909			1.30				NE¼NE¼	16	30	56	4-15—8-15	.016	3.90
	1909			1.00				NW¼NW¼	15	30	56	4-15—8-15	.012	3.00

Claimant—**Drown Bros.** Proof No. 00385
Source—**South Fork of Humboldt River.** Ditch—**Drown Bros. Ditches.**

								S½NW¼	10	31	56			
	1906			80.00				SW¼	10	31	56			
	1907			26.00				W½SE¼	10	31	56			
	1909			75.00				SE¼NW¼	11	31	56			
								S½NE¼	11	31	56	4-15—8-15	.984	240.00
								E½SW¼	11	31	56	4-15—8-15	.320	78.00
								SE¼	11	31	56	4-15—8-15	.923	225.00
	1906			....		38.80		N¼	22	31	56	4-15—5-15	.477	29.10
	1906			20.00				S½NW¼	23	31	56	4-15—8-15	.246	60.00
	1907			33.50				—	—	—	—	4-15—8-15	.412	100.50
	1908			30.80				—	—	—	—	4-15—8-15	.379	92.40
	1909			....		52.70		—	—	—	—	4-15—5-15	.648	39.53
	1909			51.80				—	—	—	—	4-15—8-15	.637	155.40
	1911			15.40				—	—	—	—	4-15—8-15	.189	46.20
	1912			—	48.10			—	—	—	—	4-15—6-15	.592	72.15
	1913			...	18.40			—	—	—	—	4-15—6-15	.226	27.00
	1908			10.90				NE¼	15	31	56	4-15—8-15	.134	32.70
	1909			3.00				E½SE¼	15	31	56	4-15—8-15	.037	9.00
	1910			21.80				SW¼SE¼	15	31	56	4-15—8-15	.268	65.40
	1915			110.80				S½SW¼	15	31	56	4-15—8-15	1.363	332.40
	1917			59.50				NW¼SW¼	15	31	56	4-15—8-15	.732	178.50
	1919			21.70				SW¼NW¼	15	31	56	4-15—8-15	.267	65.10
	1918			—		12.50		NE¼NW¼	9	31	56	4-15—5-15	.154	9.38
	1919			—		50.00		NE¼	9	31	56	4-15—5-15	.615	37.50
	1920			—		88.70		NE¼SE¼	9	31	56	4-15—5-15	1.091	66.53

Claimant—**A. J. Dewar.** Proof No. 00388
Source—**South Fork Humboldt River.** Ditch—**A. J. Dewar Ditches.**

	1907			18.00				S½S½	17	31	57			
	1908			17.32				S½	18	31	57			
	1910			6.78				SE¼NE¼	19	31	57	4-15—8-15	.221	54.00
								N½NE¼	19	31	57	4-15—8-15	.218	51.96
								NE¼NW¼	19	31	57	4-15—8-15	.083	20.34

Claimant—**Chris Baumbach.** Proof No. 00394
Source—**Rattlesnake Creek.** Ditch—**Chris Baumbach Ditches.**

Year of priority	Culture—Acres: Harvest crops	Meadow pasture	Diversified pasture	Location: Subdivision	Section	Tp.N.	R.E.	Length of season	Duty of water: C.F.S.	Acre-feet
1910	37.15			S½NW¼	19	31	57			
				SW¼NE¼	19	31	57			
				NE¼SW¼	19	31	57			
				SE¼	19	31	57			
				SW¼SW¼	20	31	57	4-15—8-15	.457	111.45

Claimant—**W. R. Bellinger.** Proof No. 00401
Source—**Lamoille Creek.** Ditch—**W. R. Bellinger Ditches.**

Year of priority	Harvest crops	Meadow pasture	Diversified pasture	Subdivision	Section	Tp.N.	R.E.	Length of season	C.F.S.	Acre-feet
1907	30.00			W½W½	30	33	58	4-15—8-15	.369	90.00
1908	11.00			S½SW¼	19	33	58	4-15—8-15	.135	33.00
1909	10.00							4-15—8-15	.123	30.00
1910	9.20							4-15—8-15	.113	27.60
1911	26.50							4-15—8-15	.326	79.50
1914	105.00							4-15—8-15	1.292	315.00
1915	8.00							4-15—8-15	.098	24.00
1918	42.00							4-15—8-15	.517	126.00

Claimant—**Hankins-Bellinger Co.** Proof No. 00405
Source—**Lamoille Creek.** Ditch—**Hankins-Bellinger Ditches.**

Year of priority	Harvest crops	Meadow pasture	Diversified pasture	Subdivision	Section	Tp.N.	R.E.	Length of season	C.F.S.	Acre-feet
1911	10.00			E½NE¼	24	33	57	4-15—8-15	.123	30.00
1912	20.00			NW¼SW¼	19	33	58	4-15—8-15	.246	60.00
1914	15.00			SW¼SW¼	19	33	58	4-15—8-15	.185	45.00

Claimant—**Samuel McIntyre Investment Company.** Proof No. 00409
Source—**Lamoille Creek.** Ditch—**Samuel McIntyre Investment Company Ditches.**

Year of priority	Harvest crops	Meadow pasture	Diversified pasture	Subdivision	Section	Tp.N.	R.E.	Length of season	C.F.S.	Acre-feet
1910	60.00			S½	9	35	58	4-15—8-15	.738	180.00
1909	—		131.50	SW¼	10	35	58	4-15—5-15	1.617	98.63
					15	35	58			

Claimant—**R. B. Stewart.** Proof No. 00446
Source—**Rabbit Creek.** Ditch—**Stewart Ditches.**

Year of priority	Harvest crops	Meadow pasture	Diversified pasture	Subdivision	Section	Tp.N.	R.E.	Length of season	C.F.S.	Acre-feet
1907	30.00			S½	26	33	57	4 15—8 15	.738	180.00
1909	30.00			N½N½	35	33	57	4-15—8-15	.738	180.00
				S½NW¼	35	33	57			

Claimant—**Albert Trescartes.** Proof No. 00459
Source—**Lamoille Creek.** Ditch—**Albert Trescartes Ditches.**

1911	87.00		N½	26	33	57	4-15—8-15	1.070	261.00
1912	61.70			...	...	...	4-15—8-15	.759	185.10

Water right initiated prior to 1905 on Sec. 25 and transferred by permit to Sec. 26.

Claimant—**Chas. Trescartes.** Proof No. 00459
Source—**Lamoille Creek.** Ditch—**Chas Trescartes Ditches.**

1907	59.20		W½NE¼	24	33	57	4-15—8-15	.728	177.60
1913	18.00		SE¼NE¼	24	33	57	4-15—8-16	.221	54.00
1916	11.00			...	...	...	4-15—8-15	.135	33.00

Claimant—**W. W. Alles.** Proof No. 00477
Source—**Springs, Swamps and Natural Draw on Secs. 5 and 6, T. 36 N, R. 60 E.**
Ditch—**W. W. Alles Ditches.**

1911	18.06		S½NE¼	6	36	60	4-15—8-15	.222	54.18

NOTE—Source is as shown above. Claimant not to take water from Ackler or Herder Creek in case of shortage.

Claimant—**Phil Harney.** Proof No. 00484
Source—**Soldier Creek.** Ditch—**McDermott 1-4, incl.**

1906	20.20*		SW¼	20	34	59	4-15—8-15	.250	60.60
1915	...	11.30†	W½SE¼	20	34	59	4-15—5-15	.139	33.90
1915	...	10.00†		...	...	...	4-15—5-15	.123	30.00

***Was pasture in 1896. †Was pasture in 1902.**

Claimant—**W. J. Smiley.** Proof No. 00491
Source—**Herder Creek.** Ditch—**W. J. Smiley Ditches.**

1910	73.00		NW¼	7	36	60	4-15—8-15	.898	213.00
1910	9.80		N½SW¼	7	36	60	4-15—8-15	.121	29.40

"This land was subirrigated from irrigation of older land, but water not directly applied on surface until 1910. No water to be applied directly to this land until all vested rights are served, nor until all permits with date prior to 1910 have been served. Agreed to by all users in settlement of disputes."

Claimant—**Hylton & Mentz.** Proof No. 00502
Source—**Herder Creek.** Ditch—**Hylton & Mentz Ditches.**

1909	5.60		SE¼	6	36	60	4-15—8-15	.069	16.80
1909	15.00		NE¼SW¼	6	36	60	4-15—8-15	.185	45.00
1909	1.00			...	...	...	4-15—8-15	.012	3.00

Claimant—**W. J.' Black.** Proof No. 00505

Source—**Ackler Creek, Brennen Gulch, and Herder Creek.** Ditches—**Nos. 1-14, incl.**

Year of priority	Culture—Acres: Harvest crops	Meadow pasture	Diversified pasture	Location: Subdivision	Section	Tp.N.	R.E.	Length of season	Duty of water: C.F.S.	Acre-feet
1909	10.00			E½	8	36	60			
				S½NW¼	8	30	60			
				NE¼SW¼	8	36	60	4-15—8-15	.123	30.00

Source—**Ackler Creek.** Ditches—**Nos. 1-14, incl.**

Year of priority	Harvest crops	Meadow pasture	Diversified pasture	Subdivision	Section	Tp.N.	R.E.	Length of season	C.F.S.	Acre-feet
1909	5.10			E½	8	36	60			
				SE¼NW¼	8	36	60			
				NE¼SW¼	8	36	60	4-15—8-15	.063	15.30

Claimant—**Isaac Griswold.** Proof No. 00519

Source—**Branch of Boulder Creek.** Ditch—**Isaac Griswold Ditches.**

Year of priority	Harvest crops	Meadow pasture	Diversified pasture	Subdivision	Section	Tp.N.	R.E.	Length of season	C.F.S.	Acre-feet
1909	7.00			SW¼NW¼	13	36	59	4-15—8-15	.086	21.00
1910	7.00			W½SW¼	13	36	59	4-15—8-15	.086	21.00
				E½E½	14	36	59			

Claimant—**Diana Morgan-Hill** (Deed to J. J. Hylton in escrow). Proof No. 00552

Source—**North Fork.** Ditch—**McKee & Clayton.**

Year of priority	Harvest crops	Meadow pasture	Diversified pasture	Subdivision	Section	Tp.N.	R.E.	Length of season	C.F.S.	Acre-feet
1913	83.50			E½NE¼	35	40	56			
				NE¼SE¼	35	40	56			
				NW¼	36	40	56			
				N½SW¼	36	40	56			
				SW¼NE¼	36	40	56			
				NW¼SE¼	36	40	56	4-15—8-15	1.027	250.50

Claimant—**C. A. & L. M. Laing.** Proof No. 00556

Source—**Pratt Creek.** Ditch—**Laing Ditches.**

Year of priority	Harvest crops	Meadow pasture	Diversified pasture	Subdivision	Section	Tp.N.	R.E.	Length of season	C.F.S.	Acre-feet
1914	53.00			NW¼SE¼	36	42	54			
				S½SE¼	36	42	54			
				S½SW¼	31	42	55			
				SE¼NW¼	1	41	54			
				NE¼	1	41	54			
					6	41	55			
				W½SW¼	5	41	55			
				NE¼NE¼	7	41	55			
				NW¼NW¼	8	41	55	4-15—8-15	.652	159.00

Claimant—**Union Land and Cattle Co.** **Proof No. 00601**

Source—**Taber Creek.** Ditch—**Nos. 1, 2, and 3.**

Year of priority	Harvest crops	Meadow pasture	Diversified pasture	Subdivision	Section	Tp.N.	R.E.	Length of season	C.F.S.	Acre-feet
1911	34.07			N½	6	40	61	4-15—8-15	.420	104.01

Claimant—**Metropolis Land Company.** Proof No. 00608
Source—**Bishop Creek.** Ditch—**Nos. 1, 2, and 3.**

1911	9.09	NW¼SE¼	28	39	62		
		N½SW¼	28	39	62		
		S½SE¼	29	39	62		
		E½NE¼	31	39	62		
		NE¼SE¼	31	39	62		
		N½	32	39	62		
		N½SW¼	32	39	62		
		NW¼SE¼	32	39	62	4-15—8-15	.112	27.27

Claimant—**John H. Cazier & Sons Co.** Proof No. 00609
Source—**Trout Creek.** Ditch—**John H. Cazier.**

1914	10.40	SE¼&SW¼	5	37	61	4-15—8-15	1.280	31.2
1915	136.50	SW¼NE¼&NW¼SE¼	8	37	61	4-15—8-15	1.679	409.5

Claimant—**Ambrose Truett.** Proof No. 00611
Source—**Tom Cain Creek.** Ditch—**Ambrose Truett Ditches.**

1908	31.43	E½SW¼	31	42	61			
		S½SE¼	31	42	61	5-1—8-31	.400	

Decree in Case 2580, records of District Court of Elko County, is binding as between parties to such suit.

Claimant—**Chas. Toyn.** Proof No. 00664
Source—**South Fork Smith Creek.** Ditch—**Chas. Toyn Ditches.**

1907	9.75	E½NW¼	35	29	56			
		W½NE¼	35	29	56			
		SE¼NE¼	35	29	56			
		E½SE¼	35	29	56			
		S½S½	36	29	56			
		N½N½	1	28	56			
		NE¼NE¼	2	28	56	4-15—8-15	.120	29.25

Claimant—**Thomas Griffin.** Proof No. 00224
Source—**Maggie Creek.** Ditch—**Griffin Ditch.**

1908	4.41	NE¼SW¼	26	33	52	4-15—8-15	.054	13.23
1908	3.55	NW¼SE¼	26	33	52	4-15—8-15	.044	10.65
1908	6.20	SW¼SE¼	26	33	52	4-15—8-15	.076	18.60
1908	4.43	SE¼SW¼	26	33	52	4-15—8-15	.054	13.29

PERMITS—Lovelock District

Claimant—**Humboldt-Lovelock Irrigation, Light and Power Co.** Permit No. 1098
Source—**Humboldt River.** Ditch—**H. L. I. L. & P. Co. Dam.**

Year of priority	Culture—Acres: Harvest crops	Meadow pasture	Diversified pasture	Location: Subdivision	Section	Tp.N.	R.E.	Length of season	Duty of water: C.F.S.	Acre-feet
1918	16960							3-15—9-15		32500

NOTE—This permit is for storage of water used on certain lands in Lovelock Valley as required to satisfy the needs of certain water users from seasonal decrease in the flow of the river.

Claimant—**A. E. Allen.** Permit No. 1240*
Source—**Humboldt River.** Ditch—**Schaefel's Ditch.**

Year of priority	Harvest crops	Meadow pasture	Diversified pasture	Subdivision	Section	Tp.N.	R.E.	Length of season	C.F.S.	Acre-feet
1909	1.00			SE¼SW¼	20	25	31	3-15—9-15	.01	

*Certificate No. 356.

Claimant—**John Holmstrom.** Permit No. 1650†
Source—**Humboldt River.** Ditch—**Young or Tunnel (Holstrom Lateral).***

Year of priority	Harvest crops	Meadow pasture	Diversified pasture	Subdivision	Section	Tp.N.	R.E.	Length of season	C.F.S.	Acre-feet
*1910	55			W¼SE¼	31	28	32	3-15—9-15	.55	

†Certificate No. 77.

Claimant—**Stefan Herzog.** Permit No. 2511*
Source—**Humboldt River.** Ditch—**Herzog Ditch.**

Year of priority	Harvest crops	Meadow pasture	Diversified pasture	Subdivision	Section	Tp.N.	R.E.	Length of season	C.F.S.	Acre-feet
1912	6.9			NE¼SE¼	36	25	30			
1912	12.6			SE¼SE¼	36	25	30			
1912	9.5			SW¼SE¼	36	25	30	3-15—9-15	.29	

*Certificate No. 466.

Claimant—**Hiram Stoker.** Permit No. 2588*
Source—**Underground Water and Sub-flow of the Humboldt River.** Ditch—**Stoker Ditch.**

Year of priority	Harvest crops	Meadow pasture	Diversified pasture	Subdivision	Section	Tp.N.	R.E.	Length of season	C.F.S.	Acre-feet
1912	.75			SW¼NW¼	24	27	31			
1912	35.37			NW¼SW¼	24	27	31			
1912	24.93			SW¼SW¼	24	27	31			
1912	31.76			NE¼SW¼	24	27	31			
1912	18.88			SE¼SW¼	24	27	31			
1912	13.94			SE¼NW¼	24	27	31			
1912	2.43			SW¼NE¼	24	27	31	3-15—9-15	1.2805	

NOTE—The water is pumped from a well by means of a ten-inch centrifugal pump driven by a 50 H.P. motor.
*Certificate No. 565.

Claimant—**A. E. Allen.** Permit No. 5205*
Source—**Humboldt River.** Ditch—**Schaefels, Allen and Harrison.**

Year of priority	Harvest crops	Meadow pasture	Diversified pasture	Subdivision	Section	Tp.N.	R.E.	Length of season	C.F.S.	Acre-feet
1918	19.34			SW¼SE¼	20	25	31			
1918	38.42			SE¼SW¼	20	25	31			
1918	37.60			SW¼SW¼	20	25	31	1-1—9-1	.9530	460.01

*Certificate No. 640.

Winnemucca District

Claimant—**The Golconda Gold Ledge Mining Co.** Permit No. 1988*
Source—**Pole Creek. Pipeline.**

†1911						1-1—12-31	†.1

*Certificate No. 234. †Right to 0.1 c.f.s. of water granted for mining, milling, and domestic purposes.

Claimant—**John G. Taylor & J. Sheehan.** Permit No. 2641*
Source—**Humboldt River.** Ditch—**Golconda Dam.**

1913						1-1—12-31	†375.0

*Certificate No. 395. †No irrigation; power purposes only.

Battle Mountain District

Claimant—**W. T. Jenkins Co.** Permit No. 19*
Source—**Rock Creek.** Ditch—**Rock Creek Ditches.**

1905	2.00	NW¼NE¼	24	37	46		
1905	11.72	SW¼NE¼	24	37	46		
1905	20.77	NW¼SE¼	24	37	46		
1905	29.03	SW¼SE¼	24	37	46		
1905	28.10	NW¼NE¼	25	37	46		
1905	0.28	SW¼NE¼	25	37	46		
1905	4.68	NW¼NE¼	25	37	46		
1905	39.72	SW¼NE¼	25	37	46		
1905	12.80	NW¼SE¼	25	37	46	4-1—10-1	1.5

*Certificate No. 97.

Claimant—**Ellison Ranching Co.** Permit No. 1486*
Source—**Fraser Creek and Tributaries.** Ditch—**Fraser Creek Ditch.**

1909	4.60	SW¼NE¼	7	39	47		
1909	34.20	W½SE¼	7	39	47		
1909	7.30	SW¼NW¼	17	39	47		
1909	15.40	N½SW¼	17	39	47		
1909	16.60	SW¼SE¼	17	39	47		
1909	20.30	N½NE¼	18	39	47		
1909	9.00	SE¼NE¼	18	39	47		
1909	34.30	NW¼NE¼	20	39	47		
1909	38.50	SW¼NE¼	20	39	47		
1909	15.20	SE¼NE¼	20	39	47		
1909	3.65	SE¼SE¼	20	39	47		
1909	36.00	NE¼NE¼	29	39	47		
1909	1.40	SE¼NE¼	29	39	47	5-1—6-20	2.3645

*Certificate No. 256.

Claimant—**W. T. Jenkins Co.** Permit No. 1905*
Source—**Rock Creek.** Ditch—**Rock Creek Ditch.**

Year of priority	Culture—Acres: Harvest crops	Meadow pasture	Diversified pasture	Location: Subdivision	Section	Tp.N.	R.E.	Length of season	Duty of water: C.F.S.	Acre-feet
1910	1.46			SW¼NE¼	24	37	46			
1910	5.16			NW¼SE¼	24	37	46			
1910	3.87			W½SW¼SE¼	24	37	46			
1910	4.07			W½NW¼NE¼	25	37	46			
1910	0.30			NE¼NW¼	25	37	46			
1910	3.09			E½SE¼NW¼	25	37	46			
1910	2.85			E½NE¼SW¼	25	37	46			
1910	2.00			E½SE¼SW¼	25	37	46			
1910	40.00			SW¼SE¼	25	37	46			
1910	27.20			NW¼SE¼	25	37	46	4-1—10-1	.9	

*Certificate No. 140.

Claimant—**E. A. Duvivier.** Permit No. 1929*
Source—**Eyrand Spring.** Ditch—**Eyrand.**

Year of priority	Harvest crops	Meadow pasture	Diversified pasture	Subdivision	Section	Tp.N.	R.E.	Length of season	C.F.S.	Acre-feet
1911	9.12			SE¼SE¼	30	35	43	3-1—10-1	.0912	
1911	31.88			NE¼SE¼	30	35	43	6-13—10-1	.3188	
1911	17.40			SE¼SE¼	30	35	43	6-13—10-1	.174	122.14

*Amended Certificate No. 451.

Claimant—**Knud Nelson.** Permit No. 3035
Source—**Boulder Creek.** Ditch—**Unnamed.**

Year of priority	Harvest crops	Meadow pasture	Diversified pasture	Subdivision	Section	Tp.N.	R.E.	Length of season	C.F.S.	Acre-feet
1914	160.00			NE¼	28	36	49			
1914	155.43			SW¼	22	36	49	4-1—7-1	3.1543	

Claimant—**Almond C. Fox.** Permit No. 3146
Source—**Boulder Creek.** Ditch—**Unnamed.**

Year of priority	Harvest crops	Meadow pasture	Diversified pasture	Subdivision	Section	Tp.N.	R.E.	Length of season	C.F.S.	Acre-feet
1914	26.50			NE¼SW¼	8	35	49			
1914	35.768			NW¼SW¼	8	35	49			
1914	26.30			SW¼SW¼	8	35	49			
1914	32.00			SE¼SW¼	8	35	49	4-1—7-1	1.2057	

Claimant—**Almond C. Fox.** Permit No. 3147
Source—**Boulder Creek.** Ditch—**Unnamed.**

Year of priority	Harvest crops	Meadow pasture	Diversified pasture	Subdivision	Section	Tp.N.	R.E.	Length of season	C.F.S.	Acre-feet
1914	37.25			NE¼NE¼	18	35	49			
1914	27.00			NW¼NE¼	18	35	49			
1914	80.00			S½NE¼	18	35	49	4-1—7-1	1.4425	

Elko District

Claimant—**George J. Hunter and George D. Banks.** Permit No. 82
Source—**South Fork Humboldt River.** Ditch—**South Side.**

1906	18.00	NE¼SE¼	8	33	54			
1906	0.50	NW¼SE¼	8	33	54			
1906	36.50	SW¼SE¼	8	33	54			
1906	8.50	SE¼SW¼	8	33	54			
1906	39.50	NE¼NW¼	17	33	54			
1906	5.00	NW¼NW¼	17	33	54			
1906	28.70	SW¼NW¼	17	33	54			
1906	41.00	NW¼SW¼	17	33	54			
1906	12.70	NE¼SE¼	18	33	54			
1906	36.00	SE¼SE¼	18	33	54			
1906	33.00	NE¼NE¼	19	33	54	4-15—8-15	2.594	778.2

Claimant—**E. C. Riddell.** Permit No. 979
Source—**Starr Creek.** Ditch—**Unnamed.**

1908	35.19	NW¼SE¼	35	37	59		
1908	38.79	SW¼SE¼	35	37	59		
1908	14.49	NE¼SW¼	35	37	59		
1908	17.63	SE¼SW¼	35	37	59	4-15—8-15	1.061

Claimant—**John Henderson.** Permit No. 1114*
Source—**Dry or Seitz Creek.** Ditch—**Henderson Dry.**

1908	0.90	NE¼SW¼	34	33	57		
1908	5.30	SE¼SW¼	34	33	57		
1908	0.30	NW¼SE¼	34	33	57		
1908	25.00	SW¼SE¼	34	33	57		
1908	2.30	SE¼SE¼	34	33	57	5-1—9-1	.34

*Certificate No. 76.

Claimant—**C. W. Griswold.** Permit No. 1115*
Source—**Dry or Seitz Creek.** Ditch—**Griswold Dry Creek.**

1908	17.80	NW¼NE¼	34	33	57		
1908	9.61	NE¼NE¼	34	33	57		
1908	11.30	SW¼NE¼	34	33	57		
1908	13.30	SE¼NE¼	34	33	57	5-1—9-1	.55

*Certificate No. 78.

Claimant—**Albert Hankins.** Permit No. 1271*
Source—**Carville Creek.** Ditch—**Carville Creek Ditches.**

Year of priority	Culture—Acres: Harvest crops	Meadow pasture	Diversified pasture	Location: Subdivision	Section	Tp. N.	R. E.	Length of season	Duty of water: C.F.S.	Acre-feet
1909	2.30			NW¼SW¼	3	29	56			
1909	6.60			SW¼SW¼	3	29	56			
1909	2.30			SE¼SW¼	3	29	56			
1909	17.60			NE¼NE¼	10	29	56			
1909	25.50			NW¼NE¼	10	29	56			
1909	31.50			SW¼NE¼	10	29	56			
1909	35.20			SE¼NE¼	10	29	56			
1909	26.10			NE¼NW¼	10	29	56			
1909	10.40			SE¼NW¼	10	29	56			
1909	30.80			NE¼SE¼	10	29	56			
1909	1.80			NW¼SE¼	10	29	56			
1909	18.30			SE¼SE¼	10	29	56			
1909	0.90			NW¼NW¼	11	29	56			
1909	16.20			SW¼NW¼	11	29	56			
1909	7.60			NW¼SW¼	11	29	56	4-1—10-1	2.331	

*Certificate No. 196.

Claimant—**Albert Hankins.** Permit No. 1272*
Source—**Smith Creek.** Ditch—**Smith Creek Ditch.**

Year of priority	Harvest crops	Meadow pasture	Diversified pasture	Subdivision	Section	Tp. N.	R. E.	Length of season	C.F.S.	Acre-feet
1909	9.80			NW¼NE¼	4	29	56			
1909	24.60			SW¼NE¼	4	29	56			
1909	6.80			NW¼SE¼	4	29	56	†5-15—8-15	.412	92.7

*Certificate No. 197. †Water right from 4-15—5-15 allowed as a vested right. (See page 190 of this order). Water right for the remainder of the irrigation season allowed hereunder.

Claimant—**Albert Hankins.** Permit No. 1273*
Source—**McCutcheon Creek.** Ditch—**McCutcheon Creek Ditch.**

Year of priority	Harvest crops	Meadow pasture	Diversified pasture	Subdivision	Section	Tp. N.	R. E.	Length of season	C.F.S.	Acre-feet
1909	0.70			NW¼SW¼	3	29	56			
1909	6.70			SW¼SW¼	3	29	56			
1909	25.30			SE¼SW¼	3	29	56			
1909	7.03			SW¼SE¼	3	29	56			
1909	2.60			NE¼NW¼	10	29	56	4-1—10-1	.4233	

*Certificate No. 198.

Claimant—**Albert Hankins.** Permit No. 1274*
Source—**Hankins or Adams Creek.** Ditch—**Hankins Creek Ditch.**

Year of priority	Harvest crops	Meadow pasture	Diversified pasture	Subdivision	Section	Tp. N.	R. E.	Length of season	C.F.S.	Acre-feet
1909	10.00			SW¼NW¼	1	29	56			
1909	0.80			SE¼NW¼	1	29	56			
1909	14.90			NW¼SW¼	1	29	56			
1909	21.00			NE¼SW¼	1	29	56	4-1—10-1	.470	

*Certificate No. 199.

Claimant—**Edward U. McDermott.** Permit No. **1299***
Source—**Lamoille Creek.** Ditch—**Ed. McDermott.**

1909	82.60	SE¼	32	34	58			
1909	14.10	NW¼SE¼	32	34	58			
1909	6.30	SW¼SE¼	32	34	58			
1909	30.70	SE¼SE¼	32	34	58			
1909	17.30	NE¼SE¼	32	34	58	4 15—8 15	1.51	302.1

*Certificate No. 620.

NOTE—Water is diverted from Lamoille Creek through ditch which empties into Talbot Creek; then another ditch takes the water out of Talbot Creek just below where the Lamoille Creek ditch empties into said Talbot Creek.

Claimant—**George W. Byers.** Permit No. **1439***
Source—**Herer (Herder) Creek.** Ditch—**Byers.**

1909	38.50	NE¼NE¼	4	36	60		
1909	11.30	NW¼NE¼	4	36	60		
1909	0.30	SW¼NE¼	4	36	60		
1909	6.10	SE¼NE¼	4	36	60	4-1—9-1	.568

*Certificate No. 254.

Claimant—**Horace A. Agee.** Permits Nos. **1548, 2613***
Source—**Tom Cain Creek.** Ditch—**Unnamed.**

1909	15.00	NW¼NW¼	1	41	60		
1909	13.48	NE¼NW¼	1	41	60		
1909	21.92	NW¼NE¼	1	41	60		
1909	2.90	NE¼NE¼	1	41	60		
1909	33.00	SE¼NE¼	1	41	60		
1909	25.70	SW¼NE¼	1	41	60		
1909	40.00	SE¼NW¼	1	41	60		
1909	40.00	SW¼NW¼	1	41	60	5-1—9-1	1.92

*Certificate No. 350.

Claimant—**Wilson J.** Forbes & Oliver C. **McCall.** Permit No. **1631***
Source—**Secret Creek.** Ditch—Forbes.

1910	33.60	NE¼SE¼	16	35	59		
1910	24.10	NW¼SE¼	16	35	59		
1910	29.50	SE¼SE¼	16	35	59		
1910	38.40	SW¼SE¼	16	35	59		
1910	20.00	SE¼SW¼	16	35	59		
1910	5.00	NE¼SW¼	16	35	59	4-1—10-1	1.506

*Certificate No. 330.

Claimant—**Herman W. Finck.** Permit No. **1635***
Source—**Trough Canyon & Springs.** Ditch—**Finck.**

1910	0.73	SW¼NE¼	16	39	62	5 1—10 1	.0375

*Certificate No. 166.

Claimant—**C. H. Black.** Permit No. 1714
Source—**Herder Creek.** Ditch—**McMullen.**

Year of priority	Culture—Acres: Harvest crops	Meadow pasture	Diversified pasture	Location: Subdivision	Section	Tp. N.	R. E.	Length of season	Duty of water: C. F. S.	Acre-feet
1910	34.10			NW¼NW¼	4	36	60			
1910	26.60			NE¼NW¼	4	36	60			
1910	6.20			SE¼NW¼	4	36	60			
1910	1.10			SW¼NW¼	4	36	60	4-15—8-15	.68	

Claimant—**L. D. Hylton and H. C. Mentz.** Permit No. 1716
Source—**Ackler and Herder Creeks.** Ditch—**Brennen Gulch.**

Year of priority	Harvest crops	Meadow pasture	Diversified pasture	Subdivision	Section	Tp. N.	R. E.	Length of season	C. F. S.	Acre-feet
1910	9.49			NE¼SW¼	6	36	60			
1910	1.10			NW¼SE¼	6	36	60			
1910	23.89			SW¼SE¼	6	36	60			
1910	19.44			SE¼SW¼	6	36	60			
1910	7.00			SW¼SW¼	6	36	60	4-15—8-15	.609	

Claimant—**Wm. Smiley.** Permit No. 1717
Source—**Ackler and Herder Creek.** Ditch—**Smiley.**

Year of priority	Harvest crops	Meadow pasture	Diversified pasture	Subdivision	Section	Tp. N.	R. E.	Length of season	C. F. S.	Acre-feet
1910	26.00			NW¼NW¼	34	37	60			
1910	21.40			NW¼NE¼	3	36	60			
1910	5.10			SE¼SE¼	34	37	60			
1910	38.00			SW¼NW¼	34	37	60			
1910	10.50			SE¼NW¼	34	37	60	4-15—8-15	1.01	

Claimant—**W. J. Black.** Permit No. 1718
Source—**Ackler Creek.** Ditch—**McMullen.**

Year of priority	Harvest crops	Meadow pasture	Diversified pasture	Subdivision	Section	Tp. N.	R. E.	Length of season	C. F. S.	Acre-feet
1910	17.70			NE¼SW¼	8	36	60	4-15—8-15	.177	

Claimant—**Joseph Jeanney.** Permit No. 1721
Source—**Ackler Creek.** Ditch—**Goodale.**

Year of priority	Harvest crops	Meadow pasture	Diversified pasture	Subdivision	Section	Tp. N.	R. E.	Length of season	C. F. S.	Acre-feet
1910	7.40			SW¼SW¼	8	36	60			
1910	28.40			SE¼SW¼	8	36	60			
1910	3.40			SW¼SE¼	8	36	60			
1910	3.50			NE¼NE¼	17	36	60			
1910	13.00			NE¼NW¼	17	36	60			
1910	9.10			NW¼NE¼	17	36	60			
1910	22.50			SW¼NE¼	17	36	60			
1910	10.10			SE¼NE¼	17	36	60	4-15—8-15	.974	

Claimant—**J. W. Johnston.** Permit No. 1734
Source—**Left Branch Boulder Creek.** Ditch **Carlson.**

Year of priority	Harvest crops	Meadow pasture	Diversified pasture	Subdivision	Section	Tp. N.	R. E.	Length of season	C. F. S.	Acre-feet
1910	7.08			NW¼NW¼	30	39	60			
1910	10.80			NE¼NW¼	30	39	60			
1910	15.07			SE¼NW¼	30	39	60	4-15—8-15	.3374	

Claimant—**W. W. Weathers and Guy E. Weathers.** Permit No. 1743

Source—**Ackley (Ackler) Creek.** Ditch—**Co-op. Ditch.**

1910	19.10	NE¼NE¼	12	36	59			
1910	2.20	SE¼NE¼	12	36	59			
1910	14.80	NW¼NE¼	12	36	59	4-15—8-15	.361	

Claimant—**Daniel F. Drumheller.** Permit No. 1750*

Source—**Secret Creek.** Ditch—**Cummins No. 1.**

1910	5.00	SW¼SW¼	22	35	59			
1910	12.70	NW¼SW¼	22	35	59			
1910	5.00	SW¼NW¼	22	35	59	5-1—8-15	.227	

*Certificate No. 192.

Claimant—**Griswold Henderson Livestock Co.** Permit No. 1831

Source—**Griswold Lake. Ditches and Storage Reservoir.**

1910	40.00	NE¼NE¼	3	32	57			
1910	39.20	NW¼NE¼	3	32	57			
1910	37.84	SE¼NE¼	3	32	57			
1910	21.21	SW¼NE¼	3	32	57			
1910	3.00	NE¼SE¼	3	32	57			
1910	38.51	NE¼NW¼	3	32	57			
1910	24.01	NW¼NW¼	3	32	57			
1910	3.67	SE¼NW¼	3	32	57			
1910	9.70	NE¼NE¼	4	32	57	4-15—8-15	2.1714	651.42

NOTE—Proof of beneficial use under this permit gives the storage capacity of Griswold Lake as 150 acre-feet. By the allowance, therefore, of the above amount of water, the lake could be filled approximately 4½ times each year, provided there were no seepage or evaporation losses. It is intended that the permittee shall have the right to store water at all times of the year.

Claimant—**Mary J. Henry.** Permit No. 1837

Source—**Deering Creek.** Ditch—**Henry.**

1910	15.80	NW¼SE¼	18	36	60			
1910	0.70	SE¼SE¼	18	36	60			
1910	29.00	SW¼SE¼	18	36	60	4-15—8-15	.455	

Claimant—**D. F. Drumheller.** Permit No. 1849*

Source—**Springs (three in number).** Ditch—**Drumheller.**

1910	20.00	N½NW¼NW¼	22	35	59	4-1—10-1	.2	

*Certificate No. 85.

Claimant—**William C. Mills.** Permit No. **1969**
Source—**Deering Creek.** Ditch—**Stone Ditch No. 1.**

Year of priority	Culture—Acres: Harvest crops	Culture—Acres: Meadow pasture	Culture—Acres: Diversified pasture	Location: Subdivision	Location: Section	Location: Tp.N.	Location: R.E.	Length of season	Duty of water: C.F.S.	Duty of water: Acre-feet
1911	0.13			Lot 2	28	36	60			
1911	6.51			Lot 3	28	36	60	4-15—8-15	.0664	

Claimant—**Matthew Gooch.** Permit No. **2059**
Source—**Humboldt River.** Ditch—**Gooch Ditch.**

Year of priority	Harvest crops	Meadow pasture	Diversified pasture	Subdivision	Section	Tp.N.	R.E.	Length of season	C.F.S.	Acre-feet
1911	25.50			NE¼NW¼	34	36	58			
1911	25.00			SE¼NW¼	34	36	58			
1911	6.50			NE¼SW¼	34	36	58			
1911	2.50			SE¼SW¼	27	36	58	4-15—8-15	.595	

Claimant—**Elko-Lamoille Power Company.** Permit No. **2090**
Source—**Lamoille Creek.** Ditch—**Power Ditch.**

Year of priority	Harvest crops	Meadow pasture	Diversified pasture	Subdivision	Section	Tp.N.	R.E.	Length of season	C.F.S.	Acre-feet
*1911									*11	

*Water used for development 415 H.P.

Claimant—**Chris Eshleman.** Permit No. **2172***
Source—**Humboldt River.** Ditch—**Dam and Reservoir.**

Year of priority	Harvest crops	Meadow pasture	Diversified pasture	Subdivision	Section	Tp.N.	R.E.	Length of season	C.F.S.	Acre-feet
†1911								†11 1—3-1		†10

*Certificate No. 172. †Water impounded in dam in Humboldt River during nonirrigating season for cutting ice.

Claimant—**Gerhart S. Schoer.** Permit No. **2188***
Source—**Cold Spring.** Ditch—**Schoer.**

Year of priority	Harvest crops	Meadow pasture	Diversified pasture	Subdivision	Section	Tp.N.	R.E.	Length of season	C.F.S.	Acre-feet
1911	9.70			Lot 3	35	42	62			
1911	1.50			NE¼NW¼	2	41	62	4-1—10-1	.112	40.32

*Amended Certificate No. 813.

Claimant—**George Walther.** Permit No. **2194***
Source—**Ruby Mineral Spring.** Ditch—**Pipe Line.**

Year of priority	Harvest crops	Meadow pasture	Diversified pasture	Subdivision	Section	Tp.N.	R.E.	Length of season	C.F.S.	Acre-feet
†1911									†0.025	

*Certificate No. 401. †Water diverted through 4-inch pipeline 60 feet in length to bottling works where it is bottled for commercial use.

Claimant—**Horace A. Agee.** Permit No. **2225***
Source—**Stony Creek in Spring Gulch.** Ditch—**Stony Creek Ditch.**

Year of priority	Harvest crops	Meadow pasture	Diversified pasture	Subdivision	Section	Tp.N.	R.E.	Length of season	C.F.S.	Acre-feet
1911	10.70			NE¼NE¼	24	42	60			
1911	18.30			NW¼NE¼	24	42	60			
1911	31.30			SW¼NE¼	24	42	60			
1911	32.00			SE¼NE¼	24	42	60	5-1—9-1	.913	

*Certificate No. 208.

Claimant—**Pacific Fruit Express Co.** Permit No. **2286***
Source—**Humboldt River.** Ditch—**P. F. E. Co. Flume.**

†1911						11 1—3-1	7.57 †150

*Certificate No. 346. †Water pumped from Humboldt River during nonirrigation season and impounded in reservoir for production of ice; 7.57 cubic feet per second allowed, but total amount stored during period above given limited to 150 acre-feet.

Claimant—**Saval Livestock Co.** Permit No. **2294***
Source—**Sixteen Mile Station Creek.** Ditch—**Main Ditch.**

1911	25.10	NE¼NW¼	26	36	54		
1911	15.00	SE¼NW¼	26	36	54	4-15—8-1	.41

*Certificate No. 314.

Claimant—**James E. Fraiser.** Proof No. 2392
Source—**Rabbit Creek.** Ditch—**Unnamed.**

1912	39.50	NW¼SE¼	14	33	57		
1912	2.00	NE¼SE¼	14	33	57		
1912	31.50	SW¼SE¼	14	33	57		
1912	0.50	SE¼SE¼	14	33	57	4-15—8-15	.735

Claimant—**Jas. E. Myers.** Permit No. 2393
Source—**Rabbit Creek.** Ditch—**Unnamed.**

1912	20.00	NW¼NE¼	14	33	57		
1912	23.50	SW¼NE¼	14	33	57	4-15—8-15	.435

Claimant—**Daniel F. Drumheller.** Permit No. 2404*
Source—**Secret Creek.** Ditch—**McCall & Forbes.**

*1910	7.60	NW¼NW¼	22	35	59		
1910	21.00	SW¼NW¼	22	35	59		
1910	21.30	NW¼SW¼	22	35	59		
1910	8.00	SW¼SW¼	22	35	59	5-1—8-15	.579

*Certificate No. 193 under permit No. 2404 which granted right to change point of diversion for part of land under permit No. 1750. Date of priority relates back to priority of permit No. 1750.

Claimant—**W. T. Jenkins Company.** Permit No. 2473
Source—**Coon Creek.** Ditch—**Coon Creek.**

1912	2.50	NE¼NW¼	33	38	53		
1912	5.71	NW¼NW¼	33	38	53		
1912	12.28	NE¼NE¼	32	38	53		
1912	5.17	NW¼NE¼	32	38	53	4-15—8-15	.2566

Claimant—**George D. Banks.** Permit No. 2480
Source—**Spring.** Ditch—**Banks Ditch.**

1912	12.00	NE¼SW¼	21	37	53		
1912	12.00	NW¼SW¼	21	37	53	4-15—8-15	.24

Claimant—**Charles H. Mickel.** Permit No. 2581
Source—**Secret Creek.** Ditch—**Unnamed.**

Year of priority	Culture—Acres: Harvest crops	Meadow pasture	Diversified pasture	Location: Subdivision	Section	Tp.N.	R.E.	Length of season	Duty of water: C.F.S.	Acre-feet
1912	81.40			SW¼	18	35	59			
1912	51.00			S½SE¼	18	35	59	4-15—8-15	1.354	

Claimant—**Ray Barriger.** Permit No. 2586
Source—**Spring Creek.** Ditch—**Unnamed.**

Year of priority	Harvest crops	Meadow pasture	Diversified pasture	Subdivision	Section	Tp.N.	R.E.	Length of season	C.F.S.	Acre-feet
1912	5.30			NW¼NW¼	36	37	58			
1912	24.70			NE¼NW¼	36	37	58			
1912	5.00			SE¼NW¼	36	37	58	4-15—8-15	.35	

Claimant—**Domingo and Jose Arrascada.** Permit No. 2671*
Source—**South Fork Humboldt River.** Ditch—**Unnamed.**

Year of priority	Harvest crops	Meadow pasture	Diversified pasture	Subdivision	Section	Tp.N.	R.E.	Length of season	C.F.S.	Acre-feet
1913	28.20			NW¼SW¼	16	33	54			
1913	30.10			NE¼SW¼	16	33	54	5-1—11-1	.673	242.28

*Certificate No. 639.

Claimant—**George Arthur, A. W. Arthur, A. B. Phillips, F. A. Fulkerson.** Permit No. 2711*
Source—**Lynn Creek.** Ditch—**Unnamed.**

Year of priority	Harvest crops	Meadow pasture	Diversified pasture	Subdivision	Section	Tp.N.	R.E.	Length of season	C.F.S.	Acre-feet
*1913									*10	

*Water used for placer mining thence returned to the stream undiminished in quantity.

Claimant—**Ralph McCoy.** Permit No. 2727
Source—**Snell Canyon Creek.** Ditch—**McCoy.**

Year of priority	Harvest crops	Meadow pasture	Diversified pasture	Subdivision	Section	Tp.N.	R.E.	Length of season	C.F.S.	Acre-feet
1913	29.60			NE¼NE¼	29	33	58			
1913	27.50			SE¼NE¼	29	33	58			
1913	2.50			NE¼SE¼	29	33	58			
1913	6.50			SE¼SE¼	29	33	58	4-15—8-15	.661	

Claimant—**Manuel Mashado.** Permit No. 2729*
Source—**Mashado Spring.** Ditch—**Unnamed.**

Year of priority	Harvest crops	Meadow pasture	Diversified pasture	Subdivision	Section	Tp.N.	R.E.	Length of season	C.F.S.	Acre-feet
1913	3.50			NE¼SE¼	28	33	53			
1913	8.40			SE¼SE¼	28	33	53			
1913	2.00			NW¼SW¼	27	33	53	4-1—9-1	.18	

*Certificate No. 407.

Claimant—**Gerhard S. Schoer.** Permit No. 2739*
Source—**Willow Creek.** Ditch—**Schoer Ditches.**

1913	32.70	NW¼SW¼	35	42	62			
1913	25.10	NE¼SW¼	35	42	62			
1913	14.10	Lot 3	35	42	62			
1913	25.40	Lot 2	35	42	62			
1913	25.30	Lot 1	35	42	62			
1913	2.30	NW¼SE¼	35	42	62			
1913	1.80	NE¼SE¼	35	42	62			
1913	0.20	E½SW¼	35	42	62			
1913	1.20	Lot 4	36	42	62			
1913	3.20	NE¼NE¼	2	41	62			
1913	2.60	NW¼NE¼	2	41	62	4-15—7-1	1.339	200.85

*Certificate No. 622.

Claimant—**George Arthur.** Permit No. 2771*
Source—**James Creek. Ditches and Storage Reservoir.**

*1882	6.85	SE¼SW¼	2	33	51			
*1882	13.10	SW¼SW¼	2	33	51			
*1882	4.16	NW¼NW¼	11	33	51			
*1882	3.98	NE¼NE¼	10	33	51	4-15—8-15	.346	84.27

*This is not an additional appropriation, but merely a permit to change the manner of use of water from direct irrigation to irrigation through storage in a reservoir. The basis of the right for this change is that listed on page 187 of this Order.

Claimant—**Frank B. Smith.** Permit No. 2772*
Source—**South Branch Coon Creek.** Ditch—**Smith Ditches Nos. 1 and 2.**

1913	10.10	SW¼NW¼	33	38	53		
1913	1.30	SE¼NW¼	33	38	53		
1913	16.40	NE¼SW¼	33	38	53		
1913	2.30	NW¼SW¼	33	38	53	5-1—10-1	.301

*Certificate No. 285.

Claimant—**W. T. Jenkins Co.** Permit No. 2781*
Source—**Coon Creek.** Ditch—**Unnamed.**

1913	6.77	SW¼SW¼	36	38	52			
1913	1.44	SE¼SE¼	35	38	52	4-15—9-1	.082	22.16

*Certificate No. 623.

Claimant—**Mrs. Mary Campbell.** Permit No. 2862
Source—**Bradley Creek.** Ditch—**Unnamed.**

1913	19.10	SE¼NE¼	6	29	57		
1913	4.50	SE¼SW¼	31	30	57		
1913	4.25	SW¼SW¼	31	30	57	4-15—8-15	.28

Claimant—**Western Pacific Ry. Co.** Permit No. **2926***
Source—**Mary's River Slough.** Ditch—**Pump and Pipeline.**

Year of priority	Culture—Acres: Harvest crops	Meadow pasture	Diversified pasture	Location: Subdivision	Section	Tp.N.	R.E.	Length of season	Duty of water: C.F.S.	Acre-feet
1914								1-1—12-31	.15	

*Certificate No. 338 issued for .15 cubic feet per second for use the entire year for transportation and railroad purposes.

Claimant—**Hyrum Brunson.** Permit No. **3008***
Source—**Brunson Spring.** Ditch—**Unnamed.**

Year of priority	Harvest crops	Meadow pasture	Diversified pasture	Subdivision	Section	Tp.N.	R.E.	Length of season	C.F.S.	Acre-feet
1914	5.80			NE¼SE¼	20	37	60	4-15—9-15	.058	

*Certificate No. 337.

Claimant—**Emeterio Plaza.** Permit No. 3027
Source—**Lamoille Creek.** Ditch—**Rockwell Plaza.**

Year of priority	Harvest crops	Meadow pasture	Diversified pasture	Subdivision	Section	Tp.N.	R.E.	Length of season	C.F.S.	Acre-feet
1914	32.00			NE¼ NE¼	16	34	58			
1914	40.00			NW¼ NE¼	16	34	58			
1914	36.00			SW¼ NE¼	16	34	58			
1914	40.00			SE¼ NE¼	16	34	58			
1914	35.00			NE¼ NW¼	16	34	58			
1914	31.50			SE¼ NW¼	16	34	58			
1914	5.60			SW¼ NW¼	15	34	58	4-15—8-15	2.201	

Claimant—**Harry A. Day.** Permit No. **3068***
Source—**Unnamed Springs.** Ditch—**Unnamed.**

Year of priority	Harvest crops	Meadow pasture	Diversified pasture	Subdivision	Section	Tp.N.	R.E.	Length of season	C.F.S.	Acre-feet
1914	11.00			NW¼ NW¼	32	40	63			
1914	36.80			SW¼ NW¼	32	40	63			
1914	21.40			SE¼ NW¼	32	40	63			
1914	20.70			NE¼ SW¼	32	40	63	5-1—7-15	.899	134.85

*Certificate No. 619.

Claimant—**Mike Koriojianakes.** Permit No. 3074
Source—**Lamoille Creek.** Ditch—**Koriojianakes and Economy.**

Year of priority	Harvest crops	Meadow pasture	Diversified pasture	Subdivision	Section	Tp.N.	R.E.	Length of season	C.F.S.	Acre-feet
1914	39.50			NE¼ NE¼	34	35	58			
1914	35.00			NW¼ NE¼	34	35	58			
1914	15.00			SW¼ NE¼	34	35	58	4-15—8-15	.895	

Claimant—**Albert Hankins.** Permit No. 3091
Source—**Smith Creek.** Ditch—**Unnamed.**

Year of priority	Harvest crops	Meadow pasture	Diversified pasture	Subdivision	Section	Tp.N.	R.E.	Length of season	C.F.S.	Acre-feet
1914	10.30			NE¼ NW¼	3	29	50	4-15—8-15	.103	

Claimant—**W. M. Weathers.** Permit No. 3095
Source—**West Fork Stevens Creek.** Ditch—**Unnamed.**

1914	74.00	NE¼NE¼	34	38	59		
1914	31.00	NW¼NE¼	34	38	59		
1914	0.50	NW¼NW¼	35	38	59	4-15—8-15	.655

Claimant—**Adelaide E. Martin.** Permit No. 3188
Source—**Grays Creek.** Ditch—**Martin.**

1914	1.60	SE¼SE¼	10	37	60		
1914	10.00	NE¼SE¼	10	37	60		
1914	1.80	SE¼NE¼	10	37	60	4-15—8-15	.14

Claimant—**George Economy.** Permit No. 3284
Source—**Lamoille Creek.** Ditch—**McIntyre, Koriojianakes and Economy.**

1915	73.00	W½SE¼	22	35	58		
1915	79.50	E½SW¼	22	35	58	4-15—8-15	1.525

Claimant—**Ella L. Chick.** Permit No. 3299
Source—**Bradley Creek.** Ditch—**Unnamed.**

1915	19.00	Lot 2	6	29	57		
1915	29.10	Lot 3	6	29	57		
1915	31.00	SW¼NE¼	6	29	57		
1915	8.50	SE¼NW¼	6	29	57		
1915	0.50	Lot 4	6	29	57		
1915	1.00	Lot 5	6	29	57	4 15—8 15	.891

Claimant—**C. H. A. Gerding, Jr.** Permit No. 3474
Source—**Soap Creek.** Ditch—**Unnamed.**

1915	6.40	NW¼NW¼	28	34	51		
1915	9.98	SW¼NW¼	28	34	51		
1915	3.80	SE¼NE¼	29	34	51	4-15—8-15	.3

Claimant—**Richard L. Wood.** Permit No. 3486*
Source—**Woods Creek.** Ditch—**Woods Creek Ditch.**

1915	19.70	SW¼NW¼	8	38	63		
1915	2.50	SW¼NW¼	8	38	63		
1915	0.50	SE¼NW¼	8	38	63		
1915	8.00	NW¼SW¼	8	38	63		
1915	10.60	NW¼SW¼	8	38	63		
1915	14.00	NW¼SW¼	8	38	63	4 1—11-1	.503

*Certificate No. 577.

Claimant—**Jas. E. Fraiser.** Permit No. 3530*

Source—**Lamoille Creek.** Ditch—**Bowers-Fraiser.**

Year of priority	Culture—Acres: Harvest crops	Meadow pasture	Diversified pasture	Location: Subdivision	Section	Tp.N.	R.E.	Length of season	Duty of water: C.F.S.	Acre-feet
†1911	30.75			NE¼NW¼	24	33	57			
†1911	38.00			NW¼NW¼	24	33	57			
†1911	40.00			SW¼NW¼	24	33	57			
†1911	38.00			SE¼NW¼	24	33	57			
†1911	40.00			NE¼SW¼	24	33	57			
†1911	38.20			NW¼SW¼	24	33	57			
†1911	35.75			SW¼SW¼	24	33	57			
†1911	36.30			SE¼SW¼	24	33	57			
†1911	3.00			SW¼SE¼	24	33	57	5-1—9-1	3.00	728.00

*Certificate No. 656. †Permit No. 3530 granted for change in point of diversion of No. 2201; hence this priority relates back to the date of filing of application No. 2201.

Cloimant—**Desidirio Martinez.** Permit No. 3562*

Source—**Beaver Springs.** Ditch—**Martinez Ditches.**

Year of priority	Harvest crops	Meadow pasture	Diversified pasture	Subdivision	Section	Tp.N.	R.E.	Length of season	C.F.S.	Acre-feet
1915	3.45			SE¼NW¼	27	41	57			
1915	27.45			SW¼NE¼	27	41	57			
1915	0.69			SW¼NE¼	27	41	57			
1915	5.61			NW¼SE¼	27	41	57			
1915	1.40			NE¼SE¼	27	41	57	4-1—10-1	.386	

*Certificate No. 482.

Claimant—**Gracien Eyroz.** Permit No. 3708

Source—**Eyroz Creek.** Ditch—**Eyroz.**

Year of priority	Harvest crops	Meadow pasture	Diversified pasture	Subdivision	Section	Tp.N.	R.E.	Length of season	C.F.S.	Acre-feet
1915	12.40			SE¼NE¼	28	43	56			
1915	0.04			NE¼SE¼	28	43	56			
1915	4.95			SW¼NW¼	27	43	56			
1915	10.27			NW¼SW¼	27	43	56			
1915	3.10			SW¼SW¼	27	43	56			
1915	5.56			SE¼SW¼	27	43	56			
1915	12.30			NE¼NW¼	34	43	56			
1915	14.23			SE¼NW¼	34	43	56			
1915	10.07			NW¼NE¼	34	43	56			
1915	9.03			SW¼NE¼	34	43	56			
1915	5.45			NE¼SW¼	34	43	56			
1915	6.32			NW¼SW¼	34	43	56	4-15—8-15	.9302	

Claimant—Harry E. Webb. Permit No. 3780*
Source—Padelford Creek. Ditch—**Webb.**

1916		18.52		SE¼NE¼	14	31	52		
1916		3.20		SW¼NE¼	14	31	52		
1916		3.00		NE¼SE¼	14	31	52		
1916		0.51		SW¼NW¼	24	31	52		
1916		3.50		SE¼NW¼	24	31	52		
1916		0.46		SW¼NE¼	24	31	52		
1916		0.10		NW¼SE¼	24	31	52	4-15—9-15	.2929	87.87

*Certificate No. 621.

Claimant—**Charles W. Mitchell.** Permit No. 3834
Source—**Browns Creek.** Ditch—**Unnamed.**

1916		14.20		SW¼NW¼	28	28	56	4-15—8-15	.143

Claimant—**L. M. Jones.** Permit No. 4060
Source—**Humboldt River. Jones Pipeline.**

1916		25.14		SE¼NW¼	20	34	55		
1916		3.92		SW¼NW¼	20	34	55		
1916		15.40		NW¼SW¼	20	34	56		
1916		9.45		NE¼SW¼	20	34	55	4 15—8-15	.5391

Claimant—**Geo. B. Russell.** Permit No. 4070*
Source—**Hot Springs.** Ditch—**Unnamed.**

1916		5.37		SW¼NW¼	22	34	55	4-1—10-1	.0537	19.33

*Certificate No. 657.

Claimant—**Geo. B. Russell.** Permit No. 4180*
Source—**Hot Springs.** Ditch—**Pipe and Flume.**

†1916				....	....	...	....	....	†.5

*Certificate No. 658. †Water granted for natatorium purposes.

Except as herein stated, it is recommended the duty of water on the lands irrigated from the Humboldt River Stream-System should be as follows:

Class A, Harvest Crops, etc.—3 acre-feet per acre.
Class B, Meadow Pasture—1½ acre-feet per acre.
Class C, Diversified Pasture—¾ acre-foot per acre.

The Humboldt River Stream-System is determined to be the Humboldt River and such other creeks or streams, the names of which are set forth in this Order of Determination.

In the foregoing tabulations the calculated rate of flow in Districts 1, 2 and 3 is based upon an irragating season of the following approximate lengths: 180 days for Class A lands, 90 days for Class B lands, and 45 days for Class C lands. In District 4 the calculated rate of flow is based upon an irrigating season of the following approximate lengths: 120 days for Class A lands, 60 days for Class B lands, and 30 days for Class C lands. Due to the wide variations in conditions of irrigation practice, season, soil, crops, etc., the State Engineer deems it necessary to reserve the right as given under section 36a, Chapter 106, Nevada Statutes of 1921, to modify his findings on the duty of water or rate of flow as allocated, where it is afterwards found that such modification is desirable and consistent with the principle that actual and beneficial use is the measure and limit of the right.

In defining the distribution of water to appropriators the State Engineer and Water Commissioners of the various districts shall give due consideration to the head required to distribute the water over the land and to the water which returns to the stream-system and becomes available for the use of other appropriators.

Upon lands where conditions render it impossible to measure the amount of water diverted upon the land, the duty of water as allotted will be modified and based upon that time-limit of irrigation which is found to be most consistent with good husbandry.

The parties named in this Order of Determination, or their successors in interest, shall not be required to take or use the amount of water allotted to them in a continuous flow, but may cumulate the same or any part thereof in rotation or periodic turn, within the season limits, with the approval of the Water Commissioner, and subject to the control and direction of the State Engineer.

The irrigation season as fixed in this Order of Determination is not to be considered as being absolute. It is and must of necessity be flexible, and vary as to the beginning and end of the season, depending upon the seasons, climatic conditions, water supply, run-off, and other matters of like character necessarily affecting the practical operation and conduct of irrigation.

In addition to water used during the irrigating season, each user should be entitled, in his proper proportion and priority, to the use of water in such reasonable amounts as necessary for fall and spring irrigation and for stock-watering purposes during the nonirrigating season.

In case any water user is dissatisfied with the duty of water as allotted in this Order of Determination, he may, at any time not later than three years from date of issuance of the court decree, submit to the State Engineer such authenticated measurements as may be neces-

sary to prove the actual and beneficial use of water on his lands. Upon approval of the proof submitted, the State Engineer will accordingly apply to the Court for a modification of the duty of water allotment in conformity with the proof submitted.

All measurements of amounts diverted are to be made at the point where the main ditch enters or becomes adjacent to the land to be irrigated or as near thereto as practicable, the location if not selected by the State Engineer to be approved by him. Each water user shall install and maintain substantial headgates and weirs in his ditch or ditches. Due allowance for losses in ditches will be made by the State Engineer in case it becomes necessary to divert additional water into said ditches.

The State Engineer hereby establishes and designates the districts of the Humboldt River Stream-System as follows:

1. Lovelock Valley.
2. Oreana to Pinson's Bridge.
3. Pinson's Bridge to Palisade.
4. Elko County and Pine Valley.

All decrees and contracts are hereby recognized as between the parties, and water will be distributed accordingly, in so far as the rights of the parties affected by such decrees or contracts are concerned.

Priorities are fixed by years, and, where the years are the same, priorities are found and determined to be equal unless otherwise specifically set forth.

The Faris Estate, the William Dunphy Estate and the Humboldt Land and Development Company have claimed a prescriptive right or a right by adverse possession to the use of all of the waters of the Humboldt River, as against all appropriators lower on the stream-system, though holders or owners of priorities earlier in period of time. I find, however, that they have not established the necessary elements showing prescriptive right or a right to the use of said water by adverse possession, and therefore find against each and all of them in this regard.

In determining and fixing priorities the doctrine of relation has been applied in this Order of Determination wherever the proofs and claims of the appropriators and the evidence presented before the State Engineer have justified.

Where in the foregoing order of determination acreages irrigated are bracketed with legal subdivisions, the water allotted is appurtenant to the legal subdivisions indicated as a unit, but limited to the acreage and culture indicated, and with a priority for the respective acreages as indicated.

As between the Union Canal, the Southwest Ditch, and the Old Channel Ditch, a certain contract dated September 10, 1910, and recorded in Book ...., page ...., of Humboldt County Records, may be recognized as between the parties, and water distributed accordingly, unless the rights of other claimants not parties to the contract are affected.

Made and filed in office this 29th day of September, 1922.

J. G. SCRUGHAM,
State Engineer.

INDEX

Waters Of The Humboldt River And Its Tributaries

Nevada. State Engineer